ENCYCLOPEDIA
OF
WORLD CRIME

ENCYCLOPEDIA OF WORLD CRIME

Criminal Justice, Criminology, and Law Enforcement

Volume VI
INDEX

Jay Robert Nash

CrimeBooks, Inc.
Wilmette, IL 1990

Publisher and **Editor-in-Chief**: Jay Robert Nash; **Associate Publisher** and **Executive Editor**: Oksana L. Creighton; **Managing Editor:** Joseph Anthony Reich (Production/Database/CD-ROM Services); **Senior Editors:** Jim McCormick, Richard C. Lindberg, Jennifer S. Harris, Richard E. Stark, Jean Blashfield Black; **Associate Editors**: Cordelia Maloney, Marck L. Bailey, Kristina Lawson, C.R. Green, Laura A. McKee, Bill Young, Eric Murphy; Jeff Carlson, Mary Anne Maloney; **Art Director:** Curtis W. Randell; **Art Consultants:** Cathy Anetsberger-Edens, Wm. O. Boze Harz; **Art Production Assistant**: Doreen J. Kozak; **Assistant Editors:** Marydeanne Wildman, John Leacock, Lawrence Eric Buhl, Marcy Firmiss, Constance Kuehn, David Foe, Amy Schroeder, Vincent M. Tornatore, John A. Koehlinger, Andrew D. Schmit, Leslie A. Krampf, Bennett H. Merens, Carol Hanson, Annie C. Higgins, Joni Overton, Clifford Tarrance, Mary Keegan Mathie, Joe Scheringer, Elizabeth Hansen, Katie Maloney, Jodi L. Schenck, Karen M. Hurley, KAri Phelps; **Research** and **Editorial Assistants**: Paul Adee, Martha Keefe, Kevin P. Pierce, Chad R. Well, Timothy A. Walsh, Angela L. Johnson, Andrea Nash, Carmel Carroll, Celia Carroll, Kymber Whitney, Inga Johnson, Leslie Haines, Daniel P. Bakula, Darryl Fox, Aaron Epstein, Christopher B. DeZutter, Michael Doorley, M. Andrew Conaway; **Bureau Chief** (Washington, D.C.): John E. Vetter; **Foreign Correspondents:** Paul Allen (Paris), Roger Madden (London), David Halliday (Berlin), G. Caetani (Rome); **Editorial Consultants**: Mitchel H. Tobin (Legal Editorial), Robert A. Janet (Law Enforcement).

Business Group: Judith A. Nash, Business Director and Associate Publisher; Patrice Tracy, Business and Sales Manager; Cordelia Maloney, Publicity and Promotion; **Consultants:** Robert Lee Ganchiff, Associate Publisher/Finance; Marc Davis, Advertising and Marketing; George C. de Kay, Publishing and Distribution; E. Leonard Rubin, David Canmann, Legal; **Associate Publishers**: Stanley Ralph Ross, Lawrence Ferguson, Barbara Browne Cramer, Marc B. Benson, Robert D. and Claudette Endacott, Peter Barrett, Lynn C. Maddox, James Baxter, Robert Champion, Ralph E. Dieckmann, James L. Anderson, Marsh Blackburn, Jeanne Nathan, Ira N. Kudish, Helen C. Creighton, James and Carole Creighton, Michael and Susan Creighton, David and Marilyn Wallace, Jeffery A. Harris, Stephanie Bemler, Jean E. Oyen, George Manny.

Editorial and **Sales Offices**: CrimeBooks, Inc., 1213 Wilmette Avenue, Wilmette, IL 60091-2557. Telephone: 1-708-251-8350. FAX: 1-708-251-5289.

Library of Congress Catalog Card Number: 88-92729
ISBN:0-923582-00-2 ENCYCLOPEDIA OF WORLD CRIME
        (6 Vols.)
        0-923582-06-1 ENCYCLOPEDIA OF WORLD CRIME,
        Vol. VI (Index)

Printed in the United States
First Edition

1 2 3 4 5 6 7 8 9 10

TABLE OF CONTENTS

BIBLIOGRAPHY

Hundreds of thousands of sources have been consulted by the author in researching the *Encyclopedia of World Crime* over the last twenty-five years. What follows are book references in excess of 25,000 entries, the largest single bibliography in the crime field. For reasons of space it is impossible to cite periodical, newspaper, and other sources indicated in our reference paragraphs following text entries as "*CBA*" (CrimeBooks Archives).

A

Aaron, Daniel (ed.). *America in Crisis.* New York: Alfred A. Knopf, 1952.
____. *Men of Good Hope.* New York: Oxford University Press, 1951.
____, and Bendiner, Robert (eds.). *The Strenuous Decade.* Garden City, N.Y.: Anchor Books, 1970.
____. *Writers on the Left.* New York: Avon, 1961.
Abadinsky, Howard. *The Criminal Elite: Professional and Organized Crime.* Westport, Conn.: Greenwood, 1983.
____. *Organized Crime.* Chicago: Nelson-Hall, 1985.
Abbait, A.H. *Italy and the Abyssinian War.* London: General Press, 1936.
____. *The Mafia in America: An Oral History.* New York: Praeger, 1981.
____. *Organized Crime.* Chicago: Nelson-Hall, 1990.
____. *Probation and Parole: Theory and Practice.* Englewood Cliffs, N.J.: Prentice-Hall, 1977.
Abbell, Aaron I. *The Urban Impact on American Protestantism, 1865-1900.* Cambridge, Mass.: Harvard University Press, 1943.
Abbot, Willis J. *Blue Jackets of '61. A History of the Navy in the War of the Secession.* New York: Dodd, Mead, 1886.
____. *Life of Carter H. Harrison.* New York: Dodd, Mead, 1895.
Abbott, E.C., and Smith, Helena Huntington. *We Pointed Them North: Recollections of a Cow Puncher.* New York: Farrar & Rinehart, 1939.
Abbott, Edith. *The Tenements of Chicago.* Chicago: University of Chicago Press, 1936.
____. *Women in Industry.* New York: D. Appleton, 1910.
Abbott, Jack Henry. *In the Belly of the Beast: Letters from Prison.* New York: Random House, 1981.
Abbott, John C., and Conwell, R.H. *Lives of the Presidents.* Portland, Maine: H. Hollett, 1896.
Abbott, John Reginald. *Footwear Evidence.* Springfield, Ill.: Charles C. Thomas, 1964.
Abbott, Lawrence F. *Impressions of Theodore Roosevelt.* New York: Doubleday, 1920.
Abbott, Lyman. *Reminiscences.* Boston: Houghton Mifflin, 1915.
Abbott, Newton Carl. *Montana in the Making.* Billings, Mont.: Gazette Printing Co., 1931.
Abbott, Wilbur C. *New York in the American Revolution.* New York: Charles Scribner's Sons, 1929.
Abel, Annie Heloise (ed.). *The Official Correspondence of James S. Calhoun, While Indian Agent at Santa Fe and Superintendent of Indian Affairs in New Mexico, 1849-1852.* Washington, D.C.: U.S. Government Printing Office, 1915.
Abel, Elie. *The Missile Crisis.* Philadelphia: J.B. Lippincott, 1966.
Abel, Ernest L. *Marihuana, The First Twelve Thousand Years.* New York: McGraw-Hill, 1982.
____. *The Scientific Study of Marihuana.* Chicago: Nelson-Hall, 1978.

Abell, L.E. *Recollections of the Emperor Napoleon.* London: John Murray, 1848.
Abell, Tyler (ed.). *Drew Pearson: Diaries, 1949-1959.* New York: Holt, Rinehart & Winston, 1974.
Abels, Jules. *Man on Fire: John Brown and the Cause of Liberty.* New York: Macmillan, 1971.
____. *The Parnell Tragedy.* London: Bodley Head, 1966.
____. *The Rockefeller Millions.* London: Frederick Muller, 1967.
Abend, Hallet, and Billingham, Anthony J. *Can China Survive?* New York: Ives Washburn, 1936.
____. *Chaos in Asia.* New York: Ives Washburn, 1939.
____. *My Life in China, 1926-41.* New York: Harcourt, 1943.
____. *Treaty Ports.* Garden City, N.Y.: Doubleday, 1944.
Abernathy, John R. *"Catch-'Em-Alive Jack": The Life and Adventures of an American Pioneer.* New York: Association Press, 1936.
____. *In Camp with Roosevelt; or, the Life of John R. (Jack) Abernathy.* Oklahoma City, Okla.: Times-Journal, 1933.
Abernethy, Thomas P. *The Burr Conspiracy.* New York: Oxford University Press, 1954.
____. *From Frontier to Plantation in Tennessee.* Chapel Hill: University of North Carolina, 1932.
Abinger, Edward. *Forty Years at the Bar.* London: Hutchinson, 1930.
Abney, H.A. *Life and Adventures of L.D. Lafferty.* New York: H.S. Goodspeed, 1875.
Abott, Abott A. *The Assassination and Death of Abraham Lincoln.* New York: American News, 1865.
Abraham, Abie. *Ghost of Bataan Speaks.* New York: Vantage Press, 1971.
Abraham, Henry J. *The Judicial Process.* New York: Oxford University Press, 1975.
Abraham, Karl. *Selected Papers.* trans. Douglas Bryan and Alix Strachey. London: Hogarth Press, 1942.
Abrahams, Gerald. *According to the Evidence.* London: Cassell, 1958.
Abrahams, I. (ed.). *The Literary Remains of the Rev. Simeon Singer: Lectures and Addresses.* London: Routledge, 1908.
Abrahams, Roger D. *Deep Down in the Jungle.* Chicago: Aldine, 1970.
____. *Positively Black.* Englewood Cliffs, N.J.: Prentice-Hall, 1970.
Abrahamsen, David. *Confessions of Son of Sam.* New York: Columbia University Press, 1985.
____. *Crime and the Human Mind.* New York: Columbia University Press, 1949.
____. *The Murdering Mind.* New York: Harper & Row, 1973.
____. *Nixon vs. Nixon: A Psychoanalytic Inquest.* New York: Farrar, Straus & Girous, 1977.
____. *The Psychology of Crime.* New York: Columbia University Press, 1960.
____. *Report on a Study of 102 Sex Offenders at Sing Sing Prison.* Utica, N.Y.: State Hospital Press, 1950.
Abrahamson, E.M., and Pezet, A.W. *Body, Mind and Sugar.* New York: Holt, Rinehart & Winston, 1951.
Abrahamson, Julia. *A Neighborhood Finds Itself.* New York: Harper & Brothers, 1959.
Abramovitch, Raphael R. *The Soviet Revolution.* New York: International Universities Press, 1962.
Abrantés, Duchesse d'. *Mémoires.* Paris: Mame, 1835.
Abrecht, Mary Ellen, and Stern, Barbara L. *The Making of a Woman Cop.* New York: William Morrow, 1976.
Abrikossow, Dmitrii I. *Revelations of a Russian Diplomat.* Seattle: University of Washington Press, 1964.
Abshagen, Karl Heinz. *Canaris, Patriot und Weltbürger.* Stuttgart, Ger.: Union Deutsche Verlagsanstalt, 1950.
Abt Associates. *An Evaluation of the Training Provided in Correc-*

tional Institutions Under the Manpower Development Act, Section 251, Final Summary Report. Cambridge, Mass.: Abt Associates, 1971.

_____. *Prison Populations and Policy Choices.* Washington, D.C.: Law Enforcement Assistance Administration, 1977.

Abuor, C.O. *White Highlands No More.* Nairobi, Kenya: Pan African Researchers, 1972.

An Account of the Curtis Homicide. Richmond, Va.: Dispatch Steam Presses, 1879.

An Account of the Execution of Samuel Green. Boston: N. Coverly, 1822.

An Account of the Murder of Richard Jennings. Newburgh, N.Y.: Benjamin F. Lewis, 1819.

An Account of the Murder of Thomas Williams. Trenton, N.J.: Sherman & Mershon, 1803.

Account of the Terrific and Fatal Riot at the New York Astor Place Opera House. New York: n.p., 1849.

Account of the Trial of Joseph Andrews. New York: n.p., 1769.

Account of the Trial of Lucian Hall, Bethuel Roberts and William H. Bell for Murder, at the Middlesex Superior Court, Connecticut. Middletown, Conn.: Charles H. Pelton, 1844.

The Accused—The Accusers: The Speeches of the Eight Chicago Anarchists in Court. Chicago: Socialistic, n.d.

Acerbo, Giacomo. *Fascism in the First Year of Governmment.* Rome: Giorgio Berlutti, 1923.

_____. *Fra due plotoni di esecuzione.* Bologna, Italy: Cappelli, 1969.

Acheson, Dean. *Present at the Creation.* New York: W.W. Norton, 1969.

Acheson, Patricia C. *The Supreme Court.* New York: Dodd, Mead, 1961.

Acland, Sir Richard. *The Forward March.* London: George Allen & Unwin, 1941.

Acland, Theodore Dyke. *William Withey Gull, A Biographical Sketch.* London: Adlard & Son, 1896.

Acton, Lord. *Essays on Church and State.* New York: Thomas Y. Crowell, 1968.

Acton, William. *The Functions and Disorders of the Reproductive Organs in Childhood, Youth, Adult Age and Advanced Life, Considered in their Physiological, Social and Moral Relations.* Philadelphia: Blakiston, 1857.

_____. *Prostitution.* London: Frederick A. Praeger, 1968.

Adair, James, *James Adair, The History of the American Indians.* London: Johnson Reprint, 1968.

Adam, H. Pearl. *Paris Sees It Through: A Diary, 1914-19.* London: Hodder & Stoughton, 1919.

Adam, Hargrave Lee. *C.I.D.* London: Sampson, Low, 1931.

_____. *The Indian Criminal.* London: John Milne, 1909.

_____. *Murder by Persons Unknown.* London: Collins, 1931.

_____. *Murder Most Mysterious.* London: Sampson, Low, 1932.

_____ (ed.). *Notable British Trials: Trial of George Chapman.* London: William Hodge, 1930.

_____. *The Police Encyclopedia.* London: Blackfriars, n.d.

_____. *Trial of George Chapman.* London: William Hodge, 1930.

_____. *Woman and Crime.* London: T.W. Laurie, 1912.

Adami, Eugenio. *La lingua di Mussolini.* Modena, Italy: Società Tipografica Modenese, 1939.

Adamic, Louis. *Dynamite: The Story of Class Violence in America.* New York: Viking Press, 1931.

_____. *The Native's Return.* New York: Harper, 1934.

Adams, A.V., and Mangum, G.L. *The Lingering Crisis of Youth Unemployment.* Kalamazoo, Mich.: W.E. Upjohn Institute for Employment Research, 1978.

Adams, Alexander B. *Geronimo.* New York: G.P. Putnam's Sons, 1971

_____. *John James Audubon.* New York: G.P. Putnam's Sons, 1966.

Adams, Andrew. *Ninja: The Invisible Assassins.* Burbank, Calif.: Ohara, 1976.

Adams, Arthur E. *Bolsheviks in the Ukraine: The Second Cam-paign, 1918-1919.* New Haven, Conn.: Yale University Press, 1963.

Adams, Brooks. *Emancipation of Massachusetts: The Dream and the Reality.* Boston: Houghton Mifflin, 1919.

Adams, Caren, and Fay, Jennifer. *No More Secrets.* San Luis Abispo, Calif.: Impact, 1981.

Adams, Charles Francis, Jr. and Henry. *Chapters of Erie.* New York: Henry Holt, 1886.

_____. *Charles Francis Adams 1835-1915: An Autobiography.* Boston: Houghton Mifflin, 1916.

_____. (ed.). *Memoirs of John Quincy Adams.* 12 vols. Philadelphia: J.B. Lippincott, 1874-1877.

_____. *Three Episodes of Massachusetts History.* Boston: Houghton Mifflin, 1892.

Adams, Cindy. *Lee Strasberg.* New York: Doubleday, 1980.

Adams, Eliphalet. *A Sermon Preached on the Occasion of the Execution of Katherine Garret.* New London, Conn.: T. Green, 1783.

Adams, Ephraim Douglass. *Great Britain and the American Civil War.* 2 vols. London: Longmans, Green, 1925.

Adams, Franklin P. *The Diary of Our Own Samuel Pepys.* New York: Simon & Schuster, 1935.

_____. *Nods and Becks.* New York: Whittlesey House, 1944.

Adams, Graham, Jr. *Age of Industrial Violence 1910-15: The Activities and Findings of the U.S. Commission on Industrial Relations.* New York: Columbia University Press, 1966.

Adams, H. Austin. *The Man, John D. Spreckles.* San Diego, Calif.: Frye & Smith, 1924.

Adams, Henry. *The Degradation of the Democratic Dogma.* New York: Macmillan, 1919.

_____. *The Education of Henry Adams.* Boston: Houghton Mifflin, 1918.

_____. *History of the United States During the Administrations of Thomas Jefferson and James Madison.* 9 vols. New York: Charles Scribner's Sons, 1889-91.

_____. *The Letters of Henry Adams.* Boston: Houghton Mifflin, 1930.

Adams, James Truslow. *The Adams Family.* Boston: Little, Brown, 1930.

_____, et al. *Album of American History.* 4 vols. New York: Charles Scribner's Sons, 1944-1948.

_____. *America's Tragedy.* New York: Charles Scribner's Sons, 1934.

_____. *The Founding of New England.* Boston: Atlantic Monthly Press, 1921.

_____. *Provincial Society 1690-1763.* New York: Macmillan, 1927.

Adams, John (ed.). *The Life and Works of Charles Francis Adams.* 10 vols. Boston: Little, Brown, 1856.

Adams, John Quincy. *Dermott MacMorrogh.* Boston: Carter, Hendee, 1832.

_____. *Life in a New England Town: 1787, 1788; Diary of John Quincy Adams.* Boston: Little, Brown, 1903.

_____. *The Lives of James Madison and James Monroe.* Boston: Phillips, Sampson, 1850.

_____. *Memoirs.* Philadelphia: J.B. Lippincott, 1874-77

Adams, P.R. *A Treatise on the Prohibitory Law of Michigan.* Romeo, Mich.: Peninsular Herald Office, 1866.

Adams, Ramon F. (ed.). *The Best of the American Cowboy.* Norman: University of Oklahoma Press, 1957.

_____. *Burs Under the Saddle.* Norman: University of Oklahoma Press, 1964.

_____. *A Fitting Death for Billy the Kid.* Norman: University of Oklahoma Press, 1960.

_____. *From the Pecos to the Powder.* Norman: University of Oklahoma Press, 1965.

_____. *The Old-Time Cowhand.* New York: Macmillan, 1961.

_____. *Six-Guns and Saddle Leather.* Norman: University of Oklahoma Press, 1969.

_____. *Western Words.* Norman: University of Oklahoma Press, 1968.

Adams, Randolph (ed.). *Selected Political Essays of James Wilson.* New York: Alfred A. Knopf, 1930.

Adams, S. *The Sociology of Punishment and Corrections.* New York: John Wiley & Sons, 1962.

Adams, Samuel Hopkins. *Alexander Woollcott: His Life and His World.* New York: Reynal & Hitchcock, 1945.

_____. *The Great American Fraud.* Chicago: Press of the American Medical Association, 1907.

_____. *Incredible Era, The Life and Times of Warren Gamaliel Harding.* Boston: Houghton Mifflin, 1939.

Adams, Thomas F. *Police Patrol.* Englewood Cliffs, N.J.: Prentice-Hall, 1971.

Adams, Virginia. *Crime.* New York: Time-Life, 1976.

Adams, W.S. *Edwardian Portraits.* London: Secker, 1957.

Adams, Ward R. *History of Arizona.* Phoenix, Ariz.: Record, 1930.

Adams, William Henry Davenport. *Witch, Warlock, and Magician.* London: Chatto & Windus, 1889.

Adams, William S. *Henry Ford and Greenfield Village.* New York: Frederick A. Stokes, 1938.

Adamson, Hans Christian. *Keepers of the Lights.* Philadelphia: Chilton-Book, 1955.

Adamson, Iain. *The Great Detective.* London: Frederick Muller, 1966.

_____. *A Man of Quality: A Biography of the Hon. Mr. Justice Cassels.* London: F. Muller, 1964.

Adcock, F.E. *The Roman Art of War under the Republic.* Cambridge, Mass.: Harvard University Press, 1940.

Adcock, Thomas Larry. *Precinct 19.* Garden City, N.J.: Doubleday, 1984.

Addams, Jane. *My Friend, Julia Lathrop.* New York: Macmillan, 1935.

_____. *A New Conscience and an Ancient Evil.* New York: Macmillan, 1913.

_____, et al. *Philanthropy and Social Progress.* New York: Thomas Y. Crowell, 1893.

_____. *The Second Twenty Years at Hull House.* New York: Macmillan, 1930.

_____. *Twenty Years at Hull House.* New York: Macmillan, 1923.

Addison, Christopher, et al. *Problems of a Socialist Government.* London: Victor Gollancz, 1933.

The Address of Abraham Johnstone. Philadelphia: n.p., 1797.

Addy, Ted. *The Dutch Schultz Story.* New York: Tower, 1962.

Ade, George. *The Old-Time Saloon: Not Wet-Nor Dry-Just History.* New York: Ray Long & Richard Smith, 1931.

Adey, R. *Locked Room Murders and Other Impossible Crimes.* London: Ferret, 1979.

Adleman, Robert H. *Alias Big Cherry.* New York: Dial Press, 1973.

_____. *The Bloody Benders.* New York: Stein & Day, 1970.

Adler, Alfred. *Billy the Kid: A Case Study in Epic Origins.* Berkeley: University of California Press, 1951.

Adler, Bill (ed.) *Washington: A Reader.* New York: Meredith Press, 1967.

_____ (ed.) *The Wisdom of Martin Luther King.* New York: Lancer Books, 1968.

Adler, Freda, and Simon, R.J. (eds.). *The Criminology of Deviant Women.* Boston: Hughton Mifflin, 1979.

_____. *Sisters in Crime: The Rise of the New Female Criminal.* New York: McGraw-Hill, 1975.

Adler, Friedrich. *The Witchcraft Trial in Moscow.* New York: Pioneer, 1937.

Adler, H.G. *Theresienstadt 1941-1945.* Tübingen, Ger.: J.C.B. Mohr, 1955.

Adler, J.A. *Elsevier's Dictionary of Criminal Science in Eight Languages.* Amsterdam, Neth.: Elsevier, 1960.

Adler, Jacob. *Claus Spreckles: The Sugar King in Hawaii.* Honolulu: University of Hawaii Press, 1966.

Adler, Mortimer J., and Van Doren, Charles (eds.). *The Negro in American History.* 3 vols. New York: William Benton,

Adler, Polly. *A House is Not a Home.* New York: Rinehart, 1953.

Adler, Renata. *Toward A Radical Middle.* New York: Random House, 1969.

Adler, Ruth (ed.). *The Working Press.* New York: G.P. Putnam's Sons, 1966.

Adorno, Theodor W., et al. *The Authoritarian Personality.* New York: Harper & Brothers, 1950.

Advertising Age. *Magazine: A Focus on the Seventies.* New York: Magazine Publishers Association, 1969.

Advisory Committee on Drug Dependence. *Cannabis.* London: H.M. Stationery Office, 1968.

Ady, Thomas. *A Candle in the Dark.* London: T. Newberry, 1656.

_____. *A Perfect Discovery of Witches.* London: H. Browne, 1661.

Aeschylus. *Oresteia.* trans. Richard Lattimore. Chicago: University of Chicago Press, 1973

Afanasyev, L., et al. *The Political Economy of Capitalism.* Moscow: Progress, 1974.

Africa, Thomas W. *Rome of the Caesars.* New York: John Wiley & Sons, 1965.

Agabekov, Georges. *OGPU: The Russian Secret Terror.* New York: Brentano's, 1931.

Agar, Herbert. *The Price of Union.* Boston: Houghton Mifflin, 1966.

Agawa Hiroshi. *Yamamoto Isoroku.* Tokyo: Shincho Shahan, 1965.

Agee, George W. *Rube Burrows, King of Outlaws, and His Band of Train Robbers.* Chicago: Hennebery, 1890.

Agee, James, and Jones, Walker. *Let Us Know Praise Famous Men.* Boston: Houghton Mifflin, 1960.

Agee, Phillip, and Wolf, Louis (eds.). *Dirty Work: The CIA in Western Europe.* Secaucus, N.J.: Lyle Stuart, 1978.

_____. *Inside the Company: CIA Diary.* New York: Stonehill, 1975.

Agee, Warren K. *Mass Media in a Free Society.* Lawrence: University of Kansas Press, 1969.

Agehanada Bharati. *The Tantric Tradition.* London: Rider, 1965.

Agel, Jerome, and Boe, Eugene. *22 Fires.* New York: Bantam Books, 1977.

Agirre, Julen. *Operation Ogro: The Execution of Admiral Luis Carrero Blanco.* trans. Barbara Probst Solomon. New York: Quadrangle New York Times Books, 1974.

Aglion, Raoul. *War in the Desert.* New York: Henry Holt, 1941.

Agoncillo, Teodoro A. *The Fateful Years: Japan's Adventure in the Philipines, 1941-45.* 2 vols. Quezson City, Phil.: R.P. Garcia, 1965.

Agourtine, Léon. *Le Général Soukhomlinov.* Clichy, Fr.: l'Auteur, 1951.

Aguilar Olmos, Rafael. *Madero sin máscara.* Mexico City: Imprenta Popular, 1911.

Ahearn, Danny. *How to Commit a Murder.* New York: Ives Washburn, 1930.

Ahern, James F. *Police in Trouble.* New York: Hawthorn, 1972.

Ahern, L. Dale. *Down One Hundred Years.* Des Moines, Iowa: Wallace-Homestead, 1938.

Ahern, M.L. *The Great Revolution.* Chicago: Lakeside, 1874.

_____. *Political History of Chicago, 1837-1887.* Chicago: Donohue & Henneberry, 1886.

Ahlstrom, Sydney E. *A Religious History of the American People.* New Haven, Conn.: Yale University Press, 1972.

Ahlstrom, W.M., and Havighurst, R.J. *Four Hundred Losers: Delinquent Boys in High School.* San Francisco: Jossey-Bass, 1971.

Ahuja, Ram. *Female Offenders in India.* Meerut, India: Menanakshi Prakashan, 1969.

Aichhorn, August. *Wayward Youth.* New York: Viking Press, 1935.

Aiken, Albert W. *Rocky Mountain Rob, the California Outlaw; or the Vigilantes of Humburg Bar.* New York: Beadle & Adams,

1871.

Aiken, Michael, and Mott, Paul E. (eds.) *The Structure of Community Power*. New York: Random House, 1970.

Aikman, Duncan. *Calamity Jane and the Lady Wildcats*. New York: Henry Holt, 1927.

_____ (ed.) *The Taming of the Frontier*. New York: Prospect Press, 1925.

Aimé-Martin, Louis. *De l'Education des meres de familles*. Paris: Gosselin, 1834.

Ainslie, Rosalynde. *The Press in Africa*. New York: Walker, 1966.

Ainsworth, M.D.S., et al. *Patterns of Attachment*. Hillsdale, N.J.: Lawrence Erlbaum, 1978.

Ainsworth, William Harrison. *The Lancashire Witches*. London: H. Colburn, 1849.

Aitken, Frank W., and Hilton, Edward. *A History of the Earthquake and Fire in San Francisco*. San Francisco: Edward Hilton, 1906.

Akagi, Roy H. *The Town Proprieters of the New England Colonies: A Study of Their Development, Organization, Activities, and Controversies*. Philadelphia: University of Philadelphia Press, 1924.

Akeny, Nesmith. *The West as I Knew It*. Lewiston, Idaho: R.G. Bailey Printing, 1938.

Akers, Ronald L., and Hawkins, Richard (eds.). *Law and Control in Society*. Englewood Cliifs, N.J.: Prentice-Hall, 1975.

Aketo Nakamura. *Hotoke no shireikan: Chu-tai kaiso-roku. [Buddha's Commander: Reminiscences of Garrison Duty in Thailand]*. Tokyo: Nihon Shuho-sha, 1958.

Akimoto Shunkichi. *Exploring the Japanese Ways of Life*. Tokyo: Tokyo News Service, 1961.

Akita, George. *Foundations of Constitutional Government in Modern Japan, 1868-1900*. Cambridge, Mass.: Harvard University Press, 1967.

Alan, A.J. *Great Unsolved Crimes*. London: Hutchinson, 1935.

Alastos, Doros. *Venizelos: Patriot, Statesman, Revolutionary*. London: P. Lund, Humphries, 1942.

Alatri, Paolo. *L'antifascismo italiano*. 2 vols. Rome: Editori Riuniti, 1956.

_____. *Le origini del fascismo*. Rome: Editori Riuniti, 1956.

Alba, Victor. *The Mexicans*. London: Pall Mall Press, 1967.

Albach, James R. *The Annals of the West*. Pittsburgh, Pa.: W.S. Haven, 1857.

Albanese, Jay S. *Organizational Offenders: Why Solutions Fall to Political, Corporate, and Organized Crime*. Niagara Falls, N.Y.: Apocalypse, 1982.

_____. *Organized Crime in America*. Cincinnati, Ohio: Anderson, 1989.

Albe, Edmond. *Hughes Géraud, évêque de Cahors: l'affaire des poisons et des envoûtements en 1317*. Cahors, Fr.: J. Girma, 1904.

Alberghini, Giovanni. *Manuale Qualificatorum Sanctae Inquisitionis*. Palermo, Italy: D. Cyrillum, 1642.

Albert, P., and, Terrou, F. *Histoire de la Presse*. Paris: Presses Universitaires de France, 1970.

Albertini, Luigi. *The Origins of the War of 1914*. London: Oxford University Press, 1952-57.

Albertson, Chris. *Bessie*. New York: Stein & Day, 1974.

Albini, Joseph L. *The American Mafia: Genesis of a Legend*. New York: Appleton-Century-Crofts, 1971.

Albion, Robert G. *The Rise of New York Port 1815-1860*. New York: Charles Scribner's Sons, 1939.

Albizzi, Cardinal. *De Inconstantia in Jure Admittenda vel Non*. Rome: Ioannis Antonii Higuetan, 1683.

Albrecht, Robert C. *Theodore Parker*. New York: Twayne, 1971.

Albrecht-Carrié, René. *Italy from Napoleon to Mussolini*. New York: Columbia University Press, 1960.

Album of American History. 3 vols. New York: Charles Scribner's Sons, 1945.

Alcatraz. San Francisco: E. Crowell Mensch, 1937.

Alciati, Andrea. *Parergon Juris Libri*. Lugduni: Sebastianum Gryphium, 1538.

Alciphron. *Letters of Courtesans*. eds. Allen Rogers Benner and Frances H. Forbes. London: William Heinemann, 1962.

Alden, John Richard. *The American Revolution, 1775-1783*. New York: Harper & Row, 1962.

Alderson, Nannie. *A Bride Goes West*. New York: Farrar & Rinehart, 1942.

Aldington, Richard. *Frauds*. London: William Heinemann, 1957.

Aldrich, Mrs. Thomas Bailey. *Crowding Memories*. Boston: Houghton Mifflin, 1920.

Aldridge, Alfred Owen. *Jonathan Edwards*. New York: Washington Square Press, 1966.

Aler, F.V. *History of Martinsburg*. Hagerstown, Md.: Mail, 1889.

Alessi, Rino. *Calda era la terra*. Bologna, Italy: Cappelli, 1958.

Alessio, Giulio. *La crisi dello stato parlamentare e l'avvento del facismo*. Padua, Italy: CEDAM, 1946.

Alessio Robles, Miguel. *Historia Politica de la Revolución*. Mexico City: Botas, 1938.

Alex, Nicholas. *Black in Blue: A Study of the Negro Policeman*. New York: Appleton-Century-Crofts, 1969.

_____. *New York Cops Talk Back: A Study of a Beleaguered Minority*. New York: John Wiley & Sons, 1976.

Alexander, C.W. *Career and Adventures of John H. Surratt*. Philadelphia: Published by Author, 1866.

Alexander, Charles C. *The Ku Klux Klan in the Southwest*. Lexington: University of Kentucky Press, 1965.

Alexander, David. *Panic! The Day the Money Stopped*. Evanston, Ill.: Regency Books, 1962.

_____. *Terror on Broadway*. New York: Random House, 1954.

Alexander, DeAlva Stanwood. *Four Famous New Yorkers: The Political Careers of Cleveland, Platt, Hill, and Roosevelt*. New York: Henry Holt, 1923.

_____. *A Political History of the State of New York*. 3 vols. New York: Henry Holt, 1906.

Alexander, Franz. *Fundamentals of Psychoanalysis*. New York: W. W. Norton, 1951.

_____, and Healy, William. *Roots of Crime*. New York: Alfred A. Knopf, 1935.

Alexander, Gilchrist. *After Court Hours*. London: Butterworth, 1950.

_____, and Staub, M. *The Criminal, the Judge and the Public*. Glencoe, Ill.: Free Press, 1956.

Alexander, Grand Duke of Russia. *Always a Grand Duke*. New York: Farrar & Rinehart, 1933.

_____. *Once a Grand Duke*. New York: Garden City, 1932.

Alexander, H.G. *The Indian Ferment*. London: Williams & Norgate, 1929.

Alexander, H.H. *The Life and Trial of Guiteau the Assassin*. Detroit, Mich.: F.H. Drake, 1882.

Alexander, Henry A. *Some Facts About the Murder Notes in the Phagan Case*. Atlanta, Ga.: Published by Author, n.d.

Alexander, Herbert E., and Caiden, Gerald E. *The Politics and Economics of Organized Crime*. Lexington, Mass.: D.C. Heath, 1985.

Alexander, Holmes. *Aaron Burr, the Proud Pretender*. New York: Harper & Brothers, 1937.

_____. *The American Talleyrand: Martin Van Buren*. New York: Harper & Brothers, 1935.

Alexander, Karl. *Time After Time*. London: Granada, 1980.

Alexander, M.E. *Jail Administration*. Springfield, Ill.: Charles C. Thomas, 1957.

Alexander, Marc. *Royal Murder*. London: Frederick Muller, 1978.

Alexander, Shana. *Anyone's Daughter*. New York: Viking Press, 1978.

_____. *The Pizza Connection: Lawyers, Money, Drugs, Mafia*. New York: Weidenfeld & Nicolson, 1988.

_____. *When She Was Bad: The Story of Bess, Hortense, Sukhreet and Nancy*. New York: Random House, 1990.

- Allen

Alexander, William Menzies. *Demonic Possession in the New Testament.* Edinburgh, Eng.: T. and T. Clara, 1902.

Alexander, William T. *History of the Colored Race in America.* Kansas City: Palmetto, 1887.

Alexander, Yonah (ed.). *International Terrorism: National, Regional and Global Perspectives.* New York: AMS Press, 1976.

_____, and Kilmarx, Robert A. (eds.). *Political Terrorism and Business: Threat and Response.* New York: Praeger, 1979.

_____, and Finger, Seymour Maxwell (eds.). *Terrorism: Interdisciplinary Perspectives.* New York: John Jay Press, 1977.

_____. *Terrorism in Italy.* New York: Crane, Russak, 1979.

Alexandra, Empress of Russia. *Letters of the Tsaritsa to the Tsar, 1914-16.* London: Duckworth, 1923.

Alexandrov, Vistor. *Journey Through Chaos.* New York: Crown, 1945.

Alfange, Dean. *The Supreme Court and the National Will.* Garden City, N.Y.: Doubleday, 1937.

Alfers, Kenneth. *Law and Order in the Capital City: A History of the Washington Police 1800-1886.* Washington, D.C.: George Washington University Press, 1976.

Alfieri, Dino. *Dictators Face to Face.* trans. David Moore. London: Elek Books, 1954.

_____, and Freddi, Luigi. *Mostra della rivoluzione fasciista.* Rome: PNF, 1933.

Alger, Horatio, Jr. *From Canal Boy to President, or the Boyhood and Manhood of James A. Garfield.* New York: J.R. Anderson, 1881.

Alger, John Goldworth. *Paris in 1789-94.* London: G. Allen, 1902.

Alice, Princess of Great Britain. *For My Grandchildren.* Cleveland: World, 1967.

Aline. *Lénine à Paris: Souvenirs inédits.* Paris: Les Revues, 1929.

Alinsky, Saul D. *Reveille for Radicals.* New York: Vintage Books, 1969.

_____. *Rules for Radicals.* New York: Random House, 1971.

Alioshin, Dmitri. *Asian Odyssey.* New York: Henry Holt, 1940.

Ali Shah, Sirdah Ikbal. *Mohammed the Prophet.* London: Wright & Brown, 1932.

Alix, Ernest Kahlar. *Ransom Kidnapping in America, 1874-1974.* Carbondale: Southern Illinois University Press, 1975.

Allan, A.A. *Gold, Men and Dogs.* New York: G.P. Putnam's Sons, 1931.

Allason, Barbara. *Memorie di un antifascista.* Milan, Italy: Avanti!, 1961.

Allbury, A.G. *Bamboo and Bushido.* London: Robert Hale, 1955.

Allbutt, R.C. *A System of Medicine.* New York: Macmillan, 1900.

Alldredge, Eugene Perry. *Cowboys and Coyotes.* Nashville, Tenn.: Marshall & Bruce, 1945.

Alleman, Tillie Pierce. *At Gettysburg.* New York: W. Lake Borland, 1889.

Allen, A. *Personal Descriptions.* London: Butterworth, 1950.

Allen, Allyn. *The Real Book About the Texas Rangers.* Garden City, N.Y.: Garden City Books, 1952.

Allen, Clifford. *Sexual Perversions and Abnormalities.* London: Oxford University Press, 1949.

_____. *A Textbook of Psychosexual Disorders.* London: Oxford University Press, 1962.

Allen, D.H. (ed.). *Essex Quarter Sessions Order Book, 1652-1661.* Chelmsford, Eng.: n.p., 1974.

Allen, David D. *The Nature of Gambling.* New York: Coward-McCann, 1952.

Allen, Edward J. *Merchants of Menace: The Mafia.* Springfield, Ill.: Charles C. Thomas, 1962.

Allen, Everett S. *The Black Ships.* Boston: Little, Brown, 1965.

Allen, F. *Whitechapel Murder.* New York: Ogilvie, 1927.

Allen, Francis A. *The Borderland of Criminal Justice.* Chicago: University of Chicago Press, 1974.

Allen, Fred. *Treadmill to Oblivion.* Boston: Little, Brown, 1954.

Allen, Frederick Lewis. *Alcoholics Anonymous Comes of Age.* New York: Alcoholics Anonymous, 1957.

_____, and Rogers, Agnes. *The American Procession, American Life Since 1860 in Photographs.* New York: Harper, 1933.

_____. *The Big Change.* New York: Harper & Brothers, 1952.

_____. *The Great Pierpont Morgan.* New York: Harper & Brothers, 1949.

_____. *The Lords of Creation.* New York: Harper & Brothers, 1935.

_____. *Only Yesterday, An Informal History of the Nineteen Twenties.* New York: Harper & Brothers, 1931.

_____. *Since Yesterday.* New York: Harper & Brothers, 1940.

Allen, G.C. *A Short Economic History of Modern Japan.* London: George Allen & Unwin, 1962.

_____, and Donnithorne, Audrey. *Western Enterprise in Far Eastern Economic Development: China and Japan.* New York: Macmillan, 1954.

Allen, Gardner W. *Our Navy and the West Indian Pirates.* Salem, Mass.: Essex Institute, 1929.

Allen, H.C. *Great Britain and the United States.* London: Odhams, 1954.

Allen, H. Warner. *Italy from End to End.* London: Methuen, 1927.

Allen, Harry E., and Simonsen, Clifford E. *Corrections in America: An Introduction.* Beverly Hills, Calif.: Glencoe, 1975.

_____, et al. *Crime and Punishment: An Introduction to Criminology.* New York: Free Press, 1981.

Allen, Hervey. *Israfel: The Life and Times of Edgar Allan Poe.* New York: G.H. Doran, 1926.

Allen, J.L. *The Reign of Law: A Tale of Kentucky Hemp Fields.* New York: Macmillan, 1900.

Allen, James. *New England's Choicest Blessing.* Boston: John Foster, 1679.

Allen, James B. *The Company Town in the American West.* Norman: University of Oklahoma Press, 1966.

Allen, John. *Assault with a Deadly Weapon: The Autobiography of a Street Criminal.* New York: Pantheon Books, 1977.

Allen, John Logan. *Passage Through the Garden: Lewis and Clark and the American Northwest.* Urbana: University of Illinois Press, 1975.

Allen, Lee. *The American League Story.* New York: Hill & Wang, 1962.

_____. *The National League Story.* New York: Hill & Wang, 1961.

Allen, Leslie H. *Bryan and Darrow at Dayton: The Record and Documents of the "Bible-Evolution" Trial.* New York: Arthur Lee, 1925.

Allen, Louis. *Japan: The Years of Triumph.* London: Purnell & Sons, 1971.

Allen, Lucas Benjamin. *Brief Considerations on the Present State of the Police of the Metropolis.* London: J. Butterworth & Son, 1821.

Allen, Mary S. *The Pioneer Policewoman.* London: Chatto & Windus, 1925.

Allen, Robert L. *Black Awakening in Capitalist America: An Analytic History.* Garden City, N.Y.: Doubleday, 1969.

Allen, Robert S., and Shannon, William. *The Truman Merry-Go-Round.* New York: Vanguard Press, 1950.

Allen, Ruth. *The Great Southwest Strike.* Austin: University of Texas, 1942.

Allen, Stookie. *Men of Daring.* New York: Cupples & Leon, 1933.

Allen, Trevor. *Ivar Kreuger.* London: John Long, 1932.

Allen, W.E.D., and Muratoff, Paul. *Caucasian Battlefields: A History of the Wars on the Turco-Caucasian Border, 1821-1921.* New York: Cambridge University Press, 1953.

_____. *The Ukraine: A History.* Cambridge, Eng.: Cambridge University Press, 1941.

Allen, William. *Starkweather: The Story of a Mass Murderer.* Boston: Houghton Mifflin, 1976.

Allen, Dr. William A. *Adventures with Indians and Game; or Twenty Years in the Rocky Mountains.* Chicago: A.W. Bowen, 1903.

Allen, William Harvey. *Al Smith's Tammany Hall, Champion Political Vampire.* New York: Institute For Public Service, 1928.

_____. *Rockefeller, Giant, Dwarf, Symbol.* New York: Institute for Public Service, 1930.

_____. *Why Tammanies Revive.* New York: Institute For Public Service, 1937.

Alley, John. *City Beginnings in Oklahoma Territory.* Norman: University of Oklahoma Press, 1939.

Allman, James J. *Police and the Changing Community.* Washington, D.C.: International Association of Chiefs of Police, 1965.

Allou, Roger (ed.). *Discours et plaidoyers d'Edouard Allou.* 2 vols. Paris: Durand et Pedone-Lauriel, 1884.

_____, and Chenu, Charles. *Grands avocats du siécle.* Paris: A. Pedone, 1894.

Allport, G.W. *Becoming.* New Haven, Conn.: Yale University Press, 1955.

_____. *The Nature of Prejudice.* Garden City, N.Y.: Doubleday/Anchor Books, 1958.

_____. *Personality: A Psychological Interpretation.* New York: Henry Holt, 1937.

_____, and Vernon, P. *Studies in Expressive Movements.* London: Macmillan, 1933.

Allsop, Kenneth. *The Bootleggers.* Garden City, N.Y.: Doubleday, 1961.

Allsopp, Frederick William. *Folklore of Romantic Arkansas.* 2 vols. New York: Grolier Society, 1931.

An Almanac of Jim Garrison's Investigation: The Crime of Silence. Austin, Texas: Research, 1968.

Almandos, Luis. *Bertillon et Vucetich.* La Plata, Argen.: n.p., 1928.

Almedingen, E.M. *The Emperor Alexander I.* London: Bodley Head, 1964.

_____. *The Emperor Alexander II.* London: Allen Lane, 1962.

_____. *The Empress Alexandra.* London: Hutchinson, 1961.

_____. *The Romanovs, Three Centuries of an Ill-Fated Dynasty.* New York: Holt, Rinehart & Winston, 1966.

_____. *An Unbroken Unity.* London: Bodley Head, 1964.

Almira, J., and Stojan, Z. *Le déclic de Sarajevo.* Paris: n.p., 1934.

Alois, Louis. *The Homicidal Maniac, Ten Studies.* Paris: Published by Author, 1967.

Aloutte. *Quantrell: The Terror of the West.* New York: M.J. Ivers, 1881.

Alper, Benedict. *Prisons Inside-Out: Alternatives in Correctional Reform.* Cambridge, Mass.: Ballinger, 1974.

Alphonsus de Spina. *Fortalicium Fidei.* Strasbourg, Fr.: Johann Mentelin, 1497.

Alphonsus de Vera Cruz. *Speculum Conjugiorum.* Milan, Italy: Ioannes Paulus Brissensis, 1556.

Alsop, Em Bowles (ed.). *The Greatness of Woodrow Wilson: 1856-1956.* New York: Rinehart, 1956.

Alsop, Joseph, and Catledge, Turner. *The 168 Days.* Garden City, N.Y.: Doubleday, 1938.

Alsop, Stewart. *The Center.* New York: Harper & Row, 1968.

Alsop, Susan Mary. *Lady Sackville.* Garden City, N.Y.: Doubleday, 1978.

Altavilla, Enrico. *The Art of Spying.* Englewood Cliffs, N.J.: Prentice-Hall, 1967.

Altekar, A.S., and Srivinas, M.N. *Marriage and Family in Mysore.* Bombay, India: New Book, 1942.

_____. *The Position of Women in Hindu Civilization.* Delhi, India: Motilal Banarasidass, 1956.

Alternative Draft of the German Penal Code. South Hackensack, N.J.: Fred B. Rothman, 1977.

Altgeld, John Peter. *Live Questions.* New York: Humbold, 1890.

_____. *Our Penal Machinery and Its Victims.* Chicago: Janson, McClurg, 1884.

Altick, Richard D. *The English Common Reader.* Chicago: University of Chicago Press, 1963.

_____. *Victorian Studies in Scarlet.* London: J.M. Dent & Sons, 1970.

Altman, Edward I., and Sametz, Arnold W. (eds.). *Financial Crisis: Institutions and Markets in a Fragile Environment.* New York: Wiley-International, 1977.

Altman, Jack, and Ziporyn, Marvin. *Born to Raise Hell.* New York: Grove Press, 1967.

Altrocchi, Julia Cooley. *The Spectacular San Franciscans.* New York: E.P. Dutton, 1949.

_____. *Traces of Folklore and Furrow.* Caldwell, Idaho: Caxton Printers, 1945.

Altrocchi, Rudolph. *Sleuthing in the Stacks.* Cambridge, Mass.: Harvard University Press, 1944.

Alvarez, A. *The Savage God: A Study of Suicide.* New York: Bantam Books, 1973.

Alvarez, Alfredo. *El limantourismo de Francisco Mader.* Mexico City: Talleres Tipográficos de la Casa de Orientación para Varones, 1934.

Alvarez, N. *The James Boys in Missouri.* Clyde, Ohio: Ames, 1907.

Alvaro, Corrado. *Quasi una vita: Giornale di uno scrittore.* Milan, Italy: Bompiani, 1951.

Alverstone, Viscount. *Recollections of Bar and Bench.* London: Arnold, 1914.

Alvesi, Fabrizio. *La ribellione degli Italiani.* Rome: Fratelli Bocca, 1956.

Alvisi, Eduardo. *Cesare Borgia.* Imola, Italy: Tip d'Ignazio Galeati e Figlio, 1878.

Alvord, Clarence Walworth, and Bidgood, Lee. *The First Explorations of the Trans-allegheny Region By the Virginians, 1650-1674.* Cleveland: Arthur H. Clark, 1912.

_____. *The Mississippi Valley in British Politics.* 2 vols. Cleveland: Arthur H. Clark, 1917.

Amado, Enrique. *La Revolucion Mexicana de 1913.* Valencia, Spain: Prometeo Sociedad Editorial, 1914.

Amaya, General Juan Gualberto. *Madero y los Auténticos Revolucionarios de 1910.* 3 vols. Mexico City: Published by Author, 1946.

_____. *Venustiano Carrangza: caudillo constitucionalista.* Mexico City: Published by Author, 1947.

Amaya Morán, Arturo. *Examen histórico-juridico del gobierno de Herta.* Mexico City: Published by Author, 1952.

Ambedkar, B.R. *Ranade, Gandhi and Jinnah.* Bombay, India: Thacker, 1943.

Ambler, Charles Henry. *A History of Transportation in the Ohio Valley.* Glendale, Calif.: Arthur H. Clark, 1932.

Ambler, Eric. *The Ability to Kill and Other Pieces.* London: Bodley Head, 1963.

Ambrose, Stephen E. *Eisenhower, The President.* New York: Simon & Schuster, 1984.

Ambrosino, Lillian. *Runaways.* Boston: Beacon Press, 1971.

Ame, Gen. Cesare. *Guerra segreta in Italia, 1940-43.* Rome: Gherardo Casini, 1954.

America: Great Crises in Our History Told by Its Makers. 12 vols. Chicago: Veterans of Foreign Wars, 1925.

American Anti-Slavery Almanac For 1838. New York: American Anti-Slavery Society, 1839.

American Bar Association. *Code of Professional Responsibility and Canons of Judicial Ethics.* Washington, D.C.: American Bar Association, 1970.

_____. *Final Report of the Committee on Economic Offenses.* Washington, D.C.: American Bar Association, 1976.

_____. *The Prosecution Function and the Defense Function.* New York: Institute for Judicial Administration, 1970.

_____. *Report on Organized Crime.* New York: American Bar

Association, 1952.

The American Bloody Register. Boston: W. Russell, 1784.

"*American Business Activity Since 1790*". Cleveland: Cleveland Trust Company, 1950.

American Correctional Association. *Correctional Officers' Training Guide*. College Park, Md.: American Correctional Association, 1959.

American Enterprise Institute. *The American Presidency: A Discussion with Gerald R. Ford*. Washington, D.C.: AEI, 1977.

American Friends Service Committee. *Struggle for Justice: A Report on Crime and Punishment in America*. New York: Hill & Wang, 1971.

American Guide Series (compiled by WPA writers).

_____. *Arizona; A State Guide*. New York: Hastings House, 1940.

_____. *Arkansas; A Guide to the State*. New York: Hastings House, 1941.

_____. *California; A Guide to the Golden State*. New York: Hastings House, 1939.

_____. *Cincinnati; A Guide to the Queen City and Its Neighbors*. Cincinnati, Ohio: Weiesen-Hart Press, 1943.

_____. *Colorado; A Guide to the Highest State*. New York: Hastings House, 1941.

_____. *Idaho; A Guide in Word and Picture*. New York: Oxford University Press, 1937.

_____. *Iowa; A Guide to the Hawkeye State*. New York: Viking Press, 1938.

_____. *Kansas; A Guide to the Sunflower State*. New York: Viking Press, 1939.

_____. *Kentucky; A Guide to the Bluegrass State*. New York: Harcourt, Brace, 1939.

_____. *Louisana; A Guide to the State*. New York: Hastings House, 1945.

_____. *Minnesota; A State Guide*. New York: Viking Press, 1938.

_____. *Mississipppi; A Guide to the Magnolia State*. New York: Hastings House, 1938.

_____. *Missouri; A Guide to the "Show Me" State*. New York: Duell, Sloan & Pearce, 1941.

_____. *Montana; A State Guide*. New York: Viking Press, 1939.

_____. *Nebraska; A Guide to the Cornhusker State*. New York: Viking Press, 1939.

_____. *New Mexico; A Guide to the Colorful State*. New York: Hasting House, 1940.

_____. *New Orleans City Guide*. Boston: Houghton Mifflin, 1938.

_____. *Oklahoma; A Guide to the Sooner State*. Norman: University of Oklahoma Press, 1941.

_____. *The Oregon Trail*. New York: Hastings House, 1939.

_____. *Provo; Pioneer Mormon City*. Portland, Ore.: Binfords & Mort, 1942.

_____. *Santa Barbara; A Guide to the Channel City and Its Environs*. New York: Hastings House, 1941.

_____. *A South Dakota Guide*. Pierre, S.D.: Pierre, 1938.

_____. *Tennessee; A Guide to the State*. New York: Hastings House, 1939.

_____. *Texas; A Guide to the Lone Star State*. New York: Hastings House, 1940.

_____. *Tulsa; A Guide to the Oil Capital*. Tulsa, Okla.: Mid-West Printing, 1938.

_____. *Utah; A Guide to the State*. New York: Hastings House, 1941.

_____. *Vermont; A Guide to the Green Mountain State*. Boston: Houghton Mifflin, 1937.

_____. *West Virginia; A Guide to the Mountain State*. New York: Oxford University Press, 1941.

_____. *Wyoming; A Guide to Its History, Highways, and People*. New York: Oxford University Press, 1941.

American Heritage. *American Heritage Picture History of the Civil War*. New York: American Heritage, 1960.

American Historical Association. *Papers of the American Histori-cal Association*. New York: G.P. Putnam's Sons, 1886.

American Humane Association Children's Division. *Trends in Officially Reported Child Neglect and Abuse in the United States*. Denver: American Humane Association, 1984.

American Law Institute. *Model Penal Code*. Philadelphia: American Law Institute, 1962.

_____, and American Bar Association. Joint Committee on Continuing Legal Education. *The Problem of Punishing Homicide*. Philadelphia: American Law Institute, 1962.

American Medical Association. *Digest of Official Action: 1846-1958*, Chicago: American Medical Association, 1959.

_____. *Drug Dependence: A Guide for Physicians*. Chicago: American Medical Association, 1969.

American Patriotism: Speeches, Letters and Other Papers. New York: John B. Alden, 1864.

American Psychiatric Association. *Biographical Directory of the Fellows and Members*. New York: R.R. Bowker, 1973.

American Racehorses of 1936. New York: Sagamore Press, 1937.

American vs. Italian Brigandage. Philadelphia: Barclay, 1875.

Ameringer, Oscar. *If You Don't Weaken*. New York: Henry Holt, 1940.

Ames, James E. *Theodore Roosevelt: Hero to His Valet*. New York: John Day, 1927.

Ames, J.W. *Co-operative Sweden Today*. Manchester, Eng.: Co-operative Union, 1956.

Ames, Walter L. *Police and Community in Japan*. Berkeley: University of California Press, 1981.

Amicucci, Ermanno. *I 600 giorni di Mussolini*. Rome: Faro, 1948.

Amir, Menachem. *Patterns in Forcible Rape*. Chicago: University of Chicago Press, 1971.

Amory, Cleveland, and Bradlee, F. *Cavalcade of the 1920's and 30's*. London: Bodley Head, 1961.

_____. *The Last Resorts*. New York: Harper & Brothers, 1948.

_____. *The Proper Bostonians*. New York: E.P. Dutton, 1947.

_____. *Who Killed Society?* New York: Harper & Brothers, 1960.

Amrine, Michael. *This Awesome Challenge: The Hundred Days of Lyndon Johnson*. New York: G.P. Putnam's Sons, 1964.

_____. *The Great Decision: The Secret History of the Atomic Bomb*. New York: G.P. Putnam's Sons, 1959.

An Analysis of Outline of the Life and Character of Josiah Burn-ham. Hanover, N.H.: Moses Davis, 1806.

Anania, Giovanni Lorenzo. *De Natura Demonum*. Naples, Italy: I.B. Cappellum, 1582.

Anatomy of a Murder. London: John Lane, 1936.

Anche l'Italia ha vinto. Rome: Mercurio, 1945.

Andenaes, Johannes. *Punishment and Deterrence*. Ann Arbor: University of Michigan Press, 1974.

Anders, Wladyslaw. *Hitler's Defeat in Russia*. Chicago: Regnery, 1953.

Andersen, Christopher P. *The Serpent's Tooth*. New York: Harper & Row, 1987.

Anderson, Abraham C. *The Pioneer Life of George W. Goodhart, and His Association with the Hudson's Bay and American Fur Company's Traders and Trappers*. Caldwell, Idaho: Caxton Printers, 1940.

Anderson, Annelise G. *The Business of Organized Crime: A Cosa Nostra Family*. Stanford, Calif.: Hoover Institution Press, 1979.

Anderson, Clinton H. *Beverly Hills Is My Beat*. New York: Popular Library, 1962.

Anderson, David, and Benjaminson, Peter. *Investigative Reporting*. Bloomington: Indiana University Press, 1976.

Anderson, E. *A Place on the Corner*. Chicago: University of Chicago Press, 1978.

Anderson, E.T. *A Quarter-Inch of Rain*. Emporia, Kan.: n.p., 1962.

Anderson, Ed H. (ed.). *History of Sherman and Grayson County*. Sherman, Texas: Lewis Printing, 1947.

Anderson, Frank W. *Bill Miner: Train Robber*. Calgary, Alberta,

Can.: Frontiers, 1963.

Anderson, Galuska. *A Border City during the Civil War.* Boston: Little, Brown, 1908.

Anderson, George B. (ed.). *History of New Mexico: Its Resources and People.* Los Angeles: Pacific States, 1907.

Anderson, J. *This Was Harlem: A Cultural Portrait, 1900-1950.* New York: Farrar, Straus, Giroux, 1982.

Anderson, Jack. *The Anderson Papers.* New York: Random House, 1973.

_____, and Boyd, James. *Confessions of a Muckraker.* New York: Random House, 1979.

_____, and Blumenthal, Fred. *The Kefauver Story.* New York: Dial Press, 1956.

Anderson, Jervis. *A. Philip Randolph.* New York: Harcourt Brace Jovanovich, 1973.

Anderson, Kristin. and DeBreuil, Linda. *The Wholesome Hooker.* New York: W.W. Norton, 1973.

Anderson, M.S. *The Eastern Question, 1774-1923.* New York: Macmillan, 1966.

_____. *18TH Century Europe: 1713-1789.* New York: Oxford University Press, 1966.

Anderson, Margaret. *My Thirty Year's War.* New York: Alfred A. Knopf, 1930.

Anderson, Oscar E., Jr. *The Health of a Nation: Harvey W. Wiley and the Fight for Pure Food.* Chicago: University of Chicago Press, n.d.

Anderson, Paul Russell. *Science in Defense of Liberal Religion.* New York: G.P. Putnam's Sons, 1933.

Anderson, Sir Robert. *Criminals and Crime: Some Facts and Suggestions.* London: James Nisbet, 1907.

_____. *The Lighter Side of My Official Life.* London: Hodder & Stoughton, 1910.

Anderson, Sherwood. *Dark Laughter.* New York: Boni & Liveright, 1925.

_____. *A Story Teller's Story.* New York: Grove Press, 1958.

Anderson, Thornton (ed.). *Masters of Russian Marxism.* New York: Appleton-Century-Crofts, 1963.

Anderson, William S. (ed.). *Ballentine's Law Dictionary.* Rochester, N.Y.: Lawyers Cooperative, 1969.

Andics, H. *Fuenfzig Jahre unseres Lebens.* Vienna, Aust.: Molden, 1968.

_____. *Rule of Terror: Russia Under Lenin and Stalin.* New York: Holt, Rinehart & Winston, 1969.

_____. *Der Staat, den keiner wollte.* Vienna, Aust.: Herder, 1962.

Andorsen, Harold F. (ed.). *Memoirs of Lord Salvesen.* London: W. & R. Chambers, 1949.

Ando Yoshio (ed.). *Showa Keizai-shi e no shogen. [Evidence Pertaining to Economic Hisoty in the Reign of Hirohito].* Tokyo: Mainichi Shinbun-sha, 1966.

Andréadès, A. *History of the Bank of England.* London: P.S. King, 1909.

Andreae, Percy. *The Prohibition Movement in its Broader Bearings upon our Social, Commercial and Religious Liberties.* Chicago: Felix Mendelsohn, 1915.

Andreas, A.T. *History of Chicago.* 3 vols. Chicago: Published by Author, 1884-86.

_____. *History of Cook County, Illinois.* Chicago: Published by Author, 1884.

_____, and Cutler, W.G. *History of the State of Kansas.* Chicago: n.p., 1883.

_____. *History of the State of Nebraska.* Chicago: Western Historical, 1882.

Andreas-Friedrich, Ruth. *Berlin Underground 1939-1945.* London: Latimer House, 1948.

Andreski, Stanislav. *The African Predicament.* New York: Atherton, 1968.

Andrew, C.F. *Mahatma Gandhi: At Work.* London: George Allen & Unwin, 1931.

_____. *Mahatma Gandhi: His Own Story.* New York: Macmillan, 1931.

_____. *Mahatma Gandhi's Ideas.* London: George Allen & Unwin, 1929.

Andrew, Roland G. *Through Fascist Italy.* London: George Harrap, 1935.

Andrewes, Antony. *The Greek Tyrants.* London: Hutchinson's University Library, 1965.

Andrews, Bert and Peter. *A Tragedy of History.* Washington, D.C.: Roberty B. Luce, 1962

Andrews, C.C. (ed.). *Minnesota in the Indian and Civil Wars.* 2 vols. St. Paul: State of Minnesota, 1890-93.

Andrews, C.L. *The Story of Alaska.* Caldwell, Idaho: Caxton Printers, 1938.

Andrews, C.M. *The Colonial Period of American History.* 4 vols. New Haven, Conn.: Yale University Press, 1934.

_____. *England's Commercial and Colonial Policy.* New Haven, Conn.: Yale University Press, 1938.

_____. *River Towns of Conneticut.* Baltimore: Johns Hopkins University Press, 1889.

Andrews, E. Benjamin. *The History of the Last Quarter-Century in the United States, 1870-1895.* 2 vols. New York: Charles Scribner's Sons, 1896.

Andrews, Frank, and Dickens, Albert. *Over the Wall.* New York: Pyramid, 1974.

Andrews, George, and Vinkenoog, Simon (eds.). *The Book of Grass.* New York: Grove Press, 1967.

_____, and Solomon, David. *The Coca Leaf and Cocaine Papers.* New York: Harcourt, Brace, 1975.

Andrews, K.H. *Elizabethan Privateering: English Privateering During the Spanish War, 1585-1603.* New York: Cambridge University Press, 1964.

Andrews, Marrietta M. *My Studio Window.* New York: E.P. Dutton, 1928.

Andrews, Matthew Page. *The Women of the South in War Times.* Baltimore: Norman Remington, 1920.

Andrews, Ralph W. *Historic Fires of the West.* New York: Bonanza Books, 1966.

Andrews, Wayne. *Battle for Chicago.* New York: Harcourt, Brace, 1946.

_____. *The Vanderbilt Legend.* New York: Harcourt, Brace, 1941.

Andrews, William. *Old-Time Punishments.* London: Tabard Press, 1960.

Andreyev, A. *Lenin v Kremle.* Moscow: Politicheskoi Literaturi, 1960.

Andric, Ivo. *Bosnian Story.* London: Lincolns-Praeger, 1948.

_____. *The Bridge on the Drina.* New York: New American Library, 1961.

Anelli, Marco. *L'Etiopia.* Chieti, Italy: Bonnani, 1935.

Anfuso, Filippo. *Du Palais de Venise au Lac de Garde.* Paris: Calmann-Lévy, 1949.

Angel, Myron (ed.). *History of Nevada.* Oakland, Calif.: Thompson & West, 1881.

_____. *History of Placer County.* Oakland, Calif.: Thompson & West, 1882.

_____. *History of San Luis Obispo County, California.* Oakland, Calif.: Thompson & West, 1883.

Angel, S. *Discouraging Crime Through City Planning.* Berkeley: University of California Press, 1969.

Angelelia, Michael. *Trial of Blood.* New York: Bobbs-Merrill, 1980.

Angell, Norman. *The Story of Money.* New York: Frederick A. Stokes, 1929.

Angell, Robert Cooley. *The Family Encounters the Depression.* New York: Charles Scribner's Sons, 1936.

Anger, Kenneth. *Hollywood Babylon.* New York: Dell, 1965.

Angle, Paul M. *Bloody Williamson: A Chapter in American Lawlessness.* New York: Alfred A. Knopf, 1952.

_____ (ed.). *Created Equal? The Complete Lincoln-Douglas Debates of 1858.* Chicago: University of Chicago Press, 1958.

_____. *The Great Chicago Fire.* Chicago: Chicago Historical Society, 1946.

_____, and Miers, Earl Schenck (eds.). *The Living Lincoln.* New Brunswick, N.J.: Rutgers University Press, 1955.

_____ (ed.). *A Portrait of Abraham Lincoln in Letters by His Oldest Son.* Chicago: Chicago Historical Society, 1968.

_____. *A Shelf of Lincoln Books.* New Brunswick, N.J.: Rutgers University Press, 1946.

_____ (ed.). *These Words.* Chicago: Rand McNally, 1954.

Anglés, Josephus. *Flores Theologicarum Quaestionum in Quartum Librum Sententiarum.* Venice, Italy: Ioannem Baptistam Somaschum, 1584.

Angly, Edward. *Oh, Yeah?* New York: Viking Press, 1931.

Anhorn, Bartholomäus. *Magiologia: Christliche Warnung für dem Aberglauben und Zauberey.* Basel, Switz.: Johann Heinrich Meyer, 1674.

Ankeny, Nesmith. *The West as I Knew It.* Lewiston, Idaho: R.G. Bailey, 1953.

Anker, Kurt. *Kronprinz Wilhelm.* Berlin: E.S. Mittler & Sohn, 1919.

Annals of San Francisco. New York: Western Press, 1855.

Annan, N.G. *Leslie Stephen.* London: MacGibbon & Kee, 1951.

Annin, Robert E. *Woodrow Wilson: A Character Study.* New York: Dodd, Mead, 1924.

Annual Report of Commissioners of Prisons and Directors of Convict Prisons 1911-12. London: H.M. Stationery Office, 1912.

Anslinger, Harry J., and Oursler, Will. *The Murderers.* New York: Farrar, Straus & Cudahy, 1961.

_____. *The Protectors.* New York: Farrar, Straus, 1964.

_____, and Tompkins, W.F. *The Traffic in Narcotics.* New York: Funk & Wagnalls, 1953.

Anson, Robert Sam. *"They've Killed the President".* New York: Bantam Books, 1975.

Anthiny, Evelyn. *The Assassin.* New York: Coward McCann, 1970.

Anthony, E.J., and Koupernik, C. (eds.). *The Child in His Family.* New York: John Wiley & Sons, 1970.

Anthony, Irving. *Paddle Wheels and Pistols.* Philadelphia: Macrae Smith, 1929.

Anthony, K.S. *Catherine the Great.* Garden City, N.Y.: Alfred A. Knopf, 1925.

_____ (ed.). *Memoirs of Catherine the Great.* New York: Alfred A. Knopf, 1927.

Anthony, Katherine. *Mothers Who Must Earn.* New York: Russell Sage Foundation, 1914.

Anti-Masonic Almanac for 1833. Baltimore: n.p., 1834.

Antommarchi, Dr. F. *The Last Days of Napoleon.* London: H. Colburn, 1826.

Antonius, George. *The Arab Awakening.* London: Hamish Hamilton, 1938.

Aoyama Koji. *Yakuza no Seikai: Kanka, Jingi, Tobaku, Sono Onna [Yakuza Society: Fighting, Chivalry, Gambling, and Women].* Tokyo: Kofusha, 1979.

Apell, George C. *Belle's Castle.* New York: MacMillan Co., 1959.

Appian. *Roman History: The Wars in Spain.* trans. Horace White. Cambridge, Mass.: Harvard University Press, 1964.

Appleby, Paul H. *Re-examination of India's Administrative System.* New Delhi: Government of India Press, 1956.

Applegate, Frank G. *The Apache Kid: "Folk-Say: A Regional Miscellany."* Norman: University of Oklahoma Press, 1931.

_____. *Native Tales of New Mexico.* Philadelphia: J.B. Lippincott, 1932.

Applegate, Rex. *Riot Control.* Harrisburg, Pa.: Stackpole, 1969.

Appleman, P., Madden, W.A., and Wolf, M. (eds.). *1859: Entering an Age of Crisis.* Bloomington: Indiana University Press, 1959.

Appleman, Roy E. *Charlie Siringo, Cowboy Detective.* Washington, D.C.: Potomac Corral, the Westerners, 1968.

Appler, Augustus C. *The Guerrillas of the West; or The Life, Character and Daring Exploits of the Younger Brothers.* St. Louis: Eureka, 1876.

_____. *The Younger Brothers.* New York: Frederick Fell, 1955.

Appleton's Dictionary of New York And Its Vicinity. New York: D. Appleton, 1898.

Aptheker, Herbert. *American Negro Slave Revolts.* New York: International, 1943.

_____. *History and Reality.* New York: Cameron, 1955.

_____. *Nat Turner's Slave Rebellion.* New York: Grove Press, 1966.

_____. *Negro Slave Revolts in the United States, 1526-1860.* New York: International, 1939.

_____. *To Be Free: Studies in American Negro History.* New York: International, 1948.

Aragón, Alfredo. *El Desarme del Ejército Federal por la Revolucion de 1913.* Paris: Imprimeries Wellhoff et Roche, 1915.

Arahara Bokusui. *Dai Uyoku Shi [Great History of the Right Wing].* Tokyo: Dai Nippon Kokumin To, 1966.

Araquistain, Luis. *La Revolución Mejicana. Sus Origenes, Sus Hombres, Su Obra.* Madrid: Renacimiento, 1929.

Arbman, Holger. *The Vikings.* New York: Praeger, 1961.

Archambault, F., and Lemoine, J.F. *4 Milliards de Journeaux.* Paris: Alain Moreau, 1977.

Archambeau, Ernest R. (ed.). *Old Tascosa, 1885-1888.* Canyon, Texas: Panhandle Plains Historical Society, 1966.

Archer, Fred. *Ghost Detectives: Crime and the Psychic World.* London: W.H. Allen, 1970.

_____. *Killers in the Clear.* New York: W.H. Allen, 1971.

Archer, Jules. *Angry Abolitionist: William Lloyd Garrison.* New York: Julian Messner, 1969.

_____. *The Extremists.* New York: Hawthorn Books, 1969.

_____. *Fighting Journalist: Horace Greeley.* New York: Julian Messner, 1966.

_____. *Hawks, Doves and the Eagle.* New York: Hawthorn Books, 1970.

_____. *Mexico and the United States.* New York: Hawthorn Books, 1973.

_____. *1968: Year of Crisis.* New York: Julian Messner, 1971.

_____. *The Plot to Seize the White House.* New York: Hawthorn Books, 1973.

_____. *Resistance.* Philadelphia: Macrae Smith, 1973.

_____. *Revolution In Our Time.* New York: Julian Messner, 1971.

_____. *Riot! A History of Mob Action in the United States.* New York: Hawthorn Books, 1974.

_____. *Strikes, Bombs and Bullets.* New York: Julian Messner, 1972.

_____. *They Made a Revolution: 1776.* New York: Scholastic, 1973.

_____. *Treason in America.* New York: Hawthorn Books, 1971.

_____. *The Unpopular Ones.* New York: Crowell-Collier, 1968.

Archer, William. *America Today.* London: William Heinemann, 1900.

Archibald, G.C. (ed.). *The Theory of the Firm.* Middlesex, Eng.: Penguin, 1971.

Ardemagni, Mirko. *Supremazia di Mussolini.* Milan, Italy: Treves, 1936.

Ardragh, John. *The New France.* Harmondsworth, Eng.: Penguin, 1973.

Ardrey, Robert. *African Genesis.* New York: Atheneum, 1963.

_____. *The Territorial Imperative.* New York: Atheneum, 1966.

Arenberg, Gerald S. *Crime Prevention Handbook.* Washington, D.C.: National Association of Chiefs of Police, 1979.

Arendt, Hannah. *Between Past and Future.* New York: Meridian Books, 1963.

_____. *Crisis of the Republic.* Harmondsworth, Eng.: Pelican, 1973.

_____. *Eichmann in Jerusalem: A Report on the Banality of Evil.* New York: Viking Press, 1963.

_____. *On Revolution.* New York: Viking Press, 1963.

_____. *On Violence.* New York: Harcourt Brace & World, 1969.

_____. *The Origins of Totalitarianism*. London: George Allen & Unwin, 1958.

Arens, Richard, and Lasswell, Harold D. *In Defense of Public Order*. New York: Columbia University Press, 1961.

Arensberg, Conrad. *The Irish Countryman: An Anthropological Study*. New York: P. Smith, 1950.

Aretin, Erwein Freiherr von. *Fritz Michael Gerlich: Ein Märtyrer unserer Tage*. Munich: Verlag Schnell & Steiner, 1949.

_____. *Krone und Ketten*. Munich: Süddeutscher Verlag, 1955.

Aretino, Pietro. *Dialogues*. trans. Raymond Rosenthal. New York: Stein & Day, 1971.

Argall, Phyllis. *The Truth About Jesse James*. Sullivan, Mo.: Lester B. Dill & Rudy Turilli, 1953.

Argenton, Mario, and Piasenti, Paride. *L'Italia dal Fascismo alla Costituzione Repubblicana*. Rome: 'Fondazione del Corpo Volontari della Liberta', 1966.

An Argument in the Case of the United States versus Philemon T. Herbert, Tried for the Murder of Thomas Keating. Washington: C. Alexander, 1856.

Argument of Hon. Edward Pierrepont to the Jury on the Trial of John H. Surratt for the Murder of President Lincoln. Washington, D.C.: U.S. Government Printing Office, 1867.

Argyle, M. *Social Interaction*. London: Tavistock, 1969.

Argyll, J.G.E.H.D.S. Campbell, Ninth Duke of. *V.R.I. Queen Victoria*. New York: Harper & Brothers, 1901.

Ariès, Phillipe. *Western Attitudes Toward Death: From the Middle Ages to the Present*. trans. Patricia M. Ranum. Baltimore: Johns Hopkins University Press, 1974.

Arieti, S., and Meth, J.A. *American Handbook of Psychiatry*. New York: Basic Books, 1959.

Ariosto, Lodovico. *The Frenzy of Orlando*. 2 vols. trans. Barbara Reynolds. London: Penquin Books, 1975.

_____. *Satires*. trans. Peter De Sa Wiggins. Athens: Ohio University Press, 1976.

Aristophanes. *The Acharnians*. trans. Benjamin Beickley Rogers. London: William Heinemann, 1950.

Aristotle. *Metaphysics*. trans. Hugh Tredennick. London: William Heinemann, 1936.

_____. *Politics*. trans. Benjamin Jowett. New York: Modern Library, 1943.

Arizona, The Grand Canyon State. New York: Hastings House, 1940.

Arizpe, Miguel Ramos. *Report to the August Congress on National, Political, and Civil Conditions of the Provinces of Coahuila, Neuvo León, Nuevo Santander, and Texas of the Four Eastern Provinces of the Kingdom Of Mexico*. Austin: University of Texas Press, 1950.

Arlacchi, Pino. *Mafia Business: The Mafia Ethic and the Spirit of Capitalism*. London: Verso, 1986.

Arlen, Michael. *Hell! Said the Duchess: A Bed-Time Story*. London: William Heinemann, 1934.

Arlen, Michael J. *Living-room War*. New York: Viking Press, 1969.

Arles y Andosilla, Martin de. *Tractatus de Superstitionibus*. Rome: Vincentium Luchinum, 1559.

Arm, Walter. *Pay-Off*. New York: D. Appleton, 1951.

Armbruster, Eugene L. *Brooklyn's Eastern District*. New York: Brooklyn, 1942.

Armellini, Gen Quirino. *Con Badgolio in Etiopia*. Milan, Italy: Mondadori, 1937.

_____. *Diario di Guerra*. Milan, Italy: Garzanti, 1946.

_____. *La crisi dell'esercito*. Rome: Pricilla, 1945.

Armes, Roy. *A Critical History of the British Cinema*. London: Oxford University Press, 1978.

Armitage, G. *History of the Bow Street Runners*. London: Wishart, 1932.

Armitage, Harold. *Russell and Rye House*. Letchworth, Eng.: Letchworth Printers, 1948.

Armor, D.J. *Measuring the Effects of Television on Aggressive Behavior*. Santa Monica, Calif.: Rand, 1975.

Armor, Samuel (ed.). *History of Orange County, California*. Los Angeles: Historic Record, 1911.

Armour, W.S. *Facing the Irish Question*. London: Gerald Duckworth, 1935.

Arms, Mear. *The Samuel Colt Biography*. New York: Beinfield, 1978.

Armstrong, Donald. *The Reluctant Warrior*. New York: Thomas Y. Crowell, 1966.

Armstrong, F.E. *The Book of the Stock Exchange*. London: Sir Isaac Pitman & Sons, 1934.

Armstrong, Hamilton Fish. *The New Balkans*. New York: Harper & Brothers, 1926.

_____. *Peace and Counter-Peace*. New York: Harper & Row, 1971.

_____. *Tito and Goliath*. New York: Macmillan, 1951.

_____. *Where the East Begins*. New York: Harper & Brothers, 1929.

Armstrong, J.B. *The Raw Edge*. Missoula: Montana State University Press, 1964.

Armstrong, John A. *The Politics of Totalitarianism*. New York: Random House, 1961.

_____. *Ukrainian Nationalism 1939-1945*. New York: Columbia University Press, 1955.

Armstrong, Lebbeus. *The Signs of the Times*. New York: R. Carter, 1848.

_____. *The Temperence Reformation: Its History from the organization of the first temperance society to the adoption of the Liquor Law of Main, 1851: and the consequent influence of the promulgation of that law on the state of New York*. New York: Fowler & Wells, 1883.

Armstrong, Leroy, and Denny, J.O. *Financial California*. San Francisco: Coast Banker, 1916.

Armstrong, Louise. *Kiss Daddy Goodnight*. New York: Hawthorn Books, 1978.

Armstrong, William M. *E.L. Godkin and American Foreign Policy, 1865-1900*. New York: Bookman Associates, 1957.

_____. *The Gilded Age Letters of E.L. Godkin*. Albany: State University of New York, 1974.

Arneson, Ben Albert. *The Democratic Monarchies of Scandinavia*. New York: Van Nostrand, 1939.

Arnett, Alex Mathews. *The Populist Movement in Georgia*. New York: Columbia University Press, 1922.

Arnim, Hans Von. *Prince Louis Ferdinand von Preussen*. Berlin: Haude & Spener, 1966.

Arnold, David O. (ed.). *The Sociology of Subcultures*. Berkeley, Calif.: Glendessary Press, 1970.

Arnold, Oren, and Hale, John P. *Hot Irons: Heraldry of the Range*. New York: Macmillan, 1940.

_____. *Thunder in the Southwest: Echoes from the Wild Frontier*. Norman: University of Oklahoma, 1937.

_____. *Wild Life in the Southwest*. Dallas: Banks Upshaw, 1935.

Arnold, Peter. *How To Protect Your Child Against Crime*. New York: Association Press, 1977.

Arnold, S.G. *Rhode Island*. 2 vols. New York: Taylor, 1860.

Arnold, Samuel Bland. *Defense and Prison Experiences of a Lincoln Conspirator: Statements and Autobiographical Notes*. Hattiesburg, Miss.: Book Farm, 1943.

Arnold, Thurman. *Fair Fights and Foul*. New York: Harcourt Brace & World, 1965.

_____. *The Folklore of Capitalism*. New Haven, Conn.: Yale University Press, 1937.

Arnot, Hugo. *A Collection and Abridgement of Celebrated Criminal Trials in Scotland, 1563-1784*. Edinburgh, Scot.: W. Smellie, 1785.

Arnstein, W.L. *Protestant versus Catholic in Mid-Victorian England*. Colombia: University of Missouri Press, 1982.

Aron, Robert. *The Vichy Regime: 1940-1944*. Boston: Beacon Press, 1969.

Aronfreed, J. *Conduct and Conscience: The Socialization of Internalized Control over Behavior*. New York: Academic

Press, 1968.

Aronson, Harvey. *Deal*. New York: Ballantine Books, 1978.

_____. *The Killing of Joey Gallo*. New York: G.P. Putnam's Sons, 1973.

Arpee, Edward. *Lake Forest Illinois*. Lake Forest, Ill.: Rotary Club of Lake Forest, 1963.

Arribavene, Count Charles. *Italy under Victor Emmanuel*. London: Hurst & Blackett, 1862.

Arrington, A.W. *Desperadoes of the Southwest*. New York: W.H. Graham, 1847.

_____. *The Rangers and Regulators of the Tanaha*. New York: R.M. Dewitt, 1856.

Arrington, Leonard. *Great Basin Kingdome: An Economic History of the Latter-day Saints, 1830-1900*. Cambridge, Mass.: Harvard University Press, 1958.

Arthur, George. *George V*. New York: Cape, 1930.

_____. *Life of Lord Kitchener*. New York: Macmillan, 1920.

Arthur, George Clinton. *Bushwhacker*. Rolla, Mo.: Rolla Printing, 1938.

Arthur, Herbert. *All the Sinners*. London: John Long, 1931.

Arthur, Timothy Shay. *Grappling with the Monster*. New Haven, Conn.: Edgewood, 1877.

_____. *Six Nights With the Washingtonians*. Philadelphia: T.B. Peterson & Brothers, 1871.

Arthur-Lévy. *Les dissentiments de la famille impériale*. Paris: Calmann-Lévy, 1932.

Artieri, Giovanni (ed.). *Le Quattro Giornate*. Naples, Italy: Alberto Marotta, 1963.

_____. *Il tempo della Regina*. Rome: Sestante, 1950.

_____. *Tre ritratti politici e quattro attentati*. Rome: Atlante, 1953.

Artrip, Louise and Fullen. *Memoirs of Daniel Fore (Jim) Chisholm and the Chisholm Trail*. Boonville, Ark.: Published by Authors, 1949.

Arvidson, Lloyd A. (ed.). *Hamlin Garland: Centennial Tributes and a Checklist of the Hamlin Garland Papers in the University of Southern California Library*. Los Angeles: University of Southern California Library, 1962.

Asbury, Herbert. *The Barbary Coast: An Informal History of the San Francisco Underworld*. New York: Garden City, 1933.

_____. *Carry Nation*. New York: Alfred A. Knopf, 1929.

_____. *The French Quarter, An Informal History of the New Orleans Underworld*. New York: Alfred A. Knopf, 1936.

_____. *The Gangs of New York*. New York: Alfred A. Knopf, 1927.

_____. *Gem of the Prairie: An Informal History of the Chicago Underworld*. New York: Alfred A. Knopf, 1940.

_____. *The Great Illusion: An Informal History of Prohibition*. New York: Doubleday, 1950.

_____. *A Methodist Saint: The Life of Bishop Asbury*. New York: Alfred A. Knopf, 1927.

_____. *Sucker's Progress: An Informal History of Gambling in America From the Colonies to Canfield*. New York: Dodd & Mead, 1938.

_____. *Up from Methodism*. New York: Alfred A. Knopf, 1926.

_____. *Ye Olde Fire Laddies*. New York: Alfred A. Knopf, 1930.

Asch, Sidney H. *Criminal Investigation Rights of the Individual*. New York: Arco, 1967.

Aschaffenburg, G. *Crime and Its Repression*. Boston: Little, Brown, 1913.

Ascoli, Max, and Feiler, Arthur. *Fascism for Whom?* New York: W.W. Norton, 1938.

_____, and _____. *Fascism: who benifits?* London: George Allen & Unwin, 1939.

_____ (ed.). *Our Times: The Best from the Reporter*. New York: Farrar, Straus & Cudahy, 1960.

Asell, S., et al. *Histoire d'Algérie*. Paris: Bouvoin, 1927.

Asfa Yilma, Princess. *Haile Selassie*. London: Sampson Low, 1936.

Ashbaugh, Don. *Nevada's Turbulent Yesterday*. Los Angeles:

Westernlore Press, 1963.

Ashby, E., and Anderson, M. *The Rise of the Student Estate in Britain*. London: Macmillan, 1970.

Ashby, Thomas A. *The Valley Campaign*. New York: Neale, 1914.

Ashe, Geoffrey. *Gandhi*. New York: Stein & Day, 1968.

Ashe, Samuel A'Court. *History of North Carolina*. Greensboro, N.C.: E.M. Uzzell, 1908.

Ashe, Thomas. *Travel in America, Performed in the Year 1806, for the Purpose of Exploring the Rivers Alleghany, Monongahela, Ohio and Mississippi*. New York: R. Phillips, 1808.

The Ashland Tragedy...A History of the Killing of Fanny Gibbons. Ashland, Ky.: J.M. Huff, 1883.

Ashley, F.W. *My Sixty Years in the Law*. London: Bodley Head, 1936.

Ashley, Richard. *Cocaine: Its History, Uses and Effects*. New York: St. Martin's Press, 1975.

_____. *Heroin: The Myths and the Facts*. New York: St. Martin's Press, 1972.

Ashley, W.J. *The Railroad Strike of 1894: The Statements of the Pullman Company and the Report of the Commission, Together with an Analysis of the Issues*. Cambridge, Mass.: Church Social Union, 1894.

Ashman, Charles. *The CIA-Mafia Link: The Inside Secrets of Assassination*. New York: Manor Books, 1975.

_____. *The Finest Judges Money Can Buy*. Los Angeles: Nash, 1973.

Ashman, Chuck, and Trescott, Pamela. *Diplomatic Crime*. Washington, D.C.: Acropolis Books, 1987.

Ashmore, Harry S. *Fear in the Air*. New York: W.W. Norton, 1973.

Ashton, John. *The Devil in Britain and America*. London: Ward & Downey, 1896.

Ashton, T.S. *Economic Fluctuations in England, 1700-1800*. Oxford, Eng.: Oxford University Press, 1959.

Ashton, Wendall J. *The Voice of the West: Biography of a Pioneer Newspaper*. New York: Duell, Sloan, & Pearce, 1950.

Ashton-Wolfe, H. *The Cask of Death*. New York: E.P. Dutton, 1932.

_____. *Crimes of Love and Hate*. Boston: Houghton Mifflin, 1927.

_____. *Crimes of Violence and Revenge*. New York: E.P. Dutton, 1932.

_____. *The Forgotten Clue*. Boston: Houghton Mifflin, 1930.

_____. *Outlaws of Modern Days*. London: Cassell, 1927.

_____. *The Underworld*. New York: George H. Doran, 1926.

Ashurst, Henry Fountain. *The Diary of Henry Fountain Ashurst*. Tucson: University of Arizona, n.d.

_____. *A Many-Colored Toga*. Tucson: University of Arizona Press, 1962.

Asinof, Eliot. *Eight Men Out: The Black Sox Scandal*. New York: Holt, Rinehart & Winston, 1963.

Askew, Garrett L. *The Pageant of the Packets*. New York: D. Appleton, 1929.

Askins, Charles. *Texans: Guns and History*. New York: Winchester Press, 1970.

Askwith, T.G. *Kenya's Progress*. Nairobi, Kenya: East African Literature Bureau/Eagle Press, 1958.

Asmodeus in New York. New York: Longchamp, 1868.

Aspinal, A. *Politics and the Press, 1780-1850*. London: Home & Van Thal, 1849.

Asprey, Robert. *War in the Shadows*. New York: Doubleday, 1975.

Asquith, Earl of Oxford and. *Memories and Reflections*. 2 vols. London: Cassell, 1928.

The Assassination and History of the Conspiracy. New York: J.R. Hawley, 1865.

The Assassination Story: Newspaper Clippings from the Two Dallas Dailes. Dallas: American Eagle, 1964.

Assassination U.S.A. New York: Herald House, 1968.

The Assassin's Doom, Full Account of the Jail Life, Trial and Sentence of Charles J. Guiteau. New York: Richard K. Fox, 1882.

Assersohn, Roy. *The Biggest Deal: Bankers, Politics, and the Hostages of Iran.* London: Methuen, 1982.

Assier, Alexandre. *Le diable en Champagne.* Paris: Dumoulin, 1869.

Associated Press (ed.). *The Torch Is Passed.* New York: Associated Press, 1963.

Associated Press Managing Editors Red Book, 1972. New York: Associated Press, 1972.

Associated Press Managing Editors Red Book, 1973. New York: Associated Press, 1973.

Associated Professional Services (ed.) *The Complete Kennedy Saga.* Los Angeles: Associated Professional Services, 1964.

_____. *Four Dark Days in History.* Los Angeles: Special Publications, 1963.

_____. *Highlights of the Warren Report.* Hollywood, Calif.: Associated Professional Services, 1964.

_____. *In Memoriam . . . 365 Days Later.* Los Angeles: Matador Magazine, 1964.

_____. *A Salute to Jacqueline Kennedy.* Los Angeles: James P. Matthews, 1964.

_____. *Who Killed Kennedy?* Covina, Calif: Collectors, 1964.

Aston, Sir George. *Biography of the Late Marshal Foch.* London: Hutchinson, 1930.

Astor, Gerald. *The Charge is Rape.* New York: Playboy Press, 1974.

_____. *The New York Cops.* New York: Charles Scribner's Sons, 1971.

Athearn, Robert G. *High Country Empire.* New York: McGraw-Hill, 1953.

_____. *Rebel of the Rockies.* New Haven, Conn.: Yale University, 1962.

_____. *Westward the Briton.* New York: Charles Scribner's Sons, 1953.

_____. *William Tecumseh Sherman and the Settlement of the West.* Norman: University of Oklahoma Press, 1956.

Atherton, Gertrude. *California, an Intimate History.* New York: Harper & Brothers, 1914.

_____. *My San Francisco.* Indianapolis, Ind.: Bobbs-Merrill, 1946.

Atherton, Lewis. *The Cattle Kings.* Bloomington: Indiana University Press, 1961.

Atholl, Justin. *The Reluctant Hangman: The Story of James Berry, Executioner 1884-1892.* London: John Long, 1956.

_____. *Shadow of the Gallows.* London: John Long, 1954.

Atiyah, Edward. *The Arabs.* London: Penguin Books, 1955.

_____. *The Thin Line.* New York: Harpers, 1952.

Atkin, Ronald. *Revolution! Mexico 1910-20.* New York: John Day, 1970.

Atkins, Burton M., and Glick, Henry R. *Prisons, Protest and Politics.* Englewood Cliffs, N.J.: Prentice-Hall, 1972.

Atkins, Gordon. *Health, Housing, and Poverty in New York City, 1865-1898.* Ann Arbor, Mich.: Edwards Brothers, 1947.

Atkinson, A.B. *The Economics of Inequality.* New York: Oxford University Press, 1983.

Atkinson, Charles Milner. *Jeremy Bentham: His Life and Work.* London: Methuen, 1905.

Atkinson, Eleanor. *Story of Chicago.* Chicago: Little Chronicle, 1911.

Atkinson, S.W. *Adventures of Oklahoma Bill.* n.p., 1906.

Atkinson, T.W. *Oriental and Western Siberia.* New York: Harpers, 1858.

Atlay, James Beresford. *Famous Trials of the Century.* London: G. Richards, 1899.

The Attempted Assassination of President Garfield: A Full Graphic and Only Complete Account, with the Life of Our President, and the Life of Guiteau, the Assassin. Philadelphia: Barclay, 1881.

Attending the Mysterious Disappearance of Samuel Field. Providence, R.I.: H.H. Brown, 1830.

Attica Commission. *Attica: The Official Report of the New York State Special Commission on Attica.* New York: Bantam Books, 1973.

Attiwill, Kenneth. *The Singapore Story.* London: Frederick Muller, 1959.

Attlee, Clement R. *As It Happened.* New York: Viking Press, 1954.

_____. *The Labor Party in Perspective and Twelve Years Later.* London: Victor Gollancz, 1949.

_____. *Labor's Aims in War and Peace.* New York: Rand School, 1941.

_____, and Williams, Francis. *Twilight of Empire: Memoirs of Prime Minister Clement R. Attlee.* New York: Barnes, 1962.

Attorney General's Task Force on Organized Crime. *Phase I, Phase II Recommendations.* Washington, D.C.: U.S. Department of Justice, 1981.

Attwood, William. *The Reds and the Blacks: A Personal Adventure.* New York: Harper & Row, 1967.

Atwell, Benjamin H. *The Great Harry Thaw Case.* Chicago: Laird & Lee, 1907.

Aubin, Nicholas. *The Cheats and Illusions of Romish Priests and Exorcists Discovered in the History of the Devils of London.* Trans. Daniel Defoe. London: W. Turner, 1703.

_____. *Cruels effects de la vengeance du Cardinal de Richelieu ou histoire des diables de Loudun.* Amsterdam: E. Roger, 1716.

Aubrey, Arthur S. Jr., and Caputo, Rudolph R. *Criminal Interrogation.* Springfield, Ill.: Charles C. Thomas, 1965.

Aubrey, Octave. *Sainte-Hélène.* Paris: Flammarion, 1835.

Auchampaugh, Philip Gerald. *James Buchanan and His Cabinet on the Eve of Secession.* Boston: J.S. Canner, 1956.

Audett, James Henry ("Blackie"). *Rap Sheet: My Life Story.* New York: William Sloane, 1954.

Audubon, John James. *Delineation of American Scenery and Character.* New York: G.A. Bakerer, 1926.

Auerbach, Jerold S. *Labor and Liberty: The LaFollette Committee and the New Deal.* Indianapolis, Ind.: Bobbs-Merrill, 1966.

_____. *Unequal Justice: Lawyers and Social Change in Modern America.* New York: Oxford University Press, 1976.

Augenti, F.P., et al. *Il dramma di Graziani.* Bologna, Italy: Cesare Zuffi, 1950.

Auger, Helen. *Passage to Glory: John Ledyard's America.* Garden City, N.Y.: Doubleday, 1946.

Augustin-Thierry, A. *Madame Mére.* Paris: Albin Michel, 1939.

Auletta, Ken. *The Underclass.* New York: Random House, 1982.

Ault, Phillip H. (ed.). *The Home Book of Western Humor.* New York: Dodd, Mead, 1967.

Ault, W.O. *Open-Field Farming in Medieval New England: A Study of Village By-Laws.* New York: Barnes & Noble, 1972.

Austin, John. *Hollywood's Unsolved Mysteries.* New York: Ace Star, 1970.

Ausubel, David P. *Drug Addiction.* New York: Random House, 1958.

_____. *What Every Well-Informed Person Should Know About Drug Addiction.* Chicago: Nelson-Hall, 1978.

Ausubel, Herman. *John Bright, Victorian Reformer.* New York: John Wiley & Sons, 1966.

Ausubel, Nathan. *Superman: The Life of Frederick the Great.* New York: Ives Washburn, 1931.

An Authentic and Particular Account of the Life of Francis Burdett Personal. New York: n.p., 1773.

The Authentic Confession of Jesse Strang. New York: E.M. Murden & A. Ming, Jr., 1827.

Authentic History of Sam Bass and His Gang. Denton, Texas: Monitor Job Office, 1878.

The Authentic Life of John C. Colt. Boston: S.N. Dickinson, 1842.

The Authentic Life of Mrs. Mary Ann Bickford, Who was Murdered in the City of Boston. Boston: Published by author, 1846.

Authentic Narrative of the Murder of Mrs. Rademacher. Philadelphia: G.B. Zieber, 1848.

An Authentic Report of the Trial of Myers and Others, for the Murder of Dudley Marvin Hoyt. New York: Richards, 1846.

An Autobiography of Gerald Toole. Hartford, Conn.: Lockwood & Co., 1862.

Automne, Bernard. *La conférence du droit français avec le droit roman.* Paris: Robert Foüet, 1615.

Autun, Jacques d'. *L'incrédulité savante et la crédulité ignorante au sujet des magiciens et des soriciers.* Lyons: Jean Molin, 1671.

Auzies, Célestin. *De la surveilance de la haunte police.* Paris: E. Thorin, 1869.

Avalon, A. *Tantra of the Great Liberation.* New York: Dover, 1972.

Avary, M.L. (ed.). *A Virginia Girl in the Civil War.* New York: D. Appleton, 1903.

Aveling, Edward and Eleanor. *The Working Class Movement in America.* London: Swann Sonnenschein, 1891.

Averbuch, Bernard, and Noble, John Wesley. *Never Plead Guilty.* New York: Straus & Cudahy, 1955.

Averso, Nino. *Napoli sotto il terrore tedesco.* Naples, Italy: 'Le Quattro Giornate', 1943.

Avetta, Ida. *Mussolini e la folla.* Mantua, Italy: Paladino, 1927.

Avey, Elijah. *The Capture and Exeuction of John Brown, a Tale of Martyrdom.* Chicago: Hyde Park Bindery, 1906.

Avinov, Marie. *Marie Avinov: Pilgrimage Through Hell.* Englewood Cliffs, N.J.: Prentice-Hall, 1968.

Avner. *Memoirs of an Assassin.* New York: Yoseloff, 1959.

Avrich, Paul. *Kronstadt: 1921.* Princeton, N.J.: Princeton University Press, 1970.

_____. *The Russian Anarchists.* Princeton, N.J.: Princeton University Press, 1967.

An Awful Warning to the Intemperate: Trial, Conviction, Sentence, and Only True Copy of the Confession of Catherine Cashiere to the Murder of Susan Anthony. New York: C. Brown, 1829.

An Awful Warning to the Youth of America. Report of the Trial of Octavius Baron. Rochester, N.Y.: Shepard, Strong & Dawson, 1838.

Axelson, G.W. *Commy.* Chicago: Reilly & Lee, 1919.

Axenfeld, Alexandre. *Jean Wier et la sorcellerie.* Paris: Germer Bailliére, 1866.

Axford, Joseph Mack. *Around Western Campfires.* New York: Pageant Press, 1964.

Aydelotte, Frank. *Elizabethan Rogues and Vagabonds.* Oxford, Eng.: Clarendon Press, 1913.

Ayer, Frederick Jr. *Yankee G-Man.* Chicago: Henry Regnery, 1957.

Ayer, I. Winslow. *The Great North-Western Conspiracy in All Its Startling Details.* Chicago: Baldwin & Bamford, 1865.

Ayer, Mary Fannell. *Early Days on Boston Common.* Boston: Privately Printed, 1910.

Ayers, Bradley Earl. *The War That Never Was.* New York: Bobbs-Merrill, 1976.

Ayers, Col. James J. *Gold and Sunshine.* Boston: Richard G. Badger, 1922.

Ayers, John H., and Bird, Carol. *Missing Men, The Story of The Missing Persons Bureau of the New York Police Department.* New York: G.P. Putnam's Sons, 1932.

Ayers, Nathaniel M. *Building a New Empire.* New York: Broadway, 1910.

Ayerst, D. *The Guardian.* London: Collins, 1971.

Ayres, Anne. *The Life and Work of William Augustus Muhlenberg, Doctor in Divinity.* New York: Thomas Whitaker, 1889.

Ayrinhac, H.A. *Marriage Legislation in the New Code of Canon Law.* New York: Benzigner Brothers, 1919.

Ayscough, Florence. *Chinese Women Yesterday and Today.* Boston: Houghton Mifflin, 1937.

B

Baader Meinhof Report, Der. Mainz, Ger.: Hase & Köhler Verlag, 1972.

Baarlag, Karl. *Island of Adventure.* New York: Farrar & Rinehart, 1940.

Babbie, Earl R. *The Practice of Social Research.* Belmont, Calif.: Wadsworth, 1975.

Baber, Daisy F., as told by Bill Walker. *Injun Summer.* Caldwell, Ohio: Caxton Press, 1952.

_____. *The Longest Rope: The Truth About the Johnson County Cattle War.* Caldwell, Idaho: Caxton Printers, 1940.

Babington, Anthony. *The English Bastille: A History of Newgate Gaol and Prison Conditions in Britain, 1188-1902.* London: Macdonals, 1971.

_____. *A House in Bow Street: Crime and the Magistracy in London, 1740-1881.* London: McDonald, 1969.

Babst, Dean V., and Gale, Joseph C. *Wisconsin County Jails, 1958-1960.* Madison: Wisconsin Division of Corrections, 1962.

Bac, Ferdinand. *Promenades dans l'Italie Nouvelle.* Paris: Hachette, 1933.

Baca, Carlos Cabeza de. *Vicente Silva, New Mexico's Vice King of the Nineties.* n.p., 1938.

Baca, Fabiola Cabeza de. *We Fed Them Cactus.* Albuquerque: University of New Mexico Press, 1954.

Bacchelli, Riccardo. *La Congiura di Don Giulio d'Este.* Rome: Arnoldo Mondadori, 1966.

Bach, Adolf. *Hexenprozesse in der Vogtei Ems.* Bad Ems, Ger.: G. Heil, 1923.

Bach, George R. *The Intimate Enemy.* New York: Avon, 1968.

Bachman, J.G. *Adolescence to Adulthood--Change and Stability in the Lives of Young Men.* Ann Arbor: University of Michigan Institute for Social Research, 1978.

_____, et al. *Dropping Out-Problem or Sympton?* Ann Arbor: University of Michigan Institute for Social Research, 1971.

Bacon, Alexander S. *The Enemies of Woodrow Wilson.* New York: n.p., 1912.

Bacon, Charles Reade. *The People Awakened.* Garden City, N.Y.: Doubleday, Page, 1912.

Bacon, G.W. *Life of Andrew Johnson.* London: Bacon, n.d.

Bacon, James. *Hollywood Is a Four-Letter Town.* New York: Avon Books, 1977.

Bacon, Sir Reginald. *Life of Lord Fisher.* London: Hodder & Stoughton, 1929.

Baddeley, A. *The Psychology of Memory.* New York: Harper, 1976.

Baddeley, John H. *Russia, Mongolia, China.* Two vols. London: Macmillan, 1919.

Bade, William Frederick. *Life and Letters of John Muir.* Boston: Houghton Mifflin, 1924.

Badel, Emile. *D'une sorcière qu'aultrefois on brusla dans Sainct-Nicholas.* Nancy, Fr.: Berger-Levrault, 1891.

Baden, Prince Max von. *Erinnerungen.* Stuttgart, Ger.: Deutsche Verlags-Anstalt, 1927.

Badian, Ernest. *Foreign Clientele, 264-70 B.C.* Oxford, Eng.: Clarendon Press, 1968.

Badillo, Herman, and Haynes, Milton. *A Bill of No Rights: Attica and the American Prison System.* New York: Outerbridge & Lazard, 1972.

Badoglio, Marshal Pietro. *Italy in the Second World War.* trans. Muriel Currey. London: Oxford University Press, 1948.

_____. *The War in Abyssinia.* London: Methuen, 1937.

Baedeker, Karl. *United States: With an Excursion Into Mexico.* New York: Da Capo Press, 1971.

Baehr, Harry W., Jr. *The New York Tribune Since the Civil War.* New York: Dodd, Mead, 1936.

Baerlein, Henry. *The Birth of Yugoslavia.* London: Parsons, 1922.

_____. *Mexico, the Land of Unrest: Being Chiefly an Account of What Produced the Outbreak of 1910.* London: Herbert & Daniel, 1913.

Baetzmann, Frederick. *Hexavaesen og Troldskab i Norge.* Oslo, Nor.: B.M. Bentzen, 1865.

Bagby, G.W. *John Brown and William Mahone.* Richmond, Va.: C.F. Johnston, 1880.

Bagdikian, Ben H. *The Shame of the Prisons.* New York: Pocket Books, 1972.

Bagdikian, Helen. *The Information Machines.* New York: Harper & Row, 1971.

Bagehot, Walter. *The English Constitution.* Boston: Little, Brown, 1873.

Bagehot, Walter. *Lombard Street: A Description of the Money Market.* London: John Murray, 1917.

Bagger, Eugene S. *Eminent Europeans.* New York: G.P. Putnam's Sons, 1922.

Baghdadi, Abdul Latif al-. *The Eastern Key.* London: Allen & Unwin, 1965.

Baier, Kurt. *The Moral Point of View: A Rational Basis of Ethics.* New York: Random House, 1965.

Bailey, Derrick Sherwin. *Common Sense About Sexual Ethics: A Christian View.* London: Victor Gollancz, 1962.

_____. *The Man-Woman Relation in Christian Thought.* London: Longmans, 1959.

_____. *Sexual Relation in Christian Thought.* New York: Harper & Brothers, 1959.

_____. *British Policy and the Turkish Reform Movement: A Study in Anglo-Turkish Relations 1826-1853.* Cambridge, Mass.: Harvard University Press, 1942.

Bailey, F. Lee, and Rothblatt, Henry B. *Crimes of Violence, Rape and Other Sex Crimes.* Rochester, N.Y.: Lawyers Co-Operative, 1973.

_____. *Defending Business and White Collar Crimes: Federal and State.* Rochester, N.Y.: Lawyer's Co-operative, 1969.

_____. *The Defense Never Rests.* New York: Signet Books, 1972.

_____, and Greenya, John. *For the Defense.* New York: Atheneum, 1975.

Bailey, Guy. *The Fatal Chance.* London: Peter Davies, 1969.

Bailey, Harry H. *When New Mexico Was Young.* Las Cruces, N.M.: Las Cruces Citizen, 1948.

Bailey, Kenneth. *Methods of Social Research.* New York: Free Press, 1978.

Bailey, Kenneth P. *The Ohio Company of Virginia and the Westward Movement, 1748-1792.* Glendale, Calif.: Arthur H. Clark, 1939.

Bailey, Robert G. *River of No Return. (The Great Salmon River of Idaho).* Lewiston, Idaho: Bailey-Blake, 1935.

Bailey, Ronald H. *Violence and Aggression.* New York: Time-Life Books, 1976.

Bailey, Sarah Loring. *Historical Sketches of Andover.* Boston: Houghton, Mifflin, 1880.

Bailey, Thomas A. *America Faces Russia.* Ithaca, N.Y.: Cornell University Press, 1950.

_____. *The American Pageant.* Boston: D.C. Heath, 1956.

_____. *A Diplomatic History of the American People.* New York: Crofts, 1944.

_____. *The Man in the Street: The Impact of American Public Opinion on Foreign Police.* New York: Macmillan, 1948.

_____. *Presidential Greatness.* New York: Appleton-Century, 1966.

_____. *Wilson and the Peacemakers.* New York: Macmillan, 1944.

_____. *Woodrow Wilson and the Great Betrayal.* New York: Macmillan, 1945.

Baillie, Hugh. *High Tension.* New York: Harper & Brothers, 1959.

Bailyn, Bernard. *The Ideological Origins of the American Revolution.* Cambridge, Mass.: Harvard University Press, 1967.

_____. *The New England Merchants in the Seventeenth Century.* Cambridge, Mass.: Harvard University Press, 1979.

_____, and Bailyn, Lotte. *Massachusetts Shipping, 1697-1714.* Cambridge, Mass.: Harvard University Press, 1959.

_____ (ed.). *Pamphlets of the American Revolution, 1750-1776.* Cambridge, Mass.: Belknap Press of Harvard University Press, 1965.

Bain, Donald. *War in Illinois.* Englewood Cliffs, N.J.: Prentice-Hall, 1978.

Bain, R.N. *The Daughter of Peter the Great.* London: Constable, 1899.

_____. *Peter III, Emperor of Russia.* London: Constable, 1902.

Bainbridge, Henry Charles. *Peter Car Fabergé: An Illustrated Record and Review of His Life and Work.* London: Batsford, 1949.

Bainder, Herman. *Maryland's Reaction to Andrew Johnson.* College Park: University of Maryland Press, 1949.

Bainton, Roland H. (ed.). *Castellioniana.* Leiden: E. J. Brill, 1951.

_____. *Hunted Heretic: The Life and Death of Michael Servetus.* Boston: Beacon, 1953.

Bair, Everett. *This Will be an Empire.* New York: Pageant Press, 1959.

Baird, Josie. *Tom Bond, Bronc-Buster, and Trail Driver.* Sweetwater, Texas: Watson-Focht, 1960.

Baird, Rev. Robert. *A View of the Valley of the Mississippi.* Philadelphia: H.S. Tanner, 1834.

Baissac, Jules. *Le Diable.* Paris: M. Dreyfus, 1882.

_____. *Les grands jours de la sorcellerie.* Paris: Klincksieck, 1890.

_____. *Historie de la diablerie chrétienne.* Paris: M. Dreyfus, 1882.

_____. *Satan ou le diable.* Paris: Maisonneuve, 1876.

Bakal, Carl. *The Right to Bear Arms.* New York: McGraw-Hill, 1966.

Bakal, Yitzhak (ed.). *Closing Correctional Institutions: New Strategies for Youth Services.* Lexington, Mass.: D.C. Heath, 1973.

Bakan, David. *The Slaughter of the Innocents.* San Francisco: Jossey-Bass, 1975.

Bakarich, Sarah Grace. *Empty Saddles: A New Version of the Earp-Clanton Fight.* n.p., 1946.

_____. *Gunsmoke.* n.p., 1947.

_____, and Bennett, Kathelen M. *There's Treasure in Our Hills.* n.p., 1947.

Bakeless, John. *Lewis and Clark: Partners in Discovery.* New York: William Morrow, 1947.

Baker, Bobby. *Wheeling and Dealing.* New York: Norton, 1978.

Baker, Dean C. *The Assassination of President Kennedy: A Study of the Press Coverage.* Ann Arbor: University of Michigan Press, 1965.

Baker, George Melville. *Mysterious Disappearances.* Boston: Published by Author, 1876.

Baker, J.E. *The Right to Participate: Inmate Involvement in Prison Administration.* Metuchen, N.J.: Scarecrow Press, 1974.

Baker, Joseph E. (ed.). *Past and Present of Alameda County, California.* Chicago: S.J. Clarke, 1914.

Baker, Gen. Lafayette C. *History of the United States Secret Service.* Philadelphia: John E. Potter, 1889.

_____. *Spies, Traitors and Conspirators of the Late Civil War.* Philadelphia: John E. Porter, 1894.

Baker, Leonard. *Back to Back: The Duel Between FDR and the Supreme Court.* New York: Macmillan, 1967.

_____. *The Johnson Eclipse.* New York: Macmillan, 1966.

Baker, Marilyn. *Exclusive.* New York: Macmillan, 1974.

Baker, Mark. *Cops.* New York: Simon and Schuster, 1985.

Baker, Nancy C. *Baby Selling.* New York: Vanguard, 1978.

Baker, Pearl. *The Wild Bunch at Robbers Roost.* New York: Abelard-Schuman, 1971.

Baker, Peter. *Time Out of Life.* London: Heinemann, 1961.

Baker, R.K., and Ball, S.J. *Mass Media and Violence.* Washington, D.C.: Government Printing Office, 1969.

Baker, Ray S. *Following the Color Line.* New York: Doubleday, Page, 1908.

Baker, Ray Stannard. *American Chronicle. The Autobiography of Ray Stannard Baker (David Grayson).* New York: Charles Scribner's Sons, 1945.

_____. *The Capture, Death and Burial of J. Wilkes Booth.* Chicago: The Poor Richard Press, 1940.

_____. *Woodrow Wilson, Life and Letters.* London: Heinemann, 1932.

Baker, Richard Terrill. *Darkness of the Sun.* New York: Abingdon-Cokesbury, 1947.

Bakir, Abd El-Mohsen. *Slavery in Pharaonic Egypt.* Cairo, Egypt: Imprimerie de l'institut Français d'archéologie Orientale, 1952.

Bakken, H.H. *Cooperation to the Finnish?* Madison, Wis.: Mimir, 1939.

Bakos, Susan Crain. *Appointment for Murder: The Story of the Killing Dentist.* New York: G.P. Putnam's Sons, 1988.

Bakunin, Michael A. *The Political Philosophy of Bakunin: Scientific Anarchism.* Glencoe, Ill.: Free Press, 1953.

Balabanoff, Angelica. *My Life as a Rebel.* London: H. Hamilton, 1938.

Balandier, Georges. *Sociologie Actuelle de l'Afrique Noire.* Paris: Presses Universitaires de France, 1955.

Balbo, Italo. *La centuria alata.* Milan, Italy: Mondadori, 1934.

_____. *Diario 1922.* Milan, Italy: Mondadori, 1932.

_____. *Stormi in volo sull'Oceano.* Milan, Italy: Mondadori, 1931.

Balchin, Nigel. *The Anatomy of Villainy.* London: St. James's Place, 1950.

_____. *Fatal Fascination.* Boston: Little, Brown, 1964.

Balcon, Michael. *Michael Balcon Presents...A Lifetime of Films.* London: Hutchinson, 1969.

Baldick, Robert. *The Duel.* London: Chapman & Hail, 1965.

Baldwin, Charles C. *Stanford White.* New York: Dodd, Mead, 1938.

Baldwin, Rev. George C. *Awful Disclosures: The Life and Confessions of Andreas Hall.* Troy, N.Y.: J.C. Kneeland, 1849.

Baldwin, Gordon. *The Warrior Apaches.* Tucson, Ariz.: Dale S. King, 1966.

Baldwin, H.W., and Stone, Shepard. *We Saw It Happen.* New York: Simon & Schuster, 1938.

Baldwin, J., and Bottoms, A.E. *The Urban Criminal.* London: Tavistock, 1976.

Baldwin, James. *The Fire Next Time.* New York: Dial Press, 1963.

Baldwin, Joseph G. *The Flush Times of Alabama and Mississippi.* San Francisco: Sumer Whitney, 1883.

Baldwin, Leland D. *Keelboat Age on Western Waters.* Pittsburgh, Pa.: University of Pittsburgh Press, 1941.

_____. *Whiskey Rebels: The Story of a Frontier Uprising.* Pittsburgh, Pa.: University of Pittsburgh Press, 1939.

Baldwin, W.W. *Mau Mau Manhunt: The Adventures of the Only American Who Fought the Terrorists in Kenya.* New York: E.P. Dutton, 1957.

Bales, William Alan. *A Tiger in the Streets.* New York: Dodd, Mead, 1962.

Balfour, Arthur J. *Speeches on Zionism.* London: Arrowsmith, 1928.

Balfour, J.S. *My Prison Life.* London: Chapman & Hall, 1907.

Balfour, Michael. *The Kaiser and His Times.* Boston: Houghton Mifflin, 1964.

Balfour, Neil, and Mackay, Sally. *Paul of Yugoslavia.* London: Hamish Hamilton, 1980.

Balfour, Patrick. *Society Racket: A Critical Survey of Modern Social Life.* London: John Long, 1933.

The Balham Mystery: A Complete Record of the "Bravo" Poisoning Case. London: The Daily Telegraph, 1876.

Balicki, Asen. *The Netsilik Eskimo.* Garden City, N.Y.: Natural History Press, 1970.

Balkan, S., Berger, R.J., and Schmidt, J. *Crime and Deviance in America.* Belmont, Calif: Wadsworth, 1980.

Ball, Eve. *Ma'am Jones of the Pecos.* Tucson: University of Arizona Press, 1968.

_____. *Ruidoso, The Last Frontier.* San Antonio, Texas: Naylor, 1963.

Ball, John C., and Chambers, Carl D. (eds.). *The Epidemiology of Opiate Addiction in the United States.* Springfield, Ill.: Charles C. Thomas, 1970.

_____. *Social Deviancy and Adolescent Personality: An Analytic Study with the MMPI.* Lexington: University of Kentucky Press, 1962.

Ball, Larry D. *The United States Marshals of New Mexico and Arizona Territories, 1846-1912.* Albuquerque: University of New Mexico Press, 1978.

Ballagh. *History of Slavery in Virginia.* New York: Johnson Reprints, 1968.

Ballard, Everett Guy. *Captain George Wellington Streeter.* Chicago: Emery, 1914.

Ballenger, T.H. *Around Tahlequah Council Fires.* Muskogee, Okla.: Motter Bookbinding, 1935.

Ballentine, James A. *Ballentine's Law Dictionary.* Rochester, N.Y.: Lawyer's, 1930.

Ballantine, William. *Some Experiences of a Barrister's Life.* London: Richard Bentley and Sons, 1822.

Ballert, Marion. *Billy the Kid: A Date with Destiny.* Seattle, Wash.: Superior, 1970.

_____. *Complete & Authentic Life of Jesse James.* New York: Frederick Fell, 1953.

_____. *Younger Brothers.* San Antonio, Texas: Naylor, 1961.

Ballinari, Libero. *Carciere Fuorilegge.* Milano, Italy: Sugarco Edizioni, n.d.

Ballinger, Kenneth. *Miami Millions.* New York: Hastings House, 1936.

Ballou, Jenny. *Period Piece: Ella Wheeler Wilcox and Her Times.* Boston: Houghton Mifflin, 1940.

Ballow, Robert O. *Early Klickitat Valley Days.* Goldendale, Wash.: Goldendale Sentinel, 1938.

_____. *Shinto: The Unconquered Enemy.* New York: Viking Press, 1945.

Balsan, Consuelo Vanderbilt. *The Glitter and the Gold.* New York: Harper & Brothers, 1952.

Balsdon, J.P.V.D. *The Emperor Gaius.* New York: Oxford University Press, 1934.

_____ (ed.). *The Romans.* New York: Basic Books, 1965.

Balsinger, David, and Sellier, Charles E., Jr. *The Lincoln Conspiracy.* Los Angeles: Schick Sunn Classic Books, 1977.

Baltzell, Digby E. *Philadelphia Gentlemen: The Making of a National Upper Class.* Glencoe, Ill.: Free Press, 1973.

_____. *The Protestant Establishment: Aristocracy and Caste in America.* New York: Vintage, 1964.

Balzac, Honore de. *Letters to Madame Hanska.* Boston: Little, Brown, 1900.

_____. *The Physiology of Marriage.* New York: Liverlight, 1932.

Bamm, Peter. *Alexander the Great: Power as Destiny.* New York: McGraw-Hill, 1968.

Banay, Ralph S. *We Call Them Criminals.* New York: Appleton-Century-Crofts, 1957.

Banchelli, Umberto. *Le memorie di un fascista.* Florence, Italy: Sassaiola Fiorentina, 1922.

Bancroft, Edgar A. *Chicago Strike of 1894.* Chicago: Gunthrop-Warren, 1895.

Bancroft, Frederic. *Slave-Trading in the Old South.* Baltimore: T.H. Furst, 1931.

_____ (ed.). *Speeches, Correspondence and Political Papers of Carl Schurz.* New York: G.P. Putnam's Sons, 1913.

Bancroft, George Pleydell. *Stage and Bar.* London: Hutchinson, 1936.

Bancroft, Hubert Howe. *California Inter Pocula.* San Francisco: The History Company, 1888.

———. *History of Arizona and New Mexico.* San Francisco: Bancroft, 1889.

———. *History of California.* 7 vols. San Francisco: San Francisco History, 1884-1890.

———. *History of Nevada, Colorado, and Wyoming, 1540-1888.* San Francisco: The History Company, 1889.

———. *History of the North Mexican States and Texas.* San Francisco: History, 1889.

———. *History of the Pacific States.* 39 vols. San Francisco: Bancroft-Whitney, 1883-92.

———. *History of Washington, Idaho and Montana.* San Francisco: History, 1887.

———. *Outlaws.* San Francisco: Historical, 1887.

———. *Popular Tribunals.* San Francisco: History, 1887.

———. *Works.* San Francisco: History, 1887.

Bandini, Franco. *Claretta.* Milan, Italy: Sugar, 1960.

———. *Tecnica della sconfitta.* Milan, Italy: Sugar, 1963.

———. *Le ultime 95 ore di Mussolini.* Milan, Italy: Sugar, 1959.

Bandura, A., and Walters, R.H. *Adolescent Aggression.* New York: Ronald Press, 1959.

———. *Aggression: A Social Learning Approach.* Engleood Cliffs, N.J.: Prentice-Hall, 1973.

———. *Social Learning Theory.* New York: General Learning Press, 1977.

Bane, Bernard M. *The Bane in Kennedy's Existence.* Boston: BMB, 1967.

———. *Is John F. Kennedy Alive...And Well?* Boston: BMB, 1973.

Banfield, Edward C. *Big City Politics: A Comparative Guide to the Political Systems of Nine American Cities.* New York: Random House, 1965.

———. *The Moral Basis of a Backward Society.* Glencoe, Ill.: The Free Press, 1958.

———. *Political Influence.* New York: The Free Press, 1961.

———. *The Unheavenly City.* Boston: Little, Brown, 1970.

Bang, Vilhelm. *Hexevaesen og Hexelforfelgelser isaer i Danmark.* Copenhagen, Den.: J. Frimodt, 1896.

Bankes, W.J. (ed.). *The Life of Giovanni Finati.* Vols. 1 and 2. London: John Murray, 1830.

Bankhead, Tallulah. *Tallulah: My Autobiography.* London: Victor Gollancz, 1952.

Bankoff, George Alexis. *Rasputin Speaks.* London: Faber & Faber, 1941.

Banks, J.A. *Prosperity and Parenthood.* London: Routledge & Kegan Paul, 1954.

Banks, Joseph. *The Endeavor Journal of Joseph Banks.* Sydney, Aus.: Trustees of the Public Library of New South Wales in association with Angus Robertson, 1962.

Banks, Reverend Louis Albert. *The Lincoln Legion: The Story of its Founder and Forerunners.* New York: Mershon, 1903.

Banks, Olive and J.A. *Feminism and Family Planning.* New York: Schocken, 1972.

Bankson, Russell A. *The Klondike Nugget.* Caldwell, Idaho: Caxton Printers, 1935.

Banning, Captain William, and George Hugh. *Six Horses.* New York: Century, 1930.

Bannorris, Amanda. *The Female Land Pirate.* Cincinnati, Ohio: E.E. Barclay, 1848.

Banta, R.E. *The Ohio.* New York: Rinehart, 1949.

Banton, Michael. *Policeman in the Community.* New York: Basic Books, 1964.

Baragwanath, John. *A Good Time Was Had.* New York: Appleton-Century-Crofts, 1962.

Baral, Robert. *Revue: A Nostalgic Reprise of the Great Broadway Period.* New York: Fleet, 1962.

Baran, Paul A., and Sweezy, Paul M. *Monopoly Capital: An Essay on the American Economic and Social Order.* New York: Monthly Review Press, 1966.

Barante, Amable G.P.B., Baron de. *Jeanne d'Arc.* Paris: Payot, 1935.

Baraoche, Céleste. *Second Empire, notes et souvenirs de seize années, 1855-1871.* Paris: G. Crés, 1921.

Baravelli, G.C. *Land Reclamation Schemes in Italy.* Rome: Novissima, 1935.

Barbagallo, Corrado. *Lettere a John.* Naples, Italy: Fiorentino, 1946.

———. *Napoli contro il terrore Nazista.* Naples, Italy: Moranok 1944.

Barbagallo, Salvo. *Randazzo, 17 Giugno 1945: Anatomia di una strage.* Catania, Italy: Nuovo Mondo, 1976.

Barba González, Silvano. *La lucha por la tierra. Emiliano Zapata.* Mexico City: n.p., 1960.

Barbash, Jack. *The Practice of Unionism.* New York: Harper & Row, 1956.

Barbé-Marbois, Francois, Marquis de. *Our Revolutionary Forefathers.* New York: Duffield, 1929.

Barber, Elinor G. *The Bourgeoisie in the 18th Century France.* Princeton, N.J.: Princeton University Press, 1955.

Barber, James David. *The Presidential Character.* Englewood Cliffs, N.J.: Prentice-Hall, 1972.

Barber, Richard. *The Knight and Chivalry.* London: Longman, 1970.

Barbey d'Aurevilly, Jules. *Polemiques d'hier.* Paris: Albert Savine, 1889.

Barbican, James. *The Confessions of a Rum-Runner.* New York: Ives Washburn, 1928.

Barbier, Edmond Jean François. *Chronique de la régence et du règne de Louis XV, 1718-1763.* Paris: Charpentier, 1857-1885.

Barbieri, Orazio. *Ponti sull'Arno.* Rome: Editori Riuniti, 1958.

Barbour, Philip L. *Dimitry, Called the Pretender: Tsar and Great Prince of All Russia, 1605-1606.* Boston: Houghton, Mifflin, 1966.

Barboza, Joe, and Messick, Hank. *Barboza.* New York: Dell Books, 1975.

Barbusse, Henri (ed.). *I Saw It Myself.* New York: E.P. Dutton, 1928.

———. *Soviet Union and Peace.* New York: International, 1929.

Barclay, S. *Bondage.* New York: Funk and Wagnalls, 1968.

Barclay, Thomas Swain. *The Liberal Republican Movement in Missouri, 1865-1871.* Columbia: State Historical Society of Missouri, 1926.

Bard, Floyd. *Horse Wrangler: Sixty Years in the Saddle in Wyoming and Montana.* Norman: University of Oklahoma Press, 1960.

Bard, Morton, and Sangrey, Daw. *The Crime Victims Book.* New York: Basic Books, 1979.

———, and Shellow, Robert. *Issues in Law Enforcement.* Reston, Va.: Reston, 1976.

Bardens, Dennis. *The Ladykiller.* London: P. Davies, 1972.

———. *Lord Justice Birkett.* London: Robert Hale, 1962.

Bardi, Adelmo. *Dall'Etiopia selvaggia all'impero d'Italia.* Sanremo, Italy: Privately Printed, 1936.

Bardolph, Richard. *The Negro Vanguard.* New York: Vintage, 1959.

Bargellini, Piero. *Il pastore angelico, Pio XII.* Florence, Italy: Sansoni, 1948,

Baridon, Philip C. *Addiction, Crime and Social Policy.* Lexington, Mass.: Lexington Books, 1976.

Baringer, William E. *A House Dividing. Lincoln as President Elect.* Springfield, Ill.: Abraham Lincoln Association, 1945.

———. *Lincoln's Rise to Power.* Boston: Little, Brown, 1937.

Baring-Gould, Sabine. *The Book of Werewolves.* London: Smith, Elder, 1865.

Baring-Gould, William S. *Sherlock Holmes: A Biography of the World's First Consulting Detective.* London: Hart-Davis, 1962.

Barja, Julio Caro. *World of Witches.* Chicago: University of

Chicago Press, 1965.

Barkas, J.L. *Victims.* New York: Charles Scribner's Sons, 1978.

Barkau, Captain Roy. *The Great Steamboat Race.* Cincinnati, Ohio: n.p., 1952.

Barker, A.J. *Pearl Harbor.* New York: Ballantine Books, 1969.

Barker, Charles Albro. *Henry George.* New York: Oxford University Press, 1955.

Barker, Dudley. *Lord Darling's Famous Cases.* London: Hutchinson, 1936.

Barker, Elizabeth. *Macedonia: Its Place in Balkan Power Politics.* London: Royal Institute of International Affairs, 1950.

Barker, Eugene C. *The Life of Stephen F. Austin.* Nashville, Tenn.: Cokesbury Press, 1925.

Barker, Frances. *From the Green Mountains to the Prairies.* Great Barrington, Mass.: Berkshire Courier Press, 1955.

Barker, John Marshall. *The Saloon Problem and Social Reform.* Boston: Everett Press, 1905.

Barker, John T. *Missouri Lawyer.* Philadelphia: Dorrance, 1949.

Barker, R.G. *Ecological psychology.* Stanford: Stanford University Press, 1968.

Barker, Richard H. (ed.). *The Fatal Caress and Other Accounts of English Murders from 1551 to 1881.* New York: Duell, Sloan and Pearce, 1947.

Barker-Benfield, G.J. *The Horros of the Half-Known Life.* New York: Harper & Row, 1976.

Barkley, Alben W. *That Reminds Me.* Garden City, N.Y.: Doubleday, 1954.

Barkley, Mary Starr. *History of Travis County and Austin, 1839-1899.* Waco, Texas: Texian Press, 1963.

Barksdale, Richard, and Kinnamon, Kenneth (eds.). *Black Writers of America.* New York: Macmillan, 1972.

Barlay, Stephen. *The Secret Business.* New York: Thomas Y. Crowell, 1973.

Barlett, Donald L., and Steele, James H. *Empire: The Life, Legend, and Madness of Howard Hughes.* New York: W.W. Norton, 1979.

Barlow, Edward. *Barlow's Journal.* London: Hurst and Blackett, 1934.

Barlow, Hugh D. *Introduction to Criminology.* Boston: Little, Brown, 1984.

Barnard, Allan (ed.). *The Harlot Killer: The Story of Jack the Ripper in Fact and Fiction.* New York: Dodd, Mead, 1953.

Barnard, Evan G. *A Rider of the Cherokee Strip.* Boston: Houghton Mifflin, 1936.

Barnard, George G. *Proceedings of the Court of Impeachment in the Matter of George G. Barnard, A Justice of the Supreme Court of the State of New York.* 3 vols. Albany, N.Y.: Weed, Parsons, 1874.

Barnard, Harry. *Eagle Forgotten: The Life of John Peter Altgeld.* Indianapolis: Bobbs-Merrill, 1938.

_____. *Rutherford B. Hayes and His America.* Indianapolis, Ind.: Bobbs-Merrill, 1954.

Barnard, Henry. *Armsmear the Samuel Colt Biography.* New York: Beinfeld, 1976.

Barnard, William F. *Forty Years at the Five Points.* New York: Five Points House of Industry, 1893.

Barnes, David. *The Draft Riots in New York. July, 1863. The Metropolitan Police: Their Services During Riot Week. Their Honorable Record.* New York: Baker & Godwin, 1863.

_____. *Trial of John Hendrickson, Jr.* Albany, N.Y.: Barnes & Hevenor, 1853.

Barnes, Gilbert Hobbes. *The Antislavery Impulse: 1830-1844.* New York: Harcourt, Brace & World, 1964.

Barnes, Harry Elmer. *The Evolution of Penology in Pennsylvania: A Study in American Social History.* Indianapolis, Ind.: Bobbs-Merrill, 1927.

_____. *Genesis of the World War.* New York: Alfred A. Knopf, 1926.

_____. *The Repression of Crime: Studies in Historical Penology.* New York: George H. Doran, 1926.

_____. *The Story of Punishment: A Record of Man's Inhumanity to Man.* Montclair, N.J.: Patterson Smith, 1972.

_____, and Teeters, Negley K. *New Horizons in Criminology.* Englewood Cliffs, N.J.: Prentice-Hall, 1959.

Barnes, Margaret. *Murder in Coweta County.* New York: Pocketbooks, 1976.

Barnes, Margaret Ayer, and Fairbank, Janet Ayer. *Julia Newberry's Diary.* New York: W.W. Norton, 1933.

Barnes, Robert Earl. *Are You Safe From Burglars?* Garden City, N.Y.: Doubleday, 1971.

Barnes, T.S. *Memoir of Thurlow Weed.* Boston: Houghton Mifflin, 1884.

Barnes, Thomas G. *Papers Read at a Clark Library Seminar, November 3, 1973.* Los Angeles: n.p., 1975.

_____. *Somerset, 1625-1640: A County's Government during the "Personal Rule."* Cambridge, Mass.: Harvard University Press, 1961.

Barnes, Viola F. *The Dominion of New England: A Study in British Colonial Policy.* New Haven, Conn.: Yale University Press, 1923.

Barnes, William Croft. *Apaches & Longhorns.* Los Angeles: Ward Ritchie Press, 1941.

Barnet, Richard J., and Muller, Ronald E. *Global Reach: The Power of the Multinational Corporations.* New York: Simon & Schuster, 1974.

Barnett, A. Doak. *Communist China and Asia.* London: Oxford University Press, 1960.

_____. *Communist China in Perspective.* New York: Praeger, 1962.

Barnett, Corelli. *The Desert Generals.* London: William Kimbe, 1960.

Barnett, D.L., and Njama, Karari. *Mau Mau for Within: Autobiography and Analysis on Kenya's Peasant Revolt.* New York: Monthly Review Press, 1966.

Barnett, Henrietta Octavia Weston. *Canon Barnett: His Life, Work and Friends by His Wife.* London: Murray, 1918.

Barnett, S.A. *Instinct and Intelligence: Behavior of Animals and Man.* Englewood Cliffs, N.J.: Prentice-Hall, 1967.

Barnett, Samuel and Henrietta. *Practicable Social: Essays on Social Reform.* London: Longmans, 1888.

Barnett, Richard J. *The Alliance.* New York: Simon & Schuster, 1983.

Barney, Libeus. *Letter's of the Pike's Peak Gold Rush.* San Jose, Calif.: Talisman Press, 1959.

Barnhart, Russell T. *Casino Gambling.* New York: E.P. Dutton, 1978.

Barnouw, Erik. *A Tower in Babel: A History of Broadcasting in the United States.* Vol. 1. New York: Oxford University Press, 1966.

Barnstone, Willis. *Greek Lyric Poetry.* New York: Schocken Books, 1972.

Barnum, G.H. *Rube Burrow, The Famous Outlaw, Murderer, and Train Robber.* Chicago: Published by Author, 1890.

Barnum, P.T. *Life of P.T. Barnum, including his Golden Rules for Money-Making. Brought up to 1888.* Buffalo, N.Y.: Courier Printers, 1888.

_____. *The Wild Beasts, Birds and Reptiles of the World: The Story of Their Capture.* New York: R.S. Peale, 1888.

Baroja, Julio Caro. *The World of the Witches.* Chicago: University of Chicago Press, 1965.

Baron, Joseph L. (ed.). *A Treasury of Jewish Quotations.* New York: Crown, 1956.

Baron, R.A. *Human Agression.* New York: Plenum, 1977.

Baron, Roger, and Feeney, Floyd. *An Exemplary Project: Juvenile Diversion Through Family Counseling.* Washington, D.C.: National Institute of Law Enforcement and Criminal Justice, 1976.

Baron, Samuel H. *Plekhanov: The Father of Russian Marxism.* Stanford, Calif.: Stanford University Press, 1963.

Baron, Stanley. *Brewed in America.* Boston: Little, Brown, 1962.

Baron, Wendy. *Sickert.* London: Phaidon, 1973.

Barone, Francesco. *Una vita per Giuliano.* Genoa, Italy: Immordino, 1968.

Barr, Jennifer. *Within a Dark Wood.* New York: Doubleday, 1979.

Barr, Martin. *Mental Defectives.* Philadelphia: Blackerson's and Sons, 1904.

Barr, Pat. *The Coming of the Barbarians: The Opening of Japan to the West, 1853-1870.* New York: E. P. Dutton, 1967.

Barr, Stringfellow. *The Mask of Jove.* New York: J.B. Lippincott, 1966.

Barracato, John. *Arson.* New York: Avon Books, 1976.

Barraclough, Geoffrey. *The Medieval Empire: Idea and Reality.* London: Historical Association, 1950.

Barragán, Juan. *Historia del ejército y de la revolución constitucionalista.* Mexico City: Talleres de la Editorial Stylo, 1946.

The Barrel Mystery, or the Career, Tragedy, and Trial of Henry Jumpertz. Chicago: Norris & Hyde, 1859.

Barrera, Alberto Calzadiaz. *Villa Contra Todos.* Mexico City: Editores Mexicanos Unidos, S.A., 1965.

Barret, Edward L., Jr., Bruton, Paul W. and Honnold, John. *Constitutional Law.* New York: The Foundation Press, 1963.

Barrett, David A., and Shaeffer, C. (eds.). *Play Safe: A Simplified Guide to Our Sex Laws.* Kansas City: Pioneer Associates, 1939.

Barrett, Ethel. *A Street Cop Who Cared.* Old Tappan, N.J.: Rerell, 1978.

Barrett, Francis. *The Magus or Celestial Intelligencer, Being a Complete System of Occult Philosophy.* London: Lackington, Allen, 1801.

Barrett, James Wyman (ed.). *The End of the World.* New York: Harper & Bros., 1931.

_____. *Joseph Pulitzer and His World.* New York: Vanguard, 1941.

_____. *The World, the Flesh, and Messrs. Pulitzer.* New York: Vanguard Press, 1941.

Barrett, Marvin. *The Jazz Age.* New York: G.P. Putnam's Sons, 1959.

Barrett, Walter. *The Old Merchants of New York City.* New York: Carleton, 1864.

Barrett, Wilfred Phillips. *The Trial of Jeanne d'Arc.* New York: Gotham House, 1932.

Barrett, William. *Irrational Man.* Garden City, N.Y.: Doubleday, 1962.

Barrett, William E., et al. *Denver Murders.* Duell, Sloan, & Pearce, 1946.

Barron, C.W. *More They Told Barron.* New York: Harper & Brothers, 1931.

_____. *They Told Barron, Notes of the Late Clarence W. Barron.* New York: Harper & Brothers, 1930.

Barron, John. *KGB: The Secret Work of Soviet Secret Agents.* New York: Dutton, 1974.

Barros, James. *The Corfu Incident of 1923.* Princeton, N.J.: Princeton University Press, 1965.

Barrow, Edward Grant, with Kahn, James M. *My Fifty Years in Baseball.* New York: Coward-McCann, 1951.

Barrow, Sir John. *The Eventful History of the Mutiny on the Bounty.* London: John Murray, 1831.

_____. *A Voyage to Cochinchina, 1792-1793.* London: T. Cadell and W. Davies, 1806.

Barrows, John R. *Ubet.* Caldwell, Idaho: Caxton Printers, 1936.

Barrows, William. *The United States of Yesterday and of Tomorrow.* Boston: Roberts Brothers, 1887.

Barry, Brian. *The Liberal Theory of Justice: A Critical Examination of the Principle Doctrines in a Theory of Justice by John Rawls.* New York: Oxford University, 1972.

Barry, Iris. *D.W. Griffith, American Film Master.* New York: Museum of Modern Art, 1940.

Barry, James P. *The Noble Experiment, 1919-1933.* New York: Franklin Watts, 1972.

Barry, John Brooks. *The Michaelmas Girls.* London: Deutsch, 1975.

Barry, Richard. *Mr. Rutledge of South Carolina.* New York: Duell, Sloan & Pearce, 1942.

Barry, Commandant General Tom. *Guerilla Days in Ireland.* Cork: Mercier Press, 1955.

Barry, Vincent. *Philosophy: A Text with Readings.* Belmont, Calif.: Wadsworth, 1983.

Barrymore, Ethel. *Memories.* New York: Harper & Brothers, 1955.

Barrymore, John. *Confessions of an Actor.* Indianapolis, Ind.: Bobbs-Merrill, 1926.

Barsness, Larry. *Gold Camp.* New York: Hastings House, 1962.

Bartell, G.D. *Group Sex: A Scientist's Eyewitness Account of the American Way of Swinging.* New York: Wyden, 1971.

Barth, Alan. *Government by Investigation.* New York: Viking, 1952.

_____. *The Loyalty of Free Men.* New York: The Viking Press, 1951.

_____. *Prophets with Honor.* New York: Alfred A. Knopf, 1974.

Barthel, Joan. *A Death in Canaan.* New York: E.P. Dutton, 1977.

Barthèty, Hilarion. *La sorcellerie en Béarn et dans le pays Basque.* Pau, Fr.: L. Ribaut, 1879.

Bartholomew, Ed. *A Biographical Album of Western Gunfighters.* Houston: Frontier Press of Texas, 1958.

_____. *Black Jack Ketchum: Last of the Hold-Up Kings.* Houston: Frontier Press of Texas, 1955.

_____. *Cullen Baker: Premier Texas Gunfighter.* Houston: Frontier Press of Texas, 1954.

_____. *Henry Plummer: Montana Outlaw Boss.* Ruidoso, N.M.: Frontier Books, 1960.

_____. *Jesse Evans: A Texas Hideburner.* Houston: Frontier Press of Texas, 1955.

_____. *Kill or Be Killed: A Record of Violence in the Early Southwest.* Houston: The Frontier Press of Texas, 1953.

_____. *Some Western Gunfighters.* Toyahvale, Texas: Frontier Book, n.d.

_____. *Western Hardcases.* Ruidoso, N.M.: Frontier Book, 1960.

_____. *Wild Bill Longley: A Texas Hard-Case.* Houston: Frontier Press of Texas, 1953.

_____. *Wyatt Earp, 1879-1882: The Man and the Myth.* Toyahvale, Texas: Frontier Book, 1964.

_____. *Wyatt Earp, 1848-1880: The Untold Story.* Toyahvale, Texas: Frontier Books, 1963.

Bartholomew, Paul C. *Summaries of Leading Cases on the Constitution.* N.J.: Littlefield, Adams, 1961.

Bartholow, Roberts. *A Manual of Hypodermatic Medication.* Philadelphia: J.B. Lippincott, 1891.

Bartlett, Arthur. *Baseball and Mr. Spalding.* New York: Farrar, Straus & Young, 1951.

Bartlett, F. *Remembering.* London: Cambridge University Press, 1932.

Bartlett, I.S. (ed.). *History of Wyoming.* Chicago: S.J. Clarke, 1918.

Bartlett, John Russell. *Personal Narrative of Explorations and Incidents in Texas, New Mexico, California, Sonora and Chihuahua.* New York: D. Appleton, 1854.

Bartol, C.L. *Criminal Behavior: A Psychosocial Approach.* Englewood Cliffs, N.J.: Prentice-Hall, 1986.

Bartoli, Domenico. *Da Vittorio Emanuele a Gronchi.* Milan, Italy: Longanesi, 1961.

_____. *La fine della Monarchia.* Milan, Italy: Mondadori, 1947.

Bartollas, Clemens, Miller, Stuart J., and Dinitz, Simon. *Juvenile Victimization.* New York: Sage & Halsted Press, 1976.

Barton, Elmer E. *A Business Tour of Chicago.* Chicago: E.E. Barton, 1887.

Barton, George. *The True Stories of Celebrated Crimes.* New York: McKinlay Stone & Mackenzie, 1909.

Barton, Joseph J. *Peasants and Strangers.* Cambridge, Mass.: Harvard University Press, 1975.

Barton, O.S., and McCorkle, John. *Three Years with Quantrell.* Armstrong, Mo.: Armstrong Herald Printing, 1914.

Barton, Roy F. *The Half-Way Sun.* New York: Brewer & Warren, 1930.

Barton, William E. *The Life of Abraham Lincoln.* 2 vols. Indianapolis, Ind.: Bobbs-Merrill, 1925.

Bartram, William. *Travels Through North and South Carolina, Georgia, East and West Florida.* New Haven, Conn.: Yale University Press, 1958.

Bartz, Karl. *Die Tragödie der deutschen Abwehr.* Salzburg, Aust.: Pilgram Verlag, 1955.

Baruch, Bernard. *M. Baruch: My Own Story.* New York: Henry Holt, 1957.

_____. *The Public Years.* New York: Holt, Rinehart & Winston, 1960.

Bary, Nee de, Victor G. and Brett. *Longtime Califom'.* Boston: Houghton Mifflin, 1974.

Barzini, Luigi. *From Caesar to the Mafia.* New York: The Library Press, 1971.

_____. *The Italians.* New York: Atheneum, 1964.

_____. *O America!* London: Hamish Hamilton, 1977.

Barzman, Sol. *Madmen and Geniuses.* Chicago: Follett, 1974.

Bar-Zohar, Michael. *Armed Prophet.* London: Davis & Poynton, 1966.

_____. *Spies in the Promised Land.* London: Davis & Poynton, 1972.

Barzun, Jacques. *Burke and Hare: The Resurrection Men.* Metuchen, N.J.: Scarecrow, 1974.

Basedow, H. *The Australian Aboriginal.* Adelaide, Aus.: F.W. Preece & Sons, 1925.

Basham, A.L. *The Wonder That Was India.* New York: Grove Press, 1954.

Basichis, Gordon. *Beautiful Bad Girl.* Santa Barbara, Calif.: Santa Barbara Press, 1985.

Basin, Thomas (ed.). *Histoire de Louis XI.* trans. Charles Samaran. Paris: Société d'Édition "Les Belles Lettres," 1963.

Baskerville, Beatrice. *What next, O Duce?* London: Longmans, 1937.

Baskin, R.N. *Reminiscences of Early Utah.* Salt Lake City, Utah: Tribune-Reporter, 1914.

Basler, Roy P. *Abraham Lincoln: His Speeches and Writings.* New York: World, 1946.

_____ (ed.). *The Collected Works of Abraham Lincoln.* 8 vols. New Brunswick, N.J.: Rutgers University Press, 1953.

_____ (ed.). *The Collected Works of Abraham Lincoln, Supplement 1832-1865.* Westport, Conn.: Greenwood Press, 1974.

Bass, Herbert J. *"I Am A Democrat": The Political Career of David Bennett Hill.* Syracuse, N.Y.: Syracuse University Press, 1961.

Bass, Robert D. *The Gamecock.* New York: Holt, Rinehart & Winston, 1961.

_____. *The Green Dragoon.* New York: Henry Holt, 1937.

_____. *The Swamp Fox.* Henry Holt, 1959.

Bass, U.F., et al. *A Study of Narcotics Addicted Offenders at the D.C. Jail.* Washington, D.C.: Narcotics Treatment Administration, 1971.

Basserman, Lujo. *The Oldest Profession: the History of Prostitution.* New York: Stein & Day, 1968.

Bassett, John Spencer. *The Federalist System.* New York: Harper & Brothers, 1906.

Bassett, Samuel Clay. *Buffalo County, Nebraska, and Its People.* Chicago: S.J. Clarke, 1916.

Bassiouni, M. Cherif. *Criminal Law and Its Process.* Springfield, Ill.: Charles C. Thomas, 1969.

_____. *International Terrorism and Political Crimes.* Springfield, Ill.: Charles C. Thomas, 1975.

Bassman, Herbert J. (ed.). *Riverside Then and Now.* Riverside, Ill.: Riverside News, 1936.

Basso, Antonia. *L'armistizio del settembre 43 in Sardegna.* Naples, Italy: Rippoli, 1947.

Basso, Hamilton. *Beauregard the Great Creole.* New York: Charles Scribner's Sons, 1933.

_____ (ed.). *Exploration of the Valley of the Amazon by William Lewis Herndon.* New York: McGraw-Hill, 1952.

Bassompierre, Baron Alfred de. *The Night of August 2-3, 1914, at the Belgian Foreign Office.* London: Hodder & Stoughton, 1916.

Bastianini, Giuseppe. *Uonini, cosi, fatti.* Milan, Italy: Vitagliano, 1959.

Basutoland Medicine Murder. London: Her Majesty's Stationary Office, 1958.

Bataille, A. *Les Causes criminelles et mondaines.* 18 vols. Paris: Dentu, 1881-1898.

Bataille, Georges. *Death and Sensuality.* New York: Walker, 1962.

_____. *Le Proces de Gilles de Rais.* Paris: Jean-Jacques Pauvert, 1965.

Bataille, Michel. *Gilles de Rais.* Paris: Editions Planete, 1966.

Batal, James. *Zionist Influence on the American Press.* Beirut, Leb.: Nasser Press, 1956.

Bates, Mrs. D.B. *Incidents on Land and Water.* Boston: James French, 1857.

Bates, David Homer. *Lincoln in the Telegraph Office.* New York: Century, 1907.

Bates, Edmund Franklin. *History and Reminiscences of Denton County.* Denton, Texas: McNitzky, 1918.

Bates, Edward. *The Diary of...* Washington, D.C.: U.S. Government Printing Press, 1933.

Bates, Ernest, and Carlson, Oliver. *Hearst: Lord of San Simeon.* New York: Viking, 1936.

Bates, Ernest Sutherland. *The Story of the Supreme Court.* New York: Bobbs-Merrill, 1936.

Bates, Finis L. *The Escape & Suicide of John Wilkes Booth; or The First True Account of Lincoln's Assassination.* Atlanta: J.L. Nichols, 1907.

Bates, Harbin E.H. (ed.). *Quarter Sessions Records for the County of Somerset.* London: Harrison and Sons, 1907.

Bates, J.C. (ed.). *History of the Bench and Bar of California.* San Francisco: Bench and Bar, 1912.

Bateson, Charles. *The Convict Ships, 1787-1868.* Glasgow, Scot.: Brown, Son & Ferguson, 1959.

Batista i Roca, J.M., and Ady, Cecilia M. *The New Cambridge Modern History.* Cambridge, Mass.: University Press, 1957.

Batsell, Walter R. *Soviet Rule in Russia.* New York: Macmillan, 1929.

Battaglia, Roberto. *Story of the Italian Resistance.* trans. P.D. Cummins. London: Odhams Press, 1958.

Battersea, C. *Reminiscences.* London: Macmillan, 1923.

Battiscombe, Georgina. *Queen Alexandra.* London: Constable, 1969.

Battle, Brendan P., and Weston, Paul B. *Arson: Detection and Investigation.* New York: Arco, 1978.

Battles and Leaders of the Civil War. New York: Century, 1884-1887.

Battley, H. *Single Finger Prints.* London: H.M. Stationery Office, 1930.

Baudin, Louis. *Daily Life in Peru Under the Last Incas.* trans. Winifred Bradford. London: Allen & Unwin, 1961.

_____. *The Socialist Empire, The Incas of Peru.* trans. Katherine Woods. Princeton, N.J.: D. Van Nostrand, 1961.

Baudin, Robert. *Confessions of a Promiscuous Counterfeiter.* New York: Harcourt Brace, 1979.

Baudrillart, Henri. *Jean Bodin.* Paris: Guillaumin, 1853.

Bauer, Bernhard A. *Woman.* London: Jonathan Cape, 1927.

Bauer, Charles J. *So I Killed Lincoln.* New York: Vantage, 1976.

Bauer, Jack. *The Mexican War 1846-1848.* New York: Macmillan, 1974.

Bauer, Yehuda. *From Diplomacy to Resistance: A History of Jewish Palestine, 1939-1945.* trans. Alton M. Winters. New

York: Atheneum, 1973.

Baugh, Jack W., and Morgan, Jefferson. *Why Have They Taken Our Children?* New York: Delacorte Press, 1978.

Baughman, E.U., and Robinson, Leonard Wallace. *Secret Service Chief.* New York: Harper & Brothers, 1961.

Baughman, Laurance. *Southern Rape Complex.* Atlanta: Pendulum Books, 1966.

Baulch, Lawrence. *Return to the World.* Valley Forge, Pa.: Judson Press, 1968.

Baur, Hans. *Hitler's Pilot.* London: Frederick Muller, 1958.

Baverstock, Keith. *Footsteps Through London's Past.* London: Shire, 1972.

Bavoux, Francis. *La Sorcellerie au pays de Quingey.* Besançon, Fr.: Editions Servir, 1947.

Baxter, Beverley. *Men, Martyrs and Mountebanks.* London: Hutchinson, 1940.

Baxter, John. *The Gangster Film.* New York: A. S. Barnes, 1970.

Baxter, Richard. *The Certainty of the World of Spirits.* London: T. Parchurst & J. Salusbury, 1691.

Baxter, Robert. *The Panic of 1866, With Its Lessons on the Currency Act.* New York: Burt Franklin, 1969.

Bayer, Oliver Weld (ed.). *Cleveland Murders.* New York: Duell, Sloan & Pearce, 1947.

Bayle, François, and Grangeron, Henri. *Relation de l'état de quelques personnes préetendues possédées faite d'auctorité du Parlement de Toulouse.* Toulouse, Fr.: Fouchac & Bely, 1682.

Bayley, David H. *Forces of Order: Police Behavior in Japan and the United States.* Berkeley: University of California Press, 1976.

_____. *The Police and Political Development in India.* Princeton, N.J.: Princeton University Press, 1969.

_____ (ed.). *Police and Society.* Beverly Hills, Calif.: Sage, 1977.

_____, and Mendelsohn, Harold. *Minorities and the Police.* New York: Free Press, 1968.

Baynes, N.H. *Byzantine Studies and Other Essays.* New York: DeGraff, 1955.

_____, and Moss, H.St.L.B. *Byzantium: An Introduction to East Roman Civilization.* New York: Oxford Press University, 1948.

Bayor, Ronald H. *Neighbors in Conflict: The Irish, Germans, Jews and Italians of New York City.* Baltimore: The Johns Hopkins University Press, 1978.

Beach, David. *A Statement of the Facts Concerning the Death of Samuel Lee and the Prosecution of David Sanford for Murder.* New Haven, Conn.: Beach, 1807.

Beach, Frank A. (ed.) *Sex and Behavior.* New York: Wiley, 1965.

Beach, Sylvia. *Shakespeare and Company.* New York: Harcourt, Brace & World, 1959.

The Beach Tragedy, The Trial of Dr. L.U. Beach. Altoona, Pa.: Call Steam Printing House, 1884.

Beadle, J.H. *The Undeveloped West; or, Five Years in the Territories.* Philadelphia: National, 1873.

_____. *Western Wilds and the Men Who Redeem Them.* Cincinnati, Ohio: Jones Brothers, 1877.

Beaglehole, J.C. *The Exploration of the Pacific.* Stanford, Calif.: Stanford University Press, 1966.

_____. *The Life of Captain James Cook.* London: Hakluyt Society, 1974.

Beal, Erica. *Royal Cavalcade.* London: Paul, 1939.

Beal, Fred. *Proletarian Journey.* New York: De Capo, 1971.

Beal, John P. *John Fuster Dulles.* New York: Harper, 1957.

Beal, M.D. *A History of Southeastern Idaho.* Caldwell, Idaho: Caxton Printers, 1942.

Beal, S. *Fo-sho-hing-tsan-king.* Oxford, Eng.: Clarendon Press, 1883.

Beale, Howard K. *The Critical Year.* New York: Harcourt, Brace, 1930.

_____ (ed.). *Diary of Gideon Wells.* New York: W.W. Norton,

1960.

_____. *Theodore Roosevelt and the Rise of America to World Power.* Baltimore: Johns Hopkins Press, 1956.

Beales, A.C.F. *The Pope and the Jews.* London: 'Sword of the Spirit', 1945.

Bealle, Morris A. *Guns of the Regressive Right.* Washington, D.C.: Columbia, 1964.

Beals, Carleton. *American Earth.* Philadelphia: J.B. Lippincott, 1939.

_____. *Brass Knuckle Crusade: The Great Know-Nothing Conspiracy, 1820-1860.* New York: Hastings House, 1960.

_____. *Nomads and Empire Builders, Native People and Cultures of South America.* New York: Chilton, 1961.

_____. *Porfirio Diaz, Dictator of Mexico.* New York: J.B. Lippincott, 1932.

_____. *Rome or Death!* New York: Century Press, 1923.

_____. *The Story of Huey P. Long.* Westport, Conn.: Greenwood Press, 1971.

Beals, Frank Lee. *Buffalo Bill.* Chicago: Wheeler, 1943.

Bean, Philip. *The Social Control of Drugs.* New York: Wiley, 1974.

Bean, Walton. *Boss Ruef's San Francisco.* Berkeley: University of California Press, 1952.

_____. *California: An Interpretive History.* New York: McGraw-Hill, 1968.

Beaney, William M. *The Right to Counsel in American Courts.* Binghampton, N.Y.: Vail-Ballow Press, 1955.

Bear, Robert L. *Delivered Unto Satan.* Carlisle, Pa.: Bear, 1974.

Beard, Charles Austin, and Mary R. *America in Midpassage.* 2 vols. New York: Macmillan, 1939.

_____. *An Economic Interpretation of the Constitution of the United States.* New York: Macmillan, 1913.

_____. *Economic Origins of Jeffersonian Democracy.* New York: Macmillan, 1915.

_____. *New Basic History of the United States.* Garden City, N.Y.: Doubleday, 1968.

_____. *President Roosevelt and the Coming of the War.* New Haven, Conn.: Yale University Press, 1948.

_____. *The Rise of American Civilization.* 2 vols. New York: Macmillan, 1927.

_____. *The Supreme Court and the Constitution.* New York: Macmillan, 1912

Beard, Dan. *Hardly a Man Is Now Alive.* New York: Doubleday, Doran, 1939.

Beard, George M. *American Nervousness: Its Causes and Consequences.* New York: G.P. Putnam's Sons, 1881.

_____. *A Practical Treatise on Nervous Exhaustion (Neurasthenia).* New York: E.B. Treat, 1894.

_____. *Psychology of the Salem Witchcraft Excitement of 1692.* New York: G.P. Putnam's Sons, 1882.

Beard, James Melville. *K.K.K. Sketches: Humorous and Didactic.* Philadelphia: Claxton, 1877.

Beard, Ross E., Jr. *Carbine, the Story of David Marshall Williams.* Lexington, S.C.: The Sandlapper Store, 1977.

Beardsley, Aubrey. *The Story of Venus and Tannhauser.* New York: Award, 1967.

Beardsley, Isaac. *Echoes From Peak and Plain.* Cincinatti, Ohio: Curts & Jennings, 1898.

Bearss, Edwin C., and Gibson, A.M. *Fort Smith, Little Gibraltar on the Arkansas.* Norman: University of Oklahoma Press, 1969.

Beaslai, Piaras. *Michael Collins.* Dublin, Ire.: Phoenix, 1926.

Beasley, Norman. *Frank Knox, American.* New York: Doubleday, 1936.

Beasley, W.G. *The Modern History of Japan.* New York: Frederick A. Praeger, 1963.

_____. *Modern Japan.* London: Allen & Unwin, 1975.

Beatly, George W. *The Background and Causes of the 1943 Detroit Race Riot.* Princeton, N.J.: n.p., 1954.

_____, and Beattie, Helen Pruitt. Heritage of the Valley: San Ber-

nardino's First Century. Oakland, Calif.: Biobooks, 1951.

Beattie, John. *The Yorkshire Ripper Story.* London: Quartet, 1981.

Beattie, Kim. *Brother! Here's A Man.* New York: Macmillan, 1940.

Beatty, Bessie. *The Red Heart of Russia.* New York: Century, 1918.

Beatty, John. *Memoirs of a Volunteer.* New York: W.W. Norton, 1946.

Beauchamp, Thomas L. (ed.). *Case Studies in Business, Society and Ethics.* Englewood Cliffs, N.J.: Prentice-Hall, 1983.

____, and Bowie, Norman E. *Ethical Theory and Business.* Englewood Cliffs, N.J.: Prentice-Hall, 1983.

Beaumont, Charles (ed.). *The Fiend in You.* New York: Ballantine, 1962.

Beaumont, F.A. *The Fifty Most Amazing Crimes of the Last 100 Years.* London: Odhams, 1936.

Beaumont, G.H. *G.H. Beaumont's Railroad Stories.* Kansas City: Seip Printing, 1912.

Beaumont, Gustave, and de Tocqueville, Alexis. *On the Penitentiary System in the United States and Its Application in France.* Carbondale, Ill.: Southern Illinois University Press, 1964.

Beaumont, John. *An Historical, Physiological, and Theological Treatise of Spirits, Apparitions, Witchcrafts, and Other Magical Practices.* London: D. Browne, 1705.

Beaune, Henri. *Les sorciers de Lyon.* Dijon, Fr.: Rabutot, 1868.

Beauvallet, Léon. *Rachel and the New World.* New York: Dix, Edwards, 1856.

Beauvoir, Simone de. *America, Day by Day.* New York: Grove Press, 1953.

____. *The Long March.* London: Deutsch & Weidenfeld & Nicolson, 1958.

____. *The Second Sex.* New York: Random House, 1974.

Beaver, Ninette. *Caril.* New York: Bantam, 1976.

Beaverbrook, Lord. *The Decline and Fall of Lloyd George.* London: Collins, 1963.

____. *Men and Power.* London: Hutchinson, 1956.

____. *Politicians and the War, 1914-16.* New York: Doubleday, Doran, 1928.

Bebel, August. *Women under Socialism.* New York: Schocken Books, 1971.

Beccaria, Cesare Bonesana. *An Essay on Crime and Punishments.* Philadelphia: Philip H. Nicklin, 1819.

____. *On Crimes and Punishment.* trans. Henry Paolucci. Indianapolis, Ind.: Bobbs-Merrill, 1963.

Bechdolt, Frederick Ritchie. *Tales of the Oldtimers.* New York: Century, 1924.

____. *When the West Was Young.* New York: Century, 1924.

Bechhart, Benjamin H. (ed.). *The New York Money Market.* 4 vols. New York: Columbia University Press, 1932-1934.

Bechhofer, Robert. *Famous American Trials.* London: Jarrolds, 1947.

Bechhofer Roberts, C.E. *Lord Mirkenhead.* London: Mills & Boon, 1926.

____. *Sir Travers Humphreys.* London: The Bodley Head, 1936.

Beck, Bertram M. *Five States, A Study of the Youth Authority Program as Promulgated by the American Law Institute.* Philadelphia: American Law Institute, 1951.

Beck, F., and Godin, W. *Russian Purge and the Extraction of Confession.* trans. Eyre Mosbacker and David Porter. New York: Viking Press, 1951.

Beck, Warren A. *New Mexico: A History of Four Centuries.* Norman: University of Oklahoma Press, 1962.

Becker, Carl Lotus. *The Declaration of Independence.* New York: Harcourt, Brace, 1922.

____. *The Eve of the Revolution.* New Haven, Conn.: Yale University Press, 1921.

Becker, Ernest. *Escape From Evil.* New York: Free Press, 1975.

Becker, Gary S. *The Economic Appproach to Human Behavior.* Chicago: University of Chicago Press, 1976.

____, and Landes, William M. (eds.). *Essays in the Economics of Crime and Punishment.* New York: National Bureau of Economic Research, 1974.

____. *Human Capital: A Theoretical and Empirical Analysis.* New York: Columbia University Press, 1975.

____. *A Treatise on t.* Cambridge, Mass.: Harvard University Press, 1981.

Becker, Howard. *German Youth: Bond or Free.* London: Routledge & Kegan Paul, 1946.

Becker, Howard S. (ed.). *Campus Power Struggle.* Chicago: Aldine, 1970.

____. *The Other Side: Perspectives on Deviance.* New York: The Free Press, 1964.

____. *Outsiders: Studies in the Sociology of Deviance.* New York: Free Press, 1963.

____. *Sociological Work.* London: Allen Lane, 1971.

____. *Through Values to Social Interpretation.* Durham, N.C.: Duke University Press, 1950.

Becker, Jillian. *Hitler's Children: The Story of the Baader-Meinhof Terrorist Gang.* New York: J.B. Lippincott, 1977.

Becker, Stephen D. *Marshall Field III.* New York: Simon & Schuster, 1964.

Becker, Theodore, L. *Comparative Judicial Politics: The Political Functioning of Courts.* Chicago: Rand McNally, 1970.

Beckett, V.B. *Baca's Battle.* Houston, Texas: Stagecoach Press, n.d.

Bedau, Hugo Adam, and Pierce, Chester M. (eds.). *Capital Punishment in the United States.* New York: AMS Press, 1976.

____. *The Case against the Death Penalty.* New York: American Civil Liberties Union, 1973.

____ (ed.). *The Death Penalty in America.* New York: Oxford University Press, 1982.

Bedeschi, Edoardo, and Alessi, Rino. *Gli anni giovanili di Mussolini.* Milan, Italy: Mondadori, 1939.

Bedford, Sybille. *The Faces of Justice.* New York: Simon & Schuster, 1961.

____. *The Trial of Dr. Adams.* New York: Time Books, 1958.

Bedini, Silvio A. *Thinkers and Tinkers: Early American Men of Science.* New York: Charles Scribner's Sons, 1975.

Bedlington, Stanley S. *Malaysia and Singapore.* Ithaca, N.Y.: Cornell University Press, 1978.

Beebe, Lucius, and Clegg, Charles. *The American West.* New York: E.P. Dutton, 1955.

____. *The Big Spenders.* New York: Doubleday, 1966.

____. *Boston and the Boston Legend.* New York: Appleton-Century, 1935.

____. *Comstock Commotion, The Story of Territorial Enterprise.* Palo Alto, Calif.: Stanford University Press, 1954.

____. *Hear the Train Blow.* New York: E.P. Dutton, 1952.

____. *Shoot if You Must.* New York: D. Appleton Century, 1943.

____. *U.S. West: The Saga of Wells Fargo.* New York: E.P. Dutton, 1949.

Beebe, Ruth. *Reminiscing Along the Sweetwater.* Boulder, Colo.: Johnson, 1973.

Beecher, Henry K. *Research and the Individual.* Boston: Little, Brown, 1970.

Beecher, Henry Ward. *Lectures to Young Men on Various Important Subjects.* Boston: John P. Jewett, 1846.

Beecher, Lyman. *Autobiography, Correspondence, Etc.* 2 vols. New York: Harper & Bros., 1865.

____. *Narrative of Riots at Alton: In Connection with the Death of Rev. Elijah P. Lovejoy.* New York: E.P. Dutton, 1965.

____. *Six Sermons on the Nature, Occasions, Signs, Evils, and Remedy of Intemperence.* New York: The American Tract Society, 1827.

Beecher, William C., and Scoville, Rev. Samuel. *A Biography of Rev. Henry Ward Beecher.* New York: Charles L. Webster, 1888.

Beeching, Jack. *The Chinese Opium Wars.* New York: Harcourt, Brace, Jovanovich, 1975.

Beechy, Captain F.W. *Narrative of the Voyage to the Pacific in H.M.S. Blossom.* London: Henry Colburn & Richard Bentley, 1831.

Beeding, Francis. *Death Walks in Eastrepps.* London: Hodder & Stoughton, 1931.

Beedle, Susannah. *An Essay on the Advisability of Total Abolition of Capital Punishment.* London: Nichols & Son, 1867.

Beer, George Louis. *The Old Colonial System 1660-1688.* 2 vols. New York: Macmillan, 1912.

Beer, M. *Fifty Years of International Socialism.* New York: Macmillan, 1935.

_____. *A History of British Socialism.* 2 vols. London: G. Bell, 1919-1920.

Beer, Thomas. *Hanna.* New York: Alfred A. Knopf, 1929.

_____. *The Mauve Decade.* New York: Alfred A. Knopf, 1926.

Beers, George A. *Vasquez; or the Hunted Bandits of San Joaquin.* New York: Robert M. DeWitt, 1875.

Beers, J.H. *History of the Great Lakes.* Chicago: n.p., 1899.

Beeson, John. *A Plea for the Indians.* New York: Published by Author, 1858.

Beeton, Isabella. *The Book of Household Management.* London: Beeton, 1861.

Beggs, Thomas. *The Royal Commission and the Punishment of Death.* London: Society for the Abolition of Capital Punishment, 1866.

Begin, Menachem. *The Revolt: Story of the Irgun.* New York: Henry Schuman, 1951.

Begnac, Yvon de. *Palazzo Venezia.* Rome: 'La Rocca', 1950.

_____. *Trent'anni di Mussolini.* Rome: Arti Grafiche Menaglia, 1934.

_____. *Vita di Mussolini.* 3 vols. Milan, Italy: Mondadori, 1936-40.

Beheim-Schwarzbach, Max. *Friedrich Wilhelms I. Colonisationwerk in Lithauen, vornehmlich die Salzburger Colonie.* Konigsburg, Ger.: Hartung, 1878.

Behn, Noel. *Big Stick-up at Brinks.* New York: Putnam, 1977.

Behrens, John C. *Reporting Work Test.* Columbus: GRID, 1974.

_____. *The Typewriter Guerrillas.* Chicago: Nelson-Hall, 1977.

Beidler, X. *Vigilante.* Norman: University of Oklahoma Press, 1965.

Beigel, Herbert and Allan. *Beneath the Badge.* New York: Harper & Row, 1977.

Beigel, Hermann. *The Examination and Confession of Certain Witches at Chelmsford.* London: Philobiblon Society, 1864.

Beigel, Hugo G. (ed.). *Advances in Sex Research.* New York: Harper & Row, 1963.

Beirne, Francis F. *Shout Treason: The Trial of Aaron Burr.* New York: Hastings House, 1959.

Beisner, Robert L. *Twelve Against Empire: The Anti-Imperialists, 1898-1900.* New York: McGraw-Hill, 1968.

Bejerot, Nils. *Addiction: An Artificially Induced Drive.* Springfield, Ill.: Charles C. Thomas, 1972.

_____. *Addiction and Society.* Springfield, Ill.: Charles C. Thomas, 1970.

Bekker, Balthasar. *De Betoverde Weereld.* Amsterdam, Neth.: D. von der Dalen, 1691.

_____. *The World Bewitched.* London: R. Baldwin, 1695.

Bekker, Cajus. *Hitler's Naval War.* New York: Doubleday, 1975.

Belbenott, Rene. *Dry Guillotine.* New York: Dutton, 1938.

_____. *Hell on Trial.* New York: Dutton, 1940.

Belcher, Edward. *Narrative of a Voyage Around the World.* 2 vols. London: H. Colburn, 1843.

Belcher, Lady. *The Mutineers of the Bounty and Their Descendants on Pitcairn and Norfolk Islands.* London: John Murray, 1870.

Belden, H.M. (ed.). *Ballads and Songs Collected by the Missouri Folk-Lore Society.* Columbia: University of Missouri, 1940.

Belden, Jack. *China Shakes the World.* New York: Harper and Bros., 1949.

Belden, John J. *Life of David Belden.* New York: Belden Brothers, 1891.

Beletti, F.M.G. *Identificando a Impressao Palmar.* Rio de Janeiro, Braz.: Inst. de Ident., 1934.

Belfrage, Cedric. *The American Inquisition 1945-1960.* Indianapolis, Ind.: Bobbs-Merrill, 1973.

Belfry Murder in Boston. Philadelphia: Old Franklin, 1875.

Belgrave, Sir Charles. *The Pirate Coast.* New York: Roy, 1967.

Belin, David W. *November 22, 1963: You Are the Jury.* New York: Quadrangle Books, 1973.

Belin, Jean. *My Work at the Sûreté.* trans. Eric Whelpton. London: Harrap, 1950.

_____. *Secrets of the Sureté.* New York: Putnam, 1950.

Bell, A.H. (ed.). *Practical Dowsing.* London: G. Bell, 1965.

Bell, Alan P., and Hall, Calvin S. *The Personality of a Child Molester: An Analysis of Dreams.* Chicago: Aldine-Atherton, 1971.

Bell, Arthur. *Kings Don't Mean a Thing.* New York: William Morrow, 1978.

Bell, Daniel (ed.). *The End of Ideology.* New York: Free Press, 1962.

_____. *Marxian Socialism in the United States.* Princeton, N.J.: Princeton University Press, 1967.

_____ (ed.). *The New American Right.* New York: Criterion, 1955.

_____. *The Radical Right.* New York: Anchor, 1964.

_____. *Toward the Year 2000.* Boston: Houghton Mifflin, 1968.

Bell, Edward A. *Those Meddlesome Attorneys.* London: Martin Secker, 1939.

Bell, Edward I. *The Political Shame of Mexico.* New York: McBride, Nast, 1914.

Bell, Ernest A. *Fighting the Traffic in Young Girls.* New York: Walter, 1911.

_____. *War on the White Slave Trade.* Chicago: Thompson, 1909.

Bell, Horace. *On the Old West Coast.* New York: William Morrow, 1930.

_____. *Reminiscences of a Ranger.* Los Angeles: Yarnell, Caystile, & Mathes, 1881.

Bell, J. Bowyer. *Assassin!: The Theory and Practice of Political Violence.* New York: St. Martin's Press, 1979.

_____. *The Secret Army: The IRA, 1916-1979.* Cambridge, Mass.: MIT Press, 1980.

_____. *Terror Out of Zion.* New York: St. Martin's Press, 1977.

_____. *Transnational Terror.* Washington, D.C.: American Enterprise Institute for Public Policy Research, 1975.

Bell, John C. *The Pilgrim and the Pioneer.* Lincoln, Neb.: International Publishing Association, 1906.

Bell, Katherine M. *Swinging the Censer. Reminiscences of Old Santa Barbara.* Santa Barbara, Calif.: n.p., 1931.

Bell, Maria. *The Life and Times of Lucrezia Borgia.* trans. Bernard and Barbara Wall. New York: Harcourt Brace, 1953.

_____. *Lucrezia Borgia.* Rome: Arnoldo Mondadori Editore, 1974.

_____. *Lucrezia Borgia la sua vita e i suoi tempi.* Rome: Arnoldo Mondadori Editore, 1967.

Bell, Millicent. *Edith Wharton and Henry James: The Story of Their Friendship.* New York: George Braziller, 1965.

Bell, Quentin. *Virginia Woolf.* London: Hogarth Press, 1972.

Bell, Roderick, Edwards, David V., and Wagner, R. Harrison. (eds.) *Political Power: A Reader in Theory and Research.* New York: Free Press, 1969.

Bell, T.P. *Our Nuptial Ode and Welcome.* London: Hamilton, Adams, 1874.

Bellamy, J.G. *Crime and the Public Order in England in the Later Middle Ages.* London: Routledge & Kegan Paul, 1973.

Bellanger, C., et al. *Histoire Générale de la Presse Francaise.* 4 vols. Paris: Presse Universitaires de France, 1969.

Belle, Frances P. *Life and Adventures of the Celebrates Bandit*

Joaquin Murieta. Chicago: Reagan, 1925.

Belli, Melvin. *Blood Money.* New York: Grosset & Dunlap, 1956.

_____, and Carroll, Maurice C. *Dallas Justice.* New York: David McKay, 1964.

_____. *The Law Revolution.* Los Angeles: Sherbourne Press, 1968.

_____, and Kaiser, Robert Blair. *My Life on Trial.* New York: William Morrow, 1976.

Bellini, Delle Stelle, et al. *Dongo: The Last Act.* London: MacDonald, 1964.

Belloc, Hilaire. *The French Revolution.* New York: Oxford University Press, 1966.

_____. *Joan of Arc.* New York: Declan X. McMullen, 1929.

_____. *Richelieu.* Philadelphia: J.B. Lippincott, 1929.

Bellotti, Felice. *La Repubblica di Mussolini.* Milan, Italy: Zagara, 1947.

Bellows, Henry W. *Historical Sketch of the Union League Club of New York.* New York: The Club, 1879.

Bellows, Roger. *Psychology of Personnel in Business and Industry.* Englewood Cliffs, N.J.: Prentice-Hall, 1961.

The Bellville Tragedy, Story of the Trial and Conviction of Rev. W.E. Hinshaw for the Murder of His Wife. Indianapolis, Ind.: Sentinel Printing Company, 1895.

Beloff, Max. *The Foreign Policy of Soviet Russia, 1929-1941.* 2 vols. London: Oxford University Press, 1947-1949.

_____. *Soviet Policy in the Far East, 1944-1951.* New York: Oxford University Press, 1953.

Belon, Marie Joseph. *Jean Bréhal, grand inquisiteur de France et la réhabilitation de Jeanne d'Arc.* Paris: P. Lethielleux, 1893.

Belote, James H., and William, M. *Corregidor, Saga of a Fortress.* New York: Harper & Row, 1967.

Belson, William A. *Juvenile Theft: The Causal Factors.* London: Harper & Row, 1975.

_____. *The Public and the Police.* London: Harper & Row, 1975.

_____. *Television Violence and the Adolescent Boy.* Farnborough, Eng.: Saxon House, 1978.

Beltramelli, Antonio. *L'uomo nuovo.* Milan, Italy: Mondadori, 1923.

Beltrami, Giacomo Constantine. *A Pilgrimage in Europe and America.* London: Hunt & Clarke, 1828.

Beman, Lemar T. (ed.). *Selected Articles on Captial Punishment.* Minneapolis, Minn.: H. W. Wilson, 1913.

Bembo, Pietro. *Fil Asolani.* trans. Rudolph B. Gottfried. Bloomington: Indiana University Press, 1954.

Bemis, George. *Report of the Case of John W. Webster.* Boston: Little, Brown, 1850.

Bemis, Samuel Flagg. *The Diplomacy of the American Revolution.* New York: Appleton-Century, 1935.

_____. *A Diplomatic History of the United States.* New York: Holt, Rinehart & Winston, 1965.

_____. *Jay's Treaty.* New York: Macmillan, 1923.

_____. *John Quincy Adams and the Foundations of American Foreign Policy.* New York: Knopf, 1949.

_____. *The Latin American Policy of the United States.* New York: Harcourt, Brace, 1943.

_____. *Pinckney's Treaty.* Baltimore: Johns Hopkins Press, 1926.

Benchley, Nathaniel. *Robert Benchley: A Biography.* New York: McGraw Hill, 1955.

Benckendorff, Count Paul. *Last Days at Tsarskoe Selo.* London: Heinemann, 1927.

Benda, Harry J. *The Crescent and the Rising Sun: Indonesian Islam Under the Japanese Occupation, 1942-1945.* The Hague, Neth.: W. van Hoeve, 1958.

Bendiner, Robert. *Just Around the Corner.* New York: Harper & Row, 1967.

Bendz, Ernest. *Oscar Wilde, a Retrospect.* Vienna: n.p., 1921.

Benedetti, Arrigo. *Paura all'alba.* Milan, Italy: Il Saggiatore, 1965.

Benedetti, Jean. *Gilles de Rais.* New York: Stein & Day, 1971.

Benedict, John D. *Muskogee and Northeastern Oklahoma.* Chicago: S.J. Clarke, 1922.

Benedict, Michael Les. *A Compromise of Principle: The Politics of Radicalism.* New York: W.W. Norton, 1974.

_____. *The Impeachment and Trial of Andrew Johnson.* New York: W.W. Norton, 1973.

Benedict, Omar K. (ed.). *The Roundup. Dewey, Oklahoma: Held Annually Week of July Fourth.* Joe A. Bettles, 1916.

Benedict, Ruth. *The Chrysanthemum and the Sword.* Boston: Houghton Mifflin, 1946.

_____. *Patterns of Culture.* Boston: Houghton Mifflin, 1959.

Benedikt, H. *Geschichte der Republik Oesterreich.* Munich: R. Oldenbourg, 1954.

Benefield, Hattie Stone. *For the Good of the Country.* Los Angeles: Lorrin L. Morrison, 1951.

Benelli, Sem. *Io in Africa.* Milan, Italy: Mondadori, 1936.

Benét, Stephen Vincent. *John Brown's Body.* Doubleday, Doran, 1928.

Benet, William Rose. *Golden Fleece.* New York: Dodd, Mead, 1935.

Benezet, Anthony. *The Mighty Destroyer Displayed, in some account of the Dreadful Havock made by the mistaken Use as well as Abuse of Distilled Spiritous Liquors.* Philadelphia: Joseph Cruikshank, 1774.

_____. *The Pennsylvania Spelling-Book, or Youth's Friendly Instructor and Monitor.* Philadelphia: Joseph Cruikshank, 1779.

Benger, G. *Rumania in 1900.* London: Asher, 1900.

Bengham, Theodore A. *The Girl That Disappears.* New York: Gorham, 1911.

Bengis, Ingrid. *Combat in the Erogenous Zone.* New York: Alfred A. Knopf, 1972.

Bengston, Hermann. *The Greeks and the Persians.* New York: Delacorte Press, 1965.

Ben Gurion, David. *Israel: A Personal History.* New York: Funk & Wagnalls, 1971.

_____. *Israel: Years of Challenge.* New York: Holt, Rinehart & Winston, 1963.

_____. *Rebirth and Destiny of Israel.* New York: Philosophical Library, 1954.

Benham, W. Gurney. *Playing Cards: History of the Pack and Explanations of its Many Secrets.* London: Ward, Lock, 1931.

Benham, William Burton. *Life of Osborn H. Oldroyd.* Washington, D.C.: O.H. Oldroyd, 1927.

Ben-Hanan, Eli. *Our Man in Damascus: Eli Cohen.* New York: Steinmatsky-World Wide, 1976.

Benini, Zenone. *Vigilia a Verona.* Milan, Italy: Garzanti, 1949.

Benjamin, Harry, and Masters, R.E.L. *Prostitution and Morality.* New York: Julian, 1964.

_____. *The Transsexual Phenomenon.* New York: Julian, 1966.

Benjamin, René. *Mossolini et son Peuple.* Paris: Plon, 1937.

Bennecke, Heinrich. *Hitler und die SA.* Munich: Günter Olzog Verlag, 1962.

Bennet, H.S. *Life on the English Manor: A Study of Peasant Conditions, 1150-1400.* Cambridge, Eng.: University Press, 1960.

Bennet, J.H.E., and Dewhurst, J.C. (eds.) *Quarter Sessions Records with Other Records of the Justices of the Peace for the County Palatine of Chester, 1559-1760.* Chester, Eng.: n.p., 1940.

Bennet, Richard. *The Black and Tans.* London: Paperback Four Square, 1959.

Bennett, Arnold. *Jackie, Bobby and Manchester: The Story Behind the Headlines.* New York: Bee-Line Books, 1967.

Bennett, Benjamin. *The Evil That Men Do.* Cape Town, S. Afri.: Howard B. Timmins, n.d.

_____. *Famous South African Murders.* London: T. Werner Laurie, 1938.

_____. *Freedom or the Gallows.* Cape Town, S.Afri.: Howard B. Timmins, 1956.

_____. *Genius for the Defense, Life of Harry Morris, K.C.* Cape Town, S.Afri.: Howard B. Timmins, 1959.

_____. *Murder is my Business.* London: Hodder and Stoughton Ltd., 1951.

_____. *Murder Will Speak.* Cape Town, S.Afri.: Howard B. Timmins, 1962.

_____. *The Noose Tightens.* Cape Town, S.Afri.: Howard B. Timmins, 1974.

_____. *This Was a Man.* Cape Town, S.Afri.: H.B. Timmins, 1958.

_____. *Too Late for Tears.* Cape Town, S.Afri.: Howard B. Timmins, 1948.

_____. *Up for Murder.* London: Hutchinson, 1934.

_____. *Was Justice Done?.* Cape Town, S.Afri.: Howard B. Timmins, 1975.

_____. *Why Did They Do It?* Capetown, S.Afri.: Howard Timmins, 1953.

Bennett, Daphne. *Vicki, Princess Royal of England and German Empress.* New York: St. Martin's Press, 1971.

Bennett, David H. *The Party of Fear: From Nativist Movements to the New Right in American History.* Chapel Hill: University of North Carolina Press, 1988.

Bennett, Edwin Lewis. *Boom Town Boy in Old Creede Colorado.* Chicago: Sage Books, 1966.

Bennett, Estelline. *Old Deadwood Days.* New York: J.H. Sears, 1928.

Bennett, Fremont O. *Politics and Politicians of Chicago, Cook County, and Illinois.* Chicago: Blakely, 1886.

Bennett, Georgette. *A Safe Place to Live.* New York: Insurance Information Institute, 1982.

Bennett, H. Gordon. *Why Singapore Fell.* Sydney, Aus.: Angus and Robertson, 1944.

Bennett, Harry Herbert. *We Never Called Him Henry.* New York: Gold Medal Books, 1951.

Bennett, James V. *I Chose Prison.* New York: Alfred A. Knopf, 1970.

_____. *Of Prisons and Justice.* Washington, D.C.: U.S. Government Printing Office, 1964.

_____. *Proceedings of the American Correctional Association.* n.p., 1953.

Bennett, Lerone, Jr. *What Manner of Man.* New York: Pocket Books, 1968.

Bennett, Richard. *The Black and Tans.* Boston: Houghton, Mifflin, 1960.

Bennett, Vito, and Clazett, Cricket. *1001 Ways to Avoid Getting Mugged.* New York: Mason/Charter, 1977.

Bennett, Wendell C., and Zing, Robert M. *The Tarahumara.* Chicago: University of Chicago Press, 1935.

Bennett, William P. *The First Baby in Camp.* Salt Lake City, Utah: Rancher, 1893.

Benoist-Méchin, Jacques. *Alexander the Great: The Meeting of East and West.* New York: Hawthorn Books, 1966.

_____. *Histoire de l'armée allemande.* Paris: Albin Michel, 1964-1966.

_____. *Le Roi Saud.* Paris: Editions Albin Michel, 1960.

_____. *Sixty Days That Shook the West: The Fall of France 1940.* New York: G.P. Putnam's Sons, 1963.

Benoit-Lévy, Edmond. *Jules Favre.* Paris: Picard-Bernheim, 1884.

Ben-Porath, Yoram. *The Arab Labor Force in Israel.* Jerusalem: Israeli University Press, 1966.

Benscholter, George E. *Book of Facts Concerning the Early Settlements of Sherman County.* Loup City, Nebr.: Loup City Northwestern Print, 1897.

Benson, Allan L. *The Truth About Socialism.* New York: Huebsch, 1913.

Benson, E.F. *The Kaiser and English Relations.* London: Longmans, 1936.

_____. *Queen Victoria's Daughters.* New York: D. Appleton-Century, 1938.

Benson, Henry C. *Life Among the Choctaw Indians and Sketches of the Southwest.* Cincinnati, Ohio: L. Swormstedt & A Poe, 1860.

Benson, Captain L. *The Book of Remarkable Trials.* London: Chatto and Windus, 1924.

Benson, Lee. *The Concept of Jacksonian Democracy: New York as a Test Case.* Princeton: Princeton University Press, 1961.

_____. *Merchants, Farmers, and Railroads: Railroad Regulation and New York Politics, 1850-1887.* Cambridge, Mass.: Harvard University Press, 1955.

Benson, Luther. *Fifteen Years in Hell; An Autobiography.* Indianapolis, Ind.: Tilford & Carlon, 1877.

Bent, Alan Edward. *The Politics of Law Enforcement.* Lexington, Mass.: D.C. Heath, 1974.

Bent, Silas. *Ballyhoo: The Voice of the Press.* New York: Boni & Liveright, 1927.

_____. *Justice Oliver Wendell Holmes.* Garden City, N.Y.: Vanguard Press, 1932.

_____. *Newspaper Crusaders.* New York: McGraw-Hill, 1939.

_____. *Strange Bedfellows.* New York: Horace Liveright, 1928.

Bentham, J. *An Introduction to the Principles of Morals and Legislation.* Oxford, Eng.: Basil Blackwell, 1948.

Bentham, Jeremy. *Theory of Legislation.* trans. R. Hildbreth. London: Trubner & co., 1864.

_____. *The Works of Jeremy Bentham.* 11 vols. New York: Russell & Russell, 1962.

Bentinck, Lady Norah Ida Emily. *The Ex-Kaiser in Exile.* London: Hodder & Stoughton, 1921.

Bentley, Elizabeth. *Out of Bondage.* New York: Devin-Adair, 1951.

Bentley, George R. *A History of the Freedmen's Bureau.* Philadelphia: University of Pennsylvania Press, 1955.

Bentley, W.G. *My Son's Execution.* London: W.H. Allen, 1957.

Benton, E.J. *International Law and the Diplomacy of the Spanish-American War.* Baltimore: Johns Hopkins Press, 1908.

_____. *The Movement for Peace without a Victory during the Civil War.* New York: Da Capo Press, 1972.

Benton, Jesse James. *Cow by the Tail.* Boston: Houghton Mifflin, 1943.

Benton, Rita. *Franklin and Other Plays.* New York: Writers, 1924.

Benton, Roger. *Where Do I Go from Here?* New York: Lee Furman, 1936.

Benton, Thomas Hart. *Thirty Years' View; or, A History of the Workings of the American Government...From 1820 to 1850.* 2 vols. New York: D. Appleton, 1854.

Bentwich, Norman. *Israel.* New York: McGraw-Hill, 1953.

Ben-Veniste, Richard, and Frampton, George Jr. *Stonewall.* New York: Tuchstone, 1978.

Bequai, August. *Computer Crime.* Lexington, Mass.: Lexington Books, D.C. Heath, 1978.

_____. *Organized Crime: The Fifth Estate.* Lexington, Mass.: D.C. Heath, 1979.

_____. *White Collar Crime: A Twentieth Century Crisis.* Lexington, Mass.: Lexington Books, D.C. Heath, 1978.

Berardi, Paolo. *Memorie di un capo di Stato Maggiore.* Bologna, Italy: ODCU, 1954.

Beraud, Henri. *Ce Que f'ai Vu à Rome.* Paris: Les Editions de France, 1930.

_____. *Men of the Aftermath.* trans. F.Whyte. London: Grant Richards & Humphrey Toulmin, 1929.

Berber, John. *Historical Collections of the State of New York.* New York: Austin, 1851.

Bercovici, Konrad. *That Royal Lover.* New York: Brer & Warren, 1931.

Berdayev, Nicholas. *The Russian Idea.* New York: Macmillan, 1948.

Berelson, Bernard, and Janowitz, Morris. *Reader in Public Opinion and Communication.* New York: Free Press, 1966.

Bérence, Fred. *Les Borgias.* Paris: Pierre aliffe, 1966.

____. *Lucrèce Borgia.* Paris: Payot, 1937.

Berendt, Joachim-Ernst. *Jazz: A Photo History.* New York: Schirmer, 1978.

Beresford, Lord Charles. *The Break-up of China.* London: Harper & Bros., 1899.

____. *The Memoirs of Admiral Lord Charles Beresford.* 2 vols. London: Lethuen, 1914.

Beresford, S.R. *Beresford's Monte Carlo.* London: Nice, 1923.

____. *The Future at Monte Carlo.* London: Palmer, Sutton, 1926.

Berg, Charles, and Allen, Clifford. *The Problem of Homosexuality.* New York: Citadel, 1958.

Berg, Karl. *The Sadist.* London: Heinemann, 1932.

Berg, L.L., Hahn, H., and Scmidhauser, J.R. *Corruption in the American Political System.* Morristown, N.J.: General Learning Press, 1976.

Bergamini, David. *Japan's Imperial Conspiracy.* New York: William Morrow, 1971.

Berger, Carl. *B-29: The Superfortress.* New York: Ballantine Books, 1970.

Berger, Earl. *The Covenant and the Sword.* Toronto, Ontario, Can.: University of Toronto Press, 1965.

Berger, Elmer. *Judaism or Jewish Nationalism.* New York: Bookman, 1957.

____. *Who Knows Better Must Say So.* New York: American Council for Judaism, 1955.

Berger, Max. *The British Traveller in America, 1836-1860.* New York: Columbia University Press, 1943.

Berger, Meyer. *The Eight Million.* New York: Simon & Schuster, 1942.

____. *The Story of the New York Times.* New York: Simon & Schuster, 1951.

Berger, Morroe. *The Arab World Today.* Garden City, N.Y.: Doubleday, 1962.

Berger, Peter L. *Invitation to Sociology.* New York: Doubleday Anchor, 1963.

____, and Luckman, Thomas. *The Social Construction of Reality: A Treatise in the Sociology of Knowledge.* Garden City, N.Y.: Doubleday, 1966.

Berger, Raoul. *Death Penalties: The Supreme Court's Obstacle Course.* Cambridge, Mass.: Harvard University Press, 1984.

Berger, Victor L. *Voice and Pen of Victor L. Berger.* Milwaukee, Wis.: Socialist Party, 1929.

Bergier, Jacques. *Secret Armies: The Growth of Corporate and Industrial Espionage.* trans. Harold J. Salemson. Indianapolis, Ind.: Bobbs-Merrill, 1975.

Berglar, Peter. *Walther Rathenau: Seine zeit, sein Werk, seine Persönlichkeit.* Bremen: Universitatsverlag, 1970.

Bergman, Andrew. *We're in the Money.* New York: New York University Press, 1972.

Bergman, Ingrid, and Burgess, Alan. *Ingrid Bergman: My Story.* New York: Delacorte, 1980.

Bergstrand, Carl Martin. *Trolldom och klokskap i Västergötland under 1800-talet.* Borås, Swed.: H. Borgströms, 1932.

Berio, Alberto. *Missione Segreta.* Milan, Italy: Dall'Oglio, 1947.

Berkeley, Edmund and Dorothy S. *John Clayton, Pioneer of American Botany.* Chapel Hill: University of North Carolina Press, 1963.

Berkeley, George. *The Democratic Policeman.* Boston: Beacon Press, 1969.

Berkinow, Louise. *Abel.* New York: Trident Press, 1970.

Berkman, Alexander. *Prison Memoirs of an Anarchist.* New York: Mother Earth, 1912.

Berkow, Ira. *The Man Who Robbed the Pierre.* New York: Atheneum, 1987.

Berkowitz, Leonard. *Aggression: A Social Psychological Analysis.* New York: McGraw-Hill, 1962.

Berkson, Seymour. *Their Majesties!* New York: Stackpole Sons, 1938.

Berky, Andrew S., and Shenton, James P. *The Historian's History of the United States.* New York: G.P. Putnam's Sons, 1966.

Berle, Adolf, and Means, Gardiner. *The Modern Corporation and Private Property.* New York: Harcourt, 1932.

Berle, Beatrice B., and Jacobs, Travis B. (eds.). *Navigating the Rapids, 1918-1971: From the Papers of Adolf A. Berle.* New York: Harcourt Brace Jovanovich, 1973.

Berlinguer, Mario. *La crisi della giustizia nel regime fascista.* Rome: Migliaresi, 1944.

Berlo, David K. *The Process of Communication.* New York: Holt, Rinehart, & Winston, 1960.

Berman, Harold J. *Justice in Russia.* Cambridge, Mass.: Harvard University Press, 1950.

____ (ed.). *Soviet Criminal Law and Procedure.* Cambridge, Mass.: Harvard University Press, 1972.

____ (ed.). *Talks on American Law.* New York: Random House, 1961.

Berman, Louis. *New Creations in Human Beings.* New York: Doran, Doubleday, 1938.

Bermant, Chaim. *Point of Arrival: A Study of London's East End.* London: Methuen, 1975.

Bermant, G., et al. *Psychology and the Law.* Toronto, Ontario, Can.: Lexington Books, 1976.

Bernadotte, Count Folke. *The Fall of the Curtain.* London: Cassell, 1945.

____. *Instead of Arms.* Stockholm: Bonniers, 1948.

____. *To Jerusalem.* London: Hodder & Stoughton, 1951.

Bernal, J.D. *Science in History.* Cambridge, Mass.: MIT Press, 1971.

Bernaldo de Quiros, C. *Modern Theories of Criminality.* trans. Alfonso de Salvio. Boston: Little, Brown, 1911.

Bernard, Richard. *A Guide to Grand Jurymen.* London: E. Blackmore, 1627.

Bernardus Comensis de Como. *Lucerna Inquisitorum Haereticae Pravitatis... et Eiusdem Tractatus de Strigiis.* Milan: Valerium & Hieronymum, 1566.

Bernardy, Francoise de. *Albert and Victoria.* New York: Harcourt, Brace, 1953.

Bernays, Robert. *Naked Fakir.* London: Victor Gollancz, 1931.

Berne, Eric E. *Games People Play.* New York: Grove Press, 1964.

____. *Principles of Group Treatment.* New York: Oxford University Press, 1966.

____. *Transactional Analysis in Psychotherapy.* New York: Grove Press, 1961.

Bernelle, Frédéric Henri. *La Psychose de Gilles de Rais.* Paris: Jouvet et Cie., 1910.

Berner, Ernst. *Geschichte des preussischen Staates.* Munich: Verlagsanstalt fur Kunst & Wissenschaft, 1891.

Bernhart, Joseph. *The Vatican as a World Power.* London: Longmans, 1939.

Bernheimer, Richard. *Wild Men in the Middle Ages: A Study in Art, Sentiment, and Demonology.* Cambridge, Mass.: Harvard University Press, 1952.

Bernikow, Louise (ed.). *The World Split Opens.* New York: Vintage, 1974.

Bernou, Jean. *La chasse aux sorcières dans le Labourd, 1609.* Agen, Fr.: Calvet et Célérié, 1897.

Berns, Walter. *For Capital Punishment: Crime and the Morality of the Death Penalty.* New York: Basic Books, 1979.

Bernstein, Barton J. (ed.). *Towards a New Past: Dissenting Essays in American History.* New York: Vintage Books, 1969.

Bernstein, Carl, and Woodward, Bob. *All the President's Men.* New York: Simon & Schuster, 1974.

____. *The Final Days.* New York: Simon & Schuster, 1976.

Bernstein, David. *The Philippine Story.* New York: Farrar, Straus, 1947.

Bernstein, Irving. *Turbulent Years.* Boston: Houghton Mifflin, 1970.

Bernstein, Marver H. *The Politics of Israel.* Princeton, N.J.: Princeton University Press, 1957.

Bernstein, Marvin D. *The Mexican Mining Industry.* Albany: State University of New York, 1964.

Bernstein, Richard J. *The Restructuring of Social and Political Theory.* New York: Harcourt Brace Jovanovich, 1976.

Bernstein, Saul. *Youth on the Streets: Work with Alienated Youth Gangs.* New York: Association Press, 1964.

Bernstorff, Count Johann Von. *My Three Years in America.* New York: Charles Scribner's Sons, 1920.

Berretta, Alfio. *Amedeo d'Aosta.* Milan, Italy: Beretta, 1956.

Berrett, James. *When I Was at Scotland Yard.* London: Sampson, Low, Marston, 1932.

Berridge, Virginia and Edwards, Griffin. *Opium and the People.* New York: St. Martin's Press, 1961.

Berrigan, Darrel. *Yakuza no Sekai: Nihon no Uchimaku (Yakuza Society: Behind the Japanese Curtain).* Tokyo: Kindai Shisosha, 1948.

Berro, Huertas. *La Pena de Muerte.* Montevideo, Urug.: Private Edition, 1961.

Berry, C.B. *The Other Side, How It Struck Us.* London: Griffith & Farran, 1880.

Berry, Gerald L. *The Whoop-Up Trail.* Edmonton, Alberta, Can.: Applies Art Productions, 1953.

Berry, J. *My Experiences as an Executioner.* Devon, Eng.: David & Charles Reprints, 1972.

Berry, L.V., and Van den Bark, M. *The American Thesaurus of Slang.* London: Harrap, 1954.

Berry, Robert Elton. *Yankee Stargazer: The Life of Nathaniel Bowditch.* New York and London: Whittlesey House, Mcgraw-Hill, 1944.

Berry, Wendell, and Shahn, Ben. *November Twenty-Six Nineteen Hundred Sixty-Three.* New York: George Braziller, 1964.

Berryer, Pierre-Antoine. *Les Oeuvres conplètes.* 9 vols. Paris: Didier, 1872-1878.

Berryhill, Jefferson. *Indian-Pioneer History.* Oklahoma City: Indian Archives Division, Oklahoma Historical Society, n.d.

Berteaut, Simone. *Piaf.* New York: Dell, 1973.

Berthet, Elie. *Le loup-garou.* Brussels: Hetitiens Doorman, 1843.

Berthoff, Rowland T. "The American Social Order: A Conservative Hypothesis." *American Historical Review* 69, 1960.

Bertie, Lord. *Diary of Lord Bertie of Thame.* Vol. I. London: Hodder & Stoughton, 1922.

Bertoldi, Silvio. *Mussolini tale e quale.* Milan, Italy: Longanesi, 1965.

_____. *I tedeschi in Italia.* Milan, Italy: Rizzoli, 1964.

_____. *La guerra parallela.* Milan, Italy: Sugar, 1963.

Berton, Peter, Langer, Paul, and Swearingen, Rodger. *Japanese Training and Research in the Russian Field.* Los Angeles: University of Southern California Press, 1956.

Berton, Pierre. *The Klondike Fever.* New York: Alfred A. Knopf, 1958.

Bertram, James. *Beneath the Shadow.* New York: John Day, 1947.

_____. *First Act in China: The Story of the Sian Mutiny.* New York: Viking, 1938.

Bertrand, Amédée. *Etude Médico-légale au sujet de Troppmann.* Paris: Published by Author, 1869.

Bertrand, Général. *Cahiers de Sainte-Hélène.* Paris: Flammarion, Albin Michel & Sulliver, 1959.

Bertrand, Isidore. *Les possédées de Loudun et Urbain Grandier.* Paris: Bloud, 1905.

Bertrand, L., and Petrie, C. *The History of Spain.* London: Appleton Century, 1945.

Berve, Helmut. *Die Tyrannis bei den Griechen.* 2 vols. Munich: C. H. Beck'sche Verlagsbuchhandlung, 1967.

Besant, Annie. *Law of Population.* London: Freethought, 1879.

Besant, Walter. *East London.* Chatto & Windus, 1903.

_____. *London in the Time of the Stuarts.* London: Adam & Black, 1903.

Besgen, Achim. *Der stille Befehl. Medizinalrat Kersten und das Dritte Reich.* Munich, Ger.: Nymphenburger Verlagshandlung, 1960.

Besharov, Douglas J. *Juvenile Justice Advocacy.* New York: Practicing Law Institute, 1974.

Beshoar, Michael. *All About Tinidad.* Denver: n.p., 1882.

Best, Geoffrey. *Mid-Victorian Britain, 1851-1875.* New York: Schocken, 1972.

Best, Harry. *Crime and the Criminal Law in the United States.* New York: Macmillan, 1930.

Best, S. Payne. *The Venlo Incident.* London: Hutchinson, 1950.

Best, Werner. *Die Deutsche Polizei.* Darmstadt, Ger.: L.C. Wittich, 1941.

Besterman, Lujo. *Men Against Women: A Study of Sexual Relations.* London: Methuen, 1924.

Besterman, Theodore. *Voltaire Essays, and Another.* New York: Oxford University Press, 1962.

Betenson, Lula. *Butch Cassidy, My Brother.* Provo, Utah: Brigham Young University Press, 1975.

Bethell, Nicholas. *The Last Secret.* New York: Basic Books, 1974.

Bettelheim, Bruno. *The Uses of Enchantment.* New York: Alfred A. Knopf, 1976.

Bettenson, Henry (ed.). *The City of God.* Harmondsworth, Eng.: Penquin, 1972.

Betts, E.M. *Thomas Jefferson's Farm Book.* Princeton, N.J.: Princeton University Press, 1953.

Betts, Ernest. *The Film Business: A History of British Cinema 1896-1972.* London: George Allen & Unwin, 1973.

Betts, Tony. *Across the Board.* New York: Citadel Press, 1956.

Beucler, André, and Alexinsky, G. *Les amours secrètes de Lénine.* Paris: Editions Baudinière, 1937.

Beurdeley, Michel, et al. *Chinese Erotic Art.* Rutland, Vt.: Charles E. Tuttle, 1969.

Bevan, Edwyn. *German Social Democracy During the War.* New York: E.P. Dutton, 1919.

_____. *Indian Nationalism.* New York: Macmillan, 1914.

Beveridge, Albert Jeremiah. *Abraham Lincoln, 1809-1858.* 2 vols. Boston: Houghton Mifflin, 1928.

_____. *The Life of John Marshall.* 4 vols. Boston: Houghton Mifflin, 1916.

_____. *The Russian Advance.* New York: Harper & Row, 1903.

Beveridge, Peter. *Inside the C.I.D.* London: Evans, 1957.

Beveridge, Sir William H. *Full Employment in a Free Society.* London: Allen & Unwin, 1945.

_____. *The Pillars of Security.* New York: Macmillan, 1943.

Beverly, Bob. *Hobo of the Rangeland.* Lovington, N.M.: n.p., 1941.

Bevin, Ernest. *The Balance Sheet of the Future.* New York: McBride, 1941.

Bevion, Giuseppe. *Due settimane di passione.* Milan, Italy: Poligr. degli Operai, 1930.

Beyen, J.W. *Money in a Maelstrom.* New York: Macmillan, 1949.

Beyens, Baron. *Deux Années à Berlin, 1912-14.* 2 vols. Paris: Plon, 1931.

_____. *Quatre Ans à Rome.* Paris: Plon, 1934.

Beyer, William Gilmore. *On Hazardous Service.* New York: Harper & Brothers, 1912.

Beyle, Marie Henri. *Oeuvres Complètes.* Paris: Librairie Honoré Champion, 1932.

Beymer, William G. *On Hazardous Service.* New York: Harper and Brothers, 1912.

Bezymenski, Lev A. *The Death of Adolf Hitler: Unknown Documents from Soviet Archives.* New York: Harcourt, Brace & World, 1968.

_____. *Martin Bormann.* Zurich, Switz.: Aurora Verlag, 1965.

Biagi, Enzo. *Il crepuscolo degli dei.* Milan, Italy: Rizzoli, 1961.

Bialer, Seweryn (ed.). *Stalin and His Generals: Soviet Military Memoirs of World War Two.* New York: Pegasus, 1969.

Bianchi, Gianfranco. *25 luglio, crollo di un regime.* Milan, Italy: Ugo Mursia, 1963.

Bianchi, Giuseppe. *The Work of the Fascist Government and the*

Economic Reconstruction of Italy. Milan, Italy: Unione Economica Italiana, 1925.

Bianchi, Lorenzo. *Mussolini scrittore e oratore*. Bologna, Italy: Zanichelli, 1937.

Bianco, Mirella. *Gadaffi, Voice from the Desert*. London: Longman, 1975.

Bibesco, Martha Lucie. *Royal Portraits*. New York: D. Appleton, 1928.

_____. *Some Royalties and a Prime Minister*. New York: D. Appleton, 1930.

Bickel, Alexander M. *The Least Dangerous Branch: The Supreme Court at the Bar of Politics*. New York: Bobbs-Merrill, 1962

_____. *Politics and the Warren Court*. New York: Harper & Row, 1965.

_____. *The Supreme Court and the Idea of Progress*. New Haven, Conn.: Yale University Press, 1978.

Bickerman, E.J. *The Maccabees*. trans. Moses Hadas. New York: Schocken, 1947.

Biddle, Bruce, and Thomas, E.J. (eds.). *Role Theory: Concepts and Research*. New York: Wiley, 1966.

Biddle, Francis. *In Brief Authority*. New York: Doubleday, 1962.

_____. *Mr. Justice Holmes*. New York: Charles Scribner's Sons, 1942.

Biddulph, Colonel John. *The Pirates of Malabar*. London: Smith, Elder, 1907.

Biderman, A., and Zimmer, H. (eds.). *The Manipulation of Human Behavior*. New York: John Wiley & Sons, 1961.

Bidwell, Austin. *From Wall Street to Newgate Via the Primrose Way*. Hertford, Conn.: Bidwell, 1895.

Bidwell, Percy, and Falconer, John I. *History of Agriculture in the Northern United States*. New York: P. Smith, 1941.

Biegel, Herbert and Allan. *Beneath the Badge: A Story of Police Corruption*. New York: Harper & Row, 1977.

Bienert, Walther. *Die Philosophie des Christian Thomasius*. Halle, Belg.: E. Klinz, 1934.

Bienstock, J.W. *Rasputin la fin d'un régime*. Paris: A. Michel, 1918.

Bierstadt, Edward Hale. *Curious Trials and Criminal Cases*. Garden City, N.Y.: Garden City Publishing, 1928.

_____. *Enter Murderers!* Garden City, N.Y.: Doubleday, Doran, 1934.

_____. *Satan Was a Man*. New York: Doubleday, Doran, 1935.

Bigelow, John. *France and the Confederate Navy (1862-1868)*. New York: Bergman, 1968.

_____ (ed.) *Letters and Literary Memorials of Samuel Jones Tilden*. New York: Harper & Brothers, 1908.

_____. *The Life of Samuel J. Tilden*. New York: Harper & Brothers, 1895.

_____. *Retrospections of an Active Life*. New York: Baker & Taylor, 1909.

_____. *The Writings and Speeches of Samuel J. Tilden*. New York: Harper and Brothers, 1885.

Bigelow, L.J. *Bench and Bar*. New York: Harper & Bros., 1871.

Bigelow, Poultney. *History of the German Struggle for Liberty*. New York: Harper & Brothers, 1896-1903.

Bigelow, W.E. *The Boston Tragedy: An Expose of the Parkman Murder*. Boston: n.p., 1850.

Biggers, Don H. *German Pioneers in Texas*. Fredericksburg, Texas: Fredericksburg, 1925.

_____. *Shackleford County Sketches*. Albany, Texas: Albany News Office, 1908.

Biggini, Carlo. *Storia inedita della conciliazione*. Milan, Italy: Garzanti, 1942.

Biggs, Earl R. *How to Protect Your Child From the Sex Criminal*. Portland, Ore.: New Science Book, 1950.

Biggs, J., Jr. *The Guilty Mind*. New York: Harcourt, 1955.

Bilby, Kenneth. *New Star in the East*. Garden City, N.Y.: Doubleday, 1950.

Bilderman, Albert D., et al. *Report on A Pilot Study in the District of Columbia on Victimization and Attitudes Toward Law Enforcement*. Commission on Law Enforcement and Administration of Justice. Washington, D.C.: U.S. Government Printing Office, 1967.

Biles, J. Hugh. *The Early History of Ada*. Ada: Oklahoma State Bank, 1954.

Billias, George Athan (ed.). *The American Revolution: How Revolutionary Was It?* New York: Holt, Rinehart & Winston, 1965.

_____. *George Washington's Generals*. New York: Morrow, 1964.

_____. *Washington's Opponents*. New York: William Morrow, 1969.

Billings, John S., et al. *The Liquor Problem*. Boston: Houghton Mifflin, 1905.

_____. *Physiological Aspects of the Liquor Problem; investigations made for and under the direction of The Committee of Fifty*. Boston: Houghton Mifflin, 1903.

Billingsley, A. *Black Families in White America*. Englewood Cliffs, N.J.: Prentice-Hall, 1969.

Billington, James H. *The Icon and the Axe: An Interpretive History of Russian Culture*. New York: Alfred A. Knopf, 1966.

_____. *Mikhailovsky and Russian Populism*. Oxford, Eng.: Oxford University Press, 1958.

Billington, Ray A. *America's Frontier Heritage*. New York: Holt, Rinehart & Winston, 1966.

_____. *The Far Western Frontier 1830-1860*. New York: Harper & Brothers, 1956.

_____. *The Protestant Crusade, 1800-1860: A Study of the Origins of American Nativism*. New York: Macmillan, 1938.

_____ (ed.). *The Reinterpretation of Early American History: Essays in Honor of John E. Pomfret*. San Marino, Calif.,: Huntington Library, 1966.

_____. *Westward Expansion*. New York: Macmillan, 1949.

Billroth, Theodore. *Historical Studies on the Nature and Treatment of Gunshot Wounds from the Fifteenth Century to the Present Time*. New Haven, Conn.: Nathan Smith Medical Club, 1933.

Billy the Kid: Las Vegas Newspaper Account of His Career, 1880-81. Waco, Texas: W.M. Morrison, 1958.

Binchy, D.A. *Church and State in Fascist Italy*. Oxford, Eng.: Oxford University Press, 1941.

Binder, Leonard. *The Ideological Revolution in the Middle East*. New York: John Wiley & Sons, 1964.

Binet, A. *La Suggestibilité*. Paris: Scheicher Fréres, 1900.

Bing, Stephen R., and Rosenfeld, S. Stephen. *The Quality of Justice in the Lower Criminal Courts of Metropolitan Boston*. Boston: Lawyers' Committee for Civil Rights Under Law to the Governor's Committee on Law Enforcement and the Administration of Justice, 1970.

Binger, Carl. *Revolutionary Doctor*. New York: W.W. Norton, 1966.

Bingham, Alfred M. *Man's Estate*. New York: W.W. Norton, 1939.

_____. *The Techniques of Democracy*. New York: Duell, Sloan, & Pearce, 1942.

Bingham, Caroline. *The Life and Times of Edward II*. London: Weidenfeld & Nicolson, 1973.

Bingham, Helen. *In Tamal Land*. San Francisco: Calkins, 1906.

Bingham, Hiram. *Lost City of the Incas*. New York: Atheneum, 1963.

_____. *A Residence of Twenty-one Years in the Sandwich Islands*. Canandaigua, N.Y.: H.D.Goodwin, 1855.

Bingham, J.A. *Trial of the Conspirators for the Assassination of President Lincoln*. Washington, D.C.: U.S. Government Printing Office, 1865.

Bingham, General Theodore A. *The Girl That Disappears. The Real Facts About the White Slave Traffic*. Boston: R.G. Badger, 1911.

Binkley, Wilfred E. *American Political Parties. Their Natural History*. New York: Alfred A. Knopf, 1944.

Binney, Cecil. *Crime and Abnormality*. Oxford, Eng.: Oxford

University Press, 1949.

Binney, Horace. *The Privilege of the Writ of Habeas Corpus Under the Constitution.* Philadelphia: C. Sherman & Sons, 1862.

Binsfield, Peter. *Tractatus de Confessionibus Maleficorum et Sagarum.* Treves: Henricus Bock, 1591.

Binz, Carl. *Doctor Johann Weyer.* Bonn, Ger.: A. Marcus, 1885.

Biographical Dictionary of the American Congress 1774-1927. Washington, D.C.: U.S. Government Printing Office, 1928.

Biographical and Historical Memoirs of Louisiana. 2 vols. Chicago: Goodspeed, 1892.

Biography of Mr. Jason Fairbanks and Miss Elizabeth Fales. Boston: n.p., n.d.

Biondi, Dino. *La Fabbrica del Duce.* Florence, Italy: Vallecchi, 1967.

Biondi, Serafino. *Le tappe della Marcia su Roma rievocate un anno dopo l'evento.* Cono, Italy: La Provincia di Como, 1923.

Bird, Caroline. *The Invisible Scar.* New York: David McKay, 1966.

Bird, Eric, and Docking, Stanley. *Fire in Buildings.* London: Adam & Charles Black, 1949.

Bird, Harrison. *The March to Saratoga.* New York: Oxford University Press, 1963.

Bird, Robert Montgomery. *Nick of the Woods; or, The Jibbenainosay.* New Haven, Conn.: College & University Press, 1967.

Birdwhistell, A. *Kinesics and Context.* London: Penguin Press, 1971.

Birdwood, Lord. *Nuti es-Said.* London: Cassell, 1959.

Bireley, Robert. *The Peace of Prague (1635) and the Counterreformation in Germany.* Ann Arbor, Mich.: University Microfilms International, 1976.

Birkbeck, Morris. *Letters from Illinois.* London: Sherwood, Nelley & Jones, 1818.

_____. *Notes on a Journey in America.* London: Severn, 1818.

Birkby, Carel. *It's a Long Way to Addis.* London: Frederick Muller, 1942.

Birkenhead, Lord. *America Revisited.* Boston: Little, Brown, 1924.

_____. *Contemporary Personalities.* London: Cassell, 1924.

_____. *Famous Trials of History.* London: Hutchinson, 1926.

_____. *F.E.: The Life of F.E. Smith, First Earl of Birkenhead.* London: Eyre & Spottiswoode, 1960.

_____. *Frederick Edwin Earl of Birkenhead.* London: Thornton Butterworth, 1933.

_____. *More Famous Trials.* London: Hutchinson, 1928.

_____. *My American Visit.* London: Hutchinson, 1918.

_____. *Points of View.* London: Hodder & Stoughton, 1922.

Birket-Smith, Kaj. *The Eskimos.* London: Methuen, 1959.

Birmingham, George A. *From Dublin to Chicago.* New York: George H. Doran, 1914.

_____. *Murder Most Foul!* London: Chatto & Windus, 1929.

_____. *Pleasant Places.* London: William Heinemann, 1934.

Birmingham, Stephen. *California Rich.* New York: Simon & Schuster, 1980.

_____. *Our Crowd.* New York: Harper & Row, 1967.

_____. *Right People.* Boston: Little, Brown, 1958.

Birney, Herman Hoffman. *Vigilantes.* Philadelphia: Penn, 1929.

Birnbaum, Martin. *Oscar Wilde: Fragments and Memories.* London: n.p., 1920.

Biron, Sir Chartres. *Without Prejudice.* London: Faber, 1936.

Bishop, C. *Women and Crime.* London: Chatto & Windus, 1931.

Bishop, Cecil. *From Information Received.* London: Hutchinson, 1932.

Bishop, Ernest S. *The Narcotic Drug Problem.* New York: Macmillan, 1919.

Bishop, George. *Executions.* Los Angeles: Sherbourne Press, 1965.

_____. *Witness to Evil.* Los Angeles: Nash, 1971.

Bishop, J.L. *A History of American Manufactures.* New York:

Augustus M. Kelley, 1966.

Bishop, Jim. *A Bishop's Confession.* Boston: Little, Brown, 1981.

_____. *The Day Kennedy Was Shot.* New York: Funk & Wagnalls, 1968.

_____. *The Day Lincoln Was Shot.* New York: Harper & Brothers, 1955.

_____. *The Days of Martin Luther King, Jr.* New York: G.P. Putnam's Sons, 1971.

_____. *FDR's Last Year.* New York: William Morrow, 1974.

_____. *The Mark Hellinger Story.* Englewood Cliffs, N.J.: Prentice-Hall, 1952.

_____. *The Murder Trial of Judge Peel.* New York: Simon & Schuster, 1962.

Bishop, Joseph B. *Chronicle of One Hundred and Fifty Years: The Chamber of Commerce of the State of New York.* New York: Charles Scribner's Sons, 1918.

_____. *Theodore Roosevelt and His Time.* New York: Charles Scribner's Sons, 1923.

Bishop, Morris. *Petrarch and His World.* Bloomington: Indiana University Press, 1963.

Bishop, N thaniel H. *Four Months in a Sneak Box.* Boston: Lee & Shephard, 1879.

Bishop, William. *Old Mexico and Her Lost Provinces.* New York: Harper, 1883.

Bismarck-Sconhausen, Prince Otto Eduard Leopold von. *Bismarck: The Man and the Statesman.* trans. A.J. Butler. London: Smith, Elder, n.d.

Biss, Andreas. *Der Stopp der Endlösung. Kampf gegen Himmler und Eichmann in Budapest.* Stuttgart, Ger.: Seewald, 1966.

Bisson, T.A. *Japan in China.* New York: Macmillan, 1938.

Bithell, Jethro. *Germany: A Companion to German Studies.* London: Methuen, 1955.

Bittner, Egon. *The Functions of the Police in Modern Society.* Rockville, Md.: National Institute of Mental Health Center for Studies of Crime and Delinquency, 1970.

Bixley, William. *The Guilty and the Innocent: My Fifty Years at the Old Bailey.* London: Souvenir Press, 1957.

Bizouard, Joseph. *Les rapports de l'homme avec le démon.* Paris: Gaume frères et J. Duprey, 1863.

Black, A.P. *End of the Long Horn Trail.* Selfridge, N.D.: Selfridge Journal, 1936.

Black, Algernon D. *The People and the Police.* New York: McGraw-Hill, 1968.

Black, B.J., and Glick, S.J. *Recidivism at the Hawthorne Cedar Knolls School: Predicted vs. Actual Outcome for Delinquent Boys.* New York: Jewish Board of Guardians, 1952.

Black, C.E. *The Establishment of Constitutional Government in Bulgaria.* Princeton, N.J.: Princeton University Press, 1943.

Black, Charles L., Jr. *Capital Punishment: The Inevitability of Caprice and Mistake.* New York: W.W. Norton, 1974.

_____. *The People and the Court: Judicial Review in a Democracy.* New York: Macmillan, 1960.

Black, Cyril (ed.). *Transformation of Russian Society: Aspects of Social Change Since 1861.* Cambridge, Mass.: Harvard University Press, 1960.

Black, David. *Murder at the Met.* Garden City, N.Y.: Doubleday, 1984.

Black, Donald. *The Behavior of Law.* New York: Academic Press, 1976.Burn

Black, George F. *A Calendar of Cases of Witchcraft in Scotland, 1510-1727.* New York: New York Public Library, 1938.

_____. *List of Works in the New York Public Library Relating to Witchcraft in Europe.* New York: New York Public Library, 1911.

_____. *List of Works in the New York Public Library Relating to Witchcraft in the United States.* New York: New York Public Library, 1908.

_____. *Some Unpublished Scottish Witchcraft Trials.* New York: New York Public Library, 1941.

Black, Henry Campbell (ed.). *Black's Law Dictionary.* St. Paul,

Minn.: West, 1968.

Black, Hugo. *One Man's Stand for Freedom.* New York: Alfred A. Knopf, 1973.

Black, J.B. *The Reign of Queen Elizabeth, 1558-1603.* Oxford, Eng.: Clarendon Press, 1936.

Black, Jack. *You Can't Win.* New York: Macmillan, 1926.

Blacker, Erwin R. (ed.). *The Old West in Fact.* New York: Ivan Obolensky, 1962.

_____. *Prescott's Histories: The Rise and Decline of the Spanish Empire.* New York: Viking Press, 1963.

Blackmar, Frank W. *Charles Robinson. The First Free-State Governor of Kansas.* Topeka, Kan.: Crane, 1900.

Blackmore, John. *The London by Moonlight Mission.* London: Robson & Avery, 1860.

Blackstock, Nelson. *Cointelpro: The FBI's Secret War on Political Freedom.* New York: Random House, 1976.

Blackstone, William. *Commentaries on the Laws of England.* 4 vols. London: A. Strahan, 1809.

Blackwell, Alice Stone. *Lucy Stone: Pioneer of Woman's Rights.* Boston: Little, Brown, 1930.

Blackwell, William L. *The Beginnings of Russian Industrialization, 1800-1860.* Princeton, N.J.: Princeton University Press, 1968.

Blackwood, A. *The Tales of Algernon Blackwood.* New York: E.P. Dutton, 1939.

Blaine, James G. *Twenty Years of Congress from Lincoln to Garfield.* Norwich, Conn.: Henry Bill, 1884.

Blair, Clay, Jr. and Joan. *The Search for JFK.* New York: Berkeley-Putnam, 1976.

_____. *The Strange Case of Jame Earl Ray.* New York: Bantam Books, 1969.

Blair, Henry William. *The Temperence Movement.* Boston: William Smythe, 1888.

Blair, John. *Seeds of Destruction: A Study of the Functional Weakness of Capitalism.* New York: Covici Friede, 1938.

Blair, John M. *Economic Concentration.* New York: Harcourt, Brace, Jovanovich, 1972.

Blair, Lawrence. *Rhythems of Vision.* New York: Schocken, 1976.

Blair, Walter, and Meine, Franklin J. (eds.). *Half Horse, Half Alligator: The Growth of the Mike Fink Legend.* Chicago: University of Chicago Press, 1956.

_____. *Mike Fink.* New York: Henry Holt, 1933.

_____. *A Raft Pilot's Log.* Glendale, Calif.: Arthur H. Clark, 1930.

Blaisdell, D.C. *European Financial Control in the Ottoman Empire: A Study of the Establishment, Activites, and Significance of the Administration of the Ottoman Public Debt.* New York: Columbia University Press, 1929.

Blake, Aldrich. *The Ku Klux Kraze.* Oklahoma City: n.p., 1924.

Blake, Euphemia Vale. *History of the Tammany Society From Its Organization to the Present Time, 1901.* New York: Souvenir, 1901.

Blake, James. *The Joint.* Garden City, N.Y.: Doubleday, 1971.

Blake, Robert. *Disraeli.* Garden City, N.Y.: Doubleday, 1968.

_____ (ed.). *Haig: Private Papers, 1914-18.* London: Eyre & Spottiswood, 1952.

Blakeley, T. *Soviet Scholasticism.* Dordrecht, Holland: D. Riedel, 1961.

Blakeney, T.S. *Sherlock Holmes: Fact or Fiction?* Morristown, N.J.: Baker Street Irregulars, 1954.

Blakeslee, G.H. (ed.). *Mexico and the Caribbean.* New York: G. E. Stechert, 1920.

Blakey, G. Robert. *The Development of the Law of Gambling: 1776-1976.* Washington, D.C.: National Institute of Law Enforcement and Criminal Justice, 1977.

_____, and Billings, Richard. *The Plot to Kill the President.* New York: Times Books, 1981.

_____, Goldstock, Ronald, and Rogovin, Charles H. *Rackets Bureau: Investigation and Prosecution of Organized Crime.* Washington D.C. U.S. Government Printing Office, 1978.

Blanc, Marie Therese. *The Condition of Woman in the United States.* Boston: Roberts Brothers, 1895.

Blanch, Lesley. *The Game of Hearts.* New York: Simon and Schuster, 1955.

_____. *Pavilion's of the Heart.* New York: G.P. Putnam's Sons, 1974.

_____. *Under a Lilac-Bleeding Star.* New York: Atheneum, 1964.

Blanchard, Claude. *Dames de Coeur.* Paris: Editions du Pré aux clercs, 1946.

Blanchard, Leola Howard. *The Conquest of Southwest Kansas.* Wichita, Kan.: Wichita Eagle Press, 1931.

Blanchard, Robert E. *Introduction to the Administration of Justice.* New York: John Wiley & Sons, 1975.

Blanchard, Rufus. *Discovery and Conquests of the Northwest with History of Chicago.* Chicago: Cushing, Thomas, 1881.

Blanchet, Maurice. *Lautréamont et Sade.* Paris: Les Editions de Minuit, 1949.

Blancké, W. Wendell. *Juárez of Mexico.* New York: Frederick A. Praeger, 1971.

Blanco Moheno, Roberto. *Crónica de la Revolución Mexicana: de la Decena Trágica a los campos de Celaya.* Mexico: Libros Mexicana, 1957.

Bland, J.O.P. *China: The Pity of It.* New York: Doubleday, 1932.

Bland, T.A. *Life of Albert B. Meacham.* Washington D.C.: T.A. & M.C. Bland, 1883.

Blankenship, Russell. *And There Were Men.* New York: Alfred A. Knopf, 1942.

Blanshard, Paul. *An Outline of the British Labor Movement.* New York: Doran, 1923.

Blanshard, Paul. *Personal and Controversial.* Boston: Beacon Press, 1973.

Blasco, E. *Historia de Corte de Madrid.* Madrid: n.p., 1904.

Blasco Ibáñez, Vicente. *In the Land of Art.* trans. Frances Douglas. London: T. Fisher Unwin, 1924.

_____. *Mexico in Revolution.* New York: E.P. Dutton, 1920.

Blau, Joseph Leon. *The Christian Interpretation of the Cabala in the Renaissance.* New York: Columbia University Press, 1944.

Blau, Peter M. *The American Occupational Structure.* New York: John Wiley & Sons, 1967.

_____. *Bureaucracy in Modern Society.* New York: Random House, 1956.

_____. *The Dynamics of Bureaucracy.* Chicago: University of Chicago Press, 1956.

_____. *Exchange and Power in Social Life.* New York: John Wiley & Sons, 1964.

_____, and Richard, Scott W. *Formal Organizations.* San Francisco: Chandler, 1962.

Blau, Zena Smith. *Black Children/White Children: Competence, Socialization, and Social Structure.* New York: Free Press, 1981.

Blaustein, A., and Porter, C. *The American Lawyer.* Chicago: University of Chicago Press, 1954.

Blauvelt, Mary Taylor. *Oliver Cromwell: A Dictator's Tragedy.* New York: G. P. Putnam's & Sons, 1937.

Blaxland, G. *The Regiments Depart: A History of the British Army, 1945-1970.* London: William Kimber, 1963.

Bleackley, Horace. *The Hangmen of England.* London: Chapman & Hall, 1929.

_____. *Ladies Fair & Frail: Sketches of the Demi-Monde During the Eighteenth Century.* London: Bodley Head, 1909.

_____. *Some Distinguished Victims of the Scaffold.* London: Kegan Paul, Trench, Trubner, 1905.

Blease, W.L. *Suvorov.* London: Constable, 1920.

Bleau, Alphonse. *Précis d'histoire sur la ville et les possédées de Loudun.* Poitiers, Fr.: H. Oudin, 1877.

Bledstein, Burton J. *The Culture of Professionalism.* New York: W.W. Norton, 1976.

Blesh, Rudi. *Keaton.* New York: Macmillan, 1966.

Bleyer, Willard Grosvenor. *Main Events in the History of Ameri-*

can Journalism. New York: Houghton Mifflin, 1927.

Blied, Benjamin J. *Catholics and the Civil War.* Milwaukee, Wis.: Published by Author, 1945.

Bligh, Lieutenant William. *A Narrative of the Mutiny on Board H.M.S. Bounty and the Subsequent Voyage of Part of the Crew in the Ship's Boat from Tofoa... to Timor.* London: George Nichol, 1790.

Blinder, M. *Lovers, Killers, Husbands and Wives.* New York: St. Martin's Press, 1985.

Bliss, Douglas Percy (ed.). *The Devil In Scotland.* London: A. MacLehose, 1934.

Bliss, E.L. (ed.). *Roots of Behavior.* New York: Harper & Row, 1962.

Bliss, Frank E. *The Life of Hon. William F. Cody Known as Buffalo Bill, the Famous Hunter, Scout and Guide.* Hartford, Conn.: Published by Author, 1879.

Bliss, W.D.P. *Encyclopedia of Social Reform.* New York: Funk and Wagnalls, 1907.

Bloch, H.S., and Niederhofer, A. *The Gang.* New York: Philosophical Library, 1958.

Bloch, Herbert A. (ed.). *Crime in America.* New York: Philosophical Library, 1961.

_____, and Geis, Gilbert. *Man, Crime, and Society.* New York: Random House, 1962.

Bloch, Ian. *The Sexual Extremities of the World.* New York: Award, 1964.

Bloch, Ivan. *Anthropological Studies in the Strange Sexual Practices of All Races in All Ages.* New York: Anthropological Press, 1933.

_____. *Marquis de Sade.* trans. James Bruce. New York: Brittany Press, 1948.

_____. *120 Days of Sodom and the Sex life of the French Age of Debauchery.* trans. Raymond Sabatier. New York: Falstaff Press, 1934.

_____. *Die Prostitution.* Berlin: L. Marcus, 1912.

_____. *Sexual Life in England Past and Present.* London: Aldor, 1938.

_____. *The Sexual Life of Our Time.* New York: Rebman, 1914.

_____. *The Sexual Life of Our Time in Its Relation to Modern Civilization.* trans. M.E. Paul. London: Rebman, 1908.

Bloch, Marc. *Feudal Society.* trans. L.A. Manyon. Chicago: University of Chicago Press, 1961.

Bloch, Max, and Kenner, Ron. *Max the Butcher.* Secaucus, N.J.: Lyle Stuart, 1982.

Bloch, Michael (ed.). *Wallis and Edward: Letters 1931-1937.* New York: Summit Books, 1986.

Bloch, Peter B., and Specht, David. *Neighborhood Team Policing.* Washington, D.C.: National Institute of Law Enforcement and Criminal Justice, 1973.

Bloch, Robert. *American Gothic.* New York: Simon & Schuster, 1974.

Block, Alan A. *East Side-West Side: Organizing Crime in New York, 1930-1950.* Swansea, U.K.: Christopher Davis, 1979.

_____, and Chambliss, William J. *Organizing Crime.* New York: Elsevier, 1981.

_____, and Scarpitti, Frank R. *Poisoning for Profit: The Mafia and Toxic Waste.* New York: William Morrow, 1985.

Block, Eugene B. *And May God Have Mercy...The Case Against Capital Punishment* San Francisco: Fearon, 1962.

_____. *The Fabric of Guilt.* Garden City, N.Y.: Doubleday, 1968.

_____. *Fifteen Clues.* Garden City, N.Y.: Doubleday, 1965.

_____. *Great Stagecoach Robbers of the West.* New York: Doubleday, 1962.

_____. *Great Train Robberies of the West.* New York: Coward-McCann, 1959.

_____. *Lie Detectors.* New York: David McKay, 1977.

_____. *Science Vs. Crime.* New York: Caroline House, 1980.

_____. *Voiceprinting.* New York: McKay, 1975.

_____. *The Wizard of Berkeley.* New York: Coward-McCann, 1958.

Block, Irvin. *Violence in America.* New York: Public Affairs Committee, 1970.

Block, Peter, Anderson, Deborah, and Gervais, Pamela. *Policewomen on Patrol.* Washington, D.C.: Police Foundation, 1973.

Block, S. *Lives Through Time.* Berkeley, Calif.: Bancroft, 1971.

Blodgett, Geoffrey. *The Gentle Reformers: Massachusetts Democrats in the Cleveland Era.* Cambridge, Mass.: Harvard University Press, 1966.

Blodgett, Rush Maxwell. *Little Dramas of Old Bakersfield.* Los Angeles: Carl A. Bundy Quill & Press, 1931.

Blok, Anton. *The Mafia of a Sicilian Village, 1860-1960.* New York: Harper & Row, 1975.

Blom-Cooper, Louis (ed.). *The Law as Literature.* London: Bodley Head, 1961.

Blom, Eric. *Mozart.* New York: Collier, 1966.

Bloom, Herbert I. *The Economic Activities of the Jews of Amsterdam in the Seventeenth and Nineteenth Centuries.* Williamsport, Pa.: Bayard Press, 1937.

Bloom, M.T. *The Trouble With Lawyers.* New York: Simon & Schuster, 1969.

Bloom, Monroe A. *A Century of Pioneering: A Brief History of the Crocker-Citizens National Bank.* San Francisco: n.p., 1970.

Bloom, Murray Teigh. *The Man Who Stole Portugal.* New York: Charles Scribner's Sons, 1953.

_____. *Money of Thier Own.* New York: Charles Scribner's Sons, 1957.

_____. *Rogues to Riches.* New York: Warner, 1973.

Bloomfield, L.M. *Egypt, Israel and the Gulf of Aqaba in International Law.* Toronto, Ontario, Can.: Carswell, 1957.

Bloomgarden, Henry S. *The Gun: A "Biography" of the Gun That Killed John F. Kennedy.* New York: Grossman, 1975.

Bloomquist, Edward R. *Marijuana.* New York: Macmillan, 1970.

Blos, Peter. *On Adolescence.* New York: Free Press, 1962.

Bloss, Roy S. *Pony Express-the Great Gamble.* Berkeley, Calif.: Howell-North, 1939.

Bloyd, Levi. *Jefferson County History.* Fairbury, Neb.: Holloway, n.d.

Blücher, Evelyn. *An English Wife in Berlin.* London: Constable, 1920.

Blum, A. *On the Origins of Paper.* New York: R.R. Bowker, 1934.

Blum, J. *Lord and Peasant in Russia from the 9th to the 19th Century.* New York: Atheneum, 1964.

Blum, John M. *From the Morgenthau Diaries.* 3 vols. Boston: Houghton Mifflin, 1959-1967.

_____. *Joe Tumulty and the Wilson Era.* Boston: Houghton Mifflin, 1951.

_____. *V was for Victory.* New York: Harcourt Brace Jovanovich, 1976.

_____. *Woodrow Wilson and the Politics of Morality.* Boston: Little, Brown, 1956.

Blum, Leon. *For All Mankind.* New York: Viking Press, 1946.

_____. *Les Radicaux et Nous (1932-1934).* Paris: Librairie Populaire, 1934.

_____. *Le Socialisme devant la Crise.* Paris: Librairie Populaire du Parti Socialiste, 1933.

_____. *L'Exercice du Pouvoir.* Paris: Librairie Gallimard, 1937.

Blum, Richard H. *Deceivers and Deceived.* Springfield, Ill.: Charles C. Thomas, 1972.

_____, et al. *The Dream Sellers.* San Francisco: Jossey-Bass, 1972.

_____. *Horatio Alger's Children: The Role of the Family in the Origin and Prevention of Drug Risk.* San Francisco: Jossey-Bass, 1973.

_____. *Offshore Haven Banks, Trusts, and Companies: The Business of Crime in the Euromarket.* New York: Frederick A. Praeger, 1984.

_____, et al. *Society and Drugs.* San Francisco: Jossey-Bass, 1969.

_____, et al. *Students and Drugs.* San Francisco: Jossey-Bass,

1969.

_____. *Surveillance and Espionage in a Free Society*. New York: Praeger, 1972.

Blumberg, Abraham S. *Criminal Justice*. Chicago: Quadrangle Books, 1970.

_____. (ed.). *Current Perspectives on Criminal Behavior*. New York: Alfred A. Knopf, 1974.

_____. *Problems of American Society Criminal Justice*. Chicago: Quadrangle Books, 1967.

_____. (ed.). *The Scales of Justice*. Chicago: Aldine, 1970.

Blumberg, Dorothy Rose. *Florence Kelley: The Making of a Social Pioneer*. New York: Augustus M. Kelley, 1966.

Blumenson, Martin. *Anzio*. London: Weidenfeld & Nicolson, 1963.

_____. *Sicily: Whose Victory?* London: n.p.,1960.

Blumenthal, Ralph. *Last Days of the Sicilians: At War with the Mafia: The FBI Assault on the Pizza Connection*. New York: Times Books, 1988.

Blumenthal, Sid, and Yazijian, Harvey (eds.). *Government by Gunplay: Assassination Conspiracy Theories From Dallas to Today*. New York: Signet Books, 1976.

Blumenthal, Walter Hart. *Brides from Bridewell: Female Felons Sent to Colonial America*. Westport, Conn.: Greenwood Press, 1962.

Blumer, H.A., Sutter, S. Ahmed, and Smith, R. *The World of Youthful Drug Use*. Berkeley: University of California, 1967.

Blumstein, Alfred, Cohen, Jacqueline, and Nagin, Daniel (eds.). *Deterrence and Incapacitation: Estimating the Effects of Criminal Sanctions on Crime Rates*. Washington, D.C.: National Academy of Sciences, 1978.

_____, and Cohen, Jacqueline. *An evaluation of a College-Level Program in a Maximum Security Prison*. Pittsburgh, Pa.: Urban Systems Institute, Carnegie-Mellon University, 1974.

Blundell, Sir M. *So Rough a Wind: Kenya Memoirs*. London: Weidenfeld & Nicholson, 1964.

Blundell, Nigel. *The World's Greatest Mysteries*. London: Octopus, 1980.

Blundell, William E. *Crime at the Top*. Philadelphia: J.B. Lippincott, 1978.

Blunt, W.J. *Desert Hawk: Abd el-Kader*. Paris: Presse Universitaires de France, 1947.

Blyth, A.W. *Poisons: Their Effects and Detection*. London: Charles Griffin, 1884.

Blyth, Henry. *Hell and Hazard*. Chicago: Regnery, 1969.

Blythe, Ronald. *The Age of Illusion: England in the Twenties and Thirties*. London: Hamish Hamilton, 1963.

Blythe, T. Roger (ed.). *A Pictorial Souvenir and Historical Sketch of Tombstone, Arizona*. Tombstone, Ariz.: Tombstone Epitaph, 1946.

Boar, Roger, and Blundell, Nigel. *The World's Most Infamous Murders*. New York: Exeter Books, 1983.

Boas, Franz. *The Central Eskimo*. Lincoln: University of Nebraska Press, 1964.

Boas, Ralph P. and Louise. *Cotton Mather, Keeper of the Puritan Conscience*. Hamden, Conn.: Archon, 1964.

Boas, T.S.R. *St. Francis of Assisi*. Bloomington: Indiana University Press, 1969.

Bobbé, Dorothie. *Mr. and Mrs, John Quincy Adams*. New York: Minton, Balch, 1930.

Bobby: The Robert F. Kennedy Story . . . The Man and His Dream. New York: Macfadden-Bartell, 1968.

Bober, M.M. *Karl Marx's Interpretation of History*. Cambridge, Mass.: Harvard University Press, 1927.

Bocca, Geofrey. *Kings Without Thrones*. London: Weidenfeld & Nicolson, 1959.

Boddam-Whetham, John. *Western Wanderings*. R. Bentley and Son, 1874.

Bodde, Derk. *China's Cultural Tradition*. New York: Rinehart, 1957.

Bode, Carl. *The American Lyceum: Town Meeting of the Mind.* New York: Oxford University Press, 1956.

_____. *Anatomy of American Popular Culture 1840-1861*. Berkeley: University of California Press, 1959.

Bode, Janet. *Fighting Back, How To Cope With The Medical, Emotional and Legal Consequences of Rape*. New York: Macmillan, 1978.

Bode, William. *Lights and Shadows of Chinatown*. San Francisco: H.S. Crocker, 1896.

Bodenheimer, Edgar. *Treatise on Justice*. New York: Philosophical Library, 1967.

Bodge, George Madison. *Soldiers in King Philip's War, Being a Critical Account of that War With a Concise History of the Indian War of New England, from 1620-1627*. Leominster, Mass.: Published by Author, 1896.

Bodin, Jean. *De la démonomanie des sorciers*. Paris: I. du Puys, 1580.

Bodine, Major Roy L., Jr. *Jap POW Diary*. Unpublished.

Boerhaave, Hermann. *Opera Medica Universa*. Geneva, Switz.: Fratres de Tournes, 1728.

Boettcher, Robert. *Gifts of Deceit: Sun Myung Moon, Tongsun Park, and the Korea Scandal*. New York: Holt, Rinehart & Winston, 1980.

Boettiger, John. *Jake Lingle*. New York: E.P. Dutton, 1931.

Boettner, Loraine. *Roman Catholicism*. Philadelphia: Presbyterian & Reform, 1962.

Boffa, Guiseppe. *Inside the Khrushchev Era*. New York: Marzani & Munsell, 1963.

Bogard, Milo T. (ed.) *The Redemption of New York*. New York: R.F. McBreen & Sons, 1902.

Bogardus, E.S. *The Mexican in the United States*. Berkeley: University of California Press, 1934.

Bogdanovich, Peter. *The Cinema of Alfred Hitchcock*. New York: Doubleday, 1963.

_____. *The Killing of the Unicorn: Dorothy Stratten, 1960-1980*. New York: William Morrow, 1984.

Boggs, Mae Helene Bacon. *My Playhouse was a Concord Coach*. Oakland, Calif.: Howell-North Press, 1942.

Boguet, Henri. *Discours des sorciers*. Lyons: Jean Pillehotte, 1602.

_____. *An Examen of Witches*. trans. Montague Summers. London: J. Rodker, 1929.

Bohannan, P. *African Homicide and Suicide*. Princeton, N.J.: Princeton University Press, 1960.

_____. (ed.). *Law & Warfare*. Austin: University of Texas Press, 1967.

Bohlen, Charles E. *Witness to History: 1929-1969*. New York: W.W. Norton, 1973.

Bohman, Nils. *Present Day Sweden*. Stockholm: Pope Förlag, 1937.

Böhmler, Rudolf. *Monte Cassino*. London: Cassell,1964.

Bois, Jules. *Le Satanisme et la magie*. Paris: L. Chailley, 1895.

Boissardus, Jean Jacques. *De Divinatione et Magicis*. Oppenheim: J.T. DeBry, 1616.

Boisser, Le Sieur A. *Recueil de lettres au sujet de malefices et du sortilége, servant de réponse aux lettres du Sieur de Saint André, médecin á Countaces, sur le même sujet*. Paris: C. Osmont, 1731.

Boissevain, Jeremy. *Friends of Friends: Networks, Manipulators and Coalitions*. Oxford, Mass.: Basil Blackwell, 1974.

Bojano, Filippo. *In the Wake of the Goose-Step*. London: Cassell, 1944.

Bok, Curtis. *Star Wormwood*. New York: Alfred A. Knopf, 1959.

Bok, Edward William. *The Americanization of Edward Bok*. New York: Charles Scribner's Sons, 1920.

Bok, Sissela. *Lying*. New York: Vintage Books, 1978.

Boland, Charles Michael. *They All Discovered America*. Garden City, N.Y.: Doubleday, 1963.

Boldt, Gerhard. *In the Shelter With Hitler*. London: Citadel Press, 1948.

Bolitho, Hector. *A Biographer's Notebook*. New York: Macmillan, 1950.

_____ (ed.). *Further Letters of Queen Victoria from the House of Brandenburg-Prussia.* London: Thornton Butterworth, 1938.

_____. *Jinnah.* London: John Murray, 1954.

_____. *Roumania Under King Carol.* London: Eyre & Spottis-wood, 1939.

Bolitho, William. *Italy Under Mussolini.* New York: Macmillan, 1926.

_____. *Murder for Profit.* New York: Harper & Brothers, 1926.

Bolla, Nino. *Colloqui con Umberto II - Colloqui con Vittorio Emanuele III.* Rome: Fantera, 1949.

_____. *Dieci mesi di Governo Badoglio.* Rome: La Nuova Epoca, 1944.

_____. *Processo alla Monarchia.* Rome: Nardini-Nobel, 1944.

Boller, Henry A. *Among the Indians.* Philadelphia: T. Ellwood Zell, 1868.

Bolling, Richard. *House Out of Order.* New York: E.P. Dutton, 1965.

Bolton, Herbert E. *Athanase de Mezieres and the Louisiana-Texas Frontier, 1768-1780.* Cleveland: Arthur H. Clark, 1914.

_____. *Coronaldo: Knight of the Pueblos and Plains.* Albuquerque: Whittlesey House and University of New Mexico Press, 1949.

_____. *Texas in the Middle Eighteenth Century.* Berkeley: University of California, 1915.

_____. *Spanish Exploration in the Southwest, 1542-1706.* New York: Charles Scribner's Sons, 1916.

Bolz, Frank, and Hershey, Edward. *Hostage Cop.* New York: Rawson Wade, 1980.

Bonacci, Giovanni. *L'Italia d'offi e le forze economiche mondiali.* Florence, Italy: Arti Grafiche, 1931.

Bonanno, Joseph. *A Man of Honor: The Autobiography of Joseph Bonanno.* New York: Simon & Schuster, 1983.

Bonaparte, Joseph. *Lettres d'exil.* Paris: Charpentier, 1912.

Bonaparte, Louis-Napoleon. *Oeuvres de Napoleon III.* 5 vols. Paris: Henri Plon, 1869.

_____. *The Political and Historical Works of Louis Napoleon Bonaparte, President of the French Republic, with an Original Memoir of His Life, brought down to the Promulgation of the Constitution of 1852.* 2 vols. London: Illustrated London Library, 1852.

Bonavita, Francesco. *Mussolini Svelato.* Milan, Italy: Sonzogno, 1933.

_____. *Il Padre del Duce.* Rome: Pinciana, 1933.

Bond, E.A. (ed.). *Russia at the Close of the Sixteenth Century.* London: Hakluyt Society, 1856.

Bond, Harold. *Return to Cassino.* London: J.M. Dent, 1964.

Bond, John. *An Essay on the Incubus or Nightmare.* London: D. Wilson & T. Durham, 1753.

Bond, John. *Mussolini the Wild Man of Europe.* Washington, D.C.: Independent Publicity, 1929.

Bone, Jan. *The Thompson Indictment.* New York: Public Interest Press, 1978.

Bonelli, Bondetto. *Animavversioni critiche.* Venice, Italy: S. Occhi, 1751.

Bonewits, P.E.I. *Real Magic.* New York: Coward, McCann & Geoghegan, 1971.

Bonger, W.A. *Race and Crime.* New York: Columbia University Press, 1943.

Bonger, Willem. *Criminality and Economic Conditions.* Bloomington: Indiana University Press, 1969.

Bonhoeffer, Dietrich. *Letters and Papers From Prison.* London: S.C.M. Press, 1953.

_____. *Prayers From Prison.* Philadelphia: Fortress Press, 1977.

Bonilla, Policarpo. *Wilson Doctrine.* New York: Published by Author, 1914.

Bonino, Antonio. *Mussolini mi ha detto.* Buenos Aires, Arg.: Ed Risorgimento, 1950.

Bonjean, Charles, et al. (eds.) *Community Politics: A Behavioral Approach.* New York: Free Press, 1971.

Bonn, John L. *The Gates of Dannemora.* New York: Doubleday, 1951.

Bonner, Judy Whitson. *Investigation of a Homicide: The Murder of John F. Kennedy.* Anderson, S.C.: Droke House, 1969.

Bonner, Thomas Neville. *Medicine in Chicago, 1850-1950.* Madison, Wis.: American History Research Center, 1957.

Bonnet, Theodore F. *The Regenrators: A Study of the Graft Prosecution in San Francisco.* San Francisco: Pacific Printing, 1911.

Bonney, Catharina V.R. *A Legacy of Historical Gleanings.* Albany, N.Y.: J. Munsell, 1875.

Bonney, Edward. *Banditti of the Prairies.* Chicago: Homewood, 1890.

Bonnie, Richard J., and Whitebread, Charles H., II. *The Marihuana Conviction: A History of Marihuana Prohibition in the Unites States.* Charlottesville: University of Virginia Press, 1974.

Bonnin, Charles (ed.). *Bismarck and the Hohenzollern Candidature for the Spanish Throne.* trans. Isabella M. Massey. London: Chatto & Windus, 1957.

Bonomi, Ivanoe. *Diario di unanno.* Milon, Italy: Garzanti, 1947.

_____. *From Socialism to Fascism: A Study of Contemporary Italy.* trans. John Murray. London: Martin Hopkinson, 1924.

Bonsal, Stephen. *Edward Fitzgerald Beale: A Pioneer in the Path of Empire, 1822-1903.* New York: G.P. Putnam's Sons, 1912.

Bontecou, Eleanor. *The Federal Loyalty-Security Program.* Ithaca, N.Y.: Cornell University Press, 1953.

Bontemps, Arna W. *Black Thunder.* New York: Macmillan, 1936.

_____. *100 Years of Negro Freedom.* New York: Dodd, Mead, 1961.

Bontham, Alan. *Sex Crimes and Sex Criminals.* New York: Wisdom House, 1961.

Booker, Anton S. *Wildcats in Petticoats.* Girard, Kan.: Haldeman-Julius, 1945.

Booker, Edna Lee. *News Is My Job.* New York: Macmillan, 1940.

Boole, Ella A. *Give Prohibition Its Chance.* New York: Fleming H. Revell, 1929.

Boorman, Howard L. (ed.). *Biographical Dictionary of Republican China.* New York: Columbia University Press, 1967.

Boorstin, Daniel J. *America and the Image of Europe: Reflections on American Thought.* New York: Meridian Boods, 1960.

_____. *The Americans: The Colonial Experience.* New York: Random House, 1958.

_____. *The Americans: The Democratic Experience.* New York: Random House, 1973.

_____. *The Americans: The National Experience.* New York: Random House, 1965.

_____. *The Lost World of Thomas Jefferson.* Boston: Beacon Press, 1948.

_____. *The Mysterious Science of the Law.* Gloucester, Mass.: Peter Smith, 1941.

Booth, Charles. *Conditions and Occupations of the People of the Tower Hamlets, 1886-7.* London: Stanford, 1887.

_____. *Life and Labour of the People of London.* London: Macmillan, 1897.

Booth, Ernest. *Stealing Through Life.* New York: Alfred A. Knopf, 1929.

Booth, Mary L. *History of the City of New York.* New York: E.P. Dutton, 1880.

Booth, William. *In Darkest England and the Way Out.* Montclair, N.J.: Patterson Smith, 1974.

Boothe, Clare. *Europe in the Spring.* New York: Alfred A. Knopf, 1940.

Bopp, William J. *O.W. Wilson and the Search for a Police Profession.* Port Washington, N.Y.: Kennikat Press, 1977.

_____. *Police Administration: Selected Readings.* Boston: Holbrook Press, 1975.

Bor, Peter. *Gespräche mit Halder.* Wiesbaden, Ger.: Limes,

1950.

Borah, William Edgar. *Haywood Trial: Closing Arguments of W.E. Borah*. Boise, Idaho: Statesman Shop, 1907.

Borchard, Edwin Montefiore. *Convicting the Innocent*. New Haven, Conn.: Yale University Press, 1932.

Bordelon, Laurent. *The History of the Ridiculous Extravagances of Monsieur Oufle*. London: J. Morphew, 1711.

Bordeux, Henri. *L'air de Rome et do la Mer*. Paris: Plon, 1938.

Bordeux, V.J. *Benito Mussolini-The Man*. London: Hutchinson, 1927.

_____. *Margherita of Savia*. London: Hutchinson, 1929.

Bordman, Gerald. *American Musical Theater: A Chronicle*. New York: Oxford University Press, 1979.

Bordoni, Francesco. *Sacrum Tribunal Judicum in Causis Sanctae Fidei*. Rome: Haeredum Corbelletti, 1648.

Bordua, David J. (ed.). *The Police: Six Sociological Essays*. New York: John Wiley & Sons, 1967.

Borel, Thomas. *The White Slavery of Europe*. trans. Joseph Edmondson. London: Dyer Brothers, 1880.

Borelli, Siegfied, and Starck, Willy. *Die Prostitution als Psychologischen Problem*. Berlin, Ger.: Springer-Verlag, 1957.

Boren, Henry C. *The Gracchi*. New York: Twayne, 1968.

Borg, Dorothy. *American Policy and the Chinese Revolution, 1925-28*. New York: Institute of Pacific Relations, 1947.

_____. *The United States and the Far Eastern Crisis of 1933-38*. Cambridge, Mass.: Harvard University Press, 1964.

Borgese, G.A. *Goliath, The March of Fascism*. New York: Viking Press, 1938.

Borghese, Junio Valerio. *Decima Flottiglia Mas*. Milan, Italy: Garzanti, 1950.

Borghi, Armando. *Mussolini Red and Black*. London: Wishart Books, 1935.

Boring, E. *A History of Experimental Psychology*. New York: Appleton-Century-Crofts, 1950.

Borkenau, Franz. *Austria and After*. London: Faber & Faber, 1938.

_____. *European Communism*. New York: Harper, 1953.

_____. *The New German Empire*. New York: Viking Press, 1939.

_____. *Socialism, National and International*. London: Routledge, 1942.

_____. *The Spanish Cockpit*. London: Faber & Faber, 1937.

Borkin, Joseph. *The Crime and Punishment of I.G. Farben*. New York: Free Press, 1978.

Bormann, Martin. *The Bormann Letters*. London: Nicolson & Weidenfeld, 1954.

Borniche, Roger. *Flic Story*. Garden City: Doubleday, 1975.

Bornstein, Joseph. *The Politics of Murder*. New York: William Sloan, 1950.

Borow, H. (ed.). *Man in a World at Work*. Boston: Houghton Mifflin, 1964.

Borowitz, Albert. *Innocence and Arsenic Studies in Crime and Literature*. New York: Harper & Row, 1977.

_____. *The Woman Who Murdered Black Satin*. Columbus: Ohio State University Press, 1981.

Borrell, Clive, and Cashinella, Brian. *Crime in Britain Today*. London: Routledge & Paul, 1975.

Borreson, Ralph. *When Lincoln Died*. New York: Appleton-Century, 1965.

Borthwick, J.D. *The Gold Hunters*. New York: Outing, 1927.

Bortner, M.A. *Inside a Juvenile Court*. New York: New York University Press, 1984.

Bortolotto, Guido. *Storia del fascismo*. Milan, Italy: Ulrico Hoepli, 1938.

Borton, Hugh. *Japan's Modern Century*. New York: Ronald Press, 1955.

Bosanquet, Ronald. *The Oxford Circuit*. London: Thames Bank, 1951.

Bosca, Quirino C. *Cronistoria della campagna italo-etiopica*. Rome: Guanella, 1937.

Böse, Ernest. *Politik und Demokrati*. Hamburg, Ger.: Deutsche Polizei Verlag, GMBH, n.d.

Bose, Nirmal Kumar. *My Days With Gandhi*. Clacutta, India: Nishana, 1953.

_____. *Selections From Gandhi*. Ahmedabad, India: Navajivan, 1948.

_____. *Studies in Gandhism*. Calcutta, India: Indian Associated, 1947.

Bose, Subhas Chandra. *The Indian Struggle*. London: Wishart, 1935.

Bosher, J.F. (ed.). *French Government and Society, 1500-1850: Essays in Memory of Alfred Cobban*. London: Athlone, 1973.

Bosis, Lauro. *Storia della mia morte*. Turin, Italy: De Silva, 1948.

Bosman, Leonard. *The Meaning and Philosophy of Numbers*. London: Rider, 1932.

Bosman, William. *A New and Accurate Description of the Coast of Guinea*. New York: Barnes & Noble, 1967.

Bossard, l'Abbé Eugene. *Gilles de Rais, Marechal de France Dit Barbe-Bleue*. Paris: H. Champion, 1886.

The Boston Fiend! Many Long Hidden Mysteries at Last Disclosed! Full Account of the Atrocious Crimes of Thomas W. Piper. Boston: n.p., 1875.

Boston Women's Health Collective. *Our Bodies, Ourselves*. New York: Simon & Schuster, 1973.

Boswell, Charles, and Thompson, Lewis. *Advocates of Murder*. New York: Collier Books, 1962.

_____. *The Girl in Lovers Lane*. New York: Fawcett, 1953.

_____. *The Girls in Nightmare House*. New York: Gold Medal, 1955.

_____. *Practitioners of Murder*. New York: Collier Books, 1962.

Boswell, James. *London Journal: 1762-1763*. New York: McGraw-Hill, 1950.

Bosworth, Patricia. *Montgomery Clift*. New York: Harcourt, Brace, Jovanovich, 1977.

Botein, Bernard, and Gordon, Murray A. *The Trial of the Future: Challenge to the Law*. New York: Cornerstone Library, 1963.

Botkin, Benjamin A. (ed.). *Folk-Say: A Regional Miscellany*. Norman: University of Oklahoma, 1929.

_____ (ed.). *Sidewalks of America*. New York: Bobbs-Merrill, 1954.

_____. *A Treasury of American Folklore*. New York: Crown, 1951.

_____. *A Treasury of Mississippi River Folklore*. New York: Crown, 1955.

_____, and Harlow, Alvin F. *A Treasury of Railroad Folklore*. New York: Crown, 1953.

_____. *A Treasury of Southern Folklore*. New York: American Legacy Press, 1984.

_____. *A Treasury of Western Folklore*. New York: Crown, 1951.

Botkin, Gleb. *The Real Romanovs*. New York: G.P. Putnam's Sons, 1931.

Botkina, Tatiana Melnik. *Vospominanya o Tsarskoy Sem'ye*. Belgrade, Yug.: Stefanonivich, 1921.

Bottai, Giuseppe. *Vent'anni e un giorno*. Milan, Italy: Garzanti, 1949.

Botting, Douglas. *Humboldt and the Cosmos*. New York: Harper & Row, 1973.

_____. *The Pirates*. New York: Time-Life, 1978.

Bottomley, A. Keith. *Criminology in Focus: Past Trends and Future Prospects*. New York: Barnes & Noble, 1979.

_____. *Decisions in the Penal Process*. London: Martin Robertson, 1973.

_____. *Prison Before Trial*. London: Bell, 1970.

Bottons, A.E., and McClintock, F.H. *Criminals Coming of Age*. London: Heinemann Educational, 1973.

_____, and McClean, J.D. *Defendants in the Criminal Process*. London: Routledge & Kegan Paul, 1978.

Bouchardon, Pierre. *L'Assassinat de l'archevêque*. Paris: Arthème Fayard, 1926.

_____. *Troppmann*. Paris: Albin Michel, 1932.

Boucher, Anthony (ed.). *The Pocket Book of True Crime Stories.* New York: Pocket Books, 1943.

_____. *Police Intelligence.* New York: AMS Press, 1976.

_____. *The Quality of Murder.* New York: E.P. Dutton, 1962.

Boudin, Louis B. *Government by Judiciary.* New York: William Godwin, 1932.

Boudreau, John F. et al. *Arson and Arson Investigations: Survey and Assessment.* Washington, D.C.: U.S. Department of Justice, 1977.

Bougainville, Louis Antoine de. *Voyage Round the World.* trans. J.R. Forster. London: J. Norse, 1772.

Bouhler, Philipp. *Kampf um Deutschland.* Berlin: Zentralverlag der NSDAP, 1939.

Boulger, Demetrius C. *The History of China.* London: W. Thacker, 1898.

Boulting, William. *Woman in Italy.* London: Methuen, 1910.

Boulton, David. *The Grease Machine.* New York: Harper & Row, 1979.

_____. *The Making of Tania: The Patty Hearst Story.* London: New English Library, 1975.

_____. *The UVF 1966-73.* Dublin: Tore Books, 1973.

Boulton, Richard. *A Complete History of Magic.* London: E. Curll & W. Taylor, 1715.

Bourdeaut, l'Abbé, Fr. M.A. *Champtocé, Gilles de Rais et les Ducs de Bretagne.* Brest: Mémoires de la Société de l'Histoire et de l'Archéologie de Brest, 1924.

Bourdrel, Philippe. *Histoire des juifs en France.* Paris: Albin Michel, 1974.

_____. *La Cagoule.* Paris: Albin Michel, 1970.

Bourg, Edme-Théodore. *Procès du prince Napoléon-Louis et de ses coaccusés devant la Xour des Pairs.* Paris: A. Levavasseur, 1840.

Bourgin, Hubert. *De Jaurès à Léon Blum.* Paris: A. Fayard, 1938.

Bourjaily, Vance Nye. *The Man Who Knew Kennedy.* New York: Dial Press, 1967.

Bourke, John G. *On the Border with the Crook.* Lincoln: University of Nebraska Press, 1971.

Bourne, Kenneth. *Britain and the Balance of Power in North America 1815-1908.* London: Longmans, Greene, 1967.

Bourne, L. *Cognition and Learning.* New York: John Wiley & Sons, 1972.

Bourne, Randolph S. *Youth and Life.* New York: Houghton Mifflin, 1913.

Bourneville, Désiré Magliore, and Tenturier, E. *Le sabbat des sorciers.* Paris: Aux Bureaux du Progrès Médical, 1882.

_____. *Louise Lateau ou la stigmatisée belge.* Paris: Delahaye, 1878.

Boutwell, George S. *The Crisis of the Republic.* Boston: Dana Estes, 1900.

_____. *Reminiscences of Sixty Years in Public Affairs.* New York: McClure, Phillips, 1902.

Bouvet, Le Sieur. *Les maniéres admirables pour découvrir toutes sortes de crimes et sortilèges avec l'instruction solide pour bien juger un procès criminel.* Paris: I. de la Caille, 1659.

Bouza, Anthony V. *Police Administration, Organization & Performance.* New York: Pergamen Press, 1979.

_____. *Police Intelligence: The Operations of an Investigative Unit.* New York: AMS Press, 1976.

Bova-Scoppa, Renato. *Colloqui con due Dittatori.* Rome: Ruffolo, 1949.

Boveri, Margret. *Treason in the Twentieth Century.* New York: G.P. Putnam's Sons, 1963.

Bovet, Richard. *Pandaemonium, or the Devil's Cloister, Being a Further Blow to Modern Sadducism, Proving the Existence of Witches and Spirits.* London: Malthus, 1684.

Bowart, Walter. *Operation Mind Control.* New York: Delacorte, 1977.

Bowden, Tom. *The Men in the Middle--The UK Police.* London: Institute for the Study of Conflict, 1976.

Bowditch, Nathaniel. *Early American-Philippine Trade: The Journal of Nathaniel Bowditch in Manila 1796.* New Haven, Conn.: Yale University Press, Southeast Asia Studies, 1962.

Bowen, Catherine D. *John Adams and the American Revolution.* Boston: Little, Brown, 1950.

_____. *Miracle at Philadelphia.* Boston: Little, Brown, 1966.

_____. *Yankee from Olympus.* Boston: Little, Brown, 1905.

Bowen, Croswell. *The Elegant Oakey.* New York: Oxford University Press, 1956.

Bowen, Walter S., and Neal, Harry Edward. *The United States Secret Service.* Philadelphia: Chilton, 1960.

Bowen-Rowlands, Ernest. *In Court and Out of Court.* London: Hutchinson, 1925.

_____. *In the Light of the Law.* London: Grant Richards, 1931.

_____. *Seventy-Two Years at the Bar.* London: Macmillan, 1924.

Bower, Robert T. *Television and the Public.* New York: Holt, Rinehart, & Winston, 1973.

Bowers, Claude Gernade. *Beveridge and the Progressive Era.* Boston: Houghton Mifflin, 1932.

_____. *Jefferson and Hamilton.* Boston: Houghton Mifflin, 1925.

_____. *Jefferson In Power.* Boston: Houghton Mifflin, 1936.

_____. *My Life: The Memoirs of Claude Bowers.* New York: Simon & Schuster, 1962.

_____. *The Party Battles of the Jackson Period.* Boston: Houghton Mifflin, 1922.

_____. *The Tragic Era.* Boston: Houghton Mifflin, 1929.

Bowers, William. *Executions in America.* Lexington, Mass.: D.C. Heath, 1974.

Bowker, A.E. *Behind the Bar.* London: Staples Press, 1949.

_____. *A Lifetime with the Law.* London: W.H. Allen, 1961.

Bowlby, J.H. *Maternal Care and Mental Health.* Geneva, Switz.: World Health Organization, 1951.

_____. *Attachment and Loss.* New York: Basic Books, 1969.

Bowles, Jane. *Collected Works.* New York: Farrar, Straus & Giroux, 1966.

Bowles, Paul. *The Delicate Prey and Other Stories.* New York: Random House, 1950.

_____. *Without Stopping.* London: Peter Owen, 1972.

Bowles, Samuel. *Across the Continent.* Springfield, Ill.: Published by Author, 1866.

Bowman, H.E. *Vissarion Belinski: A Study in the Origin of Social Criticism in Russia.* Cambridge, Mass.: Harvard University Press, 1954.

Bowman, Hank W. *Famous Guns from the Smithsonian Collection.* New York: Arco, 1967.

Bowman, Lynn. *Los Angeles, Epic of a City.* Berkeley, Calif.: Howell-North Books, 1974.

Bowne, Eliza Southgate. *A Girl's Life Eighty Years Ago.* Williamstown, Mass.: Corner House, 1980.

Bowrey, T. *A Geographical Account of Countries Round the Bay of Bengal.* Nendeln, Liechtenstein: Kraus Reprint, 1967.

Bowring, J. (ed.). *Complete Works of Jeremy Bentham with a Biography.* Edinburgh, Scot.: Tait, 1838.

Bowyer, J. Barton. *Cheating.* New York: St. Martin's Press, 1982.

Bowyer Bell, J. *Transnational Terror.* Washington, D.C.: AEI Hoover Policy Studies, 1975.

Box, Pelham H. *Three Master Builders.* London: Jarrolds, 1925.

Box, Steven. *Deviance, Reality and Society.* London: Holt, Rinehart & Winston, 1971.

Boyce, S.S. *Hemp.* New York: Orange & Judd, 1900.

Boyd, Belle. *In Camp and Prison.* New York: Blelock, 1867.

Boyd, James. *Above the Law.* New York: New American Library, 1968.

Boyd, Kier T. *Gambling Technology.* Washington D.C.: U.S. Government Printing Office, 1977.

Boyd, Thomas. *Lighthorse Harry Lee.* New York: Charles Scribner's Sons, 1931.

_____. *Poor John Fitch, Inventor of the Steamboat.* New York: G.P. Putnam's Sons, 1935.

Boyd, William Harland, and Rodgers, Glendon J. (eds.). *San Joaquin Vignettes*. Bakersfield, Calif.: Kern County Historical Society, 1955.

Boydstun, John F., and Sherry, Michael E. *San Diego Community Profile: Final Report*. Washington, D.C.: Police Foundation, 1975.

Boyer, Glenn G. (ed.) *I Married Wyatt Earp: The Recollections of Josephine Sarah Marcus Earp*. Tucson: University of Arizona Press, 1976.

_____. *An Illustrated Life of Doc Holliday*. Glenwood Springs, Colo.: Reminder, 1966.

_____. *Suppressed Murder of Wyatt Earp*. San Antonio: Naylor, 1967.

Boyer, Paul S. *Purity in Print*. New York: Charles Scribner's Sons, 1968.

_____, and Nissenbaum, Stephen. *Salem Possessed: The Social Origins of Witchcraft*. Cambridge, Mass.: Harvard University Press, 1974.

_____. *Urban Masses and Moral Order in America, 1820-1920*. Cambridge, Mass.: Harvard University Press, 1978.

Boyer, Richard O., and Morais, Herbert M. *A History of the American Labor Movement*. London: John Calder, 1955.

_____. *The Legend of John Brown: A Biography and a History*. New York: Alfred A. Knopf, 1973.

_____, Morais, Herbert M. *Labor's Untold Story*. New York: Cameron Associates, 1955.

Boylan, John. *The Old Lincoln County Courthouse*. Lincoln, N.M.: n.p., n.d.

Boyle, Andrew. *Montagu Norman*. London: Cassell, 1967.

Boyle, Kay. *My Next Bride*. New York: Harcourt, Brace, 1934.

Boyle, Kevin. *Law and the State: The Case of Northern Ireland*. London: Martin Robertson, 1975.

Boyle, Martin. *Yanks Don't Cry*. New York: Random House, 1963.

Boynton, Percy Holmes. *The Rediscovery of the Frontier*. Chicago: University of Chicago Press, 1931.

Boys, Reverand J. *The Case of Witchcraft at Coggeshall, Essex, 1699*. London: A.R. Smith, 1901.

Bozzi, Carlo. *La tragedia degli italiani vissuta da un italiano*. Rome: Leonardo, 1947.

Braatoy, Bjarne. *Labor and War*. London: George Allen & Unwin, 1934.

_____. *The New Sweden; a Vindication of Democracy*. New York: Thomas Nelson, 1939.

Brace, Charles Loring. *The Dangerous Classes of New York and Twenty Years' Work Among Them*. New York: Wynkoop & Hallenbeck, 1880.

_____. *The New West*. New York: G.P. Putnam's Sons, 1869.

Bracher, Karl Dietrich. *Die Auflösung der Weimarer Republik*. Stuttgart, Ger.: Ring-Verlag, 1955.

_____. *Die nationalsozialistische Machtergreifung*. Köln, Ger.: Westdeutscher, 1060.

Bracke, William B. *Wheat Country*. New York: Duell, Sloan & Pearce, 1950.

Brackett, Albert Gallatin. *General Lane's Brigade in Central Mexico*. Cincinnati, Ohio: H.W. Derby, 1854.

Brackett, L.P. *Our Western Empire*. Philadelphia: Bradley, Garretson, 1881.

Brackman, Arnold C. *The Last Emperor*. New York: Charles Scribner's Sons, 1975.

Bradburn, George. *A Statement by George Bradburn of His Connection with the "True Democrat" and John C. Vaughan*. Cleveland: George Bradburn, 1853.

Bradbury, John. *Travels in the Interior of America in the Years 1809, 1810, and 1811*. Cleveland: A.H. Clark, 1904.

Braddon, Russell. *The Naked Island*. London: Werner Laurie, 1952.

Braddy, Haldeen. *Cock of the Walk: The Legend of Pancho Villa*. Alburquerque: University of New Mexico Press, 1955.

_____. *Pancho Villa at Columbus*. El Paso: Texas Western College Press, 1965.

_____. *Pershing's Mission in Mexico*. El Paso: Texas Western College Press, 1966.

Bradford, Ernle. *The Sundered Cross: The Story of the Fourth Crusade*. Englewood Cliffs, N.J.: Prentice-Hall, 1967.

Bradford, Gamaliel. *D.L. Moody: A Worker In Souls*. Garden City, N.Y.: Doubleday, Doran, 1928.

_____. *Union Portraits*. New York: Houghton Mifflin, 1916.

Bradford, Kermit. *Miracle on Death Row*. Waco, Texas: Chosen Books, 1977.

Bradford, Sarah. *Cesare Borgia*. New York: Macmillan, 1976.

Bradford, S.B. *Prohibition in Kansas and the Kansas Prohibitory Law*. Topeka, Kan.: Crane, 1889.

Bradford, William. *An Enquiry How Far the Punishment of Death is Necessary in Pennsylvania*. Philadelphia: T. Dobson, 1793.

_____. *History of Plymouth Plantation*. Boston: Houghton Mifflin, 1896.

_____. *Of Plymouth Plantation, 1620-1647*. New York: Alfred A. Knopf, 1952.

Bradlee, Benjamin. *That Special Grace*. Philadelphia: J.B. Lippincott, 1964.

Bradlee, Ben, Jr. *The Ambush Murders*. New York: Dodd, Mead, 1979.

Bradlee, Francis B.C. *Piracy in the West Indies and Its Suppression*. Salem, Mass.: Essex institute, 1923.

Bradley, Glenn Danford. *The Story of the Santa Fe*. Boston: R. G. Badger, 1920.

Bradley, Hugh. *Such Was Saratoga*. Garden City, N.Y.: Doubleday Doran, 1940.

Bradley, John L. (ed.). *Rogues Progress*. Boston: Houghton Mifflin, 1965.

Bradley, Preston. *Along the Way*. New York: David McKay, 1962.

Bradley, R.T. *Lives of Frank and Jesse James*. St. Louis: J.W. Marsh, 1882.

_____. *The Outlaws of the Border*. St. Louis: J.W. Marsh, 1880.

Bradshaw, C.M., et al. (eds.). *Quantification of Steady-State Operant Behavior*. Amsterdam: Elsevier/North Holland Biomedical Press, 1981.

Bradshaw, Jon. *Dreams That Money Can Buy*. New York: William Morrow, 1985.

Brady, Cyrus Townsend. *Recollections of a Missionary in the Great West*. New York: Charles Scribner's Sons, 1900.

Brady, Jasper Ewing. *Tales of the Telegraph*. New York: Doubleday & McClure, 1899.

Brady, Katherine. *Father's Days: A True Story of Incest*. New York: Seaview Books, 1979.

Brady, Robert A. *The Spirit and Structure of German Fascism*. New York: Viking Press, 1937.

Bragadin, Commander Marc'Antonio. *The Italian Navy in World War II*. trans. Gale Hoffman. Annapolis, Md.: United States Naval Institute, 1957.

Bragge, Francis. *A Defense of the Proceedings Against Jane Wenham*. London: E. Curll, 1712.

_____. *A Full and Impartial Account of the Discovery of Sorcery and Witchcraft Practiced by Jane Wenham*. London: E. Curll 1712.

_____. *Witchcraft Further Diaplayed*. London: E. Curll, 1712.

Bragin, Charles. *Dime Novels, Bibliography, 1860-1928*. New York: Published by Author, 1938.

Brailsford, Henry Noel. *Macedonia, Its Races and Their Future*. London: Methuen, 1906.

Brainerd, Charles. *My Diary*. New York: Egbert, Bourne, 1868.

Braithwaite, J. *Inequality, Crime and Public Policy*. London: Rouledge & Kegan Paul, 1979.

Braithwaite, Max. *The Hungry Thirties*. Toronto, Can.: McClelland, 1977.

Brakel, Samuel J., and Rock, Ronald S. (eds.). *The Mentally Disabled and the Law*. Chicago: University of Chicago Press, 1971.

Braly, Malcolm. *False Starts*. Boston: Little, Brown, 1976.

———. *On the Yard*. Greenwich, Conn.: Fawcett Publications, 1967.

Braly, William C. *The Hard Way Home*. Washington, D.C.: Infantry Journal Press, 1947.

Brampton, Baron Henry Hawkins. *The Reminiscences of Sir Henry Hawkins*. London: E. Arnold, 1904.

Bramstedt, Ernest Kohn. *Dictatorship and Political Police: The Technique and Control of Fear*. London: Keagan Paul, 1945.

Branca, Patricia. *Silent Sisterhood*. Pittsburgh, Pa.: Carnegie-Mellon University Press, 1975.

———, and Stearns, Peter. *Modernization of Women in the Nineteenth Century*. St. Charles, Mo.: Forum, 1973.

Brancale, Ralph, and Ellis, Arthur. *Psychology of Sex Offenders*. Springfield, Ill.: Charles C. Thomas, 1956.

Branch, Edgar Marquess. *The Literary Apprenticeship of Mark Twain*. Urbana: University of Illinois Press, 1950.

Branch, Edward Douglas. *The Cowboy and His Interpreters*. New York: D. Appleton, 1926.

———. *The Hunting of the Buffalo*. New York: D. Appleton, 1929.

———. *The Sentimental Years*. New York: Appleton Century, 1934.

———. *Westward: The Romance of the American Frontier*. New York: D. Appleton, 1930.

Branch, Taylor, and Propper, Eugene M. *Labyrinth*. New York: Viking Press, 1982.

Brand, Carl F. *British Labor's Rise to Power*. Stanford, Calif.: Stanford University Press, 1941.

Brand, Christianna. *Heaven Knows Who*. New York: Charles Scribner's Sons, 1960.

Brand, Donald D. *Mexico: Land of Sunshine and Shadow*. New York: D. Van Nostrand, 1966.

Brand, John. *Observations on Popular Antiquities*. London: J. Johnson, 1777.

Brandeis, L.D. *Other People's Money and How the Bankers Used It*. New York: Frederick A. Stokes, 1932.

Brandenburg, Erich. *From Bismarck to the World War*. trans. Annie Elizabeth Adams. London: Oxford University Press, 1927.

Brandenburg, Frank. *The Making of Modern Mexico*. Englewood Cliffs, N.J.: Prentice-Hall, 1964.

Brandes, Georg. *Impressions of Russia*. New York: Thomas Y. Crowell, 1966.

Brandom, V., and Katash, S. (eds.). *Enclyclopedia of Criminology*. New York: Philosophical Library, 1949.

Brandon, Edgar Ewing. *A Pilgrimage of Liberty*. Athens, Ohio: Lawhead Press, 1944.

Brandon, R., and Davies, C. *Wrongful Imprisonment*. London: George Allen & Unwin, 1973.

Brandt, Conrad, Schwartz, Benjamin, and Fairbank, John K. *A Documentary History of Chinese Communism*. Cambridge, Mass.: Harvard University Press, 1952.

———. *Stalin's Failure in China, 1924-1927*. Cambridge, Mass.: Harvard University Press, 1958.

Brandt, Fred. *Fascinating San Francisco*. San Francisco: Published by Author, 1924.

Branham, Vernon, and Kytash, Samuel B. *Encyclopedia of Criminology*. New York: Philosophical Library, 1949.

Brann, Reverend Henry A. *Most Reverend John Hughes*. New York: Dodd, Mead, 1892.

Brannon, William T. *The Fabulous Drake Swindle*. New York: Mercury Press, 1955.

Brant, House. *Crimes That Shocked America*. New York: Ace, 1961.

Brant, Irving. *The Bill of Rights*. Indianapolis, Ind.: Bobbs-Merrill, 1965.

———. *Madison*. 5 vols. New York: Bobbs-Merrill, 1941-56.

Brant, Isaac. *History of John Brown*. Des Moines, Iowa: Watters-Talbott, 1895.

Brant, Stefan. *The East German Rising*. New York: Frederick A. Praeger, 1957.

Brantingham, Paul and Patricia. *Patterns in Crime*. New York: Macmillan, 1984.

Brantley, C. *The Giriama and Colonial Resistance in Kenya, 1800-1920*. Berkeley: University of California Press, 1981.

Brashear, Minnie M. *Mark Twain, Son of Missouri*. Chapel Hill: University of North Carolina Press, 1934.

Brasol, Boris. *Oscar Wilde: The Man, The Artist, The Martyr*. New York: n.p., 1938.

Bratt, John. *Trails of Yesterday*. Lincoln, Neb.: University Publishing, 1921.

Braude, M.C., and Szara, S. (eds.). *Pharmacology of Marihuana*. New York: Raven Press, 1976.

Braudel, Fernand. *The Mediterranean and the Mediterranean World in the Age of Philip II*. trans. Sian Reynolds. New York: Harper & Row, 1972.

Braverman, Harry. *Labor and Monopoly Capital: The Degradation of Work in the Twentieth Century*. New York: Monthly Review Press, 1974.

Brawley, Benjamin A. *Social History of the American Negro*. London: Collier-Macmillan, 1970.

Brayer, Garnet M. and Herbert O. *American Cattle Trails*. Bayside, N.Y.: Western Range Cattle Industry Studies, 1952.

Brayer, Herbert O. *Range Murder*. Evanston, Ill.: Branding Iron Press, 1955.

———. *William Blackmore: the Spanish-Mexican Land Grants of New Mexico and Colorado 1863-1878*. Denver: Bradford-Robinson, 1949.

Brayley, F.A. *Arrangement of Finger Prints*. Boston: Worcester Press, 1910.

Brayman, Harold. *The President Speaks Off the Record*. Princeton, N.J.: Dow Jones Books, 1976.

Breakenridge, William M. *Helldorado: Bringing the Law to the Mesquite*. Boston: Houghton Mifflin, 1928.

Brearley, H.C. *Homicide in the United States*. Chapel Hill: University of North Carolina Press, 1932.

Breasted, James Henry. *Ancient Records of Egypt*. Chicago: University of Chicago Press, 1907.

———. *A History of Egypt*. New York: Charles Scribner's Sons, 1951.

Breasted, Mary. *Oh! Sex Education*. New York: Frederick A. Praeger, 1970.

Breatnach, Seamus. *The Irish Police*. Dublin, Ire.: Anvil Books, 1974.

Breazeale, H.S. *Life As It Is*. Knoxville, Tenn.: James Williams, 1842.

Brebner, John Bartlett. *The Explorers of North America*. Garden City, N.Y.: Doubleday, 1955.

———. *North Atlantic Triangle*. London: Ryerson Press, 1946.

Breceda, Alfredo. *México Revolucionario, 1913-1917*. Madrid: Tipografia Artistica Cervantes, 1920.

Brecher, Edward M. *Licit and Illicit Drugs*. Boston: Little, Brown, 1972.

———. *Treatment Programs for Sex Offenders*. Washington, D.C.: National Institute of Law Enforcement and Criminal Justice, 1977.

Brecher, Jeremy. *Strike!* Greenwich, Conn.: Fawcett, 1972.

Breck, Samuel. *Historical Sketch of Continental Paper*. Philadelphia: J.C. Clark, 1843.

Breckenridge, William M. *Helldorado*. Boston: Houghton Mifflin, 1928.

Breen, Matthew P. *Thirty Years of New York Politics Up-To-Date*. New York: Published by Author, 1899.

Breen, Timothy H. *The Character of the Good Ruler: A Study of Puritan Political Ideas in New England, 1630-1730*. New Haven, Conn.: Yale University Press, 1970.

Brehm, B. *Der boehmische Gefreite*. Graz, Aus.: Styria, 1960.

Brehm, J., and Cohen, A. *Explorations in Cognitive Dissonance*. New York: John Wiley & Sons, 1962.

Breihan, Carl W. *Badmen of Frontier Days.* New York: Robert M. McBride Co., 1957.

_____. *The Complete and Authentic Life of Jesse James.* New York: Frederick Fell, 1953.

_____. *The Day Jesse James Was Killed.* New York: Frederick Fell, 1961.

_____. *Escapades of Frank & Jesse James.* New York: Frederick Fell, 1974.

_____. *Great Gunfighters of the West.* San Antonio, Texas: Naylor, 1962.

_____. *Great Lawmen of the West.* New York: Signet, 1978.

_____. *The Killer Legions of Quantrill.* Seattle, Wash.: Hangman Press, 1971.

_____. *The Man Who Shot Jessie James.* New York: A.S. Barnes, 1979.

_____. *The Outlaw Brothers: The True Story of Missouri's Younger Brothers.* San Antonio, Texas: Naylor, 1961.

_____. *Outlaws of the Old West.* New York: Bonanza Books, 1967.

_____. *Quantrill and His Civil War Guerrillas.* Denver: Sage Books, 1959.

_____. *Younger Brothers.* San Antonio: Naylor, 1961.

Bremer, Arthur. *An Assassin's Diary.* New York: Harper Magazine Press, 1972.

Bremer, Johan. *Asexualization: A Followup Study of 244 Cases.* New York: Macmillan, 1959.

Bremner, Robert H. (ed.). *Essays on History and Literature.* Columbus: Ohio State University Press, 1966.

_____. *From the Depths.* New York: New York University Press, 1956.

Brémond, Henri. *Histoire littéraire du sentiment religieux en France.* Paris: Bloud et Gay, 1916.

Brenan, Gerald. *The Spanish Labyrinth.* New York: Macmillan, 1943.

Brend, W.A. *A Handbook of Medical Jurisprudence and Toxicology.* Griffin, 1941.

Brendan, Rev. J. *Life, Crimes and Confession of Bridget Durgan, the Fiendish Murderess of Mrs. Coriell.* Philadelphia: C.W. Alexander, 1867.

Brener, Milton E. *The Garrison Case.* New York: Clarkson N. Potter, 1969.

Brennan, Howard L., and Cherryholmes, J. Edward. *Eyewitness To History.* Waco, Texas: Texian Press, 1987.

Brennan, John C. *Pictorial Primer Having to Do With the Assassination of Abraham Lincoln and With the Assassin, John Wilkes Booth.* Laurel, Md.: Minuteman Press, 1979.

Brennan, Robert. *Allegiance.* Dublin, Ire.: Browne & Nolan, 1950.

_____. *Irish Diary.* Westminster, Md.: Newman, 1962.

Brenner, Anita R., and Leighton, George. *The Wind That Swept Mexico.* New York: Harper, 1943.

Brenner, Charles. *An Elementary Textbook in Psychoanalysis.* Garden City, N.Y.: Doubleday/Anchor Books, 1974.

Brenner, Joseph H., et al. *Drugs and Youth.* New York: Liveright, 1970.

Brenner, M.H. *Estimating the Effects of Economic Change on National Health and Social Well-Being.* Washington, D.C.: United States Congress, 1984.

Brenner, Walter C. *The Ford Theatre Lincoln Assassination Playbills.* Los Angeles: American Scene, 1985.

Brent, Rafer (ed.). *Great Western Heroes.* New York: Bartholomew House, 1957.

Brent, William. *The Complete and Factual Life of Billy the Kid.* New York: Frederick Fell, 1964.

_____, and Brent, Milarde. *The Hell Hole.* Yuma, Ariz.: Southwest Printers, 1962.

Brenton, Myron. *The Privacy Invaders.* New York: Coward-McCann, 1964.

Brereton, Ledwis H. *The Brereton Diaries: 3 October 1941-8 May 1945.* New York: William Morrow, 1946.

Breshko-Breshkovskaya. *Hidden Springs of the Russian Revolution.* Stanford, Calif.: Stanford University Press, 1931.

Bresler, Fenton. *The Chinese Mafia.* New York: Stein & Day, 1981.

_____. *Reprieve: A Study of a System.* London: Harrap, 1965.

_____. *Lord Goddard.* London: Harrap, 1971.

_____. *Scales of Justice.* London: Weidenfeld & Nicholson, 1973.

Breslin, Jimmy. *The Gang That Couldn't Shoot Straight.* New York: Viking Press, 1969.

Bressler, F. *Reprieve.* London: Harrap, 1965.

Breton, Pierre. *Klondike Fever.* New York: Alfred A. Knopf, 1958.

Brett, E.A. *Colonialism and Underdevelopment in East Africa: The Politics of Economic Change, 1919-1939.* London: William Heinemann, 1973.

Brévannes, Roland. *L'orgie satanique á travers les siècles.* Paris: C. Offenstadt, 1904.

Breve storia di cinque mesi. Rome: Quaderni Liberi, 1944.

Brewer, E. Cobham. *A Dictionary of Phrase and Fable.* London: Cassell, 1970.

Brewer, John Francis. *The Curse Upon Mitre Square AD 1530-1888.* London: Simpkin Marshall, 1888.

Brewerton, G. Douglas. *The War in Kansas.* New York: Derby & Jackson, 1856.

Brewster, Sir David. *Letters on Natural Magic.* London: John Murray, 1832.

Brian, Denis. *Tallulah, Darling.* London: Sidgwick & Jackson, 1972.

Briand, Paul, Jr. *Daughter of the Sky.* New York: Duell, Sloan & Pearce, 1960.

Bricaud, Joanny. *J.K. Huysmans et le satanisme.* Paris: Bibliothèque Chacornac, 1913.

Brice, A.H.M. *Look Upon the Prisoner: Studies in Crime.* London: Hutchinson, 1933.

Brice, R. *Le secret de Napoléon.* Paris: Payot, 1936.

Bridenbaugh, Carl. *Cities in Revolt: Urban Life in America, 1743-1776.* New York: Alfred A. Knopf, 1965.

_____. *Cities in the Wilderness: The First Century of Urban Life in America 1625-1742.* New York: Ronald, 1938.

_____. *Cities in the Wilderness: Urban Life in America, 1625-1742.* New York: Capricorn, 1966.

_____. *Mitre and Sceptre.* New York: Oxford University Press, 1962.

_____. *Vexed and Troubled Englishmen 1590-1642.* New York: Oxford University Press, 1968.

Bridge, J.H. *The Inside History of the Carnegie Steel Company.* Chicago: Aldine, 1903.

Bridges, B.C. *Practical Fingerpainting.* New York: Funk & Wagnalls, 1942.

_____, and Boolsen, F.M. *Fifty-one Fingerprint Systems.* Privately Printed, 1935.

Bridges, Horace James. *The God of Fundamentalism and Other Studies.* Chicago: Pascal Covici, 1925.

Bridges, Robert. *Woodrow Wilson, a Personal Tribute.* New York: Privately printed, 1924

Bridges, Yseult. *How Charles Bravo Died.* London: Jarrolds, 1956.

_____. *Poison and Adelaide Bartlett.* London: Hutchindon, 1962.

_____. *Saint with Red Hands.* London: Jarrolds, 1954.

_____. *The Tragedy at Road-Hill House.* New York: Rinehart, 1955.

_____. *Two Studies in Crime.* London: Hutchinson, 1959.

Bridgman, E.P., and Parsons, L.F. *With John Brown in Kansas; the Battle of Ossawatomie.* Madison, Wis.: J.N. Davidson, 1915.

Bridwell, J.W. *The Life and Adventures of Robert McKemie.* Hillsboro, Ohio: Hillsboro Gazette, 1878.

A Brief Account of the Life, Christian Experience and Execution of Courtland C. Johnson. Harrisburg, Pa.: Hamilton Printers, 1854.

A Brief Account of the Life, Trial, Sentence, Last Words and Dying Speech of James Hamilton. Albany, N.Y.: n.p., 1818.

A Brief Account of the Murder of Marcus Lyon. Palmer, Mass.: Ezekiel Terry, 1806.

A Brief and Impartial Narrative of the Life of Sarah Maria Cornell. New York: G. Williams, 1833.

A Brief Narrative of the Life and Confession of Barnett Davenport. Hartford, Conn.: n.p., 1780.

A Brief Relation of the Cruel Murder of Betsy Van Amburgh. Jersey City, N.J., n.p., 1805.

A Brief Summary of Some of the Principal Incidents Relative to the Life of Ursula Newman and the Intercourse Subsisting Between Her and Richard Johnson. New York: Elam Bliss, 1829.

Brien, Steve. *Azaria, the Trial of the Century.* Cammeray, Aus.: QB Books, 1984.

Briffault, Robert. *The Mothers.* New York: Macmillan, 1927.

Briggs, Asa. *The Age of Improvement.* London: Green, 1939.

Briggs, C.W. *The Reign of Terror in Kansas.* Boston: n.p., 1856.

Briggs, Harold Edward. *Frontiers of the Northwest.* New York: Appleton-Century, 1940.

Briggs, I. Vernon. *The Manner of Man That Kills: Spencer, Czolgosz, Richeson.* Boston: Richard G. Badger, The Gorman Press, 1921.

Briggs, L. Vernon. *Arizona and New Mexico, 1882.* Boston: Privately Printed, 1932.

Briggs, Leslie J. *Instructional Media.* American Institute for Research, 1969.

Brighenti, Angelo. *Uomini ed episodi del tempo di Mussolini.* Milan, Italy: SEN, 1938.

Bright, John. *A History of Israel.* London: SCM Press, 1972.

_____. *Hizzoner Big Bill Thompson.* New York: J. Cape & H. Smith, 1930.

Brill, A.A. *Sexuality and Its Role in the Neuroses.* New York: International Universities Press, 1944.

Brill Associates. *Comprehensive Security Planning.* Washington, D.C.: Department of Housing and Urban Development, Office of Policy Development and Research, 1977.

Brill, Steven. *The Teamsters.* New York: Simon & Schuster, 1978.

Brim, O.G., and Kagan, J. (eds.). *Constancy and Change in Heman Development.* Cambridge, Mass.: Harvard University Press, 1980.

_____, and Wheeler, Stanton. *Socialization after Childhood.* New York: John Wiley & Sons, 1968.

Brimble, E. Lillian. *In the Eyrie of the Hohenzollern Eagle.* London: Hodder & Stoughton, 1916.

Brines, Russell. *MacArthur's Japan.* Philadelphia: J.B. Lippincott, 1948.

Bringuier, Carlos. *Red Friday: November 22, 1963.* Chicago: C. Hallberg, 1969.

Brininstool, Earl Alonzo. *Fighting Red Cloud's Warriors.* Columbus, Ohio: Hunter-Trader-Trapper, 1926.

Brink, Carol. *Harps in the Wind: The Story of the Singing Hutchinsons.* New York: Macmillan, 1947.

Brinkley, Roland A., Jr., et al. *The Laws Against Homosexuality.* Huntsville, Texas: Sam Houston State University, 1970.

Brinley, John. *A Discovery of the Impostures of Witches and Astrologers.* London: J. Wright, 1680.

Brinton, Crane. *The Anatomy of Revolution.* New York: Prentice-Hall, 1952.

Briscoe, Robert. *For the Life of Me.* Boston: Little, Brown, 1958.

Brissard, André. *Les Agents de Lucifer.* Paris: Périn, 1975.

Brissenden, Paul F. *The I.W.W.: A Study of American Syndicalism.* New York: Columbia University Press, 1919.

Bristed, Charles Astor. *The Upper Ten Thousand.* New York: Stinger & Townsend, 1852.

Bristol, Sherlock. *The Pioneer Preacher: An Autobiography.* New York: F.H. Revell, 1887.

Bristow, E.J. *Prostitution and Prejudice: The Jewish Fight Against White Slavery 1870-1939.* New York: Oxford University Press, 1982.

Bristow, G.O. *Lost on Grand River.* Nowater, I.T.: Cherokee Air, 1900.

Bristow, Joseph Quayle. *Tales of Old Fort Gibson.* New York: Exposition Press, 1961.

British Museum. *Murders (A Collection of Broadsides Containing Accounts in Prose and Verse of Murders and Executions).* London: n.p. 1794-1860.

Britton, Nan. *The President's Daughter.* New York: Elizabeth Ann Guild, 1927.

Brixton, Charles (ed.). *Memoirs of Sir Thomas Fowell Buston.* London: J.M. Dent & Sons, 1925.

Brizzolesi, Vittorio. *Giolitti.* Novara, Italy: Istituto Geografico De Agostini, 1921.

Broad, Lewis. *The Innocence of Edith Thompson.* London: Hutchinson, 1952.

Broadbent, D. *Decision and Stress.* New York: Academic Press, 1971.

Broaddus, J. Morgan. *The Legal Heritage of El Paso.* El Paso: Texas Western Press, 1963.

Broadfoot, Barry. *Ten Lost Years, 1929-1939.* Toronto, Ontario, Can.: Doubleday, 1973.

Brock, Alan. *A Casebook of Crime.* London: Watmoughs, 1948.

Brock, Arthur J. *Greek Medicine.* New York: E.P. Dutton, 1929.

Brock, W.R. *Lord Liverpool and Liberal Toryism, 1820-1827.* Cambridge, Eng.: Cambridge University Press, 1941.

Brockelmann, Carl. *History of the Islamic Peoples.* New York: G.P. Putnam's Sons: 1947.

Brockunier, S.H. *The Irrepressible Democrat: Roger Williams.* New York: Ronald, 1940.

Brockway, A. Fenner. *African Socialism.* Chester Springs, Pa.: Dufour, 1963.

_____. *The Next Step Toward Working-Class Unity.* London: I.L.P., 1933.

Brockway, F. *African Journeys.* London: Victor Gollancz, 1955.

Brockway, Z.R. *Fifty Years of Prison Service.* New York: Charities Publication Committee, 1912.

Brodeur, Paul. *Expendable Americans.* New York: Viking Press, 1974.

_____. *The Zapping of America.* New York: W.W. Norton, 1977.

Brodie, Fawn. *Thaddeus Stevens, Scourge of the South.* New York: W.W. Norton, 1959.

Brodie-Innes, John William. *Scottish Witchcraft Trials.* London: Chiswick Press, 1891.

Brodsky, Annette, M. (ed.). *The Female Offender.* Beverly Hills, Calif.: Sage, 1975.

Brody, Stephen R. *The Effectiveness of Sentencing.* London: H.M. Stationery Office, 1976.

Broehl, Wayne. *The Molly Maguires.* Cambridge, Mass.: Harvard University Press, 1964.

Broeker, Galen. *Rural Disorder and Police Reform in Ireland.* London: Routledge & Kegan Paul, 1970.

Brogan, D.W. *France Under the Republic.* New York: Harper, 1940.

_____. *Proudhon.* London: Hamish Hamilton, 1934.

Brogan, Denis W. *The Era of Franklin D. Roosevelt.* New Haven, Conn.: Yale University Press, 1950.

Brogger, A.W., and Shetelig, Haakon. *The Viking Ships.* trans. Katherine John. Oslo, Nor.: Dreyer, 1953.

Brognolo, Candido. *Alexicacon, Hoc Est de Maleficiis.* Venice, Italy: Baptistae Catamei, 1668.

_____. *Manuale Exorcistarum.* Bergamo, Italy: M.A. Rubei, 1651.

Brolaski, Harry. *Easy Money.* Cleveland: Searchlight Press, 1911.

Bromage, Mary C. *De Valera and the March of a Nation.* London: Hutchinson, 1956.

Bromberg, Walter. *Crime and the Mind.* Philadelphia: J.B. Lippincott, 1948.

Brommel, Bernard. *Eugene V. Debs: A Spokesman for Labor and Socialism.* Chicago: Charles H. Kerr, 1978.

Bronaugh, Warren C. *The Youngers' Fight for Freedom.* Columbia, Mo.: E.W. Stephens, 1906.

Brondsted, Johannes. *The Vikings*. Baltimore: Penguin Books, 1970.

Bronowski, J. *The Face of Violence*. New York: World, 1967.

Bronson, Edgar Beecher. *The Red-Blooded Heroes of the Frontier*. New York: A.C. McClurg, 1910.

_____. *The Vanguard*. New York: George H. Doran, 1914.

Bronson, John. *The Earth Shook, The Sky Burned*. New York: Doubleday, 1959.

Bronson, William. *The Earth Shook, the Sky Burned*. Garden City, N.Y.: Doubleday, 1959.

Brooke, Henry K. *Booke of Pirates*. New York: J.B. Perry, 1847.

_____. *The Highwaymen and Pirates' Own Book*. New York: J.B. Perry, 1845.

Brooke, Hugh. *Man Made Angry*. New York: Longmans, 1932.

Brooke, John. *King George III*. New York: McGraw-Hill, 1972.

Brooke, Sir Robert. *La Graunde Abridgement, Collect and Escrit per le Iudge tresreuerend Syr Robert Brooke*. London: Richard Tottyl, 1573.

Brooke, T.H. *A History of the Island of St. Helena*. London: Black, Parry & Kingsbury, 1808.

Brookes, Cannon J.R. *Murder in Fact and Fiction*. London: Hurst & Blackett, 1926.

Brookes, Dame Mabel. *St. Helena Story*. London: William Heinemann, 1960.

Brookes, George S. *Friend Anthony Benezet*. Philadelphia: University of Pennsylvania Press, 1937.

Brooks, Benjamin S. *Appendix to the Opening Statement and Brief of B.S. Books, on the Chinese Question*. San Francisco: Women's Cooperative Printing Union, 1877.

_____. *Brief of the Legislation and Adjudication Touching the Chinese Question*. San Francisco: Women's Cooperative Printing Union, 1877.

Brooks, Eugene C. *Woodrow Wilson as President*. New York: Row, Peterson, 1916.

Brooks, Graham (ed.). *Trial of Captain Kidd*. London: William Hodge, 1930.

Brooks, Jim. *Origins of Life*. Belleville, Mich.: Lion, 1985.

Brooks, John Nixon. *The Go-Go Years*. New York: Weybright & Talley, 1973.

_____. *Once in Golconda*. New York: Harper & Row, 1969.

_____. *The Seven Fat Years*. London: Victor Gollancz, 1959.

Brooks, Juanita. *The Moutain Meadows Massacre*. Stanford, Calif.: Stanford Universtiy Press, 1962.

Brooks, Lester. *Behind Japan's Surrender: The Secret Struggle That Ended an Empire*. New York: McGraw-Hill Book, 1968.

Brooks, Noah. *Washington in Lincoln's Time*. New York: Holt, Rinehart & Winston, 1958.

Brooks, Robert C. *Corruption in American Politics and Life*. New York: Dodd, Mead, 1910.

Brooks, Stuart M. *Our Assassinated Presidents*. New York: Bell, 1985.

_____. *Our Murdered Presidents: The Medical Story*. New York: Frederick Fell, 1966.

Brooks, Thomas R. *Toil and Trouble: A History of American Labor*. New York: Dell Books, 1971.

Brooks, Van Wyck. *The Confident Years*. New York: E.P. Dutton, 1952.

_____. *Fenollosa and His Circle*. New York: E.P. Dutton, 1953.

_____. *The Flowering of New England 1815-1865*. New York: Random House, 1936.

_____. *New England: Indian Summer 1865-1915*. New York: E.P. Dutton, 1940.

_____. *Our Literary Heritage*. New York: E.P. Dutton, 1956.

_____. *The Times of Melville & Whitman*. New York: E.P. Dutton, 1953.

Brook-Shepherd, Gordon. *The Anschluss*. Philadelphia: J.B. Lippincott, 1963.

_____. *Prelude to Infamy*. New York: Ivan Obolensky, 1961.

_____. *Uncle of Europe*. New York: Harcourt, Brace, Jovano-

vich, 1976.

Broomberger, Merry and Serg. *The Secrets of Suez*. London: Sedgwick and Jackson, 1957.

Brophy, Frank Cullen. *Arizona Sketch Book: Fifty Historical Sketches*. Phoenix, Ariz.: Ampco Press, 1952.

Brophy, John. *The Meaning of Murder*. London: Ronald Whiting & Wheaton, 1966.

Brosnan, Cornelius James. *History of the State of Idaho*. New York: Charles Scribner's Sons, 1918.

Bross, Werner. *Gespräche mit Hermann Göring während des Nürnberger Prozesses*. Flensburg, Ger.: Wolff, 1950.

Bross, William. *History of Chicago*. Chicago: Jansen, McClurg, 1880.

Brosse, Jacques. *Great Voyages of Discovery: Circumnavigators and Scientists, 1764-1843*. trans. Stanley Hochman. New York: Facts on File, 1983.

Broszat, Martin. *Nationalsozialistische Polenpolitik 1939-45*. Stuttgart, Ger.: Deutsche Verlagsanstalt, 1961.

Brothers, Mary Hudson. *Billy the Kid*. Farmington, N.M.: Hustler Press, 1949.

_____. *A Pecos Pioneer*. Albuquerque: University of New Mexico Press, 1943.

Broudy, Eric, Haliburton, Warren, and Swinburne, Laurence. *They Had A Dream*. New York: Pyramid Books, 1969.

Brough, James. *The Ford Dynasty-an American Story*. Garden City, N.Y.: Doubleday, 1977.

Brougher, William E. *The Long Dark Road*. Privately Published, 1946.

_____. *South to Bataan, North to Mukden*. Athens, Ga.: University of Georgia Press, 1971.

Broughton, Lord. *Recollections of a Long Life*. London: John Murray, 1911.

Broun, Heywood, and Leech, Margaret. *Anthony Comstock: Roundsman of the Lord*. New York: Boni, 1927.

_____. *The Boy Grew Older*. New York: G.P. Putnam's Sons, 1922.

_____. *Collected Edition of Heywood Broun*. New York: Harcourt, Brace, 1941.

_____. *It Seems to Me*. New York: Harcourt, Brace, 1935.

Browder, Earl R. *Communism in the United States*. Urbana, University of Illinois Press, 1967.

_____. *The Communist Party of the U.S.; Its History, Role, and Organization*. New York: Workers' Library, 1941.

_____. *The People's Front*. New York: International, 1938.

_____. *Teheran and America*. New York: Workers' Library, 1944.

_____. *Victory and After*. New York: John Day, 1942.

Browder, Robert P., and Kerensky, Alexander F. (eds.). *The Russian Provisional Government Documents*. 3 vols. Stanford. Calif.: Stanford University Press, 1961.

Brower, Brock. *Other Loyalties*. New York: Atheneum, 1968.

Brown, A. Theodore. *The Politics of Reform: Kansas City's Municipal Government, 1925-1950* Kansas City: Community Studies, 1958.

Brown, Bertram S., et al. *Psychosurgery: Perspectives on a Current Problem*. Washington, D.C.: U.S. Government Printing Office, 1973.

Brown, Brenda. *Crimes Against Women Alone*. Memphis, Tenn.: Published by Author, 1974.

Brown, Charles T. *Bilibid Prison: "The Devil's Cauldron, a Fragment from That Mosaic."* San Antonio, Texas: Naylor, 1957.

Brown, Christian. *Trial and Confession of William Hill*. New York: Brown, 1826.

Brown, Claude. *Manchild in the Promised Land*. New York: New American Library, 1965.

Brown, Dee. *The Gentle Tamers: Women of the Old West*. New York: G.P. Putnam's Sons, 1958.

_____, and Schmitt, Martin F. *Trail Driving Days*. New York: Charles Scribner's Sons, 1952.

Brown, Delmer M. *Nationalism in Japan*. New York: Russell

& Russell, 1955.

Brown, Eve. *Chapagne Cholly*. New York: E.P. Dutton, 1947.

Brown, Everett Somervile (ed.). *The Missouri Compromises and Presidential Politics, 1820-1825*. St. Louis: Missouri Historical Society, 1926.

Brown, F. Yeats (ed.). *Escape*. New York: Macmillan, 1933.

Brown, Fredric. *The Screaming Mimi*. New York: E.P. Dutton, 1949.

Brown, George L., and Peebles, John. *Trial and Confession of Robert McConaghy, The Inhuman Butcher of Mr. Brown's Family*. Huntington County, Pa.: n.p., 1840.

Brown, George Rothwell (ed.). *Reminiscences of Senator William M. Stewart, of Nevada*. New York: Neale, 1908.

Brown, Henry Collins. *Brownstone Fronts and Saratoga Trunks*. New York: E.P. Dutton, 1935.

_____ (ed.). *Valentine's Manual of Old New York*. New York: Valentine's Manual, 1919.

Brown, Ivor. *Dickens in His Time*. New York: Thomas Nelson, 1963.

Brown, J.A.C. *Techniques of Persuasion*. New York: Penguin Books, 1963.

Brown, James Cabell. *Calabaza*. San Francisco: Valleau & Peterson, 1892.

Brown, Jesse, and Willard, A.M. *The Black Hills Trails*. Rapid City, S.D.: Rapid City Journal, 1924.

Brown, John. *Twenty-Five Years a Parson in the Wild West*. Fall River, Mass.: n.p., 1896.

Brown, John Henry. *Reminiscences and Incidents of the Early Life of San Francisco*. San Francisco: Mission Journal, 1929.

Brown, John P. *Old Frontiers*. Kingsport, Tenn.: Southern, 1938.

Brown, L.G. *Sex Pathologies*. New York: Social Path, 1942.

Brown, Lee. *The Reluctant Reformation: On Criticizing the Press in America*. New York: David McKay, 1974.

Brown, Leland. *Effective Business Report Writing*. Englewood Cliffs, N.J.: Prentice-Hall, 1963.

Brown, Lester. *By Bread Alone*. New York: Frederick A. Praeger, 1974.

Brown, Mark H., and Felton, W.R. *Before Barbed Wire*. New York: Henry Holt, 1956.

_____. *The Frontier Years*. New York: Henry Holt, 1955.

_____. *The Plainsmen of the Yellowstone*. New York: G.P. Putnam's Sons, 1961.

Brown, Michael. *Marked to Die*. New York: Simon & Schuster, 1984.

Brown, Michael K. *Working the Street*. New York: Russell Sage Foundation, 1981.

Brown, Porter Emerson. *On "Keeping Out of War" and "Swapping Horses."* New York: National Hughes Alliance, 1916.

Brown, R. *Words and Things*. Glencoe: Illionis Press, 1958.

_____. *Social Psychology*. New York: Free Press, 1965

Brown, R.E. *Charles Beard and the Constitution*. Princeton, N.J.: Princeton University Press, 1956.

_____. *Middle-Class Democracy and the Revolution in Massachusetts 1691-1780*. Ithaca, N.Y.: Cornell University Press, 1955.

Brown, Ralph. *Loyalty and Security*. New Haven, Conn.: Yale University Press, 1958.

Brown, Richard M. *The South Carolina Regulators*. Cambridge, Mass.: Belknap Press of Harvard University Press, 1963.

Brown, Richard Maxwell. *Strain of Violence*. New York: Oxford, 1977.

Brown, Robert. *Demonology and Witchcraft*. London: J.F. Shaw, 1889.

Brown, Robert L. *An Empire of Silver*. Caldwell, Idaho: Caxton Printers, 1965.

_____. *Ghost Towns of the Colorado Rockies*. Caldwell, Idaho: Caxton Printers, 1968.

Brown, Robert R. (ed.). *History of Kings County*. Handford, Calif.: A.H. Canoston, 1940.

Brown, Rollo Walter. *Harvard Yard in the Golden Age*. New York: Current Books, 1948.

Brown, Stuart G. *Conscience and Politics: Adlai E. Stevenson in the 1950s*. Syracuse, N.Y.: Syracuse University Press, 1961.

_____. *Thomas Jefferson*. New York: Washington Square Press, 1966.

Brown, Warren. *Chicago White Sox*. New York: G.P. Putnam's Sons, 1952.

Brown, Wenzell. *Introduction to Murder: The Unpublished Facts behind the Lonelyhearts Killers, Martha Beck and Raymond Fernandez*. New York: Greenberg, 1952.

Brown, Will C. *Sam Bass and Company*. New York: New American Library, 1960.

Brown, William Adams. *Morris Ketchum Jesup: A Character Sketch*. New York: Charles Scribner's Sons, 1910.

Brown, William G. *Life of Oliver Ellsworth*. New York: Macmillan, 1905.

Browne, Douglas G., and Tullett, E. V. *Bernard Spilsbury: His Life and Cases*. London: Harrap, 1951.

_____, and Brock, Alan. *Fingerprints, Fifty Years of Scientific Crime Detection*. New York: E.P. Dutton, 1954.

_____. *The Rise of Scotland Yard*. New York: G.P. Putnam's Sons, 1956.

_____. *The Scalpel of Scotland Yard*. New York: E.P. Dutton, 1952.

_____. *Sir Travers Humphreys*. London: Harrap, 1960.

Browne, Henry J. *The Catholic Church and the Knights of Labor*. Washington, D.C.: Catholic University of America Press, 1949.

Browne, G. Lathom, and Stewart, C.G. *Trials for Murder by Poisoning*. London: Stevens & Sons, 1883.

Browne, J. Ross. *Adventures in Apache Country: A Tour Through Arizona and Sonora, 1864*. Tucson: University of Arizona Press, 1974.

Browne, Jefferson. *Key West: The Old and the New*. St. Augustine: Florida Record, 1912.

Browne, Junius Henri. *The Great Metropolis: A Mirror of New York*. Hartford, Conn.: American Publishing, 1869.

Browne, Malcolm. *The New Face of War*. London: Cassell, 1966.

Browne, Waldo Ralph. *Altgeld of Illinois: A Record of His Life and Work*. New York: B.W. Huebsch, 1924.

Brownell, Baker. *The Other Illinois*. New York: Duell, Sloan & Pearce, 1958.

Brownell, Blaine A, and Stickle, Warren E. *Bosses and Reformers: Urban Politics in America 1880-1920*. Boston: Houghton Mifflin, 1973.

Brownell, Emery A. *Legal Aid in the United States*. Rochester, N.Y.: Lawyers' Cooperative Publishing, 1951.

Brownfield, Charles A. *The Brain Benders*. Hicksville, N.Y.: Exposition Press, 1965.

Browning, B.L. *Chemistry of Wood*. New York: John Wiley & Sons, 1963.

Browning, Frank, and Gerassi, John. *The American Way of Crime*. New York: G.P. Putnam's Sons, 1980.

Browning, Orville Hickman. *The Diary of...* Springfield: Illinois State Historical Library, 1933.

Brownlee, Fambrough L. *Winston-Salem: A Pictorial History*. Norfolk, Va.: Donning, 1979.

Brownlee, Richard S. *Gray Ghosts of the Confederacy*. Baton Rouge: Louisiana State University Press, 1958.

Brownlee, W.E. (ed.) *Dr. Graves: His Trial and His Suicide*. Denver: Denver Times, 1893.

Brownlow, Kevin. *The Parade's Gone By*. New York: Alfred A. Knopf, 1968.

Brownlow, W.G. *Sketches of the Rise, Progress, and Decline of Secession*. Philadelphia: George W. Childs, 1862.

Brownmiller, Susan. *Against Our Will: Men, Women, and Rape*. New York: Simon & Schuster, 1975.

Browse, Lillian. *Sickert*. London: Hart-Davis, 1960.

Bruce, George. *The Stranglers: The Cult of Thugee and Its Overthrow in British India*. London: Longmans, Green, 1968.

Bruce, J. Campbell. *Escape from Alcatraz.* New York: McGraw-Hill, 1963.

Bruce, John. *Gaudy Century.* New York: Random House, 1948.

Bruce, Leona. *Banister Was There.* Fort Worth, Texas: Branch-Smith, 1968.

Bruce, Philip Alexander. *Economic History of Virginia in the Seventeeth Century.* 2 vols. New York: Macmillan, 1907.

_____. *Institutional History of Virginia in the Seventeeth Century.* 2 vols. New York: G.P. Putnam's Sons, 1910.

_____. *Social Life in the Seventeeth Century.* Lynchburg, Va.: J.P. Bell, 1927.

Bruce, Robert. *The Fighting Norths and Pawnee Scouts.* New York: Privately Printed, 1932.

Bruce, Robert V. *1877: Year of Violence.* Indianapolis, Ind.: Bobbs-Merrill, 1959.

Bruce, Ronald (ed.). *The Pot Report.* New York: Universal-Award House, 1971.

Bruce, William Cabell. *John Randolph of Roanoke.* 2 vols. New York: G.P. Putnam's Sons, 1922.

Bruce Lockhart, R.H. *British Agent.* New York: G.P. Putnam's Sons, 1933.

Bruchey, Stuart. *The Roots of American Economic Growth, 1607-1861.* New York: Harper & Row, 1968.

_____ (ed.) *Small Business in American Life.* New York: Columbia University Press, 1980.

Bruffey, George A. *Eighty-One Years in the West.* Butte, Mont.: Butte Miner, 1925.

Brugmann, Bruce G., et al. *The Ultimate Highrise.* San Francisco: San Francisco Bay Guardian Books, 1971.

Bruhns, Karl. *Life of Alexander von Humboldt.* trans. June and Caroline Larsell. London: Longmans, Green, 1873.

Brun, V.P. *My Years with Coldwell Banker.* Los Angeles: Privately Printed, n.d.

Bruner, J., et al. *A Study of Thinking.* New York: John Wiley & Sons, 1956.

Brunet, J.M.H. *Trial of William Dandridge Epes for the Murder of Francis Adolphus Muir.* Petersburg, Va.: Published by Author, 1849.

Brunet-Moret, Jean. *Le Général Trochu 1815-1896.* Paris: Haussmann, 1955.

Bruns, Carl G. *Fontes Juris Romani.* Tubingen, Ger.: J.C.B. Mohrii, 1909.

Brunswig, H., Montroe, Charles E., and Kibler, Alton L. *Explosives.* New York: John Wiley & Sons, 1922.

Brunswik, E. *Perception and the Representative Design of Psychological Experiments.* Berkley: University of California Press, 1956.

Brusher, Joseph S. *Consecrated Thunderbolt.* Hawthorne, N.J.: Joseph F. Wagner, 1973.

Brussel, James A. *Casebook of a Crime Psychiatrist.* New York: Bernard Geis Associates, 1968.

Bruttini, Alessandro, and Puglisi, Guiseppe. *L'Impero tradito.* Florence, Italy: La Fenice, 1957.

Bruun, Kettil, et al. *The Gentlemen's Club: International Control of Drugs and Alcohol.* Chicago: University of Chicago Press, 1976.

Bryan, George S. *The Great American Myth.* New York: Carrick & Evans, 1940.

Bryan, Helen. *Inside.* New York: Houghton Mifflin, 1953.

Bryan, J. Ingram. *Japan from Within: An Inquiry into the Political, Industrial, Commercial, Financial, Agricultural, Armamental and Educational Conditions of Modern Japan.* New York: Frederick A. Stokes, 1924.

Bryan, Jerry. *An Illinois Gold Hunter in the Black Hills.* Springfield, Ill.: State Historical Society, 1960.

Bryan, Mary Baird (ed.). *The Memoirs of William Jennings Bryan.* Philadelphia: John C. Winston, 1925.

Bryan, W.B. *A History of the National Capital.* 2 vols. New York: Macmillan, 1914.

Bryan, William Jennings. *The First Battle. A Story of the Campaign of 1896.* Chicago: W.B. Conkey, 1896.

_____. *In His Image.* New York: Fleming H. Revell, 1922.

_____. and Bryan, Mary Baird. *Memoirs of William Jennings Bryan.* Philadelphia: Winston, 1925.

_____. *A Tale of Two Conventions.* New York: Funk & Wagnall, 1912.

Bryant, G.E., and Baker, G.P. *A Quaker Journal: Being a Diary and Reminiscences of William Lucas, 1804-1861.* 2 vols. London: Hutchinson, 1933.

Bryant, Louise. *Mirrors of Moscow.* New York: Thomas Seltzer, 1923.

Bryant, Samuel. *The Sea and the States: A Maritime History of the American People.* New York: Thomas Y. Crowell, 1947.

Bryant, Will. *Great American Guns and Frontier Fighters.* New York: Grossett & Dunlap, 1961.

Bryant, William Cullen *Letters of a Traveller.* New York: G.P. Putnam's Sons, 1951.

_____, and Gay, Sidney Howard. *A Popular History of the United States...Fully Illustrated.* 4 vols. New York: Charles Scribner's Sons, 1880.

Bryce, James. *The American Commonwealth.* 3 vols. London: Macmillan, 1888.

Bryce, John. *The Gaudy Century: The Story of San Francisco's Hundred Years of Robust Journalism.* New York: Random House, 1948.

Brynes, Asher. *Government Against the People.* New York: Dodd, Mead, 1946.

Brynes, Thomas. *Professional Criminals in America.* New York: Chelsea House, 1969.

Bryson, John. *Evil Angels.* New York: Summit Books, 1985.

Bryson, Lyman. *Which Way America? Communism-Fascism-Democracy?* New York: Macmillan, 1939.

Brzezinski, Zbigniew K. *Permanent Purge, Politics in Soviet Totalitarianism.* Cambridge, Mass.: Harvard University Press, 1966.

_____. *The Soviet Bloc: Unity and Conflict.* New York: Frederick A. Praeger, 1962.

Buchan, John (ed.). *Bulgaria and Romania.* Boston: Houghton Mifflin, 1924.

Buchanan, A. Russell. *David S. Terry of California.* San Marino, Calif.: Huntington Library, 1956.

Buchanan, Edna. *Carr.* New York: E.P. Dutton, 1979.

Buchanan, Sir George. *My Mission to Russia.* 2 vols. London: Cassell, 1923.

Buchanan, James. *Mr. Buchanan's Administration on the Eve of Rebellion.* New York: D. Appleton, 1866.

Buchanan, Lamont. *A Pictorial History of the Confederacy.* New York: Crown, 1961.

Buchanan, Meriel. *The Dissolution of an Empire.* London: John Murray, 1932.

_____. *Queen Victoria's Relations.* London: Cassell, 1954.

Buchanan, Thomas. *Who Killed Kennedy?* New York: G.P. Putnam's Sons, 1964.

Buchheim, Hans. *Glaubenkrise im Dritten Reich.* Stuttgart, Ger.: Deutsche Verlagsanstalt, 1953.

_____. *SS und Polizei im Ns-Staat.* Duisdorf nr Bonn, Ger.: Selbstverlag der Studiengesellschaft für Zeitprobleme, 1964.

_____. *Totalitäre Herrschaft.* Munich, Ger.: Kösel, 1962.

Buchheit, Gert. *Der deutsche Geheimdienst.* Munich, Ger.: List, 1966.

Buchholz, E., et al. *Socialist Criminology.* Lexington, Mass.: D.C. Heath, 1974.

Buck, Frederick. *Horse Race Betting: A Complete Account of Parimutuel and Bookmaking.* New York: Greenburg, 1946.

Buck, Paul H. *The Road to Reunion.* New York: Vintage Books, 1959.

Buckbee, Edna Bryan. *Pioneer Days of Angel's Camp.* Angel's Camp: Calaveras Califonian, 1932.

_____. *The Saga of Old Tuolumne.* New York: Press of the Pioneers, 1935.

Buckingham, J.E. *Reminiscences and Souvenirs of the Assassination of Abraham Lincoln.* Washington, D.C.: Darby, 1894.

Buckingham, James Silk. *The Eastern and Western States of America.* London: Fisher, Son, 1842.

Buckle, George Earle (ed.). *The Letters of Queen Victoria: Third Series.* London: John Murray, 1930.

Buckler, Helen. *Doctor Dan: Pioneer in American Surgery.* Boston: Little, Brown, 1954.

Buckley, Christopher. *The Road to Rome.* London: Hodder & Stoughton, 1945.

Buckley, Margaret. *The Jangle of Keys.* Dublin, Ire.: James Duffy, 1938.

Buckley, Marie. *Breaking Into Prison.* Boston: Beacon Press, 1974.

Buckley, William F., et al. *The Committe and Its Critics: A Calm Review of the House Committe on Un-American Activities.* New York: G.P. Putnam's Sons, 1962.

_____, and Bozell, L. Brent. *McCarthy and His Enemies.* Chicago: Henry Regnery, 1954.

Buckmaster, Henrietta. *Let My People Go.* Boston: Beacon Press, 1959.

Bucknill, Sir Alfred. *The Nature of Evidence.* London: Skeffington, 1953.

Budenz, Louis F. *Men Without Faces.* New York: Harper & Brothers, 1950.

_____. *This Is My Story.* Dublin, Ire.: Browne & Nolan, 1948.

Buder, Stanley. *Pullman: An Experiment in Industrial Order and Community Planning 1880-1930.* New York: Oxford University Press, 1967.

Budge, E.A. Wallis. *History of Ethiopia.* London: Methuen, 1928.

_____ (ed.) *The Queen of Sheba and Her Only Son Menyelek:...A Complete Translation of the KEBRA NAGAST.* London: Martin Hopkinson, 1922.

Buehlman, William. *Saint with a Gun.* New York: New York University Press, 1974.

Buehrig, Edward H. (ed.). *Wilson's Foreign Policy in Perspective.* Bloomington: Indiana University Press, 1957.

_____. *Woodrow Wilson and the Balance of Power.* Bloomington: Indiana University Press, 1955.

Buel, James William. *The Border Bandits.* Chicago: Donohue, Henneberry, 1893.

_____. *The Border Outlaws.* St. Louis: Historical, 1881.

_____. *Heroes of the Plains.* St. Louis: Historical, 1881.

_____. *The James Boys.* Chicago: M.A. Donohue, n.d.

_____. *Jesse and Frank James and Their Comrades in Crime, the Younger Brothers, the Notorious Border Outlaws.* Baltimore: I. & M. Ottenheimer, 1902.

_____. *Life and Marvelous Adventures of Wild Bill, the Scout.* Chicago: Belford, Clarke, 1880.

_____. *The True Story of Wild Bill Hickok.* New York: Atomic Books, 1946.

Buell, Raymond L. (ed.). *Democratic Governments in Europe.* New York: T. Nelson & Sons, 1935.

Buenker, John D. *Urban Liberalism and Progressive Reform.* New York: Charles Scribner's Sons, 1973.

Buffum, Edward Gould. *Six Months in the Gold Mines.* Philadelphia: Lea & Blanchard, 1850.

Buffum, George Tower. *On Two Frontiers.* Boston: Lothrop, Lee & Shepard, 1918.

_____. *Smith of Bear City.* New York: Grafton Press, 1906.

Buffum, Peter C. *Homosexuality in Prison.* Washington, D.C.: U.S. Government Printing Office, 1971.

Bugge, Brian K. *The Mystique of Conspiracy.* New York: Published by Author, 1978.

Bugliosi, Vincent. *Helter Skelter.* New York: W.W. Norton, 1974.

_____. *Till Death Us Do Part.* New York: Norton, 1978.

Bühler, G. (ed.). *Sacred Books of the East.* Delhi, India: Motilala Banarasidass, 1964.

Buisseret, François. *La possession de Jeanne Fery, religieuse professe du couvent des soeurs noires de la ville de Mons, 1584.* Ed. Désiré Magliore Bourneville. Paris: Delahaye et Lacrosnier, 1886.

Buisson, H. *La police, son histoire.* Allier, Fr.: Vichy, 1949.

Buist, Martin G. *At Spes non Fracta, Hope & Co., 1770-1815: Merchant Bankers and Diplomants at Work.* The Hague, Neth.: Martinus Nijhoff, 1974.

Buitrago, Ann Mari, and Immerman, Leon Andrew. *Are You Now or Have You Ever Been in the F.B.I. Files.* New York: Grove Press, 1980.

Buley, R.C. *The Old Northwest: Pioneer Period, 1815-1840.* 2 vols. Indianapolis: Indiana Historical Society, 1950.

Bulfinch, John. *The Trial of Moses Adams.* Boston: E.B. Tilston, 1815.

Bull, Edvard. *Historie og Politikk.* Oslo, Nor.: Tiden Norsh, 1933.

Bullard, Sir Reader. *Britain and the Middle East.* London: Hutchinson, 1951.

Bullard, Scott R., and Collins, Michael Leo. *Who's Who in Sherlock Holmes.* New York: Taplinger, 1980.

Bullitt, William C., and Freud, Sigmund. *Thomas Woodrow Wilson: A Psychological Study.* Boston: Houghton Mifflin, 1967.

Bullock, Alan. *Hitler: A Study in Tyranny.* New York: Harper & Row, 1962.

Bullock, Cecil. *Etajima: The Dartmouth of Japan.* London: Sampson, Low, Marston, 1942.

Bullock, Hugh. *The Story of Investment Companies.* New York: Columbia University Press, 1959.

Bullock, Paul. *Aspiration vs. Opportunity: "Careers" in the Inner City.* Ann Arbor: Institute of Labor and Industrial Relations, University of Michigan -- Wayne State University, 1973.

Bullough, Vern L. and Bonnie. *The Emergence of Modern Nursing.* New York: Macmillan, 1964.

_____. *The History of Prohibition.* New Hyde Park, N.Y.: University Books, 1965.

_____. *The History of Prostitution.* New Hyde Park, N.Y.: University Books, 1964.

_____, and Bonnie. *An Illustrated Social History of Prostitution.* New York: Crown, 1978.

_____. *Sexual Variance in Society and Culture.* New York: Wiley Interscience, 1976.

_____. *Sin, Sickness and Sanity.* New York: New American Library, 1977.

_____. *The Subordinate Sex.* Urbana: University of Illinois Press, 1973.

Bullough, William A. *The Blind Boss and His City: Christopher Augustine Buckley and Nineteenth-Century San Francisco.* Berkeley: University of California Press, 1979.

Bulnes, Francisco. *El verdadero Diaz y la revolución.* Mexico City: E. Gómez de la kPuente, 1920.

_____. *The Whole Truth About Mexico: President Wilson's Responsibility.* New York: M. Bulnes Book, 1916.

Bülow, Prince Bernhard. *Denkwürdigkeiten.* 4 vols. Berlin: Ullstein, 1930-31.

_____. *Memoirs.* 4 vols. Boston: Little, Brown, 1931-32.

Bulygin, Paul, and Kerensky, Alexander. *The Murder of the Romanovs.* London: Hutchinson, 1935.

Bunau-Varilla, Philippe Jean. *The Great Adventure of Panama.* New York: Doubleday, 1920.

Bunce, William K. (ed.). *Religions in Japan: Buddhism, Shinto, Christianity.* Rutland, Vt.: Charles E. Tuttle, 1955.

Buncher, Judith F. (ed.). *Crime and Punishment in America.* New York: Facts on File, 1978.

Bundy, Mary Lee, and Harmon, Kenneth R. (eds.). *The National Prison Directory.* College Park, Md.: Urban Information Interpreters, 1975.

Bungay, George W. *The Maine Law Museum; and Temperance Anecdotes, Original and Selected.* Boston: Stacy & Richardson, 1852.

Bunker, Edward. *No Beast So Fierce*. New York: W.W. Norton, 1973.

Bunn, Ronald F. *German Politics and the Spiegel Affair: A Case Study of the Bonn System*. Baton Rouge: Louisiana State University Press, 1968.

Bunyan, James, and Fisher, H.H. *The Bolshevik Revolution, 1917-1921*. 2 vols. Stanford, Calif.: Stanford University Press, 1934.

Buranelli, Vincent, and Nan. *Spy/Counterspy*. New York: McGraw-Hill, 1982.

_____ (ed.). *The Trial of John Peter Zenger*. New York: New York University Press, 1957.

Burch, John P. *Charles W. Quantrell: A True History of Guerrilla Warfare on the Missouri and Kansas Border During the Civil War of 1861-1865 as Told by Capt. Harrison Trow*. Vegas, Texas: Privately Printed, 1923.

Burchard, Johann. *At the Court of the Borgia*. trans. and ed. Geoffrey Parker. London: Folio Society, 1963.

_____. *Pope Alexander and His Court*. New York: N.L. Brown, 1921.

Burchell, Robert A. *The San Francisco Irish, 1848-1880*. Berkeley: University of California Press, 1980.

Burcher, Fanny. *Many Lives, One Love*. New York: Harper & Row, 1972.

Burchett, W.G. *Wingate Adventure*. Melbourne: F. Cheshire, 1944.

Burckhardt, Carl J. *Meine Danziger Mission 1937-1939*. Munich: Georg D.W. Callwey, 1960.

_____. *Richelieu and His Age*. trans. Bernard Hoy, 4 vols. London: George Allen & Unwin, 1967.

Burckhardt, Jacob. *The Age of Constantine*. Garden City, N.Y.: Doubleday, 1956.

_____. *The Civilization of the Renaissance in Italy*. trans. S.G.C. Middlemore. New York: Oxford University Press, 1944.

Burckhardt, Titus. *Alchemy*. Baltimore: Penguin, 1971.

Bürckstümmer, Christian. *Geschichte der Reformation und Gegenreformation in der ehemaligen freien Ruchsstadt Dinkelstühl*. Leipzig, Ger.: Im Konnissionverlag con Rudolf Haupt, 1914.

Burdick, Usher Lloyd. *Jim Johnson, Pioneer*. Williston, N.D.: Privately Printed, 1941.

_____. *Life and Exploits of John Goodall*. Watford City, N.D.: McKenzie County Farmer, 1931.

_____. *Tales from Buffalo Land*. Baltimore: Wirth Brothers, 1939.

Bureau of the Census. *Characteristics of American Children and Youth:1976*. Washington, D.C.: U.S. Government Printing Office, 1978.

_____. *Historical Statistics of the United States*. Washington, D.C.: U.S. Government Printing Office, 1975.

_____. *Statistical Abstract of the United States*. Washington, D.C.: U.S. Government Printing Office, 1984.

Bureau of Justice Statistics. *Computer Crime: Criminal Justice Resource Manual*. Washington, D.C.: U.S. Department of Justice, 1979.

_____. *Criminal Victimization, 1983*. Washington, D.C.: Government Printing Office, 1984.

_____. *Family Violence-Special Report*. Washington, D.C.: Government Printing Office, 1984.

_____. *Report to the Nation on Crime and Justice*. Washington, D.C.: Government Printing Office, 1983.

Bureau of Municipal Research, New York. *Report on a Survey of the Government of the City and County of San Francisco Prepared by the San Francisco Real Estate Board*. San Francisco: Rincon, 1916.

Burges, S.H. (ed.). *The New Police Surgeon*. London: Hutchinson, 1978.

Burgess, Anne Wolbert, and Holmstrom, Lynda Lytle. *Rape: Victims of Crisis*. Bowie, Md.: Robert J. Brady, 1974.

_____, et al. *Sexual Assault of Children and Adolescents*. Lexington, Mass.: Lexington Books, 1975.

Burgess, Anthony. *A Clockwork Orange*. New York: W.W. Norton, 1963.

Burgess, John W. *Reconstruction and the Constitution*. New York: Charles Scribner's Sons, 1902.

Burgess, Opie Rundle. *Bisbee Not So Long Ago*. San Antonio, Texas: Naylor, 1967.

Burgoyne, Elizabeth. *Carmen Sylva*. London: Thronton Butterworth, 1940.

Burke, James Wakefield. *David Crockett: The Man Behind the Myth*. Austin, Texas: Eakin Press, 1984.

Burke, John M. *"Buffalo Bill" From Prairie to Palace*. Chicago: Rand McNally, 1893.

Burke, Kenneth. *Permanance and Change: An Anatomy of Purpose*. Indianapolis, Ind.: Bobbs-Merrill, 1954.

Burke, Martha Jane. *Life and Adventures of Calamity Jane By Herself*. Livingston, Mont.: Post Print, 1936.

Burke, Merle. *United States History*. Chicago: American Technical Society, 1970.

Burke, T. *Limehouse Nights*. New York: Robert M. McBride, 1926.

Burkitt, Miles C. *Our Early Ancestors*. Cambridge, Eng.: University Press, 1924.

Burks, A.L. *The Mayberry Murder Mystery of Bonita City*. Alamogordo, N.M.: Alamogordo News, n.d.

Burks, Richard V. *The Dynamics of Communism in Eastern Europe*. Princeton, N.J.: Princeton University Press, 1961.

Burland, C.A. *The Arts of the Alchemist*. New York: Macmillan, 1968.

Burlingame, Merrill G., and Toole, K. Ross. *A History of Montana*. New York: Lewis Historical, 1957.

_____. *The Montana Frontier*. Helena: Montana State, 1942.

Burn, James Dawson. *Three Years among the Working Classes in the United States during the War*. London: Smith, Elder, 1865.

Burn, William L. *The Age of Equipoise: A Study of the Mid-Victorian Generation*. New York: W.W. Norton, 1964.

Burnaby, Evelyn. *Memories of Famous Trials*. London: Sisley's, 1907.

Burnet, Gilbert. *Incidents in the Life of Matthew Hale*. Boston: J. Loring, 1832.

Burnett, E.C. *The Continental Congress*. New York: Macmillan, 1941.

Burnett, H.L. *The Controversy between President Johnson and Judge Holt*. New York: D. Appleton, 1891.

_____. *Some Incidents in the Trial of President Lincoln's Assassins*. New York: D. Appleton, 1891.

Burney, James. *The History of the Buccaneers of America*. New York: W.W. Norton, 1950.

Burnham, Daniel H. *Report on a Plan for San Francisco*. San Francisco: Rincon, 1916.

_____, and Bennett, Edward H. *Plan of Chicago*. Chicago: Commercial Club, 1909.

Burnham, Daniel H., Jr., and Kingery, Robert. *Planning the Region of Chicago*. Chicago: Chicago Regional Planning, 1956.

Burnham, David. *The Role of the Media in Controlling Corruption*. New York: John Jay Press, 1976.

Burnham, Frederick Russell. *Scouting on Two Continents*. Garden City, N.Y.: Doubleday, Page, 1926.

_____. *Taking Chances*. Los Angeles: Haynes, 1944.

Burnham, George Pickering. *American Counterfeits*. Boston: A.W. Lowering, 1879.

Burnham, James. *Congress and the American Tradition*. Chicago: Regnery, 1959.

_____. *The Web of Subversion: Underground Networks in the U.S. Government*. New York: John Day, 1954.

Burnham, John C. *Psychoanalysis and American Medicine, 1894-1918*. New York: International Universities Press, 1967.

Burnley, James. *Millionaires and Kings of Enterprise*. Philadelphia: J.B. Lippincott, 1901.

Burns, Alan. *The Angry Brigade.* London: Quartet, 1973.

Burns, Arthur F., and Mitchell, Wesley C. *Measuring Business Cycles.* New York: H. Wolff, 1946.

Burns, E.L. *Between Arab and Israeli.* London: Harrap, 1962.

Burns, Emile. *Abyssinia and Italy.* London: Victor Gollancz, 1935.

Burns, Eugene. *Then There Was One: The U.S.S. Enterprise and the First Year of the War.* New York: Harcourt, Brace, 1944.

Burns, Henry, Jr. *Corrections: Organization and Administration.* Stl Paul, Minn.: West, 1975.

Burns, James MacGregor. *Congress on Trial.* New York: Harper, 1949.

_____. *John Kennedy.* New York: Harcourt, Brace, 1959.

_____. *Roosevelt: The Lion and the Fox.* New York: Harcourt, Brace, 1956.

Burns, Robert E. *I Am A Fugitive From A Georgia Chain Gang.* New York: Vanguard Press, 1932.

Burns, Robert Homer, Gillespie, Andrew Springs, and Richardson, Willing Gay. *Wyoming's Pioneer Ranches.* Laramie, Wyo.: Top-of-the-World Press, 1955.

Burns, W.F. *The Pullman Boycott: A Complete History of the Great R.R. Strike.* St. Paul, Minn.: McGill Printing, 1894.

Burns, Walter Noble. *The One-Way Ride: The Red Trail of Chicago Gangland from Prohibition to Jake Lingle.* Garden City, N.Y.: Doubleday, Doran, 1931.

_____. *The Robin Hood of El Dorado.* New York: Coward-McCann, 1932.

_____. *The Saga of Billy the Kid.* New York: Grosset & Dunlap, 1926.

_____. *Tombstone, An Iliad of the Southwest.* Garden City, N.Y.: Doubleday, Page, 1927.

Burns, William J. *The Masked War: The Story of a Peril That Threatened the U.S., by the Man Who Uncovered the Dynamite Conspirators and Sent Them to Jail.* New York: George H. Doran, 1913.

Burnstein, Jules Quentin. *Conjugal Visits in Prison: Psychological and Social Consequences.* Lexington, Mass.: D.C. Health, 1977.

Burr, A.R. *Portrait of a Banker: James Stillman.* New York: Duffield, 1927.

Burr, George Lincoln (ed.). *Narratives of Witchcraft Cases, 1648-1706.* New York: Barnes & Noble, 1959.

Burr, Harold Saxton. *The Fields of Life.* New York: Ballantine, 1972.

Burroughs, Burt E. *Tales of an Old "Border Town".* Fowler, Ind.: Benton Review, 1925.

Burroughs, John Rolfe. *Where the Old West Stayed Young.* New York: William Morrow, 1962.

Burroughs, William S. *Naked Lunch.* New York: Grove Press, 1959.

_____. *Nova Express.* New York: Grove Press, 1962.

Burrows, Millar. *Palestin Is Our Business.* Philadelphia: Westminster Press, 1949.

Burrows, William E. *Vigilante!* New York: Harcourt Brace Jovanovich, 1976.

Burt, A.L. *The United States, Great Britain and British North America.* New Haven, Conn.: Yale University Press, 1940.

Burt, Cyril. *The Young Delinquent.* London: University of London Press, 1944.

Burt, Commander Leonard. *Commander Burt of Scotland Yard.* London: William Heinemann, 1959.

Burt, Maxwell Struthers. *The Diary of A Dude Wrangler.* New York: Charles Scribner's Sons, 1924.

_____. *Powder River: Let 'Er Buck.* New York: Farrar & Rinehart, 1938.

Burt, Olive Woolley. *American Murder Ballads.* New York: Oxford University Press, 1958.

Burtle, Meriel, et al. *The District Handbook: A Coro Foundation Guide to San Francisco's Supervisorial Districts.* San Francisco: Coro Foundation, 1979.

Burton, Anthony M. *Urban Terrorism.* London: Leo Cooper, 1975.

Burton, E. Milby. *The Siege of Charleston, 1861-1865.* Columbia: University of South Carolina Press, 1970.

Burton, Jean. *Lydia Pinkham Is Her Name.* New York: Farrar, Straus, 1949.

Burton, Jeff. *Black Jack Christian, Outlaw.* Santa Fe, N.M.: Press of the Territorian, 1967.

_____. *Dynamite and Six-Shooter.* Santa Fe, N.M.: Palomino Press, 1970.

Burton, Katherine. *The Dream Lives Forever: The Story of St. Patrick's Cathedral.* New York: Longmans, Green, 1960.

Burton, Lindy. *Vulnerable Children.* London: Routledge & Kegan Paul, 1968.

Burton, Richard Francis. *The City of the Saints.* London: Longman, Green, Longman & Roberts, 1861.

Burton, Robert. *Anatomy of Melancholy.* London: Henry Cripps, 1621.

Burton, Theodore E. *Financial Crises and Periods of Industrial and Commercial Depression.* New York: D. Appleton, 1902.

Burtt, M. *Legal Psychology.* Englewood Cliffs, N.Y.: Prentice-Hall, 1931.

Buruma, Ian. *Behind the Mask.* New York: Pantheon Books, 1984.

Bury, J.B. *A History of the Freedom of Thought.* London: Oxford University Press, 1913-52.

Bury, J.C. *The Cambridge Ancient History.* Cambridge, Mass. Cambridge University Press, 1927.

_____. *The History of the Eastern Roman Empire.* London: Macmillan, 1912.

_____. *The History of the Later Roman Emprie.* London: Macmillan, 1889.

_____. *The History of the Roman Empire.* New York: Harper & Brothers, 1893.

Busch, Francis X. *Casebook of the Curios and True.* Indianapolis, Ind.: Bobbs-Merrill, 1957.

_____. *Enemies of the State.* Indianapolis, Ind.: Bobbs-Merrill, 1954.

_____. *Guilty or Not Guilty.* Indianapolis, Ind.: Bobbs-Merrill, 1952.

_____. *In and Out of Court.* Chicago: De Paul University Press, 1942.

_____. *Prisoners at the Bar.* Indianapolis, Ind.: Bobbs-Merrill, 1952.

_____. *They Escaped the Hangman.* London: Arco, 1957.

Busch, Moritz. *Bismarck.* New York: Macmillan, 1898-1899.

Busch, Noel F. *Briton Hadden: A Biography of the Co-Founder of TIME.* New York: Farrar, Straus, 1949.

_____. *The Emperor's Sword.* New York: Funk & Wagnalls, 1969.

_____. *T.R.: The Story of Theodore Roosevelt and His Influence on Our Times.* New York: Reynal, 1963.

Buse, Renee. *The Deadly Silence.* Garden City, N.Y.: Doubleday, 1965.

Buse, William H. *The Life, Confessions and Adventures of William H. Buse.* Memphis, Tenn.: Hutton & Clark, 1859.

Busey, Samuel C. *Pictures of the City of Washington in the Past.* Washington: Ballantyne & Sons, 1898.

Bush, Ira Jefferson. *Gringo Doctor.* Caldwell, Idaho: Caxton Press, 1939.

Bush, Lewis. *Clutch of Circumstance.* Tokyo: Bungei Shunju, 1956.

_____. *Japanalia, A Concise Cyclopedia.* Tokyo: Tokyo News Service, 1965.

_____. *Land of the Dragon Fly.* London: Robert Hale, 1959.

_____. *The Road to Inamura.* London: Robert Hale, 1961.

Bushick, Frank H. *Glamorous Days.* San Antonio, Texas: Naylor, 1934.

Bushman, Richard. *From Puritan to Yankee: Character and the*

Social Order in Conneticut, 1690-1715. Cambridge, Mass.: Harvard University Press, 1967.

Bushnell, G.H.S. *The First Americans: The Pre-Columbian Civilizations.* New York, McGraw-Hill, 1968.

Businelli, Alberto. *Octtobre 1922.* Rome: Novissima, 1932.

Buss, Arnold H. *The Psychology of Aggression.* New York: John Wiley & Sons, 1961.

Buss, Henry. *Wanderings in the West, During the Year 1870.* London: Thomas Danks, 1870.

Bussy, Frederick Moir. *Irish Conspiracies.* London: Everett, 1910.

Bustamante, Luis F. *Bajo el terror Huertista.* San Luis Potosi, Mexico: Published by Author, 1916.

Butcher, H. *Human Intelligence.* London: Methuen, 1968.

Butcher, Captain Harry C. *Three Years with Eisenhower.* New York: Simon & Schuster, 1946.

Butcher, Solomon D. *Pioneer History of Custer County.* Denver: Merchants, 1901.

Butler, A.S.G. *Portrait of Josephine Butler.* London: Faber & Faber, 1954.

Butler, B.F. *Butler's Book.* Boston: A.M. Thayer, 1892.

Butler, Charles. *Travel from Detroit to Chicago in 1833.* Chicago: Railway Library, 1912.

Butler, Charles Henry. *A Century at the Bar of the Supreme Court of the United States.* New York: G.P. Putnam's Sons, 1942.

Butler, Eliza Marian. *Ritual Magic.* Cambridge, Eng.: University Press, 1949.

Butler, Ivan. *Murderers' England.* London: Robert Hale, 1973.

Butler, Josephine. *A Letter to the Mothers of England.* Liverpool, Eng.: Brakell, 1881.

_____. *Recollections of George Butler.* Bristol, Eng.: Arrowsmith, 1892.

_____. *Woman's Work and Woman's Culture.* London: Macmillan, 1869.

Butler, Nicholas Murray. *Across the Busy Years: Recollections and Reflections.* New York: Charles Scribner's Sons, 1939.

Butler, Pierce. *The Unhurried Years.* Baton Rouge: Louisiana State University Press, 1948.

Butler, P.T.T., and Lord Dunboyne (eds.). *The Trial of John George Haigh.* London: Hodge, 1953.

Butler, Richard J., and Driscoll, Joseph. *Dock Walloper.* New York: G.P. Putnam's Sons, 1933.

Butler, Rohan. *The Roots of National Socialism.* New York: E.P. Dutton, 1942.

Butler, Samuel. *Erewhon.* New York: New American Library, 1960.

Butler, Sandra. *Conspiracy of Silence: The Trauma of Incest.* San Fransco: New Glide, 1978.

Butler, W.E. *The Magician.* London: Aquarian, 1963.

Butow, Robert J.C. *Japan's Decision to Surrender.* Stanford, Calif.: Stanford University Press, 1954.

_____. *Tojo and the Coming of the War.* Princeton, N.J.: Princeton University Press, 1961.

Butt, Archie. *Letters.* New York: Doubleday, 1924.

Butt, Ernest. *Chicago Then and Now.* Chicago: Aurora, Finch & McCullouch, 1933.

Butterfield, Herbert. *The Origins of History.* New York: Basic Books, 1981.

Butterfield, Roger. *The American Past.* New York: Simon & Schuster, 1947.

Buttrick, Tilly, Jr. *Voyages, Travels and Discoveries.* Louisville, Ky.: Lost Cause Press, 1958.

Buxhoeveden, Baroness Sophie. *During the Revolution.* New York: Longmans, Green, 1929.

_____. *Left Behind: Fourteen Months in Siberia.* New York: Longmans, Green, 1928.

_____. *The Life and Tragedy of Alexandra Feodorovna, Empress of Russia.* New York: Longmans, Green, 1928.

Buxton, Thomas Fowell. *An Inquiry Whether Crime and Misery are Produced or Prevented by Our Present State of Prison Discipline.* London: J. M'Creery, 1818.

Buzek, Antonin. *How the Communist Press Works.* New York: Frederick A. Praeger, 1964.

Byas, Hugh. *Government By Assassination.* New York: Alfred A. Knopf, 1942.

_____. *The Japanese Enemy: His Power and His Vulnerability.* New York: Alfred A. Knopf, 1942.

Byck, Robert (ed.). *Cocaine Papers: Sigmund Freud.* New York: Stonehill, 1974.

Bye, Raymond T. *Capital Punishment in the United States.* Philadelphia: Committee on Philanthropic Labor of Philadelphia Yearly Meeting of Friends, 1919.

Byers, Major S.H.M. *With Fire and Sword.* New York: Neale, 1911.

Byington, Lewis F., and Lewis, Oscar (eds.). *The History of San Francisco.* San Francisco: S.J. Clarke, 1931.

Bykov, P.M. *The Last Days of Tsar Nicholas.* New York: International, 1934.

Byloff, Fritze. *Hexenglaube und Hexenverjolgung in den österreichischen Alpenländern.* Berlin: Walter de Gruyten, 1934.

Byrdsall, Fitzwilliam. *The History of the Loco Foco or Equal Rights Party, Its Movements, Conventions and Proceedings, With Short Characteristic Sketches of Its Prominent Men.* New York: Clemment & Packard, 1842.

Byrne, Frank L. *Prophet of Prohibition: Neal Dow and His Crusade.* State Historical Society of Wisconsin, 1961.

Byrne, W.E.R. *Tale of the Elk.* Charleston: West Virginia, 1940.

Byrnes, Clara. *Block Sketches of New York City.* New York: Radbridge, 1918.

Byrnes, James F. *All in One Lifetime.* New York: Harper, 1958.

_____. *Speaking Frankly.* New York: Harper, 1947.

Byrnes, Robert F. *Pobedonostsev.* Bloomington: Indiana University Press, 1968.

_____ (ed.). *Yugoslavia.* New York: Mid-European Studies Center, 1957.

Byrnes, Thomas. *Professional Criminals of America.* New York: G.W. Dillingham, 1895.

Byron, John. *Byron's Journal of His Circumnavigation, 1764-1766.* Cambridge, Eng.: Hakluyt Society, 1964.

Byron, Robert. *The Byzantine Achievement.* New York: Alfred A. Knopf, 1929.

Byrum, E.E. *Behind Prison Bars.* Moundsville, W.Va.: Gospel Trumpet, 1901.

Byzantine and Modern Greek Studies: Essays Presented to Sir Steven Runciman. Oxford, Eng.: Basil Blackwell, 1978.

C

Cabal, Juan. *Piracy and Pirates.* London: Jarrolds, 1957.

Cabanès, Dr. *Au Chevet de l'Empereur.* Paris: Albin Michel, 1943.

Cabanès, Augustin. *Moeurs intimes du passé: le sabbat a-t-il existé?* Paris: A. Michel, 1935.

Cabaniss, Allen. *Charlemagne's Cousins: Contemporary Lives of Adalard and Wala.* Syracuse, N.Y.: Syracuse University Press, 1967.

Cabella, G.G. *Testamento politico di Mussolini.* Rome: Tose, 1948.

Cable, George W. *The Negro Question.* New York: Doubleday, 1958.

_____. *The Silent South.* New York: Charles Scribner Sons, 1885.

Cabrera, Luis. *Obras politicas del Lic. Blas Urrea.* Mexico City: Imprenta Nacional, 1921.

Cadiou, Yves, and Richard, Alphonse. *Modern Firearms.* New York: William Morrow, 1977.

Cadogan, Edward. *The Roots of Evil*. London: John Murray, 1937.

Cadorna, Gen Raffaele. *La Riscossa*. Milan, Italy: Rizzoli, 1948.

La caduta del fascismo el'armistizio de Roma. Rome: Azione Letteraria Italiana, 1944.

Cady, John Henry. *Arizona's Yesterday*. Los Angeles: Privately Published, 1916.

Caesar, Gene. *Incredible Detective: The Biography of William J. Burns*. Englewood Cliffs, N.J.: Prentice-Hall, 1968.

Caetani, Vittoria. *Sparkle Distant Worlds*. London: Hutchinson, 1947.

Cagan, Philip. *Determinants and Effects of Changes in the Stock of Money, 1875-1960*. New York: Columbia University Press, 1965.

Cahalane, Cornelius F. *The Policeman*. New York: E.P. Dutton, 1923.

_____. *The Policeman's Guide*. New York: Harper & Brothers, 1952.

Cahan, Abraham. *The Rise of David Levinsky*. New York: n.p., 1971.

Cahn, Edmond *The Crest Rights*. New York: Macmillan, 1963.

_____ (ed.). *Supreme Court and Supreme Law*. Bloomington: Indiana University Press, 1954.

Cahn, William. *Good Night, Mrs. Calabash*. New York: Duell, Sloan & Pearce, 1963.

Cahuet, Albéric. *Après la mort de l'Empereur*. Paris: Emile-Paul, 1913.

_____. *Napoléon délivré: Le Coup de théâtre de 1840*. Paris: Émile-Paul, 1914.

_____. *Retours de Saint-Hélène, 1821-1840*. Paris: Fasquell, 1932.

Caidin, Martin. *The Ragged, Rugged Warriors*. New York: E.P. Dutton, 1966.

_____. *Zero Fighter*. New York: Ballantine Books, 1969.

Caillet, Albert L. *Manuel bibliographique des sciences psychiques*. Paris: L. Dorbon, 1912.

Caimpenta, Ugo. *Il Maresciallo Badoglio*. Milan, Italy: Aurora, 1936.

Cain (or Calin), Ella M. *The Story of Bodie*. Sonora, Calif.: Mother Lode Press, 1956.

Calabrese, Arnaldo. *25 Luglio*. Naples, Italy: STEM, 1962.

Calahan, E.W. (ed.). *List of Officers of the Navy of the United States, 1775-1900*. New York: L.R. Hamersly, 1900.

Calamandrei, Pietro. *Uomini e città della resistenza*. Bari, Italy: Laterza, 1955.

Caldwell, Robert Graham. *Criminology*. New York: Ronald Press, 1965.

_____. *Red Hannah, Delaware's Whipping Post*. London: Oxford University Press, 1947.

Caldwell, W.V. *LSD Psychotherapy*. New York: Grove Press, 1968.

Calef, Robert. *More Wonders of the Invisible World*. London: N. Hillar & J. Collyer, 1700.

Calero, Manuel. *The Mexican Policy of President Wilson As It Appears to a Mexican*. New York: Press of Smith & Thomson, 1916.

_____. *Un decenio de politica Mexicana*. New York: Middleditch, 1920.

Calhoon, Richard P. *Personnel Management and Supervision*. Englewood Cliffs, N.J.: Prentice-Hall, 1967.

Calhoon, Robert McCluer. *The Loyalists in Revolutionary America*. New York: Harcourt Brace Jovanovich, 1973.

Calhoun, Arthur W. *A Social History of the American Family from Colonial Times to the Present*. 3 vols. Cleveland: Arthur H. Clark, 1917-1919.

Calibano (pseud). *Le ultime ore di un dittatore*. Milan, Italy: PWB, n.d.

Calic, Edouard (ed.). *Secret Conversations with Hitler*. New York: John Day, 1971.

California Assembly Judiciary Committee. Subcommittee on Capital Punishment. *Report....Pertaining to the Problems of the Death Penalty and Its Administration in California*. Sacramento: State of California, 1957.

California Board of Corrections. *Prison Gangs in the Community*. Sacramento, Calif.: n.p., 1978.

California Senate Judiciary Committee. *Report and Testimony...[on a proposed bill] to Abolish the Death Penalty*. Sacramento: State of California, 1960.

Calincourt, Gen. *Mémoires*. Paris: Plon, 1933.

Calkins, Alonzo. *Opium and the Opium Appetite*. Philadelphia: J.B. Lippincott, 1871.

Calkins, Ernest E. *They Broke the Prairie*. New York: Charles Scribner's Sons, 1937.

Calkins, Raymond. *Substitutes for the Saloon: An Investigation Made for the Committee of Fifty under the Direction of Francis G. Peabody, Elgin R.L.Gould and William R.Sloan*. Boston: Houghton Mifflin, 1901.

Callaghan, Dean P. *Directory of State, Regional, National and International Planners and Coordinators of Volunteer Programs in Corrections*. Boulder, Colo.: National Information Center for Volunteers in Courts, 1972.

Callaghan, Morley. *That Summer in Paris*. New York: Coward-McCann, 1963.

Callahan, James Morton. *American Foreign Policy in Mexican Relations*. New York: Macmillan, 1932.

_____. *The Diplomatic History of the Southern Confederacy*. New York: Greenwood Press, 1968.

Callahan, North. *Daniel Morgan: Ranger of Revolution*. New York: AMS Press, 1961.

_____. *Henry Knox*. New York: Rinehart, 1958.

Callan, Luke B. *Ireland After Forty Years*. Boston: Angel Guardian, 1933.

Callaway, Lewis L. *Montana's Righteous Hangmen*. Norman: University of Oklahoma Press, 1982.

Callcott, George H. *A History of the University of Maryland*. Baltimore: Maryland Historical Society, 1966.

Callcott, Wilfred Hardy. *The Caribbean Policy of the United States 1890-1920*. Baltimore: Johns Hopkins University Press, 1942.

_____. *Liberalism in Mexico*. Palo Alto, Calif.: Stanford University Press, 1931.

Callimachi, Anne-Marie, Princess. *Yesterday Was Mine*. London: Falcon Press, 1952.

Callison, John J. *Bill Jones of Paradise Valley, Oklahoma*. Chicago: M.A. Donohue, 1914.

Callon, Milton W. *Las Vegas, New Mexico, the Town That Wouldn't Gamble*. Las Vegas, N.M.: Las Vegas Daily Optic, 1962.

Callow, Alexander (ed.). *The City Boss in America: An Interpretive Reader*. New York: Oxford University Press, 1976.

_____. *The Tweed Ring*. New York: Oxford University Press, 1965.

Calmeil, Louis François. *De la folie*. Paris: J.B. Baillière, 1845.

Calmer, Alan. *Labor Agitator, The Story of Albert R. Parsons*. New York: International, 1937.

Calmet, Augustin. *Dissertations sur les apparitions...et vampires*. Einsidlen: J.E. Kalin, 1749.

_____. *The Phantom World*. trans. Henry Christmas. London: R. Bentley, 1850.

Calvert, Peter. *The Mexican Revolution, 1910-1914: The Diplomacy of Anglo-American Conflict*. Cambridge, Eng.: University Press, 1968.

Calvert, Roy. *Capital Punishment in the Twentieth Century*. New York: G.P. Putnam's Sons, 1936.

_____. *The Death Penalty Inquiry*. London: Victor Gollancz, 1931.

_____. *Executions*. London: National Council for the Abolition of the Death Penalty, 1926.

Calvin, Ross. *Sky Determines*. New York: Macmillan, 1934.

Calvocoresses, George M. (ed.). *A Scientist with Perry in Japan*. Chapel Hill: University of North Carolina Press, 1947.

_____ (ed.) *Yankee Surveyors in the Shogun's Seas*. Princeton,

N.J.: Princeton University Press, 1947.

Camboid, Giselle. *Chessman i.e. Dozo Años A Espera de Morte.* Rio De Janerio, Braz.: Editorial Veechi, 1960.

Cambon, Henri. *Histoire du Monde.* Paris: Hachette, 1952.

Cambria, Adele. *Maria José.* Milan, Italy: Longanesi, 1966.

Cambriare, Celestin Pierre. *East Tennessee and Western Virginia Mountain Ballads.* London: The Mitre Press, n.d.

Cambride Department of Criminal Science. *Sexual Offenses.* New York: St. Martin's Press, 1957.

Cambridge Ancient History. London: Cambridge University Press, 1970.

Camerero, Julio. *Yo hablé Con Chessman.* Madrid: Pueblo, 1960.

Cameron, Charlotte. *Mexico in Revolution.* New York: Seeley, 1925.

Cameron, Ian. *To the Farthest Ends of the Earth: 150 Years of World Exploration by the Royal Geographical Society.* New York: E.P. Dutton, 1980.

Cameron, J. *The African Revolution.* London: Thames & Hudson, 1961.

Cameron, James. *Mandarin Red.* London: Michael Joseph, 1955.

Cameron, Mary Owen. *The Booster and the Snitch: Department Store Shoplifing.* New York: Free Press, 1964.

Cameron, Norman. *Poems of François Villon.* London: Jonathan Cape, 1952.

Cameron, William E. (ed.). *History of the World's Columbian Exposition.* Chicago: Columbian History, 1893.

Camfield, Benjamin. *A Theological Discourse of Angels and Their Ministries.* London: H. Brome, 1678.

Caminda, Jerome. *Twenty-Five Years of Detective Life.* London: John Heywood, 1895.

Cammaerts, Emile. *Albert of Belgium.* New York: Macmillan, 1935.

Cammell, Charles R. *Aleister Crowley: The Man, The Magic, The Poet.* New Hyde Park, N.Y.: University Books, 1962.

Campaign Text Book. Why the People Want a Change. The Republican Party Viewed. Its Sins of Omission and Commission...etc. New York: Democratic National Committee, 1876.

Campanelli, Paolo. *Mussolini.* London: Pallas, 1939.

Campbell, A.E. *Great Britain and the United States, 1895-1903.* London: Longmans, Green, 1960.

Campbell, Anne. *The Girls in the Gang: A Report From New York City.* New York: Basil Blackwell, 1984,

Campbell, C.S., Jr. *Anglo-American Understanding, 1898-1903.* Baltimore: Johns Hopkins Press, 1957.

_____. *Special Business Interests and the Open Door Policy.* New Haven, Conn.: Yale University Press, 1951.

Campbell, Donald T., and Stanley, Julian C. *Experimental and Quasi-Experimental Designs for Research.* Chicago: Rand McNally, 1963.

Campbell, Edna Fay, Smith, Fanny R., and Jones, Clarence F. *Our City—Chicago.* New York: Charles Scribner's Sons, 1930.

Campbell, Helen, Knox, Thomas W., and Byrnes, Thomas. *Darkness and Daylight.* Hartford, Conn.: A.D. Worthington, 1897.

_____. *Prisoners of Poverty.* Boston: Roberts Brothers, 1887.

_____. *Women Wage-Earners.* Boston: Roberts Brothers, 1893.

Campbell, Helen Jones. *The Case for Mrs. Surratt.* New York: G.P. Putnam's Sons, 1943.

_____. *Confederate Courier.* New York: St. Martin's Press, 1964.

Campbell, John Gregorson. *Superstitions of the Highlands.* Glasgow, Scot.: J. MacLehose & Sons, 1900.

_____. *Witchcraft and Second Sight in the Highlands and Islands of Scotland.* Glasgow, Scot.: J. MacLehose & Sons, 1902.

Campbell, Joseph. *The Hero with a Thousand Faces.* Princeton, N.J.: Princeton University Press, 1972.

Campbell, Leroy A. *Mithraic Iconography and Ideology.* Leiden, Neth.: E.J. Brill, 1968.

Campbell, Marjorie Freeman. *A Century of Crime.* Toronto, Can.: McLelland & Stewart, 1970.

Campbell, N. Reason. *Dead Man Walking.* New York: Marek, 1978.

Campbell, Rodney. *The Luciano Project.* New York: McGraw-Hill, 1977.

Campbell, T.J. *Records of Rhea.* Dayton, Tenn.: Rhea, 1940.

_____. *The Upper Tennessee.* Chattanooga, Tenn.: Published by Author, 1932.

Campbell, Thomas M. *Masquerade Peace: America's UN Policy, 1944-1945.* Tallahassee: Florida State University Press, 1973.

Campbell, W.P. *Oklahoma, the Mecca for the Men of Mystery. John Wilkes Booth, Escape and Wanderings Until Final Ending of the Trial by Suicide in Enid, Oklahoma, January 12, 1903.* Oklahoma City: Published by Author, 1922.

Campbell, Will D., and Holloway, James Y. (eds.). *". . .And the criminals with him . . .," Luke 23:33.* New York: Paulist Press, 1973.

Campbell, William C. *From the Quarries of Last Chance Gulch.* Helena: Montana Record, 1951.

Campbell-Johnson, Alan. *Mission With Mountbatten.* London: Robert Hale, 1951.

Campini, Dino. *El Alamein Quota 33.* Milan, Italy: Italpress, 1952

_____. *Mussolini, Churchill, i carteggi.* Milan, Italy: Italpress, 1952.

_____. *Strano gioco di Mussolini.* Milan, Italy: Studio Editoriale PG, 1952.

Campobello, Nellie. *Apuntes Sobre la Vida Militar de Francisco Villa.* Mexico City: n.p., 1940.

Campos, German Guzman, Borda, Orlando Fals, and Luna, Eduardo Umana. *La Violencia en Colombia: Estudio de un Proces-Social, Tomo Primo.* Bogota, Col.: Ediciones Tercer Mundo, 1962.

Campos, Rubén M. *El folklore literario de México.* Mexico: Talleres Gráficos de la Nación, 1929.

Camps, Professor Francis E. *Camps on Crime.* Newton Abbot, Eng.: David & Charles, 1973.

_____, and Barber, Richard. *The Investigation of Murder.* London: Michael Joseph, 1966.

_____. *Medical and Scientific Investigations in the Christie Case.* London: Medical Publications, 1953.

Camus, Albert. *The Rebel: An Essay on Man in Revolt.* trans. Anthony Bower. New York: Vintage Books, 1956.

_____. *The Stranger.* trans. Stuart Gilbert. New York: Vintage Books, 1954.

Canada Joint Committee of the Senate and House of Commons on Capital and Corporal Punishment and Lotteries. *Reports.* Ottawa, Ontario, Can.: Edmund Cloutier, 1956.

Canales, José T. *Juan N. Cortina, Bandit or Patriot?* San Antonio, Texas: Artes Gráficas, 1951.

Canby, Courtland (ed.). *Lincoln and the Civil War.* New York: Dell, 1958.

Canby, Henry Seidel. *American Memoir.* Cambridge, Mass.: Houghton Mifflin, 1947.

Cancogni, Manlio. *Storia dello squadrismo.* Milan, Italy: Longanesi, 1959.

Canevari, Emilio. *Grazizni mi ha detto.* Rome: Magi-Spinetti, 1947.

Canfield, Alyce. *God in Hollywood.* New York: Wisdom House, 1961.

Canfield, Chauncey L. *Diary of a Forty-Niner.* New York: M. Shephard, 1906.

Canfield, Kid. *Gambling And Card-Sharper's Tricks Exposed.* New York: n.p., n.d.

Canfield, Michael, and Weberman, Alan J. *Coup d'Etat in America; The C.I.A. and the Assassination of John F. Kennedy.* New York: Third Press, 1975.

Caniglia, Renato. *Razzismo italiano.* Milan, Italy: Italia Industriale, 1938.

Canler, Louis. *Mémoires de Canler, ancien chef du service du süeté*. Paris: J. Herzel, 1862.

Cannaert, Joseph Bernard. *Olim: Procès des sorcières en Belgique sous Philippe II*. Ghent, Belg.: C. Anoot-Braeckman, 1847.

Cannell, J.C. *When Fleet Street Calls*. London: Jarrolds, 1932.

Canning, John. *50 True Tales of Terror*. New York: Bell, 1972.

Cannon, James, Jr. *Bishop Cannon's Own Story*. Durham, N.C.: Duke University Press, 1955.

Cannon, Miles. *Toward the Setting Sun*. Portland, Ore.: Columbian Press, 1953.

Cantalupo, Roberto. *Fu la Spagna*. Milan, Italy: Mondadori, 1948.

Cantine, Holley, and Rainer, Dachine (eds.). *Prison Etiquette*. New York: Retort Press, 1950.

Canton, Frank M. *The Autobiography of Frank M. Canton*. Norman: University of Oklahoma Press, 1954.

_____. *Frontier Trails*. Boston: Houghton Mifflin, 1930.

Cantonwine, Alexander. *Star Forty-Six, Oklahoma*. Oklahoma City: Pythian Times, 1911.

Cantor, Eddie. *Caught Short!* New York: Simon & Schuster, 1929.

_____, as told to David Freeman. *My Life Is In Your Hands*. New York: Blue Ribbon Books, 1932.

Cantor, Norman. *The Age of Protest*. London: George Allen & Unwin, 1970.

Capaldi, Nicholas. *Clear and Present Danger: The Free Speech Controversy*. New York: Western, 1969.

Capellanus, Andreas. *The Art of Courtly Love*. New York: W.W. Norton, 1960.

Capital Punishment: Material relating to Its Purpose and Value. Ottawa, Ontario, Can.: Queen's Printer, 1965.

Caplan, Lincoln. *The Insanity Defense and the Trial of John W. Hinckley, Jr*. Boston: David R. Godine, 1984.

Capon, Paul. *The Seventh Passenger*. London: Ward Lock, 1953.

Capote, Truman. *In Cold Blood*. New York: Random House, 1965.

Capozzi, Gennaro. *Venti giorni di terrore*. Naples, Italy: 'La Floridiana', 1943.

Cappon, Lester J. *Adams-Jefferson Letters*. Chapel Hill: University of North Carolina Press, 1959.

Capra, Frank. *The Name Above the Title*. New York: Macmillan, 1971.

Caprio, Frank S., and Brenner, Donald R. *Sexual Behavior: Psycholegal Aspects*. New York: Citadel, 1961.

Capstick, J. *Given in Evidence*. London: John Long, 1960.

Caputo, David A. *Organized Crime and American Politics*. Morristown, N.J.: General Learning Press, 1974.

Caracciolo, Filipo. *'43-44: Diaro di Napoli*. Florence, Italy: Vallecchi, 1964.

Caracciolo di Feroleto, Gen. Mario. *E poi?* Rome: Corso, 1948.

_____. *Sette carceri di u generale*. Rome: Corso, 1947.

Carano, Paul, and Sanchez, Pedro C. *A Complete History of Guam*. Rutland, Vermont: Charles E. Tuttle, 1964.

Caravaglios, Cesare. *I canti delle trincee*. Rome: CCSM, 1934.

Carbery, Mary. *Happy World*. New York: Longmans, 1941.

Carboni, Gen Giacomo. *L'Armistizio e la difesa di Roma*. Rome: De Luigi, 1945

_____. *Memorie Segrete, 1935-48*. Florence, Italy: Parenti, 1955.

_____. *La verità di u generale distratto sull'8 settembre '43*. Bologna, Italy: Beta, 1966.

Carbutt, J. *Biographical Sketches of the Leading Men of Chicago*. Chicago: Wilson & St. Clair, 1868.

Carcopino, Jérome. *Daily Life in Ancient Rome*. New Haven, Conn.: Yale University Press, 1940.

Cardano, Girolamo. *De Subtilitate Libri XXI*. Nuremberg, Ger.: I. Petreium, 1550.

Cardi, Paulus Maria. *Ritualis Romani Documenta de Exorcizandis Obsessis a Daemonio*. Venice, Italy: Corma, 1733.

Cardozo, Benjamin N. *The Nature of the Judical Process*. New Haven, Conn.: Yale University Press, 1921.

Careless, J.M.J., and Brown, R. Craig (eds.). *The Canadians, 1867-1967*. Toronto, Ontario, Can.: Macmillan, 1967.

Carell, Paul. *The Foxes of the Desert*. London: Macdonald, 1961

_____. *Hitler Moves East 1941-1943*. New York: Little, Brown, 1941.

_____. *Scorched Earth: The Russian-German War 1943-1944*. trans. Ewald Osers. New York: Ballantine Books, 1971.

_____. *Unternehmen Barbarossa*. Berlin: Ullstein, 1963.

Carena, Caesar. *Tractatus de Officio Sanctissimae Inquisitionis et Modo Procendo in Causis Fidei*. Cremona, Italy: M.A. Balpierum, 1631.

Carerio, Luigi. *Practica Causarum Criminalium...Tractatus de Haereticis*. Lyons, Fr.: Gulielmum Rouillium, 1550.

Carewe-Hunt, R.N. *The Theory and Practice of Communism*. New York: Macmillan, 1950.

Carey, Arthur A. *Memoirs of a Murder Man*. Garden City, N.Y.: Doubleday, Doran, 1930.

Carey, George G. *Maryland Folklore and Folklife*. Cambridge, Md.: Tidewater, 1970.

Carey, Henry L. (ed.). *The Thrilling Story of Famous Boot Hill and Modern Dodge City*. Dodge City, Kan.: Herbert Etrick, 1937.

Carey, James T. *The College Drug Scene*. Englewood Cliffs, N.J.: Prentice-Hall, 1968.

_____. *Introduction to Criminology*. Englewood Cliffs, N.J.: Prentice-Hall, 1978.

_____. *Sociology and Public Affairs: The Chicago School*. Beverly Hills, Calif.: Sage, 1975.

Carey, John (ed.). *Eye-Witness to History*. Cambridge, Mass.: Harvard University Press, 1988.

Carey Estes Kefauver, Late a Senator from Tennessee: Memorial Addresses Delivered in Congress. Washington, D.C.: U.S. Government Printing Office, 1964.

Carey-Jones, N.S. *The Anatomy of Uhuru: An Essay on Kenya's Independence*. Manchester, Eng.: Manchester University Press, 1966.

Cargill, David, and Holland, Julian. *Scenes of Murder: A London Guide*. London: Heinemann, 1964.

Cargill, Oscar. *Intellectual America: Ideas on the March*. New York: Macmillan, 1941.

Carlbos Félix. *Génesis de la Revolución Mexicana*. La Paz, Bol.: Litografia e Imprenta Moderna, 1918.

Carlen, Pat. (ed.). *Criminal Women*. Oxford, Eng.: Polity Press, 1985.

Carleton, James Henry. *Battle of Buena Vista*. New York: Harper & Brothers, 1848.

Carli-Ballola, R. *Storia della Resistenza*. Milan, Italy: Avanti!, 1957.

Carlin, Jerome E. *Lawyers' Ethics: A Survey of the New York City Bar*. New York: Russell Sage Foundation, 1966.

_____. *Lawyers on Their Own*. New Brunswick, N.J.: Rutgers University Press, 1962.

Carlisle, William L. *Bill Carlisle, Lone Bandit: An Autobiography*. Pasadena, Calif.: Trail's End, 1946.

Carlson, John Roy. *Undercover*. New York: E.P. Dutton, 1943.

Carlson, Kenneth. *American Prisons and Jails. Population Trends and Projections*. Cambridge, Mass.: Abt Associates, 1980.

Carlson, Kurt. *One American Must Die*. New York: Congdon & Weed, 1986.

Carlson, Oliver. *Brisbane, A Candid Biography*. New York: Stackpole Sons, 1937.

_____, and Bates, Ernest Sutherland. *Hearst: Lord of San Simeon*. New York: Viking Press, 1936.

Carlyle, R.W. and A.J. *A History of Medieval Political Theory in the West*. New York: Barnes & Noble, 1932.

Carlyle, Thomas. *The French Revolution: A History*. New York: American Book Exchange, 1881.

_____. *History of Frederick II of Prussia*. 6 vols. London: Chapman & Hall, 1858-1865.

Carman, H.J., and Luthin, R.H. *Lincoln and the Patronage*. New York: Columbia University Press, 1943.

Carmer, Carl. *Stars Fell on Alabama*. New York: Farrar & Rinehart, 1934.

Carnegie, Andrew. *An American Four-in-Hand in Britain*. New York: Charles Scribner's Sons, 1884.

———. *Triumphant Democracy of Fifty Years' March of The Republic*. Garden City, N.Y.: Doubleday, Doran, 1933.

Carney, Louis. *Introduction to Correctional Science*. New York: McGraw-Hill, 1974.

Caro, Robert A. *The Years of Lyndon Johnson: The Path to Power*. New York: Vintage Books, 1983.

Caroll, John Alexander (ed.). *Pioneering in Arizona*. Tucson: Arizona Pioneers Historical Society, 1964.

Caron, Roger. *Go Boy*. Toronto, Ontario, Can.: McGraw-Hill, 1978.

Carone, Pasquale A., and Krinsky, Leonard W. (eds.). *Drug Abuse in Industry*. Springfield, Ill.: Charles C. Thomas, 1973.

Carosso, Vincent P. *Investment Banking in America*. Cambridge, Mass.: Harvard University Press, 1970.

Carothers, J.C. *The Psychology of Mau Mau*. Nairobi, Kenya: Government Printer, 1955.

Carp, E.A. (ed.). *Psychic Treatment in Sexual Perversions*. London: Mederl, 1929.

Carpenter, Frances (ed.). *Carp's Washington*. New York: McGraw-Hill, 1960.

Carpenter, Frank B. *Six Months at the White House*. New York: Hurd & Houghton, 1866.

Carpenter, Frank G. *Canada and New Foundland*. Garden City, N.Y.: Doubleday, Page, 1924.

Carpenter, J.T. *The South as a Conscious Minority*. New York: New York University Press, 1930.

Carpenter, Mary. *Our Convicts*. London: W. & F. G. Cash, 1864.

Carpenter, Rhys. *Beyond the Pillars of Hercules*. New York: Delacorte Press, 1966.

Carpenter, S.C. *Report on the Trial of Joshua Nettles and Elizabeth Cannon for the Murder of John Cannon*. Charleston, S.C.: Charleston Courier, 1905.

———. *Report of the Trial of Richard Dennis*. Charleston, S.C.: G.M. Bounetheau, 1805.

Carpozi, George Jr. *Bugsy*. New York: Pinacle, 1973.

———. *Gangland Killers*. New York: Manor Books, 1979.

———. *Ordeal By Trial: The Alice Crimmins Case*. New York: Walker, 1972.

———. *Red Spies In The U.S.* New York: Arlington House, 1973.

Carpzov, Benedict. *Practica Nova Rerum Crimilanum Imperiis Saxonica in Tres Partes Divisa*. Wittenberg: Tobiae Mevij, 1652.

Carr, Edward Hallett. *A History of Russia: The Bolshevik Revolution, 1917-1923*. 3 vols. New York: Macmillan, 1951.

———. *The Interregnum, 1923-1924*. New York: Macmillan, 1954.

———. *Michael Bakunin*. London: Macmillan, 1937.

———. *Socialism in One Country, 1924-1926*. New York: Macmillan, 1958.

———. *Studies in Revolution*. London: Macmillan, 1950.

Carr, Gordon. *The Angry Brigade*. London: Victor Gollancz, 1975.

Carr, Harry. *Los Angeles, City of Dreams*. New York: D. Appleton-Century, 1935.

———. *Riding the Tiger: An American Newspaperman in the Orient*. Boston: Houghton Mifflin, 1934.

———. *The West Is Still Wild*. Boston: Houghton Mifflin, 1932.

Carr, John. *Pioneer Days in California*. Eureka, Calif.: Times, 1891.

Carr, John Dickson. *The Life of Sir Arthur Conan Doyle*. New York: Harper, 1949.

Carr, R. Comyns. *The Nineteenth Century and After*. n.p., 1934.

Carr, Robert K. *Federal Protection of Civil Rights*. Ithaca, N.Y.: Cornell University Press, 1947.

———, et al. *American Democracy in Theory and Practice*. New York: Holt, Rinehart & Winston, 1959.

———. *The House Committee on Un-American Activities, 1945-1950*. Ithaca, N.Y.: Cornell University Press, 1952.

———. *The Supreme Court and Judicial Review*. New York: Holt, Rinehart & Winston, 1942.

Carr, William H.A. *Hollywood Tragedy*. New York: Fawcett-Crest, 1962.

———. *JFK: A Complete Biography 1917-1963*. New York: Lancer Books, 1968.

Carranza, Venustiano. *Informe del C. Venustiano Carranza, Primer Jefe del Ejército Constitucionalista, encargado del poder ejecutivo de la República. Leido ante el Congreso de la Unión, en la sesión de 15 de abril de 1917*. Mexico City: Imprenta del Gobierno, 1917.

Carrier, L. *The Beginnings of Agriculture in America*. New York: Johnson Reprint, 1962.

Carrigan, ElCl *John P. Phair, A Complete History of Vermont's Celebrated Murder Case*. Boston: Carrigan, 1879.

Carriker, Robert C. *Fort Supply, Indian Territory: Frontier Outpost On the Plains*. Norman: University of Oklahoma Press, 1970.

Carrington, Frank G. *Crime and Justice: A Conservative Strategy*. Washington, D.C.: Heritage Foundation, 1983.

———. *Neither Cruel nor Unusual*. New Rochelle, N.Y.: Arlington House, 1978.

———. *The Victims*. New Rochelle, N.Y.: Arlington House, 1977.

Carrington, Henry Beebee. *Battles of the American Revolution*. New York: A.S. Barnes, 1877.

Carrington, Hereward. *Gambler's Crooked Tricks: A Complete Exposure of Their Methods*. Girard, Kan.: Haldeman-Julius, 1928.

———, and Fodor, Nandor. *Haunted People*. New York: E.P. Dutton, 1951.

———. *The Story of the Poltergeist Down the Centuries*. London: Rider, 1953.

Carroll, J. *Language and Thought*. Englewood Cliffs, N.J.: Prentice-Hall, 1964.

Carroll, Joseph C. *Slave Insurrections in the United States, 1800-1865*. Boston: Chapman & Grimes, 1938.

Carroll, Leo. *Hacks, Blacks, and Cons: Race Relations in a Maximum Security Prison*. Lexington, Mass.: Lexington Books, 1974.

Carroll, Mollie Ray. *Labor and Politics*. Boston: Houghton Mifflin, 1923.

Carruthers, Douglas. *Beyond the Caspian*. London: Edinburgh, Oliver & Boyd, 1949.

Carse, Robert. *Rum Row*. New York: Holt, Rinehart & Winston, 1959.

Carson, Gerald. *Cornflake Crusade: From the Pulpit to the Breakfast Table*. New York: Rinehart, 1957.

Carson, Hampton L. *The Supreme Court of the United States: Its History*. Philadelphia: John Y. Huber, 1891.

Carson, John. *Doc Middleton, the Unwickedest Outlaw*. Santa Fe, N.M.: Press of the Territorian, 1966.

———. *The Union Pacific: Hell on Wheels*. Santa Fe, N.M.: Press of the Territorian, 1968.

Carson, Rachel. *Silent Spring*. New York: Houghton Mifflin, 1962.

Carsten, F.L. *The Origins of Prussia*. London: Oxford University Press, 1954.

Carswell, John. *The South Sea Bubble*. Stanford, Calif.: Stanford University Press, 1960.

Carte, Gene E. and Elaine H. *Police Reform in the United States: the Era of August Vollmer*. Berkeley: University of California Press, 1975.

Cartel, Michael. *Serial Mass Murder*. Toluca Lake, Cal.: Pepperbox Books, 1985.

Carter, Dr. Alan Barham. *All About Strokes*. New York: Nelson, 1968.

Carter, Clarence E., and Bloom, John Porter (eds.). *The Territorial Papers of the United States*. Washington, D.C.: U.S. Government Printing Office, 1934.

Carter, Boake, and Healy, Thomas. *Why Meddle in the Orient?* New York: Dodge, 1938.

Carter, Dagny. *The Symbol of the Beast.* New York: Ronald Press, 1957.

Carter, Dan T. *Scottsboro: A Tragedy of the American South.* New York: Oxford University Press, 1969.

Carter, Dyson. *Sin and Society.* New York: Heck Cattell, 1946.

Carter, Hodding. *The Angry Scar.* New York: Doubleday, 1959.
_____. *Lower Mississippi.* New York: Farrar & Rinehart, 1942.
_____ (ed.). *The Past as Prelude, New Orleans, 1718-1968.* New Orleans, La.: Tulane University Press, 1968.

Carter, Jacob. *My Drunken Life from 1825 to 1847.* Boston: Published by Author, 1849.

Carter, Lief H. *The Limits of Order.* Lexington, Mass.: D.C. Heath, 1974.

Carter, Paul A. *Little America, Town at the End of the World.* New York: Columbia University Press, 1979.

Carter, Robert, et al. (eds.). *Correctional Institutions.* Philadelphia: J.B. Lippincott, 1972.

Carter, Capt. Robert Goldthwaite. *The Old Sergeant's Story.* New York: Frederick H. Hitchcock, 1926.

Carter, Robert M., and Klein, Malcolm W. *Back on the Streets.* Englewood Cliffs, N.J.: Prentice-Hall, 1976.

Carter, Robert M., and Wilkins, Leslie T. (eds.). *Probation and Parole: Selected Readings.* New York: John Wiley & Sons, 1970.

Carter, Ronald L. *The Criminals Image of the City.* New York: Pergamon, 1980.

Carter, Rubin. *Hurricane, the Sixteenth Round.* New York: Warner, 1975.

Carter, Samuel, III. *The Riddle of Dr. Mudd.* New York: G.P. Putnam's Sons, 1974.

Carter, T.F. *The Invention of Paper in China.* New York: Columbia University Press, 1925.

Carter, W.A. *McCurtain County and Southeast Oklahoma.* Idabel, Okla.: Published by Author, 1923.

Carter, W.N. *Harry Tracy, The Desperate Outlaw.* Chicago: Laird & Lee, 1902.

Cartland, Barbara. *The Scandalous Life of King Carol.* London: Frederick Muller, 1957.

Carton de Wiart, Henry. *Souvenirs Politiques.* Brussels, Belg.: Brouwer, 1948.

Cartwright, Dorwin, and Zander, Alvin. *Group Dynamics: Research and Theory.* New York: Harper & Row, 1960.

Cartwright, Frederick F., and Biddiss, Michael D. *Disease and History.* New York: Thomas Y. Crowell, 1972.

Cartwright, Gary. *Blood Will Tell.* New York: Harcourt Brace, 1979.

Cartwright, Joe, and Patterson, Jerry. *Been Taken Lately?* New York: Grove Press, 1974.

Cartwright, Otho G. *The Middle West Side: A Historical Sketch.* New York: Survey Associates, 1914.

Cartwright, Peter. *Autobiography of Peter Cartwright.* Cincinnati: Cranston & Curts, 1856.

Carty, James. *Ireland.* Dublin, Ire.: C.J. Fallon, 1957.

Carus, Paul. *The History of the Devil and the Idea of Evil.* New York: Bell, 1969.

Caruthers, William. *Loafing Along the Death Valley Trails.* Ontario, Calif.: Death Valley, 1951.

Carver, Charles. *Brann and the Iconoclast.* Austin: University of Texas Press, 1957.

Carver, Leonard D. *Capital Punishment.* Augusta, Ga.: n.p., 1899.

Carver, Michael. *Tobruk.* London: Macdonald, 1961.

Carwardine, William H. *The Pullman Strike.* Chicago: Charles H. Kerr, 1894.

Cary, Edgar. *George William Curtis.* Boston: Houghton Mifflin, 1895.

Casady, Klina E. *Once Every Five Years: A History of Cheyenne, Oklahoma, 1892-1972.* Oklahoma City: Metro Press, 1974.

Casamayor, Serge Fuster. *Le bras séculier-justice et police.* Paris: Editions de Sueil, 1960.

Casas, Bartolome de las. *Historia de las Indias.* Madrid: Imprenta de Miguel Ginestra, 1876.

Casasola, Gustavo. *Historia Grafica de Mexico.* Mexico City: Archivo Casasola, 1954.

Casaubon, Meric. *Of Credultiy and Incredulity.* London: T. Garthwait, 1668.
_____. *A Treatise Concerning Enthusiasm As It Is an Effect of Nature, But is Mistaken by Many for Either Divine Inspiration or Diabolical Possession.* London: R. Daniel & T. Johnson, 1655.

Case, Alden Buell. *Thirty Years with the Mexicans in Peace and Revolution.* New York: Fleming H. Revell, 1917.

Case, Lee. *Lee's Official Guide Book to the Black Hills and the Badlands.* Sturgis, S.D.: Black Hills & Badlands Association, 1952.

Case, Nelson. *History of Labette County, Kansas, From the First Settlement to the Close of 1892.* Topeka, Kan.: Crane, 1893.

Case, Theodore (ed.). *History of Kansas City, Missouri.* Syracuse, N.Y.: Mason, 1880.

The Case of the Hertfordshire Witchcraft Considered. London: J. Pemberton, 1712.

Casey, Lee (ed.). *Denver Murders.* New York: Duell, Sloan & Pearce, 1947.

Casey, Ralph D. *The Press in Perspective.* Baton Rouge: Louisiana State University Press, 1963.

Casey, Robert J. *The Black Hills and Their Incredible Characters.* Indianapolis, Ind.: Bobbs-Merrill, 1949.
_____. *Chicago, Medium Rare.* Indianapolis, Ind.: Bobbs-Merrill, 1949.
_____, and Douglas, W.A.S. *The Midwesterner: The Story of Dwight H. Green.* Chicago: Wilcox & Follett, 1948.
_____. *Pioneer Railroad.* New York: McGraw-Hill, 1948.
_____. *The Texas Border and Some Borderliners.* New York: Bobbs-Merrill, 1950.

Cash, W.J. *The Mind of the South.* London: Thames & Hudson, 1971.

Cashman, John. *The Gentleman from Chicago: Being an Account of the Doings of Thomas Neill Cream.* London: Hamish Hamilton, 1974.
_____. *The LSD Story.* Greenwich, Conn.: Fawcett, 1966.

Cashman, Sean D. *Prohibition.* New York: Free Press, 1981.

Caso, Alfonso. *The Aztecs: People of the Sun.* trans. Lowell Dunham. Norman: University of Oklahoma Press, 1958.

Casper, Jonathan D. *American Criminal Justice: The Defendant's Perspective.* Englewood Cliffs, N.J.: Prentice-Hall, 1972.

Cassels, Lavender. *The Struggle for the Ottoman Empire 1717-1740.* New York: Thomas Y. Crowell, 1966.

Casserly, John J. *The Ford White House, Diary of a Speechwriter.* Boulder: Colorado Associated University Press, 1977.

Cassin, Herbert N. *Cyrus Hall McCormick.* Chicago: McClurg, 1909.

Cassinelli, Guido. *Appunti sul 25 luglio 1943.* Rome: SAPPI, 1944.

Cassity, John Holland. *The Quality of Murder.* New York: Julian Press, 1958.

Casson, Herbert N. *Cyrus Hall McCormick.* Chicago: McClurg, 1909.

Casswell, J.D. *Lance for Liberty.* London: Harrap, 1961.

Castel, Albert. *A Frontier State at War: Kansas, 1861-1865.* Ithaca, N.Y.: Cornell University Press, 1958.
_____. *William Clarke Quantrill: His Life and Times.* New York: Frederick Fell, 1962.

Castellan, G. *Le réarmement clandestin du Reich, 1930-35.* Paris: Plon, 1954.

Castellane, Esprit-Victor de.. *Journal du Maréchal de Castellane, 1804-1862.* 5 vols. Paris: Plon-nourrit, 1895-97.

Castellani, Aldo. *Microbes, Men and Monarchs.* London: Victor Gollancz, 1960

Castellano, Guiseppe. *Roma Kaputt.* Rome: Casini, 1967.

Castellanos, I. *Identification Problems, Criminal and Civil.* New York: R.V. Basuino, 1939.

Castelli, Enrico. *Il Demoniaco nell' arte.* Milan, Italy: Electa, 1952.

Castelli, Giulio. *Storia segreta di Roma 'città aperta'.* Rome: Quattrucci, 1959.

Castellucci, John. *The Big Dance.* New York: Dodd, Mead, 1986.

Castiglioni, Arturo. *Adventures of the Mind.* New York: Alfred A. Knopf, 1946.

Castiglioni, Baldassare. *The Book of the Courtier.* trans. Charles S. Singleton. New York: Anchor Books, 1959.

Castilio, Ernesto Rodan. *Chessman, El Chivo Expiato.* Mexico City: Editorial Artulguy, 1960.

Castille, Charles-Hippolyte. *Histoire de la seconde république française.* 4 vols. Paris: Victor Lecou, 1854-56.

Castillo, Jose R. del. *Historia de la revolución social de México.* Mexico City: n.p., 1915.

Castle, H.G. *Case for the Prosecution.* London: Naldrett Press, 1956.

Castleman, Harvey N. *The Bald Knobbers.* Girard, Kan.: Haldeman-Julius, 1944.

_____. *Sam Bass, The Train Robber.* Girard, Kan.: Haldeman-Julius, 1944.

_____. *The Texas Rangers.* Girard, Kan.: Haldeman-Julius, 1944.

Castleman, Michael. *Crime Free.* New York: Simon & Schuster, 1984.

Castronovo, V., and Tranfaglia, N. *Storia della Stampa Italiana.* 5 vols. Bari, Italy: Laterza Editori, 1976.

Catalano, Michele. *Lucrezia Borgia, duchessa di Ferrara.* Ferrara, Italy: A. Taddie, 1920.

Catechism on the Twin Evils, Intemperance and Tobacco. New York: R.H. McDonald Drug, n.d.

Cater, D. *The Fourth Branch of Government.* Boston: Houghton Mifflin, 1959.

_____. *TV Violence and the Child: The Evolution and Fate of the Surgeon General's Report.* New York: Russell Sage Foundation, 1975.

Cathcart, Helen. *Lord Snowdon.* London: W.H. Allen, 1968.

Cather, Helen Virginia. *The History of San Francisco's Chinatown.* San Francisco: R&E Research Associates, 1974.

Catledge, Turner. *My Life and the Times.* New York: Harper & Row, 1971.

Catlin, G.E.G. *New Trends in Socialism.* London: Lovat, Dickson & Thompson, 1935.

Catlin, George. *In the Path of Mahatma Gandhi.* London: Macdonald, 1948.

_____. *The Letters of George Catlin and His Family.* Berkeley: University of California Press, 1966.

_____. *Letters and Notes on the Manners, Customs and Conditions of North American Indians.* 2 vols. New York: Dover, 1973.

Catt, Henri Alexandre de. *Frederick the Great.* trans. F.S. Flint. London: Constable, 1916.

_____. *Unterhaltungen mit Friedrich dem Grossen.* Leipzig, Ger.: S. Hirzel, 1884.

Cattell, David T. *Communism and the Spanish Civil War.* Berkeley: University of California Press, 1956.

Cattell R.B. *Abilities: Their Structure, Growth, and Action.* Boston: Houghton Mifflin, 1971.

_____. *The Inheritance of Personality and Ability: Research Methods and Findings.* New York: Academic, 1982.

Catterall, R.D. *The Veneral Diseases.* London: Evans, 1967.

Cattermole, E.G. *Famous Frontiersmen, Pioneers and Scouts.* Chicago: Coburn & Newman, 1883.

Catton, Bruce. *The Army of the Potomac.* 3 vols. New York: Doubleday, 1962.

_____. *The Coming Fury.* New York: Pocket Books, 1967.

_____. *Glory Road.* Garden City, N.Y.: Doubleday, 1952.

_____. *Mr. Lincoln's Army.* Garden City, N.Y.: Doubleday, 1951.

_____. *A Stillness at Appomattox.* Garden City, N.Y.: Doubleday, 1954.

_____. *This Hallowed Ground.* Garden City, N.Y.: Doubleday, 1956.

_____. *The War Lords of Washington.* New York: Harcourt Brace, 1948.

Caudana, Mino. *Il Figlio del Fabbro.* 2 vols. Rome: CEN, 1960.

_____. *I Fucilati di Verona.* Rome: CEN, 1961.

Caudemberg, Girard de. *Le Monde Spirituel.* Paris: E. Dentu, 1857.

Caudill, William A. *The Psychiatric Hospital as a Small Society.* Cambridge, Mass.: Harvard University Press, 1958.

Caughey, John Walton. *California.* New York: Prentice Hall, 1953.

_____. *History of the Pacific Coast.* Los Angeles: Published by Author, 1933.

_____. *Their Majesties the Mob.* Chicago: University of Chicago Press, 1960.

Caughey & Caughey. *Los Angeles: Biography of a City.* Berkeley: University of California Press, 1976.

Caulaincourt, General de, Duke of Vicenza. *With Napoleon in Russia: Memoirs.* New York: William Morrow, 1935.

Caulfield, Max. *The Easter Rebellion.* London: Frederick Muller, 1964.

Caute, David. *The Fellow Travellers.* New York: Macmillan, 1973.

_____. *The Great Fear: The Anti-Communist Purge Under Truman and Eisenhower.* New York: Simon & Schuster, 1978.

Cauzons, Thomnas de. *Les Albigeois et l'Inquisition.* Paris: Bloud, 1908.

_____. *Histoire de l'Inquisition en France.* Paris: Bloud, 1909.

_____. *La Magie et la Sorcellerie en France.* Paris: Dourbon-aimé, 1910.

Cavallero, Carlo. *Il dramma del maresciallo Cavallero.* Milan, Italy: Mondadori, 1952.

Cavallero, Marshal Ugo. *Comando supremo.* Bologna, Italy: Cappelli, 1948.

Cavan, Ruth Shonle. *Criminology.* New York: Thomas Y. Crowell, 1955.

_____, and Ranck, Katherine Howland. *The Family and the Depression.* Chicago: University of Chicago Press, 1938.

_____. *Juvenile Delinquency: Development, Treatment, Control.* Philadelphia: J.B. Lippincott, 1969.

_____, et al. *Personal Adjustment in Old Age.* Chicago: Science Research Associates, 1949.

_____. *Suicide.* Chicago: University of Chicago Press, 1928.

Cavan, Sherri. *Liquor License: An Ethnography of Bar Behavior.* Chicago: Aldine, 1966.

Cavanaugh, Sandy. *Airborne to Suez.* London: Kimber, 1965.

Cave Brown, Anthony. *Bodyguard of Lies.* New York: Harper & Row, 1975.

Cavendish, Lady Frederick. *Diary.* ed. J. Bailey. London: John Murray, 1927.

Cavendish, Richard. *The Black Arts.* New York: G.P. Putnam's Sons, 1967.

_____ (ed.). *Encyclopedia of the Unexplained.* New York: McGraw-Hill, 1974.

_____. *A History of Magic.* London: Weidenfeld & Nicolson, 1977.

_____. *King Arthur & The Grail.* New York: Taplinger, 1979.

_____. *The Powers of Evil.* New York: G.P. Putnam's Sons, 1975.

Caviglia, Marshal Enrico. *Diario (1925-45).* Rome: Casini, 1952.

Cawelti, John G. *Focus on Bonnie and Clyde.* Englewood Cliffs, N.J.: Prentice-Hall, 1973.

Cawley, Elizabeth Hoon. *American Diaries.* Princeton, N.J.: Princeton University Press, 1952.

Cayton, H.R. *Long Old Road.* New York: Trident Press, 1965.

Ceballos Dosamantes, Jesús. *Antinomia Politica de D. Francisco I. Madero.* Mexico City: Imprenta de A. Carranza é Hijos,

1911.

_____. *La Gran Mistificación Maderista*. Mexico City: Imprenta de A. Carranza é Hijos, 1911.

Cecil, Lamar. *Albert Ballin: Business and Politics in Imperial Germany, 1888-1918*. Princeton, N.J.: Princeton University Press, 1967.

Cecilie, Augusta Mary. *Erinnerungen*. Leipzig, Ger.: K.F. Koehler, 1930.

_____. *The Memoirs of the Crown Princess Cecilie*. trans. Emile Burns. London: Victor Gollancz, 1931.

Cederblom, J.B., and Blizek, William L. (eds.). *Justice and Punishment*. Cambridge, Mass.: Ballinger, 1977.

The Celebrated Chicago Anarchists' Case. Rochester, N.Y.: Lawyers Cooperative, 1887.

Celebrated Murders. Chicago: Belford, Clarke, 1879.

Celebrated Trials of All Countries. Philadelphia: E.L. Carey & A. Hart, 1843.

Celler, Emanuel. *You Never Leave Brooklyn*. New York: John Day, 1953.

Celnart, Elisabeth F. *Manuel des dames*. Paris: Roret, 1830.

Celsus. *De Medicina*. trans. W.G. Spencer. London: William Heinemann, 1935-1938.

Centennial History of Illinois. Springfield: Illinois Centennial Association, 1919.

Center for Research on Criminal Justice. *The Iron Fist and the Velvet Glove: An Analysis of the U.S. Police*. Berkeley, Calif.: Center for Research on Criminal Justice, 1975.

Centorrino, Mario, and Sgroi, Emanuele. *Economia e classi sociali in Sicilia: La stagione delle scelte (1943-47)*. Palermo, Italy: Vittorietti, 1979.

Ceram, C.W. *Gods, Graves and Scholars: The Story of Archeology*. New York: Alfred A. Knopf, 1967.

Cerf, Bennett. *Try and Stop Me*. New York: Simon & Schuster, 1944.

Cerruti, Elisabetta. *Ambassador's wife*. London: George Allen & Unwin, 1952.

Cersosimo, Vincenzo. *Dall'istruttoria alla fucilazione: storia del processo di Verona*. Milan, Italy: Garzanti, 1949.

Cerulli, Enrico. *Il Libro etiopico dei miracoli di Maria*. Rome: Giovanna Bardi, 1943.

Cervantes, Federico. *Francisco Villa y la Revolucion*. Mexico City: Ediciones Alonso, 1960.

Cesarini, Paolo. *Elena, la moglie del Re*. Florence, Italy: La Voce, 1953.

Cetti, Carlo. *Cronaca dei fatti di Dongo*. Commo, Italy: Published by Author, 1959.

Ceva, Bianca. *5 anni di storia italiana, 1940-45, da lettere e diari di caduti*. Milan, Italy: Comunità, 1964.

_____. *Storia di una passione*. Milan, Italy: Garzanti, 1948.

Ceylon Commission of Inquiry on Capital Punishment. *Report*. Colombo, Sri.: Government Press, 1959.

Chabloz, Fritz. *Les sorciéres neuchâteloises*. Neuchâtel, Switz.: J. Attinger, 1868.

Chabod, Federico. *A History of Italian Fascism*. trans. Muriel Grindrod. London: Weidenfeld & Nicholson, 1963.

Chacornac, Paul. *Eliphas Lévi: Rénovateur de l'occultisme en France 1810-1875*. Paris: Chacornac freres, 1926.

Chadbourn, James Harmon. *Lynching and the Law*. Chapel Hill: North Carolina University Press, 1933.

Chadwick, N.K. *Celtic Britain*. London: Thames & Hudson, 1963.

Chaffee, Zechariah. *Free Speech in the United States*. Cambridge, Mass.: Harvard University Press, 1946.

_____. *Freedom of Speech*. New York: Harcourt, Brace & Howe, 1920.

_____. *Government and Mass Communications*. 2 vols. Chicago: University of Chicago Press, 1947.

_____. *The Mooney-Billings Report Suppressed by the Wickersham Commission*. New York: Gotham House, 1932.

Chafetz, Henry. *Play the Devil: A History of Gambling in the United States from 1692 to 1955*. New York: Clarkson N. Potter, 1960.

Chaffin, Lorah B. *Sons of the West: Biographical Account of Early-Day Wyoming*. Caldwell, Idaho: Caxton Printers, 1941.

Chaiken, J.M. and M.R. *Varieties of Criminal Behavior*. Santa Monica, Calif.: Rand, 1982.

Chaiken, Marcia R., and Johnson, Bruce D. *Characteristics of Different Types of Drug-Involved Offenders*. Washington, D.C.: National Institute of Justice, 1988.

Chaix-d'Est-Ange, Gustave-Louis. *Discours et Plaidoyers*. 2 vols. Paris: Didot, 1862.

Chakravarty, Amiya. *Mahatma Gandhi and the Modern World*. Calcutta, India: Book House, 1945.

Chalfant, Willie Arthur. *Gold, Guns & Ghost Towns*. Stanford, Calif.: Stanford University Press, 1947.

_____. *Outposts of Civilization*. Boston: Christopher, 1928.

_____. *The Story of Inyo*. Chicago: W.B. Conkey, 1922.

Chalidze, Valery. *Criminal Russia*. New York: Random House, 1977.

_____. *To Defend These Rights: Human Rights and the Soviet Union*. New York: Random House, 1975.

Chalmers, Allan Knight. *They Shall Be Free*. Garden City, N.Y.: Doubleday, 1951.

Chalmers, David Mark. *Hooded Americanism*. New York: Doubleday, 1965.

_____. *The Social and Political Ideas of the Muckrakers*. New York: Citadel Press, 1964.

Chamber of Commerce of the United States. *Marshaling Citizen Power Against Crime*. Washington, D.C.: n.p., 1970.

Chamberlain, Austin. *Down the Years*. London: Cassell, 1935.

Chamberlain, B.P. *The Negroes and Crime in Virginia*. Charlottesville: University of Virginia, 1936.

Chamberlain, Everett. *Chicago and Its Suburbs*. Chicago: n.p., 1894.

Chamberlain, John. *Farewell to Reform*. New York: Liveright, 1932.

Chamberlain, Newell D. *The Call of Gold: True Tales on the Gold Road to Yosemite*. Mariposa, Calif.: Gazette Press, 1936.

Chamberlin, Joseph Edgar. *John Brown*. Boston: Small, Maynard, 1899.

Chamberlin, William Henry. *Blueprint for World Conquest*. Washington, D.C.: Human Events, 1946.

_____. *Japan over Asia*. Garden City, N.Y.: Blue Ribbon, 1942.

_____. *The Russian Enigma*. New York: Charles Scribner's Sons, 1943.

_____. *The Russian Revolution, 1917-1921*. 2 vols. New York: Macmillan, 1952.

_____. *Russia's Iron Age*. London: Duckworth, 1935.

_____. *Soviet Russia: A Living Record and a History*. Boston: Little, Brown, 1930.

Chambers, Henry E. *Mississippi Valley Beginnings*. New York: G.P. Putnam's Sons, 1922.

Chambers, Homer S. *The Enduring Rock*. Blackwell, Okla.: Blackwell Publications, 1954.

Chambers, J.S. *The Conquest of Cholera*. New York: Macmillan, 1938.

Chambers, Julius. *The Book of New York*. New York: Book of New York, 1912.

Chambers, Robert. *Domestic Annals of Scotland*. Edinburgh, Scot.: W. & R. Chambers, 1858.

Chambers, Robert. *Secret Service Operator 13*. New York: D. Appleton Company, 1934.

_____. *Special Messenger*. New York: D. Appleton Company, 1909.

Chambers, Walter. *Samuel Seabury*. New York: Century, 1932.

Chambers, Whittaker. *Cold Friday*. New York: Random House, 1964.

_____. *Odyssey of a Friend*. New York: G.P. Putnam's Sons, 1969.

_____. *Witness*. New York: Random House, 1952.

Chambers, William. *Things as They Are in America.* London: William and Robert Chambers, 1857.

Chambers, William Nisbet. *Old Bullion Benton, Senator from the New West.* Boston: Little, Brown, 1956.

_____. *Political Parties in a New Nation: The American Experience, 1776-1809.* New York: Oxford University Press, 1963.

Chambers' Guide to London The Secret City. London: Ocean Books, 1974.

Chambliss, William J. *Box Man: A Professional Thief's Journey.* New York: Harper & Row, 1972.

_____. *Crime and the Legal Process.* New York: McGraw-Hill, 1969.

_____. *Functional and Conflict Theories of Crime.* New York: MSS Modular Publications, 1973.

_____, and Seidman, Robert B. *Law, Order, and Power.* Reading, Mass.: Addison-Wesley, 1971.

_____. *On the Take.* Bloomington: Indiana University Press, 1978.

_____ (ed.). *Problems of Industrial Society.* Reading, Mass.: Addison-Wesley, 1973.

Champier, Symphorien. *Dialogus in Magicarum Artium Destructionem.* Lyons: Guillaume Balsarin, 1500.

Champion, Pierre. *Splendeurs et Miseres de Paris.* Paris: Calmann-Lévy, 1934.

Chandler, Alfred D., Jr. *Henry Varnum Poor: Business Editor, Analyst and Reformer.* Cambridge, Mass.: Harvard University Press, 1956.

_____. *The Visible Hand.* Cambridge, Mass.: Harvard University Press, 1977.

Chandler, Billy Jaynes. *The Bandit King: Lampião of Brazel.* College Station: Texas A & M University Press, 1978.

_____. *King of the Mountain: The Life and Death of Giuliano the Bandit.* DeKalb: Northern Illinois University Press, 1988.

Chandler, David Leon. *Brothers in Blood: The Rise of the Criminal Brotherhoods.* New York: E.P. Dutton, 1975.

_____. *Criminal Brotherhoods.* London: Constable, 1976.

Chandler, Edna Walker. *Women in Prison.* Indianapolis, Ind.: Bobbs-Merrill, 1973.

Chandler, Frank W. *The Literature of Roguery.* 2 vols. Boston: Houghton Mifflin, 1907.

Chandler, Lester V. *America's Greatest Depression.* New York: Harper & Row, 1970.

_____. *Benjamin Strong-Central Banker.* Washington, D.C.: Brookings Institution, 1958.

Chandler, Peleg W. *American Criminal Trials.* Boston: Little, Brown, 1841-1844.

Chandler, R. *Raymond Chandler Speaking.* London: Hamish Hamilton, 1962.

Chang, K. *The Archeology of Ancient China.* New Haven, Conn.: Yale University Press, 1968.

Chang, K.C. *Food in Chinese Culture.* New Haven, Conn.: Yale University Press, 1977.

Chang Chung-li. *The Chinese Gentry, Studies on Their Role in Nineteenth-Century Chinese Society.* Seattle: University of Washington Press, 1955.

Chaninov, Nicholas Brian. *History of Russia.* trans. C.J. Hogarth. New York: E.P. Dutton, 1930.

Channing, Edward. *History of the United States.* 6 vols. New York: Macmillan, 1905-25.

Channing, Henry. *The Execution of Hannah Ocuish.* New London, Conn.: T. Green, 1786.

Channing, William Ellery. *John Brown and the Heroes of Harper's Ferry.* Boston: Cupples Upham, 1886.

Chapel, Charles Edward. *Fingerprinting.* New York: Coward-McCann, 1941.

_____. *Guns of the Old West.* New York: Coward-McCann, 1961.

_____. *Levi's Gallery of Long Guns and Western Riflemen.* San Francisco: Levi Strauss, n.d.

_____. *Levi's Gallery of Western Guns and Gunfighters.* San Francisco: Levi Strauss, n.d.

Chapin, Bradley. *Provincial America.* New York: Free Press, 1966.

Chapin, Charles. *Charles Chapin's Story.* New York: G.P. Putnam's Sons, 1920.

Chapin, Louella. *Round About Chicago.* Chicago: Unity, 1907.

Chapin, Robert Coit. *The Standard of Living Among Workingmen's Families in New York City.* New York: Russell Sage Foundation, 1909.

Chaplain, Ray. *God's Prison Gang.* Old Tappan, N.J.: Fleming H. Revell, 1977.

Chaplin, Dr. A. *A St. Helena Who's Who.* London: A. Humphreys, 1919.

Chaplin, Charles. *My Autobiography.* New York: Simon & Schuster, 1964.

Chaplin, J.P. *Rumor, Fear and the Madness of Crowds.* New York: Ballantine Books, 1959.

Chaplin, Patrice. *By Flower and Dean Street and the Love Apple.* London: Duckworth, 1976.

Chaplin, Ralph. *Wobbly: The Rough-and-Tumble Story of an American Radical.* Chicago: University of Chicago Press, 1948.

Chapman, Arthur. *The Pony Express.* New York: G.P. Putnam's Sons, 1932.

Chapman, Berlin Basil. *The Founding of Stillwater.* Oklahoma City: Times-Journal, 1948.

Chapman, Brian. *Police State.* New York: Praeger, 1970.

Chapman, Gil and Ann. *Was Oswald Alone?* San Diego, Calif.: San Diego Export, 1967.

Chapman, Guy. *The Dreyfus Case.* London: Rupert Hart-Davis, 1955.

Chapman, John. *Incredible Los Angeles.* New York: Harper & Row, 1960.

_____. *Tell It to Sweeney.* Garden City, N.Y.: Doubleday, 1961.

Chapman, John Jay. *William Lloyd Garrison.* Boston: Atlantic Monthly Press, 1921.

Chaponnière, Paul. *Voltaire chez les Calvinistes.* Geneva, Switz.: Editions du Journal de Genève, 1932.

Chappell, Duncan, et al. (eds.). *Forcible Rape: The Crime, the Victim, and the Criminal.* New York: Columbia University Press, 1977.

_____, and Monahan, John (eds.). *Violence and Criminal Justice.* Lexington, Mass.: Lexington Books, D.C. Heath, 1975.

Chappell, Joseph Mitchell. *Life and Times of Warren G. Harding.* Boston: Chapple, 1924.

A Chapter in the History of Robert Matthews, Otherwise Known as Matthias, the Prophet, together with His Trial for the Murder of Mr. Pierson. Utica, N.Y.: n.p., 1835.

Charcot, J.M., and Richer, Paul. *Les Démoniaques dans l'art.* Paris: Delahaye et Lecrosnier, 1887.

Chard, Chester S. *Man in Prehistory.* New York: McGraw-Hill, 1969.

Charles, Joseph. *The Origins of the American Party System.* Williamsburg, Va.: Insitutute for Early American Culture, 1956.

Charles, Mrs. Tom. *More Tales of Tularosa.* Alamogordo, N.M.: Bennett Printing, 1961.

_____. *Tales of the Tularosa.* Alamogordo, N.M.: n.p., 1963.

Charles-Picard, Gilbert. *Augustus and Nero: The Secret of Empire.* New York: Thomas Y. Crowell, 1965.

Charles-Roux, Francois. *Huit ans au Vatican (1932-40).* Paris: Flammarion, 1947.

Charlevoix, Pierre Francois Xavier de. *Journal D'un Voyage Dans L'amerique Septentrionale.* Paris: Nyon fils, 1744.

Charnwood, Lord. *Abraham Lincoln.* Garden City, N.Y: Garden City, 1917.

Charques, R.D. *Short History of Russia.* New York: E.P Dutton, 1956.

_____. *The Twilight of Imperial Russia.* Fairlawn, N.Y.: Essential Books, 1959.

Charriere, Henri. *Papillon.* trans. June P. Wilson and Walter

B. Michaels. New York: Morrow, 1970.

Charroux, Robert. *Forgotten Worlds.* New York: Walker, 1973.

_____. *Security and Liberty: The Problem of Native Communists.* Garden City, N.Y.: Doubleday, 1955.

Chase, Harold, and Lerman, Allen H. (eds.). *Kennedy and the Press: The News Conferences.* New York: Thomas Y. Crowell, 1965.

Chase, Stuart. *Goals for America.* New York: Twentieth Century Fund, 1942.

_____. *Idle Money, Idle Men.* New York: Harcourt, 1940.

_____. *The Most Probable World.* New York: Harper & Row, 1968.

_____. *Where's the Money Coming From?* New York: Twentieth Century Fund, 1944.

Chassaigne, M. *La lieutenance générale de police à Paris.* Paris: Arthur Rousseau, 1906.

Le Château de Gilles de Retz et Son Histoire. Olonne-Beauvoir, Fr.: Lussaud Freres, 1957.

Chatfield, W.H. *The Twin Cities of the Border.* New Orleans, La.: E.P. Brandao, 1893.

Chatfield-Taylor, Hobart C. *Chicago.* New York: Houghton Mifflin, 1917.

Chatov, Robert. *Corporate Financial Reporting: Public or Private Control?* New York: Free Press, 1975.

Chatterton, E. Keble. *The Romance of Piracy.* Philadelphia: J.B. Lippincott, 1915.

Chatterton, Fenimore C. *Yesterday's Wyoming.* Aurora, Colo.: Powder River, 1957.

Chavardès, Maurice. *La Droite Française et le 6 Février 1934.* Paris: Flammarion, 1970.

Chavarria-Aguilar, O.L. (ed.). *Traditional India.* Englewood Cliffs, N.J.: Prentice-Hall, 1964.

Cheape, Charles W., III. *Moving the Masses: Urban Public Transit in New York, Boston and Philadelphia, 1880-1912.* Cambridge, Mass.: Harvard University Press, 1981.

Cheek, W. Raymond. *The Story of an American Pioneer Family.* New York: Exposition Press, 1960.

Cheetham, James. *A View of the Political Conduct of Aaron Burr, Esp., Vice-President of the United States.* New York: Denniston & Cheetham, 1802.

Cheever, George B. *Capital Punishment: The Argument of Rev. George B. Cheever in Reply to J.L. O'Sullivan, Esq.* New York: Saxton & Miles, 1843.

_____. *A Defence of Capital Punishment and an Essay on the Ground and Reason of Punishment, with Special Reference to the Penalty of Death.* New York: Wiley & Putnam, 1846.

Chein, Isidor, et al. *The Road to H: Narcotics, Delinquency, and Social Policy.* New York: Basic Books, 1964.

Chelsea House Publishers. *The Chief Executive: Inaugural Addresses of the Presidents of the United States.* New York: Crown, 1965.

Chenault, Price. *Diagnostic and Remedial Teaching in Correctional Insitutions.* Albany: New York State Department of Correction, 1945.

Chenery, William L. *Freedom of the Press.* New York: Harcourt, Brace, 1953.

_____. *So It Seemed.* New York: Harcourt, Brace, 1952.

Cheney, M. *The Coed Killer.* New York: Walker, 1976.

Chennells, E. *Recollections of an Egyptian Princess by Her English Governess.* London: W. Blackwood & sons, 1893.

Cherniak, Laurence. *The Great Book of Hashish.* Berkeley, Calif.: University Press, 1979.

Cherniavsky, Michael. *Tsar and People.* New Haven, Conn.: Yale University Press, 1961.

Chernov, Victor M. *The Great Russian Revolution.* trans. P.E. Mosely. New Haven, Conn.: Yale University Press, 1936.

Chernyshevsky, Nikolai Gavrilovich. *Selected Philosophical Essays.* Moscow: Foreign Language Publishing House, 1953.

_____. *What Is To Be Done? Tales about New People.* trans. Benjamin R. Tucker and L.B. Turkevich. New York:

Vintage Books, 1961.

Cherrill, Fred. *Cherrill of the Yard.* London: Popular Book Club, 1955.

Cherrington, Ernest Hurst. *The Evolution of Prohibition in the United States of America: A Chronological History of the Liquor Problem and the Temperance Reform in the United States from the Earliest Settlements to the Consummation of National Prohibition.* Westerville, Ohio: American Issue Press, 1920.

Chéruel, Pierre. *Histoire de France pendant la minorité de Louis XIV.* 4 vols. Paris: Hachette, 1880.

Cheshire, Maxine. *Reporter.* Boston: Houghton Mifflin, 1978.

Chesler, P. *Women and Madness.* London: Allen Lane, 1974.

Chesney, Kellow. *The Anti-Society: An Account of the Victorian Underworld.* Boston: Gambit, 1970.

Chesnut, Mary Boykin. *A Diary from Dixie.* New York: Peter Smith, 1929.

Chesser, Eustace. *Is Chastity Outmoded?* London: William Heinemann, 1960.

_____. *Live and Let Live.* London: William Heinemann, 1958.

_____. *Strange Loves: The Human Aspects of Sexual Deviation.* New York: William Morrow, 1971.

Chessman, Caryl. *Cell 2455, Death Row.* Englewood Cliffs, N.J.: Prentice-Hall, 1954.

_____. *The Face of Justice.* Englewood Cliffs, N.J.,: Prentice-Hall, 1957.

_____. *Trial by Ordeal.* Englewood Cliffs, N.J.: Prentice-Hall, 1956.

Chester, Giraund. *Embattled Maiden.* New York: G.P.Putnam's Sons, 1951.

Chester, Lewis, Leitch, David, and Simpson, Colin. *The Cleveland Street Affair.* London: Weidenfeld & Nicolson, 1976.

Chestnut, Mary Boykin. *Diary from Dixie.* New York: D. Appleton, 1906.

Chetwynd-Hayes, R. *The Unbidden.* London: Tandem, 1971.

Chevigny, Hector. *Lord of Alaska.* New York: Viking Press, 1943.

_____. *Lost Empire.* New York: Macmillan, 1937.

_____. *Russian American: The Great Alaskan Adventure, 1741-1867.* New York: Viking Press, 1965.

Chevigny, Paul. *Police Power: Public Abuse in New York City.* New York: Random House, 1969.

Cheyney, E.P. *The Dawn of a New Era, 1250-1453.* New York: Harper & Brothers, 1936.

Chiang, Monlin. *Tides from the West: A Chinese Autobiography.* New Haven, Conn.: Yale University Press, 1947.

The Chicago Anarchists and the Haymarket Massacre. Chicago: Blakely, 1887.

Chicago Association of Commerce. *Chicago, The Great Central Market.* Chicago: R.L. Polk, 1923.

Chicago Board of Trade. *Annual Report of the Trade and Commerce of Chicago.* 1858-90.

Chicago Commision on Race Relations. *The Negro in Chicago.* Chicago: University of Chicago Press, 1922.

Chicago in 1860. Chicago: W. Thorn, 1860.

Chicago and Northwestern Railway Company. *Yesterday and Today.* Chicago: Rand, McNally, 1905.

Chicago Tribune. *A Century of Tribune Editorials, 1847-1947.* Chicago: Chicago Tribune, 1947.

_____. *Pictured Encyclopedia of the World's Greatest Newspaper.* Chicago: Chicago Tribune, 1928.

_____. *The WGN: History of the Chicago Tribune, 1847-1922.* Chicago: Chicago Tribune, 1922.

Chick, N.A. *In Memoriam. . .a Complete Record of the Assassination of Lord Mayo.* Calcutta, India: T.S. Smith, 1872.

Chidsey, Donald Barr. *On and Off the Wagon.* New York: Cowles, 1969.

Chien, I. *Narcotics, Delinquency and Social Policy.* London: Tavistock, 1964.

Chikao Fujisawa. *Kotonarism: An Introduction to the Study of*

Japanese Global Philosophy or Kotonarism. Tokyo: Society for the Advancement of Global Democracy, 1954.

Chilcote, Ronald H. *Portugese Africa.* Englewood Cliffs, N.J.: Prentice-Hall, 1967.

Child, Richard Washburn. *A Diplomat looks at Europe.* New York: Duffield, 1925.

Child Study Association of America. *What to Tell Your Children About Sex.* New York: Pocket Books, 1970.

Childers, Erskine B. *Commonsense about the Arab World.* London: Victor Gollancz, 1960.

_____. *The Road to Suez.* London: MacGibbon & Kee, 1962.

Childers, James Saxon. *Witnes to Power.* New York: McGraw-Hill, 1975.

Children in Custody: A Report on the Juvenile Detention and Correctional Facility Census of 1971. Washington, D.C.: National Criminal Justice Information and Statistics Service, 1974.

Children's Defense Fund. *Children Without Homes: An Examination of Public Responsibility to Children in and out of Home Care.* Washington, D.C.: Children's Defense Fund, 1977.

Childs, Harwood L. *Public Opinion: Nature, Formation and Role.* Princeton, N.J.: Van Nostrand, 1965.

Childs, John L., and Counts, George S. *America, Russia, and the Communist Party in the Postwar World.* New York: John Day, 1943.

Childs, Marquis W. *Sweden: The Middle Way.* New Haven, Conn.: Yale University Press, 1936.

_____. *This Is Democracy.* New Haven, Conn.: Yale University Press, 1938.

Childs, Sir Wyndham. *Episodes and Reflections.* London: Cassell, 1930.

Chilton, Charles. *The Book of the West.* Indianapolis, Ind.: Bobbs-Merrill, 1962.

Chinard, Gilbert. *Honest John Adams.* Boston: Little, Brown, 1933.

_____. *Washington as the French Knew Him.* Princeton, N.J.: Princeton University Press, 1940.

Ching, Choukai (ed.). *An Economic History of the Republic of China.* Taiwan: Jin Hua Books, n.d.

Chiniquy, Charles. *Fifty Years in the Church of Rome.* London: Robert Banks & Son, 1886.

Chinoy, Ely. *Automobile Workers and the American Dream.* New York: Doubleday, 1955.

Chintamani, C.Y. *Indian Politics Since the Mutiny.* London: George Allen & Unwin, 1939.

Chisholm, Joe. *Brewery Gulch.* San Antonio, Texas: Naylor, 1949.

_____, and Cohn, Alfred. *Take the Witness.* New York: Frederick A. Stokes, 1934.

Chittenden, Hiram Martin. *The American Fur Trade of the Far West.* 2 vols. Stanford, Calif.: Academic Reprints, 1954.

_____. *History of Early Steamboat Navigation on the Missouri River.* New York: Francis P. Harper, 1903.

Chittenden, L.E. *Recollections of President Lincoln and his Administration.* New York: Harper & Brothers, 1891.

Chittenden, Luciius. *Invisible Siege.* San Diego, Calif.: Americana Exchange Press, 1969.

Chittick, William O. *State Department, Press and Pressure Groups.* New York: John Wiley & Sons, 1970.

Chitwood, Oliver Perry. *Justice in Colonial Virginia.* Baltimore: Johns Hopkins Press, 1905.

Chiurco, G.A. *Storia della Rivoluzione Fascista.* 5 vols. Forence, Italy: Vallecchi, 1929.

Choisy, Maryse. *A Month Among the Girls.* trans. Lawrence G. Blockman. New York: Pyramid Books, 1960.

_____. *Psychoanalysis of the Prostitute.* New York: Philosophical Library, 1961.

Chomsky, N. *Aspects of the Theory of Syntax.* Cambridge, Mass.: M.I.P. Press, 1965.

_____. *Syntactic Structures.* The Hague, Neth.: Mouton, 1957.

Chrisman, Harry E. *Fifty Years on the Owl Hoot Trail.* Chicago: Sage Books, 1969.

_____. *The Ladder of Rivers: The Story of I.P. (Print) Olive.* Denver: Sage Books, 1962.

_____. *Lost Trails of the Cimarron.* Denver: Sage Books, 1961.

Christian, John T. *America or Rome, Which?* Louisville, Ky.: Baptist Book Concern, 1895.

Christie, Agatha. *An Autobiography.* New York: Dodd, Mead, 1977.

_____. *Evil under the Sun.* New York: Pocket Books. 1975,

Christie, John (ed.). *Witchcraft in Kenmore (Perthshire), 1730-57: Extracts from Kirk Session Records.* Aberfeldy: D. Cameron & son, 1893.

Christie, Nils (ed.) *Scandanavian Studies in Criminology: Aspects of Social Control in Welfare States.* Oslo, Norway: Scandanavian University Books, 1968.

Christie, Octavius F. *Dickens and His Age.* London: Heath, Cranton, 1939.

Christie, Richard, and Jahoda, Marie. *Studies in the Scope and Method of 'The Authoritarian Personality.'* Glencoe, Ill.: Free Press, 1954.

Christie, Trevor L. *Etched in Arsenic.* Philadelphia: J.B. Lippincott, 1968.

Christoff, Peter K. *An Introduction to Nineteenth-Century Russian Slavophilism: A Study in Ideas of A.S. Khomiakov.* The Hague, Neth.: Mouton, 1961.

Christoph, James B. *Capital Punishment and British Politics.* Chicago: University of Chicago Press, 1962.

Christopher, Milbourne. *ESP, Seers and Psychics.* New York: Thomas Y. Crowell, 1970.

_____. *Houdini: The Untold Story.* New York: Thomas Y. Crowell, 1969.

_____. *Mediums, Mystics and the Occult.* New York: Thomas Y. Crowell, 1975.

Chronology of Japan's Foreign Relations and Major Documents. Tokyo: Diet Library, 1955.

Chroust, Anton-Hermann. *The Rise of the Legal Profession in America.* 2 vols. Norman: University of Oklahoma Press, 1965.

Chrysler, Walter P. *The Life of an American Workman.* New York: Dodd, Mead, 1950.

Chubb, Judith. *Patronage, Power and Poverty in Southern Italy.* Cambridge, Eng.: Cambridge University Press, 1982.

Chunder, Pratap Chandra. *Kautilya on Love and Morals.* Calcutta: Jayanti, 1970.

Chunn, Calvin E. *Of Rice and Men.* Los Angeles: Veteran's, 1946.

Church, Thomas. *An Essay Toward Vindicating the Literal Sense of the Demoniacs in the New Testament.* London: J. Roberts, 1737.

The Church Belfry Murder in Boston. Philadelphia: Old Franklin, 1875.

Churchill, Allen. *The Incredible Ivan Kreuger.* London: Weidenfeld & Nicolson, 1957.

_____. *Park Row.* New York: Rinehart, 1958.

_____. *A Pictorial History of American Crime 1849-1929.* New York: Holt, Rinehart & Winston, 1964.

_____. *The Theatrical Twenties.* New York: McGraw-Hill, 1975.

_____. *They Never Came Back.* Garden City, N.Y.: Doubleday, 1960.

_____. *The Year the World Went Mad.* New York: Thomas Y. Crowell, 1960.

Churchill, John G.S. *Crowded Canvas.* London: Odhams Press, 1961.

Churchill, R.P. *The Anglo-Russian Convention of 1907.* Cedar Rapids, Iowa.: Torch Press, 1939.

Churchill, Randolph. *Twenty-One Years.* London: Weidenfeld & Nicolson, 1962.

Churchill, W.S. *My African Journey.* London: Holland Press, 1908.

Churchill, Wainwright. *Homosexual Behavior among Males: A Cross-Cultural and Cross-Species Investigation.* New York: Hawthorn, 1967.

Churchill, Winston. *The Aftermath.* London: Butterworth, 1935.

———. *Great Contemporaries.* New York: G.P. Putnam's Sons, 1937.

———. *A History of the English Speaking Peoples.* New York: Dodd, Mead, 1957.

———. *The Second World War.* 6 Vols. New York: Macmillan, 1948.

———. *Thoughts and Adventures.* London: Macmillan, 1942.

———. *The Unknown War.* New York: Charles Scribner, Sons, 1931.

———. *The World Crisis: The Aftermath.* London: Charles Scribner, Sons, 1931.

Chute, William J. *The American Scene: 1600-1860.* New York: Bantam Books, 1964.

———. *The American Scene: 1860 to the Present.* New York: Bantam Books, 1966.

Ciampini, Raffaele. *Barba-Blu.* Firenze: Fussi, 1948.

Ciano, Count Galeazzo. *Ciano's Diaries, 1939-1943.* New York: Doubleday, 1946.

———. *Ciano's Diplomatic Papers.* trans. Stuart Hood. London: Odhams Press, 1948.

———. *Diary, 1937-8.* trans. Andreas Mayor. London: Methuen, 1952.

Ciarlantini, Franco. *Mussolini immaginario.* Milan, Italy: Sonzogno, 1933.

Ciba Foundation. *Medical Care of Prisoners and Detainees.* Amsterdam, Neth.: Elsevier, 1973.

Cicero. *Murder Trials (c. 80-60 B.C.).* trans. Michael Grant. Harmondsworth, Middlesex, Eng.: Penguin Books, 1975.

———. *Pro Caelio.* trans. R. Gardner. London: William Heinemann, 1965.

Cicourel, A.V. *The Social Organization of Juvenile Justice.* New York: John Wiley & Sons, 1968.

Ciechanowski, Jan. *Defeat in Victory.* New York: Doubleday, 1947.

Cignogna, Strozzi. *Magia Omniferae.* Cologne: C. Butgeni, 1606.

Cilibrizzi, Saverio. *Pietro Badoglio rispetto a Mussolini e di fronte alla storia.* Naples, Italy: Conte, 1949.

Cinel, Dino. *From Italy to San Francisco: The Immigrant Experience.* Palo Alto, Calif.: Stanford University Press, 1982.

Cini, Zelda, and Crane, Bob. *Hollywood, Land & Legend.* New Rochelle, N.Y.: Arlington House, 1980.

Cione, Edmondo. *Storia della Repubblica Sociale Italiana.* Rome: Latinita, 1950.

Cipes, Robert M. *The Crime War.* New York: New American Library, 1967.

Cipolla, Arnaldo. *Da Baldissera a Badoglio.* Florence, Italy: Bemporad, 1936.

Cippico, Count Antonio. *Italy, the Central Problem of the Mediterranean.* New Haven, Conn.: Yale University Press, 1926.

Ciraq Estopañán, Sebastian. *Los Procesos de hechicerias en la Inquisición de Castilla la Nueva.* Madrid: Diana, 1942.

Cirillo, Guiseppe. *Casi e cose.* Naples, Italy: Ala, 1948.

Cirino, Robert. *Don't Blame the People.* New York: Random House, 1971.

Cirvelo, Pedro. *Reprobación de las supersticiones y hechizerias.* Salamanca, Mex.: Pedro de Castro, 1538.

Cist, Henry M. *The Army of the Cumberland.* New York: Charles Scribner's Sons, 1882.

Citizens' Budget Commission. *A Better Government for a Better City.* New York: Citizens' Budget Commission, 1948.

Citizens Police Committee. *Chicago Police Problems.* Chicago: University of Chicago Press, 1931.

Citizens' Research and Investigating Committee, and Tackwood, Louis E. *The Glass House Tapes.* New York: Avon Books, 1973.

Citrine, Walter M. *The Trade-Union Movement of Great Britain.* Amsterdam, Neth.: International Federation of Trade Unions, 1926.

City of Charleston Yearbook, 1886. Charleston, S.C.: Walker, Evans & Cogswell, 1886.

City Council of Women's Clubs. *Pioneer Stories.* Meade County, Kan.: n.p., 1950.

City of New York Criminal Justice Coordinating Council. *A Community Self-Study of Organized Crime.* New York: Institute for Social Analysis, 1974.

Claessens, August. *The Democratic Way of Life.* New York: Rand School, 1940.

Clairmonte, Glenn. *Calamity Jane Was Her Name.* Denver: Sage Books, 1959.

Clampitt, John Wesley. *Echoes From the Rocky Mountains.* Chicago: Clarke, 1888.

Clancy, Herbert J. *The Presidential Election of 1880.* Chicago: Loyola University Press, 1958.

Clancy, Thomas H. *Papist Pamphleteers: The Allen Person Party and the Political Thought of the Counter-Reformation in England, 1572-1615.* Chicago: Loyola University Press, 1964.

Clapham, Sir John. *The Bank of England: A History.* Cambridge, Eng.: University Press, 1945.

Clappe, Mrs. Louise Amelia Knapp Smith. *The Shirley Letters From California Mines in 1851-52.* San Francisco: Grabhorn Press, 1933.

Clark, Aaron. *Trial of James Graham.* Albany, N.Y.: J. Bull, 1814

Clark, Alan. *Barbarossa: The Russian-German Conflict 1941-1945.* New York: William Morrow, 1965.

Clark, Allen C. *Abraham Lincoln in the National Capitol.* Washington, D.C.: W.F. Roberts, 1925.

Clark, Barzilla W. *Bonneville County in the Making.* Idaho Falls, Idaho: Published by Author, 1941.

Clark, Bennett Champ. *John Quincy Adams.* Boston: Little, Brown, 1932.

Clark, Champ. *My Quarter Century of American Politics.* New York: Harper & Brothers, 1920

Clark, Charles L., and Eubank, Earle E. *Lockstep and Corridor.* Cincinnati, Ohio: University of Cincinnati Press, 1927.

Clark, Charles M. *A Trip to Pike's Peak.* San Jose, Calif.: Talisman Press, 1958.

Clark, D.M. *British Opinion and the American Revolution.* New Haven, Conn.: Yale University Press, 1930.

Clark, David G., and Hutchinson, Earl R. *Mass Media and the Law.* New York: John Wiley & Sons, 1970.

Clark, Eleanor. *The Bitter Box.* Garden City, N.Y.: Doubleday, 1946.

Clark, Emmons. *History of the Seventh Regiment of New York, 1806-1889.* New York: The Seventh Regiment, 1890.

Clark, G. (ed.). *Notable British Trials: Trial of James Camb.* London: William Hodge, 1949.

Clark, Sir George. *The Later Stuarts, 1660-1714.* Oxford, Eng.: Clarendon Press, 1955.

Clark, George T. *Leland Stanford: War Governor of California., Railroad Builder, and Founder of Stanford University.* Palo Alto, Calif.: Stanford University Press, 1931.

Clark, Gerald. *Impatient Giant: Red China Today.* London: W.H. Allen, 1960.

Clark, Henry W. *History of Alaska.* New York: Macmillan, 1930.

Clark, Homer H., Jr. *The Law of Domestic Relations.* St. Paul, Minn.: West, 1975.

Clark, Ira G. *Then Came the Railroads.* Norman: University of Oklahoma Press, 1958.

Clark, John Alonzo. *Gleanings by the Way.* New York: R. Carter, 1842.

Clark, Kenneth B. *Dark Ghetto: Dilemmas of Social Power.* New York: Harper & Row, 1965.

———. *Youth in the Ghetto: A Study of the Consequences of Powerlessness and a Blueprint for Change.* New York: Harlem Youth Opportunities, 1964.

Clark, Loremne. *Rape*. Toronto, Ontario, Can.: Womens Press, 1977.

Clark, Marjorie Ruth. *Organized Labor in Mexico*. Chapel Hill: University of North Carolina Press, 1934.

Clark, Gen. Mark. *Calculated Risk*. New York: Harper, 1950.

Clark, Martin. *Modern Italy, 1871-1982*. London: Longman, 1984.

Clark, Norman H. *Deliver Us from Evil: An Interpretation of American Prohibition*. New York: W.W. Norton, 1976.

_____. *The Dry Years*. Seattle: University of Washington Press, 1965.

Clark, O.S. *Clay Allison of the Washita*. Attica, Ind.: G.M. Williams, 1920.

Clark, Phyllis Elperin, and Lehrman, Robert. *Doing Time*. New York: Hastings House, 1980.

Clark, R.T. *The Fall of the German Republic*. London: George Allen & Unwin, 1935.

Clark, Ramsey. *Crime in America*. New York: Simon & Schuster, 1970.

Clark, Ronald William. *The Birth of the Bomb*. New York: Horizon Press, 1961.

Clark, Ted. *The Oppression of Youth*. New York: Harper & Row, 1975.

Clark, Thomas D., and Kirwan, Albert D. *The South Since Appomattox: A Century of Regional Change*. New York: Oxford University Press, 1967.

Clark, Tim, and Penycate, John. *Psychopath*. London: Routledge & Paul, 1976.

Clark, Tom. *The World of Damon Runyon*. New York: Harper & Row, 1978.

Clark, V.S. *A History of Manufactures in the United States*. New York: McGraw-Hill, 1929.

Clark, Walter van Tilburg. *The Ox-Bow Incident*. New York: New American Library, 1960.

Clarke, Asia Booth. *Booth Memorials*. New York: Carleton, 1866.

_____. *The Elder and the Younger Booth*. Boston: James R. Osgood, 1882.

_____. *The Unlocked Book: A Memoir of John Wilkes Booth by His Sister*. New York: G.P. Putnam's Sons, 1938.

Clarke, Comer. *Eichmann: The Man and His Crimes*. New York: Ballantine Books, 1960.

Clarke, Donald Henderson. *Autobiography of Frank Tarbeaux*. New York: Vanguard Press, 1930.

_____. *In the Reign of Rothstein*. New York: Vanguard Press, 1929.

_____. *Man of the World: Recollections of an Irreverent Reporter*. New York: Vanguard Press, 1950.

Clarke, Edward H. *Sex in Education*. Boston: James R. Osgood, 1874.

Clarke, Elizabeth Dodge Huntington. *The Joy of Service*. New York: National Board of the Young Women's Christian Association, 1979.

Clarke, F.G. *Scarlet and Ermine*. London: William Kimber, 1960.

Clarke, James W. *American Assassins: The Darker Side of Politics*. Princeton, N.J.: Princeton University Press, 1982.

Clarke, Joseph I.C. *My Life and Memories*. New York: Dodd, Mead, 1925.

Clarke, Mary Whatley. *The Palo Pinto Story*. Fort Worth, Texas: Manney, 1956.

Clarke, R.V.G., and Cornish, D.B. *The Controlled Trial in Institutional Research: Paradigm or Pitfall for Penal Evaluators?* London: H.M. Stationery Office, 1972.

Clarke, Samuel. *A General Martyrology*. London: T. Underhill & J. Rothwell, 1651.

Clarke, Stevens H. *The New York City Criminal Court*. New York: Report to the Mayor's Criminal Justice Coordinating Council, 1970.

Clarke, Thurston, and Tigue, John J., Jr. *Dirty Money, Swiss Banks, The Mafia, Money Laundering, and White Collar Crime*. New York: Simon & Schuster, 1975.

Clarkson, Jesse D. *A History of Russia*. New York: Random House, 1961.

Clary, Prince. *A European Past*. New York: St. Martin's Press, 1978.

Claude, Antoine-Francois. *Mémoires de Monsieur Claude, chef do al police do Sûeté sous de second empire*. Paris: Jules Rouff, 1881-82.

Claussen, W. Edmunds. *Cimarron-"Last of the Frontier."* Boyertown, Pa.: n.p., 1948.

Claveau, Anotole. *Souvenirs plitiques et parlementaires s'un témoin*. 2 vols. Paris: Plon-Nourrit, 1913-14.

Clay, Henry. *Lord Norman*. London: Macmillan, 1957.

Clay, John. *My Life on the Range*. Norman: University of Oklahoma Press, 1962.

_____. *The Tragedy of Squaw Mountain*. Chicago: Traders Print, n.d.

Clay, Lucius D. *Decision in Germany*. New York: Doubleday, 1950.

Clay-Clopton, Virginia. *A Belle of the Fifties*. New York: Da Capo Press, 1969.

Clayton, A. *Counter-Insurgency in Kenya, 1952-1960*. Nairobi, Kenya: Transafrica, 1975.

Clayton, Gerald Fancourt. *The Wall Is Strong*. London: John Long, 1958.

Clayton, James E. *The Making of Justice: The Supreme Court in Action*. New York: E.P. Dutton, 1964.

Clayton, Merle. *Union Station Massacre*. Indianapolis, Ind.: Bobbs-Merrill, 1975.

Clayton, R.R., and Voss, H.L. *Young Men and Drugs in Manhattan: A Causal Analysis*. Rockville, Md.: National Institute of Drug Abuse, 1981.

Cleary, James. *The Colonel and the Captain Take Command*. Chicago: Tribune Archives, n.d.

Cleary, James Mansfield (ed.). *Proud Are We Irish*. Chicago: Quadrangle Books, 1966.

Cleaveland, Agnes Morley. *No Life for a Lady*. Boston: Houghton Mifflin, 1941.

_____. *Satan's Paradise, from Lucien Maxwell to Fred Lambert*. Boston: Houghton Mifflin, 1952.

Cleaveland, Norman, and Fitzpatrick, George. *The Morleys*. Albuquerque, N.M.: Calvin Horn, 1971.

Cleaver, Charles. *Early Chicago Reminiscences*. Chicago: Fergus, 1882.

Cleaver, Eldridge. *Soul on Ice*. New York: McGraw-Hill, 1968.

Cleaves, Freeman. *Old Tippecanoe: William Henry Harrison*. New York: Charles Scribners Sons, 1939.

Clébert, Jean-Paul. *The Gypsies*. Middlesex, Eng.: Penguin Books, 1970.

Cleckley, H. *The Mask of Sanity*. St. Louis: Mosby, 1964.

Clegg, A. and Megson, B. *Children in Distress*. London: Penguin Books, 1968.

Clegg, Eric. *Return Your Verdict*. Sydney, Aus.: Angus & Robertson, 1965.

Clegg, Reed K. *Probation and Parole: Principles and Practices*. Springfield, Ill.: Charles C. Thomas, 1975.

Cleland, Robert Glass. *California in Our Time: 1900-1940*. New York: Alfred A. Knopf, 1947.

_____. *California Pageant, the Story of Four Centuries*. New York: Alfred A. Knopf, 1946.

_____. *The Cattle on a Thousand Hills: Southern California, 1850-1870*. San Marino, Calif.: Huntington Library, 1941.

_____. *From Wilderness to Empire*. New York: Alfred A. Knopf, 1949.

_____. *History of California: The American Period*. New York: Macmillan, 1922.

_____. *The Irvine Ranch of Orange County, 1810-1950*. San Marino, Calif.: Huntington Library, 1952.

_____, and Putnam, Frank B. *Isaias W. Hellman and the Farmers and Merchants Bank.* San Marino, Calif.: Huntington Library, 1965.

Clemens, Samuel Langhorne (Mark Twain, Pseud.). *The Adventures of Huckleberry Finn.* New York: Charles L. Webster, 1885.

———. *Life on the Mississippi.* Boston: James R. Osgood, 1883.

———. *Roughing It.* Chicago: F.G. Gilmer, 1872.

Clement, Trover, and Symes, Lillian. *Rebel America: The Story of Social Revolt in the United States.* New York: Harper & Brothers, 1934.

Clements, Kedrick A. *Frontiers of Change.* New York: Oxford University Press, 1981.

Clemmer, Donald. *The Prison Community.* Boston: Christopher, 1940.

Clendenen, Clarence C. *The United States and Pancho Villa: A Study in Unconventional Diplomacy.* Ithaca, N.Y.: Cornell University Press, 1961.

Clerget, Marcel. *Le Caire: Etude de Géographie Urbaine.* Cairo, Egypt: E. & R. Schindler, 1934.

Cleugh, James. *Love Locked Out.* New York: Crown, 1963.

———. *Prince Rupert: A Biography.* London: Geoffrey Bles, 1934.

Cleveland, Grover. *The Government in the Chicago Strike of 1894.* Princeton, N.J.: Princeton University Press, 1913.

Clews, Henry. *Fifty Years in Wall Street.* New York: Irving, 1908.

———. *Twenty-Eight Years in Wall Street.* New York: Irving, 1888.

Clifford, Brian R. *The Psychology of Person Identification.* London: Kegan Paul, 1978.

Clifford, W. *Crime Control in Japan.* Lexington, Mass.: Lexington Books, 1976.

Clifton, Alan S. *Time of Fallen Blossoms.* London: Cassell, 1950.

Clinard, Marshall B. (ed.). *Anomie and Deviant Behavior.* New York: Free Press of Glencoe, 1964.

———. *The Black Market: A Study of White Collar Crime.* New York: Holt, Rinehart & Winston, 1952.

———, and Yeager, Peter C. *Corporate Crime.* New York: Macmillan, 1978.

———, and Abbott, Daniel J. *Crime in Developing Countries.* New York: John Wiley & Sons, 1973.

———, and Quinney, Richard. *Criminal Behavior Systems: A Typology.* New York: Holt, Rinehart & Winston, 1967.

———, et al. *Illegal Corporate Behavior.* Washington, D.C.: U.S. Government Printing Office, 1979.

———. *Sociology of Deviant Behavior.* New York: Holt, Rinehart & Winston, 1962.

Cline, Gloria G. *Peter Skene Ogden.* Norman: University of Oklahoma Press, 1974.

Cline, Howard F. *The United States and Mexico.* Cambridge, Mass.: Harvard Univeristy Press, 1963.

Cline, Ray S. *Secrets, Spies & Scholars.* Washington, D.C.: Acropolis Books, 1976.

Clinton, Henry Lauren. *Celebrated Trials.* New York: Harper & Brothers, 1896.

———. *Extraordinary Cases.* New York: Harper & Brotheres, 1896.

Clinton, Sir Henry. *The American Rebellion.* New Haven, Conn.: Yale University Press, 1954.

Clissold, Stephen. *The Barbary Slaves.* Totowa, N.J.: Rowman & Littlefield, 1977.

Clokey, Richard M. *William H. Ashley: Enterprise and Politics in the Trans-Mississippi West.* Norman: University of Oklahoma Press, 1980.

Clor, H.M. *Obscenity and Public Morality: Censorship in a Liberal Society.* Chicago: University of Chicago Press, 1969.

Close, Upton. *Behind the Face of Japan.* New York: Appleton-Century-Crofts, 1951.

Clough, Rev. Arthur Hugh. *Lives: The Dryden Plutarch.* New York: Everyman's Library, 1910.

Clough, Frank C. *William Allen White of Emporia.* New York: McGraw-Hill, 1941.

Clough, M.S. *Chiefs and Politicians: Local Politics and Social Change in Kiambu, Kenya 1918-1936.* Palo Alto, Calif.: Stanford University Press, 1977.

Clough, Shepard B. *The Economic History of Modern Italy.* New York: Columbia University Press, 1964.

Clover, Samuel Travers. *On Special Assignment: Being the Further Adventures of Paul Travers.* Boston: Lothrop, 1903.

Cloward, Richard A., and Ohlin, Lloyd E. *Delinquency and Opportunity.* New York: Free Press, 1960.

———, et al. *Theoretical Studies in Social Organization of the Prison.* New York: Social Science Research Council, 1960.

Clubb, Henry S. *The Maine Liquor Law, Including a Life of the Hon. Neal Dow.* New York: Fowler & Wells, 1856.

Clubb, O. Edmund. *Twentieth Century China.* New York: Columbia University Press, 1966.

———. *The Witness and I.* New York: Columbia University Press, 1974.

Club-Fellow & Washington Mirror Consalidated. *To The City of Chicago.* New York: Club-Fellow, 1912.

Clugston, W.G. *Rascals in Democracy.* New York: Richard R. Smith, 1940.

Clum, John P. *It All Happened in Tombstone.* Flagstaff, Ariz.: Northland Press, 1965.

Clum, Woodworth. *Apache Agent.* Boston: Houghton Mifflin, 1936.

Clune, F. *The Kelly Hunters: The Authentic Impartial Histotry of the Life and Times of Edward Kelly, the Ironclad Outlaw.* Sydney, Aus.: Angus & Robertson, 1955.

Clurman, Harold. *The Fervent Years.* New York: Alfred A. Knopf, 1945.

Cluseret, Gustave Paul. *Mémoires.* 3 vols. Paris: Jules Lévy, 1888.

Clutterbuck, Richard. *Guerrillas & Terrorists.* London: Faber & Faber, 1977.

———. *Kidnap & Ransom.* Boston: Faber & Faber, 1978.

———. *Living with Terrorism.* New Rochelle, N.Y.: Arlington House, 1975.

———. *The Media and Political Violence.* London: Macmillan, 1981.

———. *Riot and Revolution in Singapore and Malaya.* London: Faber & Faber, 1973.

Cluverius, Thomas J. *My Life, Trial and Conviction.* Richmond, Va.: Andrews, Baptist & Clemmitt, 1887.

Clyde, P.H. *The Far East.* Englewood Cliffs, N.J.: Prentice-Hall, 1958.

Clyne, Peter. *An Anatomy of Skyjacking.* London: Abelard-Schuman, 1973.

Coakley, Leo J. *Jersey Troopers.* New Brunswick, N.J.: Rutgers University Press, 1971.

Coale, Ansley J., and Zeinik, Melvin. *New Estimates of Fertility and Population in the United States.* Princeton, N.J.: Princeton University Press, 1963.

Coale, Edward J. *Trials of the Mail Robbers.* Baltimore: E.J. Coale, 1818.

Coan, Charles Florus. *A History of New Mexico.* Chicago: American Historical Society, 1925.

Coates, Robert M. *The Outlaw Years: The History of the Land Pirates of the Natchez Trace.* New York: Literary Guild of America, 1930.

Coatman, J. *Police.* New York: Oxford University Press, 1959.

Cobb, Belton. *Critical Years at the Yard.* London: Faber & Faber, 1956.

———. *The First Detectives.* London: Faber & Faber, 1957.

———. *Murdered on Duty: A Chronicle of the Killing of Policemen.* London: W.H. Allen, 1961.

———. *Trials and Errors, 11 Miscarriages of Justice.* London: W.H. Allen, 1962.

Cobb, Irvin S. *Exit Laughing.* Indianapolis, Ind.: Bobbs-Merrill, 1941.

———. *Paths of Glory: Impressions of War Written at and near the*

Front. New York: E.P. Dutton, 1914.

Cobb, Joseph B. *Mississippi Scenes.* Baltimore: A. Hart, 1851.

Cobbe, Hugh. *Cook's Voyages and Peoples of the Pacific.* London: British Museum, 1974.

Cobbe, William Rosser. *Doctor Judas: A Portrayal of the Opium Habit.* Chicago: S.C. Griggs, 1895.

Cobbett, William. *A Years's Residence in America.* Boston: Small, Maynard, 1818.

Coben, Stanley. *A. Mitchell Palmer, Politician.* New York: Columbia University Press, 1963.

Coblentz, Edmund D. (ed.). *William Randolph Hearst: A Portrait in His Own Words.* New York: Simon & Schuster, 1952.

Coblentz, Stanton Arthur. *Villains and Vigilantes.* New York: Thomas Yoseloff, 1957.

Coburn, Walt. *Pioneer Cattleman in Montana: The Story of Circle C Ranch.* Norman: University of Oklahoma Press, 1968.

_____. *Stirrup High.* New York: Julian Messner, 1957.

Cocchia, Admiral Aldo. *Submarines Attacking.* trans. Margaret Gwyer. London: William Kimber, 1956.

Cochran, Hamilton. *Freebooters of the Red Sea.* Indianapolis, Ind.: Bobbs-Merrill, 1965.

Cochran, John S. *Bonnie Belmont: A Historical Romance of the Days of Slavery and the Civil War.* Wheeling, W.Va.: Wheeling News, 1907.

Cochran, Louis. *FBI Man: A Personal History.* New York: Duell, Sloan & Pearce, 1966.

Cochran, Thomas C., and Miller, William. *The Age of Enterprise, A Social History of America.* New York: Macmillan, 1942.

_____, and Andrews, Wayne (eds.). *A Concise Dictionary of American History.* New York: Charles Scribner's Sons, 1962.

Cockayne, Oswald. *Leechdoms, Wortcunning, and Starcraft of Early England.* London: Longman, Roberts, & Green, 1864.

Cockburn, A., and Blackburn, R. (eds.). *Student Power.* London: Penguin Books, 1969.

Cockburn, Claude. *In Time of Trouble.* London: Rupert Hart-Davis, 1956.

Cockburn, J.S. (ed.). *Crime in England, 1550-1800.* London: Methuen, 1977.

_____. *A History of English Assizes, 1558-1714.* Cambridge, Eng.: University Press, 1964.

Cockburn, John. *Bourignianism Detected, or The Delusions and Errors of Antonia Bourignon and Her Growing Sect...Narrative I.* London: C. Brome, 1698.

Cockburn, Leslie. *Out of Control: The Story of the Reagan Administrations's Secret War in Nicaragua, the Illegal Arms Pipeling, and the Contra Drug Connection.* New York: Morgan Entrekin/Atlantic Monthly Press, 1987.

Cockcroft, James D., Gunder Frank, André, and Johnson, Dale L. (eds.). *Dependence and Underdevelopment: Latin America's Political Economy.* New York: Doubleday, 1972.

Cocke, General John H.. *Treatise on Tobacco.* Albany, N.Y.: Van Benthuysen's Steam Printing House, 1869.

Cody, Louisa Frederici. *Memories of Buffalo Bill.* New York: D. Appleton, 1919.

Cody, William Frederick. *An Autobiography of Buffalo Bill.* New York: Cosmopolitan Book, 1920.

_____. *Buffalo Bill's Own Story of His Life and Deeds.* Chicago: John R. Stanton, 1917.

_____. *Life and Adventures of "Buffalo Bill".* Chicago: John R. Stanton, 1917.

_____. *The Life of the Hon. William F. Cody, Known as Buffalo Bill.* Hartford, Conn.: F.E. Bliss, 1879.

_____. *Story of Wild West and Camp-Fire Chats.* Richmond, Va.: B.F. Johnson, 1888.

_____. *True Tales of the Plains (William F. Cody), Frontiersman and Late Chief of Scouts, U.S. Army.* New York: Empire Books, 1908. •

Coe, Charles H. *Juggling a Rope.* Pendleton, Ore.: Hamley, 1927.

Coe, George Washington. *Frontier Fighter: The Autobiography of George W. Coe.* Boston: Houghton Mifflin, 1934.

Coe, Urling C. *Frontier Doctor.* New York: Macmillan, 1939.

Coe, Wilber. *Ranch on the Ruidoso: The Story of a Pioneer Family in New Mexico, 1871-1968.* New York: Alfred A. Knopf, 1968.

Coffey, Alan R., et al. *Administration of Criminal Justice.* Englewood Cliffs, N.J.: Prentice-Hall, 1974.

_____, et al. *Human Relations.* Englewood Cliffs, N.J.: Prentice-Hall, 1976.

Coffey, Thomas M. *The Long Thirst: Prohibition in America: 1920-1933.* New York: W.W. Norton, 1975.

Coffin, Joshua. *An Account of Some of the Principal Slave Insurrections.* New York: American Anti-Slavery Society, 1860.

Coggeshall, E.W. *Assassination of Lincoln.* Chicago: W.M. Hill, 1920.

Cogley, John. *Report on Blacklisting.* New York: Fund for the Republic, 1956.

Cogswell, Jonathan. *A Treatise on the Necessity of Capital Punishment.* Hartford, Conn.: E. Geer, 1843.

Cohen, Albert K. *Delinquent Boys: The Culture of the Gang.* Glencoe, Ill.: Free Press, 1955.

_____. *Deviance and Control.* Englewood Cliffs, N.J.: Prentice-Hall, 1966.

_____, et al. *The Sutherland Papers.* Bloomington: Indiana University Press, 1956.

Cohen, Bernard. *Police Internal Administration of Justice in New York City.* Santa Monica, Calif.: Rand, 1970.

_____, and Chaiken, Jan M. *Police Background Characteristics and Performance.* Santa Monica, Calif.: Rand, 1972.

Cohen, Daniel. *ESP, The Search Beyond the Senses.* New York: Harcourt, Brace, Jovanovich, 1973.

_____. *The Far Side of Consciousness.* New York: Dodd, Mead, 1974.

_____. *Mysteries of the World.* Garden City, N.Y.: Doubleday, 1979.

Cohen, Felix (ed.). *Felix Cohen's Handbook of Federal Indian Law.* Albuquerque: University of New Mexico Press, 1971.

Cohen, Fred. *The Legal Challenge to Corrections.* Washington, D.C.: Joint Commission on Correctional Manpower and Training, 1969.

Cohen, I.B. *Franklin and Newton.* Philadelphia: American Philosophical Society, 1956.

Cohen, Israel. *Contemporary Jewry.* London: Methuen, 1950.

_____. *The Zionist Movement.* New York: Zionist Organization of America, 1946.

Cohen, Jerry, and Murphy, William S. *Burn, Baby, Burn!* New York: Avon Books, 1966.

Cohen, John. *Chance, Skill and Luck.* New York: Penguin, 1960.

Cohen, Lawrence E. *Delinquency Dispositions: An Empirical Analysis of Processing Decisions in Three Juvenile Courts.* Washington, D.C.: U.S. Government Printing Office, 1975.

Cohen, Louis H. *Murder, Madness and the Law.* New York: World, 1952.

Cohen, M.R. and F.S. *Readings in Jurisprudence and Legal Philosophy.* Boston: Little, Brown, 1951.

Cohen, Mickey. *In My Own Words.* Englewood Cliffs, N.J.: Prentice-Hall, 1975.

Cohen, Morris R. *Reason and Law.* Glencoe, Ill.: Free Press, 1950.

Cohen, R. *Patterns of Personality Judgement.* New York: Academic Press, 1973.

Cohen, S. *The Beyond Within.* New York: Atheneum, 1965.

_____, and Taylor, L. *Psychological Survival.* Harmondsworth, Eng.: Penguin Books, 1972.

_____, and Stillman, R.C. (eds.). *The Therapeutic Potential of Marihuana.* New York: Plenum, 1976,

Cohen, S.A. *British Zionists and British Jews.* Princeton, N.J.: Princeton University Press, 1982.

Cohen, Sam. D. *100 True Crime Stories.* New York: World, 1946.

Cohen, Sidney. *The Beyond Within*. New York: Atheneum, 1964

Cohen, Stanley. *Folk Devils and Moral Panics*. London: Paladin, 1973.

_____. *The Game They Played*. New York: Farrar, Straus and Giroux, 1977.

_____. *Images of Deviance*. London: Penguin Books, 1971.

Cohen, Stephan. *Reporting Child Abuse and Neglect*. Cambridge, Mass.: Ballinger, 1975.

Cohn, Alfred, and Chisholm, Joe. *Take the Witness!* New York: Frederick A. Stokes, 1934.

Cohn, Alvin W., and Viano, Emilio. *Police Community Relations*. New York: J.B. Lippincott, 1976.

Cohn, Art. *The Joker Is Wild: The Story of Joe E. Lewis*. New York: Random House, 1955.

Cohn, D.L. *Life and Times of King Cotton*. New York: Oxford University Press, 1956.

Cohn, E. *Human Behaviour in the Concentration Camps*. trans. M.H. Braaksma. New York: W.W. Norton, 1953.

Cohn, Norman. *Europe's Inner Demons*. New York: Basic Books, 1975.

Cohn, S.I. (ed.). *Law Enforcement Science and Technology*. Washington, D.C.: Port City Press, 1969.

Coit, Margaret L. *John C. Calhoun*. Boston: Houghton Mifflin, 1950.

_____. *Mr. Baruch*. Boston: Houghton Mifflin, 1957.

Coke, Edward. *Institutes of the Laws of England*. London: E.& R. Brooke, 1797.

Colbert, Elias. *Chicago: Historical and Statistical Sketch*. Chicago: P.T. Sherlock, 1868.

_____, and Chamberlain, Everett. *Chicago and the Great Conflagration*. Chicago: Vent, 1871.

Colby, Robert. *The California Crime Book*. New York: Pyramid Books, 1971.

The Cold Springs Tragedy. Indianapolis, Ind.: A.C. Roach, 1869.

Coldwell, M.J. *Canadian Progressives on the March*. New York: League for Industrial Democracy, 1944.

Cole, A.C. *Era of the Civil War, 1848-1870*. Springfield: Illinois Centennial Commision, 1919.

_____. *The Irrepressible Conflict 1850-1865*. New York: Macmillan, 1934.

Cole, C.W. *Colbert and a Century of French Mercantilism*. New York: Columbia University Press, 1939.

Cole, Cornelius. *Memoirs of Cornelius Cole, Ex-Senator of the United States from California*. New York: McLoughlin, 1908.

Cole, David. *The Theatrical Event: A Mythos, A Vocabulary, A Perspective*. Middletown, Conn.: Wesleyan University, 1975.

Cole, George Douglas Howard, and Postgate, Raymond. *The British Common People: 1746-1946*. New York: Methuen, 1961.

_____. *The Case for Industrial Partnership*. New York: St. Martin's Press, 1957.

_____. *A History of the Labour Party from 1914*. London: Routledge, 1941.

_____. *The People's Front*. London: Victor Gollancz, 1937.

_____. *The Simple Case for Socialism*. London: Victor Gollancz, 1935.

Cole, George R. (ed.). *Criminal Justice: Law and Politics*. North Scituate, Mass.: Duxbury Press, 1976.

Cole, Hubert. *Christophe: King of Haiti*. New York: Viking Press, 1967.

_____. *Laval*. London: William Heinemann, 1963.

Cole, Margaret. *Beatrice Webb*. New York: Harcourt, Brace, 1946.

_____. *The Fabian Society*. London: Fabian Society, 1952.

_____. *Growing Up Into Revolution*. London: Longmans, Green, 1949.

_____. *The Story of Fabian Socialism*. London: William Heinemann, 1961.

Cole, Peter, and Pringle, Peter. *Can You Positively Identify This Man?*. London: Deutsch, 1974.

Cole, Philip G. *Montana in Miniature*. Kalispell, Mont.: O'Neill Printers, 1966.

Cole, S. *Counterfeit*. London: John Murray, 1955.

Cole, Stewart G. *The History of Fundamentalism*. New York: Richard R. Smith, 1931.

Cole, Wayne S. *Senator Gerald P. Nye and American Foreign Relations*. Minneapolis: University of Minnesota Press, 1962.

Cole, William Graham. *Sex in Chrisianity and Pschoanalysis*. New York: Oxford University Press, 1955.

Colean, Miles L. *Renewing Our Cities*. New York: Twentieth Century Fund, 1953.

Coleman, Charles H. *The Election of 1868: The Democratic Effort to Regain Control*. New York: Columbia University Press, 1933.

Coleman, J.S. *Bataan and Beyond*. College Station: Texas A & M Press, 1978.

_____. *The Criminal Elite*. New York: St. Martin's Press, 1985.

_____, et al. *High School Achievement*. New York: Basic Books, 1982.

Coleman, J.W. *Slavery Times in Kentucky*. Chapel Hill: University of North Carolina Press, 1940.

Coleman, James Covington. *Abnormanl Psychology and Modern Life*. Glenview, Ill.: Scott, Foresman, 1976.

Coleman, James S. *Power and the Structure of Society*. New York: W.W. Norton, 1974.

Coleman, John Winston, Jr. *Stage Coach Days in the Bluegrass*. Louisville, Ky.: Standard Press, 1935.

Coleman, Jonathan. *At Mother's Request*. New York: Atheneum, 1985.

Coleman, Lee. *The Reign of Terror*. Boston: Beacon Press, 1984.

Coleman, McAlister. *Eugene V. Debs: A Man Unafraid*. New York: Greenberg, 1930.

Coleman, Max M. *From Mustanger to Lawyer*. San Antonio, Texas: Carleton Printing, 1952.

Coleman, William. *A Collection of the Facts and Documents Relative to the Death of Alexander Hamilton*. New York: I. Riley, 1804.

_____. *Remarks and Criticisms on the Hon. John Quincy Adams's Letter to the Hon. Harrison Gray Otis*. Boston: Joshua Cushing, 1808.

_____. *Report of the Trial of Levi Weeks, On an Indictment for the Murder of Gulielma Sands, on Monday the thirty-first day of March, and Tuesday the first day of April, 1800. Taken in Short Hand by the Clerk of the Court*. New York: John Furman, 1800.

Coleridge, Lord. *This For Remembrance*. London: T. Fisher Unwin, 1925.

Coles, H.L. *The War of 1812*. Chicago: University of Chicago Press, 1965.

Coles, Robert. *Children of Crisis*. Boston: Atlantic-Little, Brown, 1977.

_____, Brenner, Joseph H., and Meagher, Dermot. *Drugs and Youth*. New York: Liveright, 1970.

_____. *The Grass Pipe*. Boston: Little, Brown, 1969.

_____. *The Old Ones of New Mexico*. Garden City, N.Y.: Anchor Books, 1975.

Coletta, Paolo E. *William Jennings Bryan*. 3 vols. Lincoln: University of Nebraska Press, 1964-1969.

Colina, Federico de la. *Madero y el Gral Diaz*. Mexico City: Guerra y Vaquez, 1913.

A Collection of Rare and Curious Tracts on Witchcraft and the Second Sight. Edinburgh, Scot.: D. Webster, 1820.

Colleoni, Angelo. *Claretta Petacci: rivelazioni sulla vita, gli amore, la morte*. Milan, Italy: Lucchi, 1945.

_____. *Porfirio Diza, Su Vida Militar, Sus Perfidias Politicas*. Mexico City: Talleres del Diario Republicano, 1911.

_____. *La verità sulla fine di Mussolini e della Petacci*. Milan, Italy: Privately Printed, 1945.

Colles, Christopher. *Roads of the U.S.A.* Cambridge, Mass.: Harvard University Press, 1961.

Collier, Basil. *The War in the Far East, 1941-1945: A Military History.* New York: William Morrow, 1969.

Collier, John. *Indians of the Americas.* New York: New American Library, 1947.

Collier, Peter, and Horowitz, David. *The Rockefellers—An American Dynasty.* London: Jonathan Cape, 1976.

Collier, R. *Ten Thousand Eyes.* New York: E.P. Dutton, 1958.

Collier, Richard. *The Great Indian Mutiny.* New York: E.P. Dutton, 1964.

Collier, William Ross-Westrate, and Victor, Edwin. *Dave Cook of the Rockies.* New York: Rufus Rockwell Wilson, 1936.

_____, and Westrate, Edwin Victor. *The Reign of Soapy Smith, Monarch of Misrule.* Garden City, N.Y.: Doubleday, Doran, 1935.

Colling, Alfred. *La Prodigieuse Histoire de la Bourse de Paris.* Paris: Société d'Éditions Économiques et Financières, 1949.

Collins, Dabney Otis. *Great Western Rides.* Denver: Sage Books, 1961.

_____. *The Hanging of Bad Jack Slade.* Denver: Golden Ball Press, 1963.

Collins, Dennis. *The Indians' Last Fight; or The Dull Knife Raid.* Girard, Kan.: Appeal of Reason, 1915.

Collins, Douglas Cecil. *A Handlist of News Pamphlets.* London: Southwest Essex Technical College, 1943.

Collins, Frederick Lewis. *The F.B.I. in Peace and War.* New York: G.P. Putnam's Sons, 1943.

_____. *Glamorous Sinners.* New York: Ray Long & Richard R. Smith, 1932.

Collins, Hubert E. *Warpath and Cattle Trail.* New York: William Morrow, 1928.

Collins, Irene. *The Government and the Newspaper Press in France.* London: Oxford University Press, 1959.

Collins, James J. Jr. (ed.). *Drinking and Crime.* New York: Guilford Press, 1981.

Collins, Lewis. *History of Kentucky.* Covington, Ky.: Collins, 1874.

Collins, Michael. *The Path to Freedom.* Dublin, Ire.: Talbot, 1922.

Collins, Philip. *Dickens and Crime.* New York: Macmillan, 1962.

Collins, Randall. *Conflict Sociology.* New York: Academic Press, 1975.

Collins, Robert O., and Tignor, Robert L. *Egypt and the Sudan.* Englewood Cliffs, N.J.: Prentice-Hall, 1967.

Collins, Ted (ed.). *New York Murders.* New York: Duell, Sloan & Pearce, 1944.

Collins, Winfield H. *The Truth About Lynching and the Negro in the South.* New York: Neale, 1918.

Collinson, Frank. *Life in the Saddle.* Norman: University of Oklahoma Press, 1963.

Collinson, Patrick. *The Elizabethan Puritan Movement.* London: Jonathon Cape, 1967.

Collison-Morley, Lacy. *The Story of the Sforzas.* New York: E.P. Dutton, 1934.

Collotti, Enzo. *L'amministrzione tedesca dell'Italia occupata.* Milan, Italy: Lerici, 1963.

Colman, Edna M. *Seventy-Five Years of White House Gossip.* Garden City, N.Y.: Doubleday Page, 1925.

Colman, Elizabeth. *Chinatown U.S.A.* New York: John Day, 1946.

Colombos, C. John. *The International Law of the Sea.* London: Longmans & Greene, 1954.

Colquhoun, Ithell. *Sword of Wisdom.* New York: G.P. Putnam's Sons, 1975.

Colquhoun, Patrick. *A Treatise on the Commerce and Police of the River Thames.* Montclair, N.J.: Patterson Smith, 1969.

_____. *A Treatise on the Police of the Metropolis.* Montclair, N.J.: Patterson Smith, 1969.

_____. *A Treatise on the Public Metropolis.* London: Joseph Mawman, 1800.

Colson, Charles W. *Born Again.* Lincoln, Va.: Chosen Books, 1976.

Colton, Calvin. *The Last Seven Years of Henry Clay.* New York: A.S. Barnes, 1856.

Colton, Joel. *Léon Blum: Humanist in Politics.* New York: Alfred A. Knopf, 1966.

Colum, Mary. *Life and the Dream.* New York: Doubleday, 1947.

Colum, Padraic. *Anthology of Irish Verse.* New York: Liveright, 1948.

_____. *Arthur Griffith.* Dublin, Ire.: Browne & Nolan, 1959.

_____. *Ourselves Alone!* New York: Crown, 1959.

_____. *The Road Round Ireland.* New York: Macmillan, 1926.

Columbus, Ferdinand. *The Life of Admiral Chistopher Columbus by His Son Ferdinand.* trans. Benjamin Keene. New Brunswick, N.J.: Rutgers University Press, 1959.

Colver, Anne. *Thedosia.* New York: Farrar, 1941.

Colvin, D. Leigh. *Prohibition in the United States: A History of the Prohibition Party and of the Prohibition Movement.* New York: George H. Doran, 1926.

Colvin, Ian. *Chief of Intelligence.* London: Victor Gollancz, 1951.

Comandini, Federico. *Responsabilità di Graziani nel ripiegamento libico del 1940.* Rome: Quaderni Liberi, 1944.

Combs, Joseph F. *Gunsmoke in the Redlands.* San Antonio, Texas: Naylor, 1968.

Comfort, W.W. *William Penn.* Philadelphia: University of Pennsylvania Press, 1944.

Comines, Philippe de. *The History of Comines.* trans. Thomas Danett. New York: AMS Press, 1967.

Commager, Henry Steele. *The American Mind.* New Haven, Conn: Yale University Press, 1950.

_____. *The Empire of Reason: How Europe Imagined and America Realized the Enlightenment.* Garden City, N.Y.: Doubleday, 1977.

_____. *Freedom and Order.* New York: World, 1968.

_____, and Morris, Richard. *The Spirit of '76.* 2 vols. New York: Bobbs-Merrill, 1958.

_____. *Theodore Parker: Yankee Crusader.* Boston: Beacon Press, 1960.

Commission on Obscenity and Pornography. *Report.* New York: Random House, 1970.

Commission on the Review of the National Policy Toward Gambling. *Gambling in America.* Washington, D.C.: U.S. Government Printing Office, 1976.

Committee for Economic Development. *Reducing Crime and Assuring Justice.* New York: Committee for Economic Development, 1972.

Committee of Fifteen. *The Social Evil.* New York: G.P. Putnam's Sons, 1902.

Committee of Fifty. *The Liquor Problem. A Summary of Investigations.* Boston: Houghton Mifflin, 1905.

Committee on Un-American Activities. *Guerrilla Warfare Advocates in the United States.* Washington, D.C.: U.S. Government Printing Office, 1968.

Commons, John R., et al. *A Documentary History of American Industrial Society.* 10 vols. Cleveland: Arthur H. Clark, 1910.

_____ (ed.). *History of Labor in the United States.* 6 vols. New York: Macmillan, 1918.

_____. *Social Reform and The Church.* New York: Thomas Y. Crowell, 1894.

Commons, M.L., et al. (eds.). *Quantitative Analyses of Behavior.* Cambridge, Mass.: Ballinger, 1982.

Commonwealth of Massachusetts by Indictment vs. Thomas W. Piper. Boston: Alfred Mudge & Son, 1876.

Commonwealth v. George Baker. Boston: Frank P. Hill, 1887

Complete Account of the Horrid Murder of James Murray! New York: n.p., 1823.

A Complete History of the Murder of Mrs. Ruth Fyler. Syracuse, N.Y.: Smith & Hough, 1855.

Complete Official History of Rube Burrows and His Celebrated Gang. Birmingham, Ala.: Lyman & Stone, n.d.

Compton, Arthur Holly. *Atomic Quest*. New York: Oxford University Press, 1956.

Comstock, Anthony. *Frauds Exposed; or How the People are Deceived and Robbed, and Youth Corrupted*. New York: J. Howard Brown, 1880.

_____. *Traps for the Young*. New York: Funk & Wagnalls, 1883.

Comte, Auguste. *A System of Positive Polity*. London: Longmans, 1877.

Conant, Ralph W. *Problems in Research: Community Violence*. Washington, D.C.: Institute on Mental Health, Research Branch, 1969.

_____. *The Prospects for Revolution*. New York: Harper & Row, 1971.

Conard, Howard L. (ed.). *Encyclopedia of the History of Missouri, a Compendium of History and Biography for Ready Reference*. 6 vols. New York: Haldeman, Conard, 1901.

_____. *Uncle Dick Wootton: The Pioneer Frontiersman of the Rocky Mountains*. Chicago: R.R. Donnelley & Sons, 1957.

Conaty, Thomas J. *Temperance and Total Abstinence*. Worcester, Mass.: Charles Hamilton, 1887.

Conconi, Charles, and House, Toni. *The Washington Sting*. New York: Coward, McCann & Geoghegan, 1979.

A Condensed History of the Prohibition Party. Chicago: National Prohibitionist, 1944.

A Condensed Report of the Trial of James Albert Trefethen, and William H. Smith for the Murder of Deltena J. Davis. Boston: Wright & Potter, 1895.

Condon, John F. *Jafsie Tells All*. New York: Jonathan Lee, 1936.

Condon, Richard. *The Manchurian Candidate*. New York: Random House, 1958

_____. *Winter Kills*. New York: Dial Press, 1974.

Condor, Stella. *Woman on the Beat*. London: Hale, 1960.

The Confession and Dying Words of Samuel Frost. Worcester, Mass.: Thomas, n.d.

Confession of Adam Horn. Baltimore: James Young, 1843.

Confession of Adam Jones. Louisville, Ky.: D. Holcomb, 1837.

Confession of Augustus Otis Jennings. St. Joseph, Mo.: K.J. Bastin, 1853.

The Confession of Benjamin Bailey. Reading, Pa.: J. Schneider, 1798.

Confession of Charles Gibbs, the Pirate. New York: Christian Brown, 1831.

Confession of Edward Donnelly. Carlisle, Pa.: A. Louden, 1808.

Confession of Elizabeth Van Valkenburgh. Johnstown, N.Y.: G. Henry & W.N. Clark, 1847.

Confession of Henry Green. Troy, N.Y.: R. Rose & R. Belcher, 1845.

Confession of John Battus. Philadelphia: Richard Folwell, 1800.

Confession of John Haggerty. Lancaster, Pa.: John H. Persol, 1847.

Confession of John Joyce. Philadelphia: Bethel Church, 1808.

Confession of Joseph Baker. Philadelphia: Richard Folwell, 1800.

Confessions of an American Opium Eater. Boston: J.H. Earle, 1895.

Confessions of Two Malefactors, Teller & Reynolds. Hartford, Conn.: Hamer & Comstock, 1833.

Congdon, Don (ed.). *Combat: European Theater, World War II*. New York: Dell, 1958.

_____ (ed.) *Combat: Pacific Theater, World War II*. New York: Dell, 1958.

_____. *Combat: The War With Japan*. New York: Dell, 1962.

_____. *The Thirties*. New York: Simon & Schuster, 1962.

Conger, John J., and Miller, W.C. *Personality, Social Class, and Delinquency*. New York: John Wiley & sons, 1966.

Conger, Roger N. *Texas Rangers: Sesquicentennial Anniversary, 1823-1973*. Fort Worth, Texas: Heritage Publications, 1973.

Congress and the Nation, 1945-1964. Washington, D.C.: Congressional Quarterly Service, 1965.

Congressional Committee Staff Study. *Political Kidnappings 1968-1973*. Washington, D.C.: n.p., 1973.

Les conjurations faites à un démon possédant le corps d'une grande dame. Paris: I Mesnier, 1619.

Conklin, John E. *The Crime Establishment*. Englewood Cliffs, N.J.: Prentice-Hall, 1977.

_____. *Illegal But Not Criminal*. Englewood Cliffs, N.J.: Spectrum Books, 1977.

_____. *The Impact of Crime*. New York: Macmillan, 1975.

_____. *Robbery and the Criminal Justice System*. Philadelphia: J.B. Lippincott, 1972.

Conkling, Roscoe P., and Conkling, Margaret B. *The Butterfield Overland Mail, 1857-1869*. Glendale, Calif.: Arthur H. Clark, 1947.

Conlin, Joseph. *Bread and Roses Too*. Westport, Conn.: Greenwood, 1969.

Conn, William. *Cow-Boys and Colonels*. London: Griffith, Farran, Okeden & Welsh, 1887.

Connable, Alfred, and Silberfarb, Edward. *Tigers of Tammany Hall: Nine Men Who Ran New York*. New York: Holt, Rinehart & Winston, 1967.

Connell, Brian. *Knight Errant: A Biography of Douglas Fairbanks, Jr.* London: Hodder & Stoughton, 1955.

Connell, John and Sutherland, Douglas. *Fraud*. New York: Stein & Day, 1979.

_____. *The Most Important Country*. London: Cassell, 1957.

Connell, Noreen, and Wilson, Cassandra (eds.). *Rape: The First Sourcebook for Women*. New York: Plume Books, 1974.

Connell, Robert, Sr. *Arkansas*. New York: Paebar, 1947.

Connelley, William Elsey. *John Brown*. Topeka, Kans.: Crane, 1900.

_____. *Quantrill and the Border Wars*. Cedar Rapids, Iowa: Torch Press, 1909.

_____. *Wild Bill and His Era*. New York: Press of the Pioneers, 1933.

Conner, Daniel Ellis. *Joseph Reddeford Walker and the Arizona Adventure*. Norman: University of Oklahoma Press, 1956.

Conners. Bernard F. *Don't Embarrass the Bureau*. Indianapolis, Ind.: Bobbs-Merrill, 1972.

Connery, Donald S. *Guilty Until Proven Innocent*. New York: G.P. Putnam's Sons, 1977.

_____. *The Scandinavian*. New York: Simon & Schuster, 1966.

Connolly, C.P. *The Truth About the Frank Case*. New York: Vail-Ballou, 1915.

Connolly, Christopher P. *The Devil Learns to Vote*. New York: Covici Friede, 1938.

Connolly, James. *Labour and Easter Week 1916*. Dublin, Ire.: Three Candles, 1949.

_____. *Labour in Ireland*. Dublin, Ire.: Maunsel, 1917.

_____. *Socialism and Nationalism*. Dublin, Ire.: Three Candles, 1948.

_____. *The Worker's Republic*. Dublin, Ire.: Three Candles, 1951.

Connor, Walter. *Deviance in Soviet Society*. New York: Columbia University Press, 1972.

Conot, Robert. *Rivers of Blood, Years of Darkness*. New York: Bantam Books, 1967.

Conquest, Robert. *The Great Terror: Stalin's Purge of the Thirties*. London: Macmillan, 1968.

_____. *Power and Policy in the USSR*. New York: St. Martin's, 1961.

Conrad, Barnaby. *A Revolting Transaction*. New York: Arbor House, 1983.

Conrad, David Eugene. *The Forgotten Farmers: The Story of Sharecroppers in the New Deal*. Urbana: University of Illinois Press, 1965.

Conrad, Earl. *Scottsboro Boy*. Garden City, N.Y.: Doubleday, 1950.

Conrad, J.P., and Dintz, S. (eds.). *In Fear of Each Other*. Lexington, Mass.: Lexington Books, 1977.

Conrad, John P. *Crime and Its Correction: An International Survey of Attitudes and Practices*. Berkeley: University of California

Press, 1967.

Conrad, Joseph. *The Secret Agent.* New York: Doubleday, 1953.

Conrad, Thomas N. *A Confederate Spy.* New York: J.S. Ogilvie, 1892.

_____. *The Rebel Scout.* Washington, D.C.: National, 1904.

Conrow, Robert. *Field Days.* New York: Charles Scribner's Sons, 1974.

Consantelos, Demetrios J. *Byzantine Philanthropy and Social Welfare.* New Brunswick, N.J.: Rutgers University Press, 1968.

Considine, Bob. *The Man Who Robbed Brinks.* New York: Random House, 1961.

Consortium for Longitudinal Studies. *As the Twig Is Bent: The Lasting Effects of Preschool Programs.* Hiillsdale, N.J.: Lawrence Erlbaum, 1983.

Constant, l'abbé Alphonse-Louis. *La Clef des grands mystères.* Paris: G. Baillière, 1861.

Constantine, King of Greece. *A King's Private Letters.* Everleigh Nash & Grayson, 1925.

Constantine-Quinn, Max. *Doctor Crippen.* London: Duckworth, 1935.

Contamine, Philippe. *Guerre, Etat et Société a la Fin du Moyen Age: Etudes sur les Armées des Rois de France, 1337-1494.* Paris: Mouton et Cie., 1972.

Contarini, A. *Travels to Tana and Persia.* London: Hakluyt Society, 1873.

Conway, Moncure Daniel. *Demonology and Devil Lore.* London: Chatto & Windus, 1879.

Conwell, Russell H. *Acres of Diamonds.* New York: Harper & Brothers, 1915.

_____. *Why and How. Why the Chinese Emigrate.* Boston: Lee & Shepard, 1871.

Coogan, Tim Pat. *The I.R.A.* London: Fontana, 1980.

Cook, Adrian. *The Armies of the Streets.* Lexington: University Press of Kentucky, 1974.

Cook, David J. *Hands Up; or Twenty Years of Detective Life in the Mountains and on the Plains.* Denver: W.F. Robinson Printing, 1897.

Cook, E.T. *Delane of the Times.* London: Constable, 1915.

Cook, Ezra A. *Ku Klux Klan Secrets Exposed.* Chicago: Published by Author, 1922.

Cook, Fred J. *The Corrupted Land: The Social Morality of Modern America.* New York: Macmillan, 1966.

_____. *The FBI Nobody Knows.* New York: Macmillan, 1964.

_____. *The Great Energy Scam.* New York: Macmillan, 1982.

_____. *Mafia!* Greenwich, Conn.: Fawcett, 1973.

_____. *The Nightmare Decade.* New York: Random House, 1971.

_____. *The Secret Rulers: Criminal Syndicates and How They Control the U.S. Underworld.* New York: Duell, Sloan & Pearce, 1966.

_____. *A Two Dollar Bet Means Murder.* New York: Dial Press, 1961.

_____. *The Unfinished Story of Alger Hiss.* New York: William Morrow, 1958.

_____. *The Warfare State.* New York: Macmillan, 1962.

Cook, Frederick Francis. *Bygone Days in Chicago.* Chicago: McClurg, 1910.

Cook, James. *The Journals of Capain James Cook in His Voyages of Discovery: The Voyage of the Resolution and Discovery 1776-1780.* 3 vols. Cambridge, Eng.: Hakluyt Society, 1955-67.

Cook, James Henry. *Fifty Years on the Old Frontier, as Cowboy, Hunter, Guide, Scout and Ranchman.* New Haven, Conn.: Yale University Press, 1923.

_____. *Longhorn Cowboy.* New York: G.P. Putnam's Sons, 1942.

Cook, Jim (Lane). *Lane on the Llano, Being the Story of Jim (Lane) Cook.* Boston: Little, Brown, 1936.

Cook, John R. *The Border and the Buffalo.* Topeka, Kan.: Crane, 1907.

Cook, Theodore P. *The Life and Public Services of the Hon.*

Samuel J. Tilden. New York: D. Appleton, 1876.

Cook, Warren. *Flood Tide of Empire.* New Haven, Conn.: Yale University Press, 1973.

Cooke, Alistair. *A Generation on Trial.* New York: Alfred A. Knopf, 1950.

_____ (ed.). *The Vintage Mencken.* New York: Vintage Books, 1955.

Cooke, Bob (ed.). *Wake Up the Echoes.* New York: Hanover House, 1956.

Cooke, Jacob E. *Alexander Hamilton: A Profile.* New York: Hill & Wang, 1967.

Cooke, T. Dickerson. *The Blue Book of Crime.* Chicago: Institute of Applied Science, 1959.

Cookridge, E.H. *The Baron of Arizona.* New York: John Day, 1967.

_____. *Set Europe Ablaze.* London: Author Baker, 1966.

Cooley, Charles Horton. *Human Nature and the Social Order.* New York: Charles Scribner's Sons, 1902.

Cooley, John K. *Libyan Sandstorm.* New York: Holt, Rinehart & Winston, 1982.

Coolidge, Calvin. *Autobiography.* New York: Cosmopolitan Book, 1929.

Coolidge, Dane. *Arizona Cowboys.* New York: E.P. Dutton, 1938.

_____. *Fighting Men of the West.* New York: E.P. Dutton, 1932.

_____. *Gringo Gold: A Story of Joaquin Murieta, the Bandit.* New York: E.P. Dutton & Co., 1939.

Coolidge, Mary Roberts. *Chinese Immigration.* New York: Henry Holt, 1909.

Cooney, John. *The American Pope.* New York: Times Books, 1984.

Coons, William R. *Attica Diary.* New York: Stein & Day, 1972.

Cooper, Alfred Duff. *Old Men Forget.* London: Hart-Davis, 1953.

Cooper, C.R. *Here's to Crime.* Boston: Little, Brown, 1937.

Cooper, C.S. *Understanding Italy.* New York: Century, 1923.

Cooper, Courtney Riley. *Designs in Scarlet.* Boston: Little, Brown, 1939.

_____. *Here's to Crime.* Boston: Little, Brown, 1937.

_____. *High Country, the Rockies Yesterday and Today.* Boston: Little, Brown, 1926.

_____. *Ten Thousand Public Enemies.* Boston: Little, Brown, 1935.

Cooper, David D. *The Lesson of the Scaffold.* Athens: Ohio University Press, 1974.

Cooper, Frank C. *Stirring Lives of Buffalo Bill, Colonel Wm. F. Cody, Last of the Great Scouts, and Pawnee Bill, Major Gordon W. Lillie, White Chief of the Pawnees.* New York: Parsons, 1912.

Cooper, James F. *Technique of Contraception.* New York: Day-Nichols, 1928.

Cooper, Jerome A. *"Sincerely Your Friend": Letters of Mr. Justice Hugo L. Black to Jerome A. Cooper.* Tuscaloosa: University of Alabama Press, 1973.

Cooper, R.W. *The Nuremberg Trial.* Harmondsworth, Eng.: Penguin Books, 1947.

Cooper, Thomas. *The Mystery of Witchcraft.* London: N. Oakes, 1617.

Cooper, William. *Shall We Ever Know? The Trial of the Hosein Brothers For the Murder of Mrs. McKay.* London: Hutchinson, 1971.

Coopers and Lybrand. *The Cost of Incarceration in New York City.* Hackensack, N.J.: National Council on Crime and Delinquency, 1978.

Copeland, Miles. *Without Cloak or Dagger: The Truth About New Espionage.* New York: Simon & Schuster, 1974.

Coote, A., and Gill, T. *The Rape Controversy.* London: NCCL, 1975.

Coox, Alvin. *Japan: The Final Agony.* New York: Ballantine Books, 1970.

Cope, Alfred Haines, and Krinsky, Fred. *Franklin D. Roosevelt and The Supreme Court*. Boston: D.C. Heath, 1952.

Copetas, A. Craig. *Metal Men*. New York: G.P. Putnam's Sons, 1985.

Copleston, Frederick. *A History of Philosophy, Volume I: Greece and Rome*. Westminster, Md.: Newman Press, 1946.

Coppeck, Robert W. and Barbara. *How to Recruit and Select Policemen and Firemen*. Chicago: Public Personnel Association, 1957.

Copple, Neale. *Depth Reporting*. Englewood Cliffs, N.J.: Prentice-Hall, 1964.

Coppolino, Carl A. *The Crime That Never Was*. Tampa, Florida: Justice Press, 1980.

Coquerel, Charles. *Historire des Eglises du Désert*. Paris: Ab. Cherbuliez et Cie, 1841.

Coquerel Fils, Athanase. *Jean Calas et sa famille*. Paris: Joel Cherbuliez, 1858.

Corbett, James J. *The Roar of the Crowd*. New York: Gosset & Dunlap, 1925.

Corbin, Charles R. *Why News Is News*. New York: Roland Press, 1928.

Corbitt, Robert L. *The Holmes Castle*. Chicago: Corbitt & Morrison, 1895.

Corcoran, Jean. *Folk Tales of England*. Indianapolis, Ind.: Bobbs-Merrill, 1968.

Cordasco, Francisco. *Jacob Riis Revisited: Poverty and the Slum in Another Era*. Garden City, N.Y.: Doubleday, 1968.

Cordell, Eugene F. *Historical Sketch of the University of Maryland School of Medicine*. Baltimore: Friedenwalk Press, 1891.

Corder, Eric (ed.). *Murder My Love*. Chicago: Playboy Press, 1973.

Cordley, Rev. Richard D. *History of Lawrence, Kansas*. Lawrence, Kan.: E.F. Caldwell, 1895.

Coremans, P. *Van Meegeren's Faked Vermeers and de Hooghs: A Scientific Examination*. trans. C.M. Hutt. London: Cassell, 1949.

Corey, Herbert. *Farewell, Mr. Gangster!* New York: Appleton-Century-Crofts, 1936.

Corey, Lewis. *The Decline of American Capitalism*. New York: Covici Friede, 1934.

_____. *The House of Morgan*. New York: Grosset & Dunlap, 1930.

_____. *The Unfinished Task*. New York: Viking Press, 1942.

Corfe, Tom. *The Phoenix Park Murders: Conflict, Compromise and Tragedy in Ireland 1979-1882*. London: Hodder & Stoughton, 1968.

Corfield, I.D. *Historical Survey of the Origins and Growth of Mau Mau*. London: H.M. Stationery Office, 1960.

Corle, Edwin. *Billy the Kid*. New York: Duell, Sloane, & Pearce, 1953.

_____. *Desert Country*. New York: Duell, Sloan & Pearce, 1941.

_____. *The Gila River of the Southwest*. New York: Rinehart, 1951.

_____. *The Royal Highway (El Camino Real)*. New York: Bobbs-Merrill, 1949.

Corley, T.A.B. *Democratic Despot: A Life of Napoleon III*. London: Barrie & Rockliff, 1961.

Corliss, Carlton J. *Main Line of Mid-America*. New York: Creative Age, 1950.

Cornelius, Wayne A. *Mexican Migration to the United States: Causes, Consequences and U.S. Responses*. Cambridge, Mass.: MIT Press, 1978.

Cornell, Robert J. *The Anthracite Coal Strike*. Washington, D.C.: Catholic University of America Press, 1957.

Corner, William (ed.). *San Antonio de Bexar: A Guide and History*. San Antonio, Texas: Bainbridge & Corner, Christmas, 1890.

Cornforth, Maurice. *Historical Materialism*. New York: International, 1962.

Cornise, Titus Fey. *The Natural Wealth of California*. San Francisco: H.H. Bancroft, 1868.

Cornish, Derek B., and Clarke, R.V.G. *Residential Treatment and Its Effects on Delinquency*. London: H.M. Stationery Office, 1975.

Cornish, G.W. *Cornish of the "Yard"*. London: John Lane, 1935.

Cornish, M. *An Introduction to Violence*. London: Cassell, 1960.

Cornwallis-West, Mrs. George. *The Reminiscences of Lady Randolph Churchill*. New York: Century, 1908.

Cornwell, John. *Earth To Earth*. New York: Ecco Press, 1982.

Corpechot, L. *Memories of Queen Amélie of Portugal*. London: Evelyn Nash, 1915.

Corpuz, Orofre D. *The Philippines*. Englewood Cliffs, N.J.: Prentice-Hall, 1965.

A Correct and Concise Account of the Interesting Trial of Jason Fairbanks, for the Barbarous and Cruel Murder of Elizabeth Fales. Boston: n.p., 1801.

A Correct Copy of the Trial & Conviction of Richard Johnson, for the Murder of Ursula Newman. New York: Christian Brown, 1829.

The Correct, Full and Impartial Report on the Trial of Rev. Ephraim K. Avery. Providence, R.I.: Marshall & Brown, 1833.

A Correct Journal of the Conduct of the Two Unfortunate Prisoners Sinclair and Johnson, from the Time of Their Conviction Until Their Execution, With a Biographical Sketch of Their Lives, As Delivered by Themselves, the Day Previous to Which They Were to Be Executed. New York: n.p., 1811.

Correspondence between Frederick Engels and Paul and Laura Lafargue. Moscow: Foreign Languages, 1960.

Correspondence de Madame Lafarge. Paris: Mercure de France, 1913.

Corry, John. *The Manchester Affair*. New York: G.P. Putnam's Sons, 1967.

Corsini, Vinceczo. *Il capo del governo nello stato fascista*. Bologna, Italy: Zanichelli, 1935.

Cortés, J.B., and Gatti, F.M. *Delinquency and Crime*. New York: Seminar Press, 1972.

Corti, Egon Caesar, Count. *The Downfall of Three Dynasties*. New York: Books for Libraries Press, 1970.

_____. *The English Empress*. London: Cassell, 1957.

_____. *Maximilian and Carlotta*. trans. Catherine Alison Philips. New York: Alfred A. Knopf, 1928.

_____. *The Romanovs*. New York: Harper & Row, 1971.

_____. *The Russian Dagger*. New York: Harper & Row, 1969.

Cortwright, David. *Soldiers in Revolt*. New York: Doubleday, 1975.

Corum, Bill. *Off and Running*. New York: Holt, Rinehart & Winston, 1959.

Corwin, Edward Samuel. *Court Over Constitution*. Princeton, N.J.: Princeton University Press, 1928.

_____. *French Policy and the American Alliance*. Princeton, N.J.: Princeton University Press, 1916.

_____. *John Marshall and the Constitution*. New York: United States Publishers Association, 1919.

_____. *The President, Office and Powers*. New York: New York University Press, 1948.

_____. *Total War and the Constitution*. New York: Alfred A. Knopf, 1947.

Cory, Donald Webster. *The Homosexual in America*. New York: Greenberg, 1951.

Coseneau, E. *Le Connétable de Richemont*. Paris: Librairie Hachette et Cie., 1886.

Coser, Lewis A. *The Functions of Social Conflict*. Glencoe, Ill.: Free Press, 1956.

_____. *Men of Ideas*. New York: Free Press, 1965.

Cosgrave, E.D. *The True History of the Phoenix Park Murders*. 1937.

Cosgrove, Nicholas. *The Cosgrove Report: Being the Private Inquiry of a Pinkerton Detective into the Death of President Lincoln*. New York: Rawson, Wade, 1979.

Cosio Villegas, Daniel (ed.). *Historia moderna de México*. 7 vols.

Mexico City: Editorial Hermes, 1955.

Cossley-Batt, Jill Lillie Emma. *The Last of the California Rangers*. New York: Funk & Wagnalls, 1928.

Cossu, Antonio. *The Sardinian Hostage*. trans. Isabel Quigly. London: Hollis & Carter, 1971.

Costello, Augustine E. *History of the Police Department of Jersey City*. Jersey City, N.J.: Published by Author, 1891.

_____. *Our Firemen: A History of the New York Fire Departments*. New York: Published by Author, 1887.

_____. *Our Police Protectors: A History of the New York Police*. New York: C.F. Roper, 1885.

Costello, John Benjamin (ed.). *Swindling Exposed: From the Diary of William B. Morrow*. Syracuse, N.Y.: Published by Author, 1907.

Costigan, Giovanni. *A History of Modern Ireland, with a Sketch of Earlier Times*. New York: Pegasus, 1969.

Costikyan, Edward N. *Behind Closed Doors: Politics in the Public Interest*. New York: Harcourt, Brace & World, 1966.

Cosulich, Gilbert. *Adult Probation Laws of the United States*. New York: National Probation Association, 1940.

Cotner, Robert C. *James Stephen Hogg: A Biography*. Austin: University of Texas Press, 1954.

Cotta, John. *The Trial of Witchcraft Showing the True and Right Method of Discovery*. London: Samuel Rand, 1616.

Cottenham, M.E.P. *Mine Host, America*. London: Collins, 1937.

Cottle, Thomas J. *Children in Jail*. Boston: Beacon Press, 1977.

Cotton, John. *The Churches Resurrection*. London: R.O. & G.D., 1642.

Cottrell, John. *Anatomy of an Assassination: The Murder of Abraham Lincoln*. New York: Funk & Wagnalls, 1966.

_____. *Assassination! The World Stood Still*. London: New English Library, 1964.

Couchoud, P.L. *Voix de Napoléon*. Geneva, Switz.: Milieu du Monde, 1949.

Coudert, Louis L. *Security Printing*. New York: American Bank Note, 1929.

Couisnot, J. *Chronique de la Pucelle ou Chronique de Cousinot*. Paris: Adophe de la Hays, 1859.

Coulange, Louis. *The Life of the Devil*. London: Alfred A. Knopf, 1929.

Coulson, Thomas. *Joseph Henry*. Princeton, N.J.: Princeton University Press, 1950.

Coulter, Ellis Merton. *The Confederate States of America 1861-1865*. Baton Rouge: Louisiana State University Press, 1950.

_____. *A History of the South*. Baton Rouge: Louisiana State University Press, 1950.

_____. *John Jacobus Flournoy: Champion of the Common Man in the South*. Savannah: Georgia Historical Society, 1942.

_____. *A Short History of Georgia*. Chapel Hill: University of North Carolina Press, 1933.

Coulter, J. *Approaches to Insanity: A Philosophical and Sociological Study*. London: Martin Robertson, 1973.

Coulton, George C. *Christ, St. Francis, and Today*. Cambridge, Eng.: University Press, 1919.

_____. *The Death Penalty for Heresy*. London: Simpkin, Marshall, Hamilton, & Kant, 1924.

_____. *Five Centuries of Religion*. Cambridge, Eng.: Cambridge University Press, 1927

_____. *The Inquisition and Liberty*. London: William Heinemann, 1938.

_____. *Medieval Panorama*. Cambridge, Eng.: Cambridge University Press, 1949.

Countant, C.G. *The History of Wyoming*. Laramie, Wyo.: Chaplin, Spafford & Mathison, 1899.

Countryman, Vern (ed.). *Douglas of the Supreme Court*. Garden City, N.Y.: Doubleday, 1959.

_____, and Finman, T. *The Lawyer in Modern Society*. Boston: Little, Brown, 1966.

Counts, George S. *Prospects of American Democracy*. New York: John Day, 1938.

_____. *School and Society in Chicago*. New York: Harcourt, Brace, 1928.

Coupland, R. *The Constitutional Problem in India: A Restatement*. London: Oxford University Press, 1944.

Courlander, Harold (ed.). *A Treasury of Afro-American Folklore*. New York: Crown, 1976.

Course, Capt. A.G. *Pirates of the Eastern Seas*. London: Frederick Muller, 1968.

Coursey, O.W. *Beautiful Black Hills: A Comprehensive Treatise on the Black Hills of South Dakota*. Mitchell, S.D.: Educator Supply, 1926.

_____. *Wild Bill (James Butler Hickok)*. Mitchell, S.D.: Educator Supply, 1924.

The Courtesan's Jewel Box. trans. Yang Hsien-Yi and Gladys Yang. Peking, China: Foreign Language Press, 1957.

Courtwright, David T. *Dark Paradise: Opiate Addiction in America Before 1940*. Cambridge, Mass.: Harvard University Press, 1982.

Cousins, Sheila. *To Beg I Am Ashamed*. London: Richards Press, 1953.

Coutney, Marguerite. *Laurette*. New York: Rinehart, 1955.

Covarrubias, Miguel. *The Eagle, the Jaguar, and the Serpent*. New York: Alfred A. Knopf, 1954.

Coveney, Peter. *The Image of Childhood*. Baltimore: Penguin, 1967.

Cowan, C.D. (ed.). *The Economic Development of China and Japan*. New York: Frederick A. Praeger, 1964.

Cowan, Frank. *Andrew Johnson*. Greensburg, Pa.: n.p., 1894.

Cowan, Paul, et al. *State Secrets*. New York: Holt, Rinehart & Winston, 1974.

Cowan, Robert Ellsworth. *Range Rider*. Garden City, N.Y.: Doubleday, Doran, 1930.

_____, and Boutwell Dunlap. *Bibliography of the Chinese Question in the United States*. San Francisco: A.M. Robertson, 1909.

Coward, Noël. *Future Indefinite*. London: William Heinemann, 1954.

_____. *Present Indicative*. London: William Heinemann, 1937.

Cowburn, Philip. *The Warship in History*. New York: Macmillan, 1965.

Cowdery, Ray R. *Capone's Chicago*. Lakeville, Minn.: Northstar-Maschek, 1987.

Cowen, Robert C. *Frontiers of the Sea: The Story of Oceanography Exploration*. New York: Doubleday, 1960.

Cowen, Thomas. *The Russo-Japanese War*. London: Edward Arnold, 1904.

Cowherd, Raymond J. *The Politics of English Dissent: The Religious Aspects of Liberal and Humanitarian Reform Movements from 1915 to 1848*. New York: New York University Press, 1956.

Cowie, J., Cowie, V., and Slater, E. *Delinquency in Girls*. London: William Heinemann, 1968.

Cowles, Calvin Duvall. *Genealogy of the Cowles Family in America*. 2 vols. New Haven, Conn.: Tuttle, Morehouse & Taylor, 1929.

Cowles, Virginia. *The Great Swindle*. New York: Harper & Brothers., 1960.

_____. *The Kaiser*. New York: Harper & Row, 1963.

_____. *No Cause for Alarm: The Story of the Labor Government*. New York: Harper, 1940.

Cowles Education, and UPI. *Assassination, Robert F. Kennedy, 1925-1968*. New York: Cowles Education, 1968.

Cowley, Malcolm. *Exile's Return*. New York: W.W. Norton, 1922.

Cowling, Mary Jo. *Geography of Denton County*. Dallas: Banks Upshaw, 1936.

Cox, Archibald. *The Warren Court*. Cambridge, Mass.: Harvard University Press, 1968.

Cox, Arthur Macy. *The Myths of National Security*. Boston: Beacon Press, 1975.

Cox, Edward R., et al. *Nader's Raiders: Report on the Federal*

Trade Commission. New York: Grove Press, 1969.

Cox, Eugene. *The Green Count of Savoy: Amadeus VI and Transalpine Savoy in the Fourteenth Century.* Princeton, N.J.: Princeton University Press, 1967.

Cox, J. Charles. *The Marriage of the Duke of Edinburgh.* London: E. Truelove, 1873.

Cox, J.R. *Kenyeatta's Country.* London: Hutchinson, 1965.

Cox, James. *My Native Land.* St. Louis: Blair, 1895.

Cox, James M. *Journey Through My Years, An Autobiography.* New York: Simon & Schuster, 1947.

Cox, John Harrington. *Folk-Songs of the South.* Cambridge, Mass.: Harvard University Press, 1925.

Cox, Robert V. *Deadly Pursuit.* New York: Cameron House, 1977.

_____, and Peiffer, Kenneth L. *Missing Person.* Harrisburg, Pa.: Stackpole Books, 1979.

Cox, Samuel Hanson. *Interviiews, Memorable and Useful.* New York: Harper & Brothers, 1855.

Cox, William R. *Luke Short and His Era.* Garden City, N.Y.: Doubleday, 1961.

Coxe, William. *Account of the Russian Discoveries Between Asia and America.* London: T. Cadell, 1780.

Coynart, Charles de. *Une Sorcière au xviii siècle: Marie-Anne de la Ville, 1680-1725.* Paris: Hachette, 1902.

Coyne, F.E. *In Reminiscence: Highlights of Men and Events in the Life of Chicago.* Chicago: Excella Press, 1941.

Cozier, Brian. *Annual of Power and Conflict 1976, 1977, 1978.* London: Institute for Study of Conflict, n.d.

Crabb, Richard E. *Empire on the Platte.* New York: World, 1967.

Crafts, Rev. Wilbur F. *Why Dry? Briefs for Prohibition Local, State National and International.* Washington, D.C.: International Reform Bureau, 1918.

Craig, Albert M. *Choshu in the Meiji Restoration.* Cambridge, Mass.: Harvard University Press, 1967.

Craig, Gordon A. *The Battle of Königgrätz.* London: Weidenfeld & Nicholson, 1964.

_____, and Gilbert, Felix. *The Diplomats, 1919-39.* Princeton, N.J.: Princeton University Press, 1953.

_____. *The Politics of the Prussian Army 1640-1945.* New York: Oxford University Press, 1964.

Craig, Newton N. *Thrills 1861 to 1887.* Oakland, Calif.: Published by Author, 1931.

Craig, Richard B. *The Bracero Program: Interest Groups and Foreign Policy.* Austin: University of Texas Press, 1951.

Craig, William. *The Fall of Japan.* New York: Dial Press, 1967.

Craighead, Erwin. *Mobile: Fact and Tradition.* Mobile, Ala.: Powers Printing, 1930.

Craigie, Sir Robert. *Behind the Japanese Mask.* London: Hutchinson, 1945.

Craigmyle, Lord. *John Marshall in Diplomacy and Law.* New York: Charles Scribner's Sons, 1933.

Craine, J.V. *The Conspirators' Victims.* Sacramento, Calif.: Gardiner & Kirk, 1855.

Cramer, James. *The World's Police.* London: Cassell, 1964.

Cramer, James A. (ed.). *Preventing Crime.* Beverly Hills, Calif.: Sage, 1978.

Cramer, Zadok. *The Navigator.* Pittsburgh, Pa.: Cramer & Spear, 1811.

Crandall, A.W. *The Early History of the Republican Party 1854-1856.* Boston: R.G. Badger, 1930.

_____. *The Growth of Southern Nationalism 1848-1861.* Baton Rouge: Louisiana State University Press, 1953.

Crandall, Allen. *The Man from Kinsman.* Sterling, Colo.: published by the author, 1933.

Crane, Milton (ed.). *Sins of New York.* New York: Boni & Gaer, 1947.

Crane, Paul S. *Korea Patterns.* Seoul, S.Kor.: Royal Asiatic Society, 1978.

Crane, Stephen. *Maggie.* Gainesville, Fla.: Scholars' Facsimiles

and Reprints, 1966.

Crane, Verner Winslow. *The Southern Frontier 1670-1732.* Durham, N.C.: Duke University Press, 1928.

Crane, Walter R. *Gold and Silver.* New York: John Wiley & Sons, 1908.

Cranfill, James Britton. *Dr. J.B. Cranfill's Chronicle.* New York: H. Revell, 1916.

_____. *From Memory.* Nashville, Tenn.: Boardman Press, 1931.

Crankshaw, Edward. *Cracks in the Kremlin Wall.* New York: Viking Press, 1951.

_____. *Gestapo, Instrument of Tyranny.* New York: Viking Press, 1956.

_____. *Khruscev Remembers.* Boston: Little, Brown, 1970.

Cranworth, L.A. *Colony in the Making, or Sport and Profit in British East Africa.* London: Macmillan, 1912.

Crapsey, Edward. *The Nether Side of New York; or The Vice, Crime and Poverty of the Great Metropolis.* New York: Sheldon, 1872.

Crater, Stella Force, with Fraley, Oscar. *The Empty Robe.* Garden City, N.Y.: Doubleday, 1961.

Craton, Michael. *A History of the Bahamas.* London: Collins, 1962.

Craven, A.O. *The Coming of the Civil War.* New York: Charles Scribner's Sons, 1942.

Craven, Avery. *Memories of the White House.* Boston: Little, Brown, 1911.

_____. *Through Five Administrations.* New York: Harper & Brothers, 1910.

Craven, John J. *Prison Life of Jefferson Davis.* New York: Dillingham, 1866.

Craven, Wesley Frank. *The Colonies in Transition 1660-1713.* New York: Harper & Row, 1967.

_____, and Cate, James Lea (eds.). *Plans and Early Operations: January 1939 to August 1942.* Chicago: University of Chicago Press, 1948.

_____. *The Southern Colonies in the Seventeenth Century.* Baton Rouge: Louisiana State University Press, 1949.

Crawford, Alan. *Thunder on the Right: The New Right and the Politics of Resentment.* New York: Pantheon, 1980.

Crawford, Francis Marion. *Southern Italy and Sicily and the Rulers of the South.* London: Macmillan, 1900.

Crawford, Lewis Ferandus. *Rekindling Camp Fires: The Exploits of Ben Arnold (Connor).* Bismarck, N.D.: Capital Books, 1926.

Crawford, Mary Caroline. *Famous Families of Massachusetts.* Boston: Little, Brown, 1930.

Crawford, P.L., et al. *Working with Teenage Gangs.* New York: Welfare Council of New York City, 1950.

Crawford, Samuel J. *Kansas in the Sixties.* Chicago: A.C. McClurg, 1911.

Crawford, Thomas Edgar. *The West of the Texas Kid, 1881-1910.* Norman: University of Oklahoma Press, 1962.

Crawford, William. *Report on the Penitentiaries of the United States.* Montclair, N.J.: Patterson Smith, 1969.

Crawley, C.W. *The Question of Greek Independence: A Study of British Policy in the Near East, 1821-1833.* Cambridge, Eng.: Cambridge Universtiy Press, 1930.

Crawley, Ernest. *The Mystic Rose.* New York: Meridian Books, 1960.

Cray, Ed. *The Big Blue Line.* New York: Coward McCann, 1967.

_____. *Burden of Proof.* New York: MacMillian, 1973.

Creel, George. *Ireland's Fight for Freedom.* New York: Harper, 1919.

_____. *The People Next Door.* New York: John Day, 1926.

_____. *Rebel at Large: Recollections of Fifty Crowded Years.* New York: G.P. Putnam's Sons, 1947.

_____. *Wilson and the Issues.* New York: Century, 1916.

Creelman, James. *Diaz, Master of Mexico.* New York: D. Appleton, 1911.

Creer, Leland. *Utah and the Nation.* Seattle: University of Washington Press, 1929.

Creger, Ralph and Carl. *This Is What We Found.* New York: Lyle Stuart, 1960.

Creighton, Mandell. *A History of the Papacy From the Great Schism to the Sack of Rome.* New York: Longmans, Green, 1911.

_____. *Memoir of Sir George Grey Bart.* London: Longmans, Green, 1901.

Crelinstein, Ronald D., and Szabo, Denis. *Hostage-Taking.* Lexington, Mass.: Lexington Books, 1979.

_____, et al. *Terrorism and Criminal Justice.* Lexington, Mass.: D.C. Heath, 1978.

Cremeans, Charles D. *The Arabs and the World.* New York: Praeger, 1963.

Crenshaw, Files, and Miller, Kenneth A. *Scottsboro: The Firebrand of Communism.* Montgomery, Ala.: Brown Printing, 1936.

Crenshaw, Ollinger. *The Slave States in the Presidential Election of 1860.* Baltimore, Md.: Johns Hopkins Press, 1945.

Crépet, M.J. (ed.). *Oeuvres complétes de Charles Baudelaire.* Paris: Louis Conard, 1928.

Crespet, Pierre. *De la Hayne de Sathan et malins esprits contre l'homme.* Paris: Guillaume de la Novë, 1590.

Cressey, Donald R. *Crime and Criminal Justice.* New York: Quadrangle, 1971.

_____. *Criminal Organization: Its Elementary Forms.* New York: Harper & Row, 1972.

_____. *Criminal Psychology.* Philadelphia: J.B. Lippincott, 1974.

_____. *Delinquency, Crime and Differential Association.* The Hague, Neth.: Martinus Nijhoff, 1964.

_____, and McDermott, Robert A. *Diversion from the Juvenile Justice System.* Washington, D.C.: National Institute of Law Enforcement and Criminal Justice, 1974.

_____. *Organized Crime Task Force Report.* Washington, D.C.: U.S. Government Printing Office, 1967.

_____. *Other People's Money.* New York: Free Press, 1953.

_____ (ed.). *The Prison: Studies in Institutional Organization and Change.* New York: Holt, Rinehart & Winston, 1961.

_____. *Theft of the Nation.* New York: Harper & Row, 1969.

Cresson, Ernest. *Cent jours du siège à la prèfecture de police.* Paris: Plon-Nourrit, 1901.

Cresson, W.P. *James Monroe.* Chapel Hill: University of North Carolina Press, 1946.

Crew, Albert. *The Old Bailey.* London: Ivor Nicholson & Watson, 1933.

Crichton, Kyle S. *Law and Order, Ltd.: The Rousing Life of Elfego Baca of New Mexico.* Glorieta, N.M.: Rio Grande Press, 1928.

Crichton, Michael. *Terminal Man.* New York: Alfred A. Knopf, 1972.

Crichton, Robert. *The Great Impostor.* New York: Random House, 1959.

The Crime Avenged or Guiteau on the Gallows. New York: Richard K. Fox, 1882.

Crime Prevention Officers' Handbook. Santa Rosa, Calif.: California Crime Prevention Institute, 1978.

Crimes and Punishment. London: BPC Publishing, 1973.

Crimes and Victims: A Report on the Dayton-San Jose Pilot Survey of Victimization. Washington, D.C.: National Criminal Justice Information and Statistics Service, 1974.

The Criminal Investigation Process: A Dialogue on Research Findings. Washington, D.C.: National Institute of Law Enforcement and Criminal Justice, 1977.

Criminal Statistics, England and Wales. London: H.M. Stationery Office, 1950.

Criminal Victimization in the United States. National Criminal Justice Information and Statistics Service, annual volumes since 1973.

Criminal Victimization in the United States, 1973. A National Crime Survey Report. U.S. Department of Justice, Law Enforcement Assistance Administration. Washington, D.C.: U.S. Government Printing Office, 1976.

Criminal Victimization in the United States, A Comparison of 1973 and 1974 Findings. A National Crime Survey Report. Washington, D.C.: Government Printing Office, 1976.

Cripps, Sir Stafford. *Democracy Up-to-Date.* London: George Allen & Unwin, 1939.

_____. *Why This Socialism?* London: Victor Gollancz, 1934.

Crisis at Columbia: Criminal Victimization in the United States, A Comparison of 1974 and 1975 Findings. National Crime Survey Report. Washington, D.C.: U.S. Government Printing Office, 1977.

Crispe, T.E. *Reminiscences of a K.C.* London: Methuen, 1909.

Crispoldi, Filippo. *Politici, Guerrieri, Poeti.* Milan, Italy: Treves, 1939.

Crissey, Elwell. *Lincoln's Lost Speech: The Pivot of His Career.* New York: Hawthorn Books, 1967.

Critchley, M. (ed.). *The Trial of Neville George Clevely Heath.* London: Hodge, 1951.

_____, and James. P.D. *The Maul and the Pear Tree.* London: Constable, 1971.

Critchley, T.A. *The Conquest of Violence.* London: Constable, 1970.

_____. *A History of Police in England and Wales 1900-1966.* London: T. & A. Constable, 1967.

Crites, Arthur S. *Pioneer Days in Kern County.* Los Angeles: Ward Ritchie Press, 1951.

Crites, Laura (ed.). *The Female Offender.* Lexington, Mass.: D.C. Heath, 1976.

Critical Reactions to the Warren Report. New York: Marzani & Munsell, 1965.

Crittenden, Henry Huston. *The Crittenden Memoirs.* New York: G.P. Putnam's Sons, 1936.

Crocker, W.C. *Far From Humdrum: A Lawyer's Life.* London: Hutchinson, 1967.

Crockett, Albert Stevens. *Peacocks on Parade.* New York: Sears, 1931.

Crockett, George Louis. *Two Centuries in East Texas.* Dallas: Southwest Press, 1932.

Crockett, W.S. *The Scott Originals, An Account of Notables & Worthies; The Originals of Characters in the Waverley Novels.* New York: Charles Scribner's Sons, 1913.

Croft-Cook, Rupert, and Meadmore, W.S. *Buffalo Bill, the Legend, the Man of Action, the Showman.* London: Sidwick & Jackson, 1952.

Croffut, W.A. *The Vanderbilts, and the Story of Their Fortune.* New York: Belford, Clarke, 1886.

Crofutt, George A. *Crofutt's Grip Sack Guide of Colorado.* Omaha, Neb.: Overland, 1881.

Croghan, George. *George Croghan's Journal of His Trip to Detroit in 1767.* Ann Arbor: University of Michigan Press, 1939.

Croker, John W. *The Croker Papers. The Correspondence and Diaries of the Late Right Honourable J.W. Croker.* 3 vols. London: John Murray, 1885.

Croker, Richard. *Some Things Richard Croker Has Said and Done.* New York: City Club of New York, 1901.

Croly, David G. *Seymour and Blair: Their Lives and Services.* New York: Richardson, 1868.

Croly, H.A. *Marcus Alonzo Hanna.* New York: Macmillan, 1912.

Cromer, Earl of. *Modern Egypt.* 2 vols. London: Macmillan, 1908.

Cromie, Robert. *The Great Chicago Fire.* New York: McGraw-Hill, 1958.

_____, and Pinkston, Joseph. *Dillinger, A Short and Violent Life.* New York: McGraw-Hill, 1962.

Cromwell, Helen, and Dougherty, Robert. *Dirty Helen.* Los Angeles: Sherbourne Press, 1966.

Cromwell, John Wesley. *The Negro in American History.* New York: Johnson Reprints, 1968.

Cronin, Bernard Cornelius. *Father Yorke and the Labor Movement in San Francisco, 1900-1910.* Washington, D.C.: Catholic University of America Press, 1943.

Cronin, Harley. *The Screw Turns.* London: Long, 1967.

Cronin, John F. *Communism: A World Menace.* Washington, D.C.: National Catholic Welfare Conference, 1947.

Cronin, John William, and Wise, W. Harvey. *A Bibliography of John Adams and John Quincy Adams.* Washington, D.C.: Riverford, 1935.

Cronin, Thomas E., et al. *U.S. v. Crime in the Streets.* Bloomington: Indiana University Press, 1981.

Cronon, E. David (ed.). *The Cabinet Diaries of Josephus Daniels: 1913-1921.* Lincoln: University of Nebraska Press, 1963.

Crook, G.T., and Rayner, John L. (eds.). *The Complete Newgate Calendar.* London: Navarre Society, 1926.

Crook, Wilfred H. *The General Strike.* Chapel Hill: University of North Carolina, 1931.

_____. *Memories of the White House.* Boston: Little, Brown, 1911.

_____. *Through Five Administrations.* New York: Harper & Brothers, 1907.

Crook, William. *Through Five Administrations.* New York: Harper & Brothers, 1907.

Crookall, Robert. *Out-of-the-Body Experiences.* New Hyde Park, N.Y.: University Books, 1970.

Crosby, A.W. *America, Russia, Hemp and Napoleon.* Columbus: Ohio State University Press, 1965.

Crosby, Caresse. *The Passionate Years.* Carbondale: Southern Illinois University Press, 1968.

Cross, A.R.N. *Punishment, Prison and the Public.* London: Stevens & Sons, 1971.

Cross, Colin. *The Fall of the British Empire, 1918-1968.* New York: Coward-McCann, 1968.

Cross, Ira Brown. *Financing an Empire.* 4 vols. Chicago: S.J. Clarke, 1927.

_____. *A History of the Labor Movement in California.* Berkeley: University of California Press, 1935.

Cross, R. *The English Sentencing System.* London: Butterworth, 1971.

_____. *Evidence.* London: Butterworth, 1958.

_____, and Jones, P.A. *An Introduction to Criminal Law.* London: Butterworth, 1959.

_____. *Precedent in English Law.* Oxford, Eng.: Clarendon, 1968.

Cross, S.H. *Slavic Civilization through the Ages.* Cambridge, Mass.: Harvard University Press, 1948.

Crosskey, W.C.S. *The Single Fingerprint Identification System.* San Francisco: Privately Printed, 1923.

Crossman, Richard (ed.). *The God That Failed.* New York: Bantam, 1954.

_____. *Palestine Mission.* New York: Harper, 1947.

Crosthwait, William L., and Fisher, Ernest G. *The Last Stitch.* Philadelphia: J.B. Lippincott, 1956.

Crothers, Thomas D. *Morphinism and Narcomanias From Other Drugs.* Philadelphia: W.B. Saunders, 1902.

Crotty, William J. (ed.). *Assassination and the Political Order.* New York: Harper & Row, 1972.

Crouch, Carrie J. *A History of Young County, Texas.* Austin: Texas State Historical Association, 1956.

Crouch, Nathaniel. *The Kingdom of Darkness.* London: A. Bettesworth, 1738.

Crouse, Russell. *It Seems Like Yesterday.* Garden City, N.Y.: Doubleday, Doran, 1931.

_____. *Murder Won't Out.* Garden City, N.Y.: Doubleday, Doran, 1932.

_____. *Twelve Unsolved New York Murders.* Garden City, N.Y.: Doubleday, Doran, 1936.

Crouse, Timothy. *The Boys on the Bus.* New York: Random House, 1972.

Crouthamel, James L. *James Watson Webb: A Biography.* Middletown, Conn.: Wesleyan University Press, 1969.

Crow, Carl. *Foreign Devils in the Flowery Kingdom.* New York: Harper, 1940.

_____. *400 Million Customers.* New York: Harper, 1937.

_____ (ed.). *Japan's Dream of World Empire: The Tanaka Memorial.* New York: Harper & Brothers, 1942.

Crow, Duncan. *The Victorian Woman.* London: Allen & Unwin, 1972.

Crow, W.B. *A History of Magic, Witchcraft, and Occultism.* London: Aquarian, 1968.

Crowe, Catherine. *The Night Side of Nature.* London: T.C. Newby, 1848.

Crowe, Pat. *Pat Crowe, His Story, Confession and Reformation.* New York: G.W. Dillingham, 1906.

_____. *Spreading Evil.* New York: Branwell, 1927.

Crowell, Chester Theodore. *Liquor, Loot and Ladies.* New York: Alfred A. Knopf, 1930.

Crowinshield, Francis W. *Manners for the Metropolis.* New York: Appleton, 1908.

Crowley, Aleister. *The Book of Thoth.* New York: Lancer Books, 1971.

_____. *The Confessions of Aleister Crowley: An Autohagiography.* London: Cape, 1969.

_____. *Diary of a Drug Fiend.* London: William Collins Sons, 1922.

Crowley, James B. *Japan's Quest for Autonomy: National Security and Foreign Policy 1930-1938.* Princeton, N.J.: Princeton University Press, 1966.

Crown, James Tracy. *The Kennedy Literature.* New York: New York University Press, 1968.

Crowne, D., and Marlow, D. *The Approval Motive.* New York: Wiley, 1964.

Crowninshield, Mary Boardman. *Letters.* Cambridge, Mass.: Riverside Press, 1935.

Croy, Homer. *Corn Country.* New York: Duell, Sloan & Pearce, 1947.

_____. *He Hanged Them High.* New York: Duell, Sloan & Pearce, 1952.

_____. *Jesse James Was My Neighbor.* New York: Duell, Sloan & Pearce, 1949.

_____. *Last of the Great Outlaws: The Story of Cole Younger.* New York: Duell, Sloan & Pearce, 1956.

_____. *Trigger Marshall: The Story of Chris Madden.* New York: Duell, Sloan & Pearce, 1958.

Crozier, Brian (ed.). *Annual of Power and Conflict.* London: Institute for the Study of Conflict, 1976.

_____. *Strategy of Survival.* New Rochelle, N.Y.: Arlington House, 1978.

Crozier, C.W. *Life and Trial of Dr. Abner Baker, Jr.* Louisville, Ky.: Prentice & Weissinger, 1846.

Crozier, Emmet. *Yankee Reporters, 1861-65.* New York: Oxford University Press, 1956.

Crozier, Frank P. *Ireland Forever!* London: Cape, 1932.

_____. *The Men I Killed.* New York: Doubleday, Doran, 1938.

Crozier, Michael. *The Bureaucratic Phenomenon.* Chicago: University of Chicago Press, 1964.

Crozier, R.H. *The Bloody Junto.* Little Rock, Ark.: Woodruff & Blocher, 1869.

Crum, Bartley. *Behind the Silken Curtain.* New York: Simon & Schuster, 1947.

Crumbine, Samuel J. *Frontier Doctor.* Philadelphia: Dorrance, 1948.

Crump, Irving, and Newton, John W. *Our G-Men.* New York: Dodd, Mead, 1937.

Cruse, Harold. *The Crisis of the Negro Intellectual.* New York: William Morrow, 1967.

Cruttwell, C.R.M. *A History of the Great War, 1914-18.* New York: Oxford University Press, 1936.

Cruz, Nicky. *Satan on the Loose.* Old Tappan, N.J.: Fleming H. Revell, 1973.

Csida, J.B., and Csida, J. *Rape: How to Avoid It and What to Do if You Can't.* Chatsworth, Calif.: Books for Better Living,

1974.

Cucco, Alfredo. *Non volevamo perder.* Bologna, Italy: Cappelli, 1950.

Cuddihy, R.J., and Shuster, G.N. *Pope Pius XI and American Public Opinion.* New York: Funk & Wagnalls, 1939.

Cudet, Francoil. *Histoire des corps de troupe qui ont été spéciale-ment chargés de service de la ville de Paris depuis son origine jusqu'à nos jours.* Paris: Léon Pillet, 1887.

Culin, Stewart. *A Trooper's Narrative of Service in the Anthracite Coal Strike, 1902.* Philadelphia: George W. Jacobs, 1903.

Cull, John G., and Hardy, Richard E. (eds.). *Types of Drug Abusers and Their Abuses.* Springfield, Ill.: Charles C. Thomas, 1970.

Cullen, Tom. *Autumn of Terror: Jack the Ripper, His Crimes and Times.* London: Bodley Head, 1965.

_____. *The Mild Murderer: The True Story of the Dr. Crippen Case.* Boston: Houghton Mifflin, 1977.

_____. *A Playful Panther: The Story of J. Maundy Gregory.* Boston: Houghton Mifflin, 1975.

_____. *When London Walked In Terror.* Boston: Houghton Mifflin, 1965.

Culley, John Henry. *Cattle, Horses & Men of the Western Range.* Los Angeles: Ward Ritchie Press, 1940.

Cullom, Shelby M. *Fifty Years of Public Service.* Chicago: A.C. McClurg, 1911.

Cullop, Charles P. *Confederate Propaganda in Europe, 1861-1865.* Coral Gables, Fla.: University of Miami Press, 1969.

Culpin, Howard. *The Newgate Noose.* London: Frederick Muller, Ltd. 1951.

Cumberland, Charles Curtis. *Mexican Revolution: The Con-stitutionalist Years.* Austin: University of Texas Press, 1974.

_____. *Mexican Revolution: Genesis Under Madero.* Austin: University of Texas Press, 1952.

_____. *Mexico: The Struggle for Modernity.* New York: Oxford University Press, 1968.

Cumings, Samuel. *The Western Pilot.* Cincinnati, Ohio: Morgan, Lodge & Fisher, 1825.

Cumming, Sir John (ed.). *Political India, 1832-1932.* New York: Oxford University Press, 1932.

Cumming, John, and Elaine. *Ego and Milieu.* New York: Atherton Press, 1962.

Cumming, W.P., et al. *The Exploration of North America, 1630-1776.* New York: G.P. Putnam's Sons, 1974.

Cummings, C.L. *The Great War Relic.* Harrisburg, Pa.: Meyers, n.d.

Cummings, Homer, and McFarland, Carl. *Federal Justice: Chap-ters in the History of Justice in the Federal Executive.* New York: Da Capo, 1970.

_____. *Selected Papers.* New York: Charles Scribner's Sons, 1939.

Cummins, Jim. *Jim Cummins' Book.* Denver: Reed, 1903.

_____. *Jim Cummins the Guerrilla.* Excelsior Springs, Mo.: The Daily Journal, 1908.

Cummins, Harold, and Midlo, Charles. *Finger Prints, Palms and Soles.* New York: Dover Publications, 1961.

Cumont, Franz. *Les religions orientales dans le paganisme romain.* Paris: E. Leroux, 1906.

Cunha, W. de B. *Eight Centuries of Portugese Monarchy: A Political Study.* London: Stephen Swift, 1911.

Cunliffe, Marcus. *The Age of Expansion: 1848-1917.* Springfield, Mass.: G. and C. Merriam, 1873.

_____. *Soldiers & Civilians: The Martial Spirit in America, 1775-1865.* Boston: Little, Brown, 1968.

Cunningham, Barry, Pearl, and Mike. *Mr. District Attorney.* New York: Mason/sharter, 1977.

Cunningham, Eugene. *Famous in the West.* El Paso, Texas: Hicks-Haywood, 1926.

_____. *Triggernometry: A Gallery of Gunfighters.* New York: Press of the Pioneers, 1934.

Cunningham, James Charles. *The Truth About Murietta: Aneco-dotes and Facts Related by Those Who Knew Him and*

Disbelieve His Capture. Los Angeles: Wetzel, 1938.

Cunningham, N.E., Jr. *The Jeffersonian Republicans: The Forma-tion of Party Organization, 1789-1801.* Chapel Hill: Univer-sity of North Carolina Press, 1958.

_____. *The Jeffersonian Republicans in Power: Party Operations 1801-1809.* Chapel Hill: University of North Carolina Press, 1963.

Cunningham, Robert E. *Trial by Mob.* Stillwater, Okla.: Redland Press, 1957.

Cunnington, C. Willett. *Feminine Attitudes in the Nineteenth Century.* London: Heinemann, 1935.

Cunynghame, Sir Arthur Augustus Thurlow. *A Glimpse at the Great Western Republic.* London: R. Bentley, 1851.

Cupta, Manmathnat. *History of the Indian Revolutionist Move-ment.* Bombay: Somaiya Publications, 1972.

Curbing the Repeat Offender: A Strategy for Prosecutors. Washing-ton, D.C.: Institute for Law and Social Research, 1977.

Curina, Antonio. *Fuochi sui monti dell' Appennino toscano.* Arezzo, Italy: Badiali, 1957.

Curley, James Michael. *I'd Do It Again.* Englewood Cliffs, N.J.: Prentice-Hall, 1957.

Curling, J. *Janus Weathercock: The Life of Thomas Griffiths Wainewright.* New York: Nelson, 1938.

Curran, Henry H. *Pillar to Post.* New York: Charles Scribner's Sons, 1941.

Curran, J.J. *Mr. Foley, of Salmon.* San Jose, Calif.: Published by Author, 1907.

Curran, James, Boyce, George, and Wingate, Pauline (eds.). *Newspaper History.* London: Constable, 1978.

Current, Richard N., et al. *American History: A Survey.* New York: Alfred A. Knopf, 1975.

_____. *Daniel Webster and the Rise of National Conservatism.* Boston: Little, Brown, 1955.

_____. *John C. Calhoun.* New York: Washington Square, 1966.

Currey, Cecil B. *Road to Revolution.* Garden City, N.Y.: Doubleday, 1968.

Currey, J. Seymour. *Chicago: Its History and Builders.* 5 vols. Chicago: S.J. Clarke, 1912.

Currey, Muriel. *Italian Foreign Policy, 1918-32.* London: Ivor Nicholson & Watson, 1932.

_____. *A Woman at the Abyssinian War.* London: Hutchinson, 1936.

Currier, Frederick A. *A Trip to the Great Lakes.* Fitchburg, Mass.: Sentimental, 1904.

Curry, Mrs. Bell. *Parsons, Labette County, Kansas.* Parson, Kan.: Bell Bookcraft Shop, n.d.

Curry, J.C. *The Indian Police.* London: Faber & Faber, 1935.

Curry, Jesse. *Personal JFK Assassination File.* Dallas: American Poster and Printing, 1969.

Curry, Leroy A. *The Ku Klux Klan under the Searchlight.* Kansas City, Mo.: Western Baptist, 1924.

Curry, Richard O. (ed.). *The Abolitionists: Reformers or Fanatics?* New York: Holt, Rinehart & Winston, 1965.

Curry, Roy M. *Woodrow Wilson and Far Eastern Policy, 1913-1921.* New York: Bookman Associates, 1957.

Curry, S.H., and Joyce, C.B.R. (eds.). *Botany and Chemistry of Cannabis.* London: Churchill, 1970.

Curtayne, Alice. *The Irish Story.* Dublin, Ire.: Clonmore & Reynolds, 1962.

Curti, Merle. *The American Struggle, 1636-1936.* New York: W.W. Norton, 1936.

_____. *Austria and the United States 1848-1852,* Northampton, Mass.: Smith College Studies in History, 1926.

_____. *The Growth of American Thought.* New York: Harper & Brothers, 1943.

Curtin, Jeremiah. *A Journey in Southern Siberia.* Boston: Little, Brown, 1909.

_____. *The Mongols: A History.* Boston: Little, Brown, 1908.

Curtin, Philip (Marie Belloc-Lowndes). *Noted Murder Mysteries.* London: Simpkin, Marshall, Hamilton, Kent, 1914.

Curtin, Philip D. *Africa Remembered: Narratives by West Africans from the Era of the Slave Trade.* Madison: University of Wisconsin Press, 1967.

Curtis, Albert. *Fabulous San Antonio.* San Antonio, Texas: Naylor, 1955.

Curtis, Charles P. *It's Your Law.* Cambridge, Mass.: Harvard University Press, 1954.

_____. *The Law as Large as Life: A Natural History for Today and the Supreme Court as Its Prophet.* New York: Simon & Schuster, 1959.

_____. *Lions Under the Throne.* Boston: Houghton, Mifflin, 1947.

_____. *Oppenheimer Case.* New York: Simon & Schuster, 1955.

Curtis, George Ticknon. *Life of James Buchanan.* New York: Harper & Brothers, 1883.

Curtis, Gerald L. *Election Campaigning Japanese Style.* Tokyo: Kodansha, 1983.

Curtis, J. *The Murder of Maria Marten.* New York: Pellegrini & Cudahy, 1948.

Curtis, Lynn A. *Criminal Violence: National Patterns and Behavior.* Lexington, Mass.: D.C. Heath, 1974.

_____. *Violence, Race, and Culture.* Lexington, Mass.: D.C. Heath, 1975.

Curtis, Nathaniel Cortland. *New Orleans.* Philadelphia: n.p., 1933.

Curtis, Winterton C. *Fundamentalism vs. Evolution at Danton, Tennessee.* Private Printing, 1956.

Curtiss, Arthur F. *The Law of Arson.* Buffalo, N.Y.: Dennis, 1936.

Curtiss, John S. *Church and State in Russia: The Last Years of the Empire, 1900-1917.* New York: Columbia University Press, 1940.

_____. *The Russian Army Under Nicholas I (1825-1855).* Durham, N.C.: Duke University Press, 1965.

_____. *The Russian Church and Soviet State, 1917-1950.* Boston: Little, Brown, 1953.

_____. *The Russian Revolutions of 1917.* Princeton, N.J.: Van Nostrand, 1957.

Curvin, Robert, and Porter, Bruce. *A Report on the Blackout Looting.* Unpublished report to the Ford Foundation, 1978.

Curzon, Sam. *Legs Diamond.* New York: Tower, 1962.

Cushing, Marshall. *The Story of Our Post Office.* Boston: A.N. Thayer, 1893.

Cushman, Dan. *The Great North Trail.* New York: McGraw-Hill, 1966.

Cusket, Walter, et al. *Drug-Trip Aboad: American Drug Refugees in Amsterdam and London.* Philadelphia: University of Pennsylvania Press, 1972.

Cust, Robert Needham. *Pictures of Indian Life: Sketched with the Pen from 1852 to 1881.* London: Trübner, 1881.

Cust, Sir Lionel. *King Edward and His Court: Some Reminiscences.* London: Murray, 1930.

Custer, George Armstrong. *My Life on the Plains.* New York: Sheldon, 1874.

Custine, Astolphe L.L. *The Empire of the Czar.* London: Longmans, 1843.

Custis, John and Freeman, Thomas. *Jefferson and Southwestern Expansion: The Freeman and Custis Accounts of the Red River Expedition of 1806.* Norman: University of Oklahoma Press, 1984.

Cuthbert, C.R.M. *Science and the Detection of Crime.* New York: Philosophical Lib., 1958.

Cuthbert, Norma B. (ed.). *Lincoln and the Baltimore Plot 1861.* San Marino, Calif.: Huntington Library, 1949.

Cutler, James E. *Lynch-Law: An Investigation into the History of Lynching in the United States.* New York: Longmans, Green, 1905.

Cutler, John Henry. *Honey Fitz: Three Steps to the White House.* Indianapolis: Bobbs-Merrill, 1962.

Cutler, Leland W. *America is Good to a Country Boy.* Palo Alto, Calif.: Stanford University Press, 1954.

Cutler, R.B. *Crossfire: Evidence of Conspiracy.* Beverly, Mass.: Omni-Print, 1972.

_____. *The Flight of CE 399: Evidence of Conspiracy.* Manchester, Mass.: published by the author, 1969.

_____. *Mr. Chairman: Evidence of a Conspiracy.* Manchester, Mass: Cutler Designs, 1978.

_____. *Seventy-Six Seconds in Dealey Plaza.* Manchester, Mass.: Cutler Designs, 1978.

_____. *The Umbrella Man: Evidence of a Conspiracy.* Manchester, Mass.: Cutler Designs, 1975.

Cutrera, Antonio. *La Mafia e i mafiosi: origini e manifestazioni studio di sociologia criminale.* Palermo, Italy: Alberto Reber, 1900.

Cutright, Paul Russell. *Lewis and Clark: Pioneering Naturalists.* Urbana: University of Illinois Press, 1969.

Cutting, Rose Marie. *John and William Bartram, William Byrd II and St. John de Crèvecoeur: A Reference Guide.* Boston: G.K. Hall, 1976.

Cuyler, Jacob S. *Trial of Reuben Dunbar for the Murder of Stephen V. Lester and David L. Lester.* Albany, N.Y.: P.L. Gilbert, 1850.

Cuyler, Theodore Ledyard. *Recollections of a Long Life.* New York: American Tract Society, 1902.

Cyril Vladimirovitch, Grand Duke of Russia. *My Life in Russia's Service.* London: Selwyn & Blount, 1939.

Czernin, Count Ferdinand. *This Salzburg.* New York: Greystone Press, 1938.

Czernin, Count Ottokar. *In the World War.* London: Cassell, 1919.

D

Dabney, Virginius. *Dry Messiah—The Life of Bishop James Cannon, Jr.* New York: Alfred A. Knopf, 1949.

Dacheux, J. *Jean Geiler von Kaisersberg.* Freiberg, Ger.: Herder, 1877.

Dacus, Joseph A. *Annals of the Great Strikes in the United States.* Chicago: L.T. Palmer, 1877.

_____. *Life and Adventures of Frank and Jesse James, the Noted Western Outlaws.* St. Louis: N.D. Thompson, 1880.

_____. *Illustrated Lives and Adventures of Frank and Jesse James and the Younger Brothers, The Noted Western Outlaws.* St. Louis: N.D. Thompson, 1882.

D'Agata, Rosario. *Mussolini, l'uomo, l'idea, l'opera.* Palermo, Si.: Sandron, 1927.

Daggett, Mabel Potter. *Marie of Roumania.* New York: George H. Doran, 1926.

Daggett, Stuart. *Chapters on the History of the Southern Pacific.* New York: Ronald Press, 1922.

Daggett, Thomas F. *Billy LeRoy, the Colorado Bandit; or the King of American Highwaymen.* New York: Richard K. Fox, Police Gazette, 1881.

_____. *The Outlaw Brothers, Frank and Jesse James.* New York: Richard K. Fox, Police Gazette, 1881.

D'Agostini, Bruno. *Colloqui con Rachele Mussolini.* Rome: OET, 1946.

Dahl, Robert A. *A Preface to Democratic Theory.* Chicago: University of Chicago Press, 1963.

_____. *Who Governs: Democracy and Power in the American City.* New Haven, Conn.: Yale University Press, 1961.

Dahlberg, Jane. *The New York Bureau of Municipal Research: Pioneer in Government Administration.* New York: New York University Press, 1966.

Dahlerup, Verner. *Hexe og Hexeprocesler i Dammark.* Copenhagen: Studentersam fundets Forlag, 1888.

Dahlgren, J.V. *Memoirs of Colonel Dahlgren.* Philadelphia: J. Lippincott Company, 1872.

Dahlinger, John Cote. *The Secret Life of Henry Ford.* New York: Bobbs-Merrill, 1978.

Dahrendorf, Ralf. *Class and Class Conflicts in Industrial Society.* Stanford: Stanford University Press, 1959.

Daigon, Arthur. *Violence U.S.A.* New York: Bantam, 1975.

Daim, Wilfried. *Der Mann, der Hitler die Ideen Gab.* Munich: Isar Verlag, 1958.

Daisy, Princess of Pless. *Better Left Unsaid.* New York: E.P. Dutton, 1931.

Dakin, Douglas. *British and American Philhellenes During the War of Greek Independence, 1821-1833.* Thessaloniki, Gr.: Institute for Balkan Studies, 1955.

D'Albas, Andrieu. *Death of a Navy: Japanese Naval Action in World War II.* New York: Devin-Adair, 1957.

Dale, Edward Everett. *Cow Country.* Norman: University of Oklahoma Press, 1965.

____, and Lytton, Gaston. *Cherokee Cavaliers.* Norman: University of Oklahoma Press, 1939.

____, and Wardell, Morris L. *History of Oklahoma.* New York: Prentice-Hall, 1948.

____. *The History of the Ranch Cattle Industry in Oklahoma.* Washington, D.C.: American Historical Association, 1920.

____. *The Range Cattle Industry.* Norman: University of Oklahoma Press, 1960.

Dale, Henry. *Adventures and Exploits of the Younger Brothers, Missouri's Most Daring Outlaws, and Companions of the James Boys.* New York: Street & Smith, 1890.

D'Alessandro, Enzo. *Brigantaggio e mafia in Sicilia.* Florence, Italy: G. D'Anna, 1959.

Daley, Robert. *Prince of the City.* Boston: Houghton Mifflin, 1978.

____. *Target Blue.* New York: Dell, 1971.

____. *The Year of the Dragon.* New York: Signet Books, 1981.

Dall, Caroline Wells Healey. *The College, The Market, and the Court.* Boston: Lee and Shepard, 1867.

____. *Woman's Right to Labor.* Boston: Walker, Wise, 1860.

Dall, William Healy. *Alaska and Its Resources.* Boston: Lea & Shepherd, 1870.

Dalla Costa, Cardinal Elia. *Storia vera su Firenze 'città aperta'.* Florence, Italy: Rinaldi, 1945.

Dallas, R. C. *The History of the Maroons.* 2 vols. London: T. N. Longman and O. Rees, 1803.

Dalla Torre, Giuseppe. *Memorie.* Milan, Italy: Mondadori, 1965.

Dallin, Alexander. *German Rule in Russia, 1941-1945.* New York: Macmillan, 1957.

Dallin, David J. *The Changing World of Soviet Russia.* New Haven, Conn.: Yale University Press, 1956.

____, and Nicolaevsky, B.I. *Forced Labor in Soviet Russia.* New Haven, Conn.: Yale University Press, 1947.

____. *The Real Soviet Russia.* New Haven, Conn.: Yale University Press, 1944.

____. *Rise of Russia in Asia.* New Haven, Conn.: Yale University Press, 1949.

____. *Soviet Espionage.* New Haven, Conn.: Yale University Press, 1955.

____. *Soviet Russia and the Far East.* New Haven, Conn.: Yale University Press, 1948.

d'Alquen, Gunter. *Die SS, Geschichte, Aufgabe und Organisation der Schutzstaffel der NSDAP.* Berlin: Junker & Dünnhaupt, 1939.

Dalton, Emmett. *Beyond the Law.* New York: J.S. Ogilvie, 1918.

____. *The Dalton Brothers and Their Astounding Career of Crime.* New York: Frederick Fell, 1954.

____, and Jungmeyer, Jack. *When the Daltons Rode.* Garden City, N.Y.: Doubleday, Doran, 1931.

Dalton, Hugh. *Practical Socialism for Britain.* London: Routledge, 1935.

Dalton, Kit. *Under the Black Flag.* Memphis, Tenn.: Lockhart, 1914.

Dalton, Michael. *Country Justice.* London: Society of Stationers, 1618.

Dalton, Rev. William J. *The Life of Father Bernard Donnelly.* Kansas City: Grimes-Joyce Printing, 1921.

Daly, Maria Lydig. *Diary of a Union Lady, 1861-1865.* New York: Funk & Wagnalls, 1962.

Daly, Mary. *Gyn/Ecology.* Boston: Beacon Press, 1978.

Dalyell, Sir John Graham. *The Darker Superstitions of Scotland.* Edinburgh, Scot.: Waugh and Innes, 1834.

Dalzell, George W. *Benefit of Clergy in America.* Winston-Salem, N.C.: J.F. Blair, 1955.

Dalzell, Robert F., Jr. *Daniel Webster and the Trial of American Nationalism.* Boston: Houghton Mifflin, 1973.

Damhouder, Joost. *Enchiridion, Praxis Rerum Criminalium.* Louvain, Belg.: S. Gualther & J. Bathenii, 1554.

Damiano, Andrea. *Rosso e grigio.* Milan, Italy: Muggiani, 1947.

Damon, A., et al. *The Human Body in Equipment Design.* Cambridge, Mass.: Harvard Univesity Press, 1966.

Damore, Leo. *The Crime of Dorothy Sheridan.* New York: Arbor House, 1978.

Dampier, William. *Dampier's Voyages.* New York: E.P. Dutton, 1906.

____. *A Voyage to New Holland, etc. in the Year 1699...* London: The Crown in St. Paul's Church-Yard, 1703.

Dana, Charles A. *Recollections of the Civil War.* New York: D. Appleton, 1898.

Dana, Charles W. *The Garden of the World.* Boston: Wentworth, 1856.

Dana, James. *The Intent of Capital Punishment: A Discourse.* New Haven, Conn.: T.& S. Green, 1790.

Dana, Julian. *A.P. Giannini—Giant in the West.* New York: Prentice-Hall, 1947.

Dana, J.G. *The Man Who Built San Francisco.* New York: Macmillan, 1937.

____, and Thomas, R.S. *A Report of the Trial of Jereboam O. Beauchamp.* Frankfort, Ky.: Albert G. Hodges, 1826.

____. *Sutter of California.* New York: Halcyon House, 1938.

Dana, Richard Henry. *Two Years Before the Mast.* New York: Modern Library, 1936.

Dana, Rocky, and Harrington, Marie. *The Blonde Ranchero.* Los Angeles: Dawson's Book Shop, 1960.

Danaceau, Paul. *Methadone Maintenance.* Washington, D.C.: The Drug Abuse Council, 1973.

Dancy, J.C. *A Commentary on I Maccabees.* Oxford, Eng.: Basil Blackwell, 1954.

Dando, S. *The Japanese Law of Criminal Procedure.* trans. F.J. George. South Hackensack, N.J.: F.B. Rothman, 1965.

Dandolo, Tullio. *La Signiora di Monza e le Streghe del Tirolo, processi famosi des secolo decimosettimo.* Milan, Italy: E. Besozzi, 1855.

D'Andrea, Ugo. *La fine del regno.* Turin, Italy: SE Torinese, 1951.

Dane, G. Ezra. *Ghost Town.* New York: Tudor, 1941.

Daneau, Lambert. *Les Sorciers.* Geneva, Switz.: I. Bourgeois, 1574.

Danelski, David J., and Tulchin, Joseph S. (eds.). *The Autobiographical Notes of Charles Evans Hughes.* Cambridge, Mass.: Harvard University Press, 1973.

____. *A Supreme Court Justice is Appointed.* New York: Random House, 1964.

Danese, Orlando. *Il Re Fascista.* Mantua, Italy: Paladino, 1923.

____. *Mussolini, il Papa e la Massoneria.* Mantua, Italy: Paladino, 1923.

d'Anethan, Baroness E.M. *Fourteen Years of Diplomatic Life in Japan.* New York: McBride, Mast, 1912.

Danforth, Harold R., and Horan, James D. *The D.A.'s Man.* New York: Crown, 1957.

Danforth, J.N. *An Alarm to the Citizens of Washington: or An*

Exposure of the Evils of Intemperence. Washington, D.C.: Way and Gideon, 1830.

Dangerfield, George. *The Awakening of American Nationalism 1815-1828.* New York: Harper & Row, 1965.

_____. *Era of Good Feelings.* New York: Harcourt, Brace, 1952.

Daniels, Douglas Henry. *Pioneer Urbanites.* Philadelphia: Temple University Press, 1980.

Daniels, Jonathan. *The Devil's Backbone.* New York: McGraw-Hill, 1962.

_____. *Frontier on the Potomac.* New York: Macmillan, 1946.

_____. *Prince of Carpetbaggers.* Philadelphia: Lippincott, 1958.

_____. *The Time Between the Wars: Armistice to Pearl Harbor.* Garden City, N.Y.: Doubleday, 1966.

Daniels, Josephus. *The Wilson Era: Years of Peace, 1910-1917.* Chapel Hill: University of North Carolina Press, 1944.

Daniels, Les. *Living in Fear: A History of Horror in the Mass Media.* New York: De Capo Press, 1983.

Daniels, Robert (ed.). *A Documentary History of Communism.* New York: Random House, 1960.

Daniels, Robert V. *The Conscience of the Revolution.* Cambridge, Mass.: Harvard University Press, 1960.

_____. *Red October: The Bolshevik Revolution of 1917.* New York: Charles Scribner's Sons, 1965.

Daniels, W.H. *The Temperence Reform and Its Great Reformers.* New York: Nelson & Philips, 1879.

Daniels, Zeke. *The Life and Death of Julia C. Bulette.* Virginia City, Nev.: Lamp Post, 1958.

D'Annunzio, Mario. *Mio padre comandante di Fiume.* Genoa, Italy: Siglaeffe, 1956.

Dansette, Adrian. *L'Attentat d'Orsini.* Paris: Editions Mondiales, 1964.

_____. *Louis-Napoléon à la conquête du pouvoir.* Paris: Hachette, 1961.

_____. *Religious History of Modern France.* 2 vols. Freiburg, Ger.: Herder, 1961.

The Dansville Poisoning Case. Dansville, N.Y.: George A. Sanders, 1858.

Danto, B.L., et al. *The Human Side of Homicide.* New York: Columbia University Press, 1982.

Dantwalala, M.L. *Gandhism Reconsidered.* Bombay, India: Padma Publications, 1944.

Danzig, Allison, and Brandewein, Peter (eds.). *The Greatest Sports Stories From the New York Times.* New York: A.S. Barnes, 1951.

Da Orta, G. *Colloquies on the Simples and Drugs of India.* London: Henry Southern, 1913.

Daraul, Arkon. *A History of Secret Societies.* New York: Pocket Books, 1969.

Darby, Ada Claire. *"Show Me" Missouri.* Kansas City: Burton, 1938.

D'Arcy, William. *The Fenian Movement in the United States, 1858-1886.* Washington, D.C.: Catholic University Press, 1947.

Darimon, Alfred. *Histoire de douze ans, 1857-1869.* Paris: E. Dentu, 1883.

_____. *Histoire d'un parti.* 5 vols. Paris: E. Dentu, 1885-89.

_____. *A Travers une revolution.* Paris: E. Dentu, 1884.

Darley, George M. *Pioneering in the San Juan.* Chicago: F.H. Revell, 1899.

Darling, Arthur B. (ed.). *The Public Papers of Francis G. Newlands.* 2 vols. Boston: Houghton Mifflin, 1932.

Darmester, J. (ed.). *The Zend-Avesta.* London: Oxford University Press, 1883.

D'Aroma, Nino. *Mussolini segreto.* Bologna, Italy: Cappelli, 1957.

_____. *Vent'anni insieme.* Bologna, Italy: Cappelli, 1957.

_____. *Vite Parallele.* Rome: CEN, 1962.

Darrah, William Culp. *Pithole: The Vanished City.* Gettysburg, Pa.: n.p., 1972.

_____. *Powell of the Colorado.* Princeton, N.J.: Princeton University Press, 1962.

Darrell, John. *A Brief Narrative of the Possession, Dispossession, and Repossession of William Somers.* London: n.p., 1598.

Darrow, Clarence. *Crime, Its Cause and Treatment.* New York: Thomas Y. Crowell, 1922.

_____. *Crime and Criminals.* Chicago: Charles H. Kerr, 1902.

_____, and Yarros, V.S. *The Prohibition Mania.* New York: Boni & Liveright, 1927.

_____. *The Story of My Life.* New York: Charles Scribner's Sons, 1932.

_____. *Verdicts Out of Court.* Chicago: Quadrangle, 1963.

Darwin, Charles. *The Descent of Man, and Selection in Relation to Sex.* New York: D. Appleton, 1876.

Das, Bhagavan. *The Science of the Self.* Benares, India: Indian Bookshop, 1939.

Dash, S., et al. *The Eavesdroppers.* New Brunswick, N.J.: Rutgers University Press, 1959.

Datta, Dhirendra M. *The Philosophy of Mahatma Gandhi.* Madison: University of Wisconsin Press, 1961.

Dauer, M.J. *The Adams Federalists.* Baltimore: Johns Hopkins Press, 1953.

Daughen, Joseph R., and Binzen, Peter. *The Cop Who Would Be King.* Boston: Little, Brown, 1977.

Daugherty, Harry M. *The Inside Story of the Harding Tragedy.* New York: Churchill, 1932.

Daugis, Antoine Louis. *Traite sur la magie, le sortilège, les possessions.* Paris: P. Prault, 1732.

Daumard, Adeline. *La Bourgeosie de Parisienne de 1815 a 1848.* Paris: S.E.V.P.E.N., 1963.

Davanzati, Archbishop Gioseppe. *Dissertazione sopra Vampiri.* Naples, Italy: Fratelli Raimondi, 1774.

Davenport, Alfred. *Camp and Field Life of the Fifth New York Volunteer Infantry.* New York: Dick and Fitzgerald, 1879.

Davenport, E.H., and Cooke, Sidney Russell. *The Oil Trusts and Anglo-American Relations.* New York: Macmillan, 1924.

Davenport, Guiles. *Zaharoff: High Priest of War.* Boston: Lothrop, Lee and Shepard, 1934.

Davenport, Jacob. *The Witches of Huntingdon.* London: R. Clutterbuck, 1646.

Davenport, John I. *The Election and the Naturalization Frauds in New York City, 1860-1870.* New York: n.p., 1894.

Davenport, Montague. *Under the Gridiron.* London: Tinsley Brothers, 1876.

Davenport, Walter. *Power and Glory, the Life of Boies Penrose.* New York: G.P. Putnam's Sons, 1931.

David, Andrew. *Famous Criminal Trials.* Minneapolis, Minn.: Lerner Publications, 1979.

David, David Brian. *The Problem of Slavery in Western Culture.* Ithaca, N.Y.: Cornell University Press, 1966.

_____. *The Slave Power Conspiracy and the Paranoid Style.* Baton Rouge: Louisiana State University Press, 1970.

David, Henry. *The History of the Haymarket Affair.* New York: Farrar & Rinehart, 1936.

David, Jay. *The Scarsdale Murder.* New York: Leisure Books, 1980.

_____ (ed.). *The Weight of the Evidence.* New York: Meredith Press, 1968.

David, Paul T., et al. *Presidential Nominating Politics in 1952.* 5 vols. Baltimore: Johns Hopkins University Press, 1954.

David, Rene, and Brierley, John E.C. *Major Legal Systems in the World Today.* New York: Free Press, 1978.

David, Richard Beale. *Intellectual Life in the Colonial South 1585-1767.* 3 vols. Knoxville: University of Tennessee Press, 1978.

David, Robert B. *Malcolm Campbell, Sheriff.* Casper, Wyo.: Wyomingana, 1932.

Davidoff, Leonore. *The Best Circles.* London: Croom Helm, 1973.

Davidson, B. *The People's Cause: A History of Guerillas in Africa.* London: Longman, 1981.

Davidson, Bill. *Collura.* New York: Simon & Schuster, 1977

_____. *To Keep and Bear Arms.* Boulder, Colo.: SIB, 1979.

Davidson, Donald. *The Tennessee.* 2 vols. New York: Rinehart, 1948.

Davidson, Eugene. *The Making of Adolf Hitler.* New York: Macmillan, 1977.

_____. *The Nuremberg Fallacy.* New York: Macmillan, 1973.

_____. *The Trial of the Germans.* New York: Macmillan, 1966.

Davidson, Jo. *Between Sittings: An Informal Autobiography.* New York: Dial Press, 1951.

Davidson, Levette J. and Blake, Forrester (eds.). *Rocky Mountain Tales.* Norman, Okla.: University of Oklahoma Press, 1947.

Davidson, Marion. *Making It Legal.* New York: McGraw-Hill, 1979.

Davidson, Philip. *Propaganda and the American Revolution 1763-1783.* Chapel Hill: University of North Carolina Press, 1941.

Davidson, R. Theodore. *Chicano Prisoners: The Key to San Quentin.* New York: Holt, Rinehart & Winston, 1974.

Davidson, Terry. *Conjugal Crime.* New York: Hawthorn, 1978.

Davidson, Thomas Douglas. *Rowan Tree and Red Thread.* Edinburgh, Scot.: Oliver and Boyd, 1949.

Davidson-Houston, J.V. *Russia and China From the Huns to Mao Tse-tung.* London: Robert Hale, 1960.

Davie, Ronald N., et al. *From Birth to Seven.* London: Longmans, 1972.

Davies, Emil. *The Case for Nationalization.* London: Allen & Unwin, 1920.

Davies, Hunter (ed.). *The New London Spy.* London: Blond, 1967.

_____, et al. *Further Studies of Female Offenders.* London: HMSO, 1976.

Davies, J., and Goodman, N. *Girl Offenders Aged 17 to 20 Years.* London: HMSO, 1972.

Davies, James C. *When Men Revolt And Why.* New York: Free Press, 1969.

Davies, John D. *Phrenology, Fad and Science.* New Haven, Conn.: Yale University press, 1955.

Davies, Reginald Trevor. *Four Centuries of Witch-Beliefs; with Special Reference to the Great Rebellion.* London: Methuen, 1947.

Davies, T. Witton. *Magic, Divination, and Demonology Among the Hebrews and Their Neighbors.* London: J. Clarke, 1898.

Davies, Wallace E. *Patriotism on Parade: The Story of Veterans' and Hereditary Organizations in America, 1783-1900.* Cambridge, Mass.: Harvard University Press, 1955.

Davis A., and Dollard, J. *Children of Bondage.* Washington, D.C.: American Council on Education, 1940.

Davis, Allen F. *American Heroine: The Life and Legend of Jane Addams.* New York: Oxford University Press, 1973.

_____, and Haller, Mark H. (eds.). *The Peoples of Philadelphia.* Philadelphia: Temple University Press, 1973.

_____. *Spearheads for Reform.* New York: Oxford University Press, 1967.

Davis, Bernice Freeman. *Assignment San Quentin.* London: Peter Davies, 1962.

_____, and Hirschberg, Al. *The Desperate and the Damned.* New York: Thomas Y. Crowell, 1961.

Davis, Burke. *Get Yamamoto.* New York: Random House, 1969.

Davis, Calvin DeArmond. *The United States and the First Hague Peace Conference.* Ithaca, N.Y.: Cornell University Press, 1962.

Davis, Carlyle C. *Olden Times in Colorado.* Los Angeles: Phillips, 1916.

Davis, Judge Charles G. *The Conduct of the Law in the Borden Case.* Boston: Boston Daily Advertiser, 1893.

_____. *Report of the Trial of Samuel M. Andrews.* New York: Hurd & Houghton, 1869.

Davis, Christopher. *Waiting For It.* New York: Harper & Row, 1980.

Davis, Clyde. *The Arkansas.* New York: Farrar & Rinehart, 1940.

Davis, Mrs. Edith Smith. *A Compendium of Temperance Truth.* Evanston, Ill.: National Woman's Christian Temperance Union, 1916.

Davis, Edwin Adams. *Fallen Guidon.* Santa Fe, N.M.: Stagecoach Press, 1962.

Davis, Elmer. *But We were Born Free.* Indianapolis, Ind.: Bobbs-Merrill, 1954.

_____. *History of the New York Times, 1851-1921.* New York: New York Times, 1921.

Davis, F. James, and Stivers, Richard (eds.). *The Collective Definition of Deviance.* New York: The Free Press, 1975.

Davis, Forrest, and Lindley, Ernest K. *How War Came: An American White Paper from the Fall of France to Pearl Harbor.* New York: Simon and Schuster, 1942.

Davis, Hamilton E. *Mocking Justice.* New York: Crown, 1978.

Davis, Helen Black. *Uncle Hugo.* Amarillo, Texas: Privately Published, 1965.

Davis, Hugh, and Gurr, Ted. *Violence in America: Historical and Comparative Perspectives.* New York: The New American Library, 1969.

Davis, James D. *History of the City of Memphis.* Memphis, Tenn.: Crumpton & Kelly, 1873.

Davis, Jean. *Shallow Diggin's.* Caldwell, Idaho: Caxton Printers, 1963.

Davis, Jefferson. *The Rise and Fall of the Confederate Government.* 2 vols. New York: D. Appleton, 1881.

Davis, Jerome. *Capitalism and Its Culture.* New York: Farrar and Rinehart, 1935.

Davis, John H. *The Bouviers.* New York: Farrar, Straus & Giroux, 1969.

_____. *The Kennedys: Dynasty and Disaster.* New York: McGraw-Hill, 1984.

Davis, John H. *Mafia Kingfish: Carlos Marcello and the Assassination of John F. Kennedy.* New York: McGraw-Hill, 1989.

Davis, Kenneth C. *Discretionary Justice.* Baton Rouge: Louisiana State University Press, 1969.

_____. *Discretionary Justice in Europe and America.* Urbana: University of Illinois Press, 1976.

_____. *FDR: The Beckoning of Destiny, 1882-1928.* New York: G.P. Putnam's Sons, 1971.

_____. *Police Discretion.* St. Paul, Minn.: West, 1975.

Davis, Kenneth S. *The Hero: Charles A. Lindbergh and the American Dream.* Garden City, N.Y.: Doubleday, 1959.

Davis, Marc, and Matthews, Jim. *Highlights of the Warren Report.* Los Angeles: Associated Professional Services, 1964.

Davis, Mary Lee. *Sourdough Gold.* Boston: W.A. Wilde, 1933.

Davis, Matthew L. *Aaron Burr.* New York: Harper & Brothers, 1838.

Davis, Michael. *The Image of Lincoln in the South.* Knoxville: University of Tennessee Press, 1971.

Davis, Rebecca Harding. *Margaret Howth.* Boston: Ticknor & Fields, 1862.

Davis, Richard Harding. *Queen's Jubilee, in a Year from a Reporter's Handbook.* New York: Harper & Brothers, 1903.

_____. *With the Allies.* New York: Charles Scribner's Sons, 1914.

Davis, Richard S. *The Best of Davis.* Milwaukee, Wisc.: Milwaukee Journal, 1961.

_____. *The West from a Car-Window.* New York: Harper & Brothers, 1892.

Davis, Reuben. *Recollections of Mississippi and the Mississippians.* Boston: Houghton Mifflin, 1889.

Davis, Susan Lawrence. *Authentic History: Ku Klux Klan, 1865-1877.* New York: American Library Service, 1924.

Davis, T. Frederick. *History of Jacksonville, Florida.* Gainesville: University of Florida Press, 1964.

Davis, Varina H. *Jefferson Davis.* New York: Belford, 1890.

Davis, W.W.H. *El Gringo: Or New Mexico and Her People.* Santa Fe, N.M.: Rydal Press, 1938.

Davis, W. Hardy. *Aiming for the Jugular in New Orleans.* Port Washington, N.Y.: Ashley Books, 1976.

Davis, Winfield J. *History of Political Conventions in California,*

1849-1892. Sacramento: California State Library, 1893.

Davis, William Watson. *The Civil War and Reconstruction in Florida.* New York: Columbia University Press, 1913.

Davison, Jean. *Oswald's Game.* New York: W.W. Norton, 1983.

Davison, M. H. Armstrong. *The Casket Letters.* Washington, D.C.: University of Washington Press, 1965.

Davison, R.H. *Reform in the Ottoman Empire, 1856-1876.* Princeton, N.J.: Princeton University Press, 1963.

Davisson, William I. *Essex Institute Historical Collections.* Salem, Mass: Harvard Univeristy Press, 1960.

Davitt, Michael. *The Fall of Feudalism in Ireland.* London: Harper, 1919.

Davray, Henry. *Oscar Wilde: La Tragédie Finale.* Paris: n.p., 1928.

Dawdley, David. *A Nation of Lords: An Autobiography of the Vice Lords.* Garden City, N.Y.: Doubleday/Anchor Books, 1973.

Dawes, Anna L. *Lend a Hand.* Philadelphia: Indian Rights Associatinon, 1886.

Dawes, C.R. *The Marquis de Sade: His Life and Works.* London: Holdern, 1927.

Dawson, Christopher (ed.). *The Mongol Mission.* New York: Sheed & Ward, 1955.

Dawson, John D. (ed.). *American State Trials.* St. Louis: Thomas Law, 1923.

Dawson, John P. *A History of Lay Judges.* Cambridge, Mass.: Harvard University Press, 1960.

Dawson, Raymond. *The Chinese Chameleon.* London: Oxford University Press, 1967.

Dawson, Robert MacGregor. *William Lyon Mackenzie King.* London: Methuen, 1959.

Dawson, Robert O. *Sentencing.* Boston: Little, Brown, 1969.

Dawson, William Harbut. *The German Empire, 1867-1914, and the Unity Movement.* London: George Allen & Unwin, 1919.

Day, B.F. *Gene Rhodes, Cowboy.* New York: Julian Messner, 1954.

Day, Donald. *Will Rogers: A Biography.* New York: David McKay, 1962.

Day, George Martin. *The Russians in Hollywood.* Los Angeles: University of Southern California Press, 1934.

Day, Horace B. *The Opium Habit, With Suggestions As To the Remedy.* New York: Harper & Brothers, 1868.

Day, Jack Hays. *The Sutton-Taylor Feud.* San Antonio, Texas: Sid Murray & Sons, 1937.

Day, Oscar F.G. *The Ging Murder and the Great Hayward Trial.* Minneapolis: Minnesota Tribune, 1895.

Dayan, Moshe. *The Story of My Life.* London: Weidenfeld & Nicolson, 1976.

Dayton, Frederick E. *Steamboat Days.* New York: Stokes, 1947.

Deacon, John, and Walker, John. *Dialogical Discourses of Spirits and Devils.* London: G. Bishop, 1601.

_____. *A Summary Answer.* London: G. Bishop, 1601.

Deacon, Richard. *The Chinese Secret Service.* New York: Taplinger, 1972.

_____. *A History of the British Secret Service.* New York: Taplinger, 1969.

_____. *A History of the Russian Secret Service.* London: Muller, 1972.

_____. *Kempei Tai: A History of the Japanese Secret Service.* New York: Berkley Books, 1985.

de Acosta, Mercedes. *Here Lies the Heart.* New York: Reynal, 1960.

Deakin, F.W. *The Brutal Friendship.* New York: Anchor Books, 1966.

_____, and Storry, G.W. *The Case of Richard Sorge.* New York: Friends of the Soviet Union, 1935.

_____. *The Six Hundred Days of Mussolini.* New York: Anchor Books, 1966.

Deale, Kenneth E.L. *Beyond Any Reasonable Doubt.* Dublin, Ire.: Gill & Macmillan, 1971.

_____. *Memorable Irish Trials.* London: Constable, 1960.

Dean, Arthur L. *Alexander & Baldwin, Ltd.* Honolulu, Hawaii: Alexander & Baldwin, 1950.

Dean, Henry Clay. *Crimes of the Civil War.* Baltimore: William T. Smithson, 1868.

Dean, John W. *Blind Ambition.* New York: Simon & Shuster, 1976.

_____. *The Indiana Torture Slaying.* Chicago: Beeline Books, 1967.

Dean, Stanley R. (ed.). *Psychiatry and Mysticism.* Chicago: Nelson-Hall, 1975.

Dean, Vera Micheles. *Fascist Rule in Italy.* London: Nelson, 1934.

Deane, John R. *The Strange Alliance.* New York: Viking Press, 1946.

Deans, R. Story. *Notable Trials: Difficult Cases.* London: Chapman & Hall, 1932.

Dearden, Harold. *Aspects of Murder.* London: Staples Press, 1951.

_____. *Death Under a Microscope.* London: Hutchinson, 1934.

_____. *The Mind of the Murderer.* London: Geoffrey Bles, 1930.

_____. *Queer People.* London: Hutchinson, 1935.

_____. *Some Cases of Sir Bernard Spilsbury and Others.* London: Hutchinson, 1934.

Dearden, R.L. *The Autobiography of a Crook.* New York: Dial Press, 1925.

Dearing, Mary R. *Veterans in Politics; the Story of the G.A.R.* Baton Rouge: Louisiana State University Press, 1952.

The Dearing Tragedy. Philadelphia: C.W. Alexander, 1866.

Dearment, Robert K. *Bat Masterson: The Man and the Legend.* Norman: University of Oklahoma Press, 1979.

DeBary, W.T., Jr. (ed.). *Sources of Chinese Tradition.* New York: Columbia University Press, 1960.

de Beaumont, Gustave, and de Tocqueville, Alexis. *On the Penitentiary System in the United States and Its Application in France.* Carbondale: Southern Illinois University Press, 1964.

de Beauvoir, Simone. *The Second Sex.* New York: Bantam, 1968.

DeBekker, Leander Jan. *The Plot Against Mexico.* New York: Alfred A. Knopf, 1919.

Debo, Angie. *The Cowman's Southwest.* Glendale, Calif.: Arthur H. Clark, 1953.

_____. *A History of the Indians of the United States.* Norman: University of Oklahoma Press, 1970.

_____. *The Rise and Fall of the Choctaw Republic.* Norman: University of Oklahoma Pres, 1934.

_____. *The Road to Disappearance.* Norman: University of Oklahoma Press, 1941.

_____. *And Still the Waters Run.* Princeton, N.J.: Princeton University Press, 1940.

_____. *Tulsa: From Creek Town to Oil Capital.* Norman: University of Oklahoma Press, 1943.

De Bono, Gen Emilio. *Anno XIII.* London: Cresset Press, 1937.

de Bracton, Henry. *Bracton On the Laws and Customs of England.* trans. Samuel E. Thorne. 4 vols. Cambridge, Mass.: Harvard University press, 1968.

Debray, Régis. *Che's Guerrilla War.* London: Penguin Books, 1975.

_____. *Revolution in the Revolution.* New York: Grove Press, 1967.

_____. *Strategy for a Revolution: Essays on Latin America.* New York: Monthly Review, 1970.

De Brouckère, Louis. *Émile Vandervelde, L'homme et son oeuvre.* Brussels, Belg.: L'Eglantine, 1928.

Debs, Eugene V. *His Life, Writings and Speeches.* New York: Hermitage Press, 1948.

_____. *Walls and Bars.* Chicago: Socialist Party, 1927.

A Debt Paid in Full, The Mass Killing of the Newall Family. New York: n.p., n.d.

De Camp, L. Sprague. *The Great Monkey Trial.* New York: Garden, 1968.

_____. *Lost Continents.* New York: Dover, 1970.

De Castro, J.P. *The Gordon Riots*. London: Oxford University Press, 1926.

de Chambrun, Clara Longworth. *The Making of Nicholas Longworth*. New York: Ray Long & Richard R. Smith, 1933.

Decker, D., et al. *Urban Structure and Victimization*. Lexington, Mass.: D.C. Heath, 1982.

Decker, Malcolm. *Benedict Arnold: Son of the Havens*. New York: Antiquarian Press, 1961.

Decker, Peter R. *Fortunes and Failures*. Cambridge, Mass.: Harvard University Press, 1978.

A Declaration in Answer to Several Lying Pamphlets Concerning the Witch of Wapping. London: n.p., 1652.

DeConde, Alexander. *Entangling Alliance: Politics & Diplomacy under George Washington*. Durham, N.C.: Duke University Press, 1958.

Dedijer, Vladmir. *The Road to Sarajevo*. New York: Simon & Schuster, 1966.

Dedmon, Emmett. *Fabulous Chicago*. New York: Random House, 1953.

Dee. D. *Lowdown on Calamity Jane*. Rapid City, S.D.: Rapid City Guide, 1932.

Dee, John. *Autobiographical Tracts of Dr. John Dee*. Manchester, Eng.: Chetham Society, 1851.

_____. *The Private Diary*. London: Camden Society, 1842.

_____. *A True and Faithful Relation of What Passed for Many Years between Dr. John Dee...and Some Spirits*. London: J. Garthwait, 1659.

A Deed of Horror! Trial of Jason Fairbanks. Salem, Mass.: W.Carlton, 1801.

Deeley, Peter. *The Manhunters*. London: Hodder & Stoughton, 1970.

_____, and Walker, Christopher. *Murder in the 4th Estate*. New York: McGraw-Hill, 1971.

Deese, J. *Psychology as Science and Art*. New York: Harcourt Brace Jovanovich, 1972.

De Felice, Renzo. *Mussolini il fascista*. Turin, Italy: Einaudi, 1966.

_____. *Mussolini il Rivoluzionario*. Turin, Italy: Einaudi, 1965.

_____. *Storia degli ebrei italiani sotto il fascismo*. Turin, Italy: Giulio Einaudi, 1961.

The Defense of Father John Baptist Girard. London: J. Roberts, 1731.

De Filippi, Filippo (ed.). *An Account of Tibet: The Travels of Ippolito Desideri of Pistoia, S.J. (1712-1727)*. London: George Routledge & Sons, 1932.

De Fiori, Vittorio. *Italia incandescente*. New York: English Book Shop, 1937.

_____. *Mussolini: Man of Destiny*. London: J.M. Dent, 1928.

Defoe, Daniel. *The Anatomy of Change-Alley*. London: E. Smith, 1719.

_____. *A General History of the Robberies and Murders of the Most Notorious Pirates, 1717-1724*. Columbia: University of South Carolina Press, 1972.

_____. *History of the Devil*. London: T. Warner, 1726.

de Ford, Miriam Allen. *Murderers Sane & Mad!* New York: Abelard-Schuman, Ltd., 1965.

_____. *The Real Ma Barker*. New York: Ace, 1970.

_____. *Stone Walls*. Philadelphia: Chilton Books, 1962.

_____. *They Were San Franciscans*. Boise, Idaho: Caxton Printers, 1947.

DeFrancis, Vincent. *Protecting the Child Victim of Sex Crimes Committed by Adults*. Denver: The American Humane Society, 1969.

DeFranco, Edward J. *Anatomy of a Scam: A Case Study of a Planned Bankruptcy by Organized Crime*. Washington, D.C.: U.S. Government Printing Office, 1973.

De Gaulle, Charles. *The Army of the Future*. Philadelphia: J.B. Lippincott, 1941.

De Givry, E.G. *Illustrated Anthology of Sorcery, Magic and Alchemy*. New York: Causeway Books, 1973.

De Givry, Grillot. *Witchcraft, Magic & Alchemy*. Boston: Houghton Mifflin, 1931.

Degler, Carl N. *Labor in the Economy and Politics of New York City, 1850-1860*. New York: Columbia University Press, 1952.

Degli Espinosa, Agostino. *Il regno del Sud*. Rome: Migliaresi, 1946.

De Gourmont, Rémy. *The Physiology of Love*. New York: Rarity Press, 1932.

de Gramont, Sanche. *The Secret War*. New York: G.P. Putnam's Sons, 1962.

De Grazia, Edward. *Censorship Landmarks*. New York: R.R. Bowker, 1969.

De Grazia, Sebastian. *The Political Community*. Chicago: University of Chicago Press, 1948.

Degrelle, Leon. *Die Verlorene Legion*. Stuttgart, Ger.: Veritas, 1952.

De Gruchy, F.A.L. *War Diary*. Aldershot, Eng.: Gale & Polden, 1949.

de Grunwald. *Peter the Great*. trans. Viola Garvin. New York: Macmillan, 1956.

de Guistino, David. *Conquest of Mind, Phrenology and Victorian Social Thought*. London: Croom Helm, 1975.

Dehn, Lili. *The Real Tsaritsa*. London: Thornton Butterworth, 1922.

Deichmann, Baroness. *Impressions and Memories*. London: John Murray, 1926.

Deighton, Len. *London Dossier*. London: Cape, 1967.

Deindorfer, Robert G. *The Spies*. New York: Fawcett, 1949.

Deiss, Joseph Jay. *Captains of Fortune: Profiles of Six Italian Condottieri*. New York: Thomas Y. Crowell, 1967.

de Jong, Louis. *Die deuts che Fünfte Kolonne im Zweiten Weltkreig*. Stuttgart, Ger.: Deutsche Verlagsanstalt, 1959.

DeJonge, Alex. *The Life and Times of Grigori Rasputin*. New York: Coward, McCann & Geoghegan, 1982.

Dekel, Efraim. *Shai: Exploits of Haganah Intelligence*. London: Yoseloff, 1959.

Delacroix, Frédéric. *Les procès de sorcellerie au xvii siècle*. Paris: Librarie de la Nouvelle Revue, 1894.

Deladurantey, J., and Sullivan D. *Criminal Investigation Standards*. New York: Harper & Row, 1980.

Delair, Paul. *Silhouetted du Palais*. Paris: E. Dentu, 1891.

Delano, Anthony. *Slip-up*. New York: Quadrangle, 1975.

Delano, Rev. Kenneth J. *Astrology, Fact or Fiction*. Huntington, Ind.: Our Sunday Visitor, 1973.

Delaney, John P. *The Blue Devils in Italy*. Washington, D.C.: Infantry Journal Press, 1947.

Delany, Ed, and Rice, M. T. *The Blood Stained Trail. A History of Militant Labor in the United States*. Seattle, Wash.: The Industrial Worker, 1927.

Delany, Edmund T. *New York's Greenwich Village*. Barre, Mass.: Barre Publishers, 1967.

Delaporte, L. *La Mesopotamie*. Paris: La Renaissance du livre, 1932.

Delarue, Jacques. *The History of the Gestapo*. trans. Marvyn Savill. London: Macdonald, 1964.

Delassus, Jules. *Les incubes et les succubes*. Paris: Sociéte du Mercure de France, 1897.

De la Torre, Lillian. *Elizabeth Is Missing*. London: Michael Joseph, 1947.

_____. *Goodbye, Miss Lizzie Borden*. New York: Sheridan House, 1948.

_____. *The Truth About Belle Gunness*. New York: Gold Medal Books, 1955.

_____. *Villainy Detected*. London: D. Appleton-Century, 1947.

Delavan, Edward Cornelius (ed.). *Temperance Essays*. South Ballston, N.Y.: National Temperance Society and Publication House, 1869.

Delay, Peter J. *History of Yuba and Sutter Counties*. Los Angeles: Historic Record, 1924.

Delbene, Thomas. *De Officio Sanctae Inquisitionis Circa Haeresim*. Lyons, Fr.: Jaomis Antoni Hugueton, 1666.

Delcambre, Etienne. *Le concept de la sorcellerie dans le Duché de Lorraine*. Nancy, Fr.: Société d'Archéologie Lorraine, 1948.

Delcroix, Carlo. *Un uomo e un popolo*. Florence, Italy: Vallecchi, 1928.

De Leeuw, Hendrik. *Sinful Cities of the Western World*. New York: Julian Messner, Inc., 1938.

_____. *Underworld Story: The Rise of Organized Crime and Vice-rackets in the U.S.A.* New York: Burns MacEachern, 1955.

Delehanty, Randolph. *Walks and Tours in the Golden Gate City*. New York: Dial Press, 1980.

DeLeon, Solon (ed.). *American Labor's Who's Who*. New York: Hanford Press, 1925.

Delin, Bart. *The Sex Offender*. Boston: Beacon, 1978.

Dell, Robert. *Socialism and Personal Liberty*. New York: Seltzer, 1922.

Dell, Roberta E. *The United States Against Bergdoll*. New York: Barnes, 1977.

Dell, S. *Silent in Court*. London: Bell, 1971.

Dellhora, Guillermo. *Iglesia Catolica*. Mexico City, Mex.: Ediciones Dellhora, 1929.

Dellin, L.A.D. (ed.). *Bulgaria*. New York: Mid-European Studies Center, 1957.

Dellinger, Dave. *More Power Than We Know*. New York: Anchor Press/Doubleday, 1975.

Delobsom, A.A.D. *L'empire du Mongho-Naba, coutoumes des Mossi de la Haute-Volta*. Paris: Domat-Montchrestien, 1932.

Delogne, Théodore. *L'Ardenne méridionale belge, suivi du procès des sorcières de Sugny en 1637*. Brussels, Belg.: H. Lamertin, 1914.

De Long, T.C. *Four Years in Rebel Capitols*. Mobile, Ala.: Gossip Printing, 1890.

Delony, Lewis S. *40 Years a Peace Officer*. Abilene, Texas.: Published by Author, 1937.

Delord, Taxile. *Histoire du second empire*. 6 vols. Paris: Germer Baillière, 1869-75.

Deloria, Vine. *Custer Died For Your Sins*. New York: Macmillan, 1969.

Del Rio, Martin Antoine. *Disquisitionum Magicarum*. Louvain, Belg.: Gerardi Rivii, 1599.

Del Vayo, J. Alvarez. *Freedom's Battle*. New York: Alfred A. Knopf, 1940.

Del Vita, Alessandro. *La Marcia su Roma con la centura scelta di Arezzo*. Arezzo, Italy: FPF, 1924.

Delzwll, C.F. *Mussolini's Enemies*. Princeton, N.J.: Princeton University Press, 1961.

De Madaraiga, Salvador. *Bolivar*. Coral Gables, Fla.: University of Miami Press: 1952.

_____. *Hernan Cortés: Conqueror of Mexico*. Coral Gables, Fla.: University of Miami Press, 1942.

Demaris, Ovid. *America the Violent*. New York: Cowles Book, 1970.

_____. *American Military History*. Washington, D.C.: U.S. Government Printing Office, 1956.

_____. *Brothers In Blood: The International Terrorist Network*. New York: Charles Scribner's Sons, 1977.

_____. *Captive City: Chicago in Chains*. New York: Lyle Stuart, 1969.

_____. *Dillinger*. New York: Tower, 1968.

_____. *The Dillinger Story*. Derby, Conn.: Monarch Books, 1961.

_____. *The Director: An Oral Biography of J. Edgar Hoover*. New York: Harper's Magazine Press, 1976.

_____. *Dirty Business*. New York: Harper's, 1974.

_____, and Reid, Ed. *The Green Felt Jungle*. New York: Trident Press, 1963.

_____. *The Last Mafioso: The Treacherous World of Jimmy Fratianno*. New York: Times Books, 1981.

_____. *The Lindbergh Kidnaping Case*. Derby, Conn.: Monarch, 1961.

_____. *Lucky Luciano*. Derby, Conn.: Monarch Books, 1960.

Demblon, Celestin. *La Guerre à Liege: Pages d'un Témoin*. Paris: Lib. Anglo-Francaise, 1915.

Demeter, Anna. *Legal Kidnapping*. Boston: Beacon Press, 1977.

Demeter, Karl. *The German Officer Corps*. trans. Angus Malcolm. London: Weidenfeld & Nicolson, 1965.

de Mille, Agnes. *Dance to the Piper*. New York: Grosset & Dunlap, 1952.

Deming, Richard. *Women: The New Criminals*. New York: Thomas Nelson, 1977.

Demos, John Putnam. *Entertaining Satan*. New York: Oxford University Press, 1982.

_____. *A Little Commonwealth*. New York: Oxford University Press, 1970.

Demosthenes. *The Crown, The Philippics, and Ten Other Orations*. trans. C. Rann Kennedy. New York: Everyman's Library, 1911.

Dempewolf, Richard. *Famous Old New England Murders*. Brattleboro, Vt.: Stephen Daye Press, 1942.

Denarques, Edmond. *Ravachol: Crimes Anarchistes*. Paris: Bernardin-Bechet, 1931.

De Nerval, G. *The Women of Cairo, Scenes of Life in the Orient*. New York: Harcourt & Brace, 1956.

DeNevi, Don. *Alcatraz "46"*. San Rafael, Calif.: Leswing Press, 1974.

Denfield, Duane. *Streetwise Criminology*. Cambridge, Mass.: Schenkman, 1974.

Denham, Reginald, and Percy, Edward. *Suspect, a Play in Three Acts*. New York: Dramatists Play Service, 1940.

Denikin, Anton. *The Russian Turmoil*. London: Hutchinson, 1922.

_____. *The White Army*. London: Cape, 1930.

Denis, Albert. *La sorcellerie à Toul*. Toul, Fr.: T. Lemaire, 1888.

Denis, Hector. *La Depression Economique et Sociale et L'Histoire des prix*. Brussels, Belg.: G.J. Huysmans, 1895.

Denisoff, R. Serge, and McCaghy, Charles H. (eds.). *Deviance, Conflict, and Criminality*. Chicago: Rand McNally, 1973.

Denison, Daniel. *Irenicon, or a Salve for New Englands Sore*. Boston: Samuel Green, 1684.

Denison, Merrill. *Klondike Mike*. New York: Morrow & Co., 1943.

Denne, Ludwig. *Das Danzig-Problem in der deutschen Aussenpolitik 1934-1939*. Bonn, Ger.: Ludwig Röhrscheid, 1959.

Dennen, Leon. *White Guard Terrorists in the U.S.A.* New York: Friends of the Soviet Union, 1935.

Dennett, Tyler. *Americans in Eastern Asia*. New York: Macmillan, 1922.

_____. *John Hay*. New York: Dodd Mead, 1933.

_____ (ed.). *Lincoln and the Civil War in the Diaries and Letters of John Hay*. New York: Dodd, Mead, 1939.

_____. *Roosevelt and the Russo-Japanese War*. New York: Doubleday, 1925.

Dennis, A.L.P. *Adventures in American Diplomacy, 1896-1906*. New York: E.P. Dutton. 1928.

Dennis, Charles H. *Victor Lawson, His Time and His Work*. Chicago: University of Chicago Press, 1935.

Dennler, J. *Ein Hexenprozess im Elass vom Jahre 1616*. Zabern: A. Fuchs, 1896.

Denson, R.B. *Destiny in Dallas*. Dallas: Denco, 1964.

Densmore, G.B. *The Chinese in California*. San Francisco: Pettit & Russ, 1880.

Dent, Harry S. *The Prodigal South Returns to Power*. New York: John Wiley & Sons, 1978.

Denton, B.E. *A Two-Gun Cyclone*. Dallas: B.E. Denton, 1927.

de Oliveira Santos, Guilherme G. *O caso dos Távoras*. Lisbon: Libraria Portugal, 1958.

de Parmiter, G. C. *Casement*. London: Barker, 1936.

Department of Health, Education, and Welfare. *The Institutional Guide to DHEW Policy on Protection of Human Subjects*.

Washington, D.C.: U.S. Government Printing Office, 1971.

Department of Health and Human Services. *For Patients Only: What You Need to Know About Marijuana.* Washington, D.C.: U.S. Government Printing Office, 1981.

_____. *Television and Behavior.* Washington, D.C.: U.S. Government Printing Office, 1982.

Department of Justice. *Report on the National Conference on Organized Crime.* Washington D.C.: U.S. Government Printing Office, 1975.

_____, and Department of Transportation. *Cargo Theft and Organized Crime.* Washington D.C.: U.S. Government Printing Office, 1972.

Department of the Treasury, Internal Revenue Service. *Estimates of Income Unreported on Individual Income Tax Returns.* Washington, D.C.: U.S. Government Printing Office, 1979.

Departmental Committee on the Employment of Prisoners. *Department Committee on the Employment of Prisoners Report.* London: H.M. Stationery Office, 1933.

Depew, Chauncey M. (ed.). *One Hundred Years of American Commerce.* 2 vols. New York: D.O. Haynes, 1895.

de Pina, L. *Dactiloscopia.* Lisbon, Port.: Bertrand, 1938.

Depperman, W.H. *Shooter's Choice.* New York: World, 1952.

de Quille, Dan. *The Big Bonanza.* New York: Thomas Y. Crowell, 1947.

De Quincey, T. *Confessions of an Opium Eater.* New York: American Library, 1966.

De Quincey, Thomas. *Miscellaneous Essays.* Boston: Ticknor, Reed, Fields, 1851.

de Quirós, C Bernaldo. *Modern Theories of Criminality.* Boston: Little, Brown, 1911.

Derby, Caroline Rosina. *Salem.* New York: Harper & Brothers, 1874.

De Renzis, Raffaelllo. *Mussolini musicista.* Mantua, Italy: Paladino, 1926

deRhram, Edith. *How Could She Do That?* New York: Clarkson N. Potter, 1969.

Deriabin, Peter, and Gibney, Frank. *The Secret World.* Garden City, N.Y.: Doubleday, 1959.

De River, J. Paul. *Crime and the Sexual Psychopath.* Springfield, Ill.: Charles C. Thomas, 1968.

_____. *The Sexual Criminal: A Psychoanalytic Study.* Springfield, Ill.: Charles C. Thomas, 1950.

D'Erlanger, B.H. *The Last Plague of Egypt.* London: Lovat Dickson & Thompson, 1936.

Derleth, August. *Wisconsin Murders.* Sauk City, Wis.: Mycroft & Moran, 1968.

Dermenghem, Emile. *La vie admirable et les révélations de Marie des Vallées.* Paris: Plon-Nourrit, 1926.

Dermenghem, Emile. *The Life of Mohammed.* London: George Routledge & Sons, 1930.

De Roo, P. *Materials for a History of Alexander VI.* 5 vol. Bruges: Desclee, DeBrower, 1924.

de Ropp, Robert S. *Drugs and the Mind.* New York: Saint Martin's Press, 1957.

de Ropp, Robert S. *Sex Energy.* New York: Delta, 1969.

Dershowitz, Alan M. *The Best Defense.* New York: Vintage Books, 1983.

_____. *Reversal of Fortune.* New York: Random House, 1986.

Derthick, Martha. *City Politics and Public Policy.* New York: John Wiley & Sons, 1968.

De Sade, Marquis. *The 120 Days of Sodom.* New York: Grove Press, 1966.

Desai, Mahadev. *Gandhi In Indian Villages.* Madras, India: S. Ganesan, 1928.

_____. *The Gita According to Gandhi.* Ahmedabad, India: Navajivan Publishing House, 1946.

_____. *A Righteous Struggle.* Ahmedabad, India: Navajivan Publishing House, 1951.

_____. *With Gandhi in Ceylon.* Madras, India: S. Ganesan, 1928.

De Sanctis, Francesco. *History of Italian Literature.* 2 vols. trans.

Joan Redfern. New York: Basic Books, 1959.

Des Glajeux, A.-Bérard. *Souvenirs d'un président d'assises.* 2 vols. Paris: Plon-Nourrit, 1892-93.

Deshpande P.G. *Gandhiana.* Ahmedabad, India: Navajivan Publishing House, 1948.

Desmond, Hugh. *Death Let Loose.* London: Wright & Brown, 1956.

_____. *A Scream in the Night.* London: Wright & Brown, 1955.

Desmond, Shaw. *The Drama of Sinn Fein.* New York: Charles Scribner's Sons, 1923.

De Sola, Ralph. *Crime Dictionary.* New York: Facts on File, 1982.

Despert, Louise J. *The Emotionally Disturbed Child.* New York: Doubleday Anchor, 1970.

Després, A. *La Prostitution en France.* Paris: J.B. Bailliére et fils, 1883.

Destler, Chester McArthur. *Henry Demarest Lloyd and the Empire of Reform.* Philadelphia: University of Pennsylvania Press, 1963.

De Sumichrast, F.C. (ed.). *The Works of Théophile Gautier.* New York: George D. Sproul, 1890.

de Tex, John. *Oldenbarnevelt.* trans. R.B. Powell. Cambridge, Eng.: The University Press, 1973.

Dethloff, Henry C. (ed.). *Huey P. Long.* New York: Heath, 1967.

De Tocqueville, Alexis. *Democracy in America.* Trans. Henry Reeve. New York: Schocken, 1961.

Dettling, Alois. *Die Hexenprozesse im Kanton Schwyz.* Schwyz: C. Triner, 1907.

Dettlinger, Chet, with Prugh, Jeff. *The List.* Atlanta, Ga.: Philmay Enterprises, 1983.

Detzer, Dorothy. *Appointment on the Hill.* New York: Henry Holt, 1948.

Detzer, Karl W. *Carl Sandburg: A Study in Personality and Background.* New York: Harcourt, Brace, 1941.

Deutsch, Albert. *The Trouble With Cops.* New York: Crown Publishers, 1954.

Deutsch, Helene. *The Psychology of Women.* New York: Grune & Stratton, 1944.

Deutsch, Hermann B. *The Huey Long Murder Case.* New York: Doubleday, 1969.

Deutsch, Julius. *The Civil War in Austria.* New York: Socialist Party, 1934.

Deutscher, Isaac. *The Prophet Armed; Trotsky: 1879-1921.* New York: Oxford University Press, 1954.

_____. *The Prophet Outcast.* London: Oxford University Press, 1963.

_____. *The Prophet Unarmed.* New York: Oxford University Press, 1959.

_____. *Stalin: A Political Biography.* New York: Oxford University Press, 1949.

_____. *The Unfinished Revolution, Russia, 1917-1967.* New York: Oxford University Press, 1967.

Deutschmann, Paul J. *Communication and Change in Latin America.* New York: Frederick A. Praeger, 1968.

de Valera, Sinead. *The Emerald Ring and Other Fairy Tales.* New York: Dodd, Mead, 1951.

Devens, R. M., Hon. *American Progress: or the Great Events of the Greatest Century.* London: Hugh Heron, 1882.

_____. *Our First Century...One Hundred Great and Memorable Events in the History of Our Country.* Springfield, Mass.: C.A. Nichols, 1879.

De Veny, William. *The Establishment of Law and Order on Western Plains.* Portland, Ore.: Optimist Print, 1915.

Devereux, George. *Abortion in Primitive Society.* New York: Julian, 1955.

Devereux, Robert. *The First Ottoman Constitutional Period: A Study of the Midhat Constitution and Parliament.* Baltimore: John Hopkins Press, 1963.

De Vincentis, Luigi. *Io sono te.* Rome: Cebes, 1946.

Devine, Philip E. *The Ethics of Homicide.* London: Cornell

University Press, 1978.

Devlin, Patrick. *The Enforcement of Morals.* London: Oxford University Press, 1965.

_____. *The Judge.* Chicago; University of Chicago Press 1981.

_____. *Trial by Jury.* London: Stevens, 1956.

de Voinovitch, L. *L'Histoire de Dalmatie.* Paris: Hachette, 1934.

DeVol, George. *Forty Years a Gambler on the Mississippi.* New York: Henry Holt, 1926.

Devol, Kenneth. *Mass Media and the Supreme Court.* New York: Hastings House, 1976.

Devonshire, R.L. *Rambles in Cairo.* Cairo, Egypt: Constable, 1917.

DeVoto, Bernard. *Across the Wide Missouri.* Boston: Houghton Mifflin, 1947.

DeVoto, Bernard. *The Course of Empire.* Boston: Houghton Mifflin, 1952.

_____. *Mark Twain's America.* Boston: Little, Brown, 1932.

_____. *We Accept With Pleasure.* Boston: Little, Brown, 1934.

_____. *The Year of Decision: 1846.* Boston: Little, Brown, 1943.

Devoy, John. *Recollections of an Irish Rebel.* New York: Chas. P. Young, 1929.

Dew, Walter. *I Caught Crippen.* London: Blackie & Son, 1938.

Dewar, Douglas. *Bygone Days in India.* London: John Lane, 1922.

_____. *In the Days of the Company.* Calcutta: Thacker, Spink, 1920.

Dewar, Hugo. *Assassins at Large.* Boston: Beacon Press, 1952.

Dewar, Michael. *Internal Security Weapons and Equipment of the World.* London: Ian Allan, 1979.

Dewar, Thomas R. *A Ramble Round the Globe.* London: Chatto and Windus, 1894.

Dewees, W.B. *Letters from Texas.* Louisville, Ky.: New Albany Tribune Plant, 1852.

Dewes, Simon. *Doctors of Murder.* London: John Long, 1962.

Dewey, G. *Autobiography of George Dewey.* New York: Charles Scribner's Sons, 1913.

Dewey, John. *The Case of Leon Trotsky, Preliminary Commission of Inquiry.* New York: Harper & Row, 1937.

_____. *Freedom and Culture.* New York: G.P. Putnam's Sons, 1939.

Dewey, Thomas E. *In the Two-Party System.* New York: Doubleday, 1966.

_____. *Twenty Against the Underworld.* Garden City, N.Y.: Doubleday, 1974.

Dewhurst, Jack. *Royal Confinements.* New York: St. Martin's Press, 1980.

DeWilde, J.C. *Building the Third Reich.* New York: Foreign Policy Association, 1939.

de Wit, Jan, and Hartup, Willard W. (eds.). *Determinants and Origins of Aggressive Behavior.* The Hague, Neth.: Mouton, 1974.

Dewitt, David Miller. *The Assassination of Abraham Lincoln and Its Expiation.* New York: Macmillan, 1909.

_____. *The Impeachment and Trial of Andrew Johnson.* Madison: State Historical Society of Wisconsin, 1967.

_____. *The Judicial Murder of Mary E. Surratt.* Baltimore: John Murphy, 1895.

De Wyss, M. *Rome Under The Terror.* London: Robert Hale, 1945.

Dexter, Lewis, and White, David Manning. *People, Society and Mass Communications.* New York: Free Press, 1964.

Dexter, Robert C. *The Social Obligation of Liberal Religion.* Boston: American Unitarian Association, 1939.

Dexter, Walter (ed.). *The Letters of Charles Dickens, 1845-1847.* 3 vols. London: Nonesuch Press, 1938.

Déy, Aristide. *Histoire de la sorcellerie au compté de Borgogne.* Vesoul, Fr.: L. Suchaux, 1861.

DeYoung, John E. *Village Life in Modern Thailand.* Berkeley: University of California, 1955.

Dhawan, G.N. *The Political Philosophy of Mahatma Gandhi.* Ahmedabad, India: Navajivan Publishing House, 1951.

Diamond, Martin. *Socialism and the Decline of the American Socialist Party.* Chicago: University of Chicago Press, 1956.

Diamond, Sander A. *The Nazi Movement in the United States, 1924-1941.* Ithaca, N.Y.: Cornell University Press, 1974.

Diamond, William. *The Economic Thought of Woodrow Wilson.* Baltimore: Johns Hopkins University Press, 1943.

Diamond, William. *Industrial Rehabilitation in Italy.* Rome: UNRRA European Regional Office, 1947.

Diapoulos, Peter, and Linakis, Steven. *The Sixth Family.* New York: E.P. Dutton, 1981.

Diaz, Carlos Félix. *Génesis de la revolución mexicana.* La Paz, Bolivia: Litografia é Imprenta "Moderna," 1918.

Dibb, Djamabatan. *The Arab Bloc in the United Nations.* Amsterdam, Hol.: Djambatan, 1956.

Dibble, Roy Floyd. *Strenuous Americans.* New York: Boni & Liveright, 1923.

Dibdin, Michael. *The Last Sherlock Holmes Story.* London: Cape, 1978.

Dice, Charles Amos. *New Levels in the Stockmarket.* New York: McGraw-Hill, 1929.

Dicey, Albert Venn. *Lectures on the Relation Between Law and Public Opinion in England During the Nineteenth Century.* London: Macmillan, 1914.

Dick, Everett. *The Sod-House Frontier, 1854-1890.* New York: D. Appleton-Century, 1937.

_____. *Vanguards of the Frontier.* New York: D. Appleton-Century, 1941.

Dickens, Charles. *American Notes For General Circulation.* London: Oxford University Press, 1957.

_____. *The Complete Writings of Charles Dickens.* 40 vols. Boston: C.E. Lauriat, 1923.

_____. *The Life and Adventures of Martin Chuzzlewit.* Boston: Estes, 1885.

_____. *Miscellaneous Papers.* 2 vols. London: Chapman and Hall, 1908.

_____. *Oliver Twist.* New York: Books, 1930.

Dickens, Henry Fielding. *Recollections.* London: William Heinemann, 1934.

Dicker, Herman. *Wandlers and Settlers in the Far East.* New York: Twayne, 1962.

Dicker, Laverne Mau. *The Chinese in San Francisco.* New York: Dover, 1979.

Dickerson, Robert B., Jr. *Final Placement: A Guide to the Deaths, Funerals and Burials of Notable Americans.* Algonac, Mich.: Reference, 1982.

Dickinson, P.L. *The Dublin of Yesterday.* London: Methuen, 1929.

Dickinson, S.N. *The Boston Almanac for the Year 1838.* Boston: S.N. Dickinson, 1838.

Dicks, Henry V. *Licensed Mass Murder; A Socio-Psychological Study of Some S.S. Killers.* New York: Basic Books, 1972.

Dickson, Arthur Jerome (ed.). *Covered Wagon Days.* Cleveland: Arthur H. Clark, 1929.

Dickson, Grierson. *Murder By Numbers.* London: Robert Hale, 1958.

Dickson, Col. H.R.P. *The Arab of the Desert.* London: Allen & Unwin, 1952.

Dictionary of American Biography. New York: Charles Scribner's Sons, 1944.

Dictionary of National Biography. London: Smith, Elder, 1898.

Diederich, Bernard. *Trujillo, The Death of the Goat.* Boston: Little, Brown, 1978.

Diefenbach, Johann. *Der Hexenwahn vor und nach der Glaubensspaltung in Deutschland.* Mainz, Ger.: F. Kirchheim, 1886.

_____. *Der Zauberglaube.* Mainz, Ger.: F. Kirchheim, 1900.

Diels, Rudolf. *Lucifer ante portas.* Stuttgart, Ger.: Deutsche Verlagsanstalt, 1950.

Dies, Luigi Maria. *Istantanea Mussoliniana a Ponza.* Rome:

Messaggerie Romane, 1949.

Dies, Martin. *Trojan Horse in America.* New York: Dodd, Mead, 1940.

Diesbach, Ghislain de. *Secrets of the Gotha.* New York: Meredith Press, 1967.

Diesel, Eugen. *Germany and the Germans.* London: Macmillan, 1931.

Dietz, Howard. *Dancing in the Dark.* New York: Quadrangle, 1974.

Diggins, John P. *Mussolini and Fascism: The View from America.* Princeton, N.J.: Princeton University Press, 1972.

_____. *Up from Communism: Conservative Odysseys in American Intellectual History.* New York: Harper & Row, 1975.

Dill, Sir Samuel. *Roman Society from Nero to Marcus Aurelius.* New York: Meridian, 1956.

_____. *Roman Society in the Last Century of the Western Empire.* New York: Macmillan, 1899.

Dillard, J.L. *American Talk.* New York: Random House, 1976.

Dilliard, Irving (ed.). *One Man's Stand for Freedom, Mr. Justice Black and the Bill of Rights.* New York: Alfred A. Knopf, 1963.

Dillmann, John. *The French Quarter Killers.* New York: Macmillan, 1987.

Dillon, Dr. E.J. *The Inside Story of the Peace Conference.* New York: Harper & Brothers, 1920.

_____. *Mexico on the Verge.* London: Hutchinson, 1922.

_____. *President Obregón, A World Reformer.* London: Hutchinson, 1922.

Dillon, M., and Chadwick, N.K. *The Celtic Realms.* London: Weidenfeld & Nicolson, 1967.

Dillon, M., and Lehane, D. *Political Murder in Northern Ireland.* London: Penguin Books, 1973.

Dillon, Merton L. *Elijah P. Lovejoy, Abolitionist Editor.* Urbana: University of Illinois Press, 1961.

Dillon, Millicent. *A Little Original Sin.* New York: Holt, Rinehart & Winston, 1981.

Dillon, Richard. *California Trail Herd.* Los Gatos, Calif.: Talisman Press, 1961.

Dillon, Richard H. *The Hatchet Men.* New York: Coward-McCann, 1972.

_____. *Wells Fargo Detective, A Biography of James B. Hume.* New York: Coward-McCann, 1969.

Dilnot, George. *The Bank of England Forgery.* New York: Charles Scribner's Sons, 1929.

_____. *Celebrated Crimes.* London: Stanley Paul, 1925.

_____. *Great Detectives and Their Methods.* Boston: Houghton Mifflin, 1928.

_____. *Man Hunters: Great Detectives and Their Achievements.* London: Robert Hale, 1937.

_____. *The Real Detective.* London: Geoffrey Bles, 1933.

_____. *Rogues' March.* London: Geoffrey Bles, 1934.

_____. *Scotland Yard: Its History and Organization, 1829-1929.* London: Geoffrey Bles, 1929.

_____. *The Story of Scotland Yard.* Boston: Houghton, Mifflin, 1927.

_____. *Triumphs of Detection.* London: Geoffrey Bles, 1929.

DiMona, Joseph. *Last Man at Arlington.* New York: Arthur Fields Books, 1973.

Dimsdale, Thomas J. *The Vigilantes of Montana.* Helena, Mont.: State Publishing, 1915.

Dinale, Ottavio. *Tempo di Mussolini.* Verona, Italy: Mondadori, 1934.

_____. *La rivoluzione che vince.* Rome: Campitelli, 1934.

_____. *Quarant'anni di colloqui con lui.* Milan, Italy: Ciarrocca, 1953.

Dineen, Joseph. *The Purple Shamrock.* New York: W.W. Norton, 1949.

Dineen, Michael P. (ed.). *Great Fires of America.* Waukesha, Wis.: Country Beautiful, 1972.

Diner, Stephen J. *A City and Its Universities.* Chapel Hill: University of North Carolina Press, 1980.

Dinerstein, Herbert S. *Intervention Against Communism.* Baltimore: Johns Hopkins Press, 1967.

Dinesen, I. *Out of Africa.* New York: Random House, 1938.

Dinges, John, and Landau, Paul. *Assassination on Embassy Row.* New York: Pantheon, 1980.

Dinneen, Joseph F. *Underworld U.S.A.* New York: Farrar, Straus, 1956.

Dinnerstein, Leonard. *The Leo Frank Case.* New York: Columbia University Press, 1968.

Dintzer, Lucien. *Nicholas Remy et son oeuvre démonologique.* Lyons, Fr.: L'imprimerie de Lyon, 1936.

Dio Cassius. *Roman History.* trans. Ernest Cary. New York: Loeb Classical Library, 1927.

DiPerna, Paula. *Juries On Trial.* New York: Dembner Books, 1984.

Diricq, Edouard. *Maléfices et sortilèges.* Lausanne, Switz.: Payot, 1910.

Dirks, Raymond L., and Gross, Leonard. *The Great Wall Street Scandal.* New York: McGraw-Hill, 1974.

DiSalle, Michael V. *The Power of Life or Death.* New York: Random House, 1965.

Discipline of the Yearly Meeting of Friends, held in New York For the State of New York and Parts Adjacent. New York: Collins and Perkins, 1810.

Divall, Tom. *Scoundrels and Scallywags.* London: Benn, 1929.

Divine, David. *Indictment of Incompetence.* London: MacDonald, 1970.

Divine, Robert A. *American Immigration Policy, 1924-1952.* New York: Da Capo Press, 1972.

Diwakar, R.R. *Glimpses of Gandhi.* Bombay, India: Hind Kitabs, 1949.

_____. *Satyagraha-Its Technique and History.* Bombay, India: Hind Kitabs, 1946.

Dix, Dorothea L. *Remarks on Prisons and Prison Discipline in the United States.* Philadelphia: Joseph Kite, 1845.

Dix, Morgan (ed.). *Memoirs of John Adams Dix.* New York: Harper Brothers, 1883.

Dix, Tenille. *The Black Baron.* Indianapolis, Ind.: Bobbs-Merrill, 1930.

Dixon, C. Aubrey, and Heilbrunn, Otto. *Communist Guerrilla Warfare.* London: Allen & Unwin, 1954.

Dixon, Clive K. *The Life of "Billy" Dixon.* Dallas: P.L. Turner, 1914.

Dixon, Harry Vernor. *Something for Nothing.* New York: Harper, 1950.

Dixon, Thomas. *The Clansman.* New York: William Heinemann, 1906.

Djemal, Pasha. *Memoirs of a Turkish Statesman.* New York: Doran, 1922.

Djilas, Milovan. *Conversations with Stalin.* New York: Harcourt, Brace & World, 1962.

_____. *The New Class: An Analysis of the Communist System.* New York: Frederick A. Praeger, 1957.

Dmytryshyn, Basil (ed.). *Imperial Russia: A Source Book, 1700-1917.* New York: Holt, Rinehart & Winston, 1967.

_____. *Moscow and the Ukraine, 1918-1953.* New York: Bookman Associates, 1956.

_____. *USSR: A Concise History.* New York: Charles Scribner's Sons, 1965.

Dobash, R. E., and Dobash, R. *Violence Against Wives.* New York: Free Press, 1979.

Dobbs, Maurice. *Studies in the Development of Capitalism.* New York: International, 1963.

Dobell, Clifton. *Antony van Leewenhoek and His "Little Animals".* New York: Russell & Russell, 1958.

Dobie, Charles Caldwell. *San Francisco's Chinatown.* New York: D. Appleton-Century, 1936.

_____. *San Francisco: A Pageant.* New York: D. Appleton Century, 1939.

Dobie, Edith. *The Political Carrer of Stephen Mallory White.* Stanford, Calif.: Stanford University Press, 1927.

Dobie, James Frank. *Coronado's Children.* Garden City, N.Y.: Garden City, 1930.

_____. *The Flavor of Texas.* Dallas: Dealey and Lowe, 1936.

_____. *Guide to Life and Literature of the Southwest.* Dallas: Southern Methodist University Press, 1952.

_____. *The Longhorns.* Boston: Little, Brown, 1941.

_____. *The Mustangs.* New York: Bantam Books, 1954.

_____. *A Vaquero of the Brush Country.* Dallas: Southwest Press, 1929.

Dobkins, J. Dwight, and Hendricks, Robert J. *Winnie Ruth Judd: The Trunk Murders.* New York: Grosset & Dunlap, 1973.

Doblado, Manuel. *México para los Mexicanos: El Presidente Wilson y su gobierno.* Mexico: Imprenta de Antonio Enriquez, 1913.

Dobroliubov, N.A. *Selected Philosophical Essays.* Moscow: Foreign Languages Publishing House, 1956.

Dobson, Christopher. *Black September: Its Short, Violent History.* New York: Macmillan, 1974.

_____, and Payne, Ronald. *The Carlos Complex: A Study in Terror.* New York: Putnam, 1977.

_____. *Counterattack: The West's Battle Against the Terrorists.* New York: Facts on File, 1982.

_____. *The Terrorists: Their Weapons, Leaders and Tactics.* New York: Facts on File, 1982.

Dobson, Terry, and Shepherd-Chow, Judith. *Safe and Alive.* Los Angeles: Tarcher, 1981.

Dobyns, Fletcher. *The Amazing Story of Repeal.* Chicago: Willett, Clark, 1940.

_____. *The Underworld of American Politics.* New York: Published by Author, 1932.

I Documenti Diplomatici Italiani. Rome: Ministero degli Esteri, 1952.

Documents of American History. New York: Crofts, 1946.

Documents on British Foreign Policy, 1918-45. London: HMSO, 1946-.

Documents on German Foreign Policy, 1918-45. London: HMSO, 1948-.

Dodd, C. H. *New Testament Studies.* Manchester, Eng.: Manchester University Press, 1933.

Dodd, S.C.T. *Combinations, Their Uses and Abuses, with a History of the Standard Oil Trust.* New York: George F. Nesbitt, 1888.

Dodd, William Edward. *The Cotton Kingdom.* New Haven, Conn.: Yale University Press, 1921.

_____. *Jefferson Davis.* Philadelphia: G.W. Jacobs, 1907.

_____. *Statesmen of the Old South.* New York: Macmillan, 1911.

Dodge, Calvert R. (ed.). *A Nation Without Prisons.* Lexington, Mass.: D.C. Heath, 1975.

Dodge, Daniel. *Trial of Peter Robinson.* Newark, N.J.: Aaron Guest, 1841.

Dodge, Ernest. *Northwest by Sea.* New York: Oxford University Press, 1961.

Dodge, Grenville M. *The Battle of Atlanta and Other Campaigns, Addresses, Etc.* Council Bluffs, Iowa: Monarch, 1911.

Dodge, Harry P. *Fifty Years at the Card Table: The Autobiography of an Old Sport.* Syracuse, N.Y.: n.p., 1885.

Dodge, I.F. *Our Arizona.* New York: Scribner's, 1929

Dodge, Richard Irving. *Our Wild Indians.* Hartford, Conn.: A.D. Worthington, 1883.

_____. *The Plains of the Great West.* New York: G.P. Putnam's Sons, 1877.

Dodwell, Henry. *Founder of Modern Egypt.* London: Cambridge University Press, 1931.

Dogan, M., and Rokkan, S. (eds.). *Quantitative Ecological Analysis in the Social Sciences.* Cambridge, Mass.: MIT Press, 1969.

Doherty, Edward J. *Gall and Honey.* New York: Sheed and Ward, 1941.

Doke, Joseph J. *M.K. Gandhi.* Madras, India: G.A. Natesan, 1909.

Dolan, J.R. *The Yankee Peddlers of Early America.* New York: Clarkson N. Potter, 1964.

Dolan, Jay. *The Immigrant Church.* Baltimore: Johns Hopkins University Press, 1975.

Dolci, Danilo. *The Man Who Plays Alone.* trans. Antonia Cowan. New York: Pantheon, 1968.

Dolfin, Giovanni. *Con Mussolini nella tragedia.* Milan, Italy: Garzanti, 1949.

Dolgoff, Sam (ed.). *Bakunin on Anarchy: Selected Works by the Activist-Founder of World Anarchism.* New York: Alfred A. Knopf, 1972.

Dollard, John. *Caste and Class in a Southern Town.* Garden City, N.Y.: Harper & Row, 1949.

_____, *Frustration and Aggression.* New Haven, Conn.: Yale University Press, 1939.

Dolléans, Edouard. *Histoire du Mouvement Ouvrier.* Paris: A. ohm, 1936.

Dollinger, Hans. *The Decline and Fall of Nazi Germany and Imperial Japan: A Pictorial History of the Final Days of World War II.* New York: Crown, 1968.

Dollmann, Eugen. *Call Me Coward.* London: William Kimber, 1956.

_____. *The Interpreter.* trans. F. Maxwell-Brownjohn. London: Hutchinson, 1967.

Dombrowski, James. *The Early Days of Christian Socialism in America.* New York: Columbia University Press, 1935.

Dombrowski, Roman. *Twilight and Fall.* London: Heinemann, 1956.

Domènech, Gabriel. *Lurs Toute L'Affaire Dominici.* Forcalquier: Editions Charles Testanière, 1956.

Domestic Council Drug Abuse Task Force. *White Paper on Drug Abuse.* Washington D.C.: U.S. Government Printing Office, 1975.

Domhoff, G. William. *The Higher Circles: The Governing Class in America.* New York: Random House, 1970.

_____. *Who Really Rules.* Santa Monica, Calif.: Goodyear, 1978.

_____. *Who Rules America?* Englewood Cliffs, N.J.: Prentice-Hall, 1967.

Domino, Ignazio. *Italo Balbo.* Florence, Italy: All'insegna del Libro, 1940.

Donahue, William A. *The Politics of the American Civil Liberties Union.* New Bruswick, N.J.: Transaction Books, 1985.

Donald, David. *Charles Sumner and the Coming of the Civil War.* New York: Alfred A. Knopf, 1960.

_____. *Charles Sumner and the Rights of Man.* New York: Alfred A. Knopf, 1970.

_____. *Lincoln Reconsidered.* New York: Alfred A. Knopf, 1956.

_____. *Lincoln's Herndon.* New York: Alfred A. Knopf, 1948.

Donald, Jay. *Outlaws of the Border.* Philadelphia: Douglas Brothers, 1882.

Donaldson, Gordon. *The Edinburgh History of Scotland.* New York: Frederick A. Praeger, 1966.

Donaldson, Thomas. *Idaho of Yesterday.* Caldwell, Idaho: The Caxton Printers, 1941.

Donaldson, William. *Don't Call Me Madam.* New York: Mason/Charter, 1975.

Doncoeur, Paul. (ed.). *La minute française.* Melun, Fr.: Librarie d'Argences, 1952.

Dönitz, Karl. *Memoirs, Ten Years and Twenty Days.* trans. R.H. Stevens. London: Weidenfeld & Nicolson, 1959.

Donnell, J. *The Corporate Counsel: A Role Study.* Bloomington: Indiana University Bureau of Business Research, 1970.

Donnelly, Edward J. *Trial of James Nutt for the Killing of N.L. Dukes.* Pittsburgh, Pa.: Stephenson & Foster, 1884.

Donnelly, Ignatius. *Atlantis: The Antediluvian World.* London: Sidgwick and Jackson, 1950.

_____. *Caesar's Column. A Story of the Twentieth Century.* Chicago: F.J. Schulte, 1890.

Donnelly, Richard C., Goldstein, Joseph, and Schwartz, Richard D. *Criminal Law*. New York: The Free Press, 1962.

Donner, Frank J. *The Age of Surveillance*. New York: Alfred A. Knopf, 1980.

_____. *The Un-Americans*. New York: Ballantine, 1961.

Donoghue, Mary Agnes. *Assassination: Murder in Politics*. Chatsworth, Calif. Major Books, 1975.

Donosti, Mario. *Mussolini e l'Europa*. Rome: Leonardo, 1945.

Donovan, Robert J. *The Assassins*. New York: Harper & Brothers, 1955.

_____. *The Assassins of American Presidents*. New York: Harper & Brothers, 1956.

_____. *Conflict and Crises: The Presidency of Harry S. Truman, 1945-1948*. New York: W.W. Norton, 1977.

_____. *Tumultuous Years: The Presidency of Harry S. Truman, 1949-1953*. New York: W.W. Norton, 1982.

Donovan, Frank. *River Boats of America*. New York: Thomas Y. Crowell, 1966.

_____. *The Thomas Jefferson Papers*. New York: Dodd, Mead, 1963.

Donovan, J. (ed.). *Catechism of the Council of Trent*. Dublin, Ire.: James Duffy, 1908.

Donovan, Mike. *The Roosevelt That I Knew*. New York: B.W. Dodge, 1909.

Doob, Leonard W. *The Plans of Men*. New Haven, Conn.: Yale University Press, 1940.

_____. Public Opinion and Propaganda. Hamden, Conn.: Archon, 1966

1966.Doolittle, J. *Social life of the Chinese*. New York: Harper & Brothers, 1865.

Dorchester, Daniel. *The Liquor Problem in All Ages*. New York: Phillips & Hunt, 1884.

Dore, R.P. *Aspects of Social Change in Modern Japan*. Princeton, N.J.: Princeton University Press, 1967.

_____. *Education in Tokugawa Japan*. Berkeley: University of California Press, 1965.

Doresse, Jean. *The Secret Books of the Egyptian Gnostics*. trans. Philip Mairet. London: Hollis and Carter, 1960.

D'Orleans, P.J. *History of the Two Tartar Conquerors of China*. London: Hakluyt Society, 1854.

Dorman, Michael. *King of the Courtroom: Percy Foreman for the Defense*. New York: Delacorte Press, 1969.

_____. *The Secret Service Story*. New York: Delacorte Press, 1967.

_____. *We Shall Overcome*. New York: Delacorte Press, 1964.

Dorman, Peter. *Dictionary of the Law*. Philadelphia: Running Press, 1978.

Dornberger, Walter. *V2-Der Schuss ins Weltall*. Esslinger, Ger.: Bechtle, 1952.

Dorough, C. Dwight. *Mr. Sam*. New York: Random Huse, 1962.

Dorr, Rheta Childe. *Drink: Coercion or Control*. New York: Frederick A. Stokes, 1929.

_____. *The Woman Who Changed the Mind of a Nation*. New York: Frederick A. Stokes, 1928.

Dorsen, N., and Friedman, L. *Disorder in the Courts*. New York: Pantheon, 1973.

_____, and Gillers, Stephen (eds.). *None of Your Business*. New York: Penguin Books, 1975.

Dorsen, Norman, Bender, Paul, and Neuborne, Burt. *Political and Civil Rights in the United States*. Boston: Little, Brown, 1976.

Dorsett, Lyle W. *The Pendergast Machine*. New York: Oxford University Press, 1968.

_____. *The Queen City*. Boulder, Colo.: Pruet Publishers, 1977.

Dorsey, Florence. *Master of the Mississippi*. Boston: Houghton Mifflin, 1941.

_____. *Road to the Sea*. New York: Rinehart, 1947.

Dorsey, George A. *Traditions of the Arikara*. Washington, D.C.: Carnegie Institution, 1904.

Dorso, Guido. *Mussolini alla conquista del potere*. Turin, Italy: Einaudi, 1949.

Dorson, Richard M. (ed.). *American Rebels*. New York: Pantheon, 1953.

Dorst, Tankred, with Ehler, Ursula. *Sand: Ein Szenarium*. Cologne: Kiepenheuer & Witsch, 1971.

Dosch, Henry Ernst. *Vigilante Days at Virginia City*. Portland, Ore.: Fred Lockley, 1924.

Dos Passos, John. *In All Countries*. New York: Harcourt, Brace, 1934.

Doster, William E. *Lincoln and Episodes of the Civil War*. New York: G.P. Putnam's Sons, 1915.

Dostoevski, Fëdor. *Crime and Punishment*. Middlesex, Eng.: Penguin, 1966.

_____. *The House of the Dead*. New York: Dell, 1959.

Doty, Duane (Mrs.). *The Town of Pullman: Its Growth with Brief Accounts of Its Industries*. Pullman, Ill.: T. P. Struhsacker, 1893.

Doughitt, Katherine Christian. *Romance and Dim Trails*. Dallas: William Tardy, 1938.

Doughty, Charles. *Travels in Arabia Deserta*. London: Jonathan Cape, 1936.

Douglas, Alfred. *The Oracle of Change*. Hammondsworth, England: Penguin, 1972.

_____. *The Tarot: The Origins, Meaning and Use of the Cards*. London: Victor Gollancz, 1973.

Douglas, Alfred Bruce, Lord. *The City of the Soul*. London: John Crane, 1911.

_____. *Without Apology*. London: M. Secker, 1938.

Douglas, Arthur. *Will the Real Jack the Ripper*. Chorley, Eng.: Countryside, 1979.

Douglas, Clarence Brown. *History of Tulsa, Oklahoma*. Chicago: S.J. Clarke, 1921.

_____. *Territory Tales*. El Reno, Okla.: El Reno American, 1951.

Douglas, Claude Leroy. *Cattle Kings of Texas*. Dallas: Cecil Baugh, 1939.

_____. *Famous Texas Feuds*. Dallas: Turner, 1936.

_____. *The Gentlemen in White Hats*. Dallas: South-West Press, 1934.

Douglas, F.A.K., Marquess of Queensbury, and Colson, P. *Oscar Wilde and the Black Douglas*. London: Hutchinson, 1949.

Douglas, Ford. *The Cattle Rustlers of Wyoming*. Nwe York: J.S. Ogilvie, 1916.

Douglas, George William. *The Many-Sided Roosevelt, An Anecdotal Biography*. New York: Dodd, Mead, 1907.

Douglas, Henry Kyd. *I Rode with Stonewall*. Chapel Hill: University of North Carolina Press, 1940.

Douglas, Jack. *Veterans on the March*. New York: Workers Library Publishers, 1934.

Douglas, Jack D. (ed.). *Deviance and Respectability*. New York: Basic Books, 1970.

_____. *Investigative Social Research*. Beverly Hills, Calif.: Sage, 1976.

_____, and Johnson, John M. (eds.). *Official Deviance*. Philadelphia: J.B. Lippincott, 1977.

_____. *The Social Meanings of Suicide*. Princeton, N.J.: Princeton University Press, 1967.

Douglas, James G. *President de Valera and the Senate*. Dublin, Ire.: Eason, 1934.

Douglas, James W.B., Ross, J.M., and Simpson, H.R. *All Our Future*. London: Peter Davies, 1968.

_____. *The Home and the School*. London: MacGibbon & Kee, 1964.

Douglas, Lord Alfred. *My Friendship with Oscar Wilde: Being the Autobiography of Lord Alfred Douglas*. New York: Charles Scribner's Sons, 1932.

Douglas, Marjory Stoneman. *The Everglades: River of Grass*. New York: Rinehart, 1947.

Douglas, Mary. *Purity and Danger*. London: Routledge and K. Paul, 1966.

Douglas, Paul H. *Social Security in the United States*. New York: McGraw-Hill, 1939.

Douglas, William O. *An Almanac of Liberty*. New York; Doubleday, 1954.

———. *Beyond the High Himalayas*. Garden City, N.Y.: Doubleday, 1953.

———. *The Court Years 1939-1975*. New York: Random House, 1980.

———. *The Douglas Opinions*. New York: Random House, 1977.

———. *Go East, Young Man: The Early Years, the Autobiography of William O. Douglas*. New York: Random HOuse, 1974.

———. *We the Judges*. Garden City, N.Y.: Doubleday, 1956.

Douglas-Hamilton, James. *Motive for a Mission: The Story Behind Hess's Flight to Britain*. New York: St. Martin's Press, 1971.

Douglass, Earl L. *Prohibition and Commonsense*. New York: Alcohol Information Committee, 1931.

Douglass, Frederick. *Life and Times of Frederick Douglass: His Early Life as A Slave, His Escape from Bondage, and His Complete History*. London: Collier-Macmillan, 1962.

———. *Narrative of the Life of Frederick Douglass*. New York: Signet Books, 1968.

Dousset, Roselene and Taillemite, Etienne. *The Great Book of the Pacific*. trans. Andrew Mouravieff-Apostal and Edita Lausanne. Secaucus, N.J.: Chartwell Books, 1979.

Doussinague, José M. *España tenia Razon 1939-1945*. Madrid: Espasa-Calpe S.A., 1950.

Douthit, Nathan. *Police Forces in History*. Beverly Hills, Calif.: Dage, 1975.

Douthwaite, L. C. *Mass Murder*. New York: Holt, 1929.

Dow, George Francis, and Edmonds, John Henry. *The Pirates of the New England Coast*. New York: Argosy-Antiquarian, 1968.

Dow, George Francis (ed.). *The Probate Records of Essex County, Mass.* Newbrury, Mass.: Parker River Reaserchers, 1988.

Dow, Lorenzo. *The Dealings of God, Man and the Devil*. 2 vols. New York: Sheldon, Lamport & Blakeman, 1856.

Dow, Neal. *The Reminiscences of Neal Dow*. Portland, Maine: Evening Express, 1898.

Dowd, Douglas F. *The Twisted Dream: Capitalist Development in the United States Since 1776*. Cambridge, Mass.: Winthrop, 1974.

Dowdy, Clifford. *Experiment in Rebellion*. Gardern City, N.Y.: Doubleday, 1946.

———. *The Land They Fought For*. Garden City, N.Y.: Doubleday, 1955.

———. *The Seven Days: The Emergence of Lee*. Boston: Little, Brown, 1964.

———. *The Wartime Papers of R.E. Lee*. Boston: Little, Brown, 1961.

Dowell, Eldridge Foster. *A History of Criminal Syndicalism Legislation in the United States*. Baltimore: Johns Hopkins Press, 1939.

Dower, J.W. *Empire and Aftermath: Yoshida Shigeru and the Japanese Experience*. Cambridge, Mass.: Harvard University Press, 1979.

Dower, K.C.G. *The First to be Freed*. London: HMSO, 1944.

Down, Thomas. *Murder Man*. New York: Dell, 1984.

Downer, Edward T. *Stonewall Jackson's Shenandoah Valley Campaign*. Lexington, Va.: Stonewell Jackson Memorial, 1959.

Downes, David M. *The Delinquent Solution*. London: Routledge & Kegan Paul, 1966.

Downes, Donald. *The Scarlet Thread*. London: Derek Verschoyle, 1953.

Downie, Leonard, Jr. *The New Muckrakers*. Washington, D.C.: New Republic, 1976.

Downie, Robert Angus. *Murder in London: A Topographical Guide to Famous Crimes*. London: A. Barker, 1973.

Doyle, Adrian Conan. *The True Conan Doyle*. New York: Coward McCann, 1946.

Doyle, James. *Not Above the Law*. New York: Morrow, 1977.

Dozier, Edward P. *The Pueblo Indians of North America*. New

York: Holt, Rinehart and Winston, 1970.

Dozy, Rinehart. *Spanish Islam*. London: Chatto & Windus, 1913.

Drage, William W. *Daimonomageia*. London: J. Dover, 1665.

———. *A Relation of Mary Hall, Possessed of Two Devils*. London: Miller, 1668.

Dragnich, Alex N. *Tito's Promised Land: Yugoslavia*. New Brunswick, N.J.: Rutgers University Press, 1954.

Drago, Harry Sinclair. *Great American Cattle Trails*. New York: Dodd, Mead, 1965.

———. *The Great Range Wars*. New York: Dodd, Mead, 1970.

———. *Lost Bonanzas*. New York: Dodd, Mead, 1966.

———. *Notorious Ladies of the Frontier*. New York: Dodd, Mead, 1969.

———. *Outlaws on Horseback*. New York: Dodd, Mead, 1964.

———. *Red River Valley*. New York: Clarkson N. Potter, 1962.

———. *Road Agents and Train Robbers*. New York: Dodd, Mead, 1973.

———. *Roads to Empire*. New York: Dodd, Mead, 1968.

———. *The Steamboaters*. New York: Dodd, Mead, 1967.

———. *Wild, Woolly & Wicked*. New York: Clarkson N. Potter, 1960.

Draine, Edwin H. *Import Traffic of Chicago and Its Hinterland*. Chicago: University of Chicago Department of Geography, 1950.

Drake, Alvin, et al. *Analysis of Public Systems*. Cambridge, Mass.: MIT Press, 1972.

Drake, St. Clair, and Cayton, Horace R. *Black Metropolis*. New York: Harcourt, Brace, 1945.

Drake, Samuel G. *Annals of Witchcraft in New England*. Boston: W.E. Woodward, 1866.

———. *Biography and History of the Indians of North America*. Philadelphia: Charles de Silver, 1860.

——— (ed.). *The Witchcraft Delusion in New England*. Roxbury, Mass.: W. Elliot Woodward, 1866.

Drake, W.D. *The Connoisseur's Handbook of Marijuana*. San Francisco: Straight Arrow Books, 1971.

Drannan, Capt. William F. *Thirty-One Years on the Plains and in the Mountains*. Chicago: Rhodes & McClure, 1899.

Draper, Theodore. *American Communism and Soviet Russia*. New York: Viking, 1960.

———. *Castroism: Theory and Practice*. New York: Praeger, 1965.

———. *The Roots of American Communism*. New York: Viking, 1957.

Draper, William R. *A Cub Reporter in the Old Indian Territory*. Girard, Kan.: E. Haldeman-Julius, 1946.

———. *Exciting Adventures Along the Indian Frontier*. Girard, Kan.: E. Haldeman-Julius, 1946.

———, and Mabel. *Old Grubstake Days in Joplin*. Girard, Kan.: E. Haldeman-Julius, 1946.

Drapkin, Israel, and Viano, Emilio (eds.) *Victimology*. Lexington, Mass.: Lexington Books, D.C. Heath, 1974.

———. *Victimology: A New Focus*. Lexington, Mass.: Lexington Books, D.C. Heath, 1975.

Dred Scott Case, The; In the Supreme Court of the United States, December Term, 1856. Washington D.C.: n.p., n.d.

Dreher, Robert H., and Kammler, Linda. *Criminal Registration Statutes and Ordinances in the United States: A Compilation*. Carbondale: Center for the Study of Crime, Delinquency and Corrections, Southern Illinois University, 1969.

Dreifus, Claudia. *Woman's Fate*. New York: Bantam, 1973.

Dreiser, Theodore. *An Amercan Tragedy*. New York: New American Library, 1964.

———. *A Book About Myself*. New York: Boni & Liveright, 1922.

———. *The Color of a Great City*. New York: Boni and Liveright, 1923.

Dresler, Adolf. *Rasputin*. München, Ger.: B. Funck-verlag, 1929.

Dresser, Albert. *California's Pioneer Mountaineer of Rabbit Gulch*. San Francisco: Published by Author, 1930.

Dressler, David. *Practice and Theory of Probation and Parole.*

New York: Columbia University Press, 1969.

Drew, Thomas. *The John Brown Invasion: An Authentic History of the Harper's Ferry Tragedy.* Boston: J. Campbell, 1860.

Drewry, W.S. *Slave Insurrections in Virginia, 1830-1865.* Washington, D.C.: Neale, 1900.

Dreyfus, Mathieu. *L'Affaire telle que je l'ai vécue.* Paris: Grasset, 1978.

Dreyfus, Pierre (ed.). *Capitaine Alfred Dreyfus: Souvenirs et Correspondence.* Paris: Grasset, 1936.

Driggs, Benjamin Woodbury. *History of Teton Valley, Idaho.* Caldwell, Idaho: Caxton Printers, 1926.

Driggs, Howard Roscoe. *Westward America.* New York: G.P. Putnam's Sons, 1942.

The Drinker's Farm Tragedy. Richmond, Va.: V.L. Fore, 1868.

Drinnon, Richard. *Rebel in Paradise: A Biography of Emma Goldman.* Chicago: University of Chicago Press, 1961.

Driscoll, R.E. *Seventy Years of Banking in the Black Hills.* Rapid City, S.D.: Gate City Guide, 1948.

Driver, G.R., and Miles, John C. (eds.) *The Assyrian Laws.* Oxford, Eng.: Clarendon Press, 1955.

Driver, Harold E. *Indians of North America.* Chicago: Chicago University Press, 1961.

Droge, Edward. *The Patrolman: A Cop's Story.* New York: New American Library, 1973.

Dromundo, Baltasar. *Francisco Villa y la Adelita.* Mexico City, Mex.: n.p., 1920.

Droysen, Johann Gustav. *Das Leben des Feldmarschalls Grafen Yorck von Wartenburg.* 3 vols. Berlin: Veit, 1851-52

Droz, Gustave. *Monsieur, Madame et Bébé.* Paris: Hetzel, 1866.

Drucker, Peter F. *The Effective Executive.* New York: Harper & Row, 1967.

_____. *The End of Economic Man.* New York: John Day, 1939.

_____. *Management.* New York: Harper & Row, 1973.

Drucker, Philip. *Indians of the Northwest Coast.* Garden City, N.Y.: The Natural History Press, 1963.

Drucker, S., and Hexter, H.B. *Children Astray.* Cambridge, Mass.: Harvard University Press, 1923.

Drug Abuse Council. *The Facts About "Drug Abuse".* New York: Free Press, 1980.

Drug Use and Crime. Report of the Panel on Drug Use and Criminal Behavior. Washington, D.C.: The National Institute on Drug Abuse, assisted by Research Triangle Institute, 1976.

Drug Use in America: Problem in Perspective. 2nd Report of the National Commission on Marijuana and Drug Abuse. Washington, D.C.: U.S. Government Printing Office, 1973.

Drumheller, Daniel. *"Uncle Dan".* Spokane, Wash.: Inland-American Printing, 1925.

Drummon, A.L. *True Detective Stories.* Chicago: M.A. Donohue, 1909.

Drummond, Isabel. *The Sex Paradox.* New York: G.P. Putnam's Sons, 1953.

Drury, Aubrey. *California, An Intimate Guide.* New York: Harper & Brothers, 1935.

_____. *John A. Hooper and California's Robust Youth.* San Francisco: Arthur W. Hooper, 1952.

Drury, John. *Historic Midwest Houses.* Minneapolis: University of Minnesota Press, 1947.

Drury, Luke. *A Report of the Examination of Rev. Ephraim K. Avery, Charged with the Murder of Sarah Maria Cornell.* Providence, R.I.: n.p., 1833.

Drury, Robert. *Madagascar.* Westport, Conn.: Greenwood, 1970.

Drury, Wells. *An Editor on the Comstock Lode.* San Francisco: Elder, 1913.

Drutman, Irving. *Good Company.* Boston: Little Brown, 1976.

Drysdale, George. *The Elements of Social Science.* London: Truelove, 1886.

Drzazga, John. *Sex Crimes and Their Legal Aspects.* Springfield, Ill.: Charles C. Thomas, 1960.

_____. *Wheels of Fortune.* Springfield, Ill.: Charles C. Thomas,

1963.

Duberman, Martin B. (ed.). *The Antislavery Vanguard: New Essays on the Abolitionists.* Princeton, N.J.: Princeton University Press, 1965.

_____. *Charles Francis Adams, 1807-1886.* Boston: Houghton Mifflin, 1961.

Dublin, Louis I., Lotka, Alfred J., and Spiegelman, Mortimer. *Length of Life.* New York: The Ronald Press Company, 1949.

_____, and Bunzel, Bessie. *To Be or Not To Be.* New York: Harrison, Smith, and Robert Haas, 1933.

Dubnov, Simon. *History of the Jews.* New York: Thomas Yoseloff, 1971.

Dubo, René. *Man Adapting.* New Haven, Conn.: Yale University Press, 1965.

Dubofsky, Melvyn, and Theoharis, Athan. *Imperial Democracy: The United States Since 1945.* Englewood Cliffs, N.J.: Prentice-Hall, 1983.

_____. *When Workers Organize.* Amherst: University of Massachusetts Press, 1968.

Duboin, Eloy. *La justice et sorciers au xvi siècle.* Nimes, Fr.: Clavel-Ballivet, 1880.

Dubois, Abbé J.A. *Hindu Manners and Customs.* Oxford, Eng.: Oxford University Press, 1906.

Du Bois, W.E.B. *The Autobiography of W.E.B. Du Bois.* New York: International Publishers, 1968.

_____. *Black Reconstruction.* New York: Harcourt, Brace, 1935.

_____. *Dusk of Dawn.* New York: Harcourt Brace Jovanovich, 1940.

_____. *John Brown.* Philadelphia: George W. Jacobs, 1909.

Dubreuil, Auguste. *Cours d'assises du Rhône. Assassinat de M. Carnot.* Lyon, Fr.: Mougin-Rusand, 1894.

Dubu, Marc. *Gilles de Rays, magicien et sodomiste.* Paris: Les Presses de la Cité, 1945.

Du Camp, Maxime. *Paris: Ses organes, ses fonctions et sa vie dans la second moitié du xixé siécle.* Paris: Hachette, 1875.

du Cane, Sir Edmund. *An Account of the Manner in Which Sentences of Penal Servitude Are Carried Out in England.* London: Millbank Prison, 1882.

_____. *The Punishment and Prevention of Crime.* London: Macmillan, 1885.

Ducasse, C. J. *The Belief in a Life After Death.* Springfield, Ill.: Charles C. Thomas, 1961.

Ducasse, Isidore. *Les Chants de Maldoror.* New York: New Directions, 1965.

Du Chaillu, Paul Belloni. *Explorations and Adventures in Equatorial Africa.* London: John Murray, 1861.

_____. *Stories of the Gorilla Country.* New York: Harper's, 1867.

Duchess of Atholl. *Searchlight on Spain.* London: Penguin Books, 1938.

Duckett, Eleanor. *Death and Life in the Tenth Century.* Ann Arbor: University of Michigan Press, 1967.

_____. *Gateway to the Middle Ages: France and Britain.* Ann Arbor: University of Michigan Press, 1938.

Dudden, F. Homes. *Henry Fielding: His Life, Work and Times.* 2 vols. London: Oxford University Press, 1952.

Dudley, Ernest. *Bywaters and Mrs. Thompson.* London: Odhams Press, 1953.

Dudycha, G. (ed.). *Pschology for Law Enforcement Officals.* Springfield, Ill.: C.C. Thomas, 1955.

Due anni di guerra. Rome: Ministero Cultura Popolare, 1942.

Duer, William A. *Reminiscences of an Old Yorker.* New York: W.L. Andres, 1867.

Duff, A.M. *Freedmen in the Early Roman Empire.* Cambridge, Eng.: Heffer, 1958.

Duff, C. *Ireland and the Irish.* New York: Boardman, 1952.

Duff, Charles. *A New Handbook on Hanging.* Chicago: Regnery, 1955.

Duff, David. *Hessian Tapestry.* London: Frederick Muller, 1967.

_____. *Victoria and Albert.* New York: Taplinger, 1972.

Duffee, David. *Using Correctional Officers in Planned Change.* Washington, D.C.: National Institute of Law Enforcement, National Technical Information Service, 1972.

Duffus, Robert L. *The Santa Fe Trail.* New York: Tudor Publishing, 1930.

_____. *The Tower of Jewels: Memories of San Francisco.* New York: W. W. Norton, 1960.

Duffy, Clinton D., and Jennings, Dean. *San Quentin Story.* New York: Doubleday, 1950.

Duffy, John. *A History of Public Health in New York City, 1866-1966.* New York: Russell Sage Foundation, 1974.

Duffy, Warden Clinton T. *The San Quentin Story, As Told to Dean Jennings.* Garden City, N.Y.: Doubleday, 1950.

_____, with Hirschberg, Al. *88 Men and Two Women.* Garden City, N.Y.: Doubleday, 1962.

Duffy, John. *A History of Public Health in New York City, 1625-1866.* New York: Russell Sage Foundation, 1968.

Dugdale, Blanche E.C. *Arthur James Balfour.* 2 Vols. New York: Putnam, 1937.

Dugdale, Richard L. *The Jukes.* New York: Putnam, 1910.

Duggan, Christopher. *Fascism and the Mafia.* New Haven, Conn.: Yale University Press, 1989.

Duhamel, Pierre. *Henry of Guise.* Paris: Librairie Académique Perrin, 1974.

Duhr, Bernard. *Geschichte der Jesuiten in den Ländern deutscher Zunge.* Freiburg, Ger.: Herden, 1907.

_____. *Die Stellung der Jesuiten in den deutschen Hexenprozessen.* Cologne, Ger.: J.P. Bachem, 1900.

Du Jarric, P. *Akbar and the Jesuits.* trans. C.H. Payne. New York: Harper and Brothers, 1926.

Duke, Thomas S. *Celebrated Criminal Cases of America.* San Francisco: James H. Barry, 1910.

Duke, Winifred (ed.). *Notable British Trials: Trial of Field and Gray.* London: William Hodge, 1939.

_____. *Notable British Trials: Trials of Frederick Nodder.* London: William Hodge, 1950.

_____. *Six Trials.* London: Victor Gollancz, 1934.

_____. *Skin for Skin.* London: Gollancz, 1935.

_____. *The Stroke of Murder.* London: R. Hale, 1937.

Dull, Paul S., and Umemura, Michael T. *The Tokyo Trials: A Functional Index to the Proceedings of the International Military Tribunal for the Far East.* Ann Arbor: University of Michigan Press, 1957.

Dulles, Allen. *The Craft of Intelligence.* New York: Harper & Row, 1963.

_____. *Germany's Underground.* New York: Macmillan, 1947.

_____. *The Secret Surrender.* London: Weidenfeld & Nicolson, 1946.

Dulles, Eleanor L. *Depression and Reconstruction.* Philadelphia: University of Pennsylvania Press, 1937.

_____. *America in the Pacific: A Century of Expansion.* Boston: Houghton Mifflin, 1938.

Dulles, Foster Rhea. *America Learns to Play.* New York: D. Appleton-Century, 1940.

_____. *China and America: The Story of Their Relations Since 1784.* Princeton, N.J.: Princeton University Press, 1946.

_____. *The Imperial Years.* New York: Thomas Y. Crowell, 1956.

_____. *Labor in America.* New York: Crowell, 1960.

_____. *The Road to Teheran: The Story of Russia and America, 1781-1943.* Princeton, N.J.: Princeton University Press, 1944.

_____. *The United States Since 1865.* Ann Arbor: University of Michigan Press, 1959.

Dulles, John W. *Yesterday in Mexico: A Chronicle of the Revolution, 1919-1936.* Austin: University of Texas Press, 1961.

Dumas, Alexandre. *Celebrated Crimes.* Translator: Jacques Wagrez. Philadelphia: Rittenhouse Press, 1895.

_____ (père). *Le meneur des loups.* Paris: Michel Lévy frères, 1860.

_____. *Urbain Grandier.* Paris: Dondey-Dupré, 1850.

Dumcke, Julius. *Zauberei und Hexenprozessen.* Berlin: A. Scherl, 1912.

Dumenil, Lynn. *Freemasonry and American Culture.* Princeton, N.J.: Princeton University Press, 1985.

Dumini, Amerigo. *17 colpi.* Milan, Italy: Longaneso. 1958.

Dumond, Dwight Lowell. *America in Our Time 1896-1946.* New York: Henry Holt, 1947.

_____. *Antislavery Origins of the Civil War.* Ann Arbor: University of Michigan Press, 1939.

_____. *A History of the United States.* New York: Henry Holt, 1942.

Dumont, René. *False Start in Africa.* London: Sphere Books, 1966.

Dunaway, W.F. *A History of Pensylvania.* New York: Prentice-Hall, 1948.

Dunbar, Dorothy. *Blood in the Parlor.* New York: A.S. Barnes, 1964.

Dunbar, Edward D. *Social Life in the Former Days, Chiefly in the Provinces of Moray.* Edinburgh, Scot.: Edmonston & Douglas, 1865.

Dunbar, Seymour. *History of Travel in America.* Indianapolis, Ind.: Bobbs-Merrill, 1915.

Dunboyne, Lord (ed.). *Notable British Trials: Trial of J.G. Haigh.* London: William Hodge, 1953.

Duncan, Arnold. *The Confession of Edward Donnelly.* Carlisle, Pa.: A. Loudon Whitehall, 1808.

Duncan, E.H. *Night-Duty Social Worker.* New York: Elsevier/Nelson, 1979.

Duncan, Hugh Dalziel. *The Rise of Chicago as a Literary Center from 1885-1920.* Totowa, N.J.: Bedminster Press, 1964.

Duncan, L. Wallace (ed.). *History of Montgomery County, Kansas, by Its Own People.* Iola, Kan.: Iola Register, 1903.

Duncan, Lee. *Over the Wall.* New York: E.P. Dutton, 1936.

Duncan, Otis Dudley and Beverly. *The Negro Population of Chicago.* Chicago: University of Chicago Press, 1957.

Duncan, Richard R. *The Social and Economic Impact of the Civil War on Maryland.* Columbus: Ohio State University, 1963.

Duncan, Ronald, and Weston-Smith, Miranda (eds.). *The Encyclopedia of Ignorance.* New York: Pergamon Press, 1977.

Duncan, Ronald (ed.). *Selected Writings of Mahatma Gandhi.* London: Faber & Faber, 1951.

Dundes, Alan (ed.). *Mother Wit from the Laughing Barrel.* Englewood Cliffs, N.J.: Prentice-Hall, 1973.

Dunham, Allison, and Kurland, Philip B. (eds.). *Mr. Justice.* Chicago: University of Chicago Press, 1964.

Dunham, Chester Forrester. *The Attitude of the Northern Clergy toward the South, 1860-1865.* Philadelphia: Porcupine Press, 1974.

Dunham, Dick, and Vivian. *Our Strip of Land: A History of Daggett County, Utah.* Manila, Utah: Daggett County Lions Club, 1947.

Dunlap, Carol. *California People.* Salt Lake City, Utah: Peregrene Smith Books, 1982.

Dunlop, Anne B. *The Approved School Experience.* London: H.M. Stationery Office, 1974.

Dunlop, Richard. *Doctors of the American Frontier.* Garden City, N.Y.: Doubleday, 1965.

Dunn, Allan. *Carefree San Francisco.* San Francisco: Elder, 1913.

Dunn, Arthur Wallace. *From Harrison to Harding.* 2 vol. New York: Putnam, 1922.

Dunn, Christopher S. *Patterns of Robbery Characteristics.* Washington, D.C.: National Criminal Justice Information and Statistics Service, 1976.

Dunn, Delmer. *Public Officials and the Press.* Reading, Mass.: Addison-Wesley, 1969.

Dunn, Donald H. *Ponzi, the Boston Swindler.* New York: McGraw-Hill, 1975.

Dunn, H.H. *The Crimson Jester: Zapata of Mexico.* London: Harrap, 1939.

Dunn, J.B. *Perilous Trails of Texas.* Dallas: Southwest Press,

1952.

Dunn, Rev. James B. *Band of Hoppe Manual*. New York: National Temperance Society and Publication House, 1867.

_____. *Moody's Talks on Temperance with Anecdotes and Incidents in Connection with the Tabernacle Temperance Work in Boston*. New York: National Temperance Society and Publication House, 1878.

Dunn, John P. *Massacres of the Mountains*. New York: Harper and Brothers, 1886.

Dunn, M.M. *William Penn: Politics and Conscience*. Princeton, N.J.: Princeton University Press, 1967.

Dunn, Richard S. *Puritans and Yankees: The Winthrop Dynasty of New England 1630-1717*. Princeton: Princeton University Press, 1962.

Dunn, W.H. *James Anthony Froude, A Biography (1857-1894)*. Oxford, Eng.: Clarendon Press, 1963.

Dunne, Edward F. *Illinois: The Heart of the Nation*. 5 vols. Chicago: Lewis, 1933.

Dunne, Finley Peter. *Mr. Dooley In the Hearts of His Countrymen*. Boston: Small, Maynard, 1899.

_____. *Mr. Dooley In Peace and In War*. Boston: Small, Maynard, 1899.

_____. *Mr. Dooley's Opinions*. New York: Harper, 1906.

Dunne, Gerald T. *Hugo Black and the Judicial Revolution*. New York: Touchstone, 1978.

Dunner, Joseph. *The Republic of Israel*. New York: McGraw-Hill, 1950.

Dunning, Harold Marion. *The Life of Rocky Mountain Jim (James Nugent)*. Boulder, Colo.: Johnson, 1967.

Dunning, John. *The Arbor House Treasury of True Crime*. New York: Arbor House, 1981.

Dunning, William A. *Essays on the Civil War and Reconstruction and Related Topics*. New York: Macmillan, 1898.

_____. *Reconstruction, Political and Economic, 1865-1877*. New York: Harper & Brothers, 1907.

Dunphy, Thomas, and Cummins, Thomas J. *Remarkable Trials*. New York: Ward & Peloubet, 1878.

Dunraven, Earl of (Windham, Thomas Wyndham-Quin). *Hunting in the Yellowstone*. New York: Macmillan, 1925.

_____. *Past Times and Pastimes*. London: Hodder & Stoughton, 1922.

Dunsany, E.J.M.D. Plunkett, 18th Baron. *Patches of Sunlight*. London: William Heinemann, 1938.

Dunshee, Kenneth Holcomb. *As You Pass By*. New York: Hastings House, 1952.

Dunshee, Tom, and Duncan, Richard. *Motorcade: November 22, 1963*. Trenton, N.J.: Published by Author, 1975.

Dunton, Alvin R. *The True Story of the Hart-Meservey Murder Trial*. Boston: Dunton, 1882.

Duplés-Agier, H. *Registre criminel du Châtelet de Paris*. Paris: C. Lahure, 1861.

Du Plessis, comte Joachim. *Berryer*. Paris: La Bonne Presse, 1946.

Dupuy, Aimée. *1870-1871, la guerre, la commune et la press*. Paris: Armand Colin, 1959.

Duràn, Fray Diego. *The Aztecs: The History of the Indies of New Spain*. Trans. Doris heyden and Fernando Horcasitas. New York: Orion, 1963.

Durand, E. Dana. *The Finances of New York City*. New York: Macmillan, 1928.

Durand, Mortimer. *Crazy Campaign*. London: George Routledge, 1936.

Durant, M.,et al. *Crime, Criminals and the Law*. London: Office of Population Censuses and Surveys, 1972.

Durant, Will. *The Renaissance*. New York: Simon and Schuster, 1953.

Duranty, Walter. *I Write as I Please*. New York: Simon and Schuster, 1935.

Durbin, E.F.M. *The Politics of Democratic Socialism*. London: Routledge, 1940.

Durden, Robert F. *The Gray and the Black*. Baton Rouge: Louisiana State University Press, 1972.

_____. *James Sheperd Pike: Republicanism and the American Negro*. Durham, N.C.: Duke University Press, 1957.

Durgnant, Raymond. *The Crazy Mirror: Hollywood Comedy and the American Image*. London: Faber & Faber, 1969.

Durham, George. *Taming the Neuces Strip*. Austin: University of Texas Press, 1962.

Durham, M.E. *The Sarajevo Crime*. London: G. Allen & Unwin, 1925.

Durham, Philip, and Jones, Everett L. *The Negro Cowboys*. New York: Dodd, Mead, 1965.

Durk, David, and Silverman, Ira. *The Plesant Avenue Connection*. New York: Harper & Row, 1977.

Durkheim, Emile. *The Division of Labor in Society*. trans. George Simpson. Glencoe, Ill.: The Free Press, 1947.

_____. *The Rules of Sociological Method*. Glencoe, Ill.: The Free Press, 1938.

_____. *Sociology and Philosophy*. Glencoe, Ill.: The Free Press, 1953.

_____. *Suicide*. Trans. John A. Spaulding and George Simpson. Glencoe, Ill.: Free Press, 1951.

DuRose, John. *Murder Was My Business*. London: W.H. Allen, 1971.

Dusinberre, William. *Civil War Issues in Philadelphia, 1856-1865*. Philadelphia: University of Pennsylvania Press, 1965.

Duster, Troy. *The Legislation of Morality: Law, Drugs, and Moral Judgement*. New York: Free Press, 1970.

Dutch, Andrew K. *Hysteria*. Philadelphia: Dorrance, 1975.

Dutcher, George M. *Disenthralled: A Story of my Life. A Vivid Portrayal of the Evils of Intemperance*. Hartford, Conn.: Colombian Book Company, 1872.

Dutt, R. Palmer. *Fascism and Social Revolution*. New York: International Publishers, 1935.

Dutt, Romesh. *India in the Victorian Age*. London: Kegan Paul, Trench, Trubner, 1904.

Dutton, Bertha P. (ed.). *Indians of the Southwest*. Santa Fe, N.M.: Southwestern Association of Indian Affairs, 1963.

Duus, Peter. *The Rise of Modern Japan*. Boston: Houghton Mifflin, 1976.

Duval, John C. *The Adventures of Big Foot Wallace, the Texas Ranger and Hunter*. Macon, Ga.: J.W. Burke, 1871.

_____. *Early Times in Texas*. Austin, Texas: H.P.N. Gammel, 1892.

Duvallon, Berquin. *Vue de la Colonie Espagnole du Mississippi*. Paris: Suvallon, 1803.

Dvornik, Francis. *The Slavs in European History and Civilization*. New Brunswick, N.J.: Rutgers University Press, 1962.

Dwight, Timothy. *Travels in New England and New York*. London: W. Baynes & Sons, 1923.

Dwivedy, S., and Bhargava, G.S. *Political Corruption in India*. New Delhi: Popular Book Services, 1967.

D'Ydewalle, Charles. *Albert and the Belgians*. New York: Morrow, 1935.

Dye, John Smith. *History of the Plots and Crimes to Overthrow Liberty in America*. Freeport, N.Y.: Books for Librairies Press, 1969.

Dyer, Alfred. *The European Slave Trade in English Girls*. London: Dyer Brothers, 1880.

_____. *Six Years' Labour and Sorrow*. London: Syer Brothers, 1885.

Dyer, John L. *The Snow-Show Itinerant*. Cincinnati, Ohio: Cranston & Stowe, 1890.

Dyess, William E. *Death March from Bataan*. Sydney, Aus.: Angus and Robertson, 1945.

_____. *The Dyess Story*. New York: G.P. Putnam's Sons, 1944.

The Dying Confession of John Lechler. Lancaster, Pa.: S.T. Stambaugh, 1822.

The Dying Declaration of James Buchanan, Ezra Ross, and William Brooks. Worcester, Mass.: n.p., 1778.

Dykes, Jefferson C. *Billy the Kid: The Bibliography of a Legend.* Albuquerque: University of New Mexico Press, 1952.

Dykstra, Robert R. *The Cattle Towns.* New York: Alfred A. Knopf, 1968.

Dymond, Alfred H. *The Law on Trial, or Personal Recollections of the Death Penalty and its Opponents.* London: Society for the Abolition of Capital Punishment, 1865.

Dyne, D.G. *Famous New Zealand Murders.* London: Collins, 1969.

Dyos, Harold James, and Wolff, Michael (eds.). *The Victorian City.* Boston: Routledge & Kegan Paul, 1973.

Dyson, James L. *The World of Ice.* New York: Alfred A. Knopf, 1962.

Dyson-Hudson, Neville. *Karamojong Politics.* London: Clarendon Press, 1966.

E

Eads, Lyle. *Survival Amidst the Ashes.* New York: Carlton Press, 1978.

Ealy, Ruth R. *Water in a Thirsty Land.* Pittsburgh: n.p., 1955.

Eames, Hugh. *Sleuths, Inc.* Philadelphia: J.B. Lippincott, 1978.

Earhart, Amelia. *Last Flight by Amelia Earhart.* New York: Harcourt, Brace, 1937.

Earhart, Mary. *Frances Willard.* Chicago: University of Chicago Press, 1944.

Earl, D.C. *Tiberius Gracchus: A Study in Politics.* Brussels, Belgium: Collection Latomus, LXVI, 1963.

Earl, David Mafarey. *Emperor and Nation in Japan.* Seattle: University of Washington Press, 1964.

Earle, Alice Moore. *Stage Coach and Tavern Days.* London: Macmillan, 1927.

_____. *Two Centuries of Costume.* New York: Macmillan, 1903

Earle, J.P. *History of Clay County and Northwest Texas.* Henrietta, Texas: n.p., 1900.

Earle, Peter. *Corsairs of Malta and Barbary.* Annapolis, Md.: U.S. Naval Institute, 1970.

East, John M. *'Neath the Mask: The Story of the East Family.* London: George Allen and Unwin, 1967.

East, N. *Society and the Criminal.* Springfield, Ill.: Charles C. Thomas, 1950.

East, Norwood. *Sexual Offenders.* London: Delisle, 1955.

_____. *Society and the Criminal.* London: H.M. Stationery Office, 1949.

East, William. *Society and the Criminal.* Springfield, Ill.: Charles C. Thomas, 1951.

Easterlin, R.A. *Birth and Fortune.* New York: Basic Books, 1980.

Easterman, A.L. *King Carol, Hitler and Lupescu.* London: Victor Gollancz, 1942.

Eastman, George D. (ed.). *Municipal Police Administration.* Washington, D.C.: International City Management Association, 1973.

Eastman, Mary F. *The Biography of Dio Lewis.* New York: Fowler & Wells, 1891.

Eastman, Max. *Enjoyment of Living.* New York: Harper & Brothers, 1948.

_____. *Love and Revolution.* New York: Random House, 1964.

_____. *Reflections on the Failure of Socialism.* New York: Devin Adair, 1955.

Easton, David. *A Framework for Political Analysis.* Englewood Cliffs, N.J.: Prentice-Hall, 1965.

Easum, Chester Verne. *The Americanization of Carl Schurz.* Chicago: University of Chicago Press, 1929.

Easum, Chester. *Prince Henry of Prussia, Brother of Frederick the Great.* Madison: University of Wisconsin Press, 1984.

Eaton, Clement. *Freedom of Thought in the Old South.* Durham, N.C.: Duke University Press, 1940.

_____. *Henry Clay and the Art of American Politics.* Boston: Little, Brown, 1957.

_____. *A History of the Old South.* New York: Macmillan, 1949.

_____. *A History of the Southern Confederacy.* New York: Macmillan, 1954.

Eaton, Dorman B. *The Government of Municipalities.* New York: Macmillan, 1899.

Eaton, Frank. *Pistol Pete, Veteran of the Old West.* Boston: Little, Brown, 1952.

Eaton, Harold. *Famous Poison Trials.* London: W. Collins Sons, 1923.

Eaton, Jeanette. *Bucky O'Neill of Arizona.* New York: William Morrow, 1949.

_____. *Gandhi, Fighter Without a Sword.* New York: William Morrow, 1950.

Eaton, Joseph W., and Polk, Kenneth. *Measuring Delinquency.* Pittsburgh, Pa.: University of Pittsburgh Press, 1961.

Eaton, Peggy. *Autobiography.* New York: Charles Scribner's Sons, 1932.

Eaves, Lucile. *A History of California Labor Legislation with an Introductory Sketch of the San Francisco Labor Movement.* Berkeley: University of California Press, 1910.

Eayrs, James (ed.). *The Commonwealth and Suez.* London: Oxford University Press, 1963.

Eban, Abba. *The Tide of Nationalism.* New York: Harper, 1959.

Ebbinghaus, H. *Memory.* trans. H. Ruyer and C.E. Bussenius. New York: Teachers College Press, 1913.

_____. *The Voice of Israel.* New York: Harper, 1957.

Ebenstein, William. *Fascist Italy.* New York: American Book, 1939.

Eberland, W. *The local cultures of South and East China.* Leiden, Neth.: E.J.Brill, 1968.

Ebin, D. (ed.). *The Drug Experience.* New York: Orion, 1961.

Ebner, Theodor. *Friedrich von Spee und die Hexenprozesse seiner Zeit.* Hamburg, Ger.: J.F. Richter, 1898.

Ebon, Martin (ed.). *The Psychic Scene.* New York: Signet, 1974.

_____. *Reincarnation in the Twentieth Century.* New York: Signet, 1967.

_____. *The Satan Trap.* New York: Doubleday, 1976.

Eccentricities and Anecdotes of Albert John Tirrell. Boston: n.p., 1846.

Echardt, Carl C. *The Papacy and World Affairs.* Chicago: University of Chicago Press, 1937.

Eckart, Dietrich. *Der Bolshewismus von Moses bei Lenin: Zwiegespräch zwischen Adolf Hitler und mir.* Munich: Hoheneichen Verlag, 1924.

Eckemorde, Hamilton James. *The Revolution in Virginia.* New York: Houghton Mifflin, 1916.

Eckenrode, H.J. *Rutherford B. Hays: Statesman of Reunion.* New York: Dodd, Mead, 1930.

Eckhardstein, Baron H. von. *Ten Years at the Court of St. James, 1895-1905.* London: Butterworth, 1921.

Eckhardt, H. *Ivan the Terrible.* New York: Charles Scribner's Sons, 1949.

Eddowes, Michael. *Khruschev Killed Kennedy.* Dallas: Published by Author, 1975.

_____. *The Man on Your Conscience,* London: Cassell, 1955.

_____. *November 22: How They Killed Kennedy.* London: Neville Spearman, 1976.

_____. *The Oswald File.* New York: Potter, 1977.

Eddy, George Sherwood. *Revolutionary Christianity.* New York: Willett, Clark, 1939.

Eddy, J.P. *Mystery of Peter the Painter.* London: Stevens & Sons, 1946.

_____. *Scarlett and Ermine.* London: William Kimber, 1960.

Eddy, Paul, Sabogal, Hugo, and Walden, Sara. *The Cocaine Wars.* New York: W.W. Norton, 1988.

Eddy, Richard. *Alcohol in Society.* New York: The National

Temperance Society and Publication House, 1888.

Eddy, Ruth Story Devereaux. *The Eddy Family in America.* Boston: The Eddy Family Association, 1930.

Eddy, Thomas. *An Account of the State Prison or Penitentiary House in the City of New York:* New York: Isaac Collins & Son, 1801.

Eddy, T.M. *The Patriotism of Illinois: A Record of Civil and Military History of the State in the War for the Union.* 2 vols. Chicago: Clarke, 1865.

Eddy, William A. *FDR Meets Ibn Saud.* New York: American Friends of the Middle East, 1957.

Edelhertz, Herbert. *The Nature, Impact and Prosecution of White-Collar Crime.* Washington D.C.: Government Printing Office, 1970.

_____. and Geis, Gilbert. *Public Compensation to Victims of Crime.* New York: Praeger, 1974.

Edelman, Murray. *The Symbolic Uses of Politics.* Urbana: University of Southern Illinois Press, 1964.

Edelstein, Tilden G. *Strange Enthusiasm: A Life of Thomas Wentworth Higginson.* New Haven, Conn.: Yale University Press, 1963.

Eden, Anthony. *Facing the Dictators.* London: Cassell, 1962.

Edgar, P. *Children and Screen Violence.* St. Lucia, Aus.: University of Queensland Press, 1977.

Edge, L.L. *Run The Cat Roads.* New York: Dembner Books, 1981.

Edgell, David P. *William Ellery Channing: An Intellectual Portrait.* Boston: Beacon Press, 1955.

Eden, Sir Anthony. *Full Circle.* London: Cassel, 1960.

Eden, William (First Baron Auckland). *Principles of Penal Law.* London: B. White & T. Codell, 1771.

Edgar, William Crowell. *Judson Moss Bemis, Pioneer.* Minneapolis Minn.: The Bellman Company, 1926.

Edgarr, W.F. *Trial of Allen C. Lavos.* Easton, Pa.: Cole & Morwitz, 1877.

Edgerton, Robert B. *The Cloak of Competence.* Berkeley: University of California Press, 1967.

_____. *Mau Mau: An African Crucible.* New York: The Free Press, 1989.

Edgeworth, Maria. *Castle Rackrent.* New York: Oxford University Press, 1964.

Edholm, Charlton. *Traffic in Girls and Work of Rescue Missions.* Oakland, Calif.: Sierra, 1900.

Edinburgh, K.G. Duke of. *A Guide to the Works of Art and Science Collected by Captain His Royal Highness The Duke of Edinburgh, K.G., during His Five-Years Cruise Round the World in H.M.S. Galatea (1867-1871).* London: Strangeways, 1872.

Edman, Irwin. *Philosopher's Holiday.* New York: The Viking Press, 1938.

Edmonds, C.J. *Kurds, Turks and Arabs.* London: Cambridge University Press, 1957.

Edmonds, Emma S. *Nurse and Spy.* Philadelphia: W.S. Williams, 1865.

Edmonds, I.G. *Hollywood R.I.P.* New York: Regency Books, 1963.

Edmonds, S. Emma E. *Nurse and Spy in the Union Army.* Harford, Conn.: W.S. Williams, 1865.

Edwardes, Allen. *The Royal Whore.* New York: Chilton Books, 1970.

Edwards, Allen. *The Jewel in the Lotus.* New York: Lancer, 1969.

_____, and Masters, R.E.L. *The Cradle of Erotica.* London: Odyssey Press, 1970.

_____. *Techniques of Attitudes Scale Construction.* New York: D. Appelton, 1957.

Edwards, Alison. *Rape, Racism, and the White Woman's Movement.* Chicago: Sojourner Truth Organization, 1976.

Edwards, B. *Sources of Social Statistics.* London: William Heinemann, 1974.

Edwards, Ellen. *Maryland During the Reconstruction Period.* Minneapolis: University of Minnesota Press, 1928.

Edwards, Eugene. *Jack Pots, Stories of the Great American Game.* Chicago: Jamieson-Higgins, 1900.

Edwards, Francis. *The Dangerous Queen.* London: G. Chapman, 1964.

Edwards, Jennie. *Biography of John N. Edwards.* Kansas City: Published by Author, 1889.

Edwards, Jerome. *The Foreign Policy of Colonel McCormick's Tribune.* Reno: University of Nevada Press, 1971.

Edwards, J.B. *Early days in Abilene.* Abilene, Texas: C.W. Wheeler, 1896.

Edwards, John Newman. *Noted Guerrillas, or the Warfare of the Border.* St. Louis: Bryan, Brand, 1877.

_____. *Shelby and His Men.* Cincinnati, Ohio: Miami Printing, 1867.

_____. *Shelby's Expedition to Mexico.* Kansas City: Kansas City Times, 1872.

Edwards, Justin. *Letter to the Friends of Temperance in Massachusetts.* Boston: Seth Bliss, 1836.

Edwards, Kenneth. *The Grey Diplomatists.* London: Rich & Cowan, 1938.

Edwards, L. Fielding. *Profane Pilgrimage.* London: Duckworth, 1938.

_____. *A Wayfarer in Yugoslavia.* New York: McBride, 1939.

Edwards, Loren E. *Shoplifting and Shrinkage Protection for Stores.* Springfield, Ill.: Charles C. Thomas, 1958.

Edwards, Monroe. *The Life and Adventures of the Accomplished Forger and Swindler, Colonel Monroe Edwards.* New York: H. Long & Brother, 1848.

Edwards, Richard C., Reich, Michael, and Weisskopf, Thomas E. *The Capitalist System: A Radical Analysis of American Society.* Englewood Cliffs, N.J.: Prentice-Hall, 1972.

Edwards, Ruth Dudley. *Patrick Pearse: The Triumph of Failure.* New York: Taplinger, 1977.

Edwards, Samuel. *The Vidoca Dossier.* Boston: Houghton Mifflin, 1977.

Eells, George. *The Life That Late He Led.* New York: G.P. Putnam & Sons, 1967.

Egan, Ferol. *Frèmont, Explorer for a Restless Nation.* Garden City, N.Y.: Doubleday, 1977.

Egen, Frederick W. *Plainclothesman: Handbook of Vice and Gambling Investigation.* New York: Arco Publishing Co., 1959.

Eggan, Fred. *Social Organization of the Western Pueblos.* Chicago: University of Chicago Press, 1950.

Eggenberger, David. *A Dictionary of Battles.* New York: Thomas Y. Crowell, 1967.

Eggert, Gerald G. *Richard Olney: Evolution of a Stateman.* University Park: Pennsylvania State University Press, 1974.

Egginton, Joyce. *From Cradle to Grave.* New York: W. Morrow, 1989.

Eglinton, J.Z. *Geek Love.* New York: Oliver Layton, 1965.

Egyptian Society of International Law. *Egypt and the United Nations.* New York: Manhattan, 1957.

Ehlers, Dieter. *Technik und Moral einer Verschwörung, 20 Juli 1944.* Frankfurt, Ger.: Athenäum, 1964.

Ehrenwald, Jan. *The ESP Experience: A Psychiatric Validation.* New York: Basic Books, 1978.

Ehrlich, Blake. *London on the Thames.* London: Cassell, 1968.

Ehrlich, J.W. *A Life in My Hands.* New York: Putnam, 1965.

Ehrlich, Leonard. *God's Angry Man.* Modern Age Books, 1938.

Ehrlich, Paul R. *The End of Affluence.* New York: Ballantine Books, 1974.

_____. and Feldman, S. Shirley. *The Race Bomb.* New York: Quadrangle, 1977.

_____. *The Population Bomb.* New York: Ballantine Books, 1971.

Ehrlich, Richard (ed.). *Immigrants in Industrial America, 1850-1920.* Charlottesville, Va.: University of Virginia Press, 1977.

Ehrlichman, John. *Witness to Power.* New York: Simon & Schuster, 1982.

Ehrmann, Herbert B. *The Untried Case: The Sacco-Vanzetti Case and the Morelli Gang.* New York: Vanguard, 1933.

Eichelberger, Robert L. *Our Jungle Road to Tokyo.* New York: Viking Press, 1950.

Eichmann in Jerusalem: A Report on the Banality of Evil. New York: Viking, 1964.

Eichner, H.W. *Basic Reasearch on Pyrolysis and Combustion of Wood.* Madison, Wisc.: U.S. Forest Products Laboratory, 1962.

Eichstaedt, J. *Von Dollfuss zu Hitler.* Wiesbaden: F. Steiner, 1955.

Eidelberg, Paul. *The Philosophy of the American Constitution.* New York: Free Press, 1968.

Eikemeyer, Carl. *Over the Great Navajo Trail.* New York: J.J. Little, 1900.

Einstein, Alfred. *Mozart: His Character, His Work.* trans. Arthur Mendel and Nathan Broder. New York: Oxford University Press, 1945.

Einstein, Izzy. *Prohibition Agent No. 1.* New York: Frederick A. Stokes, 1932.

Einzig, P. *The Economic Foundations of Fascism.* London: Macmillan, 1933.

Eisele, Mrs. Fannie L. *A History of Noble County, Oklahoma.* Covington, Okla.: Published By Author, 1958.

Eisele, Wilbert E. *The Real "Wild Bill" Hickok.* Denver: William H. Andre, 1931.

Eisenberg, Daniel M., as told to Beffel, John Nicholas. *I Find the Missing.* New York: Farrar & Rinehart, 1938.

Eisenberg, Dennis, Dan, Uri, Landau, and Landau, Eli. *Meyer Lansky.* London: Paddington Press, 1979.

Eisenbud, J. *Psi and Psychoanalysis.* New York: Grune and Stratton, 1970.

_____. *The World of Ted Serios.* New York: William Morrow, 1967.

Eisenhower, Dwight D. *Crusade in Europe.* New York: Doubleday, 1948.

_____. *Mandate for Change: 1953-1956.* Garden City, N.Y.: Doubleday, 1963.

_____. *The White House Years: Waging Peace, 1956-1961.* Garden City, N.Y.: Doubleday, 1965.

Eisenmenger, V. *Archduke Francis Ferdinand.* London: Selwyn & Blount, 1931.

Eisenschiml, Otto, and Bishop, Jim. *The Day Lincoln Was Shot.* New York: Harper & Brothers, 1955.

_____. *The Drama of Lincoln's Assassination.* Harrogate: Tennesse, 1937.

_____. *In the Shadow of Lincoln's Death.* New York: Wilfred Funk, 1940.

_____. *O.E. Historian Without an Armchair.* Indianapolis, Ind.: Bobbs-Merrill, 1963.

_____. *The Story of Shiloh.* Chicago: Civil War Round Table, 1946.

_____. *Why Was Lincoln Murdered?* Boston: Little, Brown, 1937.

_____. *Without Fame: The Romance of a Profession.* Chicago: Alliance, 1942.

_____, and Newman, R.G. *The Civil War: The American Iliad.* New York: Grosset & Dunlap, 1956.

Eisenstadt, S.N. *The Decline of Empires.* Englewood Cliffs, N.J.: Prentice-Hall, 1967.

_____. *From Generation to Generation: Age Groups and Social Structure.* Glencoe, Ill.: The Free Press, 1956.

Eisenstein, James, and Jacob, Herbert. *Felony Justice.* Boston: Little, Brown, 1977.

Eisenstein, Louis, and Rosenberg, Elliot. *A Stripe of Tammany's Tiger.* New York: R. Speller, 1966.

Eisler, Robert. *Man into Wolf: An Anthropological Interpretation of Sadism, Masochism and Lycanthropy.* London: Routledge, 1951.

_____. *The Royal Art of Astrology.* London: Herbert Joseph, 1946.

Eisner, Lotte. *The Haunted Screen.* Berkeley: University of California Press, 1974.

Eissler, K. R. *Searchlights on Delinquency.* New York: Int. Univs. Press, 1949.

Ejiri Susumu. *Characteristics of the Japanese Press.* Nihon Shinbun Kyokai, 1972.

Ekins, H. R., and Wright, Theon. *China Fights for Her Life.* New York: McGraw-Hill, 1938.

Ekman, P., et al. *Emotion in the Human Face.* New York: Pergamon Press, 1972.

Ela, Richard. *Trial of Amos Furnald.* Concord, N.H.: Jacob B. Moore, 1825.

Elath, Eliahu. *Israel and Her Neighbors.* Cleveland: World, 1957.

Elazar, Daniel. *American Federalism: A View from the States.* New York: Thomas Y. Crowell, 1972.

Elder, Donald. *Ring Lardner.* Garden City, N.Y.: Doubleday, 1956.

Elder, G.H. *Children of the Great Depression.* Chicago: University of Chicago Press, 1974.

Elder, Rob. *Chiodo 2.* Chicago: Playboy Press, 1975.

Elderkin, John, et al. (eds.) *After Dinner Speeches at the Lotos Club.* New York: Printed for the Lotos Club, 1911.

Eldridge, Benjamin P., and Watts, William B. *Our Rival the Rascal.* Boston: Pemberton, 1897.

Eldridge, William Butler. *Narcotics and the Law: A Critique of the American Experiment in Narcotic Drug Control.* Chicago: University of Chicago Press, 1967.

Eliade, Mircea. *Rites and Symbols of Initiation.* New York: Harper & Row, 1958

_____. *Shamanism.* New York: Pantheon Books, 1964

Elias, Christopher. *Fleecing the Lambs.* Chicago: Henry Regnery, 1971.

Elias, C.E. Jr., et al. *Metropolis: Values in Conflict.* Belmont, Calif.: Wadsworth, 1964.

Elias, R. *Victims of the System.* New Brunswick, N.J.: Transaction, 1983.

Elich, Philipp Ludwig. *Daemonomagia.* Frankfort, Ger.: C. Nebemii, 1607.

Eliel, Paul. *The Waterfront and General Strikes, San Francisco, 1934.*

Eliot, Sir Charles. *Hinduism and Buddhism: An Historical Sketch.* 3 vols. New York: Longmans, Green, 1921.

_____. *Turkey in Europe.* London: Edward Arnold, 1908.

Ellen, Mary, Murphy, Mark, and Weld, Ralph Foster. *A Treasury of Brooklyn.* New York: William Sloane Associates, 1949.

Ellenberger, Henri. *Criminologie du Passé et du Present.* Montreal, Can.: Presses de L'Universite de Montreal, 1965.

The Ellery C. Decision: A Case Study of Judicial Regulation of Juvenile Status Offenders. New York: Institute of Judicial Administration, 1975.

Ellet, Charles. *The Mississippi and Ohio Rivers.* Philadelphia: J.B. Lippincott, Grambo, 1853.

Ellett, Elizabeth Fries Lummis. *Summer Rambles in the West.* New York: J.C. Riker, 1853.

Elliff, John T. *Crime, Dissent, and the Attorney General: The Justice Department in the 1960s.* Beverly Hills, Calif.: Sage, 1971.

Elliff, John T. *The Reform of F.B.I. Intelligence Operations.* New Jersey: Princeton, 1979.

Elliot, James F. *Interception Patrol.* Springfield, Ill.: Charles C. Thomas, 1973.

Elliot, James L. *Red Stacks Over the Horizon.* Grand Rapids, Mich.: William B. Eerdsman, 1967.

Elliott, Bateman M. *Revolt to Revolution.* Manchester, Eng.: Manchester University Press, 1974.

Elliott, Charles Wyllys. *Mysteries, or glimpses of the Supernatural.* New York: Harper and Bros., 1852.

Elliott, David Stewart. *Last Raid of the Daltons.* Coffeyville, Kan.: Coffeyville Journal, 1892.

Elliott, Delbert S., and Voss, H.L. *Delinquency and Dropout.* Lexington, Mass.: Lexington, 1974.

Elliott, James W. *Transport to Disaster.* New York: Holt, Rinehart & Winston, 1962.

Elliott, John. *The Revolt of the Catalans.* Cambridge, Eng.: The University Press, 1963.

Elliott, Mabel A. *Conflicting Penal Theories in Statutory Criminal Law.* Chicago: University of Chicago Press, 1931.

_____. *Coercion in Penal Treatment.* Ithaca, N.Y.: Pacifist Research Bureau, 1947.

Elliott, Margaret Axson. *My Aunt Louisa and Woodrow Wilson.* Chapel Hill: University of North Carolina Press, 1944.

Elliott, Robert G., and Beatty, Albert R. *Agent of Death: The Memoirs of an Executioner.* New York: E. P. Dutton, 1940.

Ellis, Albert. *The Folklore of Sex.* New York: Charles Boni, 1951.

_____, and Abarbanel, Albert (eds.). *The Encyclopedia of Sexual Behavior.* New York: Hawthorn, 1961.

_____, and Brancale, Ralph. *The Psychology of Sex Offenders.* Springfield, Ill.: Charles C. Thomas, 1956.

_____, and Gullo, John. *Murder and Assassination.* New York: Lyle Stuart, 1971.

_____. and Harper, Robert A. *A New Guide to Rational Living.* Englewood Cliffs, N.J.: Prentice-Hall, 1975.

Ellis, Amanda M. *Bonanza Towns: Leadville and Cripple Creek.* Colorado Springs, Colo.: Dentan Printing, 1954.

_____. *Pioneers.* Colorado Springs, Colo.: Dentan Printing, 1955.

Ellis, Anne. *Life of an Ordinary Woman.* Boston: Houghton, 1929.

Ellis, Anthony L. *Prisoner at the Bar.* London: Heath Cranton, 1934.

Ellis, C.M. *The Power of the Commander-in-Chief to Declare Martial Law, and Decree Emancipation.* Boston: A. Williams, 1862.

Ellis, David, et al. *A Short History of New York State.* Ithaca, N.Y.: Cornell University Press, 1957.

Ellis, Edward Robb. *The Epic of New York City.* New York: Coward-McCann, 1966.

_____. *A Nation in Torment: The Great American Depression, 1929-1939.* New York: Coward-McCann, 1970.

Ellis, Elmer. *Mr. Dooley's America.* New York: Alfred A. Knopf, 1941.

Ellis, Harry B. *Challenge in the Middle East.* New York: Ronald, 1960.

_____. *Heritage of the Desert.* New York: Ronald, 1956.

_____. *Israel and the Middle East.* New York: Ronald, 1957.

Ellis, Havelock. *The Criminal.* New York: Scribner's, 1900.

_____. *On Life and Sex: Essays of Love and Virtue.* Garden City, N.Y.: Garden City Publishing, 1937.

_____. *Sex in Relation to Society.* New York: Random House, 1936.

_____. *Studies in the Psychology of Sex.* 2 vols. New York: Random House, 1936.

Ellis, J.C. *Black Fame: Stories of Crime and Criminals.* London: Hutchinson, 1926.

_____. *Blackmailers & Co.* London: Selwyn and Blount, 1928.

Ellis, John. *The Social History of the Machine Gun* New York: Pantheon Books, 1976.

Ellis, Dr.John B. *The Sights and Secrets of the National Capital.* New York: U.S. Publishing, 1869.

Ellis, Peter Berresford. *Hell or Connaught.* London: Hamish Hamilton, 1975.

Ellis, Sarah. *The Daughters of England.* London: Fisher, 1843.

_____. *The Mothers of England.* London: Fisher, 1843.

_____. *The Wives of England.* London: Fisher, 1843.

Ellis, Steve. *Alcatraz Number 1172.* Los Angeles: Holloway House Publishing Co., 1969.

Ellis, William T. *Billy Sunday.* Philadelphia: John C. Winston, 1914.

Ellison, E. Jerome, and Brock, Frank W. *The Run for Your Money.* New York: Dodge, 1935.

Ellison, Herbert J. *History of Russia.* New York: Holt, Rinehart & Winston, 1964.

Ellms, Charles. *The Pirates Own Book, or Authentic Narratives of the Lives, Exploits and Executions of the Most Celebrated Sea Robbers.* Salem, Mass.: Marine Research Society, 1924.

Ellsburg, Edward. *Hell on Ice: The Saga of the "Jeannette".* New York: Dodd, Mead, 1938.

Ellsler, John Adam. *The Stage Memories of John A. Ellsler.* Cleveland: Rowfant Club, 1950.

Ellsworth, Lincoln. *Beyond Horizons.* London: William Heinemann, 1938.

Ellwein, Thomas. *Das Erbe der Monarchie in der Deutschen Staatskise.* Munich: Isar Verlag, 1954.

Ellwood, David W. *Italy 1943-1945.* New York: Holmes and Meier, 1986.

Elman, Robert. *Fired in Anger: The Personal Handguns of American Heroes and Villains.* Garden City, N.Y.: Doubleday, 1968.

_____. *Badmen of the West.* Secaucus, N.J.: Ridge Press, 1974.

Elmer, E. *Children in Jeopardy: A Study of Abused Minors and Their Families.* Pittsburgh, Pa.: University of Pittsburgh Press, 1967

Elmhirst, Capt. Pennell. *Fox-Hound, Forest and Prairie.* New York: George Routledge & Sons, 1892.

Elsberry, Terence. *Marie of Romania.* New York: St. Martin's, 1972.

Elsbree, Willard H. *Japan's Role in Southeast Asian Nationalist Movements, 1940-45.* Cambridge, Mass: Harvard University Press, 1953.

Elson, Robert T. *The World of Time Inc.* New York: Atheneum, 1973.

Elst, Baron Joseph van der. *The Last Flowering of the Middle Ages.* Port Washington, N.Y.: Kennikat Press, 1969.

Elton, G.R. (ed.). *The Tudor Constitution.* New York: Cambridge University Press, 1982.

Elton, Lord. *Gordon of Khartoum: The Life of General Charles George Gordon.* New York: Alfred A. Knopf, 1955.

Elwin, V., and Winslow, J. *The Dawn of Indian Freedom.* London: Allen & Unwin, 1931.

Elworthy, Frederic Thomas. *The Evil Eye.* London: J. Murray, 1895.

Ely, Richard T. *French and German Socialism.* New York: Harper, 1898.

_____. *Social Aspects of Christianity, and Other Essays.* New York: Thomas Y. Crowell, 1889.

Ely, William. *The Big Sandy Valley: A History of the People and Country from the Earliest Settlement to the Present Time.* Cattlesburg, Ky.: Central Methodist, 1887.

Elzner, Jonnie Ross. *Lamplighters of Lampasas County, Texas.* Austin, Texas: Form Foundation, 1951.

Emard, Paul, and Fournier, Suzanne. *Les années criminelles de Madame de Montespan.* Paris: Les editions Denoël, 1939.

Emboden, W.A. *Flesh of the gods.* New York: Praeger, 1974.

Emerit, Marcel. *L'Algérie a l'Epoque d'Abd el-Kader.* Paris: Editions Larose, 1951.

Emerson, K.C. *Guest of the Emperor.* Privately published, 1977.

Emerson, R. *Judging Delinquents: Context and Process in the Juvenile Court.* Chicago: Aldine Press, 1969.

Emerson, Thomas. *The System of Freedom of Expression.* New York: Vintage Books, 1970.

_____. *Toward a General Theory of the First Amendment.* New York: Random House, 1963.

Emery, Edwin, and Smith, Henry Ladd. *The Press and America.* New York: Prentice-Hall, 1954.

Emery, Fred E. *Freedom and Justice Within Walls.* London: Tavistock Publications, 1970.

Emery, J. Gladston. *Court of the Damned.* New York: Comet

Press, 1959.

Emery, Richard W. *Heresy and the Inquisition in Norbonne.* New York: Columbia University Press, 1941.

Emery, Walter B. *Broadcasting and Government.* East Lansing: Michigan State University Press, 1961.

_____. *National and International Systems of Broadcasting.* East Lansing: Michigan State University Press, 1969.

Emmett, Chris. *Fort Union and the Winning of the Southwest.* Norman: University of Oklahoma Press, 1965.

_____. *Shanghai Pierce, a Fair Likeness.* Norman: University of Oklahoma Press, 1953.

Emmons, Dr. Robert. *The Life and Opinions of Walter Richard Sickert.* London: Faber and Faber, 1941.

Emory, B.B. *Life, Trial and Confession of Rees W. Evans, Tried and Convicted for the Murder of Louis Reese.* Wilkes-Barre, Pa.: Times, 1853.

Empey, Lamar T., and Lubeck, Steven G. *Delinquency Prevention Strategies.* Washington, D.C.: U.S. Government Printing Office, 1970.

_____, and Erickson, M.L. *The Provo Experiment.* Lexington, Mass.: Lexington Books, 1972.

_____, and Lubeck, Steven G. *The Silverlake Experiment.* Chicago: Aldine, 1971.

Emrich, Duncan. *It's An Old Wild West Custom.* New York: Vanguard Press, 1949.

Encyclopedia Americana. 30 vols. Montreal: Americana Corporation of Canada, 1962.

Endelman, T.M. *The Jews of Georgian England 1714-1830.* Philadelphia: Jewish Publication Society of America, 1979.

Endore, Guy. *Satan's Saint: A Novel About the Marquis de Sade.* New York: Crown, 1965.

Engram, E. *Science, Myth, and Reality.* Westport, Conn.: Greenwood Press, 1982.

Enfield, Dr. J.E. *The Man From Packsaddle.* Hollywood, Calif.: House-Warven, 1951.

Engberg, E. *The Spy in the Corporate Structure.* Cleveland: World, 1967

Engel, Barbara Alpern, and Rosenthal, Clifford N. (eds. and trans.). *Five Sisters: Women Against the Tsar.* New York: Alfred A. Knopf, 1975.

Engel, Lehman. *The American Musical Theater.* New York: A CBS Legacy Collection Book, 1967.

Engel, Madeline H. *The Drug Scene.* Rochelle Park, N.J.: Hayden Book, 1974.

Engel, Major. *Heeresadjutant bei Hitler, 1938-1943.* Stuttgart, Ger.: Deutsche Verlags-Anstalt, 1974.

Engelbrecht, H.C. *Merchants of Death.* New York: Dodd, Mead, 1934.

Engelmann, Bernt. *Deutschland Report.* Berlin: Ex-libris Buchhandlung GmbH-Verlag, 1965.

Engelmann, Larry. *Intemperence: The Lost War Against Liquor.* New York: Free Press, 1979.

Engels, Friedrich. *The Condition of the Working Class in England in 1844.* trans. Florence Kelley Wischnewetzky. New York: J.W. Lovell, 1887.

_____. *The Origin of the Family, Private Property, and the State.* New York: International, 1942.

England, George A. *Isles of Romance.* New York: Century, 1929.

England, Ralph W. *Prison Labour.* New York: United Nations Department of Economic and Social Affairs, 1955.

Englehardt, Father Zephyrin. *San Francisco, of Mission Dolores.* Chicago: Franciscan Herald Press, 1924.

Engler, Robert. *The Politics of Oil, A Study of Private Power and Democratic Directions.* New York: Macmillan, 1961.

English, David, et al. *Dicided They Stand.* Englewood Cliffs, N.J.: Prentice-Hall, 1969.

English. O.S., and Pearson, G.H.J. *Common Neuroses of Children and Adults.* New York: W.W. Norton, 1937.

Ennen, L. *Geschichte de Stadt Köln.* Cologne, Ger.: L. Schwann, 1863.

Ennis, Philip H. *Criminal Victimization in the United States: A Report of a National Survey.* Washington, D.C.: U.S. Government Printing Office, 1967.

Enrich, Norbert Lloyd. *Management Planning: A Systems Approach.* New York: McGraw-Hill, 1967.

Enright, Richard T. (Earl Buell). *Al Capone on the Spot.* Graphic Arts, 1931.

Ensor, David. *I Was a Public Prosecutor.* London: Robert Hale, 1958.

Ensor, R.C.K. *England, 1870-1914.* London: Cambridge University Press, 1936.

Eptein, Robin, et al. *The Legal Aspects of Contract Parole.* College Park, Md.: American Correctional Association, 1976.

Epois, Jean. *L'affaire Corday-Marat: Prelude a la Terreur.* Les Sables d'Olonne: Cercle d'Or, 1980.

Epstein, Benjamin R., and Forster, Arnold. *The Radical Right.* New York: Vintage Books, 1967.

Epstein, Edward Jay. *Agency of Fear: Opiates and Political Power in America.* New York: G.P. Putnam's Sons, 1977.

_____. *Counterplot.* New York: The Viking Press, 1969.

_____. *Inquest.* New York: The Viking Press, 1966.

_____. *Legend: The Secret World of Lee Harvey Oswald.* New York: Readers Digest Press, 1978.

_____. *News From Nowhere.* New York: Random House, 1973.

Epstein, Israel. *The Unfinished Revolution in China.* Boston: Little, Brown, 1947.

Epstein, Jason. *The Great Conspiracy Trial.* New York: Random House, 1970.

Epstein, Klaus. *Matthias Erzberger and the Dilemma of German Democracy.* Princeton, N.J.: Princeton University Press, 1959.

Epstein, Leo D. *British Politics in the Suez Crisis.* Urbana: University of Illinois Press, 1964.

Epstein, Louis M. *Sex Laws and Customs in Judaism.* New York: KTAV, 1967.

Epstein, Melech. *The Jew and Communism.* New York: Trade Union Sponsoring Committee, 1959.

_____. *Jewish Labor in U.S.A.* 2 vols. New York: Trades Union Sponsoring Committee, 1950-53.

Epton, Nina. *Love and the English.* Cleveland: World, 1960.

-----. *Love and the French.* London: Cassell, 1959.

Erasmus, Desidemun. *The Colloquies.* trans. Craig R. Thompson. Chicago: University of Chicago Press, 1965.

-----. *Julius II. Exclusus. A Dialogue. Voices of the Past Readings in Medieval and Early Modern History.* New York: Macmillan, 1967.

Erastus, Thomas. *Disputatio de Lamiis seu Strigibus.* Basel, Switz.: Petrum Pernam, 1578.

Erath, George Bernard. *Memoirs of Major George Bernard Erath.* Austin: Texas State Historical Association, 1923.

Erbstein, Charles E. *The Show-Up: Stories Before the Bar.* Chicago: Pascal Covici, 1926.

Ercole, F. *Storia del Fascismo.* Milan, Italy: Mondadori, 1939.

Ercoli, E.M. (pseud. Palmiro Togliatti). *Inside Italy.* New York: Worker's Library, 1942.

Erdman, Paul E. *The Billion Dollar Sure Thing.* New York: Scribner's Sons, 1973.

Erdstein, Erich. *Inside the Fourth Reich.* New York: St. Martins Press, 1977.

Ergang, Robert. *The Potsdam Fuhrer.* New York: Columbia University Press, 1941.

Erickson, Gladys A. *Warden Ragen of Joliet.* New York: Dutton, 1957.

Ericson, Richard V. *Making Crime: A Study of Detective Work.* Toronto, Ontario, Can.: Buttersworth, 1981.

Erie, Steven P. *Rainbow's End: Irish-Americans and the Dilemmas of Urban Machine Politics, 1840-1985.* Berkeley: University of California Press, 1988.

Erikson, Erik. H. *Childhood and Society.* New York: W.W.

Norton, 1950.

Erikson, Kai T. *Everything in Its Path*. New York: Simon & Schuster, 1976.

_____. *Wayward Puritans*. New York: John Wiley, 1966.

Eriksson, Torsten. *The Reformers*. New York: Elsevier, 1976.

Erlanger, Rachel. *Lucrezia Borgia: A Biography*. New York: Dutton, 1978.

Erman, Adolf. *The Ancient Egyptians*. trans. Aylward M. Blackman. New York: Harper Torchbooks, 1966.

Ermann, M. David, and Lundmann, Richard J. *Corporate Deviance*. New York: Holt, Rinehart, Winston, 1982.

Ernest II, Duke Saxe-Coburg-Gotha. *Memoirs*. 4 vols. London: Remington, 1888.

Ernst, B.M., and Carrington, Hereward. *Houdini and Conan Doyle*. New York: Boni and Liveright, 1932.

Ernst, Morris L. *A Love Affair with the Law: A Legal Sampler*. New York: Macmillan, 1968.

_____. *Privacy*. New York: Macmillan, 1962.

_____. *The Ultimate Power*. New York: Doubleday, Doran, 1937.

_____, and Loth, David. *Report on the American Communist*. New York: Holt, 1952.

_____, and Schwartz, Alan U. *Censorship: The Search for the Obscene*. New York: Macmillan, 1964.

Ernst, Robert A. *Immigrant Life in New York City, 1825-1863*. New York: King's Crown Press, 1949.

Eron, Leonard D., Walder, L.O., and Lefkowitz, M.M. *Learning Aggression in Children*. Boston: Little, Brown, 1971.

Erskine, Gladys. *Broncho Charlie: A Saga of the Saddle*. New York: Thomas Y. Crowell, 1934.

Erskine, Margaret. *Give Up the Ghost*. London: Hammond, 1949.

Ervin, Charles W. *Homegrown Liberal: The Autobiography of Charles W. Ervin*. New York: Dodd, Mead, 1954.

Ervin Sam J., Jr. *The Whole Truth: The Watergate Conspiracy*. New York: Random House, 1980.

Erwin, Allen A. *The Southwest of John H. Slaughter, 1841-1922*. Glendale, Calif.: Arthur H. Clark, 1965.

Erwin, Carol, and Miller, Floyd. *The Orderly Disorderly House*. Garden City, N.Y.: Doubleday, 1960.

Erwin, John R. *The Man Who Keeps Going to Jail*. Fullerton, Calif.: Cook Press, 1978.

Erzberger, Matthias. *Souvenirs de Guerre*. Paris: Payot, 1921.

Esco Foundation for Palestine. *Palestine: A Study of Jewish, Arab and British Policies*. New Haven, Conn.: Yale University Press, 1947.

Escott, T.H.S. *Masters of English Journalism*. London: T. Fisher Unwin, 1911.

Eshelman, Byron. *Death Row Chaplain*. Englewood Cliffs, N.J.: Prentice-Hall, 1962.

Esher, Reginald. *The Influence of King Edward and Other Essays*. London: Murray, 1915.

_____. *The Tragedy of Lord Kitchener*. New York: Dutton, 1921.

Eskew, Garnett. *The Pageant of the Packets*. New York: Henry Holt, 1929.

Esmein, A. *A History of Continental Criminal Procedure*. Boston: Little, Brown, 1913.

Esposito, John C. and Silverman, Larry J. *Vanishing Air: The Nadar Report on Air Pollution*. New York: Grossman, 1970.

Esquirol, Jean Étienne. *Des maladies mentales*. Paris: J. and B. Baillière, 1838.

Esquivel Obregón, Toribio. *La Influencia de España y los Estados Unidos sobre México*. Madrid: Casa Editorial Calleja, 1918.

Essas, Bey. *Nicholas II Prisoner of the Purple*. London: Hutchinson, 1936.

Essen, Léon Van Der. *The Invasion and the War in Belgium from Liege to the Yser*. London: Unwin, 1917.

Essien-Udom, E.U. *Black Nationalism*. Chicago: University of Chicago Press, 1962.

Estabrook, Arthur H. *The Jukes in 1915*. Washington, D.C.: Carnegie Institution, 1916.

_____, and Davenport, Charles P. *The Nam Family*. Cold Spring Harbor, N.Y.: Eugenics Record Office, 1912.

Estol, Horacio. *Realidad y Leyenda de Pancho Villa*. Buenos Aires, Arg.: Libreria Hachette, 1944.

Estorick, Eric. *Stafford Cripps*. New York: John Day, 1941.

Estournelles de Constant, Paul Henri Benjamin, Baron d'. *Les Etats-Unis d'AMerique*. Paris: A. Colin, 1913.

Estrada, Rogue. *La Revolucion y Francisco I. Madero*. Guadalajara, Mex.: Impreta Americana, 1912.

Estrella, Manuel M. Jr., and Forest, Martin L. *The Family Guide to Crime Prevention*. New York: Beaufort Books, 1981.

Etnasi, Fernando. *Cronache col mitra*. Milan, Italy: Giordano, 1965.

Ettinger, Clayton. *The Problem of Crime*. New York: Ray Long and Richard R. Smith, 1932.

Ettlinger, Harold. *The Axis on the Air*. Indianapolis, Ind.: Bobbs-Merrill, 1943.

Etzioni, Amitai. *A Comparative Analysis of Complex Organizations*. New York: Free Press, 1975.

Eudin, Xenia Joukoff, and North, Robert C. *Soviet Russia and the East, 1920-1927*. Stanford, Calif.: Stanford University Press, 1957.

Eudin, Xenia Joukoff, and Fisher, Harold H. *Soviet Russia and the West*. Stanford, Calif.: Stanford University Press, 1957.

Eugénie de Gréce. *Pierre-Napoléon Bonaparte, 1815-1881*. Paris: Hachette. 1963./

Eulalia, H.R.H. *Court Life from Within*. London: Cassell, 1915.

_____. *Courts and Countries After the War*. New York: Dodd, Mead, 1925.

Eulenberg, Herbert. *The Hohenzollerns*. London: George Allen & Unwin, 1929.

Evan, William M. *Law and Sociology, Exploratory Essays*. New York: Free Press of Glencoe, 1962.

_____. (ed.) *The Sociology of the Law*. New York: Free Press, 1980.

Evans, Alona, and Murphy, John (eds.). *Legal Aspects of International Terrorism*. London: Heath, 1978.

Evans, Sir Arthur. *Through Bosnia and Herzegovina on Foot During the Insurrection, 1875, With Historical Review of Bosnia*. London: Longman, 1876.

Evans, Cerinda W. *Collis Potter Huntington*. 2 vols. Newport News, Va.: Mariner's Museum, 1954.

Evans, Christopher. *Cults of Unreason*. New York: Farrar, Straus and Giroux, 1973.

Evans, Clyde (ed.). *Adventures of Great Crime Busters*. New York: New Power, 1943.

Evans, Daniel. *When Crime Strikes*. Olympia, Wash.: State Printing Plant, 1974.

Evans, Edward Payson. *The Criminal Prosecution and Capital Punishment of Animals*. London: William Heinemann, 1904.

Evans, F.B. (ed.). *Worldwide Communist Propaganda*. New York: Macmillan, 1955.

Evans, George G. *Illustrated History of the United States Mint*. Philadelphia: George G. Evans, 1890.

Evans, Henry H. *Curious Lore of San Francisco's Chinatown*. San Francisco: Purpoise Bookshop, 1955.

Evans, Joan (ed.). *The Flowering of the Middle Ages*. London: Thames & Hudson, 1966.

_____. *John Ruskin*. New York: Oxford University Press, 1955.

Evans, Max. *Long John Dunn of Taos*. Los Angeles: Westernlore Press, 1959.

Evans, M. Stanton. *The Law Breakers*. New Rochelle, New York: Arlington House, 1968.

Evans, P. *Law and Disorder, or Scenes of Life in Kenya*. London: Secker & Warburg, 1956.

Evand, Peter (ed.). *The Police Revolution*. London: George Allen & Unwin, 1974.

Evans, Rosalie. *Letters from Mexico*. Indianapolis, Ind.: Bobbs-Merrill, 1926.

Evans-Pritchard, E.E. *The Nuer*. London: Oxford University

Press, 1940.

Evatt, Herbert V. *Australian Labor Leader, the Story of W.A. Holman and the Labor Movement.* London: Angus and Robertson, 1940.

Everest, Allen S. *Rum Across the Border.* New York: Syracuse Univ., 1978.

Everson, William K. *The Detective in Film.* Secaucus, N.J.: Citadel Press, 1972.

Everett, Edward. *A Eulogy on the Life and Character of John Quincy Adams.* Boston: Dutton and Wentworth, 1848.

Everett, Marshall. *Life of William McKinley and Story of His Assassination.* Chicago: Donohue, 1901.

_____. *Great Chicago Theater Disaster.* Chicago: Publishers Union of America, 1904.

Every, Edward Van. *Sins of America as 'Exposed' by the Police Gazette.* New York: Frederick A. Stokes, 1931.

Evica, George Michael. *And We Are All Mortal.* West Hartford, Conn.: Published by Author, 1978.

Ewen, Cecil H. L'Estrange. *Some Witchcraft Criticism.* London: Published by Author, 1938.

_____. *The Trials of John Lowes, Clerk.* London: Published by Author, 1937.

_____. *Witchcraft and Demonianism.* London: Heath, Crouton, 1933.

_____. *Witchcraft in the Norfolk Circuit.* London: Published by Author, 1939.

_____. *Witchcraft in the Star Chamber.* London: Published by Author, 1939.

_____. *Witch Hunting and Witch Trials.* New York: Dial, 1930.

Ewen, David. *Richard Rodgers.* New York: Henry Holt, 1957.

-----. *Panorama of American Popular Music.* Englewood Cliffs, N.J.: Prentice-Hall, 1957.

Ewens, G.F.W. *Insanity in India.* Calcutta, India: Thacker, Spink, 1908.

Ewers, John C. *The Blackfeet: Raiders on the Northwestern Plains.* Norman: University of Oklahoma Press, 1958.

_____., et al. *Views of a Vanishing Frontier.* Omaha, Neb.: Center for Western Studies, Joslyn Art Museum, 1984.

Ewing, A.C. *The Morality of Punishment.* London: K. Paul, Trench, Trubner, 1929.

The Examination and Confession of Edward Fitzpatrick. Rutland, Mass.: Gray, 1744.

The Examination, Confession, Trial and Execution of Joan Williford. London: F.G., 1645

The Examination of John Walsh. London: John Awdely, 1566.

Examination of Joseph Antoine, Johan Fransoeis Wohlfahrt and Joanna Susan Wohlfahrt. Providence, R.I.: H.H. Brown, 1828.

The Execution and Last Moments of Henry G. Green. New York: n.p., 1845.

Execution of Richard Johnson. New York: n.p., n.d.

Exner, Judith. *My Story.* New York: Grove, 1977.

_____. *The Rorschach.* New York: Wiley, 1978.

Exquemelin, Alexander. *The Buccaneers of America.* Baltimore: Penguin Books, 1969.

The Extraordinary Life and Character of Mary Bateman, the Yorkshire Witch. Leeds, Eng.: Edward Baines, 1809.

The Extraordinary Life and Trial of Madame Rachel. London: Diprose and Bateman, 1868.

Eyck, Erich. *Bismarck: Leben und Werk.* New York: Macmillan, 1950.

Eyman, Joy Satterwhite. *How to Convict a Rapist.* New York: Stein & Day, 1980.

Eymeric, Nicolas. *Directorium Inquisitorum.* Rome: G. Ferrarium, 1587.

Eysenck, H.J. *Crime and Personality.* London: Routledge and Kegan Paul, 1977.

_____. *Dimensions of Personality.* London: Routledge & Kegan Paul, 1947.

_____. *The Structure of Human Personality.* London: Methuen, 1953.

_____. *The Structure and Measurement of Intelligence.* Berlin: Springer, 1979.

_____. and Nias, D.K.B. *Sex, Violence and the Media.* New York: Harper Colophon Books, 1978.

Eytan, Walter. *The First Ten Years: A Diplomatic History of Israel.* New York: Simon & Schuster, 1958.

Ezell, J. *Fortune's Merry Wheel: The Lottery in America.* Cambridge, Mass.: Harvard University Press, 1960.

F

Faber, Harold (ed.). *The Luftwaffe: A History.* New York: Times Books, 1977.

Fable, Edmund Jr. *Billy the Kid, the New Mexican Outlaw.* Denver: Denver, 1881.

Fabela, Isidro. *Historia Diplomática de la Revolución Mexicana.* 2 vols. Mexico: Fondo de Cultura Económica, 1959.

Fabian, Robert. *Fabian of the Yard.* London: Naldrett Press, 1950.

_____. *London After Dark.* London: Naldrett Press, 1954.

Fabian International Bureau. *Labor and Europe.* London: Fabian Society, 1943.

Fabre, J. Henri. *Study in Entomology.* trans. Alexander Teixiera De Mattos. New York: Dodd, Mead, 1917.

Fabre, Joseph. *Procés de condamnation de Jeanne d'Arc.* Paris: C. Delagrave, 1884.

_____. *Procés de réhabilitation de Jeanne d'Arc.* Paris: Hachette, 1913.

Fabre, Lucien. *Jeanne d'Arc.* Paris: J. Tallandier, 1948.

Fabre, M.A. *Jérôme Bonaparte.* Paris: Hachette, 1952.

Fabre, Maurice. *A History of Communication.* New York: Hawthorn Books, 1963.

Fact Sheet in the Rosenberg Case. New York: National Committee to Secure Justice in the Rosenberg Case, 1953.

Facts Relating to the Murder of Joseph Green. Rutland, Vt.: n.p., n.d.

Fader, Daniel N., and McNeil, Elton. *Hooked on Books: Program & Proof.* New York: Berkley, 1968.

Fadiman, Clifton (ed.). *The American Treasury, 1455-1955.* New York: Harper, 1955.

Fadiman, J.A. *An Oral History of Tribal Warfare: The Meru of Mt. Kenya.* Athens: Ohio University Press, 1982.

Faenza, Liliano. *Communismo e Cattolicesimo in una parrachia di campagna.* Milan, Italy: Feltrinelli, 1959.

Fagg, John Edwin. *Cuba, Haiti and The Dominican Republic.* Englewood Cliffs, N.J.: Prentice-Hall, 1965.

Fa-Hsien. *The Travels of Fa-Hsien (391-414 A.D.) or Record of the Buddhist Kingdoms.* trans. H.A. Giles. Cambridge, Eng.: Cambridge University Press, 1923.

Fain, Baron. *Manuscrit de 1814.* Paris, Bossange, 1825.

Fain, Tyrus G. (ed.). *The Intelligence Community.* New York: R.R. Bowker, 1977.

Fainsod, Merle. *How Russia is Ruled.* Cambridge, Mass.: Harvard University Press, 1953.

_____. *Smolensk Under Soviet Rule.* Cambridge, Mass.: Harvard University Press, 1958.

Fair, Laura D. *Wolves in the Fold.* San Francisco: n.p., 1873.

Fair and Certain Punishment. Report of the Twentieth Century Task Force on Criminal Sentencing. New York: McGraw-Hill, 1976.

Fairbairn, W.R.D. *An Object Relations Theory of the Personality.* New York: Basic Books, 1962.

Fairbank, J.K., Reischauer, E.O., and Craig, A.M. *East Asia: The Modern Transformation.* Boston: Houghton Mifflin, 1965.

_____. *A History of East Asian Civilization*. Boston: Houghton Mifflin, 1964.

Fairbank, John K. *Trade and Diplomacy on the China Coast: the Opening of the Treaty Ports 1842-1854*. Cambridge, Mass.: Harvard University Press, 1953.

_____. *The United States and China*. Cambridge, Mass.: Harvard University Press, 1948.

Fairbanks, Jason. *The Solemn Declaration of the Late, Unfortunate Jason Fairbanks*. Dedham, Mass.: Minevera Press, H. Mann, 1801.

Fairchild, Henry Pratt. *The Melting Pot Mistake*. Boston: Little, Brown, 1926.

_____. *This Way Out*. New York: Harper, 1936.

Fairfax, Edward. *A Discourse on Witchcraft*. London: Philobiblon Society, 1858.

Fairfield, Asa Merrill. *Fairfield's Pioneer History of Lassen County, California*. San Francisco: H.S. Crocker, 1916.

Fairfield, L. (ed.). *Notable British Trials: Trial of Peter Barnes and Others*. London: William Hodge, 1953.

Fairfield, Ula King. *Pioneer Lawyer: A Story of the Western Slope of Colorado*. Denver: W.H. Kistler Stationery, 1946.

Fairlie, Gerard. *The Reluctant Cop*. London: Hodder & Stoughton, 1958.

Fairman, Charles. *Mr. Justice Miller and the Supreme Court, 1862-1890*. Cambridge, Mass.: Harvard University Press, 1939.

Faithfull, Emily. *Three Visits to America*. New York: Fowler & Wells, 1884.

Fajon, Étienne. *Les Grands Problèmes de la Politique Contemporaine*. Paris: Bureau d'Éditions, 1938.

Falco, Mario. *The Legal Position of the Holy See before and after the Lateran Treaty*. Oxford, Eng.: Oxford University Press, 1935.

Falcon, W.D. (ed.). *Witness Cooperation*. Lexington, Mass.: D.C. Heath, 1976.

Faldella, Gen. Emilio. *L'Italia e la seconda gur\erra mondiàle*. Bologna, Italy: Cappelli, 1959.

Falgairolle, Edmond. *Un envoûtement en Gévaudan en l'année 1347*. Nimes, Fr.: Catélan, 1892.

Falk, Candace. *Love, Anarchy, and Emma Goldman*. New York: Holt, Rinehart & Winston, 1984.

Falk, Doris V. *Lillian Hellman*. New York: Frederick Ungar, 1978.

Falk, Stanley L. *Bataan: The March of Death*. New York: W. W. Norton, 1962.

Fall, Bernard. *Street Without Joy: Insurgency in Indo-China 1946-63*. London: Pall Mall, 1964.

_____. *The Two Vietnams*. London: Pall Mall, 1963.

Falle, Philip. *An Account of the Isle of Jersey*. London: J. Newton, 1694.

Falls, C.B. *The Birth of Ulster*. London: Methuen, 1936.

Fallwell, Gene. *The Texas Rangers*. Texarkana, Texas: Connell Printing, 1959.

Falzone, Gaetano. *Histiore de la Mafia*. Paris: Fayard, 1973.

Fang, John T. *Chinatown Handy Guide*. San Francisco: Chinese Publishing House, 1959.

Fanning, Clara E. (ed.). *Selected Articles on Capital Punishment*. Minneapolis, Minn.: H.W. Wilson, 1913.

Fanning, Pete. *Great Crimes of the West*. San Francisco: Ed Barry, 1929.

Fanon, Frantz. *Black Faces, White Masks*. New York: Bantam Books, 1966.

_____. *The Wretched of the Earth*. New York: Grove Press, 1963.

Farago, Ladislas. *Abyssinia on the Eve*. London: Putnam, 1935.

_____. *Abyssinian Stop Press*. London: Robert Hale, 1936.

_____. *The Broken Seal: The Story of "Operation Magic" and the Pearl Harbor Disaster*. New York: Random House, 1967.

Faralicq, René. *The French Police from Within*. London: Cassell, 1933.

Farb, Peter. *Word Play*. New York: Alfred A. Knopf, 1974.

Farber, James. *Texans with Guns*. San Antonio, Texas: Naylor, 1950.

_____. *Those Texans*. San Antonio, Texas: Naylor, 1945.

Farber, Maurice L. *Theory of Suicide*. New York: Funk & Wagnalls, 1968.

Farconnet, Francois. *Relation véritable contenant ce qui s'est passé aux exorcismes d'une fulle appellé Elisabeth Allier*. Paris: P. Serestre, 1649.

Farina, Savatore. *Le truppe d'assalto italiane*. Rome: FNAI, 1938.

Farinacci, Roberto. *In difea di Dumini*. Rome: Libreria dell'Ottocento, 1945.

_____. *Un periodo aurea del partito nazionale fascista*. Foligno, Italy: Franco Campitelli, 1926.

_____. *Squadrismo: dal mio diario della vigilia*. Rome, Ardita, 1933.

_____. *Storia del Fascismo*. 3 vols. Cremona, Italy: Cremona Nuova, 1937.

_____. *Da Vittorio Veneto a Piazza San Sepolcro*. Verona, Italy: Mondadori, 1933

Faris, Robert E.L. *Chicago Sociology 1920-32*. San Francisco: Chandler, 1967.

Farish, G.H. *History of Arizona*. San Francisco: Filmer, 1915.

Farish, T.E. *The Gold Hunters of California*. Chicago: M.A. Donohue, 1904.

_____. *History of Arizona*. San Francisco: Filmer Brothers Electrotype, 1915-18.

Farjeon, Eleanor (ed.). *The Unlocked Door*. New York: G.P. Putnam's Sons, 1938.

Farley, James A. *Behind the Ballots*. New York: Harcourt, 1938.

_____. *Jim Farley's Story: The Roosevelt Years*. New York: McGraw-Hill, 1948.

Farley, Philip. *Criminals of America; or Tales of the Lives of Thieves*. New York: Published by author, 1876.

Farmer, Daniel Davis. *The Life and Confessions of Daniel Davis Farmer*. Amherst, N.H.: Elijah Mansur, 1822.

Farmer, Elihu J. *The Resources of the Rocky Mountains*. Cleveland: Leader Printing, 1883.

Farmer, John, and Moore, Jacob B. *A Gazetteer of the State of New Hampshire*. Concord, N.H.: Jacob B. Moore, 1823.

Farmer, John Stephen, and Henley, W.E. *A Dictionary of Slang and Colloquial English*. New York: E.P. Dutton, 1905.

Farmer, Philip Jose. *A Feast Unknown*. New York: Essex House, 1969.

_____. *Lord of the Trees*. London: Severn House, 1982.

Farmer, William R. *Maccabees, Zealots and Josephus*. New York: Columbia University Press, 1956.

Farnsworth, Harley (ed.). *China*. Berkeley, Calif.: University of California Press, 1951.

Farnsworth, Majorie. *The Ziegfeld Follies: A History in Text and Pictures*. New York: G.P. Putnam's Sons, 1956.

Farnworth, Richard. *Witchcraft Cast Out from the Religious Seed and Israel of God*. London: G. Calvert, 1655.

Farquhar, Franklin S. *History of Livingston, California*. Livingston, Calif.: Chronicle, 1945.

Farquhar, J.N. *Modern Religious Movements in India*. London: Macmillan, 1929.

Farr, Finis. *Chicago*. New Rochelle, N.Y.: Arlington House, 1973.

_____. *Fair Enough: The Life of Westbrook Pegler*. New Rochelle, N.Y.: Arlington House, 1975.

_____. *Frank Lloyd Wright*. New York: Charles Scribner's Sons, 1961.

_____. *O'Hara*. Boston: Little Brown, 1973.

Farran, Roy. *Winged Dagger*. London: Collins, 1948.

Farrand, Max. *The Fathers of the Constitution*. New Haven, Conn.: Yale University Press, 1921.

_____. *Framing of the Constitution*. New Haven, Conn.: Yale University Press, 1913.

_____. *The Legislation of Congress for the Government of the Organized Territories of the United States, 1879-1895*. Newark,

N.J.: Wm.A. Baker, 1896.

Farrell, Cullom Holmes. *Incidents in the Life of General Pershing.* New York: Rand, McNally, 1918.

Farrell, James T. *My Baseball Diary.* New York: A.S. Barnes, 1957.

_____. *Bernard Clare.* New York: Vanguard, 1946.

Farrer, Reginald. *On the Eaves of the World.* London: Edward Arnold, 1917.

Farrow, Marion Humphreys. *Troublesome Times in Texas.* San Antonio, Texas: Glegg, 1957.

Farson, Daniel. *The Hamlyn Book of Horror.* London: Hamlyn, 1977.

_____. *Jack the Ripper.* London: Michael Joseph, 1972.

Farson, N. *Last Chance in Africa.* London: V. Gollancz, 1953.

Farston, Richard. *Birthrights.* New York: Macmillan, 1974.

Farwell, Byron. *The Man Who Presumed: A Biography of Henry M. Stanley.* New York: Henry Holt, 1957.

Farwell, Willard B. *The Chinese at Home and Abroad.* San Francisco: A.L. Bancroft, 1885.

Fast, Howard. *The Passion of Sacco Vanzetti.* New York: Blue Heron Press, 1953.

Fast, Howard Melvin. *The Last Frontier.* New York: Duell, Sloan & Pearce, 1942.

Fast, J. *Body Language.* London: Souvenir Press, 1971.

Faulds, H. *Guide to Finger Print Identification.* Hanley: Wood, Mitchell, 1905.

_____. *A Manual of Practical Dactylography.* London: Police Review, 1923.

Faulk, Odie B. *Dodge City.* New York: Oxford Univ. Press, 1977.

_____. *The Geronimo Campaign.* New York: Oxford University Press, 1969.

_____. *Tombstone: Myth and Reality.* New York: Oxford University Press, 1972.

Faulkner, Harold Underwood. *American Economic History.* New York: Harper, 1931.

_____. *American Political and Social History.* New York: Crofts, 1941.

_____. *The Quest for Social Justice.* New York: Macmillan, 1931.

Faulkner, Virginia. *Roundup: A Nebraska Reader.* Lincoln: University of Nebraska Press, 1957.

Faulkner, William. *Big Woods.* New York: Random House, 1955.

_____. *The Faulkner Reader.* New York: Random House, 1959.

Faure, Edgar. *The Serpent and the Tortoise.* London: Macmillan, 1958.

Faure, Paul. *Le Socialisme dans la Bataille Electorale.* Paris: Librairie Populaire, 1936.

Faurie, General. *Souvenirs.* Rodez, Fr.: Georges Subervie, 1937.

Favagrossa, Gen Carlo. *Perchè perdemmo la guerra: Mussolini e la produzione bellica.* Milan, Italy: Rizzoli, 1946.

Favre, Mme. Jules (ed.). *Plaidoyers Politiques et judiciaires de Jules Favre.* 2 vols. Paris: E. Plon, 1882.

Fawcett, Edgar. *The Evil That Men Do.* New York: Belford, 1889.

Fawcett, Jan (ed.). *Dynamics of Violence.* Chicago: American Medical Association, 1972.

Fawcett, Millicent. *Josephine Butler.* London: The Association for Moral and Social Hygiene, 1927.

Fawkes, Sandy. *Killing Time.* New York: Taplinger, 1979.

Fay, B. Sidney. *Origins of the World War.* London: Macmillan, 192

Fay, Bernard. *Louis XVI, or The End of a World.* Chicago: Henry Regnery, 1966.

_____. *The Revolutionary Spirit in France and America, A Study of Moral and Intellectual Relations between France and the United States at the End of the Eighteenth Century.* New York: Harcourt, Brace, 1927.

Fay, Brian. *Social Theory and Political Practice.* London: George

Allen & Unwin, 1975.

Fay, E.S. *The Life of Mr. Justice Swift.* London: Methuen, 1939.

Fay, Peter W. *The Opium War: 1840-1842.* Chapel Hill: University of North Carolina Press, 1975.

Fay, Sidney B. *The Rise of Brandenburg-Prussia to 1786.* New York: Holt, Rinehart & Winston, 1964.

Fay, Stephen, et al. *Hoax: The Inside Story of the Howard Hughs Affair.* New York: Viking Press, 1972.

Fay, Theodore S. *Norman Leslie.* New YorK: Harper & Bros., 1835.

Fea, Allan. *Secret Chambers and Hiding Places.* London: Bousfield, 1901.

Featherston, Edward Baxter. *A Pioneer Speaks.* Dallas: Cecil Baugh, 1940.

Feck, Luke. *Yesterday's Cincinnati.* Miami: E.A. Seemann, 1975.

Feder, Sid. *Longhorns and Short Tales of Victoria and the Gulf Coast.* Victoria, Texas: Victoria Advocate, 1958.

_____, and Joesten, Joachim. *The Luciano Story.* New York: David McKay, 1954.

Federal Bureau of Investigation. *Classification of Fingerprints.* Washington, D.C.: U.S. Government Printing Office, 1941.

_____. *Crime in the United States.* Washington, D.C.: U.S. Government Printing Office, 1983.

_____. *Handbook of Forensic Science.* Washington, D.C.: U.S. Government Printing Office, 1984.

_____. *Uniform Crime Reports.* Washington, D.C.: U.S. Government Printing Office, n.d.

Federal Writer's Project-Illinois-Work Project Administration. *Baseball in Old Chicago.* Chicago: A.C. McClurg, 1939.

Federzoni, Luigi. *Italia di ieri per la storia di domani.* Milan, Italy: Mondadori, 1967.

Feeley, Malcolm M. *Court Reform on Trial.* New York: Basic Books, Twentieth Century Fund, 1983.

_____, and Sarat, Austin D. *The Policy Dilemma.* Minneapolis: University of Minnesota Press, 1980.

Fehlandt, August F. *A Century of Drink Reform in the United States.* Cincinnati, Ohio: Jennings & Graham, 1904.

Fehrenbacher, Don E. *Prelude to Greatness: Lincoln in 1850s.* Stanford, Calif.: Stanford University, 1962.

Fehrenberg, Don E. *Chicago Giant.* Madison, Wis.: American History Research Center, 1957.

Feifer, George. *Justice in Moscow.* New York: Delta, 1965.

Fei Hsiao-tung. *China's Gentry, Essays in Rural-Urban Relations.* Chicago: University of Chicago Press, 1953.

_____. *Peasant Life in China: A Field Study of Country Life in the Yangtze Valley.* New York: Dutton, 1939.

Feiling, Keith. *Neville Chamberlain.* London: Macmillan, 1946.

Fein, Judith. *Are You a Target?* Belmont, Calif.: Wadsworth, 1981.

Fein, Leonard J. *Politics in Israel.* Boston: Little, Brown, 1967.

Feinberg, Joel. *Doing and Deserving.* Princeton, N.J.: Princeton University Press, 1970.

Feis, Herbert. *Between War and Peace: The Potsdam Conference.* Princeton, N.J.: Princeton University Press, 1960.

_____. *The China Tangle.* New York: Atheneum, 1965.

_____. *Churchill-Roosevelt-Stalin.* Princeton, N.J.: Princeton University Press, 1957.

_____. *Europe the World's Banker, 1870-1914.* New York: A.M. Kelley, 1961.

_____. *Japan Subdued: The Atomic Bomb and the End of the War in the Pacific.* Princeton, N.J.: Princeton University Press, 1961.

_____. *1933: Characters in Crisis.* Boston: Little, Brown, 1966.

_____. *The Road to Pearl Harbor.* Princeton, N.J.: Princeton University Press, 1950.

Feitz, Leland. *Myers Avenue.* Colorado Springs, Colo.: Dentan-Berkeland Printing, 1967.

Feldman, David M. *Marital Relations, Birth Control, and Abortion in Jewish Law.* New York: Schocken Books, 1974.

Feldman, Harold. *Fifty-One Witnesses: The Grassy Knoll.* San

Francisco: Idlewild, 1965.

Feldman, Herman. *Prohibition*. New York: D. Appleton, 1927.

Feldman, M.P. *Criminal Behaviour*. New York, John Wiley, 1977.

Félice, Paul de. *Lambert Dancau*. Paris: G. Fishbacher, 1881.

Felix, David. *Protest*. Bloomington: Indiana University Press, 1965.

Fell, James. *British Merchant Seamen in San Francisco, 1892-1898*. London: E. Arnold, 1899.

Felletti, Leonida. *Soldati senz'armi*. Rome: Donatello De Luigi, 1944.

Fellows, Dexter, and Freeman, Andrew A. *This Way to the Big Show: The Life of Dexter Fellows*. New York: Halcyon House, 1936.

Fell-Smith, Charlotte. *John Dee*. London: Constable, 1909.

Felony Arrests: Their Prosecution and Disposition in New York City's Courts. New York: The Vera Institute of Justice, 1977.

Felstead, Sidney Theodore. *Sir Richard Muir*. London: John Lane, 1927.

_____. *Shades of Scotland Yard*. London: John Long, 1950.

Felt, Jeremy P. *Hostages of Fortune*. Ithaca, N.Y.: Cornell University Press, 1965.

Felt, Joseph B. *The Annals of Salem from Its First Settlement*. Salem, Mass.: W. & S.B. Ives, 1827.

Felt, Mark. *The FBI Pyramid*. New York: G.P. Putnam's Sons, 1979.

Fenichel, Otto. *The Psychoanalytic Theory of Neurosis*. New York: W.W. Norton, 1945.

Fenley, Florence. *Grandad and I*. Leakey, Texas: John Leakey, 1951.

Fennell, J.L.I. (ed.). *The Correspondence Between Prince A. M. Kurbsky and Tsar Ivan IV of Russia, 1564-1569*. Cambridge, Mass.: Cambridge University Press, 1963.

_____. *Ivan the Great of Muscovy*. New York: St. Martin's Press, 1961.

Fensterwald, Bernard, Jr. *Coincidence or Conspiracy?* New York: Zebra Books, 1977.

Fenton, Norman. *Treatment in Prison: How the Family Can Help*. Sacramento: State of California, 1959.

Fenwick, Robert W. *Alfred Packer*. Denver: Denver Post, 1963.

Fenyvesi, Charles. *Splendor in Exile*. Washington, D.C.: New Republic Books, 1970.

Ferber, Edna. *A Peculiar Treasure*. New York: Doubleday, 1960.

Ferber, Nat. *I Found Out*. New York: Dial Press, 1939.

Fere, C.S. *Sexual Degeneration in Mankind and in Animals*. trans. Ulrich van der Horst. New York: Anthropological Press, 1932.

Ferenczi, S. *Contributions to Psychoanalysis*. Boston: Richard G. Badger, 1916.

Fergus, Robert. *Fergus' Directory of the City of Chicago, 1839*. Fergus Printing, 1876.

_____. *Fergus Historical Sketches of Chicago*. Chicago: Published by Author, 1876-1896.

Ferguson, Charles D. *The Experiences of a Forty-Niner During Thirty-Four Years' Residence in California and Australia*. Cleveland, Ohio: Williams, 1888.

Ferguson, Fergus. *From Glasgow to Missouri and Back*. Glasgow, Scot.: T.D. Morison, 1878.

Ferguson, Ian. *The Philosophy of Witchcraft*. London: G.G. Harrap, 1924.

Ferguson, Mrs. Tom B. *They Carried the Torch*. Kansas City: Burton, 1937.

Ferguson, W.J. *I Saw Booth Shoot Lincoln*. New York: Houghton Mifflin, 1930.

Ferguson, William. *America by River and Rail*. London: J. Nisbet, 1856.

Fergusson, Adam. *When Money Dies-The Nightmare of the Weimer Collapse*. London: William Kimber, 1975.

Fergusson, Erna. *Erna Fergusson's Albuquerque*. Albuquerque, N.M.: Armitage Editions, 1947.

_____. *Murder & Mystery in New Mexico*. Albuquerque, N.M.: Armitage Editions, 1948.

_____. *Our Southwest*. New York: Alfred A. Knopf, 1940.

Fergusson, Harvey. *Rio Grande*. New York: Alfred A. Knopf, 1933.

Ferman, Louis A., Kornbluh, Joyce L., and Haber, Alan (eds.). *Poverty in America*. Ann Arbor: University of Michigan Press, 1965.

Fermé, Albert. *Les Grands procés politiques: Boulogne d'aprés les socuments authentiques*. Paris: A. Le Chevalier, 1869.

Fermi, Laura. *Mussolini*. Chicago: University of Chicago Press, 1963.

Fernández Güell, Rogelio. *Episodios de la Revolución Mexicana*. San José, Costa Rica: Imprenta Trejos Hermanos, 1915.

_____. *El Moderno Juárez, Estudio Sobre la Personalidad de D. Francisco I. Madero*. Mexico City: Tipografia Artistica, 1913.

Fernandez Rojas, José. *De Porfirio Diaz a Victoriano Huerta, 1910-1913*. Mexico City: F.P. Rojas y Campañia, 1913.

Ferracuti, Franco, Lazzari, Renato, and Wolfgang, Marvin E. *Violence in Sardinina*. Rome: Mario Bulzoni, 1970.

Ferraironi, Francesco. *Le Streghe e l'Inquisizione*. Rome: Sallustiann, 1955.

Ferrara, Orestes. *The Borgia Pope*. trans. F.J. Sheed. New York: Sheed and Ward, 1940.

_____. *The Last Spanish Pope*. London: Williams & Norgate, 1937.

Ferrari, Santo. *L'Italia Fascista*. Turin, Italy: Ed Libraria Italiana, 1942.

Ferraris, Efrem. *La Marcia su Roma veduta dal Viminale*. Rome: Leonardo, 1946.

Ferrarotti, Franco. *Rapporto sulla mafia*. Naples, Italy: Liguori, 1978.

Ferrer, R. *Manual de Identificación Judicial*. Madrid: Reus, 1921.

Ferrer de M., Gabriel. *Vida de Francisco I. Madero*. Mexico City: Secretaria de Educacion Pública, 1945.

Ferrero, Guglielmo. *Four Years of Fascism*. trans. E.W. Dickes. London: P.S. King, 1942.

Ferri, Enrico. *Criminal Sociology*. New York: D. Appleton, 1896.

Ferrier, William Warren. *Ninety Years of Education in California*. Berkeley, Calif.: Sather Gate Book Shop, 1937.

Ferris, Robert G. (ed.). *Soldier and Brave: Historical Places Associated with Indian Affairs and the Indian Wars of the Trans-Mississippi West*. Washington: National Park Service, 1971.

Feshback, S., and Singer, R.D. *Television and Agression*. San Francisco: Jossey-Bass, 1971.

Fessler, Ignaz A. *Geschicht von Ungarn*. Leipzig, Ger.: F.A. Brockhaus, 1883.

Fest, Joachim C. *Das Gesicht des Dritten Reiches*. Munich: R. Piper, 1963.

_____. *Hitler*. London: Weidenfeld & Nicolson, 1974.

Festa Campanile, Raffaele and Fittipaldi R. *Mussolini e la battaglia del grano*. Rome: SNFTA, 1931.

Fethering, Doug. *The Five Lives of Ben Hecht*. London: Lester & Orpen, 1977.

Fetherstonhough, R.C. *The Royal Canadian Mounted Police*. New York: Carrick & Evans, 1938.

Fetridge, William Harrison. *With Warm Regards*. Chicago: Dartnell, 1976.

Feuchtwanger, Lion. *Wahn oder der Terfel in Boston*. Los Angeles: Pacific Press, 1948.

Feuerlicht, Roberta S. *The Desperate Act*. New York: McGraw-Hill, 1968.

Feuerwerker, Albert (ed.). *Modern China*. Englewood Cliffs, N.J.: Prentice-Hall, 1964.

Fewtrell, Malcolm. *The Train Robbers*. London: Arthur Barker, 1964.

Fiaschetti, Michael. *You Gotta Be Rough*. Garden City, N.Y.: Doubleday, Doran, 1930.

Fiedler, George. *The Illinois Law Courts in Three Centuries 1673-*

1973. Berwyn, Ill.: Physicians' Record, 1973.

Fiedler, Leslie. *An End to Innocence: Essays on Culture and Politics.* Boston: Beacon, 1955.

_____. *On Being Busted.* New York: Stein & Day, 1970.

Fiedler, Mildred. *Wild Bill and Deadwood.* New York: Bonanza Books, 1965.

Field, Carter. *Bernard Baruch.* New York: Whittlesey House, 1944.

Field, E.W. *Correspondence on the Present Relations Between Great Britain and the U.S. of A.* Boston: Little, Brown, 1862.

Field, G. Lowell. *The Syndical and Corporative Institutions of Fascism.* New York: Columbia University Press, 1938.

Field, Henry M. *Our Western Archipelago.* New York: Charles Scribner's Sons, 1895.

Fielder, Mildred (ed.). *Lawrence Country for the Dakota Territory Centennial.* Lead: Seaton Printing, 1960.

_____. *Wild Bill and Deadwood.* Seattle, Wash.: Superior, 1965.

Fieldhouse, D.K. *The Colonial Empires.* New York: Delacorte Press, 1965.

Fielding, Cecil. *Justice Triumphant.* London: John Long, 1958.

Fielding, Henry. *An Enquiry into the Causes of the Late Increase in Robbers.* New York: AMS Press, 1975.

Fielding, John. *An Account of the Origin and Effects of a Police Set on Foot by His Grace the Duke of Newcastle in the Year 1753.* London: A. Millar, 1758.

Fielding, William J. *Strange Customs of Courtship and Marriage.* New York: Hart, 1942.

Fielding, Xan. *The Money Spinner.* Boston: Little, Brown, 1977.

Fields, Howard. *High Crimes and Misdemeanors.* New York: W.W. Norton, 1978.

Fierman, Floyd D., and West, John. *Billy the Kid, the Cowboy Outlaw.* Philadelphi: Maurice Jacobs Press, 1965.

Fifteenth Army Group. *Finito!: the Po Valley campaign.* Milan, Italy: Rizzoli, 1945.

Figgis, Darrell. *A Chronicle of Jails.* Dublin, Ire.: Talbot, 1918.

_____. *Recollections of the Irish War.* Garden City, N.Y.: Doubleday, Doran, 1927.

_____. *A Second Chronicle of Jails.* Dublin, Ire.: Talbot, 1919.

Figner, Vera. *Memoirs of a Revolutionist.* trans. A.S. Kaum. New York: International Publishers, 1927.

Figuier, Guillaume Louis. *Histoire du merveilleux dans les temps modernes.* Paris: L. Hachete, 1860.

Filene, Peter Gabriel. *Him/Her/Self.* New York: Harcourt Brace Jovanovich, 1974.

Filler, Louis. *The Anxious Years: America in the Nineteen Thirties.* New York: Capricorn, 1964.

_____. *The Crusade Against Slavery.* New York: Harper & Row, 1960.

_____. *The Muckrakers.* University Park: Pennsylvania State University Press, 1976.

Filmer, Sir Robert. *An Advertisement ot the Juryment of England Touching Witches.* London: R. Royston, 1653.

_____. *Patriarcha.* Oxford, Eng.: B. Blackwell, 1949.

Filson, John. *The Discovery, Settlement and Present State of Kentucky.* Wilmington, Del.: J. Adams, 1784.

_____. *Kentucky and the Adventures of Col. Daniel Boone.* Louisville, Ky.: John P. Morton, 1934.

Final Report, Commission to Investigate Allegations of Police Corruption and the City's Anti-Corruption Procedures. New York: The Fund for the City of New York, 1972.

Finch, Sir Henry. *Law.* London: Henry Lintot, 1759.

Finckenauer, James. *Scared Straight and the Panacea Phenomenon.* Englewood Cliff, N.J.: Prentice-Hall, 1982.

Fine, Nathan. *Labor and Farm Parties in the United States, 1828-1928.* New York: Rand School of Social Service, 1928.

Fine, Ralph Adam. *Escape of the Guilty.* New York: Dodd, Mead, 1986.

Fine, William M. (ed.). *That Day With God.* New York: McGraw-Hill, 1965.

Finegan, James E. *Tammany at Bay.* New York: Dodd, 1933.

Finer, Herman. *Mussolini's Italy.* New York: Holt, 1935.

_____. *Road to Reaction.* Boston: Little, Brown, 1945.

Fines and Imprisonments in Counterfeiting Cases. Washington, D.C.: U.S. Government Printing Office, 1935.

Finestone, Harold. *Victims of Change.* Westport, Ct.: Greenwood, 1976.

Fingall, Elizabeth M.M.B., Plunkett, Countess of, and Hinkson, Pamela. *Seventy Years Young.* London: Collins, 1937.

Fingarette, Herbert. *The Meaning of Criminal Insanity.* Berkeley: University of California Press, 1972.

_____, and Hasse, A.F. *Mental Disabilities and Criminal Responsibility.* Berkeley: University of California Press, 1979.

Finger, Charles Joseph. *Adventures Under Sapphire Skies.* New York: William Morrow, 1931.

_____. *The Distant Prize.* New York: Appleton-Century, 1935.

_____. *Foot-Loose in the West.* New York: William Morrow, 1932.

_____. *Frontier Ballards.* Garden City, N.Y.: Doubleday, Page, 1927.

Fink, Arthur E. *Causes of Crime: Biological Theories in the United States, 1800-1915.* Philadelphia: University of Pennsylvania Press, 1938.

Fink, Joseph, and Sealy, Lloyd G. *The Community and the Police.* New York: John Wiley & Sons, 1974.

Finkelhor, David. *Sexually Victimized Children.* New York: Free Press, 1979.

Finkelstein, M. Marvin, et al. *Prosecution in the Juvenile Court: Guidelines for the Future.* Washington, D.C.: National Institute of Law Enforcement and Criminal Justice, 1973.

Finlay, George. *A History of Greece from its Conquest by the Romans to the Present Time, 146 B.C. to 1864 A.D.* Oxford, Eng.: Clarendon Press, 1877.

Finley, James B. *Autobiography of Reverend James B. Finley or Pioneer Life in the West.* Cincinnati, Ohio: Cranston & Curtis, 1853.

Finley, John H. *Thucydides.* Cambridge, Mass.: Harvard University Press, 1942.

Finley, M.I., Smith, Denis Mack, and Duggan, Christopher. *A History of Sicily.* New York: Viking Press, 1987.

Finley, Martha. *Elsie Dinsmore.* New York: A.L. Burton, 1896.

Finn, John T. *History of the Chicago Police.* Chicago: Police Book Fund, 1887.

Finney, Ben. *Feet First.* New York: Crown, 1971.

Finney, Charles G. *The Old China Hands.* New York: Doubleday, 1961.

Fino, Edoardo. *La tragedia di Rodi e dell'Egeo.* Rome: EICA, 1957.

Fiori, Giuseppe. *La Società del Malessere.* Bari, Italy: Laterza, 1968.

Firmin-Didot, G. *La captivité de Sainte-Hélène, rapports du marquis de Montchenu.* Paris: Firmin-Didot, 1894.

Firmin, Stanley. *Crime Man.* New York: Hutchinson, 1950.

_____. *Murderers in Our Midst.* London: Hutchinson, 1955.

_____. *Scotland Yard: The Inside Story.* London: Hutchinson, 1948.

Firth, Charles H. *The Last Years of the Protectorate.* London: Longman, Green, 1909.

_____. *Oliver Cromwell and the Rule of the Puritans in England.* New York: G.P. Putnam's Sons, 1900.

Firth, James Brierley. *A Scientist Turns to Crime.* London: W. Kimber, 1960.

Firth, Raymond. *Elements of Social Organization.* London: Watts, 1961.

Fischer, Fritz. *German's Aims in the First World War.* New York: W.W. Norton, 1967.

Fischer, George. *Russian Emigré Politics.* New York: Free Russia Fund, 1951.

_____. *Russian Liberalism.* Cambridge, Mass.: Harvard University Press, 1958.

_____. *Soviet Opposition to Stalin.* Cambridge, Mass.: Harvard

University Press, 1952.

Fischer, Louis. *The Life and Death of Stalin*. New York: Harper & Brothers, 1962.

_____. *The Life of Lenin*. New York: Harper & Row, 1964.

_____. *The Life of Mahatma Gandhi*. New York: Harper & Brothers, 1950.

_____. *Russia Revisited*. Garden City, N.Y.: Doubleday, 1957.

_____. *The Soviets and World Affairs*. New Jersey: Princeton University Press, 1951.

Fischer, Ruth. *Stalin and German Communism*. Cambridge, Mass.: Harvard University Press, 1948.

Fischer, Wilhelm. *Aberglaube aller Zeiten*. Stuttgart: Strecker & Schröder, 1906.

Fischer-Galanti, Stephen. *Eastern Europe in the Sixties*. New York: Frederick A. Praeger, 1963.

_____ (ed.). *Romania*. New York: Mid-European Studies Center, 1957.

_____. *Twentieth Century Rumania*. New York: Columbia University Press, 1970.

Fischle, Ernst. *Kidnapped in China*. trans. Marie S. Christlieb. Mangalore, India: Basel Mission Book & Tract Depository, 1932.

Fish, Carl Russell. *The American Civil War*. New York: Longmans, Green, 1937.

_____. *The Civil Service and the Patronage*. New York: Longmans, Green, 1905.

_____. *The Rise of the Common Man 1830-1850*. New York: Macmillan, 1927.

Fishbein, Morris. *Fads and Quackery in Healing*. New York: Covici, Friede, 1932.

Fishburne, Patricia, et al. *National Survey on Drug Abuse*. Washington, D.C.: U.S. Government Printing Office, 1980.

Fisher, Anne B. *The Salinas, Upside-Down River*. New York: Farrar & Rinehart, 1945.

Fisher, Carol, and Krinsky, Fred. *Middle East in Crisis*. Syracuse, N.Y.: Syracuse University Press, 1959.

Fisher, Sir Godfrey. *Barbary Legend: War, Trade and Piracy in North Africa, 1415-1830*. Oxford, Eng.: Clarendon Press, 1957.

Fisher, Harold H. *The Famine in Soviet Russia, 1919-1923*. New York: Macmillan, 1927.

Fisher, Irving. *The Nobel Experiment*. New York: Alcohol Information Committee, 1930

_____. *Prohibition at Its Worst*. New York: Macmillan, 1926.

_____, and Brougham, H.B. *Prohibition Still at Its Worst*. New York: Alcohol Information Committee, 1928.

_____. *The Purchasing Power of Money: Its Determination and Relation to Credit, Interest and Crises*. New York: Macmillan, 1911.

_____. *The Stock Market Crash-and After*. New York: Macmillan, 1930.

Fisher, John. *The Elysian Fields: France in Ferment, 1789-1804*. London: Cassell, 1966.

Fisher, Lord. *Memories*. London: Hodder & Stoughton, 1919.

Fisher, M.J. *Communist Doctrine and the Free World; the Ideology of Communism According to Marx, Engels, Lenin, and Stalin*. Syracuse, N.Y.: Syracuse University Press, 1952.

Fisher, O.C. *It Occurred In Kimble*. Houston, Texas: Anson Jones Press, 1937.

_____, with Dykes, J.C. *King Fisher: His Life and Times*. Norman: University of Oklahoma Press, 1966.

_____. *The Texas Heritage of the Fishers and the Clarks*. Salado, Texas: Anson Jones Press, 1963.

Fisher, Paul L, and Lowenstein, Ralph L. (eds.). *Race and the News Media*. Frederick A. Praeger, 1967.

Fisher, R.H. *Russian Fur Trade, 1550-1700*. Berkeley, Calif.: University of California Press, 1943.

Fisher, S.G. *The Making of Pennsylvania*. Philadelphia: J.B. Lippincott, 1932.

Fisher, Sydney. *The Middle East: A History*. New York: Alfred A. Knopf, 1959.

_____ (ed.). *The Military in the Middle East*. Columbus: Ohio State University Press, 1963.

Fisher, Vardis, and Holmes, Opal Laurel. *Gold Rushes and Mining Camps of the Early American West*. Caldwell, Idaho: Caxton Printers, 1968.

Fisher, W.B. *The Middle East*. New York: E.P. Dutton, 1950.

Fishman, Joseph F. *Sex in Prison*. National Library Press, 1934.

Fishman, William J. *East End Jewish Radicals 1875-1914*. London: Duckworth, 1975.

_____. *Jewish Radicals*. New York: Pantheon Books, 1974.

_____. *The Streets of East London*. London: Duckworth, 1979.

Fishwick, Marshall W. *American Heroes: Myth and Reality*. Washington, D.C.: Public Affairs Press, 1954.

_____. *Lee: After the War*. New York: Dodd, Mead, 1963.

Fisk, James G. *The Police Community*. Pacific Palisades, Calif.: Palisades, 1974.

Fiske, Horace Spencer. *Chicago in Picture and Poetry*. Chicago: R.F. Seymour, 1903.

Fiske, John. *The Critical Period of American History 1783-1789*. Boston: Houghton Mifflin, 1898.

_____. *The Dutch and Quaker Colonies in America*. Boston: Houghton Mifflin, 1899.

_____. *The Mississippi Valley in the Civil War*. Boston: Houghton, Mifflin, 1900.

Fiske, John. *Old Virginia and Her Neighbors*. New York: Houghton, Mifflin, 1897.

Fiske, Stephen. *Off-hand Portraits of Prominent New Yorkers*. New York: G.R. Lockwood & Son, 1884.

_____. *Tobacco and Alcohol*. New York: Leypoldt & Holt, 1869.

Fitch, J.A. *The Pittsburgh Survey*. New York: Russell Sage Foundation, 1911.

Fithian, J.B. *The Assassination of J. Clarke Swayze*. Topeka, Kan.: Blade Printing, 1877.

Fitzgerald, C.P. *The Birth of Communist China*. Baltimore: Penguin, 1964.

_____. *Flood Tide in China*. London: Cresset Press, 1958.

_____. *Revolution in China*. London: Cresset Press, 1952.

Fitzgerald, F. Scott. *The Crack-Up*. New York: New Directions, 1945.

_____. *The Great Gatsby*. New York: Charles Scribner's Sons, 1925.

Fitzgerald, John D. *Papa Married a Mormon*. Englewood Cliffs, N.J.: Prentice-Hall, 1955.

Fitzgerald, Maurice. *Criminal Investigations*. New York: Greenberg, 1953.

Fitzgerald, P.H. *Chronicles of the Bow Street Police Office*. London: Chapman & Hall, 1888.

Fitzgerald, Percy. *Chronicles of Bow Street*. Montclair, N.J.: Patterson Smith, 1972.

Fitzharris, Timothy L. *The Desirability of a Correctional Ombudsman*. Berkeley, Calif.: Institute of Governmental Studies, 1973.

Fitzjames Stephen, Sir James. *A History of the Criminal Law of England*. London: Macmillan, 1883.

Fitzpatrick, George (ed.). *This Is New Mexico*. Santa Fe, N.M.: Rydal Press, 1948.

Fitzpatrick, George (ed.). *This Is New Mexico*. Santa Fe, N.M.: Rydal Press, 1948.

Fitzpatrick, John C. (ed.). *The Writings of George Washington*. Washington, D.C.: U.S. Government Printing Office, 1931-1944.

Fitzpatrick, Joseph P. *Puerto Rican Americans*. Englewood Cliffs, N.J.: Prentice-Hall, 1971.

The Five Friends, or the Bender Hotel Horror in Kansas. Philadelphia: Old Franklin, 1874.

Flagg, Jared. *Flagg's Flats*. New York: n.p., 1907.

Flagg, Oscar H. *A Review of the Cattle Business in Johnson County, Wyoming, Since 1882*. Cheyenne, Wyo.: Vic Press, 1967.

Flaherty, David H. *Essays in the History of Early American Law.* Chapel Hill: University of North Carolina Press, 1969.

_____. *Privacy in Colonial New England.* Charlottesville: University Press of Virginia, 1972.

Flamm, Jerry. *Good Life in Hard Times.* San Francisco: Chronicle Books, 1978.

Flammonde, Paris. *The Kennedy Conspiracy.* New York: Meredith Press, 1969.

Flanagan, Mike. *Out West.* New York: Harry N. Abrams, 1987.

Flanders, Henry. *Lives and Times of the Chief Justices of the Supreme Court of the United States.* 2 vols. Philadelphia: Lippincott, Crambo, 1855-1858.

Flandrau, Charles Macomb. *Viva Mexico!* New York: D. Appleton, 1908.

Flannery, L.G. (ed.). *John Hunton's Diary.* Lingle, Wyo.: Guide-Review, 1958.

Flaubert, Gustave. *Madame Bovary.* New York: International Collectors Library, 1949.

Fleckles, Elliot V. *Willie Speaks Out: The Psychic World of Abraham Lincoln.* St. Paul, Minn.: Llewellyn, 1974.

Fleischer, Nat. *The Heavyweight Championship.* New York: G.P. Putnam's Sons, 1949.

Fleischman, Harry. *Norman Thomas.* New York: W.W. Norton, 1964.

Fleischmann, Max. *Christian Thomasius Leben und Lebenwerk.* Halle, Ger.: M. Niewmeyer, 1930.

Fleisher, B.M. *The Economics of Delinquency.* Chicago: Quadrangle Books, 1966.

Fleisher, Wilfred. *Volcanic Isle.* New York: Doubleday, Doran, 1941.

Fleming, Alice. *New on the Beat: Woman Power in the Police Force.* New York: Coward, McCann & Geoghegan, 1975.

Fleming, D.F. *The United States and the League of Nations, 1918-20.* New York: G.P. Putnam's Sons, 1932.

Fleming, E. McClung. *R.R. Bowker, Militant Liberal.* Norman: University of Oklahoma Press, 1952.

Fleming, John S. *What Is Ku Kluxism?* Goodwater, Ala.: Masonic Weekly Recorder, 1923.

Fleming, Karl and Anne Taylor. *The First Time.* New York: Simon & Schuster, 1975.

Fleming, Macklin. *The Price of Perfect Justice.* New York: Basic Books, 1974.

Fleming, Peter. *The Fate of Admiral Kolchak.* London: Hart Davis, 1963.

Fleming, Walter Lynwood. *Civil War and Reconstruction in Alabama.* New York: Columbia University Press, 1905.

_____. *Documentary History of Reconstruction.* 2 vols. Cleveland: Arthur H. Clarke, 1906-1907.

Fletcher, Baylis John. *Up the Trail in '79.* Norman: University of Oklahoma Press, 1968.

Fletcher, Ernest M. *The Wayward Horseman.* Denver: Sage Books, 1958.

Fleuret, Fernand. *De Gilles de Rais a Guillaume Apollinaire.* Poitiers, Fr.: Marc Tézier, 1933.

_____. *Le Proces Inquisitorial de Gilles de Rais avec un Essai de Réhabilitation.* Paris: Bibliotheque des Curieux, 1921.

Fleury de Chaboulon. *Mémoires.* Paris: Rouveyre, 1901.

Fleury, Marurice, comte (ed.). *Memoirs of the Empress Eugénie.* 2 vols. New York: D. Appleton, 1920.

_____, and Sonolet. *Le Société du second empire.* 4 vols. Paris: A. Michel, 1911.

Flew, Antony. *Crime or Disease?* London: Macmillan, 1973.

Flexner, Abraham. *Prostitution in Europe.* New York: Century, 1914.

Flexner, Eleanor. *Century of Struggle.* Cambridge, Mass.: Harvard University Press, 1959.

Flexner, James T. *Steamboats Come True: American Inventors in Action.* New York: Viking Press, 1944.

_____. *The Traitor and the Spy.* New York: Little, Brown, 1953.

Flick, Alexander C. (ed.). *The History of the State of New York.* New York: Columbia University Press, 1933.

_____. *Samuel Jones Tilden: A Study in Political Sagacity.* New York: Dodd, 1939.

Flinn, John. *A History of the Chicago Police.* Chicago: W.B. Conkey, 1887.

Flinn, John J., and Wilkie, John E. *History of the Chicago Police.* Montclair, N.J.: Patterson Smith, 1973.

Flint, Leon Nelson. *The Editorial: A Study in Effectiveness of Writing.* New York: D. Appleton, 1920.

Flint, Timothy. *A Condensed Geography and History of the Western States, or The Mississippi Valley.* 2 vols. Cincinnati, Ohio: E.H. Flint, 1828.

_____. *Recollections of the Last Ten Years.* Boston: Cummings, Hilliard, 1826.

Flippen, Charles C., II. *Liberating the Media.* Washington, D.C.: Acropolis Books, 1974.

Flohery, John J. *Inside the F.B.I.* Philadelphia: J.B. Lippincott, 1943.

Flora, Francesco. *Appello al Re.* Bologna, Italy: Edizioni alfa, 1965.

_____. *Ritratto di un ventennio.* Naples, Italy: Macchiaroli, 1944.

Florence, Ronald. *Fritz, The Story of a Political Assassin.* New York: Dial Press, 1971.

Florida. Special Commission for the Study of Abolition of Death Penalty in Capital Cases. *Report.* Tallahassee: State of Florida, 1965.

Florin, Lambert. *Boot Hill: Historic Graves of the Old West.* Seattle, Wash.: Superior, 1966.

_____. *Ghost Town Album.* Seattle, Wash.: Superior, 1962.

Florinsky, Michael T. *The End of the Russian Empire.* New York: Collier Books, 1961.

_____. *Fascism and National Socialism.* New York: Macmillan, 1938.

_____. *Russia, a History and an Interpretation.* 2 vols. New York: Macmillan, 1953.

Flourens, Gustave. *Paris Livré.* Paris: Lacroix, Verboeckhove, 1871.

Flower, Benjamin Orange. *Civilization's Inferno.* Boston: Arena, 1893.

Flower, Desmond, and Mans, Henry. *The Letters of Ernest Dowson.* London: Cassell, 1967.

_____. *Voltaire's England.* London: Folio Society, 1950.

Flower, Frank A. *Edwin McMasters Stanton.* New York: Saalfield, 1905.

Floyd, N.J. *Thorns in the Flesh.* Philadelphia: Edwards & Broughton, 1884.

Flusser, Martin. *The Squeal Man.* New York: William Morrow, 1977.

Flynn, Edward J. *You're the Boss.* New York: Viking Press, 1947.

Flynn, Elizabeth Gurley. *The Rebel Girl.* New York: International Press, 1955.

Flynn, J. *You're The Boss.* New York: Harcourt, Brace, 1947.

Flynn, John T. *God's Gold: John D. Rockefeller and His Times.* New York: Harcourt, Brace, 1932.

_____. *Men of Wealth: The Story of Twelve Significant Fortunes from the Renaissance to the Present Day.* New York: Simon & Schuster, 1941.

_____. *The Roosevelt Myth.* New York: Devin-Adair, 1948.

_____. *Security Speculation-Its Economic Effects.* New York: Harcourt, Brace, 1934.

Flynn, Robert DeShields. *The Poor Man in Politics.* Danville, Va.: Dance Brothers, 1894.

Flynt, Josiah. *World of Graft.* New York: McClure Phillips, 1901.

Foat, Ginny. *Never Guilty, Never Free.* New York: Random House, 1985.

Fodor, M.W. *The Revolution Is On.* Boston: Houghton Mifflin, 1940.

Foerster, Robert. *Italian Emigration of out Times.* Cambridge, Mass: Harvard University Press, 1919.

Foerster, Wolfgang. *Generaloberst Ludwig Beck.* Munich: Isar, 1953.

Foertsch, Hermann. *Schuld und Verhängnis. Die Fritsch-Krise im Frühjahr 1938.* Stuttgart, Ger.: Deutsche Verlagsanstalt, 1951.

Fogarty, Kate Hammond. *The Story of Montana.* New York: A.S. Barnes, 1916.

Fogel, David. *". . .We Are the Living Proof. . ."* Cincinnati, Ohio: W.H. Anderson, 1975.

Fogelman, Ken (ed.). *Britain's 16-Year-Olds.* London: National Children's Bureau, 1976.

Fogelson, Robert M. *Big City Police.* Cambridge, Mass.: Harvard University Press, 1977.

_____. *The Los Angeles Riots.* New York: Arno Press & The New York Times, 1969.

_____, and Rubenstein, Richard (eds.). *Mass Violence in America: Invasion at Harper's Ferry.* New York: Arno Press & New York Times, 1969.

_____. *Violence as Protest: A Study of Riots and Ghettos.* New York: Doubleday, 1971.

Foght, Harold Waldstein. *The Trail of the Loup.* Ord, Nebr.: n.p., 1906.

Foix, Pere. *Pancho Villa.* Mexico City: Ediciones Xochitl, 1950.

Foley, Doris. *The Divine Eccentric: Lola Montez and the Newspapers.* Los Angeles: Westernlore, 1969.

Folley, Vern F. *American Law Enforcement.* Boston: Holbrook Press, 1973.

Folmsbee, Stanley J., et al. *History of Tennessee.* New York: Lewis Historical, 1960.

Folsom, Burton W., Jr. *Urban Capitalists.* Baltimore: Johns Hopkins University Press, 1981.

Folwell, William Watts. *A History of Minnesota.* St. Paul: Minnesota Historical Society, 1921-30.

Foner, Philip S. *The Bolshevik Revolution: It's Impact on American Radicals, Liberals, and Labor.* New York: International, 1967.

_____. *Business and Slavery: The New York Merchants and the Irrepressible Conflict.* Chapel Hill: Univeristy of North Carolina Press, 1941.

_____. *Frederick Douglass.* New York: Citadel Press, 1964.

_____. *History of the Labor Movement in the United States: From Colonial Times to the Founding of the American Federation of Labor.* New York: International, 1947.

_____. *The Industrial Workers of the World, 1905-1917.* New York: International, 1965.

Fong, Mak Lau. *The Sociology of Secret Societies: A Study of Chinese Secret Societies in Singapore and Peninsular Malaysia.* Oxford, Eng.: Oxford University Press, 1981.

Fontaine, Felix G. *Trial of the Honorable Daniel E. Sickles.* New York: R.M. DeWitt, 1859.

Fontaine, Jacques. *Discours des marques des sorciers et de la réelle possession que le diable prend sur le corps des hommes.* Lyons, Fr.: C. Larjet, 1611.

Fontana, Vincent J. *Somewhere a Child Is Crying.* New York: Macmillan, 1973.

Fontane, Theodor. *Von Zwanzig bis Dreissig.* Berlin: S. Fischer Verlag, 1925.

Fontenay, Charles. *Estes Kefauver.* Knoxville, Tenn: 1980.

Fontenelle, Monsignor René. *His Holiness Pope Pius XI.* London: Burns, Oates & Washbourne, 1933.

Fooner, Michael. *A Guide to Interpol.* Washington, D.C.: U.S. Government Printing Office, 1985.

_____. *INTERPOL.* Chicago: Henry Regnery, 1973.

Foord, John. *The Life and Public Services of Andrew H. Green.* New York: Doubleday, Page, 1913.

_____. *The Life and Publice Services of Simon Sterne.* New York: Macmillan, 1903.

Foot, M.R.D. *Resistance.* New York: McGraw-Hill, 1977.

Foot, Michael, and Jones, Mervy. *Guilty Men.* London: Victor Gollancz, 1957.

Foot, Paul. *Who Killed Hanratty?* London, Cape, 1971.

Foote, Edward B. *Plain Home Talk.* New York: Murray Hill, 1887.

Foote, H.C. *Universal Counterfeiter and Bank Note Detector, at Sight.* New York: Oliver & Brother, 1851.

Foote, Henry Leander. *A Sketch of the Life and Adventures of Henry Leander Foote.* New Haven, Conn.: T.J. Stafford, 1850.

Foote, Henry S. *Casket of Reminiscences.* Washington, D.C.: Chronicle, 1874.

Foote, Shelby. *The Civil War, a Narrative: Fort Sumter to Perryville.* New York: Random House, 1958.

_____. *The Civil War, a Narrative: Fredericksburg to Meridian.* New York: Random House, 1963.

Foote, Stella Adelyne. *Letters from Buffalo Bill.* Billings, Mont.: Foote, 1954.

Footman, David. *Balkan Holiday.* London: William Heinemann, 1935.

_____. *Civil War in Russia.* New York: Frederick A. Praeger, 1962.

_____. *Red Prelude.* New Haven: Yale University Press, 1945.

_____ (ed.). *Soviet Affairs.* London: Chatto & Windus, 1962.

Foraker, Joseph Benson. *Notes of a Busy Life.* Cincinnati, Ohio: Stewart & Kidd, 1916.

Foran, W.R. *The Kenya Police, 1887-1960.* London: R. Hale, 1962.

Forberg, Fred. *Classical Erotilogy.* New York: Grove Press, 1966.

Forbes, Abner, and Green, J.W. *The Rich Men of Massachusetts.* Boston: W.V. Spencer, 1851.

Forbes, Allan, and Cadman, Paul. *France and New England.* New York: State Street Trust, 1925.

Forbes, Archibald. *William of Germany.* New York: Cassell, 1888.

Forbes, Colin. *The Palermo Ambush.* London: William Collins & Sons, 1972

Forbes, Edward W., and Finley, John W. (eds.). *The Saturday Club.* Boston: Houghton Mifflin, 1958.

Forbes, Esther. *A Mirror for Witches.* New York: Houghton Mifflin, 1928.

_____. *Paul Revere and the World He Lived In.* Boston: Houghton Mifflin, 1942.

Forbes, Gerald. *Guthrie: Oklahoma's First Capital.* Norman: Univesity of Oklahoma Press, 1938.

Forbes, Ian. *Squad Man.* London: W.H. Allen, 1973.

Forbes, Nevill, et al. *The Balkans.* London: Oxford, 1915.

Ford, Alice (ed.). *Audubon by Himself.* Garden City, N.Y.: Natural History Press, 1969.

Ford, Betty., and Chase, Chris. *The Times of My Life.* New York: Harper Row/Readers Digest, 1978.

Ford, Clelland S., and Beach, Frank A. *Patterns of Sexual Behavior.* New York: Harper, 1951.

Ford, Cory. *Short Cut to Tokyo: The Battle for the Aleutians.* New York: Charles Scribner's Sons, 1943.

Ford, Ford Madox. *Return to Yesterday.* London: Victor Gollancz, 1931.

Ford, Franklin L. *Political Murder.* London: Harvard University Press, 1985.

Ford, Gerald R. *A Time To Heal: The Autobiography of Gerald R. Ford.* New York: Harper & Row, 1979.

_____, and Stiles, John. *Portrait of the Assassin.* New York: Simon & Schuster, 1965.

Ford, Worthington C. (ed.) *The Writings of John Quincy Adams.* New York: Macmillan, 1913-1917.

Fordfox, Henry Jones. *The Scotch-Irish in America.* Princeton, N.J.: Princeton University Press, 1915.

_____. *Washington and His Colleagues.* New Haven, Conn.: Yale University Press, 1921.

Ford, James. *Slums and Housing With Special Reference to New York City.* Cambridge, Mass. Harvard University Press, 1936.

Ford, John Salmon. *Rip Ford's Texas.* Austin: University of Texas Press, 1963.

Ford, Patrick H. (ed.). *The Darrow Bribery Trial with Background Facts of McNamara Case and Including Darrow's Address to the Jury.* Whittier, Calif.: Western Printing, 1956.

Ford, Paul Leicester. *The Many-Sided Franklin.* New York: Century, 1921.

_____ (ed.). *The Writings of Thomas Jefferson.* New York: G.P. Putnam's Sons, 1892-99.

Ford, Tirey L. *Dawn and the Dons: The Romance of Monterey.* San Francisco: A.M. Robertson, 1936.

Fordham, Edward Wilfred. *Notable Cross-Examinations.* London: Constable, 1951.

Fordham, Peta. *The Robbers' Tale.* London: Hodder & Stoughton, 1965.

Fordin, Hugh. *Getting to Know Him.* New York: Random Huse, 1977.

Forel, August. *The Sexual Question.* New York: Rebman, 1908.

Foreman, Carolyn Thomas. *Oklahoma Imprints 1835-1907.* Norman: University of Oklahoma Press, 1936.

Foreman, Grant. *Advancing the Frontier.* Norman: University of Oklahoma Press, 1933.

_____. *The Five Civilized Tribes.* Norman: University of Oklahoma Press, 1934.

_____. *Fort Gibson.* Norman: University of Oklahoma Press, 1936.

_____. *A History of Oklahoma.* Norman: University of Oklahoma Press, 1942.

_____. *Indian Removal.* Norman: University of Oklahoma Press, 1932.

_____. *Muskogee: The Biography of an Oklahoma Town.* Norman: University of Oklahoma Press, 1943.

_____ (ed.). *A Pathfinder in the Southwest, The Itinerary of Lt. A.W. Whipple.* Norman: University of Oklahoma Press, 1940.

_____. *Pioneer Days in the Early Southwest.* Cleveland: Arthur H. Clark, 1926.

Forensic Science Society. *World List of Forensic Science Laboratories.* North Yorkshire, Eng.: n.p., n.d.

Forer, Lois G. *Criminals and Victims.* New York: W.W. Norton, 1980.

_____. *No One Will Lissen.* New York: John Day, 1970.

Forester, C.S. *The Barbary Pirates.* New York: Random House, 1953.

_____. *Union of Italy.* New York: Dodd, 1927.

Fornaro, Carlo de. *Carranza and Mexico.* New York: Mitchell Kennerley, 1915.

Forneron, Henri. *Louise de Kéroualle.* London: Sonnenschein, 1887.

Forney, John W. *Anecdotes of Public Men.* New York: Harper, 1873.

Forrest, Alan. *Italian Interlude.* London: Bailey Brothers & Swinfen, 1964.

Forrest, Earle R. *Arizona's Dark and Bloody Ground.* Caldwell, Idaho: Caxton Printers, 1953.

_____, and Hill, Edwin B. *Lone War Trail of Apache Kid.* Pasadena, Calif.: Trail's End, 1947.

_____. *Missions and Pueblos of the Old Southwest.* Cleveland: Arthur H. Clark, 1929.

Forrest, Jay W., and Malcolm, James. *Tammany's Treason.* Albany, N.Y.: Fort Orange Press, 1913.

Forrestal, James. *The Forrestal Diaries.* New York: Viking Press, 1951.

Forrester, Izola. *This One Mad Act; the Unknown Story of John Wilkes Booth and his Family.* Boston: Hale, Cushman & Flint, 1937.

Forsee, Peter A. *Five Years of Crime in California.* Ukiah City, Calif.: Forsee, 1867.

Forshufvud, Sten. *Napoléon a-t-il été empoisonné.* Paris: Plon, 1961

_____. *Who Killed Napoleon?* London: Hutchinson, 1962.

Forster, Arnold, and Epstein, Benjamin R. *Danger on the Right.* New York: Random House, 1964.

Forster, E.M. *Abinger Harvest.* New York: Harcourt, Brace, 1936.

Forster, E.S. *A Short History of Modern Greece, 1821-1956.* London: Methuen, 1958.

Forster, Johann Reinhold. *The "Resolution" Journal of Johann Reinhold Forster, 1772-1775.* 4 vols. London: Hakluyt Society, 1982.

Forster, John. *The Life of Charles Dickens.* 3 vols. London: Chapman & Hall, 1873.

Forster, Joseph. *Studies in Black and Red.* London: Ward & Downey, 1896.

Forsyth, Frederick. *Day of the Jackal.* London: Hutchinson, 1971.

Forsyth, J.S.F. *Demonologia.* London: A.K. Newton, 1831.

Forsyth, William. *History of the Capivity of Napoleon at St. Helena.* London: John Murray, 1853.

Fort, Charles. *Wild Talents.* New York: Kendall, 1932.

Fort, George. *History of Medical Ecomony During the Middle Ages.* New York: J.W. Bouton, 1883.

Fortas, Abe. *Concerning Dissent and Civil Disobedience.* New York: Signet Press, 1968.

Forter, Norman L., and Rostovsky, Demeter B. *The Roumanian Handbook.* London: Simpkin Marshall, 1931.

Fortes, M., and Evans-Pritchard, E.E. (eds.). *African Political Systems.* London: Oxford University Press, 1940.

Forti, Raul, and Ghedini, Giuseppe. *L'avvento del Fascismo.* Ferrara, Italy: Taddel, 1922.

Fortier, Alcée. *A History of Louisiana.* New York: Manz & Joyand, 1904.

Fortier, Malcom V. *Life of a POW Under the Japanese.* Spokane, Wash.: G.W. Hill, 1946.

Fortini, Franco. *Sere in Valdossola.* Milan, Italy: Mondadori, 1963.

Fortson, John. *Pott County and What Has Come of It.* Shawnee, Okla.: Pottawatomie County Historical Society, 1936.

Fortune, Jan I. (ed.). *The True Story of Bonnie & Clyde: As Told by Bonnie's Mother and Clyde's Sister.* New York: Signet Books, 1968.

Forzano, Giovacchino. *Mussolini, autore drammatico.* Florence, Italy: Barbera, 1954.

Fosburgh, Lacey. *Closing Time.* New York: Delacourt Press, 1977.

Fosdick, Raymond B. *American Police Systems.* New York: Century, 1920.

_____. *Chronicle of a Generation.* New York: Harper, 1958.

_____. *European Police Systems.* Montclair, N.J.: Patterson Smith, 1969.

Foss, B.M. (ed.). *Determinants of Infant Behavior.* New York: John Wiley & Sons, 1963.

Fossett, Frank. *Colorado: A Historical, Descriptive and Statistical Work.* Denver: Daily Tribune Steam Printing House, 1876.

_____. *Colorado: Its Gold and Silver Mines.* New York: C.G. Crawford, 1879.

Foster, Frank. *Comrades in Bondage.* London: Skeffington & Son, 1946.

Foster, George G. *Fifteen Minutes around New York.* New York: De Witt & Davenport, 1954.

_____. *New York by Gas-Light.* New York: M.J. Ivers, 1850.

Foster, Stephen. *Their Solitary Way.* New Haven, Conn.: Yale University Press, 1971.

Foster, William Z. *History of the Three Internationals.* New York: International, 1955.

_____. *Outline History of the World Trade Union Movement.* New York: International, 1956.

_____. *Toward Soviet America.* New York: Coward-McCann, 1932.

Foster-Harris. *The Look of the Old West.* New York: Viking Press, 1955.

Fotieva, Lydia. *Pages from Lenin's Life.* Moscow: Foreign Languages Publishing House, 1960.

Foucault, Maurice. *Les procés de sorcellerie dans l'ancienne France devant les jurisdictions séculiéres.* Paris: Bonvalot-Jouve, 1907.

Foucault, Michel. *Discipline & Punishment: The Birth of the Prison.* New York: Vintage Books, 1979.

_____. *The History of Sexuality.* New York: Pantheon, 1978.

_____. *Madness and Civilization.* New York: Random House, 1965.

Foulke, Roy A. *The Sinews of American Commerce.* New York: Dun and Bradstreet, 1941.

Foulke, William Dudley. *A Hoosier Autobiography.* New York: Oxford University Press, 1922.

Fouquier, Armand. *Les Cause celebres de tous les peuples.* 9 vols. Paris: Lebrun, 1858-1874.

Fournier, Paul. *Les officialités au moyen àge.* Paris: E. Plon, 1880.

Fowler, F.J., and Magione, T.W. *Neighborhood Crime, Fear and Social Control.* Washington, D.C.: National Institute of Justice, 1982.

Fowler, Gene. *Beau James: The Life and Times of Jimmy Walker.* New York: The Viking Press, 1949.

_____. *Father Goose: The Story of Mack Sennett.* New York: Civici-Friede, 1934.

_____. *Goodnight, Sweet Prince: The Life and Times of John Barrymore.* New York: Viking, 1944.

_____. *The Great Mouthpiece: The Life Story of William J. Fallon.* New York: Covici-Friede, 1931.

_____. *Skyline: A Reporter's Reminiscences of the 1920's.* New York: Macmillan Books, 1962.

_____. *Timber Line.* New York: Covici-Friede, 1933.

Fowler, Kenneth. *The Age of Plantaget and Valois.* New York: G.P. Putnam's Sons, 1967.

_____. *The Hundred Years War.* New York: Macmillan, 1971.

Fowler, O.S. *Temperance Founded on Phrenology and Physiology, or The Laws of Life, and the Principles of the Human Constitution as developed by the sciences of phrenology and physiology, applied to total abstinence from all alcoholic and intoxicating drinks.* New York: Fowler & Wells Phrenological Cabinet, 1846.

Fowler, Robert H. *Album of the Lincoln Murder.* Harrisburg, Pa.: Stackpole Books, 1965.

Fowler, Samuel Page. *Salem Witchcraft.* Salem, Mass.: H.P. Ives & A.A. Smith, 1861.

Fowler, Will. *The Young Man from Denver.* Garden City, N.Y.: Doubleday, 1962.

Fowles, A.J. *Prison Welfare.* London: H.M. Stationery Office, 1978.

Fowles, John. *Shipwreck.* London: Jonathan Cape, 1974.

Fox, A.W. *The Earl of Halsbury, Lord High Chancellor.* London: Chapman & Hall, 1929.

Fox, Dixon Ryan. *The Decline of Aristocracy in the Politics of New York, 1801-1840.* New York: Columbia University Press, 1919.

Fox, Ebenezer. *The Revolutionary Adventures.* Boston: Monroe & Francis, 1838.

Fox, Frank. *The Balkan Peninsula.* London: A. & C. Black, 1915.

Fox, Sir Frank. *Italy Today.* London: Herbert Jenkins. 1927.

Fox, George. *A Declaration of the Ground of Error.* London: Giles Calvert, 1657.

Fox, James. *White Mischief.* New York: Random House, 1982.

Fox, James Allen. *Forecasting Crime Data.* Lexington, Mass.: Lexington/D.C. Heath, 1978.

_____, and Levin, Jack. *Mass Murder: America's Growing Menace.* New York: Plenum Press, 1985.

Fox, Lionel. *English Prison and Borstal Systems.* London: Routledge, 1952.

Fox, R.M. *Green Banners: The Story of the Irish Struggle.* London: Secker & Warburg, 1938.

_____. *History of the Irish Citizen Army.* Dublin, Ire.: Duffy, 1943.

_____. *Louie Bennett: Her Life and Times.* Dublin, Ire.: Talbot, 1958.

_____. *Rebel Irishwomen.* Dublin, Ire.: Talbot, 1935.

Fox, Ralph. *Lenin, A Biography.* New York: Harcourt, Brace, 1934.

Fox, Ralph W. *France Faces the Future.* London: Lawrence & Wishart, 1936.

Fox, Richard Kyle. *The History of the Whitechapel Murders.* New York: Fox, 1888.

Fox, Stephen. *Blood and Power: Organized Crime in the Twentieth Century.* New York: William Morrow, 1989.

Fox, Sylvan. *The Unanswered Questions About President Kennedy's Assassination.* New York: Award Press, 1965.

Fox, Vernon. *Introduction to Corrections.* Englewood Cliffs, N.J.: Prentice-Hall, 1985.

_____. *Introduction to Criminology.* Englewood Cliffs, N.J.: Prentice-Hall, 1976.

Fox, Victor J. *The White House Case.* Pleasantville, N.Y.: Fargo Press, 1968.

Foxe, Arthur N. *Crime and Sexual Development.* Glens Falls, N.Y.: The Monogram Editions, 1936.

Foy, Eddie, and Harlow, Alvin F. *Clowning Through Life.* New York: E.P. Dutton, 1928.

Fracastor. *Contagion.* trans. W.C. Wright. New York: G.P. Putnam's Sons, 1930.

Fracastoro, Girolamo. *The Sinister Shepherd.* trans. William van Wyck. Los Angeles: Primavera Press, 1934.

Frackelton, Will. *Sagebrush Dentist.* Chicago: A.C. McClurg, 1941.

Fraenkel, Franz. *Missing Persons.* Dobbs Ferry, N.Y.: Oceana, 1950.

Fraenkel, Osmond K. *The Sacco and Vanzetti Case.* New York: Alfred A. Knopf, 1931.

Fraley, Oscar. *Four Against the Mob.* New York: Popular Library, 1961.

Frame, Donald M. *Montaigne: A Biography.* New York: Harcourt, Brace & World, 1965.

Francais, J. *L'église et la sorcellerie.* Paris: E. Nourry, 1910.

France, Johnny, and McConnell, Malcolm. *Incident at Big Sky.* New York: W.W. Norton, 1986.

Frances, Jose-Maria. *Vida y Aventuras de Pancho Villa.* Mexico City: Olimpa, 1956.

Francis, Dorothy B. *Shoplifting.* New York: Elsevier-Nellen, 1980.

_____. *Vandalism.* New York: E.P. Dutton, 1983.

Francis, Francis, Jr. *Saddle and Moccasin.* London: Chapman & Hall, 1887.

Francois-Poncet, André. *The Fateful Years.* trans. Jacques Le Clercq. London: Victor Gollancz, 1948.

_____. *Au Palais Farnese, 1938-40.* Paris: Fayard, 1961.

Francovich, Carlo. *La resistenza a Firenze.* Florence, Italy: La Nuova Italia, 1961.

Frank, Anne. *Diary of a Young Girl.* New York: Doubleday, 1952.

Frank, Gerold. *An American Death: The True Story of the Assassination of Dr. Martin Luther King, Jr. and the Greatest Manhunt of Our Time.* Garden City, N.Y.: Doubleday, 1972.

_____. *The Boston Strangler.* New York: New American Library, 1966.

_____. *The Deed.* New York: Simon & Schuster, 1963.

Frank, J. and B. *Not Guilty.* London: Victor Gollancz, 1957.

Frank, Jerome. *Courts on Trial.* Princeton, N.J.: Princeton University Press, 1950.

_____. *Law and the Modern Mind.* New York: Brentano, 1930.

_____, and Frank, Barbara. *Not Guilty.* New York: Doubleday, 1957.

Frank, John P. *Marble Palace.* New York: Alfred A. Knopf,

1958.

_____. *Mr. Justice Black: The Man and His Opinions.* New York: Alfred A. Knopf, 1949.

_____, and Karsh, Yousuf. *The Warren Court.* New York: Macmillan, 1964.

Frank, Joseph. *The Beginnings of the English Newspaper, 1620-1660.* Cambridge, Mass.: Harvard University Press, 1961.

Frank, T. *An economic survey of ancient Rome.* Patterson, N.J.: Pageant Books, 1959.

Frank, Tenney (ed.). *An Economic survey of Ancient Rome.* 5 vols. Baltimore: Johns Hopkins Press, 1940.

Franke, David. *The Torture Doctor.* New York: Hawthorn Books, 1975.

Franke, Paul. *They Plowed Up Hell in Old Cochise.* Douglas, Ariz.: Douglas Climate Club, 1950.

Frankel, Marvin E. *Criminal Sentences: Law without Order.* New York: Hill & Wang, 1973.

_____, and Naftalis, Gary P. *The Grand Jury: Institution on Trial.* New York: Hill & Wang, 1977.

Frankel, William. *Home Security.* Alexandria, Va.: Time-Life Books, 1979.

_____. *Israel Observed.* London: Thames & Hudson, 1980.

Frankenberg, Lloyd (ed.). *A James Stephens Reader.* New York: Macmillan, 1962.

Frankfurter, Felix, and Landis, James. *The Business of the Supreme Court.* New York: Macmillan, 1927.

_____. *The Case of Sacco and Vanzetti.* Boston: Little, Brown & Little, 1927.

_____, and Phillips, Dr. Harlow B. *Felix Frankfurter Reminiscences.* New York: Reynal, 1960.

_____. *Law and Politics.* New York: Harcourt, Brace, 1939.

_____. *Mr. Justice Brandeis.* New Haven, Conn.: Yale University Press, 1932.

_____ (ed.). *Mr. Justice Holmes.* New York: Coward-McCann, 1931.

_____. *Mr. Justice Holmes and the Supreme Court.* Cambridge, Mass.: Harvard University Press, 1938.

_____. *Of Law and Men.* New York: Harcourt, Brace & World, 1956.

Frankfurter, Marion, and Gardner, Jackson (ed.). *The Letters of Sacco and Vanzetti.* New York: Viking Press, 1928.

Frankland, Mark. *Khrushchev.* New York: Stein & Day, 1967.

Frankland, Noble. *Imperial Tragedy.* New York: Coward-McCann, 1961.

Franklin, Benjamin. *Autobiography.* New York: Washington Square Press, 1975.

_____. *Satires and Bagatelles.* Detroit, Mich.: Fine Book Circle, 1937.

Franklin, Charles. *Woman in the Case.* New York: Taplinger, 1968.

_____. *World Famous Acquittals.* London: Odhams Books, 1970.

_____. *The World's Worst Murderers: Exciting and Authentic Accounts of the Great Classics of Murder.* New York: Taplinger, 1965.

Franklin, Fabian. *What Prohibition Has Done to America.* New York: Harcourt, Brace, 1922.

Franklin, J. *A Dictionary of Rhyming Slang.* London: Routledge & Kegan Paul, 1960.

Franklin, John Hope. *From Slavery to Freedom.* New York: Alfred A. Knopf, 1947.

_____. *The Militant South 1800-1861.* Cambridge, Mass.: Harvard University Press, 1956.

_____. *Reconstruction after the Civil War.* Chicago: University of Chicago Press, 1961.

Franklin, Julian H. *Jean Bodin.* New York: Columbia University Press, 1963.

Franks, J.M. *The American Cowboy: The Myth and the Reality.* Norman, Okla.: University of Oklahoma Press, 1955.

Frantz, Joe B., and Choate, Julian Ernest, Jr. *The American Cowboy: The Myth and the Reality.* Norman: University of Oklahoma Press, 1955.

Franzero, C.M. *Inside Italy.* London: Hodder & Stoughton, 1941.

Franzius, Enno. *History of the Order of Assassins.* New York: Funk & Wagnalls, 1969.

Frarken, Glenn L. *Inside Nevada Gambling.* New York: Exposition, 1965.

Frasca, Don. *Vito Genovese: King of Crime.* New York: Avon Books, 1963.

Fraser, Antonia. *Cromwell, The Lord Protector.* New York: Alfred A. Knopf, 1973.

Fraser, George MacDonald. *Flashman: From the Flashman Papers, 1839- 1842.* New York: World, 1969.

Fraser, John Foster. *America at Work.* London: Cassell, 1907.

Fraser, Mrs. Hugh and Hugh C. *Seven Years on the Pacific Slope.* New York: Dodd, Mead, 1914.

Fraser, Morris. *Children in Conflict.* Harmondsworth, Middlesex, Eng.: Penguin Books, 1974.

Frazer, Sir James G. *Balder the beautiful.* London: Macmillan, 1920.

_____. *The Golden Bough, A Study in Magic and Religion.* New York: Macmillan, 1922.

_____. *The Magic art.* London: Macmillan, 1920.

_____. *The Scapegoat.* London: Macmillan, 1920.

Frazer, Robert W. *Forts of the West.* Norman: University of Oklahoma Press, 1965.

Frazier, E. Franklin. *The Negro Family in Chicago.* Chicago: University of Chicago Press, 1932.

Frederick II. *Memoirs of the House of Brandenborg from the Earliest Accounts to the Death of Frederick I, Knig of Prussia.* London: J. Nourse, 1757.

_____. *Posthumous Works of Frederick II, King of Prussia.* trans. Thomas Holcroft. 13 vols. London: G.G.J. & J. Robinson, 1789.

Frederick III. *The Crown Prince, Frederick William, A Diary.* London: Sampson Low, 1886.

_____. *Das Kriegstagebuch von 1870/71.* Berlin: K.F. Koehler, 1926.

_____. *Diaries of the Emperor Frederick During the Campaigns of 1866 and 1870-71 as Well as His Journeys to the East and to Spain.* London: Chapman & Hall, 1902.

_____. *The Emperor Frederick: A Diary.* London: Sampson Low, 1888.

_____. *Tagebucher von 1848-1866.* Leipzig: K.F. Koehler, 1929.

_____. *The War Diary of the Emperor Frederick III, 1870-1871.* London: Stanley Paul, 1927.

Frederick, James Vincent. *Ben Holladay, the Stagecoach King.* Glendale, Calif.: Arthur H. Clark, 1940.

Fredericks, Pierce G. (ed.). *The Civil War As They Knew It.* New York: Bantam Books, 1961.

Freeborn, Richard. *A Short History of Modern Russia.* New York: Hodder & Stoughton, 1966.

Freed, Donald, and Lane, Mark. *Executive Action.* New York: Dell Books, 1973.

_____. *The Killing of RFK.* New York: Dell Books, 1975.

Freed, Leonard. *Police Work.* New York: Simon & Schuster, 1980.

Freedland, Michael. *Jolson.* Briarcliff Manor, N.Y.: Stein & Day, 1972.

Freedman, Allan M., et al. *Modern Synopsis of Comprehensive Textbook of Psychiatry II.* Baltimore: Williams & Wilkins, 1976.

Freedman, D.G. *Human Infancy: An Evolutionary Perspective.* New York: John Wiley/Halstead Press, 1974.

Freedman, Marcia, and Pappas, Nick. *The Training and Employment of Offenders.* Washington, D.C.: President's Commission on Law Enforecement and Administration of Justice, 1967.

Freedman, Marlene. *Alcatraz.* San Francisco, Calif.: Smith Novelty, n.d.

Freedman, Max (ed.). *Roosevelt and Frankfurter: Their Correspondence.* Boston: Little, Brown, 1967.

Freeland, Richard M. *The Truman Doctrine and the Origins of McCarthyism.* New York: Alfred A. Knopf, 1972.

Freeman, D.S. *George Washington: A Biography.* 6 vols. New York: Charles Scribner's Sons, 1948-1954.

_____. *Lee's Lieutenants.* 3 vols. New York: Charles Scribner's Sons, 1942-1944.

_____. *R.E. Lee, A Biography.* 4 vols. New York: Charles Scribner's Sons, 1934-1935.

_____. *Washington and His Generals.* New York: Charles Scribner's Sons, 1951-1957.

_____. *Young Washington.* New York: Charles Scribner's Sons, 1948.

Freeman, E.H. *The Veil of Secrecy Removed, The Only True and Authentic History of Edward H.Ruloff.* Binghamton, N.Y.: Carl & Freeman, 1871.

Freeman, G.D. *Midnight and Noonday, or Dark Deeds Unraveled.* Caldwell, Kan.: G.D. Freeman, 1890.

Freeman, Howard E., and Sherwood, Clarence C. *Social Research and Social Policy.* Englewood Cliffs, N.J.: Prentice-Hall, 1970.

Freeman, James W. (ed.). *Prose and poetry of the live stock industry of the United States.* Denver: Franklin Hudson, 1905.

Freeman, John R. *A Report on the Proposed Use of the Hetch Hetchy, Eleanor and Cherry Valleys.* San Francisco: Rincon, 1912.

Freeman, Kathleen. *The Murder of Herodes and Other Trials from the Athenian Law Courts.* New York: W.W. Norton, 1963.

Freeman, Lewis Ransome. *Down the Yellowstone.* New York: Dodd, Mead, 1922.

Freeman, Lucy. *Before I Kill More.* New York: Crown, 1955.

_____, and Hulse, Wilfred C. *Children Who Kill.* New York: Berkley, 1962.

_____. *Ordeal of Stephen Dennison.* Englewood Cliffs, N.J.: Prentice-Hall, 1970.

Freeman, R.B., and Wise, D.A. *The Youth Labor Market Problem: Its Nature, Causes, and Consequences.* Chicago: University of Chicago Press, 1982.

Freemantle, Brian. *The Fix, Inside the World Drug Trade.* New York: Tom Doherty Associates, 1986.

Freidel, Frank. *Franklin D. Roosevelt: The Apprentice Years.* Boston: Little, Brown, 1952.

_____ (ed.). *Union Pamphlets of the Civil War, 1861-1865.* 2 vols. Cambridge, Mass.: Belknap Press of Harvard University, Press, 1967.

Fremantle, Anne. *This Little Band of Prophets-The British Fabians.* New York: New American Library, 1960.

Fremantle, Lt. Col. Arthur. *Three Months in the Southern States: April-June, 1863.* New York: John Bradburn, 1864.

French, Allen. *Charles I and the Puritan Upheaval.* London: George Allen & Unwin, 1955.

French, Chauncey Del. *Railroadman.* New York: Macmillan, 1938.

French, George (ed.). *Indianola Scrap Book.* Victoria, Texas: Victoria Advocate, 1936.

French, Harvey M. *The Anatomy of Arson.* New York: Arco, 1979.

French, John A. *Trial of Professor John W. Webster for the Murder of Dr. Geourge Parkman in the Medical College.* Boston: Herald Steam Press, 1850.

French, Joseph Lewis. *The Book of the Rogue.* New York: Boni & Liveright, 1926

_____ (ed.). *A Gallery of Old Rogues.* New York: Alfred H. King, 1931.

_____. *Gray Shadows.* New York: Century, 1931.

_____ (ed.). *The Pioneer West.* Boston: Little, Brown, 1923.

French, Stanley. *Crime Every Day.* Chichester, Eng.: Rose, 1976.

French, Wild James. *Wild Jim, the Texas Cowboy and Saddle King.* Antioch, Ill.: W.J. French, 1890.

French, William John. *Some Recollections of a Western Ranchman: New Mexico, 1883-1899.* London: Methuen, 1927.

Freuchen, Peter. *Book of the Eskimos.* New York: Fawcett, 1961.

Freud, Anna. *The Ego and the Mechanisms of Defense.* trans. Cecil Baines. New York: International Universities Press, 1946.

_____. *Psychoanalytic Study of the Child.* New York: International Universities Press, 1958.

Freud, J. Richard. *New Charter Catechism.* San Francisco: Charter Association, 1896.

Freud, Sigmund. *Civilization and Its Discontents.* New York: W.W. Norton, 1962.

_____. *Cocaine Papers.* New York: Stonehill, 1974.

_____. *Collected Papers.* London: Hogarth Press, 1953.

_____. *The Complete Introductory Lectures on Psychoanalysis.* New York: W.W. Norton, 1966.

_____. *The Ego and the Id.* trans. Joan Riviere. London: Hogarth Press, 1947.

_____. *A General Introduction to Psychoanalysis.* trans. Joan Riviere. New York: Garden City, 1943.

_____. *A Neuosis of Demoniacal Possession in the Seventeenth Century.* London: International Pscycho-Analytical Press, 1924.

_____. *The Origins of Psycho-Analysis, Letters to Wilhelm Fliess.* New York: Basic Books, 1954.

_____. *The Sexual Enlightenment of Children.* New York: Collier, 1963.

_____. *Studies on Hysteria.* trans. A.A. Brill. New York: Nervous and Mental Disease Publishing, 1920.

_____. *Three Contributions to the Theory of Sex.* New York: E.P. Dutton, 1962.

_____. *Totem and Taboo.* trans. James Strachey. New York: W.W. Norton, 1950.

Freund, Paul. *On Understanding the Supreme Court.* Boston: Little, Brown, 1949.

_____. *The Supreme Court of the United States, Its Business, Purposes and Performance.* Cleveland: World, 1961.

Fréville, Jean. *Inessa Armand.* Paris: Editions Sociales, 1957.

Freyre, Gilberto. *The Masters and the Slaves.* New York: Alfred A. Knopf, 1956.

Freytag, Gustav. *The Crown Prince and the German Imperial Crown: Reminiscences.* London: G. Bell & Sons, 1890.

Fribourg, Marjorie. *The Bill of Rights.* New York: Avon, 1967.

Frick, Ford. *Games, Asterisks and People.* New York: Crown, 1973.

Fricke, Charles W. *California Criminal Evidence.* Los Angeles: O.W. Smith, 1957.

_____. *California Criminal Law.* Los Angeles: O.W. Smith, 1956.

_____. *California Criminal Procedure.* Los Angeles: O.W. Smith, 1955.

_____. *California Peace Officers Manual.* Los Angeles: O.W. Smith, 1955.

_____. *5000 Criminal Definitions, Terms and Phrases.* Los Angeles: Legal Book, 1968.

_____. *Planning and Trying Cases.* St. Paul: West, 1959.

_____. *Sentence and Probation: The Imposition of Penalties Upon Convicted Criminals.* Los Angeles: Legal Book, 1950.

Fridge, Ike. *History of the Chisum war.* Electra, Texas: J.D. Smith, 1927.

Fried, Albert. *The Rise and Fall of the Jewish Gangster in America.* New York: Holt, Reinhart & Winston, 1980.

Fried, Charles. *Right and Wrong.* Campbridge, Mass.: Harvard University Press, 1977.

Friedan, Betty. *The Feminine Mystique.* New York: W.W. Norton, 1974.

Friede, Donald. *The Mechanical Angel.* New York: Alfred A. Knopf, 1948.

Friedel, Hans. *Der Tyrannenmord in Gesetzgebung und Volksmein-*

ung der Griechen. Stuttgart, Ger.: W. Kohlhammer, 1937.

Friedheim, Robert L. *The Seattle General Strike*. Seattle, Wash.: University of Washington Press, 1964.

Friedl, Ernestine. *Vasilika: A Village in Modern Greece*. New York: Holt, Rinehart & Winston, 1962.

Friedland, M.L. *Detention before Trial*. Toronto, Ontario, Can.: University of Toronto Press, 1965.

Friedland, Martin. *The Trials of Israel Lipski*. New York: Beaufort Books, 1984.

Friedlander, Kate. *The Psychoanalytic Approach to Juvenile Delinquency*. London: Kegan Paul, 1947.

Friedlander, Ludwig. *Roman Life and Manners Under the Early Empire*. trans. Leonard Magnus. London: Routledge, 1940.

Friedlander, Saul. *Prelude to Downfall: Hitler and the United States, 1939-1941*. New York: Alfred A. Knopf, 1967.

Friedman, Bruce Jay. *About Harry Towns*. New York: Alfred A. Knopf, 1974.

Friedman, K., et al. *Victims and Helpers: Reactions to Crime*. Washington, D.C.: National Institute on Crime, 1982.

Friedman, Lawrence M. *A History of American Law*. New York: Simon & Schuster, 1973.

_____. *The Legal System*. New York: Russell Sage Foundation, 1975.

Friedman, Leon, and Israel, Fred (eds.). *The Justices of the Supreme Court of the United States*. New York: Chelsea House, 1969.

_____. *The Wise Minority*. New York: Dial Press, 1971.

Friedman, Michael (ed.). *The New Left of the Sixties*. Berkeley, Calif.: Independent Socialist Press, 1972.

Friedman, Milton. *Capitalism and Freedom*. Chicago: University of Chicago Press, 1962.

_____, and Schwartz, Anna J. *The Great Contraction*. Princeton, N.J.: Princeton University Press, 1965.

_____. *A Monetary History of the United States, 1867-1960*. Princeton, N.J.: Princeton University Press, 1963.

_____. *The Optimum Quantity of Money and Other Essays*. Chicago: Aldine, 1969.

Friedman, Morris. *The Pinkerton Labor Spy*. New York: Wilshire Book, 1907.

Friedman, Saul S. *Pogromchik, The Assassination of Simon Petlura*. New York: Hart, 1976.

Friedrich, Carl J. *The Pathology of Politics*. New York: Harper & Row, 1972.

Friedrich, Otto. *Before the Deluge-A Portrait of Berlin in the 1920's*. New York: Harper & Row, 1972.

Friedson, Elliot. *Medical Men and Their Work*. Chicago: Aldine, 1972.

_____. *The Profession of Medicine*. New York: Dodd Mead, 1970.

Friend, Llerena B. *Sam Houston: The Great Designer*. Austin: University of Texas Press, 1954.

Friend, Theodore. *Between Two Empires: The Ordeal of the Philippines, 1929-1946*. New Haven, Conn.: Yale University Press, 1965.

Friendly, Alfred, and Goldfarb, Ronald L. *Crime & Publicity*. New York: Twentieth Century Fund, 1967.

Friendly, Fred W., and Elliot, Martha J.H. *The Constitution: That Delicate Balance*. New York: Random House, 1984.

_____. *The Good Guys, the Bad Guys and the First Amendment*. New York: Random House, 1976.

Frieze, Irene H., et al. *Women and Sex Roles*. New York: W.W. Norton, 1978.

Frignet, Ernest, and Carrey, Edmund. *Etats-Unis d'Amerique: les Etats du Northwest et Chicago*. Paris: Jouast, 1871.

Friis, Herman. *The Pacific Basin*. New York: American Geographical Society, 1967.

Frillman, Paul, and Peck, Graham. *China: The Remembered Life*. Boston: Houghton Mifflin, 1968.

Frink, Maurice. *Cow Country Cavalcade*. Denver: Old West, 1954.

_____, Jackson, W. Turrentine, and Spring, Agnes W. *When Grass Was King*. Boulder: University of Colorado Press, 1956.

Frischauer, Willi. *Himmler*. London: Oldhams, 1953.

Frischbier, Hermann. *Hexenspruch und Zauberbann...in der Provinz Preussen*.

Frison, Paul. *First White Woman in the Big Horn Basin*. Worland, Wyo.: Worland Press, 1962.

_____. *Grass Was Gold*. Worland, Wyo.: Worland Press, 1966.

Fritz, Henry E. *The Movement for Indian Assimilation, 1860-1890*. Philadelphia: Pennsylvania State University Press, 1963.

Fritz, Percy Stanley. *Colorado, the Centennial State*. New York: Prentice-Hall, 1941.

Froissart, Syr Jean. *The Chronicle of Froissart*. New York: AMS Press, 1967.

Fromm, Erich. *The Anatomy of Human Destructiveness*. New York: Holt, Rinehart & Winston, 1973.

Frost, John. *The Pictorial History of the United States, From the Discovery by the Northmen in the Tenth Century to the Present Time...with 400 Engravings*. Columbus, Ohio: J. & W. Miller, 1857.

Frost, R. *Race Against Time: Human Relations and Politics in Kenya Before Independence*. London: Rex Collings, 1978.

Frost, Richard H. *The Mooney Case*. Stanford, Calif.: Stanford University Press, 1968.

Frothingham, Charles W. *The Convent's Doom: A Tale of Charlestown in 1834*. Boston: Graves & Weston, 1854.

Frothingham, Octavius Brooks. *Gerrit Smith*. New York: G.P. Putnam's Sons, 1878.

Frullini, Bruno. *Squadrismo Fiorentino*. Florence, Italy: Vallecchi, 1933.

Fry, James B. *Military Miscellanies*. New York: Brentano's, 1889.

_____. *New York and the Conscription of 1863*. New York: G.P. Putnam's Sons, 1885.

Fry, J. Reese. *A Life of Gen. Zachary Taylor*. Philadelphia: Grigg, Elliot, 1947.

Fry, M. *Sex, Vice and Business*. New York: Ballantine, 1959.

Fry, Margery. *Arms of the Law*. London: Victor Gollancz, 1951.

Frye, Richard N. *The Heritage of Persia*. Cleveland: World, 1963.

_____ (ed.). *Islam and the West*. The Hague, Neth.: Mouton, 1957.

_____ (ed.). *The Near East and the Great Powers*. Cambridge, Mass.: Harvard University Press, 1951.

Fryer, Peter. *The Birth Controllers*. London: Secker & Warburg, 1965.

Fuchida Mutsuo, and Okumiya Masatake. *Midway: The Japanese Navy's Story*. Annapolis, Md.: U.S. Naval Institute, 1955.

Fuchmann, Philip David. *De Conventu Sagorum ad Sua Sabbbata*. Wittenburg, Ger.: Christiani Schröderi, 1678.

Fuchs, Martin. *A Pact with Hitler*. trans. Charles Hope Lumley. London: Victor Gollancz, 1939.

Fuchs, V.R. *How We Live: An Economic Perspective on Americans from Birth to Death*. New York: Basic Books, 1983.

Fuess, Claude M. *Carl Schurz, Reformer, 1829-1906*. New York: Dodd, Mead, 1932.

_____. *Daniel Webster*. Boston: Little, Brown, 1930.

Fugate, F.L. *The Spanish Heritage of the Southwest*. El Paso, Texas: Western Press, 1952.

Fugina, Captain Frank J. *Lore and Lure of the Upper Mississippi River*. Winona, Minn.: Privately Printed, 1945.

Fugitive Slave Law and Its Victims, Anti-Slavery Tracts. No. 15. New York: American Anti-Slavery Society, 1861.

Fujimoto Harutake. *Ningen Ishiwara Kanji*. Tokyo: Taisen Sangyo-sha, 1959.

Fujishima Taisuke. *Nihon no joryu shakai*. Tokyo: Kobun-sha, 1965.

Fujita Goro. *Koan Daiyouran (Great Directory of Public Security)*. Tokyo: Kasakura Shuppan, 1983.

_____. *Koan Hyakunenshi (The 100 Year History of Public Security)*. Tokyo: Koan Mondai Kenkyu Kyokai, 1979.

_____. *Ninkyo Hyakunenshi (The 100 Year History of Chivalry)*. Tokyo: Kasakura Shuppan, 1980.

Fulcher, Walter. *The Way I Heard It: Tales of the Big Bend*. Austin: University of Texas Press, 1959.

Fuld, Leonard. F. *Police Administration*. New York: G.P. Putnam's Sons, 1910.

Fulford, Roger (ed.). *Dearest Child*. London: Evans Brothers, 1964.

_____ (ed.). *Dearest Mama*. New York: Holt, Rinehart & Winston, 1969.

_____. *Hanover to Windsor*. New York: Macmillan, 1960.

_____ (ed.). *Your Dear Letter: Private Correspondence of Queen Victoria and the Crown Prince of Prussia, 1865-1871*. London: Evans Brothers, 1971.

Fulkerson, H.S. *Early Days in Mississippi*. Vicksburg, Miss.: Vicksburg Printing, 1885.

_____. *Random Recollections of Early Days in Mississippi*. Vicksburg, Miss.: Vicksburg, 1885.

Full Account of the Atrocious Crimes of Thomas W. Piper. Boston: n.p., 1875.

A Full Account of the Awful Murder of the Winston Family. Richmond, Va.: John D. Hammersley, 1852.

A Full Account, The Lives and Crimes of the "Molly Maguires". Philadelphia: Barclay, 1877.

A Full and True Relation of the Trial...of Ann Foster. London: D.M., 1674.

A Full Confutation of Witchcraft. London: J. Baker, 1712.

Fuller, Daniel. *Trial of John Lechler*. Lancaster, Pa.: Hugh Maxwell, 1822.

Fuller, Edgar I. *The Visible of the Invisible Empire*. Denver: Maelstrom, 1925.

Fuller, George W. *A History of the Pacific Northwest*. New York: Alfred A. Knopf, 1931.

_____. *The Inland Empire of the Pacific Northwest*. Denver: H.G. Linderman, 1928.

Fuller, Henry C. *Adventures of Bill Longley*. Nacogdoches, Texas: Baker Printing, n.d.

_____. *A Texas Sheriff*. Nacogdoches, Texas: Baker Printing, 1931.

Fuller, John. *Arigo, Surgeon of the Rusty Knife*. New York: Thomas Y. Crowell, 1974.

_____. *The Gentleman Conspirators*. New York: McGraw-Hill, 1971.

Fuller, Maj-Gen. J.F.C. *The First of the League Wars*. London: Victor Gollancz, 1939.

_____. *The Second World War*. London: Eyre & Spottiswoode, 1948.

Fuller, John G. *The Gentlemen Conspirators: The Story of Price-Fixers in the Electrical Industry*. New York: Grove Press, 1962.

Fuller, Loie. *Fifteen Years of a Dancer's Life*. Boston: Small, Maynard, 1913.

Fuller, Margaret. *Woman in the Nineteenth Century*. New York: W. W. Norton, 1971.

Fuller, Robert H. *Jubilee Jim: The Life of Colonel James Fisk, Jr.* New York: Macmillan, 1928.

Fuller, Sarah Margaret. *Summer on the Lakes, in 1843*. New York: C.S. Francis, 1844.

Fullerton, W.Y. *The Romance of Pitcairn Island*. London: Harrap, 1923.

Full Report of the Trial of Samuel M. Andrews for the Murder of Cornelius Holmes. Plymouth, Mass.: Memorial & Rock Press, 1868.

Fülöp-Müller, René. *Power and Secret of the Jesuits*. New York: George Braziller, 1956.

_____. *Rasputin, The Holy Devil*. New York: Viking Press, 1928.

Fulton, John. *Laws of Marriage*. London: Weel, Gardner, Darton, 1883.

Fulton, Maurice Garland. *History of the Lincoln County War*. Tucson: University of Arizona Press, 1968.

_____ (ed.). *Maurice Garland Fulton's History of the Lincoln County War*. Tucson: University of Arizona Press, 1968.

_____, and Horgan, Paul. *New Mexico's Own Chronicle*. Dallas: Banks Upshaw, 1937.

_____. *Roswell in Its Early Years*. Roswell, N.M.: Hall-Poorbaugh Press, 1963.

Fultz, Hollis B. *Famous Northwest Manhunts and Murder Mysteries*. Elma, Wash.: Elma Chronicle, 1955.

Funck-Brentano, Frantz. *Lucrèce Borgia*. Paris: La Nouvelle Revue Critique, 1930.

_____. *The Middle Ages*. London: William Heinemann, 1922.

_____. *Princes and Poisoners*. London: Duckworth, 1901.

Furer, Howard B. *Chicago: A Chronological and Documentary History: 1784-1970*. Dobbs Ferry, N.Y.: Oceana, 1974.

_____. *William Frederick Havemeyer: A Political Biography*. New York: American Press, 1965.

Furlong, Thomas. *Fifty Years A Detective*. St. Louis: C.E. Barnett, 1912.

Furnas, J.C. *The Life and Times of the Late Demon Rum*. New York: G.P. Putnam's Sons, 1965.

_____. *The Road to Harpers Ferry*. New York: William Sloane, 1959.

Furneaux, Rupert. *Courtroom USA-1*. Baltimore: Penguin Books, 1963.

_____. *Courtroom USA-2*. Baltimore: Penguin Books, 1963.

_____. *Famous Criminal Cases, Vols. I - VII*. London: Allan Wingate, 1959.

_____. *Guenther Podola*. London: Stevens, 1960.

_____. *The Medical Murderer*. London: Elek Books, 1957.

_____. *The Murder of Lord Erroll*. London: Stevens, 1961.

_____. *Robert Hoolhouse*. London: Stevens, 1960.

_____. *They Died By A Gun*. London: Herbert Jenkins, 1962.

_____. *The World's Most Intriguing True Mysteries*. New York: Arco, 1966.

Furniss, Norman F. *The Fundamentalist Controversy, 1918-1931*. New Haven, Conn.: Yale University Press, 1954.

Furnivall, J.S. *Colonial Policy and Practice: A Comparative Study of Burma and Netherlands India*. London: Cambridge University Press, 1957.

Fusco, Giancarlo. *Le rose del ventennio*. Turin, Italy: Einaudi, 1958.

Fusero, Clemente. *The Borgias*. trans. Peter Green. New York: Frederick A. Praeger, 1972.

Fusti Carofiglio, Mario. *Vitta di Mussolini e storia del Fascismo*. Turin, Italy: S.E. Torinese, 1949.

Futara Yoshinori, Count, and Sawada Setsuzo. *The Crown Prince's European Tour*. Osaka, Japan: Osaka Mainichi, 1926.

Fyfe, H. Hamilton. *The Real Mexico*. London: William Heinemann, 1914.

G

Gabbay, Rony E. *A Political Study of the Arab-Jewish Conflict*. Paris: Libraire Minard, 1959.

Gabert of Bruges. *The Murder of Charles the Good*. trans. James Bruce Ross. New York: Columbia University Press, 1960.

Gablentz, Otto Heinrich, von der. *Die Tragik des Preussentums*. Munich, Ger.: Verlag Franz Hanfstaengel, 1948.

Gabory, Emile. *Alias Bluebeard*. trans. Alvah C. Bessie. New York: Brewer & Warren, 1930.

_____. *La vie et la mort de Gilles de Rais*. Paris: Perrin et Cie, 1926.

Gaddis, John Lewis. *The United States and the Origins of the Cold War*. New York: Columbia University Press, 1972.

Gaddis, Thomas E. *The Birdman of Alcatraz.* New York: Random House, 1955.

_____, and Long, James O. *Killer, A Journal of Murder.* New York: Macmillan, 1970.

Gaddis, Vincent H. *Invisible Horizons.* Philadelphia: Chilton Books, 1965.

Gage, Jack R. *The Johnson County War Is a Pack of Lies.* Cheyenne, Wyo.: Flintlock, 1967.

_____. *Tensleep and No Rest.* Casper, Wyo.: Prairie, 1958.

Gage, Matilda J. *Woman, Church and State.* Chicago: C.H. Kerr, 1893.

Gage, Nicholas. *The Mafia Is Not an Equal Opportunity Employer.* New York: McGraw-Hill, 1971.

_____. *Mafia, USA.* Chicago: Playboy Press, 1972.

Gager, Nancy, and Schurr, Cathleen. *Sexual Assault: Confronting Rape in America.* New York: Grosset & Dunlap, 1976.

Gagnon, John H., and Simon, William. *Sexual Conduct: The Social Sources of Human Sexuality.* Chicago: Aldine, 1973.

_____ (eds.). *Sexual Deviance.* New York: Harper & Row, 1967.

_____ (eds.). *The Sexual Scene.* Chicago: Aldine, 1970.

Gainer, B. *The Alien Invasion.* London: Heinemann, 1972.

Galaway, B., and Hudson, J. *Perspectives on Crime Victims.* St. Louis: C.V. Mosby, 1981.

Galbiati, Maj-Gen. Enzo. *Il 25 luglio e la MVSN.* Milan, Italy: Bernabo', 1950.

Galbraith, John Kenneth. *The Affluent Society.* Boston: Houghton Mifflin, 1958.

_____. *The Great Crash, 1929.* Boston: Houghton Mifflin, 1955.

_____. *The New Industrial State.* New York: Signet Books, 1968.

Gale, Edwin O. *Reminiscences of Early Chicago.* Chicago: Revell, 1902.

Galewitz, Herb. *Great Comics.* New York: Crown, 1972.

Gallagher, Frank. *The Anglo-Irish Treaty.* London: Hutchinson, 1965.

_____. *Days of Fear.* New York: Harpers, 1929.

_____. *The Invisible Island.* London: Gollancz, 1957.

Gallagher, O.D. *Retreat in the East.* London: George C. Harrap, 1942.

Gallagher, Robert S. *If I Had It to Do Over Again.* New York: Dutton, 1969.

Gallant, Roy A. *Astrology, Sense or Nonsense.* Garden City, N.Y.: Doubleday, 1974.

Galler, Meyer, and Marquess, Harlan E. *Soviet Prison Camp Speech.* Madison: University of Wisconsin Press, 1972.

Galli, Giogio. *Storia del Partito Comunista Italiano.* Milan, Italy: Schwarz, 1958.

Gallico, Paul. *Farewell to Sport.* New York: Alfred A. Knopf, 1938.

_____. *The Golden People.* Garden City, N.Y.: Doubleday, 1965.

Galliher, Hohn F., and McCartney, James L. *Criminology.* Homewood, Ill.: Dorsey, 1977.

Gallo, Max. *Mussolini's Italy, Twenty Years of the Fascist Era.* trans. Charles Lam Markmann. New York: Macmillan, 1973.

Gallo, Patrick J. *Old Bread, New Wine: A Portrait of the Italian-American.* Chicago: Nelson-Hall, 1981.

Galloway, George B. *History of the House of Representatives.* New York: Crowell, 1962.

Galloway, John. *Criminal Justice & the Berger Court.* New York: Facts on File, 1978.

Galton, F. *Finger Prints.* London: Macmillan, 1892.

_____. *Fingerprint Directories.* London: Macmillan, 1895.

_____. *Hereditary Genius.* London: Macmillan, 1869.

_____. *Inquiries into Human Faculty.* New York: Dent, 1906.

_____. *Method of Indexing Finger-Marks.* London: Proc. Royal Society of London, 1891.

Galvin, John. *The Minute Men.* New York: Hawthorn, 1967.

Gambetti, Fidia. *1919-45: inchiesta seul fascismo.* Milan, Italy: Mastellone, 1953.

Gambino, Richard. *Blood of My Blood: The Dilemma of the Italian-American.* Garden City, N.Y.: Doubleday, 1974.

_____. *Vendetta.* Garden City, N.Y.: Doubleday, 1977.

Gambino, Sharo. *La Mafia in Calabria.* Reggio Calabria, Italy: Edizioni Parallelo, 1971.

Gamel, Thomas W. *Life of Thomas W. Gamel.* n.p., n.d.

Gamio, Manuel. *Mexican Immigration to the United States.* New York: Dover, 1971.

Gandhi, Mohandas K. *All Men Are Brothers: Life and Thoughts of Mahatma Gandhi As Told in His Own Words.* New York: Columbia University Press, 1958.

_____. *Bapu's Letters to Mira (1924-1948).* Ahmedabad, India: Navajivan Publishing House, 1949.

_____. *Basic Education.* Ahmedabad, India: Navajivan Publishing House, n.d.

_____. *Christian Missions.* Ahmedabad, India: Navajivan Publishing House, 1948.

_____. *Community Unity.* Ahmedabad, India: Navajivan Publishing House, 1949.

_____. *Constructive Programme.* Ahmedabad, India: Navajivan Publishing House, 1948.

_____. *Delhi Diary.* Ahmedabad, India: Navajivan Publishing House, 1948.

_____. *Diet and Diet Reform.* Ahmedabad, India: Navajivan Publishing House, 1949.

_____. *Economics of Khadi.* Ahmedabad, India: Navajivan Publishing House, 1941.

_____. *Ethical Religion.* Madras, India: S. Ganesan, 1922.

_____. *For Pacifists.* Ahmedabad, India: Navajivan Publishing House, 1949.

_____. *From Yiravda Mandir.* Ahmedabad, India: Navajivan Publishing House, 1937.

_____. *Gandhi's Correspondence With the Government (1942-1944).* Ahmedabad, India: Navajivan Publishing House, 1945.

_____. *A Guide to Health.* Madras, India: S. Ganesan, 1921.

_____. *Hind Swaraj, or Indian Home Rule.* Ahmedabad, India: Navajivan Publishing House, 1938.

_____. *Indian Opinion.* Natal, India: n.p., 1915.

_____. *Jail Experiences.* Madras, India: Tagore, 1922.

_____. *My Early Life.* Bombay, India: Oxford University Press, 1932.

_____. *My Soul's Agony.* Ahmedabad, India: Navajivan Publishing House, 1932.

_____. *Non-violence in Peace and War.* Ahmedabad, India: Navajivan Publishing House, 1945.

_____. *Rebuilding Our Villages.* Ahmedabad, India: Navajivan Publishing House, 1952.

_____. *Rowlatt Bills and Satyagraha.* Madras, India: G.A. Natesan, 1919.

_____. *Sarvodaya.* Ahmedabad, India: Navajivan Publishing House, 1951.

_____. *Satyagraha.* Ahmedabad, India: Navajivan Publishing House, 1951.

_____. *Satyagraha Ashram's History.* Madras, India: G.A. Natesan, 1933.

_____. *Satyagraha in South Afica.* Madras, India: S. Ganesan, 1928.

_____. *Self-restraint vs. Self-indulgence.* Ahmedabad, India: Navajivan Publishing House, 1947.

_____. *Songs From Prison.* London: Allen & Unwin, 1934.

_____. *Speeches and Writings.* Madras, India: G.A. Natesan, 1933.

_____. *The Story of My Experiments With Truth.* Washington D.C.: Public Affairs Press, 1960.

_____. *To Ashram Sisters.* Ahmedabad, India: Navajivan Publishing House, 1952.

_____. *To a Gandhian Capitalist.* Bombay, India: Hind Kitabs, 1951.

_____. *To the Students.* Ahmedabad, India: Navajivan Publishing House, 1949.

_____. *Towards New Education.* Ahmedabad, India: Navajivan Publishing House, 1953.

_____. *Towards Non-Violent Socialism.* Ahmadabad, India: Navajivan Publishing House, 1951.

_____. *Unto This Last.* Ahmedabad, India: Navajivan Publishing House, 1951.

_____. *Women and Social Injustice.* Ahmedabad, India: Navajivan Publishing House, 1942.

_____. *Young India.* Ahmedabad, India: n.p., 1934.

Gandy, Lewis Cass. *The Tabors: A Footnote of Western History.* New York: Press of the Pioneers, 1934.

Gankin, O.H., and Fisher, H.H. (eds.). *The Bolsheviks and the World War.* Stanford, Calif.: Stanford University Press, 1940.

Gann, Walter. *Tread of the Longhorns.* San Antonio, Texas: Naylor, 1949.

Ganoe, William Addleman. *The History of the United States Army.* New York: D. Appleton, 1924.

Gans, H. *People and Plans.* New York: Basic Books, 1968.

Gans, Herbert J. *The Urban Villagers.* New York: Free Press, 1962.

Gantt, Paul H. *The Case of Alfred Packer, the Man Eater.* Denver: University of Denver, 1952.

Ganzhorn, Jack. *I've Killed Men.* London: Robert Hale, 1940.

Gaponenko, L.S. *Velikiy Oktyabr: Sbornik dokumentov.* Moscow: Izdatelstvo Akademii Nauk S.S.S.R., 1960.

Gara, Larry. *The Liberty Line.* Lexington: University of Kentucky Press, 1961.

Garabedian, P.G., and Gibbons, D.C. (eds.). *Becoming Delinquent.* Chicago: Aldine Press, 1970.

Garcia-Granados, Jorge. *The Birth of Israel.* New York: Alfred A. Knopf, 1948.

Garcia Granados, Richardo. *Por qué y como Cayo Porfirio Diaz.* Mexico City: Botas é Hijos, 1928.

Garcon, Maurice (ed.). *L'Affair Bernardy de Sigoyer.* Paris: Albin Michel, 1948.

_____. *The Devil.* trans. Stephen Haden Guest. New York: E.P. Dutton, 1930.

_____. *Histoires curieuses.* Paris: A. Fayard, 1959.

Gard, Wayne. *The Chisholm Trail.* Norman: University of Oklahoma Press, 1954.

_____. *Fabulous Quarter Horse: Steel Dust.* New York: Duell, Sloan & Pearce, 1958.

_____. *Frontier Justice.* Norman: University of Oklahoma Press, 1949.

_____. *The Great Buffalo Hunt.* New York: Alfred A. Knopf, 1959.

_____. *Rawhide Texas.* Norman: University of Oklahoma Press, 1965.

_____. *Sam Bass.* New York: Houghton Mifflin, 1936.

Garden, Alexander. *A Brief Account of the Deluded Dutartres.* New Haven, S.C.: James Parker, 1762.

Gardiner, A.G. *The War Lords.* London: Dent, 1915.

Gardiner, A.W. *The Life of Sir William Harcourt.* London: Constable, 1923.

Gardiner, Alexander. *Canfield, The True Story of the Greatest Gambler.* Garden City, N.Y.: Doubleday, 1930.

Gardiner, Charles Fox. *Doctor at Timberline.* Caldwell, Idaho: Caxton Printers, 1939.

Gardiner, Dorothy, and Walker, Katherine (eds.). *Raymond Chandler Speaking.* London: Hamish Hamilton, 1962.

Gardiner, Gerald. *Capital Punishment as a Deterrent and the Alternative.* London: Victor Gollancz, 1956.

Gardiner, John A. *The Politics of Corruption: Organized Crime in an American City.* New York: Russell Sage Foundation, 1970.

_____. *Traffic and the Police.* Cambridge, Mass.: Harvard University Press, 1969.

Gardiner, John, and Olson, David. *Theft of the City.* Bloomington: Indiana University Press, 1974.

Gardiner, Muriel. *The Deadly Innocents, Portraits of Children Who Kill.* New York: Basic Books, 1976.

Gardiner, Ralph. *England's Grievance Discovered in Relation to the Coal Trade.* London: R. Ibbitson and P. Stent, 1655.

Gardini, T.L. *Towards the New Italy.* London: Lindsay Drummond, 1943.

Gardner, Charles W. *The Doctor and the Devil, or Midnight Adventures of Dr. Parkhurst.* New York: Warren, 1894.

Gardner, Erle Stanley. *The Court of Last Resort.* New York: W. Sloane, 1952.

Gardner, Edmund G. *Dukes and Poets at Ferrara.* New York: E.P. Dutton, 1904.

Gardner, Gerald Brosseau. *Witchcraft Today.* New York: Citadel, 1955.

Gardner, H. *Developmental Psychology.* Boston: Little, Brown, 1978.

Gardner, John. *The Return of Moriarty.* London: Weidenfeld and Nicholson, 1974.

Gardner, Martin. *Fads and Fallacies in the Name of Science.* New York: Dover Publications, 1957.

_____. *In the Name of Science.* New York: G. P. Putnam, 1952.

Gardner, R., and Moriarty, A. *Personality Development at Preadolescence.* Seattle, Wash.: University of Washington Press, 1968.

Gardner, Raymond Hatfield. *The Old Wild West.* San Antonio, Texas: Naylor, 1944.

Gardner, Roy. *Hellcatraz, The Rock of Despair.* New York: Hearst, 1939.

Garfield, Brian (ed.). *I Witness.* New York: Quadrangle, 1978.

Garfinkel, H. *Studies in Ethnomethodology.* New York: Prentice-Hall, 1967.

Garinet, Jules. *Histoire de la magie en France.* Paris: Foulon et cie, 1818.

Garis, Howard R. *With Force and Arms: A Tale of Love and Salem Witchcraft.* New York: J.S. Ogilvie, 1902.

Garland, Hamlin. *The Captain of the Gray-Horse Troop.* New York: Harper & brothers, 1902.

_____. *A Daughter of the Middle Border.* New York: Macmillan, 1921.

_____. *Roadside Meetings.* New York: Macmillan, 1930.

Garland, Hugh A. *The Life of John Randolph of Roanoke.* 2 vol. New York: D. Appleton, 1851.

Garnel, Donald. *The Rise of Teamster Power in the West.* Berkeley: University of California Press, 1972.

Garner, James Wilford. *Reconstruction in Mississippi.* New York: Macmillan, 1901.

Garnett, David. *Lady into Fox.* New York: Alfred A. Knopf, 1923.

Garnett, Richard. *Rome and the Temporal Power.* Cambridge, Eng.: Cambridge University Press, 1907.

Garnier, Dr. Samuel. *Barbe Buvée, en religion Soeur Saint-Colombe, et la prétendue possession des Ursulines d'Auxonne 1658-63, étude historique et médicale.* Paris: F. Alcan, 1895.

Garofalo, James. *Local Victim Surveys: A Review of the Issues.* Washington, D.C.: National Criminal Justice Information and Statistics Service, 1977.

Garofalo, Raffaele. *Criminology.* Boston: Little, Brown, 1914.

Garrard, J.A. *The English and Immigration 1880-1910.* London: Oxford University Press, 1971.

Garrat, G.T. *Mussolini's Roman Empire.* London: Penguin Books, 1938.

Garraty, John A. *Henry Cabot Lodge: A Biography.* New York: Alfred A. Knopf, 1953.

_____. *Quarrels that Have Shaped the Constitution.* New York: Harper and Row, 1962.

Garrett, Charles. *The La Guardia Years: Machine and Reform Politics in New York City.* New Brunswick, N.J.: Rutgers University Press, 1961.

Garrett, Patrick Floyd, and Upson, Ash. *The Authentic Life of Billy the Kid.* New York: Macmillan, 1927.

Garretson, Martin S. *The American Bison.* New York: New

York Zoological Society, 1938.

Garrison, Jim. *A Heritage of Stone*. New York: G.P. Putnam's Sons, 1970.

_____. *The Star Spangled Contract*. New York: Warner Books, 1977.

Garrison, Omar V. *The Hidden Story of Scientology*. New York: Citadel Press, 1974.

_____. *The Secret World of Interpol*. New York: Ralston-Pilot, 1976.

Garrity, Donald. *The Prison*. New York: Holt, Rinehart & Winston, 1961.

Garrow, David J. *The FBI and Martin Luther King, Jr.: From "Solo" to Memphis*. New York: Norton, 1981.

Garrow-Gree, G. *In the Royal Irish Constabulary*. London: J. Blackwood, 1905.

Garry, Charles, and Goldburg, Art. *Streetfighter in the Courtroom*. New York: Dutton, 1977.

Garsia, Marston. *Criminal Law and Procedure in a Nutshell*. Sweet & Maxwell, 1953.

Garson, Barbara. *McBird!* Grassy Knoll Press, 1966.

Garst, Doris Shannon. *The Story of Wyoming and Its Constitution and Government*. Douglas, Wyo.: Douglas Enterprise, 1938.

_____. *When the West Was Young*. Douglas, Wyo.: Douglas Enterprise, 1942.

_____, and Garst, Warren. *Wild Bill Hickok*. New York: Julian Messner, 1952.

Garthoff, R.L. *Soviet Military Doctrine*. Glencoe, Ill.: Free Press, 1953.

Gartner, L.P. *The Jewish Immigrant in England 1870-1914*. Detroit, Mich.: Wayne State University Press, 1960.

Gartner, Michael (ed.). *Crime and Business*. Princeton, N.J.: Dow Jones, 1971.

Garvin, J.L. *The Life of Joseph Chamberlain*. London: Macmillan, 1932.

Garwood, Darrel. *Crossroads of America: The Story of Kansas City*. New York: W.W. Norton, 1948.

Garza Treviño, Ciro de la. *Wilson y Huerta, Tampico y Veracruz; ensayo de divulgación histórica*. Mexico City: Published by Author, 1933.

Gasciogne, Bamber. *The Great Moghuls*. London: Cape, 1971.

Gash, Norman. *Mr. Secretary Peel: The Life of Sir Robert Peel to 1830*. Cambridge, Mass.: Harvard University Press, 1961.

_____. *Reaction and Reconstruction in English Politics, 1832-1852*. Clarendon Press, 1965.

Gasparotto, Luigi. *Diario di un deputato*. Milan, Italy: Dall' Oglio, 1945.

Gates, John D. *The Du Pont Family*. New York: Doubleday, 1979.

Gates, Paul Wallace. *The Farmer's Age: Agriculture 1815-1860*. New York: Holt, Rinehart & Winston, 1960.

_____. *Fifty Million Acres: Conflicts Over Kansas Land Policy 1854-1890*. Ithaca, N.Y.: Cornell University Press, 1954.

_____. *Illinois Central Railroad and Its Colonization Work*. Cambridge, Mass.: Harvard University Press, 1934.

Gatewood, Willard B. *Preachers, Pedagogues & Politicians: Evolution Controversy in North Carolina, 1920-1927*. Chapel Hill: University of North Carolina Press, 1966.

_____. *Theodore Roosevelt and the Art of Controversy*. Baton Rouge, La.: Louisiana University Press.

Gath, A. *Down's Syndrome and the Family*. New York: Academic Press, 1978.

Gatheru, Reuel Mugo. *Child of Two Worlds*. London: Routledge & K. Paul, 1964.

Gathorne-Hardy, A.E. (ed.). *Gathorne Hardy, First Earl of Cranbrook: A Memoir*. 2 vols. London: Longman, 1910.

Gattegno, Caleb. *Towards a Visual Culture*. New York: Outerbridge & Dienstfrey, 1969.

Gatti, Arthur. *The Kennedy Curse*. Chicago: Henry Regnery, 1976.

Gatto, Alfonso (ed.). *Il coro della guerra*. Bari, Italy: Laterza,

1963.

Gauché, Général. *Le deuxième bureau au travail*. Paris: Amiot-Dumont, 1954.

Gaucher, Roland. *The Terrorists: From Tsarist Russia to the O.A.S.* trans. Albin Michel. London: Secker & Warburg, 1968.

Gaule, John. *Mysmantia, the Mag-astromancer*. London: Joshua Kirton, 1652.

_____. *Select Cases of Conscience Touching Witches and Witchcraft*. London: W. Wilson, Richard Clutterbuck, 1646.

Gaunt, Mary. *A Broken Journey*. London: Lippincott, 1919.

Gaunt, William. *The Pre-Raphaelite Tragedy*. London: Cape, 1965.

Gauquelin, Michel. *The Scientific Basis of Astrology*. New York: Stein and Day, 1969.

Gaustad, E.S. *The Great Awakening in New England*. New York: Harper & Brothers, 1957.

Gavagnin, Armando. *Vent'anni di resistenza al Fascismo*. Turin, Italy: Einaudi, 1957.

Gavshon, Arthur L. *The Mysterious Death of Dag Hammerskjold*. New York: Walker, 1962.

Gaxotte, Pierre. *Frederick the Great*. New Haven, Conn.: Yale University Press, 1942.

_____. *German Diplomatic Documents, 1871-1914*. trans. E.T.S. Dugdale. London: Methuen, 1928.

Gay, Antoinette G. *Calle de Alvarado*. Monterey, Calif.: Monterey Trade Press, 1936.

Gay, Felix M. *History of Nowata County*. Stillwater, Okla.: Redlands Press, 1957.

Gay, H. Nelson. *Strenuous Italy*. Boston: Houghton Mifflin, 1927.

Gay, Peter. *The Dilemma of Democratic Socialism*. New York: Columbia University Press, 1952.

_____. *Voltaire's Politics*. Princeton, N.J.: Princeton University Press, 1959.

Gay, Vicente. *Madre Roma*. Barcelona, Spain: Bosch, 1935.

Gay, William G., and Theodore, H., and Schack, Stephen. *Improving Patrol Productivity*. Vol.I, *Routine Patrol*. Washington, D.C.: National Institute of Law Enforcement and Criminal Justice, Office of Technology Transfer, 1977.

Gayer, Arthur D., Rostow, W.W., and Schwartz, Anna J. *The Growth and Fluctuation of the British Economy, 1790-1850*. Oxford, Eng.: Oxford University Press, 1953.

Gaylin, Willard. *In the Service of Their Country: War Resisters in Prison*. New York: Viking Press, 1970.

_____. *The Killing of Bonnie Garland*. New York: Simon & Schuster, 1982.

_____. *Partial Justice*. New York: Alfred A. Knopf, 1974.

_____. *The Rage Within: Anger in Modern Life*. New York: Simon & Schuster, 1984.

Gaylord, Chic. *Handgunner's Guide: Including the Art of the Quick-Draw and Combat Shooting*. New York: Hasting House, 1960.

Gaylord, Otis H. *The Rise and Fall of Legs Diamond*. New York: Bantam Books, 1960.

Gayn, Mark J. *Japan Diary*. New York: William Sloan Associates, 1948.

Gaynor, William J. *Some of Mayor Gaynor's Letters and Speeches*. New York: Greaves, 1913.

Gazely, John Gerow. *American Opinion of German Unification, 1848-1871*. New York: Columbia University Press, 1926.

Gazzaniga, Rodolfo. *Mussolini come l'ho visto io*. Mantua, Italy: Paladino, 1927.

Gebhard, Paul H., Gagnon, John H., Pomeroy, Wardell B., and Christenson, Cornelia V. *Sex Offenders: An Analysis of Types*. New York: Harper & Row, 1965.

Geertz, Clifford. *Ideology and Discontent*. New York: Free Press of Glencoe, 1964.

Gehl, J. *Austria, Germany and the Anschluss*. New York: Oxford University Press, 1963.

Geiler von Kaysersberg, Johann. *Die Emeis*. Strassburg: Jehannes Grieninger, 1516.

Geis, Gilbert. *Not the Law's Business: An Examination of Homosexuality, Abortion, Prostitution, Narcotics, and Gambling in the United States*. Rockville: National Institute of Mental Health, 1972.

_____. (ed.). *White Collar Crime*. New York: Atherton, 1968.

_____, and Meier, Robert F. (eds.). *White-Collar Crime: Offenses in Business, Politics, and the Professions*. New York: Free Press, 1977.

Geiser, Robert L. *Hidden Victims*. Boston: Beacon Press, 1979.

Gelb, Arthur and Barbara. *O'Neill*. New York: Harper & Bros., 1962.

Gelb, Barbara. *On the Track of Murder*. New York: William Morrow, 1975.

Gelber, L.M. *The Rise of Anglo-American Friendship*. London: Oxford University Press, 1938.

Geller, Alan, and Boas, Maxwell. *The Drug Beat*. New York: Cowles, 1971.

Geller, Uri. *My Story*. New York: Praeger, 1975.

Gelles, Richard J., and Cornell, C.P. *Intimate Violence in Families*. Newbury Park, Calif.: Sage, 1985.

_____. *The Violent Home*. Beverly Hills, Calif.: Sage, 1974.

Gellhorn, Ernest. *Administrative Law and Process in a Nutshell*. St. Paul: West, 1972.

Gellhorn, Walter. *American Rights*. New York: Macmillan, 1960.

_____. *Ombudsmen and Others*. Cambridge, Mass.: Harvard University Press, 1966.

_____. *When Americans Complain*. Cambridge, Mass.: Harvard University Press, 1966.

Gellner, John. *Bayonets in the Streets*. Canada: Collier Macmillan, 1974.

Gelluis, Aulus. *Attic Nights*. trans. John C. Rolfe. London: William Heinemann, 1952-1960.

Gelzer, Matthias. *Caesar: Politician and Statesman*. Cambridge, Mass.: Harvard University Press, 1968.

Gemmill, W.N. *Salem Witchtrials*. Chicago: A.C. McClurg, 1924.

Genealogy of the Cutts Family in America. Albany, N.Y.: Joel Munsells Sons, 1892.

Genet, Jean. *The Thief's Journal*. New York: Grove Press, 1964.

Génies et Réalistes. *Napoléon*. Paris: Hachette, 1962.

Genkina, E.B. *Lenin: Predsedatel Sovnarkoma*. Moscow: Izdatelstvo Akademmii Nauk S.S.S.R.,1960.

Genoud, Francois (ed.). *The Testament of Adolf Hitler*. trans. Col. R.H. Stevens. London: Cassell, 1961.

Genov, Georgi P. *Bulgaria and the Treaty of Neuilly*. Sofia, Bul.: H.G. Danov, 1935.

Genthe, Arnold. *As I Remember*. New York: Reynal & Hitchcock, 1936.

_____, and Irwin, Will. *Pictures of Old Chinatown*. New York: Mills College, 1908.

Gentry, Curt. *Frame-Up: The Incredible Case of Tom Mooney and Warren Billings*. New York: Norton, 1967.

_____. *The Madams of San Francisco*. New York: Doubleday, 1964.

Genung, Abram Polhemus. *The Frauds of the New York City Government Exposed. Sketches of the Members of the Ring and Their Confederates*. New York: Published by Author, 1871.

Geoffrey of Monmouth. *The History of the Kings of Britain*. Penguin Books, 1966.

Georg, Enno. *Die wirtschaftlichen Unternehmungen der SS*. Stuttgart, Ger.: Deutsche Verlagsanstalt, 1963.

George, Alexander and Juliet. *Woodrow Wilson and Colonel House: A Personality Study*. New York: John Day, 1956.

George, Andrew L. *The Texas Convict: Thrilling and Terrible Experiences of a Texas Boy*. Austin, Texas: Ben C. Jones, 1893.

George, Earl Lloyd. *Lloyd George*. London: Muller, 1960.

George, Edward Augustus. *Seventeenth Century Men of Latitude*. New York: Charles Scribner's Sons, 1908.

George, Henry. *Progress and Poverty*. New York: Modern Library, 1929.

George, Henry, Jr. *The Life of Henry George*. New York: Doubleday, McClure, 1900.

George, S.K. *Gandhi's Challenge to Christianity*. London: Allen & Unwin, 1939.

George, Susan. *How the Other Half Dies: The Real Reasons for World Hunger*. Montclair, N.J.: Allanheld, Osmun, 1977.

George, Todd Menzies. *Just Memories, and Twelve Years with Cole Younger*. Kansas City: Quality Hill Printing, 1959.

Georgetown University Law Center. *The Role of Prison Industries Now and In the Future*. Washington, D.C.: Institute of Criminal Law and Procedure, 1974.

Geraghty, Tony. *Who Dares Win*. London: Arms & Armour Press, 1980.

Gerard, A.G. *Itineraire de Quebec à Chicago*. Montreal, Quebec, Can.: C.O. Beauchemin & Valois, 1868.

Gerard, James. *My First 83 Years in America*. Garden City, N.Y.: Doubleday, 1951.

_____. *My Four Years in Germany*. New York: Doran, 1917.

Gerard, James W. *Face to Face with Kaiserism*. New York: George H. Doran, 1918.

Gerard, John. *The Autobiography of a Hunted Priest*. New York: Pellegrini & Cudahy, 1952.

Gerassi, John. *Boys of Boise*. New York: Macmillan, 1966.

Gerber, Albert B. *Bashful Billionaire*. New York: Lyle Stuart, 1967.

Gerenson, Alvin. *Kennedy and Big Business*. Beverly Hills, Calif.: Book Company of America, 1964.

Gerhart, Eugene C. *America's Advocate: Robert H. Jackson*. Indianapolis, Ind.: Bobbs-Merril, 1958.

Germann, A.C., et al. *Introduction to Law Enforcement and Criminal Justice*. Springfield, Ill.: Charles C. Thomas, 1968.

_____. *Police Personnel Management*. Springfield, Ill.: Thomas, 1958.

Germino, Dante L. *The Italian Fascist Party in Power*. Minneapolis: University of Minnesota Press, 1959.

Gernsheim, Helmut. *Lewis Carroll*. New York: Dover, 1969.

Gernsheim, Helmut and Alison. *Victoria R*. New York: G.P. Putnam's Sons, 1959.

Gerry, Elbridge, Jr. *Diary*. New York: Brentano's, 1927.

Gerry, Margarita Spalding. *Through Five Administrations: Reminiscences of Colonel William H. Crook*. New York: Harper & Brothers, 1907.

Gerschenkron, Alexander. *Economic Backwardness in Historical Perspective*. Cambridge, Mass.: Harvard University Press, 1962.

Gerson, Noel B. *Light-Horse Harry: A Biography of Washington's Great Cavalryman, General Henry Lee*. Garden City, N.Y.: Doubleday, 1966.

Gertsenzon, A.A. *Vvedenie v sovetskuyu kriminologiyu*. Moscow: n.p., 1965.

Gertz, Elmer. *A Handful of Clients*. Chicago: Follett, 1965.

_____. *Henry Miller*. DeKalb: Southern Illinois University Press, 1978

_____. *Moment of Madness: The People vs. Jack Ruby*. Chicago: Follett, 1968.

_____. *To Life*. New York: McGraw Hill, 1974.

Gervais of Tilbury. *Otia Imperialia*. Hanover: C. Rumpler, 1856.

Gessi, Leone. *Roma, la guerra, il Papa*. Rome: Standerini, 1945.

Gest, John Marshall. *The Old Yellow Book*. Philadelphia: University of Pennsylvania Press, 1927.

Geva, Tamara. *Split Seconds*. New York: Harper & Row, 1972.

Gével, Claude. *Deux carbonari: Orsini et Napoléon III*. Paris: Emile-Paul fréres, 1934.

Geyer, Frank P. *The Holmes-Pitezel Case*. Philadelphia: Frank Geyer, 1896.

Geyl, Pieter. *The Netherlands in the Seventeenth Century, pt. l: 1609-1648*. New York: Barnes & Noble, 1961.

_____. *The Revolt of the Netherlands, 1555-1609*. London: Ernest

Benn, 1962.

Geytenbeck, A.C. Van. *Musonius Rufus and Greek Diatribe.* trans. B.L. Hijamans, Jr. Assen, Neth.: Van Gorcum, 1963.

Ghent, William James. *Our Benevolent Feudalism.* New York: Macmillan, 1902.

_____. "William Barclay Masterson". *The Dictionary of American Biography.* New York: Charles Scribner's Sons, 1933.

Ghezzi, Raoul. *Comunisti, industriali e fascisti a Torino, 1920-23.* Turin, Italy: Vega, 1945.

Ghirotti, Gigi. *Mitra e Sardegna.* Milan, Italy: Longanesi, 1968.

Ghirshman, Roman. *Iran from the Earliest Times to the Islamic Conquest.* London: Penguin, 1954.

Ghisalberti, Alberto M. (ed.). *Lettere di Felice Orsini.* Rome: Vittoriano, 1936.

Giachette, Cipriano. *Fascismo liberatore.* Florence, Italy: Bemporad, 1922.

Giallombardo, Rose. *The Social World of Imprisoned Girls.* New York: Wiley, 1974.

_____. *Society of Women: A Study of a Women's Prison.* New York: Wiley, 1966.

Giancana, Antoinette, and Renner, Thomas C. *Mafia Princess: Growing Up in Sam Giancana's Family.* New York: Avon, 1985.

Gianeri, Enrico. *Il cesare di cartapesta.* Turin, Italy: Vega, 1945.

_____. *Il piccolo re.* Turin, Italy: Fiorini, 1946.

Giannini, Alberto. *Le memorie di un fesso.* Milan, Italy: Corbaccio, 1941.

Gibb, Hamilton A.R., and Bowen, H. *Islamic Society and the West: A Study of the Impact of Western Civilization on Moslem Culture in the Near East.* London: Oxford University Press, 1950.

_____. *Modern Trends in Islam.* Chicago: University of Chicago Press, 1947.

_____. *Studies on the Civilization of Islam.* London: Routledge & Keegan Paul, 1962.

Gibbens, T.C.N., and Prince, J. *Child Victims of Sex Offences.* London: Instutute for the Study and Treatment of Delinquency, 1963.

_____, and Ahrenfeldt, R.H. (eds.). *Cultural Factors in Delinquency.* Philadelphia: J.B. Lippincott, 1966.

_____. *Psychiatric Studies of Borstal Lads.* London: Oxford University Press, 1963.

_____. *Shoplifting.* London: ISTD, 1962.

Gibbes, R.W. *Documentary History of the American Revolution.* Columbia, S.C.: Banner Steam-Power Press, 1853.

Gibbings, Robert. *Lovely Is the Lee.* New York: Dutton, 1945.

Gibbon, Edward. *The History of the Decline and Fall of the Roman Empire.* New York: Everyman's Library, 1936.

Gibbon, Thomas Edward. *Mexico Under Carranza.* New York: Doubleday, Page, 1919.

Gibbons, Don C. *Changing the Lawbreaker.* Englewood Cliffs, N.J.: Prentice-Hall, 1965.

_____. *Crime and Criminal Careers.* Englewood Cliffs, N.J.: Prentice-Hall, 1968.

_____. *The Criminological Enterprise.* Englewood Cliffs, N.J.: Prentice-Hall, 1979.

_____. *Delinquent Behavior.* Englewood Cliffs, N.J.: Prentice-Hall, 1970.

_____. *Society, Crime, and Criminal Careers.* Englewood Cliffs, N.J.: Prentice-Hall, 1977.

_____, and Garrity, Donald L. *The Study of Deviance.* Englewood Cliffs, N.J.: Prentice-Hall, 1975.

Gibbons, Edward. *Floyd Gibbons: Your Headline Hunter.* New York: Exposition Press, 1953.

Gibbons, Floyd. *And They Thought We Wouldn't Fight.* New York: Doran, 1918.

Gibbons, Herbert Adams. *Paris Reborn.* New York: Century, 1915.

Gibbons, Rev. James Joseph. *In the San Juan, Colorado: Sketches.* Chicago: Press of Calumet Book & Engraving, 1898.

Gibbons, James S. *The Banks of New York, Their Dealers, the Clearing House, and the Panic of 1857.* New York: D. Appleton, 1859.

Gibbons, Lois Oliphant. (ed.). *Liberty and Persecution, Essays in Honor of George Lincoln Burr.* Ithaca, N.Y.: Cornell University Press, 1931.

_____. *Some Rhenish Foes of Credulity and Cruelty 1620-40.* Ithaca, N.Y.: Cornell University Press, 1920.

Gibbs, Angelica. *New York Murders.* New York: Duell, Sloan & Pearce, 1944.

Gibbs, George Sweet, and Knowlton, Evelyn H. *The Resurgent Years: 1911-1927.* II. *The History of Standard Oil.* 2 vols. New York: Harper & Row, 1956.

Gibbs, Jack P. *Crime, Punishment, and Deterrence.* New York: Elsevier, 1975.

Gibbs, Josiah F. *The Mountain Meadow Massacre.* Salt Lake City, Utah: Salt Lake Tribune, 1910.

Gibbs, Peter. *Crimean Blunder.* New York: Holt, Rinehart & Winston, 1960.

Gibbs, Sir Philip. *Since Then.* London: William Heinemann, 1930.

Gibney, B. *The Beauty Queen Killer.* New York: Pinnacle, 1984.

Gibney, Frank. *Five Gentlemen of Japan: The Portrait of a Nation's Character.* New York: Farrar, Straus & Young, 1953.

_____. *Japan: The Fragile Superpower.* New York: W.W. Norton, 1975.

_____. *The Operators.* New York: Harper & Bros., 1960.

Gibran, Kahlil. *The Prophet.* New York: Alfred A. Knopf, 1963.

Gibson, Arrell M. *The Life and Death of Colonel Albert Jennings Fountain.* Norman: University of Oklahoma Press, 1965.

_____. *A Political Crime. The History of the Great Fraud.* New York: William S. Gottsberger, 1885.

Gibson, Brian. *The Birmingham Bombs.* London: Barry Rose, 1976.

Gibson, E. *Principles of Perceptual Learning and Development.* New York: Appleton-Century-Crofts, 1969.

Gibson, Evelyn, and McClintock, W.H. *Robbery in London.* London: Macmillan, 1961.

_____. *Time Spent Awaiting Trial.* London: Her Majesty's Stationery Office, 1960.

Gibson, George Rutledge. *Journal of a Soldier Under Kearny and Doniphan, 1846-1847.* Glendale, Calif.: Arthur H. Clark, 1935.

Gibson, Hugh. *A Journal from Our Legation in Belgium.* New York: Doubleday, 1917.

Gibson, Rev. Otis. *Chinaman or White Man, Which?* San Francisco: Alta Printing House, 1873.

_____. *The Chinese in America.* Cincinnati, Ohio: Hitchcock & Walden, 1877.

Gibson, Sonny. *Mafia Kingpin.* New York: Grossett & Dunlop, 1981.

Gibson, Walter B. and Litzka R. *The Complete Illustrated Book of Divination and Prophecy.* New York: Doubleday, 1973.

_____. *The Fine Art of Swindling.* New York: Grosset & Dunlap, 1966.

Gicaru, M. *Land of Sunshine: Scenes of Life in Kenya Before Mau Mau.* London: Lawrence & Wishart, 1958.

Giddens, Anthony. *The Class Structure of the Advanced Societies.* New York: Harper & Row, 1975.

Giddens, Edward. *Anti-Masonic Almanac For the Year 1833.* Utica, N.Y.: William Williams, 1982.

Giddens, Paul H. *The Birth of the Oil Industry.* New York: Macmillan, 1938.

Giddings, Luther. *Sketches of the Campaign in Northern Mexico by an Officer of the First Ohio Volunteers.* New York: G.P. Putnam, 1853.

Gide, André. *Journals.* trans. Justin O'Brien. London: Secker & Warburg, 1949.

_____. *Ne Jugez Pas.* Paris: Gallimard, 1930.

_____. *Oscar Wilde: A Study*. Oxford, Eng.: Hollywell, 1905.

Gieroff, Alex K. *Sexual Deviations in the Criminal Law: Homosexual, Exhibitionistic, and Pedophilic Offences in Canada*. Toronto, Ontario, Can.: University of Toronto Press, 1968.

Gies, Joseph. *The Colonel of Chicago: A Biography of the Chicago Tribune's Legendary Publisher Colonel Robert McCormick*. New York: E.P. Dutton, 1979.

Giesler, Jerry, as told to Pete Martin. *Hollywood Lawyer--The Jerry Giesler Story*. New York: Simon & Schuster, 1960.

Gifford, Denis. *Chapin*. Garden City, N.Y.: Doubleday, 1974.

Gifford, Edward S., Jr. *The Evil Eye*. New York: n.p., 1958.

Gifford, George. *A Dialogue Concerning Witches and Witchcrafts*. London: H. Milford, 1931.

_____. *A Discourse of the Subtle Practices of Devils by Witches and Sorcerers*. London: Toby Cooke, 1587.

Giglio, Giovanni. *The Triumph of Barabbas*. London: Victor Gollancz, 1937.

Giglio, James N. *Harry M. Daugherty and the Politics of Expediency*. Kent, Ohio: Kent State University Press, 1978.

Gigon, Fernand. *Jeudi Noir*. Paris: Laffont, 1976.

Gil, David C. *Violence Against Children*. Cambridge, Mass.: Harvard University Press, 1970.

Gilbert, Bill. *The Trailblazers*. New York: Time-Life Books, 1973.

_____. *Westering Man: The Life of Joseph Walker*. New York: Atheneum, 1983.

Gilbert, Clinton W. *The Mirrors of Washington*. New York: Putnam, 1921.

Gilbert, Emile. *Les plantes magiques et la sorcellerie*. Moulins: H. Durond, 1899.

_____. *Sorciers et magiciens*. Moulins: n.p., 1895.

Gilbert, Felix (ed.). *Hitler Directs His War*. New York: Oxford University Press, 1950.

_____. *Machiavelli and Guicciardini*. Princeton, N.J.: Princeton University Press, 1965.

Gilbert, Frank. *Centennial History of the City of Chicago: Its Men and Institutions*. Chicago: Inter Ocean, 1905.

Gilbert, G.M. *Nuremberg Diary*. New York: New American Library, 1947.

Gilbert, James Burkhart. *The Psychology of Dictatorship*. New York: Ronald Press, 1950.

_____. *Writers and Partisans*. New York: Wiley, 1968.

Gilbert, Martin. *The Arab-Israeli Conflict: Its History in Maps*. London: Weidenfeld and Nicolson, 1974.

_____. *Winston S. Churchill*. London: William Heinemann, 1976.

Gilbert, Michael F. *Dr. Cripppen*. London: Odhams Press, 1953.

Gilbert, Paul Thomas, and Bryson, Charles Lee. *Chicago and Its Makers*. Chicago: University of Chicago Press, 1929.

Gilbert, Robert E. *Television and Presidential Politics*. North Quincy, Mass.: Christopher, 1972.

Gilbert, Rodney. *What's Wrong with China*. London: John Murray, 1926.

Gilbert, Stirling Price. *James Clark McReynolds*. Privately Printed: 1946.

Gilbert, William. *Lucrezia Borgia*. London: Hurst & Blackett, 1864.

Gilbert, William Napier John, and Holland, Julian. *Pacific Voyages*. Garden City, N.Y.: Doubleday, 1971.

Gilchrist, David T. (ed.) *The Growth of the Seaport Cities, 1790-1825*. Charlottesville: University of Virginia Press, 1967.

Gilder, Richard Watson, *Grover Cleveland: A Record of Friendship*. New York: Century, 1919.

Gilder, Rodman. *The Battery*. Boston: Houghton Mifflin, 1956.

Gildrie, Richard. *Salem, Massachusetts*. Charlottesville: University of Virginia, 1975.

Giles, F.T. *The Criminal Law*. London: Penguin Books, 1954.

Gilfillan, Archer B. *A Goat's Eye View of the Black Hills*. Rapid City, S.D.: Dean & Dean, 1953.

Gililov, C.V.I. *Lenin, Organizer*. Moscow: Gosudarstvennoe Izdatelstvo, 1960.

Gilio, Maria Esther. *The Tupamaros*. London: Secker & Warburg, 1972.

_____. *The Tupamaro Guerrillas*. trans. Anne Edmondson. New York: Saturday Review Press, 1972.

Gill, Brendan. *Tallulah*. New York: Holt, Rinehart & Winston, 1972.

Gill, G. Hermon. *Royal Australian Navy, 1939-42*. Canberra: Australian War Memorial, 1957.

Gill, John. *Tide Without Turning: Elijah P. Lovejoy and Freedom of the Press*. Boston: Starr King Press, 1958.

Gill, Obadiah. *Some Few Remarks Upon a Scandalous Book against the Government and Ministry of New England*. Boston: T. Green, 1701.

Gille, Bertrand. *Le banque et le crédit en France de 1815 à 1848*. Paris: University of France Press, 1959.

_____. *Histoire économique et sociale de la Russie du moyen age au vingtieme siècle*. Paris: Payot, 1949.

Gillelen, F.M.L. *The Oil Regions of Pennsylvania*. Pittsburgh, Pa.: John P. Hunt, 1864.

Gillen, Mollie. *Assassination of the Prime Minister: The Shocking Death of Spencer Perceval*. New York: St. Martin's Press, 1972.

Gillers, Stephen. *Getting Justice; The Rights of People*. New York: New American Library, 1971.

Gillespie, Joan. *Algeria: Rebellion and Revolution*. London: Ernest Benn, 1960.

Gillespie, R.W. *Economic Factors in Crime and Delinquency*. Washington, D.C.: National Institute of Law Enforcement and Criminal Justice, 1975.

Gillet, Louis. *Londres et Rome*. Paris: Bernard Grasset, 1936.

Gillett, Charlie. *The Sound of the City*. New York: Outerbridge & Dienstfrey, 1972.

Gillett, Frederick H. *George Frisbie Hoar*. Boston: Houghton Mifflin, 1934.

Gillett, James Buchanan. *Six Years With the Texas Rangers, 1875 to 1881*. Lincoln: University of Nebraska Press, 1976.

Gillette, John Morris. *Culture Agencies of a Typical Manufacturing Group*. Chicago: University of Chicago Press, 1901.

Gillette, Paul J. *The Encyclopedia of Erotica*. New York: Award, 1969.

_____, and Tillinger, Eugene. *Inside the Ku Klux Klan*. New York: Pyramid Books, 1965.

_____. *The Lopinosn Case*. Los Angeles: Holloway House, 1967.

Gilliam, Harold. *San Francisco Bay*. Garden City, N.Y.: Doubleday, 1957.

Gilliam, Olive Kuntz. *The Memoirs of Augustus*. New York: Vantage Press, 1965.

Gilliard, Pierre. *Thirteen Years at the Russian Court*. New York: Doran, 1921.

Gillin, John. *For a Science of Man*. New York: Macmillan, 1954.

Gillis, O.J. *To Hell and Back Again, Its Discovery, Description, and Experiences; or, Life in the Penitentiary of Texas and Kansas*. Little Rock, Ark.: Democrat Printing, 1906.

Gilliver, L. *Select Trials at the Sessions-House in the Old Bailey*. London: n.p., 1747.

Gillmor, Donald M. *Free Press and Fair Trial*. Washington, D.C.: Public Affairs Press, 1966.

Gilman, Daniel Coit. *The Life of James Dwight Dana*. New York: Harper & Brothers, 1899.

Gilmore, Al-Tony. *Bad Nigger!*. Port Washington, N.Y.: Kennikat Press, 1975.

Gilmore, Harry. *Four Years in the Saddle*. New York: Harper and Brothers, 1866.

Gilmore, James R. *Personal Recollections of Abraham Lincoln and the Civil War*. Boston: L. C. Page, 1898.

Gilsinan, James F. *Doing Justice, How the System Works - As seen by the Participants*. Englewood Cliffs, N.J.: Prentice-Hall, 1982.

Gineste, Raoul. *Les grandes victimes de l'hystérie: Louis Gaufridi curé des Accoules et Magdeleine de la Palud*. Paris: L. Michaud, 1907.

Ging, Eng Ying, and Grant, Bruce. *Tong War*. Boston: Little, Brown, 1924.

The Ging Murder: Being a Complete Version of the Most Horrible Event in the Criminal History of the World. Minneapolis, Minn.: Tribune, 1894.

Ginger, Raymond. *The Age of Excess*. New York: Macmillan, 1965.

_____. *Altgeld's America*. Chicago: Quadrangle Books, 1965.

_____. *The Bending Cross: A Biography of Eugene Victor Debs*. New Brunswick, N.J.: Rutgers University Press, 1949.

_____. *Eugene V. Debs: The Making of an American Radical*. New York: Macmillan, 1949.

_____. *Six Days or Forever? Tennesse v. John Thomas Scopes*. Boston: Beacon Press, 1958.

Ginsberg, Eli, et al. *The Pluralistic Economy*. New York: McGraw-Hill, 1965.

Ginsberg, Morris. *On Justice in Society*. Baltimore: Penguin Books, 1965.

Ginty, Elizabeth Beall. *Missouri Legend*. New York: Random House, 1938.

Ginzberg, E. *Sex and Class Behavior*. New York: New American Library of World Literature, 1948.

Ginzburg, Ralph. *100 Years of Lynchings*. New York: Lancer Books, 1962.

Giolitti, Giovanni. *Memoirs of my life*. trans. Edward Storer. London: Chapman & Dodd, 1923.

Giovio, P. *La Vita di Alfonso d' Este Duca di Ferrara*. trans. G.B. Filli. Venice, Italy: Venezia, 1597.

Gipson, Fred. *Fabulous Empire: Colonel Zack Miller's Story*. Boston: Houghton Mifflin, 1946.

Gipson, Larence Henry. *The British Empire before the American Revolution*. 9 vols. New York: Alfred A. Knopf, 1936-56.

_____. *The Coming of the Revolution, 1763-1775*. New York: Harper & Brothers, 1954.

_____. *Lewis Evans*. Philadelphia: Historical Society of Pennsylvania, 1939.

Girace, Piero. *Diario di uno squadrista*. Naples, Italy: Rispoli Anonima, 1940.

Giraldo, Le Pére Mathias de. *Histoire curieuse et pittoresque des sorciers*. Paris: Librarie populaire des Villes et des campagnes, 1854.

Giraud, Victor. *Vie de Jeanne d'Arc*. Avignon: G. Aubanel, 1948.

Girling, J.L.S. *People's War*. London: George Allen & Unwin, 1969.

Giron, Aimé. *Les Amours étranges*. Paris: Michel-Lévy Frères, 1864.

_____, and Tozza, Albert. *La Bête de luxure*. Paris: Ambert, 1903.

Gisevius, Hans Bernd. *Adolf Hitler: Versuch einer Deuting*. Munich: Rutten-Loening Verlag, 1963.

_____. *To the Bitter End*. trans. Richard and Clara Winston. Boston: Houghton Mifflin, 1947.

_____. *Wo ist Nebe?*. Zurich, Switz.: Droemersche Verlagsanstalt, 1966.

Gish, Anthony. *American Bandits*. Girard, Kan.: Haldeman-Julius, 1938.

Gish, Lillian, with Pinchot, Ann. *The Movies, Mr. Griffith and Me*. New York: Prentice-Hall, 1969.

Gitlow, Benjamin. *I Confess: The Truth About American Communism*. New York: E.P. Dutton, 1940.

_____. *The Whole of Their Lives*. New York: Charles Scribner's Sons, 1948.

Gittinger, Roy. *The Formation of the State of Oklahoma*. Norman: University of Oklahoma Press, 1939.

Giurescu, Constantin C. *La Transylvanie*. Boston: N. Stroila, 1943.

Glaab, Charles N., and Brown, A. Theodore. *A History of Urban America*. New York: Macmillan, 1967.

Glad, Paul W. *The Trumpet Soundeth: William Jennings Bryan and His Democracy, 1896-1912*. Lincoln: University of Nebraska Press, 1960.

Gladden, Washington. *Christianity and Socialism*. New York: Eaton & Means, 1905.

Gladstone, W.E. *Rome and the Newest Fashions in Religion*. New York: Harpers, 1875.

Glaister, John. *Final Diagnosis*. London: Hutchinson, 1964.

_____., and Rentoul, E. *Medical Jurisprudence and Toxicology*. London: Livingstone Press, 1953.

_____. *The Power of Poison*. New York: William Morrow, 1954.

_____., and Smith, S.A. *Recent Advances in Forensic Medicine*. London: Churchill, 1931.

Glanvill, Joseph. *A Blow at Modern Saducism*. London: E.C., J. Collins, 1668.

_____. *Saducismus Triumphatus*. (trans. Anthony Horneck). London: A. Bettesworth, J. Batley, 1726.

_____. *Some Philosophical Considerations Touching the Being of Witches and Witchcraft*. London: J. Collins, 1667.

Glaser, Barney and Strauss, Anselm. *The Discovery of Grounded Theory*. Chicago: Aldine, 1967.

Glaser, D. *Adult Crime and Social Policy*. Englewood Cliffs, N.J.: Prentice-Hall, 1972.

Glaser, Daniel. (ed.). *Crime in the City*. New York: Harper & Row, 1970.

_____. *Crime in Our Changing Society*. New York: Holt, Rinehart, Winston, 1978.

_____. *The Effectiveness of a Prison and Parole System*. Indianapolis: Bobbs-Merrill, 1964.

_____. (ed.). *The Handbook of Criminology*. Chicago: Rand-McNally, 1974.

_____. *Strategic Criminal Justice Planning*. Rockville, Md.: National Institute of Mental Health Center for Studies of Crime and Delinquency, 1975.

_____, et al. *The Violent Offender*. Washington, D.C.: U.S. Printing Office, 1968.

Glaser, Kurt. *Die Tschechoslowakei*. Bonn, Ger.: Athenäum, 1964.

Glasgow, J. Ewing. *The Harper's Ferry Insurrection*. Edinburgh, Scot.: Myles MacPhail, 1860.

Glassco, John. *Memoirs of Montparnasse*. New York: Oxford University Press, 1970.

Glasscock, Carl Burgess. *Bandits of the Southwest Pacific*. New York: Frederick A. Stokes, 1929.

_____. *Big Bonanza: The Story of the Comstock Trade*. Indianapolis, Ind.: Bobbs-Merrill, 1931.

_____. *Gold in Them Hills: The Story of the West's Last Wild Mining Days*. Indianapolis, Ind.: Bobbs-Merrill, 1932.

_____. *A Golden Highway: Scenes of History's Greatest Gold Rush Yesterday and Today*. Indianapolis, Ind.: Bobbs-Merrill, 1934.

_____. *Lucky Baldwin*. Indianapolis, Ind.: Bobbs-Merrill, 1933.

_____. *Then Came Oil*. New York: Bobbs-Merrill, 1938.

_____. *The War of the Copper Kings: Builders of Butte and Wolves of Wall Street*. Indianapolis, Ind.: Bobbs-Merrill, 1935.

Glasser, William. *Reality Therapy*. New York: Harper & Row, 1965.

Glatzle, Mary, and Fiore, Evelyn. *Muggable Mary, My Life with the Street Crime Unit*. Englewood Cliffs, N.J.: Prentice-Hall, 1980.

Glazer, Nathan, and Moynihan, Daniel Patrick. *Beyond the Melting Pot: The Negroes, Puerto Ricans, Jews, Italians, and Irish of New York City*. Cambridge, Mass.: M.I.T. Press, 1964.

Glazier, Willard. *Down the Great River*. Philadelphia: Hubbard Brothers, 1883

_____. *Ocean to Ocean on Horseback*. Philadelphia: Hubbard, 1896.

_____. *Peculiarities of American Cities*. Philadelphia: Hubbard, 1886.

Gleason, Arthur. *What the Workers Want*. New York: Harcourt,

1920.

Gleason, John H. *The Genesis of Russophobia in Great Britain.* Cambridge, Eng.: Harvard University Press, 1950.

_____. *The Justices of the Peace in England.* Oxford, Eng.: Clarendon Press, 1969.

Gleeson, James. *Bloody Sunday.* London: Davies, 1962.

Glenn, N.D. *Cohart Analysis.* Beverly Hills, Calif.: Sage, 1977.

Glenn, William Wilkins. *Between North and South.* Rutherford: Fairleigh Dickenson University Press, 1976.

Glib, Corinne L. *Hidden Hierarchies.* New York: Harper & Row, 1966.

Glick, Carl, and Hong, Sheng-Hwa. *Chinese Secret Societies.* New York: Whittlesey House, 1947.

Glick, Edward B. *Latin America and the Palestine Problem.* New York: Herzl Foundation, 1958.

Glick, Rush G., and Newsom, Robert S. *Fraud Investigation.* Springfield, Ill.: Charles C. Thomas, 1974.

Glikes, Erwin A., and Schwaber, Paul, (eds.). *Of Poetry and Power: Poems Occasioned by the Presidency and by the Death of John F. Kennedy.* New York: Basic Books, 1964.

Glover, E. *The Psycho-pathology of Prostitution.* London: Instutute for Study and Treatment of Delinquency, 1945.

_____. *The Roots of Crime.* New York: International Universities Press, 1960.

Glubb, Lt. Gen. Sir John. *Britain and the Arabs.* London: Hodder & Stoughton, 1957.

_____. *The Empire of the Arabs.* London: Hodder & Stoughton, 1963.

_____. *The Great Arab Conquests.* London: Hodder & Stoughton, 1963.

_____. *A Soldier with the Arabs.* London: Hodder & Stoughton, 1957.

_____. *The Story of the Arab Legion.* London: Hodder & Stoughton, 1948.

Glubb, J.B., and Clines, Walter. *Notes on the People of Siwah and El Garah in the Libyan Desert.* Menasha, Wis.: George Banta, 1936.

_____. *The Sulubba and Other Ignoble Tribes of Southwestern Asia.* Menasha, Wis.: George Banta, 1936.

Glück, Elsie. *John Mitchell, Miner: Labor's Bargain with the Gilded Age.* New York: John Day, 1929.

Gluckman, Max. *Custom and Conflict in Africa.* New York: Barnes & Nobel, 1973.

Glueck, B. *Studies in Forensic Psychiatry.* London: Heinemann, 1916.

Glueck, B.C., Jr. *New York Final Report on Deviated Sex Offenders.* Albany, N.Y.: Department of Mental Hygiene, 1956.

Glueck, S. *Crime and Justice.* Boston: Little, Brown, 1936.

Glueck, Sheldon, and Eleanor T. *Criminal Careers in Retrospect.* New York: Commonwealth Fund, 1943.

_____. *Criminal Law and Its Enforcement.* St. Paul: West, 1951.

_____. *Delinquents and Nondelinquents in Perspective.* Cambridge, Mass.: Harvard University Press, 1968.

_____. *500 Criminal Careers.* New York: Alfred A. Knopf, 1930.

_____. *500 Delinquent Women.* New York: Alfred A. Knopf, 1934.

_____. *Juvenile Delinquents Grown Up.* New York: Commonwealth Fund, 1940.

_____. *Later Criminal Careers.* New York: Commonwealth Fund, 1937.

_____. *1000 Juvenile Delinquents.* Cambridge, Mass.: Harvard University Press, 1934.

_____. *Physique and Delinquency.* New York: Harper, 1956.

_____, and Eleanor T. *Predicting Delinquency and Crime.* Cambridge, Mass.: Harvard University Press, 1959.

_____. *Toward a Typology of Juvenile Offenders.* New York: Grune and Stratton, 1970.

_____. *Unravelling Juvenile Delinquency.* Cambridge, Mass.: Harvard University Press, 1950.

Goad, H.E. *The Making of the Corporate State.* London: Chris-

tophers, 1932.

Gobetti-Marchesini, Prospero A. *Diario partigiano.* Turin, Italy: Einaudi, 1956.

Gobright, Lawrence A. *Recollections of Men and Things at Washington during the Third of a Century.* Philadelphia: Claxton, Ramsen, 1869.

Goddard, Donald. *Joey.* New York: Harper & Row, 1974.

Goddard, Henry. *The Memoirs of a Bow Street Runner.* New York: William Morrow, 1956.

Goddard, Henry H. *Feeble-Mindedness.* New York: Macmillan, 1914.

_____. *Juvenile Delinquency.* New York: Dodd, Mead, 1921.

_____. *The Kallikak Family.* New York: Macmillan, 1912.

Godden, Gertrude M. *Mussolini.* London: Burns & Oates, 1923.

Godelmann, Johann Georg. *Tractatus de Magis.* Frankfort: Ex officina typographica Nicolai Bassei, 1591.

_____. *Von Zauberern, Hexen und Unholden wahrhaftiger und wohlgegründeter Bericht.* trans. Georgius Nigrinus. Frankfort, Ger.: N. Bassaeum, 1592.

Godfrey, E. Drexel, Jr., and Harris, Don R. *Basic Elements of Intelligence.* Washington, D.C.: U.S. Government Printing Office, 1971.

Godfrey, Samuel E. *A Sketch of the Life of Samuel E. Godfrey.* Hanover, Vt.: David Watson, 1818.

Godkin, Edwin Lawrence. *Problems of Modern Democracy, Political and Economic Essays.* New York: Charles Scribner's Sons, 1897.

_____. *Reflections and Comments, 1865-1895.* New York: Charles Scribner's Sons, 1896.

_____. *The Triumph of Reform: November 6, 1894.* New York: Souvenir, 1895.

_____. *Unforeseen Tendencies of Democracy.* Boston: Houghton Mifflin, 1898.

Godkin, G.S. *Life of Victor Emmanuel II.* London: Macmillan, 1880.

Godoy, Jose Francisco. *Porfirio Diaz, President of Mexico: The Master Builder.* New York: G.P. Putnam's Sons, 1910.

Godspeed, G. S. *A History of the Babylonians and Assyrians.* New York: Charles Scribner's Sons, 1906.

Godwin, George. *Crime and Social Action.* London: Watts, 1956.

_____. *Killers Unknown.* London: Jenkins, 1960.

_____. *Peter Kurten, A Study in Sadism.* London: Acorn Press, 1938.

Godwin, John. *Alcatraz 1868-1963.* New York: Doubleday, 1963.

_____. *Killers in Paradise.* London: Herbert Jenkins, 1962.

_____. *Murder U.S.A.: The Ways We Kill Each Other.* New York: Ballantine Books, 1978.

_____. *Occult America.* New York: Doubleday, 1972.

_____. *Unsolved, The World of the Unknown.* New York: Doubleday, 1976.

Godwin, William. *Lives of the Necromancers.* New York: Harper Brothers, 1847.

Goebbels, Josef. *Diaries.* trans. Louis P. Lochner. London: Hamish Hamilton, 1948.

_____. *The Early Goebbels Diaries.* London: Nicolson & Weidenfeld, 1962.

Goebel, Julius, and Naughton, T. Raymond. *Law Enforcement in Colonial New York: A Study in Criminal Procedure.* Montclair, N.J.: Patterson Smith, 1970.

_____ (ed.). *The Law Practice of Alexander Hamilton.* New York: Columbia University Press, 1964.

Goer, Geoffrey. *Exploring English Character.* New York: Criterion Books, 1955.

Goerlitz, Walter. *History of the German General Staff, 1657-1945.* trans. Brian Battershaw. New York: Fredrick A. Praeger, 1953.

Goerner, Fred. *The Search of Amelia Earhart.* Garden City, N.Y.: Doubleday, 1966.

Goethe, C.M. *"What's In a Name?".* Sacramento, Calif.: Keystone Press, 1949.

Goette, John. *Japan Fights for Asia*. New York: Harcourt, 1943.

Goetz, Albrecht, and Meek, Theophile J. *The Ancient Near East.* Princeton, N.J.: Princeton University Press, 1965.

Goetzmann, William H. *Army Exploration in the American West, 1803-1863.* New Haven, Conn.: Yale University Press, 1959.

_____. *Exploration and Empire: The Explorer and the Scientist in the winning of the American West.* New York: Alfred A. Knopf, 1966.

_____. *Exploring the American West, 1803-1879.* Washington: Division of Publications, National Park Service, U.S. Department of the Interior, 1966.

_____, and Sloan, Kay. *Looking Far North: The Harriman Expedition to Alaska, 1899.* New York: Viking, 1982.

_____. *New Lands, New Men: America and the Second Great Age of Discovery.* New York: Viking Penguin, 1986.

_____. *When the Eagle Screamed: The Romantic Horizon in American Diplomacy 1800-1860.* New York: John Wiley & Sons, 1966.

Goff, John S. *Robert Todd Lincoln.* Norman: University of Oklahoma Press, 1969.

Goff, Kenneth. *Crackpot or Crackshot.* Englewood, Colo.: Published by Author, 1965.

Goffman, Erving. *Asylums.* New York: Doubleday, 1961.

_____. *Encounters.* Indianapolis, Ind.: Bobbs-Merrill, 1961..

_____. *Essays on the Social Situation of Mental Patients and Other Inmates.* New York: Doubleday, 1961.

_____. *Frame Analysis.* New York: Harper & Row, 1974.

_____. *Interaction Ritual.* Garden City, N.Y.: Doubleday, 1967.

_____. *The Presentation of Self in Everyday Life.* Garden City, N.Y.: Doubleday, 1959.

_____. *Relations in Public.* New York: Basic Books, 1971.

_____. *Stigma.* Englewood Cliffs, N.J.: Prentice Hall, 1963.

_____. *Strategic Interaction.* Philadelphia: University of Pennsylvania Press, 1969.

Going, C.B. *David Wilmont Free Soiler.* New York: D. Appleton, 1924.

Gold, Gerald (ed.). *Watergate Tapes.* New York: Viking Press, 1973.

Gold, Mark S. *800-Cocaine.* New York: Bantam Books, 1984.

Gold, Martin. *Delinquent Behavior in an American City.* Belmont, Calif.: Brooks/Cole, 1970.

_____. *Deviant Behavior in an American City.* Belmont, Calif.: Brooks-Cole, 1970.

Gold, Victor. *PR as in President.* New York: Doubleday, 1977.

Goldberg, Alfred. *Conspiracy Interpretations of the Assassination of President Kennedy.* Los Angeles: University of California Security Studies Project, 1968.

Goldberg, B.Z. *The Sacred Fire.* New York: University Books, 1958.

Goldberg, Harvey. *American Radicals: Some Problems and Personalities.* New York: Monthly Review Press, 1957.

Goldberg, Isaac. *Queen of Hearts.* New York: Day, 1936.

Goldberg, Jacob A., and Rosamond W. *Girls of the City Streets.* New York: Foundation Books, 1940.

Goldberg, Robert Alan. *Hooded Empire.* Chicago: The University of Illinois Press, 1981.

Goldberg, S. *The Inevitability of Patriarchy.* New York: Morrow, 1973.

Golden, Harry. *A Little Girl Is Dead.* New York: World Publishing, 1965.

_____. *The Right Time: An Autobiography.* New York: G.P. Putnam's Sons, 1969.

Golden, Harry L. *Carl Sandburg.* Cleveland: World Publishing, 1961.

Golden, Hyman E., O'Leary, Frank, and Lipsius, Morris (eds.). *Dictionary of American Underworld Lingo.* New York: Citadel Press, 1962.

Golden, Sandy. *Driving The Drunk Off The Road.* Washington, D.C.: Acropolis Books, 1983.

Goldenberg, Boris. *The Cuban Revolution and Latin America.* New York: Frederick A. Praeger, 1965.

Golder, Frank A. (ed.). *Documents of Russian History, 1914-1917.* New York: Appleton Century Crofts, 1927.

_____. *Russian Expansion on the Pacific, 1641-1850.* London: Clark, 1914.

Goldfarb, Ronald L. *Jails: The Ultimate Ghetto.* Garden City, N.Y.: Anchor Press/Doubleday, 1975.

_____, and Singer, Linda R. *After Conviction.* New York: Simon & Schuster, 1973.

Goldman, Alex J. *John Fitzgerald Kennedy: The World Remembers.* New York: Fleet Press, 1968.

Goldman, E. *The Traffic in Women and Other Essays on Feminism.* Washington, D.C.: Times Change Press, 1970.

Goldman, Emma. *Anarchism and Other Essays.* New York: Mother Earth Publishing, 1911.

_____. *Living My Life.* New York: Alfred A. Knopf, 1931.

Goldman, Eric F. *The Crucial Decade.* New York: Alfred A. Knopf, 1956.

_____. *Rendezvous with Destiny: A History of Modern American Reform.* New York: Alfred A. Knopf, 1952.

_____. *The Tragedy of Lyndon Johnson.* New York: Alfred A. Knopf, 1969.

Goldman, Marion S. *A Portrait of the Black Attorney in Chicago.* Chicago: American Bar Foundation, 1972.

Goldman, Marshall. *Soviet Foreign Aid.* New York: Frederick A. Praeger, 1967.

Goldman, Nathan. *The Differential Selection of Juvenile Defenders for Court Appearance.* New York: National Council on Crime and Delinquency, 1963.

Goldmark, Josephine. *Democracy in Denmark.* Washington, D.C.: National Home Library Foundation, 1936.

Goldring, Douglas. *Odd Man Out: The Autobiography of a "Propaganda Novelist".* London: Chapman & Hall, 1935.

Goldsborough, William W. *The Maryland Line in the Confederate States Army.* Baltimore: Kelly, Piet, 1869.

Goldschmidt, Harvey, Mann, H. Michael, and Weston, Fred (eds.). *Industrial Concentration: The New Learning.* New York: Columbia University Press, 1974.

Goldschmidt, Richard. *The Mechanism and Physiology of Sex Determination.* trans. William J. Dakin. London: Methuen, 1923.

Goldsmith, Donald (ed.). *Scientists Confront Velikovsky.* Ithaca, N.Y.: Cornell University Press, 1977.

Goldsmith, Gloria. *Rape.* Beverly Hills, Calif.: Wollstonecraft, 1974.

Goldsmith, Jack and Sharon (eds.). *The Police Community.* Pacific Palisades, Calif. Palisades, 1974.

Goldsmith, Lewis. *Procés de Buonaparte.* Paris: J. Moronval, 1815.

Goldstein, Abraham S., and Joseph (eds.). *Crime, Law and Society.* New York: The Free Press, 1971.

_____. *The Insanity Defense.* New Haven, Conn.: Yale University Press, 1967.

Goldstein, Arnold P. *Police & The Elderly.* New York: Pergamon, 1980.

Goldstein, Herman. *Police Corruption: A Perspective on its Nature and Control.* Washington, D.C.: Police Foundation, 1975.

_____. *Policing a Free Society.* Cambridge, Mass.: Ballinger, 1977.

Goldstein, Jeffry H. *Aggression and Crimes of Violence.* New York: Oxford University Press, 1975.

Goldstein, Joseph, Freud, Anna, and Solnit, Albert J. *Beyond the Best Interests of the Child.* New York: The Free Press, 1973.

Goldstein, Michael J., and Kant, Harold S. *Pornography and Sexual Deviance: A Report of the Legal and Behavioral Institute, Beverly Hills, California.* Berkeley: University of California Press, 1973.

Goldstein, Robert J. *Political Repression in Modern America.* Cambridge, Mass.: Schenkman/Two Continents, 1978.

Goldstock, Ronald, and Coenan, Dan T. *Extortionate and Usuri-*

ous Credit Transactions: Background Materials. Ithaca, N.Y.: Cornell Institute on Organized Crime, 1978.

Goldston, Robert. *Satan's Disciples.* New York: Ballantine Books, 1962.

_____. *The Negro Revolution.* New York: Signet Books, New American Library, 1968.

Goldsworthy, D. *Tom Mboya: The Man Kenya Wanted to Forget.* London: William Heinemann, 1982.

Goldwyn, Samuel. *Behind the Screen.* New York: George H. Doran, 1923.

Gollmar, Judge Robert H. *Edward Gein: America's Most Bizarre Murderer.* Delavan, Wis.: Chas. Hallberg, 1981.

Gollomb, Joseph. *Crimes of the Year.* New York: Liveright, 1931.

_____. *Master Highwaymen.* New York: Macaulay, 1927.

Golovin, Ivan. *Stars and Stripes.* New York: D. Appleton, 1856.

Golovine, Nicholas. *The Russian Army in World War.* New Haven, Conn.: Yale University Press, 1931.

Gomez, Laureano. *El Cuadrilatero.* Bogota, Col.: Libreria Colombiana, 1935.

Gompers, Samuel. *The McNamara Case.* Washington, D.C.: American Federation of Labor, 1911.

_____. *Seventy Years of Life and Labor: An Autobiography.* 2 vols. New York: E.P. Dutton, 1925.

Gonella, Guido. *The Papacy and World Peace.* London: Hollis & Carter, 1945.

Gong, Eng Ying, and Grant, B. *Tong War.* Boston: Little, Brown, 1930.

Gonzalez Blanco, Andrés. *Un déspota y un libertador.* Madrid: Imprenta Helénica, 1916.

González Blanco, Edmundo. *Carranza y la Revolución de Mexico.* Madrid: Imprenta Helénica, 1916.

Gonzalez Blanco, Pedro. *De Porfirio Diaz a Carranza.* Madrid: Imprenta Helenica, 1916.

Gonzalez Garza, Federico. *El Testamento Politico de Madero.* Mexico City: Imprenta Victoria, 1921.

_____. *La Revolución Mexicana.* Mexico City: A. del Bosque, 1936.

_____. *La Revolución Politico-Literaria.* Mexico City: A. del Bosque, 1936.

Gonzalez, Manuel. *Contra Villa: Relatos de la campana de 1914-1915.* Mexico City: Botas, 1935.

Gonzalez Ramirez, Manuel. *La Revolución Social de México.* Mexico City: Fondo de Cultura Económica, 1960.

Gooch, George P. *Catherine the Great and Other Studies.* New York: Longmans, 1954.

_____. *Franco-German Relations, 1871-1914.* New York: Russell & Russell, 1923.

_____. *Frederick the Great: The Ruler, the Writer, the Man.* New York: Alfred A. Knopf, 1947.

_____. *Germany.* London: Ernest Benn, 1925.

_____. *Germany and the French Revolution.* New York: Russell & Russell, 1920.

_____. *History of Modern Europe.* New York: Henry Holt, 1923.

Good, Milton. *Twelve Years in a Texas Prison.* Amarillo, Texas: Russell Stationery, 1935.

Goode, E. (ed.). *Marijuana.* New York: Atherton Press, 1969.

Goode, Erich. *Deviant Behavior.* Englewood Cliffs, N.J.: Prentice-Hall, 1984.

_____. *The Drug Phenomenon: Social Aspects of Drug Taking.* New York: Bobbs-Merrill, 1973.

_____. *Drugs in American Society.* New York: Alfred A. Knopf, 1972.

_____. *The Marijuana Smokers.* New York: Basic Books, 1970.

Goode, Stephen. *Affluent Revolutionaries.* New York: Franklin Watts, 1974.

Goodell, Charles. *Political Prisoners in America.* New York: Random House, 1973.

Goodhart, Arthur L. *Five Jewish Lawyers of the Common Law.* London: Oxford University Press, 1949.

Goodhart, C.A.E. *The New York Money Market and the Finance of Trade, 1900-1913.* Cambridge, Mass.: Harvard University Press, 1969.

Goodman, Derick. *Crime of Passion.* New York: Greenberg, 1958.

_____. *Villainy Unlimited.* London: Elek Books, 1957.

Goodman, Edward J. *The Explorers of South America.* New York: Macmillan, 1972.

Goodman, Ezra. *The Fifty-Year Decline and Fall of Hollywood.* New York: Simon & Schuster, 1961.

Goodman, J.M. *POW.* New York: Exposition Press, 1972.

Goodman, Jonathon. *Bloody Versicles: The Rhymes of Crime.* Newton Abbot, Eng.: David & Charles, 1971.

_____. *The Burning of Evelyn Foster.* New York: Charles Scribner's Sons, 1977.

_____. *The Killing of Julia Wallace.* New York: Charles Scribner's Sons, 1969.

_____. *The Railway Murders.* London: Allison & Busby, 1984.

_____. *Posts-Mortem: The Correspondence of Murder.* New York: St. Martin's Press, 1971.

Goodman, Louis S., and Gilman, Alfred. *The Pharmacological Basis of Therapeutics.* New York: Macmillan, 1956.

Goodman, N., and Price, J. *Studies of Female Offenders.* London: Home Office Research Unit Report no. II, 1967.

Goodman, Nathan G. *Benjamin Rush: Physician and Citizen, 1746-1813.* Philadelphia: University of Pennsylvania Press, 1934.

Goodman, Ray. *The New Danish Constitution.* London: n.p., 1939.

Goodman, Walter. *All Honorable Men: Corruption and Compromise in American Life.* Boston: Little, Brown, 1963.

_____. *The Committee: the Extraordinary Career of the White House Committee on Un-American Activities.* New York: Farrar, Straus & Giroux, 1968.

Goodnow, Frank J., and Bates, Frank G. *Municipal Government.* New York: Century, 1919.

Goodrich, Charles Augustus. *The Land We Live In.* Cincinnati, Ohio: H.M. Rulison, 1857.

Goodrich, Frederick E. *Life of Winfield Scott Hancock.* Boston: B.B. Russell, 1886.

Goodsmith, Elliott S. *The Story of a Forty-Niner.* Chicago: n.p., 1930.

Goodspeed, E.J. *A Full History of the Wonderful Career of Moody Sankey.* New York: Henry S. Goodspeed, 1876.

_____. *History of the Great Fire in Chicago and the West.* New York: Published by Author, 1871.

Goodspeed, Thomas Wakefield. *A History of the University of Chicago.* Chicago: University of Chicago, 1916.

_____. *Story of the University of Chicago.* Chicago: University of Chicago Press, 1925.

_____. *University of Chicago Biographical Sketches.* Chicago: University of Chicago Press, 1922.

Goodspeed, Westin Arthur, and Healy, Daniel D. (eds.). *History of Cook County Illinois.* Chicago: Goodspeed Historical Association, 1909.

_____. *The Province and the States.* Madison, Wis.: Western Historical Association, 1904.

Goodstone, Tony (ed.). *The Pulps.* New York: Chelsea House, 1970.

Goodwin, Cardinal. *The Trans-Mississippi West.* New York: D. Appleton, 1927.

Goodwin, D.W. *Is Alchoholism Hereditary?* New York: Oxford University Press, 1976.

Goodwin, Jean, et al. *Sexual Abuse.* Boston: John Wright, 1982.

Goodwin, John G. *Insanity and the Criminal.* London: Hutchinson, 1923.

Goodwin, Leonard. *Do the Poor Want to Work?.* Washington, D.C.: Brookings Institution, 1972.

Goodwin, Nat C. *Nat Goodwin's Book.* Boston: Richard G. Badger, 1914.

Goodwin, Ralph. *Passport to Eternity*. London: Arthur Barker, 1956.

Goodwin, William B. *The Truth About Leif Ericsson and the Greenland Voyages*. Boston: Meador, 1941.

Goodykoontz, Colin B. *Home Missions on the American Frontier*. Caldwell, Idaho: Caxton, 1939.

Goplen, Arnold O. *The Career of the Marquis de Mores in the Badlands of North Dakota*. Bismarck: State Historical Society of North Dakota, 1946.

Gora, Joel. *The Rights of Reporters*. New York: Discus, Avon, 1974.

Goran, Morris. *Fact, Fraud and Fantasy: The Occult and Pseudo-sciences*. New York: A.S. Barnes, 1979.

Gordeaux, Paul. *Le Docteur Petiot*. Paris: Editions J'ai lu, 1970.

Gordon, Alexander. *The Lives of Pope Alexander VI and his Son Caesar Borgia*. 2 vols. London: C. Davis & T. Green, 1929.

Gordon, Anna A. *The Beautiful Life of Frances Willard*. Chicago: Woman's Temperance Association, 1898.

Gordon, B.L. *Medicine throughout Antiquity*. Philadelphia: T.A. Davis, 1949.

Gordon, Charles. *The Old Bailey and Newgate*. London: T. Fisher Unwin, 1903.

Gordon, Daniel N. (ed.). *Social Change and Urban Politics: Readings*. Englewood Cliffs, N.J.: Prentice-Hall, 1973.

Gordon, David F. *Decolonization and the State in Kenya*. Boulder, Colo.: Westview, 1986.

Gordon, David M., Edwards, Richard, and Reich, Michael. *Segmented Work, Divided Workers*. New York: Cambridge University Press, 1982.

Gordon, Ernest. *The Maine Law*. New York: Fleming H. Revell, 1919.

_____. *Through the Valley of the Kwai*. New York: Harper & Brothers, 1962.

_____. *When the Brewer Had the Stranglehold*. New York: Alcohol Information Committee, 1930.

_____. *The Wrecking of the 18th Amendment*. Francestown, N.H.: Alcohol Information Press, 1943.

Gordon, Harold J. *The Austrian Empire, Abortive Federation?* Lexington, Mass.: D.C. Heath, 1974.

_____. *The Reichswehr and the German Republic*. London: Oxford University Press, 1947.

Gordon, John J. *Unmasked*. New York: Self-Published, 1924.

Gordon, Manya. *How to Tell Progress From Reaction*. New York: E.P. Dutton, 1944.

_____. *Workers Before and After Lenin*. New York: Macmillan, 1948.

Gordon, Max. *Max Gordon Presents*. New York: Bernard Geis Associates, 1963.

Gordon, Mike. *I Arrest Pearl Starr, and Other Stories of Adventure as a Policeman in Fort Smith, Arkansas, for 40 Years*. Fort Smith, Ark.: Press-Atgus, 1958.

Gordon, R.A. *Proceedings of the II International Sympsium on Criminology*. San Paulo, Braz.: International Center for Biological and Medico-forensic Criminology, 1975.

Gordon, Rosalie. *Nine Men Against America*. New York: Devon-Adair, 1958.

Gordon, Ruth. *Over Twenty-one*. New York: Random House, 1944.

Gordon, S. *Recollections of Old Milestown*. Miles City, Mont.: Independent Printing, 1918.

Gordon, Welche. *Jesse James and His Band of Notorious Outlaws*. Chicago: Laird & Lee, 1891.

Gordon, Wendell C. *The Expropriation of Foreign-Owned Property in Mexico*. Washington, D.C.: American Council on Public Affairs, 1941.

Gordon, Mrs. Will. *Roumania Yesterday and Today*. London: John Lane, The Bodley Head, 1919.

Gore, John. *King George V*. London: John Murray, 1941.

Gore, Leroy. *Joe Must Go*. New York: Julian Messner, 1954.

Gore-Booth, Eva. *The Death of Finovar from the Triumph of Maeve*. London: Erskine MacDonald, 1916.

Goren, Arthur A. *New York Jews and the Quest for Community*. New York: Columbia University Press, 1970.

Gorer, G. *The Life and Ideas of the Marquis de Sade*. London: Peter Owen, 1953.

Gorer, Geoffrey. *Himalayan Village*. London: Michael Joseph, 1938.

_____, and Rickman, John. *The People of Great Russia: A Psychological Study*. New York: W.W. Norton, 1962.

Gores, Joe. *Hammett*. New York: G.P. Putnam's Sons, 1975.

Goriachkin, F.T. *Pervy Russky Fashist: Pyotor Arkadievich Stolypin*. Harbin, U.S.S.R.: Merkury, 1928.

Goring, Charles. *The English Convict*. London: H.M. Stationery Office, 1913.

Gorky, Maxim. *Days with Lenin*. trans. V.I. Lenin. New York: International Publishers, 1932.

Görlitz, Walter, and Quint, Herbert A. *Adolf Hitler. Eine Biographie*. Stuttgart, Ger.: Steingruben Verlag GmbH, 1952.

_____. *Generalfeldmarschall Keitel. Verbrecher oder Offizier?* Berlin: Musterschmidt, 1961.

_____. *Die Waffen-SS*. Berlin: Arani, 1960.

Gorman, Harry M. *My Memoires of the Comstock*. New York: Sutton-House, 1939.

Gorman, Joseph Bruce. *Kefauver: a Political Biography*. New York: Oxford University Press, 1971.

Gornick, V., and Moran, B.K. (eds.). *Woman in Sexist Society*. New York: Basic Books, 1971.

Gorresio, Vittorio. *Un anno di libertà*. Rome: OET, 1945.

Gorz, André. *Socialism and Revolution*. New York: Doubleday, 1973.

_____. *Strategy for Labor: A Radical Proposal*. Boston: Beacon Press, 1967.

Gosch, Martin A., and Hammer, Richard. *The Last Testament of Lucky Luciano*. Boston: Little, Brown, 1974.

Gosling, John, and Craig, Dennis. *The Great Train Robbery*. Indianapolis, Ind.: Bobbs Merrill, 1964.

_____, and Warner, Douglas. *The Shame of a City*. London: W.H. Allen, 1960.

Gosnell, H. Allen. *Guns on the Western Waters*. Baton Rouge, La.: Louisiana State University Press, 1949.

Gosnell, Harold F. *Boss Platt and His New York Machine*. Chicago: F. Mendelsohn, 1933.

_____. *Machine Politics: The Chicago Model*. Chicago: F. Mendelsohn, 1937.

_____. *Negro Politicians: The Rise of Negro Politics in Chicago*. Chicago: University of Chicago Press, 1967.

Goss, Helen Rocca. *The Life and Death of a Quicksilver Mine*. Los Angeles: Historical Society of Southern California, 1958.

Gosse, Philip. *The History of Piracy*. New York: Longmans, Green, 1932.

_____. *The Pirates' Who's Who*. Boston: E. Lauriat, 1924.

Gosset, Pierre, and Gosset, Renée. *Adolph Hitler*. Paris: Juillard, 1961.

Gossett, Thomas F. *Race: The History of an Idea in America*. New York: Schocken Books, 1965.

Gotlieb, Alan M. *The Rights of Gun Owners*. Aurora, Ill.: Caroline House, 1981.

Goto Takao. *Koria Uochiya (Korea Watcher)*. Tokyo: Gendai no Rironsha, 1982.

Gott, Richard. *Guerrilla Movements in Latin America*. Garden City, N.Y.: Doubleday, 1971.

Gottfredson, Don M., Wilkins, Leslie T., and Hoffman, Peter B. *Parole Decision Making*. Washington, D.C.: National Institute of Law Enforcement and Criminal Justice, 1973.

Gottfried, Alex. *Boss Cermak of Chicago*. Seattle, Wash.: University of Washington Press, 1962.

Gottlieb, Gerald H. *Capital Punishment*. Santa Barbara, Calif.: Center for the Study of Democratic Insitutions, 1967.

Gottman, John, et al. *A Couple's Guide to Communication.* Champaign, Ill.: Research Press, 1976.

Gottschalk, Louis Moreau. *Notes of a Pianist.* Philadelphia: J.B. Lippincott, 1881.

Goubert, Pierre. *Louis XIV and the Twenty Million Frenchmen.* New York: Random House, 1972.

Gough, Barry. *The Royal Navy and the Northwest Coast of North America.* Vancouver: University of British Columbia Press, 1971.

Gough, John B. *Platform Echoes: or, Living Truths for Head and Heart.* Hartford, Conn.: A.D. Worthington, 1886.
_____. *Sunlight and Shadow, or Gleanings From my Life Work.* Hartford, Conn.: A.D. Worthington, 1881.

Gough, William Charles. *From Kew Observatory to Scotland Yard.* London: Hurst & Blackett, 1927.

Goulart, Ron. *An Informal History of the Pulp Magazine.* New York: Ace Books, 1972.
_____. *Line Up, Tough Guys.* Nashville, Tenn.: Sherbourne Press, 1966.

Gould, E.W. *Fifty Years on the Mississippi.* St. Louis, Mo.: Nixon-Jones, 1889.

Gould, Leroy C., and Walker, Andrew L., and Crane, Lansing E. *Connections: Notes from the Heroin World.* New Haven, Conn.: Yale University Press, 1974.
_____, et al. *Crime as a Profession.* Washington, D.C.: Final Report to the Office of Law Enforcement Assistance and President's Commission on Law Enforcement and Administration of Justice, 1967.

Gould, Leslie. *The Manipulators.* New York: David McKay, 1966.

Gould, Rupert T. *Enigmas.* New York: University Books, 1965.

Gould, S.J. *The Mismeasure of Man.* New York: W.W. Norton, 1981.

Goulden, Joseph C. *The Benchwarmers: The Private World of thePowerful Federal Judges.* New York: Ballantine, 1974.
_____. *The Best Years, 1945-1950.* New York: Atheneum, 1976.
_____. *Million Dollar Lawyers.* New York: G.P. Putnam's Sons, 1978.
_____. *The Superlawyers.* New York: Weybright & Talley, 1972.

Goulder, W.A. *Reminiscences of a Pioneer.* Boise, Idaho: Timothy Regan, 1909.

Gouldner, Alvin W. *The Coming Crisis of Western Sociology.* London: Heinemann Educational, 1971.
_____. *Patterns of Industrial Bureaucracy.* New York: Free Press, 1954.

Gourgaud, Général. *Journal de Sainte-Hélène, 1815-1818.* Paris, Flammarion, 1947.

Gourko, Basil. *War and Revolution in Russia, 1914-1917.* New York: Macmillan, 1919.

Gourko, Vladimir. *Features and Figures of the Past.* Palo Alto, Calif.: Stanford University Press, 1939.

Gourley, Douglas. *Public Relations and the Police.* Springfield, Ill.: Charles C. Thomas, 1953.

Gourley, G. Douglas., and Bristow, Allen P. *Patrol Administration.* Springfield, Ill.: Charles C. Thomas, 1967.

Govan, T.P. *Nicholas Biddle: Nationalist and Public Banker 1786-1844.* Chicago: University of Chicago Press, 1959.

Government of India. *Congress Responsibility for the Disturbances (1942-1943).* New Delhi: Government of India, 1943.
_____. *Gandhian Outlook and Techniques.* New Delhi: Government of India, 1953.
_____. *Homage to Gandhi.* New Delhi: Government of India, 1948.

Governor's Commission on the Los Angeles Riots. *Watts Report: Violence in the City-An End of a Beginning.* Los Angeles: Published by Author, 1965.

Gower, Lord Ronald. *Joan of Arc.* London: J.C. Nimmo, 1893.

Gowers, Sir Ernest. *A Life for a Life.* London: Chatto & Windus, 1956.

Grace, Clive, and Wilkinson, Philip. *Negotiating the Law.* London: Routledge, 1978.

Gradet, Roger. *Images du Far-west.* n.p., 1936.

Grady, Henry F., and Carr, Robert M. *The Port of San Francisco.* Berkeley: University of California Press, 1934.

Graebner, N.A. *Empire on the Pacific.* New York: Ronald, 1955.

Graf, Arturo. *Il Diavolo.* Milan, Italy: Fratelli Treves, 1890
_____. *Geschichte des Terfelsglaubens.* trans. R. Teuscher. Jena: Costenoble, 1893.
_____. *The Story of the Devil.* trans. Edward Noble Stone. New York: MacMillan, 1931.

Graff, Henry F. (ed.). *Bluejackets with Perry in Japan.* New York: New York Public Library, 1952.

Graham, Evelyn. *Fifty Years of Famous Judges.* London: John Long, 1930.
_____. *Lord Darling and His Famous Trials.* London: John Long, 1953.

Graham, Fred P. *The Alias Program.* Boston: Little, Brown, 1978.
_____. *The Self-Inflicted Wound.* New York: Dell, 1972.

Graham, Hugh D., and Gurr, Ted Robert. *The History of Violence in America: A Report to the National Commission on the Causes and Prevention of Violence.* New York: Bantam Books, 1969.
_____(ed.). *Huey Long.* Englewood Cliffs, N.J.: Prentice-Hall, 1970.
_____, and Gurr, Ted Robert. *Violence in America: Historical and Comparitive Perspective.* A Report to the National Commission on the Causes and Prevention of Violence. Washington, D.C.: U.S. Government Printing Office, 1969.

Graham, I.C.C. *Colonists from Scotland: Emigration to North America 1707-1783.* Ithaca, N.Y.: Cornell University Press, 1956.

Graham, Jean. *Tales of the Ozark River Country.* Clinton, Mo.: Press of Martin Printing, 1929.

Graham, Jory. *Chicago, an Extraordinary Guide.* Chicago: Rand McNally, 1967.

Graham, Lloyd. *Niagra Country.* New York: Duell, Sloan & Pearce, 1949.

Graham, Loren R. *The Soviet Acadamy of Sciences and the Communist Party, 1927-1932.* Princeton, N.J.: Princeton University Press, 1967.

Graham, Matthew J. *The Ninth Regiment New York Volunteers (Hawkins Hawk' Zouaves) being a History of the Regiment and Veteran Association from 1860 to 1900.* New York: E.P. Colby, 1900.

Graham, Philip. *Showboats: The History of an American Institution.* Austin: University of Texas Press, 1951.

Graham, Stephen. *Alexander of Yugoslavia.* New Haven, Conn.: Yale University Press, 1939.
_____. *New York Nights.* New York: G.H. Doran, 1927.
_____. *Peter the Great.* London: Benn, 1929.
_____. *St. Vitus' Day.* New York: D. Appleton, 1931.
_____. *Tsar of Freedom: Life and Reign of Alexander II.* New Haven, Conn.: Yale University Press, 1935.

Graham, Sylvester. *Lecture to Young Men.* Providence, R.I.: Weeden & Cory, 1834.

Graham-Mulhall, Sara. *Opium: The Demon Flower.* New York: Harold Vinal, 1926.

The Graham Tragedy and the Molloy-Lee Examination: The Only Authentic History of the Murder of Sarah Graham by Her Husband, George E. Graham. Springfield, Mo.: Ozark, 1886.

Gramling, Oliver. *AP: The Story of the News.* New York: Farrar & Rinehart, 1940.

Gramont, Sanche de. *The Secret War.* New York: G.P. Putnam's Sons, 1962.

Granding, Mme. Léon. *Impressions d'une Parisienne à Chicago.* Paris: E. Flammarion, 1894.

Granet, Marcel. *Chinese Civilization.* New York: Meridian Books, 1958.

Granier, Camille. *La Femme criminelle.* Paris: Doin, 1906.

Granlund, Nils T. *Blondes, Brunettes and Bullets.* New York: David McKay, 1957.

Grant, Bruce. *The Cowboy Encyclopedia.* New York: Rand McNally, 1951.

Grant, C.S. *Democracy on the Connecticut Frontier Town of Kent.* New York: Columbia University Press, 1961.

Grant, Frederick C., and Rowley, H.H. (eds.). *Dictionary of the Bible.* New York: Charles Scribner's Sons, 1963.

Grant, Hamil. *Spies and Secret Service.* New York: Frederick A. Stokes, 1915.

Grant, Jack. *Trail Dust and Gun Smoke: Factual Stories of a Cowboy's Life.* New York: Vantage Press, 1965.

Grant, Jesse R. *In the Days of My Father, General Grant.* New York: Harper & Brothers, 1925.

Grant, Joanne. *Black Protest.* Greenwich, Conn.: Fawcett, 1968.

Grant, Joseph D. *Redwoods and Reminiscences.* San Fransisco: Save the Redwoods League & the Menninger Foundation, 1973.

Grant, Julia Dent. *The Personal Memoirs of...* New York: G.P. Putnam's Sons, 1975.

Grant, Madison, and Davison, Charles S. (eds.). *The Alien in Our Midst: Or Selling Our Birthright for a Mess of Pottage.* New York: Galton, 1930.

Grant, Michael. *The Jews in the Roman World.* London: Weidenfeld & Nicolson, 1973.

_____. *The World of Rome.* New York: Mentor, 1960.

Grant, Robert. *The Convictions of a Grandfather.* New York: Charles Scribner's Sons, 1912.

Grant, Ulysses S. *Personal Memoirs.* 2 vols. New York: Charles L. Webster, 1885.

Graper, Elmer D. *American Police Administration.* Montclair, N.J.: Patterson Smith, 1969.

Grässe, Johann George Theodor. *Bibliotheca Magica et Pneumatica.* Leipzig: W. Englemann, 1843.

_____. *Trésor de livres rare.* New York: S. Hacker, 1951.

Grasso, Franco (ed.). *Girolamo Li Causi e la sua azione politica per la Sicilia.* Palermo, Italy: Libri Siciliani, 1966.

Gratacap, Louis Pope. *The Political Mission of Tammany Hall.* New York: A.B. King, 1894.

Grathwohl, Larry. *Bringing Down America.* New Rochelle, N.Y.: Arlington House, 1976.

Grattan, Hartley. *Introducing Australia.* New York: John Day, 1942.

Gravel, Senator Mike (ed.). *The Pentagon Papers.* Boston: Beacon Press, 1971.

Gravelli, Asvero. *Mussolini Aneddotico.* Rome: Latinità, 1951.

_____. *I canti della rivoluzione.* Rome: Nuova Europa, 1926.

_____ (ed.). *Marcia su Roma.* Rome: Nuova Europa, 1934.

Graves, Charles. *None But the Rich.* London: Cassell, 1963.

_____. *Royal Riviera.* London: William Heinemann, 1957.

Graves, Richard. *Experiment in Anarchy.* London: Victor Gollancz, 1949.

Graves, Richard S. *Oklahoma Outlaws.* Fort Davis, Texas: Frontier Books, 1968.

Graves, Robert. *They Hanged My Saintly Billy; the Life and Death of Dr. William Palmer.* New York: Doubleday, 1957.

_____. *The Twelve Caesars.* Baltimore: Penguin Books, 1957.

Graves, Robert, and Hodge, Alan. *The Long Week-End: A Social History of Great Britain, 1918-1939.* London: Faber & Faber, 1940.

Graves, Sally. *A History of Socialism.* London: Hogarth Press, 1939.

Graves, W.W. *Life and Letters of Rev. Father John Shoemaker.* St. Paul, Kan.: Commercial, 1928.

Gray, Albert (ed.). *The Voyage of François Pyrard.* London: Hakluyt Society, 1887.

Gray, Alexander. *The Socialist Tradition.* London: Longmans, 1946.

Gray, Arthur Amos. *Men Who Built the West.* Caldwell, Idaho: Caxton Printers, 1945.

Gray, F.C. *Prison Discipline in America.* London: John Murray, 1848.

Gray, Frank S. *Pioneering in Southwest Texas.* Austin, Texas: Steck, 1949.

Gray, James H. *The Roar of the Twenties.* Toronto, Ontario, Can.: Macmillan, 1975.

_____. *The Winter Years.* Toronto, Ontario, Can.: Macmillan, 1966.

Gray, L.C. *History of Agriculture in the Southern United States.* Gloucester, Mass.: Peter Smith, 1958.

Gray, Robert K. *Eighteen Acres Under Glass.* Garden City, N.Y.: Doubleday, 1962.

Gray, Wood. *The Hidden Civil War.* New York: Viking Press, 1942.

Graybar, Lloyd J. *Albert Shaw of the Review of Reviews.* Lexington: University of Kentucky Press, 1974.

Grayson, Admiral Cary Travers. *Woodrow Wilson: An Intimate Memoir.* New York: Holt, Rinehart & Winston, 1960.

Grazia, Alfred de. *The Western Public, 1952 and Beyond.* Stanford, Calif.: Stanford University Press, 1954.

Graziani, Marshal Rodolfo. *Graziani.* Rome: Rivista Romana, 1956.

_____. *Ho difeso la patria.* Milan, Italy: Garzanti, 1948.

_____. *Processo Graziani.* Rome: Ruffolo, 1948.

_____. *Il fronte sud.* Milan, Italy: Mondadori, 1938.

Grazzi, Emanuele. *Il principio della fine.* Rome: Faro, 1945.

Great Britain. *Report...Together With the Proceedings...and the Minutes of Evidence, Taken Before the Select Committee. 1929-1930.* London: H.M. Stationery Office, 1931.

Great Britain, Home Office. *The Length of Prison Sentences: Interim Report of the Advisory Council on the Penal System.* London: H.M. Stationary Office, 1977.

_____. *A Review of Criminal Justice Policy 1976.* London: H.M. Stationary Office, 1977.

_____. *The Sentence of the Court: A Handbook for Courts on the Treatment of Criminal Offenders.* London: H.M. Stationary Office, 1964.

Great Britain, Royal Commission on Capital Punishment. *Report, Together With the Minutes of Evidence and Appendix.* London: H.M. Stationery Office, 1866.

_____. *Minutes of Evidence.* London: H.M. Stationery Office, 1949-1951.

_____. *Report.* London: H.M. Stationery Office, 1953.

The Great Guiteau Trial. Philadelphia: Barclay, 1882.

The Great Impeachment and Trial of Andrew Johnson, President of the United States. Philadelphia: J.B. Peterson & Brothers, 1868.

The Great Murder Trial of Lindsey Gibson in Western Arkansas. Alma, Ark.: Alma Book, 1981.

Great Palace of the Byzantine Emperors: Being A First Report on the Excavations Carried Out in Istanbul, 1935-1938. London, Oxford University Press, 1947.

Great True Stories of Crime, Mystery and Detection. Pleasantville, N.Y.: Reader's Digest Association, 1965.

The Great Trunk Mystery of New York. Philadelphia: Barclay, 1871.

Greaves, C. Desmond. *The Life and Times of James Connolly.* London: Lawrence & Wishart, 1961.

Grebstein, Sheldon Norman. *Monkey Trial: The State of Tennessee vs. John Thomas Scopes.* Boston: Houghton Mifflin, 1960.

Greco, Eugenio. *Il Ministro Alverto de'Stefani.* Milan, Italy: Ceschina, 1959.

The Greek Anthology. trans. W.R. Paton. Cambridge, Mass.: Harvard University Press, 1918.

Greeley, Gene. *Bankers and Cattlemen.* New York: Alfred A. Knopf, 1966.

Greeley, Horace. *The American Conflict.* Hartford, Conn.: O.D. Case, 1864.

_____. *Greeley on Lincoln.* New York: Baker & Taylor, 1893.

_____. *Hints Toward Reforms.* New York: Fowler & Wells, 1853.

_____. *An Overland Journey from New York to San Francisco in the Summer of 1859.* New York: C.M. Saxon, Barker, 1860.

_____. *Recollections of a Busy Life.* New York: J.B. Ford, 1868.

Greely, Maj. Gen. Adolphus W. *Earthquake in California, April 18, 1906, Special Report....* Washington, D.C.: U.S. Government Printing Office, 1906.

Green, Alice Sophie Amelia. *Ourselves Alone in Ulster.* Dublin, Ire.: Maunsel, 1918.

Green, Abel, and Lauri, Joe, Jr. *Show Biz: From Vaude to Video.* New York: Henry Holt, 1951.

Green, Adwin Wigfall. *The Man Bilbo.* Baton Rouge: Louisiana State University Press, 1963.

Green, Celia. *Out-of-the-Body Experiences.* New York: Ballantine, 1973.

Green, Constance McLaughlin. *Washington: Capital City, 1879-1950.* Princeton, N.J.: Princeton University Press, 1963.

_____. *Washington: Village and Capitol, 1800-1878.* Princeton, N.J.: Princeton University Press, 1962.

Green, E. *Psychology for Law Enforcement.* New York: John Wiley & Sons, 1976.

Green, Edward. *Judicial Attitudes in Sentencing.* London: Macmillan, 1961.

Green, Gil. *Cold War Fugitive.* New York: International, 1984.

Green, J.H. *Gambling Unmasked! or The Personal Experience of J. H. Green, the Reformed Gambler.* Philadelphia: Privately Published, 1847.

_____. *Report of Gambling in New York.* New York: Privately Published, 1851.

_____. *The Secret Band of Brothers; or The American Outlaws.* Philadelphia: Privately published, 1847.

Green, Jonathon. *The Directory of Infamy: The Best of the Worst.* London: Mills and Boon, 1980.

Green, Mark J., and Moore, B., and Wasserstein, B. *The Closed Enterprise System.* New York: Grossman, 1972.

_____., et al. *The Monopoly Makers.* New York: Grossman, 1973.

_____. *The Other Government: The Unseen Power of Washington Lawyers.* New York: Grossman, 1975.

_____. *Who Runs Congress.* New York: Bantam/Grossman Book, 1972.

Green, Paul D. *Fabulous Freddie and the Saints and Sinners.* New York: Wilfred Funk, 1951.

Green, Robert L. *The Urban Challenge-Poverty and Race.* Chicago: Follet Publishing, 1977.

Green, Samuel Abbot. *Groton in the Witchcraft Times.* Groton, Mass.: J. Wilson & Son, 1883.

Green, Stanley. *Ring Bells, Sing Songs.* New Rochelle, N.Y.: Arlington House, 1971.

_____. *The World of Musical Comedy.* New York: A.S. Barnes, 1974.

Green, Thomas J. *Journal of the Texian Expedition against Mier.* New York: Harper & Brothers, 1845.

Green, V.H.H. *Medieval Civilization in Western Europe.* New York: St. Martin's Press, 1971.

Greenberg, Bradley S., and Parker, Edwin B. (eds.). *The Kennedy Assassination and the American Public: Social Communication in Crisis.* Stanford, Calif.: Stanford University Press, 1965.

Greenberg, David F. *Crime and Capitalism.* Palo Alto, Calif.: Mayfield, 1981.

_____. (ed.). *Corrections and Punishment.* Beverly Hills, Calif.: Sage, 1977.

Greenberg, Edward S. *Serving the Few: Corporate Capitalism and the Bias of Government Policy.* New York: John Wiley & Sons, 1974.

Greenberg, J., and Cohen, R.L. (eds.). *Equity and Justice in Social Behavior.* New York: Academic Press.

Greenberg, Michael. *British Trade and the Opening of China 1800-1842.* Cambridge, Eng.: Cambridge University Press, 1951.

Greenberg, Norman. *The Man with a Steel Guitar: Portrait of Desperation, and Crime.* Hoover, N.H.: University Press of New England, 1981.

Greenberger, Richard. *Red Rising in Bavaria.* New York: St. Martin's Press, 1973.

Greenbie, Marjorie Barstow. *Lincoln's Daughters of Mercy.* New York: G.P. Putnam's Sons, 1944.

Greene, A.C. *The Santa Claus Bank Robbery.* New York: Alfred A. Knopf, 1972.

Greene, E.B. *The Revolutionary Generation 1763-1790.* New York: Macmillan, 1943.

Greene, Felix. *China: The Country Americans Are Not Allowed to Know.* New York: Ballantine Books, 1962.

Greene, Francis Vinton. *Nathanael Greene.* New York: D. Appleton, 1893.

Greene, George Washington. *Nathanael Greene.* Boston: Houghton Mifflin, 1900.

Greene, Capt. Jonathan H. *A Desperado in Arizona, 1858-1860.* Santa Fe, N.M.: Stagecoach, 1964.

Greene, Laurence. *America Goes to Press, The News of Yesterday.* Indianapolis, Ind.: Bobbs Merrill, 1936.

_____. *The Era of Wonderful Nonsense: A Casebook of the 'Twenties.* Indianapolis, Ind.: Bobbs Merrill, 1939.

Greene, Mark H., Kozel, Nicholas J., and Hunt, Leon G. *An Assessment of the Diffusion of Heroin Abuse to Medium Sized American Cities.* Washington, D.C.: U.S. Government Printing Office, 1974.

Greene, Nathanael. *European Socialism Since World War I.* Chicago: Quadrangle Books, 1971.

Greene, Robert W. *The Sting Man.* New York: E.P. Dutton, 1981.

Greenhaw, Wayne. *Flying High.* New York: Dodd, Mead, 1984.

_____. *Watch Out for George Wallace.* Englewood Cliffs, N.J.: Prentice-Hall, 1976.

Greenhow, Rose O'Neil. *My Imprisonment and the First Year of Abolition Rule at Washington.* London: R. Bentley, 1863.

Greeno, Edward. *War On the Underworld.* London: John Long, 1960.

Greenslet, Ferris. *Joseph Glanvill.* New York: Columbia University Press, 1900.

Greenstone, James L., and Leviton, Sharon. *Hotline Crisis Intervention Directory.* New York: Facts on File, 1981.

Greenwald, Dr. Harold. *The Call Girl: A Social and Psycho-analytic Study.* New York: Ballantine, 1958.

_____. *The Elegant Prostitute.* New York: Walker, 1970.

_____. (ed.). *The Prostitute in Literature.* New York: Ballantine, 1960.

Greenwall, Harry J. *Mediterranean Crisis.* London: Nicholson & Watson, 1939.

_____. *They Were Murdered in France.* London: Jarrolds, 1957.

Greenwood, Arthur. *Why We Fight Labor's Case.* London: Routledge, 1940.

Greenwood, Colin. *Police Tactics in Armed Operations.* Boulder, Colo.: Paladin Press, 1979.

Greenwood, Grace. *New Life in New Lands.* New York: J.B. Ford, 1873.

Greenwood, James. *The Seven Curses of London.* London: Stanley Rivers, 1869.

Greenwood, Peter W. *An Analysis of the Apprehension Activities of the New York City Police Department.* New York: New York City Rand Institute, 1970.

_____, et al. *The Criminal Investigation Process, Observations and Analysis.* Santa Monica, Calif.: Rand, 1975.

_____, et al. *Prosecution of Adult Felony Defendants in Los Angeles County: A Policy Perspective.* Washington, D.C.: Law Enforcement Assistance Administration, 1973.

_____. *Selective Incapacitation.* Santa Monica, Calif.: Rand, 1982.

Greenwood, Robert. *The California Outlaw, Tiburcio Vásquez.* Los Gatos, Calif.: Talisman Press, 1960.

Greenwood, Thomas. *A Tour in the States and Canada.* London: L.U. Gill, 1883.

Greenwood, William. *Guilty or Not Guilty*. London: Hutchinson, 1931.

Greenwood, William. *Curia Comitatus Rediviva*. London: John & William Place, 1657.

Greenya, John. *Blood Relations*. New York: Harcourt Brace Jovanovich, 1987.

Greer, Donald. *The Incidence of the Terror During the French Revolution*. Cambridge, Mass.: Harvard University Press, 1935.

Greer, Germaine. *The Female Eunich*. New York: McGraw-Hill, 1971.

Greer, James K. *Grand Prairie*. Dallas, Texas: Tardy, 1935.

Greer, James Kimmins. *Bois d'arc to Barb'd Wire; Ken Carey: Southwestern Frontier Born*. Dallas, Texas: Dealey & Lowe, 1936.

_____ (ed.). *Buck Barry: A Texas Ranger and Frontiersman*. Dallas, Texas: Southwest Press, 1932.

_____ . *Colonel Jack Hays: Texas Frontier Leader and California Builder*. New York: E.P. Dutton, 1952.

Greever, William S. *The Bonanza West: The Story of the Western Mining Rushes, 1848-1900*. Norman: University of Oklahoma Press, 1963.

Gregg, Andrew K. *New Mexico in the Nineteenth Century: A Pictorial History*. Albuquerque: University of New Mexico Press, 1968.

Gregg, Andy. *Drums of Yesterday: The Forts of New Mexico*. Santa Fe, N.M.: Press of the Territorian, 1968.

Gregg, Jacob Ray. *Pioneer Days in Malheur County*. Los Angeles: Lorrin L. Morrison, 1950.

Gregg, Josiah. *The Commerce of the Prairies*. Lincoln: University of Nebraska, 1967.

Gregg, Kate L. (ed.). *The Road to Santa Fe*. Albuquerque: University of New Mexico Press, 1952.

Gregg, Richard B. *A Discipline for Non-violence*. Ahmedabad, India: Navajivan, 1941.

Gregor, A. James. *The Fascist Persuasion in Radical Politics*. Princeton, N.J.: Princeton University Press, 1974.

Gregorie, Anne King. *Thomas Sumter*. Columbia, S.C.: R.L. Bryan, 1931.

Gregorovius, Ferdinand. *History of the City of Rome in the Middle Ages*. trans. Mrs. Gustavus W. Hamilton. London: G. Bell, 1903-12.

_____ . *Lucrèce Borgia*. Paris: Sandoz et Fischbacher, 1876.

_____ . *Lucretia Borgia*. trans. John Leslie Garner. New York: D. Appleton, 1903.

Gregory, Charles O., and Katz, Harold A. *Labor and the Law*. New York: London: Norton, 1979.

Gregory, J.D. *Dollfuss and His Times*. London: Hutchinson, 1935.

Gregory, Lester. *True Wild West Stories*. London: Andrew Dakers, n.d.

Gregory of Tours. *History of the Franks*. trans. Ernest Brehaut. New York: W.W. Norton, 1969.

Gregory of Tours. *The History of the Franks*. trans. O.M. Dalton. Oxford, Eng.: Clarendon Press, 1937.

Gregory, R. *Concepts and Mechanisms of Perception*. London: Duckworth, 1974.

Greiner, Helmuth. *Die Oberste Wehrmachführung 1939-1943*. Wiesbaden, Ger.: Limes, 1951.

Greiner, Josef. *Das Ende des Hitler-Mythos*. Zürich, Switz.: Amalthea Verlag, 1947.

Grellin, Richard. *J'Accuse*. New York: Doran, 1915.

Grenfell, Russell. *Main Fleet to Singapore*. London: Faber & Faber, 1951.

Gresham, Otto. *The Greenbacks*. Chicago: Book Press, 1927.

Greven, Philip. *Four Generations*. Ithaca, N.Y.: Cornell University Press, 1970.

Greville, Charles Cavendish Fulke. *The Greville Memoirs: Second Part: A Journal of the Reign of Queen Victoria, 1837-1852*. 3 vols. London: Longman, Green, 1885.

Grew, Joseph C. *The Diary of Joseph C. Grew* and *The Papers of Joseph C. Grew*. Cambridge, Mass.: Houghton Library, Harvard University, n.d.

_____ . *Ten Years in Japan*. New York: Simon & Schuster, 1944.

_____ . *Turbulent Era*. New York: Houghton Mifflin, 1952.

Grey, Sir Edward. *Twenty-Five Years: 1892-1916*. New York: Frederick A. Stokes, 1925.

Grey, Frederick W. *Seeking a Fortune in America*. London: Smith, Elder, 1912.

Grey, Ian. *Catherine the Great: Autocrat and Empress of All Russia*. New York: J.B. Lippincott, 1961.

_____ . *The First Fifty Years*. New York: Coward-McCann, 1967.

_____ . *Ivan the Terrible*. New York: J.B. Lippincott, 1964.

_____ . *Peter the Great, Emperor of All Russia*. New York: J.B. Lippincott, 1960.

Greyre, G. *The Masters and the Slaves*. New York: Alfred A. Knopf, 1968.

Gribaudi, Piero. *La Piu' frande Italia*. Turin, Italy: SEI, 1925.

Gribble, Francis H. *Emperor and Mystic: The Life of Alexander I of Russia*. London: Nash & Grayson, 1931.

Gribble, Leonard. *Adventures in Murder*. London: John Long, 1954.

_____ . *The Black Maria or the Criminal's Omnibus*. London: Victor Gollancz, 1935.

_____ . *Clues That Spelled Guilty*. London: John Long, 1961.

_____ . *Compelled to Kill*. London: John Long, 1977.

_____ . *The Dead End Killers*. London: John Long, 1978.

_____ . *The Deadly Professionals*. London: John Long, 1978.

_____ . *Detection and Deduction*. Garden City, N.Y.: Doubleday, 1934.

_____ . *Famous Feats of Detection and Crime*. Garden City, N.Y.: Doubleday, Doran, 1934.

_____ . *Famous Judges and Their Trials*. London: John Long, 1957.

_____ . *Famous Manhunts: A Century of Crime*. London: John Long, 1953.

_____ . *Famous Stories of the Murder Squad*. London: Barker, 1974.

_____ . *Great Detective Exploits*. London: John Long, 1958.

_____ . *Great Manhunters of the Yard*. New York: Roy, 1966.

_____ . *Hallmark of Horror*. London: John Long, 1973.

_____ . *Murders Most Strange*. London: John Long, 1959.

_____ . *Queens of Crime*. London: Hurst & Blackett, 1932.

_____ . *Sisters of Cain*. London: John Long, 1972.

_____ . *Stories of Famous Detectives*. New York: Hill & Wang, 1963.

_____ . *Stories of Famous Modern Trials*. London: Barker, 1973.

_____ . *Strange Crimes of Passion*. London: John Long, 1970.

_____ . *Such Was Their Guilt*. London: John Long, 1974.

_____ . *Such Women are Deadly*. London: John Long, 1965.

_____ . *They Challenged the Yard*. London: John Long, 1963.

_____ . *They Conspired to Kill*. London: John Long, 1975.

_____ . *They Got Away with Murder*. London: John Long, 1971.

_____ . *They Had A Way with Women*. London: John Long, 1967.

_____ . *Triumphs of Scotland Yard*. London: John Long, 1955.

_____ . *When Killers Err*. London: John Long, 1962.

Grieb, Kenneth J. *The United States and Huerta*. Lincoln: University of Nebraska Press, 1969.

Grier, William H., and Cobbs, Price M. *Black Rage*. New York: Bantam Books, 1969.

Grierson, Francis. *Famous French Crimes*. London: Frederick Muller, 1959.

_____ . *The Valley of the Shadows, The Coming of the Civil War in Lincoln's Midwest*. New York: Harper & Row, 1948.

Griesinger, Theodor. *The Jesuits*. London: W.H. Allen, 1883.

Griffin, Bulkley S. (ed.). *Offbeat History*. New York: World, 1967.

Griffin, Clifford S. *Their Brothers' Keepers: Moral Stewardship in the United States, 1800-1865*. New Brunswick, N.J.: Rutgers University Press, 1960.

Griffin, John I. *Statistics Essential for Police Efficiency.* Springfield, Ill.: Charles C. Thomas, 1958.

Griffin, Susan. *Rape.* New York: Harper & Row, 1979.

Griffis, Joseph K. *Tahan: Out of Savagery Into Civiliazation.* New York: George H. Doran, 1915.

Griffith, A. Kinney. *Mickey Free: Manhunter.* Caldwell, Idaho: Caxton Press, 1969.

Griffith, Lippon R. *Mugging.* Englewood Cliffs, N.J.: Spectrum, 1978.

Griffith, Robert. *The Politics of Fear: Joseph McCarthy and the Senate.* Lexington: University of Kentucky Press, 1970.

_____, and Theoharis, Athan. *The Specter: Original Essays on the Cold War and the Origins of McCarthyism.* New York: New Viewpoints, 1974.

Griffith, William E. *Albania and the Sino-Soviet Rift.* Cambridge, Mass.: M.I.T. Press, 1963.

Griffiths, Major Arthur. *Early French Prisons.* London: Grolier Society, n.d.

_____. *English Prisons.* Vols. I, II, III. London: Grolier Society, n.d.

_____. *German and Austrian Prisons.* London: Grolier Society, n.d.

_____. *Italian Prisons.* London: Grolier Society, n.d.

_____. *Modern French Prisons.* London: Grolier Society, n.d.

_____. *Mysteries of Police and Crime.* Vols. I, II, III. London: Cassell, 1902.

_____. *Non-Criminal Prisons.* London: Grolier Society, n.d.

_____. *Oriental Prisons.* London: Grolier Society, n.d.

_____. *Over Seas Prisons.* London: Grolier Society, n.d.

_____. *Russian Prisons.* London: Grolier Society, n.d.

_____. *Secrets of the Prison-House or Gaol Studies and Sketches.* London: Chapman & Hall, 1894.

_____. *Spanish Prisons.* London: Grolier Society, n.d.

_____. *The World's Famous Prisons.* 12 vols. London: Grolier Society, 1894.

Griggs, George. *History of Mesilla Valley.* Las Cruces, N.M.: Bronson Printing, 1930.

Gril, Etienne. *Madame Lefarge devant ses juges.* Paris: Gallimard, 1958.

Grillandus, Paulus. *Tractatus de Hereticis et Sortilegiis.* Lyons: J. Givch, 1536.

Grillot de Givry, Emile Angelo. *La musée des sorciers, mages et alchimistes.* Paris: Librarie de France, 1929.

_____. *A Pictorial Anthology of Witchcraft, Magic and Alchemy.* trans. J. Courtenay Locke. New York: University Books, 1958.

Grimal, Pierre (ed.). *Hellenism and the Rise of Rome.* trans. A.M. Sheridan Smith. New York: Delacorte Press, 1965.

Grimes, Alan Pendleton. *The Political Liberalism of the New York Nation.* Chapel Hill: University of North Carolina Press, 1953.

Grimley, O. *The New Norway; A People with the Spirit of Co-operation.* Oslo, Nor.: Griff-Forlaget, 1937.

Grimshaw, Allen A. (ed.). *Racial Violence in the United States.* Chicago: Aldine, 1969.

Grimshaw, Eric, and Jones, Glyn. *Lord Goddard: His Career and Cases.* London: Allan Wingate, 1958.

Grimstad, Kirsten, and Rennier, Susan (eds.). *The New Woman's Survival Catalog.* New York: Coward, McCann, & Geoghegan/Berkeley, 1973.

The Grinder Poisoning Case. Pittsburgh, Pa.: John P. Hunt, 1866.

Grindrod, Muriel. *The New Italy.* London: Royal Institute of International Affairs, 1947.

Grinnell, George B. *The Cheyennes: Their History and Ways of Life.* 2 vols. New York: Cooper Square, 1962.

_____. *The Fighting Cheyennes.* New York: Charles Scribner's Sons, 1915.

Grinspoon, Lester, and Bakalar, James B. *Cocaine: A Drug and Its Evolution.* New York: Basic Books, 1976.

_____. *Marihuana Reconsidered.* Cambridge, Mass.: Harvard University Press, 1977.

_____. *Psychodelic Drugs Reconsidered.* New York: Basic Books, 1979.

_____, and Hedblom, Peter. *The Speed Culture: Amphetamine Use and Abuse in America.* Cambridge, Mass.: Harvard University Press, 1975.

Grisham, Noel. *Tame the Reckless Wind: The Life and Legends of Sam Bass.* Austin, Texas: San Felipe Press, 1968.

Grison, Georges. *Souvenirs de la place de la Roquette.* Paris: E. Dentu, 1883.

Griswold, A. Whitney. *The Far Eastern Policy of the United States.* New York: Harcourt, 1938.

Griswold, Don and Jean. *The Carbonate Camp Called Leadville.* Denver: University of Denver Press, 1951.

Griswold, E.N. *The Fifth Amendment Today.* Cambridge, Mass.: Harvard University Press, 1955.

Griswold, H. Jack, et al. *An Eye for an Eye.* New York: Henry Holt, Rinehart & Winston, 1970.

Grodzins, Morton. *Americans Betrayed, Politics and the Japanese Evacuation.* Chicago: University of Chicago Press, 1949.

Gronsky, P.P., and Astrov, N.J. *The War and The Russian Government.* New Haven, Conn.: Yale University Press, 1929.

Gropp, Ignatz. *Collectio Scriptorum et Rerum Wircebургensium.* Frankfort, Ger.: ex officina Weidmanniana, 1741-1750.

Groppe, Theodor. *Ein Kampf um Recht und Sitte.* Trier, Ger.: Paulinus, 1947.

Gross, Bertram. *Friendly Fascism.* New York: M. Evans, 1980.

Gross, Feliks. *The Seizure of Political Power.* New York: Philosophical Library, 1958.

Gross, Felix. *Violence in Politics.* New York: Mouton, 1972.

Gross, Gerald (ed.). *Masterpieces of Murder: An Edmund Pearson True Crime Reader.* Boston: Little, Brown, 1963.

_____. *The Responsiblity of the Press.* New York: Fleet, 1966.

Gross, H.G.A. *Criminal Investigation: A Practical Textbook for Magistrates, Police Officers and Lawyers.* trans. J. Adam and J. Collyer Adam. London: Sweet & Maxwell, 1949.

Gross, Hans. *Criminology Psychology.* Boston: Little, Brown, 1915.

Gross, Kenneth. *The Alice Crimmins Case.* New York: Alfred A. Knopf, 1975.

Gross, L. *Sexual Behaviour.* New York: John Wiley & Sons, 1974.

Gross, Robert D. *The Emergence of Liberal Catholicism in America.* Cambridge, Mass.: Harvard University Press, 1958.

Gross, S.L. and Hardy, J.E. (eds.). *Images of the Negro in American Literature.* Chicago: University of Chicago Press, 1966.

Gross, Theodore L. *Albion W. Tourgée.* New York: Twayne, 1963.

Grosser, Alfred. *Germany in Our Time.* London: Pelican Books, 1974.

Grossman, Edwina Booth. *Edwin Booth: Recollections by His Daughter.* New York: Century, 1894.

Grosso, Sonny, and Devaney, John. *Murder at the Harlem Mosque.* New York: Crown, 1977.

Grosvernor, Melville Bell. *The Last Full Measure: The World Pay Tribute to President Kennedy.* Washington, D.C.: National Geographic, 1964.

Grote, George. *History of Greece.* London: John Murray, 1853.

Grote, Otto Freiherr. *Ortia Lundeman oder der Zaubereiprocess zu Egeln, 1612.* Osterweick: A.W. Zickfeldt, 1877.

Groth, A. Nicholas. *Men Who Rape.* London: Plenum, 1980.

Groth-Marnat, Gary. *Handbook of Pschological Assessment.* New York: Van Nostrand, Reinhold, 1984.

Grover, David H. *Debaters and Dynamiters: The Story of the Haywood Trial.* Corvallis, Ore.: Oregon State University Press, 1964.

_____. *Diamondfield Jack: A Study in Frontier Justice.* Reno: University of Nevada Press, 1968.

Grover, G.W. *Shadows lifted or sunshine restored on the hori-*

of human lives. Chicago: Stromberg, Allen, 1894

Grover, William C. *The Tammany Hall Democracy of the City of New York, and the General Committee for 1875.* New York: n.p., 1875.

Grube, Oswald W. *One Hundred Years of Architecture in Chicago.* Chicago: Follett, 1977.

Gruening, Ernest. *Mexico and Its Heritage.* London: Stanley Paul, 1928.

_____. *The State of Alaska.* New York: Random House, 1968.

_____., and Beaser, Herbert W. *Vietnam Folly.* Washington: National Press, 1968.

Gruesser, O. (ed.). *Pattern Recognition in Biological and Technical Systems.* New York: Springer-Verlag, 1971.

Grunberger, Richard. *A Social History of the Third Reich.* London: Penguin Books, 1974.

Grund, Francis J. *Aristocracy in America.* New York: Harper & Brothers, 1959.

Grunder, Garel A., and Livezey, William E. *The Philippines and the United States.* Norman: University of Oklahoma Prss, 1951.

Grünebaum, Gustave E. von. *Medieval Islam.* Chicago: University of Chicago Press, 1946.

Grünhut, Max, *Penal Reform.* Oxford, Eng.: Clarendon Press, 1948.

_____, Sieverts, Rudolf, and Bemmelen, Jacob M. *Sexual Crime Today.* The Hague, Neth.: Martinus Nijhoff, 1960.

Grunwald, Constantine. *Peter the Great.* Philadelphia: Saunders, 1956.

_____. *Tsar Nicholas I.* New York: Macmillan, 1955.

Grupp, Stanley E. (ed.). *Theories of Punishment.* Bloomington: University of Indiana Press, 1972.

Gsovski, V., and Grzybowski, K. *Government, Law and Courts in the Soviet Union and Eastern Europe.* London: Stevens, 1959.

Guaita, Stanislas de. *Essais des sciences maudites.* Paris: Chamuel, 1891-97.

Gualerni, Gualtiero. *La politica industriale fascista.* Milan, Italy: Istituto Sociale Ambrosiano, 1956.

Guard, William J. *The Soul of Paris.* New York: Sun, 1914.

Guardian Newspapers. *Windscale: A Summary of the Evidence and the Argument.* London: Guardian Newspapers, 1977.

Guariglia, Baron Raffaele. *La Diplomatie Difficile.* Paris: Plon, 1955.

Guarino, Vincent J. *Everyman's Guide to Better Home Secuity.* Boulder, Colo.: Paladin Press, 1981.

Guazzo, Francesco-Maria. *Compendium Maleficarum.* trans. E.A. Ashwin) London: J. Rodker, 1929.

Guderian, Heinz. *Panzer Leader.* trans. Constantine Fitzgibbon. London: Michael Joseph, 1952.

Gue, Benjamin F. *History of Iowa.* New York: Century History, 1903.

Guedalla, Philip. *The Queen and Mrs. Gladstone.* Garden City, N.Y.: Doubleday, Doran, 1934.

Guenther, H.V. *Yuganaddha.* Varanasi, India: Chokhambra Sanscrit Series Studies, 1969.

Guépin, M.A. *Histoire de Nantes.* Nantes, Fr.: Librairie Prosper Sébire, 1839.

Guerin, Daniel. *Fascism and Big Business.* New York: Pioneer, 1929.

Guerin, Eddie. *I Was a Bandit.* Garden City, N.Y.: Doubleday, Doran, 1929.

Guerin, Thomas. *Caps and Crowns of Europe.* Montreal, Quebec, Can.: Louis Carrier, 1929.

Guériot, Paul. *Napoléon III.* 2 vols. Paris: Payot, 1933-34.

Guernsey, Alfred H., and Alden, Henry M. *Harper's Pictorial History of the Great Rebellion.* 2 vols. New York: Harper, 1866.

Guernsey, Charles Arthur. *Wyoming Cowboy Days.* New York: G.P. Putnam's Sons, 1936.

Guest, Ivor. *Napoleon III in England.* London: British Technical & General Press, 1952.

Guest, S.H. *Russia in Flux.* New York: Macmillan, 1948.

Guettée, René-Francois-Wladimir. *Souvenirs d'un prêtre romain devenue prêtre orthodoxe.* Paris: Fischbacher, 1889.

Guevera, Che. *Guerrilla Warfare.* New York: Random House, 1968.

Gugas, Chris. *The Silent Witness.* Englewood Cliffs, N.J.: Prentice-Hall, 1979.

Gugliotta, Guy, and Leen, Jeff. *Kings of Cocaine: Inside the Medellin Cartel-An Astonishing True Story of Murder, Money, and International Corruption.* New York: Simon & Schuster, 1989.

Guicciardini, Francesco. *History of Italy and History of Florence.* New York: Washington Square Press, 1964.

_____. *Ricordi (Maxims and Reflections of a Renaissance Statesman).* New York: Harper & Row, 1965.

Guild, June Purcell. *Black Laws of Virginia.* New York: Negro University Press, 1969.

Guild, Josephus Conn. *Old Times in Tennessee.* Nashville, Tenn.: Eastman & Howell, 1878.

Guild, Leo. *The Fatty Arbuckle Case.* New York: Paperback Library, 1962.

Guiles, Fred Lawrence. *Marion Davies.* New York: McGraw Hill, 1972.

Guilford, J.P. *The Nature of Human Intelligence.* New York: McGraw-Hill, 1967.

Guillemain, Bernard. *La cour pontifical d'Avignon, 1309-1376.* Paris: E. De Boccard, 1966.

Guilty or Not Guilty, The True Story of the Manhattan Well. New York: Carleton, 1870.

Guinn, J.M. *A History of California, and an Extended History of Its Southern Coast Counties.* Los Angeles: Historic Record, 1907.

_____. *Historical and Biographical Record of Southern California.* Chicago: Chapman, 1902.

_____. *History of the State of California and Biographical Record of Sacramento Valley, California.* Chicago: Chapman, 1906.

_____. *History of the State of California and Biographical Record of San Joaquin County.* Los Angeles: Historic Record, 1909.

Guiteau's Confession: The Garfield Assassination, Being a Full History of the Cruel Crime. Philadelphia: Old Franklin, 1881.

Guiteau's Crime: The Full History of the Murder of President James A. Garfield. New York: Richard K. Fox, 1881.

Guiteau Trial. New York: John Polhemus, 1882.

Guizot, François. *A Popular History of France.* trans. Robert Black. Boston: Colonial Press, 1870.

Gull, Cyril. *Oscar Wilde: Some Reminiscences.* London: T.W. Laurie, 1978.

Gullick, C.A. *Austria from Habsburg to Hitler.* Berkeley: University of California, 1950.

Gully, James M. *An Exposition of the Symptoms, Essential Nature and Treatment of Neuropathy or Nervousness.* London: Churchill, 1837.

Gumbel, E.J. *Vier Jahre Politscher Mord.* Berlin: Malik Verlag, 1922.

Gumina, Deanna Paoli. *The Italians of San Francisco, 1850-1930.* New York: Center for Migration Studies, 1978.

Gummere, Amelia Mott. *Witchcraft and Quakerism.* Philadelphia: Biddle, 1908.

Gun, Nerin. *Eva Braun: Hitler's Mistress.* New York: Hawthorne Books, 1968.

_____. *Red Roses From Texas.* London: Fredrick Muller, 1964.

Gunn, John. *Violence.* New York: Frederick A. Praeger, 1973.

Gunn, John W. *Wisdom of Clarence Darrow.* Girard, Kan.: Haldeman-Julius, 1947.

Gunther, Jack D., and Charles O. *The Identification of Firearms.* New York: John Wiley & Sons, 1935.

Gunther, John. *Inside Asia.* New York: Harper & Brothers, 1939.

_____. *Inside Europe.* New York: Harper & Brothers, 1938.

_____. *Inside U.S.A.* New York: Harper & Brothers, 1947.

_____. *Riddle of MacArthur: Japan, Korea and the Far East.* New York: Harper & Brothers, 1951.

_____. *Roosevelt in Retrospect.* New York: Harper and Brothers, 1950.

_____. *Taken at the Flood.* New York: Harper, 1960.

Gunther, Max. *D.B. Cooper, What Really Happened?* Chicago: Contemporary Books, 1985.

Gurko, Miriam. *Clarence Darrow.* New York: Thomas Y. Crowell, 1965.

Gurko, V.I. *Features and Figures of the Past.* Stanford, Calif.: Stanford University Press, 1939.

Gurley, Dr. *Sermon at the Funeral of Abraham Lincoln.* Philadelphia: Presbyterian Church of Philadelphia, 1940.

Gurowski, Adam. *Diary.* 3 vols. Boston: n.p., 1862-66.

Gurr, Ted Robert. *Rogues, Rebels, and Reformers: A Political History of Urban Crime and Conflict.* Beverly Hills, Calif.: Sage, 1976.

_____. *Why Men Rebel.* Princeton, N.J.: Princeton University Press, 1970.

Gurr, Tom, and Cox, H.H. *Famous Australasian Crimes.* London: Frederick Muller, 1957.

Gurvitch, Georges. *Sociology of Law.* New York: Philosophical Library, 1941.

Gurwell, John K. *Mass Murder in Houston.* Houston, Texas: Cordovan Press, 1974.

Gurwitsch, Aron. *The Field of Consciousness.* Pittsburgh, Pa.: Duquesne University Press, 1964.

Gusfield, Joseph. *Symbolic Crusade: Status Politics and the American Temperance Movement.* Urbana: University of Illinois Press, 1963.

Gussow, Mel. *Don't Say Yes Until I Finish Talking: A Biography of Darryl F. Zanuck.* New York: Doubleday, 1971.

Gustafsson, Karl Erik, and Hadenius, Stig. *Swedish Press Policy.* Stockholm: Swedish Institute, 1976.

Gustin, Lawrence R. *Billy Durant.* Grand Rapids, Mich.: William B. Eerdmans, 1973.

Gutheim, Frederick A. *The Potomac.* New York: Rinehart, 1949.

Guthman, Edwin. *We Band of Brothers.* New York: Harper & Row, 1964.

Gutierres de Lara, L. and Pinchon, Edgcumb. *The Mexican People: Their Struggle for Freedom.* New York: Doubleday, Page, 1914.

Gutkind, Curt (ed.) *Mussolini e il suo fascismo.* Florence, Italy: Le Monnier, 1927.

Gutman, Herbert G. *The Black Family in Slavery and Freedom, 1750-1925.* New York: Pantheon, 1976.

Gutman, Richard J.S., and Kellie O. *John Wilkes Booth Himself.* Dover, Mass.: Hired Hand Press, 1979.

Guttmacher, Manfred. *The Mind of the Murderer.* New York: Farrar, Straus, 1960.

_____, and Weihofen, Henry. *Psychiatry and the Law.* New York: W.W. Norton, 1952.

_____. *Sex Offenses: The Problem, Causes and Prevention.* New York: W.W. Norton, 1951.

Guttmann, Allen. *The Wound in the Heart.* New York: Free Press of Glencoe, 1962.

Guyer, James S. *Pioneer life in west Texas.* Brownwood, Texas: n.p., 1938.

Guyon, René. *The Ethics of Sexual Acts.* New York: Alfred A. Knopf, 1934.

Guyton, Pearl Vivian. *Campaign and Siege of Vicksburg.* Vicksburg, Pa.: n.p., 1945.

_____. *Sexual Freedom.* New York: Alfred A. Knopf, 1950.

Guzman, Martin Luis. *The Eagle and the Serpent.* New York: Doubleday, 1965.

_____. *Memoirs of Pancho Villa.* trans. Virginia H. Taylor. Austin: University of Texas Press, 1965.

Guzman, Ramón. *El Intervencionismo de Mr. Wilson en México.* New Orleans: Published by Author, 1915.

Guzmán Esparza, Ropberto. *Memoirias de Don Adolfo de la Huerta según su propio dictado.* Mexico City: Ediciones "Guzmán," 1957.

Gwatkin, H.M. and Whitney J.P. (eds.). *The Cambridge Medieval History.* New York: Macmillan, 1911-1936.

Gwynn, D.R. *Pius XI.* London: Holme Press, 1932.

Gwynn, Stephen (ed.). *The Letters and Friendships of Sir Cecil Spring-Rice.* London: Constable, 1929.

H

Haas, Ben. *KKK.* Evanston, Ill.: Regency, 1963.

Haas, Carl. *Die Hexenprozesse: ein cultur-historischer Versuch, nebst Dokumenten.* Tübingen, Ger.: H. Laupp'sche Buchhandlung, 1865.

Habas, Bracha. *The Gate Breakers.* New York: Thomas Yoseloff, 1963.

Habe, Hans. *Der Tod in Texas: Eine Amerikansche Tragodie.* Munich: K. Desch, 1964.

_____. *The Wounded Land: Journey Through a Divided America.* New York: Coward-McCann, 1964.

Haber, Samuel. *Efficiency and Uplift: Scientific Management in the Progressive Era.* Chicago: University of Chicago Press, 1964.

Habermas, Jürgen. *Legitimation Crisis.* Boston: Beacon Press, 1975.

_____. *Theory and Practice.* Boston: Beacon Press, 1974.

_____. *Toward a Rational Society: Student Protest, Science and Politics.* Boston: Beacon Press, 1971.

Hacker, Frederick J. *Crusaders, Criminals, Crazies: Terror and Terrorism in Our Time.* New York: W.W. Norton, 1976.

Hacker, Louis M. *Alexander Hamilton, in the American Tradition.* New York: McGraw-Hill, 1957.

_____. *The Shaping of American Tradition.* New York: Columbia University Press, 1947.

_____, and Kendrick, B.B. *The United States Since 1865.* New York: F.S. Crofts, 1932.

Hackett, Charles Wilson. *The Mexican Revolution and the United States, 1910-1926.* New York: World Peace Commission, 1926.

Hackett, Francis. *I Chose Denmark.* New York: Doubleday, 1941.

_____. *Ireland: A Study in Nationalism.* New York: Huebsch, 1920.

Hackney, Francis S. *From Populism to Progressivism in Alabama, 1890-1910.* Princeton, N.J.: Princeton University Press, 1969.

Hadawi, Sami. *The Arab-Israeli Conflict.* Beirut, Leb.: Institute for Palestine Studies, 1967.

_____. *Palestine Before the United Nations: Annual Documentary, 1965.* Beirut, Leb.: Institute for Palestine Studies, 1965.

_____. *UN Resolutions on Palestine, 1947-1972.* Beirut, Leb.: Institute for Palestine Studies, 1974.

Hadfield, R.L. *Picturesque Rogues.* London: H.F. & G. Witherby, 1931.

Hadley, Harold. *Come See Them Die.* New York: Julian Messner, 1934.

Hadley, Henry H. *The Blue Badge of Courage.* Akron, Ohio: Saalfield, 1902.

Hadley, Norman. *The Viking Process.* New York: Avon Books, 1977.

Hadley, Samuel H. *Down in Water Street.* New York: Fleming H. Revell, 1902.

Haen, Anton von. *De Magia.* Naples, Italy: F. Ippoliti, 1777.

Haestier, Richard. *Dead Men Tell Tales.* London: John Long,

1934.

Haestrup, Jorgen. *Til Landets Bedste.* Copenhagen, Den.: Gyldendal, 1966.

Hafen, Leroy R. (ed.). *Colorado Gold Rush: Contemporary Letters and Reports, 1858-1859.* Glendale, Calif.: Arthur H. Clark, 1941.

_____, and Young, Francis Marion. *Fort Laramie and the Pageant of the West.* Glendale, Calif.: Arthur H. Clark, 1938.

_____ and Ann. *Handcrafts for Zion.* Glendale, Calif.: Arthur H. Clark, 1860.

_____, and Rister, Carl Coke. *Western America.* New York: Prentice-Hall, 1941.

Haft, Marilyn G., and Hermann, Michelle (eds.). *Prisoners' Rights.* New York: Practicing Law Institute, 1972.

Hagan, Frank E. *Introduction to Criminology.* Chicago: Nelson-Hall, 1986.

_____. *Research Methods in Criminal Justice and Criminology.* New York: Macmillan, 1982.

Hagan, William T. *American Indians.* Chicago: University of Chicago Press, 1961.

_____. *Indian Police and Judges: Experiences in Acculturation and Control.* New Haven, Conn.: Yale University Press, 1966.

Hagedorn, Hermann. *Roosevelt in the Badlands.* Boston: Houghton Mifflin, 1921.

_____. *The Roosevelt Family at Sagamore Hill.* New York: Macmillan, 1954.

_____. *The Theodore Roosevelt Treasury.* New York: G.P. Putnam's Sons, 1957.

Hagemann, Gerard. *Man on the Bench.* Notre Dame, Ind.: Dujarie Press, 1962.

Hagen, Paul. *Will Germany Crack?* New York: Harper, 1942.

Hagen, Walter. *Die geheime Front.* Linz, Aust.: Nibelungen, 1950.

Hagood, Margaret. *Statistics for Sociologists.* New York: Henry Holt, 1941.

Hahn, Emily. *The Soong Sisters.* New York: Doubleday, 1943.

Hahn, Jon K., and McKenney, Harold C. *Legally Sane.* Chicago: Regnery, 1972.

Haider, C. *Capital and Labor Under Fascism.* New York: Columbia University Press, 1930.

_____. *Do We Want Fascism?* New York: John Day, 1934.

Haight, Anne Lyon, and Grannis, Chandler. *Banned Books: 387 B.C. to 1978 A.D.* New York: R.R. Bowker, 1978.

Haight, Elizabeth Hazelton. *Italy Old and New.* London: Stanley Paul, 1923.

Hailey, John. *The History of Idaho.* Boise, Idaho: Syms-York, 1910.

Haiman, Franklyn. *Freedom of Speech.* Skokie, Ill.: National Textbook, 1976.

Haimson, Leopold H. *Russian Marxists and the Origins of Bolshevism.* Cambridge, Mass.: Harvard University Press, 1955.

Hainari, Oskar A., and Grotenfelt, Kustavi. *Suomen historia Ruostin Mahtavuuden aikakaudella, 1617-1721.* Jyväskylä, Fin.: K.J. Gummerus, 1922.

Haines, Charles G. *The American Doctrine of Judicial Review.* Berkeley: University of California Press, 1932.

_____. *The Role of the Supreme Court in American Government and Politics, 1789-1835.* Berkeley: University of California Press, 1944.

_____, and Foster, Sherwood. *The Role of the Supreme Court in American Government and Politics, 1835-1864.* Berkeley: University of California Press, 1944.

Haines, John E. *Automatic Controls.* New York: McGraw-Hill, 1961.

Haines, Max. *Bothersome Bodies.* Toronto, Ontario, Can.: McClelland & Stewart, 1977.

_____. *Crime Flashback.* Toronto, Ontario, Can.: Toronto Sun, 1981.

Haining, Peter. *Witchcraft and Black Magic.* New York: Grosset & Dunlap, 1972.

Haire, N., et al. *Encyclopedia of Sexual Knowledge.* New York: Eugenics, 1937.

Hakluyt, R. *The Principall Navigations, Voiages and Discoveries of the English Nation.* London: Hakluyt Society, 1903.

Halasz, Nicholas. *Captain Dreyfus.* New York: Simon & Schuster, 1955.

_____. *In the Shadow of Russia.* New York: Ronald, 1959.

_____. *The Rattling Chains: Slave Unrest and Revolt in the Antebellum South.* New York: McKay, 1966.

Halbwachs, Maurice. *Les Causes du Suicide.* Paris: Libraire Felix Alcan, 1930.

Haldane, Richard Burdon. *An Autobiography.* New York: Doubleday, Doran, 1929.

Haldeman, H.R., and Di Mona, Joseph. *The Ends of Power.* New York: Times, 1978.

Haldeman-Julius, Emanue. *John Brown, the Facts of His Life and Martyrdom.* Girard, Kan.: Haldeman-Julius, 1925.

Haldeman-Julius, Marcet. *Clarence Darrow's Two Great Trials.* Girard, Kan.: Haldeman-Julius, 1927.

Hale, Charles A. *Mexican Liberalism in the Age of Mora, 1821-1853.* New Haven, Conn.: Yale University Press, 1968.

Hale, Horace. *Education in Colorado 1861-1885.* Denver: News, Printing, 1885.

Hale, John. *A Modest Inquiry into the Nature of Witchcraft and How Persons Guilty of that Crime may be Convicted.* Boston: B. Eliot, 1702.

_____. *Narratives of the Witchcraft Cases, 1648-1706.* New York: Barnes & Noble, 1959.

Hale, Leslie. *Hanged in Error.* London: Penguin Books, 1961.

_____. *Hanging in the Balance.* London: Jonathan Cape, 1962.

Hale, Sir Matthew. *Pleas of the Crown.* London: Richard Tonson, 1678.

Hale, Nathan G., Jr. *Freud and the Americans: The Beginnings of Psychonalysis in the United States, 1876-1917.* New York: Oxford University Press, 1972.

Hale, Richard W., Jr. *Democratic France.* New York: Coward-McCann, 1941.

Hale, William Bayard. *Woodrow Wilson: The Story of His Life.* Garden City, N.Y.: Doubleday, Page, 1911.

Hale, William Harlan. *Horace Greeley: Voice of the People.* New York: Harper, 1950.

Hales, E.E.Y. *Pio Nono: A Study of European Politics and Religion in the Nineteenth Century.* London: Eyre & Spottiswoode, 1954.

Halévy, Elie. *The Growth of Philosophic Radicalism.* Boston: Beacon Press, 1955.

_____. *A History of The English People in the Nineteenth Century.* Ernest Benn, 1961.

_____. *L'ère des Tyrannies.* Paris: Gallimard, 1938.

Haley, Alex. *Autobiography of Malcolm X.* New York: Grove Press, 1964.

Haley, J. Evetts. *Charles Goodnight: Cowman and Plainsman.* Boston: Houghton Mifflin, 1936.

_____, and Holden, William Curry. *The Flamboyant Judge: James D. Hamlin.* Canyon, Texas: Palo Duro Press, 1972.

_____. *George W. Littlefield, Texan.* Norman: University of Oklahoma Press, 1943.

_____. *Jeff Milton: A Good Man with a Gun.* Norman: University of Oklahoma Press, 1948.

_____. *Jim East: Trailhand and Cowboy.* Canyon, Texas: n.p., 1931.

_____. *A Texan Looks at Lyndon: A Study in Illegitimate Power.* Canyon, Texas: Palo Duro Press, 1964.

_____. *The XIT Ranch of Texas and the Early Days of the Llano Estacado.* Chicago: Lakeside Press, 1929.

Haley, Kenneth H.D. *The First Earl of Shaftsbury.* Oxford, Eng.: Clarendon Press, 1968.

Haley, P. Edward. *Revolution and Intervention: The Diplomacy of Taft and Wilson with Mexico, 1910-1917.* Cambridge, Mass.: MIT Press, 1970.

Halifax, Lord. *Fullness of Days*. London: Collins, 1957.

Hall, A.C. *Crime in Its Relation to Social Progress*. New York: Columbia University Press, 1902.

Hall, Angelo. *Forty-One Thieves: A Tale of California*. Boston: Cornhill, 1919.

Hall, Angus (ed.). *The Crime Busters*. London: Verdict Press, 1976.

Hall, Benjamin F. *The Trial of William Freeman for the Murder of John G. Van Nest*. Auburn, N.Y.: Derby, Miller, 1848.

Hall, C.S., and Lindzey, G. *Theories of Personality*. New York: John Wiley & Sons, 1978.

Hall, Clifton R. *Andrew Johnson, Military Governor of Tennessee*. Princeton, N.J.: Princeton University Press, 1916.

Hall, David. *The Faithful Shepherd*. Chapel Hill: University of North Carolina Press, 1972.

Hall, E. Hagaman. *The Second City of the World*. New York: Republic Press, 1898.

Hall, Francis. *Travels in Canada and the United States in 1816 and 1817*. Boston: Wells & Lilly, 1818.

Hall, Frank. *History of the State of Colorado*. Chicago: Blakeley Printing, 1889.

Hall, Frank O., and Whitten, Lindsey H. *Jesse James Rides Again*. Lawton, Okla.: LaHoma, 1948.

Hall, Gerald. *How To Completely Secure Your Home*. Blue Ridge Summit, Penn.: Tab Books, 1978.

Hall, Gladys M. *Prostitution in the Modern World*. New York: Emerson Books, 1965.

Hall, Gordon Langley. *The Two Lives of Baby Doe*. Philadelphia: Macrae Smith, 1962.

Hall, Gus. *For a Radical Change-The Communist View*. New York: New Outlook, 1966.

Hall, Henry and James. *Cayunga in the Field: A Record of the 19th New York Volunteers*. Auburn, N.Y.: Truair, Smith, 1873.

Hall, J.M. *The Beginnings of Tulsa*. Tulsa, Okla.: n.p., 1933.

Hall, James. *The Harpe's Head: A Legend of Kentucky*. Philadelphia: Key & Biddle, 1833.

_____. *Sketches of History: Life and Manners in the West*. Philadelphia: H. Hall, 1835.

_____. *Statistics of the West, At the Close of the Year 1836*. Cincinnati, Ohio: J.A. James, 1836.

_____. *The West: Its Commerce and Navigation*. Cincinnati: H.W. Derby, 1848.

Hall, James O. *Notes on the John Wilkes Booth Escape Route*. Clinton, Md.: Surratt Society, 1980.

Hall, Jerome, and Mueller, G.O.W. *Cases and Readings on Criminal Law and Procedure*. Indianapolis, Ind.: Bobbs-Merrill, 1965.

_____. *General Principles of Criminal Law*. Indianapolis, Ind.: Bobbs-Merrill, 1947.

_____. *Theft, Law and Society*. Indianapolis, Ind.: Bobbs-Merrill, 1952.

Hall, John. *The Bravo Mystery and Other Cases*. London: Bodley Head, 1923.

_____ (ed.). *Notable British Trials: Trial of Abraham Thornton*. London: William Hodge, 1926.

_____ (ed.). *The Trial of Adelaide Bartlett*. London: William Hodge, 1927.

Hall, Livingston, et al. *Modern Criminal Procedure*. St. Paul, Minn.: West, 1969.

Hall, Michael G. *Edward Randolph and the American Colonies, 1676-1703*. Chapel Hill: University of North Carolina Press, 1960.

Hall, Newman. *From Liverpool to St. Louis*. London: George Routledge & Sons, 1870.

Hall, Reis H., Milazzo, Mildred, and Posner, Judy. *A Descriptive and Comparative Study of Recidivism in Pre-Release Guidance Center Releasees*. Washington, D.C.: U.S. Department of Justice, Bureau of Prisons, n.d.

Hall, Susan. *Gentlemen of Leisure*. New York: New American Library, 1972.

Hall, Thomas Cuming. *The Religious Background of American Culture*. Boston: Little, Brown, 1930.

Hall, Trevor H. *The Late Mr. Sherlock Holmes and Other Literary Studies*. New York: St. Martin's Press, 1971.

_____. *Sherlock Holmes and His Creator*. New York: St. Martin's Press, 1977.

_____. *The Spiritualists*. New York: Garret-Helix, 1963.

_____. *The Strange Case of Edmund Gurney*. London: Gerald Duckworth, 1964.

Hall, Trowbridge. *California Trails: Intimate Guide to the Old Mission*. New York: Macmillan, 1920.

Hallberg, Charles. *The Suez Canal*. New York: Columbia University Press, 1931.

Halleck, Seymour L. *Psychiatry and the Dilemmas of Crime: A Study of Causes, Punishment and Treatment*. New York: Harper & Roe/Hoeber, 1967.

Hallett, Benjamin F. *Trial of Rev. Mr. Avery*. Boston: Daily Commercial Gazette, 1833.

Halliday, Samuel B. *The Lost and Found; Or, Life Amongst the Poor*. New York: Blakeman & Mason, 1859.

Halloran, J. *The Effects of Mass Communication*. Leicester, Eng.: Leicester University Press, 1965.

Hall-Quest, Olga W. *Wyatt Earp, Marshal of the Old West*. New York: Farrar, Straus & Cudahay, 1956.

Hall-Williams, J.E. *The English Penal System in Transition*. London: Butterworth, 1970.

Hallywell, Henry. *Melampronoea...With a Solution of the Chiefest Objections Brought Against the Being of Witches*. London: W. Kettilby, 1681.

Halper, Albert (ed.). *The Chicago Crime Book*. Cleveland: World, 1967.

_____. *Goodbye, Union Square*. Chicago: Quadrangle, 1970.

Halper, Andrew, and Ku, Richard. *New York City Police Street Crime Unit*. Washington, D.C.: U.S. Department of Justice, 1972.

Halperin, Ernst. *Terrorism in Latin America*. Washington, D.C.: Sage, 1976.

Halperin, Morton H., et al. *The Lawless State: The Crimes of the U.S. Intelligence Agencies*. New York: Penguin, 1976.

_____, and Hoffman, Daniel N. *Top Secret: National Security and the Right to Know*. Washington, D.C.: New Republic Books, 1977.

Halperin, S.W. *Mussolini and Italian Fascismus*. Princeton, N.J.: Van Nostrand, 1964.

Halperin, Samuel. *The Political World of American Zionism*. Detroit, Mich.: Wayne State University Press, 1961.

Halpern, Ben. *The American Jew*. New York: Theodore Herzl Foundation, 1956.

_____. *The Idea of the Jewish State*. Cambridge, Mass.: Harvard University Press, 1961.

Halpern, Joel M. *A Serbian Village*. New York: Columbia University Press, 1958.

Halpern, John. *Los Angeles, Improbable City*. New York: E.P. Dutton, 1963.

Halsell, Grace. *The Illegals*. New York: Stein & Day, 1978.

Halsell, H.H. *The Old Cimarron*. Lubbock, Texas: Published by Author, 1944.

_____. *Cowboys and Cattleland*. Nashville, Tenn.: Parthenon Press, 1937.

Halsey, Margaret. *The Psuedo-Ethic*. New York: Simon & Schuster, 1963.

Halstead, Murat. *The Illustrious Life of William McKinley*. Chicago: n.p., 1901.

_____, and Beale, J.F. *Life of Jay Gould: How He Made His Fortune*. New York: Edgewood, 1892.

_____. *Life and Distinguished Services of William McKinley, Our Martyr President*. Chicago: Vosbrink Mercantile, 1901.

Halsted, Dennis. *Doctor in the Nineties*. London: Johnson, 1959.

Haltom, Richard W. *History and Description of Nacogdoches County.* Nacogdoches, Texas: *Nacogdoches News*, 1880.

Hambleton, Chakley J. *A Gold Hunter's Experience.* Chicago: Published by Author, 1898.

Hambloch, Ernest. *Italy Militant.* London: Duckworth, 1941.

Hambly, Charles R. *Hold Your Money.* Los Angeles: Monitor, 1932.

Hambrook, Walter. *Hambrook of the Yard.* London: R. Hale, 1937.

Hamburg, D.A., and Trudeau, M.B. (eds.). *Biobehavioral Aspects of Aggression.* New York: A.R. Liss, 1981.

Hamby, Alonzo L. *Beyond the New Deal: Harry S. Truman and American Liberalism.* New York: Columbia University Press, 1973.

_____ (ed.). *Harry S. Truman and the Fair Deal.* Lexington, Mass.: Heath, 1974.

Hamel, Ernest. *Histoire illustrée du second empire.* Paris: Degorce-Cadot, 1873.

Hamel, Frank. *Human Animals.* London: W. Rider & Son, 1915.

Hamer, Alvin C. (ed.). *Detroit Murders.* New York: Duell, Sloan & Pearce, 1948.

Hamer, Philip M. *Tennessee: A History.* New York: American Historical Society, 1933.

Hamerow, Theodore S. (ed.). *Otto von Bismarck: A Historical Assessment.* Boston: D.C. Heath, 1962.

Hamilton, Alastair. *The Appeal of Fascism.* New York: Macmillan, 1971.

Hamilton, Alexander, Jay, John, and Madison, James. *The Federalist Papers.* New York: Washington Square Press, 1971.

_____. *Gentelman's Progress.* Chapel Hill: University of North Carolina Press, 1948.

Hamilton, Alice. *Exploring the Dangerous Trades.* Boston: Little, Brown, 1943.

Hamilton, Allan McLane. *The Intimate Life of Alexander Hamilton.* London: Duckworth, 1910.

Hamilton, Charles (ed.). *Men of the Underworld.* New York: Macmillan, 1952.

Hamilton, Cicely Mary. *Modern Italy as Seen by an English-woman.* London: J.M. Dent, 1932.

Hamilton, Edward. *The War in Abyssinia.* London: John Heritage, 1936.

Hamilton, Gerald. *The Way It Was With Me.* London: Leslie Frewin, 1969.

Hamilton, Henry Raymond. *The Epic of Chicago.* Chicago: Willett, Clarke, 1932.

Hamilton, James. *Negro Plot.* Boston: Ingraham, 1822.

Hamilton, James McClellan. *From Wilderness to Statehood: A History of Montana, 1805-1900.* Portland, Ore.: Binsford & Mort, 1957.

Hamilton, John Church. *History of the Republic of the United States of America as Traced in the Writings of Alexander Hamilton and His Contemporaries.* Philadelphia: D. Appleton, 1864.

Hamilton, Jonathan Newman. *A Storeboat on the Ohio River.* Cincinnati, Ohio: Published by Author, n.d.

Hamilton, Mary E. *Policewoman: Her Service and Ideals.* New York: A. Stokes, 1924.

Hamilton, Patrick. *Resources of Arizona.* San Francisco: Bancroft, 1884.

Hamilton, Peter. *Espionage and Subversion in an Industrial Society.* London: Hutchinson, 1967.

Hamilton, Thomas Marion. *The Young Pioneer: When Captain Tom Was a Boy.* Washington D.C.: Library Press, 1932.

Hamilton, Virginia V. *Hugo Black: The Alabama Years.* Baton Rouge: Louisiana State University Press, 1972.

Hamilton, William Baskerville. *Anglo-American Law on the Frontier.* Durham, N.C.: Duke University Press, 1953.

Hamilton, Winifred Oldham. *Wagon Days on Red River.* Raton, N.M.: Daily Range, 1947.

Hamlin, Charles E. *The Life and Times of Hannibal Hamlin.* Cambridge, Mass.: Riverside Press, 1899.

Hamlin, David. *The Nazi/Skokie Conflict.* Boston: Beacon, 1980.

Hamlin, Lloyd and Rose. *Hamlin's Tombstone Picture Gallery.* Glendale, Calif.: Western Americana Press of Glendale, 1960.

Hamlin, William Lee. *The True Story of Billy the Kid.* Caldwell, Idaho: Caxton Printers, 1959.

Hammack, David C. *Power and Society.* New York: Russell Sage Foundation, 1982.

Hammer, Richard. *The CBS Murders.* New York: William Morrow, 1987.

_____. *Gangland U.S.A.* Chicago: Playboy Press, 1975.

_____. *Playboy's Illustrated History of Organized Crime.* Chicago: Playboy Press, 1975.

_____. *The Vatican Connection.* New York: Holt, Rinehart & Winston, 1982.

Hammerschlag, H.E. *Hypnotism and Crime.* London: Rider, 1956.

Hammon, J.L. *Gladstone and the Irish Nation.* London: Longmans, 1938.

Hammond, Bray. *Banks and Politics in America from the Revolution to the Civil War.* Princeton, N.J.: Princeton University Press, 1957.

Hammond, David. *The Search for Psychic Power.* New York: Bantam, 1975.

Hammond, Dorothy M., and Hendricks, George. *The Dodge City Story.* Indianapolis, Ind.: Bobbs-Merrill, 1964.

Hammond, G.P. (ed.). *The Larkin Papers.* Berkeley: University of California Press, 1951.

Hammond, J.L. *C.P. Scott of the Manchester Guardian.* New York: Harcourt-Brace, 1934.

Hammond, John Hays. *The Autobiography of John Hays Hammond.* New York: Farrar & Rinehart, 1935.

Hammond, John L. and Foot, M.R. *Gladstone and Liberalism.* London: English University Press, 1952.

Hammond, Mason. *The Antonine Monarchy.* Rome: The American School, 1959.

Hammond, Phillip (ed.). *Sociologists at Work.* New York: Basic Books, 1964.

Hammond, S.H. *The Closing Argument in the Case of the People vs. Reuben Dunbar for Murder.* Albany, N.Y.: Joel Munsell, 1851.

Hammond, W.H., and Chayen, E. *Persistent Criminals.* London: H.M. Stationery Office, 1963.

Hammond, William. *The Trial of Daniel McFarland for the Shooting of Albert D. Richardson.* New York: American News Company, 1870.

Hamner, Laura V. *Light n'Hitch.* Dallas: American Guild Press, 1958.

_____. *The No-Gun Man of Texas.* Amarillo, Texas: Published by Author, 1935.

_____. *Short Grass and Longhorns.* Norman: University of Oklahoma Press, 1942.

Hampden-Turner, Charles. *Sane Asylum: Inside the Delancy Street Foundation.* San Francisco: San Francisco Books, 1976.

Hamperian, D.R., et al. *The Violent Few.* Lexington, Mass.: Lexington, 1978.

Hanayama Shinsho. *The Way of Deliverance: Three Years With the Condemned Japanese War Criminals.* New York: Charles Scribner's Sons, 1950.

Hanbury-Williams, Sir John. *The Emperor Nicholas as I Knew Him.* New York: E.P. Dutton, 1923.

Hanchett, Lafayette. *The Old Sheriff.* New York: Margent Press, 1937.

Hanchett, William. *Irish: Charles G. Halpine in Civil War America.* Syracuse, N.Y.: Syracuse University Press, 1970.

_____. *The Lincoln Murder Conspiracies.* Chicago: University of Illinois Press, 1983.

Hand, Learned. *The Bill of Rights.* Cambridge, Mass.: Harvard

University Press, 1958.

A Handbook of Public Discipline. London: Police Federation, 1965.

Handerich, Ted. *Punishment: The Supposed Justifications.* Baltimore, Md.: Penguin, 1971.

Handleman, Howard. *Bridge to Victory: Story of the Reconquest of the Aleutians.* New York: Random House, 1954.

Handlin, Oscar. *Al Smith and His America.* Boston: Little, Brown, 1958.

_____. *Boston's Immigrants.* Cambridge, Mass.: Harvard University Press, 1941.

_____, and Mary F. *Facing Life: Youth and the Family in American History.* Boston: Little, Brown, 1971.

_____ (ed.). *Immigration as a Factor in American History.* Englewood Cliffs, N.J.: Prentice-Hall, 1959.

_____. *The Newcomers: Negroes and Hispanics in a Changing Metropolis.* Cambridge, Mass.: Harvard University Press, 1969.

_____. *The Newcomers: Negroes and Puerto Ricans in a Changing Metropolis.* Cambridge, Mass.: Harvard University Press, 1959.

_____. *Race and Nationality in American Life.* Boston: Little, Brown, 1948.

_____ (ed.). *Readings in American History.* New York: Alfred A. Knopf, 1957.

_____. *This Was America.* New York: Harper & Row, 1949.

_____. *The Uprooted.* New York: Grosset & Dunlap, 1955.

Handy, Isaac W.K. *United States Bonds, or Duress by Federal Authorities.* Baltimore: Turnbull Brothers, 1874.

Handy, Robert T. *A Christian America: Protestant Hopes and Historical Realities.* New York: Oxford University Press, 1984.

Hane, Michiso. *Peasants, Rebels, and Outcasts: The Underside of Modern Japan.* New York: Random House, 1982.

Hanes, Colonel Bailey C. *Bill Doolin Outlaw O.T.* Norman: University of Oklahoma Press, 1968.

Haney, Lewis. *A Congressional History of Railways in the United States.* Madison: University of Wisconsin Press, 1910.

Hanff, Helene. *John F. Kennedy: Young Man of Destiny.* Garden City, N.Y.: Nelson Doubleday, 1965.

Hanfstaengl, Ernst. *Unheard Witness.* Philadelphia: J.B. Lippencott, 1957.

Hanged by the Neck Until You Be Dead. Brooklyn, N.Y.: W.C. Wilton, 1877.

Hankins, Leonard. *Nineteen Years Innocent.* New York: Exposition Press, 1956.

Hanna, D. O'D. *The Face of Ulster.* New York: Devin-Adair, 1952.

Hanna, Paul. *British Policy in Palestine.* Washington, D.C.: American Council on Public Affairs, 1942.

Hannah, Walton. *Darkness Visible: A Revelation and Interpretation of Freemasonry.* London: Augustine Press, 1952.

Hannerz, Ulf. *Soulside.* New York: Columbia University Press, 1969.

Hannibal, Edward, and Boris, Robert. *Blood Feud.* New York: Ballantine, 1979.

Hanny, David. *Diaz.* London: Constable, 1917.

Hans, N.A. *History of Russian Educational Policy, 1701-1917.* London: King, 1931.

Hanscom, Elizabeth. *The Friendly Craft.* New York: Macmillan, 1908.

Hansel, C.E.M. *ESP: A Scientific Evaluation.* New York: Charles Scribner's Sons, 1966.

Hansen, Alvin H. *Business Cycles and National Income.* New York: W.W. Norton, 1957.

Hansen, Chadwick. *Witchcraft at Salem.* New York: New American Library, 1970.

Hansen, Gladys C., and Heintz, William F. *The Chinese in California.* Portland, Ore.: Richard Abel, 1970.

_____. *San Francisco Almanac.* San Rafael, Calif.: Presidio Press, 1980.

Hansen, Harry. *The 1959 World Almanac and Book of Facts.* New York: New York *World-Telegram & Sun*, 1959.

Hansen, Harvey J., and Miller, Jeanne Thurlow. *Wild Oat in Eden: Sonoma County in the 19th Century.* Santa Rosa, Calif.: n.p., 1962.

Hansen, Joseph. *Quellen und Untersuchungen zur Geschichte des Hexenwahns und der Hexenverfolgung im Mittelalter.* Bonn, Ger.: C. Georgi, 1901.

_____. *Westdeutsche Zeitschrift für Geschichte und Kunst.* Trier, Ger.: F. Lintz, 1882.

_____. *Zauberwahn, Inquisition und Hexenprozess im Mittelalter.* Munich: R. Oldenbourg, 1900.

Hansen, Marcus L. *The Atlantic Migration 1607-1860.* Cambridge, Mass.: Harvard University Press, 1940.

_____. *The Immigrant in American History.* Cambridge, Mass.: Harvard University Press, 1940.

Hanser, Richard. *Putsch: How Hitler Made a Revolution.* New York: Peter H. Wyden, 1970.

Hanson, Joseph Mills. *The Conquest of the Missouri.* New York: Murray Hill, 1946.

Hanson, R.P.C. *Saint Patrick: His Origins and Career.* New York: Oxford University Press, 1968.

Hanson, William H. *The Shooting of John F. Kennedy: One Assassin, Three Shots, Three Hits—No Misses.* San Antonio, Texas: Naylor, 1969.

Hansson, Per Albin. *Demokrati.* Stockholm: Tidens, 1935.

Hansson, Sigfrid. *The Trade Union Movement of Sweden.* Amsterdam, Neth.: International Federation of Trade Unions, 1927.

Han Suyin. *And the Rain My Drink.* London: Jonathan Cape, 1956.

_____. *Birdless Summer.* New York: G.P. Putnam's Sons, 1968.

Hanway, Jonas. *Letters Written Occasionally on the Customs of Foreign Nations in Regards to Harlots.* London: John Rivington, 1761.

Hapgood, D. *The Screwing of the Average Man.* New York: Doubleday, 1974.

Hapgood, Hutchins. *Autobiography of a Thief.* New York: Fox, Duffield, 1903.

_____. *The Spirit of the Ghetto.* New York: Funk & Wagnalls, 1902.

_____. *The Spirit of Labor.* New York: Duffield, 1907.

_____. *A Victorian in the Modern World.* New York: Harcourt, Brace, 1939.

Hapgood, Norman (ed.). *Professional Patriots.* New York: Boni, 1927.

_____, and Moskowitz, Henry. *Up From the Streets: Alfred E. Smith.* New York: Harcourt, Brace, 1927.

Harbaugh, William H. *Lawyer's Lawyer: The Life of John W. Davis.* New York: Oxford University Press, 1973.

Harbinson, R. *No Surrender.* London: Faber & Faber, 1960.

Harcave, Sidney. *First Blood: The Russian Revolution of 1905.* New York: Macmillan, 1964.

_____. *Russia: A History.* Chicago: J.B. Lippincott, 1952.

Hardesty, Don. *Kansas Correctional Officer Selection Study.* Topeka, Kan.: Consulting for Business, Industry & Government, 1970.

_____. *A One Year Personal Study of the Correctional Officer and His Work in the Kansas Penal System.* Topeka, Kan.: Consulting for Business, Industry & Government, 1969.

Hardie, James. *An Impartial Account of the Trial of Mr. Levi Weeks for the Supposed Murder of Miss Julianna Elmore Sands at a Court Held in the City of New York.* New York: N. McFarlane, 1800.

Hardin, John Wesley. *The Life of John Wesley Hardin.* Norman: University of Oklahoma Press, 1961.

Harding, Alan. *A Social History of English Law.* Baltimore: Penguin Books, 1966.

Harding, Berita. *Age Cannot Wither.* Philadelphia: J.B. Lippincott, 1947.

Harding, Thomas Swann. *Aren't Men Rascals?* New York: Dial Press, 1930.

———. *Fads, Frauds and Physicians.* New York: Dial Press, 1930.

———. *The Popular Practice of Fraud.* London: Longmans, Green, 1935.

Hardinge, Arthur. *A Diplomatist in Europe.* London: Jonathan Cape, 1927.

Hardman, J.B.S. (ed.). *American Labor Dynamics.* New York: Harcourt, Brace, 1928.

Hardmon, William. *A Trip To America.* London: T.V. Wood, 1884.

Hardwick, Elizabeth. *Seduction and Betrayal.* New York: Random House, 1974.

Hardwick, Michael. *Doctors on Trial.* London: Herbert Jenkins, 1961.

Hardwick, Mollie. *Emma, Lady Hamilton.* New York: Holt, Rinehart & Winston, 1969.

Hardy, Allison. *Kate Bender, The Kansas Murderess.* Girard, Kan: Haldeman-Julius, 1944.

———. *Wild Bill Hickok, King of Gun-Fighters.* Girard, Kan.: Haldeman-Julius, 1943.

Hardy, Mary Duffus. *Through Cities and Prairie Lands.* New York: R. Worthington, 1881.

Hare, F.A. *The Last of the Bushrangers: The Capture of the Kelly Gang.* Chicago: Weeks, 1892.

Hare, R.D., and Schalling, D. (eds.). *Psychopathic Behaviour.* Chichester, Eng.: John Wiley & Sons, 1978.

Hare, Richard. *Pioneers of Russian Social Thought.* New York: Random House, 1964.

———. *Portraits of Russian Personalities Between Reform and Revolution.* New York: Oxford University Press, 1959.

Harel, Isser. *The House on Garibaldi Street.* London: Andre Duetsch, 1975.

Harenberg, Johann Christoph. *Vernunftige und Christliche Gedancken über die Vampirs oder bluhtsugende Todten.* Wolffen-büttel, Ger.: Meissner, 1733.

Hargrave, Catherine Perry. *A History of Playing Cards.* Boston: Houghton Mifflin, 1930.

Hargrave, Francis (ed.). *A Collection of Tracts Relative to the Laws of England.* Dublin, Ire.: E. Lynch, W. Colles, 1787.

Hargreaves, Reginald. *Red Sun Rising: The Siege of Port Arthur.* Philadelphia: J.B. Lippincott, 1962.

Hargreaves, William. *Our Wasted Resources: The Missing Link in the Temperance Reform.* New York: National Temperance Society, 1878.

Haring, C.H. *The Buccaneers in the West Indies in the Seventeenth Century.* New York: E.P. Dutton, 1910.

Haring, J.V. *The Hand of Hauptmann: The Handwriting Expert Tells the Story of the Lindbergh Case.* Plainfield, N.J.: Hamer, 1937.

Harkey, Dee. *Mean as Hell.* Albuquerque: University of New Mexico Press, 1948.

Harlow, Alvin. *Murders Not Quite Solved.* New York: Julian Messner, 1938.

———. *Old Bowery Days: The Chronicles of a Famous Street.* New York: D. Appleton, 1931.

———. *Old Waybills.* New York: Appleton-Century, 1934.

———. *Weep No More My Lady.* New York: McGraw-Hill, 1942.

Harlow, Ralph Volney. *Gerrit Smith, Philanthropist and Reformer.* New York: Russell & Russell, 1972.

Harlow, Victor Emmanuel. *The Most Picturesque Personality in Oklahoma, Al Jennings.* Oklahoma City, Okla.: Harlow, 1912.

Harman, Samuel W. *Belle Starr, the Female Desperado.* Houston: Frontier Press of Texas, 1954.

———. *Cherokee Bill, the Oklahoma Outlaw.* Houston: Frontier Press of Texas, 1954.

———. *Hell on the Border.* Fort Smith, Ark.: Phoenix, 1898.

Harmer, Ruth Mulvey. *American Medical Avarice.* New York:

Abelard-Schuman, 1975.

Harmon, Jim. *The Great Radio Heroes.* New York: Ace, 1967.

Harms, Ernest. *Drugs and Youth.* New York: Pergamon, 1973.

Harnden, Harvey. *Narrative of the Apprehension in Rindge, N.H. of the Rev. E.K. Avery, Charged with the Murder of Sarah M. Cornell.* Providence, R.I.: W. Marshall, 1833.

Harney, Malachi L., and Cross, John C. *The Informer in Law Enforcement.* Springfield, Ill.: Charles C. Thomas, 1960.

Harolds Club. *Pioneer Nevada.* Reno, Nev.: Harolds Club, 1951.

Harolow, Ralph Volney. *The Growth of the United States.* New York: Henry Holt, 1943.

Harpending, Asbury. *The Great Diamond Hoax.* San Francisco: James Barry, 1913.

Harper, Allen D. *The Politics of Loyalty: The White House and the Communist Issue, 1946-1952.* Westport, Conn.: Green-wood, 1969.

Harper, Charles G. *Half-Hours with the Highwaymen.* London: Chapman & Hall, 1908.

Harper, Fowler V. *Justice Rutledge and the Bright Constellation.* Indianapolis, Ind.: Bobbs-Merrill, 1965.

Harper, J. Henry. *The House of Harper: A Century of Publishing in Franklin Square.* New York: Harper & Brothers, 1912.

Harper, L.A. *The English Navigation Laws: A Seventeenth Century Experiment in Social Engineering.* New York: Columbia University Press, 1939.

Harper, Lillie DuPuy VanCulin. *Colonial Men and Times.* Philadelphia: Innes & Sons, 1916.

Harper, Minnie Timms, and Dewey, George. *Old Ranches.* Dallas: Dealey & Lowe, 1936.

Harper, Robert S. *Lincoln and the Press.* New York: McGraw-Hill, 1951.

Harper, Samuel N. *The New Electoral Law for the Russian Duma.* Chicago: University of Chicago Press, 1908.

———. *The Russia I Believe In.* Chicago: University of Chicago Press, 1945.

Harper, William Hudson (ed.). *Chicago: A History and Forecast.* Chicago: Chicago Association of Commerce, 1921.

Harrelson, Walter. *From Fertility Cult to Worship.* New York: Doubleday, 1969.

Harriman, Alice. *Pacific History Stories.* San Francisco: Whitaker & Ray, 1903.

Harriman, Margaret Case. *The Vicious Circle.* New York: Rinehart, 1951.

Harrington, Alan. *Psychopaths.* New York: Simon & Schuster, 1972.

Harrington, Fred Harvey. *Fighting Politician: Major General N.P. Banks.* Philadelphia: University of Pennsylvania Press, 1948.

———. *Hanging Judge.* Caldwell, Idaho: Caxton Printers, 1951.

Harrington, Michael. *The Accidental Century.* New York: Macmillan, 1965.

———. *The Other America.* New York: Macmillan, 1962.

Harrington, Virginia. *The New York Merchant on the Eve of the Revolution.* New York: Columbia University Press, 1935.

Harris, C.R.S. *Allied Administration of Italy, 1943-1945.* London: HMSO, 1957.

Harris, Carl M. *Statistical Analysis of Recedivism Data.* Washington, D.C.: George Washington University, 1973.

Harris, Carl V. *Political Power in Birmingham, 1871-1921.* Knoxville: University of Tennessee Press, 1977.

Harris, Charles Townsend. *Memories of Manhattan in the Sixties and Seventies.* New York: Derrydale Press, 1928.

Harris, Frank. *My Reminiscences As a Cowboy.* New York: Charles Boni, 1930.

Harris, George W. *Sut Lovingood.* New York: Dick & Fitzger-ald, 1867.

Harris, Janet. *Crisis in Corrections: The Prison Problem.* New York: McGraw-Hill, 1973.

Harris, Joel Chandler. *Gabriel Tolliver: A Story of Reconstruction.* New York: McClure, Phillips, 1902.

Harris, Larry A. *Pancho Villa and the Columbus Raid.* El Paso,

Texas: McMath, 1949.

Harris, Larry R., and Shaw, J. Gary. *Cover-Up: The Governmental Conspiracy to Conceal the Facts About the Public Execution of John Kennedy.* Cleburne, Texas: Shaw, 1976.

Harris, Leon. *Upton Sinclair: American Rebel.* New York: Thomas Y. Crowell, 1975.

Harris, Louis, et al. *Corrections 1968: A Climate for Change.* Washington, D.C.: Joint Commission on Correctional Manpower & Training, 1968.

_____. *The Public Looks at Crime and Corrections.* Washington, D.C.: Joint Commission on Correctional Manpower & Training, 1968.

Harris, M. Kay, and Spiller, Dudley P. *After Decision: Implementation of Judicial Decrees in Correctional Settings.* Washington, D.C.: American Bar Association Commission on Correctional Facilities & Services, 1976.

Harris, Mark. *Mark the Glove Boy.* New York: Curtis Books, 1972.

Harris, N.D. *Europe and the East.* Boston: Houghton Mifflin, 1926.

Harris, Phil. *This Is Three Forks Country.* Muskogee, Okla.: Hoffman Printing, 1965.

Harris, Richard. *The Fear of Crime.* New York: Praeger, 1969.
_____. *Freedom Spent.* Boston: Little, Brown, 1976.
_____. *Justice: The Crisis of Law, Order, and Freedom in America.* New York: E.P. Dutton, 1970.
_____. *The Police Academy: An Inside View.* New York: John Wiley & Sons, 1973.
_____. *The Real Voice.* New York: Macmillan, 1964.

Harris, Robert J. *Judicial Power of the United States.* Baton Rouge: Louisiana State University Press, 1940.

Harris, Robert T., McIsaac, William M., and Chuster, Charles R., Jr. (eds.). *Drug Dependence.* Austin: University of Texas Press, 1970.

Harris, Sallie B. *Hide Town in the Texas Panhandle: 100 Years in Wheeler County and Panhandle of Texas.* Hereford, Texas: Pioneer Books, 1968.

Harris, Sara. *Father Divine: Holy Father.* Garden City, N.J.: Doubleday, 1953.
_____. *House of Ten Thousand Pleasures.* New York: E.P. Dutton, 1962.
_____. *Nobody Cries for Me.* New York: Signet Library, 1959.
_____. *They Sell Sex.* Greenwich, Conn.: Fawcett, 1960.

Harris, Seymour E. *Twenty Years of Federal Reserve Policy.* Cambridge, Mass.: Harvard University Press, 1933.
_____. *Rome's Responsibility for the Assassination of Lincoln.* Pittsburg, Pa.: Williams, 1897.

Harris, T.M. *Assassination of Lincoln: A History of the Great Conspiracy.* Boston: American Citizen, 1892.

Harris, Thomas A. *I'm OK—You're OK: A Practical Guide to Transactional Analysis.* New York: Harper & Row, 1969.

Harris, Thomas L. *The Trent Affair.* Indianapolis, Ind.: Bowen-Merrill, 1896.

Harris, Thomas O. *The Kingfish: Huey P. Long, Dictator.* Baton Rouge, La.: Baton Rouge Clator, 1938.

Harrison, B. *Education, Training, and the Urban Ghetto.* Baltimore, Md.: Johns Hopkins University Press, 1978.

Harrison, Benjamin S. *Fortune Favors the Brave: The Life and Times of Horace Bell.* Los Angeles: Ward Ritchie Press, 1953.

Harrison, Mrs. Burton. *Recollections Grave and Gay.* New York: Charles Scribner's Sons, 1911.

Harrison, Carter H. *Growing Up With Chicago.* Indianapolis, Ind.: Bobbs-Merrill, 1944.
_____. *Recollections of Life and Doings in Chicago.* Chicago: Normandie House, 1945.
_____. *Stormy Years.* Indianapolis, Ind.: Bobbs-Merrill, 1935.

Harrison, Charles Yale. *Clarence Darrow.* New York: Jonathan Cape & Harrison Smith, 1931.

Harrison, E.J. *Fighting Spirit of Japan.* London: W. Foulsham, 1955.

Harrison, Frase. *The Dark Angel: Aspects of Victorian Sexuality.* London: Sheldon, 1977.

Harrison, Fred. *Hell Holes and Hangings.* New York: Ballentine Books, 1968.
_____. *The West's Territorial Prisons, 1861-1912.* New York: Ballantine Books, 1973.

Harrison, George Bagshawe. *Elizabethan Journal, 1591-94.* New York: Cosmopolitan, 1929.

Harrison, H.D. *The Soul of Yugoslavia.* London: Hodder & Stoughton, 1941.

Harrison, Harry P. *Culture Under Canvas: The Story of Tent Chautauqua.* New York: Hastings House, 1958.

Harrison, Henry. *The Neutrality of Ireland: Why It Was Inevitable.* London: R. Hale, 1942.
_____. *Ulster and the British Empire.* London: R. Hale, 1939.

Harrison, Jane. *Prolegomena to the Study of Greek Religion.* New York: Meridian Books, 1955.

Harrison, John A. *Japan's Northern Frontier.* Gainesville: University of Florida Press, 1953.

Harrison, Leonard V. *Police Administration in Boston.* Cambridge, Mass.: Harvard University Press, 1934.

Harrison, Michael. *Clarence: The Life of the Duke of Clarence and Avondale.* London: W.H. Allen, 1972.
_____. *In the Footsteps of Sherlock Holmes.* London: Cassell, 1958.
_____. *The London of Sherlock Holmes.* New York: Drake, 1972.
_____. *The World of Sherlock Holmes.* New York: Drake, 1973.

Harrison, R.H. *Healing Herbs of the Bible.* Leiden, Neth.: E.J. Brill, 1966.

Harrison, Richard. *Criminal Calendar.* London: Jarrolds, 1951.
_____. *Criminal Calendar II.* London: Jarrolds, 1952.
_____. *Foul Deeds Will Rise.* London: John Long, 1958.
_____. *Whitehall 1212: The Story of the Police of London.* London: Jarrolds, 1947.

Harrison, Tom. *World Within: A Borneo Story.* London: The Cresset Press, 1959.

Harrison, Walter M. *Me and My Big Mouth.* Oklahoma City: Briton, 1954.

Harry Hayward: Life, Crimes, Dying Confession and Execution of the Celebrated Minneapolis Criminal. Minneapolis, Minn.: Calhoun, 1896.

Harsnett, Samuel. *A Declaration of Egregious Popish Impostures...under the Pretense of Casting out Devils.* London: James Roberts, 1603.
_____. *Discovery of Fraudulent Practices of John Darrell.* London: John Wolfe, 1599.

Hart, Adolphus M. *History of the Valley of the Mississippi.* New York: Newman & Ivison, 1853.

Hart, Albert Bushnell (ed.). *American History Told by Contemporaries.* New York: Macmillan, 1910.

Hart, B.H. Liddell (ed.). *The Red Army.* New York: Harcourt-Brace, 1956.

Hart, Charles Henry. *Browere's Life Masks of Great Americans.* New York: DeVinne Press, 1899.

Hart, Dorothy. *Thou Sell, Thou Witty.* New York: Harper & Row, 1976.

Hart, Harold (ed.). *Drugs: For and Against.* New York: Hart, 1970.

Hart, Henry H. *Marco Polo.* Norman: University of Oklahoma Press, 1967.

Hart, Herbert L.A. *Law, Liberty, and Morality.* London: Oxford University Press, 1963.
_____. *Punishment and Responsibility.* Oxford, Eng.: Oxford University Press, 1968.

Hart, Herbert M. *Old Forts of the Southwest.* Seattle, Wash.: Superior, 1964.

Hart, J.M. *The British Police.* New York: Macmillan, 1951.

Hart, Sara L. *The Pleasure is Mine.* Chicago: Valentine-Newman, 1947.

Hart, Smith. *The New Yorkers*. New York: Sheridan House, 1938.

Hart, W.C. *Confessions of an Anarchist*. London: Richards, 1906.

Hart, William Surrey. *My Life East and West*. Boston: Houghton Mifflin, 1929.

Hartendorp, A.V.H. *The Santo Tomas Story*. New York: McGraw-Hill, 1964.

Hartjen, Clayton A. *Crime and Criminalization*. New York: Holt, Rinehart, Winston, 1978.

_____. *Possible Trouble: An Analysis of Social Problems*. New York: Praeger, 1977.

Hartlieb, W. Von. *Parole: Das Reich*. Vienna, Aust.: A. Luser, 1939.

Hartman, Chester. *The Transformation of San Francisco*. Totowa, N.J.: Rowman & Allenheld, 1984.

_____. *Yerba Buena*. San Francisco: Glide, 1974.

Hartman, Mary S., and Banner, Lois W. (eds.). *Clio's Consciousness Raised*. New York: Harper & Row, 1974.

_____. *Victorian Murderesses*. New York: Schocken Books, 1977.

Hartman, Susan. *Truman and the 80th Congress*. Columbia: University of Missouri Press, 1971.

Hartmann, Franz. *Buried Alive*. Boston: Occult, 1895.

_____. *Magic: White and Black*. New Hyde Park, N.Y.: University Books, 1970.

Hartmann, L. M. *The Cambridge Medieval History*. Cambridge, Eng.: Cambridge University Press, 1926.

Hartmann, Robert T. *Palace Politics*. New York: McGraw-Hill, 1980.

Hartmann, Wilhelm. *Die Hexenprozesse in der Stadt Hildesheim*. Hildesheim, Ger.: A. Lax, 1927.

Hartogs, Retanus. *The Two Assassins*. New York: Thomas Y. Crowell, 1965.

_____, and Artzi, Eric. *Violence*. New York: Dell, 1970.

Hartsough, Mildred. *From Canoe to Steel Barge on the Upper Mississippi*. Minneapolis: University of Minnesota Press, 1934.

Hartung, Frank E. *Crime, Law, and Society*. Detroit, Mich.: Wayne State University, 1965.

Hartung, Fritz. *Deutsche Verfassungsgeschichte vom 15. Jahrhundert bis zur Gegenwart*. Stuttgart, Ger.: K.F. Koehler, 1950.

_____. *König Friedrich Wilhelm I, der Begründer des preussischen Staates*. Berlin: De Gruyter, 1942.

Hartwell, Samuel W. *A Citizen's Handbook of Sexual Abnormalities*. Lansing: State of Michigan, 1950.

Hartz, Louis. *The Liberal Tradition in America: An Interpretation of American Political Thought Since the Revolution*. New York: Harcourt, Brace, 1955.

Harumi Maeda. *History of Rebellion in the Reign of Hirohito*. Tokyo: Nihon-sho Hosha, 1964.

Harvald, B., and Hauge, M. *Genetics and the Epidemiology of Chronic Diseases*. Washington, D.C.: U.S. Public Health Service, 1965.

Harvey, Allen. *Israfel: The Life and Times of Edgar Allen Poe*. New York: Rinehart, 1934.

Harvey, Clara Toombs. *Not So Wild the Old West*. Denver: Golden Bell Press, 1961.

Harvey, G.B. *Henry Clay Frick, the Man*. New York: Charles Scribner's Sons, 1928.

Harvey, Rowland Hill. *Samuel Gompers*. Palo Alto, Calif.: Stanford University Press, 1935.

Harvison, C. W. *The Horsemen*. Toronto, Ontario, Can.: McClellan & Stewart, 1967.

Harwell, Fred. *A True Deliverance: The Joan Little Case*. New York: Alfred A. Knopf, 1980.

Harwick, J.M.D. *The Sherlock Holmes Companion*. London: John Murray, 1962.

Hasbrouck, Louise S. *Mexico From Cortez to Carranza*. New York: D. Appleton, 1918.

Hasenfeld, Yeheskel, and English, Richard A. (eds.). *Human Service Organizations*. Ann Arbor: University of Michigan Press, 1974.

Hashimoto Mochitsura. *Sunk: The Story of the Japanese Submarine Fleet 1942-1945*. trans. E.H.M. Colegrave. London: Cassell, 1954.

Haskell, Daniel C. *The United States Exploring Expedition, 1838-1842*. New York: Greenwood Press, 1968.

Haskell, E. Luscomb. *The Life of Jesse Harding Pomeroy, the Most Remarkable Case in the History of Crime or Criminal Law*. Boston: n.p., 1892.

Haskell, Frank A. *The Battle of Gettysburg*. Boston: Houghton Mifflin, 1958.

Haskell, Henry C., and Fowler, Richard B. *City of the Future: A Narrative History of Kansas City, 1850-1950*. Kansas City: Frank Glenn, 1950.

Haskell, Martin R., and Yablonsky, Lewis. *Crime and Delinquency*. Chicago: Rand-McNally, 1974.

_____. *Criminology: Crime and Criminality*. Chicago: Rand-McNally, 1974.

Haskell, Molly. *From Reverance to Rape*. New York: Holt, Rinehart & Winston, 1974.

Haskell, Thomas Nelson. *Young Konkaput, the King of the Utes*. Denver: Collier & Cleaveland, 1889.

Haskins, C.H. *The Renaissance of the Twelfth Century*. Cambridge, Mass.: Harvard University Press, 1927.

Haskins, George Lee. *Law and Authority in Early Massachusetts*. New York: Macmillan, 1960.

Haskins, James. *Profiles in Black Power*. Garden City, N.Y.: Doubleday, 1972.

_____. *Street Gangs*. New York: Hastings House, 1974.

Haskins, Jim. *The Cotton Club*. New York: Random House, 1977.

Haslip, Joan. *Catherine the Great*. New York: G.P. Putnam's Sons, 1977.

_____. *The Crown of Mexico*. New York: Holt, Rinehart & Winston, 1971.

Hassard, John R.G. *The Life of...John Hughes*. New York: D. Appleton, 1866.

Hassell, Ulrich von. *Vom anderen Deutschland*. Frankfurt, Ger.: Fischer Bücherei, 1964.

_____. *The Von Hassell Diaries 1938-1944*. New York: Doubleday, 1947.

Hassler, Alfred. *Diary of a Self-Made Convict*. Chicago: Regnery, 1954.

Hastings, Macdonald. *The Other Mr. Churchill: A Lifetime of Shooting and Murder*. New York: Dodd, Mead, 1963.

Hastings, Max. *Yoni, Hero of Entebbe*. New York: Dial Press, 1979.

Hastings, Michael. *Lee Harvey Oswald: A Far Mean Streak of Indepence (sic.) Brought on by Negleck (sic.)*. Baltimore: Penguin Books, 1966.

Hastings, Sir Patrick. *The Autobiography of Sir Patrick Hastings*. London: William Heinemann, 1948.

_____. *Cases in Court*. London: William Heinemann, 1947.

Haswell, Jock. *Spies & Spymasters*. New York: Thames & Hudson, 1977.

Hata Ikuhiko. *Army Fascism*. Tokyo: Kawade Shobo, 1962.

_____. *History of the Sino-Japanese War*. Tokyo: Kawade Shobo, 1962.

_____. *Reality and Illusion*. New York: East Asian Institute, Columbia University, 1967.

Hatch, Alden P. *The Byrds of Virginia*. New York: Holt, Rinehart & Winston, 1969.

_____. *Citizen of the World: Franklin D. Roosevelt*. London: Skeffington & Son, 1948.

_____. *Edith Bolling Wilson*. New York: Dodd, Mead, 1961.

Hatcher, Harlan. *The Western Reserve*. Indianapolis, Ind.: Bobbs-Merrill, 1949.

Hatcher, Julian S., and Jury, Frank J., and Weller, Jac. *Firearms Investigation, Identification, and Evidence*. Harrisburg, Pa.: Stackpole, 1957.

Hathaway, S.R., and Monachesi, E.D. *Analyzing and Predicting Juvenile Deliquency with the MMPI*. Minneapolis: University of Minnesota Press, 1953.

_____, and McKinley, J.C. *Minnesota Multiphasic Personality Inventory*. Minneapolis: University of Minnesota Press, 1942.

Hatherill, George H. *A Detective's Story*. New York: McGraw Hill, 1972.

Hatie, Joseph C. *Commonwealth of Pennsylvania vs. Blasius Pistorius*. Norristown, Pa.: Stephen S. Remark, 1876.

Hatry, Cecil. *The Hatry Case: Eight Current Misconceptions*. London: Published by Author, 1938.

Hatry, Clarence C. *Light Out of the Darkness*. London: Rich & Cowan, 1939.

Hatta, Mohammad. *The Cooperative Movement in Indonesia*. Ithaca, N.Y.: Cornell University Press, 1957.

Hattich, William. *Pioneer Magic*. New York: Vantage Press, 1964.

Hattori Takushiro. *Complete History of the Greater East Asia War*. Tokyo: Hara Shobo, 1965.

Hauber, Eberhard David. *Bibliotheca, Acta et Scripta Magica*. Lemgo, Ger.: J.H. Meyer, 1738.

Haughland, Vern. *The AAF Against Japan*. New York: Harper & Brothers, 1948.

Haupe, Theodore. *Crime and Punishment in Germany*. New York: E.P. Dutton, 1926.

Hauser, Philip H. *Rapid Growth: Key to Understanding Metropolitan Problems*. Washington, D.C.: Washington Center for Metropolitan Studies, 1961.

Hauser, Philip M., and Kitagawa, Evelyn M. *Local Community Fact Book for Chicago, 1950*. Chicago: University of Chicago, 1953.

Hauser, Stuart L. *Black and White Identity Formation*. New York: Wiley-Interscience, 1971.

Hausser, Paul. *Soldaten wie andere auch*. Osnabrück, Ger.: Munin, 1966.

_____. *Waffen-SS im Einsatz*. Göttingen, Ger.: Plesse Verlag K.W. Schütz, 1953.

Haussmann, Georges Eugène. *Mémoires*. Paris: Victor-Havard, 1890.

Hauterive, E. d'. *Sainte-Hélène au temps de Napoléon et aujourd'hui*. Paris: Calmann-Lévy, 1903.

Havas, Laslo. *Hitler's Plot to Kill the Big Three*. New York: Bantam, 1971.

Haven, Charles, and Belden, Frank. *A History of the Colt Revolver and Other Arms by Colt's Patent Fire Arms Manufacturing Co. from 1936 to 1940*. New York: William Morrow, 1940.

Haven, Violet Sweet. *Gentlemen of Japan*. New York: Ziff-Davis, 1944.

Havens, Murray, Leiden, Carl, and Schmitt, Karl. *The Politics of Assassination*. Englewood Cliffs, N.J.: Prentice-Hall, 1970.

Havighurst, R.J., et al. *Growing Up in River City*. New York: Wiley, 1962.

Havighurst, Walter. *Annie Oakley of the Wild West*. New York: Macmillan, 1954.

_____. *Voices on the River, The Story of the Mississippi Waterways*. New York: Macmillan, 1964.

Havins, T.R. *Something About Brown (A History of Brown County, Texas)*. Brownwood, Texas: Banner Printing, 1958.

Hawes, Frances. *Henry Brougham*. London: Jonathan Cape, 1957.

Hawes, Harry B. *Frank and Jesse James in Review for the Missouri Society*. Washington D.C.: n.p., 1939.

Hawk, P.B., Oser, B.L., and Summerson, W.H. *Practical Physiological Chemistry*. Blakinston's Sons, 1947.

Hawke, David Freeman. *Benjamin Rush: Revolutionary Gadfly*. Indianapolis, Ind.: Bobbs-Merrill, 1971.

Hawkeye, Harry. *The Dalton Brothers and Their Gang: Fearsome Bandits of Oklahoma and the Southwest*. Philadelphia: Kerner & Getts, 1908.

_____. *Rube Burrows, the Outlaw*. Baltimore: I.& M. Ottenheimer, 1908.

_____. *Tracy, the Outlaw, King of Bandits*. Baltimore: I.& M. Ottenheimer, 1908.

Hawkins, Gordon J., and Zimring, Franklin E. *Deterrance: The Legal Threat in Crime Control*. Chicago: University of Chicago Press, 1973.

_____. *The Prison: Policy and Practice*. Chicago: University of Chicago Press, 1977.

Hawkins, Hugh (ed.). *The Abolitionists: Immediatism and the Question of Means*. Boston: D.C. Heath, 1964.

_____. *The Abolitionists: Means, Ends and Motivations*. Boston: D.C. Heath, 1972.

_____. *Booker T. Washington and His Critics: The Problem of Negro Leadership*. Boston: D.C. Heath, 1962.

Hawkins, Jack. *Never Say Die*. Philadelphia: Dorrance, 1961.

Hawkins, Peter. *Prince Rainier of Monaco*. London: William Kimber, 1966.

Hawkins, Walter. *Old John Brown*. London: Charles H. Kelly, 1913.

Hawks, Francis L. *History of North Carolina*. Fayetteville, N.C.: E.J. Hale, 1857.

_____. *Narrative of the Expedition of an American Squadron to the China Seas and Japan*. New York: D. Appleton, 1856.

Hawley, James H. (ed.). *History of Idaho, the Gem of the Mountains*. Chicago: S.J. Clarke, 1920.

Hawley, Lowell S., and Bushnell, Ralph Potts. *Counsel for the Damned*. Philadelphia: J.B. Lippincott, 1953.

Hawley, Willis D., and Wirt, Frederick M. (eds.). *The Search for Community Power*. Englewood Cliffs, N.J.: Prentice-Hall, 1968.

_____, and Svara, James H. *The Study of Community Power*. Santa Barbara, Calif.: ABC-CLIO Press, 1972.

_____, et al. *Theoretical Perspectives on Urban Politics*. Englewood Cliffs, N.J.: Prentice-Hall, 1976.

Hawthorne, Nathaniel. *American Note-Books*. Boston: James R. Osgood, 1817.

_____. *The House of the Seven Gables*. Boston: Ticknor, Reed, & Fields, 1851.

Hawtrey, R.G. *The Art of Central Banking*. London: Longmans, Green, 1932.

_____. *Currency and Credit*. New York: Longmans, Green, 1930.

Haxthausen-Abbenburg, August F. *The Russian Empire: Its People, Institutions and Resources*. London: Chapman & Hall, 1856.

Hay, Denys. *The Italian Renaissance in Its Historical Background*. Cambridge, Eng.: University Press, 1961.

Hay, Donald, and Morris, Derek. *Industrial Economics: Theory and Evidence*. Oxford, Eng.: Oxford University Press, 1979.

Hay, Douglas. *Albion's Fatal Tree*. New York: Pantheon Books, 1975.

Hay, John. *The Bread-Winners*. New York: Harper & Bros., 1884.

_____. *Lincoln and the Civil War in the Diaries and Letters of John Hay*. New York: Dodd, Mead, 1939.

Hayashi Fusao. *Affirmative Discussion of the Greater East Asia War*. Tokyo: Bancho Shobo, 1965.

Hayashi Masayoshi (ed.). *Hidden History of Hirohito's Regime*. Tokyo: Mainichi Shimbun-ki, 1965.

Hayashi Shigeru, et al. *The History of the End of Japan's War*. Tokyo: Yomiuri Shimbun-sha, 1965.

Haycraft, Howard. *Murder for Pleasure*. New York: Appleton-Century, 1941.

Hayden, Tom. *Rebellion in Newark: Official Violence and Ghetto Response*. New York: Vintage Books, 1967.

Haydn, Hiram. *Words and Faces*. New York: Harcourt Brace Jovanovich, 1974.

Haydon, Arthur Lincoln. *The Riders of the Plains*. Chicago: A.C.

McClurg, 1910.

Hayek, F.A. (ed.). *Capitalism and the Historians.* Chicago: University of Chicago Press, 1974.

_____. *Law, Legislation, and Liberty.* Chicago: University of Chicago Press, 1973.

Hayes, Augustus Allen, Jr. *New Colorado and the Santa Fe Trail.* New York: Harper & Brothers, 1880.

Hayes, Benjamin. *Pioneer Notes From the Diaries of Judge Benjamin Hayes, 1849-1875.* Los Angeles: Marjorie Tisdale Walcott, 1929.

Hayes, Dorsha. *Chicago: Crossroads of American Enterprise.* New York: J. Messner, 1944.

Hayes, Harold. *Smiling Through the Apocalypse.* New York: McCall, 1969.

Hayes, Jeff W. *Paradise on Earth.* Portland, Ore.: F.W. Bates, 1913.

Hayes, Jess G. *Apache Vengeance.* Albuquerque: University of New Mexico Press, 1954.

_____. *Boots and Bullets: The Life and Times of John W. Wentworth.* Tucson: University of Arizona Press, 1968.

_____. *Sheriff Thompson's Day-Turbulence in the Arizona Territory.* Tucson: University of Arizona Press, 1968.

Hayes, Samuel P. *Conservation and the Gospel of Efficiency.* New York: Atheneum, 1974.

_____. *The Response to Industrialism, 1885-1914.* Chicago; University of Chicago Press, 1957.

Hayes, William C. *The Scepter of Egypt.* Cambridge, Mass.: Harvard University Press, 1953.

Hayes, William Edward. *Iron Road to Empire: The History of 100 Years of Progress and Achievements of the Rock Island Lines.* New York: Simmons-Boardman, 1953.

Hayes-McCoy, G.A. (ed.). *The Irish At War.* Cork, Ire.: Mercier, 1964.

Hayman, Leroy. *The Assassination of John and Robert Kennedy.* New York: Scholastic Book Service, 1976.

_____. *The Death of Lincoln: A Picture History of the Assassination.* New York: Scholastic Book Service, 1968.

_____. *O Captain! The Death of Abraham Lincoln.* New York: Four Winds Press, 1968.

Haynes, Fred E. *The American Prison System.* New York: McGraw-Hill, 1939.

_____. *Social Politics in the United States.* Boston: Houghton Mifflin, 1924.

Haynes, Roy A. *Prohibition Inside Out.* Garden City, N.Y.: Doubleday, Page, 1923.

Hays, Arthur Garfield. *City Lawyer.* New York: Simon & Schuster, 1942.

_____. *Democracy Works.* New York: Random House, 1939.

_____. *Let Freedom Ring.* New York: Boni & Liveright, 1928.

_____. *Trial By Prejudice.* New York: Covici, Friede, 1933.

Hays, Will. *The Memoirs of Will Hays.* New York: Doubleday, 1955.

Hayter, Alethea. *Opium and the Romantic Imagination.* Berkeley: University of California Press, 1968.

Hayward, Arthur L. (ed.). *A Complete History of the Lives and Robberies of the Most Notorious Highwaymen, Footpads, Shoplifts, and Cheats of Both Sexes.* London: George Routledge & Sons, 1926.

_____. *Lives of the Most Remarkable Criminals Who Have Been Condemned and Executed.* London: George Routledge & Sons, 1927.

Hayward, Brooke. *Haywire.* New York: Alfred A. Knopf, 1977.

Hayward, C. *The Courtesan.* London: Casanova Society, 1926.

Hayward, J. *The Case of Israel Lipski, Now Lying Under Sentence of Death for the Murder of Miriam Angel.* London: n.p., 1887.

Haywood, William D. *Bill Haywood's Book.* New York: International, 1929.

Hazard, Lucy Lockwood. *In Search of America.* New York: Thomas Y. Crowell, 1930.

Hazelrigg, Lawrence (ed.). *Prison Within Society.* New York: Doubleday, 1968.

Hazeltine, Rachel C. *Aimee Semple McPherson's Kidnapping.* New York: Carlton Press, 1965.

Hazen, R.W. *History of the Pawnee Indians.* Fremont, Neb.: Fremont Tribune, 1893.

Head, Franklin Harvey. *Untrodden Fields in History and Literature, and Other Essays.* Cleveland: The Rowfant Club, 1923.

Head, Richard. *The English Rogue.* London: George Routledge & Sons, 1874.

Headlam, Stewart P. *Christian Socialism.* London: Fabian Society, 1897.

Headley, Joel Tyler. *The Great Riots of New York: 1712-1873.* New York: E.B. Treat, 1873.

_____. *Napoleon and His Marshals.* New York: Baker & Scribner, 1847.

_____. *Pen and Pencil Sketches of the Great Riots.* New York: E. B. Treat, 1882.

_____. *Washington and His Generals.* New York: Baker & Scribner, 1847.

Headley, John W. *Confederate Operations in Canada and New York.* New York: Neale, 1906.

Healy, Paul F. *Cissy, A Biography of Eleanor M. "Cissy" Paterson.* Garden City, N.Y.: Doubleday, 1966.

Healy, T.M. *Letters and Leaders of My Day.* London: Butterworth, 1928.

Healy, William. *The Individual Delinquent.* Boston: Little, Brown, 1914.

_____. *Mental Conflict and Misconduct.* Boston: Little, Brown, 1917.

_____, and Bronner, Augusta F. *New Light on Delinquency and its Treatment.* New Haven, Conn.: Yale University Press, 1936.

Heaney, Frank, and Machado, Gay. *Inside the Walls of Alcatraz.* Palo Alto, Calif.: Bull, 1987.

Heaps, Willard A. *Assassination: A Special Kind of Murder.* New York: Meredith, 1969.

_____. *Riots U.S.A., 1765-1965.* New York: Seabury Press, 1966.

Heard, Alexander. *The Costs of Democracy.* Chapel Hill: University of North Carolina Press, 1960.

Hearings Before the Subcommittee on Civil and Constitutional Rights of the Committee of the Judiciary. Washington, D.C.: U.S. Government Printing Office, 1976.

Hearn, Lafcadio. *Japan: An Interpretation.* New York: Grosset & Dunlap, 1904.

Hearn, Walter. *Killing of Apache Kid.* n.p, n.d.

Hearns, Rudolph S. *Handwriting, an Analysis Through Its Symbolism.* New York: Vantage Press, 1966.

Hearnshaw, Fossey John Cobb (ed.). *The Social and Political Ideas of Some English Thinkers.* London: G.G. Harrap, 1928.

Hearst, Patricia Campbell. *Every Secret Thing.* Garden City, N.Y.: Doubleday, 1982.

Heath, Carl. *Gandhi.* London: Allen & Unwin, 1944.

Heath, James. *Eighteenth Century Penal Theory.* New York: Oxford University Press, 1963.

Heath, Peter. *Assassins From Tomorrow.* New York: Prestige Books, 1967.

Heathcote, Dudley. *My Wanderings in the Balkans.* London: Hutchinson, 1925.

Heaton, John L. *The Story of a Page: Thirty Years of Public Service and Public Discussion in the Editorial Columns of the New York World.* New York: Harper & Brothers, 1913.

Hebard, Grace Raymond. *The Pathbreakers From River to Ocean.* Chicago: Lakeside Press, 1911.

Hebbel, Friedrich. *Gyges und sein Ring.* Frankfurt, Ger.: Ullstein Bücher, 1965.

Heberle, Rudolf. *Zur Geschichte der Arbeiter-bewegung in Schweden.* Jena, Ger.: Fischer, 1925.

Hebert, Frank. *40 Years Prospecting and Mining in the Black Hills of South Dakota.* Rapid City, S.D.: Rapid City *Daily Journal,* 1921.

Hebrew University of Jeruslaem. *Israel and the United Nations.* New York: Manhattan, 1956.

Hechinger, Fred and Grace. *Growing Up in America.* New York: McGraw-Hill, 1975.

Hechler, Ken. *Working with Truman: A Personal Memoir of the White House Years.* New York: G.P. Putnam's Sons, 1982.

Hecht, Ben. *Charlie: The Improbable Life and Times of Charles MacArthur.* New York: Harper & Bros., 1957.

_____. *A Child of the Century.* New York: Simon & Schuster, 1954.

_____. *Gaily, Gaily, The Memoirs of a Cub Reporter in Chicago.* New York: Doubleday, 1963.

Hecht, David. *Russian Radicals Look to America, 1825-1894.* Cambridge, Mass.: Harvard University Press, 1947.

Hechtlinger, A. *The Great Patent Medecine Era.* New York: Grosset & Dunlap, 1970.

Hecker, Justus Friederich Karl. *The Epidemics of the Middle Ages.* trans. B.G. Babington. London: Sherwood, Gilbert, & Piper, 1835.

Heckerthorn, Charles. *The Secret Societies of All Ages and Countries.* New Hyde Park, N.Y.: University Books, 1965.

Heckman, William L. *Steamboating: Sixty-Five Years on Missouri's Rivers.* Kansas City: Burton, 1950.

Heckstall-Smith, Anthony. *Company of Strangers.* New York: Coward, 1960.

_____. *Sacred Cowes.* London: Anthony Blond, 1965.

Hedayat, Sadeq. *Haji Agha.* Austin, Tex.: CRMS, 1979.

Hedges, J.B. *Henry Villard and the Railways of the Northwest.* New Haven, Conn.: Yale University Press, 1930.

Hedgpeth, Nelie McGraw. *My Early Days in San Francisco.* San Francisco: Victorian Alliance, 1974.

Hedley, F.Y. *Marching through Georgia.* Chicago: n.p., 1890.

Heermans, Forbes. *Thirteen Stories of the Far West.* Syracuse, N.Y.: C.W. Bardeen, 1887.

Heffernan, E. *Making it in Prison.* New York: John Wiley & Sons, 1972.

Heffner, Richard D. *A Documentary History of the United States.* New York: New American Library, 1965.

_____, and Wallace, Michael (eds.) *American Violence.* New York: Vintage Books, 1971.

Hegemann, W. *Napolean, or Prostration Before the Hero.* London: Constable, 1931.

Heiber, Helmut. *Adolf Hitler: Eine Biographie.* Berlin: Colloquium, 1960.

_____. *Hitlers Lagebesprechungen.* Stuttgart, Ger.: Deutsche Verlagsanstalt, 1962.

_____. *Walter Frand and His National Institute for the History of the New Germany.* Stuttgart, Ger.: Deutsche Verlagsanstalt, 1967.

Heidel, Alexander. *The Gilgamesh Epic and Old Testament Parallels.* Chicago: University of Chicago Press, 1949.

Heiden, Konrad. *The Birth of the Third Reich.* Zurich, Switz.: Europa, 1934.

_____. *Der Fuehrer.* Boston: Houghton Mifflin, 1944.

_____. *A History of National Socialism.* Berlin: Rowohlt, 1932.

Heidenheimer, Arnold J. (ed.). *Political Corruption: Readings in Comparative Analysis.* New York: Holt, Rinehart & Winston, 1970.

Heijenoort, Jan Van. *With Trotsky in Exile: From Prinkipo to Coyoacan.* Cambridge, Mass.: Harvard University Press, 1978.

Heilbron, W.C. *Convict Life at the Minnesota State Prison.* St. Paul, Minn.: W.C. Heilbron, 1909.

Heilbroner, Robert. *The Limits of American Capitalism.* New York: Harper & Row, 1966.

_____, et al. *In The Name of Profit: Profiles in Corporate Irresponsibility.* New York: Warner Paperback Library, 1973.

Heilbrunn, O.J. *Soviet Secret Service.* New York: Praeger, 1956.

Heimann, Eduard. *Communism, Fascism, or Democracy?* New York: W.W. Norton, 1938.

Heimbuchner, Max. *Die Orden und Kongregationen der Katholischen Kirche.* Munich: F. Schöningh, 1965.

Heimer, Mel. *The Cannibal: The Case of Albert Fish.* New York: Lyle Stuart, 1971.

Heimert, Alan. *Religion and the American Mind: From the Great Awakening to the Revolution.* Cambridge, Mass.: Harvard University Press, 1966.

Heindel, R.H. *The American Impact on Great Britain, 1898-1914.* Philadelphia: University of Pennsylvania Press, 1940.

Heindl, R. *System und Praxis der Daktyloskopie.* Berlin: de Gruyter, 1927.

Heine, Heinrich. *Poésies.* Paris: Mercure de France, 1924.

Heinig, Curt. *Hohenzollern: Wilhelm II und sein Haus—Der Kampf um den Kronbesitz.* Berlin: n.p., 1921.

Heinrichs, Waldo H., Jr. *American Ambassador: Joseph C. Grew and the Development of the U.S. Diplomatic Tradition.* Boston: Little, Brown, 1966.

Heintz, William F. *San Francisco's Mayors: 1850-1880.* Woodside, Calif.: Gilbert Richards, 1975.

Heinz, G., and Donnay, H. *Lumumba: The Last Fifty Days.* New York: Grove Press, 1969.

Heinz, Heinz A. *Germany's Hitler.* London: Hurst & Blackett, 1934.

Heinzeler, Gerhard. *Das Bild des Tyrannen bei Platon.* Stuttgart, Ger.: W. Kohlhammer, 1927.

Heise, Kenan and Frazel, Mark. *Hands on Chicago.* Chicago: Bonus Books, 1987.

_____. *Is There Only One Chicago?* Richmond, Va.: Westover, 1973.

_____. *This Is Chicago.* Richmond, Va.: Westover, 1973.

Heiss, Robert. *Engels, Kierkegaard, and Marx.* New York: Dell, 1975.

Heitmann, Francis B. *Historical Register and Dictionary of the U.S. Army, 1789-1903.* Washington, D.C.: U.S. Government Printing Office, 1903.

Heizer, Robert F., and Almquist, Alan F. *The Other Californians: Prejudice and Discrimination Under Spain, Mexico, and the United States to 1920.* Berkeley: University of California Press, 1971.

Helbrant, Maurice. *Narcotic Agent.* New York: Vanguard Press, 1941.

Held, Gerrit Jean. *Magie, Hekserij, Entoverij.* Groningen, Neth.: J.B. Wolters, 1950.

Helfer, Ray E., and Kempe, C. Henry (eds.). *The Battered Child.* Chicago: University of Chicago Press, 1974.

Hellerman, Michael, and Renner, Thomas C.. *Wall Street Swindler.* Garden City, N.Y.: Doubleday, 1977.

Hellman, George S. *Benjamin S. Cardozo.* New York: McGraw-Hill, 1940.

Hellman, Lillian. *Pentimento.* Boston: Little, Brown, 1973.

_____. *Scoundrel Time.* Boston: Little, Brown, 1976.

_____. *An Unfinished Woman.* Boston: Little, Brown, 1969.

Helm, P.J. *Alfred the Great.* New York: Thomas Y. Crowell, 1963.

Helm, Peter J. *Jeffreys.* London: Hales, 1966.

Helmer, John. *Drugs and Minority Oppression.* New York: Seabury Press, 1975.

Helmer, William J. *The Gun That Made the Twenties Roar.* New York: Macmillan, 1969.

Helmreich, Ernst C. *The Diplomacy of the Balkan Wars, 1912-1913.* Cambridge, Mass.: Harvard University Press, 1938.

Hélot, Charles. *Névroses et possessions diaboliques.* Paris: Bloud et Barrel, 1898.

Helper, Hinton. *The Land of Gold.* Baltimore: H. Taylor, 1855.

Helpern, Milton, and Knight, Bernard. *Autopsy.* New York: St. Martin's Press, 1977.

Hemingway, Ernest. *By-Line.* New York: Charles Scribner's Sons, 1967.

_____. *A Moveable Feast.* New York: Charles Scribner's Sons, 1964.

Hemm, G. *St. George's Hall, Liverpool.* London: Northern, 1949.

Hemphill, Charles F. *The Dictionary of Practical Law.* Englewood Cliffs, N.J.: Prentice-Hall, 1979.

Hemphill, Vivia. *Down the Mother Lode.* Sacramento, Calif.: Purnell's, 1922.

Hendel, Samuel. *Charles Evans Hughes and the Supreme Court.* New York: King's Crown Press, 1951.

Henderson, Bruce, and Summerlin, Sam. *In Memoriam: John F. Kennedy.* New York: Cowles Education, 1968.

_____. *The Super Sleuths.* New York: Macmillan, 1976.

Henderson, Fred. *The Case for Socialism.* New York: Socialist Party, 1934.

Henderson, G.F.R. *Stonewall Jackson and the American Civil War.* New York: David McKay, 1961.

Henderson, George C. *Keys to Crookdom.* New York: D. Appleton, 1924.

Henderson, Harry B., and Morris, Herman C. *War in Our Time.* Garden City, N.Y.: Doubleday, Doran and Company, 1942.

Henderson, I., and Goodhart, P. *Man Hunt in Kenya.* Garden City, N.Y.: Doubleday, 1958.

Henderson, Jeff S. (ed.). *100 Years in Montague County, Texas.* Saint Jo, Texas: Ipta Printers, 1958.

Henderson, Sir Neville. *Failure of a Mission.* London: Hodder & Stroughton, 1940.

Henderson, Nicholas. *Prince Eugen of Savoy.* London: Weidenfeld & Nicholson, 1964.

Henderson, Richard B. *Maury Maverick: A Political Biography.* Austin: University of Texas Press, 1970.

Henderson, Yandell. *A New Deal in Liquor: A Plea for Dilution.* New York: Doubleday, Doran, 1934.

Hendin, David. *Life Givers.* New York: William Morrow, 1976.

Hendrick, Burton J. *The Age of Big Business.* New Haven, Conn.: Yale University Press, 1919.

_____. *Life of Andrew Carnegie.* New York: Doubleday, Doran, 1932.

_____. *Life and Letters of Walter H. Page.* Garden City, N.Y.: Doubleday, Page, 1922.

_____. *Lincoln's War Cabinet.* Garden City, N.Y.: Dolphin, 1961.

_____. *Lost Cause: Jefferson Davis and his Cabinet.* Boston: Little, Brown, 1939.

_____. *Statesmen of the Lost Cause.* New York: Literary Guild, 1939.

_____. *The Training of an American.* New York: Houghton Mifflin, 1928.

Hendricks, George David. *The Bad Man of the West.* San Antonio, Texas: Naylor, 1941.

Hendrickson, Robert. *Hamilton, 1789-1804.* New York: Mason/Charter, 1976.

Hendrix, John M. *If I Can Do It on Horseback: A Cow-Country Sketchbook.* Austin: University of Texas Press, 1964.

Hendron, J.W. *The Story of Billy the Kid.* Santa Fe, N.M.: Rydal Press, 1948.

Hening, H.B. (ed.). *George Curry, 1861-1947: An Autobiography.* Albuquerque: University of New Mexico Press, 1958.

Henkys, Richard. *Die nationalsozialistischen Gewaltverbrechen.* Berlin: Kreuz, 1964.

Hennen, Gerhard. *Ein Hexenprozess aus der Umgegend von Trier aus dem Jahre, 1592.* St. Wendel, Ger.: Published by Author, 1887.

Hennessey, John A. *What's the Matter with New York? A Story of the Waste of Millions.* New York: O'Connell Press, 1916.

Hennessy, W.B. *Tracy, the Bandit; or, the Romantic Life and Crimes of a Twentieth Century Desperado.* Chicago: M.A. Donohue, 1902.

Hennings, Beth. *Gustav III: En Biografi.* Stockholm: Norstedts, 1957.

Henriques, Fernando. *Modern Sexuality: Prostitution and Society.* London: MacGibbon, 1968.

_____. *Prostitution and Society.* London: MacGibbon, 1968.

_____. *Prostitution in Europe and the Americas.* New York: Citadel Press, 1965.

Henriques, Robert. *A Hundred Hours to Suez.* New York: Viking, 1957.

Henry, Alexander. *Travels and Adventures in Canada and the Indian Territories Between the Years 1760 and 1776.* New York: I. Riley, 1809.

Henry, Andrew F., and Short, James F. *Suicide and Homicide.* Glencoe, Ill.: Free Press, 1954.

Henry, E.R. *Classification and Uses of Finger Prints.* London: H.M. Stationery Office, 1937.

Henry, Jack. *Detective-Inspector Henry's Famous Cases.* London: Hutchinson, 1942.

Henry, James Dodds. *History and Romance of the Petroleum Industry.* London: Bradbury, Agnew, 1914.

Henry, Jules. *Pathways to Madness.* New York: Random House, 1965.

Henry, Mellinger Edward. *Folk-Songs from the Southern Highlands.* New York: J.J. Augustin, 1938.

Henry, Robert Mitchell. *The Evolution of Sinn Fein.* Dublin, Ire.: Talbot Press, 1920.

Henry, Stuart Oliver. *Conquering Our Great American Plains.* New York: E.P. Dutton, 1930.

Henry, W.S. *Campaign Sketches of the War with Mexico.* New York: Harper & Brothers, 1847.

Henry, Will. *Death of A Legend.* New York: Random House, 1954.

_____. *The Raiders.* New York: Bantam Books, 1956.

Henslin, James M. (ed.) *Studies in the Sociology of Sex.* New York: Appleton-Century-Crofts, 1971.

Henson, Allen L. *Confessions of a Criminal Lawyer.* New York: Vantage Press, 1959.

Hentig, Hans von. *Crime: Causes and Conditions.* New York: McGraw-Hill, 1947.

_____. *The Criminal and His Victim.* New Haven, Conn.: Yale University Press, 1948.

_____. *Punishment: Its Origin, Purpose, and Psychology.* London: Hodge, 1937.

Hentoff, Nat. *A Doctor Among the Addicts.* New York: Grove Press, 1968.

_____. *The First Freedom: The Tumultuous History of Free Speech in America.* New York: Delacorte Press, 1980.

Hentze, Margot. *Pre-Fascist Italy.* London: George Allen & Unwin, 1939.

Henze, Paul B. *The Plot to Kill the Pope.* New York: Charles Scribner's Sons, 1983.

Hepburn, A. *Complete Guide to the Southwest.* New York: Doubleday, 1963.

Hepburn, James. *Farewell America.* Vaduz, Liechtenstein: Frontiers, 1968.

Heppenstall, Rayner. *Bluebeard and After, Three Decades of Murder in France.* London: Peter Owen, 1972.

_____. *French Crime in the Romantic Age.* London: Hamish Hamilton, 1970.

_____. *A Little Pattern of French Crime.* London: Hamish Hamilton, 1969.

_____. *The Sex War and Others.* London: Peter Owen, 1973.

Herald, George W., and Rabin, Edward D. *The Big Wheel.* New York: William Morrow, 1963.

Herberg, Will. *Protestant, Catholic, Jew.* Garden City, N.Y.: Doubleday, 1960.

Herbertstein, Sigismund von. *Notes Upon Russia.* trans. R.H. Major. London: Hakluyt Society, 1851.

Herbst, Josephine. *New Green World.* New York: Hastings House, 1954.

Herdon, William H., and Weik, Jesse W. *Abraham Lincoln: The True Story of a Great Life.* New York: D. Appleton, 1893.

Hereford, Robert A. *Old Man River.* Caldwell, Idaho: Caxton, 1943.

Hergesheimer, Joseph. *Swords and Roses.* New York: Alfred A. Knopf, 1929.

Heritage of Freedom. New York: Lion, 1984.

Héritier, Jean. *Catherine De Midici.* trans. Charlotte Haldane. New York: St. Martin's Press, 1963.

Herlihy, David. *The History of Feudalism.* New York: Walker, 1971.

Herling, A.K. *Soviet Slave Empire.* New York: Funk, 1951.

Herling, John. *The Great Price Conspiracy.* Westport, Conn.: Greenwood Press, 1962.

Herman, Judith Lewis. *Father-Daughter Incest.* Cambridge, Mass.: Harvard University Press, 1981.

Herman, Robert D. *Gambling.* New York: Harper & Row, 1967.

Hermann, Donald H.J. *The Insanity Defence.* Springfield, Ill. Charles C. Thomas, 1983.

Hermann, Ernst. *Die Hexen von Baden-Baden.* Karlsruhe, Ger.: Macklot, 1890.

Hermann, Kai, and Koch, Peter. *Entscheidung in Mogadishyu: Die 50 Tage nach Schleyers Entführung.* Hamburg, Ger.: Grunner, 1977.

Hermann, Michele G. *Search and Seizure Checklist.* London: Clark Boardman, 1979.

Hernandez, Ludovico. *Le Procès Inquisitorial de Gilles de Rais avec un Essai de Réhabilitation.* Paris: Bibliothèque des Curieux, 1921.

Hernández Chávez, Salvador. *La Angustia Nacional en 16 Meses del Gobierno de Don Francisco I. Madero.* Mexico City: Alfonso López, 1913.

Herndon, Booton. *Ford: An Unconventional Biography of the Men and Their Times.* New York: Weybright & Tally, 1969.

_____. *The President.* New York: Alfred A. Knopf, 1975.

Hersh, Seymour. *Cover-up.* New York: Random House, 1972.

Hershkowitz, Leo. *Tweed's New York: Another Look.* New York: Anchor, 1978.

Herskovitz, Melville J. *The Anthropometry of the American Negro.* New York: Columbia University Press, 1930.

_____. *Man and His Works.* New York: Alfred A. Knopf, 1956.

Hertell, Thomas. *An Exposé of the Causes of Intemperate Drinking and the Means By Which It May Be Obviated.* New York: E. Conrad, 1819.

Hertogs, Renatus, and Freeman, Lucy. *The Two Assassins.* New York: Thomas Y. Crowell, 1965.

Hertz, Emmanuel. *The Hidden Lincoln: From the Letters and Papers of William H. Herndon.* Garden City, N.Y.: Blue Ribbon Books, 1940.

Hertz, Wilhelm. *Der Werwolf.* Stuttgart, Ger.: A Kröner, 1862.

Hertzberg, Rafaël. *Kulturbilder ur Finlands historia II.* Helsinki, Fin.: G.W. Edlund, 1885.

Hertzog, Peter. *A Dictionary of New Mexico Desperadoes.* Santa Fe, N.M.: Press of the Territorian, 1965.

_____. *Legal Hangings.* Sante Fe, N.M.: Press of the Territorian, 1966.

_____. *Little Known Facts About Billy the Kid.* Santa Fe, N.M.: Press of the Territorian, 1963.

_____. *Old Town Albuquerque.* Santa Fe, N.M.: Press of the Territorian, 1962.

Hervez, Jean. *Ruffians at Ribaudes au moyen âge.* Paris: Bibliothéque des Curieux, 1913.

Herzen, Alexander. *The Memoirs of Alexander Herzen.* New Haven, Conn.: Yale University Press, 1923.

_____. *My Past and Thoughts.* trans. Constance Garnett. New York: Alfred A. Knopf, 1968.

Herzog, Arthur. *Vesco.* New York: Doubleday, 1987.

Herzog, Asa S., and Erickson, A. J. *Camera, Take the Stand.* Englewood Cliffs, N.J.: Prentice-Hall, 1940.

Herzog, E. *Identifying Potential Delinquents.* Washington, D.C.: U.S. Government Printing Office, 1960.

Herzog, Robert. *Die Volksdeutschen in der Waffen-SS.* Tübingen, Ger.: Institut für Besatzungsfragen, 1955.

Herzog, Wilhelm (ed.). *Der Kampf einer Republik: Die Affare Dreyfus.* Zürich, Switz.: Europa-Verlag, 1933.

_____. *From Dreyfus to Petain.* New York: Creative Age Press, 1947.

Hess, Henner. *Mafia and Mafiosi: The Structure of Power.* trans. Ewald Osers. Lexington, Mass.: D.C. Heath, 1970.

Hess, Rudolf. *Reden.* Munich: Eher Verlag, 1938.

Hesseltine, W.B. *Lincoln and the War Governors.* New York: Alfred A. Knopf, 1948.

_____. *Lincoln's Plan of Reconstruction.* Gloucester, Mass.: Peter Smith, 1963.

_____. *Ulysses S. Grant, Politician.* New York: Dodd, Mead, 1935.

Hessling, Peter. *Trois monstres.* Paris: Gallimard, 1958.

Heuman, William. *The Indians of Carlisle.* New York: G.P. Putnam's Sons, 1965.

Heumann, Milton. *Plea Bargaining: The Experience of Prosectors, Judges and Defense Attorneys.* Chicago: University of Chicago Press, 1978.

Heusinger, Adolf. *Befehl im Widerstreit.* Tübingen, Ger.: Rainer Wunderlich Hermann Leinz, 1950.

Heuston, R.F.V. *Lives of the Lord Chancellors, 1885-1940.* Oxford, Eng.: Clarendon Press, 1964.

Hewart, Lord. *Not Without Prejudice.* London: Hutchinson, 1937.

Hewett, Edgar L. *Ancient Life in the American Southwest.* Indianapolis, Ind.: Bobbs-Merrill, 1930.

Hewins, Ralph. *Quisling: Prophet without Honour.* London: W.H. Allen, 1965.

Heydrich, Reinhard. *Wandlungen unseres Kampfes.* Munich: Verlag Franz Eher II, 1935.

Heymann, Robert. *Rasputin.* Leipzig, Ger.: P. List, 1917.

Heyward, DuBose. *Porgy.* New York: Doubleday, 1953.

Heywood, Thomas. *The Heirarchy of the Blessed Angels.* London: Adam Islip, 1635.

Hezlet, Sir Arthur. *The B-Specials.* London: Tom Stacey, 1972.

Hibben, Paxton. *Henry Ward Beecher: An American Portrait.* New York: Press of the Reader's Club, 1942.

_____. *The Peerless Leader: William Jennings Bryan.* New York: Farrar & Rinehart, 1929.

Hibbert, Christopher. *Benito Mussolini.* London: Longmans, Green, 1962.

_____. *Garibaldi and His Enemies.* Boston: Little, Brown, 1966.

_____. *Highwaymen.* New York: Delacorte Press, 1967.

_____. *King Mob: The Story of Lord George Gordon and the London Riots of 1780.* New York: World, 1958.

_____. *The Roots of Evil.* Boston: Little, Brown, 1963.

Hichborn, Franklin. *The System: The San Francisco Graft Prosecution.* Montclair, N.J.: Patterson Smith, 1969.

Hickey, John J. *Our Police Guardians: History of the Police Department of the City of New York Compiled and Written by Officer "787" John J. Hickey, Retired.* New York: Published by Author, 1925.

Hickey, Neal. *The Gentleman Was A Thief.* New York: Holt, Rinehart, Winston, 1962.

Hickey, Neil and Edwin (ed.). *Adam Clayton Powell and the Politics of Race.* New York: Fleet, 1965.

Hickman, Warren Edwin. *An Echo From the Past.* Denver: Western Newspaper Union, 1914.

Hickman, William. *Brigham's Destroying Angels: Being the Life, Confession and Startling Disclosures of the Notorious Bill Hickman, the Dante Chief of Utah.* Salt Lake City, Utah: Shepard, 1904.

Hickox, John H.A. *A History of the Bills of Credit or Paper Money Issued in New York, from 1709 to 1780.* Albany, N.Y.: J.H. Hickox, 1866.

Hicks, Edwin P. *Belle Starr and Her Pearl.* Little Rock, Ark.: Pioneer Press, 1963.

Hicks, Frederick C. (ed.). *Arguments and Addresses of Joseph Hodges Choate.* St. Paul, Minn.: West, 1926.

Hicks, Granville. *Part of the Truth*. New York: Harcourt, Brace, 1965.

_____. *Small Town*. New York: Macmillan, 1946.

Hicks, John D. *The Populist Revolt*. Minneapolis: University of Minnesota Press, 1931.

_____, and Mowry, George E. *A Short History of American Democracy*. Boston: Houghton Mifflin, 1956.

Hicks, John Edward. *Adventures of a Tramp Printer, 1880-1890*. Kansas City: Mid-Americana Press, 1950.

Hicks, Seymour. *Not Guilty M'Lord*. London: Cassell, 1939.

Hidalgo, O.C. *Spy for Fidel*. Miami: Seeman, 1971.

Hidetoshi Matsumura. *Tenno to hanran gun*. Tokyo: Nihon Shuho, 1957.

Hidy, Muriel E. and Ralph W. *Pioneering in Big Business, 1882-1911: The History of the Standard Oil Company*. New York: Harper & Row, 1955.

Hiebert, Ray Eldon, Ungurait, Donald F., and Bohn, Thomas W. *Mass Media: An Introduction to Modern Communication*. New York: David McKay, 1974.

_____, et al. *The Political Image Merchants*. Washington, D.C.: Acropolis Books, 1971.

_____. *The Press in Washington*. New York: Dodd, Mead, 1966.

_____, and Spitzer, Carlton E. *The Voice of Government*. New York: John Wiley & Sons, 1968.

Higdon, Hal. *The Crime of the Century*. New York: G.P. Putnam's Sons, 1975.

_____. *The Union vs. Dr. Mudd*. Chicago: Follett, 1964.

Higgins, Robert. *In the Name of the Law*. London: John Long, 1958.

Higgins, Thomas G. *An Autobiography*. New York: n.p., 1965.

Higginson, John. *Our Dying Saviour's Legacy of Peace to His Disciples in a Troublesome World*. Boston: John Usher, 1686.

Higham, Charles. *The Adventures of Conan Doyle: The Life of the Creator of Sherlock Holmes*. New York: W.W. Norton, 1976.

_____. *Marlene: The Life of Marlene Dietrich*. New York: W.W. Norton, 1977.

_____. *Trading with the Enemy*. New York: Delacorte Press, 1982.

_____. *Ziegfeld*. Chicago: Regnery, 1972.

Higginson, Thomas Wentworth. *Travellers and Outlaws: Episodes in American History*. New York: C.T. Dillingham, 1888.

Higham, John. *Strangers in the Land: Patterns of American Nativism, 1860-1925*. New York: Atheneum, 1973.

Highsmith, Patricia. *Strangers on a Train*. New York: Harper & Brothers, 1950.

Higinbotham, H.N. *Report of the President to the Board of Directors of the World's Columbian Exposition*. Chicago: Rand-McNally, 1898.

Hilary Skinner, John E. *After the Storm; or, Jonathan and his Neighbors in 1865-66*. London: Richard Bentley, 1866.

Hilberg, Raul. *The Destruction of the European Jews*. Chicago: Quadrangle, 1961.

Hilberman, Elaine. *The Rape Victim*. Washington, D.C.: American Psychiatric Association, 1976.

Hildebrand, Wolfgang. *Goetia vel Theurgia*. Leipzig, Ger.: J. Francken, S. Erben, und S. Scheiben, 1631.

Hildreth, Richard. *Japan As It Was and Is*. Chicago: A.C. McClure, 1906.

_____. *A Report on the Trial of Emphraim K. Avery*. Boston: Russell, Odiorne, 1833.

Hildreth, S.P. *History of an Early Voyage Down the Ohio and Mississippi Rivers*. Pittsburgh: n.p., 1856.

Hilger, G., and Meyer, A.G. *The Incompatible Allies; a Memoir History of German-Soviet Relations, 1918-1941*. New York: Macmillan, 1953.

Hill, Rev. Albert Fay. *The North Avenue Irregulars: A Suburb Battles the Mafia*. New York: Cowles, 1968.

Hill, Alice Polk. *Tales of the Colorado Pioneers*. Denver: Pierson & Gardner, 1884.

Hill, Christopher. *The Century of Revolution, 1603-1714*. New York: W.W. Norton, 1982.

_____. *Lenin and the Russian Revolution*. London: English Universities Press, 1957.

_____. *Society and Puritanism*. New York: Schocken Books, 1964.

Hill, Daniel Harvey. *Hal Bridges, Lee's Maverick General*. New York: McGraw-Hill, 1961.

Hill, Douglas, and Williams, Pat. *The Supernatural*. New York: Hawthorn, 1966.

Hill, Edwin C. *The American Scene*. New York: M. Witmark & Sons, 1933.

Hill, Elizabeth, and Mudie, Doris (eds.). *The Letters of Lenin*. New York: Harcourt, Brace, 1937.

Hill, Elwin C. *The American Scene*. New York: M. Witmark & Sons, 1933.

Hill, Forest G. *Roads, Rails and Waterways*. Norman: University of Oklahoma Press, 1957.

Hill, Frederic. *An Autobiography of Fifty Years in Times of Reform*. London: R. Bentley & Son, 1894.

_____. *The Substitute for Capital Punishment*. London: Society for the Abolition of Capital Punishment, 1866.

Hill, George A. *Go Spy the Land*. London: Cassell, 1932.

Hill, J.L. *End of the Cattle Trail*. Long Beach, Calif.: George W. Moyle, 1920.

Hill, James M. *Mining Districts of the Western United States*. Washington, D.C.: U.S. Government Printing Office, 1912.

Hill, John, Jr. *Gold Bricks of Speculation*. Chicago: Lincoln Books, 1904.

Hill, John Alexander. *Stories of the Railroad*. New York: Doubleday & McClure, 1899.

Hill, Judah. *Class Analysis: United States in the 1970s*. Emeryville, Calif.: Class Analysis, 1975.

Hill, Matthew Davenport. *Suggestions for the Repression of Crime*. London: John W. Parker & Sons, 1837.

Hill, Paul. *Portrait of a Sadist*. New York: Avon, 1960.

Hill, R.D. *The Strengths of Black Families*. New York: Emerson Hall, 1972.

Hill, Richard. *The Blessings of Polygamy Displayed*. London: J. Mathews, 1781.

Hill, Rita. *Then and Now, Here and Around Shakespeare*. n.p., 1963.

Hill, Robert A. (ed.). *Marcus Garvey and Universal Negro Improvement Association Papers*. Berkeley: University of California Press, 1983.

Hill, W.A. *Historic Ways...* Hays, Kan.: News, 1938.

_____. *Rome, the Predecessor of Hays*. Hays, Kan.: n.p, n.d.

Hill, William Boyle. *A New Earth and a New Heaven*. London: Watts, 1936.

Hillard-Steinbömer, Gustav. *Herren und Narren der Welt*. Munich: List, 1954.

Hillebrand, Karl. *France and the French in the Second Half of the Nineteenth Century*. London: Trübner, 1881.

Hillel, Marc, and Henry, Clarissa. *Children of the SS*. London: Hutchinson, 1976.

_____. *Of Pure Blood*. trans. Eric Mossmacher. New York: McGraw-Hill, 1977.

Hillmayr, Heinrich. *Roter und Weisser Terror in Bayern*. Munich: Nusser, 1974.

Hillquit, Morris. *History of Socialism in the United States*. New York: Funk & Wagnalls, 1910.

_____. *Loose Leaves from a Busy Life*. New York: Macmillan, 1934.

_____. *Socialism in Theory and Practice*. New York: Macmillan, 1909.

Hills, Stuart L. (ed.). *Corporate Violence: Injury and Death for Profit*. New York: Barnes & Noble, 1987.

_____. *Crime, Power and Morality*. Scranton, Pa.: Chandler, 1971.

Hilsman, Roger. *To Move a Nation*. New York: Doubleday,

1967.

Hilton, Conrad. *Be My Guest.* Englewood Cliffs, N.J.: Prentice-Hall, 1957.

Hilton, J. *A Popular Account of the Thugs and Dacoits, ther Hereditary Gang Robbers and Garrotters of India.* London: Allen, 1857.

Hilton-Young, Wayland. *The Italian Left.* London: Longmans, 1949.

Himes, Norman E. *Medical History of Contraception.* New York: Schocken Books, 1970.

Himmelstein, Jerome L. *The Strange Career of Marijuana: Politics and Ideology of Drug Control in America.* Westport, Conn.: Greenwood, 1983.

Himmler, Heinrich. *Die Schutzstaffel als antibolschewistische Kampf-organisation.* Munich: Zentralverlag der NSDAP, Franz Eher II, 1936.

Hinchley, Vernon. *Spies Who Never Were.* New York: Dodd, Mead, 1965.

Hinckle, Warren, and Turner, William. *The Fish is Red: The Story of the Secret War Against Castro.* New York: Harper & Row, 1981.

Hinckley, Jack and Jo Ann, and Sherrill, E. *Breaking Points.* New York: Berkley Books, 1986.

Hinde, R.S.E. *The British Penal System, 1773-1950.* London: Duckworth, 1951.

Hindelang, M.J., and McDermott, M.J. *Juvenile Criminal Behavior.* Washington, D.C.: U.S. Government Printing Office, 1981.

_____. *Measuring Delinquency.* Beverly Hills, Calif.: Sage, 1981.

_____, Gottfredson, M.R., and Garofalo, J. *Sourcebook of Criminal Justice Statistics, 1976.* Washington, D.C.: National Criminal Justice Information & Statistics Service, 1977.

_____. *Victims of Personal Crime: An Empirical Foundation for a Theory of Personal Victimization.* Cambridge, Mass.: Ballinger, 1978.

Hindenburg, Field Marshal Paul von. *Aus meinem Leben.* Leipzig, Ger.: S. Hirzel, 1920.

_____. *Briefe, Reden, Berichte.* Munich: W. Langwiesche-Brandt, 1934.

_____. *Out of My Life.* New York: Harper's, 1921.

Hindle, Brooke. *David Rittenhouse.* Princeton, N.J.: Princeton University Press, 1964.

_____. *The Pursuit of Science in Revolutionary America, 1735-1789.* Chapel Hill: University of North Carolina Press, 1956.

Hindlip, L. *British East Africa: Past, Present, and Future.* London: T. Fisher Unwin, 1905.

Hindus, Maurice. *Broken Earth.* New York: International, 1926.

_____. *The House Without a Roof: Russia After Forty-Three Years of Revolution.* Garden City, N.Y.: Doubleday, 1961.

Hine, Robert V. *The American West: An Interpretive History.* Boston: Little, Brown, 1973.

Hingley, Ronald. *Nihilists: Russian Radicals and Revolutionaries in the Reign of Alexander II, 1855-1881.* London: Weidenfeld & Nicolson, 1967.

Hinken, Victor. *Illinois in the Civil War.* Urbana: University of Illinois, 1966.

Hinkson, Katherine. *Father Mathew.* London: Macdonald & Evans, 1908.

Hinrichs, Karl. *Friedrich Wilhelm I.* Hamburg, Ger.: Hanseatische Verlagsanstalt, 1941.

_____. *Der Kronprinzenprozess: Friedrich und Katte.* Hamburg, Ger.: Hanseatische Verlagsanstalt, 1936.

Hinschius, Paul. *System des katholischen Kirchenrechts.* Berlin: L. Guttentag, 1869.

Hinshaw, David. *A Man From Kansas: The Story of William Allen White.* New York: G.P. Putnam's Sons, 1974.

Hinshaw, William Wade. *Encyclopedia of Quaker Geneology.* Ann Arbor, Mich.: Edwards Brothers, 1940.

Hinton, Arthur Cherry, and Godsell, Philip H. *The Yukon.* New York: Macrae Smith, 1955.

Hinton, Richard J. *Hand-Book of Arizona.* San Francisco: Upham, 1878.

_____. *John Brown and His Men.* New York: Funk & Wagnalls, 1894.

Hintze, Otto. *Die Hohenzollern und ihr Werk.* Berlin: P. Parey, 1915.

Hippler, A.E. *Hunter's Point.* New York: Basic Books, 1974.

Hirning, L. Clovis. *The Sex Offender in Custody: Handbook of Correctional Psychology.* New York: Philosophical Library, 1947.

Hiroshima Plus 20. New York: Delacorte Press, 1965.

Hirsch, Arthur Henry. *The Huguenots of Colonial South Carolina.* Durham, N.C.: Duke University Press, 1928.

Hirsch, Foster. *The Dark Side of the Screen: Film Noir.* Cranbury, N.J.: A.S. Barnes, 1981.

Hirsch, Kurt. *SS, Gestern, heute und...* Darmstadt, Ger.: Progress Verlag Johann Fladung, 1960.

Hirsch, Mark D. *William C. Whitney, Modern Warwick.* New York: Dodd, Mead, 1948.

Hirsch, Nathaniel. *Dynamic Causes of Juvenile Crime.* Cambridge, Eng.: Sci-Art, 1937.

Hirsch, Phil. *Death House.* New York: Pyramid Books, 1966.

_____. *Fires.* New York: Pyramid Books, 1971.

_____. *Hollywood Uncensored.* New York: Pyramid Books, 1965.

_____. *The Killers.* New York: Pyramid Books, 1971.

_____. *The Law Enforcers.* New York: Pyramid Books, 1969.

_____. *Men Behind Bars.* New York: Pyramid Books, 1962.

_____. *The Racketeers.* New York: Pyramid Books, 1969.

Hirsch, Richard. *The Soviet Spies.* New York: Duell, Sloan, & Pearce, n.d.

Hirschfeld, Magnus. *Sexual Anomalies and Perversions.* London: Encyclopedic Press, 1938.

Hirschi, Travis. *Causes of Delinquency.* Berkeley: University of California Press, 1969.

_____, and Selvin, Hanan. *Delinquency Research.* New York: Free Press, 1967.

Hirshson, Stanley P. *Farewell to the Bloody Shirt: Northern Republicans and the Southern Negro, 1877-1893.* Bloomington: Indiana University Press, 1962.

_____. *Grenville M. Dodge: Soldier, Politician, Railroad Pioneer.* Bloomington: Indiana University Press, 1967.

Hirst, David. *The Gun and the Olive Branch.* London: Faber & Faber, 1977.

Hirst, Derek. *The Representative of the People? Voters and Voting in England under the Early Stuarts.* Cambridge, Eng.: Cambridge University Press, 1975.

Hirst, Francis W. *The Six Panics and Other Essays.* London: Methuen, 1913.

Hiss, Alger. *In the Court of Public Opinion.* New York: Alfred A. Knopf, 1957.

Hiss, Tony. *Laughing Last.* Boston: Houghton Mifflin, 1977.

The History and Confession of the Young Felon, Edward W. Hawkins. Louisville, Ky.: n.p., 1857.

History of Bayard: The Good Chevalier Sans Peur et Sans Reproche. trans. Loredan Larchey. London: Chapman & Hall, 1883.

The History of Napa and Lake Counties. San Francisco: Slocum, Bowen, 1880.

History of Placer County. Oakland, Calif.: Thompson & West, 1882.

History of the Arkansas Valley, Colorado. Chicago: O.L. Baskin, 1881.

History of the Crime and True Confessions of William Seely Hopkins. Philadelphia: n.p., 1890.

History of the Eleventh Pennsylvania Cavalry. Philadelphia: Franklin, 1902.

History of the Fifth New York Cavalry. Albany, N.Y.: S.R. Gray, 1865.

The History of the Murder of Hiram Sawtell by His Brother, Isaac Sawtell. Laconia, N.H.: John H. Lane, n.d.

History of the New Orleans Police Department. New Orleans: n.p.,

1900.

A History of the O'Mara Murder Trial. Montrose, Pa.: E.B. Hawley, 1874.

Hitchcock, Ethan Allen. *Fifty Years in Camp and Field.* New York: G.P. Putnam's Sons, 1909.

Hitchcock, Frank. *A True Account of the Capture of Frank Rande, "The Noted Outlaw".* Peoria, Ill.: J.W. Franks & Sons, 1897.

Hitchcock, Mary E. *Two Women in the Klondike: The Story of a Journey to the Gold-Fields of Alaska.* New York: G.P. Putnam's Sons, 1899.

Hitler, Adolf. *Hitler's Secret Book.* New York: Grove Press, 1961.

_____. *Mein Kampf.* trans. Ralph Manheim. Boston: Houghton Mifflin, 1943.

Hitler e Mussolini: lettre e documenti. Rome: Rizzoli, 1946.

Hittell, John S. *The Commerce and Industries of the Pacific Coast.* San Francisco: A.L. Bancroft, 1882.

_____. *A History of the City of San Francisco.* San Francisco: A.L. Bancroft, 1878.

Hittell, Theodore H. *History of California.* San Francisco: N.J. Stone, 1898.

Hitti, Philip. *History of the Arabs.* London: Macmillan, 1937.

_____. *History of Syria.* London: Macmillan, 1951.

Hixson, Fred. *The Age of Will Cummings.* Published by Author, 1962.

Hjersman, Peter. *The Stash Book.* Berkeley, Calif.: And/Or Press, 1978.

Hoan, Daniel W. *City Government.* New York: Harcourt, Brace, 1936.

Hoar, George F. *Autobiography of Seventy Years.* New York: Charles Scribner's Sons, 1906.

Hoare, Sir Samuel. *Nine Troubled Years.* London: William Collins, 1954.

Hobart, Mrs. Garret A. *Memories.* Published by Author, 1930.

Hobart, Pasha. *Sketches From My Life.* New York: D. Appleton, 1887.

Hobbes, Thomas. *Leviathan.* Oxford, Eng.: Basil Blackwell, 1957.

Hobbs, James. *Wild Life in the Far West: Personal Adventures of a Border Mountain Man.* Hartford, Conn.: Wiley, Waterman & Eaton, 1872.

Hobbs, Richard Gear. *Glamorland: The Ozarks.* Manhattan, Kan.: n.p., 1944.

Hobby, E.W. *Eastern Uganda.* London: Anthropological Institute of Great Britain, 1902.

Hobhouse, S., and Brockway, A.F. *English Prisons Today.* London: Longmans, 1922.

Hobley, C.W. *Kenya: From Chartered Company to Crown Colony.* London: H.F. & G. Witherby, 1929.

Hobsbawm, Eric J. *The Age of Revolution, 1789-1848.* New York: New American Library, 1962.

_____. *Bandits.* New York: Delacorte Press, 1969.

_____. *Primitive Rebels: Studies in Archaic Forms of Social Movement in the 19th and 20th Centuries.* New York: W.W. Norton, 1965.

_____. *The Revolutionaries.* New York: New American Library, 1975.

_____. *Social Bandits and Primitive Rebels.* Glencoe, Ill.: Free Press, 1959.

Hobson, H., et al. *The Pearl of Days: An Intimate Memoir of the Sunday Times.* London: Hamish Hamilton, 1972.

Hobson, John A. *Confessions of an Economic Heretic.* London: George Allen & Unwin, 1938.

_____. *Economics and Ethics.* Boston: Heath, 1929.

_____. *The Evolution of Modern Capitalism.* New York: Charles Scribner's Sons, 1926.

_____. *Free Thought in the Social Sciences.* New York: Macmillan, 1926.

_____. *Imperialism: A Study.* Ann Arbor: University of Michigan Press, 1965.

_____. *Incentives and the New Industrial Order.* New York: Seltzer, 1922.

Hobson, Richmond Pearson. *Alcohol and the Human Race.* New York: Fleming H. Revell, 1919.

_____. *The Great Destroyer.* Washington, D.C.: n.p., 1911.

Hochberg, J.E. *Perception.* Englewood Cliffs, N.J.: Prentice-Hall, 1978.

Hochstedler, Ellen C. *Corporations as Criminals.* Beverly Hills, Calif.: Sage, 1984.

Hodder, Alfred. *A Fight for the City.* New York: Macmillan, 1903.

Hodder, Edwin. *The Life and Work of the Seventh Earl of Shaftesbury.* London: Cassell, 1886.

Hodge, Frederick Webb (ed.). *Handbook of American Indians North of Mexico.* Washington D.C.: U.S. Government Printing Office, 1907.

Hodge, Harry. *The Black Maria, or the Criminal's Omnibus.* London: Victor Gollancz, 1935.

_____ (ed.). *Famous Trials.* Baltimore: Penguin Books, 1941.

Hodges, D.C. (ed.). *Philosophy of the Urban Guerrilla: The Revolutionary Writings of Abraham Guillen.* New York: William Morrow, 1973.

Hodgetts, Edward A.B. *The House of Hohenzollern.* London: Methuen, 1911.

_____. *Life of Catherine the Great of Russia.* London: Methuen, 1914.

Hodgson, M.G.S. *The Order of Assassins.* The Hague, Neth.: Mouton, 1959.

Hodson, James Lansdale. *The Sea and the Land.* London: Victor Gollancz, 1945.

Hodson, H.V. *Slump and Recovery, 1929-1937.* Oxford, Eng.: Oxford University Press, 1938.

Hoebel, E. Adamson. *Anthropology.* New York: McGraw-Hill, 1972.

_____. *The Cheyennes.* New York: Henry Holt, 1960.

_____. *The Law of Primitive Man.* Cambridge, Mass.: Harvard University Press, 1954.

Hoegner, Wilhelm. *Die verratene Republik.* Munich: Isar, 1958.

Hoehling, Mary D. *The Real Sherlock Holmes.* New York: Julian Messner, 1965.

Hoensbroech, Count Paul von. *Fourteen Years a Jesuit.* London: Cassell, 1911.

Hoetzsch, Otto. *Grundzuge der Geschichte Russlands.* Stuttgart, Ger.: K.F. Koehler, 1949.

Hoff, Harry Summerfield. *Shall We Ever Know? The Trial of the Brothers Hosein for the Murder of Mrs. McKay.* New York: Harper & Row, 1971.

Hoffer, A., and Osmond, H. *The Hallucinogens.* New York: Academic Press, 1967.

Hofman, Hans Hubert. *Der Hitlerputsch.* Munich: Nymphenburger Verlagshandlung, 1961.

Hoffman, A. *Unwanted Mexican Americans.* Tucson: University of Arizona Press, 1974.

Hoffman, Charles Fenno. *A Winter in the West.* Chicago: Fergus, 1882.

Hoffman, F.L. *The Homicide Problem.* Newark, N.J.: Prudential Press, 1925.

Hoffman, Frederick J. *The Twenties: American Writing in the Postwar Decade.* New York: Free Press, 1962.

Hoffman, George W. *The Balkans in Transition.* New York: D. Van Nostrand, 1963.

_____, and Neal, Fred Warner. *Yugoslavia and the New Communism.* New York: Twentieth Century Fund, 1962.

Hoffman, J.J. *The Twenties.* New York: Viking Press, 1949.

Hoffman, O. *Reports on Land Cases.* San Francisco: Numa Hubert, 1892.

Hoffman, P. *Lions in the Street.* New York: Saturday Review Press, 1973.

Hoffman, Paul. *Courthouse.* New York: Hawthorn Books, 1979.

_____. *To Drop a Dime.* New York: G.P. Putnam's Sons, 1976.

Hoffman, Robert. *More Than a Trial: The Struggle of Captain Dreyfus.* New York: Free Press, 1980.

Hoffmann, Martin. *The Gay World.* New York: Bantam, 1971.

Hoffmann, Peter. *The History of the German Resistance, 1933-1945.* trans. Richard Barry. Cambridge, Mass.: MIT Press, 1977.

_____. *Hitler's Personal Security.* London: Macmillan, 1979.

Hoffmann, Peter, and Wallace, Michael. *American Violence.* New York: Alfred A. Knopf, 1970.

Hofstadter, Richard. *The Age of Reform.* New York: Random House, 1955.

_____. *The American Political Tradition and the Men Who Made It.* New York: Vintage Books, 1955.

_____, and Wallace, Michael (eds.). *American Violence: A Documentary History.* New York: Vintage Books, 1971.

_____. *Anti-Intellectualism in American Life.* New York: Alfred A. Knopf, 1963.

_____. *Great Issues in American History.* New York: Vintage Books, 1969.

_____. *The Paranoid Style in American Politics.* New York: Alfred A. Knopf, 1965.

Hogan, David. *The Four Glorious Years.* Dublin, Ire.: Irish Press, 1953.

Hogan, Ray. *The Life and Death of Clay Allison.* New York: New American Library, 1961.

_____. *The Life and Death of Johnny Ringo.* New York: New American Library, 1963.

Hogan, William Ransom. *The Texas Republic.* Norman: University of Oklahoma Press, 1946.

Hogarth, Georgina (ed.). *The Letters of Charles Dickens, 1833-1870.* London: Chapman & Hall, 1909.

Hogarth, John. *Sentencing as a Human Process.* Toronto, Ontario, Can.: University of Toronto Press, 1971.

Hogg, Gary. *Cannibalism and Human Sacrifice.* New York: Citadel Press, 1966.

Hogg, Ian V. *The Complete Encyclopedia of World Firearms.* New York: A & W, 1978.

_____. *Guns.* New York: Everest House, 1979.

_____, and Weeks, John. *Military Small Arms of the 20th Century.* New York: Hippocrene Books, 1977.

Hogg, James. *Private Memoirs and Confessions of a Justified Sinner.* London: Oxford University Press, 1981.

Hogg, Thomas E. *Authentic History of Sam Bass and His Gang.* Denton, Texas: Monitor Job Office, 1878.

Hohenberg, John. *The New Front Page.* New York: Columbia University Press, 1966.

_____. *The Professional Journalist.* New York: Holt, Rinehart & Winston, 1961.

Hohenlohe-Schillingfürst, Alexander von. *Denkwürdigkeiten der Reichskanzlerzeit.* Stuttgart, Ger.: Deutsche Verlags-Anstalt, 1931.

Hohimer, Frank. *The Home Invaders.* Chicago: Chicago Review Press, 1975.

Hohler, Sir Thomas B. *Diplomatic Petrel.* London: John Murray, 1942.

Höhn, Reinhard. *Arthur Mahraun, der Wegweiser zur Nation.* Rendsburg, Ger.: Schleswig-Holsteinische Verlagsanstalt, 1929.

Hohne, Heinz. *The Order of the Death's Head.* New York: Coward-McCann, 1970.

Holand, Hjalmar R. *America, 1355-1364.* New York: Duell, Sloan & Pearce, 1946.

_____. *Explorations in America Before Columbus.* New York: Twayne, 1956.

_____. *The Kensington Stone.* Ephraim, Wis.: Published by Author, 1932.

_____. *My First Eighty Years.* New York: Twayne, 1957.

_____. *A Pre-Columbian Crusade to America.* New York: Twayne, 1962.

_____. *Westward From Vinland.* New York: Duell, Sloan & Pearce, 1940.

Holbrook, D. *Sex and Dehumanization.* London: Pitman, 1972.

Holbrook, Stewart H. *The Age of Moguls.* Garden City, N.Y.: Doubleday, 1954.

_____. *Dreamers of the American Dream.* Garden City, N.Y.: Doubleday, 1957.

_____. *Far Corner: A Personal View of the Northwest.* New York: Macmillan, 1952.

_____. *Holy Old Mackinaw: A Natural History of the American Lumberjack.* New York: Macmillan, 1938.

_____. *Let Them Live.* New York: Macmillan, 1938.

_____. *Little Annie Oakley and Other Rugged People.* New York: Macmillan, 1948.

_____. *Murder Out Yonder.* New York: Macmillan, 1941.

_____ (ed.). *Promised Land: A Collection of Northwest Writings.* New York: McGraw-Hill Books, 1945.

_____. *The Rocky Mountain Revolution.* New York: Henry Holt, 1956.

_____. *The Story of American Railroads.* New York: Crown, 1947.

_____. *Wild Bill Tames the West.* New York: Random House, 1952.

Holcombe, Arthur N. *The Spirit of the Chinese Revolution.* New York: Alfred A. Knopf, 1930.

Holcombe, R.I. (ed.). *History of Marion County, Missouri.* St. Louis: E.F. Parkins, 1884.

Holden, W.C. *Alkali Trails.* Dallas: The Southwest Press, 1930.

Holdredge, Helen. *Mammy Pleasant.* New York: G.P. Putnam's Sons, 1953.

_____. *The Woman in Black.* New York: G.P. Putnam's Sons, 1955.

Holdsworth, W.S. *A History of English Law.* London: Methuen, 1903.

Hole, Christina. *Haunted England.* London: B.T. Batsford, 1940.

_____. *A Mirror of Witchcraft.* London: Chatto & Windus, 1957.

_____. *Witchcraft in England.* New York: Charles Scribner's Sons, 1947.

Holiday, Billie. *Lady Sings the Blues.* New York: Doubleday, 1956.

Holland, Claude V. *Tortugas Run.* Bonita Springs, Fla.: Holland Books, 1972.

Holland, Gustavus Adolphus. *History of Parker County and the Double Log Cabin.* Weatherford, Texas: Herald, 1937.

_____. *The Man and His Monument: The Man Was J.R. Couts, His Monument the Citizens National Bank.* Weatherford, Texas: Herald, 1924.

Holland, Henry. *A Treatise Against Witchcraft.* Cambridge, Eng.: J. Legatt, 1590.

Holland, J.G. *Life of Abraham Lincoln.* New York: Paperback Library, 1961.

Hollander, Gayle Durham. *Soviet Political Indoctrination: Development in Mass Media and Propaganda Since Stalin.* New York: Frederick A. Praeger, 1972.

Hollick, F. *Murder Made Moral: Or An Account of the Thugs and Other Secret Murderers of India.* Manchester, Eng.: A. Heywood, 1840.

Holliday, Charles W. *The Valley of Youth.* Boise, Idaho: Caxton Printers, 1948.

Hollingsworth, Claire. *The Arabs and the West.* London: Methuen, 1952.

Hollingsworth, Ellen Jane. *Dimensions in Urban History.* Madison: University of Wisconsin Press, 1979.

Hollis, C. *Shadow of the Gallows.* London: Victor Gollancz, 1951.

Hollis, Christopher. *The American Heresy.* London: Sheed & Ward, 1927.

Hollon, W. Eugene. *Frontier Violence: Another Look.* New York: Oxford University Press, 1974.

_____. *The Southwest Old and New.* New York: Alfred A. Knopf, 1961.

Holloway, Carroll C. *Texas Gun Lore*. San Antonio, Texas: Naylor, 1951.

Holloway, Jean. *Hamlin Garland*. Austin: University of Texas Press, 1960.

Holloway, Laura C. *The Ladies of the White House; or, In the Homes of the Presidents*. Philadelphia: Bradley, 1886.

Holloway, Mark. *Heavens on Earth*. London: Turnstile Press, 1951.

Holman, D. *Bwana Drum*. London: W.K. Allen, 1964.

Holmes, the Arch Fiend. Cincinnati, Ohio: Barclay, 1890.

Holmes, Clive. *The Eastern Association in the English Civil War*. Cambridge, Eng.: Cambridge University Press, 1974.

Holmes, Colin. *Anti-Semitism in British Society, 1876-1939*. London: Edward Arnold, 1979.

Holmes, John Haynes. *The Christ of Today*. Madras, India: Tagore, 1922.

_____. *My Gandhi*. New York: Harper & Brothers, 1953.

Holmes' Own Story. Philadelphia: Burke & McFetridge, 1895.

Holmes, Oliver Wendell. *The Common Law*. Cambridge, Mass.: Belknap, 1963.

Holmes, Paul. *The Candy Murder Case*. New York: Bantam, 1966.

Holmes, Ronald M., and DeBurger, James. *Serial Murder*. Newbury Park, Calif.: Sage, 1988.

Holmes, Thomas James. *Cotton Mather*. Cambridge, Mass.: Harvard University Press, 1940.

_____. *Cotton Mather and His Writings on Witchcraft*. Chicago: University of Chicago Press, 1926.

Holmes, William Gordon. *The Age of Justinian and Theodora*. London: G. Bell & Sons, 1912.

Holroyd, James Edward. *Baker Street Byways: A Book about Sherlock Holmes*. London: George Allen & Unwin, 1959.

_____. *The Gaslight Murders*. London: George Allen & Unwin, 1960.

_____. *The Sheppard Murder Case*. New York: David McKay, 1961.

Holroyd, Michael. *Lytton Strachey*. New York: Holt, Rinehart & Winston, 1968.

Holt, Arthur E. *Christian Roots of Democracy in America*. New York: Friendship Press, 1941.

Holt, Don. *The Justice Machine*. New York: Ballantine, 1972.

Holt, Edgar. *Protest in Arms: The Irish Troubles, 1916-1923*. London: G.P. Putnam's Sons, 1960.

Holt, J. *Finger Prints Simplified*. Chicago: F.J. Drake, 1941.

Holt, J. *Report of the Judge Advocate General on the Order of American Knights, or Sons of Liberty*. Washington, D.C.: U.S. Government Printing Office, 1864.

Holt, Sir John. *Modern Cases Argued and Adjudged*. London: J. Walthoe, 1725.

_____. *A Report of All the Cases Determined by Sir John Holt, 1681-1710*. London: J. Hazard, 1738.

Holton, Leonard T., and Longstreth, Edward. *What'll We Do Now?* New York: Simon & Schuster, 1928.

Holtzman, Jerome (ed.). *No Cheering in the Press Box*. New York: Holt, Rinehart & Winston, 1973.

Holtzoff, H. (ed.). *Encyclopedia of Criminology*. New York: Philosophical Library, 1949.

Holyoake, George Jacob. *Sixty Years of an Agitator's Life*. London: Unwin, 1893.

Holyst, B. *Comparative Criminology*. Lexington, Mass.: Lexington Books, 1979.

Holz, Denice (ed.). *Conspiracy in Dallas*. Shreveport, La.: Fairchild, 1981.

Holzer, Hans. *The Truth About Witchcraft*. New York: Doubleday, 1969.

Holzinger, J.B. *Zur Naturgeschichte der Hexen*. Graz, Aust.: Steiermark, 1883.

Holzman, Robert S. *The Romance of Firefighters*. New York: Bonanza Books, 1971.

Holzner, Burkart. *Reality Construction in Society*. Cambridge, Mass.: Schenkman, 1968.

Homans, George C. *The Human Group*. New York: Harcourt, Brace, 1950.

_____. *Social Behavior: Its Elementary Forms*. New York: Harcourt, Brace & World, 1961.

Home Office. *Report of the Departmental Committee on Legal Aid in Criminal Proceedings*. London: HMSO, 1966.

_____. *Report of the Working Party on Bail in Magistrates' Courts*. London: HMSO, 1974.

_____. *The Sentence of the Court*. London: HMSO, 1969.

Homer. *The Iliad*. trans. William Cowper. New York: G.P. Putnam's Sons, 1850.

_____. *The Odyssey*. trans. W.H.D. Rouse. New York: New American Library, 1963.

Homer, Frederick D. *Guns and Garlic*. West Lafayette, Ind.: Purdue University Press, 1974.

Homes, Nathaniel. *Demonology and Theology*. London: J. Martin & J. Ridley, 1650.

Homsher, Lola M. (ed.). *South Pass, 1868: James Chisholm's Journal of the Wyoming Gold Rush*. Lincoln: University of Nebraska Press, 1960.

Hone, J.M. *William Butler Yeats: The Poet in Contemporary Ireland*. Dublin, Ire.: Maunsel, 1915.

Honeycombe, Gordon. *The Murders of the Black Museum, 1870-1970*. London: Hutchinson, 1982.

Honigman, John J. *Culture and Ethos of Kaska Society*. New Haven, Conn.: Yale University Press, 1949.

Honour, Hugh. *The New Golden Land*. New York: Pantheon Books, 1975.

Hood, R.G. *Sentencing in Magistrates' Courts*. London: Stevens, 1962.

_____. *Sentencing the Motoring Offender*. London: Heinemann Educational, 1972.

Hood, Roger, and Sparks, Richard. *Key Issues in Criminology*. New York: McGraw-Hill, 1970.

Hoogenboom, Ari. *Outlawing the Spoils*. Urbana: University of Illinois Press, 1961.

Hook, Sidney. *Common Sense and the Fifth Amendment*. New York: Criterion, 1957.

_____. *From Hegel to Marx: Studies in the Intellectual Development of Karl Marx*. Ann Arbor: University of Michigan Press, 1962.

_____. *Heresy, Yes-Conspiracy, No*. New York: John Day, 1953.

_____ (ed.). *John Dewey*. New York: Dial Press, 1950.

_____. *Marx and the Marxists*. Princeton, N.J.: D. Van Nostrand, 1955.

_____. *The Paradoxes of Freedom*. Berkeley: University of California Press, 1962.

_____. *Political Power and Personal Freedom*. New York: Criterion Books, 1959.

Hooker, Richard J. (ed.). *The Carolina Backcountry on the Eve of the Revolution*. Chapel Hill, N.C.: University of North Carolina Press, 1953.

Hooker, Thomas. *The Application of Redemption*. London: Peter Cole, 1659.

Hooker, William Francis. *The Prairie Schooner*. Chicago: Saul Brothers, 1918.

Hoole, W. Stanley. *The James Boys Rode South*. Tuscaloosa, Ala.: Published by Author, 1955.

Hooper, Osman C. *History of Ohio Journalism, 1793-1933*. Columbus, Ohio: Published by Author, 1933.

_____. *Ohio Journalism Hall of Fame*. Columbus: Ohio State University, 1929.

Hooper, William Eden. *The History of Newgate and the Old Bailey*. London: Underwood Press, 1935.

Hooton, Earnest A. *The American Criminal*. Cambridge, Mass.: Harvard University Press, 1939.

_____. *Crime and the Man*. Cambridge, Mass.: Harvard University Press, 1939.

Hoover, Calvin B. *Germany Enters the Third Reich*. New York:

Macmillan, 1933.

Hoover, H.A. *Early Days in the Mogollons.* El Paso, Texas: Western Press, 1958.

Hoover, Herbert. *Addresses Upon the American Road, 1941-1945.* New York: Charles Scribner's Sons, 1946.

_____. *The Memoirs of Herbert Hoover: The Cabinet and the Presidency, 1920-1933.* New York: Macmillan, 1952.

_____. *The Memoirs of Herbert Hoover: The Great Depression, 1929-1941.* New York: Macmillan, 1941.

_____. *The Memoirs of Herbert Hoover: Years of Adventure, 1874-1920.* New York: Macmillan, 1952.

Hoover, Irwin Hood. *Forty-two Years in the White House.* Boston: Houghton Mifflin, 1934.

Hoover, J. Edgar. *Criminal Identification and the Functions of the Identification Division.* Washington, D.C.: U.S. Department of Justice, 1938.

_____. *J. Edgar Hoover on Communism.* New York: Random House, 1969.

_____. *J. Edgar Hoover Speaks.* Washington, D.C.: Capitol Hill, 1971.

_____. *Masters of Deceit.* New York: Henry Holt, 1958.

_____. *Persons in Hiding.* Boston: Little, Brown, 1938.

_____. *A Study of Communism.* New York: Holt, Rinehart & Winston, 1962.

Hoover, Mildred Brooks. *Historic Spots in California: Counties of the Coast Range.* Palo Alto, Calif.: Stanford University Press, 1937.

Hopkins, Alphonso. *Profit and Loss in Man.* New York: Funk & Wagnalls, 1909.

Hopkins, Charles H. *The Rise of the Social Gospel in American Protestantism.* New Haven, Conn.: Yale University Press, 1940.

Hopkins, Ernest Jerome. *Our Lawless Police.* New York: Viking Press, 1931.

_____. *What Happened in the Mooney Case?* New York: Brower, Warren & Putnam, 1932.

Hopkins, Harry L. *Spending to Save.* New York: W.W. Norton, 1936.

Hopkins, J.F. *A History of the Hemp Industry in Kentucky.* Lexington: University of Kentucky Press, 1951.

Hopkins, James H. *A History of Political Parties in the United States.* New York: G.P. Putnam's Sons, 1900.

Hopkins, Mark. *Mass Media in the Soviet Union.* New York: Pegasus Books, 1970.

Hopkins, Matthew. *The Discovery of Witches.* Great Toham, Eng.: Charles Clark, 1837.

Hopkins, R.C. *Muniments of Title of the Barony of Arizona and Translation into English.* San Francisco: Bancroft, 1893.

Hopkins, R. Thurston. *Life and Death at the Old Bailey.* London: Herbert Jenkins, 1935.

Hopkins, Robert S. *Darwin's South America.* New York: John Day, 1969.

Hopkins, Robert Thurston. *Oscar Wilde: A Study of the Man and His Work.* London: Lynwood, 1913.

Hoppé, E.O. *In Gypsy Camp and Royal Palace.* New York: Charles Scribner's Sons, 1924.

Hopper, Columbus B. *Sex in Prisons.* Baton Rouge: Louisiana State University Press, 1969.

Hopper, Vincent Foster. *Medieval Number Symbolism.* New York: Columbia University Press, 1938.

Hopper, W.L. *Famous Texas Landmarks.* Dallas: Arrow Press, 1966.

Hopping, Richard C. *A Sheriff-Ranger in Chuckwagon Days.* New York: Pageant Press, 1952.

Hopson, Justice. *The Confession of the Terrible Pirate, Charles Gibbs.* New York: n.p., 1831.

Hoptner, Jacob B. *Yugoslavia in Crisis, 1934-1941.* New York: Columbia University Press, 1962.

Horan, James D. *Across the Cimmaron.* New York: Crown, 1956.

_____. *The Authentic Wild West—The Gunfighters.* New York: Crown, 1976.

_____. *The Authentic Wild West—The Lawmen.* New York: Crown, 1980.

_____. *The Authentic Wild West—The Outlaws.* New York: Crown, 1977.

_____. *Confederate Agent.* New York: Crown, 1954.

_____. *Desperate Men: Revelations from the Sealed Pinkerton Files.* New York: G.P. Putnam's Sons, 1949.

_____. *Desperate Women.* New York: G.P. Putnam's Sons, 1952.

_____. *The Desperate Years.* New York: Crown, 1962.

_____. *The Great American West.* New York: Crown, 1959.

_____. *The Life of Tom Horn.* New York: Crown, 1978.

_____. *The Mob's Man.* New York: Bantam, 1966.

_____, and Sann, Paul. *Pictorial History of the Wild West.* New York: Crown, 1954.

_____. *The Pinkertons, The Detective Dynasty That Made History.* New York: Crown, 1967.

_____, and Swiggett, Howard. *The Pinkerton Story.* New York: G.P. Putnam's Sons, 1951.

_____. *The Trial of Frank James Brown.* New York: Crown, 1978.

_____. *The Wild Bunch.* New York: New American Library, 1958.

Horan, J.W. *On the Side of the Law: Biography of J.D. Nicholson.* Edmonton, Alberta, Can.: Institute of Applied Arts, 1944.

Horchem, Hans Josef. *Extremisten in Einer Selbsbewussten Demokratie.* Freiburg, Ger.: Verlag Herder KG, 1975.

_____. *West German's Red Army Anarchists.* London: Conflict Studies No. 46, 1974.

Horman, Richard E., and Fox, Allen M. *Drug Awareness: Key Documents on LSD, Marijuana and the Drug Culture.* New York: Avon Books, 1970.

Horn, Calvin. *New Mexico's Troubled Years: The Story of the Early Territorial Governors.* Albuquerque, N.M.: Horn & Wallace, 1963.

Horn, David Bayne. *Frederick the Great and the Rise of Prussia.* Mystic, Conn.: Verry Lawrence, 1964.

Horn, Stanley F. *Invisible Empire: The Story of the Ku Klux Klan 1866-1871.* Boston: Houghton Mifflin, 1939.

Horn, Tom. *Life of Tom Horn: A Vindication.* Denver: Louthan, 1904.

Hornby, George (ed.). *The Great Americana Scrap Book.* New York: Crown, 1975.

Horner, Harlan Hoyt. *Lincoln and Greeley.* Urbana: University of Illinois Press, 1953.

Horner, John Willard. *Silver Town.* Caldwell, Idaho: Caxton, 1950.

Horney, Karen. *Feminine Psychology.* London: Routledge & Kegan Paul, 1967.

_____. *New Ways in Psychoanalysis.* New York: W.W. Norton, 1939.

Horos, Carol. *Rape: The Private Crime, a Social Horror.* New Canaan, Conn.: Tobey, 1974.

Horowitz, Daniel L. *The Italian Labour Movement.* Cambridge, Mass.: Harvard University Press, 1963.

Horowitz, David. *State in the Making.* New York: Alfred A. Knof, 1953.

Horowitz, Donald L. *The Courts and Social Policy.* Washington, D.C.: Brookings Institute, 1977.

Horowitz, Elinor. *Capital Punishment, U.S.A.* Philadelphia: J.B. Lippincott, 1973.

Horowitz, Helen Lefkowitz. *Culture and the City.* Lexington: University Press of Kentucky, 1976.

Horowitz, Irvin, et al. (eds.). *The Whitehouse Transcripts.* New York: Viking Press, 1974.

Horowitz, Irvin M. *Assassination.* New York: Harper & Row, 1972.

Horrid Assassination: Sketches of the Life, and a Narrative of the Trial of James Hamilton. New York: n.p., 1818.

Horrid Massacre! Sketches of the Life of Captain James Purrington. Augusta, Me.: Peter Edes, 1806.

Horsky, C. *The Washington Lawyer.* Boston: Little, Brown, 1952.

Horst, Georg Conrad. *Daemonomagie, oder Geschichte des Glaubens an Zauberei und daemonische Wunder.* Frankfort, Ger.: Gebrüdern Wilmans, 1818.

_____. *Zauberbibliothek.* Mainz, Ger.: F. Kupferberg, 1821.

Hort, Gertrude M. *Dr. John Dee.* London: W. Rider & Sons, 1922.

Hortense, Queen. *Mémoires.* Paris: Plon, 1927.

Horthy, Nikolaus von. *Ein Leben für Ungarn.* Bonn, Ger.: Athenäum, 1953.

Horton, Philip. *Hart Crane: The Life of an American Poet.* New York: Compass Books, 1957.

Horton, Rushmore G. *A Brief Memorial of the Origin and Earlier History of the Tammany Society, or Columbian Order.* New York: New York Printing, 1867.

_____. *The Life and Public Services of James Buchanan.* New York: Derby & Jackson, 1856.

_____. *A Youth's History of the Great Civil War.* New York: Van Evrie, Horton, 1867.

Horton, Thomas F. *History of Jack County.* Jacksboro, Texas: Gazette, 1932.

Horwell, John E. *Horwell of the Yard.* London: Andrew Melrose, 1947.

Hoskins, H.L. *British Routes to India.* New York: Longmans, Green, 1928.

_____. *The Middle East.* New York: Macmillan, 1957.

Hoskins, Percy. *The Sound of Murder.* London: Long, 1973.

_____. *They Almost Escaped.* London: Hutchinson, 1938.

Höss, Rudolf. *Kommandant in Auschwitz.* Munich: Deutscher Taschenbuch, 1965.

Hossbach, Friedrich. *Zwischen Wehrmacht und Hitler, 1934-1938.* Wolfenbüttel, Ger.: Wolfenbütteler Verlagsanstalt, 1949.

Hostetter, Gordon L., and Beesley, Thomas Quinn. *It's A Racket.* Chicago: Les Quin Books, 1929.

Hotchkiss, A.S. *The Manchester Homocide.* Hartford, Conn.: Hartford *Daily Courant*, 1866.

Hot Corn. Boston: Jewett, 1854.

Ho-t'ien Ma. *Chinese Agent in Mongolia.* trans. John De Francis. Baltimore: Johns Hopkins Press, 1949.

Höttl, Wilhelm. *The Secret Front: The Story of Nazi Political Espionage.* trans. R.H. Stevens. New York: Frederick A. Praeger, 1954.

Houden, Robert. *The Card Sharper Exposed.* London: Chapman & Hall, 1863.

Houdini, Harry. *A Magician Among the Spirits.* New York: Harper, 1924.

Hougan, James. *Spooks.* New York: William Morrow, 1978.

Hough, Emerson. *The Story of the Cowboy.* New York: D. Appleton, 1897.

_____. *The Story of the Outlaw.* New York: Outing, 1907.

Hough, John T., Jr. *A Peck of Salt: A Year in the Ghetto.* Boston: Little, Brown, 1970.

Hough, Richard (ed.). *Advice to a Grand-Daughter: Letters from Queen Victoria to Princess Victoria of Hesse.* London: William Heinemann, 1975.

Hough, Richard. *The Potemkin Mutiny.* Englewood Cliffs, N.J.: Prentice-Hall, 1960.

Houghton, Norris. *But Not Forgotten.* New York: William Sloan, 1951.

Houghton, Robert A. *Special Unit Senator.* New York: Random House, 1970.

Hourani, Albert. *Great Britain in the Arab World.* London: John Murray, 1946.

House, Boyce. *City of Flaming Adventure.* San Antonio, Texas: Naylor, 1949.

_____. *Cowtown Colonist.* San Antonio, Texas: Naylor, 1946.

_____. *Oil Field Fury.* San Antonio, Texas: Naylor, 1954.

_____. *Texas Treasure Chest.* San Antonio, Texas: Naylor, 1956.

House, Brant (ed.). *Crimes That Shocked America.* New York: Ace Books, 1961.

House, E. *A Narrative of the Captivity of Mrs. Horn and Her Two Children, With That of Mrs. Harris, by the Comanche Indians.* St. Louis: C. Keemle, 1839.

House, Edward M. *Philip Dru: Administrator.* New York: B.W. Huebsch, 1912.

House, Edward Mandell. *Riding For Texas.* New York: Reynal & Hitchcock, 1936.

_____, and Seymour, Charles (eds.). *What Really Happened at Paris.* New York: Charles Scribner's Sons, 1921.

House, Humphry. *The Dickens World.* London: Oxford University Press, 1960.

House, Jack. *Square Mile of Murder.* London: W. & R. Chambers, 1961.

Houseman, John. *Front and Center.* New York: Simon & Schuster, 1979.

Housman, Clemence. *The Werewolf.* London: J. Lane, 1896.

Houston, David Franklin. *Eight Years with Wilson's Cabinet: 1913-1920.* Garden City, N.Y.: Doubleday, Page, 1926.

Houts, Marshall. *From Gun to Gavel: The Courtroom Recollections of James Mathers of Oklahoma.* New York: William Morrow, 1954.

_____. *They Asked for Death.* New York: Cowles, 1970.

_____. *Where Death Delights: The Story of Dr. Milton Helpern and Forensic Medicine.* New York: Dell, 1968.

Hovland, C., et al. *Communication and Persuasion.* New Haven, Conn.: Yale University Press, 1953.

_____. *The Order of Presentation in Persuasion.* New Haven, Conn.: Yale University Press, 1957.

How, W.W., and Wells, J. *A Commentary on Herodotus.* Oxford, Eng.: Clarendon, 1936.

Howard, Clark. *American Saturday.* New York: Richard Marek, 1981.

_____. *Brothers in Blood.* New York: St. Martin's/Marek, 1983.

_____. *Six Against the Rock.* New York: Dial, 1977.

_____. *Zebra.* New York: Richard Marek, 1979.

Howard, D.L. *John Howard, Prison Reformer.* London: Johnson, 1958.

Howard, Dick, and Kannensohn, Michael. *A State-Supported Local Correctional System: The Minnesota Experience.* Lexington, Ky.: Council of State Governments, 1977.

Howard, Donald Stevenson. *The WPA and Federal Relief Policy.* New York: Russell Sage, 1943.

Howard, Ethel. *Potsdam Princes.* London: Methuen, 1916.

Howard, H.R. *The History of Virgil A. Stewart.* New York: Harper & Brothers, 1836.

_____. *The Life and Adventures of Joseph T. Hare, the Bold Robber and Highwayman.* New York: Hillong and Brother, 1847.

Howard, Hamilton. *Civil War Echoes.* Washington, D.C.: Howard, 1907.

Howard, Harry N. *The King-Crane Commission.* Beirut, Leb.: Khayat, 1963.

_____. *The Partition of Turkey: A Diplomatic History 1913-1923.* Norman: Oklahoma University Press, 1931.

Howard, Helen Addison. *Northwest Trail Blazers.* Caldwell, Idaho: Caxton Printers, 1963.

Howard, John. *The State of the Prisons.* New York: E.P. Dutton, 1929.

Howard, John R. (ed.). *Awakening Minorities.* New Brunswick, N.J.: Transaction Books, 1970.

Howard, Joseph Kinsey. *Montana, High, Wide and Handsome.* New Haven, Conn.: Yale University Press, 1943.

_____ (ed.). *Montana Margins: A State Anthology.* New Haven, Conn.: Yale University Press, 1946.

Howard, Leslie Ruth. *A Quite Remarkable Father.* New York: Harcourt, Brace, 1959.

Howard, Michael. *The Franco-Prussian War.* London: Rupert Hart-Davis, 1960.

Howard, Milford W. *Fascism: A Challenge to Democracy.* New York: Fleming H. Revell, 1928.

Howard, Robert P. *Illinois: A History of the Prairie State.* Grand Rapids, Mich.: William B. Eerdman's, 1972.

Howard, Robert West. *The Downseekers.* New York: Harcourt Brace Jovanovich, 1975.

_____ (ed.). *This Is the West.* New York: Rand McNally, 1957.

Howard, Sarah Elizabeth. *Pen Pictures of the Plains.* Denver: Reed, 1902.

Howard, W.V. *Authority in TVA Land.* Kansas City: Frank Glenn, 1948.

Howarth, Henry. *History of the Mongols Part III: Mongols of Persia.* London: Longmans Green, 1888.

Howbert, Irving. *Memories of a Lifetime in the Pike's Peak Region.* New York: G.P. Putnam's Sons, 1925.

Howe, Charles Willis. *Timberleg of the Diamond Trail.* San Antonio, Texas: Naylor, 1949.

Howe, Cliff. *Scoundrels, Fiends and Human Monsters.* New York: Ace Books, 1958.

Howe, Daniel Walker. *The Unitarian Conscience: Harvard Moral Philosophy 1805-1861.* Cambridge, Mass.: Harvard University Press, 1970.

_____ (ed.). *Victorian America.* Philadelphia: University of Pennsylvania Press, 1976.

Howe, Elvon L. (ed.). *Rocky Mountain Empire.* Garden City, N.Y.: Doubleday, 1950.

Howe, Frederic C. *The Confessions of a Reformer.* New York: Charles Scribner's Sons, 1926.

_____ . *Denmark: The Land of Co-operation.* New York: Coward-McCann, 1936.

Howe, Helen. *The Gentle Americans.* New York: Harper & Row, 1965.

_____ . *We Happy Few.* New York: Simon & Schuster, 1946.

Howe, Henry. *Historical Collections of Ohio.* Cincinnati, Ohio: Derby, Bradley, 1847.

Howe, Irving and Coser, Lewis. *The American Communist Party: A Critical History.* New York: Frederick A. Praeger, 1962.

_____ . *Politics and the Novel.* Cleveland: World, 1962.

_____ (ed.). *The Radical Imagination.* New York: New American Library, 1967.

_____ . *The World of Our Fathers.* New York: Harcourt Brace Jovanovich, 1976.

Howe, Julia Ward. *Reminiscences, 1819-1899.* Boston: Houghton Mifflin, 1900.

Howe, Mark De Wolfe. *George von Lengerke Meyer: His Life and Public Services.* New York: Dodd, Mead, 1920.

_____ . *Justice Oliver Wendell Holmes.* Cambridge, Mass.: Harvard University Press, 1957.

_____ . *Later Years in the Saturday Club.* Boston: Houghton Mifflin, 1927.

_____ . *Readings in American Legal History.* Cambridge, Mass.: Harvard University Press, 1949.

Howe, Sir Ronald. *The Pursuit of Crime.* London: A. Barker, 1962.

_____ . *The Story of Scotland Yard.* London: A. Barker, 1965.

Howe, William F., and Hummel, Abraham. *In Danger; or Life in New York, A True History of a Great City's Wiles and Temptations.* New York: J.S. Ogilvie, 1888.

Howell, Ann Chandler. *Kidnapping in the U.S.* Ann Arbor, Mich.: University Microfilms, 1975.

Howell, Joseph T. *Hard Living on Clay Street.* Garden City, N.Y.: Anchor Books, 1973.

Howell, Thomas Bayly. (ed.). *A Complete Collection of State Trials and Proceedings for High Treason.* London: Longman, 1816.

Howells, William Dean. *A Hazard of New Fortunes.* New York: Boni & Liveright, 1889.

_____ . *Impressions and Experiences.* New York: Harper & Brothers, 1896.

Howgrave-Graham, H.M. *Light and Shade at Scotland Yard.* London: John Murray, 1947.

Howison, Robert Reid. *A History of Virginia: From Its Discovery and Settlement by Europeans to the Present Time.* Philadelphia: Carey & Hart, 1846.

Howitt, William. *Visits to Remarkable Places.* Philadelphia: Carey & Hart, 1841.

Howson, Gerald. *The Thief-Taker General: The Rise and Fall of Jonathan Wild.* London: Hutchinson, 1970.

Howson, Susan, and Winch, Donald. *The Economic Advisory Council, 1930-1939: A Study in Economic Advice During Depression and Recovery.* Cambridge, Eng.: Cambridge University Press, 1977.

Hoy, William. *The Chinese Six Companies.* San Francisco: Chinese Consolidated Benevolent Association, 1942.

Hoyer, Svennik, Hadenius, Stig, and Weibull, Lennart. *The Politics and Economics of the Press: A Developmental Perspective.* Beverly Hills, Calif.: Sage, 1975.

Hoyland, John S. *Indian Crisis.* New York: Macmillan, 1944.

Hoyt, Edwin P. *The Guggenheims and the American Dream.* New York: Funk & Wagnalls, 1967.

_____ . *The House of Morgan.* London: Frederick Muller, 1968.

_____ . *The Sea Wolves: Germany's Dreaded U-Boats of WWII.* New York: Lancer Books, 1972.

_____ . *The Vanderbilts and Their Fortunes.* Garden City, N.Y.: Doubleday, 1962.

Hoyt, Henry Franklin. *Frontier Doctor.* Boston: Houghton Mifflin, 1929.

Hoyt, Homer. *One Hundred Years of Land Values in Chicago, 1830-1933.* Chicago: University of Chicago, 1933.

_____ . *The Structure and Growth of Residential Neighborhoods in American Cities.* Washington, D.C.: Federal Housing Administration, 1939.

Hoyt, Ken, and Leighton, Frances Spatz. *Drunk Before Noon: The Behind-the-Scenes Story of the Washington Press Corps.* Englewood Cliffs, N.J.: Prentice-Hall, 1979.

Hoyt, Kendall K. *Ink & Avgas.* Aviation Writers Association, 1963.

Hrdlicka, A. *Peoples of the Soviet Union.* Washington, D.C.: Smithsonian, 1942.

Hrushevsky, M.S. *History of the Ukraine.* New Haven, Conn.: Yale University Press, 1941.

Hsiung, S.I. *The Life of Chiang Kai-shek.* London: Davies, 1948.

Hsu, Francis L.K. *Under the Ancestors' Shadow: Chinese Culture and Personality.* New York: Columbia University Press, 1948.

Hsü, Immanuel C.Y. *The Rise of Modern China.* Oxford, Eng.: Oxford University Press, 1975.

Hsüan Tsang. *Buddhist Records of the Western World.* trans. Samuel Beal. London: Trübner, 1884.

Hsu Kai-yu. *Chou En-lai.* Garden City, N.Y.: Doubleday, 1968.

Hsu-Shu-hsi. *The War Conduct of the Japanese.* Shanghai, China: Kelley & Walsh, 1938.

Hubatsch, Walther. *Die Ära Tirpitz.* Berlin: Musterschmidt, 1955.

_____ . *Hohenzollern in der deutschen Geschichte.* Frankfurt, Ger.: Athenäum Verlag, 1961.

Hubbard, David G. *The Skyjacker: His Flights of Fantasy.* New York: Macmillan, 1971.

Hubbard, Frederick Heman. *The Opium Habit and Alcoholism.* New York: A.S. Barnes, 1881.

Hubbard, Freeman H. *Railroad Avenue.* New York: McGraw-Hill, 1945.

Hubbard, Gurdon S. *Autobiography of Gurdon S. Hubbard.* Chicago: Lakeside Press, 1911.

Hubbard, Harry D. *Building the Heart of an Empire.* Boston: Meador, 1937.

Hubbard, L. Ron. *Dianetics.* New York: Paperback Library, 1973.

Hubbard, Preston J. *Origins of the TVA.* Nashville, Tenn.: Vanderbilt University Press, 1961.

Hubbard, William. *The Benefit of a Well-Ordered Conversation.*

Boston: Samuel Green, 1684.

_____. *A General History of New England from the Discovery to MDCLXXX.* Boston: C.C. Little & J. Brown, 1848.

_____. *The Happiness of a People in the Wisdome of their Rulers Directing.* Boston: John Foster, 1676.

Hubbard, Wynant. *Fiasco in Ethiopia.* New York: Harper Brothers, 1936.

Hubbell, Charles Bulkeley. *Recollections of an Inconsequential Life.* New York: Charles Scribner's Sons, 1939.

Hubbell, William Wheeler. *The Commonwealth of Pennsylvania vs. George S. Twitchell, Jr.* Philadelphia: E.C. Markley & Son, 1869.

Hubbs, Barney. *Robert Clay Allison: Gentleman Gunfighter, 1840-1887.* Pecos, Texas: n.p., 1966.

Huber, Leonard V. *Louisiana.* New York: Charles Scribner's Sons, 1975.

_____. *New Orleans.* New York: Crown, 1971.

Hubert, René Riese. *The Dreyfus Affair and the French Novel.* Cambridge, Mass.: n.p., 1951.

Hübner, Alexander von (ed.). *Neuf ans de souvenirs d'un ambassadeur d'Autriche à Paris.* Paris: Plon, 1904.

Huc and Gabet. *Travels in Tartary, Thibet and China, 1844-1846.* trans. William Hazlitt. London: George Routledge & Sons, 1928.

Huckabay, Ida Lasater. *Ninety-four Years in Jack County, 1854-1948.* Austin, Texas: Steck, 1949.

Huddle, Norrie, and Reich, Michael. *Island of Dreams: Enviromental Crisis in Japan.* Tokyo: Autumn Press, 1975.

Huddleston, Sisley. *Bohemian Literary and Social Life in Paris: Salons, Cafés, Studios.* London: George G. Harrap, 1928.

_____. *What's Right with America.* Philadelphia: J.B. Lippincott, 1930.

Hudson, Frederic. *Journalism in the United States from 1690 to 1872.* New York: Harper, 1873.

Hudson, G.F. *The Sino-Soviet Dispute.* New York: Frederick A. Praeger, 1962.

Hudson, G.P. *The Far East in World Politics.* Oxford, Eng.: Clarendon Press, 1937.

Hudson, Jan. *The Sex and Savagery of the Hell's Angels.* London: New English Library, 1967.

Hudson, Joe, and Galaway, Burt (eds.). *Considering the Victim.* Springfield, Ill.: Charles C. Thomas, 1975.

Hudson, W.S. *John Ponet: Advocate of Limited Monarchy.* Chicago: University of Chicago Press, 1942.

Hudson, William C. *Random Recollections of an Old Political Reporter.* New York: Cupples & Leon, 1911.

Hudson, Wilson M. *Andy Adams, His Life and Writings.* Dallas: Southern Methodist University Press, 1964.

_____, and Maxwell, Allen (eds.). *The Sunny Slopes of Long Ago.* Dallas: Southern Methodist University Press, 1966.

Hudson Institute. *Increased Gambling in New York—A Policy Analysis.* Croton-on-Hudson, N.Y.: Hudson Institute, 1973.

Huebner, Theodore, and Voss, C.V. *This is Israel.* New York: Philosophical Library, 1954.

Hueston, Ethel. *Calamity Jane of Deadwood Gulch.* Indianapolis, Ind.: Bobbs-Merrill, 1937.

Huff, Darrell. *How to Lie with Statistics.* New York: John Wiley & Sons, 1966.

Huggett, Renee, and Berry, Paul. *Daughters of Cain.* London: George Allen & Unwin, 1956.

Huggins, Nathan I. *Protestants Against Poverty.* Westport, Conn.: Greenwood Press, 1971.

Hughan, Jessie W. *American Socialism of the Present Day.* New York: Lane, 1911.

_____. *What Is Socialism?* New York: Vanguard Press, 1928.

Hughes, Charles Evans. *The Supreme Court of the United States.* Garden City, N.Y.: Garden City, 1928.

Hughes, Dan de Lara. *South From Tombstone.* New York: Methuen, 1938.

Hughes, Everett Cherrington. *Men and Their Work.* Glencoe, Ill.: Free Press, 1958.

Hughes, H. Stuart. *The United States and Italy.* Cambridge, Mass.: Harvard University Press, 1953.

Hughes, Helen MacGill (ed.). *Delinquents and Criminals.* Boston: Holbrook Press, 1970.

_____. *News and the Human Interest Story.* Chicago: University of Chicago Press, 1940.

Hughes, J.R.T. *Fluctuations in Trade, Industry and Finance: A Study of British Economic Development, 1850-1860.* Oxford, Eng.: Oxford University Press, 1960.

Hughes, John R. *The Killing of Bass Outlaw.* Austin, Texas: Brick Row Books, 1963.

Hughes, Marion. *Oklahoma Charley.* St. Louis: John P. Wagner, 1910.

Hughes, Pennethorne. *Witchcraft.* Baltimore, Md.: Penguin, 1967.

Hughes, Philip. *Popular History of the Catholic Church.* New York: Doubleday, 1960.

Hughes, Richard B. *Pioneer Years in the Black Hills.* Glendale, Calif.: Arthur H. Clark, 1957.

Hughes, Rupert. *The Complete Detective: Being the Life and Strange and Exciting Cases of Raymond Schindler, Master Detective.* New York: Sheridan House, 1950.

Hughes, T.J., and Luard, D.E.T. *The Economic Development of Communist China, 1949-1958.* London: Oxford University Press, 1959.

Hughes, Thomas. *A Journal.* Cambridge, Eng.: Cambridge University Press, 1947.

Hughes, W.J. *Rebellious Ranger: Rip Ford and the Old Southwest.* Norman: University of Oklahoma Press, 1964.

Hugins, Walter. *Jacksonian Democracy and the Working Class: A Study of the New York Workingmen's Movement, 1829-1837.* Palo Alto, Calif.: Stanford University Press, 1960.

Huie, William Bradford. *Did the FBI Kill Martin Luther King?* Nashville, Tenn.: Thomas Nelson, 1977.

_____. *The Execution of Private Slovik.* New York: New American Library, 1954.

_____. *He Slew the Dreamer.* New York: Delacorte Press, 1968.

_____. *Hiroshima Pilot.* New York: G.P. Putnam's Sons, 1964.

_____. *Three Lives for Mississippi.* New York: Signet, 1968.

Huizinga, J. *The Waning of the Middle Ages.* London: Edward Arnold, 1955.

Hulbert, Archer Butler. *The Historic Highways of America.* Cleveland: A.H. Clark, 1905.

_____. *Waterways of Westward Expansion.* Cleveland: A.H. Clark, 1903.

Hull, C. *Aptitude Testing.* New York: Harrap, 1928.

Hull, Clifton E. *Shortline Railroads of Arkansas.* Norman: University of Oklahoma Press, 1969.

Hull, Cordell. *The Memoirs of Cordell Hull.* New York: Macmillan, 1948.

Hull, S.P. *Report on the Trial and Conviction of Antoine Le Blanc.* New York: Lewis Nichols, 1833.

Hullah, John. *The Train Robber's Career: A Life of Sam Bass.* Chicago: Belford, Clarke, 1881.

Hullinger, Edwin Ware. *The New Fascist State.* New York: Rae D. Henkle, 1928.

Hulot, Etienne Gabriel Joseph. *De l'Atlantique au Pacifique à travers le Canada et les etats-Unis.* Paris: E. Plon, Nourrit & Cie, 1888.

Hulteng, John. *The Messenger's Motives.* Englewood Cliffs, N.J.: Prentice-Hall, 1976.

Hultz, Fred S. *Range Beef Production in the Seventeen Western States.* New York: John Wiley & Sons, 1930.

Humbaaraci, Arslan. *Middle East Indictment.* London: Robert Hall, 1958.

Humbert, W.H. *The Pardoning Power of the President.* Washington, D.C.: American Council on Public Affairs, 1941.

Humboldt, Alexander von. *Alexander von Humboldt und das preussische Königshaus.* Leipzig, Ger.: K.F. Koehler, 1928.

_____. *Personal Narrative of Travels to the Equinotical Regions of the New Continent.* London: Longman, Hurst, Rees, Orme & Brown, 1814.

_____. *Political Essay on the Kingdom of New Spain.* London: Longman, Hurst, Rees, Orme & Brown, 1811.

Hume, David. *The History of England.* Boston: Little, Brown, 1850.

Hume, James B. and Thacker, John N. *Report of Jas. B. Hume and Jno. N. Thacker, Special Officers, Wells, Fargo & Co.'s Express, Covering a Period of Fourteen Years.* San Francisco: H.S. Crocker, 1885.

Hummel, A.H. *Trial and Conviction of Jack Reynolds.* New York: American News, 1870.

Humphrey, Heman. *Parallel Between Intemperance and the Slave-Trade.* New York: John P. Haven, 1829.

Humphrey, Seth King. *Following the Prairie Frontier.* Minneapolis: University of Minnesota Press, 1931.

Humphreys, A.A., and Abbot, H.L. *Report Upon the Physics and Hydraulics of the Mississippi River.* Philadelphia: J.B. Lippincott, 1861.

Humphreys, Christmas. *The Great Pearl Robbery of 1913.* London: William Heinemann, 1929.

_____. *Seven Murders.* London: William Heinemann, 1931.

Humphreys, J.R. *The Lost Towns and Roads of America.* Garden City, N.Y.: Doubleday, 1961.

Humphreys, Laud. *Tearoom Trade.* Chicago: Aldine, 1970.

Humphreys, Sir Travers. *A Book of Trials.* London: William Heinemann, 1953.

_____. *Criminal Days.* London: Hodder & Stoughton, 1946.

Hungerford, Edward. *Wells Fargo: Advancing the American Frontier.* New York: Random House, 1949.

Hunnings, Neville. *Film Censors and the Law.* New York: Hillary, 1967.

Hunt, Aurora. *Kirby Benedict.* Glendale, Calif.: Arthur H. Clark, 1961.

_____. *Major General James Henry Carleton.* Glendale, Calif.: Arthur H. Clark, 1958.

Hunt, Sir David. *A Don at War.* London: William Kimber, 1966.

_____. *On the Spot.* London: Peter Davies, 1975.

Hunt, Douglas. *Exploring the Occult.* New York: Ballantine Books, 1964.

Hunt, E. Howard. *Give Us This Day.* New York: Arlington House, 1973.

_____. *Undercover: Memoirs of an American Secret Agent.* Berkeley, Calif.: n.p., 1974.

Hunt, Frazier. *Cap Mossman, Last of the Great Cowmen.* New York: Hastings House, 1951.

_____. *The Long Trail From Texas: The Story of Ad Spaugh, Cattleman.* New York: Doubleday, Doran, 1940.

_____. *The Tragic Days of Billy the Kid.* Caldwell, Idaho: Caxton Printers, 1959.

_____. *Untold Story of Douglas MacArthur.* New York: Devin-Adair, 1954.

Hunt, Gaillard. *Impeachment Trial of Andrew Johnson.* 3 vols. Washington: U.S. Government Printing Office, 1868.

Hunt, Henry M. *The Crime of the Century: The Assassination of Dr. Patrick Henry Cronin.* Chicago: H. & D. Kochersperger, 1889.

Hunt, Henry T. *The Case of Thomas J. Mooney and Warren K. Billings.* New York: C.G. Burgoyne, 1929.

Hunt, Holloway Whitfield. *A Sermon Preached at the Execution of Matthias Gotlieb.* Newton, N.J.: n.p., 1796.

Hunt, Inez, and Draper, Wanetta W. *To Colorado's Restless Ghosts.* Denver: Sage Books, 1960.

Hunt, Lenoir. *Bluebonnets and Blood.* Houston: Texas Books, 1938.

Hunt, Leon Gibson. *Recent Spread of Heroin Use in the United States: Unanswered Questions.* Washington, D.C.: Drug Abuse Council, 1974.

_____, and Chambers, Carl D. *The Heroin Epidemics.* New York: Spectrum, 1976.

_____, and Zinberg, Norman E. *Heroin Use: A New Look.* Washington, D.C.: Drug Abuse Council, 1976.

Hunt, Marsha. *Parents, Peers, and Pot.* Rockville, Md.: National Institute On Drug Abuse, 1979.

Hunt, Morton. *The Mugging.* New York: Signet, 1972.

_____. *The Natural History of Love.* New York: Alfred A. Knopf, 1959.

_____. *Sexual Behavior in the 1970s.* New York: Dell Books, 1974.

Hunt, Peter. *The Madeleine Smith Affair.* London: Carroll & Nicholson, 1950.

Hunt, R.D. *California and the Californians.* San Francisco: Lewis, 1926.

Hunt, R.N. Carew. *The Theory and Practice of Communism.* New York: Macmillan, 1957.

Hunt, Rockwell D. *California Ghost Towns Live Again.* Stockton, Calif.: College of the Pacific, 1948.

_____. *California's Stately Hall of Fame.* Stockton, Calif.: College of the Pacific, 1950.

_____, and Van De Grift Sanchez, Nellie. *A Short History of California.* New York: Thomas Y. Crowell, 1929.

Hunt, Thomas P. *The Cold Water Army.* Boston: Whipple & Darrell, 1841.

Hunt, William R. *Arctic Passage.* New York: Charles Scribner's Sons, 1975.

_____. *Dictionary of Rogues.* New York: Philosophical Library, 1970.

The Hunter-Armstrong Tragedy. Philadelphia: Barclay, 1878.

Hunter, D. *Papermaking through Eighteen Centuries.* New York: William E. Rudge, 1930.

Hunter, Diana, and Anderson, Alice. *Jack Ruby's Girls.* Atlanta: Hallux, 1970.

Hunter, Edward. *Brain-Washing in Red China.* New York: Vanguard Press, 1951.

Hunter, Floyd. *Community Power Structure.* Garden City, N.Y.: Anchor Books, 1973.

Hunter, George William. *A Civic Biology.* New York: American Books, 1914.

_____. *New Civic Biology.* New York: American Books, 1926.

Hunter, I. *Memory.* Harmondsworth, Eng.: Penguin Books, 1964.

Hunter, John Marvin, and Rose, Noah H. *Album of Gunfighters.* Bandera, Texas: n.p., 1951.

_____. *Peregrinations of a Pioneer Printer: An Autobiography.* Grand Prairie, Texas: Frontier Times, 1954.

_____. *The Story of Lottie Deno, Her Life and Times.* Bandera, Texas: Four Hunters, 1959.

_____ (ed.). *The Trail Drivers of Texas.* Nashville, Tenn.: Cokesbury Press, 1925.

Hunter, Lillie Mae. *The Moving Finger.* Borger, Texas: Plains Printing, 1956.

Hunter, Louis C. and B.J. *Steamboats on the Western Rivers.* Cambridge, Mass.: Harvard University Press, 1949.

Hunter, Robert. *Poverty.* New York: Grosset & Dunlap, 1908.

_____. *Revolution: Why? How? When?* New York: Harper, 1940.

_____. *Socialists at Work.* New York: Macmillan, 1908.

_____. *Violence and the Labor Movement.* New York: Macmillan, 1919.

Hunter, Sir W.W. *The Life of the Earl of Mayo.* London: n.p., 1875.

Huntington, George. *Robber and Hero: The Story of the Raid on the First National Bank, Minnesota.* Northfield, Minn.: Christian Way, 1895.

Huntington, S. *Political Order in Changing Societies.* New Haven, Conn.: Yale University Press, 1968

Huntington, Samuel. *The Soldier and the State.* Cambridge, Mass.: Harvard University Press, 1957.

Huntington, William. *Bill Huntington's Both Feet in the Stirrups.* Billings, Mont.: Western Livestock Reporter Press, 1959.

_____. *Bill Huntington's Good Men and Salty Cusses.* Billings,

Mont.: Western Livestock Reporter Press, 1952.

Hunton, John. *John Hunton's Diary.* Lingle, Wyo.: Flannery, 1956.

Hurd, C.W. *Boggsville: Cradle of the Colorado Cattle Industry.* Boggsville, Colo.: Bent County *Democrat*, 1957.

Hurd, Charles and Eleanor (eds.). *A Treasury of Great American Letters.* New York: Hawthorn, 1961.

_____. *Washington Cavalcade.* New York: E.P. Dutton, 1948.

_____. *When the New Deal Was Young and Gay.* New York: Hawthorn Books, 1965.

_____. *The White House: A Biography.* New York: Harper, 1940.

Huret, Jules. *En Amérique: de San Francisco au Canada.* Paris: E. Fasquelle, 1905.

Hurewitz, J.C. *Diplomacy in the Near and Middle East.* Princeton, N.J.: Van Nostrand, 1956.

_____. *Middle East Dilemmas.* New York: Harper, 1952.

_____. *The Struggle for Palestine.* New York: W.W. Norton, 1950.

Hurlburt, Henry H. *Chicago Antiquities.* Chicago: Rudd, 1881.

Hurley, Edward N. *The Bridge to France.* Philadelphia: J.B. Lippincott, 1927.

Hurley, Victor. *Jungle Patrol: The Story of the Philippine Constabulary.* New York: E.P. Dutton, 1939.

Hursch, Carolyn. *The Trouble with Rape.* Chicago: Nelson-Hall, 1977.

Hurst, A. Herscovici. *Roumania and Great Britain.* London: Hodder & Stroughton, 1916.

Hurst, James W. *The Growth of American Law: The Law Makers.* Boston: Little, Brown, 1950.

Hurt, Henry. *Reasonable Doubt.* New York: Holt, Rinehart & Winston, 1985.

Hurwitz, Howard L. *Theodore Roosevelt and Labor in New York State, 1800-1900.* New York: Columbia University Press, 1943.

Hurwitz, Stephen. *Criminology.* London: George Allen & Unwin, 1952.

Hurwood, Bernhardt J. *Society and the Assassin.* New York: Parent's Magazine Press, 1970.

Husband, Joseph. *Story of the Pullman Car.* Chicago: McClurg, 1917.

Huson, Hobart. *Refugio: A Comprehensive History of Refugio County from Aboriginal Times to 1953.* Woodsboro, Texas: Rooke Foundation, 1933.

Huson, Richard (ed.) *Sixty Famous Trials.* London: Daily Express, 1967.

Hussein, H.M. King. *Uneasy Lies the Head.* London: William Heinemann, 1962.

Hussey, J.M. *The Byzantine World.* New York: Rinehart, 1957.

Hussey, Robert. *Murderer Scot-Free.* New York: Great Albion Books, 1972.

Hutchens, John K. *The Gambler's Bedside Book.* New York: Taplinger, 1978.

_____. *One Man's Montana: An Informal Portrait of a State.* Philadelphia: J.B. Lippincott, 1964.

Hutchinson, E. *A Model Mayor. Early Life, Congressional Career and Triumphant Municipal Administration of the Hon. Fernando Wood.* New York: American Family, 1855.

Hutchinson, Elmo. *Violent Truce.* New York: Devin-Adair, 1956.

Hutchinson, Francis. *An Historical Essay Concerning Witchcraft.* London: R. Knaplock, 1718.

_____. *Historischer Versuch von der Hexerey.* Leipzig, Ger.: J.C. Martini, 1726.

Hutchinson, H.F. *Edward II, The Pliant King.* London: Eyre & Spottiswood, 1971.

Hutchinson, J.R. *The Romance of the Regiment.* London: Sampson Low, 1898.

Hutchinson, John. *The Imperfect Union: A History of Corruption in American Trade Unions.* New York: E.P. Dutton, 1972.

Hutchinson, John Wallace. *Story of the Hutchinsons.* Boston: Lee & Shepard, 1896.

Hutchinson, Keith. *The Decline and Fall of British Capitalism.* New York: Charles Scribner's Sons, 1958.

Hutchinson, Robert H. *The Socialism of New Zealand.* New York: New Review, 1916.

Hutchinson, Thomas. *A Collection of Original Papers Relative to the History of the Colony of Massachusetts Bay.* Boston: Thomas & John Fleet, 1769.

_____. *History of the Colony of Massachusetts Bay.* London: M. Richardson, 1760.

Hutchinson, W.H. *Another Notebook of the Old West.* Chico, Calif.: Hurst & Yount, 1954.

_____. *Another Verdict for Oliver Lee.* Clarendon, Texas: Clarendon Press, 1965.

_____. *A Bar Cross Man: The Life & Personal Writings of Eugene Manlove Rhodes.* Norman: University of Oklahoma Press, 1956.

_____. *A Notebook of the Old West.* Chico, Calif.: Hurst, 1947.

_____. *The Rhodes Reader: Stories of Virgins, Villains, and Varmints.* Norman: University of Oklahoma Press, 1957.

_____, and Mullin, R.N. *Whiskey Jim and a Kid Named Billy.* Clarendon, Texas: Clarendon Press, 1967.

Hutchinson, William R. *The Modernist Impulse in American Protestantism.* Cambridge, Mass.: Harvard University Press, 1976.

Hutchinson, William T. *Lowden of Illinois.* Chicago: University of Chicago Press, 1957.

_____ (ed.). *The Marcus W. Jernegan Essays in American Historiography.* Chicago: University of Chicago Press, 1937.

Hutson, Jan. *The Chicken Ranch.* New York: Barnes, 1980.

Hutt, C. *Males and Females.* Harmondsworth, Eng.: Penguin Books, 1972.

Hutto, Nelson A. *The Dallas Story, from Buckskins to Top Hat.* Dallas: William S. Henson, 1953.

Hutton, J. Bernard. *Hess: The Man and His Mission.* London: David Bruce & Watson, 1970.

Hutton, James. *A Popular Account of the Thugs and Dacoits, and the Hereditary Garotters and Gang-Robbers of India.* London: William A. Allen, 1857.

Hutton, Peregrine. *The Life and Confession of Peregrine Hutton.* n.p., n.d.

Hutton, Ulrich von. *Of the Wood Called Guaiacum.* trans. Thomas Paynel. London: Thomas Bertheleti, 1539.

Hutzel, Eleanor. *The Policewoman's Handbook.* New York: Columbia University Press, 1933.

Huxley, Aldous. *The Devils of Loudun.* New York: Harper & Row, 1952.

_____. *The Doors of Perception.* New York: Harper & Row, 1954.

Huxley, Julian, and Kettlewell, H.B.D. *Charles Darwin and His World.* New York: Viking Press, 1965.

Huysmans, J.K. *Là-Bas, (Down There).* trans. Keene Wallace. New York: Dover, 1972.

Hyams, Edward. *A Dictionary of Modern Revolution.* New York: Allen Lane, 1973.

_____. *Killing No Murder, A Study of Assassination as a Political Means.* London: Thomas Nelson & Sons, 1969.

Hyamson, A.M. *Palestine under the Mandate.* London: Methuen, 1950.

Hyde, Albert E. *Billy the Kid and the Old Regime in the Southwest.* Ruidoso, N.M.: Frontier Books, 1961.

Hyde, George E. *Pawnee Indians.* Denver: University of Denver Press, 1951.

Hyde, H. Montgomery. *The Atom Bomb Spies.* London: Hamish Hamilton, 1980.

_____. *Carson: The Life of Sir Edward Carson, Lord Carson of Duncaim.* London: William Heinemann, 1953.

_____. *Cases That Changed The Law.* London: William Heinemann, 1951.

_____. *The Cleveland Street Scandal.* New York: Coward, McCann & Geoghegan, 1976.

_____. *Crime Has Its Heroes*. London: Constable, 1976.

_____. *A History of Pornography*. New York: Dell Books, 1966.

_____. *An International Casebook of Crime*. London: Barrie & Rockcliff, 1962.

_____. *Norman Birkett: The Life of Lord Birkett, of Ulverston*. London: Hamish Hamilton, 1964.

_____. *Room 3603*. New York: Farrar, Straus & Giroux, 1962.

_____. *Sir Patrick Hastings, His Life and Cases*. London: William Heinemann, 1960.

_____. *Their Good Names*. London: Hamish Hamilton, 1970.

_____ (ed.). *The Trials of Oscar Wilde*. London: Hodge, 1948.

_____. *United in Crime*. New York: Roy, 1955.

Hyde, Margaret O. *Hotline!* New York: McGraw-Hill, 1976.

_____. *Juvenile Justice and Injustice*. London: Watts, 1978.

Hyde, Nina and Filmore. *Russia Then and Always*. New York: Coward, McCann, 1944.

Hyer, Julien. *The Land of Beginning Again: The Romance of the Brazos*. Atlanta, Ga.: Tupper & Love, 1952.

Hylan, John Francis. *Autobiography*. New York: Rotary Press, 1922.

Hyland, William, and Shryock, Richard W. *The Fall of Krushchev*. New York: Funk & Wagnalls, 1968.

Hylton, J. Dunbar. *The Praesidicide*. New York: Howard Callen, 1884.

Hyman, Dick. *The Trenton Pickle Ordinance and Other Bonehead Legislation*. Battleboro, Vt.: Stephen Greene Press, 1976.

Hyman, Harold M. *A More Perfect Union*. New York: Alfred A. Knopf, 1973.

_____. *With Malice Toward Some*. Springfield, Ill.: Abraham Lincoln Association, 1978.

Hynd, Alan. *Brutes, Beasts and Human Fiends*. New York: Paperback Library, 1964.

_____. *Con Man*. New York: Paperback Library, 1961.

_____. *The Giant Killers*. New York: Robert M. McBride, 1945.

_____. *Murder, Mayhem and Mystery*. New York: A.S. Barnes, 1958.

_____. *Sleuths, Slayers, and Swindlers*. New York: A.S. Barnes, 1959.

_____. *Violence in the Night*. New York: Fawcett, 1955.

_____. *We are the Public Enemies*. New York: Fawcett, 1949.

Hyndman, Henry Mayers. *Commercial Crisis of the Nineteenth Century*. New York: Augustus M. Kelley, 1967.

_____. *Further Reminiscences*. London: Macmillan, 1912.

Hynds, Ernest C. *American Newspapers in the 1970s*. New York: Hastings House, 1975.

Hynes, Samuel. *The Edwardian Turn of Mind*. Princeton, N.J.: Princeton University Press, 1968.

I

Ianni, Francis A.J. *The Black Mafia: Ethnic Succession in Organized Crime*. New York: Simon & Schuster, 1974.

_____. *Ethnic Succession in Organized Crime*. Washington, D.C.: U.S. Government Printing Office, 1973.

_____, and Reuss-Ianni, Elizabeth. *A Family Business: Kinship and Social Control in Organized Crime*. New York: Russell Sage Foundation, 1972.

Iannone, N.F. *Supervision of Police Personnel*. Englewood Cliffs, N.J.: Prentice-Hall, 1975.

Ibn Batuta. *Travels in Asia and Africa, 1325-1354*. trans. H.A.R. Gibb. New York: R.M. McBride, 1929.

Ibn Duqmaq. *Kitab al-Intissar: Description de l'Egypte*. Cairo, Egypt: n.p., 1893.

Ibn Khaldun. *The Muqaddimah: An Introduction to History*. trans. Franz Rosenthal. New York: Pantheon Books, 1958.

Ibn Khallikin, Shams al-Din, Ahmed Ibn Mohammed. *Wayfayat al Ayan wa Anba Abna al-Zaman*. trans. de Slane. Paris: n.p., 1843.

Icard, S. *La Femme et la période menstruelle*. Paris: Alcan, 1890.

Icardi, Aldo. *Aldo Icardi: American Master Spy*. Pittsburgh, Pa.: Stalwart, 1954.

Iceberg Slim. *Pimp: The Story of My Life*. Los Angeles: Holloway House, 1969.

Ickes, Harold L. *America's House of Lords, An Inquiry into the Freedom of the Press*. New York: Harcourt, Brace, 1935.

_____. *Autobiography of a Curmudgeon*. New York: Reynal & Hitchcock, 1943.

_____. *The Secret Diary of Harold L. Ickes*. New York: Simon & Schuster, 1954.

Ide Hideo. *Jissho: Nihon no Yakuza (Documented Account: The Japanese Yakuza)*. Tokyo: Tatsukaze, 1972.

d'Ideville, Count. *Memoirs of Marshal Bugeaud*. London: Hurst & Blackett, 1884.

Iglehart, Ferdinand Cowle. *King Alcohol Dethroned*. Westerville, Ohio: American Issue, 1919.

Ignatieff, Michael. *A Just Measure of Pain*. New York: Pantheon Books, 1978.

Ike Nobutaka. *The Beginnings of Political Democracy in Japan*. New York: Alfred A. Knopf, 1950.

_____ (trans. and ed.). *Japan's Decision for War: Records of the 1941 Political Conferences*. Palo Alto, Calif.: Stanford University Press, 1967.

Iklé, Frank William. *German-Japanese Relations, 1936-1940*. New York: Bookman, 1956.

Ileana, Princess of Roumania and Archduchess of Austria. *I Live Again*. New York: Rinehart, 1952.

Iliodor. *The Mad Monk of Russia*. New York: Century, 1918.

Illinois Legislative Council. *Bills to Abolish the Death Penalty in Illinois*. Springfield: State of Illinois, 1951.

_____. *Capital Punishment for Serious Sex Offences*. Springfield: State of Illinois, 1954.

Illustrated Catalogue of the Centennial Exhibition, 1876. New York: John Filmer, 1876.

Illustrations of Contra Costa County. Oakland, Calif.: Smith & Elliott, 1878.

Imai Takeo. *Reminiscences of the China Affair*. Tokyo: Misuzu Shobo, 1964.

Impartial Account of the Trial of Ebenezer Mason. Dedham, Mass.: H. Mann, 1802.

Inbau, Fred, and Reid, J.E. *Criminal Interrogations and Confessions*. Baltimore: Williams & Wilkins, 1976.

_____. *Criminal Investigation and Criminal Law*. Radnor, Pa.: Chilton, 1972.

_____ (ed.). *Criminal Law for the Layman*. Randor, Pa.: Chilton, 1978.

_____. *Criminal Law for the Police*. Randor, Pa.: Chilton, 1969.

_____. *Evidence Law for the Police*. Radnor Pa.: Chilton, 1972.

_____, and Reid, J.E. *Lie Detection and Criminal Interrogation*. Baltimore: Williams & Wilkins, 1953.

_____. *Scientific Police Investigation*. Randor, Pa.: Chilton, 1972.

Inciardi, James A. *Careers in Crime*. Chicago: Rand McNally College, 1975.

_____. *The Drugs-Crime Connection*. Beverly Hills, Calif.: Sage, 1981.

_____, and Chambers, Carl D. (eds.). *Drugs and the Criminal Justice System*. Beverly Hills, Calif.: Sage, 1974.

_____. *A History and Sociology of Organized Crime*. Ann Arbor: University of Michigan Microfilms, 1974.

_____ (ed.). *Radical Criminology*. Beverly Hills, Calif.: Sage, 1980.

_____. *Reflections on Crime*. New York: Holt, Rinehart & Winston, 1979.

_____. *The War on Drugs: Heroin, Cocaine, Crime, and Public Policy*. Palo Alto, Calif.: Mayfield, 1986.

Incidents in the Life of Milton W. Streeter. Pawtucket, R.I.: H.F.

Tingley, 1850.

Ind, Allison. *Bataan: The Judgement Seat.* New York: Macmillan, 1944.

Inderwick, F.A. *Side-Lights on the Stuarts.* London: Low, Marston, Searle & Rivington, 1888.

Industrial Association of San Francisco. *San Francisco: A City That Achieved Freedom.* San Francisco: n.p., 1931.

Ingersoll, Ernest. *Knocking Around the Rockies.* New York: Harper, 1883.

Ingersoll, L.D. *A History of the War Department of the United States.* Washington, D.C.: Mohun, 1880.

_____. *The Life of Horace Greeley.* Chicago: Union, 1873.

Ingersoll, Robert G. *Great Speeches of Robert Ingersoll.* Chicago: Rhodes & McClure, 1888.

Ingham, George Thomas. *Digging Gold Among the Rockies.* Philadelphia: Hubbard Brothers, 1888.

Ingham, K. *A History of East Africa.* London: Longmans, 1962.

Ingle, Don. *Fall Forward, My Son.* New York: Carlton Press, 1974.

Ingleton, Roy D. *Police of the World.* New York: Charles Scribner's Sons, 1979.

Inglis, Brian. *The Forbidden Game: A Social History of Drugs.* New York: Charles Scribner's Sons, 1975.

_____. *Private Conscience—Public Morality.* London: André Deutsch, 1964.

_____. *The Story of Ireland.* London: Faber & Faber, 1956.

_____. *West Briton.* London: Faber & Faber, 1962.

Ingraham, Abijah A. *A Biography of Fernando Wood, A History of the Forgeries, Perjuries, and Other Crimes of Our "Model Mayor."* New York: n.p., 1856.

Ingraham, Charles A. *Elmer E. Ellsworth and the Zouaves of '61.* Chicago: University of Chicago Press, 1925.

Ingraham, Joseph H. *The South-West: By a Yankee.* New York: Harper & Brothers, 1835.

Ingraham, Prentiss. *Wild Bill, the Pistol Dead Shot.* New York: Beadle & Adams, 1882.

Inman, Henry. *The Great Salt Lake Trail.* New York: Macmillan, 1898.

_____. *The Old Santa Fe Trail.* New York: Macmillan, 1897.

Inman, Samuel Guy. *Intervention in Mexico.* New York: Charles Scribner's Sons, 1919.

Innerst, J. Stewart. *Is Capital Punishment the Answer?* Richmond, Ind.: The Five Years Meeting of Friends, 1959.

Innes, Brian. *The Book of Pirates.* London: Bancroft, 1966.

Innis, Harold A. *The Bias of Communication.* Toronto, Ontario, Can.: University of Toronto Press, 1951.

Inoguchi Rikihei, Tadashi Nakajima, and Pineau, Roger. *The Divine Wind: Japan's Kamikaze Force in World War II.* Annapolis, Md.: United States Naval Institute, 1958.

Ino Kenji. *Kodama Yoshio no Kyozo to Jitsuzo (The Image and Reality of Yoshio Kodama).* Tokyo: Sokon Shuppan, 1970.

_____. *Nihon no Uyoku (Japan's Right Wing).* Tokyo: Nisshin Godo Shuppan, 1973.

_____. *Yakuza to Nihonjin (Yakuza and the Japanese).* Tokyo: Mikasa Shoto, 1974.

In Prison and On the Scaffold. Indianapolis, Ind.: Ned Reed, 1879.

Institorius, Henricus. *Malleus Maleficarum.* trans. Rev. Montague Summers. New York: Benjamin Bolm, 1928.

Institute of Judicial Administration/ American Bar Association Juvenile Justice Standards Project. *Standards Relating to Counsel for Private Parties.* Cambridge, Mass.: Ballinger, 1977.

_____. *Standards Relating to Juvenile Delinquency and Sanctions.* Cambridge, Mass.: Ballinger, 1977.

_____. *Standards Relating to Non-Criminal Misbehavior.* Cambridge, Mass.: Ballinger, 1977.

Institute for Mediterranean Affairs. *The Palestine Refugee Problem.* New York: St. Martin's, 1958.

Institute for the Study of Drug Dependence. *Drug Abuse Briefing.* London: Published by Author, 1987.

The Interesting Trial of William F. Hooe. New York: Joseph M'Cleland, 1826.

International Association of Chiefs of Police. *An Organizational Study of the Police Department.* New York: IACP, 1967.

The Interocean. *A History of Chicago: Its Men and Institutions.* Chicago: Interocean, 1900.

The Investigation of the Assassination of President Kennedy. Washington, D.C.: U.S. Government Printing Office, 1976.

Ionescu, Ghita. *Communism in Rumania, 1944-1962.* London: Oxford University Press, 1964.

Ionides, Michael. *Divide and Lose.* London: Geoffrey Bles, 1960.

Ions, Edmond S. *James Bryce and American Democracy.* London: Macmillan, 1968.

Ireland, Alleyne. *Joseph Pulitzer: Reminiscences of a Secretary.* New York: Mitchell Kennerley, 1914.

Ireland, William Henry. *Memoirs of Jeanne d'Arc.* London: R. Triphook, 1824.

Irenholm, U.C. *The Shoshonis: Sentinels of the Rockies.* Norman: University of Oklahoma Press, 1964.

Irey, Elmer L., and Slocum, William T. *The Tax Dodgers.* Garden City, N.Y.: Doubleday, 1948.

Irish Times (ed.). *Eamon de Valera, 1882-1975.* Dublin: Irish Times Limited, 1976.

Irons, Peter. *Justice at War.* New York: Oxford University Press, 1983.

Irving, Clifford. *Fake!* New York: McGraw-Hill, 1969.

Irving, David. *Hitler's War.* New York: Viking Press, 1977.

_____. *The Mare's Nest.* London: William Kimber, 1964.

_____. *The Trail of the Fox: The Search for the True Field Marshal Rommel.* New York: E.P. Dutton, 1977.

Irving, Henry Brodribb. *A Book of Remarkable Criminals.* New York: George H. Doran, 1918.

_____. *French Criminals of the Nineteenth Century.* London: William Heinemann, 1901.

_____. *The Trial of Franz Muller.* London: William Hodge, 1911.

_____ (ed.). *The Trial of Mrs. Maybrick.* London: William Hodge, 1912.

_____. *The Trial of the Wainwrights.* London: William Hodge, 1926.

Irving, Joseph. *The Annals of Our Time, 1837-1868.* London: Macmillan, 1869.

Irving, Washington. *Life of George Washington.* New York: G.P. Putnam's Sons, 1857.

_____. *Life of Mohammed.* London: J.M. Dent, 1849.

_____. *Lives of the Successors of Mohammed.* London: John Murray, 1850.

Irwin, Inez Haynes. *Angels and Amazons: A Hundred Years of American Women.* Garden City, N.Y.: Doubleday, Doran, 1934.

Irwin, John. *The Felon.* Englewood Cliffs, N.J.: Prentice-Hall, 1970.

Irwin, Will. *The City that Was: A Requiem of Old San Francisco.* New York: B.W. Huebsch, 1906.

_____. *Confessions of a Con Man.* New York: B.W. Huebsch, 1909.

_____. *Pictures of Old Chinatown.* New York: Moffat, Yard, 1908.

Isaac, Paul E. *Prohibiton and Politics.* Knoxville: University of Tennessee Press, 1965.

Isaacs, G. R. *The South Sea Bubble.* New York: G.P. Putnam's Sons, 1933.

Isaacs, Harold R. *No Peace for Asia.* Cambridge, Mass.: MIT Press, 1967.

_____. *Scratches on Our Minds: American Images of China and India.* New York: John Day, 1958.

_____. *The Tragedy of the Chinese Revolution.* Palo Alto, Calif.: Stanford University Press, 1938.

Isely, Bliss, and Richards, W.M. *Four Centuries in Kansas.* Wichita, Kan.: McCormick-Mathers, 1936.

Isely, Jeter Allen. *Horace Greeley and the Republican Party, 1853-1861*. Princeton, N.J.: Princeton University Press, 1947.

Isidore of Seville. *History of the Kings of the Goths*. trans. Guidi Donini and Gordon B. Ford, Jr. Leiden, Neth.: E.J. Brill, 1966.

Iskander, Marwan. *The Arab Boycott of Israel*. Beirut, Leb.: Research Center, Palestine Liberation Organization, 1966.

Islemann, Sigurd von. *Der Kaiser in Holland*. Munich: Biederstein Verlag, 1967.

Isman, Felix. *Webber and Fields: Their Tribulations, Triumphs and Their Associates*. New York: Boni & Liveright, 1924.

Isocrates. trans. La Rue Van Hook. Cambridge, Mass.: Harvard University Press, 1954.

Isolani, Isidoro. *Libellus Adversus Magos, Divinatores, Maleficos*. Milan, Italy: Angeli Seinzenzeler, 1506.

Israel, Fred L. *The Chief Executive*. New York: Crown, 1965.

_____ (ed.). *1897 Sears Roebuck Catalogue*. New York: Chelsea House, 1968.

Israel, Lee. *Kilgallen*. New York: Delacorte, 1957.

_____. *Miss Tallulah Bankhead*. New York: G.P. Putnam's Sons, 1972.

Issawi, Charles. *Egypt at Mid-Century*. New York: Oxford University Press, 1954.

Issel, William, and Cherny, Robert W. *San Francisco, 1865-1932*. Berkeley: University of California Press, 1986.

Issler, Anne Roller. *Stevenson at Silverado*. Caldwell, Idaho: Caxton Printers, 1939.

Italy's Fighting Forces on Land, Sea and Air. London: Sampson Low, 1940.

Italy's Struggle for Liberation. London: International, 1944.

Italy's War Crimes in Ethiopia. Woodford Green, Eng.: *New Times & Ethiopia News*, 1945.

Ito Kanejiro. *Military Men of My Native Land*. Tokyo: Kyo no Mondai-sha, 1939.

Ito Masanori. *The End of the Imperial Japanese Navy*. trans. Andrew Y. Kuroda and Roger Pineau. New York: W.W. Norton, 1962.

Ivanov, Miroslav. *Target: Heydrich*. New York: Macmillan, 1972.

Ivansky, A.I. *Molodiye godi V.I. Lenina*. Moscow: Molodaya Gvardiya, 1960.

Ives, George. *A History of Penal Methods*. Montclair, N.J.: Patterson Smith, 1972.

Ivins, William M. *Machine Politics and Money in Elections in New York City*. New York: Harper, 1887.

Izvolsky, Alexander. *Memoirs*. trans. Charles L. Seeger. London: Hutchinson, 1920

_____. *Recollections of a Foreign Minister*. Garden City, N.Y.: Doubleday, 1921.

Izzeddin, Nejla. *The Arab World: Past, Present and Future*. Chicago: Regenery, 1953.

J

Jaastad, Ben. *Man of the West: Reminiscences of George Washington Oaks, 1840-1917*. Tucson: Arizona Pioneers' Historical Society, 1956.

Jabarti, Abdul Rahman al-. *Merveilles Biographiques et Historiques*. trans. Chefik Mansour Bey, et. al. Cairo, Egypt: Impr. Nationale, 1888.

Jabotinsky, Vladimer. *The Jewish War Front*. London: George Allen & Unwin, 1940.

Jachino, Angelo. *Gaudo e Matapan*. Milan, Italy: Mondadori, 1946.

_____. *Tramonto di una grande Marina*. Milan, Italy: Mondadori, 1959.

Jäckel, Eberhard. *Frankreich in Hitlers Europa*. Stuttgart, Ger.: Deutsche Verlagsanstalt, 1958.

Jackh, Ernest. *Background of the Middle East*. Ithaca, N.Y.: Cornell University Press, 1952.

Jacks, Irving, and Cox, Steven G. (eds.). *Psychological Approaches to Crime and Its Correction*. Chicago: Nelson-Hall, 1984.

Jackson, Anthony. *A Place Called Home*. Cambridge, Mass.: MIT Press, 1976.

Jackson, Bruce. *Death Row*. Boston: Beacon Press, 1980.

_____. *In The Life*. New York: Macmillan, 1972.

_____. *Killing Time*. Ithaca, N.Y.: Cornell University Press, 1977.

_____. *A Thief's Primer*. New York: Macmillan, 1969.

Jackson, Donald, and Spence, Mary Lee (eds.). *The Expeditions of John Charles Frémont*. Urbana: University of Illinois Press, 1970.

_____ (ed.). *Letters of the Lewis and Clark Expedition*. Urbana: University of Illinois Press, 1962.

Jackson, E.L. *St. Helena*. London: Ward, Lock, 1903.

Jackson, Geoffrey. *People's Prison*. London: Faber & Faber, 1973.

_____. *Surviving the Long Night: An Autobiographical Account of a Political Kidnapping*. New York: Vanguard Press, 1974.

Jackson, George. *Soledad Brothers: The Prison Letters of George Jackson*. New York: Coward-McCann, 1970.

Jackson, H.H. *A Century of Dishonor*. New York: Harper & Brothers, 1881.

Jackson, Helen Hunt. *Bits of Travel at Home*. Boston: Little, Brown, 1878.

Jackson, Herbert G., Jr. *The Spirit Rappers*. New York: Doubleday, 1972.

Jackson, John H. *Finland*. London: George Allen & Unwin, 1938.

Jackson, Joseph. *America's Most Historic Highway*. Philadelphia: John Wannamaker, 1926.

Jackson, Joseph Henry. *Anybody's Gold: The Story of California's Mining Towns*. New York: Appleton-Century, 1941.

_____. *Bad Company*. New York: Harcourt, Brace, 1949.

_____. *The Creation of Joaquin Murieta*. n.p., 1948.

_____. *The Portable Murder Book*. New York: Viking Press, 1945.

_____. *San Francisco Murders*. New York: Duell, Sloan & Pearce, 1947.

_____. *Tintypes in Gold: Four Studies in Robbery*. New York: Macmillan, 1939.

Jackson, Josephine A., and Salisbury, Helen M. *Outwitting Our Nerves*. New York: Century, 1932.

Jackson, Joy J. *New Orleans in the Gilded Age*. Baton Rouge: Louisiana State University Press, 1969.

Jackson, K.H. *The Gododdin*. Edinburgh, Scot.: Edinburgh University Press, 1969.

Jackson, Kenneth T. *The Ku Klux Klan in the City*. New York: Oxford University Press, 1970.

Jackson, Luther P. *Negro Office-Holders in Virginia, 1865-1895*. Norfolk, Va.: Guide Quality Press, 1945.

Jackson, Mary E. *Bank and Train Robbers*. Chicago: Henneberry, 1881.

_____. *The Life of Nellie C. Bailey*. Topeka, Kan.: R.E. Martin, 1885.

Jackson, Mason. *The Pictorial Press: Its Origins and Progress*. London: Hurst & Blackett, 1885.

Jackson, Orich. *The White Conquest of Arizona*. Los Angeles: West Coast Magazine, 1908.

Jackson, R. *The Chief*. London: Harrap, 1959.

Jackson, R.M. *The Machinery of Justice in England*. London: Cambridge University Press, 1964.

Jackson, Ralph Semmes. *Home on Double Bayou: Memories of an East Texas Ranch*. Austin: University of Texas Press, 1961.

Jackson, Sir Richard. *Occupied with Crime*. London: Harrap, 1967.

Jackson, Robert. *Airships*. Garden City, N.Y.: Doubleday, 1973.

_____. *Case for the Prosecution: A Biography of Sir Archibald Bodkin, Director of Public Prosecutions, 1920-1930*. London: Arthur Barket, 1962.

_____. *The Crime Doctors*. London: Frederick Muller, 1966.

_____. *Francis Camps: Famous Case Histories of the Celebrated Pathologist*. London: Hart Davis, 1975.

Jackson, Robert H. *The Struggle for Judicial Supremacy*. New York: Alfred A. Knopf, 1941.

_____. *The Supreme Court in the American System of Government*. Cambridge, Mass.: Harvard University Press, 1955.

Jackson, Stanley. *The Life and Cases of Mr. Justice Humphreys*. London: Odhams Press, 1951.

_____. *Mr. Justice Avory*. London: Victor Gollancz, 1935.

Jackson, T.A. *Ireland Her Own*. New York: International, 1947.

Jackson, T.G. *Dalmatia, the Quarnero and Istria, with Cettinje and the Isle of Grado*. Oxford, Eng.: Clarendon Press, 1887.

Jackson, W.A. Douglas. *Russo-Chinese Borderlands*. New York: D. Van Nostrand, 1962.

Jackson, W.G.F. *Seven Roads to Moscow*. New York: Philosophical Library, 1958.

Jackson, W.T.H. *The Literature of the Middle Ages*. New York: Columbia University Press, 1960

Jackson, W. Turrentine. *Treasure Hill*. Tucson: University of Arizona Press, 1963.

Jacob, Herbert. *Justice in America: Courts, Lawyers, and the Judicial Process*. Boston: Little, Brown, 1972.

_____ (ed.). *The Potential for Reform of Criminal Justice*. Beverly Hills, Calif.: Sage, 1974.

Jacobs, Clyde. *Justice Frankfurter and Civil Liberties*. Berkeley: University of California Press, 1961.

Jacobs, Glenn (ed.). *The Participant Observer*. New York: George Braziller, 1970.

Jacobs, Harold. *Weatherman*. New York: Ramparts Press, 1970.

Jacobs, James B. *Stateville: The Penitentiary in Mass Society*. Chicago: University of Chicago Press, 1977.

Jacobs, Jane. *The Death and Life of Great American Cities*. New York: Random House, 1961.

Jacobs, Norman (ed.). *Culture for the Millions: Mass Media in Modern Society*. Boston: Beacon Press, 1964.

Jacobs, Paul. *Prelude to Riot: A View of Urban America from the Bottom*. New York: Vintage Books, 1968.

Jacobs, T.C.H. *Aspects of Murder*. London: Stanley Paul, 1956.

_____. *Cavalcade of Murder*. London: Stanley Paul, 1955.

_____. *Pageant of Murder*. London: Stanley Paul, 1956.

Jacobson, David J. *The Affairs of Dame Rumor*. New York: Rinehart, 1948.

Jacobson, J. Mark. *The Development of American Political Thought*. New York: Century, 1932.

Jacobson, Lauri. *Hollywood Heartbreak*. New York: Simon & Schuster, 1984.

Jacobson, Richard, and Zinberg, Norman E. *The Social Basis of Drug Abuse Prevention*. Washington, D.C.: Drug Abuse Council, 1975.

Jacoby, Jean. *Raspoutine*. Paris: Flammarion, 1934.

Jacoby, Joseph E. (ed.). *Classics of Criminology*. Oak Park, Ill.: Moore, 1979.

Jacoby, Neil H., Nehemkis, Peter, and Eells, Richard. *Bribery and Extortion in World Business*. New York: Macmillan, 1977.

Jacoby, Susan. *Wild Justice*. New York: Harper & Row, 1983.

Jacomet, Daniel. *Jehanne d'Arc...documents originaux*. Paris: Librairie Floury, 1933.

Jacomet, Pierre. *Avocats rébublicains du second empire*. Paris: Denoël et Steele, 1933.

_____. *Berryer au prétoire*. Paris: Plon, 1938.

_____. *Les Drames judiciares du XIXeme siecle*. Paris: Payot, 1929.

Jacquier, Nicholas. *Flagellum Haereticorum Fascinariorum*. Frankfort, Ger.: N. Bassaeum, 1581.

Jaensch, E. *Eidetic Imagery and Topological Methods of Investigation*. trans. O. Oeser. New York: Harcourt Brace, 1930.

Jaffa, Harry V. *Crisis of the House Divided*. New York: Doubleday, 1959.

Jaffe, F.A. *A Guide to Pathological Evidence*. Toronto, Ontario, Can.: Carswell, 1976.

Jaffe, Julian F. *Crusade Against Radicalism*. Port Washington, N.Y.: Kennikat, 1972.

Jaffe, Louis. *English and American Judges as Lawmakers*. New York: Oxford, 1969.

Jaffe, Philip J. *The Rise and Fall of American Communism*. New York: Horizon, 1975.

Jäger, Karl. *Die Hexenverfolgung im Amt Homburg*. Bad Homburg, Ger.: F. Schick, 1931.

Jaher, Frederick C. *Doubters and Dissenters*. London: Free Press of Glencoe, 1964.

_____. *The Rich, the Well Born, and the Powerful*. Urbana: University of Illinois Press, 1973.

Jahns, Pat. *The Frontier World of Doc Holliday*. New York: Hastings House, 1957.

Jaksch, Wenzel. *Europas Weg nach Potsdam*. Stuttgart, Ger.: Deutsche Verlagsanstalt, 1958.

Jamal Mohammed Ahmed. *Intellectual Origins of Egyptian Nationalism*. London: Oxford University Press, 1960.

James, C.L.R. *A History of Negro Revolt*. London: Fact, 1938.

James, Daniel. *Mexico and the Americas*. New York: Frederick A. Praeger, 1963.

James, David H. *The Rise and Fall of the Japanese Empire*. London: George Allen & Unwin, 1951.

James, E.O. *Myth and Ritual in the Ancient Near East*. New York: Frederick A. Praeger, 1958.

James, Edgar. *James Boys: Deeds and Daring*. Baltimore: I. & M. Ottenheimer, 1912.

_____. *The Lives and Adventures, Daring Hold-ups, Train and Bank Robberies of the World's Most Desperate Bandits and Highwaymen— The Notorious James Brothers*. Baltimore: I. & M. Ottenheimer, 1913.

James, Edwin. *Account of an Expedition from Pittsburgh to the Rocky Mountains*. Philadelphia: H.C. Carey & I. Lea, 1822.

James, Frank. *Frank James and His Brother Jesse*. Baltimore: I. & M. Ottenheimer, 1915.

James, G., and Rosenthal, T. (eds.). *Tobacco and Health*. Springfield, Ill.: Charles C. Thomas, 1962.

James, Grace. *Japan: Recollections and Impressions*. London: George Allen & Unwin, 1936.

James, H. *Richard Olney and his Public Service*. New York: Houghton Mifflin, 1923.

James, H.K. *The Destruction of Mephisto's Greatest Web; or All Grafts Laid Bare*. Salt Lake City, Utah: Raleigh, 1914.

James, Henry. *American Scene*. New York: Charles Scribner's Sons, 1907.

_____. *The Bostonians*. New York: Macmillan, 1886.

James, Howard. *Children in Trouble: A National Scandal*. New York: David McKay, 1969.

_____. *The Little Victims: How America Treats Its Children*. New York: David McKay, 1975.

James, Jesse Edward, Jr. *Jesse James, My Father*. Independence, Mo.: Sentinel, 1899.

James, Jesse Lee. *Jesse James and the Lost Cause*. New York: Pageant Press, 1961.

James, John. *The Facts of Sex*. Princeton, N.J.: Vertex, 1970.

James, John. *My Experience With Indians*. Austin, Texas: Gammel's Book Store, 1925.

James, John T. *The Benders of Kansas*. Wichita, Kan.: Kan.-Okla., 1913.

James, Marquis. *Andrew Jackson: The Border Captain*. New York: Literary Guild, 1933.

_____, and Bessie. *Biography of a Bank*. New York: Harper & Row, 1954.

_____. *The Cherokee Strip: A Tale of an Oklahoma Boyhood*.

New York: Viking Press, 1945.

———. *The Life of Andrew Jackson*. Indianapolis, Ind.: Bobbs-Merrill, 1938.

———. *The Raven: A Biography of Sam Houston*. Indianapolis, Ind.: Bobbs-Merrill, 1929.

———. *They Had Their Hour*. Indianapolis, Ind.: Bobbs-Merrill, 1934.

James, Montague Rhode. *Lists of Manuscripts Formerly Owned by Dr. John Dee*. Oxford, Eng.: Oxford University Press, 1921.

James, Ralph and Esther. *Hoffa and the Teamsters*. Princeton, N.J.: D. Van Nostrand, 1965.

James, Robert Rhodes. *Chips*. London: Weidenfeld & Nicolson, 1967.

———. *Lord Randolph Churchill*. London: Weidenfeld & Nicolson, 1959.

James, Rosemary, and Wardlaw, Jack. *Plot or Politics?: The Garrison Case and Its Cast*. New Orleans, La.: Pelican, 1967.

James, T.E. *Prostitution and the Law*. London: William Heinemann, 1951.

James, Thomas. *Three Years Among the Indians and Mexicans*. Philadelphia: J.B. Lippincott, 1962.

James, Vinton Lee. *Frontier and Pioneer Recollections of Early Days in San Antonio and West Texas*. San Antonio, Texas: Published by Author, 1938.

James, William. *Francis Marion*. Marietta, Ga.: Continental, 1948.

James, William. *Philosophy of William James*. New York: Modern Library, 1925.

James, William F., and McMurray, George H. *History of San Jose, California*. San Jose, Calif.: Cawston, 1933.

Jameson, Henry B. *Heroes by the Dozen*. Abilene, Kan.: Shadinger-Wilson, 1961.

———. *Miracle of the Chisholm Trail*. Abilene, Kan.: Tri-State Chisholm Trail Centennial Commission, 1967.

Jameson, John Franklin. *The American Revolution Considered as a Social Movement*. Princeton, N.J.: Princeton University Press, 1967.

———. *Privateering and Piracy in the Colonial Period*. New York: Macmillan, 1923.

Janke, Peter, and Price, D.L. *Ulster: Coercion and Concensus*. London: Institute for the Study of Conflict, 1974.

Jannewein, J. Leonard. *Calamity Jane of the Western Trails*. Huron, S.D.: Dakota Books, 1953.

Janov, Arthur. *Primal Scream*. New York: G.P. Putnam's Sons, 1970.

Janowitz, M. *The Professional Solidier: A Social and Political Portrait*. New York: Free Press of Glencoe, 1964.

Janowitz, Morris. *The Last Half Century: Societal Change and Politics in America*. Chicago: University of Chicago Press, 1978.

Janowsky, Oscar I. *Foundations of Israel*. Princeton, N.J.: D. Van Nostrand, 1959.

Jansen, G.H. *Nonalignment and the Afro-Asian States*. New York: Frederick A. Praeger, 1966.

Jansen, Godfrey. *Why Robert Kennedy Was Killed*. New York: Third Press, 1970.

Jansen, Marius B. *The Japanese and Sun Yat-sen*. Cambridge, Mass.: Harvard University Press, 1954.

Janson, Carl-Gunnar. *Project Metropolitan, Research Report No. 7*. Stockholm: Stockholm University, 1977.

Janson, Charles William. *The Stranger in America, 1793-1806*. New York: Press of the Pioneers, 1935.

Janssen, Johannes. *Geschichte des deutschen Volkes seit dem Ausgang des Mittelalters*. Freiburg, Ger.: Herder'sche, 1876.

Jany, Kurt. *Geschichte der Köiglich preussischen Armee bis zum Jahre 1807*. Berlin: K. Siegismund, 1928.

Janzé, Alix de. *Berryer, souvenirs intimes*. Paris: Plon, 1881.

Japan Biographical Encyclopedia and Who's Who. Tokyo: Rengo Press, 1958.

Japan Biographical Outlines. Tokyo: Asakura Shobo, 1960.

Jaramillo, Cleofas M. *Shadows of the Past*. Santa Fe, N.M.: Seton Village Press, 1941.

Jarcke, Carl. *Carl Ludwig San, usw: Eine psychologisch-criminalistische Eroertung aus der Geschichte unserer Zeit*. Berlin: Ferdinand Dummler, 1831.

Jardin, Anne. *The First Henry Ford*. Cambridge, Mass.: MIT Press, 1970.

Jardin Birnie, Renée. *Le Cahier Rouge d'Eugène Weidmann*. Paris: Gallimard, 1968.

Jarman, T.L. *The Rise and Fall of Nazi Germany*. New York: New American Library, 1961.

Jarrett, J. *Environmental Quality in a Growing Economy*. Baltimore: Johns Hopkins Press, 1966.

Jaszi, Oscar, and Lewis, John D. *Against the Tyrant: The Tradition and Theory of Tyrannicide*. Glencoe, Ill.: Free Press, 1957.

Jaurès, Jean Léon. *Oeuvres de Jean Jaurès*. Paris: Les Editions Rieder, 1931.

———. *Pages Choisis*. Paris: Les Editions Rieder, 1922.

———. *Studies in Socialism*. New York: G.P. Putnam's Sons, 1906.

Jaworski, Leon. *Files of Evidence Connected With the Investigation of the Assassination of President John F. Kennedy*. Washington, D.C.: Microcard Editions, 1967.

———. *The Right and the Power*. Houston, Texas: Gulf, 1976.

Jay, Douglas. *Socialism and the New Society*. London: Longmans, 1962.

Jean, Albert. *Le Secret de Barbe-Bleue*. Paris: SFELT, 1950.

Jebb, Sir Joshua. *Report of the Surveyor-General of Prisons on the Construction, Ventilation and Details of Pentonville Prison*. London: W. Clowes & Sons, 1844.

Jedlicka, Ludwig. *Der 20 Juli 1944 in Österreich*. Munich: Verlag Herold, 1965.

Jefferson, Joseph. *Autobiography*. New York: Century, 1889.

Jefferson Davis and His Complicity in the Assassination of Abraham Lincoln and Where the Traitor Shall Be Tried. Philadelphia: Sherman, 1866.

Jeffery, C. Raymond. *Crime Prevention Through Environmental Design*. Beverly Hills, Calif.: Sage, 1977.

Jeffrey, John Mason. *Adobe and Iron*. La Jolla, Calif.: Prospect Avenue Press, 1969.

Jeffreys-Jones, Rhodri. *American Espionage: From Secret Service to CIA*. New York: Free Press, 1977.

Jeffries, Sir Charles. *The Colonial Police*. London: Max Parish, 1952.

Jeffries, Joseph M.N. *Palestine: The Reality*. New York: Longmans, 1939.

Jelavich, Barbara. *A Century of Russian Foreign Policy, 1814-1914*. Philadelphia: J.B. Lippincott, 1964.

———. *Russia and the Rumanian National Cause, 1858-1859*. Bloomington: Indiana University Press, 1959.

Jelavich, Charles and Barbara. *The Balkans*. Englewood Cliffs, N.J.: Prentice-Hall, 1965.

———. *Tsarist Russia and Balkan Nationalism: Russian Influence in the Internal Affairs of Bulgaria and Serbia, 1876-1886*. Berkeley: University of California Press, 1958.

Jelinek, George. *Ellsworth, Kansas, 1867-1947*. Salina, Kan.: Consolidated, 1947.

———. *90 Years of Ellsworth and Ellsworth County History*. Ellsworth, Kan.: Messenger Press, 1957.

Jelley, Herbert M., and Herrmann, Robert O. *The American Consumer*. San Francisco: McGraw-Hill, 1973.

Jellinek, E.M. *The Disease Concept of Alcoholism*. New Brunswick, N.J.: College & University Press, 1960.

Jemolo, A.C. *Church and State in Italy, 1859-1950*. trans. David Moore. Oxford, Eng.: Basil Blackwell, 1960.

Jencks, C.S. *Who Gets Ahead?* New York: Basic Books, 1979.

Jenkins, A.O. *Olive's Last Roundup*. Loup City, Nebr.: Sherman County Times, n.d.

Jenkins, Alan. *The Stock Exchange Story*. London: William

Heinemann, 1973.

_____. *The Twenties*. New York: Universe Books, 1974.

Jenkins, Brian. *Dr. Gully's Story*. New York: Coward, McCann & Geoghegan, 1972.

_____. *High Technology Terrorism and Surrogate War*. Santa Monica, Calif.: Rand, 1975.

_____. *Hostage Survival: Some Preliminary Observations*. Santa Monica: Rand, 1976.

_____, and Johnson, Janera. *International Terrorism: A Chronology 1968-1975*. Santa Monica, Calif.: Rand, 1975.

_____. *International Terrorism: A New Kind of Warfare*. Santa Monica, Calif.: Rand, 1974.

_____. *Numbered Lives: Some Statistical Observations from 77 International Hostage Episodes*. Santa Monica, Calif.: Rand, 1977.

_____. *Should Corporations Be Prevented From Paying Ransom?* Santa Monica, Calif.: Rand, 1974.

_____. *Will Terrorists Go Nuclear?* Santa Monica, Calif.: Rand, 1975.

Jenkins, Elizabeth. *Six Criminal Women*. London: Pan Books, 1949.

Jenkins, John H., and Frost, Gordon. *I'm Frank Hamer: The Life of a Texas Peace Officer*. New York: The Pemberton Press, 1968.

_____. *Neither the Fanatics nor the Faint-Hearted*. Austin, Texas: The Pemberton Press, 1963.

Jenkins, John S. *History of the War Between the United States and Mexico*. New York: C.M. Saxton, 1859.

Jenkins, Malinda, and Lilienthal, Jesse. *Gambler's Wife*. Boston: Houghton Mifflin, 1933.

Jenkins, Philip, and Potter, Gary W. *The City and the Syndicate: Organizing Crime in Philadelphia*. Lexington, Mass.: Ginn, 1985.

_____. *Crime and Justice: Issues and Ideas*. Belmont, Calif.: Brooks/Cole, 1984.

Jenkins, W.S. *Proslavery Thought in the Old South*. Chapel Hill: University of North Carolina Press, 1935.

Jenkinson, Michael. *Ghost Towns of New Mexico*. Albuquerque: University of New Mexico Press, 1967.

Jenks, Ira C. *Trial of David F. Mayberry*. Janesville, Wis.: Baker, Burnett & Hall, 1855.

Jenks, Leland H. *The Migration of British Capital to 1875*. New York: Alfred A. Knopf, 1927.

Jenness, John Scribner. *The Isles of Shoals*. New York: Hurd & Houghton, 1873.

Jennewein, J. Leonard. *Calamity Jane of the Western Trails*. Huron, S.D.: Dakota Books, 1953.

_____, and Boorman, Jane (eds.). *Dakota Panorama*. Sioux Falls, S.D.: Midwest-Beach Printing, 1961.

Jennings, Alphonso J. *Beating Back*. New York: D. Appleton, 1914.

_____. *Number 30664, by Number 31539*. Hollywood, Calif.: Pioneer Press, 1941.

_____. *Through the Shadows with O. Henry*. New York: H.K. Fly, 1921.

Jennings, Dean. *We Only Kill Each Other: The Life and Bad Times of Bugsy Siegel*. Englewood Cliffs, N.J.: Prentice-Hall, 1967.

Jennings, J.S. *Trial of James Parks*. Akron, Ohio: Laurie & Barnard, 1855.

Jennings, Jesse D., and Norbeck, Edward (eds.). *Prehistoric Man in the New World*. Chicago: University of Chicago Press, 1963.

Jennings, Napoleon A. *A Texas Ranger*. New York: Charles Scribner's Sons, 1899.

Jennings, Peter. *An End To Terrorism*. London: Lion Paperback, 1985.

Jennison, Keith W. *The Humorous Mr. Lincoln*. New York: Thomas Y. Crowell, 1965.

Jensen, A.R. *Bias in Mental Testing*. New York: Macmillan, 1980.

_____. *Straight Talk about Mental Tests*. New York: Macmillan, 1981.

Jensen, Ann (ed.). *Texas Ranger's Diary and Scrapbook*. Dallas: Kaleidograph Press, 1936.

Jensen, Joan M. *Military Surveillance of Civilians in America*. Morristown, N.J.: General Learning Press, 1975.

_____. *The Price of Vigilance*. Chicago: Rand McNally, 1968.

Jensen, Merrill. *The Founding of a Nation: A History of the American Revolution, 1763-1776*. New York: Oxford University Press, 1968.

_____. *The New Nation*. New York: Alfred A. Knopf, 1950.

Jensen, Richard. *The Winning of the Midwest*. Chicago: University of Chicago Press, 1971.

Jensen, Vernon H. *Heritage of Conflict*. Ithaca, N.Y.: Cornell University Press, 1950.

Jerome, Lawrence E. *Astrology Disproved*. Buffalo, N.Y.: Prometheus, 1977.

Jerome, Thomas J. *Ku Klux Klan No. 40*. Raleigh, N.C.: Edwards & Broughton, 1895.

Jerrett, Herman Daniel. *California's El Dorado, Yesterday and Today*. Sacramento, Calif.: Press of Jo Anderson, 1915.

Jerrold, Blanchard. *The Life of Napolean III*. London: Longmans, Green, 1874.

Jersild, Jens. *Boy Prostitution*. Copenhagen: G.E.C. Gad, 1956.

Jervis, Eustace. *Twenty-Five Years in Six Prisons*. London: T. Fisher Unwin, 1925.

Jervis, John. *On the Office and Duties of Coroners, with Forms and Procedures*. London: Sweet & Maxwell, 1957.

Jesness, Carl F. *The Fricot Ranch Study*. Sacramento: California Department of Youth Authority, 1965.

Jesse, F. Tennyson. *Comments on Cain*. London: William Heinemann, 1948.

_____. *Murder and Its Motives*. New York: Alfred A. Knopf, 1924.

_____. *Trial of Ley and Smith*. London: William Hodge, 1947.

_____ (ed.). *The Trial of Madeleine Smith*. New York: Day, 1927.

_____. *Trials of Timothy John Evans and John Reginald Halliday Christie*. London: William Hodge, 1957.

Jessor, Richard, et al. *Society, Personality, and Deviant Behavior*. New York: Holt, Rinehart & Winston, 1968.

Jessup, Philip C. *Elihu Root*. New York: Dodd, Mead, 1938.

Jetzinger, Franz. *Hitlers Jugend*. Vienna, Aust.: Europa-Verlag, 1956.

Jevons, H.S. *Italian Military Secrets*. London: Published by Author, 1937.

Jewett, Charles. *A Forty Years' Fight with the Drink Demon, or A History of the Temperance Reform as I Have Seen It, and of My Labor in Connection Therewith*. New York: National Temperance Society, 1876.

Jeyes, S.H., and How, F.D. *The Life of Sir Howard Vincent*. London: George Allen, 1912.

JFK Assassination Solved: Special Report. North West Assassination Research Committee, n.d.

JFK Murder Solved: Killing Coordinated by CIA. Los Angeles: Los Angeles Free Press, 1978.

Jimenez, Janey. *My Prisoner*. Kansas: McMillan, 1977.

Jobé, Joseph (ed.). *The Great Age of Sail*. New York: New York Graphic Society, 1967.

Jocknick, Sidney. *Early Days on the Western Slope of Colorado*. Denver: Carson-Harper, 1913.

Joël, Ernst, and Fränkel, Fritz. *Der Cocainismus*. Berlin: Springer, 1924.

Joeston, Joachim. *The Biggest Lie I Ever Told: The Kennedy Fraud and How I Helped Expose It*. Munich: Published by Author, 1968.

_____. *The Case Against the Kennedy Clan in the Assassination of President John F. Kennedy*. Munich: Published by Author, 1968.

_____. *The Case Against Lyndon B. Johnson in the Assassination of President Kennedy*. Munich: Published by Author, 1967.

_____. *The Dark Side of Lyndon Baines Johnson*. London: Peter Dawnay, 1968.

_____. *De Gaulle and His Murders*. Isle of Man, Brit.: Times Press, 1964.

_____. *The Garrison Enquiry*. London: Peter Dawnay, 1967.

_____. *Marina Oswald*. London: Peter Dawnay, 1967.

_____. *Oswald: Assassin or Fall Guy?* Marzani & Munsell, 1964.

Joey. *Hit #29*. New York: Pocket Books, 1975.

_____. *Joey Kills*. New York: Pocket Books, 1975.

_____. *Killer*. New York: Pocket Books, 1975.

Johannsen, Albert. *The House of Beadle and Adams and Its Nickel and Dime Novels*. Norman: University of Oklahoma Press, 1950.

Johannsen, Robert W. *Stephen A. Douglas*. New York: Oxford University Press, 1973.

John Fitzgerald Kennedy, 1917-1963, and the Federal City He Loved. Washington, D.C.: Tatler, 1963.

A John F. Kennedy Memorial. New York: MacFadden Books, 1964.

John of Joinville. *The Life of St. Louis*. trans. René Hague. New York: Sheed & Ward, 1955.

Johns, A. Wesley. *The Man Who Shot McKinley*. South Brunswick, N.J.: A.S. Barnes, 1970.

Johnsen, Julia E. (ed.). *Capital Punishment*. New York: H.W. Wilson, 1939.

_____. *Palestine: Jewish Homeland*. New York: H.W. Wilson, 1946.

Johnson, Allen (ed.). *Chronicles of America*. New Haven, Conn.: Yale University Press, 1918.

Johnson, Andrew: Trial of an Impeachment by the House of Representatives for High Crimes and Misdemeanor. Washington, D.C.: U.S. Government Printing Office, 1868.

Johnson, Angus James, II. *Virginia Railroads in the Civil War*. Chapel Hill: University of North Carolina Press, 1961.

Johnson, B.B. *Abraham Lincoln and Boston Corbett*. Waltham, Mass.: Byron Berkeley Johnson, 1914.

Johnson, Barry C. (ed.). *The English Westerners' 10th Anniversary Publication, 1964*. London: English Westerners' Society, 1964.

Johnson, C.S. *Growing Up in the Black Belt*. Washington, D.C.: American Council on Education, 1941.

Johnson, Chalmers. *Revolution and the Social System*. Stanford, Calif.: Hoover Institution, 1964.

Johnson Charles. *Lives of the Most Noted Highwaymen*. Dublin, Ire.: Tegg, 1839.

Johnson, Claudius O. *Borah of Idaho*. Longmans, Green, 1936.

_____. *Carter Henry Harrison I*. Chicago: University of Chicago Press, 1928.

Johnson, David R. *American Law Enforcement*. St. Louis: Forum Press, 1981.

Johnson, Diane. *Dashiell Hammett, A Life*. New York: Random House, 1983.

Johnson, Donald Bruce, and Walker, Jack L. (eds.). *The Dynamics of the American Presidency*. New York: John Wiley & Sons, 1964.

Johnson, Dorothy. *Famous Lawmen of the Old West*. New York: Dodd, Mead, 1963.

_____. *Some Went West*. New York: Dodd, Mead, 1965.

Johnson, Douglas. *France and the Dreyfuss Affair*. London: Blandford, 1966.

Johnson, E. *Justice and Reform: The Formative Years of the OEO Legal Services Program*. New York: Russell Sage Foundation, 1974.

Johnson, Edward. *Wonder-Working Providence*. New York: Barnes & Noble, 1952.

Johnson, Elmer H. *Crime, Correction, and Society*. Homewood, Ill.: Dorsey Press, 1964.

_____. *Social Problems of Urban Man*. Homewood, Ill.: Dorsey Press, 1974.

_____. *Work Release: Factors in Selection and Results*. Carbondale, Ill.: Center for the Study of Crime, Delinquency and Corrections, 1969.

Johnson, Forrest B. *Hour of Redemption: The Ranger Raid on Cabanatuan*. New York: Manor Books, 1978.

Johnson, Francis. *Famous Assassinations*. Chicago: A.C. McClurg, 1903.

Johnson, G.C. *Wagon Yard*. Dallas: William T. Tardy, 1938.

Johnson, Gerald W. *The Lunatic Fringe*. New York: J.B. Lippincott, 1957.

_____. *Randolph of Roanoke: A Political Fantastic*. New York: Minton, Balch, 1929.

_____. *Woodrow Wilson*. New York: Harpers, 1944.

Johnson, Haynes. *The Bay of Pigs*. New York: W.W. Norton, 1964.

Johnson, Hugh S. *The Blue Eagle from Egg to Earth*. Garden City, N.Y.: Doubleday, Doran, 1935.

Johnson, J.H. *The Open Book*. Kansas City: Published by Author, 1927.

Johnson, James, and Miller, Floyd. *The Man Who Sold The Eiffel Tower*. Garden City, N.Y.: Doubleday, 1961.

Johnson, James D. *A Century of Chicago Streetcars*. Wheaton, Ill.: Traction Orange, 1964.

Johnson, James Weldon. *Along This Way*. New York: Viking, 1968.

Johnson, Jeremiah Augustus. *The Life of a Citizen: At Home and in Foreign Service*. New York: Vail Ballou Press, 1915.

Johnson, John. *Trial and Sentence of John Johnson*. New York: Joseph Desnoues, 1824.

Johnson, John. *Doing Field Research*. New York: Free Press, 1974.

Johnson, John J., and Douglas, Jack D. (eds.). *Crime at the Top: Deviance in Business and the Professions*. Philadelphia: J.B. Lippincott, 1978.

Johnson, John J. (ed.). *The Role of the Military in Underdeveloped Countries*. Princeton, N.J.: Princeton University Press, 1962.

Johnson, Julia E. (ed.). *Capital Punishment*. New York: H.W. Wilson, 1939.

Johnson, K. *Guatemala: From Terrorism to Terror*. London: Institute for Study of Conflict, 1972.

Johnson, L.F. *Famous Kentucky Tragedies and Trials*. Louisville, Ky: Baldwin Law Books, 1916.

Johnson, Lyndon B. *The Vantage Point*. New York: Popular Library, 1971.

Johnson, Malcolm. *Crime on the Labor Front*. New York: McGraw-Hill, 1950.

Johnson, Pamela Hansford. *On Iniquity*. New York: Charles Scribner's Sons, 1967.

Johnson, R.A. *Report of the Surveyor General upon the Alleged Peralta Grant*. Phoenix: Arizona Gazette Book and Job Office, 1890.

Johnson, R.E. *Juvenile Deliquency and Its Origins*. Cambridge, Eng.: Cambridge University Press, 1979.

_____. *A Shopkeeper's Millennium*. New York: Hill & Wang, 1978.

Johnson, Ray. *Too Dangerous to Be at Large*. New York: Quadrangle, 1975.

Johnson, Richard A., et al. *The Theory and Management of Systems*. New York: McGraw-Hill, 1973.

Johnson, Robert, and Toch, Hans (eds.). *The Pains of Imprisonment*. Beverly Hills, Calif.: Sage, 1982.

Johnson, Robert Underwood, and Buel, Clarence C. (eds.). *Battles and Leaders of the Civil War*. New York: Century, 1887.

Johnson, Rossiter (ed.). *Campfire and Battlefield*. New York: Knight & Brown, 1896.

_____. *History of World's Columbian Exposition*. n.p., n.d.

Johnson, Vera Scott, and Wommack, Thomas. *The Secrets of Numbers*. New York: Dial, 1973.

Johnson, W.A. *History of Anderson County, Kansas*. Garnett,

Kan.: Kauffman & Iler, 1877.

Johnson, W.F. *History of Cooper County, Missouri.* Cleveland: Historical, 1919.

Johnson, Walter (ed.). *Selected Letters of William Allen White, 1899-1943.* New York: Henry Holt, 1947.

_____. *William Allen White's America.* New York: Henry Holt, 1947.

Johnson, William J. *Abraham Lincoln: The Christian.* Milford, Mich.: Mott Media, 1976.

Johnson, William Weber. *Heroic Mexico.* New York: Doubleday, 1968.

_____. *Mexico.* New York: Life World Library, 1961.

Johnston, Alva. *The Legendary Mizners.* New York: Farrar, Straus & Young, 1953.

Johnston, Charles Haven Ladd. *Famous American Athletes of Today.* Boston: L.C. Page, 1928.

_____. *Famous Scouts, Including Trappers, Pioneers, and Soldiers of the Frontier.* Boston: L.C. Page, 1910.

Johnston, Harry V. *The Last Roundup.* Minneapolis, Minn.: H.V. Johnston, 1950.

_____. *My Home on the Range: Frontier Life in the Bad Lands.* St. Paul, Minn.: Webb, 1942.

Johnston, James A. *Alcatraz Island Prison.* New York: Charles Scribner's Sons, 1949.

Johnston, James P. *Grafters I Have Met.* Chicago: Thompson & Thomas, 1906.

Johnston, Lloyd D., Bachman, Jerald G., and O'Malley, Patrick M. *Student Drug Use, Attitudes and Beliefs.* Washington, D.C.: U.S. Government Printing Office, 1983.

Johnston, Michael. *Political Corruption and Public Policy in America.* Monterey, Calif.: Brooks/Cole, 1982.

Johnston, Norman. *The Human Cage: A Brief History of Prison Architecture.* New York: Walker, 1973.

_____, Savitz, Leonard, and Wolfgang, Marvin E. (eds.). *The Sociology of Punishment and Corrections.* New York: John Wiley & Sons, 1962.

Johnston, Philip. *Lost and Living Cities of the California Gold Rush.* Los Angeles: Touring Bureau of the Automobile Club, 1948.

Johnston, Reginald F. *Twilight in the Forbidden City.* London: Victor Gollancz, 1934.

Johnston, Robert H. *Tradition Versus Revolution.* New York: Columbia University Press, 1977.

Johnston, Samuel P. (ed.). *Alaska Commercial Company, 1868-1940.* Edwin E. Wachter, 1941.

Johnston, Stanley. *Queen of the Flat-Tops: The U.S.S. Lexington and the Coral Sea Battles.* New York: E.P. Dutton, 1942.

Johnston, William Davidson. *T.R.: Champion of the Strenuous Life.* New York: Farrar, Straus & Cudahy, 1958.

Joint Center for Political Studies. *A Policy Framework for Racial Justice.* Washington, D.C.: Joint Center for Political Studies, 1983.

Joint Commission on Correctional Manpower and Training. *Offenders as a Correctional Manpower Resource.* Washington, D.C.: Joint Commission on Correctional Manpower and Training, 1968.

_____. *Perspectives on Correctional Manpower and Training.* Washington, D.C.: Joint Commission On Correctional Manpower and Training, 1970.

_____. *A Time to Act.* Washington, D.C.: Joint Commission on Correctional Manpower and Training, 1969.

Joll, James. *The Anarchists.* New York: Grosset & Dunlap, 1964.

Jolly, Cyril. *The Vengeance of Private Pooley.* London: William Heinemann, 1956.

Joly, H. *Le Crime.* Paris: Cerf, 1889.

Jonas, George, and Amiel, Barbara. *By Persons Unknown.* Toronto, Ontario, Can.: Macmillan, 1977.

_____. *The Strange Death of Christine Demeter.* Toronto, Ontario, Can.: Macmillan, 1977.

Jonas, Hans. *The Gnostic Religion.* Boston: Beacon Press, 1958.

Jonas, Klaus. *The Life of Crown Prince William.* trans. Charles W. Bangert. London: Routledge & Kegan Paul, 1961.

Jones, A.B., and Llewellyn, J. *Malingering.* London: William Heinemann, 1917.

Jones, Alfred W. *Life, Liberty, and Property.* Philadelphia: J.B. Lippincott, 1941.

Jones, Ann. *Autobiography of Mother Jones.* Chicago: Charles H. Kerr, 1925.

Jones, C. Sheridan. *The Story of the Hohenzollern.* London: Jarrold & Sons, 1915.

Jones, David A. *The Health Risks of Imprisonment.* Lexington, Mass.: D.C. Heath, 1976.

Jones, Eliot. *The Trust Problem in the United States.* New York: Macmillan, 1921.

Jones, Elwyn. *The Last Two to Hang.* New York: Stein-Day, 1966.

_____, and Lloyd, John. *The Ripper File: A Documentary Investigation.* London: Barker, 1975.

Jones, Ernest. *The Life and Work of Sigmund Freud.* New York: Basic Books, 1961.

_____. *Nightmares, Witches, and Devils.* New York: W.W. Norton, 1931.

_____. *On the Nightmare.* London: International Psycho-Analytic Library, 1931.

Jones, F.C. *Japan's New Order in Asia.* New York: Oxford University Press, 1954.

_____. *Manchuria Since 1931.* London: Royal Institute of International Affairs, 1949.

Jones, Francis P. *History of the Sinn Fein and The Irish Rebellion of 1916.* New York: P.J. Kenedy, 1917.

Jones, Gareth Stedman. *Outcast.* London: Clarendon Press, 1971.

Jones, H. *Crime, Race, and Culture.* New York: John Wiley & Sons, 1981.

Jones, Haloway R. *John Muir and the Sierra Club.* San Francisco: Sierra Club, 1965.

Jones, Hardin B. and Helen B. *Sensual Drugs.* Cambridge, Eng.: Cambridge University Press, 1977.

Jones, Harry (ed.). *The Courts, the Public, and the Law Explosion.* Englewood Cliffs, N.J.: Prentice-Hall, 1965.

Jones, Horace. *The Story of Rice County.* Wichita, Kan.: Wichita Eagle, 1928.

Jones, Howard. *Crime and Penal System.* London: University Tutorial Press, 1956.

_____. *Open Prisons.* London: RKP, 1979.

Jones, Howard Mumford. *O Strange New World.* New York: Viking/Compass, 1967.

Jones, Hugh. *Modern Denmark: Its Social, Economic, and Agricultural Life.* London: P.S. King, 1927.

Jones, J. Elbert. *The Mysteries of Famous Crimes Solved by St. Louis Policemen.* St. Louis: Moinster, 1924.

Jones, J. Harry, Jr. *The Minutemen.* Garden City, N.Y.: Doubleday, 1968.

Jones, J. William. *Christ in Camp.* Richmond, Va.: n.p., 1887.

Jones, James. *Andrew Johnson.* Greeneville: East Tennessee, 1901.

Jones, James Rees. *The First Whigs: The Politics of the Exclusion Crisis, 1678-1683.* New York: Oxford University Press, 1961.

Jones, John B. *A Rebel War Clerk's Diary at the Confederate States Capital.* New York: Old Hickory Bookshop, 1935.

Jones, John H., and Britten, Fred A. (eds.). *A Half Century of Chicago Building.* Chicago: n.p., 1910.

Jones, Katherine M. *The Plantation South.* New York: Bobbs-Merrill, 1957.

Jones, Lester W. (ed.). *A Treasury of Spices.* New York: American Spice Trade Association, 1956.

Jones, Lewis Wade. *Cold Rebellion: The South's Oligarchy in Revolt.* London: MacGibbon & Kee, 1962.

Jones, Lloyd. *Life and Adventures of Harry Tracy.* Chicago: Jewett & Lindrooth, 1902.

Jones, Maldwyn Allen. *American Immigration.* Chicago: University of Chicago Press, 1960.

Jones, M.E. *Gandhi Lives.* London: Hodder & Stoughton, 1948.

Jones, Mat Ennis. *Fiddlefooted.* Denver: Sage Books, 1966.

Jones, Pamela. *Under the City Streets.* New York: Holt, Rinehart & Winston, 1978.

Jones, Penn, Jr. *Forgive My Grief, Volume I.* Midlothian, Texas: Midlothian Mirror, 1966.

Jones, Richard Glyn (ed.). *Unsolved Classic True Murder Cases.* New York: Peter Bedrick Books, 1987.

Jones, Robert L. *The Eighteenth Amendment and Our Foreign Relations.* New York: Thomas Y. Crowell, 1933.

Jones, Robert W. *Journalism in the United States.* New York: E.P. Dutton, 1947.

Jones, S. Alfred. *Is Fascism the Answer?* Hamilton, Ontario, Can.: David-Lisson, 1933.

Jones, Thomas. *Lloyd George.* London: Oxford University Press, 1951.

_____. *Whitehall Diary, 1916-1930.* London: Oxford University Press, 1969.

Jones, Thomas A. *J. Wilkes Booth.* Port Tobacco, Md.: Society for the Restoration of Port Tobacco, 1955.

Jones, Thomas Jesse. *The Sociology of a New York City Block.* New York: Columbia University Press, 1904.

Jones, Tom B. *The Silver-Plated Age.* Sandoval, Spain: Coronado Press, 1962.

Jones, Virgil Carrington. *The Hatfields and the McCoys.* Chapel Hill: University of North Carolina Press, 1948.

Jones, W.C. *Report on the Subject of Land Titles.* Washington, D.C.: Gidgeon, 1860.

Jones, W.F. *The Experiences of a Deputy U.S. Marshal of the Indian Territory.* Tulsa, Okla.: n.p., 1937.

Jones, Willoughby. *James Fisk, Jr.: The Life of a Green Mountain Boy.* Philadelphia: W. Flint, 1872.

_____. *The Life of James Fisk, Jr.* Cincinnati, Ohio: Union, 1872.

_____. *Weighed and Found Wanting: The Stupendous Schemes and Enterprises that Make Rich Men Poor and Poor Men Rich in a Day.* Philadelphia: W. Flint, 1872.

Jones, Winfield. *Knights of the Ku Klux Klan.* New York: Tocsin, 1941.

_____. *Story of the Ku Klux Klan.* Washington, D.C.: American Newspaper Syndicate, 1921.

Jonescu, Take. *Some Personal Impressions.* London: Nisbet, 1919.

The Jones-Galentine Tragedy. Cleveland: Nevins' Brothers, 1871.

Jordan, D., and Pratt, E.J. *Europe and the American Civil War.* Boston: Houghton Mifflin, 1931.

Jordan, David P. *The King's Trial.* Berkeley: University of California Press, 1979.

Jordan, David Starr. *The Days of a Man.* New York: World Book, 1922.

Jordan, J. Glenn. *The Unpublished Inside Story of the Famous Scottsboro Case.* Huntsville, Ala.: White, 1932.

Jordan, Philip D. *The People's Health.* St. Paul: Minnesota Historical Society, 1948.

Jordan, Winthrop D. *The White Man's Burden.* New York: Oxford University Press, 1974.

_____. *White Over Black: American Attitudes Toward the Negro, 1550-1812.* Chapel Hill: University of North Carolina Press, 1968.

Jordin, John F. *Memories.* Gallatin: North Missourian Press, 1904.

Jorns, Auguste. *The Quakers as Pioneers in Social Work.* New York: Macmillan, 1931.

Jorre, Georges. *The Soviet Union: The Land and Its People.* London: Longmans, 1961.

Joselit, Jenna W. *Our Gang: Jewish Crime and the New York Jewish Community, 1900-1940.* Bloomington: Indiana University Press, 1983.

Josephson, Matthew. *Al Smith: Hero of the Cities.* Boston: Houghton Mifflin, 1969.

_____. *Life Among the Surrealists.* New York: Holt, Rinehart & Winston, 1962.

_____. *The Politicos.* New York: Harcourt, Brace, 1938.

_____. *Portrait of the Artist as American.* New York: Harcourt, Brace, 1930.

_____. *The President Makers.* New York: Harcourt, Brace, 1940.

_____. *The Robber Barons.* New York: Harcourt, Brace, 1934.

_____. *Sidney Hillman: Statesman of American Labor.* Garden City, N.Y.: Doubleday, 1952.

_____. *Union House, Union Bar.* New York: Random House, 1956.

Josephus, Flavius. *The Jewish War and Other Selections.* trans. H. St. J. Thackeray and Ralph Marcus. New York: Twayne, 1965.

Josselyn, John. *An Account of Two Voyages to New England.* Boston: W. Veazie, 1865.

Joughin, G. Louis, and Morgan, Edmund M. *The Legacy of Sacco and Vanzetti.* New York: Harcourt, Brace, 1948.

Jowitt, Earl. *The Strange Case of Alger Hiss.* London: Hodder & Stoughton, 1953.

Jowitt, William Allen. *Some Were Spies.* London: Hodder & Stoughton, 1954.

_____. *The Strange Case of Alger Hiss.* Garden City, N.Y.: Doubleday, 1953.

Joy, Maurice (ed.). *The Irish Rebellion of 1916 and its Martyrs.* New York: Devin-Adair, 1916.

Joyanx, Georges. *Prince Napolean in America, 1861.* Bloomington: Indiana University Press, 1959.

Joyce, James Avery. *Capital Punishment, A World View.* New York: Nelson, 1962.

_____. *Justice at Work.* London: Chapman & Hall, 1952.

Joyce, Michael. *Edinburgh: The Golden Age.* London: Longman, Green, 1951.

Joyneville, C. *Life of Alexander of Russia.* n.p., 1883.

Judas, Elizabeth. *Rasputin: Neither Devil nor Saint.* Los Angeles: Wetzel, 1942.

Judd, Denis. *Eclipse of Kings.* London: Macdonald & Jane's, 1976.

_____. *The Victorian Empire.* New York: Frederick A. Praeger, 1970.

Judge, Arthur V. *The Elizabethan Underworld.* London: George Routledge & Sons, 1930.

Judson, Horace Freeland. *Heroin Addiction in Britain.* New York: Harcourt Brace Jovanovich, 1974.

Judson, Katherine Berry. *Montana: The Land of Shining Mountains.* Chicago: A.C. McClurg, 1909.

Jue, George K. *Chinatown: It History, Its People, Its Importance.* San Francisco: San Francisco Chamber of Commerce, 1951.

Juergens, George. *Joseph Pulitzer and the New York World.* Princeton, N.J.: Princeton University Press, 1966.

Julian, G.W. *Political Recollections.* Chicago: Jansen, McClurg, 1884.

Jullian, Phillipe. *Oscar Wilde.* trans. Violet Wyndham. London: Constable, 1969.

Jumpertz Tried and Convicted. Chicago: Norris & Hyde, 1859.

Jung, Carl Gustav. *Psychology and Alchemy.* London: Routledge & Kegan Paul, 1953.

Jünger, Ernst. *Der Kampf als inneres Erlebnis.* Berlin: E.S. Mittler & Son, 1922.

Junkin, D.X. *The Life of Winfield Scott Hancock.* New York: D. Appleton, 1880.

Junod, H.A. *The Life of a South African Tribe.* Neuchatel, Switz.: Attinger Brothers, 1912.

Juris, Harvey A., and Feville, Peter. *Patrol Unionism.* Toronto, Ontario, Can.: Lexington, 1973.

Just, Ward S. *To What End: Report from Vietnam.* Boston: Houghton Mifflin, 1968.

Justice, Blair, and Blair, Rita. *The Abusing Family.* New York: Human Sciences Press, 1976.

Justice, Jean. *Murder vs. Murder: The British Legal System and the A.6 Murder Case.* Paris: Olympia Press, 1964.

Juvenile Violence: A Study of the Handling of Juveniles Arrested for Crimes Against Persons in New York City, July 1, 1973-June 30, 1974. New York: Office of Children's Services, Division of Criminal Justice Services, 1976.

Juviler, Peter. *Revolutionary Law and Order.* New York: Free Press, 1976.

K

Kacewicz, George V. *Great Britain, The Soviet Union and The Polish Government In Exile, 1939-1945.* The Hague, Neth.: Martinus Nijhoff, 1979.

Kadi, Leila. *Arab Summit Conferences and the Palestine Problem.* Beirut, Leb.: Research Center, Palestine Liberation Organization, 1966.

Kadish, S.H. (ed.). *Encyclopedia of Crime and Justice.* New York: Free Press, 1983.

Kaeslte, C.F., and Vinovskis, M.A. *Education and Social Change in Nineteenth-Century Massachusetts.* Cambridge, Eng.: Cambridge University Press, 1980.

_____. *The Evolution of an Urban School System.* Cambridge, Mass.: Harvard University Press, 1973.

Kagan, Jerome, and Moss, H.A. *Birth to Maturity.* New York: John Wiley & Sons, 1962.

_____. *The Growth of a Child.* New York: W.W. Norton, 1978.

_____, Kearsley, R.B., and Zelazo, P.R. *Infancy: Its Place in Human Development.* Cambridge, Mass.: Harvard University Press, 1978.

_____. *The Nature of the Child.* New York: Basic Books, 1984.

_____, and Havemann, E. *Psychology: An Introduction.* New York: Harcourt Brace Jovanovich, 1972.

Kaggia, B.M. *Roots of Freedom.* Nairobi, Kenya: East African, 1975.

Kahane, Meir. *Never Again!* Los Angeles: Nash, 1971.

Kähler, Heinz. *The Art of Rome and Her Empire.* New York: Crown, 1962.

Kahn, Albert E., and Sayers, Michael. *The Great Conspiracy.* Boston: Little, Brown, 1946.

_____. *High Treason.* New York: Hour, 1950.

Kahn, David. *The Codebreakers.* New York: Macmillan, 1967.

Kahn, E.J., Jr. *The China Hands.* New York: Viking, 1975.

_____. *Fraud.* New York: Harper & Row, 1954.

_____. *The World of Swope.* New York: Simon & Schuster, 1965.

Kahn, Edgar M. *Cable Car Days in San Francisco.* Stanford, Calif.: Stanford University Press, 1944.

Kahn, Judd. *Imperial San Francisco.* Lincoln: University of Nebraska Press, 1979.

Kahn, Roger. *How the Weather Was.* New York: Harper & Row, 1973.

Kahn, S. *Mentality and Homosexuality.* Boston: Meadow, 1937.

Kahn, Samuel. *Sing Sing Criminals.* Philadelphia: Dorrance, 1936.

Kaiser, Georg. *Gilles und Jeanne.* Potsdam, Ger.: Gustav Kiepenheuer Verlag, 1923.

Kaiser, Robert Blair. *RFK Must Die! A History of the Robert Kennedy Assassination and Its Aftermath.* New York: E.P. Dutton, 1970.

Kai-shek, Chiang. *A Summing Up at Seventy: Soviet Russia in China.* London: George C. Harrap, 1957.

Kajima Morinosuke. *Emergence of Japan as a World Power, 1895-1925.* Rutland, Vt.: Charles E. Tuttle, 1968.

Kakuzo Okakura. *The Awakening of Japan.* New York: Japan Society, 1921.

Kalb, Marvin and Bernard. *Kissinger.* Boston: Little, Brown, 1974.

Kalbfus, Joseph H. *Dr. Kalbfus's Book: A Sportsman's Experiences and Impressions in East and West.* Altoona, Pa.: Times Tribune, 1926.

Kale, Susan. *The Fire Escape.* New York: Doubleday, 1960.

Kalikar, Kakar. *Stray Glimpses of the Bapu.* Ahmedabad, India: Navajivan, 1950.

Kalven, Harry, Jr., and Zeisel, Hans. *The American Jury.* Chicago: University of Chicago Press, 1966.

Kameji Fukumoto. *True Story of the Secret Record of the February 26 Incident.* Tokyo: Ozei Shindun-sha, 1958.

Kamiyama Shigeo. *Theoretical Problems Concerning the Emperor System.* Tokyo: Ashi-kai, 1947.

Kamm, Josephine. *Hope Deferred.* London: Methuen, 1965.

Kammler, Hans. *Die Feudalmonarchienb.* Cologne, Ger.: Böhlau, 1974.

Kandel, D.B. *Longitudinal Research on Drug Use.* Washington, D.C.: Hemisphere, 1978.

Kandle, George C., and Ronnow, H. Kris. *The Fire in Today's Prisons.* New York: United Presbyterian Church, U.S.A., 1972.

_____, and Cassler, Henry H. *Ministering to Prisoners and Their Families.* Englewood Cliffs, N.J.: Prentice-Hall, 1968.

Kane, Harnett T. *Louisiana Hayride: The American Rehearsal For Dictatorship 1928-1940.* New York: William Morrow, 1941.

Kane, Harry H. *Drugs That Enslave.* Philadelphia: P. Blakiston, 1881.

_____. *The Hypodermic Injection of Morphia.* New York: C.L. Bermingham, 1880.

_____. *Opium Smoking in America and China.* New York: G.P. Putnam's Sons, 1881.

Kane, Larry. *100 Years Ago with the Law and the Outlaw.* n.p., n.d.

Kaneko Harushi. *The Face of the Imperial Family.* Tokyo: Imperial Household Ministry, 1962.

Kanfer, Stefan. *A Journal of the Plague Years.* New York: Atheneum, 1973.

Kanjia, R.K. *The Mind of Mr. Nehru.* London: George Allen & Unwin, 1960.

Kanogo, T. *Squatters and the Roots of Mau Mau, 1905-63.* London: James Currey, 1987.

Kanowitz, Leo. *Sex Roles in Law and Society.* Albuquerque: University of New Mexico Press, 1973.

_____. *Women and the Law.* Albuquerque: University of New Mexico Press, 1971.

Kantor, Seth. *The Ruby Cover-Up.* New York: Zebra Books, 1978.

_____. *Who Was Jack Ruby?* New York: Everest House, 1978.

Kantorovitch, Haim. *Problems of Revolutionary Socialism.* New York: American Socialist Monthly, 1936.

Kaplan, Chaim. *Scroll of Agony: The Warsaw Diary of Chaim Kaplan.* New York: Macmillan, 1965.

Kaplan, David E., and Dubro, Alec. *Yakuza: The Explosive Account of Japan's Criminal Underworld.* Reading, Mass.: Addison-Wesley, 1986.

Kaplan, Herbert H. *The First Partition of Poland.* New York: Columbia University Press, 1962.

Kaplan, J.D. (ed.). *The Dialogues of Plato.* New York: Washington Square Press, 1963.

Kaplan, John. *Criminal Justice: Introductory Cases and Materials.* Mineola, N.Y.: Foundation Press, 1973.

_____. *The Hardest Drug: Heroin and Public Policy.* Chicago: University of Chicago Press, 1983.

_____. *Marihuana: The New Prohibition.* New York: World, 1970.

_____, and Waltz, Jon R. *The Trial of Jack Ruby.* New York: Macmillan, 1965.

Kaplan, Justin. *Lincoln Steffens: A Biography.* New York: Simon & Schuster, 1974.

Kaplow, Jeffry. *The Names of Kings: The Parisian Laboring Poor in the Eighteenth Century.* New York: Basic Books, 1972.

Kappler, Charles J. (ed.). *Indian Affairs: Laws and Treaties.* Washington, D.C.: U.S. Government Printing Office, 1903.

Karamanski, Theodore J. *Fur Trade and Exploration.* Norman: University of Oklahoma Press, 1983.

Karamzin, A.M. *Letters of a Russian Traveler, 1789-1790.* New York: Columbia University Press, 1957.

Karanikas, Alexander. *Tillers of Myth.* Madison: University of Wisconsin Press, 1969.

Karig, Walter, Harris, Russell L., and Manson, Frank A. (eds.). *Battle Report: The End of an Empire.* New York: Rinehart, 1948.

_____, and Kelley, Welbourn (eds.). *Battle Report: Pearl Harbor to the Coral Sea.* New York: Rinehart, 1944.

Kariuki, J., and Ochieng, P. *Mau Mau Detainee: The Account by a Kenya African of his Experience in Detention Camps, 1953-1960.* London: Oxford University Press, 1963.

Karl, Berry Dean. *Executive Reorganization and Reform in the New Deal.* Cambridge, Mass.: Harvard University Press, 1963.

Karlen, Delmar. *Anglo-American Criminal Justice.* Oxford: Clarendon Press, 1967.

_____. *The Citizen in Court.* New York: Holt, Rinehart & Winston, 1964.

Karlin, Arno. *Sexuality and Homosexuality.* New York: W.W. Norton, 1971.

Karmel, Roberta S. *Regulation By Prosecution.* New York: Simon & Schuster, 1982.

Karmen, A. *Crime Victims.* Belmont, Calif.: Brooks/Cole, 1984.

Karmin, Jacob. *Myth, Fantasy, or Fact?* New York: Vantage Press, 1977.

Karol, K.S. *Guerillas in Power.* trans. Arnold Pomerans. New York: Hill & Wang, 1970.

Karolevitz, Robert F. *Newspapering in the Old West.* Seattle, Wash.: Superior, 1965.

Karpis, Alvin, and Trent, Bill. *The Alvin Karpis Story.* New York: Coward McCann & Geoghegan, 1971.

_____, and Livesey, Robert. *On The Rock.* New York: Beaufort Books, 1980.

Karpmen, Benjamin. *Case Studies in the Psychopathology of Crime.* Washington, D.C.: Mimeotorm Press, 1933.

_____. *The Individual Criminal.* Washington, D.C.: Nervous & Mental Diseases, 1935.

_____. *The Sexual Offender and His Offenses: Etiology, Pathology, Psychodynamics, and Treatment.* New York: Julian, 1954.

Karpovich, M.M. *Imperial Russia, 1801-1917.* New York: Henry Holt, 1932.

Karraker, Cyrus H. *Piracy Was a Business.* New York: Richard R. Smith, 1953.

Karski, Jan. *Story of a Secret State.* Kingsport, Tenn.: Kingsport Press, 1944.

Karsner, David. *Eugene V. Debs: Authorized Life & Letters.* New York: Boni & Liveright, 1921.

_____. *John Brown: Terrible "Saint".* New York: Dodd, Mead, 1934.

_____. *Silver Dollar: The Story of the Tabors.* New York: Covici, Friede, 1932.

Karst, Gene, and Jones, Martin. *Who's Who in Professional Baseball.* New Rochelle, N.Y.: Arlington House, 1973.

Kase Toshikazu. *Journey to the "Missouri."* New Haven, Conn.: Yale University Press, 1952.

Kassebaum, Gene, Ward, D., and Wilner, D. *Prison Treatment and Parole Survival.* New York: John Wiley & Sons, 1971.

Kaster, Joseph (trans. and ed.). *Wings of the Falcon: Life and Thought of Ancient Egypt.* New York: Holt, Rinehart & Winston, 1968.

Kastner, Joseph. *A Species of Eternity.* New York: Alfred A. Knopf, 1977.

Katchadourian, Herant A., and Lunde, Donald T. *Fundamentals of Human Sexuality.* New York: Holt, Rinehart and Winston, 1972.

Katcher, Leo. *The Big Bankroll: The Life and Times of Arnold Rothstein.* New York: Harper & Brothers, 1959.

_____. *Earl Warren: A Political Biography.* New York: McGraw-Hill, 1967.

Kates, Brian. *The Murder of a Shopping Bag Lady.* New York: Harcourt Brace Jovanovich, 1985.

Kates, George N. *The Years Were Fat: Peking, 1933-40.* New York: Harper, 1952.

Katkin, Daniel. *The Nature of Criminal Law.* Monterey, Calif.: Brooks/Cole, 1982.

Kato Masuo. *The Lost War.* New York: Alfred A. Knopf, 1946.

Katsh, Abraham (ed.). *Scroll of Agony: The Warsaw Diary of Chaim A. Kaplan.* New York: Macmillan, 1965.

Katz, Daniel, and Kahn, Robert. *The Social Psychology of Organizations.* New York: John Wiley & Sons, 1966.

Katz, Herbert and Marjorie. *Museums U.S.A.* New York: Doubleday, 1965.

Katz, Jay, et al. *Experimentation with Human Beings.* New York: Russell Sage Foundation, 1972.

Katz, L., Litwin, L., and Bamberger, R. *Justice is the Crime.* Cleveland: Case Western Reserve University Press, 1972.

Katz, Leonard. *Uncle Frank: The Biography of Frank Costello.* New York: Drake, 1973.

Katz, M. *Class, Bureaucracy, and Schools.* New York: Frederick A. Praeger, 1971.

_____. *The Irony of Early School Reform.* Cambridge, Mass.: Harvard University Press, 1968.

Katz, Martin. *Mikhail N. Katkov, 1818-1887: A Political Biography.* The Hague, Neth.: Mouton, 1966.

Katz, Robert. *Days of Wrath.* New York: Doubleday, 1980.

Katz, Sanford N. *When Parents Fail: The Law's Response to Family Breakdown.* Boston: Beacon Press, 1971.

Katz, Stanley, and Kutler, Stanley (eds.). *New Perspectives on the American Past.* Boston: Little, Brown, 1969.

Kauffman, Reginald Wright. *The House of Bondage.* New York: Grosset & Dunlap, 1912.

Kaufman, Beatrice, and Hennessey, Joseph (eds.). *The Letters of Alexander Wollcott.* New York: Viking Press, 1944.

Kaufman, George S., and Hart, Moss. *The Man Who Came to Dinner.* New York: Random House, 1939.

Kaufman, Herbert. *Administrative Feedback.* Washington, D.C.: Brookings Institute, 1973,

_____. *The Forest Ranger.* Baltimore: Johns Hopkins University Press, 1960.

Kaufman, Michael T. *The Gun.* New York: Award Books, 1974.

Kaufmann, Jacques. *L'Internationale Terroriste.* Paris: Librairie Plon, 1976.

Kaun, Alexander. *Maxim Gorky and His Russia.* New York: Jonathan Cape & Harrison Smith, 1931.

Kaus, Gina. *Catherine, Portrait of an Empress.* New York: Viking Press, 1935.

Kautsky, Benedikt. *Teufel und Verdammte.* Zurich, Switz.: Büchergilde Gutenberg, 1946.

Kautsky, Carl Johann. *The Guilt of William Hohenzollern.* London: Skeffington & Son, 1920.

Kautsky, Karl. *The Labor Revolution.* London: George Allen & Unwin, 1925.

_____. *Social Democracy vs. Communism.* New York: Rand School Press, 1946.

Kavanagh, Marcus. *The Criminal and His Allies.* Indianapolis, Ind.: Bobbs-Merrill, 1928.

_____. *You Be The Judge.* Chicago: Reilly & Lee, 1929.

Kawai Kazuo. *Japan's American Interlude.* Chicago: University of Chicago Press, 1960.

Kawakami, K.K. *Japan Speaks on the Sino-Japanese Crisis.* New York: Macmillan, 1932.

Kayser, Elmer Louis. *Bricks Without Straw: The Evolution of*

George Washington University. New York: Appleton-Century-Croft, 1970.

Kazemzadeh, Firuz. *The Struggle for Transcaucasia, 1917-1921*. New York: Philosophical Library, 1951.

Kazin, Alfred. *On Native Grounds*. New York: Reynal & Hitchcock, 1942.

_____. *Starting Out in the Thirties*. Boston: Little, Brown, 1962.

Kazuo Sakamaki. *I Attacked Pearl Harbor*. New York: Associated Press, 1949.

Kearns, Doris. *Lyndon Johnson and the American Dream*. New York: Harper & Row, 1976.

Kearns, Linda. *In Times of Peril*. Dublin, Ire.: Talbot, 1922.

Kearns, Phil, and Wead, Doug. *People's Temple—People's Tomb*. New York: Logos International, 1979.

Keating, Bern. *The Flamboyant Mr. Colt*. New York: Doubleday, 1978.

_____. *Texas Rangers*. New York: Promontory Press, 1975.

Keating, J. Michael, et al. *Grievance Mechanisms in Correctional Institutions*. Washington, D.C.: Law Enforcement Assistance Administration, 1975.

Keating, W. J., and Carter, R. *The Man Who Rocked the Boat*. New York: Harper, 1956.

Keatinge, Charles Wilbur. *Gold Miners of Hard Luck; or, Three-Fingered Jack*. Cleveland: Arthur Westbrook, 1927.

Keaton, Buster. *My Wonderful World of Slapstick*. New York: Doubleday, 1960.

Keats, John. *Howard Hughes*. New York: Random House, 1966.

Keats, John. *You Might as Well Live*. New York: Simon & Schuster, 1970.

Keayne, Robert. *The Apologia of Robert Keayne*. New York: Harper & Row, 1964.

Keckley, Elizabeth. *Behind the Scenes*. New York: G.W. Carleton, 1868.

Kedourie, Elie. *England and the Middle East*. London: Bowes & Bowes, 1956.

Kedward, H. Roderick. *The Dreyfuss Affair*. New York: Harper & Row, 1965.

_____. *Fascism in Western Europe, 1900-1945*. New York: New York University Press, 1971.

Keebler, Robert S. *The Tennessee Evolution Case*. Memphis, Tenn.: Davis, 1925.

Keeler, Bronson C. *Leadville and Its Silver Mines*. Chicago: E.L. Ayer, 1879.

Keeler, Charles. *San Francisco and Thereabout*. San Francisco: A.M. Robertson, 1912.

_____. *San Francisco Through Earthquake and Fire*. San Francisco: P. Elder, 1906.

Keeler, Ralph. *Vagabond Adventures*. Boston: Fields, Osgood, 1870.

Keeley, Joseph. *The China Lobby Man*. New Rochelle, N.Y.: Arlington House, 1969.

Keeley, Leslie E. *An Essay Upon the Morphine and Opium Habit*. Dwight, Ill.: Published by Author, 1882.

_____. *The Morphine Eater; or From Bondage to Freedom*. Dwight, Ill.: C.L. Palmer, 1881.

_____. *The Non-Heredity of Inebriety*. Chicago: S.C. Griggs, 1896.

Keene, Frances. *Neither Liberty nor Bread*. New York: Harper, 1940.

Keene, M. Lamar. *The Psychic Mafia*. New York: Dell, 1977.

Keepnews, Orrin, and Grauer, Bill, Jr. *A Pictorial History of Jazz*. New York: Crown, 1966.

Keeps, J.L.H. *The Rise of Social Democracy in Russia*. New York: Oxford University Press, 1963.

Keesing, Felix M. *Cultural Anthropology*. New York: Rinehart, 1958.

Keeton, George Williams. *Guilty But Insane*. London: MacDonald, 1961.

_____. *Lord Chancellor Jeffreys and the Stuart Cause*. London: MacDonald, 1965.

Kefauver, Estes. *Crime in America*. New York: Doubleday, 1951.

_____. *In a Few Hands*. New York: Pantheon, 1965.

_____. *Second Interim Report*. Washington, D.C.: U.S. Government Printing Office, 1951.

_____. *Third Interim Report*. Washington D.C.: U.S. Government Printing Office, 1951.

_____, and Levin, Jack. *A 20th Century Congress*. New York: Duell Sloan, 1947.

Kefauver Committee Report on Organized Crime. New York: Didier, 1951.

Kehoe, Lawrence. *John Hughes, Complete Works*. New York: Published by Author, 1866.

Keil, Charles. *Urban Blues*. Chicago: University of Chicago Press, 1966.

Keilitz, Ingo, and Fulton, Junius P. *The Insanity Defense*. Williamsburg, Va.: National Center for State Courts, 1984.

Keitel, Wilhelm. *Memoirs*. trans. David Irving. London: William Kimber, 1965.

Keith, Agnes Newton. *Three Came Home*. Boston: Little, Brown, 1947.

Keith, Billy. *Days of Anguish, Days of Hope*. New York: Doubleday, 1972.

Keith, Elmer. *Shotguns by Keith*. New York: Stackpole, 1967.

_____. *Sixguns by Keith*. Harrisburg, Pa.: Stackpole, 1955.

Keithley, Ralph. *Bucky O'Neill: He Stayed with 'Em While He Lasted*. Caldwell, Idaho: Caxton Printers, 1949.

Keleher, William A. *The Fabulous Frontier: Twelve New Mexico Items*. Santa Fe, N.M.: Rydal Press, 1945.

_____. *Maxwell Land Grant, a New Mexico Item*. Santa Fe, N.M.: Rydal Press, 1942.

_____. *Violence in Lincoln County, 1869-81*. Albuquerque, N.M.: University of New Mexico Press, 1957.

Keller, Morton. *The Art and Politics of Thomas Nash*. New York: Oxford University Press, 1968.

_____. *In Defense of Yesterday*. New York: Coward-McCann, 1958.

_____ (ed.). *Theodore Roosevelt: A Profile*. New York: Hill & Wang, 1967.

Kelley, Clarence M. *Crime in the United States, 1976*. Washington, D.C.: U.S. Government Printing Office, 1977.

Kelley, George H. *Legislative History, Arizona 1864-1912*. Phoenix, Ariz.: The Manufacturing Stationers, Inc., 1926.

Kelley, Robert. *The Transatlantic Persuasion*. New York: Alfred A. Knopf, 1969.

Kelley, Thomas P. *The Black Donnellys*. New York: Signet Books, 1955.

_____. *Jesse James*. New York: Export, 1950.

Kelling, George L., et al. *The Kansas City Patrol Experiments: A Technical Report*. Washington, D.C.: Police Foundation, 1974.

_____, et al. *The Kansas City Preventive Patrol Experiment: A Summary*. Washington, D.C.: Police Foundation, 1974.

Kellner, Bruce. *Carl Van Vechten and the Irreverent Decades*. Norman: The University of Oklahoma Press, 1963.

Kellner, Charlotte. *Alexander von Humboldt*. London: Oxford University Press, 1963.

Kellogg, Charles Flint. *National Association for the Advancement of Colored People*. Baltimore, Md.: Johns Hopkins Press, 1967.

Kellogg, Grace. *The Two Lives of Edith Wharton: The Woman and Her Work*. New York: Appleton-Century, 1965.

Kellogg, J.H. *Plain Facts for Old and Young*. Buffalo, N.Y.: Heritage Press, 1974.

Kellogg, Louise Phelps (ed.). *Early Narratives of the Northwest, 1634-1699*. New York: Charles Scribner's Sons, 1917.

_____. *The French Régime in Wisconsin and the Northwest*. Madison: State Historical Society of Wisconsin, 1925.

Kellogg, Paul, and Gleason, Arthur. *British Labor and the War*. New York: Boni & Liveright, 1919.

Kelly, Alexander. *Jack the Ripper: A Bibliography and Review of the Literature*. London: Association of Assistant Librarians,

1973.

Kelly, Alfred, et al. *The American Constitution.* New York: W.W. Norton, 1983.

Kelly, Charles, and Hoffman, Birney. *Holy Murder: The Story of Porter Rockwell.* New York: Minton, Balch, 1934.

_____. *The Outlaw Trail.* New York: Devin-Adair, 1959.

Kelly, Edmond. *Twentieth-Century Socialism.* New York: Longmans, 1916.

Kelly, Edward James. *The Crime at Ford's Theatre.* Alexandria, Va.: Action, 1944.

Kelly, Erick P. *On the Staked Plain, El Llano Estacado.* New York: Macmillan, 1940.

Kelly, Florence Finch. *Flowing Stream: The Story of Fifty-Six Years in American Newspaper Life.* New York: E.P. Dutton, 1939.

Kelly, G.A. *The Psychology of Personal Constructs.* New York: W.W. Norton, 1955.

Kelly, G.G. *The Gun in the Case.* Christchurch, N. Zea.: Whitcombe & Tombs, 1963.

Kelly, George H. *Legislative History of Arizona, 1864-1912.* Phoenix, Ariz.: Manufacturing Stationers, 1926.

Kelly, Jack. *On The Street.* Chicago: Henry Regnery, 1974.

Kelly, Joseph "Bunco". *Thirteen Years in the Oregon Penitentiary.* Portland, Ore.: Published by Author, 1908.

Kelly, Michael J. *Police Chief Selection.* Washington, D.C.: Police Foundation, 1975.

Kelly, R.S. *Ireland's Bloodless Revolution.* Chicago: Joyce & Smith, 1936.

Kelly, Robert J. (ed.). *Organized Crime: An International Perspective.* Totowa, N.J.: Rowman & Littlefield, 1986.

Kelly, Robin A. *The Sky Was Their Roof.* London: Andrew Melrose, 1955.

Kelly, Thomas P. *Jesse James, His Life and Death.* New York: Export, 1950.

Kelly, Vince. *The Charge is Murder.* London: Angus & Robertson, 1965.

Kelly, Walter Keating. *History of Russia.* London: H.G. Dohn, 1854.

Kelsen, H. *General Theory of Law and State.* Cambridge, Mass.: Harvard University Press, 1945.

Kelsey, D.M. *History of Our Wild West and Stories of Pioneer Life.* Chicago: Thompson & Thomas, 1901.

Kelso, Ruth. *Doctrine for the Lady of the Renaissance.* Urbana: University of Illinois Press, 1956.

Kemble, James. *Napolean Immortal.* London: John Murray, 1959.

Kemechey, L. *Il Duce.* trans. Magda Vamos. London: Williams & Norgate, 1930.

Kemler, Edgar. *The Irreverant Mr. Menken.* Boston: Little, Brown, 1950.

Kemmerer, Edwin W. *Inflation and Revolution: Mexico's Experience of 1912-1917.* Princeton, N.J.: Princeton University Press, 1940.

Kemp, Ben W., and Dykes, J.C. *Cow Dust and Saddle Leather.* Norman: University of Oklahoma Press, 1968.

Kemp, Louis Wiltz. *The Signers of the Texas Declaration of Independence.* Houston, Texas: Anson Jones Press, 1944.

Kemp, P. *The Healing Ritual.* London: Faber & Faber, 1935.

Kemp, P.H., and Lloyd, Christopher. *The Brethren of the Coast: Buccaneers in the South Seas.* New York: St. Martin's Press, 1961.

Kemp, T. *Prostitution: An Investigation of its Causes, Especially with Regard to Hereditary Factors.* trans. E.M. Werner. New York: Stechert, 1936.

Kempe, Ruth and C. Henry. *Child Abuse.* London: Fontana/Open Books, 1978.

Kempf, Edward J. *Abraham Lincoln's Philosophy of Common Sense.* New York: Academy of Sciences, 1965.

Kempner, Robert M.W. *Eichmann und Komplizen.* Stuttgart, Ger.: Europa-Verlag AG, 1961.

_____. *SS im Kreuzverhör.* Munich: Rütten & Loening, 1964.

Kempton, Murray. *Part of Our Time: Some Monuments and Ruins of the Thirties.* New York: Simon & Schuster, 1955.

Kendall, George Wilkins. *Narrative of the Texas Santa Fe Expedition.* New York: Harper & Brothers, 1856.

Kendall, Glenn M. *The Organization and Teaching of Social and Economic Studies in Correctional Institutions.* New York: Columbia University Press, 1939.

Kendall, John S. *History of New Orleans.* New York: Lewis, 1922.

Kendall, L. *The Phantom Prince: My Life With Ted Bundy.* Seattle, Wash.: Madrona, 1981.

Kenilworth, Walter Winston. *A Study of Oscar Wilde.* New York: R.F. Fenno, 1912.

Keniston, Kenneth. *The Uncommitted: Alienated Youth in American Society.* New York: Dell, 1967.

_____. *Youth and Dissent: The Rise of the New Opposition.* New York: Harcourt Brace Jovanovich, 1971.

Ken Kurigara. *The Emperor: Notes of the Reign of Hirohito.* Tokyo: Yushin-do Bunka Shinsho, 1955.

Kennan, George. *American Diplomacy: 1900-1950.* Chicago: New American Library, 1951.

_____. *American Foreign Policy: 1900-1950.* Chicago: University of Chicago Press, 1951.

_____. *Decision to Intervene.* Princeton, N.J.: Princeton University Press, 1958.

_____. *E.H. Harriman: A Biography.* Boston: Houghton Mifflin, 1922.

_____. *Russia Leaves the War.* Princeton, N.J.: Princeton University Press, 1956.

_____. *Russia and the West Under Lenin and Stalin.* Boston: Little, Brown, 1961.

_____. *Siberia and the Exile System.* New York: Century, 1891.

_____. *Soviet-American Relations: The Decision to Intervene.* Princeton, N.J.: Princeton University Press, 1958.

_____. *Soviet-American Relations: Russia Leaves the War.* Princeton, N.J.: Princeton University Press, 1956.

Kennard, Dorothy Katherine. *A Roumanian Diary: 1915, 1916, 1917.* New York: Dodd, Mead, 1917.

Kennaugh, Robert. *Contemporary Murder.* Johannesburg, S. Afri.: Hugh Keartland, 1968.

Kennedy, Captain. *Jesse James' Mysterious Warning: or, the Raid That Almost Failed.* Baltimore: I. & M. Ottenheimer, 1915.

_____. *Jesse James' Thrilling Raid: or the Daylight Robbery of the Harkness Bank.* Baltimore: I. & M. Ottenheimer, 1913.

_____. *Jesse James' Wild Leap: or, the Hold-Up of the Through Express.* Baltimore: I. & M. Ottenheimer, 1915.

Kennedy Confidential. Washington, D.C.: Metro, 1969.

Kennedy, D. *Islands of White: Settler Society and Culture in Kenya and Southern Rhodesia, 1890-1939.* Durham, N.C.: Duke University Press, 1987.

Kennedy, John. *Fire Investigation.* Chicago: Investigations Institute, 1977.

Kennedy, John F. *The Burden and the Glory.* New York: Harper & Row, 1964.

_____. *Profiles in Courage.* New York: Harper & Brothers, 1956.

_____. *Public Papers of the Presidents of the United States.* Washington, D.C.: U.S. Government Printing Office, 1962.

_____. *The Strategy of Peace.* New York: Harper & Brothers, 1960.

_____. *To Turn the Tide.* New York: Harper & Row, 1962.

Kennedy, Joseph Patrick. *The Story of the Films.* New York: A.W. Shaw, 1927.

Kennedy, Lionel, and Parker, Thomas. *An Official Report of the Trials of Sundry Negroes Charged with an Attempt to Raise an Insurrection in the State of South Carolina.* Charleston, S.C.: Published by Authors, 1822.

Kennedy, Ludovic. *The Airman and the Carpenter.* New York: Viking Penguin, 1985.

_____. *Ten Rillington Place.* New York: Simon & Schuster, 1961.

Kennedy, Malcolm D. *A History of Japan.* London: Weidenfeld

& Nicolson, 1963.

_____. *The Problem of Japan.* London: Nisbet, 1935.

_____. *Some Aspects of Japan and Her Defense Forces.* Kobe, Japan: J.L. Thompson, 1928.

Kennedy, Michael S. (ed.). *Cowboys and Cattleman.* New York: Hastings House, 1964.

Kennedy, P.G. *An Irish Sanctuary.* London: Hutchinson, 1956.

Kennedy, Robert F. *The Enemy Within.* New York: Popular Library, 1960.

_____. *Thirteen Days: A Memoir of the Cuban Missle Crisis.* New York: New American Library, 1969.

Kennedy, Rose Fitzgerald. *Times to Remember.* Garden City, N.Y.: Doubleday, 1974.

Kennedy, William Sloane. *Italy in Chains.* West Yarmouth, Mass.: Stonecroft Press, 1927.

Kennelly, Ardythe. *Good Morning, Young Lady.* Boston: Houghton Mifflin, 1953.

_____. *The Spur.* New York: Julian Messner, 1951.

Kenner, Charles L. *A History of New Mexican-Plains Indian Relations.* n.p., n.d.

Kennett, Lee, and Anderson, James Laverne. *The Gun in America.* Westport, Conn.: Greenwood Press, 1975.

Kenney, John P. *The California Police.* Springfield, Ill.: Charles C. Thomas, 1964.

_____, and Pursuit, Dan G. *Police Work with Juveniles and the Administration of Juvenile Justice.* Springfield, Ill.: Charles C. Thomas, 1954.

Kenny, C.S. *Outlines of Criminal Law.* London: Cambridge University Press, 1947.

Kent, Arthur. *The Death Doctors.* London: New English Library, 1975.

Kent, Lewis. *Leadville in Your Pocket.* Denver: Daily Times Steam Printing House, 1880.

Kent, William. *Reminiscences of Outdoor Life.* San Francisco: A.M. Robertson, 1929.

Kent-Hughes, W.S. *Slaves of the Samurai.* Melbourne, Aus.: Ramsey Ware, 1946.

Kentucky Legislative Research Commission. *Capital Punishment.* Frankfort: State of Kentucky, 1965.

Kenworthy, Aubrey Saint. *The Tiger of Malaya: The Inside Story of the Japanese Atrocities.* New York: Exposition Press, 1953.

Kenworthy, J.M. *The Conquest of Italy.* London: Hutchinson, 1944.

Kenyatta, J. *Facing Mt. Kenya: The Tribal Life of the Gikuyu.* New York: Vintage Books, 1962.

_____. *Suffering Without Bitterness: The Founding of the Kenya Nation.* Nairobi, Kenya: East African, 1968.

Kenyon, F.W. *The Naked Sword: The Story of Lucrezia Borgia.* New York: Dodd, Mead, 1968.

Kenyon, John Philippe. *The Popish Plot.* New York: St. Martin's Press, 1972.

Keogh, James Edward. *Burglarproof.* New York: McGraw-Hill, 1976.

Keonig, Louis W. *The Invisible Presidency.* New York: Rinehart, 1960.

Kephart, William M. *Racial Factors and Urban Law Enforcement.* Philadelphia: University of Pennsylvania Press, 1957.

Kératry, Emile, comte de. *Le 4 septembre.* Paris: Lacroix-Verboeckhoven, 1872.

Kerby, R.L. *The Confederate Invasion of New Mexico and Arizona.* Los Angeles: Westernlore, 1958.

Kerensky, Alexander. *The Catastrophe: Kerensky's Own Story.* New York: D. Appleton, 1927.

_____. *The Crucifixion of Liberty.* New York: John Day, 1934.

_____, and Bulygin, Paul. *The Murder of the Romanovs.* London: Hutchinson, 1935.

_____. *Russia and History's Turning Point.* New York: Duell, Sloan & Pearce, 1965.

Kern, Erich. *Dance of Death.* New York: Charles Scribner's Sons, 1951.

_____. *Der grosse Rausch.* Württemberg, Ger.: Verlag Lothar Leberecht, 1948.

Kerner, Dieter, Dalchow, Johannes, and Duda, Gunther. *Mozart's Tod: 1791-1971.* Pahl, Verlag Hohe Warte Bebenberg, 1971.

Kerner, Otto. *Supplemental Studies for the National Advisory Commission on Civil Disorders.* Washington, D.C.: U.S. Government Printing Office, 1968.

Kerner, Robert J. *The Urge to the Sea.* Berkley: University of California Press, 1942.

Kerner Committee. *Report of the National Advisory Commission on Civil Disorders.* New York: E.P. Dutton, 1968.

Kerney, James. *The Political Education of Woodrow Wilson.* New York: Century, 1926.

Kernot, Henry. *Bibliotheca Diabolica.* New York: Scribner, Welford & Armstrong, 1874.

Kerns, Phil. *People's Temple, People's Tomb.* Plainfield, N.J.: Logos, 1979.

Kerr, E. Bartlett. *Surrender and Survival: The Experience of American POWs in the Pacific 1941-1945.* New York: William Morrow, 1985.

Kerr, W.S. *John Sherman: His Life and Public Service.* Boston: Sherman, French, 1908.

Kerry, The Earl of (ed.). *The Secret of the Coup D'Etat.* New York: G.P. Putnam's Sons, 1924.

Kershaw, Alister. *A History of the Guillotine.* London: J. Calder, 1958.

_____. *Murder In France.* London: Constable, 1955.

Kersten, Felix. *The Kersten Memoirs, 1940-1945.* trans. Constantine Fitzgibbon and James Oliver. London: Hutchinsons, 1956.

Kertesz, Stephan. *The Fate of East Central Europe.* South Bend, Ind.: University of Notre Dame Press, 1956.

Kerzhentsev, P. *Life of Lenin.* New York: International, 1939.

Kessel, Joseph. *The Man with Miraculous Hands.* trans. Helen Weaver and Leo Raditsa. New York: Farrar, Straus & Cudahy, 1961.

Kesselring, Albert. *Gedanken zum Zweiten Weltkrieg.* Bonn, Ger.: Athenäum, 1955.

_____. *Memoirs.* trans. Lynton Hudson. London: William Kimber, 1953.

Kessler, Count Harry. *Walther Rathenau: His Life and Work.* New York: Harcourt, Brace, 1930.

Kessner, Thomas. *The Golden Door.* New York: Oxford University Press, 1976.

Ketcham, Ralph L. *Benjamin Franklin.* New York: Washington Square Press, 1966.

Ketchiva, Paul. *The Devil's Playground.* London: Sampson Low, 1934.

Kett, J.F. *Rites of Passage.* New York: Basic Books, 1977.

Kettle, L.J. *The Material for Victory: Being the Memoirs of Andrew J. Kettle.* Dublin, Ire.: Fallon, 1958.

Keun, Odette. *Trumpets Bray.* London: Constable, 1943.

Keup, Wolfram (ed.). *Drug Abuse: Current Concepts and Research.* Springfield, Ill.: Charles C. Thomas, 1972.

Keve, Paul W. *Prison Life and Human Worth.* Minneapolis: University of Minnesota Press, 1974.

Kevorkian, Jack. *Medical Research and the Death Penalty.* New York: Vantage Press, 1960.

Key, Della Tyler. *In the Cattle County: History of Potter County, 1887-1966.* Quanah-Witchita Falls, Texas: Nortex Offset, 1972.

Key, V.O., Jr. *A Primer of Statistics for Political Scientists.* New York: Thomas Y. Crowell, 1954.

Key, Wilson Bryan. *Media Sexploitation.* Englewood Cliffs, N.J.: Prentice-Hall, 1976.

Keyes, E.D. *Fifty Years Observation of Men and Events.* New York: Charles Scribner's Sons, 1884.

Keyes, Edward. *The Michigan Murders.* New York: Thomas Y.

Crowell, 1976.

Keyes, Harold C. *Tales of the Secret Service.* Cleveland: Britton Gardner, 1927.

Keylin, Arleen, and DeMirjian, Arto, Jr. *Crime: As Reported by the New York Times.* New York: Arno Press, 1976.

_____. *The Fabulous Fifties.* New York: Arno Press, 1978.

Keynes, John Maynard. *The End of Laissez Faire.* London: L. & V. Wolff, 1926.

_____. *The General Theory of Employment, Interest and Money.* London: Macmillan, 1936.

_____. *Laissez Faire and Communism.* New York: New Republic, 1926.

_____. *The Means to Prosperity.* London: Macmillan, 1933.

_____. *A Treatise on Money.* London: Macmillan, 1930.

Khaled, Leila. *Autobiography.* London: Hodder & Stoughton, 1973.

_____. *My People Shall Live.* London: Hodder & Stoughton, 1973.

Khalaf, Samir. *Prostitution in a Changing Society.* Beirut, Leb.: Khayats, 1965.

Khalil, Mohammed. *The Arab States and the Arab League.* Beirut, Leb.: Khayat, 1962.

Khouri, Fred J. *The Arab-Israeli Dilemma.* Syracuse, N.Y.: Syracuse University Press, 1968.

Khueller, Sebastian. *Murke Bund warhafftige Historia.* Munich: Wein, 1885.

Kiaulehn, Walther. *Berlin: Schicksal einer Weltstadt.* Berlin: Biederstein Verlag, 1958.

Kibera, S. *Voices in the Dark.* Nairobi, Kenya: East African, 1970.

Kidd, W.R. *Police Interrogation.* New York: Basuino, 1940.

Kidder, Jonathan Edward. *Japan Before Buddhism.* New York: Frederick A. Praeger, 1959.

Kidder, Reuben. *The Life and Adventures of John Dahmen.* Jeffersonville, Ind.: Smith & Bolton, 1821.

Kidder, Robert L. *Connecting Law and Society.* Englewood Cliffs, N.J.: Prentice-Hall, 1983.

Kidder, T. *The Road to Yuba City: A Journey Into the Juan Corona Murders.* New York: Doubleday, 1974.

Kidner, John. *Crimaldi: Contract Killer.* Washington, D.C.: Acropolis Books, 1976.

Kido Koichi. *Additional Writings.* Tokyo: Tokyo University Press, 1966.

_____. *Diary of Koichi Kido.* Tokyo: Tokyo University Press, 1966.

Kiefer, Otto. *Sexual Life in Ancient Rome.* London: Routledge & Kegan Paul, 1934.

Kielmansegg, Adolf Graf von. *Der Fritschprozess 1938.* Hamburg, Ger.: Hoffmann & Campe, 1949.

Kieran, John. *The American Sporting Scene.* New York: Macmillan, 1941.

Kiernan, Thomas. *Yasir Arafat.* London: Abacus Books, 1976.

Kiesewetter, Carl. *John Dee: ein Spiritist des 16. Jahrhunderts.* Leipzig, Ger.: M. Spohr, 1893.

Kiesler, C. *The Psychology of Commitment.* New York: Academic Press, 1971.

Kiester, Edwin. *Crimes With No Victims.* New York: Alliance for a Safer New York, 1972.

Kieve, J.L. *The Electric Telegraph.* New York: David & Charles, Newton Abbot, and Harper & Row, 1973.

Kilbracken, Lord. *Van Meegeren: Master Forger.* New York: Charles Scribner's Sons, 1967.

Kilby, Clyde S. *Minority of One: The Biography of Jonathan Blanchard.* Grand Rapids, Mich.: William B. Eerdmans, 1959.

Kilduff, Marshall, and Javers, Ron. *The Suicide Cult.* New York: Bantam Books, 1978.

Kilgallen, Dorothy. *Murder One.* New York: Random House, 1967.

Kilian, Michael, Fletcher, Connie, and Ciccone, F. Richard. *Who Runs Chicago?* New York: St. Martin's Press, 1979.

Killanin, Michael (ed.). *Four Days.* London: William Heinemann, 1938.

Killinger, George G., and Cromwell, Paul F., Jr. (eds.). *Penology: The Evolution of Corrections in America.* St. Paul, Minn.: West, 1973.

Kilroe, Edwin P. *Saint Tammany and the Origin of the Society of Tammany or Columbian Order in the City of New York.* New York: M.B. Brown, 1913.

Kimball, I.G. *Recollections.* Washington: Carnahan Press, 1912.

Kimball, Nell. *Her Life as an American Madam, by Herself.* New York: Macmillan, 1970.

Kimball, Penn. *The File: The Chilling True Account of Government Spying on an Innocent Man.* New York: Harcourt Brace, 1983.

Kimche, Jon and David. *A Clash of Destinies.* New York: Frederick A. Praeger, 1960.

_____. *General Guisans Zweifrontenkreig.* Berlin: Verlag Ullstein, 1962.

_____ and David. *The Secret Roads.* London: Secker & Warburg, 1955.

_____. *Seven Fallen Pillars.* New York: Frederick A. Praeger, 1953.

Kimeldorf, Howard. *Reds or Rackets? The Making of Radical and Conservative Unions on the Waterfront.* Berkeley: University of California Press, 1988.

Kimmel, Stanley. *The Mad Booths of Maryland.* Indianapolis, Ind.: Bobbs-Merrill, 1940.

_____. *Mr. Lincoln's Washington.* New York: Bramhall House, 1957.

Kimmens, A.C. (ed.). *Tales of Hashish.* New York: William Morrow, 1977.

Kinberg, Olof. *Basic Problems of Criminology.* Copenhagen: Levin & Munkgaard, 1935.

Kinchen, Oscar A. *Confederate Operations in Canada and the North.* North Quincy, Mass.: Christopher, 1970.

Kind, Stewart. *Science Against Crime.* New York: Doubleday, 1972.

Kinder, Gary. *Victim: The Other Side of Murder.* New York: Delacorte Press, 1982.

Kindleberger, Charles P. *Manias, Panics and Crashes.* New York: Basic Books, 1978.

_____. *The World in Depression: 1929-1939.* Berkeley: University of California Press, 1973.

King, Bolton. *Fascism in Italy.* London: William & Norgate, 1931.

King, Cecil. *Strictly Personal.* London: Weidenfeld & Nicolson, 1969.

King, Coretta Scott. *My Life With Martin Luther King, Jr.* New York: Holt, Rinehart & Winston, 1969.

King, Dick. *Ghost Towns of Texas.* San Antonio, Texas: Naylor, 1953.

King, Edward. *The Southern States of North America.* London: Blackie & Son, 1875.

King, Ernest L. *Main Line: Fifty Years of Railroading with the Southern Pacific.* Garden City, N.Y.: Doubleday, 1948.

King, Ethel M. *Reflections of Reedy: A Biography of William Marion Reedy of Reedy's Mirror.* Brooklyn, N.Y.: Gerald J. Richard, 1961.

King, Francis. *The Magical World of Aleister Crowley.* New York: Coward, McCann & Geoghegan, 1977.

King, Frank M. *Mavericks: The Salty Comments of an Old-Time Cowpuncher.* Pasadena, Calif.: Trail's End, 1947.

_____. *Pioneer Western Empire Builders.* Pasadena, Calif.: Trail's End, 1946.

_____. *Wranglin' the Past: Being Reminiscences of Frank M. King.* Pasadena, Calif.: Trail's End, 1946.

King, Grace. *New Orleans: The Place and the People.* New York: Macmillan, 1937.

King, Harry. *Box Man.* New York: Harper & Row, 1972.

King, Hoyt. *Citizen Cole of Chicago*. Chicago: Horder's, 1931.

King, Leonard. *From Cattle Rustler to Pulpit*. San Antonio, Texas: Naylor, 1943.

King, Leonard. *A History of Babylon*. New York: Frederick A. Stokes, 1915.

King, Lester S. *The Medical World of the Eighteenth Century*. Chicago: University of Chicago Press, 1958.

King, M. *Bail or Custody*. London: Cobden Trust, 1971.

King, Martin Luther, Jr. *Stride Toward Freedom*. New York: Harper & Row, 1964.

———. *Where Do We Go From Here: Chaos or Community?* Boston: Beacon Press, 1968.

———. *Why We Can't Wait*. New York: New American Library, 1964.

King, Moses. *Handbook of New York City*. Boston: Published by Author, 1893.

———. *King's Handbook of the United States*. Buffalo, N.Y.: Published by Author, 1891.

———. *Views of New York*. Boston: Benjamin Bloom, 1896.

King, P.D. *Law and Society in the Visigothic Kingdom*. Cambridge, Eng.: Cambridge University Press, 1972.

King, Rosa E. *Tempest Over Mexico: A Personal Chronicle*. New York: Methuen, 1936.

King, Rufus. *The Drug Hang-Up: America's Fifty Year Folly*. New York: W.W. Norton, 1972.

———. *Gambling and Organized Crime*. Washington, D.C.: Public Affairs Press, 1969.

King, Veronica and Paul. *Problems of Modern American Crime*. London: Heath Cranton, 1924.

King, W.C.T. *History of the London Discount Market*. London: George Routledge & Sons, 1936.

King, Willard L. *Lincoln's Manager*. Cambridge, Mass.: Harvard University Press, 1960.

———. *Melville Weston Fuller*. New York: Macmillan, 1950.

King-Hall, Sir Stephen. *Three Dictators*. London: Faber & Faber, 1964.

Kingsford, William. *Impressions of the West and South during a Six Weeks' Holiday*. Toronto, Ontario: A.H. Armour, 1888.

Kingsley, Charles. *Lectures Delivered in America in 1874*. Philadelphia: Joseph H. Coates, 1875.

Kingsmill, Joseph. *Chapters on Prisons and Prisoners and the Prevention of Crime*. London: Longman, Brown & Green, 1854.

———. *A History of the Guillotine*. New York: Taplinger, 1959.

Kingston, Charles. *The Bench & The Dock*. London: Stanley Paul, 1925.

———. *Dramatic Days At the Old Bailey*. New York: Frederick A. Stokes, 1927.

———. *Enemies of Society*. London: Stanley Paul, 1927.

———. *Famous Judges and Famous Trials*. New York: Frederick A. Stokes, 1923.

———. *A Gallery of Rogues*. London: Stanley Paul, 1924.

———. *The Judges and the Judged*. London: John Lane, Bodley Head, 1926.

———. *Law-Breakers*. London: John Lane, Bodley Head, 1930.

———. *Remarkable Rogues: Some Notable Criminals of Europe and America*. New York: John Lane, 1921.

———. *Rogues and Adventuresses*. London: John Lane, Bodley Head, 1928.

Kinnaird, Lawrence. *History of the Greater San Francisco Bay Region*. New York: Lewis Historical, 1966.

Kinney, Jay, and Mavrides, Paul. *Cover-Up Lowdown*. San Fransico: Rip Off Press, 1977.

Kinsey, Alfred C., et al. *Sexual Behavior in the Human Female*. London: Saunders, 1953.

———, Pomeroy, W.B., and Martin, C.E. *Sexual Behavior in the Human Male*. London: Saunders, 1948.

Kinsley, David R. *The Sword and the Flute: Kali and Krasna*. Berkley: University of California Press, 1978.

Kinsley, Philip. *The Chicago Tribune: Its First Hundred Years*. Chicago: Chicago *Tribune*, 1943.

Kinyon, Edmund. *The Northern Mines*. Nevada City, Calif.: Union, 1949.

Kinzie, Mrs. John H. *Wau Bun*. Chicago: Rand, McNally, 1901.

Kiplinger, Austin H., and Knight A. *Washington Now*. New York: Harper & Row, 1975.

Kiplinger, W. M. *Washington is Like That*. New York: Harper & Brothers, 1942.

Kipnis, Ira. *The American Socialist Movement, 1897-1912*. New York: Columbia University Press, 1952.

Kirby, Cecil, and Renner, Thomas C. *Mafia Enforcer*. New York: Villard Books, 1987.

Kirby, S. Woodburn, et al. *The War Against Japan*. London: HMSO, 1957.

Kirchheimer, Otto. *Political Justice*. Princeton, N.J.: Princeton University Press, 1961.

Kirk, George E. *Contemporary Arab Politics*. New York: Frederick A. Praeger, 1961.

———. *The Middle East, 1945-50*. London: Oxford, 1954.

———. *The Middle East in the War*. London: Oxford, 1952.

———. *A Short History of the Middle East*. New York: Frederick A. Praeger, 1960.

Kirk, Hyland C. *Heavy Guns and Light: A History of the 4th New York Heavy Artillery*. New York: C.T. Dillingham, 1890.

Kirk, John. *Medicinal Drinking*. New York: National Temperance Society, 1869.

Kirk, Paul L., and Bradford, L.W. *The Crime Laboratory*. Springfield, Ill.: C.C. Thomas, 1965.

———. *Fire Investigation—Including Fire-Related Phenomena: Arson, Explosion, Asphyxiation*. New York: John Wiley & Sons, 1969.

Kirk, Robert. *Secret Commonwealth*. Edinburgh, Scot.: Longman, Hurst, Rees, Oormet & Brown, 1815.

Kirkbride, Sir Alec. *A Crackle of Thorns*. London: John Murray, 1956.

Kirke, Dorothea. *Domestic Life in Rumania*. London: John Lane, 1916.

Kirkendall, Richard S. (ed.). *The Truman Period as a Research Field*. Columbia: University of Missouri Press, 1967.

Kirkham, George. *Signal Zero*. New York: J.B. Lippincott, 1976.

Kirkham, James F. *Assassination and Political Violence*. Washington, D.C.: U.S. Goverment Printing Office, 1969.

Kirkland, Edward Chase. *Business in the Guilded Age*. Madison: University of Wisconsin Press, 1952.

———. *The Peacemakers of 1864*. New York: Macmillan, 1927.

Kirkland, Joseph. *The Story of Chicago*. Chicago: Dibble, 1892.

Kirkpatrick, Clifford. *Capital Punishment*. Philadelphia: Philadelphia Committee on Philanthropic Labor, 1945.

Kirkpatrick, Ernest E. *Crime's Paradise*. San Antonio, Tex.: Naylor, 1934.

———. *Voices from Alcatraz*. San Antonio, Tex.: Naylor, 1947.

Kirkpatrick, Sir Ivone. *Mussolini: Study of a Demagogue*. London: Odhams Books, 1964.

———. *The Inner Circle*. London: Macmillan, 1959.

Kirkpatrick, Lyman B., Jr. *The Real CIA*. New York: Macmillan, 1968.

———. *The U.S. Intelligence Community*. New York: Hill & Wang, 1973.

Kirkpatrick, Sidney D. *A Cast of Killers*. New York: E.P. Dutton, 1986.

Kirkwood, James. *American Grotesque: An Account of the Clay Shaw-Jim Garrison Affair in the City of New Orleans*. New York: Simon & Schuster, 1970.

Kirpalani, K.R. *Tagore, Gandhi and Nehru*. Bombay, India: Hind Kitabs, 1947.

Kirsch, Robert, and Murphy, William S. *West of the West*. New York: E.P. Dutton, 1967.

Kirschten, Ernest. *Catfish and Crystal*. New York: Doubleday, 1960.

Kirwan, Daniel. *Palace and Hovel*. London: Abelard-Schuman,

1963.

Kirwin, Harry W. *The Inevitable Success: Herbert R. O'Conor.* Westminster, Md.: Newman Press, 1962.

Kisch, C.H. *The Portuguese Banknote Case.* New York: Macmillan, 1932.

Kitagawa, Evelyn M., and Teauber, Karl E. (eds.). *Local Community Fact Book.* Chicago: University of Chicago, 1963.

Kitchin, John. *Jurisdictions.* London: J. Place, 1663.

Kitman, Marvin. *George Washington's Expense Account.* New York: Simon & Schuster, 1970.

Kitson, Frank. *Bunch of Five.* London: Faber & Faber, 1977.

_____. *Gangs and Counter-Gangs.* London: Barrie & Rockliffe, 1960.

_____. *Low Intensity Operations: Subversion, Insurgency, Peace-Keeping.* Hamden, Conn.: Shoe String Press, 1974.

Kittredge, George Lyman. *Studies in History of Religions Presented to Crawford Howell Toy.* New York: Macmillan, 1912.

_____. *Witchcraft in Old and New England.* Cambridge, Mass.: Harvard University Press, 1929.

Kittrel, Norman G. *Governors Who Have Been and Other Public Men of Texas.* Houston, Texas: Dealy-Adey-Elgin, 1921.

Kittrie, Nicholas N. *The Right to be Different: Deviance and Enforced Therapy.* Baltimore: Johns Hopkins Press, 1971.

Klapper, Joseph T. *The Effects of Mass Communication.* Glencoe, Ill.: Free Press, 1961.

Klapthor, M.B., and Brown, P.D. *The History of Charles County, Maryland.* La Plata, Md.: Charles County Tercentenary, 1958.

Klare, Hugh J. *Anatomy of Prison.* London: Hutchinson, 1960.

_____ (ed.). *Changing Concepts in Crime and Its Treatment.* Elmsford, N.Y.: Pergamon Press, 1966.

Klasne, William. *Street Cops.* Englewood Cliffs, N.J.: Prentice-Hall, 1980.

Klasner, Lily. *My Girlhood Among Outlaws.* Tucson: University of Arizona Press, 1972.

Klaus, Samuel (ed.). *The Molineux Case.* New York: Alfred A. Knopf, 1929.

Klausner, Lawrence D. *Son of Sam.* New York: McGraw-Hill, 1981.

Klebba, A. Joan. *Homicide Trends in the United States, 1900-1974.* Washington, D.C.: U.S. Government Printing Office, 1975.

Kleeman, Rita Halle. *Gracious Lady.* New York: D. Appleton, 1932.

Klein, Alexander (ed.). *Double Dealers.* Philadelphia and New York: J.B. Lippincott, 1958.

_____ (ed.). *The Empire City: A Treasury of New York.* New York: Rinehart, 1955.

_____. *Grand Deception.* New York: J.B. Lippincott, 1955.

Klein, Felix. *In the Land of the Strenuous Life.* Chicago: A.C. McClurg, 1905.

_____. *L'Amérique de demain.* Paris: Plon-Nourrit et Cie, 1910.

Klein, Henry H. *Sacrificed.* New York: Isaac Goldman, 1927.

Klein, Herbert T. *The Police.* New York: Crown, 1968.

Klein, Johann. *Meditatio Academica Exhibens Examen Juridicum Judicialis.* Güstrow, Ger.: John Michael Rudigeri, 1705.

Klein, Malcolm W. *Juvenile Gangs in Context.* Englewood Cliffs, N.J.: Prentice-Hall, 1967.

_____ (ed.). *The Juvenile Justice System.* Beverly Hills, Calif.: Sage, 1976.

_____. *Street Gangs and Street Workers.* Englewood Cliffs, N.J.: Prentice-Hall, 1971.

Klein, Maury. *Life and Times of Jay Gould.* Baltimore: Johns Hopkins University Press, 1986.

Klein, P. *Prison Methods in New York State.* New York: Columbia University Press, 1920.

Klein, Tim. *Die Befreiung 1813, 1814, 1815.* Munich: W. Langewiesche-Brandt, 1913.

Kleindienst, Richard. *Justice: The Memoirs of an Attorney General.* Ottawa, Ill.: Jameson, 1985.

Kleinmuntz, B. *Personality and Psychological Assessment.* New York: St. Martin's Press, 1982.

Kleist, Peter. *Zwischen Hitler und Stalin 1939-1945.* Bonn, Ger.: Athenäum, 1950.

Klélé, J. *Hexenwahn und Hexenprozesse in der ehemaligen Reichsstadt und Landvogtei Hagenau.* Hagenau, Ger.: F. Ruckstuhl, 1893.

Klement, Frank L. *The Copperheads in the Middle West.* Chicago: University of Chicago Press, 1960.

Klepper, Jochen. *Der Soldatenkönig und die Stillen im Lande.* Berlin: Eckart-Verlag, 1938.

Kleppner, Paul. *The Cross of Culture.* New York: Free Press, 1970.

Klette, Ernest. *The Crimson Trail of Joaquin Murieta.* Los Angeles: Wetzel, 1928.

Kline, Draza, and Overstreet, Helen-Mary Forbush. *Foster Care of Children.* New York: Columbia University Press, 1972.

Kline, P. *Fact and Fantasy in Freudian Theory.* London: Methuen, 1972.

Klinefelter, W. *Sherlock Holmes in Portrait and Profile.* Syracuse, N.Y.: Syracuse University Press, 1963.

Kling, Samuel G. *Sexual Behavior and the Law.* New York: Bernard Geis, 1965.

Klinkhamer, Marie C. *Edward Douglas White.* Washington, D.C.: Catholic University of America Press, 1943.

Klockars, Carl B. *The Professional Fence.* New York: Free Press, 1974.

_____, Murray, Henry A., and Schneider, David M. *Personality in Nature, Society, and Culture.* New York: Alfred A. Knopf, 1953.

Kluchevsky, V.O. *History of Russia.* trans. C.J. Hogarth. New York: Russell & Russell, 1960.

_____. *Peter the Great.* New York: E.P. Dutton, 1963.

Kluckhohn, Clyde, and Leighton, Dorthea. *The Navaho.* Garden City, N.Y.: Doubleday, 1962.

Kluger, Richard. *Simple Justice.* New York: Alfred A. Knopf, 1975.

Klurfeld, Herman. *Winchell: His Life and Times.* New York: Frederick A. Praeger, 1976.

Klüver, Heinrich. *Mescal and Mechanisms of Hallucinations.* Chicago: University of Chicago Press, 1966.

Knapp, A.E. (ed.). *Pioneers of the San Juan Country.* Durango, Colo.: Durango Printing, 1952.

Knapp, Arthur May. *Feudal and Modern Japan.* Yokohama, Japan: Kelly & Walsh, 1906.

Knapp, M. *Non-Verbal Communication in Human Interaction.* New York: Holt, Rinehart & Winston, 1972.

Knapp, Paul. *The Berengaria Exchange.* New York: Dial Press, 1972.

Knapp, Whitman. *Knapp Commission Report on Police Corruption.* New York: George Braziller, 1972.

Knappen, M.M. *Tudor Puritanism.* Chicago: University of Chicago Press, 1939.

Knappman, Edward W. (ed.). *Watergate and the White House.* New York: Facts on File, 1973.

Kneedler, H.S. *Through Storyland to Sunset Seas.* Chicago: Knight, Leonard, 1895.

Kneeland, George J. *Commercialized Prostitution in New York City.* New York: Century, 1913.

Kneier, Andrew. *Serving Two Masters: A Common Cause Study of Conflicts of Interest in the Executive Branch.* Washington, D.C.: Common Cause, 1976.

Knieriem, August von. *The Nuremberg Trials.* Chicago: Henry Regnery, 1959.

Knight, David C. *The ESP Reader.* New York: Grosset & Dunlap, 1968.

Knight, Edgar W. *Fifty Years of American Education.* New York:

Ronald, 1952.

Knight, Edward. *Wild Bill Hickok.* Franklin, N.H.: Hillside Press, 1959.

Knight, Janet M. *Three Assassinations.* New York: Fonf, 1980.

Knight, Oliver. *Fort Worth: Outpost on the Trinity.* Norman: University of Oklahoma Press, 1953.

Knight, Robert Edward Lee. *Industrial Relations in the San Francisco Bay Area, 1900-1918.* Berkley: University of California Press, 1960.

Knight, Stephen. *The Brotherhood The Secret World of the Freemasons.* London: Granada, 1984.

_____. *The Final Solution: Jack the Ripper.* New York: David McKay, 1976.

Knight, Thomas A. *The Strange Disappearance of William Morgan.* Becksville, Ohio: Published by Author, 1932.

Knightley, Philip. *The First Casualty: The War Correspondent as Hero, Propagandist and Myth Maker from Crimea to Vietnam.* New York: Harcourt Brace Jovanovich, 1975.

Knittle, W.A. *Early Eighteenth Century Palatine Immigration.* Philadelphia: Dorrance, 1936.

Knollenberg, Bernhard. *Origin of the American Revolution: 1759-1776.* New York: Free Press, 1961.

Knortz, Karl. *Hexen, Teufel und Blocksbergspuk in Geschichte, Sage und Literatur.* Annaberg, Ger.: R. Liesche, 1913.

Knott, G.H. (ed.). *The Trial of Roger Casement.* London: Hodge, 1926.

Knott, George H. (ed.). *Trial of William Palmer.* London: W. Hodge, 1912.

Knowles, Graham. *Bomb Security Guide.* Los Angeles: Security World, 1976.

Knowles, Horace (ed.). *Gentlemen, Scholars and Scoundrels.* New York: Harper & Brothers, 1959.

Knowles, Leonard. *Court of Drama: Famous Trials at Lewes Assizes.* London: John Long, 1966.

Knowlton, Charles. *Fruits of Philosophy.* Mount Vernon, N.Y.: Peter Pauper Press, 1937.

Knox, Major-General Sir Alfred. *With the Russian Army, 1914-1917.* New York: E.P. Dutton, 1921.

Knox, Bill. *Court of Murder: Famous Trials at Glascow High Court.* London: John Long, 1968.

Knox, Donald. *Death March.* New York: Harcourt Brace Jovanovich, 1981.

Knox, John. *Works.* Edinburgh, Scot.: James Thin, 1895.

Knox, John Jay. *United States Works.* London: T.F. Unwin, 1885.

Knox, Rose B. *Footlights Afloat.* New York: Doubleday, Doran, 1937.

Knox, Thomas W. *Underground, or Life Below the Surface.* Hartford, Conn.: J.B. Burr, Hyde, 1873.

Knudten, Richard D. *Crime in a Complex Society: An Introduction to Criminology.* New York: Dorsey Press, 1970.

_____ (ed.). *Criminal Controversies.* New York: Appleton-Century-Crofts, 1968.

Knuttel, W.P.C. *Balthasar Bekker die Bestijder van het Bijgeloof.* The Hague, Neth.: M. Nijhoff, 1892.

Kobetz, Richard W. *The Police Role and Juvenile Delinquency.* Gaithersburg, Md.: IACP, 1971.

_____, and Cooper, H.H.A. *Target Terrorism: Providing Protective Services.* Gaithersburg, Md.: International Association of Chiefs of Police, 1978.

Kobler, John. *Ardent Spirits: The Rise and Fall of Prohibition.* New York: G.P. Putnam's Sons, 1973.

_____. *Capone: The Life and World of Al Capone.* New York: G.P. Putnam's Sons, 1971.

_____. *Some Like It Gory.* New York: Dodd, Mead, 1940.

Kobre, Sidney. *The Development of American Journalism.* Dubuque, Iowa: William C. Brown, 1972.

_____. *The Yellow Press and Gilded Age Journalism.* Tallahassee: Florida State University, 1964.

Kobylinsky, Colonel Eugene. *The Last Days of the Romanovs.* London: Thornton Butterworth, 1920.

Koch, Hugo. *Hexenprozesse und Reste des Hexenglaubens in der Wetterau.* Giessen, Ger.: O. Kindt, 1935.

Koch, Peter, and Hermann, Kai. *Assault at Mogadishu.* London: Corgi Books, 1977.

Kochan, Lionel. *The Making of Modern Russia.* London: Jonathan Cape, 1962.

Kochman, Thomas (ed.). *Rappin' and Stylin' Out.* Urbana: University of Illinois Press, 1972.

Kodama, Yoshio. *I Was Defeated.* Tokyo: Robert Booth & Taro Fukuda, 1951.

Koehl, Robert L. *RKFVD: German Resettlement and Population Policy, 1939-1945.* Cambridge, Mass.: Harvard University Press, 1957.

Koen, Ross Y. *The China Lobby in American Politics.* New York: Macmillan, 1960.

Koenig, Louis W. *Bryan: A Political Biography of William Jennings Bryan.* New York: G.P. Putnam's Sons, 1971.

Koenigberg, Moses. *King News—An Autobiography.* New York: Frederick A. Stokes, 1941.

Koestler, Arthur. *Arrow in the Blue.* New York: Macmillan, 1952.

_____. *Darkness at Noon.* New York: Macmillan, 1941.

_____, and Rolph, C.H. *Hanged by the Neck.* New York: Penguin, 1961.

_____. *The Invisible Writing.* London: Collins, 1954.

_____. *Promise and Fulfillment: Palestine, 1917-1949.* London: Macmillan, 1949.

_____. *Reflections on Hanging.* London: Victor Gollancz, 1956.

_____. *The Roots of Coincidence.* New York: Random House, 1972.

_____. *The Sleepwalkers.* New York: Macmillan, 1959.

Kofoed, Jack. *Moon Over Miami.* New York: Random House, 1955.

Kogan, Herman, and Wendt, Lloyd. *Chicago: A Pictorial History.* New York: E.P. Dutton, 1958.

_____. *The First Century: The Chicago Bar Association, 1874-1974.* Chicago: Rand-McNally, 1974

_____, and Cromie, Robert. *The Great Fire: Chicago 1871.* New York: G.P. Putnam's Sons, 1971.

_____ and Rick. *Yesterday's Chicago.* Miami, Fla.: E.A. Seemann, 1976.

Kogan, Norman. *Italy and the Allies.* Cambridge, Mass.: Harvard University Press, 1956.

_____. *The Politics of Italian Foreign Policy.* London: Pall Mall Press, 1963.

Kogon, Eugen. *The Theory and Practice of Hell.* trans. Heinz Norden. London: Secker & Warburg, 1950.

Kohl, James, and Litt, John. *Urban Guerrilla Warfare in Latin America.* Cambridge, Mass.: MIT Press, 1974.

Kohlmeier, Louis. *The Regulators.* New York: Harper & Row, 1969.

Kohlsaat, H.H. *From McKinley to Harding: Personal Recollections of Our Presidents.* New York: Charles Scribner's Sons, 1923.

Kohn, Hans. *Basic History of Modern Russian Political, Cultural, and Social Trends.* Princeton, N.J.: Van Nostrand, 1957.

_____. *The Idea of Nationalism.* New York: Macmillan, 1952.

_____ (ed.). *Mind of Modern Russia.* New Brunswick, N.J.: Rutgers University Press, 1955.

_____. *Nationalism and Imperialism in the Hither East.* New York: Harcourt & Brace, 1932.

_____. *Pan-Slavism.* South Bend, Ind.: University of Notre Dame Press, 1953.

Kohn, Howard. *Who Killed Karen Silkwood?* New York: Summit Books, 1981.

Kohn, S., and Meyendorff, Baron A.F. *The Cost of the War to Russia.* New Haven, Conn.: Yale University Press, 1932.

Kojima Noboru. *The Pacific War.* Tokyo: Chuo Koron-sha, 1966.

Kokovtsov, V.N. *Out of My Past.* Stanford, Calif.: Stanford University Press, 1933.

Kolb, Lawrence. *Drug Addiction: A Medical Problem.* Springfield,

Ill.: Charles C. Thomas, 1962.

Kolko, Gabriel. *The Politics of War*. New York: Random House, 1968.

_____. *Wealth and Power in America: An Analysis of Social Class and Income Distribution*. New York: Frederick A. Praeger, 1962.

Koller, Larry (ed.). *The American Gun*. New York: Madison Books, 1961.

_____. *The Fireside Book of Guns*. New York: Simon & Schuster, 1959.

Komarovsky, Mirra. *The Unemployed Man and His Family*. New York: Dryden Press, 1940.

Komatsu Isao. *The Japanese People: Origins of the People and the Language*. Tokyo: Kokusai Bunka Shinkokai, 1962.

Konefsky, Samuel J. *Chief Justice Stone and the Supreme Court*. New York: Macmillan, 1945.

_____. *The Legacy of Holmes and Brandeis*. New York: Collier Books, 1961.

König, Bruno. *Ausgeburten des Menschenwahns im Spiegel der Hexenprozesse und der Auto da fé's*. Rudolfstadt, Ger.: A. Bock, 1893.

Konig, David Thomas. *Law and Society in Puritan Massachusetts, Essex County, 1629-1692*. Chapel Hill: University of North Carolina Press, 1979.

Kononenko, Konstentyn. *Ukraine and Russia: A History of the Economic Relations, 1654-1917*. Marquette, Wis.: Marquette University Press, 1958.

Konopka, Gisela. *The Adolescent Girl in Conflict*. Englewood Cliffs, N.J.: Prentice-Hall, 1966.

_____. *Young Girls: A Portrait of Adolescence*. Englewood Cliffs, N.J.: Prentice-Hall, 1976.

Konorski, J. *Integrative Activity of the Brain*. Chicago: University of Chicago Press, 1967.

Konovalov, Serge (ed.). *Russo-Polish Relations: An Historical Survey*. Princeton, N.J.: Princeton University Press, 1945.

Konoye, Fumimaro. *The Konoye Diary*. Tokyo: Kyodo Press, 1968.

_____. *My Efforts Towards Peace*. Tokyo: Nippon Dempo Tsushinsha, 1946.

Konstantin, Prince of Bavaria. *Der Pabst*. Munich: Kindler & Schiermeyer, 1950.

Konvitz, Milton. *Bill of Rights Reader*. Ithaca, N.Y.: Cornell University Press, 1968.

_____. *Civil Rights in Immigration*. Ithaca, N.Y.: Cornell University Press, 1953.

_____. *First Amendment Freedoms*. Ithaca, N.Y.: Cornell University Press, 1963.

Koop, W.E. *Billy the Kid*. Kansas City: Kansas City Posse of Westerners, 1965.

Koral, Mark. *The Zionist Conspiracy Behind the President Kennedy Assassination*. Rochester, N.Y.: Published by Author, 1976.

Korda, Michael. *Charmed Lives*. New York: Random House, 1979.

Kordt, Erich. *Nicht aus den Akcen*. Stuttgart, Ger.: Union Deutsche Verlagsgesellschaft, 1950.

Koren, John. *Alcohol and Society*. New York: Henry Holt, 1916.

_____. *Economic Aspects of the Liquor Problem*. Boston: Houghton, Mifflin, 1899.

Korff, Baron S.A. *Russia's Foreign Relations During the Last Half Century*. New York: Macmillan, 1922.

Korn, Richard R., and McCorkle, Lloyd W. *Criminology and Penology*. New York: Henry Holt, 1959.

Korngold, R. *The Last Years of Napoleon*. London: Victor Gollancz, 1960.

Kornhauser, Ruth R. *Social Sources of Delinquency: An Appraisal of Analytic Models*. Chicago: University of Chicago Press, 1978.

Kornilov, Alexander. *Modern Russian History*. New York: Alfred A. Knopf, 1952.

Kornitzer, Bela. *The Real Nixon*. New York: Rand-McNally, 1960.

Koshko, A.F. *Ocherki ugolovnogo mira tsarskoy Rossii*. Paris: n.p., 1926.

Kossuth, Count Louis. *Souvenirs et écrits de mon exil*. Paris: Plon, 1880.

Koster, F. *Het Socialisme in de Branding*. Bern, Switz.: Hollandia-Drukkerij N.V., 1935.

Koszyk, K. *Die Deutsche Presse im 19. Jahrhundert*. Berlin: Colloquium, 1966.

_____. *Die Deutsche Presse 1914-1945*. Berlin: Colloquium, 1972.

Koukoules, P. *The Private Lives of the Byzantines*. Athens, Gr.: n.p., 1947.

Kouwenhoven, John A. *Adventures of America, 1857-1900*. New York: Harper & Brothers, 1938.

_____. *The Columbia Historical Portrait of New York*. Garden City, N.Y.: Doubleday, 1953.

Kovalevski, M.M. *Russian Political Institutions*. Chicago: University of Chicago Press, 1902.

Koyama Itoko. *Nagako, Empress of Japan*. New York: John Day, 1958.

Kraditor, Aileen S. *Up From the Pedestal*. Chicago: Quadrangle, 1968.

Kraemer, William, et al. *The Normal and Abnormal Love of Children*. Kansas City: Sheed Andrews & McMeel, 1976.

Krafft-Ebing, Richard von. *Psychopathia Sexualis*. New York: G.P. Putnam's Sons, 1965.

Kraines, Oscar. *Government and Politics in Israel*. Boston: Houghton Mifflin, 1961.

Krakel, Dean F. *The Saga of Tom Horn: The Story of a Cattlemen's War*. Laramie, Wyo.: Powder River, 1954.

Kramarz, Joachim. *Stauffenberg: The Life and Death of an Officer*. trans. R.H. Barry. London: André Deutsch, 1967.

Kramer, Caspar J., Jr. (ed.). *The Complete Works of Horace*. New York: Modern Library, 1936.

Kramer, Heinrich, and Sprenger, James. *Malleus Malificarum*. New York: Dover, 1971.

Kramer, Noah Samuel. *History Begins at Sumer*. Garden City, N.Y.: Doubleday, 1959.

_____ (ed.). *Mythologies of the Ancient World*. New York: Doubleday Anchor, 1961.

_____. *Sumerian Mythology*. New York: Harper, 1961.

Krannhals, Hanns von. *Der Warschauer Aufstand 1944*. Frankfurt, Ger.: Bernard & Graefe Verlag für Wehrwesen, 1962.

Krantz, Sheldon, et al. *Right to Counsel in Criminal Cases: The Mandate of Argersinger v. Hamlin*. Cambridge, Mass.: Ballinger, 1976.

Kranz, H. *Lebensschicksale Krimineller Zwillinge*. Berlin: Springer, 1936.

Krasnow, Erwin G., and Longley, Lawrence D. *The Politics of Broadcast Regulation*. New York: St. Martin's Press, 1973.

Kraus, Adolf. *Reminiscences and Comments: The Immigrant, the Citizen, a Public Office, the Jew*. Chicago: Toby Rubovits, 1925.

Kraus, Michael. *The Atlantic Civilization: Eighteenth Century Origins*. Ithaca, N.Y.: Cornell University Press, 1949.

_____. *A History of American History*. New York: Farrar & Rinehart, 1937.

_____. *Immigration: The American Mosaic*. Princeton, N.J.: Princeton University Press, 1966.

_____. *Intercolonial Aspects of American Culture on the Eve of the Revolution*. New York: Columbia University Press, 1928.

_____. *The United States to 1865*. Ann Arbor: University of Michigan Press, 1959.

Krause, Aurel. *The Tlingit Indians*. trans. Erna Gunther. Seattle: University of Washington, 1956.

Krause, Charles. *Guyana Massacre*. New York: Berkley, 1978.

Krause, Lawrence B., and Dam, Kenneth W. *Federal Tax Treatment of Foreign Income*. Washington, D.C.: Brookings Institution, 1964.

Krausse, Alexis. *Russia in Asia, 1558-1899*. New York: Henry

Holt, 1900.

Kravchinski, S.M. *Russian Under the Tsars*. New York: Charles Scribner's Sons, 1885.

_____. *Underground Russia*. New York: Charles Scribner's Sons, 1883.

Krebs, Albert. *Fritz-Dietlof Graf von der Schulenburg*. Hamburg, Ger.: Leibnitz, 1964.

_____. *Tendenzen und Gestalten der NSDAP*. Stuttgart, Ger.: Deutsche Verlagsanstalt, 1959.

Krehbiel, Henry Edward. *Mozart: The Man and the Artist Revealed in His Own Words*. New York: Dover, 1965.

Kreighbaum, Hillier. *Pressures on the Press*. New York: Thomas Y. Crowell, 1972.

Kretschmer, Ernst. *Physique and Character*. trans. W.J.H. Sprott. New York: Harcourt, Brace, 1926.

Krippner, S. *Song of the Siren*. New York: Harper & Row, 1975.

Krisberg, Barry. *Crime and Privilege*. Englewood Cliffs, N.J.: Prentice-Hall, 1975.

Krivitsky, Walter. *I Was Stalin's Agent*. Bristol, Eng.: Right Book Club, 1940.

Krock, Arthur. *In the Nation: 1932-1966*. New York: McGraw-Hill, 1966.

_____. *Memoirs*. New York: Funk & Wagnalls, 1968.

Kroeber, Theodora. *Ishi in Two Worlds*. Berkeley: University of California Press, 1961.

Kroll, Harry Harrison. *Rogue's Company: A Novel of John Murrell*. Indianapolis, Ind.: Bobbs-Merrill, 1943.

Kronenberger, Louis. *No Whippings, No Gold Watches*. Boston: Atlantic, Little Brown, 1970.

Kronhayssen, Eberhard and Phyllis. *Pornography and the Law*. New York: Ballantine, 1959.

Kroninger, Robert H. *Sarah and the Senator*. Berkeley, Calif.: Howell-North, 1964.

Krooss, Herman E. (ed.). *Documentary History of Banking and Currency in the United States*. New York: Chelsea House, 1969.

Kropotkin, Piotr A. *Conquest of Bread*. New York: G.P. Putnam's Sons, 1907.

_____. *In Russian and French Prisons*. London: Ward & Downey, 1887.

_____. *Memoirs of a Revolutionist*. Boston: Houghton Mifflin, 1930.

Krotz, David. *How to Hide Almost Anything*. New York: William Morrow, 1975.

Krout, John Allen. *Annals of American Sport*. New Haven, Conn.: Yale University Press, 1929.

_____, and Fox, Dixon Ryan. *The Completion of Independence*. New York: Macmillan, 1944.

_____. *The Origins of Prohibition*. New York: Alfred A. Knopf, 1925.

Krueger, Thomas A. *And Promises to Keep: The Southern Conference for Human Welfare*. Nashville, Tenn.: Vanderbilt University Press, 1967.

Krummer, R. *Rasputin ein Werkzeug der Juden*. Berlin: n.p., 1939.

Krumrey, Kate Warner. *Saga of Sawlog*. Denver: Big Mountain Press, 1965.

Krupskaya, N.K. *Izbrannie Pedagogicheskie Proizvedeniya*. Moscow: Izdatelstvo, Akademii Pedagogicheskikh Nauk, 1955.

_____. *O Lenine: Sbornik Statei*. Moscow: Gosudarstvennoe Izdatelstvo, 1960.

_____. *Vospominaniya o Lenine*. Moscow: Partizdat, 1933.

Krushchev, Nikita Sergeevich. *Krushchev Remembers*. trans. Strobe Talbott. Boston: Little, Brown, 1970.

Krutch, Joseph Wood. *The Modern Temper*. New York: Harcourt, Brace, 1929.

_____. *More Lives Than One*. New York: William Sloan, 1962.

K.S. *Agent in Italy*. London: Hutchinson, 1943.

Kschessinska, Mathilde. *Dancing in Petersburg*. trans. Arnold Haskel. Garden City, N.Y.: Doubleday, 1961.

Kubizek, August. *Young Hitler: The Story of Our Friendship*. Maidstone, Eng.: Mann, 1973.

Kübler-Ross, Elisabeth. *On Death and Dying*. New York: Macmillan, 1976.

Kubly, Herbert. *Italy*. New York: Time, 1961.

Kuby, Erich. *The Russians and Berlin, 1945*. New York: Hill & Wang, 1968.

Kucherow, Samuel. *Courts, Lawyers, and Trials under the Last Three Tsars*. New York: Frederick A. Praeger, 1953.

Kuczynski, Jurgen. *The Rise of the Working Class*. New York: McGraw-Hill, 1967.

Kuebert, Hans. *Zauberwahn, die Greuel der Inquisition und Hexenprozesse*. Munich: Buchhandlung Nationalverein, 1913.

Kugel, Yerachmiel, and Gruenberg, Gladys W. *International Payoffs: Dilemma for Business*. Lexington, Mass.: Lexington Books, 1977.

Kugler, Franz Theodor. *Life of Frederick the Great*. trans. E.A. Moriarty. New York: George Routledge & Sons, 1877.

Kuhn, Thomas S. *The Structure of Scientific Revolutions*. Chicago: University of Chicago Press, 1962.

Kuhne, F. *The Finger Print Instructor*. New York: Munn, 1942.

Kumarappa, J.M. *Our Begger Problem: How To Tackle It*. Bombay, India: Padma, 1945.

Kung, C.T. *Archaeology in China*. Toronto, Ontario: University of Toronto Press, 1959.

Kunhardt, Dorothy and Philip, Jr. *Twenty Days*. New York: Castle Books, 1965.

Kunnes, Richard. *The American Heroin Empire*. New York: Dodd, Mead, 1972.

Kunstler, William M. *Beyond A Reasonable Doubt? The Original Trial of Caryl Chessman*. New York: William Morrow, 1961.

_____. *The Case for Courage*. New York: William Morrow, 1962.

_____. *First Degree*. New York: Ocean Press, 1960.

_____. *The Minister and the Choir Singer*. New York: William Morrow, 1964.

Kuper, Leo. *Genocide: Its Political Use in the Twentieth Century*. New Haven, Conn.: Yale University Press, 1981.

Kupper, Winifred. *The Golden Hoof: The Story of the Sheep of the Southwest*. New York: Alfred A. Knopf, 1945.

Kupperman, Robert, and Trent, Darrell (eds.). *Terrorism: Threat, Reality, Response*. Stanford, Calif.: Hoover Institution Press, 1979.

Kurenberg, Joachim von. *The Kaiser*. trans. Russell and Hagen. New York: Simon & Schuster, 1955.

Kurland, Gerald. *Clarence Darrow, Attorney for the Damned*. Charlotteville, N.Y.: SamHar Press, 1972.

Kurland, Philip. *The Constitution and the Warren Court*. Chicago: University of Chicago Press, 1970.

_____. *Supreme Court Review*. Chicago: University of Chicago Law School, 1960.

Kurth, Ann. *Prescriptions: Murder*. New York: Signet, 1976.

Kurtz, Harold. *The Empress Eugénie, 1826-1920*. London: Hamish Hamilton, 1964.

Kurtz, Michael L. *Crime of the Century: The Kennedy Assassination From a Historian's Perspective*. Knoxville: University of Tennessee, 1982.

Kurtz, S.G. *The Presidency of John Adams: The Collapse of Federalism*. Philadelphia: University of Pennsylvania Press, 1957.

Kurzman, Dan. *Kishi and Japan: The Search for the Sun*. New York: Ivan Obolensky, 1960.

_____. *The Race for Rome*. New York: Doubleday, 1975.

Kutler, Stanley I. *The American Inquisition: Justice and Order in the Cold War*. New York: Hill & Wang, 1982.

Kuykendall, Ivan Lee. *Ghost Riders of the Mogollon*. San Antonio, Texas: Naylor, 1954.

Kuykendall, William Littlebury. *Frontier Days: A True Narrative of Striking Events on the Western Frontier*. Published by Author, 1917.

Kuznetsov, Edward. *Prison Diaries*. New York: Stein & Day, 1980.

Kwartler, Richard (ed.). *Behind Bars*. New York: Random House, 1974.

Kwitney, Jonathan. *The Fountainhead Conspiracy*. New York: Alfred A. Knopf, 1971.

_____. *The Mullendore Murder Case*. New York: Warner Books, 1976.

_____. *Vicious Circles: The Mafia in the Marketplace*. New York: W.W. Norton, 1979.

Kyemba, Henry. *A State of Blood*. New York: Ace, 1977.

Kyle, Otto R. *Abraham Lincoln in Decatur*. New York: Vantage, 1957.

Kyner, James H. *End of the Tracks*. Caldwell, Idaho: Caxton Printers, 1937.

L

Labaree, Benjamin W. *The Boston Tea Party*. New York: Oxford University Press, 1964.

Labaree, L.W. *Conservation in Early American History*. New York: New York University Press, 1948.

_____. *Royal Government in America*. New Haven, Conn.: Yale University Press, 1930.

Labat, Père. *Memoirs 1693-1705*. London: Frank Cass, 1970.

Labedz, Leopold (ed.). *Revisionism*. New York: Frederick A. Praeger, 1962.

La Bern, Arthur. *The Life and Death of a Ladykiller*. London: Published by Author, 1967.

Laborde, Jean. *The Dominici Affair*. New York: William Morrow, 1974.

Lachman, S., and Singer, B. *The Detroit Riot of July 1966: A Psychological, Sociological and Economic Profile of 500 Arrestees*. Detroit: Behavior Research Institute, 1968.

Lackey, B. Roberts. *Stories of the Texas Rangers*. San Antonio, Texas: Naylor, 1955.

Lacky, William E.H. *History of European Morals*. 2 vols. New York: Harper, 1958.

La Condamine, Charles-Marie de. *A Succinct Abridgement of a Voyage Made Within the Inland Parts of South America*. London: E. Withers, 1747.

Lacquer, Walter Z. *Communism and Nationalism in the Middle East*. New York: Frederick A. Praeger, 1956.

_____. *The Middle East in Transition*. New York: Frederick A. Praeger, 1958.

_____. *The Soviet Union and the Middle East*. New York: Frederick A. Praeger, 1959.

Lacroix, Paul. *France in the Middle Ages*. New York: Frederick Ungar, 1963.

_____. *History of Prostitution*. trans. Samuel Putnam. New York: Covici-Friede, 1931.

_____. *Military and Religious Life in the Middle Ages and the Renaissance*. New York: Frederick Ungar, 1964.

La Croix, Arda. *Billy the Kid*. New York: J.S. Ogilvie, 1907.

Ladame, Paul. *Procés criminel de la demière sorcière brulée à Genève le 6 avril 1652*. Paris: Delahaye et Lacrosnier, 1888.

Ladd, Robert E. *Eight Ropes to Eternity*. Tombstone, Ariz.: Tombstone Epitaph, 1965.

Ladder, Lawrence. *Abortion*. Indianapolis, Ind.: Bobbs-Merrill, 1966.

Lader, Lawrence. *The Bold Brahmins, New England's War Against Slavery*. New York: E.P. Dutton, 1961.

Ladies of the Mission. *The Old Brewery and the New Mission House at Five Points*. New York: Arno Press, 1970.

Ladner, Joyce A. *Tomorrow's Tomorrow*. New York: Doubleday, Anchor, 1972.

Lafarge, Marie. *Heures de prison*. New York: Lasalle, 1854.

_____. *Mémoires de Marie Cappelle, veuve LaFarge, écrits par elle-même*. Brussels, Belg.: Jamar, 1841.

La Farge, Oliver. *A Pictorial History of the American Indian*. New York: Crown, 1956.

_____. *Santa Fe: The Autobiography of a Southwestern Town*. Norman: University of Oklahoma Press, 1959.

LaFave, Wayne R. *Arrest*. Boston: Little, Brown, 1965.

_____, and Scott, A.W., Jr. *Handbook on Criminal Law*. St. Paul, Minn.: West, 1972.

LaFeber, Walter. *America, Russia, and the Cold War, 1945-1971*. New York: John Wiley & Sons, 1972.

_____. *The New Empire*. Ithaca, N.Y.: Cornell University Press, 1963.

Laferte, V. *Alexandre II*. Bale, Fr.: H. Georg, 1882.

Laffan, Robert George. *The Serbs, Guardians of the Gates*. Oxford, Eng.: Clarendon Press, 1918.

Laffin, John. *Fedayeen: The Arab Israeli Dilemma*. London: Cassell, 1973.

La Follette, Belle Case and Fola. *Robert M. La Follette*. New York: Macmillan, 1953.

La Follette, Robert Hoath. *Eight Notches, "Lawlessness and Disorder, Unlimited"*. Albuquerque, N.M.: Valiant Printing, 1950.

La Font, Don. *Rugged Life in the Rockies*. Casper, Wyo.: Prairie, 1951.

Lagardelle, Hubert. *Mission à Rome*. Paris: Plon, 1955.

La Gorce, Pierre de. *Histoire du second empire*. Paris: Plon-Nourrit, 1894.

Lagrange, Francis, and Murray, William. *Flag on Devil's Island*. Garden City, N.Y.: n.p., 1961.

Lagrange, François. *Vie de M. Duganloup, évêque d'Orleans*. Paris: Pousielgue frères, 1883.

La Guardia, Robert. *Monty*. New York: Arbor House, 1977.

Laguer, Walter. *Terrorism*. Boston: Little, Brown, 1977.

Lahue, Kalton C. *Dreams for Sale: The Rise and Fall of the Triangle Film Corporation*. New York: Thomas Yoseloff, 1971.

_____. *Mack Sennett's Keystone: The Man, the Myth and the Comedies*. New York: A.S. Barnes, 1971.

_____. *Motion Picture Pioneer: The Selig Polyscope Company*. New York: A.S. Barnes, 1973.

_____, and Gill, Samuel. *Clown Princes and Court Jesters: Some Great Comics of the Silent Screen*. New York: A.S. Barnes, 1970.

_____, and Brewer, Terry. *Kops and Custards: The Legend of Keystone Films*. Norman: University of Oklahoma Press, 1967.

Laidler, Harry W. *American Socialism*. New York: Harper, 1937.

_____. *The Federal Government and Functional Democracy*. New York: League for Industrial Democracy, 1940.

_____. *History of Socialism*. New York: Crowell, 1968.

_____. *A Program for Modern America*. New York: Crowell, 1936.

_____. *Socialism in Thought and Action*. New York: Macmillan, 1920.

_____, and Thomas, N. (eds.). *The Socialism of Our Times*. New York: Vanguard Press, 1929.

_____, and Thomas, N. *Socialist Planning and a Socialist Program*. New York: Falcon Press, 1932.

_____. *Toward a Farmer-Labor Party*. New York: League for Industrial Democracy, 1938.

Laine, Tanner. *Campfire Stories*. Lubbock, Texas: Ranch House, 1965.

Laing, R.D. *The Divided Self*. Baltimore: Penguin Books, 1965.

Lait, Jack, and Mortimer, Lee. *Chicago Confidential*. New York: Crown, 1950.

_____. *New York Confidential*. Chicago: Ziff-Davis, 1948.

_____. *U.S.A. Confidential*. Crown, 1952.

_____. *Washington Confidential*. New York: Crown, 1951.

Lajpat, Rai Lala. *Ideals of Non-co-operation*. Madras, India: S. Ganesan, 1924.

_____. *Unhappy India*. Calcutta, India: Banna, 1928.

Lake, Carolyn (ed.). *Under Cover for Wells Fargo*. Boston: Houghton Mifflin, 1969.

Lake, Stuart N. *He Carried a Six-Shooter: The Biography of Wyatt Earp*. New York: Peter Nevill, 1952.

_____. *Wyatt Earp, Frontier Marshal*. Boston: Houghton Mifflin, 1931.

Lallemand, Claude-François. *On Involuntary Seminal Discharges*. trans. William Wood. Philadelphia: A. Waldie, 1839.

Lalor, John J. (ed.). *Cyclopedia of Political Science, Political Economy, and of the Political History of the United States*. New York: Maynard, Merrill, 1895.

Lamar, Howard Roberts. *Dakota Territory, 1861-1889: A Study of Frontier Politics*. New Haven, Conn.: Yale University Press, 1956.

_____. *The Far Southwest, 1846-1912: A Territorial History*. New Haven, Conn.: Yale University Press, 1966.

_____ (ed.). *A Reader's Encyclopedia of the American West*. New York: Thomas Y. Crowell, 1977.

Lamartine, Alphonse de. *Méditations Poétiques Suivies de Poésies Diverses*. Paris: Livre de Poche, 1963.

Lamb, Arthur H. *Tragedies of the Osage Hills*. Pawhuska, Okla.: Osage Printery, 1935.

Lamb, Charles. *Witches*. London: M. Dent & Sons, 1929.

Lamb, Harold. *New Found World*. Garden City, N.Y.: Doubleday, 1955.

Lamb, Martha, and Harrison, Burton. *History of the City of New York*. New York: A.S. Barnes, 1877.

Lamb, Ruth DeForest. *American Chamber of Horrors*. New York: Farrar & Rinehart, 1936.

Lambarde, William. *Eirenarcha*. London: R. Newbery & H. Bynneman, 1581.

_____. *William Lambarde and Local Government*. Ithaca, N.Y.: Cornell University Press, 1962.

Lambert, Oscar Doane. *Stephen Benton Elkins*. Pittsburgh, Pa.: University of Pittsburgh Press, 1955.

Lambert, R.S. *When Justice Faltered*. London: Methuen, 1935.

_____. *The Universal Provider*. London: Harrap, 1938.

Lambrino, Jeanne. *Mon Marie Le Roi Carol*. Paris: Calmann-levy, 1950.

Lambton, Arthur. *Echoes of Causes Celebres*. London: Hurst & Blackett, 1931.

_____. *Thou Shalt Do No Murder*. London: Hurst & Blackett, 1930.

Lamon, Ward H. *Life of Abraham Lincoln*. Boston: Osgood, 1872.

_____. *Recollections of Abraham Lincoln*. Washington, D.C.: Dorothy Lamon Teillard, 1911.

Lamond, John. *Arthur Conan Doyle*. London: John Murray, 1931.

Lamont, Corliss (ed.). *The Thomas Lamonts in America*. New York: A.S. Barnes, 1971.

Lamont, Thomas W. *Across World Frontiers*. New York: Harcourt, Brace, 1951.

_____. *My Boyhood in a Parsonage*. New York: Harper & Brothers, 1946.

Lamothe-Langon, Etienne Léon de. *Histoire de l'Inquisition en France*. Paris: J.G. Dentu, 1829.

Lamott, K. *The Moneymakers: The Great Big New Rich in America*. Boston: Little, Brown, 1969.

LaMotte, E.N. *The Ethics of Opium*. New York: Century, 1924.

Lamour, Catherine, and Lamberti, Michael R. *The International Connection: Opium From Growers to Pushers*. New York: Pantheon, 1974.

Lamparski, Richard. *Whatever Became of...?* New York: Crown, 1967.

Lampert, E. *Studies in Rebellion*. New York: Frederick A. Praeger, 1957.

Lampman, Ben Hur. *Centralia Tragedy and Trial*. Tacoma, Wash.: n.p., 1920.

Lampman, Robert J. *The Share of Top Wealth-Holders in National Wealth, 1922-1956*. Princeton, N.J.: Princeton University Press, 1956.

Lancellotti, Arturo. *D'Annunzio nella luce di domani*. Rome: Staderini, 1938.

Lancre, Pierre de. *L'incrédulité et mécréance du sortilège*. Paris: Nicolas Bvon, 1622.

_____. *Tableau de l'inconstance des mauvais anges et démons*. Paris: Nicolas Bvon, 1612.

Landau, Henry. *The Enemy Within*. New York: G.P. Putnam's Sons, 1937.

Landau, Jacob M. *Radical Politics in Modern Turkey*. Leiden, Neth.: E.J. Brill, 1974.

Landau, Ron. *Moroccan Drama*. London: Robert Hale, 1956.

_____. *Morocco Independent*. London: George Allen & Unwin, 1961.

Landauer, Carl. *European Socialism*. 2 vols. Berkeley: University of California Press, 1959.

Landauer, T. *Psychology: A Brief Overview*. New York: McGraw-Hill, 1972.

Lander, B. *Towards an Understanding in Juvenile Delinquency*. New York: Columbia University Press, 1954.

Lander, C. *My Kenya Acres: A Woman Farms in Mau Mau Country*. London: Harrap, 1957.

Lander, Ernest McPherson, Jr. *A History of South Carolina, 1865-1960*. Chapel Hill: University of North Carolina Press, 1960.

Landesco, John. *Organized Crime in Chicago*. Chicago: University of Chicago Press, 1968.

Landis, Charles K. *The Founder's Own Story of the Founding of Vineland, New Jersey*. Vineland, N.J.: Vineland Historical and Antiquarian Society, 1903.

Landress, M.M., with Dobler, Bruce. *I Made It Myself*. New York: Grosset & Dunlap, 1973.

Landreth, Helen. *Dear Dark Head*. New York: Whittlesey House, 1936.

_____. *The Pursuit of Robert Emmett*. New York: Whittlesey House, 1948.

Landru, H.C. *The Blue Parka Man*. New York: Dodd, Mead, 1980.

Landrum, Graham. *Grayson County*. Fort Worth, Texas: University Supply & Equipment, 1960.

Landsburg, Alan. *In Search of Magic and Witchcraft*. New York: Bantam, 1976.

_____. *In Search of Strange Phenomena*. New York: Bantam, 1977.

Lane, Allen Stanley. *Emperor Norton, the Mad Monarch of America*. Caldwell, Idaho: Caxton Printers, 1939.

Lane, Anne W., and Wall, Louis H. (eds.). *The Letters of Franklin K. Lane*. Boston: Houghton Mifflin, 1922.

Lane, Arthur Bliss. *I Saw Poland Betrayed*. Indianapolis, Ind.: Bobbs-Merrill, 1948.

Lane, Edward William. *The Manners and Customs of the Modern Egyptians*. London: Everyman's Library, 1860.

_____. *The Thousand and One Nights*. London: Routledge, 1889.

Lane, Margaret. *Edgar Wallace: The Biography of a Phenomenon*. London: William Heinemann, 1938.

Lane, Mark. *A Citizen's Dissent: Mark Lane Replies*. New York: Holt, Rinehart & Winston, 1968.

_____, and Gregory, Dick. *Code Name "Zorro."* Englewood Cliffs, N.J.: Prentice-Hall, 1973.

_____. *Rush to Judgment*. New York: Holt, Rinehart & Winston, 1966.

_____. *The Strongest Poison*. New York: Hawthorn Books, 1980.

Lane, R. *Violent Death in the City: Suicide, Accident, and Murder in Nineteenth-Century Philadelphia*. Cambridge, Mass.: Harvard University Press, 1979.

Lane, Robert E., and Sears, David O. (eds.). *Public Opinion.*

Englewood Cliffs, N.J.: Prentice-Hall, 1964.

Lane, Robert R. *The Regulation of Business: Social Conditions of Government Economic Control.* New Haven, Conn.: Yale University Press, 1954.

Lane, Roger. *Policing the City: Boston, 1822-1885.* Cambridge, Mass.: Harvard University Press, 1967.

Lane, Wheaton J. *Commodore Vanderbilt, An Epic of the Steam Age.* New York: Alfred A. Knopf, 1942.

Lane-Poole, Stanley. *Cairo: Sketches of Its History, Monuments and Social Life.* London: J.S. Virtue, 1892.

_____. *The Speeches and Table-Talk of the Prophet Mohammed.* London: Macmillan, 1882.

_____. *The Story of Cairo.* London: J.M. Dent, 1902.

Lanfranchi, Ferruccio. *La Resa degli ottocentomila.* Rome: Rizzoli, 1948.

Lang, Andrew. *Book of Dreams and Ghosts.* London: Longmans, Green, 1897.

_____. *Cock Lane and Common Sense.* London: Longmans, Green, 1894.

_____. *Magic and Religion.* London: Longman, Green, 1901.

_____. *The Maid of France.* London: Longman, Green, 1924.

_____. *The Making of Religion.* London: Longmans, Green, 1898.

Lang, David. *The First Russian Radical: Alexander Radishchev, 1749-1802.* London: George Allen & Unwin, 1959.

Lang, Rev. Gordon. *Mr. Justice Avory.* London: Herbert Jenkins, 1935.

Lang, Kurt and Gladys. *Politics and Television.* Chicago: Quadrangle Books, 1968.

Lang, John. *Wanderings in India.* London: Routledge, Warne and Routhorpe, 1859.

Lang, Lincoln A. *Ranching With Roosevelt.* Philadelphia: J.B. Lippincott, 1926.

Lang, Lucy Robins. *Tommorow is Beautiful.* New York: Macmillan, 1948.

Langbein, Hermann. *Im Namen des deutschen Volkes.* Zurich, Switz.: Europa Verlag AG, 1963.

Langdon, Emma F. *Labor's Greatest Conflict.* Denver: Denver Press, 1908.

Lange, Johannes. *Crime and Destiny.* New York: Charles Boni, 1930.

Langeluttig, Albert G. *Department of Justice in the United States.* Baltimore: Johns Hopkins University Press, 1927.

Langer, W.L. *Franco-Russian Alliance, 1890-1894.* Cambridge, Mass.: Harvard University Press, 1929.

Langer, William L. *European Alliances and Alignments, 1871-1890.* New York: Alfred A. Knopf, 1956.

Langford, Gerald. *Alias O. Henry: A Biography of William Sidney Porter.* New York: Macmillan, 1957.

Langford, Gerald. *The Murder of Stanford White.* Indianapolis: Bobbs-Merrill, 1962.

Langford, Nathaniel Pitt. *Vigilante Days and Ways.* Chicago: A.L. Burt, 1890.

Langguth, A.J. *Hidden Terrors: The Truth About U.S. Police Operations in Latin America.* New York: Pantheon Books, 1978.

Längin, Georg. *Religion und Hexenprozesse.* Leipzig, Ger.: O. Wigand, 1888.

Langmaid, Rowland. *"The Med": The Royal Navy in the Mediterranean, 1939-1945.* London: Batchworth Press, 1948.

Langsam, W.C. *Historic Documents of World War Two.* Princeton, N.J.: D. van Nostrand, 1958.

Langton, Edward. *Satan, a Portrait.* London: Skeffington & Son, 1945.

Langtry, Lillie. *The Days I Knew.* New York: George H. Doran, 1925.

Lano, Pierre de. *Le Secret d'un empire.* Paris: V. Havard, 1892.

Lanphear, Roger Glenn. *Freedom From Crime.* New York: Nellen, n.d.

Lansford, William Douglas. *Pancho Villa.* Los Angeles: Sher-

bourne Press, 1965.

Lansing, Robert. *War Memoirs of Robert Lansing.* New York: Bobbs-Merrill, 1935.

Lapide, Pinchas. *The Last Three Popes and the Jews.* London: Souvenir Press, 1967.

Lapidus, Edith J. *Eavesdropping on Trial.* Rochelle Park, N.J.: Hayden, 1974.

Lappé, Frances M., and Collins, Joseph. *Food First: Beyond the Myth of Scarcity.* New York: Ballantine Books, 1977.

Lapping, B. *End of Empire.* New York: St. Martin's Press, 1985.

Laqueur, T.W. *Religion and Respectability.* New Haven, Conn.: Yale University Press, 1976.

Laqueur, Walter. *Guerrilla.* London: Weidenfeld & Nicolson, 1976.

_____. *The Guerilla Reader.* Philadelphia: Temple University Press, 1977.

_____, and Labedz, Leopold. *Polycentrism.* New York: Frederick A. Praeger, 1962.

_____. *The Road to War.* London: Penguin, 1969.

_____. *Terrorism.* Boston: Little, Brown, 1977.

_____ (ed.). *The Terrorism Reader: A Historical Anthology.* New York: Meridian, 1978.

_____. *Young Germany.* London: Routledge & Paul Kegan, 1962.

Lara Pardo, Luis. *De Porfirio Diaz a Francisco I. Madero.* New York: Polyglot Publishing and Commercial, 1912.

Lara Pardo, Dr. Luis. *Marcha de Dictadores: Wilson contra Heurta: Carranza contra Wilson.* Mexico City: A.P. Marquez, 1942.

Larcom, Lucy. *A New England Girlhood.* Magnolia, Mass.: Peter Smith, 1973.

Lardner, Ring, Jr. *The Lardners: My Family Remembered.* New York: Harper & Row, 1976.

Lardner, W.B., and Brock, M.J. *History of Placer and Nevada Counties, California.* Los Angeles: Historic Record, 1924.

Lardy, Charles. *Les procédures de sorcellerie à Neuchâtel.* Neuchâtel, Fr.: J. Sandoz, 1866.

Larken, P.M. *An Account of the Zande.* Khartoum, Sudan: McCorquodale, 1926.

Larkin, Margaret. *Singing Cowboys.* New York: Alfred A. Knopf, 1931.

Larkin, Maurice. *Church and State After the Dreyfuss Affair.* New York: Harper & Row, 1974.

Larkin, Oliver. *Art and Life in America.* New York: Rinehart, 1949.

Larned, Edward C., and Knowles, William. *A Full Report of the Trial of John Gordon and William Gordon.* Providence, R.I.: Daily Transcript, 1844.

Larner, Jeremy, and Tefferteller, Ralph. *The Addict in the Street.* New York: Grove Press, 1964.

The Laros Murder: A Whole Family Poisoned by an Ungrateful Son. Easton, Pa.: West & Hilburn, 1876.

Larrieu, L. *Histoire de la kgendarmerie.* Paris: Charles-Lavauzelle, 1920.

Larrowe, Charles P. *Harry Bridges.* New York: Lawrence Hill, 1972.

Larry "The Silver Fox". *My Life with Xaviera.* New York: Warner Books, 1974.

Larsen, Charles. *The Good Fight.* Chicago: Quadrangle Books, 1972.

Larsen, Lawrence H. *The Urban West at the End of the Frontier.* Lawrence: Regents Press of Kansas, 1978.

Larsen, Otto. *Violence and the Mass Media.* New York: Harper & Row, 1968.

Larsen, Richard W. *Bundy, The Deliberate Stranger.* Englewood Cliffs, N.J.: Prentice-Hall, 1980.

Larson, J.A. *A Single Fingerprint System.* New York: D. Appleton, 1924.

Larson, Orvin. *American Infidel: Robert G. Ingersoll.* New York: Citadel Press, 1962.

Larson, Richard C. *Urban Police Patrol Analysis.* Cambridge, Mass.: M.I.T. Press, 1972.

Larson, Robert W. *New Mexico Populism.* Boulder: Colorado Associated University Press, 1974.

Larson, T.A. *History of Wyoming.* Lincoln: University of Nebraska Press, 1965.

Larue, André. *Les Flics.* Paris: Fayard, 1969.

Las Cases, Emmanuel de. *Notice.* Paris: Remquet, 1854.

Lasch, Christopher. *The Agony of the American Left.* New York: Vintage Books, 1969.

———. *The Culture of Narcissism.* New York: Warner Books, 1979.

———. *The New Radicalism in America, 1889-1963.* New York: Alfred A. Knopf, 1965.

Laserson, M.M. *The American Impact on Russia: Diplomatic and Ideological, 1784-1917.* New York: Macmillan, 1950.

———, and Shotwell, J.T. *Russia and Poland, 1919-1945.* New York: King's Crown, 1945.

Lash, Joseph P. (ed.). *From the Diaries of Felix Frankfurter.* New York: W.W. Norton, 1975.

Laski, Harold J. (ed.). *A Defense of Liberty Against Tyrants.* New York: Peter Smith, 1963.

———. *Democracy in Crisis.* Chapel Hill: University of North Carolina Press, 1933.

———. *Faith, Reason and Civilization.* New York: Viking Press, 1944.

———. *The Labor Party, the War, and the Future.* London: Labor Party, 1939.

———. *Marx and Today.* London: Fabian Research Bureau, 1943.

———. *Reflections on the Revolution of Our Time.* New York: Viking Press, 1943.

Lasky, Jesse, with Weldon, Don. *I Blow My Own Horn.* New York: Doubleday, 1957.

Lasky, Victor. *It Didn't Start With Watergate.* New York: Dell, 1978.

———. *Jimmy Carter: The Man & the Myth.* New York: Richard Marek, 1979.

Laslett, John H.M. *Labor and the Left.* New York: Basic Books, 1970.

Laslett, Peter. *The World We Have Lost.* New York: Charles Scribner's Sons, 1984.

Lass, William E. *A History of Steamboating on the Upper Missouri River.* Lincoln: University of Nebraska Press, 1962.

Lasswell, Harold D., and McKenna, Jerimiah B. *The Impact on Organized Crime on an Inner-City Community.* New York: Policy Sciences Center, 1972.

———, and Rogow, Arnold A. *Power, Corruption, and Rectitude.* Englewood Cliffs, N.J.: Prentice-Hall, 1963.

———. *Power and Personality.* New York: W.W. Norton, 1948.

———, and Blumenstock, Dorothy. *World Revolutionary Propaganda.* New York: Alfred A. Knopf, 1939.

The Last Dying Confessions and Remains of Michael Jones. Louisville, Ky.: n.p., 1834.

The Last Dying Speech and Confession of Joseph Andrews. New York: L. Swiney and J. Stewart, 1769.

The Last Dying Speech & Confession of the Mormon Bishop. Salt Lake City, Utah: n.p., 1875.

Last Dying Words and Confession of Charles Gibbs, the Pirate. New York: n.p., 1831.

The Last Speech and Confession of Henry Halbert. Philadelphia: Anthony Armbruster, n.d.

The Last Words and Dying Speech of Edmund Fortis. Exeter, Maine: n.p., 1795.

Latané, B., and Darley, J.M. *The Unresponsive Bystander.* New York: Appleton, 1970.

Latham, Earl *The Communist Controversy in Washington.* Cambridge, Mass.: Harvard University Press, 1966.

——— (ed.). *The Meaning of McCarthyism.* Lexington, Mass.: Heath, 1973.

——— (ed.). *The Philosophy and Policies of Woodrow Wilson.* Chicago: University of Chicago Press, 1958.

Latham, Edward. *Crisis in the Middle East.* New York: Wilson, 1952.

Lathrop, Amy. *Tales of Western Kansas.* Kansas City: La Rue Printing, 1948.

Lathrop, Gilbert A. *Little Engines and Big Men.* Caldwell, Idaho: Caxton Printers, 1954.

Latimer, Dean, and Goldberg, Jeff. *Flowers in the Blood: The Story of Opium.* New York: Franklin Watts, 1981.

La Torre, Ferdinando. *Del conclave di Alessandro VI, papa Borgia.* Rome: Olschki, 1933.

Latouche, Robert. *Histoire des Francs.* Paris: Les Belles Lettres, 1963.

Latour, Anny. *The Borgias.* trans. Neil Mann. New York: Abelard-Schuman, 1963.

Latrobe, Charles Joseph. *The Rambler in North America, 1832-1833.* New York: Harper & Brothers, 1835.

Latta, Estelle. *Controversial Mark Hopkins.* New York: Greenberg, 1953.

Lattimer, Dr. John K. *Kennedy and Lincoln: Medical and Ballistic Comparisons of Their Assassinations.* New York: Harcourt, Brace, Jovanovich, 1980.

Lattimore, Owen. *Manchuria, Cradle of Conflict.* New York: Macmillan, 1932.

———. *Ordeal by Slander.* Boston: Little Brown, 1950.

———, and Eleanor (eds.). *Silks, Spices and Empire: Asia Seen Through the Eyes of Its Discoverers.* New York: Delacorte Press, 1968.

Latourette, Kenneth S. *The Chinese: Their History and Culture.* New York: Macmillan, 1934.

Lauck, W. Jett. *The Causes of the Panic of 1893.* Boston: Houghton Mifflin, 1907.

———. *Political and Industrial Democracy, 1776-1926.* New York: Funk & Wagnalls, 1926.

Lauder, Ronald S. *Fighting Violent Crime in the United States.* New York: Dodd, Mead, 1985.

Laufer, B. *Annual Report.* Washington, D.C.: Smithsonian Institute, 1912.

Laugel, Auguste. *Les Etats-Unis pendant la guerre (1861-65).* Paris: Germer Baillière, 1866.

Laughlin, Clara E. *The Death of Lincoln: The Story of Booth's Plot, His Deed, and the Penalty.* New York: Doubleday, Page, 1909.

———. *Traveling Through Life.* Boston: Houghton Mifflin, 1934.

Laughlin, Clarence John, and Cohn, David L. *New Orleans and Its Living Past.* Boston: Houghton Mifflin, 1941.

Laughlin, Ruth. *Caballeros.* New York: D. Appleton, 1931.

Laune, Seigniora Russell. *Sand in Your Eyes.* Philadelphia: J.B. Lippincott, 1956.

Laurence, John A. *Extraordinary Crimes.* London: Low, Marston, 1931.

Laurence, John. *A History of Capital Punishment.* New York: Citadel Press, 1963.

Laurens, John. *Correspondence.* New York: Arno Press, 1969.

Laurent, Charles. *Sainte Jeanne d'Arc.* Paris: Haton, 1920.

Laurie, B. *The Newgate Calendar.* New York: G.P. Putnam's Sons, 1932.

Laurie, Peter. *Drugs.* Middlesex, Eng.: Penguin, 1967.

———. *Scotland Yard: A Study of the Metropolitan Police.* Middlesex, Eng.: Penguin, 1972.

Laurie, T. Werner. *The Newgate Calendar.* New York: G.P. Putnam's Sons, 1932.

Laut, Agnes C. *Pilgrims of the Santa Fe.* New York: Frederick A. Stokes, 1931.

———. *The Romance of the Rails.* New York: Robert M. McBride, 1928.

Lauterpacht, E. (ed.). *The Suez Canal Settlement.* New York: Praeger, 1960.

——— (ed.). *The United Nations Emergency Force: Basic Docu-*

ments. London: Stevens, 1960.

Lautréamont, Comte de. *Les Chants de Maldoror.* New York: New Directions, 1965.

LaValley, Albert (ed.). *Focus on Hitchcock.* Englewood Cliffs, N.J.: Prentice-Hall, 1972.

Lavater, Ludwig. *Von Gespänsten vaghüren fälen und anderen wunderbaren Dingen.* Zurich, Switz.: C. Froschower, 1569.

Lavelle, Patricia O'Mara. *James O'Mara.* Dublin: Clonmore & Reynolds, 1961.

Lavender, David. *The American Heritage History of the Great West.* New York: American Heritage, 1965.

_____. *The Big Divide.* Garden City, N.Y.: Doubleday, 1948.

_____. *Land of Giants, The Drive to the Pacific Northwest.* New York: Doubleday, 1958.

_____. *Nothing Seemed Impossible.* Palo Alto, Calif.: American West, 1975.

_____. *The Rockies.* New York: Harper & Row, 1968.

Laver, James. *The Age of Optimism, 1848-1914.* New York: Harper & Row, 1966.

LaVey, Anton Szandor. *The Satanic Bible.* New York: Avon, 1969.

Lavigne, Frank C. *Crimes, Criminals and Detectives.* Helena, Mont.: State, 1921.

Lavigne, Yves. *Hells Angels: Taking Care of Business.* Toronto, Can.: Deneua and Wayne, 1987.

Lavine, Emanuel H. *Gimme—or How Public Officials Get Rich.* New York: Vanguard Press, 1931.

Lavine, Sigmund. *Allan Pinkerton, America's First Private Eye.* New York: Dodd, Mead, 1963.

Lavisse, Ernest. *Histoire de France.* Boston: D.C. Heath, 1919.

_____. *Youth of Frederick the Great.* London: Bentley & Son, 1891.

Law Enforcement Assistance Administration. *Criminal Justice Monograph.* Washington, D.C.: U.S. Department of Justice, 1973.

Lawes, Warden Lewis Edward. *Cell 202 Sing-Sing.* New York: Farrar & Rinehart, 1935.

_____. *Man's Judgment of Death.* New York: G. P. Putnam's Sons, 1924.

_____. *Meet the Murderer!* New York: Harper & Bros., 1932.

_____. *Twenty Thousand Years In Sing Sing.* New York: R. Long & R. R. Smith, 1932.

Lawrence, D.H. *The Letters of D.H. Lawrence.* New York: Viking Press, 1932.

Lawrence, David. *Beyond the New Deal.* New York: McGraw-Hill, 1934.

_____. *Nine Honest Men.* New York: D. Appleton-Century, 1936.

_____. *The True Story of Woodrow Wilson.* New York: George H. Doran, 1924.

Lawrence, Lt.-Gen. Sir George. *Forty Years' Service in India.* London: John Murray, 1874.

Lawrence, Gertrude. *A Star Danced.* New York: Doubleday, 1945.

Lawrence, J. *A History of Capital Punishment with Special Reference to Capital Punishment in Britain.* Port Washington, N.Y.: Kennikat Press, 1932.

Lawrence, Jerome, and Lee, Robert E. *Inherit the Wind.* N.Y.: Random House, 1955.

Lawrence, John, Sir. *A History of Russia.* New York: New American Library, 1978.

Lawrence, Joseph Stagg. *Wall Street and Washington.* Princeton, N.J.: Princeton University Press, 1929.

Lawrence, Lincoln. *Were We Controlled?* New Hyde Park, N.Y.: University Books, 1967.

Lawrence, T.E. *The Seven Pillars of Wisdom.* London: Cape, 1973.

Lawrenson, Helen. *Stranger at the Party.* New York: Random House, 1974.

The Laws of Manu. trans. Georg Bühler. New York: Dover, 1969.

Lawson, Deodat. *A Brief and True Narrative.* Boston: Benjamin Harris, 1692.

Lawson, John. *History of North Carolina.* London: n.p., 1718.

_____. *A Voyage to Carolina.* Chapel Hill: University of North Carolina Press, 1967.

Lawson, John D. (ed.). *American State Trials.* 17 vols. St. Louis: Thomas, 1914-1937.

Lawson, R. Alan. *The Failure of Independent Liberalism, 1930-1941.* New York: G.P. Putnam's Sons, 1971.

Lawson, W.B. *The Indian Outlaw, or Hank Starr: the Log Cabin Bandit.* Orville, Ohio: Frank T. Fries, n.d.

_____. *Jesse James at Long Branch; or, Playing for a Million.* New York: Street & Smith, 1898.

Lawton, Harry. *Willie Boy, a Desert Manhunt.* Balboa Island, Calif.: Paisano Press, 1960.

Lawton, Lancelot. *The Russian Revolution.* London: Macmillan, 1927.

Layman, Richard. *Shadow Man: The Life of Dashiell Hammett.* New York: Harcourt, Brace, Jovanovich, 1981.

Laymann, Paul. *Theologia Moralis.* Antwerp, Belg.: Johannem Meursium, 1634.

Layne, J. Gregg. *Annals of Los Angeles, From the Arrival of the First White Man to the Civil War, 1769-1861.* San Francisco: California Historical Society, 1935.

Layres, Augustus. *Both Sides of the Chinese Question.* San Francisco: A.F. Woodbridge, 1877.

_____. *The Other Side of the Chinese Question.* San Francisco: n.p., 1876.

Lazanga, G.B. *Ponte Rotto.* Genoa, Italy: Edizioni del Partigiano, 1946.

Lazarovitch-Hrbelianovitch, Prince and Princess. *The Serbian People.* New York: Charles Scribner's Sons, 1910.

Lazerson, M. *Origins of the Public School.* Cambridge, Mass.: Harvard University Press, 1971.

Lea, Henry Charles. *History of the Inquisition in Spain.* New York: Macmillan, 1906.

_____. *History of the Inquisition of the Middle Ages.* New York: Harper & Brothers, 1887.

_____. *History of Sacerdotal Celibacy in the Christian Church.* Secaucus, N.J.: University Books, 1966.

_____. *Materials Toward a History of Witchcraft.* Philadelphia: University of Pennsylvania Press, 1939.

_____. *Minor Historical Writings.* Philadelphia: University of Pennsylvania Press, 1942.

_____. *Studies in Church History.* London: S. Low & Son, & Marston, 1869.

_____. *Superstitions and Force.* Philadelphia: Published by Author, 1866.

Leach, A.J. *A History of Antelope County, Nebraska.* Chicago: Lakeside Press, 1909.

Leach, Charles E. *On Top of the Underworld.* London: Sampson, Low, Marston, 1933.

Leach, Douglas E. *Flintlock and Tomahawk: New England in King Philip's War.* New York: Norton, 1966.

_____. *The Northern Colonial Frontier, 1607-1763.* New York: Holt, Rinehart & Winston, 1966.

Leach, Harold. *The Crime of Century, or the Mystery of Emanuel Baptist Church.* San Francisco: Yosemite, 1895.

Leacock, Eleanor Burke (ed.). *The Culture of Poverty: A Critique.* New York: Simon & Schuster, 1971.

League of Nations. *Prostitutes: Their Early Lives.* The League of Nations Report, 1938.

Leahy, William. *The Catholic Church in New England.* Boston: Hurd and Everts, 1899.

Leahy, William D. *I Was There.* New York: McGraw Hill, 1950.

Leake, Chauncey. *The Amphetamines.* Springfield, Ill.: Charles C. Thomas, 1959.

Leakey, John. *The West that was from Texas to Montana.* Dallas: Southern Methodist University Press, 1958.

Leakey, L.S.B. *Defeating Mau Mau*. London: Methuen, 1954.
____. *Mau Mau and the Kikuyu*. London: Methuen, 1953.
____. *White African*. London: Hodder and Stoughton, 1937.
Leakey, Richard E., and Lewin, Roger. *Origins*. New York: E.P. Dutton, 1977.
Learsi, Rufus. *The Jews in America: A History*. Cleveland: World, 1954.
Leary, John J., Jr. *Talks With T.R.* Boston: Houghton Mifflin, 1920.
Leary, Timothy. *The Politics of Ecstacy*. New York: G.P. Putnam's Sons, 1969.
LeAveux, William. *Things I Know About Kings, Celebrities and Crooks*. London: Everleigh, Nash & Grayson, 1923.
Leavitt, Ruby Rohrlich. *The Puerto Ricans*. Tucson: University of Arizona Press, n.d.
Lebey, André. *Les Trois coups d'état de Louis-Napoléon Bonaparte*. Paris: Perrin, 1906.
LeBlanc, Jerry, and Davis, Ivor. *5 to Die*. Los Angeles: Holloway House, 1970.
LeBon, G. *The Crowd: A Study of the Popular Mind*. London: T. Fisher, Unwin, 1922.
Le Brun, George P. *Call Me If It's Murder*. New York: William Morrow, 1962.
____. *It's Time to Tell*. New York: William Morrow, 1962.
Lecanu, Auguste François. *Histoire du Satan*. Paris: Parent-Des Barres, 1861.
Le Caron, Maj. Henri (Thomas Beach). *Twenty-five Years in the Secret Service: The Recollections of a Spy*. London: William Heinemann, 1892.
Lechartier, G. *Intrigues et Diplomaties à Washington, 1914-1917*. Paris: Plon-Nourrit et Cie, 1919.
Lechford, Thomas. *Note-Book Kept by Thomas Lechford, Esq., Lawyer, in Boston, Massachusetts Bay, from June 27, 1638 to July 1641*. Cambridge, Mass.: J. Wilson & Sons, 1885.
____. *Plain Dealing, or News from New-England*. New York: Garrett Press, 1970.
Leckenby, Charles H. *The Tread of the Pioneers...Some Highlights in the Dramatic and Colorful History of Northwestern Colorado*. Steamboat Springs, Colo.: Pilot Press, 1945.
Leckie, William H. *The Buffalo Soldiers*. Norman: Oklahoma University Press, 1967.
Lecky, W.E.H. *History of European Morals*. New York: D. Appleton, 1917.
____. *History of the Rise and Influence of the Spirit of Rationalism in Europe*. New York: D. Appleton, 1866.
Le Clère, Marcel. *L'Assassinat de Jean Jaurès*. Paris: Mame, 1969.
____. *Histoire de la police*. Paris: Presses Universitaires de France, 1947.
Lecocq, Ad. *Les sorciers de la Beauce*. Chartres, Fr.: Petrot-Garnier, 1861.
Lecomte, Maurice. *Le Prince des Dandys*. Paris: Lemerre, 1928.
Ledda, Alberto. *La Civiltà Fuorilegge. Natura e Storia del Banditismo Sardo*. Milano, Italy: Mursia, 1971.
Ledeen, Michael Arthur. *Universal Fascism*. New York: Howard Fertig, 1972.
Lederer, Emil. *State of the Masses*. New York: Norton, 1940.
Lederer, Ivo J. (ed.). *Russian Foreign Policy: Essays in Historical Perspective*. New Haven, Conn.: Yale University Press, 1962.
____. *Yugoslavia at the Paris Peace Conference: A Study in Frontier-Making*. New Haven, Conn.: Yale University Press, 1963.
Lederer, Laura (ed.). *Take Back the Night: Women on Pornography*. New York: William Morrow, 1980.
Lederer, Wolfgang. *The Fear of Women*. New York: Grune & Stratton, 1968.
Le Duc, L. Leouzon. *Gustave III, Roi de Suede*. Paris: Amyot, 1856.
Le Duc, Thomas. *Piety and Intellect at Amherst College, 1865-1912*. New York: Columbia University Press, 1946.

Lee, Alan J. *The Origins of the Popular Press, 1855-1914*. Totowa, N.J.: Rowman & Littlefield, 1976.
Lee, Alfred McClung. *The Daily Newspaper in America: The Evolution of a Social Instrument*. New York: Macmillan, 1937.
____, and Humphrey, Norman Daymond. *Race Riot*. New York: Dryden, 1943.
Lee, Arthur Gould. *Crown Against Sickle*. New York: Hutchinson, 1950.
____. *Empress Frederick Writes to Sophie, Her Daughter, Crown Princess and later Queen of the Hellenes: Letters 1889-1901*. London: Faber & Faber, 1955.
____. *Helen, Queen Mother of Rumania*. London: Faber & Faber, 1956.
Lee, Changsoo. *Koreans in Japan*. Brekeley: University of California Press, 1981.
Lee, Charles (ed.). *North, East, South, West: A Regional Anthology of American Writing*. New York: Howell Soslin, 1945.
Lee, Clark. *Douglas MacArthur: An Informal Biography*. New York: Henry Holt, 1952.
Lee, Francis Bazley. *New Jersey as a Colony and as a State*. New York: Publishing Society of New Jersey, 1903.
Lee, Henry. *How Dry We Were: Prohibition Revisited*. Englewood Cliffs, N.J.: Prentice-Hall, 1963.
Lee, Henry. *Memoirs of the War in the Southern Department*. New York: University, 1870.
Lee, Ida. *Captain Bligh's Second Voyage to the South Seas*. London: Longmans, Green, 1920.
Lee, James Melvin. *History of American Journalism*. New York: Houghton Mifflin, 1917.
Lee, John A. *Socialism in New Zealand*. London: T. Werner Laurie, 1938.
Lee, John Doyle. *The Lee Trial! An Expose of the Mountain Meadow Massacre*. Salt Lake City, Utah: Tribune Printing, 1875.
____. *The Mormon Menace, being the Confession of John D. Lee, Danite*. New York: Home Protection, 1905.
Lee, Mabel Barbee. *Cripple Creek Days*. New York: Doubleday, 1958.
Lee, Maurice, Jr. *James I and Henry IV*. Urbana: University of Illinois Press, 1970.
Lee, Peter G. *Interpol*. New York: Stein and Day, 1976.
Lee, Raymond. *Those Scandalous Sheets of Hollywood*. Venice, Calif.: Venice, 1972.
Lee, Raymond, and Van Hecke, B. C. *Gangsters and Hoodlums, The Underworld and the Cinema*. New York: Barnes & Noble, 1971.
Lee, Robert E. *Blackbeard the Pirate*. Winston-Salem, Mass.: John F. Blair, 1974.
Lee, Robert E. *The Wartime Papers of Robert E. Lee*. Boston: Little, Brown, 1961.
Lee, Rose Hum. *The Chinese in the United States of America*. Hong Kong: Hong Kong University Press, 1960.
Lee, Samuel D. *San Francisco's Chinatown*. San Francisco: Central District Coordinating Council, 1940.
Lee, Susan E. *These Also Served: Brief Histories of Pioneers*. Las Lunas, N.M.: Published by Author, 1960.
Lee, Sir Sydney. *King Edward VII*. New York: Macmillan, 1925.
Lee, W.L.M. *A History of Police in England*. London: Methuen, 1901.
Leech, Arthur B. *Irish Riflemen in America*. New York: Van Nostrand, 1875.
Leech, Margaret. *In the Days of McKinley*. New York: Harper & Brothers, 1959.
____. *Reveille in Washington 1860-1865*. New York: Harper, 1941.
Leech, Rev. Samuel Vanderlip. *The Raid of John Brown at Harper's Ferry as I Saw It*. Washington: Published by Author, 1909.
Leedy, Carl H. *Golden Days in the Black Hills, by "The Old Tim-*

er". n.p., n.d.

Leek, Sybil and Sugar, Bert R. *The Assassination Chain*. New York: Corwin Books, 1976.

_____. *Phrenology*. New York: Macmillan, 1970.

Leenhouts, Keith J. *A Father...A Son...And A Three Mile Run*. New York: Zondervan, 1975.

Lees-Milne, James. *Harold Nicolson, A Biography, vol. 2, 1930-1968*. New York: Archon Books, 1981.

Leeson, Benjamin. *Lost London: The Memoirs of an East End Detective*. London: S. Paul, 1934.

Leeson, Francis. *Kama Shilpa*. Bombay, India: D.B. Taraporevala Sons, 1962.

Leeson, Michael A. *History of Montana*. Chicago: Warner, Beers, 1885.

LeFave, Wayne. *Arrest: The Decision to Take a Suspect Into Custody*. Boston: Little, Brown, 1965.

Lefébure, Constant. *Souvenirs d'un ancien directeur des prisons de Paris*. Paris: H. Louvet, 1894.

Lefebure, Molly. *Evidence for the Crown*. London: Heinemann, 1955.

_____. *Murder with a Difference*. London: Heinemann, 1958.

Lefevre, Edwin. *Reminiscences of a Stock Operator*. Garden City, N.Y.: Doubleday, Doran, 1931.

_____. *Stock Market Manipulator*. New York: Traders Press, 1967.

Lefevre, Ernest W. *Uncertain Mandate*. Baltimore: Johns Hopkins Press, 1967.

Lefkowitz, B. *The Victims*. New York: G.P. Putnam's Sons, 1969.

Lefkowitz, Monroe M., et al. *Growing Up to be Violent: A Longitudinal Study of the Development of Aggression*. New York: Pergamon Press, 1977.

Lefler, Hugh T. *North Carolina History Told by Contemporaries*. Chapel Hill: University of North Carolina Press, 1934.

LeFors, Joe. *Wyoming Peace Officer*. Laramie, Wyo.: Laramie Printing, 1953.

Lefkowitz, Bernard, and Gross, Kenneth G. *The Victims*. New York: G.P. Putnam's Sons, 1969.

Leftkowitz, N.M., et al. *Growing Up to Be Violent*. New York: Pergamon, 1977.

Leftwich, Bill. *Tracks Along the Pecos*. Pecos, Texas: Pecos Press, 1957.

Legends and Traditionary Stories. London: E. Lumley, 1843.

Legué, Gabriel. *Médecins et empoisonneurs au xvii siécle*. Paris: Bibliothéque-Charpentier, 1895.

_____, and de la Tourette, Gilles. *Soeur Jeanne des Anges*. Paris: Bureaux du Progrès Médical, 1886.

_____. *Urbain Grandier et les possédées de Loudun*. Paris: Charpentier, 1884.

LeHardy, William (ed.). *County of Middlesex: Calendar to the Sessions Records*. London: Sir E. Hart, 1935.

Lehman, R.C. (ed.) *Charles Dickens as Editor. Being Letters Written by Him to William Henry, His Sub-editor*. London: Smith, Elder, 1912.

Lehmann, Alfred G.L. *Aberglaube und Zauberei*. Stuttgart, Ger.: F. Enke, 1925.

Lehovich, Dimitry V. *White Against Red*. New York: W.W. Norton, 1974.

Lehrman, Hal. *Israel, the Beginning and Tomorrow*. New York: William Sloane, 1952.

Leib, Johann. *Consilia*. Frankfort, Ger.: H. à Sande, 1666.

Leigh, I. *In the Shadow of the Mau Mau*. London: W.H. Allen, 1955.

Leigh, Norman. *Thirteen Against the Bank*. London: Weidenfeld & Nicolson, 1976.

Leighton, George R. *Five Cities. The Story of Their Youth and Old Age*. New York: Harper, 1939.

Leighton, Isabel (ed.). *The Aspirin Age, 1919-1941*. New York: Simon and Schuster, 1949.

Leinwand, Gerald (ed.). *Civil Rights and Civil Liberties*. New

York: Washington Square Press, 1968.

Leiss, William. *The Domination of Nature*. Boston: Beacon Press, 1974.

Leitch, David. *The Discriminating Thief*. New York: Holt, Rinehart & Winston, 1968.

Leitenberg, H. (ed.). *Handbook of Behavior Modification and Behavior Therapy*. Englewood Cliffs, N.J.: Prentice-Hall, 1976.

Leiter, Kenneth. *Telling It Like It Is: A Study of Teachers' Accounts*. Santa Barbara: University of California Press, 1971.

Leiter, Robert D. *The Teamsters Union*. New York: Bookman Associates, 1957.

Leites, Nathan. *Operational Code of the Politburo*. New York: McGraw-Hill, 1951.

_____. *Study of Bolshevism*. Glencoe, Ill.: Free Press, 1953.

Leith, Rod. *The Prostitute Murders*. New York: Pinnacle, 1983.

Leitschuh, Friederich. *Beiträge zur Geschichte des Hexenwesens in Franken*. Bamberg, Ger.: C. Hübscher, 1883.

Lekachman, Robert. *The Age of Keynes*. New York: Random House, 1966.

_____. *Greed Is Not Enough*. New York: Pantheon Books, 1982.

Leland, Charles Godfrey. *Arcadia or the Gospel of the Witches*. London: D. Nutt, 1899.

Le Loyer, Pierre. *Discours et histories des spectres*. Paris: N. Bvon, 1605.

Lely, Gilbert. *The Marquis de Sade: A Biography*. New York: Grove Press, 1961.

Lemarchand, M.G. *Procès du prince Pierre-Napoléon Bonaparte devant la Haute Cour de Justice*. Tours, Fr.: Mazereau, 1870.

LeMasters, E.E. *Blue Collar Aristocrat*. Madison: University of Wisconsin Press, 1975.

Lemert, Edwin M. *Human Deviance, Social Problems, and Social Control*. Englewood Cliffs, N.J.: Prentice-Hall, 1967.

_____. *Social Action and Legal Change: Revolution with the Juvenile Court*. Chicago: Aldine Press, 1970.

_____. *Social Pathology*. New York: McGraw-Hill, 1951.

Lemire, Charles. *L'Episode de Barbe-Bleue au Théâtre*. Paris: Trebse et Stock, 1898.

_____. *Un Maréchal et un Connétable de France*. Paris: E. Leroux, 1886.

Lemke, William. *The Crime Against Mexico*. Minneapolis, Minn.: Great-West Printing, 1915.

Lemkin, Raphael. *Axis Rule in Occupied Europe*. Washington, D.C.: Carnegie Endowment for International Peace, 1944.

Lemley, Vernon. *The Old West, 1849-1929*. Osborne, Kan.: n.p., 1929.

Lemon, John J. *The Northfield Tragedy; or, the Robber's Raid*. St. Paul, Minn.: Published by Author, 1876.

Lempens, Carl. *Geschichte der Hexen und Hexenprozesse*. Jena, Ger.: H.W. Schmidt, 1904.

Lenczowski, George. *The Middle East in World Affairs*. Ithaca, N.Y.: Cornell University Press, 1962.

Lend, Evelyn. *The Underground Struggle in Germany*. New York: League for Industrial Democracy, 1938.

LeNeve, Ethel. *Ethel LeNeve: Her Life Story*. Manchester, Eng.: Daisy Bank Printing, 1910.

Lengyel, Emil. *Siberia*. New York: Random House, 1943.

Lenin, Nikolai. *Marx, Engels, Marxism*. Moscow: Foreign Languages Publishing House, 1947.

Lenin, V.I. *Collected Works*. trans. Bernard Isaacs and Isidor Laker. Moscow: Progress, 1962.

_____. *Pisma k rodnim*. Moscow: Gosizdat, 1930.

Lening, Gustav. *The Dark Side of New York Life*. New York: F. Gerhard, 1873.

Lennon, Florence Brecher. *The Life of Lewis Carroll*. New York: Dover, 1972.

Lenotre, G. *The Guillotine and Its Servants*. trans. Mrs. Rudolph Stawell. London: Hutchinson, 1929.

Lens, Sydney. *The Labor Wars*. Garden City, N.Y.: Doubleday, 1974.

_____. *Poverty Yesterday and Today*. New York: Thomas Y. Crowell, 1973.

_____. *Radicalism in America*. New York: Thomas Y. Crowell, 1966.

Lensen, George A. *The Damned Inheritance*. Tallahassee, Fla.: The Diplomatic Press, 1974.

_____. *Report From Hokkaido*. Hakodate: Municipal Library, 1954.

_____. *The Russian Push Toward Japan: Russo-Japanese Relations, 1697-1875*. Princeton, N.J.: Princeton University Press, 1959.

_____. *Russia's Eastward Expansion*. Englewood Cliffs, N.J.: Prentice-Hall, 1964.

_____. *Russia's Japan Expedition of 1852 to 1855*. Gainesville: University of Florida Press, 1955.

_____. *The Strange Neutrality*. Tallahassee, Fla.: The Diplomatic Press, 1972.

Lenton, H.T. *German Warships of the Second World War*. London: Arco, 1969.

Lenz, Robert. *Explosives and Bomb Disposal Guide*. Springfield: C.C. Thomas, 1976.

Leo, Africanus. *History and Description of Africa*. trans. Pory. London: Hakluyt Society, 1896.

Leo, C. *Land and Class in Kenya*. Toronto, Ontario, Can.: University of Toronto Press, 1984.

Leonard, Charles C. *The History of Pithole*. Pithole City, Pa.: Morton Longwell, 1867.

Leonard, Delavan L. *The Story of Oberlin*. Boston: Pilgrim Press, 1898.

Leonard, Elizabeth Jane, and Goodman, Julia Cody. *Buffalo Bill: King of the Old West*. New York: Library, 1955.

Leonard, George. *The Silent Pulse*. New York: Bantam, 1981.

Leonard, John C., et al. *History of Davies and Gentry Counties, Missouri*. Topeka, Kan.: Historical, 1922.

Leonard, Jonathan N. *Three Years Down*. New York: Carrick and Evans, 1939.

Leonard, Larry. *The United Nations and Palestine*. New York: Carnegie Endowment for International Peace, 1949.

Leonard, Royal. *I Flew for China: Chiang Kai-shek's Personal Pilot*. New York: Doubleday, 1942.

Leonard, V.A. *The Police, the Judiciary and the Criminal*. Springfield: Charles C. Thomas, 1969.

Leonard, V.A. *Police Organization and Management*. New York: Foundation Press, 1951.

Leonard, Wolfgang. *The Kremlin Since Stalin*. New York: Praeger, 1962.

Leonardi, Dante Ugo. *Luglio 1943 in Sicilia*. Modena, Italy: Soc Tip Modenese, 1947.

Leonardi, Dell. *The Reincarnation of John Wilkes Booth: A Study in Hypnotic Regression*. Old Greenwich, Conn.: Devin-Adair, 1975.

Leone, Mario, and Pasetti, John. *Inchiesta sulla morte di Mussolini*. Rome: Aletti, 1962.

Leong, Gor Yum. *Chinatown Inside Out*. New York: B. Mussey, 1936.

Leon-Portilla, Miguel (ed.). *The Broken Spears: The Aztec Account of the Conquest of Mexico*. Boston: Beacon Press, 1962.

Leopold, Nathan F. *Life Plus 99 Years*. Garden City, N.Y.: Doubleday, 1958.

Leopold, Richard W. *The Growth of American Foreign Policy*. New York: Alfred A. Knopf, 1962.

Leovell, John. *Memoirs of John Yates Beall*. Montreal, Quebec, Can.: Published by Author, 1865.

Lepper, J.H. *Famous Secret Societies*. London: Low, Marston, 1932.

Le Queux, William. *Things I Know about Kings, Celebrities and Crooks*. London: Everleigh, Nash & Grayson, 1923.

Lerman, Paul. *Community Treatment and Social Control*. Chicago: University of Chicago Press, 1975.

Lermolo, Elizabeth. *Face of a Victim*. New York: Harper & Brothers, 1955.

Lermontov, Mikhail. *A Hero of our Time*. trans. Vladimir Nabokov. New York: Doubleday Anchor Books, 1958.

Lerner, Max. *America as a Civilization*. New York: Simon & Schuster, 1957.

_____. *Ideas Are Weapons*. New York: The Viking Press, 1939.

_____. *Ideas for the Ice Age*. New York: The Viking Press, 1941.

_____. *It Is Later Than You Think*. New York: The Viking Press, 1938.

_____. (ed.). *The Mind and Faith of Justice Holmes*. Boston: Little, Brown, 1943.

_____. *The Unfinished Country*. New York: Simon & Schuster, 1959.

Le Roux, Louis N. *Patrick H. Pearse*. Dublin, Ire.: Talbot, 1932.

LeRoy, Dave. *Gerald Ford: Untold Story*. Arlington, Va.: R.W. Beatty, 1974.

Leroy-Beaulieu, Anatole. *The Empire of the Tsars*. trans. Z. Ragozin. New York: Putnam, 1898.

Lesberg, Sandy. *Assassination in Our Times*. London: Peebles Press, 1976.

Lescadieu, A., and Laurant, A. *Histoire de Nantes*. Paris: A. Pougin, 1836.

Le Shan, Edna. *The Roots of Crime*. New York: Four Winds Press, 1981.

Le Shan, Lawrence. *The Medium, the Mystic and the Physicist*. New York: Viking, 1974.

Leslie, Anita. *Mrs. Fitzherbert*. New York: Charles Scribner's Sons, 1960.

_____. *The Remarkable Mr. Jerome*. New York: M. Holt, 1954.

Leslie, R.F. *Reform and Insurrection in Russian Poland, 1856-1865*. London: University of London Press, 1963.

Leslie, Robert C. (ed.). *The Journal of Captain Woodes Rogers 1708-11*. London: Chapman and Hall, 1894.

Leslie, Shane. *The Irish Tangle*. London: MacDonald, 1946.

_____. *Sir Evelyn Ruggles-Brise*. London: John Murray, 1938.

Leslie, Warren. *Dallas Public and Private: Aspects of an American City*. New York: Grossman, 1964.

Lessa, William, and Vogt, Evon (eds.). *Reader in Comparative Religion*. New York: Harper & Row, 1965.

Lesson, Michael A. *History of Montana, 1739-1885*. Chicago: Warner, Beer, 1885.

Lessona, Alessandro. *Memoire*. Florence, Italy: Sansoni, 1958.

_____. *Verso l'Impero*. Florence, Italy: Sansoni, 1939.

Lessor, G. (ed.). *Psychology and Educational Practice*. London: Foresman, 1970.

Lester, David, and Lester, Gene. *Crime of Passion*. Chicago: Nelson-Hall, 1975.

Lester, John C., and Wilson, D.C. *Ku Klux Klan: It's Origin, Growth and Disbandment*. New York: Neale, 1905.

Lester, Muriel. *Entertaining Gandhi*. London: Ivor Nicholson & Watson, 1932.

Le Strange, G. *Baghdad during the Abbasid Caliphate*. Oxford, Eng.: Clarendon, 1900.

Le Sueur, Meridel. *North Star County*. New York: Duell, Sloan, & Pearce, 1945.

Lesure, Thomas B. *Adventures in Arizona*. San Antonio, Texas: Naylor, 1956.

Letere edite ed inedite de Felice Orsini. Milan: Francesco Sanvito, 1962.

Lethbridge, Alice. *Halfway to Yesterday*. n.p., 1974.

_____. *Well Do I Remember*. Flint, Mich.: Berwyn-London, 1976.

Lethbridge, Thomas Charles. *Witches: Investigating an Ancient Religion*. London: Routledge & Kegan Paul, 1962.

Letkemann, Peter. *Crime as Work*. Englewoods, N.J.: Prentice-Hall, 1973.

Leto, Guido. *OVRA, Fascismo e antifascismo*. Bologna, Italy: Cappelli, 1951.

_____. *Polizia segreta in Italia*. Rome: Vito Bianco, 1961.

A Letter from Richard P. Robinson, as Connected with the Murder of Ellen Jewett. New York: n.p., 1837.

Leuchtenburg, William E. *Franklin D. Roosevelt and the New Deal.* New York: Harper & Row, 1963.

_____. *The Perils of Prosperity 1914-1932.* Chicago: University of Chicago Press, 1958.

Leuret, François. *Fragments Psychologiques sur la Folie.* Paris: Crochard, 1834.

Levant, Oscar. *A Smattering of Ignorance.* New York: Doubleday, Doran, 1940.

Levasseur, A. *Lafayette in America.* trans. J.D. Godman, Philadelphia: Carey & Lea, 1829.

Levenstein, Aaron. *The Atomic Age: Suicide, Slavery of Social Planning.* New York: League for Industrial Democracy, 1946.

Lever, Harry, and Young, Joseph. *Wartime Racketeers.* New York: G.P. Putnam's Sons, 1945.

Leverkuehn, Paul. *German Military Intelligence.* trans. R.H. Stevens and C. Fitzgibbon. New York: Praeger, 1954.

Levi, Eliphas. *The History of Magic.* London: Rider, 1913.

Levin, Alfred. *The Second Duma.* New Haven, Conn.: Yale University Press, 1940.

Levin, David. *What Happened in Salem?* New York: Harcourt, Brace, 1956.

Levin, Harry. *Jerusalem Embattled.* London: Gallancz, 1950.

Levin, Jack, and Fox, James Alan. *Mass Murder.* New York: Plenum, 1985.

Levin, Meyer. *Compulsion.* New York: Simon & Schuster, 1956.

_____. *The Obsession.* New York: Simon & Schuster, 1973.

Levin, Murray. *Political Hysteria in America: The Democratic Capacity for Repression.* New York: Basic Books, 1971.

Levin, Nora. *The Holocaust, The Destruction of European Jewry, 1933-1945.* New York: Thomas Y. Crowell, 1968.

Levine, Alan, and Carey, Eve. *The Rights of Students.* New York: Discus, Avon Books, 1977.

Levine, Edward M. *The Irish and Irish Politicians.* Notre Dame, Ind.: University of Notre Dame Press, 1966.

Levine, Gary. *Anatomy of a Gangster.* New York: Barnes, 1979.

Levine, Irving R. *Main Street U.S.S.R.* New York: Doubleday, 1959.

Levine, Issac Don. *Eyewitness to History.* New York: Hawthorn, 1973.

_____. *The Man Lenin.* New York: Thomas Seltzer, 1924.

_____. *The Mind of an Assassin.* New York: New American Library, 1960.

Levine, Lawrence W. *Defender of the Faith.* New York: Oxford University Press, 1965.

Levine, Richard M. *Bad Blood.* New York: New American Library, 1982.

Levine, Stephen (ed.). *Death Row.* San Francisco: Glide, 1972.

Levinson, Horace C. *The Science of Chance.* London: Faber, 1952.

Levitan, Sar A., Magnum, G.L., and Marshall, R. *Human Resources and Labor Markets.* New York: Harper & Row, 1976.

_____, Johnston, William B., and Taggart, Robert. *Still A Dream.* Cambridge, Mass.: Harvard University Press, 1974.

Levitsky, Serge L. *The Russian Duma: Studies in Parliamentary Procedure, 1906-1917.* New York: Fordham, 1958.

Levitt, Morton and Michael. *A Tissue of Lies: Nixon vs. Hiss.* New York: McGraw-Hill, 1979.

Levy, Frank, Meltsner, Arnold, and Wildavsky, Aaron. *Urban Outcomes.* Berkeley: University of California Press, 1974.

Levy, Harriet Lane. *920 O'Farrell Street.* New York: Doubleday, 1947.

Levy, J.E., and Kunitz, S.J. *Indian Drinking.* New York: Wiley, 1974.

Levy, J.H. *The Necessity for Criminal Appeal as Illustrated by the Maybrick Case.* London: King, 1899.

Levy, Jo Ann L. *Behind the Western Skyline.* Los Angeles: Coldwell Banker, 1981.

Levy, Leonard, and Nelson, Harold. *Freedom of the Press. Vol.* 1, *From Zenger to Jefferson; Vol. 2, From Hamilton to the Warren Court.* New York: Bobbs-Merrill, 1966.

_____. *Jefferson and Civil Liberties: The Darker Side.* New York: Quadrangle Books, 1973.

Levy, Marion J. *The Family Revolution in Modern China.* Cambridge, Mass.: Harvard University Press, 1949.

Levy, Newman. *My Double Life.* Garden City, N.Y.: Doubleday, 1958.

_____. *The Nan Patterson Case.* New York: Simon & Schuster, 1959.

Levy, Reuben. *The Social Structure of Islam.* Cambridge, Eng.: Cambridge University Press, 1957.

Lewin, Henry Grote. *The Railway Mania and Its Aftermath, 1845-1852.* New York: Augustus M. Kelley, 1968.

Lewin, K. *Field Theory in the Social Sciences.* New York: Harper & Row, 1951.

Lewin, Louis. *Phantastica, Narcotic and Stimulating Drugs.* New York: Dutton, 1964.

Lewin, Malcolm. *The Government of the East India Company and Its Monopolies.* London: James Ridgway, 1857.

Lewinsohn, Richard. *A History of Sexual Customs.* New York: Harper & Bros., 1959.

_____. *The Mystery Man of Europe: Sir Basil Zaharoff.* Philadelphia: J.B. Lippincott, 1929.

Lewinson, Edwin A. *John Purroy Mitchell: The Boy Mayor of New York.* New York: Astra Books, 1965.

Lewis, Alfred Allan, with Mac Donell, Herbert Leon. *The Evidence Never Lies.* New York: Holt, Rinehart and Winston, 1984.

Lewis, Alfred Henry. *The Apaches of New York.* New York: G.W. Dillingham, 1912.

_____. *The Boss: And How He Came to Rule New York.* New York: A. S. Barnes, 1903.

_____. *Confessions of a Detective.* New York: A.S. Barnes, 1906.

_____. *Nation-Famous New York Murders.* New York: G.W. Dillingham, 1914.

_____. *Richard Croker.* New York: Life, 1901.

_____. *The Sunset Trail.* New York: A.S. Barnes, 1905.

Lewis, Alonzo. *The History of Lynn.* Boston: J.H. Eastburn, 1829.

_____, and Newhall, J.R. *History of Lynn, Including Lynnfield, Saugus, Swampscott, and Nahant.* Boston: Shorey, 1865.

Lewis, Anthony. *Gideon's Trumpet.* New York: Random House, 1964.

_____. *Portrait of a Decade.* New York: Random House, 1964.

Lewis, Bernard. *The Arabs in History.* London: Hutchinson, 1956.

_____. *The Assassins.* New York: Oxford University Press, 1967.

_____. *The Emergence of Modern Turkey.* London: Oxford University Press, 1961.

_____. *The Origins of Ismailism.* Cambridge, Eng.: W. Heffner & Sons, 1940.

Lewis, C.S. *Allegory of Love.* Oxford, Eng.: Galaxy Books, 1958.

Lewis, Charles E. *Two Lectures on a Short Visit to America.* London: Blades, East, and Blades, 1876.

Lewis, Charles Lee. *The Romantic Decatur.* Philadelphia: University of Pennsylvania Press, 1937.

Lewis, David, and Scott, Frank. *Make This Your Canada.* Toronto, Ontario, Can.: Central Canada, 1943.

Lewis, Commander David D. *The Fight for the Sea: The Past, Present and Future of Submarine Warfare in the Atlantic.* New York: First Collier, 1961.

Lewis, David L. *Prisoners of Honor: The Dreyfuss Affair.* New York: Morrow, 1973.

_____. *The Public Image of Henry Ford.* Detroit, Mich.: Wayne State University Press, 1976.

_____. *When Harlem Was in Vogue.* New York: Alfred A. Knopf, 1981.

Lewis, Dioclesian. *The New Gymnastics for Men, Women and Children.* New York: Clarke Bros., 1867.

_____. *Our Girls.* New York: Harper, 1871.

_____. *Prohibition, a Failure.* Boston: James R. Osgood, 1875.

Lewis, Dominic B. Wyndham. *François Villon.* New York: Literary Guild, 1928.

_____. *The Soul of Marshal Gilles de Raiz.* London: Eyre & Spottiswoode, 1952.

Lewis, Eugene. *Public Entrepreneurship: Toward a Theory of Bureaucratic Political Power.* Bloomington: Indiana University Press, 1984.

Lewis, Felice Flannery. *Literature, Obscenity and Law.* Carbondale: Southern Illinois University Press, 1976.

Lewis, Flannery. *Suns Go Down.* New York: Macmillan, 1937.

Lewis, Flora. *Red Pawn: The Story of Noel Field.* Garden City, N.J.: Doubleday, 1965.

Lewis, Gifford. *Somerville and Ross.* New York: Viking, 1985.

Lewis, James. *The Consumer's Fight-Back Book.* New York: Award Books, 1972.

Lewis, Jerry D. *Crusade Against Crime.* New York: Bernard Geis Associates, 1962.

Lewis John B., and Bombaugh, Charles C. *The Goss-Undderzook Tragedy.* Baltimore: James H. McClellan, 1896.

Lewis, John L., et al. *Heywood Broun As He Seemed to Us.* New York: Random House, 1940.

Lewis, John Wilson. *Leadership in Communist China.* Ithaca, N.Y.: Cornell University Press, 1963.

_____. *Major Doctrines of Communist China.* New York: Norton, 1964.

Lewis, John Woodruff. *The True Life of Billy the Kid.* New York: Frank Tousey, 1881.

Lewis, Leonard. *Trunk Crimes Past and Present.* London: Hutchinson, 1934.

Lewis, Lloyd, and Smith, Henry Justin. *Chicago: The History of Its Reputation.* New York: Harcourt, Brace, 1929.

_____, and Pargellis, S.M. *Granger County.* Boston: Little, Brown, 1949.

_____. *It Takes All Kinds.* New York: Harcourt, Brace, 1947.

_____. *Myths After Lincoln.* New York: Harcourt, Brace, 1929.

_____, and Smith, Henry Justin. *Oscar Wilde Discovers America.* New York: Harcourt, Brace, 1936.

Lewis, Meriwether, and Clark, William. *The Journals of Lewis and Clark.* Boston: Houghton Mifflin, 1953.

_____. *The Letters of the Lewis and Clark Expedition.* Urbana: University of Illinois Press, 1962.

Lewis, Mildred and Milton. *Famous Modern Newspaper Writers.* New York: Dodd, Mead, 1962.

Lewis, Nolen D. C., and Yarnell, Helen. *Pathological Firesetting.* New York: Coolidge Foundation, 1951.

Lewis, Norman. *The Honored Society.* New York: G.P. Putnam's Sons, 1964.

Lewis, Orlando F. *The Development of American Prisons and Prison Customs, 1776-1845.* Montclair, N.J.: Patterson Smith, 1967.

Lewis, Oscar. *Bay Window Bohemia.* New York: Doubleday, 1956.

_____. *The Big Four.* New York: Alfred A. Knopf, 1938.

_____, and Hall, Carroll D. *Bonanza Inn.* New York: Alfred A. Knopf, 1959.

_____. *The Children of Sanchez.* New York: Random House, 1961.

_____. *Five Families.* New York: Basic Books, 1959.

_____. *High Sierra Country.* New York: Duell, Sloan & Pearce, 1955.

_____. *La Vida: A Puerto Rican Family in the Culture of Poverty-San Juan and New York.* New York: Random House, 1966.

_____. *Silver Kings.* New York: Alfred A. Knopf, 1947.

_____. *This Was San Francisco.* New York: David McKay, 1962.

Lewis, R.W.B. *Edith Wharton: A Biography.* New York: Harper & Row, 1975.

Lewis, Richard Warren, and Schiller, Lawrence. *The Scavengers and Critics of the Warren Report.* New York: Delacorte Press, 1967.

Lewis, Sasha G. *American Exploitation of Illegal Aliens.* Boston: Beacon Press, 1979.

Lewis, Tracy Hammond. *Along the Rio Grande.* New York: Lewis, 1916.

Lewis, W. David. *From Newgate to Dannemora: The Rise of the Penitentiary in New York, 1796-1848.* Ithaca, N.Y.: Cornell University Press, 1965.

Lewis, W.H. *The Splendid Century.* New York: Sloane, 1953.

Lewis, Willie Newberry. *Between Sun and Sod.* Clarendon, Texas: Clarendon Press, 1938.

Lewisham, Richard. *The Man Behind the Scenes.* London: Gollancz, 1929.

Lewiston, Robert R. *Hit From Both Sides.* London: Abelard-Schuman, 1967.

Lexow Investigation. *Report and Proceedings of the Senate Committee Appointed to Investigate the Police Department of the City of New York.* 5 vols. Albany, N.Y.: J.B. Lyon, 1895.

Ley, Willy. *For Your Information on Earth and in the Sky.* Garden City, N.Y.: Doubleday, 1967.

Leys, N.M. *A Last Chance in Kenya.* London: Hogarth, 1931.

Libby, Charles Thornton (ed.). *Province and Court Records of Maine.* Portland: Maine Historical Society, 1928.

Liberati, M. *La Repubblica di Salò.* Rome: Nuova, 1952.

Liberman, Simon. *Building Lenin's Russia.* Chicago: Chicago University Press, 1945.

Library of Congress. *Capital Punishment: Pro and Con Arguments.* Washington, D.C.: Legislative Reference Service, 1966.

Li, Choh-ming. *Economic Development of Communist China: An Appraisal of the First Five Years of Industrialization.* Berkeley, Calif.: University of California Press, 1959.

Liceaga, Luis. *Félix Diaz.* Mexico City: Editorial Jus, 1958.

Li Chih-Ch'ang. *The Travels of an Alchemist.* trans. Arthur Waley. London: George Routledge & Sons, 1931.

Licht, Hans. *Sexual Life of Ancient Greece.* London: The Abbey Library, 1971.

Lickona, R. (ed.). *Moral Development and Behavior.* New York: Holt, Rinehart & Winston, 1976.

Liddell Hart, Sir Basil (ed.). *The Red Army.* London: Weidenfeld & Nicolson, 1956.

Liddell, R. *Byzantium and Istanbul.* New York: Macmillan, 1956.

Lie, Trygve. *In the Cause of Peace.* New York: Macmillan, 1954.

Lieb, Fred. *Baseball As I Have Known It.* New York: Coward, McCann & Geoghegan, 1977.

_____. *The Story of the World Series.* New York: G.P. Putnam's Sons, 1949.

Lieberman, Jethro. *How the Government Breaks the Law.* Baltimore: Penguin, 1973.

Lieberson, Goddard (ed.). *The Columbia Records Legacy Collection.* n.p., n.d.

Lieberstein, Stanley. *Who Owns What Is In Your Head? Trade Secrets and the Mobile Employee.* New York: Hawthorne, 1979.

Liebling, Abbott J. *Chicago: Second City.* New York: Alfred A. Knopf, 1952.

_____. *The Press.* New York: Ballantine, 1964.

Liebow, Elliot. *Tally's Corner: A Study of Negro Streetcorner Men.* Boston: Little Brown, 1967.

Lieck, Albert (ed.). *Notable British Trials: Trial of Benjamin Knowles.* London: William Hodge, 1933.

Lief, Alfred. *Democracy's Norris.* New York: Stackpole Sons, 1939.

_____. *The Social and Economic Views of Mr. Justice Brandeis.* New York: Vanguard Press, 1930.

Lietzmann, Hans. *A History of the Early Church.* New York: Meridian Books, 1961.

Life, Adventures and Confessions of Albert Teufel. Doylestown, Pa.: W.W.H. Davis, 1867.

Life and Adventures of Henry Thomas. Philadelphia: T.B. Peterson, 1848.

Life and Adventures of Manuel Fernandez. New York: New York Sun, 1835.

Life and Awful Confessions of Reuben Dunbar. Albany, N.Y.: n.p., n.d.

Life and Career of the Most Skillful and Noted Criminal of His Day, Charles Mortimer. Sacramento, Calif.: Record Steambook, 1873.

Life and Confession of Arnold. Albany, N.Y.: G. Hooker, n.d.

Life and Confession of Cato. Johnstown, N.Y.: Abraham Romyen, 1803.

The Life and Confession of Daniel Shaeffer. Lancaster, Pa.: Peter Reed, Jr., & A.F. Osterloh, 1832.

Life and Confession of George Acker: The Murderer of Isaac Gordon. New York: Baker & Godwin, 1860.

The Life and Confession of George B. Jarman. New Brunswick, N.J.: Jacob Edmonds, William Packer & Aaron Slack, n.d.

Life and Confession of Henry Wyatt. Auburn, N.Y.: J.C. Merrell, 1846.

The Life and Confession of Isaac Heller. Liberty, Iowa: C.V. Duggins, 1836.

The Life and Confession of John D. Lee, the Mormon, with a Full Account of the Mountain Meadow Massacre and the Execution of Lee: Helpless Women and Children Butchered in Cold Blood by Merciless Mormon Assassins. Philadelphia: Barclay, 1877.

The Life and Confession of John E. Lovering. McAlisterville, Pa.: n.p., n.d.

Life and Confession of John Johnson: The Murderer of James Murray. New York: Brown & Tyrell, 1824.

The Life and Confession of Joseph Drew. Northampton, Mass.: n.p., 1808.

Life and Confession of Miner Babcock. New London, Conn.: Samuel Green, 1816.

Life and Confession of Moses W. Keen. Maysville, K.Y.: n.p., 1842.

Life and Confession of Stephen Lee Richards. Lincoln, Neb.: State Journal, 1879.

Life and Dying Confession of James Hamilton. Albany, N.Y.: Printing Office, 1818.

Life and Dying Confession of John Van Alstine. Cooperstown, N.Y.: H. & E. Phinney, 1819.

The Life and Confessions of Charles E. Jones. Montpelier, Vt.: Ballou, Loveland, 1860.

Life and Confessions of Henry G. Green. Troy, N.Y.: n.p., 1845.

The Life and Confessions of Martha Grinder. Pittsburgh, Pa.: John P. Hunt, 1866.

The Life and Confessions of Mrs. Henrietta Robinson, the Veiled Murderess. Boston: Dr. H.B. Skinner, 1855.

The Life and Conversations of Richard P. Robinson, the Supposed Murderer of Ellen Jewett. New Haven, Conn.: n.p., 1840.

The Life and Death of Mrs. Maria Bickford, a Beautiful Female Who was Inhumanly Murdered in the Moral and Religious City of Boston. Boston: n.p., 1845.

Life and Dying Confession of James Hamilton. Albany, N.Y.: Printing Office, 1818.

Life and Dying Confession of John Van Alstine. Cooperstown, N.Y.: H. & E. Phinney, 1819.

Life and Execution of Jack Kehoe, King of the "Mollie Maguires." Philadelphia: Barclay, 1881.

Life and History Together with the Details of the Trial of Bill Fox. Sedalia, Mo.: J. West Goodwin, 1884.

Life and Trial for Murder of Wilson Howard. Lebanon, Mo.: F.A. Erwin, 1893.

The Life and Trial of John Hughes for the Murder of Miss Tamzen Parsons. Cleveland: John K. Stetler, 1866.

Life and Trial of Perry Bowsher. Chillicothe, Ohio: Edward Kauffman, 1878.

Life and Writings of Adolphus F. Monroe. Cincinnati, Ohio: N.B. Aulick, 1857.

The Life, Character and Career of Edward W. Green, Postmaster of Malden. Boston: Benjamin F. Russell, 1864.

The Life, Confession, and Atrocious Crimes of Antoine Probst. Philadelphia: Barclay, 1866.

Life, Confession and Execution of Bishop John D. Lee, the Mormon Fiend. Philadelphia: Old Franklin, 1877.

Life, Confession, and Letters of Courtship of Rev. Jacob S. Harden. Hackettstown, N.J.: E. Winton, 1860.

Life, Crimes and Confession of Mrs. Julia Fortmeyer. Philadelphia: Barclay, 1875.

Life, Crimes and Confessions of Bridget Durgan. Philadelphia: C.W. Alexander, 1867.

Life, Flight, Capture, Trial and Execution of Edward Alonzo Pennington. Cincinnati: E. Shepard, 1846.

Life, Letters and Last Conversation of John Caldwell Colt, Who Committed Suicide in the New York City Prison. New York: Sun, 1841.

The Life of Andrew Hellman, Alias Adam Horn. Philadelphia: John P. Perry, 1844.

Life of Augustus von Kotzebue. London: Boosey & Sons, 1820.

Life of the Chicago Banker, George W. Green. Chicago: Mellen, 1855.

Life of Elizabeth Sowers. Philadelphia: P. Augustus Sage, 1839.

The Life of Ellen Jewett. New York: n.p., 1836.

Life of Henry Phillips. Boston: Russell, Cutler, 1817.

Life of Jesse H. Pomeroy, the Boy Fiend. Taunton, Mass.: Taunton, 1875.

Life of Leonard Howard, Alias Edward Thomas. Auburn, N.Y.: n.p., 1877.

Life of Samuel Green. Boston: David Felt, 1822.

Life of the Chicago Banker, George W. Green. Chicago: Mellen, 1855.

The Life of Ursula Newman, and the Intercourse Subsisting Between Her and Richard Johnson. New York: Elam Bliss, 1829.

Life, Secret Confession and Execution of Rugg, the Fiend. Philadelphia: Barclay, 1885.

Life, Trial and Adventures of John H. Surratt, the Conspirator. Port Tobacco, Md.: James L. Barbour, 1988.

Life, Trial and Confession of Frank C. Almy. Laconia, N.H.: John J. Lane, 1892.

Life, Trial and Confession of Thomas Jones. New York: Christian Brown, 1824.

Life, Trial and Conviction of Edward Stokes. Philadelphia: Barclay, 1873.

Life, Trial and Execution of Edward H. Ruloff. Philadelphia: Barclay, 1871.

The Life, Trial & Execution of John Dahmen. Jeffersonville, Ind.: Cuthbert, 1825.

Life, Trial, Confession and Conviction of John Hanlon. Philadelphia: Barclay, 1870.

Life, Trial, Confession and Execution of Albert W. Hicks. New York: Robert M. DeWitt, 1860.

Lifflander, Mathew L. *Final Treatment, The File on Dr. X.* New York: W. W. Norton, 1979.

Lifton, David S. *Best Evidence: Disguise and Deception in the Assassination of John F. Kennedy.* New York: Macmillan, 1980.

Lifton, Robert Jay. *Thought Reform and the Psychology of Totalism.* New York: W.W. Norton, 1969.

Liggett, J. *The Human Face.* London: Constable, 1974.

Liggett, William Sr. *My Seventy-Five Years Along the Mexican Border.* New York: Exposition Press, 1964.

Likhachev, S.S. and Lur'ye, Ya. S. *Letters of Ivan the Terrible.* Moscow: n.p., 1951.

Likimani, M. *Passbook Number F.47927: Women and Mau Mau in Kenya.* London: Macmillan, 1985.

Lilienthal, Alfred M. *The Other Side of the Coin.* New York: Devon-Adair, 1965.

_____. *There Goes the Middle East.* New York: Devin-Adair, 1957.

_____. *What Price Israel.* Chicago: Henry Regnery, 1953.

Lilienthal, David. *Journals.* New York: Harper & Row, 1964.

Lilienthal, J.A. *Die Hexenprocesse der beiden Städte Braunsberg.*

Kaliningrad, U.S.S.R.: T. Theile, Ferdinand Beyer, 1861.

Lilienthal, Lillie Bernheimer. *In Memoriam: Jesse Warren Lilienthal.* San Francisco: John Henry Nash, 1921.

Lillard, Richard G. *Desert Challenge.* New York: Alfred A. Knopf, 1942.

Lillie, Beatrice. *Every Other Inch a Lady.* New York: Doubleday, 1972.

Lillie, Gordon William. *Life Story of Pawnee Bill.* Topeka, Kan., n.p., 1916.

Lilly, Marjorie. *Sickert, The Painter and His Circle.* London: Elek, 1971.

Liman, Paul. *Der politische Mord im Wandel der Geschichte.* Berlin: A. Hofmann, 1912.

Limborch, Philip van. *Historia Inquisitionis.* Amsterdam, Neth.: H. Westenium, 1692.

Limet, Charles. *Un Vétéran du Barreau Parisien, Quatre-vingts Ans de Souvenirs.* Paris: Lemerre, 1908.

Limpus, Lowell J. *Honest Cop: Lewis J. Valentine.* New York: Dutton, 1939.

Lincoln, Abraham. *The Collected Works of Abraham Lincoln.* New Brunswick, N.J.: Rutgers University, 1953.

Lincoln, C. Eric. *The Black Muslims in America.* Boston: Beacon Press, 1961.

Lincoln, F.S. *Charleston.* New York: Corinthian, 1946.

Lincoln, Victoria. *Disgrace: Lizzie Borden by Daylight.* New York: G. P. Putnam's Sons, 1967.

Lindberg, Richard C. *Chicago Ragtime: Another Look at Chicago, 1880-1920.* South Bend, Ind.: Icarus Press, 1985.

_____. *To Serve and Collect: Chicago Politics and Police Corruption from the Lager Beer Riot to the Summerdale Scandal: 1855-1920.* New York: Praeger Press, 1991.

_____. *Who's On Third?: The Chicago White Sox Story.* South Bend, Ind.: Icarus Press, 1983.

Lindbergh, Anne Morrow. *The Flower and the Nettle: Diaries and Letters, 1936-1939.* New York: Harcourt Brace Jovanovich, 1974.

_____. *Hour of Gold, Hour of Lead: Diaries and Letters, 1929-1932.* New York: Harcourt, Brace, Jovanovich, 1973.

_____. *Listen, the Wind.* New York: Harcourt Brace, 1938.

_____. *Locked Rooms and Open Doors: Diaries and Letters, 1933-1935.* New York: Harcourt Brace Jovanovich, 1974.

_____. *North to the Orient.* New York: Harcourt Brace, 1935.

_____. *War Within and War Without: Diaries and Letters, 1939-1944.* New York: Harcourt Brace Jovanovich, 1980.

Lindbergh, Charles. *Boyhood on the Upper Mississippi.* Minnesota Historical Society, 1972.

_____. *The Spirit of St. Louis.* New York: Charles Scribner's Sons, 1953.

_____. *We.* New York: G.P. Putnam's Sons, 1927.

Lindblom, Charles E. *Politics and Markets.* New York: Basic Books, 1977.

Lindemann, Albert S. *The Red Years: European Socialism versus Bolshevism, 1919-1921.* Berkeley: University of California Press, 1974.

Linden, Carl A. *Khrushchev and the Soviet Leadership, 1957-1964.* Baltimore: Johns Hopkins Press, 1966.

Lindeqvist, K.O. *Taikausto ja Noitavainot.* Porvoo, Swed.: Söderström, 1903.

Linder, Ronald L., Lerner, Steven E., and Burns, R. Stanley. *PCP: The Devil's Dust.* Belmont, Calif.: Wadsworth, 1981.

The Linder Tragedy: History of Nelson E. Wade, the McBride Murderer. Williamsport, Pa.: Gazette & Bulletin, 1873.

Linderholm, Emanuel. *De Stora Häxprocesserna i Sverige.* Uppsala, Swed.: J.A. Lindblad, 1918.

Lindesmith, Alfred C. *Addiction and Opiates.* Chicago: Aldine, 1968.

_____. *The Drug Addict and the Law.* Bloomington: University of Indiana Press, 1965.

Lindley, Ernest K. *Franklin D. Roosevelt: A Career in Progressive Democracy.* New York: Bobbs Merrill, 1931.

_____. *The Roosevelt Revolution: First Phase.* New York: Viking, 1933.

Lindner, Robert. *The Fifty-Minute Hour.* New York: Rinehart, 1955.

_____. *Must You Conform?* New York: Grove, 1956.

Lindquist, Allan Sigvard. *Jess Sweeten, Texas Lawman.* San Antonio, Texas: Naylor, 1961.

Lindsay, Charles. *Big Horn Basin.* Lincoln: University of Nebraska Press, 1932.

Lindsay, Jack. *Cleopatra.* London: Constable, 1971.

_____. *Origins of Astrology.* New York: Barnes and Noble, 1971.

Lindsay, John V. *The City.* New York: W.W. Norton, 1969.

Lindsay, Philip. *The Mainspring of Murder.* London: John Long, 1958.

Lindsey, Almont. *The Pullman Strike: The Story of a Unique Experiment and of a Great Labor Upheaval.* Chicago: University of Chicago Press, 1971.

Lindsey, Benjamin B., and O'Higgins, Harvey J. *The Beast.* New York: Doubleday, Page, 1911.

Linebarger, Paul, *The China of Chiang Kai-shek.* Boston: World Peace Foundation, 1941.

Linedecker, Clifford L. *The Man Who Killed Boys.* New York: St. Martin's Press, 1980.

Linford, Velma. *Wyoming, Frontier State.* Denver: Old West, 1947.

Lingle, Robert T., and Linford, Dee. *The Pecos River Commission of New Mexico and Texas.* Santa Fe, N.M.: Rydal Press, 1961.

Link, Arthur S. *Wilson: Campaigns for Progressivism and Peace, 1916-1917.* Princeton, N.J.: Princeton University Press, n.d.

_____. *Wilson: Confusions and Crises, 1915-1916.* Princeton, N.J.: Princeton University Press, 1964.

_____. *Wilson: The Diplomatist.* Baltimore, Md.: The Johns Hopkins University Press, 1957.

_____. *Wilson: The New Freedom.* 2 vols. Princeton, N.J.: Princeton University Press, 1956.

_____. *Wilson: The Road to the White House.* Princeton, N.J.: Princeton University Press, 1947.

_____. *Wilson: The Struggle for Neutrality, 1914-1915.* Princeton, N.J.: Princeton University Press, 1960.

_____. *Woodrow Wilson: A Look at His Major Foreign Policies.* Baltimore, Md.: Johns Hopkins Press, 1957.

_____. (ed.). *Woodrow Wilson: A Profile.* New York: Hill & Wang, 1968.

_____. *Woodrow Wilson and the Progressive Era, 1910-1917.* New York: Harper & Bros., 1954.

Link, Eugene Perry. *Democratic-Republican Societies, 1790-1800.* New York: Octagon Books, 1965.

Linklater, Eric. *The Conquest of England.* New York: Dell, 1966.

_____. *The Corpse on Clapham Common.* London: Macmillan, 1971.

Linn, James Weber. *James Keeley, Newspaperman.* New York: Bobbs-Merrill, 1937.

_____. *Jane Addams.* New York: Greenwood Press, 1968.

Linton, Calvin D. (ed.). *American Headlines Year by Year.* New York: Thomas Nelson, 1985.

Linton, E. Lynn. *The Girl of the Period, and Other Social Essays.* London: Bentley, 1883.

_____. *Witch Stories.* London: Chatto & Windus, 1883.

Lintott, Andrew W. *Violence, Civil Strife and Revolution in the Classical City, 750-330 B.C.* Baltimore: Johns Hopkins Press, 1982.

_____. *Violence in Republican Rome.* Oxford: Clarendon Press, 1968.

Lin Yutang. *My Country and My People.* New York: Reynal & Hitchcock, 1935.

Linzee, E.H. *Development of Oklahoma Territory.* Oklahoma City, Okla.: n.p., 1941.

Lipemann, Heinz. *Rasputin, a New Judgement.* n.p., 1955.

Lipman, Eugene (ed. and trans.). *The Mishna*. New York: W.W. Norton, 1970.

Lipman, Mark, and Daley, Robert. *Stealing*. New York: Harper's Magazine Press, 1973.

Lipman, V.D. *A Century of Social Service, 1859-1959*. London: Routledge & Kegan Paul, 1959.

Lippincott, Sara Jane. *New Life in New Lands*. New York: J.B. Ford, 1873.

Lippmann, Walter. *American Inquisitors: A Commentary on Dayton and Chicago*. New York: Macmillan, 1928.

_____. *Drift and Mastery*. New York: Mitchell Kennerley, 1914.

_____. *Early Writings*. New York: Liveright, 1970.

_____. *The Good Society*. Boston: Little, Brown, 1943.

_____. *A Preface to Morals*. New Brunswick, N.J.: Transaction, 1982.

_____. *Public Opinion*. New York: Free Press, 1965.

Lipset, Seymour Martin. *Political Man*. Garden City, N.Y.: Anchor Books, Doubleday, 1963.

_____, et al. *Union Democracy*. New York: Anchor Books, 1962.

Lipsig, Frances. *Murder-Family Style*. New York: Collier Books, 1962.

Lipsky, George A. *John Quincy Adams: His Theory and Ideas*. New York: Thomas Y. Crowell, 1950.

Lipsky, Michael. *Street-Level Bureaucracy*. New York: Russell Sage Foundation, 1980.

Lipton, Dean. *Malpractice, An Autobiography of a Victim*. New York: A. S. Barnes, 1978.

_____. *The Truth About Simon Girty*. New York: Pyramid Press, 1957.

Lipton, Douglas, Martinson, Robert, and Wilks, Judith, *The Effectiveness of Correctional Treatment: A Survey of Treatment Evaluation Studies*. New York: Praeger, 1975.

Lipton, Lawrence. *The Erotic Revolution*. Los Angeles: Sherbourne Press, 1965.

Lischi, Dario. *La Marcia su Roma con la colonna Lamarmora*. Florence, Italy: Florentia, 1923.

Lisio, Donald J. *The President and Protest: Hoover, Conspiracy and the Bonus Riot*. Columbia: University of Missouri Press, 1973.

Liska, George. *Imperial America: The International Politics of Primacy*. Baltimore, Md.: Johns Hopkins Press, 1967.

Lister, Richard Percival. *The Secret History of Genghis Khan*. London: P. Davies, 1969.

Liston, Robert H. *The Edge of Madness: Prisons and Prison Reform in America*. New York: Franklin Watts, 1972.

_____. *Great Detectives*. New York: Platt & Munk, 1966.

_____. *Terrorism*. New York: Thomas Nelson, 1977.

Litt, Edgar. *The Political Culture of Massachusetts*. Cambridge, Mass.: MIT Press, 1965.

Little, Arthur D. *The State of the Art of Traffic Safety*. New York: Praeger, 1970.

Little, Bryan. *Crusoe's Captain*. London: Odhams Press, 1960.

_____. *The Monmouth Episode*. London: Werner Laurie, 1956.

Little, David B. *Religion, Order, and Law*. New York: Harper & Row, 1970.

Little, James A. *Jacob Hamlin*. Salt Lake City, Utah: Juvenile Instructor, 1881.

Little, Kenneth L. *The Mende of Sierra Leone*. London: Routledge & Kegan Paul, 1951.

Little, Tom. *Egypt*. New York: Praeger, 1959.

Littlepage, J.D., and Bess, Demaree. *In Search of Soviet Gold*. New York: Harcourt Brace, 1938.

Litvinoff, Barnett. *Ben Gurion of Israel*. New York: Praeger, 1954.

Litwack, Leon F. *North of Slavery: The Negro in the Free States, 1790-1860*. Chicago: University of Chicago Press, 1961.

Liu, F.F. *A Military History of Modern China, 1924-1949*. Princeton, N.J.: Princeton University Press, 1956.

Livermore, H.V. *A History of Portugal*. Cambridge: Cambridge University Press, 1947.

Livermore, Jesse Lauriston. *How to Trade in Stocks*. New York: Duell, Sloan, & Pearce, 1940.

Livermore, Mary A. *The Story of My Life, or, The Sunshine and Shadow of Seventy Years*. Hartford, Conn.: A.D. Worthington, 1899.

Lives and Confessions of Henry Fife and Charlotte Jones. Pittsburgh, Pa.: Hunt & Miner, 1857.

The Lives and Confessions of James M'Gowan & James Jameson. Philadelphia: James O'Hara, 1807.

Lives and Trial of Gibbs and Wansley. Boston: n.p., 1832.

The Lives, Last Words and Dying Speeches of Ezra Ross, James Buchanan, and William Brooks. Worcester, Mass.: n.p., 1778.

The Lives of Helen Jewett, and Richard P. Robinson. New York: Police Gazette, 1836.

Lives: The Dryden Plutarch. New York: Everyman's Library, 1910.

Livingston, Armstrong, and Stein, Captain John G. *The Murdered and the Missing*. New York: Stephen-Paul, 1947.

Livingston, Edward. *A Personal History of the San Francisco Earthquake and Fire*. San Francisco: Windsor Press, 1941.

Livingstone, Belle. *Belle Out of Order*. London: Heinemann, 1960.

Livingstone, Neil C. *The War Against Terrorism*. London: Heath, 1982.

Livsey, Clara. *The Manson Women*. New York: Marek, 1980.

Livy. *Summary*. trans. B.O. Foster. Cambridge, Mass.: Harvard University Press, 1963.

Llewellyn, K. *The Brabble Bush*. Dobbs Ferry, N.Y.: Oceana, 1960.

Llorente, Juan Antonio. *Histoire critique de l'Inquisition d'Espagne*. Paris: Treuttel et Wurtz, 1817.

Lloyd, Alan. *The Making of the King: 1066*. New York: Holt, Rinehart and Winston, 1966.

Lloyd, Benjamin Estelle. *Lights and Shadows in San Francisco*. San Francisco: Published by Author, 1876.

_____. *Lights and Shadows of Chinatown*. San Francisco: Published by Author, 1896.

Lloyd, Caroline Augusta. *Henry Demarest Lloyd 1847-1903: A Biography*. 2 vols. New York: G.P. Putnam's Sons, 1912.

Lloyd, Christopher. *Sir Francis Drake*. London: Faber and Faber, 1957.

_____. *William Dampier*. Hamden, Conn.: Archon Books, 1966.

Lloyd, Everett. *Law West of the Pecos: The Story of Roy Bean*. San Antonio, Texas: Naylor, 1936.

Lloyd George, David. *War Memoirs: 1916-17*. Boston: Little, Brown, 1934.

Lloyd George, Earl. *Lloyd George*. London: Frederick Muller, 1960.

Lloyd, H.E. *Alexander I*. London: Treuttel & Wurtz, 1826.

Lloyd, Henry Demarest. *Men, the Workers*. New York: Doubleday, Page, 1909.

_____. *Wealth Against Commonwealth*. New York: Harper, 1894.

Lloyd, James T. *Steamboat Directory and Disasters on the Western Waters*. Cincinnati: J.T. Lloyd, 1856.

Lloyd, John. *The Invaders: A Story of the "Hole-in-the-Wall" Country*. New York: R.F. Fenno, 1910.

Lloyd, Lord. *Egypt Since Cromer*. London: Macmillan, 1933.

Lloyd, Robin. *For Money or Love: Boy Prostitution in America*. New York: Vanguard, 1976.

Lloyd, William. *Wealth Against Commonwealth*. New York: Harper & Brothers, 1894.

Lloyd-Owen, Frances. *Gold Nugget Charlie: A Narrative Compiled From the Notes of Charles E. Masson*. London: George C. Harrap, 1939.

Lobanov-Rostovsky, Andrei A. *The Grinding Mill*. New York: Macmillan, 1935.

_____. *Russia and Asia*. Ann Arbor, Mich.: Wahr, 1951.

_____. *Russia and Europe, 1789-1825*. Durham, N.C.: Duke University Press, 1947.

Lobineau, Dom Gui Aléxis. *Histoire de Bretagne.* Paris: La Veuve François Muguet, 1707.

Locard, E. *L'Enquête Criminelle et les Méthodes Scientifiques.* Paris: Flammarion, 1920.

_____. *La Preuve Judiciaire par les Empreintes Digitales.* Lyons, Fr.: A. Rey, 1914.

_____. *Traité de Criminalistique.* Lyons, Fr.: Desvigne, 1931.

Lochner, Louis Paul. *Always the Unexpected.* New York: Macmillan, 1956.

_____ (ed. & trans.). *The Goebbels Diaries.* Garden City, N.Y.: Doubleday, 1948.

_____. *What About Germany?* New York: Dodd, 1942.

Locke, John. *Two Treatises of Government.* New York: New American Library, 1963.

Locke, Raymond Friday (ed.). *The Birth of America.* New York: Hawthorn Books, 1971.

_____ (ed.). *The Human Side of History: Man's Manners, Morals and Games.* New York: Hawthorn Books, 1970.

Lockhart, B.H. Bruce. *British Agent.* New York: G.P. Putnam's Sons, 1933.

Lockhart, Robert Bruce. *Scotch: The Whiskey of Scotland in Fact and Story.* London: Putnam, 1951,

Lockhart, William B., Kamisar, Yale, and Choper, Jesse H. *Constitutional Rights and Liberties.* St. Paul, Minn.: West, 1975.

Lockley, Fred. *Oregon Folks.* New York: Knickerbocker Press, 1927.

Lockridge, Kenneth A. *A New England Town, The First Hundred Years: Dedham, Massachusetts, 1636-1736.* New York: W.W. Norton, 1985.

Lockwood, Francis Cummins. *Arizona Characters.* Los Angeles: Times-Mirror, 1928.

_____. *Pioneer Days in Arizona.* New York: Macmillan, 1932.

Lodge, Senator Henry Cabot. *Daniel Webster.* Boston: Houghton Mifflin, 1884.

_____. *The Senate and the League of Nations.* New York: Charles Scribner's, 1925.

_____. *The War with Spain.* New York: Harper, 1899.

Lodge, Juliet (ed.). *Terrorism, A Challenge to the State.* London: Martin Robertson, 1981.

Loeb, Richard H. *Your Legal Rights as a Minor.* New York: Franklin Watts, 1974.

Loehlin, J.C., Lindzey, G., and Spuhler, J.N. *Race Differences in Intelligence.* San Francisco: W.H. Freeman, 1975.

Loeser, Herta. *Women, Work, and Volunteering.* Boston: Beacon, 1974.

Loewy, Arnold H. *Criminal Law in a Nutshell.* St. Paul, Minn.: West, 1975.

Lofland, John. *Analyzing Social Settings.* Belmont, Calif.: Wadsworth, 1971.

_____. *Deviance and Social Identity.* Englewood Cliffs, N.J.: Prentice-Hall, 1969.

Lofton, John. *Insurrection in South Carolina: The Turbulent World of Denmark Vesey.* Yellow Springs, Ohio: Antioch Press, 1964.

_____. *Justice and the Press.* Boston: Beacon Press, 1966.

Lofts, Norah, and Weiner, Margery. *Eternal France.* Garden City, N.Y.: Doubleday, 1968.

Logan, Andy. *Against the Evidence: The Becker-Rosenthal Affair.* New York: McGraw-Hill, 1970.

_____. *The Man Who Robbed the Robber Barons.* New York: W.W. Norton, 1965.

Logan, Frenise A. *The Negro in North Carolina, 1876-1894.* Chapel Hill, N.C.: University of North Carolina Press, 1964.

Logan, Guy. *Dramas of the Dock.* London: Stanley Paul, 1928.

_____. *Great Murder Mysteries.* London: Stanley Paul, 1931.

_____. *Guilty or Not Guilty?* London: Stanley Paul, 1928.

_____. *Masters of Crime: Studies of Multiple Murders.* London: Stanley Paul, 1928.

_____. *Rope, Knife and Chair.* London: Stanley Paul, 1930.

_____. *Verdict and Sentence.* London: Eldon Press, 1935.

_____. *Wilful Murder.* London: Eldon Press, 1935.

Logan, Herschel C. *Buckskin and Satin.* Harrisburg, Pa.: Stackpole, 1954.

Logan, James. *Notes of a Journey Through Canada, the United States of America, and the West Indies.* Edinburgh, Scot.: Fraser, 1838.

Logan, John A. *The Great Conspiracy.* Philadelphia: Barclay, 1866.

Logan, Mrs. John A. *Reminiscences of a Soldier's Wife.* New York: Charles Scribner's Sons, 1916.

Logan, Joshua. *Josh.* New York: Delacorte Press, 1976.

Logan, Rayford W. *The Betrayal of the Negro.* New York: Collier, 1965.

Loggins, Vernon. *The Negro Author.* New York: Kennikat Press, 1931.

Logio, George C. *Bulgaria Past and Present.* Manchester, Eng.: Sheratt and Hughes, 1936.

Logsdon, Joseph. *Horace White: Nineteenth Century Liberal.* Westport, Conn.: Greenwood Press, 1971.

Logue, Roscoe. *Tumbleweeds and Barb Wire Fences.* Amarillo, Texas: Russell Stationery, 1935.

_____. *Under Texas and Border Skies.* Amarillo, Texas: Russell Stationery, 1935.

Lohbeck, Don. *Patrick J. Hurley.* Chicago: Regnery, 1956.

Lohr, Lennox R. *Fair Management.* Chicago: Cuneo Press, 1952.

Lomask, Milton. *Aaron Burr.* New York: Farrar, Straus & Giroux, 1979.

_____. *Andrew Johnson, President on Trial.* New York: Farrar, Straus & Cudahy, 1960.

Lomax, Elizabeth L. *Leaves From an Old Washington Diary.* New York: Dutton, 1943.

Lomax, Virginia. *The Old Capitol and Its Inmates.* New York: E.J. Hale & Sons, 1867.

Lombardi, Gabrio. *Il Corpo Italiano di Liberazione.* Rome: Magi-Spinetti, 1945.

Lombardo Toledano, Vicente. *La libertad sindical en México.* Mexico City: Talleres Linotipograficos "La Lucha," 1926.

Lombroso, Caesar. *Crime, Its Causes and Remedies.* Boston: Little, Brown, 1911.

_____. *Criminal Man According to the Classification of Cesare Lombroso.* New York: Putnam, 1911.

_____, and Ferrero, William. *The Female Offender.* New York: Appleton, 1897.

London, Jack. *John Barleycorn.* New York: Century, 1913.

_____. *Revolution and Other Essays.* New York: Macmillan, 1912.

_____. *War of the Classes.* New York: The Regent Press, 1912.

London Labor Party. *What Labor Has Done for London.* London: London Labor, 1936.

Long, E.B. *The Civil War Day by Day.* New York: Doubleday, 1971.

Long, E. Hudson. *Mark Twain Handbook.* New York: Hendricks House, 1957.

_____. *O. Henry, the Man and His Work.* Philadelphia: University of Pennsylvania Press, 1949.

Long, Gavin. *The Final Campaigns.* Vol. VII, Series 1 (Army.) Canberra: Australian War Memorial, 1963.

_____. *MacArthur as Military Commander.* New York: Van Nostrand Reinhold, 1969.

Long, Haniel. *Piñon Country.* New York: Duell, Sloan & Pearce, 1941.

Long, Huey P. *Every Man a King. The Autobiography of Huey P. Long.* New Orleans: National Books, 1933.

Long, J.C. *Bryan: The Great Commoner.* New York: D. Appleton, 1928.

Long, Katherine W., and Siciliano, Samuel A. *Yuma From Hell-Hole to Haven.* Yuma, Ariz.: Yuma County Chamber of Commerce, 1950.

Longchamp et Wagnière, *Mémoires sur Voltaire.* Paris: A. André,

1826.

Longford, Earl of. *Pornography: The Longford Report*. London: Hodder, 1972.

Longford, Elizabeth. *Queen Victoria: Born to Succeed*. New York: Harper, 1965.

Longford, Joseph H. *The Evolution of New Japan*. Cambridge: Cambridge University Press, 1913.

Longgood, William. *Suez Story: Key to the Middle East*. New York: Greenberg, 1957.

Longhitano, R. *La politica religiosa di Mussolini*. Rome: Cremonese Libraio Editore, 1938.

Longman, F.W. *Frederick the Great and the Seven Years War*. London: Longmans, 1888.

Longo, Luigi. *Un popolo alla macchia*. Milan, Italy: Mandadori, 1947.

Longrigg, Stephen H. *Iraq, 1900-1950*. London: Oxford University Press, 1953.

Longsford, Elizabeth (ed.). *Louisa, Lady in Waiting*. London: Jonathan Cape, 1979.

_____. *Queen Victoria*. New York: Harper & Row, 1964.

Longstreet, James. *From Manassas to Appomattox*. Bloomington: Indiana University Press, 1969.

Longstreet, Stephen. *All Star Cast, an Anecdotal History of Los Angeles*. New York: Thomas Y. Crowell, 1977.

_____. *Chicago, 1860-1919*. New York: McKay, 1973.

_____. *Sportin' House*. Los Angeles: Sherbourne Press, 1965.

_____. *The Wilder Shore*. New York: Doubleday, 1968.

_____. *Win or Lose*. Indianapolis: The Bobbs-Merrill, 1977.

Longstreth, T. Morris. *In Scarlet and Plain Clothes*. New York: Macmillan, 1933.

_____. *The Silent Force: Scenes From the Life of the Mounted Police of Canada*. New York: Century, 1927.

Longworth, Alice Roosevelt. *Crowded Hours*. New York: Charles Scribner's Sons, 1933.

Longworth, David. *A Brief Narrative of the Trial for the Bloody and Mysterious Murder of the Unfortunate Young Woman in the Famous Manhattan Well*. New York: Published by Author, 1800.

_____. *New York Register and City Directory for the Twenty-Fifth Year of American Independence*. New York: D. Longworth, 1800.

Longworth, Philip. *The Cossacks*. New York: Holt, Rinehart and Winston, 1969.

Look, Al. *Unforgettable Characters of Western Colorado*. Boulder, Colo.: Pruett Press, 1966.

Looker, Earle. *The White House Gang*. Old Tappan, N.J.: Fleming H. Revell, 1929.

Loomis, Samuel Lane. *Modern Cities and Their Religious Problems*. New York: Baker & Taylor, 1887.

Loomis, Stanley. *A Crime of Passion*. Philadelphia: Lippincott, 1967.

_____. *Du Barry*. Philadelphia: J.B. Lippincott, 1959.

_____. *Paris In The Terror*. New York: J. B. Lippincott, 1964.

Looney, Ralph. *Haunted Highways: The Ghost Towns of New Mexico*. New York: Hastings House, 1968.

Loos, Anita. *A Girl Like I*. New York: Viking, 1966.

López Portillo y Rojas, José. *Elevación y caída de Porfirio Díaz*. Mexico City: Librería española, 1921.

Lopez-Ray, Manuel. *Crime: An Analytical Appraisal*. New York: Praeger, 1970.

Lorain, Pierre, and Marquiset, Robert. *Armes à Feu Françaises Modèles Rélementaires*. Paris: J. Boudriot, 1969.

Lorant, Stefan. *The Glorious Burden: The American Presidency*. New York: Harper & Row, 1969.

_____. *The Life and Times of Theodore Roosevelt*. New York: Doubleday, 1959.

_____. *Lincoln: His Life in Photographs*. New York: Duell, Sloan and Pearce, 1941.

_____. *Lincoln: A Picture Story of His Life*. New York: W. W. Norton, 1952.

Lord, Jess R. *Marijuana and Personality Change*. Lexington, Mass.: D.C. Heath, 1971.

Lord, John. *Frontier Dust*. Hartford, Conn.: E.V. Mitchell, 1926.

Lord, R.H. *Second Partition of Poland*. Cambridge, Mass.: Harvard University Press, 1915.

Lord, Walter. *Day of Infamy*. New York: Holt, Rinehart & Winston, 1961.

_____. *The Fremantle Diary*. Boston: Little, Brown, 1954.

_____. *The Good Years, From 1900 to the First World War*. New York: Harper & Bros., 1960.

_____. *Incredible Victory*. New York: Harper & Row, 1967.

_____. *The Past That Would Not Die*. New York: Harper & Row, 1964.

Lorédan, Jean. *Un Grand Procès de Sorcelerie au XVII Siècle*. Paris: Perrin, 1912.

Lorenz, Konrad. *On Aggression*. New York: Harcourt, Brace & World, 1966.

Lorenz, R. *Der Staat wider Willen*. Berlin: Junker and Duennhaupt, 1941.

Lorgion, Everard Jan Dienst. *Balthazar Bekker in Amsterdam*. Groningen, Neth.: H.R. Roelfsema, 1848.

_____. *Balthazar Bekker in Francken*. Groningen, Neth.: H.R. Roelfsema, 1848.

Lorwin, Lewis Levitzki with Flexner, Jean Atherton. *The American Federation of Labor: History, Policies, and Prospects*. Washington, D. C.: The Brookings Institution, 1933.

_____. *The International Labor Movement*. New York: Harper & Brothers, 1953.

_____. *Labor and Internationalism*. New York: Macmillan, 1929.

Los Angeles, City of. *Dangerous Chemicals Code*. Los Angeles: Los Angeles Fire Department, 1951.

Loseby, Charles Edgar. *Witches, Mediums, Vagrants, and Law*. Manchester, Eng.: Spiritualists' National Union, 1946.

Loskeil, George Henry. *History of the Mission of the United Brethren Among the Indians in North America*. London: Brethren's Society for the Furtherance of the Gospel, 1794.

Lossing, Benson J. *Field-Book of the American Revolution*. New York: Harper, 1850.

_____. *Our Country*. 3 vols. New York: Henry J. Johnson, 1878.

_____. *Pictorial History of the Civil War*. Hartford, Conn.: T. Belknap, 1868.

_____. *Washington and the American Republic*. 3 vols. New York: Virtue and Yorston, 1870.

Lot, Ferdinand. *Les Invasions Barbares*. Paris: Paynot, 1937.

Lotchin, Roger W. *San Francisco - 1846-1856*. New York: Oxford University Press, 1974.

Loth, David. *Alexander Hamilton: Portait of a Prodigy*. New York: Carrick & Evans, 1939.

_____. *Public Plunder: A History of Graft in America*. New York: Carrick & Evans, 1938.

_____. *Swope of G.E.* New York: Simon & Schuster, 1958.

Loti, Pierre. *Carmen Sylva and Sketches from the Orient*. trans. Fred Rothwell. New York: Macmillan, 1912.

_____. *Egypt*. tran. W.P. Baines. London: T. Werner Laurie, 1909.

Lott, Davis Newton (ed.). *The Presidents Speak*. New York: Holt, Rinehart & Winston, 1961.

Loucks, Emerson Hunsberger. *The Ku Klux Klan in Pennsylvania*. Harrisburg, Pa.: Telegraph Press, 1936.

Louderback, Lew. *The Bad Ones*. New York: Fawcett, 1968.

Loudon, John Baird. *A Tour through Canada and the United States*. Coventry, Eng.: Curtis & Beamish, 1879.

Louis Ferdinand of Hohenzollern, Prince of Prussia. *The Rebel Prince*. Chicago: Regnery, 1952.

Louise Sophia, Princess of Prussia. *Behind the Scenes at the Prussian Court*. London; John Murray, 1939.

Louise, Théophile. *De la Sorcellerie et de la Justice Criminelle à Valenciennes*. Valenciennes, Fr.: E. Prignet, 1861.

Lounsberry, Clement A. *History of North Dakota*. Chicago: S.J. Clarke, 1917.

Louria, Donald B. *The Drug Scene*. New York: McGraw-Hill, 1968.

_____. *Nightmare Drugs*. New York: Pocket Books, 1966.

Love, Nat. *The Life and Adventures of Nat Love, Better Known in the Cattle Country as "Deadwood Dick", by Himself*. Los Angeles: Wayside Press, 1907.

Love, Robertus. *The Rise and Fall of Jesse James*. New York: G. P. Putnam's Sons, 1926.

Lovejoy, Joseph C. and Owen. *Memoirs of the Rev. Elijah P. Lovejoy; Who Was Murdered in Defence of the Liberty of the Press, at Alton, Illinois, Nov. 7, 1837*. New York: John S. Taylor, 1838.

Lovell, Emily Kalled. *A Personalized History of Otero County, New Mexico*. Alamorgordo, N.M.: Star, 1963.

Lovesey, Peter. *Swing, Swing Together*. London: MacMillan, 1976.

Lovett, Sir H. Verney. *The Cambridge History of India*. Cambridge: The University Press, 1932.

Lovett, Robert Morss. *All Our Years*. New York: Viking, 1948.

Low, Alfred. *Lenin on the Question of Natonality*. New York: Bookman Associates, 1958.

Low, Benjamin R.C. *Seth Low*. New York: G.P. Putnam's Sons, 1925.

Low, Frederick F. *Some Reflections of an Early California Governor*. Sacramento, Calif.: Sacramento Book Collectors Club, 1959.

Low, Seth. *New York in 1850 and 1890. A Political Study. An Address Delivered Before the New York Historical Society on its Eighty-seventh Anniversary*. New York: New York Historical Society, 1892.

Lowdermilk, Walter C. *Palestine Land of Promise*. New York: Harper, 1944.

Lowe, David. *KKK: Invisible Empire*. New York: W.W. Norton, 1967.

Lowe, David. *Lost Chicago*. Boston: Houghton Mifflin, 1975.

Lowe, Frank M., Jr. *A Warrior Lawyer*. New York: Fleming H. Revell, 1942.

Lowe, Joyce Egerton. *Magic in Greek and Latin Literature*. Oxford: Basil Blackwell, 1929.

Lowe, Pardee. *Father and Glorious Descendant*. Boston: Little, Brown, 1943.

Lowenthal, M. (ed.). *The Diaries of Theodor Herzl*. New York: Dial Press, 1956.

Lowenthal, Max. *The Federal Bureau of Investigation*. New York: William Sloane Associates, 1950.

Lowi, Theodore. *At the Pleasure of the Mayor*. New York: Free Press, 1964.

Lowie, Robert H. *The Crow Indians*. New York: Farrar & Rinehart, 1935.

_____. *Indians of the Plains*. New York: McGraw-Hill, 1954.

Lowitt, Richard. *A Merchant Prince of the Nineteenth Century: William E. Dodge*. New York: Columbia University Press, 1954.

Lowndes, Marie Belloc. *Lizzie Borden: A Study in Conjecture*. New York: Longmans, Green, 1930.

_____. *The Lodger*. New York: Scribner, 1911.

Lowndes, Susan (ed.). *Diaries and Letters of Marie Belloc Lowndes 1911-1947*. London: Windus, 1971.

Lowrey, G.P. *English Neutrality: Is the "Alabama" a British Pirate?* New York: Anson D.F. Randolph, 1863.

Lowry, Edward G. *Washington Close-ups*. Boston: Houghton Mifflin, 1921.

Lowther, Charles C. *Dodge City, Kansas*. Philadelphia: Dorrance, 1940.

Lu, David J. *From the Marco Polo Bridge to Pearl Harbor*. Washington, D.C.: Public Affairs Press, 1961.

Lubbock, Percy. *Portrait of Edith Wharton*. New York: D. Appleton-Century, 1947.

Lubin, Martin, (as told to Coe, Phyllis). *Good Guys, Bad Guys*. New York: McGraw-Hill Book, 1982.

Lubove, Roy. *The Progressives and the Slums*. Pittsburgh, Pa.: University of Pittsburgh Press, 1936.

Lucas, A. *Forensic Chemistry and Scientific Criminal Investigation*. New York: Longmans, Green, 1935.

Lucas, Daniel B. *Memoirs of John Yates Beall*. Montreal: J. Lovell, 1865.

Lucas, Norman. *The Child Killers*. London: Barker, 1972.

_____. *Laboratory Detectives*. New York: Taplinger, 1972.

_____. *The Sex Killers*. New York: W. H. Allen, 1974.

Lucas, Scott. *The FDA*. Millbrae, Calif.: Celestial Arts, 1978.

Lucas-Dubreton, J. *The Borgias*. trans. Philip John Stead. New York: E.P. Dutton, 1956.

Luce, Gay Gaer. *Biological Rhythms in Human and Animal Physiology*. New York: Dover, 1971.

Lucia, Ellis. *Klondike Kate: The Life and Legend of Kitty Rockwell, the Queen of the Yukon*. New York: Hastings House, 1962.

_____. *The Saga of Ben Holladay, Giant of the Old West*. New York: Hastings House, 1959.

_____. *Tough Men, Tough Country*. Englewood Cliffs, N.J.: Prentice-Hall, 1963.

Lucia, Salvatore Pablo (ed.). *Alcohol and Civilization*. New York: McGraw-Hill, 1963.

Luciano, Celso. *Rapporto al Duce*. Rome: Società Editrice "Giornale del Mezzogiorno", 1948.

Lucie-Smith, Edward. *The Dark Pageant: A Novel About Gilles de Rais*. London: Blond & Briggs, 1977.

_____. *Eroticism in Western Art*. London: Thames & Hudson, 1972.

_____. *Joan of Arc*. London: Allen Lane, 1976.

Luckenbill, David. *Other People's Lives*. Santa Barbara: University of California, Santa Barbara, 1973.

Lucretius. *De Rerum Natura*. trans. W.H.D. Rouse. London: William Heinemann, 1924.

Ludecke, Winifred. *Behind the Scenes of Espionage*. London: Mellifont Press, 1949.

Ludeke, Kurt. *I Knew Hitler*. New York: Charles Scribner's Sons, 1937.

Ludendorff, General Erich. *Ludendorff's Own Story, August 1914-November 1918*. New York: Harper's, 1919.

_____. *My War Memories, 1914-1918*. London: Hutchinson, 1919.

Ludlow, Fitzhugh. *The Hasheesh Eater*. New York: Harper Brothers, 1857.

_____. *The Heart of the Continent*. New York: Hurd and Houghton, 1870.

Ludlow, J.M. *British India: Its Races and Its History*. 2 vols. Cambridge, Eng.: Macmillan, 1858.

Ludlum, David M. *Social Ferment in Vermont. 1791-1850*. Montpelier, Vt.: Vermont Historical Society, 1948.

Ludlum, Stuart D. (ed.). *Great Shooting Stories*. Garden City, N.Y.: Doubleday, 1947.

Ludwig, Emil. *The Davos Murder*. trans. Eden and Cedar Paul. New York: Viking Press, 1936.

_____. *The Germans*. trans. Heinz and Ruth Norden. Boston: Little, Brown, 1941.

_____. *Napoleon*. Garden City, N.Y.: Garden City, 1926.

_____. *Roosevelt: A Study in Fortune and Power*. New York: Viking Press, 1938.

_____. *Talks with Mussolini*. trans. Eden and Cedar Paul. London: George Allen & Unwin, 1933.

_____. *Three Portraits*. London: Alliance, 1940.

_____. *Wilhelm Hohenzollern*. New York: G.P. Putnam's Sons, 1926.

Luhan, Mabel Dodge. *Intimate Memoirs*. 4 vols. New York: Harcourt, Brace, 1933.

Luján, Manuel L. *Reconocimiento de la Revolución Mexicana de 1912, por el Gobierno de Francisco I. Madero*. El Paso, Tex.: n.p., 1913.

Lukacs, George. *Solzhenitsyn*. London: Merlin, 1971.

Lukas, J. Anthony. *Don't Shoot - We Are Your Children!* New York: Dell, 1972.

_____. *Nightmare, the Underside of the Nixon Years.* New York: Viking Press, 1976.

Lukens, John. *The Sanger Story.* London: Hodder & Stoughton, 1956.

Lunday, Todd. *The Mystery Unveiled: The Truth about the Borden Tragedy.* Providence: J.A. & R.A. Reid, 1893.

Lum, Dyer D. *A Concise History of the Great Trial of the Chicago Anarchists in 1886.* Chicago: Socialistic, 1886.

Lundberg, Ferdinand. *America's 60 Families.* New York: Citadel Press, 1937.

_____. *Imperial Hearst.* New York: Modern Library, 1937.

_____, and Farnham, Marynia F. *Modern Women, The Lost Sex.* New York: Harper & Brothers, 1947.

_____. *The Rich and the Super-Rich: A Study of Power and Money Today.* New York: Lyle Stuart, 1969.

_____. *Who Controls Industry?* New York: Vanguard Press, 1938.

Lunde, Donald T. *The Die Song.* New York: Playboy Press, 1980.

_____. *Murder and Madness.* New York: W.W. Norton, 1975.

Lunden, Walter A. *The Death Penalty.* Anamosa, Iowa: Iowa State Reformatory Printing Department, 1960.

Lundsgaarde, Henry P. *Murder in Space City: A Cultural Analysis of Houston Homicide Patterns.* New York: Oxford University Press, 1977.

Luraghi, Raimondo. *Il Movimento Operaio Torinese Durante la Resistenza.* Turin, Italy: Einaudi, 1958.

Lussu, Emilio. *Diplomazia clandestina.* Rome: Nuova Italia, 1956.

_____. *Enter Mussolini.* trans. Marion Rawson. London: Methuen, 1936.

_____. *Un anno sull'altipiano.* Turin, Italy: Einaudi, 1964.

Lustgarten, Edgar. *The Business of Murder.* New York: Charles Scribner's Sons, 1968.

_____. *A Case to Answer.* London: Eyre and Spottiswoode, 1947.

_____. *A Century of Murders.* London: Eyre Methuen, 1975.

_____. *Defender's Triumph.* London: Wingate, 1951.

_____. *The Illustrated Story of Crime.* Chicago: Follett, 1976.

_____. *The Judges and the Judged.* London: Odhams, 1961.

_____. *The Murder and the Trial.* New York: Charles Scribner's Sons, 1958.

_____. *Prisoner at the Bar.* London: Andre Deutsch, 1951.

_____. *Verdict in Dispute.* New York: Scribner, 1950.

_____. *The Woman in the Case.* London: Andre Deutsch, 1955.

Luther, Martin. *Letters of Spiritual Counsel.* trans. Theodore G. Trapper. Philadelphia: Westminster Press, 1955.

_____. *Works.* Philadelphia: Muhlenberg & Concordia, 1955.

Luthin, R.H. *The First Lincoln Campaign.* Cambridge, Mass.: Harvard University Press, 1944.

_____. *The Real Abraham Lincoln.* Englewood Cliffs, N.J.: Prentice-Hall, 1960.

Luttwak, Edward. *Coup D'Etat: A Practical Handbook.* New York: Alfred A. Knoff, 1969.

_____, and Horwitz, Dan. *The Israeli Army.* New York: Harper & Row, 1975.

Lutyens, G. *Letters.* London: J. Lane, 1915.

Lutz, Alma. *Created Equal: A Biography of Elizabeth Cady Stanton, 1815-1902.* New York: John Day, 1940.

_____. *Susan B. Anthony.* Boston: Beacon Press, 1959.

Lutz, Ralph Haswell (ed.). *The Fall of the German Empire, 1914-1918.* Stanford, Calif.: Stanford University Press, 1932.

Luxemburg, Rosa. *The Russian Revolution.* Ann Arbor: University of Michigan Press, 1961.

Luzio, Alessandro, and Renier, Rodolfo. *Mantova e Urbino.* Turin, Italy: L. Roux, 1893.

Lybyer, Albert Howe. *The Government of the Ottoman Empire in the Time of Suleiman the Magnificent.* Cambridge, Mass.: Harvard University Press, 1913.

Lydolph, Paul E. *Geography of the USSR.* New York; Wiley, 1964.

Lydon, James G. *Pirates, Privateers and Profits.* Upper Saddle River, N.J.: Gregg Press, 1971.

Lydston, G. Frank. *Panama and the Sierras: A Doctor's Wander Days.* Chicago: Riverton Press, 1900.

Lyell, Sir Charles. *A Second Visit to the United States of North America.* New York: Harper & Brothers, 1850.

Lyford, Joseph P. *The Airtight Cage.* New York: Harper & Row, 1966.

Lyle, Jack. *The News in Megalopolis.* San Fransisco: Chandler, 1967.

Lyle, Judge John H. *The Dry and Lawless Years.* Englewood Cliffs, N.J.: Prentice-Hall, 1960.

Lyle, Katie Letcher. *The Man Who Wanted Seven Wives.* Chapel Hill, N.J.: Algonquin Books, 1986.

Lyman, Abbott. *Reminiscences.* Boston: Houghton Mifflin, 1923.

Lyman, Albert R. *Indians and Outlaws: Settling of the San Juan Frontier.* Salt Lake City, Utah: Bookcraft, 1962.

Lyman, George Dunlap. *John Marsh, Pioneer: The Life Story of a Trail-Blazer on Six Frontiers.* New York: Charles Scribner's Sons, 1930.

_____. *Ralston's Ring.* New York: Charles Scribner's Sons, 1937.

_____. *The Saga of the Comstock Lode.* New York: Charles Scribner's Sons, 1934.

Lyman, Henry M. *Artificial Anaesthesia and Anaesthetics.* New York: William Wood, 1881.

Lyman, Stanford M. *Chinese Americans.* New York: Random House, 1974.

_____, and Scott, Marvin B. *A Sociology of the Absurd.* New York: Appleton-Century-Crofts, 1970.

Lyman, Susan Elizabeth. *The Story of New York.* New York: Crown, 1964.

Lynch, Charles H. *The Civil War Diary, 1862-1865, of Charles H. Lynch.* Hartford, Conn.: Published by Author, 1915.

Lynch, Denis Tilden. *Boss Tweed, the Story of a Grim Generation.* New York: Boni and Liveright, 1927.

_____. *Criminals and Politicians.* New York: Macmillan, 1932.

_____. *An Epoch and a Man. Martin Van Buren and His Times.* New York: Horace Liveright, 1929.

_____. *The Wild Seventies.* New York: Appleton-Century, 1941.

Lynch, Diarmuid. *The I.R.B. and the 1916 Insurrection.* Cork: Mercier, 1957.

Lynch, Florence Monteith. *The Mystery Man of Banna Strand.* New York: Vantage Press, 1959.

Lynch, James D. *Kemper County Vindicated, and a Peep at Radical Rule in Mississippi.* New York: E.J. Hale & Son, 1879.

Lynch, K. *The Image of the City.* Cambridge, Mass.: MIT Press, 1960.

Lynch, P.P. *No Remedy for Death.* London: Long, 1970.

Lynch, W. Ware. *Rape! One Victim's Story.* Chicago: Follett, 1974.

Lynd, Kenneth S. (ed.). *The Professionals in America.* Boston: Beacon Press, 1965.

Lynd, Robert S., and Helen M. *Middletown: A Study in Contemporary American Culture.* London: Constable, 1929.

_____. *Middletown in Transition: A Study in Cultural Conflicts.* London: Constable, 1937.

Lynd, Staughton. *Class Conflict, Slavery and the United States Constitution.* Indianapolis: Bobbs-Merrill, 1968.

Lynes, Russell. *The Tastemakers.* New York: Harper, 1949.

Lynn, Kenneth S. *The Dream of Success.* Boston: Little, Brown, 1955.

_____. *William Dean Howells: An American Life.* New York: Harcourt Brace Jovanovich, 1970.

Lynx, J. J. *The Prince of Thieves.* New York: Atheneum, 1964.

Lyon, Peter. *The Wild, Wild West.* New York: Funk & Wagnalls, 1969.

Lyons, Arthur. *The Second Coming, Satanism in America.* New York: Dodd, Mead, 1970.

Lyons, B.J. *Thrills and Spills of a Cowboy Rancher.* New York:

Vantage Press, 1959.

Lyons, Eugene. *Assignment in Utopia*. New York: Harcourt, Brace, 1937.

_____. *Herbert Hoover: A Biography*. New York: Doubleday, 1964.

_____. *The Life and Death of Sacco and Vanzetti*. New York: International, 1927.

_____. *Worker's Paradise Lost*. New York: Funk & Wagnalls, 1967.

Lyons, Maurice F. *William F. McCombs: The President Maker*. Cincinnati: Bancroft, 1922.

Lytle, Andrew Nelson. *Bedford Forrest and His Critter Company*. New York: Minton, Balch, 1931.

M

Maas, Peter. *King of the Gypsies*. New York: Bantam, 1975.

_____. *Manhunt*. New York: Random House, 1986.

_____. *Serpico*. New York: Viking Press, 1973.

_____. *The Valachi Papers*. New York: G.P. Putnam's Sons, 1968.

Maas, Walter B. *Assassination in Vienna*. New York: Charles Scribner's Sons, 1972.

Maasburg, Friederich von. *Theresianische Halsgerichtsordnung*. Vienna, Aust.: Manz, 1880.

Mabry, William A. *The Negro in North Carolina Politics Since Reconstruction*. Durham, N.C.: Duke University Press, 1940.

MacAdam, George. *The Little Church Around the Corner*. New York: G.P. Putnam's Sons, 1925.

McAdoo, Eleanor R.W. *The Woodrow Wilsons*. New York: Macmillan, 1937.

McAdoo, William. *Guarding a Great City*. New York: Harper & Brothers, 1906.

_____. *When the Court Takes a Recess*. New York: E.P. Dutton, 1924.

McAdoo, William G. *Crowded Years*. Boston: Houghton Mifflin, 1931.

McAfee, Joseph Ernest. *College Pioneering*. Kansas City: Alumni Parkana Committee, 1938.

McAfee, Ward. *California's Railroad Era*. San Marino, Calif.: Golden West Books, 1973.

McAleavy, Henry. *A Dream of Tartary: The Origins and Misfortunes of Henry Pu Yi*. London: George Allen & Unwin, 1963.

McAllister, Robert. *The Kind of Guy I Am*. London: Hammond & Hammond, 1959.

McAllister, Ward. *Society as I Have Found It*. New York: Cassell, 1890.

McAlmon, Robert. *Being Geniuses Together*. Garden City, N.Y.: Doubleday, 1968.

McAlpine, R.W. *The Life and Times of Col. James Fisk, Jr.* New York: New York Books, 1872.

MacAndrew, C., and Edgerton, R.B. *Drunken Comportment*. Chicago: Aldine, 1969.

McAnear, Beverly. *The Income of the Colonial Governors of British North America*. New York: Pageant Press, 1967.

Macardle, Dorothy. *The Irish Republic*. New York: Farrar, Straus & Giroux, 1965.

Macarthur, Douglas. *Reminiscences*. New York: McGraw-Hill, 1964.

Macartney, C.A. *The Habsburg Empire: 1790-1918*. New York: Macmillan, 1969.

_____, and Palmer, A.W. *Independent Eastern Europe: A History*. London: Macmillan, 1962.

Macartney, Maxwell H. *One Man Alone*. London: Chatto & Windus, 1944.

Macartney, M.H.H., and Cremona, Paul. *Italy's Colonial and Foreign Policy, 1914-1937*. Oxford, Eng.: Oxford University Press, 1938.

McAuley, Jerry. *Jerry McAuley: His Life and Work*. New York: New York Observer, 1885.

McBain, Howard Lee. *Prohibition: Legal and Illegal*. New York: Macmillan, 1928.

McBath, Will R., and Adkins, E.W. *Life, Trial and Confession of John Nance*. Knoxville, Tenn.: Brownlow & Haws, 1867.

McBride, George M. *The Land Systems of Mexico*. New York: American Geographical Society, 1923.

McBride, Maud Gonne. *A Servant of the Queen*. Dublin, Ire.: Golden Eagle, 1950.

McBride, Robert W. *Personal Recollections of Abraham Lincoln*. Indianapolis, Ind.: Bobbs-Merrill, 1926.

McBride, Theresa M. *The Domestic Revolution: The Modernisation of Household Service in England and France*. London: Croom Helm, 1976.

McCabe, James D. *The History of the Great Riots*. Philadelphia: National, 1877.

_____. *Lights and Shadow of New York Life*. Philadephia: National, 1872.

McCabe, John. *Charlie Chaplin*. Garden City, N.Y.: Doubleday, 1978.

McCabe, Joseph. *Decay of the Church of Rome*. London: Methuen, 1909.

_____. *The Story of the World's Oldest Profession*. Kansas City: Girard, 1932.

McCabe, S., and Purves, R. *By-passing the Jury*. Oxford, Eng.: Basil Blackwell, 1972.

McCafferty, James A. (ed.). *Capital Punishment*. Chicago: Aldine, Atherton, 1972.

McCaffrey, Lawrence J. *The Irish Diaspora in America*. Bloomington: Indiana University Press, 1976.

McCaghy, C.H. *Crime in American Society*. New York: Macmillan, 1980.

_____. *Deviant Behaviour*. New York: Macmillan, 1976.

McCague, James. *The Second Rebellion: The Study of the New York City Draft Riots of 1863*. New York: Dial Press, 1968.

McCaleb, Walter Flavius. *Present and Past Banking in Mexico*. New York: Harper & Brothers, 1920.

McCall, George. *Observing the Law*. New York: Free Press, 1978.

McCall, Samuel W. *The Life of Thomas Brackett Reed*. Boston: Houghton Mifflin, 1914.

McCallum, Henry D., and Frances T. *The Wire That Fenced the West*. Norman: University of Oklahoma Press, 1965.

McCallum, John D. *Crime Doctor*. Mercer Island, Wash.: Writing Works, 1978.

_____. *Dave Beck*. Vancouver, British Columbia, Can.: Writing Works/Soules, 1978.

McCann, Alfred. *God--or Gorilla?* New York: Devin-Adair, 1922.

McCarry, Charles. *The Tears of Autumn*. Greenwich, Conn.: Fawcett, n.d.

McCartan, Patrick. *With De Valera in America*. Dublin, Ire.: Fitzpatrick, 1932.

McCarthy, Burke. *The Suppressed Truth about the Assassination of Abraham Lincoln*. Washington, D.C.: Published by Author, 1922.

McCarthy, Charles H. *Lincoln's Plan of Reconstruction*. New York: AMS Press, 1966.

McCarthy, Dennis V.N., and Smith, Philip W. *Protecting the President: The Inside Story of a Secret Service Agent*. New York: William Morrow, 1985.

McCarthy, Dudley. *South-West Pacific Area--First Year: Kokoda to Wau*. Canberra, Aus.: Australian War Memorial, 1959.

McCarthy, E. Ray. *The Crisis of 1873*. Minneapolis, Minn.: Burgess, 1935.

McCarthy, Joe. *McCarthyism: The Fight for America.* New York: Devin-Adair, 1952.

_____. *Major Speeches and Debates Delivered in the U.S. Senate, 1950-51.* Washington, D.C.: U.S. Government Printing Office, 1953.

McCarthy, Raymond G. (ed.). *Drinking and Intoxication.* New Haven, Conn.: Yale Center of Alcohol Studies, 1959.

McCarty, D. *Psychology for the Lawyer.* Englewood Cliffs, N.J.: Prentice-Hall, 1929.

McCarty, John L. *Adobe Walls Bride.* San Antonio, Texas: Naylor, 1955.

_____. *The Enchanted West.* Dallas: Doctor Pepper, 1944.

_____. *Maverick Town: The Story of Old Tascosa.* Norman: University of Oklahoma Press, 1946.

_____ (ed.). *Some Experiences of Boss Neff in the Texas and Oklahoma Panhandle.* Amarillo, Texas: Globe News, 1941.

McCarty, Lea Franklin. *The Gunfighters.* Berkeley, Calif.: Mike Roberts, 1959.

Mccarty, Rev. *Account of the Behavior of Mrs. Spooner After Her Commitment and Condemnation for Being Accessory in the Murder of Her Husband.* Brookfield, Mass.: n.p., 1778.

Maccarty, Thaddeus. *The Guilt of Innocent Blood Put Away.* Norwich, Conn.: John Trumbull, 1778.

McCauley, James Emmitt. *A Stove-Up Cowboy's Story.* Dallas: University of Texas Press, 1943.

McClane, Charles B. *Soviet Policy and the Chinese Communists 1931-1946.* New York: Columbia University Press, 1958.

McCleery, Richard H. *Policy Change in Prison Management.* East Lansing: Michigan State University Bureau of Social and Political Research, 1957.

McClellan, George B., Jr. *The Gentleman and The Tiger: The Autobiography of George B. McClellan, Jr.* Philadelphia: J.B. Lippincott, 1956.

_____. *McClellan's Own Story-A War for the Union.* New York: Charles L. Webster, 1887.

McClellan, Grant S. (ed.). *Capital Punishment.* New York: H.W. Wilson, 1961.

McClellan, John L. *Crime Without Punishment.* New York: Duell, Sloan & Pearce, 1962.

McClellan, Woodford D. *Svetozar Markovic and the Origins of Balkan Socialism.* Princeton, N.J.: Princeton University Press, 1964.

McClement, Fred. *The Strange Case of Ambrose Small.* Toronto, Ontario, Can.: McClelland and Stewart, 1974.

McClintick, David. *Stealing From the Rich.* New York: Quill, 1983.

McClintock, Frederick H. *Crimes of Violence.* New York: St. Martin's Press, 1963.

_____, and Avison, N.H. *Crime in England and Wales.* London: William Heinemann, 1968.

_____, and Gibson, Evelyn. *Robbery in London.* New York: St. Martin's Press, 1961.

McClintock, James H. *Arizona, Prehistoric-Aboriginal-Pioneer-Modern.* Chicago: S.J. Clarke, 1916.

McClintock, John S. *Pioneer Days in the Black Hills.* Deadwood, S.D.: Published by Author, 1939.

McClintock, Miller. *Report and Recommendations of the Metropolitan Street Traffic Survey.* Chicago: Chicago Association of Commerce, 1926.

McCloskey, Robert J. *The American Supreme Court.* Chicago: University of Chicago Press, 1960.

_____. *The Modern Supreme Court.* Cambridge, Mass.: Harvard University Press, 1972.

McClosky, Herbert, and Turner, John E. *The Soviet Dictatorship.* New York: McGraw-Hill, 1960.

McCloy, John J. *The Great Gulf Oil Spill: The Inside Report; Gulf Oil's Bribery and Political Chicanery.* New York: Chelsea House, 1976.

McClure, Alexander Kelly. *Abraham Lincoln and Men of War-Times.* Philadelphia: Times, 1892.

_____. *Recollections of a Half Century.* Salem, Mass.: n.p., n.d.

_____. *Three Thousand Miles Through the Rocky Mountains.* Philadelphia: J.B. Lippincott, 1869.

McClure, James. *Killers.* London: Fontana, 1976.

_____. *Spike Island.* New York: Pantheon, 1980.

McClure, James Baird (ed.). *Stories and Sketches of Chicago: An Interesting, Entertaining, and Instructive Sketch History of the Wonderful City "By the Sea".* Chicago: Rhodes & McClure, 1880.

McClure, Stanley W. *Ford's Theatre and the House Where Lincoln Died.* Washington, D.C.: U.S. Government Printing Office, 1969.

_____. *The Lincoln Museum and the House Where Lincoln Died.* Washington, D.C.: National Park Service Historical Handbook, 1949.

Maccoby, E.E., and Jacklin, C.N. *The Psychology of Sex Differences.* Stanford, Calif.: Stanford University Press, 1974.

Maccoby, Hyam. *Revolution in Judaea: Jesus and the Jewish Resistance.* New York: Taplinger, 1980.

Maccoby, Simon (ed.). *The English Radical Tradition, 1763-1914.* London: Nichols Kaye, 1952.

McColl, R. *Roger Casement: A New Judgement.* London: Hamish Hamilton, 1956.

McComas, J. Francis. *The Graveside Companion.* New York: Obelensky, 1962.

McCombs, William F. *Making Woodrow Wilson President.* New York: Fairview, 1921.

_____. *Some Reasons Why Woodrow Wilson Should be the Democratic Nominee.* New York: Editorial Review, 1912.

McConaughy, John. *From Cain to Capone: Racketeering Down the Ages.* New York: Brentano's, 1931.

McConnell, Brian. *Assassination.* London: Leslie Frewin, 1969.

_____. *Found Naked and Dead.* London: New English Library, 1974.

_____. *The History of Assassination.* Nashville, Tenn.: Aurora, 1969.

McConnell, Grant. *Private Power and American Democracy.* New York: Alfred A. Knopf, 1956.

McConnell, H.H. *Five Years a Cavalryman; or, Sketches of Regular Army Life on the Texas Frontier.* Jacksboro, Texas: J.N. Rogers, 1889.

McConnell, J.L. *Western Characters.* New York: Redfield, 1853.

McConnell, Jean. *The Detectives: Turning Points in Criminal Investigation.* Newton Abbot, Eng.: David & Charles, 1976.

McConnell, William J. *Early History of Idaho.* Caldwell, Idaho: Caxton Printers, 1913.

McConnell, William John. *Frontier Law: A Story of Vigilante Days.* New York: World Book, 1924.

McConville, Michael, and Baldwin, John. *Courts, Prosecution and Conviction.* Oxford, Eng.: Clarendon Press, 1981.

McCool, Grace. *So Said the Coroner: How They Died in Old Cochise.* Tombstone, Ariz.: Tombstone Epitaph, 1968.

McCord, W., and McCord, J. *Origins of Crime.* New York: Columbia University Press, 1959.

_____. *The Psycopath: An Essay on the Criminal Mind.* Princeton, N.J.: D. Van Nostrand, 1964.

McCorkle, John. *Three Years with Quantrill: A True Story.* Armstrong, Mo.: Armstrong Herald, 1914.

McCorkle, Lloyd, Elias, Albert, and Lovell, Bixby F. *The Highfields Story: An Experimental Treatment Project for Youthful Offenders.* New York: Henry Holt, 1958.

_____, and Korn, Richard. *The Sociology of Punishment and Correction.* New York: John Wiley & Sons, 1970.

MacCorkle, Stuart A. *American Policy of Recognition Towards Mexico.* Baltimore, Md.: Johns Hopkins University Press, 1933.

MacCorkle, William Alexander. *Recollections of Fifty Years of West Virginia.* New York: G.P. Putnam's Sons, 1928.

MacCormick, A.H. *Education of Adult Prisoners.* New York: National Society of Penal Information, 1931.

McCormick, Anne O'Hare. *Vatican Journal, 1921-1954.* New York: Ferrar, Straus & Cudahy, 1957.

McCormick, Donald, *The Identity of Jack the Ripper.* London: Arrow Books, 1970.

_____. *Murder by Witchcraft.* London: John Long, 1968.

_____. *Peddlar of Death.* London: Macdonald, 1965.

McCormick, Ken. *Sprung: The Release of Willie Calloway.* New York: St. Martin's 1964.

McCormick, R.P. *The History of Voting in New Jersey.* New Brunswick, N.J.: Rutgers University Press, 1953.

McCormick, Robert R. *The American Empire.* Chicago: Chicago Tribune, 1952.

_____. *The American Revolution and its Influence on World Civilization.* Chicago: Chicago Tribune, 1945.

_____. *The Army of 1918.* New York: Harcourt, Brace, 1920.

_____. *Freedom of the Press.* New York: D. Appleton-Century, 1936.

_____. *How We Acquired Our National Territory.* Chicago: Chicago Tribune, 1942.

_____. *Ulysses S. Grant: The Great Soldier of America.* New York: D. Appleton-Century, 1934.

_____. *The War Without Grant.* New York: Bond Wheelwright, 1950.

_____. *With the Russian Army, Being the Experiences of a National Guardsman.* New York: Macmillan, 1915.

McCoy, Alfred W. *The Politics of Heroin in Southeast Asia.* New York: Harper & Row, 1972.

McCoy, Donald. *Angry Voices: Left-of Center Politics in the New Deal Era.* Lawrence: University of Kansas Press, 1958.

McCoy, Joseph G. *Historic Sketches of the Cattle Trade.* Kansas City: Ramsey Millet & Hudson, 1874.

McCracken, Alan. *Very Soon Now, Joe.* New York: Hobson Book Press, 1947.

McCracken, Harold. *Hunters of the Stormy Sea.* Garden City, N.Y.: Doubleday, 1957.

McCrady, Edward. *History of South Carolina in the Revolution.* 2 vols. New York: Macmillan, 1901.

McCready, Albert L. *Railroads in the Days of Steam.* New York: American Heritage, 1960.

MacCreary, Henry. *A Story of Durant, "Queen of Three Valleys".* Durant, Okla.: Democrat Printing, 1946.

McCullagh, Francis. *Red Mexico: A Reign of Terror in America.* New York: L. Carrier, 1928.

McCullogh, Hugh. *Men and Measures of Half a Century.* New York: Charles Scribner's Sons, 1889.

McCune, Bily. *The Autobiography of Bily McCune.* New York: Popular Biographies, 1973.

McCune, Wesley. *The Nine Young Men.* New York: Harper & Row, 1947.

McCurdy, A.C. *Win Who Will.* Philadelphia: Barclay, 1872.

MacCurdy, J.T. *Germany, Russia and the Future.* Cambridge, Eng.: Cambridge University Press, 1944.

McCutcheon, John T. *Drawn from Memory.* Indianapolis, Ind.: Bobbs-Merrill, 1950.

McDade, Thomas. *Annals of Murder.* Norman: University of Oklahoma Press, 1961.

McDaniel, Ruel. *Vinegaroon.* Kingsport, Tenn.: Southern, 1936.

McDearmon, Ray. *Without the Shedding of Blood: The Story of Dr. U.D. Uzell, and of Pioneer Life at Old Kimball.* San Antonio, Texas: Naylor, 1953.

McDermott, John D. *The French in the Mississippi Valley.* Urbana: University of Illinois Press, 1965.

McDermott, John Francis (ed.). *Frenchmen and French Ways in the Mississippi Valley.* Chicago: University of Illinois Press, 1969.

_____. *The Lost Panoramas of the Mississippi.* Chicago: University of Chicago Press, 1958.

Macdermott, Mercia. *A History of Bulgaria, 1393-1885.* London: George Allen & Unwin, 1962.

McDermott, M.J., and Hindelang, M.J. *Juvenile Criminal Behavior in the United States.* Washington, D.C.: Office of Juvenile Justice and Delinquency Prevention, 1981.

_____. *Rape Victimization in 26 American Cities.* Washington, D.C.: U.S. Government Printing Office, 1979

MacDonagh, Michael. *The Irish at the Front.* London: Hodder & Stoughton, 1916.

_____. *In London During the Great War: Diary of a Journalist.* London: Eyre & Spottiswoode, 1935.

MacDonald, A.B. (ed.). *Hands Up! True Stories of the Six-Gun Fighters of the Old Wild West.* New York: Bobbs-Merrill, 1927.

MacDonald, Arthur. *Criminology.* New York: Funk & Wagnalls, 1893.

_____. *Le criminel type dans quelques formes graves de la criminalité.* Lyons, Fr.: Storck, 1893.

Macdonald, Bruce J.S. *The Trial of Kurt Meyer.* Toronto, Ontario, Can.: Clarke Irwin, 1954.

McDonald, Donald. *The Police.* Santa Barbara, Calif.: Center for the Study of Democratic Institutions, 1962.

Macdonald, Dwight. *The Ford Foundation.* New York: Reynal, 1955.

_____. *Henry Wallace: The Man and the Myth.* New York: Vanguard Press, 1947.

MacDonald, Fergus. *The Catholic Church and the Secret Societies in the United States.* New York: U.S. Catholic Historical Society, 1946.

McDonald, Forrest. *Insull.* Chicago: University of Chicago Press, 1962.

_____. *We the People: The Economic Origins of the Constitution.* Chicago: University of Chicago Press, 1958.

McDonald, Hugh C., and Bocca, Geoffrey. *Appointment in Dallas: The Final Solution to the Assassination of JFK.* New York: Published by Author, 1975.

_____, and Moore, Robin. *L.B.J. and the J.F.K. Conspiracy.* Westport, Conn.: Condon, 1979.

_____. *Survival.* New York: Ballantine, 1982.

MacDonald, J. Fred. *Television and the Red Menace: The Video Road to Vietnam.* New York: Frederick A. Praeger, 1985.

McDonald, James G. *My Mission in Israel.* New York: Simon & Schuster, 1951.

McDonald, James Ramsay. *American Speeches.* London: Jonathan Cape, 1930.

_____. *The Socialist Movement.* New York: Henry Holt, 1911.

MacDonald, John. *Secrets of the Great Whiskey Ring; and Eighteen Months in the Penitentiary. . . etc.* St. Louis: W.S. Bryan, 1880.

MacDonald, John M. *Armed Robbery.* Springfield, Ill.: Charles C. Thomas, 1975.

_____. *Homicidal Threats.* Springfield, Ill.: Charles C. Thomas, 1968.

_____. *Indecent Exposure.* Springfield, Ill: Charles C. Thomas, 1973.

_____. *The Murderer and His Victim.* Springfield, Ill.: Charles C. Thomas, 1961.

_____. *Psychiatry and the Criminal.* Springfield, Ill.: Charles C. Thomas, 1958.

_____. *Rape: Offenders and Their Victims.* Springfield, Ill.: Charles C. Thomas, 1971.

MacDonald, Philip. *Mystery of the Dead Police.* New York: Doubleday, 1933.

MacDonald, Robert. *The League of Arab States.* Princeton, N.J.: Princeton University Press, 1965.

McDonald, William A. *Progress Into the Past: The Rediscovery of Mycenaean Civilization.* Bloomington, Ind.: Indiana University Press, 1967.

McDonald, William F. (ed.). *Criminal Justice and the Victim.* Beverly Hills, Calif.: Sage, 1976.

McDougal, Henry Clay. *Recollections, 1844-1909.* Kansas City: Franklin Hudson, 1910.

MacDougall, A. Kent. *The Press.* Princeton, N.J.: Dow Jones,

1972.

MacDougall, Alexander William. *The Maybrick Case, a Settlement of the Case As a Whole.* London: Balliére, Tindall, and Cox, 1896.

MacDougall, Curtis D. *Hoaxes.* New York: Macmillan, 1940.

MacDougall, Ernest D. (ed.). *Crime for Profit: A Symposium on Mercenary Crime.* Boston: Statford, 1933.

MacDougall, Malcolm D. *We Almost Made It.* New York: Crown, 1977.

MacDougall, Michael, and Furnas, F.C. *Gamblers Don't Gamble.* New York: Greystone Press, 1939.

McDougall, Walt. *This Is the Life!* New York: Alfred A. Knopf, 1926.

McDougall, William H., Jr. *By Eastern Windows: The Story of a Battle of Souls and Minds in the Prison Camps of Sumatra.* London: Arthur Barker, 1951.

McDowell, Robert. *The Irish Administration: 1801-1914.* Westport, Conn.: Greenwood Press, 1976.

Macé, Gustave. *Les Femmes criminelles.* Paris: Charpentier, 1904.

_____. *My First Crime.* London: Vizetelly, 1886.

_____. *La Police parisienne.* Paris: Charpentier, 1884.

Mace, Ellis C. *River Steamboats and Steamboat Men.* Cynthiana, Ky.: Hobson Book Press, 1944.

Mace, Vera and David. *Marriage East and West.* Garden City, N.Y.: Doubleday, 1960.

Mace, William H. *American History.* Skokie, Ill.: Rand McNally, 1925.

McElderry, Andrea Lee. *Shanghai Old-Style Banks 1800-1935.* Ann Arbor: University of Michigan Press, 1935.

McElroy, John. *Andersonville: A Story of Rebel Military Prisons.* New York: Arno, 1879.

McElroy, Robert. *Grover Cleveland. The Man and the Statesman.* 2 vols. New York: Harper, 1923.

_____. *Levi Parsons Morton: Banker, Diplomat, and Statesman.* New York: G.P. Putnam's Sons, 1930.

McElroy, Robert, et al. *The Retrospect.* San Francisco: A. Buswell, 1883.

McEntee, Col. Girard L. *Military History of the World War.* New York: Charles Scribner's Sons, 1937.

McFall, J.E.W. (ed.). *Buchanan's Text-Book of Forensic Medicine and Toxicology.* London: Livingstone, 1925.

McFarland, Raymond. *A History of the New England Fisheries.* New York: D. Appleton, 1911.

Macfarlane, A.D.J. *Witchcraft in Tudor and Stuart England.* New York: Harper & Row, 1970.

McFarlane, Ian. *Proof of Conspiracy in the Assassination of President Kennedy.* Melbourne: Book Distributors, 1974.

Macfarlane, Jean W., and Allen, L., and Honzik, M.P. *A Developmental Study of the Behavior Problems of Normal Children between 21 Months and 14 Years.* Berkeley: University of California Press, 1954.

Macfarlane, Leslie. *Violence and the State.* London: Nelson, 1974.

McGarvey, Patrick J. *C.I.A.: The Myth and the Madness.* Baltimore, Md.: Penguin Books, 1973.

McGeary, M. Nelson. *Gifford Pinchot: Forester Politician.* Princeton, N.J.: Princeton University Press, 1960.

McGee, John H. *Rice and Salt.* San Antonio, Texas: Naylor, 1962.

McGeeney, P.S. *Down at Stein's Pass: A Romance of New Mexico.* Boston: Angel Guardian Press, 1909.

McGehee, Edward G., and Hildebrand, William H. (eds.). *The Death Penalty: A Literary and Historical Approach.* Boston: D.C. Heath, 1964.

McGhee, J.D. *Running the Gauntlet.* New York: National Urban League, 1984.

McGiffin, Lee. *Ten Tall Texans.* New York: Lothrop, Lee & Shepard, 1956.

McGillycuddy, Julia B. *McGillycuddy, Agent: A Biography of Dr.*

Valentine T. McGillycuddy. Stanford, Calif.: Stanford University Press, 1941.

McGinnis, Edith B. *The Promised Land.* Boerne, Texas: Topperwein, 1947.

McGinnis, Joe. *The Selling of the President, 1968.* New York: Pocket Books, 1968.

McGinty, Billy, and Eyler, Glenn, Jr. *The Old West.* Stillwater, Okla.: Redlands Press, 1958.

McGinty, Garnie W. *A History of the Great Reform Movement in New Orleans.* n.p., n.d.

McGivena, Leo E., et al. (eds.). *The News: The First Fifty Years of New York's Picture Newspaper.* New York: News Syndicate, 1960.

McGivern, Edward. *Ed McGivern's Book on Fast and Fancy Revolver Shooting and Police Training.* Springfield, Mass.: King-Richardson, 1938.

McGlinchee, Claire. *The First Decade of the Boston Museum.* Boston: Bruce Humphries, 1940.

McGloin, John Bernard. *San Francisco: The Story of a City.* San Rafael, Calif.: Presidio Press, 1978.

McGory, Mary. *In Memoriam.* Washington, D.C.: Washington Evening Star Newspaper, n.d.

McGovern, James. *Martin Bormann.* New York: William Morrow, 1968.

MacGovern, William. *From Luther to Hitler.* London: George Harrap, 1946.

McGowan, Helen. *Big City Madam.* New York: Lancer Books, 1965.

Macgowan, Kenneth. *Behind the Screen: The History and Techniques of the Motion Picture.* New York: Delacorte Press, 1965.

McGrady, Mike. *Crime Scientists.* Philadelphia: J.B. Lippincott, 1961.

McGrath, John H., and Scarpitti, Frank R. *Youth and Drugs.* Glenview, Ill.: Scott, Foresman, 1970.

McGrath, W.T. *Should Canada Abolish the Gallows and the Lash?* Winnipeg, Manitoba, Can.: Stovel-Advocate Press, 1956.

McGregor, Douglas. *The Human Side of Enterprise.* New York: McGraw-Hill, 1960.

MacGregor, F., et al. *Facial Deformities and Plastic Surgery.* Springfield, Ill.: Charles C. Thomas, 1953.

MacGregor, Geddes. *Thundering Scot.* London: Macmillan, 1958.

_____. *The Tichborne Impostor.* Philadelphia: J.B. Lippincott, 1957.

MacGregor, George. *The History of Burke and Hare.* Glasgow, Scot.: T.D. Morison, 1884.

McGregor, O.R. *Divorce in England.* Toronto, Ontario, Can.: William Heinemann, 1957.

MacGregor-Hastie, Roy. *The Day of the Lion, The Rise and Fall of Fascist Italy, 1922-1945.* New York: Coward-McCann, 1963.

McGuigan, Patrick B., and Rader, Randall R. (eds.). *Criminal Justice Reform.* Chicago: Henry Regnery, 1983.

McGuire, Constantine E. *Italy's International Economic Position.* London: George Allen & Unwin, 1927.

McGuire, E. Patrick. *The Forgers.* Bernardsville, N.J.: Padrie, 1969.

Macguire, H.N. *The Black Hills of Dakota: A Miniature History of Their Settlement, Resources, Production and Prospects.* Chicago: Jacob S. Gantz, 1879.

_____. *The Coming Empire: A Complete and Reliable Treatise on the Black Hills, Yellowstone and Big Horn Regions.* Sioux City, Iowa: Watkins & Snead, 1878.

McGuire, Maria. *To Take Arms.* London: Macmillan, 1973.

McGurrin, James. *Bourke Cockran: A Free Lance in American Politics.* New York: Charles Scribner's Sons, 1958.

McHenry, Dean E. *The Labor Party in Transition, 1931-1938.* London: George Routledge & Sons, 1938.

Machiavelli, Niccolò. *The History of Florence and Other Selections.* trans. Judith A. Rawson. New York: Washington Square Press, 1940.

_____. *The Prince and the Discourses.* New York: Modern Library, 1940.

Machlin, Milton. *Libby.* New York: Tower, 1980.

_____, and Woodfield, William Read. *Ninth Life.* New York: G.P. Putnam's Sons, 1961.

McHugh, Hugh [George Vere Hobart]. *You Can Search Me.* New York: G. W. Dillingham, 1905.

McIlvaine, Mabel (ed.). *Reminiscences of Chicago during the Civil War.* Chicago: R.R. Donnelley, 1914.

_____ (ed.). *Reminiscences of Chicago during the Forties and Fifties.* Chicago: R.R. Donnelley, 1913.

_____ (ed.). *Reminiscences of Chicago during the Great Fire.* Chicago: R.R. Donnelley, 1915.

_____. *Reminiscences of Early Chicago.* Chicago: Lakeside Press, 1912.

McIlwain, C.H. *The Growth of Political Thought in the West.* New York: Macmillan, 1932.

McIlwaine, Shields. *Memphis Down in Dixie.* New York: E.P. Dutton, 1948.

MacInnes, Colin. *The London Novels of Colin MacInnes.* New York: Farrar, Straus & Giroux, 1969.

McInnis, Edgar. *The War, Third Year.* New York: Oxford University Press, 1942.

McIntire, James. *Early Days in Texas: A Trip to Hell and Heaven.* Kansas City: McIntire, 1902.

McIntire, Josephine. *Boot Hill.* Boston: Chapman & Grimes, 1945.

McIntyre, J.W. (ed.). *The Writings and Speeches of Daniel Webster.* Boston: Little, Brown, 1903.

McIntosh, Arthur T. *Chicago.* Chicago: Press of G.G. Renneker, 1921.

McIntosh, Mary. *The Organization of Crime.* London: Macmillan, 1975.

MacIsaac, John. *Half the Fun Was Getting There.* Englewood Cliffs, N.J.: Prentice-Hall, 1968.

MacIver, R.M. *The Ramparts We Guard.* New York: Macmillan, 1950.

_____. *Social Causation.* Boston: Ginn, 1940.

_____. *The Web of Government.* New York: Macmillan, 1947.

Mackaness, George. *The Life of Vice-Admiral William Bligh.* New York: Farrar & Rinehart, 1936.

MacKay, Charles. *Extraordinary Popular Delusions and the Madness of Crowds.* Boston: L.C. Page, 1932.

McKay, Claude. *Home to Harlem.* New York: Pocket Books, 1965.

McKay, Henry D., and Shaw, Clifford R. *Juvenile Delinquency and Urban Areas.* Chicago: University of Chicago Press, 1942.

Mackay, Margaret. *Los Angeles Proper and Improper.* New York: Goodwin, 1938.

McKay, Richard C. *South Street: A Maritime History.* New York: G.P. Putnam's Sons, 1934.

McKay, Robert B. *Reapportionment: The Law and Politics of Equal Representation.* New York: Twentieth Century Fund, 1965.

MacKaye, James. *Americanized Socialism.* New York: Doubleday, Page, 1916.

Mackaye, Milton. *Dramatic Crimes of 1927.* Garden City, N.Y.: Crime Club, 1928.

_____. *The Tin Box Parade.* New York: Robert M. McBride, 1934.

McKean, Dayton. *The Boss.* Boston: Houghton Mifflin, 1940.

McKee, Alexander. *H.M.S. Bounty.* New York: William Morrow, 1962.

McKee, Claude G. *Producing Maryland Tobacco.* College Park, Md.: University of Maryland, 1963.

McKee, Irving. *"Ben-Hur" Wallace.* Berkeley: University of California Press, 1947.

MacKellar, Jean Scott. *Rape: The Bait and the Trap.* New York: Crown, 1975.

McKelvey, Blake. *American Prisons.* Montclair, N.J.: Patterson Smith, 1977.

_____. *The Emergence of Metropolitan America, 1915-1966.* New Brunswick, N.J.: Rutgers University Press, 1968.

McKelvie, Martha. *The Fenceless Range.* Philadelphia: Dorrance, 1960.

McKelway, St. Clair. *The Big Little Man Brooklyn.* Boston: Houghton Mifflin, 1969.

_____. *True Tales from the Annals of Crime and Rascality.* New York: Random House, 1950.

_____. *True Tales of Crime and Rascality.* New York: Random House, 1933.

Macken, Walter. *The Scorching Wind.* New York: Macmillan, 1964.

McKenna, Marion C. *Borah.* Ann Arbor: University of Michigan Press, 1961.

McKenna, Stephen. *While I Remember.* New York: Doran, 1921.

McKenney, Thomas L., and Hall, James. *History of the Indian Tribes of North America.* Philadelphia: Daniel Rice & James G. Clark, 1842.

McKennon, C.H. *Iron Men: A Saga of the Deputy United States Marshals Who Rode the Indian Territory.* Garden City, N.Y.: Doubleday, 1967.

Mackenzie, Colin. *Biggs, The World's Most Wanted Man.* New York: William Morrow, 1975.

McKenzie, Donald. *Occupation: Thief.* Indianapolis, Ind.: Bobbs-Merrill, 1955.

Mackenzie, Frederic A. *Landru.* New York: Charles Scribner's Sons, 1928.

_____. *"Pussyfoot" Johnson.* New York: Fleming H. Revell, 1920.

_____. *The Trial of Harry Thaw.* London: Geoffrey Bles, 1928.

_____. *Twentieth Century Crimes.* Boston: Little, Brown, 1927.

_____. *World Famous Crimes.* London: Geoffrey Bles, 1927.

Mackenzie, Sir George. *Laws and Customs of Scotland in Matters Criminal.* Edinburgh, Scot.: George Swinton, 1678.

Mackenzie, Jeanne and Norman. *The Murder of Maria Marten.* New York: Pellegrini & Cudahy, 1948.

MacKenzie, K.P. *Operation Rangoon Jail.* London: Christopher Johnson, 1954.

Mackenzie, Sir Morell. *The Fatal Illness of Frederick the Noble.* London: Sampson Low, 1888.

Mackenzie, Muir. *Travels in the Slavonic Provinces of Turkey in Europe.* London: Bell & Daldy, 1867.

Mackenzie, Norman. *Secret Societies.* New York: Holt, Rinehart & Winston, 1967.

McKeon, Richard (ed.). *The Basic Works of Aristotle.* New York: Random House, 1941.

McKeown, Martha Ferguson. *The Trail Led North: Mont Hawthorne's Story.* New York: Macmillan, 1948.

McKernan, Maureen. *The Amazing Crime and Trial of Leopold and Loeb.* New York: New American Library, 1957.

MacKey, Philip English. *Voices Against Death.* New York: Artemis, 1978.

McKie, Ronald. *Proud Echo.* Sydney, Aus.: Angus & Robertson, 1953.

McKinley, Brian. *Royal Tour.* Adelaide, Aus.: Rigby, 1970.

McKinley, James. *Assassination in America.* New York: Harper & Row, 1977.

McKinney, John C. *Constructive Typology and Social Theory.* New York: Appleton-Century-Crofts, 1966.

Mackinnon, Flora Isabel (ed.). *Philosophical Writings of Henry More.* New York: Oxford University Press, 1925.

Mackinnon, Lord Justice. *On Circuit.* London: Cambridge University Press, 1940.

McKitrick, Eric L. *Andrew Johnson and the Reconstruction.* Chicago: University of Chicago Press, 1960.

McKittrick, Myrtle M. *Vallejo, Son of California.* Portland, Ore.:

Binfords & Mort, 1944.

McKnight, Gerald. *The Mind of the Terrorist*. London: Michael Joseph, 1974.

_____. *The Murder Squad*. London: W.H. Allen, 1967.

_____. *The Terrorist Mind*. Indianapolis, Ind.: Bobbs-Merrill, 1975.

Mack, Effie Mona. *Mark Twain in Nevada*. New York: Charles Scribner's Sons, 1947.

Mack, John A. *The Crime Industry*. Westmead, Eng.: Saxon House, 1974.

Mack, Mary Peter. *A Bentham Reader*. New York: Western, 1969.

Mack Smith, Denis. *A History of Sicily: Modern Sicily after 1713*. New York: Viking Press, 1968.

_____. *Italy: A Modern History*. Ann Arbor: University of Michigan Press, 1969.

McLain, John Scudder. *Alaska and the Klondike*. New York: McClure, Phillips, 1905.

MacLane, John F. *A Sagebrush Lawyer*. New York: Pandick Press, 1953.

McLaren, Malcolm, Jr. "Tyranny," *The Greek Political Experience*. Princeton, N.J.: Princeton University Press, 1941.

McLaughlin, James Fairfax. *The Life and Times of John Kelly, Tribune of the People*. New York: American News, 1885.

Maclay, Edgar Stanton. *A History of American Privateers*. New York: D. Appleton, 1899.

Maclean, Don. *Pictorial History of the Mafia*. New York: Pyramid, 1974.

McLean, Evalyn Walsh. *Father Struck It Rich*. Boston: Little, Brown, 1936.

Maclean, Fitzroy. *Take Nine Spies*. New York: Atheneum, 1978.

McLean, John H. *Reminiscences*. Nashville, Tenn.: Smith & Lamar, 1918.

MacLeish, Archibald. *The Irresponsibles*. New York: Duell, Sloan & Pearce, 1940.

McLellan, Hugh (ed.). *Journal of Thomas Nye Written during a Journey between Montreal and Chicago in 1837*. Champlain, Quebec, Can.: Moorsfield Press, 1932.

McLellan, Vin, and Avery, Paul. *The Voices of Guns*. New York: G.P. Putnam's Sons, 1977.

McLennon, John. *The Patriarchal Theory*. London: Macmillan, 1885.

McLeod, Alexander. *Pigtails and Gold Dust*. Caldwell, Idaho: Caxton Printers, 1947.

MacLeod, Donald. *Biography of Hon. Fernando Wood, Mayor of the City of New York*. New York: O.F. Parsons, 1858.

Macleod, Malcolm. *History of Witches*. Washington, D.C.: C.A. Beckert, 1894.

Macleod, William Christie. *The American Indian Frontier*. New York: Alfred A. Knopf, 1928.

McLoughlin, Emmett. *An Inquiry into the Assassination of Abraham Lincoln*. New York: Lyle Stuart, 1963.

McLoughlin, William G., Jr. *Billy Sunday Was His Real Name*. Chicago: University of Chicago Press, 1955.

McMahon, Edward B., and Curry, Leonard. *Medical Cover-Ups in the White House*. Washington, D.C.: Farragut, 1987.

MacManus, M.J. *Eamon de Valera*. Dublin, Ire.: Talbot, 1944-1962.

MacManus, Seumas. *The Story of the Irish Race*. New York: Irish, 1921.

McManus, Virginia. *Not For Love*. London: Frederick Muller, 1961.

McMaster, John Bach. *A History of the People of the United States from the Revolution to the Civil War*. 8 vols. New York: D. Appleton, 1904.

_____. *With the Fathers, Studies in the History of the United States*. New York: D. Appleton, 1896.

McMaster, S.W. *Sixty Years on the Upper Mississippi*. Rock Island: n.p., 1893.

McMillan, George. *The Making of an Assassin*. Boston: Little,

Brown, 1976.

Macmillan, H. *Pointing the Way, 1959-1961*. London: Macmillan, 1972.

_____, *Riding the Storm, 1956-1959*. London: Macmillan, 1959.

Macmillan, Harold. *The Blast of War*. London: Macmillan, 1967.

Macmillan, James. *The Honours Game*. London: Leslie Frewin, 1969.

McMillan, Priscilla Johnson. *Marina and Lee*. New York: Harper & Row, 1977.

Macmillan, Richard. *Twenty Angels over Rome*. London: Jarrolds, 1945.

MacMinn, George R. *The Theatre of the Golden Era in California*. Caldwell, Idaho: Caxton Printers, 1941.

McMullen, Jerry. *Paddle Wheel Days in California*. Palo Alto, Calif.: Stanford University Press, 1944.

McMullen, Thomas. *Hand-book of Wines*. New York: D. Appleton, 1852.

Macmunn, G.F. *Religions and Hidden Cults of India*. London: Sampson, Low, 1931.

McMurray, Donald L. *Coxey's Army*. Seattle: University of Washington Press, 1929.

McMurray, Floyd L. *Westbound*. New York: Charles Scribner's Sons, 1943.

MacNaghten, Sir Melville. *Days of My Years*. London: Edward Arnold, 1914.

MacNair, Harley Farnsworth (ed.). *China*. Berkeley: University of California Press, 1951.

MacNamara, Donald E.J., and Sagarin, Edward. *Sex, Crime and the Law*. New York: Free Press, 1978.

McNamara, Joseph D. *Safe and Sane*. New York: G.P. Putnam's Sons, 1984.

McNeal, Robert H. (ed.). *Lenin, Stalin, Khrushchev: Voices of Bolshevism*. New York: Prentice-Hall, 1963.

McNeal, Thomas Allen. *When Kansas Was Young*. New York: Macmillan, 1922.

MacNeice, Louis. *Astrology*. New York: Doubleday, 1964.

McNeil, Cora. *Mizzoura*. Minneapolis, Minn.: Mizzoura, 1898.

McNeill, John T., and Gamer, Helena M. *Medieval Handbooks of Penance*. New York: Columbia University Press, 1938.

McNeill, William H. *The Greek Dilemma: War and Aftermath*. Philadelphia: J.B. Lippincott, 1947.

_____. *A World History*. New York: Oxford University Press, 1967.

McNelly, Theodore. *Politics and Government in Japan*. Boston: Houghton Mifflin, 1972.

Macnish, Robert. *The Philosophy of Sleep*. Glasgow, Scot.: W.R. M'Phun, 1830.

McNitt, Frank. *The Indian Traders*. Norman: University of Oklahoma Press, 1962.

Macomb, John N. *Exploring Expedition from Santa Fe, New Mexico, to the Junction of the Grand and Green Rivers of the Great Colorado of the West*. Washington, D.C.: U.S. Government Printing Office, 1876.

Macomber, Ben. *The Jewel City*. San Francisco: J.H. Williams, 1915.

McPartland, J. *Sex in Our Changing World*. New York: Rinehart, 1947.

McPhaul, John J. *Deadlines and Monkeyshines: The Fabled World of Chicago Journalism*. Englewood Cliffs, N.J.: Prentice-Hall, 1962.

_____. *Johnny Torrio*. New Rochelle, N.Y.: Arlington House, 1970.

McPherren, Ida. *Empire Builders*. Sheridan, Wyo.: Star, 1942.

_____. *Imprints on Pioneer Trails*. Boston: Christopher, 1950.

_____. *Trail's End*. Casper, Wyo.: Prairie, 1938.

McPherson, Edward. *The Political History of the United States During the Period of Reconstruction*. Washington, D.C.: Solomons & Chapman, 1876.

MacPherson, J.S. *Eleven-Year-Olds Grow Up*. London: University of London Press, 1958.

McPherson, J.W. *The Moulids of Egypt.* Cairo, Egypt: Ptd. N.M. Press, 1941.

McQuaid, Clement (ed.). *Gamblers' Digest.* Chicago: Follett, 1961.

McRandle, James H. *The Track of the World.* Evanston, Ill.: Northwestern University Press, 1965.

Macready, Nevil. *Annals of an Active Life.* 2 vols. London: Hutchinson, 1924.

McReynolds, Robert. *Thirty Years on the Frontier.* Colorado Springs, Colo.: El Paso Publishing, 1906.

McRill, Albert. *And Satan Came Also.* Oklahoma City, Okla.: Britton, 1955.

McSeveney, Samuel T. *The Politics of Depression: Political Behavior in the Northeast, 1893-1896.* New York: Oxford University Press, 1972.

MacShane, Frank. *The Life of John O'Hara.* New York: E.P. Dutton, 1980.

_____. *The Life of Raymond Chandler.* London: Jonathan Cape, 1976.

MacStiofean, Sean. *Memoirs of a Revolutionary.* London: Gordon Cremonesi, 1975.

McTaggart, Lynne. *The Baby Brokers.* New York: Dial Press, 1980.

MacVicker, Charles P. *Titoism: Pattern for International Communism.* New York: St. Martin's Press, 1957.

McWatters, George S. *Detectives of Europe and America, or Life in the Secret Service.* Chicago: Laird & Lee, 1892.

_____. *Forgers and Confidence Men, or The Secrets of the Detective Service Divulged.* Chicago: Laird & Lee, 1892.

_____. *The Gambler's Wax Finger and Other Startling Detective Experiences.* Chicago: Laird & Lee, 1892.

_____. *Knots Untied, or Ways and Byways in the Hidden Life of American Detectives.* Hartford, Conn.: J.B. Burr & Hyde, 1871.

McWilliams, Carey. *Ambrose Bierce, A Biography.* New York: A. & C. Boni, 1929.

_____. *Factories in the Fields.* Boston: Little, Brown, 1943.

_____. *North from Mexico.* New York: Greenwood Press, 1948.

_____. *Southern California Country: The Cults of California.* New York: Duell, Sloan & Pearce, 1946.

_____. *Witch Hunt: The Revival of Heresy.* Boston: Little, Brown, 1950.

Macy, Christy, and Kaplan, Susan. *Documents.* New York: Penguin Books, 1980.

Macy, John. *Socialism in America.* New York: Doubleday, Page, 1916.

Madariaga, Isabel de. *Britain, Russia and the Armed Neutrality of 1780.* New Haven, Conn.: Yale University Press, 1962.

Madden, David (ed.). *Tough Guy Writers of the Thirties.* Carbondale: Southern Illinois University Press, 1968.

Madden, R.R. *Travels in Turkey, Egypt, Nubia and Palestine in 1824-1827.* London: H. Colburn, 1829.

Madden, Richard Robert. *The Literary Life and Correspondence of the Countess of Blessington.* New York: Harper, 1856.

_____. *Phantasmata, or Illusions and Fanaticism.* London: T.C. Newby, 1857.

Madelin, Louis. *Histoire du Consulat et de l'Empire.* 16 vols. Paris: Hachette, 1937-54.

Mader, Julius. *Who's Who in CIA.* Berlin: Published by Author, 1968.

Madero, Franciso I. *Las memorias y las mejores cartas de Francisco I. Madero.* Mexico City: Libro Mexicana, 1956.

Madison, Arnold. *Great Unsolved Cases.* London: Franklin Watts, 1978.

Madison, Charles A. *Critics and Crusaders: A Century of American Protest.* New York: Henry Holt, 1947.

Madison, James. *Notes of Debates in the Federal Convention of 1787.* Athens: Ohio University Press, 1966.

Madison, Virginia. *The Big Bend Country of Texas.* Albuquerque: University of New Mexico Press, 1955.

_____, and Stillwell, Hallie. *How Come It's Called That?* Albuquerque: University of New Mexico Press, 1958.

Madow, Leo, et al. *The Dangerous Sex Offender.* Philadelphia: General Assembly of the Commonwealth of Pennsylvania, 1963.

Maeder, Thomas. *Crime and Madness.* New York: Harper & Row, 1985.

Maeder, Thomas. *The Unspeakable Crimes of Dr. Petiot.* Toronto, Ontario, Can.: Atlantic, Little, Brown, 1980.

Maestro, Marcello. *Cesare Beccaria and the Origins of Penal Reform.* Philadelphia: Temple University Press, 1973.

_____. *Voltaire and Beccaria as Reformers of the Criminal Law.* New York: Columbia University Press, 1942.

Magaña, Gildardo, and Guerrero, Carlos Perez. *Emiliano Zapata y el Agrarismo en Mexico.* 5 vols. Mexico City: Editorial Ruta, 1951.

Magee, D. *What Murder Leaves Behind: The Victim's Family.* New York: Dodd, Mead, 1983.

Magee, John. *Northern Ireland: Crisis and Conflict.* London: Routledge & Kegan Paul, 1974.

Mager, N.H. and Katel, Jacques (eds.). *Conquest Without War.* New York: Simon & Schuster, 1961.

Mager, N.H. and S.K. *Protect Yourself.* New York: Dell, 1978.

Magidoff, Robert. *Kremlin vs. the People.* New York: Doubleday, 1953.

Magistrati, Count Massimo. *L'Italia a Berlino, 1937-1939.* Milan, Italy: Mondadori, 1956.

Magnus, Leonard A. *Roumania's Cause and Ideals.* London: Kegan Paul, Trench, Trubner, 1917.

Magnus, Philip. *Gladstone: A Biography.* London: John Murray, 1954.

_____. *King Edward the Seventh.* London: John Murray, 1964.

_____. *Kitchener.* New York: E.P. Dutton, 1959.

Magrath, C. Peter. *Morrison R. Waite.* New York: Macmillan, 1963.

Maguire, John Francis. *Father Mathew: A Biography.* London: Longman, Roberts & Green, 1863.

_____. *The Irish in America.* London: Longmans, Green, 1868.

MaGuire, Maria. *To Take Arms.* London: Macmillan, 1973.

Mahan, Rear Admiral Alfred T. *On Naval Warfare.* Boston: Little, Brown, 1942.

Mahdi, M. *Ibn Khaldun's Philosophy of History.* London: George Allen & Unwin, 1957.

Maher, George F. *Hostage: A Police Approach to a Contemporary Crisis.* Springfield, Ill.: Charles C. Thomas, 1977.

Mahin, Helen Ogden. *The Development and Significance of the Newspaper Headline.* Ann Arbor, Mich.: G. Wahr, 1924.

Mahoney, Dennis A. *The Prisoner of State.* New York: G.W. Caleton, 1863.

Mahoney, Ella V. *Sketches of Tudor Hall and the Booth Family.* Bel Air, Md.: Franklin Printing, 1925.

Mahoney, Irene. *Royal Cousin.* Garden City, N.Y.: Doubleday, 1970.

Maier, Hans W. *Der Kokainismus.* Leipzig, Ger.: Georg Thieme, 1926.

Maiken, Peter T. *Rip-Off.* Kansas City: Andrews & McMeel, 1979.

Mailer, Norman. *The Executioner's Song.* Boston: Little, Brown, 1979.

Main, J.T. *The Antifederalists: Critics of the Constitution, 1781-1788.* Chapel Hill: University of North Carolina Press, 1961.

_____. *The Social Structure of Revolutionary America 1763-1783.* Princeton, N.J.: Princeton University Press, 1965.

Maina, P. *Six Mau Mau Generals.* Nairobi, Kenya: Gazelle Books, 1977.

Maine, C.E. (ed.). *The World's Strangest Crimes.* New York: Hart, 1967.

Maine, Sir Henry Sumner. *Ancient Law.* London: John Murray, 1883.

Mainwaring, George. *Observations on the Present State of the Po-*

lice. London: John Murray, 1821.

Maire, G.F. *Raspoutine*. Paris: n.p., 1934.

Mairowitz, David Zane. *The Radical Soap Opera*. New York: Avon, 1974.

Mairs, G.T. *Fingerprint Study Data*. New York: Dlehanty Institute, 1938.

Maisch, Herbert. *Incest*. New York: Stein & Day, 1972.

Maitland, Frederic William. *The Constitutional History of England*. Cambridge, Eng.: Cambridge University Press, 1908.
_____. *The History of the English Law*. Cambridge, Eng.: Cambridge University Press, 1895.

Majdalany, Fred. *The Battle of El Alamein*. London: Weidenfeld & Nicolson, 1965.
_____. *Cassino*. London: Longmans, Green, 1957.
_____. *The Fall of Fortress Europe*. New York: Doubleday, 1968.
_____. *State of Emergency: The Full Story of Mau Mau*. Boston: Houghton Mifflin, 1963.

Majors, Alexander. *Seventy Years on the Frontier*. Chicago: Rand McNally, 1893.

Majumdar, R.C., et al. *An Advanced History of India*. New York: Macmillan, 1946.

Maki, John M. *Conflict and Tension in the Far East: Key Documents, 1894-1960*. Seattle: University of Washington Press, 1961.

Makins, John R. (ed.). *Boston Murders*. New York: Duell, Sloan & Pearce, 1947.

Malaparte, Curzio. *Kaputt*. trans. Cesare Foligno. New York: E.P. Dutton, 1946.
_____. *Technique du Coup d'Etat*. Paris: Bernard Grasset, 1948.

Malcolm, Andrew. *The Tyranny of the Group*. Totowa, N.J.: Littlefield, Adams, 1975.

Malcolm, Ian (ed.). *Scraps of Paper: German Proclamations in Belgium and France*. New York: Doran, 1916.
_____. *Trodden Way, 1895-1930*. London: Macmillan, 1930.

Malcolm, Lady. *A Diary of St. Helena*. London: George Allen & Unwin, 1899.

Malcovati, Enrica (ed.). *Oratorum Romanorum Fragmenta*. Taurinorum, Italy: Paravial et Sociorum, 1955.

Maldonado R., Calixto. *Los asesinatos de los Señores Madero y Pino Suárez*. Mexico City: n.p., 1922.

Malgeri, Alfredo. *L'occupazione di Milano e la Liberazione*. Milan, Italy: Editori Associati, 1947.

Malia, Martin E.. *Alexander Herzen and the Birth of Russian Socialism*. Cambridge, Mass.: Harvard University Press, 1961.

Malin, James C. *John Brown and the Legend of Fifty-Six*. Philadelphia: American Philosophical Society, 1942.

Malinowski, Bronislaw. *Crime and Custom in Savage Society*. Totowa, N.J.: Littlefield, Adams, 1966.
_____. *Magic, Science and Religion*. New York: Doubleday Anchor Books, 1954.
_____. *Sex and Repression in Savage Society*. London: Kegan, Paul, Trench, Trubner, 1927.
_____. *The Sexual Life of Savages*. London: George Routledge & Sons, 1932.

Malkiel, Burton G. *A Random Walk Down Wall Street*. New York: W.W. Norton, 1973.

Malkin, Maurice L. *Return to My Father's House*. New Rochelle, N.Y.: Arlington House, 1972.

Malko, George. *Scientology, The Now Religion*. New York: Dell, 1970.

Mallet, M.E. *The Borgias*. London: Bodley Head, 1969.

Mallet, Victor (ed.). *Life with Queen Victoria: Marie Mallet's Letters from Court 1887-1901*. Boston: Houghton Mifflin, 1968.

Mallory, John A. *United States Compiled Statutes: Annotated*. St. Paul, Minn.: West, 1916.

Mallory, Walter H. (ed.). *Political Handbook of the World*. New York: Harper & Row, 1927.

Malone, Dumas. *Jefferson the Virginian*. Boston: Little, Brown, 1948.

Malory, Thomas. *Le Morte D'Arthur*. trans. Keith Baines. New York: New American Library, 1962.

Malozemoff, Andrew. *Russian Far Eastern Policy, 1881-1904*. Berkeley: University of California Press, 1958.

Maltby, W.J. *Captain Jeff, or Frontier Life in Texas with the Texas Rangers*. Colorado, Texas: Whipkey, 1906.

Maltz, Michael D. *Evaluation of Crime Control Programs*. Washington, D.C.: National Institute of Law Enforcement and Criminal Justice, 1972.

Mamatey, Victor S. *The United States and East Central Europe 1914-1918: A Study in Wilsonian Diplomacy and Propaganda*. Princeton, N.J.: Princeton University Press, 1957.

Managing for Effective Police Discipline: A Manual of Rules, Procedures, Supportive Law and Effective Management. Gaithersburg, Md.: International Association of Chiefs of Police, 1976.

Manakee, Harold R. *Maryland in the Civil War*. Baltimore: Maryland Historical Society, 1961.

Manatt, Marsha. *Parents, Peers and Pot*. Rockville, Md.: National Institute on Drug Abuse, 1979.

Manceron, C. *Le dernier choix de Napoléon*. Paris: Robert Laffont, 1960.

Manchester, A.H. *A Modern Legal History of England and Wales, 1750-1950*. London: Butterworths, 1980.

Manchester, William. *American Caesar: Douglas MacArthur, 1880-1964*. Boston: Little, Brown, 1978.
_____. *The Death of a President*. New York: Harper & Row, 1967.
_____. *Disturber of the Peace*. New York: Harper & Bothers, 1951.
_____. *The Glory and the Dream*. Boston: Little, Brown, 1973.
_____. *Portrait of a President - John F. Kennedy in Profile*. Boston: Little, Brown, 1962.

Mancini, Jean-Gabriel. *Prostitutes and Their Parasites*. London: Elek Books, 1963.

Mancuso, Edward T. *The Public Defender System in the State of California*. Chicago: National Legal Aid and Defender Association, 1959.

Mandelbaum, Seymour J. *Boss Tweed's New York*. New York: John Wiley & Sons, 1965.

Manetti, Dante. *Gente di Romagna*. Bologna, Italy: Cappelli, 1924.

Maney, Richard. *Fanfare*. New York: Harper & Brothers, 1957.

Mangam, William Daniel. *The Clarks: An American Phenomenon*. New York: Silver Bow Press, 1941.
_____. *The Clarks of Montana*. New York: Silver Bow Press, 1939.

Mangan, Frank J. *Bordertown*. El Paso, Texas: Carl Hertzog, 1964.

Mangione, Jerre. *A Passion for Sicilians: The World Around Danilo Dolci*. New Brunswick, N.J.: Transaction Books, 1985.

Mangum, C.S. *The Legal Status of the Negro*. Chapel Hill: University of North Carolina Press, 1940.

The Manheim Tragedy. Lancaster, Pa.: H.A. Rockafield, 1858.

A Man and His Friends: A Life Story of Milton H. Esberg. San Francisco: Recorder-Sunset Press, 1953.

Manicas, Peter T. *The Death of the State*. New York: G.P. Putnam's Sons, 1974.

Mankiewicz, Frank, and Jones, Kirby. *With Fidel: A Portrait of Castro and Cuba*. New York: Ballantine, 1975.

Mankoff, Allan H. *Mankoff's Lusty Europe*. New York: Viking Press, 1973.

Manly, William Lewis. *Death Valley in 1840*. Santa Barbara, Calif.: Wallace Hebberd, 1929.

Mann, Arthur. *Baseball Confidential*. New York: David McKay, 1951.

Mann, Arthur. *La Guardia Comes to Power: 1933*. Philadelphia: J.B. Lippincott, 1965.

_____. *Yankee Reformers in the Urban Age*. Cambridge, Mass.: Harvard University Press, 1954.

Mann, Etta Donnan. *Four Years in the Governor's Mansion in Virginia, 1910-1914*. Richmond, Va.: Diet Press, 1937.

Mann, Golo. *Wallenstein: His Life Narrated*. trans. Charles Kessler. New York: Holt, Rinehart & Winston, 1976.

Mann, Kenneth. *Defending White-Collar Crime*. New Haven, Conn.: Yale University Press, 1985.

Mann, W. Edward. *Orgone, Reich and Eros*. New York: Simon & Schuster, 1973.

Mann, William B. *Trial, Life and Execution of Anton Probst*. Philadelphia: T.P. Peterson & Brothers, 1866.

Mannheim, Hermann. *Comparative Criminology*. Boston: Houghton Mifflin, 1965.

_____. *Criminal Justice and Social Reconstruction*. New York: Oxford University Press, 1946.

_____. *The Dilemma of Penal Reform*. London: George Allen & Unwin, 1939.

_____. *Group Problems in Crime and Punishment*. New York: Humanities Press, 1955.

_____ (ed.). *Pioneers in Criminology*. London: Stevens, 1961.

_____, and Wilkins, L.T. *Prediction Methods in Relation to Borstal Training*. London: H.M. Stationery Office, 1955.

_____. *Social Aspects of Crime in England Between the Wars*. London: George Allen & Unwin, 1940.

Manning, Clarence A. *Story of the Ukraine*. New York: Philosophical Library, 1947.

_____. *Twentieth Century Ukraine*. New York: Bookman Associates, 1951.

Manning, Olivia. *The Balkan Trilogy*. New York: Penguin, 1981.

Manning, Peter K. *The Narc's Game*. Cambridge, Mass.: MIT Press, 1980.

_____. *Police Work: The Social Organization of Policing*. Cambridge, Mass.: MIT Press, 1977.

_____, and Truzzi, Marcello (eds.). *Youth and Sociology*. Englewood Cliffs, N.J.: Prentice-Hall, 1972.

Manning, Thomas G. (ed.). *The Chicago Strike of 1894*. New York: Holt, 1960.

Mannino, Stefano. *Mitra e poltrone*. Palermo, Italy: G. Denaro, 1964.

Mannix, Daniel P., and Cowley, Malcolm. *Black Cargoes: A History of the Atlantic Slave Trade, 1518-1865*. New York: Viking Press, 1962.

_____. *The Hell Fire Club*. New York: Ballantine, 1959.

Manocchio, Anthony J., Dunn, Jimmy, and Empey, Lamar T. *The Time Game*. New York: Delta Books, 1970.

The Man of Two Lives. New York: American News, 1871.

Manoni, Mary. *Bedford-Stuyvesant*. New York: Quadrangle/New York Times Book, 1973.

Mansergh, Nicholas. *Britain and Ireland*. New York: Longmans, Green, 1942.

_____. *The Coming of the First World War*. New York: Longmans, Green, 1949.

Mansfield, John Brandt. *History of the Great Lakes*. 2 vols. Chicago: J.H. Beers, 1899.

Mansfield, Justine. *True Tales of Kidnappings in America - in China - in Mexico*. New York: Business Bourse Press, 1932.

Mansfield, Peter. *Nasser's Egypt*. Baltimore: Penguin Books, 1965.

Manson, I., and Palmer, J. *The Dirty Old Man on the Last Tube: The Social Response to Pornography*. London: Davis-Poynter, 1973.

Manstein, Erich von. *Lost Victories*. trans. A.G. Powell. London: Methuen, 1958.

Mantegazza, P. *Physiology of Love*. trans. H. Alexander. New York: Eugenics, 1936.

Manual of Military Law. London: H.M. Stationery Office, 1956-1958.

Manunta, Ugo. *La caduta degli angeli: storia intima della RSI*. Rome: Italiana, 1947.

Manvell, Roger, and Fraenkel, Heinrich. *The Conspirators: 20th July, 1944*. London: Bodley Head, 1964.

_____, and _____. *Goebbels*. New York: Pyramid Books, 1960.

_____. *Heinrich Himmler*. New York: G.P. Putnam's Sons, 1965.

_____. *Hermann Göring*. London: William Heinemann, 1962.

_____, *Hess*. London: MacGibbon & Kee, 1972.

_____, *The Men Who Tried to kill Hitler*. New York: Coward-McCann, 1964.

_____. *SS and Gestapo: Rule by Terror*. London: Macdonald, 1970.

Manzini, Carlo. *Il Duce a Verona*. Verona, Italy: Albaretti-Marchesetti, 1938.

Manzour, Anatole G. *Rise and Fall of the Romanovs*. Princeton, N.J.: D. Van Nostrand, 1960.

_____. *Russia, Past and Present*. New York: D. Van Nostrand, 1951.

Mao Tse-tung. *On Practice*. Peking, China: Foreign Language Press, 1952.

Maple, Eric. *The Dark World of Witches*. New York: A.S. Barnes, 1962.

_____. *The Domain of Devils*. New York: A.S. Barnes, 1966.

Maqrizi, Taqi al-Din. *Description topographique et historique de l'Egypte*. Cairo, Egypt: Bouriant & Casanova, 1895-1920.

Marandon, Sylvaine. *L'Image de la France dans l'Angleterre victorienne*. Paris: Colin, 1967.

Marc-Bonnet, Henry. *Les Papes de La Renaissance*. Paris: Presses Universitaires de France, 1969.

March, James G., and Simon, Herbert A. *Organizations*. New York: John Wiley & Sons, 1958.

March, John. *Actions for Slaunder...to which is added Awards or Arbitrements*. London: M. Wolbank & R. Best, 1647.

Marchal, Charles. *Les Conspirateurs en Angleterre*. Paris: Lebigre-Duquesne, 1858.

Marchand, Jean. *Le procès de condamnation de Jeanne d'Arc*. Paris: Plon, 1955.

Marchand, Louis. *Les Idées de Berryer*. Paris: Nouvelle Librairie Nationale, 1917.

_____. *Mémoires*. Paris: Plon, 1955.

Marchenko, Anatoly. *My Testimony*. New York: E.P. Dutton, 1969.

Marchetti, U. *Mussolini, i prefetti e i podestà*. Mantua, Italy: Paladino, 1928.

Marchetti, Victor, and Marks, John D. *The CIA and the Cult of Intelligence*. New York: Alfred A. Knopf, 1974.

_____. *The Rope-Dancer*. New York: Grossett & Dunlap, 1971.

Marcu, Valeriu. *Lenin*. London: Victor Gollancz, 1928.

Marcus, Edward. *Canada and the International Business Cycle, 1927-1939*. New York: Brookman Associates, 1954.

Marcus, Jacob Rader (ed.). *Memoirs of American Jews, 1775-1865*. 3 vols. Philadelphia: Jewish Publication Society, 1955-1956.

Marcus, Raymond. *The Bastard Bullet: A Search for Legitimacy for Commission Exhibit 399*. Los Angeles: Randall, 1966.

Marcus, Sheldon. *Father Coughlin*. Boston: Little, Brown, 1973.

Marcus, Steven (ed.). *The Continental Op*. New York: Random House, 1974.

_____. *Engels, Manchester, and the Working Class*. New York: Random House, 1974.

_____. *The Other Victorians*. New York: Basic Books, 1966.

Marcuse, F. (ed.). *Areas of Psychology*. New York: Harper, 1954.

Marcuse, Maxwell F. *This Was New York*. New York: Lim Press, 1969.

Mardaan, A. *Deva-Dasi*. New York: Macauley, 1959.

Marden, Charles F. *Minorities in American Society*. New York: American Book, 1952.

Mardin, Serif. *The Genesis of Young Ottoman Thought: A Study in the Modernization of Turkish Political Ideas*. Princeton, N.J.: Princeton University Press, 1962.

Margolies, Edward. *Which Way Did He Go?* New York: Holmes & Meier, 1982.

Margolis, J.S., and Clorfene, R. *A Child's Garden of Grass.* North Hollywood, Calif.: Contact Books, 1969.

Mariana, Juan de. *The King and the Education of the King.* trans. George Albert Moore. Washington, D.C.: Country Dollar Press, 1948.

Mariani, Angelo. *Coca and Its Theraputic Application.* New York: J.N. Jaros, 1890.

Mariani, Pietro. *Le tre giornate di Roma.* Rome: Studio Romano, 1922.

Mariano, John Horace. *The Second Generation of Italians in New York.* Boston: Christopher, 1921.

Maria y Campos, Armando de. *Episodios de la Revolución: de la caida de Porfirio Diaz a la Decena Trágica.* Mexico City: Libro Mexicana, 1957.

Marie de France. *Lai de Bisclaveret.* Paris: L. Curmer, 1842.

Marie, Grand Duchess of Russia. *Education of a Princess: A Memoir.* trans. Russell Lord. New York: Viking Press, 1931.

_____. *A Princess in Exile.* New York: Viking Press, 1932.

_____. *Things I Remember.* trans. Russell Lord. London: Cassell, 1931.

Marie, Queen of Romania. *The Country That I Love: An Exile Memories.* London: Duckworth, 1925.

_____. *Crowned Queens.* London: Heath Cranton, 1929.

_____. *The Dreamer of Dreams.* London: Hodder & Stoughton, 1915.

_____. *The Magic Doll of Roumania.* New York: Frederick A. Stokes, 1929.

_____. *Masks.* New York: E.P. Dutton, 1937.

_____. *My Country.* London: Hodder & Stoughton, 1916.

_____. *Ordeal: The Story of My Life.* New York: Charles Scribner's Sons, 1935.

_____. *The Queen of Rumania's Fairy Book.* New York: Frederick A. Stokes, 1926.

_____. *The Story of My Life.* New York: Charles Scribner's Sons, 1934.

_____. *The Story of Naughty Kildeen.* New York: Harcourt, Brace, 1926.

_____. *Why? A Story of Great Longing.* Stockholm: Svenska Tryckeriaktiebolaget, 1923.

Marie, Linda. *I Shall Not Rock.* New York: Daughters, 1977.

Marie-Louise, Princess. *My Memories of Six Reigns.* New York: E.P. Dutton, 1957.

Marighela, Carlos. *For the Liberation of Brazil.* London: Penguin, 1971.

The Marijuana Problem in the City of New York. New York: Mayor's Committee on Marijuana, 1944.

Marine, Gene. *The Black Panthers.* New York: New American Library, 1969.

Marinoni, Antonio. *Italy: Yesterday and Today.* New York: Macmillan, 1931.

Marion, John Francis. *The Charleston Story.* Harrisburg, Pa.: Stackpole Books, 1978.

Maritain, Paul. *Jules Favre.* Paris: A. Rousseau, 1882.

Marjoribanks, Edward. *For The Defence The Life of Sir Edward Marshall Hall.* London: Victor Gollancz, 1926.

_____. *The Life of Lord Carson.* Volume one. London: Victor Gollancz, 1932.

_____. *The Life of Sir Edward Marshall Hall.* London: Victor Gollancz, 1931.

Mark, Irving. *Agrarian Conflicts in Colonial New York.* New York: Columbia University Press, 1942.

Mark, Vernon H., and Ervin, Frank R. *Violence and the Brain.* New York: Harper & Row, 1970.

Markens, Issac. *President Lincoln and the Case of John Yeates Beall.* New York: Published by Author, 1911.

Markham, James W. *Voices of the Red Giants.* Ames: Iowa State University Press, 1967.

Markham, S.F. *A History of Socialism.* London: A. & C. Black, 1930.

Markiewicz, Casimir Dunin. *The Memory of the Dead: A Romantic Drama of '98 in Three Acts.* Dublin, Ire.: Tower, 1910.

Markmann, Charles Lam. *The Buckleys: A Family Examined.* New York: William Morrow, 1973.

_____. *The Noblest Cry.* New York: St. Martin's Press, 1965.

Marks, Harry H. *Small Change, or Lights and Shadows of New York.* New York: Standard, 1882.

Marks, Jeannette. *Thirteen Days.* New York: A. & C. Boni, 1929.

Marks, John. *The Search for the Manchurian Candidate.* New York: Times Books, 1979.

Marks, Laurence, and Van den Bergh, Tony. *Ruth Ellis: A Case of Diminished Responsibility?* London: Macdonald and Janes, 1977.

Marks, Percy Leman. *Chimneys and Flues.* London: Technical Press, 1935.

Marks, R.F., Leswing, K., and Fortinsky, B. *The Lawyer, the Public and Professional Responsibility.* Chicago: American Bar Foundation, 1972.

Marks, Stanley J. *Coup d'Etat! Three Murders That Changed the Course of History: President Kennedy, Reverend King, and Senator Robert F. Kennedy.* Los Angeles: Bureau of International Affairs, 1970.

_____. *Murder Most Foul! The Conspiracy That Murdered President Kennedy.* Los Angeles: Bureau of International Affairs, 1967.

_____. *Two Days of Infamy: Relating to the Murder of President Kennedy.* Los Angeles: Bureau of International Affairs, 1969.

Marlow, Joyce. *The Peterloo Massacre.* London: Rapp & Whiting, 1969.

Marlowe, George Francis. *Coaching Roads of Old New England.* New York: Macmillan, 1945.

Marlowe, John. *Arab Nationalism and British Imperialism.* New York: Frederick A. Praeger, 1961.

_____. *A History of Modern Egypt and Anglo-Egyptian Relations.* New York: Frederick A. Praeger, 1954.

_____. *The Making of the Suez Canal.* London: Cresset Press, 1964.

_____. *The Seat of Pilate: An Account of the Palestine Mandate.* London: Cresset Press, 1959.

Maroger, D. (ed.). *The Memoirs of Catherine the Great.* New York: Macmillan, 1955.

Marquardt, Dorothy A. *A Guide to the Supreme Court.* Indianapolis, Ind.: Bobbs-Merrill, 1977.

Marquand, H.A., et al. *Organized Labor in Four Continents.* New York: Longmans, Green, 1939.

Marqués, René. *The Docile Puerto Rican.* Philadelphia: Temple University Press, 1976.

Márquez, J.M. *El vientiuno. Hombres de la revolución y sus hechos.* Mexico City: n.p., 1916.

Márquez Sterling, Manuel. *Los Ultimos Dias del Presidente Madero.* Havana, Cuba: Imprenta El Siglo XX, 1917.

Marriott, John A.R. *The Eastern Question: A Historical Study in European Diplomacy.* Oxford, Eng.: Clarendon Press, 1951.

_____. *The Makers of Modern Italy.* London: Oxford University Press, 1937.

Marryat, Francis Samuel. *Mountains and Molehills.* Stanford, Calif.: Stanford University Press, 1952.

Mariotti, Giulio. *Verità sugli avvenimenti del 25 luglio e '8 settembre 1943.* Leghorn: Pozzolini, 1946.

Markevitch, Igor. *Made in Italy.* trans. Darina Silone. London: Harvill Press, 1949.

Marryat, Captain. *Diary in America.* Philadelphia: Carey & Hart, 1839.

Marsden, B.A and J.A. *Geneological Memoirs of the Family of Marsden.* Birkenhead, Eng.: Griffith, 1914.

Marsden, G.V. *Rasputin and Russia, the Tragedy of a Throne.* n.p., 1920.

Marsden, James Loftus. *The Action of the Mind on the Body.*

Great Malvern: Lamb, 1859.

_____. *Notes on Homeopathy.* London: Headland, 1849.

Marsden, John Buxton. *History of the Early Puritans.* London: Hamilton, Adams, 1850.

Marsh, Charles W. *Recollections, 1837-1910.* Chicago: Farm Implement News, 1910.

Marsh, John. *A Narrative of the Life of William Beadle.* Hartford, Conn.: Bavil Webster, 1783.

Marsh, John. *Hannah Hawkins.* New York: American Temperance Union, 1844.

_____. *The Napolean of Temperance.* New York: American Temperance Union, 1852.

_____. *Temperance Recollections.* New York: Charles Scribner's Sons, 1866.

_____. *The Triumphs of Temperance.* New York: John P. Prall, 1855.

Marsh, Ngaio. *Singing in the Shrouds.* Boston: Little, Brown, 1958.

Marsh, Thomas O. *Roots of Crime.* Newton, N.J.: Nellen, 1981.

Marshall, Carrington T. *A History of Courts and Lawyers of Ohio.* New York: American Historical Society, 1934.

Marshall, F. *A Brief History of Witchcraft with Especial Reference to the Witches of Northamptonshire.* Northampton, Eng.: J. Taylor, 1866.

Marshall, J. *Law and Psychology in Conflict.* New York: Anchor Books, 1966.

Marshall, James. *Elbridge A. Stuart, Founder of Carnation Company.* Los Angeles: Carnation, 1949.

_____. *Santa Fe, The Railroad That Built an Empire.* New York: Random House, 1945.

Marshall, Jim. *Swinging Doors.* Seattle, Wash.: Frank McCaffrey, 1949.

Marshall, John A. *American Bastille.* Philadelphia: Thomas W. Hartley, 1877.

Marshall, J.T. *The Miles Expedition of 1874-1875.* Austin, Texas: Encino Press, 1971.

Marshall, Otto Miller. *The Wham Paymaster Robbery.* Pima, Ariz.: Pima Chamber of Commerce, 1967.

Marshall, S.L. *Sinai Victory.* New York: William Morrow, 1958.

_____. *Swift Sword: The Historical Record of Israel's Victory, June, 1967.* New York: American Heritage, 1967.

Marshall, T.H. *Citizenship and Social Class.* Cambridge, Eng.: Cambridge University Press, 1950.

Marshall, T.M. *A History of the Western Boundary of the Louisiana Purchase, 1819-1841.* Berkeley: University of California Press, 1924.

Marshall, Theodora Britton, and Evans, Gladys Crail. *They Found It In Natchez.* New Orleans, La.: Pelican, 1939.

Marshall, Thomas Francis. *Speeches and Writings of Thomas Francis Marshall.* Cincinnati, Ohio: Applegate, 1858.

Marshall, Thomas M. *Early Records of Gilpin County, Colorado, 1859-1861.* Boulder: University of Colorado Press, 1920.

Marshall, Thomas R. *Recollections of Thomas R. Marshall.* Indianapolis, Ind.: Bobbs-Merrill, 1925.

Marshall, Walter Gore. *Through America, or Nine Months in the United States.* London: S. Low, Marston, Searle & Rivington, 1881.

Martelli, George. *Italy Against the World.* London: Chatto & Windus, 1937.

_____. *Whose Sea?* London: Chatto & Windus, 1938.

Marten, Manuel Edward. *The Doctor Looks at Murder.* Garden City, N.Y.: Doubleday, Doran, 1937.

Martienssen, Anthony. *Crime and the Police.* London: Martin Secker & Warbury, 1951.

_____. *Hitler and His Admirals.* London: Secker & Warburg, 1948.

Marti-Ibáñez, Felix. *The Epic of Medicine.* New York: Clarkson N. Potter, 1962.

Martin, Charles L. *A Sketch of Sam Bass, The Bandit.* Norman: University of Oklahoma Press, 1956.

Martin, David C. *Wilderness of Mirrors.* New York: Harper & Row, 1980.

Martin, Del. *Battered Wives.* New York: Pocket Books, 1977.

Martin, Douglas D. *An Arizona Chronology: The Territorial Years, 1846-1912.* Tucson: University of Arizona Press, 1963.

_____. *The Earps of Tombstone.* Tombstone, Ariz.: Tombstone Epitaph, 1959.

_____. *Silver, Sex and Six Guns: Tombstone Sage of the Life of Buckskin Frank Leslie.* Tombstone, Ariz.: Tombstone Epitaph, 1962.

_____. *Tombstone's Epitaph.* Albuquerque: University of New Mexico Press, 1951.

Martin, Edward Sanford. *The Life of Joseph Hodges Choate: As Gathered Chiefly from His Letters.* New York: Charles Scribner's Sons, 1921.

Martin, Edward Winslow. *History of the Grange Movement; or, the Farmer's War Against Monopolies. . . etc.* Chicago: National, 1874.

_____. *The Secrets of the Great City.* Philadelphia: n.p., 1868.

Martin, Edwin M. *The Allied Occupation of Japan.* New York: American Institute of Pacific Relations, 1948.

Martin, E.P. and J.M. *The Black Extended Family.* Chicago: University of Chicago Press, 1978.

Martin, Frederick Townsend. *The Passing of the Idle Rich.* Garden City, N.Y.: Doubleday, Page, 1912.

_____. *Things I Remember.* New York: John Lane, 1913.

Martin, George. *Causes and Conflicts: The Centennial History of the Association of the Bar of the City of New York, 1870-1970.* Boston: Houghton Mifflin, 1970.

_____. *Madam Secretary: Frances Perkins.* Boston: Houghton Mifflin, 1976.

Martin, George Washington. *The First Two Years in Kansas.* Topeka, Kan.: State Printing Office, 1907.

Martin, Jack. *Border Boss: Captain John R. Hughes.* San Antonio, Texas: Naylor, 1942.

Martin, John Bartlow. *Break Down the Walls.* New York: Ballantine, 1954.

_____. *Butcher's Dozen and Other Murders.* New York: Harper & Row, 1950.

_____. *My Life in Crime.* New York: Harper & Brothers, 1952.

Martin, John M., and Fitzpatrick, Joseph P. *Delinquent Behaviour.* New York: Random House, 1965.

Martin, John P. *Juvenile Vandalism.* Springfield, Ill.: Charles C. Thomas, 1961.

_____. *Offenders as Employees.* London: Macmillan, 1962.

_____, and Webster, D. *The Social Consequences of Conviction.* London: William Heinemann, 1971.

Martin, K. *Editor.* London: Hutchinson, 1968.

Martin, L. John. *International Propaganda.* Minneapolis: University of Minnesota Press, 1958.

Martin, Mildred Crowl. *Chinatown's Angry Angel.* Palo Alto, Calif.: Pacific Books, 1977.

Martin, M.K., and Voorhies, B. *Female of the Species.* New York: Columbia University Press, 1975.

Martin, Olga. *Hollywood's Movie Commandments.* New York: H.W. Wilson, 1937.

Martin, Ralph G. *Ballots and Bandwagons.* Chicago: Rand McNally, 1964.

Martin, Raymond V. *Revolt in the Mafia.* New York: Duell, 1963.

Martin, Roscoe C. (ed.). *TVA: The First Twenty Years.* Knoxville: University of Tennessee Press, 1956.

Martin, Sir Theodore. *Life of the Prince Consort.* London: Smith, Elder, 1875.

Martin, V. Covert. *Stockton Album Through the Years.* Stockton, Calif.: Simard Printing, 1959.

Martineau, Gilbert. *Napoleon's St. Helena.* trans. Frances Partridge. Chicago: Rand McNally, 1968.

Martineau, Harriet. *The History of England During the Thirty Years' Peace, 1816-1846.* 2 vols. London: Charles Knight,

1849.

_____. *Society in America.* 3 vols. London: Saunders & Otley, 1837.

Martineau, Mrs. Philip. *Roumania and Her Rulers.* London: Stanley Paul, 1927.

Martinez, Al. *Jigsaw John.* Los Angeles: J.P. Tarcber, 1975.

Martinez, Rafael, and Guerra, E. *Madero, su vida y su obra.* Monterrey: n.p., 1914.

_____, et al. *La Revolución y sus Hombres.* Mexico City: Talleres Tipográficos de El Tiempo, 1912.

Martinson, Robert M., Palmer, Ted, and Adams, Stuart. *Rehabilitation, Recidivism, and Research.* Hackensack, N.J.: National Council on Crime and Deliquency, 1976.

Martyn, Carlos. *John B. Gough: The Apostle of Cold Water.* New York: Funk & Wagnalls, 1894.

Maruyama Masao. *Thought and Behavior in Modern Japanese Politics.* London: Oxford University Press, 1963.

Marvin, Richard. *The Kennedy Curse.* New York: Belmont Books, n.d.

Marwick, Christine M. (ed.). *Litigation Under the Amended Federal Freedom of Information Act.* Washington, D.C: Center for National Security Studies, 1978.

Marwitz, Freidrich August Ludwig von der. *Lebensbeschreibung.* Berlin: E.S. Mittler und Sohn, 1908.

Marx, Harpo, and Barber, Rowland. *Harpo Speaks!* New York: Bernard Geis Associates, 1961.

Marx, Jean. *L'Inquisition en Dauphiné.* Paris: E. Champion, 1913.

Marx, Karl. *The Class Struggles in France.* New York: International, 1963.

_____, and Engels, Frederick. *The Communist Manifesto.* New York: International, 1965.

_____. *A Contribution to the Critique of Political Economy.* New York: International, 1970.

_____. *The Eighteenth Brumaire of Louis Bonaparte.* New York: International, 1963.

_____. *Theories of Surplus-Value.* Moscow: Progress, 1963.

Marx, Samuel, and Clayton, Jan. *Rodgers and Hart.* New York: G.P. Putnam's Sons, 1976.

Mary, André. *Paroles authentiques de Jeanne d'Arc tirées du procès du 1431.* Paris: Fernand Roches, 1931.

Marye, George Thomas. *Nearing the End in Imperial Russia, 1914-1916.* Philadelphia: Dorance, 1929.

_____. *Secrets of the Great City; the Virtues and the Vices, the Mysteries, Miseries and Crimes at New York City.* New York: Published by Author, 1968.

Maryland Legislative Council Committee. *Report on Capital Punishment.* Baltimore: State of Maryland, 1962.

Masani, R.P. *Dadabhai Naoroji.* London: George Allen & Unwin, 1939.

Masaryk, T.G. *The Spirit of Russia.* 2 vols. New York: Macmillan, 1955.

Masefield, John. *On the Spanish Main.* New York: Macmillan, 1925.

Maser, Werner. *Adolf Hitler: Legende, Mythos, Wirchlichkeit.* Munich: Bechtle, 1971.

_____. *Die Frühgeschichte der NSDAP.* Frankfurt, Ger.: Athenäum, 1965.

_____. *Hitler: Legend, Myth and Reality.* New York: Harper & Row, 1974.

_____. *Hitlers Briefe und Notizen.* Düsseldorf, Ger.: Econ Verlag, 1973.

_____. *Hitler's Mein Kampf: An Analysis.* London: Faber & Faber, 1970.

_____. *Naissance du parti national-socialiste.* Paris: Fayard, 1967.

_____. *Nuremberg: A Nation on Trial.* trans. Richard Barry. New York: Charles Scribner's Sons, 1979.

Mashruwala, K.G. *Gandhi and Marx.* Ahmedabad, India: Kitabistan, 1942.

Maskelyn, John Nevil. *Sharps and Flats, A Complete Revelation of the Secrets of Cheating at Games of Chance and Skill.* New York: Longmans, Green, 1894.

Maslow, Abraham. *Motivation and Personality.* New York: Harper & Row, 1954.

_____. *Personnel: The Human Problems of Management.* Englewood Cliffs, N.Y.: Prentice-Hall, 1972.

Mason, Alpheus Thomas. *Brandeis: A Free Man's Life.* New York: Viking Press, 1946.

_____. *Harland Fiske Stone: Pillar of the Law.* New York: Viking Press, 1956.

_____. *Security through Freedom.* Ithaca, N.Y.: Cornell University Press, 1955.

_____. *The Supreme Court from Taft to Warren.* Baton Rouge: Louisiana State University Press, 1958.

_____, and Beaney, William M. *The Supreme Court in a Free Society.* Englewood Cliffs, N.J.: Prentice-Hall, 1959.

Mason, David. *U-Boat: The Secret Menace.* London: Ballantine, 1960.

Mason, Edward Gay (ed.). *Early Chicago and Illinois.* Chicago: Fergus Printing, 1890.

Mason, Herbert. *To Kill the Devil, Attempts on the Life of Adolf Hitler.* New York: W.W. Norton, 1978.

Mason, James. *The Anatomy of Sorcery.* London: I. Legatte, 1612.

Mason, John Alden. *The Ancient Civilizations of Peru.* London: Penguin Books, 1957.

Mason, Philip. *Call the Next Witness.* New York: Harcourt, Brace, 1945.

Mason, Thomas Alpheus. *Brandeis: A Free Man's Life.* New York: Viking Press, 1946.

_____. *Harlan Fiske Stone: Pillar of the Law.* New York: Viking Press, 1966.

Maspero, Gaston. *Popular Stories of Ancient Egypt.* trans. A.S. Johns. New Hyde Park, N.Y.: University Books, 1967.

Massachusetts, Commonwealth of. *Historical Data Relating to Counties, Cities, and Towns in Massachusetts.* Boston: Commonwealth of Massachusetts, 1948.

_____. *Laws.* Boston: Wright & Potter, 1836.

Massachusetts General Court. *Record of Public Hearing before Joint Committee on the Judiciary of Massachusetts Legislature on the Resolution . . . Recommending a Posthumous Pardon for Nichola Sacco and Bartolomeo Vanzetti.* Boston: Boston Committee for the Vindication of Sacco and Vanzetti, 1959.

Massachusetts Special Commission Established for the Purpose of Investigating and Studying the Abolition of the Death Penalty in Capital Cases. *Report and Recommendations.* Boston: Commonwealth of Massachusetts, 1958.

Massarik, Fred. *A Report on the Jewish Population of San Francisco, Marin County, and the Peninsula: 1959.* San Francisco: Jewish Welfare Federation, 1959.

Massé, Pierre. *De l'imposture et tromperie des diables.* Paris: I. Poupy, 1576.

Masserman, Jules H. (ed.). *The Dynamics of Dissent: Scientific Proceedings of the American Academy of Psycholanalysis.* New York: Grune & Stratton, 1968.

Massie, Robert K. *Nicholas and Alexandra.* New York: Atheneum, 1967.

Massing, Hede. *This Deception.* New York: Duell, Sloan & Pearce, 1951.

Massok, R.G. *Italy fron Within.* London: Macmillan, 1943.

Masson, Albert. *La sorcellerie et la science des poisons au xvii siècle.* Paris: Librairie Hachette, 1904.

Masson, F. *Une jounée de Napoléon.* Paris: Flammarion, 1934.

Masson, René. *Number One: A Story of Landru.* trans. Gillian Tindall. London: Hutchinson, 1964.

Massu, Georges-Victor. *L'Enquête Petoit.* Paris: Librairie Arthème Fayard, 1959.

Mast, Blaine. *K.K.K. Friend or Foe: Which?* Pittsburgh, Pa.: Herbrick & Held Printing, 1924.

Masterman, J.C. *The Double Cross System in the War of 1939 to*

1945. New Haven, Conn.: Yale University Press, 1972.

Masterpieces of American Eloquence. New York: Christian Herald, 1900.

Masters, Anthony. *The Devil's Dominion: The Complete Story of Hell and Satanism in the Modern World.* New York: G.P. Putnam's Sons, 1978.

Masters, Brian. *Killing For Company.* New York: Stein & Day, 1985.

Masters, Edgar Lee. *Across Spoon River.* New York: Farrar & Rinehart, 1936.

_____. *Lincoln the Man.* New York: Dodd, Mead, 1931.

_____. *The New Star Chamber.* Chicago: Hammersmark, 1904.

_____. *The Role of the Bar in Electing the Bench in Chicago.* Chicago: University of Chicago Press, 1936.

_____. *Songs and Satires.* New York: Macmillan, 1916.

_____. *The Tale of Chicago.* New York: G.P. Putnam's Sons, 1933.

Masters, R.E.L. *Patterns of Incest.* New York: Ace, 1963.

_____, and Lea, Eduord. *Perverse Crimes in History.* New York: Julian Press, 1963.

_____. *Sex Crimes in History: Evolving Concepts of Sadism, Lust-Murder, and Necrophilia from Ancient to Modern Times.* New York: Julian Press, 1963.

Masters, Roger D. *The Nation Is Burdened.* New York: Alfred A. Knopf, 1957.

Masters, William H., and Johnson, Virginia E. *Human Sexual Inadequacy.* Boston: Little, Brown, 1970.

_____. *Human Sexual Response.* Boston: Little, Brown, 1966.

Masterson, Vincent Victor. *The Katy Railroad and the Last Frontier.* Norman: University of Oklahoma Press, 1952.

Masterson, William Barclay ("Bat"). *Famous Gunfighters of the Frontier.* Houston: Frontier Press of Texas, 1957.

_____. *The Tenderfoot's Turn.* Utica, N.Y.: Savage Arms, 1909.

Mastny, Vojtch. *The Czechs under Nazi Rule: The Failure of the National Resistence, 1939-1942.* New York: Columbia University Press, 1971.

Masudi, Abu al-Hassan al-. *Murju al-Dhahab was Mahdin al-Jawhar.* 9 vols. trans. De Maynard and De Courteille. Paris: n.p., 1861-1877.

Masur, Norbert. *En Jud talar med Himmler.* Stockholm: Hoffman und Campe, 1946.

Matarazzo, Francesco. *Chronicles of the City of Perugia.* trans. E.S. Morgan. New York: Harper & Row, 1969.

Matheny, H.W. *Major General Thomas Maley Harris.* Parsons, W.Va.: McClain Printing, 1963.

Mather, Cotton. *Detur Dignori: The Righteous Man Described as the Excellent Man.* Boston: B. Green, 1720.

_____. *Diary.* Boston: Society, 1911.

_____. *Magnalia Christi Americana.* London: T. Parkhurst, 1702.

_____. *Memorable Providences Relating to Witchcrafts and Possessions.* Boston: R.P., 1689.

_____. *Nunc Dimittis Briefly Descanted On.* Boston: B. Green, 1709.

_____. *The Present State of New England.* Boston: S. Green, 1690.

_____. *Wonders of the Invisible World.* Boston: J. Dunton, 1693.

Mather, Frederick C. *Public Order in the Age of Chartists.* Manchester, Eng.: Manchester University Press, 1959.

Mather, Increase. *Cases of Conscience Concerning Evil Spirits.* Boston: B. Harris, 1693.

_____. *An Essay for the Recording of Illustrious Providences.* Boston: S. Green, 1684.

Mathew, A.H. *The Life and Times of Rodrigo Borgia.* London: St. Paul, 1912.

Mathew, Theobald. *For Lawyers and Others.* London: William Hodge, 1937.

Mathews, Alfred. *Ohio and Her Western Reserve.* New York: Appleton-Century, 1902.

Mathews, Donald G. *Agitation for Freedom: The Abolitionist Movement.* New York: John Wiley & Sons, 1972.

Mathewson, R.W., Jr. *The Positive Hero in Russian Literature.* New York: Columbia University Press, 1958.

Mathiesen, Thomas. *Beyond the Boundaries of Organization.* California: Glendessary Press, 1972.

_____. *The Defences of the Weak: A Study of a Norweigan Correctional Institution.* London: Tavistock, 1965.

Mathiessen, F.O. *American Renaissance: Art and Expression in the Age of Emerson and Whitman.* New York: Oxford University Press, 1941.

Matlin, Matthew (ed.). *Should We Build More Prisons?* Hackensack, N.J.: National Council on Crime and Delinquency, 1977.

Matlock, J. Eugene. *Gone Beyond the Law.* Dallas: Mathis, Van Nort, 1940.

Matson, A.T. *The Nandi Campaign Against the British, 1895-1906.* Nairobi, Kenya: Transafrica, 1974.

Matsumoto Seicho. *Nihon no Kuroikiri* (Black Mist over Japan). Tokyo: Bungei Shunju, 1974.

Matteo, Pat. *This Captive Land.* Yonkers, N.Y.: Published by Author, 1968.

Matteotti, Giacomo. *The Fascisti Exposed.* trans. E.W. Dickes. London: ILP, 1924.

_____. *Matteotti.* Rome: ANPPIA, 1957.

_____. *Relique.* Milan, Italy: Corbaccio, 1924.

Matters, Leonard. *The Mystery of Jack the Ripper.* London: W.H. Allen, 1948.

Matthews, Herbert L. *The Education of a Correspondent.* New York: Harcourt, Brace, 1946.

_____. *The Fruits of Fascism.* New York: Harcourt, Brace, 1943.

_____. *Two Wars and More to Come.* New York: Carrick & Evans, 1938.

_____. *A World in Revolution.* New York: Charles Scribner's Sons, 1971.

Matthews, Jim. *Four Dark Days in History: November 22, 23, 24 and 25, 1963.* Los Angeles: Special, 1963.

Matthews, Lillian R. *Women in Trade Unions in San Francisco.* Berkley: University of California Press, 1913.

Matthews, R.C.O. *A Study in Trade-Cycle History: Economic Fluctuations in Great Britain, 1832-1842.* Cambridge, Eng.: Cambridge University Press, 1954.

Matthews, Sallie Reynolds. *Interwoven: A Pioneer Chronicle.* El Paso, Texas: Carl Hertzog, 1958.

Matthews, T.S. *Name and Address.* New York: Simon & Schuster, 1960.

Matthiesen, Thomas. *The Defences of the Weak.* London: Tavistock, 1965.

Mattick, Hans W., and Caplan, Nathan S. *The Chicago Youth Development Project.* Ann Arbor, Mich.: Institute for Social Research, 1964.

_____ (ed.). *The Future of Imprisonment in a Free Society.* Chicago: St. Leonard's House, 1965.

_____, and Sweet, Ronald P. *Illinois Jails.* Chicago: University of Chicago Law School, 1969.

_____. *The Prosaic Sources of Prison Violence.* Chicago: University of Chicago, 1972.

_____. *The Unexamined Death.* Chicago: John Howard, 1963.

Mattingly, Garrett. *Armada.* Boston: Houghton Mifflin, 1959.

Mattioli, Guido. *Mussolini aviatore.* Rome: Pinciana, 1936.

Mattison, Ray H. *Roosevelt and the Stockmen's Association.* Bismarck: State Historical Society of North Dakota, 1950.

Matusow, Allen J. (ed.). *Joseph McCarthy.* Englewood Cliffs, N.J.: Prentice-Hall, 1971.

Matz, Mary Jane. *The Many Lives of Otto Kahn.* New York: Macmillan, 1963.

Matza, David. *Becoming Deviant.* Englewood Cliffs, N.J.: Prentice-Hall, 1969.

_____. *Delinquency and Drift.* New York: John Wiley & Sons, 1964.

Maugeri, Franco. *From the Ashes of Disgrace.* New York: Reynal & Hitchcock, 1948.

Maugham, F.H. *The Case of Jean Calas.* London: William Heinemann, 1928.

Maughan-Brown, D. *Land, Freedom, and Fiction: History and Ideology in Kenya.* London: Zed Books, 1985.

Maule, Thomas. *New England's Persecutors Mauled with Their Own Weapons.* New York: William Bradford, 1697.

_____. *The Truth Held Forth and Maintained.* New York: William Bradford, 1695.

Maupas, Charlemagne-Emile de. *Mémoires sur le second empire.* Paris: E. Dentu, 1884.

Maurain, Jean. *La Politique ecclésiastique du second empire de 1852 à 1869.* Paris: Félix Alcan, 1930.

Maurer, Armand A. *Medieval Philisophy.* New York: Random House, 1962.

Maurer, David W. *The Big Con.* New York: Bobbs-Merrill, 1940.

_____. *Whiz Mob.* Gainesville, Fla.: American Dialect Society, 1955.

Maurer, James H. *It Can Be Done.* New York: Rand School Press, 1938.

Maurice, Arthur Bartlett. *New York in Fiction.* New York: Dodd, Mead, 1901.

Maurice, C. Edmund. *The Revolutionary Movement of 1848-9 in Italy, Austria-Hungary, and Germany with Some Explanation of the Previous Thirty Years.* New York: G.P. Putnam's Sons, 1887.

Maurice, Frederick Denison. *The Life of Frederick Denison Maurice.* 2 vols. New York: Charles Scribner's Sons, 1884.

Maurice, J.F., and Long, Wilfred J. *The Franco-Prussian War.* London: Swan Sonnenschein, 1900.

Maurois, André. *Edwardian Era.* New York: Appleton-Century, 1933.

_____. *Histoire de la France.* Paris: D. Wapler, 1947.

_____. *Tragedy in France.* New York: Harper, 1940.

Maurois, Simone Andre. *Miss Howard and the Emperor.* New York: Alfred A. Knopf, 1957.

Maurras, Charles. *Au signe de Flore: Souvenirs de vie politique, Affaire Dreyfus, la fondation de l'Action Francaise, 1898-1900.* Paris: Les Oeuvres Représentatives, 1931.

_____. *Promenade Italienne.* Paris: Flammarion, 1929.

Maury, General Dabney Herndon. *Recollections of a Virginian in the Mexico, Indian and Civil Wars.* New York: Charles Scribner's Sons, 1894.

Maverick, Augustus. *Henry J. Raymond and the New York Press.* Hartford, Conn.: A.S. Hale, 1870.

Mavity, Nancy Barr. *Sister Aimee.* Garden City, N.Y.: Doubleday, Doran, 1931.

Mavor, J. *An Economic History of Russia.* 2 vols. New York: E.P. Dutton, 1925.

Mavrogordato, John. *Modern Greece: A Chronicle and a Survey 1800-1931.* London: Macmillan, 1931.

Maxa, Rudy. *Dare to Be Great.* New York: William Morrow, 1977.

Maxim, Sir Hiram. *Monte Carlo Facts and Fallacies.* London: Grant Richards, 1904.

Maxton, James. *Lenin.* London: Peter Davies, 1932.

Maxwell, Constantia E. *Dublin Under the Georges.* London: Faber & Faber, 1956.

_____. *The Stranger in Ireland.* London: Jonathan Cape, 1954.

Maxwell, Elsa. *I Married the World.* London: William Heinemann, 1955.

Maxwell, G.S. *Highwayman's Heath.* London: Middlesex Chronicle, 1935.

Maxwell, Gavin. *Bandit.* New York: Harper & Brothers, 1956.

_____. *God Protect Me from My Friends.* New York: Longmans, Green, 1956.

Maxwell, Gilbert. *Helen Morgan: Her Life and Legend.* New York: Hawthorn Books, 1974.

May, Betty. *Tiger-Woman: My Story.* London: Duckworth, 1929.

May, Ernest R. *Imperial Democracy.* New York: Harcourt, Brace & World, 1961.

May, Henry F. (ed.). *The Discontent of Intellectuals: A Problem of the Twenties.* Chicago: Rand-McNally, 1963.

_____. *The End of American Innocence.* Chicago: Quadrangle Books, 1964.

_____. *The Enlightenment in America.* New York: Oxford University Press, 1976.

_____. *Protestant Churches and Industrial America.* New York: Harper, 1949.

May, Henry John. *Murder by Consent.* London: Hutchinson 1968.

May, Rollo. *Power and Innocence.* New York: W.W. Norton, 1972.

Maybrick, Florence Elizabeth. *Mrs. Maybrick's Own Story.* New York: Funk & Wagnalls, 1905.

Maycock, Sir Willoughby. *Celebrated Crimes and Criminals.* Maidstone, Eng.: George Mann, 1973.

Mayer, Arno J. *Political Origins of the New Diplomacy, 1917-1918.* New Haven, Conn.: Yale University Press, 1959.

Mayer, Edwin Justus. *Children of Darkness: An Original Tragi-Comedy.* New York: H. Liverlight, 1929.

Mayer, Frank H., and Roth, Charles B. *The Buffalo Harvest.* Denver: Sage Books, 1958.

Mayer, Grace M. *Once Upon a City: New York From 1890 to 1910 as Photographed by Byron.* New York: Macmillan, 1958.

Mayer, Harold M. *Chicago: City of Decisions.* Chicago: The Geographical Society of Chicago, 1955.

_____, and Richard C. Wade. *Chicago: Growth of a Metropolis.* Chicago: University of Chicago Press, 1969.

_____. *The Port of Chicago and the St. Lawrence Seaway.* Chicago: University of Chicago Press, 1957.

Mayer, Henry. *The Press in Australia.* New Rochelle, N.Y.: Soccer Associates, 1964.

Mayer, J.E., and Timms, N. *The Client Speaks.* London: Routledge & Kegan Paul, 1970.

Mayer, Martin. *The Bankers.* New York: Ballantine Books, 1974.

_____. *The Lawyers.* New York: Harper & Row, 1967.

_____. *Today and Tomorrow in America.* New York: Harper & Row, 1976.

_____. *Wall Street—The Inside Story of American Finance.* London: Bodley Head, 1959.

Mayer, Meyer. *Corporate and Legal History of United Air Lines and Its Predecessors and Subsidiaries, 1925-1945.* Chicago: Twentieth Century Press, 1953.

Mayer, Robert. *The Dreams of Ada.* New York: Viking Press, 1987.

_____ (ed.). *San Francisco.* Dobbs Ferry, N.Y.: Oceana Publications, 1974.

_____. *Los Angeles, a Chronological and Documentary History.* Dobbs Ferry, N.Y.: Oceana, 1978.

Mayers, Lewis. *The American Legal System.* New York: Harper & Row, 1964.

Mayfield, Eugene O. *The Backbone of Nebraska.* Omaha, Neb.: Burkley Printing, 1916.

Mayhew, Athol. *The Emperor of Germany, William I: A Life Sketch.* London: T. Nelson & Sons, 1887.

Mayhew, Henry, and Binny, John. *The Criminal Prisons of London and Scenes of Prison Life.* London: Griffin, Bohn, 1862.

_____. *London Labour and the London Poor.* London: Frank Cass, 1967.

_____. *London's Underworld.* London: William Kimber, 1950.

Mayhew, Leon. *Law and Equal Opportunity.* Cambridge, Mass.: Harvard University Press, 1968.

Maynard, Sir John. *Russia in Flux.* New York: Collier, 1962.

Maynard, Louis. *Oklahoma Panhandle: A History and Stories of No Man's Land.* Privately Printed, 1956.

Maynard, R. *The Impact of Supported Work on Young School Dropouts.* New York: Manpower Demonstration Research, 1980.

Maynard, Theodore. *The Story of American Catholicism.* New York: Macmillan, 1941.

Mayo, A.D. *Southern Women in the Recent Educational Movement in the South.* Washington, D.C.: U.S. Government Printing Office, 1892.

Mayo, Bernard. *Henry Clay, Spokesman of the New West.* Boston: Houghton Mifflin, 1937.

Mayo, H.B. *Democracy and Marxism.* New York: Oxford University Press, 1955.

Mayo, Herbert. *On the Truths Contained in Popular Superstitions.* London: W. Blackwood & Sons, 1851.

Mayo, John B. *Bulletin from Dallas: The President is Dead.* New York: Exposition Press, 1967.

Mayo, Katherine. *The Face of Mother India.* New York: Harper & Brothers, 1936.

———. *Justice to All: The Story of the Pennsylvania State Police.* Boston: Houghton Mifflin, 1920.

———. *Mother India.* New York: Harcourt, Brace, 1927.

———. *Mounted Justice.* Boston: Houghton Mifflin, 1922.

———. *Slave of the Gods.* New York: Harcourt, Brace, 1929.

———. *The Standard Bearers.* Boston: Houghton Mifflin, 1918.

Mayo, Lawrence (ed.). *America of Yesterday as Reflected in the Journal of John Davis Long.* Boston: Atlantic Monthly Press, 1923.

———. *John Endecott: A Biography.* Cambridge, Mass.: Harvard University Press, 1936.

Mayo, Morrow. *Los Angeles.* New York: Alfred A. Knopf, 1933.

Mayor's Committee on Marihuana. *The Marihuana Problem in the City of New York.* Lancaster, Pa.: Jaques Cattell, 1944.

Maytorena, José Maria. *Algunas verdades sobre el General Alvaro Obregón.* Los Angeles: Iprenta de "El Heraldo de México," 1919.

Mazedier, René. *Histoire de la Presse Parisienne.* Paris: Editions du Pavois, 1945.

Mazlish, Bruce. *In Search of Nixon: A Psychohistorical Inquiry.* New York: Basic Books, 1972.

Mazo, Earl. *Richard Nixon: A Political and Personal Portrait.* New York: Harper & Brothers, 1959.

Mazour, Anatole G. *The First Russian Revolution, 1825.* Berkeley: University of California Press, 1937.

———. *The Rise and Fall of the Romanovs.* Princeton, N.J.: D. Van Nostrand, 1960.

———. *Russia Past and Present.* Princeton, N.J.: D. Van Nostrand, 1951.

———. *Russia: Tsarist and Communist.* Princeton, N.J.: D. Van Nostrand, 1962.

Mazzanovick, Anton. *Trailing Geronimo.* Los Angeles: Gem, 1926.

Mazzucchelli, Mario. *I segreti del processo di Verona.* Milan, Italy: Cino del Duca, 1963.

Mazzula, Fred and Jo. *Al Packer, a Colorado Cannibal.* Denver: Published by Authors, 1968.

———. *Brass Checks and Red Lights.* Denver: Published by Authors, 1966.

———. *Outlaw Album.* Denver: A.B. Hirschfeld Press, 1966.

Mboya, T. *Freedom and After.* London: Andre Deutsch, 1963.

Mead, George Herbert. *Mind, Self and Society.* Chicago: University of Chicago Press, 1934.

Mead, M., and Wolfenstein, M. (eds.). *Childhood in Contemporary Cultures.* Chicago: University of Chicago Press, 1955.

Mead, Margaret, and Bunzel, Ruth L. *The Golden Age of American Anthropology.* New York: George Braziller, 1960.

———. *Male and Female.* New York: William Morrow, 1975.

Meade, George (ed.). *The Life and Letters of George Meade.* Amber, Pa.: G.G. Meade, 1924.

Meade, Robert D. *Judah P. Benjamin, Confederate Statesman.* London: Oxford University Press, 1943.

Meagher, Sylvia. *Accessories After the Fact.* New York: Bobbs-Merrill, 1967.

———. *Subject Index to the Warren Report and Hearings and Exhibits.* New York: Scarecrow Press, 1966.

Meakin, Annette M.B. *A Ribbon of Iron.* London: Archibald & Constable, 1901.

Means, Gaston B. *The Strange Death of President Harding.* New York: Gold Label Books, 1930.

Mearns, A. *The Bitter Cry of Outcast London.* New York: Humanities Press, 1970.

Mearns, David C. *The Lincoln Papers.* 2 vols. Garden City, N.Y.: Doubleday, 1948.

Mecham, John Lloyd. *Church and State in Latin America: A History of Politico-Ecclesiastical Relations.* Chapel Hill: University of North Carolina Press, 1934.

Mechoulam, Raphael (ed.). *Marijuana: Chemistry, Pharmacology, Metabolism and Clinical Effects.* New York: Academic Press, 1973.

Mecklin, John M. *The Ku Klux Klan: A Study of the American Mind.* New York: Russell & Russell, 1963.

Medalie, Richard J. *From Escobedo to Miranda.* Washington, D.C.: Lerner Law Book, 1966.

Medbery, J.K. *Men and Mysteries of Wall Street.* New York: Osgood, 1870.

Medea, Andrea, and Thompson, Kathleen. *Against Rape.* New York: Farrar, Straus & Giroux, 1974.

Medley, Julius George. *An Autumn Tour in the United States and Canada.* London: H.S. King, 1873.

Mednick, S.A., and Christiansen, K.O. (eds.). *Biosocial Bases of Criminal Behavior.* New York: Gardner Press, 1977.

———, and Baert, A.E. (eds.). *Prospective Longitudinal Research.* Oxford, Eng.: Oxford University Press, 1981.

Mee, Charles L., Jr. *Meeting at Potsdam.* New York: M. Evans, 1975.

———. *The Ohio Gang.* New York: M. Evans, 1981.

Meecham, A.B. *Wigwam and War-Path; or, the Royal Chief in Chains.* Boston: John P. Dale, 1875.

Meek, Victor. *Cops and Robbers.* London: G. Duckworth, 1962.

———. *Private Enquiries: A Handbook for Detectives.* London: G. Duckworth, 1967.

Meeker, Arthur. *Chicago With Love.* New York: Alfred A. Knopf, 1955.

Meekes, J. Edward. *The Work of the Stock Exchange.* New York: Ronald Press, 1930.

Meenan, J.F. *A View of Ireland.* Dublin, Ire.: British Association for the Advancement of Science, 1957.

Megargee, E.I. *The California Psychological Inventory Handbook.* San Francisco: Jossey-Bass, 1972.

———, and Bohn, M.J., Jr. *Classifying Criminal Offenders.* Beverly Hills, Calif.: Sage, 1979.

Megaro, Gaudens. *Mussolini in the Making.* Boston: Houghton, Mifflin, 1938.

Megarry, R.E. *A Manual of the Law of Real Property.* London: Stevens, 1955.

Mehdi, Mohammad T. *Peace in the Middle East.* New York: Wilson, 1956.

Mehling, Harold. *The Scandalous Scamps.* New York: Henry Holt, 1959.

Mehnert, Klaus. *Twilight of the Young.* New York: Holt, Rinehart & Winston, 1976.

Meier, August. *Negro Thought in America, 1880-1915: Racial Ideologies in the Age of Booker T. Washington.* Ann Arbor: University of Michigan Press, 1963.

Meier, Matt S., and Rivera, Feliciano. *The Chicanos.* New York: Hill & Wang, 1972.

Meiklejohn, Alexander. *Free Speech and Its Relationship to Self-Government.* New York: Harper, 1960.

Meinecke, Friedrich. *Preussisch-deutsche Gestalten und Probleme.* Leipzig, Ger.: Koehler und Amelang, 1940.

———. *Das Zeitatler der deutschen Erhebung, 1785 bis 1815.* Bielefeld, Ger.: Veldhagen und Klasing, 1924.

Meinhold, Wilhelm. *Mary Schweidler, the Amber Witch.* trans. Lady Duff Gordon. London: Oxford University Press, 1928.

Meir, Golda. *My Life*. New York: G.D. Putnam's Sons, 1975.

Melchior-Bonnet, C. *Dictionnaire de la Révolution et de l'Empire*. Paris: Larousse, 1965.

A Melancholy Narrative of the Late, Unhappy Samuel Brand. Lancaster, Pa.: Francis Bailey, 1774.

Meléndez, José T. (ed.). *Historia de la Revolución Mexicana*. 2 vols. Mexico City: Talleres gráficos de La Nación, 1936.

Melendy, H. Brett, and Gilbert, Benjamin F. *The Governors of California*. Georgetown, Calif.: Talisman Press, 1965.

Melgarejo Randolph, Antonio Damaso. *Los Crimens del Zapatismo*. Mexico City: F.P. Rojas y Compañia, 1913.

Melish, Howard. *Bishop J.L. Spaulding*. New York: Macmillan, 1917.

Mellen, Joan. *Privilege: The Enigma of Sasha Bruce*. New York: New American Library, 1982.

Mellini Ponce de Leon, Count Alberto. *Guerra diplomatica a Sàlo*. Bologna, Italy: Cappelli, 1950.

_____. *L'Italia entra in guerra*. Bologna, Italy: Cappelli, 1963.

Mellis, J.C. *St. Helena*. London: n.p., 1872.

Mellnik, Brigadier General Steve. *Philippine Diary, 1939-1945*. New York: Van Nostrand, Reinhold, 1969.

Mellor, Alex. *La torture*. Paris: Horizons Littéraires, 1949.

Mellwain, David. *The Bizarre and the Bloody*. London: Hart, 1972.

Melnicoe, William B., and Menning, Jan. *Elements of Police Supervision*. New York: Glencoe Press, 1969.

Melograni, Piero. *Corriere della Sera*. Bologna, Italy: Cappelli, 1965.

Melton, A., and Martin, E. (eds.). *Coding Process in Human Memory*. New York: John Wiley & Sons, 1972.

Meltsner, Michael. *Cruel and Unusual: The Supreme Court and Capital Punishment*. New York: Random House, 1973.

Meltzer, Milton (ed.). *In Their Own Words: A History of the American Negro, 1619-1865*. New York: Thomas Y. Crowell, 1964.

_____ (ed.). *In Their Own Words: A History of the American Negro, 1865-1916*. New York: Thomas Y. Crowell, 1965.

_____. *Milestones to American Liberty: The Foundations of the Republic*. New York: Thomas Y. Crowell, 1965.

_____. *World of Our Fathers*. New York: Farrar, Straus & Giroux, 1974.

Melville, Herman. *The Confidence Man*. London: Constable, 1923.

Melville, L. *The South Sea Bubble*. Boston: Small, Maynard, 1923.

Melville, Lewis, and Hargreaves, Reginald. *Famous Duels and Assassinations*. New York: J.H. Sears, 1930

Melville, Samuel. *Letters from Attica*. New York: William Morrow, 1972.

Melville-Lee, Capt. W.L. *A History of Police in England*. London: Methuen, 1901.

Memminger, Anton. *Das verhexte Kloster*. Würzburg, Ger.: Published by Author, 1904.

Memoirs of King Abdullah of Transjordan. New York: Philosophical Library, 1950.

Memorial and Genealogical Record of Texas. Chicago: Goodspeed Brothers, 1894.

Memorial to Greatness: The Presidential Years of John F. Kennedy. Island Park, N.Y.: Aspen, 1964.

Mena Brito, Bernardino. *Carranza: sus amigos, sus enemigos*. Mexico City: Ediciones Botas, 1935.

Ménager, Georges. *Les Quatre Vérités de Papillon*. Paris: La Table Ronde, 1970.

Menard, Peter. *Certain Connections of Affinities with Jack the Ripper*. Edinburgh, Scot.: Nimmo, 1903.

Mencken, August. *By the Neck*. New York: Hastings House, 1942.

Mencken, H.L. *The American Language*. New York: Alfred A. Knopf, 1945.

_____. *The Bathtub Hoax*. New York: Alfred A. Knopf, 1958.

_____. *A Carnival of Buncombe*. Baltimore: Johns Hopkins University Press, 1956.

_____. *The Days of H.L. Mencken (Heathen Days: 1890-1936)*. New York: Alfred A. Knopf, 1947.

_____. *A Mencken Chrestomathy*. New York: Alfred A. Knopf, 1949.

_____. *A New Dictionary of Quotations*. New York: Alfred A. Knopf, 1942.

_____. *Newspaper Days, 1899-1906*. New York: Alfred A. Knopf, 1941.

_____. *Prejudices*. New York: Alfred A. Knopf, 1926.

_____. *The Vintage Mencken*. New York: Vintage Books, 1955.

Mend, Hans. *Adolf Hitler im Felde*. Munich: Hober, 1931.

Mende, Tibor. *China and Her Shadow*. London: Thames & Hudson, 1961.

Mendel, Arthur P. *Dilemmas of Progress in Tsarist Russia: Legal Marxism and Legal Populism*. Cambridge, Mass.: Harvard University Press, 1961.

Mendelson, Jack H., Rossi, A. Michael, and Meyer, Roger E. *The Use of Marihuana: A Psychological and Physiological Inquiry*. New York: Plenum Press, 1974.

Mendelson, Mary A. *Tender Loving Greed*. New York: Vintage Books, 1975.

Mendelson, Wallace. *Capitalism, Democracy and the Supreme Court*. New York: Appleton-Century-Crofts, 1960.

_____ (ed.). *Felix Frankfurter: A Tribute*. New York: Reynal, 1964.

_____. *Justices Black and Frankfurter: Conflicts in the Court*. Chicago: University of Chicago Press, 1961.

Mendelson, Wallace B. *The Use and Misuse of Sleeping Pills: A Clinical Guide*. New York: Plenum, 1980.

Mendelssohn, Peter de. *Japan's Political Warfare*. London: George Allen & Unwin, 1944.

_____. *The Nuremberg Documents*. London: George Allen & Unwin, 1946.

_____. *Zeitungsstadt Berlin*. Berlin: Ullstein, 1959.

Mendershausen, Horst. *Changes in Income Distribution During the Great Depression*. New York: National Bureau of Economic Research, 1946.

Mendiola, Gabriel Ferrer de. *Historia del la Revolución Mexicana*. Mexico City: Ediciones de El Nacional, 1956.

Menefee, Eugene L., and Dodge, Fred A. *History of Tulare and Kings Counties California*. Los Angeles: Historic Record, 1913.

Meng, John, and Gergely, E.J. *American History for Catholic High Schools*. New York: W.H. Sadlier, 1955.

Menghi, Girolamo. *Compendio dell'arte essorcistica*. Bologna, Italy: Giovanni Rossi, 1576.

_____. *Flagellum Daemonum*. Bonn, Ger.: Giovanni Rossi, 1582.

_____. *Fustum Daemonis*. Bonn, Ger.: Giovanni Rossi, 1584.

Ménière. *Mémoires anecdotiques sur les salons du second empire*. Paris: Plon-Nourrit, 1903.

Mennel, Robert M. *Thorns and Thistles*. Hanover, N.H.: University Press of New England, 1973.

Menninger, Karl. *The Crime of Punishment*. New York: Viking Press, 1969.

_____. *Love Against Hate*. New York: Harcourt, Brace, 1942.

_____. *Man Against Himself*. New York: Harcourt, 1938.

_____. *Whatever Became of Sin?* New York: Hawthorn Books, 1973.

Mennini, S. (ed.). *Le tre giornate di Roma*. Borgo San Lorenzo, Italy: Toccafreddi, 1922.

Mensch, Earnest Cromwell. *Alcatraz*. San Francisco: San Francisco, 1937.

Menshutkin, B.N. *Russia's Lomonosov: Chemist, Courtier, Physicist, Poet*. Princeton, N.J.: Princeton University Press, 1952.

Menuhin, Moshe. *The Decadence of Judaism in Our Time*. New York: Exposition Press, 1965.

Mercer, Asa Shinn. *The Banditti of the Plains*. Cheyenne, Wyo.: Published by Author, 1894.

Mercier, C. *Criminal Responsibility.* London: Oxford, 1935.

Meredith, M. *The First Dance of Freedom: Black Africa in the Postwar Era.* London: Hamish Hamilton, 1984.

Meredith, Roy. *Mr. Lincoln's Camera Man, Mathew B. Brady.* New York: Charles Scribner's Sons, 1946.

_____. *Mr. Lincoln's Contemporaries: An Album of Portraits by Mathew S. Brady.* New York: Charles Schribner's Sons, 1951.

Meredith, Scott. *George Kaufman and His Friends.* New York: Doubleday, 1974.

Merilees, William. *The Short Arm of the Law.* London: John Long, 1960.

Meriwether, Lee. *Jim Reed, "Sartorial Immortal".* Webster Grove, Mo.: International Mark Twain Society, 1948.

_____. *The Tramp at Home.* New York: Harper, 1889.

Meriwether, Louise. *Daddy Was a Number Runner.* New York: Pyramid Books, 1971.

Merk, Frederick. *The Oregon Question.* Cambridge, Mass.: Harvard University Press, 1967.

Merli, Frank J. *Great Britain and the Confederate Navy, 1861-1865.* Bloomington: Indiana University Press, 1965.

Merlon, M.D. *Man and Marihuana.* Rutherford, N.J.: Fairleigh Dickinson University Press, 1972.

Merriam, Charles Edward. *The American Party System.* New York: Macmillan, 1922.

_____. *American Political Ideas, Studies in the Development of American Political Thought, 1865-1917.* New York: Macmillan, 1920.

_____. *Chicago: A More Intimate View of Urban Politics.* Chicago: University of Chicago Press, 1929.

Merrick, George Byron. *Old Times on the Upper Mississippi.* Cleveland: Arthur H. Clark, 1909.

Merrill, Frederick T. *Japan and the Opium Menace.* New York: Institute of Pacific Relations and the Foreign Policy Association, 1942.

Merrill, George P. *The First One Hundred Years of American Geology.* New Haven, Conn.: Yale University Press, 1924.

Merrill, James M. *Target Tokyo: The Halsey-Doolittle Raid.* Chicago: Rand McNally, 1964.

Merrill, John C. *The Elite Press: Great Newspaper of the World.* New York: Pitman, 1968.

Merrill, M.A. *Problems of Child Delinquency.* Boston: Houghton Mifflin, 1947.

Merrill, Walter M. *Against Wind and Tide.* Cambridge, Mass.: Harvard University Press, 1963.

Merrow, Smith, Harris, L.W., and Harris, James. *Prison Screw.* London: Jenkins, 1962.

Merry, S.E. *Urban Danger.* Philadelphia: Temple University Press, 1981.

Mersereau, John, Jr. *Mikhail Lermontov.* Carbondale: Southern Illinois University Press, 1962.

Mersky, Roy M., and Jacobstein, J. Myron. *Ten Year Index to Periodical Articles Relating to Law.* Dobbs Ferry, N.Y.: Blanville, 1970.

Mertens, Corneille. *The Trade-Union Movement in Belgium.* Amsterdam: International Federation of Trade Unions, 1925.

Merton, Robert K., and Nisbet, Robert A. *Contemporary Social Problems.* New York: Harcourt, Brace & World, 1961.

_____, and Lazarsfeld, Paul F. (eds.). *Continuities in Social Research.* Glencoe, Ill.: Free Press, 1950.

_____. *Continuities in the Theory of Social Structure and Anomie.* Glencoe, Ill.: Free Press, 1957.

_____. *Social Theory and Social Structure.* New York: Free Press, 1968.

Mertz, Leon Claire. *John Selman, Texas Gunfighter.* New York: Hastings House, 1966.

Meryman, Richard. *Mank.* New York: William Morrow, 1978.

Merz, Charles. *The Dry Decade.* New York: Doubleday, Doran, 1931.

_____. *The Great American Bandwagon.* New York: John Day, 1928.

Meserve, Frederick and Sandburg, Carl. *The Photographs of Abraham Lincoln.* New York: Harcourt, Brace, 1944.

Meskil, Paul S., with Callahan, Gerard M. *Cheesebox.* Prentice-Hall, 1974.

_____. *Don Carlo: Boss of Bosses.* New York: Popular Library, 1973.

Messaiu, Mario. *Mesina Perchè?* n.p.: Editrice Sarda Fossatoro, 1976.

Messick, Hank. *John Edgar Hoover.* New York: David McKay, 1972.

_____, and Goldblatt, Burt. *Kidnapping.* New York: Dial Press, 1974.

_____. *Lansky.* New York: G.P. Putnam's Sons, 1971.

_____. *The Mobs and the Mafia.* New York: Ballantine Books.

_____. *Of Grass and Snow: The Secret Criminal ELite.* Englewood Cliffs, N.J.: Prentice-Hall, 1979.

_____. *The Only Game in Town.* New York: T.Y. Crowell, 1976.

_____. *The Politics of Prosecution.* Ottawa, Ill.: Caroline House Books, 1978.

_____. *The Private Lives of Public Enemies.* New York: P.H. Wyden, 1973.

_____. *Secret File.* New York: G.P. Putnam's Sons, 1969.

_____. *The Silent Syndicate.* New York: Macmillan, 1967.

_____. *Syndicate in the Sun.* New York: Macmillan, 1968.

Messkill, Johanna Menzel. *Hitler and Japan: The Hollow Alliance.* New York: Atherton Press, 1966.

Metternich, Pauline von. *Souvenirs d'enfance et de jeunesse.* Paris: Plon-Nourrit, 1924.

Metternich, Richard (ed.). *Memoirs of Prince Metternich, 1773-1815.* 2 vols. New York: Charles Scribner's Sons, 1880.

Metz, Leon Claire. *Dallas Stoudenmire: El Paso Marshall.* New York: Pemberton Press, 1969.

_____. *John Selman: Texas Gunfighter.* New York: Hastings House, 1966.

_____. *Pat Garrett: The Story of a Western Lawman.* Norman: University of Oklahoma Press, 1974.

Meunier, Georges. *Gilles de Rais et son temps.* Paris: Nouvells Éditions Latines, 1949.

Meuret, F.C. *Annales de Nantes.* Nantes, Fr.: C. Merson, 1840.

Mewshaw, Michael. *Life for Death.* Garden City, N.Y.: Doubleday, 1980.

Meyer, Alfred G. *Communism.* New York: Random House, 1960.

_____. *Leninism.* Cambridge, Mass.: Harvard University Press, 1957.

Meyer, Annie. *Woman's Work in America.* New York: Henry Holt, 1891.

Meyer, Charles. *Full Account of the Life, Adventures, and Execution of Ernst William Gross.* Philadelphia: Fairbanks & Glessner, 1852.

Meyer, Håkon. *Den Politiske Arbeiderbevegelse i Norge.* Oslo, Norway: Det Norske Arbeiderpartis Förlag, 1931.

Meyer, Hermann H.B. *Select List of References on Capital Punishment.* Washington, D.C.: G.P.O., 1912.

Meyer, Howard N. *XIV the Amendment That Refused to Die.* Boston: Beacon, 1978.

Meyer, Johann Jacob. *Sexual Life in Ancient India.* New York: Barnes & Noble, 1953.

Meyer, Kurt. *Grenadiere.* Munich: Schild, 1965.

Meyer, Leland Winfield. *The Life and Times of Colonel Richard M. Johnson of Kentucky.* New York: Columbia University Press, 1932.

Meyer, M. (ed.). *Third Western Symposium on Learning.* Bellingham: Western Washington State College, 1972.

Meyer, Martin A. *Western Jewry.* San Francisco: Emanu-El, 1916.

Meyer, Michael C. *Huerta: A Political Portrait.* Lincoln: University of Nebraska, 1972.

Meyer, Peter. *The Yale Murder.* New York: Berkley Books, 1983.

Meyer, Philip. *Precision Journalism*. Bloomington: Indiana University Press, 1973.

Meyerholt, Paul. *The Strategy of Persuasion*. New York: Berkeley Medallion Books, 1968.

Meyers, Gustavus. *Great American Fortunes*. New York: Modern Library, 1936.

Meyers, William, and Newton, Walter (eds.). *The Hoover Administration*. New York: Charles Scribner's Sons, 1936.

Meyerson, Martin, and Banfield, Edward C. *Politics, Planning, and the Public Interest*. Glencoe, Ill.: Free Press, 1955.

Meyfart, Johann Matthäus. *Christliche Erinnerung*. Schleusingen, Ger.: Peter Schmincken, 1636.

Meyrick, Mrs. Kate. *Secrets of the 43*. London: John Long, 1933.

Mezerik, A.G. *Arab-Israeli Conflict*. New York: International Review Service, 1962.

_____ (ed.). *The Refugee Problem in the Middle East*. New York: International Review Service, 1957.

Mezzrow, Milton, and Wolfe, Bernard. *Really the Blues*. New York: Random House, 1946.

Michael, Jerome, and Adler, Mortimer J. *Crime, Law and Social Science*. New York: Harcourt, Brace, 1933.

Michaëlis, Sebastian. *The Admirabel History of the Possession and Conversion of a Penitent Woman*. London: W. Aspley, 1613.

_____. *A Discourse of Spirits*. London: W. Aspley, 1613.

Michalowski, Raymond J. *Order, Law, and Crime*. New York: Random House, 1985.

Michaud et Poujoulat. *Mémoires pour Servir à l'Histoire de France*. Paris: Edouard Proux, 1837.

Michaud, Stephen G., and Aynesworth, Hugh. *The Only Living Witness*. New York: Simon and Schuster, 1983.

Michaux, Henri. *Light through Darkness*. trans. Haakon Chevalier. New York: Orion Press, 1961.

_____. *Miserable Miracle*. trans. L. Varese. San Francisco: City Lights Books, 1953.

Michelet, Jules. *Histoire de France*. 5 vols. Paris: Hetzel et cie, 1870.

_____. *Joan of Arc*. trans. Albert Guérard. Ann Arbor: University of Michigan Press, 1957.

_____. *La Sorcière*. Paris: Librairie Marcel Didier, 1952.

_____. *Louis XIV et la Révolution*. Paris: Chamerot, 1860.

_____. *Satanism and Witchcraft*. trans. A.R. Allinson. New York: Citadel Press, 1930.

Michels, Robert. *Political Parties*. New York: Free Press, 1962.

Michelson, Charles. *The Ghost Talks*. New York: G.P. Putnam's Sons, 1944.

_____. *Mankillers at Close Range*. Houston: Frontier Press of Texas, 1958.

Michigan Department of Corrections. *The Use of Correctional Trade Training*. Lansing: Michigan Department of Corrections, 1969.

Micromegas. *I 7 responsabili del Fascismo*. Campione, Italy: Pagine di Campione, 1943.

Middagh, John. *Frontier Newspaper: The El Paso Times*. El Paso, Texas: Western College Press, 1958.

Middlebrook, Martin. *Convoy*. New York: William Morrow, 1976.

The Middle East. London: Europa, 1948.

Middlekauff, Robert. *The Mathers: Three Generations of Puritan Intellectuals*. New York: Oxford University Press, 1971.

Middleton, J., and Winter, E.H. (eds.). *Witchcraft and Sorcery in East Africa*. London: Routledge & Kegan Paul, 1963.

Miers, Earl Schenck (ed.). *Lincoln Day by Day: A Chronology 1809-1865*. 3 vols. Washington, D.C.: Lincoln Sesquicentennial Commission, 1960.

Mighill, Benjamin P., and Blodgette, George B. (eds.). *The Early Records of the Town of Rowley, Massachusetts*. Rowley, Mass.: Published by Author, 1894.

Migne, J.P. *Patrologiae cursuscompletus, Series Graeco Latina*. Paris: Garnier, 1887.

Mijatovich, C. *A Royal Tragedy: Assassination of King Alexander and Queen Draga of Serbia*. London: Eveleigh Nash, 1906.

Mikolajczyk, Stanislaw. *The Rape of Poland*. New York: Whittlesey House, 1948.

Miler, Arthus Selwyn. *The Supreme Court and American Capitalism*. New York: Free Press, 1968.

Miles. *Socialism's New Beginning*. New York: League for Industrial Democracy, 1934.

Miles, Michael W. *The Radical Probe*. New York: Atheneum, 1971.

Miles, Nelson A. *Personal Recollections and Observations of General Nelson A. Miles*. Chicago: Werner, 1896.

Milgram, Stanley. *Obedience ot Authority*. New York: Harper & Row, 1974.

_____, and Shotland, R.L. *Television and Anti-Social Behavior*. New York: Academic Press, 1973.

Miliukov, Pavel N. *Outlines of Russian Culture*. 3 vols. Philadelphia: University of Pennsylvania Press, 1941.

_____. *Political Memoirs, 1905-1917*. Ann Arbor: University of Michigan Press, 1967.

_____. *Russia and Its Crisis*. Chicago: University of Chicago Press, 1906.

_____. *Russia To-day and To-morrow*. New York: Macmillan, 1922.

Mill, John Stuart. *Essays on Politics and Culture*. New York: Doubleday, 1962.

_____. *On Liberty*. New York: W.W. Norton, 1975.

_____. *Principle of Political Economy, with Some of Their Applications to Social Philosophy*. London: Longmans, Green, 1929.

_____. *Utilitarianism, Liberty and Representative Government*. New York: E.P. Dutton, 1951.

Millar, Mara. *Hail to Yesterday*. New York: Farrar & Rinehart, 1941.

Millard, Bailey. *History of the San Francisco Bay Region*. Chicago: American Historical Society, 1924.

Millard, Mara. *Hail to Yesterday*. New York: Farrar & Rinehart, 1941.

Millard, Joseph. *No Law But Their Own*. Evanston, Ill.: Regency Books, 1967.

Millard, Oscar E. *Burgomaster Max*. London: Hutchinson, 1936.

Millen, Ernest. *Specialist in Crime*. London: Harrap, 1972.

Miller, Arthur. *The Crucible*. New York: Bantam Books, 1959.

Miller, Arthur R. *The Assault on Privacy*. Ann Arbor: University of Michigan Press, 1971.

Miller, Benjamin S. *Ranch Life in Southern Kansas and the Indian Territory*. New York: Fless & Ridge Printing, 1896.

Miller, C. *The Lunatic Express: An Entertainment in Imperialism*. New York: Macmillan, 1971.

Miller, Charles A. *The Supreme Court and the Uses of History*. Cambridge, Mass.: Harvard University Press, 1969.

Miller, Curt. *Total Home Protection*. Farmington, Mich.: Structures, 1976.

Miller, Douglas T. *The Fifties: The Way We Really Were*. Garden City, N.Y.: Doubleday, 1977.

_____. *Jacksonian Aristocracy: Class and Democracy in New York 1830-1860*. New York: Oxford University Press, 1967.

Miller, E.P. *A Treatise on the Cause of Exhausted Vitality*. New York: John A. Gray & Green, 1867.

Miller, Ernest B. *Bataan Uncensored*. Long Prairie, Minn.: Hart, 1949.

Miller, Ernest C. *John Wilkes Booth in the Pennsylvania Oil Region*. Warren, Pa.: Crawford County Historical Society, 1987.

Miller, F.J.W., et al. *Growing Up in Newcastle upon Tyne*. London: Oxford University Press, 1974.

Miller, Floyd. *Bill Tilghman: Marshal of the Last Frontier*. New York: Doubleday, 1968.

_____. *The School Years in Newcastle Upon Tyne*. London: Oxford University Press, 1974.

Miller, Francis Trevelyan. *The Photographic History of the Civil War*. New York: Review of Reviews, 1911.

Miller, Frank W. *Prosecution: The Decision to Charge a Suspect With a Crime*. Boston: Little, Brown, 1969.

Miller, Gene, with Mackle, Barbara Jane. *83 Hours Till Dawn*. Garden City, N.Y.: Doubleday, 1971.

Miller, George, Jr. *Missouri's Memorable Decade*. Columbia, Mo.: E.W. Stephens, 1898.

_____. *Trial of Frank James for Murder*. Columbus, Mo.: E.W. Stephens, 1898.

Miller, H. *The Wisdom of the Heart*. New York: New Directions, 1941.

Miller, Harry, and Cooper, Page. *Footloose Fiddler*. New York: McGraw-Hill Book, 1945.

Miller, Henry S. *Price Control in Fascist Italy*. New York: Columbia University Press, 1938.

Miller, Herman P. *Rich Man, Poor Man*. New York: Thomas Y. Crowell, 1966.

Miller, Irving. *Israel: The Eternal Ideal*. New York: Farrar, Straus & Cudahy, 1955.

Miller, James Edward. *The United States and Italy, 1940-1950*. Chapel Hill: University of North Carolina Press, 1986.

Miller, Joaquin. *An Ilustrated History of the State of Montana*. Chicago: Lewis, 1894.

Miller, John Anderson. *Fares, Please! From Horse-Cars to Streamliners*. New York: D. Appleton-Century, 1941.

Miller, John C. *Crisis in Freedom: The Alien and Sedition Acts*. Boston: Little, Brown, 1951.

_____. *Origins of the American Revolution*. Stanford, Calif.: Stanford University Press, 1959.

_____. *Sam Adams: Pioneer in Propaganda*. Boston: Little, Brown, 1936.

_____. *The Triumph of Freedom*. Boston: Little, Brown, 1948.

_____. *Arizona Cavalcade: The Turbulent Times*. New York: Hastings House, 1962.

Miller, Joseph. *Arizona, A State Guide*. New York: Hastings House, 1956.

_____. *Arizona, The Last Frontier*. New York: Hastings House, 1956.

_____. *The Arizona Rangers*. New York: Hastings House, 1972.

_____. *The Arizona Story*. New York: Hastings House, 1952.

Miller, L.L. (ed.). *Marijuana*. New York: Academic Press, 1974.

Miller, Margaret S. *The Economic Development of Russia, 1905-1914*. London: King, 1926.

Miller, Max. *Holladay Street*. New York: Signet Books, 1962.

Miller, Merle. *The Judges and the Judged Report for the American Civil Liberties Union*. Garden City, N.Y.: Doubleday, 1952.

Miller, N., and Dollard, J. *Social Learning and Imitation*. New Haven, Conn.: Yale University Press, 1941.

Miller, N.M. *Kenya: The Quest for Prosperity*. Boulder, Colo.: Westview Press, 1984.

Miller, Nina Hull. *Shutters West*. Denver: Sage Books, 1962.

Miller, Nyle H., and Snell, Joseph W. *Great Gunfighters of the Kansas Cowtowns, 1867-1886*. Lincoln: University of Nebraska Press, 1963.

_____, Langsdorf, Edgar, and Richmond, Robert W. *Kansas, a Pictorial History*. Topeka: Kansas State Historical Society, 1961.

_____. *Kansas Frontier Police Officers Before TV*. Topeka: Kansas State Historical Society, 1958.

_____. et al. *Kansas in Newspapers*. Topeka: Kansas State Historical Society, 1963.

_____. *Some Widely Publicized Western Police Officers*. Lincoln, Neb.: n.p., 1958.

_____, and Snell, Joseph W. *Why the West Was Wild*. Topeka: Kansas State Historical Society, 1963.

Miller, Perry. *Errand into the Wilderness*. New York: Harper & Row, 1964.

_____. *The Life of the Mind in America: From the Revolution to the Civil War*. New York: Harcourt, Brace & World, 1965.

_____. *The New England Mind: From Colony to Province*. Cambridge, Mass.: Harvard University Press, 1954.

_____. *The New England Mind: The Seventeenth Century*. Cambridge, Mass.: Harvard University Press, 1953.

_____, and Johnson, T.H. *The Puritans*. New York: American Book, 1938.

_____. *Roger Williams: His Contribution to the American Tradition*. New York: Atheneum, 1962.

Miller, Richard R. *Slavery and Catholicism*. Durham, N.C.: North State, 1957.

Miller, Ronald Dean. *Shady Ladies of the West*. Los Angeles: Westernlore Press, 1964.

Miller, Stuart Creighton. *The Unwelcome Immigrant*. Berkley: University of California Press, 1969.

Miller, Thomas Lloyd. *The Public Lands of Texas, 1519-1970*. Norman: University of Oklahoma Press, 1972.

Miller, Tom. *The Assassination Please Almanac*. Chicago: Henry Regnery, 1977.

Miller, W. Henry. *Pioneering North Texas*. San Antonio, Texas: Naylor, 1953.

Miller, Walter B. *Violence by Youth Gangs and Youth Groups as a Crime Problem in Major American Cities*. Washington, D.C.: U.S. Government Printing Office, 1975.

Miller, Webb. *I Found No Peace*. London: Victor Gollancz, 1937.

Miller, Wilbur R. *Cops and Bobbies: Police Authority in New York and London, 1830-1870*. Chicago: University of Chicago Press, 1973.

Miller, William. *The Balkans: Roumania, Bulgaria, Serbia, and Montenegro*. London: T. Fisher Unwin, 1923.

_____. *A History of the Greek People, 1821-1921*. London: Methuen, 1922.

Miller, William Alexander. *Early Days in the Wild West*. n.p., 1943.

Miller, William D. *Mr. Crump of Memphis*. Baton Rouge: Louisiana State University Press, 1964.

Miller, William R. *Nonviolence: A Christian Interpretation*. New York: Association Press, 1964.

Millett, Kate. *Flying*. New York: Alfred A. Knopf, 1974.

Milliband, Ralph. *The State in Capitalist Society*. New York: Basic Books, 1969.

Milligan, Maurice M. *The Inside Story of the Pendergast Machine by the Man Who Smashed It*. New York: Charles Scribner's Sons, 1948.

_____. *Missouri Waltz*. New York: Charles Scribner's Sons, 1948.

Milliot, Louis. *Introduction á l'édude du droit Muselman*. Paris: Recueil Sirey, 1953.

Millis, Walter (ed.). *The Forrestal Dairies*. New York: Viking Press, 1951.

_____. *The Martial Spirit: A Study of Our War with Spain*. Boston: Houghton Mifflin, 1931.

_____. *The Road to Pearl*. Cambridge, Mass.: Riverside Press, 1935.

_____. *This is Pearl! The United States and Japan--1941*. New York: William Morrow, 1947.

Mills, C. Wright. *The Power Elite*. New York: Oxford University Press, 1956.

Mills, Edward Laird. *Plains, Peaks and Pioneers*. Portland, Ore.: Binfords & Mort, 1947.

Mills, James. *The Prosecutor*. New York: Pocket Books, 1970.

_____. *The Underground Empire: Where Crime and Governments Meet*. New York: Dell, 1986.

Mills, James Cooke. *Our Inland Seas*. Chicago: McClurg, 1910.

Mills, Jeannie. *Six Years With God*. New York: A. & W., 1979.

Mills, Joseph Travis. *Bright and the Quakers*. 2 vols. New York: Methuen, 1935.

Mills, Lester W. *A Sagebrush Saga*. Springfield, Utah: Art City, 1956.

Mills, William W. *Forty Years at El Paso, 1858-1898*. El Paso, Texas: Carl Hertzog, 1962.

Millspaugh, Arthur. *Crime Control by the National Government*. Washington, D.C.: Brookings, 1937.

Milner, Alan (ed.). *African Penal Systems*. London: Routledge & Kegan Paul, 1969.

Milner, Christina and Richard. *Black Players*. Boston: Little, Brown, 1972.

Milner, Duncan C. *Lincoln and Liquor*. New York: Neale, 1920.

Milner, Joe E., and Forrest, Earle R. *California Joe, Noted Scout and Indian Fighter*. Caldwell, Idaho: Caxton Printers, 1935.

Milner, Lucille. *Education of an American Liberal*. New York: Horizon, 1954.

Milner, Michael. *Sex on Celluloid*. New York: McFadden, 1964.

Milton, Catherine. *Women in Policing*. Washington, D.C.: Police Foundation, 1972.

Milton, George Fort. *Abraham Lincoln and the Fifth Column*. New York: Vanguard Press, 1942.

_____. *Age of Hate*. New York: Coward-McCann, 1930.

_____. *Conflict: The American Civil War*. New York: Coward-McCann, 1941.

_____. *The Eve of Conflict: Stephen A. Douglas and the Needless War*. New York: Octagon Books, 1963.

Mines, John Flavel. *A Tour Around New York*. New York: Harper and Brothers, 1893.

Minear, Richard H. *Victors' Justice: The Tokyo War Crimes Trial*. Princeton, N.J.: Princeton University Press, 1973.

Minehan, Thomas. *Boy and Girl Tramps of America*. New York: Farrar, 1934.

Miner, Frederick Roland. *Outdoor Southland of California*. Los Angeles: Times-Mirror Press, 1923.

Miner, Maude E. *Slavery of Prostitution*. New York: Macmillan, 1916.

Minney, Rubeigh James. *Rasputin*. London: Cassell, 1972.

Minnigerode, Meade. *Certain Rich Men*. New York: G.P. Putnam's Sons, 1927.

_____. *The Fabulous Forties 1840-1850*. Garden City, N.Y.: Garden City, 1924.

Minogue, Kenneth R. *The Concept of a University*. Berkeley: University of California Press, 1973.

Minor, Charles L.C. *The Real Lincoln, from the Testimony of his Contemporaries*. Gastonia, N.C.: Atkins-Rankin, 1928.

Minot, G.E. *Murder Will Out*. Boston: Marshall Jones, 1928.

Minow, Newton N., Martin, John Bartlow, and Mitchell, Lee M. *Presidential Television*. New York: Basic Books, 1973.

Minton, Robert J. (ed.). *Inside Prison American Style*. New York: Random House, 1971.

Mintz, Ilse. *Deterioration in the Quality of Bonds Issued in the United States, 1920-1930*. New York: National Bureau of Economic Research, 1951.

Mintz, Morton, and Cohen, Jerry S. *America, Inc.* New York: Dial Press, 1971.

_____, and Cohen, Jerry. *Power, Inc.* New York: Viking Press, 1976.

_____. *The Therapeutic Nightmare*. Boston: Houghton Mifflin, 1965.

A Minute and Correct Account of the Trial of Lucian Hall. Middletown, Conn.: Charles H. Pelton, 1844.

Mirabehn. *Bapu's Letters to Mira*. Ahmedabad, India: Navajivan, 1949.

_____. *Gleanings*. Ahmedabad, India: Navajivan, 1949.

Miron, Murry S., and Goldstein, Arnold P. *Hostage*. New York: Pergamon Press, 1979.

Mirskii, Dmitri Petrovich. *Russia, a Social History*. London: Cresset, 1931.

Mirsky, Dimitrii S. *Contemporary Russian Literature, 1881-1925*. New York: Alfred A. Knopf, 1926.

Mirsky, Jeannette and Nevins, Allan. *The World of Eli Whitney*. New York: Macmillan, 1952.

Mirville, Jules Eudes, Marquis de. *Des Espirits*. Paris: F. Wattelier, 1868.

Misciatelli, P. *Lettere de Letizia Buonaparte*. Milan, Italy: U. Hoepli, 1936.

Mishlove, Jeffrey. *The Roots of Consciousness*. New York: Random House, 1975.

Missiroli, Mario. *L'Italia d'oggi*. Bologna, Italy: Zanichelli, 1932.

_____. *What Italy Owes to Mussolini*. London: John Heritage, 1938.

Mississippi River Commission. *Flood Control and Navigation Maps of the Mississippi River*. Vicksburg, Miss.: Mississippi River Commission, 1961.

Misuri, Alfredo. *Ad bestias!* Rome: Catacombe, 1944.

Mitau, G. Theodore. *Decade of Decision*. New York: Charles Scribner's Sons, 1967.

Mitchel, John. *Jail Journal*. Dublin, Ire.: M.H. Gill & Son, 1913.

Mitchell, Alexander R.K. *Drugs: The Parent's Dilemma*. London: Priory Press, 1972.

Mitchell, Allan. *Revolution in Bavaria, 1918-1919*. Princeton, N.J.: Princeton University Press, 1965.

Mitchell, Broadus. *Alexander Hamilton: A Concise Biography*. New York: Oxford University Press, 1976.

_____. *Alexander Hamilton: The National Adventure, 1788-1804*. New York: Macmillan, 1962.

_____, and Louise. *A Biography of the Constitution*. New York: Oxford University Press, 1964.

_____. *Depression Decade: From the New Era through the New Deal*. New York: Rinehart, 1947.

Mitchell, C. Ainsworth. *Science and the Criminal*. London: Pitman, 1911.

_____. *The Scientific Detective and the Expert Witness*. London: Heffer, 1931.

Mitchell, David. *The Light of Synomon*. New York: Seaview Books, 1980.

_____. *1919: Red Mirage*. New York: Macmillan, 1970.

_____. *Pirates, An Illustrated History*. New York: Dial Press, 1976.

Mitchell, David W. *Ten Years in the United States. . . etc.* London: Smith, Elder, 1862.

Mitchell, Edward P. *Memoirs of an Editor: Fifty Years of Journalism*. New York: Charles Scribner's Sons, 1941.

Mitchell, Edwin Valentine (ed.) *The Newgate Calendar*. Garden City, N.Y.: Garden City, 1926.

Mitchell, J. *Psychoanalysis and Feminism*. London: Allen Lane, 1974.

Mitchell, John D. *Lost Mines of the Southwest*. Phoenix, Ariz.: Journal, 1933.

Mitchell, John. *Organized Labor*. Philadelphia: American Book and Bible House, 1903.

Mitchell, Lt. Col. Joseph B. *Decisive Battles of the Civil War*. Greenwich, Conn.: Fawcett, 1962.

Mitchell, Julia Post. *St. Jean de Crèvecoeur*. New York: Columbia University Press, 1916.

Mitchell, Lee Clark. *Witness to a Vanishing America*. Princeton, N.J.: Princeton University Press, 1981.

Mitchell, Lige. *Daring Exploits of Jesse James and His Band of Border Train and Bank Robbers*. Baltimore: I. & M. Ottenheimer, 1912.

Mitchell, Mairin. *Maritime History of Russia, 848-1948*, London: Sidgwick & Jackson, 1949.

Mitchell, Silas Weir. *Doctor and Patient*. Philadelphia: J.B. Lippincott, 1988.

Mitchell, Stewart. *Horatio Seymour of New York*. Cambridge, Mass.: Harvard University Press, 1938.

Mitchell, Wesley C. *Business Cycles*. New York: National Bureau of Economic Research, 1927.

Mitchell, William Ansel. *Linn County, Kansas: A History*. Kansas City, Kan.: Campbell-Gates, 1928.

Mitchell, William G. *The American Polity*. New York: Free Press of Glencoe, 1962.

Mitchison, G.R. *The First Workers' Government*. London: Victor Gollancz, 1934.

Mitford, Jessica. *The American Way of Death*. New York: Paperback Library, 1963.

_____. *A Fine Old Conflict*. New York: Alfred A. Knopf, 1977.

_____. _Kind and Usual Punishment: The Prison Business._ New York: Alfred A. Knopf, 1973.

_____. _The Trial of Dr. Spock._ New York: Vintage Books, 1970.

Mitford, Nancy. _Frederick the Great._ New York: Harper & Row, 1970.

_____. _Madame de Pompadour._ London: Reprint Society, 1954.

Mitgang, Herbert. _America at Random._ New York: Coward-McCann, 1969.

_____. (ed.). _The Letters of Carl Sandburg._ New York: Harcourt, Brace & World, 1968.

_____. _Lincoln as They Saw Him._ New York: Holt, Rinehart & Winston, 1956.

_____. _The Man Who Rode the Tiger, The Life and Times of Judge Samuel Seabury._ Philadelphia: J.B. Lippincott, 1963.

Mitrany, D. _The Land and the Peasant in Rumania: The War and Agrarian Reform (1917-1921)._ London: Oxford University Press, 1930.

Mitrany, David. _Marx Against the Peasant._ Chapel Hill: University of North Carolina Press, 1951.

Mitscherlich, Alexander, and Mielke, Fred. _Das Diktat der Menschlichkeit._ Heidelberg, Ger.: Verlag Lambert Schneider, 1947.

_____. _Medizin ohne Menschlichkeit._ Frankfurt, W. Ger.: Fischer Bücherei, 1960.

Mitsuko, Iolana. _Honolulu Madame._ Los Angeles: Holloway House, 1969.

Mix, Olive Stokes, and Heath, Eric. _The Fabulous Tom Mix._ Englewood Cliffs, N.J.: Prentice-Hall, 1957.

Mix, Tom. _The West of Yesterday._ Los Angeles: Times-Mirror Press, 1923.

Miyanokochi Kentaro. _Sino-Japanese Dictionary._ Tokyo: Obunsha, 1957.

Miyatovitch, Cheddo. _A Royal Tragedy._ London: E. Nash, 1906.

_____. _Serbia of the Serbians._ London: Pitman, 1915.

Mizener, Arthur. _The Far Side of Paradise._ Boston: Houghton Mifflin, 1951.

Mizner, Addison. _The Many Mizners._ New York: Sears, 1932.

Moaks, Sim. _The Last of the Mill Creek and Early Life in Northern California._ Chico, Calif.: n.p., 1923.

Moats, Alice-Leone. _Lupescu._ New York: Henry Holt, 1955.

Moats, Leone B. _Thunder In Their Veins._ London: George Allen and Unwin, 1933.

Mochulsky, Knostantin. _Dostoevsky: His Life and Work._ trans. Michael A. Minihan. Princeton, N.J.: Princeton University Press, 1967.

Model, F. Peter, and Groden, Robert J. _JFK: The Case for Conspiracy._ New York: Manor Books, 1976.

Modiglani, Vera. _Esilio._ Milan, Italy: Garzanti, 1946.

Moe, Finn. _Does Norwegian Labor Seek the Middle Way?_ New York: League for Industrial Democracy, 1937.

Moenssens, Andre A. _Fingerprint Techniques._ Radnor, Pa.: Chilton, 1971.

Moers, Ellen. _The Dandy._ New York: Viking, 1960.

Moffett, Cleveland. _True Detective Stories._ New York: G.W. Dillingham, 1898.

Moffitt, Dona (ed.). _Swindled._ New Jersey: Dow Jones Books, 1976.

Mogelever, Jacob. _Death to Traitors: The Story of General Lafayette C. Baker, Lincoln's Forgotten Secret Service Chief._ Garden City, N.Y.: Doubleday, 1960.

Moggeridge, D.E. _The Return to Gold, 1925: The Formation of Policy and Its Critics._ Cambridge, Eng.: Cambridge University Press, 1972.

Mohammed Ali. _The Prophet Mohammed._ London: Cassell, 1947.

Mohr, James C. _The Radical Republicans in New York During Reconstruction._ Ithaca, N.Y.: Cornell University Press, 1973.

Mohr, Johan W., et al. _Pedophilia and Exhibitionism._ Toronto, Ontario, Can.: University of Toronto Press, 1964.

Mohrenschildt, Dimitri von. _Russia in the Intellectual Life of the Eighteennth-Century France._ New York: Columbia University Press, 1936.

Moiseiwitsch, Maurice. _Five Famous Trials._ Connecticut: New York Graphic Society, 1962.

Mokhiber, Russell. _Corporate Crime and Violence: Big Business Power and the Abuse of the Public Trust._ San Francisco: Sierra Club Books, 1988.

Mokler, Alfred James. _History of Natrona County, Wyoming._ Chicago: Lakeside Press, 1923.

Moland, Louis. _Oeuvres Complètes de Voltaire._ Paris: Garneir Frères, 1881.

Moldea, Dan E. _The Hoffa Wars._ New York: Charter Books, 1978.

Molesworth, William N. _The History of England From the Year 1830._ (3 vols.) London: Chapman & Hall, 1874.

Moley, Raymond. _After Seven Years._ New York: Harper & Cross, 1939.

_____. _The First New Deal._ New York: Harcourt, Brace & World, 1966.

_____. _Politics and Criminal Prosecution._ New York: Minton, Balch, 1929.

_____. _Tribunes of the People._ New Haven, Conn.: Yale University Press, 1932.

Molfese, Franco. _Storia del brigantaggio dodo l"unita._ Milan, Italy: Feltrinelli, 1976.

Molinier, Charles. _L'Inquisition dans le midi de la France au xiii et au xiv siècle._ Paris: Sandoz & Fischbacher, 1880.

Molitor, Ulrich. _De Lamiis et Phitonicis Mulieribus._ Strassburg, Ger.: J. Prüss, 1849.

Moll, A. _Libido Sexualis._ New York: American Ethnological Press, 1933.

_____. _Perversions of the Sex Instinct._ trans. M. Popkin. Newark, N.J.: Julian Press, 1931.

_____. _The Sexual Life of the Child._ New York: Macmillan, 1921.

Moll, Kendall D. _Arson, Vandalism and Violence: Law Enforcement Problems Affecting Fire Departments._ Washington, D.C.: U.S. Department of Justice, 1974.

Mollenhoff, Clark R. _The Man Who Pardoned Nixon._ New York: St. Martin's Press, 1976.

_____. _Strike Force: Organized Crime and the Government._ Englewood Cliffs, N.J.: Prentice-Hall, 1972.

_____. _Tentacles of Power._ Cleveland: World, 1965.

Mollenkopf, John H. _The Contested City._ Princeton, N.J.: Princeton University Press, 1983.

Möllhausen, E.F. _La carta perdente._ Rome: Sestante, 1948.

The Mollie Maquires. Tamagua, Pa.: Eveland & Harris, 1876.

Molloy, Robert. _Charleston: A Gracious Heritage._ New York: D. Appleton-Century, 1947.

Molony, J.C. _The Riddle of the Irish._ London: Methuen, 1927.

Moltke, Count Helmuth Carl Bernhard von. _Ausgewählte Werke._ Berlin: Reimar Hobbing, 1925.

_____. _Essays, Speeches, and Memoirs._ trans. C.F. McClumpha, et al. London: Osgood & McIlvaine, 1893.

_____. _The Franco-German War of 1870-71._ trans. C. Bell and H.W. Fischer. London: Osgood & McIlvaine, 1891.

_____. _Gesammelte Schriften und Denkwürdigkeiten._ Berlin: E.S. Mittler & Sohn, 1891.

Momigliano, Arnaldo. _Claudius, the Emperor and his Achievement._ New York: Barnes & Noble, 1961.

Momigliano, E. _Storia tragica e grottesca del razzismo fascista._ Florence, Italy: Mondadori, 1946.

Mommsen, Wolfgang, and Hirschfeld, Gerhard (eds.). _Social Protest, Violence and Terror in Nineteenth and Twentieth Century Europe._ London: Macmillan, 1982.

Monaghan, Frank. _John Jay, Defender of Liberty._ New York: Bobbs-Merrill, 1935.

_____, and Lowenthal, Marvin. _This Was New York._ New York: Doubleday, Doran, 1943.

Monaghan, James Charles. _Is Woodrow Wilson A Bigot?_ New York: n.p., 1912.

Monaghan, Jay (ed.). *The Book of the American West.* New York: Julian Messner, 1963.

_____. *Civil War on the Western Border 1854-1865.* Boston: Little, Brown, 1955.

_____. *The Great Rascal.* New York: Bonanza Books, 1951.

_____. *Last of the Bad Men.* New York: Bobbs-Merrill, 1946.

_____. *The Legend of Tom Horn, Last of the Bad Men.* New York: Bobbs-Merrill, 1946.

_____. *The Man Who Elected Lincoln.* Indianapolis, Ind.: Bobbs-Merrill, 1956.

_____. *The Overland Trail.* New York: Bobbs-Merrill, 1947.

Monahan, Florence. *Women in Crime.* New York: Washburn, 1941.

Monahan, J. *Predicting Violent Behaviour.* Beverly Hills, Calif.: Sage, 1981.

Monahan, John and Steadman, Henry J. (eds.). *Mentally Disordered Offenders: Perspectives from Law and Social Science.* New York: Plenum Press, 1983.

Monahan, M. (ed.). *A Text-Book of True Temperance.* New York: U.S. Brewers Association, 1911.

Monas, Nicholas I. Sidney. *The Third Section: Police and Society in Russia under Nicholas I.* Cambridge, Mass.: Harvard University Press, 1961.

Monat, Pawel, with Dille, John. *Spy in the U.S.* New York: Harper & Row, 1961.

Monelli, Paolo. *Mussolini: An Intimate Life.* trans. Brigid Maxwell. London: Thames & Hudson, 1953.

_____. *Roma, 1943.* Rome: Longanesi, 1963.

Mongrédien, Georges. *L'affaire Foucquet.* Paris: Hachette, 1956.

_____. *Leonora Galigai: Un proces de sorcellerie sous Louis XIII.* Paris: Hachette, 1968.

_____. *Madame de Montespan et l'affaire des poisons.* Paris: Hachette, 1953.

Monkkonen, E.H. *Police in Urban America, 1860-1920.* Cambridge, Eng.: Cambridge University Press, 1981.

Mon-lin, Chiang. *Tides from the West.* Taipei, Taiwan: China Publication Foundation, 1957.

Monnerot, Jules. *The Sociology and Psychology of Communism.* Boston: Beacon, 1953.

Monoghan, James. *The Great Rascal.* Boston: Little, Brown, 1952.

Monroe, Arthur Worley. *San Juan Silver.* Grand Junction, Colo.: Grand Junction Sentinel, 1940.

Monroe, David G. *State and Provincial Police.* Evanston, Ill.: International Association of Chiefs of Police and Northwestern University Traffic Institute, 1941.

Monroe, Elizabeth. *The Mediterranean in Politics.* London: Oxford University Press, 1939.

Monroe, Robert. *Journeys Out-of-the-Body.* New York: Doubleday, 1972.

Monroe, Russell R. *Brain Dysfunction in Aggressive Criminals.* Lexington, Mass.: D.C. Heath, 1978.

Montagna, Renzo. *Mussolini e il processo di Verona.* Milan, Italy: Edizioni Omnia, 1949.

Montagu, Ashley. *The Anatomy of Swearing.* New York: Macmillan, 1967.

_____. *Human Heredity.* New York: World, 1959.

_____. *Man and Aggression.* New York: Oxford University Press, 1968.

Montagu, Basil (ed.). *The Opinions of Different Authors Upon the Punishment of Death.* 3 vols. London: Longman, Hurst, Rees & Orme, 1809.

Montague, Edwin S. *An Indian Diary.* London: William Heinemann, 1930.

Montague, G.H. *Trusts of Today.* New York: McClure, Phillips, 1904.

Montague, Joseph. *Wild Bill, a Western Story.* New York: Chelsea House, 1926.

Montalban, Charles. *La Petite Bible des jeunes époux.* Paris: Flammarion, 1885.

Montanelli, Indro. *Le Bonhomme Mussolini.* Paris: Francoy, 1947.

Montarron, Marcel. *Histoire des Crimes Sexuels.* Paris: Plon, 1970.

_____. *Histoire du Milieu.* Paris: Plon, 1969.

_____. *Les Grande Procès d'Assises.* Paris: Planète, 1967.

_____. *Tout Ce Joli Monde.* Paris: La Table Ronde, 1965.

Monteil, Vincent. *Les Officiers.* Paris: Editions du Seuil, 1958.

Monteilhet, J. *Les Institutions militaires de la France, 1814-1932.* Paris: Félix Alcan, 1932.

Monteiro, John B. *Corruption: Control and Maladministration.* Bombay, India: P.C. Manaktla & Sons, 1966.

Monteith, Robert. *Casement's Last Adventure.* Dublin, Ire.: Moynihan, 1953.

Montelera, Luigi Rossi di. *Racconto di un Sequestro.* Torino, Italy: Dossiers Sei, 1977.

Montell, William Lynwood. *Killings Folk Justice in the Upper South.* Lexington: University Press of Kentucky, 1986.

Montespan, Madame. *Memoirs of Madame la Marquise de Montespan.* trans. P.E.P. London: Grover Society, 1904.

Monteval, Marion. *The Klan Inside Out.* Claremore, Okla.: Monarch, 1924.

Montgomerie, Hastings Seton. *William Bligh of the Bounty in Fact and Fable.* London: Williams & Norgate, 1937.

Montgomery, Bernard L. *The Second World War.* London: Hutchinson, 1946.

Montgomery, Cora. *Eagle Pass.* New York: G.P. Putnam's Sons, 1852.

Montgomery, John. *The Twenties.* London: George Allen & Unwin, 1957.

Montgomery, Robert H. *Sacco-Vanzetti: The Murder and the Myth.* New York: Devin-Adair, 1960.

Montgomery, Ruth. *Hail to the Chiefs.* New York: Coward-McCann, 1970.

Montijo, Eugénie de. *Lettres familières de l'impératice Eugénie.* Paris: Le Devan, 1935.

Montross, Lynn. *Ragtag and Bobtail.* New York: Harper, 1952.

_____. *The Reluctant Rebels.* New York: Harper & Brothers, 1950.

_____. *War Through the Ages.* New York: Harper & Brothers, 1944.

Moody, John. *The Masters of Capital.* New Haven, Conn.: Yale University Press, 1919.

_____. *The Railroad Builders.* New Haven, Conn.: Yale University Press, 1919.

_____. *The Truth About Trusts.* New York: Moody, 1904.

Moody, Ralph. *Stagecoach West.* New York: Thomas Y. Crowell, 1967.

_____. *Wells Fargo.* Boston: Houghton Mifflin, 1961.

Moody, Richard. *The Astor Place Riot.* Bloomington: Indiana University Press, 1958.

_____. *Lillian Hellman Playwright.* New York: Pegasus, 1972.

Moody, Robert E. *The Saltonstall Papers.* Boston: Massachusetts Historical Society, 1972.

Moody, Samuel. *Summary Account of the Life and Death of Joseph Quasson.* Boston: S. Gerrish, 1726.

Moody, Samuel B. *Reprieve From Hell.* New York: Pageant Press, 1961.

Moody, Walter D. *What of the City?* Chicago: McClurg, 1919.

Mook, Hubertus J. van. *The Netherlands Indies and Japan: Battle on Paper, 1940-1941.* New York: W.W. Norton, 1944.

Moon, Parker Thomas. *Imperialism and World Politics.* New York: Macmillan, 1944.

Mooney, M. *Crime Incorporated.* New York: McGraw-Hill, 1935.

Mooney, M. *Crime, Unincorporated.* New York: Whittlesey House, 1935.

Mooney, Michael Macdonald. *Evelyn Nesbit and Stanford White, Love and Death in the Gilded Age.* New York: William Morrow, 1976.

Mooney-Billings Report Suppressed by the Wickersham Commission.

New York: Gotham House, 1932.

Moorad, George. *Lost Peace in China.* New York: Dutton, 1949.

Moore, B. *A Modest Proposal for the Reform of the Capitalist System (Part A).* Washington, D.C.: Center for the Study of Capitalist Institutions, 1974.

Moore, Barrington Jr. *Soviet Politics: The Dilemma of Power.* Cambridge, Mass.: Harvard University Press, 1950.

_____. *Terror and Progress U.S.S.R.* Cambridge, Mass.: Harvard University Press, 1954.

Moore, Brian. *The Revolution Script.* New York: Holt, Rinehart and Winston, 1971.

Moore, Charles. *Daniel Hudson Burnham, Architect, Planner of Cities.* Boston: Houghton Mifflin, 1921.

Moore, Dan Tyler. *Wolves, Widows and Orphans, An Expose of the Ways and Wiles of Con Men, Card Sharps, Swindlers and Rogues.* New York: World, 1967.

Moore, Doris Langley. *The Child in Fashion.* London: B.T. Batsford, 1953.

Moore, Edward C. *William James.* New York: Washington Square Press, 1966.

Moore, Frank L. (ed.). *The Rebellion Record.* New York: D. Van Nostrand, 1861.

_____. *Souls and Saddlebags, the Diaries and Correspondence of Frank L. Moore, Western Missionary, 1888-1896.* Denver: Big Mountain Press, 1963.

_____. *Women of the War.* Hartford, Conn.: S.S. Scranton, 1867.

Moore, Frederick. *With Japan's Leaders: An Intimate Record of Fourteen Years as Counsellor to the Japanese Government, Ending Dec. 7, 1941.* New York: Charles Scribner's Sons, 1942.

Moore, George. *Confessions of a Young Man.* London: William Heinemann, 1926.

_____. *Parnell and His Island.* London: Swan Sonnenschein, Lowrey, 1887.

Moore, Glover. *The Missouri Controversy.* Lexington: University of Kentucky Press, 1953.

Moore, Guy W. *The Case of Mrs. Surratt: Her Controversial Trial and Execution for Conspiracy in the Lincoln Assassination.* Norman: University of Oklahoma Press, 1954.

Moore, J.W. *Homeboys.* Philadelphia: Temple University Press, 1978.

Moore, James and Dahl, Norman. *Famous Lives: Crime and Justice.* London: Hamlyn, 1980.

Moore, John M. *The West.* Wichita Falls, Texas: Wichita Printing, 1935.

Moore, John R. *Senator Josiah William Bailey of North Carolina.* Durham, N.C.: Duke University Press, 1968.

Moore, Jonathan, and Fraser, Janet (eds.). *The Managers Look at '76.* Cambridge, Mass.: Ballinger, 1977.

Moore, Kenneth C. *Airport, Aircraft and Airline Security.* Los Angeles: Security World, 1976.

Moore, Langdon W. *His Own Story of His Eventful Life.* Boston: L.W. Moore, 1893.

Moore, Mark Harrison. *Buy and Bust.* Lexington, Mass.: Lexington Books, 1977.

Moore, Maurice E. *Frauds and Swindles.* London: Gee, 1933.

Moore, Nathanial Fish. *Diary: A Trip from New York to the Falls of St. Anthony in 1845.* Chicago: University of Chicago Press, 1946.

Moore, R. Laurence. *In Search of White Crows: Spiritualism, Parapsychology, and American Culture.* New York: Oxford University Press, 1977.

Moore, Robin, with Barbara Fuca. *Mafia Wife.* New York: Macmillan, 1977.

Moore, Sally Falk, and Myerhoff, Barbara C. (eds.). *Symbol and Politics in Communal Ideology.* Ithaca, N.Y.: Cornell University Press, 1975.

Moore, U., and Callahan, C.C. *Law and Learning Theory.* New Haven, Conn.: Yale Law Journal, 1943.

Moore, William H. *The Kefauver Committee and the Politics of Crime.* Columbia: University of Missouri Press, 1974.

Moore, William T. *Dateline Chicago.* New York: Taplinger, 1973.

Moore-Anderson, Arthur P. *Sir Robert Anderson and Lady Agnes Anderson.* London: Marshall, Morgan and Scott, 1947.

Moorehead, Alan. *African Trilogy.* London: Hamish Hamilton, 1965.

_____. *The Blue Nile.* London: Hamish Hamilton, 1962.

_____. *The Russian Revolution.* New York: Harper, 1958.

_____. *The White Nile.* London: Hamish Hamilton, 1960.

Moorehead, Caroline. *Hostages To Fortune.* New York: Atheneum, 1980.

Moorhouse, Geoffrey. *India Britannica.* New York: Harper & Row, 1983.

Moorthy, M.V. (ed.). *Beggar-Problem in Greater Bombay.* Bombay, India: Indian Conference of Social Work, 1959.

Mootz, Herman Edwin. *The Blazing Frontier.* Dallas: Tardy, 1936.

_____. *"Pawnee Bill." A Romance of Oklahoma.* Los Angeles: Excelsior, 1928.

Moquin, Wayne. *The American Way of Crime.* New York: Frederick A. Praeger, 1976.

_____, and Van Doren, Charles (eds.) *A Documentary History of the Mexican Americans.* New York: Frederick A. Praeger, 1972.

Morain, Alfred. *The Underground of Paris.* New York: Blue Ribbon Books, 1931.

_____. *The Underworld of Paris.* London: Jarrolds, 1929.

Morales, Armando. *Ando Sangrando.* La Puente, Calif.: Perspectiva, 1972.

Morales Hesse, José. *El general Pablo González. Datos para la historia, 1910-1916.* Mexico City: n.p., 1916.

Morales Jiménez, Alberto. *Hombres de la Revolución Mexicana.* Mexico City: Biblioteca del Instituto Nacional de Estudios Históricos de la Revolución Mexicana, 1960.

Moran, Richard. *Knowing Right from Wrong: The Insanity Defence of Daniel McNaughtan.* New York: Free Press, 1981.

Moray, Alastair. *The Diary of a Rum Runner.* London: Philip, Alan, 1929.

Mordden, Ethan. *Better Foot Forward.* New York: Grossman, 1976.

Mordecai, Samuel. *Richmond in Bygone Days.* Richmond, Va.: Dietz Press, 1946.

Mordell, Albert. *Clarence Darrow, Eugence V. Debs and Haldeman-Julius: Incidents in the Career of an Author, Editor and Publisher.* Girard, Kan.: Haldeman-Julius, 1950.

More, Henry. *An Antidote Against Atheism.* London: Roger Daniel, 1653.

More, Louise Bolard. *Wage-Earners' Budgets: A Study of Standards and Costs of Living in New York City.* New York: Henry Holt, 1907.

More, Thomas. *Ideal Commonwealths.* New York: Colonial Press, 1901.

_____. *Utopia.* Harmondsworth, Eng.: Penguin Books, 1965.

Moreau, Georges. *Souvenirs de la Petite et de la Grande Roquette.* Paris: J. Rouff, 1884.

Moreau, J. *Du hachisch et de l'alienation mentale.* Paris: Masson, 1845.

Morehouse, Clifford P. (ed.) *A History of Trinity Church in the City of New York.* New York: Seaburg Press, 1978.

Moreland, Nigel. *Background to Murder.* London: Werner Laurie, 1955.

_____. *Hangman's Clutch.* London: Werner Laurie, 1954.

_____. *Science in Crime Detection.* London: Robert Hale, 1958.

Moreland, Roy. *The Law of Homocide.* Indianapolis, Ind.: Bobbs-Merrill, 1952.

Moreland, W.H. and Chatterjee, Atul Chandra. *A Short History of India.* London: Longmans, 1957.

Morelle, Paul. *Histoire de la sorcellerie.* Paris: Richard-Masse, 1946.

Moreno, Daniel A. *Francisco I. Madero, José M. Pino Suárez, el crimen de la* embajada. Mexico City: Libros Mexicana, 1960.

_____. *Los Hombres de la Revolución: 40 Estudios Biográficos.* Mexico City: Libro Mex Editores, 1960.

Morgan, C.R. *The Commonwealth of Pennsylvania versus Edward Parr.* Phildelphia: Gillen & Nagle, 1879.

Morgan, Charles, Jr. *A Time to Speak.* New York: Harper & Row, 1964.

Morgan, Dale L. *The Humboldt, Highroad of the West.* New York: Farrar & Rinehart, 1943.

Morgan, Donald G. *Justice William Johnson: The First Dissenter.* Columbia: University of South Carolina Press, 1954.

Morgan, E.D., and Coote, C.H. (eds.). *Early Voyages and Travels in Russia and Persia.* London: Hakluyt Society, 1886.

Morgan, E. Victor. *Studies in British Financial Policy, 1914-1925.* London: Macmillan, 1952.

Morgan, Edmund S. (ed.). *The American Revolution: Two Centuries of Interpretation.* Englewood Cliffs, N.J.: Prentice-Hall, 1965.

_____. *The Birth of the Republic 1763-1789.* Chicago: University of Chicago Press, 1956.

_____. *The Gentle Puritan: A Life of Ezra Stiles, 1727-1795.* New Haven, Conn.: Yale University Press, 1962.

_____. *Prologue to Revolution.* Chapel Hill: University of North Carolina Press, 1959.

_____. *The Puritan Dilemma: The Story of John Winthrop.* Boston: Little, Brown, 1958.

_____. *The Puritan Family.* New York: Harper & Row, 1966.

_____. and Helen M. *The Stamp Act Crisis: Prologue to Revolution.* New York: Collier Books, 1963.

_____. *Visible Saints: The History of a Puritan Idea.* New York: New York University Press, 1963.

Morgan, Edward E.P. *God's Loaded Dice; Alaska, 1897-1930.* Caldwell, Idaho: Caxton Printers, 1948.

_____. *The Theory and Practices of Central Banking, 1797-1913.* Cambridge, Eng.: Cambridge University Press, 1943.

Morgan, H. Wayne. *William McKinley and His America.* Syracuse, N.Y.: Syracuse University Press, 1963.

Morgan, Helen M. *A Season in New York.* Pittsburgh, Penn.: University of Pittsburgh Press, 1969.

Morgan, John. *Prince of Crime.* New York: Stein and Day, 1985.

Morgan, John P. *Reprints of Statements Submitted by Members of J.P. Morgan and Company to Senate Committee on Banking and Currency at Its Hearings in Washington May 23 to 9 June 1933.* Privately printed, 1933.

Morgan, Jonnie R. *The History of Wichita Falls.* Oklahoma City, Okla.: Economy, 1931.

Morgan, Leon. *Shooting Sheriffs of the Wild West.* Racine, Wis.: Whitman, 1936.

Morgan, Lewis Henry. *Ancient Society.* Cleveland: World, 1877.

Morgan, Murray. *Skid Road: An Informal Portrait of Seattle.* New York: Viking Press, 1951.

Morgan, Richard E. *Domestic Intelligence: Monitoring Dissent in America.* Austin, Tex.: University of Texas Press, 1980.

Morgan, Richard P. *The Decline of Commerce of the New York Port.* Urbana: University of Illinois Press, 1901.

Morgan, Robin. *Lady of the Beasts.* New York: Random House, 1976.

Morgan, Ted. *FDR: A Biography.* New York: Simon and Schuster, 1985.

Morgan, Thomas B. *Spurs on the Boot.* New York: Longmans, 1941.

Morgan, W.P. *Triad Societies in Hong Kong.* Hong Kong: Government Press, 1960.

Morgan, Wallace M. *History Kern County, California.* Los Angeles: Historic Record, 1914.

Morgan, Wayne H. *Drugs in America.* New York: Syracuse University Press, 1981.

_____. *The Gilded Age: A Reappraisal.* Syracuse, N.Y.: Syracuse University Press, 1970.

_____. *William McKinley and His America.* Syracuse, N.Y.: Syracuse University Press, 1963.

_____. *Yesterday's Addicts.* Norman: University of Oklahoma, 1980.

Morgan, William. *Morgan's Freemasonry Exposed and Explained.* New York: L. Fitzgerald, 1882

Morganstern, Oskar. *International Financial Transactions and Business Cycles.* Princeton, N.J.: Princeton University Press, 1959.

Morganthau, Hans J. *In Defense of the National Interest: A Critical Examination of American Foreign Policy.* New York: Alfred A. Knopf, 1951.

_____. *The Purpose of American Politics.* New York: Random House, Vintage Books, 1960.

Morgenstern, George E. *Pearl Harbor: The Story of the Secret War.* New York: Devin-Adair, 1947.

Morgenthau, Henry. *All in a Life-Time.* Garden City, N.Y.: Doubleday, Page, 1922.

_____. *Ambassador Morgenthau's Story.* New York: Doubleday, Page, 1918.

Morgenthau, Henry, Jr. *Morgenthau Diary, China.* 2 vols. Washington, D.C.: GPO, 1965.

Mori, Cesare. *The Last Struggle of the Mafia.* trans. Orlo Williams. New York: G.P. Putnam's Sons, 1933.

Moriarty, C.C.H. *Police Procedure and Administration.* London: Spottiswoode, Ballantyne, 1950.

Moriarty, Florence. *True Confessions.* New York: Simon and Schuster, 1979.

Morice, Dom H. *Histoire de Bretagne.* Paris: Imprimerie de la Guette, 1750.

Mori Ei. *Kurokikan* (Black Chamber). Tokyo: Daiyamondo, 1977.

Morier Evans, D. *The History of the Commercial Crisis, 1857-1858, and the Stock Exchange Panic of 1859.* New York: Augustus M. Kelley, 1969.

Morikawa Tetsuro. *Chi no Senkoku: Don Taoka Sogeki Jiken* (Bloody Verdict: The Shooting Incident of Don Taoka). Tokyo: Sanichi Shubo, 1979.

Morin, André Saturnin. *Le prêtre et le sorcier.* paris: A. Le Chevalier, 1872.

Morin, Relman. *Assassination: The Death of President John F. Kennedy.* New York: New American Library, 1968.

Morison, Elting E. et al. (eds.). *Letters of Theodore Roosevelt.* Cambridge, Mass.: Harvard University Press, 1951.

_____. *Turmoil and Tradition: The Life and Times of Henry L. Stimson.* Boston: Houghton Mifflin, 1960.

Morison, S. *The English Newspaper, 1622-1932.* New York: Macmillan, 1932.

Morison, Samuel Eliot. *Admiral of the Ocean Sea.* Boston: Little, Brown, 1942.

_____. *Builders of the Bay Colony.* Boston: Houghton Mifflin, 1930.

_____, and Commager, Henry Steele. *The Growth of the American Republic.* New York: Oxford University Press, 1942.

_____. *Harvard College in the Seventeenth Century.* Cambridge, Mass.: Harvard University Press, 1936.

_____. *John Paul Jones: A Sailor's Biography.* New York: Time, 1959.

_____. *The Maritime History of Massachusetts 1783-1860.* Boston: Houghton Mifflin, 1921.

_____. *The Oxford History of the American People.* New York: Oxford University Press, 1965.

_____. *The Parkman Reader.* Boston: Little, Brown, 1955.

_____. *The Rising Sun in the Pacific.* Volume 4. Boston: Little, Brown, 1948.

_____. *The Story of the Old Colony of New Plymouth.* New York: Knopf, 1956.

_____. *The Two Ocean War.* Boston: Little Brown, 1963.

Morland, Nigel. *Background to Murder.* London: Werner Laurie,

1955.

___. *Death for Sale.* London: Hale, 1957.

___. *Hangman's Clutch.* London: Werner Laurie, 1954.

___. *An Outline of Scientific Criminology.* London: Cassell, 1950.

___. *An Outline of Sexual Criminology.* New York: Hart, 1967.

___. *Pattern of Murder.* London: Elek Books, 1966.

___. *Science In Crime Detection.* London: Robert Hale, 1958.

___. *That Nice Miss Smith.* London: Muller, 1957.

___. *This Friendless Lady.* London: Frederick Muller, 1957.

Morleigh. *Life in the West....* London: Saunders & Otley, 1842.

Morley, C.F. *Guide to Research in Russian History.* Syracuse, N.Y.: Syracuse University Press, 1951.

Morley, Christopher. *Fifth Avenue Bus.* Philadelphia: J. B. Lippincott, 1931.

Morley, James William. *The Japanese Thrust into Siberia, 1918.* Ner York: Columbia University Press, 1957.

Morley, John. *The Life of Richard Cobden.* London: T.F. Unwin, 1903.

___. *Life of William Ewart Gladstone.* New York: Macmillan, 1903.

___. *Voltaire.* London: Macmillan, 1872.

Morley, Sylvanus G. *The Ancient Maya.* Stanford, Calif.: Stanford University Press, 1946.

Morny, Charles-Auguste. *Un Ambassade en Russie, 1856.* Paris: Ollendorff, 1892.

Morrel, Ed. *The Twenty-fifth Man.* Montclar, N.J.: New Era, 1924.

Morrell, Parker. *Diamond Jim.* New York: Simon & Schuster, 1934.

Morrell, William P. *Gold Rushes.* New York: Macmillan, 1941.

Morrell, Z.N. *Flowers and Fruits.* Boston: Gould & Lincoln, 1872.

Morris, B.F. (ed.). *Memorial Record of the Nation's Tribute to Abraham Lincoln.* Washington D.C.: W.H. & O.H. Morrison, 1865.

Morris, Charles, and Halstead, Murat. *Life and Reign of Queen Victoria.* Chicago: International Publishing Society, 1901.

Morris, Clara. *Life on the Stage: My Personal Experiences and Recollections.* New York: McClure, 1901.

Morris, Constance Lily. *On Tour with Queen Marie.* New York: Robert M. McBride, 1927.

Morris, Eastin. *The Tennessee Gazetteer.* Nashville, Tenn.: W. Hassell Hunt, 1834.

Morris, Ed. *Born to Lose.* New York: Mason & Lipscomb, 1974.

Morris, Eric. *Corregidor: The End of the Line.* New York: Stein & Day, 1981.

Morris, F. Baldwin. *The Panorama of a Life. . .* Philadelphia: G.W. Ward, 1878.

Morris, Henry Curtis. *Desert Gold and Total Prospecting.* Washington D.C.: Published by Author, 1955.

Morris, Dr. I.I. *Nationalism and the Right Wing in Japan.* London: Oxford University Press, 1960.

Morris, Ira N. *Heritage from My Father.* New York: Private Printing, 1947.

Morris, Ivan. (ed.). *Japan, 1931-1945: Militarism, Fascism, Japanism?* Boston: D.C. Heath, 1963.

___. *The World of the Shining Prince.* New York: Alfred A. Knopf, 1964.

Morris, J. *The Age of Arthur.* London: Weidenfeld & Nicolson, 1973.

Morris, James. *The Hashemite Kings.* New York: Pantheon, 1959.

Morris, Joe Alex. *First Offender.* New York: Funk & Wagnalls, 1970.

___. *What a Year!* New York: Harper Bros., 1956.

Morris, John. *An Exposure of the Arts & Miseries of Gambling.* Cincinatti: n.p., 1843.

___. *Wanderings of A Vagabond.* New York: Published by Author, 1873.

Morris, Leopold. *Pictorial History of Victoria and Victoria County "Where the History of Texas Began".* San Antonio, Texas: Clements, 1953.

Morris, Lerona Rosamond (ed.). *Oklahoma-Yesterday, Today, Tomorrow.* Guthrie, Okla.: Co-Operative, 1930.

Morris, Lloyd R. *Incredible New York.* New York: Random House, 1951.

___. *Not So Long Ago.* New York: Random House, 1949.

___. *Postscript to Yesterday.* New York: Random House, 1947.

Morris, Lucile. *Bald Knobbers.* Caldwell, Idaho: Caxton Printers, 1939.

Morris, Maurice. *Rambles in the Rocky Mountains.* London: Smith, Elder, 1864.

Morris, Norval, and Tonry, Michael. *Crime and Justice.* Chicago: University of Chicago Press, 1980.

___. *The Future of Imprisonment.* Chicago: University of Chicago Press, 1974.

___. *The Habitual Criminal.* Cambridge, Mass.: Harvard University Press, 1951.

___, and Hawkins, Gordon. *The Honest Politician's Guide to Crime Control.* Chicago: University of Chicago Press, 1970.

___, and Hawkins, Gordon. *Letter to the President on Crime Control.* Chicago: University of Chicago Press, 1977.

___. *Madness and the Criminal Law.* Chicago: University of Chicago Press, 1982.

Morris, Richard B. *Alexander Hamilton and the Founding of the Nation.* New York: Dial Press, 1957.

___. *The American Revolution Reconsidered.* New York: Harper & Row, 1967.

___. *Fair Trial.* New York: Alfred A. Knopf, 1952.

___. *Government and Labor in Early America.* New York: Columbia University Press, 1946.

___ (ed). *Great Presidential Decisions.* Greenwich, Conn.: Fawcett Publications, 1966.

___. *The Peacemakers: The Great Powers and American Independence.* New York: Harper & Row, 1965.

___. *Select Cases of the Mayor's Court of New York City.* Washington, D.C.: American Historical Society, 1935.

___. *Studies in the History of American Law.* New York: Columbia University Press, 1930.

Morris, Robert. *Encyclopedia of American History.* New York: Harper, 1953.

___. *No Wonder We Are Losing.* New York: Bookmailer, 1956.

Morris, Roger. *The Devil's Butcher Shop.* New York: Franklin Watts, 1983.

Morris, Terence, and Blom-Cooper, Louis. *A Calendar of Murder.* London: Michael Joseph, 1964.

___. *The Criminal Area.* New York: The Humanities Press, 1958.

___, and Pauline. *Pentonville: A Sociological Study of an English Prison.* London: Routledge & Kegan Paul, 1963.

Morris, W.R. *The Men Behind the Guns.* Lexington, Tenn.: Angel Lea Books, 1975.

Morrison, Anne L., and Haydon, John H. *History of San Luis Obispo County and Environs, California.* Los Angeles: Historic Record, 1917.

Morrison, Arthur. *A Child of the Jago.* New York: Duffield, 1896.

Morrison, Charles C. *The Social Gospel and the Christian CUlts.* New York: Harper, 1933.

Morrison, Herbert. *Forward from Victory.* London: Gollancz, 1946.

___. *Socialization of Transport.* London: Constable, 1933.

Morrison, Ian. *Malaya Postscript.* Sydney: Angus and Robertson, 1943.

Morrison, John H. *History of American Steam Navigation.* New York: Frederick Ungar, 1958.

Morrison, Joseph L. *W.J. Cash, Southern Prophet.* New York: Alfred A. Knopf, 1967.

Morrison, Samuel Elliot. *The Story of the Old Colony of New*

Plymouth. New York: Alfred A. Knopf, 1956.

Morrison, William Brown. *Military Posts and Camps in Oklahoma*. Oklahoma City: Harlow, 1936.

Morrissey, John. *John Morrissey, His Life, Battles and Wrangles, from His Birth in Ireland Until He Died a State Senator*. New York: n.p., 1881.

Morrow, Honore W. *Tiger! Tiger! The Life Story of John B. Gough*. New York: William Morrow, 1930.

Morrow, Ralph E. *Nothern Methodism and Reconstruction*. East Lansing: Michigan State University Press, 1956.

Morrow, Robert D. *Betrayal*. Chicago: Henry Regnery, 1976.

Morse, Arthur D. *While Six Million Died: A Chronicle of American Apathy*. New York: Hart, 1967.

Morse, Frank P. *Cavalcade of Rails*. New York: E.P. Dutton, 1940.

Morse, H.B., and MacNair, H.F. *Far Eastern International Relations*. Boston: Houghton Mifflin, 1931.

Morse, John T. *Abraham Lincoln*. 2 vols. Boston: Houghton Mifflin, 1893.

_____. *John Quincy Adams*. New York: Houghton, Mifflin, 1883.

Morse, John Torrey. *Famous Trials: The Tichborne Claimant*. Boston: Little, Brown, 1874.

Morse, Samuel B. *Foreign Conspiracy Against the Liberties of the United States*. New York: Leavitt, Lord, 1835.

Mortimer, Lee. *Washington Confidential Today*. New York: Paperback Library, 1962.

Mortimer, W. Golden. *Peru: History of Coca*. New York: J.H. Vail, 1901.

Morton, A.A. *Literary Detection*. New York: Scribners, 1980.

Morton, D., and Fuller, D. *Human Locomotion and Body Form*. New York: Williams & Wilkins, 1952.

Morton, Louis. *The Fall of the Philippines*. U.S. Army in World War II, Washington D.C.: Government Printing Office, 1953.

Morton, Robert H. *Territory of New Mexico Map*. Washington, D.C.: A.B. Graham, 1896.

Morton, R.S. *Venereal Diseases*. London: Peguin Books, 1966.

Morton, Thomas. *The New English Canaan*. Boston: Prince Society, 1883.

Morton, W. Scott. *Japan: Its History and Cultures*. New York: Thomas Y. Crowell, 1970.

Mosca, Gaetano. *Encyclopedia of the Social Sciences*. New York: Macmillan, 1933.

Moscheles, Felix S. *Fragments of an Autobiography*. New York: Harper & Brothers, 1899.

Moscow, Alvin. *The Rockefeller Inheritance*. Garden City, N.Y.: Doubleday, 1977.

Moscow, Warren. *Politics in the Empire State*. New York: Knopf, 1948.

_____. *What Have You Done for Me Lately? The Ins and Outs of New York City Politics*. Englewood Cliffs, N.J.: Prentice-Hall, 1961.

Mosedale, John. *The Men Who Invented Broadway*. New York: Richard Marek, 1981.

Moseley, Leonard. *On Borrowed Time: How World War Two Began*. New York: Random House, 1959.

Mosely, Philip E. *Russian Diplomacy and the Opening of the Eastern Question in 1838 and 1839*. Cambridge, Mass.: Harvard University Press, 1934.

Moser, C.A., and Kalton, G. *Survey Methods in Social Investigation*. London: Heinemann Educational, 1971.

Moser, Don, and Cohen, Jerry. *The Pied Piper of Tucson*. New York: Signet Books, 1967.

Moses, David. *Who Shot Kennedy?* England: Church of God, 1973.

Moses, John, and Kirkland, Joseph. *History of Chicago*. 2 vols. Chicago: Munsell, 1895.

Moses, Joseph L., and Byham, William C. *Applying the Assessment Center Method*. Elmsford, N.Y.: Pergamon Press, 1977.

Mosher, Gouverneur. *Kyoto: A Contemporary Guide*. Rutland, Vt.: Charles E. Tuttle, 1964.

Mosier, Richard D. *Making the American Mind*. New York: King's Crown Press, 1947.

Moskalev, M. *V.I. Lenin v Sibiri*. Moscow: Gospolitizdat, 1957.

Moskowitz, Henry. *Alfred E. Smith. An American Career*. New York: Thomas Seltzer, 1924.

Mosley, Leonard. *Haile Selassie: The Conquering Lion*. Englewood Cliffs, N.J.: Prentice-Hall, 1964.

_____. *Hirohito: Emperor of Japan*. Englewoood Cliffs, N.J.: Prentice-Hall, 1966.

_____. *Lindbergh*. New York: Doubleday, 1976.

Mosley, Nicholas. *The Assassination of Trotsky*. London: Michael Joseph, 1972.

Mosley, Philip. *Russian Diplomacy and the Opening of the Eastern Question in 1838 and 1839*. Cambridge, Mass.: Harvard University Press, 1934.

Mosolov (Mossolov, A.A.) *At the Court of the Last Tsar*. London: Methuen, 1935.

Moss, Frank. *The American Metropolis, From Knickerbocker Days to the Present Time, New York City Life in All Its Various Phases*. 3 vols. New York: Peter Fenelon Collier, 1897.

Moss, Robert. *Urban Guerrillas*. London: Temple Smith, 1972.

Moss, Thelma. *The Probability of the Impossible*. Los Angeles: J. P. Tarcher, 1974.

Moss, William Paul. *Rough and Tumble: The Autobiography of a West Texas Judge*. New York: Vantage Press, 1954.

Mosse, Werner E. *Alexander II and the Moderization of Russia*. New York: Macmillan, 1958.

Mossiker, Frances. *The Affair of the Poisons*. New York: Knopf, 1969.

The Most Foul and Unparalleled Murder in the Annals of Crime: Life and Confession of Reuben A. Dunbar. Albany, N.Y.: John D. Parsons, Parsons, Weed, Parsons, 1851.

Motley, John Lothrop. *The Life and Death of John Barneveld, Advocate of Holland*. New York: Harper & Bros., 1902.

_____. *The Rise of the Dutch Republic*. New York: Harper & Bros., 1883.

Moton, Robert R. *What the Negro Thinks*. Garden City, N.Y.: Doubleday, 1929.

Mott, Mrs. D.W. (ed.). *Legends and Lore of Long Ago (Ventura County, California)*. Los Angeles: Wetsel, 1929.

Mott, Frank Luther. *American Journalism: A History, 1690-1960*. New York: Macmillan, 1969.

_____. *American Journalism: A History of Newspapers in the United States*. New York: Macmillan, 1950.

_____. *Golden Multitudes*. New York: Macmillan, 1947.

_____. *A History of American Magazines 1741-1850*. New York: D. Appleton-Century, 1930.

_____. *Jefferson and the Press*. Baton Rouge: Louisiana State University Press, 1943.

Mott, Harper Striker. *The New York of Yesterday*. New York: G.P. Putnam's Sons, 1908.

Mott, Colonel T. Bentley. *Twenty Years as a Military Attaché*. New York: Oxford University Press, 1937.

Mottram, R.H. *Trader's Dream: The Romance of the East India Company*. New York: Appleton-Century, 1939.

Mouland, W.H. and Atul Chatterjee. *A Short History of India*. New York: Longmans, Green, 1936.

Moulin, Leo. *Socialism of the West*. London: Gollancz, 1945.

Moulton, H. Fletcher. *The Trial of Steinie Morrison*. London: William Hodge, 1922.

Moultrie, William. *Memoirs*. New York: Longworth, 1802.

Mouneyrat, Edmond. *La Préfecture de police*. Paris: Bonvalot-Jouve, 1906.

Mousnier, Roland. *The Assassination of Henry IV*. trans. Joan Spencer. New York: Scribner, 1973.

Mousset, Albert. *L'Attentat de Sarajevo*. Paris: Payot, 1930.

Mowat, C.L. *Britain Between the Wars, 1918-1940*. London: Methuen, 1955.

Mowat, R.B. *The American Entente*. London: Oxford University Press, 1939.

_____. *The Diplomatic Relations of Great Britain and the United States.* London: Arnold, 1925.

_____. *Life of Lord Pauncefote, First Ambassador to the United States.* London: Houghton, 1929.

Mowrer, Edgar. *Immortal Italy.* New York: D. Appleton, 1922.

Mowrer, O. Hobart. *Learning Theory and Behavior.* New York: John Wiley & Sons, 1960.

Mowry, George E. *The California Progressives.* Berkeley: University of California Press, 1951.

_____. *The Era of Theodore Roosevelt 1900-1912.* New York: Harper & Bros., 1958.

_____. *Theodore Roosevelt and the Progressive Movement.* Madison: University of Wisconsin Press, 1946.

Mowry, Sylvester. *Arizona and Sonora.* New York: Harper & Brothers, 1864.

Moyer, Kenneth E. *The Psychobiology of Aggression.* New York: Harper & Row, 1976.

The Moyer-Haywood Case and the United States Supreme Court. New York: n.p., 1907.

Moyes, John F. *Mighty Midgets.* Sydney: N.S.W. Bookstall, 1946.

Moylan, John F. *Scotland Yard and the Metropolitan Police.* London: Putnam, 1929.

Moyniham, Daniel P. (ed.). *On Understanding Poverty.* New York: Basic Books, 1969.

Moynihan, James H. *The Life of Archbishop Ireland.* New York: Harper & Brothers, 1853.

Mozley, Thomas. *Reminiscences Chiefly of Oriel College and the Oxford Movement.* 2 vols. London: Longmans, 1882.

Mrs. Hull's Murder. Philadelphia: Old Franklin, 1880.

Muarte, Eulogio Zudaire. *El conde-duque y Cataluña.* Madrid: Consejo Superior de Investigaciones Cientificas, 1964.

Muck, Otto. *The Secret of Atlantis.* New York: New York Times, 1978.

Mudd, Nettie. *The Life of Dr. Samuel A. Mudd.* Saginaw, Mich.: Richard D. Mudd, 1962.

Mudd, Dr. Richard D. *Dr. Samuel Alexander Mudd and His Descendants.* Freeland, Mich.: Bastian Brothers, 1982.

_____. *The Mudd Family of the United States.* 2 vols. Saginaw, Mich.: Published by Author, 1951.

Mudd, Samuel A. *The Life of Dr. Samuel A. Mudd.* ed. Nettie Mudd. New York: Neale, 1906.

Muddiman, J.G. (ed.). *The Bloody Assizes.* Edinburgh: William Hodge, 1929.

Mudge, Zachariah Atwell. *Witch Hill: A History of Salem Witch-craft.* New York: Carlton & Lanahan, 1870.

Mudgett, Herman. *Holmes' Own Story.* Philadelphia: Burk & McFetridge, 1895.

Mueller, Gerhard O.W. (ed.). *Essays in Criminal Science.* New York: Rothman, 1961.

_____. *Legal Regulation of Sexual Conduct.* New York: Oceana, 1961.

_____. *Sentencing.* Springfield, Ill.: Charles Thomas, 1977.

Muggeridge, Malcolm. *The Thirties.* London: Hamish Hamilton, 1940.

_____. *Tread Softly for You Are Treading on My Jokes.* London: Collins, 1966.

Mugglebee, Ruth. *Father Coughlin of the Shrine of the Little Flower.* Boston: L.C. Page, 1933.

Muhlon, Wilhelm. *L'Europe devastée: notes prises dans le premiers mois de la guerre.* Paris: Payot, 1918.

Muir, Florabel. *Headline Happy.* New York: Henry Holt 1950.

Muir, Helen. *Miami, U.S.A.* New York: Holt, 1953.

Muir, Mackenzie and Irby. *Travels in the Slavonic Provinces of Turkey in Europe.* London: Bell & Daldy, 1867.

Muir, Sir William. *The Caliphate, Its Rise, Decline and Fall.* Edinburgh, Scot.: John Grant, 1924.

_____. *The Mameluke Dynasty of Egypt.* London: Smith & Elder, 1896.

Muir, William Ker, Jr. *Police: Streetcorner Politicians.* Chicago: The University of Chicago Press, 1977.

Muirden, James. *Stars and Planets.* New York: Thomas Y. Crowell, 1965.

Muirhead, James F. *America, the Land of Contrasts: A Briton's View of his American Kin.* New York: J. Lane, 1907.

Mukerjee, Dilip. *Zulfikar Ali Bhutto: Quest for Power.* Delhi-Bombay: Vikes Publishing House, 1972.

Mukerjee, Hirendranath. *Indian Struggle for Freedom.* Bombay: Kutub, 1946.

Muldoon, Sylvan and Carrington, Hereword. *The Projection of the Astral Body.* New York: Samuel Weiser, 1970.

Mulé, S.J., and Brill, Henry (eds.). *Chemical and Biological Aspects of Drug Dependence.* Cleveland: CRC Press, 1972.

Mullane, William H. (ed.). *This Is Silver City, 1882-1891.* 4 vols. Silver City, N.M.: Silver City Enterprise, 1963-1967.

Mullen, Arthur F. *Western Democrat.* New York: Wilfred Funk, 1940.

Müller, Friederich. *Beirträge zur Geschichte des Hexenglaubens und des Hexenprocesses in Siebenbürgen.* Brunswick, Ger.: C.A. Schwetschke & Sohn, 1854.

Müller, Georg Alexander von. *The Kaiser and His Court.* tran. Mervyn Savill. London: Macdonald, 1961.

Muller, Herbert J. *Adlai Stevenson: A Study in Values.* New York: Harper & Row, 1967.

Muller, Max. *The Mythologies of All Races.* Boston: Marshall Jones, 1918.

Müller-Hillebrand, Burkhart. *Das Heer 1933-1945.* 2 vols. Frankfort: E.S. Mittler & Son, 1954-56.

Mullin, Robert N. *The Boyhood of Billy the Kid.* El Paso, Texas: Texas Western Press, 1967.

_____. *A Chronology of the Lincoln County War.* Santa Fe, N.M.: Press of the Territorian, 1966.

_____ (ed.). *Maurice Garland Fulton's History of the Lincoln County War.* Tucson: University of Arizona Press, 1968.

Mullins, Claud. *Fifteen Years' Hard Labour.* London: Victor Gollancz, 1949.

_____. *Why Crime?* Philadelphia: Saunders, 1945.

Mulvihill, Donald J., Tumin, Melvin M., and Curtis, Lynn A. *Crimes of Violence.* Washington D.C.: U.S. Government Printing Office, 1969.

Mumey, Nolie. *Calamity Jane, 1852-1903: A History of Her Life and Adventure in the West.* Denver: Range Press, 1950.

_____. *Creede, Colorado.* Denver: Artcraft Press, 1949.

_____. *Hoofs to Wings: The Pony Express.* Boulder, Colo.: Johnson, 1960.

_____. *Poker Alice.* Denver: Artcraft Press, 1951.

Mumford, Beverly Bland. *Virginia's Attitude Toward Slavery and Secession.* New York: Negro University Press, 1969.

Mumford, Lewis. *The Golden Day.* New York: Boni and Liveright, 1926.

Mundy, John H. *Liberty and Political Power in Toulouse.* New York: Columbia University Press, 1954.

Munford, W.A. *William Ewart, M.P., 1788-1869: Portrait of a Radical.* London: Grafton, 1960.

Munn, N. *Psychology: The Fundamentals of Human Adjustment.* New York: Harrap, 1961.

Munoz, Rafael F. *Pancho Villa: Rayo y Azote.* Mexico City: Populibros La Prensa, 1955.

Munro, Andrew Keith. *Autobiography of a Thief.* London: Michael Joseph, 1972.

Munro, Dana Carleton. *The Middle Ages.* New York: Century, 1922.

Munro, Dana Gardner. *The United States and the Caribbean Area.* Boston: World Peace Foundation, 1934.

Munro, Ion S. *Beyond the Alps.* London: Alexander Macelhose, 1934.

_____. *Through Fascism to World Power.* London: Alexander Maclehose, 1933.

Munro, Jim L. *Administrative Behavior and Police Organization.* Cincinnati, Ohio: W.H. Anderson, 1974.

Munro, William Bennett. *Personality in Politics, Reformers, Bosses and Leaders, What They Do and How They Do It.* New York: Macmillan, 1924.

_____. *Personality in Politics: A Study of Three Types in American Public Life.* New York: Macmillan, 1934.Munsell, M.E. *Flying Sparks.* Kansas City: Tierman-Dart, 1914.

Munsell, Joel. *Annals of Albany.* Albany, N.Y.: J. Munsell, 1850.

Munson, Lyle H. *Stifle the Legend.* New York: Bookmailer, 1964.

Munsterberg, H. *On the Witness Stand.* New York: Clark, Boardman, 1908.

Murasaki, Lady. *The Tales of Gengi.* New York: Doubleday Anchor, 1955.

Murat, Princess Marie. *Raspoutine et l'aube sanglante.* Paris: E. deBoccard, 1917.

Muratore, Guiseppe, and Persia, Carmine. *I dodici giorni di Mussolini a Ponza.* Rome: STEB, 1945.

Murbarger, Nell. *Ghosts of the Adobe Walls.* Los Angeles: Westernlore Press, 1964.

_____. *Sovereigns of the Sage.* Palm Desert, Calif.: Desert Magazine Press, 1958.

Murchison, C. *Criminal Intelligence.* Worcester, Mass.: Clark University, 1926.

_____. *A Handbook of Child Psychology.* Worcester, Mass.: Clark University Press, 1931.

Murchison, Carl (ed.). *The Case For and Against Psychical Belief.* New York: Arno Press, 1975.

The Murder of the Geogles and Lynching of the Fiend Snyder. Philadelphia: Barclay, 1881.

Murder of the Meek Family. Kansas City: Ryan Walker, 1896.

The Murder on Dr. Tideman's Farm. Philadelphia: John Campbell, 1867.

The Murderer, Allen C. Laros. Easton, Pa.: n.p., 1876.

Murdock, Eugene Converse. *Patriotism Limited, 1862-1865: The Civil War Draft and the Bounty System.* Kent, Ohio: Kent State University Press, 1967.

Murdock, John C. *Under the Covenant: The Story of the Mormons.* New York: Vantage Press, 1966.

Murdock, K.M. *Literature and Theology in Colonial New England.* Cambridge, Mass.: Harvard University Press, 1949.

Murdock, Kenneth B. *Increase Mather: The Foremost American Puritan.* New York: Russell & Russell, 1966.

_____. *Selections from Cotton Mather.* New York: Harcourt, Brace, 1926.

Muret, Maurice. *L'archduc François-Ferdinand.* Paris: B. Grasset, 1932.

Muriithi, J.K., Ndoria, P.N. *War in the Forest: An Autobiography of a Mau Mau Leader.* Nairobi: East African Publishing House, 1971.

Murofushi Tetsuro. *Japan's Terrorists.* Tokyo: Kobunsho, 1963.

Murphy, Celeste G. *The People of the Pueblo; or, the Story of Sonoma.* Sonoma, Calif.: Published by Author, 1935.

Murphy, Harry J. *Where's What: Sources of Information for Federal Investigators.* New York: Warner Books, 1979.

Murphy, J.G. *Retribution, Justice, and Therapy.* Dordrecht, Neth.: D. Reidel, 1979.

Murphy, John T. *A Manual on the Rise and Fall of italy's Fascist Empire.* London: Crowther, 1943.

_____. *Stalin, 1879-1944.* London: Lane, 1945.

_____. *Trade Unions and Socialism.* London: National Council of the Socialist League, 1936.

Murphy, Patrick T. *Our Kindly Parent-The State.* New York: The Viking Press, 1974.

Murphy, Patrick V., and Plate, Thomas. *Commissioner.* New York: Simon & Schuster, 1977.

Murphy, Paul. *The Constitution in Crisis Times.* New York: Harper & Row, 1972.

Murphy, Rhoads. *Shanghai: Key to Modern China.* Cambridge, Mass.: Harvard University Press, 1953.

Murphy, Robert. *Diplomat Among Warriors.* New York: Doubleday, 1964.

Murphy, Thomas F. *The Hearts of the West.* Boston: Christopher, 1928.

Murphy, Walter F. *Congress and the Court.* Chicago: University of Chicago Press, 1962.

Murray, Albert. *The Omni-Americans.* New York: Outerbridge & Dienstfrey, 1970.

Murray, Charles A., and Cox, I.A. *Beyond Probation.* Beverly Hills, Calif.: Sage, 1979.

_____. *Days in Court.* Washington, D.C.: American Institutes for Research, 1980.

_____. *The Link Between Learning Disabilities and Juvenile Delinquency.* Washington, D.C.: National Institute for Juvenile Justice and Delinquency Prevention, 1976.

_____. *Losing Ground.* New York: Basic Books, 1984.

Murray, Charles Augustus. *Travels in North America During the Years 1834, 1835 & 1836.* New York: Harper & Brothers, 1839.

Murray, George. *The Legacy of Al Capone.* New York: Putnam, 1975.

_____. *The Madhouse on Madison Street.* Chicago: Follett, 1965.

Murray, H. *Explorations in Personality.* New York: Oxford University Press, 1938.

Murray, John Courtney. *We Hold These Truths.* New York: Sheed & Ward, 1960.

Murray, Margaret Alice. *The God of the Witches.* London: Faber & Faber, 1931.

_____. *The Witchcult in Western Europe.* Philadelphia: Pennsylvania University Press, 1939.

Murray, Norbert. *Legacy of an Assassination.* New York: Pro-People Press, 1964.

Murray, R.H. *The Political Consequences of the Reformation.* New York: Russell & Russell, 1960.

Murray, Robert H. *The History of Political Science from Plato to the Present.* Cambridge, Eng.: W. Heffer & Sons, 1926.

Murray, Robert K. *Red Scare: A Study in National Hysteria, 1919-1920.* New York: McGraw-Hill, 1964.

Murray-Brown, J. *Kenyatta.* London: George Allen, 1972.

Murrell, John A. *Life and Adventures of John A. Murrell.* Philadelphia: T.B. Peterson & Brothers, 1845.

Murrell, William. *A History of American Graphic Humor.* 2 vols. New York: Volume I, Whitney Museum of American Art, 1933. Volume II, Macmillan, 1938.

Murrow, Edward R (ed.). *Talks.* New York: Columbia Broadcasting System, 1937.

Murtagh, John M., and Harris, Sara. *Cast the First Stone.* New York: McGraw-Hill, 1957.

_____. *Who Live in Shadow.* New York: McGraw-Hill, 1959.

Murton, Thomas, and Hyams, Joe. *Accomplices to the Crime: The Arkansas Prison Scandal.* New York: Grove Press, 1969.

_____. *The Dilemma of Prison Reform.* New York: Holt, Rinehart & Winston, 1976.

Muschler, Reinhold. *Philipp zu Eulenburg, sein Leben und seine Zeit.* Leipzig, Ger.: F.W. Grunhow, 1930.

Mushanga, Tibamanya. *Crime and Deviance.* Nairobi, Kenya: East African Literature Bureau, 1976.

Mushkat, Jerome. *Tammany: The Evolution of a Political Machine, 1789-1865.* Syracuse, N.Y.: Syracuse University Press, 1971.

Musick, John R. *Mysterious Mr. Howard.* New York: G.W. Dillingham, 1896.

_____. *Stories of Missouri.* New York: American Book, 1897.

Musmanno, Michael A. *After Twelve Years.* New York: Alfred A. Knopf, 1939.

_____. *Verdict!* Garden City, N.Y.: Doubleday, 1958.

Mussen, P.H., Conger, J.J., and Kagan, J. *Child Development and Personality.* New York: Harper & Row, 1979.

Mussolini, Benito. *The Corporate State.* Florence, Italy: Vallecchi, 1938.

_____. *Fascism: Doctrines and Institutions.* Rome: Ardita, 1935.

_____. *Il mio diaro di guerra.* Rome: Imperia, 1923.

_____. _Je Parle avec Bruno_. Montreux, Fr.: Editions de l'Aigle, 1942.

_____. _La mia Vita_. Rome: Faro, 1947.

_____. _My Autobiography_. trans. Richard Washburn Child. London: Hutchinson, 1928.

_____. _Storia di un anno_. Verona, Italy: Mondadori, 1944.

_____. _Vita de Sandro e di Arnaldo_. Milan, Italy: Hoepli, 1934.

Mussolini, Edvige. _Mio fratello Benito_. Florence, Italy: La Fenice, 1957.

Mussolini, Rachele, and Pensotti, Anita. _Benito il mio uomo_. Milan, Italy: Rizzoli, 1956.

_____, and Chinigo, Michele. _My Life with Mussolini_. London: Hale, 1959.

Mussolini, Vittorio. _Due donne nella tempesta_. Milan, Italy: Mondadori, 1958.

_____. _Vita con mio padre_. Milan, Italy: Mondadori, 1957.

Mustain, Gene, and Capeci, Jerry. _Mob Star: The Story of John Gotti, the Most Powerful Criminal in America_. New York: Franklin Watts, 1988.

Musto, David. _The American Disease: Origins of Narcotic Control_. New Haven, Conn.: Yale University Press, 1973.

_____. _Narcotics and America_. New Haven, Conn.: Yale University Press, 1972.

Muusmann, Carl. _Hvem var Jack the Ripper?_ Copenhagen: Hermann-Petersen, 1908.

Muzumdar, H.T. _Gandhi Triumphant! The Inside Story of the Historic Fast_. New York: Universal, 1939.

Muzzey, David Saville. _History of the American People_. Boston: Ginn, 1929.

_____. _James G. Blaine: A Political Idol of Other Days_. New York: Dodd, Mead, 1934.

_____. _Readings in American History_. Boston: Ginn, 1915.

Mydans, Carl. _More Than Meets the Eye_. New York: Harper & Brothers, 1959.

Myers, Gustavus. _History of Bigotry in the United States_. ed. Henry M. Christman. New York: Random House, 1943.

_____. _History of Public Franchises in New York City_. New York: The Reform Club, 1900.

_____. _History of the Great American Fortunes_. 3 vols. New York: Charles H. Kerr, 1910.

_____. _History of the Supreme Court of the United States_. Chicago: Charles H. Kerr, 1918.

_____. _History of Tammany Hall_. New York: Boni & Liveright, 1901.

Myers, Hugh N. _Prisoner of War, World War II_. Portland, Ore.: Metropolitan Press, 1965.

Myers, James. _Churches in Social Action_. New York: Federal Council of Churches, 1943.

Myers, John Myers. _The Death of the Bravos_. Boston: Little, Brown, 1962.

_____. _Doc Holliday_. Boston: Little, Brown, 1955.

_____. _The Last Chance: Tombstone's Early Years_. New York: E.P. Dutton, 1950.

_____. _San Francisco's Reign of Terror_. New York: Doubleday 1966.

Myers, Margaret G. _A Financial History of the United States_. New York: Columbia University Press, 1970.

_____. _The New York Money Market_. New York: Columbia University Press, 1931.

Myers, S.D. (ed.). _Pioneer Surveyor, Frontier Lawyer: The Personal Narrative of O.W. Williams, 1877-1902_. El Paso, Texas: Texas Western College Press, 1966.

Myers, Starr, and Newton, Walter H. _The Hoover Administration_. New York: Charles Scribner's Sons, 1936.

Myers, W.H. _Human Personality and Its Survival of Bodily Death_. New York: Longmans Green, 1954.

Mylar, Isaac L. _Early Days at the Mission San Juan Bautista_. Watsonville, Calif.: Evening Pajaronian, 1929.

Myrdal, Alva. _Nation and Family; The Swedish Experiment in Democratic Family and Population Policy_. New York: Harper, 1942.

Myrdal, Gunnar. _An American Dilemma_. New York: Harper & Row, 1962.

_____. _Asian Drama: An Inquiry Into the Poverty of Nations_. New York: Twentieth Century Fund, 1968.

My Secret Life. New York: Grove Press, 1966.

The Mysteries and Miseries of San Francisco. New York: Dick & Fitzgeraldm 1853.

The Mysterious Murder of Pearl Bryan, or The Headless Horror. Cincinnati, Ohio: Barclay, n.d.

N

Nabonne, B. _Joseph Bonaparte_. Paris: Hachette, 1949.

Nadeau, Maurice. _The History of Surrealism_. trans. Richard Howard. New York: Macmillan, 1965.

Nadeau, Reni. _City-Makers: The Men Who Transformed Los Angeles from Village to Metropolis During the First Great Boom, 1868-76_. Garden City, N.Y.: Doubleday, 1948.

_____. _Los Angeles, from Mission to Modern City_. New York: Longmans, Green 1960.

Nadel, Siegfried F. _A Black Byzantium: The Kingdom of Nupe in Nigeria_. London: Oxford University Press, 1942.

Nader, Ralph. _The Consumer and Corporate Accountability_. New York: Harcourt Brace Jovanovich, 1973.

_____, and Green, Mark J. (eds.). _Corporate Power in America_. New York: Grossman, 1973.

_____, Green, Mark J., and Seligman, Joel. _Taming the Giant Corporation_. New York: W.W. Norton, 1976.

_____. _Unsafe at Any Speed_. New York: Grossman, 1965.

_____, Petkas, Peter J, and Blackwell, Kate (eds.). _Whistle Blowing_. New York: Viking Penguin, 1972.

Nadler, Susan. _Good Girls Gone Bad_. New York: Freundlich Books, 1987.

Nag, Kalidas. _Tolstoy and Gandhi_. Patna, India: Pustak Bhandar, 1950.

Nagel, William G. _An American Archipelago....: The United States Bureau of Prisons_. Philadelphia: The American Foundation, 1974.

_____. _The New Red Barn: A Critical Look at the Modern American Prison_. New York: The American Foundation, 1973.

Nagy, Ferenc. _The Struggle Behind the Iron Curtain_. New York: Macmillan, 1948.

Nahal, Chaman (ed.). _Drugs and the Other Self_. New York: Harper & Row, 1971.

Nahas, Gabriel G. _Keep Off the Grass_. New York: Reader's Digest Press, 1976.

_____, and Paton, W.D.M. (eds.). _Marihuana: Biological Effects-Analysis, Metabolism, Cellular Response, Reproduction and Brain_. Oxford, Eng.: Pergamon Press, 1979.

_____. _Marihuana, Deceptive Weed_. New York: Raven Press, 1973.

Nahm, Milton C. _Las Vegas and Uncle Joe_. Norman: University of Oklahoma Press, 1964.

Naimark, Norman M. _Terrorists and Socialists: The Russian Revolutionary Movement Under Alexander III_. Cambridge, Mass.: Harvard University Press, 1983.

Nair, C. Sankaran. _Gandhi and Anarchy_. Madras, India: Tagore, 1922.

Nakane, Chie. _Japanese Society_. Berkeley: University of California, 1973.

Namier, L.B. _England in the Age of the American Revolution_. New York: Macmillan, 1930.

Nanda, B.R. _Mahatma Gandhi: A Biography_. Boston: Beacon Press, 1958.

Nantet, Jacques. *Histoire du Liban*. Paris: Les Editions de Minuit, 1963.

Naotoshi Todani. *Walk in the Mountains, Rot as a Corpse in the Grass*. Osaka, Japan: Bunsho-in, 1965.

Napoléon I. *Dictionnaire des opinions et jugements*. Paris: Club de l'Honnête Homme, 1964.

Napoléon, Prince, and Hanoteau, J. *Lettres personelles des souverains à l'Empereur Napoléon*. Paris: Plon, 1939.

Narell, Irena. *Our City: The Jews of San Francisco*. San Diego, Calif.: Howell-North, 1981.

Narishkin-Kurakin, Elizabeth. *Under Three Tsars*. New York: E.P. Dutton, 1931.

Narrative of the Life and Dying Speech of John Ryer. Danbury, Conn.: Nathan Douglas, 1793.

Narrative of the Life of James Lane. Chillicothe, Ohio: John Bailhache, 1817.

Narrative of the Murder of James Murray, and the Circumstances of Its Detection with the Trial of John Johnson. New York: S. King, 1824.

A Narrative of Part of the Life and Adventures of Joseph Andrews. New York: n.p., 1769.

The Narrative of Whiting Sweeting. Lansingburgh, N.Y.: Sylvester Tiffany, 1791.

Nash, George. *The Conservative Intellectual Movement in America Since 1945*. New York: Basic Books, 1975.

Nash, Harry C. *Citizen's Arrest: The Dissent of Penn Jones, Jr., in the Assassination of JFK*. Austin, Texas: Latitudes Press, 1977.

Nash, Jay Robert. *Almanac of World Crime*. New York: Doubleday, 1981.

_____. *Among the Missing, An Anecdotal History of Missing Persons from the 1800s to the Present*. New York: Simon & Schuster, 1978.

_____. *Bloodletters and Badmen, A Narrative Encyclopedia of American Criminals From the Pilgrims to the Present*. New York: M. Evans, 1973.

_____. *Citizen Hoover, A Critical Study of J. Edgar Hoover and His FBI*. Chicago: Nelson-Hall, 1972.

_____. *Crime Chronology*. New York: Facts on File, 1984.

_____. *A Crime Story*. New York: Delacorte Press, 1981.

_____. *The Dark Fountain*. New York: A & W, 1982.

_____. *Darkest Hours, A Narrative Encyclopedia of Worldwide Disasters from Ancient Times to the Present*. Chicago: Nelson-Hall, 1976.

_____. *Dillinger: Dead or Alive?* Chicago: Henry Regnery, 1970.

_____. *The Dillinger Dossier*. Highland Park, Ill.: December Press, 1983.

_____. *Hustlers and Con Men, An Anecdotal History Of the Confidence Man and His Games*. New York: M. Evans, 1976.

_____. *The Innovators*. Chicago: Regnery Gateway, 1982.

_____. *Look for the Woman*. New York: M. Evans, 1981.

_____. *The Mafia Diaries*. New York: Delacorte Press, 1984.

_____. *Murder, America, Homicide in the United States from the Revolution to the Present*. New York: Simon & Schuster, 1980.

_____. *Murder Among the Mighty*. New York: Delacorte Press, 1983.

_____. *Open Files*. New York: McGraw-Hill, 1983.

_____. *People to See*. Piscataway, N.J.: New Century, 1981.

_____. *Zanies*. Piscataway, N.J.: New Century, 1982.

Nash, Roderick. *Wilderness and the American Mind*. New Haven, Conn.: Yale University Press, 1967.

Nash, Walter. *New Zealand - A Working Democracy*. New York: Duell, Sloan and Pearce, 1943.

Nass, Lucien. *Les empoisonnements sous Louis XIV*. Paris: n.p., 1898.

Nassau Daily Tribune (eds.). *The Murder of Sir Harry Oakes, BT*. Nassau, Bah.: Nassau Daily Tribune, 1959.

Nasser, Gamal Abdel. *Egypt's Liberation: The Philosophy of the Revolution*. Washington, D.C.: Public Affairs Press, 1959.

Nathan, George Jean. *The Intimate Notebooks of George Jean Nathan*. New York: Alfred A. Knopf, 1932.

Nation, Carry A. *The Use and Need of the Life of Carry A. Nation*. Topeka, Kan.: F.M. Steves & Sons, 1905.

The Nation Encyclopedia of American Biography. New York: White, 1904.

National Advisory Commission on Civil Disorders. *U.S. Riot Commission Report*. New York: Bantam, 1968.

National Advisory Committee on Criminal Justice Standards and Goals. *Community Crime Prevention*. Washington, D.C.: U.S. Government Printing Office, 1973.

_____. *Criminal Justice Research and Development*. Washington, D.C.: National Institute of Law Enforcement and Criminal Justice, 1976.

_____. *A National Strategy to Reduce Crime*. Washington, D.C.: U.S. Government Printing Office, 1973.

_____. *Organized Crime*. Washington, D.C.: Law Enforcement Assistance Administration, 1976.

_____. *Report of the Task Force on Disorders and Terrorism*. Washington, D.C.: U.S. Government Printing Office, 1976.

_____. *Task Force Report on Corrections*. Washington, D.C.: U.S. Government Printing Office, 1973.

National Broadcasting Company. *There Was a President*. New York: Random House, 1966.

National Commission on the Causes and Prevention of Violence. Staff Report. *Crimes of Violence*. Washington, D.C.: U.S. Government Printing Office, 1969.

_____. Staff Report. *Law and Order Reconsidered*. Washington, D.C.: U.S. Printing Office, 1969-71.

_____. *Task Force on Violent Aspects of Protest and Confrontation*. Washington, D.C.: U.S. Government Printing Office, 1969.

_____. Staff Report. *To Establish Justice, To Insure Domestic Tranquility*. Washington, D.C.: U.S. Government Printing Office, 1969.

_____. *Violence in America: Historical and Comparative Perspectives*. Washington D.C.: U.S. Government Printing Office, 1969.

_____. *Walker Report*. Washington, D.C.: U.S. Government Printing Office, 1969.

National Commission on Law Observance and Enforcement. *Report on Penal Institutions, Probation and Parole*. Washington, D.C.: U.S. Government Printing Office, 1931.

National Commission on Obscenity and Pornography. *Commission on Obscenity and Pornography Report*. New York: Bantam Books, 1970.

National Council on Crime and Delinquency. *Four Thousand Lifetimes: A Study of Time Served and Parole Outcomes*. Davis, Calif.: NCCD Research Center, 1973.

_____. *Guided Group Interaction*. Hackensack, N.J.: Training Center, 1972.

_____. *Model Act for the Protection of Rights of Prisoners*. Washington, D.C.: National Council on Crime and Delinquency, 1972.

_____. *Residential Corrections: Alternatives to Incarceration*. Davis, Calif.: NCCD Research Group, 1973.

_____. *Standard Act for State Correctional Services*. Washington, D.C.: National Council on Crime and Delinquency, 1966.

National Crime Survey. *Criminal Victimization in the United States, 1979*. Washington, D.C.: U.S. Government Printing Office, 1981.

National Criminal Justice Reference Service. *We Are All the Victims of Arson*. Washington, D.C.: U.S. Government Printing Office, 1979.

The National Cyclopedia of American Biography. New York: J.J. White, 1893.

National Fire Protection Association. *Arson: Some Problems and Solutions*. Boston: NFPA Publications, 1976.

_____. *National Fire Codes*. Boston: National Fire Protection Association, 1977.

National Institute on Drug Abuse. *National Household Survey on Drug Abuse.* Washington, D.C.: U.S. Government Printing Office, 1982.

National Institute on Law Enforcement and Criminal Justice. *The Development of the Law of Gambling, 1776-1976.* Washington, D.C.: Law Enforcement Assistance Administration, 1977.

_____. *The Role of Correctional Industries.* Washington, D.C.: U.S. Government Printing Office, 1972.

National Moratorium on Prison Construction. *The Moratorium on Prison Construction: Some Questions and Answers.* Boston: Unitarian Universalist Service Committee, 1978.

National Parole Institutes. *The Sentencing and Parole Process.* New York: National Council on Crime and Delinquency, 1964.

National Press Club. *shrdlu.* Washington, D.C.: Colortone Press, 1958.

National Probation and Parole Association. *Parole in Principle and Practice.* New York: National Probation and Parole Association, 1957.

Natori Junichi. *A Short History of Nippon.* Tokyo: Hokuseido Press, 1943.

Naudé, Gabriel. *Apologie pour les grands hommes soupçonnez de magie.* Amsterdam: J.F. Bernard, 1712.

_____. *The History of Magic By Way of Apology for All the Wise Men Who Have Unjustly Been Reputed Magicians.* trans. J. Davies. London: J. Streater, 1657.

Naumann, Viktor. *Argumente und Dokumente.* Berlin: Rowohlt, 1928.

_____. *Profile.* Munich: Duncker & Humblot, 1925.

Nauroy, Charles. *Le Curieux.* Paris: 6 rue de Seine, 1883-88.

_____. *Les Secrets des Bonaparte.* Paris: Emile Boullion, 1889.

Navarra, Quinto. *Memorie del cameriere di Mussolini.* Milan, Italy: Longanesi, 1946.

Navasky, Victor S. *Kennedy Justice.* New York: Atheneum, 1971.

_____. *Law Enforcement: The Federal Role.* New York: McGraw-Hill, 1976.

_____. *Naming Names.* New York: Viking, 1980.

Naylor, M.J. *Four Sermons Preached at All Saints Church.* Cambridge, Eng.: J. Deighton & W.H. Lunn, 1795.

Naylor, Robert A. *Across the Atlantic.* Westminster, Mass.: The Roxburge Press, 1893.

Neal, Daniel. *The History of the Puritans.* London: R. Hett, 1732.

Neal, Dorothy Jensen. *Captive Mountain Waters: A Story of Pipe Line and People.* El Paso, Texas: Western Press, 1961.

Neale, A.D. *The Antitrust Laws of the United States of America.* Cambridge, Eng.: Cambridge University Press, 1960.

Neale, John C. *A Terrible Tragedy, The Execution, Life and Crime of Felix Kampf.* Charleston, W.Va.: *Charleston Dailey Star*, 1890.

Neale, R.G. *Great Britain and United States Expansion: 1898-1900.* Lansing: Michigan State University Press, 1966.

Neale, Walter. *The Life of Ambrose Bierce.* New York: W. Neale, 1929.

Nearing, Scott. *The British General Strike.* New York: Vanguard, 1926.

_____. *Economics for the Power Age.* New York: John Day, 1952.

Neatby, H. Blair. *Mackenzie King, Vol. II., 1924-1932.* London: Methuen, 1963.

_____. *The Politics of Chaos.* Toronto, Canada: Macmillan, 1972.

Neatby, Leslie H. *Conquest of the Last Frontier.* Athens: Ohio University Press, 1966.

_____. *In Quest of the Northwest Passage.* New York: Thomas Y. Crowell, 1958.

Neave, Airey. *On Trial at Nuremberg.* Boston: Little, Brown, 1979.

Nechkina, M.V. (ed.). *Russia in the Nineteenth Century.* Ann Arbor, Mich.: Edwards, 1953.

Ned, Nebraska. *Buffalo Bill and His Daring Adventures in the Romantic Wild West.* Baltimore: I. & M. Ottenheimer, 1913.

Nee, Victor G., and deBary, Brett. *Longtime Californ': A Documentary Study of an American Chinatown.* New York: Pantheon Books, 1973.

Needham, Joseph. *Science and Civilization in China.* Cambridge, Eng.: Cambridge University Press, 1956.

Needham, Ted and Howard. *Alcatraz.* Millbrae, Calif.: Celestial Arts, 1976.

Neely, Mark E., Jr. *The Abraham Lincoln Encyclopedia.* New York: McGraw-Hill, 1982.

Neely, Richard. *How Courts Govern America.* New Haven, Conn.: Yale University Press, 1981.

_____. *Why Courts Don't Work.* New York: McGraw-Hill, 1983.

Neese, Robert. *Prison Exposures.* New York: Chilton, 1959.

Neff, Boss S. *Some Experiences in the Texas and Oklahoma Panhandle.* Amarillo, Texas: The Globe News, 1941.

The Negro in Chicago: A Study of Race Relations and a Race Riot. Chicago: University of Chicago Press, 1922.

Neguib, Mohammed. *Egypt's Destiny.* London: Victor Gollancz, 1953.

Negulesco, Gogu. *Rumania's Sacrifice: Her Past, Present and Future.* trans. Mrs. C. de S. Wainright. New York: Century, 1918.

Nehru, Jawaharlal. *An Autobiography.* London: John Lane, 1936.

_____. *The Discovery of India.* Calcutta, India: Signet, 1941.

_____, *Eighteen Months in India.* Allahabad, India: Kitabistan, 1938.

_____. *Mahatma Gandhi.* Calcutta, India: Signet Press, 1949.

_____. *The Unity of India.* London: Lindsay Drummond, 1941.

Neider, Charles (ed.) *The Great West.* New York: Coward-McCann, 1958.

Neiderhoffer, Arthur, and Blumberg, Abraham S. (eds.). *The Ambivalent Force: Perspectives on the Police.* San Francisco: Rinehart Press, 1973.

_____. *Behind the Shield: The Police in Urban Society.* New York: Doubleday, 1967.

Neier, Aryeh. *Crime and Punishment: A Radical Solution.* New York: Stein & Day, 1975.

Neil, Arthur Fowler. *Forty Years of Man-Hunting.* London: Jarrolds, 1932.

_____. *Man-Hunters of Scotland Yard.* New York: Doubleday, Doran, 1933.

Neisser, U. *Cognitive Psychology.* New York: Appleton-Century-Crofts, 1967.

Nelli, Humbert S. *The Business of Crime: Italians and Syndicate Crime in the United States.* New York: Oxford University Press, 1976.

Nelson, Bruce. *Land of the Dacotahs.* Minneapolis: University of Minnesota Press, 1946.

Nelson, Harold L., and Teeter, Dwight L. *Law of Mass Communications: Freedom and Control of Print and Broadcasting Media.* Mineola, N.Y.: Foundation Press, 1969.

Nelson, Jack E., and Ostrow, Ronald J. *The FBI and the Berrigans.* New York: Coward, McCann, 1972.

_____, et al. *Guide to Drug Abuse Research Terminology.* Rockville, Md.: National Institute on Drug Abuse, 1982.

_____, and Bass, Jack. *The Orangeburg Massacre.* New York: World, 1970.

Nelson, John C. *Renaissance Theory of Love.* New York: Columbia University Press, 1958.

Nelson, John G. *Preliminary Investigation and Police Reporting: A Complete Guide to Police Written Communication.* Beverly Hills: Glencoe Press, 1970.

Nelson, Oliver M., and Debo, A. *The Cowman's Southwest.* Glendale, Calif.: Arthur H. Clark, 1953.

Nelson, Rick. *The Cop Who Wouldn't Quit.* New York: Ballantine, 1983.

Nelson, Victor. *Prison Days and Nights.* Boston: Little, Brown, 1933.

Nelson, Walter Henry. *The Berliners: Their Saga and Their City.* New York: McKay, 1969.

_____. *The Soldier Kings, The House of Hohenzollern.* New York: G.P. Putnam's Sons, 1970.

Nelson, William (ed.). *Out of the Crocodile's Mouth.* Washington, D.C.: Public Affairs Press, 1949.

Nenni, Pietro. *Ten Years of Tyranny in Italy.* trans. Anne Steele. London: George Allen & Unwin, 1932.

_____. *Vent'anni di Fascismo.* Milan, Italy: Avanti!, 1964.

Nère, Jacques. *La crise de 1929.* A. Colin, 1968.

Nesbit, Charles Francis. *An American Family, the Nesbits of St. Clair.* Washington D.C.: n.p., 1932.

Nese, Marco. *Nel Segno della Mafia Storia di Luciano Liggio.* Milan, Italy: Rizzoli, 1975.

Ness, Eliot, with Fraley, Oscar. *The Untouchables.* New York: Julian Messner, 1957.

Nessen, Ron. *It Sure Looks Different From the Inside.* Chicago: Playboy Press, 1978.

Nettl, John P. *The Eastern Zone and Soviet Policy in Germany.* New York: Oxford University Press, 1951.

Nettlebeck, Joachim. *Lebensgeschichte.* Halle, Ger.: Rengersche Buchhandlung, 1820.

Nettler, Gwynn. *Criminal Careers.* Cincinnati, Ohio: Anderson, 1982.

_____. *Explaining Crime.* New York: McGraw-Hill, n.d.

_____. *Killing One Another.* Cincinnati, Ohio: Anderson, 1982.

Nettles, C.P. *George Washington and American Independence.* Boston: Little, Brown, 1951.

_____. *The Roots of American Civilization.* New York: Crofts, 1938.

Netzer, Hans-Joachim (ed.). *Preussen: Porträt einer politischen Kultur.* Munich: Paul List, 1968.

Neubauer, David W. *Criminal Justice in Middle America.* Morristown, N.J.: General Learning Press, 1974.

Neufield, E. *The Hittite Laws.* London: Luzac, 1951.

Neumann, Eric. *The Great Mother: An Analysis of the Archetype.* trans. Ralph Manheim. New York: Pantheon Books, 1955.

Neumann, Franz. *Behemoth: The Structure and Practice of National Socialism.* New York: Oxford University Press, 1942.

Neumann, Robert. *Zaharoff, the Armaments King.* trans. R.T. Clark. George Allen & Unwin, 1938.

Neumann, William L. *America Encounters Japan: From Perry to MacArthur.* Baltimore, Md.: The Johns Hopkins Press, 1963.

Neustatter, W. Lindsay. *The Mind of the Murderer.* London: Christopher Johnson, 1957.

_____. *Psychological Disorder and Crime.* London: Christopher Johnson, 1953.

Neusüss-Hunkel, Ermenhild. *Die SS.* Hannover, Ger.: Norddeutsche, 1956.

Neutzel, Charles. *Whodunit? Hollywood Style.* Beverly Hills: California Book Company of America, 1965.

Neville, A.W. *The History of Lamar County (Texas).* Paris, Texas: Texas, 1937.

_____. *The Red River Valley, Then and Now.* Paris, Texas: Texas, 1948.

Neville, Amelia Ransome. *The Fantastic City: Memoirs of the Social and Romantic Life of Old San Francisco.* Boston: Houghton Mifflin, 1932.

Nevins, Allan. *Abram S. Hewitt, With Some Account of Peter Cooper.* New York: Harper & Brothers, 1935.

_____ (ed.). *American Press Opinion: Washington to Coolidge.* New York: D.C. Heath, 1928.

_____. *The American States During and After the Revolution 1775-1789.* New York: Macmillan, 1924.

_____, and Weitenkampf, Frank. *A Century of Political Cartoons. Caricature in the United States from 1800 to 1900.* New York: Charles Scribner's Sons, 1944.

_____. *The Constitution Makers and the Public, 1785-1790.* New York: Foundation for Public Relations Research and Education, 1962.

_____. *A Diary of Battle: The Personal Journals of Colonel Charles S. Wainwright, 1861-1865.* New York: Harcourt, Brace & World, 1962.

_____ (ed.). *The Diary of John Quincy Adams, 1794-1845.* New York: Longmans, Green, 1919.

_____ (ed.). *The Diary of Philip Hone, 1828-1851.* New York: Dodd, Mead, 1936.

_____. *The Emergence of Lincoln.* 2 vols. New York: Charles Scribner's Sons, 1950.

_____. *The Emergence of Modern America, 1865-1878.* New York: Macmillan, 1927.

_____. *The Evening Post: A Century of Journalism.* New York: Boni & Liveright, 1922.

_____, and Hill, Frank E. *Ford - The Times, the Man, the Company.* New York: Charles Scribner's Sons, 1950.

_____. *Ford - Decline and Rebirth, 1933-1962.* New York: Charles Scribner's Sons, 1963.

_____. *Ford - Expansion and Challenge, 1915-1933.* New York: Charles Scribner's Sons, 1957.

_____. *Frémont: Pathmarker of the West.* New York: D. Appleton-Century, 1955.

_____, and Kraut, John A. *The Greater City: New York, 1898-1948.* New York: Columbia University Press, 1948.

_____. *Grover Cleveland: A Study in Courage.* New York: Dodd, Mead, 1932.

_____. *Hamilton Fish: The Inner History of the Grant Administration.* New York: Dodd, Mead, 1936.

_____. *Henry White: Thirty Years of American Diplomacy.* New York: Harper & Brothers, 1930.

_____. *Herbert H. Lehman and His Era.* New York: Charles Scribner's Sons, 1963.

_____. *A House Dividing, 1852-1857.* 2 vols. New York: Charles Scribner's Sons, 1947.

_____. *John D. Rockefeller: The Heroic Age of American Enterprise.* New York: Charles Scribner's Sons, 1940.

_____. *Letters of Grover Cleveland, 1850-1908.* Boston: Houghton Mifflin, 1933.

_____ (ed.). *Letters and Journal of Brand Whitlock.* New York: D. Appleton-Century, 1936.

_____. *Ordeal of the Union.* New York: Charles Scribner's Sons, 1947.

_____. *Times of Trial.* New York: Alfred A. Knopf, 1958.

_____. *The War for the Union: The Improvised War, 1861-1862.* New York: Charles Scribner's Sons, 1959-1971.

Nevins, Winfield Scott. *Witchcraft in Salem Village in 1692.* Boston: Lee & Shepard, 1892.

Nevinson, Henry W. *Last Changes, Last Chances.* London: Nisbet, 1928.

Nevius, John Livingston. *Demon Possession and Allied Themes.* Chicago: F.H. Revell, 1894.

Newall, Albert. *All My People Gone: The Tragedy at the Newall Farm.* Billings, Mont.: n.p., n.d.

Newell, Barbara W. *Chicago and the Labor Movement: Metropolitan Unionism in the 1930's.* Urbana: University of Illinois Press, 1961.

Newfield, Jack. *The Abuse of Power.* New York: Viking, 1977.

_____. *A Prophetic Minority.* New York: New American Library, 1967.

_____. *Robert Kennedy: A Memoir.* New York: E.P. Dutton, 1969.

New Forms of Juvenile Delinquency, Their Origin, Prevention, and Treatment. New York: United Nations, 1960.

The Newgate Calendar. London: T. Werner Laurie, 1932.

The Newgate Calendar, or Malefactors' Bloody Register. London: Capricorn Books, 1961.

New Jersey Commission to Study Capital Punishment. *Report.* Trenton: State of New Jersey, 1964.

Newman, Albert H. *The Assassination of John F. Kennedy: The Reasons Why.* New York: Clarkson N. Potter, 1970.

Newman, Barclay Moon. *Japan's Secret Weapon.* New York: Current, 1944.

Newman, Donald J. *Conviction: The Determination of Guilt or Innocence Without Trial.* Boston: Little, Brown, 1966.

_____. *Introduction to Criminal Justice.* Philadelphia: J.B. Lippincott, 1975.

Newman, E.W. Polson. *Ethiopian Realities.* London: George Allen & Unwin, 1936.

_____. *Italy's Conquest of Abyssinia.* London: Thornton Butterworth, 1937.

Newman, G. *Comparative Deviance.* New York: Elsevier, 1976.

Newman, Graeme. *Just and Painful: A Case for the Corporal Punishment of Criminals.* New York: Macmillan, 1983.

_____. *The Punishment Response.* Philadelphia: J.B. Lippincott, 1978.

_____. *Understanding Violence.* New York: J.B. Lippincott, 1978.

Newman, O. *Defensible Space: Crime Prevention through Urban Design.* New York: Macmillan, 1972.

Newman, R.A. (ed.). *Equity in the World's Legal Systems.* Brussels, Belg.: Establishments Emile Bruyant, 1973.

Newman, Ralph G., and Long, E.B. *The Civil War: Picture Chronicle of the Events, Leaders, and Battlefields of the War.* New York: Grosset & Dunlap, 1956.

Newmark, Harris. *Sixty Years in Southern California.* New York: Knickerbocker Press, 1916.

Newmark, Marco R. *Jottings in Southern California History.* Los Angeles: Ward Ritchie Press, 1955.

Newsam, Sir Frank Aubrey. *The Home Office.* London: George Allen & Unwin, 1954.

Newsom, J.A. *The Life and Practice of the Wild and Modern Indian.* Oklahoma City, Okla.: Harlow, 1923.

Newton, A.P. *A Hundred Years of the British Empire.* London: Methuen, 1940.

Newton, D., and Hampshire, A.C. *Taranto.* London: William Kimber, 1959.

Newton, George D., and Zimring, Franklin E. *Firearms and Violence in American Life.* Washington D.C.: U.S. Government Printing Office, 1969.

Newton, H. Chance. *Crime and the Drama or Dark Deeds Dramatized.* London: Stanley Paul, 1927.

Newton, Harry J. *Yellow Gold of Cripple Creek.* Denver: Nelson, 1928.

Newton, Henry, and Jenney, Walther P. *Report on the Geology and Resources of the Black Hills of Dakota with Atlas.* Washington D.C.: U.S. Government Printing Office, 1880.

Newton, John. *Captain John Brown of Harper's Ferry.* London: T. Fisher Unwin, 1902.

Newton, Joseph Fort. *The Builders: A Story and Study of Masonry.* London: George Allen & Unwin, 1918.

Newton, Thomas. *Lord Lansdowne.* London: Macmillan, 1929.

New York, City of. *Annual Report.* New York: Department of Correction, 1968.

New York, City of. *The Melrose Report: A Neighborhood Plans for Change.* New York: City Planning Commission, 1969.

New York, City of. *Plan for New York City: 2: The Bronx.* New York: City Planning Commission, 1969.

New York, City of. *Progress Through Crisis, 1954-1965.* New York: Department of Correction, 1965.

New York, City of. *Two Year Report.* New York: Mayor's Criminal Justice Coordinating Council, 1969.

New York City Youth Board. *Reaching the Fighting Gang.* New York: New York City Youth Board, 1960.

New York Commission on Capital Punishment. *Report.* Albany, N.Y.: Argus, 1888.

New York Legislature. *Report and Proceedings of the Senate Committee on the Police Department of the City of New York.* Albany, N.Y.: State Printing Office, 1932.

New York Radical Feminists. *Rape: The First Sourcebook for Women.* New York: New American Library, 1974.

New York in Slices, by an Experienced Carver. New York: W.F. Burgess, 1849.

New York, State of. *The Code of Criminal Procedure.* New York: The Eagle Library, 1965.

New York, State of. *The Penal Law of the State of New York.* New York: The Eagle Library, 1965.

New York State Special Commission on Attica. *Attica.* New York: Bantam, 1972.

New York. Temporary Commission on Revision of the Penal Law and Criminal Code. *Special Report on Capital Punishment.* Albany: State of New York, 1965.

Ney, Richard. *The Wall Street Jungle.* New York: Grove Press, 1971.

Nézondet, René. *Petiot "le possédé."* Paris: Published by Author, 1950.

Ngugi, J.A. *Grain of Wheat.* London: William Heinemann, 1967.

NiCarthy, Ginny. *Getting Free: A Handbook for Women in Abusive Relationships.* Seattle, Wash.: Seal Press, 1982.

Nice, Richard (ed.). *Crime and Insanity.* New York: Philosophical Library, 1958.

_____. *Dictionary of Criminology.* New York: Philosophical Library, 1965.

Nicholas, H.R.H. *My Fifty Years.* London: Hutchinson, 1926.

Nicholl, Edith M. *Observations of a Ranch Woman in New Mexico.* New York: Macmillan, 1898.

Nicholls, Ernest. *Crime Within the Square Mile.* London: John Long, 1935.

Nichols, Alice. *Bleeding Kansas.* New York: Oxford University Press, 1954.

Nichols, Beverley. *The Sweet and Twenties.* London: Weidenfeld & Nicolson, 1958.

Nichols, C.W. *The Ulta-Fashionable Peerage of America.* New York: George Harjes, 1904.

Nichols, Egbert Ray, and Baccus, Joseph. (eds.). *Selected Articles on Minimum Wages and Maximum Hours.* New York: H.W. Wilson, 1937.

Nichols, Jeanette P., and Roy F. *The Growth of American Democracy.* New York: D. Appleton-Century, 1939.

_____. *Twentieth Century United States.* New York: D. Appleton-Century, 1943.

Nichols, John Wesley. *The People's Candidate for President.* New York: n.p., 1872.

Nichols, R.F. *The Disruption of American Democracy.* New York: Macmillan, 1948.

Nichols, Ray Franklin. *Franklin Pierce, Young Hickory of the Granite Hills.* Philadelphia: University of Pennsylvania Press, 1958.

Nichols, Roger L., and Halley, Patrick L. *Stephen Long and American Frontier Exploration.* Newark: University of Delaware Press, 1980.

Nichols, Roy. *The Stakes of Power 1845-1877.* New York: Hill & Wang, 1961.

Nichols, Thomas Low. *Esoteric Anthropology: The Mysteries of Man.* New York: Arno, 1972.

_____. *Forty Years of American Life.* New York: Stackpole, 1937.

_____, and Mary Gove. *Marriage: Its History, Character and Results.* Cincinnati, Ohio: Nicholson, 1854.

Nicholson, George, Condit, Thomas W., Greenbaum, Stuart. *Forgotten Victims.* Sacramento, Calif.: California District Attorneys Association, 1977.

Nicholson, Harold. *King George the Fifth: His Life and Reign.* London: Constable, 1952.

_____. *Peacemaking.* New York: Grosset & Dunlap, 1965.

Nicholson, Irene. *The x in Mexico: Growth Within Tradition.* London: Faber and Faber, 1965.

Nicholson, Isaac. *A Sermon Against Witchcraft Preached in Great Paxton, Huntingdon, July 17, 1808.* London: J. Mawman, 1808.

Nicholson, Michael. *The Yorkshire Ripper.* London: W. H. Allen, 1979.

Nickerson, Hoffman. *The Turning Point of the Revolution.* Boston: Houghton Mifflin, 1928.

Nicolaevsky, Boris I. (ed.). *The Crimes of the Stalin Era.* New York: The New Leader, 1962.

Nicolai, Christopher Friedrich. *Anekdoten von Friedrich dem Grossen.* Leipzig, Ger.: Insel-Bücherei, 1915.

Nicolas, Augustin. *Si la torture est un moyen seur à verifier les crimes secrets.* Amsterdam, Neth.: Abraham Wolfgang, 1681.

Nicolay, Helen. *Lincoln's Secretary: A Biography of John G. Nicolay.* New York: Longmanns, Green, 1949.

Nicolay, John G., and Hay, John. *Abraham Lincoln, A History.* New York: Century, 1890.

_____. *A Short Life of Abraham Lincoln.* New York: Century, 1902.

Nicolosi, Salvatore. *La leggenda di Giuiano: Vita di un fuorilegge.* Naples, Italy: "Il Tripode," 1977.

Nicolson, Harold. *King George the Fifth.* London: Constable, 1952.

_____. *Peacemaking: 1919.* Boston: Houghton Mifflin, 1933.

_____. *Portrait of a Diplomatist: Being the Life of Sir Arthur Nicolson, First Lord Carnock.* Boston: Houghton Mifflin, 1930.

Nicolson, Nigel (ed.). *Harold Nicolson, Diaries and Letters 1930-1939.* New York: Atheneum, 1966.

Nicotri, G., and Nicotri, F. *Freedom for Italy.* New York: Italian-American Press, 1942.

Nic Shiublaigh, Marie. *The Splendid Years.* Dublin, Ire.: Duffy, 1955.

Nider, Johannes. *Formicarius.* Cologne, Ger.: Ulrich Zel, 1475.

_____. *Praeceptorium.* Basel, Switz.: Berthold Ruppel, 1438.

Niebuhr, Rienhold. *Moral Man and Immoral Society.* New York: Charles Scribner's Sons, 1933.

_____. *Reflections on the End of an Era.* New York: Charles Scribner's Sons, 1934.

Niederhoffer, Arthur. *Behind the Shield: The Police in Urban Society.* Garden City, N.Y.: Anchor Doubleday, 1969.

Niehues, Bernard. *Zur Geschichte des Hexenglaubens.* Münster, Ger.: Coppenrath, 1875.

Niemann, Alfred. *Die Entthronung Kaiser Wilhelms II.* Leipzig, Ger.: K.F. Koehler, 1924.

_____. *Kaiser und Revolution: Die entscheidenden Ereignisse im Grossen Hauptquartier.* Berlin: A. Scherl, 1922.

_____. *Wanderungen mit Kaiser Wilhelm II.* Berlin: K.F. Koehler, 1924.

Niemetschek, Franz Xaver. *W.A. Mozart's Laben, nach Originalquallen Beschreiben.* Prague: Taussig, 1905.

Niemeyer, Gerhart and Reshetar, J.S. *Inquiry into Soviet Mentality.* New York: Frederick A. Praeger, 1956.

Niemoeller, Adolph F. *Sexual Slavery in America.* New York: Panurge Press, 1935.

Nietzel, Michael T. *Crime and Its Modification.* New York: Pergamon, 1980.

Nietzsche, Friedrich. *The Birth of Tragedy and the Genealogy of Morals.* Garden City, N.Y.: Doubleday, 1956.

Niles, Blair. *Condemned to Devil's Island.* New York: Grosset & Dunlap, 1928.

Nimmer, Raymond T. *Diversion: The Search for Alternative Forms of Prosecution.* Chicago: American Bar Foundation, 1974.

_____. *Two Million Unnecessary Arrests.* Chicago: American Bar Foundation, 1971.

Nintchitch, M. *La Crise bosniaque (1908-9).* Paris: Alfred Costes, 1937.

Nisbet, Ada. *Dickens and Ellen Ternan.* Berkeley: University of California Press, 1952.

Nisbet, Robert. *Prejudices: A Philosophical Dictionary.* Cambridge, Mass.: Harvard University Press, 1982.

Nishi, Toshio. *Unconditional Democracy.* Stanford, Calif.: Hoover Institute Press, 1982.

Niskanen, William A., Jr. *Bureaucracy and Representative Government.* Chicago: Aldine, 1971.

Nitti, F.F. *Escape.* New York: G.P. Putnam's Sons, 1930.

Nix, Evett Dumas. *Oklahombres.* St. Louis: Eden, 1929.

Nixon, Edgar B. *Franklin D. Roosevelt and Foreign Affairs.* Cambridge, Mass.: Harvard University Press, 1969.

Nixon, Edna. *Voltaire and the Calas Case.* London: Victor Gollancz 1961.

Nixon, Raymond B. *Henry W. Grady: Spokesman for the New South.* New York: Alfred A. Knopf, 1943.

Nixon, Richard M. *RN: The Memoirs of Richard Nixon.* New York: Grosset & Dunlap, 1978.

_____. *Six Crises.* New York: Doubleday, 1962.

Nizer, Louis. *The Implosion Conspiracy.* Garden City, N.Y.: Doubleday, 1973.

_____. *The Jury Returns.* New York: Pocket Books, 1968.

_____. *My Life in Court.* New York: Pyramid, 1963.

Nobile, Philip (ed.). *The Con III Controversy: The Critics Look at the Greening of America.* New York: Pocket Books, 1971.

Noble, John, and Cronin, John F. (eds.). *Records of the Court of Assistants of the Colony of Massachusetts Bay.* Boston: Published by Author, 1901.

Noble, John Wesley, and Averbuch, Bernard. *Never Plead Guilty.* New York: Farrar, Strauss, Cudahy, 1955.

Noble, Ransome E., Jr. *New Jersey Progressivism before Wilson.* Princeton, N.J.: Princeton University Press, 1946.

Nock, Arthur D. *Conversion.* Oxford, Eng.: Clarendon Press, 1933.

Nodé, Pierre. *Déclamation contre l'erreur exécrable des maléficiers.* Paris: J. Du Carroy, 1578.

Noel, Mary. *Villain's Galore.* New York: Macmillan, 1954.

Nogales, General Rafael de. *Four Years Beneath the Crescent.* New York: Charles Scribner's Sons, 1926.

_____. *Memoirs of a Soldier of Fortune.* New York: Harrison Smith, 1932.

Noggle, Burl. *Teapot Dome: Oil and Politics in the 1920's.* Baton Rouge: Louisiana State University Press, 1962.

Noguchi, Yoné. *The Story of Yoné Noguchi, Told by Himself.* Philadelphia: G.W. Jacobs, 1915.

Nolan, Frederick W. *The Life & Death of John Henry Tunstall.* Albuquerque: University of New Mexico Press, 1965.

_____. *The Sound of Their Music.* New York: Walter, 1978.

Nolan, J. Bennett. *Lafayette in America Day by Day.* Baltimore: The Johns Hopkins Press, 1934.

Nolan, William A. *Communism Versus the Negro.* Chicago: Henry Regner, 1951.

Nolan, William F. *Hammett: A Life at the Edge.* New York: Congdon and Weed, 1983.

Nolen, Oren Warder. *Galloping Down the Texas Trail.* Odem, Texas: Privately Printed, 1947.

Nolen, William A. *Healing, A Doctor in Search of A Miracle.* New York: Random House, 1975.

Nolte, Ernst. *Three Faces of Fascism.* New York: Holt, Rinehart & Winston, 1965.

Nolte, Richard H. (ed.). *The Modern Middle East.* New York: Atherton, 1963.

Nomad, Max. *Rebels and Renegades.* New York: Macmillan, 1932.

Nonte, Maj. George C., Jr. *Handgun Competition.* New York: Winchester, 1979.

Noonan, E.A. *The Trunk Tragedy, A Complete History of the Murder of Preller and the Trial of Maxwell.* St. Louis, Mo.: St. Lewis News, 1886.

Noonan, John T., Jr. *Persons and Masks of the Law.* New York: Farrar, Straus & Giroux, 1976.

Norbeck, Edward. *Religion in Primitive Society.* New York: Harper & Row, 1961.

Nord, David Jr. *Dallas Conspiracy.* Hollis, N.H.: n.p., 1968.

Nord, P. *Mes camarades sont morts.* Paris: Librairie des Champes Elysées, 1947.

Nordhoff, Charles. *California, For Health, Pleasure and Residence.* New York: Harper, 1882.

Nordholt, J.W. Schulte. *The People That Walk in Darkness.* New

York: Ballantine Books, 1960.

Nordon, Pierre. *Conan Doyle, A Biography*. New York: Holt, Rinehart & Winston, 1966.

Nordyke, Lewis T. *The Angels Sing*. Clarendon, Texas: Clarendon Press, 1964.

_____. *Cattle Empire: The Fabulous Story of the 3,000,000 Acre XIT*. New York: William Morrow, 1949.

_____. *The Great Roundup*. New York: William Morrow, 1955.

_____. *John Wesley Hardin, Texas Gunman*. New York: William Morrow, 1957.

_____. *The Truth About Texas*. New York: Thomas Y. Crowell, 1957.

Norfleet, J. Frank. *The Amazing Experiences of An Intrepid Texas Rancher With an International Swindling Ring (as told to Gordon Hines)*. Sugar Land, Texas: Imperial Press, 1927.

_____. *Norfleet: The Actual Experiences of a Texas Rancher's 30,000-Mile Transcontinental Chase after Five Confidence Men*. Fort Worth: W.F. White, 1924.

Norman, Charles. *Discoverers of America*. New York: Thomas Y. Crowell, 1968.

Norman, D. (ed.). *Models of Human Memory*. New York: Academic Press, 1970.

Norman, Frank. *Bang to Rights*. London: Seeker & Warburg, 1958.

_____. *Stand on Me*. London: Pan Books, 1959.

Norman, Sherman. *The Youth Service Bureau: A Brief Description of Five Current Programs*. Paramus, N.J.: National Council of Crime and Delinquency, 1970.

Norris, Clarence, and Washington, Sybil D. *The Last of the Scottsboro Boys*. New York: G.P. Putnam's Sons, 1979.

Norris, Frank. *McTeague: A Story of San Francisco*. New York: W.W. Norton, 1977.

Norris, Gordon W. *Golden Empire*. Boston: Bruce Humphries, 1949.

Norris, Harold. *Mr. Justice Murphy and the Bill of Rights*. Dobbs Ferry, N.Y.: Oceana, 1965.

Norris, Marianna. *Father and Son for Freedom*. New York: Dodd, Mead, 1968.

North Carolina. Board of Charities and Public Welfare. *Capital Punishment in North Carolina*. Raleigh: State of North Carolina, 1929.

North, Escott. *The Saga of the Cowboy*. London: Jarrolds, 1942.

North, Robert C. *Moscow and Chinese Communists*. Palo Alto, Calif.: Stanford University Press, 1953.

Northrop, H.D. *The Life and Achievements of Jay Gould*. New York: National, 1892.

Northrup, William B., and Northrup, John B. *The Insolence of Office: The Story of the Seabury Investigation*. New York: G.P. Putnam's Sons, 1932.

The Northwood Murder. Manchester, N.H.: n.p., 1873.

Norton, Mary. *The Borrowers*. New York: Harcourt, Brace, 1952.

Norton, Richard H.B. *Silver Spoon*. London: Hutchinson, 1954.

Norton, Sara, and Howe, M.A. DeWolfe (eds.). *Letters of Charles Eliot Norton with Biographical Comment*. Boston: Houghton Mifflin, 1913.

Norton, Samuel Wilber. *Chicago Traction: A History Legislative and Political*. Chicago: A.C. McClurg, 1907.

Norvell, Saunders. *Forty Years of Hardware*. New York: Hardware Age, 1924.

Nose, Abe (ed.) *Tenno no insho*. Tokyo: Sogen-sha, 1949.

Noske, Gustav. *Erlebtes aus Aufstieg und Niedergang einer Demokratie*. Offenbach, Ger.: Bollwerk, 1947.

Notestein, W. *A History of English Witchcraft from 1558-1718*. Washington, D.C.: American Historical Association, 1911.

Notestein, Wallace. *The English People on the Eve of Colonization, 1603-1660*. New York: Harper and Brothers, 1954.

Nott, Eliphalet. *Lectures on Temperance*. New York: Cheldon, Blakeman, 1857.

Nott-Bower, Sir William. *Fifty-two Years a Policeman*. London: Edward Arnold, 1926.

Notter, Harley. *The Origins of the Foreign Policy of Woodrow Wilson*. Baltimore: Johns Hopkins Press, 1937.

Novak, Maximillian E. *Economics and the Fiction of Daniel Defoe*. Berkeley: University of California Press, 1962.

Novak, William. *High Culture: Marihuana and the Lives of Americans*. New York: Alfred A. Knopf, 1980.

Novikoff-Priboy, A. *Tsushima*. New York: Alfred A. Knopf, 1937.

Novoselov, P.I. *Grigorii Rasputin i misticheskoe rasputstvo*. Moscow: n.p., 1912.

Novotny, Ann. *Strangers at the Door*. Riverside, Conn.: Chatham Press, 1972.

Nowak, Frank. *Medieval Slavdom and the Rise of Russia*. New York: Henry Holt, 1930.

Nowlis, Helen H. *Drugs on the College Campus*. New York: Doubleday, 1969.

Noyes, A. *The Accusing Ghost of Roger Casement*. New York: Citadel, 1957.

Noyes, Alexander Dana. *Forty Years of American Finance*. New York: G.P. Putnam's Sons, 1939.

_____. *The Market Place*. Boston: Little, Brown, 1938.

Noyes, Alva Josiah. *In the Land of the Chinook*. Helena, Mont.: State, 1917.

_____. *The Story of Ajax: Life in the Big Hole Basin*. Helena, Mont.: State, 1914.

Noyes, Arthur, and Kalb, Lawrence. *Modern Clinical Psychiatry*. Philadelphia: Saunders, 1958.

Noyes, Ella. *Story of Ferrara*. London: J.M. Dent, 1904.

Noyes, Peter. *Legacy of Doubt*. New York: Pinnacle, 1963.

Nozick, Robert. *Anarchy, State, and Utopia*. New York: Basic Books, 1974.

Nugent, Donald. *Ecumenism in the Age of Reformation: The Colloquy of Poissy*. Cambridge, Mass.: Harvard University Press, 1974.

Nugent, John Peer. *White Night*. New York: Rawson, Wade, 1979.

Nulli, Siro Attilio. *Lodovico il Moro*. Milan, Italy: Casa editrice ambrosiana, 1949.

Nunan, Thomas. *Diary of an Old Bohemian*. San Francisco: Harr Wagner, 1927.

Núñez de Pardo, Guillermo. *Revolución de México: la Decena Trágica*. Barcelona: F. Granada, 1913.

Nunis, Doyce B., Jr. (ed.). *The Golden Frontier: The Recollections of Herman Francis Reinhart, 1851-1869*.

Nunn, W.C. *Texas Under the Carpetbaggers*. Austin: University of Texas Press, 1962.

Nunnelley, Lela S. *Boothill Grave Yard*. Tombstone, Ariz.: Tombstone Epitaph, 1952.

Nuseibeh, Hazem Z. *The Idea of Arab Nationalism*. Ithaca, N.Y.: Cornell University Press, 1956.

Nute, Grace Lee. *Caesars of the Wilderness*. New York: D. Appleton-Century, 1943.

Nu Thakin (U Nu). *Burma Under the Japanese: Pictures and Portraits*. London: Macmillan, 1954.

Nuttall, Chris P., et al. *Parole in England and Wales*. London: H.M. Stationery Office, 1977.

Nuttall, Thomas. *A Journal of Travels into the Arkansas Territory During the Year 1819*. Norman: University of Oklahoma Press, 1980.

Nutting, Anthony. *The Arabs: A Narrative History from Mohammed to the Present*. New York: Clarkson N. Potter, 1964.

_____. *I Saw For Myself: The Aftermath of Suez*. Garden City, N.Y.: Doubleday, 1958.

_____. *No End of a Lesson: The Inside Story of the Suez Crisis*. New York: Published by Author, 1967.

Nye, F.I. *Family Relationships and Delinquent Behavior*. New York: John Wiley & Sons, 1958.

Nye, Nelson C. *Pistols for Hire: A Tale of the Lincoln County War and the West's Most Desperate Outlaw William (Billy the Kid) Bonney*. New York: Macmillan, 1941.

Nye, Russel B. *The Cultural Life of the New Nation 1776-1830.* New York: Harper and Row, 1960.
_____. *Fettered Freedom.* East Lansing: Michigan State College Press, 1945.
_____. *William Lloyd Garrison and the Humanitarian Reformers.* Boston: Little, Brown, 1955.
Nye, Captain W.S. *Carbine and Lace.* Norman: University of Oklahoma Press, 1937.
Nynauld, Jean de. *De la lycanthropie, transformation, et extase des sorciers.* Paris: N. Rousset, 1615.

O

Oakes, Cecil George. *Sir Samuel Romilly: 1757-1818.* London: George Allen & Unwin, 1935.
Oakley, Amy. *Scandinavia Beckons.* New York: D. Appleton, 1938.
Oakley, Ann. *Sex, Gender and Society.* London: Temple Smith, 1972.
_____. *The Sociology of Housework.* London: Martin Robertson, 1974.
Oaks, Dallin H., and Lehman, Warren. *A Criminal Justice System and the Indigent.* Chicago: University of Chicago Press, 1968.
Oates, Stephen B. *Confederate Cavalry West of the River.* Austin: University of Texas Press, 1961.
_____. *To Purge This Land With Blood: A Biography of John Brown.* New York: Harper & Row, 1970.
_____. *With Malice Towards None.* New York: Harper & Row, 1977.
O'Ballance, Edgar. *The Arab-Israeli War, 1948.* New York: Frederick A. Praeger, 1957.
_____. *Language of Violence: The Blood Politics of Terrorism.* San Rafael, Calif.: Presidio Press, 1979.
_____. *The Sinai Campaign, 1956.* London: Faber & Faber, 1959.
_____. *Terror in Ireland: The Heritage of Hate.* Novato, Calif.: Presidio Press, 1981.
Oberholtzer, Ellis Paxson. *Abraham Lincoln.* Philadelphia: George W. Jacobs, 1904.
_____. *A History of the United States since the Civil War.* New York: Macmillan, 1917-1937.
_____. *Jay Cooke, Financier of the Civil War.* 2 vols. New York: George W. Jacobs, 1907.
Oberholzer, Emil. *Delinquent Saints.* New York: Columbia University Press, 1956.
Obieta, J.A. *The International Status of the Suez Canal.* The Hague, Neth.: M. Nijhoff, 1960.
Obolensky, Serge. *One Man in His Time.* New York: McDowell Obolensky, 1958.
Obregon, Alvaro. *Ocho Mil Kilometros en Campana.* El Paso, Texas: El Paso del Norte, 1915.
_____. *Partes Oficiales de las Batallas de celaya.* Mexico City: n.p., n.d.
O'Brian, John L. *National Security and Industrial Freedom.* Cambridge, Mass.: Harvard University Press, 1955.
O'Brien, Barry. *Life of Lord Russell of Killowen.* London: Smith, Elder, 1901.
O'Brien, C. Bickford. *Muscovy and the Ukraine.* Berkeley: University of California Press, 1963.
_____. *Russia Under Two Tsars, 1682-1689, Regency of Sophia Alekseevna.* Berkeley: University of California Press, 1952.
O'Brien, Conor Cruise. *Herod, Reflections on Political Violence.* London: Hutchinson, 1978.
_____. *Parnell and His Party, 1880-1890.* Oxford, Eng.: Oxford University Press, 1957.
_____. *The Shaping of Modern Ireland.* London: Routledge & Kegan Paul, 1960.
_____. *States of Ireland.* New York: Pantheon, 1972.
O'Brien, Frank M. *Murder Mysteries of New York.* New York: W.F. Payson, 1932.
_____. *The Story of the Sun, 1833-1918.* New York: George H. Doran, 1918.
O'Brien, John T. *Crime and Justice in America.* New York: Pergamon, 1980.
O'Brien, Nora Connolly. *Portrait of a Rebel Father.* Dublin, Ire.: Talbot, 1935.
O'Brien, P.J. *Forward with Roosevelt.* Chicago: Winston, 1936.
O'Brien, R.B. *The Life of Parnell.* 2 vols. London: Smith, Elder, 1898.
O'Brien, Robert. *California Called Them: A Saga of Golden Days and Roaring Camps.* New York: McGraw-Hill, 1951.
_____. *This Is San Francisco.* New York: Whittlesey House, 1948.
O'Brien, Robert, and Cohen, Sidney. *Encyclopedia of Drug Abuse.* New York: Facts on File, 1984.
O'Brien, William, and Ryan, Desmond (eds.). *Devoy's Post Bag, 1871-1928.* Dublin, Ire.: Fallon, 1953.
O'Broin, Leon. *The Prime Informer: A Suppressed Scandal.* London: Sidgwick & Jackson, 1971.
O'Byrne, John. *"Pike's Peak or Bust," and Historical Sketches of the Wild West.* Colorado Springs, Colo.: n.p., 1922.
O'Callaghan, Edmund Bailey. *Documentary History of the State of New York.* Albany, N.Y.: Weed, Parsons, 1849.
O'Callaghan, Sean. *Damaged Baggage: The White Slave Trade and Narcotics Trafficking in the Americas.* New York: Roy, 1969.
_____. *The Jackboot in Ireland.* London: Wingate, 1958.
_____. *The Slave Trade Today.* New York: Crown, 1961.
_____. *The Triads.* London: W.H. Allen, 1978.
_____. *The Yellow Slave Trade.* London: Anthony Blond, 1968.
O'Casey, Sean. *Drums Under the Windows.* New York: Macmillan, 1947.
_____. *Inishfallen Fare Thee Well.* New York: Macmillan, 1949.
_____. *The White Slave Trade.* London: Robert Hale, 1965.
O'Cathasaigh, P. (Sean O'Casey). *The Story of the Irish Citizen Army.* Dublin, Ire.: Maunsel, 1919.
Ochieng', W.R. *A History of Kenya.* London: Macmillan, 1985.
O'Connell, Marvin R. *The Counter Reformation, 1559-1610.* New York: Harper & Row, 1974.
O'Connor, Edwin. *The Last Hurrah.* Boston: Little, Brown, 1956.
O'Connor, Elizabeth. *Call to Commitment.* New York: Harper & Row, 1963.
O'Connor, Frank. *The Big Fellow.* New York: Nelson, 1937.
_____. *Michael Collins and the Irish Revolution.* Dublin, Ire.: Clonmore & Reynolds, 1965.
_____. *An Only Child.* New York: Alfred A. Knopf, 1961.
O'Connor, Harvey. *The Astors.* New York: Alfred A. Knopf, 1941.
_____. *Mellon's Millions.* New York: John Day, 1933.
O'Connor, Irma. *Edward Gibbon Wakefield: The Man Himself.* London: Selwyn & Blount, 1928.
O'Connor, James. *The Fiscal Crisis of the State.* New York: St. Martin's Press, 1973.
O'Connor, John J. *Broadway Racketeers.* New York: Liveright, 1928.
O'Connor, Len. *Clout: Mayor Daley and His City.* Chicago: Henry Regnery, 1974.
O'Connor, Richard. *Ambrose Bierce.* London: Victor Gollancz, 1968.
_____. *Bat Masterson.* New York: Doubleday, 1957.
_____. *Black Jack Pershing.* New York: Doubleday, 1961.
_____. *The Cactus Throne: The Tragedy of Maximilian and Carlotta.* New York: G.P. Putnam's Sons, 1971.
_____. *Courtroom Warrior: The Combative Career of William Travers Jerome.* Boston: Little, Brown, 1963.

_____. *Gould's Millions.* Garden City, N.Y.: Doubleday, 1962.

_____. *Hell's Kitchen.* Philadelphia: J.B. Lippincott, 1958.

_____. *Heywood Brown.* New York: G.P. Putnam's Sons, 1975.

_____. *High Jinks on the Klondike.* Indianapolis, Ind.: Bobbs-Merrill, 1954.

_____. *Pat Garrett.* New York: Ace Books, 1960.

_____. *The Scandalous Mr. Bennett.* Garden City, N.Y.: Doubleday, 1962.

_____. *Wild Bill Hickok.* New York: Doubleday, 1959.

O'Connor, Ulick. *The Times I've Seen; Oliver St. John Gogarty, A Biography.* New York: Ivan Obolensky, 1963.

Oddie, S. Ingleby. *Inquest.* London: Hutchinson, 1941.

Oddone, Jacinto. *Historia de Socialismo Argentine.* Buenos Aires: La Vanguardia, 1934.

O'Dea, John C. *The Matrimonial Impediment of Nonage.* Washington, D.C.: Catholic University of America Press, 1944.

Odegard, Peter H. *Pressure Politics: The Story of the Anti-Saloon League.* New York: Columbia University Press, 1928.

O'Dell, Paul, with Slide, Anthony. *Griffith and the Rise of Hollywood.* New York: A.S. Barnes, 1970.

Odell, Robin. *Exhumation of Murder: The Life and Trial of Major Armstrong.* London: Harrap, 1975.

_____. *Jack the Ripper in Fact and Fiction.* London: Harrap, 1965.

O'Dell, Scott. *Country of the Sun: Southern California, an Informal History and Guide.* New York: Thomas Y. Crowell, 1957.

Oden, Bill. *Early Days on the Texas-New Mexico Plains.* Canyon, Texas: Palo Duro Press, 1965.

Odens, Peter. *Outlaws, Heroes and Jokers of the Old Southwest.* Yuma, Ariz.: Southwest Printers, 1964.

Odes to Pindar. trans. Sir John Sandys. Cambridge, Mass.: Harvard University Press, 1968.

Odhe, Thorstein. *Finland, A Nation of Cooperators.* London: Williams & Norgate, 1931.

O'Doherty, Katherine. *Assignment: America.* New York: de Tanko, 1957.

O'Donnell, Bernard. *Cavalcade of Justice.* London: Clerke & Cockeran, 1951.

_____. *Crimes That Made News.* London: Burke, 1954.

_____. *Great Thames Mysteries.* London: Harrap, 1965.

_____. *The Old Bailey and Its Trials.* London: Clerke & Cockeran, 1950.

_____. *Should Women Hang?* London: W.H. Allen, 1956.

_____. *The Trials of Mr. Justice Avory.* London: Rich & Cowan, 1935.

_____. *The World's Strangest Murders.* London: Frederick Muller, 1957.

_____. *The World's Worst Women.* London: W.H. Allen, 1953.

O'Donnell, Elliott. *Confessions of a Ghost Hunter.* London: Thornton Butterworth, 1928.

_____. *Great Thames Mysteries.* London: Selwyn & Blount, 1929.

_____. *Haunted Britain.* London: Rider, 1948.

_____. *Strange Disappearances.* New Hyde Park, N.Y.: University Books, 1972.

_____. *Trial of Kate Webster.* London: William Hodge, 1925.

_____. *Werewolves.* London: Methuen, 1912.

O'Donnell, Frank J. Hugh. *The Dawn Mist: A Play of the Rebellion.* Dublin, Ire.: Thomas Kiersey, 1919.

O'Donnell, John A., and Ball, J.C. (eds.). *Narcotic Addiction.* New York: Harper & Row, 1966.

_____. *Narcotic Addicts in Kentucky.* Washington, D.C.: U.S. Public Health Service, 1969.

O'Donnell, Kenneth P., Powers, David F., with McCarthy, Joe. *"Johnny, We Hardly Knew Ye."* Boston: Little, Brown, 1972.

O'Donnell, M.K. *You Can Hear the Echo.* New York: Simon & Schuster, 1966.

O'Donnell, Peadar. *There Will Be Another Day.* Dublin, Ire.: Dolmen, 1963.

O'Donoghue, Florence. *No Other Law (The Story of Liam Lynch and the Irish Republican Army, 1916-1923).* Dublin, Ire.: Irish Press, 1954.

Odorico, Federico. *Le Streghe di Valtellina e la Santa Inquisizione.* Milan, Italy: n.p., 1862.

Odum, Howard W., and Johnson, Guy B. *The Negro and His Songs.* Chapel Hill: University of North Carolina Press, 1925.

O'Dwyer, Paul. *Counsel for the Defense.* New York: Simon & Schuster, 1979.

Oesterreich, Traugott Konstantin. *Possession, Demoniacal and Other.* New York: R.R. Smith, 1930.

Oettinger, Katherine B. *Not My Daughter: Facing Up to Adolescent Pregnancy.* Englewood Cliffs, N.J.: Prentice-Hall, 1979.

O'Faolain, Julian, and Martines, Laura. *Not in God's Image.* New York: Harper Torchbooks, 1973.

O'Faolain, Sean. *Constance Markievicz or The Average Revolutionary.* London: Jonathan Cape, 1934.

_____. *De Valera.* Harmondsworth, Eng.: Penguin, 1939.

_____. *An Irish Journey.* London: Longmans, 1940.

_____. *Vive Moi!* Boston: Little, Brown, 1963.

Ofer, Yehuda. *Operation Thunderbolt: The Entebbe Raid.* London: Penguin Books, 1976.

Office of Management and Budget. *Social Indicators.* Washington, D.C.: U.S. Government Printing Office, 1973.

Official Report of the National Commission on Marihuana and Drug Abuse. *Marihuana: A Signal of Misunderstanding.* New York: The New American Library, 1972.

The Official Report of the Trial of Henry K. Goodwin. Boston: Wright & Potter, 1887.

Official Report of the Trial of Laura D. Fair. San Francisco: San Francisco Cooperative Printing, 1871.

Official Report of the Trial of Mary Harris. Washington: W.H. & O.H. Morrison, 1865.

Official Report on the Trial of John O'Neil. Boston: Wright & Potter, 1901.

Offstein, Jerrold. *Self-Defense for Women.* Palo Alto, Calif.: National Press Books, 1972.

O'Flaherty, Daniel. *General Jo Shelby.* Chapel Hill: University of North Carolina Press, 1954.

O'Flaherty, Liam. *The Informer.* London: Jonathan Cape, 1949.

_____. *Insurrection.* London: Victor Gollancz, 1950.

O'Flaherty, Wendy D. *The Origins of Evil in Hindu Mythology.* Berkeley: University of California Press, 1978.

Ogata, Sadako N. *Defiance in Manchuria: The Making of Japanese Foreign Policy, 1931-1932.* Berkeley: University of California Press, 1964.

Ogburn, Charlton, Jr. *The Marauders.* New York: Harper, 1959.

Ogden, Rollo (ed.). *Life and Letters of Edwin L. Godkin.* New York: Macmillan, 1907.

Ogg, Frederick Austin. *The Opening of the Mississippi.* New York: Macmillan, 1904.

Ogilvie, J.S. *History of the Assassination of J.A. Garfield.* New York: Published by Author, 1881.

Ogle, Ralph Hedrick. *Federal Control of the Western Apaches.* Albuquerque: University of New Mexico Press, 1970.

Oglesby, Carl. *The Yankee and Cowboy War.* Mission, Kan.: Sheed, Andrews & McMeel, 1976.

O'Hara, Albert R. *Position of Women in Early China.* Washington, D.C.: Catholic University of America Press, 1945.

O'Hara, Charles. *Fundamentals of Criminal Investigation.* Springfield, Ill.: Charles C. Thomas, 1969.

O'Hea, Patrick. *Reminiscences of the Mexican Revolution.* Mexico City, Mex.: Editorial Fournier, 1966.

O'Hegarty, P.S. *A History of Ireland Under the Union.* Dublin, Ire.: Talbot, 1922.

_____. *A Short Memoir of Terence MacSwiney.* Dublin, Ire.: Talbot, 1922.

_____. *Ulster.* Dublin, Ire.: Maunsel, 1919.

_____. *The Victory of Sinn Fein.* Dublin, Ire.: Talbot, 1924.

Ohio. Legislative Service Commission. *Capital Punishment.* Columbus: State of Ohio, 1961.

Ohle, Rudolf. *Die Hexen in und um Prenzlau.* Prenzlau: Mitteilungen, 1908.

Ohlin, Lloyd E. (ed.). *Prisoners in America.* Englewood Cliffs, N.J.: Prentice-Hall, 1973.

_____. *Selection for Parole.* New York: Russell Sage, 1951.

Ohrwalder, Joseph. *Ten Years Captivity in the Mahdi's Camp.* London: Sampson Low, Marston, 1893.

Ohtani Keijiro. *The Beginning of Sunset: History of the Japanese Army in the Reign of Hirohito.* Tokyo: Yakumo Shoten, 1959.

_____. *History of the Secret Police During the Reign of Hirohito.* Tokyo: Misuzu Shobo, 1966.

Oh Yeah? compl. Edward Angly. New York: Viking, 1932.

Ojetti, Ugo. *I Taccuini, 1914-1943.* Florence, Italy: Sansoni, 1954.

Okamoto Aisuke. *White Paper on the Emperor.* Tokyo: Bungei Shunju, 1956.

Okey, Thomas. *A Basketful of Memoirs: An Autobiographical Sketch.* London: Dent, 1930.

Oklahoma: A Guide to the Sooner State. Norman, Okla.: U.S. W.P.A., 1945.

Okun, S.B. *The Russian-American Company.* Cambridge, Mass.: Harvard University Press, 1951.

Olcott, C. *The Life of William McKinley.* 2 vols. New York: Houghton Mifflin, 1916.

Oldekop, Justus. *Observationes Criminales Practicae.* Frankfort, Ger.: J.Schrey & John Christ, 1698.

Olden, Marc. *Cocaine.* New York: Lancer Books, 1973.

Olden, Rudolf. *Hitler.* New York: Covici-Friede, 1936.

Oldenberg, Hermann. *Buddha: His Life, His Doctrine, His Order.* trans. William Hoey. London: Williams & Norgate, 1882.

Oldenburg, Zöé. *Catherine the Great.* New York: Pantheon Press, 1965.

Oldenburger, Philipp Andreas. *Thesaurus Rerum Publicarum.* Geneva, Switz.: Sauvelem de Tournes, 1675.

Oldenburg-Januschau, Elard von. *Erinnerungen.* Leipzig, Ger.: Hase & Koehler, 1938.

Older, Cora. *Love Stories of Old California.* New York: Coward-McCann, 1940.

_____. *San Francisco: Magic City.* New York: Longmans, Green, 1961.

_____. *William Randolph Hearst, American.* New York: D. Appleton-Century, 1936.

Older, Fremont and Cora. *George Hearst: California Pioneer.* Los Angeles: Westernlore, 1966.

_____. *Growing Up.* San Francisco: Call-Bulletin, 1931.

_____. *My Own Story.* New York: Macmillan, 1926.

Oldroyd, Osborn H. *The Assassination of Abraham Lincoln.* Washington D.C.: Published by Author, 1901.

_____. *Words of Lincoln.* Washington D.C.: Published by Author, 1895.

Olearius, Adam. *The Voyages and Travels of the Ambassadors.* London: Thomas Dring, John Starkey, 1662.

Oliva, Lawrence Jay. *Misalliance: A Study of French Policy in Russia During the Seven Years' War.* New York: New York University Press, 1964.

_____ (ed.). *Russia and the West From Peter to Khrushchev.* Boston: Heath, 1965.

Oliver, James H. *The Ruling Power.* Philadelphia: American Philosophical Society, 1953.

Oliver, John Rathbone. *Foursquare.* New York: Macmillan, 1929.

Oliver, N.T. *The Whitechapel Mystery: Jack the Ripper, A Psychological Problem.* Chicago: Continental, 1891.

Oliver, Roland and Caroline. *Africa in the Days of Exploration.* Englewood Cliffs, N.J.: Prentice-Hall, 1965.

Ollestad, Norman. *Inside the FBI.* New York: Lancer, 1968.

Ollivier, Emile. *L'Empire libéral, études, récits, souvenirs.* Paris: Garnier frères, 1895-1918.

_____. *Journal, 1846-1869.* Paris: René Julliard, 1961.

Ollman, Bertell. *Alienation: Marx's Conception of Man in Capitalist Society.* New York: Cambridge University Press, 1971.

Olmstead, A.T. *History of Assyria.* New York: Charles Scribner's Sons, 1923.

Olmsted, Frederick Law. *The Cotton Kingdom.* New York: Alfred A. Knopf, 1953.

_____. *A Journey in the Seaboard Slave States.* New York: Dix & Edwards, 1856.

_____. *A Journey Through Texas.* New York: Dix & Edwards, 1857.

Olmsted, Roger, and Watkins, T.H. *Here Today: San Francisco's Architectural Heritage.* San Francisco: Chronicle Books, 1968.

Olschki, L. *The Grail Castle and Its Mysteries.* trans. J.A. Scott. Manchester, Eng.: Manchester University Press, 1966.

Olsen, Alten L., and Green, John W. *Laboratory of Explosive Chemistry.* London: John Wiley & Sons, 1943.

Olsen, Jack. *The Man with the Candy: The Story of the Houston Mass Murders.* New York: Simon & Schuster, 1974.

_____. *Son: A Psychopath and His Victims.* New York: Dell, 1983.

Olsen, Sidney. *Young Henry Ford.* Detroit, Mich.: Wayne State University Press, 1963.

Olson, Edmund T. *Utah, a Romance in Pioneer Years.* Salt Lake City, Utah: Published by Author, 1931.

Olson, James C. *History of Nebraska.* Lincoln: University of Nebraska Press, 1955.

Olsson, Jan Olof. *Welcome to Tombstone.* trans. Maurice Michael. London: Elek Books, 1956.

Olszewski, George J. *Restoration of Ford's Theatre.* Washington D.C.: U.S. Government Printing Office, 1963.

Oltmans, Willem. *Reportage over de Moordenaars.* Utrecht, Holland: Bruna & Zoon, 1977.

O'Mahony, Peter Tynan (ed.). *Eamon de Valera 1882-1975.* Dublin, Ire.: The Irish Times, 1979.

O'Malley, Ernie. *On Another Man's Wound.* London: Rich & Cowan, 1936.

O'Malley, Tom. *My Life in Little Russia.* New York: Vantage Press, 1966.

Oman, C. *English Silver in the Kremlin 1557-1663.* London: Methuen, 1961.

Oman, C.W.C. *The History of the Art of War, Middle Ages.* 2 vols. New York: Burt Franklin, 1959.

Oman, Sir Charles. *Seven Roman Statesmen of the Later Republic.* Freeport, N.Y.: Books for Libraries, 1971.

O'Meara, James. *The Vigilance Committee of 1856.* San Francisco: Nash, 1932.

Omura Bunji. *The Last Genro: Prince Saionji, The Man Who Westernized Japan.* Philadelphia: J.B. Lippincott, 1938.

Omura Takeshi. *Prince Saionji in the Full Moon of Life.* Tokyo: Denki Kanko-kai, 1937.

O'Neal, Bill. *Encyclopedia of Western Gunfighters.* Norman: University of Oklahoma Press, 1979.

Oneal, James. *American Communism.* New York: Rand School, 1927.

O'Neal, James Bradas. *They Die But Once.* New York: Knight, 1935.

One Hundred Years of Progress in the United States. . . by Eminent Literary Men. . . with 280 Engravings. Hartford, Conn.: L. Stebbens, 1873.

O'Neil, William L. *The Woman Movement.* Chicago: Quadrangle, 1969.

O'Neill, Bard E. *Armed Struggle in Palestine: A Political-Military Analysis.* Boulder, Colo.: Westview Press, 1978.

_____. *Revolutionary Warfare in the Middle East.* Boulder, Colo.: Palatine Press, 1974.

O'Neill, F. Gordon. *Ernest Reuben Lilienthal and His Family.* Palo Alto, Calif.: Stanford University Press, 1949.

O'Neill, Gerard, and Lehr, Dick. *The Underboss: The Rise and Fall of a Mafia Family.* New York: St. Martin's, 1989.

O'Neill, William L. *Coming Apart: An Informal History of America in the 1960s*. New York: Quadrangle, 1971

_____. *Divorce in the Progressive Era*. New York: New Viewpoints, 1973.

The Only True Confession: The Last Words and Dying Confession of William Gross. Philadelphia: n.p., 1823.

Opium Eating: An Autobiographical Sketch by an Habituate. Philadelphia: Claxton, Remsen, Haffelfinger, 1876.

Opler, Morris E. *An Apache Life-Way*. Chicago: University of Chicago Press, 1941.

Oppenheim, Felix E. *Dimensions of Freedom*. New York: St. Martin's Press, 1961.

Oppenheimer, Ernest J. *The Inflation Swindle*. Englewood Cliffs, N.J.: Prentice-Hall, 1978.

Oppenheimer, H. *The Rationale of Punishment*. London: University of London Press, 1913.

Oprea, I.M. *Nicholae Titulescu's Diplomatic Activity*. Bucharest: Publishing House of the Academy of the Socialist Republic of Romania, 1968.

Orano, Paolo. *Mussolini da vicino*. Rome: Pinciana, 1928.

_____. *Rodolfo Graziani, generale scipionico*. Rome: Pinciana, 1936.

Orb, Heinrich. *Nationalsozialismus, 13 Jahre Machtrausch*. Olten, Switz.: Otto Walter, 1945.

Orchard, Harry (Albert E. Horsley). *The Confessions and Autobiography of Harry Orchard*. New York: Doubleday, Page, 1907.

O'Reilly, Edward S. *Roving and Fighting: Adventures Under Four Flags*. New York: Century, 1918.

O'Reilly, Harrington. *Fifty Years on the Trail: A True Story of Western Life*. London: Chatto & Windus, Piccadilly, 1889.

O'Reilly, James T. *Federal Information Disclosure: Procedures, Forms and the Law*. Springs, Colo.: Shepard's, 1977.

O'Reilly, Kenneth. *Hoover and the Un-Americans*. Philadelphia: Temple University Press, 1983.

O'Rell, Max. *Les Filles de John Bull*. Paris: Lévy, 1884.

Orfali, John, and Van Young, Sayre (ed.). *Marijuana Datebook, 1980*. Berkeley, Calif.: And/Or Press, 1979.

Orfield, Lester. *Criminal Appeals in America*. Boston: Little, Brown, 1939.

_____. *Criminal Procedure from Arrest to Appeal*. New York: New York University Press, 1947.

_____. *Criminal Procedure from Arrest to Trial*. New York: New York University Press, 1947.

_____. *Criminal Procedure Under Federal Rules*. Rochester, N.Y.: Lawyers Cooperative, 1967.

Organizations: Structure and Process. Englewood Cliffs, N.J.: Prentice-Hall, 1977.

Organized Crime Task Force Report. Washington, D.C.: U.S. Government Printing Office, 1967.

Origen (Origenes Adimantius). *The Ante-Nicene Christian Library*. Edinburgh, Scot.: T. & T. Clark, 1867.

Origo, Marchioness Iris. *War in Wal d'Orcia*. London: Jonathan Cape, 1947.

Orland, Leonard. *Prisons: Houses of Darkness*. New York: The Free Press, 1975.

Orlando, Francesco. *Mussolini volle il 25 luglio*. Milan, Italy: SPES, 1946.

Orlando, Gen Taddeo. *Vittoria di un popolo*. Rome: Corso, 1946.

Orlansky, Harold. *The Harlem Riot: A Study in Mass Frustration*. New York: Social Analysis, 1943.

Orloski, Richard J. *Criminal Law*. Chicago: Nelson-Hall, 1977.

Orlov, Alexander. *Handbook of Intelligence and Guerrilla Warfare*. Ann Arbor: University of Michigan Press, 1965.

Orlow, Dietrich. *The History of the Nazi Party*. 2 vols. Pittsburgh, Pa.: University of Pittsburgh Press, 1969.

Orman, Richard A. van. *A Room for the Night: Hotels of the Old West*. Bloomington: Indiana University Press, 1966.

Ormerod, Henry. *Piracy in the Ancient World*. London: Hodder & Stoughton, 1924.

Ormsby, W.L.A. *A Description of Bank Note Engraving*. New York: Published by Author, 1852.

Ornstein, R.E. *The Psychology of Consciousness*. San Francisco: Freeman, 1972.

Oron, Yitzhak (ed.). *Middle East Record*. New York: Daniel Davey, 1966.

O'Rorke, T. *The History of Sligo: Town and Country*. Dublin, Ire.: James Duffy, 1889.

Orsi, Count Giuseppe. *Recollections of the Last Half-Century*. London: Longmans, 1881.

Orsini, Felice. *The Austrian Dungeons of Italy*. Trans. J. Meriton White. London: George Routledge & Sons, 1856.

_____. *Memoirs and Adventures of Felice Orsini*. Trans. George Carbonel. Edinburgh, Scot.: Thomas Constable, 1857.

Ortega Y Gassett, Jose. *Revolt of the Masses*. New York: W.W. Norton, 1932.

Orth, Samuel P. *The Boss and the Machine: A Chronicle of the Politicians and Party Organizations*. New Haven, Conn.: Yale University Press, 1920.

_____. *Five American Politicians*. Cleveland: Burrows Brothers, 1906.

_____. *Socialism and Democracy in Europe*. New York: Henry Holt, 1913.

Orton, Samuel Torrey. *Reading, Writing and Speech Problems in Children*. New York: W.W. Norton, 1937.

Osbert, Reuben. *Freud and Marx*. New York: Equinox Co-operative Press, 1937.

Osborn, Albert D. *Questioned Document Problems*. Albany, N.Y.: Boyd Printing, 1944.

Osborn, Campbell. *Let Freedom Ring*. Tokyo: Inter-Nation, 1954.

Osborne, Francis. *Miscellaneous Works*. London: E. Bell, 1722.

_____. *Miscellany of Sundry Essays*. London: Grismond, 1659.

Osborne, John. *The Second Year of the Nixon Watch*. New York: Liveright, 1971.

_____. *The White House Watch: The Ford Years*. Washington, D.C.: New Republic, 1977.

Osborne, R.T. *Twins: Black and White*. Athens, Ga.: Foundation for Human Understanding, 1980.

Osborne, Thomas Mott. *Prisons and Common Sense*. Philadelphia: J.B. Lippincott, 1924.

Osgood, C., Suci, G., and Tannenbaum, P. *The Measurement of Meaning*. Urbana: The University of Illinois Press, 1957.

Osgood, Cornelius. *The Koreans and Their Culture*. New York: The Ronald Press, 1951.

Osgood, Ernest Staples. *The Day of the Cattleman*. Minneapolis: University of Minnesota Press, 1929.

Osgood, Herbert Levi. *The American Colonies in the Eighteenth Century*. New York: Columbia University Press, 1924.

_____. *The American Colonies in the Seventeenth Century*. 3 vols. New York: Macmillan, 1904-07.

Osgood, Robert E., and Tucker, Robert W. *Force, Order, and Justice*. Baltimore: Johns Hopkins Press, 1967.

O'Shaughnessy, Edith. *A Diplomat's Wife in Mexico*. New York: Harper, 1916.

_____. *Intimate Pages of Mexican History*. New York: Doran, 1920.

_____. *Marie Adelaide*. New York: Harrison Smith, 1932.

O'Shaughnessy, Michael M. *The Hetch Hetchy Water Supply and Power Project of San Francisco*. San Francisco: n.p., 1931.

Oshinsky, David M. *A Conspiracy So Immense: The World of Joe McCarthy*. New York: Free Press, 1983.

Osofsky, Gilbert. *Harlem: The Making of a Ghetto*. New York: Harper & Row, 1968.

Ossendowski, Ferdinand. *Beasts, Men and Gods*. New York: E.P. Dutton, 1922.

Oster, John E. *Political and Economic Doctrines of John Marshall*. New York: Neals, 1914.

Osterburg, James W. *The Crime Laboratory*. Bloomington: Indiana University Press, 1968.

Ostermann, Peter. *Commentarius Juridicus.* Cologne, Ger.: Petrum Metternich, 1659.

Ostermann, Robert. *Crime in America.* New York: Dow Jones, 1966.

Osterweis, R.G. *Romanticism and Nationalism in the Old South.* New Haven, Conn.: Yale University Press, 1949.

Ostrander, Gilman M. *The Prohibition Movement in California, 1848-1933.* Los Angeles: University of California Press, 1957.

Ostrander, Shield and Schroeder, Lynn. *Psychic Discoveries Behind the Iron Curtain.* New York: Bantam, 1971.

_____. *Handbook of Psychic Discoveries.* New York: Berkley, 1974.

Ostrogorski, Moisei. *Democracy and the Organization of Political Parties.* 2 vols. New York: Macmillan, 1902.

Ostrogorsky, Georgije. *History of the Byzantine State.* New Brunswick, N.J.: Rutgers University Press, 1957.

Ostrom, Vincent. *The Intellectual Crisis in American Public Administration.* Tuscaloosa: University of Alabama Press, 1973

O'Sullivan, A.M. *The Last Serjeant.* London: Macdonald, 1952.

O'Sullivan, Donal. *The Irish Free State and Its Senate.* London: Faber & Faber, 1940.

O'Sullivan, F. Dalton. *Crime Detection.* Chicago: O'Sullivan, 1928.

O'Sullivan, Noel (ed.). *Terrorism, Ideology,and Revolution.* Boulder, Colo.: Westview Press, 1986.

O'Sullivan, Vincent. *Aspects of Wilde.* New York: H. Holt, 1936.

Oswald, Marguerite. *Aftermath of an Execution: The Burial and Final Rights of Lee Harvey Oswald as Told by His Mother.* Dallas: Published by Author, 1964.

Oswald, Robert L., Myrick, and Land, Barbara. *Lee: A Portrait of Lee Harvey Oswald.* New York: Coward-McCann, 1967.

Oswald, Russel G. *Attica: My Story.* Garden City, N.Y.: Doubleday, 1972.

Oswald: Assassin or Fall Guy? New York: Marzani & Munsell, 1964.

Oswandel, J.J. *Notes on the Mexican War, 1846-47-48.* Philadelphia: n.p., 1885.

Otero, Caroline. *My Story.* London: Philpot, 1927.

Otero, Pear Miquel Antonio. *My Life on the Frontier, 1864-1882.* 2 vols. New York: The Press of the Pioneers, 1935.

_____. *My Nine Years as Governor of the Territory of New Mexico, 1897-1906.* Albuquerque: University of New Mexico Press, 1940.

_____. *The Real Billy The Kid.* New York: Rufus Rockwell Wilson, 1936.

Otis, Elwell S. *The Indian Question.* New York: Sheldon, 1878.

O'Toole, George. *The Assassination Tapes: An Electronic Probe into the Murder of John F. Kennedy and the Dallas Cover-up.* New York: Penthouse Press, 1975.

_____. *The Private Sector.* New York: W.W. Norton, 1978.

Ottaviani, Giovanni Battista. *La politica rurale di Mussolini.* Rome: Littorio, 1929.

Ottenberg, Miriam. *The Federal Investigators.* Englewood Cliffs, N.J.: Prentice-Hall, 1962.

Otto, James, and Towle, Albert. *Modern Biology.* New York: Holt, Rinehart & Winston, 1965.

Oukhtomsky, E.E. *Voyage en Orient, 1890-1891, de Son Altesse Imperiale le Tsarevitch.* Paris: Delegrave, 1893.

Oulton, John E.L., and Chadwick, Henry. *Alexandrian Christianity.* Philadelphia: Westminster Press, 1954.

Oursel, Raymond. *Jeanne d'Arc.* Tours, Fr.: Maue, 1952.

_____. *Le procès de condamnation de Jeanne d'Arc.* Paris: Club du meilleur livre, 1953.

Ousler, W. *Marijuana: The Facts, The Truth.* New York: Paul S. Eriksson, 1968.

Outerbridge, Henry. *Captain Jack: His Story as Told to Henry Outerbridge.* New York: Century, 1928.

Outlawry and Justice in Old Arizona. Tucson, Ariz.: L.A. Printers, 1965.

Outler, Albert C. (ed.). *Confessions.* London: SCM Press, 1955.

Ovazza, Carla. *Cinque Ciliege Rosse: Una Notte Lunga Trenta-cinque Giorni.* Milan, Italy: Mursia, 1978.

Overholser, Joel F. *A Souvenir History of Fort Benton, Montana.* Fort Benton, Mont.: The River Press, n.d.

Overholser, Winfred. *The Psychiatrist and the Law.* New York: Harcourt, Brace, 1953.

Overly, Don H., and Schell, Theodore H. *New Effectiveness Measures for Organized Crime Control Efforts.* Washington, D.C.: U.S. Government Printing Office, 1973.

Overstreet, Harry A. *A Declaration of Interdependence.* New York: W.W. Norton, 1937.

_____, and Overstreet, Bonaro. *The FBI in an Open Society.* New York: W.W. Norton, 1969.

Overton, Grant (ed.). *Mirrors of the Year.* New York: F.A. Stokes, 1927-28.

Ovid. *Amores.* trans. Grant Showerman. London: William Heinemann, 1950.

Ovitt, Mabel. *Golden Treasure.* Dillon, Mont.: Privately Printed, 1952.

Owen, A.R.G. *Can We Explain the Poltergeist?* New York: Taplinger, 1964.

_____. *Psychic Mysteries of the North.* New York: Harper & Row, 1975.

Owen, Collinson. *King Crime, an English Study of America's Greatest Problem.* New York: Henry Holt, 1932.

Owen, David E. *English Philanthropy, 1660-1960.* Cambridge, Mass.: Harvard University Press, 1964.

Owen, Frank. *Tempestuous Journey: Lloyd George, His Life and Times.* London: Hutchinson, 1954.

_____. *The Three Dictators.* London: George Allen & Unwin, 1941.

Owen, Henry, and Schultze, Charles L. (eds.). *Setting National Priorities: The Next Ten Years.* Washington D.C.: The Brookings Institution, 1976.

Owen, Launcelot A. *The Russian Peasant Movement, 1906-1917.* London: King, 1937.

Owen, Mary Cameron. *The Booster and the Snitch.* New York: Free Press, 1964.

Owen, Robert Dale. *Footfalls on the Boundary of Another World.* Philadelphia: J.B. Lippincott, 1860.

Owens, Meroe J. *A Brief History of Sherman County, Nebraska.* Norfolk, Neb.: Norfolk News, 1952.

Owens, William A. *Slave Mutiny.* New York: John Day, 1953.

Owing, Chloe. *Women Police.* Montclair, N.J.: Patterson Smith, 1968.

Owls-Glass. *Rebel Brag and British Bluster.* The American News, 1865.

Owsley, F.L. *Plain Folk of the Old South.* Baton Rouge: Louisiana State University Press, 1949.

_____. *States Rights in the Confederacy.* Chicago: University of Chicago Press, 1925.

Oxford Regional Economic Atlas. The U.S.S.R. and Eastern Europe. New York: Oxford University Press, 1956.

Oya Soichi. *Japan's Longest Day.* Tokyo: Bungei Shunju, 1965.

Ozaki Yoshiharu. *The Men Who Moved the Army.* Odawara, Japan: Hachi-ko-do Shoten, 1960.

P

Pace, Denny F. *Handbook of Vice Control.* Englewood Cliffs, N.J.: Prentice-Hall, 1971.

Pace, Dick. *Golden Gulch: The Story of Montana's Fabulous Alder*

Gulch. Butte, Mont.: n.p., 1962.

Packard, George R. *Protest in Tokyo: The Security Treaty Crisis of 1960.* Princeton, N.J.: Princeton University Press, 1966.

Packard, Reynolds and Eleanor. *Balcony Empire.* London: Chatto & Windus, 1943.

Packard, Vance. *The Hidden Persuaders.* New York: Simon & Schuster, 1966.

_____. *The Naked City.* New York: David McKay, 1964.

Packe, Michael St. John. *The Bombs of Orsini.* London: Secker & Warburg, 1957.

_____. *Orsini: The Story of a Conspirator.* Boston: Little, Brown, 1957.

Packer, Herbert L. *Ex-Communist Witnesses.* Palo Alto, Calif.: Stanford University Press, 1962.

_____. *The Limits of the Criminal Sanction.* Palo Alto, Calif.: Stanford University Press, 1968.

Packer, William F. *Report on the Trial and Conviction of John Earls.* Williamsport, Pa.: n.p., 1836.

Pacq, Hilary. *Le Proces d'Oscar Wilde.* Paris: Gallimaud, 1933.

Paddock, Capt. B.B. *A Twentieth Century History and Biographical Record of North and West Texas.* Chicago: Lewis, 1906.

Paden, Irene D., and Schlichtmann, Margaret E. *The Big Oak Flat Road: An Account of Freighting From Stockton to Yosemite Valley.* San Francisco: n.p., 1955.

Padoan, Giovanni. *Abbiamo lottato insieme.* Udine, Italy: Del Bianco, 1965.

Padover, Saul K. (ed.). *Thomas Jefferson On Democracy.* New York: New American Library, 1946.

_____. *The Living U.S. Constitution.* New York: New American Library, 1983.

Page, Bruce, Leitch, David, and Knightley, Phillip. *The Philby Conspiracy.* Garden City, N.Y.: Doubleday, 1968.

Page, Elizabeth. *Wagons West.* New York: Farrar & Rinehart, 1930.

Page, Henry Markham. *Pasadena; Its Early Years.* Los Angeles: Lorrin L. Morrison, 1964.

Page, Joseph A., and O'Brien, Mary-Win. *Bitter Wages: Ralph Nader's Study Group Report on Disease and Injury on the Job.* New York: Grossman, 1973.

Page, Thomas J. *La Plata, the Argentine Confederation and Paraguay.* New York: Harper & Brothers, 1859.

Page, Thomas Nelson. *Red Rock.* London: William Heinemann, 1898.

The Pageant of America. 15 vols. New Haven, Conn.: Yale University Press, 1925.

Paget, R.T., and Silverman, Sydney. *Hanged-And Innocent?* London: Victor Gollancz, 1953.

Paget, Walpurga Ehrengarde Helena (von Hohenthal). *Embassies of Other Days and Further Recollections.* 2 vols. New York: George H. Doran, 1923.

Paine, Albert Bigelow. *Captain Bill McDonald, Texas Ranger.* New York: J.J. Little & Ives, 1909.

_____. *Mark Twain's Notebook.* New York: Harper & Brothers, 1935.

_____. *The Nast: His Period and His Pictures.* New York: Macmillan, 1904.

Paine, Bayard H. *Pioneers, Indians and Buffaloes.* Curtis, Neb.: Curtis Enterprise, 1935.

Paine, Lauran. *The Assassin's World.* New York: Taplinger, 1975.

_____. *Texas Ben Thompson.* Los Angeles: Westernlore Press, 1966.

_____. *Tom Horn, Man of the West.* Barre, Mass.: Barre, 1963.

Paine, Ralph D. *Lost Ships and Lonely Seas.* New York: Century, 1922.

Paine, Swift. *Eilley Orrum, Queen of the Comstock.* New York: Bobbs-Merrill, 1929.

Painter, Sidney. *French Chivalry.* Ithaca, N.Y.: Cornell University Press, 1940.

Paivio, A. *Imagery and Verbal Processes.* New York: Holt, Rinehart, Winston, 1971.

Pakenham, F.A., (assisted by R. Opie). *Causes of Crime.* London: Weidenfeld & Nicholson, 1958.

_____. *The Idea of Punishment.* London: Chapman, 1961.

_____. *Peace by Ordeal.* London: Jonathan Cape, 1935.

Pakenham, Simona. *Pigtails and Pernod.* London: Macmillan, 1962.

Pakula, Hannah. *The Last Romance: A Biography of Queen Marie of Roumania.* New York: Simon & Schuster, 1984.

Palacios, Porfirio. *Emiliano Zapata.* Mexico City: n.p., 1960.

Palavicini, Félix Fulgencio. *Mi vida revolucionaria.* Mexico City: Ediciones Botas, 1937.

Palazzeschi, Aldo. *Tre imperi mancati.* Florence, Italy: Vallecchi, 1945.

Paléologue, Maurice. *An Embassador's Memoirs.* 3 vols. trans. F.A. Holt. New York: Doran, 1925.

_____. *The Enigmatic Czar: The Life of Alexander I of Russia.* London: Harper & Brothers, 1938.

_____. *The Tragic Empress.* New York: Harper & Brothers, 1928.

_____. *The Tragic Romance of Alexander II.* London: Hutchinson, 1926.

Palfrey, John Goodman. *History of New England During the Stewart Dynasty.* Boston: Little, Brown, 1897.

Palingh, Abraham. *Het afgerukt mom-aangezicht der Tooverij.* Amsterdam: Andries van Danne, 1725.

Pallavicino, Ferrante. *The Whore's Rhetorick.* New York: Ivan Obolensky, 1961.

Pallis, A.A. *Greece's Anatolian Venture and After.* London: Hutchinson, 1937.

Palm, A.J. *The Death Penalty.* New York: G.P. Putnam's Sons, 1891.

Palmer, A. Emerson. *The New York Public School.* New York: Macmillan, 1905.

Palmer, Benjamin W. *Marshall and Taney.* Minneapolis: University of Minnesota Press, 1939.

Palmer, E.L., and Dorr, A. (eds.). *Children and the Faces of Television: Teaching, Violence, Selling.* New York: Academic Press, 1980.

Palmer, Edward W. (ed.). *The Communist Problem in American.* New York: Thomas Y. Crowell, 1951.

Palmer, Edwin O. *History of Hollywood.* Hollywood, Calif.: Arthur H. Cawston, 1937.

Palmer, H.A., and Palmer, H. (eds.). *Wilsheve's Criminal Procedure.* London: Sweet & Maxwell, 1954.

Palmer, John. *Journal of Travels.* London: Sherwood, Neely & Sons, 1818.

Palmer, N. Dunbar. *The Irish Land League.* New Haven: Yale University Press, 1940.

Palmer, R.R. *The Age of the Democratic Revolution: A Political History of Europe and America, 1760-1800.* 2 vols. Princeton, N.J.: Princeton University Press, 1959.

Palmer, S. *The Prevention of Crime.* New York: Behavioral, 1973.

Palmer, Stuart. *The Psychology of Murder.* New York: Thomas Y. Crowell, 1960.

Palmer, T. *Correctional Intervention and Research.* Lexington, Mass.: Lexington Books/D.C. Heath, 1978.

Palmer, Vivien M. *Social Backgrounds of Chicago's Local Communities.* Chicago: University of Chicago Press, 1930.

Palomares, Justino. *La invasión yanqui en 1914.* Mexico City, Mex.: n.p., 1940.

Paltsits, Victor Hugo. *Minutes of the Executive Council of the Province of New York.* Albany, N.Y.: State of New York, 1910.

Panati, Charles (ed.). *The Geller Papers.* Boston: Houghton Mifflin, 1976.

_____. *Supersenses.* New York: Quadrangle, 1974.

Panel for the Evaluation of Crime Surveys. *Surveying Crime.* Washington, D.C.: National Academy of Sciences, 1976.

Paneth, Donald. *News Dictionary.* New York: F.A.F., 1979.

Panikkar, K.M. *Asia and Western Dominance.* London: George Allen & Unwin, 1953.

_____. *In Two Chinas: Memoirs of a Diplomat.* London: George Allen & Unwin, 1955.

Pannell, Walter. *Civil War on the Range.* Los Angeles: Welcome News, 1943.

Pansini, Edoardo. *Goliardi a scugnizzi nelle quattro giornate.* Naples, Italy: Cimento, 1944.

Pantaleo, Paolo. *Il fascismo cremonese.* Cremona, Italy: Cremona Nuova, 1931.

Pantaleone, Michele. *The Mafia and Politics.* New York: Coward-McCann, 1966.

Pantazzi, Ethel Greening. *Roumania in Light and Shadow.* London: T.F. Unwin, 1921.

Paolucci, Raffaele. *Il mio piccolo mondo perduto.* Bologna, Italy: Cappelli, 1947.

Papadatos, Peter. *The Eichmann Trial.* New York: Frederick A. Praeger, 1964.

Papen, Franz von. *Memoirs.* trans. Brian Connell. New York: E.P. Dutton, 1953.

Pappworth, H.M. *Human Guinea Pigs.* Boston: Beacon Press, 1967.

Paredes, Americo. *With a Pistol in his Hand: A Border Ballad and Its Hero.* Austin: University of Texas Press, 1958.

Parent-Duchâtelet, A.J.B. *De la Prostitution dans la ville de Paris.* Paris: J.B. Baillière, 1836.

_____. *La Syphilis et les autres maladies veneriennes chez les prostitutées de Paris.* Paris: Pierre Fort, 1900.

Parenti, Michael. *Democracy for the Few.* New York: St. Martin's Press, 1980.

Pares, Sir Bernard. *The Fall of the Russian Monarchy.* New York: Alfred A. Knopf, 1939.

_____. *A History of Russia.* New York: Alfred A. Knopf, 1953.

_____. *Russia and Reform.* London: Constable, 1907.

Pares, Richard. *King George III and the Politicians.* Oxford, Eng.: Clarendon Press, 1953.

_____. *Yankees and Creoles.* Cambridge, Mass.: Harvard University Press, 1956.

Paris, Comte De. *History of the Civil War in America.* Philadelphia: Porter & Coates, 1875.

Pariset, Madame (pseud.). *nouveau Manuel complet de la maitresse de maison.* Paris: Roret, 1852.

Parish, Joe. *Coffins, Cactus and Cowboys.* El Paso, Texas: Superior, 1954.

Park, Alexander. *Bolshevism in Turkestan, 1917-1927.* New York: Columbia University Press, 1957.

Park, Robert. *History of Oklahoma State Penitentiary at McAlester, Okla.* McAlester, Okla.: McAlester Printing, 1914.

Park, Robert E., Burgess, Ernest W., and MacKensie, Roderick D. *The City.* Chicago: University of Chicago Press, 1925.

_____. *Human Communities.* Glencoe, Ill.: Free Press, 1952.

_____. *The Immigrant Press and Its Control.* New York: Harper & Brothers, 1922.

Parke, Adelia. *Memoirs of an Old Timer.* Weiser, Idaho: Signal-American, 1955.

Parkenham, Frank. *Causes of Crime.* London: Weidenfeld, 1948.

Parker, Alfred E. *August Vollmer: Crime Fighter.* New York: Macmillan, 1961.

_____. *The Berkeley Police Story.* Springfield, Ill.: Charles C. Thomas, 1972.

Parker, Amos Andrew. *Trip to the West and Texas.* Concord, N.H.: White & Fisher, 1835.

Parker, Carleton H. *The Casual Laborer and Other Essays.* New York: Harcourt, Brace & Howe, 1920.

Parker, Donn B. *Crime by Computer.* New York: Scribners, 1976.

Parker, Frank. *Caryl Chessman, the Red Light Bandit.* Chicago: Nelson-Hall, 1975.

Parker, Frank J. *The Law and the Urban Poor.* Maryknoll, N.Y.: Orbis Books, 1973.

Parker, James. *The Old Army Memories, 1872-1918.* Philadelphia: Dorrance, 1929.

Parker, John Lloyd. *Unmasking Wall Street.* Boston: Stratford, 1932.

Parker, L. Craig, Jr. *The Japanese Police System Today.* New York: Kodansha International, 1984.

Parker, Lew. *Odd People I Have Met.* n.p., n.d.

Parker, Robert Allerton. *The Transatlantic Smiths.* New York: Random House, 1959.

Parker, Theodore. *Sermon of the Dangerous Classes in Society.* Boston: Spear, 1847.

Parker, Rev. Theodore. *John Brown's Expedition Reviewed in a Letter from Rev. Theodore Parker at Rome to Francis Jackson.* Boston: The Fraternity, 1960.

Parker Tony, and Allerton, Robert. *The Courage of His Convictions.* New York: W.W. Norton, 1962.

_____. *The Hidden World of Sex Offenders.* New York: Bobbs-Merrill, 1969.

Parker, Watson. *Gold in the Black Hills.* Norman: University of Oklahoma Press, 1966.

Parker, Willie J. *Halt! I'm A Federal Game Warden.* New York: McKay, 1977.

Parkes, Henry Bamford. *A History of Mexico.* London: Eyre & Spottiswoods, 1962.

Parkes, James W. *A History of Palestine from 135 A.D. to Modern Times.* New York: Oxford University Press, 1949.

Parkhill, Forbes. *The Law Goes West.* Denver: Sage Books, 1956.

_____. *The Wildest of the West.* New York: Henry Holt, 1951.

Parkhurst, Rev. Charles H. *My Forty Years in New York.* New York: Macmillan, 1923.

_____. *Our Fight with Tammany.* New York: Charles Scribner's Sons, 1895.

Parkinson, C. Northcote. *Parkinson's Law.* New York: Ballantine, 1957.

Parkinson, Maude. *Twenty Year in Roumania.* London: George Allen & Unwin, 1921.

Parkinson, Roger. *Zapata.* New York: Stein & Day, 1975.

Parkinson, Sydney. *A Journal of a Voyage to the South Seas, in His Majesty's Ship, the Endeavour.* London: Published by Author, 1773.

Parkman, Francis. *La Salle and the Discovery of the Great West.* Boston: Little, Brown, 1880.

_____. *The Oregon Trail.* New York: Modern Library, 1949.

Parks, Charles Caldwell. *A Plaything of the Gods.* Boston: Sherman, Finch, 1912.

Parks, Ed Winfield. *Segments of Southern Thought.* Athens: University of Georgia Press, 1938.

Parks, Melvin. *Musicals of the 1930s.* New York: Museum of the City of New York, 1966.

The Parks and Property Interests of the City of Chicago. Chicago: Western News, 1869.

Parmelee, Maurice. *Bolshevism, Fascism, and the Liberal Democratic State.* New York: John Wiley & Sons, 1934.

Parmer, Charles B. *For Gold and Glory.* New York: Carrick & Evans, 1939.

Parmet, Herbert S., and Hecht, Marie B. *Aaron Burr, Portrait of an Ambitious Man.* New York: Macmillan, 1967.

_____. *Eisenhower and the American Crusades.* New York: Macmillan, 1972.

_____. *Jack: The Struggles of John F. Kennedy.* New York: Dial, 1980.

_____. *JFK: The Presidency of John F. Kennedy.* New York: Dial, 1983.

Parminter, Geoffrey de C. *Reasonable Doubt.* London: Arthur Baker, 1938.

_____. *Roger Casement.* London: Arthur Baker, 1936.

Parquin, Denis Charles. *Souvenirs du Capitaine Parquin, 1803-1814.* Paris: Boussod-Valadon, 1892.

Parrillo, Ornella, and Nese, Marco. *Parola d'Ordine. Roma Uno: Cronaca di un Rapimento*. Milan, Italy: Rizzoli, 1976.

Parrinder, Geoffrey. *Witchcraft: European and African*. Baltimore: Penguin Books, 1958.

Parrington, Vernon Louis. *The Colonial Mind 1620-1800*. New York: Harcourt, Brace, 1927.

_____. *Main Currents in American Thought*. 3 vols. New York: Harcourt, Brace, 1927-1930.

Parrish, J.M., and Crossland, J.R. *The Fifty Most Amazing Crimes of the Last Hundred Years*. London: Odhams, 1936.

Parris, John. *Most of My Murders*. London: Frederick Muller, 1960.

Parrish, Joe. *Coffins, Cactus and Cowboys: The Exciting Story of El Paso, 1536 to Present*. El Paso, Texas: Superior, 1964.

Parrish, Lydia. *Slave Songs of Georgia Sea Islands*. New York: Creative Age Press, 1942.

Parrish, Randall. *The Great Plains: The Romance of Western American Exploration, Warfare and Settlement, 1527-1870*. Chicago: A.C. McClurg, 1907.

Parrish, William E. *David Rice Atchison of Missouri: Border Politician*. Columbia: University of Missouri Press, 1961.

_____. *Turbulent Partnership: Missouri and the Union, 1861-1865*. Columbia: University of Missouri Press, 1963.

Parrot, Cecil. *The Tightrope*. London: Faber & Faber, 1975.

Parry, Albert. *Terrorism: From Robespierre to Arafat*. New York: The Vanguard Press, 1976.

Parry, Sir Edward Abbott. *The Drama of the Law*. New York: Charles Scribner's Sons, 1924.

Parry, John Horace, and Sherlock, P.M. *A Short History of the West Indies*. New York: St. Martin's Press, 1956.

_____. *Trade and Dominion*. London: Weidenfeld & Nicolson, 1971.

Parry, Dr. Leonard. *Some Famous Medical Trials*. Perkus, Cathy (ed.). *Cointelpro: The FBI's Secret War on Political* London: Churchill, 1927.

Parson, John E. *The Peacemaker and Its Rivals: An Account of the Single Action Colt*. New York: William Morrow, 1950.

Parson, Mabel. *A Courier of New Mexico*. n.p., n.d.

Parsons, Alice Beal. *The Trial of Helen McLeod*. New York: Funk & Wagnalls, 1938.

Parsons, Chuck. *The Capture of John Wesley Hardin*. College Station, Texas: Young West, n.d.

Parsons, George Frederick. *Life and Adventures of James W. Marshall*. Sacramento, Calif.: J.W. Marshall & W. Burke, 1870.

Parsons, George W. *The Private Journal of George Whitwell Parsons*. Phoenix: Arizona Statewide Archival and Records Project, 1939.

Parsons, John E. *The Peacemaker and Its Rivals*. New York: William Morrow, 1950.

Parsons, Louella A. *The Gay Illiterate*. New York: Doubleday, Doran, 1944.

Parsons, Lucy E. *Life of Albert R. Parsons, with Brief History of the Labor Movement in America*. Chicago: Published by Author, 1889.

Parsons, Philip Archibald. *Crime and the Criminal*. New York: Alfred A. Knopf, 1926.

Parsons, Talcott. *On Institutions and Social Evolution*. Chicago: University of Chicago Press, 1982.

_____, and Shils, Edward A. *Toward a General Theory of Action*. Cambridge, Mass.: Harvard University Press, 1951.

_____, Bales, Robert F., and Shils, Edward A. *Working Papers in the Theory of Action*. Glencoe, Ill.: The Free Press, 1953.

Partisan Review. *America and the Intellectuals: A Symposium*. New York: Partisan Review, 1953.

Parton, James. *The Life and Times of Aaron Burr*. New York: Mason Brothers, 1858.

_____. *The Life of Andrew Jackson*. 3 vols. New York: Mason Brothers, 1861.

_____. *The Life of Horace Greeley*. New York: Mason Brothers, 1855.

Parton, Margaret. *Journey Through a Lighted Room*. New York: Viking Press, 1973.

Partridge, Bellamy, and Bettmann, Otto. *As We Were. Family Life in America 1850-1900*. New York: Whittlesey House, 1946.

_____. *Country Lawyer*. New York: McGraw-Hill, 1939.

_____. *Sir Billy Howe*. New York: Longmans, Green, 1932.

Partridge, Burgo. *A History of Orgies*. New York: Avon, 1958.

_____. *Memoirs of an Assassin, Confessions of a Stern Gang Killer*. New York: Thomas Yoseloff, 1959.

Partridge, Eric. *A Dictionary of the Underworld, British and American*. London: Routledge & Kegan Paul, 1949.

_____. *Here, There and Everywhere*. London: Routledge & Kegan Paul, 1950.

_____. *Slang Today and Yesterday*. New York: Macmillan, 1950.

Partridge, Ralph. *Broadmoor: A History of Criminal Lunacy and its Problems*. London: Chatto & Windus, 1953.

Pascal, Harold. *The Marijuana Maze*. Canfield, Ohio: Alba House Communications, 1976.

Pascal, Pierre. *Mussolini alla vigilia della sua morte e l'Europa*. Rome: L'Arnia, 1948.

Paschal, Joel F. *Mr. Justice Sutherland*. Princeton, N.J.: Princeton University Press, 1951.

Pasley, Fred D. *Al Capone: The Biography of A Self-Made Man*. New York: Ives Washburn, 1930.

_____. *Muscling In*. New York: Ives Washburn, 1931.

Passant, Ernest J. *A Short History of Germany 1815-1945*. New York: Columbia University Press, 1962.

Passy, Colonel. *Deuxième bureau--Londres*. Monte Carlo, Monaco: Solar, 1947.

Pasternack, S.A. (ed.). *Violence and Victims*. New York: Spectrum, 1975.

Pastor, Ludwig. *The History of the Popes*. London: Routledge & Kegan Paul, 1950.

_____. *La Storia dei Papi*. Rome: Desclee, 1912.

Pasvolsky, Leo. *Agricultural Russia on the Eve of the Revolution*. London: George Routledge & Sons, 1930.

_____. *Russia in the Far East*. New York: Macmillan, 1922.

Patai, Raphael. *Israel Between East and West*. Philadelphia: Jewish Publication Society, 1953.

_____. *Sex and Family in the Bible and the Middle East*. New York: Doubleday, 1959.

Patch, Joseph Dorst. *Reminiscences of Fort Huachuca, Arizona*. n.p., n.d.

Pate, H. Clay. *John Brown as Viewed by H. Clay Pate*. New York: Published by Author, 1959.

Pate, Tony, et al. *Police Response Time: Its Determinants and Effects*. Washington, D.C.: The Police Foundation, 1976.

_____, and Bowers, Robert A., and Parks, Ron. *Three Approaches to Criminal Apprehension in Kansas City: An Evaluation Report*. Washington, D.C.: The Police Foundation, 1976.

Patel, G.I. *Life and Times of Vithalbhai*. Bombay: Hind Katabs, 1947.

Patel, Manibehn. *Letters to Sardar Patel*. Ahmedabad: Navajivan, 1950.

Paterson, A. *Legal Aid as a Social Service*. London: Cobden Trust, 1970.

Paterson, Thomas G. (ed.). *The Origins of the Cold War*. Lexington, Mass.: Heath, 1974.

Patmore, Derek. *Balkan Correspondent*. New York: Harper & Brothers, 1941.

_____. *Invitation to Roumania*. London: Macmillan, 1939.

Paton, Alan. *Too Late the Phalarope*. New York: Charles Scribner's Sons, 1953.

Patrick, Ted. *Let Our Children Go!* New York: E.P. Dutton, 1976.

Pattenden, Rosemary. *The Judge, Discretion, and the Criminal Trial*. Oxford, Eng.: Clarendon Press, 1982.

Patterns of Global Terrorism: 1983. Washington, D.C.: U.S. Dept. of State, 1984.

Patterson, C.L. *Sensational Texas Manhunt.* San Antonio, Texas: Sid Murray & Son, 1939.

Patterson, G.R. *Coercive Family Process.* Eugene, Ore.: Castalia, 1982.

Patterson, Haywood, and Conrad, Earl. *Scottsboro Boy.* Garden City, N.Y. Doubleday, 1950.

Patterson, James T. *Congressional Conservation and the New Deal.* Lexington: University of Kentucky Press, 1967.

Patterson, Jerry E. *The City of New York.* New York: Harry N. Abrams, 1978.

Patterson, Joseph Medill. *A Little Brother of the Rich.* Chicago: Reilly & Britton, 1908.

_____. *A Notebook of a Neutral.* New York: Duffield, 1915.

Patterson, Robert T. *The Great Boom and Panic, 1921-1929.* Chicago: Henry Regnery, 1965.

Patti, Ercole. *Roman Chronicle.* London: Chatto & Windus, 1965.

Patton, Clifford W. *The Battle for Municipal Reform: Mobilization and Attack, 1875-1900.* Washington, D.C.: American Council on Public Affairs, 1940.

Patton, Fred J. *History of Fort Smith, Arkansas.* Ft. Smith, Ark.: Chamber of Commerce, n.d.

Paul, Henry N. *The Royal Play of Macbeth.* New York: Macmillan, 1950.

Paul, Rodman W. *California Gold: The Beginning of Mining in the Far West.* Cambridge, Mass.: Harvard University Press, 1947.

_____. *Mining Frontiers of the Far West 1848-1880.* New York: Holt, Rinehart & Winston, 1963.

Paul-Dubois, L. *The Irish Struggle and Its Results.* trans. T.P. Gill. London: Longmans, Green, 1934.

Paulsen, Monrad G., and Whitebread, Charles H. *Juvenile Law and Procedure.* Reno, Nev.: National Council of Juvenile Court Judges, 1974.

Paul the Deacon. *History of the Lombards.* trans. William Dudley Folke. Philadelphia: University of Pennsylvania Press, 1974.

Pauwels, Louis and Bergier, Jacques. *The Morning of the Magicians.* New York: Stein and Day, 1964.

Pavalko, Ronald M. *The Sociology of Occupations and Professions.* Itasca, Ill.: F.E. Peacock, 1971.

Pavlovsky, George. *Agricultural Russia on the Eve of the Revolution.* London: George Routledge & Sons, 1930.

Paxson, Frederick L. *The Civil War.* New York: Henry Holt, 1911.

_____. *History of the American Frontier, 1763-1793.* Boston: Houghton Mifflin, 1924.

_____. *The Last American Frontier.* New York: Macmillan, 1910.

Paxton, W.M. *Annals of Platte County.* Kansas City, Mo.: Hudson Kimberley, 1897.

Payne, Albert Bigelow. *Captain Bill McDonald, Texas Ranger.* New York: Little & Ives, 1909.

Payne, Doris Palmer. *Captain Jack, Modoc Renegade.* Portland, Ore.: Binford & Mort, 1938.

Payne, Edwin F., and Harper, Henry H. *The Charity of Charles Dickens.* Boston: Bibliophile Society, 1929.

Payne, Howard C. *The Police State of Louis Napoleon Bonaparte, 1851-1860.* Seattle: University of Washington Press, 1966.

Payne, Les, and Findley, Tim. *The Life and Death of the SLA.* New York: Ballantine Books, 1976.

Payne, Ransom. *The Dalton Brothers and Their Astounding Career of Crime.* Chicago: Laird & Lee, 1892.

Payne, Robert. *Chungking Diary.* London: William Heinemann, 1945.

_____. *The Holy Sword.* London: Robert Hale, 1961.

_____. *The Life and Death of Adolf Hitler.* New York: Frederick A. Praeger, 1973.

_____. *The Life and Death of Lenin.* New York: Simon & Schuster, 1964.

_____. *Portrait of a Revolutionary: Mao Tse-tung.* New York: Abelard-Schuman, 1961.

Payne, William. *Deep Cover: An FBI Agent Infiltrates the Radical Underground.* New York: Newsweek Books, 1979.

Paz, Ireneo. *Porfirio Diaz.* 2 vols. Mexico City, Mex.: Imprenta y Encuadernación de Ireneo Paz, 1911.

Peabody, James E., and Hunt, Arthur E. *Biology & Human Welfare.* New York: Macmillan, 1924.

Peabody, Richard R. *The Common Sense of Drinking.* Boston: Little, Brown, 1931.

Peabody, Robert L. *Organizational Authority.* New York: Atherton Press, 1964.

Peak, Howard W. *A Ranger of Commerce; or, 52 Years on the Road.* San Antonio, Texas: Naylor, 1929.

Peake, Ora Brooks. *The Colorado Range Cattle Industry.* Glendale, Calif.: Arthur H. Clark, 1937.

Pearce, Charles. *Unsolved Murder Mysteries.* New York: Stokes, 1924.

Pearl Bryan, or A Fatal Ending. Cincinnati, Ohio: Barclay, n.d.

Pearl, Cyril. *The Girl With the Swansdown Seat.* Indianapolis, Ind.: Bobbs, 1955.

Pearl, Jack. *The Dangerous Assassins.* Derby, Conn.: Monarch Books, 1964.

Pearlman, Maurice. *Mufti of Jerusalem.* London: Victor Gollancz, 1947.

Pearlman, Moshe. *Ben-Gurion Looks Back.* New York: Simon & Schuster, 1965.

Pearsall, Ronald. *The Worm in the Bud: The World of Victorian Sexuality.* New York: Macmillan, 1969.

Pearson, Drew. *Diaries 1949-1959.* New York: Holt, Rinehart, Winston, 1974.

_____, and Allen, Robert S. *The Nine Old Men.* Garden City, N.Y.: Doubleday, Doran, 1936.

_____, and Anderson, Jack. *The Case Against Congress.* New York: Simon & Schuster, 1968.

Pearson, Edmund. *Five Murders.* Garden City, N.Y.: Doubleday, Doran, 1928.

_____. *Instigation of the Devil.* New York: Charles Scribner's Sons, 1930.

_____. *Masterpieces at Murder.* Boston: Little, Brown, 1924.

_____. *More Studies in Murder.* New York: Smith & Haas, 1936.

_____. *Murder at Smutty Nose and Other Murders.* Garden City, N.Y.: Doubleday, 1927.

_____. *Studies in Murder.* New York: Macmillan, 1924.

_____ (ed.). *The Trial of Lizzie Borden.* New York: Doubleday, Doran, 1937.

Pearson, Geoffrey. *The Deviant Imagination.* London: Macmillan, 1975.

_____. *The New Heroin Users.* Oxford, Eng.: Basil Blackwell, 1987.

Pearson, H. *The Life of Oscar Wilde.* New York: Grosset, 1954.

Pearson, H. *The Life of John A. Andrew, Governor of Massachusetts, 1861-65.* Boston: Houghton Mifflin, 1904.

Pearson, Jim Berry. *The Maxwell Land Grant.* Norman: University of Oklahoma Press, 1961.

Pearson, John. *The Profession of Violence.* London: Weidenfeld & Nicolson, 1972.

Pearson, Michael. *Age of Consent.* London: David & Charles, 1972.

_____. *Five Pound Virgins.* New York: Saturday Review Press, 1972.

_____. *The Millionaire Mentality.* London: Secker & Warburg, 1961.

Pease, E.R. *The History of the Fabian Society.* New York: E.P. Dutton, 1925.

Pease, Margaret. *Jean Jaurès, Socialist and Humanitarian.* New York: Huebsch, 1917.

Pease, Theodore Calvin (ed.). *The Diary of Orville Hickman.* Springfield: Illinois State Historical Library, 1925.

Peattie, Donald Culross (ed.). *Audubon's America.* Boston: Houghton Mifflin, 1940.

Peattie, Mark R. *Ishiwara Kanji and Japan's Confrontation with the West.* Princeton, N.J.: Princeton University Press, 1975.

Peattie, Roderick (ed.). *The Black Hills.* New York: Vanguard Press, 1952.

_____. *The Inverted Mountain; Canyons of the West.* New York: Vanguard Press, 1948.

Peavey, John R. *From the Thorny Hills of Duval to the Sleepy Rio Grande.* Brownsville, Texas: Springman-King, 1963.

Peavy, Charles D. *Charles A. Siringo, a Texas Picaro.* Austin, Texas: Steck-Vaughn, 1967.

Pechel, Rudolf. *Deutscher Widerstand.* Zurich, Switz.: Eugen Rentsch Verlag, Erlenbach, 1947.

Pechman, Joseph A., and Okner, Benjamin A. *Who Bears the Tax Burden?* Washington, D.C.: The Brookings Institution, 1974.

Peck, Anne Merriman. *Southwest Roundup.* New York: Dodd, Mead, 1950.

Peck, Graham. *Two Kinds of Time.* Boston: Houghton Mifflin, 1950.

Peck, Harry Thurston. *Twenty Years of the Republic 1885-1905.* New York: Dodd, Mead, 1906.

Peck, Joseph H. *What Next, Doctor Peck?* Englewood Cliffs, N.J.: Prentice-Hall, 1959.

Peckham, H.H. *Pontiac and the Indian Uprising.* Princeton, N.J.: Princeton University Press, 1947.

Pecora, Ferdinand. *Wall Street Under Oath.* New York: Simon & Schuster, 1939.

Peddie, James. *All About Monte Carlo.* London: Comet, 1893.

Pedrick, W.E. *New Orleans As It Was.* Cleveland: W.W. Williams, 1885.

Peel, Mrs. C.S. *How We Lived Then, 1914-1918.* London: John Lane, 1929.

Peel, Dorothy. *Life's Enchanted Cup.* London: John Lane, 1933.

Peel, Roy V. *The Political Clubs of New York.* New York: G.P. Putnam's Sons, 1935.

Peers, William R., and Brelis, Dean. *Behind the Burma Road.* Boston: Little, Brown, 1963.

Peffer, Nathaniel. *The Far East.* Ann Arbor: University of Michigan Press, 1958.

Peggs, James. *Capital Punishment: The Importance of its Abolition.* London: n.p., 1839.

Peixotto, Edgar D. *Report on the Trial of William Henry Theodore Durrant.* Detroit, Mich.: Collector, 1899.

Peixotto, Jessica B. *The French Revolution and Modern French Socialism.* New York: Thomas Y. Crowell, 1901.

Pekelis, Alexander H. *Law and Social Action.* Ithaca, N.Y.: Cornell University Press, 1950.

Pekkanen, John. *Victims: An Account of Rape.* New York: Popular Library, 1976.

Pekrovskii, Mikhail Nikolaevich. *Brief History of Russia.* trans. D.S. Mirsky. London: M. Lawrence, 1933.

Pelcovits, N.A. *Old China Hands and the Foreign Office.* New York: King's Crown Press, 1948.

Pelfrey, William V. *The Evolution of Criminology.* Cincinnati, Ohio: Anderson, 1980.

Pelham, Camden. *The Chronicles of Crime, or the New Newgate Calendar.* 2 vols. London: Reeves and Turner, 1886.

Pelissier, Roger (ed.). *The Awakening of China, 1783-1949.* New York: Putnam, 1967.

Pell, Eve (ed.). *Maximum Security: Letters from Prison.* New York: E.P. Dutton, 1972.

Pellew, J. *The Home Office 1848-1914: from Clerks to Bureaucrats.* London: Heinemann Educational Books, 1982.

Pellizzi, C. *Italy.* London: Longmans, 1939.

Pells, Richard H. *Radical Visions and American Dreams.* New York: Harper & Row, 1973.

Peltason, Jack Walter. *Fifty-Eight Lonely Men.* Harcourt, Brace & World, 1961.

Pelzer, Louis. *The Cattlemen's Frontier.* Glendale, Calif.: Arthur H. Clark, 1936.

Pember, A. *Ivan the Terrible.* London: A.P. Marsden, 1895.

Pember, Ron, and de Marne, Denis. *Jack the Ripper: A Musical Play.* London: French, 1976.

Pemberton, John C. *Pemberton: Defender of Vicksburg.* Chapel Hill: University of North Carolina Press, 1942.

The Penal Code of the RSFSR. London: H.M. Stationery Office, 1925.

Penal Reform in England: Introductory Essays on Some Aspects of English Criminal Policy. London: Macmillan, 1946.

Pence, Mary Lou, and Homsher, Lola M. *The Ghost Towns of Wyoming.* New York: Hastings House, 1956.

Pendel, Tom. *Thirty-Six Years in the White House.* Washington, D.C.: Neale, 1900.

Penfield, Thomas. *Dig Here!* San Antonio, Texas: Naylor, 1962.

_____. *Western Sheriffs and Marshals.* New York: Grossett & Dunlap, 1955.

Penn, I. Garland. *The Afro-American Press and Its Editors.* Springfield, Mass.: Willey, 1891.

Penn, James. *Remarks on Thelyphthora.* London: Published by Author, 1781.

Pennsylvania Crime Commission. *A Decade of Organized Crime: 1980 Report.* St. Davids, Pa.: Pennsylvania Crime Commission, 1980.

_____. *Report on Organized Crime.* Harrisburg, Pa.: Commonwealth of Pennsylvania, 1970.

_____. *Report on Police Corruption and the Quality of Law Enforcement in Philadelphia.* St. Davids, Pa.: Pennsylvania Crime Commission, 1974.

Pennsylvania. Joint Legislative Committee on Capital Punishment. *Report.* Harrisburg: Commonwealth on Pennsylvania, 1961.

Pennypacker, Samuel. *The Autobiography of a Pennsylvanian.* Philadelphia: John C. Winston, 1918.

Penrose, Barrie, and Courtior, Roger. *The Pencourt File.* New York: Harper & Row, 1978.

Penrose, Charles Bingham. *The Johnson County War.* Laramie: University of Wyoming, 1939.

_____. *The Rustler Business.* Douglas, Wyo.: Douglas Budget, 1959.

Penrose, Matt R. *Pots O' Golds.* Reno, Nev.: A. Carlisle, 1935.

Penry, J. *Looking at Faces and Remembering Them.* London: Elek Books, 1971.

Pensa, Henri. *Sorcellerie et religion.* Paris: Felix Alcon, 1933.

Penseè editors. *Velikovsky Reconsidered.* Garden City, N.Y.: Doubleday, 1976.

The People Against Edward H. Ruloff. New York: Drossy, 1872.

People Against Rowell. New York: George S. Diossy, Law Publishers, n.d.

The People vs. Elijah Gray & James Gray. New York: n.p., n.d.

Pepinsky, Harold. *Crime and Conflict.* New York: Academic Press, 1976.

_____. *Crime Control Strategies.* New York: Oxford, 1980.

Pepper, Curtis Bill. *Kidnapped! 17 Days of Terror.* New York: Harmony Books, 1978.

Percival, A.E. *The War in Malaya.* London: Eyre and Spottiswoode, 1949.

Percy, Adrian. *Twice Outlawed; a Personal History of Ed and Lon Maxwell, Alias the Williams Brothers.* Chicago: W.B. Conkey, 1884.

Percy, William Alexander. *Lanterns on the Levee.* New York: Alfred A. Knopf, 1941.

Peres, Shimon. *David's Sling.* New York: Random House, 1970.

Peretz, Don. *Israel and the Palestine Arabs.* Washington, D.C.: Middle East Institute, 1958.

_____. *The Middle East Today.* New York: Holt, Rinehart & Winston, 1963.

Perey, Lucien, and Maugras, Gaston. *Vie intime de Voltaire aux Délices et à Ferney, 1754-1778.* Paris: C. Lévy, 1885.

Perkin, Harold J. *The Origins of Modern English Society, 1780-1880.* London: Routledge & Kegan Paul, 1969.

Perkins, Bradford. *Castlereagh and Adams: England and the United States, 1812-1823.* Berkeley: University of California Press, 1964.

_____. *The First Rapprochement: England and the United States 1795-1805*. Philadelphia: University of Pennsylvania Press, 1955.

_____. *Prologue to War: England and the United States, 1805-1812*. Berkeley: University of California Press, 1961.

Perkins, Dexter. *A History of the Monroe Doctrine*. Boston: Little, Brown, 1955.

Perkins, Frances. *The People at Work*. New York: John Day, 1934.

_____. *The Roosevelt I Knew*. New York: Viking Press, 1946.

Perkins, Jacob R. *Trails, Rails and War: The Life of General Grenville M. Dodge*. Indianapolis, Ind.: Bobbs-Merrill, 1929.

Perkins, Whitney T. *Denial of Empire: The United States and Its Dependencies*. Leyden, Neth.: A.W. Sythoff, 1962.

Perkins, William. *A Discourse of the Damned Art of Witchcraft*. Cambridge, Eng.: Thomas Pickering, 1608.

Perkus, Cathy (ed.). *Cointelpro: The FBI's Secret War on Political Freedom*. New York: Monad, 1975.

Perlamutter, Amos. *The Military and Politics of Modern Times*. New Haven, Conn.: Yale University Press, 1977.

Perles, Anthony. *The People's Railway: The History of the Municipal Railway of San Francisco*. Glendale, Calif.: Interurban Press, 1981.

Perley, Sidney. *The History of Salem, Massachusetts*. Salem, Mass.: Published by Author, 1924.

Perlman, Mark. *The Machinists: A New Study in American Trade Unionism*. Cambridge, Mass.: Harvard University Press, 1961.

Perlman, Robert, and Jones, David. *Neighborhood Service Centers*. Washington, D.C.: U.S. Government Printing Office, 1967.

Perlman, Selig, and Taft, Philip. *History of Labor in the United States 1896-1932*. New York: Macmillan, 1935.

Perloff, Harvey S., and Wingo, Lowdon, Jr. (eds.). *Issues in Urban Economics*. Baltimore: The Johns Hopkins University Press, 1968.

Perlstein, Gary R., and Phelps, Thomas R. (eds.). *Alternatives to Prison: Community-Based Corrections*. Pacific Palisades, Calif.: Goodyear, 1975.

Pernikoff, Alexandre. *Bushido: The Anatomy of Terror*. New York: Liveright, 1943.

Pernoud, Régine. *Joan of Arc*. trans. Edward Hyams. New York: Stein & Day, 1966.

Perone Capano, Renato. *La resistenza in Roma*. 2 vols. Naples, Italy: Gaetano Macchiaroli, 1963.

Perowne, Stewart. *Death of the Roman Republic*. Garden City, N.Y.: Doubleday, 1968.

Perrett, Geoffrey. *America in the Twenties*. New York: Simon & Schuster, 1982.

_____. *Days of Sadness, Years of Triumph*. New York: Coward, McCann, 1973.

_____. *Dream of Greatness*. New York: Coward, McCann, 1979.

Perreux, Gabriel. *Les Conspirations de Louis Napoleon Bonaparte*. Paris: Hachette, 1926.

Perrigo, Lynn I. *Our Spanish Southwest: Its Peoples and Cultures*. New York: Holt, Rinehart, Winston, 1971.

Perrin, Noel. *Giving Up the Gun*. Boston: Shambhala, 1979.

Perrow, Charles. *Complex Organizations*. Glenview, Ill.: Scott, Foresman, 1979.

Perroy, Edouard. *The Hundred Years War*. Bloomington: Indiana University Press, 1962.

Perruchon, Jules (ed. and trans.) *Vie de Lalibala, roi d'Ethiopie*. Paris: Ernest Leroux, 1892.

Perry, Bliss. *The Heart of Emerson's Journal*. New York: Houghton Mifflin, 1926.

Perry, George Sessions. *The Story of Texas A&M*. New York: McGraw-Hill Book, 1951.

_____. *Texas, a World in Itself*. New York: McGraw-Hill Book, 1942.

Perry, J., and Chabert, J. *L'Affaire Petiot*. Paris: Gallimard, 1957.

Perry, Lewis. *Radical Abolitionism: Anarchy and the Government of God in Antislavery Thought*. Ithaca, N.Y.: Cornell University Press, 1973.

Perry, Louis B., and Perry, Richard S. *A History of the Los Angeles Labor Movement, 1911-1941*. Berkeley: University of California Press, 1963.

Perry, Martha Derby (ed.). *Letters from a Surgeon of the Civil War*. Boston: Little, Brown, 1906.

Perry, Matthew Calbraith. *The Japan Expedition, 1852-1854; The Personal Journal of Commodore Matthew C. Perry*. Washington, D.C.: Smithsonian Institute Press, 1968.

Perry, Thomas Sergeant (ed.). *The Life and Letters of Francis Lieber*. Boston: James R. Osgood, 1882.

Pershing, Gen. John J. *My Experiences in the World War*. 2 vols. New York: Frederick A. Stokes, 1931.

Persons, Stow. *The Decline of Gentility*. New York: Columbia University Press, 1973.

Perticone, Giacomo. *La Repubblica di Salò*. Rome: Leonardo, 1947.

Peskett, S. John. *Grim, Gruesome, and Grisly*. London: Leslie Frewin, 1974.

Pessen, Edward. *Most Uncommon Jacksonians: The Radical Leaders of the Early Labor Movement*. Albany, N.Y.: State University of New York Press, 1968.

Petacci, Clara. *Il mio diario*. Milan, Italy: Editori Associati, 1946.

Petacco, Arrigo. *Joe Petrosino*. New York: Macmillan, 1974.

Peter II, King of Yugoslavia. *A King's Heritage*. New York: G.P. Putnam's Sons, 1954.

Peter, Laurence J. (ed.). *Peter's Quotations*. New York: William Morrow, 1977.

Peters, Charles, and Branch, Taylor. *Blowing the Whistle*. New York: Frederick A. Praeger, 1972.

Peters, Hugh. *Good Work for a Good Magistrate*. London: W. Du Gard, 1651.

Petersdorf, Egon von. *Daemonologie*. Munich, Ger.: Verlag für Kultur und Geschichte, 1956.

Petersen, David M., and Truzzi, Marcello (eds.). *Criminal Life: Views from the Inside*. Englewood Cliffs, N.J.: Prentice-Hall, 1972.

Petersen, William. *Japanese Americans*. New York: Random House, 1971.

Petersen, William J. *Steamboating on the Upper Mississippi*. Iowa City: Iowa State Historical Society, 1937.

Petersilia, Joan, Greenwood, Peter W., Lavin, Marvin. *Criminal Careers of Habitual Felons*. Santa Monica, Calif.: The Rand Corporation, 1977.

_____, et al. *Granting Felons Probation*. Santa Monica, Calif.: The Rand Corporation, 1985.

_____. *Racial Disparities in the Criminal Justice System*. Santa Monica, Calif.: The Rand Corporation, 1983.

Peterson, Arnold. *Daniel DeLeon*. New York: New York Labor News, 1941.

Peterson, E. *Rhode Island*. New York: Taylor, 1853.

Peterson, Harold L. *A History of Firearms*. New York: Charles Scribner's Sons, 1961.

Peterson, Horace Cornelius, and Fite, Gilbert C. *Opponents of War, 1917-1918*. Madison: University of Wisconsin Press, 1957.

Peterson, J. *Early Conceptions and Tests of Intelligence*. Yonkers, N.Y.: World Book, 1925.

Peterson, Mark A. *Doing Crime: A Survey of California Prison Inmates*. Santa Monica, Calif.: The Rand Corporation, 1980.

_____, and Braiker, Harriet B. *Who Commits Crimes*. Cambridge: Oelgeschlager, Gunn & Hain, 1981.

Peterson, P.D. *Through the Black Hills and Bad Lands of South Dakota*. Pierre, S.D.: Fred Orlander, 1929.

Peterson, T.B. *The Trial of the Alleged Assassins and Conspirators*. Philadelphia: T.B. Peterson & Brothers, 1865.

Peterson, V.W. *Crime Commissions in the United States*. Chicago: Chicago Crime Commission, 1945.

Peterson, Virgil. *Barbarians in Our Midst: A History of Chicago Crime and Politics.* Boston: Little, Brown, 1952.

_____. *The Mob: 200 Years of Organized Crime in New York.* Ottawa, Ill.: Green Hill, 1983.

_____. *A Report on Chicago Crime for 1956.* Chicago: Chicago Crime Commission, 1957.

_____. *A Report on Chicago Crime for 1958.* Chicago: Chicago Crime Commission, 1959.

_____. *A Report on Chicago Crime for 1961.* Chicago: Chicago Crime Commission, 1962.

_____. *A Report on Chicago Crime for 1963.* Chicago: Chicago Crime Commission, 1964.

_____. *A Report on Chicago Crime for 1965.* Chicago: Chicago Crime Commission, 1966.

_____. *A Report on Chicago Crime for 1967.* Chicago: Chicago Crime Commission, 1968.

Petherick, Maurice. *Restoration Rogues.* London: Hollis Carter, 1951.

Petitot, M. *Collection Complète des Mémoires Rélatifs à l'Histoire de France.* Paris: Foucault, 1825.

Petri, Glen. *A Singular Iniquity-the Campaigns of Josephine Butler.* New York: Viking Press, 1971.

Petrie, Sir Charles. *Lords of the Inland Sea.* London: Lovat Dickson, 1937.

_____. *Mussolini.* London: Holme Press, 1931.

Petrie, W. M. Flinders. *Social Life in Ancient Egypt.* New York: Houghton Mifflin, 1923.

Petrocelli, William. *Low Profile, How to Avoid the Privacy Invaders.* New York: McGraw-Hill, 1982.

Petronius. *New York Unexpurgated.* New York: Matrix House, 1966.

_____. *The Satyricon.* trans. W.C. Firebaugh. New York: Washington Square Press, 1966.

Petrov, V.M., and E. *Empire of Fear.* New York: Frederick A. Praeger, 1956.

Petrov, Vladimir. *My Retreat from Russia.* New Haven, Conn.: Yale University Press, 1950.

Petrovich, Michael Boro. *The Emergence of Russian Panslavism, 1856-1870.* New York: Columbia University Press, 1956.

Pettigrew, R.F. *The Course of Empire: An Official Record.* New York: Boni & Liveright, 1920.

Petty, George Eugene. *The Narcotic Drug Diseases and Allied Ailments.* Philadelphia: F.A. Davis, 1913.

Petuchoqski, Jacob J. *Zion Reconsidered.* New York: Twayne, 1967.

Peucer, Kaspar. *Commentarius de Praecipuis Divinationum Generibus.* Wittenberg, Ger.: Johannes Crato, 1953.

Peyton, George. *How to Detect Counterfeit Bank Notes.* New York: Published by Author, 1856.

Peyton, Green. *San Antonio, City in the Sun.* New York: McGraw-Hill Book, 1946.

Peyton, John Lewis. *Over the Alleghanies and Across the Prairies.* London: Simkin, Marshall, 1869.

Pfeffer, Leo. *Church, State, and Freedom.* Boston: Beacon Press, 1953.

_____. *God, Caesar, and the Constitution.* Boston: Beacon Press, 1975.

_____. *The Liberties of an American: The Supreme Court Speaks.* Boston: Beacon Press, 1963.

_____. *Religious Freedom.* Skokie, Ill.: National Textbook, 1977.

_____. *This Honorable Court.* Boston: Beacon Press, 1965.

Pfister, Christian. *Nicolas Remy et la sorcellerie en Lorraine á la fin du XVI siècle.* Paris: n.p., 1907.

Pfister, Oscar. *Calvins Eingreifen in die Hexenprozesse 1545.* Zurich, Switz.: Artemis, 1947.

Phares, Ross. *Bible in Pocket, Gun in Hand.* Garden City, N.Y.: Doubleday, 1964.

_____. *Reverend Devil, A Biography of John A. Murrell.* New Orleans, La.: Pelican, 1941.

_____. *Texas Tradition.* New York: Henry Holt, 1954.

Phelan, James. *History of Tennessee.* Boston: Houghton Mifflin, 1888.

Phelan, John (ed.). *Communications Control.* New York: Sheed & Ward, 1969.

Phelps, Alonzo. *Contemporary Biography of California's Representative Men.* 2 vols. San Francisco: A.L. Bancroft, 1881-1882.

Phelps, H.P. *Players of a Century.* Albany, N.Y.: J. McDonough, 1880.

Phelps, Robert H., and Hamilton, E. Douglass. *Libel: A Guide to Rights, Risks, Responsibilities.* New York: Collier-Macmillan, 1966.

Philadelphia Society for Alleviating the Miseries of Public Prisons. *Extracts and Remarks on the Subjects of Punishment and Reformation of Criminals.* Philadelphia: Z. Poulson, 1790.

Philbrick, Herbert. *I Led Three Lives: Citizen, "Communist," Counterspy.* New York: McGraw-Hill, 1952.

Philby, H. St. John. *Arabian Jubilee.* London: Robert Hale, 1952.

Philby, Kim. *My Silent War.* New York: Grove, 1968.

Phillips, Alan. *The Living Legend.* Boston: Little, Brown, 1957.

Phillips, C. Coffin. *Portsmouth Plaza.* San Francisco: Nash, 1932.

Phillips, Cabell. *Dateline Washington.* Garden City, N.Y.: Doubleday, 1949.

_____. *From the Crash to the Blitz 1929-1939: The New York Times Chronicle of American Life.* New York: Macmillan, 1969.

_____. *The 1940's: Decade of Triumph and Trouble.* New York: Macmillan, 1975.

Phillips, Charles. *Vacation Thoughts on Capital Punishment.* London: W.& F.G. Cash, 1856.

Phillips, Conrad. *Murderer's Moon.* London: Arthur Baker, 1956.

Phillips, David. *Skyjack: The Story of Air Piracy.* London: Harrap, 1973.

Phillips, Harlan B. *Felix Frankfurter Reminisces.* New York: Reynal, 1960.

Phillips, Henry. *Historical Sketches of the Paper Currency of the American Colonies, Prior to the Adoption of the Federal Constitution.* Roxbury, Mass.: W. Elliot Woodward, 1865.

Phillips, James Duncan. *Salem in the Seventeenth Century.* Boston: Houghton Mifflin, 1933.

Phillips, Mark. *Francesco Guicciardini: The Historian's Craft.* Toronto, Ontario, Can.: University of Toronto Press, 1977.

Phillips, Michael James. *History of Santa Barbara County, California.* Chicago: S.J. Clarke, 1927.

Phillips, O. Hood. *Constitutional and Administrative Law.* London: Sweet & Maxwell, 1967.

Phillips, Paul Chrisler. *The Fur Trade.* 2 vols. Norman: University of Oklahoma Press, 1961.

Phillips, Sir Percival. *The Red Dragon and the Black Shirts.* London: Daily Mail, 1923.

Phillips, Steven. *No Heroes, No Villains.* New York: Random House, 1977.

Phillips, Ulrich Bonnell. *American Negro Slavery.* Baton Rouge: Louisiana State University Press, 1966.

_____. *Life and Labor in the Old South.* New York: Grosset & Dunlap, 1929.

Phillips, W. Alison. *The Revolution in Ireland 1906-1923.* London: Longmans, Green, 1926.

Phillips, Wendell. *Oman a History.* New York: William Morrow, 1967.

_____. *Speeches, Lectures and Letters.* Boston: Lee & Shepard, 1892.

Phillips, William. *The Conquest of Kansas, by Missouri and Her Allies.* Boston: Phillips, Sampson, 1856.

Phillips, William. *The Short Stories of Dostoevsky.* trans. Constance Garnett. New York: Dial Press, 1946.

Phillips, William. *Ventures in Diplomacy.* Boston: Beacon Press, 1952.

Phillipson, Coleman. *Three Criminal Law Reformers: Beccaria, Bentham, Romilly.* London: J.M. Dent & Sons, 1923.

Phillipson, M. *Sociological Aspects of Crime and Delinquency.*

London: Routledge & Kegan Paul, 1971.

Phillipson, Martin. *Der Grosse Kurfürst Friedrich Wilhelm von Brandenburg.* 3 vols. Berlin: S. Cronbach, 1897-1903.

Philo. *On the Special Laws.* trans. F.H. Colson. London: William Heinemann, 1958.

Piaget, J., and Inhelder, B. *The Child's Conception of Space.* New York: W.W. Norton, 1967.

_____. *The Psychology of the Child.* New York: Basic Books, 1969.

Piatnitsky, O. *Memoirs of a Bolshevik.* New York: International, 1934.

Piatt, Donn. *Memories of the Men Who Saved the Union.* Chicago: Belford, Clarke, 1887.

Pichon, J.E. *Le complot de Sarajevo, 1914.* Paris: Bossard, 1918.

Picht, Werner. *Vom Wesen des Krieges und vom Kriegwesen der Deutschen.* Stuttgart, Ger.: Friedrich Vorwerk, 1952.

Picigallo, Philip R. *The Japanese on Trial: Allied War Crimes Operations in the East, 1945-1951.* Austin: University of Texas Press, 1979.

Picker, Dr. Henry. *Hitlers Tischgeprache im Führerhauptquartier, 1941-42.* Bonn, Ger.: Athenaum-Verlag, 1951.

Pickering, Clarence R. *The Early Days of Prohibition.* New York: Vantage Press, 1964.

Pickett, Calder M. *Ed Howe: Country Town Philosopher.* Lawrence: Unviersity Press of Kansas, 1968.

Pickett, Elbert Deets (ed.). *The Cyclopedia of Temperance, Prohibition and Public Morals.* New York: Methodist Book Concern, 1917.

Pico della Mirandola, Gianfrancesco. *Libro detto Strega o delle Illusioni del Demonio.* Bologna, Italy: Germimo de Beneditti du Bologna, 1524.

_____. *Strix, sive de Ludificatione Daemonum.* Bologna, Italy: P. Ledertz, 1612.

Pierard, Louis. *Belgian Problems Since the War.* New Haven, Conn.: Yale University Press, 1929.

Pierce, Bessie Louise. *As Others See Chicago: Impressions of Visitors, 1673-1933.* Chicago: University of Chicago Press, 1932.

_____. *A History of Chicago.* 3 vols. New York: Alfred A. Knopf, 1937.

Pierce, Edward L. *Memoir and Letters of Charles Sumner.* Boston: Roberts Brothers, 1893.

Pierce, Frank Cushman. *A Brief History of the Lower Rio Grande Valley.* Menasha, Wis.: George Banta, 1917.

Pierce, N.H., and Brown, Nugent E. *The Free State of Menard: A History of the County.* Menard, Texas: Menard News Press, 1946.

Pierce, Richard A. (ed.). *Rezanov Reconnoiters California, 1806.* San Francisco: Book Club of San Francisco, 1972.

_____. *Russian Central Asia, 1867-1917.* Berkeley: University of California Press, 1960.

Pierce, Richard D. *Records of the First Church in Salem, Massachusetts, 1629-1736.* Salem, Mass.: Essex Institute, 1974.

Pierrepont, Edward W. *Fifth Avenue to Alaska.* New York: G.P. Putnam's Sons, 1884.

Pierson, George Wilson. *Tocqueville and Beaumont in America.* New York: Oxford University Press, 1938.

Pies, Herman. *Kaspar Hauser.* Stuttgart, Ger.: Lutz, 1926.

Piggot, Gen. F.S.G. *Broken Thread: An Autobiography.* London: Gale & Polden, 1950.

Pigors, Paul, and Myers, Charles A. *Personnel Administration: A Point of View and a Method.* New York: McGraw Hill, 1973.

Pigou, A.C. *Aspects of British Economic History, 1918-25.* London: Macmillan, 1948.

Pike, Frederick B. *Chile and the United States: 1880-1962.* South Bend, Ind.: University of Notre Dame Press, 1963.

Pike, James S. *The Prostrate State.* New York: D. Appleton, 1874.

Pike, Luke Owen. *A History of Crime in England.* 2 vols. Montclair, N.J.: Patterson Smith, 1962.

Pike, Royston. *Hard Times.* New York: Frederick A. Praeger, 1966.

Pike, Ruth. *Aristocrats and Traders.* Ithaca, N.Y.: Cornell University Press, 1972.

Pilat, Oliver. *The Atom Spies.* New York: G.P. Putnam's Sons, 1952.

_____, and Rabson, Jo. *Sodom by the Sea.* Garden City, N.Y.: Garden City, 1943.

Pileggi, Nicholas. *Blye, Private Eye.* Chicago: Playboy Press, 1977.

_____. *Wiseguy, Life in a Mafia Family.* New York: Simon & Schuster, 1985.

Piliavin, I., and Gartner, R. *The Impact of Supported Work on Ex-Offenders.* New York: Manpower Demonstration Research, 1981.

Pilkington, Ian D.B. *The King's Pleasure.* London: Jarrolds, 1957.

Pilling, D., and Pringle, M.K. *Controversial Issues in Child Development.* New York: Schocken Books.

Pilot, Oliver. *Drew Pearson.* New York: Harper's Magazine Press, 1973.

Pilpel, Robert H. *Churchill in America.* New York: Harcourt Brace Jovanovich, 1976.

Pimlott, John Alfred Ralph. *Toynbee Hall: Fifty Years of Social Progress, 1884-1934.* London: Dent, 1935.

Pin, Tao Hsu. *A History of Shanghai.* Taiwan: China Book Translation, 1968.

Pinchon, Edgcumb. *Dan Sickles, Hero of Gettysburg and Yankee King of Spain.* Garden City, N.Y.: Doubleday, 1945.

_____. *Viva Villa! A Recovery of the Real Pancho Villa, Peon, Bandit, Soldier, Patriot.* New York: Harcourt, 1933.

_____. *Zapata, the Unconquerable.* New York: Doubleday, Doran, 1941.

Pinckney, Josephine. *Three O'Clock Dinner.* New York: The Viking Press, 1945.

Pini, Giorgio. *Filo diretto con Palazzo Venezie.* Bologna, Italy: Cappelli, 1950.

_____. *Itinerario tragico.* Milan, Italy: Ed Omnia, 1956.

_____. *Mussolini.* trans. Luigi Villari. London: Hutchinson, 1939.

_____, and Susmel, Duilio. *Mussolini: l'uomo e l'opera.* 4 vols. Florence, Italy: La Fenice, 1953-1955.

Pink, Louis Heaton. *Gaynor: The Tammany Mayor Who Swallowed the Tiger.* New York: International Press, 1931.

Pinkerton, A. Frank. *Jim Cummins: Or, the Great Adams Express Robbery.* Chicago: Laird & Lee, 1887.

_____. *The Whitechapel Murders: or and American Detective in London.* New York: Laird & Lee, 1889.

Pinkerton, Allan. *Bankrobbers and the Detectives.* New York: G.W. Carleton, 1883.

_____. *Criminal Reminiscences and Detective Sketches.* New York: G.W. Dillingham, 1878.

_____. *History and Evidence of the Passage of Abraham Lincoln from Harrisburg, Pa., to Washington D.C., on the Twenty Third of February, 1861.* New York: Rode & Bravel, 1868.

_____. *Mississippi Outlaws and the Detectives.* New York: G.W. Carleton 1881.

_____. *The Mollie Maguires and the Detectives.* New York: G.W. Carleton, 1877.

_____. *Professional Thieves and Detectives.* New York: G.W. Carleton, 1880.

_____. *The Somnambylist and Detectives.* New York: G.W. Dillingham, 1903.

_____. *Spy of the Rebellion.* New York: G.W. Carleton, 1883.

Pinkerton, Matthew W. *Murder in All Ages.* Chicago: A.E. Pinkerton 1898.

Pinkerton, William A. *Train Robbers.* Jamestown, Va.: International Chiefs of Police Association, 1907.

Pinkney, Alphonso. *The American Way of Violence.* New York: Random House, 1972.

Pinkowski, Edward. *The Latimer Massacre.* Philadelphia: Sunshine Press, 1950.

Pinner, Walter. *How Many Arab Refugees?* London: MacGibbon & Kee, 1960.

Pinter, Rudolph. *Intelligence Testing: Methods and Results.* New York: Henry Holt, 1923.

Piotrowski, Stanislav. *Hans Franks Tagebuch.* Warsaw, Pol.: Polnischer Verlag der Wissenschaften, 1963.

Piper: His Life, His Crimes and His Execution. Boston: New England News, 1876.

Piper, Edwin Ford. *Barbed Wire and Wayfarers.* New York: Macmillan, 1924.

Pipes, Richard N. *Formation of the Soviet Union: Communism and Nationalism, 1917-1923.* Cambridge, Mass.: Harvard University Press, 1954.

_____ (ed.). *Karamzin's Memoir on Ancient and Modern Russia.* Cambridge, Mass.: Harvard University Press, 1959.

_____ (ed.). *The Russian Intelligentsia.* New York: Columbia University Press, 1961.

_____. *Social Democracy and the St. Petersburg Labor Movement, 1885-1897.* Cambridge, Mass.: Harvard University Press, 1963.

Pipkin, Charles W. *The Idea of Social Justice; A Study of Legislation and Administration and the Labor Movement in England and France: 1900-1926.* New York: Macmillan, 1927.

Pisarev, Dimitri I. *Selected Philosophical, Social and Political Essays.* Moscow: Foreign Languages Publishing House, 1958.

Piscitelli, Enzo. *Storia della Resistenza romana.* Bari, Italy: Laterza, 1965.

Pistelli, Ermenegildo. *Eroi, uomini e ragazzi.* Florence, Italy: Sansoni, 1927.

Pistone, Joseph D. *Donnie Brasco: My Undercover Life in the Mafia.* New York: New American Library, 1987.

Pistrak, Lazar. *The Great Tactician: Khrushchev's Rise to Power.* New York: Frederick A. Praeger, 1961.

Pitcairn, R. (ed.). *Criminal Trials in Scotland from A.D. 1488 to A.D. 1624.* Edinburgh, Scot.: William Tait, 1833.

Pitigliani, Fausto. *The Italian Corporative state.* London: P.S. King, 1933.

Pitkin, John. *The Prison Cell in Its Lights and Shadows.* London: S. Low, Marston, 1918.

Pitkin, Thomas M., and Cordasco, Francesco. *The Black Hand: A Chapter in Ethnic Crime.* Totawa, N.J.: Littlefield, Adams, 1977.

Pitman, Benn. *The Assassination of President Lincoln and the Trial of the Conspirators.* New York: Funk & Wagnalls, 1954.

Pitt, Roxane. *The Courage of Fear.* London: Jarrolds, 1957.

Pittau, Joseph. *The Meiji Political System.* Tokyo: Sophia University, 1963.

Pittenger, W. *Secret Service.* Philadelphia: J.B. Lippincott, 1882.

Pittman, Benn. *The Assassination of President Lincoln and the Trial of the Conspirators.* New York: Moore, Wilstach, Baldwin, 1865.

Pittman, David J. and Snyder, Charles R. *Society, Culture and Drinking Patterns.* New York: John Wiley & Sons, 1961.

Pitts, Dr. J.R.S. *Life and Bloody Career of the Executed Criminal James Copeland.* Jackson, Miss.: Pilot, 1874.

Pitts, John Linwood. *Witchcraft and Devil Lore in the Channel Islands.* Guernsey, Can.: Guille-Allès Library, 1886.

Pius XII, Pope. *The Pope Speaks.* London: Faber, 1940.

_____. *Selected letters and addresses.* London: Catholic Truth Society, 1949.

Pivar, David J. *The Purity Crusade.* Westport, Conn.: Greenwood, 1973.

Piven, Frances Fox, and Cloward, Richard A. *Regulating the Poor: The Functions of Public Welfare.* New York: Random House, 1971.

Pizer, Donald (ed.). *Hamlin Garland's Diaries.* San Marino, Calif.: Huntington Library, 1968.

Pizzey, Erin. *Scream Quietly.* Short Hills, N.J.: Ridley Easlow, 1977.

Place, Francis. *Illustrations and Proofs of the Principle of Population.* London: George Allen & Unwin, 1930.

Planel, Alomée. *Docteur Satan ou l'Affaire Petiot.* Paris: Editions Robert Laffont, 1978.

Plantsch, Martinus. *Opusculum de Sagis Maleficis.* Pforzheim: Thome Anshelni, 1507.

Plass, Hermann Gottlob. *Die Tyrannis in ihren beiden Perioden bei den alten Griechen.* Bremen: Franz Schlochtmann, 1852.

Platanov, S.F. *Boris Godunov.* trans. L. Rex Pyles. Gulf Breeze, Fla.: Academic International Press, 1973.

_____. *History of Russia.* trans. E. Aronsberg. New York: Macmillan, 1929.

_____. *Ivan the Terrible.* trans. J.L. Wieczynski. Gulf Breeze, Fla.: Academic International Press, 1974.

_____. *The Time of Troubles.* trans. John T. Alexander. Lawrence: University Press of Kansas, 1970.

Plate, Thomas. *Crime Pays!* New York: Simon and Schuster, 1975.

_____. *The Mafia at War.* New York: Magazine Press, 1972.

_____, and Darvi, Andrea. *Secret Police.* Garden City, N.Y.: Doubleday, 1981.

Platel, Félix. *Portraits d'Ignotus.* Paris: Meaux, impr. ch. Chochet, 1878.

Platnick, Kenneth B. *Great Mysteries of History.* Harrisburg, Pa.: Stackpole, 1971.

Plato. *Cratyllus 400C.* trans. H.N. Fowler. London: William Heinemann, 1953.

_____. *The Last Days of Socrates.* trans. Hugh Tredennick. Baltimore: Penguin Books, 1969.

_____. *Phaedrus and the Seventh and Eighth Letters.* trans. Walter Hamilton. Baltimore: Penguin, 1973.

_____. *The Republic.* trans. Benjamin Jowett. New York: Colonial Press, 1901.

_____. *Symposium.* trans. W.R.M. Lamb. London: William Heinemann, 1953.

_____. *Thirteen Epistles.* trans. L.A. Post. Oxford, Eng.: Clarendon Press, 1925.

Platt, Anthony M. *The Child Savers: The Invention of Delinquency.* Chicago: University of Chicago Press, 1969.

_____, and Cooper, Lynn. *Policing America.* Englewood Cliffs, N.J.: Prentice Hall, 1974.

Platt, Jerome J., and Labate, Christina. *Heroin Addiction: Theory, Research and Treatment.* New York: John Wiley & Sons, 1976.

Platt, Sir T.C. *The Abyssinian Storm.* London: Jarrolds, 1935.

Platt, Thomas Collier. *The Autobiography of Thomas Collier Platt.* New York: B.W. Dodge, 1910.

Plautus. *Mostellaria.* trans. Paul Nixon. London: William Heinemann, 1963.

Playfair, Giles, and Sington, Derrick. *Crime, Punishment and Cure.* London: Secker & Warburg, 1965.

_____. *The Offenders.* New York: Simon & Schuster, 1957.

Playfair, Sir Robert Lambert. *The Scourage of Christendom; Annals of British Relations with Algiers Prior to the French Conquest.* London: Smith, Elder, 1884.

Pleasants, Mrs. J.E. *History of Orange County, California.* Los Angeles: J.R. Finnell & Sons, 1931.

Pleasants, J. Hall (ed.). *Proceedings of the Court of Chancery of Maryland.* Baltimore: Maryland Archives, 1934.

Pleasants, Samuel Augustus. *Fernando Wood of New York.* New York: Columbia University Press, 1948.

Pleasants, William James. *Twice Across the Plains, 1849, 1856.* San Francisco: W.M. Brunt Co., 1906.

Plenn, Jaime H., and LaRoche, C.J. *The Fastest Gun in Texas.* New York: American Library, 1956.

_____. *Mexico Marches.* Indianapolis, Ind.: Bobbs-Merrill, 1939.

_____. *Saddle in the Sky: The Lone Star State.* Indianapolis, Ind.: Bobbs-Merrill, 1940.

_____. *Texas Hellion: The True Story of Ben Thompson.* New York: American Library, 1955.

Plimpton, George (ed.). *American Journey: Interviews by Jean Stein.* New York: Harcourt Brace Jovanovich, 1970.

Plomin, R., and DeFries, J.C., and McClearn, G.E. *Behavioral Genetics.* San Francisco: W.H. Freeman, 1980.

Ploscowe, Morris. *Organized Crime and Law Enforcement.* New York: Grosby Press, 1952-53.

_____. *Sex and the Law.* New York: Prentice-Hall, 1951.

Plotinus. *The Enneads.* trans. Stephen MacKenna. London: Faber & Faber, 1956.

Plowden, David. *Lincoln and His America 1809-1865.* New York: Viking Press, 1970.

Plum, William R. *The Military Telegraph During the Civil War in the United States.* 2 vols. Chicago: Jansen, McClurg, 1882.

Plumb, J.H. *England in the Eighteenth Century, 1714-1815.* London: Penguin Books, 1959.

_____. *The Horizon Book of the Renaissance.* New York: American Heritage, 1961.

Plumbe, George E. *Chicago.* Chicago: Chicago Association of Commerce, 1912.

Plummer, Jonathon. *Dying Confession of Plumb.* Newburyport, Mass.: Blunt & March, 1795.

Plunkitt, George W. *Plunkitt of Tammany Hall.* New York: Alfred A. Knopf, 1948.

Plutarch. *On Love, the Family and the Good Life.* New York: New American Library, 1957.

Pobedonostsev, Konstantin P. *Reflections of a Russian Statesman.* Ann Arbor: University of Michigan Press, 1965.

Pocock, Roger S. *Following the Frontier.* New York: McClure, Phillips, 1903.

Podmore, Frank. *The Newer Spiritualism.* New York: Arno Press, 1975.

Poe, Edgar Allan. *The Complete Works of Edgar Allan Poe.* 17 vols. New York: G.D. Sproul, 1902.

_____. *The Letters of Edgar Allan Poe.* 2 vols. Cambridge, Mass.: Harvard University Press, 1948.

Poe, John William. *The Death of Billy the Kid.* Boston: Houghton Mifflin, 1933.

Poe, Sophie A. *Buckboard Days.* Caldwell, Idaho: Caxton Printers, 1936.

Pogue, Forrest C. *George C. Marshall: Ordeal and Hope.* New York: Viking, 1963.

Pohl, Frederick J. *Atlantic Crossings Before Columbus.* New York: W.W. Norton, 1961.

_____. *The Lost Discovery.* New York: W.W. Norton, 1952.

_____. *The Viking Explorers.* New York: Thomas Y. Crowell, 1966.

_____. *The Vikings on Cape Cod.* Pictou, Nova Scotia, Can.: n.p., 1957.

Pointer, Larry. *In Search of Butch Cassidy.* Norman: University of Oklahoma, 1977.

Pointer, Michael. *The Public Life of Sherlock Holmes.* New York: Drake, 1975.

The Poison Fiend! Life, Crimes, and Conviction of Lydia Sherman. Philadelphia: Barclay, 1872.

Pol, Heinz. *Suicide of a Democracy.* New York: Reynal and Hitchcock, 1940.

Poldervaart, Arie W. *Black-Robed Justice.* Albuquerque, N.M.: Historical Society of New Mexico, 1948.

Polenberg, Richard. *War and Society: The United States, 1941-1945.* Philadelphia: J.B. Lippincott, 1972.

Poliakov, Leon, *Das Dritte Reich und die Juden.* Berlin-Grünewald, 1955.

_____. *Das Dritte Reich und seine Denker.* Berlin-Grünewald, 1959.

_____, and Wulf, Josef. *Das Dritte Reich und seine Diener.* Berlin-Grünewald: Arani, 1956.

Police Foundation. *Domestic Violence and the Police.* Washington, D.C.: Police Foundation, 1977.

_____. *Guidelines and Papers from the National Symposium on Police Labor Relations IACP.* Washington, D.C.: Police Foundation, 1974.

Police Gazette, Editor of. *The Pictorial Life and Adventures of John A. Murrel.* Philadelphia: T.B. Peterson & Brothers, 1848.

Politics and Political Parties in Roumania. London: International Reference Library, 1936.

Polk, James Knox. *The Diary of James K. Polk.* Chicago: A.C. McClurg, 1910.

Polk, K., and Schafer, W.E. *Schools and Delinquency.* Englewood Cliffs, N.J.: Prentice-Hall, 1972.

Polk, Stella Gipson. *Mason and Mason County: A History.* Austin, Texas: Pemberton Press, 1966.

Polk, William. *The United States and the Arab World.* Cambridge, Mass.: Harvard University Press, 1965.

Polk, William R., Stamler, David M., and Asfour, Edmund. *Backdrop to Tragedy.* Boston: Beacon Press, 1957.

Pollack, Emanuel. *The Kronstadt Rebellion.* New York: Philosophical, 1959.

Pollack, Sir Frederick. *Essays in Jurisprudence and Ethics.* London: Macmillan, 1882

Pollock, George. *Mr. Justice McCardie.* London: J. Lane, 1934.

Pollack, Heinrich. *Mittheilungen über den Hexenprozess in Deutschland.* Berlin: F. Siemenroth, 1886.

Pollack, Jack Harrison. *Dr. Sam, an American Tragedy.* Chicago: Henry Regnery, 1972.

Pollack, Otto. *The Criminality of Women.* Philadelphia: University of Pennsylvania Press, 1950.

Pollack, Sam. *Mutiny for the Cause.* London: Paper Back Sphere Books, 1969.

Pollak, Gustav. *Fifty Years of American Idealism: The New York Nation, 1865-1915.* Boston: Houghton Mifflin, 1915.

Pollak, Otto. *The Criminality of Women.* Philadelphia: University of Pennsylvania Press, 1950.

Pollard, Edward A. *Observations in the North.* Richmond, Va.: E.W. Ayrres, 1865.

Pollard, Henry Robinson. *Memories and Sketches.* Richmond, Va.: Lewis Printing, 1923.

Pollard, Hugh B.C. *A Busy Time in Mexico.* New York: Duffield, 1913.

_____. *The Secret Societies of Ireland.* London: P. Allan, 1922.

Pollard, James E. *The Presidents and the Press,* New York: Macmillan, 1947.

Pollard, Joseph. *Mr. Justice Cardozo.* New York: Yorktown Press, 1935.

Pollens, B. *The Sexual Criminal.* New York: Macaulay, 1938.

Polley, Robert L. (ed.). *Lincoln, His Words and His World.* New York: Hawthorn Books, 1965.

Pollock, Channing. *Harvest of My Years.* New York: Bobbs-Merrill, 1943.

Pollock, Frederick, and Maitland, Frederic William. *The History of English Law.* Cambridge, Mass.: Cambridge University Press, 1899.

Polo, Marco. *Travels.* New York: Book League of America, 1929.

Polsky, Howard W. *Cottage Six.* New York: Russell Sage Foundation, 1962.

Polsky, Ned. *Hustlers, Beats, and Others.* Chicago: Aldine, 1967.

Polybius. *The Histories.* trans. W.R. Paton. Cambridge, Mass.: Harvard University Press, 1922.

Pomerantz, Sidney I. *New York, An American City: 1783-1803.* New York: Columbia University Press, 1938.

Pomeroy, Earl S. *The Territories and the United States.* Philadelphia: The Pennsylvania State University Press, 1947.

Pomeroy, Jesse H. *Autobiography of Jesse H. Pomeroy.* Boston: J.A. Cummings, 1875.

Pomeroy, Wardell B. *Dr. Kinsey and the Institute for Sex Research.* New York: New American Library, 1973.

Pomfret, John E. *Founding the American Colonies, 1583-1660.* New York: Harper & Row, 1970.

Pomper, Gerald M., et al. *The Election of 1976.* New York: David McKay, 1977.

Pomponazzi, Pietro. *De Naturalium Effectuum Causis.* Basel, Switz.: Henricum Petri, 1556.

Pomroy, ha. *What Every Woman Needs to Know About the Law.* Garden City, N.Y.: Doubleday 1980.

Ponsonby, Arthur. *Henry Ponsonby, Queen Victoria's Private Secretary: His Life from His Letters.* New York: Macmillan, 1943.

_____ (ed.). *Letters of the Empress Frederick.* New York: Macmillan, 1930.

Ponsonby-Fane, Richard A.B. *Imperial House of Japan.* Kyoto, Japan: Ponsonby Memorial Society, 1959.

_____. *Sovereign and Subject.* Kyoto, Japan: Ponsonby Memorial Society, 1962.

_____. *Studies in Shinto and Shrines.* Kyoto, Japan: Ponsonby Memorial Society, 1962.

_____. *The Vicissitudes of Shinto.* Kyoto, Japan: Ponsonby Memorial Society, 1963.

_____. *Visiting Famous Shrines in Japan.* Kyoto, Japan: Ponsonby Memorial Society, 1964.

Pontell, Henry N. *A Capacity to Punish.* Bloomington: University of Indiana Press, 1984.

Ponzinibio, Giovanni Francesco. *Subtilis et Utilis Tractatus de Lamiis.* n.p., n.d.

Poock, L.D. *"Headless, Yet Identified," A Story of the Solution of the Pearl Bryan, or Fort Thompson Mystery.* Columbus, Ohio: Hann & Adair, 1897.

Poole, Ernest. *Giants Gone: Men Who Made Chicago.* New York: McGraw-Hill, 1943.

Poor Mary Stannard!: A Full and Thrilling Story of the Circumstances Connected with Her Murder. New Haven, Conn.: Stafford Printing, 1879.

Poore, Ben Perley (ed.). *The Conspiracy Trial for the Murder of the President.* New York: Arno Press, 1972.

_____. *Perley's Reminiscences of Sixty Years in the National Metropolis.* 2 Vols. Philadelphia: Hubbard Brothers, 1886.

Pope, Jennie Barnes. *The Rise of New York Port.* New York: Charles Scribner's Sons, 1939.

Pope, Jesse E. *The Clothing Industry in New York.* Columbia: University of Missouri, 1905.

Pope, John. *A Tour Through the Southern and Western Territories of the United States of America.* New York: C.L. Woodward, 1888.

Pope-Hennessy, James. *Queen Mary: 1867-1953.* New York: Alfred A. Knopf, 1960.

Popkin, Richard H. *The Second Oswald.* New York: Avon Books, 1966.

Popov, Dusko. *Spy Counter-Spy.* New York: Grosset & Dunlap, 1974.

Popper, Karl. *The Poverty of Historicism.* London: Routledge & Kegan Paul, 1960.

Porambo, Ron. *No Cause For Indictment.* New York: Holt, Rinehart and Winston, 1971.

Porche, F. *Charles Baudelaire.* trans. J. Mavin. New York: Horace Liveright, 1928.

Porée, Charles Gabriel. *Le pour et le contre de la possession des filles de la parroisse de Landes.* Antioche: Chez les hértiers de la bonne foy, 1738.

Poretsky, Elizabeth. *Our Own People.* Ann Arbor: University of Michigan Press, 1969.

Porges, Irwin. *The Violent Americans.* Derby, Conn.: Monarch Books, 1963.

Porphyry. *Abstinence from Animal Food.* trans. Thomas Taylor. London: Thomas Rodd, 1823.

Porta, Giovanni Battista della. *Magiae Naturalissive.* Naples, Italy: M. Cancer, 1558.

Porter, A. Toomer. *Led On!* New York: G.P. Putnam's Sons, 1898.

Porter, David D. *The Naval History of the Civil War.* New York: Sherman, 1886.

Porter, Edwin H. *The Fall River Tragedy.* Fall River, Mass.: George R.H. Buffington, 1893.

Porter, Garnett Clay. *Strange and Mysterious Crimes.* New York: McFadden, 1929.

Porter, Glenn, and Livesay, Harold C. *Merchants and Manufacturers: Studies in the Changing Structure of Nineteenth Century Marketing.* Baltimore: Johns Hopkins University Press, 1971.

Porter, Henry M. *Pencilings of an Early Western Pioneer.* Denver: World Press, 1929.

Porter, Mae Reed, and Davenport, Odessa. *Scotsman in Buckskin: Sir William Drummond Stewart and the Rocky Mountain Fur Trade.* New York: Hastings House, 1963.

Porter, Mary W. *The Surgeon in Charge.* Concord, N.H.: Rumford Press, 1949.

Porter, Millie Jones. *Memory Cups of Panhandle Pioneers.* Clarendon, Texas: Clarendon Press, 1945.

Porterfield, Austin L., and Talbert, Robert W. *Crime, Suicide and Social Well-Being in Your State and City.* Fort Worth: Texas Christian University, 1948.

_____. *Cultures of Violence.* Ft. Worth, Texas: Manney, 1965.

_____. *Current Approaches to Delinquency.* New York: National Probation and Parole Association, 1949.

Porteus, S.D. *The Maze Test and Mental Differences.* Vineland, N.J.: Smith, 1933.

Portigliotti, Giuseppe. *The Borgias.* trans. Bernard Miall. London: George Allen & Unwin, 1928.

Portmann, Adolf. *Animals as Social Beings.* New York: Viking Press, 1961.

Poschinger, Margaretha von. *Life of the Emperor Frederick.* New York: Harper & Brothers, 1901.

Posey, Calvert R., and Judith L. *A History of the Role Charles County Played in the Civil War.* La Plata, Md.: Times Crescent, 1960.

Posner, Gerald L. *Warlord of Crime: Chinese Secret Societies - The New Mafia.* New York: McGraw-Hill, 1988.

Posner, Richard. *The Economics of Justice.* Cambridge, Mass.: Harvard University Press, 1981.

_____. *The Federal Courts: Crisis and Reform.* Cambridge: Harvard University Press, 1985.

Pospelov, P.N. (ed.). *Vladimir Ilyich Lenin: Biographiya.* Moscow: Institut Marksizma-Lenina, 1960.

Post, Louis F. *The Deportations Delirium of Nineteen-Twenty.* Chicago: C.H. Kerr, 1923.

_____, and Leubuscher, Fred C. *Henry George's 1886 Campaign: An Account of the George-Hewitt Campaign in the New York Municipal Election of 1886.* Westport, Conn.: Hyperion Press, 1976.

Postan, M.M. *The Medieval Economy and Society.* Berkeley: University of California Press, 1972.

Postgate, Raymond. *Murder, Piracy and Treason.* New York: Houghton Mifflin, 1925.

Postman, L. (ed.). *Psychology in the Making.* New York: Alfred A. Knopf, 1962.

Poston, Richard W. *The Gang and the Establishment.* New York: Harper & Row, 1971.

Pott, Johann Heinrich. *Specimen Juridicum.* Jena: Tobian Oehrlingium, 1689.

Potter, Arthur Gray. *I Can Go Home Again.* Chapel Hill: University of North Carolina Press, 1943.

Potter, C.E. *Report on the Trial of Bradbury Ferguson.* Concord, N.H.: Morrill, Silsby, 1841.

Potter, Charles Francis. *The Preacher and I: An Autobiography.* New York: Crown, 1951.

Potter, David M. *Lincoln and His Party in the Secession Crisis 1860-1861.* New Haven, Conn.: Yale University Press, 1942.

Potter, George. *To the Golden Door.* Boston: Little, Brown, 1960.

Potter, Colonel Jack. *Cattle Trails of the Old West.* Clayton, N.M.: Laura R. Krehbiel, 1939.

_____. *Lead Steer and Other Tales.* Clayton, N.M.: Leader Press, 1939.

Potter, John Deane. *The Art of Hanging.* New York: A.S. Barnes, 1969.

_____. *A Solider Must Hang: The Biography of an Oriental General.* London: Frederick Miller, 1963.

_____. *Yamamoto: The Man Who Menaced America.* New York: Viking Press, 1965.

Potter, John Mason. *Plots Against Presidents.* New York: Astor-Honor, 1968.

_____. *The Fatal Gallows Tree.* London: Elek Books, 1965.

_____. *13 Desperate Days.* New York: Ivan Obslensky, 1964.

Potter, Theodore Edgar. *The Autobiography of Theodore Edgar Potter.* Concord, N.H.: Rumford Press, 1913.

Potter, Rev. William J. *A History of the Pocasset Tragedy.* New Bedford, Mass.: Charles W. Knight, 1879.

Potts, Thomas. *The Wonderful Discovery of the Witches in the County of Lancaster.* London: John Barnes, 1613.

_____. *The Trial of the Lancaster Witches.* London: P. Davies, 1929.

Poujoulot, Jean-Joseph-François. *Vie de Mgr. Sibour.* Paris: E. Repos, 1857.

Poulantzas, Nicos. *Classes in Contemporary Capitalism.* London: New Left Books, 1975.

Pound, Arthur. *The Golden Earth: The Story of Manhattan's Landed Wealth.* New York: Macmillan, 1935.

_____, and Day, R.E. *Johnson of the Mohawks: A Biography of Sir William Johnson.* New York: Macmillan, 1930.

_____. *The Turning Wheel.* Garden City, N.Y.: Doubleday, Doran, 1934.

Pound, R., and Harmsworth, G. *Norhtcliffe.* New York: Frederick A. Praeger, 1960.

Pound, Roscoe. *Criminal Justice in America.* New York: Da Capo Press, 1972.

_____. *An Introduction to the Philosophy of Law.* New Haven, Conn.: Yale University Press, 1959.

_____. *The Lawyer from Antiquity to Modern Times.* St. Paul, Minn.: West, 1953.

_____. *Social Control Through Law.* New Haven, Conn.: Yale University Press, 1942.

Pourrat, Henri. *L'homme à la peau de loup.* Neuchâtel, Switz.: V. Attinger, 1950.

Powderly, Terence V. *Thirty Years of Labor, 1859-1889.* Columbus, Ohio: Excelsior, 1889.

Powel, Gretchen and Peter. *New York 1929.* Paris: Black Sun Press, 1930.

Powell, Addison M. *Trailing and Camping in Alaska.* New York: A. Wessells, 1909.

Powell, D.M. *The Peralta Grant.* Norman: University of Oklahoma Press, 1960.

Powell, Hickman. *Lucky Luciano: Ninety Times Guilty.* New York: Citadel Press, 1975.

Powell, John B. *My 25 Years in China.* New York: Macmillan, 1945.

Powell, John Wesley. *Exploration of the Colorado River of the West and Its Tributaries.* Washington, D.C.: U.S. Government Printing Office, 1875.

Powell, Philip Wayne. *Soldiers, Indians, and Silver.* Berkeley: University of California Press, 1952.

Power, Rex. *How to Beat Police Radar.* New York: Arco, 1980.

Power, Tyrone. *Impressions of America.* London: Richard Bentley, 1836.

Powers, Alfred. *Redwood Country: The Lava Region and the Redwoods.* New York: Duell, Sloan & Pearce, 1949.

Powers, Edwin. *Crime and Punishment in Early Massachusetts.* Boston: Beacon Press, 1966.

_____, and Witmer H. *An Experiment in the Prevention of Delinquency.* New York: Columbia University Press, 1951.

Powers, Laura Bride. *Old Monterey, California's Adobe Capital.* San Francisco: San Carlos Press, 1934.

Powers, Michael. *Life of Michael Powers.* Boston: Russell & Gardner, 1820.

Powers, Pat G., and Baskin, Wade. *Sex Education: Issues and Directions.* New York: Philosophical Library, 1969.

Powers, Richard Gid. *Secrecy and Power: The Life of J. Edgar Hoover.* New York: The Free Press, 1987.

Powers, Thomas. *The Man Who Kept Secrets.* New York: Alfred A. Knopf, 1979.

Powicke, Frederick J. *A Life of the Reverend Richard Baxter.* New York: Houghton Mifflin, 1924.

Poynter, J.W. *Forgotten Crimes.* New York: Macaulay, 1928.

Pozner, Vladimir. *Bloody Baron: The Story of Ungern-Sternberg.* New York: Random House, 1938.

Pozzi, Arnaldo. *Come li ho visti io.* Milan, Italy: Mondadori, 1947.

Prabhu, R.K. and Rao, U.R. *India of My Dreams.* Bombay, India: Hind Kitabs, 1947.

_____. *The Mind of Mahatma Gandhi.* Bombay, India: Oxford University Press, 1945.

_____. *Mahatma Gandhi and Bihar.* Bombay, India: Hind Kitabs, 1949.

Praetorius, Antonius. *Gründlicher Bericht von Zauberey and Zauberern.* Frankfort, Ger.: J.C. Vackles, 1629.

Prakke, H., Lerg, W.B., and Schmolke, M. (eds.). *Handbuch der Weltpresse.* Opladen, Ger.: Westdeutscher, 1970.

Prall, Robert H., and Mockridge, Norton. *This is Costello.* New York: Gold Medal Books, 1951.

Prasad, Rajendra. *Autobiography.* Mazaffarpur, India: Bharti Sadan, 1947.

_____. *Gandhiji in Champaran.* Madras, India: S. Ganesan, 1928.

_____. *India Divided.* Bombay, India: Hind Kitabs, 1947.

_____. *Satyagraha in Champaran.* Ahmedabad, India: Navajivan, 1949.

Prassel, Frank Richard. *The Western Peace Officer. A Legacy of Law and Order.* Norman: University of Oklahoma Press, 1972.

Prasteau, Jean. *The Lady of the Camellias.* trans. Stella Rodway. London: Hutchinson, 1965.

Prather, H. Bryant. *Come Listen to My Tale.* Tahlequah, Okla.: Pan Press, 1964.

_____. *Texas Pioneer Days.* Dallas: Egan, 1965.

Pratt, Sister Antoinette Marie. *Attitude of the Catholic Church to Witchcraft.* Washington, D.C.: National Capital Press, 1915.

Pratt, Edward Ewing. *Industrial Causes of Congestion of Population in New York City.* New York: Columbia University Press, 1911.

Pratt, Fletcher. *Civil War on Western Waters.* New York: Henry Holt, 1956.

_____. *The Compact History of the United States Navy.* New York: Hawthorn, 1967.

_____. *The Cunning Mulatto and Other Cases of Ellis Parker, American Detective.* New York: Smith & Haas, 1930.

_____. *Stanton: Lincoln's Secretary of War.* New York: W.W. Norton, 1953.

Pratt, J.G. *ESP Research Today.* Metuchen, N.J.: Scarecrow Press, 1973.

_____. *Parapsychology: An Insider's View of ESP.* New York: E.P. Dutton, 1966.

Pratt, John Webb. *Religion, Politics, and Diversity: The Church-State Theme in New York History.* Ithaca, N.Y.: Cornell University Press, 1967.

Pratt, Julius W. *American Secretaries of State and Their Diplomacy.* 2 vols. New York: Cooper-Square, 1964.

_____. *America's Colonial Experiment: How the United States Gained, Governed, and In Part Gave Away a Colonial Empire.* New York: Prentice-Hall, 1950.

Pratt, Sarah S. *The Old Crop in Indiana.* Indianapolis, Ind.: Pratt Poster, 1928.

Pratt, Walter Merriam. *The Burning of Chelsea.* Boston: Sampson, 1908.

Prawdin, Michael. *The Mongol Empire*. London: George Allen & Unwin, 1953.

_____. *The Unmentionable Nechaev: A Key to Bolshevism*. London: Ray, 1961.

Praz, Mario. *The Romantic Agony*. New York: Meridian, 1956.

Preble, George Henry. *The Opening of Japan: A Diary of Discovery in Far East, 1853-1856*. Norman: University of Oklahoma Press, 1962.

Pred, Allan R. *Urban Growth and the Circulation of Information: The United States System of Cities, 1790-1840*. Cambridge, Mass.: Harvard University Press, 1973.

_____. *Urban Growth and City-Systems in the United States, 1840-1860*. Cambridge, Mass.: Harvard University Press, 1980.

Preece, Harold. *The Dalton Gang, End of An Outlaw Era*. New York: Hastings House, 1963.

_____. *Living Pioneers: The Epic of the West by Those Who Lived It*. New York: World, 1952.

_____. *Lone Star Man: Ira Aten*. New York: Hastings House, 1963.

Prélot, Marcel. *L'Evolution Politique du Socialisme Français 1789-1934*. Paris: Editions Ipes, 1939.

Prendergrass, W. *The Z-Car Detective*. London: John Long, 1964.

Prendergast, Thomas F. *Forgotten Pioneers: Irish Leaders in Early California*. San Francisco: Trade, 1942.

Prentis, Noble L. *Southwestern Letters*. Topeka: Kansas Publishing House, 1882.

Presbrey, Frank S. *The History and Development of Advertising*. Garden City, N.Y.: Doubleday, Doran, 1929.

Prescott, Marjorie Wiggin. *New England Son*. New York: Dodd, Mead, 1949.

Prescott, William Hinkling. *Histories: The Rise and Decline of the Spanish Empire*. New York: The Viking Press, 1963.

President's Commission on the Assassination of President John F. Kennedy. *Investigation of the Assassination of President John F. Kennedy: Hearings Before the President's Commission*. 26 vols. Washington, D.C.: U.S. Government Printing Office, 1964.

President's Commission on Law Enforcement and Administration of Justice. *The Challenge of Crime in a Free Society*. Washington, D.C.: U.S. Government Printing Office, 1967.

_____. *Task Force Report: Corrections*. Washington, D.C.: U.S. Government Printing Office, 1967.

_____. *Task Force Report: Crime and Its Impact: An Assessment*. Washington, D.C.: U.S. Government Printing Office, 1967.

_____. *Task Force Report: Juvenile Delinquency and Youth Crime*. Washington, D.C.: U.S. Government Printing Office, 1967.

_____. *Task Force Report: Organized Crime*. Washington, D.C.: U.S. Government Printing Office, 1967.

_____. *Task Force Report: Science and Technology*. Washington, D.C.: U.S. Government Printing Office, 1967.

_____, Task Force on the Police. *Task Force Report: The Police*. Washington, D.C.: U.S. Government Printing Office, 1969.

President's Science Advisory Committee. *Youth: Transition to Adulthood*. Washington, D.C.: U.S. Government Printing Office, 1973.

President's Task Force on Prisoner Rehabilitation. *The Criminal Offender*. Washington, D.C.: U.S. Government Printing Office, 1970.

President's Task Force on Victims of Crime. *Final Report*. Washington, D.C.: U.S. Government Printing Office, 1982.

Presidenza della Regione Siciliana. *Le elezioni in Sicilia, 1946-1956*. Milan: A. Guiffrè, 1956.

Presley, James, and Getty, Gerald W. *Public Defender*. New York: Grosset & Dunlap, 1974.

Press, S. James. *Some Effects of An Increase in Police Manpower in the 20th Precinct of New York City*. Santa Monica, Calif.: Rand Corporation, 1971.

Presseisen, Ernst L. *Germany and Japan: A Study in Totalitarian Diplomacy, 1933-1941*. The Hague, Neth.: Martinus Nijhoff, 1958.

Pressel, Wilhelm. *Hexen und Hexenmeister*. Stuttgart, Ger.: C. Belser, 1860.

Preston, John Hyde. *A Short History of the American Revolution*. New York: Pocket Books, 1952.

Preston, Paul. *Wild Bill, the Indian Slayer*. New York: Robert M. DeWitt, n.d.

Preston, Richard Arthur (ed.). *For Friends at Home*. London: McGill-Queen's University Press, 1974.

_____, Wise, Sydney F., and Werner, Herman O. *Men in Arms*. New York: Frederick A. Praeger, 1956.

Preston, William, Jr. *Aliens and Dissenters*. Cambridge, Mass.: Harvard University Press, 1963.

Prettyman, Barrett, Jr. *Death and the Supreme Court*. New York: Harcourt, Brace & World, 1961.

Prettyman, J.R. *Dispauperization*. London: Longmans, Green, 1878.

Prettyman, W.S. *Indian Territory*. Norman: University of Oklahoma Press, 1957.

Preuss, Johann David Erdmann. *Friedrich der Grosse mit seinen Verwandten und Freunden: Eine historische Skizze*. Berlin: Duncker & Humblot, 1838.

_____ (ed.). *Oeuvres de Frédéric le Grand*. 30 vols. Berlin: n.p., 1846-1857.

Prévost, Abbé. *Manon Lescaut*. New York: Modern Library, 1920.

Prezzolini, Giuseppe. *Fascism*. London: Methuen, 1926.

_____. *I Trapiantati*. Milan, Italy: Longanesi, 1958.

Price, Con. *Memories of Old Montana*. Hollywood, Calif.: Highland Press, 1945.

Price, D.L. *Jordan and Palestinians: The PLO's Prospects*. London: Instutute for the Study of Conflict, 1975.

Price, Ernest Batson. *The Russo-Japanese Treaties of 1907-1916 Concerning Manchuria and Mongolia*. Baltimore: The Johns Hopkins Press, 1933.

Price, G.G. *Death Comes to Billy the Kid*. Greenburg, Kan.: Signal, 1940.

Price, G. Ward. *Extra Special Correspondent*. London: Harrap, 1957.

_____. *I Know These Dictators*. London: Harrap, 1937.

_____. *Year of Reckoning*. London: Cassell, 1939.

Price, George McReady. *The New Geology*. Moutain View, Calif.: Pacific Press, 1923.

Price, H. *The Most Haunted House in England*. New York: Longmans, Green, 1940.

Price, Harry. *Fifty Years of Psychical Research*. New York: Arno Press, 1975.

_____. *Poltergeist Over England*. London: Country Life, 1945.

Price, Morgan Philips. *America after Sixty Years: The Travel Diaries of Two Generations of Englishmen*. London: George Allen & Unwin, 1936.

Price, Sir Rose Lambart. *A Summer in the Rockies*. London: Sampson Low, Marston, 1898.

Price, S. Goodale. *Black Hills, the Land of Legend*. Los Angeles: De Vorrs, 1935.

_____. *Ghosts of Golconda: A Guide Book to Historical Characters and Locations in the Black Hills of South Dakota*. Deadwood, S.D.: Western, 1952.

_____. *Saga of the Hills*. Hollywood, Calif.: Cosmo, 1940.

Price, Willard. *Japan and the Son of Heaven*. New York: Duell, Sloan & Pearce, 1945.

Pride, W.F. *The History of Fort Riley*. n.p, 1926.

Pridham, Francis. *Close of a Dynasty*. London: Wingate, 1956.

Prieur de Laval, Claude. *Dialogue de la Lycanthrope ou Transformations D'Hommes en Loups*. Louvain, Belg.: I. Maes and P. Zangre, 1596.

Priest, Loring Benson. *Uncle Sam's Stepchildren*. New Brunswick, N.J.: Rutgers University Press, 1942.

Priestland, Gerald. *The Future of Violence*. London: Hamish

Hamilton, 1974.

Priestley, Herbert Ingram. *The Coming of the White Man, 1492-1848*. New York: Macmillan, 1929.

Priet, Guillermo. *San Francisco in the Seventies: The City as Viewed by a Mexican Political Exile*. trans. Edwin S. Marby. San Francisco: John Henry Nash, 1938.

Prime, Nathaniel S. *The Pernicious Effects of Intemperance in the Use of Ardent Spirits and the Remedy for the Evil*. New York: Alden Spooner, 1812.

Prince, L. Bradford. *A Concise History of New Mexico*. Cedar Rapids, Iowa: Torch Press, 1912.

_____. *Historical Sketches of New Mexico*. New York: Leggat Brothers, 1883.

_____. *The Student's History of New Mexico*. Denver: Publishers Press, 1913.

Pringle, Henry F. *Alfred E. Smith: A Critical Study*. New York: Macy-Masius, 1927.

_____. *The Life and Times of William Howard Taft*. 2 vols. New York: Farrar & Rinehart, 1939.

_____. *Theodore Roosevelt: A Biography*. New York: Harcourt, Brace, 1931.

Pringle, Patrick. *Hue & Cry, The Birth of the British Police*. London: Museum Press, 1955.

_____. *Jolly Roger: The Story of the Great Age of Piracy*. New York: W.W. Norton, 1953.

_____. *Stand and Deliver*. London: Museum Press, 1951.

Prisoners in America. New York: American Assembly, Columbia University, 1973.

Pritchard, F.H. (ed.). *More Essays of Today*. London: George G. Harrup, 1928.

Pritchard, James B. (ed.). *The Ancient Near East*. Princeton, N.J.: Princeton University Press, 1973.

Pritchett, C. Herman. *Civil Liberties and the Vinson Court*. Chicago: University of Chicago Press, 1954.

_____. *Congress versus the Supreme Court, 1957-1960*. Minneapolis: University of Minnesota Press, 1961.

_____. *The Roosevelt Court*. New York: Macmillan, 1948.

_____, and Westin, Alan F. (eds.). *The Third Branch of Government*. New York: Harcourt, Brace & World, 1963.

Pritchett, V.S. *Midnight Oil*. New York: Random House, 1972.

Pritt, D.N. *Spies and Informers in the Witness Box*. London: Bernard Harison, 1958.

Proal, Louis. *Political Crime*. New York: D. Appleton, 1898.

Proceedings of the White House Conference on Narcotic and Drug Abuse. Washington, D.C.: U.S. Government Printing Office, 1962.

Procès verbal du crime détestable de trois sorcières. Paris: Imprimerie Motteroz, 1876.

Processo originale degli Untori nella peste del 1630. Milan, Italy: Tipografia Merati e comp., 1839.

Procopius. *Anecdota*. trans. H.B. Dewing. London: William Heinemann, 1935.

Proctor, Richard. *Chance and Luck*. London: Longmans, 1887.

A Prodigious and Tragical History of Six Witches at Maidstone. London: R. Harper, 1629.

Profiles from the New Yorker. New York: Alfred A. Knopf, 1938.

Program Material for Temperence Day or Frances E. Willard Day. Evanston, Ill.: National W.C.T.U., n.d.

Prokopf, D. *Urban Core and Inner City*. Amsterdam, Neth.: Leinder, 1967.

Propertius. *Elegies*. trans. H.F. Butler. London: William Heinemann, 1956.

Proskauer, Joseph M. *A Segment of My Times*. New York: Farrar, Straus, 1950.

Prosser, William L. *Handbook of the Law of Torts*. St. Paul, Minn.: West, 1964.

Prothero, James Warren. *The Dollar Decade*. Baton Rouge: Louisiana State University Press, 1954.

Prothero, Margaret. *The History of the Criminal Investigation Department of Scotland Yard from Earliest Times until Today*.

London: Jenkins, 1931.

Prouty, L. Fletcher. *The Secret Team: The CIA and Its Allies in Control of the World*. n.p., n.d.

Provence, S., and Lipton, R.C. *Infants in Institutions*. New York: International University Press, 1962.

Prucha, Francis Paul. *A Guide to the Military Posts of the United States, 1789-1895*. Madison: State Historical Society of Wisconsin, 1964.

Pruiett, Moman. *Moman Pruiett: Criminal Lawyer*. Oklahoma City, Okla.: Harlow, 1944.

Psellus, Michaelis. *Chronographia*. trans. E.R.A. Sewter. New Haven, Conn.: Yale University Press, 1953.

Psellus, Michaelis. *De Operatione Daemonum Dialogus*. trans. Gilbertus Gaulminus Molinensis. Paris: H. Drovart, 1615.

Public Papers of the President. Washington, D.C.: U.S. Government Printing Office, 1974.

Puckett, James L., and Ellen. *History of Oklahoma and Indian Territory and Homeseekers Guide*. Vinita, Okla.: Chieftan, 1906.

Puente, Ramón. *La dictadura, la Revolución, y sus hombres*. Mexico City, Mex.: Ediciones Bocetas, 1938.

_____. *Pascual Orozco y la revulta de Chihuahua*. Mexico City, Mex.: Eusebio Gómez de la Puente, 1912.

_____. *Vida de Francisco Villa, Contada por El Mismo*. Los Angeles: O. Paz, 1919.

_____. *Villa en Pie*. Mexico City, Mex.: n.p., 1937.

Pugh, Marshall. *Frogman, Commander Crabb's Story*. New York: Charles Scribner's Sons, 1956.

Pugh, Ralph B. *Imprisonment in Medieval England*. Cambridge, Eng.: Cambridge University Press, 1968.

Pugliese, Gen. Emanuele. *L'esercito e la cosidetta marcia su Roma*. Rome: Tipografia Regionale, 1958.

Puharich, Andrija. *Beyond Telepathy*. Garden City, N.Y.: Doubleday, 1973.

_____. *Uri: The Journal of the Mystery of Uri Geller*. Garden City, N.Y.: Doubleday, 1974.

Pullen, John J. *Patriotism in America*. New York: American Heritage Press, 1971.

Pulling, Christopher. *Mr. Punch and the Police*. London: Butterworths, 1964.

Pumpelly, Raphael. *Across America and Asia*. New York: Leypoldt & Holt, 1870.

_____. *My Reminiscences*. 2 vols. New York: Henry Holt, 1918.

Puntoni, Gen. Paolo. *Parla Vittorio Emanuele III*. Milan, Italy: Aldo Palazzi, 1958.

Purdy, Ross L. *Factors in the Conviction of Law Violators: The Drinking Driver*. Ann Arbor, Mich.: University Microfilms, 1971.

Purishkevich, Vladimir. *Comme j'ai tué Raspoutine*. Paris: Povolozky, 1923.

Pursell, C.W., Jr. (ed.). *The Military-Industrial Complex*. New York: Harper & Row, 1972.

Pursley, Robert D. *Introduction to Criminal Justice*. Encino, Calif.: Glencoe, 1977.

Purvis, James. *Great Unsolved Mysteries*. New York: Grosset & Dunlap, 1978.

Purvis, Melvin. *American Agent*. New York: Doubleday, Doran, 1936.

Puryear, Vernon J. *England, Russia and the Straits Question, 1844-1856*. Berkeley: University of California Press, 1931.

Pusey, Merlo J. *Charles Evans Hughes*. 2 vols. New York: Macmillan, 1952.

_____. *The Supreme Court Crisis*. New York: Macmillan, 1937.

Pusey, William Allen. *The History and Epidemiology of Syphilis*. Springfield, Ill.: Charles C. Thomas, 1933.

Pushkarev, Sergei. *The Emergence of Modern Russia, 1801-1919*. trans. R.H. McNeal and T. Yedlin. New York: Holt, Rinehart & Winston, 1963.

Putnam, Allen. *Witchcraft of New England Explained by Modern Spiritualism*. Boston: Colby and Rich, 1888.

Putnam, Carleton. *Race and Reason*. Washington, D.C.: Public Affairs Press, 1961.

Putnam, Carleton. *Theodore Roosevelt: The Formative Years.* New York: Charles Scribner's Sons, 1958.

Putnam, Emily Jane. *The Lady.* Chicago: University of Chicago, 1970.

Putnam, George Plamer. *Soaring Wings, A Biography of Amelia Earhart.* New York: Harcourt, Brace, 1939.

Putnam, George R. *Lighthouses and Lightships of the United States.* Boston: Houghton Mifflin, 1923.

Putnam, James William. *Illinois and Michigan Canal.* Chicago: University of Chicago Press, 1918.

Putnam, Peter. *Seven Britons in Imperial Russia.* Princeton, N.J.: Princeton University Press, 1952.

Putnam, Samuel. *History of Prostitution.* 3 vols. Chicago: P. Covici, 1926.

_____. *Paris Was Our Mistress.* Carbondale: Southern Illinois University Press, 1970.

Putterman, Jaydie, and Lesur, Rosalyn. *Police.* New York: Holt, Rinehart and Winston, 1983.

Putzel, Max. *The Man in the Mirror: William Marion Reedy and His Magazine.* Cambridge, Mass.: Harvard University Press, 1963.

Pu Yi, Aisin Gioro. *From Emperor to Citizen.* 2 vols. Peking: Foreign Language Press, 1965.

Pyarelal. *The Epic Fast.* Ahmedabad, India: Navajivan, 1950.

_____. *Gandhian Techniques in the Modern World.* Ahmedabad, India: Navajivan,1953.

_____. *Mahatma Gandhi, The Last Phase.* 2 vols. Ahmedabad, India: Navajivan, 1956.

_____. *A Nation Builder at Work.* Ahmedabad, India: Navajivan, 1953.

_____. *A Pilgrimage For Peace.* Ahmedabad, India: Navajivan, 1950.

Pye, Lucian. *Guerrilla Communism in Malaya.* Princeton, N.J.: Princeton University Press, 1956.

Pyle, G.F. et al. *The Spatial Dynamics of Crime.* Chicago: University of Chicago Department of Geography Research Paper, 1974.

Pyle, J.G. *The Life of James J. Hill.* New York: Doubleday, Doran, 1917.

Pyzur, Eugene. *The Doctrine of Anarchism of Michael A. Bukunin.* Milwaukee, Wis.: Marquette University Press, 1955.

Q

Quackery in Twentieth Century America. Princeton, N.J.: Princeton University Press, 1967.

Quaife, Milo Milton. *Checagou: From Indian Wigwam to Modern City, 1673-1835.* Chicago: University of Chicago Press, 1933.

_____. *Chicago and the Old Northwest, 1673-1835: A Study of the Evolution of the Northwestern Frontier, Together with a History of Fort Dearborn.* Chicago: University of Chicago Press, 1913.

_____. *Chicago's Highways Old and New: From Indian Trails to Motor Road.* Chicago: D.F. Keller, 1923.

_____. *Lake Michigan.* Indianapolis, Ind.: Bobbs Merrill, 1944.

Quaranta di San Serverino, Baron Bernardo (ed.). *Mussolini as Revealed in his Political Speeches.* London: Dent, 1923.

Quarles, Benjamin (ed.). *Blacks on John Brown.* Urbana: University of Illinois Press, 1972.

_____. *The Negro in the American Revolution.* Chapel Hill: University of North Carolina Press, 1961.

_____. *The Negro in the Civil War.* Boston: Little, Brown, 1953.

Quazza, Guido (ed.). *Fascismo e Societa Italiana.* Einaudi, 1973.

_____, Valiani, Leo, Volterra, Eduardo. *Il Governo del CLN.* Turin, Italy: Giappichelli, 1966.

Queen, Ellery. *A Study in Terror.* New York: Lancer, 1966.

Queens, S.A. *The Passing of the Country Jail.* Menasha, Wis.: Banta, 1920.

Queens Bench Foundation. *Rape: Prevention and Resistance.* San Francisco: Queens Bench Foundation, 1976.

Quertermous, R.S. *Modern Guns.* New York: Crown, 1979.

Quetelet, L.A.J. *A Treatise on Man and the Development of His Facilities.* Edinburgh, Scot.: William & Robert Chambers, 1842.

Queux, William Le (ed.). *The Secret Life of the Ex-Tsaritza.* London: Odhams, 1918.

Quicherat, J. *Procès de Condemnation et de Réhabilitation de Jeanne d'Arc.* 5 vols. Paris: Renouard, 1841-1849.

Quick, Herbert. *One Man's Life: An Autobiography.* Indianapolis, Ind.: Bobbs-Merrill, 1925.

Quiett, Glenn Chesney. *Pay Dirt, A Panorama of American Gold Rushes.* New York: D. Appleton-Century, 1936.

_____. *They Built the West.* New York: D. Appleton Century, 1934.

Quigg, Lemuel Ely. *"Gentleman" George Ives, a Montana Desperado.* Houston: Frontier Press of Texas, 1958.

Quigley, Harold S. *Far Eastern War, 1937-1941.* Boston: World Peace Foundation, 1942.

Quimby, Myron J. *The Devil's Emissaries.* New York: Modern Library, 1969.

Quinby, G.W. *The Gallows, the Prison and the Poor House.* Cincinatti, Ohio: Quinby, 1856.

Quinby, Ione. *Murder for Love.* New York: Covici-Friede, 1931.

Quincy, Josiah. *Memoir of the Life of John Quincy Adams.* Boston: Crosby, Nichols, Lee, 1860.

_____. *Memoir of the Life of Josiah Quincy.* Boston: Cummings, Hilliard, 1825.

Quinn, Arthur Hobson. *Edgar Allan Poe: A Critical Biography.* New York: Alfred A. Knopf, 1941.

Quinn, David B. *Raleigh and the British Empire.* London: Hodder & Stoughton, 1947.

Quinn, John Philip. *Fools of Fortune, or Gambling and Gamblers.* Chicago: W.B. Conkey, 1890.

_____. *Gambling and Gambling Devices.* Canton, Ohio: J.P. Quinn, 1912.

Quinn, Vernon. *War-Paint and Powder-Horn.* New York: Frederick A. Stokes, 1929.

Quinney, Richard. *Class, State and Crime: On the Theory and Practice of Criminal Justice.* New York: David McKay, 1977.

_____. *Crime and Justice in Society.* Boston: Little, Brown, 1969.

_____. *Criminal Justice in America: A Critical Understanding.* Boston: Little, Brown, 1974.

_____. *Criminology: Analysis and Critique of Crime in America.* Boston: Little, Brown, 1975.

_____. *Critique of Legal Order: Crime Control in Capitalist Society.* Boston: Little, Brown, 1974.

_____, and Wildeman, John. *The Problem of Crime.* New York: Harper & Row, 1977.

_____. *The Social Reality of Crime.* Boston: Little, Brown, 1970.

Quinton, René. *Die Stimme des Krieges.* Berlin: Der graue Verlag, 1936.

Quirk, Robert E. *An Affair of Honor: Woodrow Wilson and the Occupation of Veracruz.* Lexington: University of Kentucky Press, 1962.

_____. *The Mexican Revolution, 1914-1915: The Convention of Aguascalientes.* Bloomington: Indiana University Press, 1960.

R

Raab, Selwyn. *Justice in the Back Room.* New York: World,

1967.

Rabasa, Emilio. *La evolución histórica de México*. Mexico City: Libreria de la Vda. de Ch. Bouret, 1920.

Rabb, Theodore, and Rothberg, Robert (eds.). *The Family in History*. New York: Harper & Row, 1973.

Rabin, Yitzhak. *The Rabin Memoirs*. Boston: Little, Brown, 1979.

Rabinowicz, Oscar K. *Fifty Years of Zionism*. London: Robert Anscome, 1952.

Rabinowitch, Alexander. *Prelude to Revolution: The Petrograd Bolsheviks and the July 1917 Uprising*. Bloomington: Indiana University Press, 1968.

Rabitsch, Hugo. *Aus Adolf Hitlers Jugendzeit*. Munich: Deutscher Volksverlag, 1938.

Rabutaux, A.P.E. *De la Prostitution en Europe*. Paris: Lebigre-Duquesne Frères, 1851.

Raby, R. Cornelius. *Fifty Famous Trials*. Washington, D.C.: Washington Law Books, 1937.

Rachauskas, Constantine, and the Committee on World Order. *The Internationalization of Jerusalem*. Washington D.C.: Catholic Association for International Peace, n.d.

Rachleff, Owen S. *The Occult Conceit*. Chicago: Cowles-Regnery, 1971.

_____. *The Secrets of Superstitions*. Garden City, N.Y.: Doubleday, 1976.

Rachlin, Harvey. *The Kennedys: A Chronological History, 1823-Present*. New York: World Almanac Books, 1986.

Rachlis, Eugene, and Marqusee, John E. *The Land Lords*. New York: Random House, 1963.

Radano, Gene. *Walking the Beat*. Cleveland: World, 1968.

Radcliffe-Brown, A.R. *Method in Social Anthropology*. Chicago: University of Chicago Press, 1958.

Radelet, Louis A., Reed, Hoy, and Reed, Coe. *The Police and the Community*. Encino, Calif.: Glencoe Press, 1977.

Rader, Erich. *Struggle for the Sea*. trans. E. Fitzgerald. London: Kimber, 1959.

Radhakrishnan, Sarvepalli. *Indian Philosophy*. 2 vols. London: George Allen & Unwin, 1931.

_____ (ed.). *Mahatma Gandhi: Essays and Reflections*. London: George Allen & Unwin, 1939.

_____, and Moore, Charles A. (eds.). *A Sourcebook in Indian Philosophy*. Princeton, N.J.: Princeton University Press, 1957.

Radin, Edward D. *Crimes of Passion*. New York: G.P. Putnam's Sons, 1953.

_____. *Headline Crimes of the Year*. Boston: Little, Brown, 1952.

_____. *The Innocents*. New York: William Morrow, 1964.

_____. *Lizzie Borden: The Untold Story*. New York: Simon & Schuster, 1961.

_____. *12 Against Crime*. New York: G.P. Putnam's Sons, 1953.

_____. *12 Against the Law*. New York: Duell, Sloan & Pearce, 1942.

Radin, Max. *The Law and You*. New York: New American Library, 1948.

Radkey, Oliver Henry. *The Agrarian Foes of Bolshevism: Promise and Default of the Russian Socialist Revolutionaries*. New York: Columbia University Press, 1958.

_____. *The Elections to the Russian Constituent Assembly of 1917*. Cambridge, Mass.: Harvard University Press, 1950.

_____. *The History of the Russian Revolution*. Ann Arbor: University of Michigan Press, 1957.

_____. *The Sickle under the Hammer*. New York: Columbia University Press, 1963.

Rado, Sandor. *An Adaptational View of Sexual Behavior in Psychosexual Development in Health and Disease*. New York: Grune & Stratton, 1949.

_____. *Psychoanalysis of Behavior*. New York: Grune & Stratton, 1956.

Radosh, Ronald (ed.). *Debs*. Englewoood Cliffs, N.J.: Prentice-Hall, 1971.

Radosh, Ronald, and Milton, Joyce. *The Rosenberg File: A Search for the Truth*. New York: Holt, Rinehart & Winston, 1983.

Radwanski, George. *Trudeau*. Toronto: Macmillan of Canada, 1978.

Radzinowicz, Leon, and Wolfgang, Marvin E. (eds.). *Crime and Justice*. 3 vols. New York: Basic Books, 1971.

_____. *Crime and Society*. New York: Basic Books, 1977.

_____, and Hood, Roger. *Criminology and the Administration of Criminal Justice*. London: Mansen Information, 1976.

_____, and King, Joan. *The Growth of Crime*. New York: Basic Books, 1977.

_____. *A History of English Criminal Law and Its Administration from 1750*. 4 vols. London: Stevens & Sons, 1948-68.

_____. *Ideology and Crime*. New York: Columbia University Press, 1966.

_____. *In Search of Criminology*. Cambridge, Mass.: Harvard University Press, 1962.

_____, and Turner, J.W.C. (eds.). *The Modern Approach to Criminal Law, English Studies in Criminal Science*. London: Macmillan, 1945.

_____ (ed.). *Sexual Offences*. London: Macmillan, 1957.

_____. *Sir James F. Stephens and his Contributions to the Development of Criminal Law*. London: B. Quaritch, 1957.

Radziweill, Catherine. *The Intimate Life of the Last Tsarina*. London: Cassell, 1929.

_____. *Nicholas II: The Last of the Tsars*. London: Cassell, 1931.

_____. *Royal Marriage Market of Europe*. New York: Funk & Wagnalls, 1915.

_____. *Secrets of Dethroned Royalty*. London: John Lane, 1920.

_____. *Sovereigns and Statesmen of Europe*. New York: Funk & Wagnalls, 1916.

_____. *Those I Remember*. London: Cassell, 1924.

Radziwill, Princess Marie Dorothée Elisabeth. *Briefe vom deutschen Kaiserhof 1889-1915*. Berlin: Deutscher, 1936.

_____. *This Was Germany: An Observer at the Court of Berlin*. ed. and trans. Cyril Spencer Fox. Forest Hills, N.Y.: Transatlantic Arts, 1938.

Raeff, Marc. *The Decembrist Movement*. Englewood Cliffs, N.J.: Prentice-Hall, 1966.

_____. *Michael Speransky: Statesman of Imperial Russia, 1772-1839*. The Hague, Neth.: Martinius Nijhoff, 1957.

_____ (ed.). *Plans for Political Reform in Imperial Russia, 1730-1905*. Englewood Cliffs, N.J.: Prentice-Hall, 1965.

_____. *Siberia and the Reforms of 1822*. Seattle: University of Washington Press, 1956.

Rafael, Ruth Kelson. *Continuum-A Selective History of San Francisco Eastern European Jewish Life, 1880-1940*. Berkeley, Calif.: Judah L. Magnes Museum, 1977.

Rafanelli, Leda. *Una donna e Mussolini*. Milan, Italy: Rizolli, 1946.

Raffalovich, George. *Benito Mussolini*. Florence, Italy: Owl, 1923.

Raftis, J. Ambrose. *Tenure and Mobility: Studies in the Social History of the Medieval English Village*. Toronto, Ontario, Can.: Institute of Medieval Studies, 1964.

Ragen, Joseph E., and Finston, Charles. *Inside the World's Toughest Prison*. Springfield, Ill.: Charles C. Thomas, 1962.

Ragon, Michel. *L'Avant-Guerre*. Paris: Planète, 1968.

Rahn, Rudolf. *Ambasciatore di Hitler a Vichy e a Salò*. Milan, Italy: Garzanti, 1950.

_____. *Ruheloses Leben*. Düsseldorf, Ger.: Deiderichs, 1959.

Raht, Carlyse Graham. *The Romance of the Davis Mountains and the Big Bend Country*. El Paso, Texas: Rahtbooks, 1919.

Raine, William McLeod, and Barnes, Will C. *Cattle*. New York: Doubleday, Doran, 1930.

_____. *Famous Sheriffs and Western Outlaws*. Garden City, N.Y.: Doubleday, Doran, 1929.

_____. *45-Caliber Law: The Way of Life of the Frontier Peace Officer*. Evanston, Ill.: Row, Peterson, 1941.

_____. *Guns of the Frontier: The Story of How Law Came to the*

West. Boston: Houghton Mifflin, 1940.

Rainey, George. *The Cherokee Strip.* Guthrie, Okla.: Cooperative, 1933.

_____. *No Man's Land.* Guthrie, Okla.: Cooperative, 1937.

Rainsford, William S. *The Story of a Varied Life.* Garden City, N.Y.: Doubleday, Page, 1922.

Rainwater, Lee. *Behind Ghetto Walls.* Chicago: Aldine, 1970.

_____, and Yancey, William L. *The Moynihan Report and the Politics of Controversy.* Cambridge, Mass.: MIT Press, 1967.

Rajagopalachari, C. *The Nation's Voice.* Ahmedabad, India: Navajivan, 1932.

Rajski, Raymond B. (ed.). *A Nation Grieved: The Kennedy Assassination in Editorial Cartoons.* Rutland, Vt.: Charles E. Tuttle, 1967.

Rak, Mary Kidder. *Border Patrol.* Boston: Houghton Mifflin, 1938.

Rakov, Milton L. *Don't Make No Waves, Don't Back No Losers.* Bloomington: Indiana University Press, 1975.

Ralph, Julian E. *Our Great West: A Study of the Present Conditions and Future Possibilites of the New Commonwealths and Capitals of the United States.* New York: Harper & Brothers, 1893.

Ramachandran, G. *A Sheaf of Gandhi Anecdotes.* Bombay, India: Hind Kitabs, 1946.

Raman, T.A. *What Does Gandhi Want?* New York: Oxford University Press, 1942.

Rambo, Ralph. *Trailing the California Bandit Tiburcio Vásquez, 1835-1875.* San Jose, Calif.: Rosicrucian Press, 1968.

Ramirez Plancarte, Francisco. *La Ciudad de México durante la revolución constituciónalista.* Mexico City: Ediciones Botas, 1941.

Rammelkamp, Julian S. *Pulitzer's Post-Dispatch 1878-1883.* Princeton, N.J.: Princeton University Press, 1967.

Ramparts Magazine (ed.). *In the Shadow of Dallas: A Primer on the Assassination of President Kennedy.* San Francisco: Ramparts, 1967.

Ramsauer, E.E. *The Young Turks: Prelude to the Revolution of 1908.* Princeton, N.J.: Princeton University Press, 1957.

Ramsay, David. *History of South Carolina.* Newberry, S.C.: W.J. Duffie, 1858.

Ramsay, Marion Livingston. *Pyramids of Power: The Story of Roosevelt, Insull, and the Utility Wars.* New York: Bobbs-Merrill, 1937.

Ramsdell, Charles. *San Antonio, a Historical and Pictorial Guide.* Austin: University of Texas Press, 1959.

Ramsdell, Charles W. *Reconstruction in Texas.* New York: Columbia University Press, 1910.

Ramsey, James G.M. *Annals of Tennessee.* Philadelphia: Lippincott, Grambo, 1853.

Rand, Christopher. *The Puerto Ricans.* New York: Oxford University Press, 1958.

Rand, Edward Kennard. *Founders of the Middle Ages.* New York: Dover, 1928.

Rand, Michael, Loxton, Howard, and Deighton, Len. *The Assassination of President Kennedy.* London: Jonathan Cape, 1967.

Randall, Donald A., and Glickman, Arthur P. *The Great American Auto Repair Robbery.* New York: Charterhouse, 1972.

Randall, Frank A. *History of the Development of Building Construction in Chicago.* Urbana: University of Illinois, 1949.

Randall, George M. *First Report of Bishop Randall of Colorado.* New York: Sanford, Harroun, 1866.

Randall, James G., and Donald, David. *The Civil War and Reconstruction.* New York: D.C. Heath, 1937.

_____. *Consitutional Problems Under Lincoln.* Urbana: University of Illinois Press, 1964.

_____. *Lincoln the President: Midstream.* New York: Dodd, Mead, 1952.

_____. *Lincoln the President: Springfield to Gettysburg.* New York: Dodd, Mead, 1945.

Randall, Leslie. *The Famous Cases of Sir Bernard Spilsbury.* London: I. Nicholson & Watson, 1936.

Randall, Ruth Painter. *Colonel Elmer Ellsworth: A Biography of Lincoln's Friend and First Hero of the Civil War.* Boston: Little, Brown, 1960.

_____. *Mary Lincoln: Biography of a Marriage.* Boston: Little, Brown, 1953.

Randall, Richard. *Censorship of the Movies.* Madison: University of Wisconsin Press, 1968.

Randall, Terry. *Hooker.* New York: Award Books, 1969.

Randel, William Pierce. *The Ku Klux Klan: A Century of Infamy.* New York: Chilton Books, 1965.

Randell, Captain Jack. *I'm Alone.* London: Jonathan Cape, 1931.

Randi, James. *The Magic of Uri Geller.* New York: Ballantine, 1975.

Randolph, Edward. *Edward Randolph: His Letters and Official Papers.* Boston: Prince Society, 1898.

Randolph, Vance. *Ozark Folksongs.* 4 vols. Columbia: State Historical Society of Missouri, 1946-1950.

_____. *Ozark Superstitions.* New York: Columbia University Press, 1947.

_____. *Who Blowed Up the Church House?* New York: Columbia University Press, 1952.

Ranger, T. *Peasant Consciousness and Guerilla War in Zimbabwe.* London: James Currey, 1985.

Rank, Otto. *The Double: A Psychoanalytic Study.* trans. Harry Tucker, Jr. New York: New American Library, 1979.

Ranke, Kurt (ed.). *Folktales of Germany.* Chicago: University of Chicago Press, 1968.

Ranke, Leopold von. *Hardenberg und die Geschichte des preussischen Staates, 1793-1813.* Berlin: Duncker & Humblot, 1879.

_____. *History of the Popes.* London: George Bell & Sons, 1891.

_____. *Zwölf Bücher preussischer Geschichte.* Leipzig, Ger.: Duncker & Humblot, 1874.

Rankin, Henry B. *Personal Recollections of Abraham Lincoln.* New York: G.P. Putnam's Sons, 1916.

Rankin, Hugh F. *Criminal Trial Proceedings in the General Court of Colonial Virginia.* Williamsburg: University Press of Virginia, 1965.

_____. *The Golden Age of Piracy.* New York: Holt, Rinehart & Winston, 1969.

Rankin, L. *No. 6847; or, the Horrors of Prison Life.* n.p, 1897.

Rankin, M. Wilson. *Reminiscences of Fronter Days, Including an Authentic Account of the Thornburg and Meeker Massacre.* Denver: Smith-Brooks, 1938.

Ransom, Rev. A. *A Terrible History of Fraud and Crime: The Twin Brothers of Texas.* Philadelphia: M.A. Milliette, 1858.

Ransom, Harry Howe. *Central Intelligence and National Security.* Cambridge, Mass: Harvard University Press, 1959.

_____. *The Intelligence Establishment.* Cambridge, Mass.: Harvard University Press, 1970.

Ransome, Arthur. *Russia in 1919.* New York: B.W. Huebsch, 1919.

Rantoul, Robert, Jr. *Memoirs, Speeches and Writings of Robert Rantoul, Jr.* Boston: J.P. Jewett, 1854.

Ranulf, Svend. *Moral Indignation and Middle Class Psychology.* New York: Schocken, 1964.

Rao, K.R. *Experimental Parapsychology: A Review and Interpretation.* Springfield, Ill.: Charles C. Thomas, 1966.

Rao, R. Venugopal. *Facets of Crime in India.* Bombay, India: Allied, 1963.

_____. *Gandhian Institutions of Wardha.* Bombay, India: Thackus, 1947.

_____. *Murder: A Pilot Study with Particular Reference to the City of Delhi.* New Delhi: Government of India, 1968.

Raper, A.F. *The Tragedy of Lynching.* Chapel Hill: University of North Carolina Press, 1933.

Rapoport, Daniel. *Inside the House.* Chicago: Follett, 1975.

Rapp, Ludwig. *Die Hexenprozesse und ihre Gegner in Tirol.* Innsbruck, Austria: n.p., 1874.

Rappaport, Armin. *Henry L. Stimson and Japan, 1931-1933.* Chicago: University of Chicago Press, 1963.

Rappard, William E. *The Government of Switzerland.* New York: D. Van Nostrand, 1936.

_____, et al. *Source Book on European Governments, Switzerland, France, Italy, Germany, the Soviet Union.* New York: D. Van Nostrand, 1937.

Rapoport, David C. *Assassination and Terrorism.* Toronto, Ontario, Can.: Canadian Broadcasting, 1971.

Rascoe, Burton. *Before I Forget.* Garden City, N.Y.: Doubleday, Doran, 1937.

_____. *Belle Starr, The Bandit Queen.* New York: Random House, 1941.

_____. *We Were Interrupted.* Garden City, N.Y.: Doubleday, 1947.

Rascoe, Jesse Ed. *Some Western Treasures.* Cisco, Texas: Frontier Books, 1964.

Rashke, Richard. *The Killing of Karen Silkwood.* Boston: Houghton Mifflin, 1981.

Rasmussen, A.H. *China Trader.* New York: Thomas Y. Crowell, 1954.

Rasmussen, Knud. *Across Arctic America.* New York: Greenwood Press, 1969.

_____. *Eskimo Folk Tales.* London: Gyldendal, 1921.

Rasputin, Maria and Barham, Patte. *Rasputin: The Man Behind the Myth.* London: W.H. Allen, 1977.

_____. *The Real Rasputin.* London: John Long, 1929.

Rath, Ida Ellen. *Early Ford County.* North Newton, Kan.: Mennonite Press, 1964.

_____. *The Rath Trail.* Wichita, Kan.: McCormick-Armstrong, 1961.

Rathbone, Perry T. (ed.). *Mississippi Panorama.* St. Louis, Mo.: St. Louis City Art Museum, 1950.

Rathenau, Walther. *Der Kaiser: Eine Betrachtung.* Berlin: S. Fischer, 1919.

_____. *Walther Rathenau in Brief und Bild.* Frankfort, Ger.: M.A. Leber, 1967.

Rather, Dan, and Herskowitz, Mickey. *The Camera Never Blinks.* New York: William Morrow, 1977.

_____, and Gates, Gary Paul. *The Palace Guard.* New York: Warner, 1975.

Rathjen, Frederick W. *The Texas Panhandle Frontier.* Austin: University of Texas Press, 1973.

Rathlef-Keilmann, Harriet von. *Anastasia, Survivor of Ekaterinberg.* New York: Putnam, 1928.

Rathus, Spenser. *Human Sexuality.* New York: Holt, Rinehart, & Winston, 1983.

Ratledge, Marcus Wayne. *Don't Become the Victim.* Boulder, Colo.: Paladin Press, 1981.

Rattigan, Frank. *Diversions of a Diplomat.* London: Chapman & Hall, 1924.

Rauch, Basil. *The History of the New Deal 1933-1938.* New York: Creative Age, 1944.

Rauch, Georg Von. *A History of Soviet Russia.* New York: Frederick A. Praeger, 1957.

Rauschning, Hermann. *Hitler Speaks.* London: Thornton Butterworth, 1939.

Raushenbush, Stephen. *The March of Fascism.* New Haven, Conn.: Yale University Press, 1940.

Rautenstrauch, Walter. *Who Gets the Money?* New York: Harper, 1934.

Rautert, Fr. *Etwas Näheres über die Hexenprozesse der Vorzeit.* Essen, Ger.: G.D. Bädecker, 1827.

Ravaisson, Francois. *Archives de La Bastille.* Paris: A Durant Et Pedone-Lauriel, Libraires, 1873.

Ravdin, Dr. Isidor. *Reminiscences.* New York: East Asian Institute, Columbia University, n.d.

Raven, S.S. *The Feathers of Death.* London: Anthony Blond, 1959.

Ravenel, Mazyck P. (ed.). *A Half Century of Public Health.* New York: American Public Health Association, 1921.

Ravenel, Mrs. St. Julien (Harriott Hörry). *Charleston: The Place and the People.* New York: Macmillan, 1906.

_____. *Eliza Pinckney.* New York: Charles Scribner's Sons, 1896.

Ravenstein, E.G. *The Russians on the Amur.* London: Trübner, 1861.

Raviart, Georges. *Sorcières et possédées.* Lille, Fr.: E. Raoust, 1936.

Ravitch, Diane. *The Great School Wars: New York City, 1805-1973.* New York: Basic Books, 1974.

Ravitz, Abe C. *Clarence Darrow and the American Literary Tradition.* Cleveland: Press of Western Reserve University, 1962.

Ravoof, A.A. *Meet Mr. Jinnah.* Lahore, Pak.: Sheikh Muhammad Ashraf, 1947.

Rawcliffe, D.H. *Illusions and Delusions of the Supernatural and Occult.* New York: Dover, 1959.

_____. *The Struggle for Kenya.* London: Victor Gollancz, 1954.

Rawley, James A. *Edwin D. Morgan, 1811-1883.* New York: Columbia University Press, 1955.

Rawls, John. *A Theory of Justice.* Cambridge, Mass.: Harvard University Press, 1971.

Rawson, Geoffrey. *Bligh of the "Bounty".* London: Philip Allan, 1930.

Rawson, Philip. *Erotic Art of the East.* New York: G.P. Putnam's Sons, 1968.

Rawson, Tabor. *I Want to Live.* New York: Signet Books, 1958.

Ray, Bright. *Legends of the Red River Valley.* San Antonio, Texas: Naylor, 1941.

Ray, Chaplain, with Wagner, Walter. *God's Prison Gang.* Old Tappan, N.J.: Revell, 1976.

Ray, Clarence E. *The Alabama Wolf: Rube Burrow and His Desperate Gang of Highwaymen.* Chicago: Regan, 1910.

_____. *The Border Outlaws, Frank & Jesse James.* Chicago: Regan, n.d.

_____. *Buffalo Bill, the Scout.* Chicago: Regan, n.d.

_____. *The Dalton Brothers.* Chicago: Regan, n.d.

_____. *Famous American Scouts.* Chicago: Regan, n.d.

_____. *Harry Tracy, Bandit, Highwayman and Outlaw of the Twentieth Century.* Chicago: Regan, n.d.

_____. *The James Boys.* Chicago: Regan, n.d.

_____. *The James Boys and Bob Ford.* Chicago: Regan, 1893.

_____. *Jesse James' Daring Raid.* Chicago: Regan, n.d.

_____. *Jesse James and His Gang of Train Robbers.* Chicago: Regan, n.d.

_____. *Life of Bob and Cole Younger with Quantrell.* Chicago: Regan, 1916.

_____. *The Oklahoma Bandits: The Daltons and Their Desperate Gang.* Chicago: Regan, n.d.

_____. *Rube Burrow, King of Outlaws and Train Robbers.* Chicago: Regan, n.d.

_____. *The Younger Brothers.* Chicago: Regan, n.d.

Ray, Elizabeth L. *The Washington Fringe Benefit.* New York: Dell Books, 1976.

Ray, G.B. *Murder at the Corners.* San Antonio, Texas: Naylor, 1957.

Ray, Grace Ernestine. *Wily Women of the West.* San Antonio, Texas: Naylor, 1972.

Ray, James Earl. *Tennessee Waltz: The Making of a Political Prisoner.* Saint Andrews, Tenn.: Saint Andrew's Press, 1987.

Ray, Oakley. *Drugs, Society, and Human Behavior.* St. Louis: C.V. Mosby, 1978.

Ray, Sam Hill. *Border Tales: Stories of Texas-New Mexico.* El Paso, Texas: Commercial, 1964.

Ray, Worth S. *Down in the Cross Timbers.* Austin, Texas: Published by Author, 1947.

Rayburn, Otto Ernest. *The Eureka Springs Story.* Eureka Springs, Ark.: Times-Echo Press, 1954.

_____. *Ozark Country.* New York: Duell, Sloan & Pearce, 1941.

Rayfield, Alma C. *The West That's Gone.* New York: Carleton Press, 1962.

Raymar, Robert George. *Montana, the Land and the People.* Chicago: Lewis, 1930.

Raymond, Dora Neill. *Captain Lee Hall of Texas.* Norman: University of Oklahoma Press, 1940.

Raymond, Henry J. *The Life and Public Services of Abraham Lincoln.* New York: Derby & Miller, 1865.

Raymond, John (ed.). *Victoria's Early Letters.* New York: Macmillan, 1963.

Raynor, Ted. *Old Timers Talk in Southwestern New Mexico.* El Paso: Texas Western Press, 1960.

Re, Emilio. *Storia di un archivo: Le carte di Mussolini.* Milan, Italy: Milione, 1946.

Rea, Ralph. *Boone County and Its People.* Van Buren, Ark.: Press-Argus, 1955.

Read, Donald. *Peterloo: The Massacre and Its Background.* Manchester, Eng.: Manchester University Press, 1958.

Read, Frederick Brent. *Up the Heights to Fame and Fortune.* Cincinnati, Ohio: Moore, 1873.

Read, John. *The Alchemist.* London: Thomas Nelson & Sons, 1947.

Read, Opie. *Mark Twain and I.* Chicago: Reilly & Lee, 1940.

Read, Piers Paul. *The Train Robbers.* New York: J.B. Lippincott, 1978.

Reade, Brian. *Sexual Heretics.* New York: Coward-McCann, 1970.

Reading, D.K. *The Anglo-Russian Commercial Treaty of 1734.* New Haven, Conn.: Yale University Press, 1938.

Reading, Gerald Rufus Isaacs. *Rufus Isaacs, First Marquess of Reading.* New York: Putnam, 1940.

Reaney, P.H. *A Dictionary of British Surnames.* London: Routledge & Kegan Paul, 1958.

Reagen, Michael V., and Stoughton, Donald M. *School Behind Bars.* Metuchen, N.J.: Scarecrow Press, 1976.

Reasons, Charles E. *The Criminologist: Crime and the Criminal.* Pacific Palisades, Calif.: Goodyear, 1974.

_____, and Kuykendall, Jack L. (eds.). *Race, Crime and Justice.* Pacific Palisades, Calif.: Goodyear, 1972.

Rebel Cork's Fighting Story from 1916 to the Truce with Britain. Tralee, Ire.: Kerryman, n.d.

Rebérioux, Madeleine. *La République radicale? 1898-1914.* Paris: Editions du Seuil, 1975.

Récit véritable de ce qui s'est fait et passé à Louviers touchant les religieuses possedées. Paris: I. Mesnier, 1621.

Reckless, Walter. *American Criminology: New Directions.* New York: Appleton-Century-Crofts, 1973.

_____. *The Crime Problem.* New York: D. Appleton, 1950.

_____. *The Etiology of Delinquent and Criminal Behavior.* New York: Social Science Research Council, 1943.

_____, and Smith, M. *Juvenile Delinquency.* New York: Mc-Graw-Hill, 1932

_____, and Dinitz, S. *The Prevention of Juvenile Delinquency.* Columbus: Ohio State University Press, 1972.

_____. *Vice in Chicago.* Chicago: University of Chicago Press, 1933.

The Record of Crimes in the U.S. Buffalo, N.Y.: Faxon, 1834.

Records of the Monthly Meeting of the Society of Friends. New York: Havilland Records Room, n.d.

Rector, William Gerald. *Log Transportation in the Lake States Lumber Industry.* Glendale, Calif.: Arthur H. Clark, 1953.

Recueil général des pièces contenues au procez du père Jean-Baptiste Girard, Jésuite. Aix-en-Provence, Fr.: J. David, 1731.

Redd, D. (ed.). *Speech Recognition.* New York: Academic Press, 1974.

Reddaway, W.F., et al. (eds.). *Cambridge History of Poland.* Cambridge, Eng.: Cambridge University Press, 1941.

_____ (ed.). *Documents on Catherine the Great.* Cambridge, Eng.: Cambridge University Press, 1931.

_____. *Frederick the Great and the Rise of Prussia.* New York: Haskell House, 1904.

Reddig, William M. *Tom's Town.* New York: J.B. Lippincott, 1947.

Redding, Jay Saunders. *The Lonesome Road; the Story of the Negro's Part in America.* New York: Doubleday, 1958.

_____. *They Came in Chains.* Philadelphia: J.B. Lippincott, 1950.

Redfield, Horace V. *Homicide: North and South.* Philadelphia: J.B. Lippincott, 1880.

Redford, Polly. *Billion Dollar Sandbar.* New York: E.P. Dutton, 1970.

Redford, Robert. *The Outlaw Trail.* New York: Grosset & Dunlap, 1979.

Redgrove, H. Stanley. *Alchemy: Ancient and Modern.* New York: Barnes & Noble, 1973.

_____. *Joseph Glanvill and Psychical Research in the Seventeenth Century.* London: Rider & Son, 1921.

Redl, Fritz, and Wineman, David. *Children Who Hate.* Glencoe, Ill.: Free Press, 1951.

Redlich, Fritz. *The Molding of American Banking: Men and Ideas.* New York: Johnson Reprint, 1968.

Redmond, Dennis M. *"Four Sixes to Beat".* El Paso, Texas: n.p, 1965.

Redmond, Frank. *The Younger Brothers.* St. Louis: Dramatic, 1901.

Redmond-Howard, L.G. *Six Days of the Irish Republic: A Narrative and Critical Account of the Latest Phase of Irish Politics.* Boston: John W. Luce, 1916.

Redpath, James. *The Public Life of Captain John Brown.* Boston: Thayer & Eldridge, 1860.

Redston, George, and Crossen, Kendall F. *The Conspiracy of Death.* New York: Random House, 1952.

Reed, Adolf Frank. *The Case of General Yamashita.* Chicago: University of Chicago Press, 1949.

Reed, Douglas. *Nemesis: The Story of Otto Strasser and the Black Front.* Boston: Houghton Mifflin, 1940.

Reed, George Irving (ed.). *Bench and Bar of Ohio.* Chicago: Century Publishing and Engraving, 1897.

Reed, John. *Ten Days That Shook the World.* New York: Modern Library, 1935.

Reed, John Silas. *Insurgent Mexico.* New York: D. Appleton, 1914.

Reed, Lear B. *Human Wolves: Seventeen Years of War on Crime.* Kansas City, Mo.: Brown-White, Lowell Press, 1941.

Reedy, George E. *The Twilight of the Presidency.* New York: New American Library, 1970.

Reeling, Viola Crouch. *Evanston: Its Land and its People.* Evanston, Ill.: Fort Dearborn Chapter, Daughters of the American Revolution, 1928.

Rees, David. *Harry Dexter White: A Study in Paradox.* New York: Coward, McCann & Geoghegan, 1973.

Rees, Goronwy. *The Great Slump - Capitalism in Crisis, 1929-1933.* London: Weidenfeld & Nicholson, 1970.

_____. *The Multi-Millionaires.* London: Chatto & Windus, 1961.

Rees, J.R. *Sexual Perversions.* London: Practitioner, 1936.

Rees, J. Taylor, and Usill, Harley V. (eds.). *They Stand Apart.* London: William Heinemann, 1955.

Rees, James. *The Life of Edwin Forrest.* Philadelphia: T.B. Peterson & Brothers, 1874.

Reese, John Walter and Lillian Estelle. *Flaming Feuds of Colorado County.* Salado, Texas: Anson-Jones Press, 1962.

Reeves, Col. Ira L. *Ol' Rum River.* Chicago: Rockwell, 1931.

Reeves, Richard. *A Ford, Not a Lincoln.* New York: Harcourt Brace Jovanovich, 1975.

Reeves, Thomas C. *Foundations Under Fire.* Ithaca, N.Y.: Cornell University Press, 1970.

Regan, Robert. *Poe: A Collection of Critical Essays.* Englewood Cliffs, N.J.: Prentice-Hall, 1967.

Regenstein, Lewis. *America the Poisoned.* Washington, D.C.: Acropolis Books, 1982.

Regino. *De Ecclesiasticis Disciplinis.* Vienna, Aus.: T-Thome, 1765.

Regis, E. *Les régicides dans l'histoire.* Lyon, Fr.: A. Storck, 1890.

Regler, Gustav. *A Land Bewitched.* New York: G.P. Putnam's Sons, 1955.

Regnault, Elias. *L'Histoire de huit ans, 1840-1848.* Paris: Pabnerre, 1860.

Régné, Jean. *La Sorcellerie en Vivarais.* Paris: F. Alcan, 1913.

Rehearsal both Strange and True of the Heinous and Horrible Acts Committed by Elizabeth Stile. London: E. White, 1579.

Reich, Albert. *Aus Adolf Hitlers Heimat Land.* Munich: Verlag Frz. Eher, 1933.

Reich, Charles A. *The Greening of America.* New York: Random House, 1970.

Reich V., and Rohwig, O. *Der Freiheitskampf der Ostmark Deutschen.* Graz, Ger.: L. Stocker, 1942.

Reich, Wilhelm. *The Sexual Revolution.* New York: Octagon, 1971.

Reichard, Gladys A. *Navaho Religion.* New York: Bollingen Foundation, 1950.

Reiche, Johann. *Untershiedliche Schrifften vom Unfug des Hexen-Processes.* Halle, Ger.: Mandelburg, 1703.

Reichler, Joe (ed.). *The Game and the Glory.* Englewood Cliffs, N.J.: Prentice-Hall, 1976.

Reid, Ed. *The Green Felt Jungle.* New York: Cardinal, 1964.
_____. *The Grim Reapers, The Anatomy of Organized Crime in America.* Chicago: Henry Regnery, 1969.
_____. *Mafia.* New York: Random House, 1952.
_____. *The Mistress and the Mafia.* New York: Bantam, 1972.
_____. *The Shame of New York.* New York: Random House, 1953.

Reid, I.D.A. *The Negro Immigrant.* New York: Columbia University Press, 1939.

Reid, Col. J.M. *Sketches and Anecdotes of the Old Settlers and New Comers.* Keokuk, Iowa: R.R. Ogden, 1876.

Reid, John E., and Inbau, Fred E. *Truth and Deception, the Polygraph.* Baltimore: Williams & Wilkins, 1977.

Reid, Mildred I. *The Devil's Handmaidens.* Boston: Humphries, 1951.

Reid, Samuel C., Jr. *The Scouting Expeditions of McCulloch's Texas Rangers.* Philadelphia: G.B. Zieber, 1848.

Reid, Susan Titus. *Crime and Criminology.* New York: Holt, Rinehart, 1976.
_____. *Crime and Criminology.* New York: Holt, Rinehart & Winston, 1982.

Reid, T.W. *The Life, Letters and Friendships of Richard Monckton Milnes, First Lord Houghton.* 2 vols. London: Cassell, 1890.

Reid, Whitelaw. *After the War: A Southern Tour May 1, 1865 to May 1, 1866.* Cincinnati, Ohio: Moore, Wilstach & Baldwin, 1866.

Reiff, R., and Scheerer, M. *Memory and the Hypnotic Age of Regression.* New York: International University Press, 1959.

Reiff, Robert. *The Invisible Victim.* New York: Basic Books, 1979.

Reiffenberg, Baron de. *Mémoires de Jacques du Clercq.* Paris: J.A. Buchen, 1826-27.

Reik, Theodor. *The Compulsion to Confess.* New York: Farrar, Straus, 1959.
_____. *Myth and Guilt.* New York: Braziller, 1957.

Reilly, Michael F., and Slocum, William J. *I Was Roosevelt's Shadow.* London: W. Foulsham, 1946.

Reiman, Jeffrey H. *In Defense of Political Philosophy.* New York: Harper & Row, 1972.
_____. *The Rich Get Richer and the Poor Get Prison.* New York: John Wiley & Sons, 1979.

Reinach, Joseph. *Histoire de l'affaire Dreyfus.* 7 vols. Paris: Fasquelle, 1901-11.

Reinach, Lucien de. *Le Laos.* Paris: A. Charles, 1901.

Reiners, Ludwig. *Bismarck.* 3 vols. Munich: Beck, 1956-1958.
_____. *Frederick the Great: An Informal Biography.* trans.

Lawrence P.R. Wilson. London: Oswald Wolff, 1960.

Reinhardt, James Melvin. *The Murderous Trail of Charles Starkweather.* Springfield, Ill.: Charles C. Thomas, 1962.
_____. *The Psychology of Strange Killers.* Springfield, Ill.: Charles C. Thomas, 1962.
_____. *Sex Perversions and Sex Crimes.* Springfield, Ill.: Charles C. Thomas, 1957.

Reinhard, Marcel R., Armengaud, André, and Dupaquier, Jacques. *Histoire Génerale de la Population Mondiale.* Paris: Editions Montchrestien, 1968.

Reinhardt, Richard. *Out West on the Overland Train.* Palo Alto, Calif.: American West, 1967.

Reinhart, Herman Francis. *The Golden Frontier: The Recollections of Herman Francis Reinhart, 1851-1869.* Austin: University of Texas, 1962.

Reinsch, Paul S. *An American Diplomat in China, 1913-19.* New York: Doubleday, Page, 1922.

Reischach, Baron Hugo von. *Under Three Emperors: Being Court Reminiscences Under William I, Frederick III and William II.* trans. Prince Blücher. London: Constable, 1927.

Reischauer, Edwin O. *Japan Past and Present.* New York: Alfred A. Knopf, 1964.
_____. *Japan: The Story of a Nation.* New York: Alfred A. Knopf, 1970.
_____. *The Japanese.* Cambridge, Mass.: Harvard University Press, 1977.
_____, *The United States and Japan.* Cambridge, Mass.: Harvard University Press, 1950.

Reisman, W. Michael. *Folded Lies: Bribery, Crusades, and Reforms.* New York: Free Press, 1979.

Reisner, Robert George. *Show Me the Good Parts.* New York: Citadel Press, 1964.

Reiss, Albert J., Jr. *The Police and the Public.* New Haven, Conn.: Yale University Press, 1971.
_____. *Studies in Crime and Law Enforcement in Major Metropolitan Areas.* Washington, D.C.: U.S. Government Printing Office, 1967.

Reiss, Erna. *Rights and Duties of Englishwomen.* Manchester, Eng.: Sherrat & Hughes, 1934.

Reiter, P.J. *Antisocial or Criminal Acts and Hypnosis.* Springfield, Ill.: Charles C. Thomas, 1958.

Reith, Charles. *The Blind Eye of History.* London: Faber & Faber, 1952.
_____. *A New Study of Police History.* London: Oliver, 1956.
_____. *The Police Idea; its History and Evolution in England in the Eighteenth Century and After.* London: Oxford University Press, 1938.
_____. *A Short History of the British Police.* London: Oxford University Press, 1940.

Reitlinger, Gerald. *The Final Solution.* New York: Thomas Yoseloff, 1961.
_____. *The House Built on Sand.* New York: Viking Press, 1960.
_____. *The SS. Alibi of a Nation.* London: William Heinemann, 1956.

Reitman, Ben L. *The Second Oldest Profession.* New York: Vanguard Press, 1931.
_____. *Sister of the Road: The Autobiography of Boxcar Bertha.* New York: Sheridan House, 1937.

Reitsch, Hanna. *Flying is My Life.* New York: G.P. Putnam's Sons, 1954.

Reiwald, P. *Society and Its Criminals.* New York: International University Press, 1950.

A Relation of the Diabolical Practices of above Twenty Wizards and Witches of the Sheriffdom of Renfrew. London: H. Newman, 1697.

Remak, Joachim. *The First World War: Causes, Conduct, Consequences.* New York: John Wiley & Sons, 1971.
_____. *The Origins of World War I, 1871-1914.* Hinsdale, Ill.: Dryden Press, 1967.
_____. *The Nazi Years.* Englewood Cliffs, N.J.: Prentice-Hall,

1969.

_____. *Sarajevo: The Story of a Political Murder.* New York: Criterion Press, 1959.

Remarkable Trials of all Countries. New York: S.S. Peloubet, 1882.

Remault, J. Edwards. *The Car-Hook Tragedy.* Philadelphia: Barclay, 1873.

Rembar, Charles. *The Law of the Land.* New York: Simon & Schuster, 1980.

Remick, Peter as told to Shuman, James B. *In Constant Fear.* New York: Reader's Digest Press, 1975.

Remi, Nicholas. *Demonalatreiae Libri Tres.* Lyons, Fr.: In officina Vincentii, 1595.

_____. *Demonolatry.* London: John Rodker, 1930.

Remini, Robert V. *Martin Van Buren and the Making of the Democratic Party.* New York: Columbia University Press, 1959.

Reminiscences of Chicago During the Civil War. Chicago: Lakeside Press, 1914.

Reminiscences of Chicago During the Forties and Fifties. Chicago: Lakeside Press, 1913.

Reminiscences of Early Chicago. Chicago: R.R. Donnelley & Sons, 1912.

Rémusat, Madame de. *Mémoires.* Paris: Calmann-Lévy, 1881.

Remy, Nicholas. *Demonalatry.* Secaucus, N.J.: University Books, 1947.

Remy, Oliver E., et al. *The Attempted Assassination of Ex-President Theodore Roosevelt.* Milwaukee: Progressive, 1912.

Renaissance Reader. New York: Viking Press, 1958.

Renda, Francesco. *Socialisti e cattolici in Sicilia 1900-1904: Le lotte agrarie.* Caltanisetta-Rome: Sciascia, 1972.

Rendu, Ambroise. *Deux grand avocats: M. Allou et M. Rousse.* Paris: Durand et Pedone-Lauriel, 1885.

Rennert, Vincent Paul. *The Cowboy.* New York: Crowell-Collier Press, 1966.

-----. *Western Outlaws.* New York: Crowell-Collier Press, 1968.

Reno, John. *Life and Career of John Reno.* Indianapolis , Ind.: Indianapolis Journal, 1879.

Rensch, Hero Eugene and Ethel Grace. *Historic Spots in California: The Southern Counties.* Stanford, Calif.: Stanford University Press, 1932.

_____. *Historic Spots in California: Valley and Sierra Counties.* Stanford, Calif.: Stanford University Press, 1933.

Renshaw, Patrick. *The General Strike.* London: Eyre & Methuen, 1975.

_____. *The Wobblies.* Garden City, N.Y.: Doubleday, 1967.

Rentoul, Sir Gervaise. *Sometimes I Think.* London: Hodder & Stoughton, 1940.

_____. *This Is My Case.* London: Hutchinson, 1944.

Renvoize, Jean. *Web of Violence.* London: Rootledge, 1978.

Repaci, Antonino. *La Marcia su Roma.* Rome: Canesi, 1963.

Report of the Case of Ephraim Gilman. Portland, Maine: Stephen Barry, 1863.

The Report of the Commission on Obscenity and Pornography. New York: Bantam, 1970.

Report of Commission on Race Relations. *Negro in Chicago.* Chicago: University of Chicago Press, 1922.

Report of the Committee Appointed to Investigate Revolutionary Conspiracies in India. Parliamentary Papers, No. 9190. London: H.M. Stationery Office, 1918.

Report of the Committee of Merchants for the Relief of Colored People Suffering from the Late Riots in the City of New York. New York: Whitehorne, 1863.

Report on the Evidence and Points of Law arising in the Trial of John Francis Knapp for the Murder of Joseph White. Salem, Mass.: W & S.B. Ives, 1830.

Report on the Manhattan Company. New York: John Furman, 1799.

Report of the National Advisory Commission on Civil Disorders. New York: Bantam, 1968.

Report of the Trial and Conviction of John Haggerty. Lancaster, Pa.: J.H. Pearsol, 1847.

Report on the Trial and Conviction of Louis H.F. Wagner. Saco, Maine: William S. Noyes, 1874.

Report of the Trial of Abraham Prescott. Concord, N.H.: M.G. Atwood & Currier & Hall, 1834.

Report of the Trial of Albert S. Field. Providence, R.I.: Miller & Grattan, 1826.

Report of the Trial of Dominic Daley and James Halligan for the Murder of Marcus Lyon. Northampton, Mass.: S. & E. Butler, 1806.

Report of the Trial of James M. Lowell, Indicted for the Murder of His Wife, Mary Elizabeth Lowell. Portland, Me.: Dresser, McLellan, 1875.

Report of the Trial of Jason Fairbanks. Boston: Russell & Cutler, 1801.

Report of the Trial of John McKinney. Newark, N.J.: n.p., n.d.

Report of the Trial of Martin Posey. Edgefield, S.C.: Advertiser Print, 1850.

Report on the Trial of Adonijah Bailey. Windham, Conn.: n.p., 1825.

Report on the Trial of Edward Williams. Westchester, Pa.: Harnum & Hempill, 1830.

Report on the Trial of Richard D. Croucher on an Indictment for the Rape on Margaret Miller. Minutes of the Court of Oyer and Terminer and General Gaol Delivery, 1796-1801.

Report on the Trial of William F. Comings. Boston: S.N. Dickinson, 1844.

Reporter, The. *The Trial of John H. Surratt.* Washington D.C.: The Reporter, 1867.

Reports of the Committee of Investigation sent in 1873 by the Mexican Government to the Frontier of Texas. New York: Baker & Godwin, 1875.

Reppetto, Thomas A. *The Blue Parade.* New York: Free Press, 1978.

_____. *Residential Crime.* Cambridge, Mass.: Ballinger Press, 1974.

Reps, John W. *Cities of the American West: A History of Frontier Urban Planning.* Princton, N.J.: Princeton University Press, 1979.

_____. *The Making of Urban America: A History of City Planning in the United States.* Princeton, N.J.: Princeton University Press, 1965.

Rerick, Roland H. *Memoirs of Florida.* Atlanta: Southern Historical Association, 1902.

Reshetar, John S., Jr. *A Concise History of the Communist Party of the Soviet Union.* New York: Frederick A. Praeger, 1960.

_____. *The Ukranian Revolution, 1917-1920, A Study in Nationalism.* Princeton, N.J.: Princeton University Press, 1952.

Resnick, H.L.P. and Wolfgang, Marvin E. (eds.). *Sexual Behaviors: Social, Clinical, and Legal Aspects.* Boston: Little, Brown, 1972.

Reston, James Jr. *The Innocence of Joan Little.* New York: Quadrangle Books, 1977.

_____. *Our Father Who Art in Hell.* New York: Times Books, 1981.

Reuben, William A. *The Atom Spy Hoax.* New York: Action Books, 1960.

_____. *The Honorable Mr. Nixon and the Alger Hiss Case.* New York: Action Books, 1956.

_____. *The Mark Fein Case.* New York: Dial, 1967.

Reuss, Rodolphe Ernest. *La Sorcellerie.* Paris: J. Cherbuliez, 1871.

Reuter, B.A. *Anglo-American Relations During the Spanish-American War.* New York: Macmillan, 1924.

Reuter, Peter. *Disorganized Crime.* Cambridge, Mass.: Massachusetts Institute of Technology, 1983.

_____, and Rubinstein, Jonathan. *Illegal Gambling in New York.* Washington, D.C.: National Institute of Justice, 1982.

_____. *Racketeering in Legitimate Industries: A Study in the Eco-

nomics of Intimidation. Santa Monica, Calif.: Rand, 1987.

_____, Rubinstein, Jonathan, and Wynn, Simon. *Racketeering in Legitimate Industries: Two Case Studies. Executive Summary.* Washington, D.C.: U.S. Government Printing Office, 1983.

Revelli, Nuto. *La guerra dei poveri.* Turin, Italy: Giulio Einaudi, 1962.

The Review of Criminal Police. London: n.p., 1958.

Revised Standard Version: Old Testament Section. New York: Thomas Nelson & Sons, 1952.

Revoil, Benedict. *The Hunter and Trapper in North America.* trans. W.H. Davenport Adams, New York: Thomas Nelson & Sons, 1874.

Revolutionary Socialist Congress. *A New Hope for World Socialism.* London: International Bureau for Revolutionary Socialist Unity, 1938.

Rey, J. *The Whole Art of Dining.* London: Carmona & Baker, 1914.

Reyes, Victor. *Cabalgando Con Villa.* Mexico City: Populibros La Prensa, 1961.

Reynolds, George M. *Machine Politics in New Orleans.* New York: Columbia University Press, 1936.

Reynolds, Gerald W., and Judge, Anthony. *The Night the Police Went on Strike.* London: Weidenfeld & Nicholson, 1968.

Reynolds, John N. *The Twin Hells: A Thrilling Narrative of Life in the Kansas and Missouri Penitentiaries.* Chicago: Bee, 1890.

Reynolds, Marcus T. *The Housing of the Poor in American Cities.* Baltimore: American Economic Association, 1893.

Reynolds, M.G. *Spanish and Mexican Land Laws.* St. Louis: Buxton, 1895.

Reynolds, Quentin R. *Courtroom: The Story of Samuel S. Leibowitz.* New York: Farrar, Straus & Cudahy, 1950.

_____. *I, Willie Sutton.* New York: Farrar, Straus, 1953.

_____. *Minister of Death. The Eichmann Story.* New York: Viking Press, 1960.

_____. *Police Headquarters.* New York: Harper, 1955.

Reynolds, Robert L. *Commodore Perry in Japan.* New York: American Heritage, 1963.

Reynolds, Ruth. *Murder 'Round the World.* New York: Justice Books, 1953.

Rhamm, Albert. *Hexenglaube und Hexenprocesse.* Wolfenbüttel, Ger.: J. Zwissler, 1882.

Rhett, Robert Goodwyn. *Charleston: An Epic of Carolina.* Richmond, Va.: Garrett & Massie, 1940.

Rhine, J.B. *New World of the Mind.* New York: William Sloane, 1971.

-----, and Pratt, J.G. *Parapsychology: Frontier Science of the Mind.* Springfield, Ill.: Charles C. Thomas, 1962.

_____ (ed.). *Progress in Parapsychology.* Durham, N.C.: Parapsychology Press, 1971.

Rhine, L.E. *Mind Over Matter.* New York: Macmillan, 1970.

Rhoades, William. *Recollections of Dakota Territory.* Fort Pierre, S.D.: n.p., 1931.

Rhode, John. *The Case of Constance Kent.* New York: Charles Scribner's Sons, 1928.

Rhoden, Harold. *High Stakes.* New York: Crown, 1980.

Rhodes, Anthony. *The Poet as Superman.* London: Weidenfeld & Nicolson, 1959.

Rhodes, Eugene Manlove. *The Trusty Knaves.* Boston: Houghton Mifflin, 1933.

Rhodes, Henry Taylor-Fowkes. *Alphonse B. Bertillon.* New York: Abelard-Schumann, 1956.

_____. *Clues and Crime.* London: John Murray, 1933.

_____. *The Criminals We Deserve.* London: Methuen, 1937.

_____. *In the Tracks of Crime.* London: Turnstile Press, 1952.

_____. *The Satanic Mass: A Sociological and Criminological Study.* London: Rider, 1954.

_____. *Science and the Police Officer.* London: Police Chronicle, 1934.

Rhodes, James A., and Jauchius, Dean. *The Trial of Mary Todd*

Lincoln. Indianapolis, Ind.: Bobbs-Merrill, 1959.

Rhodes, James Ford. *History of the United States from the Compromise of 1850.* New York: Macmillan, 1900.

Rhodes, James Ford. *History of the United States from the Compromise of 1850 to the McKinley-Bryan Campaign of 1898.* 8 vols. New York: Macmillan, 1920.

Rhodes, May D. *The Hired Man on Horseback.* Boston: Houghton Mifflin, 1938.

Rhodes, Robert P. *The Insoluble Problem of Crime.* New York: John Wiley & Sons, 1977.

_____. *Organized Crime: Crime Control vs. Civil Liberties.* New York: Random House, 1984.

Riasanovsky, Nicholas V. *A History of Russia.* New York: Oxford University Press, 1969.

_____. *Nicholas I and Official Nationality in Russia, 1825-1855.* Berkeley: University of California Press, 1959.

_____. *Russia and the West in the Teachings of the Slavophiles.* Cambridge, Mass.: Harvard University Press, 1952.

Ribbentrop, Joachim von. *The Ribbentrop Memoirs.* trans. Oliver Watson. London: Weidenfeld & Nicolson, 1954.

Ribot, Héctor. *Félix Diaz en Vera Cruz. El Movimiento Revolucionario del 16 al 25 de Octobre, 1912.* Mexico City: Imprenta Calle de Humboldt, 1912.

Riccardi, Raffaello. *Pagine squadriste.* Rome: Unione Editoriale d'Italia, 1940.

Ricci, Scipio. *Female Convents: The Secrets of Nunneries Disclosed.* New York: D. Appleton, 1834.

Riccieri, Lodovico. *Lectionum Antiquarum.* Basel, Switz.: Ioannem Frobenium, 1517.

Rice, Allen Thorndike. *Reminiscences of Abraham Lincoln by Distinguished Men of His Time.* New York: North America, 1886.

Rice, Arnold S. *The Ku Klux Klan in American Politics.* Washington D.C.: Public Affairs Press, 1962.

Rice, Craig. *45 Murderers.* New York: Simon & Schuster, 1952.

_____. *Los Angeles Murders.* New York: Sloan & Pearce, 1947.

Rice, Cy. *Defender of the Damned: Gladys Trowles Root.* New York: Citadel Press, 1964.

_____. *Nick the Greek.* New York: Funk & Wagnalls, 1969.

Rice, D. Talbot. *The Art of Byzantium.* New York: Harry N. Abrams, 1959.

_____. *The Byzantines.* New York: Frederick A. Praeger, 1962.

Rice, Damon. *Seasons Past.* New York: Frederick A. Praeger, 1976.

Rice, George G. *My Adventure With Your Money.* Boston: R.G. Badger, 1913.

Rice, Grantland. *The Tumult and the Shouting.* New York: A.S. Barnes, 1954.

Rice, John R. *What Was Back of Kennedy's Murder?* Murfreesboro, Tenn.: Sword of the Lord, 1964.

Rice, Otis K. *The Hatfields and the McCoys.* Lexington: University Press of Kentucky, 1979.

Rice, Robert. *The Business of Crime.* New York: Farrar, Straus & Cudahy, 1956.

Rice, Stuart A. *Farmers and Workers in American Politics.* New York: Columbia University Press, 1924.

Rice, Wallace. *The Chicago Stock Exchange.* Chicago: Chicago Stock Exchange, 1928.

Rich, Bennett M. *The Presidents and Civil Disorder.* Washington D.C.: Brookings Institution, 1941.

Rich, Everett (ed.). *The Heritage of Kansas.* Lawrence: University of Kansas Press, 1961.

Rich, Everett. *William Allen White, the Man from Emporia.* New York: Farrar & Rinehart, 1941.

Richard, Emile. *La Prostitution à Paris.* Paris: J.B. Baillière, 1890.

Richards, David. *Sex, Drugs and the Law.* Totowa, N.J.: Rowman & Littlefield, 1982.

Richards, George. *The Trial of Alpheus Hitchcock.* Utica, N.Y.:

Seward & Williams, 1807.

Richards, Guy. *The Hunt for the Czar*. Garden City, N.Y.: Doubleday, 1971.

Richards, Laura E., and Elliott, Maud Howe. *Julia Ward Howe*. 2 vols. Boston: Houghton Mifflen, 1916.

Richards, Stanley. *Black Bart*. Wolfeboro, N.H.: Christopher Davies, 1966.

Richards, William C. *Great in Goodness: A Memoir of George N. Briggs*. Boston: Gould & Lincoln, 1866.

Richards, William C. *The Last Billionaire*. New York: Charles Scribner's Sons, 1948.

Richardson, A. *Mental Imagery*. New York: Springer, 1969.

Richardson, Albert D. *Beyond the Mississippi*. Hartford, Conn.: American, 1867.

_____. *The Secret Service: The Field, The Dungeon, and Escape*. Hartford, Conn,: American, 1865.

Richardson, Anthony. *Nick of the River*. London: Harrap, 1955.

Richardson, Edgar P., Hindle, Brooke, and Miller, Lillian B. *Charles Willson Peale and His World*. New York: Harry N. Abrams, 1982.

Richardson, Ernest Cushing. *Nicene and Post-Nicene Fathers*. Grand Rapids, Mich.: Wm. B. Eerdmans, 1952.

Richardson, Gladwell. *Two Guns, Arizona*. Santa Fe, N.M.: Press of the Territorian, 1968.

Richardson, H. *Adolescent Girls in Approved Schools*. London: Routledge & Kegan Paul, 1969.

Richardson, Jack. *Memoir of a Gambler*. New York: Simon & Schuster, 1979.

Richardson, James D. *A Compilation of the Messages and Papers of the Presidents 1789-1897*. 10 vols. Washington, D.C.: Published by Authority of Congress, 1899.

_____ (ed.). *Messages and Papers of Jefferson Davis and the Confederacy*. 2 vols. New York: Chelsea House-Robert Kector, 1966.

_____ (ed.). *Messages and Papers of the Presidents*. 11 vols. Washington D.C.: Bureau of National Literature and Art, 1907.

Richardson, James F. *The New York Police: Colonial Times to 1901*. New York: Oxford University Press, 1970.

_____. *Urban Police in the United States*. Port Washington, N.Y.: Kennikat Press, 1974.

Richardson, Jane, and Kroeber, A.L. *Three Centuries of Women's Dress Fashions*. Berkley: University of California Press, 1940.

Richardson, Joanna. *The Courtesans*. Cleveland: World, 1967.

Richardson, Joseph Hall. *From the City to Fleet Street: Some Journalistic Experiences*. London: Stanley Paul, 1927.

Richardson, R.N. *Texas, the Lone Star State*. New York: Prentice-Hall, 1943.

Richardson, Rupert Norval. *Adventuring With a Purpose: Life Story of Arthur Lee Wasson*. San Antonio, Texas: Naylor, 1951.

_____. *The Comanche Barrier to South Plains Settlement*. Glendale, Calif.: Arthur H. Clark, 1933.

_____, and Rister, Carl Coke. *The Greater Southwest*. Glendale, Calif.: Arthur H. Clark, 1934.

Richardson, William Payson. *The Law of Evidence*. Brooklyn, N.Y.: Prince, 1955.

The Richardson-McFarland Tragedy. Philadelphia: Barclay, 1870.

Richelieu. *Memoires*. Paris: Collection des memoires relatifs a l'histoire de France, 1823.

Richelmy, Carlo. *Cinque Re*. Rome: Casini, 1952.

Richental, Ulrich. *Chronicle of the Council of Florence*. trans. Louise Rope Loomis. New York: Columbia University Press, 1961.

Richer, Paul Marie Louis Pierre. *Etudes Cliniques sur la Grande Hystérie ou Hystéro-épilepsie*. Paris: A Delahaye et É. Lecresnier, 1885.

Richette, Lisa Aversa. *The Throwaway Children*. Philadelphia: J.B. Lippencott, 1969.

Richland, W. Bernard. *You Can Beat City Hall*. New York: Rawson, 1980.

Richman, Harry. *A Hell of a Life*. New York: Duell, Sloan & Pearce, 1966.

Richman, N., Stevenson, J., and Graham, P.J. *Pre-School to School*. London: Academic Press, 1982.

Richmond, A.B. *Leaves from the Diary of an Old Lawyer*. New York: American Book Exchange, 1880.

Richmond, W. *The Adolescent Boy*. New York: Farrar & Rinehart, 1933.

_____. *The Adolescent Girl*. New York: Macmillan, 1925.

Richter, D.C. *The Riotous Victorians*. n.p.: Ohio University Press, 1981.

Rickaby, Frank. *Ballads and Songs of the Shanty Boy*. Cambridge, Mass.: Harvard University Press, 1926.

Rickard, T.A. *A History of American Mining*. New York: McGraw, 1932.

_____. *Through the Yukon and Alaska*. San Francisco: Mining & Scientific Press, 1909.

Rickard, Mrs. "Tex", with Oboler, Arch. *Everything Happened to Him*. New York: Frederick A. Stokes, 1936.

Rickards, Colin. *"Buckskin Frank" Leslie: Gunman of Tombstone*. El Paso, Texas: Western College Press, 1964.

_____. *Charles Littlepage Ballard, Southwesterner*. El Paso: Texas Western Press, 1966.

_____. *The Gunfight at Blazer's Mill*. El Paso: Texas Western Press, 1974.

_____. *The Man from Devil's Island*. London: Dawnay, 1968.

_____. *Mysterious Dave Mathers*. Santa Fe, N.M.: Press of the Territorian, 1968.

Rickenbacker, Edward V. *Rickenbacker*. Englewood Cliffs, N.J.: Prentice-Hall, 1967.

Ricketts, William Pendleton. *50 Years in the Saddle*. Sheridan, Wyo.: Star, 1942.

Rickles, N.K. *Exhibitionism*. Philadelphia: J.B. Lippincott, 1950.

Rickman, John. *Journal of Captain Cook's Last Voyage to the Pacific Ocean*. New York: Da Capo Press, 1967.

Riddell, Lord. *Intimate Diary of the Peace Conference and After, 1918-1923*. London: Victor Gollancz, 1924.

Riddle, Albert Gallatin. *Recollections of War Times, Reminiscences of Men and Events in Washington, 1860-1865*. New York: G.P. Putnam's Sons, 1895.

Riddle, Jeff C. *The Indian History of the Modoc War, and the Cause That Led to It*. n.p, 1914.

Rider, Arthur Fremont. *Rider's New York City*. New York: Henry Holt, 1916.

Ridge, John Rollin (Yellow Bird). *The Life and Adventure of Joaquin Murieta, the Celebrated California Bandit*. Norman: University of Oklahoma Press, 1969.

Ridings, Sam P. *The Chisholm Trail*. Guthrie, Okla.: Cooperative, 1936.

Ridolfi, Roberto. *The Life of Niccolò Machiavelli*. trans. Cecil Grayson. Chicago: University of Chicago Press, 1963.

Ridpath, John Clark. *Life and Trial of Guiteau the Assassin*. Cincinnati, Ohio: Jones Brothers, 1882.

Riegel, Robert E. *America Moves West*. New York: Henry Holt, 1930.

_____. *The Story of the Western Railroads*. New York: Macmillan, 1926.

Riegelman, Harold. *Caves of Biak: An American Officer's Experiences in the Southwest Pacific*. New York: Dial Press, 1955.

Riegger, Paul Josef. *Dissertatio de Magia*. Vienna, Aust.: Ionnem Thomae nob de Trattnem, 1773.

Riegler, Ferdinand. *Hexenprozesse*. Graz, Aust.: U. Moser, 1926.

Riencourt, Amaury de. *The Coming Caesars*. New York: Capricorn, 1964.

Rieseberg, Felix Jr. *Golden Gate: The Story of San Francisco Harbor*. New York: S. Paul, 1940.

Riesman, David. *Abundance for What? and Other Essays*. New

York: Doubleday, 1964.

_____. *Individualism Reconsidered.* Glencoe, Ill.: Free Press, 1954.

_____, Glazer, Nathan, and Denney, Reuel. *The Lonely Crowd.* New York: Doubleday, 1953.

Riess, Curt (ed.). *There They Were.* New York: G.P. Putnam's Sons, 1944.

_____. *Total Espionage.* New York: G.P. Putnam's Sons, 1941.

Riezler, Sigmund. *Geschichte der Hexenprozesse in Bayern.* Stuttgart, Ger.: J.G. Cotta, 1896.

Rife, Clarence W. *Essays in Colonial History Presented to Charles McLean Andrews.* New Haven, Conn.: Yale University Press, 1931.

Rifkin, Shepard. *King Fisher's Road.* Greenwich, Conn.: Fawcet, 1963.

Rigault, Abel. *Le Procès de Guichard.* Paris: Picard et fils, 1896.

Rignall, Jeff, and Wilder, Ron. *29 Below.* Chicago: Wellington Press, 1979.

Riha, Thomas (ed.). *Readings in Russian Civilization.* Chicago: University of Chicago Press, 1964.

Rihan, Ameen. *Ibn Saud of Arabia.* London: Constable, 1928.

Riis, Jacob August. *The Battle With the Slum.* New York: Macmillan, 1902.

_____. *The Children of the Poor.* New York: Charles Scribner's Sons, 1892.

_____. *Children of the Tenements.* New York: Macmillan, 1903.

_____. *How the Other Half Lives.* New York: Charles Scribner's Sons, 1890.

_____. *The Making of an American.* New York: Macmillan, 1901.

_____. *Theodore Roosevelt the Citizen.* New York: Macmillan, 1904.

Riker, T.W. *The Making of Rumania: A Study of an International Problem, 1856-1866.* Oxford, Eng.: Oxford University Press, 1941.

Ringel, W. *Identification and Police Line-Ups.* New York: Gould, 1968.

Ringger, Peter. *Das Problem der Besessenheit.* Zurich, Switz.: Verlag Neue Wissenschaft, 1953.

Ringgold, Gene, and LaManna, Roger. *Assassin: The Lee Harvey Oswald Biography.* Hollywood, Calif.: Associated Professional Services, 1964.

Ringgold, Jennie Parks. *Frontier Days in the Southwest: Pioneer Days in Old Arizona.* San Antonio, Texas: Naylor, 1952.

Rink, Paul. *Building the Bank of America - A.P. Giannini.* Chicago: Encyclopedia Britannica Press, 1963.

Rintelen, A. *Erinnerungen an Oesterreichs Weg.* Munich: F. Bruckmann, 1941.

Rintelen, Enno von. *Mussolini l'alleato.* Rome: Corso, 1952.

Riordan, William L. *Plunkitt of Tammany Hall.* New York: E.P. Dutton, 1963.

Ripka, Hubert. *Czechoslovakia Enslaved.* London: Victor Gollancz, 1950.

Ripley, Roswell Sabine. *The War with Mexico.* New York: Harper & Brothers, 1849.

Ripley, Thomas. *They Died with Their Boots On.* Garden City, N.Y.: Doubleday, Doran, 1935.

Ripley, W.Z. (ed.). *Railway Problems.* New York: Ginn, 1916.

_____. *Trusts, Pools, and Corporations.* New York: Ginn, 1916.

Rippy, J. Fred, Vasconcelos, José, and Stephens, Guy. *American Policy Abroad: Mexico.* Chicago: University of Chicago Press, 1928.

_____. *Latin America in World Politics.* New York: Alfred A. Knopf, 1931.

_____. *The United States and Mexico.* New York: Alfred A. Knopf, 1926.

Rischin, Moses. *The Promised City: New York's Jews, 1870-1914.* Cambridge, Mass.: Harvard University Press, 1962.

Rister, Carl Coke. *Fort Griffin on the Texas Frontier.* Norman: University of Oklahoma Press, 1956.

_____. *Land Hunger.* Norman: University of Oklahoma Press,

_____. *No Man's Land.* Norman: University of Oklahoma Press, 1948.

_____. *The Southern Plainsmen.* Norman: University of Oklahoma Press, 1938.

_____. *The Southwestern Frontier: 1865-1881.* Cleveland: Arthur H. Clark, 1928.

Rittenhouse, Jack D. *Cabezon: A New Mexico Ghost Town.* Santa Fe, N.M.: Stagecoach Press, 1963.

_____. *The Man Who Owned Too Much: Together with an 1895 Newspaper Account of the Life of Lucien Maxwell.* Houston, Texas: Stagecoach Press, 1958.

_____. *Outlaw Days at Cabezon.* Santa Fe, N.M.: Stagecoach Press, 1964.

Ritter, Gerhard. *Carl Goerdeler und die deutsche Widerstandsbewegung.* Stuttgart, Ger.: Deutsche Verlagsanstalt, 1956.

_____. *Frederick the Great: A Historical Profile.* trans. Peter Paret. Berkeley: University of California Press, 1968.

Ritter, Lawrence. *The Glory of Their Times.* New York: Macmillan, 1966.

Ritthaler, Anton. *Die Hohenzollern: Ein Bildwerk.* Frankfurt, Ger.: Athenäum, 1961.

_____. *Kaiser Wilhelm II: Herrscher in einer Zeitwende.* Cologne, Ger.: Tradition und Leben, 1958.

River, J. Paul (ed.). *Crime and the Sexual Psychopath.* Springfield, Ill.: Charles C. Thomas, 1958.

_____. *The Sexual Criminal.* Springfield, Ill.: Charles C. Thomas, 1950.

Rivero, Gonzalo. *Hacia la Verdad, Episodios de la Revolución.* Mexico City: Compañia Editora Nacional, 1911.

Rivers, William L. *The Adversaries: Politics and the Press.* Boston: Beacon Press, 1970.

_____. *The Mass Media.* New York: Harper & Row, 1975.

_____. *The Opinionmakers.* Boston: Beacon Press, 1967.

Rivett, Rohan D. *Behind Bamboo: An Inside Story of the Japanese Prison Camps.* Sydney, Aus: Angus & Robertson, 1946.

Riviere, Joan, et al. (eds.). *Collected Papers.* New York: Basic Books, 1959.

Roads, Samuel, Jr. *History and Traditions of Marblehead.* Boston: Houghton Mifflin, 1881.

Roark, Garland. *The Coin of Contraband.* Garden City, N.Y.: Doubleday, 1964.

Roatta, Mario. *Otto Milioni di Baionette.* Milan, Italy: Mondadori, 1946.

Roazen, Paul. *Freud and His Followers.* New York: Alfred A. Knopf, 1975.

Robb, F.H. *Negro in Chicago.* Chicago: Intercollegiate Club of Chicago, 1927.

Robbins, James J. *The Government of Labor Relations in Sweden.* Chapel Hill: University of North Carolina Press, 1942.

Robbins, Jhan. *Front Page Marriage.* New York: G.P. Putnam's Sons, 1982.

Robbins, Lionel. *The Great Depression.* New York: Macmillan, 1934.

Robbins, Paul R. *Marijuana: A Short Course.* Boston: Branden Press, 1976.

Robbins, Roy M. *Our Landed Heritage: The Public Domain.* Lincoln: University of Nebraska Press, 1962.

Robbins, Russell Hope. *The Encyclopedia of Witchcraft and Demonology.* New York: Crown, 1965.

Robert, Clémence. *La Famille Calas.* Paris: Michel Lévy Frères, 1876.

Robert, H. *Les Grands Procès de l'Histoire.* Paris: Payot, 1926.

Robert, Joseph C. *The Story of Tobacco in America.* Chapel Hill: University of North Carolina Press, 1949.

Robert, Marthe. *The Psychoanalytic Revolution.* trans. Kenneth Morgan. London: George Allen & Unwin, 1966.

Robert of Clari. *The Conquest of Constantinople.* trans. Edgar Holmes McNeal. New York: W.W. Norton, 1964.

Roberts, Albert R. (ed.). *Readings in Prison Education.* Springfield, Ill.: Charles C. Thomas, 1973.

Roberts, Alexander. *A Treatise of Witchcraft.* London: N.O., Samuel Man, 1616.

Roberts, Bruce. *Springs from Parched Ground.* Uvalde, Texas: Hornby Press, 1950.

Roberts, C.E.B. *The New World of Crime, Famous American Trials.* London: Burrows, Eyre & Spottiswoode, 1933.

Roberts, Cecil. *The Bright Twenties.* London: Hodder & Stoughton, 1970.

Roberts, Chalmers M. *Washington, Past and Present.* Washington D.C.: Public Affairs Press, 1949-50.

_____. *The Washington Post: The First 100 Years.* Boston: Houghton Mifflin, 1977.

Roberts, Charles. *The Truth About the Assassination.* New York: Grosset & Dunlap, 1967.

Roberts, Daniel Webster. *Rangers and Sovereignty.* San Antonio, Texas: Wood Printing and Engraving, 1914.

Roberts, Ellis H. *New York.* Boston: Houghton Mifflin, 1897.

Roberts, Elmer. *Monarchial Socialism in Germany.* New York: Charles Scribner's Sons, 1913.

Roberts, Henry L. *Rumania: Political Problems of an Agrarian State.* New Haven, Conn.: Yale University Press, 1951.

Roberts, Jane. *The Seth Material.* Englewoood Cliffs, N.J.: Prentice-Hall, 1970.

Roberts, John. *Mitsui: Three Centuries of Japanese Business.* Tokyo: John Weatherhill, 1973.

Roberts, Kenneth. *Black Magic.* Indianapolis, Ind.: Bobbs-Merrill, 1924.

Roberts, Kenneth (ed.). *March to Quebec, Journals of the Members of Arnold's Expedition.* New York: Down East Books, 1980.

_____ and Anna M. *Moreau de St. Mery's American Journey: 1793-98.* New York: Doubleday, 1947.

Roberts, Lou Conwary. *A Woman's Reminiscences of Six Years im Camp with Texas Rangers.* Austin, Texas: Press of von Boechmann-Jones, 1928.

Roberts, M. Elizabeth. *Outlines of Balkan History.* London: Arthur H. Stockwell, 1943.

Roberts, Stephen H. *The House That Hitler Built.* New York: Harper, 1938.

Roberts, Sydney. *Holmes and Watson: A Miscellany.* New York: Oxford University Press, 1953.

Roberts, W. Adolphe. *Sir Henry Morgan.* New York: Covici, Friede, 1933.

Robertson, Angus. *Mussolini and the New Italy.* London: Allenson, 1929.

_____. *Victor Emmanuel.* London: George Allen & Unwin, 1925.

Robertson, E. Arnot. *The Spanish Town Papers.* London: Cresset Press, 1959.

Robertson, Frank. *Triangle of Death.* London: Rootledge, 1977.

Robertson, Frank C., and Harris, Beth Kay. *Soapy Smith, King of the Frontier Con Men.* New York: Hastings House, 1961.

Robertson, George. *The Discovery of Tahiti: A Journal of the Second Voyage of H.M.S. Dolphin...Written by Her Master George Robertson.* London: Hakluyt Society, 1948.

Robertson, Mrs. Harriet M. (ed.). *Dishonest Elections and Why We Have Them.* Chicago: Published by Author, 1934.

Robertson, John A. *Rough Justice: Perspectives on Lower Criminal Courts.* Boston: Little, Brown, 1974.

Robertson, Pauline Durrett, and R.L. *Panhandle Pilgrimage: Illustrated Tales Tracing History in the Texas Panhandle.* Canyon, Texas: Staked Plains Press, 1976.

Robertson, Ruth T. *Famous Bandits; Brief Accounts of the Lives of Jesse James, Cole Younger, Billy the Kid and Others...* Washington D.C.: Washington Bureau, 1928.

Robertson, Terence. *Crisis: The Inside Story of the Suez Conspiracy.* New York: Atheneum, 1965.

Robertson, William. *Our American Tour, Being a Run of Ten Thousand Miles from the Atlantic to the Golden Gate in the Autumn of 1869.* Edinburgh, Scot.: n.p., 1869.

Robins, Lee N. *Deviant Children Grown Up.* Baltimore, Md.: Williams & Wilkins, 1966.

_____. *A Followup of Vietnam Drug Users.* Washington, D.C.: U. S. Government Printing Office, 1973.

_____. *The Vietnam Drug User Returns.* Washington, D.C.: U.S. Government Printing Office, 1974.

Robins, Natalie, and Aronson, Steven. *Savage Grace.* New York: William Morrow, 1985.

Robinson, Alfred. *Life in California.* Santa Barbara, Calif.: Peregrine, 1970.

Robinson, Charles. *The Kansas Conflict.* New York: Harper & Brothers, 1882.

Robinson, Clark. *Explosives: Their Anatomy and Destructiveness.* New York: McGraw-Hill, n.d.

Robinson, Corinne Roosevelt. *My Brother Theodore Roosevelt.* New York: Charles Scribner's Sons, 1921.

Robinson, Cyril E. *Apollo History of Greece.* New York: Thomas Y. Crowell, 1965.

_____. *Apollo History of the Roman Republic.* New York: Thomas Y. Crowell, 1965.

_____. *Apollo History of Rome.* New York: Thomas Y. Crowell, 1965.

Robinson, Daniel N. *Psychology and the Law: Can Justice Survive the Social Sciences?* Oxford, Eng.: Oxford University Press, 1980.

Robinson, David. *The Great Funnies.* New York: E.P. Dutton, 1969.

_____. *Hollywood in the Twenties.* New York: A.S. Barnes, 1968.

Robinson, Doane. *Doane Robinson's Encyclopedia of South Dakota.* Pierre, S.D.: Published by Author, 1925.

Robinson, Duncan W. *Judge Robert McAlpin Williamson, Texas' Three-Legged Willie.* Austin: Texas State Historical Association, 1948.

Robinson, E.S. *Law and the Lawyers.* Toronto Ontario, Can.: Macmillan, 1935.

Robinson, Edgar E., and West, Victor J. *The Foreign Policy of Woodrow Wilson.* New York: Macmillan, 1917.

Robinson, F.E., and Morgan, W.E. *Why Dayton-of All Places.* Chattanooga, Tenn.: Andrews Printery, 1925.

Robinson, Geroid T. *Rural Russia under the Old Regime.* New York: Macmillan, 1949.

Robinson, Henry Morton. *Fantastic Interim.* New York: Harcourt, Brace, 1943.

_____. *Science Catches the Criminal.* Indianapolis, Ind.: Bobbs-Merrill, 1935.

Robinson, Jacob. *Palestine and the United Nations.* Washington D.C.: Public Affairs Press, 1947.

Robinson, Jerry. *The Comics: An Illustrated History of Comic Strip Art.* New York: G.P. Putnam's Sons, 1974.

Robinson, L.N. *Penology in the United States.* Philadelphia: Winston, 1921.

_____. *Should Prisoners Work?* Philadelphia: Winston, 1931.

Robinson, Lennox. *A Gold Treasury of Irish Verse.* New York: Macmillan, 1925.

_____. *Lady Gregory's Journals.* London: G.P. Putnam's Sons, 1946.

Robinson, Louis Newton. *History and Organization of Criminal Statistics in the United States.* New York: Hart, Schaffner & Marx, 1911.

Robinson, Sara T.L. *Kansas: Its Interior and Exterior Life.* Boston: Crosby, Nichols, 1856.

Robinson, Stuart. *Infamous Perjuries of the Bureau of Military Justice.* Louisville, Ky.: Published by Author, 1865.

Robinson, Vandaleur. *Albania's Road to Freedom.* London: George Allen & Unwin, 1941.

Robinson, Victor. *An Essay on Hasheesh.* New York: Dingwall-Rock, 1925.

Robinson, W.W. *Bombs and Bribery.* Los Angeles: Dawson's Book Shop, 1969.

_____. *Lawyers of Los Angeles.* Los Angeles: Los Angeles Bar

Association, 1959.

_____. *Panorama, a Picture History of Southern California.* Los Angeles: Title Insurance and Trust, 1953.

Robinson, William A. *Thomas B. Reed, Parliamentarian.* New York: Dodd, Mead, 1930.

Robinson, William Henry. *The Story of Arizona.* Phoenix, Ariz.: Berryhill, 1919.

Robitscher, Jonas. *The Powers of Psychiatry.* Boston: Houghton Mifflin, 1980.

Robleto, Hernan. *La Mascota de Pancho Villa.* Mexico City: Ediciones Botas, 1934.

Robson, Eric. *The American Revolution 1763-1783.* New York: Oxford University Press, 1955.

Robson, John S. *How a One-Legged Rebel Lives.* Durham, N.C.: Education, 1898.

Robson, William A. *Civilization and the Growth of Law.* New York: Macmillan, 1935.

Roche, John P. *The Quest for the Dream: The Development of Civil Rights and Human Relations in Modern America.* New York: Macmillan, 1963.

Roche, Philip Q. *The Criminal Mind.* New York: Farrar, Straus & Cudahy, 1958.

Rochefort, Henri. *Les Aventures du ma vie.* Paris: Paul DuPont, 1896.

Roches, A. (ed.). *Encyclopédie nationale de la police.* Paris: Compagnie Nationale de Diffusion du Livre, 1955.

Rochester, Anna. *The Populist Movement in the United States.* New York: International, 1943.

Rochette, Edward C. *The Medallic Portraits of John F. Kennedy.* Iola, Wis.: Krause, 1966.

Rochow, Caroline Louise Albertine von, and de la Motte-Fouqué, Marie. *Leben am preussischen Hofe 1815-1852.* Berlin: E.S. Mittler & Sohn, 1908.

Rock, Marion Tuttle. *Illustrated History of Oklahoma.* Topeka, Kan.: C.B. Hamilton & Son, 1890.

Rock, Paul, and McIntosh, Mary (eds.). *Deviance and Social Control.* London: Tavistock, 1973.

_____. *A Sociology of Deviance.* London: Hutchinson, 1973.

Rockafield, H.A. *The Manheim Tragedy: A Complete History of the Double Murder of Mrs. Garber and Mrs. Ream.* Lancaster, Pa.: Evening Express, 1858.

Rockefeller Commission Report. *Report to the President by the Commission on CIA Activities Within the United States.* New York: Manor Books, 1975.

Rockefeller, J.D. *Random Reminiscences of Men and Events.* New York: Doubleday, Page, 1909.

Rockfellow, John Alexander. *The Log of an Arizona Trailblazer.* Tucson, Ariz.: Acme Printing, 1933.

Rockhill, William W. *The Land of the Lamas.* New York: Century, 1891.

Rockwell, Wilson (ed.) *Memoirs of a Lawman: Autobiography of Cyrus Wells Shores.* Denver: Sage Books, 1962.

_____. *New Frontier: Saga of the North Fork.* Denver: World Press, 1938.

_____. *Sunset Slope: True Epics of Western Colorado.* Denver: Big Mountain Press, 1955.

_____. *Utes: A Forgotten People.* Denver: Sage Books, 1956.

Rocquain, Félix. *Notes et fragments d'histoire.* Paris: Plon, 1906.

Rodd, Sir James Rennell. *Frederick, Crown Prince and Emperor: A Biographical Sketch Dedicated to His Memory.* London: David Scott, 1888.

Rodell, Fred. *Nine Men.* New York: Random House, 1955.

_____. *Woe Unto You, Lawyers!* Brooklyn: Pageant-Poseidon, 1937.

Rodell, Marie F. (ed.). *Boston Murders.* New York: Duell, Sloan & Pearce, 1948.

_____. *Charleston Murders.* New York: Duell, Sloan & Pearce, 1947.

_____. *Chicago Murders.* New York: Duell, Sloan & Pearce, 1945.

_____. *Cleveland Murders.* New York: Duell, Sloan & Pearce, 1947.

_____. *Denver Murders.* New York: Duell, Sloan & Pearce, 1946.

_____. *Detroit Murders.* New York: Duell, Sloan & Pearce, 1948.

_____. *Los Angeles Murders.* New York: Duell, Sloan & Pearce, 1947.

_____. *New York Murders.* New York: Duell, Sloan & Pearce, 1944.

_____. *San Francisco Murders.* New York: Duell, Sloan & Pearce, 1947.

Rodgers, Cleveland. *Robert Moses: Builder of Democracy.* New York: Henry Holt, 1952.

Rodgers, Richard. *Musical Stages.* New York: Random House, 1975.

Rodgers, William W. *The One Gallused Rebellion.* Baton Rouge: Louisiana State University Press, 1970.

Rodney, William. *Joe Boyle: King of the Klondike.* Toronto, Ontario, Can.: McGraw-Hill Ryerson, 1974.

Rodocanachi, Emmanuel. *Histoire de Rome. Une cour princière au Vatican pendant la renaissance.* Paris: Hachette, 1925.

Rodwell, Sir Cecil. *Report on a Visit to Pitcairn Island.* London: H.M. Stationary Office, 1921.

Rodzianko, M.V. *The Reign of Rasputin.* New York: Frederick A. Stokes, 1927.

_____, and Steadwell, B.S. *The Great War on White Slavery.* Oakland, Calif.: Smithsonian, 1911.

Roe, Clifford. *Panderers and Their White Slaves.* Chicago: Revell Pub., 1910.

Roe, Edward Thomas. *The James Boys.* Chicago: A.E. Weeks, 1893.

Roe, Frank G. *The Indian and the Horse.* Norman: University of Oklahoma Press, 1955.

_____. *The North American Buffalo.* Toronto, Ontario, Can.: University of Toronto Press, 1951.

Roe, G.M. (ed.). *Our Police: A History of the Cincinnati Police Force, From the Earliest Period Until the Present Day.* Cincinnati: n.p., 1890.

Roeburt, John. *Sex Life and Criminal Law.* New York: Belmont Books, 1963.

Roebuck, Julian B. *Criminal Typology.* Springfield, Ill.: Charles C. Thomas, 1967.

_____, and Frese, Wolfgang. *The Rendezvous: A Case Study of an After Hours Club.* New York: Free Press, 1976.

Roeburt, John. *Al Capone.* New York: Pyramid, 1959.

_____. *Tough Cop.* New York: Simon & Schuster, 1949.

Roeder, Ralph. *The Man of the Renaissance.* New York: Viking Press, 1933.

Roemer, Theodore. *Catholic Church in the United States.* St. Louis: B. Herder, 1950.

Roenigk, Adolph. *Pioneer History of Kansas.* Lincoln, Kan.: Publish by Author, 1933.

Roesche, Roberta with De La Roche, Harry, Jr. *Anyone's Son.* Kansas City, Kan.: Andrews & McNeel, 1979.

Roff, Joe T. *A Brief History of Early Days in North Texas and the Indian Territory.* Allen, Okla.: Pontotoc County Democrat, 1930.

Roffman, Howard. *Presumed Guilty: How and Why the Warren Commission Framed Lee Harvey Oswald.* New York: A.S. Barnes, 1976.

Rogers, Agnes, and Allen, Frederick Lewis. *I Remember Distinctly.* New York: Harper & Brothers, 1947.

Rogers, Artemas, and Chase, Henry H. *Trial of Daniel Davis Farmer.* Concord, N.H.: Hill & Moore, 1821.

Rogers, Cameron (ed.). *A County Judge in Arcady: Selected Private Papers of Charles Fernald, Pioneer California Jurist.* Glendale, Calif.: Arthur H. Clark, 1954.

_____. *Gallant Ladies.* New York: Harcourt, Brace, 1928.

Rogers, Fred B. *Soldiers of the Overland: Being Some Account of the Services of General Patrick Edward Conner & His Volunteers in the Old West.* San Francisco: Grabhorn Press, 1938.

Rogers, James Edwin Thorold (ed.). *Bright's Speeches on Questions of Public Policy*. 2 vols. London: Macmillan, 1869.

Rogers, James Grafton. *American Bar Leaders: Biographies of the Presidents of the American Bar Association 1878-1928*. Chicago: American Bar Association, 1932.

Rogers, John William. *The Lusty Texans of Dallas*. New York: E. P. Dutton, 1951.

Rogers, Justus H. *Colusa Country*. Orland, Calif.: Published by Author, Justus H. Rogers, 1891.

Rogers, Kenneth Paul. *For One Sweet Grape*. New York: Playboy Press, 1974.

Rogers, Rev. Patrick. *Father Theobald Mathew*. New York: Longmans, Green, 1945.

Rogers, Robert. *Journals of Major Robert Rogers*. New York: Corinth Books, 1961.

Rogers, Robert W. *A History of Babylonia and Assyria*. Cincinnati: Abingdon Press, 1915.

Rogers, R.S. *Studies in the Reign of Tiberius*. Baltimore: Johns Hopkins Press, 1943.

Rogers, W.A. *America's Black and White Book*. New York: Cupples & Leon, 1917.

Rogers, W.C. *Ladies Bountiful*. New York: Harcourt, Brace & World, 1968.

Rogers, Will. *The Autobiography of Will Rogers*. Boston: Houghton Mifflin, 1949.

Rogge, O. John. *Why Men Confess*. New York: Nelson, 1959.

Roggendorf, Joseph (ed.). *Studies in Japanese Culture*. Tokyo: Sophia University Press, 1963.

Rogger, Hans. *National Consciousness in Eighteenth-Century Russia*. Cambridge, Mass.: Harvard University Press, 1960.

Roggeveen, Jacob. *The Journal of Jacob Roggeveen*. Oxford, Eng.: Clarendon Press, 1970.

Rogin, Michael Paul. *The Intellectuals and McCarthy: The Radical Specter*. Cambridge, Mass.: M.I.T. Press, 1967.

_____, and Shover, John L. *Political Change in California: Critical Elections and Social Movements, 1890-1966*. Westport, Conn.: Greenwood Press, 1970.

Rogo, D. Scott. *Parapsychology: A Century of Inquiry*. New York: Taplinger, 1975.

Rogoff, H. *An East Side Epic - Meyer London*. New York: Vanguard Press, 1930.

Rogow, Arnold A., and Lasswell, Harold D. *Power, Corruption and Rectitude*. Englewood Cliffs, N.J.: Prentice-Hall, 1963.

Röhl, Klaus Rainer. *Fünf Finger sind keine Faust*. Cologne: Verlg Keipenheuer & Witsch, 1974.

Röhm, Ernst. *Die Geschichte eines Hochverräters*. Munich: Verlag Franz Eher II, 1933.

Rohmer, Sax, and Ward, Arthur. *The Romance of Sorcery*. New York: E.P. Dutton, 1924.

Röhricht, Edgar. *Pflict und Gewissen*. Stuttgart: W. Kohlhammer, 1965.

Rohr, Philippus. *De Masticatione Moruorum*. Leipzig, Ger.: Michaelis Vogtii, 1679.

Röhrs, Hans-Dietrich. *Hitler, L'Autodestruction d'une Personnalité*. Paris: La Table Ronde, 1970.

Rojas, Arnold R. *California Vaquero*. Fresno, Calif.: Academy Library Guild, 1953.

Rojas, Luis Manuel. *Epocas de Porfirio Diaz y Francisco I. Madero en el proceso histórico de nuestra nación*. Mexico City: Publicaciones de la revista "Irrigación de Mexico," 1931.

_____. *La culpa de Henry Lane Wilson en el gran desastre de México*. Mexico City: Compañia Editoria "La Verdad," 1928.

Rolfe, F.W. *Chronicles of the House of Borgia*. New York: Dover, 1962.

Roll, William G. *The Poltergeist*. New York: Signet, 1974.

Rolland, Romain. *Mahatma Gandhi*. London: George Allen & Unwin, 1924.

Rolle, Andrew F. *California, A History*. Arlington Heights, Ill.: Harlan Davidson, 1978.

_____ (ed.). *The Road to Virginia City: The Diary of James Knox Polk Miller*. Norman: University of Oklahoma Press, 1960.

Rollins, Alfred B., Jr. *Woodrow Wilson and the New America*. New York: Dell, 1965.

Rollins, Frank. *School Administration in Municipal Government*. New York: Columbia University Press, 1902.

Rollins, Philip Ashton. *The Cowboy*. New York: Charles Scribner's Sons, 1922.

Rollison, John K. *Hoofprints of a Cowboy and U.S. Ranger; Pony Trails in Wyoming*. Caldwell, Idaho: Caxton Printers, 1941.

Rollinson, John K. *Wyoming Cattle Trails*. Caldwell, Idaho: Caxton Printers, 1948.

Rolph, C. *Personal Identity*. New York: Thomas, 1957.

Rolph, Cecil Hewitt. *Common Sense About Crime and Punishment*. London: Victor Gollancz, 1961.

_____ (ed.). *The Police and the Public*. London: William Heinemann, 1962.

_____. *Women of the Streets*. London: Secker & Warburg, 1955.

Rolt-Wheeler, Francis William. *The Book of Cowboys*. Boston: Lothrop, Lee & Shepard, 1921.

Romain, Wiley-Paul. *Le dossier de la police*. Paris: Librairie Académique Perrin, 1966.

The Romance of Lust. New York: Grove Press, 1972.

Romano, Salvatore Francesco. *Storia dei Fasci Siciliani*. Bari, Italy: Laterza, 1959.

Romanov, Boris A. *Russia in Manchuria, 1892-1906*. Ann Arbor, Mich.: Edwards, 1952.

Romanus, Charles, and Sunderland, Riley. *Stilwell's Mission to China*. Washington, D.C.: Dept. of the Army, Historical Division, 1953.

Romaswamy, M. *Creative Role of the Supreme Court of the United States*. Stanford, Calif.: Stanford University Press, 1956.

Rombauer, Robert J. *The Union Cause in St. Louis in 1861*. St. Louis: Nixon-Jones Press, 1909.

Rome, Florence. *The Tatooed Men*. New York: Delacorte, 1975.

Romer, F. *Makers of History: A Story of the Development of the History of Our Country at the Muzzle of a Colt*. Hartford, Conn.: Colt's Patent Firearms Manufacturing, 1926.

Roméro Flores, Jesús. *Anales históricos de la Revolución Mexicana*. Mexico City: Ediciones Encuadernales, 1939.

Romeyn, Herman M. *Report on the Trial of Nathan Foster*. Kingston, N.Y.: Joseph S. Smith, 1819.

Romilly, Samuel. *Memoirs of the Life of Sir Samuel Romilly, Written by Himself*. 3 vols. London: John Murray, 1840.

_____. *Observations on the Criminal Law of England as it Relates to the Capital Punishments, and on the Mode in Which it is Administered*. London: McCreery, 1810.

Rommel, Erwin. *The Rommel Papers*. trans. Paul Finley. New York: Harcourt, Brace, 1953.

Romoli, Kathleen. *Columbia*. Garden City, N.Y.: Doubleday, Doran, 1941.

Romualdi, Pino. *L'ora di Catilina*. Rome: TER, 1963.

Romualdi, Serafino. *Presidents and Peons: Recollections of a Labor Ambassador in Latin America*. New York: Funk & Wagnalls, 1967.

Romulo, Carlos. *I Saw the Fall of the Philippines*. New York: Doubleday, Doran, 1943.

Roney, Frank. *Frank Roney: Irish Rebel and California Labor Leader: An Autobiography*. Berkeley: University of California Press, 1931.

Roosa, William V. *The Significance of Excorcism in the Gospel of Mark*. Chicago: University of Chicago Libraries, 1937.

Roosevelt, Blanche. *Elisabeth of Roumania: A Study*. London: Chapman & Hall, 1891.

Roosevelt, Eleanor. *Autobiography*. New York: Harper & Row, 1961.

_____. *This I Remember*. New York: Harper & Row, 1949.

_____. *This Is My Story*. New York: Harper, 1936.

Roosevelt, Elliott. *As He Saw It*. New York: Duell, Sloane &

Pearce, 1946.

Roosevelt, Franklin D. *His Personal Letters*. ed. Elliott Roosevelt. 2 vols. New York: Duell, Sloan & Pearce, 1950.

____. *Public Papers and Addresses of F.D.R.* New York: Random House, 1938-1950.

Roosevelt, James and Shalett, Sidney. *Affectionately, F.D.R.* New York: Harcourt, Brace, 1959.

Roosevelt, Kermit. *The Happy Hunting Grounds*. New York: Charles Scribner's Sons, 1921.

____. *The Overseas Target: War Report of the OSS*. New York: Walker, 1976.

Roosevelt, Theodore. *All in the Family*. New York: G.P. Putnam's Sons, 1929.

____. *American Ideals*. New York: AMS Press, 1969.

____. *Autobiography*. New York: Macmillan, 1913.

____. *Essays on Practical Politics*. New York: G.P. Putnam's Sons, 1887.

____. *The Hunting and Exploring Adventures of Theodore Roosevelt*. ed. Donald Day. New York: Dial Press, 1955.

____. *Works*. 24 vols. New York: Charles Scribner's Sons, 1923.

Root, Frank A., and Connelley, William Elsey. *The Overland Stage to California*. Topeka, Kan.: Published by Authors, 1901.

Root, Gladys and Rice, Cy. *Defender of the Damned*. New York: Citadel Press, 1964.

Root, Grace C. *Women and Repeal*. New York: Haper & Brothers, 1934.

Root, Jonathan. *Halliburton, The Magnificent Myth*. New York: Coward-McCann, 1965.

____. *The Life and Bad Times of Charlie Becker*. London: Secker & Warburg, 1962.

____. *One Night in July*. New York: Coward-McCann, 1961.

Rootham, Helen. *Kossovo: A Translation of the Heroic Songs of the Serbs*. London: Blackwell, 1920.

Roper, A.F. *The Tragedy of Lynching*. Chapel Hill: North Carolina University Press, 1933.

Roper, Elmo. *You and Your Leaders*. New York: William Morrow, 1957.

Roper, Esther (ed.). *Prison Letters of Countess Markievicz*. London: Longmans, Green, 1934.

Ropp, Theodore. *War in the Modern World*. Chapel Hill, N.C.: Duke University Press, 1962.

Rorabaugh, W.J. *The Alcoholic Republic*. New York: Oxford University Press, 1979.

Rorem, Ned. *The Final Diary*. New York: Holt, Rinehard, Winston, 1974.

____. *The New York Diary*. New York: George Braziller, 1967.

Rorick, Eleanor. *The Notorious Benders*. Cherryvale, Kan.: n.p., n.d.

Rorschach, H. *Psychodiagnostik*. Leipzig, Ger.: Bircher, 1921.

Rorty, James, and Decter, Moshe. *McCarthy and the Communists*. Boston: Beacon Press, 1954.

Rosa, Joseph G. *Alias Jack McCall: A Pardon or Death?*. Kansas City: Kansas City Posse of the Westerners, 1967.

____. *The Gunfighter, Man or Myth?* Norman: University of Oklahoma Press, 1969.

____. *They Called Him Wild Bill*. Norman: University of Oklahoma Press, 1964.

____. *The West of Wild Bill Hickok*. Norman: University of Oklahoma Press, 1982.

Rosa, Joseph, and May, Robin. *Gun Law*. Chicago: Contemporary Books, 1977.

Rosales, Ramón M. *El 20 de noviembre de 1910 y el patriota ciudano doctor Francisco Vásquez Gómez*. San Antonio, Texas: Editorial Ramón M. Rosales, 1921.

Rosas y Reyes, Román. *Las imposturas de Vicente Blasco Ibáñez*. Barcelona, Spain: Sintes, 1922.

Rosberg, Robert R. *Game of Thieves*. New York: Everest House, 1980.

Roscher, G. *Handbuch der Daktyloskopie*. Leipzig, Ger.: C.L. Hirschfeld, 1905.

Roscoe, Jesse. *The Treasure Album of Pancho Villa*. El Paso, Tex.: Toyahvale Press, 1962.

Roscoe, Theodore. *The Lincoln Assassination, April 14, 1865*. New York: Franklin Watts, 1971.

____. *True Tales of Bold Escapes*. Englewood Cliffs, N.J.: Prentice-Hall, 1965.

____. *The Web of Conspiracy: The Complete Story of the Men Who Murdered Lincoln*. Englewood Cliffs, N.J.: Prentice-Hall, 1959.

Roscoe, William. *The Life and Pontificate of Leo the Tenth*. 2 vols. London: Henry G. Bohn, 1853.

Rose, Andrew. *Stinie, Murder on the Common*. London: Bodley Head, 1985.

Rose, Clarkson. *Red Plush and Greasepaint*. London: Museum Press, 1964.

Rose, Colin (ed.). *The World's Greatest Rip-Offs*. New York: Sterling, 1978.

Rose, Dan. *Prehistoric and Historic Gila County, Arizona*. Phoenix, Ariz.: Republic and Gazette, n.d.

Rose, Elliot. *A Razor for a Goat*. Toronto, Ontario, Can.: University of Toronto Press, 1962.

Rose, G.N.G. *Royal Commission on Assizes and Quarter Sessions 1966-69*. London: Special Statistical Survey, HMSO, 1971.

Rose, Gordon. *The Struggle for Penal Reform*. Chicago: Quadrangle Books, 1961.

Rose, H.M. *Lethal Aspects of Urban Violence*. Lexington, Mass.: D.C. Heath, 1979.

Rose, J.H. *Life of Napoleon*. London: George Bell, 1901.

Rose, Kenneth. *King George V*. London: Weidenfeld & Nicolson, 1983.

Rose, Louis. *Faith Healing*. Middlesex, Eng.: Penguin, 1971.

Rose, Peter I., Glazer, Myron, and Glazer, Penina Migdal. *Sociology: Inquiry into Society*. New York: St. Martin's Press, 1982.

Rose, T. *Violence in America*. New York: Random House, 1969.

Rose, Victor M. *The Life and Services of Gen. Ben McCulloch*. Philadelphia: Pictorial Bureau of the Press, 1888.

____. *The Texas Vendetta, or the Sutton-Taylor Feud*. New York: J.J. Little, 1880.

Rose, William Ganson. *Cleveland: The Making of a City*. Cleveland: World, 1950.

Rose-Ackerman, Susan. *The Economics of Corruption: An Essay in Political Economy*. New York: Academic Press, 1978.

Rosebery, Lord. *Napoleon, The Last Phase*. London: A. Humphreys, 1900.

Rosebury, Theodore. *Microbes and Morals*. New York: Viking Press, 1971.

Rosefsky, Robert S. *Frauds, Swindles, and Rackets*. Chicago: Follett, 1973.

Rosen, Baron R.R. *Forty Years of Diplomacy*. 2 vols. New York: Alfred A. Knopf, 1922.

Rosen, Charles. *Scandals of '51: How Gamblers Almost Killed College Basketball*. New York: Holt, Rinehart & Winston, 1978.

Rosen, George. *Madness in Society*. New York: Harper & Row, 1968.

Rosen, Rev. Peter. *Pa-ha-sa-pah; or the Black Hills of South Dakota*. St. Louis: Nixon-Jones, 1895.

Rosen, Ruth. *The Last Sisterhood: Prostitution in America, 1900-1918*. Baltimore: Johns Hopkins University Press, 1983.

Rosen, Ruth, and Davidson, Sue (eds.). *The Maimie Papers*. New York: Feminist Press, 1977.

Rosenbaum, H. Jon, and Sederberg, Peter C. (eds.). *Vigilante Politics*. Philadelphia: University of Philadelphia, 1976.

Rosenbaum, Julius. *The Plague of Lust*. New York: Frederick Publications, 1955.

Rosenbaum, Kurt. *Community of Fate: German-Soviet Diplomatic Relations, 1922-1928*. Syracuse, N.Y.: Syracuse University

Press, 1965.

Rosenberg, Alfred. *Letzte Aufzeichnungen.* Göttingen, Ger.: Plesse, 1955.

Rosenberg, Arthur. *Democracy and Socialism.* New York: Alfred A. Knopf, 1939.

_____. *A History of the German Republic.* London: Methuen, 1936.

Rosenberg, Bernard, and White, David Manning (eds.). *Mass Culture Revisited.* New York: Van Nostrand Reinhold, 1971.

Rosenberg, B., and Silverstein, H. *The Varieties of Delinquent Experience.* Waltham, Mass.: Blaisdell, 1969.

Rosenberg, Charles E. *The Trial of the Assassin Guiteau.* Chicago: University of Chicago Press, 1968.

Rosenberg, Hans. *Bureaucracy, Aristocracy and Autocracy: The Prussian Experience 1660-1815.* Cambridge, Mass.: Beacon Press, 1966.

_____. *Die Weltwirtschaftskrise von 1857-59.* Stuttgart, Ger.: W. Kohlhammer, 1934.

Rosenberg, M. *Attitude Organization and Change.* New Haven, Conn.: Yale University Press, 1960.

Rosenberg, Philip. *The Spivey Assignment.* New York: Holt, Rinehart & Winston, 1979.

Rosenblatt, Stanley M. *Trial Lawyer.* Secaucus, N.J.: Lyle Stuart, 1984.

Rosenbloom, Morris V. *Peace Through Strength: Bernard Baruch and a Blueprint for Security.* New York: Farrar, Straus & Young, 1953.

Rosenburg, Samuel. *Naked is the Best Disguise: The Death and Resurrection of Sherlock Holmes.* Indianapolis, Ind.: Bobbs-Merrill, 1974.

Rosengarten, Theodore. *All God's Dangers: The Life of Nate Shaw.* New York: Alfred A. Knopf, 1974.

Rosenheim, Margaret K. (ed.). *Pursuing Justice for the Child.* Chicago: University of Chicago Press, 1976.

Rosenman, Judge Samuel I. *Working With Roosevelt.* New York: Harper & Row, 1952.

Rosenquist, C.M., and Megargee, E.I. *Delinquency in Three Cultures.* Austin: University of Texas Press, 1969.

Rosenstein, Jaik. *Hollywood Leg Man.* Los Angeles: Madison Press, 1950.

Rosenstone, Robert A. *Romantic Revolutionary: John Reed.* New York: Alfred A. Knopf, 1975.

Rosenthal, D. *Genetic Theory and Abnormal Behavior.* New York: McGraw-Hill, 1970.

Rosenthal, E.I.J. *Political Thought in Medieval Islam.* Cambridge: Cambridge University Press, 1962.

Rosenthal, Eric. *The Fall of Italian East Africa.* London: Hutchinson, 1942.

_____. *Gold Bricks and Mortar.* Johannesburg, S. Afri.: Printing House, 1946.

Rosenthal, F. *The Herb.* Leiden, Neth. E.J. Brill, 1971.

Rosenthal, M.A. *Thirty-Eight Witnesses.* New York: McGraw-Hill, 1964.

Rosenthal, Robert. *Experimenter Effects in Research.* New York: D. Appleton, 1966.

_____, and Jacobson, Lenore. *Pygmalion in the Classroom.* New York: Holt, Rinehart & Winston, 1968.

Rosett, Arthur, and Cressey, Donald R. *Justice by Consent.* Philadelphia: J.B. Lippincott, 1976.

Rosevear, J. *Pot: A Handbook of Marihuana.* New York: University Books, 1967.

Rosinski, Herbert. *The German Army.* London: Hogarth, 1939.

Roskoff, Gustav. *Geschichte des Teufels.* Leipzig, Ger.: F.A. Brockhaus, 1869.

Rosmond, Babette. *Robert Benchley, His Life and Good Times.* New York: Doubleday, 1970.

Rosow, Eugene. *Born to Lose, The Gangster Film in America.* New York: Oxford University Press, 1978.

Ross, Anne. *Everyday Life of the Pagan Celts.* New York: G.P. Putnam's Sons, 1970.

Ross, Caroline, and Lawrence, Ken. *J. Edgar Hoover's Detention Plan.* Jackson, Miss.: American Friends Service Committee, 1978.

Ross, D. *Hitler und Dollfuss.* Hamburg, Ger.: Leibniz, 1966.

Ross, Dorothy G. *G. Stanley Hall: The Psychologist as Prophet.* Chicago: University of Chicago Press, 1972.

Ross, Edith Connelley. *The Bloody Benders.* Kansas State Historical Society, 1926-28.

Ross, Edmund G. *History of the Impeachment of Andrew Johnson.* Santa Fe, N.M.: New Mexican Printing, 1896.

Ross, Joel H. *What I Saw in New York; Or, A Bird's eye View of City Life.* Auburn, N.Y.: Derby & Miller, 1852.

Ross, Lloyd. *Labor in Australia.* New York: American Council, Institute of Pacific Relations, 1943.

Ross, Marvin C. *The West of Alfred Jacob Miller.* Norman: University of Oklahoma Press, 1951.

Ross, Nancy Wilson. *Westward the Women.* New York: Alfred A. Knopf, 1944.

Ross, Robert. *The Trial of Al Capone.* Chicago: Robert Ross, 1933.

Ross, Stanley R. *Francisco I. Madero: Apostle of Mexican Democracy.* New York: Columbia University Press, 1955.

Ross, Susan C. *The Rights of Women.* New York: Avon, 1973.

Ross, W.D. (ed.). *The Works of Aristotle.* Oxford, Eng.: Clarendon Press, 1921.

Ross, Walter S. *The Last Hero.* New York: Harper & Row, 1976.

Rossani, Ottavio. *Intervista sui Rapimenti.* Milan, Italy: Edizioni Elle, 1978.

_____. *L'industria dei Sequestri: dalla Mafia alle Brigate Rosse: la Storia, le Techniche, i Nomi.* Milan: Longanesi, 1978.

Rossi, Angelo T. *The Rise of Italian Fascism.* trans. Peter and Dorothy Wait. London: Methuen, 1938.

Rossi, Cesare. *Il Delitto Matteotti.* Milan, Italy: Ceschina, 1965.

_____. *Mussolini com'era.* Rome: Ruffolo, 1947.

_____. *Personaggi di ieri e di oggi.* Milan, Italy: Ceschina, 1965.

Rossi, Gen. Francesco. *Come arrivammo all' armistizio.* Milan, Italy: Garzanti, 1946.

_____. *Mussolini e lo Stato Maggiore.* Milan, Italy: Regionale, 1951.

Rossi, Peter, Berk, Richard A., and Eidson, Bettye K. *The Roots of Urban Discontent.* New York: John Wiley & Sons, 1974.

Rossiter, Clinton. *Seedtime of the Republic.* New York: Harcourt, Brace, 1953.

Rosskam, Edwin and Louise. *Towboat River.* New York: Duell, Sloan & Pearce, 1948.

Rossner, Judith. *Looking for Mr. Goodbar.* New York: Simon & Schuster, 1975.

Rossum, Ralph A. *The Politics of the Criminal Justice System.* New York: Marcel Dekker, 1978.

Rosten, Leo C. *The Washington Correspondents.* New York: Harcourt Brace, 1937.

Rostovtzeff, Michael I. *The Social and Economic History of the Roman Empire.* 2 vols. Oxford, Eng.: Clarendon Press, 1957.

Rostow, W.W. and Levin, Alfred. *Dynamics of Soviet Society.* New York: W.W. Norton, 1953.

Roszak, Theodore. *The Making of a Counter Culture: Reflections on the Technocratic Society and Its Youthful Opposition.* Garden City, N.Y.: Doubleday, 1969.

_____. *Unfinished Animal.* New York: Harper & Row, 1975.

Roth, Andrew. *Japan Strikes South.* New York: American Council, Institute of Pacific Relations, 1941.

Rothbard, Murray N. *America's Great Depression.* Princeton, N.J.: D. Van Nostrand, 1963.

Rothblatt, Henry B. *That Damned Lawyer.* New York: Dodd, Mead, 1983.

Rothert, Otto A. *The Outlaws of Cave-in-Rock.* Cleveland: Arthur H. Clark, 1924.

Rothery, Agnes E. *Norway, Changing and Changeless.* New York:

Viking Press, 1935.

Rothfels, Hans. *Bismarck, der Osten und das Reich.* Stuttgart, Ger.: Kohlhammer, 1960.

_____. *The German Opposition to Hitler: An Assessment.* Krefeld, Ger.: Scherpe-Verlag, 1949.

Rothman, David J. *Conscience and Convenience.* Boston: Little, Brown, 1980.

_____. *The Discovery of the Asylum: Social Order and Disorder in the New Republic.* Boston: Little, Brown, 1971.

Rothschild, Joseph. *Communist Eastern Europe.* New York: Walker, 1964.

_____. *The Communist Party of Bulgaria: Origins and Development, 1883-1936.* New York: Columbia University Press, 1959.

Rothstein, William G. *American Physicians in the Nineteenth Century: From Sects to Science.* Baltimore: Johns Hopkins University Press, 1973.

Rottenberg, Simon (ed.). *The Economics of Crime and Punishment.* Washington, D.C.: American Enterprise Institute for Public Policy Research, 1973.

Roucek, Joseph S. *Contemporary Roumania and Her Problems: A Study in Modern Nationalism.* London: Oxford University Press, 1932.

Roueché, Berton. *Alcohol: Its History, Folklore and Its Effect on the Human Body.* New York: Grove Press, 1962.

Rougement, Denis de. *Love in the Western World.* trans. Montgomery Belgion. New York: Pantheon, 1956.

Roughead, William. *The Art of Murder.* New York: Sheridan House, 1943.

_____. *Bad Companions.* New York: Duffield & Green, 1931.

_____. *Burke and Hare.* London, Hodge, 1948.

_____. *Classic Crimes.* London: Cassell, 1951.

_____. *Famous Crimes.* London: Faber & Faber, 1935.

_____. *The Fatal Countess.* London: Green, 1924.

_____. *In Queer Street.* London: Green, 1924.

_____. *Mainly Murder.* London: Cassell, 1937.

_____. *Malice Domestic.* New York: Doubleday, Doran, 1929.

_____. *The Murderer's Companion.* New York: Readers Club, 1941.

_____. *Neck or Nothing.* London: Cassell, 1939.

_____. *Reprobates Reviewed.* London: Cassell, 1941.

_____. *The Riddle of Ruthvens.* Edinburgh, Scot.: W. Green & Son, 1919.

_____. *Rogues Walk Here.* London: Cassell, 1934.

_____. *The Seamy Side.* London: Cassell, 1938.

_____. *Tales of the Criminous.* London: Cassell, 1956.

_____. *Twelve Scots Trials.* London: Green, 1913.

Rounds, Frank. *Window on Red Square.* Boston: Houghton Mifflin, 1953.

Roundy, William Noble. *The Visit of Apollo...* Chicago: Hack & Anderson, 1907.

Rourke, Constance Mayfield. *Trumpets of Jubliee.* New York: Harcourt, Brace, 1927.

Rouse, M.C. *A History of Cowboy Flat-Campbell-Pleasant Valley.* Guthrie, Okla.: Privately Printed, 1960.

Rousseau, J.J. *Discourse on Inequality.* trans. G.D.H. Cole. London: J.M. Dent, 1973.

_____. *Emile.* trans. B. Foxely. London: Dent/Everyman's Library, 1974.

Rousselet, Marcel. *Les souverains devant la justice, de Louis XVI à Napoléon III.* Paris: A. Michel, 1946.

Rout, Leslie B., and Bratzel, John F. *The Shadow War: German Espionage and United States Counterespionage in Latin America During World War II.* Frederick, Md.: University Publications, 1986.

Routledge, Mrs. Scoresby. *The Mystery of Easter Island.* London: Sifton, Praed, 1919.

Rovere, Franco. *Vita amorosa di Claretta Petacci.* Milan, Italy: Lucchi, 1946.

Rovere, Richard H. *The American Establishment and Other Reports, Opinions, and Speculations.* New York: Harcourt, Brace & World, 1962.

_____. *Howe and Hummell: Their True and Scandalous History.* New York: Farrar, Straus, 1947.

_____. *Senator Joe McCarthy.* New York: Harcourt, Brace, 1959.

_____. *The Weeper and the Blackmailer.* New York: New American Library, 1950.

Rowan, David. *Famous American Crimes.* London: Frederick Muller, 1957.

_____. *Famous European Crimes.* London: Frederick Muller, 1956.

Rowan, Ford. *Techno Spies.* New York: G.P. Putnam's Sons, 1978.

Rowan, Richard Wilmer. *A Family of Outlaws.* Fort Wayne, Ind.: n.p., 1955.

_____. *The Pinkertons, A Detective Dynasty.* Boston: Little, Brown, 1931.

_____, with Deindorfer, Robert. *Secret Service, 33 Centuries of Espionage.* New York: Hawthorn Books, 1967.

_____. *The Story of Secret Service.* New York: Garden City, 1939.

Rowan, Roy. *The Four Days of Mayaguez.* New York: W.W. Norton, 1975.

Rowe, Gary Thomas, Jr. *My Undercover Years With the Ku Klux Klan.* New York: Bantam Books, 1976.

Rowe, Richard. *Total Self-Protection.* New York: Morrow Quill, 1979.

Rowell, Earle A. and Robert. *On the Trail of Marijuana: The Weed of Madness.* Mountain View, Calif.: Pacific Press, 1939.

Rowell, Henry T. *Rome in the Augustan Age.* Norman: University of Oklahoma Press, 1962.

Rowen, Herbert (ed.). *The Low Countries in Early Modern Times.* New York: Walker, 1972.

Rowen, Herbert H. *John de Witt, Grand Pensionary of Holland, 1625-1672.* Princeton, N.J.: Princeton University Press, 1978.

Rowland, B.M. (ed.). *Balance of Power vs. Hegemony: The Interwar Monetary System.* New York: New York University Press, 1976.

Rowland, Desmond, and Bailey, James. *The Law Enforcement Handbook.* New York: Facts on File, 1985.

Rowland, Dunbar. *History of Mississippi.* Chicago: S.J. Clarke, 1925.

Rowland, John. *A Century of Murder.* London: Home & Van Thal, 1950.

_____. *Criminal Files.* London: Arco, 1957.

_____. *More Criminal Files.* London: Arco, 1958.

_____. *Murder by Persons Unknown.* London: Mellifont Press, 1941.

_____. *Murder Mistaken.* London: J. Long, 1963.

_____. *Murder Revisited: A Study of Two Poisoning Cases.* London: John Long, 1961.

_____. *Poisoner in the Dock.* London: Arco, 1960.

_____. *The Wallace Case.* London: Carroll & Nicholson, 1949.

_____. *Unfit to Plead?* London: John Long, 1965.

Rowntree, Joseph, and Sherwell, Arthur. *The Temperance Problem and Social Reform.* London: Hodder & Stoughton, 1901.

Rowntree, Maurice L. *Mankind Set Free.* London: Jonathan Cape, 1939.

Rowse, Arthur Edward. *Slanted News.* Boston: Beacon Press, 1957.

Roy, Claude. *Les Arts Fantastiques.* Paris: Encyclopédie Essentielle, 1960.

Roy, Jules. *The War in Algeria.* New York: Grove Press, 1961.

Roy, Maurice. *1929: La Grand Crise.* Paris: Denoël, 1969.

Royal College of Psychiatrists. *Drug Scenes: A Report on Drug Dependence.* London: Gaskell, 1987.

The Royal Commission and the Punishment of Death. London: Society for the Abolition of Capital Punishment, 1866.

Royal Commission On Capital Punishment, 1949-1953: Report.

London: H.M. Stationery Office, 1953.

Royal, H.W. *Gambling and Confidence Games Exposed: showing How the Proprietors of Gambling Houses and the Players can be Cheated.* Chicago: Published by Author, 1896.

Royal Institute of International Affairs. *Great Britain and Palestine, 1915-1945.* London: Oxford University Press, 1946.

_____. *The Impact of the Russian Revolution, 1917-1967.* London: Institute, 1967.

_____. *The Middle East: A Political and Economic Survey.* London: Oxford University Press, 1958.

_____. *Survey of International Affairs.* London: Oxford University Press, 1953.

Royce, Josiah. *California From the Conquest in 1846 to the Second Vigilance Committee in San Francisco.* New York: Houghton Mifflin, 1886.

Royce, Sarah. *A Frontier Lady's Recollections of the Gold Rush and Early California.* New Haven, Conn.: Yale University Press, 1932.

Royko, Mike. *Boss: Richard J. Daley of Chicago.* New York: E.P. Dutton, 1971.

_____. *I May Be Wrong, But I Doubt It.* Chicago: Henry Regnery, 1968.

_____. *Up Against It.* Chicago: Henry Regnery, 1967.

Royster, Charles. *Light-Horse Harry Lee and the Legacy of the American Revolution.* New York: Alfred A. Knopf, 1981.

Royster, Vermont. *A Pride of Prejudices.* New York: Alfred A. Knopf, 1968.

Ruark, R. *Something of Value.* New York: Doubleday, 1955.

Rubenstein, or The Murdered Jewess. Philadelphia: Old Franklin, 1876.

Rubenstein, Richard E. *Rebels in Eden: Mass Political Violence in the United States.* Boston: Little, Brown, 1970.

Rubin, David. *The Rights of Teachers.* New York: Discus, Avon Books, 1972.

Rubin, Sol. *Crime and Juvenile Delinquency.* New York: Oceana, 1958.

_____. *The Law of Criminal Corrections.* St. Paul, Minn.: West, 1963.

Rubin, Vera (ed.). *Cannabis and Culture.* The Hague, Neth.: Mouton, 1975.

_____, and Comitas, Lambros. *Ganja in Jamaica.* Garden City, N.Y.: Anchor Press/Doubleday, 1976.

Rubington, Earl, and Weinberg, Martin S. (eds.). *Deviance: The Interactionist Perspective.* New York: Macmillan, 1973.

Rubinstein, Jonathan. *City Police.* New York: Ballantine, 1973.

_____, and Reuter, Peter. *Numbers: The Routine Racket.* New York: Policy Sciences Center, 1977.

Rubinstein, Nicolai. *Lucrezia Borgia.* Rome: Istituto della Enciclopedia Italiana, 1971.

Rublowsky, John. *The Stoned Age: A History of Drugs in America.* New York: G.P. Putnam's Sons, 1975.

Rubner, Alex. *The Economy of Israel.* New York: Frederick A. Praeger, 1960.

Ruchames, Louis (ed.). *The Abolitionists: A Collection of Their Writings.* New York: G.P. Putnam's Sons, 1963.

Ruchames, Louis. *A John Brown Reader.* New York: Abelard-Schuman, 1959.

Ruck, S.K. (ed.). *Paterson on Prisons.* London: Frederick Muller, 1951.

Rucker, Bryce W. *The First Freedom.* Carbondale: Southern Illinois University Press, 1968.

Rude, George F.E. *The Crowd in History: A Study of Popular Disturbances in France and England, 1730-1848.* New York: John Wiley & Sons, 1964.

_____. *Hanoverian London 1714-1808.* Berkeley: University of California Press, 1971.

Rudenko, S.I. *Frozen Tombs of Siberia.* Berkeley: University of California Press, 1970.

Rudensky, Morris ("Red"), and Riley, Don. *The Gonif.* Blue Earth, Minn.: Piper, 1970.

Rudin, Harry R. *Armistice 1918.* New Haven, Conn.: Yale University Press, 1944.

Rudwick, Elliott M. *Race Riot at East St. Louis: July 2, 1917.* Carbondale: Southern Illinois University Press, 1964.

Rueff, Jacques. *The Age of Inflation.* Chicago: Henry Regnery, 1964.

Ruehlmann, William. *Saint with a Gun.* New York: New York University Press, 1974.

Ruelher, Rosemary Radford (ed.). *Religion and Sexism. Images of Woman in the Jewish and Christian Traditions.* New York: Simon & Schuster, 1974.

Ruggles, Eleanor. *Prince of Players: Edwin Booth.* New York: W.W. Norton, 1953.

Ruggles-Brise, Sir Evelyn. *The English Prison System.* London: Macmillan, 1938.

Rugoff, Milton. *Prudery and Passion.* New York: G.P. Putnam's Sons, 1971.

Ruhm, Herbert (ed.). *The Hard-Boiled Detective.* New York: Vintage Books, 1977.

Ruinas, Stanis. *Pioggia sulla Repubblica.* Rome: Corso, 1946.

Rule, Ann. *The Stranger Beside Me.* New York: W.W. Norton, 1980.

Rumbelow, Donald. *The Complete Jack the Ripper.* Boston: New York Graphic Society, 1975.

_____. *The Houndsditch Murders: The Siege of Sidney Street.* London: Macmillan, 1973.

_____. *I Spy Blue: Police and Crime in the City of London from Elizabeth I to Victoria.* London: Macmillan, 1971.

_____. *The Siege of Sidney Street.* New York: St. Martin's Press, 1973.

Rummel, R.J. *Applied Factor Analysis.* Evanston, Ill.: Northwestern University Press, 1970.

Rumney, Jay, and Murphy, J.P. *Probation and Social Adjustment.* New Brunswick, N.J.: Fordham University Press, 1952.

Runciman, Steven. *Byzantine Civilization.* New York: Longmans, Green, 1933.

_____. *History of the Crusaders.* 3 vols. London: Cambridge University Press, 1951-1954.

Runyon, Damon. *Guys and Dolls.* New York: Frederick A. Stokes, 1931.

_____. *More Guys and Dolls.* New York: Garden City Books, 1951.

_____. *A Treasury of Damon Runyon.* New York: Random House, 1958.

_____. *Trials and Other Tribulations.* New York: J.B. Lippincott, 1933.

Runyon, Damon, Jr. *Father's Footsteps.* New York: Random House, 1953.

Rusca, Antonio. *De Inferno et Statu Daemonum ante Mundi Exitum.* Milan, Italy: ex Collegij ambrosiam typographia, 1621.

Rusche, George, and Kirchheimer, Otto. *Punishment and Social Structure.* New York: Russell & Russell, 1939.

Rush, Benjamin. *Autobiography.* Princeton, N.J.: Princeton University Press, 1948.

Rush, Florence. *The Best Kept Secret.* Englewood Cliffs, N.J.: Prentice-Hall, 1980.

Rush, M. *Khrushchev and the Stalin Succession.* Santa Monica, Calif.: Rand, 1957.

Rush, N. Orwin. *Mercer's Banditti of the Plains.* Tallahassee: Florida State University Library, 1961.

Rusher, William. *Special Counsel.* New Rochelle, N.Y.: Arlington House, 1968.

Rushing, William (ed.). *Deviant Behavior and Social Process.* Chicago: Rand McNally, 1969.

Rusk, Ralph L. *The Life of Ralph Waldo Emerson.* New York: Columbia University Press, 1949.

Russ, William A., Jr. *The Hawaiian Revolution (1893-1894) and Its Struggle To Win Annexation.* Selinsgrove, Pa.: Susquehanna University Press, 1959.

Russel, Robert Royal. *Economic Aspects of Southern Sectionalism 1840-1861.* Urbana: University of Illinois Press, 1924.

Russell, Bertrand. *The Autobiography of Bertrand Russell 1914-1944.* Boston: Little, Brown, 1968.

_____, et al. *Dare We Look Ahead?* New York: Macmillan, 1942.

_____. *Freedom vs. Organization.* New York: W.W. Norton, 1934.

_____. *The History of Western Philosophy.* New York: Simon & Schuster, 1945.

_____. *Marriage and Morals.* London: George Allen & Unwin, 1967.

_____. *Power: A New Social Analysis.* New York: W.W. Norton, 1938.

_____. *Proposed Roads to Freedom.* New York: Harcourt, Brace, 1919.

Russell, Brian, and Sellier, Charles E. *Conspiracy to Kill a President.* New York: Bantam Books, 1982.

Russell, Carl Parcher. *One Hundred Years in Yosemite.* Palo Alto, Calif.: Stanford University Press, 1931.

Russell, Charles Edmund. *Adventures of the DCI.* London: Hurst & Blackett, 192-.

Russell, Charles Edward. *A-Rafting on the Mississipp'.* New York: Century, 1928.

_____. *Bare Hands and Stone Walls: Some Reflections of a Side-Line Reformer.* New York: Charles Scribner's Sons, 1933.

_____. *Blaine of Maine. His Life and Times.* New York: Cosmopolitan, 1931.

_____. *The Greatest Trust in the World.* New York: Ridgway-Thayer, 1905.

_____. *The Story of the Non-Patisan League.* New York: Harper, 1920.

_____. *Why I Am a Socialist.* New York: George H. Doran, 1910.

Russell, C.W. (ed.). *Memoirs of Colonel John S. Mosby.* Boston: Little, Brown, 1917.

Russell, Charles M. *Good Medicine.* Garden City, N.Y.: Garden City, 1930.

Russell, Diana E.H. *Crimes Against Women.* Millbrae, Calif.: Les Femmes, 1977.

_____. *The Politics of Rape.* New York: Stein & Day, 1975.

Russell, Dick. *Closing In: The Search for JFK's Assassins.* New York: Dial Press, 1977.

Russell, Don. *The Lives and Legends of Buffalo Bill.* Norman: University of Oklahoma Press, 1960.

Russell, Donn (ed.). *Best Murder Cases.* London: Faber & Faber, 1958.

_____. *Lizzie Borden, The Untold Story.* New York: Simon & Schuster, 1961.

Russell, Lady Dorothea. *Medieval Cairo and the Monasteries of the Wadi Natrun.* London: Weindenfeld & Nicolson, 1962.

Russell, Edward Frederick Langley, Baron, of Liverpool. *The French Corsairs.* London: Robert Hale, 1970.

_____. *Knights of Bushido: The Shocking History of Japanese War Atrocities.* New York: E.P. Dutton, 1958.

_____. *Though the Heavens Fall.* London: Cassell, 1956.

Russell, Francis. *A City in Terror.* New York: Viking Press, 1975.

_____. *The Shadow of Blooming Grove: Warren G. Harding in His Times.* New York: McGraw-Hill, 1968.

_____. *Tragedy in Dedham.* New York: McGraw-Hill, 1962.

Russell, George K. *Marihuana Today.* New York: Myrin Institute, 1976.

Russell, George William. *The National Being: Some Thoughts on an Irish Polity by A.E.* London: Macmillan, 1925.

Russell, Guy. *Guilty or Not Guilty?* London: Hutchinson, 1931.

Russell, Harold E., and Beigel, Allan. *Understanding Human Behavior For Effective Police Work.* New York: Basic Books, 1982.

Russell, Jeffrey Burton. *The Devil.* Ithaca, N.Y.: Cornell University Press, 1977.

Russell, Jesse Lewis. *Behind These Ozark Hills.* New York: Hobson Book Press, 1947.

Russell, John. *An Essay on the History of the English Government and Constitution from the Reign of Henry VIII to the Present Time.* London: Green, Longman, 1865.

Russell, L.B. *Grandpa's Autobiography.* Comanche, Texas: Comanche, 1927.

Russell, Oland D. *The House of Mitsui.* Boston: Little, Brown, 1939.

Russell, Phillip. *Mexico in Transition.* Austin, Texas: Colorado River Press, 1977.

Russell, R.V., and Lal, Hira. *Tribes and Castes of the Central Provinces of India.* London: Macmillan, 1916.

Russell, Ray. *Unholy Trinity.* New York: Bantam, 1967.

Russell, Thomas H. *The Illustrious Life and Work of Warren G. Harding.* Chicago: n.p., 1923.

Russo, Robert J. *Amphetamine Abuse.* Springfield, Ill.: Charles C. Thomas, 1972.

Ruth, Kent. *Great Day in the West: Forts, Posts, and Rendezvous Beyond the Mississippi.* Norman: University of Oklahoma Press, 1963.

_____. *Oklahoma, A Guide to the Sooner State.* Norman: University of Oklahoma Press, 1957.

Rutherford, Andrew, et al. *Prison Population and Policy Choices.* Washington, D.C.: National Institute of Law Enforcement and Criminal Justice, 1977.

Rutherford, L. *John Peter Zenger.* New York: Peter Smith, 1941.

Rutherford, Ward. *Fall of the Philippines.* New York: Ballantine Books, 1971.

Rutledge, Col. Dick. *A Few Stirring Events in the Life of Col. Dick Rutledge, Only Living Indian Scout of the Early Frontier Days of the West.* Denver: n.p., 1930.

Rutledge, Lyman V. *Moonlight at Murder Smuttynose.* Boston: Star King Press, 1958.

Rutman, Darrett B. *Husbandmen of Plymouth: Farms and Villages in the Old Colony, 1620-1692.* Boston: Beacon Press, 1967.

_____. *Winthrop's Boston: Portrait of a Puritan Town, 1630-1649.* Chapel Hill: University of North Carolina Press, 1963.

Rüttenauer, Isabelle. *Friedrich von Spee.* Freiburg, Ger.: Herder, 1951.

Rutter, M., Maughan, B., Mortimore, P., and Ouston, J. *Fifteen Thousand Hours.* Cambridge, Mass.: Harvard University Press, 1979.

_____, and Giller, H. *Juvenile Delinquency.* New York: Guilford Press, 1984.

_____. *Maternal Deprivation Reassessed.* New York: Penguin, 1972.

Rutter, Owen. *The Pirate Wind: Tales of the Sea Robbers of Malaya.* London: Hutchinson, 1930.

Rutter, Owen (ed.). *Notable British Trials: Trial of Bounty Mutineers.* London: William Hodge, 1931.

Ryan, Cornelius. *The Last Battle.* New York: Simon & Schuster, 1966.

Ryan, Desmond. *James Connolly: His Life, Work and Writing.* Dublin, Ire.: Talbot, 1924.

_____. *Remembering Sion.* London: Arthur Barker, 1934.

_____. *Sean Tracy and the Third Tipperary Brigade I.R.A.* Tralee, Ire.: Kerryman, 1945.

_____. *The Rising: The Complete Story of Easter Week.* Dublin, Ire.: Golden Eagle, 1957.

Ryan, Ed. *Me and the Black Hills.* Custer, S.D.: Published by Author, 1951.

Ryan, Frederick L. *Industrial Relations in the San Francisco Building Trades.* Norman: University of Oklahoma Press, 1935.

Ryan, J.C. *A Skeptic Dude in Arizona.* San Antonio, Texas: Naylor, 1952.

Ryan, John A. *Distributive Justice.* New York: Macmillan, 1942.

Ryan, Mark F. *Fenian Memories.* Dublin, Ire.: Gill, 1946.

Ryan, Michael. *Prostitution in London.* London: Bailliere, 1838.

Ryan, N.J. *A History of Malaysia and Singapore.* Oxford University Press, 1976.

Ryan, William. *Blaming the Victim*. New York: Vintage Books, 1976.

Ryder, David Warren. *A Century of Hardware and Steel*. San Francisco: Historical 1949.

_____. *Great Citizen: A Biography of William H. Crocker*. San Francisco: Historical, 1962.

Rye, Edgar. *The Quirt and the Spur*. Chicago: W.B. Conkey, 1909.

Ryerson, Ellen. *The Best Laid Plans*. New York: Hill & Wang, 1978.

Rynning, Thomas H. *Gun Notches*. New York: Frederick A. Stokes, 1931.

Rysan, Joseph. *Wilhelm Meinhold's Bernsteinhexe*. Chicago: University of Chicago, 1948.

S

Saarinen, Aline B. *The Proud Possessors*. New York: Random House, 1958.

Sa'b, Husan. *Zionism and Racism*. Beirut, Leb.: Research Center, Palestine Liberation Organization, 1965.

Sabatini, Rafael. *The Life of Cesare Borgia*. New York: Brentano's, 1923.

Sabetti, Filippo. *Political Authority in a Sicilian Village*. New Brunswick, N.J.: Rutgers University Press, 1984.

Sabin, Edwin LeGrand. *Wild Men of the Wild West*. New York: Thomas Y. Crowell, 1929.

Sabine, George H. *A History of Political Theory*. New York: Henry Holt, 1937.

Saburo Hayashi. *A History of Land Warfare Conditions in the Pacific War*. Toyko: Iwanami Shinsho, 1951.

The Sacco-Vanzetti Case: Transcript of the Record of the Trial. New York: Henry Holt, 1928-1929.

Sacher, Harry. *Israel and the Establishment of a State*. London: Wiedenfield & Nicolson, 1952.

Sacher, Howard M. *The Course of Modern Jewish History*. Cleveland: World, 1958.

Sachs, Emanie. *"The Terrible Siren." Victoria Woodhull (1838-1927)*. New York: Harper, 1932.

Sack, A.J. *The Birth of the Russian Democracy*. New York: Russian Information Bureau, 1918.

Sacks, Benjamin. *Arizona's Angry Man*. Tempe: Arizona Historical Foundation, 1970.

Sackville-West, Vita. *Saint Joan of Arc*. New York: Doubleday, Doran, 1936.

The Sad Case of Mrs. Kate Southern. Philadelphia: Old Franklin House, 1878.

Sadat, Anwar. *Revolt on the Nile*. New York: Day, 1957.

Sadler, A.L. *The Maker of Modern Japan: The Life of Tokugawa Ieyasu*. New York: W.W. Norton, 1937.

Sadler, William S. *Theory and Practice of Psychiatry*. St. Louis: C.V. Mosby, 1936.

Sáenz, Aarón. *La Politica Internacional de la Revolución: Estudios y Documentos*. México City, Méx.: Fondo de la Cultura Económica, 1960.

Sáenz, Moisés, and Priestley, Herbert Ingram. *Some Mexican Problems*. Chicago: University of Chicago Press, 1926.

Saferstein, R. *Criminalistics: An Introduction to Forensic Science*. Englewood Cliffs, N.J.: Prentice-Hall, 1977.

Safire, William. *Before the Fall*. New York: Tower, 1975.

Sagarin, Edward. *Criminology: New Concerns*. Beverly Hills, Calif.: Sage, 1979.

_____ (ed.). *Taboos in Criminology*. Beverly Hills, Calif.: Sage, 1980.

Sage, Lee. *The Last Rustler: The Autobiography of Lee Sage*. Boston: Little, Brown, 1930.

Saggs, H.W.F. *The Greatness That Was Babylon*. New York: New American Library, 1968.

Sahula-Dyckes, Ignatz. *Alias Linson; or, the Ghost of Billy the Kid*. New York: Pageant Press, 1963.

Saini, Ezio. *La notte di Dongo*. Rome: Corso, 1950.

Sainsbury, W.N., and Fortescue, J.W. *Calendar of State Papers*. London: Longman, Green, Longman, Roberts, 1860-1902.

Saint André, François de. *Lettres*. Paris: R.M. Despilly, 1725.

St. Aubyns, Giles. *Edward VII: Prince and King*. New York: Atheneum, 1979.

_____. *Infamous Victorians*. London: Constable, 1971.

Saint-Aulaire, Auguste Félix Charles de Beaupoil, Comte de. *Confession d'un Vieux Diplomate*. Paris: Flammarion, 1953.

St. Clair, William. *Trelawny: The Incurable Romancer*. New York: Vanguard Press, 1978.

Saint-Gaudens, Homer (ed.). *The Reminiscences of Augustus Saint-Gaudens*. New York: Century, 1913.

St. German, Christopher. *Doctor and Student*. London: R. & E. Atkins, 1709.

St. John, Robert. *Ben Gurion*. Garden City, N.Y.: Doubleday, 1959.

_____. *The Boss: The Story of Gamal Abdel Nasser*. New York: McGraw-Hill, 1960.

_____. *This Was My World*. New York: Doubleday, 1953.

St. John Packe, M. *The Life of John Stuart Mill*. London: Secker & Warburg, 1954.

St. Johns, Adela Rogers. *Final Verdict*. Garden City, N.Y.: Doubleday, 1962.

St. John-Stevas, N. *Life, Death and the Law: Law and Christian Morals in England and the United States*. Bloomington: Indiana University Press, 1961.

_____. *Obscenity and the Law*. New York: Macmillan, 1956.

St. Ledger, A.J. *Australian Socialism*. London: Macmillan, 1919.

Saito, Dr. Yoshie. *Deceived History: An Inside Account of Matsuoka and the Tripartite Pact*. Tokyo: Yomiuri Shimbun, 1955.

Sakai Saburo, Caidin, Martin, and Saito, Fred. *Samurai!*. New York: E.P. Dutton, 1957.

Sakolski, A.M. *The Great American Land Bubble*. New York: Harper & Brothers, 1932.

Sakomizu, Hisatsune. *The Prime Minister's Official Residence under Machine-Gun Fire*. Tokyo: Kobun Sha, 1965.

Sakran, Frank C. *Palestine Dilemma: Arab Rights versus Zionist Aspirations*. Washington, D.C.: Public Affairs Press, 1948.

Sala, George Augustus. *My Diary in America in the Midst of War*. London: Tinsley Brothers, 1865.

Salandra, Antonio. *Memorie politiche, 1916-25*. Milan, Italy: Garzanti, 1951.

Sale, Kirkpatrick. *SDS*. New York: Vintage Books , 1974.

Saleilles, R. *The Individualization of Punishment*. trans. R.S. Jastrow. Boston: Little, Brown, 1911.

Salerno, Ralph, and Tompkins, John. *The Crime Confederation*. New York: Doubleday, 1969.

Sales, Bruce Dennis. *The Criminal Justice System*. New York: Plenum, 1977.

_____. *Psychology in the Legal Process*. Englewood Cliffs, N.J.: Prentice-Hall, 1976.

Salgado, Gamini. *Cony-Catchers and Bawdy Baskets*. New York: Penguin Books, 1972.

_____. *The Elizabethan Underworld*. London: J.M. Dent & Sons, 1977.

Salillas, Raphael. *La Fascinación en España*. Madrid: E. Arias, 1905.

Salinger, Pierre, and Vanocur, Sander. *A Tribute to John F. Kennedy*. Chicago: Encyclopedia Britannica, 1964.

Salisbury, Albert and Jane. *Here Rolled the Covered Wagons*. Seattle, Wash.: Superior, 1948.

Salisbury, Allen. *The Civil War and the American System. Ameri-*

ca's Battle with Britain, 1860-1876. New York: Campaigner, 1978.

Salisbury, Harrison. *American in Russia.* New York: Harper, 1955.

_____. *Black Night White Snow.* London: Cassell, 1978.

Salk, Erwin A. *A Layman's Guide to Negro History.* New York: McGraw-Hill, 1967.

Salley, Alexander S. (ed.). *Narratives of Early Carolina, 1650-1708.* New York: Charles Scribner's Sons, 1911.

Sallust. *The War with Jugurtha.* trans. R.C. Rolfe. Cambridge, Mass.: Harvard University Press, 1971.

Salmon, Lucy Maynard. *The Newspaper and the Historian.* New York: Oxford University Press, 1923.

Salomies, Ilmari. *Noitausko ja noitavainot.* Helsinki, Fin.: Kustannusosakeyhtiö Otava, 1944.

Salomon, Ernst von. *Der Fragebogen.* New York: Doubleday, 1955.

Salsbury, Stephen. *No Way to Run A Railroad.* New York: McGraw-Hill, 1982.

Salt, H.S. *The Life of James Thomson.* London: Reeves & Turner, 1889.

Salter, C. *Introducing Portugal.* London: Methuen, 1956.

Salter, John Thomas. *The American Politician.* Chapel Hill: University of North Carolina Press, 1938.

Saltman, Jules. *Marijuana and Your Child.* New York: Grosset & Dunlap, 1970.

Salusbury, G.T. *Street Life in Medieval England.* Oxford, Eng.: Pen-in-Hand, 1948.

Salvadori, Max. *Brief History of the Patriot Movement in Italy.* trans. Giacinto Salvadori-Paleotti. Chicago: Clemente, 1954.

_____. *The Labour and the Wounds.* London: Pall Mall Press, 1958.

Salvatorelli, Luigi, and Mira, Giovanni. *Storia d'Italia nel periodo fascista.* Turin, Italy: Einaudi, 1956.

_____. *Vent'anni fra due guerre.* Rome: Italiana, 1946.

Salvatori, Renato. *Nemesi.* Milan, Italy: Baldassarre Gnocchi, 1945.

Salvemini, Gaetano. *The Fascist Dictatorship in Italy.* New York: Holt, Rinehart & Winston, 1927.

_____. *Italia scombinata.* Turin, Italy: Einaudi, 1959.

_____. *Prelude to World War II.* London: Victor Gollancz, 1953.

_____. *Under the Axe of Fascism.* New York: Viking Press, 1936.

Samenow, Stanton E. *Inside the Criminal Mind.* New York: Times Books, 1984.

Samora, Julian, and Simon, Patricia Vandel. *A History of the Mexican-American People.* Notre Dame, Ind.: University of Notre Dame Press, 1977.

_____. *Los Mojados: The Wetback Story.* Notre Dame, Ind.: University of Notre Dame Press, 1966.

Sampson, Anthony. *The Arms Bazaar.* London: Coronet Books, 1977.

Sampson, E.E. (ed.). *Approaches, Contexts, and Problems of Social Psychology.* Englewood Cliffs, N.J.: Prentice-Hall, 1964.

Samuel, Herbert Louis. *Memoirs.* London: Cresset Press, 1945.

Samuel, Raphael. *East End Underworld.* Boston: Routledge & Kegan Paul, 1981.

Samuel, Ray, Huber, Leonard, and Ogden, Warren C. *Tales of the Mississippi.* New York: Hastings House, 1955.

Samuels, Charles. *Death was the Bridegroom.* New York: Fawcett, 1955.

_____ and Louise. *The Girl in the House of Hate.* New York: Fawcett, 1953.

_____. *The Girl in the Red Velvet Swing.* New York: Fawcett, 1955.

_____. *The Magnificent Rube: The Life and Gaudy Times of Tex Rickard.* New York: McGraw-Hill, 1957.

_____ and Louise. *Night Fell on Georgia.* New York: Dell, 1956.

Samuels, Charles Thomas. *Encountering Directors.* New York: Capricorn/Putnam's, 1972.

Sanborn, Franklin Benjamin. *The Life and Letters of John Brown.*

Boston: Roberts Bors, 1885.

_____. *Recollections of Seventy Years.* 2 vols. Boston: Gorham Press, 1909.

Sanborn, Margaret. *Robert E. Lee: A Portrait, 1807-1861.* Philadelphia: J.B. Lippincott, 1966.

Sand, Charles Louis. *Memoir of Charles Louis Sand.* London: G. & W.B. Whittaker, 1819.

Sandbach, J.B. *This Old Wig.* London: Hutchinson, n.d.

Sandburg, Carl. *Abraham Lincoln: The Prairie Years.* 2 vols. New York: Harcourt, Brace, 1926.

_____. *Abraham Lincoln: The War Years.* 4 vols. New York: Harcourt, Brace, 1939.

_____. *Always the Young Strangers.* New York: Harcourt, Brace, 1953.

_____. *The American Songbag.* New York: Harcourt, Brace, 1927.

_____. *The Chicago Race Riots, July, 1919.* New York: Harcourt, Brace & Howe, 1919.

_____. *The Letters of Carl Sandburg.* New York: Harcourt, Brace & World, 1968.

_____. *Lincoln Collector. The Story of Oliver R. Barrett's Great Private Collection.* New York: Harcourt, Brace, 1949.

Sanders, Bruce. *Murder Behind the Bright Lights.* London: Herbert Jenkins, 1958.

_____. *Murder in Big Cities.* New York: Roy, 1962.

_____. *Murder in Lonely Places.* London: Jenkins, 1960.

_____. *They Caught These Killers.* New York: Roy, 1968.

_____. *They Couldn't Lose the Body.* London: Jenkins, 1966.

Sanders, Ed. *The Family.* New York: E.P. Dutton, 1971.

Sanders, Gwendoline Paul. *The Sumner County Story.* North Newton, Kan.: Mennonite Press, 1966.

Sanders, Helen Fitzgerald. *A History of Montana.* 3 vols. Chicago: Lewis, 1913.

_____, and Bertsche, William H., Jr. (eds.). *X. Beidler: Vigilante.* Norman: University of Oklahoma Press, 1957.

Sanders, Irwin T. *Balkan Village.* Lexington: University of Kentucky Press, 1949.

_____ (ed.). *Collectivization of Agriculture in Eastern Europe.* Lexington: University of Kentucky Press, 1959.

_____. *Rainbow in the Rock: the People of Rural Greece.* Cambridge, Mass.: Harvard University Press, 1961.

Sanders, Joan. *La Petite: The Life of Louise de la Vallière.* Boston: Houghton Mifflin, 1959.

Sanders, Cmdr. M.G. *The Soviet Navy.* New York: Prager, 1958.

Sanders, Ronald. *The Downtown Jews: Portraits of an Immigrant Generation.* New York: Harper & Row, 1966.

Sanders, Wiley B. *Juvenile Offenders of 1000 Years.* Durham: University of North Carolina Press, 1970.

Sanders, William B. *Criminology.* Reading, Mass.: Addison Wesley, 1983.

_____. *Detective Work.* New York: Free Press, 1977.

_____ (ed.). *The Sociologist as Detective.* New York: Praeger, 1976.

Sandford, Mrs. John. *Female Improvement.* London: Longman, 1836.

Sandmeyer, Elmer C. *The Anti-Chinese Movement in California.* Urbana: University of Illinois Press, 1939.

Sandoe, James (ed.). *Murder: Plain & Fanciful.* New York: Sheridan, 1948.

Sandoz, Mari. *The Buffalo Hunters.* New York: Hastings House, 1954.

_____. *The Cattlemen.* New York: Hastings House, 1958.

_____. *Love Song of the Plains.* New York: Harper & Brothers, 1961.

Sands, Bill. *My Shadow Ran Fast.* Englewood Cliffs, N.J.: Prentice-Hall, 1964.

Sands, Frank. *A Pastoral Prince.* Santa Barbara, Calif.: n.p., 1893.

San Francisco Chamber of Commerce. *Law and Order in San Francisco: A Beginning.* San Francisco: H.S. Crocker, 1916.

_____. *The San Francisco-Oakland Metropolitan Area: An Industrial Study*. San Francisco: Published by Author, 1931.

San Francisco Chamber of Commerce Research Department. *San Francisco Economic Survey, 1938*. San Francisco: Published by Author, n.d.

San Francisco Citizen's Alliance. *A Few of the Things Done by the Citizens' Alliance of San Francisco*. San Francisco: Published by Author, n.d.

San Francisco: Its Builders, Past and Present. 2 vols. Chicago: S.J. Clarke, 1913.

San Francisco Labor Council. *The New Charter: Why It Should Be Defeated*. San Francisco: Published by Author, 1896.

San Francisco Merchants' Association. *Seventeenth Annual Review: A Year of Civic Work*. San Francisco: Published by Author, 1911.

Sanger, Joan. *The Case of the Missing Corpse*. New York: Green Circle Books, 1936.

Sanger, Margaret. *Autobiography*. New York: W.W. Norton, 1938.

Sanger, Richard H. *Where the Jordan Flows*. Washington, D.C.: Middle East Institute, 1963.

Sanger, William W. *History of Prostitution*. New York: Harper, 1858.

Sangier, Félix. *Plaidoyers de Charles Lachaud*. Paris: Charpentier, 1885.

Sann, Paul. *The Angry Decade: The Sixties*. New York: Crown, 1979.

_____. *Kill the Dutchman!* New Rochelle, N.Y.: Arlington House, 1971.

_____. *The Lawless Decade*. New York: Crown, 1957.

Sansom, George. *A History of Japan*. 3 vols. Stanford, Calif.: Stanford University Press, 1958.

_____. *Japan: A Short Cultural History*. New York: Appleton-Century-Crofts, 1962.

_____. *The Western World and Japan*. New York: Alfred A. Knopf, 1950.

Sanson, Henri. *Sept générations d'exécuteurs 1688-1847*. Paris: Dupray de La Mahérie, 1862-63.

Sansone, Vito, and Gastone, Ingrasci. *Sei anni di banditismo in Sicilia*. Milan, Italy: Le Edizioni Sociale, 1950.

Santayana, George. *Character and Opinion in the United States*. New York: Charles Scribner's Sons, 1920.

_____. *Dominations and Powers*. New York: Charles Scribner's Sons, 1951.

_____. *Egotism in German Philosophy*. New York: Charles Scriber's Sons, 1940.

_____. *The Genteel Tradition at Bay*. New York: Charles Scribner's Sons, 1931.

_____. *The Last Puritan*. New York: Charles Scribner's Sons, 1937.

_____. *Persons and Places*. New York: Charles Scribner's Sons, 1944.

Santee, Ross. *Apache Land*. New York: Charles Scribner's Sons, 1947.

_____. *Lost Pony Tracks*. New York: Charles Scribner's Sons, 1953.

Santerre, George H. *Dallas' First Hundred Years, 1856-1956*. Dallas: Book Craft, 1856.

Santesson, H.S. *The Locked Room Reader: Stories of the Impossible Crimes and Escapes*. New York: Random House, 1968.

Santoro, Cesare. *Hitler Germany as Seen by a Foreigner*. Berlin: Internationaler, 1938.

Saporiti, Piero. *Empty Balcony*. London: Victor Gollancz, 1947.

Saposs, David Joseph. *Communism in American Politics*. Washington, D.C.: Public Affairs Press, 1960.

_____. *The Labor Movement in Postwar France*. New York: Columbia University Press, 1931.

Sapte, W. *A Century's Sensations*. London: George Routledge, 1893.

Saragat, Giuseppe. *40 anni di lota per la democrazia*. Milan, Italy: Ugo Mursia, 1966.

Sardi, Alessandro. *La Marcia su Roma*. Rome: Instituto Poligrafico dello Stato, 1932.

_____. *...Ma, non si imprigiona la storia*. Rome: CEN, 1958.

Sardou, Victorien. *Les Papiers de Victorien Sardou*. Paris: A. Michel, 1934.

Sarfatti, Margherita. *Dux: The Life of Benito Mussolini*. trans. Frederic Whyte. London: Thornton Butterworth, 1925.

Sargent, Epes. *Planchette; or, the Despair of Science*. Boston: Robert Brothers, 1887.

Sargent, F.W. *England, the United States, and The Southern Confederacy*. New York: Negro Universities Press, 1969.

Sargent, Nathan. *Public Men and Events*. Philadelphia: J.B. Lippincott, 1875.

Sarkar, S.C. *Some Aspects of the Earliest Social History of India*. London: Oxford University Press, 1928.

Sarles, Frank B., Jr., and Shedd, Charles E. *Colonials and Patriots*. Washington, D.C.: U.S. Department of the Interior, National Park Service, 1964.

Sarmiento, F.L. *Pauline Cushman, Union Spy and Scout*. New York: John E. Potter, 1865.

Sarnoff, Paul. *Jesse Livermore - Speculator King*. Palisades Park, N.J.: Investors' Press, 1967.

Sarri, Rosemary C. *Under Lock and Key: Juveniles in Jails and Detention*. Ann Arbor: National Assessment of Juvenile Corrections, University of Michigan, 1974.

_____, and Hasenfeld, Yeheskel (eds.). *Brought to Justice? Juveniles, the Courts and the Law*. Ann Arbor: National Assessment of Juvenile Corrections, University of Michigan, 1976.

Sartain, John. *The Reminiscences of a Very Old Man, 1808-1897*. New York: D. Appleton, 1899.

Sarton, George. *Galen of Pergamon*. Lawrence: University of Kansas Press, 1954.

Sartre, Jean-Paul. *Being and Nothingness*. trans. Hazel E. Barnes. New York: Philosophical Library, 1965.

_____. *Le Mur*. Paris: Librairie Gallimard, 1939.

Sarytschew, Gawrila. *Account of a Voyage of Discovery to the Northeast of Siberia*. London: Richard Phillips, 1806.

Sato, Naotake. *My Eighty Years Reminiscences*. Tokyo: Jiji Press, 1964.

Sattler, J.M. *Assessment of Children's Intelligence and Special Abilities*. Boston: Allyn & Bacon, 1982.

Saunders, Arthur C. *The History of Bannock County, Idaho*. Pocatello, Idaho: Tribune, 1915.

_____. *Jersey before and after the Norman Conquest of England*. Jersey, Channel Islands: J.T. Bigwood, 1935.

_____. *Jersey in the Fifteenth and Sixteenth Centuries*. Jersey, Channel Islands: J.T. Bigwood, 1933.

Saunders, Charles Francis. *The Southern Sierras of California*. Boston: Houghton Mifflin, 1923.

Saunders, Edith. *The Mystery of Marie Lefarge*. Paris: Pagnerre, 1840.

Saunders, Welch. *A Proposal to Render Effectual a Plan to Remove the Nuisance of Common Prostitution from the Streets of this Metropolis*. London: C. Henderson, 1758.

Sauter, Johann Georg. *Zur Hexenbulle, 1448*. Ulm, Ger.: J. Ebner, 1884.

Sauvage, Leo. *The Oswald Affair: An Examination of the Contradictions and Omissions of the Warren Report*. Cleveland: World, 1966.

Sauvin, Georges. *Autour de Chicago: Notes sur les Etats-Unis*. Paris: E. Plon, Nourrit et Cie, 1893.

Sauzé, Jean Charles. *Essai médico-historique*. Paris: Regnoux, 1839.

Savage, C. *The Policy of the United States Towards Maritime Commerce in War*. Washington, D.C.: U.S. Government Printing Office, 1934.

Savage, Edward H. *Police Records and Recollections or Boston by Daylight and Gaslight*. Montclair, N.J.: Patterson Smith,

1971.

Savage, Henry, Jr. *Discovering America, 1700-1875.* New York: Harper & Brothers, 1979.

Savage, James. *A Genealogical Dictionary of the First Settlers of New England.* Boston: Little, Brown, 1860.

Savage, James Woodruff, et al. *History of the City of Omaha, Nebraska.* New York: Munsell, 1894.

Savage, John. *Life of Andrew Johnson.* New York: Derby & Miller, 1866.

Savage, Pat. *One Last Frontier: A Story of Indians, Early Settlers and Old Ranches of Northern Arizona.* New York: Exposition Press, 1964.

Savage, Percy. *Savage of Scotland Yard.* London: Hutchinson, 1934.

Savant, J. *La vie fabuleuse et authentique de Vidocq.* Paris: Éditions du Seuil, 1950.

Savelle, Max. *Seeds of Liberty.* New York: Alfred A. Knopf, 1948.

Savitz, Leonard D., and Johnston, Norman. *Crime in Society.* New York: John Wiley & Sons, 1978.

_____. *Dilemmas in Criminology.* New York: McGraw-Hill, 1967.

Sawyer, Eugene Taylor. *The Life and Career of Tiburcio Vasquez.* San Francisco: Bacon, 1875.

Sawyer, Joseph Dillaway. *Washington.* 2 vols. New York: Macmillan, 1927.

Saxon, Lyle. *Fabulous New Orleans.* New York: D. Appleton-Century, 1928.

_____. *Father Mississippi.* New York: Century, 1927.

Saxton, Alexander. *The Indispensable Enemy: Labor and the Anti-Chinese Movement in California.* Berkeley: University of California Press, 1971.

Sayegh, Fayez (ed.). *The Dynamics of Neutralism in the Arab World.* San Francisco: Chandler, 1964.

Sayer, James Edward. *Clarence Darrow: Public Advocate.* Dayton, Ohio: Wright State University, 1978.

Sayers, Dorothy L. *Tales of Detection, Mystery and Horror.* London: Gollancz, 1928.

Sayers, R.C. *A History of Economic Change in England, 1880-1939.* Oxford, Eng.: Oxford University Press, 1967.

Sayre, Wallace, and Kaufman, Herbert. *Governing New York City: Politics in the Metropolis.* New York: Russell Sage Foundation, 1960.

Sazonov, Serge. *Fateful Years.* New York: Stokes, 1928.

Scacco, Anthony M. *Rape in Prison.* Springfield, Ill.: Charles C. Thomas, 1975.

Scaduto, Anthony. *Scapegoat: The Truth about the Lindbergh Kidnapping.* New York: G.P. Putnam's Sons, 1976.

Scalapino, Robert A. *Democracy and the Party Movement in Prewar Japan.* Berkeley: University of California Press, 1952.

Scanland, John Milton. *Life of Pat F. Garrett and the Taming of the Border Outlaw.* El Paso, Texas: Carleton F. Hodge, 1952.

Scanlon, Detective Robert A. (ed.). *Law Enforcement Bible.* South Hackensack, N.J.: Stoeger, 1978.

Scanzoni, J.H. *The Black Family in Modern Society.* Boston: Allyn & Bacon, 1971.

Scarne, John. *Scarne's Complete Guide to Gambling.* New York: Simon & Schuster, 1974.

Scarr, Harry A. *Patterns of Burglary.* Washington, D.C.: Department of Justice, 1972.

Schaack, Michael J. *Anarchy and the Anarchists.* Chicago: F.J. Schulte, 1889.

Schaar, John H. *Loyalty in America.* Berkeley: University of California Press, 1957.

Schachner, Nathan. *Aaron Burr.* New York: A.S. Barnes, 1961.

_____. *Alexander Hamilton.* New York: Appleton-Century, 1946.

Schachner von Inwil, Joseph. *Das Hexenwesen im Kanton Luzern.* Lucerne, Switz.: Räber, 1947.

Schacht, Hjalmar. *My First Seventy-six Years.* London: Allen Wingate, 1955.

Schack, Johan. *Disputatio Juridica Ordinaria de Probatione*

Criminis Magae. Greifswald, Ger.: D.B. Starkii, 1706.

Schadow, Gottfried. *Biographie in Aufsätzen und Briefen.* Stuttgart, Ger.: Ebner & Seubert, 1890.

Schaefer, Jack. *Heroes Without Glory: Some Good Men of the Old West.* Boston: Houghton Mifflin, 1965.

Schaefer, Walter V. *The Suspect and Society.* Evanston, Ill.: Northwestern University Press, 1967.

Schafer, E.H. *The Golden Peaches of Samrkand.* Berkeley: University of California Press, 1970.

Schafer, R.J. *The Economic Societies in the Spanish World.* Syracuse, N.Y.: Syracuse University Press, 1958.

Schafer, Robert S. *Introduction to Criminology.* Englewood Cliffs, N.J.: Prentice-Hall, 1926.

Schafer, Stephen. *Introduction to Criminology.* Reston, Va.: Reston, 1976.

_____. *The Political Criminal.* New York: Free Press, 1974.

_____. *The Political Prisoner: The Problem of Morality and Crime.* New York: Free Press, 1974.

_____. *Restitution to Victims of Crime.* London: Stevens & Sons, 1960.

_____. *Theories in Criminology.* New York: Random House, 1969.

_____. *The Victim and His Criminal: A Study in Functional Responsibility.* New York: Random House, 1968.

Schakovsky, Zinäida. *Precursors of Peter the Great.* London: Jonathan Cape, 1964.

Schallmeyer, Wilhelm. *Verrbung und Auslese im Lebenslauf der Völker.* Jena, Ger.: Gustav Fischer, 1903.

Schapiro, Jacob S. *Movements of Social Dissent in Modern Europe.* New York: Anvil, 1962.

Schapiro, Leonard. *The Communist Party of the Soviet Union.* New York: Random House, 1960.

Schapsmeier, E.L., and Schapsmeier, F.H. *Henry A. Wallace of Iowa: The Agrarian Years, 1910-1940.* Ames: Iowa State University Press, 1968.

Scharf, John Thomas. *History of the Confederate States Navy.* New York: Rogers & Sherwood, 1887.

_____, and Westcott, Thompson. *History of Philadelphia 1609-1884.* 3 vols. Philadelphia: L.H. Everts, 1884.

Scharf, Maggie. *Body, Mind, Behavior.* Washington, D.C.: New Republic, 1976.

Schatz, August Herman. *Opening a Cow Country: A History of the Pioneer's Struggle in Conquering the Prairie South of the Black Hills.* Ann Arbor, Mich.: Edwards Brothers, 1939.

Schauss, Alexander. *Diet, Crime, and Delinquency.* Berkeley, Calif.: Parker House, 1980.

Schechter, Betty. *The Dreyfus Affair: A National Scandal.* Boston: Houghton Mifflin, 1965.

Schechtman, J.B. *The Arab Refugee Problem.* New York: Philosophical Library, 1952.

_____. *The United States and the Jewish State Movement: The Crucial Decade, 1939-1949.* New York: Herzl Press, 1966.

Schecter, Leonard, and Phillips, William. *On the Pad.* New York: Berkeley, 1973.

Scheer, George F., and Randkin Hugh F. *Rebels and Redcoats.* New York: New American Library, 1959.

Scheflin, Alan W., and Opton, Jr., Edward M. *The Mind Manipulators.* New York: Paddington Press, 1978.

Scheidemann, Philipp. *Memoiren eines Sozialdemokraten.* 2 vols. Dresden, Ger.: C. Reissner, 1928.

Scheidenhelm, Richard (ed.). *The Response to John Brown.* Belmont, Calif.: Wadsworth, 1972.

Scheier, Ivan H., et al. *Guidelines and Standards for the Use of Volunteers in Correctional Programs.* Washington, D.C.: U.S. Department of Justice, 1972.

_____, and Jorgenson, James D. *Volunteer Training for Courts and Corrections.* Metuchen, N.J.: Scarecrow Press, 1973.

Scheim, David E. *Contract on America: The Mafia Murders of John and Robert Kennedy.* Silver Springs, Md.: Argyle Press, 1983.

Schein, Edgar. *Coercive Persuasion.* New York: W.W. Norton, 1971.

Scheiner, Seth M. *Negro Mecca: A History of the Negro in New York City, 1865-1920.* New York: New York University Press, 1965.

Scheir, Walter and Miriam. *Invitation to an Inquest.* Garden City, N.Y.: Doubleday, 1965.

Schell, Herbert Samuel. *South Dakota, Its Beginnings and Growth.* New York: American Book, 1942.

Schell, Theodore H., et al. *Traditional Preventive Patrol.* Washington, D.C.: Law Enforcement Assistance Administration, National Institute of Law Enforcement and Criminal Justice, 1976.

Schellenberg, Walter. *The Labyrinth.* New York: Harper & Brothers, 1956.

_____. *The Schellenberg Memoirs.* trans. Louis Hagen. London: André Deutsch, 1961.

Schellie, Don. *Vast Domain of Blood.* Los Angeles: Westernlore Press, 1968.

Schelling, Thomas. *The Strategy of Conflict.* London: Oxford University Press, 1963.

Scheltema, Jacobus. *Geschiedenis der Heksenprocessen.* Haarlem, Neth.: V. Loosjés, 1828.

Scherer, Frederick. *Industrial Market Structure and Market Performance.* Chicago: Rand McNally, 1970.

Scherer, James A.B. *The First Forty-Niner.* New York: Minton Balch, 1925.

_____. *"The Lion of the Vigilantes": William T. Coleman and the Life of Old San Francisco.* Indianapolis, Ind.: Bobbs-Merrill, 1939.

_____. *Manchukuo: A Bird's Eye View.* Tokyo: Hokuseido Press, 1933.

_____. *Three Meiji Leaders.* Tokyo: Hokuseido Press, 1936.

Scherr, Johannes. *Hammerschläge und Historien.* Zurich, Switz.: C. Schmidt, 1872.

Schevill, Ferdinand. *The Great Elector.* Hamden, Conn.: Shoe String Press, 1947.

_____. *Medieval and Renaissance Florence.* 2 vols. New York: Harper Torchbooks, 1961.

Schiano, Anthony, with Burton, Anthony. *Solo.* New York: Warner, 1974.

Schiano, Pasquale. *La rezistenza nel Napoletano.* Naples, Italy: CESP, 1965.

Schiavi, Allessandro. *La vita e l'opera di Giacomo Matteotti.* Rome: Opere Nuove, 1957.

Schiavo, Giovanni. *The Truth About the Mafia.* El Paso, Texas: Vigo Press, 1962.

Schiavo, Giovanni Erminegildo. *Italians in Chicago.* Chicago: Italian-American, 1928.

Schieder, Theodor. *Das deutsche Kaiserreich von 1871 als Nationalstaat.* Cologne, Ger.: Westdeutscher, 1961.

Schiller, Herbert I. *Mass Communications and American Empire.* Boston: Beacon Press, 1971.

_____. *The Mind Managers.* Boston: Beacon Press, 1973.

Schilling, John H. *Scenic Trips to the Geologic Post No. 5.* Socorro: New Mexico Institute of Mining and Technology, 1959.

Schimmel, David, and Fischer, Louis. *The Civil Rights of Students.* New York: Harper & Row, 1975.

Schimmel-Falkenau, Walther. *Kommen und Gehen Unter den Linden.* Berlin: Rembrandt, 1963.

Schiesl, Martin J. *The Politics of Efficiency: Municipal Administration and Reform in America, 1800-1920.* Berkeley: University of California Press, 1977.

Schlabrendorff, Fabian von. *The Secret War Against Hitler.* New York: Pitman, 1965.

Schlapp, Max G., and Smith, Edward H. *The New Criminology: A Consideration of the Chemical Causation of Abnormal Behavior.* New York: Boni & Liveright, 1928.

Schlesinger, Arthur Meier. *The American as Reformer.* Cambridge, Mass.: Harvard University Press, 1951.

_____. *The Colonial Merchants and the American Revolution 1763-1776.* New York: Columbia University Press, 1918.

_____. *Paths to the Present.* New York: Macmillan, 1949.

_____. *The Rise of the City, 1878-1898.* New York: Macmillan 1933.

Schlesinger, Arthur M., Jr. *The Age of Jackson.* Boston: Little, Brown, 1945.

_____. *The Age of Roosevelt.* London: William Heinemann, 1957.

_____. *The Coming of the New Deal.* Boston: Houghton Mifflin, 1960.

_____ (ed.). *The Cotton Kingdom.* New York: Alfred A. Knopf, 1953.

_____. *The Crisis of the Old Order 1919-1933.* Boston: Houghton Mifflin, 1957.

_____. *History of American Presidential Elections.* New York: McGraw-Hill, 1971.

_____. *The Imperial Presidency.* Boston: Houghton Mifflin, 1973.

_____. *The Politics of Upheaval.* Boston: Houghton Mifflin, 1960.

_____. *Prelude to Independence: The Newspaper War on Britain, 1764-1776.* New York: Alfred A. Knopf, 1958.

_____. *Robert Kennedy and His Times.* Boston: Houghton Mifflin, 1978.

_____. *A Thousand Days: John F. Kennedy in the White House.* Boston: Houghton Mifflin, 1965.

_____. *Violence: America in the Sixties.* New York: New American Library, 1968.

_____. *The Vital Center: The Politics of Freedom.* New York: Houghton Mifflin, 1949.

Schlesinger, Steven R. *Exclusionary Injustice.* New York: Marcel Dekker, 1977.

Schlessinger, Ken. *This is Hollywood.* Los Angeles: Ken Schlessing Productions, 1984.

Schieler, Caspar. *Magister Johannes Nider.* Mainz, Ger.: F. Kirchheim, 1885.

Schiess, Emil. *Die Hexenprozesse und das Gerichtswesen im Lande Appenzell.* Trogan, Ger.: O. Kübler, 1919.

Schiff, Harriet Sarnoff. *The Bereaved Parent.* New York: Crown, 1977.

Schlierbach, Helmut. *Die politische Polizei in Preussen.* Emsdetten, Ger.: Heinrich & J. Lechte, 1938.

Schloss, B., and Giesbrecht, N.A. *Murder in Canada: A Report on Capital and Non-Capital Murder Statistics, 1961-1970.* Toronto, Ontario, Can.: Centre of Criminology, University of Toronto, 1972.

Schlossberg, Joseph. *The Workers and Their World.* New York: A.L.P. Committee, 1935.

Schlossman, Steven L. *Love and the American Delinquent: Theory and Practice of "Progressive" Juvenile Justice, 1825-1920.* Chicago: University of Chicago Press, 1977.

Schmalhausen, Samuel D., and Calverton, V. F. (eds.). *Woman's Coming of Age: A Symposium.* New York: Horace Liveright, 1931.

Schmeckebier, Laurence F. *The Bureau of Prohibition: Its History, Activities and Organization.* Washington, D.C.: Brookings Institution, 1929.

_____. *History of the Know-Nothing Party in Maryland.* Baltimore: Johns Hopkins Press, 1899.

Schmedding, Joseph. *Cowboy and Indian Trader.* Caldwell, Idaho: Caxton Printers, 1951.

Schmidhauser, John R. *The Supreme Court as Final Arbiter in Federal-State Relations, 1789-1857.* Chapel Hill: University of North Carolina Press, 1958.

Schmidt, Carl T. *The Plough and the Sword.* New York: Columbia University Press, 1938.

Schmidt, Heinie. *Ashes of My Campfire.* Dodge City, Kan.: Journal, 1952.

Schmidt, Johann Georg. *Die gestriegelte Rocken Philosophia.* Chemnitz, Ger.: Conrad Stosseln, 1706.

Schmidt, Karl. *Henry Wallace: Quixotic Crusade.* Syracuse, N.Y.:

Syracuse University Press, 1960.

Schmidt, Paul. *Hitler's Interpreter.* New York: Macmillan, 1951.

Schmidt-Paulie, E.V. *We Indians.* London: Butterworth, 1931.

Schmitt, Bernadotte E. *The Annexation of Bosnia, 1908-1909.* Cambridge, Eng.: Cambridge University Press, 1937.

Schmitt, Jo Ann. *Fighting Editors: The Story of Editors Who Faced Six-Shooters with Pen and Won.* San Antonio, Texas: Naylor, 1958.

Schmitt, Martin F. (ed.). *General George Crook: His Autobiography.* Norman: University of Oklahoma Press, 1946.

_____, and Brown, Dee. *The Settler's West.* New York: Charles Scribner's Sons, 1955.

Schmitz, Eugene E. *The Fate of the San Francisco Grafters: Benedict Arnold of His Native City.* San Francisco: n.p., 1908.

Schneid, Hayyim. *Marriage.* Philadelphia: Jewish Publication Society of America, 1973.

Schneider, David M., and Deutsch, Albert. *The History of Public Welfare in New York State, 1609-1866.* Chicago: University of Chicago Press, 1938.

Schneider, H.W. *Making the Fascist State.* New York: Oxford University Press, 1928.

Schneider, Herbert and Clough, Shepard. *Making Fascists.* Chicago: Chicago University Press, 1929.

Schneider, Jane and Peter. *Culture and Political Economy in Western Sicily.* New York: Academic Press, 1976.

Schneider, Kurt. *The Psychopathic Personality.* Springfield, Ill.: Charles C. Thomas, n.d.

Schneider, Marcel. *La Littérature Fantastique en France.* Paris: Fayard, 1964.

Schneider, Reinhold. *Die Hohenzollern.* Leipzig, Ger.: Hegner, 1933.

Schneir, Walter and Miriam. *Invitation to an Inquest.* Garden City, N.Y.: Doubleday, 1965.

Schnell, Eugen. *Zur Geschicte der Criminal-Justiz.* n.p., 1873.

Schnepper, Jeff A. *Inside the IRS.* New York: Stein & Day, 1978.

Schoberlin, Melvin. *From Candles to Footlights: A Biography of the Pike's Peak Theatre, 1859-76.* Denver: Old West, 1941.

Schoenbaum, David. *Hitler's Social Revolution: Class and Status in Nazi Germany, 1933-1939.* Garden City, N.Y.: Doubleday, 1966.

_____. *The Spiegel Affair.* Garden City, N.Y.: Doubleday, 1968.

Schoenberger, Dale T. *The Gunfighters.* Caldwell, Idaho: Caxton Printers, 1971.

Schoenbrun, David. *The Three Lives of Charles De Gaulle.* New York: Atheneum, 1966.

Schoeps, Hans Joachim. *Das andere Preussen.* Stuttgart, Ger.: Friedrich Vorwerk, 1952.

_____. *Die Ehre Preussens.* Stuttgart, Ger.: Friedrich Vorwerk, 1951.

_____. *Das war Preussen: Zeugnisse der Jahrhunderte, Eine Anthologie.* Hanau, Ger.: Dr. Hans Peter, 1955.

Schofer, Jerry P. *Urban and Rural Finnish Communities in California: 1860-1960.* San Francisco: R & E Research Associates, 1975.

Schofield, George A. *The Ancient Records of the Town of Ipswich.* Ipswich, Mass.: Chronicle Motor Press, 1890.

Schofield, Lieut.Gen. John M. *Forty-six Years in the Army.* New York: Century, 1897.

Scholem, Gershom Gerhard. *Major Trends in Jewish Mysticism.* New York: Schocken Books, 1946.

_____. *On the Kabbalah and Its Symbolism.* New York: Schocken Books, 1965.

Schomackers, Günter. *The Wild West.* London: Macdonald & Jane's, 1977.

Schon, Donald. *Beyond the Stable State.* New York: Random House, 1971.

Schonfield, Hugh J. *Italy and Suez.* London: Hutchinson, 1940.

_____. *The Suez Canal in World Affairs.* New York: Philosophi-cal Library, 1953.

Schoolcraft, Henry Rowe. *Narrative of an Expedition through the Upper Mississippi to Itasca Lake.* New York: Harper & Brothers, 1834.

_____. *Travels in the Central Portions of the Mississippi Valley.* New York: Collins & Hannay, 1825.

Schoolfield, F.E. *Captain Alex F. Boss, Western Rivers Pilot from 1824-1850.* Cincinnati, Ohio: Public Library of Cincinnati, n.d.

Schoonmaker, Paul D. *The Prison Connection.* Valley Forge, Pa.: Judson Press, 1978.

Schorer, Mark. *Sinclair Lewis: An American Life.* New York: McGraw-Hill, 1961.

Schorn, Hubert. *Der Richter im Dritten Reich.* Frankfort, Ger.: Vittorio Klostermann, 1959.

Schorr, Alvin L. (ed.). *Children and Decent People.* New York: Basic Books, 1974.

Schorr, Daniel. *Clearing the Air.* Boston: Houghton Mifflin, 1977.

Schott, Gaspar. *Physica Curiosa.* Würzberg, Ger.: A. Endter, 1667.

Schott, Joseph L. *No Left Turns, the FBI in Peace and War.* New York: Frederick A. Praeger, 1975.

Schouler, James. *History of the United States of America under the Constitution.* New York: Dodd, Mead, 1899.

Schrag, Clarence. *Crime and Justice: American Style.* Rockville, Md.: National Institute of Mental Health Center for Studies in Crime and Delinquency, 1971.

Schram, Stuart R. *The Political Thought of Mao Tse-tung.* New York: Praeger, 1963.

Schramm, Percy Ernst. *Hitler: The Man and the Military Leader.* Chicago: Quadrangle Books, 1971.

Schramm, Wilbur (ed.). *Mass Communications.* Chicago: University of Illinois Press, 1959.

_____. *Men, Messages and Media: A Look at Human Communica-tion.* New York: Harper & Row, 1973.

Schramm, Wilhelm von. *Conspiracy among Generals.* trans. R.T. Clark. London: George Allen & Unwin, 1956.

Schrantz, Ward L. *Jasper County, Missouri, in the Civil War.* Carthage, Mo.: Carthage Press, 1923.

Schreiber, Flora Rheta. *The Shoemaker, Anatomy of a Psychotic.* New York: Simon & Schuster, 1983.

Schreiber, Heinrich. *Die Hexenprozesse.* Freiburg, Ger.: L. Waizenegger, 1837.

Schrieber, Jan. *The Ultimate Weapon.* New York: William Morrow, 1978.

Schriftgiesser, Karl. *The Lobbyists.* Boston: Little, Brown, 1951.

_____. *This Was Normalcy.* Boston: Atlantic, Little, Brown, 1948.

Schroeder, Douglas. *The Issue of the Lakefront: An Historical Critical Survey.* Chicago: Heritage Committee, 1963.

Schroeder, John Frederick. *Life and Times of Washington.* 2 vols. New York: Johnson, Fry, 1857.

_____. *The Maxims of Washington.* New York: n.p., 1845.

Schroyer, Trent. *The Critique of Domination: The Origins and Development of Critical Theory.* New York: George Brazil-ler, 1973.

Schubert, Glendon S. *Quantitative Analysis of Judicial Behavior.* Glencoe, Ill.: Free Press, 1960.

Schuschnigg, Kurt von. *Dreimal Oesterreich.* Vienna, Aust.: Hegner, 1937.

Schwaeble, René. *Le problème du mal.* Paris: Librarie du magnetisme, 1911.

_____. *Le sataniste flagellé.* Paris: R. Outaire, 1912.

Schwager, Johann Moriz. *Versuch einer Geschichte der Hexenpro-cesse.* Berlin: J.F. Unger, 1784.

Schwarz, Klaus. *Psychologische Fibel fur die Polizei.* Munchen, Ger.: Verlag W. Jungling KG, n.d.

Shubert, Glendon. *The Constitutional Politics.* Boston: Boston University Press, 1970.

_____ (ed.). *Judicial Decision-Making.* New York: Free Press, 1963.

Schüddekopf, Otto-Ernst. *Fascism.* New York: Frederick A. Praeger, 1973.

Schudson, Michael. *Discovering the News: A Social History of American Newspapers.* New York: Basic Books, 1978.

Schuessler, Karl (ed.). *Edwin H. Sutherland: On Analyzing Crime.* Chicago: University of Chicago Press, 1973.

Schuker, Stephen A. *The End of French Predominance in Europe, The Financial Crisis of 1924 and the Adoption of the Dawes Plan.* Chapel Hill: University of North Carolina Press, 1976.

Schulman, Sidney. *Toward Judicial Reform in Pennsylvania.* Philadelphia: University of Pennsylvania Law School, 1962.

Schultz, Alfred P. *Race or Mongrel.* Boston: L.C. Page, 1908.

Schultz, Donald O., and Scott, Stanley K. *The Subversive.* Springfield, Ill.: Charles C. Thomas, 1973.

Schultz, Duane. *Hero of Bataan: The Story of General Jonathan M. Wainwright.* New York: St. Martin's Press, 1981.

Schultz, Gladys Denny. *How Many More Victims, Society and the Sex Criminal.* Philadelphia: J.B. Lippincott, 1966.

Schultz, Harry D., and Coslow, Samson. *A Treasury of Wall Street Wisdom.* Palisades Park, N.J.: Investors' Press, 1966.

Schultz, Leroy G. *Rape Victimology.* Springfield, Ill.: Charles C. Thomas, 1975.

Schultz, R.L. *Crusader in Babylon: W.T. Stead and the Pall Mall Gazette.* Omaha: University of Nebraska Press, 1972.

Schultz, Richard, and Sloan, Stephen (eds.). *Responding to the Terrorist Threat: Security and Crisis Management.* Elmford, N.Y.: Pergamon Press, 1980.

Schultz, S.K. *The Culture Factory: Boston Public Schools.* New York: Oxford University Press, 1973.

Schultz, Vernon B. *Southwestern Town: The Story of Willcox, Arizona.* Tucson: University of Arizona Press, 1964.

Schuman, Frederick L. *Europe on the Eve.* London: Robert Hale, 1939.

_____. *The Nazi Dictatorship.* New York: Alfred A. Knopf, 1936.

_____. *Russia Since 1917.* New York: Alfred A. Knopf, 1957.

Schuman, Julian. *Assigment China.* New York: Whittier Books, 1956.

Schumpeter, Joseph A. *Business Cycles: A Theoretical, Historical and Statistical Analysis of the Capitalist Process.* New York: McGraw-Hill, 1939.

_____. *Capitalism, Socialism, and Democracy.* New York: Harper, 1942.

Schur, Edwin M. *Crimes Without Victims: Deviant Behavior and Public Policy.* Englewooed Cliffs, N.J.: Prentice-Hall, 1965.

_____. *Labeling Deviant Behavior: Its Sociological Implications.* New York: Harper & Row, 1971.

_____. *Law and Society: A Sociological View.* New York: Random House, 1968.

_____. *Our Criminal Society: The Social and Legal Sources of Crime in America.* Englewood Cliffs: Prentice-Hall, 1969.

_____. *Radical Non-Intervention.* Englewood Cliffs, N.J.: Prentice-Hall, 1973.

_____, and Bedau, Hugo Adam. *Victimless Crimes.* Englewood Cliffs, N.J.: Prentice-Hall, 1974.

Schur, Max. *Freud, Living and Dying.* New York: International Universities, 1972.

Schurz, Carl. *The Autobiography of Carl Schurz.* New York: Charles Scribner's Sons, 1961.

Schuschnigg, Kurt von. *Austrian Requiem.* New York: G.P. Putnam's Sons, 1946.

_____. *Im Kampf gegen Hitler.* Vienna, Aust.: Molden, 1969.

_____. *My Austria.* New York: Alfred A. Knopf, 1938.

Schüssler, Wilhelm. *Kaiser Wilhelm II, Schicksal und Schuld.* Göttingen, Ger.: Musterschmidt, 1962.

Schuster, Ernest Otto. *Pancho Villa's Shadow.* New York: Exposition Press, 1947.

Schuster, George Naumann. *The Germans: An Enquiry and an Estimate.* New York: n.p., 1932.

Schuster, Ildefonso. *Gli ultimi tempi di un regime.* Milan, Italy: La Vita, 1946.

Schutz, Alfred. *Collected Papers: The Problem of Social Reality.* The Hague, Neth.: Martinus Nijhoff, 1971.

Schuyler, Eugene. *Peter the Great, Emperor of Russia.* 2 vols. New York: Charles Scribner's Sons, 1890.

Schuyler, Robert Livingston. *The Constitution of the United States.* New York: Macmillan, 1923.

Schwab, Arnold T. *James Gibbons Huneker.* Stanford, Calif.: Stanford University Press, 1963.

Schwartz, Alfred I., and Clarren, Sumner N. *The Cincinnati Team Policing Experiment: A Summary Report.* n.p., n.d.

Schwartz, Benjamin I. *Chinese Communism and the Rise of Mao.* Cambridge, Mass.: Harvard University Press, 1951.

Schwartz, Bernard. *The Great Rights of Mankind: A History of the American Bill of Rights.* New York: Oxford University Press, 1956.

_____. *The Law in America.* New York: American Heritage, 1974.

_____. *Super Chief.* New York: New York University Press, 1983.

_____. *The Supreme Court: Constitutional Revolution in Retrospect.* New York: Ronald Press, 1957.

Schwartz, Charles. *Cole Porter.* New York: Dial Press, 1977.

Schwartz, Dr. Fred. *The Three Faces of Revolution.* Washington, D.C.: Captial Hill Press, 1972.

Schwartz, Harold. *Samuel Gridley Howe 1801-1876.* Cambridge, Mass.: Harvard University Press, 1976.

Schwartz, Harry. *The Red Phoenix. Russia Since World War II.* New York: Frederick Praeger, 1961.

Schwartz, Herman. *Taps, Bugs, and Fooling the People.* New York: Field Foundation, 1977.

Schwartz, Richard, and Skolnick, Jerome. *Society and the Legal Order.* New York: Basic Books, 1970.

Schwartz, Ted. *The Hillside Strangler: A Murderer's Mind.* Garden City, N.Y.: Doubleday, 1981.

Schwartz, Walter. *The Arabs in Israel.* London: Faber & Faber, 1959.

Schwartzchild, Leopold. *Red Prussian.* New York: Charles Scribner's Sons, 1947.

Schwebel, Stephen M. *The Secretary-General of the United Nations.* Cambridge, Mass.: Harvard University Press, 1952.

Schwechlers, K. *Die Oesterreichische Socialdemokratie.* Graz, Aust.: "Styria," 1907.

Schwendinger, Herman and Julia R. *The Sociologists of the Chair: A Radical Analysis of the Formative Years of North American Sociology, 1883-1922.* New York: Basic Books, 1974.

Schwerin von Krosigk, Lutz Graf. *Es geschah in Deutschland.* Tübingen, Ger.: Rainer Wunderlich Verlag Hermann Leins, 1951.

Schwickerath, Robert. *Attitude of the Jesuits in the Trials for Witchcraft.* Philadelphia: n.p., 1902.

Schwipps, Werner. *Die Garnisonkirchen von Berlin und Potsdam.* Berlin: Haude & Spenersche, 1964.

Schwitzgebel, Ralph K. *Development and Legal Regulation of Coercive Behavior Modification Techniques with Offenders.* Rockville, Md.: National Institute of Mental Health, 1971.

Sciascia, Leonard. *L'Affaire Moro.* Palermo, Italy: Sellerio Editore, 1978.

_____. *Mafia Vendetta.* New York: Alfred A. Knopf, 1963.

Scigliano, Robert. *The Supreme Court and the Presidency.* New York: Free Press, 1971.

Scobee, Barry. *Fort Davis, Texas, 1583-1960.* El Paso, Texas: Published by Author, 1960.

_____. *Old Fort Davis.* San Antonio, Texas: Naylor, 1947.

_____. *The Steer Branded Murder.* Houston: Frontier Press of Texas, 1952.

Scomp, H.A. *King Alcohol in the Realm of King Cotton, or, a History of the Liquor Traffice and Temperance Movement in Georgia.* New York: Press of Blakely Printing, 1888.

Scopes, John T, and Presley, James. *Center of the Storm: Memoirs of John T. Scopes.* New York: Holt, Rinehart & Winston, 1967.

Scorza, Carlo. *Il segreto di Mussolini.* Lanciano, Italy: Carabba, 1933.

Scot, Reginald. *The Discoverie of Witchcraft.* New York: Dover, 1972.

Scotellaro, Rocco. *L'uva puttanella.* Bari, Italy: Laterza, 1955.

Scott, Anne Firor. *The Southern Lady from Pedestal to Politics 1830-1930.* Chicago: University of Chicago Press, 1970.

Scott, Arthur P. *Criminal Law in Colonial Virginia.* Chicago: University of Chicago Press, 1930.

Scott, Benjamin. *A State Iniquity: Its Rise, Extension, and Overthrow.* New York: Augustus M. Kelley, 1968.

Scott, Craig. *The Houses They Lived In.* North Hollywood, Calif.: Brandon House Books, 1963.

Scott, D.J.R. *Russian Political Institutions.* New York: Rhinehart, 1958.

Scott, George Ryley. *The History of Capital Punishment.* London: Torchstream Books, 1950.

_____. *A History of Prostitution.* London: T. Werner Laurie, 1936.

_____. *Such Outlaws as Jesse James.* London: Gerald S. Swann, 1943.

Scott, George W. *The Black Hills Story.* Fort Collins, Colo.: Published by Author, 1953.

Scott, Sir Harold (ed.). *The Concise Encyclopedia of Crime and Criminals.* New York: Hawthorn Books, 1961.

_____. *Scotland Yard.* London: Andre Deutsch, 1954.

Scott, Gen. Hugh Lennox. *Some Memories of a Soldier.* New York: Century, 1928.

Scott, J.W. Robertson. *The Life and Death of a Newspaper.* London: Methuen, 1952.

_____. *The Story of the Pall Mall Gazette.* London: Oxford University Press, 1950.

Scott, James C. *Comparative Political Corruption.* Englewood Cliffs, N.J.: Prentice-Hall, 1972.

Scott, John. *Behind the Urals.* New York: Houghton Mifflin, 1942.

Scott, John A. *Living Documents in American History.* New York: Washington Square Press, 1964.

Scott, John Finley. *Internalization of Norms: A Sociological Theory of Moral Commitment.* Englewood Cliffs, N.J.: Prentice-Hall, 1971.

Scott, Kenneth D. *Belle Starr in Velvet.* Tahlequah, Okla.: Pan Press, 1963.

Scott, Marvin B. *The Racing Game.* Chicago: Aldine, 1968.

Scott, Mary Wingfield. *Houses of Old Richmond.* Richmond, Va.: Valentine Museum, 1941.

Scott, Mel G. *The San Francisco Bay Area: A Metropolis in Perspective.* Berkeley: University of California Press, 1959.

Scott, Nancy F. (ed.). *Roots of Bitterness.* New York: E.P. Dutton, 1972.

Scott, Peter Dale, et al. (eds.). *The Assassinations: Dallas and Beyond - A Guide to Cover-ups and Investigations.* New York: Random House, 1976.

_____. *Crime and Cover-Up: The CIA, the Mafia, and the Dallas-Watergate Connection.* Berkeley, Calif.: Westworks, 1977.

Scott, Otto. *The Secret Six: John Brown and the Abolitionist Movement.* New York: Times Books, 1979.

Scott, Rachel. *Muscle and Blood.* New York: E.P. Dutton, 1974.

Scott, Robert A., and Douglas, Jack D. (eds.). *Theoretical Perspectives on Deviance.* New York: Basic Books, 1972.

Scott, Robert William. *The Constitution and Finance of English, Scottish and Irish Joint-Stock Companies to 1720.* Cambridge, Eng.: Cambridge University Press, 1911.

Scott, W.S. *Jeanne d'Arc.* London: George G. Harrap, 1974.

Scott, Sir Walter. *Fair Maid of Perth.* New York: John B. Alden, 1831.

_____. *Letters on Demonology and Witchcraft.* New York: J. & J. Harper, 1830.

_____. *Life of Napoleon.* n.p., n.d.

Scott, William B. *Some Memoires of a Palaeontologist.* Princeton, N.J.: Princeton University Press, 1939.

Scott, William G. *The Management of Conflict.* Homewood, Ill.: Richard D. Irwin & Dorsey Press, 1965.

Scott, Winfield. *Memoirs of Lieut. General Scott, LL.D., Written by Himself.* New York: Sheldon, 1864.

Scoundrels & Scalawags. New York: Reader's Digest, 1968.

Scoville, W.C. *The Persecution of the Huguenots and French Economic Development.* Berkeley: University of California Press, 1960.

Scribonius, Wilhelm Adolf. *De Sagarum Natura.* Marburg, Ger.: Pauli Egenolphi, 1558.

Scripps, John Locke. *Life of Abraham Lincoln.* Chicago: Chicago Press and Tribune, 1860.

Scrivener, Jane. *Inside Rome with the Germans.* New York, Macmillan, 1945.

Scudder, Kenyon J. *Prisoners Are People.* Garden City, N.Y.: Doubleday, 1952.

Scull, Andrew T. *Decarceration: Community Treatment and the Deviant.* Englewood Cliffs, N.J.: Prentice-Hall, 1977.

Seabrook, William. *Witchcraft: Its Power in the World Today.* New York: Harcourt, Brace, 1940.

Seaburg, Carl. *Boston Observed.* Boston: Beacon Press, 1971.

Seabury, Paul. *The Wilhelmstrasse.* Berkeley: University of California Press, 1954.

Seagle, William. *Acquitted of Murder.* Chicago: Henry Regnery, 1958.

_____. *Law, the Science of Inefficiency.* New York: Macmillan, 1952.

_____. *The Quest for Law.* New York: Alfred A. Knopf, 1941.

Seagrave, Sterling. *The Soong Dynasty.* New York: Harper & Row, 1985.

Seale, Patrick, and McConville, Maureen. *Philby: The Long Road to Moscow.* New York: Simon & Schuster, 1973.

Seale, William. *Sam Houston's Wife: A Biography of Margaret Lea Houston.* Norman: University of Oklahoma Press, 1970.

Searcher, Victor. *The Farewell to Lincoln.* New York: Abingdon Press, 1965.

_____. *Lincoln's Journey to Greatness.* Philadelphia: Winston, 1960.

Sears, Clara Endicott. *Days of Delusion.* Boston: Houghton Mifflin, 1924.

Sears, John Henry. *The Physical Geography, Geology, Mineralogy and Paleontology of Essex County, Massachusetts.* Salem, Mass.: Essex Institute, 1905.

Sears, Louis Martin. *Jefferson and the Embargo.* Durham, N.C.: Duke University Press, 1927.

Sears, R.R., Macoby, E.E., and Levin, H. *Patterns of Child Rearing.* Evanston, Ill.: Row, Peterson, 1957.

Seaton, Sir Thomas. *From Cadet to Colonel.* London: Hurst & Blackett, 1866.

Sebald, William J., and Brines, Russell. *With MacArthur in Japan: A Personal History of the Occupation.* New York: W.W. Norton, 1965.

Secchia, Pietro, and Moscatelli, Cino. *Il Monte Rosa e sceso a Milano.* Turin, Italy: Einaudi, 1958.

Seccombe, Thomas (ed.). *Lives of Twelve Bad Men.* London: T. Fisher Unwin, 1894.

Sechrest, L., White, S.O., and Brown, E.D. (eds.). *The Rehabilitation of Criminal Offenders.* Washington, D.C.: National Academy of Sciences.

The Second Part of the Boy of Bilson or a True and Particular Relation of the Impostor Susannah Fowler. London: E. Whitlock, 1698.

Secrest, William B. *Joaquin.* Fresno, Calif.: Saga-West, 1967.

_____. *Juanita.* Fresno, Calif.: Saga-West, 1967.

The Secular Spirit: Life and Art at the End of the Middle Ages. New York: E.P. Dutton, 1975.

Sedgwick, Henry Dwight. *In Praise of Gentlemen*. Boston: Little, Brown, 1935.

Seduction of the Innocent. New York: Rinehart, 1954.

Seedman, Albert A., and Hellman, Peter. *Chief!* New York: Avon, 1974.

Seeger, Alan. *Poems*. New York: Charles Scribner's Sons, 1916.

Seeger, Eugen. *Chicago, the Wonder City*. Chicago: n.p., 1893.

Seeley, Charles Livingstone. *Pioneer Days in the Arkansas Valley in Southern Colorado*. Denver: Published by Author, 1932.

Segal, Charles M. (ed.). *Conversations With Lincoln*. New York: G.P. Putnam's Sons, 1961.

Segal, Ronald. *Race War*. New York: Viking Press, 1967.

Segale, Sister Blandina. *At the End of the Santa Fé Trail*. Columbia, Ohio: Columbia Press, 1932.

Segin, W. *Geschichte der Wewelsburg*. Westphalia, Ger.: Druck u. Verlag P.N. Esser, Büren, 1925.

Segur, Count Philippe-Raul de. *Napoleon's Russia Campaign*. Boston: Houghton Mifflin, 1958.

Seidenberg, D.A. *Uhuru and the Kenya Indians: The Role of a Minority Community in Kenya Politics, 1939-1963*. Delhi, India: Vikas, 1983.

Seidler, Lee J., Andrews, Frederick, and Epstein, Marc J. *The Equity Funding Papers*. New York: Wiley/Hamilton, 1977.

Seidler, Murray B. *Norman Thomas; Respectable Rebel*. Syracuse, N.Y.: Syracuse University Press, 1961.

Seidman, Harold. *Labor Czars: A History of Labor Racketeering*. New York: Liveright, 1938.

Seidman, Joel. *The Needle Trades*. New York: Farrar & Rinehart, 1942.

Seigenthaler, John. *In Search of Justice*. Nashville, Tenn.: Aurora, 1971.

Seitz, Don Carlos. *The Dreadful Decade...1869-1879*. Indianapolis, Ind.: Bobbs-Merrill, 1926.

_____. *The James Gordon Bennetts: Father and Son, Proprietors of the New York Herald*. Indianapolis, Ind.: Bobbs-Merrill, 1928.

_____. *Joseph Pulitzer, His Life & Letters*. New York: Simon & Schuster, 1924.

_____. *Lincoln the Politician: How the Rail-Splitter and Flat-Boatman Played the Great American Game*. New York: Coward-McCann, 1931.

_____. *Uncommon Americans*. Indianapolis, Ind.: Bobbs-Merrill, 1925.

_____. *Under the Black Flag*. New York: Gryphon Books, 1971.

Seldes, George. *Lords of the Press*. New York: Julian Messner, 1938.

_____. *Sawdust Caeser*. New York: Harper, 1938.

_____. *The Vatican: Yesterday, Today and Tomorrow*. London: Kegan Paul, Trench, Trubner, 1934.

_____. *You Can't Print That*. New York: Payson & Clarke, 1929.

Seldes, Gilbert. *The New Mass Media: Challenge to a Free Society*. Washington, D.C.: Public Affairs Press, 1968.

_____. *The Stammering Century*. New York: Harper Colophon Books, 1965.

_____. *Witch Hunt: The Technique and Profits of Redbaiting*. New York: Modern Age, 1940.

Select Committee on Intelligence. *The Investigation of the Assassination of President John F. Kennedy: Performance of the Intelligence Agencies*. Washington, D.C.: U.S. Government Printing Office, 1976.

Seligman, Edwin. *The Social Evil*. New York: G.P. Putnam's Sons, 1912.

Seligman, M.E. *Helplessness: On Depression, Development, and Death*. San Francisco: W.H. Freeman, 1975.

Seligmann, Kurt. *Magic, Supernaturalism and Religion*. New York: Pantheon Books, 1971.

_____. *The Mirror of Magic*. New York: Pantheon, 1948.

Seligmann, Siegfried. *Der böse Blick und Verwandtes*. Berlin: H. Barsdorf, 1910.

Sell, Henry Blackman, and Weybright, Victor. *Buffalo Bill and the Wild West*. New York: Oxford University Press, 1955.

Sellers, Alvin V. *Classics of the Bar: Stories of the World's Greatest Legal Trials and Forensic Masterpieces*. Washington, D.C.: Washington Law Books, 1942.

Sellers, C.C. *Benedict Arnold*. New York: Minton, Balch, 1930.

Sellers, C.G. *James K. Polk, Jacksonian 1795-1843*. Princeton, N.J.: Princeton University Press, 1957.

Sellin, Thorsten (ed.). *Capital Punishment*. New York: Harper & Row, 1967.

_____. *Culture Conflict and Crime*. New York: Social Science Research Council, 1938.

_____. *The Death Penalty*. Philadelphia: American Law Institute, 1959.

_____, and Wolfgang, M. (eds.). *Deliquency: Selected Studies*. New York: John Wiley & Sons, 1969.

_____, *The Measurement of Delinquency*. New York: John Wiley & Sons, 1964.

_____. *Research Memorandum on Crime in the Depression*. New York: Social Science Research Council, 1937.

Selmier, Dean, and Dram, Mark. *Blow Away*. New York: Viking Press, 1979.

Selsam, Howard. *Socialism and Ethics*. London: Lawrence & Wishart, 1947.

Selvin, David F. *Eugene Debs*. New York: Lothrop, Lee & Shepard, 1967.

_____. *A Place in the Sun: A History of California Labor*. San Francisco: Boyd & Fraser, 1981.

_____. *Sky Full of Storm: A Brief History of California Labor*. San Francisco: California Historical Society, 1975.

Selznick, Philip. *Organizational Weapon, Study of Bolshevik Strategy and Tactics*. New York: McGraw-Hill, 1952.

_____. *TVA and the Grass Roots*. Berkeley: University of California Press, 1949.

Semelaigne, Dr. René. *Les Pionniers de la psychiatrie français avant et aprés Pinel*. Paris: Baillière et fils, 1930-32.

Semmes, Raphael. *The Confederate Raider Alabama*. Greenwich, Conn.: Fawcett, 1962.

_____. *Crime and Punishment in Early Maryland*. Baltimore: Johns Hopkins Press, 1938.

Semmler, Rudolf. *Goebbels: The Man Next to Hitler*. London: Westhouse, 1947.

Sen, Gertrude Emerson. *Voiceless India*. Toronto, Ontario, Can.: Longmans, Green, 1946.

Seneca. *Ad Lucilium Epistulae Morales*. trans. R.M. Gummere. London: William Heinemann, 1953.

Seng, R.A., and Gilmour, J.V. *Brink's the Money Movers*. Chicago: R.R. Donnelley & Sons, 1959.

Senger, Frido von. *Neither Fear Nor Hope*. New York: E.P. Dutton, 1964.

Senior, Nassau William. *Conversations with Distinguished Persons During the Second Empire from 1860-1863*. London: Hurst & Blackett, 1880.

Senise, Carmine. *Quando ero capo della polizia*. Rome: Ruffolo, 1946.

Senn, Edward L. *"Wild Bill" Hickok, "Prince of Pistoleers"*. Deadwood, S.D.: n.p., 1939.

Sennett, Mack, as told to Shipp, Cameron. *King of Comedy*. New York: Doubleday, 1954.

Senzel, Howard T. *Cases: A Courthouse Chronicle of Crime and Wit*. New York: Viking Press, 1982.

Serge, Victor. *Mémoires d'un Revolutionnaire*. Paris: Editions de Seuil, 1951.

_____. *Men in Prison*. London: Writers & Readers, 1969.

Sergeant, Philip Walsingham. *Witches and Warlocks*. London: Hutchinson, 1936.

Serling, Robert J. *The Only Way to Fly*. Garden City, N.Y.: Doubleday, 1976.

Sermons Preached in Boston on the Death of Abraham Lincoln. Boston: J.E. Tilton, 1865.

Servadio, Gaia. *Angelo LaBarbera: The Profile of a Mafia Boss*.

London: Quartet Books, 1974.

_____. *Mafioso: A History of the Mafia from Its Origins to the Present Day.* New York: Dell, 1976.

Servan-Schreiber, Jean-Louis. *The Power to Inform.* New York: McGraw-Hill, 1974.

Serven, James E. *The Collecting of Guns.* Harrisburg, Pa.: Stackpole Books, 1964.

_____. *Colt Firearms From 1836.* Harrisburg, Pa.: Stackpole Books, 1979.

Service, John S. *The Amerasia Papers: Some Problems in the History of US-China Relations.* Berkeley: University of California Press, 1971.

Seth, Ronald. *Encyclopedia of Espionage.* London: New English Library, 1972.

_____. *Petiot, Victim of Chance.* London: Hutchinson, 1963.

_____. *The Sleeping Truth.* New York: Hart, 1968.

_____. *Unmasked: The Story of Soviet Espionage.* New York: Hawthorn Books, 1965.

_____. *Witches and Their Craft.* New York: Taplinger, 1967.

Seton-Watson, Hugh. *Decline of Imperial Russia, 1855-1914.* New York: Frederick A. Praeger, 1953.

_____. *Eastern Europe Between the Wars, 1918-1941.* Hamden, Conn.: Archon, 1962.

_____. *The East European Revolution.* New York: Frederick A. Praeger, 1956.

_____. *From Lenin to Malenkov: The History of World Communism.* New York: Frederick A. Praeger, 1953.

Seton-Watson, Hugh. *The Russian Empire, 1801-1917.* Oxford, Eng.: Clarendon, 1967.

Seton-Watson, R.W. *A History of the Rumaninas from Roman Times to the Completion of Unity.* Cambridge, Eng.: Cambridge University Press, 1934.

_____. *Roumania and the Great War.* London: Constable, 1915.

_____. *Sarajevo: A Study in the Origins of the Great War.* London: Hutchinson, 1925.

_____. *The Southern Slav Question and the Habsburg Monarchy.* London: Constable & Son, 1911.

_____. *Transylvania: A Key-Problem.* London: Classic Press, 1943.

Seton-Williams, M.V. *Britain and the Arab States.* London: Luzac, 1948.

Settimelli, Emilio. *Colpo di stato fascista?* Milan, Italy: Facchi, 1922.

_____. *Edda contro Benito.* Rome: Corso, 1952.

_____. *Mussolini visto da Settimelli.* Rome: Pinciana, 1929.

Settle, Irving. *A Pictorial History of Radio.* New York: Citadel Press, 1960.

Settle, Raymond W., and Lund, Mary. *Empire on Wheels.* Palo Alto, Calif.: Stanford University Press, 1949.

Settle, William A., Jr. *Jesse James Was His Name.* Columbia: University of Missouri Press, 1966.

Severin, Timothy. *Explorers of the Mississippi.* New York: Alfred A. Knopf, 1968.

_____. *The Golden Antilles.* New York: Alfred A. Knopf, 1970.

Severn, William. *Toward One World: The Life of Wendall Willke.* New York: I. Washburn, 1967.

Sévigné, Madame de. *Lettres.* Paris: F. Didot frères, 1856.

Sewall, Samuel. *The Diary of Samuel Sewall.* New York: Farrar, Straus, & Giroux, 1973.

_____. *The Trial of Alpheus Livermore and Samuel Angier...for the Murder of Nicholas John Crevay.* Boston: Watson & Bangs, 1813.

Sewall, William W. *Bill Sewall's Story of T.R.* New York: Harper & Brothers, 1919.

Seward, Desmond. *The First Bourbon.* Boston: Gambit, 1971.

Seward, Frederick W. *Andrew Johnson.* Philadelphia: J.B. Lippincott, 1890.

_____. *Reminiscences of a War-Time Statesman and Diplomat.* New York: G.P. Putnam's Sons, 1916.

_____. *Seward at Washington.* New York: Derby & Miller, 1891.

Seward, William Henry. *Life and Public Services of John Quincy Adams, Sixth President of the United States.* New York: Miller, Orton, & Mulligan, 1856.

Sex Information and Educational Council of the United States. *Sexuality and Man.* New York: Charles Scribner's Sons, 1970.

Seyfried, Vincent F. *The Long Island Rail Road: A Comprehensive History,* part 2, *The Flushing, North Shore & Central Railroad.* Garden City, N.Y.: Privately Published, 1963.

Seymour, Charles (ed.). *The Intimate Papers of Colonel House.* 2 vols. Boston: Houghton Mifflin, 1926.

Seymour, Flora Warren. *Indian Agents of the Old Frontier.* New York: D. Appleton-Century, 1941.

_____. *The Story of the Red Man.* Longmans, Green, 1929.

Seymour, L. *Finger Print Classification.* Los Angeles: Privately Printed, 1913.

Seymour, St. John Drelincourt. *Irish Witchcraft and Demonology.* Baltimore: Norman, Remington, 1682.

Seymour, W. *Why Justice Fails.* New York: William Morrow, 1973.

Seymour-Smith, Martin. *Fallen Women.* London: Thomas Nelson, 1969.

Seymour-Ure, Colin. *The Political Impact of Mass Media.* Beverly Hills, Calif.: Sage, 1974.

Sforza, Count Carlo. *L'Italia dal 1914 al 1944 quale io la vidi.* Rome: Mondadori, 1944.

_____. *Noi e gli altri.* Milan, Italy: Gentile, 1945.

Sforza, M.C. *Gli attentati a Mussolini.* Milan, Italy: Mondadori, 1965.

Shaaber, M.A. *Some Forerunners of the Newspaper in England, 1476-1622.* New York: Octagon Books, 1966.

Shabad, Theodore. *Geography of the USSR: A Regional Survey.* New York: Columbia University Press, 1951.

Shackleford, William Yancey. *Belle Starr, The Bandit Queen.* Girard, Kan.: Haldemann-Julius, 1943.

_____. *Buffalo Bill Cody, Scout and Showman.* Girard, Kan.: Haldemann-Julius, 1944.

_____. *Gunfighters of the Old West.* Girard, Kan.: Haldemann-Julius, 1943.

Shackleton, B. Close. *Handbook of Frontier Days of Southeast Kansas.* Privately Printed, 1961.

Shackleton, Robert. *The Book of Chicago.* Philadelphia: n.p., 1920.

Shadowitz, Albert, and Walsh, Peter. *The Dark Side of Knowledge: Exploring the Occult.* Reading, Mass.: Addison-Wesley, 1976.

Shadwell, Arthur. *Drink in 1914-1922: A Lesson in Control.* New York: Longmans, Green, 1923.

Shadwell, Thomas. *The Lancaster Witches.* London: J.Starkey, 1682.

Shaffer, Ron. *Surprise! Suprise!* New York: Viking Press, 1977.

Shaginyan, Mariette. *Semya Ulyanovikh.* Moscow: Molodaya Gvardiya, 1958.

Shah, S.A. *Report on the XYZ Chromosomal Abnormality.* Washington, D.C.: U.S. Government Printing Office, 1970.

Shah, Sayed Idries. *Oriental Magic.* London: Octagon Press, 1968.

Shakespeare, Geoffrey. *Let Candles Be Brought In.* London: Macdonald, 1949.

Shalloo, J.P. *Private Police: With Special Reference to Pennsylvania.* Philadelphia: American Academy of Political and Social Science, 1933.

Shanahan, Donald T. *Patrol Administration.* Boston: Holbrook Press, 1975.

Shanani, Ranju. *Mr. Gandhi.* New York: Macmillan, 1961.

Shaner, Dolph. *The Story of Joplin.* New York: Stratford House, 1948.

Shannon, David A. (ed.). *Beatrice Webb's American Diary, 1898.* Madison: University of Wisconsin Press, 1963.

_____. *The Decline of American Communism.* New York: Harcourt, Brace, 1959.

_____. *The Great Depression.* Englewood Cliffs, N.J.: Prentice-Hall, 1960.

_____ (ed.). *The Great Imposter.* New York: Prentice-Hall, 1960.

_____. *The Socialist Party of America.* New York: Macmillan, 1955.

_____. *Twentieth Century America, The United States Since the 1890's.* Chicago: Rand McNally, 1963.

Shannon, Elaine. *Desperados: Latin Drug Lord, U.S. Lawmen, and the War America Can't Win.* New York: Viking Press, 1988.

Shannon, Fred A. *The Organization and Administration of the Union Army, 1861-1865.* Cleveland: Arthur H. Clark, 1928.

Shannon, William V. *The American Irish.* New York: Macmillan, 1963.

_____. *The Heir Apparent: Robert Kennedy and the Struggle for Power.* New York: Macmillan, 1967.

Shapiro, Fred C. *Whitmore.* New York: Pyramid, 1970.

_____, and Sullivan, James W. *Race Riots: New York 1964.* New York: Thomas Y. Crowell, 1964.

Shapiro, Harry Lionel. *Descendants of the Mutineers of the Bounty.* Honolulu, Hawaii: The Museum, 1929.

Shapiro, Lionel. *They Left the Back Door Open.* London: Jarrolds, 1945.

Shapiro, Nat, and Hentoff, Nat. *Hear Me Talkin' to Ya: The Story of Jazz and the Men Who Made It.* New York: Rinehart, 1955.

Shapiro, Stanley. *A Time to Remember.* New York: Random House, 1986.

Shapland, J.J. Williams, and Duff, P. *Victims in the Criminal Justice System.* Brookfield, Vt.: Gower, 1985.

Shaplen, Robert. *Kreuger: Genius and Swindler.* New York: Alfred A. Knopf, 1960.

_____. *The Lost Revolution: The Story of Twenty Years of Neglected Opportunities in Vietnam and of America's Failure to Foster Democracy There.* New York: Harper & Row, 1965.

Sharabi, Hisham B. *Nationalism and Revolution in the Arab World.* Princeton, N.J.: D. Van Nostrand, 1966.

Sharman, Lyon. *Sun Yat-sen.* New York: John Day, 1934.

Sharp, Donald B. *Commentaries on Obscenity.* Metuchen, N.J.: Scarecrow Press, 1970.

Sharp, Paul F. *Whoop-Up Country: The Canadian-American West, 1865-1885.* Minneapolis: University of Minnesota Press, 1955.

Sharp, V. *Palm Prints.* Cape Town: Mercantile-Atlas, 1937.

Sharpe, Charles Kirkpatrick. *Witchcraft in Scotland.* New York: Barnes & Noble, 1972.

Sharpe, Malcolm P. *Was Justice Done?: The Rosenberg-Sobell Case.* New York: Monthly Review Press, n.d.

Sharpe, May Churchill. *Chicago May: Her Story.* New York: Macaulay, 1928.

Shattuck, Roger. *The Banquet Years: 'The Origins of the Avant-Garde in France: 1885 to World War I.'* New York: Vintage Books, 1968.

Shaw, A.G.L. *Convicts and the Colonies.* London: Faber & Faber, 1966.

Shaw, Albert H. *Abraham Lincoln...A Cartoon History.* 2 vols. New York: Review of Reviews, 1929.

_____ (ed.). *The Lincoln Encyclopedia.* New York: Macmillan, 1950.

_____. *Municipal Government in Continental Europe.* New York: Century, 1895.

_____. *Municipal Government in Great Britain.* New York: Century, 1895.

Shaw, Arnold. *The Street That Never Slept.* New York: Coward, McCann & Geoghegan, 1971.

Shaw, Clifford R. *Brothers in Crime.* Chicago: University of Chicago Press, 1938.

_____, et al. *Delinquency Areas.* Chicago: University of Chicago Press, 1929.

_____. *The Jackroller.* Chicago: University of Chicago Press, 1930.

_____, and McKay, Henry D. *Juvenile Delinquency and Urban Areas.* Chicago: University of Chicago Press, 1972.

Shaw, David. *Press Watch.* New York: Macmillan, 1984.

Shaw, Frederick. *History of the New York City Legislature.* New York: Columbia University Press, 1954.

Shaw, George Bernard, *Bernard Shaw and Fascism.* London: Favil Press, 1927.

_____. *The Crime of Imprisonment.* New York: Philosophical Library, 1946.

_____ (ed.). *The Doctor's Dilemma.* New York: Dodd, Mead, 1941.

_____. *Everybody's Political What's What.* New York: Dodd, Mead, 1944.

Shaw, J. Gary, and Harris, Larry R. *Cover-Up: 'The Governmental Conspiracy to Conceal the Facts About the Public Execution of John Kennedy.'* Cleburne, Texas: Published by Authors, 1976.

Shaw, Luella. *True History of Some of the Pioneers of Colorado.* Hotchkiss, Colo.: Published by Author, 1909.

Shaw, Margaret. *Social Work in Prison.* London: H.M. Stationery Office, 1974.

Shawcross, Tim, and Young, Martin. *Men of Honour: The Confessions of Tommaso Buscetta.* London: Collins, 1987.

Shay, Frank. *More Pious Friends and Druken Companions.* New York: Macaulay, 1928.

_____, and Held, John, Jr. *My Pious Friends and Drunken Companions.* New York: Macaulay, 1927.

Shea, John. *History of the Catholic Church in the United States.* New York: Published by Author, 1886-1892.

Shea, John Gilmary (ed.). *The Lincoln Memorial: A Record of the Life, Assassination, and Obsequies of the Martyed President.* New York: Bruce & Huntington, 1865.

Shea, Robert, and Wilson, Robert Anton. *Illuminatus, Part I: The Eye in the Pyramid.* New York: Dell, 1975.

Sheahan, James W., and Upton, George P. *Great Conflagration: Chicago, Its Past, Present and Future.* Philadelphia: Union, 1871.

Shealey, C. Norman. *Occult Medicine Can Save Your Life.* New York: Dial, 1975.

Shearing, Joseph. *Airing in a Closed Cottage.* New York: Harper & Brothers, 1943.

_____. *So Evil My Love.* New York: Harper, 1947.

_____. *The Strange Case of Lucile Cléry.* New York: Harper and Brothers, 1932.

Shears, Richard. *Mother on Trial.* New York: St. Martin's Press, 1988.

Shecter, Leonard. *On the Pad.* New York: G.P. Putnam's Sons, 1973.

Sheed, F.J. *The Irish Way.* New York: Kennedy, 1932.

Sheehan, P. (ed.). *The Function and Nature of Imagery.* London: Academic Press, 1972.

Sheehan, Susan. *A Prison and a Prisoner.* Boston: Houghton, 1978.

Sheehan, Vincent. *Between the Thunder and the Sun.* New York: Random, 1943.

_____. *Mahatma Gandhi.* New York: Alfred A. Knopf, 1955.

_____. *Personal History.* New York: Doubleday, 1935.

Sheehy, Eugene. *May It Please the Court.* Dublin, Ire.: C.J. Fallon, 1951.

Sheehy, Gail. *Hustling: Prostitution in Our Wide Open Society.* New York: Delacorte Press, 1973.

Sheer, George, and Rankin, Hugh. *Rebels and Redcoats.* New York: World, 1957.

Sheffens, L. *The Shame of Cities.* New York: McClure, 1904.

Sheffy, Lester Fields. *The Francklyn Land and Cattle Company: A Panhandle Enterprise, 1882-1957.* Austin: University of Texas Press, 1963.

Sheldon, Addison Erwin. *Nebraska Old and New: History, Stories, Folklore.* Lincoln: University of Nebraska, 1937.

Sheldon, George W. *The Story of the Volunteer Fire Department of the City of New York.* New York: Harper & Brothers, 1882.

Sheldon, Walter J. *The Honorable Conquerors: The Occupation of Japan 1945-1952.* New York: Macmillan, 1965.

Sheldon, William H. *Atlas of Men.* New York: Harper, 1949.

_____. *Varieties of Delinquent Youth.* New York: Harper, 1949.

_____, Stevens, S.S., and Tucker, W.B., *Varieties of Human Physique.* New York: Harper, 1940.

_____, Stevens, S.S. *Varieties of Temperament.* New York: Harper, 1949.

Sheley, J.F. *Understanding Crime: Concepts, Issues, Decisions.* Belmont, Calif.: Wadsworth, 1979.

Shell, Leslie Doyle, and Hazel M. *Forgotten Men of Cripple Creek.* Denver: Big Mountain Press, 1959.

Sheller, Roscoe. *Bandit to Lawman.* Yakima, Wash.: Franklin Press, 1966.

_____. *Ben Snipes: Northwest Cattle King.* Portland, Ore.: Binsford & Mort, 1957.

Shelley, L.E. *Crime and Modernization.* Carbondale: Southern Illinois University Press, 1981.

Shelton, Vaughan. *Mask for Treason: The Lincoln Murder Trial.* Harrisburg, Pa.: Stackpole Books, 1965.

Shenton, James P. *The Reconstruction: A Documentary History of the South after the War: 1865-1877.* New York: G.P. Putnam's Sons, 1963.

Shepard, Gordon. *Dollfus.* New York: Macmillan, 1961.

Shepard, Odell. *Connecticut, Past and Present.* London: Alfred A. Knopf, 1939.

Sheperd, Charles R. *The Ways of Ah Sin.* New York: Revell, 1923.

Sheppard, William. *Of Corporations, Fraternities and Guilds.* London: J.S., 1659.

_____. *The Court-keepers Guide.* London: W.G. for G., 1641.

_____. *England's Balme.* London: Bedel & T. Collins, 1662.

Shepro, Richard Warren. *The Reconstruction of Chicago after the Great Fire of 1871.* Cambridge, Mass.: Harvard University Press, 1975.

Sheps, Mindel C., and Menken, Jane A. *Mathmatical Models of Conception and Birth.* Chicago: University of Chicago Press, 1973.

Sherard, Robert Harborough. *Life of Oscar Wilde.* New York: M. Kennerly, 1906.

_____. *Oscar Wilde, the Story of an Unhappy Friendship.* London: Hermes, 1902.

_____. *The Real Oscar Wilde.* Norwood, Pa.: Norwood, 1975.

Sheresky, Norman. *On Trial.* New York: Viking Press, 1977.

Sherick, L.G. *Freedom of Information Act.* New York: Arco, 1980.

Sheridan, Clare. *In Many Places.* London: Jonathan Cape, 1923.

Sheridan, James E. *Chinese Warlord: The Careen of Feng Yu-hsiang.* Stanford, Calif.: Stanford University Press, 1966.

Sheridan, Leo W. *I Killed for the Law.* New York: Stackpole Sons, 1938.

Sheridan, Martin. *Comics and Their Creators.* Boston: Hale, Cushman & Flynt, 1942.

Sheridan, P.H. *Personal Memoirs of P.H. Sheridan, General United States Army.* New York: Charles L. Webster, 1888.

Sheridan, Sol N. *History of Ventura County, California.* Chicago: S.J. Clarke, 1926.

Sheridan, Walter. *The Rise and Fall of Jimmy Hoffa.* New York: Saturday Review Press, 1972.

Sherif, Muzafer and Carolyn. *Groups in Harmony and Tension.* New York: Octagon, 1966.

_____ (eds.). *Interdisciplinary Relationships in the Social Sciences.* Chicago: Aldine, 1969.

_____, et al. *Intergroup Conflict and Cooperation.* Norman: University of Oklahoma Press, 1961.

_____. *Reference Groups.* New York: Harper & Row, 1964.

Sherlock, Herbert Arment. *Black Powder Snapshots.* Huntington, W.Va.: Standard, 1946.

Sherman, Edwin. *Engineer Corps of Hell.* San Francisco: Privately Printed, 1833.

Sherman, James E., and Barbara H. *Ghost Towns of Arizona.* Norman: University of Oklahoma Press, 1969.

Sherman, John. *Recollections of Forty Years in the House, Senate and Cabinet: An Autobiography.* Chicago: Werner, 1895.

Sherman, Lawrence W. *The Control of Official Misconduct in Louisville, Kentucky.* Louisville, Ky.: Department of Public Safety, 1976.

_____. *Police Corruption: A Sociological Perspective.* Garden City, N.Y.: Doubleday, 1974.

_____. *The Quality of Police Education: A Critical Review with Recommendations for Improving Programs in Higher Education.* San Francisco: Jossey Bass, 1978.

_____. *Scandal & Reform: Controlling Police Corruption.* Berkeley: University of California, 1978.

_____, Milton, Catherine H., and Kelley, Thomas V. *Team Policing: Seven Case Studies.* Washington, D.C.: Police Foundation, 1973.

Sherman, Michael, and Hawkins, Gordon. *Imprisonment in America.* Chicago: University of Chicago Press, 1982.

Sherman, Philemon Tecumseh. *Inside the Machine, Two Years in the Board of Alderman, 1898-1899.* New York: Cooke & Fry, 1901.

Sherman, William Tecumseh. *Home Letters of General Sherman.* New York: Charles Scribner's Sons, 1909.

_____. *Memoirs.* 2 vols. New York: D. Appleton, 1875.

_____. *The Sherman Letters.* New York: Charles Scribner's Sons, 1894.

Sherrard, P. *Constantinople.* New York: Oxford University Press, 1965.

Sherrill, Robert. *Gothic Politics in the Deep South.* New York: Grossman, 1968.

_____. *The Saturday Night Special.* New York: Charterhouse, 1973.

Sherwell, Samuel. *Old Recollections of an Old Boy.* New York: Knickerbocker Press, 1923.

Sherwin, Martin J. *A World Destroyed.* New York: Alfred A. Knopf, 1975.

Sherwin, Oscar. *Prophet of Liberty: The Life and Times of Wendell Phillips.* New York: Bookman Associates, 1958.

Sherwin, Robert Veit. *Sex and the Statutory Law.* New York: Oceana, 1949.

Sherwood, Robert E. *Roosevelt and Hopkins.* New York: Harper & Brothers, 1948.

Sheth, Hansa. *Juvenile Delinquency in an Indian Setting.* Bombay: Popular Book Depot, 1961.

Shew, E. Spencer. *A Companion to Murder.* New York: Alfred A. Knopf, 1960.

_____. *Hands of the Ripper.* London" Sphere, 1971.

_____. *A Second Companion to Murder.* New York: Knopf, 1961.

Shields, Pete. *Guns Don't Die-People Do.* New York: Priam/Arbor House, 1981.

Shields, Robert William. *Seymour, Indiana and the Famous Story of the Reno Gang.* Indianapolis, Ind.: H. Lieber, 1939.

Shigemitsu, Mamoru. *Japan and Her Destiny: My Struggle for Peace.* New York: E.P. Dutton, 1958.

Shihab, Aziz. *Sirhan.* San Antonio, Texas: Naylor, 1969.

Shils, Edward Albert. *Center and Periphery.* Chicago: University of Chicago Press, 1975.

_____, and Finch, H.A. *Max Weber on the Methodology of the Social Sciences.* Glencoe, Ill.: Free Press, 1949.

_____. *The Torment of Secrecy: The Background and Consequences of American Security Policies.* Glencoe, Ill.: Free Press, 1956.

Shimada Toshihiko. *The Kwantung Army.* Tokyo: Chuo Koronsha, 1965.

Shimkin, D.B., Shimkin, E.M., and Frate, D.A. *The Extended Family in Black Societies.* The Hague, Neth.: Mouton, 1978.

Shinkle, James D. *Fifty Years of Roswell History, 1867-1917.* Roswell, N.M.: Hall-Poorbaugh Press, 1964.

_____. *Reminiscences of Roswell Pioneers*. Roswell, N.M.: Hall-Poorbaugh Press, 1966.

Shinn, Charles Howard. *Graphic Description of Pacific Coast Outlaws*. Los Angeles: Westernlore Press, 1958.

_____. *Mining Camps: A Study in American Frontier Government*. New York: Alfred A. Knopf, 1948.

Shipley, Maynard. *The War on Modern Science: A Short History of the Fundamentalist Attacks on Evolution and Modernism*. New York: Alfred A. Knopf, 1927.

Shipman, Margaret. *Mexico's Struggle toward Democracy: The Mexican Revolutions of 1857 and 1910*. New York: Published by Author, 1926.

Shipman, Mrs. O.L. *Letters, Past and Present...* n.p., n.d.

_____. *Taming the Big Bend: A History of the Extreme Western Portion of Texas from Fort Clark to El Paso*. Marfa, Texas: n.p., 1926.

Shippey, Lee. *It's an Old California Custom*. New York: Vanguard Press, 1948.

Shirer, William L. *Berlin Diary*. New York: Alfred A. Knopf, 1941.

_____. *The Collapse of the Third Republic*. New York: Simon & Schuster, 1969.

_____. *End of a Berlin Diary*. New York: Alfred A. Knopf, 1947.

_____. *Gandhi: A Memoir*. New York: Simon & Schuster, 1979.

_____. *The Rise and Fall of the Third Reich*. New York: Simon & Schuster, 1960.

_____. *20th Century Journey: A Memoir of a Life and the Times of William L. Shirer*. New York: Simon & Schuster, 1976.

Shirk, George H. *Oklahoma Place-Names*. Norman: University of Oklahoma Press, 1965.

Shirley, Glenn. *Belle Starr and Her Times*. Norman: University of Oklahoma Press, 1982.

_____ (ed.). *Buckskin Joe; Being the Unique and Vivid Memoirs of Edward Jonathan Hoyt*. Lincoln: University of Nebraska Press, 1966.

_____. *Buckskin and Spurs: A Gallery of Frontier Rogues and Heroes*. New York: Hastings House, 1958.

_____. *Heck Thomas, Frontier Marshal*. Philadelphia: Chilton, 1962.

_____. *Henry Starr, Last of the Real Bad Men*. New York: David McKay, 1965.

_____. *Law West of Fort Smith*. New York: Henry Holt, 1957.

_____. *Outlaw Queen: The Fantastic True Story of Belle Starr*. Derby, Conn.: Monarch Books, 1960.

_____. *Pawnee Bill: A Biography of Major Gordon W. Lillie*. Albuquerque: University of New Mexico Press, 1958.

_____. *Shotgun for Hire: The Story of "Deacon" Jim Miller, Killer of Pat Garrett*. Norman: University of Oklahoma Press, 1970.

_____. *Six-Gun and Silver Star*. Albuquerque: University of New Mexico Press, 1955.

_____. *Temple Houston*. Norman: University of Oklahoma Press, 1980.

_____. *Toughest of Them All*. Albuquerque: University of New Mexico Press, 1953.

_____. *West of Hell's Fringe: Crime, Criminals, and the Federal Peace Officer in Oklahoma Territory, 1889-1907*. Norman: University of Oklahoma Press, 1978.

Shirovama Saburo. *War Criminal*. Tokyo: Kodansha, 1980.

Shirreff, Patrick. *A Tour through North America; Together with a Comprehensive View of the Canadas and United States*. Edinburgh, Scot.: Oliver & Boyd, 1835.

Shnayerson, Robert. *The Illustrated History of the Supreme Court of the United States*. New York: Harry N. Abrams, 1986.

Shneour, Elie. *The Malnourished Mind*. Garden City, N.Y.: Anchor Press/Doubleday, 1974.

Shockley, Martin. *Southwest Writers Anthology*. Austin, Texas: Steck-Vaughn, 1967.

Shoell, Rudolf, and Kroll, Juilelem (eds.). *Corpus Juris Civilis*. Berlin: Weidmann, 1959.

Shoemaker, Floyd (ed.). *Missouri, Day by Day*. 2 vols. Jefferson City, Mo.: Mid-State Printing, 1942.

_____. *Missouri and Missourians: Land of Contrasts and People of Achievements*. 5 vols. Chicago: Lewis, 1943.

Shoenfeld, Dudley D. *The Crime and the Criminal: A Psychiatric Study of the Lindbergh Case*. New York: Covici-Friede, 1936.

Shogan, Robert, and Craig, Tom. *The Detroit Race Riot: A Study in Violence*. Philadelphia: Chilton Books, 1964.

_____. *A Question of Judgement*. Indianapolis, Ind.: Bobbs-Merrill, 1972.

Shoham, S. *Crime and Social Deviation*. Chicago: Henry Regnery, 1966.

_____. *Society and the Absurd*. Oxford, Eng.: Blackwell, 1974.

Shonle Cavan, Ruth. *Criminology*. New York: Thomas Y. Crowell, 1955.

Shore, W. Teignmouth (ed.). *Crime and It's Detection*. London: Gresham, 1931.

_____. *The Trial of Browne and Kennedy*. London: William Hodge, 1930.

_____. *The Trials of Charles Frederick Peace*. London: William Hodge, 1926.

_____. *Trial of Thomas Neill Cream*. London: Hodge, 1923.

A Short Account of the Trial of the Cyrus Emlay. Burlington, N.J.: S.C. Ustick, 1801.

Short, Anthony. *The Communist Insurrection in Malaya*. Princeton, N.J.: Princeton University Press, 1956.

Short, James F., Jr. (ed.). *Delinquency, Crime and Society*. Chicago: University of Chicago Press, 1976.

_____ (ed.). *Gang Delinquency and Delinquent Subcultures*. New York: Harper & Row, 1968.

_____, and Strodtbeck, F.L. *Group Process and Gang Delinquency*. Chicago: University of Chicago Press, 1965.

Shorter, C. *Napoleon and His Fellow Travellers*. London: Cassell, 1908.

Shorter, Dora Sigerson. *Sixteen Dead Men and Other Poems of Easter Week*. New York: Mitchell Kennerley, 1919.

Shotwell, W.G. *Driftwood*. New York: Longmans, Green, 1927.

Shover, John L. *Cornbelt Rebellion*. Urbana: University of Illinois Press, 1965.

The Show of Violence. New York: Doubleday, 1949.

Shridharani, Krishnalal. *The Mahatma and the World*. New York: John Day, 1939.

_____. *War Without Violence*. New York: Harcourt, Brace, 1939.

Shub, David. *Lenin, A Biography*. New York: Doubleday, 1948.

Shuey, A.M. *The Testing of Negro Intelligence*. New York: Social Science Press, 1966.

Shugg, Roger W. *Origins of the Class Struggle in Louisana*. New York: n.p, 1953.

Shukairy, Ahmed. *Dialogues and Secrets with Kings*. (In Arabic) Beirut, Leb.: n.p., 1971.

Shukla, Chandrashankar (ed.). *Incidents of Gandhiji's Life*. Bombay, India: Vora, 1949.

Shulman, Alix Kates (ed.). *Red Emma Speaks*. New York: Vintage Books, 1972.

Shulman, Harry M. *Juvenile Delinquency in American Society*. New York: Harpers, 1961.

_____. *A Study of Problem Boys and Their Brothers*. Albany: New York State Crime Commission, 1929.

Shulman, Marshall D. *Stalin's Foreign Policy Reappraised*. Cambridge, Mass.: Havard University Press, 1963.

Shultz, Earle, and Simmons, Walter. *Offices in the Sky*. Indianapolis, Ind.: Bobbs-Merrill, 1959.

Shultz, Gladys Denny. *How Many More Victims?* New York: J.B. Lippincott, 1965.

Shulvass, Moses A. *The History of the Jewish People*. Chicago: Regnery Gateway, 1982.

Shumaker, Wayne. *The Occult Sciences in the Renaissance*. Berkeley: University of California Press, 1972.

Shumard, George. *The Ballard and History of Billy the Kid*. Clovis, N.M.: Tab, 1966.

Shumate, Albert. *A Visit to Rincon Hill and South Park*. San

Francisco: Tamalpais Press, 1963.

Shurtleff, Nathaniel B. (ed.). *Records of the Governor.* Boston: W. White, 1853-54.

Shutes, Milton H. *Lincoln and the Doctors: A Medical Narrative of the Life of Abraham Lincoln.* New York: Pioneer Press, 1933.

____. *Lincoln's Emotional Life.* Philadelphia: Dorrance, 1957.

Siberman, Charles E. *Crisis in Black and White.* New York: Random House, 1964.

Sichel, Joyce L., et al. *Women on Patrol. A Piot Study of Police Performance in New York City.* New York: Vera Institute of Justice, 1977.

Sichel, Walter. *Emma Lady Hamilton.* New York: Dodd, Mead, 1907.

Siciliano, Vincent. *Unless They Kill Me First.* New York: Hawthorne Books, 1970.

Sickels, H.E. *Reports on the Cases decided in the Court of Appeals of the State of New York.* Albany, N.Y.: James B. Lyons, 1893.

Sickler, Joseph S. (ed.). *Rex et Regina v. Lutherland.* Woodstown, N.J.: Seven Stars Press, 1948.

Sicot, Marcel. *Servitude et Grandeur Policières.* Paris: Les Productions de Paris, 1959.

Sideman, Belle Becker, and Friedman, Lillian (eds.). *Europe Looks at the Civil War.* New York: Collier Books, 1962.

Sidey, Hugh, and Ward, Fred. *Portrait of a President.* New York: Harper & Row, 1975.

Sidran, Ben. *Black Talk.* New York: Holt, Rinehart & Winston, 1971.

Siebert, Wilbur H. *The Underground Railroad from Slavery to Freedom.* New York: Macmillan, 1898.

Sieburg, F. *Napoléon.* Paris: Robert Laffont, 1957.

Siegel, Larry J. *Criminology.* St. Paul, Minn.: West, 1983.

Siegfried, Andre. *Suez and Panama.* New York: Harcourt & Brace, 1940.

Sienkiewicz, Henry. *Portrait of America: Letters.* trans. Charles Morley. New York: Columbia University Press, 1959.

Sifakis, Carl. *A Catalogue of Crime.* New York: New American Library, 1979.

Sigal, Leon. *Reporters and Officials.* Lexington, Mass.: D.C. Heath, 1973.

Sigaud, Louis A. *Belle Boyd, Confederate Spy.* Richmond, Va.: Dietz Press, 1945.

Sigler, Robert T. *Furlough Programs for Inmates.* Washington, D.C.: National Institute for Law Enforcement and Criminal Justice, 1976.

____. *Furlough Programs for Inmates: Final Report.* Washington, D.C.: National Institute for Law Enforcement and Criminal Justice, 1976.

Silber, Irwin (ed.). *Songs of the Civil War.* New York: Columbia University Press, 1960.

Silberer, Victor. *The Games of Roulette and Trente-et-Quarante as Played at Monte Carlo.* London: Harrison, 1910.

Silberman, Charles E. *Criminal Violence, Criminal Justice.* New York: Random House, 1978.

____. *Crisis in Black and White.* New York: Random House, 1974.

____. *The Myths of Automation.* New York: Harper & Row, 1966.

Silbey, Joel, et al. *American Electoral History: Quantitative Studies in Popular Voting Behavior.* Princeton, N.J.: Princeton University Press, 1978.

Silenzi, Fernando. *Pasquino Quattro secoli di satira romana.* Florence, Italy: Vallecchi, 1968.

Silj, Alessandro. *Mai più senza fucile! alle Origini dei NAP e delle BR.* Firenze, Italy: Vallecchi, 1977.

Silk, L. Howard, and Vogel, David. *Eithics and Profits: The Crisis of Confidence in American Business.* New York: Simon & Schuster, 1976.

Sillman, Leonard. *Here Lies Leonard Sillman.* New York:

Citadel Press, 1959.

Silva Herzog, Jesús. *Breve historia de la Revolución Mexicana.* 2 vols. Mexico City, Mex.: Fondo de Cultura Económica, 1962.

____. *Un ensayo sobre la revolución mexicana.* Mexico City, Mex.: Cuadernos Americanos, 1946.

Silva, Pietro. *Io difendo la Monarchia.* Rome: De Fonseca, 1946.

Silver, Aba. *Visions of Victory.* New York: Zionist Organization of America, 1949.

Silver, Gary (ed.). *The Dope Chronicles.* New York: Harper & Row, 1979.

Silvera, Alain. *Daniel Halévy and His Times.* Ithaca, N.Y.: Cornell University Press, 1966.

Silverman, David. *Pitcairn Island.* New York: World, 1967.

Silverman, Kenneth. *The Life and Times of Cotton Mather.* New York: Harper & Row, 1970.

Silverman, R. *Psychology.* Philadelphia: W.B. Saunders, 1971.

Silversparre, Axel. *Appendix to New Map of Colorado.* Chicago: J.M. Jones Stationery & Printing, 1882.

Silverstein, Lee. *The Defense of the Poor in Criminal Cases in American State Courts.* Chicago: American Bar Foundation, 1965.

Silvestri, Carlo. *Contro la Vendetta.* Milan, Italy: Longanesi, 1948.

____. *I reponsabili della catastrofe italiana.* Milan, Italy: CEBES, 1946.

____. *Matteotti, Mussolini e il dramma italiano.* Rome: Ruffolo, 1947.

____. *Mussolini, Graziani e l'antifascismo.* Milan, Italy: Longanesi, 1949.

____. *Turati l'ha detto.* Milan, Italy: Rizzoli, 1947.

Silvestri, Giuseppe. *Albergo agli Scalzi.* Verona, Italy: Neri Pozza, 1963.

Simanovich, Aron. *Rasputin der allmächtige Bauer.* Berlin: Hensel, 1928.

Simenon, Georges. *Maigret and the Black Sheep.* trans. Helen Thomson. New York: Harcourt Brace Jovanovich, 1976.

Simiani, Carlo. *I giustiziati fascisti dell'aprile 1945.* Milan, Italy: Omnia, 1949.

Simis, Konstantin M. *The Corrupt Society: The Secret World of Soviet Capitalism.* New York: Simon & Schuster, 1982.

Simkins, Francis Butler, and Woody, R.H. *South Carolina during Reconstruction.* Chapel Hill: University of North Carolina Press, 1932.

____, and Tatton, J.W. *The Women of the Confederacy.* Richmond, Va.: Garrett & Massey, 1936.

Simmel, Georg. *Conflict and the Web of Group Affiliations.* trans. Kurt H. Wolff and Reinhard Bendix. New York: Free Press, 1955.

____. *The Sociology of Georg Simmel.* ed. and trans. Kurt Wolff. New York: Free Press, 1950.

Simmons, Edward Henry Harriman. *The Principal Causes of the Stock Market Crisis of Nineteen Twenty-nine.* Privately Printed, 1930.

Simmons, J.L. *Marihuanna: Myths and Realities.* North Hollywood, Calif.: Brandon House, 1967.

Simmons, Jerry L. *Deviants.* Berkeley, Calif.: Glendessary Press, 1969.

Simmons, Lee. *Assignment Huntsville: Memoirs of a Texas Prison Official.* Austin: University of Texas Press, 1957.

Simmons, William J. *Men of Mark: Eminent, Progressive and Rising.* Cleveland: Rewell, 1887.

Simms, H.H. *A Decade of Sectional Controversy.* Chapel Hill: University of North Carolina Press, 1942.

Simms, William Gilmore. *Francis Marion.* New York: J.C. Derby, 1854.

____. *Nathanael Greene.* New York: Derby & Jackson, 1858.

____. *The Partisan.* New York: Lovell, Coryell, 1850.

Simon. *La Peine de mort.* Paris: Lacroix, Verboeckhoven, 1869.

Simon, Carl, and Witte, Ann. *Beating the System.* Cambridge,

Mass.: Auburn House, 1982.

Simon, David R., and Eitzen, D. Stanley. *Elite Deviance*. Boston: Allyn & Bacon, 1982.

Simon, Edith. *The Making of Frederick the Great*. Boston: Little, Brown, 1963.

Simon, F., and Weatheritt, M. *The Use of Bail and Custody*. London: H.M. Stationery Office, 1974.

Simon, H. *Sciences of the Artificial*. Cambridge, Mass.: MIT Press, 1969.

Simon, Herbert. *Administration Behavior*. New York: Free Press, 1976.

Simon, Jordan. *Die Nichtigkeit der Hexerey und Zauberkunst*. Frankfort, Ger.: J.J. Stahel, 1766.

Simon, Kate. *Fifth Avenue*. New York: Harcourt Brace Jovanovich, 1978.

_____. *London: Places and Pleasures*. London: McGibbon & Kee, 1968.

Simon, M.J. *The Law for Advertising and Marketing*. New York: W.W. Norton, 1956.

Simon, Paul. *Lovejoy, Martyr to Freedom*. St. Louis: Concordia, 1964.

Simon, Rita James. *As We Saw the Thirties*. Urbana: University of Illinois Press, 1967.

_____. *The Contemporary Women and Crime*. Rockville, Md.: National Institute of Mental Health, 1975.

_____. *The Jury System in America: A Critical Overview*. Beverly Hills, Calif.: Sage, 1975.

_____. *Women and Crime*. Lexington, Mass.: D.C. Heath, 1978.

Simon, William E. *A Time for Truth*. New York: Reader's Digest Press, 1978.

Simond, Lieutenant-Colonel Émile. *Histoire de la Troisième République*. 4 vols. Paris, H. Charles-Lavauzelle, 1913.

Simonds, William Adams. *Henry Ford and Greenfield Village*. New York: Frederick A. Stokes, 1938.

Simoni, Leonardo. *Berlin, Ambassade d'Italie*. trans. C.D. Jonquiére. Paris: Robert Laffont, 1947.

Simonin, Louis Laurent. *Le monde américain: Souvenirs de mes voyages aux Etats-Unis*. Paris: Hachette & Cie, 1877.

Simons, Henry. *Economic Policy for a Free Society*. Chicago: University of Chicago Press, 1948.

Simpson, A.W.B. *An Introduction to the History of the Land Law*. New York: Oxford University Press, 1961.

Simpson, Alan. *Puritanism in Old and New England*. Chicago: University of Chicago Press, 1955.

Simpson, Anthony. *The Literature of Police Corruption*. New York: John Jay Press, 1977.

Simpson, C.H. *Life in the Far West; or, a Detective's Thrilling Adventures Among the Indians and Outlaws of Montana*. Chicago: Rhodes & McClure, 1893.

Simpson, C. Keith. *Modern Trends in Forensic Medicine*. London: Butterworth, 1952.

Simpson, Eyler Newton. *The Ejido--Mexico's Way Out*. Chapel Hill: University of North Carolina Press, 1937.

Simpson, F.A. *Louis Napoleon and the Recovery of France*. London: Longmans, Green, 1923.

_____. *The Rise of Louis Napoleon*. London: Longmans, Green, 1909.

Simpson, Helen (ed.). *The Anatomy of Murder*. New York: Macmillan, 1934.

Simpson, Sir John Hope. *The Refugee Problem*. London: Oxford University Press, 1939.

Simpson, Keith. *Forensic Medicine*. London: Arnold, 1964.

_____. *Forty Years of Murder*. New York: Charles Scribner's Sons, 1979.

Simpson, Lesley Byrd. *Many Mexicos*. Berkeley: University of California Press, 1952.

Simpson, S.R. *Llano Estacado; or, the Plains of West Texas*. San Antonio, Texas: Naylor, 1957.

Sims, George Robert. *The Mysteries of Modern London*. London: Pearson, 1906.

Sims, Judge Orland L. *Gun-Toters I Have Known*. Austin, Texas: Encino Press, 1967.

Sims, Patsy. *The Klan*. New York: Stein & Day, 1978.

Sinan, A. *Le Vieux Nantes*. Paris: Floch, 1935.

Sinclair, Andrew. *The Available Man*. New York: Macmillan, 1965.

_____. *Era of Excess: A Social History of the Prohibition Movement*. New York: Harper & Row, 1964.

_____. *Prohibition: The Era of Excess*. Boston: Little, Brown, 1962.

Sinclair, George. *Hydrostaticks*. Edinburgh, Scot.: G. Swintown, J. Glen, T. Brown, 1672.

_____. *Satan's Invisible World Discovered*. London: J. Bailey, 1915.

Sinclair, Upton. *The Autobiography of Upton Sinclair*. New York: Harcourt, Brace & World, 1962.

_____. *The Book of Life*. Long Beach, Calif.: Published by Author, 1926.

_____. *Boston*. Pasadena, Calif.: Published by Author, 1928.

_____. *The Brass Check: A Study of American Journalism*. Pasadena, Calif.: Published by Author, 1920.

_____. *The Cup of Fury*. Great Neck, N.Y.: Channel Press, 1956.

_____. *I, Candidate for Governor and How I Got Licked*. Pasadena, Calif.: Published by Author, 1935.

_____. *The Jungle*. New York: Doubleday Page, 1906.

_____. *My Lifetime in Letters*. Columbia: University of Missouri Press, 1960.

_____. *Presidential Agent*. New York: Viking Press, 1944.

Sindler, Allan P. *Huey Long's Louisiana*. Baltimore,: Johns Hopkins, 1956.

Singer, Charles Joseph (ed.) *Studies in the History and Method of Science*. Oxford, Eng.: Clarendon Press, 1917-1921.

Singer, Isidore. *Social Justice*. New York: I. Goldmann, 1923.

Singer, J.L., and D.G. *Television, Imagination, and Agression*. Hillsdale, N.J.: Lawrence Erlbaum Associates, 1981.

Singer, Kurt (ed.). *Crime Omnibus*. London: W.H. Allen, 1961.

_____, and Sherrod, Jane. *Great Adventures in Crime*. Minneapolis, Minn.: T.S. Denison, 1962.

_____. *Mata Hari*. New York: Universal, 1967.

_____ (ed.). *My Greatest Crime Story*. London: W.H. Allen, 1956.

_____. *My Strangest Cases*. Garden City, N.Y.: Doubleday, 1958.

_____. *Spies Who Changed History*. New York: Ace-Star, 1960.

Singer, Neil M. *The Value of Adult Inmate Manpower*. Washington, D.C.: American Bar Association Commission on Correctional Facilities and Services, 1973.

Singh, Anup. *Nehru, The Rising Star of India*. New York: John Day, 1939.

Singh, Rev. J.A.L, and Zingg, Robert M. *Wolf-Children and Feral Man*. New York: Harper & Row, 1942.

Singletary, Otis A. *Negro Militia and Reconstruction*. Austin: University of Texas Press, 1957.

Sinise, Jerry. *Pink Higgins: The Reluctant Gunfighter*. Quanah, Texas: Nortex Press, 1974.

Sinistrari, Ludovico Maria. *De Daemonialitate et Incubis et Succubis*. trans. I. Liseaux. Paris: I. Liseaux, 1876.

_____. *Demoniality*. trans. Montague Summers. London: Fortune Press, 1927.

Sinkler, George. *The Racial Attitudes of American Presidents*. New York: Doubleday, 1971.

Sion, Abraham. *Prostitution and the Law*. Winchester, Mass.: Faber, 1977.

Sir Arthur Conan Doyle Centenary: 1859-1959. London: John Murray, 1959.

Siragusa, Charles. *The Trail of the Poppy*. Englewood Cliffs, N.J.: Prentice-Hall, 1966.

Sirghebo, Arcese. *Edda Ciano e il 25 luglio 1943*. Leghorn, Italy: Moderna, 1945.

Sirica, John J. *To Set the Record Straight*. London: W.W. Norton, 1979.

Siringo, Charles A. *A Cowboy Detective, an Autobiography*. Chicago: W.B. Conkey, 1912.

_____. *The History of Billy the Kid*. Santa Fe, N.M.: Published by Author, 1920.

_____. *A Lone Star Cowboy*. Sante Fe, N.M.: Published by Author, 1919.

_____. *Riata and Spurs: The Story of a Lifetime Spent in the Saddle as a Cowboy and Ranger*. Boston: Houghton Mifflin, 1927.

_____. *A Texas Cowboy, or Fifteen Years on the Hurricane Deck of A Spanish Pony*. Chicago: M. Umbdenstock, 1885.

_____. *Two Evil Isma, Pinkertonism and Anarchism*. Chicago: Published by Author, 1915.

Sitaramayza, Pattabhi. *History of the Indian National Congress*. Bombay, India: Padma, 1947.

Sites, Paul. *Lee Harvey Oswald and the American Dream*. New York: Pageant Press, 1967.

Sitwell, Sir Osbert. *A Free House! or The Artist as Craftsman, being the Writings of Walter Richard Sickert*. London: Macmillan, 1947.

_____ (ed.). *Noble Essences or Courteous Revelations: Being a Book of Characters and the Fifth and Last Volume of Left Hand, Right Hand*. London: Macmillan, 1950.

_____. *The Scarlet Tree*. London: Macmillan, 1946.

Sitwell, Sacheverell. *Poltergeists*. London: Faber & Faber, 1940.

_____. *Roumanian Journey*. London: B.T. Batsford, 1938.

Size, Mary. *Prison I Have Known*. London: George Allen & Unwin, 1957.

Sjorquist, Captain Arthur W. *Los Angeles Police Department, 1869-1984*. Los Angeles: LAPD Revolver and Athletic Club, 1984.

Sjowal, Maj. and Wahloo, Per. *Roseanna*. New York: Random House, 1967.

Skaggs, Jimmy M. *The Cattle-Training Industry*. Lawrence: University Press of Kansas, 1973.

Skelton, Charles L. *Riding the Pony Express West*. New York: Macmillan, 1937.

Skendi, Stavro (ed.). *Albania*. New York: Mid-European Studies Center, 1956.

_____. *The Albanian National Awakening, 1878-1912*. Princeton, N.J.: Princeton University Press, 1967.

Skene, Anthony. *The Ripper Returns*. Manchester, Eng.: Pemberton, 1948.

Sketch of the Life and Adventures of Guy C.Clark. Ithaca, N.Y.: n.p., 1832.

Sketch of the Life of Miss Ellen Jewett. New York: n.p.,n.d.

Sketch of the Trial of Mary Cole. New Brunswick, N.J.: J.W. Kirn, 1812.

Sketches of the Life and a Narrative of the Trial of James Hamilton. Albany, N.Y.: n.p., 1818.

Skinner, B.F. *Beyond Freedom and Dignity*. New York: Alfred A. Knopf, 1971.

_____. *Science and Human Behavior*. New York: Macmillan, 1953.

Skinner, Cornelia Otis. *Elegant Wits and Grand Horizontals*. Boston: Houghton Mifflin, 1962.

Skinner, Emory Fiske. *Reminiscences*. Chicago: Vestal Printing, 1908.

Skinner, Otis. *The Mad Folk of the Theater*. New York: Bobbs-Merrill, 1928.

Skinnider, Margaret. *Doing My Bit For Ireland*. New York: Century, 1917.

Sklansky, Gloria J., and Algazi, Linda P. *Helping Women*. Groupwork Today, 1981.

Sklar, Kathryn Kish. *Catharine Beecher: A Study in American Domesticity*. New Haven, Conn.: Yale University Press, 1973.

Skogan, W.G. *Issues in the Measurement of Victimization*. Washington, D.C.: Bureau of Justice Statistics, 1981.

_____ (ed.). *Sample Surveys of the Victims of Crime*. New York: Ballinger, 1976.

_____. *Victimization Surveys and Criminal Justice Planning*. Washington, D.C.: National Institute of Law Enforcement and Criminal Justice, 1978.

Skolnick, Jerome H., Forst, Martin L., and Scheiber, Jane L. (eds.). *Crime and Justice in America*. Del Mar, Calif.: Publishers, 1977.

_____, and Currie, Elliot (eds.). *Crisis in American Institutions*. Boston: Little, Brown, 1982.

_____. *House of Cards: Legalization and Control of Casino Gambling*. Boston: Little, Brown, 1978.

_____. *Justice Without Trial*. New York: John Wiley and Sons, 1966.

_____. *The Police and the Urban Ghetto*. Chicago: American Bar Foundation, 1968.

_____. *The Politics of Protest*. New York: Ballantine Books, 1969.

Skorzeny, Otto. *Skorzeny's Special Missions*. London: Robert Hale, 1957.

Skousen, Mark. *Mark Skousen's Complete Guide to Financial Privacy*. Alexander, Va.: Alexandria House, 1979.

Skrine, Francis H. *Expansion of Russia, 1815-1900*. Cambridge: Cambridge University Press, 1904.

Slade, Daniel Denison. *Major Daniel Denison*. Boston: n.p., 1869.

Sladek, John. *Black Aura*. London: Jonathan Cape, 1974.

Slane, Baron M. de. *Les Prolegomenes d'Ibn Khaldun*. Paris: Imprimerie Imperiale, 1863.

Slate, Sam, and Cook, Joe. *It Sounds Impossible*. New York: Macmillan, 1965.

Slater, M. *Trial of Jomo Kenyatta*. London: Secker & Warburg, 1955.

Slater, Philip E. *The Glory of Hera*. Boston: Beacon Press, 1868.

Slatin, Rudolph C. *Fire and Sword in the Sudan*. New York: Edward Arnold, 1896.

Sleeman, W.H. *A Journey Through the Kingdom of Oude*. London: Richard Bentley, 1858.

_____. *Ramaseeana, or A Vocabulary of the Peculiar Language Use by the Thugs*. Calcutta, India: G.H. Huttmann, Military Orphan Press, 1836.

_____. *Rambles and Recollections*. London: Hatchard, 1884.

_____. *Report on the Budhuk Dacoits*. Calcutta, India: J.C. Sheriff, 1949.

_____. *Report on the Depredations Committed by the Thug Gangs of Upper and Central India*. Calcutta, India: G.H. Huttmann, Bengal Military Orphan Press, 1840.

_____. *The Thugs or Pansigars of India, Comprising a History of the Rise and Progress of That Extraordinary Fraternity of Assassins*. Philadelphia: Carey & Hart, 1839.

Slesinger, Tess. *The Unpossessed*. New York: Avon, 1934.

Slesser, Sir Henry. *Judgement Reserved*. London: Hutchinson, 1941.

Slim, Iceberg. *Pimp: The Story of My Life*. Los Angeles: Holloway House, 1969.

Slim, Viscount Sir William. *Defeat into Victory*. New York: David MacKay, 1961.

Slingerland, Peter van. *Something Terrible Has Happened: The Account of the Sensational Thalia Massie Affair which Burst from Prewar Hawaii to Incense the Nation*. New York: Harper & Row, 1966.

Sliwa, Curtis, and Schwartz, Murray. *Streetsmart: The Guardian Angel Guide to Safe Living*. Reading, Mass.: Addison-Wesley, 1982.

Sloan, Alfred P. *My Years with General Motors*. Garden City, N.Y.: Doubleday, 1963.

Sloan, Irving J. *Our Violent Past: An American Chronicle*. New York: Random House, 1970.

_____. *Youth and the Law*. Dobbs Ferry, N.Y.: Ocean, 1970.

Sloan, Richard E. (ed.). *History of Arizona*. Phoenix, Ariz.: Record, 1930.

_____. *Memoires of an Arizona Judge*. Stanford, Calif.: Stanford University Press, 1932.

Sloan, Stephen. *The Anatomy of Non-Territorial Terrorism.* Gaithersburg, Md.: Bureau of Operations and Research, International Association of Chiefs of Police, 1978.
_____. *Simulating Terrorism.* Norman: University of Oklahoma Press, 1981.
_____. *A Study in Political Violence: The Indonesian Experience.* Chicago: Rand McNally, 1971.
Sloane, Eugene A. *The Complete Book of Locks, Keys, Burglar and Smoke Alarms, and Other Devices.* New York: William Morrow, 1977.
Sloane, Howard N. and Lucille L. *A Pictorial History of American Mining.* New York: Crown, 1970.
Slobin, D. *Psycholinguistics.* New York: Scott, Foresman, 1971.
Slocombe, George. *The Dangerous Sea.* London: Hutchinson, 1938.
_____. *A Mirror to Geneva.* London: Jonathan Cape, 1937.
_____. *The Tumult and the Shouting.* London: William Heinemann, 1936.
Slocum, Victor. *Captain Joshua Slocum.* New York: Sheridan House, 1950.
Slonim, Marc. *The Epic of Russian Literature.* New York: Oxford University Press, 1964.
Slosson, Preston William. *The Great Crusade and After, 1914-1928.* New York: Macmillan, 1930.
Slotkin, Richard. *Regeneration Through Violence.* Middletown, Conn.: Wesleyan University Press, 1974.
Slovenko, Ralph. *Sexual Behavior and the Law.* Springfield, Ill.: Charles C. Thomas, 1965.
Small, Floyd B. *Autobiography of a Pioneer.* Seattle, Wash.: Published by Author, 1916.
Small, Joe Austell (ed.). *The Best of True West.* New York: Julian Messner, 1964.
Small, Kathleen Edwards, and Smith, J. Larry. *History of Tulare County, California.* Chicago: S.J. Clarke, 1926.
Small, William. *Political Power and the Press.* New York: Hastings House, 1972.
Smalley, George W. *Anglo-American Memories.* New York: G.P. Putnam's Sons, 1911.
Smallwood, Charles A. *The White Front Cars of San Francisco.* Glendale, Calif.: Interurbans, 1978.
Smallwood, William Martin. *Natural History and the American Mind.* New York: Columbia University Press, 1941.
Smart, Carol. *Women, Crime and Criminology.* London: RKP, 1977.
Smart, Charles Allen. *Viva Juarez!* London: Eyre & Spottiswoode, 1964.
Smart, William. *Economic Annals of the Nineteenth Century.* New York: Augustus M. Kelley, 1964.
Smedley, Agnes. *Daughters of Earth.* New York: Feminist Press, 1973.
Smelser, Neil J., and Lipset S.M. (eds.). *Social Structure and Mobility in Economic Development.* Chicago: Aldine, 1966.
Smigel, Erwin O., and Ross, H. Laurence (eds.). *Crimes Against Bureaucracy.* New York: Van Nostrand Reinhold, 1970.
_____. *The Wall Street Lawyer: Professional Organization Man?* New York: Free Press of Glencoe, 1964.
Smith, A. *Theory of Moral Sentiments.* Indianapolis, Ind.: Liberty Classics, 1976.
Smith, A.C.H. *Paper Voices: The Popular Press and Social Change, 1935-1965.* Totowa, N.J.: Rowman & Littlefield, 1975.
Smith, A.E. *Colonists in Bondage.* Chapel Hill: University of North Carolina Press, 1947.
Smith, A.E.W. *The Drug Users: The Psychopharmacology of Turning on.* Wheaton, Ill.: Harold Shaw, 1969.
Smith, A. Hassell. *County and Court: Government and Politics in Norfolk.* Oxford, Eng.: Clarendon Press, 1974.
Smith, A. Robert. *An American Rape.* Washington, D.C.: New Republic, 1977.
Smith, Adam. *An Inquiry into the Nature and Causes of the Wealth of Nations.* New York: Modern Library, 1937.

Smith, Adam. *Supermoney.* New York: Random House, 1972.
Smith, Alan G.R. *The Government of Elizabethan England.* New York: W.W. Norton, 1967.
Smith, Captain Alexander. *History of the Highwaymen.* London: George Routledge & Sons, 1926.
Smith, Alexander B., and Pollack, Harriet. *Crime and Justice in a Mass Society.* Waltham, Mass.: Xerox, 1972.
Smith, Alfred (ed.). *Communication and Culture.* New York: Holt, Rinehart & Winston, 1966.
Smith, Alfred E. *Up to Now: An Autobiography.* New York: Viking Press, 1929.
Smith, Alson Jesse. *Brother Van, a Biography of the Rev. William Wesley Van Orsdel.* New York: Abingdon-Cokesbury, 1948.
_____. *Syndicate City: The Chicago Crime Cartel and What to Do about It.* Chicago: Henry Regnery, 1954.
Smith, Ann D. *Women in Prison.* Chicago: Quandrangle, 1962.
Smith, Anthony. *The Newspaper An International History.* London: Thames & Hudson, 1979.
_____. *Subsidies and the Press in Europe.* London: Political and Economic Planning, 1976.
Smith, Arthur. *Lord Goddard.* London: Weidenfeld and Nicolson, 1959.
Smith, Arthur D. Howden. *Commodore Vanderbilt: An Epic of American Achievement.* New York: Robert M. McBride, 1927.
_____. *John Jacob Astor: Landlord of New York.* Philadelphia: J.B. Lippincott, 1929.
_____. *Mr. House of Texas.* New York: Funk & Wagnalls, 1940.
_____. *Old Fuss and Feathers.* New York: Greystone, 1937.
Smith, Arthur H. *China and America Today.* New York: Revell, 1907.
Smith, Bill. *A Hog Story: From the Aftermire of the Kennedy Assassination.* Washington, D.C.: L'Avant Garde, 1968.
Smith, Bradley F. *Adolf Hitler: His Family, Childhood and Youth.* Stanford, Calif.: Stanford University Press, 1967.
_____. *Reaching Judgment at Nuremberg.* New York: Meridian, 1979.
_____. *The Shadow Warriors.* New York: Basic Books, 1983.
Smith, Bruce. *Police Systems in the U.S.* New York: Harper, 1960.
_____. *The State Police.* Montclair, N.J.: Patterson Smith, 1969.
Smith, C. Alphonso. *Edgar Allan Poe.* Indianapolis, Ind.: Bobbs-Merrill, 1921.
_____. *O. Henry Biography.* Garden City, N.Y.: Doubleday, Page, 1916.
Smith, Cecil. *Musical Comedy in America.* New York: Theatre Arts Books, 1950.
Smith, Chard Powers. *Yankees and God.* New York: Hermitage House, 1954.
Smith, Charles A. *A Comprehensive History of Minnehaha County, South Dakota.* Mitchell, S.D.: Educator Supply, 1949.
Smith, Charles Edward. *Papal Enforcement of Some Medieval Marriage Laws.* Baton Rouge: Louisiana State University, 1940.
Smith, Charles P. *James Wilson.* Chapel Hill: University of North Carolina Press, 1956.
Smith, Colin. *Carlos: Portrait of a Terrorist.* New York: Holt, Rinehart & Winston, 1977.
Smith, Cornelius C., Jr. *Emilio Kosterlitzky.* Glendale, Calif.: Arthur H. Clarke, 1970.
_____. *William Sanders Oury: History Maker of the Southwest.* Tucson: University of Arizona Press, 1968.
Smith, D.B. *Two Years in the Slave-Pen of Iowa.* Kansas City: H.N. Farey, 1885.
Smith, David E. (ed.). *Amphetamine Use, Misuse, and Abuse.* Boston: G.K. Hall, 1979.
Smith, Dennis Mack. *Garibaldi.* New York: Alfred A. Knopf, 1956.
_____. *A History of Sicily: Modern Sicily (after 1713).* London: Chatto & Windus, 1968.

Smith, Don. *Peculiarities of the Presidents: Strange Facts Not Usually Found in History*. Van Wert, Ohio: Wilkinson Press, 1938.

Smith, Duane A. *Rocky Mountain Mining Camps*. Bloomington: Indiana University Press, 1967.

Smith, Dwight C., Jr. *The Mafia Mystique*. New York: Basic Books, 1975.

Smith, E.B. *Magnificent Missourian: The Life of Thomas Hart Benton*. Philadelphia: J.B. Lippincott, 1958.

Smith, E.D. *The Battles for Cassino*. London: Ian Allen, 1975.

Smith, E.W. *Baker Street and Beyond: A Sherlockian Gazetteer*. New York: Pamphlet House, 1940.

_____. *The Incunabular Sherlock Holmes*. New York: Morrison, 1957.

_____. *Profile by Gaslight: An Irregular Reader about the Private Life of Sherlock Holmes*. New York: Simon & Schuster, 1944.

Smith, Edgar. *Getting Out*. New York: Coward, McCann, Geoghegan, 1972.

Smith, Edward Henry. *Famous American Poison Mysteries*. New York: Dial Press, 1927.

_____. *Mysteries of the Missing*. New York: Dial Press, 1927.

_____. *You Can Escape*. New York: Macmillan, 1929.

Smith, Elbert B. *The Death of Slavery: The United States 1837-65*. Chicago: University of Chicago Press, 1967.

Smith, Elizabeth Oakes. *The Newsboy*. New York: J.C. Derby, 1854.

Smith, Frank Meriweather (ed.). *San Francisco Vigilance Committee of '56*. San Francisco: Barry, Baird, 1883.

Smith, G. *The Treaty of Washington, 1871*. Ithaca, N.Y.: Cornell University Press, 1941.

Smith, Gene. *High Crimes and Misdemeanors: The Impeachment and Trial of Andrew Jackson*. New York: William Morrow, 1977.

_____, and Smith, Jayne Barry. *The National Police Gazette*. New York: Simon & Schuster, 1972.

_____. *When the Cheering Stopped*. New York: William Morrow, 1964.

Smith, Gibbs M. *Joe Hill*. Salt Lake City: University of Utah Press, 1969.

Smith, Geoffrey S. *To Save a Nation*. New York: Basic Books, 1973.

Smith, George H. *Martin Luther King, Jr.: Drum Major for Justice*. New York: Lancer Books, n.d.

Smith, George Winston, and Judah, Charles. *Life in the North During the Civil War*. Albuquerque: University of New Mexico Press, 1966.

Smith, Gerald L.K. *The Mysterious and Unpublicized Facts Behind the Assassination of John F. Kennedy*. Los Angeles: Christian Nationalist Crusade, 1965.

Smith, Grant H. *The History of the Comstock Lode 1850-1920*. Reno: University of Nevada Bulletin, 1943.

Smith, H. *Sensitivity to People*. New York: McGraw-Hill, 1966.

Smith, H. Allen. *The Life and Legend of Gene Fowler*. New York: William Morrow, 1977.

Smith, Harold S. *I Want to Quit Winners*. Englewood Cliffs, N.J.: Prentice-Hall, 1961.

Smith, Harvey H. *Shelter Bay: Tales of the Quebec North Shore*. Toronto, Ontario, Can.: McClelland & Stewart, 1964.

Smith, Helena Huntington. *The War on Powder River*. New York: McGraw-Hill, 1966.

Smith, Sir Henry. *From Constable to Commissioner: The Story of Sixty Years, Most of Them Misspent*. London: Chatto & Windus, 1910.

Smith, Henry Justin. *Chicago's Great Century, 1833-1933*. Chicago: Consolidated, 1933.

_____. *Deadlines and Josslyn*. Chicago: Sterling North, 1934.

Smith, Henry Nash, and Gibson, William M. (eds.). *Mark Twain-Howells Letters: The Correspondence of Samuel L. Clemens and William D. Howells, 1872-1910*. Cambridge, Mass.:

Belknap Press, 1960.

_____. *Virgin Land*. Cambridge, Mass.: Harvard University Press, 1950.

Smith, Homer W. *Man and His Gods*. Boston: Little, Brown, 1952.

Smith, Horace. *Crooks of the Waldorf*. New York: Macaulay, 1929.

Smith, J. Barnett. *The Life and Speeches of the Right Hon. John Bright, M.P.* 2 vols. London: Hodder & Stoughton, 1881.

Smith, J.C., and Hogan, B. *Criminal Law*. London: Butterworth, 1973.

Smith, James Morton. *Freedom's Fetters: The Alien and Sedition Laws and American Civil Liberties*. Ithaca, N.Y.: Cornell University Press, 1956.

Smith, Jedediah S. *The Southwestern Expedition of Jedediah S. Smith: His Personal Account of the Journey to California, 1826-1827*. Glendale, Calif.: Arthur H. Clark, 1977.

Smith, John. *The Generall Historie of Virginia, New-England, and the Summer Isles*. Ann Arbor, Mich.: University Microfilms, 1966.

Smith, John Chabot. *Alger Hiss: The True Story*. New York: Holt, Rinehart & Winston, 1976.

Smith, John Talbot. *The Catholic Church in New York: A History of the New York Diocese from Its Establishment in 1808 to the Present Time*. New York: Hall & Locke, 1905.

Smith, Joseph H. *Appeals to the Privy Council from the American Plantations*. New York: Columbia University Press, 1950.

Smith, Joseph H. (ed.). *Colonial Justice in Western Massachusetts*. Cambridge, Mass.: Harvard University Press, 1961.

Smith, Justin Harvey. *Our Struggle for the Fourteenth Colony*. 2 vols. New York: G.P. Putnam's Sons, 1907.

_____. *The War With Mexico*. 2 vols. New York: Macmillan, 1919.

Smith, Laurence Dwight. *Counterfeiting, Crime Against the People*. New York: W.W. Norton, 1944.

Smith, Malcolm E. *The Real Marijuana Danger*. Smithtown, N.Y.: Suffolk House, 1981.

Smith, Margaret Bayard. *The First Forty Years of Washington Society*. New York: Charles Scribner's Sons, 1906.

Smith, Matthew Hale. *Sunshine and Shadow in New York*. Hartford, Conn.: J.B. Burr, 1868.

Smith, Merriman, et al. *Four Days*. New York: United Press International & American Heritage, 1964.

Smith, Mortimer. *William Jay Gaynor: Mayor of New York*. Chicago: Henry Regnery, 1951.

Smith, Page. *John Adams*. New York: Doubleday, 1962.

Smith, Pauline, and Blake, Brian. *Portrait of a Young Girl*. London: Hutchinson, 1965.

Smith, Pauline C. *The End of the Line*. Cranbury, N.J.: A.S. Barnes, 1970.

Smith, Preserved. *The Age of Reformation*. New York: Henry Holt, 1920.

Smith, R.H. *Justice and the Poor*. New York: Carnegie Foundation, 1919.

Smith, R. Harris. *OSS: The Secret History of America's First Central Intelligence Agency*. Berkeley: University of California Press, 1972.

Smith, Ralph Lee. *The Tarnished Badge*. New York: Thomas Y. Crowell, 1965.

Smith, Randolph Wellford. *Benighted Mexico*. New York: John Lane, 1916.

_____. *The Sober World*. Boston: Marshall Jones, 1919.

Smith, Richard Furnald. *Prelude to Science*. New York: Charles Scribner's Sons, 1975.

Smith, Richard Norton. *Thomas E. Dewey and His Times*. New York: Simon & Schuster, 1982.

_____. *An Uncommon Man: The Triumph of Herbert Hoover*. New York: Simon & Schuster, 1984.

Smith, Rixey, and Beasley, Norman. *Carter Glass*. New York: Longmans, Green, 1939.

Smith, Robert Ellis. *Privacy: How to Protect What's Left of It.* Garden City, N.Y.: Anchor Press/Doubleday, 1979.

Smith, Robert R. *Triumph in the Philippines.* Washington, D.C.: U.S. Government Printing Office, 1963.

Smith, Samuel D. *The Negro in Congress, 1870-1901.* Chapel Hill: University of North Carolina Press, 1940.

Smith, Mrs. Samuel Harrison. *The First Forty Years of Washington Society.* New York: Charles Scribner's Sons, 1906.

Smith, Sarah Tappan. *History of the Establishment and Progress of the Christian Religion in the Islands of the South Sea.* Boston: Tappan & Dennet, 1841.

Smith, Sir Sidney. *Mostly Murder.* New York: David McKay, 1959.

Smith, Soloman F. *Theatrical Journey-Work and Anecdotal Recollections.* Philadelphia: T.B. Peterson, 1854.

_____. *Theatrical Management in the West and Southwest for Thirty Years.* New York: n.p., 1868.

Smith, Stephen. *The City That Was.* New York: Frank Allaben, 1911.

Smith, Susy. *Ghosts Around the House.* New York: World, 1970.

Smith, Sydney. *The Works of Rev. Sydney Smith.* London: Longman, 1869.

Smith, Sydney. *Mostly Murder.* London: Harrap, 1959.

-----, and Cook, W.G.H. (eds.). *Taylor's Principles and Practices of Medical Jurisprudence.* London: Churchill, 1928.

Smith, T. Marshall. *Legends of the War of Independence and of the Earlier Settlements in the West.* Louisville, Ky: J.F. Brenan, 1855.

Smith, T.V. *Live Without Fear.* New York: New American Library, 1956.

_____. *A Non-Existent Man.* Austin: University of Texas Press, 1962.

Smith, Tevis Clyde, Jr. *From the Memories of Men.* Brownwood, Texas: Published by Author, 1954.

_____. *Frontier's Generation.* Brownwood, Texas: Published by Author, 1931.

Smith, Thomas. *Vitae Eruditissimorum ac Illustrium Vivorum.* London: David Mortier, 1707.

Smith, Thomas E. *Political Parties and Their Places of Meeting in New York City.* New York: Published by Author, 1893.

Smith, Thomas E.V. *The City of New York in the Year of Washington's Inauguration.* Riverside, Conn.: Chatham Press, 1972.

Smith, Vincent A. *The Oxford History of India.* Oxford, Eng.: Oxford University Press, 1920.

_____. *The Oxford Student's History of India.* New York: Oxford University Press, 1951.

Smith, W.L.J. *The Life and Times of Lewis Cass.* New York: Derby & Jackson, 1856.

Smith, W. Eugene and Aileen. *Minamata.* New York: Holt, Rinehart & Winston, 1975.

Smith, W. Lynn, and Kling, Arthur (eds.). *Issues in Brain/Behavior Control.* New York: Spectrum, 1976.

Smith, W. Robertson. *Kinship and Marriage in Early Arabia.* Cambridge, Eng.: Cambridge University Press, 1885.

Smith, Waddell F. (ed.). *The Story of the Pony Express.* San Francisco: Hesperian House, 1960.

Smith, Walker C. *The Everett Massacre.* Chicago: I.W.W., 1917.

Smith, Wallace. *Garden of the Sun.* Los Angeles: Lymanhouse, 1939.

_____. *Prodigal Sons: The Adventures of Christopher Evans and John Sontag.* Boston: Christopher, 1951.

Smith, Wallace. *Oregon Sketches.* New York: G.P. Putnam's Sons, 1925.

Smith, Wilfred Cantwell. *Islam in Modern History.* Princeton, N.J.: Princeton University Press, 1957.

_____. *Modern Islam in India.* London: Victor Gollancz, 1947.

Smith, William Fielding. *Diamond Six.* Garden City, N.Y.: Doubleday, 1958.

Smith, Zay N., and Zekman, Pamela. *The Mirage.* New York: Random House, 1980.

Smith-Hughes, Jack. *Eight Studies in Justice.* London: Cassell, 1953.

_____. *Unfair Comment Upon Some Victorian Murder Trials.* London: Cassell, 1951.

_____. *Nine Verdicts on Violence.* London: Cassell, 1956.

_____. *Six Ventures in Villainy.* London: Cassell, 1956.

Smithson, Annie M.P. *Myself-and Others.* Dublin, Ire.: Talbot, 1944.

Smithwick, Noah. *The Evolution of a State.* Austin, Texas: Gammel Book, 1900.

Smoot, R.M. *The Unwritten History of the Assassination of Abraham Lincoln.* Baltimore: John Murphy, 1904.

Smythe, William E. *The Conquest of Arid America...* New York: Macmillan, 1905.

Snares of New York, or Tricks and Traps at the Great Metropolis, Being a Complete, Vivid and Truthful Exposure of the Swindles, Humbugs and Pitfalls of the Great City. New York: n.p., 1879.

Snelgrave, Captain William. *A New Account of Some Parts of Guinea, And the Slave Trade.* Lanham, Md.: Biblio Distribution, 1971.

Snell, John L. *Illusion and Necessity: The Diplomacy of Global War, 1939-45.* Boston: Houghton Mifflin, 1963.

_____ (ed.). *The Meaning of Yalta: Big Three Diplomacy and the New Balance of Power.* Baton Rouge: Louisiana State University Press, 1956.

_____. *Wartime Origins of the East-West Dilemma over Germany.* New Orleans, La.: Hauser Press, 1959.

Snell, Joseph W. *Painted Ladies of the Cowtown Frontier.* Kansas City: Kansas City Posse of Westerners, 1965.

Snell, Otto. *Hexenprozesse und Geistesstörung.* Munich: J.F. Lehmann, 1891.

Snibbe, John, and Homer. *The Urban Policeman in Transition.* Springfield, Ill.: Charles C. Thomas, 1973.

Snorre, Sturlason. *The Heimskringla: A History of the Norse Kings.* New York: Norroena, 1907-1911.

Snow, Edgar. *Far Eastern Front.* New York: Smith & Haas, 1933.

_____. *Random Notes on Red China, 1936-1945.* Cambridge, Mass.: Harvard University Press, 1957.

_____. *Red Star over China.* New York: Random House, 1938.

Snow, Edward Rowe. *Great Gales and Dire Disasters.* New York: Dodd, Mead, 1952.

_____. *Mysteries and Adventures Along the Atlantic Coast.* New York: Dodd, Mead, 1948.

_____. *Mysterious Tales of the New England Coast.* New York: Dodd, Mead, 1961.

_____. *Piracy, Mutiny and Murders.* New York: Dodd, Mead, 1959.

_____. *True Tales and Curious Legends.* New York: Dodd, Mead, 1969.

_____. *Unsolved Mysteries of Sea and Shore.* New York: Dodd, Mead, 1963.

Snow, Peter, and Phillips, David. *Leila's Hijack War.* London: Pan, 1965.

Snyder, C.R. *Alcohol and the Jews.* New York: Free Press, 1958.

Snyder, LeMoyne. *Homicide Investigation: Practical Information for Coroners, Police Officers, and Other Investigators.* Springfield, Ill.: Charles .C. Thomas, 1973.

Snyder, Louis (ed.). *The Dreyfus Case: A Documentary History.* New Brunswick, N.J.: Rutgers University Press, 1973.

Snyder, Louis L., and Morris, Richard B. (eds.). *They Saw it Happen.* Harrisburg, Pa.: Stackpole Books, 1951.

_____, and Morris, Richard B. (eds.). *A Treasury of Great Reporting.* New York: Simon & Schuster, 1949.

Sobel, Lester A. *Corruption in Business.* New York: Facts on File, 1977.

_____. *Pornography, Obscenity & the Law.* New York: Facts on File, 1979.

Sobel, Robert. *The Age of Giant Corporations.* Westport, Conn.:

Greenwood Press, 1972.

_____. *The Big Board - A History of the New York Stock Market.* New York: Free Press, Macmillan, 1965.

_____. *The Great Bull Market - Wall Street in the 1920's.* New York: W.W. Norton, 1968.

_____. *The Manipulators.* Garden City, N.Y.: Anchor Press/Doubleday, 1976.

_____. *Panic on Wall Street.* New York: Macmillan, 1972.

Sobell, Morton. *On Doing Time.* New York: Bantam, 1976.

Sobieski, John. *The Life-Story and Personal Reminiscences of Col. John Sobieski.* Shelbyville, Ill.: J.L. Douthit & Son, 1900.

Sobol, Louis. *Along the Broadway Beat.* New York: Avon, 1951.

_____. *The Longest Street.* New York: Crown, 1968.

Soboul, Albert. *The French Revolution, 1787-1799.* trans. Alan Forrest and Colin Jones. New York: Random House, 1974.

The Social Evil in New York City, A Study of Law Enforcement by the Research Committee of the Committee of Fourteen. New York: A.H. Kellogg, 1910.

The Social Evil, With Special Reference to Conditions Existing in the City of New York. A Report Prepared under the Direction of the Committee of Fifteen. New York: G.P. Putnam's Sons, 1912.

Socialist Union. *Twentieth Century Socialism.* Baltimore: Penguin Books, 1956.

Society of Friends. Conference on Crime and the Treatment of Offenders. *What Do the Churches Say on Capital Punishment?* Philadelphia: Friends World Committee, 1961.

A Socio-Economic Profile of Puerto Rican New Yorkers. New York: U.S. Department of Labor, Bureau of Labor Statistics, 1975.

Soderman, Harry, and O'Connell, J.J. *Modern Criminal Investigation.* New York: Funk & Wagnalls, 1952.

_____. *Policeman's Lot.* New York: Funk & Wagnalls, 1956.

Sogoro Tanaka. *Tenno no kenkyu.* Tokyo: Kawabe Shobo, 1951.

Sokolow, Nahum. *History of Zionism, 160-1918.* 2 vols. London: Longmans & Greene, 1919.

Sold to Satan, Holmes-A poor wife's sad story, not a mere rehash, but something new never before published. A living victim. Philadelphia: Old Franklin, 1896.

Soldan, Wilhelm Gottlieb. *Geschichte der Hexenprozesse aus der Quellen dargestelt.* Munich: G. Muller, 1912.

Soleri, Marcello. *Memorie.* Turin, Italy: Einaudi, 1949.

Sollid, Roberta Beed. *Calamity Jane, a Study in Historical Criticism.* Helena, Mont.: Western Press, 1958.

Sollis, Roberta Beed. *Calamity Jane: A Study in Historical Criticism.* Helena, Mont.: Western Press, 1958.

Solomon, Barbara Miller. *Ancestors and Immigrants: A Changing New England Tradition.* Cambridge, Mass.: Harvard University Press, 1956.

Solomon, David (ed.). *LSD: The Consciousness Expanding Drug.* New York: G.D. Putnam's Sons, 1964.

_____. *The Marihuana Papers.* New York: Bobbs-Merrill, 1966.

Solomon, Ezra, and Bilbija, Zarko G. *Metropolitan Chicago: An Economic Analysis.* Glencoe, Ill.: Free Press, 1959.

Solomon, G.A. *Lenin i evo semya.* Paris: Travailleurs Intellectuels, 1931.

Solomon, George. *Among the Red Autocrats.* New York: Arno C. Gaebelein, 1935.

Solomon, Peter H. Jr. *Soviet Criminologists and Criminal Policy.* New York: Columbia, 1978.

Solov'ev, sergei Mikhailovich. *History of Russia.* trans. Hugh F. Graham. Gulf Breeze, Fla.: Acedemic International, 1976.

Soloveytchik, George. *Potemkin: A Picture of Catherine's Russia.* New York: W.W. Norton, 1947.

Solso, R. (ed.). *Theories in Cognitive Psychology.* Potomac, Md.: Lawrence Erbaum Associates, 1974.

Solzhenitsyn, Alexander. *The Gulag Archipelago.* New York: Harper & Row, 1973.

Soman, Alfred (ed.). *The Massacre of St. Bartholomew: Reappraisals and Documents.* The Hague, Neth.: Nijhoff, 1974.

Sombart, Werner. *A New Social Philosophy.* Princeton, N.J.: Princeton University Press, 1937.

Some Circumstances in Consequence of the French Settling Colonies on the Mississippi. London: n.p., 1720.

Some Particulars of the Life of Thomas W. Daniels, Alias Danial H. Thomas. Boston: William Chamberlain, 1819.

Somerset, Susan M. *Impressions of a Tenderfoot.* London: John Murray, 1890.

Somerville, Charles. *The Master Rogue.* Philadelphia: J.B. Lippincott, 1935.

Sommer, Robert. *The End of Imprisonment.* New York: Oxford University Press, 1976.

Sommerfeldt, Martin H. *Ich war dabei.* Darmstadt, Ger.: Drei Quellen, 1949.

Sommerville, John. *The Communist Trials and the American Tradition.* New York: Cameron Associates, 1956.

Sondern, Frederic, Jr. *Brotherhood of Evil: The Mafia.* New York: Farrar, Straus & Cudahy, 1959.

Sonkin, Daniel Jay, and Durphy, Michael. *Learning How to Live Without Violence: A Handbook for Men.* San Francisco: Volcano Press, 1982.

Sonney, Louis S. *The American Outlaw.* n.p, n.d.

Sonnichsen, Charles Leland. *Alias Billy the Kid.* Albuquerque: University of New Mexico Press, 1955.

_____. *Billy King's Tombstone: The Private Life of an Arizona Boom Town.* Caldwell, Idaho: Caxton Printers, 1942.

_____. *Cowboys and Cattle Kings.* Norman: University of Oklahoma Press, 1950.

_____. *The Grave of John Wesley Hardin.* College Station: Texas A & M University Press, 1979.

_____. *I'll Die Before I'll Run.* New York: Harper & Brothers, 1951.

_____. *Outlaw: Bill Mitchell Alias Baldy Russell.* Denver: Sage Books, 1965.

_____. *Pass of the North.* El Paso: Texas Western Press, 1968.

_____. *The Story of Roy Bean, Law West of the Pecos.* New York: Macmillan, 1943.

_____. *Ten Texas Feuds.* Albuquerque: University of New Mexico Press, 1951.

_____. *Tularosa.* New York: Devin-Adair, 1960.

Sontag, Raymond J., and James S. Beddie (eds.). *Nazi-Soviet Relations, 1939-1941.* Washington, D.C.: State Department, 1948.

Sopher, Sharon. *Up From the Walking Dead.* New York: Doubleday, 1978.

Soranus. *Gynecology.* trans. O.W. Temkin. Baltimore: John Hopkins Press, 1956.

Sorel, Georges. *Reflections on Violence.* Glencoe, Ill.: Free Press, 1950.

_____. *The Kennedy Legacy.* New York: New American Library, 1970.

Sorenson, Alfred R. *Early History of Omaha; or, Walks and Talks Among the Old Settlers.* Omaha, Neb.: Daily Bee, 1876.

_____. *Hands Up! or The History of a Crime.* Omaha, Neb.: Barkalow Brothers, 1877.

_____. *The Story of Omaha from the Pioneer Days to the Present Time.* Omaha, Neb.: National, 1923.

Sorenson, Charles E. *My Forty Years with Ford.* New York: W.W. Norton, 1956.

Sorenson, Theodore C. *Kennedy.* New York: Harper, 1965.

Sorokin, Pitirim A. *The American Sex Revolution.* Boston: Porter Sargent, 1956.

_____. *Leaves from a Russian Diary.* New York: E.P. Dutton, 1924.

_____. *Social and Cultural Dynamics.* New York: American, 1937.

_____, Zimmerman, Carle C., and Galpin, Charles J. *A Systematic Source Book in Rural Sociology.* Minneapolis: University of Minnesota Press, 1930.

Sorrentino, Joseph N. *The Concrete Cradle.* Los Angeles: Wollstonecraft, 1975.

Sotelo Inclan, Jesús. *Raiz y razón de Zapata: Anenecuilco Investigacion Histórica.* Mexico City: n.p., 1943.

Soule, Frank, and Gilran, John H, and Nisbet, James. *The Annals of San Francisco.* New York: D. Appleton, 1855.

Soule, George H. *The Future of Liberty.* New York: Macmillan, 1936.

_____. *Prosperity Decade.* New York: Rinehart, 1947.

_____. *The Stength of Nations.* New York: Macmillan, 1942.

Soulé, Gihon, John H., and Misbet, James. *Annals of San Francisco.* New York: D. Appleton, 1855.

Sources of Conflict in the Middle Soule, Frank, and Gilran, John H, and Nisbet, James. The AnnalsEast. London: Institute for Strategic Studies, 1966.

Sourdeval, Mourain de. *Les Sires de Retz.* Tours, Fr.: Imprimerie de Marne, 1845.

Soustelle, Jacques. *The Daily Life of the Aztecs on the Eve of the Spanish Conquest.* trans. Patrick O'Brian. New York: Macmillan, 1962.

South, Colon. *Out West; or, From London to Salt Lake City and Back.* London: Wyman & Sons, 1884.

Southall, A.W., and Gutkind, P.C.W. *Townsmen in the Making: Kampala and Its Suburbs.* London: Kegan Paul Trench Trubner, 1957.

Southey, Robert. *The Life of John Wesley.* London: Hutchinson, 1904.

Southwood, John. *"Beauty and Booty," the Watchword of New Orleans.* New York: M. Doolady, 1867.

Souvarine, Boris. *Stalin, A Critical Survey of Bolshevism.* New York: Longmans, Green, 1939.

Sowell, Thomas. *Ethnic America.* New York: Basic Books, 1981.

_____. *Knowledge and Decisions.* New York: Basic Books, 1980.

_____. *Race and Economics.* New York: David McKay, 1975.

Sowle, Claude R. (ed.). *Police Power and Individual Freedom.* Chicago: Aldine, 1962.

Spaeth, Sigmund. *A History of Popular Music in America.* New York: Random House, 1948.

Spaggiari, Albert. *Fric-Frac.* Boston: Houghton Mifflin, 1979.

Spagnuolo, Giovanni. *Ceka fascista.* Rome: Ruffolo, 1947.

Spahr, Charles B. *An Essay on the Present Distribution of Wealth in the United States.* New York: Thomas Y. Crowell, 1896.

Spalding, J. Willett. *The Japan Expedition.* New York: Redfield, 1855.

Spalding, Thomas Alfred. *Elizabethan Demonology.* Chatto & Windus, 1880.

Spampanato, Bruno. *Contromemoriale.* Rome: L'illustrato, 1952.

Spanò, Aristide. *Faccia a faccia con la mafia.* Milan, Italy: Mondadori, 1978.

Spargo, John. *The Bitter Cry of the Children.* New York: Macmillan, 1916.

Sparhawk, E.V. *Report of the Trial of Richard Johnson.* New York: n.p., 1829.

Sparks, Jared. *John Sullivan.* Boston: Little, Brown, 1848.

_____. *Life of George Washington.* Boston: Tappen & Dennet, 1843.

Sparks, R.F. *Local Prisons: The Crisis in the English Penal System.* London: Heinemann Educational, 1971.

_____, Genn, Hazel G., and Dodd, David J. *Surveying Victims.* New York: John Wiley & Sons, 1977.

Sparks, William. *The Apache Kid, a Bear Fighter and Other True Stories of the Old West.* Los Angeles: Skelton, 1926.

Sparling, Earl. *Mystery Men of Wall Street.* New York: Greenburg, 1930.

Sparrow, Judge Gerald. *Crimes of Passion.* London: Barker, 1973.

_____. *The Great Assassins.* New York: Arco, 1969.

_____. *The Great Swindlers.* London: John Long, 1959.

_____. *Murder Parade.* London: Robert Hale, 1957.

_____. *Satan's Children.* London: Odhams, 1966.

_____. *Vintage Edwardian Murder.* London: Arthur Barker, 1971.

_____. *Vintage Victorian Murder.* New York: Hart, 1972.

_____. *Women Who Murder.* New York: Abelard-Schuman, 1970.

Sparrow, John. *After the Assassination: A Positive Appraisal of the Warren Report.* New York: Chilmark Press, 1967.

Spaulding, William A. *History and Reminiscences: Los Angeles City and County, California.* 3 vols. Los Angeles: J.R. Finnell & Sons, 1931.

Spear, Percival. *The History of India.* London: Penguin Books, 1965.

Spears, J.R. *The Saga of No Man's Land.* Beaver, Okla.; Herald-Deomcrat, 1956.

Spears, John R. *The American Slave Trade.* New York: Ballantine Books, 1960.

Spector, Ivar. *The First Russian Revolution: Its Impact on Asia.* Englewood Cliffs, N.J.: Prentice-Hall, 1962.

_____. *The Soviet Union and the Muslim World, 1917-1956.* Seattle: University of Washington Press, 1956.

Spector, Sherman David. *Rumania at the Paris Peace Conference: A Study of the Diplomacy of Ioan I.C. Bratianu.* New York: Bookman Associates, 1962.

Spedding, James Ellis, R.L., and Heath, D.D. (eds.). *The Works of Francis Bacon.* 14 vols. London: Longman, 1857-74.

Spee, Friedrich von. *Cautio Criminalis.* Weimar, Ger.: H. Böhlaus, 1939.

Speech of Henry L. Clinton. Westchester, N.Y.: n.p., 1871.

Speech of Paul David Brown. Philadelphia: Robb, Pile, M'Elroy, 1858.

Speed, Thomas. *The Wilderness Road.* Louisville, Ky.: John P. Morton, 1886.

Speek, Peter Alexander. *The Singletax and the Labor Movement.* Madison: University of Wisconsin Press, 1917.

Speer, Albert. *Infiltration: How Heinrich Himmler Schemed to Build an SS Industrial Empire.* New York: Macmillan, 1981.

_____. *Inside the Third Reich.* New York: Macmillan, 1970.

Speer, Marion A. *Western Trails.* Huntington Beach, Calif.: Huntington Beach News, 1931.

Speer, W. Harold. *The Secret History of Great Crimes.* London: Arthur H. Stockwell, 1931.

Speer, William. *China and California.* San Francisco: Marvin & Hitchcock, 1853.

_____. *A Humble Plea in Behalf of the Immigrants from the Empire of China.* San Francisco: Office of the *Oriental,* 1856.

_____. *The Oldest and the Newest Empire: China and the United States.* Hartford, Conn.: S.S. Scranton, 1870.

Speer, William S., and Brown, John Henry (eds.). *The Encyclopedia of the New West.* Marshall, Texas: United States Biographical, 1881.

Speidel, Hans. *Invasion 1944: Rommel and the Normandy Campaign.* trans. Ian Colvin. Chicago: Regnery, 1950.

_____. *We Defended Normandy.* trans. Ian Colvin. London: Herbert Jenkins, 1951.

Speiser, E.A. *The United States and the Near East.* Cambridge, Mass.: Harvard University Press, 1950.

Spence, Lewis. *The Encyclopedia of Occultism.* London: Routledge & Sons, 1920.

Spencer, Mrs. George E. *Calamity Jane: A Story of the Black Hills.* New York: Cassell, 1887.

Spencer, J.A. *A History of the United States from the Earliest Settlement to the Administration of James Buchanan.* New York: Johnson, Fry, 1858.

Spencer, John Wallace. *Limbo of the Lost.* Westfield, Mass.: Phillips, 1969.

_____. *No Earthly Explanation.* Westfield, Mass.: Phillips, 1974.

Spencer, Philip. *Political Beliefs in Nineteenth Century France.* London: Faber & Faber, 1954.

Spencer, Samuel R., Jr. *Booker T. Washington and the Negro's Place in American Life.* Boston: Little, Brown, 1955.

Spencer, William. *Political Evolution in the Middle East.* Philadelphia: J.B. Lippincott, 1962.

Spender, Harold. *A Briton in America*. London: William Heinemann, 1921.

Spender, John A., and Asquith, Cyril. *Life of Herbert Henry Asquith, Lord Oxford and Asquith*. London: Hutchinson, 1932.

_____. *Weetman Pearson: First Viscount Cowdray--1856-1927*. London: Cassell, 1930.

Spender, Stephen. *The Year of the Young Rebles*. New York: Vintage Books, 1969.

Spengler, Oswald. *Preussentum und Sozialismus*. Munich: C.H. Beck, 1920.

Sperco, Willy. *L'Ecroulement d'une Dictature*. Paris: Hachette, 1946.

_____. *Tel fut Mussolini*. Paris: Fasquelle, 1955.

Spergel, Irving. *Racketville, Slumtown, Haulberg*. Chicago: University of Chicago Press, 1964.

_____. *Street Gang Work*. Reading, Mass.: Addison-Wesley, 1966.

Speriglio, Milo, and Eubanks, S. Thomas. *How to Protect Your Life and Property*. Sherman Oaks, Calif.: Seville, 1982.

Spewack, Bella and Samuel. *Clear All Wires*. New York: Samuel French, 1932.

Spice, Robert Paulton. *The Wanderings of the Hermit of Westminster between New York & San Francisco in the Autumn of 1881*. London: Metchim & Son, 1882.

Spicer, Edward H. *Cycles of Conquest*. Tucson: University of Arizona Press, 1960.

Spiegel, Lawrence D. *A Question of Innocence*. Parsippany, N.J.: Unicorn, 1986.

Spiel, Hilde. *The Congress of Vienna*. trans. Richard H. Weber. Philadelphia: Chilton Book, 1968.

Spielmann, Karl Heinz. *Die Hexenprozesse in Kurhessen*. Marburg, Ger.: N.G. Elwert, 1932.

Spielmann, Marion Harry. *The History of Punch*. London: Cassell, 1895.

Spier, Hans. *Social Order and the Risks of War*. Cambridge, Mass.: MIT Press, 1969.

Spiering, Frank. *Lizzie*. New York: Random House, 1984.

_____. *The Man Who Got Capone*. Indianapolis, Ind.: Bobbs-Merrill, 1976.

_____. *Prince Jack: The True Story of Jack the Ripper*. New York: Doubleday, 1978.

Spigelgass, Leonard. *Hello, Hollywood*. Garden City, N.Y.: Doubleday, 1962.

Spindler, Will Henry. *Rim of the Sandhills: A True Picture of the Old Holt County Horse Thief-Vigilante Days*. Mitchell, S.D.: Educator Supply, 1941.

_____. *Yesterday's Trails*. Gordon, Neb.: Gordon Journal, 1961.

Spink, J.G. Taylor. *Judge Landis and Twenty-Five Years of Baseball*. New York: Thomas Y. Crowell, 1947.

Spinka, Matthew. *A History of Christianity in the Balkans*. Chicago: American Society of Church History, 1933.

Spiridovitch, Gen. Alexandre. *Les Dernières Années de la Cour de Tsarkoie-Selo*. 2 vols. Paris: Payot, 1928.

_____. *Raspoutine, 1863-1916*. Paris: Payot, 1935.

Spiro, Edward. *From Battenberg to Mountbatten*. London: Arthur Barker, 1966.

Spivak, J.L. *Europe under the Terror*. London: Victor Gollancz, 1936.

Splawn, Andrew Jackson. *Ka-Mi-Akin, the Last Hero of the Yakimas*. Portland, Ore.: Press of Kilham, 1917.

Spock, Benjamin. *A Teenager's Guide to Life and Love*. New York: Pocket Books, 1971.

Spofford, Harriet E.P. *New England Legends*. Boston: James R. Osgood, 1871.

Spolansky, Jacob. *The Communist Trail in America*. New York: Macmillan, 1951.

Spoto, Donald. *The Dark Side of Genius: The Life of Alfred Hitchcock*. New York: Ballantine, 1983.

Sprague, A.P. *Speeches, Arguments, and Miscellaneous Papers of David Dudley Field*. New York: D. Appleton, 1884.

Sprague, Marshall. *Massacre, the Tragedy at White River*. Boston: Little, Brown, 1957.

_____. *Money Mountain: The Story of Cripple Creek Gold*. Boston: Little, Brown, 1953.

Sprague, O.M.W. *History of the Crises Under the National Banking System*. New York: Augustus M. Kelley, 1968.

Sprague, Richard E. *The Taking of America 1-2-3*. Hartsdale, N.Y.: Published by Author, 1976.

Sprague, William F. *Women and the West: A Short Social History*. Boston: Christopher, 1940.

Spray, John Campbell (ed.). *The Book of Woodlawn*. Chicago: Published by Author, 1920.

_____. *Chicago's Great South Shore*. Chicago: South Shore, 1930.

Sprenger, James, and Kramer, Henry. *Malleus Maleficarum*. London: John Rodker, 1928.

Spriegel, William R., and Schultz, Ed. *Elements of Supervision*. New York: John Wiley & Sons, 1942.

Sprigge, C.J.S. *The Development of Modern Italy*. London: Duckworth, 1943.

_____. *Karl Marx*. New York: Macmillan, 1957.

Spring, Agnes Wright. *The Cheyenne and Black Hills Stage and Express Routes*. Glendale, Calif.: Arthur H. Clark, 1949.

_____. *Colorado Charley, Wild Bill's Pard*. Boulder, Colo.: Pruett Press, 1968.

_____ (ed.). *Pioneer Years in the Black Hills*. Glendale, Calif.: Arthur H. Clark, 1957.

_____. *Seventy Years: A Panoramic History of the Wyoming Stock Growers' Association*. Cheyenne, Wyo.: Privately Printed, 1942.

_____. *William Chapin Deming, of Wyoming, Pioneer Publisher, and State and Federal Official*. Glendale, Calif.: Arthur H. Clark, 1944.

Springfield, Lincoln. *Some Piquant People*. London: Fisher Unwin, 1924.

Sproat, John G. *"The Best Men": Liberal Reformers in the Gilded Age*. New York: Oxford University Press, 1968.

Sprott, W.J.H. *The Social Background of Delinquency*. Nottingham, Eng.: University of Nottingham, 1954.

Sprout, Harold and Margaret. *The Rise of American Naval Power, 1776-1918*. Princeton, N.J.: Princeton University Press, 1939.

Spulber, Nicolas. *The Economics of Communist Eastern Europe*. Cambridge, Mass.: MIT Press, 1957.

Spurr, Josiah Edward. *Through the Yukon Gold Diggings*. Boston: Eastern, 1900.

Squiers, Granville. *Secret Hiding Places*. Tower, 1971.

Srole, Leo, and Fisher, Anita K. (eds.). *Mental Health in the Metropolis: The Midtown Manhattan Study*. New York: New York University Press, 1978.

Ssu-ma Ch'ien. *Records of the Grand Historian of China*. 2 vols. trans. Burton Watson. New York: Columbia University Press, 1961.

Stack, Andy. *The I-5 Killer*. New York: Signet, 1984.

_____. *Lust Killer*. New York: Signet, 1983.

_____. *The Want-Ad Killer*. New York: Signet, 1983.

Stack, C.B. *All Our Kin*. New York: Harper & Row, 1974.

Stackpole, Edouard A. *Mutiny at Midnight: The Adventures of Cyrus Hussey of Nantucket Aboard the Whale Ship "Globe" in the South Pacific, from 1822-1826*. London: F. Miller, 1944.

Stacton, David. *The Judges of the Secret Court*. New York: Pantheon Books, 1961.

Stade, Reinhold. *Barbara Elizabeth Schulzin*. Arnstadt, Ger.: E. Protscher, 1904.

Staffe, Baronne. *Les Usages du Monde*. Paris: Havard, 1890.

Stafford, Ann. *The Age of Consent*. London: Hodder & Stoughton, 1964.

Stafford, Jean. *A Mother in History: Mrs. Marguerite Oswald*. New York: Farrar, Straus & Giroux, 1966.

Stafford, Marshall P. *A Life of James Fisk, Jr.* New York: Polhemus, 1873.

Stafford, Peter. *Sexual Behavior in the Communist World*. New

York: Julian, 1967.

Stagg, Lawrence Joseph. *Wall Street and Washington*. Princeton, N.J.: Princeton University Press, 1929.

Stahl, O'Glen. *Public Personnel Administration*. New York: Harper & Row, 1976.

Stalin, J.V., et al. *The History of the Civil War in the U.S.S.R.* Moscow: Foreign Languages, 1946.

Stambaugh, J. Lee and Lillian J. *A History of Collin County, Texas*. Austin: Texas State Historical Association, 1958.

Stampp, K.M. *And the War Came: The North and the Secession Crisis 1860-1861*. Baton Rouge: Louisiana State University Press, 1950.

_____. *The Peculiar Institution*. New York: Alfred A. Knopf, 1956.

Stanard, Mary Mann Page. *Richmond, Its People and Its Story*. Philadelphia: J.P. Lippincott, 1923.

Standford, Barbara. *Myths and Modern Man*. New York: Pocket Books, 1972.

Stanford, Rev. John. *Trial, Conviction, Sentence, and Only True Copy of the Confession of Catherine Cashiere*. New York: C. Brown, 1829.

_____. *A True Account of the Confessions and Contra Confessions of John Johnson*. New York: C. Brown & R. Tyrell, 1824.

Stanford, Sally. *The Lady of the House*. New York: G.P. Putnam's Sons, 1966.

Stang, Alan. *They Killed the President: Lee Harvey Oswald Wasn't Alone*. Belmont, Mass.: American Opinion, 1976.

Stanley, David T. *Prisoners Among Us*. Washington, D.C.: Brookings Institution, 1976.

Stanley, Edwin J. *Life of Rev. L.B. Stateler; or, Sixty-Five Years on the Frontier*. Nashville, Tenn.: M.E. Church South, 1907.

Stanley, F. (pseud. for Father Stanley Crocchiola). *The Alma (New Mexico) Story*. n.p., n.d.

_____. *The Antonchico (New Mexico) Story*. n.p, n.d.

_____. *Clay Allison*. Denver: World Press, 1956.

_____. *The Clayton (New Mexico) Story*. n.p, n.d.

_____. *Dave Rudabaugh: Border Ruffian*. Denver: World Press, 1961.

_____. *Desperadoes of New Mexico*. Denver: World Press, 1953.

_____. *The Duke City: The Story of Albuquerque, New Mexico, 1706-1956*. Pampa, Texas: Pampa Print, 1963.

_____. *The Elizabethtown (New Mexico) Story*. n.p., 1961.

_____. *The Folsom (New Mexico) Story*. Pantex, Texas: Published by Author, 1962.

_____. *Fort Bascom Comanche-Kiowa Barrier*. Pampa, Texas: Pampa Print, 1961.

_____. *Fort Stanton*. Pampa, Texas: Pampa Print, 1964.

_____. *Fort Union (New Mexico)*. n.p, 1953.

_____. *The Grant That Maxwell Bought*. Denver: World Press, 1952.

_____. *The Kingston (New Mexico) Story*. Pantex, Texas: Published by Author, 1961.

_____. *The La Belle (New Mexico) Story*. Pantex, Texas: n.p., 1962.

_____. *The Lake Valley (New Mexico) Story*. Pep, Texas: n.p, 1964.

_____. *The Lamy (New Mexico) Story*. Pep, Texas: n.p., 1966.

_____. *The Las Vegas Story*. Denver: World Press, 1951.

_____. *The Lincoln (New Mexico) Story*. Pep, Texas: n.p., 1964.

_____. *Longhair Jim Courtright: Two Gun Marshal of Fort Worth*. Denver: World Press, 1957.

_____. *The Mogollon (New Mexico) Story*. Pep, Texas: n.p., 1968.

_____. *No More Tears for Black Jack Ketchum*. Denver: World Press, 1958.

_____. *One Half Mile from Heaven; or, the Cimarron Story*. Denver: World Press, 1949.

_____. *The Otero (New Mexico) Story*. Pantex, Texas: n.p., 1962.

_____. *The Private War of Ike Stockton*. Denver: World Press, 1959.

_____. *Raton Chronicle*. Denver: World Press, 1948.

_____. *Rodeo Town*. Denver: World Press, 1953.

_____. *The Seven Rivers (New Mexico) Story*. Pep, Texas: n.p., 1963.

_____. *The Shakespeare (New Mexico) Story*. Pantex, Texas: Published by Author, 1961.

_____. *Socorro: The Oasis*. Denver: World Press, 1950.

_____. *The Springer (New Mexico) Story*. Pantex, Texas: Published by Author, 1962.

_____. *Story of the Texas Panhandle Railroads*. Borger, Texas: Hess, 1976.

_____. *The White Oaks (New Mexico) Story*. n.p., 1961.

Stanley, Henry M. *My Early Travels and Adventures in America and Asia*. 2 vols. London: Sampson Low, Marston, 1895.

_____. *Through the Dark Continent*. 2 vols. New York: Harper & Brothers, 1878.

Stanley, Leo. *Men at Their Worst*. New York: D. Appleton-Century, 1940.

Stansbery, Lon R. *The Passing of the 3D Ranch*. Tulsa, Okla.: George W. Henry, 1930.

Stansky, Peter. *Gladstone: A Progress in Politics*. Boston: Little, Brown, 1979.

Stanton, Alfred H., and Schwartz, M.S. *The Mental Hospital*. New York: Basic Books, 1954.

Stanton, Elizabeth Cady, Anthony, Susan B., and Gage, Matilda Joslyn. *History of Woman's Suffrage*. New York: Fowler & Wells, 1881.

Stanton, G. Smith. *When the Wildwood Was in Flower*. New York: J.S. Ogilvie, 1910.

Stanton, Irving W. *Sixty Years in Colorado*. Denver: n.p., 1922.

Staples, William R. *A Correct Report of the Examination of Rev. Ephraim K. Avery*. Providence, R.I.: Marshall & Brown, 1833.

Stapleton, Joseph W. *The Great Crime of 1860*. London: Marlborough, 1861.

Starhemberg, E.R. Von. *Between Hitler and Mussolini*. London: Hodder & Stoughton, 1941.

Stark, Francis R. *The Abolition of Privateering and the Declaration of Paris*. New York: Columbia University Press, 1897.

Stark, W. *The Social Bond*. New York: Fordham University Press, 1976-80.

Starkey, Larry. *Wilkes Booth Came to Washington*. New York: Random House, 1976.

Starkey, Marion L. *The Cherokee Nation*. New York: Alfred A. Knopf, 1946.

_____. *The Devil in Massachusetts*. New York: Alfred A. Knopf, 1949.

_____. *Land Where Our Fathers Died*. Garden City, N.Y.: Doubleday, 1962.

_____. *A Little Rebellion*. New York: Alfred A. Knopf, 1955.

Starkie, Enid *Baudelaire*. Norfolk, Conn.: New Directions, 1958.

_____. *Flaubert*. London: Weidenfeld & Nicolson, 1967.

Starkie, Walter. *The Waveless Plain*. London: John Murray, 1938.

Starling, Edmund W. *Starling of the White House*. New York: Simon & Schuster, 1946.

Starobin, Joseph R. *American Communism in Crisis, 1943-1957*. Cambridge, Mass.: Harvard University Press, 1972.

Starr, Frederick. *Mexico and the United States: A Story of Revolution, Intervention and War*. Chicago: Bible House, 1914.

Starr, John. *The Purveyor: Shocking Story of Today's Illicit Liquor Empire*. New York: Holt, Rinehart & Winston, 1961.

Starr, John W. *Lincoln's Last Day*. New York: Frederick A. Stokes, 1922.

Starr, Lando. *Blue Book of San Franciscans in Public Life*. San Francisco: McLaughlin, 1941.

Starr, Louis M. *Bohemian Brigade: Civil War Newsmen in Action*. New York: Alfred A. Knopf, 1954.

Starr, Stephen Z. *Colonel Grenfell's Wars*. Baton Rouge: Louisiana State University Press, 1971.

Starrett, Vincent. *The Private Life of Sherlock Holmes*. New

York: Macmillan, 1933.

Statement of James E. Eldredge, Convicted for the Murder of Sarah Jane Gould. New York: S.P. Remington, 1859.

Statler, Oliver. *Japanese Inn*. New York: Harcourt Brace Jonvanovich, 1961.

Staudenraus, P.J. (ed.). *Mr. Lincoln's Washington: Selections from the Writings of Noah Brooks, Civil War Correspondent*. New York: Thomas Yoseloff, 1967.

Stave, Bruce M. (ed.). *Urban Bosses, Machines, and Progressive Reformers*. Lexington, Mass.: D.C. Heath, 1972.

Stavenhagen, Lee (ed.). *A Testament of Alchemy*. Hanover, N.H.: University Press of New England, 1974.

Stavrianos, Leften S. *Balkan Federation: A History of the Movement Toward Balkan Unity in Modern Times*. Northampton, Mass.: Smith College, 1944.

_____. *The Balkans, 1815-1914*. New York: Holt, Rinehart & Winston, 1963.

_____. *The Balkans since 1453*. New York: Holt, Rinehart & Winston, 1958.

_____. *Greece: American Dilemma and Opportunity*. Chicago: Henry Regnery, 1952.

Stavrou, Theofanis G. *Russian Interests in Palestine, 1882-1914*. Thessaloniki, Gr.: Institute for the Balkan Studies, 1963.

Stead, Christina. *House of All Nations*. New York: Alfred A. Knopf, 1938.

Stead, E.W. *My Father: Personal and Spiritual Reminiscences*. London: William Heinemann, 1913.

Stead, Philip J. (ed. and trans.). *Second Bureau*. London: Evans, 1959.

_____. *The Memoirs of Lacenaire*. London: Staples, 1952.

_____. *Pioneers in Policing*. Montclair, N.J.: Patterson Smith, 1977.

_____. *The Police of Paris*. London: Staples, 1951.

_____. *Vidocq*. New York: Roy, 1954.

Stead, William T. *If Christ Came to Chicago: A Plea for the Union of All Who Love in the Service of All Who Suffer*. Chicago: Laird & Lee, 1894.

_____. *Satan's Invisible World Displayed*. New York: R.F. Fenno, 1897.

Steadman, Henry J. *Beating a Rap?* Chicago: University of Chicago Press, 1960.

Steadman, J.C., and Leonard, R.A. *The Workingmen's Party of California: An Epitome of Its Rise and Progress*. San Francisco: n.p., 1878.

Steadman, Robert F. (ed.). *The Police and the Community*. Baltimore: John Hopkins University Press, 1972.

Stealey, O.O. *Twenty Years in the Press Gallery*. Published by Author, 1906.

Stearn, Gerald Emanuel, and Fried, Albert (eds.). *The Essential Lincoln*. New York: Collier Books, 1962.

Stearn, Jess. *Edgar Cayce--The Sleeping Prophet*. New York: Bantam, 1968.

Stearne, John. *A Confirmation and Discovery of Witchcraft*. London: W. Wilson, 1648.

Stearns, Harold E. (ed.). *America Now*. New York: Charles Scribner's Sons, 1938.

_____. *Civilization in the U.S.* New York: Harcourt, Brace, 1922.

Stebel, S.L. *The Shoe Leather Treatment*. New York: St. Martins, 1980.

Steck, Rudolf. *Die Akten des Jetzerprozess*. Basel, Switz.: Verlag der Basler Buchund Antiquariatshandlung Vormals A. Geering, 1904.

_____. *Der Berner Jetzerprozess 1507-09*. Bern, Switz.: Schmid & Franck, 1902.

Steckmesser, Kent Ladd. *The Western Hero in History and Legend*. Norman: University of Oklahoma Press, 1965.

Steed, Henry Wickham. *The Habsburg Monarchy*. London: Constable, 1913.

_____. *Through Thirty Years*. New York: Doubleday, Doran, 1929.

Steegmuller, Francis. *Flaubert and Madame Bovary*. London: Collins, 1947.

Steel, Ronald. *Pax Americana*. New York: Viking Press, 1967.

Steele, A.T. *The American People and China*. New York: McGraw-Hill, 1966.

Steele, Matthew Forney. *American Campaigns*. 2 vols. Washington, D.C.: Byron S. Adams, 1909.

Steele, Robert V.P. *Between Two Empires: The Life Story of California's First Senator*. Boston: Houghton Mifflin, 1969.

_____. *The Vanishing Evangelist: The Aimee Semple McPherson Kidnapping Affair*. New York: Viking Press, 1959.

Steele, S.B. *Forty Years in Canada*. New York: Dodd, Mead, 1915.

Steeman, W.H. *Report on Budhuk, Alias Bagee, Dacoits and Other Gang Robbers by Heredity Profession*. Calcutta, India: Bengal Military Orphan Press, 1843.

Steen, Ralph W. (ed.). *The Texas News: A Miscellany of Texas History in Newspaper Style*. Austin, Texas: Steck, 1955.

Steer, G.L. *Caeser in Abyssinia*. London: Hodder & Soughton, 1936.

Steevens, George Washington. *The Land of the Dollar*. New York: Dodd, Mead, 1897.

Steffan, Jack. *The Long Fellow: The Story of the Great Irish Patriot, Eamon De Valera*. New York: Macmillan, 1966.

Steffen, Jerome Q. *The American West*. Norman: University of Oklahoma Press, 1979.

Steffens, Lincoln. *Autobiography*. New York: Harcourt, Brace, 1931.

_____. *The Letters of Lincoln Steffens*. New York: Harcourt, Brace, 1938.

_____. *The Shame of the Cities*. New York: McClure, Phillips, 1904.

_____. *The Struggle for Self-Government*. New York: McClure, Phillips, 1906.

_____. *The World of Lincoln Steffens*. New York: Hill & Wang, 1962.

Stegner, Wallace. *Beyond the Hundreth Meridan*. Boston: Houghton Mifflin, 1953.

_____. *Gathering of Zion*. New York: McGraw-Hill, 1964.

_____. *Mormon Country*. New York: Duell, Sloan & Pearce, 1942.

Steiger, Brad. *The Mass Murderer*. New York: Award Books, 1967.

_____. *A Roadmap of Time*. Englewoood Cliffs, N.J.: Prentice-Hall, 1975.

Stein, David Lewis. *Living the Revolution: The Yippies in Chicago*. New York: Bobbs-Merrill, 1969.

Stein, George H. *The Waffen-SS*. Ithaca, N.Y.: Cornell University Press, 1966.

Stein, Gertrude. *The Autobiography of Alice B. Toklas*. New York: The Literary Guild, 1933.

_____. *Paris France*. New York: Liveright, 1970.

Stein, Harold (ed.). *Public Administration and Policy Development*. New York: Harcourt, Brace, & World, 1948.

Stein, Leon. *The Triangle Fire*. Philadelphia: J.B. Lippincott, 1962.

Stein, Leonard. *The Balfour Declaration*. London: Vallentine-Mitchell, 1961.

Stein, Sir Mark Aurel. *Sand Buried Ruins of Khotan*. London: T. Fisher Unwin, 1903.

Stein, Martha L. *Lovers, Friends, Slaves...* Berkeley, Calif.: Berkeley, 1974.

Stein, Maurice. *The Eclipse of Community*. New York: Harper & Row, 1964.

Stein, Meyer L. *Under Fire: The Story of American War Correspondents*. New York: Simon & Schuster, 1968.

Steinberg, Alfred. *The Bosses*. New York: Macmillan, 1972.

Steinberg, I.N. *In the Workshop of the Revolution*. New York: Rinehart, 1953.

Steinberg, Peter L. *The Great "Red Menace": United States*

Prosecution of American Communists, 1947-1952. Westport, Conn.: Greenwood, 1984.

Steinbruner, John. *The Cybernetic Theory of Decision.* Princeton, N.J.: Princeton University Press, 1974.

Steinbrunner, Chris, and Penzler, Otto (eds.). *Encyclopedia of Mystery and Detection.* New York: McGraw-Hill, 1976.

Steinel, Alvin T. *History of Agriculture in Colorado.* Ft. Collins, Colo.: State Agricultural College, 1926.

Steiner, Bernard C. *Life of Reverdy Johnson.* Baltimore: Norman Remington, 1914.

_____. *The Life of Roger Brooke Taney, Chief Justice of the United States Supreme Court.* Westport, Conn.: Greenwood Press, 1970.

Steiner, Felix. *Die Armee der Geächteten.* Göttingen, Ger.: Plesse, 1963.

_____. *Die Freiwilligen.* Göttingen, Ger.: Plesse, 1958.

_____. *von Clausewitz bis Bulganin.* Bielefeld, Ger.: Deutsche Heimat-Verlag, 1956.

Steiner, H.A. *Government in Fascist Italy.* New York: McGraw Hill, 1938.

Steiner, Jesse F., and Brown, Roy M. *The North Carolina Chain Gang.* Chapel Hill: University of North Carolina Press, 1927.

Steiner, Stan. *La Raza.* New York: Harper & Row, 1970.

Steinman, D.B. *The Builders of the Bridge: The Story of John Roebling and His Son.* New York: Harcourt, Brace, 1945.

Steinmetz, Charles P. *America and the New Epoch.* New York: Harper, 1916.

Steinmetz, Suzanne K., and Straus, Murray A. (eds.). *Violence in the Family.* New York: Dodd, Mead, 1974.

Stekel, Wilhelm. *Compulsion and Doubt.* New York: Liveright, 1950.

_____. *Peculiarities of Behavior.* New York: Liveright, 1924.

_____. *Sadism and Masochism.* New York: Liveright, 1929.

_____. *Sexual Aberrations: The Phenomena of Fetishism in Relation to Sex.* trans. S. Parker. 2 vols. New York: Liveright, 1930.

Stellman, Jeanne M., and Daum, Susan M. *Work Is Dangerous to Your Health.* New York: Vintage Books, 1973.

Stellman, Louis J. *Mother Lode: The Story of California's Gold Rush.* San Francisco: Harr Wagner, 1934.

Stelzle, Charles. *Why Prohibition?* New York: George H. Doran, 1918.

Stemman, Roy. *Spirits and Spirit Worlds.* Garden City, N.Y.: Doubleday, 1976.

Stendhal. *Napoleon.* Paris: H. Champion, 1929.

_____. *The Red and the Black: A Chronicle of the Nineteenth Century.* trans. Lloyd C. Parks. New York: New American Library, 1970.

Stengel, Erwin. *Suicide and Attempted Suicide.* Harmondsworth, Eng.: Penguin Books, 1969.

_____, and Cook, N.G., and Kreeger, I.S. *Attempted Suicide; Its Social Significance and Effects.* London: Chapman & Hall, 1958.

Stephan, John J. *The Russian Fascists: Tragedy and Farce in Exile, 1925-1945.* New York: Harper & Row, 1978.

Stephen, J.F. *A Digest of Criminal Law.* London: L.F. Struge, 1950.

_____. *A History of the Criminal Law in England.* London: Macmillan, 1893.

Stephen, Leslie. *The Life of Sir James Fitzjames Stephens, A Judge of the High Court of Justice.* London: Smith, Elder, 1895.

Stephen, Otis H., Jr. *The Supreme Court and Confessions of Guilt.* Knoxville: University of Tennessee Press, 1973.

Stephens, C.L. McCluer. *Famous Crimes and Criminals.* London: Stanley Paul, 1924.

Stephens, Edward. *A Collection of Modern Relations of Matter and Fact Concerning Witches and Witchcraft.* London: John Harris, 1693.

Stephenson, George M. *John Lind of Minnesota.* Minneapolis: University of Minnesota Press, 1935.

Stephenson, James. *The Insurrection in Dublin.* New York: Macmillan, 1917.

Stephenson, John (ed.). *A Royal Correspondence: Letters of King Edward VII and King George V to Admiral Sir Henry F. Stephenson.* London: Macmillan, 1938.

Stephenson, Nathaniel Wright. *Texas and the Mexican War.* New Haven, Conn.: Yale University Press, 1921.

Stephenson, Richard M., and Scarpitti, Frank R. *Group Interaction As Theory.* Westport, Conn.: Greenwood Press, 1976.

Stepniak, S.M. (pseud. for Sergei Kravchinsky). *Russia Under the Tsars.* New York: Charles Scribner's Sons, 1885.

_____. *Underground Russia: Revolutionary Profiles and Sketches from Life.* New York: Scribner, 1883.

Steranko, James. *History of Comics.* Reading, Pa.: Supergraphics, 1970.

Sterling, Claire. *The Masaryk Case.* New York: Harper & Row, 1969.

_____. *The Terror Network.* New York: Holt, Rinehart & Winston, 1981.

_____. *The Time of Assassins.* New York: Holt, Rinehart & Winston, 1983.

Sterling, Hank. *Famous Western Outlaw-Sheriff Battles.* New York: Rainbow Books, 1954.

Sterling, William Warren. *Trails and Trials of a Texas Ranger.* n.p., 1959.

Stern, August (ed.). *The USSR vs. Dr. Mikhail Stern.* New York: Urizen Books, 1978.

Stern, Fritz. *Gold and Iron: Bismarck, Bleichröder and the Building of German Empire.* London: George Allen & Unwin, 1977.

Stern, Jean. *Voltaire et sa Nièce, Madame Denis.* Paris: La Palatine, 1957.

Stern, L.W. *General Psychology from the Personalistic Standpoint.* New York: Macmillan, 1938.

_____. *Psychology of Early Childhood.* London: George Allen & Unwin, 1924.

Stern, Michael. *No Innocence Abroad.* New York: Random House, 1953.

Stern, Philip M. *Lawyers on Trial.* New York: Time Books, 1980.

_____. *The Rape of the Taxpayer.* New York: Vintage Books, 1974.

Stern, Philip Van Doren. *The Man Who Killed Lincoln: The Story of John Wilkes Booth and His Part in the Assassination.* New York: Random House, 1939.

_____. *Tin Lizzie.* New York: Simon & Schuster, 1955.

Stern, Samuel. *Thrilling Mysteries of the Rubenstein Murder.* New York: S. Stern & Cohn, 1876.

Stern, Susan. *With The Weatherman.* New York: Doubleday, 1975.

Stern, W. *Die psychologische Methoden der Intelligenzprufung.* Leipzig, Ger.: Barth, 1912.

Sterne, R.S. *Delinquent Conduct in Broken Homes.* New Haven, Conn.: College and University Press Services, 1964.

Stetler, Alfred. *Psi Healing.* New York: Bantam, 1976.

Stetson, James B. *San Francisco During the Eventful Days of April 1906.* San Francisco: Murdock Press, 1906.

Stettinius, Edward R., Jr. *The Diaries of Edward R. Stettinius, Jr., 1943-1946.* New York: New Viewpoints, 1975.

_____. *Lend-Lease. Weapon for Victory.* New York: Macmillan, 1944.

_____. *Roosevelt and the Russians: The Yalta Conference.* New York: Doubleday, 1949.

Steuart, Justin. *Wayne Wheeler, Dry Boss: An Uncensored Biography of Wayne B. Wheeler.* New York: Fleming H. Revell, 1928.

Steven, Stewart. *Operation Splinter Factor.* Philadelphia: J.B. Lippincott, 1974.

Stevens, Brevet-Major Isaac I. *Campaigns of the Rio Grande and of Mexico.* New York: D. Appleton, 1851.

Stevens, C.L. McCluer. *Famous Crimes and Criminals*. London: Stanley Paul, 1924.

_____. *From Clue to Dock*. London: Stanley Paul, 1927.

Stevens, E.A. *Here Comes Pancho Villa: The Anecdotal History of a Genial Killer*. New York: Frederick A. Stokes, 1930.

Stevens, George Warrington. *The Tragedy of Dreyfus*. New York: Harper, 1899.

Stevens, Georgiana G. *Jordan River Partition*. Stanford, Calif.: Hoover Institute, 1965.

_____ (ed.). *The United States and the Middle East*. Englewood Cliffs, N.J.: Prentice-Hall, 1964.

Stevens, Jay. *Storming Heaven: LSD and the American Dream*. New York: Atlantic Monthly Press, 1987.

Stevens, John. *Medieval Romance*. London: Hutchinson, 1973.

Stevens, Dr. L.L. *Lives, Crimes and Confessions of the Assassins*. Troy, N.Y.: Daily Times Stream Printing Establishment, 1865.

Stevens, Richard E. *National Fire Code*. Boston: National Fire Protection Association, 1973.

Stevens, Richard P. *American Zionism and U.S. Foreign Policy 1942-1947*. New York: Pageant Press, 1962.

Stevens, Rosemary. *American Medicine and the Public Interest*. New Haven, Conn.: Yale University Press, 1971.

Stevens, Shane. *By Reason of Insanity*. London: Weidenfeld & Nicholson, 1979.

Stevens, William O. *Pistols at Ten Paces*. Boston: Houghton Mifflin, 1940.

_____. *The Shenandoah and Its Byways*. New York: Dodd, Mead, 1941.

Stevenson, Burton (ed.). *The Macmillan Book of Proverbs, Maxims, and Famous Phrases*. New York: Macmillan, 1948.

Stevenson, Ian. *Twenty Cases Suggestive of Reincarnation*. Charlottesville: University of Virginia Press, 1974.

Stevenson, Janet. *The Undiminished Man*. Novato, Calif.: Chandler & Sharp, 1980.

Stevenson, John, and Cook, Chris. *The Slump - Society and Politics During the Depression*. London: Jonathan Cape, 1977.

Stevenson, Robert Louis. *Across the Plains*. New York: Charles Scribner's Sons, 1892.

Stevenson, R.S. *Morell Mackenzie: The Story of a Victorian Tragedy*. London: William Heinemann, 1946.

Stevenson, W. *Strike Zion*. New York: Bantam Books, 1967.

Stevenson, William. *A Man Called Intrepid*. New York: Harcourt Brace Jovanovich, 1976.

_____. *90 Minutes at Entebbe*. New York: Bantam Books, 1976.

Stevenson-McDermott, Myra E. *Lariat Letters*. Liberal, Kan.: n.p., 1907.

Steward, A.J.D. (ed.). *The History of the Bench and Bar of Missouri*. St. Louis: Legal, 1898.

Stewart, A.T.Q. *The Ulster Crisis*. London: Faber Paperback, 1967.

Stewart, C.P., and Stolman, A. *Toxicology: Mechanisms and Analytical Methods*. New York: Academic Press, 1960-1961.

Stewart, Caroline Taylor. *The Origin of Werewolf Superstitions*. Columbia: University of Missouri Press, 1909.

Stewart, Charles D. *Fellow-Creatures*. Boston: Little, Brown, 1935.

Stewart, Charles J., and Kendell, Bruce (eds.). *A Man Named John F. Kennedy: Sermons on His Assassination*. Glen Rock, N.J.: Paulist Press, 1964.

Stewart, Desmond. *Cairo: 5500 Years*. New York: Thomas Y. Crowell, 1968.

_____. *Young Egypt*. London: Wingate, 1958.

Stewart, Dora Ann. *Government and Development of Oklahoma Territory*. Oklahoma City: Harlow, 1933.

Stewart, E.W. *The Troubled Land*. New York: McGraw-Hill, 1972.

Stewart, Edgar I. *Custer's Luck*. Norman: University of Ok-lahoma Press, 1955.

Stewart, George R. *U.S. 40*. Boston: Houghton Mifflin, 1953.

Stewart, Julian H., and Faron, Louis C. *Native Peoples of South America*. New York: McGraw-Hill, 1959.

Stewart, Margaret. *Reform Under Fire - Social Progress in Spain 1931-1938*. London: New Fabian Research Bureau,1938.

Stewart, Oliver. *Danger in the Air*. New York: Philosophical Library, 1958.

Stewart, Robert. *Sam Steele*. Garden City, N.Y.: Doubleday, 1979.

Stewart, Robert C. *Identification and Investigation of Organized Criminal Activity*. Houston, Texas: National College of District Attorneys, 1980.

Stewart, Robert E., Jr. and Mary Frances. *Adolph Sutro: A Biography*. Berkeley, Calif.: Howell-North, 1962.

Stewart, Sidney. *Give Us This Day*. New York: W.W. Norton, 1957.

Stewart, Walter A. *Psychoanalysis: The First Ten Years: 1888-1898*. London: George Allen & Unwin, 1969.

Stewart, William. *Jack the Ripper: A New Theory*. London: Quality Press, 1939.

Stewart, William J. *The Era of Franklin D. Roosevelt: A Selected Bibliography*. Washington D.C.: National Archives and Records Service, 1971.

Stewart, Senator William M. *Reminiscences*. New York: Neale, 1908.

Stewart, William Rhinelander. *The Philanthropic Work of Josephine Shaw Lowell*. New York: n.p., 1905.

Stick, David. *The Outer Banks of North Carolina*. Chapel Hill, N.C.: University of North Carolina Press, 1958.

Stickles, Arndt Mathias. *Simon Bolivar Buckner: Borderland Knight*. Chapel Hill: University of North Carolina Press, 1940.

Stidger, Felix G. *Treason History of the Order of the Sons of Liberty*. Chicago: Published by Author, 1903.

Still, Bayrd. *Mirror for Gotham: New York as Seen by Contemporaries from Dutch Days to the Present*. New York: New York University Press, 1956.

Still, William. *The Underground Railroad*. Philadelphia: Porter & Coates, 1872.

Stillé, Charles Janeway. *The Life and Times of John Dickinson 1732-1808*. Philadelphia: Historical Society of Pennsylvania, 1891.

Stillman, Edmund, and Pfaff, William. *Power and Impotence: The Failure of America's Foreign Policy*. New York: Random House, 1966.

Stilwell, Joseph W. *The Stilwell Papers*. New York: Sloane, 1948.

Stimmel, Smith. *Personal Reminiscences of Abraham Lincoln*. Minneapolis, Minn.: William H.M. Adams, 1928.

Stimpson, George W. *A Book about American Politics*. New York: Harper, 1952.

Stimson, Gerry V., and Oppenheimer, Edna. *Heroin Addiction: Treatment and Control in Britain*. London: Tavistock, 1982.

_____. *Heroin and Behavior*. New York: John Wiley & Sons, 1973.

Stimson, Grace Heilman. *Rise of the Labor Movement in Los Angeles*. Berkeley: University of California Press, 1955.

_____, and Bundy, McGeorge. *On Active Service in Peace and War*. New York: Harper & Row, 1947.

Stimson, Henry L. *The Diary of Henry L. Stimson* and *The Papers of Henry L. Stimson*. New Haven, Conn.: Yale University Library, 1973.

_____. *The Far Eastern Crisis: Recollections and Observations*. New York: Harper, 1936.

Stinchcombe, A. *Crime and Punishment: Changing Attitudes in American Society*. San Francisco: Jossey-Bass, 1980.

Stirling, James. *Letters from the Slave States*. London: J.W. Parker & Son, 1857.

Stirling, Nora. *Your Money or Your Life*. Indianapolis, Ind.: Bobbs-Merril, 1974.

Stock, Ernest. *Israel on the Road to Sinai, 1949-1956.* Ithaca, N.Y.: Cornell University Press, 1967.

Stocking, George, and Watkins, Myron. *Cartels in Action.* New York: Twentieth Century Fund, 1946.

Stoddard, Charles Warren. *A Bit of Old China.* San Francisco: A.M. Richardson, 1912.

Stoddard, Ellwyn R. *Mexican Americans.* New York: Random House, 1973.

Stoddard, Francis Hovey (ed.). *Life and Letters of Charles Butler, Financier and Philanthropist.* New York: Charles Scribner's Sons, 1903.

Stoddard, Henry Luther. *As I Knew Them.* New York: Harper & Brothers, 1927.

_____. *Horance Greeley: Printer, Editor, Crusader.* New York: G.P. Putnam's Sons, 1946.

Stoddard, Lothard. *The Revolt Against Civilisation.* New York: Charles Scribner's Sons, 1923.

_____. *The Rising Tide of Color.* New York: Charles Scribner's Sons, 1922.

Stoddard, Theodore Lothrop. *Master of Manhattan: The Life of Richard Croker.* New York: Longmans Green, 1931.

Stoddard, William L. *Financial Racketeering and How To Stop It.* New York: Harper & Brothers, 1931.

Stoddard, William O. *Inside the White House in War Times.* New York: Charles L. Webster, 1890.

_____. *The Volcano Under the City.* New York: Fords, Howard & Hulbert, 1887.

Stoddard, William O., Jr. *Lincoln's Third Secretary: The Memoirs of William O. Stoddard.* New York: Exposition Press, 1955.

Stoessinger, J.G. *The Refugee and the World Community.* Minneapolis: University of Minnesota Press, 1956.

Stoker, Bram. *Famous Impostors.* New York: Sturgis & Walton, 1910.

Stoker, Charles. *Thicker 'N Thieves.* Santa Monica, Calif.: Sidereal, 1949.

Stokes, Isaac Newton Phelps, and Haskell, Daniel C. *American Historical Prints, Early Views of American Cities. . .etc.* New York: Public Library, 1932.

_____. *The Iconography of Manhattan Island, 1498-1909.* New York: R.H. Dodd, 1915-1928.

Stokoe, Dr. J. *With Napoleon at St. Helena.* London: n.p., 1902.

Stolberg, Benjamin. *Tailor's Progress: The Story of a Famous Union and the Men Who Made It.* New York: Doubleday, 1944.

Stoll, William T. *Silver Strike: The True Story of Silver Mining in the Coeur d'Alenes.* Boston: Little, Brown, 1932.

Stoller, Robert J. *Perversion: The Erotic Form of Hatred.* New York: Random House, 1975.

Stolman, E.S., and Khauslovich, G.P. *Mechanations and Methods.* New York: Academic Press, 1960.

Stone, Arthur L. *Following Old Trails.* Missoula, Mont.: Morton John Elrod, 1913.

Stone, Calvin P. (ed.). *Comparative Psychology.* New York: Prentice-Hall, 1951.

Stone, Candace. *Dana and the Sun.* New York: Dodd, Mead, 1938.

Stone, Christopher D. *Where the Law Ends: The Social Control of Corporate Behavior.* New York: Harper & Row, 1975.

Stone, Edward (ed.). *Incident at Harper's Ferry.* Englewood Cliffs, N.J.: Prentice-Hall, 1956.

Stone, I.F. *The Haunted Fifties.* New York: Vintage Books, 1969.

_____. *The Killings at Kent State.* New York: New York Review Book, 1971.

_____. *The Truman Era.* New York: Vintage Books, 1973.

Stone, Irving. *Clarence Darrow for the Defense.* Garden City, N.Y.: Doubleday, 1941.

_____. *Earl Warren.* New York: Prentice-Hall, 1948.

_____. *They Also Ran. The Story of the Men Who Were Defeated for the Presidency.* Garden City, N.Y.: Doubleday, Doran, 1943.

Stone, Dr. James W. *Report of the Trial of Professor John W. Webster.* Boston: Phillips, Sampson, 1850.

Stone, Kate. *Brokenbum.* Baton Rouge: Louisiana State University Press, 1955.

Stone, Melville E. *Fifty Years a Journalist.* Garden City, N.Y.: Doubleday, Page, 1923.

Stone, W.G., and Hirliman, G. *The Hate Factory.* New York: Dell, 1982.

Stone, Will Hale. *Twenty-Four Years a Cowboy and Ranchman in Southern Texas and Old Mexico.* Published by Author, 1905.

Stone, William L. *History of New York City.* New York: Virtue & Yorston, 1872.

Stoneham, C.T. *Mau Mau.* London: Museum Press, 1953.

_____. *Out of Barbarism.* London: Museum Press, 1955.

Stong, Phil. *Gold in Them Hills.* Garden City, N.Y.: Doubleday, 1957.

Storaska, Frederick. *How to Say No to a Rapist.* New York: Warner, 1976.

Storey, Moorfield. *The Reform of Legal Procedure.* New Haven, Conn.: Yale University Press, 1911.

Storr, Anthony. *Human Aggression.* New York: Bantam Books, 1968.

Storrs, Sir Ronald. *Orientations.* London: Nicholson & Watson, 1939.

Storry, Richard. *The Double Patriots: A Study of Japanese Nationalism.* Boston: Houghton Mifflin, 1957.

_____. *A Modern History of Japan.* New York: Penguin Books, 1960.

Story, Charles. *Alcohol: Its Nature and Efects.* New York: National Temperance Society, 1879.

The Story of the FBI: The Official Picture History. New York: Dutton, 1947.

Story of the Old Homestead: 1732-1932. Cornwall, N.Y.: The Two Hundredth Anniversary Committee, 1932.

Story, Charles. *Alcohol: Its Nature and Effects.* New York: National Temperance Society, 1879.

Story, William W. (ed.). *Life and Letters of Joseph Story.* Boston: C.C. Little & J. Brown, 1851.

Stott, William. *Documentary Expression and Thirties America.* New York: Oxford University Press, 1973.

Stouffer, Samuel A., et al. *The American Soldier.* Princeton, N.J.: Princeton University Press, 1949.

_____, and Lazarsfeld, Paul. *Research Memorandum on the Family in the Depression.* New York: Social Science Research Council, 1937.

Stoughton, William. *New England's True Interest.* Cambridge, Mass.: S.G. & M.J., 1970.

Stout, Charles Taber. *The Eighteenth Amendment and the Part Played by Organized Medicine.* New York: Mitchell Kennerley, 1921.

Stout, Ernest. *The Younger Brothers.* Chicago: Dramatic, 1902.

_____. *The Younger Brothers' Last Raid.* Chicago: Dramatic, 1902.

_____. *The Youngers' Last Stand.* Chicago: Dramatic, 1902.

_____. *The Youngers Out West.* Chicago: Dramatic, 1902.

Stout, F.E. *Rube Burrows; or, Life, Exploits and Death of the Bold Train Robber.* Aberdeen, Miss.: n.p., 1890.

Stout, Tom (ed.). *Montana, Its Story and Biography.* Chicago: American Historical Society, 1921.

Stover, Elizabeth Matchett (ed.). *Son-of-a-Gun Stew; a Sampling of the Southwest.* Dallas: University of Dallas Press, 1945.

Stow, E.W. *The Native Races of South Africa.* Cape Town, S. Afri.: Juta, 1910.

Stow, John. *The Survey of London.* London: J.M. Dent, 1912.

Stowe, Lyman Beecher. *Saints, Sinners and Beechers.* Indianapolis, Ind.: Bobbs-Merrill, 1934.

Stowers, Carlton. *Careless Whispers.* Dallas: Taylor, 1984.

Stoyan, P.B. *World Without End.* New York: Reynal & Hitchcock, 1939.

Stoyanovitch, M.D. *The Great Powers and the Balkans (1875-78)*. Cambridge, Eng.: Cambridge University Press, 1938.

Stoyanovitch, N. *La Serbie d'hier et de demain*. Paris: Berger-Levrault, 1927.

Strachey, John. *A Faith to Fight For*. London: Victor Gollancz, 1940.

———. *How Socialism Works*. New York: Moder Age Books, 1939.

———. *Socialism Looks Forward*. New York: Philosophical Library, 1945.

Strachey, Lytton. *Eminent Victorians*. London: Collins, 1920.

———. *Queen Victoria*. New York: Harcourt, Brace, 1921.

Strachey, William. *History of the Travaile into Virginia Britannia*. London: Hakluyt Society, 1849.

Strahorn, Carrie Adell. *Fifteen Thousand Miles by Stage*. New York: G.P. Putnam's Sons, 1911.

Strahorn, Robert E. *To the Rockies and Beyond*. Omaha: New West, 1879.

———. *Wyoming, Black Hills and Big Horn Region*. Cheyenne, Wyo.: Western Press, 1877.

Straight, Michael. *Make This the Last War*. New York: Harcourt, Brace, 1943.

———. *Trial by Television*. Boston: Beacon Press, 1954.

Strakhovsky, L.I. *Alexander I of Russia*. New York: W.W. Norton, 1947.

Strange and Mysterious Crimes. New York: MacFadden, 1929.

Strasberg, Lee (ed.). *Famous American Plays of the 1950s*. New York: Dell, 1962.

Strasburg, Paul A. *Violent Delinquents*. New York: Simon & Schuster, 1978.

Strassels, Paul N. *All You Need to Know about the IRS*. New York: Random House, 1979.

Strasser, Otto. *Hitler and I*. Boston: Houghton Mifflin, 1940.

Strate, David K. *Sentinel to the Cimarron*. Dodge City, Kansas: Cultural Heritage and Arts Center, 1970.

Straton, John Roach. *The Famous New York Fundamentalist-Modernist Debates*. New York: George H. Doran, 1925.

Stratton, David H. (ed.). *The Memoirs of Albert B. Fall*. El Paso: University of Texas Press, 1966.

Strauch, Rudi. *Sir Neville Henderson*. Bonn, Ger.: Ludwig Röhrscheid, 1959.

Straus, M., Gelles, R., and Steinmetz, S. *Behind Closed Doors: Violence in the American Family*. Garden City, N.Y.: Anchor-Doubleday, 1980.

Straus, Ralph. *Coaches and Carriages*. London: M. Secher, 1912.

Strauss, G.L.M. *Emperor William: The Life of a Great King and Good Man*. London: Ward & Downey, 1888.

Strauss, George, and Sayles, Leonard R. *Personnel*. Englewood Cliffs, N.J.: Prentice-Hall, 1972.

Strauss, Levi. *Levi's Round-Up of Western Sheriffs*. San Francisco: Levi Strauss, n.d.

Strauss, Patricia. *Bevin and Co*. New York: G.P. Putnam's Sons, 1941.

———. *Cripps, Advocate Extraordinary*. New York: Duell, Sloan & Pearce, 1942.

Strawson, John. *Hitler as Military Commander*. London: B.T. Batsford, 1971.

Strecker, A.M. *Clinical Psychiatry*. Philadelphia: P. Blackeston Sons, n.d.

Street, David, Vintner, Robert D., and Perrow, Charles. *Organization for Treatment: A Comparative Study on Institutions for Delinquents*. New York: Free Press, 1966.

Street, Julian Leonard. *Abroad at Home: American Ramblings, Observations, and Adventures of Julian Street*. New York: Century, 1914.

———. *The Most Interesting American*. New York: Century, 1915.

Streeter, Floyd Benjamin. *Ben Thompson, Man With A Gun*. New York: Frederick Fell, 1957.

———. *The Kaw: The Heart of a Nation*. New York: Farrar & Rinehart, 1941.

———. *Prairie Trails and Cow Towns*. Boston: Chapman & Grimes, 1936.

Street-Porter, Janet. *Scandal*. New York: Dell, 1981.

Streetwalker. London: The Bodley Head, 1959.

Strevey, Tracy Elmer. *Joseph Medill and the Chicago Tribune During the Civil War Period*. Chicago: Chicago University Press, 1930.

Stribling, T.S. *Teeftallow*. Garden City, N.Y.: Doubleday, Page, 1926.

Strickland, Stephen Parks (ed.). *Hugo Black and the Supreme Court*. Indianapolis, Ind.: Bobbs-Merrill, 1967.

Strictures on the Case of Ephraim K. Avery. Providence, R.I.: William Simons, Jr., 1833.

Strik-Strikfeldt, Wilfried. *Against Hitler and Stalin*. New York: John Day, 1973.

Stripling, Robert E. *The Red Plot Against America*. New York: Bell, 1949.

Strobel, Martin. *A Report on the Trial of Michael & Martin Toohey*. Charleston, S.C.: A.E. Miller, 1819.

Strode, Hudson. *Finland Forever*. New York: Harcourt, 1941.

———. *Jefferson Davis: American Patriot 1808-1861*. New York: Harcourt, Brace, 1955.

———. *Jefferson Davis: Confederate President*. New York: Harcourt, Brace, 1959.

———. *Timeless Mexico*. New York: Harcourt, Brace, 1944.

Strong, Benjamin. *Interpretations of Federal Reserve Policy*. New York: Harper & Brothers, 1930.

Strong, George Templeton. *Diary, 1820-1875*. 4 vols. New York: Macmillan, 1952.

Strong, Capt. Henry W. *My Frontier Days & Indian Fights on the Plains of Texas*. Dallas: n.p, 1926.

Strong, Josiah. *The New Era or The Coming Kingdom*. New York: Baker & Taylor, 1893.

Stryker, Lloyd Paul. *Andrew Jackson. A Study in Courage*. New York: Macmillan, 1929.

———. *The Art of Advocacy*. New York: Cornerstone Library, 1965.

Stryker, William. *Battles of Trenton and Princeton*. Boston: Houghton Mifflin, 1898.

Stuart, George R. *The Stump Digger*. Westerville, Ohio: American Issue, 1896.

Stuart, Graham H. *The Department of State*. New York: Macmillan, 1949.

Stuart, Granville. *Forty Years on the Frontier*. 2 vols. Cleveland: Arthur H. Clark, 1925.

Stuart, Hix C. *The Notorious Ashley Gang*. Stuart, Fla.: St. Lucie Printing, 1928.

Stuart, John Leighton. *Fifty Years in China*. New York: Random, 1946.

Stuart, Phyllis L., and Cantor, Muriel G. (eds.). *Varieties of Work Experience*. New York: Halsted Press, John Wiley & Sons, 1974.

Stuart, Theodore M. *Past and Present of Lucas and Wayne Counties, Iowa*. 2 vols. Chicago: S.J. Clarke, 1913.

Stuart, William H. *The 20 Incredible Years*. Chicago: M.A. Donohue, 1935.

Stubbs, Stanley A. *Bird's-Eye View of the Pueblos*. Norman: University of Oklahoma Press, 1950.

Stuckey, G.B. *Evidence for the Law Enforcement Officer*. New York: McGraw-Hill, 1968.

Studt, Elliot, Messinger, Sheldon, and Wilson, Thomas P. *C-Unit: Search for Community in Prison*. New York: Russell Sage Foundation, 1974.

Stuerwald, John E. *Fire and Arson Investigator*. International Association of Arson Investigators, 1977.

Stumpff, Johann. *Histoire véritable*. Geneva, Switz.: J.G. Fick, 1868.

Sturgkh, General Graf Josef. *Im Deutschen Grossen Hauptquartier*. Leipzig, Ger.: List, 1921.

Sturmthal, Adolf. *The Tragedy of European Labor*. New York:

Columbia University Press, 1943.

Styles, George. *Bombs Have No Pity.* London: Lustcombe, 1975.

A Succinct Narrative of the Life and Character of Abel Clemmons. Morgantown, Va.: J. Campbell, 1806.

Suchey, John T. and Tipton, Howard O. *Arson: America's Malignant Crime.* Columbus, Ohio: Battelle Columbus Laboratories, 1976.

Suchman, Edward A. *Evaluative Research.* New York: Russel Sage Foundation, 1967.

Suda Teichi. *Kazami Akira and Those Times.* Tokyo: Shobo, 1965.

Sudhoff, Karl. *Der Ursprung der Syphilis.* Leipzig, Ger.: F.C.W. Vogel, 1913.

Sudnow, David (ed.). *Studies in Social Interaction.* New York: Free Press, 1972.

Suetonius Tranquillus, Gaius. *Lives of the Caesars.* trans. Robert Graves. London: Penguin Books, 1957.

_____. *The Twelve Caesars.* trans. Robert Graves. Baltimore, Md.: Penguin Books, 1957.

The Sugar Creek Tragedy, Life and Confessions of John Goodman. Ottawa, Ohio: Sentinel, 1875.

Sugar, Peter F. *Industrialization of Bosnia-Hercegovina, 1878-1918.* Seattle: University of Washington Press, 1964.

Suhl, Yuri (ed. and trans.). *They Fought Back: The Story of the Jewish Resistance in Nazi Europe.* New York: Crown, 1967.

Suhrawardy, Sir Abdullah al-Mamun al-. *The Sayings of Mohammed.* London: John Murray, 1941.

Sukhanov, N.N. *Russian Revolution, 1917.* New York: Oxford University Press, 1955.

Suliashvili, David. *Vstrechi s V.I. Leninim v emigratsii.* Tiflis, U.S.S.R.: Izdatelstvo Zarya Vostoka, 1957.

Sullerot, Evelyn. *Women, Change and Society.* New York: McGraw-Hill, 1971.

Sullivan, Clyde E., and Mandell, Wallace. *Restoration of Youth Through Training: A Final Report.* Staten Island, N.Y.: Wakoff Research Center, 1967.

Sullivan, Dulcie. *The LS Brand: The Story of a Texas Panhandle Ranch.* Austin: University of Texas Press, 1968.

Sullivan, Edward Dean. *Chicago Surrenders: A Sequel to Rattling the Cup on Chicago Crime.* New York: Vanguard Press, 1930.

_____. *The Fabulous Wilson Mizner.* New York: Henkle, 1935.

_____. *Rattling the Cup on Chicago Crime.* New York: Vanguard Press, 1929.

_____. *The Snatch Racket.* New York: Vanguard Press, 1932.

Sullivan, Frank S. *A History of Meade County, Kansas.* Topeka, Kan.: Crane, 1916.

Sullivan, Gerald E. (ed.). *The Story of Englewood, 1835-1923.* Chicago: Foster & McDonnell, 1924.

Sullivan, Gerard, and Aronson, Harvey. *High Hopes: The Amityville Murders.* New York: Coward, McCann & Geohegan, 1981.

Sullivan, Harry Stack. *The Interpersonal Theory of Psychology.* New York: W.W. Norton, 1953.

Sullivan, Lawrence. *Prelude to Panic.* Washington, D.C.: Statesman Press, 1936.

Sullivan, Mark. *Our Times: The United States.* New York: Charles Scribner's Sons, 1926-1935.

Sullivan, Robert. *The Disappearance of Dr. Parkman.* New York: Prentice-Hall, 1960.

Sullivan, Terry, with Maiken, Peter T. *Killer Clown.* New York: Grosset & Dunlap, 1983.

Sullivan, W.A. *The Industrial Worker in Pennsylvania 1800-1840.* Harrisburg: Pennsylvania Historical and Museum Commission, 1955.

Sullivan, W. John L. *Twelve Years in the Saddle for Law and Order on the Frontiers of Texas.* Austin, Texas: Von Boeckman-Jones, 1909.

Sullivan, William C. *The Bureau.* New York: W.W. Norton, 1979.

Sulzberger, C.L. *A Long Row of Candles: Memoirs and Diaries.* New York: Macmillan, 1969.

Summers, Anne. *Damned Whores and God's Police.* Ringwood, N.J.: Penguin, 1975.

Summers, Anthony. *Conspiracy.* New York: McGraw-Hill, 1980.

_____. *Goddess: The Secret Lives of Marilyn Monroe.* New York: Macmillan, 1985.

Summers, Marvin R., and Barth, Thomas E. (eds.). *Law and Order in a Democratic Society.* New York: Charles E. Merrill, 1970.

Summers, Montague. *An Examen of Witches.* London: J. Rodker, 1929.

_____. *The Geography of Witchcraft.* London: Routledge & Kegan Paul, 1927.

_____. *The History of Witchcraft and Demonology.* New Hyde Park, N.Y.: University Books, 1956.

_____. *Popular History of Witchcraft.* New York: E.P. Dutton, 1937.

_____. *The Vampire in Europe.* New York: E.P. Dutton, 1929.

_____. *The Vampire: His Kith and Kin.* New York: E.P. Dutton, 1929.

_____. *The Werewolf.* New York: E.P. Dutton, 1934.

_____. *Witchcraft and Black Magic.* New York: Rider, 1934.

Sumner, Benedict H. *Peter the Great and the Emergence of Russia.* New York: Macmillan, 1951.

_____. *Peter the Great and the Ottoman Empire.* Oxford, Eng.: Blackwell, 1949.

_____. *Russia and the Balkans, 1870-1880.* London: Milford, 1937.

_____. *Tsardom and Imperialism in the Far and Middle East.* Oxford, Eng.: Oxford University Press, 1940.

Sumner, Charles. *The Crime Against Kansas.* Washington, D.C.: Buell & Blanchard, 1856.

_____. *Speech of Hon. Charles Sumner Before the Citizens of New York at Cooper Institute, September 10, 1863.* Boston: William V. Spencer, 1863.

Sumner, William Graham. *Essays of William Graham Sumner.* 2 vols. New Haven, Conn.: Yale University Press, 1934.

_____. *Folkways.* Boston: Ginn, 1906.

_____. *A History of Banking in the United States.* New York: Journal of Commerce and Commercial Bulletin, 1896.

The Sun's Guide to New York. New York: New York Sun, 1893.

Sunset Club. *Echoes, 1889-1891.* Chicago: n.p., n.d.

_____. *Yearbooks.* Chicago: n.p., various dates.

Surface, William. *Inside Internal Revenue.* New York: Coward-McCann, 1967.

Surgeon General's Scientific Advisory Committee on Television and Social Behavior. *Television and Growing Up: The Impact of Televised Violence.* Washington, D.C.: U.S. Government Printing Office, 1972.

Surieu, Robert. *Saru-é naz: An Essay on Love and Representation of Erotic Themes in Ancient Iran.* trans. James Hogarth. Geneva, Switz.: Nagel, 1967.

Surin, Jean Joseph. *Histoire abregée de la possession des Ursalines de Loudun et des peines du père Surin.* Paris: au Bureau du l'Association Catholique du Sacré-Coeur, 1828.

Surrency, Edwin C. (ed.). *A Marshall Reader.* New York: Oceana, 1955.

Survey of Inmates of Local Jails, 1972. Washington, D.C.: National Criminal Justice Information and Statistics Service, 1976.

Susman, Jackwell (ed.). *Crime and Justice, 1971-1972.* New York: AMS Press, 1974.

Susmel, Duilio. *Vita sbagliata di Galeazzo Ciano.* Milan, Italy: Aldo Palazzi, 1962.

Susmel, Edoardo. *Mussolini e il suo tempo.* Milan, Italy: Garzanti, 1950.

_____, and Dulio (eds.). *Opera omnia di Benito Mussolini.* Florence, Italy: La Fenice, 1951-1957.

_____. *Scritti e discorsi di Benito Mussolini.* Florence, Italy: La

Fenice, 1934-39.

Susskind, Richard. *The Crusades*. New York: Ballantine, 1962.

Sussman, Frederick B. *Laws of Juvenile Delinquency*. New York: Oceana, 1950.

Sussman, Les, and Bordwell, Sally. *The Rapist File*. New York: Chelsea House, 1981.

Sutch, W.B. *New Zealand's Labor Government at Work*. New York: League for Industrial Democracy, 1940.

Sutcliffe, Alice. *Robert Fulton and the "Clermont"*. New York: Century, 1909.

Sutherland, Edwin H. *Criminology*. Philadelphia: J.D. Lippincott, 1924.

_____. *On Analyzing Crime*. Chicago: University of Chicago Press, 1973.

_____, and Cressy, Donald R. *Principles in Criminology*. Philadelphia: J.D. Lippincott, 1966.

_____, and Cressey, Donald R. *Principles of Criminology*. Philadelphia: J.B. Lippincott, 1955.

_____. *The Professional Thief*. Chicago: University of Chicago Press, 1937.

_____ (ed.). *White Collar Crime*. New York: Holt, Rinehart & Winston, 1949.

Sutherland, Millicent. *Six Weeks at the War*. Chicago: McCluny, 1915.

Sutherland, Sidney. *Ten Real Murder Mysteries*. New York: G.P. Putnam's Sons, 1929.

Sutherland, William Alexander. *Out Where the West Be-Grins*. Las Cruces, N.M.: Southwest, 1942.

Suthers, John W., and Shupp, Gary L. *Fraud & Deceit: How To Stop Being Ripped Off*. New York: Arco, 1982.

Sutley, Jack T. *The Last Frontier*. New York: Macmillan, 1930.

Sutley, Zachary Taylor. *The Last Frontier*. New York: Macmillan, 1933.

Suttles, Gerald D. *The Social Order of the Slum*. Chicago: University of Chicago Press, 1968.

Sutton, Charles Warden. *The New York Tombs; Its Secrets and Mysteries*. New York: U.S., 1874.

Sutton, Ernest V. *A Life Worth Living*. Pasadena, Calif.: Trail's End, 1948.

Sutton, Fred Ellsworth. *Hands Up! Stories of the Six Gun Fighters of the Old West*. Indianapolis, Ind.: Bobbs-Merrill, 1926.

Sutton, Robert C., Jr. *The Sutton-Taylor Feud*. Quanah, Texas: Nortex Press, 1974.

Sutton, Willie, and Reynolds, Quentin. *I, Willie Sutton*. New York: Farrar, Straus, & Young, 1953.

_____. *Where the Money Was*. New York: Viking Press, 1976.

Svensson, Arne, and Wendell, Otto. *Crime Detection*. London: Cleaver-Hume, 1955.

Sveri, K. *Kriminalitet og Older*. Stockholm: Almquist & Wiksell, 1960.

Swados, Harvey. *Standing up for the People: The Life and Work of Estes Kefauver*. New York: E.P. Dutton, 1972.

Swain, John. *A History of Torture*. New York: Award, 1969.

Swaine, R.T. *The Cravath Firm*. New York: n.p., 1946.

Swallow, Alan (ed.). *The Wild Bunch*. Denver: Sage Books, 1966.

Swan, A.M. *Life, Trial, Conviction, Confession, and Execution of John Marion Osborne, The Murderer of Mrs. Adelia M. Mathews*. Peoria, Ill.: A.C. Bloomer, 1873.

Swan, Oliver G. *Covered Wagon Days*. New York: Grosset & Dunlap, 1928.

_____ (ed.). *Frontier Days*. Philadelphia: Macrae-Smith, 1928.

Swanberg, William A. *Citizen Hearst: A Biography of William Randolph Hearst*. New York: Charles Scribner's Sons, 1961.

_____. *Dreiser*. New York: Charles Scribner's Sons, 1965.

_____. *First Blood: The Story of Fort Sumter*. New York: Charles Scribner's Sons, 1957.

_____. *Jim Fisk, The Career of An Improbable Rascal*. New York: Charles Scribner's Sons, 1961.

_____. *Luce and His Empire*. New York: Charles Scribner's

Sons, 1972.

_____. *Pulitzer*. New York: Charles Scribner's Sons, 1967.

_____. *Sickles the Incredible*. New York: Charles Scribner's Sons, 1956.

Swaney, W.B. *Safeguards of Liberty*. New York: Oxford University Press, 1920.

Swann, Thomas. *Ernest Dowson*. New York: Twayne, 1964.

Swansea, A. Schofield. *Notes on Canada and the United States of America*. London: Cambria Daily Leader, 1888.

Swanson, C., Chamelin, N., and Territo, L. *Criminal Investigation*. Santa Monica, Calif.: Goodyear, 1977.

Swanton, John R. *The Indians of the Southeastern United States*. New York: Greenwood Press, 1969.

Sward, Keith. *The Legend of Henry Ford*. New York: Rinehart, 1948.

Swarthouth, Glendon. *The Shootist*. Garden City, N.Y.: Doubleday, 1975.

Swayze, Mrs. J.C. *Ossawatomie Brown, or the Insurrection at Harper's Ferry*. New York: Samuel French, 1859.

Swearingen, Rodger. *Red Flag in Japan*. Cambridge, Mass.: Harvard University Press, 1952.

Sweeney, Thomas J., and Ellingsworth, William (eds.). *Issues in Police Patrol*. Washington, D.C.: Police Foundation, 1973.

Sweet, Alex E., and Knox, J. Amory. *On a Mexican Mustang Through Texas, from the Gulf to the Rio Grande*. Hartford, Conn.: S.S. Scranton, 1883.

Sweet, P.R. *Mussolini and Dollfuss*. London: Victor Gollancz, 1948.

Sweet, William W. *Religion in Colonial America*. New York: Charles Scribner's Sons, 1942.

Sweet, Willis. *Carbonate Camps, Leadville and Ten-Mile of Colorado*. Kansas City: Ramsey, Millett & Hudson, 1879.

Sweet-Escott, Bickham. *Greece: A Political and Economic Survey, 1939-1953*. London: Royal Institute of International Affairs, 1954.

Sweetman, Luke D. *Back Trailing on Open Range*. Caldwell, Idaho: Caxton Printers, 1951.

Sweezy, Paul M. *Socialism*. New York: McGraw-Hill, 1949.

_____. *The Theory of Capitalist Development*. New York: Monthly Review Press, 1968.

Swessinger, Earl A. *Texas Trail to Dodge City*. San Antonio, Texas: Naylor, 1950.

Swift, Arthur. *New Frontiers of Religion*. New York: Macmillan, 1938.

Swift, David W. (ed.). *Ninety Li a Day*. Taipei, Tai.: Orient Cultural Service, 1975.

Swiggert, Howard. *The Rebel Raider*. Indianapolis, Ind.: Bobbs-Merrill, 1934.

_____ (ed.). *A Rebel War Clerk's Diary*. New York: Barnes & Noble, 1935.

Swinburne. *Lucretia Borgia*. London: Golden Cockerel Press, 1942.

Swinburne, John. *Poisoning by Aconite: Synopsis of the Trial of Hendrickson for the Murder of His Wife*. Philadelphia: n.p., 1862.

Swing, Raymond G. *Forerunners of American Fascism*. New York: Julian Messner, 1935.

Swinston, William. *History of the Seventh Regiment, National Guard, State of New York . . . etc*. New York: Fields, Osgood, 1870.

Swint, Henry L. *The Northern Teacher in the South, 1862-1870*. Nashville, Tenn.: Vanderbilt University Press, 1941.

Swinton, John. *Striking for Life, Labor's Side to the Labor Question. The Right of the Workingman to a Fair Living*. Philadelphia: A.R. Keller, 1894.

Swire, Joseph. *Albania: the Rise of a Kingdom*. London: Williams & Ungate, 1929.

Swisher, Carl Brent. *American Constitutional Development*. Boston: Houghton Mifflin, 1943.

_____. *Motivation and Political Technique in the California*

Constitutional Convention, 1878-1879. Claremont, Calif.: Pomona College, 1930.

_____. *Roger B. Taney.* New York: Macmillan, 1935.

_____ (ed.). *Selected Papers of Homer Cummings.* New York: Charles Scribner's Sons, 1939.

_____. *Stephen J. Field: Craftsman of the Law.* Washington, D.C.: Brookings Institute, 1930.

_____. *The Supreme Court in Modern Role.* New York: New York University Press, 1958.

Switzler, William F. *Switzler's Illustrated History of Missouri, from 1541 to 1877.* St. Louis: C.R. Barns, 1879.

Swope, Herbert Bayard. *Inside the German Empire.* New York: Century, 1917.

Sydnor, C.S. *The Development of Southern Sectionalism 1819-1848.* Baton Rouge: Louisiana State University Press, 1948.

_____. *Gentlemen Freeholders: Political Practices in Washington's Virginia.* Chapel Hill: University of North Carolina Press, 1952.

Sykes, Christopher. *Cross Roads to Israel.* London: Williams Collins, 1965.

_____. *Nancy: The Life of Lady Astor.* London: William Collins Sons, 1972.

Sykes, Godfrey. *A Westerly Trend.* Tucson: Arizona Pioneer's Historical Society, 1944.

Sykes, Gresham M. *Crime and Society.* New York: Random House, 1956.

_____. *Criminology.* New York: Harcourt, Brace, Jovanovich, 1978.

_____. *The Future of Crime.* Rockville, Md.: National Institute of Mental Health, 1980.

_____. *The Society of Captives.* New York: Atheneum, 1969.

Syme, A.V. *The Assassins.* Sydney, Aus.: Horwitz, 1967.

Syme, Sir Ronald. *Colonial Elites.* New York: Oxford University Press, 1958.

_____. *The Roman Revolution.* Oxford, Eng.: Clarendon Press, 1939.

_____. *Tacitus.* 2 vols. Oxford, Eng.: Clarendon Press, 1958.

Symes, Lillian and Clement, Travers. *Rebel America.* New York: Harper, 1934.

Symon, J.D. and Bensusan, S.L. *The Renaissance and Its Makers.* London: T.C. & E.C. Jack, 1913.

Symonds, John. *The Great Beast: The Life and Magick of Aleister Crowley.* London: MacDonald, 1971.

Symonds, John Addington. *The Age of Despots.* London: Smith, Elder, 1898.

Symons, A. *Baudelaire: Prose and Poetry.* New York: Albert & Charles Boni, 1926.

Symons, Arthur. *A Study of Oscar Wilde.* London: C.J. Sawyer, 1930.

Symons, J. *Horatio Bottomley.* London: Cresset, 1955.

Symons, Julian. *A.J.A. Symons: His Life and Speculations.* London: Eyre & Spottiswoode, 1950.

_____. *A Pictorial History of Crime.* New York: Crown, 1966.

_____. *A Reasonable Doubt.* London: Cresset Press, 1960.

Synon, Mary. *McAdoo.* Indianapolis, Ind.: Bobbs-Merrill, 1924.

Synopsis of the Trial of John and William Gordon for the Murder of Amasa Sprague. Boston: Skinner & Blanchard, 1845.

Syrett, Harold C. (ed.). *American Historical Documents.* New York: Barnes & Noble, 1960.

_____ (ed.). *The City of Brooklyn, 1865-1898.* New York: Columbia University Press, 1944.

_____. *The Gentleman and the Tiger: Autobiography of G.B. McClellan Jr.* Philadelphia: J.B. Lippincott, 1956.

_____ (ed.). *The Papers of Alexander Hamilton.* New York: Columbia University Press, 1961.

Szarowski, John (ed.). *Storyville Portraits; Photographs Taken from the New Orleans Red Light District by E.J. Bellocq.* New York: Museum of Modern Art, 1970.

Szasz, Thomas S. *Ceremonial Chemistry: The Ritual Persecution of Drugs, Addicts, and Pushers.* Garden City, N.Y.: Anchor Press, 1974.

_____. *Law, Liberty, and Psychiatry.* New York: Macmillan, 1963.

_____. *The Manufacture of Madness.* New York: Harper & Row, 1970.

_____. *The Myth of Mental Illness.* New York: Paul B. Hoeber, 1961.

_____. *Pain and Pleasure.* New York: Basic Books, 1957.

_____. *Psychiatric Justice.* New York: Collier, 1965.

Szulc, Tad. *The Illusion of Peace.* New York: Viking Press, 1978.

T

Tabb, William K., Sawers, Larry (eds.). *Marxism and the Metropolis: New Perspectives in Urban Political Economy.* New York: Oxford University Press, 1984.

Tabbora, Lina. *Suvivre dans Beyrouth.* Paris: Olivier Orban, 1977.

Taber, Robert. *The War of the Flea.* London: Paladin, 1970.

Tablada, José Juan. *Historia de la campaña de la división del norte.* Mexico City: Imprenta del Gobierno Federal, 1913.

Tabor, Pauline. *Pauline's.* New York: Fawcett Crest Book, 1973.

Tabori, Paul. *Crime and the Occult.* New York: Taplinger, 1974.

Tacitus. *The Annals.* trans. A.J. Church and W.J. Brodribb. New York: Twayne, 1964.

_____. *The Germania.* trans. Hugh Mattingly. New York: Penguin, 1971.

Tackwood, Louis, and C.R.I.C. *The Glass House Tapes.* New York: Avon, 1973.

Taeuber, Irene and Conrad. *People of the United States in the 20th Century.* Washington, D.C.: U.S. Department of Commerce, Bureau of the Census, 1971.

Taft, Donald R. *Criminology.* New York: J.B. Lippincott, 1954.

Taft, Lorado. *History of American Sculpture.* New York: Macmillan, 1924.

Taft, Philip. *The A.F. of L. in the Time of Gompers.* New York: Harper & Brothers, 1957.

_____. *Labor Politics American Style: The California State Federation of Labor.* Cambridge, Mass.: Harvard University Press, 1968.

Taft, Robert. *Artists and Illustrators of the Old West.* New York: Charles Scribner's Sons, 1953.

_____. *Photography and the American Scene.* New York: Macmillan, 1938.

Tagart, Edward. *Memoir of the Late Captain Peter Heywood.* London: Effingham Wilson, 1832.

Tagiuri, R., and Petrullo, L. (eds.). *Person Perception and Interpersonal Behavior.* Palo Alto, Calif.: Stanford University Press, 1958.

Tagore, Radindranath. *Mahatmaji and the Depressed Humanity.* Calcutta, India: Vishna-Bharati, 1932.

_____. *Sadhana.* New York: Macmillan, 1916.

Taillepied, Noel. *Histoire de l'etat et république des druides.* Paris: Jean Sarant, 1585.

_____. *Treatise of Ghosts.* trans. M. Summers. London: Fortune Press, 1933.

Taine, Hippolyte Adolphe. *The French Revolution.* trans. John Durand. New York: H. Holt, 1878.

Takahashi Masaye. *The 2/26 Incident.* Tokyo: Chuo Koron Sha, 1965.

Takamiya Taihei. *Pacific Record of a Nation.* Tokyo: Takenawa-to-sha, 1951.

Takeda Taijun. *Notes on Politicians.* Tokyo: Iwanami Shinsho, 1960.

Takemori, Hisaakira. *Miezaru Seifu (Invisible Government).* Tokyo: Shiraishi Shoten, 1976.

Takeuchi, Tatsuji. *War and Diplomacy in the Japanese Empire.* Chicago: University of Chicago Press, 1935.

Taku-ichiro Kamada. *Ugaki Kazushige: A Biography.* Tokyo: Chuo Koron-sha, 1937.

Talbot, Ethelbert. *My People of the Plains.* New York: Harper, 1906.

Talbot, F.L. (ed.). *St. Louis Police Department.* St. Louis: Woodward & Tiernan, n.d.

Talbot, J.H. *A Biographical History of Medicine.* New York: Grune & Stratton, 1970.

Talese, Gay. *Honor Thy Father.* New York: World, 1971.

_____. *The Kingdom and the Power.* New York: World, 1966.

_____. *Thy Neighbor's Wife.* Greenwich, Conn.: Fawcett Crest Books, 1979.

Tallant, Robert. *Murder in New Orleans.* London: William Kimber, 1952.

_____. *Ready to Hang.* New York: Harper & Brothers, 1952.

_____. *The Romantic New Orleanians.* New York: E.P. Dutton, 1950.

_____. *Voodoo in New Orleans.* New York: Macmillan, 1946.

Tallent, Annie D. *The Black Hills: or, The Last Hunting Ground of the Dakotahs.* St. Louis: Nixon-Jones Printing, 1899.

Talleyrand, Prince de. *Mémoires.* Paris: Plon, 1957.

Talmage, T. DeWitt. *The Abominations of Modern Society.* New York: Adams, Victor, 1872.

_____. *The Masque Torn Off.* Chicago: J. Fairbanks, 1880.

Tamaro, Attilio. *Due anni di storia, 1943-1945.* Rome: Tosi, 1948.

_____. *Vent' anni di storia.* 3 vols. Rome: Tiber, 1954-1955.

Tamassia, Mirella. *L'attesa nell'ombra.* Padua, Italy: Zanocco, 1946.

Tammany, A Patriotic History. New York: New York County Democratic Committee, 1924.

Tamrat, Tadesse. *Church and State in Ethiopiea, 1270-1527.* Oxford, Eng.: Clarendon Press, 1972.

Tamura Yoshio (ed.). *Secret History of the Greater East Asia War.* 12 vols. Tokyo: Fuji Shoen, 1953.

Tanay, F. *The Murderers.* Indianapolis, Ind.: Bobbs-Merrill, 1976.

Tancred, Sir Thomas. *Suggestions on the Treatment and Disposal of Criminals.* London: T. Hatchard, 1857.

Tandlero, Tobia. *Dissertatio de Fascino et Incantatione.* Wittenberg, Ger.: Schmidt, 1606.

Tanenbaum, Robert, and Rosenberg, Philip. *Badge of the Assassin.* New York: E.P. Dutton, 1979.

_____, and Greenberg, Peter S. *The Piano Teacher.* New York: New American Library, 1987.

Tang Leang-li. *The Inner History of the Chinese Revolution.* New York: E.P. Dutton, 1930.

Tang, Peter S.H. *Russian and Soviet Policy in Manchuria and Outer Mongolia 1911-1931.* Durham, N.C.: Duke University Press, 1959.

Tannenbaum, Arnold S. *Control in Organizations.* New York: McGraw-Hill, 1968.

Tannenbaum, Frank. *Crime and the Community.* New York: Columbia University Press, 1938.

_____. *The Mexican Agrarian Revolution.* New York: Macmillan, 1929.

_____. *Mexico: The Struggle for Peace and Bread.* New York: Alfred A. Knopf, 1950.

_____. *Peace by Revolution: An Interpretation of Mexico.* New York: Columbia University Press, 1933.

_____. *Wall Shadows.* New York: G.P. Putnam's Sons, 1922.

Tanner, Louise. *All the Things We Were.* Garden City, N.Y.: Doubleday, 1968.

Tanner, R.E.S. *The Witch Murders in Sukumaland - A Sociological Commentary. Crime in Africa Series No. 4.* Uppsala, Swed.: Scandinavian Institute of African Studies, 1970.

Tanon, Celestin Louis. *Histoire des tribunaux de l'Inquisition en France.* Paris: L. Larose & Forcel, 1893.

Tansill, Charles Callan. *Back Door to War.* Chicago: Henry Regnery, 1952.

Taoka Kazuo. *Yamaguchi Gumi Sandaime: Taoka Kazuo Jiten. (Yamaguchigumi Third Generation: The Autobiography of Kazuo Taoka).* Tokyo: Tokukan Shoten, 1973.

Tapié, Victor L. *France in the Age of Louis XIII and Richlieu.* trans. D. McN. Lockie. New York: Macmillan, 1974.

_____. *The Rise and Fall of the Habsburg Monarchy.* trans. Stephen Hardman. New York: Frederick A. Praeger, 1971.

Tapley, Charles Sutherland. *Rebecca Nurse.* Boston: Marshall Jones, 1930.

Tappan, Paul W. *Crime, Justice, and Correction.* New York: McGraw-Hill, 1960.

_____. *The Habitual Sex Offender.* Trenton: State of New Jersey, 1950.

_____. *Juvenile Delinquency.* New York: McGraw-Hill, 1960.

Taracena, Alfonso. *Carranza contra Madero.* Mexico City: Editorial Bolivar, 1934.

_____. *Francisco I. Madero y la verdad.* Mexico City: Editorial "Bolivar," 1933.

_____. *Madero, victima del imperialismo Yanqui.* Mexico City: Editorial Jus, 1960.

_____. *Madero, Vida del hombre y del politico.* Mexico City: Botas, 1937.

_____. *La verdadera Revolución Mexicana.* 6 vols. Mexico City: Editorial Jus, 1960.

Taracouzio, T.A. *War and Peace in Soviet Diplomacy.* New York: Macmillan, 1940.

Tarbell, Ida M. *History of the Standard Oil Company.* New York: Macmillan, 1904.

_____. *In the Footsteps of the Lincolns.* New York: Harper & Brothers, 1924.

_____. *The Life of Abraham Lincoln.* 2 vols. New York: Doubleday Page, 1909.

_____. *The Life of Elbert H. Gary: The Story of Steel.* New York: D. Appleton, 1925.

Tarchi, Angelo. *Teste dure.* Milan, Italy: SELC, 1967.

Tarde, Gabriel. *Penal Philosophy.* Boston: Little, Brown, 1912.

Targ, Russell, and Puthoff, Harold. *Mind-Reach: Scientists Look at Psychic Ability.* New York: Delacorte, 1977.

Targ, William. *The Great American West.* New York: World, 1946.

Tarlé, Eugene. *Napoleon's Invasion of Russia, 1812.* New York: Oxford University Press, 1942.

Tarling, Nicholas. *Southeast Asia, Past and Present.* Melbourne: Cheshire, 1966.

Tarnovecky, Joseph. *Purchase of Alaska: Background and Reactions.* Montreal, Quebec, Can.: McGill University Press, 1968.

Tarsaidze, Alexander. *Czars and Presidents: The Story of a Forgotten Friendship.* New York: McDowell, Obolensky, 1958.

Tarshis, Maurice S. *The LSD Controversy: An Overview.* Springfield, Ill.: Charles C. Thomas, 1972.

Tarsia in Curia, Angelo. *La verità sulle 'quattro giornate' di Napoli.* Naples, Italy: Genovese, 1950.

Tart, Charles (ed.). *Altered States of Consciousness.* New York: John Wiley & Sons, 1969.

Tartarotti, Girolamo. *Apologia del Congresso notturno delle Lammie.* Venice, Italy: S. Occhi, 1751.

Tastmona, Thothnu N. *It Is As If: Curious Aspects Concerning the Matter of President Kennedy's Death.* New York: Thothmona Book, 1966.

Tate, Allen. *Stonewall Jackson.* New York: Minton, Balch, 1928.

Tate, Charles Spencer. *Pickway, a True Narrative.* Chicago: Golden Rule, 1905.

Tate, Merze. *The United States and the Hawaiian Kingdom: A Political History.* New Haven, Conn.: Yale University Press, 1965.

Tateno Nobuyuki. *Army Fractions in the Reign of Hirohito: An*

Anthology of Upheaval. Tokyo: Kodan-sha, 1963.

Tatu, Michel. *Power in the Kremlin.* trans. Helen Katel. New York: Viking Press, 1969.

Tatum, Edward Howland, Jr. *The United States and Europe, 1815-1823: A Study in the Background of the Monroe Doctrine.* Berkeley: University of California Press, 1936.

Taube, Otto von. *Rasputin.* Müchen: C.H. Beck, 1925.

Taubman, Bryna. *Lady Cop.* New York: Warner Books, 1987.

Taussig, F.W. *The Tariff History of the United States.* New York: G.P. Putnam's Sons, 1931.

Taussig, Jacob. *Letter F or Starling Revelations in the Durrant Case.* San Francisco: N. Savier, 1895.

Tavenner, Eugene. *Studies in Magic from Latin Literature.* New York: Columbia University Press, 1916.

Tavernier, René. *Alors rôdait dans l'ombre le docteur Petoit.* Paris: Presses de la Cité, 1974.

Tawney, R.H. *The Acquisitive Society.* New York: Harcourt, 1920.

_____. *The Agrarian Problem in the Sixteenth Century.* New York: Longmans, Green, 1912.

_____. *The British Labor Movement.* New Haven, Conn.: Institute of Politics, 1925.

_____. *Land and Labour in China.* London: George Allen & Unwin, 1932.

_____. *Religion and the Rise of Capitalism.* New York: Harcourt, Brace, 1922.

Taylor, A.J.P. *Beaverbrook.* New York: Simon & Schuster, 1972.

_____. *Bismarck: The Man and the Statesman.* New York: Alfred A. Knopf, 1955.

_____. *The Course of German History.* New York: Coward-McCann, 1946.

_____. *The Habsburg Monarchy, 1809-1918: A History of the Austrian Empire and Austria-Hungary.* New York: Macmillan, 1949.

_____. *The Last of Old Europe: A Grand Tour.* New York: Quadrangle Books, 1976.

_____. *The Origins of the Second World War.* London: Hamish Hamilton, 1961.

_____. *The Struggle for Mastery in Europe 1848-1918.* London: Clarendon Press, 1954.

Taylor, Alan R. *Prelude to Israel: An Analysis of Zionist Diplomacy 1897-1947.* New York: Philosophical Library, 1959.

Taylor, Arnold H. *American Diplomacy and the Narcotics Traffic, 1900-1939.* Durham, N.C.: Duke University Press, 1969.

Taylor, Bayard. *Colorado: A Summer Trip.* New York: G.P. Putnam's Sons, 1867.

_____. *Eldorado, or Adventures in the Path of Empire.* New York: G.P. Putnam's Sons, 1850.

_____. *A Journey to Central Africa.* New York: G.P. Putnam's Sons, 1970.

_____. *The Land of the Saracens.* New York: G.P. Putnam's Sons, 1855.

_____. *A Visit to India, China and Japan.* New York: G.P. Putnam's Sons, 1855.

Taylor, David Wooster. *The Life of James Rolph, Jr.* San Francisco: Recorder Printing, 1934.

Taylor, Deems. *Some Enchanted Evenings.* New York: Harper & Brothers, 1953.

Taylor, Drew Kirksey. *Taylor's Thrilling Tales of Texas.* San Antonio, Tex.: Guaranty Bond Printing, 1926.

Taylor, Edmund L. *The Fall of Dynasties: The Collapse of the Old Order, 1905-1922.* Garden City, N.Y.: Doubleday, 1963.

Taylor, Frank J. *High Horizons: Daredevil Flying Postman to Modern Magic Carpets, The United Air Lines Story.* New York: McGraw, 1951.

Taylor, George E. *The Struggle for North China.* New York: Institute of Pacific Relations, 1940.

Taylor, Graham. *Pioneering on Social Frontiers.* Chicago: University of Chicago Press, 1930.

Taylor, Ian, Walton, Paul, and Young, Jock. *Critical Criminology.* London: Routledge & Kegan Paul, 1975.

_____. *The New Criminology.* New York: Harper & Row, 1973.

_____. *For a Social Theory of Deviance.* New York: Harper & Row, 1973.

Taylor, Rev. John. *Dictionary of the Bible.* New York: Charles Scribner's Sons, 1963.

Taylor, John G. *Superminds.* New York: Viking Press, 1975.

Taylor, John Metcalfe. *The Witchcraft Delusion in Colonial Connecticut 1647-97.* New York: Grafton Press, 1908.

Taylor, John Russell. *Hitch: The Life and Times of Alfred Hitchcock.* New York: Pantheon, 1978.

Taylor, John Sydney. *Selections from the Writings of John Sydney Taylor.* London: Charles Gilpin, 1843.

Taylor, Joseph Henry. *Kaleidoscopic Lives.* Washburn, N.D.: Published by Author, 1896.

Taylor, Laurie, and Cohen, Stanley. *Psychological Survival: The Experience of Long Term Imprisonment.* Harmondsworth, Eng.: Penguin, 1972.

Taylor, Morris F. *Trinidad, Colorado Territory.* Trinidad, Colo.: Trinidad State Junior College, 1966

Taylor, Norman. *Narcotics: Nature's Dangerous Gifts.* New York: Dell, 1963.

Taylor, Paul S. *The Sailors' Union of the Pacific.* New York: Ronald Press, 1923.

Taylor, Ralph C. *Colorado, South of the Border.* Denver: Sage Books, 1963.

Taylor, Ray W. *Hetch Hetchy: The Story of San Francisco's Struggle to Provide a Water Supply for Her Future Needs.* San Francisco: Ricardo J. Orozco, 1927.

Taylor, Rex. *Assassination.* London: Hutchinson, 1961.

_____. *Michael Collins.* London: Hutchinson, 1958.

Taylor, Richard. *Destruction and Reconstruction.* New York: Longmans, Green, 1955.

Taylor, Robert Lewis. *Vessel of Wrath: The Life and Times of Carry Nation.* New York: New American Library, 1966.

Taylor, Robert S. *The Improvement of the Mississippi River.* St. Louis: n.p., 1884.

Taylor, Telford. *Grand Inquest.* New York: Ballantine, 1961.

_____. *Sword and Swastika: Generals and Nazis in the Third Reich.* Chicago: Quadrangle Books, 1969.

Taylor, Thomas Ulvan. *Bill Longley and His Wild Career.* Bandera, Texas: Frontier Times, 1925.

_____. *The Chisholm Trail and Other Routes.* San Antonio, Texas: Naylor, 1936.

Taylor, Timothy Alden. *The Bible View of the Death Penalty.* Worcester, Mass.: Howland, 1850.

Taylor, William. *California Life Illustrated.* New York: n.p., 1860.

_____. *Seven Years' Street Preaching in San Francisco, California.* New York: Published By Author, 1856.

Taylor, Zachary. *The Surey Impostor.* London: John Jones, 1698.

Tchernoff, J. *Le Parti républican au coup d'état et sous le second empire.* Paris: Pedone, 1906.

Tead, Orway. *The Art of Administration.* New York: McGraw-Hill, 1951.

_____. *The Case for Democracy.* New York: Association Press, 1938.

Tebbel, John. *An American Dynasty: The Story of the McCormicks, Medills and Pattersons.* New York: Doubleday, 1947.

_____. *The American Magazine: A Compact History.* New York: Hawthorn Books, 1969.

_____. *The Compact History of the American Newspaper.* New York: Hawthorn Books, 1963.

_____. *George Horace Lorimer and the Saturday Evening Post.* Garden City, N.Y.: Doubleday, Doran, 1941.

_____. *The Inheritors.* New York: G.P. Putnam's Sons, 1962.

_____. *The Life and Good Times of William Randolph Hearst.* New York: E.P. Dutton, 1952.

_____. *The Marshall Fields: A Study in Wealth.* New York: E.P. Dutton, 1947.

_____. *The Media in America.* New York: Thomas Y. Crowell,

1975.

Tedrow, Richard J., and Thomas, L. *Death At Chappaquiddick.* New York: Caroline House, 1980.

Teeters, Negley K. *The Cradle of the Penitentiary: The Walnut Street Jail at Philadelphia 1773-1835.* Philadelphia: Temple University Press, 1955.

_____, and Hedblom, Jack H. *"...Hang By the Neck..."* Springfield, Ill.: Charles C. Thomas, 1967.

_____. *Scaffold and Chair: A Compilation of Their Use in Pennsylvania, 1682-1962.* Philadelphia: Pennsylvania Prison Society, 1963.

_____. *They Were in Prison: A History of the Pennsylvania Prison Society.* Philadelphia: John C. Winston, 1937.

Tefft, B.F. *Life of Daniel Webster.* Philadelphia: Porter & Coates, 1854.

Tegner, G. *Security in Sweden.* Stockholm: Swedish Institute, 1956.

Teichmann, Howard. *Smart Aleck: The Wit, World and Life of Alexander Woollcott.* New York: William Morrow, 1976.

Teirlinck, Isidoor. *Flora Magica.* Antwerp, Belg.: C.A. Mees, 1925.

Teitelbaum, Louis W. *Woodrow Wilson and the Mexican Revolution, 1913-1916: A History of United States-Mexican Relations from the Murder of Madero until Villa's Provocation Across the Border.* New York: Exposition Press, 1967.

Teja Zabre, Alfonso. *Guide to the History of Mexico.* Mexico City: Press of the Ministry of Foreign Affairs, 1935.

Telfair, Alexander. *A New Confirmation of Sadducism.* London: A. Bell, 1696.

_____. *A True Relation of an Apparition.* Edinburgh, Scot.: George Mosman, 1696.

Teller, Walter. *Joshua Slocum.* New York: Sheridan House, 1950.

Temin, Peter. *Did Monetary Forces Cause the Great Depression?* New York: W.W. Norton, 1976.

_____. *The Jacksonian Economy.* New York: W.W. Norton, 1969.

Temperley, H.W.V. *England and the Near East: the Crimea.* London: Longmans, Green, 1936.

_____. *Frederick the Great and Kaiser Joseph: An Episode of War and Diplomacy in the Eighteenth Century.* New York: Barnes & Noble, 1968.

_____ (ed.). *A History of the Peace Conference of Paris.* London: Frowder & Stoughton, 1924.

_____. *History of Serbia.* London: G. Bell & Sons, 1917.

Temple, Sir Richard. *The Century for the Mutiny.* Bombay: n.p., n.d.

Templewood, Lord Samuel. *Nine Troubled Years.* London: Collins, 1954.

Templewood, Viscount. *The Shadow of the Gallows.* London: Victor Gollancz, 1951.

Ten Eyck, John. *The Life of John Ten Eyck.* Pittsville, Mass.: David O'Connell, 1878.

Tendulkar, D.G., et al (ed.) *Gandhiji: His Life and Work.* Bombay, India: Karnatak, 1944.

_____. *Mahatma.* 8 vols. Bombay: Times of India Press, 1951-54.

Tenemura Sako. *Secret Diary of Imperial Headquarters.* Tokyo: Diamond Sha, 1952.

Tenenti, Alberto. *Piracy and the Decline of Venice.* Berkeley: University of California Press, 1967.

Teng, Ssu-yü, and Fairbank, John K. *China's Response to the West.* Cambridge, Mass.: Harvard University Press, 1954.

Tengler, Ulric. *Layenspiegel.* Strasbourg, Fr.: H. Knoblouch den Jungen, 1530.

_____. *Der neu Layenspiegel.* Colophon, Fr.: Gednuckt du Strassburg, durch Johannem Knoblouch, 1527.

Tenyson, Jesse F. *Comments on Cain.* London: William Heinemann, 1948.

Terasaki, Gwen. *Bridge to the Sun.* Chapel Hill: University of

North Carolina Press, 1957.

Teresa, Vincent. *My Life in the Mafia.* New York: Doubleday, 1973.

TerHorst, Jerald F. *Gerald Ford and the Future of the Presidency.* New York: Third Press, 1974.

Terhune, Albert Payson. *Famous Hussies of History.* New York: World, 1943.

Terkel, Studs. *Hard Times.* New York: Pantheon Books, 1970.

Terman, L.M., and Oden, M.H. *The Gifted Group at Mid-Life.* Stanford, Calif.: Stanford University Press, 1959.

Terra, Helmut de. *Humbolt.* New York: Alfred A. Knopf, 1955.

Terraine, John. *The Great War, 1914-1918.* New York: Macmillan, 1965.

Terraneo, Sacr Ecclesio. *Il Servo di Dio, Cardinale Ildefonso Schuster.* Milan, Italy: Daverio, 1962.

Terrell, Charles Vernon. *The Terrells: Eighty-Five Years, from Indian to Atomic Bomb...* Dallas: Wilkinson Printing, 1948.

Terret, Charles. *Traffic in Innocents.* New York: Bantam Books, 1961.

Terrett, Courtenay. *Only Saps Work: A Ball for Racketeering.* New York: Vanguard Press, 1930.

The Terrible Haystack Murder: Life and Trial of the Rev. Ephraim K. Avery for the Murder of the Young and Beautiful Miss Sarah M. Cornell, a Factory Girl of Fall River, Mass. Philadelphia: Barclay, 1876.

The Terrible Tragedy at Washington: The Assassination of President Lincoln. Port Tobacco, Md.: James L. Barbour, 1988.

Terrot, Charles. *Traffic in Innocents: The Shocking Story of White Slavery in England.* New York: E.P. Dutton, 1960.

Terry, Charles E., and Pellens, Mildred. *The Opium Problem.* New York: The Committee on Drug Addictions, in Collaboration with the Bureau of Social Hygiene, 1928.

Terry, Sarah M. *Poland's Place in Europe: General Sikorki and the Origin of the Oder-Neisse Line.* Princeton, N.J.: Princeton University Press, 1982.

Tertz, Abram. *A Voice form the Chorus.* New York: Farrar, Straus & Giroux, 1976.

Tessandori, Vicenzo. *BR: Imputazione Banda Armata.* Milan, Italy: Garzanti, 1977.

Testimony of Sandford Conover, Dr. J.B. Merritt, and Richard Montgomery before the Military Court at Washington. Toronto, Ontario, Can.: Lovell & Gibson, 1865.

Tetsuma Hashimoto. *The Emperor and the Officers of the Rebellion.* Tokyo: Nihon Shuho-sha, 1954.

Tevis, James. *Arizona in the 50s.* Albuquerque: University of New Mexico Press, 1954.

Texas Commission on Alcohol and Drug Abuse (TCADA). *Drug Abuse Trends in Texas.* Austin, Texas: TCADA, 1987.

Texas Corrections Department. *A National Survey of Good Time Laws and Adminstrative Procedures.* Huntsville, Texas: Research and Development Division, 1973.

Thaden, Edward C. *Conservative Nationalism in 19th Century Russia.* Seattle: University of Washington Press, 1964.

Thamm, Melchior. *Fehmgericht und Hexenprozesse.* Leipzig, Ger.: Bibliographisches Institut, 1903.

Thane, Elswyth. *The Fighting Quaker: Nathanael Greene.* New York: Hawthorn Books, 1972.

Thane, Eric. *High Border Country.* New York: Duell, Sloan & Pearce, 1942.

_____. *The Majestic Land: Peaks, Parks & Prevaricators of the Rockies & Highlands of the Northwest.* Indianapolis, Ind.: Bobbs-Merrill, 1950.

Tharp, Louise Hall. *Three Saints and a Sinner: Julia Ward Howe, Louisa, Anne and Sam Ward.* Boston: Little, Brown, 1956.

Tharp, R.G., and Wetzel, R.J. *Behavior Modification in the Natural Environment.* New York: Academic Press, 1969.

Thaw, Harry K. *The Traitor.* New York: Dorrance, 1926.

Thaxter, Celia. *Among the Isles of Shoals.* Boston: Houghton Mifflin, 1873.

Thayer, Eli M. *A History of the Kansas Crusade.* New York:

Harper & Brother, 1889.

_____. *The New England Emigrant Aid Society.* Worcester, Mass.: Franklin P. Rice, 1887.

Thayer, George. *The Farther Shores of Politics.* New York: Simon & Schuster, 1967.

_____. *The War Business. The International Trade in Armaments.* New York: Simon & Schuster, 1969.

Thayer, J.B. *Cases on Evidence.* Cambridge, n.p., 1900.

Thayer, Philip W. (ed.). *Tension in the Middle East.* Baltimore: Johns Hopkins Press, 1958.

Thayer, Theodore. *Nathanael Greene.* New York: Twayne, 1960.

_____. *Pennsylvania Politics and the Growth of Democracy 1740-1776.* Harrisburg, Pa.: Historical and Museum Commission, 1953.

Thayer, W.R. *The Life and Letters of John Hay.* 2 vols. Boston: Houghton, 1915.

Theobald, Robert. *The Guaranteed Income.* New York: Doubleday, 1966.

Theodoli, Alberto. *A cavallo di due secoli.* Rome: La Navicella, 1950.

Theoharis, Athan G. (ed.). *Beyond the Hiss Case.* Philadelphia: Temple University Press, 1982.

_____. *Seeds of Repression.* Chicago: Quadrangle Books, 1971.

_____, and Griffith, Robert (eds.). *The Specter: Original Essays on the Cold War and McCarthyism.* New York: Watts, 1974.

_____. *Spying on Americans.* Philadelphia: Temple University Press, 1978.

_____. *The Truman Presidency: The Origins of the Imperial Presidency and the National Security State.* Stanfordville, N.Y.: Coleman, 1979.

_____. *The Yalta Myths.* Columbia: University of Missouri Press, 1970.

Thera, Narada. *The Buddha and His Teachings.* Colombo. Sri.: Vajirarama, 1964.

Thernstrom, Stephan. *The Other Bostonians: Poverty and Progress in the American Metropolis, 1880-1970.* Cambridge, Mass.: Harvard University Press, 1973.

Thiaucourt, Paul. *La sorcellerie au Ban de Ramonchamp.* Remiremont, Fr.: H. Haut, 1906.

Thicknesse, S.G. *Arab Refugees: A Study of Resettlement Possibilities.* London: Chatham House, 1949.

Thielmann, Bonnie, and Merrill, Dean. *The Broken God.* New York: David C. Cook, 1979.

Thiery, Maurice. *Bouganville, Soldier and Sailor.* London: Grayson, 1932.

Thirteen Epistles. trans. L.A. Post. Oxford, Eng.: Clarendon Press, 1925.

Thirty Years of Lynching in the U.S., 1889-1918. New York: NAACP, Arno Press, 1969.

Thisle, J., and Cook, J.P. (eds.). *Seventeenth Century Economic Documents.* Oxford, Eng.: Claredon Press, 1972.

Thoburn, Joseph B., and Wright, Muriel H. *Oklahoma: A History of the State and Its People.* 4 vols. New York: Lewis Historical, 1929.

_____. *A Standard History of Oklahoma.* 5 vols. Chicago: American Historical Society, 1916.

Thomas, A., Chess, S., and Birch, H.G. *Temperament and Behavior Disorders in Children.* New York: New York University Press, 1968.

Thomas, Benjamin P. *Abraham Lincoln.* New York: Alfred A. Knopf, 1952.

_____. *Russo-American Relations, 1815-1876.* Baltimore: Johns Hopkins Press, 1930.

_____, and Hyman, Harold M. *Stanton: The Life and Times of Lincoln's Secretary of War.* New York: Alfred A. Knopf, 1962.

_____. *Theodore Weld: Crusader for Freedom.* New Brunswick, N.J.: Rutgers University Press, 1950.

Thomas, Bob. *King Cohn.* New York: G.P. Putnam's Sons, 1967.

_____. *Selznick.* New York: Doubleday, 1970.

_____. *Thalberg.* New York: Doubleday, 1969.

_____. *Winchell.* Garden City, N.Y.: Doubleday, 1971.

Thomas, Brinley. *Migration and Economic Growth.* Cambridge, Eng.: Cambridge University Press, 1954.

Thomas, Charles W., and Hepburn, John R. *Crime, Criminal Law, and Criminology.* Dubuque, Iowa: William C. Brown, 1983.

_____, and Peterson, David M. *Prison Organization and Inmate Subcultures.* Indianapolis, Ind.: Bobbs Merrill, 1977.

Thomas, D.A. *Principles of Sentencing.* London: Heinemann Educational Books, 1970.

Thomas, D.K. *Wild Life in the Rocky Mountains; or, the Lost Million Dollar Gold Mine.* C.E. Thomas, 1917.

Thomas, D.S. *Social Aspects of the Business Cycle.* London: George Routledge & Sons, 1925.

Thomas, Dana L. *The Plungers and the Peacocks.* New York: G.P. Putnam's Sons, 1967.

Thomas, David. *Seek Out the Guilty.* London: John Long, 1969.

Thomas, Donald. *A Long Time Burning: The History of Literary Censorship in England.* New York: Frederick A. Praeger, 1969.

Thomas, Elizabeth Marshall. *Warrior Herdsmen.* London: Secker & Warburg, 1965.

Thomas, Gordon and Morgan, and Witts, Max. *The Day the Bubble Burst: A Social History of the Wall Street Crash of 1929.* Garden City, N.Y.: Doubleday, 1979.

Thomas, Gough. *Shotgun Shooting Facts.* New York: Winchester, 1979.

Thomas, Helen. *Dateline: White House.* New York: Macmillan, 1975.

Thomas, Hugh. *Cuba: The Pursuit of Freedom, 1762-1969.* New York: Harper & Row, 1971.

_____. *The Spanish Civil War.* London: Eyre & Spottiswoode, 1961.

_____. *Suez.* New York: Harper & Row, 1967.

Thomas, Ivor. *Who Mussolini Is.* London: Oxford University Press, 1942.

Thomas, J.E. *The English Prison Officer Since 1850: A Study in Conflict.* London: Routledge & Kegan Paul, 1972.

Thomas, John L. (ed.). *John C. Calhoun: A Profile.* New York: Hill & Wang, 1968.

_____. *The Liberator: William Lloyd Garrison, A Biography.* Boston: Little, Brown, 1963.

Thomas, John N. *The Institute of Pacific Relations.* Seattle: University of Washington Press, 1974.

Thomas, Keith. *Religion and the Decline of Magic.* London: Wiedenfeld & Nicolson, 1971.

Thomas, Lately. *A Debonair Scoundrel.* New York: Holt, Rinehart & Winston, 1962.

_____. *The First President Johnson.* New York: William Morrow, 1968.

_____. *The Mayor Who Mastered New York: The Life and Opinions of William J. Gaynor.* New York: William Morrow, 1969.

_____. *Storming Heaven.* New York: William Morrow, 1970.

_____. *The Vanishing Evangelist.* New York: Viking Press, 1959.

Thomas, Lloyd J. *Reading Disability: Developmental Dyslexia.* Springfield, Ill.: Charles C. Thomas, 1969.

Thomas, Lowell. *Book of the High Mountains.* New York: Julian Messner, 1964.

_____. *Old Gimlet Eye: The Adventures of Smedley Butler.* New York: Farrar & Rinehart, 1933.

Thomas, Marcel. *L'Affaire sans Dreyfus.* Paris: Fayard, 1961.

Thomas, Norman. *America's Way Out.* New York: Macmillan, 1932.

_____. *As I See It.* New York: Macmillan, 1932.

_____. *The Choice Before Us.* New York: Macmillan, 1934.

_____. *Democratic Socialism - A New Appraisal.* New York: League for Industrial Democracy, n.d.

_____. *A Socialist's Faith.* New York: W.W. Norton, 1951.

_____. *Socialism on the Defensive.* New York: Harper, 1938.

_____. *Socialism Re-examined*. New York: W.W. Norton, 1963.

_____. *We Have a Future*. Princeton, N.J.: Princeton University Press, 1941.

_____. *What is Our Destiny?* New York: Doubleday, Doran, 1944.

Thomas, P.W. *Sir John Berkenhead, 1617-1679*. Oxford, Eng.: Clarendon Press, 1969.

Thomas, Piri. *Down These Mean Streets*. New York: New American Library, 1967.

The Thomas Street Tragedy: Trial of Robinson! Murderer of Ellen Jewett. New York: n.p., 1836.

Thomas, Trevor. *This Life We Take*. Washington, D.C.: Friends Committee on Legislation, 1965.

Thomas, W. Hugh. *The Murder of Rudolf Hess*. New York: Harper & Row, 1979.

Thomas, W.I. and Dorothy S. *The Child in America*. New York: Alfred A. Knopf, 1928.

Thomas, William H. *The American Negro*. New York: Macmillan, 1901.

Thomas, William Henry. *The Whaleman's Adventures in the Sandwich Islands and California*. Boston: Lee & Shepard, 1872.

_____. *Sex and Society*. Chicago: University of Chicago Press, 1907.

_____. *The Unadjusted Girl*. New York: Harper & Row, 1970.

Thomasius, Christian. *De Crimine Magiae*. Halle, Ger.: Litteris Salfeldiamis, 1730.

Thomasius, Jacob. *De Transformatione Hominum in Bruta*. Leipzig, Ger.: John Eric Hahn, 1673.

Thompson, Albert W. *The Story of Early Clayton, New Mexico*. Clayton, N.M.: Clayton News, 1933.

_____. *They Were Open Range Days; Annals of a Western Frontier*. Denver: World Press, 1946.

Thompson, Sir Basil. *The Criminal*. London: Hodder & Stoughton, 1925.

_____. *The Story of Scotland Yard*. London: Grayson & Grayson, 1925.

_____. *Voyage of the H.M.S. Pandora*. London: Francis Edwards, 1915.

Thompson, C.J.S. *Poison Mysteries in History*. Philadelphia: J.B. Lippincott, 1932.

_____. *Poison Mysteries Unsolved*. London: Hutchinson, 1937.

_____. *Poisons and Poisoners*. London: Harold Shaylor, 1931.

Thompson, C.V.R. *Trousers Must Be Worn*. New York: G.P. Putnam's Sons, 1941.

Thompson, Charles H., and Shattuck, Frances M. *The 1956 Presidential Campaign*. Washington, D.C.: Brookings Institute, 1960.

Thompson, Charles T. *The Peace Conference Day by Day*. New York: Brentano's, 1920.

Thompson, Charles W. *President's I've Known and Two Near Presidents*. Indianapolis, Ind.: Bobbs-Merrill, 1929.

Thompson, Craig, and Raymond, Allen. *Gang Rule in New York*. New York: Dial Press, 1940.

Thompson, Edward Palmer. *The Making of the English Working Class*. New York: Random House, 1963.

_____. *The Poverty of Theory and Other Essays*. New York: Monthly Review Press, 1978.

Thompson, Eliza Jane Trimble, et al. *Hillsboro Crusade Sketches*. Cincinnati, Ohio: n.p., 1906.

Thompson, Fred D. *At That Point in Time: The Inside Story of the Senate Watergate Committee*. New York: Quadrangle Books, 1975.

Thompson, G. *Travels and Adventures in Southern Africa*. Cape Town, S. Afri.: Von Riebeeck Society, 1967.

Thompson, G.S. *Catherine the Great and the Expansion of Russia*. New York: Macmillan, 1950.

Thompson, George. *Der Zar Raspoutine und die Juden*. Hamburg: A. Götting, 1922.

Thompson, George. *Impressions of America*. Arbrath, Scot.: T. Bunele, 1916.

Thompson, George G. *Bat Masterson, The Dodge City Years*. Topeka: Kansas State Printing Plant, 1943.

Thompson, Goldianne. *History of Clayton and Union County, New Mexico*. Denver, Colo.: Monitor, 1962.

Thompson, Henry C. *Sam Hildebrand Rides Again*. Bonne Terre, Mo.: Steinbeck, 1950.

Thompson, Henry T. *Ousting the Carpetbagger from South Carolina*. Columbia, S.C.: R.L. Bryan Press, 1926.

Thompson, Hunter S. *Fear and Loathing in Las Vegas*. New York: Warner Books, 1971.

_____. *Hell's Angels: A Strange and Terrible Saga*. New York: Random House, 1966.

Thompson, J.M. *The French Revolution*. New York: Oxford University Press, 1966.

_____. *Louis-Napoleon and the Second Empire*. Oxford, Eng.: Blackwell, 1954.

_____. *Napoleon Bonaparte, His Rise and Fall*. Oxford, Eng.: Blackwell, 1958.

Thompson, James D. *Organization in Action*. New York: McGraw-Hill, 1967.

Thompson, James Westfall, et al. *The Civilization of the Renaissance*. New York: Frederick Ungar, 1929.

Thompson, John Eric Sidney. *Maya Hieroglyphic Writing: An Introduction*. Norman: University of Oklahoma Press, 1960.

_____. *The Rise and Fall of Maya Civilization*. Norman: University of Oklahoma Press, 1954.

Thompson, Josiah. *Six Seconds in Dallas*. New York: Bernard Geis Associates, 1967.

Thompson, Mary, et al. *Clayton: The Friendly Town of Union County, New Mexico*. Denver: Monitor, 1962.

Thompson, Norman. *Fire Behavior and Sprinklers*. Boston: National Fire Protection Association, 1964.

Thompson, Paul. *Socialists, Liberals, and Labour: The Struggle for London*. Toronto, Ontario, Can.: University of Toronto Press, 1967.

Thompson, Peter E. (ed.). *Contemporary Chronicles of the Hundred Years War*. London: Folio Society, 1966.

Thompson, Sir Robert. *Defeating Communist Insurgency*. London: Chatto & Windus, 1969.

_____. *Peace is Not at Hand*. London: Chatto & Windus, 1974.

Thompson, Robert Lowe. *History of the Devil*. London: K. Paul, Trench, Trubner, 1929.

Thompson, R.W. *Footprints of the Jesuits*. New York: Hunt & Eaton, 1894.

Thompson, Slason. *A Short History of American Railways: Covering Ten Decades*. New York: D. Appleton-Century, 1925.

Thompson, Thomas. *Blood and Money*. Garden City, N.Y.: Doubleday, 1976.

_____. *Serpentine*. Garden City, N.Y.: Doubleday, 1979.

Thompson, Vance. *Drink*. New York: E.P. Dutton, 1918.

Thompson, Virginia. *French Indo China*. New York: Macmillan, 1937.

Thompson, William Hale. *Chicago: Eight Years of Progress: January, 1923...* Chicago: n.p., 1923.

Thompson, William Irwin. *The Imagination of an Insurrection*. New York: Oxford University Press, 1967.

Thomson, Elizabeth McClure (ed.). *The Chamberlain Letters*. New York: G.P. Putnam's Sons, 1965.

Thomson, George C. *The Quest for Truth: A Quizzical Look at the Warren Report-Or How President Kennedy Really Was Assassinated*. Glendale, Calif.: Published by Author, 1964.

Thomson, Helen. *Murder at Harvard*. Boston: Houghton Mifflin, 1971.

Thorez, Maurice. *Son of the People*. London: Lawrence & Wishart, 1938.

Thorn, W. *Chicago in 1860: A Glance at Its Business Houses...* Chicago: Published by Author, 1860.

Thornberry, Terence Patrick. *Punishment and Crime: The Effect of Legal Dispositions on Subsequent Criminal Behavior*. Ann

Arbor, Mich.: University Microfilms, 1972.

Thorndike, Joseph J. *The Very Rich: A History of Wealth*. New York: American Heritage, 1976.

Thorndike, Lynn. *A History of Magic and Experimental Science*. New York: Columbia University Press, 1934.

_____. *The Place of Magic in Intellectual History of Europe*. New York: Columbia University Press, 1905.

Thorndike, Thaddeus. *Lives and Exploits of the Daring Frank and Jesse James*. Baltimore: I.& M. Ottenheimer, 1909.

Thornley, Kerry Wendell. *Oswald*. Chicago: Allied, 1965.

Thornton, Willis. *Fable, Fact and History*. Philadelphia: Chilton, 1939.

Thorp, Arthur. *Calling Scotland Yard*. London: Allan Wingate, 1954.

Thorp, Jack, and Clark, Neil McCullough. *Pardner of the Wind*. Caldwell, Idaho: Caxton Printers, 1945.

Thorp, Margaret Farrand. *Charles Kingsley*. Princeton, N.J.: Princeton University Press, 1937.

Thorp, Nathan Howard. *Story of the Southwestern Cowboy, Pardner of the Wind*. Caldwell, Idaho: Caxton Printers, 1945.

Thorp, Raymond W., and Bunker, Robert. *Crow Killer*. New York: Signet, 1958.

_____. *Spirit Gun of the West; the Story of Doc W.F. Carver*. Glendale, Calif.: Arthur H. Clark, 1957.

Thorp, Willard L. *Business Annals*. New York: National Bureau of Economic Research, 1926.

Thorwald, Jürgen. *The Century of the Detective*. New York: Harcourt, Brace & World, 1964.

_____. *Crime and Science*. Orlando, Fla.: Harcourt, Brace & World, 1967.

_____. *Dead Men Tell Tales*. London: Thames & Hudson, 1966.

_____. *The Illusion: Soviet Soldiers in Hitler's Armies*. trans. Richard and Clara Winston. New York: Harcourt Brace Jovanoich, 1975.

_____. *The Marks of Cain*. London: Thames & Hudson, 1965.

_____. *Proof of Poison*. London: Thames & Hudson, 1966.

Thouless, Robert. *From Anecdote to Experiment in Psychical Research*. London: Routledge & Kegan Paul, 1972.

Thrapp, Dan L. *Al Sieber: Chief of Scouts*. Norman: University of Oklahoma Press, 1964.

Thrasher, Frederick. *The Gang: A Study of 1,313 Gangs in Chicago*. Chicago: University of Chicago Press, 1927.

Throup, D.W. *Economic and Social Origins of Mau Mau, 1945-1953*. London: James Currey, 1988.

Thucydides. *The Pelopennesian Wars*. trans. Hubert Wetmore Wells. Baltimore: Penguin Books, 1959.

_____. trans. B. Jowett. Oxford, Eng.: Clarendon Press, 1881.

Thumm, Theodor. *Tractatus Theologicus de Sagarum Impietate*. John Henry Reis, 1667.

Thurber, James. *The Years with Ross*. New York: Grosset & Dunlap, 1957.

Thurston, Gavin. *The Clerkenwell Riot*. London: George Allen & Unwin, 1967.

_____. *Coroner's Practice*. London: Butterworth, 1958.

Thurston, Herbert, and Attwater, Donald (eds.). *Butler's Lives of the Saints*. London: Burns & Oates, 1956.

Thwaites, Reuben Gold. *The Colonies*. London: Longmans, Green, 1913.

_____. *The Ohio Valley Press before the War of 1812-15*. Worcester, Mass.: Davis Press, 1909.

Thyraeus, Pierre. *Daemoniaci cum Locis Infestis*. Lyons, Fr.: J. Pillehotte, 1640.

Thyssen, Fritz. *I Paid Hitler*. Port Washington, N.Y.: Kennikat, 1971.

Tibbles, Thomas Henry. *Buckskin and Blanket Days: Memories of a Friend of the Indians*. Garden City, N.Y.: Doubleday, 1957.

Tice, J.H. *Over the Plains and on the Mountains*. St. Louis: Industrial Age Printing, 1872.

Tidyman, Ernest. *Big Bucks*. New York: W.W. Norton, 1982.

Tiedemann, Arthur. *Modern Japan*. Princeton, N.J.: D. Van Nostrand, 1962.

Tierney, Kevin. *Darrow, A Biography*. New York: Thomas Y. Crowell, 1979.

Tiersort, Francis J. *Temperance or Prohibition?* New York: J.J Little, 1929.

Tiffany, Francis. *Life of Dorthea Lynde Dix*. New York: Houghton Mifflin, 1890.

Tiffany, Lawrence P., McIntyre, Donald M., and Rottenburg, Daniel L. *Detection of Crime*. Boston: Little, Brown, 1967.

Tiger, Edith (ed.). *In re Alger Hiss: Petition for a Writ of Error Coram Nobis*. New York: Wang & Hill, 1979.

Tilden, Freeman. *Following the Frontier With F. Jay Haynes*. New York: Alfred A. Knopf, 1964.

Tilden, Samuel J. *Letters and Literary Memorials*. New York: Harper & Brothers, 1908.

_____. *The New York City Ring, Its Origin, Maturity and Fall*. New York: Press of J. Polhemus, 1873.

Tilea, R.V. *The Last Century of Roumania History*. Cambridge, Eng.: n.p., 1943.

Tilghman, Zoe A. *Marshal of the Last Frontier*. Glendale, Calif.: Arthur H. Clark, 1949.

_____. *Outlaw Days*. Oklahoma City: Harlow, 1926.

_____. *Spotlight: Bat Masterson and Wyatt Earp as U.S. Deputy Marshals*. San Antonio, Texas: Naylor, 1960.

Tilley, Arthur. *The Dawn of the French Renaissance*. Cambridge, Eng.: Cambridge University Press, n.d.

_____. *Medieval France*. Cambridge, Eng.: Cambridge University Press, 1922.

Tillman, Seth P. *Anglo-American Relations at the Paris Peace Conference of 1919*. Princeton, N.J.: Princeton University Press, 1961.

Tillotson, F.H. *How To Be A Detective*. Kansas City: Hailman Printing, 1909.

Tilly, Charles. *The Vendee*. Cambridge, Mass.: Harvard University Press, 1964.

Tilly, Richard. *The Rebellious Century, 1830-1930*. Cambridge, Mass.: Harvard University Press, 1975.

Tiltman, Hessell. *The Terror in Europe*. London: Jarrolds, 1931.

Timasheff, Nicholas S. *The Great Retreat*. New York: Macmillan, 1940.

_____. *One Hundred Years of Probation*. New York: Fordham University Press, 1941.

Timberlake, James H. *Prohibition and the Progressive Movement, 1900-1920*. Cambridge, Mass.: Harvard University Press, 1963.

Time Capsule/1927. Alexandria, Va.: Time-Life Books, 1968.

Timerman, Jacobo. *Prisoner without a Name, Cell without a Number*. trans. Toby Talbot. New York: Alfred A. Knopf, 1981.

Timewell, James. *Is Stinie Morrison Innocent?* London: Published by Author, 1914.

_____. *The Prison Life of Stinie Morrison*. London: Published by Author, 1914.

Timmons, Bascom N. *Garner of Texas*. New York: Harper & Brothers, 1948.

Timmons, William. *Twilight on the Range: Recollections of a Latterday Cowboy*. Austin: University of Texas Press, 1962.

Timms, N. *The Receiving End*. London: Routledge & Kegan Paul, 1973.

Timperlaey, H.J. *Japanese Terror in China*. New York: Modern Age Books, 1958.

Tinbergen, N. *The Study of Instinct*. London: Oxford University Press, 1951.

Tindall, George B. *America: A Narrative History*. New York: W.W. Norton, 1988.

_____. *The Emergence of the New South, 1913-1945*. Baton Rouge: Louisiana State University Press, 1967.

_____. *South Carolina Negroes, 1877-1900*. Columbia: University of South Carolina Press, 1952.

Tinkham, George H. *California Men and Events: Time 1769-1890.* Stockton, Calif.: Record, 1915.

_____. *History of San Joaquin, California.* Los Angeles: Historic Record, 1923.

_____. *A History of Stockton from Its Organization Up to the Present Time.* San Francisco: W.H. Hinton, 1880.

Tinklenburg, J.R. *Marijuana and Health Hazards.* New York: Academic Press, 1975.

Tinnin, David B. *Hit Team.* London: Weidenfeld & Nicholson, 1976.

Tirpitz, Alfred Peter Friedrich von. *Deutschlands Ohnmachtpolitik im Weltkriege.* Hamburg, Ger.: Hanseatische, 1926.

_____. *My Memoirs.* 2 vols. New York: Dodd, Mead, 1919.

Tisdall, E.E.P. *Marie Fedorovna: Empress of Russia.* New York: John Day, 1958.

_____. *Queen Victoria's Private Life.* London: Jarrolds, 1961.

_____. *Royal Destiny: The Royal Hellenic Cousins.* New York: S. Paul, 1955.

Tissot, S.A.D. *A Treatise Upon the Disorders of Masturbation.* trans. A. Hume. London: J. Pridden, 1766.

Titler, Dale. *Wings of Mystery.* New York: Dodd, Mead, 1966.

Tittle, C.R. *Sanctions and Social Deviance.* New York: Frederick A. Praeger, 1980.

Tittsworth, W.G. *Outskirt Episodes.* Avoca, Iowa: Published by Author, 1927.

Tobias, Fritz. *The Reichstag Fire.* New York: G.P. Putnam's Sons, 1964.

Tobias, J.J. *Crime and Industrial Society in the 19th Century.* New York: David McKay, 1965.

_____. *Urban Crime in Victorian England.* New York: Schocken, 1972.

Tobin, A.I., and Gertz, Elmer. *Frank Harris, A Study in Black and White.* Chicago: M. Mendelsohn, 1931.

Toch, Hans, Grant, J. Douglas, and Galvin, Raymond T. *Agents of Change: A Study in Police Reform.* New York: John Wiley & Sons, 1975.

_____. *Living in Prison: The Ecology of Survival.* New York: Free Press, 1977.

_____. *Police, Prisons, and the Problem of Violence.* Rockville, Md.: National Institute of Mental Health Center for Studies of Crime and Delinquency, 1977.

_____. *Psychology of Crime and Criminal Justice.* New York: Holt, Rinehart & Winston, 1979.

_____. *Violent Men.* Chicago: Aldine, 1969.

Tocqueville, Alexis de. *De la Démocratie en Amérique.* Paris: Librairie de Medicis, 1835.

_____. *Democracy in America.* 2 vols. New York: Alfred A. Knopf, 1958.

_____. *Journey to America.* Garden City, N.Y.: Anchor Books, 1971.

_____. *The Old Regime and the French Revolution.* trans. S. Gilbert. Garden City, N.Y.: Doubleday Anchor Books, 1955.

Todd, A.L. *Justice on Trial.* New York: McGraw-Hill, 1964.

Todd, Charles Burr. *History of Redding, Connecticut.* New York: John A. Gray Press, 1880.

_____. *Story of the City of Washington.* New York: G.P. Putnam's Sons, 1889.

Todd, Frank Morton. *The Story of the Exposition.* 5 vols. New York: G.P. Putnam's Sons, 1921.

Toennies, Ferdinand. *Community and Society.* trans. Charles Loomis. East Lansing: Michigan State University, 1957.

Toffler, Alvin. *Future Shock.* New York: Random House, 1970.

Togo, Shigenori. *The Cause of Japan.* New York: Simon & Schuster, 1956.

Toland, John. *Adolf Hitler.* Garden City, N.Y.: Doubleday, 1976.

_____. *But Not in Shame: The Six Months After Pearl Harbor.* New York: Random House, 1961.

_____. *The Dillinger Days.* New York: Random House, 1963.

_____. *The Last 100 Days.* New York: Random House, 1966.

_____. *The Rising Sun: The Decline and Fall of the Japanese Empire, 1936-1945.* New York: Random House, 1970.

Tolbert, Frank X. *An Informal History of Texas: From Cabeza de Vaca to Temple Houston.* New York: Harper & Brothers, 1961.

Tolchin, Martin and Susan. *To the Victor: Political Patronage from the Clubhouse to the White House.* New York: Random House, 1971.

Toledano, Ralph de. *J. Edgar Hoover: The Man in His Time.* New Rochelle, N.Y.: Arlington House, 1973.

_____. *Lament for a Generation.* New York: Farrar, Straus & Cudahy, 1960.

_____, and Lasky, V. *The Seeds of Treason: The Strange Case of Alger Hiss.* New York: Funk & Wagnalls, 1956.

_____. *Spies, Dupes and Diplomats.* New Rochelle, N.Y.: Arlington House, 1967.

Tolischus, Otto D. *Tokyo Record.* New York: Reynal & Hitchcock, 1943.

Toliver, Raymond F., and Constable, Trevor F. *Fighter Aces.* New York: Macmillan, 1965.

Toller, Ernst. *I Was a German.* London: John Lane, 1934.

Tolles, F.B. *James Logan and the Culture of Provincial America.* Boston: Little, Brown, 1957.

_____. *Meeting House and Counting House, the Quaker Merchants of Colonial Philadelphia.* Chapel Hill: University of North Carolina Press, 1948.

Tolman, William Howe, and Hull, William I. (eds.). *Handbook of Sociological Information with Especial Reference to New York City.* New York: n.p., 1894.

_____. *Municipal Reform Movements in the United States: The Textbook of the New Reformation.* New York: Fleming H. Ravell, 1895.

Tolstoy, Nicolai. *The Night of the Long Knives.* New York: Ballantine Books, 1972.

_____. *Stalin's Secret War: A Startling Expose of His Crimes Against the Russian People.* New York: Holt, Rinehart & Winston, 1981.

Tomalin, Nicholas, and Hall, Ron. *The Strange Last Voyage of Donald Crowhurst.* New York: Stein & Day, 1970.

Tomasevich, Jozo. *Peasants, Politics, and Economic Change in Yugoslavia.* Stanford, Calif.: Stanford University Press, 1955.

Tombstone Map and Guide. Tombstone, Ariz.: Devere, 1969.

Tomkins, Calvin. *Living Well is the Best Revenge.* New York: Viking Press, 1971.

Tomkins, Jerry R. (ed.). *D-Days at Dayton.* Baton Rouge: Louisiana State University Press, 1965.

Tomlinson, William P. *Kansas in Eighteen Fifty-Eight.* New York: H. Dayton, 1859.

Tompkins, Dorothy C. *Juvenile Gangs and Street Groups - A Bibliography.* Berkeley: University of California Institute of Governmental Studies, 1966.

_____. *The Supreme Court of the United States: A Bibliography.* Berkeley: University of California Press, 1959.

Tompkins, Maj. Frank. *Chasing Villa.* Harrisburg, Pa.: Military Service, 1934.

Tompkins, Jerry R. (ed.). *D-days at Dayton: Reflections on the Scopes Trial.* Baton Rouge: Louisiana State University Press, 1965.

Tompkins, Pauline. *American-Russian Relations in the Far East.* New York: Macmillan, 1949.

Tompkins, Peter. *Italy Betrayed.* New York: Simon & Schuster, 1966.

_____. *Secrets of the Great Pyramid.* New York: Harper & Row, 1971.

Tompkins, Stuart R. *Alaska from Promyshlennik to Sourdough.* Norman: University of Oklahoma Press, 1945.

_____. *Russia Through the Ages.* New York: Prentice-Hall, 1940.

_____. *The Russian Intelligentsia: Makers of the Revolutionary State.* Norman: University of Oklahoma Press, 1957.

_____. *The Russian Mind from Peter the Great through the Enlightenment.* Norman: University of Oklahoma Press, 1953.

Tompkins, Walker A. *Santa Barbara's Royal Rancho, the Fabulous History of Los Dos Pueblos.* Berkeley, Calif.: Howell-North, 1960.

Tomsich, John. *A Genteel Endeavor: American Culture and Politics in the Gilded Age.* Stanford, Calif.: Stanford University Press, 1971.

Tonquédoc, J. de. *Les maladies nerveuses ou mentales et les manifestations diaboliques.* Paris: Beauchesne et ses fils, n.d.

Toole, Gerald. *An Autobiography of Gerald Toole.* Hartford, Conn.: Lockwood, 1862.

Toole, K. Ross. *Montana: An Uncommon Land.* Norman: University of Oklahoma Press, 1959.

Toponce, Alexander. *Reminiscences of Alexander Toponce, Pioneer.* Ogden, Utah: Century Printing, 1923.

Torchiana, Henry Albert William van Coenen. *California Gringos.* San Francisco: Paul Elder, 1930.

_____. *Story of the Mission Santa Cruz.* San Francisco: Paul Elder, 1933.

Torgersen, Don Arthur. *People of Destiny: Ghandhi.* Chicago: Regensteiner, 1968.

Tormes, Yvonne. *Child Victims of Incest.* Denver: American Humane Association, 1969.

Toro, Carlos. *La caida de Madero por la revolución felicista.* Mexico City: F. Garcia y Alva, 1913.

Torrera, General Juan Manuel. *La Decena Trágica, apuntes para la historia del ejército Mexicano.* 2 vols. Mexico City: Ediciones, Joloco, 1939.

Torres, Elias L. *La Cabeze de Villa.* Mexico City: El Libro Español, 1947.

_____. *Veinte Vibrante Episodos de la Vida de Villa.* Mexico City: n.p., n.d.

Torsiello, Mario. *Settembre 1943.* Milan, Italy: Cisalpina, 1963.

Toscano, Mario. *Le origini diplomatiche del Patto d'Acciaio.* Florence, Italy: Sansoni, 1948.

_____. *Pagine di storia diplomatica contemporanea.* 2 vols. Milan, Italy: A. Giuffrè, 1963.

Tosti, Amedeo. *Pietro Badoglio.* Milan, Italy: Mondadori, 1956.

Total Home Security. New York: Butterick, 1979.

Toth, Max, and Nielsen, Greg. *Pyramid Power.* New York: Freeway Press, 1974.

Toughy, Roger. *The Stolen Years.* Cleveland, Ohio: Pennington, 1959.

Toulmin, Col. H.A. *With Pershing in Mexico.* Harrisburg, Pa.: Military Service, 1935.

Toulouse, Joseph H. and James R. *Pioneer Posts of Texas.* San Antonio, Texas: Naylor, 1936.

Tourtellot, Arthur Bernon. *The Presidents on the Presidency.* Garden City, N.Y.: Doubleday, 1964.

Towbridge, John Townsend. *My Own Story: With Recollections of Noted Persons.* Boston: Houghton Mifflin, 1903.

Towle, Virginia Rowe. *Vigilante Woman.* South Brunswick, N.Y.: A.S. Barnes, 1966.

Towler, J.E. *The Police Role in Racial Conflicts.* Springfield, Ill.: Charles C. Thomas, 1964.

Town Records of Manchester, from the Earliest Grants of Land, 1636...until 1736. Salem, Mass.: Salem Press, 1889.

Towne, Charles Hanson. *The Rise and Fall of Prohibition.* New York: Macmillan, 1923.

Towne, Charles Wayland, and Wentworth, Edward Norris. *Shepherd's Empire.* Norman: University of Oklahoma Press, 1945.

Townsend, E.D. *Anecdotes of the Civil War.* New York: D. Appleton, 1884.

Townsend, Edward W. *A Daughter of the Slums.* New York: Lovell, Coryell, 1895.

Townsend, George Alfred. *Katy of Catoctin.* New York: D. Appleton, 1886.

_____. *The Life, Crime and Capture of John Wilkes.* New York: Dick & Fitzgerald, 1865.

_____. *Rustics in Rebellion: A Yankee Reporter on the Road to Richmond, 1861-1865.* Chapel Hill: University of North Carolina Press, 1950.

Townsend, Irving. *John Hammond, On Record.* New York: Ridge Press, 1977.

Townsend, John D. *New York in Bondage.* New York: n.p., 1901.

Townsend, Robert S. (ed.). *Decade of Decision 1855-1865.* Kansas City: Kansas City Life Insurance, 1960.

Townsend, W., and Townsend, L. *Black Cap: Murder Will Out.* London: Albert E. Marriott, 1930.

Townshend, R.B. *The Tenderfoot in New Mexico.* London: John Lane, 1923.

Towster, Julian. *Political Power in the U.S.S.R., 1917-1947.* New York: Oxford University Press, 1948.

Toynbee, Arnold. *A Journey to China.* London: Constable, 1931.

_____. *A Study of History.* New York: Oxford University Press, 1946.

Toynbee, William (ed.). *The Diaries of William Charles Macready, 1833-1851.* New York: G.P. Putnam's Sons, 1912.

Tozer, Basil. *Confidence Crooks and Blackmailers.* Boston: Stratford, 1930.

Trabucchi, Alessandro. *I vinti hanno sempre torto.* Turin, Italy: Francesco da Silva, 1947.

Tracey, Herbert. *Social-Democracy in Britain; Fifty Years of the Socialist Movement.* London: Social Democratic Federation, 1935.

Trachtenberg, Alan (ed.). *Memoirs of Waldo Frank.* Amherst: University of Massachusetts Press, 1973.

Trachtenberg, Joshua. *The Devil and the Jews.* New Haven, Conn.: Yale University Press, 1943.

_____. *Jewish Magic and Superstition.* New York: Behrman's, 1939.

Trachtman, Paul. *The Gunfighters.* New York: Time-Life Books, 1974.

Traffic in Opium and Other Dangerous Drugs. Washington, D.C.: U.S. Treasury Dept., Bureau of Narcotics, 1940.

Train, Arthur. *The Confessions of Artemas Quibble.* New York: Charles Scribner's Sons, 1925.

_____. *Courts, Criminals, and Camorra.* New York: Charles Scribner's Sons, 1922.

_____. *Courts and Criminals.* New York: Charles Scribner's Sons, 1925.

_____. *My Day in Court.* New York: Charles Scribner's Sons, 1939.

_____. *On the Trail of the Bad Men.* New York: Charles Scribner's Sons, 1925.

_____. *The Prisoner at the Bar.* New York: Charles Scribner's Sons, 1925.

_____. *True Stories of Crime from the District Attorney's Office.* New York: McKinley, Stone & MacKenzie, 1908.

_____. *Tutt and Mr. Tutt.* New York: Charles Scribner's Sons, 1925.

_____. *Yankee Lawyer: The Autobiography of Ephraim Trutt.* New York: Charles Scribner's Sons, 1943.

Train, George Francis. *American Merchant in Europe, Asia, and Australia: A Series of Letters.* New York: G.P. Putnam's Sons, 1857.

_____. *In a British Jail. England Bombarded With Bastile Epigrams.* New York: Fenian Brotherhood, 1868.

_____. *My Life in Many States and in Foreign Lands.* New York: D. Appleton, 1902.

_____. *Spread Eagleisms.* New York: Derby & Jackson, 1859.

Traini, Robert. *Murder for Sex.* London: William Kimber, 1960.

Tramerage, Pierre L'Espagnol de la. *The World Struggle for Oil.* trans. C. Leonard Lesse. New York: Alfred A. Knopf, 1924.

Transcript of the Record of the Trial of Niccolo Sacco and Bartolomeo Vanzetti. New York: Henry Holt, 1929.

Trask, Willard. *Joan of Arc, Self Portrait.* New York: Stackpole Sons, 1936.

Trasler, G. *The Explanation of Criminality.* London: Routledge & Kegan Paul, 1962.

Trattner, Walter I. *Homer Folks: Pioneer in Social Welfare*. New York: Columbia University Press, 1968.

The Travels of Marco Polo. London: Everyman's Library, 1954.

Traver, Robert. *Anatomy of a Murder*. New York: Saint Martin's Press, 1958.

Travers, James W. *California: Romance of Clipper Ships and Gold Rush Days*. Los Angeles: Wetzel, 1949.

Travers, l'Abbé. *Histoire Civile, Politique et Religieuse de la Ville de Nantes*. Nantes, Fr.: Vincent Forest, 1836.

Travesi, Gonzalo G. *La Revolución Mexicana y el imperialismo Yanqui*. Barcelona, Spain: Case Editorial Maucci, 1914.

Treadgold, Donald W. *The Great Siberian Migration: Government and Peasant in Resettlement From Emancipation to the First World War*. Princeton, N.J.: Princeton University Press, 1959.

_____. *Lenin and His Rivals: The Struggle for Russia's Future, 1898-1906*. New York: Frederick A. Praeger, 1955.

_____. *Twentieth Century Russia*. Chicago: Rand McNally, 1964.

Treadwell, C.A.L. *Notable New Zealand Trials*. New Plymouth, N.Zea.: T. Avery & Sons, 1936.

Treadwell, Gordon W. *Myron Buel, The Murderer of Catherine Mary Richards*. Binghamton, N.Y.: Republican Print, 1879.

Trease, Geoffrey. *Portrait of a Cavalier: William Cavendish, First Duke of Newcastle*. New York: Taplinger, 1979.

Treasury Department, Special Narcotics Committee. *Traffic in Narcotic Drugs: Report of the Special Committee Investigation Appointed March 25, 1918, by the Secretary of Treasury*. Washington, D.C.: U.S. Government Printing Office, 1919.

Trebach, Arnold S. *The Great Drug War: Radical Proposals That Could Make America Safe Again*. New York: Macmillan, 1987.

_____. *The Heroin Solution*. New Haven, Conn.: Yale University Press, 1982.

_____. *The Rationing of Justice*. New Brunswick, N.J.: Rutgers University Press, 1964.

Trefethen, James B., and Serven, James E. (eds.). *Americans and Their Guns*. Harrisburg, Pa.: Stackpole Books, 1967.

Tredgold, A.F. *Mental Deficiency*. New York: William Wood, 1920.

_____, and Soddy, K. *A Textbook of Mental Deficiency*. London: Balliere, Tindall & Cox, 1956.

Tregaskis, Richard. *Invasion Diary*. New York: Random House, 1944.

Tregonning, K.G. *A History of Modern Sabah (North Borneo, 1881-1963)*. Singapore: University of Malaya Press, 1965.

Tréguiz, Louis. *L'Irlande dans la Crise Universelle*. Paris: Librairie Félix Alcan, n.d.

Treitschke, Heinrich von. *Treitschke's Origins of Prussianism: The Teutonic Knights*. trans. Eden and Cedar Paul. London: George Allen & Unwin, 1942.

Trelawney-Ansell, E.C. *I Followed Gold*. London: Peter Davies, 1938.

Trelease, Allen W. *White Terror*. New York: Harper & Row, 1971.

Tremble, H.M., and Allison, F.A. *The Langston Tragedy: A History of the Fiendish Murder of Mrs. Nancy Langston*. Mattoon, Ill.: Mattoon Journal, 1873.

Trenery, Walter N. *Murder in Minnesota*. St. Paul: Minnesota Historical Society, 1962.

Trenholm, Virginia Cole. *Footprints on the Frontier: Saga of the La Ramie Region of Wyoming*. Douglas, Wyo.: Douglas Enterprise, 1945.

_____, and Carley, Maurine. *Wyoming Pageant*. Casper, Wyo.: Prairie, 1946.

Trent, Lucia, and Cheyney, Ralph. *America Arraigned*. New York: Dean, 1928.

Trentin, Silvio. *L'Aventure Italienne*. Paris: Les Presses Universitaires de France, 1928.

Tresolini, Rocco J. *Justice and the Supreme Court*. Philadelphia: J.B. Lippincott, 1963.

Treutlein, Theodore E. *San Francisco Bay: Discovery and Colonization, 1769-1776*. San Francisco: California Historical Society, 1968.

Trevelyan, George Macaulay. *English Social History*. New York: Longmans, Green, 1942.

_____. *Grey of Fallodon: The Life and Letters of Sir Edward Grey*. Boston: Houghton Mifflin, 1937.

_____. *History of England*. New York: Harper, 1962.

_____. *The Life of John Bright*. London: Constable, 1913.

Trevelyan, George Otto. *The American Revolution*. New York: David McKay, 1964.

Trevelyan, Janet Penrose. *A Short History of the Italian People*. London: George Allen & Unwin, 1956.

Treves, Paolo. *What Mussolini Did to Us*. trans. Casimiro Isolani. London: Victor Gollancz, 1940.

Trevor, Daphne. *Under the White Paper*. Jerusalem, Isr.: Jerusalem Press, 1948.

Trevor-Roper, H.R. *Blitzkrieg to Defeat: Hitler War Directives 1939-1945*. New York: Holt, Rinehart & Winston, 1971.

_____. *The Bormann Letters*. London: Weidenfeld & Nicolson, 1954.

_____. *The Crisis of the Seventeenth Century*. New York: Harper & Row, 1966.

_____. *The European Witch-Craze of the 16th and 17th Centuries*. Harmondsworth, Eng.: Penguin, 1969.

_____. (ed.). *The Golden Age of Europe*. New York: Bonanza Books, 1987.

_____. *Hermit of Peking*. New York: Alfred A. Knopf, 1977.

_____. *Hitler's Table Talk, 1941-44*. London: Weidenfeld & Nicolson, 1953.

_____. *The Last Days of Hitler*. New York: Crowell-Collier, 1962.

Trewin, J.C. *Benson and the Bensonians*. London: Barrie & Rockliff, 1960.

Treyvaud, Otto. *La tragédie de Sarajevo*. Lausanne, Switz.: Payot, 1934.

Trial of the Assassins and Conspirators for the Murder of Abraham Lincoln. Port Tobacco, Md.: James L. Barbour, 1981.

Trial and Confession of Andrew P. Potter. New Haven, Conn.: William Goodwin, 1845.

Trial and Confession of John Funston. New Philadelphia, Ohio: S. Patric, 1825.

The Trial and Confession of John Johnson. Philadelphia: n.p., n.d.

Trial and Confession of William Hill. New York: Christian Brown, 1836.

Trial and Conviction of Abraham Casler. Schoharie, N.Y.: n.p., 1817.

Trial and Conviction of Jack Reynolds. New York: American News, 1870.

Trial and Dying Confession of Henry Evans. Watertown, N.Y.: S.A. Abbey, 1828.

Trial and Execution of Thomas Barrett. Boston: Skinner & Blanchard, 1845.

Trial and Execution of Washington Goode. Boston: Skinner, n.d.

Trial and Sentence of Thomas J. Wansley and Charles Gibbs for Murder and Piracy Aboard the Brig Vineyard. New York: Christian Brown, 1831.

Trial and a Sketch of the Life of Amos Miner. Providence, R.I.: H.H. Brown, 1833.

The Trial at Large of the Rev. Ephraim K. Avery for the Wilful Murder of Sarah Maria Cornell. New York: n.p., 1833.

Trial, Confession and Execution of Isobel Insh, John Stewart, Margaret Barclay, and Isobel Crawford for Witchcraft. Ardrossan, Scot.: Herald Office, 1855.

Trial, Conviction and Sentence of Richard Johnson. New York: C. Brown, n.d.

The Trial for Murder of James E. Eldredge. Ogdensburgh, N.Y.: Hitchcock, Tollotson & Stilwell, 1857.

Trial, Life, and Confessions of Charles Cook. Schenectady, N.Y.: E.M. Packard, 1840.

Trial, Life, and Confession of John Van Patten. Schenectady, N.Y.:

Mohawk Sentinel, 1825.

Trial of Abraham Prescott. Philadelphia: C. Alexander, 1866.

Trial of Albert J. Tirrell. Boston: Boston Daily Mail, 1846.

Trial of Albert John Tirrell. Boston: Times, 1846.

Trial of Alpheus Livermore. Boston: Watson & Bangs, 1813.

Trial of Andreas Hall for the Murder of Mrs. Amy Smith. Troy, N.Y.: J.C. Kneeland, 1849.

The Trial of Carlyle W. Harris for Poisoning His Wife, Helen Potts. New York: n.p., 1892.

Trial of Charles Getter for the Murder of His Wife. Philadelphia: Alexander, 1833.

The Trial of Cyrus B. Dean for the Murder of Jonathan Ormsby and Asa Marsh. Burlington, Vt.: Samuel Mills, 1808.

Trial of Daniel Giddings for Shooting Benjamin Wiltshire. Hillsboro, Ohio: n.p., 1885.

The Trial of Daniel McFarland for the Shooting of Albert D. Richardson. New York: American News, 1870.

Trial of Emil Lowenstein. Albany, N.Y.: W. Gould & Son, 1874.

Trial of German Major War Criminals. 22 parts. London: H.M. Stationery Office, 1946-1950.

Trial of Capt. Henry Whitby. New York: Gould, Banks, Gould, 1812.

Trial of Capt. John Windsor. Milford, Del.: J.H. Emerson, 1851.

Trial of Charles Lewis. Princeton, N.J.: Standard Office, 1863.

Trial of Edward Tinker. Newbern, N.C.: Hall, Bryan & Watson, 1811.

Trial of Emile Lowenstein. Albany, N.Y.: William Gould & Son, 1874.

The Trial of Frank Kelly for the Assassination and Murder of Octavius V. Catto. Philadelphia: n.p., n.d.

Trial of George Miller. Boston: n.p., 1876.

Trial of George Travers. Boston: T.G. Bangs, 1815.

Trial of Henry G. Green for the Murder of His Wife. New York: n.p., 1845.

Trial of Henry Ward. Tunkhannock, Pa.: Tunkhannock Republican, 1871.

The Trial of Herman W. Mudgett. Philadelphia: George T. Bisel, 1897.

Trial of the Hon. Daniel E. Sickles for the Murder of Philip Barton Key. New York: R.M. De Witt, 1859.

Trial of James Anthony for the Murder of Joseph Green. Rutland, Vt.: Fay & Davison, 1814.

Trial of James P. Donnelly. Freehold, N.J.: Monmouth Inquirer, 1857.

Trial of John C. Colt for the Murder of Samuel Adams. New York: Sun, 1842.

Trial of John Fox. New Brunswick, Conn.: Freedonian, 1856.

Trial of John H. Surratt in the Criminal Court for the District of Columbia. 2 vols. Washington D.C.: U.S. Government Printing Office, 1867.

Trial of John H. Surratt...on an Indictment for Murder of President Lincoln. Washington D.C.: R. Sutton, 1867.

The Trial of John K. Hardenbrook. Rochester, N.Y.: D.M. Dewey, 1849.

Trial of John Y. Bealle As A Spy and Guerrilla. New York: D. Appleton, 1865.

Trial of Joseph LaPage, The French Monster. Philadelphia: Old Franklin, 1876.

Trial of Levi Kelley. Cooperstown, N.Y.: Watch Tower, 1827.

Trial of Maurice Antonio. Rochester, N.Y.: Dmn M. Dewey, 1852.

Trial of Medad M'Kay. Albany, N.Y.: Websters & Skinners, 1821.

Trial of Mrs. Elizabeth Wharton on a Charge of Poisoning General W.S. Ketchum. Baltimore: Baltimore Gazette, 1872.

Trial of Mrs. Margaret Howard for the Murder of Miss Mary Ellen Smith. Cincinnati, Ohio: n.p., 1849.

Trial of Mrs. Rebecca Peake. Montpelier, Vt.: E.P. Walton & Sons, 1836.

Trial of Orrin De Wolf. Worcester, Mass.: Thomas Drew, Jr., 1845.

Trial of Pasach HN. Rubenstein. New York: Baker, Voorhis, 1876.

The Trial of Rev. Ephraim K. Avery. New York: n.p., 1833.

Trial of Rev. George W. Carawan. New York: n.p., 1854.

Trial of Richard Johnson for the Murder of Mrs. Ursula Newman. New York: J. M'Cleland, 1829.

Trial of Robert Douglass. Bath, N.Y.: B.F. Smead, 1825.

Trial of Robert McConaghy, Together with His Confession and Execution. Philadelphia: n.p., 1840.

Trial of Robert Swan, Charged with the Murder of William O. Sprigg. Hagerstown, Md.: Heard & Williams, 1853.

The Trial of Rufus Hill for the Murder of Mary Sisson. Salem, N.Y.: n.p., 1808.

Trial of Sager for the Murder of his Wife. Augusta, Maine: Luther Severance, 1834.

Trial of Samuel Daviess for the Murder of Henry Pendleton Smith. Frankfurt, Ky.: Kendall & Russells, 1819.

Trial of Samuel M. Andrews for the Murder of Cornelius Holmes. Plymouth, Mass.: True Plymouth Rock Office, 1868.

Trial of Sheldon Pond. Middlebury, Vt.: W. Clark, 1855.

Trial of Stephen Arnold. Cooperstown, N.Y.: E. Phinney, 1805.

Trial of Stephen Videto. Malone, N.Y.: Telegraph Office, 1825.

Trial of U-2. Chicago: Translation World, 1960.

Trial of William Dandredge Epes. Petersburg, Va.: J.M.H. Brunet, 1849.

Trial of William E. Sturtivant for the Murder of Simeon Sturtivant. Plymouth, Mass.: Old Colony Memorial Office, 1874.

The Trial of William Holmes, Thomas Warrington and Edward Rosewain on an Indictment for Murder on the High Seas. Boston: Joseph C. Spear, 1820.

Trial of William Stewart. Baltimore: Bull & Tuttle, 1838.

The Trial, Sentence and Confession of Antoine Le Blanc. Morristown, N.Y.: n.p., 1833.

A Tribute to Robert Francis Kennedy. New York: Stanley, 1968.

The Tricks and Traps of Chicago. New York: Dinsmore, 1859.

Triffin, Robert. *Gold and the Dollar Crisis: The Future of Convertibility*. New Haven, Conn.: Yale University Press, 1960.

Triggs, J.H. *History of Cheyenne and Northern Wyoming*. Omaha, Neb.: Herald Printing House, 1876.

_____. *History and Directory of Laramie City, Wyoming Territory*. Laramie City, Wyo.: Daily Sentinel Print, 1875

Trillin, Calvin. *Killings*. New York: Penguin Books, 1984.

Trilling, Diana. *Mrs. Harris, the Death of the Scarsdale Diet Doctor*. New York: Harcourt Brace Jovanovich, 1981.

_____. *We Must March My Darlings*. New York: Harcourt, Brace, Jovanoich, 1977.

Trilling, Lionel. *The Middle of the Journey*. Garden City, N.Y.: Doubleday, 1957.

Trimble, William. *The Mining Advance into the Inland Empire*. Madison: University of Wisconsin History Series, 1914.

Trinka, Zena Irma. *Out Where the West Begins, Being the Early and Romantic History of North Dakota*. St. Paul, Minn.: Pioneer, 1920.

Triplett, Col. Frank. *Conquering the Wilderness*. New York: N.D. Thompson, 1883.

_____. *History, Romance and Philosophy of Great American Crimes and Criminals*. Hartford, Conn.: Park, 1885.

_____. *The Life, Times, and Treacherous Death of Jesse James*. St. Louis: J.H. Chambers, 1882.

Tripp, C.A. *The Homosexual Matrix*. New York: McGraw-Hill, 1975.

Trizzino, Antonio. *Navi e poltrone*. Milan, Italy: Longanesi, 1966.

_____. *Settembre nero*. Milan, Italy: Longanesi, 1959.

Trochu, Louis-Jules. *L'Armée française en 1867*. Paris: Amyot, 1867.

_____. *Oeuvres posthumes*. Tours, Fr.: A. Mame, 1896.

_____. *Pour la vérité et pour la justice*. Paris: J. Hetzel, 1873.

Troelstra, Pieter J. *Troelstra, de Ziener*. Amsterdam. Neth.: N.V.E. Querido's Uitgevers Mij., 1935.

Trohan, Walter. *Political Animals*. Garden City, N.Y.: Double-day, 1975.

Trojanowicz, Robert C. *An Evaluation of the Neighborhood Foot Patrol Program in Flint, Michigan*. East Lansing: Michigan State University, 1984.

_____, and Dixon, Samuel L. *Criminal Justice and the Community*. Englewood Cliffs, N.J.: Prentice-Hall, 1974.

Trollope, Anthony. *The Three Clerks*. New York: Harper & Brothers, 1860.

Trollope, Frances. *Domestic Manners of the Americans*. New York: Dodd, Mead, 1901.

_____. *Great Crimes and Criminals in America*. New York: R.K. Fox, 1881.

_____. *Paris and the Parisians in 1835*. Paris: Galignani, 1836.

Trotsky, Leon. *The Defence of Terrorism*. London: George Allen & Unwin, 1921.

_____. *Diary in Exile, 1935*. trans. Elena Zarudnaya. Cambridge, Mass.: Harvard University Press, 1958.

_____. *History of the Russian Revolution*. 3 vols. Ann Arbor: University of Michigan Press, 1957.

_____. *Lenin*. New York: Grosset & Dunlap, 1960.

_____. *My Life*. New York: Charles Scribner's Sons, 1930.

_____. *Stalin*. New York: Harper & Brothers, 1941.

_____. *Terrorism and Communism*. Ann Arbor, University of Michigan Press, 1961.

_____. *Whither France?* New York: Pioneer, 1936.

Trotter, Eleanor. *Seventeenth Century Life in the Country Parish, with Special Reference to the Local Government*. Cambridge, Eng.: Cambridge University Press, 1919.

Troup, E. *The Home Office*. London: John Murray, 1938.

Trowbridge, J.T. *A Picture of the Desolated States; and the Work of Restoration*. Hartford, Conn.: L. Stebbins, 1868.

_____. *The South: A Tour of Its Battlefields and Ruined Cities*. Hartford, Conn.: L. Stebbins, 1866.

Truc, Gonzague. *Madame de Montespan*. Paris: A. Colin, 1936.

True and Authentic Life and Confession of Joel Clough. Philadelphia: Robert Desilver, 1833.

A True and Exact Relation of the Several Informations, Examinations, and Confessions of the Late Witches...in Essex. London: H. Overton, 1645.

The True and Genuine Confession of William Gross. Philadelphia: A. Guild, 1823.

A True and Impartial Relation of the Informations Against Three Witches. London: Freeman Collins, 1682.

A True and Just Record of the Information, Examination, and Confession of All the Witches Taken at St. Edmundsbury. London: London: T. Dawson, 1582.

A True Discourse, Declaring the Damnable Life and Death of One Stubbe Peter. London: E. Venge, 1590.

A True Relation of the Arraignment of Eighteen Witches at St. Edmundsbury. London: I.H., 1645.

A True Relation of a Very Strange and Wonderful Thing That Was Heard in the Air. London: L. Chapman, 1658.

Trufanov, Sergyei. *The Mad Monk of Russia*. New York: Century, 1918.

Truffaut, François. *Hitchcock*. New York: Simon & Schuster, 1967.

The Truly Remarkable Life of the Beautiful Helen Jewett Who was So Mysteriously Murdered. Philadelphia: Barclay, 1878.

Truman, Benjamin Cummings. *Life, Adventures and Capture of Tiburcio Vasquez*. Los Angeles: Los Angeles Star, 1874.

Truman, David. *The Governmental Process: Political Interests and Public Opinion*. New York: Alfred A. Knopf, 1951.

Truman, Harry S. *Memoirs*. 2 vols. New York: Doubleday, 1955.

_____. *Year of Decisions*. New York: New American Library, 1965.

_____. *Years of Trial and Hope*. New York: New American Library, 1965.

Trumble, Alfred. *Crooked Life in New York, The Mysteries of Metropolitan Crime and Criminals Unveiled!* New York: R. K. Fox, 1882.

_____. *Famous Frauds: Or the Sharks of Society*. New York: R.K. Fox, 1883.

_____. *Faro Exposed, or The Gambler and His Prey*. New York: R.K. Fox, 1883.

_____. *The Female Sharpers of New York*. New York: R.K. Fox, 1882.

Trumpener, Ulrich. *Germany and the Ottoman Empire, 1914-1918*. Princeton, N.J.: Princeton University Press, 1968.

Truth Stranger Than Fiction, Lydia Sherman, Confession of the Arch Murderess of Connecticut. Philadelphia: T.R. Callender, 1873.

Trzenbinski, E. *The Kenya Pioneers*. New York: W.W. Norton, 1986.

Tschudi, C. de. *La mère de Napoléon*. Paris: Fontemoing, 1910.

Tschuppik, Karl. *The Reign of the Emperor Franz Josef*. London: G. Bell, 1930.

t'Serstevens, A. *Mexico: Three-Storyed Land*. London: Hutchinson, 1959.

Tsien, T.H. *Written on Bamboo and Silk*. Chicago: University of Chicago Press, 1962.

Tsuji Masanobu. *Singapore: The Japanese Version*. trans. Margaret E. Lake. New York: St.Martin's Press, 1960.

_____. *Underground Escape*. Tokyo: Robert Booth & Taro Fukada, 1952.

Tsunoda, Ryusaku, de Bary, William Theodore, and Keene, Donald, (comps.). *Sources of Japanese Tradition*. New York: Columbia University Press, 1958.

Tsurumi Shunsuke, et. al. *Japan's Century*. 10 vols. Tokyo: Chikuma Shobo, 1964.

Tucci, Giuseppe. *Rati Lilà: An Interpretation of the Tantric Imagery of the Temples of Nepal*. trans. James Hogarth. Geneva, Switz.: Nagel, 1966.

_____. *Theory and Practice of the Mandala*. trans. Alan Houghton Broderick. London: Rider, 1969.

_____. *Tibetan Painted Scrolls*. Rome: Libreria dell Stato, 1949.

Tuchman, Barbara W. *A Distant Mirror*. New York: Alfred A. Knopf, 1978.

_____. *The Guns of August*. New York: Macmillan, 1962.

_____. *The Proud Tower*. New York: Macmillan, 1966.

_____. *Stilwell and the American Experience in China 1911-45*. New York: Macmillan, 1971.

_____. *The Zimmermann Telegram*. New York: Viking Press, 1958.

Tucker, Glenn. *Hancock the Superb*. Indianapolis, Ind.: Bobbs-Merrill, 1960.

_____. *Tecumseh, Vision of Glory*. Indianapolis, Ind.: Bobbs-Merril, 1956.

Tucker, Howard. *History of Gov. Walton's War*. Oklahoma City: Southwest, 1923.

Tucker, William. *Vigilante, the Backlash Against Crime in America*. New York: Stein & Day, 1985.

Tuckerman, Bayard (ed.). *The Diary of Philip Hone*. New York: Dodd, Mead, 1889.

Tuckerman, Bayard. *Lafayette*. New York: Dodd, Mead, 1889.

Tuckwell, Reverend William. *A.W. Kingslake: A Biographical and Literary Study*. London: G. Bell, 1902.

Tufts, Henry. *The Autobiography of a Criminal*. New York: Duffield, 1930.

Tugwell, Rexford G. *Battle for Democracy*. New York: Columbia University Press, 1935.

_____. *The Brains Trust*. New York: Viking Press, 1968.

_____. *The Democratic Roosevelt*. Garden City, N.Y.: Doubleday, 1957.

Tuke, A.W., and Gillman, R.J.H. *Barclays Bank Ltd., 1926-1969*. London: Privately Printed, 1972.

Tuker, Sir Francis. *While Memory Serves*. London: Cassell, 1950.

_____. *The Yellow Scarf, The Story of the Life of Thuggee Sleeman*. London: J.M. Dent & Sons, 1961.

Tulchin, S.H. *Intelligence and Crime.* Chicago: University of Chicago Press, 1939.

Tullett, Tom. *Portrait of a Bad Man.* New York: Rinehart, 1956.

_____. *Strictly Murder.* New York: St. Martin's Press, 1979.

Tullock, Gordon. *Economics of Income Redistribution.* Boston: Kluwer-Nijhoff, 1983.

_____. *The Politics of Bureaucracy.* Washington, D.C.: Public Affairs Press, 1965.

Tully, Andrew. *CIA, the Inside Story.* Greenwich, Conn.: Fawcett, 1962.

_____. *Era of Elegance.* New York: Funk & Wagnalls, 1947.

_____. *The FBI's Most Famous Cases.* New York: William Morrow, 1965.

_____. *Inside the FBI.* New York: McGraw-Hill, 1980.

_____. *Inside Interpol.* New York: Walker, 1965.

_____. *Treasury Agent.* New York: Simon & Schuster, 1958.

Tully, Grace. *FDR, My Boss.* New York: Charles Scribner's Sons, 1949.

Tulsky, S. *Manchzhuriya.* Moscow: Voenizdat, 1932.

Tulving, E., and Donaldson, W. (eds.). *Organization of Memory.* New York: Academic Press, 1972.

Tumulty, Joseph Patrick. *Woodrow Wilson as I Know Him.* Garden City, N.Y.: Doubleday, Page, 1921.

Tuni, Edwin. *The Young United States.* New York: Thomas Y. Crowell, 1969.

Tunnard, Christopher, and Reed, Henry Hope. *American Skyline: The Growth and Form of Our Cities and Towns.* Boston: Houghton Mifflin, 1955.

Tupper, Harmon. *To the Great Ocean.* Boston: Little, Brown, 1965.

Turberville, Arthur Stanley. *Medieval Heresy and the Inquisition.* London: George Allen & Unwin, 1920.

Turchi, Franz. *Prefetto con Mussolini.* Rome: Latinità, 1950.

Turk, Austin T. *Criminality and the Legal Order.* Chicago: Rand McNally, 1969.

_____. *Legal Sanctioning and Social Control.* Washington D.C.: U.S. Government Printing Office, 1972.

_____. *Political Criminality.* Beverly Hills, Calif.: Sage, 1982.

Turkus, Burton B., and Feder, Sid. *Murder, Inc.: The Story of the Syndicate.* New York: Farrar, Straus & Young, 1951.

Turland, Ephraim. *Notes of a Visit to America: Eleven Lectures.* Manchester, Eng.: Johnson & Rawson, 1877.

Turlington, Edgar W. *Mexico and her Foreign Creditors.* New York: Columbia University Press, 1930.

Turmel, Joseph. *Histoire du diable.* Paris: Rieder, 1931.

Turnbull, Robert J. *A Visit to the Philadelphia Prison.* Philadelphia: Budd & Bartram, 1796.

Turner, Cecil Howard. *The Inhumanists.* London: Alexander Crouseley, 1932.

Turner, E.M. *Josephine Butler: An Appreciation.* London: Association for Moral and Social Hygiene, 1928.

Turner, Ernest Sackville. *The Shocking History of Advertising.* New York: E.P. Dutton, 1953.

_____. *The Shocking History of Social Reform.* London: Michael Joseph, 1950.

Turner, F.J. *The Frontier in American History.* New York: Henry Henry Holt, 1920.

_____. *The United States, 1830-1850.* New York: Holt, 1935.

Turner, Fitzhugh. *Dirty Little Coward of Fauquier County.* Warrentonn, Va.: n.p., 1953.

Turner, Frederick Jackson. *Rise of the New West 1819-1829.* New York: Harper & Brothers, 1906.

Turner, J.W.C. (ed.). *Kenny's Outlines of Criminal Law.* Cambridge, Eng.: Cambridge University Press, 1952.

Turner, James S. *The Chemical Feast.* New York: Grossman, 1970.

Turner, John Kenneth. *Barbarous Mexico.* Chicago: C.H. Kerr, 1911.

_____. *Hands Off Mexico.* New York: Rand School of Social Science, 1920.

Turner, John Peter. *The North-West Mounted Police, 1873-1893.* 2 vols. Ottawa, Ontario, Can.: Edmund Cloutier, 1950.

Turner, Jonathan. *The Structure of Sociological Theory.* Homewood, Ill.: Dorsey, 1974.

Turner, Justin G., and Levitt, Linda. *Mary Todd Lincoln: Her Life and Letters.* New York: Alfred A. Knopf, 1972.

Turner, Louis. *Invisible Empires.* New York: Harcourt Brace Jovanovich, 1970.

Turner, Mary Honeyman Ten Eyck. *Avery Turner, Pioneer Railroad and Empire Builder of the Great Southwest.* Amarillo, Texas: Southwestern, 1933.

_____. *These High Plains.* Amarillo, Texas: Russell Stationery, 1941.

Turner, Mertyn. *Safe Lodging.* London: Hutchinson, 1961.

Turner, Nat. *The Confessions of Nat Turner.* Richmond, Va.: T.R. Gray, 1832.

Turner, R.F. *Forensic Science and Laboratory Techniques.* Springfield, Ill.: Charles C. Thomas, 1949.

Turner, Thomas R. *Beware the People Weeping: Public Opinion and the Assassination of Abraham Lincoln.* Baton Rouge: Louisiana State University Press, 1982.

Turner, Wallace. *Gambler's Money.* Boston: Houghton Mifflin, 1965.

Turner, William. *Complete History of the Most Remarkable Providences.* London: John Dunton, 1697.

Turner, William (ed.). *Traffic Investigation.* San Francisco: Aqueduct, 1965.

Turner, William W. *Hoover's FBI.* New York: Dell, 1970.

_____. *The Police Establishment.* New York: G.P. Putnam's Sons, 1968.

Turrou, Leon G. *Where My Shadow Falls.* Garden City, N.Y.: Doubleday, 1949.

Tuska, Jon. *The Detective in Hollywood.* Garden City: Doubleday, 1978.

_____, and Piekarski. *Encyclopedia of Frontier and Western Fiction.* New York: McGraw-Hill, 1983.

Tutorow, Norman E. *Leland Stanford: Man of Many Careers.* Menlo Park, Calif.: Pacific Coast, 1971.

Tuttle, Charles R. *History of Kansas.* Madison, Wis.: Interstate, 1876.

Tuttle, Daniel S. *Reminiscences of a Missionary Bishop.* New York: Thomas Whittaker, 1906.

Tuttle, Elizabeth Orman. *The Crusade Against Captial Punishment in Great Britain.* Chicago: Quadrangle Books, 1961.

Tuttle, William M., Jr. *Race Riot: Chicago in the Red Summer of 1919.* New York: Atheneum, 1970.

Twain, Mark [Samuel Clemens]. *Following the Equator: A Journey Around the World.* New York: Harper & Brothers, 1899.

_____. *Life on the Mississippi.* Boston: J.R. Osgood, 1883.

_____. *Roughing It.* Hartford, Conn.: American, 1872.

Tweedie, Ethel Brilliana. *America As I Saw It; or America Revisited.* New York: Macmillan, 1913.

_____. *Mexico As I Saw It.* London: Hurst and Blackett, 1902.

_____. *Mexico from Diaz to the Kaiser.* New York: George H. Doran, 1918.

_____. *Porfirio Diaz.* London: Hurst and Blackett, 1906.

Twentieth Century Task Force on Criminal Sentencing. *Fair and Certain Punishment.* New York: McGraw-Hill, 1976.

Twining, Thomas. *Travels in America 100 Years Ago.* New York: Harper & Brothers, 1893.

Twitchell, Ralph E. *Historical Sketch of Governor William Carr Lane.* Santa Fe: New Mexico Historical Society, 1917.

_____. *The History of Military Occupation of the Territory of New Mexico.* Chicago: Rio del Grande Press, 1963.

_____. *The Leading Facts of New Mexican History.* Cedar Rapids, Iowa: Torch Press, 1911-1917.

Two Centuries Growth of American Law, 1701-1901. New York: Charles Scribner's Sons, 1902.

Twyman, H.W. *The Best Laid Schemes.* London: Harold Shayler, 1931.

Tyack, David B. *The One Best System: A History of American Urban Education.* Cambridge, Mass.: Harvard University Press, 1974.

Tylen, Alice Felt. *The Foreign Policy of James G. Blaine.* Minneapolis: University of Minnesota Press, 1927.

Tyler, Alice Felt. *Freedom's Ferment: Phases of American Social History to 1860.* Minneapolis: University of Minnesota Press, 1944.

Tyler, Froom. *Gallows Parade.* London: Lorat Dickson, 1933.

Tyler, George C. *Whatever Goes Up.* Indianapolis, Ind.: Bobbs-Merrill, 1934.

Tyler, George W. *The History of Bell County.* San Antonio, Texas: Naylor, 1936.

Tyler, Gus (ed.). *Organized Crime in America.* Ann Arbor: University of Michigan Press, 1962.

Tyler, Helen E. *Where Prayer and Purpose Meet: The W.C.T.U. Story.* Evanston, Ill.: Signal Press, 1949.

Tyler, J.E. *The Struggle for Imperial Unity.* London: Longman, 1938.

Tyler, Moses Colt. *The Literary History of the American Revolution 1763-1783.* 2 vols. New York: G.P. Putnam's Sons, 1897.

Tyler, Samuel. *Memoir of Rogers Brooke Taney.* Baltimore: John Murphy, 1872.

Tynan, Katherine. *Twenty-five Years: Reminiscences.* London: Smith, Elder, 1913.

_____. *The Years of the Shadow.* London: Constable, 1919.

Tynan, P.J.P. *The Irish National Invincibles and Their Times.* New York: Irish National Invincible, 1894.

Tyng, Dudley Atkins. *Digest of the Cases Decided in the Supreme Judicial Court of the Commonwealth of Massachusetts.* Boston: Richardson & Lord, 1825.

Tyrner-Tyrnauer, A.R. *Lincoln and the Emperors.* New York: Harcourt, Brace & World, 1962.

Tyron, George. *Fire Protection Handbook.* Boston: National Protection Association, 1962.

U

Ubbelohde, Carl. *The Vice-Admiralty Courts and the American Revolution.* Chapel Hill: University of North Carolina Press, 1960.

Udall, David King, and Pearl Udall Nelson. *Arizona Pioneer Mormon.* Tucson: Arizona Silhouettes, 1959.

Uelmen, Gerald F., and Haddox, Victor G. (eds.). *Drug Abuse and the Law.* New York: Clark, Boardman, 1983.

_____. *Varieties of Police Policy.* Beverly Hills, Calif.: Institute on Law and Urban Studies, 1972.

Ugaki Kazushige. *Ugaki Diary.* Tokyo: Asahi Shinbunsha, 1954.

Uhnak, Dorothy. *Policewoman.* New York: Simon & Schuster, 1964.

Ulam, Adam B. *The Bolsheviks.* New York: Macmillan, 1965.

_____. *Expansion and Coexistence.* New York: Frederick A. Praeger, 1968.

_____. *Ideologies and Illusions.* Cambridge, Mass.: Harvard University Press, 1976.

_____. *In the Name of the People.* New York: Viking Press, 1977.

_____. *The Rivals: America and Russia Since World War II.* New York: Viking Press, 1971.

_____. *Stalin: The Man and His Era.* New York: Viking, 1973.

_____. *Titoism and the Cominform.* Cambridge, Mass.: Harvard University Press, 1952.

Ulanov, Ann Bedford. *The Feminine in Jungian Psychology and on Christian Theology.* Evanston. Ill.: Northwestern University Press, 1971.

Ular, Alexander. *A Russo-Chinese Empire.* Westport, Conn.: Greenwood, 1975.

Ullerstam, Lars. *The Erotic Minorities.* New York: Grove Press, 1966.

Ullman, Joe. *What's The Odds?* New York: n.p., 1903.

Ullman, Leonard P., and Krasner, Leonard. *A Psychological Approach to Abnormal Behavior.* Englewood Cliffs, N.J.: Prentice-Hall, 1975.

Ullman, Montague, et al. *Dream Telepathy.* New York: Macmillan, 1973.

Ullman, Richard H. *Britain and the Russian Civil War.* Princeton, N.J.: Princeton University Press, 1968.

Ulloa, Antonio de, and Santarcilia, Jorge Juan y. *A Voyage to South America.* London: J. Stockdale, 1806.

Ulman, Albert. *Maiden Lane--The Story of a Single Street.* New York: Maiden Lane Historical Society, 1931.

Ulyanova-Elizarova, Anna Ilyinicha. *Aleksandr Ilyich Ulyanov i delo I Marta, 1887.* Moscow: Gosizdat, 1927.

_____. *Vospominaniya ob Ilyiche.* Moscow: Parinoe Izdatelstvo, 1934.

Umashima Takeshi. *Secret History of Hidden Factional Feuds in the Army.* Tokyo: Kyodo, 1946.

The Umberger Tragedy, with a Criminal History of Somerset County. Somerset, Pa.: Highland Farmer, 1890.

Umbreit, Kenneth B. *Our Eleven Chief Justices: A History of the Supreme Court in Terms of Their Personalities.* New York: Harper & Row, 1940.

Underhill, H.C. *Criminal Evidence.* New York: Bobbs-Merrill, 1973.

Underhill, Lonnie E., and Littlefield, Daniel F., Jr. (eds.). *Hamlin Garland's Observations on the American Indian 1895-1905.* Tucson: University of Arizona Press, 1976.

Underhill, Ruth Murray. *The Navajos.* Norman: University of Oklahoma Press, 1958.

_____. *Red Man's America.* Chicago: University of Chicago Press, 1953.

Underwood, John L. *The Women of the Confederacy.* New York: Neale, 1906.

Ungar, Sanford J. *FBI.* Boston: Little, Brown, 1975.

Unger, Roberto Mangabeira. *Law in Modern Society.* New York: Free Press, 1976.

Uniform Crime Reports for the United States. Washington, D.C.: U.S. Government Printing Office, 1976.

United Nations Department of Economic and Social Affairs. *Capital Punishment.* New York: United Nations, 1962.

United Nations Educational, Scientific, and Cultural Organization. *All Men Are Brothers: Life and Thoughts of Mahatma Gandhi.* Paris: UNESCO, 1958.

United Press International (ed.). *John F. Kennedy, From Childhood to Martyrdom.* Washington D.C.: Tatler, 1963.

United States Adjutant General's Office, Military Commission. *Trial of John Yates Beall.* New York: D. Appleton, 1865.

United States Advisory Commission on Intergovernmental Relations. *State-Local Relations in the Criminal Justice System.* Washington D.C.: U.S. Government Printing Office, 1971.

The United States and Canada As Seen by Two Brothers in 1858 and 1861. London: E. Stanford, 1862.

United States Army Air Forces. *Mission Accomplished: Interrogations of Japanese Industrial, Military and Civil Leaders of World War II.* Washington, D.C.: U.S. Government Printing Office, 1946.

United States Bureau of Labor. *The Slums of Baltimore, Chicago, New York, and Philadelphia.* Washington D.C.: U.S. Government Printing Office, 1894.

United States Bureau of Prisons. *Handbook of Correctional Institution Design and Construction.* Washington, D.C.: n.p., 1949.

_____. *Recent Prison Construction 1950-1960.* Washington, D.C.: n.p., 1960.

United States Central Intelligence Agency. *International and*

Transnational Terrorism: Diagnosis and Prognosis. Langley, Va.: U.S. Central Intelligence Agency, 1977.

United States Corps of Engineers. *Navigation Bulletins.* Memphis, Tenn.: U.S. Army Engineer District, 1961.

United States Department of Commerce, Bureau of the Census. *Prisoners in State and Federal Prisons and Reformatories, 1927.* Washington D.C.: U.S. Government Printing Office, 1931.

United States Department of Justice, Federal Bureau of Investigation. *Uniform Crime Reports for the United States.* Washington, D.C.: U.S. Government Printing Office, 1950-1970.

United States Department of Justice, Law Enforcement Assisstance Administration. *Expenditure and Employment Data for the Criminal Justice System, 1968-1969.* Washington, D.C.: U.S. Government Printing Office, 1970.

_____. *National Jail Census.* Washington, D.C.: U.S. Government Printing Office, 1971.

United States Eighty-sixth Congress, second session. House of Representatives. Committee of the Judiciary. *Hearing...on H.R. 870 to Abolish the Death Penalty.* Washington, D.C.: U.S. Government Printing Office, 1960.

United States Government. *Combatting Crime in the United States.* Washington, D.C.: U.S. Government Printing Office, 1967.

United States Government Commission on Violence. *Causes and Prevention of Violence.* Washington, D.C.: U.S. Government Printing Office, n.d.

United States Government General Services Administration. *Transportation of Explosive Compounds, title 49.* Washington, D.C.: General Administration Archives, n.d.

United States House of Representatives. *Pardon of Richard M. Nixon and Related Matters.* Washington, D.C.: n.p., 1974.

_____. *Report of the Select Committee on Assassinations: Findings and Recommendations.* Washington D.C.: U.S. Government Printing Office, 1979.

_____. *Select Committee on Assassinations.* Washington D.C.: U.S. Government Printing Office, 1979.

United States House of Representatives, Select Committed on Crime. Hearings: *Crime in America—Aspects of Organized Crime, Court Delay, and Juvenile Justice.* Washington, D.C.: U.S. Government Printing Office, 1970.

_____. Hearings: *Crime in America—A Mid-American View.* Washington, D.C.: U.S. Government Printing Office, 1969.

_____. Hearings: *Crime in America—Response of a Midsouth Community.* Washington, D.C.: U.S. Government Printing Office, 1970.

_____. Hearings: *Crime in America—The Nations Capital.* Washington, D.C.: U.S. Government Printing Office, 1970.

_____. Hearings: *The Improvement and Reform of Law Enforcement and Criminal Justice in the United States.* Washington, D.C.: U.S. Government Printing Office, 1969.

United States National Archives. *Inventory of the Records of the President's Commission on the Assassination of President Kennedy.* Washington D.C.: General Services Administration, 1973.

_____. *Public Papers of the Presidents of the United States.* Washington D.C.: U.S. Government Printing Office, 1962-1964.

United States Senate. *Final Report of the Select Committee to Study Governmental Operations With Respect to Intelligence Activities.* Washington D.C.: U.S. Government Printing Office, 1976.

_____. *Memorial Addresses in the Congress of the United States and Tributes in Eulogy of John Fitzgerald Kennedy, A Late President of the United States.* Washington D.C.: U.S. Government Printing Office, 1964.

United States Senate, Committee on the District of Columbia. *Report of the Advisory Panel Against Armed Violence.* Washington, D.C.: U.S. Government Printing Office.

_____. *Staff Study on Drug Abuse in the Washington Area.* Washington, D.C.: U.S. Government Printing Office, 1969.

United States Senate, Committee on the Judiciary, Subcommittee on Criminal Laws and Procedures. *Controlling Crime.* Washington, D.C.: U.S. Government Printing Office, 1967.

Upham, Charles W. *Salem Witchcraft.* Boston: Wiggin & Lunt, 1867.

Upham, Thomas C. *The Manual of Peace.* New York: Leavitt, Lord, 1836.

Upham, W.P. *Wenham Town Records.* Wenham, Mass.: Wenham Historical Society, 1930.

Upshur, George Lyttleton. *As I Recall Them, Memories of Crowded Years.* New York: Wilson-Erickson, 1936.

Upton, Harriet Taylor. *A Twentieth Century History of Turnbull County, Ohio.* Chicago: Lewis, 1909.

Underhill, Ruth Murray. *Papago Indian Religion.* New York: Columbia University Press, 1946.

Ungar, Sanford J. *FBI.* Boston: Atlantic Monthly Press, 1976.

Unger, Irwin. *The Movement.* New York: Dodd, Mead, 1974.

Unger, Sanford J. *FBI, an Uncensored Look Behind the Walls.* Boston: Little, Brown, 1976.

Unterberger, B. M. *America's Siberian Expedition, 1918-1920.* Durham, N.C.: Duke University Press, 1956.

Unterecker, John. *Voyager: A Life of Hart Crane.* New York: Farrar, Straus & Giroux, 1969.

Unwin, J.D. *Sex and Culture.* London: Oxford University Press, 1934.

_____. *Sexual Regulations and Human Behavior.* London: Williams & Norgate, 1933.

Upham, Charles Wentworth. *Lectures on Witchcraft.* Boston: Carter, Hendee, Babcock, 1831.

_____. *Salem Witchcraft.* Boston: Wiggin & Lunt, 1867.

Upshur, George Lyttleton. *As I Recall Them: Memories of Crowded Years.* New York: Wilson-Erickson, 1936.

Upton, Charles Elmer. *Pioneers of El Dorado.* Placerville, Calif: Published by Author, 1906.

Ure, P.N. *The Origin of Tyranny.* New York: Russell & Russell, 1962.

Urofsky, Melvin I. and Levy, David W. *Letters of Louis D. Brandeis.* Albany: State University of New York Press, 1971.

_____. *A Mind of One Piece: Brandeis and American Reform.* New York: Charles Scribner's Sons, 1971.

Urquhart, Lena M. *Roll Call: The Violent and Lawless.* Denver: Golden Bell Press, 1967.

Urquizo, Francisco L. *Carranza.* Mexico City: n.p., 1954.

_____. *Páginas de la revolución.* Mexico City: Talleres Gráficos de la Nación, 1956.

Usdin, Earl (ed.). *Neuropharmacology of Monoamines and Their Regulatory Enzmes.* New York: Raven Press, 1974.

Usher, Roland G. (ed.). *The Presbyterian Movement in the Reign of Queen Elizabeth.* London: Royal Historical Society, 1905.

Utley, Freda. *Will the Middle East Go West?* Chicago: Henry Regnery, 1957.

Uviller, H. *The Processes of Criminal Justice: Investigation.* St. Paul, Minn.: West, 1979.

Uyehara, Cecil H. (comp.) *Checklist of Archives in the Japanese Ministry of Foreign Affairs, Tokyo, Japan 1868-1945.* Washington, D.C.: Library of Congress, 1954.

V

Vacandard, Abbé Elphège. *L'Inquisition: A Critical and Historical Study of the Coercive Power of the Church.* trans. Bertrand L. Conway. New York: Longmans, Green, 1926.

Vacaresco, Helene. *Kings and Queens I Have Known.* New York: Harper & Brothers, 1904.

Vacha, Robert (ed.). *The Kaiser's Daughter.* Englewood Cliffs,

N.J.: Prentice-Hall, 1977.

Vaillant, G.E. *The Natural History of Alcoholism*. Cambridge, Mass.: Harvard University Press, 1983.

Vaillant, George C. *Aztecs of Mexico*. Garden City, N.Y.: Doubleday, 1941.

Vairo, Leonardo. *De Fascino*. Venice, Italy: Aldum, 1589.

Valderramo, Pedro. *Histoire générale du monde*. Paris: chez Isaac Mesmer, 1617-19.

Vale, M.G.A. *Charles VII*. Berkeley: University of California Press, 1974.

Valency, Maurice. *In Praise of Love*. New York: Macmillan, 1956.

Valentin, Veit. *The German People from the Holy Roman Empire to the Third Reich*. trans. O. Marx. New York: Alfred A. Knopf, 1946.

_____. *Geschichte der Deutschen*. Berlin: Pontes, 1947.

Valentine, Alan. *Lord Stirling*. New York: Oxford University Press, 1969.

_____. *Vigilante Justice*. New York: Reynal, 1956.

Valentine, Betty Lou. *Hustling and Other Hard Work*. New York: Free Press, 1978.

Valentine, David T. *Manuals of the Corporation of the City of New York*. New York: n.p., 1861.

Valentine, Ferdinand C. *Gotham and the Gothamites*. London: Field & Tuer, 1887.

Valentine, Lewis J. *Nightstick*. New York: Dial Press, 1947.

Valentine's Manual of Old New York. New York: Valentine's Manual, 1916.

Valentinov, N. *Vstrechi s Leninim*. New York: Izdatelstvo imeni Chekhova, 1953.

Valera, Paolo. *Mussolini*. Milan, Italy: La Folla, 1924.

Valeri, Antonio. *Da Giolitti a Mussolini*. Florence, Italy: Parenti, 1956.

Valéry, Paul. *Masters and Friends*. trans. Martin Turnell. Princeton, N.J.: Bollingen Foundation, 1968.

Vallandigham, Rev. James L. *A Life of Clement L. Vallandigham*. Baltimore: Turnbull Brothers, 1872.

Valler, Walton, and McNear, Robert. *The Night Chief*. South Bend, Ind.: Regnery/Gateway, 1980.

Vallet de Viriville, M. (ed.). *Chronique de la Pucelle ou Chronique de Cousinot*. Paris: Adolphe de la Hays, 1859.

Valletta, Niccola. *Cicalata sul Fascino volgamente detto Jettatura*. Milan, Italy: A. Fidi, 1925.

Valverde, Custodio. *Julián Blanc y la revolución en el estado de Guerrero*. Mexico City: Imprenta de J. Chávez é Hijos, 1916.

Valzelli, L. *Psychobiology of Aggression and Violence*. New York: Raven Press, 1981.

Vanauken, Wilhemus. *The Trial of Wilhemus Vanauken*. Kingston, N.J.: Plebian Office, 1822.

Van Bergen, R. *The Story of China*. New York: American, 1902.

Vance, James E., Jr. *Geography and Urban Evolution in the San Francisco Bay Area*. Berkeley, Calif.: Institute of Governmental Studies, 1964.

Vance, John R. *Doomed Garrison—The Philippines. (A POW Story)*. Ashland, Ore.: Cascade House, 1974.

Van Cise, Philip S. *Fighting the Underworld*. Boston: Houghton Mifflin, 1936.

Vancouver, George. *A Voyage of Discovery to the North Pacific Ocean and Round the World*. London: J. Stockdale, 1801.

Vandenbosch, Amry. *The Dutch Communities of Chicago*. Chicago: Knickerbocker Society of Chicago, 1927.

Van Den Bruck. *Germany's Third Reich*. New York: Europe, 1940.

Van Den Haag, Ernest, and Conrad, John P. *The Death Penalty: A Debate*. New York: Plemum Press, 1983.

_____. *Political Violence and Civil Disobedience*. New York: Harper & Row, 1972.

_____. *Punishing Criminals: Concerning a Very Old and Painful Question*. New York: Basic Books, 1978.

Van Der Bergh, Ernst. *Der Polizeigedanke einst und jetzt*. Frankfort, Ger.: Heinrich Reinhardt Verlag, 1949.

Vanderbilt, Cornelius, Jr. *Farewell to Fifth Avenue*. New York: Simon & Schuster, 1935.

Vanderbilt, Kermit. *Charles Eliot Norton: Apostle of Culture in a Democracy*. Cambridge, Mass.: Belknap Press of Harvard University Press, 1959.

Van Der Haag, Ernest. *Political Violence and Disobedience*. New York: Harper & Row, 1972.

Van der Valk, M. *Conservatism in Modern Chinese Family Law*. Leiden, Neth.: E.J. Brill, 1956.

Vandervelde, Emile. *Jean L. Jaurès*. Paris: F. Alcan, 1929.

_____. *Le Parti Ouvrier Belge, 1885-1925*. Brussells: L'Eglantine, n.d.

Van der Zee, John, and Jacobson, Boyd. *The Imagined City: San Francisco in the Minds of Its Writers*. San Francisco: California Living Books, 1980.

Van Deusen, Glyndon G. *Henry Clay*. Boston: Little, Brown, 1937.

_____. *Horace Greeley: Nineteenth-Century Crusader*. Philadelphia: University of Pennsylvania Press, 1953.

_____. *The Jacksonian Era 1828-1848*. New York: Harper & Brothers, 1958.

_____. *Thurlow Weed: Wizard of the Lobby*. Boston: Little, Brown, 1947.

_____. *William Henry Seward*. New York: Oxford University Press, 1967.

Van Devander, Charles W. *The Big Bosses*. New York: Howell, Soskin, 1944.

Van de Water, Frederic F. *The Real McCoy*. Garden City, N.Y.: Doubleday, Doran, 1931.

Vandor, Paul E. *History of Fresno County, California*. Los Angeles: Historic Record, 1919.

Van Doren, Carl. *Benjamin Franklin*. New York: Viking Press, 1938.

_____. *The Great Rehearsal*. New York: Viking Press, 1948.

_____. *Mutiny in January*. New York: Viking Press, 1943.

_____. *Secret History of the American Revolution*. New York: Kelley, 1973.

Van Doren, Mark (ed.). *An Autobiography of America*. New York: Albert & Charlie Boni, 1929.

Van Doren, Mark. *The Autobiography of Mark Van Doren*. New York: Harcourt, Brace, 1958.

Van Druten, John. *The Widening Circle*. London: William Heinemann, 1951.

Van Every, Dale. *Ark of Empire*. New York: New American Library, 1963.

Van Every, Edward. *Sins of America as "Exposed" by the Police Gazette*. New York: Frederick A. Stokes, 1931.

_____. *Sins of New York*. New York: Frederick A. Stokes, 1930.

Van Gelder, Lawrence. *The Untold Story: Why the Kennedys Lost the Book Battle*. New York: Award Books, 1967.

Van Gulik, R.H. *Sexual Life in Ancient China*. Leiden, Neth.: E.J. Brill, 1961.

Van Hagen, Victor Wolfgang. *The Ancient Sun Kingdoms of the Americas*. Cleveland: World, 1961.

_____. *The Incas, People of the Sun*. Cleveland: World, 1961.

Van Horn, Maj. Gen Carl. *Soldiering for Peace*. New York: David McKay, 1967.

Vanier, Henriette. *La Mode et ses métiers: Frivolités et luttes des classes, 1830-1870*. Paris: Colin, 1960.

Van Kleeck, Mary. *Creative America*. New York: Covici Friede, 1936.

Van Kleek, Rev. Robert B. *Confession of Henry G. Green*. Troy, N.Y.: R. Rose, 1845.

Van Kley, Dale K. *The Damiens Affair and the Unraveling of the Ancien Regime*. Princeton, N.J.: Princeton University Press, 1984.

Van Metre, T.W. *Economic History of the United States*. New York: Henry Holt, 1921.

Van Nada, M.L. (ed.). *The Book of Missourians.* Chicago: T.J. Steele, 1906.

Van Passen, Pierre. *Days of Our Years.* New York: Dial Press, 1940.

_____. *To Number Our Days.* New York: Charles Scribner's Sons, 1964.

Van Rensselaer, Mrs. John King. *The Devil's Picture Books.* New York: Dodd, Mead, 1890.

_____, and Van de Water, F.F. *The Social Ladder.* New York: Henry Holt, 1924.

Van Slingerland, Peter. *Something Terrible Has Happened.* New York: Harper & Row, 1966.

Van Thal, Herbert (ed.). *The Prime Ministers, Volume Two.* London: George Allen & Unwin, 1975.

Van Tramp, John C. *Plain and Rocky Mountain Adventure.* Columbus, Ohio: Gilmore & Segner, 1866.

_____. *Prairie and Rocky Mountain Adventures.* Columbus, Ohio: Segner & Condit, 1867.

Van Tyne, Claude Halstead. *The War of Independence.* Boston: Houghton Mifflin, 1929.

Van Vechten, C. *Peter Whiffle: His Life and Works.* New York: Alfred A. Knopf, 1925.

Van Vleck, George W. *The Panic of 1857.* New York: Columbia University Press, 1953.

Van Voris, Jacqueline. *Constance de Markievicz: In the Cause of Ireland.* Amherst: University of Massachusetts Press, 1967.

Van Winkle, Marshall, and Wolff, H. *Sixty Famous Cases.* Summertown, Tenn.: Book Manufacturing, 1956.

Van Wyck, Frederick. *Recollections of an Old New Yorker.* New York: Liverlight, 1933.

Varaut, Jean-Marc. *L'Abominable Dr. Petiot.* Paris: Balland, 1974.

Varg, P.A. *Open Door Diplomat: The Life of W.W. Rockhill.* Urbana: University of Illinois Press, 1952.

Varneck, Elena, and Fisher, H.H. *The Testimony of Kolchak and other Siberian Materials.* Palo Alto: Stanford University Press, 1935.

Varney, Glen H. *Management by Objectives.* Chicago: Dartnell, 1971.

Vasconcelos, José. *Breve historia de México.* Mexico City: Ediciones Botas, 1937.

_____. *La caida de Carranza: De la dictadura a la libertad.* Mexico City: Imprenta de Muguia, 1920.

Vasiliev, A.A. *History of the Byzantine Empire.* Madison: University of Wisconsin Press, 1928.

_____. *Justin the First.* Cambridge, Mass.: Harvard University Press, 1950.

Vassilyev, A.T. *The Okhrana: The Russian Secret Police.* Philadelphia: J.B. Lippincott, 1930.

Vatikiotis, P.J. *The Egyptian Army in Politics.* Bloomington: Indiana University Press, 1961.

Vatsyana. *Kama Sutra.* trans. Richard F. Burton. New York: E.P. Dutton, 1962.

Vaughan, Alden. *New England Frontier.* Boston: Little, Brown, 1965.

Vaughan, Joe. *The Only True History of Frank James, Written by Himself.* Pine Bluff, Ark.: Sarah E. Snow, 1926.

Vaughn, Miles W. *Under the Japanese Mask.* London: Lovat Dickson, 1937.

Vaughn, Robert. *Then and Now or Thirty-Six Years in the Rockies.* Minneapolis, Minn.: Tribune, 1900.

Vaulabelle, A. de. *Histoire des deux restaurations.* Paris: Perrotin, 1855.

Vay, Petér Gróf. *The Inner Life of the United States by Monsignor Count Vay de Vaya and Luskod.* London: John Murray, 1908.

Vaz, E. (ed.). *Middle Class Juvenile Delinquency.* New York: Harper & Row, 1967.

Veale, F.J.P. *William Herbert Wallace.* London: Merrymeade, 1950.

Veall, Donald. *The Popular Movement for Law Reform.* Oxford, Eng.: Clarendon Press, 1970.

Veblen, Thorstein. *Absentee Ownership.* New York: Viking Press, 1923.

_____. *The Engineers and the Price System.* New York: Huebsch, 1921.

_____. *Instinct of Workmanship.* New York: Macmillan, 1914.

_____. *Theory of Business Enterprise.* New York: Charles Scribner's Sons, 1904.

_____. *The Theory of the Leisure Class.* New York: Viking Press, 1948.

Vedder, C., and Somerville, D. *The Delinquent Girl.* Springfield, Ill.: Charles C. Thomas, 1970.

Vedder, H. *Southwest Africa in Early Times.* New York: Barnes & Noble, 1966.

Veheyne, C. *Horror.* London: Brown, Watson, 1962.

Vehse, Dr. Carl Eduard. *Memoirs of the Court of Prussia.* trans. Franz C.F. Demmler. London: T. Nelson & Sons, 1854.

The Veiled Lady, or The Mysterious Witness in the McFarland Trial. Philadelphia: C.W. Alexander, 1870.

Veith, I. (ed.). *The Yellow Emperor's Classic Internal Medicine.* Baltimore: Williams & Wilkins, 1949.

Velasquez, Loreta Janeta. *The Woman in Battle.* Hartford, Conn.: T. Belknap, 1876.

Velázquez, José Victor. *Apuntes para la historia de la revolución felicista.* Mexico City: Libreria de la Viuda de Ch. Bouret, 1913.

Velie, Lester. *Desperate Bargain.* New York: Readers Digest Press, 1977.

Velikovsky, Immanuel. *Worlds in Collision.* New York: Doubleday, 1950.

Velikovsky and Establishment Science. Glassboro, N.J.: Krones Press, 1977.

Venturi, Franco. *Roots of Revolution.* New York: Alfred A. Knopf, 1960.

Venys, L. *A History of the Mau Mau Movement.* Prague, Czech.: Charles University, 1970.

Vera Estañol, Jorge. *Carranza and His Bolshevik Regime.* Los Angeles: Wayside Press, 1920.

_____. *La Revolución Mexicana: origenes y resultados.* Mexico City: Editorial Porrúa, 1957.

Vera Institute of Justice. *Bail and Parole Jumping in Manhattan in 1967.* New York: n.p., 1970.

Verbit, Gilbert P. *International Monetary Reform and the Developing Countries: The Rule of Law Problem.* New York: Columbia University Press, 1975.

Verckler, Stewart P. *Cowtown-Abilene: The Story of Abilene, Kansas, 1867-1875.* New York: Carlton Press, 1961.

Verdun, Paul. *Le diable dans la vie des saints.* Paris: Delhomme & Briguet, 1896.

Veretennikov, Nikolay. *Vospominaniya.* Moscow: Izdatdetlit, 1941.

Vergani, Guido. *Mesina.* Milan, Italy: Longanesi, 1968.

Verger, Jean-Louis. *Réflexions impartiales d'un auditeur aux débats de la cour d'assises de Seine-et-Marne.* Paris: Cosse et Dumaine, 1856.

Verhaeren, Emile. *La Belgique sanglante.* Paris: Nouvelle Revue Francaise, 1915.

Verkko, Veli. *Homicides and Suicides in Finland and Their Dependence on National Character.* Copenhagen: G.E.C. Gads Forlag, 1951.

Vermaseren, M.J. *Mithras: The Secret God.* New York: Barnes & Noble, 1959.

Vermorel, Auguste-Jean-Marie. *La Police contemporaire.* Paris: Lebigre-Duquesne, 1864.

Vernadsky, George. *Ancient Russia.* New Haven, Conn.: Yale University Press, 1943.

_____. *Ancient Russia and Kievan Russia.* New Haven, Conn.: Yale University Press, 1948.

_____. *A History of Russia.* New Haven, Conn.: Yale University

Press, 1961.

———. *Mongols and Russians.* New Haven, Conn.: Yale University Press, 1953.

———. *The Origins of Russia.* Oxford, Eng.: Clarendon Press, 1959.

———. *Political and Diplomatic History of Russia.* Boston: Houghton Mifflin, 1936.

———. *Russia at the Dawn of the Modern Age.* New Haven, Conn.: Yale University Press, 1959.

Verner, Elizabeth O'Neill. *Mellowed By Time.* Columbia, S.C.: Bostick & Thornley, 1941.

Verner, Gerald (ed.). *The Prince of Darkness.* New York: Rider, 1951.

Vernon, Joseph S., and Booth, Capt. Henry. *Along the Old Trail: A History of the Old and a Story of the New Santa Fe Trail.* Cimarron, Kan.: Tucker-Vernon, 1910.

———. *Dodge City and Ford County, Kansas.* Larned, Kan.: Tucker-Vernon, 1911.

Vernon, P.E. *Intelligence: Heredity and Environment.* San Francisco: Freeman, 1979.

Verstegen, Richard. *Theatrum Crudelitatum Haereticorum.* Antwerp, Belg.: Adrian Huberti, 1588.

Vervorst, Chanoine Firmin. *Autographe de Louis Verger.* Paris: Les principaux librairies, 1857.

Vestal, Bud. *Jerry Ford Up Close.* New York: Coward, McCann & Geoghegan, 1974.

Vestal, Stanley (pseud. of Walter S. Campbell). *Bigfoot Wallace.* Boston: Houghton Mifflin, 1942.

———. *Dodge City, Queen of Cow Towns.* New York: Harper & Brothers, 1951.

———. *Jim Bridger, Mountain Man.* New York: William Morrow, 1946.

———. *Joe Meek, The Merry Moutain Man.* Caldwell, Idaho: Caxton Printers, 1952.

———. *The Missouri.* New York: Farrar & Rinehart, 1945.

———. *The Old Santa Fe Trail.* Boston: Houghton Mifflin, 1939.

———. *Queen of Cowtowns, Dodge City.* New York: Harper & Brothers, 1952.

———. *Short Grass Country.* New York: Duell, Sloan & Pearce, 1941.

———. *Sitting Bull.* New York: Houghton Mifflin, 1932.

———. *Wagons West: Story of the Old Trail to Santa Fe.* New York: American Pioneer Trails Association, 1946.

———. *Warpath and the Council Fire.* New York: Random House, 1948.

Vetter, H.J., and Silverman, I.J. *The Nature of Crime.* Philadelphia: W.B. Saunders, 1978.

Viano, Emilio C., and Reiman, Jeffrey H. (eds.). *The Police in Society.* Lexington, Mass.: Lexington Books, 1975.

———. *Victims and Society.* Washington D.C.: Visage, 1976.

Vice Commission of Chicago. *The Social Evil in Chicago.* Chicago: Gunthorp-Warren, 1911.

Vicinus, Martha (ed.). *Suffer and Be Still: Women in the Victorian Age.* Bloomington: Indiana University Press, 1972.

Vickers, C.L. (ed.). *History of the Arkansas Valley, Colorado.* Chicago: O.L. Baskin, 1881.

Vickers, Sir Geoffrey. *The Art of Judgement.* New York: Basic Books, 1965.

Victor, Orville J. *History of American Conspiracies.* New York: James D. Torrey, 1863.

Victor, Sarah M. *The Life Story of Sarah M. Victor.* Cleveland: Williams, 1887.

Vicuña, Francisco Orrego (ed.). *Chile: The Balanced View: A Recopilation of Articles about the Allende Years and After.* Santiago: University of Chile Institute of International Affairs, 1975.

Vidal, Jean Marie. *Bullaire de l'Inquisition française.* Paris: Librarie Letouzey et Ané, 1913.

Vidal-Naquet, Pierre. *Le Chasseur noir: Formes de pensée et formes de société dans le monde grec.* Paris: Maspero, 1981.

Vidnes, Jacob. *Norway.* Oslo, Nor.: M. Johansens, 1935.

Vidocq, Eugène-François. *Les Mémoires de Vidocq.* Paris: Editions Baudelaire, 1967.

Viel Castel, Horace de Salviac, Count de. *Memoirs.* London: Remington, 1888.

Viereck, George Sylvester. *The Kaiser on Trial.* London: Duckworth, 1938.

Viereck, Peter. *Metapolitics: The Roots of the Nazi Mind.* New York: G.P. Putnam's Sons, 1961.

———. *Shame and Glory of the Intellectual.* Boston: Beacon, 1953.

Viertel, Salka. *The Kindness of Strangers.* New York: Holt, Rinehart & Winston, 1969.

Viglotti, Gabriel R. *The Girls of Nevada.* Secaucus, N.J.: Citadel Press, 1975.

Vigny, Alfred de. *Cinq mars.* Paris: Urbain Canel, 1826.

Villano, Anthony. *Brick Agent.* Chicago: Quadrangle Books, 1977.

Villard, Henry. *Memoirs of Henry Villard, Journalist and Financier, 1835-1900.* Boston: Houghton Mifflin, 1904.

Villard, Oswald Garrison. *John Brown 1800-1859: A Biography Fifty Years After.* New York: Alfred A. Knopf, 1943.

———. *Some Newspapers and Newspaper-Men.* Alfred A. Knopf, 1933.

Villari, Luigi. *The Awakening of Italy.* London: Methuen, 1924.

———, *The Fascist Experiment.* London: Faber & Gwyer, 1926.

Villari, Pasquale. *Niccolò Machiavelli e i suoi tempi.* 3 vols. Milano, Italy: Hoepli, 1895.

Villars, Nicolas Pierre Henri de Montfaucon, abbé de. *Le Comte de Gabalis.* Paris: Chez Claude Barbin, 1671.

Villehardouin, Geoffrey de. *Chronicles of the Crusades.* London: Penguin Books, 1963.

Villeneuve, Roland. *Le Diable: Erotologie de Satan.* Paris: Jean-Jacques Pauvert, 1963.

———. *Gilles de Rays" Une Grande Figure Diabolique.* Verviers, Belg.: Editions Gérard & Cie., 1973.

———. *Le Poison et les empoisonneurs célèbres.* Paris: La Palatine, 1960.

Villette, John. *The Annals of Newgate; or, Malefactors Register.* London: J. Wenman, 1776.

Villiers, Alan. *Posted Missing.* New York: Charles Scribner's Sons, 1956.

Villiers, Broughain, and Chesson, W.H. *Anglo-American Relations, 1861-1865.* New York: Charles Scribner's Sons, 1920.

Villiers, Elizabeth. *Riddles of Crime.* London: Werner Laurie, 1928.

Villiers, Gérard de. *Papillon Épinglé.* Paris: Presses de la Cité, 1970.

Villon, François. *The Complete Works.* trans. Anthony Bonner. New York: David McKay, 1960.

Vinacke, Harold M. *A History of the Far East in Modern Times.* New York: Appleton-Century-Crofts, 1959.

Vincent, Arthur (ed.). *Lives of Twelve Bad Women.* Boston: L. C. Page, 1897.

Vincent, C. *Unmarried Mothers.* New York: Free Press, 1961.

Vincent, Louis, and Binns, Clare. *Gilles de Rais: The Original Bluebeard.* Boston: Small, Maynard, 1926.

Viner, Charles. *A General Abridgement of Law and Equity.* London: G.G.J. & J. Robinson, 1791-95.

Viner, Jacob. *Studies in the Theory of International Trade.* New York: Harper, 1937.

Vingt ans de police, souvenirs et anecdotes d'un ancien officier de paix. Paris: E. Dentu, 1881.

Vining, Elizabeth Gray. *Return to Japan.* Philadelphia: J.B. Lippincott, 1960.

———. *Windows for the Crown Prince.* Philadelphia: J.B. Lippincott, 1952.

Vinogradoff, Sir Paul. *Self-Government in Russia.* London: Constable, 1915.

Vinson, J. Chal. *Thomas Nast: Political Cartoonist.* Athens:

University of Georgia Press, 1967.

Vinter, Robert D., Downs, George, and Hall, John. *Juvenile Corrections in the States: Residential Programs and Deinstitutionalization*. Ann Arbor: National Assessment of Juvenile Corrections, University of Michigan, 1975.

_____ (ed.). *Time Out: A National Study of Juvenile Correctional Programs*. Ann Arbor: National Assessment of Juvenile Corrections, University of Michigan, 1976.

Violette, Eugene Morrow. *A History of Missouri*. New York: D.C. Heath, 1918.

Vioux, Marcelle. *Henry of Navarre*. trans. J.L. May. New York: E.P. Dutton, 1937.

Viret, Pierre. *The World Possessed with Devils*. trans. Thomas Stocker. London: I. Perin, 1583.

Viroubova, Anna Aleksandrovna. *Memories of the Russian Court*. New York: Macmillan, 1923.

Vishinsky, Andrei. *The Law of the Soviet State*. New York: Macmillan, 1948.

Visscher, William Lightfoot. *Buffalo Bill's Own Story of His Life and Deeds*. n.p., 1917.

Visser, Cassimir K. *Van de Heksenwaag te Oudewater*. Lochem: De Tijdstroom, 1941.

Vitray, Laura. *The Great Lindbergh Hullabaloo: An Unorthodox Account*. New York: William Fargo, 1932.

Vivian, A. Pendarves. *Wanderings in a Western Land*. London: Sampson Low, Marston, Searle & Rivington, 1880.

Vivian, Herbert. *The Servian Tragedy, with Impressions of Macedonia*. London: Grant Richards, 1904.

Vivian, Martha Campbell. *Down the Avenue of Ninety Years*. Privately Printed, 1924.

Vizetelly, Ernest Alfred. *The Anarchists*. New York: John Lane, 1911.

_____. *Bluebeard*. London: Chatto & Windus, 1902.

_____. *Court Life of the Second French Empire*. New York: Charles Scribner's Sons, 1907.

Voge, Cecil I.B. *The Chemistry and Physics of Contraceptives*. London: Jonathon Cape, 1933.

Vogel, E.G. *Japan as Number One: Lessons for America*. Cambridge, Mass.: Harvard University Press, 1979.

Vogel, Morris J., and Rosenberg, Charles E. (eds.). *The Therapeutic Revolution: Essays in the Social History of American Medicine*. Philadelphia: University of Pennsylvania Press, 1979.

Vogeler, R., and Sanders, E. *R. Vogeler, E. Sanders and Their Accomplices Before the Criminal Court*. Budapest, Hungary: Hungarian State Publishing House, 1950.

Vogt, Evon A., and Hyman, Ray. *Water Watching U.S.A*. Chicago: University of Chicago Press, 1959.

Vogt, Gottlob Heinrich. *Kurtzes Bedencken von denen Actenmässigen Relationen wegen derer Vampiren*. Leipzig, Ger.: Bey A. Martini, 1732.

Vogt, Hannah. *The Burden of Guilt: A Short History of Germany, 1914-1945*. New York: Oxford University Press, 1964.

The Volcano Under the City. New York: Ford, Howard, and Hulbert, 1887.

Volckmann, R.W. *We Remained*. New York: W.W. Norton, 1954.

Vold, George B. *Theoretical Criminology*. New York: Oxford University Press, 1958.

Volgelsang, Thilo. *Reichswehr, Staat und NSDAP*. Stuttgart, Ger.: Deutsch Verlagsanstalt, 1962.

Volk, Franz. *Hexen in der Landvogtei Ortenau und Reichsstadt Offenburg*. Lahr, Ger.: Moritz Schauenburg, 1882.

Vollmer, August, and Parker, Alfred E. *Crime, Crooks and Cops*. New York: Funk & Wagnalls, 1937.

_____, *The Criminal*. New York: Foundation Press, 1949.

_____. *The Police and Modern Society*. Montclair, N.J.: Smith, 1971.

Vollmer, Bernhard. *Volksopposition in Polizeistaat*. Stuttgart, Ger.: Deutsche Verlagsanstalt, 1957.

Vollmer, Howard M., and Mills, Donald M. (eds.). *Professionalization*. Englewood Cliffs, N.J.: Prentice-Hall, 1966.

Volpe, et al. *La vita mediovale italiana nella miniatura*. Roma, Italy: Bestetti, 1960.

Volta, Ornella. *The Vampire*. trans. Raymond Rudorff. London: Tandem, 1965.

Voltaire, Fraçois-Marie Arouet de. *Lettres inédites sur la Tolérance*. Paris: Joel Cherbuliez, 1863.

_____. *Traité sur la Tolérance*. Genève, Switz.: Les Editions du Cheval Ailé, n.d.

Volwiler, Albert Tangeman (ed.). *The Correspondence Between Benjamin Harrison and James G. Blaine, 1882-1893*. Phildelphia: American Philosophical Society, 1940.

_____. *George Croghan and the Westward Movement 1741-1782*. Cleveland: Arthur H. Clark, 1926.

Volz, Joseph, and Bridge, Peter J. (eds.). *The Mafia Talks: Here are the Secret Cosa Nostra Coversations Recorded by the FBI*. Greenwich, Conn.: Fawcett, 1969.

von Block, B.W. *Super Detective*. Chicago: Playboy Press, 1972.

von Cranach, M., and Vine, I. (eds.). *Social Communication and Movement*. London: Academic Press, 1973.

von Däniken, Erich. *Chariots of the Gods?* New York: Bantam, 1971.

_____. *Miracles of the Gods*. New York: Delacorte Press, 1975.

Von der Hoven, Helena. *King Carol of Romania*. London: Hutchinson, 1940.

von Gaevernitz, Gero (ed.). *They Almost Killed Hitler*. New York: Macmillan, 1953.

Von Hagen, Victor Wolfgang. *The Ancient Sun Kingdoms of the Americas*. Cleveland: World, 1961.

_____. *The Aztec: Man and Tribe*. New York: New American Library, 1958.

_____. *The Incas: People of the Sun*. Cleveland: World, 1961.

_____. *World of the Maya*. New York: New American Library, 1960.

von Hammer-Purgstall, Joseph. *History of the Assassins*. trans. Oswald Charles Wood. London: Smith & Elder, Corhill, 1935.

von Hentig, Hans. *The Criminal and His Victim*. New York: Schocken Books, 1979.

_____. *Punishment: The Origin, Purpose and Psychology*. London: William Hodge, 1937.

von Hirsch, Andrew. *Doing Justice: The Choice of Punishments*. New York: Hill & Wang, 1976.

_____, and Hanrahan, Kathleen. *The Question of Parole*. Cambridge, Mass.: Ballinger, 1979.

von Hoensbroech, Paul Kajus. *Fourteen Years a Jesuit*. trans. Alice Zimmern. New York: Cassell, 1911.

von Holst, Dr. Hermann Eduard. *The Constitutional Law of the United States*. Chicago: A.B. Mason, 1887.

_____. *John Brown*. Boston: Cupples & Hurd, 1889.

von Kotzebue, Wilhelm (ed.). *August von Kotzebue: Urtheile de Zeitgenossen und der Gegenwart*. Dresden, Ger.: Wilhelm Baensch, 1881.

Von Laue, Theodore H. *Sergei Witte and the Industrialization of Russia*. New York: Columbia University Press, 1963.

von Ludendorff, F.M. *My War Memories, 1914-1918*. 2 vols. London: Hutchinson, 1919.

von Müller. *Karl Ludwig San*. Munich: Beck, 1925.

von Ranke, Leopold. *Geschichte Wallensteins*. Leipzig, Ger.: Duncker & Humblot, 1880.

_____. *A History of Servia and the Servian Revolution*. London: John Murray, 1847.

von Rauch, Georg. *History of Soviet Russia*. New York: Frederick A. Praeger, 1957.

von Samson-Himmelstierna, H. *Russia under Alexander III*. New York: Macmillan, 1893.

von Schlabrendorff, Fabian. *Offiziere gegen Hitler*. Zurich, Switz.: Europa, 1946.

_____. *The Secret War Against Hitler*. New York: Pitman, 1965.

Von Schwartz, Dr. Karl. *Fire and Explosion Risks.* trans. Charles T.C. Salter. London: Charles Griffin, 1926.

von Sosnosky, T. *Franz Ferdinand, Erzherzog.* n.p., 1920.

von Srbik, Heinrich. *Wallensteins Ende.* Salzburg, Aust.: O. Müller, 1952.

von Sternberg, Josef. *Fun in a Chinese Laundry.* New York: n.p., 1965.

von Wissenman, H. *My Second Journey Through Equatorial Africa.* London: Chatto & Windus, 1891.

Vööbus, A. *Celibacy.* Stockholm: Estonian Theological Society in Exile, 1951.

Voorhees, Luke. *Personal Recollections of Pioneer Life on the Mountains and Plains of the Great West.* Cheyenne, Wyo.: Privately Printed, 1920.

Vopicka, Charles J. *Secrets of the Balkans.* Chicago: Rand McNally, 1921.

Vorres, Ian. *The Last Grand Duchess.* New York: Charles Scribner's Sons, 1964.

Vorse, Mary Heaton. *Footnote to Folly.* New York: Farrar & Rinehart, 1935.

Vrba, Rudolf, and Bestic, Alan. *I Cannot Forgive.* New York: Grove Press, 1964.

Vreeland, Frank. *Foremost Films of 1938.* New York: Pitman, 1939.

Vucetich, J. *dactiloscopia Comparada.* La Plata, Arg.: Peuser, 1904.

Vucinich, Alexander. *Science in Russian Culture: A History to 1860.* Stanford, Calif.: Stanford University Press, 1963.

Vucinich, Wayne S. (ed.). *The Peasant in Nineteenth-Century Russia.* Stanford, Calif.: Stanford University Press, 1968.

_____. *Serbia Between East and West: the Events of 1903-1908.* Stanford, Calif.: Stanford University Press, 1954.

Vulliamy, C. E. (ed.) *Red Archives [Krasny Arkhiv].* trans. A.L. Hynes. London: Bles, 1929.

Vyrubeva, Anna. *Memories of the Russian Court.* New York: Macmillan, 1933.

Vyshinsky, A.Y. *The Law of the Soviet State.* New York: Macmillan, 1948.

W

Waagenaar, Sam. *The Murder of Mata Hari.* London: Arthur Barker, 1964.

Wachanga, H.K. *The Swords of Kirinyaga: The Fight for Land and Freedom.* Nairobi: East African Publishing House, 1975.

Wachira, G. *Ordeal in the Forest.* Nairobi: East African Publishing House, 1968.

Waddell, D.A.G. *The West Indies & the Guianas.* Englewood Cliffs, N.J.: Prentice-Hall, 1967.

Wade, Carlson. *Great Hoaxes and Famous Impostors.* New York: Jonathan David, 1976.

Wade, John. *A Treatise on the Police and Crimes of the Metropolis.* Montclair, N.J.: Patterson Smith, 1972.

Wade, Louise C. *Graham Taylor Pioneer for Social Justice, 1851-1938.* Chicago: University of Chicago Press, 1964.

Wade, Richard C. *Slavery in the Cities: The South 1820-1860.* New York: Oxford University Press, 1964.

_____. *The Urban Frontier.* Chicago: University of Chicago Press, 1964.

Wade, Stuart C. *Harry T. Hayward's Life, Trial, Confession, and Execution.* Chicago: E.A. Weeks, 1896.

Wadsworth, M.E.J. *Roots of Delinquency.* New York: Barnes & Noble/Harper & Row, 1979.

Wagenheim, Kal. *Puerto Rico: A Profile.* New York: Frederick A. Praeger, 1970.

Wagenknecht, Edward C. *Edgar Allan Poe: The Man Behind the Legend.* New York: Oxford University Press, 1963.

_____ (ed.). *Joan of Arc: An Anthology of History and Literature.* New York: Creative Age Press, 1948.

_____. *John Greenleaf Whittier: A Portrait in Paradox.* New York: Oxford University Press, 1967.

_____ (ed.) *John Greenleaf Whittier's The Supernaturalism of New England.* Norman: University of Oklahoma Press, 1969.

_____. *The Seven Worlds of Theodore Roosevelt.* New York: Longmans, Green, 1958.

_____. *William Dean Howells: The Friendly Eye.* New York: Oxford University Press, 1969.

Wagner, Charles R. *The CPA and Computer Fraud.* New York: Lexington Books, 1979.

Wagner, Diane. *Corpus Delicti.* New York: St. Martin's/Marek, 1986.

Wagner, Henry R. *Bullion to Books.* Los Angeles: Zamorano Club, 1942.

Wagner, Margaret Seaton. *The Monster of Dusseldorf, The Life and Trial of Peter Kurten.* London: Faber & Faber, 1932.

Wagner, Robert Léon. *Sorcier et magicien.* Paris: E. Droz, 1939.

Wagner, Walter. *The Golden Fleecers.* Garden City, N.Y.: Doubleday, 1966.

Wagoner, Jay J. *Arizona Territory, 1863-1912.* Tucson: University of Arizona Press, 1970.

_____. *History of the Cattle Industry.* Tucson: University of Arizona, 1952.

Wagstaffe, John. *The Question of Witchcraft Debated.* London: Edward Millington, 1671.

Wainwright, Jonathan. *General Wainwright's Story.* Garden City, N.Y.: Doubleday, 1946.

Wainwright, Nicholas B. *George Croghan, Wilderness Diplomat.* Chapel Hill: University of North Carolina Press, 1959.

_____ (ed.). *A Philadelphia Perspective: The Diary of Sidney George Fisher Covering the Years, 1834-1871.* Philadelphia: Historical Society of Pennsylvania, 1967.

Waissenberger, Robert (ed.). *Vienna 1890-1920.* Secaucus, N.J.: Wellfleet Press, 1984.

Waite, Edward Arthur. *Alchemists through the Ages.* New York: Rudolf Stein, 1970.

_____. *The Book of Ceremonial Magic.* New York: University Books, 1961.

_____. *Devil Worship in France.* London: G. Redway, 1896.

_____. *The Pictorial Key to the Tarot.* London: William Rider & Son, 1911.

_____. *The Secret Tradition in Alchemy.* New York: Alfred A. Knopf, 1926.

Waite, John B. *The Prevention of Repeated Crime.* Ann Arbor: University of Michigan Press, 1943.

Wakefield, Dan. *Island in the City: The World of Spanish Harlem.* Boston: Houghton Mifflin, 1957.

Wakefield, Edward Gibbon. *Facts Relating to the Punishment of Death in the Metropolis.* London: n.p., 1831.

_____. *The Hangman and the Judge, or a Letter from Jack Ketch to Mr. Justice Alderson.* London: Effingham Wilson, 1833.

_____. *Terrorstruck Town.* London: Steill, 1833.

Wakefield, H. Russell. *The Green Bicycle Case.* London: Philip Allan, 1930.

_____. *Landru: The French Bluebeard.* London: Duckworth, 1936.

Wakefield, Harold. *New Prints for Japan.* New York: Oxford University Press, 1948.

Wakeman, Abram. *History and Reminiscences of Lower Wall Street and Vicinity.* New York: Spice Mill, 1914.

Wakin, Edward. *Children Without Justice: A Report by the National Council of Jewish Women.* New York: National Council of Jewish Women, 1975.

Walbrook, H.M. *Detective Days.* London: Cassell, 1931.

_____. *Murders and Murder Trials, 1812-1912.* London: Constable, 1932.

Waldbrühl, Wilhelm von. *Naturforschung und Hexenglaube*. Berlin: C.G. Lüderitz, 1867.

Waldeck, R.G. *Athene Palace*. Garden City, N.Y.: Blue Ribbon Books, 1942.

Waldegg, Richard, and Werner, Heinz. *Geschichte und Wesen der Prostitution*. Stuttgart, Ger.: Weltspiegel Verlag, 1956.

Walden, Arthur Treadwell. *A Dog-Puncher on the Yukon*. Boston: Houghton Mifflin, 1928.

Waldhorn, Judith Lynch, and Woodbridge, Sally B. *Victoria's Legacy*. San Francisco: 101 Publications, 1978.

Waldo, Dwight. *The Administrative State*. New York: Ronald Press, 1948.

Waldo, Edna La Moore. *Dakota, an Informal Study of Territorial Days Gleaned from Contemporary Newspapers*. Bismarck, N.D.: Capital, 1932.

Waldron, J. Milton, and Harkless, J.D. *The Political Situation in a Nut-Shell, Some Un-Colored Truths for Colored Voters*. Washington, D.C.: National Independent Political League, 1912.

Waldron, Ronald J., et al. *The Criminal Justice System: An Introduction*. Boston: Houghton Mifflin, 1976.

Waldrop, Frank C. *McCormick of Chicago: An Unconventional Portrait of a Controversial Figure*. Englewood Cliffs, N.J.: Prentice-Hall, 1966.

Waley, Arthur. *The Opium War Through Chinese Eyes*. London: George Allen & Unwin, 1958.

_____. *Translations from the Chinese*. New York: Alfred A. Knopf, 1941.

Walgamott, Charles Shirley. *Six Decades Back*. Caldwell, Idaho: Caxton Printers, 1936.

Waliszewski, Kazimierz. *Ivan the Terrible*. trans. Lady Mary Lloyd. London: William Heinemann, 1904.

_____. *Paul the First of Russia, the Son of Catherine the Great*. London: William Heinemann, 1913.

_____. *Peter the Great*. London: William Heinemann, 1898.

_____. *The Story of a Throne (Catherine II of Russia)*. London: William Heinemann, 1895.

Walker, Alexander. *Sex in the Movies*. London: Penquin Books, 1968.

Walker, Benjamin. *The Hindu World*. New York: Frederick A. Praeger, 1968.

Walker, Bill. *The Case of Barbara Graham*. New York: Ballantine Books, 1961.

_____. *The True Story of the Barbara Graham Case*. Los Angeles: Ace Books, 1961.

Walker, C.R., and Guest, R.H. *The Man on the Assembly Line*. Cambridge, Mass.: Harvard University Press, 1952.

Walker, Charles R. *American City*. New York: Farrar & Rinehart, 1937.

Walker, Daniel. *Rights in Conflict*. New York: Signet-Broadside, 1968.

Walker, Franklin. *San Francisco's Literary Frontier*. New York: Alfred A. Knopf, 1939.

Walker, Henry J. *Jesse James "the Outlaw," Jesse Woodson James alias J. Frank Dalton 1848-1951*. Des Moines, Iowa: Wallace Homestead, 1961.

Walker, James Blaine. *Fifty Years of Rapid Transit, 1864-1917*. New York: Law Printing, 1918.

Walker, Kenneth M. *Sex Difficulties in the Male*. London: Jonathan Cape, 1934.

Walker, Lenore E. *The Battered Woman*. New York: Harper & Row, 1979.

Walker, Marcia J., and Brodsky, Stanley L. (eds.) *Sexual Assault: The Victim and the Rapist*. Lexington, Mass.: Heath, 1976.

Walker, Mrs. *Untrodden Paths in Roumania*. London: Chapman & Hall, 1888.

Walker, Nigel. *Crimes, Courts and Figures*. Harmondsworth, Eng.: Penguin Books, 1971.

_____. *Crime and Insanity in England*. Edinburgh, Scot.: Edinburgh University Press, 1968.

_____. *Crime and Punishment in Britain*. Edinburgh, Scot.: Edinburgh University Press, 1973.

Walker, P. *Identification Parade*. London: Hale, 1972.

Walker, Roy. *Sword of Gold*. London: Indian Independence Union, 1945.

_____. *The Wisdom of Gandhi*. London: Andrew Pakers, 1943.

Walker, Samuel. *Sense and Nonsense About Crime*. Belmont, Calif.: Brooks/Cole, 1985.

Walker, E. Samuel. *Popular Justice: A History of American Criminal Justice*. New York: Oxford University Press, 1980.

Walker, Stanley. *Dewey: An American of This Century*. New York: Whittlesley House, McGraw-Hill, 1944.

Walker, Stanley. *Home to Texas*. New York: Harper & Brothers, 1956.

Walker, Stanley. *The Night Club Era*. New York: Frederick A. Stokes, 1933.

Walker, T. Mike. *Voices From the Bottom of the World, A Policeman's Journal*. New York: Grove Press, 1969.

Walker, Tacetta B. *Stories of Early Days in Wyoming*. Casper, Wyo.: Prairie, 1936.

Walker, Tom. *Fort Apache*. New York: Avon, 1977.

Walker Report. National Commission on the Causes and Prevention of Violence. Washington, D.C.: U.S. Government Printing Office, 1969.

Walker-Smith, Derek. *The Life of Mr. Justice Darling*. London: Cassell, 1938.

_____. *Lord Reading and His Cases*. New York: Macmillan, 1934.

Walkin, Jacob. *The Rise of Democracy in Pre-Revolutionary Russia: Political and Social Institutions Under the Last Three Czars*. New York: Frederick A. Praeger, 1962.

Wall, Joseph Frazier. *Andrew Carnegie*. New York: Oxford University Press, 1970.

Wall, P. *Eyewitness Identification in Criminal Cases*. New York: Thomas, 1965.

Wall, Robert E. *Massachusetts Bay*. New Haven, Conn.: Yale University Press, 1972.

Wall, W.D., and Williams, H.L. *Longitudinal Studies and the Social Sciences*. London: William Heinemann, 1970.

Wallace, Andrew (ed.). *Sources & Readings in Arizona History*. Tucson: Arizona Pioneers' Historical Society, 1965.

Wallace, Betty. *Gunnison County*. Denver: Sage Books, 1960.

_____. *History With the Hide Off*. Denver: Sage Books, 1965.

Wallace, C.H. *Witchcraft in the World Today*. London: Universal-Tandem, 1967.

Wallace, Clark. *Wanted: Donald Morrison*. Garden City, N.Y.: Doubleday, 1977.

Wallace, D.D. *The History of South Carolina*. 3 vols. New York: American Historical Society, 1934.

Wallace, Sir Donald Mackenzie. *Russia on the Eve of War and Revolution*. New York: Vintage Books, 1961.

Wallace, Edgar. *A Short Autobiography*. London: Hodder & Stoughton, 1923.

Wallace, Edward S. *Destiny and Glory*. New York: Coward-McCann, 1957.

Wallace, Elizabeth. *The Unending Journey*. Minneapolis: University of Minnesota Press, 1952.

Wallace, Ernest, and Hoebel, E.A. *The Comanches*. Norman: University of Oklahoma Press, 1952.

Wallace, Irving. *The Fabulous Showman*. London: Pan Books, 1962.

Wallace, John. *Carpetbag Rule in Florida: The Inside Workings of the Reconstruction of Civil Government in Florida after the Close of the Civil War*. Jacksonville, Fla.: DaCosta Printing, 1888.

Wallace, Lew. *Lew Wallace: An Autobiography*. New York: Harper & Brothers, 1906.

Wallace, Paul A. *Conrad Weiser, 1696-1760*. Philadelphia: University of Pennsylvania Press, 1945.

Wallace, Willard M. *Appeal to Arms: A Military History of the*

American Revolution. New York: Harper, 1951.

_____. *Traitorous Hero: The Life and Fortunes of Benedict Arnold.* New York: Harper, 1954.

Wallace, William H. *Speeches and Writings of William H. Wallace; an Autobiography.* Kansas City: Western Baptist, 1914.

Wallack, L.R. *American Pistol and Revolver.* New York: Winchester Press, 1979.

Wallack, Walter M., Kendall, Glenn M., Briggs, Howard L. *Education Within Prison Walls.* New York: Columbia University Press, 1939.

Wallance, Gregory. *Papa's Game.* New York: Rawson, Wade, 1981.

Wallas, G. *Jeremy Bentham.* London: University College, 1922.

Wallas, Graham. *The Life in Francis Place.* London: George Allen & Unwin, 1918.

Wallbank, T. Walter. *A Short History of India and Pakistan.* New York: Mentor, 1958.

Waller, Brown. *Last of the Great Western Train Robbers.* South Brunswick, N.Y.: A.S. Barnes, 1968.

Waller, George. *Kidnap: The Story of the Lindbergh Case.* New York: Dial Press, 1961.

_____. *Saga of an Imposing Era.* Englewood Cliffs, N.J.: Prentice-Hall, 1966.

Waller, Irle. *Chicago Uncensored: Firsthand Stories about the Al Capone Era.* New York: Exposition Press, 1965.

Waller, Irvin. *Men Released from Prison.* Toronto, Ontario, Can.: University of Toronto Press, 1974.

Waller, John. *A Treatise on the Incubus or Nightmare.* London: E. Cox & Son, 1816.

Walling, E.A.J. (ed.). *The Diaries of John Bright.* London: Cassell, 1930.

Walling, George. *Recollections of a New York Chief of Police.* New York: Caxton Book Concern, 1887.

Walling, William English. *Socialism as It Is.* New York: Macmillan, 1912.

_____, et. al. *The Socialism of Today.* New York: Henry Holt, 1916.

_____. *Socialists and the War.* New York: Henry Holt, 1915.

Wallis, George A. *Cattle Kings of the Staked Plains.* Dallas: American Guide Press, 1957.

Wallis, Roy. *The Road to Total Freedom: A Sociological Analysis of Scientology.* New York: Columbia University Press, 1977.

Wallnöfer, Heinrich, and Rottauscher, Anna von. *Chinese Folk Medicine.* trans. Marion Palmedo. New York: Crown, 1965.

Walls, H.J. *Forensic Science.* New York: Frederick Praeger, 1968.

Walls, Jim and Phil. *Chinatown, San Francisco.* Stanford, Calif.: Howell-North, 1960.

Walpole, Spencer. *A History of England from the Conclusion of the Great War in 1815.* (6 vols.) London: Longman, 1890.

Walsh, Edmund A. *The Fall of the Russian Empire.* New York: Blue Ribbon Books, 1927.

Walsh, James P. *Ethnic Militancy: An Irish Catholic Prototype.* Sna Francisco: R & E Research Associates, 1972.

_____ (ed.). *The San Francisco Irish: 1850-1976.* San Francisco: Irish Literary & Historical Society, 1978.

Walsh, Marilyn E. *The Fence.* Westport, Conn.: Greenwood, 1977.

Walsh, Ray. *The Mycroft Memoranda.* London: Deutsch, 1984.

Walsh, Richard John. *The Making of Buffalo Bill.* Indianapolis, Ind.: Bobbs-Merrill, 1928.

Walsh, Warren Bartlett. *Readings in Russian History.* Syracuse, N.Y.: Syracuse University Press, 1958.

_____. *Russia and the Soviet Union.* Ann Arbor: University of Michigan Press, 1968.

Walster, E., G.W., Berschied, E. *Equity: Theory and Research.* Boston: Allyn & Bacon,

Walter, Eugene Victor. *Terror and Resistance: A Study of Political Violence, with Case Studies of Some Primitive African Com-*
munities. New York: Oxford Univeristy Press, 1969.

Walter, G. *The Living Brain.* New York: W.W. Norton, 1953.

Walter, George W. *The Loomis Gang.* Prospect, N.Y.: Prospect Books, 1953.

Walter, Gérard. *Histoire du Communisme.* Paris: Payot, 1931.

Walter, Ingo. *Secret Money: The World of International Financial Secrecy.* Lexington, Mass.: D.C. Heath, 1985.

Walter, William W. *The Great Understander: True Life Story of the Last of the Wells, Fargo Shotgun Express Messengers.* Aurora, Ill.: Published by Author, 1931.

Walters, Alexander. *My Life and Work.* New York: Revel, 1917.

Walters, Lorenzo D. *Tombstones's Yesterday.* Tucson, Ariz.: Acme Printing, 1928.

Walters, Raymond. *Stephen Foster: Youth's Golden Gleam.* Princeton, N.J.: Princeton University Press, 1936.

Walters, Raymond, Jr. *Albert Gallatin: Jeffersonian Financier and Diplomat.* New York: Macmillan, 1957.

Waltersdorf, M.C. *Regulation of Public Utilities in New Jersey.* Baltimore: Waverly Press, 1936.

Walton, Augustus. *A History of Detection, Conviction, Life and Designs of John A. Murrel, The Great Western Land Pirate.* Athens, Tenn.: George White, 1835.

Walton, Clyde C. (ed.). *An Illinois Reader.* DeKalb: Northern Illinois University, 1970.

Walton, R.P. *Marihuana, America's New Drug Problem.* Philadelphia: J.B. Lippincott, 1938.

Walton, William M. *The James Boys of Old Missouri.* Cleveland: Arthur Westbrook, 1907.

_____. *Life and Adventures of Ben Thompson, the Famous Texan.* Houston, Texas: Frontier Press, 1954.

Waltrip, Lela, and Rufus. *Cowboys and Cattlemen.* New York: David McKay, 1967.

Walworth, Arthur. *Black Ships Off Japan.* New York: J.B. Lippincott, 1960.

_____. *Woodrow Wilson.* Baltimore: Penguin Books, 1965.

The Walworth Parricide! New York: Thomas O'Kane, 1873.

Walzer, Michael L. *Regicide and Revolution: Speeches at the Trial of Louis XVI.* trans. Marian Rothstein. New York: Cambridge University Press, 1979.

_____. *The Revolution of the Saints: A Study in the Origin of Radical Politics.* New York: Atheneum, 1968.

Walzer, Richard. *Galen on Jews and Christians.* London: Oxford University Press, 1949.

Wambaugh, Joseph. *The Blue Knight.* New York: Dell Books, 1972.

_____. *The Onion Field.* New York: Delacorte Press, 1973.

Wamweya, J. *Freedom Fighter.* trans. Ciira Cerere. Nairobi: East African Publishing House, 1971.

Wandell, Samuel H., and Minnegerode, Meade. *Aaron Burr.* 2 vols. New York: G.P. Putnam's Sons, 1925.

Wang, James C.F. *Hawai'i State and Local Politics.* Hilo: University of Hawaii Press, 1982.

Wanner, E. *On Remembering, Forgetting and Understanding Sentences.* Paris: Mouton, 1974.

War Department Official Records of the Union and Confederate Armies. Washington, D.C.: U.S. Government Printing Office, 1880-1901.

War Department Official Records of the Union and Confederate Navies. Washington, D.C.: U.S. Government Printing Office, 1894-1919.

Warbey, William, et. al. *Modern Norway: A Study in Social Democracy.* London: Fabian Society, 1953.

Warburg, Paul M. *The Federal Reserve System - Its Origins and Growth.* New York: Macmillan, 1930.

Warburton, Clark. *The Economic Results of Prohibition.* New York: Columbia University Press, 1932.

Ward, Sir Adolphus William. *The Cambridge Modern History.* London: Cambridge University Press, 1902-1911.

Ward, Arthur. *Stuff and Silk.* London: Gansey, n.d.

Ward, Christopher. *The War of the Revolution.* New York:

Macmillan, 1952.

Ward, David. *Cities and Immigrants*. New York: Oxford University Press, 1971.

Ward, David A., and Kassebaum, Gene G. *Women's Prison: Sex and Social Structure*. Chicago: Aldine, 1965.

Ward, Don (ed.). *Bits of Silver: Vignettes of the Old West*. New York: Hastings House, 1961.

Ward, Estolv E. *Harry Bridges on Trial*. New York: Modern Age, 1940.

Ward, Geoffrey C. *Before the Trumpet: Young Franklin Roosevelt, 1882-1905*. New York: Harper & Row, 1985.

Ward, Harry F. *In Place of Profit*. New York: Charles Scribner's Sons, 1933.

Ward, J.W. *Andrew Jackson, Symbol for an Age*. New York: Oxford University Press, 1953.

Ward, Joseph O. *My Grandpa Went West*. Caldwell, Idaho: Caxton Printers, 1956.

Ward, Margaret. *Cimarron Saga*. n.p., 1940.

Ward, Marion. *The Dubarry Inheritance*. New York: Crowell, 1967.

Ward, Martindale C. *A Trip to Chicago: What I Saw, What I Heard, What I Thought*. Glasgow: A. Malcolm, 1895.

Ward, R. Gerard. *American Activities in the Central Pacific, 1790-1870*. Ridgewood, N.J.: Gregg, 1966-1969.

Ward, Richard. *The Life of the Learned and Pious Dr. Henry Moore*. London: J. Downing, 1710.

Ward, Richard H. *Introduction to Criminal Investigation*. Reading, Mass.: Addison-Wesley, 1975.

Ward, Robert. *Asia for the Asiatics? The Techniques of Japanese Occupation*. Chicago: University of Chicago Press, 1945.

Ward, Robert E., and Rustow, Dankwart A. (eds.) *Political Modernization in Japan and Turkey*. Princeton, N.J.: Princeton University Press, 1964.

Ward, William. *The Dalton Gang, the Bandits of the Far West*. Cleveland: Arthur Westbrook, n.d.

_____. *Harry Tracy, the Death Dealing Oregon Outlaw*. Cleveland: Arthur Westbrook, 1908.

_____. *The James Boys of Old Missouri*. Cleveland: Arthur Westbrook, 1907.

_____. *Jesse James' Blackest Crime*. Cleveland: Arthur Westbrook, 1909.

_____. *Jesse James' Dash for Fortune*. Cleveland: Arthur Westbrook, n.d.

_____. *Jesse James' Midnight Attack*. Cleveland: Arthur Westbrook, 1910.

_____. *Jesse James' Mid-Winter Lark*. Cleveland: Arthur Westbrook, n.d.

_____. *Jesse James' Race for Life*. Cleveland: Arthur Westbrook, n.d.

_____. *The Younger Brothers, the Border Outlaws*. Cleveland: Arthur Westbrook, 1908.

"Warden". *His Majesty's Guests: Secrets of the Cells*. London: Jarrolds, 1929.

Warden, A.J. *The Linen Trade*. New York: A.M. Kelley, 1968.

Warden, Ernest A. *Infamous Kansas Killers*. Wichita, Kan.: McGuin, 1944.

_____. *Thrilling Tales of Kansas*. Wichita, Kan.: Wichita Eagle Press, 1932.

Warden, Robert B. *Private Life & Public Services of Salmon P. Chase*. Cincinnati, Ohio: Wilsatch, Baldwin, 1874.

Wardlaw, Reverend Ralph. *Lectures on Magdalenism*. New York: J.S. Redfield, 1843.

Wardman, Cy. *Frontier Stories*. New York: Charles Scribner's Sons, 1898.

_____. *The Story of the Railroad*. New York: D. Appleton, 1911.

Ware, Captain Eugene F. *The Indian War of 1864*. New York: St. Martin's Press, 1960.

Ware, Timothy. *The Orthodox Church*. London: Penguin, 1964.

Waring, L.F. *Serbia*. London: Henry Holt, Home University Library, 1917.

Warlimont, Walter. *Inside Hitler's Headquarters*. trans. R.H. Barry. London: Weidenfeld & Nicholson, 1964.

Warman, Cy. *Frontier Stories*. New York: Charles Scribner's Sons, 1898.

_____. *The Story of the Railroad*. New York: D. Appleton, 1898.

Warne, Coleston E. (ed.). *The Pullman Boycott of 1894: The Problem of Federal Intervention*. Boston: D.C. Heath, 1955.

Warne, Frank Julian. *The Coal Mine Workers*. New York: Longmans, Green, 1905.

Warner, Dale G. *Who Killed the President?* New York: American Press, 1964.

Warner, Emily Smith and Daniel, Hawthorne. *The Happy Warrior: A Biography of My Father*. Garden City, N.Y.: Doubleday, 1956.

Warner, Matt. *The Last of the Bandit Riders*. Caldwell, Idaho: Caxton Printers, 1940.

Warner, Opie L. *A Pardoned Life: Life of George Sontag*. San Bernardino, Calif.: Index Print, 1909.

Warner, Philip. *The Special Air Service*. London: William Kimber, 1971.

Warner, Sam B., Jr. *The Private City: Philadelphia in Three Periods of Its Growth*. Philadelphia: University of Pennsylvania Press, 1968.

Warner, W. Lloyd and Lunt, Paul S. *The Social Life of a Modern Community*. New Haven, Conn.: Yale University Press, 1941.

Warr, P., and Knapper, C. *The Perception of People and Events*. Chichester, Eng.: Wiley, 1968.

Warren, Austin. *New England Saints*. Ann Arbor: University of Michigan Press, 1956.

Warren, Charles. *A History of the American Bar*. Cambridge, Eng.: Cambridge University Press, 1912.

_____. *The Supreme Court in United States History*. Boston: Little, Brown, 1922.

Warren Commission. *Report of the Warren Commission on the Assassination of President Kennedy*. New York: Bantam, 1964.

Warren, David M. *The Plot to Kill JFK*. Chicago: Novel Books, 1965.

Warren, Earl, et al. *Hearings Before the President's Commission on the Assassination of President Kennedy*. 26 vols. Washington, D.C.: U.S. Government Printing Office, 1964.

_____. *Report of the President's Commission on the Assassination of President Kennedy*. Washington, D.C.: U.S. Government Printing Office, 1964.

Warren, Frank A. *Liberals and Communism: The 'Reed Decade' Revisited*. Bloomington: Indiana University Press, 1946.

Warren, John H., Jr. *Thirty Years Battle with Crime, or The Crying Shame of New York As Seen Under the Broad Glare of An Old Detective's Lantern*. Poughkeepsie, N.Y.: A.J. White, 1874.

Warren, Paul. *Next Time Is For Life*. New York: Dell Books, 1953.

Warren, Robert Penn. *John Brown: The Making of a Martyr*. New York: Payson & Clarke, 1929.

Warren, Viola Lockhart. *Dragoons on Trial*. Los Angeles: Dawson Book Shop, 1965.

Warren, W. Preston. *Masaryk's Democracy*. Chapel Hill: University of North Carolina Press, 1941.

Warshow, Robert. *Bet A Million Gates*. New York: Greenberg, 1932.

_____. *Jay Gould: The Story of a Fortune*. New York: Greenberg, 1928.

_____. *The Story of Wall Street*. New York: Greenberg, 1929.

Warth, Robert D. *The Allies and the Russian Revolution*. Durham, N.C.: Duke University Press, 1954.

Warwick, Donald P. *A Theory of Public Bureaucracy*. Cambridge, Mass.: Harvard University Press, 1975.

Washburn, Charles. *Come Into My Parlor: A Biography of the Aristocratic Everleigh Sisters of Chicago.*. New York: National Library Press, 1936.

Washburn, Emory. *Sketches of the Judicial History of Massachusetts.* Boston: Little Brown, 1840.

Washburn, Wilcomb E. *The Governor and the Rebel: A History of Bacon's Rebellion in Virginia.* Chapel Hill: University of North Carolina Press, 1957.

_____ (ed.). *The Indian and the White Man.* Garden City, N.Y.: Anchor Books, 1964.

Washburton, Watson, and De Long, Edmund. *High and Low Financiers.* Indianapolis, Ind.: Bobbs-Merrill, 1932.

Washington, Brenda. *The Deployment of Female Police Officers in the United States.* Gaithersburg, Md.: International Association of Chiefs of Police, 1974.

Washington, E.D. (ed.). *Selected Speeches of Booker T. Washington.* New York: Doubleday, 1932.

Washington, Joseph R., Jr. *Black Religion: The Negro and Christianity in the United States.* Boston: Beacon Press, 1964.

Washington Merry Go Round. New York: Horace Liveright, 1931.

Washington Research Project. *The Case Against Capital Punishment.* Washington, D.C.: Washington Research Project, 1971.

Washnis, G.J. *Citizen Involvement in Crime Prevention.* Lexington, Mass.: Lexington Books, 1976.

Waskow, Arthur I. *From Race Riot to Sit-In: 1919 and the 1960s.* Garden City, N.Y.: Doubleday, 1966.

Wasserstein, Bruce. *With Justice for Some.* Boston: Beacon, 1980.

Wasserstrom, William. *Civil Liberties and the Arts.* Syracuse, N.Y.: Syracuse University Press, 1964.

Wasson, Robert Gordon and Valentina Pavlovna. *Mushrooms, Russia and History.* New York: Pantheon Books, 1957.

_____. *Soma, The Divine Mushroom of Immortality.* New York: Harcourt Brace Jovanovich, 1975.

Watanabe Ryusaku. *Bandits on Horseback.* Tokyo: Chuo Koronsha, 1964.

Waterman, A.N. *Washington at the Time of the First Bull Run.* Washington, D.C.: Military Order of the Loyal Legion of the United States, n.d.

Waterman, Elijah. *A Sermon Preached at Windham.* Windham, Conn.: John Byrne, 1803.

Waterman, L. *Royal Correspondence of the Assyrian Empire.* Ann Arbor: University of Michigan Press, 1930.

Waterman, William Randall. *Frances Wright.* New York: Columbia University Press, 1924.

Waterman, Willoughby C. *Prostitution and Its Repression in New York City: 1900-1931.* New York: Columbia University Press, 1932.

Waters, Ethel. *His Eye is on the Sparrow.* New York: Doubleday, 1950.

Waters, Frank. *The Colorado.* New York: Rinehart, 1946.

_____. *Midas of the Rockies.* Newbury Park, Calif: Sage, Swallow, 1972.

_____. *The Story of Mrs. Virgil Earp: The Earp Brothers of Tombstone.* New York: Clarkson N. Potter, 1960.

Waters, Harold. *Adventure Unlimited: My Twenty Years of Experience in the United States Coast Guard.* New York: Prentice-Hall, 1955.

_____. *Smugglers of Spirits.* New York: Hastings House, 1971.

Waters, James F. *The Court of Missing Heirs.* New York: Modern Age Books, 1941.

Waters, L.L. *Steel trails to Santa Fe.* Lawrence: University of Kansas Press, 1951.

Waters, R. *Undiscovered Crimes.* London: n.p., 1862.

Waters, William. *A Gallery of Western Badmen.* Covington, Ky. Americana, 1954.

Watkins, Sam R. *"Co.Aytch".* New York: Collier Books, 1962.

Watkins, T.H., and Olmsted, Roger R. *Mirror of the Dream: An Illustrated History of San Francisco.* San Francisco: Scrimshaw Press, 1976.

Waters, Thomas Franklin. *Ipswich in the Massachusetts Bay Colony.* Ipswich, Mass.: Ipswich Historical Society, 1905.

Watrous, Ansel. *History of Larimer County, Colorado.* Fort Collins, Colo.: Courier, 1911.

Watson, E.R. *The Trial of Eugene Aram.* London: Hodge, 1913.

Watson, Frederick. *A Century of Gunmen; a Study in Lawlessness.* London: Ivor Nicholson & Watson, 1931.

Watson, John F. *Annals and Occurrences of New York City and State in the Olden Time.* Philadelphia: H.F. Anners, 1846.

_____. *Annals of Philadelphia and Pennsylvania in the Olden Time.* Philadelphia: n.p., 1857.

Watson, John Selby. *Justin, Cornelius Nepos and Eutropius.* London: Henry G. Bohn, 1853.

Watson, Lyall. *The Romeo Error.* Garden City, N.Y.: Doubleday, 1973.

_____. *Supernature.* New York: Doubleday, 1973.

Watson, Peter. *War on the Mind.* New York: Basic Books, 1978.

Watson, Tex. *Will You Die For Me.* New Jersey: Revell, 1978.

Watt, D.C. *Britain and the Suez Canal.* London: Oxford, 1956.

Watt, J.M., and Breyer-Brandwijk, M.G. *The Medicinal and Poisonous Plants of Southern Africa.* Edinburgh, Scot.: E. & S. Livingstone, 1932

Watt, John H. *National Fire Protection Association Handbook of the Electrical Code.* Boston: National Fire Protection Association, n.d.

Watt, Richard M. *The King's Depart.* New York: Simon & Schuster, 1969.

Watters, Pat, and Gillers, Stephen. *Investigating the FBI.* New York: Doubleday, 1973.

_____, and Cleghorn, Reese. *Climbing Jacob's Ladder: The Arrival of Negroes in Southern Politics.* New York: Harcourt, Brace & World, 1967.

Watterson, Henry. *"Marse Henry," An Autobiography.* New York: George H. Doran, 1929.

Watts, Hamp B. *The Babe of the Company.* Fayette, Mo.: Democrat Leader Press, 1913.

Watts, Marthe. *The Men in My Life.* London: Christopher Johnson, 1960.

Watts, Judge R.A. *The Trial and Execution of the Lincoln Conspirators.* Lansing: Michigan History Magazine, 1922.

Watts, William Courtney. *The Chronicles of a Kentucky Settlement.* New York: G.P. Putnam's Sons, 1897.

Wauchope, Robert. *Lost Tribes and Sunken Continents.* Chicago: University of Chicago Press, 1962.

Waugh, Alec. *A History of the West Indies from 1492 to 1898.* Garden City, N.Y.: Doubleday, 1964.

Waugh, Edgar Wiggins. *Second Consul.* Indianapolis, Ind.: Bobbs-Merrill, 1956.

Wavell, Col. A.P. *The Palestine Campaign.* London: Constable, 1928.

Way, Fredrick, Jr. *She Takes the Horns.* Cincinnati, Ohio: Picture Marine, 1953.

Way, Thomas E. *Frontier Arizona.* New York: Carlton Press, 1950.

_____. *Sgt. Fred Platten's Ten Years on the Trail of Redskins.* Williams, Ariz.: Williams News Press, 1963.

Way, W.J. (Jack). *The Tombstone Story.* Tucson, Ariz.: Livingston Press, 1965.

Wayland, John W. *The Washingtons and Their Homes.* Staunton, Va.: McClure, 1944.

Weadock, Jack. *Dust of the Desert: Plain Tales of the Desert and the Border.* New York: D. Applton-Century, 1936.

Weaver, James. *Political Economy: Radical and Orthodox Approaches.* Rockleigh, N.J.: Allyn & Bacon, 1972.

Weaver, John. *El Pueblo Grande.* Los Angeles: Ward Ritchie Press, 1973.

Weaver, Richard. *Ideas Have Consequences.* Chicago: University of Chicago Press, Phoenix Books, 1948.

_____. *Warren, the Man, the Court, the Era.* Boston: Little, Brown, 1967.

Webb, Beatrice. *American Diary, 1898.* Madison: University of Wisconsin Press, 1963.

____. *My Apprenticeship.* New York: Longmans, Green, 1926.

Webb, Duncan. *Crime Is My Business.* London: Muller, 1953.

____. *Deadline for Crime.* London: Muller, 1955.

Webb, Eugene J., et al. *Nonreactive Measures in the Social Sciences.* New York: Houghton Mifflin, 1981.

____. *Unobtusive Measures: Nonreactive Research in the Social Sciences.* Chicago: Rand McNally, 1966.

Webb, Jack. *The Badge.* Englewood Cliffs, N.J.: Prentice-Hall, 1958.

Webb, James. *The Occult Underground.* LaSalle, Ill.: Open Court, 1974.

Webb, Lucas. *The Attempted Assassination of John F. Kennedy.* San Bernardino, Calif.: R. Reginald, 1976.

Webb, May Folk, and Estes, Patrick Mann. *Carey-Estes Genealogy.* Rutland, Vt.: Tuttle, 1939.

Webb, Richard D. *Life and Letters of Captain John Brown.* London: Smith, Elder, 1861.

Webb, R.K. *The British Working-Class Reader, 1780-1848.* London: Chatto & Windus, 1955.

Webb, Sidney and Beatrice. *The Development of English Local Government 1689-1835.* London: Oxford University Press, 1963.

____. *English Prisons Under Local Government.* Hamden, Conn.: Archon Books, 1963.

____. *The History of the Trade Unionism.* New York: Longmans, 1920.

Webb, Thomas H. *Information for Kansas Immigrants.* Boston: Afred Mudge, 1855.

Webb, Walter Prescott. *The Great Frontier.* Boston: Houghton Mifflin, 1952.

____. *The Great Plains.* Boston: Ginn, 1931.

____ (ed.). *The Handbook of Texas.* 2 vols. Austin: Texas State Historical Society, 1952.

____. *The Story of the Texas Rangers.* New York: Grossett & Dunlap, 1957.

____. *The Texas Rangers, A Century of Frontier Defense.* Boston: Houghton Mifflin, 1935.

Webb, W.E. *Buffalo Land; an Authentic Account of the Discoveries, Adventures, and Mishaps of a Scientific and Sporting Party in the Wild West.* Chicago: E. Hannaford, 1872.

Weber, Brom (ed.). *The Letters of Hart Crane.* New York: Hermitage House, 1952.

Weber, David. *The Lost Trappers.* Albuquerque: University of New Mexico Press, 1970.

____. *The Taos Trappers.* Norman: University of Oklahoma Press, 1968.

Weber, Eugen. *Varieties of Fascism.* Princeton, N.J.: Van Nostrand, 1964.

Weber, Max. *From Max Weber: Essays in Sociology.* trans. Hans Gerth and C.W. Mills. New York: Oxford University Press, 1946.

____. *On Law in Economy and Society.* trans. Edward Shils and Max Rheinstein. New York: Simon & Schuster, 1954.

____. *On Methodology of the Social Sciences.* trans. Edward A. Shils, and Henry A. Finch. New York: Free Press, 1949.

____. *The Protestant Ethic and the Spirit of Capitalism.* New York: Charles Scribner's Sons, 1930.

____. *The Theory of Social and Economic Organization.* trans. Alexander M. Henderson and Talcott Parsons. New York: Oxford University Press, 1947.

Webster, Daniel. *Argument on the Trial of John Francis Knapp, The Works of Daniel Webster.* Boston: Little, Brown, 1951.

Webster, David. *A Collection of Rare and Curious Tracts on Witchcraft and the Second Sight.* Edinburgh, Scot.: D. Webster, 1820.

Webster, John. *The Displaying of Supposed Witchcraft.* London: J.M., 1677.

Webster, Nesta H. *Secret Societies and Subversive Movements.* London: Boswell Printing, 1924.

Webster, Samuel C. (ed.). *Mark Twain, Business Man.* Boston: Little, Brown, 1946.

Webster, William H. *Crime in the United States.* Washington, D.C.: U.S. Government Printing Office, 1984.

Wechsburg, Joseph. *The Merchant Bankers.* Boston: Little, Brown, 1966.

Wechsler, D. *The Measurement of Adult Intelligence.* Baltimore: Williams & Wilkins, 1944.

Wechsler, James A. *The Age of Suspicion.* New York: Random House, 1953.

____. *Reflections of an Angry, Middle-Aged Editor.* New York: Random House, 1960.

Wecter, Dixon. *The Age of the Great Depression: 1929-1941.* New York: Macmillan, 1941.

____. *The Hero in America.* Ann Arbor: University of Michigan Press, 1963.

____. *The Saga of American Society: A Record of Social Aspiration, 1607-1937.* New York: Charles Scribner's Sons, 1937.

____. *Samuel Clemens of Hannibal.* Boston: Houghton Mifflin, 1952.

Wedded and Murdered within an Hour!: The Cruel Murder of Mina Miller by Kenkowsky, Alias Kettler. Philadelphia: Barclay, 1881.

Wedeck, Harry E. *Dictionary of Magic.* New York: Philosophical Library, 1956.

Wedgwood, Cicely V. *The Thirty Years War.* New Haven, Conn.: Yale University Press, 1939.

____. *The Trial of Charles I.* London: Collins, 1964.

____. *William the Silent.* New Haven, Conn.: Yale University Press, 1944.

Wee, Herman van der. *The Great Depression, Revisited.* The Hague, Neth.: M. Nijoff, 1972.

Weed, Thurlow. *Autobiography and Memoirs.* Boston: Houghton Mifflin, 1925.

Weeden, William B. *Economic and Social History of New England.* New York: Hilary House, 1963.

Weeks, Edward. *My Green Age.* Boston: Atlantic Monthly Press, 1973.

Weeks, J.E.P. *Trial of Albert John Tirrell.* Boston: Times, 1846.

Weeks, Robert P. (ed.). *Commonwealth vs. Sacco and Vanzetti.* Englewood Cliffs, N.J.: Prentice-Hall, 1958.

Wei, Henry. *China and Soviet Russia.* Princeton, N.J.: Princeton University Press, 1956.

Weichmann, Louis J., and Arnold, Samuel B. *Defence and Prison Experiences of a Lincoln Conspirator.* Hattiesburg, Miss.: Book Farm, 1943.

____. *A True History of the Assassination of Abraham Lincoln and of the Conspiracy of 1865.* New York: Alfred A. Knopf, 1975.

Weidenfield, Sheila R. *First Lady's Lady.* New York: G.P. Putnam's Sons, 1979.

Weider, Ben. *Assassination at St. Helena.* Vancouver, British Columbia, Can.: Mitchell Press, 1978.

____, and Hapgood, David. *The Murder of Napoleon.* New York: Congdon & Lattes, 1982.

Weiger, L. *Moral Tenets and Customs of China.* trans. L. Davrout. Hokien-fu, China: Catholic Mission Press, 1913.

Weigley, Russell. *The Partisans' War.* Columbia: South Carolina Tricentennial Commission, 1970.

Weihofen, H. *The Urge to Punish.* New York: Farrar, Straus & Cudahy, 1956.

Weil, Joseph as told to W.T. Brannon. *"Yellow Kid" Weil.* Chicago: Ziff-Davis, 1948.

Weill, Georges. *Le Parti républicain de 1814 à 1870.* Paris: Félix Alcan, 1900.

Weinbaum, Martin (ed.). *British Burrough Charters, 1307-1660.* Cambridge, Eng.: University Press, 1943.

Weinberg, A.K. *Manifest Destiny.* Baltimore, Md.: Johns Hopkins Press, 1935.

Weinberg, Arthur (ed.). *Attorney for the Damned.* New York: Simon & Schuster, 1957.

_____ and Lila. *Clarence Darrow*. New York: G.P. Putnams Sons, 1980.

_____ and Lila (eds.). *Verdicts Out of Court*. Chicago: Quadrangle Books, 1963.

Weinberg, Kirson S. *Incest Behavior*. New York: Citadel Press, 1965.

Weiner, Ed. *The Damon Runyon Story*. New York: David McKay, 1948.

_____. *Let's Go to Press*. New York: G.P. Putnam's Sons, 1955.

Weiner, Herbert. *9 1/2 Mystics: The Kabbala Today*. New York: Holt, Rinehart & Winston, 1969.

Weiner, Margery. *Matters of Felony: A Reconstruction*. London: William Heinemann, 1967.

_____. *Matters of Felony: A True Tale of 18th Century Ireland*. New York: Atheneum, 1967.

Weingart, George W. *Pyrotechnics*. New York: Chemical, 1947.

Weingarten, Arthur. *The Sky is Falling*. London: Hodder & Stoughton, 1977.

Weingast, David Elliot. *Walter Lippmann: A Study in Personal Journalism*. New Brunswick, N.J.: Rutgers University Press, 1949.

Weinreb, L.L. *Criminal Law: Cases, Comments, Questions*. Mineola, N.Y.: Foundation Press, 1975.

Weinstein, Alfred A. *Barbed Wire Surgeon*. New York: Macmillan, 1948.

Weinstein, Allen. *Perjury: The Hiss-Chambers Case*. New York: Vintage Books, 1979.

Weinstein, Harold R. *Jean Jaurès; A Study of Patriotism in the French Socialist Movement*. New York: Columbia University Press, 1936.

Weinstein, James. *The Corporate Ideal in the Liberal State*. Boston: Beacon Press, 1968.

_____. *The Decline of Socialism in America, 1912-1925*. New York: Monthly Review Press, 1967.

Weinstock, Matt. *My LA*. New York: Current Books, A.A. Wyn, 1947.

Weintraub, Hyman. *Andrew Furuseth: Emancipator of the Seamen*. Berkeley: University of California Press, 1959.

Weir, James. *Lonz Powers*. Philadelphia: Lippincott, Grambo, 1850.

Weis, Frederick Lewis. *The Colonial Clergy and the Colonial Churches of New England*. Lancaster, Mass.: Publications of the Society of the Desendants of the Colonial Clergy, 1936.

Weisberg, Bernard A. *The American Newspaperman*. Chicago: University of Chicago Press, 1961.

Weisberg, Harold. *Frame-Up: The King/Ray Case*. New York: Outerbridge & Dienstfrey, 1971.

_____. *Oswald in New Orleans*. New York: Canyon Books, 1967.

_____. *Photographic Whitewash: Suppressed Kennedy Assassination Pictures*. Hyattstown, Md.: Published by Author, 1967.

_____. *Post Mortem*. Frederick, Md.: Published by Author, 1971.

_____. *Whitewash: The Report on the Warren Report*. Hyattstown, Md.: Published by Author, 1965.

_____. *Whitewash II: The FBI - Secret Service Cover-up*. Hyattstown, Md.: Published by Author, 1966.

_____. *Whitewash IV: Top Secret JFK Assassination Transcript*. Frederick, Md.: Published by Author, 1974.

Weisberger, Bernard A. (ed.). *Abolitionism: Disrupter of the Democratic System or Agent of Progress?* Chicago: Rand McNally, 1963.

_____. *The American Newspaperman*. Chicago: University of Chicago Press, 1961.

Weisman, Thomas. *Drug Abuse and Drug Counseling*. New York: Jason Aronson, 1972.

Weiss, Carl, and Frair, David James. *Terror in the Prisons: Homosexual Rape and Why Society Condones It*. Indianapolis, Ind.: Bobbs-Merrill, 1974.

Weiss, Harry B. and Grace M. *An Introduction to Crime and Punishment in Colonial New Jersey*. Trenton, N.J.: Past Times, 1960.

Weiss, Karel (ed.). *The Prison Experience: An Anthology*. New York: Delacorte Press, 1976.

Weiss, Nancy J. *Charles Francis Murphy, 1858-1924: Respectability and Responsibility in Tammany Politics*. Northampton, Mass.: Smith College, 1968.

Weissberg, Alexander. *The Accused*. New York: Simon & Schuster, 1951.

Weitenkampf, Frank. *American Graphic Art*. New York: Macmillan, 1924.

Weizäcker, Siegfried. *Erinnerungen*. Munich: Paul List, 1950.

Welch, Moses C. *The Gospel to be Preached to All Men*. Windham, Conn.: John Byrne, 1805.

Weld, Charles Richard. *A Vacation Tour in the United States and Canada*. London: Longman, Brown, Green & Longmans, 1855.

Weld, Ralph Foster. *Brooklyn Is American*. New York: Columbia University Press, 1950.

Weller, John L. *The New Haven Railroad: The Rise and Fall*. New York: Hastings House, 1969.

Welles, Gideon. *Diary of Gideon Welles*. 3 vols. Boston: Houghton Mifflin, 1911.

Welles, Patricia. *Angel in the Snow*. New York: Pocket Books, 1980.

Welles, Sumner. *Time of Decision*. New York: Harper & Brothers, 1944.

_____. *We Need Not Fail*. Boston: Houghton Mifflin, 1948.

Wellesley, F.A. *Secrets of the Second Empire*. New York: Harper & Brothers, 1929.

Wellford, Harrison. *Sowing and Wind*. New York: Grossman, 1972.

Welling, Richard W.G. *As the Twig is Bent*. New York: G.P. Putnam's Sons, 1942.

Wellman, Francis L. *The Art of Cross-Examination*. New York: Macmillan, 1903.

_____. *Gentlemen of the Jury: Reminiscences of Thirty Years at the Bar*. New York: Macmillan, 1924.

Wellman, Manly Wade. *Dead and Gone, Classic Crimes of North Carolina*. Chapel Hill: University of North Carolina Press, 1954.

Wellman, Paul I. *The Blazing Southwest*. London: W. Foulshar, 1961.

_____. *Death on Horseback*. New York: J.B. Lippincott, 1934.

_____. *A Dynasty of Western Outlaws*. Garden City, N.Y.: Doubleday, 1961.

_____. *Glory, God and Gold*. Garden City, N.Y.: Doubleday, 1954.

_____. *The Indian Wars of the West*. Garden City, N.J.: Doubleday, 1947.

_____. *Spawn of Evil*. Garden City, N.Y.: Doubleday, 1964.

_____. *The Trampling Herd*. New York: Carrick & Evans, 1939.

Wellman, William R. *Elementary Electricity*. New York: Van Nostrand Reinhold, 1947.

Wells, Brian. *Psychedelic Drugs*. New York: Jason Aronson, 1974.

Wells, Damon. *Stephen Douglas: The Last Years, 1857-1861*. Austin: University of Texas Press, 1971.

Wells, David A. *Recent Economic Changes and Their Effects on Production and Distribution of Wealth and the Well-Being of Society*. New York: D. Appleton, 1889.

Wells, Evelyn. *Champagne Days of San Francisco*. New York: D. Appleton-Century, 1939.

_____, and Peterson, Harry Austin. *The '49ers*. Garden City, N.Y.: Doubleday, 1949.

_____. *Fremont Older*. New York: D. Appleton-Century, 1936.

Wells, H.G. *Experiment in Autobiography*. New York: Macmillan, 1934.

_____. *The Future in America*. New York: Harper, 1906.

_____. *Mr. Blettsworthy on Rampole Island*. New York: Doubleday, Doran, 1928.

_____. *The Outline of History*. Garden City, N.Y.: Garden City

Books, 1949.

_____. *Russia in the Shadows*. London, Hodder, Stoughton, n.d.

_____. *The Way the World is Going*. London: Ernest Benn, 1928.

Wells, Hal M. *The Sensuous Child*. New York: Stein & Day, 1978.

Wells, James M. *The Chisolm Massacre: A Picture of "Home Rule" in Mississippi*. Washington D.C.: Chisolm Monument Association, 1877.

Wells, Polk. *Life and Adventures of Polk Wells (Charles Knox Polk Wells), the Notorious Outlaw*. Halls, Mo.: G.A. Warnica, 1907.

Welter, Rush. *The Mind of America, 1820-1860*. New York: Columbia University Press, 1975.

Weltfish, Gene. *The Lost Universe*. New York: Basic Books, 1965.

Wendell, Barrett. *Cotton Mather, the Puritan Priest*. New York: Dodd, Mead, 1891.

Wendland, Michael F. *The Arizona Project*. Kansas City: Sheed, Andrews & McMeel, 1977.

Wendt, Lloyd, and Kogen, Herman. *Bet a Million!* Indianapolis, Ind.: Bobbs-Merrill, 1948.

_____. *Big Bill of Chicago*. Indianapolis, Ind.: Bobbs-Merrill, 1953.

_____. *Bosses in Lusty Chicago*. Indianapolis: University of Indiana Press, 1943.

_____. *Chicago Tribune: The Rise of a Great American Newspaper*. Chicago: Rand McNally, 1979.

_____. *Lords of the Levee*. New York: Bobbs-Merrill, 1943.

Wendte, Charles W. *Thomas Starr King, Patriot and Preacher*. Boston: Beacon Press, 1921.

Weng, Johann F. *Die Hexenprocesse*. Nördlingen, Ger.: C.H. Beck, 1838.

Wensley, Frederick Porter. *Detective Days*. London: Cassell, 1931.

_____. *Forty Years of Scotland Yard: The Record of a Lifetime's Service in the Criminal Investigation Department*. New York: Garden City, 1930.

Wentworth, B., and Wilder, H.H. *Personal Indentification*. Chicago: T.G. Cooke, 1932.

Wentworth, Edward Norris. *America's Sheep Trails*. Ames: Iowa State College Press, 1948.

Wentworth, Harold, and Flexner, Stuart Berg. *Dictionary of American Slang*. New York: Thomas Y. Crowell, 1967.

Wepman, D. *Jomo Kenyatta*. New York: Chelsea House, 1985.

Weppner, Robert S. (ed.). *Street Ethnography*. Beverly Hills, Calif.: Sage, 1977.

Werfel, Franz. *Class Reunion*. New York: Simon & Schuster, 1929.

_____. *Twilight of a World*. trans. H.T. Lowe-Porter. New York: Viking Press, 1937.

Werkheiser, Richard M., and Barnhart, Arthur C. *Capital Punishment*. New York: National Council of the Episcopal Church, 1961.

Werner, E.E., and Smith, R.S. *Kauai's Children Come of Age*. Honolulu: University of Hawaii Press, 1977.

_____. *Vulnerable but Invincible*. New York: McGraw-Hill, 1982.

Werner, M.R. *Barnum*. New York: Harcourt, Brace, 1929.

_____. *Bryan*. New York: Harcourt, Brace, 1929.

_____. *It Happened in New York*. New York: Coward-McCann, 1957.

_____. *Privileged Characters*. New York: R.M. McBride, 1935.

_____. *Tammany Hall*. Garden City, N.Y.: Doubleday, Doran, 1928.

Werstein, Irving. *July 1863*. New York: Ace Books, 1957.

_____. *1861-1865: The Adventure of the Civil War*. New York: Cooper Square, 1964.

Wertenbaker, Charles. *The Death of Kings*. New York: Random House, 1954.

Wertenbaker, Thomas Jefferson. *Father Knickerbocker Rebels: New York City During the Revolution*. New York: Charles Scribner's Sons, 1948.

_____. *The First Americans 1607-1690*. New York: Macmillan, 1927.

_____. *The Founding of American Civilization: The Middle Colonies*. New York: Charles Scribner's Sons, 1938.

_____. *The Planters of Colonial Virginia*. Princeton, N.J.: Princeton University Press, 1922.

_____. *The Puritan Oligarchy*. New York: Charles Scribner's Sons, 1947.

_____. *Torchbearer of the Revolution*. Princeton, N.J.: Princeton University Press, 1940.

_____. *Virginia Under the Stuarts*. Princeton, N.J.: Princeton University Press, 1914.

Werth, Alexander. *France in Ferment*. London: Jarrolds, 1934.

_____. *Which Way France?* New York: Harper, 1937.

Wertham, Dr. Fredric. *The Circle of Guilt*. New York: Rinehart, 1956.

_____. *Dark Legend: A Study in Murder*. London: Victor Gollancz, 1947.

_____. *Seduction of the Innocent*. New York: Rinehart, 1954.

_____. *The Show of Violence*. New York: Doubleday, 1949.

_____. *A Sign for Cain*. New York: Paperback Library, 1969.

Wesley, Charles H. *Neglected History: Essays in Negro-American History*. Wilberforce, Ohio: Central State College Press, 1965.

Wesley, Charles H. *Negro Labor in the United States, 1850-1925: A Study in American Economic History*. New York: Vanguard Press, 1927.

Wesley, L. *Air-Guns and Air-Pistols*. New Jersey: Barnes, 1980.

Wesser, Robert F. *Charles Evans Hughes: Politics and Reform in New York, 1905-1910*. Ithaca, N.Y.: Cornell University Press, 1967.

West, Algernon. *Contemporary Portraits*. London: T. Fisher Unwin, 1920.

West, Donald J. (ed.). *Criminological Implications of Chromosome Abnormalities*. Cambridge, Eng.: University of Cambridge, 1969.

_____. *Delinquency: Its Roots, Careers, and Prospects*. Cambridge, Mass.: Harvard University Press, 1982.

_____, and Farrington, D.P. *The Delinquent Way of Life*. New York: Crane Russak, 1977.

_____. *The Habitual Prisoner*. London: Macmillan, 1963.

_____. *Murder Followed By Suicide*. London: William Heinemann, 1965.

_____. *Present Conduct and Future Delinquency*. London: William Heinemann, 1969.

_____. *Sacrifice Unto Me*. New York: Pyramid, 1974.

_____, and Farrington, D.P. *Who Becomes Delinquent?* London: William Heinemann, 1973.

_____, *The Young Offender*. London: Penguin, 1967.

West, John Anthony, and Toonder, Jan Gerhard. *The Case for Astrology*. Baltimore, Md.: Penguin, 1973.

West, John B. *The Death of the President: The Warren Report on Trial in New Orleans!* Covina, Calif.: n.p., 1967.

West, John O. *Billy the Kid, Hired Gun or Hero*. Dallas: Southern Methodist University Press, 1966.

West, Jude, and Stratton, John R. *The Role of Correctional Industries*. Iowa City: University of Iowa, 1971.

West, R.A. *The Great Mollie Maguire Trials*. Pottsville, Pa.: Chronicle, 1876.

West, Ray B., Jr. (ed.). *Rocky Mountain Cities*. New York: W.W. Norton, 1949.

West, Rebecca. *Black Lamb and Grey Falcon*. 2 vols. New York: Viking Press, 1941.

_____. *The New Meaning of Treason*. New York: Viking Press, 1967.

_____. *A Train of Powder*. New York: Viking Press, 1946.

West, William. *Simboleography*. London: Miles Flesher, 1647.

West, William Gordon. *Serious Thieves: Lower-Class Adolescent Males in a Short-Term Deviant Occupation*. Ann Arbor,

Mich.: University Microfilms, 1974.

Westarp, Count Kuno Friedrich Victor von. *Das Ende der Monarchie am 9. November 1918*. Berlin: Rauschenbusch, 1952.

Westerfield, H. Bradford. *Foreign Policy and Party Politics*. New Haven, Conn.: Yale University Press, 1955.

Westermarck, Edward. *The History of Human Marriage*. London: Macmillan, 1922.

_____. *The Origin and Development of Moral Ideas*. London: Macmillan, 1908.

Westermeier, Clifford P. *Trailing the Cowboy*. Caldwell, Idaho: Caxton Printers, 1955.

Western Kansas Cattle Growers Assoc. *Brand Book*. n.p., 1882, 1883, 1884, 1885.

Westerners, The. *Brand Book*. Los Angeles: Los Angeles Corral, 1947.

_____. *The Smoke Signal*. 13 vols. Tucson, Ariz.: Tucson Corral, n.d.

Westham, F. *Seduction of the Innocent*. New York: Museum, London & Rhinehart, 1955.

Westin, Alan F. *The Anatomy of a Constitutional Law Case*. New York: Macmillan, 1958.

_____ (ed.). *An Autobiography of the Supreme Court*. New York: Macmillan, 1963.

_____. *Computers, Health Records, and Citizens' Rights*. Washington D.C.: U.S. Government Printing Office, 1976.

_____ (ed.). *Freedom Now! The Civil Rights Struggle in America*. New York: Basic Books, 1964.

_____, and Salisbury, Stephan (eds.). *Individual Rights in the Corporation*. New York: Pantheon Books, 1980.

_____. *Privacy and Freedom*. New York: Atheneum, 1966.

_____ (ed.). *The Supreme Court: Views From Inside*. New York: W.W. Norton, 1961.

_____. *Whistle-Blowing! Loyalty and Dissent in the Corporation*. New York: McGraw-Hill, 1981.

Westley, William. *Violence and the Police: A Sociological Study of Law, Custom and Morality*. Cambridge, Mass.: MIT Press, 1970.

Westmeyer, Russell E. *Modern Economic and Social Systems*. New York: Farrar & Rinehart, 1940.

Weston, J.A. *Historic Doubts as to the Execution of Ney*. New York: T. Whittaker, 1895.

Weston, Paul B. and Wells, Kenneth M. *Criminal Investigation: Basic Perspectives*. Englewood Cliffs, N.J.: Prentice-Hall, 1974

_____. *Criminal Justice: Introduction and Guidelines*. Pacific Palisades, N.J.: Goodyear, 1976.

Westphal, Siegfried. *The German Army in the West*. London: Cassell, 1951.

Westphall, Victor. *Thomas Benton Catron and His Era*. Tucson: University of Arizona Press, 1973.

Wethern, George. *A Wayward Angel*. New York: Marek, 1978.

Wetmore, Helen Cody. *Last of the Great Scouts: The Life Story of Col. William F. Cody*. Duluth, Minn.: Duluth Press, 1899.

Wettem, Desmond. *The Lonely Battle*. London: W.H. Allen, 1960.

Weukkm Georges J. *Histoire du Mouvement Social en France, 1852-1914*. Paris: F. Alcan, 1924.

Wexley, J. *The Judgment of Julius and Ethel Rosenberg*. London: Cameron & Kahn, 1955.

Weyer, Edward, Jr. *Jungle Quest*. New York: Harper, 1955.

Weyer, Johan. *De Lamiis*. Basel, Switz.: ex officina Oporiana, 1564.

_____. *De Praestigiis Daemonum*. Basel, Switz: I. Oporinum, 1564.

_____. *Histoires*. trans. Simon Goulart. Paris: A. Delahaye & Lecrosnier, 1885.

Weyl, Nathaniel, and Marina, William. *American Statesmen on Slavery and the Negro*. New Rochelle, N.Y.: Arlington House, 1971.

_____. *The Battle Against Disloyalty*. New York: Thomas Y. Crowell, 1951.

_____ and Sylvia. *The Reconquest of Mexico*. London: Oxford University Press, 1939.

_____. *Treason: The Story of Disloyalty and Betrayal in American History*. Washington D.C.: Public Affairs Press, 1950.

Weyrauch, W.O. *The Personality of Lawyers*. New Haven, Conn.: Yale University Press, 1964.

Whalen, Grover. *Mr. New York: The Autobiography of Grover Whalen*. New York: G.P. Putnam's Sons, 1955.

Whalen, Richard J. *The Founding Father - The Story of Joseph P. Kennedy*. New York: New American Library, 1964.

Wharton, A.F. *Trial of the Crew and Officers of the Privateer Savannah on Charges of Piracy*. New York: Baker & Goodwin, 1862.

Wharton, Clarence Ray. *L'Archevêque*. Houston, Texas: Anson Jones Press, 1941.

_____. *History of Fort Bend County*. San Antonio, Texas: Naylor, 1939.

Wharton, Edith. *Age of Innocence*. New York: Modern Library, 1920.

Wharton, J.E. *History of the City of Denver*. Denver: Byers & Dailey, 1866.

Wharton, Vernon Lane. *The Negro in Mississippi 1865 to 1890*. Chapel Hill: University of North Carolina Press, 1947.

Wheaton, Eliot B. *The Nazi Revolution 1933-35: Prelude to Calamity*. Garden City, N.Y.: Doubleday, 1969.

Wheeler, Burton K., and Healy, Paul F. *Yankee from the West*. New York: Doubleday, 1962.

Wheeler, David Hilton. *Brigandage in South Italy*. London: S. Low, Son & Marston, 1864.

Wheeler, Douglas L. *Republican Portugal: A Political History, 1910-1926*. Madison: University of Wisconsin Press, 1978.

Wheeler, Col. Homer Webster. *Buffalo Days; Forty Years in the Old West*. Indianapolis, Ind.: Bobbs-Merrill, 1925.

_____. *The Frontier Trail; or, from Cowboy to Colonel*. Los Angeles: Times-Mirror Press, 1923.

Wheeler, John N. *I've Got News for You*. New York: E.P. Dutton, 1961.

Wheeler, Kenneth W. *For the Union/Ohio Leaders in the Civil War*. Columbus: Ohio State University Press, 1968.

Wheeler, Post, and Rides, Hallie Erminie. *Dome of Many-Colored Glass*. Garden City, N.Y.: Doubleday, 1965.

Wheeler, Stanton (ed.). *Controlling Delinquents*. New York: John Wiley & Sons, 1968.

_____, and Goslin, David A. (eds.). *Handbook of Socialization Theory and Research*. Chicago: Rand McNally, 1969.

_____ (ed.). *On Record: Files and Dossiers in American Life*. New Brunswick, N.J.: Transaction Books, 1969.

Wheeler-Bennett, Sir John W. *Hindenburg: The Wooden Titan*. London: Macmillan, 1936.

_____. *King George VI*. New York: St. Martin's Press, 1958.

_____. *The Nemesis of Power: The German Army in Politics 1918-1945*. New York: St. Martin's Press, 1953.

_____. *Three Episodes in the Life of Kaiser Wilhelm II*. London: Cambridge University Press, 1956.

Wheelock, Keith. *Nasser's New Egypt*. New York: Frederick A. Praeger, 1960.

Whibley, Charles. *American Sketches*. London: Blackwood & Sons, 1908.

Whibley, Charles. *A Book of Scoundrels*. New York: Benjamin Blom, 1971.

While Lincoln Lay Dying. A Facsimile Reproduction of the First Testimony Taken in Connection with the Assassination...as Recorded by Corporal James Tanner. Philadelphia: Union League of Philadelphia, 1968.

Whinery, Leo H., et al. *Predictive Sentencing: An Empirical Evaluation*. Lexington, Mass.: D.C. Health, 1976.

Whipple, Leon. *The Story of Civil Liberty in the United States*. New York: Vanguard Press, 1927.

Whipple, Sidney B. *The Lindbergh Crime*. New York: Blue Ribbon Books, 1935.

_____. *Noble Experiment*. London: Methuen, 1934.

_____ (ed.). *The Trial of Bruno Richard Hauptmann*. Garden City, N.Y.: Doubleday & Doran, 1937.

Whisenand, Emma Boge. *This Is Nebraska*. Kansas City: Burton, 1942.

Whisenand, Paul, and Ferguson, R. Fred. *The Managing of Police Organizations*. Englewood Cliffs, N.J.: Prentice-Hall, 1973.

_____. *Police Supervision: Theory and Practice*. Englewood Cliffs, N.J.: Prentice-Hall, 1971.

Whitaker, A.P. *The Mississippi Question, 1795-1803*. New York: Appleton-Century, 1934.

Whitaker, Arthur P. *The United States and the Independence of Latin America, 1800-1830*. New York: W.W. Norton, 1964.

_____. *The United States and the Southern Cone: Argentina, Chile, and Uruguay*. Cambridge, Mass.: Harvard University Press, 1976.

Whitaker, Ben. *The Police*. London: Penguin Books, 1964.

Whitbread, J.R. *The Railway Policeman*. London: Harrap, 1961.

White, A. *Efficiency and Empire*. Brighton, Eng.: Harvester Press, 1973.

White, A. *The Modern Jew*. London: William Heinemann, 1899.

_____. *The Problems of a Great City*. London: Remington, 1887.

White, Andrew Dickson. *Autobiography*. 2 vols. New York: Century, 1905.

_____. *A History of the Warfare of Science with Theology in Christendom*. New York: Dover, 1896-1960.

_____. *Seven Great Statesmen*. Garden City, N.Y.: Garden City, 1926.

White, Arnold (ed.). *Letters of S.G.O.* London: Griffith & Farren, 1890.

White, Bouck. *The Book of Daniel Drew*. New York: George H. Doran, 1910.

White, Charles T. *Lincoln and Prohibition*. New York: Abingdon Press, 1921.

White, Dale. *Bat Masterson*. New York: Julian Messner, 1960.

White, Edward G. *The American Judicial Tradition: Profiles of Leading American Judges*. New York: Oxford University Press, 1976.

White, George M. *From Boniface to Bank Burglar*. New York: Seaboard, 1907.

White, Horace. *The Life of Lyman Trumball*. Boston: Houghton Mifflin, 1913.

White, Capt. J.R. *Misfit: An Autobiography*. London: Jonathan Cape, 1930.

White, John, and Kippner, Stanley (eds.). *Future Science: Life Energies and the Physics of Paranormal Phenomena*. New York: Anchor/Doubleday, 1977.

_____ (ed.). *Psychic Exploration: A Challenge to Science*. New York: G.P. Putnam's Sons, 1974.

White, John A. *The Diplomacy of the Russo-Japanese War*. Princeton, N.J.: Princeton University Press, 1964.

_____. *The Siberian Intervention*. Princeton, N.J.: Princeton University Press, 1950.

White, John Baker. *True Blue: An Autobiography, 1902-1939*. London: Frederick Muller, 1970.

White, Judy (ed.). *Chile's Days of Terror: Eyewitness Accounts of the Military Coup*. New York: Pathfinder Press, 1974.

White, Leigh. *The Long Balkan Night*. New York: Charles Scribner's Sons, 1944.

White, Leonard D. *The Federalists: A Study in Administrative History, 1789-1801*. New York: Free Press, 1965.

_____. *The Jacksonians*. New York: Free Press, 1965.

_____. *The Jeffersonians*. New York: Free Press, 1965.

_____. *The Republican Era: 1869-1901: A Study in Administrative History*. New York: Macmillan, 1958.

White, Leslie T. *Me Detective*. New York: Harcourt, Brace, 1936.

White, Mel. *Deceived*. New York: Spire Books, 1979.

White, Michael C. *California All the Way Back to 1828*. Los Angeles: Glen Dawson, 1956.

White, Nathan I. *Harry Dexter White, Loyal American*. Waban, Mass.: n.p., 1956.

White, Osmar. *Green Armour*. Sydney, Aus.: Angus & Robertson, 1942.

White, Owen Payne. *The Autobiography of a Durable Sinner*. New York: G.P. Putnam's Sons, 1942.

_____. *Lead and Likker*. New York: Minton, Balch, 1932.

_____. *My Texas 'Tis of Thee*. New York: G.P. Putnam's Sons, 1936.

_____. *Out of the Desert: The Historical Romance of El Paso*. El Paso, Texas: McMath, 1923.

_____. *Texas, an Informal Biography*. New York: G.P. Putnam's Sons, 1945.

_____. *Them Was the Days; From El Paso to Prohibition*. New York: Minton, Balch, 1925.

_____. *Trigger Fingers*. New York: G.P. Putnam's Sons, 1926.

White, P.S., and Pleasants, H.R. *The War of Four Thousand Years*. Philadelphia: Grifft & Simon, 1846.

White, Ray Lewis (ed.). *Sherwood Anderson's Memoirs: A Critical Edition*. Chapel Hill: University of North Carolina Press, 1969.

White, Robert H. *Tennessee, Its Growth and Progress*. n.p., 1947.

White, Robert W. *The Abnormal Personality: A Textbook*. New York: Ronald Press, 1956.

White, S.E. *Arizona Nights*. New York: McClure, 1907.

White, Stephen. *Should We Now Believe the Warren Report?* New York: Macmillan, 1968.

White, Stewart Edward. *The Unobstructed Universe*. New York: E.P. Dutton, 1940.

White, Theodore H. *Breach of Faith: The Fall of Richard Nixon*. New York: Atheneum, 1975.

_____. *The Making of the President 1960*. New York: Atheneum, 1961.

_____. *The Making of the President 1964*. New York: Atheneum, 1965.

_____. *The Making of the President 1968*. New York: Atheneum, 1969.

_____, and Jacoby, Annalee. *Thunder out of China*. New York: Sloane, 1946.

White, Trumbull. *The Wizard of Wall Street and His Wealth, or the Life and Deeds of Jay Gould*. Chicago: Mid-Continent, 1892.

White, W.F. *How Far the Promised Land?* New York: Viking Press, 1955.

White, W.L. *Bernard Baruch, Portrait of a Citizen*. New York: Harcourt, Brace, 1950.

_____. *They Were Expendable*. Boston: Little, Brown, 1942.

White, Walter Francis. *A Man Called White*. New York: Viking Press, 1948.

White, William Allen. *The Autobiography of William Allen White*. New York: Macmillan, 1946.

_____. *Crimes and Criminals*. New York: Farrar & Rinehart, 1933.

_____. *Forty Years on Main Street*. New York: Farrar & Rinehart, 1937.

_____. *Masks in a Pageant*. New York: Macmillan, 1928.

_____. *A Puritan in Babylon: The Story of Calvin Coolidge*. New York: Macmillan, 1938.

_____. *Woodrow Wilson*. New York: Houghton Mifflin, 1924.

White, William C. *Lenin*. New York: Harrison Smith, 1936.

White, William S. *Citadel*. New York: Harper, 1956.

_____. *The Taft Story*. New York: Harper, 1954.

Whited, Charles. *Chiodo I*. Chicago: Playboy Press, 1974.

Whitehead, Don. *Attack on Terror: The FBI Against the Ku Klux Klan in Mississippi*. New York: Funk & Wagnalls, 1970.

_____. *Borderguard*. New York: McGraw-Hill, 1963.

_____. *The F.B.I. Story*. New York: Random House, 1956.

_____. *Journey Into Crime*. New York: Random House, 1960.

Whitehead, George G. *Clarence Darrow--the Big Minority Man.* Girard, Kan.: Haldeman-Julius, 1931.

_____. *Clarence Darrow: "Evangelist" of Sane Thinking.* Girard, Kan.: Haldeman-Julius, 1931.

Whitehead, Z.W., and McMillan, Hamilton. *The Trial of D.A. McDougald for the Murder of Simeon Conoley.* Fayetteville, N.C.: n.p., 1891.

Whitelaw, David. *Corpus Delicti.* London: Geoffrey Bles, 1936.

Whitelaw, Robert N.S., and Levkoff, Alice F. *Charleston Come Hell or High Water.* Columbia, S.C.: R.L. Bryan, 1975.

Whiteley, C.H. and W.M. *Sex and Morals.* London: Batsford, 1967.

Whiteley, Emily Stone. *Washington and His Aides.* New York: Macmillan, 1936.

Whiteside, Thomas. *Computer Capers: Tales of Electronic Thievery, Embezzlement and Fraud.* New York: Thomas Y. Crowell, 1978.

Whitfield, Stephen J. *Scott Nearing: Apostle of American Radicalism.* New York: Columbia University Press, 1974.

Whiting, Allen S. *Soviet Policies in China, 1917-1924.* New York: Columbia University Press, 1953.

Whiting, B. and J.W.M. *Children of Six Cultures.* Cambridge, Mass.: Harvard University Press, 1975.

Whiting, F.B. *Grit, Grief and Gold: A True Narrative of an Alaskan Pathfinder.* Seattle, Wash.: Peacock, 1933.

Whiting, J.W.M., and Child, I.L. *Child Training and Personality.* New Haven: Yale University Press, 1953.

Whiting, Sweeting. *The Narrative of Whiting Sweeting.* Lansingburg, N.Y.: Sylvester Tiffany, 1791.

Whitlock, Brand. *Belgium: A Personal Narrative.* New York: D. Appleton, 1910.

_____. *Forty Years of It.* New York: D. Appleton, 1914.

_____. *Lafayette.* 2 vols. New York: D. Appleton, 1929.

_____. *The Little Green Shutter.* New York: D. Appleton, 1874.

Whitman, Howard. *Terror in the Streets.* New York: Dial Press, 1951.

Whitman, Sidney. *Reminiscences of the King of Roumania.* New York: Harper & Brothers, 1899.

Whitmore, Richard. *Victorian and Edwardian Crime and Punishment from Old Photographs.* London: Batsford, 1978.

Whitmore, William H. (ed.). *The Andros Tracts.* Boston: Prince Society, 1868-1874.

Whitmore, William H. *The Colonial Laws of Massachusetts.* Boston: Rockwell & Churchill, 1890.

Whitney, Courtney. *MacArthur: His Rendezvous with History.* New York: Alfred A. Knopf, 1956

Whitney, David G. *The American President.* Garden City, N.Y.: Doubleday, 1975.

Whitney, Louisa. *The Burning of the Convent.* Cambridge: Welch, Bigelow, 1877.

Whitney, Richard. *Red in America.* New York: Beckwith, 1924.

_____, and Perkins, William R. *Short Selling - For and Against.* New York: D. Appleton, 1932.

Whitridge, Arnold. *Men in Crisis: The Revolutions of 1848.* New York: Charles Scribner's Sons, 1949.

Whitt, J. Allen. *Urban Elites and Mass Transportation: The Dialectics of Power.* Princeton, N.J.: Princeton University Press, 1982.

Whittemore, L.H. *Cop.* Greenwich, Conn.: Fawcett, 1969.

_____. *The Super Cops.* New York: Bantam, 1973.

Whittemore, Margaret. *One-Way Ticket to Kansas: The Autobiography of Frank M. Stahl.* Lawrence: University of Kansas Press, 1959.

Whittington-Egan, Richard. *A Casebook on Jack the Ripper.* London: Wildy & Sons, 1975.

_____. *Liverpool Colonnade.* London: Philip, Son, Nephew, 1955.

Whittle, Tyler. *The Last Kaiser: A Biography of Wilhelm II.* n.p., n.d.

Whitwell, J.R. *Syphilis in the Earlier Days.* London: H.K. Lewis,

1940.

Who Killed Haddock? The Famous Arensdorf Case. Minneapolis, Minn.: Harrison & Smith, 1888.

The Whole Tiral and Examination of Mrs. Mary Hicks. London: W. Mathews, 1716.

Whymper, Frederick. *Travel and Adventure in the Territory of Alaska.* London: John Murray, 1868.

Whyte, Frederick. *Japan's Purpose in Asia and the Pacific.* Melbourne: Oxford University Press, 1942.

Whyte, William Foote. *Street Corner Society.* Chicago: University of Chicago Press, 1943.

Wibberley, Leonard Patrick O'Connor. *Coming of the Green.* New York: Henry Holt, 1958.

Wice, P.B. *Freedom for Sale: A National Study of Pre-Trial Release.* Lexington, Mass.: Lexington Books, D.C. Heath, 1974.

Wicker, Tom. *Investigating the FBI.* Garden City: Doubleday, 1973.

_____. *On Press.* New York: Viking Press, 1978.

_____. *A Time to Die.* Chicago: Quadrangle Books, 1975.

Wickersham Commission. *Report on Penal Institutions, Probation and Parole.* Washington, D.C.: U.S. Government Printing Office, 1931.

Wickersham, James. *Old Yukon: Tales, Trails and Trials.* Washington D.C.: Washington Law Book, 1938.

Wickes, George. *Americans in Paris.* Garden City, N.Y.: Paris Review Editions, 1969.

Wickler, Wolfgang. *The Sexual Code.* Garden City, N.J.: Doubleday, 1972.

Wickman, Peter, and Whitten, Phillip. *Criminology.* Lexington, Mass.: D.C. Heath, 1980.

Wicksell, Knut. *Lectures on Political Economy.* New York: Macmillan, 1935.

Wickwar, John William. *Witchcraft and the Black Art.* New York: R.M. McBride, 1926.

Wickwar, W. *The Struggle for Freedom of the Press, 1819-1832.* London: George Allen & Unwin, 1928.

Wickwire, Arthur M. *The Weeds of Wall Street.* Philadelphia: John C. Winston, 1932.

Wickwire, Franklin and Mary. *Cornwallis.* Boston: Houghton Mifflin, 1970.

Wiebe, Robert H. *Businessmen and Reform: A Study of the Progressive Movement.* Chicago: Quadrangle Books, 1968.

_____. *The Search for Order: 1877-1920.* New York: Hill & Wang, 1967.

Wiegler, Paul. *William the First: His Life and Times.* trans. and ed. Constance Vesey. London: George Allen & Unwin, 1929.

Wiegman, Carl. *Trees to News: A Chronicle of the Ontario Paper Company's Origin and Development.* Toronto, Ontario, Can.: McClelland & Stewart, 1953.

Wiener, Leo (ed.). *Anthology of Russian Literature From the Earliest Period to the Present Time: The Nineteenth Century.* New York: G.P. Putnam's Sons, 1903.

Wiesenthal, S. *Grossmufti - Grossagent der Achse.* Salzburg, Aust.: Ried, 1947.

Wiet, Gaston. *Les Mosquées du Caire.* Paris: Librarie Hachette, 1966.

Wigdor, A.K., and Garner, W.R. (eds.). *Ability Testing.* Washington, D.C.: National Academy Press, 1982.

Wiggin, Kate Douglas. *My Garden of Memory: An Autobiography.* Boston: Houghton Mifflin, 1923.

Wighton, Charles. *Heydrich: Hitler's Most Evil Henchman.* London: Oldhams Press, 1962.

Wigmore, John H. *The Principles of Judicial Proof.* Boston: Little, Brown, 1931.

_____. *Wigmore on Evidence.* Boston: Little, Brown, 1940.

Wigmore, Lionel. *The Japanese Thrust.* Canberra, Aus.: Australian War Memorial, 1959.

Wilbarger, Josiah W. *Indian Depredations in Texas.* Austin,

Texas: Hutchings Printing House, 1889.

Wilber, E.J., and Eastman, E.P. *A Treatise on Counterfeit, Altered and Spurious Bank Notes.* Poughkeepsie, N.Y.: Published by Authors, 1865.

Wilberforce, Rev. Basil. *Doctors and Brandy.* London: W. Tweedie, 1874.

Wilbour, Charles E. *Trial of Charles M. Jefferds for Murder.* New York: Ross & Tousey, 1862.

Wilbur, Martin, and How, Julie Lien-ying. *Documents on Communism, Nationalism and Societ Advisers in China, 1918-1927.* New York: Columbia University Press, 1958.

Wilbur, Ray Lyman, and Hyde, Arthur Mastick. *The Hoover Policies.* New York: Charles Scribner's Sons, 1937.

Wilbur, Sibyl. *The Life of Mary Baker Eddy.* Boston: Christian Science Publishing Society, 1923.

Wilckes, Frances G. *The Inner World of Childhood.* New York: New American Library, 1966.

Wild, Roland. *Crimes and Cases of 1933.* London: Rich & Cowan, 1934.

_____. *Crimes and Cases of 1934.* London: Rich & Cowan, 1935.

_____, and Curtis-Bennett, D. *Curtis, the Life of Sir Henry Curtis-Bennett.* London: Cassell, 1930.

Wildavsky, Aaron. *Dixon-Yates: a Study in Power Politics.* New Haven: Yale University Press, 1962.

Wilde, Harry. *Politische Morde unserer Zeit.* Frankfurt-am-Main, Ger.: Societäts Verlag, 1966.

Wildeblood, Peter. *Against the Law.* New York: Messner, 1959.

Wilder, Alec. *American Popular Song.* New York: Oxford University Press, 1972.

Wilder, Daniel W. *The Annals of Kansas.* Topeka, Kans.: George W. Martin, 1875.

Wilder, Robert. *Written on the Wind.* G.P. Putnam's Sons, 1945.

Wildes, Harry Emerson. *Typhoon in Tokyo: The Occupation and its Aftermath.* New York: Macmillan, 1954.

Wile, Frederic William. *Men Around the Kaiser.* Philadelphia: J.B. Lippincott, 1913.

Wilensky, H.L. *Intellectuals in Labor Unions: Organizational Pressures on Professional Roles.* Glencoe, Ill.: Free Press, 1956.

_____. *Organizational Intelligence: Knowledge and Policy in Government and Industry.* New York: Basic Books, 1967.

Wiles, P.N.P., and Carson, W.G. (eds.). *Crime and Delinquency in Britain.* London: Martin Robertson, 1970.

Wiley, B.I. *The Life of Billy Yank.* Indianapolis, Ind.: Bobbs-Merrill, 1952.

_____. *The Life of Johnny Reb.* New York: Bobbs-Merrill, 1943.

Wiley, Margaret L. *The Subtle Knot.* Cambridge, Mass.: Harvard University Press, 1952.

Wilhelm, Paul, Duke of Württemberg. *Early Sacramento.* trans. Louis C. Butscher. Sacramento, Calif.: Sacramento Book Collectors Club, 1973.

_____. *Travels in North America, 1822-1824.* trans. W. Robert Nitske. Norman: University of Oklahoma Press, 1973.

Wilhelm, Richard. *The I Ching or Book of Changes.* Princeton, N.J.: Princeton University Press, 1950.

Wilhelm, Stephen R. *Cavalcade of Hooves and Horns.* San Antonio, Texas: Naylor, 1958.

_____. *Texas, Yesterday and Tomorrow.* Houston, Texas: Gulf, 1947.

Wilhelmine, Princess of Prussia. *Friedrich der Grosse in seiner Zeit.* ed. Georg Heinrich. Leipzig, Ger.: Georg Kummers, 1928.

_____. *Memoirs of Frederica Sophia Wilhelmina, Princess Royal of Prussia.* Boston: J.R. Osgood, 1877.

_____. *Memoirs, Written by Herself.* 2 vols. London: H. Colburn, 1812.

Wilkenson, Fred T. *The Realities of Crime and Punishment.* Springfield, Mo.: Mycroft Press, 1972.

Wilkerson, Michael, and Wilkerson, Dick. *Someone Cry for the Children.* New York: Dial Press, 1981.

Wilkes, George. *The Mysteries of the Tombs. A Journal of Thirty Days' Imprisonment in the New York City Prison; For Libel.* New York: n.p., 1844.

Wilkie, Don, and Luther, Mark Lee. *American Secret Service Agent.* New York: Frederick A. Stokes, 1934.

Wilkie, Franc B. *Pen and Powder.* Boston: Ticknor, 1888.

_____. *Personal Reminiscences of Thirty-Five Years of Journalism.* Chicago: F.J. Schulte, 1891.

_____. *Walks About Chicago: 1871-1881.* Chicago: Belford, Clarke, 1882.

Wilkins, Harold T. *Captain Kidd and His Skeleton Island.* London: Cassell, 1935.

Wilkins, Harold T. *Strange Mysteries of Time and Space.* New York: Citadel Press, 1959.

Wilkins, James H. (ed.). *The Great Diamond Hoax and Other Stirring Incidents in the Life of Asbury Harpending.* San Francisco: James H. Barry, 1913.

Wilkins, Leslie. *Delinquent Generations.* London: H.M. Stationery Office, 1960.

_____. *Evaluation of Penal Measures.* New York: Random House, 1969.

_____. *Social Deviance.* London: Tavistock, 1965.

Wilkins, Thurman. *Clarence King.* New York: Macmillan, 1958.

Wilkins, W.H. *Love of an Uncrowned Queen.* London: Longmans, Green, 1900.

Wilkinson, Alec. *Midnights, A Year with the Wellfleet Police.* New York: Random House, 1982.

Wilkinson, Doris Y. (ed.). *Social Structure and Assassination.* New Brunswick, N.J.: Transaction Books, 1976.

Wilkinson, George Theodore. *The Newgate Calendar.* London: Cornish, 1814.

Wilkinson, Sir J. Gardner. *A Popular Account of the Ancient Egyptians.* New York: Crescent Books, 1988.

_____. *Travels in Dalmatia and Montenegro: History of Dalmatia.* London: John Murray, 1848.

Wilkinson, Laurence. *Behind the Face of Crime.* London: Frederick Muller, 1957.

Wilkinson, Paul. *Political Terrorism.* New York: John Wiley & Sons, 1974.

_____. *Terrorism and the Liberal State.* London: Macmillan, 1977.

_____. *Terrorism versus Liberal Democracy: The Problem of Response.* London: Institute for the Study of Conflict, 1976.

Wilks, S., and Bettany, G.T. *Biographical History of Guy's Hospital.* London: Ward Lock, 1892.

Willan, T.S. *The Early History of the Muscovy Company 1553-1603.* Manchester, Eng.: Manchester University Press, 1956.

Willard, Charles Dwight. *The Herald's History of Los Angeles City.* Los Angeles: Kingsley-Barnes & Neuner, 1901.

Willard, David. *History of Greenfield.* Greenfield, Mass.: Kneeland & Eastman, 1838.

Willard, Francis E. *Woman and Temperance: or, the Work and Workers of the Woman's Christian Temperance Movement.* Hartford, Conn.: Park, 1883.

Willard, Josiah Flynt. *My Life.* New York: Outing, 1908.

_____. *Notes of an Itinerant Policeman.* Boston: L.C. Page, 1900.

_____. *Tramping with Tramps.* New York: Century, 1899.

_____. *The World of Graft.* New York: McClure, Phillips, 1901.

Willard, Samuel. *Some Miscellany Observations on Our Present Debates Respecting Witchcraft.* Philadelphia: William Bradford, 1692.

Willcock, H.D., and Stokes, J. *Deterrents and Incentives to Crime Among Youths Ages 15-21.* London: H.M. Stationery Office, 1968.

Willcox, Philip H.A. *"The Detective Physician" The Life and Work of Sir William Willcox.* London: William Heinemann Medical Books, 1970.

Willcox, William. *Portrait of a General.* New York: Alfred A. Knopf, 1964.

Wille, W. *Citizens Who Commit Murder.* St. Louis, Mo.: Warren

Greene, 1974.

Willebrandt, Mabel Walker. *The Inside of Prohibition.* Indianapolis, Ind.: Bobbs-Merrill, 1929.

Willeford, Charles. *Off the Wall.* Montclair, N.J.: Pegasus Rex Press, 1980.

Willemise, Captain Cornelius W. *Behind the Green Lights.* New York: Alfred A. Knopf, 1931.

Willerman, L. *The Psychology of the Individual and Group Differences.* San Francisco: W.H. Freeman, 1979.

Willets, Gilson. *Inside History of the White House.* New York: Christian Herald, 1908.

Willett, T.C. *Criminal on the Road.* London: Tavistock, 1964.

_____. *Drivers after Sentence.* London: Heinemann Educational, 1973.

Willey, Basil. *Seventeenth Century Background.* New York: Columbia University Press, 1952.

Willey, Peter. *The Castles of the Assassins.* London: G.G. Harrap, 1963.

William I, German Emperor and King of Prussia. *The Correspondence of William I and Bismarck, with other Letters from and to Prince Bismarck.* 2 vols. trans. J.A. Ford. London: William Heinemann, 1903.

_____. *Wilhelm's des Grossen, Kaiser, Briefe, Reden und Schriften.* 2 vols. Berlin: E.S. Mittler & Sohn, 1906.

_____. *Wilhelms I: Briefe an seinen Vater König Friedrich Wilhelm III (1827-1839).* Berlin: K. Curtius, 1922.

_____. *Wit and Wisdom of the Late Emperor William.* trans. J. Liebe. London: Ward & Downey, 1888.

William II, German Emperor and King of Prussia. *The Emperor's Speeches: Being a Selection from the Speeches, Edicts, Letters and Telegrams of the Emperor William II.* trans. L. Elkind. London: Longmans, 1904.

_____. *Ereignisse und Gestalten aus den Jahren 1878-1918.* Leipzig, Ger.: K.F. Koehler, 1922.

_____. *The German Emperor as Shown in His Public Utterances.* ed. Christian Gauss. New York: William Heinemann, 1915.

_____. *My Ancestors.* trans. W.W. Zambra. London: William Heinemann, 1929.

_____. *My Early Life.* London: Methuen, 1926.

_____. *The War Lord: A Character Study of Kaiser William II by Means of his Speeches, Letters and Telegrams.* London: F. & C. Palmer, 1914.

William Hohenzollern, former Crown Prince of Germany. *I Seek the Truth: A Book on Responsibility for the War.* trans. Ralph Butler. London: Faber & Gwyer, 1926.

_____. *Ich Suche die Wahrheit!-Ein Buch zur Kriegsschuldfrage.* Stuttgart, Ger.: J.G. Cotta'sche Buchhandlung Nachf., 1925.

_____. *The Memoirs of the Crown Prince of Germany.* London: Thornton Butterworth, 1922.

_____. *My War Experiences.* London: Hurst & Blackett, 1932.

Williams, Albert N. *The Black Hills, Mid-Continent Resort.* Dallas: Southern Methodist University Press, 1952.

_____. *The Holy City.* New York: Duell, Sloan & Pierce, 1954.

Williams Albert Rhys. *Lenin: The Man and His Work.* New York: Scott & Selzer, 1919.

_____. *Through the Russian Revolution.* New York: Boni & Liveright, 1921.

Williams, Alfred B. *Hampton and His Red Shirts.* Charleston, S.C.: Walker, Evans & Cogswell, 1935.

Williams, Amelia W., and Barker, Eugene C. (eds.). *The Writings of Sam Houston.* Austin: University of Texas Press, 1938-1943.

Williams, Brad. *Due Process.* New York: William Morrow, 1960.

_____, and Pepper, Choral. *Lost Legends of the West.* New York: Holt, Rinehart & Winston, 1970.

_____, and _____. *The Mysterious West.* New York: World, 1967.

Williams, Carol M. *The Organization and Practices of Police-women's Division in the United States.* Detroit: National Training School of Public Service, 1946.

Williams, Charlean Moss. *Washington, Hemstead County, Arkansas.* Houston, Texas: Anson-Jones Press, 1951.

Williams, Charles. *Descent into Hell.* New York: Pellegrini & Cudahy, 1949.

_____. *Witchcraft.* London: Faber & Faber, 1941.

Williams, Charlotte. *Hugo L. Black: A Study in the Judicial Process.* Baltimore: Johns Hopkins University Press, 1950.

Williams, David A. *David C. Broderick: A Political Portrait.* San Marino, Calif.: Huntington Library, 1969.

Williams, Edward Bennett. *One Man's Freedom.* New York: Popular Library, 1964.

Williams, Edward Huntington. *Opiate Addiction.* New York: Macmillan, 1922.

Williams, Emma Inman. *Historic Madison: The Story of Jackson and Madison Counties, Tennessee.* Jackson, Tenn.: Madison County Historical Society, 1946.

Williams, Emlyn. *Beyond Belief.* New York: Random House, 1968.

Williams, Eric. *From Columbus to Castro: The History of the Caribbean 1492-1969.* New York: Harper & Row, 1971.

Williams, Frances Leigh. *Plantation Patriot.* New York: Harcourt, Brace & World, 1967.

Williams, Francois. *Fifty Years March - The Rise of the Labor Party.* London: Odhams Press, 1949.

Williams, Frank. *No Fixed Address.* London: W.H. Allen, 1973.

Williams, Franklin. *Negroes With Guns.* New York: Marzani & Munsell, 1962.

Williams, Glanville. *The Proof of Guilt.* London: Stevens & Sons, 1955.

_____. *Salmond on Jurisprudence.* London: Sweet & Maxwell, 1957.

Williams, Guy R. *The Hidden World of Scotland Yard.* London: Hutchinson, 1972.

Williams, H. Noel. *Memoirs of Madame du Barry.* New York: Collier, 1910.

Williams, Harry. *Texas Trails; Legends of the Great Southwest.* San Antonio, Texas: Naylor, 1932.

Williams, Harry T. *Lincoln and the Radicals.* Ann Arbor: University of Wisconsin Press, 1965.

Williams, Henry Llewellyn. *"Buffalo Bill".* London: George Routledge & Sons, 1887.

Williams, Howard. *Superstitions of Witchcraft.* London: Longman, Green, Longman, Roberts, Green, 1865.

Williams, J.S. *Old Times in West Tennessee.* Memphis, Tenn.: W.G. Cheeney, 1873.

Williams, Jack K. *Vogues in Villainy.* Columbia: University of South Carolina Press, 1959.

Williams, Jay R., Redlinger, Lawrence J., and Manning, Peter K. *Police Narcotics Control: Patterns and Strategies.* Washington, D.C.: U.S. Government Printing Office, 1979.

Williams, Jean. *The Lynching of Elizabeth Taylor.* Sante Fe, N.M.: Press of the Territorians, 1967.

_____. *Hume: Portrait of a Couple Murderer.* London: The Windmill Press, 1960.

Williams, John. *A Cop Remembers.* New York: Alfred A. Knopf, 1933.

_____. *Suddenly at the Priory.* London: William Heinemann, 1957.

_____. *Heyday for Assassins.* London: William Heinemann, 1958.

Williams, John Alexander. *West Virginia and the Captains of Industry.* Morgantown: West Virginia University Library, 1976.

Williams, John B. *Vice Control in California.* Beverly Hills, Calif.: Glencoe Press, 1964.

Williams, John G. *The Adventures of a Seventeen-Year-Old Lad and the Fortunes He Might Have Won.* Boston: Collins Press, 1894.

Williams, Justin, Sr. *Japan's Political Revolution Under MacArthur.* Athens: University of Georgia Press, 1979.

Williams, K.P. *Lincoln Finds a General: A Military History of the Civil War.* 4 vols. New York: Macmillan, 1949-56.

Williams, M. Monier. *Religious Thought and Life in India.* London: John Murray, 1891.

Williams, Mary Floyd. *History of the San Francisco Committee on Vigilance of 1851.* Berkeley: University of California Press, 1921.

Williams, Montague. *Later Leaves.* London: Macmillan, 1891.
_____. *Leaves of a Life.* New York: Macmillan, 1890.
_____. *Round London: Down East and Up West.* London: Macmillan, 1892.

Williams, Neville. *Captains Outrageous: Seven Centuries of Piracy.* New York: Macmillan, 1962.
_____. *Henry VIII and His Court.* New York: Macmillan, 1971.

Williams, Judge Oscar Waldo. *A City of Refuge.* n.p., n.d.
_____. *The Old New Mexico, 1879-1880.* n.p., n.d.
_____. *Pioneer Surveyor, Frontier Lawyer: The Personal Narrative of O.W. Williams, 1877-1902.* El Paso: Texas Western College Press, 1966.

Williams, R.H. *With the Border Ruffians.* New York: E.P. Dutton, 1907.

Williams, R. Hal. *The Democratic Party and California Politics: 1880-1896.* Stanford, Calif.: Stanford University Press, 1973.

Williams, Raymond. *The Long Revolution.* London: Chatto & Windus, 1961.

Williams, Robert C. *Culture in Exile: Russian Émigrés in Germany, 1881-1941.* Ithaca, N.Y.: Cornell University Press, 1972.

Williams, Robert H. *Vice Squad.* New York: Thomas Y. Crowell, 1973.

Williams, Roger. *Key into the Language of America.* London: Gregory Dexter, 1643.

Williams, Roger L. *The French Revolution of 1870-1871.* New York: W.W. Norton, 1969.
_____. *Gaslight and Shadow: The World of Napoleon III.* New York: Macmillan, 1957.
_____. *Henri Rochefort: Prince of the Gutter Press.* New York: Charles Scribner's Sons, 1966.
_____. *Manners and Murder in the World of Louis Napoleon.* Seattle: University of Washington Press, 1975.
_____. *The Mortal Napoleon III.* Princeton, N.J.: Princeton University Press, 1971.

Williams, Roger M. *The Super Crooks.* Chicago: Playboy Press, 1973.

Williams, Samuel C. *Dawn of the Tennessee Valley and Tennessee History.* Johnson City, Tenn.: Watauga Press, 1937.

Williams, Thomas Harry. *Lincoln and His Generals.* New York: Alfred A. Knopf, 1952.
_____. *Lincoln and the Radicals.* Madison: University of Wisconsin Press, 1941.

Williams, T. Harry, Richard, N., and Freidel, Frank. *A History of the United States to 1877.* New York: Alfred A. Knopf, 1959.

Williams, T. Harry. *Huey Long.* New York: Alfred A. Knopf, 1969.

Williams, Tennessee. *Memoirs.* New York: Doubleday, 1975.

Williams, Vergil L., and Fish, Mary. *Convicts, Codes, and Contraband: The Prison Life of Men and Women.* Cambridge, Mass.: Ballinger, 1974.

Williams, W.A. *American Russian Relations, 1781-1947.* New York: Rinehart, 1947.

Williams, Walter, and Shoemaker, Floyd Calvin. *Missouri, Mother of the West.* Chicago: American Historical Society, 1930.

Williams, Watkin W. *The Life of General Sir Charles Warren.* Oxford, Eng.: Basil Blackwell, 1941.

Williams, Wayne C. *Williams Jennings Bryan.* New York: G.P. Putnam's Sons, 1936.

Williams, William Appleman. *The Contours of American History.* New York: World, 1961.

Williamson, Chilton. *American Suffrage from Property to Democracy 1760-1800.* Princeton, N.J.: Princeton University Press, 1960.

Williamson, G.A. *The World of Josephus.* London: Secker & Warburg, 1964.

Williamson, Harold F., et. al. *The American Petroleum Industry.* 2 vols. Evanston, Ill.: Northwestern University Press, 1959.
_____. *Edward Atkinson: The Biography of an American Liberal, 1827-1905.* Boston: Old Corner Book Store, 1934.

Williamson, Hugh Ross. *Historical Whodunits.* New York: Macmillan, 1956.

Williamson, James J. *Prison Life in the Old Capitol.* West Orange, N.J.: n.p., 1911.

Williamson, Jeffry G. *American Growth and the Balance of Payments, 1830-1913: A Study of the Long Swing.* Chapel Hill: University of North Carolina Press, 1964.

Williamson, Oliver. *Markets and Hierarchies.* New York: Free Press, 1975.

Williamson, Peter. *The Life and Curious Adventures of Peter Williamson.* Aberdeen: Printed for the Booksellers, 1812.

Williamson, Samuel T. *Frank Gannett.* New York: Duell, Sloan & Pearce, 1940.

Williamson, Thames. *Far North Country.* New York: Duell, Sloan & Pearce, 1944.

Williamson, W.H. *Annals of Crime: Some Extraordinary Women.* London: George Routledge & Sons, 1930.

Williard, James F., and Goodykoontz, Collin B. (eds.). *The Trans-Mississippi West.* Boulder: University of Colorado Press, 1930.

Willis, Carrie Hunter, and Walker, Etta Belle. *Legends of the Skyline Drive and of the Great Valley of Virginia.* Richmond, Va.: Dietz Press, 1937.

Willison, George Finlay. *Here They Dug the Gold.* New York: Brentano's, 1931.
_____. *Saints and Strangers.* New York: Reynal & Hitchcock, 1945.

Willoughby, Charles A., and Chamberlain, John. *MacArthur, 1941-1951.* New York: McGraw-Hill Book, 1954.
_____, *Maneuver in War.* Harrisburg, Pa.: Military Service, 1939.
_____. *Shanghai Conspiracy.* New York: E.P. Dutton, 1952.

Willoughby, Harold R. *Pagan Regeneration.* Chicago: University of Chicago Press, 1929.

Willoughby, Malcolm F. *Rum War at Sea.* Washington D.C.: U.S. Government Printing Office, 1964.

Willoughby, W.W. *Opium as an International Problem.* Baltimore: John Hopkins University Press, 1930.

Willoughby, Westel W. *Japan's Case Examined.* Baltimore: Johns Hopkins Press, 1940.

Wills, C. *Who Killed Keyna?* London: D. Dobson, 1953.

Wills, Garry, and Demaris, Ovid. *Jack Ruby: The Man Who Killed the Man Who Killed Kennedy.* New York: New American Library, 1968.
_____. *Nixon Agonistes.* Boston: Houghton Mifflin, 1970.
_____. *The Second Civil War: Arming for Armageddon.* New York: New American Library, 1968.

Wills, William. *On Principles of Circumstantial Evidence.* London: Butterworth, 1936.

Willson, Clair E. *Mimes and Miners: A Historical Study of the Theater in Tombstone.* Tucson: University of Arizona, 1935.

Willson, Roscoe G. *No Place for Angels.* Phoenix: Arizona Silhouettes, 1958.

Willwerth, James. *Jones, Portrait of a Mugger.* New York: M. Evans, 1974.

Wilmot, Chester. *The Struggle for Europe.* New York: Harper & Brothers, 1952.

Wilson, Sir Arnold T. *The Suez Canal.* London: Oxford, 1939.

Wilson, C. *Anglo-Dutch Commerce and Finance in the Eighteenth Century.* Cambridge, Eng.: Cambridge University Press, 1941.

Wilson, C.F. *Violence Against Women: An Annotated Bibliography.* Boston: G.K. Hall, 1981.

Wilson, Carlos. *The Tupamaros: The Unmentionables.* Boston: Branden Press, 1974.

Wilson, Carol Green. *Chinatown Quest: The Life and Adventure of Donaldina Cameron.* Stanford, Calif.: Stanford University Press, 1931.

Wilson, Charles. *Anglo-Dutch Commerce and Finance in the Eighteenth Century.* Cambridge, Eng.: Cambridge University Press, 1941.

Wilson, Colin. *A Casebook of Murder.* New York: Cowles, 1970.

_____. *A Criminal History of Mankind.* London: Granada, 1984.

_____, and Pitman, Patricia. *The Encyclopedia of Murder.* New York: G.P. Putnam's Sons, 1961.

_____, and Seaman, Donald. *Encyclopedia of Modern Murder, 1962-1982.* New York: G.P. Putnam's Sons, 1985.

_____. *Mysteries.* New York: Perigee, 1978.

_____. *The Occult.* New York: Random House, 1971.

_____. *Order of Assassins: The Psychology of Murder.* London: Rupert Hart-Davis, 1972.

_____. *Rasputin and the Fall of the Romanovs.* New York: Farrar Straus, 1964.

_____. *Ritual in the Dark.* Boston: Houghton Mifflin, 1960.

_____. *Witches.* New York: Crescent Books, 1981.

Wilson, D. *Henrietta Robinson.* New York: Auburn, Miller, Orton & Mulligan, 1855.

Wilson, Don W. *Governor Charles Robinson of Kansas.* Wichita: University of Kansas Press, 1975.

Wilson, Dorothy Clarke. *Lone Woman: The Story of Elizabeth Blackwell, the First Woman Doctor.* Boston: Little, Brown, 1970.

Wilson, Edith Bolling. *My Memoir.* New York: Bobbs-Merrill, 1938.

Wilson, Edmund. *The American Earthquake.* New York: Doubleday, 1958.

_____. *The American Jitters.* New York: Charles Scribner's Sons, 1932.

_____. *Axel's Castle.* London: Fontana, 1961.

_____. *I Thought of Daisy.* New York: Charles Scribner's Sons, 1929.

_____. *Patriotic Gore.* New York: Galaxie, 1966.

_____. *The Shores of Light.* New York: Farrar, Straus, Young, 1952.

_____. *The Twenties.* New York: Farrar, Straus & Giroux, 1975.

_____. *To the Finland Station.* New York: Harcourt, Brace, 1940.

Wilson, Edward. *An Unwritten History: A Record from the Exciting Days of Early Arizona.* Phoenix, Ariz.: McNeill, 1915.

Wilson, Edward O. *Sociobiology.* Cambridge, Mass.: Harvard University Press, 1975.

Wilson, F.M. Huntington. *Memoirs of an Ex-Diplomat.* Boston: Bruce Humphries, 1945.

Wilson, Forrest. *Crusader in Crinoline. The Life of Harriet Beecher Stowe.* Philadelphia: J.B. Lippincott, 1941.

Wilson, Francis. *John Wilkes Booth: Fact and Fiction of Lincoln's Assassination.* Boston: Houghton Mifflin, 1929.

Wilson, Frank J., and Day, Beth. *Special Agent.* New York: Holt, Rinehart & Winston, 1965.

Wilson, G., and Nias, D. *Love's Mysteries.* London: Open Books, 1976.

Wilson, Gordon. *Passing Institutions: A Series of Essays About Things We Used to Know.* Cynthiana, Ky.: Privately Published, 1943.

Wilson, H.B. *American Ambassadors to England, 1785-1928.* London: John Murray, 1928.

Wilson, H.W. *The Downfall of Spain: Naval History of the Spanish-American War.* London: Low, Marston, 1900.

Wilson, Harry Leon. *Ma Pettingill.* Garden City, N.Y.: Doubleday, Doran, 1919.

Wilson, Henry. *History of the Rise and Fall of the Slave Power in America.* 3 vols. Boston: Houghton Mifflin, 1872.

Wilson, Henry Lane. *Diplomatic Episodes in Mexico, Belgium, and Chile.* Garden City, New York: Doubleday, Page, 1927.

Wilson, J.C. (ed.). *An American Textbook of Applied Therapeutics.* Philadelphia: W.B. Saunders, 1896.

Wilson, James. *Capital, Currency and Banking.* London: Economist, 1847.

Wilson, James Grant. *Memorial History of the City of New York.* New York: New York History, 1893.

Wilson, James Q. *The Amateur Democrat: Club Politics in Three Cities.* Chicago: University of Chicago Press, 1962.

_____, and Herrnstein, Richard J. *Crime and Human Nature.* New York: Simon & Schuster, 1985.

_____ (ed.). *Crime and Public Policy.* San Francisco: Institute for Contemporary Studies Press, 1983.

_____. *The Investigators: Managing FBI and Narcotics Agents.* New York: Basic Books, 1978.

_____. *Thinking About Crime.* New York: Basic Books, 1976.

_____. *Varieties of Police Behavior.* Cambridge, Mass.: Harvard University Press, 1968.

Wilson, Jerry. *Police Report.* Boston: Little, Brown, 1975.

Wilson, Joan Hoff. *Herbert Hoover: Forgotten Progressive.* Boston: Little, Brown, 1975.

Wilson, John. *Equality.* New York: Harcourt, Brace & World, 1966.

Wilson, John A. *The Culture of Ancient Egypt.* Chicago: University of Chicago Press, 1951.

Wilson, John Gray. *Not Proven.* London: Secker & Warburg, 1960.

_____. *The Trial of Peter Manuel.* London: Secker & Warburg, 1959.

Wilson, John Harold. *All the King's Ladies: Actresses of the Restoration.* Chicago: University of Chicago Press, 1958.

Wilson, John Harold. *Nell Gwyn.* New York: Pellegrini & Cudahy, 1952.

Wilson, Joseph G. *Are Prisons Necessary?* Philadelphia: Dorrance, 1950.

Wilson, Lawrence. *The Incredible Kaiser: A Portrait of William II.* London: Robert Hale, 1963.

Wilson, N. *Belgrade: The White City of Death.* n.p., 1903.

Wilson, Nanci Koser. *Risk Ratios in Juvenille Deliquency.* Ann Arbor, Mich.: University Microfilms, 1972.

Wilson, Neill Compton (ed.). *Deep Roots: The History of Blake, Moffitt, and Towne, Pioneers in Paper Since 1855.* San Francisco: Privately Printed, 1955.

_____. *400 California Street: A Century Plus Five.* San Francisco: Bank of California, 1969.

_____. *Silver Stampede.* New York: Macmillan, 1936.

_____. *Silver Stampede, the Career of Death Valley's Hell-Camp.* New York: Macmillan, 1937.

_____, and Taylor, Frank J. *Southern Pacific: The Roaring Story of a Fighting Railroad.* New York: McGraw-Hill Book, 1952.

_____. *Treasure Express: Epic Days of the Wells Fargo.* New York: Macmillan, 1936.

Wilson, Orlando W. (ed.). *Parker on Police.* Springfield, Ill.: Charles C. Thomas, 1957.

_____. *Police Administration.* New York: McGraw-Hill, 1950.

_____. *Police Planning.* Springfield, Ill.: Thomas, 1968.

_____. *Power in the City: Decision Making in San Francisco.* Berkeley: University of California Press, 1974.

Wilson, Patrick. *Children Who Kill.* London: Michael Joseph, 1973.

_____. *Murderesses: A Study of the Women Executed in Britain Since 1843.* London: Michael Joseph, 1971.

Wilson, R.L. *The Colt Heritage.* New York: Simon & Schuster, 1979.

Wilson, Rufus Rockwell, and Sears, Ethel M. *History of Grant County, Kansas.* Wichita, Kan.: Wichita Press, 1950.

_____. *Intimate Memoires of Lincoln.* Elmira, N.Y.: Primavera Press, 1945.

_____. *Lincoln among his Friends.* Caldwell, Idaho: Caxton Printers, 1942.

_____. *Lincoln in Caricature.* New York: Horizon Press, 1953.

_____. *New York in Literature.* Elmira, N.Y.: Primavera Press, 1947.

_____. *New York: Old and New.* Philadelphia: J.B. Lippincott, 1902.

_____. *Out of the West.* New York: Press of the Pioneers, 1933.

Wilson, Samuel Payntor. *Chicago and Its Cesspools of Vice and Infamy.* Chicago: n.p., 1910.

Wilson, Thomas. *Bluebeard: A Contribution to Historical Folklore.* New York: G.P. Putnam's Sons, 1897.

Wilson, Thomas, and Skinner, Andrew S. (eds.). *The Market and the State: Essays in Honour of Adam Smith.* Oxford, Eng.: Oxford University Press, 1976.

Wilson, Woodrow E. *George Washington.* New York: Harper & Brothers, 1896.

_____. *A History of the American People.* 10 vols. New York: Harper & Brothers, 1917-1918.

_____. *A New American History.* Garden City, N.Y.: Garden City, 1938.

The Public Papers of Woodrow Wilson. New York: Harper & Brothers, 1925-27.

_____. *Robert E. Lee: an Interpretation.* Chapel Hill: University of North Carolina Press, 1924.

Wilstach, Frank J. *The Plainsman Wild Bill Hickok.* Garden City, N.Y.: Sun Dial Press, 1937.

_____. *Wild Bill Hickok, the Prince of Pistoleers.* New York: Doubleday, Page, 1926.

Wilston, Robert. *The Last Days of the Romanovs.* London: Thorton Butterworth, 1920.

Wilton, G.W. *Fingerprints: History, Law and Romance.* London: William Hodge, 1938.

Wiltse, C.M. *Calhoun.* 3 vols. Indianapolis, Ind.: Bobbs-Merrill, 1944-51.

Wiltz, John E. *In Search of Peace: The Senate Munitions Inquiry, 1934-1936.* Baton Rouge: Louisiana State University Press, 1963.

Winant, Lewis. *Firearms Curiosa.* New York: Bonanza Books, 1955.

Winch, Frank. *Thrilling Lives of Buffalo Bill.* New York: S.L. Parsons, 1911.

Winch, R.F. *Familial Organization: A Quest for Determinants.* New York: Free Press, 1977.

Winchell, Lilbourne Alsip. *History of Fresno County, and the San Joaquin Valley.* Fresno, Calif.: A.H. Cawston, 1933.

Winder, W.H.D. *Stephen's Commentaries on the Law of England.* London: Butterworth, 1959.

Windsor, Dean of, and Bolitho, Hector (eds.). *Later Letters of Lady Augusta Stanley 1864-1876.* London: Jonathan Cape, 1929.

Windsor, Edward, Duke of. *A King's Story.* New York: G.P. Putnam's Sons, 1947.

Wines, E.C. *Punishment and Reformation.* New York: Thomas Y. Crowell, 1895.

_____. *Report on Prisons and Reformatories of the United States and Canada.* New York: State Assembly Document No. 35, 1867.

_____. *The State of Prisons and Child-Saving Institutions in the Civilized World.* Cambridge. Mass.: J. Wilson & Sons, 1880.

Wines, Frederick Howard. *Punishment and Reformation.* New York: Thomas Y. Crowell, 1919.

Winfield, Gerald F. *China: The Land and the People.* New York: Sloan and American Institute of Pacific Relations, 1948.

Wingate, General George W. *History of the Twenty-Second Regiment of the National Guard of the State of New York from Its Organization to 1895.* New York: Edwin W. Dayton, 1896.

Wingate, Sir Reginald. *Mahdiism and the Egytian Sudan.* London: Macmillan, 1891.

Winget, Dan. *Anecdotes of Buffalo Bill.* Chicago: Historical, 1927.

Winick, Charles, and Kinsie, Paul M. *The Lively Commerce: Prostitution in the U.S.* Chicago: Quadrangle Books, 1971.

Winkler, C. *Die Hexenprozesse in Türkheim.* Colmar, Fr.: F. Waldmeyer, 1904.

Winkler, F. *Die Diktatur in Oesterreich.* Zurich, Switz.: O. Fuessli, 1935.

Winkler, Franz. *About Marijuana.* New York: Myrin Institute, 1970.

Winkler, John K. *Morgan the Magnificent.* New York: Vanguard Press, 1930.

_____. *William Randolph Hearst: An American Phenomenon.* New York: Simon & Schuster, 1928.

_____. *William Randolph Hearst: A New Appraisal.* New York: Hastings House, 1955.

Winkler, Max. *Foreign Bonds, an Autopsy: A Study of Defaults and Repudiations of Government Obligations.* Philadelphia: Roland Swain, 1933.

Winkley, J.W. *John Brown the Hero.* Boston: James K. West, 1905.

Winks, Robin W. *Canada and the United States: The Civil War Years.* Baltimore: Johns Hopkins University Press, 1960.

Winks, Robin W. (ed.). *The Historian as Detective: Essays on Evidence.* New York: Harper & Row, 1968.

Winn, D. *Prostitutes.* London: Hutchinson, 1974.

Winn, Dilys. *Murder, Inc.* New York: Workman Press, 1977.

Winn, Mary Day. *The Macadam Trail: Ten Thousand Miles by Motor Coach.* New York: Alfred A. Knopf, 1931.

Winn, Steven, and Merrill, David. *Ted Bundy: The Killer Next Door.* New York: Bantam, 1980.

Winslade, William J., and Ross, Judith Wilson. *The Insanity Plea.* New York: Charles Scribner's Sons, 1983.

Winslow, John H. *Darwin's Victorian Malady.* Philadelphia: American Philosophical Society, 1971.

Winslow, Kathryn. *Big Pan-Out.* New York: W.W. Norton, 1951.

Winslow, Lyttleton Stewart Forbes. *Recollections of Forty Years: Being an Account at First Hand of Some Famous Criminal Lunacy Cases...* London: John Ousley, 1910.

Winslow, O.E. *Master Roger Williams.* New York: Macmillan, 1957.

Winslow, Robert. *Society in Transition: A Social Approach to Deviancy.* New York: Free Press, 1970.

Winsor, Justin. *The Mississippi Basin: The Struggle Between England and France.* Boston: Houghton Mifflin, 1898.

_____. *Narrative and Critical History of America.* New York: Houghton Mifflin, 1889.

_____. *The Westward Movement.* Boston: Houghton Mifflin, 1899.

Winston, Alexander. *No Man Knows My Grave.* Boston: Houghton Mifflin, 1969.

Winston, Richard. *Thomas Becket.* New York: Alfred A. Knopf, 1967.

Winston, Robert W. *Andrew Johnson, Plebian and Patriot.* New York: Henry Holt, 1928.

Wint, Guy, and Calvocaressi, Peter. *Middle East Crisis.* Baltimore: Penguin, 1957.

Winter-Berger, Robert N. *The Gerald Ford Letters.* N.J.: Lyle Stuart, 1974.

Winter-Berger, Robert N. *The Washington Pay-Off.* New York: Dell, 1972.

Winter, Ella. *And Not to Yield.* New York: Harcourt, Brace & World, 1963.

Winter, Ella, and Hicks, Granville (eds.). *The Letters of Joseph Lincoln Steffens.* 2 vols. New York: Harcourt, Brace, 1938.

Winter, Lumen, and Degner, Glenn. *Minute Epics of Flight.* New York: Grosset & Dunlap, 1933.

Winter, William. *Vagrant Memories.* New York: George H. Doran, 1915.

Winterbotham, F.W. *The Ultra Secret.* New York: Harper & Row, 1974.

Winterich, John T. *Twenty-Three Books and the Stories Behind Them.* Philadelphia: J.B. Lippincott, 1939.

Winther, Oscar Osburn. *The Great Northwest: A History.* New York: Alfred A. Knopf, 1947.

_____. *The Old Oregon Country: A History of Frontier Trade, Transportation, and Travel*. Palo Alto, Calif.: Stanford University Press, 1950.

_____. *The Transportation Frontier; Trans-Mississippi West, 1865-1890*. New York: Rinehart & Winston, 1964.

_____. *Via Western Express & Stagecoach*. Palo Alto, Calif.: Stanford University Press, 1945.

Winthrop Family. *Correspondence of the Winthrop Family*. Boston: Massachusetts Historical Society, 1929.

Winthrop, John. *The History of New England*. Boston: Little, Brown, 1853.

Winthrop, Theodore. *Life in the Open Air, and Other Papers*. Boston: Ticknor & Fields, 1863.

Winthrop, W.W. *Military Law*. Washington, D.C.: J.J. Chapman, 1893.

_____. *Military Law and Precedents*. Washington, D.C.: U.S. Government Printing Office, 1920.

Winwar, Frances. *Gallows Hill*. New York: Henry Holt, 1937.

_____. *Oscar Wilde and the Yellow Nineties*. New York: Harper & Brothers, 1941.

_____. *The Saint and the Devil: Joan of Arc and Gilles de Rais*. New York: Harper, 1948.

Wirth, Louis. *The Ghetto*. Chicago: University of Chicago Press, 1928.

_____, and Bernert, Eleanor H. (eds.). *Local Community Fact Book of Chicago*. Chicago: University of Chicago Press, 1949.

_____, and Furez, Margaret (eds.). *Local Community Fact Book, 1938*. Chicago: Chicago Recreation Commission, 1938.

Wirth, Max. *Geschichte der Handelskrisen*. New York: Burt Franklin, 1968.

Wisan, Joseph E. *The Cuban Crisis as Reflected in the New York Press, 1895-1898*. New York: Columbia University Press, 1934.

Wisconsin. Legislative Reference Library. *Capital Punishment in the States with Special Reference to Wisconsin*. Madison: State of Wisconsin, 1962.

Wise, Dan, and Maxfield, Marietta. *The Day Kennedy Died*. San Antonio, Texas: Naylor, 1964.

Wise, David. *The American Police State*. New York: Random House, 1976.

_____, and Ross, Thomas B. *The Espionage Establishment*. New York: Random House, 1967.

_____. *The Invisible Government*. New York: Random House, 1967.

_____. *The Politics of Lying: Government Deception, Secrecy and Power*. New York: Vintage Books, 1973.

Wise, Jennings C. *Woodrow Wilson, Disciple of Revolution*. New York: Paisley Press, 1938.

Wise, John S. *The End of an Era*. Boston: Houghton Mifflin, 1899.

Wisehart, David. *The Fur Trade of the American West, 1807-1840*. Lincoln: University of Nebraska Press, 1979.

Wisehart, M.K. *Sam Houston: American Giant*. Washington D.C.: Robert B. Luce, 1962.

Wiseley, William. *A Tool of Power: The Political History of Money*. New York: Wiley-Interscience, 1977.

Wiseman, Jacqueline. *Stations of the Lost*. Englewood Cliffs, N.J.: Prentice-Hall, 1970.

Wish, Harvey. *Society and Thought in Modern America*. New York: Longmans, Green, 1952.

Wishard, William R. *Rights of the Elderly and Retired*. San Francisco: Cragmont, 1978.

Wishman, Seymour. *Confessions of a Criminal Lawyer*. New York: Penguin, 1981.

Wishy, B. *The Child and the Republic*. Philadelphia: University of Pennsylvania Press, 1968.

Wiskemann, Elizabeth. *Europe of the Dictators*. London: Collins (Fontana), 1966.

_____. *Italy Since 1945*. New York: St. Martin's, 1971.

_____. *The Rome-Berlin Axis*. London: Collins, 1969.

_____. *Undeclared War*. London: Constable, 1939.

Wismes, Armel de. *Nantes et le Pays Nantais*. Nantes, Fr.: Editions France-Empire, n.d.

Wisotsky, Steven. *Breaking the Impasse in the War on Drugs*. Westport, Conn.: Greenwood, 1987.

Wissler, Clark. *The American Indian*. New York: Oxford University Press, 1938.

Wister, Fanny Kemble (ed.). *Owen Wister Out West: His Journals and Letters*. Chicago: University of Chicago Press, 1958.

Wister, Owen. *Lady Baltimore*. New York: Macmillan, 1906.

_____. *Roosevelt, The Story of a Friendship*. New York: Macmillan, 1930.

_____. *The Virginian*. New York: Macmillan, 1902.

The Witch of Wapping. London: T. Spring, 1652.

Witchcraft in Old and New England. Cambridge, Mass.: Harvard University Press, 1929.

Witcher, W.C. *The Reign of Terror in Oklahoma*. Fort Worth, Texas: Published by Author, 1923.

_____. *The Unveiling of the Ku Klux Klan*. Fort Worth, Texas: American Constitutional League, 1922.

Witches Apprehended, Examined and Executed. London: E. Marchant, 1613.

Witches of Northhamptonshire. London: T. Purfoot, A. Johnson, 1612.

Witcover, Jules. *Marathon: The Pursuit of the Presidency, 1972-1976*. New York: Viking Press, 1977.

Witekind, Hermann. *Christlich Bedencken und Erinnerung von Zauberey*. Basel, Switz.: Gertruckdt durch Sebastianum Henricpetri, 1593.

With the I.R.A. in the Fight for Freedom. Tralee, Ire.: Kerryman, n.d.

With the Pinkertons. New York: McFadden, 1940.

Withers, William. *Freedom Through Power*. New York: John Day, 1965.

Witkamp, F.T. *The Refugee Problem in the Middle East*. The Hague, Neth.: Research Group for European Migration Problem, 1957.

Witkin, H., et al. *Psychological Differentiation: Studies in Development*. New York: John Wiley & Sons, 1962.

Witmer, Helen L., and Tufts, Edith. *The Effectiveness of Delinquency Prevention Programs*. Washington, D.C.: U.S. Government Printing Office, 1954.

_____, and Kotinsky, Ruth, (eds.). *New Perspectives for Research on Juvenile Delinquency*. Washington, D.C.: U.S. Government Printing Office, 1956.

_____ (ed.). *Parents and Delinquency*. Washington, D.C.: Department to Health, Education, and Welfare, 1954.

Witte, Count Sergius. *Memoirs*. trans. Abraham Yarmolinsky. New York: Doubleday, Page, 1921.

Wittenborn, J.R., et al. (eds.). *Drugs and Youth: Proceedings of the Rutgers Symposium on Drug Abuse*. Springfield, Ill.: Charles C. Thomas, 1969.

Wittenmyer, Annie. *History of the Woman's Temperance Crusade*. Philadelphia, Pa.: Office of Christian Women, 1878.

Witters, Weldon L., and Jones-Witters, Patricia. *Drugs and Sex*. New York: Published by Author, 1975.

Wittgenstein, Ludwig. *Lectures and Conversations on Aesthetics, Psychology and Religious Belief*. Berkeley: University of California Press, 1966.

Wittke, Carl F. *The Irish in America*. Baton Rouge: Louisiana State University Press, 1956.

_____. *We Who Built America: The Saga of the Immigrant*. New York: Prentice-Hall, 1939.

Wittrock, M., and Wiley, D. (eds.). *The Evaluation of Instruction*. New York: Holt, Rinehart, Winston, 1970.

Wofford, Harris. *Of Kennedys and Kings*. New York: Farrar, Straus, Giroux, 1980.

Wohl, A.S. *The Eternal Slum: Housing and Social Policy in Victorian London*. London: Edward Arnold, 1977.

Woldman, Albert A. *Lincoln and the Russians.* New York: Collier Books, 1961.

Wolf, Eric R. *Sons of the Shaking Earth.* Chicago: University of Chicago Press, 1959.

Wolf, George. *Frank Costello.* New York: William Morrow, 1974.

Wolf, John B. *Louis XIV.* New York: W.W. Norton, 1968.

Wolf, Leonard. *Bluebeard.* New York: Potter, 1980.

_____. *A Dream of Dracula.* Boston: Little, Brown, 1972.

_____ (ed.). *The Uses of the Present.* New York: McGraw-Hill Book, 1970.

Wolf, Marvin J., and Mader, Katherine. *Fallen Angels.* New York: Facts on File, 1986.

Wolfe, Alan. *The Seamy Side of Democracy: Repression in America.* New York: David McKay, 1973.

Wolfe, Bertram D. *Communist Totalitarianism.* Boston: Beacon Press, 1961.

_____. *Krushchev and Stalin's Ghost.* New York: Frederick A. Praeger, 1957.

_____. *Marxism: 100 Years in the Life of a Doctrine.* New York: Dell, 1967.

_____. *Three Who Made A Revolution: Lenin, Trotsky, Stalin.* New York: Dial Press, 1948.

Wolfe, Burton H. *Pileup on Death Row.* Garden City, N.Y.: Doubleday, 1973.

Wolfe, H. Ashton. *The Thrill of Evil.* London: Hurst & Blackett, n.d.

_____. *The Underworld.* London: Hurst & Blackett, n.d.

Wolfe, James Raymond. *Secret Writing.* New York: McGraw-Hill, 1970.

Wolfe, John B. *Louis XIV.* New York: W.W. Norton, 1968.

Wolfe, W.C. (ed.). *Men of California.* San Francisco: Western Press Reporter, 1925.

Wolfenden, John, et al. *Report of the Departmental Committee on Homosexual Offences and Prostitution.* London: H.M. Stationery Office, 1956.

Wolfenstein, Martha, and Kliman, Gilbert. *Children and the Death of a President.* Garden City, N.Y.: Doubleday Anchor, 1966.

Wolfers, Arnold. *Discord and Collabration: Essays on International Politics.* Baltimore: Johns Hopkins Press, 1962.

Wolff, Albert. *Mémoires d'un Parisien.* Paris: V. Havard, 1884-88.

Wolff, Anthony. *Unreal Estate.* Los Angeles: Sierra Club, 1974.

Wolff, Geoffrey. *Black Sun: The Brief Transit and Violent Eclipse of Harry Crosby.* New York: Random House, 1976.

Wolff, H.D. *Rambling Recollections.* London: Macmillan, 1908.

Wolff, Leon. *Little Brown Brother: America's Forgotten Bid for Empire which Cost 250,000 Lives.* London: Longmans, Green, 1961.

Wolff, Leon. *Lockout: The Story of the Homestead Strike.* New York: Harper & Row, 1965.

Wolff, Robert Lee. *The Balkans in Our Times.* Cambridge, Mass: Harvard University Press, 1956.

_____. *Byzantine and Modern Greek Studies: Essays Presented to Sir Steven Runciman.* Oxford, Eng.: Basil Blackwell, 1978.

Wolff, Robert Paul. *In Defense of Anarchism.* New York: Harper & Row, 1970.

Wolff, W. *The Expression of Personality.* New York: Harper, 1945.

Wolfgang, Marvin E. *Crime and Race.* New York: Institute of Human Relations Press, 1964.

_____, Figlio, R.M., and Sellin, T. *Delinquency in a Birth Cohort.* Chicago: University of Chicago Press, 1972.

_____, et al. *Evaluating Criminology.* New York: Elsevier, 1978.

_____. *Patterns in Criminal Homicide.* Philadelphia: University of Pennsylvania Press, 1958.

_____, Savitz, Leonard, and Johnston, Norman (eds.). *The Sociology of Crime and Delinquency.* New York: John Wiley & Sons, 1970.

_____. *Studies in Homicide.* New York: Harper & Row, 1967.

_____, and Ferracuti, Franco. *The Subculture of Violence: Towards an Integrated Theory in Criminology.* Newbury, Calif.: Sage, 1982.

Wolfle, Joan L., and Heaphy, John. (eds.). *Readings on Productivity in Policing.* Washington, D.C.: Police Foundation, 1975.

Wolfskill, George. *The Revolt of the Conservatives.* Boston: Houghton Mifflin, 1962.

Wolin, Simon, and Slusser, Robert M. (eds.). *The Soviet Secret Police.* New York: Frederick A. Praeger, 1957.

Wolle, Muriel Sibell. *The Bonanza Trail, Ghost Towns and Mining Camps of the West.* Bloomington: Indiana University Press, 1953.

_____. *Montana Pay Dirt: A Guide to the Mining Camps of the Treasure State.* Denver: Sage Books, 1963.

_____. *Stampede to Timberline, the Ghost Towns and Mining Camps of Colorado.* Denver: Artcraft Press, 1949.

Wollenberg, Charles M. *All Deliberate Speed: Segregation and Exclusion in California Schools, 1855-1975.* Berkeley: University of California Press, 1976.

Wolman, Benjamin B. (ed.). *Handbook of Parapsychology.* New York: Van Nostrand Reinhold, 1978.

Wolseley, Vicompte. *Le déclin et la chute de Napoléon.* Paris: Ollendorff, 1894.

Wolsey, Serge G. *Call House Madam.* San Francisco: Martin Tudordale, 1942.

Wolstenholme, G.E.W., and Knight, Julie (eds.). *Hashish.* London: J. & A. Churchill, 1965.

Womack, John, Jr. *Zapata and the Mexican Revolution.* New York: Alfred A. Knopf, 1968.

The Wonderful Discovery of the Witchcrafts of Margaret and Philip Flower. London: G. Eld, I. Barnes, 1619.

Wong, K.C., and Lien-Teh, W. *History of Chinese Medicine.* Shanghai, China: National Quarantine Service, 1936.

Wood, Arthur. *Criminal Lawyer.* New Haven, Conn.: College & University Press, 1967.

Wood, Clive, and Suitters, Beryl. *The Fight For Acceptance.* Aylesbury, Eng.: Medical and Technical, 1970.

Wood, Elmer. *English Theories of Central Banking Control, 1819-1858.* Cambridge, Mass.: Harvard University Press, 1939.

Wood, Fernando. *Oration Delivered by Hon. Fernando Wood, on the Anniversary of Washington's Birthday, February 22, 1862, at Scranton, Pa.* New York: George H. Clark, 1862.

Wood, Frederick S. (ed.). *Roosevelt as We Knew Him.* New York: John C. Winston, 1927.

Wood, Fremont. *The Introductory Chapter to the History of the Trials of Moyer, Haywood, and Pettibone, and Harry Orchard.* Caldwell, Idaho: Caxton Printers, 1931.

Wood, George B., and Bache, Franklin. *The Dispensatory of the United States.* Philadelphia: J.B. Lippincott, 1899.

Wood, Jim. *The Rape of Inez Garcia.* New York: G.P. Putman's Sons, 1976.

Wood, John Maxwell. *Witchcraft and Superstitious Record in The Southwestern District of Scotland.* Dumfries, Scot.: J. Maxwell & Sons, 1911.

Wood, Jones F. *The Principles of Anatomy as Seen in the Hand.* London: J. & A. Churchill, 1920.

Wood, Margaret M. *Paths of Loneliness.* New York: Columbia University Press, 1953.

Wood, R.E. *Life and Confessions of James Gilbert Jenkins.* Napa City, Calif.: C.H. Allen, 1864.

Wood, Raymund F. *California's Agua Fria: The Early History of Mariposa County.* Fresno, Calif.: Academy Library Guild, 1954.

Wood, Richard Coke. *Calaveras, the Land of Skulls.* Sonora, Calif.: Mother Lode Press, 1955.

_____. *Murphys, Queen of the Sierra: A History of Murphys, Calaveras County, California.* Angel's Camp, Calif.: Calaveras Californian, n.d.

Wood, Richard G. *Stephen Harriman Long, 1784-1864.* Glendale, Calif.: Arthur H. Clark, 1966.

Wood, W.B., and Edmonds, J.S. *Military History of the Civil War.* New York: G.P. Putnam's Sons, 1937.

Wood, Walter (ed.). *Survivor's Tales of Famous Crimes.* London: Cassell, 1916.

Woodall, William Otter (ed.). *A Collection of Reports of Famous Trials.* London: Shaw & Sons, 1873.

Woodberry, George E. *The Life of Edgar Allan Poe.* Boston: n.p., 1885.

Woodbridge, John. *Severals Relating to a Fund.* Boston: Samuel Green, 1682.

Woodbury, George. *The Great Days of Piracy.* New York: W.W. Norton, 1951.

Woodcock, George. *The Anarchist Prince.* London: T.V. Boardman, 1950.

Wooden, Kenneth. *The Children of Jonestown.* New York: McGraw-Hill, 1981.

_____. *Weeping in the Playtime of Others.* New York: McGraw-Hill, 1976.

Woodford, Howard J. *Mr. Justice Murphy: A Political Biography.* Princeton, N.J.: Princeton University Press, 1968.

Woodhall, Edwin T. *Crime and the Supernatural.* London: Long, 1935.

_____. *Detective and Secret Service Days.* London: Jarrolds, 1929.

_____. *Jack the Ripper: or When London Walked in Terror.* London: Mellifont Press, 1937.

_____. *Secrets of Scotland Yard.* London: The Bodley Head, 1936.

Woodham-Smith, Cecil. *The Great Hunger.* New York: Harper, 1962.

Woodhouse, Christopher M. *The Greek War of Independence: Its Historical Setting.* London: Hutchinson, 1952.

Woodhull, Victoria C. *The Elixir of Life.* New York: Woodhull & Claflin, 1873.

Woodland, W. Lloyd. *Assize Pageant: Fifty Years in the Criminal Courts.* London: George G. Harrap, 1952.

Woodley, Richard A. *Dealer: Portrait of a Cocaine Merchant.* New York: Holt, Rinehart, Winston, 1971.

Woodmason, Charles. *The Carolina Backcountry on the Eve of the Revolution.* Chapel Hill: University of North Carolina Press, 1953.

Woodruff, Douglas. *The Tichborne Claimant.* London: Hullis & Charter, 1967.

Woodruff, Ephraim T. *The Sovereignty of God.* Warren, Ohio: Hapgood & Sprague, 1820.

Woodruff, Leonard. *The Infernal Machine, Trial of William Arrison.* Cincinnati, Ohio: H.H. Robinson, 1854.

Woodruff, Philip. *The Men Who Ruled India.* London: Jonathan Cape, 1953.

Woods, Arthur. *Crime Prevention.* Princeton, N.J.: Princeton University Press, 1918.

_____. *Policemen and Public.* Montclair, N.J.: Patterson Smith, 1975.

Woods, Betty. *Ghost Towns and How to Get to Them.* Santa Fe, N.M.: Press of the Territorian, 1964.

Woods, Henry F., and Morgan, Edward E.P. *God's Loaded Dice: Alaska, 1897-1930.* Caldwell, Idaho: Caxton Printers, 1948.

Woods, Rufus. *The Wierdest Story in American History: The Escape of John Wilkes Booth.* Wenatchee, Wash.: Published by Author, 1944.

Woods, S.D. *Lights and Shadows of Life on the Pacific Coast.* New York: Funk & Wagnalls, 1910.

Woodson, C.G., and Wesley, C.H. *The Story of the Negro Retold.* Washington, D.C.: Associated, 1959.

Woodson, William H. *History of Clay County, Missouri.* Topeka, Kan.: Historical, 1920.

Woodward, Bob, and Armstrong, Scott. *The Brethren, Inside the Supreme Court.* New York: Simon & Schuster, 1979.

_____, and Bernstein, Carl. *All the President's Men.* New York: Simon & Schuster, 1974.

_____. *The Final Days.* New York: Simon & Schuster, 1976.

Woodward, C. Vann. *The Burden of Southern History.* Baton Rouge: Louisiana State University Press, 1960.

_____. *Origins of the New South, 1877-1913.* Baton Rouge: Louisiana State University Press, 1951.

_____. *Reunion and Reaction.* New York: Doubleday, 1956.

_____. *The Strange Career of Jim Crow.* New York: Oxford University Press, 1957.

_____. *Tom Watson, Agrarian Rebel.* New York: Macmillan, 1938.

Woodward, David. *The Russians at Sea: A History of the Russian Navy.* New York: Frederick A. Praeger, 1966.

Woodward, Ian. *The Werewolf Delusion.* New York: Paddington Press, 1979.

Woodward, W.E. *Meet General Grant.* New York: Sun Dial Press, 1928.

_____. *A New American History.* New York: Farrar & Rinehart, 1936.

_____. *The Way Our People Lived: An Intimate American History.* New York: E.P. Dutton, 1944.

Woodward, W. Elliot. *Records of the Salem Witchcraft.* Roxbury, Mass.: Published by Author, 1864.

Woodward, W.H. *Cesare Borgia.* London: Chapman & Hall, 1913.

Woolacott, J.E. *India on Trial: A Study of Present Conditions.* New York: Macmillan, 1929.

Wooldridge, Clifton R. *Hands Up! In the World of Crime or Twelve Years a Detective.* Chicago: Police, 1901.

Wooldridge, Maj. J.W. *History of Sacramento Valley, California.* Chicago: Pioneer Historical, 1931.

Wooley, Basil M. *The Opium and Whiskey Habits and Their Cure.* Atlanta: Franklin, 1888.

_____. *The Opium Habit and Its Cure.* Atlanta: Atlanta Constitution Press, 1879.

Woolf, S.J. (ed.). *The Nature of Fascism.* New York: Vintage Books, 1969.

Woollcott, Alexander. *Enchanted Aisles.* New York: G.P. Putnam's Sons, 1924.

_____. *Going to Pieces.* New York: G.P. Putnam's Sons, 1928.

_____. *Long, Long Ago.* New York: Viking Press, 1943.

_____. *While Rome Burns.* New York: Grosset & Dunlap, 1934.

Woolley, Bryan. *November 22.* New York: Seaview Books, 1981.

Woolley, Reginald Maxwell. *Exorcism and the Healing of the Sick.* London: Society for Promoting Christian Knowledge, 1932.

Woolrych, Humphrey William. *On the Report of the Capital Punishment Commission of 1866.* London: Society for the Abolition of Capital Punishment, 1866.

Woolston, Howard B. *Prostitution in the United States.* New York: D. Appleton, 1921.

Wooten, Dudley G. (ed.). *A Comprehensive History of Texas.* Dallas: William G. Scarff, 1898.

Wooten, Mattie Lloyd (ed.). *Women Tell the Story of the Southwest.* San Antonio, Texas: Naylor, 1940.

Wooton, Barbara. *Social Science and Social Pathology.* New York: Macmillan, 1959.

Wootton, B.F., et al. *Social Science and Social Pathology.* London: George Allen & Unwin, 1959.

Worker, Dwight, and Worker, Barbara. *Escape.* San Francisco: San Francisco Books, 1977.

Workman, Boyle. *Boyle Workman's the City That Grew.* Los Angeles: Southland, 1935.

Works Progress Administration, Federal Writers Project. *New York City Guide.* New York: Random House, 1939.

The World's Most Famous Court Trial: Tennessee Evolution Case. Cincinnati, Ohio: National, 1925.

Wormser, René A. *The Story of the Law and the Men Who Made It.* New York: Simon & Schuster, 1962.

Wormser, Richard. *The Yellowlegs, The Story of the United States Cavalry.* Garden City, N.Y.: Doubleday, 1966.

Worral, Olga and Ambrose. *The Gift of Healing.* New York: Harper & Row, 1965.

Wortham, Louis J. *A History of Texas: From Wilderness to Commonwealth.* 5 vols. Fort Worth, Texas: Wortham-Molyneaux, 1924.

Worthley, Harold F. (ed.). *An Inventory of the Records of the Particular (Congregational) Churches of Massachusetts.* Cambridge, Mass.: Harvard University Press, 1970.

Wortley, Mrs. E. Stuart. *A Prime Minister and His Son.* New York: E.P. Dutton, 1925.

Woytinsky, W.S. *Additional Workers and the Volume of Unemployment in the Depression.* Washington, D.C.: Committee on Social Security, Social Science Research Council, 1940.

Wraith, Ronald, and Simpkins, Edgar. *Corruption in Developing Countries.* London: George Allen & Unwin, 1953.

Wrangel, Baron Nicholas. *Memoirs, 1847-1920.* Philadelphia: J.B. Lippincott, 1927.

Wrangel, General Baron Peter N. *Always with Honor.* New York: Robert Speller & Sons, 1957.

_____. *The Memoirs of General Wrangel.* London: Williams & Norgate, 1929.

Wraxall, Sir Lascelles. *Criminal Celebrities: A Collection of Notable Trials.* London: n.p., 1861.

_____. *Remarkable Adventure and Unrevealed Mysteries.* London: W.H. Allen, 1865.

Wren, Lassiter. *Masterstrokes of Crime Detection.* Garden City, N.Y.: Doubleday, Doran, 1929.

Wren, Melvin C. *The Course of Russian History.* New York: Macmillan, 1963.

Wright, Arnold. *Annesley of Surat and His Times.* London: Andrew Melrose, 1918.

_____. *Disturbed Dublin: The Story of the Great Strike of 1913-1914.* London: Longmans, Green, 1914.

Wright, Carolyn and Clarence. *Tiny Hinsdale of the Silvery San Juan.* Denver: Big Mountain Press, 1964.

Wright, Carroll D. *New Century Book of Facts.* Springfield, Mass.: King Richardson, 1911.

Wright, Charles Alan. *Federal Practice and Procedure.* St. Paul, Minn.: West, 1969.

Wright, Christopher. *The Art of the Forger.* New York: Dodd, Mead, 1985.

Wright, Conrad. *Three Prophets of Religious Liberalism: Channing-Emerson-Parker.* Boston: Beacon Press, 1961.

Wright, Constance. *Beautiful Enemy: A Biography of Queen Louise of Prussia.* New York: Dodd, Mead, 1969.

Wright, Dudley. *Vampires and Vampirism.* London: W. Rider, 1924.

Wright, Erik Olin (ed.). *The Politics of Punishment: A Critical Analysis of Prisons in America.* New York: Harper & Row, 1973.

Wright, Frank Lloyd. *An Autobiography.* New York: Duell, Sloan & Pearce, 1943.

Wright, George F. *History of Sacramento County.* Oakland, Calif.: Thompson & West, 1880.

Wright, George Frederick. *Asiatic Russia.* 2 vols. New York: McClure, Phillips, 1902.

Wright, Gordon. *Between the Guillotine and Liberty.* New York: Oxford University Press, 1983.

Wright, H.B. *Insiders and Outliers: The Individual in History.* San Francisco: W.H. Freeman, 1980.

_____. *When a Man Was a Man.* New York: Burt, 1918.

Wright, James D., et al. *Under the Gun: Weapons, Crime and Violence in America.* Hawthorne, N.Y.: Aldine, 1983.

Wright, John Stephen. *Chicago: Past, Present, and Future.* Chicago: Western News, 1863.

Wright, L.B. *The Atlantic Frontier.* New York: Alfred A. Knopf, 1947.

_____. *The Cultural Life of the American Colonies 1607-1763.* New York: Harper & Brothers, 1956.

_____. *Middle-Class Culture in Elizabethan England.* Chapel Hill:

University of North Carolina Press, 1935.

Wright, Lord. *Legal Essays and Addresses.* London: Cambridge, 1939.

Wright, Malcolm. *If I Die: Coastwatching and Guerrilla Warfare Behind Japanese Lines.* Melbourne: Landsdown Press, 1965.

Wright, Mary C. *The Last Stand of Chinese Conservatism: The T'ung-chih Restoration, 1862-1874.* Stanford, Calif.: Stanford University Press, 1957.

Wright, Muriel H. *The Story of Oklahoma.* Oklahoma City: Webb, 1930.

Wright, Richard O. (ed.). *Whose FBI?* La Salle, Ill.: Open Court, 1974.

Wright, Richardson. *Hawkers and Walkers in Early America.* Philadelphia: J.B. Lippincott, 1927.

Wright, Robert M. *Dodge City, The Cowboy Capital and the Great Southwest.* Wichita, Kan.: Wichita Eagle Press, 1913.

_____. *Dodge City, the Cowboy Capital.* Wichita, Kan.: Wichita Eagle Press, 1917.

Wright, S.F. *Hart and the Chinese Customs.* Belfast, Ire.: Queens University, 1950.

Wright, Sewell Peaslee (ed.). *Chicago Murders.* New York: Duell, Sloan & Pearce, 1945.

Wright, Theon. *Rape in Paradise.* New York: Hawthorne Books, 1966.

_____. *In Search of the Lindbergh Baby.* New York: Tower, 1981.

Wright, Thomas. *Narratives of Sorcery and Magic.* New York: Redfield, 1852.

Wright, William. *History of the Big Bonanza.* San Francisco: A.L. Bancroft, 1876.

Wright, William. *The Von Bulow Affair.* New York: Delacorte Press, 1983.

Wrong, George McKinnon. *The Rise and Fall of New France.* 2 vols. New York: Macmillan, 1928.

Wu, A.K. *China and the Soviet Union.* New York: John Day, 1950.

Wu, Felix L. (ed.). *The Asia Who's Who, 1958.* Hong Kong: Pan-Asia Newspaper Alliance, 1958.

Wulf, Josef. *Das Dritte Reich und seine Vollstrecker.* Berlin-Grünewald, 1961.

_____. *Heinrich Himmler.* Berlin-Grünewald: Arani, 1960.

Wulffen, Erich. *Woman as Sexual Criminal.* trans. David Berger. New York: American Ethnological Press, 1934.

Wurm, Ted. *Hetch Hetchy and Its Dam Railroad.* Berkeley, Calif.: Howell-North, 1973.

Wycherley, George. *Buccaneers of the Pacific.* Indianapolis, Ind.: Bobbs-Merrill, 1928.

Wyckoff, Richard D. *Wall Street Ventures and Adventures Through Forty Years.* New York: Harper Brothers, 1930.

Wyden, Peter. *The Hired Killers.* New York: William Morrow, 1963.

Wykes, Alan. *Hitler.* New York: Ballantine Books, 1971.

_____. *Nuremberg Rallies.* New York: Ballantine Books, 1969.

Wyler, Seymour B. *The Book of Old Silver.* New York: Crown, 1937.

Wyles, Lilian. *Women at Scotland Yard.* London: Faber & Faber, 1952.

Wyllie, Irvin Gordon. *The Self-Made Man in America.* New Brunswick N.J.: Rutgers University Press, 1954.

Wyllys, Rufus Kay. *Arizona, the History of a Frontier State.* Phoenix, Ariz.: Hobson & Herr, 1950.

Wyman, Mark. *Immigrants in the Valley: Irish, Germans, and Americans in the Upper Mississippi Country, 1830-1860.* Chicago: Nelson Hall, 1984.

Wyman, Walker D. *Nothing But Prairie and Sky: Life on the Dakota Range in the Early Days.* Norman: University of Oklahoma Press, 1954.

Wyndham, Horace. *Consider Your Verdict.* London: W.H. Allen, 1946.

_____. *Crime on the Continent.* Boston: Little, Brown, 1928.

_____. *Dramas of the Law.* London: Hutchinson, 1936.

_____. *Famous Trials Re-told.* London: Hutchinson, 1925.
_____. *Feminine Frailty.* London: Ernest Benn, 1929.
Wyndham-Brown, W.F. *The Trial of Herbert Wallace.* London: Gollancz, 1933.
Wynn, Marcia Rittenhouse. *Desert Bonanza: Story of Early Randeburg, Mojave Desert Mining Camp.* Culver City, Calif.: M.W. Samelson, 1949.
Wynn, Wilton. *Nasser of Egypt.* Cambridge, Mass.: Adington Books, 1959.

X

Xenophon. *Memoirs of Socrates.* trans. Hugh Tredennick. Harmondsworth, Eng.: Penguin, 1970.
_____. *Xenophon's Minor Works.* trans. John Selby Watson. London: George Bell & Sons, 1891.
Xydis, Stephen G. *Greece and the Great Powers, 1944-1947: Prelude to the Truman Doctrine.* Thessaliniki: Institute for Balkan Studies, 1963.

Y

Yablonsky, Lewis. *George Raft.* New York: McGraw-Hill, 1974.
_____. *Synanon: The Tunnel Back.* New York: Macmillan, 1965.
_____. *The Violent Gang.* New York: Macmillan, 1963.
Yaffe, James. *Nothing But the Night.* New York: Bantam Books, 1959.
Yakhontoff, V.A. *Russia and the Soviet Union in the Far East.* New York: Coward, McCann, 1931.
Yale, William. *The Near East: A Modern History.* Ann Arbor: University of Michigan Press, 1958.
Yallop, David. *The Day the Laughter Stopped.* New York: St. Martin's Press, 1976.
_____. *Deliver Us From Evil.* London: MacDonald Futura, 1981.
Yallop, David A. *To Encourage the Others.* London: W.H. Allen, 1971.
Yanaga, Chitoshi. *Japan Since Perry.* New York: McGraw-Hill, 1949.
_____. *Japanese People and Politics.* New York: Wiley, 1956.
Yanitch, Voyeslav, and Hankey, C. Patrick. *The Lives of the Serbian Saints.* New York: Macmillan, 1921.
Yarbus, A. *Eye Movement and Vision.* New York: Plenum Press, 1967.
Yardley, Jonathon. *Ring: A Biography of Rand Lardner.* New York: Random House, 1977.
Yarmolinsky, Avrahm. *Road to Revolution.* New York: Collier, 1962.
Yarnell, Allen. *Democrats and Progressives.* Berkeley: University of California Press, 1974.
Yaron, Reuven. *The Laws of Eshnunna.* Jerusalem, Isr.: Hebrew University, 1969.
Yarovslavsky, E. *Biographiya Lenina.* Moscow: Partiinoe Izdatelstvo, 1934.
Yarros, Victor S. *My 11 Years with Clarence Darrow.* Girard, Kan.: Haldeman-Julius Publications, 1950.
Yarrow, M., Campbell, J., Burton, R. *Child Rearing.* San Francisco: Jossey-Bass, 1968.
Yates, Alayne. *Sex Without Shame.* New York: William Morrow, 1978.
Yates, Aubrey J. *Frustration and Conflict.* New York: Wiley, 1962.

Yates, Frances A. *Giordano Bruno and the Hermetic Tradition.* Chicago: University of Chicago Press, 1964.
Yates, W.H. *Modern History of Egypt.* London: Smith & Elder, 1843.
Yearly, Clifton K. *The Money Machines: The Breakdown and Reform of Governmental and Party Finance in the North, 1860-1920.* Albany: State University of New York Press, 1970.
Yeats-Brown, F. *Escape.* New York: Macmillan, 1933.
Yee, Min S., and Layton, Thomas N. *In My Father's House.* New York: Holt, Rinehart and Winston, 1981.
_____. *The Melancholy History of Soledad Prison.* New York: Harper's Magazine Press, 1970.
Yefsky, S.A. (ed.). *Law Enforcement Science and Technology.* Washington, D.C.: Thompson Book Company, 1967.
Yellen, Samuel. *American Labor Struggles.* New York: Harcourt, Brace, 1936.
Yellowitz, Irwin. *Labor and the Progressive Movement in New York State, 1897-1916.* Ithaca, N.Y.: Cornell University Press, 1965.
Yeomans, Henry A. *Abbott Lawrence Lowell.* Cambridge, Mass.: Harvard University Press, 1948.
Yerrington, James M.M. *The Official Report of the Trial of Henry K. Goodwin.* Boston: Wright & Potter, 1887.
_____. *The Official Report of the Trial of Sarah Jane Robinson.* Boston: Wright & Potter, 1888.
_____. *The Official Report of the Trial of Thomas W. Piper.* Boston: Wright & Potter, 1887.
_____. *Report on the Case of George C. Hersey.* Boston: A. Williams, 1862.
Yin, P. *Victimization of the Aged.* Springfield, Ill.: Charles W. Thomas, 1985.
Yin, Robert K., and Yates, Douglas. *Street-Level Governments.* Santa Monica, Calif.: The Rand Corporation, 1974.
Yoakum, Henderson K. *History of Texas.* New York: Redfield, 1856.
Yochelson, Samuel, and Samenow, Stanton E. *The Criminal Personality.* New York: Jason Aronson, 1976.
York, Mary E. *The Bender Tragedy.* Mankato, Kan.: G.W. Neff, 1875.
York, Robert M. *George B. Cheever, Religious and Social Reformer, 1807-1890.* Orono: Maine University Press, 1955.
Yoshida, Shigeru. *The Yoshida Memoirs: The Story of Japan in Crisis.* Boston: Houghton Mifflin, 1962.
Yoshihashi Takehiko. *Conspiracy at Mukden: The Rise of the Japanese Military.* New Haven, Conn.: Yale University Press, 1963.
Yost, Nellie Snyder. *The Call of the Range: The Story of the Nebraska Stock Growers Association.* Denver: Sage Books, 1966.
_____. *Medicine Lodge.* Chicago: Sage Books, 1970.
Young, A. Morgan. *Imperial Japan: 1912-1938.* New York: William Morrow, 1938.
_____. *Japan in Recent Times, 1912-1926.* New York: William Morrow, 1929.
Young, Alfred E. *Dissent: Explorations in the History of American Radicalism.* DeKalb: Northern Illinois University Press, 1968.
Young, Art. *Art Young, His Life and Times.* New York: Sheridan House, 1939.
_____. *On My Way.* New York: Horace Liveright, 1928.
Young, Arthur. *China and the Helping Hand, 1937-1945.* Cambridge, Mass.: Harvard University Press, 1963.
Young, Betty Lou. *Pacific Palisades, Where the Mountains Meet the Sea.* Los Angeles: Pacific Palisades Historical Society Press, 1983.
Young, Charles E. *Dangers on the Trail in 1865.* Geneva, N.Y.: W.Y. Humphrey, 1912.
Young, Filson. *The Trial of Hawley Harvey Crippen.* London: William Hodge, 1920.

Young, Francis C. *Echoes From Arcadia.* Denver: Lanning Brothers, 1903.

Young, Frederick R. *Dodge City.* Dodge City, Kan.: Boot Hill Museum, 1972.

Young, G.F. *The Medici.* New York: Modern Library, 1930.

A Young Girl's Diary. New York: Barnes & Noble, 1961.

Young, Harry (Sam). *Hard Knocks, A Life Story of the Vanishing West.* Portland, Ore.: Wells & Company, 1915.

Young, Herbert V. *Ghosts of Cleopatra Hill: Men and Legends of Old Jerome.* Jerome, Ariz.: Jerome Historical Society, 1964.

Young, Hugh. *My Forty Years at the Yard.* London: W.H. Allen, 1955.

Young, James Harvey. *The Medical Messiahs, A Social History of Health Quackery in Twentieth Century America.* Princeton, N.J.: Princeton University Press, 1967.

_____. *The Toadstool Millionaires.* Princeton: Princeton University Press, 1961.

Young, John P. *Journalism in California.* San Francisco: Chronicle, 1915.

_____. *San Francisco: A History of the Pacific Coast Metropolis.* San Francisco: S.J. Clarke, 1912.

Young, John Russell. *Men and Memories.* ed. May D. Russell Young. New York: F. Tennyson Nealy, 1901.

Young, Morgan. *Japan Under Taisho Tenno.* New York: William Morrow, 1929.

Young, Otis E., Jr. (ed.). *The First Military Escort on the Santa Fe Trail.* Glendale, Calif.: Arthur H. Clarke, 1952.

Young, Pauline V. *Pilgrims of Russian-Town.* Chicago: University of Chicago Press, 1932.

_____. *Social Treatment in Probation and Delinquency.* New York: McGraw-Hill, 1952.

Young, Peter. *Bedouin Command with the Arab Legion, 1953-1956.* London: Kimber, 1956.

Young, Rosalind Amelia. *Mutiny of the Bounty and Sotry of Pitcairn Island.* San Francisco: Pacific Press, 1894.

Young, S. Glenn. *Life and Exploits of S. Glenn Young, World-Famous Law Enforcement Officer.* Herrin, Ill.: Mrs. S. Glenn Young, 1924.

Young, Dr. S.O. *True Stories of Old Houston and Houstonians.* Houston, Texas: Oscar Springer, 1913.

Young, Wayland. *Eros Denied: Sex in Western Society.* New York: Grove, 1964.

Youngblood, Rufus W. *20 Years in the Secret Service: My Life With Five Presidents.* New York: Simon & Schuster, 1973.

Younger, Coleman. *The Story of Cole Younger by Himself.* Chicago: Press of the Henneberry, 1903.

Younger, Scout. *True Facts of the Lives of America's Most Notorious Outlaws.* n.p., n.d.

Younghusband, Francis E. *The Heart of a Continent.* London: John Murray, 1896.

Youngs, F.A. *The Proclamations of the Tudor Queens.* Cambridge: Cambridge University Press, 1976.

Youssoupov, Prince Felix. *Lost Splendor.* trans. Ann Green and Nicolas Katkoff. London: Jonathan Cape, 1953.

_____. *Rasputin: His Malignant Influence and His Assassination.* London: Cape, 1927.

Yriarte, Charles. *Autour des Borgia.* Paris: J. Rothschild, 1891.

_____. *Cesare Borgia.* trans. William Sterling. London: F. Aldor, 1947.

Yule, H. *The Book of Ser Marco Polo.* New York: Book League of America, 1929.

Yule, Sir Henry (ed.). *Cathay and the Way Thither.* 4 vols. London: Hakluty Society, 1915.

Yurka, Blanche. *Bohemian Girl.* Athens: Ohio University Press, 1970.

Yusupov, Feliks Feliksovich. *Rasputin.* trans. Oswald Rayner. Maidstone, Eng.: Mann, 1974.

Yves-Plessis, Robert. *Essai d'une bibliographie française.* Paris: Bibliothéque Chacornac, 1900.

Z

Zabriskie, Edward H. *American-Russian Rivalry in the Far East, 1895-1914.* Philadephia: University of Pennsylvania Press, 1946.

Zachariae, George. *Mussolini si confessa.* Milan, Italy: Garzanti, 1948.

Zaehner, R.C. *Zen, Drugs and Mysticism.* New York: Pantheon Books, 1973.

Zagoria, Donald S. *The Sino-Soviet Conflict 1956-1961.* Princeton, N.J.: Princeton University Press, 1962.

Zahniser, Marvin R. *Charles Cotesworth Pinckney.* Chapel Hill: University of North Carolina Press, 1967.

Zalba, Serapio. *Women Prisoners and Their Families.* Sacramento, Calif.: Department of Social Welfare and Department of Corrections, 1964.

Zalman, Marvin. *Indeterminate Sentence Laws: Present, Past, Future.* Dallas: Academy of Criminal Justice Sciences, 1976.

Zamora, William. *Trial By Your Peers.* New York: A. Maurice Girodias Associates, 1973.

Zancka, Herman. *Rasputin.* Kristiania: H. Erichsen, 1918.

Zanco, Aurelio. *Oscar Wilde.* Genova, Italy: Emiliano degli Orfini, 1934.

Zander, M. *Cases and Materials on the English Legal System.* London: Weidenfeld & Nicolson, 1973.

Zarchin, Michael M. *Glimpses of Jewish Life in San Francisco.* San Francisco: Willis E. Berg, 1952.

Zarudnaya, Elena (ed.). *Trotsky's Diary in Exile.* Cambridge: Harvard University Press, n.d.

Zawodny, J.K. *Death in the Forest: The Story of the Katyn Forest Massacres.* Notre Dame, Ind.: University of Notre Dame Press, 1962.

Zayas, Enrique Rafael de. *The Case of Mexico and the Policy of President Wilson.* New York: Boni, 1914.

Zedlitz-Trutzschler, Robert. *Twelve Years at the Imperial German Court.* New York: Doran, 1924.

Zehner, Ioachim. *Fünf Predigten von den Hexen.* Leipzig, Ger.: 1613.

Zeichner, Oscar. *Connecticut's Years of Controversy 1750-1776.* Chapel Hill: University of North Carolina Press, 1949.

Zeiger, Henry A. *The Jersey Mob.* New York: New American Library, 1975.

_____. *Sam the Plumber.* Bergenfield, N.J.: New American Library, 1973.

Zeine, Z.N. *Arab-Turkish Relations and the Emergence of Arab Nationalism.* Beirut, Leb.: Khayat, 1966.

_____. *The Struggle for Arab Independence.* Beirut, Leb.: Khayat, 1960.

Zeisel, Hans, Kalven, Harry, Jr, and Buchholz, Bernard. *Delay in the Court.* Boston: Little, Brown, 1959.

_____. *Say it with Figures.* New York: Harper, 1957.

Zeldin, Theodore (ed.). *Conflicts in French Society: Anti-Clericalism, Education and Morals in the Nineteenth Century.* London: George Allen & Unwin, 1970.

_____. *Emile Ollivier and the Liberal Empire of Napoleon III.* Oxford: Clarendon Press, 1963.

_____. *France 1848-1945: Ambition, Love, and Politics.* Oxford, Eng.: Clarendon Press, 1973.

Zeligs, Meyer A. *Friendship and Fratricide: An Analysis of Whittaker Chambers and Alger Hiss.* New York: The Viking Press, 1967.

Zeller, Eberhard. *Geist der Freiheit.* Munich: Hermann Rinn, Gotthold Müller, 1963.

_____. *The Flame of Freedom: The German Struggle Against Hitler.* Miami, Fla.: University of Miami Press, 1969.

Zelt, Johannes. *Proletarischer Internationalismus im Kamp um Sacco und Vanzetti.* East Berlin: Dietz Verlag, 1958.

Zeman, Z.A.B. *Germany and the Revolution in Russia, 1915-1918.* London: Oxford University Press, 1958.

Zemans, Eugene S. *Held Without Bail.* Chicago: John Howard

Association, 1949.

Zemansky, Mark W., and Sears, Francis Weldon. *College Physics.* Reading, Pa.: Addison-Wesley, 1957.

Zenkovsky, Serge. *Medieval Russia's Epics, Chronicles and Tales.* New York: Dutton, 1963.

Zenkovsky, V.V. *History of Russian Philosophy.* 2 vols. New York: Columbia University Press, 1953.

Zerbe, Jerome, and Gill, Brendan. *Happy Times.* New York: Harcourt Brace Jovanovich, 1973.

Zerman, Melvyn Bernard. *Call the Final Witness.* New York: Harper & Row, 1977.

Zerman, Z.A.B. and Scharlau, W.B. *The Merchant of Revolution: The Life of Alexander Israel Helphand (Parvus), 1867-1924.* New York: Oxford University Press, 1965.

Zernatto, G. *Die Wahrheit ueber Oesterreich.* New York: Longmans, Green, 1939.

Zernov, N. *The Russian Prophets: Khomiakov, Dostoevsky, Soloviev.* London: Macmillan, 1944.

Zetlin, Michael. *The Decembrists.* trans. G. Panin. New York: International Universities Press, 1958.

Zévaès, Alexander. *L'Affaire Pierre Bonaparte.* Paris: Hachette, 1929

Zevin, J. *Violence in America: What is the Alternative?.* Englewood Cliffs, N.J.: Prentice-Hall, 1973.

Zevort, E. *Histoire de la troisième république.* 4 vols. Paris: F. Alcan, 1896.

Ziadeh, Nicola. *Syria and Lebanon.* New York: Frederick A. Praeger, 1957.

Ziegler, Jesse. *Wave of the Gulf.* San Antonio, Texas: Naylor, 1938.

Ziemke, Earl F. *Battle for Berlin: End of the Third Reich.* New York: Ballantine Books, 1970.

Zierold, Norman. *Little Charlie Ross.* Boston: Little, Brown, 1967.

_____. *Three Sisters in Black.* Boston: Little, Brown, 1968.

Zilboorg, Gregory. *The Medical Man and the Witch during the Renaissance.* Baltimore: John Hopkins University Press, 1935.

Zilg, Gerard C. *Dupont: Behind the Nylon Curtain.* Englewood Cliffs, N.J.: Prentice-Hall, 1974.

Zilliacus, Konni. *The Russian Revolutionary Movement.* London: Rivers, 1905.

Zimmer, Lucien. *Un Septennat Policier.* Paris: Fayard, 1967.

Zimmerman, Isidore, with Bond, Francis. *Punishment without Crime.* New York: Clarkson N. Potter, 1964.

Zimring, Franklin E. *The Changing Legal World of Adolescence.* New York: Free Press, 1982.

_____, and Hawkins, Gordon J. *Deterrence: The Legal Threat in Crime Control.* Chicago: University of Chicago Press, 1973.

Zinberg, Norman E. *Drug, Set, and Setting: The Basis for Controlled Intoxicant Use.* New Haven, Conn.: Yale University Press, 1984.

_____, and Robertson, John A. *Drugs and the Public.* New York: Simon & Schuster, 1972.

Zincke, F. Barham. *Last Winter in the United States....* London: John Murray, 1868.

Zingerle, Ignaz. *Barbara Pachlerin die Santhaler Hexe und Mathias Perger der Lauterfresser.* Innsbruck, Aust.: Wagner, 1858.

Zink, Harold. *City Bosses in the United States: A Study of Twenty Municipal Bosses.* Durham, N.C.: Duke University Press, 1930.

Zink, Wilbur A. *The Roscoe Gun Battle: Younger Brothers vs. Pinkerton Detectives.* Appleton City, Mo.: Democrat, 1967.

Zinman, David H. *The Day Huey Long Was Shot.* New York: Ivan Obolensky, 1963.

Zinn, Howard (ed.). *Justice Eyewitness Accounts.* Boston: Beacon, 1974.

_____ (ed.). *Justice in Everyday Life: The Way it Really Works.* New York: William Morrow, 1974.

Zinoviev, G. *Vladimir Ilyich Ulyanov.* Petrograd: n.p., 1918.

Zins, H. *England and the Baltic in the Elizabethan Era.* Manchester, Eng.: Manchester University Press, 1972.

Zipfel, Friedrich. *Gestapo und Sicherheitsdienst.* Berlin-Grünewald: Arani, 1960.

_____. *Kirchenkampf in Deutschland 1933-1945.* Berlin: Walter de Gruyter, 1965.

Zittle, Capt. John H. *A Correct History of the John Brown Invasion.* Hagerstown, Md.: Published by his widow, 1905.

Znaniecki, F. *Social Actions.* New York: Farrar & Rinehart, 1936.

Zobel, Hiller B. *The Boston Massacre.* New York: W.W. Norton, 1970.

Zola, Emile. *La République en marche.* Paris: Fasquelle, 1956.

Zoller, Albert (ed.). *Hitler Privat. Erlebnisbericht seiner Geheimsekretärin.* Düsseldorff: Droste, 1949.

Zopft, John Heinrich. *Dissertatio de Vampiris Serviensibus.* Halle, Ger.: John Sas, 1733.

Zorbaugh, Harvey W. *The Gold Coast and the Slum.* Chicago: University of Chicago Press, 1929.

Zornow, William Frank. *Kansas: A History of the Jayhawk State.* Norman: University of Oklahoma Press, 1957.

Zua'iter, Akram. *The Palestine Question.* Damascus, Syria: Al Jadida, 1958.

Zuckerman, Michael J. *Vengeance is Mine.* New York: Macmillan, 1987.

Zukor, Adolph, with Kramer, Dale. *The Public Is Never Wrong.* New York: G.P. Putnam's Sons, 1953.

Zumoto Motosada. *Sino-Japanese Entanglements, 1931-1932: A Military Record.* Tokyo: Herald Press, 1932.

Zusne, L. *Visual Perception of Form.* New York: Academic Press, 1970.

Zwei Hexenprocesse aus dem Jahre 1688. Quedlinburg, Ger.: H.C. Huch, 1863.

Zweig, Stefan. *Amerigo.* trans. Andrew St. James. New York: Viking Press, 1942.

Zwetsloot, Hugo. *Friedrich Spee und die Hexenprozesse.* Treves, Ger.: Paulins-Verlag, 1954.

SUBJECT INDEX

Green, Bill	U.S.	1372
Green, Everett D.	U.S.	1373
Gunness, Belle	U.S.	1400
Harris, Leopold	Brit.	1462
Hatto, Moses	Brit.	1478
Hauptfleisch, Petrus S. Francois	S.Afri.	1478
Hawk, Ralph	U.S.	1491
Hereford, Anne	Brit.	1523
Hill, James	Brit.	1551
Holman, George	U.S.	1597
Ingham, Ellery P.	U.S.	1692
Jacobs, William M.	U.S.	1692
Keller, Eva	U.S.	1777
Kelley, Dillard E., Sr.	U.S.	1777
Kendig, William L.	U.S.	1692
Kierdorf, Frank	U.S.	1815
Kipnik, Erich	Ger.	2656
Koehnin, Charles	U.S.	1841
Kohout, Edward	U.S.	1842
Kohout, Henry	U.S.	1842
Kreuger, Alexander	Swed.	1849
Krüten, Peter	Ger.	1862
Lancey, John	Brit.	1883
Lawson, John D.	U.S.	1908
Lee, Bruce	Brit.	1917
Lisbon Earthquake	Port.	1970
Lopez, Hector	U.S.	783
Lopez, Jose Francisco Rivera	P.R.	138
Luddites	Brit.	2007
Lynchehaun, James	Ire.	2017
Marja	U.S.	2124
Mendez, Francisco	U.S.	783
Morgan, Edward	Brit.	2219
Mullins, Patrick	U.S.	2250
Murieta, Joaquin	U.S.	2256
Negro Conspiracy	U.S.	2296
Newitt, Harvey K.	U.S.	1692
O'Bryan, Patrick	Brit.	2357
Ohio State Penitentiary	U.S.	2366
Ohmura Ichiro	Japan	2366
Pankhurst, Emmeline	Brit.	2405
Ponce, Noratto	U.S.	422
Reichstag Fire	Ger.	2559
Rivera, Armando Jimenez	P.R.	138
Roberts, Clarence	U.S.	2591
Roy, Gilder	Scot.	2632
Ryan, Bobbie	U.S.	2646
Saffran, Fritz	Ger.	2656
Salmon, Thomas	U.S.	2671
Scarlow, Sam	U.S.	2688
Schwartz, Charles Henry	U.S.	2706
Segee, Robert Dale	U.S.	2723
Showery, Allan	U.S.	2750
Skinner, Kenneth	U.S.	2774
Small, Frederick L.	U.S.	2780
Soto, Juan	U.S.	422
Stolerman, James Bernard	Brit.	1095
Stone, John	Brit.	750
Taylor, Arthur	U.S.	1692
Taylor, Tom	Brit.	2902
Tbilisi Opera and Ballet Fire	U.S.S.R.	2906
Toole, Gerald	U.S.	2968
Vasquez, Tiburcio	U.S.	422
Von Arbin, Eric	Swed.	1849
Warren, Benjamin	U.S.	1099
Weallans, Clifford Alexander	Brit.	3106
White Cloud Arson	U.S.	3139
White, Charles Thomas	Brit.	3137
Wise, Martha Hasel	U.S.	3178
Zenner, Albert	U.S.	3219

ARSON - Case of

Kent, Perry	U.S.	2409
New Bethel African Meth. Churc	U.S.	2309
Parisi, Angelo	U.S.	2409
Pates, Robert Eugene	U.S.	2418

ARSON - Wrongly Convicted

Scampton, Thomas	Brit.	2687

ASSASSINATION

Abancourt, Charles	Fr.	1
Abbas I	Egypt	2
Abd Allah	Jor.	8
Adwan, Kamal	Fr.	36
Ahaziah	Judah	41
Ala al-Din Mujahid	India	46
Ala ud-Din Muhammad Khalji	India	46
Alamgir II	India	46
Alberic I	Roman.	47
Albert I	Ger.	47
Alexander	Rus.	75
Alexander I (Karageorgevic)	Yug.	75
Alexander I (Obrenovic)	Serb.	78
Alexander II	Rus.	84
Alfonso of Aragon	Italy	91
Ali (Ali Pasha)	Turk.	92
Ali (Ali ibn Abi Talib)	Islam	92
Amalasuntha	Tuscany	108
Amasa	Isr.	109
Amaziah	Judah	110
Amin, al-	Abassid	114
An Lushan	China	128
Andrew	Rus.	126
Andronicus I Comnenus	Roman.	127
Anno	Ger.	129
Antigonus I	Judea	133
Antiochus II	Syria	133
Antiochus V	Syria	133
Antipater	Judea	133
Antonia, Claudia	Roman.	134
Antonius, Marcus	Roman.	134
Apollodorus of Damascus	Gr.	138
Aquino, Benigno S., Jr.,	Phil.	139
Aramburu, Pedro Eugenio	Arg.	142
Arason, Jon	Ice.	143
Arboleda, Julio	Col.	143
Ardashir III	Per.	153
Aristobulus III	Cappadocia	154
Arlosoroff, Dr. Chaim	Isr.	156
Armagnac, Bernard VII d'	Fr.	156
Arrhidaeus	Mac.	166
Arses	Per.	168
Arsinoe III	Egypt	168
Arsinoe IV	Egypt	168
Artabanus	Pers.	168
Artavasdes III	Arm.	168
Artaxerxes III	Per.	168
Atahaulpa	Peru	173
Ataulphus	Visigoths	173
Athaliah	Judah	175
Aung San	Burma	185
Aurelian	Roman.	185
Avidius Cassius, Gaius	Roman.	190
Bagoas	Per.	207
Balewa, Sir Abubakar Tafewa	Nigeria	218
Balta, Jos	Peru	222
Bandaranaike, Solomon W.R.	Ceylon	224
Bandera, Stefan	Ger.	224
Bar Cocheba, Simon	Isr.	233
Bardas	Byzantium	233

Duca, Jon	Rom.	1030		Gratian	Roman.	1364
Dumas, Ren Franois	Fr.	1034		Griboedov, Aleksandr Sergeevic	Rus.	1385
Duncan I	Scot.	1035		Grimoald I	Italy	1390
Duncan II	Scot.	1035		Guardiola, Santos	Hond.	1395
Eadric Streona	Mercia	1052		Guatemotzin	Mex.	1395
Edmund	Brit.	1070		Guerrero, Vicente	Mex.	1397
Edmund I	Brit.	1070		Guevara, Ernesto	Bol.	1397
Edward	Brit.	1070		Guinness, Walter Edward	Ire.	1398
Edward II	Brit.	1071		Guise, François	Lorraine	1398
Edward V	Brit.	1071		Guise, Henri I de Lorraine	Fr.	1398
Edwards, Louis F.	U.S.	1072		Guiteras, Antonio	Cuba	1399
Eftimoff, Simeon	Bul.	1074		Gundimar II	Fr.	1400
Eichorn, Hermann von	Ger.	1077		Gustavus III	Swed.	1406
Eisner, Kurt	Ger.	1079		Gustloff, Wilhelm	Switz.	1408
Elagabulus	Roman.	1080		Gyges	Lydia	1411
Elah	Israel	1080		Habibullah Khan	Afg.	1412
Elio, Francisco Javier	Spain	1082		Halim Pasa, Said	Turk.	1420
Elizabeth	Switz.	1082		Hamaguchi Osachi	Japan	1433
Elisabeth de France	Fr.	1082		Hammarskjoeld, Dag Hjalmer A.C	Congo	1436
Elliott, John M.	U.S.	1084		Hannington, James	S.Afri.	1443
Emin Mehmed	Zaire	1091		Hara Takashi	Japan	1445
Engelbert I	Ger.	1095		Harpalus	Babylonia	1455
Enver Pasa	Turk.	1099		Harrison, Carter Henry, Sr.	U.S.	1464
Epremesnil, Jean-Jacques Duval	Fr.	1099		Hasan al-Banna	Egypt	1473
Erik IV	Den.	1101		Hatto II	Ger.	1477
Erlach, Charles Louis d'	Switz.	1101		Hazael	Syria	1500
Ernst, Karl	Ger.	1101		Heliogabalus	Roman.	1512
Erzberger, Matthias	Ger.	1102		Henry III	Fr.	1517
Essad, Pasa	Turk.	1106		Henry IV	Fr.	1518
Ethelbert	E.Anglia	1109		Henry of Cornwall	Brit.	1520
Faisal	Saud.	1127		Heraclian	Roman.	1522
Faisal II	Iraq	1128		Hermocrates	Si.	1524
Fakhr al-Din II	Leb.	1130		Hernandez, Francisco Javier O.	Mex.	1524
Fausta	Roman.	1139		Heydrich, Reinhard Tristan Eug	Ger.	1529
Fersen, Hans Axel	Swed.	1153		Hiempsal I	Numidia	1544
Fitzgerald, Gerald	Ire.	1171		Hinojosa, Pedro de	Spain	1562
Flaccus, Lucius Valerius	Roman.	1174		Hipparchus	Gr.	1562
Flaccus, Marcus	Roman.	1174		Histiaeus	Gr.	1564
Flavian	Turk.	1176		Hormizd III	Per.	1619
Flor, Roger di	Byzantium	1181		Hormizd IV	Per.	1619
Flores, Venancio	Urug.	1181		Hoyos, Carlos Mauro	Col.	1633
Ford, Francis Xavier	China	1193		Hsiao Yen	China	1633
Foullon, Joseph Franois	Fr.	1204		Humbert I	Italy	1639
Foulques	Fr.	1204		Hunt, Leamon R.	Italy	1643
Francis Ferdinand	Aust.	1210		Huscar	Peru	1634
Fyodor II	Rus.	1244		Hussein Avni Pasha	Turk.	1647
Gabaldon, Isaac	Spain	1245		Hutten, Philipp von	Venez.	1648
Gaimar V	Italy	1249		Hypatia	Gr.	1650
Gaitan, Jorge Elicer	Col.	1250		Hyperbolus	Gr.	1650
Galante, Carmine	U.S.	1250		Hyperides	Gr.	1650
Galaup, Jean-Francois de	Fr.	1251		Ibrahim Lodi	Afg.	1652
Galba, Servius Sulpicius	Roman.	1251		Igor	Rus.	1652
Gallus, Gaius Vibius Trebonian	Roman.	1257		Inukai Tsuyoshi	Japan	1660
Galswintha	Neustria	1257		Ishbosheth	Isr.	1668
Gandhi, Indira	India	1261		Iturbide, Agustin de	Mex.	1670
Gandhi, Mohandas Karamchand	India	1261		Ivan VI Antonovich	Rus.	1671
Garcia, Moreno Gabriel	Ecu.	1267		Ivanovich, Dmitri	Rus.	1671
Garfield, James Abram	U.S.	1270		Jalal ud-Din	India	1694
Gaveston, Piers	Brit.	1286		Jalal-ad-Din Mingburnu	Khwarazm	1694
George of Cappadocia	Gr.	1300		James I	Scot.	1694
Gessler	Switz.	1302		Jaurs, Jean Lon	Fr.	1712
Geta, Publius Septimius	Roman.	1303		Jehoram	Israel	1717
Giovanni	Italy	1316		Joanna I	Naples	1724
Godunov, Boris Fdorovich	Rus.	1324		John	Brit.	1726
Gordianus, Marcus Antonios III	Roman.	1342		John Hyrcanus II	Judaea	1726
Goremykin, Ivan Longinovich	Rus.	1348		John XIV	Italy	1726
Gounares, Demetrios	Gr.	1352		John of Nepomuk	Bohemia	1726
Govind Singh	India	1353		Josaphat Kuncewicz	Pol.	1744
Gracchus, Gaius Sempronius	Roman.	1355		Julia Mamaea	Roman.	1749
Gracchus, Tiberius Sempronius	Roman.	1355		Justinian II	Roman.	1750

Kapodistrias, Ioannis Antnios	Gr.	1762
Karageorge	Serbia	1762
Karami, Rashid	Leb.	1763
Karume, Abeid	Tan.	1766
Kassem, Abdul Karim	Iraq	1767
Kemal, Mustafa Pasha	Turk.	1790
Kennedy, John Fitzgerald	U.S.	1794
Kennedy, Robert Francis	U.S.	1801
Kestutis	Lithuania	1806
Khalil, al-Ashraf Salah ad-Din	Egypt	1809
Khosrau II	Persia	1811
Kim Koo	Korea	1820
King, Martin Luther, Jr.	U.S.	1823
Kirov, Sergei Mironovich	U.S.S.R.	1830
Kleber, Jean-Baptiste	Fr.	1832
Klement, Rudolf	Fr.	1833
Konishi Yukinaga	Japan	1842
Konovalec, Evhen	Neth.	1842
Ksem Sultan	Turk.	1844
Lacy, Baron Hugh de	Brit.	1870
Ladislas IV	Hung.	1870
Lamballe, Marie-Threse-Lou. de	Fr.	1877
Laporte, Pierre	Can.	1897
Launay, Bernard Rene Jordan de	Fr.	1903
Lawrence, Saint	Roman.	1906
Lee Tai Lim	Sing.	1921
Leo V	Roman.	1931
Leontius	Roman.	1932
Lepeletier de Saint-Fargeau, L	Fr.	1939
Letelier, Orlando	Int'l.	1942
Liaquat Ali Khan	Pak.	1948
Licinius, Valerius Licinianus	Roman.	1949
Liebknecht, Karl	Ger.	1950
Liege, Bishop of	Belg.	1951
Lincoln, Abraham	U.S.	1953
Liniers, Santiago Antonio Mari	Arg.	1968
Li Ssu	China	1970
Li Tachao	China	1970
Long, Huey Pierce	U.S.	1982
López, Carlos Antonio	Para.	1989
Lorraine, Louis II de	Fr.	1991
Lotf Ali Khan Zand	Per.	1991
Louis	Fr.	1992
Lumumba, Patrice Hemery	Congo	2010
Luna, Alvaro de	Spain	2012
Ly Bon	Viet.	2015
Lysias	Syria	2020
Maccabees, Jonathan	Judea	2022
Maccabees, Simon	Judea	2022
McGee, Thomas D'Arcy	Can.	2040
McIntosh, William	U.S.	2046
McKinley, William	U.S.	2049
Macnaghten, Sir William Hay	India	2062
Madero, Francisco Indlcio	Mex.	2073
Magnus III	Nor.	2087
Magnus IV	Nor.	2087
Mahmud Shevket Pasha	Turk.	2088
Majali, Hazza	Jor.	2090
Majorian	Roman.	2092
Malcolm X	U.S.	2095
Manco Inca Yupanqui	Peru	2100
Manlius Capitolinus, Marcus	Roman.	2104
Marat, Jean-Paul	Fr.	2115
Marcel, Etienne	Fr.	2117
Marcellus, Marcus Claudius	Roman.	2118
Marcum, James B.	U.S.	2119
Mariamne the Hasmonaean	Judea	2121
Masaniello	Italy	2135
Matteotti, Giacomo	Italy	2148
Maurice, Saint	Roman.	2153
Mauricius	Roman.	2153
Maximinus, Gaius Julius Verus	Roman.	2154
Medici, Alessandro	Italy	2161
Meeker, Nathan Cook	U.S.	2162
Mehemet Ali Pasha	Turk.	2162
Mejia, Toms	Mex.	2163
Membre, Zenobius	U.S.	2164
Miantonomo	U.S.	2176
Michael	Rom.	2176
Michael	Serbia	2176
Michael III	Roman.	2176
Michiel, Vitale, II	Italy	2177
Miloradovich, Mikhail Andreyev	Rus.	2186
Minamoto Tameyoshi	Japan	2187
Minamoto Yoshitomo	Japan	2187
Mindaugas	Lithuania	2187
Miramón, Miguel	Mex.	2189
Mirza Taqi Khan	Per.	2190
Mithridates III	Parthia	2193
Mithridates V Euergetes	Parthia	2193
Mitrione, Dan A.	Urug.	2193
Mohammed X	Granada	2197
Mohammed of Ghor	Per.	2197
Molay, Jacques de	Fr.	2197
Monaldeschi, Marchese Giovanni	Italy	2200
Montacute, John de		2203
Morales, Agustin	Bol.	2213
Moro, Aldo	Italy	2223
Mountbatten, Louis Fran. A.V.N	Brit.	2235
Mowbray, John I de	Brit.	2236
Moyne, Lord	Egypt	2237
Mursilis I	Syria	2261
Mussolini, Benito Amilcare And	Italy	2263
Mustafa IV	Turk.	2269
Mustasim, al-	Baghdad	2269
Mutawakkil, al-	Baghdad	2269
Nabis	Sparta	2275
Nader Khan	Afg.	2275
Nadir Shah	Per.	2275
Nagata Tetsuzan	Japan	2275
Najjar, Mohammed Yusif	Leb.	2275
Napoléon I	Fr.	2277
Napoléon III	Fr.	2279
Narai, Phra	Siam	2282
Nasir ad-Dawlah	Iraq	2287
Nasr-ed-Din	Per.	2287
Navachine, Dimitri	U.S.S.R.	2292
Neave, Airey Middleton Sheffie	Brit.	2295
Neville, Richard	Brit.	2308
Ngo Dinh Diem	Viet.	2327
Nicephorus II Phocas	Roman.	2328
Nicholas II	Rus.	2328
Niger, Pescennius	Roman.	2336
Nin, Andreas	Spain	2337
Nizam-al-Mulk	Turk.	2341
Nobunaga	Japan	2341
Nunez Vela, Blasco	Peru	2348
Obregn, Alvaro	Mex.	2355
Octavius, Gnaeus	Roman.	2360
O'Dwyer, Sir Michael	Brit.	2362
O'Higgins, Kevin Christopher	Ire.	2366
Odoacer	Roman.	2361
Okubo, Toshimichi	Japan	2367
Olid, Cristbal de	Mex.	2369
Olympio, Sylvanus	Togo	2372
Omar I	Arabia	2372
O'Neill, Shane	Ire.	2373
Ordelaffi, Pino III	Italy	2376
Orestes	Roman.	2377
Orleans, Duke of	Fr.	2378

Orleans, Louis I	Fr.	2378		Remón, José Antonio	Pan.	2566
Orleans, Louis Philippe Joseph	Fr.	2379		Retief, Pieter	S.Afri.	2570
Ormizd IV	Per.	2379		Ribaut, Jean	U.S.	2573
Ormonde, James	Brit.	2379		Ricci, Alberto Bellardi	Swed.	2574
Orodes II	Parthia	2379		Rienzi, Cola di	Italy	2582
Ortin Gil, Constantino	Spain	2380		Riggs, Elisha Francis	U.S.	2583
Othman	Per.	2385		Ritavouri, Heikki	Fin.	2585
Oxenham, John	Brit.	2389		Rivera y Orbaneja, Ant. Primo	Spain	2586
Paes, Sidnio B. Cardosa da Sil	Port.	2392		Rizzio, David	Scot.	2587
Palme, Sven Olof Joachim	Swed.	2398		Roehm, Ernst	Ger.	2607
Pando, José Manuel	Bol.	2404		Romanus III Argyrus	Roman.	2616
Pardo, Manuel	Peru	2408		Romero Menea, Jose Javier	El Sal.	2616
Parmenio	Mac.	2414		Rossi, Count Pellegrino	Italy	2625
Patterson, Albert L.	U.S.	2422		Roxana	Mac.	2632
Paul I	Rus.	2426		Rufinus, Flavius	Roman.	2638
Pedro el Cruel	Fr.	2435		Sadat, Anwar	Egypt	2653
Penda	Mercia	2439		Said Halim Pasha, Mehmet	Turk.	2657
Perceval, Spencer	Brit.	2443		Sakamoto Ryoma	Japan	2662
Perdiccas	Mac.	2444		Sakuma Shozan	Japan	2662
Pertinax, Publius Helvius	Roman.	2448		Salameh, Ali Hassan	Leb.	2663
Peter I	Fr.	2450		Salaverry, Felipe Santiago	Peru	2663
Peter III	Rus.	2451		Sam, Vilbrun Guillaume	Haiti	2674
Peter III	Rus.	2452		Sambhaji, Raja	India	2674
Peter of Castelnau	Fr.	2452		Sanchez Cerro, Luis M.	Peru	2675
Petlyura, Symon	Fr.	2454		Sancho II		2675
Phalaris	Si.	2456		Sancho IV		2675
Phaulkon, Constantine	Thai.	2456		Saturninus, Lucius Appuleius	Roman.	2681
Philip II	Mac.	2457		Savarkar, Vir Vinayak Damodar	India	2682
Philip III Arrhidaeus	Mac.	2457		Savinkov, Boris Viktorovich	Rus.	2684
Philip of Swabia	Ger.	2457		Saw, U.	Burma	2684
Philochorus	Gr.	2460		Sayadian, Aruthin	Armenia	2685
Philopoemen	Gr.	2460		Scaevola, Quintus Mucius	Roman.	2685
Phraates III	Parthia	2460		Scipio, Gnaeus Cornelius	Roman.	2708
Phraates IV	Parthia	2460		Scipio, Publius Cornelius	Roman.	2708
Phrynichus	Gr.	2460		Scipio Nasica, Publius Cornelius	Roman.	2708
Pius XI	Italy	2472		Seleucus I	Mac.	2725
Pizarro, Francisco	Peru	2472		Seleucus IV	Seleucia	2725
Plantagenet, Richard	Brit.	2475		Seleucus V	Seleucia	2725
Plateau, Marius	Fr.	2475		Selim III	Turk.	2726
Plehve, Wenzel von	Rus.	2476		Seliverstoff, Michael de	Fr.	2726
Pole, Sir Edmund de la	Brit.	2481		Sennacherib	Assyria	2728
Pompeius Magnus, Gnaeus	Roman.	2485		Seqenenre II	Egypt	2728
Portales, Diego José Victor	Chile	2490		Sertorius, Quintus	Roman.	2729
Porus	India	2492		Sevket Pasa, Mahmud	Turk.	2730
Postumus, Marcus Cassianius L.	Roman.	2492		Sforza, Galeazzo Maria	Italy	2732
Prim, Juan	Spain	2501		Shah Shoja	Afg.	2733
Probus, Marcus Aurelius	Roman.	2505		Shah Sultan Husayn	Per.	2733
Ptolemy Eupator	Egypt	2510		Shaka	Afr.	2734
Ptolemy V	Egypt	2510		Shermarke, Abdi Rashid Ali	Somalia	2745
Ptolemy VII	Egypt	2510		Sibour, Marie-Dominique-August	Fr.	2751
Ptolemy X	Egypt	2510		Sidky Pasha, Bakir	Iraq	2753
Ptolemy XI	Egypt	2510		Sigebert I	Austrasia	2759
Ptolemy XIV	Egypt	2510		Sigebert II	Gaul	2759
Ptolemy XV	Egypt	2510		Sigurd II	Nor.	2759
Puchert, George	Ger.	2510		Silverius, Saint	Italy	2761
Pupienus Maximus, Marcus Clodi	Roman.	2511		Sixtus II	Roman.	2772
Quezon, Aurora Aragon	Phil.	2523		Smerdis	Per.	2781
Quintana Lacaci, Guillermo	Spain	2523		Snorri Sturluson	Ice.	2805
Radic, Stefan	Croatia	2527		Soga Iruka	Japan	2812
Raditch, Stefan	Yug.	2527		Stack, Sir Lee Oliver Fitzmaur	Egypt	2835
Rahman, Mujibur		2529		Stafford, Humphrey	Brit.	2836
Rainsborough, Thomas	Brit.	2530		Stamboliyski, Aleksandur	Bul.	2837
Ramorino, Girolamo	Italy	2533		Stambolov, Stefan	Bul.	2837
Rasin, Alois	Czech.	2536		Starzynski, Stefan	Pol.	2844
Rasputin, Gregory	Rus.	2536		Stelescu, Michael	Rom.	2849
Rathenau, Walther	Ger.	2542		Stephen VI	Italy	2850
Raziya	India	2548		Steunenberg, Frank R.	U.S.	2851
Regulus, Marcus Atilius	Roman.	2559		Stewart, James	Brit.	2853
Reina Barrios, José Maria	Guat.	2561		Strang, James Jesse	U.S.	2866
Reiss, Ignace	Switz.	2563		Stürgkh, Karl von	Aust.	2873

ASSASSINATION ATTEMPTS - Case of

ASSASSINATION ATTEMPTS - Unsolved

ASSASSINATION PLOT

ASSAULT

Fontaine, Peter De la	Brit	1193
Goslett, Arthur Andrew Clement	Brit.	1349
Hadfield, John	Brit.	1413
Hamilton, Mary	Brit.	1435
Le Quong, Vinh	Viet.	1939
Martin, Robert H.	U.S.	2132
Menken, Adah Bertha	U.S.	2166
Moders, Mary	Brit.	2196
Montagu, Edward Wortley	Brit.	2203
Morris, Henry	Brit.	2225
Murphy, Charles	U.S.	2258
Owens, Loy Alton	U.S.	2389
Philip the Magnanimous	Ger.	2458
Poderjay, Ivan	Int'l.	2478
Raviere, Raymond la	U.S.	2546
Roediger, Fritz	Can.	2607
Russell, John Francis Stanley	Brit.	2642
Schneider, Anna	Ger.	2696
Shotton, Edward George	Brit.	2749
Smith, Cecil Brown	Int'l.	2782
Stocks, Maria	Brit.	3132
Van Wie, Francis	U.S.	3035
Von Veltheim, Franz	Brit.	3064
Watson, James P.	U.S.	3103
Watson, Lionel Rupert Nathan	Brit.	3103
Wheat, Thomas	Brit.	3132
Williams, Norman	U.S.	3164

BIGAMY - Case of

Howard, Eleanor	Brit.	1628
Jones, Catherine	Brit.	1736
Schultzenstein, Otto	Ger.	2705

BLACKMAIL

Arthur, Charles W.	Brit.	2314
Bigland, Reuben	Brit.	360
Braasch, Clarence E.	U.S.	463
Brcourt, Jeanne Amenaide	Fr.	482
Cagliostro, Count Alessandro d	Int'l.	571
Chaffers, Alexander	Brit.	669
Churchill, May Vivienne	Int'l.	713
Davidson, George Maxim	Brit.	880
Dongan, Thomas	U.S.	999
Esposito, Giuseppe	Int'l.	1105
Fox, Sidney Harry	Brit.	1206
Gaudry, Nathalis	Fr.	482
Hobbs, William Cooper	Brit.	2314
Hosein, Arthur	Brit.	1623
Hosein, Nizamodeen	Brit.	1623
Kutze, Karl Frederic Moritz L.	S. Afri.	1864
Leverson, Sarah Rachel Russell	Brit.	1943
Mann, William d'Alton	U.S.	2104
Margrove, Stephen	Brit.	2121
Merrett, John Donald	Int'l.	2167
Moders, Mary	Brit.	2196
Newton, Montague Noel	Brit.	2314
Omichund	India	2372
Stuart, Norman	Brit.	2900
Taylor, George William	Brit.	2900
Von Veltheim, Franz	Brit.	3064
Wilson, Harriette	Brit.	3171
Wood, John	Brit.	2121

BLACKMAIL - Case of

Brooks, Flossie	U.S.	499
Crowley, Aleister	Int'l.	837
Marovitz, William	U.S.	2127

BLASPHEMY

Diagoras	Gr.	934

Nayler, James	Brit.	2292

BOAT MURDERS

Baker, Joseph	U.S.	216
Bram, Thomas Mead Chambers	U.S.	469
Brown, George	U.S.	506
Brown, James	U.S.	507
Collings, Benjamin P.	U.S.	750
Dalzeel, Alexander	Brit.	864
De Graff, William	U.S.	902
de Soto, Benito	Spain	926
Fair, Laura D.	U.S.	1126
Flowery Land Mutiny	Brit.	1182
Floyd, Charles Arthur	U.S.	1182
Fly, William	U.S.	1188
Galapagos Murders	Ecu.	1251
Galbraith, James	Brit.	1251
Gibbs, Charles	U.S.	1307
Gillette, Chester	U.S.	1313
Goodere, Samuel	Brit.	1339
Gordon, Nathaniel	U.S.	1345
Gow, John	Brit.	1353
Griffin, William	U.S.	1386
Halsey, Joseph	Brit.	1432
Hargraves, Dick	U.S.	1453
Harvey, Julian	U.S.	1472
Hermione Boys, The	Brit.	1523
Hill, William	U.S.	1556
Holmes, Alexander William	U.S.	1601
Holmes, William	U.S.	1603
Jefferies, Christopher	Brit.	1715
Jones, Thomas	U.S.	1741
Kidd, Capt. William	Brit.	1811
Low, Edward	Brit.	1996
Miller, George	U.S.	2180
Monsson, Otto	Brit.	2544
Morgan, Sir Henry	Brit.	2219
Morgan, Jack	U.S.	2221
Morgan, William	U.S.	2221
Morhead, Roy	U.S.	2221
Rau, Gustav	Brit.	2544
Roche, Phillip	Brit.	2604
Rogers, George White	U.S.	2610
Rosewaine, Edward	U.S.	1603
Schmidt, Willem	Brit.	2544
Warrington, Thomas	U.S.	1603
White, Charles	Brit.	1339

BOMBING

Argentine Political Violence	Arg.	154
Armstrong, Karelton Lewis	U.S.	159
Armstrong, Karleton	U.S.	1159
Arrison, William	U.S.	167
Austin, Alice	U.S.	185
Barnes, Peter	Brit.	245
Belcastro, James	U.S.	316
Billings, Warren Knox	U.S.	2207
Bishop, Cameron David	U.S.	381
Black September Organization	Mid.East	398
Clichy Uprising	Fr.	732
Colonial Office Bombing	Brit.	755
Cripple Creek Explosion	U.S.	825
Curzi, Barbara	U.S.	2107
Dunn, Beverly Wyly	U.S.	1037
FALN	U.S.	1132
Faust, Reinhold	U.S.	1139
Fedayeen		1143
Fine, David S.	U.S.	1159
Graham, John Gilbert	U.S.	1358
Harvey's Resort Hot.-Casino Bo	U.S.	1473

Henry, Emile	Fr.	1519
Hindenburg Disaster	Ger.	1559
Jackson, Terry	U.S.	1680
Kim Hyun Hui	N.Kor.	1820
Kulak, Frank	U.S.	1861
Kurbegovic, Muharem	U.S.	1862
Laaman, Jaan Karl	U.S.	2107
Levasseur, Patricia Gros Luc	U.S.	2107
Levasseur, Raymond Luc	U.S.	2107
McNamara Brothers	U.S.	2062
McNamee, Gilbert	Brit.	2064
Manning, Carol	U.S.	2107
Manning, Thomas William	U.S.	2107
Mare Island Explosion	U.S.	2119
Metesky, George Peter	U.S.	2172
Mooney, Thomas Jeremiah	U.S.	2207
Morse, Donald Lee	U.S.	2228
Murray, Mick	Brit.	2260
Okudaira Junzo	Italy	2367
Orchard, Harry	U.S.	2375
Orgeron, Paul	U.S.	2378
Pan Am Flight 103	Scot.	2402
Pankhurst, Emmeline	Brit.	2405
Peak, Duane	U.S.	2575
Poindexter, Edwin	U.S.	2575
Police Bombing	Fr.	2481
Ravachol	Fr.	2545
Rice, David	U.S.	2575
Richards, James	Brit.	245
Scott, Ira	U.S.	185
Simmons, Ted	U.S.	185
Stoner, J.B.	U.S.	2861
Suffragettes	Brit.	2875
Surrey Pubs Bombings	Brit.	2879
Thomas, William King	Ger.	2932
U.S. Embassy Bombing	Leb.	3021
Vaillant, Auguste	Fr.	3024
Ward, Judith	Brit.	3091
Warder (Idaho) Bombing	U.S.	3094
Warr, Carl	U.S.	3095
Williams, Richard Charles	U.S.	2107

BOMBING - Case of

Freedom Riders	U.S.	1231
Linderfeld, Wolfe	U.S.	1967
Plamondon, Lawrence R.	U.S.	2474
Wall Street Bombing	U.S.	3083
World's Fair Bombing	U.S.	3187

BOMBING ATTEMPTS

Savina, Richard	U.S.	2684

BOMBING ATTEMPTS - Unsolved

Salem (Ind.) Bomb Scare	U.S.	2664

BOOTLEGGING

Ashline, Roy	U.S.	170
Audett, James Henry	U.S.	182
Barbican, James	U.S.	232
Barton, Bert	U.S.	270
Baylanch, Autry	U.S.	285
Baylanch, Gee	U.S.	285
Baylanch, Jes	U.S.	285
Billingsley, Fred	U.S.	362
Billingsley, Logan	U.S.	362
Brinkley, Dr. John Romulus	U.S.	488
Clark, Marvin J.	U.S.	724
Cochran, Garland	U.S.	735
Cohen, Monty	U.S.	742
Cool, Floyd	U.S.	772

Cretan, The	U.S.	816
Fogelman, Clay	U.S.	1190
Gagliano, Joseph	U.S.	1249
Gallant, Barney	U.S.	1255
Green, Hershey	U.S.	2123
Hackmeister, Ralph	U.S.	1413
Hardcastle Family	U.S.	1446
Jones, Brant	U.S.	1736
Kreisberg, Daniel	U.S.	2123
Ladd, Bucky	U.S.	170
La Montagne, Montaigu	U.S.	1879
La Montagne, Morgan	U.S.	1879
La Montagne, Rene	U.S.	1879
La Montagne, William	U.S.	1879
Langley, John W.	U.S.	1890
Licavoli, Thomas	U.S.	1949
Marino, Tony	U.S.	2123
Marquett, Jack	U.S.	2127
Maxwell Street Police Station	U.S.	2154
Murphy, David	U.S.	2123
Musica, Philip	U.S.	2262
O'Connor, Tommy	U.S.	2359
O'Donnell Bros. (Chicago, South)	U.S.	2361
O'Donnell Bros. (Chicago, West)	U.S.	2361
Olmstead, Roy	U.S.	2370
Pasqua, Frank	U.S.	2123
Racicot, Sam	U.S.	170
Reed, Edwin	U.S.	2556
Remus, George	U.S.	2566
Shelton Brothers	U.S.	2739
Warner, Dick	U.S.	2359

BOOTLEGGING - Case of

Dunlap, Leon A.	U.S.	1037
Means, Gaston Bullock	U.S.	2159
Riggs, David	U.S.	1037

BRIBERY

Aronowitz, Joseph	U.S.	166
Arpels, Claude	U.S.	166
Basketball Scandal	U.S.	272
Bellson, Samuel	Brit.	1436
Benintende, Joseph	U.S.	330
Berman, Jacob Bennett	U.S.	1180
Biaggi, Mario	U.S.	356
Biaggi, Richard	U.S.	356
Black Sox Scandal	U.S.	399
Brown, Nathaniel	U.S.	1097
Calpurnius Bestia	Roman.	585
Civella, Nicholas	U.S.	717
Clark, James H.	U.S.	722
Clem, Nancy E.	U.S.	728
Cleomenes I	Sparta	730
Corbitt, Michael	U.S.	2142
Crédit Mobilier	U.S.	814
Curtis, Richard L.	U.S.	722
Donegan, Edward	U.S.	998
Dutch West India Company	Neth.	1044
Duvall, John L.	U.S.	1048
Dwyer, William Vincent	U.S.	1049
Englisis, Anthony	U.S.	1097
Englisis, Nicholas	U.S.	1097
Feinberg, Saul	U.S.	1097
Flint, Motley H.	U.S.	1180
Fong Ching	U.S.	1192
Gard, Eddie	U.S.	2814
Garsson, Henry M.	U.S.	1280
Garsson, Murray	U.S.	1280
Getzoff, Ben	U.S.	1180
Goldsmith, Jack	U.S.	2814

Hynes, James	Brit.	1650
Jablonski, Kazimiriz	U.S.	1674
Jenkins, Carrie Lee	U.S.	1718
Jenkins, Thomas James	Brit.	1506
Johnson, Ray	U.S.	1731
Johnson, William	Brit.	1733
Joyce, William	Brit.	1745
Keenan, Brian Paschal	Brit.	1774
Keller, Edward	U.S.	1776
Kennedy, Mathew	Int'l.	1800
Kovalev, Ivan	U.S.	1845
Kravotney, Basil	Czech.	1847
Leboucher, Simonne	Fr.	1915
Lohbauer, John	U.S.	1072
Lowrie, Donald	U.S.	1998
Luddites	Brit.	2007
Maclean, Tony	Brit.	2057
Majors, Abe	U.S.	2092
Mallard, John	Brit.	2414
Marsh, Thomas	Brit.	2128
Maunders, Cyril Edward	Brit.	2153
Maw, Will	Brit.	2153
McCabe, John	U.S.	2022
McGraw, Alice Marie	U.S.	2042
Mead, George	U.S.	2158
Merrick, Suds	U.S.	2168
Milsom, Albert	Brit.	1204
Montos, Nick George	U.S.	2206
Moore, Alfred	Brit.	2209
Moore, Langdon W.	U.S.	2210
Morrison, Richard	U.S.	2226
Munnick, Jan Willem Hendrik	S.Afri.	2251
Munoman, Eleanor	Brit.	2251
Murphy, Jack	U.S.	2259
Neil, Harry	Brit.	2297
Panczko, Joseph	U.S.	2404
Panczko, Paul	U.S.	2404
Panther, The	Brit.	2406
Parquot, Francis	Brit.	2414
Paulson, Michael	U.S.	2427
Peace, Charles Frederick	Brit.	2429
Perkins, Josephine Amelia	Brit.	2444
Peters, Warren	U.S.	3171
Powis, Joseph	Brit.	2495
Purolator Burglary	U.S.	2512
Ramensky, Johnny	Scot.	2533
Reiser, Charles	U.S.	2562
Richardson, Charles	Brit.	1074
Richardson, Joseph	Brit.	2578
Richier, Dr. Xavier	Fr.	2579
Rizzi, William	U.S.	2587
Rulloff, Edward Howard	U.S.	2639
St. Bude, David	Brit.	2658
Sauvageot, Serge	Fr.	121
Saxton, John William	Brit.	522
Saxton, John William	Brit.	3197
Schwart, Emil	U.S.	2706
Seager, George	Brit.	2718
Seaman, William	Brit.	2718
Siege of Sidney Street	Brit.	2758
Simms, Henry	Brit.	2765
Slark, Tom	Brit.	2776
Staggs, Elizabeth	Brit.	522
Staggs, Robert	Brit.	522
Stcherbakov, Matthiew	U.S.	1845
Stevenson, Thomas	U.S.	864
Stewart, Frederick	Brit.	2852
Sugarman Gang	Brit.	2875
Sutton, Michael	U.S.	2881
Timmons, Ronald	U.S.	2956

Tsumaki, Matsukichi	Japan	2998
Vallejo, Daniel	U.S.	1072
Vicars, Henry Edward	Brit.	3044
Vox, Archie	Int'l.	1039
Wagstaff, William	Brit.	3069
Watts, Coral Eugene	U.S.	3104
Weart, James Brennan, Jr.	U.S.	3106
Weiner, Bertha	Brit.	3119
Welch, Bernard Charles, Jr.	U.S.	3123
Wheeler, John	Brit.	3133
Wilson, Charles	U.S.	3171
Wilson, Dink	U.S.	3170
Wilson, Eddie	U.S.	3171
Worth, Adam	Int'l.	3188
Wright, Cecil	U.S.	3192
Wright, Tom	Brit.	3195
Wyatt, John Arthur	Brit.	3197
Wyatt, Margaret	Brit.	522
Wynne, Thomas	Brit.	3199
Young, Joseph Louis	U.S.	3210

BURGLARY - Attempted

Agnew, John	U.S.	1581
Hobbs, William	U.S.	1581
Rose, Vincent	U.S.	1581

BURGLARY - Case of

Abraham, Jack	S.Afri.	1805
Ahlstedt, Gustave	U.S.	41
Anderson, Harry	U.S.	123
Collingwood, Percy	S.Afri.	750
Green, Cleo Joel, III	U.S.	1372
Holliday, Bertram Redvers	Brit.	1592
Kerr, Donald	S.Afri.	1805
Kirby, Walter	S.Afri.	750
Manners, Arthur	S.Afri.	750
Partridge, Tom	Brit.	2416
Soto, Erno	U.S.	2816
Vuong, Phung	U.S.	3066

BURGLARY - Unsolved

Leiva, Dr. Don Carlos	U.S.	1926

BURGLARY - Wrongly Convicted

Flechter, Victor	U.S.	1177
Preston, James W.	U.S.	2498
Usher, Cornelius	U.S.	3021

CANNIBALISM

Bean, Sawney	Scot.	289
Brown, Nichol	Scot.	515
Denke, Carl	Ger.	914
Dudley, Thomas	Brit.	1032
Fentress, Albert	U.S.	1149
Fish, Hamilton Albert Howard	U.S.	1162
Garnier, Gilles	Fr.	1275
Gein, Edward	U.S.	1289
Grossmann, George	Ger.	1393
Haarman, Fritz	Ger.	1412
Helm, Boone	U.S.	1513
Hofmann, Kuno	Ger.	1587
Johnson, John	U.S.	1730
Katist-Chen	Can.	1768
Kemper, Edmund Emil III	U.S.	1791
Kroll, Joachim	Ger.	1852
Langulet, Antoine	Fr.	1891
Packer, Alferd G.	U.S.	2390
Pierce, Alexander	Aus.	2462
Seye, Blaise Ferrage	Fr.	2730
Stephens, Edwin	Brit.	1032

Davidson, Thomas Joseph	Brit.	881		Haun's Hill Massacre	U.S.	1478
Davies, Gerald	Brit.	881		Hauptmann, Bruno Richard	U.S.	1479
Davies, John Michael	Brit.	881		Heady, Bonnie Brown	U.S.	1421
Davis, Thomas Cullen	U.S.	885		Heeber, Dr. Allen	U.S.	1507
de Rais, Gilles	Fr.	2530		Hefeldt, Paul	Brit.	1939
Detroit Child Murders	U.S.	928		Heideman, Frank	U.S.	1507
Doudet, Celestine	Fr.	1008		Heirens, William George	U.S.	1508
Drake, David H.	U.S.	1891		Heller, Isaac	U.S.	1512
Eyman, David L.	U.S.	1121		Hendricks, David	U.S.	1515
Falling, Christine	U.S.	1131		Henley, Elmer Wayne	U.S.	785
Faulkner, Richard	Brit.	1138		Hennis, Timothy Baily	U.S.	1517
Fitz, Alfred	Brit.	1171		Henry VII	Brit.	1518
Fortner, Clifford	U.S.	1200		Hepper, William Sanchez de Pin	Brit.	1522
Frank, Theodore	U.S.	1224		Hickman, William Edward	U.S.	1532
Freeman, Charles F.	U.S.	1231		Hickock, Richard Eugene	U.S.	1534
Freeman, Jeannace	U.S.	1231		Higdon, Lloyd	U.S.	1544
Freeman, John Gilbert	U.S.	1232		Higginbottom, Henry James	Brit.	1545
Freeman, William	U.S.	1232		Higgins, Patrick	Scot.	1546
Freeway Phantom Murders	U.S.	1233		Hill, Harold	Brit.	1551
Gaca, Barbara	U.S.	1246		Hill, James Douglas	U.S.	1552
Gacy, John Wayne, Jr.	U.S.	1246		Hill, Rufus	U.S.	1554
Galloway, Robert	U.S.	1257		Hinkman, William	U.S.	1561
Gandolfe, Jeanne	Fr.	1264		Hoffman, Victor Ernest	Can.	1586
Garcia, Antonio	U.S.	422		Hollis, David Lee	U.S.	1596
Garcia, Joseph	Brit.	1266		Holroyd, Susannah	Brit.	1603
Garnier, Gilles	Fr.	1275		Hood, Linda	U.S.	1608
Garret, Katherine	U.S.	1276		Hood, Vera	Brit.	1608
Gaskins, Donald Henry	U.S.	1283		Horne, William Andrew	Brit.	1620
Gebbia, Leonardo	U.S.	1287		Huberty, James Oliver	U.S.	1634
Gerghuta, Ion	Rom.	1301		Hudson, Frederick	Brit.	1634
Gibbs, Janie Lou	U.S.	1308		Hunter, Thomas	Brit.	1644
Gidley, George	Brit.	2051		Hurd, William	Brit.	2821
Girardi, James A.	U.S.	1317		Jackson, Gertrude	U.S.	1231
Giri, Laxman	India	1317		Jefferies, Christopher	Brit.	1715
Glass, Jimmie	U.S.	1321		Jeffs, Doreen	Brit.	1716
Gluskoter, Rochelle	U.S.	1323		Jenkin, William Thomas Francis	Brit.	1717
Goebbels, Paul Joseph	Ger.	1324		Johnson, Frank	U.S.	1733
Goldenson, Alexander	U.S.	1332		Johnson, Mary	U.S.	1731
Goode, Arthur Frederick, III	U.S.	1339		Johnson, Robert	U.S.	1732
Goozee, Albert	Brit.	1341		Johnson, Vateness	U.S.	1733
Gorringe, Esther	Brit.	1348		Jones, Genene	U.S.	1737
Gottfried, Gesina Margaretha	Ger.	1350		Jones, Harold	Brit.	1737
Governor, Jimmy	Aus.	1353		Jones, Jeremiah	Brit.	1739
Grabowski, Klaus	Ger.	1355		Jones, Reginal	U.S.	1740
Grasso, Santo	Fr.	1363		Jones, Willie	U.S.	1742
Green River Killer	U.S.	1378		Jordan, Clayton	U.S.	1820
Green, Ann	Brit.	1372		Joubert, John J.	U.S.	1744
Greenberg, Bertram	U.S.	1376		Judy, Steven T.	U.S.	1748
Gretzler, Douglas	U.S.	1382		Juenemann, Charlotte	Ger.	1748
Griffiths, Peter	Brit.	1388		Kaczmarczyk, Joseph	Fr.	1752
Grupen, Peter	Ger.	1394		Kalavryta Massacre	Gr.	1753
Gunness, Belle	U.S.	1400		Kantarian, Nancy Lee	U.S.	1759
Haarman, Fritz	Ger.	1412		Kavinsky, Gerald	U.S.	1770
Haga, Eric L.	U.S.	1414		Kehoe, Andrew	U.S.	1775
Haggerty, John	U.S.	1415		Kelley, Dillard E., Sr.	U.S.	1777
Haigh, John George	Brit.	1417		Kelley, Sally	U.S.	1778
Haight, Edward	U.S.	1418		Kelliher, Mary	U.S.	1778
Halbert, Henry	U.S.	1420		Kent, Constance Emilie	Brit.	1804
Hall, Carl Austin	U.S.	1421		Kines, John	U.S.	1820
Hall, George Albert	Brit.	1424		King, Alvin Lee, III	U.S.	1820
Hall, James William	Aus.	1426		Knau, Jobst	Ger.	1835
Hanlon, John	U.S.	1442		Knight, Mary	Brit.	1835
Hardaker, Betty	U.S.	1445		Knight, Virgil	U.S.	1835
Hardy, William	U.S.	1452		Knoppa, Antony Michael	U.S.	1891
Harris, Robert Alton	U.S.	1463		Knowles, Paul John	U.S.	1837
Hart, Gene Leroy	U.S.	1467		Kohout, Edward	U.S.	1842
Harvey, Julian	U.S.	1472		Kohout, Henry	U.S.	1842
Harwood, Jocelin	Brit.	1473		Kraman, Randall	U.S.	1846
Haskell, Flora Fanny	Brit.	1474		Kroll, Joachim	Ger.	1852
Hatcher, Charles Ray	U.S.	1475		Kures, Junka	Fr.	1862

Read, Richard	U.S.	2548
Rees, Melvin David	U.S.	2557
Reggettz, Paul	U.S.	2558
Rendall, Martha	Aus.	2568
Restell, Ann	U.S.	2569
Reynolds, Melvin Lee	U.S.	2571
Rhodes, Ernest	Brit.	2572
Richardson, James	U.S.	2577
Richardson, Leonard	Brit.	2578
Rivera, Antonio	U.S.	2586
Rivire, Pierre	Fr.	2586
Robinson, Sarah Jane	U.S.	2601
Roche, John Francis	U.S.	2604
Rogers, Dayton Leroy	U.S.	2608
Rogers, Kenneth Paul	U.S.	2611
Rojas, Francisca	Arg.	2613
Romer, Richard	U.S.	2616
Rosales, Maria	U.S.	2620
Ross, Charles B.	U.S.	2621
Ross, Colin Campbell	Aus.	2624
Ross, Michael B.	U.S.	2624
Ross, Perry Dean	U.S.	2624
Rottman, Arthur	N.Zea.	2629
Rousseau, Rosella	Fr.	2630
Rowland, Ferrin	U.S.	2631
Ruiz, Luis	U.S.	2638
Rulloff, Edward Howard	U.S.	2639
Ruotolo, Cynthia	U.S.	2640
Ruppert, James	U.S.	2641
Rush, James Blomfield	Brit.	2641
Rutherford, Elsie Mae	U.S.	2644
Rutherford, Howard	U.S.	2644
Ruxton, Buck	Brit.	2645
Ruzicka, James	U.S.	2646
Ryan, Michael	Brit.	2647
Ryan, Michael Ann	U.S.	2647
Sach, Amelia	Brit.	2649
Sadler, Dora Martha Spalding	Brit.	2656
Salmon, Thomas	U.S.	2671
Salvage, Arthur James Farraday	Brit.	2673
Sand Creek Massacre	U.S.	2675
Santana, Frank	U.S.	2679
Saunders, John	U.S.	2693
Schaefer, Gerard	U.S.	2689
Schmid, Charles Howard, Jr.	U.S.	2693
Schneider, Marie	Ger.	2696
Schnick, James Eugene	U.S.	2697
Schuessler, Anton	U.S.	2698
Schuessler, John	U.S.	2698
Seefeld, Adolf	Ger.	2722
Segee, Robert Dale	U.S.	2723
Sellman, Edward Leon	U.S.	2726
Sheen, William	Brit.	2738
Shelfo, Rosary	U.S.	2739
Sherman, Lydia	U.S.	2744
Shoaf, Mamie Shey	U.S.	2747
Shomette, Nancy Marie	U.S.	2647
Shuck, Douglas Paul	U.S.	2750
Simants, Erwin Charles	U.S.	2763
Simmons, Tommie Bernard	U.S.	2726
Smith, Clarice	U.S.	2783
Smith, Linda	Brit.	2798
Smith, Perry	U.S.	1534
Smith, William	Brit.	2803
Snyder, Donald	U.S.	2805
Sodeman, Arnold Karl	Aus.	2811
Soto, Erno	U.S.	2816
Soto, Juan	U.S.	422
Sparrow, William	Brit.	2821
St. Quintin, Richard	Brit.	2051

Stack, Richard	U.S.	2835
Stanciel, Elijah	U.S.	2838
Starkweather, Charles	U.S.	2840
Staunton Family	Brit.	2844
Steelman, William	U.S.	1382
Stevens, Dallas Ray	U.S.	2851
Stimson, Ann	Brit.	2855
Stinney, George Junius, Jr.	U.S.	2856
Stüllgens, Robert Wilhelm	Ger.	2873
Stone, Lawrence Clinton	U.S.	2859
Stone, Scott C.	U.S.	2860
Straffen, John Thomas	Brit.	2866
Sullivan, Howard	U.S.	2875
Swart, Marthinus Erich	S.Afri.	2886
Terpening, Oliver, Jr.	U.S.	2915
Tessnov, Ludwig	Ger.	2917
Tiernan, Helen	U.S.	2953
Tierney, Nora Patricia	Brit.	2953
Tillman, Emil	Ger.	2955
Tinning, Marybeth Roe	U.S.	2956
Treadaway, Jonathan C.	U.S.	2984
Tremamunno, Donato	Italy	2985
Troppmann, Jean-Baptiste	Fr.	2990
Truscott, Steven Murray	Can.	2998
Vasquez, Tiburcio	U.S.	422
Walpole, Merla	U.S.	2586
Walters, Annie	Brit.	2652
Washington, Allen	U.S.	3097
Watt, Miriam	U.S.	3104
Weber, Adolph	U.S.	3108
Weber, Jeanne	Fr.	3108
Werner, Karl	U.S.	3127
Westervelt, William	U.S.	3129
Wheat, Clarence	U.S.	3132
Wheeler, Mary Eleanor	Brit.	3133
Wheelock, Norman	U.S.	3134
Whelpton, George	Brit.	3135
Whiteway, Alfred Charles	Brit.	3141
Whitman, Charles Joseph	U.S.	3143
Whittle, William	Brit.	3147
Wienchowski, Joseph	U.S.	3148
Wierzbiki, Edward F.	U.S.	3148
Wild, William	Brit.	3151
Williams, Ada Chard	Brit.	3159
Williams, Edward	Aus.	3161
Williams, Thomas	Brit.	382
Williams, Wayne Bertram	U.S.	3166
Wilson, James William	U.S.	3172
Wilson, John Gleeson	Brit.	3174
Winsor, Charlotte	Brit.	3177
Wise, Olive Catherine	Brit.	3178
Wright, Jeanne Anne	U.S.	3194
Wymer, Eugene William	U.S.	3198
York, William	Brit.	3207
Zekerman, Andrew	Brit.	2051
Zu Shenatir	El-Yemen	3223

CHILD PORNOGRAPHY - Case of

Chalkley, Dr. Thomas	U.S.	670

CITIZENS GROUP

Chicago Crime Commission	U.S.	696

COINING

Bacchus, Thomas	Brit.	205
Moore, John	Brit.	2210
Roberts, Samuel	Brit.	205

COMPUTER CRIME

Zinn, Herbert D.	U.S.	3221

Noske, Gustav	Ger.	2347	Rouse, John	Brit.	3074
O'Donnell, Calvagh	Ire.	2361	Ruthven, Patrick	Scot.	2644
O'Donnell, Hugh Roe	Ire.	2361	Ruthven, William	Scot.	2644
O'Donnell, Sir Niall Garv	Ire.	2361	Rye House Plot	Brit.	2647
O'Neill, Daniel	Ire.	2373	Rykov, Aleksei Ivanovich	Rus.	2647
O'Neill, John	U.S.	2373	Ryleev, Kondrati Fdorovich	Rus.	2648
O'Neill, Shane	Ire.	2373	Saint-Germain, Comte de	Fr.	2658
O'Reilly, Alexander	Spain	2377	Sakai Toshihiko	Japan	2662
O'Reilly, John Boyle	Brit.	2377	Salan, Raoul Albin Louis	Fr.	2663
Obando, José Maria	Col.	2350	Salinas, F.A.	U.S.	2671
Odinga, Sekou	U.S.	2360	Salmon, James	Brit.	348
Og, Jacques Vincent	Haiti	2365	Salmon, Sheldon J.	U.S.	2671
Okawa Shumei	Japan	2366	Sanders, Nicholas	Ire.	2676
Olozaga, Salustiano	Spain	2371	Sandys, Sir Edwin	Brit.	2677
Omichund	India	2372	Santa Anna	Mex.	2679
Order, The	U.S.	2376	Santarosa, Santorre di	Italy	2679
Ordzhonikidze, Grigori Konstan	Rus.	2377	Savarkar, Vir Vinayak Damodar	India	2682
Orloff, Michael A.	U.S.	2379	Savinkov, Boris Viktorovich	Rus.	2684
Osborn, Albert	Brit.	2711	Saw, U.	Burma	2684
Ostermann, Andrei Ivanovich	Rus.	2384	Schall von Bell, Johann Adam	Ger.	2690
Osuna, Pedro Tllez y Girn	Spain	2385	Schindler, Michael	U.S.	2692
Otho, Marcus Salvius	Roman.	2385	Scott, Henry	Brit.	2711
Paget, William	Brit.	2394	Scott, James	Brit.	2712
Palm, Johann Philipp	Ger.	2398	Scrope, Henry le	Brit.	2716
Pan Ku	China	2405	Scrope, Richard le	Brit.	2716
Pandulph III	Italy	2405	Sejanus, Lucius Aelius	Roman.	2724
Parnell, Kenneth E.	U.S.	2414	Seneca, Lucius Annaeus	Roman.	2728
Parsons, Robert	Brit.	2416	Sertorius, Quintus	Roman.	2729
Pasic, Nikola	Serbia	2418	Seton, Baron George	Scot.	2729
Pelham, John	Brit.	495	Sewell, Frederick Joseph	Brit.	2730
Percy, Sir Henry	Brit.	2443	Seymour, Edward	Brit.	2730
Percy, Thomas	Brit.	2444	Sheiner, William	U.S.	2461
Perez, Antonio	Spain	2444	Shyres, Mark	U.S.	2379
Pestel, Pavel Ivanovich	Rus.	2450	Sigismund	Hung.	2759
Peter, Hugh	Brit.	2452	Sinclair, George	Scot.	2768
Petrucci, Pandolfo	Italy	2455	Sisk, T. Edward	U.S.	2772
Philotas	Mac.	2460	Sixtus IV	Italy	2772
Piacentile, Victor	U.S.	2461	Sjahrir, Sutan	Indo.	2772
Pichegru, Charles	Fr.	2462	Smith, Cyril Broughton	Brit.	2711
Pilsudski, Jzef	Pol.	2466	Smith, Gerrit	U.S.	2793
Pisarev, Dmitry Ivanovich	Rus.	2470	Snell, William	U.S.	1113
Piso, Gaius Calpurnius	Roman.	2470	Snider, Duke	U.S.	1512
Piso, Lucius Calpurnius Caeson	Roman.	2470	Snorri Sturluson	Ice.	2805
Plantagenet, Edward	Brit.	2475	Sohappy, David	U.S.	2812
Platshorn, Robert Elliot	U.S.	2475	Sokolnikov, Grigori Yakovlevic	Rus.	2812
Pleshcheev, Aleksei Nikolaevic	Rus.	2476	Sophia Alekseevna	Rus.	2816
Plunket, Oliver	Ire.	2477	Southampton, Henry Wriothesley	Brit.	2817
Pole, Sir Geoffrey	Brit.	2481	Sprengtporten, Jakob Magnus	Fin.	2833
Polignac, Armand Jules M.H. de	Fr.	2482	Stafford, Henry	Brit.	2836
Polignac, Auguste Jules A.M. d	Fr.	2482	Steiger, Schultheiss Niklaus F	Switz.	2847
Pompeius Magnus, Sextus	Roman.	2485	Stewart, Alexander	Scot.	2852
Potmkin, Grigori Aleksandrovic	Rus.	2492	Stewart, Andrew	Brit.	2852
Power, Michael	Brit.	495	Stewart, John	Brit.	2853
Pracey, John	Brit.	2711	Stewart, Robert	Scot.	2853
Protopopov, Aleksandr Dmitriev	Rus.	2508	Stoner, J.B.	U.S.	2861
Prusias II	Bithynia	2509	Strozzi, Giovanni Battista	Italy	2871
Psamtik III	Egypt	2510	Stuart, Esm	Brit.	2871
Ptolemy VIII	Egypt	2510	Stuart, Lady Arabella	Brit.	2871
Pyatakov, Grigori L.	Rus.	2517	Sturmer, Boris Vladimirovich	Rus.	2874
Pym, John	Brit.	2517	Sugarman Gang	Brit.	2875
Ramos, Graciliano	Braz.	2533	Svinhufvud, Pehr Evind	Fin.	2884
Ramsay, Sir John	Scot.	2533	Swendsen, Kurt	Brit.	2888
Randolph, Thomas	Brit.	2534	Tavannes, Seigneur de	Fr.	2899
Raymond, Cindy	U.S.	1512	Taylor, Charles Frederick	U.S.	2772
Renwick, James	Scot.	2569	Tellez, Hector	U.S.	2912
Ridolfi, Roberto	Brit.	2581	Theodosius	Roman.	2926
Rkosi, Mtys	Hung.	2532	Thomas, Sharon	U.S.	1512
Robertson, David	U.S.	2692	Thomas of Woodstock	Brit.	2932
Rogers, John	Brit.	2610	Thompson, Anthony	U.S.	2692
Rosenberg, Edward	U.S.	1180	Throckmorton, Francis	Brit.	2942

Ingham, Ellery P.	U.S.	1692
Jacobs, William	U.S.	483
Jacobs, William M.	U.S.	1692
Johnson, Edwin	Can.	1728
Jones, John	Brit.	916
Kendig, William	U.S.	483
Kendig, William L.	U.S.	1692
Koslov, Walter	U.S.	3124
Krger, Friedrich Walter Bernha	Ger.	1852
Lustig, Victor	U.S.	3105
Marang, Karel	Port.	2562
Maw, Will	Brit.	2153
Miassojedoff, Ivan	Liech.	2176
Mora, Frederico	Int'l.	2213
Morello, Giuseppe	U.S.	2217
Mueller, Edward	U.S.	2247
Murphy, Christian	Brit.	2259
Naylor, Francis	Int'l.	2292
Newitt, Harvey K.	U.S.	1692
Ninger, Emanuel	U.S.	2338
Nissen, Charles	Brit.	2339
Oster Gang	U.S.	2384
Parsons, William	Brit.	2416
Perreau, Daniel	Brit.	2445
Perreau, Robert	Brit.	2445
Raamat, Elmar	U.S.	3124
Reis, Arthur Virgilio Alves	Port.	2562
Reis, Maria L.J. D'Azevado	Port.	2562
Roberts, William	Brit.	2594
Salisbury, Francis	Brit.	2671
Schmidt, Hans	U.S.	2694
Sharp, Thomas	Brit.	2735
Sing Lee	U.S.	2769
Skog, John Albert	Int'l.	2774
Smolianoff, Solomon	Ger.	2804
Spencer, Barbara	Brit.	2824
Sperati, Giovanni de	Brit.	2828
Stucley, Thomas	Brit.	2873
Taylor, Arthur	U.S.	483
Taylor, Arthur	U.S.	1692
Taylor, Arthur	U.S.	2899
Ulrich, Charles	U.S.	3014
Watts, William	U.S.	3105
Wellman, Edward John	U.S.	3124
Windisch-Graetz, Ludwig	Hung.	3176

COUNTERFEITING - Case of

Neilson, Frederick	Aus.	2298
Sprinkle, Jacob	U.S.	2833
Sprinkle, Nancy	U.S.	2833
Taylor, John	Brit.	2901

COUNTERFEITING - Wrongly Convicted

Sullivan, Percy B.	U.S.	2875
Zambino, Luigi	U.S.	3215

COURTS AND TRIALS

Chastelard, Pierre de Boscosel	Fr.	690
Old Bailey	Brit.	2367
Scopes, John Thomas	U.S.	2709
Scott, Dred	U.S.	2711

CRIME & PUNISHMENT

Brady, Mary	U.S.	467
Farrett, Jane	Brit.	1136
Orbilius Pupillus	Roman.	2375
Runcorn, Ann	Brit.	2640

CRIME DISTRICT

Indian Territory	U.S.	1654

Thieves' Exchange	U.S.	2929

CRIME MUSEUM

Black Museum, The	Brit.	397

CRIME PREVENTION

Guardian Angels	U.S.	1395
Yale, Linus	U.S.	3204

CRIMINAL JUSTICE

Fox, Henry Richard Vassall	Brit.	1205
Jones, Samuel Milton	U.S.	1741
Winslow, Forbes Benignus	Brit.	3177

CRIMINALLY INSANE

Finley, Ruth	U.S.	1160

CRIMINAL NEGLIGENCE

Anatoly S. Dyatlov	U.S.S.R.	524
Bryukhanov, Viktor P.	U.S.S.R.	524
Byng, John	Brit.	564
Nikolai M. Fomin	U.S.S.R.	524

CRIMINALLY NEGLIGENT HOMICIDE

Longet, Claudine	U.S.	1987

CRIMINAL TRESPASS

Ray, Margaret	U.S.	2547
Rust, Matthias	U.S.S.R.	2643

CRIMINOLOGY

Baldwin, Roger Nash	U.S.	218
Bertillon, Alphonse	Fr.	349
Bonesana, Cesare	Italy	429
Caldwell, Charles	U.S.	579
Coffin, Thomas	U.S.	741
Cohen, Louis	U.S.	741
Colquhoun, Patrick	Brit.	759
Durkheim, Emile	Fr.	1041
Ellero, Pietro	Italy	1083
Faulds, Henry		1138
Ferri, Enrico	Int'l	1153
Fitzthedmar, Arnold	Brit.	1173
Gall, Franz Joseph	Ger.	1254
Galton, Francis	Brit.	1257
Glueck, Eleanor Touroff	U.S.	1323
Glueck, Sol Sheldon	U.S.	1323
Gonzalez, T.A.	Mex.	1338
Goring, Charles B.	Brit.	1348
Gross, Hans	Aust.	1392
Heinrich, Edward Oscar	U.S.	1508
Henry, Sir Edward Richard	Brit.	1519
Herschel, Sir William John	Brit.	1526
Hooton, Dr. Earnest A.	U.S.	1609
Keeler, Leonarde	U.S.	1773
Koehler, Arthur	U.S.	1841
Krogman, Wilton Marion	U.S.	1851
Lavater, Johan Casper	Switz.	1905
Locard, Edmond	Fr.	1974
Lombroso, Cesare	Italy	1980
Maudsley, Henry	Brit.	2151
Niceforo, Alfredo	Italy	2327
Ryan, Edward James	U.S.	2646
Sanger, Dr. William	U.S.	2677
Simon, Dr. Carleton	U.S.	2765
Spruzheim, John Casper	U.S.	2834
Vucetich, Juan	Arg.	3065
von Olshausen, Justus	Ger.	2371

CRUCIFIXION - Case of

Collins, Ed	U.S.	751

CRUELTY

Littire, Henri	Fr.	1971

COURT MARSHAL

Hall, James	U.S.	1425
Hazen, William Babcock	U.S.	1500
Hull, William	U.S.	1638
Mitchell, William	U.S.	2192
Porter, Fitz-John	U.S.	2491
Revere, Joseph Warren	U.S.	2570
Scott, John	Brit.	2712
Stesel, Anatoli Mikhailovich	Rus.	2851
Stokoe, John	Brit.	2857
Stessel, Anatoly Mikhaylovich	Rus.	2864

DEMONOLOGY

Boguet, Henri	Fr.	421

DETECTIVE

McParland, James	U.S.	2066
Norfleet, J. Frank	U.S.	2343
Parker, Ellis	U.S.	2410
Pellicano, Anthony J.	U.S.	2437
Pinkerton, Allan	U.S.	2467
Pinkerton, William Allan	U.S.	2468
Siringo, Charles Angelo	U.S.	2771

DETECTIVE AGENCY

Pinkerton Detective Agency	U.S.	2468

DISORDERLY CONDUCT

Tuck, Mark	Brit.	2998

DRAFT DODGER

Bergdoll, Grover Cleveland	U.S.	341
Rubinstein, Serge	U.S.	2633

DRUGS

Abrams, Michael	U.S.	13
Alvarez-Quiroga, Juliana	U.S.	107
Alvarez-Qurioga, Roman	U.S.	107
Alvarez-Qurioga, Roman Jr.	U.S.	107
Ansaldi, Marius	Fr.	129
Attardi, Alphonse	U.S.	179
Aunay, Pierre	Fr.	184
Autullo, Dante, Jr.	U.S.	186
Bafia, Brian	U.S.	618
Baker, Andrew	U.S.	213
Bangkok Legless Drug Smuggler	Thai.	225
Barba Hernndez, Javier	Mex.	229
Barnes, Leroy	U.S.	245
Beland, Lucy	U.S.	316
Benjamin, Victor H.	U.S.	331
Bishop, Jesse Walter	U.S.	381
Blaisdell, Steven	Fr.	892
Bourbonnais, Charles	Int'l.	2619
Bridges, Dean	U.S.	1267
Byrski, Martin	U.S.	1134
Calamaris, Nicholas	Int'l.	2619
Calamia, Leonard	U.S.	577
Cappas, John	U.S.	618
Carrasco, Fred Gomez	U.S.	637
Chagra, Jamiel Alexander	U.S.	669
Chindawongse, Sihadej	U.S.	700
Chiying	China	701
Cirillo, Louis	U.S.	716
Clark, James G.	U.S.	722
Clark, Laura Ethel	U.S.	723

Cohen, Aaron	Malaysia	741
Cohen, Lorraine	Malaysia	741
Colas, Andr	U.S.	742
Cole, Thomas Charles	Col.	743
Concannon, Jack	U.S.	763
Cro Quintero, Rafael	Mex.	634
Dean-Siddel, Elizabeth	Fr.	892
De Lorean, John Zachary	U.S.	908
DeMaro, Audrey	U.S.	2435
DeMaro, Michael	U.S.	2435
DiPalermo, Joseph	U.S.	976
DiPasquale, Diego	Can.	1252
Distefano, Luigi	Can.	1252
Doo Lew	U.S.	1002
Dorr, David L.	U.S.	2118
Dragoti, Stan	Ger.	1019
Eghise, Mauricio	Mex.	1075
Escalante, Ramon	U.S.	1102
Escobar Gaviria, Pablo	Col.	1103
Esparragoza Moreno, Juan Jos	Mex.	1104
Farmer, Jack	U.S.	1134
Farmer, Mike	U.S.	1134
Farmer, Pamela	U.S.	1134
Fine, Herman	U.S.	1159
Fiumara, Agostino	Can.	1252
Felix Gallardo, Miguel Angel	Mex.	1146
Flores, Eduardo	U.S.	1181
Foley, Carole	Fr.	892
Fonseca Carrillo, Ernesto	Mex.	1192
Fort, Jeff	U.S.	1199
Francisco, Sancho	Mex.	1210
Fucaloro, Anthony	U.S.	1134
Gagliano, Joseph	U.S.	1249
Galante, Carmine	U.S.	1250
Galifi, Nicola	Can.	1252
Gallardo Parra, José Luis	Mex.	1255
Garcia, Percy	U.S.	1267
Garcia, Rolando	U.S.	2408
Garza, Isuaro	U.S.	1282
Gotti, Gene	U.S.	1350
Herrera Family	Int'l.	1525
Hill, Virginia	U.S.	1555
Hoffman, Abbie	U.S.	1585
Impastato, Nicolo	U.S.	1653
Jefferson, Leroy	U.S.	1715
Jenkins, David	U.S.	1718
Jenkins, Ferguson	Can.	1718
Johnson, John R.	U.S.	1730
Katzenberg, Yasha	U.S.	1769
Kelley, Dillard E., Sr.	U.S.	1777
Kerridan, Michael	U.S.	618
King, Robert L.	Int'l.	1826
Kirby, George	U.S.	1828
Krupa, Gene	U.S.	1853
Lasser, Louise	U.S.	1900
Leani, Jean	Fr.	184
Lehder Rivas, Carlos Enrique	Int'l.	1924
Leifer, Gitel	Int'l.	1926
Leifer, Isak	Int'l.	1926
Li Sheung	U.S.	1970
Litteral, Robert	U.S.	1970
LoCascio, Peter	U.S.	1974
London Dog-Doping	Brit.	1980
Lopez, Agapito	U.S.	1989
Loury, Glenn C.	U.S.	1994
Lozano-Ahumada Feud	U.S.	2000
Lucente, Anthony	U.S.	1249
Luciano, Dominic	Can.	1252
McCartney, Paul	Japan	2024
MacDonald, Lynda Anne	Can.	1252

McLain, Dennis Dale	U.S.	2054
McNab, Kevin	U.S.	1134
Madonna, Matthew	U.S.	2078
Marchant, Peter A.	U.S.	2118
Matta Ballesteros, Juan Ramn	Mex.	2147
Medellin Murders	Col.	2161
Meinster, Robert Jay	U.S.	2163
Meinster, Robert Jay	U.S.	2475
Melton, Tracy	U.S.	2164
Melton, William	U.S.	2164
Milgazo, F.F.	U.S.	2179
Mines, Joseph	U.S.	2188
Minkow, Barry	U.S.	2188
Mitchum, Robert	U.S.	2192
Miyagawa Yashukichi	Brit.	2194
Myers, Eugene Arter	U.S.	2163
Nelson, Roger	U.S.	2304
Nichopoulos, Dr. George	U.S.	2334
Noriega Morena, Manuel Antonio	Pan.	2344
Ochoa Vsquez, Jorge Luis	Col.	2358
Pagano, Joseph Luco	U.S.	2392
Pagano, Pasquale A.	U.S.	2392
Palermo Connection	Si.	2397
Pardo, Manuel	U.S.	2408
Pedote, Frank	U.S.	2435
Perlowin, Bruce J.	U.S.	2445
Pizza Connection	U.S.	2472
Platshorn, Robert Elliot	U.S.	2163
Quintero Payn, Emilio	Mex.	2523
Quintero Payn, Juan Jos	Mex.	2523
Ramirez, Patrick	U.S.	2533
Reese, Walter	U.S.	2558
Roark, Mike	U.S.	2589
Rodriguez Gacha, Jose Gonzalo	Col.	2606
Rodriguez Orejuela, Gilberto	Col.	2606
Rodriguez Orejuela, Miguel Ang	Col.	2606
Rosal, Mauricio	Int'l.	2619
Salcido Uzeta, Manuel	Mex.	2663
Savides, Christ	U.S.	2683
Scalise, Frank	U.S.	2686
Scarfo, Nicodemo	U.S.	2688
Schultz, Arden	U.S.	2699
Siano, Fiore Ernest	U.S.	2751
Sibille, Serge	U.S.	742
Sica, Joseph	U.S.	2751
Smith, Cathy Evelyn	U.S.	2782
Smith, Edward	Brit.	2784
Smith, Jimmy Lee	U.S.	2796
Sobhraj, Gurmukh Charles	India	2810
Starkie, Richard	Brit.	2840
Stead, William Thomas	Brit.	2846
Stratton, Richard L.	U.S.	2868
Surez Gmez, Roberto, Sr.	Bol.	2874
Tarditi, Etienne	Int'l.	2619
Tonner, Francis Ian	U.S.	2967
Vaccaro, John	U.S.	3023
Villapando, James	U.S.	1134
Vinci, Michele	Can.	1252
Vitale, John Joseph	U.S.	3057
Yesh, Robert	U.S.	3207
Zaccaro, John A., Jr.	U.S.	3215

DRUGS - Case of

Polanski, Roman	U.S.	2481
Rasta-Coptic Smuggling Network	Jam.	2541
Soto, Erno	U.S.	2816

DUEL

Anderson, Hugh	U.S.	123
Barbot, John	W.Indies	233

Barthlemy, Emanuel	Brit.	266
Brougham, Henry	Brit.	503
Brudenell-Tuckett Duel	Brit.	519
Buckingham, Duke of	Brit.	532
Burr, Aaron	U.S.	554
Cadwalader, John	U.S.	569
Calhoun-Williamson Duel	U.S.	580
Canning, George	Brit.	599
Carrel, Nicolas Armand	Fr.	637
Cavallotti, Felice Carlo Emman	Italy	660
Christie-Scott Duel	Brit.	708
Chateauneuf	Fr.	690
Cyrano de Bergerac, Savinien d	Fr.	852
d'Amboise, Bussy	Fr.	864
D'Artois-de Bourbon Duel	Fr.	877
de Beauvallon, Rosamond	Fr.	894
Decatur-Barron Duel	U.S.	897
D'Entragues-Caylus Duel	Fr.	916
Douglas-Mahun Duel	Scot.	1009
Dupont-Fournier Duel	Fr.	1039
Finch-Hatton/Wellesley Duel	Brit.	1158
Fitzgibbon, John	Ire.	1172
Floquet, Charles Thomas	Fr.	1181
Francis, Sir Philip	Brit.	1210
Fulton, Katie	U.S.	1241
Guesclin, Bertrand du	Fr.	1397
Gwin-McCorckle Duel	U.S.	1410
Hamilton-Mohun Duel	Brit.	1435
Hastings, Warren	Brit.	1475
Jackson-Dickinson Duel	U.S.	1681
Jarnac-Chteigneraie Duel	Fr.	1711
Jeffcott-Hennis Duel	Brit.	1714
Jeffreys-Moore Duel	Brit.	1716
Knollys, Charles	Brit.	1836
Lassalle, Ferdinand	Ger.	1900
Laurens-Lee Duel	U.S.	1904
McIntosh-Gwinet Duel	U.S.	2046
Maquer, Chevalier	Fr.	2114
Martin-Wilkes Duel	Brit.	2133
Maugerin-Riberac Duel	Fr.	2151
Melcy-Castlereagh Duel	Brit.	2164
Mellant-Lenfant Duel	Fr.	2164
Neilson, George	Scot.	2298
O'Connell-D'Esterre Duel	Ire.	2358
Rameau, Jaquette	Fr.	2533
Randolph-Clay Duel	U.S.	2534
Retz, Cardinal de	Fr.	2570
Rowan-Chambers Duel	U.S.	2631
Sand Bar Gun Battle	U.S.	2675
Silks, Mattie	U.S.	2759
Stewart-Canning Duel	Brit.	2854
Stuart-Boswell Duel	Scot.	2872
Svign, Marquis Henri de	Fr.	2730
Terry, David Smith	U.S.	2916
Tierney, George	Brit.	2953
Tuckett-Brudenell Duel	Brit.	2999
Wedderburne-Stanhope Duel	Brit.	3112
Wellesley-Finch-Hatton Duel	Brit.	3124

DUEL - Case of

Wilson-Lyon Duel	Can.	3173

EMBEZZLEMENT

Bain, Robert Owen	U.S.	212
Berman, Jacob Bennett	U.S.	1180
Bloom, David	U.S.	410
Blumen, Julius	U.S.	412
Blumen, Leopold	U.S.	412
Boyle, Richard	Brit.	462
Brethauser, G. Henry	U.S.	485

Turlis, Thomas	Brit.	3003
Tyburn Tree	Brit.	3010
de Crespigny, Sir Claude	Brit.	898

EXILE

Ceawlin	Brit.	662
Cem	Turk.	663
Cerchi, Vieri dei	Italy	663
Chao Huan	China	680
Confalonieri, Federico	Italy	764
Costello, John	Ire.	796
de Ricard, Louis Xavier	Fr.	2573
Haakon VII	Nor.	1412
Hurtado de Mendoza, Diego	Spain	1646
Jovanovic, Slobodan	Yugo.	1745
Konbaung, Thibaw	Burma	1842
Leroux, Pierre	Fr.	1940
Machado, Bernardino Luis	Port.	2045
Magnus, Johannes	Swed.	2087
Marcellus I	Roman.	2118
Maret, Hugues Bernard	Fr.	2120
Mickiewicz, Adam Bernard	Pol.	2177
Milkowski, Zygmunt	Pol.	2179
Mneccimbasi, Ahmed Dede	Turk.	2251
Mnnich, Burkhard Christoph von	Rus.	2251
Mohammed I Askia	Songhai	2196
Montalvo, Juan	Ecu.	2203
Montfar y Rivera Maestre, Lore	Guat.	2206
Moreau, Jean Victor-Marie	Fr.	2216
Moses Ben Nahman	Spain	2233
Mussato, Albertino	Italy	2263
Nerva, Marcus Cocceius	Roman.	2306
Pez, José Antonio	Venez.	2392
Pushkin, Aleksander Sergeevich	Rus.	2516
Radishchev, Aleksandr Nikolaev	Rus.	2527
Saavedra R. d. Baquendano, Ang	Spain	2649
Saldanha Oliveira Daun, Joao C.	Port.	2663
Samory	Guinea	2674
Shevchenko, Taras Hryhorovych	Rus.	2745
Siqueiros, David Alfaro	Mex.	2771
Somodevilla y Bengoechea, Zen.	Spain	2815
Teresa	Port.	2914
Theodore Studites	Roman.	2926
Thompson, George	Brit.	2934
Timoleon	Gr.	2956
Ulbricht, Walter	Ger.	3014
Ursinus	Roman.	3018
Vonck, Jean-Franois	Belg.	3062

EXPLOSIVES

Munroe, Charles Edward	U.S.	2251
Oliver, Paul Ambrose	U.S.	2370

EXTORTION

Aleman, Harry	U.S.	72
Alexander, Daniel	Brit.	657
Alexander, Lee	U.S.	91
Bertolotti, Freddy	U.S.	2691
Black Hand	Int'l.	392
Blanton, Ray	U.S.	407
Bolland, James	Brit.	424
Borstein, Sydney	U.S.	2691
Bove, James V.	U.S.	1140
Boyles, Odell Carlysle	U.S.	463
Boyles, Sue Zachary	U.S.	463
Braasch, Clarence E.	U.S.	463
Byrne, Dominic P.	U.S.	2016
Campbell, Don	U.S.	593
Carter, James Y.	U.S.	644
Catalano, Anthony Joseph	U.S.	976

Cather, John	Brit.	657
Coles, Ronald R.	U.S.	745
Corallo, Anthony	U.S.	2448
Curran, James M.	U.S.	848
DeCarlo, Angelo	U.S.	896
Decavalcante, Samuel Rizzo	U.S.	898
de Contreras, Fernando	Alg.	898
Delay, Dallas Ray	U.S.	908
DiPasquale, Anthony Louis	U.S.	976
Dolabella, Publius Cornelius	Roman.	985
Donally, James	Brit.	998
Dutch West India Company	Neth.	1044
Esposito, Giuseppe	Int'l.	1105
Farese, Thomas R.	U.S.	1133
Fay, Joseph S.	U.S.	1140
Fleming, Erin	U.S.	1178
Freidland, David	U.S.	1234
Furnari, Christopher	U.S.	2448
Galante, Carmine	U.S.	1250
Gallighen, Mona	U.S.	1829
Ganev, Gantscho	Switz.	3093
Gianola, Leonard	U.S.	1307
Harper, Michael	U.S.	1456
Harvey, James	U.S.	1472
Harvey's Resort Hot.-Casino Bo	U.S.	1473
Hooper, Harney E., Jr.	U.S.	1609
Igor	Rus.	1652
Indelicato, Anthony	U.S.	2448
Ismael, Muley	Int'l.	1668
Kane, Patrick	Brit.	657
Kerrigan, Larry	U.S.	1829
Kessler, Samuel J.	U.S.	1806
Kierdorf, Frank	U.S.	1815
Kirk, James	U.S.	1829
Knight, Thomas	U.S.	1835
Koury, Leo Joseph	U.S.	1845
Kovic, Anthony C.	U.S.	1845
Langella, Gennaro	U.S.	2448
Lynch, Mel Patrick	U.S.	2016
McCormick, James, J.	U.S.	2027
McGee, John	U.S.	593
McLagan, Robert	Can.	2054
Marco, Alberto	U.S.	2118
Martin, Clestine Camille	Fr.	2131
Moore, Cory C.	U.S.	2210
Moran, James J.	U.S.	2215
Mumfre, Joseph	U.S.	2250
Order of Our Lady of Mercy	Spain	2376
Osano Kenji	Japan	2382
Persico, Carmine	U.S.	2448
Provenzano, Anthony	U.S.	2508
Roselli, John	U.S.	2620
Salerno, Anthony	U.S.	2448
Santoro, Salvatore	U.S.	2448
Schiff, Jack	U.S.	2691
Scopo, Ralph	U.S.	2448
Spilotro, Victor	U.S.	2829
Thoman, J. Clarence	U.S.	2929
Vaughan, Thomas	Brit.	3039
Wardas, Roman	Switz.	3093
Wedtech Scandal	U.S.	3112
Williams, Roy	U.S.	1829
Williams, William August Helm	U.S.	3167
Winche, Paul	Brit.	3176
Woody, Loretta	U.S.	1829

EXTORTION - Case of

Commito, Angelo	U.S.	762
Ezaki Katsuhisa	Japan	1122
Kiritsis, Anthony G.	U.S.	1829

Crafton, Paul Arthur	U.S.	805	Leone, Raymond	U.S.	1394
Crook, Japhet	Brit.	828	LeRoy, Wright	U.S.	1940
Davidson, Peter	Brit.	881	Levine, Ave	U.S.	1394
Davria, Govind Narayen	India	887	Lewis, S.C.	U.S.	1180
de Thuin, Raul	Mex.	927	LoCascio, Peter	U.S.	1974
Deupree, Jim	U.S.	930	MacKay, Henry	U.S.	1180
Dillard, E.H.	U.S.	943	Macleod, Mrs. A.	Scot.	2057
Dodd, William	Brit.	983	Mahoney, James E.	U.S.	2089
Donadieu, Alfredo-Hecktor	Int'l.	996	Malskat, Lothar	Ger.	2098
Dossena, Alceo	Int'l.	1006	Maynard, Thomas	Brit.	2157
Dougal, Samuel Herbert	Brit.	1009	Mercier, Euphrasie	Fr.	2166
Dowse, Margaret	Brit.	1014	Merrett, John Donald	Int'l.	2167
Drossner, Charles Jean	U.S.	1025	Meyer, Henry C.F.	U.S.	2174
Dyer, Ernest	Brit.	1050	Miassojedoff, Ivan	Liech.	2176
Elliott, Joe	Int'l.	1084	Montalbano, Cynthia	U.S.	2203
Engles, George	Int'l.	1096	Musica, Philip	U.S.	2262
Farese, Thomas R.	U.S.	1133	Nandakumar	India	2276
Fauntleroy, Henry	Brit.	1138	Nee, A.H.	U.S.	2295
Fey, Dietrich	Ger.	2098	Newton, Montague Noel	Brit.	2314
Finney, Warren Wesley	U.S.	1161	O'Dare, Josephine	Brit.	2360
Fletcher, Joshua	Brit.	1179	Parker, James	U.S.	2411
Flint, Motley H.	U.S.	1180	Parker, Mabel	U.S.	2411
Freeman, Morris	Brit.	3138	Patrick, Albert T.	U.S.	2419
George, Frederick Douglas	U.S.	1299	Peach, Phillip	Brit.	1636
Getzoff, Ben	U.S.	1180	Peete, Lofie Louise	U.S.	2436
Gibbons, Thomas	Brit.	3138	Perreau, Daniel	Brit.	2445
Goldblum, Stanley	U.S.	1331	Perreau, Robert	Brit.	2445
Gossage, Eben	U.S.	1349	Phipps, Thomas, Jr.	Brit.	2460
Goudie, Thomas Patterson	Brit.	1351	Phipps, Thomas, Sr.	Brit.	2460
Graham, John Gilbert	U.S.	1358	Pigott, Richard	Brit.	2465
Great Bank of England Forgery	Brit.	1366	Preston, Guy Richard	Brit.	2498
Green, Clovis Carl	U.S.	1373	Price, Charles	Brit.	2499
Griffiths, James	Brit.	1388	Reavis, James Addison	Int'l.	2550
Gruebert, Frederick	U.S.	1394	Rice, John	Brit.	2575
Hadfield, John	Brit.	1413	Ritson, Joseph	Brit.	2585
Haiat, Fred	Brit.	1416	Roberts, William	Brit.	2594
Haiat, Joe	Brit.	1416	Robinson, Herbert	Brit.	1596
Hardin, Rufus Howard	U.S.	1451	Rosenberg, Edward	U.S.	1180
Harkins, William Hamilton	U.S.	1453	Roupell, William	Brit.	2629
Harman, Mary Ann	Brit.	1596	Salisbury, Francis	Brit.	2671
Hatcher, Charles Ray	U.S.	1475	Savary, Henry	Brit.	2683
Hatry, Clarence	Brit.	1477	Savitt, Samuel Norman	U.S.	2684
Henderson, George	Brit.	1515	Scott, Leonard Ewing	U.S.	2712
Hirschorn, Stephen	U.S.	1394	Sheridan, Walter Cartman	Int'l.	2743
Hobbs, William Cooper	Brit.	1581	Simpson, Edward	Brit.	2766
Hobbs, William Cooper	Brit.	2314	Sisson Documents	U.S.	2772
Hofman, Mark W.	U.S.	1587	Skene, George	Brit.	2773
Holloway, Joseph	Brit.	1596	Stonehouse, John Thomas	Brit.	2860
Horry, George Cecil	N.Z.	1622	Strumm, Franz Felix	Brit.	2871
Houghton, Thomas	Brit.	1625	Tawell, John	Brit.	2899
Howard, Joseph	U.S.	1629	Taylor, Courtney Townsend	U.S.	2899
Howard, Mendell	Brit.	1630	Trinder, Stanley	Brit.	1014
Hughes, Mrs.	Brit.	1636	Ulrich, Charles	U.S.	3014
Huntington Library Fakes	U.S.	1645	Vaughan, H.	Brit.	519
Hunton, Joseph	Brit.	1645	Vaughan, Richard William	Brit.	3039
Innes, John	Brit.	1656	Wainewright, Thomas Griffiths	Brit.	3070
Ireland, William Henry	Brit.	1663	Walpole, Horace	Brit.	3084
Isaac, Bernard	Brit.	1667	Wellings, Edward	Brit.	1636
Jackson, Theresa	U.S.	1681	Weston, George	Brit.	3129
Jennings, George Augustine	Brit.	1721	Weston, Joseph	Brit.	3129
Jim the Penman	Brit.	1724	Westwood, William John	Aus.	3130
Jones, Charles F.	U.S.	2419	White, Henry	Brit.	3138
Kemp, John J.	U.S.	1791	Whitefoord, Dr. Caleb C.	Brit.	3139
Kennaway, Gerald	Brit.	1793	Whitehead, Philip	Brit.	3140
Kennaway, Herbert	Brit.	1793	Wilby, Ralph Marshall	U.S.	3149
King, Francis Reginald	Brit.	1667	Willing, Maud	Brit.	1636
Kuhn, Fritz	U.S.	1854	Witt, Herman	U.S.	1394
Larson, Chester N.	U.S.	1900	Woods, Dorothy	U.S.	3185
Lauder, William	Brit.	1903	Wright, Whitaker	Brit.	3195
Leone, Louis Quentin	U.S.	1394	Young, James	U.S.	3210

Young, John	Scot.	3210

FORGERY - Case of

Bismarck, Prince	Prussia	383
Dick, Jack	U.S.	939
Keating, Tom	Brit.	1772
Means, Gaston Bullock	U.S.	2159
Ryves, Mrs. Anthony T.	Brit.	2648

FORGERY - Wrongly Convicted

Campbell, Bertram	U.S.	592
Fontaine, Peter De la	Brit	1193
Shephard, Clifford	U.S.	2739

FORGERY - Wrongly Convicted (?)

Davison, William	Scot.	887

FRAUD
Art Fraud

Beckford, William	Brit.	311
Bertram, Charles Julius	Den.	351
Cremonse, Francesco	Fr.	815
De Hory, Elmyr	Spain	902
Erickson, Lewis	U.S.	1101
Fasoli, Alfredo	Italy	1138
Fioravanti, Alfredo	U.S.	1161
Irving, Clifford	U.S.	1665
Lloyd, Francis Kenneth	U.S.	1973
Lucas, Vrain	Fr.	2002
MacPherson, James	Scot.	2069
Mount, Charles Merrill	U.S.	2235
Onomacritus	Gr.	2373
Pallesi	Italy	1138
Shapira, M.W.	Int'l.	2734
Stein, David	Int'l.	2847
van Meegeren, Han	Neth.	3032

Art Fraud - Case of

Covert, Adolphe B.	U.S.	2816
Scoby, Alpheus	U.S.	2816
Scotford, James O.	U.S.	2816
Soper, Daniel E.	U.S.	2816

Bank Fraud

Angelos, Anthony G.	U.S.	127
Bain, John	U.S.	212
Barber, William Henry	Brit.	1179
Baum, Frank	U.S.	2848
Bermondt-Avalov, Pavel Mihailovich	Rus.	346
Brandl, John H.	U.S.	472
Chadwick, Constance Cassandra	U.S.	667
Clem, Nancy E.	U.S.	728
Colombo, Marc	Switz.	755
Deeming, Frederick Bayley	Int'l.	899
Doeberl, Frank A.	U.S.	1229
Ettelson, Leonard B.	U.S.	1109
Fialkow, Norman	U.S.	2657
Fletcher, Joshua	Brit.	1179
Freccia, Carmela Emily	U.S.	1229
Freccia, Frank	U.S.	1229
Freedman, Leonard	U.S.	2848
Gleason, John S., Jr.	U.S.	1109
Hartman, Silas W.	U.S.	728
House, James Arthur	U.S.	1626
Humbert, Frederic	Fr.	1640
Humbert, Therese Daurignac	Fr.	1640
Isaac, Bernard	Brit.	1667
Janus, Christopher G.	U.S.	1711
King, Francis Reginald	Brit.	1667
Klotz, Louis Lucien	Fr.	1833

Kuhrmeier, Ernst	Switz.	1854
Laffranchi, Claudio	Switz.	1854
Lea, Luke, Jr.	U.S.	1913
Lea, Luke, Sr.	U.S.	1913
Lorimer, William	U.S.	1991
Lytle, John R.	U.S.	2020
McConnell, J.R.	U.S.	2027
Marcinkus, Paul C.	Italy	2118
Mastocciolo, Joseph A.	U.S.	1229
Mecham, Evan	U.S.	2160
Merrett, John Donald	Int'l.	2167
Patterson, William	U.S.	2020
Pecoraro, Michael	U.S.	2435
Rentschler, William H.	U.S.	2569
Rifkin, Stanley Mark	U.S.	2582
Saft, Howard E.	U.S.	2657
Santowski, Donald	U.S.	2848
Sheridan, Walter Cartman	U.S.	2743
Sindona, Michele	U.S.	2768
Steinberg, Louis	U.S.	2848
Stonehouse, John Thomas	Brit.	2860
Villagran, Dovie Beams	U.S.	3054
Waggoner, Charles Delos	U.S.	3068
Walker, Daniel	U.S.	3076
Wilson, Philip Morrel	U.S.	3175

Business Fraud

Ainsworth, Ernest Albert Harri	Brit.	43
Balfour, Jabez Spencer	Brit.	218
Beall, Edward	Brit.	287
Beck, Sophie	U.S.	297
Benson, Henry	Brit.	334
Bernard, Henry Peter	Brit.	346
Bernard, Marcus Edward Septimus	Brit.	346
Binder, Aaron M.	U.S.	370
Bolland, James	Brit.	424
Bottomley, Horatio William	Brit.	449
Bowers, Donald	U.S.	2120
Brinsmead, Thomas Edward	Brit.	43
Celani, Frederick George	U.S.	370
Chambers, Wayne	Brit.	1630
Colino, Richard	U.S.	746
Crotch, Walter	Brit.	1137
Culliford, Albert	Brit.	844
Culliford, Stanley	Brit.	844
Darby, Walter	Brit.	346
Day, Raymond	U.S.	888
Dunstance, Norman Jackson	Brit.	1038
Factor, John	Int'l.	1123
Fadell, Fred	U.S.	1842
Farley, E.E.	U.S.	1134
Farrow, Thomas	Brit.	1137
Hanau, Marthe	Fr.	1440
Harper, Carey Judson	U.S.	1456
Harris, George	Brit.	2448
Howarth, Kenneth	Brit.	1630
Jacobs, John J.	U.S.	1692
Kaye, William Henry	Brit.	43
Keely, John E. Worrell	U.S.	1773
Kline, Marvin L.	U.S.	1842
Koolish, Abraham	U.S.	1842
Koolish, David	U.S.	1842
Kupfer, Gertrude	Ger.	1862
Kupfer, Martha	Ger.	1862
Lamont, Anne	U.S.	1879
Lovesay, Joseph John	Brit.	844
Margolies, Irwin	U.S.	2120
Margolis, Henry	U.S.	2121
McManus, Thomas J.	U.S.	2059
Mecham, Evan	U.S.	2160

Meyer, Augustus Wilhelm	Brit.	2174
Mitchell, Charles Edwin	U.S.	2190
Mitten, Thomas Eugene	U.S.	2194
Moreno, Anthony	Fr.	2217
Newman, Julia St. Clair	Brit.	2312
Noriega Morena, Manuel Antonio	Pan.	2344
Novick, Hyman David	Int'l.	2347
Olson, Clifford	Can.	2371
Owen, Brynar James	Brit.	2388
Perrott, John	Brit.	2445
Perryman, Charles Wilbraham	Brit.	2448
Poulson, John Garlick Llewelly	Brit.	2493
Pritchard, Harold E.	U.S.	2504
Richardson, Charles William	Brit.	2576
Richardson, Edward	Brit.	2576
Richardson, John	Brit.	2577
Rubinstein, Serge	U.S.	2633
Rutland, William	Brit.	2644
Saruco, Charles	Brit.	2680
Slatter, Herbert Shorland	Brit.	2680
Spilotro, Victor	U.S.	2829
Stavisky, Serge Alexandre	Fr.	2845
Stone, John T.	U.S.	2859
Stonehouse, John Thomas	Brit.	2860
Trippet, Robert S.	U.S.	2989
Turner, Glenn W.	U.S.	3004
Wagner, Clair C.	U.S.	3068
Wells, Charles	Brit.	3125
Zaghlul, Saad	Egypt	3215

Business Fraud - Case of

Rabhan, Erwin David	U.S.	2525

Check Fraud

Baum, Frank	U.S.	2848
Belew, George Lester	U.S.	317
Bolland, James	Brit.	424
Cummings, Lulu	U.S.	845
Deeming, Frederick Bayley	Int'l.	899
Deupree, Jim	U.S.	930
Disintegrating Checks, Case of	U.S.	978
Finney, Warren Wesley	U.S.	1161
Freedman, Leonard	U.S.	2848
Gabor, George Robert	U.S.	1245
Gordon-Baille, Mary Ann	Brit.	1346
Gray, William McKinnon	Brit.	1365
Harper, Carey Judson	U.S.	1456
Hohensee, Adolphus	U.S.	1589
Klotz, Louis Lucien	Fr.	1833
Lerwill, William Knight	Brit.	1940
Levy, Joseph	U.S.	1945
Owen, Brynar James	Brit.	2388
Parker, James	U.S.	2411
Parker, Mabel	U.S.	2411
Pencovic, Francis	U.S.	2439
Ponzi, Charles	U.S.	2485
Preston, Guy Richard	Brit.	2498
Santowski, Donald	U.S.	2848
Savitt, Samuel Norman	U.S.	2684
Schneider, Anna	Ger.	2696
Steinberg, Louis	U.S.	2848
Taylor, Courtney Townsend	U.S.	2899

Computer Fraud

Leavenworth Prison Tax Fraud	U.S.	1914
Rifkin, Stanley Mark	U.S.	2582
Schneider, Jerry Neal	U.S.	2696

Confidence Game Fraud

Banuolo, Donna	U.S.	228

Barrena, Juan	Mex.	248
Beale, Charles James	Brit.	1416
Beck, Martha Julie	U.S.	296
Berry, John	Brit.	348
Blee, Mr.	Brit.	348
Blodgett, Wilson A.	U.S.	1380
Blonger, Louis	U.S.	409
Boatright, Buck	U.S.	413
Boudes, Abb	Fr.	453
Buckminster, Fred	U.S.	533
Casanova, Giovanni G. de Seing	Italy	648
Chadwick, Constance Cassandra	U.S.	667
Chaperau, Albert Nathaniel	U.S.	680
Churchill, May Vivienne	Int'l.	713
Clarke, Mary Anne	Brit.	725
Close, Henry Colin	U.S.	733
Cole, Edwin	U.S.	743
Collins, Curly	U.S.	1424
Conwell, Chic	U.S.	768
Cook, Dr. Frederick A.	U.S.	769
Corrigan, Michael	Brit.	790
Cory, James	U.S.	792
Cox, Seymour E.J.	U.S.	769
Cummings, Lulu	U.S.	845
Davis, Jim	U.S.	1424
De Silva, Charles Percival	Brit.	925
Dean, Dickie	U.S.	1424
Debar, Ann O'Delia Diss	Brit.	893
Deeming, Frederick Bayley	Int'l.	899
Delaney, Daniel	Brit.	906
Dillard, E.H.	U.S.	943
Dutton, Stephen	U.S.	1046
Egan, James	Brit.	348
Engel, Sigmund	U.S.	1093
Estes, Billie Sol	U.S.	1107
Factor, John	Int'l.	1123
Farley, E.E.	U.S.	1134
Fernandez, Raymond Martinez	U.S.	296
Fox, Mary	Brit.	1206
Frad, Willie T.	U.S.	1207
Frost, George William	Brit.	1238
Furey, Joseph	U.S.	1243
Furguson, Arthur	Int'l.	1242
Gondorf Brothers	U.S.	1336
Gordon-Baille, Mary Ann	Brit.	1346
Gordon-Gordon	U.S.	1346
Gregory, Arthur John P. Mich.	Brit.	1379
Grenfell, T. Remington	U.S.	1380
Grey, Alice	Brit.	1382
Grierson, Alan James	Brit.	1385
Grieve, Elizabeth	Brit.	1385
Grin	Brit.	1391
Grunspavnin, Count Nikolas	Brit.	2884
Hadfield, John	Brit.	1413
Haiat, Fred	Brit.	1416
Haiat, Joe	Brit.	1416
Hall, Archibald	Brit.	1420
Hall, Eddie	U.S.	1424
Halliot, Henry	U.S.	1428
Harper, Michael	U.S.	1456
Haseltine, James	Brit.	1473
Herd, Alexander T.	U.S.	1523
Hohenau, Walter	U.S.	1589
Hooley, Ernest Terah	Brit.	1609
Johnston-Noad, Edward	Brit.	1735
Jones, William	U.S.	1741
Kitto, Michael	Brit.	1420
Las Vegas Casino Chip Scam	U.S.	1901
Las Vegas Casino Roulette Ball Scam	U.S.	1901
Leach, Harvey	U.S.	1913

Donaldson, Archibald	U.S.	1030
Dubois, Frank	U.S.	1030
Dunne, Edward	U.S.	1030
Frad, Willie T.	U.S.	1207
Francasal Fraud	Brit.	1208
Gondorf Brothers	U.S.	1336
Johnson, Enoch	U.S.	1728
Jones, William	U.S.	1741
Las Vegas Casino Chip Scam	U.S.	1901
Las Vegas Casino Roulette Ball Scam	U.S.	1901
Moore, George	U.S.	1030
Musgrave, Vernon Cecil Ellingh	Brit.	2262
Nelson, Harry	U.S.	1030
New York Lottery Swindle	U.S.	2326
Sheehan, John J.	U.S.	1030
Slack, John	U.S.	162
Smith, Jefferson Randolph	U.S.	2794
Stone, O.M.	U.S.	2860
Thomas, Alvin Clarence	U.S.	2929
Tieri, Frank	U.S.	2953
Turner, J.W.	U.S.	2860
Waggles Case	Brit.	3068

Gaming/Gambling Fraud - Case of

Chifney, Samuel	Brit.	699
Crane, William	U.S.	810
Kurr, William	Brit.	3085
Murray, Edwin	Brit.	3085
Walters, Henry	Brit.	3085
Wyatt	U.S.	810

Gaming/Gambling Fraud - Wrongly Convicted

Powell, Willard	U.S.	2494

Government Fraud

Bergman, Bernard	U.S.	342
Bigot, Franois	Fr.	361
Blackstone Rangers	U.S.	402
Bredell, Baldwin S.	U.S.	1692
Brotherton, Eric	Brit.	503
Christos, Eftihia	Brit.	710
Cotlar, Marvin L.	U.S.	2379
Curley, James Michael	U.S.	847
Delano, Columbus	U.S.	907
Estes, Billie Sol	U.S.	1107
Farouk I	Egypt	1135
Fort, Jeff	U.S.	1199
Glaze, Billy	U.S.	1322
Jacobs, William M.	U.S.	1692
Kendig, William L.	U.S.	1692
Rickson, William	U.S.	2580
Savitt, Samuel Norman	U.S.	2684
Siegel Trading Company	U.S.	2757
Sliwka, Tadeusz	U.S.	2778
Taylor, Arthur	U.S.	1692
Taylor, Linda	U.S.	2901

Government Fraud - Case of

Calandra, Joseph	U.S.	578
Commito, Angelo	U.S.	762
Donovan, Raymond J.	U.S.	1001

Heath Insurance Fraud

Abrams, Sam	U.S.	13
Alberding, Heinrich	Ger.	46
Bass, Dr. Andrew	U.S.	274
Bolber, Morris	U.S.	422
Douat, Vital	Int'l.	1008
Favato, Carino	U.S.	422
Fox, Sidney Harry	Brit.	1206

Freccia, Carmela Emily	U.S.	1229
Freccia, Frank	U.S.	1229
Gross, Martin	U.S.	3120
Hayward, Harry T.	U.S.	1499
Knoop, George F.	U.S.	1836
Larocque, Francois	Can.	1898
Messman, Dr. Hirsch L.	U.S.	3120
Meyer, Henry C.F.	U.S.	2174
Page, Robert	U.S.	2393
Petrillo, Herman	U.S.	422
Petrillo, Paul	U.S.	422
Tetzner, Kurt Erich	Ger.	2918
Udderzook, William E.	U.S.	3014
Unger, Dr. August M.	U.S.	3015
Watzl, Ernest	Aust.	3106
Weiss, Joseph J.	U.S.	3120

Health Insurance Fraud - Case of

Dwight, Walton	U.S.	1048

Impersonation Fraud

Allen, George E.	U.S.	95
Baker, Mary	Brit.	217
Bedloe, William	Brit.	313
Benson, Harry	Brit.	334
Bluffstein, Sophie	Rus.	412
Boudes, Abb	Fr.	453
Chadwick, Constance Cassandra	U.S.	667
Charlesworth, Violet	Brit.	687
Close, Henry Colin	U.S.	733
Corrigan, Michael	Brit.	790
Crook, Japhet	Brit.	828
Curley, James Michael	U.S.	847
Day, Alexander	Brit.	888
Debar, Ann O'Delia Diss	Brit.	893
Deeming, Frederick Bayley	Int'l.	899
Delaney, Daniel	Brit.	906
Demara, Ferdinand Waldo, Jr.	U.S.	910
de Moreno, Don Pedro Suarez	Fr.	913
Dillard, E.H.	U.S.	943
Domela, Harry	Ger.	994
Douglas, Philip	Brit.	1010
Douglas, Richard	Brit.	1010
Du Tilb, Arnold	Fr.	1045
Engel, Sigmund	U.S.	1093
Fox, Margaret	U.S.	1206
Fox, Sidney Harry	Brit.	1206
Francis, Charles Julius	U.S.	1209
Freccia, Carmela Emily	U.S.	1229
Freccia, Frank	U.S.	1229
Gabor, George Robert	U.S.	1245
Harold, Gille	Nor.	1455
Harris, George	Brit.	2448
Hatfield, John	Brit.	1476
Jennings, George Augustine	Brit.	1721
Johnson, Will H.	U.S.	1733
Knoop, George F.	U.S.	1836
Lancaster, Mrs. Val Edwin	Brit.	1882
Orton, Arthur	Brit.	2380
Otto, Stephen Victor	Brit.	2386
Perryman, Charles Wilbraham	Brit.	2448
Peters, Frederick Emerson	U.S.	2452
Psalmanazar, George	Brit.	2510
Remling, Dale Otto	U.S.	2565
Ricardo, Joseph	U.S.	2573
Romanoff, Michael A.D. Obelens	U.S.	2615
Schmidt, Johann	Ger.	2695
Schneider, Anna	Ger.	2696
Schneider, Jerry Neal	U.S.	2696
Simnel, Lambert	Brit.	2765

Smith, Cecil Brown	Brit.	2782
Stonehouse, John Thomas	Brit.	2860
Sutcliffe, George M.	U.S.	2879
Swendsen, Kurt	Brit.	2888
Tourbillon, Robert Arthur	U.S.	2978
Troppmann, Jean-Baptiste	Fr.	2990
Vinocur, Barry Allan	U.S.	3056
Voight, Wilhelm	Ger.	3059
Warbeck, Perkin	Brit.	3090
Weyman, Stanley Clifford	U.S.	3130
Williams, Eleazer	U.S.	3162
Williams, William August Helm	U.S.	3167
Wilson, Sarah	U.S.	3175
Wivallius, Lars	Swed.	3181

Impersonation Fraud - Case of
Cunningham, Emma Augusta	U.S.	846

Inheritance Fraud
Baker Estate Swindle	Int'l.	217
Carmody, John	Brit.	628
de Moreno, Don Pedro Suarez	Fr.	913
Drake Swindle	Int'l.	1020
Edwards, Herbert H.	U.S.	1072
Hartzell, Oscar Merril	U.S.	1471
Morris, Thomas Patrick	U.S.	2225
Orton, Arthur	Brit.	2380
Wright, David Ray	U.S.	3193
Wright, Raymond	U.S.	3193
Wright, Willye Sue	U.S.	3193

Investment Fraud
Ammon, Robert Adams	U.S.	2184
Baker, A.Y.	U.S.	213
Birrell, Lowell McAfee	U.S.	379
Bottomley, Horatio William	Brit.	449
Corrigan, Michael	Brit.	790
Culliford, Albert	Brit.	844
Culliford, Stanley	Brit.	844
DeAngelis, Anthony	U.S.	892
Deeming, Frederick Bayley	Int'l.	899
Drew, Daniel	U.S.	1022
Emma Mine	U.S.	1091
Enricht, Louis	U.S.	1098
Factor, John	Int'l.	1123
Fisk, James, Jr.	U.S.	1167
Forbes, Robert Duncan	Brit.	1193
Gold Accumulator Swindle	U.S.	1330
Gordon-Gordon	U.S.	1346
Gordon, Leroy	U.S.	2258
Gould, Jay	U.S.	1351
Harrison, Charles	Brit.	1193
Hoffman, Jerome D.	Int'l.	1585
Humbert, Frédéric	Fr.	1640
Humbert, Thérèse Daurignac	Fr.	1640
Isaacs, Charles	Brit.	1193
Konkus, Charles	U.S.	2258
Koretz, Leo	U.S.	1842
Kreuger, Ivar	Swed.	1849
Kyslant, Lord	Brit.	1865
Law, John	Int'l.	1905
Lefferdink, Allen Jonas	U.S.	1922
Lennon, Patrick Henry	U.S.	1930
Levine, Dennis	U.S.	1944
Long Island Lighting Co., The	U.S.	1987
Lorang, Francis	Brit.	1990
Lovesay, Joseph John	Brit.	844
Lyons, Sophie	U.S.	2018
Mandeville, Alexis	Brit.	2101
Mandeville, Henry	Brit.	2101

Mandeville, Walter	Brit.	2101
Markus, Edward Jules	Int'l.	2125
Miller, William Franklin	U.S.	2184
Minkow, Barry	U.S.	2188
Mitchell, Rodger	U.S.	2258
Morland, Harold	Brit.	1865
Murlas Commodities	U.S.	2258
Serhant, Robert B.	U.S.	2728
South Sea Bubble, The	Brit.	2818
Spencer, Charles	Brit.	2825
Stavisky, Serge Alexandre	Fr.	2845
Tausand, Franz	Ger.	2898
Trippet, Robert S.	U.S.	2989

Investment Fraud - Case of
Fidelity Investment Association	U.S.	1154

Mail Fraud
Allison, William Stafford	U.S.	1601
Angelos, Anthony G.	U.S.	127
Answera, Louis	Brit.	1275
Ault, Maude	U.S.	184
Ault, Robert Eugene	U.S.	184
Aust, Hans Georg	U.S.	1354
Bailey, Albert Edward	Brit.	1336
Balgar, Robert L.	U.S.	219
Baum, Frank	U.S.	2848
Beach, Charles Richard	Brit.	1336
Berroyer, Helen	U.S.	2247
Bertrams, Carl H.	U.S.	352
Binder, Aaron M.	U.S.	370
Blanton, Ray	U.S.	407
Celani, Frederick George	U.S.	370
Cook, John Clarence	U.S.	1601
Cottlieb, Nathan	Brit.	1336
Cox, Seymour Ernest J.	U.S.	803
Craig, Robert	U.S.	806
Cunningham, Alice	Brit.	1336
Curley, James Michael	U.S.	847
Dawson, Frank Albert	Brit.	3055
De Hory, Elmyr	Spain	902
Diggs, Charles C., Jr.	U.S.	943
Edwards, Kermit C.	U.S.	1637
Estes, Billie Sol	U.S.	1107
Factor, John	Int'l.	1123
Fadell, Fred	U.S.	1842
Feldman, Richard L.	U.S.	1146
Finney, Warren Wesley	U.S.	1161
Flautt, Elizabeth	U.S.	1326
Flautt, Irene	U.S.	1326
Freccia, Carmela Emily	U.S.	1229
Freccia, Frank	U.S.	1229
Freedman, Leonard	U.S.	2848
Fuchs, Bernard	U.S.	1239
Fulkerson, Samuel Cole	U.S.	1240
Galenti, Cora	U.S.	1252
Garland, Wallace Graydon	U.S.	1275
Garner, Stanley	Brit.	1275
Garvey, Marcus Aurelius	U.S.	1280
George Y. Ayling	U.S.	352
Goebel, Otto E.	U.S.	1326
Golding, Anthony	Brit.	1336
Goldstone, Charles Joseph	Brit.	1336
Gordon, Herman Hy	U.S.	1601
Graber, Roland H.	U.S.	1354
Griffith, John Ike	U.S.	1637
Grigsby, Stanley Thomas	Brit.	1336
Grossman, Israel G.	U.S.	1393
Groves, George S.	U.S.	1394
Groves, Wallace	U.S.	1394

Habib, Jacob	U.S.	1601
Harper, Carey Judson	U.S.	1456
Hartzell, Oscar Merril	U.S.	1471
Hastings, James F.	U.S.	1474
Hill, Mildred	U.S.	1554
Hoffman, Jerome D.	Int'l.	1585
Hohensee, Adolphus	U.S.	1589
Holmes, Jimmy Jack	U.S.	1601
Holsinger, Maurice Paul	U.S.	1603
Homer, John Arthur	Brit.	1336
Huie, J. Robert	U.S.	1637
Jacobs, John J.	U.S.	1692
Janus, Christopher G.	U.S.	1711
Jennings, George Augustine	Brit.	1721
Jessup, Charles	U.S.	1723
Jones, Wilfred	U.S.	2247
Jones, Wilfred Algernon	Brit.	1336
Katzen, Morris	U.S.	1769
Kaye, Herman	U.S.	1770
Kline, Marvin L.	U.S.	1842
Koolish, Abraham	U.S.	1842
Koolish, David	U.S.	1842
Lamont, Anne	U.S.	1879
LaRouche, Lyndon, Jr.	U.S.	1899
Leavey, James Joseph	Brit.	1336
Levenson, Alfred Percival	Brit.	1336
Levy, Joseph	U.S.	1945
Louisiana State University Sca	U.S.	1993
Love Letters Scandal	Italy	1996
Lucas, Vrain	Fr.	2002
Mandel, Marvin	U.S.	2100
Markert, Louis	U.S.	806
Martenson, Richard	U.S.	1146
Martino, Joseph E.	U.S.	2379
Martin-Trigona, Anthony R.	U.S.	2133
Mason, Arnold Caverly	U.S.	1275
Mass, Cecil Wallace	Brit.	1336
Means, Gaston Bullock	U.S.	2159
Minkow, Barry	U.S.	2188
Montgomery, Austin Howard	U.S.	2205
Moore, Bob, Jr.	U.S.	1637
Morrell, George	Brit.	1336
Muench, Nellie Tipton	U.S.	2247
Netherland, Robert	U.S.	2307
Orloff, Michael A.	U.S.	2379
Parker, James	U.S.	2411
Parker, Mabel	U.S.	2411
Paul, William	Brit.	1336
Piacentile, Victor	U.S.	2461
Pinkus, Joseph J.	U.S.	2468
Powers, Otto	U.S.	1601
Pritchard, Harold E.	U.S.	2504
Roberts, Dennis L.	U.S.	2591
Roth, Murray David	U.S.	2625
Sager, Harold G.	U.S.	2657
Santowski, Donald	U.S.	2848
Savitt, Samuel Norman	U.S.	2684
Scott, Elliot Nathaniel	U.S.	2711
Sheiner, William	U.S.	2461
Shelhamer, Richard K.	U.S.	352
Shyres, Mark	U.S.	2379
Sims, Loyie	U.S.	2767
Steinberg, Louis	U.S.	2848
Tannenbaum, Gershon	U.S.	1239
Varley, Joseph	Brit.	1336
Vincent, Gaius Tom	Brit.	3055
Whitten, Frank O., Jr.	U.S.	1637
Wilson, Irving	Brit.	1366
Woodward, Harry	U.S.	1770

Mail Fraud - Case of

Commito, Angelo	U.S.	762
Insull, Samuel	U.S.	1657

Media Fraud

Aeronauts in the New York World	U.S.	36
Boston *Globe* Hoax	U.S.	446

Medical Fraud

Abrams, Albert	U.S.	11
Allen, George E.	U.S.	95
Aycock, Charles	U.S.	193
Brinkley, Dr. John Romulus	U.S.	488
Cagliostro, Count Alessandro d	Int'l.	572
Colgrove, Chester Walker	U.S.	745
Drown, Ruth	U.S.	1025
Fulkerson, Samuel Cole	U.S.	1240
Galenti, Cora	U.S.	1252
Ghadiali, Dinshah Pestanji Fra	U.S.	1304
Graham, James	Brit.	1357
Harper, Robert N.	U.S.	1456
Hayes, Edward	U.S.	1494
Hohensee, Adolphus	U.S.	1589
Hoxsey, Harry M.	U.S.	1633
Jenkins, David	U.S.	1718
Kaadt, Charles Frederick	U.S.	1751
Kaadt, Peter	U.S.	1751
Katterfelto, Gustavus	Brit.	1768
Katzen, Morris	U.S.	1769
Koch, William	U.S.	1839
Long, John	Brit.	1986
Mesmer, Franz Anton	Int'l.	2170
Operation Quack Quack	U.S.	2374
Perkins, Elisha	U.S.	2444
Pinkus, Joseph J.	U.S.	2468
Radam, William	U.S.	2527
Rain, Harold K.	U.S.	2530
Rollins, Frank E.	U.S.	2614
Ward, Joshua	Brit.	3091

Medical Fraud - Case of

Calandra, Joseph	U.S.	578

Property Insurance Fraud

Allers, Katherine	U.S.	99
Brust, Julius	Brit.	1095
Clayton-Wright, Derek	Brit.	728
Douat, Vital	Int'l.	1008
Ellsworth, James	U.S.	1085
Engelstein, Joseph	Brit.	1095
Fillis, George Frederick	Brit.	1157
Harris, Leopold	Brit.	1462
Lancey, John	Brit.	1883
Lawson, John D.	U.S.	1908
Stolerman, James Bernard	Brit.	1095
Tinker, Edward	U.S.	2956
Wallace, Michael Shaw Stewart	Brit.	3081
Wallace, Patrick Maxwell Stewa	Brit.	3081

Real Estate Fraud

Bennett, Berkeley	Brit.	2314
Birchall, John Reginald	Int'l.	372
Buckminster, Fred	U.S.	533
Cadek, Louis J.	U.S.	568
Corrigan, Michael	Brit.	790
Furguson, Arthur	Int'l.	1242
Gordon-Gordon	U.S.	1346
Kaye, Herman	U.S.	1770
Manhattan Island Sale Swindle	U.S.	2103
McConnell, J.R.	U.S.	2027

Newton, Arthur	Brit.	2314
Reavis, James Addison	Int'l.	2550
Renick, William	U.S.	2568
Roupell, William	Brit.	2629
Woodward, Harry	U.S.	1770

Spiritual Fraud

Baker, George	U.S.	215
Ballard, Guy	U.S.	222
Cagliostro, Count Alessandro di	Int'l.	572
Chadwick, Constance Cassandra	U.S.	667
Clapham, Harry	Brit.	720
Davenport, Ira Erastus	U.S.	880
Davenport, William H. Harrison	U.S.	880
Debar, Ann O'Delia Diss	Brit.	893
Harris, Thomas Lake	U.S.	1463
Home, Daniel Dunglas	Brit.	1605
Jessup, Charles	U.S.	1723
Mathews, Robert	U.S.	2146
McPherson, Aimee Semple	U.S.	2066
Mokanna, al-	Per.	2197
Patten, Carl Thomas	U.S.	2421
Pencovic, Francis	U.S.	2439
Prince, Henry James	Brit.	2502
Salomen, Edith	Int'l.	2672
Schafer, James B.	U.S.	2690
Sharp, Thomas	Brit.	2735
Smith, Cecil Brown	Scot.	2782
Soulakiotis, Mariam	Gr.	2816

Spiritual Fraud - Case of

Roy, William	Brit.	2633

Stock Fraud

Ammon, Robert A.	U.S.	115
Berman, Jacob Bennett	U.S.	1180
Bernhardt, R. Jack	U.S.	347
Bob, Charles V.	U.S.	413
Boesky, F. Ivan	U.S.	418
Chicago Board of Trade Bucket Shop	U.S.	696
Cook, Dr. Frederick A.	U.S.	769
Cousins, Walter	Brit.	800
Cox, Seymour E.J.	U.S.	769
Craggs, James	Brit.	805
Cutten, Arthur William	U.S.	851
Dardi, Virgil David	U.S.	871
Day, Raymond	U.S.	888
Dillon, William	U.S.	973
Drew, Daniel	U.S.	1022
Factor, John	Int'l.	1123
Fisk, James, Jr.	U.S.	1167
Flint, Motley H.	U.S.	1180
Getzoff, Ben	U.S.	1180
Goldblum, Stanley	U.S.	1331
Goldstein, Michael	U.S.	1146
Gordon-Gordon	U.S.	1346
Gordon, Edgar	Brit.	800
Gould, Jay	U.S.	1351
Grossman, Israel G.	U.S.	1393
Guterma, Alexander L.	U.S.	1408
Guylee, Edward Harold	Brit.	1409
Hatry, Clarence	Brit.	1477
Helman, William	U.S.	2671
Hooley, Ernest Terah	Brit.	1609
Keely, John E. Worrell	U.S.	1773
Koretz, Leo	U.S.	1842
Kreuger, Ivar	Swed.	1849
Law, John	Int'l.	1905
Lefferdink, Allen Jonas	U.S.	1922
Lennon, Patrick Henry	U.S.	1930

Lewis, S.C.	U.S.	1180
MacKay, Henry	U.S.	1180
Mandeville, Alexis	Brit.	2101
Mandeville, Henry	Brit.	2101
Mandeville, Walter	Brit.	2101
Miller, William F.	U.S.	115
Mitchell, Charles Edwin	U.S.	2190
Montgomery, Austin Howard	U.S.	2205
Morse, Charles Wyman	U.S.	2228
Morton-Mandeville, Alexis	Brit.	2232
Morton-Mandeville, Henry	Brit.	2232
Morton-Mandeville, Walter	Brit.	2232
Phillips, Rubel L.	U.S.	2856
Preston, Guy Richard	Brit.	2498
Redpath, Leopold	Brit.	2554
Rentschler, William H.	U.S.	2569
Rosenberg, Edward	U.S.	1180
Ruderman, Seymour G.	U.S.	2635
Salmon, Sheldon J.	U.S.	2671
Schulz, Edwin J.	U.S.	2856
Sheridan, Walter Cartman	U.S.	2743
Shinwell, Ernest	Int'l.	2746
Siegel Trading Company	U.S.	2757
South Sea Bubble, The	Brit.	2818
Spencer, Charles	Brit.	2825
Stavisky, Serge Alexandre	Fr.	2845
Stirling, David, Jr.	U.S.	2856
Stirling, William G.	U.S.	2856
Stone, John T.	U.S.	2859
Trippet, Robert S.	U.S.	2989
Truen, Jerome	U.S.	2671
Turner, Glenn W.	U.S.	3004
Wang, Stephen Sui-Kuan, Jr.	U.S.	3089
Yanowitch, Harold M.	U.S.	2856

Stock Fraud - Case of

Bank of Taiwan Scandal	Japan	227
Boulton, Robert	Brit.	454

Tax Fraud

Atkins, Charles A.	U.S.	175
Bowers, Donald	U.S.	2120
Carlisi, Sam Anthony	U.S.	624
Carter, James Y.	U.S.	644
Hack, William S.	U.S.	175
Hart, Frederick Duncan Tabrum	Brit.	1137
Home-Stake Case	U.S.	1606
Janus, Christopher G.	U.S.	1711
Kelley, John M.	U.S.	1778
Kovic, Anthony C.	U.S.	1845
Margolies, Irwin	U.S.	2120
Margolis, Henry	U.S.	2121
Nee, A.H.	U.S.	2295
Newman, Ralph G.	U.S.	2313
Podmore, William Henry	Brit.	2478
Spilotro, Victor	U.S.	2829
Wolf, Jerome W.	U.S.	3181

Tax Fraud - Case of

Fidelity Investment Association	U.S.	1154

Wire Fraud

Callahan, Gerald Michael	U.S.	581
Cosgrove, James	U.S.	793
Dillon, William	U.S.	973
Donegan, Edward	U.S.	998
Elliott, Alfred	U.S.	1084
Feldman, Richard L.	U.S.	1146
Finney, Warren Wesley	U.S.	1161
Jessup, Charles	U.S.	1723

St. Clair, Stephanie	U.S.	2658
Sure Enuf Hotel	U.S.	2878
Tennes, Jacob	U.S.	2914
Tiplitz, William		2957
Twelfth Street, Kansas City, M	U.S.	3009
Wilson, F.	U.S.	494

Gambling - Case of

Frink, John B.	U.S.	1236
Higgins, James W.	U.S.	1545
Maltese, Frank	U.S.	2098

GENOCIDE

Artukovic, Andrija	Yugo.	169
ben Yair, Eleazer	Judea	339
Burundi Africa Massacre	Burundi	559
Christian II	Swed.	703
Dyer, Reginald Edward Harry	India	1051
Mengele, Josef	Ger.	2165
Mummius, Lucius	Rom.	2251
Mwanga	Buganda	2270
Pequot Tribe Massacre	U.S.	2443
Phao Sriyanond	Thai.	2456
Pol Pot	Kampuchea	2483
Selim I	Turk.	2726
Tokugawa Hidetada	Japan	2963
Tokugawa Iemitsu	Japan	2963

GRAFT

Abetz, Otto	Ger.	10
Abscam	U.S.	13
Addicks, John Edward O'Sullivan	U.S.	29
Agnew, Spiro	U.S.	37
Aurelio, Thomas A.	U.S.	185

GRAPHOLOGIST

Tyrrell, John F.	U.S.	3012

GRAVE ROBBERY

Ganev, Gantscho	Switz.	3093
Von Cosel, Karl Tanzler	U.S.	3062
Wardas, Roman	Switz.	3093

GRAVE ROBBERY - Case Of

Bertrand, Francois	Fr.	352
McLean, John	Scot.	2425
Munro, Robert	Scot.	2425
Pattison, Granville Sharp	Scot.	2425
Russell, Andrew	Scot.	2425

GRAVE ROBBERY- Unsolved

Romaine, Henry G.	U.S.	2615

GUN CONTROL

Helfgott, Marvin	U.S.	1512

HARASSMENT

Collins, Omester	Ger.	1967
Lindsey, Bryon	Ger.	1967

HARASSMENT - Wrongly Convicted

Krapp, John W.	U.S.	1847

HABORING FUGITIVES

de Balsham, Inetta	Brit.	893

HERESY

Abednego		2733
Aetius	Syria	36

Askew, Anne	Brit.	171
Bacon, Roger	Brit.	206
Badby, John	Brit.	206
Barclay, Robert	Scot.	233
Barnes, Robert	Brit.	246
Barrow, Henry	Brit.	263
Barton, Elizabeth	Brit.	270
Berenger	Fr.	340
Biddle, John	Brit.	359
Bilney, Thomas	Brit.	370
Bradford, John	Brit.	465
Brown, John	Scot.	509
Browne, Robert	Brit.	518
Brucioli, Antonio	Italy	519
Bruno, Giordano	Italy	521
Bruys, Pierre de	Fr.	522
Bunyan, John	Brit.	542
Burnet, Gilbert	Brit.	550
Caerularius, Michael	Const.	569
Calamy, Edmund	Brit.	577
Carnesecchi, Pietro	Italy	631
Carranza, Bartolom de	Spain	636
Cartwright, Thomas	Brit.	647
Catherine of Alexandria	Egypt	657
Cecco d'Ascoli	Italy	662
Celestius	Roman.	663
Charles V	Spain	686
Cheke, John	Brit.	691
Cheney, Charles Edward	U.S.	692
Chong Yakjong	Korea	702
Claude, Jean	Fr.	726
Clitherow, Margaret	Brit.	733
Craig, John	Scot.	806
Cranmer, Thomas	Brit.	810
Crapsey, Algernon Sidney	U.S.	810
Crell, Nikolaus	Saxony	815
Cyprian	Carthage	852
Dolet, Tienne	Fr.	986
Dunster, Henry	U.S.	1039
Dyer, Mary	U.S.	1051
Echeverria, Esteban	Arg.	1067
Edelmann, Johann Christian	Ger.	1068
Englefield, Francis	Brit.	1096
Enzinas, Francisco de	Spain	1099
Eugenikos, Markos	Gr.	1110
Featley, Daniel	Brit.	1143
Ferrar, Robert	Brit.	1151
Fisher, John	Brit.	1165
Floquet, Charles Thomas	Fr.	1181
Foster, Cuthbert Pearson	Brit.	1202
Fox, George	Brit.	1205
Frith, John	Brit.	1237
Gentili, Alberico	Brit.	1298
Goes, Damiao De	Port.	1328
Gorton, Samuel	U.S.	1348
Greenwood, John	Brit.	1379
Guyon, Jeanne-Marie de la Mott	Fr.	1409
Hakim, al-	Egypt	1419
Hamilton, Patrick	Scot.	1435
Harrison, Thomas	Brit.	1465
Henry IV	Ger.	1518
Henry of Lausanne	Fr.	1520
Hetzer, Ludwig	Switz.	1528
Hofmann, Melchior	Fr.	1588
Hooper, John	Brit.	1609
Hosius	Spain.	1624
Hubmaier, Balthasar	Aust.	1634
Huss, John	Bohemia	1646
Hutchinson, Anne	U.S.	1647
Huynh Phu So	Viet.	1648

Ibn Taymiyah	Syria	1652	Tyndale, William	Brit.	3012
Ibn al-Abbar	Tun.	1651	U'dall, John	Brit.	3014
Ibn al-Jawzi	India	1651	van Oldenbarnevelt, Johan	Neth.	2368
Ibn-Hanbal	Arabia	1651	Vincent, Saint	Roman.	3055
Jerome of Prague	Bohemia	1723	Waldis, Burkard	Ger.	3075
Joan of Arc	Fr.	1724	Ward, Margaret	Brit.	3092
John bar Qursos	Syria	1726	Warriston, Archibald J.	Scot.	3097
John of Leiden	Neth.	1726	Wheelwright, John	U.S.	3134
John of Wesel	Ger.	1727	William of Saint-Amour	Fr.	3159
Jovinian	Italy	1745	Williams, Roger	Brit.	3165
Julian of Eclanum	Italy	1749	Wishart, George	Scot.	3179
Knipperdolling, Bernhard	Ger.	1836	Wullenwever, Jrgen	Ger.	3196
Latimer, Hugh	Brit.	1902	Wycliffe, John	Brit.	3198
Lefevre d'Etaples, Jacques	Fr.	1922	Zevi, Sabbatai	Turk.	3220
Legate, Bartholomew	Brit.	1923	Zinzendorf, Nikolaus Ludwig vo	Saxony	3221
Leighton, Alexander	Scot.	1926			
Line, Anne	Brit.	1968	**HERESY - Case Of**		
Lucy, Saint	Roman.	2007	Ebel, Johann Wilhelm	Ger.	1066
Lully, Raymond	Alg.	2009			
Manes	Per.	2101	**HIJACKING**		
Maning, Frederick Edward	N.Zea.	2103	de Souto, Jorge	Port.	1258
Marbeck, John	Brit.	2117	Galvao, Henrique	Port.	1258
Maximus	Roman.	2154	Grant, Garland	Cuba	1362
Maximus	Rus.	2154	Haigler, Kate	U.S.	1419
Melville, Andrew	Scot.	2164	Haigler, Keith	U.S.	1419
Meshach		2733	Smith, Francis	U.S.	2784
Michael Cerularius	Roman.	2176	Velo, Jose	Port.	1258
Molcho, Solomon	Port.	2197	Wells, Harry	U.S.	3125
Molinos, Miguel de	Spain	2198			
Montmorency, Filips van	Neth.	2206	**HOAX**		
Muggleton, Lodowicke	Brit.	2247	Benan Letter	Ger.	323
Nestorius	Turk.	2307	Chappell, George Shepard	U.S.	686
Nicholas of Autrecourt	Fr.	2334	Charles E. Fisher	U.S.	1722
Nicholas of Hereford	Brit.	2334	Dawson, Charles	Brit.	887
Oldcastle, John	Brit.	2368	de Rougemont, Louis	Brit.	920
Overton, Richard	Brit.	2388	du Bois, Henri Pene	Int'l.	1994
Pacca, Bartolommeo	Italy	2390	Dupre, George	Can.	1039
Paleario, Aonio	Italy	2396	Ford, Corey	U.S.	686
Pamphilus of Caesarea	Caesarea	2402	Fortsas Catalogue Hoax	Belg.	1201
Pecock, Reginald	Brit.	2435	Freeman, Arthur Vectis	Brit.	1231
Pelagius I	Italy	2437	Gurdjieff, George Ivan	Fr.	1406
Penn, William	Brit.	2441	Hall, George	U.S.	2310
Peter of Bruys	Fr.	2452	Heth, Joice	U.S.	1528
Peter, Saint	Roman.	2450	Hewitt, Marvin	U.S.	1528
Peucer, Kaspar	Ger.	2455	Hitler Diary Hoax	Ger.	1580
Pico della Mirandola, Giovanni	Italy	2462	Hull, George	U.S.	1638
Pole, Reginald	Brit.	2481	Jarrell, Sanford	U.S.	1712
Polycarp, Saint	Roman.	2484	Jernegan, Prescott Ford	U.S.	1722
Polyeuctos, Saint	Roman.	2484	Joan	Italy	1724
Pontian, Saint	Roman.	2485	Kammerer, Paul	Aust.	1754
Priscillian	Spain	2503	Kreisler, Fritz	Ger.	1848
Prynne, William	Brit.	2510	Locke, Richard Adams	U.S.	1975
Quesnel, Pasquier	Belg.	2523	Logan, Dorothy Cochrane	Brit.	1977
Rene of France	Fr.	2568	Louys, Pierre	Int'l.	1994
Ridley, Nicholas	Brit.	2581	MacDonald, David Rowland	U.S.	2031
Rogers, John	Brit.	2610	Mad Anesthetist of Matoon	U.S.	2072
Rogers, John	U.S.	2610	Milne, Caleb, IV	U.S.	2185
Rutherford, Samuel	Scot.	2644	Minor, Wilma Francis	U.S.	2188
Saisset, Bernard	Fr.	2662	Moccia, Luigi	Italy	2195
Salem Witchcraft Trials	U.S.	2664	Newell, Stub	U.S.	2310
Sebastian, Saint	Roman.	2719	Pearson, Hesketh	Brit.	2433
Servetus, Michael	Spain	2729	Rogers, Hunter Charles	Fr.	2610
Severian of Gabala	Syria	2729	Satyricon Hoax	Italy	2681
Shadrach		2733	Scribner, John C.	U.S.	2716
Silva, Antnio Jos da	Port.	2761	Sigonius, Charles	Italy	2759
Somodevilla y Bengoechea, Zen.	Spain	2815	Vanderbourg, Charles	Fr.	3030
Southworth, John	Brit.	2819	Vella, Joseph	Si.	3040
Stephen, Saint	Roman.	2850	Voliva, Wilbur Glenn	U.S.	3060
Taylor, Rowland	Brit.	2902	Wagenfeld, Frederick	Ger.	3068
Tegh Bahadur	India	2912	Walpole, Horace	Brit.	3084

Anson, William Reynell	Brit.	132	Bentinck, William Cavendish	India	336
Anzilotti, Dionisio	Italy	135	Berrien, John MacPherson	U.S.	347
Armour, John Douglas	Can.	156	Berry, Charles Henry	U.S.	348
Arnold, Thurman Wesley	U.S.	163	Bertelsman, William Odis	U.S.	349
Arraj, Alfred Albert	U.S.	166	Bethell, Richard	Brit.	355
Aspen, Marvin E.	U.S.	171	Bethmann-Hollweg, Moritz A. vo	Ger.	355
Asquith of Bishopstone, Lord	Brit.	171	Betti, Ugo	Italy	355
Asser, Tobias Michael Carel	Neth.	172	Betts, Samuel Rossiter	U.S.	355
Atchison, David Rice	U.S.	174	Bibb, Charles Scott	U.S.	357
Atkin, Richard	Brit.	175	Biddle, Francis Bevereley	U.S.	359
Atkinson, George Wesley	U.S.	176	Bingham, Edward Franklin	U.S.	370
Atkinson, Cyril	Brit.	176	Birkett, Norman	Brit.	378
Atkyns, Edward	Brit.	176	Biron, Henry Chartres	Brit.	379
Atwell, William Hawley	U.S.	181	Biunno, Vincent Pasquale	U.S.	383
Aurelio, Thomas A.	U.S.	185	Black, Hugo La Fayette	U.S.	384
Austin, John	Brit.	186	Black, Jeremiah Sullivan	U.S.	385
Austin, Richard Bevan	U.S.	186	Black, Lloyd Llewellyn	U.S.	385
Avory, Horace Edmund	Brit.	191	Black, Norman William	U.S.	385
Azo	Italy	194	Black, Susan Harrell	U.S.	385
Azuni, Domenico Alberto	Sardinia	194	Blackmun, Harry Andrew	U.S.	397
Azzone	Italy	194	Blackstone, William	Brit.	402
Bachelet, Vittorio	Italy	205	Blair, Jacob Beeson	U.S.	403
Bachofen, Johann Jakob	Switz.	205	Blair, John	U.S.	403
Bacon, Nicholas	Brit.	206	Blair, Montgomery	U.S.	403
Bailhache, Clement Meacher	Brit.	212	Blair, William W.	U.S.	403
Baker, William Eli	U.S.	217	Blake, Edward	Can.	403
Baldwin, Alexander White	U.S.	218	Blake, Henry Nichols	U.S.	403
Baldwin, Henry	U.S.	218	Bland, Theodric	U.S.	405
Baldwin, James Harris	U.S.	218	Blastares, Matthew	Byzantium	408
Baldwin, Robert	Can.	218	Blatchford, Samuel Milford	U.S.	408
Baldwin, Simeon Eben	U.S.	218	Bodine, Joseph Lamb	U.S.	415
Ballou, Sidney Miller	U.S.	222	Boe, Nils Andreas	U.S.	417
Bankes, John	Brit.	227	Bogue, Andrew Wendell	U.S.	421
Bantz, Gideon D.	U.S.	228	Boguet, Henri	Fr.	421
Bar, Karl Ludwig von	Ger.	228	Boise, Reuben Patrick	U.S.	421
Barber, Orion Metcalf	U.S.	230	Boldt, George Hugo	U.S.	423
Barbour, Philip Pendleton	U.S.	233	Bond, Hugh Lennox	U.S.	428
Bard, Guy Kurtz	U.S.	233	Bonsal, Dudley Baldwin	U.S.	434
Barnes, Stanley Nelson	U.S.	246	Bonynge, Paul	U.S.	435
Barrett, James Emmett	U.S.	249	Boreman, Herbert Stephenson	U.S.	440
Barrington, Daines	Brit.	250	Boreman, Jacob Smith	U.S.	440
Barry, Redmond	Ire.	264	Bowen, Charles Synge Christoph	Brit.	456
Bartlett, Ara	U.S.	269	Boyce, Henry	U.S.	460
Bartlett, Josiah	U.S.	269	Boyd, James Edmund	U.S.	460
Bartolus	Italy	270	Boyd, Marion Speed	U.S.	460
Barton, Edmund	Aus.	270	Boyle, Charles Edmund	U.S.	462
Barwell, Henry Newman	Aus.	271	Boyle, Patricia Jean E. Pernic	U.S.	462
Batcheller, George Sherman	U.S.	280	Boynton, Charles A.	U.S.	463
Bauer, William Joseph	U.S.	284	Bracton, Henry de	Brit.	464
Bauman, Arnold	U.S.	284	Bradford, Edward Green	U.S.	464
Bazelon, David L.	U.S.	286	Bradley, Joseph P.	U.S.	466
Beamer, George N.	U.S.	287	Bradshaw, John	Brit.	466
Bean, Roy	U.S.	288	Bramwell, George Wm. Wilshere	Brit.	470
Beattie, Charlton Reid	U.S.	292	Bramwell, Henry	U.S.	470
Beaumanoir, Philippe de Rmi	Fr.	293	Brandebury, Lemuel G.	U.S.	472
Beaumont, Campbell Eben	U.S.	293	Brandeis, Louis Dembitz	U.S.	472
Beaumont, Robert de	Brit.	293	Branson, George A. Harwin	Brit.	473
Beccaria	Italy	294	Bray, Reginald More	Brit.	480
Beche Argello, Octavio	Cos.	313	Brazee, Andrew Washburne	U.S.	480
Bechtle, Louis Charles	U.S.	294	Breitenstein, Jean Sala	U.S.	484
Becker, Edward	U.S.	309	Brenger, Ren	Fr.	340
Bedford, Gunning, Jr.	U.S.	312	Brennan, William Joseph, Jr.	U.S.	485
Bedreddin	Turk.	313	Brett, Thomas Rutherford	U.S.	485
Bell, George Joseph	Scot.	317	Brewer, David Josiah	U.S.	485
Bellinger, Charles Byron	U.S.	321	Breyer, Stephen Gerald	U.S.	487
Benedict, Kirby	U.S.	330	Briant, Elijah S.	U.S.	487
Bennett, Granville Gaylord	U.S.	331	Brimmer, Clarence Addison	U.S.	488
Benson, Egbert	U.S.	334	Brinker, William H.	U.S.	488
Benson, Paul	U.S.	335	Bristol, Warren	U.S.	492
Bentham, Jeremy	Brit.	335	Bristol, William	U.S.	492

Cordova, Valdemar Aguirre	U.S.	784	Dick, Robert Paine	U.S.	939
Corn, Samuel Thompson	U.S.	785	Dickens, Henry Fielding	Brit.	939
Cornejo, Mariano Harlan	Peru	786	Dier, Richard A.	U.S.	942
Costa Cabral, Antnio Bernardo	Port.	794	Diesbach, Niklaus von	Switz.	942
Costa y Martinez, Joaquin	Spain	794	Digges, Dudley	Brit.	943
Coventry, Thomas	Brit.	801	Dimond, Anthony Joseph	U.S.	975
Covington, James Harry	U.S.	801	Dobie, Armistead Mason	U.S.	981
Cowell, John	Brit.	801	Doe, Charles	U.S.	983
Cowper, William	Brit.	802	Doherty, Charles Joseph	Can.	985
Cradlebaugh, John	U.S.	804	Domat, Jean	Fr.	994
Craig, Thomas	Scot.	807	Donahue, Maurice H.	U.S.	998
Cranch, William	U.S.	807	Dooling, John Francis, Jr.	U.S.	1004
Crawford, William	U.S.	813	Dooling, Maurice Timothy	U.S.	1004
Creasy, Edward Shepherd	Brit.	814	Dorion, Antoine Aim	Can.	1005
Creighton, William, Jr.	U.S.	815	Dorislaus, Isaac	Brit.	1005
Crocker, Myron Donovan	U.S.	827	Dorotheus	Syria	1005
Crome, Karl	Ger.	828	Douglas, Stephen Arnold	U.S.	1010
Croom-Johnson, Reginald P.	Brit.	828	Douglas, William Orville	U.S.	1010
Cross, Edward	U.S.	835	Doyle, James Edward	U.S.	1017
Cujas, Jacques	Fr.	843	Draco	Gr.	1018
Cunningham, Thomas	U.S.	846	Drago, Luis Maria	Arg.	1019
Curran, Edward Matthew	U.S.	848	Drake, Charles Daniel	U.S.	1019
Curran, John Philpot	Ire.	848	Drake, Thomas Jefferson	U.S.	1020
Curtin, John Thomas	U.S.	848	Drayton, John	U.S.	1021
Curtis, Benjamin Robbins	U.S.	848	Drayton, William	U.S.	1021
Cushing, Luther Stearns	U.S.	849	Drayton, William Henry	U.S.	1021
Cushing, William	U.S.	849	Driver, Samuel Marion	U.S.	1025
Dallas, George Mifflin	U.S.	857	Drummond, William Wormer	U.S.	1028
Dalrymple, James	Scot.	857	Duane, James	U.S.	1029
Dana, Francis	U.S.	865	Dudley, Joseph	U.S.	1031
Danaher, John Anthony	U.S.	865	Duer, John	U.S.	1032
Dane, Nathan	U.S.	866	Duer, William Alexander	U.S.	1032
Daniel, Peter Vivian	U.S.	866	Duffy, Frank Gavan	Aus.	1033
Darling, Charles John	Brit.	871	Duffy, Kevin Thomas	U.S.	1033
Davidson, Thomas Whitfield	U.S.	881	Duguit, Leon	Fr.	1034
Davies, John	Brit.	881	Duncan, Robert Morton	U.S.	1036
Davies, Louis Henry	Can.	882	Dundas, Robert	Scot.	1036
Davis, David	U.S.	883	Dunlop, James	U.S.	1037
Davis, George Breckenridge	U.S.	883	Duplantier, Adrian Guy	U.S.	1039
Davis, John A.	U.S.	884	Duport, Adrien-Jean-Franois	Fr.	1039
Davis, John Chandler Bancroft	U.S.	884	Durand, Guillaume	Fr.	1041
Davis, John Warren	U.S.	885	Duval, William Pope	U.S.	1047
Dawani	Iran	887	Duvall, Gabriel	U.S.	1047
Dawson, Charles I.	U.S.	887	Dyer, David Patterson	U.S.	1050
Day, William L.	U.S.	888	Dyer, Eliphalet	U.S.	1050
Day, William Rufus	U.S.	888	Dyer, James	Brit.	1051
Dayton, Alston Gordon	U.S.	888	Easton, Rufus	U.S.	1066
Deaver, Bascom Sine	U.S.	893	Eastwood, John Francis	Brit.	1066
Debevoise, Dickinson Richards	U.S.	894	Ebermayer, Ludwig	Ger.	1066
Decazes, Elie	Fr.	898	Eckles, Delena R.	U.S.	1067
Decker, Bernard Martin	U.S.	898	Edelstein, David Norton	U.S.	1068
De Lancey, James	U.S.	906	Edgerton, Alonzo Jay	U.S.	1069
Delbos, Yvon	Fr.	908	Edgerton, Henry White	U.S.	1069
Demascio, Robert Edward	U.S.	911	Edgerton, Sidney	U.S.	1069
Demetz, Frdric Auguste	Fr.	912	Edwards, George Clifton, Jr.	U.S.	1972
Denham, John	Ire.	913	Edwards, Ninian	U.S.	1073
Denman, George	Brit.	914	Ehrlich, Eugen	Aust.	1075
Denman, Thomas	Brit.	914	Eichhorn, Karl Friedrich	Ger.	1076
Denman, William	U.S.	914	Eike von Repgow	Ger.	1077
Denney, Robert Vernon	U.S.	914	Eisele, Garnett Thomas	U.S.	1079
De Peyster, Abraham	U.S.	917	Eldon, John Scott	Brit.	1081
Devens, Charles	U.S.	930	Elfvin, John Thomas	U.S.	1082
Deventer, Conrad Theodor van	Neth.	930	Ellery, William	U.S.	1083
De Villiers, Jacob	S. Afri.	931	Elliot, Gilbert	Scot.	1083
De Villiers, John Henry	S. Afri.	931	Elliott, George	Brit.	1084
Devitt, Edward James	U.S.	932	Elliott, James Douglas	U.S.	1084
Devlin, Patrick Arthur	Brit.	932	Elliott, John M.	U.S.	1084
Dharmavamsa	Indo.	934	Ellsworth, Oliver	U.S.	1085
Diaz, Anacleto	Phil.	938	Ellsworth, William Wolcott	U.S.	1086
Dicey, Albert Venn	Brit.	939	Ely, Walter Raleigh, Jr.	U.S.	1090

Ender, Otto	Aust.	1093		Fulton, Charles Britton	U.S.	1241
Enright, William Benner	U.S.	1098		Gaius	Roman.	1250
Epremesnil, Jean-Jacques Duval	Fr.	1099		Galvez, Jos	Spain	1258
Erskine of Carnock, John	Scot.	1102		Ganey, James Cullen	U.S.	1264
Erwin, Richard Cannon	U.S.	1102		Gardner, Archibald K.	U.S.	1268
Eschbach, Jesse Ernest	U.S.	1103		Garrecht, Francis Arthur	U.S.	1276
Espinosa, Gaspar de	Pan.	1104		Garrity, Wendell Arthur, Jr.	U.S.	1280
Estee, Morris March	U.S.	1107		Garvin, Edward Louis	U.S.	1281
Estes, Joe Ewing	U.S.	1109		Gasca, Pedro de la	Spain	1282
Estes, William Lee	U.S.	1109		Gascoigne, William	Brit.	1282
Evans, Orinda Dale	U.S.	1113		Gaston, William	U.S.	1284
Evans, Walter Howard	U.S.	1114		Gatley, Clement Carpenter	Brit.	1284
Evatt, Herbert Vere	Aus.	1114		Gesell, Gerhard A.	U.S.	1302
Ewart, Hamilton Glover	U.S.	1119		Gewin, Walter Pettus	U.S.	1304
Fairchild, Thomas Edward	U.S.	1127		Gibbons, John Joseph	U.S.	1307
Falsen, Christian Magnus	Nor.	1133		Gibson, Benjamin F.	U.S.	1308
Farinacci, Prospero	Italy	1134		Gibson, Edward	Ire.	1308
Faris, Charles Breckenridge	U.S.	1134		Gierbolini, Gilberto	U.S.	1309
Fay, Peter Thorp	U.S.	1142		Giffard, Hardinge Stanley	Brit.	1310
Feinberg, Wilfred	U.S.	1146		Gifford, Adam	Scot.	1311
Ferguson, Fenner	U.S.	1150		Gilchrist, Robert Budd	U.S.	1311
Fernandez Alonso, Severo	Bol.	1151		Giles, James Tyrone	U.S.	1312
Fernandez-Badillo, Juan B.	P.R.	1151		Gilmore, Horace Weldon	U.S.	1315
Field, Richard Stockton	U.S.	1155		Glanville, Ranulf de	Brit.	1320
Field, Stephen Johnson	U.S.	1155		Glaser, Julius	Aust.	1320
Figueras-Chiques, Jose-Maria	P.R.	1157		Gleason, William E.	U.S.	1322
Filangieri, Gaetano	Italy	1157		Glenn, Elias	U.S.	1322
Finch, Heneage	Brit.	1158		Glenn, John	U.S.	1322
Finlay, Robert Bannatyne	Brit.	1160		Gneist, Rudolf von	Ger.	1323
Finlay, William	Brit.	1160		Gny, Francois	Fr.	1298
Fiore, Pasquale	Italy	1161		Goddard, Rayner	Brit.	1323
Fischart, Johann	Ger.	1162		Godefroy, Jacques	Fr.	1323
Fisher, Frederick Charles	Phil.	1165		Goettel, Gerard Louis	U.S.	1329
Fisher, George Purnell	U.S.	1165		Goff, John W.	U.S.	1330
Fisher, Joseph Jefferson	U.S.	1166		Goff, Nathan	U.S.	1330
Fitts, Oliver	U.S.	1171		Goffe, William	Brit.	1330
Fitzgerald, William Francis	U.S.	1172		Goldberg, Arthur J.	U.S.	1331
Fitzgibbon, John	Ire.	1172		Goldsborough, Thomas Alan	U.S.	1334
Fitzherbert, Anthony	Brit.	1172		Gonzalez, Jose Alejandro, Jr.	U.S.	1337
Fitzpatrick, Charles	Can.	1172		Goodwin, Alfred Theodore	U.S.	1340
Flandrau, Charles Eugene	U.S.	1175		Gordon, Eugene Andrew	U.S.	1343
Flannery, Thomas Aquinas	U.S.	1175		Gordon, Peyton	U.S.	1345
Flaum, Joel Martin	U.S.	1175		Gordon, Walter A.	U.S.	1346
Flavius, Gnaeus	Roman.	1176		Gorman, William	Brit.	1348
Foley, James Thomas	U.S.	1190		Gouin, Lomer	Can.	1351
Foley, Roger D.	U.S.	1190		Grady, John Francis	U.S.	1355
Foley, Roger Thomas	U.S.	1190		Graham, William Johnson	U.S.	1361
Follmer, Frederick Voris	U.S.	1192		Grant, Robert Allen	U.S.	1362
Forbes, Duncan	Scot.	1193		Grantham, William	Brit.	1363
Forbes, Vernon Day	U.S.	1193		Gravina, Gian Vincenzo	Italy	1364
Ford, Francis Joseph William	U.S.	1193		Gray, George	U.S.	1364
Foreman, James L.	U.S.	1197		Gray, Horace	U.S.	1364
Forman, Phillip	U.S.	1198		Green, Ben Charles	U.S.	1372
Fortas, Abe	U.S.	1199		Greene, Albert Gorton	U.S.	1376
Fortescue, John	Brit.	1200		Greene, William	U.S.	1376
Foster, Cassius Gaius	U.S.	1202		Greenleaf, Simon	U.S.	1377
Foster, Rufus Edward	U.S.	1203		Greer, Frederick Arthur	Brit.	1379
Fournier, Tlesphore	Can.	1204		Gresham, Walter Quintin	U.S.	1382
Frank, Reinhard von	Ger.	1224		Grey, George	Brit.	1383
Frankel, Marvin E.	U.S.	1224		Grey, John de	Brit.	1383
Frankfurter, Felix	U.S.	1224		Grier, Robert Cooper	U.S.	1385
Frazer, William Clark	U.S.	1229		Griffin, Cyrus	U.S.	1386
Frear, Walter Francis	U.S.	1229		Griffith, Samuel Walker	Aus.	1387
Freed, Emerich B.	U.S.	1230		Griggs, John William	U.S.	1389
Freeman, Ralph McKenzie	U.S.	1232		Grillandus, Paulus	Rome	1389
Freisler, Roland	Ger.	1234		Grosscup, Peter Stenger	U.S.	1393
Fromentin, Eligius	U.S.	1238		Grove, William Robert	Brit.	1394
Fry, Edward	Brit.	1239		Grtner, Franz	Ger.	1406
Fuchs, Ernst	Ger.	1239		Gubow, Lawrence	U.S.	1396
Fuller, Melville Weston	U.S.	1240		Guin, Junius Foy, Jr.	U.S.	1398

Gurfein, Murray Irwin	U.S.	1406	Hoffman, Walter Edward	U.S.	1586
Guthrie, Charles John	Scot.	1409	Holden, James Stuart	U.S.	1590
Guy, Ralph B., Jr.	U.S.	1409	Holder, Cale James	U.S.	1591
Gwyer, Maurice Linford	Brit.	1411	Holland, James Buchanan	U.S.	1591
Hagerup, Georg Francis	Nor.	1415	Holloway, William Judson, Jr.	U.S.	1597
Halbert, Sherrill	U.S.	1420	Holman, Jesse Lynch	U.S.	1597
Hale, Matthew	Brit.	1420	Holmes, Nathaniel	U.S.	1602
Haliburton, Thomas Chandler	Can.	1420	Holmes, Oliver Wendell, Jr.	U.S.	1602
Hall, Augustus Caesar	U.S.	1421	Holschuh, John David	U.S.	1603
Hall, Edward Marshall	Brit.	1424	Holt, George Chandler	U.S.	1604
Hall, James	U.S.	1425	Holt, Joseph	U.S.	1604
Hall, Peirson Mitchell	U.S.	1427	Holtzendorff, Franz von	Ger.	1605
Hall, Robert Howell	U.S.	1427	Holtzoff, Alexander	U.S.	1605
Hallett, Hugh Imbert Perri	Brit.	1428	Holzheimer, William Andrew	U.S.	1605
Halsbury, Hardinge Goulburn G.	Brit.	1432	Home, Henry	Scot.	1606
Hamlin, Oliver D., Jr.	U.S.	1436	Hopkins, Richard Joseph	U.S.	1618
Han Fei (Han Fei-tzu)	China	1442	Hopkinson, Joseph	U.S.	1618
Hancock, Joseph	U.S.	1441	Horridge, Thomas Gordon	Brit.	1622
Hand, Learned	U.S.	1441	Houck, Charles Weston	U.S.	1624
Haney, Ebert Emory	U.S.	1442	Hough, Benson W.	U.S.	1624
Hanson, Richard Davies	Brit.	1445	Houghton, Joab	U.S.	1625
Hardy, Charles Leach	U.S.	1452	Howard, Charles	Brit.	1627
Harlan, John Marshall	U.S.	1454	Howard, Joseph Clemens	U.S.	1629
Harris, Oren	U.S.	1463	Howard, Sumner	U.S.	1630
Harrison, Benjamin	U.S.	1464	Howell, David	U.S.	1631
Hartigan, John Patrick	U.S.	1469	Howell, William Thompson	U.S.	1633
Hartshorne, Richard	U.S.	1470	Howry, Charles Bowen	U.S.	1633
Hartwell, Alfred Stedman	U.S.	1471	Hoyt, John Philo	U.S.	1633
Harvey, Alexander, II	U.S.	1471	Huber, Max	Switz.	1634
Hastie, William Henry	U.S.	1474	Huber, Seba Cormany	U.S.	1634
Hastings, John Simpson	U.S.	1474	Hudson, Manley Ottmer	U.S.	1634
Hatch, Carl Atwood	U.S.	1475	Hudspeth, Harry Lee	U.S.	1635
Hatchett, Joseph Woodrow	U.S.	1476	Hufstedler, Shirley Ann Mount	U.S.	1636
Hatfield, Charles Sherrod	U.S.	1476	Hughes, Charles Evans	U.S.	1636
Hatfield, Paul Gerhart	U.S.	1477	Hulen, Rubey Mosley	U.S.	1638
Hauk, A. Andrew	U.S.	1478	Humphrey, J. Otis	U.S.	1641
Haultain, Frederick Gordon	Can.	1478	Humphreys, Travers	Brit.	1642
Hawke, John Anthony	Brit.	1492	Humphreys, West Hughes	U.S.	1642
Hawkins, Henry	Brit.	1492	Hungate, William Leonard	U.S.	1642
Hawley, Thomas Porter	U.S.	1492	Hunt, Ward	U.S.	1644
Hay, George	U.S.	1493	Hunt, William Henry	U.S.	1644
Haynsworth, Clement Furman, Jr	U.S.	1498	Hunter, William	Brit.	1645
Healy, Maurice	Brit.	1501	Hurst, Cecil James Barring	Brit.	1646
Healy, William	U.S.	1501	Hutcheson, Charles Sterling	U.S.	1647
Heilbron, Rose	Brit.	1508	Hutchison, Harvey Macleary	U.S.	1648
Helvering, Guy Tresillian	U.S.	1514	Hyde, Charles Cheney	U.S.	1649
Henderson, Henry Perry	U.S.	1515	Hyde, Nicholas	Brit.	1650
Henderson, William Finley	U.S.	1515	Ibn Khallikan	Syria	1651
Henning, Edward J.	U.S.	1517	Ibn Shaddad	Syria	1651
Herbert, Edward	Brit.	1522	Ide, Henry Clay	U.S.	1652
Herbert, William	Brit.	1522	Iglesias, Jos Maria	Mex.	1652
Herlands, William Bernard	U.S.	1523	Igoe, Michael Lambert	U.S.	1652
Hernandez, Jose Conrado	U.S.	1524	Impey, Elijah	Brit.	1653
Herschel, William John	Brit.	1526	Ingersoll, Charles Anthony	U.S.	1655
Hewart, Gordon	Brit.	1528	Inskip, Thomas Walker Hobart	Brit.	1657
Hickey, John Joseph	U.S.	1532	Iredell, James	U.S.	1662
Hicks, Xenophen	U.S.	1544	Isaacs, Isaac Alfred	Aus.	1667
Higginbotham, Aloyisus Leon, J	U.S.	1545	Jackson, Howell Edmunds	U.S.	1678
Higginbotham, Patrick Errol	U.S.	1545	Jackson, John Jay, Jr.	U.S.	1678
Hilbery, Malcolm	Brit.	1550	Jackson, Robert Houghwout	U.S.	1679
Hill, Delmas Carl	U.S.	1551	Jacobus	Italy	1693
Hill, Robert Andrews	U.S.	1554	Jacquier, Nicholas	Fr.	1693
Hill, William Henry	U.S.	1556	James, Henry	Brit.	1695
Hiranuma, Kiichiro	Japan	1563	Jameson, William James	U.S.	1711
Hitchcock, Samuel	U.S.	1565	Jay, John	U.S.	1713
Hitz, William	U.S.	1581	Jeffrey, Francis	Scot.	1716
Hnel, Gustav Friedrich	Ger.	1441	Jeffreys, George	Brit.	1716
Hoar, Ebenezer Rockwood	U.S.	1581	Jelf, Arthur Richard	Brit.	1717
Hodge, Walter Hartman	U.S.	1583	Jenkins, James Graham	U.S.	1719
Hoffman, Julius Jennings	U.S.	1586	Jenkins, John James	U.S.	1719

Jenkins, Lawrence Hugh	India	1719	Landis, Frederick	U.S.	1884
Jette, Louis Amable	Can.	1724	Landis, Kenesaw Mountain	U.S.	1884
Johnson, Charles S.	U.S.	1728	Langdell, Christopher Columbus	U.S.	1889
Johnson, Frank Minis, Jr.	U.S.	1729	Laurel, Jos Paciano	Phil.	1903
Johnson, George E.Q.	U.S.	1729	Law, Edward	Brit.	1905
Johnson, Noble Jacob	U.S.	1731	Lawrance, John Compton	Brit.	1906
Johnson, Reverdy	U.S.	1731	Lawrence, Alfred Tristram	Brit.	1906
Johnson, Sam D.	U.S.	1732	Lawrence, Geoffrey	Brit.	1907
Johnson, Thomas	U.S.	1732	Lay, Donald Pomery	U.S.	1909
Johnson, W. Lee	U.S.	1734	Leavitt, Humphrey Howe	U.S.	1914
Johnson, William	U.S.	1733	Leavy, Charles Henry	U.S.	1914
Johnson, William Samuel	U.S.	1734	Lee, Charles	U.S.	1917
Joiner, Charles Wycliffe	U.S.	1735	Lee, William Little	U.S.	1921
Jones, James McHall	U.S.	1737	Leibowitz, Samuel S.	U.S.	1925
Jones, Nathaniel Raphael	U.S.	1740	Lerdo de Tejada, Sebastian	Mex.	1939
Jones, William Blakely	U.S.	1742	Leval, Pierre Nelson	U.S.	1943
Jovellanos, Gaspar Melchor de	Spain	1745	Leveson-Gower, John	Brit.	1944
Judd, John Waltus	U.S.	1746	Lewis, Joseph R.	U.S.	1946
Julian, Anthony	U.S.	1749	Lewis, Morgan	U.S.	1946
Justinian I	Roman.	1750	Lewis, Wilfred Hubert Poye	Brit.	1946
Kaess, Frederick William	U.S.	1752	Lewis, William	U.S.	1946
Kalbfleisch, Girard Edward	U.S.	1753	Lexow, Clarence	U.S.	1946
Kane, John Kintzing	U.S.	1754	Ley, James	Brit.	1947
Kantorowicz, Hermann	Ger.	1759	Li Ang	China	1948
Kashiwa, Shiro	U.S.	1767	Lieb, Joseph Patrick	U.S.	1950
Kaufman, Frank Albert	U.S.	1769	Lincoln, Levi	U.S.	1965
Kaufman, Irving Robert	U.S.	1769	Lindet, Nathaniel	Fr.	1967
Keatley, John Henry	U.S.	1773	Lindsey, Benjamin Barr	U.S.	1967
Keeling, Walter Angus	U.S.	1773	Ling, David W.	U.S.	1968
Kehoe, Joseph William	U.S.	1776	Liszt, Franz von	Ger.	1970
Keller, Friedrich Ludwig	Switz.	1777	Littleton, Edward	Brit.	1972
Kellogg, Frank Billings	U.S.	1779	Livingston, Henry Brockholst	U.S.	1972
Kennamer, Charles Brents	U.S.	1793	Lloyd, David	U.S.	1973
Kennedy, Anthony McLeod	U.S.	1794	Lockwood, Belva Ann	U.S.	1976
Kennedy, Harold	U.S.	1794	Loder, Bernard Cornelius Johan	Neth.	1976
Kennedy, James K.	U.S.	1794	Logan, James	U.S.	1979
Kennedy, William Rann	Brit.	1803	Logan, James Harvey	U.S.	1979
Kent, James	U.S.	1805	Lomen, Gudbrand J.	U.S.	1980
Kent, W. Wallace	U.S.	1805	Long, Elisha Van Buren	U.S.	1982
Kenyon, William Squire	U.S.	1805	Lord, Miles Welton	U.S.	1990
Ker, David	U.S.	1805	Lowe, Mary Johnson	U.S.	1997
Kerr, Ewing Thomas	U.S.	1805	Lowell, John	U.S.	1998
Key, David McKendree	U.S.	1808	Lucy, Richard de	Brit.	2007
Kidd, William Matthew	U.S.	1815	Lucy, Thomas	Brit.	2007
Kidder, Jefferson Parish	U.S.	1815	Lurton, Horace Harmon	U.S.	2012
Killits, John Milton	U.S.	1816	Lyle, John H.	U.S.	2015
Kilmuir of Creich	Brit.	1816	Lymer, William Barker	U.S.	2016
Kincheloe, David Hayes	U.S.	1820	Lynch, Charles	U.S.	2016
King, Samuel Pailthorpe	U.S.	1826	MacKinnon, George Edward	U.S.	2052
Kinneary, Joseph Peter	U.S.	1828	MacMahon, Lloyd Francis	U.S.	2058
Kinney, John Fitch	U.S.	1828	Mack, Julian William	U.S.	2046
Kirkpatrick, William Huntingto	U.S.	1830	Macnaghten, Malcolm Martin	Brit.	2062
Kitchen, John Joseph	U.S.	1832	Mahir Pasha, Ali	Egypt	2088
Kloeb, Frank Leblond	U.S.	1833	Mahon, Eldon Brooks	U.S.	2088
Knapp, Whitman	U.S.	1834	Maine, Henry James Sumner	Brit.	2089
Knappen, Loyal Edwin	U.S.	1835	Maitland, Frederic William	Brit.	2090
Knight, John	U.S.	1835	Malcolm, George Arthur	U.S.	2094
Knowles, Hiram	U.S.	1837	Malik ibn-Anas	Arabia	2096
Kocoras, Charles Petros	U.S.	1840	Mancini, Pasquale Stanislao	Italy	2099
Kraft, Charles William	U.S.	1846	Mann, Edward Ames	U.S.	2104
Kunzig, Robert Lowe	U.S.	1862	Mansfield, Walter Roe	U.S.	2108
Laband, Paul	Ger.	1867	Marquez, Alfredo Chavez	U.S.	2127
Labeo, Marcus Antistius	Roman.	1867	Marshall, Consuelo Bland	U.S.	2129
Labori, Fernand Gustave Gaston	Fr.	1868	Marshall, John	U.S.	2130
Lacey, Frederick Bernard	U.S.	1869	Marshall, Prentice Henry	U.S.	2130
Lafontaine, Louis Hypolite	Can.	1873	Marshall, Thurgood	U.S.	2130
Lamar, Joseph Rucker	U.S.	1875	Marten, Henry	Brit.	2130
Lamar, Lucius Quintus Cincina	U.S.	1876	Martens, Frdric Frommhold de	Rus.	2130
Lambros, Thomas D.	U.S.	1877	Martin, Boyce Ficklen, Jr.	U.S.	2131
Lancre, Pierre de	Fr.	1883	Martin, Franois Xavier	U.S.	2131

Martin, James Loren	U.S.	2131	Moreland, Sherman P.	U.S.	2216
Martinus	Italy	2133	Morison, Thomas Brash	Scot.	2223
Marvin, William	U.S.	2133	Morphonios, Ellen J.	U.S.	2224
Mason, Charles	U.S.	2136	Morris, Lewis	U.S.	2225
Mason, John Young	U.S.	2136	Morris, Michael	Ire.	2225
Mathews, Clifton	U.S.	2146	Morris, Richard	U.S.	2225
Matthews, Stanley	U.S.	2150	Morris, Robert	U.S.	2225
Maude, John Cyril	Brit.	2151	Morton, Leland Clure	U.S.	2229
Maxwell, Robert Earl	U.S.	2154	Moulton, John Fletcher	Brit.	2235
Mayer, Julius	U.S.	2157	Muecke, Charles Andrew	U.S.	2247
Mazzone, A. David	U.S.	2158	Mulock, William	Can.	2250
McAllister, Matthew Hall	U.S.	2021	Murphy, Frank	U.S.	2259
McCardie, Henry Alfred	Brit.	2023	Murray, William	Brit.	2260
McCarthy, James William	U.S.	2023	Neaher, Edward Raymond	U.S.	2293
McCarthy, William T.	U.S.	2024	Negron Fernandez, Luis	P.R.	2297
McClernand, John Alexander	U.S.	2026	Nelson, Samuel	U.S.	2304
McClure, George Buchanan	Brit.	2026	Nerva Cocceius	Roman.	2306
McConnell, William B.	U.S.	2027	Neville, Philip	U.S.	2308
McCormick, Andrew Phelps	U.S.	2027	Nevin, Robert Reasoner	U.S.	2308
McDonald, David	U.S.	2031	Newcombe, Edmund Leslie	Can.	2310
McEntee, Edward Matthew	U.S.	2037	Newcomer, Clarence Charles	U.S.	2310
McGarr, Frank James	U.S.	2040	Newman, Jon Ormond	U.S.	2312
McGohey, John F.X.	U.S.	2042	Nichol, Fred Joseph	U.S.	2328
McGranery, James Patrick	U.S.	2042	Nield, Basil Edward	Brit.	2336
McGuire, Matthew Francis	U.S.	2043	Nields, John Percy	U.S.	2336
McIlvaine, John Wilson	U.S.	2045	Nikitchenko, Iola T.	U.S.S.R.	2336
McKean, Thomas	U.S.	2048	Niles, Henry Clay	U.S.	2336
McKenna, Joseph	U.S.	2048	Noonan, Gregory Francis	U.S.	2343
McKinley, John	U.S.	2049	Norcross, Frank Herbert	U.S.	2343
McLean, John	U.S.	2057	Northcutt, Elliott	U.S.	2345
McMillan, James Bryan	U.S.	2060	Nott, Abraham	U.S.	2347
McNamee, Charles Joseph	U.S.	2064	Nys, Ernest	Belg.	2348
McNary, Charles Linza	U.S.	2064	O'Brien, Donald E.	U.S.	2357
McNaught, John Joseph	U.S.	2064	O'Connor, Sandra Day	U.S.	2359
McPherson, John Bayard	U.S.	2069	O'Hagan, Thomas	Ire.	2366
McPherson, Smith	U.S.	2069	Oaksey, Lord	Brit.	2349
McReynolds, James Clark	U.S.	2070	Odlin, Arthur Fuller	U.S.	2361
Mechene, Merritt Cramer	U.S.	2160	Ogier, Isaac Stockton Keith	U.S.	2365
Mehaffy, Pat	U.S.	2162	Oliphant, Ethelbert	U.S.	2369
Meir of Rothenburg	Ger.	2163	Oliver, Rowland Giffard	Brit.	2370
Meredith, James Hargrove	U.S.	2166	Olney, Cyrus	U.S.	2371
Merkel, Adolf	Ger.	2167	Orr, John Wellesley	Brit.	2380
Merlin, Philippe-Antoine	Fr.	2167	Orr, William Edwin	U.S.	2380
Merritt, Gilbert Stroud, Jr.	U.S.	2169	Paine, Elijah	U.S.	2394
Mersey, John Charles Bigham	Brit.	2169	Paine, Robert Treat	U.S.	2394
Michael Attaliates	Roman.	2176	Palmer, Cornelius Solomon	U.S.	2398
Mickelson, George T.	U.S.	2177	Palmer, Roundell	Brit.	2399
Miles, Wendell Alverson	U.S.	2179	Papinian	Roman.	2407
Miller, Andrew	U.S.	2180	Parke, Benjamin	U.S.	2410
Miller, Andrew Galbraith	U.S.	2180	Parker, Alton Brooks	U.S.	2410
Miller, Justin	U.S.	2182	Parker, Isaac	U.S.	2411
Miller, Samuel Freeman	U.S.	2182	Parker, Isaac C.	U.S.	2411
Miner, James Alvin	U.S.	2187	Parker, Thomas	Brit.	2412
Miner, Roger Jeffrey	U.S.	2187	Parlange, Charles	U.S.	2414
Minobe, Tatsukichi	Japan	2188	Parris, Albion Keith	U.S.	2415
Minton, Sherman	U.S.	2189	Parsons, Charles Francis	U.S.	2416
Mitchell, George John	U.S.	2191	Parsons, Theophilus	U.S.	2416
Mittermaier, Karl Joseph Anton	Ger.	2194	Paterson, William	U.S.	2418
Mller, Eduard	Switz.	2249	Patterson, Robert Porter	U.S.	2425
Moinet, Edward J	U.S.	2197	Paulus, Julius,	Roman.	2427
Monkswell, Robert Porret Collier	Brit.	2201	Pea y Pea, Manuel de la	Mex.	2439
Monroe, Thomas Bell	U.S.	2202	Peckham, Rufus Wheeler, Jr.	U.S.	2434
Montagu, Edward	Brit.	2203	Pecora, Ferdinand	U.S.	2435
Montagu, Henry	Brit.	2203	Pelletier, Charles A.P.	Can.	2437
Montgomery, Robert Morris	U.S.	2206	Pemberton, Francis	Brit.	2439
Moody, Gideon Curtis	U.S.	2207	Pendleton, Edmund	U.S.	2440
Moody, William Henry	U.S.	2207	Peters, Emil Cornelius	U.S.	2452
Moore, Alfred	U.S.	2209	Peters, Richard	U.S.	2452
Moore, John Bassett	U.S.	2210	Pettit, John	U.S.	2455
Moore, Leonard Page	U.S.	2211	Pfordten, Ludwig von der	Bav.	2456

Pfyffer, Ludwig	Fr.	2456	Rodey, Bernard Shandon	U.S.	2606
Phillimore, Walter George Fran	Brit.	2458	Rose, John Carter	U.S.	2620
Phillips, Harry	U.S.	2458	Rosenman, Samuel Irving	U.S.	2621
Pickett, John Coleman	U.S.	2462	Ross, Donald Roe	U.S.	2624
Pierrepont, Edwards	U.S.	2464	Roth, Stephen John	U.S.	2625
Piggott, Francis Taylor	Brit.	2465	Rothari	Italy	2625
Pine, David Andrew	U.S.	2466	Rowlatt, Sidney Arthur Tay	Brit.	2632
Pinelo	Spain	2467	Rusk, Thomas Jefferson	U.S.	2642
Piso, Lucius Calpurnius	Roman.	2470	Russell, Charles	Brit.	2642
Pitkin, William	U.S.	2471	Rutilius Rufus, Publius	Roman.	2644
Pitman, James Campbell	Scot.	2471	Rutledge, John	U.S.	2645
Pitman, John	U.S.	2471	Rutledge, Wiley Blount	U.S.	2645
Pitney, Mahlon	U.S.	2471	Ryan, Harold Lyman	U.S.	2646
Pittman, Thomas Virgil	U.S.	2472	Ryder, Dudley	Brit.	2647
Plumer, Thomas	Brit.	2476	Saavedra, Juan Bautista	Bol.	2649
Plunket, William Conyngham	Ire.	2477	Sabinus, Massurius	Roman.	2649
Poindexter, George	U.S.	2480	Sacheverell, William	Brit.	2653
Poindexter, Joseph Boyd	U.S.	2480	Sage, George Read	U.S.	2657
Polenta, Guido da	Italy	2481	St. John, Oliver	Brit.	2659
Pollard, Charles R.	U.S.	2483	St. Leonards, Edw. Burten-shaw	Brit.	2659
Pollock, David	India	2483	Sakuma Shozan	Japan	2662
Pollock, Frederick	Brit.	2483	Salter, Arthur Clavell	Brit.	2673
Pollock, Jonathan Frederic	Brit.	2483	Salvius Julianus	Roman.	2674
Pope, Nathaniel	U.S.	2489	Samuel	Israel	2674
Popham, John	Brit.	2489	Sanchez de B. y Sirven, Antoni	Cuba	2675
Porter, Donald James	U.S.	2491	Sanford, Edward Terry	U.S.	2677
Porter, Samuel Lowry	Brit.	2491	Sanjo II		2678
Porter, William Wood	U.S.	2491	Sankey, John	Brit.	2678
Porterie, Gaston Louis Noel	U.S.	2491	Sapru, Tej Bahadur	India	2679
Powell, Charles Lawrence	U.S.	2493	Savigny, Friedrich Karl von	Ger.	2683
Powell, Lewis Franklin, Jr.	U.S.	2494	Scaevola, Publius Mucius	Rome	2685
Powers, Orlando Woodworth	U.S.	2495	Scalera, Ralph Francis	U.S.	2686
Pratt, Philip	U.S.	2497	Scalia, Antonin	U.S.	2686
Pratt, Charles	Brit.	2497	Scarlett, James	Brit.	2688
Pray, Charles Nelson	U.S.	2497	Schmerling, Anton von	Aust.	2693
Pride, Thomas	Brit.	2501	Schultheis, Heinrich von	Ger.	2699
Proculus, Sempronius	Roman.	2505	Schwartz, Murray Merle	U.S.	2707
Putnam, Richard Johnson	U.S.	2516	Schweigaard, Anton Martin	Nor.	2707
Quackenbush, Justin Lowe	U.S.	2519	Scofield, Glenni William	U.S.	2708
Quarles, Joseph Very	U.S.	2521	Scott, William	Brit.	2713
Quesnay de Beaurepaire, Jules	Fr.	2523	Scroggs, William	Brit.	2716
Ragon, Heartsill	U.S.	2529	Scrutton, Thomas Edward	Brit.	2716
Ramirez, Raul Anthony	U.S.	2533	Seals, Woodrow Bradley	U.S.	2718
Rastell, William	Brit.	2542	Seay, Abraham Jefferson	U.S.	2719
Rau, Benegal Narsing	India	2544	Sedgwick, Theodore	U.S.	2721
Read, George	U.S.	2548	Selden, John	Brit.	2725
Read, John Meredith	U.S.	2548	Sellers, Frederick Aked	Brit.	2726
Read, Lazarus Hammond	U.S.	2548	Seneca, Lucius Annaeus	Roman.	2728
Reed, Stanley Forman	U.S.	2557	Senter, Lyonel Thomas, Jr.	U.S.	2728
Rehnquist, William H.	U.S.	2559	Severus, Lucius Septimius	Roman.	2729
Reid, Robert Threshie	Brit.	2560	Sewall, Samuel	U.S.	2730
Rentoul, Gervais	Brit.	2569	Seymour, Stephanie Kulp	U.S.	2731
Reynolds, John W.	U.S.	2571	Sharswood, George	U.S.	2736
Rice, Walter Herbert	U.S.	2575	Shaw, Lemuel	U.S.	2737
Richards, John Kelvey	U.S.	2576	Shearman, Montague	Brit.	2738
Richards, William Buell	Can.	2576	Shell, Terry Lee	U.S.	2739
Richardson, Scovel	U.S.	2579	Shepley, George Foster	U.S.	2740
Richey, Charles Robert	U.S.	2579	Sherburne, John Samuel	U.S.	2743
Ridley, Edward	Brit.	2581	Sherman, Roger	U.S.	2745
Riner, John Alden	U.S.	2584	Shipman, William Davis	U.S.	2746
Ringo, Daniel	U.S.	2584	Shippard, Sidney G. Alexander	S.Afri.	2747
Ritchie, William Johnstone	Can.	2585	Shippen, Edward	U.S.	2747
Roberts, Clarence Joseph	U.S.	2591	Shiras, George	U.S.	2747
Roberts, Jack	U.S.	2592	Sibley, Solomon	U.S.	2751
Roberts, Owen Josephus	U.S.	2593	Sifton, Charles Proctor	U.S.	2759
Robertson, Thomas Bolling	U.S.	2594	Sighibuldi, Cino dei	Italy	2759
Robinson, Aubrey Eugene, Jr.	U.S.	2595	Siler, Eugene Edward, Jr.	U.S.	2759
Rocco, Alfredo	Italy	2603	Silvela, Francisco	Spain	2761
Roche, Alexander Adair	Brit.	2603	Singleton, John Edward	Brit.	2769
Roche, Michael Joseph	U.S.	2604	Sitgreaves, John	U.S.	2772

Slick, Thomas W.	U.S.	2778	Thoravensen, Bjarni Vigfusson	Ice.	2937
Smith, Edmund Munroe	U.S.	2784	Thornberry, William Homer	U.S.	2939
Smith, James Francis	U.S.	2794	Thornton, Thomas Patrick	U.S.	2940
Smith, Jeremiah	U.S.	2795	Thurlow, Edward	Brit.	2948
Smith, Thomas	U.S.	2802	Tjoflat, Gerald Bard	U.S.	2959
Smith, William	Can.	2804	Tobin, Alfred Aspinall	Brit.	2959
Smith, William	U.S.	2804	Todd, Thomas	U.S.	2963
Smith, William Francis	U.S.	2804	Tokugawa Yoshimune	Japan	2964
Snell, Ivan Edward	Brit.	2804	Tolin, Ernest Allen	U.S.	2964
Snorri Sturluson	Ice.	2805	Torquemada, Toms de	Spain	2969
Snow, Zerubbabel	U.S.	2805	Torres, Florentino	U.S.	2969
Snyder, A. Cecil	U.S.	2805	Trapnell, John Graham	Brit.	2984
Speakman, Howard	U.S.	2821	Tribonian	Roman	2989
Speer, Emory	U.S.	2824	Trieber, Jacob	U.S.	2989
Spencer, Ambrose	U.S.	2824	Trimble, Robert	U.S.	2989
Stafford, Wendell Philips	U.S.	2836	Trimble, William	U.S.	2989
Stahl, David	U.S.	2836	Trowbridge, Edmund	U.S.	2994
Stainback, Ingram Macklin	U.S.	2836	Tubman, William Vacanarat Shad	Liberia	2998
Stanley, Edwin Monroe	U.S.	2839	Tucker, Henry St. George	U.S.	2999
Stanley, Henry	Ire.	2839	Tucker, St. George	U.S.	2999
Starr, Raymond W.	U.S.	2844	Turner, Ezekiel B.	U.S.	3004
Steger, William Merritt	U.S.	2847	Tuttle, Arthur J.	U.S.	3006
Steinbach, Emil	Aust.	2847	Twiss, Travers	Brit.	3010
Sten Sture	Swed.	2850	Tyler, John	U.S.	3011
Stephen, James Fitzjames	Brit.	2850	Tytler, Alexander Fraser	Scot.	3012
Stern, Herbert Jay	U.S.	2850	Ulpian	Roman.	3014
Sterndale, William Pickfor	Brit.	2850	Unden, Bo Osten	Swed.	3015
Stevens, John Paul	U.S.	2851	Vanartsdalen, Donald West	U.S.	3029
Stewart, Potter	U.S.	2853	Van Devanter, Willis	U.S.	3030
Steyn, Marthinus Theunis	S.Afri.	2854	Van Fleet, William Cary	U.S.	3031
Stockton, Richard	U.S.	2857	Van Orsdel, Josiah Alexander	U.S.	3034
Stone, Harlan Fiske	U.S.	2858	Van Valkenburgh, Arba Seymour	U.S.	3035
Story, Joseph	U.S.	2864	Vela, Filemon Bartolome	U.S.	3040
Stoughton, William	U.S.	2865	Villamor, Ignacio	Phil.	3054
Stout, Robert	N.Zea.	2866	Villareal, Antonio	Phil.	3054
Strathclyde, Alexander Ur	Scot.	2867	Viner, Charles	Brit.	3055
Strickland, Obed F.	U.S.	2869	Vinogradoff, Paul Gavrilov	Brit.	3056
Strong, William	U.S.	2870	Vinson, Frederick Moore	U.S.	3056
Stuart, James	Can.	2871	Von der Heydt, James Arnold	U.S.	3063
Sullivan, John	U.S.	2875	von Feuerbach, Paul Joh.Anselm	Ger.	1153
Sulpicius, Rufus, Servius	Roman.	2877	von Ficker, Julius	Ger.	1154
Sutherland, George	U.S.	2880	von Fle, Niklaus von	Switz.	1188
Swayne, Noah Haynes	U.S.	2887	von Kamptz, Karl Albert C. Hei	Prussia	1754
Sweeney, George Clinton	U.S.	2887	Waddill, Edmund, Jr.	U.S.	3067
Sweet, Willis	U.S.	2888	Waite, Morrison Remick	U.S.	3074
Swift, Rigby Philip Watson	Brit.	2888	Waldo, Henry Linn	U.S.	3075
Symes, J. Foster	U.S.	2891	Walton, George	U.S.	3087
Taft, Alphonso	U.S.	2893	Walton, Valentine	Brit.	3087
Taft, William Howard	U.S.	2893	Wapner, Joseph A.	U.S.	3090
Talbot, George John	Brit.	2894	Wardell, Robert	U.S.	3093
Talfourd, Thomas Noon	Brit.	2895	Ware, Ashur	U.S.	3094
Tamm, Edward Allen	U.S.	2896	Warren, Earl	U.S.	3096
Taney, Roger Brooke	U.S.	2896	Warren, Robert Willis	U.S.	3097
Taschereau, Henri Elzear	Can.	2898	Washington, Bushrod	U.S.	3097
Taschereau, Henri Thomas	Can.	2898	Watrous, John Charles	U.S.	3102
Tate, Albert, Jr.	U.S.	2898	Watson, Edward Minor	U.S.	3103
Tayler, Robert Walker	U.S.	2899	Watts, John Sebrie	U.S.	3105
Taylor, Anna Katherine J. Digg	U.S.	2899	Wayne, James Moore	U.S.	3106
Tazewell, Henry	U.S.	2906	Weare, Meshech	U.S.	3106
Teitelbaum, Hubert Irving	U.S.	2912	Webb, Edwin Yates	U.S.	3107
Templar, Henry George	U.S.	2913	Webb, Nathan	U.S.	3108
Thacher, Thomas Day	U.S.	2921	Weber, Randolph Henry	U.S.	3108
Thayer, Webster	U.S.	2926	Webster, John Stanley	U.S.	3109
Thomas, Alfred Delavan	U.S.	2929	Wedderburn, Alexander	Brit.	3112
Thomas, John Robert	U.S.	2931	Weick, Charles	U.S.	3113
Thomasius, Christian	Ger.	2932	Weiss, Andr	Fr.	3119
Thompson, Anne E.	U.S.	2932	Wells, Edmund William	U.S.	3125
Thompson, John Sparrow Dav	Can.	2935	Wells, Ira Kent	U.S.	3125
Thompson, Smith	U.S.	2935	Wells, Robert William	U.S.	3126
Thompson, William George	U.S.	2936	West, Samuel H.	U.S.	3129

Westenhaver, David C.	U.S.	3129
Whaley, Edward	Brit.	3131
Wheaton, Henry	U.S.	3132
Whelan, Francis C.	U.S.	3134
Whipple, Lawrence Aloysius	U.S.	3135
White, Byron Raymond	U.S.	3136
White, Edward Douglass	U.S.	3138
White, Edward Douglass, Jr.	U.S.	3138
White, Hugh Lawson	U.S.	3138
Whiteley, George Cecil	Brit.	3140
Whittaker, Charles Evans	U.S.	3146
Wilbur, Curtis Dwight	U.S.	3149
Wild, Ernest Edward	Brit.	3150
Wilde, Thomas	Brit.	3155
Wilkerson, James Herbert	U.S.	3157
Wilkey, Malcolm Richard	U.S.	3157
Wilkins, Ross	U.S.	3157
Williams, Archibald	U.S.	3160
Williams, Thomas Sutler	U.S.	3166
Williston, Samuel	U.S.	3169
Wilson, Frank Wiley	U.S.	3171
Wilson, James	U.S.	3172
Wilson, James Clifton	U.S.	3172
Wilson, Scott	U.S.	3175
Wilson, Thomas Stokeley	U.S.	3175
Winch, Joel C.C.	U.S.	3175
Wing, Francis Joseph	U.S.	3176
Wingard, Samuel Cyrus	U.S.	3176
Winthrop, John	U.S.	3177
Witmer, Charles B.	U.S.	3180
Wood, Harlington, Jr.	U.S.	3182
Woodbury, Levi	U.S.	3184
Woods, William Burnham	U.S.	3185
Wright, James Skelly	U.S.	3194
Wright, Robert Alderson	Brit.	3194
Wright, Scott Olin	U.S.	3195
Wright, Robert Samuel	Brit.	3194
Wrottesley, Frederic John	Brit.	3196
Wyche, Charles Cecil	U.S.	3198
Wyman, Alfred Lee	U.S.	3198
Wyndham, Charles	Brit.	3198
Xiphilinus, John VIII	Roman.	3200
Yankwich, Leon Rene	U.S.	3205
Yates, Robert	U.S.	3205
Yorke, Philip	Brit.	3207
Youmans, Frank A.	U.S.	3208
Young, Don John	U.S.	3208
Young, George	Scot.	3209
Young, James Scott	U.S.	3210
Youngdahl, Luther Wallace	U.S.	3211
Zaghlul Pasha, Saad	Egypt	3215
Zahle, Carl Theodor	Den.	3215
Zaleucus	Gr.	3215
Zampano, Robert Carmine	U.S.	3216
Zane, Charles Shuster	U.S.	3216
Zavatt, Joseph Carmine	U.S.	3218
Ziani, Sebastiano	Venice	3220
Zirpoli, Alfonso Joseph	U.S.	3221
Zouche, Richard	Brit.	3223

JUVENILE REFORM

| Marshall, James | U.S. | 2129 |

KIDNAPPING

Abbott, Burton W.	U.S.	4
Adkins, Orville	U.S.	436
Ah Chai	China	40
Alcorn, Gordon	U.S.	2678
Alvarez, Raul Lpez	Mex.	107
Amsler, Joseph C.	U.S.	115

Anderson, Bella	U.S.	263
Anderson, Don Benny	U.S.	123
Aramburu, Pedro Eugenio	Arg.	142
Arindell, William	Brit.	1179
Arvenitakis, Takos	Gr.	169
Ashwell, Thomas	U.S.	171
Atahaulpa	Peru	173
Bailey, Harvey John	U.S.	208
Bailey, James Warren	U.S.	211
Barrow, Addie	U.S.	263
Barrow, George	U.S.	263
Beihl, Eugen	Spain	315
Bell, Larry Gene	U.S.	318
Berenguer Gang	Italy	340
Berroyer, Helen	U.S.	2247
Biddings, Robert	U.S.	358
Bishop, Arthur Gary	U.S.	380
Blake, H.G.	U.S.	3095
Blanc, Jean	Fr.	3113
Bogle, Helen McDermott	U.S.	419
Bogle, James H.	U.S.	419
Booth, Arnett	U.S.	436
Born, Jorge	Arg.	444
Born, Juan	Arg.	444
Boschetti, Enzo	Italy	445
Bradley, Magda	Aus.	466
Bradley, Stephen Leslie	Aus.	466
Brigate Rosse	Italy	488
Brown Sisters, The	Int'l	519
Browning, William Lacy	U.S.	919
Brunette, Harry	U.S.	520
Bryan, Joseph Francis, Jr.	U.S.	523
Burton, Lee A.	U.S.	558
Bush, John Earl	U.S.	660
Busic, Julienne	U.S.	560
Busic, Zvonko	U.S.	560
Byrne, Dominic P.	U.S.	2016
Caillol, Alain	Fr.	576
Campbell, James	Brit.	1735
Campbell, Kevin	U.S.	1515
Carrasco, Fred Gomez	U.S.	637
Casanova, Eduardo	Guat.	648
Cave, Alphonso	U.S.	660
Chang Hsueh-liang	China	677
Charlton Street Gang	U.S.	688
Chaucer, Geoffrey	Brit.	690
Click, Franklin	U.S.	732
Cochise	U.S.	735
Coleman, Alton	U.S.	743
Coll, Vincent	U.S.	746
Collins, George E., Jr.	U.S.	751
Corbett, Joseph, Jr.	U.S.	781
Corsetti, Mirta	Italy	790
Croft, Curtis	U.S.	1515
Curcio, Margherita Cafol	Italy	847
Cusamano, Santos	U.S.	2123
Dainard, William J.	U.S.	855
Dainard, William J.	U.S.	3075
Dalton, John	Brit.	858
Davis, Larry Ronald	U.S.	885
De La Hoz, Licenciada M.	Mex.	905
DeBoer, Frank	U.S.	894
de Contreras, Fernando	Alg.	898
Deputy, Martin	U.S.	919
de Sade, Donatien Al. Franois	Fr.	2656
Duchateau, Daniel	Fr.	1030
Dugger, Thomas E.	U.S.	1033
Dunlevy, John	U.S.	1037
Dustin, Hannah	U.S.	1043
Edward of Norwich	Brit.	1071

Edwards, Daniel J.	U.S.	1071		Kirk, James	U.S.	1829
Edwards, Mack Ray	U.S.	1073		Klutas, Theodore	U.S.	1833
Eisemann-Schier, Ruth	U.S.	1851		Knight, Thomas	U.S.	1835
Elsas, Ferdi	Neth.	1086		Kokoraleis, Andrew C.	U.S.	1288
ERP	Arg.	1102		Kokoraleis, Thomas	U.S.	1288
Esposito, Giuseppe	Int'l	1105		Krist, Gary Steven	U.S.	1851
Evans, Michael	U.S.	1113		Kyprianou, Achilleas	Cyprus	1865
Fakkak, The	Spain	1130		LaMarca, Angelo John	U.S.	1876
FAR	Guat.	1133		Laporte, Pierre	Can.	1897
Fedayeen	Int'l.	1143		Larcher, Pierre-Marie	Fr.	2613
Fletcher, John	Brit.	1179		Lebanon Hostage Situation	Leb.	1914
Fontenot, Karl	U.S.	3092		Lee, Albert	U.S.	1917
Foreman, Leslie	Brit.	1692		Leopold, Duke	Aust.	1932
Front de Liberation du Quebec	Can.	1238		Lepidus, Jacob	Brit.	1939
Fukunaga, Myles Yutaka	U.S.	1239		Le Quong, Vinh	Viet.	1939
Gallagher, Eddie	Ire.	1254		Liggio, Luciano	Italy	1951
Gallego, Gerald	U.S.	1255		Lindwall, Richard	U.S.	1968
Gallighen, Mona	U.S.	1829		Little, Dwain Lee	U.S.	1971
Garcia, Luis	U.S.	1266		Llaguna, Roger	U.S.	1266
Gebbia, Leonardo	U.S.	1287		Logan, James	U.S.	1979
Gecht, Robin	U.S.	1288		Lu Sing-pan	China	2012
Genghis Khan	Mongolia	1291		Lynch, Mel Patrick	U.S.	2016
Getty, J. Paul III	Italy	1304		Maalot Massacre	Isr.	2021
Gooch, Arthur	U.S.	1338		McCall, Franklin Pierce	U.S.	2023
Goodere, Samuel	Brit.	1339		McElway, Marita	U.S.	2036
Gordon, Nathaniel	U.S.	1345		McGee, Walter	U.S.	2041
Gula, Demetrius	U.S.	1399		Marighella, Carlos	Braz.	2122
Haight, Edward	U.S.	1418		Marino, Antonio	U.S.	2123
Hall, Carl Austin	U.S.	1421		Matanic, Peter	U.S.	560
Hamilton, Thomas L.	U.S.	1435		Medley, Joseph Dunbar	U.S.	2161
Hardy, Joseph M.	U.S.	3095		Meek, Howard	U.S.	2161
Harper, Michael	U.S.	1456		Meins, Commando Holger	Swed.	2162
Harris, Emily	U.S.	1464		Mele, Charles	U.S.	919
Harris, William	U.S.	1464		Mesina, Giovanni	Italy	2169
Hauptmann, Bruno Richard	U.S.	1479		Mesina, Graziano	Italy	2169
Hay, Donald Alexander	Can.	1493		Mesina, Niccolo	Italy	2169
Heady, Bonnie Brown	U.S.	1421		Mesrine, Jacques	Int'l	2170
Hefeldt, Paul	Brit.	1939		Messino, William	U.S.	2172
Heirens, William George	U.S.	1508		Meyer, Robert	U.S.	2175
Henderson, Demetrius	U.S.	1515		Milani, Joseph Harry	U.S.	2178
Hickman, William Edward	U.S.	1532		Million, Roger	Fr.	3113
Higgins, William R.	Leb.	1547		Montgomery, Archibald	Brit.	1735
Hinkman, William	U.S.	1561		Moore, Cory C.	U.S.	2210
Hodzic, Shefka	Yug.	1583		Moormann, Robert Henry	U.S.	2211
Holmes, John	U.S.	1601		Muench, Nellie Tipton	U.S.	2247
Holmes, John Maurice	U.S.	2949		Muhlenbroich, Wilhelm Jakob	U.S.	2247
Holt, Thomas J., Jr.	U.S.	1605		Nai Krit	Siam	2827
Honduran Death Squads	Hond.	1607		Neilson, Donald	Brit.	2297
Hooker, Cameron	U.S.	1608		Nicolini, Sharon	U.S.	2547
Hosein, Arthur	Brit.	1623		Noah, Mordecai Manuel	U.S.	2341
Hosein, Nizamodeen	Brit.	1623		Norvell, Randal	U.S.	2346
Inkpaduta	U.S.	1656		O'Donnell, Calvagh	Ire.	2361
Irwin, John W.	U.S.	115		O'Neill, Shane	Ire.	2373
Irwin, Warren Lee	U.S.	1667		Olsson, Jan-Erik	Swed.	2372
Ismael, Muley	Int'l	1668		Oquendo, Wilfredo Roman	U.S.	2374
Jacobs, Jack	Brit.	1692		Outlaws, The	U.S.	2387
Johnson, Terry Wayne	U.S.	660		Parker, J.B.	U.S.	660
Johnston, John	Brit.	1735		Parnell, Kenneth E.	U.S.	2414
Jones, Arthur Albert	Brit.	1736		Pascal, August	U.S.	2417
Jones, Mary	U.S.	1740		Pasch, John, Jr.	U.S.	2417
Jones, Wilfred	U.S.	2247		Patrick, Ted	U.S.	2421
Jones, Willie Lee	U.S.	1742		People's Liberation Army	Turk.	2442
June 2nd Movement	Ger.	1750		People's Revolutionary Army	Arg.	2442
Karpis, Alvin	U.S.	1763		Pesut, Frane	U.S.	560
Kavinsky, Gerald	U.S.	1770		Peters, Warren	U.S.	3171
Keenan, Barry W.	U.S.	115		Peters, Warren, Jr.	U.S.	2674
Keene, John	U.S.	1774		Phillips, W.A.	Can.	2460
Kelly, George R.	U.S.	1782		Pierce, Darci Kayleen	U.S.	2463
Kerrigan, Larry	U.S.	1829		Popular Revolutionary Vanguard	Braz.	2490
Khaalis, Hamaas Abdul	U.S.	1809		Potts, Jack Howard	U.S.	2492

Name	Country	Page
Raffaelo, Robert	U.S.	2123
Raisuli	Mor.	2532
Ray, Mark	U.S.	2547
Rebel Armed Forces	Guat.	2551
Riley, Irvin George	U.S.	211
Rish, Nancy D.	U.S.	1071
Robbins, Bobby Ray	U.S.	2589
Robinson, Thomas H., Jr.	U.S.	2601
Rolland, Raymond	Fr.	2613
Ruthven, William	Scot.	2644
Sacoda, Joseph S.	U.S.	1399
Salisbury, Steven A.	U.S.	2671
Sanchez, Hector Reuben	U.S.	2674
Sankey, Verne	U.S.	2678
Sardinian Shepherds	Sardinia	2679
Savasta, Antonio	Italy	2683
Schild, Anabella	Sardinia	2692
Schoenfeld, James L.	U.S.	3185
Schoenfeld, Richard A.	U.S.	3185
Seadlund, John Henry	U.S.	2717
Sellman, Edward Leon	U.S.	2726
Seye, Blaise Ferrage	Fr.	2730
Simmons, Tommie Bernard	U.S.	2726
Singleton, Lawrence	U.S.	2769
Sioux Indian Massacre	U.S.	2770
Skobline, Nadine Plevitskaia	Fr.	2774
Smith, Michael	U.S.	2801
Socley, Gabriel	Fr.	2810
Soulder, Frank	U.S.	2817
South Moluccan Kidnappers	Neth.	2818
Spendle, Robert Courtney Frase	Siam	2827
Spreitzer, Edward	U.S.	1288
Stephenson, David Curtis	U.S.	2850
Story, John	Brit.	2864
Swendsen, Kurt	Brit.	2888
Swolley, Gale E.	U.S.	2817
Symbionese Liberation Army	U.S.	2889
Taewon-gun	Korea	2893
Taylor, Ernest	U.S.	2900
Terry, Paul	U.S.	1113
Thurmond, Thomas H.	U.S.	1601
Thurmond, Thomas Harold	U.S.	2949
Tillman, Emil	Ger.	2955
Travis, John	U.S.	436
Traxler, Roy	U.S.	2984
Trowell, Nicholas	Brit.	1692
Tuller, Bryce	U.S.	3000
Tuller, Charles A.	U.S.	3000
Tuller, Jonathan	U.S.	3000
Tupamaros, The	Urug.	3002
Unified Anti-Re-election Comma	Dom.	3015
Utter, Earl Ray	U.S.	3022
Vallanzasca, Renato	Italy	3027
Vlasic, Mark	U.S.	560
von Holleben, Ehrenfried	Braz.	3063
Wakefield, Edward Gibbon	Brit.	3074
Wakefield, Frances	Brit.	3074
Wakefield, William Hay	Brit.	3074
Waley, Harmon	U.S.	3075
Waley, Harmon Metz	U.S.	855
Waley, Margaret	U.S.	3075
Walters, Ted	U.S.	3086
Ward, Tommy	U.S.	3092
Warner, Albert S.	U.S.	3095
Webb, George W.	U.S.	3107
Weidmann, Eugen	Fr.	3113
Wein, Edward Simon	U.S.	3118
Werner, Walter	U.S.	919
West, Ronald Eugene	U.S.	3129
Westervelt, William	U.S.	3129

Name	Country	Page
White, Charles	Brit.	1339
Whyte, James Albert	U.S.	211
Wilder, Christopher Bernard	U.S.	3155
Williams, Dennis	U.S.	3161
Williams, Hernando		3162
Williams, Roy	U.S.	1829
Williams, William August Helm	U.S.	3167
Wilson, Eddie	U.S.	3171
Woodard, Alonzo	U.S.	1515
Woods, Frederick Newhall	U.S.	3185
Woody, Loretta	U.S.	1829
Yiorgalli, Dinos	Brit.	1692
Young, Danny Jerome	U.S.	3208
Zebra Killings	U.S.	3218

KIDNAPPING - Attempted

Name	Country	Page
Ball, Ian	Brit.	221

KIDNAPPING - Case Of

Name	Country	Page
Amati, Giovanna	Italy	109
Annesley, Richard	Ire	129
Battaglia, Alfredo	Italy	283
Conley, Harold	U.S.	2258
Cross, James	Can.	835
Crowe, Patrick	U.S.	836
Davis, Angela Yvonne	U.S.	882
Dikko, Umaru	Brit.	943
di Nardi, Nicolletta	Italy	975
Empain, Baron	Fr.	1092
Ezaki Katsuhisa	Japan	1122
Ford, Lord Grey of Werke	Brit.	1195
Gabaldon, Armigiro	Venez.	1245
Gordon, Lauden	Brit.	1345
Gordon, Lockhart	Brit.	1345
Gosch, John David	U.S.	1349
Grimoald III	Italy	1390
Gustavus I	Swed.	1406
Kiritsis, Anthony G.	U.S.	1829
Macino, Joseph	U.S.	2046
McKay, Muriel	Brit.	2047
Motto, Vincenzo	U.S.	2046
Murphy, Angus	U.S.	2258
Ovazza, Carla	Italy	2387
Roe, James	U.S.	2607
Waterbury, Ward	U.S.	3098
Zuno Hernandez, Jos Guadalupe	Mex.	3223

KIDNAPPING - Unsolved

Name	Country	Page
Ashley, Andrew	U.S.	170
Bialek, Robert	Ger.	356
Bitterman, Chester A., III	Col.	383
Blumer, Fred	U.S.	413
Boettcher, Charles, II	U.S.	418
Cash, Bailey	U.S.	650
Claustre, Franoise	S.Afri.	727
de Bourbon, Charles Louis	Fr.	894
Desouches, Thierry	Fr.	926
Diogenes	Gr.	976
Elbrick, Charles Burke	Braz.	1080
Esparza, Richard	U.S.	1104
Fiorentino, Claudio	Italy	1161
Fischer, Karl	Aust.	1162
Forstein, Dorothy	U.S.	1198
Fraccari, Filiberto	Italy	1207
Galindez, Jesus de	Int'l	1253
Gluskoter, Rochelle	U.S.	1323
King, Kenneth	U.S.	1822
Koutiepov, Paul Alexander	U.S.S.R.	1845
LaHaye, Aubrey	U.S.	1874
Lawzi, Salim	Leb.	1908

KIDNAPPING - Wrongly Convicted

KIDNAPPING PREVENTION

KIDNAPPING VICTIMS

LAW AGENCY

LAW COMMISSION

LAW OFFICER

Seymour, Horatio	U.S.	2731	Bahuti, al	Egypt	207
Shantz, Phyllis	U.S.	2734	Bailey, Francis Lee	U.S.	207
Simpson, John Richard	U.S.	2766	Baker, Newton Diehl	U.S.	217
Simpson, Joseph	Brit.	2766	Baldivieso, Enrique	Bol.	217
Siragusa, Charles	U.S.	2771	Ballantine, William	Brit.	222
Smith, Al	U.S.	2781	Bankhead, John Hollis	U.S.	227
Smith, Moe	U.S.	1078	Barbosa, Ruy	Braz.	233
Snyder, LeMoyne	U.S.	2806	Barbour, Oliver Lorenzo	U.S.	233
Spenser, Edmund	Brit.	2828	Barreda Laos, Felipe	Peru	248
Stoddard, William Osborn	U.S.	2857	Barrington, John Shute	Brit.	250
Stoudenmire, Dallas	U.S.	2864	Barroso, Gustavo	Braz.	250
Strom, J. Preston	U.S.	2870	Baumes, Caleb Howard	U.S.	284
Swope, Edwin B.	U.S.	2888	Bayard, James Asheton	U.S.	285
Tegart, Charles Augustus	Brit.	2912	Bcking, Eduard	Ger.	415
Temr Khan	China	2913	Beck, James Montgomery	U.S.	296
Ten Most Wanted List	U.S.	2913	Belli, Melvin	U.S.	321
Thomson, Basil Home	Brit.	2937	Benjamin, Judah Philip	U.S.	331
Tilghman, Edward J.	U.S.	2955	Bennett, Richard Bedford	Can.	334
Tolson, Clyde A.	U.S.	2964	Bernard, Mountague	Brit.	346
Trenchard, Hugh Montague	Brit.	2985	Berryer, Pierre Nicolas	Fr.	349
Turner, Maurice T., Jr.	U.S.	3004	Bez, Cecilio	Para.	207
Turow, Scott	U.S.	3005	Binney, Horace	U.S.	371
Valentine, Lewis Joseph	U.S.	3025	Birkenhead, First Earl of	Brit.	378
Veza, Daniel T.	U.S.	3044	Blackburne, Francis	Ire.	388
Vidocq, Eugne-Francois	Fr.	3047	Blount, James Henderson	U.S.	411
Vincent, Howard	Brit.	3055	Bodkin, Archibald	Brit.	417
Vollmer, August	U.S.	3061	Bootle, William Augustus	U.S.	437
Voyer, Marc-Rene	Fr.	3064	Borah, William Edgar	U.S.	437
Waldo, Rhinelander	U.S.	3075	Borno, Louis-Eus.-Ant.-Fran.-J	Haiti	445
Waldron, John Lovegrove	Brit.	3075	Bouvier, John	Italy	455
Walker, Richard D.	U.S.	3078	Boyd, Jorge Eduardo	Pan.	460
Walsingham, Francis	Brit.	3084	Bragg, Thomas	U.S.	469
Walworth, William	Brit.	3087	Bravo-Murillo, Juan Gonzalez	Spain	479
Ward, Benjamin	U.S.	3090	Brewster, Benjamin Harris	U.S.	487
Warren, Charles	Brit.	3096	Bristow, Benjamin Helm	U.S.	493
Webster, William Hedgcock	U.S.	3112	Brown, Aaron Venable	U.S.	504
Wensley, Frederick	Brit.	3126	Brown, Benjamin Gratz	U.S.	505
Whalen, Grover Michael Aloysiu	U.S.	3131	Brown, Prentiss Marsh	U.S.	515
Whalen, Lawrence E.	U.S.	3131	Brown, Walter Folger	U.S.	516
Wild, Jonathan	Brit.	3150	Browning, Orville Hickman	U.S.	518
Williams, Alexander S.	U.S.	3160	Bruce, William Cabell	U.S.	519
Williams, Grant	U.S.	3162	Bryan, William Jennings	U.S.	523
Williams, Willie L.	U.S.	3168	Bugliosi, Vincent	U.S.	534
Wilson, Frank J.	U.S.	3171	Burton, Theodore Elijah	U.S.	559
Wilson, Jerry V.	U.S.	3173	Butler, Benjamin Franklin	U.S.	561
Windham, Thomas R.	U.S.	3176	Butler, Charles	Brit.	561
Wolters, Jacob F.	U.S.	3181	Butt, Isaac	Ire.	563
Wooldridge, R. Clifton	U.S.	3186	Byrns, Joseph Wellington	U.S.	566
Worley, Claude M.	U.S.	3188	Cabrera, Luis	Mex.	568
Yoshimitsu	Japan	3207	Cairns, Hugh McCalmont	Ire.	577
Young, William	U.S.	3211	Cajetan of Thiene	Italy	577
Yung-yen	China	3214	Calhoun, John	U.S.	580

LAW PROFESSOR

			Calhoun, John Caldwell	U.S.	580
			Calhoun, William James	U.S.	580
Dwight, Theodore William	U.S.	1048	Callahan, Michael	U.S.	583
			Campos Salles, Manuel Ferraz d	Braz.	594
LAWYERS			Carlile, John Snyder	U.S.	624
Abbott, Austin	U.S.	4	Carlisle, John Griffin	U.S.	625
Abbott, Benjamin Vaughn	U.S.	4	Carrington, Henry Beebee	U.S.	637
Abbott, John Joseph Caldwe	Can.	8	Carter, James Coolidge	U.S.	644
Abinger, Edward	Brit.	10	Cartier, George tienne	Can.	646
Aitchison, Craigie Mason	Scot.	43	Casgrain, Philippe Baby	Can.	650
Akerman, Amos Tappan	U.S.	45	Cass, Lewis	U.S.	651
Alessandri Palma, Arturo	Chile	73	Casswell, Joshua David	Brit.	654
Alessandri Rodriguez, Arturo	Chile	73	Cavaignac, Jean Baptiste	Fr.	659
Allen, Elisha Hunt	U.S.	93	Chafee, Zechariah	U.S.	669
Amen, John Harlan	U.S.	113	Chalmers, George	Scot.	671
Andreyev, Leonid Nikolayevich	Rus.	127	Chandler, William Eaton	U.S.	677
Angell, Joseph Kinnicutt	U.S.	127	Chauveau-Lagarde, Claude Fran.	Fr.	691
Baer, George Frederick	U.S.	207	Child, Richard Washburn	U.S.	699

Chitty, Edward	Brit.	700	Erskine, Thomas	Brit.	1102
Chitty, Joseph	Brit.	700	Evarts, William Maxwell	U.S.	1114
Chitty, Joseph D.	Brit.	700	Fallon, William Joseph	U.S.	1131
Chitty, Thomas	Brit.	700	Favre, Jules	Fr.	1140
Choate, Joseph Hodges	U.S.	701	Fazy, Jean Jacob	Switz.	1143
Choate, Rufus	U.S.	701	Field, David Dudley, Jr.	U.S.	1154
Clarke, Edward George	Brit.	725	Folk, Joseph W.	U.S.	1191
Clay, Henry	U.S.	728	Foote, John Anderson	Brit.	1193
Clinton, DeWitt	U.S.	733	Foreman, Percy	U.S.	1197
Clinton, George	U.S.	733	Fosdick, Raymond Blaine	U.S.	1202
Cockle, James	Brit.	737	Foulke, William Dudley	U.S.	1203
Cockran, William Bourke	U.S.	737	Fouquier-Tinville, Antoine Que	Fr.	1204
Coghlan, Charles Patrick J	Rhodesia	741	Fox-Davies, Arthur Charles	Brit.	1207
Cohen, Alfred Morton	U.S.	741	Frampton, Walter	Brit.	1207
Cohen, Arthur	Brit.	741	Frank, Jerome New	U.S.	1217
Cohen, Benjamin Victor	U.S.	741	Frelinghuysen, Frederick Theod	U.S.	1234
Colby, Bainbridge	U.S.	743	Fulton, Eustace Cecil	Brit.	1241
Colden, Cadwallader David	U.S.	743	Galloway, Joseph	U.S.	1257
Coleridge, Herbert	Brit.	745	Gambetta, Lon-Michel	Fr.	1258
Collamer, Jacob	U.S.	748	Garat, Dominique Joseph	Fr.	1265
Collier, William Miller	U.S.	749	Gardner, Erle Stanley	U.S.	1269
Colquhoun, Patrick MacChombaich de	Brit.	759	Garland, Augustus Hill	U.S.	1275
Colquitt, Walter Terry	U.S.	759	Garvan, Francis Patrick	U.S.	1280
Conkling, Roscoe	U.S.	765	Gary, Elbert Henry	U.S.	1282
Cooper, Grant Burr	U.S.	776	Gay, Jean-Baptiste-Sylvre	Fr.	1286
Cooper, Henry Ernest	U.S.	776	Gerry, Elbridge Thomas	U.S.	1302
Corcoran, Thomas Gardiner	U.S.	782	Gertz, Elmer	U.S.	1302
Cormenin, Louis Marie de Lahay	Fr.	785	Giesler, Jerry	U.S.	1309
Cortelyou, George Bruce	U.S.	791	Gill, Charles Frederick	Brit.	1312
Corwin, Thomas	U.S.	792	Gillett, Frederick Huntington	U.S.	1313
Coudert, Frederic Ren	U.S.	798	Goblet, Ren	Fr.	1323
Coulter, Ernest Kent	U.S.	798	Goebel, Julius	U.S.	1326
Cox, Jacob Dolson	U.S.	803	Gregory, Thomas Watt	U.S.	1380
Cox, Samuel Sullivan	U.S.	803	Gridley, Jeremiah	U.S.	1385
Crabb, George	Brit.	804	Groesbeck, William Slocum	U.S.	1392
Crawford, William Harris	U.S.	813	Grundy, Felix	U.S.	1394
Cripps, Charles Alfred	Brit.	825	Hadley, Herbert Spencer	U.S.	1414
Cripps, Richard Stafford	Brit.	825	Hamilton, Andrew	U.S.	1434
Crisp, Charles Frederick	U.S.	825	Harcourt, Simon	Brit.	1445
Crittenden, John Jordan	U.S.	825	Harmon, Judson	U.S.	1455
Culbertson, William Smith	U.S.	843	Hawke, Edward Anthony	Brit.	1492
Cummins, Albert Baird	U.S.	845	Hawkins, Dexter Arnold	U.S.	1492
Curtis-Bennett, Henry H.	Brit.	849	Haynes, Richard	U.S.	1497
Curtis, George Ticknor	U.S.	849	Hays, Arthur Garfield	U.S.	1498
Cushing, Caleb	U.S.	849	Hemmerde, Edward George	Brit.	1514
Cutler, Lloyd	U.S.	850	Heney, Francis Joseph	U.S.	1516
Dalton, Hugh	Brit.	857	Hermippus	Gr.	1524
Daly, T.F. Gilroy	U.S.	864	Herndon, William Henry	U.S.	1525
Dana, Richard Henry	U.S.	865	Hertzog, James Barry Munnik	S.Afri.	1527
Darrow, Clarence Seward	U.S.	872	Hill, David Bennett	U.S.	1551
Davis, Julius Richard	U.S.	885	Hines, Walker Downer	U.S.	1561
Deakin, Alfred	Aus.	890	Hoffman, John Thompson	U.S.	1586
Dek, Ferenc	Hung.	890	Hogan, Frank	U.S.	1588
Del Toro Cuevas, Emilio	Spain	910	Houston, Temple L.	U.S.	1627
Dershowitz, Alan	U.S.	920	Howe, William F.	U.S.	1631
Dewey, Thomas Edmund	U.S.	932	Hughes, Hector	Brit.	1636
Dies, Martin	U.S.	942	Hume, Fergus	Brit.	1641
Dodsin, Gerald	Brit.	983	Hummel, Abraham H.	U.S.	1631
Dole, Sanford Ballard	U.S.	986	Humphreys, Travers Christmas	Brit.	1642
Donovan, William Joseph	U.S.	1001	Hutchins, Harry Burns	U.S.	1647
Dropsie, Moses Aaron	U.S.	1025	Hutchins, Robert Maynard	U.S.	1647
Dulles, John Foster	U.S.	1034	Hutchinson, St. John	Brit.	1648
Duncan, Patrick	S.Afri.	1036	Ingersoll, Robert Green	U.S.	1656
Dupin, Andr Marie Jean Jacques	Fr.	1039	Jenks, Edward	Brit.	1720
Du Ponceau, Pierre tienne	U.S.	1039	Jerome, William Travers	U.S.	1722
Dupont de l'Eure, Jacques Char	Fr.	1039	Johnson, Hiram Warren	U.S.	1729
Durant, Henry Fowle	U.S.	1041	Johnston, Douglas Harold	Brit.	1734
Edmunds, George Franklin	U.S.	1070	Jones, Wesley Livsey	U.S.	1741
Ehrlich, Jacob	U.S.	1075	Joubert, Petrus Jacobus	S.Afri.	1745
Erbstein, Charles	U.S.	1100	Jowitt, William Allen	Brit.	1745

Katzenbach, Nicholas de Bellev	U.S.	1769
Knollys, Francis	Brit.	1836
Kunstler, William	U.S.	1861
La Guardia, Fiorello Henry	U.S.	1873
La Rossa, Jimmy	U.S.	1899
Lammasch, Heinrich	Aust.	1879
Lamon, Ward Hill	U.S.	1879
Lewis, George Henry	Brit.	1946
Lincoln, Robert Todd	U.S.	1965
Livingston, Robert R., Sr.	U.S.	1973
McAdoo, William Gibbs	U.S.	2021
M'Clure, Alexander Logan	Scot.	2026
Macdonald, John Hay Athole	Scot.	2032
Mackenzie, George	Scot.	2048
MacNally, Leonard	Ire.	2062
McNutt, Paul Vories	U.S.	2065
Mann, James Robert	U.S.	2104
Marcy, William Learned	U.S.	2119
Maris, Herbert L.	U.S.	2124
Mason, Jeremiah	U.S.	2136
Mathews, Charles	Brit.	2146
Matos Guerra, Gregrio de	Braz.	2147
Meigs, Return Johnathan	U.S.	2162
Mends-France, Pierre	Fr.	2164
Meredith, William Morris	U.S.	2166
Merola, Mario	U.S.	2167
Moreau de Saint-Mery, Md. L..	Fr.	2216
Morgan, Edmund Morris, Jr.	U.S.	2219
Morrow, Dwight Whitney	U.S.	2227
Morse, John Torrey Jr.	U.S.	2228
Mosby, John Singleton	U.S.	2232
Moss, Frank	U.S.	2233
Mouton, Alexander	U.S.	2236
Muir, Richard David	Brit.	2248
O'Connor, Terence James	Brit.	2359
O'Conor, Charles	U.S.	2360
O'Sullivan, Richard	Brit.	2385
Paget, Reginald Thomas	Brit.	2394
Patterson, Robert Porter	U.S.	2425
Peckham, Wheeler Hazard	U.S.	2434
Philip, James Randall	Brit.	2457
Philip, James Randall	Scot.	2457
Pomerene, Atlee	U.S.	2484
Ponzinibio, Gianfrancesco	Italy	2488
Post, Melville Davisson	U.S.	2492
Pound, Roscoe	U.S.	2493
Pruiett, Moman	U.S.	2509
Pryor, Roger Atkinson	U.S.	2510
Purchase, William Bentley	Brit.	2511
Reeve, Tapping	U.S.	2558
Requier, Augustus Julian	U.S.	2569
Roberts, Geoffrey Dorling	Brit.	2591
Robinson, Christopher	Can.	2595
Rogers, Earl	U.S.	2609
Romilly, Samuel	Brit.	2616
Roome, Henry Delacombe	Brit.	2617
Roosevelt, Robert Barnwell	U.S.	2618
Rusk, Thomas Jefferson	U.S.	2642
Sears, Barnabas Francis	U.S.	2718
Sergeant, Jonathan Dickinson	U.S.	2728
Sewall, Jonathan Mitchell	U.S.	2730
Sherman, John	U.S.	2744
Sinha, Satyendra Prasanno	India	2770
Somers, John	Brit.	2814
Spence, Gerald L.	U.S.	2824
Stevens, Thaddeus	U.S.	2852
Stewart, William Morris	U.S.	2854
Storm, Theodor	Ger.	2864
Sullivan, Alexander Martin	Brit.	2875
Sullivan, Alexander Martin	Ire.	2875

Taft, Henry Waters	U.S.	2893
Thayer, James Bradley	U.S.	2926
Thesiger, Frederick	Brit.	2927
Tilden, Samuel Jones	U.S.	2954
Turkus, Burton B.	U.S.	3002
Vachell, Charles Francis	Brit.	3023
Vilas, William Freeman	U.S.	3050
Volstead, Andrew John	U.S.	3061
Vyshinsky, Andrey Yanuaryevich	U.S.S.R.	3066
Waldeck-Rousseau, Pierre M.R.	Fr.	3074
Wallace, Lewis	U.S.	3081
Warren, Charles	U.S.	3095
Webster, Daniel	U.S.	3108
Wei Tao-Ming	China	3122
Welch, Joseph Nye	U.S.	3123
Westlake, John	Brit.	3129
Wharton, Francis	U.S.	3131
Wheeler, Wayne Bidwell	U.S.	3134
Wheeler, William Almon	U.S.	3134
Whitelocke, Bulstrode	Brit.	3140
Wigmore, John Henry	U.S.	3149
Willebrandt, Mabel Walker	U.S.	3158
Williams, Edward Bennett	U.S.	3161
Williams, Montagu Stephen	Brit.	3164
Wingate, George Wood	U.S.	3176
Winthrop, John	U.S.	3177
Yancey, William Lowndes	U.S.	3204
Yates, Richard	U.S.	3205
Yves of Brittany, Saint	Fr.	3214

LEGAL COMPILER

Ableiges, Jacques d'	Fr.	10

LEGAL HISTORIAN

Bunge, Friedrich Georg	Rus.	542
Conring, Herman	Ger.	767

LEGAL SCHOLAR

Bluntschli, Johann Kaspar	Switz.	413
Borchard, Edwin	U.S.	437
Corwin, Edward Samuel	U.S.	792

LEGAL STATICIAN

M'Naghten Rules	Brit.	2062

LIBEL

Austin, Edward, Dr.	Brit.	186
Bache, Benjamin Franklin	U.S.	205
Bastwick, John	Brit.	278
Baxter, Richard	Brit.	285
Bigland, Reuben	Brit.	360
Bradlaugh, Charles	Brit.	465
Burdett, Francis	Brit.	543
Busembaum, Hermann	Ger.	560
Callender, James Thompson	U.S.	584
Chaffers, Alexander	Brit.	669
Chen, Eugene	China	692
Clarke, Mary Anne	Brit.	725
Cobbett, William	Brit.	735
Daily Chronicle, The	Brit.	855
Daily Express, The	Brit.	855
Daily Mail, The	Brit.	855
de Villemessant, Hippolyte-Aug	Fr.	931
Douglas, Alfred	Brit.	1009
Floyd, Edward	Brit.	1188
Gilbert, William Schwenck	Brit.	1311
Gladstone, Henry Neville	Brit.	1320
Gladstone, Herbert John	Brit.	1320
Gordon, George	Scot.	1343
Hulme, William Edward	Brit.	1638

Drew, Pearl	U.S.	1022		Sala, Peter	Can.	2662
Dunbar, Ronald Patrick	Brit.	1035		Selby, Norman	U.S.	2724
Earullo, Fred	U.S.	1063		Sharp, Michael	Brit.	2735
Edinburgh Mock Battle Death	Scot.	1069		Sliwka, Tadeusz	U.S.	2778
Edwards, Matthew	Brit.	1073		Smith, Cathy Evelyn	U.S.	2782
Fantle, Ernest	Brit.	1133		Smith, Francis	Brit.	2784
Farino, Thomas	U.S.	1942		Solomon, Alfred	Brit.	2814
Farwell, Hartwell	U.S.	1137		Soursas, Simone	Fr.	2817
Field, Albert S.	U.S.	1154		Steinberg, Joel B.	U.S.	2847
Ford, Arthur Kendrick	Brit.	1193		Stevens, Peter	Brit.	2851
Fortmeyer, Julia E.	U.S.	1200		Stolarz, John	U.S.	2857
Furnald, Amos	U.S.	1243		Sturla, Theressa	U.S.	2873
Gates, Rick L.	U.S.	1284		Sutcliffe, George M.	U.S.	2879
Gay, Marvin Pentz, Sr.	U.S.	1286		Swapp, Addam	U.S.	2886
Girard, William S.	Japan	1316		Teissier, Lazare	Fr.	2912
Goodwin, Joyce	Brit.	1340		Telling, Michael	Brit.	2913
Gribble, Kenneth	Brit.	1384		Tinsley, James	Brit.	2957
Hammer, Armand	U.S.	1436		Ward, William		3093
Harding, Arthur	Brit.	2851		Washington, Allen	U.S.	3097
Harrington, Jack	U.S.	1458		Waters, Bridget	U.S.	3101
Hastings, Jeffrey R.	U.S.	1474		Watson, Robert J.	U.S.	3104
Henson, Nicholas	Brit.	1521		Young, Joseph Louis	U.S.	3210
Hermann, Marie	Brit.	1523		Zantzinger, William Devereux	U.S.	3216
Herrin, Richard	U.S.	1525		Zeev, Israel	Isr.	3218
Hicks, Lutien Roy	Sing.	1544				
Hill, Thomas C.	U.S.	1554		**MANSLAUGHTER - Case Of**		
Horne, Brian	Brit.	1620		Allingham, Dan	U.S.	1884
Ison, Hobart	U.S.	1668		Baxter, Jeannie	Brit.	284
Jaccoud, Pierre	Switz.	1674		Carroll, Thomas	U.S.	642
James, Francis	Brit.	1695		Cheatham, Weldon J.	U.S.	691
Jordan, Gilbert Paul	Can.	1743		Cory Brothers Limited	Brit.	792
Keller, Edward	U.S.	1776		Crane, Cheryl	U.S.	807
Kelly, James R.	U.S.	1787		Folsey, George, Jr.	U.S.	1884
Kern, Scott	U.S.	1942		Jennings, Glenn	U.S.	1721
King, Henry	Brit.	1822		Landis, John	U.S.	1884
Klar, Gabriel	U.S.	342		Little, John	Brit.	1971
Klar, Gabriel	U.S.	1832		Magee, Carl C.	U.S.	2086
Knowles, James H.	U.S.	1474		McKeever, John	Brit.	2048
Ladone, Jason	U.S.	1942		Medina, Ernest L.	U.S.	2161
Larkin, Luther	U.S.	1898		Merrick, Richard L., Jr.	U.S.	2168
Lee, Adam	Brit.	1917		Nassar, James	U.S.	2287
Lee, Bruce	Brit.	1917		Nassar, Patricia	U.S.	2287
Lester, Jon	U.S.	1942		Ormond, Dougal	Brit.	2379
Liger, Jean	Fr.	1951		Payne, Frederick	Brit.	2429
Lindrfer, Friedrich	Ger.	1967		Remley, Charles	U.S.	2565
Lloyd, Owen	Brit.	1973		Selfridge, Thomas O.	U.S.	2725
Manos, John	U.S.	2107		Treloar, James Gray	U.S.	2985
Martinucci, Piero Maria	Brit.	2133		Wingo, Dorcey	U.S.	1884
Matheson, Herbert	Brit.	2146				
McKinney, John	U.S.	2052		**MANSLAUGHTER - Unsolved**		
Mines, Joseph	U.S.	2188		Brinham, George	Brit.	488
Mogni, Gregorie	Brit.	2196				
Montgomery, Gabriel de	Fr.	2205		**MANSLAUGHTER - Wrongly Convicted**		
Nafte, Jaerl	S.Afri.	2275		Fry, John	U.S.	1239
Neal, Tom	U.S.	2293		Kassim, Ahmed	U.S.	1767
Nienstedt, Lena Theresa	U.S.	2336		Maynard, William A.	U.S.	2157
Norton, Samuel	U.S.	2346		Williams, Joseph S.	U.S.	3164
O'Rourke, Anthony	Brit.	2379				
Ouyerack, Charlie	Can.	2662		**MARTYR**		
Packham, Tom	Brit.	2392		Ursula, Saint	Ger.	3018
Palmer, Charles Jackson	Brit.	2398				
Pattmore, May	U.S.	2426		**MASS MURDER**		
Pine, John	Brit.	586		Allaway, Thomas Henry	Brit.	92
Pine, William	Brit.	586		Anderson, William	U.S.	125
Plauche, Gary	U.S.	2475		Andrews, Joseph	U.S.	126
Pop, Eugene Lewis	U.S.	2489		Andrews, Lowell Lee	U.S.	126
Posey, Joseph	U.S.	2492		Andrews, William	U.S.	2464
Povinelli, James	U.S.	1942		Avinain, Charles	Fr.	190
Roberts, Luke	Brit.	2851		Ax Man of New Orleans	U.S.	192
Russell, Rosemary	Brit.	2643		Bannon, Charles	U.S.	228

Katyn Massacre	U.S.S.R.	1768		Mudgett, Herman Webster	U.S.	2240
Kehoe, Andrew	U.S.	1775		Mullin, Herbert William	U.S.	2249
Kelbach, Walter		1776		Murad IV	Turk.	2252
Kelley, Dillard E., Sr.	U.S.	1777		Murder, Inc.	U.S.	2252
Kelly, Dan	Aus.	1779		Murieta, Joaquin	U.S.	2256
Kelly, Edward	Aus.	1779		My Lai Massacre	Viet.	2272
Kelly, Tom	N.Zea.	544		Nana Sahib	India	2276
Kenosha, Wis., Killings	U.S.	1804		Nash, Stephen	U.S.	2287
Khomeini, Ayatollah Ruhollah	Iran	1810		Nero	Roman.	2305
Kim Hyun Hui	N.Kor.	1820		Nesset, Arnfinn	Nor.	2307
King, Alvin Lee, III	U.S.	1820		Ng, Benjamin K.	U.S.	2093
Kirker, James	U.S.	1830		Nilsen, Dennis Andrew	Brit.	2336
Knight, Virgil	U.S.	1835		O'Brien, George	Can.	2357
Kohout, Edward	U.S.	1842		O'Bryan, Patrick	Brit.	2357
Kohout, Henry	U.S.	1842		Oates, Reginald Vernon	U.S.	2349
Kokoraleis, Andrew C.	U.S.	1288		Oberst, Owen	U.S.	2355
Kokoraleis, Thomas	U.S.	1288		Ohmura Ichiro	Japan	2366
Lampião	Braz.	1880		Opimius, Lucius	Roman.	2374
Lance, Myron	U.S.	1776		Orchard, Harry	U.S.	2375
Laros, Allen C.	U.S.	1899		Ottoman Sultans	Int'l	2386
Latham, James Douglas	U.S.	1901		Ovechkin, Ninel	U.S.S.R.	2387
Layman, Charles Newton	U.S.	1909		Owen, John	Brit.	2388
Lüdke, Bruno	Ger.	2007		Packer, Alferd G.	U.S.	2390
Le Bon, Joseph	Fr.	1915		Panzram, Carl	U.S.	2406
Ledbetter, Huddie	U.S.	1916		Pardo, Manuel	U.S.	2408
Lefèbre, Jean-Marie	Belg.	1921		Paris, Richard James	U.S.	2409
Lego, Donald	U.S.	1731		Parker, Bonnie	U.S.	250
Lepidus, Jacob	Brit.	1939		Pasha, Jezzar	Syria	2418
Levy, Philip	N.Zea.	544		Pates, Robert Eugene	U.S.	2418
Liggio, Luciano	Italy	1951		Paul, Rene	Can.	2427
Lock Ah Tam	Brit.	1974		Pearson, Moses	U.S.	2433
Lod Airport Massacre	Isr.	1976		Pelletier, Lawrence, Jr.	U.S.	2437
Logan, James	U.S.	1979		Perry, Calvin D., III	U.S.	2446
Loomis, George Washington, Jr.	U.S.	1988		Perry, Henry	Brit.	2446
López, Francisco Solano	Para.	1989		Petiot, Marcel Andre Henri Flix	Fr.	2453
Lopez, Hector	U.S.	783		Philadelphia County Prison Dea	U.S.	2456
Lopez, Pedro Alonso	Ecu.	1989		Phillips, Morgan	Brit.	2460
Lorentzen, Robert	U.S.	1991		Pierre, Dale	U.S.	2464
Low, Edward	Brit.	1996		Piskorski, Ronald	U.S.	2470
Loy Yeung	U.S.	1999		Pitre, Marguerite	Can.	1396
Lucas, Henry Lee	U.S.	2001		Pope, Duane Earl	U.S.	2489
Maalot Massacre	Isr.	2021		Porteous, John	Scot.	2490
MacDonald Clan Massacre	Scot.	2034		Powers, Harry F.	U.S.	2495
MacDonald, Jeffrey	U.S.	2032		Pranzini, Karl	Fr.	2496
McConaghy, Robert	U.S.	2026		Price, Albert	Brit.	2499
McCoy, Russell	U.S.	2029		Prince William, Va., Slayings	U.S.	2503
McCrary Family	U.S.	2029		Probst, Antoine	U.S.	2504
McGurn, Jack	U.S.	2043		Pulliam, Mark	U.S.	2511
M'Kinlie, Peter	Brit.	2051		Purrinton, James	U.S.	2513
McNamara Brothers	U.S.	2062		Quantrill, William Clarke	U.S.	2519
Mak, Kwan Fai	U.S.	2093		Raies, Jeanne	Switz.	2530
Mankato Massacre	U.S.	2103		Ransom, Florence	Brit.	2535
Mansfield, Billy	U.S.	2108		Rau, Gustav	Brit.	2544
Manson, Charles	U.S.	2108		Reggettz, Paul	U.S.	2558
Manuel, Peter Thomas Anthony	Scot.	2113		Reiser, Charles	U.S.	2562
Martin, Lee Roy	U.S.	2131		Renczi, Vera	Rom.	2567
Mary I	Brit.	2135		Rendall, Martha	Aus.	2568
Mason, Samuel	U.S.	2136		Rhodesia Missionary Slayings	Rhodesia	2572
Matuschka, Sylvestre	Hung.	2150		Richards, Stephen Dee	U.S.	2576
Medellin Murders	Col.	2161		Richardson, James	U.S.	2577
Medina, Ernest L.	U.S.	2161		Riley, Thomas	U.S.	2584
Mendez, Francisco	U.S.	783		Rivire, Pierre	Fr.	2586
Menndez de Avils, Pedro	Spain	2165		Roberts, Harry Maurice	Brit.	2592
Mikasevich, Gennadiy	U.S.S.R.	2177		Roche, Phillip	Brit.	2604
Miller, James B.	U.S.	2181		Rogers, George White	U.S.	2610
Monsson, Otto	Brit.	2544		Rojas, Tefilo	Col.	2613
Montvoisin, Catherine	Fr.	2206		Rolle, Randal	U.S.	2614
Morando, Jose	U.S.	648		Romanian Executions	Rom.	2615
Morgan, Henry	Brit.	2219		Romer, Richard	U.S.	2616
Mors, Frederick	U.S.	2227		Roy, Gilder	Scot.	2632

MATRICIDE

Caedwalla	Brit.	569	Dalrymple, John	Scot.	857
Cain	Mid.East.	576	Dalton, John	Brit.	858
Calla, Caesar	U.S.	581	Daniel, Robert	U.S.	867
Calvert, Mrs. Louie	Brit.	586	Daniels, Thomas H.	U.S.	868
Cambyses II	Per.	588	Danilo	Montenegro	868
Campbell, John	Scot.	593	Davidson, William	Brit.	2929
Candelaria, Nev.	U.S.	595	Davies, Alfred T.	Liberia	312
Candra Gupta II	India	595	Davies, Richard	Brit.	882
Canning, Joseph	Brit.	600	Davis, Edward	Aus.	883
Capello, Bianca	Italy	603	Davis, John W.	U.S.	884
Carlton, Harry	U.S.	627	Dead Man's Alley	U.S.	889
Casander	Macedonia	648	Deering, John	U.S.	901
Casares, Jose Hilario	U.S.	648	DeJong	Neth.	903
Cascioferro, Vito	Int'l	648	De Mau Mau Gang	U.S.	911
Casey, Michael	Brit.	1980	de Rais, Gilles	Fr.	2530
Cassidy, James P.	U.S.	2056	DeSimone, Thomas	U.S.	547
Catherine II	Rus.	657	DeStefano, Mario Anthony	U.S.	926
Cenci, Beatrice	Italy	663	Devereux, Walter	Ire.	931
Chadwick, William	U.S.	1134	Devlin, Henry	Scot.	932
Chalcraft, J.	Brit.	692	Dingaan	Int'l	975
Chamblit, Rebekah	U.S.	674	Dixon, Margaret	Scot.	979
Chapel, Martha	Brit.	680	Dobbs, Johnny	U.S.	980
Chapman, Jack	Brit.	1035	Dobell, Charles Joseph	Brit.	981
Chappleau, Joseph Ernst	U.S.	686	Domby, Victor	Fr.	994
Charles IX	Fr.	687	Donahue, John Xavier	U.S.	997
Chase, Charles	U.S.	689	Doody, William	U.S.	1002
Chauncey, Henry	U.S.	691	Dorsey, Charles	U.S.	1005
Chennell, George, Jr.	Brit.	692	Dotson, Clint	U.S.	1007
Chilperic I	Neustria	699	Douglas-Mahun Duel	Scot.	1009
Christie, Balm	U.S.	705	Douglas, Jean	Scot.	1010
Christina	Swed.	709	Douglas, William	Scot.	1010
Christophe, Henri	Haiti	710	Douglas, William	Scot.	1010
Chung Yi Miao	Brit.	711	Dreamer, Robert	U.S.	1021
Clark, Mary	Brit.	724	Druse, Mary	U.S.	1028
Clarke, David K.	Liberia	312	Dudley, Richard	Brit.	1031
Clench, Martin	Brit.	730	Duell, William	Brit.	1032
Click, Franklin	U.S.	732	Dugan, Eva	U.S.	1033
Clough, Jonathan	Brit.	734	Dumollard, Marie	Fr.	1034
Cochise	U.S.	735	Dun, Timothy	Brit.	1035
Cocklain, Matthew	Brit.	737	Duncalf, William	Brit.	777
Codre, Georges	Brit.	738	Dunford, Peter Anthony	Brit.	1036
Cohen, Ronald John Vivian	S.Afri.	742	Dunsdon Brothers	Brit.	1038
Colavito, Erminia	U.S.	1751	Dyer, Amelia Elizabeth	Brit.	1050
Coleman, Jefferson	U.S.	744	Dyon, John	Brit.	1051
Colley, Thomas	Brit.	749	Dyon, William	Brit.	1051
Collins, John Baptist	U.S.	752	Eadric Streona	Mercia	1052
Collins, John Norman	U.S.	752	Edwards, Paul	U.S.	1073
Combe, Michael	U.S.	761	Edwards, William	Brit.	3179
Constantine I	Rome	767	Eisele, Joseph	U.S.	1079
Conway, John	Brit.	768	Elby, William	Brit.	1080
Cook, William Edward	U.S.	770	Elsas, Ferdi	Neth.	1086
Cooper, Calmen	U.S.	2847	Elsom, Eleanor	Brit.	1087
Cooper, James	Brit.	777	Elwell, Robert	U.S.	1090
Cooper, Ralph	U.S.	777	English, Collis	U.S.	777
Copeland, Michael	Brit.	779	Erik Bldox	Nor.	1101
Coppola, Frank J.	U.S.	779	Escobedo, Daniel	U.S.	1103
Corallo, Anthony	U.S.	2448	Estrada, Pedro Luis	U.S.	1109
Corbett, Joseph, Jr.	U.S.	781	Eutropius	Roman.	1110
Corll, Dean Allen	U.S.	785	Evans, Charles	U.S.	1111
Court, M.	Fr.	2535	Evans, Chester	U.S.	1111
Cowdrey, Thomas	Brit.	801	Evans, David	Brit.	1111
Cox, Tom	Brit.	803	Evans, Michael	U.S.	1113
Crawford, George	U.S.	812	Eyler, Larry W.	U.S.	1120
Crimes of Honor Law	Italy	818	Fairris, Hurbie Franklin, Jr.	U.S.	1127
Crokes, Willie	U.S.	828	Farley, John	U.S.	1134
Crump, Paul	U.S.	840	Farmer, Mike	U.S.	1134
Cummings, Samuel	Liberia	312	Farmer, Pamela	U.S.	1134
Curtis, Winslow	U.S.	3138	Ferguson, Champ	U.S.	1150
Cutolo, Don Raffaele	Italy	850	Fine, Louis	U.S.	1159
Daley, Dominic	U.S.	856	Fitzpatrick, Edward	U.S.	1172

Fleming, Jim	U.S.	1007	Gyges	Lydia	1411	
Fleming, Patrick	Ire.	1178	Haggart, Robert Lee	U.S.	1415	
Fly, William	U.S.	1188	Haight, Edward	U.S.	1418	
Fooy, Sam	U.S.	1193	Halligan, James	U.S.	856	
Formi, Jose	U.S.	1198	Hamilton, Ray	U.S.	1435	
Forster, George	Brit.	1199	Hammond, Geoffrey	Brit.	1438	
Fort, Jeff	U.S.	1199	Hardaker, Betty	U.S.	1445	
Foster, George	Brit.	1202	Harland, Berry	U.S.	2374	
Foster, William	U.S.	1203	Harsh, George S.	U.S.	1466	
Foster, William	S.Afri.	1203	Heldenberg, Isoline	Fr.	1512	
Foulkes, Robert	Brit.	1204	Heldenberg, Martine	Fr.	1512	
Francia, Jos Gaspar Rodriguez	Para.	1209	Henry VII	Brit.	1518	
Francis, Willie	U.S.	1210	Hicswa, Joseph	U.S.	1544	
Francisco, Sancho	Mex.	1210	Higgins, Patrick	Scot.	1546	
Frank, Theodore	U.S.	1224	Himmler, Heinrich	Ger.	1556	
Fristoe, Leonard T.	U.S.	1237	Hind, James	Brit.	1558	
Fucaloro, Anthony	U.S.	1134	Hinkle, Betty	U.S.	2380	
Fukunaga, Myles Yutaka	U.S.	1239	Hitler, Adolf	Ger.	1565	
Furnari, Christopher	U.S.	2448	Holt, Alice	Brit.	1603	
Fury, Bridget	U.S.	1243	Honduran Death Squads	Hond.	1607	
Gacy, John Wayne, Jr.	U.S.	1246	Hooe, William F.	U.S.	1608	
Galbaio, Giovanni	Italy	1251	Hooker, Cameron	U.S.	1608	
Galbraith, James	Brit.	1251	Hornig, Frank	Aus.	1621	
Gale, Sarah	Brit.	1375	Horry, George Cecil	N.Z.	1622	
Gallogly, Richard Gray	U.S.	1257	Hosein, Arthur	Brit.	1623	
Gardiner, Faikai	Liberia	312	Hosein, Nizamodeen	Brit.	1623	
Garesio, Antonio	Italy	1270	Howard, Moustache	U.S.	1888	
Garesio, Gian Battista	Italy	1270	Howard, David	U.S.	1628	
Garner, Vance	U.S.	1275	Howard, George, Jr.	U.S.	1628	
Garret, Katherine	U.S.	1276	Howard, George, Sr.	U.S.	1628	
Gaydon, Jonathan	Brit.	1286	Howard, Leonard	U.S.	1629	
Geidel, Paul	U.S.	1289	Hugon, Daniel	Fr.	1637	
Gentile, Daniel	U.S.	1038	Hull, Fred	U.S.	1638	
Gentry, Charles	U.S.	1298	Hungerford, Alys	Brit.	1642	
Gerghuta, Ion	Rom.	1301	Hunter, Jack	U.S.	1275	
Gibbony, Mortimore	U.S.	421	Hunyadi, Lszil	Hung.	1645	
Gibbs, Charles	U.S.	1307	Hussey, Charles	Brit.	1647	
Gibbs, Edward Lester	U.S.	1307	Hutton, Peregrine	U.S.	1648	
Gibons, Jacqueline	U.S.	1308	Hyde, Edward	Brit.	1649	
Glanton, John J.	U.S.	1320	Illingworth, Monty	U.S.	1652	
Glaze, Billy	U.S.	1322	Indelicato, Anthony	U.S.	2448	
Glew, John	U.S.	2180	Ingle, Carl	U.S.	1733	
Glycerius	Roman.	1323	Ings, James	Brit.	2929	
Godfrey, Samuel E.	U.S.	1324	Inkpaduta	U.S.	1656	
Goering, Hermann Wilhelm	Ger.	1326	Irwin, James	U.S.	1666	
Goodman, John	U.S.	1340	Isaacs, Billy	U.S.	1036	
Goodwin, Henry K.	U.S.	1340	Jackson, Francis	Brit	1677	
Goodwin, James	Brit.	1340	Jackson, Joseph	U.S.	1678	
Goodwin, Marvin Clyde	U.S.	1341	Jackson, Louie	Brit.	1678	
Goolde, Maria Vere	Fr.	1341	Jefferies, Christopher	Brit.	1715	
Gordon-Lennox, Ellen	S.Afri.	3034	Jeffs, Doreen	Brit.	1716	
Gorringe, Jack	Brit.	1348	Jenkins, E.B	Brit.	1718	
Gosselin, Ambroisine	Fr.	1350	Jewell, Stephen	Brit.	1724	
Gotarzes II	Parthia	1350	Joanna I	Naples	1724	
Goucher, Allen	U.S.	1351	Joanna II	Naples	1724	
Gourier, Pere	Fr.	1353	John II	Spain	1726	
Gow, John	Brit.	1353	Johnson, Christopher	Brit.	1728	
Gower, William	Brit.	981	Johnson, Edward Earl	U.S.	1728	
Graham, George E.	U.S.	1356	Johnson, Mary	U.S.	1731	
Greco, Michele	Italy	1372	Johnson, Terry Lee	U.S.	1732	
Greenwood, David	Brit.	1378	Johnson, Terry Wayne	U.S.	660	
Grey, Arthur	Brit.	1383	Johnson, Watterson	U.S.	1733	
Grogan, Daniel	U.S.	421	Johnson, Will	U.S.	1275	
Gross, Ernst William	U.S.	1392	Johnston, Bruce, Sr.	U.S.	1734	
Grumbach, Wilhelm von	Ger.	1394	Johnston, David	U.S.	1734	
Grzechowiak, Stephen	U.S.	1395	Johnston, Duncan	U.S.	1735	
Guillaume de Hauteville	Normandy	1398	Johnston, Norman	U.S.	1734	
Guillemenot, Adolphe	Fr.	121	Jon, Gee	U.S.	1736	
Gunn, Raymond	U.S.	1400	Jones, Charles E.	U.S.	1737	
Gunness, Belle	U.S.	1400	Jones, John	Brit.	1739	

Jordan, Clayton	U.S.	1743		McLaughlin, Charles	U.S.	2056
Jud, Charles	Fr.	1746		McNab, Kevin	U.S.	1134
Kaber, Eva Catherine	U.S.	1751		McPherson, John	Can.	2069
Kaloyan	Bul.	1754		Mackley, James	Brit.	730
Kashney, Roland	U.S.	1767		Macrinus	Roman.	2070
Kasper, Karl	Ger.	1767		Maggiore, Michele della	Italy	2087
Kassow, Raymond	U.S.	1733		Magnentius, Flavius Popilius	Roman.	2087
Katist-Chen	Can.	1768		Mahoney, James E.	U.S.	2089
Kelley, William Cody	U.S.	1778		Malatesta, Gianciotto	Italy	2094
Kennedy, Edmund B.	Aus.	1794		Maleno, Steven	U.S.	2813
Kidden, Frances	Brit.	1815		Manchester Martyrs	Brit.	2099
Killorain, Japonica Jack	Peru	107		Manley, George	Brit.	2103
Kirkcaldy, William	Scot.	1830		Manlius Imperiosus Torq., Titu	Roman.	2104
Kleist, Heinrich von	Ger.	1833		Manna, Louis Anthony	U.S.	2105
Knighton, William	Brit.	1836		Mansfield, Billy	U.S.	2108
Knowles, Paul John	U.S.	1837		Maquer, Chevalier	Fr.	2114
Kodaira Yoshio	Japan	1840		Marcel, tienne	Fr.	2117
Koguchi Shizu	Japan	1840		Marshall, James	Brit.	1980
Koury, Leo Joseph	U.S.	1845		Mary I	Brit.	2135
Kovalev, Ivan	U.S.	1845		Mason, Samuel	U.S.	2136
Kuwaiti Airways Skyjacking	Iran	1865		Medellin Murders	Col.	2161
Ladislas V	Hung.	1870		Medley, Joseph Dunbar	U.S.	2161
Lake, Leonard	U.S.	1874		Menndez de Avils, Pedro	Spain	2165
Lalande, John	U.S.	1875		Mesrine, Jacques	Int'l	2170
Lalemant, Gabriel	U.S.	1875		Milano, Joseph	U.S.	2056
Lamb, James	U.S.	1876		Miles, Edward	Brit.	2179
Lamb, Mary Ann	Brit.	1877		Miller, Bill	U.S.	2180
Landis, M.D.	U.S.	1885		Miller, George	U.S.	2180
Landru, Henri Desire	Fr.	1885		Miller, John	U.S.	2182
Lane, Ed	U.S.	1888		Million, Roger	Fr.	3113
Langella, Gennaro	U.S.	2448		Milo, Titus Annius Papianus	Roman.	2186
Lavin, Martin	U.S.	1905		Mla, Auguste	Fr.	2163
Lawrence, Lenox	U.S.	228		Moity, Henry	U.S.	2197
Ldke, Bruno	Ger.	2007		Monsson, Otto	Brit.	2544
Leigh, John	U.S.	1733		Montgomery, T.H.	Brit.	2206
Le Quong, Vinh	Viet.	1939		Morales, Juan Castillo	Mex.	2213
Liao Chang-Shin	China	1948		Morando, Jose	U.S.	648
Liffey, Pasha	Brit.	1951		Morgan, Davy	Brit.	2218
Lightbourne, Wendell Willis	Ber.	1953		Morgan, Samuel	Brit.	2221
Lincoln, Warren	U.S.	1965		Morgan, Henry	Brit.	2219
Linder, Sonia Jacobs	U.S.	1967		Morin, Lontine	Fr.	248
Lindsay, Alexander	Scot.	1967		Morris, Raymond Leslie	Brit.	2225
Lindsay, Wayne	U.S.	228		Morse, Frederick	Brit.	2228
Lindwall, Richard	U.S.	1968		Mowbray, Thomas I	Brit.	2236
Lineveldt, Gamat Salie	S.Afri.	1968		Mullin, Herbert William	U.S.	2249
Lingard, Anthony	Brit.	1968		Muravyov, Mikhail Nikolayevich	Rus.	2252
Link, Karen Glabe	U.S.	1968		Murder, Inc.	U.S.	2252
Link, Mitchel	U.S.	1968		Murphy, Jack	U.S.	2259
Little Pete	U.S.	1972		Murphy, James	Brit.	2259
Lonagan, Edward	Brit.	1980		Murray, Edith	Brit.	2260
Loomis, George Washington, Jr.	U.S.	1988		Myers, William J.	U.S.	2270
Lopez, Pedro Alonso	Ecu.	1989		Nash, Stephen	U.S.	2287
Loredan, Pietro	Venice	1990		Nechayev, Sergey Gennadiyevich	Rus.	2295
Louis of Taranto	Naples	1993		Newell, Susan	Scot.	2310
Lowell, James	U.S.	1998		Nicolini, Sharon	U.S.	2547
Lowther, Will	Brit.	1999		Night of the Sicilian Vespers	U.S.	2336
Lucy, Richard de	Brit.	2007		Noel, Harrison	U.S.	2342
Luddites	Brit.	2007		Northcott, Gordon Stewart	U.S.	2345
Luetgert, Adolph Louis	U.S.	2007		Northcott, Sarah Louise	U.S.	2345
Lugo, Diego	U.S.	2009		O'Brien, Sandra	U.S.	2380
Lukens, Albert B.	U.S.	2009		O'Connor, Edward	Brit.	2359
Lutherland, Thomas	Brit.	2015		O'Dell, Albert	U.S.	1876
McCall, Edward L.	U.S.	2022		O'Donnell, Leo George	Brit.	2361
McConaghy, Robert	U.S.	2026		Old Brewery	U.S.	2368
McCracken, Henry	U.S.	2029		O'Neal, Belton	U.S.	2372
McDonald, Eddie	U.S.	1131		O'Neall, Darren	U.S.	2372
MacDonald, Ewan	Brit.	2031		Oneby, John	Brit.	2373
McDonnell, James	U.S.	2034		O'Sullivan, Patrick	U.S.	2385
M'Guinness, Thomas	Scot.	2043		Onufrejczyk, Michael	Brit.	2373
Mackay, Alexander	Brit.	2046		Opimius, Lucius	Roman.	2374

Soeder, Leon	U.S.	2811		Vratz, Christopher	Brit.	3064
Soga Umako	Japan	2812		Vucetic, Slobodan	Ger.	3065
Sophia Alekseevna	Rus.	2816		Vuong, Phung	U.S.	3066
Sowrey, Alfred	Brit	2819		Wagner, Franz	Ger.	3069
Stafford, Roger Dale	U.S.	2836		Wagner, Louis	U.S.	3069
Stalin, Joseph	U.S.S.R.	2836		Wainwright, Thomas	Brit.	3071
Stanciel, Elijah	U.S.	2838		Walker, Ernest Albert	Brit.	3076
Staniak, Lucian	Pol.	2839		Walker, Isobel	Scot.	3076
Stcherbakov, Matthiew	U.S.	1845		Walker, William	U.S.	3079
Stein, Harry	U.S.	2847		Wall, Joseph	Goree	3079
Stephens, John S.	U.S.	2850		Waltham Blacks	Brit.	3086
Stephenson, David Curtis	U.S.	2850		Walworth, William	Brit.	3087
Stewart, Alexander	Scot.	2852		Ward, Frederick	Aus.	3091
Stewart, Mrs. Francis	Brit.	2852		Wareru	Burma	3094
Stewart, Glen Gold	Can.	2852		Washington, Jeffrey	U.S.	3097
Stllgens, Robert Wilhelm	Ger.	2873		Watson, James P.	U.S.	3103
Stockdale, John	Brit.	1728		Watson, John Selby	Brit.	3103
Stockwell, John Frederick	Brit.	2857		Watts, Coral Eugene	U.S.	3104
Straffen, John Thomas	Brit.	2866		Weber, Adolph	U.S.	3108
Stubb, Peter	Ger.	2872		Weber, Jeanne	Fr.	3108
Sullivan, Howard	U.S.	2875		Webster, Daniel R.	U.S.	3109
Sullivan, Robert Austin	U.S.	2876		Weidmann, Eugen	Fr.	3113
Sutcliffe, Peter William	Brit.	2879		Wells, Thomas	Brit.	3126
Sutherland, John	Brit.	2880		Werner, Louis	U.S.	547
Swart, Marthinus Erich	S.Afri.	2886		West, John	U.S.	867
Swatz, Hermanus Lambertus	S.Afri.	3030		Westervelt, William	U.S.	3129
Swearingen, George	U.S.	2887		Whelpton, George	Brit.	3135
Tamerlane the Great	Mongolia	2895		White, Alexander	U.S.	3136
Taudien, Hugo	Japan	2898		White, John	Brit.	1677
Tavannes, Seigneur de	Fr.	2899		White, John Duncan	U.S.	3138
Taylor, Gary Addison	U.S.	2900		White, Roy	Brit.	3139
Taylor, Jack S.	U.S.	2901		White, Will	Brit.	1035
Taylor, Perry Alexander	U.S.	2902		Whitman, Charles Joseph	U.S.	3143
Taylor, William G.	U.S.	2906		Whittaker, Samuel	U.S.	3146
Teach, Edward	Int'l.	2906		Whittle, William	Brit.	3147
Terry, Paul	U.S.	1113		Williams, John	Brit.	1677
Texas Strangler	U.S.	2921		Williams, Norman	U.S.	3164
Theodoric II	Italy	2926		Williams, Wayne Bertram	U.S.	3166
Thompson, George	U.S.	2934		Wilmot, Thomas	Brit.	3170
Thompson, Phil B., Jr.	U.S.	2935		Wilson, Charles	U.S.	3171
Thompson, William Paul	U.S.	2937		Wilson, Dink	U.S.	3171
Thornton, Mark	Brit.	2940		Wilson, Earl	U.S.	3171
Thrift, John	Brit.	2942		Wilson, Edwin	U.S.	3171
Thurland, Tom	Brit.	1035		Wilson, Mary Elizabeth	Brit.	3174
Tidd, Richard	Brit.	2929		Wilson, Ocie	U.S.	3174
Tiernan, Helen	U.S.	2953		Winsor, Charlotte	Brit.	3177
Tierney, Nora Patricia	Brit.	2953		Winter, Willie	Brit.	3177
Tinker, Edward	U.S.	2956		Wissner, Nathan	U.S.	2847
Tiptoft, John	Brit.	2958		Woodfield, Randall Brent	U.S.	3184
Tipu Sahib	India	2958		Woolfolk, Thomas	U.S.	3186
Toal, Gerard	Ire.	2959		Woomer, Ronald	U.S.	3187
Tokugawa Ieyasu	Japan	2964		Wright, Samuel	Brit.	3195
Toledo, Francisco de	Peru	2964		Wright, Tom	Brit.	3195
Toohey, Michael	U.S.	2968		Wynkeburn, Walter	Brit.	3198
Townsend, Harry	U.S.	2980		Wynne, Thomas	Brit.	3199
Tracy, Benjamin Franklin	U.S.	2981		Yagoda, Henrikh Gregoryevich	U.S.S.R.	3201
Traxler, Roy	U.S.	2984		Yoritomo	Japan	3207
Trefethen, James	U.S.	2985		Young, Danny Jerome	U.S.	3208
Trolle, Gustav Eriksson	Swed.	2990		Young, Earl	U.S.	3208
Tully, Samuel	U.S.	3000		Young, William Hooper	U.S.	3211
Turtletaub, Sam	U.S.	3006		Zinoviev, Grigori Evseevich	Rus.	3221
Tz'u-Hsi	China	3012		Zo	Roman.	3222
Usefof, Joseph	U.S.	2056		Zodiac Killer	U.S.	3221
van der Merwe, Dorothea	S.Afri.	3030				
Villapando, James	U.S.	1134		**MURDER - Case of**		
Viola, Giuseppe	Italy	1034		**General**		
Visconti, Gian Galeazzo	Italy	3056		Antoine, Joseph	U.S.	134
Vlad Dracul		3058		Ball, William Weekly	Brit.	222
Vlad Tepes		3058		Banks, Alf	U.S.	227
Vollaro, Luigi	Italy	3061		Bates, W.L.	U.S.	3039

Bennett, Myrtle	U.S.	333	Boniface, Saint	Brit.	429
Boorn, Jesse	U.S.	436	Borynski, Father Henry	Brit.	445
Boorn, Stephen	U.S.	436	Bowlsby, Alice Augusta	U.S.	459
Bothwell, Fourth Earl of	Scot.	448	Brach, Helen Voorhees	U.S.	464
Bowen, George	U.S.	456	Brantley, John	U.S.	474
Calamia, Leonard	U.S.	577	Browne, William George	Brit.	518
Carbone, Paul	Fr.	620	Buswell, Harriet	Brit.	561
Carmen, Jack Allen	U.S.	628	Camp, Elizabeth Annie	Brit.	591
Carpenter, Oran A.	U.S.	635	Cash, Bailey	U.S.	650
Chamberlain, Robert	Brit.	672	Chateaubriant, Franoise de	Fr.	690
Donnelly, James	Can.	999	Cohn, Lenora	U.S.	742
Estes, Cornell Avery	U.S.	1109	Coogler, Ovida	U.S.	768
Falling, Christine	U.S.	1131	Culley, Robert	Brit.	843
Francis II	Fr.	1209	Currieri, Cesar	Fr.	848
Franz, Johann Karl	Brit.	1227	Danby, Benjamin	Brit.	865
Fraser, Simon	Scot.	1227	Daniels, Winifred	Fr.	868
Gibson, Lindsey	U.S.	1308	Davys, John	Sing.	887
Goldsborough, Robert	Brit.	1334	Decken, Karl Klaus von der	Somalia	898
Gordon, John Williams	Brit.	1344	Desouches, Thierry	Fr.	926
Gould, Richard	Brit.	1352	Despenser, Hugh le	Brit.	926
Green, Ann	Brit.	1372	Diaz de Solis, Juan	Spain	938
Harpur, Charles	Brit.	1457	Dutreuil de Rhins, Jules Lon	Tibet	1046
Hicks, Edward	U.S.	227	Dympna	Belg.	1051
Jackson, Harold	U.S.	1677	Galapagos Murders	Ecu.	1251
Jensen, Thomas Peter	U.S.	1722	Glass, Jimmie	U.S.	1321
Kelly, Frank	U.S.	1781	Hand, Horace	Brit.	1441
Keseberg, Lewis	U.S.	1806	Harte, Robert Sheldon	Mex.	1469
McGuire, John Francis	Brit.	2043	Hoffa, James Riddle	U.S.	1584
McKay, Muriel	Brit.	2047	Jogues, Isaac	U.S.	1726
McKinstry, Joseph Ralph Bradle	Brit.	2053	Johnston, Erin Elizabeth	China	1735
Medina, Ernest L.	U.S.	2161	Krick, Mary	Brit.	1851
Muscau, Andrea	Italy	2261	LaHaye, Aubrey	U.S.	1874
Pay, Esther	Brit.	2428	Lairre, Marie	Brit.	1874
Price, William Joseph	Brit.	1025	Lawson, Louise	U.S.	1908
Raper, Pamela	Fr.	2535	Lee, Louisa	Brit.	1919
Read, Richard	U.S.	2548	Lee, Reginald Arthur	Fr.	1920
Rees, Rees T.	U.S.	2557	Levy, Henry	U.S.	1945
Reggettz, Paul	U.S.	2558	Lyon, Katherine	U.S.	2018
Robbins, Gary A.	U.S.	2589	Lyon, Sheila	U.S.	2018
Sander, Hermann N.	U.S.	2675	Marvin, Horace, Jr.	U.S.	2133
Santini, Donald Michael	U.S.	2679	May, Jeannette	Italy	2154
Skipwith, J.K.	U.S.	2774	McCormick, Willie	U.S.	2027
Soto, Erno	U.S.	2816	Merrill, Jane Surget	U.S.	2169
Spirito, Franois	Fr.	620	Moonlight Murderer	U.S.	2209
Stannard, Albert	Aus.	2839	Morgan, William	U.S.	2221
Stiles, Will	U.S.	3039	Munk, Kaj Harald Leininger	Den.	2251
Stout, Samuel	U.S.	2866	Nitribitt, Rosemarie	Ger.	2339
Strong, John Patrick	Aus.	2839	Nolte, Elizabeth	U.S.	2342
Tanner, John	U.S.	2897	Oakland County Murders	U.S.	2349
Tse-ne-gat	U.S.	2998	Oldham, John	U.S.	2368
Vaught, Millard	U.S.	3039	Oliver, Alfred	Brit.	2370
Votyak Tribe Murders	Rus.	3064	Palmer, Edward Henry	Brit.	2398
Weeks, Levi	U.S.	3112	Paquet, Christienne	Fr.	2408
West, Eugene	U.S.	3128	Parsons, Mrs. William H.	U.S.	2416
de Lussatz, Gaetan	Fr.	620	Peter Martyr, Saint	Italy	2452
deMarigny, Alfred M. de Foug.	Bahamas	911	Peterson, Robert	U.S.	2698
			Philip	U.S.	2457
MURDER - Unsolved			Philoxenus	Roman.	2460
General			Pickelny, Irving	U.S.	2462
Spilotro, Anthony	U.S.	2828	Powell, Charlotte Ann	U.S.	2493
Wallis, Dorothy Edith	Brit.	3083	Ramus, Petrus	Fr.	2533
Accoramboni, Vittorio	Italy	18	Reville, Jean	U.S.	2570
Alboin	Italy	47	Rivire, Henri Laurent	Viet.	2586
Arnold, Dorothy Harriet Camill	U.S.	161	Robsart, Amy	Brit.	2603
Ashley, Andrew	U.S.	170	Rogers, Mary Cecilia	U.S.	2611
Barginde, Sigrid	U.S.	234	Ross, Charles B.	U.S.	2621
Benhadad I	Damascus	330	Rosse, Edith Marion	Brit.	2625
Bernard VII	Fr.	346	Rothman, Harry	U.S.	2626
Berner, Mrs. Stewart	U.S.	347	Rubinstein, Serge	U.S.	2633
Bialek, Robert	Ger.	356	Schneider, E.L.	U.S.	2696

Schuessler, Anton	U.S.	2698		Decker, Earl	U.S.	865
Schuessler, John	U.S.	2698		Dedmond, Roger Zane	U.S.	899
Schuster, Arnold	U.S.	2705		Deveaux, Jean-Marie	Fr.	930
Setrabutra, Panep	Thai.	2729		Donnelly, James	U.S.	1000
Sheasby, June	Brit.	2738		Donovan, George Thomas	Brit.	1001
Sheasby, Royston	Brit.	2738		Dove, Frank	U.S.	1011
Southgate, Susan	Brit.	2818		Dove, Fred	U.S.	1011
Stein, Edith	Ger.	2847		Dulin, William	U.S.	1034
Ter-Petrosyan, Semyon	U.S.S.R	2915		Emmett, George	U.S.	814
Tharme, Lilian	Brit.	2921		Fay, Floyd	U.S.	1140
Todd, Thelma	U.S.	2960		Fenayrou, Gabrielle	Fr.	1147
Turner, John Virgil	U.S.	3004		Ferber, Neil	U.S.	1149
Vallint, Miles	Brit.	3028		Fewell, Stanford Ellis	U.S.	1154
Vintenon, Franois	Fr.	3056		Fisher, William	U.S.	1167
Wagner, Charles	Brit.	3068		Foster, James	U.S.	1202
Walton, Charles	Brit.	3087		Frank, Leo Max	U.S.	1217
William of Norwich, Saint	Brit.	3159		Frederick, Johnny	U.S.	1230
				Garvey, Mike	U.S.	1281
MURDER - Wrongly Convicted				Goodwin, Paul	U.S.	1341
Adams, Randall Dale	U.S.	28		Grace, Frank Parky	U.S.	1355
Amado, Christian	U.S.	108		Graham, John	Brit.	1358
Antoniewicz, Joseph	U.S.	134		Green, Robert	Brit.	1374
Arroyo, Miguel	U.S.	168		Green, William S.	U.S.	1375
Bachelor, Brett Allen	U.S.	205		Groake, Patrick	Brit.	1391
Bailey, Robert Ballard	U.S.	212		Gross, Louis	U.S.	1392
Bambrick, Thomas	U.S.	223		Growden, Gerald	U.S.	1394
Barbato, Joseph	U.S.	230		Gunter, Thomas	U.S.	1405
Barber, Arthur	U.S.	230		Habron, William	Brit.	1412
Baxwell, James	Gibraltar	285		Hacker, Larry	U.S.	814
Ben Ali, Ameer	U.S.	323		Haines, Ernest	U.S.	1419
Bennett, Louis William	U.S.	333		Hall, Gordon Robert Castillo	U.S.	1424
Bernstein, Charles	U.S.	347		Hall, James	U.S.	1425
Berry, Henry	Brit.	1374		Hall, Lindberg	U.S.	722
Bertrand, Delphine	U.S.	352		Hallowell, William A.	U.S.	134
Bhutto, Zulfikar Ali	Pak.	356		Hampton, Mary Katheryn	U.S.	1440
Bilger, George	U.S.	361		Hankins, Leonard	U.S.	1442
Boggie, Clarence Gilmore	U.S.	419		Hanratty, James	Brit.	1444
Boyd, Payne	U.S.	461		Hardy, Vance	U.S.	1452
Brite, Coke	U.S.	493		Harris, Frank	U.S.	1460
Brite, John	U.S.	493		Harris, Thomas	Brit.	1463
Broady, Thomas H., Jr.	U.S.	494		Hefner, Cecil	U.S.	1507
Brown, Bradford	U.S.	505		Hess, Walter	U.S.	805
Brown, J.B.	U.S.	508		Hicks, Larry	U.S.	1543
Bundy, Harry Dale	U.S.	537		Hill, Lawrence	Brit.	1374
Butler, Louise	U.S.	562		Hoffner, Louis	U.S.	1587
Calas, Jean	Fr.	578		Holbrook, Ernest, Jr.	U.S.	1589
Calloway, Willie	U.S.	585		Hudson, Jim	U.S.	841
Carden, Ronald Q.	U.S.	621		Imbler, Paul Kern	U.S.	1653
Carter, Nathaniel	U.S.	644		Jackson, Edmond D.	U.S.	1676
Cauvin, Louis	Fr.	659		Jackson, Sergeant H.	U.S.	1680
Chalker, Edward Poole	Brit.	670		Jaramillo, Anibal	U.S.	1711
Chambers, Isaiah	U.S.	672		Jenkins, Billy	U.S.	814
Chambers, Leon	U.S.	673		Jenkins, Lonnie	U.S.	1719
Chance, John Henry	U.S.	675		Jennings, Jasper	U.S.	1722
Charles, Earl	U.S.	687		Johnson, John A.	U.S.	1730
Chol Soo Lee	U.S.	702		Jones, Harllel	U.S.	1737
Clark, Charles Lee	U.S.	721		Jordan, Theodore	U.S.	1743
Clark, Ephraim R.	U.S.	722		Keaton, David Roby	U.S.	1230
Coleman, Richard	Brit.	744		Kirkes, Leonard	U.S.	1830
Coleman, Robert	U.S.	745		Kuykendall, Sceola	U.S.	722
Corbisiero, Carlo	Italy	782		Lang, Donald	U.S.	1889
Cox, Robert	Brit.	803		Larkman, Edward	U.S.	1898
Craig, Alvin	U.S.	805		Lee, Wilbert	U.S.	1920
Creamer, James	U.S.	814		Lesher, Harvey	U.S.	1281
Crutcher, Willie	U.S.	841		McDonald, Wilbur	U.S.	2033
Dabney, Condy	U.S.	853		Matera, Pietro	U.S.	2145
Dame, Lige	U.S.	865		Miller, Lloyd Eldon, Jr.	U.S.	2182
Davis, Charlie	U.S.	672		Murchison, John	U.S.	841
De Los Santos, George	U.S.	910		O'Neil, Jack	U.S.	2373
DeMore, Louis	U.S.	913		Owens, Aaron	U.S.	2388

Parks, Edward H.	U.S.	134
Parrott, Lemuel	U.S.	2415
Perry Family	Brit.	2448
Pine, Edmund	Brit.	2466
Pitts, Freddie	U.S.	1920
Powell, Hoyt	U.S.	814
Pyle, Harry	U.S.	2517
Qvist, Soren	Den.	2524
Roberts, Charles	U.S.	814
Robinson, Van Bering	U.S.	2601
Rodriguez, Santos	U.S.	2606
Rogers, Silas	U.S.	2612
Rohan, Phil	U.S.	1281
Ruff, Wayne	U.S.	814
Samuels, Joseph	Aus.	2674
Seaton, Terry	U.S.	2719
Seznec, Guillaume	Fr.	2731
Sheeler, Rudolph	U.S.	361
Sherman, David	U.S.	2744
Smith, Grace M.	U.S.	2793
Smith, Larry Thomas	U.S.	2798
Staten, Cleo	U.S.	841
Taylor, Percival Leonard	Brit.	1001
Thompson, Sam	U.S.	2415
Tibbs, Delbert	U.S.	2950
Torres, Pedro	U.S.	2969
Valletutti, John	U.S.	3028
Vargas, Anastacio	U.S.	3036
Vasquez, David	U.S.	3037
Venegas, Juan	U.S.	3041
Weaver, James	Brit.	1001
Weaver, Joseph	U.S.	3107
Williams, George	U.S.	1011
Williams, Robert	U.S.	3165
Williams, Samuel Tito	U.S.	3166
Williamson, Jack	U.S.	672
Wing, George Chew	U.S.	3176
Woodward, Walter	U.S.	672
Yelder, George	U.S.	562

MURDER?

Crater, Joseph Force	U.S.	810
Earhart, Amelia Mary	U.S.	1052
Orgen, Jacob	U.S.	2377
Quintillus	Roman.	2523
Adamic, Louis	U.S.	20

MURDER - Unsolved?

Sedov, Lev Lvuvich	Fr.	2722
Moore, William	U.S.	2211
Poole, William	U.S.	2488
Mozart, Wolfgang Amadeus	Aust.	2237
King, Dorothy	U.S.	1821

MURDER - Wrongly Convicted?

Brooks, Fisher	U.S.	2676
Kapatos, Thomas	U.S.	1759
Kirby, James	Ire.	1829
Lambert, Henry J.	U.S.	1877
Lamble, Harold	U.S.	1877
Lee, James	Brit.	1917
Lefley, Mary	Brit.	1922
Lindley, William Marvin	U.S.	1967
Monroe, Ronald	U.S.	2202
Pope, Ervin	U.S.	2489
Sanders, Albert	U.S.	2676
Schwartz, Harry	U.S.	2707
Stewart, James	Scot.	2853
Wan Zian Sung	U.S.	3090
Watt, Newton	U.S.	2707

Woodmansee, Ernest	U.S.	3184

MURDER BY ACID

de Kaplany, Geza	U.S.	903
Haigh, John George	Brit.	1417

MURDER BY ASPHYXIATION

Basile, Tobia	Italy	272
Bell, Larry Gene	U.S.	318
Bender Family	U.S.	324
Boulogne, Henri	Fr.	454
Bradley, Magda	Aus.	466
Bradley, Stephen Leslie	Aus.	466
Brown, Joseph	Brit.	514
Burke, William	Scot.	547
Caldwell, Roger	U.S.	579
Carr, Melvin	U.S.	636
Coleman, Alton	U.S.	743
Conlin, Charles William	Brit.	765
Conroy, Teresa Miriam	Brit.	767
Corey, Frank	U.S.	784
Cullen, John	U.S.	2747
Durrant, William Henry Theodor	U.S.	1041
Edwards, Daniel J.	U.S.	1071
Fitzgerald, Thomas Richard	U.S.	1171
Gangy, Paul W.	U.S.	1264
Glaze, Billy	U.S.	1322
Gordon, Nathaniel	U.S.	1345
Hall, Archibald	Brit.	1420
Hare, William	Scot.	547
Hatcher, Charles Ray	U.S.	1475
Hauptfleisch, Petrus S, François		
Heys, Arthur	Brit.	
Horne, William Andrew	Brit.	1620
Julian of Goathland	Brit.	1749
Kinman, Donald	U.S.	1827
Kirwan, William Bourke	Ire.	1831
Kitto, Michael	Brit.	1420
Lacenaire, Pierre Franois	Fr.	1868
Landru, Henri Desire	Fr.	1885
Lemoine, Victoire Mingot	Fr.	1928
Lipski, Israel	Brit.	1969
Longhi, Luigi	Den.	1987
Malik, Abdul	Trinidad	2096
Masset, Louise	Brit.	2139
McCall, Franklin Pierce	U.S.	2023
Messenger, Margaret	Brit.	2171
Miller, Lucille	U.S.	2182
Moormann, Robert Henry	U.S.	2211
Pearcey, Mary Eleanor	Brit.	2433
Philadelphia County Prison Deaths	U.S.	2456
Place, Martha	U.S.	2473
Price, Albert	Brit.	2499
Rees, Melvin David	U.S.	2557
Reiser, Charles	U.S.	2562
Rizzi, William	U.S.	2587
Robinson, John	Brit.	2596
Rohart, Armand	Fr.	2613
Ross, Elizabeth	Brit.	2624
Shonbrun, Eli	U.S.	2747
Smith, Edward Charles	Brit.	514
Sobhraj, Gurmukh Charles	India	2810
Thomas, Edward	U.S.	2930
Tinning, Marybeth Roe	U.S.	2956
Troppmann, Jean-Baptiste	Fr.	2990
Webb, Madeline	U.S.	2747
Williams, Wayne Bertram	U.S.	3166
Wise, Olive Catherine	Brit.	3178
Shaeffer, Daniel	U.S.	2733
Tinning, Marybeth Roe	U.S.	2956

Stockwell, John Frederick	Brit.	2857
Stout, Peter	U.S.	2865
Stowe, Louis Richard	U.S.	2866
Turner, Nat	U.S.	3004
Walker, John	Brit.	3078
Westwood, William John	Aus.	3130
Whiteway, Alfred Charles	Brit.	3141
Wightman, Donald	U.S.	2053
Williams Farm Murders	U.S.	3168
Gallagher, John	Brit.	2886
Swann, Emily	Brit.	2886
Webster, Kate	Brit.	3111

MURDER BY AX/HATCHET - Case of

Adams, Moses	U.S.	27
Borden, Lizzie	U.S.	437
Clanwaring, Thomas	Brit.	720
Covert, Clarice	Brit.	801
Gatlin, Alma Petty	U.S.	1284
Green, Cleo Joel, III	U.S.	1372
Hatfield, William	U.S.	1477
Jordano, Frank	U.S.	1744
Knott, Hester Elizabeth	S.Afri.	1836
Nau, Ralph	U.S.	2291
Robinson, Richard P.	U.S.	2598
Shaddy, Gregory	U.S.	2732

MURDER BY AX/HATCHET - Unsolved

Ax Man of New Orleans	U.S.	192
Bathurst, Benjamin	Brit.	282
Bourg, Frank	U.S.	454
DeFoor, Martin	U.S.	901
DeFoor, Susan	U.S.	901
Ferguson, Bessie	U.S.	1149
Pontiac, Chief	U.S.	2485
Tulsa Bludgeonings	U.S.	3001
Zimbabwe Missionary Massacre	Zimbabwe	3220

MURDER BY AX/HATCHET - Wrongly Convicted

Shaffer, Howard	U.S.	2733
Stevens, Charles	U.S.	2733
Troop, William	U.S.	2733

MURDER BY BEATING

Abrams, Michael	U.S.	13
Adler, Lydia	Brit.	31
Anderson, Dick	U.S.	2935
Antonio, Maurice	U.S.	134
Appo, Quimby	U.S.	139
Aram, Eugene	Brit.	141
Armour, Joseph	U.S.	156
Baniszewski, Gertrude Wright	U.S.	226
Barton, John Evert	U.S.	271
Beagles, David Ervin	U.S.	286
Belvin, Paul Augustus	Ber.	322
Bender Family	U.S.	324
Birch, Leroy	U.S.	107
Bischoff, Charles	U.S.	380
Bishop, William Bradford, Jr.	U.S.	382
Bonafous, Louis	Fr.	427
Bonney, Edward W.	U.S.	431
Bozzeli, Peter	U.S.	463
Branch, Elizabeth	Brit.	470
Branch, Mary	Brit.	470
Burns, Alfred	Brit.	551
Caligula	Rome	580
Cawley, Brian	Brit.	662
Coleman, Edward	U.S.	744
Comings, William Freeman	U.S.	762
Cretzer, Joseph Paul	U.S.	816

Crossman, George Albert	Brit.	835
Dacey, Edwin	Brit.	853
Darby, Christopher	Brit.	1463
DeCroat, Arthur	U.S.	898
DeLeon, Leoncio	U.S.	107
Dean, Laurence Michael	Brit.	891
Deeming, Frederick Bayley	Int'l	899
de Tourville, Count Henri	Aust.	928
Devlin, Edward Francis	Brit.	551
Donnell, Richard	U.S.	999
Donnelly, Edward	U.S.	999
Dorbell, Tom	Brit.	1004
Draper, William	U.S.	1020
Drew, Joseph	U.S.	1022
Dumini, Amerigo	Italy	1034
Edel, Frederick W.	U.S.	1068
Edmunds, William Charles	Brit.	1070
Edwards, Mack Ray	U.S.	1073
Edwards, Vernon David, Jr.	U.S.	1074
Egyptian Dragons	U.S.	1075
Emmett-Dunne, Frederick	Ger.	1092
Epton, George Cyril	Brit.	1100
Falleni, Eugene	Aus.	1130
Fenayrou, Marin	Fr.	1147
Ferguson, David	Brit.	1150
Filipovitz, Peter	Aust.	2994
Fisher, Lavinia	U.S.	1166
Fitzgerald, Thomas Richard	U.S.	1171
Flack, William	Brit.	1174
Flinn, Charles J.	U.S.	1179
Flowery Land Mutiny	Brit.	1182
Forsyth, Francis	Brit.	1463
Fowler, Bunny	Brit.	1204
Fox, John	U.S.	1205
Franklin, Timothy	Brit.	1226
Fratson, George	Brit.	1228
Freeman, Samuel	U.S.	1232
Gallego, Gerald	U.S.	1255
Goethe, Robert	U.S.	1328
Gonzalez Valenzuela, Delfina	Mex.	1338
Gonzalez Valenzuela, Maria de	Mex.	1338
Gordon, John	U.S.	1344
Gordon, William	U.S.	1344
Goslett, Arthur Andrew Clement	Brit.	1349
Gough, John	Brit.	1351
Graham, Adam	Brit.	1355
Graham, Barbara	U.S.	1355
Graham, James	U.S.	1357
Griffiths, James	Scot.	1388
Griffiths, Peter	Brit.	1388
Gunderman, Stacey	U.S.	1400
Hall, James W.	U.S.	1425
Halsey, Joseph	Brit.	1432
Hays, Henry Francis	U.S.	1498
Haight, Edward	U.S.	1418
Harris, Norman James	Brit.	1463
Harris, Pleasant	U.S.	1463
Hauser, Frederick I.	U.S.	1490
Heidnik, Gary M.	U.S.	1507
Hernandez, Cayetano	Mex.	2813
Hernandez, Santos	Mex.	2813
Hibner, Esther	Brit.	1532
Hill, Rufus	U.S.	1554
Hinks, Reginald Ivor	Brit.	1561
Hodapp, Jacob Frederick	U.S.	1583
Horton, Charles	U.S.	107
Howdeshell, Roy	U.S.	1631
Hsan-chi Y	China	1633
Hunter, Edward	U.S.	1644
Jacobson, Howard	U.S.	1693

Jennings, Augustus Otis	U.S.	1721
Johnson, Frank	U.S.	1733
Johnson, Vateness	U.S.	1733
Kingsmill Gang	Brit.	1827
Lee, William W.	U.S.	1921
LeGrand, Devernon	U.S.	1924
Lutt, Terence	Brit.	1463
McGee, Eddie	U.S.	2040
MacKay, Patrick David	Brit.	2047
Maddux, Ronald	U.S.	2073
Maddux, Wanda Gibson	U.S.	2073
Marino, Arthur	U.S.	2123
Marsh, Elizabeth	Brit.	2128
Mastrian, Norman	U.S.	2935
Maynard, William John	Brit.	2158
Meade, Thomas	Brit.	2159
Metyard, Sarah	Brit.	2173
Metyard, Sarah Morgan	Brit.	2173
Meyer, Robert	U.S.	2175
Mills, John	Brit.	2184
Milone, Richard	U.S.	2186
Milsom, Albert	Brit.	1204
Moore, Charles	Brit.	2209
Nero	Roman.	2305
Olson, Clifford	Can.	2371
Parker, Frederick William	Brit.	2410
Price, John	Brit.	2500
Probert, Albert	Brit.	2410
Ralph, Edward	U.S.	2533
Regan, Leonard	U.S.	2558
Rogatsch, Johann	Aust.	2608
Rutherford, Elsie Mae	U.S.	2644
Rutherford, Howard	U.S.	2644
Salmon, Thomas	U.S.	2671
Schewchuk, Peter	U.S.	1049
Shue, Erasmus Stribling Trout	U.S.	2750
Solis, Eleazor	Mex.	2813
Solis, Magdalena	Mex.	2813
Sommer, Gerhard Martin	Ger.	2814
Starkweather, Albert L.	U.S.	2840
Sturtivant, William E.	U.S.	2874
Teufel, Albert	U.S.	2918
Thick, Edwin Claude	Brit.	2928
Thompson, Gerald	U.S.	2934
Thompson, Robert J.	Mex.	2935
Thompson, Tilmer Eugene	U.S.	2935
Thorne, John Norman Holmes	Brit.	2939
Truber, Manfred	Aust.	2994
Veronica Mutineers	Brit.	3042
Wallner, Walter	Aust.	2994
Walsh, Edward	Brit.	2209
Washington, Allen	U.S.	3097
Watt, Miriam	U.S.	3104
Watt, Newton	U.S.	3104
Watts, Coral Eugene	U.S.	3104
Weatherill, Miles	Brit.	3107
Williams, John	Brit.	3162
Williamson, John	Brit.	3168

MURDER BY BEATING - Case of

Beeman, Gary L.	U.S.	314
Benquet, Jean	Fr.	2282
Cazenave, Jean	Fr.	2282
Coombs, George	U.S.	774
Corey, Daniel H.	U.S.	784
Cornock, Mrs. Cecil	Brit.	788
Dodd, Jeff	U.S.	983
Doudet, Clestine	Fr.	1008
Eastman, Robert	U.S.	1065
Ecker, Lewis C., II	U.S.	1067

Edmonds, Edmund	Brit.	1069
Hart, Gene Leroy	U.S.	1467
McDonald, Peter Alexander	Brit.	2033
Nardon, Georges	Fr.	2282
Norris, Melissa	U.S.	2345
O'Malley, James	U.S.	2372
Wilkins, Walter Keene	U.S.	3157

MURDER BY BEATING - Unsolved

Aposhian, Dalbert	U.S.	138
Baker, Rosetta	U.S.	217
D'Andrea, Nicholas J.	U.S.	866
Doze, Grace	U.S.	1017
East, Winifred	Brit.	1063
Frome, Nancy	U.S.	1237
Frome, Mrs. Weston G.	U.S.	1237
Gooding, Florence	Brit.	1339
Lovejoy, Elijah Parish	U.S.	1995
Mattson, Charles	U.S.	2150
Matulla Murders	U.S.	2150
Mills, Dorothy	Brit.	2184
Millsom, Sarah	Brit.	2185
Mogano, Penelope	Brit.	2196
Money, Mary Sophia	Brit.	2200
Pill, William John	Aus.	2466
Roberts, Jane	Brit.	2592
Scottoriggio, Joseph R.	U.S.	2714
Steele, Ann	Scot.	2847
Thomas, Elizabeth	Brit.	2930
Tulsa Bludgeonings	U.S.	3001

MURDER BY BEATING - Wrongly Convicted

Lobaugh, Ralph W.	U.S.	1974
Lyons, Ernest	U.S.	2018
Morris, Gordon	U.S.	2224
Rusnok, George	U.S.	2975
Sabol, Michael	U.S.	2975
Toth, Andrew	U.S.	2975

MURDER BY BLUNT INSTRUMENT
General

Abbandando, Frank	U.S.	1
Abbott, Burton W.	U.S.	4
Adams, Caleb	U.S.	22
Adams, James	U.S.	25
Adomeit, Kurt	Ger.	32
Adomeit, Ursula	Ger.	32
Agostini, Antonio	Aus.	37
Alexander, Frank	Canary Is.	90
Alexander, Norris	U.S.	623
Allen, Margaret	Brit.	97
Allen, Peter Anthony	Brit.	98
Allison, James	Can.	99
Anderson, Allen Leroy	U.S.	121
Antonini, Theresa	Ger.	134
Arden, Alice	Brit.	153
Arnold, Stephen	U.S.	163
Ashcroft, David	Brit.	170
Ashcroft, James	Brit.	170
Ashcroft, James, Jr.	Brit.	170
Ashwell, Thomas	U.S.	171
Athoe, Thomas, Jr.	Brit.	175
Athoe, Thomas, Sr.	Brit.	175
Ball, George	Brit.	220
Barr, Aime Thomas	Fr.	248
Boost, Werner	Ger.	436
Bowsher, Perry	U.S.	459
Bradley, James	U.S.	465
Brown, Conrad	U.S.	505
Bruneau, Albert	Fr.	520

Bundy, Theodore	U.S.	537
Butler, James	Brit.	562
Butler, William	Brit.	563
Byrnes, Thomas	U.S.	566
Caligula	Rome	580
Campbell, Peter	Scot.	593
Cargin, Freeman	U.S.	623
Cargin, Julia Ann	U.S.	623
Carter, George	Brit.	643
Carver, Donald	U.S.	647
Clarke, Morris Arthur	Brit.	726
Cluverius, Thomas J.	U.S.	734
Coleman, Alton	U.S.	743
Cummings, Joyce Lisa	U.S.	465
Cutty Sark Tragedy	Brit.	851
Deeming, Frederick Bayley	Int'l	899
Dominici, Gaston	Fr.	995
du Plessis, Andries Stephanus	S.Afri.	1039
Drysdale, Alexander	U.S.	1029
Edwards, Robert Allan	U.S.	1073
Evans, Gwynne Owen	Brit.	98
Fife, Henry	U.S.	1157
Flinn, Charles J.	U.S.	1179
Fortner, Clifford	U.S.	1200
Ganz, Jacob	Switz.	2452
Garvie, Sheila W.	Scot.	2919
Gary, Carlton	U.S.	1282
Gould, Janice Irene	U.S.	465
Gufler, Max	Aust.	1397
Gutkind, Johann	Ger.	1409
Haggerty, Owen	Brit.	1596
Haigh, John George	Brit.	1417
Hall, George Albert	Brit.	1424
Hanlon, John	U.S.	1442
Heath, Neville George Clevely	Brit.	1504
Hewett, Jack	Brit.	1528
Holden, William	Brit.	170
Holloway, John	Brit.	1596
Hulme, Juliet Marion	N.Zea.	2412
Inquisition, The	Int'l.	1656
Jggli, Margaret	Switz.	2452
Johnson, Milton	U.S.	1731
Kehoe, Andrew	U.S.	1775
Kemper, Edmund Emil III	U.S.	1791
Kenkowski, Martin	U.S.	1792
King, Reginald Frederick	Brit.	1826
Kirkwood, James Boyd	Scot.	1830
Kitto, Michael	Brit.	1420
Knight, Mary	Brit.	1835
LaPage, Joseph	U.S.	1896
Lane, James	U.S.	1889
Lang, Howard	U.S.	1889
Laurie, John Watson	Scot.	1904
Lefbre, Jean-Marie	Belg.	1921
Lego, Donald	U.S.	1731
Lewis, Harry	Brit.	1946
Lowry, James	Brit.	1998
Lucas, Henry Lee	U.S.	2001
Mayer, Earl	U.S.	2800
Morey, William	U.S.	2218
Olive, Marlene	U.S.	2370
Papin, Christine	Fr.	2407
Papin, Leah	Fr.	2407
Pappas, Rosemary	U.S.	2407
Parker, Pauline Yvonne	N.Zea.	2412
Pascoe, Russell	Brit.	3147
Peete, Lofie Louise	U.S.	2436
Pell, Max	U.S.	2218
Perry, Henry	Brit.	2446
Peter, Caspar	Switz.	2452

Peter, Elizabeth	Switz.	2452
Peter, Margaret	Switz.	2452
Phillips, Ann	U.S.	2458
Phillips, Henry	U.S.	2459
Phillips, Sylvester	U.S.	2458
Piper, Thomas W.	U.S.	2469
Pleil, Rudolf	Ger.	2476
Pollard, William	U.S.	2483
Queripel, Michael	Brit.	2522
Raven, Daniel	Brit.	2545
Rees, Melvin David	U.S.	2557
Richter, Ursula	Ger.	2580
Riley, Charles David	U.S.	2370
Roberts, David	Brit.	2591
Robertson, David	U.S.	2692
Robinson, John	Brit.	170
Rogers, George White	U.S.	2610
Rogers, Irene	U.S.	2610
Royal, David	U.S.	2218
Russell, George	Brit.	2642
Sangret, August	Brit.	2677
Schindler, Michael	U.S.	2692
Schuetz, Hans	Ger.	2698
Schwartz, Charles Henry	U.S.	2706
Seaman, William	Brit.	2718
Segee, Robert Dale	U.S.	2723
Sin, Foo	U.S.	2768
Singh Sandhu, Suchnam	Brit.	2769
Small, Frederick L.	U.S.	2780
Smart, Lee	U.S.	2273
Smith, Edgar Herbert, Jr.	U.S.	2783
Smith, Mary Eleanor	U.S.	2800
Smith, Mary Jane	U.S.	623
Snook, James Howard	U.S.	2805
Sommerhalder, Richard	U.S.	2814
Spencer, Henry	U.S.	2825
Stewart, William	Ire.	2853
Stourton, Charles	Brit.	2865
Stratton, Albert	Brit.	2867
Strodtman, Herman	Brit.	2869
Telles, Felix	Arg.	2912
Tevendale, Brian	Scot.	2919
Thomas, William F.	Brit.	2932
Thompson, Anthony	U.S.	2692
Thurtell, John	Brit.	2949
Toole, Ottis Elwood	U.S.	2001
Troppmann, Jean-Baptiste	Fr.	2990
Turner, Richard	U.S.	3005
Tyburski, Leonard	U.S.	3010
Udderzook, William E.	U.S.	3014
Vacko, Pavel	Ger.	3024
Van Wyk, Stephanus Louis	S.Afri.	3035
Vasil, George T.	U.S.	3037
Vegnaduzzi, Andre	Fr.	3040
Vereneseneckockockhoff, Alb. F	U.S.	3041
Veronica Mutineers	Brit.	3042
Voisin, Louis Marie Joseph	Brit.	3059
Waldron, William Henry, Jr.	U.S.	3075
Weber, Adolph	U.S.	3108
Webster, John White	U.S.	3109
Wheeler, Mary Eleanor	Brit.	3133
Whittemore, Richard Reese	U.S.	3146
Whitty, Dennis	Brit.	3147
Woodward, Raymond L. Jr.	U.S.	3185
Yeldham, William James	Brit.	3205
Young, John Riley	Brit.	3210

Weapon: Ashtray

Lapa, Frank Albert	U.S.	1896

Weapon: Auto crank

Brain, George	Brit.	469

Scott, William Lester	U.S.	2713		Holmyard, William John	Brit.	1603
Weapon: Baseball bat				**Weapon: Flatiron**		
Coffey, William N.	U.S.	741		Grierson, Alan James	Brit.	1385
Matthews, Rod	U.S.	2149		**Weapon: Frying pan**		
Mieske, Kenneth M.	U.S.	2177		Bradford, Priscilla	U.S.	465
Pancoast, Marvin	U.S.	2403		**Weapon: Gun handle**		
Weapon: Billiard ball				Anstadt, Achim	Fr.	2163
Mellant-Lenfant Duel	Fr.	2164		Coneys, Theodore Edward	U.S.	764
Weapon: Binoculars				Dashwood, Samuel	Brit.	877
Weger, Chester	U.S.	3113		de Praslin, Duke	Fr.	917
Weapon: Blackjack				Harrison, Daniel Paul	U.S.	1464
Borum, Alfonso	U.S.	2129		Melchert, Peter	Fr.	2163
Marshall, Franklin	U.S.	2129		Scanlan, John	Ire.	2687
Neu, Kenneth	U.S.	2307		Sullivan, Stephen	Ire.	2687
Williams, Robert	U.S.	2129		Watkins, Jesse	U.S.	3102
Weapon: Board/wood				Whitfield, John Leonard	U.S.	3141
Cook, DeWitt Clinton	U.S.	769		**Weapon: Hatchet**		
Faulkner, Richard	Brit.	1138		Greenwood, Vaughn Orrin	U.S.	1379
Fisher, Julius	U.S.	1166		Johnson, John	U.S.	1730
Hart, George	U.S.	1467		Hauptmann, Bruno Richard	U.S.	1479
Weapon: Bottle				**Weapon: Stake**		
Andrews, Norman	Aus.	1917		Otter, Tom	Brit.	2385
Clayton, Robert David	Aus.	1917		**Weapon: Hoe**		
Lee, Jean	Aus.	1917		Frost, Samuel	U.S.	1238
Strickland, Carl Willis	U.S.	2869		**Weapon: Inkwell**		
Trevor, Harold Darien	Brit.	2988		Becker, John	U.S.	309
Weapon: Brick/concrete				**Weapon: Iron**		
Holmes, John	U.S.	1601		Coneys, Theodore Edward	U.S.	764
Holmes, John Maurice	U.S.	2949		Perry, Arthur	U.S.	2446
Hulme, Juliet Marion	N.Z.	1638		Serafima	U.S.S.R.	2728
Masset, Louise	Brit.	2139		**Weapon: Iron bar**		
Meyers, Martin	U.S.	2175		Congden, Robert	Brit.	764
Nixon, Robert	U.S.	2340		Dabner, Louis	U.S.	853
Ogilvie, Adam	Brit.	2365		Garvie, Mervyn	Aus.	1281
Reiper, Pauline Yvonne	N.Z.	1638		Giffard, Miles	Brit.	1310
Thurmond, Thomas H.	U.S.	1601		Goodale, Robert	Brit.	1339
Thurmond, Thomas Harold	U.S.	2949		Green, Samuel	U.S.	1374
Weapon: Broom				Harris, Dennis	U.S.	1460
Branch, Elizabeth	Brit.	470		Ivory, Henry	U.S.	1672
Branch, Mary	Brit.	470		Manuel, Peter Thomas Anthony	Scot.	
Weapon: Candle holder				Morrison, Steinie		
Caldwell, Roger	U.S.	579		Neu, Kenneth	U.S.	2307
Weapon: Cane				Panzram, Carl	U.S.	2406
Hall, Lucian	U.S.	1426		Perry, William	U.S.	1672
Sullivan, Howard	U.S.	2875		Pratt, Dennis James	Brit.	2497
Weapon: Chisel				Rockwell, Frederick Kress	U.S.	2605
Hauptmann, Bruno Richard	U.S.	1479		Seimsen, John	U.S.	853
Horton, Kenneth	Brit.	1623		Stirling, Amos	U.S.	1672
Woolfe, George	Brit.	3186		**Weapon: Lard beater**		
Weapon: Club				Hatto, Moses	Brit.	1478
Boyd, Jabez	U.S.	460		**Weapon: Lead cable**		
Dunbar, Reuben A.	U.S.	1035		Ogorzov, Paul	Ger.	2365
Farmer, Daniel Davis	U.S.	1134		**Weapon: Lock**		
Friend, Wilbert Felix	U.S.	1236		Campbell, Gary Lee	U.S.	593
Governor, Jimmy	Aus.	1353		Craig, Daniel	U.S.	593
Green, Samuel	U.S.	1374		Glasder, James	U.S.	593
Hall, Andreas	U.S.	1420		Shine, John	U.S.	593
Jackson, Mary Jane	U.S.	1679		Shine, Joseph	U.S.	593
Johnson, Robert	U.S.	1732		**Weapon: Log**		
Jones, Adam	U.S.	1736		Green, Leslie	Brit.	1374
Personel, Francis Burdett	U.S.	2448		**Weapon: Hammer/mallet**		
Stone, John	U.S.	2859		Beck, Martha Julie	U.S.	296
Weapon: Crowbar/lug wrench				Bowen, Nancy	U.S.	456
Chrimes, Joseph	Brit.	702		Butler, William	Brit.	563
Craft, Ellis	U.S.	804		Campbell, Cecil	U.S.	592
Duchowski, Charles	U.S.	1031		Chalcraft, J.	Brit.	670
Gibbs, Edward Lester	U.S.	1307		Charlton, Porter	Italy	688
Hermle, Raymond	U.S.	1524		Chennell, George Jr.	Brit.	670
Jones, Thomas	U.S.	1741		Colt, John Caldwell	U.S.	759
Weapon: Firetongs				Coo, Eva	U.S.	768

Cossentino, Armando	U.S.	793
Crawford, James	U.S.	813
Davis, Lolita	U.S.	885
Dawson, Sie	U.S.	887
Duffy, Renee	Brit.	1033
Fearn, Donald	U.S.	1143
Gibons, Jacqueline	U.S.	1308
Gossage, Eben	U.S.	1349
Harries, Thomas Ronald Lewis	Brit.	1458
Harrison, Daniel Paul	U.S.	1464
Harvey, Llewellin Garret Talma	Brit.	1472
Heideman, Frank	U.S.	1507
Holmes, Leonard	Brit.	1602
Horton, Kenneth	Brit.	1623
Jackson, John	Brit.	1678
Jacoby, Henry Julius	Brit.	1693
Keeling, Frederick	Brit.	1773
Kidd, William	Brit.	1811
Krten, Peter	Ger.	1862
Littles, Sarah Stout	U.S.	2865
MacArthur, Malcolm	Ire.	2022
Macleod, Hugh	Scot.	2058
McEwen, Mervin Clare	Brit.	2037
Morales, Michael Angelo	U.S.	2213
Mullins, James	Brit.	2250
Murder Stones	Brit.	2256
Murphy, Charles	U.S.	2258
Myrtel, Hra	Fr.	2273
Nicholson, William Lawrence W.	S.Afri.	2334
Ortega, Ricky	U.S.	2213
Phillips, Clara	U.S.	2458
Podmore, William Henry	Brit.	2478
Richards, Stephen Dee	U.S.	2576
Rowland, Walter Graham	Brit.	2631
St. Pierre, Robert	U.S.	1308
Savage, Thomas	Brit.	2682
Scales, James I.	U.S.	2686
Seymour, Henry Daniel	Brit.	2731
Stout, Marion Ira	U.S.	2865
Sung Djang Djing	Brit.	2877
Sutcliffe, Peter William	Brit.	2879
Tierney, Nora Patricia	Brit.	2953
Watson, James P.	U.S.	3103
West, Velma	U.S.	3129
Wilson, Barry Alan	U.S.	1308
Weapon: Oar		
Goodwin, Solomon	U.S.	1341
Weapon: Pestle		
Ellis, Charles	U.S.	1084
Weapon: Iron pipe/lead pipe		
Bingham, Richard John	Brit.	370
Borum, Alfonso	U.S.	2129
Braden, Howard	U.S.	2366
Brownrigg, Elizabeth	Brit.	518
Davies, Gerald	Brit.	881
DeSalvo, Albert Henry	U.S.	921
Glaze, Billy	U.S.	1322
Hayward, George Frederick Walt	Brit.	1499
Jacks, George H.	U.S.	1674
Marshall, Franklin	U.S.	2129
Miller, George	U.S.	2180
Monsson, Otto	Brit.	2544
Ohern, Michael	U.S.	2366
Rau, Gustav	Brit.	2544
Roche, John Francis	U.S.	2604
Schmidt, Willem	Brit.	2544
Stoneley, John William	Brit.	2861
Sykes, George Ernest	Brit.	2861
Voirbo, Pierre	Fr.	3059
von Sydow, Frederick	Swed.	3063

Willows, William	U.S.	1674
Weapon: Poker		
Ashcroft, David	Brit.	1591
Ashcroft, James, Jr.	Brit.	1591
Ashcroft, James, Sr.	Brit.	1591
Blake, Daniel	Brit.	403
Goolde, Maria Vere	Fr.	1341
Goolde, Vere	Fr.	1341
Green, Leslie	Brit.	1374
Hatto, Moses	Brit.	1478
Holden, William	Brit.	1591
Lawrence, John	Brit.	1907
Litton, Donald	Brit.	1972
Taunton, William	Brit.	2898
Weapon: Rifle		
Governor, Jimmy	Aus.	1353
Weapon: Rock/stone		
Bird, Jake	U.S.	373
Caulfield, Frederick	Ire.	658
Codarre, Edwin	U.S.	738
Field, Jack Alfred	Brit.	1155
Garabedian, David	U.S.	1265
Glaze, Billy	U.S.	1322
Gray, William Thomas	Brit.	1155
Jones, Jeremiah	Brit.	1739
Jones, Michael	U.S.	1740
Keech, Mary Ann Newton	U.S.	2315
Khomeini, Ruhollah	Iran	1810
Lovett, George	U.S.	1740
Newton, William	U.S.	2315
Pierce, Alexander	Aus.	2462
Pixley, Andrew	U.S.	2472
Saunders, John	U.S.	2693
Schmid, Charles Howard, Jr.	U.S.	2693
Stuart, Rupert Max	Aus.	2872
Thomas, Sarah Harriet	Brit.	2931
Tomlinson, Richard	Brit.	2966
Weapon: Rolling pin		
Greenacre, James	Brit.	1375
True, Ronald	Brit.	2995
Weapon: Ruler		
Horton, Kenneth	Brit.	1623
Weapon: Sandbag		
Bolber, Morris	U.S.	422
Favato, Carino	U.S.	422
Petrillo, Herman	U.S.	422
Petrillo, Paul	U.S.	422
Weapon: Shoe		
Forsyth, Francis Robert George	Brit.	1199
Harris, Norman James	Brit.	1199
Maxwell, Edith	U.S.	2154
Weapon: Shovel/spade		
LeBlanc, Antoine	U.S.	1915
Mason, Ebenezer	U.S.	2136
Miller, Walter	Brit.	2183
Robinson, Peter	U.S.	2598
Weapon: Spike		
Carey, Walter Burton, III	U.S.	622
Murder Stones	Brit.	2256
Prescott, Abraham	U.S.	2497
Stinney, George Junius, Jr.	U.S.	2856
Weapon: Stool		
McDonagh, Terence	Brit.	2031
Weapon: Tennis racket		
Gillette, Chester	U.S.	1313
Weapon: Automobile jack		
Butterfield, Neale Allen	U.S.	563
Weapon: Toilet bowl		
Hardaker, Betty	U.S.	1445
Bennett, Benjamin	U.S.	331

Weapon: Tree branch/stick

Bevan, Catherine	U.S.	355
Branch, Elizabeth	Brit.	470
Branch, Mary	Brit.	470
Craig, Eric Roland	Aus.	806
Hall, James	Brit.	1425
Hays, Henry Francis	U.S.	1498
Hocker, Thomas Henry	Brit.	1582
Jameson, James	U.S.	1711
Knowles, James Llewellyn	U.S.	1498
M'Gowan, James	U.S.	1711
Toe, Gbassie	Liberia	312

Weapon: Truncheon

Dorn, Albert Edward	Brit.	2209
Moore, Brian Steven	Brit.	2209

Weapon: Vase

Green, Leslie	Brit.	1374

Weapon: Washboard

Nesbitt, Bronston	U.S.	2306

Weapon: Weights

Bishop, Oliver	U.S.	382
Edwards, Edgar	Brit.	1072
Haggerty, John F.	U.S.	1416

Weapon: Wrench

Carroll, Mario	U.S.	641
Johnston, James	U.S.	641

MURDER BY BLUNT INSTRUMENT - Case of
General

Holland, Kenneth Raymond	U.S.	1591
Kaczmarczyk, Joseph	Fr.	1752
Lamson, David Albert	U.S.	1880
Reese, Freeman	Brit.	2558
Schuldig, Winfried	Ger.	2699
Sheppard, Samuel	U.S.	2741
Smith, Henry Sydney	Brit.	2794
Turner, Aaron	U.S.	3003
Wallace, William Herbert	Brit.	3081
Warner, Charles	Brit.	3095
Williams, Joseph	Brit.	3163

Weapon: Bottle

Murray, William	Brit.	2260

Weapon: Baseball bat

Perry, Calvin D., III	U.S.	2446

Weapon: Club

Carroll, James	Can.	641

Weapon: crowbar/lug wrench

Foat, Virginia Eleanor	U.S.	1189
Jackson, Thomas Henry	Brit.	1681

Weapon: Flashlight

Diggs, Ira	U.S.	2128
Evans, Herbert	U.S.	2128
Marrero, Alex	U.S.	2128
Watts, Michael	U.S.	2128

Weapon: Hammer/mallet

Allen, Stuart Buckner	U.S.	98
Bradley, Edward E.	U.S.	465
Carroll, Francis M.	U.S.	640
Leyra, Camilo Weston, Jr.	U.S.	1947
Mancini, Tony	Brit.	2099
Pook, Edmund Walter	Brit.	2488
Rattenbury, Alma Victoria	Brit.	2544

Weapon: Iron

Radcliffe, William	U.S.	2527

Weapon: Lead pipe

Kennedy, Samuel	U.S.	1803

Weapon: Nightstick

Diggs, Ira	U.S.	2128
Evans, Herbert	U.S.	2128
Marrero, Alex	U.S.	2128

Watts, Michael	U.S.	2128

Weapon: Oar

Morhead, Roy	U.S.	2221

Weapon: Shovel/spade

Carroll, James	Can.	641

Weapon: Tree branch/stick

Bosworth, Mary	Brit.	2855
Male, Mary	Brit.	2855
Miskimen, Paul	U.S.	2190
Stimson, Ann	Brit.	2855

Weapon: Stone/concrete

Andrews, Samuel M.	U.S.	127
Halsmann, Philipp	Ger.	1433

Weapon: Tongs

Murray, William	Brit.	2260

Weapons: Weights

Healy, John	Brit.	1501

MURDER BY BLUNT INSTRUMENT - Unsolved
General

Brame, Lex, Jr.	U.S.	470
Creed, Edwin Austin	Brit.	815
Freedman, Helen	Brit.	1230
Grimes, Joseph	Brit.	1390
Jeffs, Frederick Walter	Brit.	1717
McConkey, Joseph	U.S.	2026
Ormesher, Margaret	Brit.	2379
Ormesher, May	Brit.	2379
Pye, Emily	Brit.	2517
Ridgley, Elizabeth	Brit.	2580
Ridley, Edward Albert	U.S.	2581
Rosales, Maria	U.S.	2620
Rose, Gertrude	Brit.	2620
Slaney, Sidney	Brit.	2776
Texarkana (Texas) Slayings	U.S.	2919
Walder, Arnold	Fr.	3074
Welch, Albert	Brit.	3123
Welsh, Leila	U.S.	3126

Weapon: Blackjack

Carey, Estelle Evelyn	U.S.	622

Weapon: Bottle

Collins, Shirley	Aus.	753

Weapon: Cane

Anderson, Levi E.	U.S.	123

Weapon: Crowbar/lug wrench

Nathan, Benjamin	U.S.	2288

Weapon: Firetongs

Wren, Margery	Brit.	3192

Weapon: Golf club

Moxley, Martha	U.S.	2236

Weapon: Hammer/mallet

Hogg, Mary Anne	Brit.	1588
Scharn, Kathryn	U.S.	2690

Weapon: Gun handle

Hunt, Dora	Fr.	1642
Shore, Florence Nightingale	Brit.	2748

Weapon: Poker

Milne, Jean	Scot.	2186
Shepherd, J.C.	Brit.	2740

Weapon: Solder iron

Percy, Valerie	U.S.	2444

Weapon: Shovel/spade

Donohue, Alice	U.S.	1000

Weapon: Weights

Collins, Shirley	Aus.	753

Weapon: Wood/board

Loomis, Grace	U.S.	1988
Mayer, Mabel	U.S.	2157

MURDER BY BLUNT INSTRUMENT - Wrongly Convicted

McDermott, Frederick Lincoln	Aus.	2030
Slater, Oscar	Scot.	2776
Lucas, Jesse	U.S.	2001
Lucas, Margaret	U.S.	2001

MURDER BY BURNING

Aponte, Hctor Escudero	Pu.Ric.	138
Barton, Mary	Brit.	271
Bauf, Richard	Ire.	284
Bishop, Barnell	U.S.	381
Bishop, William Bradford, Jr.	U.S.	382
Boost, Werner	Ger.	436
Borgia Family	Italy	441
Briscoe, Ricky	U.S.	492
Brown, Nichol	Scot.	515
Caligula	Roman.	580
Chigango, Chief	Rhodesia	699
Clements, Mark	U.S.	729
Close, Henry Colin	U.S.	733
Cordero, Jos Antonio	U.S.	783
Cornwell, Gerry	U.S.	788
Corrigan, Hugh	U.S.	789
Crowder, James	U.S.	836
Devann, Patrick	Ire.	930
Donnelly, Edward	U.S.	999
Dowry Murders	India	1014
Elbert, John	U.S.	1080
Epstein, Albert	U.S.	1099
Falleni, Eugene	Aus.	1130
Ferdinand, Phil	U.S.	1080
Frazier, John Linley	U.S.	1229
Gibbs, Charles	U.S.	1307
Godfrey of Bouillon	Mid.East	1324
Good, Daniel	Brit.	1338
Goulter, Sidney Bernard	Brit.	1352
Grant, Thomas	Can.	1363
Gunness, Belle	U.S.	1400
Guy, Thomas	Aus.	1409
Hawk, Ralph	U.S.	1491
Hauptfleisch, Petrus Stephanus François	S.Afri.	1478
Humphrey, Josephine	U.S.	1080
Inquisition, The	Int'l.	1656
Ivan IV Vasilyevich	Rus.	1670
Jacobson, Howard	U.S.	1693
Jewell, Joseph	U.S.	2093
John of Lancaster	Brit.	1726
Kantarian, Nancy Lee	U.S.	1759
Kelley, Dillard E., Sr.	U.S.	1777
Khomeini, Ayatollah Ruhollah	Iran	1810
Kohout, Edward	U.S.	1842
Kohout, Henry	U.S.	1842
Lopez, Hector	U.S.	783
Lopez, Jose Francisco Rivera	Pu.Ric.	138
Majors, Lloyd L.	U.S.	2093
Mankato Massacre	U.S.	2103
Marshall, Lindsay Howitt	Brit.	2130
Meacham, Jeremiah	U.S.	2158
Mendez, Francisco	U.S.	783
Menesclou, Louis	Fr.	2165
Mercier, Euphrasie	Fr.	2166
Montvoisin, Catherine	Fr.	2206
Moore, Charles	Brit.	2209
Morgan, Edward	Brit.	2219
Mudgett, Herman Webster	U.S.	2240
My Lai Massacre	Viet.	2272
Nero	Roman.	2305
Nischt, Joseph	U.S.	2338
Owens, Loy Alton	U.S.	2389
Phillips, Morgan	Brit.	2460

Pulliam, Mark	U.S.	2511
Quantrill, William Clarke	U.S.	2519
Rivera, Armando Jimenez	Pu.Ric.	138
Roberts, Clarence	U.S.	2591
Rouse, Alfred Arthur	Brit.	2629
Ryan, Bobbie	U.S.	2646
Segee, Robert Dale	U.S.	2723
Showers, John	U.S.	2093
Simaniuk, George	U.S.	2763
Simececk, James	U.S.	2763
Starkweather, Albert L.	U.S.	2840
Stone, Lawrence Clinton	U.S.	2859
Tetzner, Kurt Erich	Ger.	2918
Walsh, Edward	Brit.	2209
Warren, Benjamin	U.S.	1099
Watt, Miriam	U.S.	3104
Wilkinson, Alec	Brit.	3157

MURDER BY BURNING - Case of

Bodine, Mary	U.S.	415
Budde, Richard	U.S.	533
Franklin, Connie	U.S.	1224
Gardiner, William	Brit.	1268
Pates, Robert Eugene	U.S.	2418

MURDER BY BURNING - Unsolved

Carey, Estelle Evelyn	U.S.	622
D'Andrea, Nicholas J.	U.S.	866
Eyman, David L.	U.S.	1121
Foster, Evelyn	Brit.	1202
Grlitz	Ger.	1348
Matulla Murders	U.S.	2150

MURDER BY DECAPITATION

Christian VII	Int'l	703
Lu Sing-pan	China	2012
Oates, Reginald Vernon	U.S.	2349
Power, John	Brit.	2494

MURDER/CANNIBALISM

Fentress, Albert	U.S.	1149
Fish, Hamilton Albert Howard	U.S.	1162

MURDER BY DROWNING

Algarron, Jacques	Fr.	1867
Baker, Joseph	U.S.	216
Barker Brothers	U.S.	235
Barlow, Kenneth	Brit.	244
Bartlett, Helen	U.S.	269
Beck, Martha Julie	U.S.	296
Belvin, Paul Augustus	Ber.	322
Bishop, John	Brit.	382
Brown, George	U.S.	506
Caligula	Roman.	580
Cerny, Wenzel	Czech.	664
Chivers, Elizabeth	Brit.	700
Dalzeel, Alexander	Brit.	864
Davidson, Thomas Joseph	Brit.	881
de Soto, Benito	Spain	926
Dorn, Albert Edward	Brit.	2209
Edwards, Robert Allan	U.S.	1073
Ferguson, Walter	U.S.	1151
Fitz, Alfred	Brit.	1171
Flowery Land Mutiny	Brit.	1182
Gidley, George	Brit.	2051
Gillette, Chester	U.S.	1313
Goodwin, Solomon	U.S.	1341
Goslett, Arthur Andrew Clement	Brit.	1349
Haight, Edward	U.S.	1418
Harvey, Julian	U.S.	1472

Hill, James Douglas	U.S.	1552
Hill, William	U.S.	1556
Holmes, Alexander William	U.S.	1601
Holmes, John	U.S.	1601
Holmes, John Maurice	U.S.	2949
Holmes, William	U.S.	1603
Holzapfel, Floyd Albert	U.S.	2435
James, Robert	U.S.	1709
Jones, Jeremiah	Brit.	1739
Judy, Steven T.	U.S.	1748
Koslow, Jack	U.S.	1844
Labb, Denise	Fr.	1867
M'Kinlie, Peter	Brit.	2051
Miller, William	Brit.	2183
Moore, Brian Steven	Brit.	2209
Murad IV	Turk.	2252
Njendana, Tomo	Rhodesia	2341
O'Laughlin, Pearl	U.S.	2367
Peel, Joseph, Jr.	U.S.	2435
Raffaelo, Roberto	U.S.	2528
Richardson, John	Brit.	2577
Roche, Phillip	Brit.	2604
Rosewaine, Edward	U.S.	1603
Rowland, Ferrin	U.S.	2631
Scanlan, John	Ire.	2687
Sims, Mitchell Carleton	U.S.	2767
Slaughterford, Christopher	Brit.	2777
Smith, George Joseph	Brit.	2786
Smith, George Robert	U.S.	2793
Spooner, Bathsheba	U.S.	2832
St. Quintin, Richard	Brit.	2051
Strickland, Carl Willis	U.S.	2869
Sullivan, Stephen	Ire.	2687
Veronica Mutineers	Brit.	3042
Wardlaw Sisters	U.S.	3094
Warrington, Thomas	U.S.	1603
Wild, William	Brit.	3151
Williams Farm Murders	U.S.	3168
Williams, Thomas	Brit.	382
Wright, Jeanne Anne	U.S.	3194
Zekerman, Andrew	Brit.	2051

MURDER BY DROWNING - Case of

Clare, Philip	Brit.	720
Cowper, Spencer	Brit.	802
Gorringe, Esther	Brit.	1348
Hurd, William	Brit.	2821
Maggs, William	Brit.	2821
Marson, John	Brit.	802
Oakley, Frederick	Brit.	2349
Rogers, William	Brit.	802
Sparrow, William	Brit.	2821
Stephens, Ellis	Brit.	802
Thornton, Abraham	Brit.	2940

MURDER BY DROWNING - Unsolved

Clarence, Duke of	Brit.	720
Collings, Benjamin P.	U.S.	750
Faithfull, Starr	U.S.	1128
Love, Jack	Brit.	1995
Love, Mary	Brit.	1995
Montesi, Wilma	Italy	2204

MURDER BY ELECTROCUTION

Heidnik, Gary M.	U.S.	1507

MURDER BY EXECUTION

Abahai	China	1
Abel	Den.	10
Abimelech	Pales.	10

Absolom	Isr.	14
Adaloald	Italy	20
Amin Dada Oumee, Idi	Uganda	114
Aranguren, William	Col.	143
Aspar, Flavius Ardaburius	Italy	171
Barriobero, Eduardo	Spain	250
Bessus	Sogdiana	354
Biron, Ernst Johann	Ger.	379
Cromwell, Oliver	Brit.	828
Khomeini, Ayatollah Ruhollah	Iran	1810
Le Bon, Joseph	Fr.	1915
Lorraine, Henri I de	Fr.	1991
López, Francisco Solano	Para.	1989
MacDonald Clan Massacre	Scot.	2034
Malcolm III MacDuncan	Scot.	2094
Manguin, Andr	Fr.	2102
Messalina, Valeria	Roman.	2170
Michael IX Palaeologus	Roman.	2176
Mortimer, Roger IV de	Brit.	2229
Mustafa IV	Turk.	2269
Narcissus	Roman.	2282
Odoacer	Roman.	2361
Ottoman Sultans	Int'l	2386
Pasha, Jezzar	Syria	2418
Pedrarias	Spain	2435
Pilate, Pontius	Judea	2465
Pizarro, Hernando	Peru	2472
Rada, Juan de	Peru	2527
Saw, U.	Burma	2684
Tiberius	Roman.	2950
Danos, Abel	Fr.	869

MURDER BY EXECUTION - Case of

Mary	Scot.	2134

MURDER BY EXECUTION - Unsolved

Alcibiades	Gr.	70
Blmant, Robert	Fr.	408
Lorca, Federico Garcia	Spain	1990
Lucerno, Alitea de	Spain	2002
Percy, Henry	Brit.	2443

MURDER BY EXPLOSION

Adamson, John Harvey	U.S.	28
Argentine Political Violence	Arg.	154
Armstrong, Karelton Lewis	U.S.	159
Armstrong, Karleton	U.S.	1159
Arrison, William	U.S.	167
Austin, Alice	U.S.	185
Barnes, Peter	Brit.	245
Barrett, Michael	Brit.	249
Belcastro, James	U.S.	316
Benson, Steven	U.S.	335
Billings, Warren Knox	U.S.	2207
Bosch, Orlando	Venez.	445
Curzi, Barbara	U.S.	2107
Field, George Morton	U.S.	1155
Fine, David S.	U.S.	1159
Fugmann, Michael	U.S.	1239
Graham, John Gilbert	U.S.	1358
Guay, Albert	Can.	1396
Giuliano, Salvatore	Si.	1317
Haymarket Riot	U.S.	1495
Henry, Emile	Fr.	1519
Hofman, Mark W.	U.S.	1587
Kehoe, Andrew	U.S.	1775
Khomeini, Ayatollah Ruhollah	Iran	1810
Kim Hyun Hui	N.Kor.	1820
Kovovick, Milovar	U.S.	1845
Kreuger, Alexander	Swed.	1849

Laaman, Jaan Karl	U.S.	2107
Lacombe, Francois	Fr.	1869
Levasseur, Patricia Gros Luc	U.S.	2107
Levasseur, Raymond Luc	U.S.	2107
Lod Airport Massacre	Isr.	1976
McNamara Brothers	U.S.	2062
Magnuson, John	U.S.	2088
Manning, Carol	U.S.	2107
Matuschka, Sylvestre	Hung.	2150
Matuschka, Sylvestre	Hung.	2150
McNamara Brothers	U.S.	2062
Meins, Commando Holger	Swed.	2162
Mooney, Thomas Jeremiah	U.S.	2207
Morse, Donald Lee	U.S.	2228
Murad IV	Turk.	2252
Nesbit, William Raymond	U.S.	2306
Orchard, Harry	U.S.	2375
Paris, Richard James	U.S.	2409
Patrovick, Milovar	U.S.	1845
Payne, A.D.	U.S.	2429
Peak, Duane	U.S.	2575
Pitre, Marguerite	Can.	1396
Poindexter, Edwin	U.S.	2575
Rice, David	U.S.	2575
Richards, James	Brit.	245
Rogers, George White	U.S.	2610
Ruest, Genreaux	Can.	1396
Scott, Ira	U.S.	185
Simmons, Ted	U.S.	185
Von Arbin, Eric	Swed.	1849

MURDER BY EXPLOSION - Case of

Endrigkeit, Christiane Gabriel	Ger.	1093
Gonzales, Frank	U.S.	1337
Haywood, William Dudley	U.S.	1499
Gollum, George	U.S.	2387
Overell, Beulah Louise	U.S.	2387
Ahmed Nawaf Mansour Hazi	Ger.	1093
Endrigkeit, Christiane Gabriel	Ger.	1093

MURDER BY EXPLOSION - Unsolved

Bolles, Don	U.S.	424
Chartrand, Richard	U.S.	689
Nardi, John A.	U.S.	2282
New York World's Fair Bombing	U.S.	2327
Noble, Herbert	U.S.	2341
Wall Street Bombing	U.S.	3083
Williams, Berkeley Cecil	Brit.	3160
Pencovic, Francis	U.S.	2439
Hammons, Samuel	U.S.	1439
Farran, Rex Francis	Brit.	1135
Fraunces Tavern Explosion	U.S.	1228

MURDER BY EXPLOSION - Wrongly Convicted

Wilkinson, Robert	U.S.	3158

MURDER BY GUNSHOT

Abbandando, Frank	U.S.	1
Abdallah, Georges Ibrahim	Fr.	8
Abdullah, Mohammed	U.S.	9
Abdullah, Sameer Mohammed	Ger.	1081
Acevedo, Louis	U.S.	18
Achey, John Henry	U.S.	19
Adams, Eddie	U.S.	25
Adams, Millicent	U.S.	27
Agostini, Antonio	Aus.	37
Ahearn, Danny	U.S.	41
Alberding, Heinrich	Ger.	46
Alderman, James Horace	U.S.	72

Aldridge, Alfred Scott	U.S.	72
Aleman, Luis Antonio Colindres	El Sal.	72
Alex, Michael	U.S.	73
Allaway, Thomas Henry	Brit.	92
Allen, Floyd	U.S.	94
Allen, Joseph	U.S.	96
Allen, Kenneth	U.S.	96
Allen, William O'Meara	Brit.	98
Allison, James	Can.	99
Almarez, Stella Delores	U.S.	102
Almer, Jack	U.S.	103
Alsopp, Gunnar	U.S.	104
Amerman, Max	U.S.	113
Amiel, Jean	Fr.	113
Anargeros, Sophie	U.S.	116
Anderson, Allen Leroy	U.S.	121
Anderson, David L.	U.S.	122
Anderson, Edward	U.S.	1050
Anderson, Leroy Gene	U.S.	123
Anderson, William	U.S.	125
Andrews, Dorothy Ann	U.S.	126
Andrews, Lowell Lee	U.S.	126
Andrews, Milton Franklin	U.S.	127
Andrews, William	U.S.	2464
Angier, Samuel	U.S.	1972
Annunziata, Joseph	U.S.	129
Anstdt, Achim	Fr.	2163
Antone, Anthony	U.S.	134
Approved School Breakout, The	Brit.	139
Arcine, James	U.S.	153
Argentine Political Violence	Arg.	154
Armstrong, Thomas Jefferson	U.S.	159
Arrington, Marie Dean	U.S.	167
Artegian, Rodney	U.S.	3169
Ashe, Richard	Aust.	170
Asser	Brit.	171
Atkinson, Isaac	Brit.	176
Attebery, Ira	U.S.	179
Attica Prison Riot	U.S.	180
Attrill, Mabel Lucy	Brit.	181
Augustin, Ella	Ger.	2656
Aulisio, Joseph	U.S.	184
Austin, Tom	Brit.	186
Ayala, Samuel	U.S.	193
Badran, Ibrahim	Ger.	1081
Bailey, Benjamin	U.S.	207
Bailey, James Warren	U.S.	211
Bailey, Raymond	Aus.	211
Bailey, Robert Taylor	U.S.	212
Baker, Abner, Jr.	U.S.	213
Baker, George	U.S.	287
Baker, James	Brit.	216
Balfour, Alexander	Scot.	218
Ball, Ebenezer	U.S.	219
Ball, Joseph	U.S.	221
Banister, Debra	U.S.	226
Banks, Jerry	U.S.	227
Barany, Serge	Fr.	228
Bardlett, William	U.S.	233
Barker Brothers	U.S.	235
Baron, Joseph Octavius	U.S.	247
Barrett, George	U.S.	249
Barrow, Clyde Champion	U.S.	250
Barsi, Jozsef	U.S.	265
Bass, Andrew	U.S.	274
Bauf, Richard	Ire.	284
Baylanch, Autry	U.S.	285
Baylanch, Gee	U.S.	285
Baylanch, Jes	U.S.	285
Beadle, James	U.S.	1021

Beadle, James	U.S.	1915	Brazier, Nicola	Brit.	480
Beagles, David Ervin	U.S.	286	Brazilian Death Squad	Braz.	480
Beale, George P.	U.S.	287	Brennan, William Theodore	Brit.	485
Bean, Harold Walter	U.S.	287	Bretagna, Santo	U.S.	485
Bean, Robert M.	U.S.	288	Brewer, Rudolph	U.S.	486
Beasley, Milton	U.S.	292	Brigate Rosse	Italy	488
Beattie, Henry Clay	U.S.	292	Brink's Armored Car Robbery	U.S.	489
Beck, Douglas	U.S.	295	Brisbon, Henry, Jr.		
Beck, Martha Julie	U.S.	296	Brook, John	Brit.	497
Beck, Robert	U.S.	3097	Brooks, Henry M.	U.S.	499
Bednarski, Richard Lee	U.S.	313	Brothers, Leo Vincent	U.S.	501
Belachheb, Abdelkrim	U.S.	315	Brown, Arthur Ross	U.S.	504
Belcastro, James	U.S.	316	Brown, Ernest	Brit.	505
Bell, Herman	U.S.	317	Brown, John	U.S.	509
Bell, James E.	U.S.	317	Brown, John Whelan	Aus.	514
Bell, Sydney	U.S.	319	Brown, Leslie	U.S.	515
Bembenek, Lawrencia	U.S.	322	Browne, Frederick Guy	Brit.	516
Bentley, Derek	Brit.	336	Bruhne, Vera	Ger.	520
Berkowitz, David	U.S.	344	Bruno, Eugene	U.S.	423
Berthier, Emile	Brit.	349	Bruno, John J.	U.S.	521
Bertucci, Clarence V.	U.S.	352	Brust, Albert	U.S.	522
Beto, Joseph Anthony	U.S.	355	Bryant, Kenneth	U.S.	524
Bibeau, John T.	U.S.	357	Buck Gang	U.S.	531
Bickford, James Madison	U.S.	358	Buckhout, Isaac Van Wart	U.S.	532
Biegenwald, Richard F.	U.S.	359	Buckley, Tim	Brit.	532
Billington, John	U.S.	362	Buffet, Claude	Fr.	534
Birchall, John Reginald	Int'l.	372	Buisson, Emile	Fr.	535
Bird Cage, The	U.S.	374	Bullock, David	U.S.	536
Bird, Jack	Brit.	373	Burgunder, Robert Marcus, Jr.	U.S.	544
Bisbee, Ariz., Massacre	U.S.	380	Burke, David Augustus	U.S.	545
Bishop, Jesse Walter	U.S.	381	Burke, Fred	U.S.	546
Bjorkland, Rosemarie Diane	U.S.	383	Burkley, Bluitt	U.S.	549
Black, James W.	Scot.	385	Burkley, Thurman	U.S.	549
Black Liberation Army	U.S.	396	Burnett, Benjamin	U.S.	2393
Black Panthers, The	U.S.	398	Burnett, Melvin	U.S.	551
Black, Robert	U.S.	385	Burnworth, Edward	Brit.	554
Black September Organization	Mid.East	398	Burrows, Erskine Durrant	Berm.	2893
Blackman, William	U.S.	396	Burton, Walter William	Brit.	559
Blackstone, David Thomas	U.S.	2785	Buse, William A.	U.S.	560
Bojorques, Narciso	U.S.	422	Bush, Robert	U.S.	560
Bolgnia, Joseph	U.S.	423	Byrne, Joseph	Aus.	1779
Bolin, Patty	U.S.	423	Cady, William	Brit.	569
Bolton, Mildred Mary	U.S.	426	Caffee, William	U.S.	571
Bonnet, Stede	Brit.	430	Calbeck, Lorene	U.S.	578
Bonney, Thomas Lee	U.S.	431	Calbeck, Lorene	U.S.	578
Bonnot Gang	Fr.	432	Caldwell, John	Scot.	579
Bono, Victor Jerald	U.S.	2147	Campbell, Calif., Post Office	U.S.	592
Booher, Vernon	Can.	435	Campbell, Henry Colin	U.S.	593
Bookie Gang, The	U.S.	435	Canales, Daniel	El Sal.	72
Boost, Werner	Ger.	436	Captain Jack	U.S.	618
Born, Ronald Joseph	U.S.	445	Caravan, George Washington	U.S.	619
Bottom, Anthony	U.S.	317	Carey, Howard	U.S.	622
Bottom, Anthony	U.S.	449	Carey, James	U.S.	622
Boudin, Kathy	U.S.	453	Carey, Mary	U.S.	622
Bounds, Patra Mae	U.S.	2724	Carlson, Gladys	U.S.	627
Bouvier, Lone	Fr.	455	Carney, John	Can.	631
Bowers, Donald	U.S.	2120	Carpenter, Richard	U.S.	635
Bowers, Sam H., Jr.	U.S.	457	Carrasco, Fred Gomez	U.S.	637
Bowles, Frank	U.S.	459	Carroll, Janet Faye	U.S.	641
Bowles, Homer	U.S.	459	Carter, Frank	U.S.	643
Boyce, Arthur Robert	Brit.	460	Carter, Rubin	U.S.	645
Bracy, William	U.S.	1609	Cartier, Andre	Brit.	646
Brady, Al	U.S.	466	Case, William	U.S.	649
Brady, John	U.S.	467	Casey, James P.	U.S.	780
Brand, Samuel	U.S.	472	Castalas, Louis	Fr.	654
Brandon, Mark	Brit.	472	Cave, Alphonso	U.S.	660
Brannan, Joshua	U.S.	473	Cayson, Doyle	U.S.	662
Branson, William	U.S.	473	Cayson, Jesse	U.S.	662
Bras Coup	U.S.	474	Cesario, Sam	U.S.	665
Braun, Thomas Eugene	U.S.	475	Chancy, Harrison	U.S.	676

Chang-Jen, Tjou	S.Kor.	678	Croft, William James	Brit.	827
Chapin, Charles	U.S.	681	Cropp, Marion	U.S.	789
Chapman, Gerald	U.S.	683	Crosby, Henry Grew	U.S.	829
Chapman, Mark David	U.S.	685	Crowley, Francis	U.S.	838
Charles, Henri	Alg.	687	Crumpley, Ronald K.	U.S.	841
Charrier, Jacques Mecislas	Fr.	688	Crumpley, Ronald K.	U.S.	841
Charrire, Henri-Antoine	Fr.	688	Crumpley, Ronald K.	U.S.	841
Chase, John Paul	U.S.	689	Cruse, William	U.S.	841
Chase, Richard Trenton	U.S.	690	Culhane, Charles	U.S.	843
Chenault, Marcus Wayne	U.S.	692	Cullins, Eddie	Ire.	844
Chevez, Cleovara	U.S.	422	D'Anglemont, Germaine	Fr.	866
Childers, Jimmy	U.S.	699	D'Autremont Brothers	U.S.	878
Choate, Pearl	U.S.	701	Dague, Walter Glenn	U.S.	2698
Choice, William A.	U.S.	701	Daguebert, Achille	Fr.	854
Christie, Balm	U.S.	705	Dahman, John	U.S.	855
Christie, Isham Thomas	U.S.	705	Daniels, James	U.S.	867
Cibuku, Gazi	U.S.	714	Daniels, Murl	U.S.	867
Ciucci, Vincent	U.S.	717	Dann, Laurie Wasserman	U.S.	869
Clark, Douglas Daniel	U.S.	722	Darden, Willie Jasper	U.S.	870
Clark, Lorraine	U.S.	723	Davin, Guy	Fr.	882
Clark, Marcellus Jerome	U.S.	723	Davis, Clarence	U.S.	2889
Clark, Michael	U.S.	724	Davis, Louis	U.S.	2543
Clem, Nancy E.	U.S.	728	Davis, Nelson Grant	U.S.	2889
Clerc, Jean Pierre	Fr.	730	Davis, Ralph Orin	U.S.	885
Close, Henry Colin	U.S.	733	Davis, William	Brit.	886
Cobb, John R.	U.S.	735	Day, Jack	Brit.	888
Codreanu, Cornelius Zelea	Roman.	738	de Kerninon, Countess Suzanne	Fr.	904
Codreanu, Cornelius Zelea	Roman.	738	De La Roche, Harry, Jr.	U.S.	907
Coetzee, Jacobus Hendrik	S.Afri.	740	de Lara, Enrique	U.S.	907
Coffelt, Elijah	U.S.	740	de Leeuw, Huibrecht Jacob	S. Afri.	908
Colby, Robert A.	Ger.	743	de Tourville, Count Henri	Aust.	928
Cole, Thomas Charles	Col.	743	Dean, Dayton	U.S.	890
Coleman, Wayne	U.S.	1036	Decarnelles, Suzanne	Fr.	896
Colley, George	U.S.	749	DeFeo, Ronald Joseph, Jr.	U.S.	901
Collins, Clarence	U.S.	2724	DeGroot, Robert	U.S.	902
Collins, George	U.S.	2636	Delay, Dallas Ray	U.S.	908
Collins, James Thomas	Brit.	751	DeLuca, Frank	U.S.	760
Collins, Melvin	U.S.	752	Dennis, Richard	U.S.	915
Columbo, Patricia	U.S.	760	Desgrandschamps, Charles	Fr.	924
Colwell, Martin	U.S.	761	Desnoyers, Guy	Fr.	925
Congden, Robert	Brit.	764	Detollenaere, Jean-Baptiste	Fr.	928
Connolly, Ann	U.S.	2834	Di Donne, Theodore	U.S.	423
Contreras, Pvt. Francisco Orla	El Sal.	72	Dickman, John Alexander	Brit.	940
Cook, Thomas	U.S.	358	Dietl, Marilyn	U.S.	942
Cook, William Edward	U.S.	770	Distafano, Ralph P.	U.S.	978
Cooley, Scott	U.S.	772	Dockery, John	U.S.	1427
Coolidge, Edward H.	U.S.	773	Doelitzsch, Fritz	Egypt	983
Coons, William	U.S.	775	Doetsch, Gunter	U.S.	984
Cooper, Calman	U.S.	775	Dominici, Gaston	Fr.	995
Cooper, Ronald John	Brit.	778	Dominiquez, Orin	U.S.	996
Cooper, Thomas	Brit.	778	Dorfman, Benny	U.S.	775
Copeland, James	U.S.	779	Dorsey, Charles	U.S.	2423
Cora, Charles	U.S.	780	Dougal, Samuel Herbert	Brit.	1009
Corona, Juan Vallejo	U.S.	788	Downs, Elizabeth Diane	U.S.	1014
Corrie, Peter	U.S.	789	Doyle, Michael J.	U.S.	1781
Costa, Antone C.	U.S.	794	Dreesman, Robert	U.S.	1021
Cotter, Benny	U.S.	797	Dreher, Thomas	U.S.	1021
Cotterill, Eardley	Brit.	797	Dreher, Thomas E.	U.S.	1915
Countryman, Alfred	U.S.	798	Drew, Charles	Brit.	1022
Courtney, John	U.S.	1769	du Plessis, Andries Stephanus	S.Afri.	1039
Couture, Donald	U.S.	2437	Dubuisson, Pauline	Fr.	1030
Couture, Donna	U.S.	2437	Duck, Aug Tai	U.S.	1031
Cowan, Frederick W.	U.S.	801	Duddy, John	Brit.	2592
Cox, Edward	U.S.	802	Duffield, Austin Christopher	Gibraltar	1032
Craig, Christopher	Brit.	806	Dungee, George	U.S.	1036
Craig, Christopher	Brit.	336	Dunham, James C.	U.S.	1037
Craig, John H.	U.S.	806	Dunn, John M.	U.S.	1038
Crain, J.V.	U.S.	807	Durand, Earl	U.S.	1040
Crane, James	Brit.	810	Dutartre, Peter	U.S.	1043
Croc, Raoul	Fr.	826	Dye, Troy	U.S.	1050

Dyer, Ernest	Brit.	1050		Galloway, Robert	U.S.	1257
Eaton, Helen Spence	U.S.	1066		Gambrill, Henry	U.S.	789
Edghill, Carlos Antonio	U.S.	1069		Gambrill, Henry	U.S.	1259
Edwards, Darrell A.	U.S.	1072		Garcia, Antonio	U.S.	422
Edwards, Joseph Sinnott	U.S.	1072		Garcia, Inez	U.S.	1265
Edwards, Mack Ray	U.S.	1073		Garcia, Luis	U.S.	1266
Egyptian Well Murder Case	Egypt	1075		Garcia, Rolando	U.S.	2408
el Dnawy, Abd el-Kadir	Ger.	1081		Garside, William	Brit.	1280
Elder, Ronald	U.S.	1080		Gartside, John Edward	Brit.	1280
Ellis, Blaine	U.S.	1084		Garvie, Sheila W.	Scot.	2919
Ellis, Ruth	Brit.	1085		Gaskins, Donald Henry	U.S.	1283
Ellsworth, James	U.S.	1085		Gatti, Salvatore	U.S.	1284
Ellul, Philip Louis	Brit.	1086		Gauchet, Georges	Fr.	1284
Emmeloth, David	U.S.	1092		Gay, Clestell	U.S.	3004
Engleman, Glennon E.	U.S.	1096		Geary, Charles Russell	U.S.	1287
Enkhardt, Max	Aus.	1097		Gein, Edward	U.S.	1289
Epes, William Dandridge	U.S.	1099		Gein, Edward	U.S.	1289
Erler, Robert John	U.S.	1101		George, John	U.S.	2834
Esposito, Anthony	U.S.	1104		Geraghty, Christopher James	Brit.	1300
Esposito, William	U.S.	1105		Germano, Andro	U.S.	1301
Essex, Mark James Robert	U.S.	1106		Giberson, Ivy	U.S.	1308
Evans, Rees W.	U.S.	1113		Gilmore, Gary	U.S.	1314
Faber, Abraham	U.S.	2179		Girardi, James A.	U.S.	1317
Fairlie, Walter	Brit.	1127		Giubelli, Alfa Ricciotti	Italy	1317
Fallon, Mickey	U.S.	1131		Giuliano, Salvatore	Si.	1317
FAR	Guat.	1133		Giuliano, Salvatore	Si.	1317
Faria, Albert	U.S.	1134		Glass, Jimmy	U.S.	1321
Farley, George	U.S.	1134		Glenn, Herschel	U.S.	1322
Farmer, Jack	U.S.	1134		Goethe, Robert	U.S.	1328
Faysom, David	U.S.	1142		Gohl, Billy	U.S.	1330
Fedayeen	Mid.East.	1143		Goins Brothers	U.S.	1330
Fein, Mark	U.S.	1146		Goldenberg, Jack	Brit.	1331
Fentress, Albert	U.S.	1149		Goldenson, Alexander	U.S.	1332
Ferbach, Johann	Ger.	520		Goldsborough, Fitzhugh Coyle	U.S.	1333
Fernandez, Manuel	U.S.	1151		Goldstein, Stuart	U.S.	1335
Fernandez, Raymond Martinez	U.S.	296		Golkowski, Johann	Turk.	1336
Ferrara, Florence	U.S.	1151		Good, Earl	U.S.	2828
Ferrers, Lawrence Shirley	Brit.	1152		Gordon, James	U.S.	1344
Fesch, Jacques	Fr.	1153		Gould, William	Brit.	98
Fiedler, Paulette	U.S.	1154		Graham, Eric Stanley George	N.Zea.	1356
Fielding, Charles	U.S.	1156		Graham-Tewksbury Feud	U.S.	1361
Finch, Raymond Bernard	U.S.	1158		Grant, Thomas	Can.	1363
Finlay, Edwin	Brit.	1160		Grasso, Santo	Fr.	1363
Fisher, Dennis	U.S.	1164		Gray, Ronald Adrin	U.S.	1365
Fitzgerald, Charles J.	U.S.	1171		Gray, William John	Brit.	1365
Fleming, Jim	U.S.	1178		Gray, William McKinnon	Brit.	1365
Floyd, Charles Arthur	U.S.	1182		Green, Edward W.	U.S.	1373
Fogelman, Clay	U.S.	1190		Green, Winona	U.S.	1375
Fontenot, Karl	U.S.	3092		Greenberg, Bertram	U.S.	1376
Force, Julia	U.S.	1193		Gretzler, Douglas	U.S.	1382
Ford, Jessie	U.S.	2889		Griffiths, James	Scot.	1388
Ford, Robert	U.S.	1195		Grondkowski, Marian	Brit.	1392
Fort Pillow Massacre	U.S.	1200		Gross, Reginald R.	U.S.	1393
Forwood, Stephen	Brit.	1202		Guenzel, Guel Sultan	Turk.	1396
Fox, William	U.S.	1206		Guerin, Joseph	U.S.	1396
Franklin, Joseph Paul	U.S.	1225		Guillen, Antonio Arias	U.S.	1398
Fredericks, William M.	U.S.	1230		Guillen, Jose	U.S.	1398
Free, James	U.S.	1230		Gula, Demetrius	U.S.	1399
Freeman, John Gilbert	U.S.	1232		Guyon, Melvin Bay	U.S.	1409
French, Harry	U.S.	1235		Guzman, Rene Adolfo	U.S.	1410
French Riviera Gang Wars	Fr.	1235		Hackman, Rev. James	Brit.	1413
Fugate, Caril Ann	U.S.	2840		Hagan, Michael	U.S.	1415
Funston, John	U.S.	1242		Haggart, David	Int'l.	1415
Furnace, Samuel James	Brit.	1242		Haigh, John George	Brit.	1417
Fyler, Alfred	U.S.	1243		Haitian Death Squads	Haiti	1419
Gaither, Ernie	U.S.	1250		Haley, Carl	U.S.	1420
Galante, Carmine	U.S.	1250		Hall, Archibald	Brit.	1420
Galentine, Jay F.	U.S.	1252		Hall, Ben	Aus.	1421
Gallego, Gerald	U.S.	1255		Hall, Carl Austin	U.S.	1421
Gallo, Samuel	U.S.	1255		Hall, James W.	U.S.	1425

Hall, James William	Aus.	1426	Hooper, Murray	U.S.	1609
Hall, Leo	U.S.	1426	Hope, Edgar	U.S.	1617
Hall, William	U.S.	1427	Hopkins, William Seeley	U.S.	1618
Hamadi, Mohammad Ali	Ger.	1433	Hopwood, Edward	Brit.	1618
Hambleton, John	Brit.	1433	Houghton, Charles	Brit.	1624
Hamilton, James	U.S.	1434	Housden, Jane	Brit.	1733
Hammond, Karl	U.S.	1439	Huberty, James Oliver	U.S.	1634
Hansen, Arthur Emil	U.S.	1444	Hufnagel, Thomas E.	U.S.	1635
Hanson, William P.	U.S.	1445	Hughes, John W.	U.S.	1636
Hardin, Andrew	U.S.	1446	Hughes, Susan Piasecny	U.S.	1637
Hargraves, Dick	U.S.	1453	Huiel, Henry	U.S.	2392
Harper, Calvin	U.S.	1455	Hulten, Karl Gustav	Brit.	1639
Harper, Michael	U.S.	1456	Hume, Brian Donald	Brit.	1641
Harrelson, Charles	U.S.	1457	Humphries, John R.	U.S.	1642
Harris, Jean Struven	U.S.	1461	Hunt, Joe	U.S.	1643
Harris, Pleasant	U.S.	1463	Hunt, Richard	U.S.	1643
Harris, Robert Alton	U.S.	1463	Hunt, Virnell	U.S.	1644
Hart, Michael George	Brit.	1467	Hyderabad Massacre	Pak.	1650
Hart, Steve	Aus.	1779	Ily, Nicole	Fr.	1653
Hartman, Silas W.	U.S.	728	Ingenito, Ernest	U.S.	1655
Harvey-Bugg, William Benjamin	Aus.	1472	Irvin, Leslie	U.S.	1664
Harwood, Levi	Brit.	1473	Irwin, Andrew	U.S.	2499
Harwood, Samuel	Brit.	1473	Isaacs, Carl	U.S.	1036
Hatcher, Edward	U.S.	2834	Ives, George	U.S.	1672
Hatfield-McCoy Feud	U.S.	1477	IWW Riot	U.S.	1672
Hauer, John	U.S.	1478	Jackson-Dickinson Duel	U.S.	1681
Haun's Hill Massacre	U.S.	1478	Jackson, Florence	U.S.	2708
Hawkins, Edward W.	U.S.	1492	Jackson, Loretta	U.S.	2708
Hayes, Daniel	Ire.	1494	Jahnke, Richard J.	U.S.	1694
Haymarket Riot	U.S.	1495	James, Jesse Woodson	U.S.	1695
Haynes, Dennis E.	U.S.	1497	Janecka, Allen Wayne	U.S.	1033
Haynes, Theodore Park	U.S.	1498	Jarmain, Peter Joseph	Brit.	1711
Hayward, Harry T.	U.S.	1499	Jayne, Silas	U.S.	1713
Heady, Bonnie Brown	U.S.	1421	Jeffcott-Hennis Duel	Brit.	1714
Hearn, John Wayne	U.S.	385	Jefferds, Charles	U.S.	1715
Heeber, Allen	U.S.	1507	Jenkins, Allison	U.S.	1717
Hefeld, Paul	Brit.	1507	Jenkins, Charles Harry	Brit.	1300
Hefeldt, Paul	Brit.	1939	Jenkins, James Gilbert	U.S.	1719
Heirens, William George	U.S.	1508	Jennings, James Brandon	U.S.	1721
Helms, Henry	U.S.	2543	Jett, Curtis	U.S.	1723
Henderson, Clem	U.S.	1515	Jewell, Joseph	U.S.	2093
Henley, Elmer Wayne	U.S.	785	John Martin	Brit.	216
Hennessy, Thomas	U.S.	1516	Johnson, Courtland C.	U.S.	1728
Henriot, Michel	Fr.	1517	Johnson, Jerome	U.S.	1730
Henry, Toni Jo	U.S.	1519	Johnson, Johnny	U.S.	1730
Henwood, Frank Harold	U.S.	1521	Johnson, Nicholas de Clare	Brit.	497
Herring, Robert	U.S.	1525	Johnson, Richard	U.S.	1731
Hervouet, Pierre	Fr.	1915	Johnson, William	Brit.	1733
Heslin, Peter	U.S.	1527	Jones, Elizabeth Maud	Brit.	1639
Hetenyi, George Paul	U.S.	1527	Jones, James	Brit.	1473
Hetherington, Joseph	U.S.	1528	Jones, James Warren	Guyana	1737
Hickock, Richard Eugene	U.S.	1534	Jones, Peter	U.S.	1740
Hightower, Rudy	U.S.	1547	Jones, Reginal	U.S.	1740
Hightower, William A.	U.S.	1547	Jones, Willie	U.S.	1742
Hilaire, Marcel	Fr.	1549	Jones, Willie Lee	U.S.	1742
Hileman, Doyle	U.S.	1550	Jordan, Thomas	U.S.	1744
Hill, Clarence	U.S.	1550	Jordon, Josiah	U.S.	2834
Hill, Joe	U.S.	1552	Judd, Winnie Ruth	U.S.	1746
Hill, Robert	U.S.	2543	June 2nd Movement	Ger.	1750
Hilton, Paul Emanuel	U.S.	1556	Kagebien, Joey Newton	U.S.	1752
Hinshaw, W.E.	U.S.	1562	Kalavryta Massacre	Gr.	1753
Hoddenbach, Keith	U.S.	1583	Kalavryta Massacre	Gr.	1753
Hodzic, Shefka	Yugo.	1583	Kansas City Massacre	U.S.	1754
Hoffman, Victor Ernest	Can.	1586	Kansas City Massacre	U.S.	1754
Hofmann, Kuno	Ger.	1587	Kaplan, Joel David	U.S.	1759
Hollings, W.H.	Brit.	1595	Katz, Arthur	U.S.	1769
Holloway, William	Brit.	1597	Kaufman, William	U.S.	1769
Holmes, John Maurice	U.S.	2949	Kayser, Otto	U.S.	1770
Holt, Emory	U.S.	1603	Kearney, Frank	U.S.	1771
Holt, Frederick Rothwell	Brit.	1604	Kearney, Patrick Wayne	U.S.	1772

Keech, Mary Ann Newton	U.S.	2315	Lippart, Joseph	U.S.	1969
Keele, Richard	Brit.	1773	Lipshitz, William	U.S.	1969
Keene, John	U.S.	1774	Livermore, Alpheus	U.S.	1972
Kehoe, John	U.S.	1775	Llaguna, Roger	U.S.	1266
Kelbach, Walter	U.S.	1776	Lock Ah Tam	Brit.	1974
Keller, Eva	U.S.	1777	Lod Airport Massacre	Isr.	1976
Kelley, Levi	U.S.	1778	Lod Airport Massacre	Isr.	1976
Kelly, Dan	Aus.	1779	Lohbauer, John	U.S.	1072
Kelly, Edward	Aus.	1779	Lopez, Leonardo Ramos	U.S.	1410
Kelly, Edward	Aus.	1781	Lorentzen, Robert	U.S.	1991
Kelly, Edward O.	U.S.	1781	Low, Edward	Brit.	1996
Kelly, George	Brit.	1782	Lowenstein, Emil	U.S.	1998
Kelly, Leo E., Jr.	U.S.	1788	Lowther, William	Brit.	1773
Kemper, Edmund Emil III	U.S.	1791	Loy Yeung	U.S.	1999
Kennedy, William	Brit.	516	Lozano-Ahumada Feud	U.S.	2000
Kennedy, William	U.S.	1769	Lucas, Arthur	Can.	2001
Khaalis, Hamaas Abdul	U.S.	1809	Lucas, Henry Lee	U.S.	2001
Khomeini, Ayatollah Ruhollah	Iran	1810	Lusk, Grace	U.S.	2012
Kimes-Terrill Gang	U.S.	1819	Lyons, Daniel	U.S.	2018
Kimmel, Samuel	U.S.	423	Lyons, Lewis W.	U.S.	2018
King, Alvin Lee, III	U.S.	1820	Maalot Massacre	Isr.	2021
King, Tom	Brit.	3005	Maalot Massacre	Isr.	2021
Kinne, Sharon	Int'l	1827	M'Donald, John	Scot.	385
Kinney, David	U.S.	1828	MacKay, George	Brit.	2047
Kipnik, Erich	Ger.	2656	MacKay, George	Brit.	2046
Kitto, Michael	Brit.	1420	M'Manus, Charles	U.S.	1478
Knight, Thomas	U.S.	1835	M'Naughton, John	Ire.	2064
Knight, Virgil	U.S.	1835	Macqueer, William	Brit.	2069
Knighten, Greg	U.S.	1836	Madden, Owen	U.S.	2072
Knoppa, Antony Michael	U.S.	1891	Madsen, Yvette	U.S.	2079
Knowles, Benjamin	W.Afri.	1837	Maine, Leonard	U.S.	475
Knowles, Paul John	U.S.	1837	Mainwaring, Gerald	Brit.	2089
Krafchenko, John	Can.	1846	Majors, Abe	U.S.	2092
Kray, Ronald	Brit.	1847	Majors, Lloyd L.	U.S.	2093
Kulak, Frank	U.S.	1861	Mak, Kwan Fai	U.S.	2093
Kurtz, Walter A.	U.S.	1864	Malinowski, Henry K.	Brit.	1392
Lacroix, Georges	Brit.	1870	Maloney, James	U.S.	2098
Lahore Conspiracy	India	1874	Maltby, Cecil	Brit.	2098
LaMarr, Harley	U.S.	1876	Manning, Frederick George	Brit.	2105
Lampio	Braz.	1880	Manning, Maria	Brit.	2105
Lanahan, Michael	U.S.	1881	Manning, Thomas William	U.S.	2107
Lance, Myron	U.S.	1776	Manson, Charles	U.S.	2108
Lane, Brant	U.S.	1888	Manuel, Peter Thomas Anthony	Scot.	2113
Lanham, Harry	U.S.	1891	Marcucci, Nol	Fr.	228
Lannen, George	Brit.	2735	Margolies, Irwin	U.S.	2120
Lannen, Gordon	Brit.	1891	Markle, John	U.S.	2125
Larkin, Michael	Brit.	98	Markus, Edward	S.Afri.	3034
Latham, James Douglas	U.S.	1901	Marshall, Lindsay Howitt	Brit.	2130
Latimer, Irving	U.S.	1902	Martin, Billy	U.S.	551
Lawton, John	U.S.	1050	Martin, John	Brit.	2131
Layman, Charles Newton	U.S.	1909	Marx, Gustave	U.S.	3030
Le Boeuf, Ada	U.S.	1021	Mason, Alexander Campbell	Brit.	2135
Le Boeuf, Ada Bonner	U.S.	1915	Massie, Thomas	U.S.	2139
LeBaron, Ervil Morerel	U.S.	1914	Mathis, James R.	U.S.	2147
Lebby, Olen	U.S.	1915	Mationg, Florencio Lopez	U.S.	2147
Leboucher, Simonne	Fr.	1915	Mayer, Robert	U.S.	2157
Lechler, John	U.S.	1915	McAdoo, Anthony LaQuin	U.S.	2930
Lee, Barney	U.S.	1917	McAuliffe, Joseph Herbert	Can.	2022
Lee Chuck	U.S.	1921	McCain, Willie B.	U.S.	2940
Lee, John	U.S.	1918	McCarter, James T.	U.S.	2343
Lee, John D.	U.S.	1918	McClary, David	U.S.	2025
Lee-Peacock Feud	U.S.	1921	McCollum, Ruby	U.S.	2026
Lefroy, Percy	Brit.	1922	McCoy, Joe	U.S.	2028
Lepidus, Jacob	Brit.	1939	McCoy, Old Dick	U.S.	2028
Lewis, Al Junior	U.S.	1945	McCoy, Russell	U.S.	2029
Lewis, Charles	U.S.	1945	McCoy, Tom	U.S.	2028
Liggio, Luciano	Italy	1951	McCrary Family	U.S.	2029
Lightfoot, James	Brit.	1953	McCue, J. Samuel	U.S.	2030
Lightfoot, William	Brit.	1953	McDonald, John Edward	S.Afri.	2032
Lindh, Aaron	U.S.	1967	McDonald, Roland	U.S.	2033

McGannon, William H.	U.S.	2040	Newman, Merrit	U.S.	2312
McGivern, Gary	U.S.	843	Newman, Monte	U.S.	2312
McGloin, Michael	U.S.	2041	Newton General Massacre	U.S.	2315
McGrath, James	U.S.	2042	Newton, William	U.S.	2315
McGuigan, John	Scot.	2042	Ng, Benjamin K.	U.S.	2093
McGurn, Jack	U.S.	2043	Nicely, David	U.S.	2327
McKenzie, Pete	U.S.	2048	Nicely, Joseph	U.S.	2327
McManus, Fred Eugene	U.S.	2059	Nickols, Kevin	U.S.	2335
McMonigle, Thomas Henry	U.S.	2060	Nisby, Marcus	U.S.	2338
McNair, Lawrence	U.S.	2062	Noakes, Audrey	U.S.	3004
McQuire, George	Brit.	2069	Noor, Marvin Dean	U.S.	2343
Meins, Commando Holger	Swed.	2162	Nordlund, Herman	U.S.	2343
Melchert, Peter	Fr.	2163	Norton, Heber	U.S.	2346
Mesina, Giovanni	Italy	2169	Nuccio, Richard L.	U.S.	2347
Mesina, Graziano	Italy	2169	Nutt, James	U.S.	2348
Mesina, Niccolo	Italy	2169	Oberst, Owen	U.S.	2355
Metcalf, Danny	U.S.	2172	O'Brien, George	Can.	2357
Meyer, Jacob	Brit.	1507	O'Bryan, Patrick	Brit.	2357
Milani, Joseph Harry	U.S.	2178	O'Connell-D'Esterre Duel	Ire.	2358
Millen, Irving	U.S.	2179	O'Connor, Thomas	U.S.	2359
Millen, Murton	U.S.	2179	Odierno, Salvatore	U.S.	2360
Millen, Norma Brighton	U.S.	2179	Olive, Ison Prentice	U.S.	2369
Miller, James B.	U.S.	2181	Olive, Marlene	U.S.	2370
Miller, Jean	U.S.	2708	Oliver, Frank Miles	U.S.	2785
Milosavljeric, Ljubinka	Yug.	2186	Orrock, Thomas Henry	Brit.	2380
Minsky, Max	U.S.	2188	Ortiz, Lorna	U.S.	2380
Mitchell, Tyrone	U.S.	2192	Osborne, Alberta	U.S.	2383
Molina del Rio, Francisco	U.S.	2197	Osborne, Carl	U.S.	2383
Molqi, Magid al-	Italy	2199	Ovechkin, Ninel	U.S.S.R.	2387
Mondolini, Roger	Fr.	2200	Owens, Edgar A.	U.S.	2388
Monsson, Otto	Brit.	2544	O'Young, James	U.S.	2389
Monteneros	Arg.	2204	O'Young, Thomas	U.S.	2389
Montoya, Alfred	U.S.	2147	Packer, Alferd G.	U.S.	2390
Montoya, Harold	U.S.	2147	Padgett, John	U.S.	2392
Moodie, Duncan	S.Afri.	2206	Page, Brian	U.S.	2393
Moon, Norman	U.S.	2207	Page, Duane	U.S.	2393
Moore, Alfred	Brit.	2209	Palmer, James Gordon	U.S.	2399
Moore, Hutchie	U.S.	2210	Palmer, William	Brit.	2400
Moore, Roger	U.S.	2211	Panconi, Claude	Fr.	2403
Moreira, Manuel	Braz.	2216	Panzram, Carl	U.S.	2406
Moreno, Jose	El Sal.	72	Parchmeal, William	U.S.	153
Morgan, Derrick	U.S.	2219	Pardo, Manuel	U.S.	2408
Morgan, Jack	U.S.	2221	Parker, Bonnie	U.S.	250
Morgan, Maggie	U.S.	2724	Parker, George Henry	Brit.	2410
Moriarty, Daniel	Ire.	1494	Pasch, John, Jr.	U.S.	2417
Mortensen, Peter	U.S.	2229	Patterson, John	U.S.	2423
Moseley, Joseph	Brit.	1280	Paul, Rene	Can.	2427
Move	U.S.	2236	Payne, Clyde	U.S.	1446
Moxley, William Cyril	Aus.	2236	Peace, Charles Frederick	Brit.	2429
Mulligan, Billy	U.S.	2249	Peakes, Bayard Pfundtner	U.S.	2432
Munnick, Jan Willem Hendrik	S.Afri.	2251	Pearson, Moses	U.S.	2433
Murder, Inc.	U.S.	2252	Peete, Lofie Louise	U.S.	2436
Murieta, Joaquin	U.S.	2256	Pelletier, Lawrence, Jr.	U.S.	2437
Murray, Esther del Rosario	Phil.	2260	Peltier, Leonard	U.S.	2438
My Lai Massacre	Viet.	2272	Peltzer Brothers	Belg.	2439
Myles, Jerry	U.S.	2273	People's Liberation Army	Turk.	2442
Myrtel, Hra	Fr.	2273	Pesce, Ernesto	Arg.	2449
Nally, William	U.S.	2276	Peterson, Richard	U.S.	2453
Nash, Frank	U.S.	2283	PFLP	Int'l	2456
Nathaniel, Cathy	U.S.	2289	Phillips, William R.	U.S.	2460
Naumoff, Nicolas	Italy	2291	Phuoc Tri Nguyen	U.S.	2460
Neidemeyer, Peter	U.S.	3030	Pierce, Louis	U.S.	2463
Neilson, Donald	Brit.	2297	Pierce, William Joseph, Jr.	U.S.	2463
Nelson, Dale Merle	Can.	2298	Pierre, Dale	U.S.	2464
Nelson, George	U.S.	2301	Pierson, Cheryl	U.S.	2464
Nemechek, Francis Donald	U.S.	2305	Pierson, Howard	U.S.	2464
Nesbitt, Elbert	U.S.	2306	Pierson, Marcel	Fr.	2465
Nesbitt-Talbot Feud	U.S.	2306	Pineau, Henri	Brit.	2466
Newell, Arthur L.	U.S.	2393	Piskorski, Ronald	U.S.	2470
Newman, John	U.S.	2312	Podola, Guenther Fritz Erwin	Brit.	2478

Poindexter, John E.	U.S.	2480		Rudolph, William	U.S.	2636
Ponce, Noratto	U.S.	422		Rulloff, Edward Howard	U.S.	2639
Pond, Sheldon	U.S.	2485		Rumbold, Freda	Brit.	2639
Poole, Derek Alan	Brit.	2488		Runk, John	U.S.	2640
Poole, Peter Harold	Kenya	2488		Rupp, William F.	U.S.	2641
Pope, Duane Earl	U.S.	2489		Ruppert, James	U.S.	2641
Porteous, John	Scot.	2490		Rush, James Blomfield	Brit.	2641
Pow, Frederick	Brit.	2493		Rutherford, Norman	Brit.	2644
Prejean, Dalton	U.S.	2497		Ryan, Jack	U.S.	2646
Prewett, John T.	U.S.	2499		Ryan, Michael	Brit.	2647
Prilukoff, Donat	Italy	2291		Sacco, Nicola	U.S.	2649
Prilukoff, Donat	Italy	2501		Sacoda, Joseph S.	U.S.	1399
Profit, William	U.S.	193		Saffran, Fritz	Ger.	2656
Prudom, Barry Peter	Brit.	2509		Salabarria, Mario	Cuba	2662
Pruyn, Kenyon W.	U.S.	2509		Sanchez, Hector Reuben	U.S.	2674
Quantrill, William Clarke	U.S.	2519		Santana, Frank	U.S.	2679
Quasson, Joseph	U.S.	2522		Sarrejani, Georges Alexander	Fr.	2680
Racco, Rocco	U.S.	2526		Sawtell, Isaac	U.S.	2684
Rafferty, Anthony	U.S.	2528		Saxe, Susan Edith	U.S.	2685
Ralph, Edward	U.S.	2533		Sberna, Charles	U.S.	1284
Ransom, Florence	Brit.	2535		Scatta, Salvatore	U.S.	423
Rardon, Gary	U.S.	2536		Schader, Charles	U.S.	1031
Ratliff, Marshall	U.S.	2543		Schmidt, Patricia	U.S.	2695
Rau, Gustav	Brit.	2544		Schmidt, Willem	Brit.	2544
Ray, Mark	U.S.	2547		Schnick, James Eugene	U.S.	2697
Rayner, Horace George	Brit.	2547		Schreuder, Frances Bernice	U.S.	2697
Read, James Canham	Brit.	2548		Schreuder, Marc Frances	U.S.	2697
Red Sash Gang	U.S	2555		Schroeder, Irene	U.S.	2698
Redanies, Dedea	Brit.	2552		Schultz, Arden		2699
Redenbaugh, Joseph	U.S.	2553		Schweitzer, William	U.S.	2708
Reed, Edwin	U.S.	2556		Scott, Ronald Allen	U.S.	2713
Rees, Melvin David	U.S.	2557		Selby, Joseph Franklyn	U.S.	2724
Reiser, Charles	U.S.	2562		Sellman, Edward Leon	U.S.	2726
Remus, George	U.S.	2566		Sewell, Frederick Joseph	Brit.	2730
Rennels, Robert R.	U.S.	2568		Seye, Blaise Ferrage	Fr.	2730
Rhodesia Missionary Slayings	Rhodesia	2572		Shanklin, Thomas	U.S.	2463
Richards, Stephen Dee	U.S.	2576		Sharkey, William J.	U.S.	2734
Richardson, Virgil	U.S.	2579		Sharpe, Walter	Brit.	2735
Rickard, Christopher	U.S.	2580		Sharpe, Walter	Brit.	1891
Riley, Charles David	U.S.	2370		Sharpeville Massacre	S.Afri.	2735
Riley, Irvin George	U.S.	211		Shaw, Jill	U.S.	1073
Riley, Thomas	U.S.	2584		Sheridan, Andrew	U.S.	2743
Rivers, Benjamin	U.S.	2586		Sheridan, Andrew	U.S.	1038
Rizo, Gregorio	U.S.	1031		Sherrill, Patrick Henry	U.S.	2745
Roa, Bernardo	U.S.	1031		Shillitoni, Oresto	U.S.	2745
Roberts, Harry Maurice	Brit.	2592		Shope, Dani Lee	U.S.	2343
Robertson, Eugene	U.S.	2940		Showers, John	U.S.	2093
Robinson, Joe	U.S.	2393		Shrimpton, John	Brit.	2750
Robinson, Noah R.	U.S.	2597		Shriner, Carl Elson	U.S.	2750
Robinson, Virgil	U.S.	2602		Shutt, Barbara Jean	U.S.	2751
Rodriguez, Carlos	U.S.	2606		Silverberg, Albert I.	U.S.	2312
Roeski, Emil	U.S.	3030		Simmons, Ronald Gene	U.S.	2763
Rogers, John	Brit.	2610		Simmons, Tommie Bernard	U.S.	2726
Rolt, Terence	Brit.	1300		Simmons, William	U.S.	1134
Romanian Executions	Rom.	2615		Simonelli, Neil	U.S.	129
Romanian Executions	Rom.	2615		Simpson, Charlie	U.S.	2765
Ronconi, Susanna	Italy	2616		Sims, Mitchell Carleton	U.S.	2767
Root, John	U.S.	2618		Sirocco, Jack	U.S.	2772
Rosenberg, Willie	U.S.	485		Skingle, Arthur	Brit.	2773
Ross, Charles William	Kenya	2623		Skull, Sally	U.S.	2774
Ross, Perry Dean	U.S.	2624		Slade, Joseph Alfred	U.S.	2775
Rossouw, Marthinius	S.Afri.	2625		Slayton, Elmo	U.S.	2778
Roush, Harvey L.	U.S.	2630		Slayton, Roy	U.S.	2778
Roussel, Aime de Qurangel P.	Fr.	2522		Small, Kenneth B.	U.S.	2780
Rowan-Chambers Duel	U.S.	2631		Smart, Lee	U.S.	2273
Royal Family, The	U.S.	2633		Smith, Frederick D.	U.S.	2785
Ruby, Jack	U.S.	2634		Smith, George, Jr.	Brit.	2786
Rudge, Anthony	Brit.	2131		Smith, Jimmy Lee	U.S.	2796
Rudge, Anthony Benjamin	Brit.	216		Smith, John Thomas	Aust.	2797
Rudolf	Int'l	2635		Smith, Lucille	U.S.	2825

Smith, Perry	U.S.	1534	Tuer, William Franklin	Can.	2999
Smith, Richard	U.S.	2801	Tuller, Bryce	U.S.	3000
Smith, Robert Benjamin	U.S.	2801	Tuller, Charles A.	U.S.	3000
Smith, Russell Lee	U.S.	2802	Tuller, Jonathan	U.S.	3000
Smith, Thomas	U.S.	2834	Turner, Jouyce	U.S.	3004
Snider, Paul	U.S.	2804	Turtletaub, Sam	U.S.	3006
Sontag Brothers	U.S.	2815	Tyner, Hugh Leon, Jr.	U.S.	3012
Soto, Juan	U.S.	422	Unruh, Howard	U.S.	3016
Spada, André	Fr.	2819	Urich, Heinz Karl Gunther	Mor.	3018
Sparrow, Peter	Brit.	2773	Vallanzasca, Renato	Italy	3027
Spencer, Anthony	U.S.	2824	Vallejo, Daniel	U.S.	1072
Spencer, Bertram G.	U.S.	2825	Van Buuren, Clarence Gordon	S.Afri.	3029
Spencer, Brenda	U.S.	2825	Van Dine, Harvey	U.S.	3030
Spencer, Verlin	U.S.	2827	van Heerden, Cornelius Johanne	S.Afri.	3032
Spenkelink, John A.	U.S.	2827	Van Niekerk, Andries	S.Afri.	3034
Spicer, Edward A.	U.S.	2828	Vanzetti, Bartolomeo	U.S.	2649
Stacey, Rebecca	U.S.	2834	Varecha, James	U.S.	3036
Stacey, Robert	U.S.	2834	Vasquez, Tiburcio	U.S.	422
Staleski, Walter	U.S.	1031	Vega, Evelyn	U.S.	2437
Stanley, Arthur Cromwell	S.Afri.	2839	Velez, Luis S.	U.S.	3040
Stano, Gerald Eugene	U.S.	2839	Vernon, Roger	Int'l	3042
Starkweather, Charles	U.S.	2840	Vetsera, Maria	Int'l.	2635
Steelman, William	U.S.	1382	Vidal, Ginette	Fr.	3047
Stein, Harry	U.S.	775	Volk, Adam	U.S.	3060
Stewart, Frederick	Brit.	2852	Vontsteen, Franciscus Wynand	S.Afri.	3064
Stone, Elton M.	U.S.	2858	Wable, John Wesley	U.S.	3067
Stopa, Wanda	U.S.	2861	Wainwright, Henry	Brit.	3071
Strang, Jesse	U.S.	2866	Walden, Bernard Hugh	Brit.	3074
Stuart-Boswell Duel	Scot.	2872	Walker, Charles	U.S.	3076
Sutton-Taylor Feud	U.S.	2884	Walker, Jesse	U.S.	3077
Swancutt, Beaufort George	U.S.	2885	Walker, Thomas Ray, Jr.	U.S.	3079
Swart, Marthinus Erich	S.Afri.	2886	Walls, James Jr.	U.S.	193
Swart, Stephen	S.Afri.	2887	Walsh, Daniel	U.S.	3084
Sweeney, Dennis	U.S.	2887	Walsh, James	Brit.	3084
Swope, A.M.	U.S.	1340	Wanderer, Carl Otto	U.S.	3087
Sylvester, David Joseph	U.S.	2889	Wanka, Alfred	S.Afri.	3089
Symbionese Liberation Army	U.S.	2889	Ward, Tommy	U.S.	3092
Taborsky, Joseph	U.S.	2893	Washington, Aaron	U.S.	3097
Tacklyn, Larry Winfield	Berm.	2893	Washington, Albert	U.S.	449
Tacklyn, Larry Winfield	Ber.	558	Washington, Albert	U.S.	317
Talbot, Lug	U.S.	2895	Washington, Leon	U.S.	3098
Talbott, Albert	U.S.	2895	Watt, Newton	U.S.	3104
Talbott, Charles E.	U.S.	2895	Weatherill, Miles	Brit.	3107
Tansey, John	U.S.	2897	Weber, Adolph	U.S.	3108
Tarnowska, Marie Nicolaievna	Italy	2291	Weidmann, Eugen	Fr.	3113
Terpening, Oliver, Jr.	U.S.	2915	Weil, Levi	Brit.	3118
Terry, John Victor	Brit.	2917	Weind, James	U.S.	2383
Tevendale, Brian	Scot.	2919	Weipert, Lee	U.S.	2934
Thacker, William J.	U.S.	2921	Welch, Bernard Charles, Jr.	U.S.	3123
Thaw, Harry Kendall	U.S.	2921	Wells, Alfred	U.S.	3124
Therrien, Armand R.	U.S.	2927	Wessel, Horst	Ger.	3128
Thomas, Arthur Alan	N.Zea.	2930	West, John Coulter	U.S.	867
Thomas, Donald George	Brit.	2930	West, Ronald Eugene	U.S.	3129
Thomas, Frederick Jerome	U.S.	2930	Westwood, Billy	U.S.	3130
Thompson, George	S.Afri.	2934	Wheat, Clarence	U.S.	3132
Thompson, William	Brit.	2936	Wheeler, Bernard	Brit.	3132
Thornhill, Hillary	U.S.	2940	Whelan, John	Aus.	3134
Thurtell, John	Brit.	2949	Whitby, Roy	U.S.	3136
Tilghman, John	U.S.	2955	Whitman, Charles Joseph	U.S.	3143
Toole, Ottis Elwood	U.S.	2001	Whyte, James Albert	U.S.	211
Torrez, Robert	U.S.	1031	Willgoss, Walter William	Aus.	3158
Tracey, Frank J.	U.S.	2981	Williams, Carl	U.S.	3160
Tracy, Ann Gibson	U.S.	2981	Williams, David Marshall	U.S.	3161
Tracy, Harry	U.S.	2981	Williams, Dennis	U.S.	3161
Travers, George	U.S.	2984	Williams, Hernando		3162
Treffene, Phillip John	Aus.	2985	Williams, Matthew	U.S.	3164
Tregoff, Carole	U.S.	1158	Williams, Richard Charles	U.S.	2107
Tremamunno, Donato	Italy	2985	Williams, Thomas Joseph	Brit.	3166
Trolia, John	U.S.	2990	Williams, Wayne Bertram	U.S.	3166
Trotter, Clarence	U.S.	2994	Willis, Frances	U.S.	3169

Willner, Josephine	U.S.	3169		Corbett, Thomas P.	U.S.	782
Willock, Essie Mae	U.S.	2825		Craft, Mary Faye	U.S.	805
Wilson, James William	U.S.	3172		Crittenden, Thomas	U.S.	825
Wissner, Nathan	U.S.	775		Croker, Richard	Ire.	827
Witherspoon, William	U.S.	3179		Crump, Raymond, Jr.	U.S.	841
Witney, John	Brit.	2592		Curtis, Maurice	U.S.	849
Woo Bum Kong	Korea	3181		Dampier, Edith	Brit.	865
Woods, Frank	U.S.	1769		Daniel, Vickie	U.S.	867
Woolmington, Reginald	Brit.	3186		Davies, Idris	Brit.	881
Workman, William	U.S.	3187		Daviess, Samuel	U.S.	882
Wounded Knee Massacre	U.S.	3192		Davis, Angela Yvonne	U.S.	882
Wright, David	U.S.	3193		Davis, Thomas Cullen	U.S.	885
Wynekoop, Alice	U.S.	3198		DeKing, Lillian	U.S.	904
York, George Ronald	U.S.	1902		Delorme, Abb J. Adelard	Can.	909
Young, Gig	U.S.	3209		Denhardt, Henry H.	U.S.	913
Young, Harry	U.S.	3209		Denicke, Ernest	U.S.	914
Young, Robert	U.S.	3211		Diener, George Edward	U.S.	942
Zamp, Jerome	U.S.	355		Donohue, Thomas	U.S.	1000
Zayas, Fernando	U.S.	3218		Du Toit, Petrus Hendrik	S.Afri.	1045
Zebra Killings	U.S.	3218		Dunlap, Leon A.	U.S.	1037
Zinzigk, Perry	U.S.	3221		Dunnigan, John	U.S.	1038
Zizzio, Domenick	U.S.	423		Dupree, Lewis 17X	U.S.	1040
Zodiac Killer	U.S.	3221		Emerald Hunters Slayings	Col.	1090
				Emerson, William D.	Brit.	1090
				Eskridge, Joseph	U.S.	1103
MURDER BY GUNSHOT - Case of				Everett, Ronald James	Brit.	1300
Alford, William	U.S.	91		Fahmy, Marie-Margurite	Brit.	1125
Allaway, Edward Charles	U.S.	92		Fair, Laura D.	U.S.	1126
Allen, Edward H.B.	U.S.	93		Farrell, Edgar Joseph Raymond	Aus.	1136
Allen, Peggy	U.S.	98		Field, Stephen J.	U.S.	2292
Appel, Hans	Ger.	138		Foat, Virginia Eleanor	U.S.	1189
Arensdorf, John	U.S.	154		Foreman, Frederick	Brit.	1300
Barbaro, Anthony F.	U.S.	229		Francey, Henriette	Fr.	1209
Barney, Elvira Dolores	Brit.	246		Gant, W.C.	U.S.	1265
Barstow, Ralph Gordon	Brit.	265		Gehr, Herbert	U.S.	1289
Bedell, Penn	U.S.	312		George, Annie	U.S.	1299
Bennett, Myrtle	U.S.	333		Gerard, Alfred Robert	Brit.	1300
Benton, Wallace	Brit.	337		Giddings, Daniel	U.S.	1309
Betchel, Lawrence	U.S.	354		Goebel, William	U.S.	1326
Blumenfield, Isadore	U.S.	413		Gonzales, Frank	U.S.	1337
Bommarito, Joseph	U.S.	426		Gop, Chew Tin	U.S.	1750
Bonaparte, Pierre-Napolon	Fr.	428		Grant, James	U.S.	1362
Boyer, Ernie	U.S.	461		Green, Clement Clay	U.S.	1372
Boynton, Edward	U.S.	463		Groce, Bunt	U.S.	1391
Brady, Patrick	Aus.	468		Grupen, Peter	Ger.	1394
Braunsdorf, Eugene	U.S.	475		Hamilton, Jones S.	U.S.	1435
Broughton, Henry John Delv	Kenya	503		Hamon, Clara Smith	U.S.	1439
Brown, Anthony Silah	U.S.			Haneline, Scott Anthony	U.S.	1441
Brown, Charles T.	U.S.	505		Haneline, Scott Anthony	U.S.	1441
Brown, JoAnne	U.S.	509		Harris, Mary	U.S.	1462
Bryant, Roy	U.S.	2178		Heads, Charles	U.S.	1501
Butts, Thomas	U.S.	564		Held, Leo A.	U.S.	1511
Caillaux, Henriette Claretie	Fr.	575		Hemming, Richard	Brit.	1514
Cain, John	Brit.	576		Herbert, Philemon T.	U.S.	1522
Callaghan, Jeremiah	Brit.	1300		Hill, Miriam	Brit.	1554
Camberg, John F.	U.S.	588		Hoffman, Harry L.	U.S.	1585
Carman, Mrs. Edwin	U.S.	628		Holland, Tom	U.S.	1592
Carroll, James	Can.	641		Holman, Libby	U.S.	1597
Castro, Julie Ann	U.S.	656		Houndsditch Murders	Brit.	1625
Casuse, Larry Wayne	U.S.	656		Hurd, Roosevelt Carlos, Sr.	U.S.	1645
Cero, Gangi	U.S.	664		Hyde, Fanny	U.S.	1649
Chevallier, Yvonne	Fr.	695		Ibn-Tamas, Beverly Ann	U.S.	1651
Christie, Avril	U.S.	705		Icardi, Aldo Lorenzo	Italy	1652
Cienski, Ludomir	Brit.	715		Inukitsaq	Can.	1853
Clark, David	U.S.	721		Ippolito, Joseph	U.S.	1662
Clark, Willard	U.S.	725		Israel, Harold F.	U.S.	1668
Clever, Daniel	U.S.	732		Johnson, Peggy	U.S.	1731
Coffelt, Winford	U.S.	740		Jung, Lem	U.S.	1750
Colson, David	U.S.	759		Kakonis, Thomas D.	U.S.	1753
Cooks, Tony	U.S.	772		Katyn Massacre	U.S.S.R.	1768

Kiger, Jo Ann	U.S.	1816	Sherwood, Ella	U.S.	2745
Kitchen, George	Brit.	1832	Shipp, Thomas	U.S.	2746
Kobvello	Can.	1839	Sickles, Daniel Edgar	U.S.	2752
Kudlooktoo	Can.	1853	Simants, Erwin Charles	U.S.	2763
Lamantia, Rocco	U.S.	1875	Simmons, G.W.	U.S.	463
Lancaster, William Newton	U.S.	1882	Smith, Alfonso Francis Austin	Brit.	2781
Latourette, Patricia	U.S.	1902	Smith, Bernard	U.S.	2781
Lawrence, Edward	Brit.	1907	Smith, Jerry Paul	U.S.	2795
Lawton, Gary	U.S.	1908	Smith, Leonard	U.S.	2798
Ledru, Robert	Fr.	1916	Smith, William	Scot.	2804
Lewis, Frank	U.S.	1945	Sposato, Frank	U.S.	2833
Light, Ronald Vivian	Brit.	1952	Stefani, Jean-Paul	Fr.	2847
Link, Theodore C.	U.S.	1969	Steinman, Jacob	U.S.	2849
Livecchi, Angelo	U.S.	426	Stiltz, Moses S.	U.S.	2855
Luparelli, Joe	U.S.	2012	Stone, Louise	U.S.	2860
McCaskill, Hamby	U.S.	2025	Stone, Loy Dean	U.S.	2860
Macdonald, Alexander Bain	Scot.	2915	Stretz, Vera	U.S.	2869
McDonald, Dora Feldman	U.S.	2031	Struck, Ira G.	U.S.	2871
McDougald, Daniel A.	U.S.	2035	Swan, Robert	U.S.	2885
McDow, Thomas Ballard	U.S.	2035	Tarter-Coffelt Feud	U.S.	2898
McFarland, Daniel	U.S.	2037	Terig, Duncan	Scot.	2915
McMullen, Stewart	U.S.	2060	Thoresen, Louise	U.S.	2937
M'Naghten, Daniel	Brit.	2061	Toplis, Percy	Brit.	2968
McNamara, Cynthia Stowell	Peru	2062	Torsney, Robert	U.S.	2974
Maddox, Corinne	U.S.	2073	Toth, Robert W.	U.S.	2975
Malcolm, Douglas	Brit.	2094	Townsend, William	Can.	2980
Malcolm, Vance	U.S.	463	Vineyard, James R.	U.S.	3055
Mallalieu, Richard Louis	S.Afri.	2096	Voiss, Peter	U.S.	3059
Matranga, Charles	U.S.	2147	Walker, William L.	U.S.	3079
Matranga, Tony	U.S.	2147	Ward, Matthew F.	U.S.	3092
Means, Gaston Bullock	U.S.	2159	Ward, Robert J.	U.S.	3092
Mervin, John	U.S.	2169	Ward, Walter S.	U.S.	3093
Milam, J.W.	U.S.	2178	Waring, John U.	U.S.	3094
Milazzo, Frank	U.S.	2178	Weitzman, Irving	U.S.	3122
Miller, Robert Ingersoll	U.S.	2182	Whistlecraft, George	Brit.	3135
Mitchell, George	U.S.	2191	White, Alice	U.S.	3136
Mize, Louis	U.S.	2194	Willis, George Henry	Brit.	3169
Monson, Alfred John	Scot.	2202	Wilson-Lyon Duel	Can.	3173
Munter, Judith Marie	U.S.	2251	Wintermute, Peter P.	U.S.	3177
Myers, William R.	U.S.	2270	Wright, Charles Edward	Brit.	3193
Nash, James Lawrence	Brit.	2287	Wright, Paul	U.S.	3194
Neagle, David	U.S.	2292			
Nixon-Nirdlinger, Charlotte	Fr.	2340	**MURDER BY GUNSHOT - Unsolved**		
Noel, William	Brit.	2342	Abdinoor, George	U.S.	9
Obenchain, Madalynne	U.S.	2355	Anderson, Thomas Weldon	Brit.	124
Oesterreich, Walburga	U.S.	2363	Bas, Marvin J.	U.S.	271
Osceola, John	U.S.	2384	Beckett, Moses	U.S.	311
Paight, Carol	U.S.	2394	Berbers, Jean	Fr.	339
Patterson, Gertrude Gibson	U.S.	2422	Berg, Alan	U.S.	341
Patterson, Nan Randolph	U.S.	2423	Bintel, Joe	U.S.	371
Peltz, Greta	U.S.	2439	Bitterman, Chester A., III	Col.	383
Petrou, Theodosios	Brit.	2455	Black, George Barron	Brit.	384
Pinet, Francois	Fr.	2467	Booze, Eugene P.	U.S.	437
Pizzino, Ted	U.S.	426	Bright, James	Brit.	488
Poland, Margaret	U.S.	2480	Brogile, Prince Jean de	Fr.	497
Power, Katherine Ann	U.S.	2494	Buggy, John James	Brit.	534
Probst, Carrie	U.S.	2504	Callahan, William H.	U.S.	583
Purvis, Will	U.S.	2514	Cancel, Linda Louise	El Sal.	595
Rayne, Richard	Brit.	576	Canning, Gertrude	Scot.	599
Reickles, John H.	U.S.	2560	Cheever, Mary	U.S.	691
Reymond, Claire	Fr.	2570	Chin, Frank	U.S.	700
Reynolds, Robert G.	China	2571	Christi, Frank	U.S.	703
Riggs, David	U.S.	1037	Confessore, Alfonse	U.S.	764
Roberts, William	Brit.	2593	Connors, Charles	U.S.	766
Roma, Joe	U.S.	2615	Cosarian, Acokis	U.S.	793
Rowe, Gary Thomas, Jr.	U.S.	2631	Costa, Gaetano	Italy	794
Sanhuber, Otto	U.S.	2363	Cuccari, Pierre	Fr.	843
Scannell, John	U.S.	2688	Dahme, Father Hubert	U.S.	855
Sewell, Douglas	U.S.	2730	Dauber, Charlotte	U.S.	878
Shattuck, Jane	U.S.	2736	Dauber, William E.	U.S.	878

MURDER BY GUNSHOT - Wrongly Convicted

Walker, Lee Dell	U.S.	3078
Wallace, Ernest	U.S.	3080
Zimmerman, Isidore	U.S.	3220

MURDER BY NEGLECT

Adkins, Orville	U.S.	436
Bischoff, Charles	U.S.	380
Booth, Arnett	U.S.	436
Hauser, Frederick I.	U.S.	1490
Heidnik, Gary M.	U.S.	1507
Holy Child Orphanage Case	China	1605
Inquisition, The	Int'l.	1656
Juenemann, Charlotte	Ger.	1748
LaMarca, Angelo John	U.S.	1876
Maddux, Ronald	U.S.	2073
Maddux, Wanda Gibson	U.S.	2073
Metyard, Sarah Morgan	Brit.	2173
Nemechek, Francis Donald	U.S.	2305
Redenbaugh, Joseph	U.S.	2553
Smith, Clarice	U.S.	2783
Soulakiotis, Mariam	Gr.	2816
Staunton Family	Brit.	2844
Tamerlane the Great	Mongolia	2895
Travis, John	U.S.	436
Williamson, John	Brit.	3168

MURDER BY NEGLECT - Case of

Acton, Thomas	Brit.	19
Adams, Jani	U.S.	25
Arbuckle, Roscoe Conkling	U.S.	143
Benquet, Jean	Fr.	2282
Cazenave, Jean	Fr.	2282
Doudet, Clestine	Fr.	1008
Nardon, Georges	Fr.	2282

MURDER BY NEGLECT - Unsolved

Dawson, John	Brit.	887
Drinan, John Albert	Fr.	1024
Frome, Mrs. Weston G.	U.S.	1237
Frome, Nancy	U.S.	1237
Grimes, Barbara	U.S.	1390
Grimes, Patricia	U.S.	1390

MURDER BY NEGLECT - Wrongly Convicted

Rivera, Antonio	U.S.	2586
Walpole, Merla	U.S.	2586

MURDER BY POISON

Archer-Gilligan, Amelia	U.S.	152
Bailey, George Arthur	Brit.	208
Bevan, Catherine	U.S.	355
Bishop, John	Brit.	382
Bougrat, Pierre	Fr.	453
Brinvilliers, Marie de	Fr.	491
Britland, Mary	Brit.	493
d'Albe, Dominique	Fr.	856
Derues, Antoine Francois	Fr.	920
de Scotiney, Walter	Brit.	923
Deshayes, Catherine	Fr.	924
Drusilla, Livia	Roman.	1029
Goebbels, Paul Joseph	Ger.	1324
Harris, Charlotte	Brit.	1460
Hoch, Johann Otto	U.S.	1582
La Spara, Hieronyma	Italy	1900
Lucusta	Roman.	2007
Meyer, Henry C.F.	U.S.	2174
Monson, William	Brit.	2202
Montvoisin, Catherine	Fr.	2206
Pledge, Sarah	Brit.	3131
Raies, Jeanne	Switz.	2530

Renczi, Vera	Rom.	2567
Restell, Ann	U.S.	2569
Riembauer, Franz Sales	Ger.	2581
Rijke, Sjef	Neth.	2584
Rogers, George White	U.S.	2610
Roose, Richard	Brit.	2617
Ruopp, Siegfried	Ger.	2640
Sach, Amelia	Brit.	2649
Sadler, Dora Martha Spalding	Brit.	2656
Sejanus, Lucius Aelius	Roman.	2724
Sherman, Lydia	U.S.	2744
Sorel, Agnes	Fr.	2816
Spara, Hieronyma	Italy	2821
Tawell, John	Brit.	2899
Tiberius	Roman.	2950
Tilghman, John	U.S.	2955
Tz'u-Hsi	China	3012
van Rensburg, Smartryk Johanne	S.Afri.	3034
Walters, Annie	Brit.	2652
Whale, Anne	Brit.	2476
Williams, Mary	Brit.	3164
Williams, Thomas	Brit.	382
Wood, Isaac	U.S.	3182

Poison: E-GO5

Lehmann, Christa Ambros	Ger.	1925

Poison: Aconite

Hendrickson, John, Jr.	U.S.	1516
Lamson, George Henry	Brit.	1881
Pritchard, Edward William	Scot.	2503
Warder, Alfred William		

Poison: Ammonia

Covell, Alton	U.S.	800

Poison: Anecdine

Jones, Genene	U.S.	1737

Poison: Antimony

Chapman, George	Brit.	682
Jeanneret, Marie	Switz.	1714
Pritchard, Edward William	Scot.	2503

Poison: Arsenic

Albanese, Charles	U.S.	46
Allnutt, William Newton	Brit.	102
Appelgate, Everett	U.S.	815
Armstrong, Herbert Rowse	Brit.	156
Barber, Ann	Brit.	230
Barfield, Velma Margie	U.S.	234
Bateman, Mary	Brit.	280
Becker, Barent	U.S.	297
Bilansky, Ann	U.S.	361
Billik, Herman	U.S.	362
Black, Edward Ernest	Brit.	384
Blandig, Albert	Brit.	406
Blandy, Mary	Brit.	406
Borgia Family	Italy	441
Botkin, Cordelia	U.S.	448
Bowers, Martha	U.S.	457
Brekke, Carstein	Norway	484
Bryant, Charlotte	Brit.	523
Burdock, Mary Ann	Brit.	543
Carawan, George Washington	U.S.	619
Carew, Edith Mary Porch	Japan	621
Carter, Polk	U.S.	644
Casler, Abraham	U.S.	651
Chesham, Sarah	Brit.	693
Cotton, Mary Ann Rob. Mowbray	Brit.	797
Cotton, Mary Ann Rob. Mowbray		
Creighton, Mary Frances	U.S.	815
Cross, Philip Henry	Ire.	835
Daniloff, Jeanne	Fr.	868
Dazeley, Sarah	Brit.	889
DeMelker, Daisy L. Cowle Sproa	S. Afri.	912

Freidgood, Charles E.	U.S.	1233
Poison: Diamond Powder		
Howard, Frances	Brit.	1628
Poison: Digitalin		
Beck, Martha Julie	U.S.	296
Becker, Marie Alexander	Belg.	309
De la Pommerais, Edmond	Fr.	907
Poison: Diptheria		
O'Brien de Lacy, Patrick	Rus.	2357
Panchenko, Dr.	Rus.	2357
Poison: Drug Overdose		
Gufler, Max	Aust.	1397
Poison: Ether		
Harvey, Donald	U.S.	1471
Leboucher, Simonne	Fr.	1915
Poison: Gas		
Green, Hershey	U.S.	2123
Kreisberg, Daniel	U.S.	2123
Marino, Tony	U.S.	2123
Murphy, David	U.S.	2123
Pasqua, Frank	U.S.	2123
Poison: Gelsemine		
Fullam, Augusta Fairfield	India	1240
Poison: Hepatitis Serum		
Harvey, Donald	U.S.	1471
Poison: Hydrobromide		
Crippen, Hawley Harvey	Brit.	819
Poison: Hydrochloride		
Rendall, Martha	Aus.	2568
Poison: Insulin		
Barlow, Kenneth	Brit.	244
Hooijaijers, Frans	Neth.	1608
Poison: Laudenum		
Bird, Edward	Brit.	372
Francisco, Cornelius Henry	U.S.	1210
Jumpertz, Henry	U.S.	1749
Poison: Laurel Water		
Donellan, John	Brit.	999
Poison: Lead Acetate		
Taylor, Louisa Jane	Brit.	2902
Poison: Lidocaine		
Diaz, Robert R.	U.S.	938
Poison: Mercury		
Dean, Sarah Ruth	U.S.	891
Franklin, James	Brit.	1224
Howard, Frances	Brit.	1628
Williams, Ann	Brit.	3160
de Deurwaerder, Louis	Belg.	899
Poison: Methylphenobarbitone		
Conroy, Teresa Miriam	Brit.	767
Poison: Morphine		
Buchanan, Robert W.	U.S.	529
Castaing, Edm Samuel	Fr.	654
Clements, Robert George	Brit.	730
Harris, Carlyle W.	U.S.	1459
Jackson, Scott	U.S.	1679
Jeanneret, Marie	Switz.	1714
Joniaux, Marie Thrse	Belg.	1742
LeDoux, Emma	U.S.	1916
Swett, Jane	U.S.	2888
Toppan, Jane	U.S.	2968
Waddingham, Dorothea Nancy	Brit.	3067
Walling, Alonzo M.	U.S.	1679
Poison: Mushrooms		
Seefeld, Adolf	Ger.	2722
Poison: Nicotine		
Bocarm, Comte Hippolyte de	Belg.	414
Poison: Opium		
Chantrelle, Eugne Marie	Scot.	680
Jones, Cornelius	U.S.	1737

Poison: Paraquat		
Barber, Susan	Brit.	231
Poison: Phosphorus		
Ansell, Mary Ann	Brit.	129
Borgia Family	Italy	441
Bowers, J. Milton	U.S.	457
Merrifield, Louisa Highway	Brit.	2168
Poison: Prussic Acid		
Auriol, Joseph	Fr.	185
Brinkley, Richard	Brit.	488
Coolidge, Valorus P.	U.S.	773
Latimer, Irving	U.S.	1902
Watson, Lionel Rupert Nathan	Brit.	3103
Poison: Pyralion		
Scieri, Antoinette	Fr.	2708
Poison: Rat Poison		
Dean, Dovie	U.S.	891
Poison: Rose Algar		
Howard, Frances	Brit.	1628
Poison: Sodium Pentathol		
Clark, Ronald E.	U.S.	724
Poison: Strychnine		
Barlow, Silas	Brit.	244
Brown, Thomas Mathieson	Brit.	516
Carigiola, Luigi	Italy	624
Cream, Thomas Neill	Int'l	813
de Beer, Petrus Cornelius	S.Afri.	894
DeMelker, Daisy L. Cowle Sproa	S. Afri.	912
du Plessis, Dirkie Cathrina	S.Afri.	2346
Dove, William	Brit.	1011
Duvall, William Potts	U.S.	1048
Edmunds, Christiana	Brit.	1070
Gunness, Belle	U.S.	1400
Hartson, Dorothy	S.Afri.	1470
Hersey, George Canning	U.S.	1526
Horsford, Walter	Brit.	1622
Horton, Floyd	U.S.	1622
Hyde, Bennett Clarke	U.S.	1648
Johnston, Anna	U.S.	1622
Major, Ethel Lillie	Brit.	2092
Nortje, Jan Christian	S.Afri.	2346
Pearson, Elizabeth	Brit.	2433
Pearson, Sarah	N.Ire.	2434
Rablen, Eva	U.S.	2525
Vaquier, Jean Pierre	Brit.	3035
Wainewright, Thomas Griffiths	Brit.	3070
Weiss, Jeanne Daniloff	Alg.	3120
Zoldoske, Rose	U.S.	3222
Poison: Succinyleholine		
Coppolino, Carl	U.S.	780
Poison: Thallium		
Marek, Martha Lowenstein	Aust.	2119
Young, Graham	Brit.	3209
Poison: Toxic Whiskey		
Graves, Thomas Thatcher	U.S.	1364
Poison: Typhoid Germs		
Girard, Henri	Fr.	1316
Hyde, Bennett Clarke	U.S.	1648
Poison: Veronal		
Nozire, Violette	Fr.	2347
MURDER BY POISON - Case of		
General		
Cole, Hiram	U.S.	743
Smethurst, Thomas	Brit.	2781
Thyng, Rosalie A.	U.S.	2950
Tolomelli, Lucia	Italy	2964
Poison: Antimony		
Bravo, Florence Ricardo	Brit.	476
Livingston, Mary Alice Almont	U.S.	1973

Wharton, Elizabeth	U.S.	3131
Winslow, Thomas	Brit.	3177

Poison: Arsenic

de Poulaillon	Fr.	917
Besnard, Marie Jos. Phil. Dav.	Fr.	353
Gilmour, Christina	Scot.	1315
Greenwood, Harold	Brit.	1378
Griggs, Ronald Geeves	Aus.	1389
Hartung, Mary	U.S.	1470
Hayden, Herbert H.	U.S.	1493
Hearn, Sarah Ann	Brit.	1501
Kelliher, Mary	U.S.	1778
King, William Laurie	Scot.	1826
M'Kay, Medad	U.S.	2047
McMillan, Margaret	Scot.	2060
Meilhan, Joseph	Fr.	1869
Millington, Frank C.	U.S.	2184
Millington, Mary	U.S.	2184
Orpet, William	U.S.	2379
Pace, Beatrice Annie	Brit.	2390
Robinson, Richard P.	U.S.	2598
Smith, Madeleine Hamilton	Scot.	2799
Wilson, James	N.Zea.	3172
Ladd, Gloria Beale	U.S.	1870

Poison: Chloroform

Bartlett, Adelaide	Brit.	266

Poison: Copper Sulphate

Griffin, William	U.S.	1386

Poison: Curare

Jascalevich, Mario E.	U.S.	1712

Poison: Cyanide

Costello, Jessie	U.S.	796
Dimmig, John	U.S.	975
Icardi, Aldo Lorenzo	Italy	1652
MacFarland, William Allison	U.S.	2039
Molineux, Roland Burnham	U.S.	2198

Poison: Digitalin

Nelles, Susan	Can.	2298

Poison: Heroin

Adams, John Bodkin	Brit.	26

Poison: Insulin

La Scola, Raymond	U.S.	1900

Poison: Mercury

Butterfield, Jane	Brit.	563

Poison: Morphine

Adams, John Bodkin	Brit.	26
Crawford, Annie	U.S.	812
Rosier, Peter	U.S.	2621

Poison: Paraldehyde

Adams, John Bodkin	Brit.	26

Poison: Pavulon

Narcisco, Filipina B.	U.S.	2282
Perez, Leonara M.	U.S.	2282

Poison: Potassium

Bolding, Jane Francis	U.S.	422

Poison: Prussic Acid

Schoeppe, Paul	U.S.	2697

Poison: Seconal

Armstrong, John	Brit.	157

Poison: Barbiturates

Bayle, Blodwen	Brit.	285

Poison: Strychnine

Brand, Elizabeth	S.Afri.	471
Brand, Maria	S.Afri.	471
Budde, Richard	U.S.	533
Farrell, Edgar Joseph Raymond	Aus.	1136
Griffiths, Mrs.	S.Afri.	471
Hardenbrook, John K.	U.S.	1446
Ingersoll, Sarah	U.S.	1656

Poison: Sucostrin

Favor, Arsenio	U.S.	1139

MURDER BY POISON - Unsolved
General

Burrus, Sextus Afranius	Roman.	558
Drummond, Margaret	Scot.	1028
Dyveke	Den.	1051
Henrietta Anne	Brit.	1517
Home, George	Brit.	1606
Randolph, Thomas	Scot.	2534
d'Estres, Gabrielle	Fr.	927

Poison: Arsenic

Bingham Family Poisonings	Brit.	371
Crouch, Mary Ann	Brit.	836
Croydon Murders	Brit.	840
Duff, Edmund	Brit.	1032
Hall, Charles Francis	Greenland	1424
Kemp, Fanny	Brit.	1791
Louise, Marie	Spain	1993
Sydney, Vera	Brit.	1032
Sydney, Violet	Brit.	1032

Poison: Belladona

d'Albret, Jeanne	Fr.	856

Poison: Cyanide

Freihoff, William	U.S.	1234
Tylenol Murders	U.S.	3011

Poison: Hydrochloride

Willats, Fleetwood	Brit.	3158

Poison: Hyoscyamus

d'Albret, Jeanne	Fr.	856

Poison: Morphine

Rougier, Hilary	Brit.	2629

Poison: Opium

d'Albret, Jeanne	Fr.	856

Poison: Ricin

Markov, Georgi	Brit.	2125

Poison: Strychnine

Chevis, Hubert George	Brit.	696

MURDER BY POISON - Wrongly Convicted
Poison: Gas

Marino, Tony	U.S.	2123

Poison: Parathion

Richardson, James	U.S.	2577

MURDER BY PUSHING/SHOVING

Chambers, Robert K.	U.S.	673
Crimmins, Craig	U.S.	819
D'Arcy, Patrick	Ire.	870
Daniels, Thomas	Brit.	868
Hallam, Robert	Brit.	1427
Twitchell, George S.	U.S.	3010
Wymer, Eugene William	U.S.	3198
Zu Shenatir	El-Yemen	3223

MURDER BY STABBING
General

Abbandando, Frank	U.S.	1
Abbott, Jack Henry	U.S.	6
Abrahams, M.	Brit.	11
Abrams, Michael	U.S.	13
Adams, Caleb	U.S.	22
Adams, William Nelson	Brit.	28
Aikney, Thomas	Brit.	494
Alcott, John James	Brit.	70
Alexander, Frank	Canary Is.	90
Alexander, Harald	Canary Is.	90
Allen, Peter Anthony	Brit.	98
Allweiss, David	U.S.	102
Almarez, Stella Delores	U.S.	102

Alvarez, Louis	U.S.	107	Crowninshield, Richard	U.S.	839	
Anderson, Alexander	U.S.	121	Crump, Michael Tyrone	U.S.	840	
Anderson, Clifford	U.S.	122	Cruttenden, Ann	Brit.	842	
Anderson, Dick	U.S.	2935	Dacey, Edwin	Brit.	853	
Appo, Quimby	U.S.	139	Dalmas, Augustus	Brit.	857	
Arden, Alice	Brit.	153	Dalzeel, Alexander	Brit.	864	
Armistead, Norma Jean	U.S.	156	Davis, Vincent	Brit.	886	
Arnold, Louise	U.S.	162	DeLuca, Frank	U.S.	760	
Babcock, Miner	U.S.	204	Deo, Mrs. Josiah	U.S.	917	
Baekeland, Antony	Brit.	206	Desha, Isaac B.	U.S.	924	
Bagg, Arthur Richard	S. Afri.	207	Donnelly, Dr. James P.	U.S.	1000	
Ball, Edward	Ire.	220	Dos Santo, Francisco	U.S.	1006	
Banks, John	U.S.	227	Douglass, Robert	U.S.	1011	
Beckett, Henry	Brit.	310	Drake, David H.	U.S.	1891	
Bender Family	U.S.	324	Draw, Derrick	U.S.	1020	
Bessarabian Gang	Brit.	353	Driscoll, Daniel	Brit.	1025	
Best, Alton Alonzo	U.S.	354	Dudley, Thomas	Brit.	1032	
Bichel, Andreas	Ger.	358	Dunkins, Horace Franklin, Jr.	U.S.	1037	
Bird, Jake	U.S.	373	Durgan, Bridget	U.S.	1041	
Blanther, Joseph	U.S.	407	Edmondson, Mary	Brit.	1069	
Blazek, Frank	U.S.	408	Edwards, Mack Ray	U.S.	1073	
Bonetti, Rosina	Italy	430	Edwards, Vernon David, Jr.	U.S.	1074	
Bonmartini, Countess Linda	Italy	430	Egyptian Dragons	U.S.	1075	
Boudes, Abb	Fr.	453	Evans, Gwynne Owen	Brit.	98	
Bower, Elliot	Fr.	456	Fairbanks, Jason	U.S.	1126	
Bram, Thomas Mead Chambers	U.S.	469	Farrell, William Patrick	U.S.	1136	
Branch, Mark	U.S.	471	Fenayrou, Marin	Fr.	1147	
Bras Coup	U.S.	474	Fentress, Albert	U.S.	1149	
Breeds, John	Brit.	483	Fife, Henry	U.S.	1157	
Brinsden, Matthias	Brit.	491	Filipovitz, Peter	Aust.	2994	
Broadingham, Elizabeth	Brit.	494	Flack, William	Brit.	1174	
Buckfield, Reginald Sidney	Brit.	531	Flinn, Charles J.	U.S.	1179	
Bunyon, Sidney	Brit.	542	Flowery Land Mutiny	Brit.	1182	
Burgess, Richard	N.Zea.	544	Folkes, Robert E. Lee	U.S.	1191	
Bush, John Earl	U.S.	660	Foote, Henry Leander	U.S.	1193	
Byron, Emma	Brit.	566	Ford, James	U.S.	1195	
Cabellero, Juan	U.S.	2638	Fortis, Edmund	U.S.	1200	
Caddell, Dr. George	Brit.	568	Fortner, Clifford	U.S.	1200	
Caligula	Rome	580	Fowler, Henry	Brit.	2186	
Calla, Salvatore	U.S.	1751	Franceschini, Count Guido	Italy	1208	
Calverley, Walter	Brit.	585	Fullam, Augusta Fairfield	India	1240	
Campbell, Kevin	U.S.	1515	Fyler, Alfred	U.S.	1243	
Campbell, Peter	Scot.	593	Garcia, Joseph	Brit.	1266	
Campi, Michel	Fr.	594	Garlick, Edward Donald	Brit.	1275	
Cantero, Jonathan Eric	U.S.	601	Gecht, Robin	U.S.	1288	
Caritativo, Bart	U.S.	624	Gidley, George	Brit.	2051	
Carraher, Patrick	Scot.	636	Glabe, Karen	U.S.	1320	
Casey, John Edward	Brit.	650	Goluneff, Paul	Bul.	1336	
Cashiere, Catherine	U.S.	650	Goode, Washington	U.S.	1339	
Chalcraft, J.	Brit.	670	Goodmacher, Marks	Brit.	1340	
Chapin, Kenneth R.	U.S.	681	Goozee, Albert	Brit.	1341	
Chennell, George Jr.	Brit.	670	Gordon, Clara	U.S.	1343	
Childers, Jimmy	U.S.	699	Graham, Oaland	U.S.	1361	
Choi, David Puilum	U.S.	701	Greenacre, James	Brit.	1375	
Christensen, William Dean	U.S.	702	Gregory, James	Brit.	2682	
Clark, Dewey	U.S.	721	Greil, Hans	Ger.	1586	
Clarke, Matthew	Brit.	725	Grimm, Baltazard	Fr.	1390	
Clifton, Alice	U.S.	732	Gurga, Jeffrey	U.S.	1406	
Clough, Joel	U.S.	733	Haight, Edward	U.S.	1418	
Cole, Mary	U.S.	743	Halbert, Henry	U.S.	1420	
Columbo, Patricia	U.S.	760	Hall, Andreas	U.S.	1420	
Cook, Charles	U.S.	769	Hallman, Larry	U.S.	1428	
Cooney, Terence George	Brit.	775	Hambleton, John	Brit.	1433	
Cooper, Paula	U.S.	777	Hammond, Karl	U.S.	1439	
Cossentino, Armando	U.S.	793	Hannah, John	Brit.	1442	
Costley, Cann	U.S.	797	Hays, Henry Francis	U.S.	1498	
Courvoisier, Francois Benjamin	Brit.	800	Hayward, George Frederick Walt	Brit.	1499	
Cox, Frederick William	S.Afri.	802	Heirens, William George	U.S.	1508	
Croft, Curtis	U.S.	1515	Henderson, Demetrius	U.S.	1515	
Crowninshield, George	U.S.	839	Henson, Tom	U.S.	1521	

Roche, John Francis	U.S.	2604	Trotter, Clarence	U.S.	2994
Roche, Phillip	Brit.	2604	Truber, Manfred	Aust.	2994
Rogers, Dayton Leroy	U.S.	2608	Tucker, Charles Louis	U.S.	2998
Ross, Charles Ray	U.S.	2623	Tucker, Felix	U.S.	2999
Rowlands, Edward	Brit.	1025	Vacher, Joseph	Fr.	3023
Rowlands, John	Brit.	1025	van de Corput, Piet	U.S.	3029
Roy, Gilder	Scot.	2632	Verger, Jean-Louis	Fr.	3042
Ruiz, Luis	U.S.	2638	Vicars, John	Brit.	3045
Samples, Duane	U.S.	2674	Vitalis, Leon	Fr.	3057
Sangret, August	Brit.	2677	Vollman, John Jacob	Can.	3061
Sapwell, William	Brit.	2679	Wallner, Walter	Aust.	2994
Savage, Richard	Brit.	2682	Walter, Clarence	U.S.	3085
Scales, James I.	U.S.	2686	Ward, Charles William, Jr.	Brit.	3090
Schmidt, Hans	U.S.	2694	Ward, John	U.S.	3091
Schumacher, Petra	Ger.	2831	Watts, Coral Eugene	U.S.	3104
Secchi, Dr. Carl	Italy	430	Waye, Alton	U.S.	3106
Selhurst, John	Brit.	2725	Weinger, Mitchell	U.S.	3119
Seymour, Brian	Scot.	2730	Whitman, Charles Joseph	U.S.	3143
Seymour, Golney	U.S.	2730	Whitty, Dennis	Brit.	2417
Shafer, Russell F.	U.S.	2733	Wienchowski, Joseph	U.S.	3148
Sheward, William	Brit.	2745	Williams, Arnold Jason	U.S.	3160
Shoaf, Mamie Shey	U.S.	2747	Williams, Edward	Aus.	3161
Shobek, Michael	Bahamas	2747	Williams, John	Brit.	3162
Simmons, Theodore	U.S.	2764	Wilson, Eddie	U.S.	1428
Simpson, Willie Joe	U.S.	2767	Wilson, John Gleeson	Brit.	3174
Slade, Joshua	Brit.	2776	Wilson, John Wayne	U.S.	3174
Smith, Andrew M'Laghlin	Brit.	2781	Winstanley, Elijah	Brit.	3177
Smith, Arthur John	Brit.	2781	Withers, Jack	Brit.	3179
Smith, Mark	U.S.	2800	Woodard, Alonzo	U.S.	1515
Smith, Matthew	Brit.	2801	Woodward, Raymond L. Jr.	U.S.	3185
Smith, Perry	U.S.	1534	Woolridge, Charles Thomas	Brit.	3186
Smith, Thomas	U.S.	2802	Yarham, Samuel	Brit.	3205
Snook, James Howard	U.S.	2805	Zekerman, Andrew	Brit.	2051
Snyder, Donald	U.S.	2805	Zodiac Killer	U.S.	3221
Soderburg, Erland H.	U.S.	2811	Zon, Hans von	Neth.	3222
Soli, Salvatore	U.S.	2813	**Weapon: Bayonet**		
Splett, Norbert	Ger.	2831	Carroll, Patrick	Brit.	642
Spreitzer, Edward	U.S.	1288	Hermione Boys, The	Brit.	1523
Springer, James	U.S.	2833	Phillips, Mason	U.S.	2459
St. Quintin, Richard	Brit.	2051	Toohey, Martin	U.S.	2968
Stack, Richard	U.S.	2835	**Weapon: Can opener**		
Stano, Gerald Eugene	U.S.	2839	Cummins, Gordon Frederick	Brit.	845
Starkweather, Albert L.	U.S.	2840	**Weapon: Carving fork**		
Stephens, Edwin	Brit.	1032	Perry, Henry	Brit.	2446
Stevens, Dallas Ray	U.S.	2851	**Weapon: Chisel**		
Stevens, James	Brit.	2851	Kubal, Lawrence	U.S.	1853
Stewart, Dr. Glen Gold	Can.	2852	Leopold, Nathan F., Jr.	U.S.	1932
Stllgens, Robert Wilhelm	Ger.	2873	Loeb, Richard A.	U.S.	1932
Stourton, Lord Charles	Brit.	2865	**Weapon: Cleaver**		
Sutcliffe, Peter William	Brit.	2879	Ashcroft, David	Brit.	170
Tapner, Benjamin	Brit.	2897	Ashcroft, James	Brit.	170
Telles, Felix	Arg.	2912	Gunness, Belle	U.S.	1400
Terrell, William	U.S.	2916	Holden, William	Brit.	170
Tessnov, Ludwig	Ger.	2917	**Weapon: Crock shard**		
Testro, Angelina	U.S.	2918	Kawananakoa, David Kalakaua	U.S.	1770
Thiri Thu Dhamma	Arakan	2929	**Weapon: Duckpin**		
Thistlewood, Arthur	Brit.	2929	Watson, Clarence Edward, Jr.	U.S.	3102
Thomas, Henry	U.S.	2930	**Weapon: Harpoon**		
Thomas, Leonard Jack	Brit.	2931	Jones, Thomas	U.S.	1741
Thompson, Edith Jessie	Brit.	2933	**Weapon: Hook**		
Thompson, Tilmer Eugene	U.S.	2935	York, William	Brit.	3207
Thorn, Martin George	U.S.	2937	**Weapon: Ice pick**		
Thorne, Thomas Harold	Brit.	2939	Murder, Inc.	U.S.	2252
Thurtell, John	Brit.	2949	**Weapon: Iron last**		
Toole, Ottis Elwood	U.S.	2001	Giordano, Gregorio	U.S.	1315
Totterman, Emil	U.S.	2975	**Weapon: Ivory comb**		
Townsend, Pink Earl	U.S.	1822	Gardelle, Theodore	Brit.	1267
Tremamunno, Donato	Italy	2985	**Weapon: Knife**		
Trent, Lindbergh	U.S.	2985	Beach, Lewis U.	U.S.	286
Tripp, Grace	Brit.	2989	Beadle, William	U.S.	286

Ovet, Jack	Brit.	2388	
Paleotti, Marquis de Ferdinand	Brit.	2396	
de Praslin, Duke	Fr.	917	

MURDER BY STABBING - Case of General

Achew, James	Brit.	18
Atter, Leonard Vincent	Brit.	179
Beiliss, Mendel	Rus.	315
Cain, John	Brit.	576
Cero, Gangi	U.S.	664
Chamberlain, Alice Lynne	Aus.	671
Church, Richard J.	U.S.	712
Crews, Paul David	U.S.	818
Cunningham, Emma Augusta	U.S.	846
Day, James	U.S.	888
De Graff, William	U.S.	902
Doyle, James	Brit.	1017
Frank, J.H.W.	U.S.	1217
Freeman, William	U.S.	1232
Gardiner, William	Brit.	1268
Green, Cleo Joel, III	U.S.	1372
Griffin, Henry	Brit.	1386
Griffith, Stiles H.	U.S.	1387
Griffith, William	U.S.	1387
Haskell, Flora Fanny	Brit.	1474
Hayden, Herbert H.	U.S.	1493
Hennis, Timothy Baily	U.S.	1517
Howard, Cornelius	Brit.	1627
Hurd, Roosevelt Carlos, Sr.	U.S.	1645
Hussmann, Karl	Ger.	1647
Jacobi, Frank C., Jr.	U.S.	1692
Johnson, Thomas	U.S.	1733
Kirwan, Andrew Donaldson	U.S.	1830
Levick, Alice	Brit.	1944
Malone, Cavan John	Brit.	2098
Mariani, Paul	Fr.	2121
Mossler, Candace Grace Weather	U.S.	2233
Murdaugh, John	U.S.	3158
Nimer, Melvin Dean	U.S.	2337
Parks, Kenneth	Can.	2413
Parr, Edward	U.S.	2415
Payne, Alfred Augustus	Brit.	2429
Powers, Melvin Lane	U.S.	2233
Rayne, Richard	Brit.	576
Reilly, Peter		2560
Savino, James	U.S.	2684
Shaddy, Gregory	U.S.	2732
Smith, Henry Sydney	Brit.	2794
Smith, Michael		2801
Sykes, Troisville	U.S.	2888
Talbot, Julie	U.S.	2895
Wilkinson, Dr. Benjamin R.	U.S.	3158
Wilkinson, Edward C.	U.S.	3158
Williams, Joseph	Brit.	3163
Wood, Robert William T. Cavers	Brit.	3183

Weapon: Ice pick

Little, Joan	U.S.	

Weapon: Knife

Baretti, Joseph	Brit.	234
Freeman, Charles F.	U.S.	1231
Hessberger, George L.	U.S.	1527
Shepherd, Charles	U.S.	2739
Thay, Emily	Brit.	3206
Toole, Gerald	U.S.	2968
Yellow, Marjorie	Brit.	3206

Weapon: Pins

Bosworth, Mary	Brit.	2855
Male, Mary	Brit.	2855
Stimson, Ann	Brit.	2855

Weapon: Pitchfork

Wilson, John	U.S.	3173

Weapon: Razor

Barberi, Maria	U.S.	231
Boyle, Victor James	Brit.	462
Tirrell, Albert John	U.S.	2958

Weapon: Sword

Mohun, Charles	Brit.	2197

MURDER BY STABBING - Unsolved

Ax Man of New Orleans	U.S.	192
Bailes, Marie Ellen	Brit.	207
Banning, C. Michael	U.S.	228
Black Dahlia, The	U.S.	388
Black Doodler, The	U.S.	391
Bow Kum	U.S.	458
Bright, James	Brit.	488
Cameron, John	Scot.	589
Castillo, Dr. Richard	Brit.	655
Charlie Chopoff Slayings	U.S.	688
Clarke, George	Brit.	725
Cockrane, Kilso	Brit.	737
Coles, Frances	Brit.	745
Davis, Eliza	Brit.	883
Dawkins, Iris	Brit.	887
Delacourt, Rose	Fr.	905
de Masel, Madame	Fr.	911
Freedman, Helen	Brit.	1230
Gaca, Barbara	U.S.	1246
Giri, Laxman	India	1317
Godfrey, Edmund Berry	Brit.	1324
Grimwood, Eliza	Brit.	1391
Hall-Mills Case	U.S.	1428
Harley Street Mystery	Brit.	1454
Hauser, Kasper	Ger.	1491
Hogg, Mary Anne	Brit.	1588
Kanthack, Irene Francis	S.Afri.	1759
Kenosha, Wis., Killings	U.S.	1804
Long, John	Brit.	1986
Loo Sing	U.S.	1989
Lubienska, Teresa	Brit.	2000
Lurye, Willie	U.S.	2012
Marlowe, Christopher	Brit.	2126
Mills, Eleanor Reinhardt	U.S.	1428
Mogano, Penelope	Brit.	2196
Monster of Florence	Italy	2202
Morosov, Fedor	U.S.S.R.	2224
Morosov, Pavel	U.S.S.R.	2224
Murray, Charlie	U.S.	2260
Nicholson, John	U.S.	2334
Old Shakespeare Case	U.S.	2368
Piernicke, Dora	Brit.	2464
Prince Georges Cty., Md., Slay	U.S.	2502
Ruthven, Alexander	Scot.	2644
Ruthven, John	Scot.	2644
Ryan, Mary	U.S.	2647
Ryan, Nicholas	U.S.	2647
Savoy Hotel Murder	Brit.	2684
Sellis, Joseph	Brit.	2726
Sirikul, Taweeyos	U.S.	2771
Storrs, George Henry	Brit.	2864
Texarkana (Texas) Slayings	U.S.	2919
Thomas, Roma	Aus.	2931
Toolan, Sean	U.S.	2968
Welsh, Leila	U.S.	3126
Zwani, Fikizolo	Swaziland	3223

Weapon: Bottle

Carey, Estelle Evelyn	U.S.	622

Weapon: Metal tool

Chalinder, Jean	Brit.	670

Weapon: Stiletto

Fennick, Rachel	Brit.	1148

MURDER BY STABBING - Wrongly Convicted
General

Fowler, Walter	U.S.	2511
Merritt, George	U.S.	2169
Pellizioni, Serafino	Brit.	2438
Pugh, Earl Heywood	U.S.	2251
Shaw, William	Scot.	2737

Weapon: Cleaver

McLachlan, Jessie	Scot.	2054

MURDER BY STARVATION

Ebner, Esther		
Gonzalez Valenzuela, Delfina	Mex.	1338
Ubaldini, Ruggiero	Italy	3014

MURDER BY STRANGULATION
General

Abbandando, Frank	U.S.	1
Allen, John Edward	Brit.	96
Almodovar, Anibal	U.S.	103
Anderson, Percy Charles	Brit.	124
Anthony, James	U.S.	133
Avril, Robert	Fr.	191
Axilrod, Dr. Arnold Asher	U.S.	192
Baldonado, Augustine	U.S.	1035
Barrett, Thomas	U.S.	249
Bassot, Henri	Fr.	1317
Beard, Arthur	Brit.	290
Beck, Dieter	Ger.	295
Beck, Martha Julie	U.S.	296
Belvin, Paul Augustus	Ber.	322
Berger, Theodor	Ger.	342
Berry, Saul	U.S.	1820
Bianchi, Kenneth	U.S.	356
Boden, Wayne Clifford	Can.	415
Bolton, David	Brit.	425
Bolton, John	Brit.	425
Bompard, Gabrielle	Fr.	1121
Borgia Family	Italy	441
Boyd, Thomas	U.S.	2185
Brewer, Morris Sutton Ramsden	Aus.	485
Brookins, Louis Dwight	U.S.	497
Brumit, Lucille	U.S.	1544
Bundy, Theodore	U.S.	537
Buono, Angelo, Jr.	U.S.	356
Burger, Albert	Fr.	543
Burke, William	Scot.	547
Camb, James	Brit.	587
Carr, Thomas D.	U.S.	636
Carter, Theodore H.	U.S.	646
Carter, William	Brit.	2897
Cato	U.S.	657
Catoe, Jarvis Theodore Rooseve	U.S.	657
Chou En-lai	China	702
Christie, John Reginald Hallid	Brit.	705
Christofi, Styllou	Brit.	709
Church, Harvey	U.S.	712
Clark, Joseph Reginald Victor	Brit.	723
Clarke, Philmore	U.S.	726
Clarke, Victor	Brit.	726
Clment, Charles	Fr.	729
Cobby, John	Brit.	2897
Cochran, Willie Grady	U.S.	735
Coddington, Herbert James	U.S.	738
Cohen, Raymond	Brit.	425
Coleman, Alton	U.S.	743
Conroy, Thomas	U.S.	767
Coombes, Robert L.	U.S.	774
Cooney, Edward J., Jr.	U.S.	775
Cooper, Ray Anthony	U.S.	778
Cooper, Ronald Frank	S.Afri.	778
Corey, Frank	U.S.	784
Cox, Chastine	U.S.	802
Cox, John	Brit.	803
Cunningham, Charles	U.S.	846
Cusamano, Santos	U.S.	2123
Cvek, George	U.S.	851
Davenport, Barnett	U.S.	880
Davis, Bruce A.	U.S.	882
Davis, Gregory	U.S.	883
Davis, Larry Ronald	U.S.	885
Del Petrarca, Robert	U.S.	910
Delaitre, Pierre-Joel	Brit.	905
Dobkin, Harry	Brit.	981
Donald, Jeannie Ewen	Scot.	998
Drachman, Louis	Fr.	1018
Dumollard, Martin	Fr.	1034
Durrant, William Henry Theodor	U.S.	1041
Eberhardt, Susan	U.S.	2821
Edwards, Mack Ray	U.S.	1073
Edwards, Vernon David, Jr.	U.S.	1074
Edwardson, Derrick	Brit.	1074
Ellis, Michael	Brit.	425
Emery, Ronald	U.S.	1091
Evans, Franklin B.	U.S.	1112
Eyraud, Michel	Fr.	1121
Farrell, William Patrick	U.S.	1136
Field, Frederick Herbert Charl	Brit.	1154
Fiorenza, John	U.S.	1161
Fish, Hamilton Albert Howard	U.S.	1162
Flanagan, Sean Patrick	U.S.	1175
Flinn, Charles J.	U.S.	1179
Flittner, Anton	Ger.	1180
Fortner, Clifford	U.S.	1200
Fowler, George E.	Brit.	1205
Fox, Sidney Harry	Brit.	1206
Franklin, William	U.S.	1226
Freeman, Jeannace	U.S.	1231
Freeway Phantom Murders	U.S.	1233
Front de Liberation du Quebec	Can.	1238
Garnier, Gilles	Fr.	1275
Garrow, Robert	U.S.	1280
Gebbia, Leonardo	U.S.	1287
Gecht, Robin	U.S.	1288
Gelardi, Agostino	U.S.	1290
Getter, Charles	U.S.	1303
Gibbs, Edward Lester	U.S.	1307
Gilman, Ephraim	U.S.	1314
Giriat, Victorine	Fr.	1317
Goode, Arthur Frederick, III	U.S.	1339
Goodere, Samuel	Brit.	1339
Goulter, Sidney Bernard	Brit.	1352
Gourbin, Emile	Fr.	1353
Graham, Harrison	U.S.	1356
Gray, Henry Judd	U.S.	2810
Greenberg, Bertram	U.S.	1376
Haerm, Teet	Swed.	1414
Haga, Eric L.	U.S.	1414
Hammond, John	Brit.	2897
Hampton, Melvin	U.S.	1440
Hanlon, John	U.S.	1442
Hannah, John	Brit.	1442
Hare, William	Scot.	547
Harris, Ann	Brit.	1459
Hay, Gordon	Scot.	1493
Heideman, Frank	U.S.	1507
Hepper, William Sanchez de Pin	Brit.	1522

Soleilland, Albert	Fr.	2812		DeSalvo, Albert Henry	U.S.	921
Spann, Enoch F.	U.S.	2821		Gary, Carlton	U.S.	1282
Speck, Richard Franklin	U.S.	2822		Grabowski, Klaus	Ger.	1355
Spencer, Timothy Wilson	U.S.	2826		**Weapon: Rope**		
Spreitzer, Edward	U.S.	1288		Bowe, Alice Atte	Brit.	456
St. James, George L.	U.S.	2927		Conrad, Fritz	Ger.	766
Stansfield, Philip	Scot.	2840		Diblanc, Marguerite	Brit.	938
Starkweather, Charles	U.S.	2840		Dunbar, Reuben A.	U.S.	1035
Stevens, Dallas Ray	U.S.	2851		Dyer, Albert	U.S.	1050
Stone, Elton M.	U.S.	2858		Gerson, Robert	U.S.	1302
Stone, Scott C.	U.S.	2860		Glatman, Harvey Murray	U.S.	1321
Stout, Arthur	U.S.	2398		Holle, Edward	U.S.	1592
Straffen, John Thomas	Brit.	2866		Housden, Nina	U.S.	1626
Sutcliffe, Peter William	Brit.	2879				
Tapner, Benjamin	Brit.	2897		**MUTILATION**		
Teasdale, William	Brit.	2912		Trapia, Francisco	U.S.	2983
Texas Strangler	U.S.	2921				
Theodahad	Tuscany	2926		**MUTINY**		
Therrien, Joseph W.	U.S.	2927		Adams, John	Brit.	26
Thomas, Allgen Lars	Swed.	1414		Bakht Khan	India	217
Thomas, Edward	U.S.	2930		Burgos, Jose	Phil.	544
Tiberius	Roman.	2950		Curtis, Winslow	U.S.	3138
Tillman, Emil	Ger.	2955		Gidley, George	Brit.	2051
Toole, Ottis Elwood	U.S.	2001		Jones, Thomas	U.S.	1741
Trbert, Guy	Fr.	2985		M'Kinlie, Peter	Brit.	2051
Tremamunno, Donato	Italy	2985		Mare Island Mutiny Case	U.S.	2119
Trevor, Harold Darien	Brit.	2988		Monsson, Otto	Brit.	2544
Truscott, Steven Murray	Can.	2998		Parker, Richard	Brit.	2412
Turley, Preston	U.S.	3003		Plowden, Sir Edmund	U.S.	2476
Vacher, Joseph	Fr.	3023		Rau, Gustav	Brit.	2544
van Jaarsveld, Jacobus Frederi	S.Afri.	1903		St. Quintin, Richard	Brit.	2051
Verzeni, Vincent	Italy			Schmidt, Willem	Brit.	2544
Walls, Samuel Cornelius	U.S.	3083		Veronica Mutineers	Brit.	3042
Walter, Albert, Jr.	U.S.	3084		White, John Duncan	U.S.	3138
Watts, Coral Eugene	U.S.	3104		Zekerman, Andrew	Brit.	2051
Weber, Jeanne	Fr.	3108				
Webster, Robert	U.S.	3111		**NAZI HUNTER**		
Weidmann, Eugen	Fr.	3113		Wiesenthal, Simon	Ger.	3148
Wheeler, George	U.S.	3132				
Whelpton, George	Brit.	3135		**NECROMANCY**		
White, Charles	Brit.	1339		Bolingbroke, Roger	Brit.	424
Wierzbiki, Edward F.	U.S.	3148				
Williams, Ada Chard	Brit.	3159		**NECROPHILIA**		
Wilson, John Wayne	U.S.	3174		Blot, Henri	Fr.	411
Wilson, Otto Stephen	U.S.	3175		Bundy, Carol	U.S.	722
Wolter, Albert W.	U.S.	3181		Byrne, Patrick Joseph	Brit.	565
York, George Ronald	U.S.	1902		Clarence, Duke George	Brit.	721
Young, Earl	U.S.	3208		Clark, Douglas Daniel	U.S.	722
Youngman, William Godfrey	Brit.	3214		Dyer, Albert	U.S.	1050
Yukl, Charles	U.S.	3214		Hofmann, Kuno	Ger.	1587
Znidar, Thomas F.	U.S.	3221		Honka, Fritz	Ger.	1607
Zowkowski, John	U.S.	3223		Kemper, Edmund Emil III	U.S.	1791
Weapon: Belt				Kroll, Joachim	Ger.	1852
Gordon, Harry W.	U.S.	1343		LaPage, Joseph	U.S.	1896
Weapon: Bootlace				Ldke, Bruno	Ger.	2007
Bennett, Herbert John	Brit.	331		Little, Dwain Lee	U.S.	1971
Weapon: Cord				Sullivan, Howard	U.S.	2875
D'Iorio, Ernest	U.S.	976		Young, Robert	U.S.	3211
DeSalvo, Albert Henry	U.S.	921		Yukl, Charles	U.S.	3214
Weapon: Cloth/handkerchief						
Bevan, Catherine	U.S.	355		**NEGLIGENT HOMICIDE**		
Donovan, Conrad	Brit.	1001		Coombe, Michael	U.S.	774
Harrison, Henry	Brit.	1465				
Wade, Charles	Brit.	1001		**NOVELS**		
Weapon: Hands				*About the Murder of the Clergy*		11
Gordon, Harry W.	U.S.	1343		*After House, The*		37
Irwin, Robert	U.S.	1666		*After the Fact*		37
Weapon: Hanger				*Airing in a Closed Carriage*		43
Mattox, Jon	U.S.	2150		*All This and Heaven Too*		102
Weapon: Nylons				*All the King's Men*		102

NOVELLAS

Double Indemnity	1008
Homecoming	1606

OBSCENITY

Besant, Annie	Brit.	353
Bradlaugh, Charles	Brit.	353
Dial-A-Porn Case	U.S.	934
Flynt, Larry C.	U.S.	1189
Kelly, Peter	Brit.	1789
Smith, Jerry Lee	U.S.	2795

OBSCENITY - Case of

Broughton, William	U.S.	503
Knowlton, Charles	U.S.	1838

OBSCENITY - Wrongly Convicted

Krueger, Oscar	U.S.	1852

ORATORS

Afer, Domitius	Rome	36
Antonius, Marcus	Rome	134

ORGANIZED CRIME
General

Aguayo, Robert	U.S.	40
Alex, Gus	U.S.	73
Apalachin Conference	U.S.	136
Atlantic City Conference	U.S.	176

Beasley, Milton	U.S.	292
Blémant, Robert	Fr.	408
Bontade, Giovanni	Si.	434
Buccieri, Frank	U.S.	525
Burke, Fred	U.S.	546
Buscetta, Tommasso	U.S.	559
Caifano, Marshall Joseph	U.S.	575
Castellano, Paul	U.S.	655
Cesario, Sam	U.S.	665
Coppola, Michael	U.S.	779
Cosa Nostra	U.S.	793
Costello, Frank	U.S.	794
Daddano, William, Sr.	U.S.	854
D'Andrea, Nicholas J.	U.S.	866
Dellacroce, Aniello	U.S.	908
DiSimone, Frank	U.S.	978
Duke's Restaurant	U.S.	1034
Eastman, Edward	U.S.	1063
Enright, Maurice	U.S.	1098
Exner, Judith Campbell	U.S.	1119
Five Points Gang	U.S.	1174
Flynt, Larry C.	U.S.	1189
Franse, Steven	U.S.	1226
Frantizius, Peter von	U.S.	1227
Galante, Carmine	U.S.	1250
Genovese, Michael	U.S.	1294
Gigante, Vincent	U.S.	1311
Glick, Allen	U.S.	1322
Havana Conference	Cuba	1491
Kefauver Hearings	U.S.	1774
Kimura Tokutaro	Japan	1820
Kishi Nobusuke	Japan	1831
Kynette, Earle E.	U.S.	2736
Magliocco, Joseph	U.S.	2087
Mangano, Vincent	U.S.	2102
Mansueto, Simone	Si.	2112
Moran, Dr. Joseph Patrick	U.S.	2215
Morello, Peter	U.S.	2217
Nakasone Yasuhiro	Japan	2276
O'Dwyer, William	U.S.	2362
Orlando, Leoluca	Italy	2378
Ottumvo, Vincenzo	U.S.	2386
Pagano, Joseph Luco	U.S.	2392
Pillow Gang	U.S.	2466
Presser, Jackie	U.S.	2497
Russo, Giuseppe Genco	Si.	2643
Sasakawa Ryoichi	Japan	2681
Scarlisi, Sam Anthony	U.S.	2688
Scarne, John	U.S.	2689
Shirt Tails	U.S.	2747
Spirito, François	Fr.	2831
Sportsmen's Hall	U.S.	2832
Stacher, Joseph	U.S.	2834
Testa, Salvatore	U.S.	2918
Trafficante, Santo, Jr.	U.S.	2983
Trupiano, Matthew M., Jr.	U.S.	2995
Valachi, Joseph Michael	U.S.	3024
Zelig, Jack	U.S.	3218
Zito, Frank	U.S.	3221

Activity: Arson

Cascioferro, Vito	Int'l.	648
Cullotto, Frank	U.S.	844
Kierdorf, Frank	U.S.	1815
Lombardo, Joseph	U.S.	1980

Activity: Assassination

Kodama Yoshio	Japan	1840
Marcello, Carlos	U.S.	2117

Acitivty: Assault

Accardi, Settimo	U.S.	14

Aiuppa, Joseph	U.S.	44
Alderisio, Felix Anthony	U.S.	71
Boyd, Murray Allen	U.S.	461
Capone, Frank	U.S.	617
Comer, Jack	Brit.	761
Diamond, Jack	U.S.	934
Forty-Two Gang	U.S.	1201
Gophers	U.S.	1341
Hell's Kitchen Gang	U.S.	1513
Honeymoon Gang	U.S.	1607
Hounds	U.S.	1625
Kelly, Paul	U.S.	1788
Kerryonians	U.S.	1805
Kray, Reginald	Brit.	1847
Kray, Ronald	Brit.	1847
Labor War	U.S.	1867
Lansky, Meyer	U.S.	1892
Larocca, John Sebastian	U.S.	1898
Machii Hisayuki	Japan	2045
Madden, Owen	U.S.	2072
Maranzano, Salvatore	U.S.	2114
Market Street Gang	U.S.	2124
Miranda, Michele	U.S.	2189
Moran, George	U.S.	2213
Morton, Samuel J.	U.S.	2229
Mose, The Bowery Boy	U.S.	2232
Murphy, Timothy D.	U.S.	2259
Nineteenth Street Gang	U.S.	2338
O'Bannion, Charles Dion	U.S.	2350
O'Donnell Bros. (Chicago, Sout	U.S.	2361
Orgen, Jacob	U.S.	2377
Pisciotta, Gaspare	Si.	2470
Plant, Roger	U.S.	2474
Plug Uglies	U.S.	2476
Pranno, Rocco Salvatore	U.S.	2496
Prio, Ross	U.S.	2503
Ragen's Colts	U.S.	2529
Rastelli, Philip	U.S.	2542
Reles, Abraham	U.S.	2563
Roach Guards	U.S.	2588
Schivarelli, Peter	U.S.	2692
Telvi, Abraham	U.S.	2913

Activity: Blackmail

Galiffi, Agata	Arg.	1252
Gioe, Charles	U.S.	1315
Hell's Angels	U.S.	1512

Activity: Bombing

Alderisio, Felix Anthony	U.S.	71
Amatuna, Samuel Samuzzo	U.S.	109
Pineapple Primary	U.S.	2466
Pranno, Rocco Salvatore	U.S.	2496
Prio, Ross	U.S.	2503

Activity: Bootlegging

Adonis, Joseph	U.S.	32
Alderisio, Felix Anthony	U.S.	71
Amatuna, Samuel Samuzzo	U.S.	109
Amberg, Joseph C.	U.S.	110
Amberg, Louis	U.S.	110
Anastasia, Albert	U.S.	117
Barbara, Joseph M., Sr.	U.S.	229
Boiardo, Ruggiero	U.S.	421
Bonanno, Joseph	U.S.	427
Capone, Alphonse	U.S.	603
Carfano, Anthony	U.S.	623
Carolla, Sylvestro	U.S.	634
Circus Gang	U.S.	716
Coll, Vincent	U.S.	746
Costello, Frank	U.S.	794
Cuckoos Gang	U.S.	843
Dalitz, Morris Barney	U.S.	857

Diamond, Jack	U.S.	934
Drucci, Vincent	U.S.	1026
Druggan-Lake Gang	U.S.	1027
Eastman, Edward	U.S.	1063
Egan's Rats	U.S.	1074
Entratta, Charles	U.S.	1099
Esposito, Joseph	U.S.	1105
Fay, Larry	U.S.	1140
Fusco, Joseph Charles	U.S.	1243
Genna Brothers	U.S.	1291
Genovese, Vito	Int'l.	1295
Giancana, Sam	U.S.	1305
Gordon, Waxey	U.S.	1346
Guifoyle Gang	U.S.	1397
Higgins, Vannie	U.S.	1546
Hoff, Max	U.S.	1584
Hoffa, James Riddle	U.S.	1584
Lazia, John	U.S.	1909
Licavoli, Peter Joseph, Sr.	U.S.	1949
Licavoli, Thomas	U.S.	1949
Lombardo, Antonio	U.S.	1979
Luciano, Charles	Int'l.	2002
Madden, Owen	U.S.	2072
Magaddino, Stefano	U.S.	2086
Maranzano, Salvatore	U.S.	2114
Masseria, Joseph	U.S.	2137
McErlane, Frank	U.S.	2037
Miller, Vernon C.	U.S.	2182
Moran, George	U.S.	2213
Morton, Samuel J.	U.S.	2229
Nitti, Frank	U.S.	2339
O'Bannion, Charles Dion	U.S.	2350
O'Donnell Bros. (Chicago, South)	U.S.	2361
O'Donnell Bros. (Chicago, West)	U.S.	2361
Patriarca, Raymond L.S.	U.S.	2419
Pinelli, Anthony R., Sr.	U.S.	2467
Purple Gang	U.S.	2513
Ragen, James M.	U.S.	2529
Rothstein, Arnold	U.S.	2626
Saltis, Joseph	U.S.	2673
Schultz, Dutch	U.S.	2699
Sheldon Gang	U.S.	2739
Shelton Brothers	U.S.	2739
Siegel, Benjamin	U.S.	2753
Solomon, Charles	U.S.	2814
Stacher, Joseph	U.S.	2834
Strollo, Anthony C.	U.S.	2870
Syndicate, The	U.S.	2891
Torrio, John	U.S.	2969
Touhy, Roger	U.S.	2976
Valley Gang	U.S.	3028
Weiss, Earl	U.S.	3119
Weissman, William	U.S.	3121
White Family	U.S.	3139
Wortman, Frank	U.S.	3191
Yale, Frankie	U.S.	3203
Zerilli, Joseph	U.S.	3219
Activity: Bribery		
Adonis, Joseph	U.S.	32
Aiuppa, Joseph	U.S.	44
Alderisio, Felix Anthony	U.S.	71
Alex, Gus	U.S.	73
Civella, Nicholas	U.S.	717
Corallo, Anthony	U.S.	781
Cormack, William H.	U.S.	2736
Cáro Quintero, Rafael	Mex.	634
El Rukn Gang, The	U.S.	1086
Félix Gallardo, Angel Miguel	Mex.	1146
Fong Ching	U.S.	1192
Guzik, Jake	U.S.	1410

Heitler, Michael	U.S.	1511
Hines, James J.	U.S.	1560
Hoffa, James Riddle	U.S.	1584
Kodama Yoshio	Japan	1840
Lombardo, Joseph	U.S.	1980
Matta Ballesteros, Juan Ramón	Mex.	2147
Osano Kenji	Japan	2382
Paris, P. Alvin	U.S.	2409
Rothstein, Arnold	U.S.	2626
Sarkiyev, Ilyas	U.S.S.R.	2680
Scotto, Anthony M.	U.S.	2714
Shaw, Joseph	U.S.	2736
Stacher, Joseph	U.S.	2834
Teamsters Union	U.S.	2906
Valley Gang	U.S.	3028
Weiss, Earl	U.S.	3119
Activity: Burglary		
Alderisio, Felix Anthony	U.S.	71
Brown, Ronald	U.S.	516
Caifano, Marshall Joseph	U.S.	575
Capone, Alphonse	U.S.	603
Diamond, Jack	U.S.	934
Forty Little Thieves	U.S.	1201
Genovese, Vito	Int'l.	1295
Hell's Kitchen Gang	U.S.	1513
La Pietra, James	U.S.	1897
Lenox Avenue Gang	U.S.	1931
Montana, John	U.S.	2203
Montos, Nick George	U.S.	2206
Moran, George	U.S.	2213
O'Bannion, Charles Dion	U.S.	2350
Reles, Abraham	U.S.	2563
Tenth Avenue Gang	U.S.	2914
Torello, James Vincent	U.S.	2969
Valley Gang	U.S.	3028
Weiss, Earl	U.S.	3119
Yellow Henry Gang	U.S.	3206
Activity: Confidence Games Fraud		
Boccia, Ferdinand	U.S.	414
Cain, Richard B.	U.S.	576
Draper, Shang	U.S.	1020
Activity: Conspiracy		
Hines, James J.	U.S.	1560
Tieri, Frank	U.S.	2953
Activity: Corruption		
Kelly, Paul	U.S.	1788
Activity: Credit Card Fraud		
Alderisio, Felix Anthony	U.S.	71
Langella, Gennaro	U.S.	1889
Saietta, Ignazio		2658
Activity: Drugs		
Accardi, Settimo	U.S.	14
Adonis, Joseph	U.S.	32
Agueci, Albert	Can.	40
Agueci, Albert	U.S.	40
Agueci, Vito	U.S.	40
Agueci, Vito	Can.	40
Alderisio, Felix Anthony	U.S.	71
Alo, Vincent	U.S.	103
Amberg, Joseph C.	U.S.	110
Amberg, Louis	U.S.	110
Amuso, Victor	U.S.	116
Anastasia, Albert	U.S.	117
Araujo, Jaime	U.S.	143
Attardi, Alphonse	U.S.	179
Aunay, Pierre	Fr.	184
Badalamenti, Gaetano	Si.	206
Barba Hernández, Javier	Mex.	229
Barnes, Leroy	U.S.	245
Beasley, Milton	U.S.	292

Amberg, Joseph C.	U.S.	110		Milano, Carmen	U.S.	2178
Amberg, Louis	U.S.	110		Milano, Peter John	U.S.	2178
Anastasia, Albert	U.S.	117		Moretti, Willie	U.S.	2217
Anastasio, Anthony	U.S.	120		Nitti, Frank	U.S.	2339
Badalamenti, Gaetano	Si.	206		Ogawa Kaoru	Japan	2364
Balistrieri, Frank P.	U.S.	219		Osano Kenji	Japan	2382
Battaglia, Samuel	U.S.	283		Palermo, Nick	U.S.	2396
Belcastro, James	U.S.	316		Persico, Carmine	U.S.	2448
Bioff, William Morris	U.S.	371		Pranno, Rocco Salvatore	U.S.	2496
Borgio, Rosario	U.S.	442		Prio, Ross	U.S.	2503
Buchalter, Louis	U.S.	525		Profaci, Joseph	U.S.	2505
Bufalino, Russell	U.S.	533		Provenzano, Anthony	U.S.	2508
Caifano, Marshall Joseph	U.S.	575		Purple Gang	U.S.	2513
Cammisano, William	U.S.	589		Ragen, James M.	U.S.	2529
Campagna, Louis	U.S.	591		Rastelli, Philip	U.S.	2542
Capone, Alphonse	U.S.	603		Ricca, Paul	U.S.	2573
Carbo, Frankie	U.S.	620		Roselli, John	U.S.	2620
Cardinelli Gang	U.S.	621		Royal Family, The	U.S.	2633
Carolla, Sylvestro	U.S.	634		Salerno, Anthony	U.S.	2670
Carrollo, Charles	U.S.	642		Sarkiyev, Ilyas	U.S.S.R.	2680
Cascioferro, Vito	Int'l.	648		Scarfo, Nicodemo	U.S.	2688
D'Andrea, Philip	U.S.	866		Shapiro, Jacob	U.S.	2734
DeCarlo, Angelo	U.S.	896		Sica, Joseph	U.S.	2751
Decavalcante, Samuel Rizzo	U.S.	898		Siegel, Benjamin	U.S.	2753
DiNapoli, Vincent	U.S.	975		Solano, Vincent	U.S.	2812
Di Cristina, Paul	Int'l.	941		Squillante, James	U.S.	2834
Dio, Johnny	U.S.	976		Taoka Kazuo	Japan	2897
Dragna, Jack	U.S.	1018		Teamsters Union	U.S.	2906
Dragna, Louis Tom	U.S.	1018		Toyama Mitsuru	Japan	2980
Eastman, Edward	U.S.	1063		Twentieth Century Sporting Club	U.S.	3009
Eisen, Maxie	U.S.	1079		Unione Siciliane	U.S.	3015
El Rukn Gang, The	U.S.	1086		White Hand Gang	U.S.	3140
English, Charles Carmen	U.S.	1097		Whyos, The	U.S.	3147
Esposito, Giuseppe	Int'l.	1105		Yale, Frankie	U.S.	3203
Esposito, Joseph	U.S.	1105		Zerilli, Joseph	U.S.	3219
Fay, Larry	U.S.	1140		**Activity: Fencing**		
Fein, Benjamin	U.S.	1145		Apacalo, Anthony	U.S.	135
Forty Thieves	U.S.	1201		**Activity: Forgery**		
French Riviera Gang Wars	Fr.	1235		Vitale, John Joseph	U.S.	3057
Galiffi, Agata	Arg.	1252		**Activity: Fraud**		
Gallo Brothers	U.S.	1256		Caifano, Marshall Joseph	U.S.	575
Gambino, Carlo	U.S.	1259		Cain, Richard B.	U.S.	576
Gas House Gang	U.S.	1283		Callahan, Gerald Michael	U.S.	581
Genna Brothers	U.S.	1291		Capone, Alphonse	U.S.	603
Genovese, Vito	Int'l.	1295		Capone, Frank	U.S.	617
Giancana, Sam	U.S.	1305		Carlisi, Sam Anthony	U.S.	624
Gioe, Charles	U.S.	1315		Cicero, Ill.	U.S.	714
Hell's Kitchen Gang	U.S.	1513		DeStefano, Mario Anthony	U.S.	926
Henry Street Gang	U.S.	1520		Dio, Johnny	U.S.	976
Ianniello, Matthew	U.S.	1651		Eastman, Edward	U.S.	1063
Inagawa Kakuji	Japan	1653		Eisen, Maxie	U.S.	1079
Infelice, Ernest	U.S.	1654		El Rukn Gang, The	U.S.	1086
Jimmy Curly Gang	U.S.	1724		Franzese, Michael	U.S.	1227
Kaplan, Nathan	U.S.	1760		Grady Gang	U.S.	1355
Kastel, Phillip	U.S.	1767		Hudson Dusters, N.Y.	U.S.	1634
Kierdorf, Frank	U.S.	1815		Ianniello, Matthew	U.S.	1651
Kray, Reginald	Brit.	1847		Kastel, Phillip	U.S.	1767
Kray, Ronald	Brit.	1847		Lombardozzi, Carmine	U.S.	1980
Labor War	U.S.	1867		Machii Hisayuki	Japan	2045
Lanza, Joseph	U.S.	1896		Minkow, Barry	U.S.	2188
Liggio, Luciano	Italy	1951		Ogawa Kaoru	Japan	2364
Lombardo, Joseph	U.S.	1980		Pineapple Primary	U.S.	2466
Machii Hisayuki	Japan	2045		Spilotro, Anthony	U.S.	2828
Magaddino, Stefano	U.S.	2086		Teresa, Vincent Charles	U.S.	2914
Maine State Prison	U.S.	2089		Tieri, Frank	U.S.	2953
Manchester Gangster Plot	Brit.	2099		Tronolone, John	U.S.	2990
Mangano, Lawrence	U.S.	2102		Valachi, Joseph Michael	U.S.	3024
Masseria, Joseph	U.S.	2137		Zuta, Jack	U.S.	3223
Matranga, Charles	U.S.	2147		Zwerbach, Maxwell	U.S.	3224
Matranga, Tony	U.S.	2147		**Activity: Gambling**		

Accardo, Anthony Joseph	U.S.	15	Kastel, Phillip	U.S.	1767
Adonis, Joseph	U.S.	32	Langella, Gennaro	U.S.	1889
Aiuppa, Joseph	U.S.	44	Lansky, Meyer	U.S.	1892
Alderisio, Felix Anthony	U.S.	71	LaPietra, Angelo J.	U.S.	1897
Alex, Gus	U.S.	73	Larocca, John Sebastian	U.S.	1898
Alo, Vincent	U.S.	103	Last Chance Tavern	U.S.	1901
Annenberg, Moses L.	U.S.	128	Lazia, John	U.S.	1909
Apacalo, Anthony	U.S.	135	Le Van Vien	Indo-China	1943
Batista, Fulgencio	Cuba	282	Licavoli, James T.	U.S.	1948
Benintende, Joseph	U.S.	330	Licavoli, Peter Joseph, Sr.	U.S.	1949
Berman, Dave	U.S.	345	Liggio, Luciano	Italy	1951
Biase, Anthony Joseph	U.S.	357	Lombardozzi, Carmine	U.S.	1980
Binaggio, Charles	U.S.	370	Lucchese, Thomas	U.S.	2002
Birmingham Boys	Brit.	379	Luciano, Charles	Int'l.	2002
Boccia, Ferdinand	U.S.	414	Magaddino, Stefano	U.S.	2086
Boiardo, Ruggiero	U.S.	421	Maltese, Frank	U.S.	2098
Bompensiero, Frank	U.S.	426	Mangano, Lawrence	U.S.	2102
Bonanno, Joseph	U.S.	427	Maranzano, Salvatore	U.S.	2114
Borgio, Rosario	U.S.	442	McDonald, Michael Cassius	U.S.	2032
Bravos, George	U.S.	479	Milano, Carmen	U.S.	2178
Brazilian Death Squad	Braz.	480	Milano, Peter John	U.S.	2178
Bruno, Angelo	U.S.	521	Mirro, James	U.S.	2190
Buccieri, Frank	U.S.	525	Mock Duck	U.S.	2195
Caifano, Marshall Joseph	U.S.	575	Moran, George	U.S.	2213
Callahan, Gerald Michael	U.S.	581	Moretti, Willie	U.S.	2217
Capone, Alphonse	U.S.	603	Morton, Samuel J.	U.S.	2229
Carbo, Frankie	U.S.	620	Nicoletti, Charles	U.S.	2335
Carfano, Anthony	U.S.	623	Paris, P. Alvin	U.S.	2409
Carlisi, Sam Anthony	U.S.	624	Patrick, Leonard	U.S.	2421
Carnera Boxing Scandal	U.S.	628	Pranno, Rocco Salvatore	U.S.	2496
Carolla, Sylvestro	U.S.	634	Prio, Ross	U.S.	2503
Caruso, Frank T.	U.S.	647	Purple Gang	U.S.	2513
Cerone, Frank	U.S.	664	Ragen, James M.	U.S.	2529
Cerone, John Philip	U.S.	665	Ragen's Colts	U.S.	2529
Chichester Gang	U.S.	698	Riccobene, Harry	U.S.	2574
Cicero, Ill.	U.S.	714	Rothkopf, Louis	U.S.	2625
Civella, Nicholas	U.S.	717	Rothstein, Arnold	U.S.	2626
Cohen, Mickey	U.S.	741	St. Clair, Stephanie	U.S.	2658
Colony Sports Club	Int'l.	755	Salerno, Anthony	U.S.	2670
Colosimo, James	U.S.	755	Savides, Christ	U.S.	2683
Comer, Jack	Brit.	761	Scarpelli, Gerald Hector	U.S.	2689
Coppola, Michael	U.S.	779	Siegel, Benjamin	U.S.	2753
Costello, Frank	U.S.	794	Simmons, Zachariah	U.S.	2764
Daddano, William, Sr.	U.S.	854	Smaldone, Clarence	U.S.	2779
Dalitz, Morris Barney	U.S.	857	Smaldone, Clyde	U.S.	2779
Di Cristina, Paul	Int'l.	941	Smaldone, Eugene	U.S.	2779
DiCocco, Paul, Sr.	U.S.	940	Solano, Vincent	U.S.	2812
DiFronzo, John	U.S.	942	Solomon, Charles	U.S.	2814
DiNapoli, Vincent	U.S.	975	Strollo, Anthony C.	U.S.	2870
DiVarco, Joseph Vincent	U.S.	978	Sydney Ducks	U.S.	2888
Dragna, Louis Tom	U.S.	1018	Syndicate, The	U.S.	2891
Eastman, Edward	U.S.	1063	Taoka Kazuo	Japan	2897
Erickson, Frank	U.S.	1100	Teresa, Vincent Charles	U.S.	2914
Eto, Ken	U.S.	1109	Testa, Philip	U.S.	2918
Ferriola, Joseph	U.S.	1153	Tiplitz, William	U.S.	2957
Fong Ching	U.S.	1192	Tocco, Albert Caesar	U.S.	2959
Four Deuces	U.S.	1204	Tong Wars	U.S.	2967
French Riviera Gang Wars	Fr.	1235	Torello, James Vincent	U.S.	2969
Galiffi, Agata	Arg.	1252	Torrio, John	U.S.	2969
Gambino, Carlo	U.S.	1259	Trafficante, Santo, Sr.	U.S.	2983
Genovese, Vito	Int'l.	1295	Tronolone, John	U.S.	2990
Giancana, Sam	U.S.	1305	Valachi, Joseph Michael	U.S.	3024
Gophers	U.S.	1341	Valley Gang	U.S.	3028
Gordon, Waxey	U.S.	1346	Weissman, William	U.S.	3121
Greenbaum, Gus	U.S.	1375	West, Jack	U.S.	330
Hawthorne Inn	U.S.	1492	Wortman, Frank	U.S.	3191
Hoff, Max	U.S.	1584	Zwerbach, Maxwell	U.S.	3224
Ianniello, Matthew	U.S.	1651	Zwillman, Abner	U.S.	3225
Inagawa Kakuji	Japan	1653	**Activity: Graft**		
Jirocho Shimizu no	Japan	1724	Addonizio, Hugh J.	U.S.	30

Scarpelli, Gerald Hector	U.S.	2689
Schultz, Dutch	U.S.	2699
Scopo, Ralph	U.S.	2448
Shapiro, Jacob	U.S.	2734
Sheldon Gang	U.S.	2739
Sheridan, Andrew	U.S.	2743
Shotgun Man	U.S.	2749
Sica, Joseph	U.S.	2751
Siegel, Benjamin	U.S.	2753
Sirocco, Jack	U.S.	2772
Skar, Manny	U.S.	2773
Solano, Vincent	U.S.	2812
Spanish, Johnny	U.S.	2820
Spilotro, Anthony	U.S.	2828
Spirito, François	Fr.	620
Squillante, James	U.S.	2834
Stevens, Walter	U.S.	2852
Strauss, Harry	U.S.	2868
Strollo, Anthony C.	U.S.	2870
Sydney Ducks	U.S.	2888
Syndicate, The	U.S.	2891
Taoka Kazuo	Japan	2897
Tenuto, Frederick J.	U.S.	2914
Terranova, Ciro	U.S.	2915
Tocco, Albert Caesar	U.S.	2959
Torrio, John	U.S.	2969
Toyama Mitsuru	Japan	2980
Tri-State Gang	U.S.	2990
Turtletaub, Sam	U.S.	3006
Unione Siciliane	U.S.	3015
Vaccarizi, Raymond	Spain	3023
Valenti, Rocco	U.S.	3024
Valley Gang	U.S.	3028
Ventura, Dominique	Fr.	2216
Vignon, Henri	Fr.	3050
Vitale, John Joseph	U.S.	3057
Vizzini, Calgero	Si.	3057
Vollaro, Luigi	Italy	3061
Walsh, Johnny	U.S.	3084
Weiss, Earl	U.S.	3119
Weiss, Emmanuel	U.S.	3120
Weissman, William	U.S.	3121
White Hand Gang	U.S.	3140
White, William Jack	U.S.	3139
Whyos, The	U.S.	3147
Winkler, Gus	U.S.	3176
Workman, Charles	U.S.	3187
Yale, Frankie	U.S.	3203
Yellow Henry Gang	U.S.	3206
Zelig, Jack	U.S.	3218
Zerilli, Joseph	U.S.	3219
Zwerbach, Maxwell	U.S.	3224

Activity: Patronage

Cormack, William H.	U.S.	2736
Shaw, Frank L.	U.S.	2736
Shaw, Joseph	U.S.	2736

Activity: Pornography

Langella, Gennaro	U.S.	1889

Activity: Prostitution

Adler, John (Jakie, Jakey)	U.S.	31
Adonis, Joseph	U.S.	32
Alex, Gus	U.S.	73
Alo, Vincent	U.S.	103
Apacalo, Anthony	U.S.	135
Bioff, William Morris	U.S.	371
Borgio, Rosario	U.S.	442
Capone, Alphonse	U.S.	603
Cicero, Ill.	U.S.	714
Colosimo, James	U.S.	755
Costello, Frank	U.S.	794

DiVarco, Joseph Vincent	U.S.	978
Eastman, Edward	U.S.	1063
Four Deuces	U.S.	1204
French Riviera Gang Wars	Fr.	1235
Garfinkle, David	U.S.	3029
Gas House Gang	U.S.	1283
Genovese, Vito	Int'l.	1295
Gophers	U.S.	1341
Hart, Mike	U.S.	3029
Hart, Mollie	U.S.	3029
Heitler, Michael	U.S.	1511
Jukes Family	U.S.	1748
Kelly, Paul	U.S.	1788
Larocca, John Sebastian	U.S.	1898
Lazia, John	U.S.	1909
Le Van Vien	Indo-China	1943
Luciano, Charles	Int'l.	2002
McDonald, Michael Cassius	U.S.	2032
Mangano, Lawrence	U.S.	2102
Matranga, Charles	U.S.	2147
Matranga, Tony	U.S.	2147
Messina Brothers	Brit.	2171
Micalleff, Antony	Brit.	2176
Mock Duck	U.S.	2195
Panno, Frank	U.S.	2405
Solano, Vincent	U.S.	2812
Taoka Kazuo	Japan	2897
Tong Wars	U.S.	2967
Torrio, John	U.S.	2969
Tyler, Dick	U.S.	3029
Unione Siciliane	U.S.	3015
Van Bever, Julia	U.S.	3029
Van Bever, Maurice	U.S.	3029
White Front Cigar Store	U.S.	3139
Zwerbach, Maxwell	U.S.	3224

Activity: Racketeering

Abbandando, Frank	U.S.	1
Accardi, Settimo	U.S.	14
Acceturo, Anthony	U.S.	18
Adonis, Joseph	U.S.	32
Alderisio, Felix Anthony	U.S.	71
Alterie, Louis	U.S.	104
Amberg, Joseph C.	U.S.	110
Amberg, Louis	U.S.	110
Amuso, Victor	U.S.	116
Anastasio, Anthony	U.S.	120
Angiulo, Gennaro J.	U.S.	127
Bas, Marvin J.	U.S.	271
Berman, Otto	U.S.	345
Bioff, William Morris	U.S.	371
Boiardo, Ruggiero	U.S.	421
Bompensiero, Frank	U.S.	426
Brothers, Leo Vincent	U.S.	501
Buccieri, Frank	U.S.	525
Buchalter, Louis	U.S.	525
Bufalino, Russell	U.S.	533
Capone, Alphonse	U.S.	603
Capone, Ralph	U.S.	618
Cascioferro, Vito	Int'l.	648
Cicero, Ill.	U.S.	714
Colombo, Joseph, Sr.	U.S.	754
Colosimo, James	U.S.	755
Corallo, Anthony	U.S.	781
Dauber, William E.	U.S.	878
DeCarlo, Angelo	U.S.	896
DeStefano, Mario Anthony	U.S.	926
DiNapoli, Vincent	U.S.	975
Dragna Family	U.S.	1019
El Rukn Gang, The	U.S.	1086
English, Charles Carmen	U.S.	1097

Harrison, Carter Henry, Sr.	U.S.	1464
Herbert, Edward	Brit.	1522
Hines, James J.	U.S.	1560
Hochberg, Alan	U.S.	1582
Hodge, Orville Enoch	U.S.	1583
Hoeppel, Charles J.	U.S.	1583
Hoeppel, John Henry	U.S.	1583
Hogan, Michael J.	U.S.	1588
Holles, Denzil	Brit.	1592
Johnson, Enoch	U.S.	1728
Julia Mamaea	Roman.	1749
Kao Kang	China	1759
Küchlüq	Mongolia	1853
Kelly, Edward Joseph	U.S.	1781
Kemp, G. Leroy	U.S.	1791
Kenna, Michael	U.S.	1792
Kleindienst, Richard Gordon	U.S.	1833
Kline, Charles H.	U.S.	1833
Kálmán	Hung.	1754
Klotz, Louis Lucien	Fr.	1833
Kremlin Murder Scandal	U.S.S.R.	1848
Langer, William	U.S.	1890
Le Bon, Joseph	Fr.	1915
Liu Chin	China	1972
Lorraine, Charles de	Fr.	1991
Louderback, Harold	U.S.	1991
Lopez, Carlos Antonio	Para.	1989
Lopez, Francisco Solano	Para.	1989
Macclesfield, Earl of	Brit.	2026
Marcos, Ferdinand	Phil.	2118
Markert, Louis	U.S.	806
Mitchell, John H.	U.S.	2191
Mitchell, John Newton	U.S.	2191
Montagu, John	Brit.	2203
Moses, Sidney	U.S.	2233
Mozaffar od-Din	Per.	2237
Municipal Brothel	U.S.	2251
Musto, William V.	U.S.	2269
New York Police Scandals	U.S.	2326
Nixon, Richard Milhous	U.S.	2340
O'Brien, John Patrick	U.S.	2357
O'Dwyer, William	U.S.	2362
Ormonde, James	Ire.	2379
Pahlavi, Mohammed Riza	Iran	2394
Pendergast Machine	U.S.	2440
Pendergast, Thomas Joseph	U.S.	2439
Pern, Juan Domingo	Arg.	2445
Phao Sriyanond	Thai.	2456
Pianto, Larry	U.S.	2461
Ptolemy VIII	Egypt	2510
Ready Mix Case	U.S.	2549
Reynolds, William Henry	U.S.	2571
Ritter, Halsted L.	U.S.	2585
Robinson, Noah R.	U.S.	2597
Ruef, Abraham	U.S.	2636
Rutilius Rufus, Publius	Roman.	2644
Rynders, Isaiah	U.S.	2648
St. Leger, Sir Anthony	Brit.	2659
Salii, Lazarus	Palau	2670
Sandys, Sir Edwin	Brit.	2677
Scott, William J.	U.S.	2713
Scrope, William le	Brit.	2716
Seabury Investigations	U.S.	2717
Sforza, Lodovico	Fr.	2732
Shaftesbury, Anthony A. Cooper	Brit.	2733
Sixtus IV	Italy	2772
Small, Len	U.S.	2780
Soga Umako	Japan	2812
Spencer, Charles	Brit.	2825
Squires, Sir Richard Anderson	Can.	2834

Stewart, Matthew	Scot.	2853
Stewart, Patrick	Brit.	2853
Stigand	Brit.	2854
Stone, William Joel	U.S.	2860
Stuart, Lady Arabella	Brit.	2871
Succop, Bertram L.	U.S.	1833
Sudbury, Simon of	Brit.	2875
Sukarno	Indo.	2875
Sullivan, Timothy	U.S.	2876
Sweeny, Peter Barr	U.S.	2888
Tallien, Jean Lambert	Fr.	2895
Tammany Hall	U.S.	2896
Tanaka Kakuei	Japan	2896
Tanuma Okitsugu	Japan	2897
Teapot Dome Scandal	U.S.	2907
Thompson, William Hale	U.S.	2936
Tokugawa Tsunayoshi	Japan	2964
Toledo, Francisco de	Peru	2964
Tweed, William Marcy	U.S.	3007
Twysden, Sir Roger	Brit.	3010
Vaudreuil, Pierre Cav. de Riga	Int'l.	3038
Verres, Gaius	Roman.	3043
Voldemaras, Augustinas	Lith.	3060
Walker, James John	U.S.	3076
Watergate Scandal	U.S.	3098
Wei Chung-hsien	China	3113
Welfare Island Prison Scandal	U.S.	3123
Williams, John James	U.S.	3163
Wilson, Tug	U.S.	3175
Wood, Fernando	U.S.	3182
Yazid ibn al-Muhallab	Per.	3205
Zimmerman, Alfred F.M.	Ger.	3220

POLITCAL CORRUPTION - Case of

Anzalone, Theodore V.	U.S.	135
Burroughs, Ada L.	U.S.	600
Cannon, James, Jr.	U.S.	600
Donovan, James J.	U.S.	1001
Fasi, Frank F.	U.S.	1137
Hall, Abraham Oakey	U.S.	1420
Haro, Miguel Nassar	U.S.	1455
Hastings, Warren	Brit.	1475
Isaacs, Sir Rufus Daniel	Brit.	1667
Lloyd George, David	Brit.	1667
Means, Gaston Bullock	U.S.	2159
Montgomery, Robert	U.S.	2205
Newberry, Truman Handy	U.S.	2309
Wright, James Claude, Jr.	U.S.	3193

POLYGAMY

Cannon, George Quayle	U.S.	600
Crossman, George Albert	Brit.	835
LeBaron, Ervil Morerel	U.S.	1914
Snow, Lorenzo	U.S.	2805
Swapp, Addam	U.S.	2886
Taylor, John	U.S.	2901

PORNOGRAPHY

Collin, Frank	U.S.	749
Dial-A-Porn Case	U.S.	934
Gauthe, Gilbert	U.S.	1284
Smith, Jerry Lee	U.S.	2795
Vermilye, Claudius I.	U.S.	3042

PRIVATE DETECTIVES

Burns, William John	U.S.	553

PRISON BRUTALITY

Georgia Prison Camp Massacre	U.S.	1300

PRISON ESCAPE

Alcatraz	U.S.	47
Balfour, Alexander	Scot.	218
Balgar, Robert L.	U.S.	219
Banghart, Basil	U.S.	224
Bastille	Fr.	278
Bedford Hills Correctional	U.S.	312
Belcher, Emory Allen	U.S.	316
Biddle, Ed	U.S.	358
Biddle, Jack	U.S.	358
Blin, George	Fr.	408
Bruno, John J.	U.S.	521
Burns, Robert Elliott	U.S.	551
Callahan, Jack	U.S.	582
Cecconi, Patrick	U.S.	3041
Cellini, Benvenuto	Italy	663
Charrire, Henri-Antoine	Fr.	688
Clark, David Scott	U.S.	721
Cochise	U.S.	735
Coleman, Jefferson	U.S.	744
Cummins, Ark., Prison Farm Esc	U.S.	846
Davis, Larry Ronald	U.S.	885
Davis, Robert Earl	U.S.	1311
Docherty, Dutch	Ire.	981
Dorman, Frank	U.S.	358
Dowd, John	U.S.	2223
Duchowski, Charles	U.S.	1031
Eaton, Helen Spence	U.S.	1066
Erler, Robert John	U.S.	1101
Evans, Mary	U.S.	1113
Fielden, Don	Mex.	1156
Flinn, Charles J.	U.S.	1179
Gallegos, David, Jr.	U.S.	1311
Garrow, Robert	U.S.	1280
Gasre (Iran) Prison Escape	Iran	1284
Georgia State Prison Escape	U.S.	1300
Gilbert, William Wayne	U.S.	1311
Graterford (Pa.) State Prison	U.S.	1363
Gurin, Eddie	Fr.	1396
Haggart, David	Int'l.	1415
Hill, Gregory	U.S.	1551
Hinds, Alfie	Int'l.	1560
Jackson, John	Brit.	1678
Joliet State Penitentiary	U.S.	1735
Kaplan, Joel David	U.S.	1759
Kappler, Herbert	Ger.	1762
Kennedy, Mathew	Int'l.	1800
Kinslow, Jimmy	U.S.	1311
Legge, William	Brit.	1923
Lynchehaun, James	Ire.	2017
McCartney, Thomas Peter	U.S.	2024
McGrath, James	U.S.	2042
McKenzie, Pete	U.S.	2048
Mahaney, Jack	U.S.	2088
Maxwell, William	Brit.	2154
Meehan, Martin	Ire.	981
Miner, William	U.S.	2187
Mitchel, John	Ire.	2190
Mitchell, Frank Samuel	Brit.	2190
Moders, Mary	Brit.	2196
Montos, Nick George	U.S.	2206
Morley, Charles	U.S.	2223
Munnick, Jan Willem Hendrik	S.Afri.	2251
Myers, William J.	U.S.	2270
Nannery, James	U.S.	2277
Nelson, Victor F.	U.S.	2305
Nesbit, William Raymond	U.S.	2306
Nithsdale, Earl of	Brit.	2339
O'Connor, Thomas	U.S.	2359
O'Neill, Daniel	Ire.	2373

O'Reilly, John Boyle	Brit.	2377
Paddock, Benjamin Hoskins	U.S.	2392
Paine, Thomas	Fr.	2394
Pallister, Thomas	U.S.	2397
Pentridge Prison Escape	Aus.	2441
Peter, Saint	Roman.	2450
Remling, Dale Otto	U.S.	2565
Retz, Cardinal de	Fr.	2570
Rizo, Gregorio	U.S.	1031
Roa, Bernardo	U.S.	1031
Roberts, George Denwhite	U.S.	2592
Roche, Edward	U.S.	2603
Roehl, Frank	U.S.	2397
Romero, Michael	U.S.	1311
Ronconi, Susanna	Italy	2616
Schader, Charles	U.S.	1031
Schmidt, Michael	U.S.	1311
Scott, Francis	U.S.	2711
Sellers, Willie Foster	U.S.	2726
Sharkey, William J.	U.S.	2734
Sheppard, Jack	Brit.	2740
Smith, John Thomas	Aust.	2797
Smith, Lucille	U.S.	2825
Sobhraj, Gurmukh Charles	India	2810
Southard, Lydia	U.S.	2817
Spencer, Brenda	U.S.	2825
Staleski, Walter	U.S.	1031
Taby, Arpad	Hung.	2893
Taylor, Charles	U.S.	2223
Torres, Hector Herman	U.S.	1311
Torrez, Robert	U.S.	1031
Tower of London	Brit.	2979
Traxler, Roy	U.S.	2984
Velleff, Randy	U.S.	3041
Walters, Ted	U.S.	3086
Wanka, Alfred	S.Afri.	3089
Ward, Margaret	Brit.	3092
Whitfield, John Leonard	U.S.	3141
Wilcox, Jennie	U.S.	358
Willmott, Donna Jean	U.S.	3169
Willock, Essie Mae	U.S.	2825
Wright, Jessie	U.S.	358

PRISON ESCAPE - Case of

Good, Millard	U.S.	1339

PRISON ESCAPE ATTEMPTS

Johnson, Richard	Brit.	1731

PRISON REFORMERS

Booth-Clibborn, Catherine	Brit.	437
Buxton, Sir Thomas Fowell	Brit.	564
Carpenter, Mary	Brit.	635
Demetz, Frédéric Auguste	Fr.	912
Dix, Dorothea Lynde	U.S.	979
England, John	Aus.	1096
Fry, Elizabeth	Brit.	1239
Howard, John	Brit.	1629
Maconochie, Alexander	Brit.	2065
Morrell, Edward	U.S.	2224
Peel, Sir Robert	Brit.	2435
Phillip, Arthur	Brit.	2458
Whittington, Richard	Brit.	3147

PRISONS

Alcatraz	U.S.	47
Newgate	Brit.	2310
Tombs, The	U.S.	2964

PROSTITUTION

PROSTITUTION - Case of

PSYCHIATRISTS

PSYCHICS

RACKETEERING

Baraldini, Silvia	U.S.	2360
Bertolotti, Freddy	U.S.	2691
Binder, Aaron M.	U.S.	370
Bloom, Lloyd	U.S.	3086
Bolt, Nut & Rivet Man. Assoc.	U.S.	425
Borstein, Sydney	U.S.	2691
Bove, James V.	U.S.	1140
Brown, Nathaniel	U.S.	1097
Carrollo, Charles	U.S.	642
Carter, James Y.	U.S.	644
Celani, Frederick George	U.S.	370
Corallo, Anthony	U.S.	781
Corallo, Anthony	U.S.	2448
Corbitt, Michael	U.S.	2142
Elliott, Alfred	U.S.	1084
Englisis, Anthony	U.S.	1097
Englisis, Nicholas	U.S.	1097
Fay, Joseph S.	U.S.	1140
Feinberg, Saul	U.S.	1097
Feldman, Richard L.	U.S.	1146
Ferriola, Joseph	U.S.	1153
Fort, Jeff	U.S.	1199
Furnari, Christopher	U.S.	2448
Goldstein, Michael	U.S.	1146
Indelicato, Anthony	U.S.	2448
Jermyn, Edmund Beson	U.S.	1722
Kaye, Herman	U.S.	1770
Keating, James	U.S.	2142
Klukofsky, Eli	U.S.	1833
Kotlyar, Nikolai	U.S.S.R.	1844
Koury, Leo Joseph	U.S.	1845
Langella, Gennaro	U.S.	2448
McLain, Dennis Dale	U.S.	2054
Mansberg, Marvin	U.S.	1097
Martenson, Richard	U.S.	1146
Masters, Alan	U.S.	2142
Meinster, Robert Jay	U.S.	2475
Moriarty, Joseph Vincent	U.S.	2223
Myers, Eugene Arter	U.S.	2475
Odinga, Sekou	U.S.	2360
Panno, Frank	U.S.	2405
Perlowin, Bruce J.	U.S.	2445
Persico, Carmine	U.S.	2448
Platshorn, Robert Elliot	U.S.	2475
Provenzano, Anthony	U.S.	2508
Salerno, Anthony	U.S.	2448
Santoro, Salvatore	U.S.	2448
Scalise, George	U.S.	2687
Schiff, Jack	U.S.	2691
Scopo, Ralph		2448
Tieri, Frank	U.S.	2953
Walters, Norby	U.S.	3086
Wedtech Scandal	U.S.	3112
Woodward, Harry	U.S.	1770

RACKETEERING - Case of

De Lorean, John Zachary	U.S.	908
Gotti, Gene	U.S.	1350
Long Island Lighting Co., The	U.S.	1987
Operation Phocus	U.S.	2373

RAPE

Allweiss, David	U.S.	102
Anderson, Alexander	U.S.	121
Aquilar, Frank	U.S.	166
Arridy, Joseph	U.S.	166
Ashwell, Thomas	U.S.	171
Avril, Robert	Fr.	191
Axilrod, Dr. Arnold Asher	U.S.	192

Bailey, Robert Taylor	U.S.	212
Barton, John Evert	U.S.	271
Battus, John	U.S.	284
Baylanch, Autry	U.S.	285
Baylanch, Gee	U.S.	285
Baylanch, Jes	U.S.	285
Beagles, David Ervin	U.S.	286
Beagles, David Ervin	U.S.	735
Bean, Thomas Lee	U.S.	290
Beck, Dieter	Ger.	295
Berger, Theodor	Ger.	342
Berry, Saul	U.S.	1820
Bey, Djevet	Turk.	355
Bey, Enver	Turk.	355
Bey, Talaat	Turk.	355
Bianchi, Kenneth	U.S.	356
Biddings, Robert	U.S.	358
Boden, Wayne Clifford	Can.	415
Boost, Werner	Ger.	436
Borgia Family	Italy	441
Braden, Howard	U.S.	2366
Brudos, Jerry	U.S.	520
Brumit, Lucille	U.S.	1544
Bryant, Kenneth	U.S.	524
Buck Gang	U.S.	531
Buckley, Tim	Brit.	532
Buffet, Claude	Fr.	534
Bundy, Carol	U.S.	722
Buono, Angelo, Jr.	U.S.	356
Burke, Thomas	Can.	2069
Burton, Lee A.	U.S.	558
Campbell, Kevin	U.S.	1515
Cant, George	Brit.	600
Carr, Melvin	U.S.	636
Cato	U.S.	657
Catoe, Jarvis Theodore Rooseve	U.S.	657
Chessman, Caryl	U.S.	693
Chinese Mass Rapes	China	700
Christensen, William Dean	U.S.	702
Clark, Dewey	U.S.	721
Clark, Douglas Daniel	U.S.	722
Cleary, Joe	U.S.	728
Click, Franklin	U.S.	732
Cochran, Willie Grady	U.S.	735
Coddington, Herbert James	U.S.	738
Coleman, Alton	U.S.	743
Coleman, Wayne	U.S.	1036
Collins, Roosevelt	U.S.	752
Collinsworth, Willion	U.S.	753
Cook, DeWitt Clinton	U.S.	769
Cook, Peter	Brit.	770
Coolidge, Edward H.	U.S.	773
Coombes, Robert L.	U.S.	774
Cooper, Ray Anthony	U.S.	778
Cordeiro, John	U.S.	2762
Costello, William	Ire.	794
Croft, Curtis	U.S.	1515
Daniel, Robert	U.S.	867
Davis, Larry Ronald	U.S.	885
De Boe, William Thomas	U.S.	894
DeSalvo, Albert Henry	U.S.	921
de Sade, Donatien Al. François	Fr.	2656
de Soto, Benito	Spain	926
Dorbell, Tom	Brit.	1004
Draper, William	U.S.	1020
Duck, Aug Tai	U.S.	1031
Duell, William	Brit.	1032
Dungee, George	U.S.	1036
Dunkins, Horace Franklin, Jr.	U.S.	1037
Edmundson, Calvin Jerome	U.S.	1070

Emery, Ronald	U.S.	1091	Juricic, James	U.S.	1750
Evans, Michael	U.S.	1113	Kallinger, Joseph	U.S.	1753
Farrell, William Patrick	U.S.	1136	Kemper, Edmund Emil III	U.S.	1791
Fearn, Donald	U.S.	1143	Kines, John	U.S.	1820
Filipovitz, Peter	Aust.	2994	Knoppa, Antony Michael	U.S.	1891
Fiorenza, John	U.S.	1161	Kodaira Yoshio	Japan	1840
Fitzmaurice, Walter	Ire.	794	Koguchi Shizu	Japan	1840
Folk, Carl	U.S.	1191	Kokoraleis, Andrew C.	U.S.	1288
Foote, Henry Leander	U.S.	1193	Kokoraleis, Thomas	U.S.	1288
Fortis, Edmund	U.S.	1200	Kroll, Joachim	Ger.	1852
Garcia, Luis	U.S.	1266	Kurten, Peter	Ger.	1862
Garvie, Mervyn	Aus.	1281	Lake, Leonard	U.S.	1874
Gary, Carlton	U.S.	1282	Lanham, Harry	U.S.	1891
Gecht, Robin	U.S.	1288	Lee, William	U.S.	1921
Ghadiali, Dinshah Pestanji Fra	U.S.	1304	Leggett, Emmett Earl	U.S.	1923
Gholston, Kenneth	U.S.	1305	LeGrand, Devernon	U.S.	1924
Gilmore, Dwayne	U.S.	2233	Lennard, John	Brit.	1930
Glatman, Harvey Murray	U.S.	1321	Lieberman, Brad	U.S.	1950
Glenn, Herschel	U.S.	1322	Lightbourne, Wendell Willis	Ber.	1953
Gonzales, Edward E.	U.S.	1337	Lineveldt, Gamat Salie	S.Afri.	1968
Grasso, Santo	Fr.	1363	Little, Dwain Lee	U.S.	1971
Gray, Ronald Adrin	U.S.	1365	Llaguna, Roger	U.S.	1266
Green, Clovis Carl	U.S.	1373	Long, Bobby Joe	U.S.	1981
Green, Samuel	U.S.	1374	Lopez, Pedro Alonso	Ecu.	1989
Greenberg, Bertram	U.S.	1376	Lovat, Lord	Brit.	1994
Griffiths, Peter	Brit.	1388	Lugo, Diego	U.S.	2009
Gunn, Raymond	U.S.	1400	Maclean, Tony	Brit.	2057
Haight, Edward	U.S.	1418	Martinsville Seven	U.S.	2133
Hallman, Larry	U.S.	1428	Mattheis, Valorus	U.S.	2149
Hammerling, Peter	U.S.	1436	McCrary Family	U.S.	2029
Hammond, Karl	U.S.	1439	McFarland, Earl	U.S.	2039
Harris, E.K.	U.S.	1460	McGee, Willie	U.S.	2041
Hatcher, Charles Ray	U.S.	1475	McGuigan, John	Scot.	2042
Hay, Donald Alexander	Can.	1493	McPherson, John	Can.	2069
Heideman, Frank	U.S.	1507	Meyer, Robert	U.S.	2175
Heidnik, Gary M.	U.S.	1507	Miller, Adrian H.	U.S.	2179
Henderson, Demetrius	U.S.	1515	Miller, Frank	U.S.	2180
Henry, Leroy	Brit.	1519	Montgomery, Randolph Conrad	U.S.	2205
Hepper, William Sanchez de Pin	Brit.	1522	Morales, Juan Castillo	Mex.	2213
Hernandez, Joe Frank	U.S.	1524	Morgan, Samuel	Brit.	2221
Heys, Arthur	Brit.	1532	Morris, Raymond Leslie	Brit.	2225
Higdon, Lloyd	U.S.	1544	Moseley, Winston	U.S.	2232
Hill, Clarence	U.S.	1550	Mosley, Ronnie	U.S.	2233
Holt, Thomas J., Jr.	U.S.	1605	Moxley, William Cyril	Aus.	2236
Hooker, Cameron	U.S.	1608	Mu'Min, Dawud	U.S.	2250
Horne, Carlton	U.S.	1620	Munnick, Jan Willem Hendrik	S.Afri.	2251
Horton, William Robert	U.S.	1623	O'Bryan, Patrick	Brit.	2357
Howard, John C.	U.S.	1629	Oakes, Gregory	U.S.	2349
Howdeshell, Roy	U.S.	1631	Oakes, Jerry	U.S.	2349
Hunt, Virnell	U.S.	1644	Oakes, John Howard	U.S.	2349
Inkpaduta	U.S.	1656	Ohern, Michael	U.S.	2366
Irvin, Walter Lee	U.S.	1665	Olson, Clifford	Can.	2371
Irwin, Warren Lee	U.S.	1667	Olson, Raymond Lee	U.S.	2149
Isaacs, Billy	U.S.	1036	Osborn, John Marion	U.S.	2383
Isaacs, Carl	U.S.	1036	Paisnel, Edward John Louis	Brit.	2395
Iszard, Henry	U.S.	1670	Pantages, Alexander	U.S.	2405
Ivan IV Vasilyevich	Rus.	1670	Parker, Mack Charles	U.S.	2411
Jackson, Calvin	U.S.	1675	Penry, Johnny Paul	U.S.	2441
Jackson, Cobb	U.S.	1676	Perkins, Rudolph	U.S.	2444
Jackson, Edward Franklin, Jr.	U.S.	1676	Peters, Warren	U.S.	1428
Johnson, Billy Ray	U.S.	2349	Peters, Warren	U.S.	3171
Jones, Arthur Albert	Brit.	1736	Pommerencke, Heinrich	Ger.-Aust.	2485
Jones, Bennie	U.S.	1736	Pytsch, Cornelius	U.S.	2517
Jones, David	U.S.	2349	Ramirez, Patrick	U.S.	2533
Jones, Harold	Brit.	1737	Raposo, Victor	U.S.	2762
Jones, Henry Earl	U.S.	721	Raymond, Robert	U.S.	2547
Jones, Roger Lee	U.S.	1740	Roche, John Francis	U.S.	2604
Jones, Tom	Brit.	1741	Rogatsch, Johann	Aust.	2608
Jordan, Clayton	U.S.	1820	Rogers, Francis J.	U.S.	2610
Judy, Steven T.	U.S.	1748	Rogers, Kenneth Paul	U.S.	2611

Romulus	Roman.	2616
Ross, Colin Campbell	Aus.	2624
Ross, Michael B.	U.S.	2624
Roy, Gilder	Scot.	2632
Rupp, William F.	U.S.	2641
Russen, Benjamin	Brit.	2643
Ruzicka, James	U.S.	2646
Ryan, Jack	U.S.	2646
Scarborough, Patrick	U.S.	753
Scottsboro Case	U.S.	2714
Seye, Blaise Ferrage	Fr.	2730
Seymour, Golney	U.S.	2730
Silvia, Daniel	U.S.	2762
Singleton, Lawrence	U.S.	2769
Sioux Indian Massacre	U.S.	2770
Smith, Louis Maurice	U.S.	2799
Smith, Mark	U.S.	2800
Smith, Michael	U.S.	2801
Soleilland, Albert	Fr.	2812
Speck, Richard Franklin	U.S.	2822
Spencer, Timothy Wilson	U.S.	2826
Spires, John	U.S.	2831
Spreitzer, Edward	U.S.	1288
Staniak, Lucian	Pol.	2839
Stevens, Dallas Ray	U.S.	2851
Stllgens, Robert Wilhelm	Ger.	2873
Stone, Elton M.	U.S.	2858
Stone, Scott C.	U.S.	2860
Story, John Huntington	U.S.	2864
Stoutamire, Ollie	U.S.	753
Stuart, Rupert Max	Aus.	2872
Sutcliffe, Peter William	Brit.	2879
Sweeney, Jack	U.S.	768
Tarquinius, Sextus	Roman.	2898
Taylor, Gary Addison	U.S.	2900
Terry, Paul	U.S.	1113
Thompson, Gerald	U.S.	2934
Thompson, Robert J.	Mex.	2935
Toney, Donald	U.S.	2967
Toney, Leonard	U.S.	2967
Trent, Lindbergh	U.S.	2985
Trotter, Clarence	U.S.	2994
Truber, Manfred	Aust.	2994
Tucker, Charles Louis	U.S.	2998
Tully, Thomas Alton	U.S.	3001
Turner, Richard	U.S.	3005
Varecha, James	U.S.	3036
Vieira, Joseph	U.S.	2762
Waldron, Tom	U.S.	728
Wallner, Walter	Aust.	2994
Walls, Samuel Cornelius	U.S.	3083
Washington, Jeffrey	U.S.	3097
Watson, Clarence Edward, Jr.	U.S.	3102
Waye, Alton	U.S.	3106
Webb, George W.	U.S.	3107
Webster, Robert	U.S.	3111
Wein, Edward Simon	U.S.	3118
West, John	U.S.	867
West, Ronald Eugene	U.S.	3129
Whiteway, Alfred Charles	Brit.	3141
Wilder, Christopher Bernard	U.S.	3155
Williams, Dennis	U.S.	3161
Williams, Hernando	U.S.	3162
Wilson, Eddie	U.S.	1428
Wilson, Eddie	U.S.	3171
Wojtasik, Gerald	U.S.	3181
Woodard, Alonzo	U.S.	1515
Woodfield, Randall Brent	U.S.	3184
Wortham, Quintin	U.S.	3191
Young, Earl	U.S.	3208

RAPE - Case of

Andrews, Thomas	Brit.	127
Arbuckle, Roscoe Conkling	U.S.	143
Baltimore, Lord Frederick	Brit.	223
Blazes, Albert	U.S.	408
Brawley, Tawana	U.S.	480
Carmen, Jack Allen	U.S.	628
Ecker, Lewis C., II	U.S.	1067
Green, Cleo Joel, III	U.S.	1372
Griffenburg, Elizabeth	Brit.	223
Hadley, Charles B.	U.S.	1414
Hammond, Travis	Brit.	1439
Harvey, Anne	Brit.	223
Hennis, Timothy Baily	U.S.	1517
Hurd, William	Brit.	2821
Kaczmarczyk, Joseph	Fr.	1752
Maggs, William	Brit.	2821
Polanski, Roman.	U.S.	2481
Richardson, Leonard	Brit.	2578
Rideout, John	U.S.	2580
Shepherd, Charles	U.S.	2739
Simants, Erwin Charles	U.S.	2763
Sparrow, William	Brit.	2821
White, Bob	U.S.	3136
Williams, Patrick	U.S.	3165

RAPE - Unsolved

Bell, Shirley	U.S.	319
Foster, Evelyn	Brit.	1202
Francis, Connie	U.S.	1209
Gandolfe, Jeanne	Fr.	1264
Kanthack, Irene Francis	S.Afri.	1759
Noblett, Anne	Brit.	2341
Page, Vera	Brit.	2393
Santa Cruz, Marta	U.S.	2679
Texarkana (Texas) Slayings	U.S.	2919
Tharme, Lilian	Brit.	2921
Tulsa Bludgeonings	U.S.	3001
Winslow, Angela	U.S.	3177

RAPE - Wrongly Convicted

Coleman, Richard	Brit.	744
Cooke, Jewey	S.Afri.	772
Dillen, Bob	U.S.	943
Dotson, Gary	U.S.	1007
Forbes, Douglas	U.S.	1193
Giles, James	U.S.	1312
Giles, John	U.S.	1312
Greenlee, Charles	U.S.	1377
Hanratty, James	Brit.	1444
Holbrook, Ernest, Jr.	U.S.	1589
Hollins, Jess	U.S.	1595
Irvin, Walter Lee	U.S.	1377
Johnson, Joseph, Jr.	U.S.	1312
Labat, Edgar	U.S.	1867
Lobaugh, Ralph W.	U.S.	1974
Mansell, Alvin	U.S.	2108
Montgomery, Jim	U.S.	2205
Poret, Clifton Alton	U.S.	1867
Scott, Lindsey	U.S.	2712
Shepherd, Samuel	U.S.	1377
Silverstein, Jack	S.Afri.	772
Tibbs, Delbert	U.S.	2950
Vasquez, David	U.S.	3037
Walker, Nathaniel	U.S.	3078
Wellman, William Mason	U.S.	3124
Williams, Gene Howard	U.S.	3162

RAPE - Wrongly Convicted?

Hanratty, James	Brit.	1444	Fredericq, Paul	Belg.	1230
Kuehn, Vinzenz	Ger.	1853	Freneau, Philip Morin	U.S.	1235
			Gainus	Roman.	1249
RAPE ATTEMPTS			Garcia Lorca, Federico	Spain	1267
Gray, Arthur	Brit.	1364	Garcia, Iiguez	Cuba	1265
Hampton, Patrick	U.S.	1835	Garrett, Joao Bapt. da S.L. de	Port.	1276
Knight, Ricky	U.S.	1835	Garza, Catarino	Int'l.	1282
			Gensonn, Armand	Fr.	1298
RAPE ATTEMPTS - Unsolved			Goto Shojiro	Japan	1350
Townsend, Jean	Brit.	2980	Grenville, George	Brit.	1381
			Grigoryants, Sergei I.	U.S.S.R.	1389
REBELLION			Grimoald I	Italy	1390
Abarca de Bolea	Spain	1	Groot, Huigh	Neth.	1392
Absolom	Isr.	14	Hammond, John Hays	S.Afri.	1438
Aung San	Burma	185	Hanriot, Francois	Fr.	1444
Avvakum Petrovich	Rus.	192	Hanson, Alexander Contee	U.S.	1445
Barabbas	Pales.	228	Han Yong-un	Korea	1445
Barriobero, Eduardo	Spain	250	Har Dayal	India	1446
ben Yair, Eleazer	Judea	339	Haya de la Torre, Victor Ral	Peru	1493
Caboche, Simon	Fr.	568	Hébert, Jacques	Fr.	1505
Cabrera, Ramón	Spain	568	Helvidius Priscus	Roman.	1514
Cadoudal, Georges	Fr.	569	Henry II de Lusignan	Mid.East	1517
Cale, Guillaume	Fr.	580	Henry, Patrick	U.S.	1519
Cambon, Pierre-Joseph	Fr.	588	Heredia y Campuzano, José M. de	Cuba	1523
Cameron, Duncan	Can.	589	Hereward	Brit.	1523
Caraccioli, Francesco	Italy	619	Hermenegild	Spain	1523
Caritat, Marie-Jean-Ant.-Nicol	Fr.	624	Herndon, Angelo	U.S.	1525
Carrera, José Miguel	Chile	637	Hernández Girón, Francisco	Spain	1525
Castilla, Miguel Hidalgoy	Mex.	655	Herriot, Edouard	Fr.	1526
Chabot, François	Fr.	666	Herwegh, Georg	Ger.	1527
Chang Hsien-chung	China	677	Hidalgo y Costilla, Miguel	Mex.	1544
Charette de la Contrie, Franoi	Fr.	686	Hlinka, Andrej	Czech.	1581
Chernyshevski, Nikolai Gavrilo	Rus.	693	Hoel, Halvor Nielsen	Nor.	1583
Chester, Randulf de Gernons	Brit.	695	Hofer, Andreas	Tyrol	1584
Chilembwe, John	Nyasaland	699	Hora, Nicolae	Rom.	1619
Cho'e Cheu	Korea	701	Houchard, Jean Nicolas	Fr.	1624
Cipriani, Amilcare	Italy	716	Hsiang Y	China	1633
Claryngdon, Sir Roger	Brit.	726	Hsiao Yen	China	1633
Clavire, tienne	Fr.	727	Hs Ta	China	1633
Clementis, Vladimir	Czech.	729	Hull, William	U.S.	1638
Cloots, Jean-Bapt. du Val-de-G	Fr.	733	Humphreys, West Hughes	U.S.	1642
Cobb, Howell	U.S.	735	Hung Jenkan	China	1642
Cochise	U.S.	735	Husbands, Hermon	U.S.	1646
Comyn, John	Scot.	763	Hussein Avni Pasha	Turk.	1647
Confalonieri, Federico	Italy	764	Hutchinson, Thomas	U.S.	1648
Cottereau, François	Fr.	797	Hyde de Neuville, Jean-Guillau	Fr.	1650
Cottereau, Jean	Fr.	797	Ibn Taymiyah	Syria	1652
Davitt, Michael	Ire.	887	Jameson, Sir Leander Starr	S.Afri.	1711
Delgado, José Matias	El Sal.	908	Jem	Turk.	1717
Dost Mohammad Khan	Afg.	1007	Kallay, Mikls	Hung.	1753
Duarte, Juan Pablo	Dom.	1029	Kallrgis, Dimitrios	Gr.	1753
Dutra, Eurico Gaspar	Braz.	1046	Kamenev, Lev Borisovich	U.S.S.R.	1754
Dutthagamani	Ceylon	1046	Kapp, Wolfgang	Ger.	1762
Dzerzhinski, Feliks Edmundovic	Rus.	1051	Karageorge	Serbia	1762
Dzsa, Gyrgy	Hung.	1017	Keng Ching-Chung	China	1792
Emmet, Thomas Addis	Ire.	1092	Ket, Robert	Brit.	1807
Empecinado, El	Spain	1093	Khaz'al Khan	Per.	1810
Engelbrekt Engelbrektsson	Swed.	1095	Khosrau II	Persia	1811
Enver Pasa	Turk.	1099	Khuang Aphaiwong	Thai.	1811
Espronceda y Delgado, José de	Spain	1106	Kickham, Charles Joseph	Ire.	1811
Estrada Palma, Toms	Cuba	1109	Kolchak, Aleksandr Vasiliyevic	Rus.	1842
Eunus	Roman.	1110	Korfanty, Wojciech	Pol.	1844
Fauchet, Claude	Fr.	1138	Korosec, Anton	Yugo.	1844
Fenians	Int'l.	1147	Kossuth, Lajos	Hung.	1844
Fischhof, Adolf	Aust.	1162	Krizanic, Juraj	Rus.	1851
Flores, Venancio	Urug.	1181	Kropotkin, Pyotr Alekseevich	Rus.	1852
Flourens, Gustave-Paul	Fr.	1181	Lamoriciere, Louis Christ. Léon	Fr.	1880
Fontan, Louis Marie	Fr.	1193	Lancaster, Thomas	Brit.	1882
Forster, Thomas	Brit.	1199	Lanzo of Milan	Italy	1896
Frederick IX	Den.	1230	Laurens, Henry	Brit.	1903

West, Thomas	Neth.	3129
West, Thomas	Ire.	3129
White, Bouck	U.S.	3136
Yang Hsiu-ching	China	3205
Yazid ibn al-Muhallab	Per.	3205
Yeh T'ing	China	3205
Yellow Turban Rebellion	China	3206
Zapata, Emiliano	Mex.	3216
Zedekiah	Judah	3218
Zevi, Sabbatai	Turk.	3220

REBELLION - Case of

Spreull, John	Scot.	2833

REFORMERS

Barrows, Samuel June	U.S.	264
Bentham, Jeremy	Brit.	335
Comstock, Anthony	U.S.	763
Edgar the Peaceful	Brit.	1069
Ewart, William	Brit.	1119
Gollancz, Sir Victor	Brit.	1336
King, Martin Luther, Jr.	U.S.	1823
Nation, Carry Amelia	U.S.	2289
Parkhurst, Charles H.	U.S.	2413
Parr, Catherine	Brit.	2415
Potter, Henry Codman	U.S.	2492
Roosevelt, Robert Barnwell	U.S.	2618
Talmadge, T. DeWitt	U.S.	2895
Yazdegerd I	Per.	3205

REGICIDE

Hutchinson, John	Brit.	1648

RESTRAINT OF TRADE

Rockefeller, John Davison	U.S.	2605

RIOT

Allen, Roger	Brit.	98
B & O Railroad Strike	U.S.	224
Baltimore Bank Riot	U.S.	227
Bodmin Jail Riot	Brit.	417
Bollander, William	U.S.	1942
Bolshevik Riots	Rus.	424
Bombay Riots	India	426
Bonus Army Riot	U.S.	434
Bristol Reform Riots	Brit.	492
British Soccer Riots	Belg.	493
Brooks, James	Brit.	499
Buckman	Haiti	533
Burmese Civil Riots	Burma	550
Canal Street	U.S.	594
Chartists, The	Brit.	689
Chicago Seven Trial, The	U.S.	698
Christ Miracle Healing Center and Church	U.S.	709
Cicero, Ill., Race Riot	U.S.	714
Clichy Uprising	Fr.	732
Clinton Prison Riot	U.S.	733
Colorado State Prison Riot	U.S.	755
Dartmoor Prison Riot	Brit.	877
Davis, William	Brit.	499
Farino, Thomas	U.S.	1942
Folsom Prison Riot	U.S.	1192
Fronde Uprising	Fr.	1238
Germano, Andro	U.S.	1301
Goldman, Emma	U.S.	1332
Gordon Riots	Brit.	1347
Hawkins, William	Brit.	1492
Homestead (Pa.) Strike	U.S.	1606
Kern, Scott	U.S.	1942
Ladone, Jason	U.S.	1942

Larkin, Luther	U.S.	1898
Lester, Jon	U.S.	1942
Montana State Prison Riot	U.S.	2203
Myles, Jerry	U.S.	2273
New Mexico State Prison Riot	U.S.	2313
OP Riots	Brit.	2374
Oklahoma State Prison Riot	U.S.	2367
Orange Riots	U.S.	2375
Pall Mall Riot	Brit.	2398
Pentecost Riot	U.S.	2441
Peterloo Massacre	Brit.	2452
Portland Whorehouse Riot	U.S.	2491
Povinelli, James	U.S.	1942
Providence Race Riot	U.S.	2508
Reform League Riots	Brit.	2558
St. George's In the East Rit.	Brit.	2658
Sharpeville Massacre	S.Afri.	2735
Smart, Lee	U.S.	2273
South Korean Riots	S. Kor.	2818
Southern Michigan State Prison	U.S.	2817
Spafields Riot	Brit.	2819
Surfleet Stockade Escapes	Brit.	2878
Trenton Prison Riots	U.S.	2986
Watts Race Riots	U.S.	3105
Westwood, William John	Aus.	3130
White, John	Brit.	499

RIOT - Case of

Smith, Jerry Paul	U.S.	2795

RIOT - Wrongly Convicted

Penlez, Bosavern	Brit.	2441

ROBBERY

Abbershaw, Lewis Jeremiah	Brit.	3
Abrams, Michael	U.S.	13
Adams, Dick	Brit.	22
Adams, Eddie	U.S.	22
Adams, Kitty	U.S.	26
Adams, Mary	Brit.	27
Addison, Jack	Brit.	30
Aleman, Harry	U.S.	72
Alex, Michael	U.S.	73
Allweiss, David	U.S.	102
Almer, Jack	U.S.	103
Anderson, Billy Dean	U.S.	122
Anderson, David L.	U.S.	122
Anderson, Leroy Gene	U.S.	123
Andrews, Milton Franklin	U.S.	127
Andrews, Norman	Aus.	1917
Andrews, William	U.S.	2464
Antonini, Theresa	Ger.	134
Archer-Shee, George	Brit.	152
Arcine, James	U.S.	153
Arindell, William	Brit.	1179
Armstrong, John	Brit.	157
Armstrong, Thomas Jefferson	U.S.	159
Arnold, Joseph	U.S.	162
Arnstein (Arndstein), Jules W.	U.S.	163
Arsenault, Henry	U.S.	168
Ashcroft, David	Brit.	170
Ashcroft, David	Brit.	1591
Ashcroft, James	Brit.	170
Ashcroft, James, Jr.	Brit.	170
Ashcroft, James, Sr.	Brit.	1591
Ashline, Roy	U.S.	170
Ashton, John	Brit.	170
Atkinson, Isaac	Brit.	176
Atlanta Bond Theft	U.S.	176
Attia, Joseph Victor Bhamin	Fr.	179

Audett, James Henry	U.S.	182	Booth, Ernest	U.S.	436
Austin, John	Brit.	186	Boudin, M.	Fr.	2658
Austin, Tom	Brit.	186	Bourke, Patrick	Brit.	454
Avery	Brit.	189	Bowman, John H.	U.S.	1732
Avery, Peter	Brit.	189	Bracey, Joan	Brit.	464
Ayala, Samuel	U.S.	193	Bradshaw, Jack	Brit.	466
Bailey, Harvey John	U.S.	208	Brady, Al	U.S.	466
Bailey, Reese	U.S.	212	Brady, John	U.S.	467
Bain, Robert Owen	U.S.	212	Brady, Matthew	Brit.	468
Baker, George	U.S.	287	Bras Coup	U.S.	474
Baker, James	Brit.	216	Brennan, Ben	U.S.	485
Baker, James	Brit.	2131	Brink's Armored Car Robbery	U.S.	489
Banghart, Basil	U.S.	224	Brink's Robbery	U.S.	489
Banister, Christopher	Brit.	226	Brisbon, Henry, Jr.	U.S.	492
Barany, Serge	Fr.	228	British Bank of the Middle East	Leb.	493
Barber, Ronald L.	U.S.	230	Brletic, Joseph James	U.S.	494
Barker Brothers	U.S.	235	Brooklyn Refinery Robbery	U.S.	498
Barrack, Margaret	Scot.	248	Brown, Arthur	Peru	107
Barrington, George	Brit.	250	Brown, Bruce	Brit.	505
Barrow, Clyde Champion	U.S.	250	Brown, H. Rap	U.S.	507
Barry, Arthur	U.S.	264	Brown, Jim	U.S.	2056
Bartley, Alvis R.	U.S.	270	Brown, Joseph	Brit.	514
Barton, Mary	Brit.	271	Bruneau, Albert	Fr.	520
Barwick, Charles	Brit.	271	Brunette, Harry	U.S.	520
Basile, Tobia	Italy	272	Bryant, Kenneth	U.S.	524
Bassot, Henri	Fr.	1317	Bryon, Robert	U.S.	3085
Bates, Joseph	U.S.	765	Buchanan, Eugene	U.S.	529
Battistelli, Mathieu	Fr.	1915	Buckley, Tim	Brit.	532
Bauf, Richard	Ire.	284	Buckly, William	U.S.	533
Baynes, Andrew	Brit.	286	Buffalo Bill House	U.S.	534
Beale, George P.	U.S.	287	Buffet, Claude	Fr.	534
Bean, Harold Walter	U.S.	3085	Buisson, mile	Fr.	535
Beatson, John	Brit.	292	Bullard, Charles	U.S.	536
Becker, Charles	U.S.	297	Bullard, Charles	U.S.	536
Beckett, Henry	Brit.	310	Bunce, Stephen	Brit.	536
Beckwourth, James	U.S.	311	Burgess, Richard	N.Zea.	544
Bell, Sydney	U.S.	319	Burk, Wayne	U.S.	545
Benedetti, Jacques	Fr.	1915	Burke, Fred	U.S.	546
Bentley, Derek	Brit.	336	Burke, James	U.S.	547
Bentz, Edward Wilhelm	U.S.	337	Burnett, Benjamin	U.S.	2393
Berdue, Thomas	U.S.	340	Burns, John	U.S.	551
Berta, Charles	U.S.	349	Burnworth, Edward	Brit.	554
Bew, William	Brit.	355	Burrell, Mr.	Brit.	777
Biddings, Robert	U.S.	358	Burton, Reginald	Brit.	271
Biddle, Ed	U.S.	358	Bush, John Earl	U.S.	660
Biddle, Jack	U.S.	358	Butler, Harry Linton	U.S.	561
Biggin Hill Robbery	Brit.	360	Butler, James	Brit.	562
Biggs, Peter	U.S.	2797	Butler, Robert	Aus.	563
Bird, Jack	Brit.	373	Butler, Robert	N.Zea.	563
Bisbee, Ariz. Massacre	U.S.	380	Butler, William	Brit.	563
Bishop, Barnell	U.S.	381	Buzzard Brothers	U.S.	564
Bishop, Jesse Walter	U.S.	381	Byrne, Joseph	Aus.	1779
Bismarck Hall	U.S.	383	Byrnes, Thomas	U.S.	566
Black Bart	U.S.	385	Cady, William	Brit.	569
Black Dick	Brit.	391	Cagliostro, Count Alessandro d	Int'l.	571
Black, James W.	Scot.	385	Caldclough, James	Brit.	579
Blacket, Mary	Brit.	392	Caldwell, John	Scot.	579
Blake, Daniel	Brit.	403	Callahan, John	U.S.	582
Blake, Joseph	Brit.	404	Campbell, Calif., Post Office	U.S.	592
Blake, Lena	U.S.	404	Carlisle, William	U.S.	625
Blanck, Tom	U.S.	405	Cartouche	Fr.	647
Bliss, George Miles	U.S.	409	Caruana, Salvatore Michael	U.S.	647
Blood, Thomas	Brit.	409	Casebolt, Crawford	U.S.	649
Bojorques, Narciso	U.S.	422	Casey, Michael	Brit.	1980
Bolognini, Arnaldo	Italy	665	Cassidy, James P.	U.S.	2056
Bolton, David	Brit.	425	Castiglioni, Eros	Italy	665
Bonnet, Edward	Brit.	430	Caswell, Alex	U.S.	2056
Bonnet, Jeanne	U.S.	430	Cauty, Bill	Brit.	659
Bonnot Gang	Fr.	432	Cave, Alphonso	U.S.	660
Bookie Gang, The	U.S.	435	Cecconi, Patrick	U.S.	3041

Cesaroni, Enrico	Italy	665	Dagoe, Hannah	Brit.	854
Chambers, Arthur	Brit.	672	Dahman, John	U.S.	855
Chancy, Harrison	U.S.	676	Dainard, William J.	U.S.	855
Chapman, Gerald	U.S.	683	Daley, Dominic	U.S.	856
Chapman, Jack	Brit.	1035	Dalton, Willie	U.S.	858
Chapman, John T.	U.S.	685	Daniels, Thomas H.	U.S.	868
Charlton Street Gang	U.S.	688	Dashwood, Samuel	Brit.	877
Charrier, Jacques Mecislas	Fr.	688	Davis, Bruce A.	U.S.	882
Chase, John Paul	U.S.	689	Davis, Edward	Aus.	883
Chatham, Linwood	U.S.	1732	Davis, Jack	U.S.	884
Chaucer, Geoffrey	Brit.	690	Davis, Louis	U.S.	2543
Chevez, Cleovara	U.S.	422	Davis, William	Brit.	886
Choate, Pearl	U.S.	701	De Boe, William Thomas	U.S.	894
Chowick, William	U.S.	702	DeCroat, Arthur	U.S.	898
Churchill, Deborah	Brit.	713	Dead Man's Alley	U.S.	889
Churchill, May Vivienne	Int'l.	713	Dean, Dan	U.S.	890
Ciappina, Ugo	Italy	665	Dean, Margie	U.S.	891
Clark, Marcellus Jerome	U.S.	723	Deering, John	U.S.	901
Clark, Thomas	U.S.	724	De Jarnette, John Kinchloe	U.S.	902
Clarke, Morris Arthur	Brit.	726	DeMaria, Luciano	Italy	665
Clavel, John	Brit.	727	Demury, Lucille	Brit.	2057
Clayton, Robert David	Aus.	1917	Dennison, Stephen Heath	U.S.	915
Cleaver, Charles	U.S.	728	Denvile, Robert	Brit.	917
Clement, Robert	U.S.	765	Denvile, Sir Gosselin	Brit.	917
Clough, Jonathan	Brit.	734	De Rosa, Anthony	Brit.	919
Cock, George	Brit.	737	De Rosa, Emanuel	Brit.	919
Cocklain, Matthew	Brit.	737	DeSalvo, Albert Henry	U.S.	921
Codre, Georges	Brit.	738	Desgrandschamps, Charles	Fr.	924
Cohen, John	Brit.	741	DeSimone, Thomas	U.S.	547
Cohen, Raymond	Brit.	425	de Stamir, Victor	Brit.	926
Colarco, Ross	U.S.	742	DeTell, Hugh	U.S.	927
Coleman, Alton	U.S.	743	Dick, Frank	U.S.	939
Coleman, Jefferson	U.S.	744	Dickson, Christopher	Brit.	940
Coleman, Tommy	U.S.	745	Dillard, Norman	U.S.	943
Collet, James	Brit.	748	Dillinger, John Herbert	U.S.	943
Colley, George	U.S.	749	Diver, Jenny	Brit.	978
Collings, Jack	Brit.	750	Dixon, Fred Michael	U.S.	979
Collins, George	U.S.	2636	Doane Gang	U.S.	980
Colson, Forrest Ray	U.S.	759	Dobbs, Johnny	U.S.	980
Comfort, Robert Anthony	U.S.	762	Dombkiewicz, Peter	U.S.	994
Congden, Robert	Brit.	764	Donahoe, Jack	Brit.	997
Conlin, Charles William	Brit.	765	Dondone, John	U.S.	998
Connelly, William C.	U.S.	765	Donohue, Thomas	U.S.	1000
Connolly, Ann	U.S.	2834	Dooley, Rafer	U.S.	1002
Cook, DeWitt Clinton	U.S.	769	Dorbell, Tom	Brit.	1004
Cooney, Cecilia Roth	U.S.	774	Dorman, Frank	U.S.	358
Cooney, Edward	U.S.	774	Dorsey, Charles	U.S.	1005
Cooper, James	Brit.	777	Dorsey, Charles	U.S.	2423
Cooper, Paula	U.S.	777	Douglas, Sawney	Brit.	1010
Cooper, Ray Anthony	U.S.	778	Dowdall, James	U.S.	1013
Copeland, James	U.S.	779	Drysdale, Alexander	U.S.	1029
Corey, Frank	U.S.	784	Dubois, Aline	Fr.	1125
Cotter, Benny	U.S.	797	Dudley, Richard	Brit.	1031
Court, M.	Fr.	2535	Duell, William	Brit.	1032
Couture, Donald	U.S.	2437	Dun, Thomas	Brit.	1034
Couture, Donna	U.S.	2437	Dun, Timothy	Brit.	1035
Cowley, James D.	Int'l.	801	Dunbar, Ronald Patrick	Brit.	1035
Cox, Tom	Brit.	803	Duncalf, William	Brit.	777
Coyle, Joseph William	U.S.	804	Duncan, Mary	Scot.	248
Craig, Christopher	Brit.	336	Dunsdon Brothers	Brit.	1038
Cretzer, Joseph Paul	U.S.	816	du Plessis, Andries Stephanus	S.Afri.	1039
Crews, Paul David	U.S.	818	Durant, Jack	U.S.	1041
Crowley, Francis	U.S.	838	Duval, Claude	Brit.	1046
Cullen, John	U.S.	2747	Duval, Jean	Can.	1047
Cullum, Jack	Brit.	844	Edmundson, Calvin Jerome	U.S.	1070
Curtis, Winslow	U.S.	3138	Edwards, William	Brit.	3179
Cutpurse, Moll	Brit.	850	Egan, Robert Danny	U.S.	3085
D'Autremont Brothers	U.S.	878	Eisele, Joseph	U.S.	1079
Dabner, Louis	U.S.	853	Elby, William	Brit.	1080
Dacoity	India	853	Elliott, Joe	Int'l.	1084

Ellis, George	Brit.	454	Gholston, Kenneth	U.S.	1305
Ellis, Michael	Brit.	425	Gibson, John	Brit.	940
Esposito, Anthony	U.S.	1104	Giriat, Victorine	Fr.	1317
Esposito, William	U.S.	1105	Giuliano, Salvatore	Si.	1317
Evans, Evan	Brit.	1111	Glatman, Harvey Murray	U.S.	1321
Evans, William	Brit.	1111	Goethe, Robert	U.S.	1328
Everett, John	Brit.	1114	Goff, Sadie	U.S.	1330
Faber, Abraham	U.S.	2179	Good, Earl	U.S.	2828
Fagard, Edmond	Fr.	1125	Good, Millard	U.S.	1339
Fahy, William	U.S.	1126	Goodwin, Jack	Brit.	1340
Farr, John William	U.S.	1135	Gordon, William	Brit.	1346
Farrell, Stephen	U.S.	1136	Gould, Richard	Brit.	1352
Farrington, Hilary	U.S.	1137	Gould, William	U.S.	1352
Farrington, Levi	U.S.	1137	Gow, John	Brit.	1353
Ferguson, Champ	U.S.	1150	Grady, John	U.S.	1355
Ferguson, Richard	Brit.	1151	Gray, Thomas	Brit.	1365
Fesch, Jacques	Fr.	1153	Great Gold Robbery	Brit.	1367
Field, William	Brit.	1155	Great Mail Robbery	U.S.	1369
Filewood, James	Brit.	1157	Great Train Robbery	Brit.	1370
Filipovitz, Peter	Aust.	2994	Green, Edward W.	U.S.	1373
Fisher, Lavinia	U.S.	1166	Green, Samuel	U.S.	1374
Fisher, Margaret	Brit.	1167	Greil, Hans	Ger.	1586
Fitzgerald, Mamie	U.S.	1171	Grierson, Alan James	Brit.	1385
Fitzpatrick, James	U.S.	1172	Griffiths, James	Scot.	1388
Fleagle Gang	U.S.	1176	Grizzard, Joseph	Brit.	1391
Fleming, Patrick	Ire.	1178	Gurin, Eddie	Fr.	1396
Fletcher, John	Brit.	1179	Haggart, David	Int'l.	1415
Fletcher, Simon	Brit.	1179	Hall, Andreas	U.S.	1420
Flinn, Charles J.	U.S.	1179	Hall, Archibald	Brit.	1420
Floyd, Charles Arthur	U.S.	1182	Hall, Ben	Aus.	1421
Fogg Art Museum Coin Robbery	U.S.	1190	Hall, Jack	Brit.	1424
Fooy, Sam	U.S.	1193	Hall, James William	Aus.	1426
Ford, Emma	U.S.	1193	Halligan, James	U.S.	856
Ford, James	U.S.	1195	Halloway, Ann	Brit.	1432
Forrest, Elliot	Fr.	1198	Halsey, Jacob	Brit.	1432
Foster, William	S.Afri.	1203	Hamilton, Ray	U.S.	1435
Fox, Isaac Garrett	U.S.	1205	Hammerling, Peter	U.S.	1436
Fox, William	U.S.	1206	Hampton, Patrick	U.S.	1835
Fra Angelo	Italy	1207	Hare, Joseph Thompson	U.S.	1452
Franklyn, Rudolph	Brit.	1226	Harland, Berry	U.S.	2374
Fraser, Alfred	Brit.	1227	Harmon, Charles Preston	U.S.	1454
Fredericks, William M.	U.S.	1230	Harmond, John H.	U.S.	1455
Fromanger	Fr.	1915	Harper, Richard	U.S.	1456
Fugate, Caril Ann	U.S.	2840	Harris, Dennis	U.S.	1460
Gadesby, William	Brit.	1248	Harris, Nan	Brit.	1462
Gagliano, Joseph	U.S.	1249	Harrow, William	Brit.	1466
Gaither, Ernie	U.S.	1250	Hart, Steve	Aus.	1779
Gallus Mag	U.S.	1257	Hartley, John	Brit.	1469
Garcia, Antonio	U.S.	422	Harvey, Margaret	Brit.	1472
Garcia, Luis	U.S.	1266	Harwood, Jocelin	Brit.	1473
Gardiner, Frank	Aus.	1268	Harwood, Levi	Brit.	1473
Gardner, Roy	U.S.	1269	Harwood, Samuel	Brit.	1473
Garesio, Antonio	Italy	1270	Hatcher, Charles Ray	U.S.	1475
Garesio, Gian Battista	Italy	1270	Hatcher, Edward	U.S.	2834
Garret, Thomas	Brit.	1276	Hawes, Nathaniel	Brit.	1491
Garrison, Donald Graham	U.S.	1279	Hayward, George Frederick Walt	Brit.	1499
Gary, Carlton	U.S.	1282	Hearst, Patricia Campbell	U.S.	1501
Gasperoni, Antonio	Italy	1283	Hedgepeth, Marion	U.S.	1506
Gatti, Salvatore	U.S.	1284	Hefeldt, Paul	Brit.	1939
Gauchet, Georges	Fr.	1284	Helms, Henry	U.S.	2543
Gault, Julian	Int'l.	1284	Hereford, Anne	Brit.	1523
Gearish, Anthony	Brit.	1287	Herring, Robert	U.S.	1525
Geary, Percy	U.S.	2107	Heslin, Peter	U.S.	1527
Gense, Gerard	Fr.	1125	Hickman, William Edward	U.S.	1532
George, John	U.S.	2834	Hill, Gregory	U.S.	1551
Geraghty, Christopher James	Brit.	1300	Hill, Robert	U.S.	2543
Gerena, Victor Manuel	U.S.	1301	Hind, James	Brit.	1558
Gerrard, Thomas	Brit.	1301	Hinds, Alfie	Int'l.	1560
Gesmundo, Arnaldo	Italy	665	Hinkle, Betty	U.S.	2380
Gettings, William	Brit.	1303	Hinton, Edward	Brit.	1562

Hirasawa Sadamichi	Japan	1563	Keating, Francis L.	U.S.	728
Hirst	Brit.	2102	Kehoe, John	U.S.	1776
Hobday, Stanley Eric	Brit.	1581	Kelly, Dan	Aus.	1779
Hoffner, Anna	Ger.	1586	Kelly, Edward	Aus.	1779
Hogan, Dominick	U.S.	1776	Kelly, George	Brit.	1782
Hogan, Edward	U.S.	1776	Kelly, George R.	U.S.	1782
Holden, Thomas	U.S.	728	Kelly, Peter	Brit.	1789
Holden, Thomas	U.S.	1590	Kelly, Tom	N.Zea.	544
Holden, William	Brit.	170	Kelsey, Thomas	Brit.	1790
Holden, William	Brit.	1591	Kennedy, Mathew	Int'l.	1800
Holland, Anne	Brit.	1591	Kenyon, Michael H.	U.S.	1805
Holliday, John	Brit.	1592	Killorain, Japonica Jack	Peru	107
Hollyday, William	Brit.	1597	Kimes-Terrill Gang	U.S.	1819
Holmes, John	Brit.	1601	King, Charles	Brit.	1821
Holzhay, Reimund	U.S.	1605	King, Jack	U.S.	1776
Hope, James	U.S.	1617	Kingsmill Gang	Brit.	1827
Horne, Carlton	U.S.	1620	Kirkland, Haywood T.	U.S.	1732
Horner, Nicholas	Brit.	1621	Kitto, Michael	Brit.	1420
Hornig, Frank	Aus.	1621	Knapp, George	U.S.	1834
Horton, William Robert	U.S.	1623	Knight, Arthur B.	U.S.	1732
Houghton, Hugh	Brit.	1624	Knight, Ricky	U.S.	1835
Houndsditch Murders	Brit.	1625	Knös, Andre	Brit.	1836
Housden, Jane	Brit.	1733	Kovovick, Milovar	U.S.	1845
Howe, Michael	Int'l.	1631	Krafchenko, John	Can.	1846
Huber, Charles	U.S.	1634	Kress, Joseph	U.S.	2107
Hughes, Daniel	Brit.	1636	Lacombe, Francois	Fr.	1869
Hughes, George	U.S.	2940	Ladd, Bucky	U.S.	170
Hughes, John	U.S.	2107	Ladermann, Csar	Fr.	1317
Hughes, Richard	Brit.	1637	Lamm, Herman K.	U.S.	1877
Hume, Brian Donald	Brit.	1641	Lampião	Braz.	1880
Hunt-Gant Gang	U.S.	1645	Langley, Gilbert	Brit.	1890
Hunt, Richard	U.S.	1643	Langton, Catherine	Brit.	1891
Hutchings, Harvey	Brit.	1647	Languille, Henri	Fr.	1891
Hutton, Peregrine	U.S.	1648	Langulet, Antoine	Fr.	1891
Ingle, Carl	U.S.	1733	Lannen, Gordon	Brit.	1891
Irwin, Estelle Mae	U.S.	1666	Lapa, Frank Albert	U.S.	1896
Ivory, James	U.S.	2940	La Villette Gang	Fr.	1905
Jacks, George H.	U.S.	1674	Lavin, Martin	U.S.	1905
Jackson, Charles	U.S.	1676	Laws, Elizabeth	Brit.	1907
Jackson, Eddie	U.S.	1676	Lawson, Gordon F.	U.S.	1907
Jackson, Edwin Aubrey	Brit.	1677	Leca, Paul	Fr.	1915
James, Jesse Woodson	U.S.	1695	Ledmond, Patrick	Brit.	1916
Jameson, James	U.S.	1711	Lee, Jean	Aus.	1917
Jenkins, Charles Harry	Brit.	1300	Leigh, John	U.S.	1733
Jenkins, Harry	U.S.	1718	Lemay, Georges	Can.	1926
Jenkins, James Gilbert	U.S.	1719	Leonard, James	Brit	1931
Jenkins, Thomas	Brit.	1719	Lepidus, Jacob	Brit.	1939
Johnson, Henry	Brit.	1729	Leslie, George Leonidas	U.S.	1941
Johnson, John	U.S.	1730	Levy, Philip	N.Zea.	544
Johnson, Johnny	U.S.	1730	Lewis, Charles	U.S.	1945
Johnson, Laura	U.S.	1730	Lewis, Howard Henry	Brit.	1227
Johnson, Robert L.	U.S.	1732	Lieberman, Brad	U.S.	1950
Johnson, Terry Wayne	U.S.	660	Liebscher, William, Jr.	U.S.	1950
Johnson, Watterson	U.S.	1733	Lipa, Peter	U.S.	1969
Johnson, William	Brit.	1733	Liston, Dr. Robert	Brit.	1970
Jollivet	Fr.	1915	Llaguna, Roger	U.S.	1266
Jones, Adam	U.S.	1736	Lonagan, Edward	Brit.	1980
Jones, Calvin S.	U.S.	1732	Loomis, George Washington, Jr.	U.S.	1988
Jones, Charles E.	U.S.	1737	Lovering, John E.	U.S.	1996
Jones, James	Brit.	1473	Low, Dick	Brit.	1996
Jones, Milton E.	U.S.	2764	Lowenstein, Emil	U.S.	1998
Jones, Moll	Brit.	1740	Lowther, Will	Brit.	1999
Jones, Peter	U.S.	1740	Lufthansa Robbery	U.S.	2008
Jones, Will	Brit.	1741	Lyle, Edward	U.S.	2015
Jordon, Josiah	U.S.	2834	Lympus, Thomas	Brit.	2016
Jorgensen, Jorgen	Ice.	1744	Lyons, William	U.S.	1352
Kallinger, Joseph	U.S.	1753	McAdoo, Anthony LaQuin	U.S.	2930
Karpis, Alvin	U.S.	1763	McAuliffe, Joseph Herbert	Can.	2022
Kassow, Raymond	U.S.	1733	McCallum, McNeill Francis	Aus.	2023
Keating, Francis	U.S.	1590	McCarthy, Justin William	U.S.	2024

Parker, Frederick William	Brit.	2410
Parker, J.B.	U.S.	660
Parkyn, Arthur	Brit.	2414
Parnell, Kenneth E.	U.S.	2414
Patrovick, Milovar	U.S.	1845
Patterson, John	U.S.	2423
Patti, D.	Si.	2425
Pattmore, May	U.S.	2426
Paulson, Michael	U.S.	2427
Peare, William	Brit.	2433
Pelletier, Lawrence, Jr.	U.S.	2437
Pelletier, Nicolas-Jacques	Fr.	2437
Perkins, Rudolph	U.S.	2444
Perry, Henry	Brit.	2446
Perry, Oliver Curtis	U.S.	2447
Peruggia, Vincenzo	Fr.	2448
Peters, Warren	U.S.	3171
Phillips, Morgan	Brit.	2460
Phillips, Thomas	Brit.	2828
Philson, Robert	U.S.	2460
Phuoc Tri Nguyen	U.S.	2460
Pierre, Dale	U.S.	2464
Pierson, Marcel	Fr.	2465
Piskorski, Ronald	U.S.	2470
Plackett, John	Brit.	2474
Podmore, William Henry	Brit.	2478
Ponce, Noratto	U.S.	422
Pope, Duane Earl	U.S.	2489
Pranzini, Dr. Karl	Fr.	2496
Pratt, Dennis James	Brit.	2497
Price, John	Brit.	2500
Prior, John	Brit.	2503
Probert, Albert	Brit.	2410
Proctor, George H.	U.S.	2505
Profit, William	U.S.	193
Purdy, William	Brit.	2512
Pytsch, Cornelius	U.S.	2517
Quailes, Ian	Brit.	2519
Quinn, Thomas	U.S.	2107
Raby, Moll	Brit.	2525
Racicot, Sam	U.S.	170
Rag, Isaac	Brit.	1035
Ramirez, Patrick	U.S.	2533
Randall, Tom	Brit.	2534
Rankin, Gilman D.	U.S.	2656
Rann, John	Brit.	2534
Rao, Joseph	U.S.	2535
Raoul, Clair	Fr.	2535
Ratliff, Marshall	U.S.	2543
Ratsey, Gamaliel	Brit.	2544
Ray, Mark	U.S.	2547
Raymond, Robert	U.S.	2547
Redenbaugh, Joseph	U.S.	2553
Redmond, Patrick	Ire.	2554
Reed, Bjorn	U.S.	1136
Reed, Edwin	U.S.	2556
Reeves, Thomas	Brit.	1469
Reginald of Châtillon	Fr.	2559
Reno Brothers	U.S.	2568
Reynolds, Thomas	Brit.	2571
Reynolds, Tom	Brit.	466
Reynolds, Tom	Brit.	2364
Ricardo, Joseph	U.S.	2573
Rice, Josie	U.S.	404
Richardson, Charles William	Brit.	2576
Richardson, Edward	Brit.	2576
Riga, Michael	U.S.	2583
Riley, James	U.S.	2584
Riley, John	U.S.	2342
Rizzolo, Michael	U.S.	2588

Roach, George	Brit.	2588
Roberts, George Denwhite	U.S.	2592
Robinson, George	Brit.	2595
Robinson, Joe	U.S.	2393
Robinson, John	Brit.	170
Robinson, Virgil	U.S.	2602
Roche, Edward	U.S.	2603
Rockwood, Edward	U.S.	2605
Roderick, Audrey	Brit.	2605
Roeski, Emil	U.S.	3030
Rolley, George Harold	Scot.	2614
Rolt, Terence	Brit.	1300
Romanetti, Nonce	Italy	2615
Rose, Alfred	Brit.	2620
Ross, Charles	U.S.	2374
Ross, Elizabeth	Brit.	2624
Ross, Walter	U.S.	2374
Rowland, Tom	Brit.	2631
Roy, Gilder	Scot.	2632
Rubel Ice Company Robbery	U.S.	2633
Ruberti, Barthelemy	Fr.	1915
Rudensky, Morris	U.S.	2635
Rudge, Anthony	Brit.	2131
Rudge, Anthony Benjamin	Brit.	216
Rudolph, William	U.S.	2636
Rumbold, Thomas	Brit.	2639
Russend, Joseph	U.S.	2643
Russo, Ferdinando	Italy	665
Sacco, Nicola	U.S.	2649
Sadler, Fern L.	U.S.	2656
Salter, John	Brit.	2673
Sanna, François	Fr.	1915
Saul, Nicholas	U.S.	2681
Saunders, Howard Donald	U.S.	2682
Savage, Thomas	Brit.	2682
Saxe, Susan Edith	U.S.	2685
Sberna, Charles	U.S.	1284
Scaffa, Noel Charles	U.S.	2685
Schlagle, Harvey	U.S.	2656
Scott, Andrew George	Aus.	2710
Scott, Don	U.S.	2713
Scott, Francis	U.S.	2711
Scott, Paul	U.S.	2713
Searcy, Charles J.	U.S.	2718
Sedley, Bill	U.S.	2721
Seimsen, John	U.S.	853
Selby, Norman	U.S.	2724
Sellers, Willie Foster	U.S.	2726
Sennanedj, Roger Mardothe	Fr.	1915
Sewell, Frederick Joseph	Brit.	2730
Seye, Blaise Ferrage	Fr.	2730
Sharp, Thomas	Brit.	2735
Sharpe, Walter	Brit.	1891
Sheehan, Patrick	U.S.	2738
Sheppard, Jack	Brit.	2740
Sheridan, Walter Cartman	Int'l.	2743
Sheridan, Walter Cartman	Belg.	2743
Sherrington, Charles	Brit.	2745
Shinburn, Max	Int'l.	2746
Shinburn, Max	Belg.	2746
Shinney, Janet	Scot.	248
Shonbrun, Eli	U.S.	2747
Shouse, Minnie	U.S.	2749
Showery, Allan	U.S.	2750
Shrimpton, John	Brit.	2750
Shriner, Carl Elson	U.S.	2750
Sica, Joseph	U.S.	2751
Silverosa, George	Brit.	877
Simmons, Theodore	U.S.	2764
Simms, Henry	Brit.	2765

Simpson, Jonathan	Brit.	2766	Tripp, Grace	Brit.	2989
Sims, Mitchell Carleton	U.S.	2767	Truber, Manfred	Aust.	2994
Singh, Boysie	Trinidad	2768	Tucker, Charles Louis	U.S.	2998
Slade, Joshua	Brit.	2776	Tufts, Henry	U.S.	2999
Smith, Charles	U.S.	2783	Tuller, Bryce	U.S.	3000
Smith, Edward Charles	Brit.	514	Tuller, Charles A.	U.S.	3000
Smith, Ellsworth	U.S.	2784	Tuller, Jonathan	U.S.	3000
Smith, Jack	U.S.	2056	Turner, Richard	U.S.	3005
Smith, Joe	Brit.	2796	Turpin, Richard	Brit.	3005
Smith, John	Brit.	2796	Uckele, John Joseph	U.S.	3014
Smith, John	U.S.	2797	Underhill, Wilbur	U.S.	3015
Smith, Lucille	U.S.	2825	Usefof, Joseph	U.S.	2056
Smith, Mattie	U.S.	2801	Vacko, Pavel	Ger.	3024
Smith, Michael	U.S.	2801	Vallanzasca, Renato	Italy	3027
Smith, Pearl	U.S.	2801	Van Dine, Harvey	U.S.	3030
Smith, Thomas	U.S.	2834	Van Niekerk, Andries	S.Afri.	3034
Smith, Thomas L.	U.S.	2803	Vanzetti, Bartolomeo	U.S.	2649
Smith, William	U.S.	2804	Varnars, George	U.S.	2643
Snow, William	Brit.	2805	Vasquez, Tiburcio	U.S.	422
Sobhraj, Gurmukh Charles	India	2810	Vaughan, George	Brit.	3039
Soeder, Leon	U.S.	2811	Vaux, James Hardy	Brit.	3040
Soli, Salvatore	U.S.	2813	Vega, Evelyn	U.S.	2437
Sontag Brothers	U.S.	2815	Vegnaduzzi, Andre	Fr.	3040
Soto, Juan	U.S.	422	Velleff, Randy	U.S.	3041
Spaggiari, Albert	Fr.	2820	Viccei, Valerio	Brit.	3045
Spencer, Al	U.S.	2824	Von Veltheim, Franz	Brit.	3064
Spencer, Anthony	U.S.	2824	Vratz, Christopher	Brit.	3064
Spencer, Bertram G.	U.S.	2825	Wable, John Wesley	U.S.	3067
Spencer, Brenda	U.S.	2825	Wagoner, Frank	U.S.	2656
Spencer, Henry	U.S.	2825	Waley, Harmon Metz	U.S.	855
Spicer, Edward A.	U.S.	2828	Walker, Charles	U.S.	3076
Spiggot, William	Brit.	2828	Walker, Jonathan	U.S.	3078
St. Albans (Vt.) Robbery	U.S.	2658	Walker, William	U.S.	3079
St. Germain, M.	Fr.	2658	Wallace, Stewart	U.S.	2107
Stacey, Rebecca	U.S.	2834	Waller, John	Brit.	3082
Stacey, Robert	U.S.	2834	Wallner, Walter	Aust.	2994
Stafford, Philip	Brit.	2836	Walls, James Jr.	U.S.	193
Starkweather, Charles	U.S.	2840	Walsh, Bill	Brit.	3084
Starr, Belle	U.S.	2843	Walters, Ann Carol	U.S.	3085
Starr, Henry	U.S.	2843	Walters, Ted	U.S.	3086
Stewart, Archie	U.S.	2107	Walters, Wayne	U.S.	3085
Stockwell, John Frederick	Brit.	2857	Waltham Blacks	Brit.	3086
Stokely, John	U.S.	2797	Ward, Frederick	Aus.	3091
Stratton, Albert	Brit.	2867	Ward, William	Brit.	3093
Stratton, Alfred	Brit.	2867	Washington, Aaron	U.S.	3097
Stuart, James	U.S.	2871	Waters, Tom	Brit.	3101
Stubbs, William Morley	Brit.	2872	Watkins, Phillip Benjamin	Brit.	1677
Sutton, William Francis	U.S.	2881	Watkins, Thomas	Brit.	3102
Sverre	Nor.	2884	Watson, David	U.S.	1041
Symbionese Liberation Army	U.S.	2889	Watt, Newton	U.S.	3104
Sympson, Thomas	Brit.	2891	Webb, Madeline	U.S.	2747
Tavernier, Jean Baptiste	Burma	2899	Weber, Adolph	U.S.	3108
Taylor, Tom	Brit.	2902	Webster, Kate	Brit.	3111
Thayer, Earl	U.S.	2926	Weipert, Lee	U.S.	2934
Thomas, Frederick Jerome	U.S.	2930	Wells, Harry	U.S.	3125
Thompson, George	U.S.	2934	Wells, Nicholas	Brit.	3125
Thompson, Robert J.	Mex.	2935	Werner, Louis	U.S.	547
Thornton, Lonzo	U.S.	2940	West, Ronald Eugene	U.S.	3129
Thornton, Mark	Brit.	2940	Weston, George	Brit.	3129
Thorvik, Louis	U.S.	2940	Weston, Joseph	Brit.	3129
Throgmorton, William	Brit.	2942	Westwood, William John	Aus.	3130
Thurland, Tom	Brit.	1035	Weymouth, Charles	Brit.	940
Tieri, Frank	U.S.	2953	Whalley, William	Brit.	292
Timmons, Ronald	U.S.	2956	Wharton, Charles S.	U.S.	728
Tracey, Frank J.	U.S.	2981	Whelan, John	Aus.	3134
Tracey, Walter	Brit.	2981	White, John Duncan	U.S.	3138
Tracy, Harry	U.S.	2981	White, Will	Brit.	1035
Tracy, Martha	Brit.	2982	Whitefield, John	Brit.	3139
Trease, Edward	U.S.	2984	Whiteway, Alfred Charles	Brit.	3141
Trevor, Harold Darien	Brit.	2988	Whitfield, John	Brit.	3141

MacKay, Patrick David	Brit.	2047
Mikasevich, Gennadiy	U.S.S.R.	2177
Monster of Florence	Italy	2202
Moonlight Murderer	U.S.	2209
Nelson, Earle Leonard	Int'l.	2299
New Bedford (Mass.) Serial Mur	U.S.	2308
Oakland County Murders	U.S.	2349
Ogorzov, Paul	Ger.	2365
Olson, Clifford	Can.	2371
Palmer, William	Brit.	2400
Peete, Lofie Louise	U.S.	2436
Phillipe, Joseph	Fr.	2458
Piper, Thomas W.	U.S.	2469
Pleasant, Mary Ellen	U.S.	2475
Pleil, Rudolf	Ger.	2476
Point Reyes Murders	U.S.	2480
Pommerencke, Heinrich	Aust.	2485
Prince Georges Cty., Md., Slay	U.S.	2502
Putt, George Howard	U.S.	2517
Ralph, Edward	U.S.	2533
Rardon, Gary	U.S.	2536
Red-Haired Women Killings	U.S.	2553
Rees, Melvin David	U.S.	2557
Robinson, Sarah Jane	U.S.	2601
Roche, John Francis	U.S.	2604
Rogers, Dayton Leroy	U.S.	2608
Rogers, Kenneth Paul	U.S.	2611
Ross, Michael B.	U.S.	2624
Rudloff, Fritz	Ger.	2635
Sarrejani, Georges Alexander	Fr.	2680
Schaefer, Gerard	U.S.	2689
Schonleben, Anna Maria	Ger.	2697
Scieri, Antoinette	Fr.	2708
Seefeld, Adolf	Ger.	2722
Shobek, Michael	Bahamas	2747
Spencer, Timothy Wilson	U.S.	2826
Staniak, Lucian	Pol.	2839
Sutcliffe, Peter William	Brit.	2879
Taborsky, Joseph	U.S.	2893
Tacklyn, Larry Winfield	Ber.	558
Taylor, Gary Addison	U.S.	2900
Taylor, Louisa Jane	Brit.	2902
Texarkana (Texas) Slayings	U.S.	2919
Texas Strangler	U.S.	2921
3-X Slayer	U.S.	2941
Tinning, Marybeth Roe	U.S.	2956
Toffania, La	Italy	2963
Toppan, Jane	U.S.	2968
Tulsa Bludgeonings	U.S.	3001
Vacher, Joseph	Fr.	3023
Watson, James P.	U.S.	3103
Watts, Coral Eugene	U.S.	3104
Weber, Jeanne	Fr.	3108
Weidmann, Eugen	Fr.	3113
Whelan, John	Aus.	3134
Whiteway, Alfred Charles	Brit.	3141
Wilder, Christopher Bernard	U.S.	3155
Wilford, Thomas	Brit.	3157
Williams, Wayne Bertram	U.S.	3166
Woodfield, Randall Brent	U.S.	3184
Zebra Killings	U.S.	3218
Zodiac Killer	U.S.	3221

SEX MURDER

Abbott, Burton W.	U.S.	4
Anstädt, Achim	Fr.	2163
Aposhian, Dalbert	U.S.	138
Arbuckle, Roscoe Conkling	U.S.	143
Barrett, Thomas	U.S.	249
Barton, John Evert	U.S.	271

Battus, John	U.S.	284
Beagles, David Ervin	U.S.	286
Bean, Thomas Lee	U.S.	290
Beard, Arthur	Brit.	290
Beck, Dieter	Ger.	295
Bell, Larry Gene	U.S.	318
Bell, Shirley	U.S.	319
Bennett, Herbert John	Brit.	331
Berdella, Robert	U.S.	339
Berger, Theodor	Ger.	342
Berry, Saul	U.S.	1820
Best, Alton Alonzo	U.S.	354
Bianchi, Kenneth	U.S.	356
Bishop, Arthur Gary	U.S.	380
Bittaker, Lawrence Sigmond	U.S.	383
Boden, Wayne Clifford	Can.	415
Bonafous, Louis	Fr.	427
Bonin, William	U.S.	429
Boost, Werner	Ger.	436
Borgia Family	Italy	441
Boyd, William C.	U.S.	461
Bram, Thomas Mead Chambers	U.S.	469
Brookins, Louis Dwight	U.S.	497
Brooks, David Owen	U.S.	785
Brudos, Jerry	U.S.	520
Brumit, Lucille	U.S.	1544
Brust, Albert	U.S.	522
Buck Gang	U.S.	531
Bundy, Theodore	U.S.	537
Buono, Angelo, Jr.	U.S.	356
Burke, Thomas	Can.	2069
Burrows, Albert Edward	Brit.	558
Buss, Timothy D.	U.S.	561
Butcher, Christine	Brit.	561
Butterfield, Neale Allen	U.S.	563
Butts, Vernon	U.S.	429
Camb, James	Brit.	587
Campbell, Kevin	U.S.	1515
Carmen, Jack Allen	U.S.	628
Carr, Melvin	U.S.	636
Catoe, Jarvis Theodore Rooseve	U.S.	657
Christensen, William Dean	U.S.	702
Christie, John Reginald Hallid	Brit.	705
Clark, Dewey	U.S.	721
Clark, Douglas Daniel	U.S.	722
Clark, Ronald E.	U.S.	724
Clarke, Nelly	Brit.	726
Click, Franklin	U.S.	732
Cochran, Willie Grady	U.S.	735
Codarre, Edwin	U.S.	738
Coddington, Herbert James	U.S.	738
Cohn, Lenora	U.S.	742
Coleman, Alton	U.S.	743
Collins, John Norman	U.S.	752
Coogler, Ovida	U.S.	768
Cook, Charles	U.S.	769
Coolidge, Edward H.	U.S.	773
Coombes, Robert L.	U.S.	774
Corll, Dean Allen	U.S.	785
Corona, Juan Vallejo	U.S.	788
Craft, Ellis	U.S.	804
Croft, Curtis	U.S.	1515
Cunningham, Evelina	U.S.	846
Davis, Gregory	U.S.	883
Davis, Larry Ronald	U.S.	885
de Rais, Gilles	Fr.	2530
Detroit Child Murders	U.S.	928
Dorbell, Tom	Brit.	1004
Duell, William	Brit.	1032
Dunkins, Horace Franklin, Jr.	U.S.	1037

Walker, Nathaniel	U.S.	3078

SUBVERSION

Dies Committee Investigation	U.S.	942

SUICIDE

Adamic, Louis	U.S.	20
Alsopp, Gunnar	U.S.	104
Andrew of Carniola	Carniola	126
Andrews, Milton Franklin	U.S.	127
Arria	Roman.	166
Attebery, Ira	U.S.	179
Babeuf, Francois Emile	Fr.	204
Bailey, Norman Percival	Brit.	211
Ball, Joseph	U.S.	221
Banks, Jerry	U.S.	227
Barbaro, Anthony F.	U.S.	229
Barsi, Jozsef	U.S.	265
Beadle, William	U.S.	286
Beck, Douglas	U.S.	295
Blandig, Albert	Brit.	406
Blanther, Joseph	U.S.	407
Bolin, Patty	U.S.	423
Bolton, John	Brit.	425
Boulanger, Georges Ernest J. M	Fr.	453
Branch, Mark	U.S.	471
Brandstatter, N.L.	U.S.	473
Brooks, Henry M.	U.S.	499
Brust, Albert	U.S.	522
Burke, Charles	U.S.	545
Bush, Robert	U.S.	560
Calbeck, Lorene	U.S.	578
Campbell, Cecil	U.S.	592
Capel, Arthur	Brit.	603
Carbo, Gaius Papirius	Roman.	620
Chamfort, Sbastien-Roch Nicola	Fr.	675
Chang Soo Lee	U.S.	678
Chapman, Henry	Aus.	685
Chatterton, Thomas	Brit.	690
Chiying	China	701
Christophe, Henri	Haiti	710
Clark, Michael	U.S.	724
Clavière, Étienne	Fr.	727
Clements, Dr. Robert George	Brit.	730
Cleomenes I	Sparta	730
Clive, Robert	Int'l.	733
Clment, Charles	Fr.	729
Cole, Thomas Charles	Col.	743
Collins, Melvin	U.S.	752
Coolidge, Dr. Valorus P.	U.S.	773
Cooper, David	U.S.	2708
Cooper, Herbert	Brit.	777
Corbulo, Gnaeus Domitius	Roman.	782
Cotterill, Eardley	Brit.	797
Couturier, Delphine	Fr.	800
Cowan, Frederick W.	U.S.	701
Crawford, James	U.S.	813
Crosby, Henry Grew	U.S.	829
Crossman, George Albert	Brit.	835
Cutty Sark Tragedy	Brit.	851
D'Arcy, Patrick	Ire.	870
Daniloff, Jeanne	Fr.	868
Dann, Laurie Wasserman	U.S.	869
David, Immanuel	U.S.	880
Davidson, Jane	Brit.	881
Davis, Lolita	U.S.	885
De Silva, Charles Percival	Brit.	925
DeGroot, Robert	U.S.	902
Delaitre, Pierre-Joel	Brit.	905
Denke, Carl	Ger.	914

Detollenaere, Jean-Baptiste	Fr.	928
Deutscher, Albert	Int'l.	930
Distafano, Ralph P.	U.S.	978
Doetsch, Gunter	U.S.	984
Dolezal, Frank	U.S.	986
Downey, John	Brit.	1013
Dreesman, Robert	U.S.	1021
Duck, Aug Tai	U.S.	1031
Dwyer, R. Budd	U.S.	1049
Dyer, Ernest	Brit.	1050
Eastman, Robert	U.S.	1065
Edwards, Mack Ray	U.S.	1073
Elazar, Sasson Shalom	Brit.	1080
Ellis, John	Brit.	1085
Fairlie, Walter	Brit.	1127
Farrell, Edgar Joseph Raymond	Aus.	1136
Finlay, Edwin	Brit.	1160
Foster, William	S.Afri.	1203
Fox, Isaac Garrett	U.S.	1205
Furnace, Samuel James	Brit.	1242
Galloway, Robert	U.S.	1257
Geary, Charles Russell	U.S.	1287
Gerghuta, Ion	Rom.	1301
Germano, Andro	U.S.	1301
Girardi, James A.	U.S.	1317
Goebbels, Paul Joseph	Ger.	1324
Goering, Hermann Wilhelm	Ger.	1326
Goldsborough, Fitzhugh Coyle	U.S.	1333
Gonzales, Frank	U.S.	1337
Grasso, Santo	Fr.	1363
Gutkind, Johann	Ger.	1409
Haigler, Keith	U.S.	1419
Haley, Carl	U.S.	1420
Harvey, Julian	U.S.	1472
Hefeld, Paul	Brit.	1507
Held, Leo A.	U.S.	1511
Hickman, Sophia	Brit.	1532
Hileman, Doyle	U.S.	1550
Hoffman, Abbie	U.S.	1585
Holliday, Bertram Redvers	Brit.	1592
Hollins, Lawrence Henry	S.Afri.	1595
Holt, Emory	U.S.	1603
Hoshen	China	1624
Hsiang Y	China	1633
Hufnagel, Thomas E.	U.S.	1735
Hutchison, John James	Brit.	1648
Irwin, Warren Lee	U.S.	1667
Jones, Charles	U.S.	1736
Jones, James Warren	Guyana	1737
Jones, Willie	U.S.	1742
Kammerer, Paul	Aust.	1754
Kao Kang	China	1759
Katz, Arthur	U.S.	1769
Kayser, Otto	U.S.	1770
King, Alvin Lee, III	U.S.	1820
Kleist, Heinrich von	Ger.	1833
Knight, Virgil	U.S.	1835
Kogut, William	U.S.	1841
Kourdakov, Sergei	U.S.	1844
Kreuger, Ivar	Swed.	1849
Kubiczek, Jose	Fr.	1853
Lake, Leonard	U.S.	1874
Landis, M.D.	U.S.	1885
Lane, Brant	U.S.	1888
Lerwill, William Knight	Brit.	1940
Ley, Dr. Robert	Ger.	1947
Liu An	China	1972
Loewenstein, Alfred	Brit.	1976
Lorentzen, Robert	U.S.	1991
Love, Jack	Brit.	1995

Love, Mary	Brit.	1995
Lowther, George	Brit.	1999
Lucan	Roman.	2001
McCardie, Sir Henry Alfred	Brit.	2023
McConnell, J.R.	U.S.	2027
McElroy, Mary	U.S.	2036
MacSwiney, Terence	Ire.	2071
McVay, Charles Butler, III	U.S.	2071
Magnentius, Flavius Popilius	Roman.	2087
Maloney, James	U.S.	2098
Maltby, Cecil	Brit.	2098
Markle, John	U.S.	2125
Marshall, Lindsay Howitt	Brit.	2130
Mathis, James R.	U.S.	2147
Maximian	Roman.	2153
Mayer, Robert	U.S.	2157
Melton, Tracy	U.S.	2164
Melton, William	U.S.	2164
Meyer, Jacob	Brit.	1507
Minamoto Yoshitsune	Japan	2187
Mitchell, Tyrone	U.S.	2192
Mithradates VI Eupator	Pontus	2193
Mitten, Thomas Eugene	U.S.	2194
Mokanna, al-	Per.	2197
Moore, Roger	U.S.	2211
Myles, Jerry	U.S.	2273
Narcissus	Roman.	2282
Nero	Roman.	2305
Newbold, Thomas Gray	Brit.	2309
Nickols, Kevin	U.S.	2335
Nisby, Marcus	U.S.	2338
O'Dare, Josephine	Brit.	2360
Oneby, John	Brit.	2373
O'Regan, Brian	U.S.	2377
Ortega, Fernando	Mex.	2380
Otho, Marcus Salvius	Roman.	2385
Ovechkin, Ninel	U.S.S.R.	2387
Palach, Jan	Czech.	2396
Paris, Richard James	U.S.	2409
Paul, Rene	Can.	2427
Payne, A.D.	U.S.	2429
Pearson, Moses	U.S.	2433
Pelagia of Antioch	Roman.	2437
Perry, Calvin D., III	U.S.	2446
Petion de Villeneuve, Jérôme	Fr.	2453
Phuoc Tri Nguyen	U.S.	2460
Piso, Gaius Calpurnius	Roman.	2470
Porcia	Roman.	2490
Poulin, Robert	Can.	2492
Prudom, Barry Peter	Brit.	2509
Purrinton, James	U.S.	2513
Radford, Frederick Gordon	Brit.	2527
Ramirez, Patrick	U.S.	2533
Regan, Leonard	U.S.	2558
Rennels, Robert R.	U.S.	2568
Restell, Ann	U.S.	2569
Ritter, Kenneth	Ger.	2586
Robbins, Gary A.	U.S.	2589
Rolle, Randal	U.S.	2614
Romer, Richard	U.S.	2616
Roux, Jacques	Fr.	2630
Rudolf	Int'l.	2635
Rutledge, Dr. Robert C., Jr.	U.S.	2645
Ryan, Michael	Brit.	2647
Salii, Lazarus	Palau	2671
Sanders, Lindberg	U.S.	2676
Savinkov, Boris Viktorovich	Rus.	2684
Scarpelli, Gerald Hector	U.S.	2689
Schmidt, Helmuth	U.S.	2695
Schultz, Raymond T.	U.S.	2705

Schwartz, Charles Henry	U.S.	2706
Schweitzer, Robert	U.S.	2708
Seneca, Lucius Annaeus	Roman.	2728
Sharpe, Violet	U.S.	2735
Sherrill, Patrick Henry	U.S.	2745
Shoaf, Mamie Shey	U.S.	2747
Simpson, Charlie	U.S.	2765
Smart, Lee	U.S.	2273
Smith, Russell Lee	U.S.	2802
Socrates	Gr.	2810
Springer, James	U.S.	2833
Stopa, Wanda	U.S.	2861
Strozzi, Giovanni Battista	Italy	2871
Swancutt, Beaufort George	U.S.	2885
Thomas, William King	Ger.	2932
Tigellinus, Ofonius	Roman.	2953
Toyotomi Hidetsugo	Japan	2981
Tremamunno, Donato	Italy	2985
Turner, Richard	U.S.	3005
Tyner, Hugh Leon, Jr.	U.S.	3012
Urich, Heinz Karl Gunther	Mor.	3018
van Heerden, Cornelius Johanne	S.Afri.	3032
Vargas, Getulio	Braz.	3036
Vetsera, Maria	Int'l.	2635
Voirbo, Pierre	Fr.	3059
von Sydow, Frederick	Swed.	3063
Wagner, Gustav Franz	Ger.	3069
Wagner, John F.	U.S.	3069
Walsh, James	Brit.	3084
Warder, Alfred William	Brit.	3093
Watzl, Ernest	Aust.	3106
Webster, Daniel R.	U.S.	3109
Wei Chung-hsien	China	3113
Wheat, Clarence	U.S.	3132
Whitby, Roy	U.S.	3136
Wilkins, Walter Keene	U.S.	3157
Williams, John	Brit.	3162
Wilson, John Wayne	U.S.	3174
Winheld, Oscar	U.S.	3176
Woo Bum Kong	Korea	3181
Wright, Whitaker	Brit.	3195
Wright, William	U.S.	3196
Yang Yen	China	3205
Young, Gig	U.S.	3209
Yui Shosetsu	Japan	3214
Zaleucus	Gr.	3215
Zowkowski, John	U.S.	3223

SUICIDE?

Abd al-Aziz	Otto. Emp.	8
Krivitzky, Walter	U.S.	1851
Louis Henri Joseph	Fr.	1992
Margerison, George Frederick	Brit.	2120
Monroe, Marilyn	U.S.	2201
Pichegru, Charles	Fr.	2462
Prince, Albert	Fr.	2502
Roberts, Samuel Clifford	S.Afri.	2593
Swart, Stephen	S.Afri.	2887

SUICIDE ATTEMPTS

Gray, William McKinnon	Brit.	1365
Rayner, Horace George	Brit.	2547

TAX EVASION

Agnew, Spiro	U.S.	37
Baker, A.Y.	U.S.	213
Beck, David	U.S.	294
Biaggi, Mario	U.S.	356
Biaggi, Richard	U.S.	356
Bowers, Donald	U.S.	2120

Brown, Reese B.	U.S.	515
Capasso, Carl A.	U.S.	602
Caruana, Salvatore Michael	U.S.	647
Chagra, Jamiel Alexander	U.S.	669
Claiborne, Harry E.	U.S.	717
Cotlar, Marvin L.	U.S.	2379
Friderichs, Hans	Ger.	1877
Harper, Carey Judson	U.S.	1456
Johnson, Enoch	U.S.	1728
Kelley, John M.	U.S.	1778
Kirk, Dana	U.S.	1829
Klein, Allen	U.S.	1833
Lambsdorff, Otto	Ger.	1877
Leggett, Charles E.	U.S.	1923
Loren, Sophia	Italy	1990
Lustig, E. Allen	U.S.	2013
Lustig, Henry	U.S.	2013
McDonnell, John J.	U.S.	2034
McGarry, Dennis William	Brit.	2040
Margolies, Irwin	U.S.	2120
Martino, Joseph E.	U.S.	2379
Moon, Sun Myung	U.S.	2207
Nipon, Albert	U.S.	2338
Orloff, Michael A.	U.S.	2379
Perlowin, Bruce J.	U.S.	2445
Reed, Rex	U.S.	2557
Rich, Marc	U.S.	2575
Savitt, Samuel Norman	U.S.	2684
Scheible, Mae	U.S.	2691
Scott, William J.	U.S.	2713
Shyres, Mark	U.S.	2379
Smith, Dr. James Monroe	U.S.	2794
Sobel, Joseph	U.S.	2013
Steinman, Moe	U.S.	2849
Thomas, Gordon	Brit.	2040
Ulasewicz, Anthony T.	U.S.	3014
Wedtech Scandal	U.S.	3112
von Brauchitsch, Eberhard	Ger.	1877

TAX EVASION - Case of

Mitchell, Charles Edwin	U.S.	2190

TERRORISM
General

Aleksandrov, Todor	Macedonia	72
Billaud-Varenne, Jean-Nicolas	Fr.	362
Conspiracy of London, The	Brit.	767
de Robespierre, Maximilien F.M	Fr.	2594
Feeney, Hugh	Brit.	2500
Karakhan, Lev Mikhailovich	U.S.S.R.	1762
Kenyatta, Jomo	Kenya	1805
Kohlhase, Hans	Ger.	1841
Lod Airport Massacre	Isr.	1976
Mbeki, Govan	S.Afri.	2158
Mikhaylovsky, Nikolay, Konstan	Rus.	2178
Missile Smuggling	Belg.	2190
Palestine Liberation Organizat	Intl.	2397
Price, Dolours	Brit.	2500
Price, Marion	Brit.	2500
Ronconi, Susanna	Italy	2616

Activity: Abduction

Abdullah, Sameer Mohammed	Ger.	1081
Badran, Ibrahim	Ger.	1081
el Dnawy, Abd el-Kadir	Ger.	1081

Activity: Bombing

Arafat, Yasir	Mid.East	140
Busic, Zvonko	U.S.	560
Weather Underground Org.	U.S.	3107

Activity: Guerrilla Attacks

Arafat, Yasir	Mid.East	140

Eritrean People's Liberation F	Eth.	1101
Khalistan Commando Force	India	1809
Khler, Gundolf	Ger.	1841
Kikumura, Yu	U.S.	1816
Maalot Massacre	Isr.	2021
New People's Army	Phil.	2314
November 17	Gr.	2347
People's Liberation Front	Sri.	2442
Ravachol	Fr.	2545
Rhodesia Missionary Slayings	Rhodesia	2572
Salan, Raoul Albin Louis	Fr.	2663
Sanchez, Ilyich Ramirez	Int'l.	2674
Stern, Abraham	Isr.	2850
Tokugawa Ieyasu	Japan	2964
Tupamaros, The	Urug.	3002
Molqi, Magid al-	Italy	2199

Activity: Hijacking

South Moluccan Kidnappers	Neth.	2818

Activity: Kidnapping

Baader-Meinhof Gang	Ger.	195
Black September Organization	Mid.East	398
Brigate Rosse	Italy	488
Busic, Zvonko	U.S.	560
Curcio, Margherita Cafol	Italy	847
Franklin, Joseph Paul	U.S.	1225
Islamic Tendencies Movement	Tun.	1668
June 2nd Movement	Ger.	1750
Khaalis, Hamaas Abdul	U.S.	1809
Khomeini, Ayatollah Ruhollah	Iran	1810
Kruszyk, Florian	Switz.	1853
Kyprianou, Achilleas	Cyprus	1865
Maalot Massacre	Isr.	2021
Marighella, Carlos	Braz.	2122
Michalski, Marek	Switz.	1853
Monteneros	Arg.	2204
People's Liberation Army	Turk.	2442
People's Revolutionary Army	Arg.	2442
Plewinski, Miroslaw	Switz.	1853
Popular Revolutionary Vanguard	Braz.	2490
RAF	Ger.	2528
Rebel Armed Forces	Guat.	2551
Red Brigades	Italy	2552
Sanchez, Ilyich Ramirez	Int'l.	2674
Savasta, Antonio	Italy	2683
South Moluccan Kidnappers	Neth.	2818
Symbionese Liberation Army	U.S.	2889
Tupamaros, The	Urug.	3002
Wasilewski, Krysztoe	Switz.	1853

Activity: Murder General

Abdallah, Georges Ibrahim	Fr.	8
Abdullah, Sameer Mohammed	Ger.	1081
Ahmed Nawaf Mansour Hazi	Ger.	1093
Allen, William O'Meara	Brit.	98
Baader-Meinhof Gang	Ger.	195
Badran, Ibrahim	Ger.	1081
Bakaris, Saleh Abdullah	Yemen	213
Barnes, Peter	Brit.	245
Barrett, Michael	Brit.	249
Bitterman, Chester A., III	Col.	383
Black Liberation Army	U.S.	396
Black Muslims	U.S.	397
Black September Organization	Mid.East	398
Brigate Rosse	Italy	488
Codreanu, Cornelius Zelea	Roman.	738
Curzi, Barbara	U.S.	2107
Dimitrijevic, Dragutin	Serb.	973
Doyle, Michael J.	U.S.	1781
el Dnawy, Abd el-Kadir	Ger.	1081
Endrigkeit, Christiane Gabriel	Ger.	1093
Farran, Rex Francis	Brit.	1135

Cooper, Calman	U.S.	775	Lyons, Sophie	U.S.	2018
Crown Jewels of England, The	Brit.	840	Maple, Frank	Aust.	2114
Dague, Walter Glenn	U.S.	2698	Marvell, William	Brit.	2133
Davin, Guy	Fr.	882	Mathis, Columbus	U.S.	2147
Davis, John	U.S.	884	Maxwell, Mary	U.S.	2154
Davis, Larry Ronald	U.S.	885	Mayer, Earl	U.S.	2800
DeJong	Neth.	903	Meyer, Jacob	Brit.	1507
DeLucia, William	U.S.	910	Millard, Frederick William	Brit.	2869
Dennis, Gerard Graham	U.S.	914	Mitchel, Anthony	Brit.	2190
Dennison, Theodore	U.S.	916	Moders, Mary	Brit.	2196
Deupree, Jim	U.S.	930	Moore, Flossie	U.S.	2210
Dimmick, Walter	U.S.	974	Munnick, Jan Willem Hendrik	S.Afri.	2251
Donohue, John	U.S.	1000	Musica, Philip	U.S.	2262
Dorfman, Benny	U.S.	775	Nai Krit	Siam	2827
Doty, Sile	U.S.	1007	Newman, Julia St. Clair	Brit.	2312
Doughty, Jack	Can.	1009	O'Neall, Darren	U.S.	2372
Dowse, Margaret	Brit.	1014	Otis, Arlene	U.S.	2385
Drown, Ruth	U.S.	1025	Pace, Laud Spencer	U.S.	2390
Emery, Ronald	U.S.	1091	Parkhurst, Walter	Brit	1677
Enricht, Louis	U.S.	1098	Parnell, Kenneth E.	U.S.	2414
Farese, Thomas R.	U.S.	1133	Paulson, Michael	U.S.	2427
Feldman, Joseph	U.S.	1146	Peete, Lofie Louise	U.S.	2436
Fogelman, Clay	U.S.	1190	Perkins, Josephine Amelia	Brit.	2444
Fontenot, Karl	U.S.	3092	Pfeiffer, Anna Ursula	Ger.	2456
Fox, Sidney Harry	Brit.	1206	Philipps, Robert J.	U.S.	2457
Fratto, Frank	U.S.	1228	Pinker, S. Eric	U.S.	2467
Gault, Julian	Int'l.	1284	Plumpton, Gilbert	Brit.	2477
Gianola, Leonard	U.S.	1307	Potamitis, Christos	U.S.	2492
Gordon, Herman Hy	U.S.	1601	Powers, Otto	U.S.	1601
Gossage, Eben	U.S.	1349	Price, Amey	Brit.	2499
Graham, Oaland	U.S.	1361	Rachel, Arthur	Brit.	2687
Great Pearl Robbery	Brit.	1369	Raymond, Cindy	U.S.	1512
Green, Samuel	U.S.	1374	Rivera, Lino	U.S.	2586
Habib, Jacob	U.S.	1601	Roberts, Luke	Brit.	2851
Harding, Arthur	Brit.	2851	Scalise, Joseph Jerome	Brit.	2687
Harms, John P.	U.S.	1455	Schroeder, Irene	U.S.	2698
Hawkins, Moll	Brit.	1492	Seye, Blaise Ferrage	Fr.	2730
Hefeld, Paul	Brit.	1507	Shaw, Tom	Fr.	2737
Heldt, Henning	U.S.	1512	Shue, Erasmus Stribling Trout	U.S.	2750
Hellier, Thomas	U.S.	1512	Smith, Mary Eleanor	U.S.	2800
Hermann, Mitchell	U.S.	1512	Smith, William	U.S.	2804
Hightower, Rudy	U.S.	1547	Snider, Duke	U.S.	1512
Hoch, Johann Otto	U.S.	1582	Sobhraj, Gurmukh Charles	India	2810
Holmes, Jimmy Jack	U.S.	1601	Spendle, Robert Courtney Frase	Siam	2827
Hubbard, C.R.	U.S.	1634	St. Claire, Ruth	U.S.	2658
Hubbard, Mary Sue	U.S.	1512	Stein, David	Int'l.	2847
Inglis, James	Scot.	1656	Stein, Harry	U.S.	775
International Pearl Necklace Theft	Int'l.	1659	Stevens, Peter	Brit.	2851
Jackson, Francis	Brit	1677	Stonehouse, John Thomas	Brit.	2860
Jeffery, Henry Edward	Brit.	1715	Stride, Herbert William	Brit.	2869
Jegado, Hélène	Fr.	1717	Taylor, Courtney Townsend	U.S.	2899
Jenkins, John	U.S.	1719	Terroni, Anthony	Brit.	1715
Jones, Mary	Brit.	1739	Thomas, Sharon	U.S.	1512
Kennaway, Herbert	Brit.	1793	Thomas, William F.	Brit.	2932
Kennedy, Mathew	Int'l.	1800	Trinder, Stanley	Brit.	1014
Kepner, Graham	U.S.	1805	Troppmann, Jean-Baptiste	Fr.	2990
King, Tom	Brit.	3005	Turlis, Thomas	Brit.	3003
Krten, Peter	Ger.	1862	Turpin, Richard	Brit.	3005
LaGace, Arthur	U.S.	1873	Vaughan, Jerry	U.S.	3039
Lancaster, Mrs. Val Edwin	Brit.	1882	Vaux, James Hardy	Brit.	3040
Landis, James	U.S.	1884	Villiers, Harry	Brit.	3055
Larson, Chester N.	U.S.	1900	Walker, John	Brit.	1715
Lawrence, John	Brit.	1907	Walmsley, Martha	Brit.	3084
Lee, Mattie	U.S.	1919	Ward, Tommy	U.S.	3092
Leggett, Charles E.	U.S.	1923	Watts, Walter	Brit.	3105
Lemarchand	Fr.	699	Weigand, Richard	U.S.	1512
Lewis, Helynn R.	U.S.	1946	West, Ronald Eugene	U.S.	3129
Lowrie, William	U.S.	2154	White, John	Brit.	1677
Lozano-Ahumada Feud	U.S.	2000	White, Louise	U.S.	3138
Lucas, Vrain	Fr.	2002	Whitfield, John Leonard	U.S.	3141

Brady, Patrick	Aus.	468
Brigate Rosse	Italy	488
Brooks, Hugh M.	U.S.	499
Burke, William	Scot.	547
Carr, Melvin	U.S.	636
Domby, Victor	Fr.	994
Eyraud, Michel	Fr.	1121
Fein, Mark	U.S.	1146
Fine, Louis	U.S.	1159
Gatlin, Alma Petty	U.S.	1284
Goolde, Maria Vere	Fr.	1341
Goolde, Vere	Fr.	1341
Hare, William	Scot.	547
Judd, Winnie Ruth	U.S.	1746
Kenosha, Wis., Killings	U.S.	1804
LeDoux, Emma	U.S.	1916
M'Kay, James	Scot.	2047
Mahon, Patrick Herbert	Brit.	2088
Mahoney, James E.	U.S.	2089
Mancini, Tony	Brit.	2099
Moity, Henry	U.S.	2197
Mudgett, Herman Webster	U.S.	2240
Myrtel, Héra	Fr.	2273
Pardo, Manuel	U.S.	2408
Prestes, Luiz Carlos	Braz.	2498
Rees, Melvin David	U.S.	2557
Remedios, Patricio	Japan	2564
Reville, Jean	U.S.	2570
Robinson, John	Brit.	2596
Russell, George	Brit.	2642
Salmon, Thomas	U.S.	2671
Tal, Schlomo	U.S.	2894
Watts, Coral Eugene	U.S.	3104
Wheeler, George	U.S.	3132

UNLAWFUL ENTRY

Lynch, Patrick	U.S.	2017

VAGRANCY

Pearlstein, Charles	U.S.	2433
Smat, Benjamin	Brit.	2780

VANDALISM

Bayley, James	Brit.	286
Courbet, Gustave	Fr.	799
Guillard, Pierre	Fr.	1398
Reynolds, Thomas	Brit.	286
van Rem, Mathijis	Neth.	3034

VERBAL ASSAULT

Zind, Ludwig	Ger.	3220

VICE DISTRICTS

Canal Street	U.S.	594
Candelaria, Nev.	U.S.	595
Hole-In-The-Wall Saloon	U.S.	1591
McGuirk's Suicide Hall	U.S.	2043
Custom House Place	U.S.	849
Five Points	U.S.	1173
Gallatin Street	U.S.	1255
Haymarket, The	U.S.	1495
Julian Street	U.S.	1749
Little Water Street	U.S.	1972
Natchez-Under-the-Hill	U.S.	2288
Sands, The	U.S.	2676
Tenderloin	U.S.	2913

VIGILANTISM

Anderson, Reese	U.S.	124
Beidler, John X.	U.S.	315

Gourgues, Dominique de	U.S.	1353
Mouton, Alexander	U.S.	2236
Soc. for Rec. of Stolen Horses	U.S.	2810
Vigilantes' Executive Committe	U.S.	3049
White Caps	Int'l.	3139

VIGILANTISM - Case of

Goetz, Bernhard Hugo	U.S.	1329

WAR CRIME

Abetz, Otto	Ger.	10
Artukovic, Andrija	Yugo.	169
Bangladesh Ind. War Atrocities	Bangladesh	225
Barbie, Klaus	Fr.	232
Bataan Death March	Phil.	279
Berger, Gottlob	Ger.	342
Blaskowitz, Johannes	Ger.	407
Boger, Wilhelm	Ger.	418
Bormann, Martin Ludwig	Ger.	443
Bruno, Karl	Yugo.	521
Calley, William Laws, Jr.	U.S.	584
Caratacus	Brit.	619
Caruso, Pietro	Italy	647
Chack, Paul	Fr.	666
Darnand, Joseph	Fr.	871
de Brinon, Fernand	Ger.	895
Demjanjuk, John	Ger.	912
Dietrich, Joseph	Ger.	942
Dipo Negoro, Pangeran	Indo.	977
Doenitz, Karl	Ger.	984
Dostler, Anton	Ger.	1007
Eichmann, Karl Adolf	Ger.	1076
Ferguson, Champ	U.S.	1150
Frank, Hans	Ger.	1217
Frank, Karl Hermann	Ger.	1217
Frey, Willi	Ger.	1236
Frick, Wilhelm	Ger.	1236
Fritzsche, Hans	Ger.	1237
Funk, Walther	Ger.	1242
Grese, Irma	Ger.	1381
Hagen, Herbert	Ger.	1970
Halabja Massacre	Iraq	1419
Hcha, Emil	Ger.	1413
Heinrichsohn, Ernst	Ger.	1970
Henlein, Konrad	Ger.	1516
Hess, Rudolf	Ger.	1527
Himmler, Heinrich	Ger.	1556
Hitler, Adolf	Ger.	1565
Hoess, Rudolf Francis Ferdinan	Pol.	1583
Homma Masaharu	Japan	1606
Imredy, Bla	Ger.	1653
Ishii, Maj. Shiro	Japan	1668
Jodl, Alfred	Ger.	1725
Kalejs, Konrads	U.S.	1753
Kaltenbrunner, Ernst	Ger.	1754
Kappler, Herbert	Ger.	1762
Katyn Massacre	U.S.S.R.	1768
Kawakita, Tomaya	U.S.	1770
Keitel, Wilhelm	Ger.	1776
Kesselring, Albert	Ger.	1806
Kimura Tokutaro	Japan	1820
Kishi Nobusuke	Japan	1831
Koch, Ilse	Ger.	1839
Koch, Peter	Italy	1839
Kohn, Peter	Ger.	1841
Kramer, Josef	Ger.	1846
Krupp, Gustav	Ger.	1853
Lammers, Hans Heinrich	Ger.	1879
Langiewicz, Marjan	Aust.	1890
Laval, Pierre	Int'l.	1904

Ley, Dr. Robert	Ger.	1947
Linnas, Karl	Estonia	1969
Lischka, Kurt	Ger.	1970
List, Siegmund Wilhelm Walther	Ger.	1970
Malmedy Massacre, The	Belg.	2097
McVay, Charles Butler, III	U.S.	2071
Mengele, Josef	Ger.	2165
Menten, Pieter	Pol.	2166
Meyer, Kurt Ernst	Ger.	2175
Mihailovich, Draja	Yug.	2177
Mithradates VI Eupator	Pontus	2193
Naumann, Erich	Ger.	2291
Nebuchadnezzar II	Babylon	2295
Nuremberg Trials	Ger.	2348
Oberg, Karl	Ger.	2355
Okawa Shumei	Japan	2366
Oradour-sur-Glane Massacre	Fr.	2374
Peiper, Joachim	Fr.	2436
Pfitzner, Dr. Josef	Czech.	2456
Raeder, Erich	Ger.	2528
Rajakowitsch, Erich	Ger.	2532
Rauff, Walter Herman Julius	Ger.	2545
Roatta, Mario	Italy	2589
Rosenberg, Alfred	Ger.	2620
Ryan, Hermine Braunsteiner	Ger.	2646
S.S. Athenia Sinking	Ger.	2834
Sauckel, Fritz	Ger.	2681
Schwammberger, Josef Franz Leo	Ger.	2706
Seyss-Inquart, Arthur	Ger.	2731
Sommer, Gerhard Martin	Ger.	2814
Songgram, Philbul	Siam	2815
Speer, Albert	Ger.	2824
Stangl, Franz	Ger.	2838
Streicher, Julius	Ger.	2868
Tojo Hideki	Japan	2963
Tokuda Hisakichi	Japan	2963
Trenck, Baron Franz von der	Aust.	2985
Vehme	Ger.	3040
von Manstein, Fritz Erich	Ger.	2112
von Manstein, Fritz Erich	Ger.	3063
von Neurath, Konstantin	Ger.	3063
von Papen, Franz	Ger.	3063
von Ribbentrop, Joachim von	Ger.	2573
von Schirach, Baldur	Ger.	3063
Wagner, Gustav Franz	Ger.	3069
Wagner, Wilhelm	Ger.	3069
Wirz, Henry	U.S.	3178
Witzler, Margarete	Ger.	3180
Yamashita Tomoyuki	Japan	3204
Yazdegerd II	Per.	3205

WAR CRIME - Case of

Detlavs, Karlis	Latvia	928
Deutscher, Albert	Int'l.	930
Schacht, Hjalmar	Ger.	2689

WAX MUSEUM CURATOR

Tussaud, Marie	Int'l.	3006

WEAPONS POSSESSION

Rooum, Donald	Brit.	2619
Rowan, Carl T.	U.S.	2630

WESTERN GUNFIGHT

Guadalupe Canyon Massacres	U.S.	1395
Keating's Saloon, Battle of	U.S.	1772
OK Corral	U.S.	2366

WESTERN GUNMEN

Anderson, Hugh	U.S.	123
Anderson, Scott L.	U.S.	124
Anderson, William	U.S.	126
Augustine, Robert	U.S.	184
Averill, James	U.S.	187
Beard, Edward T.	U.S.	291
Brann, William Cowper	U.S.	473
Brewer, Richard M.	U.S.	486
Brooks, William L.	U.S.	500
Brown, Henry Newton	U.S.	506
Brown, Sam	U.S.	516
Canton, Frank M.	U.S.	601
Champion, Nathan D.	U.S.	675
Chilton, Fred	U.S.	700
Claiborne, William	U.S.	717
Clements, Emmanuel, Jr.	U.S.	729
Coe, Frank	U.S.	739
Coe, George Washington	U.S.	739
Coe, Philip Haddox	U.S.	739
Colbert, Chunk	U.S.	742
Courtright, Timothy Isaiah	U.S.	799
Cruz, Florentino	U.S.	842
Cummings, Samuel M.	U.S.	845
Daly, James	U.S.	864
Day, Alfred	U.S.	888
de Rana, Patas	U.S.	919
Dolan, James J.	U.S.	985
Dunn, Bill	U.S.	1038
Earhart, Bill	U.S.	1053
Elliott, Joe	U.S.	1084
Estabo, Tranquellano	U.S.	1106
Fisher, John King	U.S.	1165
Fountain, Albert Jennings	U.S.	1204
French, Jim	U.S.	1235
Gilliland, Fine	U.S.	1314
Gladden, George	U.S.	1320
Good, John	U.S.	1338
Grannon, Riley	U.S.	1362
Griego, Francisco	U.S.	1385
Hardin, John Wesley	U.S.	1446
Harris, Jack	U.S.	1461
Higgins, John Calhoun Pinckney	U.S.	1545
Hindman, George W.	U.S.	1559
Holliday, John Henry	U.S.	1593
Hoover, Tuck	U.S.	1617
Johnson, Jack	U.S.	1729
Johnson, William H.	U.S.	1734
Kemp, David	U.S.	1790
Leslie, Nashville Franklin	U.S.	1940
Long, John	U.S.	1986
Long, Steve	U.S.	1986
Longley, William Preston	U.S.	1987
Loving, Frank	U.S.	1996
Lowe, Joseph	U.S.	1997
McCall, John	U.S.	2023
McCluskie, Arthur	U.S.	2026
McConnell, Andrew	U.S.	2027
McDowell, Jack	U.S.	2035
McNab, Frank	U.S.	2060
Manning, James	U.S.	2106
Marlowe, Boone	U.S.	2126
Masterson, Edward J.	U.S.	2143
Masterson, James P.	U.S.	2143
Matthews, Jacob B.	U.S.	2149
Meldrum, Bob	U.S.	2164
Middleton, John	U.S.	2177
Mitchell, William	U.S.	2192
Morco, John	U.S.	2216
O'Rourke, John	U.S.	2379
Outlaw, Bass	U.S.	2386
Peacock, Lewis	U.S.	2432

Pickett, Tom	U.S.	2462	Daniels, Benjamin F.	U.S.	867
Pierce, Abel Head	U.S.	2462	Delony, Lewis S.	U.S.	908
Plummer, Henry	U.S.	2477	Donahue, Cornelius	U.S.	997
Powell, Sylvester	U.S.	2494	Downing, William	U.S.	1013
Reed, Charlie	U.S.	2556	Earp, Wyatt Berry Stapp	U.S.	1053
Richardson, Levi	U.S.	2579	Fisher, John King	U.S.	1165
Riggs, Barney	U.S.	2583	Frazer, George A.	U.S.	1229
Ringo, John	U.S.	2584	Gabriel, Peter	U.S.	1245
Roberts, Jim	U.S.	2592	Gildea, Augustus	U.S.	1312
Scurlock, Josiah G.	U.S.	2716	Gillett, James Buchanan	U.S.	1313
Selman, John	U.S.	2727	Gosling, Harold L.	U.S.	1349
Sherman, James D.	U.S.	2744	Graham, Dayton	U.S.	1356
Shonsey, Mike	U.S.	2748	Hall, Jesse Lee	U.S.	1426
Shores, Cyrus Wells	U.S.	2748	Harkey, Dee	U.S.	1453
Short, Luke	U.S.	2748	Hays, John Coffey	U.S.	1499
Smith, Jack	U.S.	2794	Helm, Jack	U.S.	1514
Standard, Jess	U.S.	2838	Hickok, James Butler	U.S.	1535
Stiles, William Larkin	U.S.	2854	Higgins, Fred R.	U.S.	1545
Stilwell, Frank C.	U.S.	2855	Hindman, George W.	U.S.	1559
Stinson, Joe	U.S.	2856	Hollister, Cassius M.	U.S.	1596
Stockton, Port	U.S.	2857	Horn, Tom	U.S.	1619
Storms, Charles	U.S.	2864	Houston, Tom	U.S.	1627
Strawhim, Samuel	U.S.	2868	Hughes, John Reynolds	U.S.	1636
Taylor, Jack Hays	U.S.	2900	Hunt, J. Frank	U.S.	1643
Taylor, Jim	U.S.	2901	Jennings, Napoleon Augustus	U.S.	1722
Taylor, Phillip	U.S.	2902	Johnson, Jack	U.S.	1729
Taylor, William	U.S.	2902	Johnson, John	U.S.	1730
Tewksbury, Edwin	U.S.	2919	Johnson, William H.	U.S.	1734
Tewksbury, Jim	U.S.	2919	Jones, Frank	U.S.	1737
Thompson, Ben	U.S.	2932	Jones, John B.	U.S.	1739
Thompson, William	U.S.	2936	Kemp, David	U.S.	1790
Tucker, Tom	U.S.	2999	King, Frank	U.S.	1822
Turner, Ben	U.S.	3003	Larn, John M.	U.S.	1898
Wait, Frederick T.	U.S.	3071	Latham, James V.	U.S.	1902
Watson, Ella	U.S.	187	Ledbetter, Bud	U.S.	1916
Watson, Jack	U.S.	3103	Lefors, Joseph	U.S.	1922
Webb, John Joshua	U.S.	3108	Lindsey, Seldon T.	U.S.	1968
Wren, William R.	U.S.	3192	Long, John	U.S.	1986
			McCall, Thomas P.	U.S.	2023
WESTERN LAW OFFICER			McIntire, James	U.S.	2046
Allison, Charles	U.S.	99	McKinney, Thomas L.	U.S.	2052
Alvord, Burton	U.S.	107	McMahon, Francis Marion	U.S.	2058
Anderson, William H.	U.S.	126	McMasters, Sherman	U.S.	2059
Andrew, Robert	U.S.	126	McNelly, Leander H.	U.S.	2065
Armstrong, John Barclay	U.S.	158	Madsen, Christian	U.S.	2078
Arrington, George W.	U.S.	167	Masterson, James P.	U.S.	2143
Aten, Ira	U.S.	174	Masterson, William Barclay	U.S.	2143
Baca, Elfego	U.S.	204	Mather, Dave H.	U.S.	2145
Beckwith, John H.	U.S.	311	Meagher, Mike	U.S.	2159
Beckwith, Robert W.	U.S.	311	Meldrum, Bob	U.S.	2164
Behan, John	U.S.	314	Milton, Jeff Davis	U.S.	2187
Bell, Hamilton	U.S.	317	Morse, Harry N.	U.S.	2228
Bell, J.W.	U.S.	318	Mossman, Burton C.	U.S.	2234
Breakenridge, William Milton	U.S.	481	Oden, Lon	U.S.	2360
Brewer, Richard M.	U.S.	486	Outlaw, Bass	U.S.	2386
Briant, Elijah S.	U.S.	487	Owens, Perry	U.S.	2389
Bridges, Jack L.	U.S.	487	Pickett, Tom	U.S.	2462
Brooks, James Abijah	U.S.	499	Plummer, Henry	U.S.	2477
Brooks, William L.	U.S.	500	Roberts, Jim	U.S.	2592
Brown, Angus	U.S.	504	Robertson, Ben F.	U.S.	2594
Brown, Henry Newton	U.S.	506	Rynning, Thomas H.	U.S.	2648
Burts, Matthew	U.S.	559	St. Leon, Ernest	U.S.	2659
Canton, Frank M.	U.S.	601	Scarborough, George W.	U.S.	2688
Carson, Thomas	U.S.	642	Selman, John	U.S.	2727
Clements, Emmanuel, Jr.	U.S.	729	Shadley, Lafe	U.S.	2732
Connelly, Charles T.	U.S.	765	Slaughter, John Horton	U.S.	2777
Cook, Thalis T.	U.S.	770	Smith, Thomas	U.S.	2802
Courtright, Timothy Isaiah	U.S.	799	Smith, Tom	U.S.	2803
Crawford, Ed	U.S.	812	Spradley, A. John	U.S.	2833
Cummings, Samuel M.	U.S.	845	Stiles, William Larkin	U.S.	2854

Stockton, Port	U.S.	2857	Delaney, William E.	U.S.	907
Tewksbury, Edwin	U.S.	2919	de Rana, Patas	U.S.	919
Thomas, Henry Andrew	U.S.	2931	Donahue, Cornelius	U.S.	997
Tilghman, William Matthew, Jr.	U.S.	2955	Doolin, William M.	U.S.	1002
Tucker, Tom	U.S.	2999	Downing, William	U.S.	1013
Tyler, Jesse	U.S.	3011	Dunlap, Jack	U.S.	1037
Watson, Jack	U.S.	3103	Dutch Henry	U.S.	1044
Webb, John Joshua	U.S.	3108	Escobar, Rafael	U.S.	1103
Wheeler, Harry	U.S.	3133	Espinosa Brothers	U.S.	1104
Whitney, Chauncey Belden	U.S.	3143	Evans, Christopher	U.S.	1111
Wren, William R.	U.S.	3192	Evans, Jesse	U.S.	1112
			Fellows, Dick	U.S.	1147
WESTERN OUTLAWS			Flores, Juan	U.S.	1181
Allison, Charles	U.S.	99	Ford, Robert	U.S.	1195
Allison, Robert A.	U.S.	99	Frisco Sue	U.S.	1237
Alvord, Burton	U.S.	107	Gallagher, Jack	U.S.	1254
Apache Kid	U.S.	135	Garcia, Manuel	U.S.	1266
Archer Brothers	U.S.	152	Goldsby, Crawford	U.S.	1334
Averill, James	U.S.	187	Gordon, Lon	U.S.	1345
Baker, Cullen Montgomery	U.S.	213	Graham Brothers	U.S.	1361
Baldwin, Thurman	U.S.	218	Gristy, Bill	U.S.	1391
Barkley, Clinton	U.S.	243	Hanks, Orlando Camillo	U.S.	1442
Barnes, Seaborn	U.S.	246	Hardin, John Wesley	U.S.	1446
Barter, Richard	U.S.	265	Harpe, Wiley	U.S.	1455
Bass, Samuel	U.S.	274	Harpe, William Micajah	U.S.	1455
Baugh, Andrew T.	U.S.	284	Hart, Pearl	U.S.	1468
Beck, H.O.	U.S.	295	Hassells, Samuel	U.S.	1474
Bell, Tom	U.S.	320	Hays, Bob	U.S.	1498
Bickerstaff, Benjamin F.	U.S.	358	Heath, John	U.S.	1504
Bideno, Juan	U.S.	359	Helm, Boone	U.S.	1513
Billee, John	U.S.	362	Hill, Tom	U.S.	1554
Billy the Kid	U.S.	363	Hite, Robert Woodson	U.S.	1565
Black, Isaac	U.S.	384	Hole-in-the-Wall	U.S.	1591
Blackburn, Duncan	U.S.	388	Horn, Tom	U.S.	1619
Blake, John	U.S.	403	Jackson, Frank	U.S.	1677
Blevins Family	U.S.	408	Jaybird-Woodpecker War	U.S.	1713
Blue Duck	U.S.	411	Jennings, Alphonso J.	U.S.	1720
Brocius, Curly Bill	U.S.	494	Johnson, Richard	U.S.	1732
Brock, Leonard Calvert	U.S.	495	Jones Brothers	U.S.	1742
Brown, Henry Newton	U.S.	506	Jones, John	U.S.	1739
Bryant, Charles	U.S.	523	Keaton, Pierce	U.S.	1773
Bunch, Eugene	U.S.	537	Kelly, Daniel	U.S.	1779
Burrow, Reuben Houston	U.S.	556	Kennedy, James	U.S.	1794
Burts, Matthew	U.S.	559	Ketchum, Thomas E.	U.S.	1807
Caballero, Guadalupe	U.S.	568	Kettle, Jack	U.S.	1808
Carver, William	U.S.	647	Kilpatrick, Benjamin	U.S.	1817
Cassidy, Butch	U.S.	651	King, Luther	U.S.	1822
Chacón, Augustin	Int'l.	666	King, Sandy	U.S.	1822
Christian, Will	U.S.	703	Kuhns, Marvin	U.S.	1854
Christianson, Willard Erastus	U.S.	704	Lacy, Robert	U.S.	1870
Christie, Ned	U.S.	708	Larn, John M.	U.S.	1898
Claiborne, William	U.S.	717	Lay, William Ellsworth	U.S.	1909
Clanton-McLowery Gang	U.S.	718	Lee, Oliver Milton	U.S.	1920
Clark, Jim Cummings	U.S.	722	Lee, Robert	U.S.	1920
Clements, Emmanuel, Sr.	U.S.	729	Leonard, Bill	U.S.	1931
Clifton, Daniel	U.S.	732	Lewis, Elmer	U.S.	1945
Collins, William	U.S.	753	Logan, Harvey	U.S.	1977
Cook, William Tuttle	U.S.	771	Logan, Lonie	U.S.	1979
Cornett, Brack	U.S.	788	Lyons, Haze	U.S.	2018
Cortez, Gregorio	U.S.	791	Mather, Dave H.	U.S.	2145
Cortina, Juan	U.S.	792	McCarty Brothers	U.S.	2025
Crane, Jim	U.S.	810	McCarty, Tom	U.S.	2025
Cravens, Ben	U.S.	811	McIntire, James	U.S.	2046
Crawford, Foster	U.S.	812	McKemie, Robert	U.S.	2048
Curry, George	U.S.	848	Miller, James B.	U.S.	2181
Dalton Brothers	U.S.	858	Murphy, Jim	U.S.	2259
Dalton, J. Frank	U.S.	857	Musgrove, Lee H.	U.S.	2262
Daly, James	U.S.	864	Newcomb, George	U.S.	2309
Daugherty, Roy	U.S.	878	Newman, Bud	U.S.	2312
Day, Alfred	U.S.	888	Parish, Frank	U.S.	2409

Pierce, Charles	U.S.	2463
Ponce, Noratto	U.S.	2485
Quantrill, William Clarke	U.S.	2519
Raidler, William	U.S.	2529
Raynor, William P.	U.S.	2548
Reed, Jim	U.S.	2556
Reed, Nathaniel	U.S.	2556
Regulator War	U.S.	2559
Reynolds Gang	U.S.	2571
Roberts, Judd	U.S.	2593
Robertson, Ben F.	U.S.	2594
Rudabaugh, David	U.S.	2635
Shepherd, Oliver	U.S.	2740
Silva, Vincente	U.S.	2761
Skinner, Cyrus	U.S.	2774
Smith, Bill	U.S.	2782
Soto, Juan	U.S.	2816
Starr, Tom	U.S.	2844
Stiles, William Larkin	U.S.	2854
Sundance Kid, The	U.S.	2877
Taylor, Jack Hays	U.S.	2900
Taylor, Phillip	U.S.	2902
Towerly, William	U.S.	2979
Vásquez, Tiburcio	U.S.	3037
Waightman, George	U.S.	3069
Walker, Joe	U.S.	3077
Walters, William E.	U.S.	3086
Watson, Ella	U.S.	187
Welch, Ed	U.S.	3123
West, Richard	U.S.	3128
Wheeler, Grant	U.S.	3133
Wild Bunch	U.S.	3151
Willis, Thomas	U.S.	362
Wyatt, Nathaniel Ellsworth	U.S.	3197
Yager, Erastus	U.S.	3201
Younger Brothers	U.S.	3212

WESTERN OUTLAW HIDEOUT

Calabaza, Ariz.	U.S.	577
Cookson Hills, Okla.	U.S.	772
Robber's Roost	U.S.	2589

WHITE SLAVERY

Allen, Ned	U.S.	98
Althers, Mr.	U.S.	106
Arnold, Andrew J.	U.S.	160
Beckett Sisters	U.S.	311
Bismarck Hall	U.S.	383
Bluestone, Jesse	U.S.	412
Bompart, Mre	Fr.	426
Box, Jack	U.S.	2572
Butler, Josephine Elizabeth	Brit.	562
Cantor, Louis	U.S.	602
Carlin, William	U.S.	624
Crouch, John	Brit.	836
DeFranzio, Louis	U.S.	901
de Nicola, Morris	U.S.	914
Dorsey, Richard	U.S.	1005
Flores, Tony	U.S.	624
Frank, Harry	U.S.	1217
Frazier, Jessie	U.S.	1725
Garfinkle, David	U.S.	3029
Gentry, Clarence	U.S.	1298
Gonzalez Valenzuela, Delfina	Mex.	1338
Gonzalez Valenzuela, Maria de	Mex.	1338
Graham, Robert J.	U.S.	1361
Grosinger, Adam	U.S.	1836
Hannon, Charles	U.S.	1443
Hart, Mike	U.S.	3029
Hart, Mollie	U.S.	3029

Heeber, Dr. Allen	U.S.	1507
Hildegard, Evelyn	U.S.	1550
Hull, Anna	U.S.	3162
Jacobson, Jacob	U.S.	1693
Jocker, Harry	U.S.	1725
Johnson, Jack	U.S.	1729
Knipschild, William	U.S.	1836
Lagerman, Gustave	U.S.	1873
Levinson, Harry	U.S.	1944
Lietke, Andrew	U.S.	1005
McCarty, Blanche	U.S.	2025
Messina Brothers	Brit.	2171
Moore, Belle	U.S.	2209
Mosenson, Samuel	U.S.	412
Needham, Mother	Brit.	2295
O'Conner, Michael J.	U.S.	2359
Outlaws, The	U.S.	2387
Purdy, Sam	U.S.	2512
Reinstein, Samuel	U.S.	2561
Rhodes, Alexander	U.S.	2572
Rodriguez, Carlos	U.S.	2606
Scalise, George	U.S.	2687
Scheible, Mae	U.S.	2691
St. Lawrence, Napoleon	U.S.	2659
Thuna, Max	U.S.	2948
Trackenburg, Max	U.S.	2981
Tyler, Dick	U.S.	3029
Van Bever, Julia	U.S.	3029
Van Bever, Maurice	U.S.	3029
Watchman, Louis	U.S.	3098
Watchman, Philip	U.S.	3098
Williams, Frank C.	U.S.	3162

WHITE SLAVERY - Case of

Chaplin, Charles Spencer	U.S.	681
Macino, Joseph	U.S.	2046
Motto, Vincenzo	U.S.	2046
Plummer, Annie	U.S.	2476
Valentino, Rudolph	U.S.	3025

WITCHCRAFT

Aberdeen Witches	Brit.	10
Aix-en-Provence Nuns	Fr.	45
Arras Witches	Fr.	166
Auxonne Nuns	Fr.	186
Bacon, Roger	Brit.	206
Bamberg Witch Trials	Ger.	223
Barclay, Margaret	Scot.	233
Barton, Elizabeth	Brit.	270
Basque Witches	Fr.	273
Bateman, Mary	Brit.	280
Bedell, Joshua	Liberia	312
Bernauer, Agnes	Ger.	347
Black Mass, The	Int'l.	396
Bodenham, Anne	Brit.	415
Bodin, Jean	Fr.	415
Bourgot, Pierre	Fr.	3041
Brattle, Thomas	U.S.	475
Buirmann, Franz	Ger.	534
Bury St. Edmunds Witches	Brit.	559
Cadire, Marie Catherine	Fr.	568
Carpzov, Benedict	Saxony	635
Cassini, Samuel de	Italy	654
Cathars	Fr.	657
Chambre Ardente Affair	Fr.	674
Channel Islands Witchcraft	Brit.	680
Chelmsford Witches	Brit.	691
Cideville Case	Fr.	715
Clarke, David K.	Liberia	312
Cobham, Eleanor	Brit.	735

Brann, William Cowper	U.S.	473
Buntline, Ned	U.S.	542
Burckhard, Max Eugen	Aust.	543
Burgess, John William	U.S.	544
Burnett, William Riley	U.S.	551
Burt, Sir Cyril Lodowic	Brit.	558
Chambers, Ernest John	Can.	672
Chandler, Raymond Thornton	U.S.	676
Cheyney, Peter	Brit.	696
Christie, Agatha	Brit.	704
Cirvelo, Pedro Sanchez	Spain	717
Cohen, Octavus Roy	U.S.	742
Coryell, John Russell	U.S.	792
Dimsdale, Thomas J.	U.S.	975
Dinneen, Joseph F.	U.S.	975
Douglas, John	Brit.	1010
Doyle, Sir Arthur Conan	Brit.	1014
Fleming, Ian Lancaster	Brit.	1178
Freeman, Richard Austin	Brit.	1232
Gaboriau, Emile	Fr.	1245
Gardner, Erle Stanley	U.S.	1269
Genet, Jean	Fr.	1291
Gosse, Philip	Brit.	1350
Green, Anna Katharine	U.S.	1372
Hake, Edward	Brit.	1419
Hammett, Samuel Dashiell	U.S.	1437
Hecht, Ben	U.S.	1505
Hornung, Ernest William	Brit.	1621
Hume, Fergus	Brit.	1641
Jovellanos, Gaspar Melchor de	Spain	1745
Leblanc, Maurice-Marie-Emile	Fr.	1915
Lee, Manfred Bennington	U.S.	1919
Le Queux, William Tufnell	Brit.	1939
Leroux, Gaston	Fr.	1940
Lincoln, Natalie Sumner	U.S.	1965
Luther, Seth	U.S.	2015
MacDonald, Arthur	U.S.	2031
MacIver, Robert Morrison	U.S.	2046
Madan, Martin	Brit.	2071
Mailer, Norman	U.S.	2089
Malone, Edmund	Ire.	2098
Marsh, Ngaio	N.Zea.	2128
Martyn, Wyndham	U.S.	2133
Mason, Francis Van Wyck	U.S.	2136
More, Henry	Brit.	2216
Morrison, Arthur	Brit.	2226
Morse, John Torrey Jr.	U.S.	2228
Nash, Thomas	Brit.	2287
Orczy, Emmuska Mag.	Brit.	2375
Oursler, Fulton	U.S.	2386
Pearson, Edmund Lester	U.S.	2433
Poe, Edgar Allan	U.S.	2479
Ponzinibio, Gianfrancesco	Italy	2488
Porter, William Sydney	U.S.	2491
Reeve, Arthur Benjamin	U.S.	2558
Rinehart, Mary Roberts	U.S.	2584
Sayers, Dorothy Leigh	Brit.	2685
Seldes, Gilbert Vivian	U.S.	2725
Simenon, Georges	Fr.	2763
Smollett, Tobias George	Brit.	2804
Spee, Friedrich von	Ger.	2824
Starrett, Vincent	U.S.	2844
Stewart, Alfred Walter	Ire.	2852
Stimson, Frederic Jesup	U.S.	2856
Stout, Rex	U.S.	2866
Street, Cecil John Charles	Brit.	2868
Summers, Montague	Brit.	2877
Taylor, Phoebe Atwood	U.S.	2902
Thiers, Louis Adolphe	Fr.	2928
Thomson, Sir Basil Home	Brit.	2937

Tocqueville, Alexis-C. Henri	Fr.	2960
Tytler, William	Scot.	3012
Tytler, William	U.S.	3012
Upfield, Arthur William	Aus.	3018
Walling, Robert Alfred John	Brit.	3083
Warren, Charles	U.S.	3095
Wells, Carolyn	U.S.	3125
Wells, Ida Bell	U.S.	3125
Wertham, Frederic	U.S.	3127
White, Isaac	U.S.	3138
Wright, Willard Huntington	U.S.	3195

WRONGFUL DEATH

Gash, Stanton	U.S.	1282

INDEX

A

Abahai, 1
Abancourt, Charles Xaxier Joseph de
    Franqueville d', 1
Abarca de Bolea, 1
Abati, Michael, 577
Abatte, Frank, 3380
Abbandando, Frank "The Dasher", 1-2, 112,
    117, 120, 2252, 2255, 2536, 3003, 3401,
    3408, 3410
Abbandando, Rocco, 2
Abbas I, 2, 114, 3241
Abbas III, 2275
Abbatemarco, Anthony, 2, 3401
Abbatemarco, Frank "Frankie Shots", 2,
    2505, 3401
Abberline, Frederick George, 2-3, 683, 1688,
    1921
Abbershaw, Jerry, 3-4
Abbott, Anthony, 436
Abbott, Austin, 4
Abbott, Benjamin Vaughan, 4
Abbott, Burton W., 4-6, 3327
Abbott, Georgia, 4-6
Abbott, Jack Henry, 6-8, 540, 2809
Abbott, Sir John Joseph Caldwell, 8
Abbott, Robert Sengstacke, 8
Abbott, Stanley, 2096
Abboud Abdul Arzzak, 3253
Abdala, 3499, 3501, 3529
Abd al-Aziz, 8, 2177
Abd al-Halim Khaddam, 3257
Abd Allah, 8
Abdallah, Allal ben 140, 3252
Abdallah, Georges Ibrahim, 8-9, 3281
Abdel-Alim, Ahmed Tarek, 3215
Abdelaziz, Mohamed, 3522
Abdel Azziz al-Shalhi, 2518
Abdelhakim Suleiman, 3520
Abdelkader Barakrok, 3253
Abderhaman, 3244
Abd es, Ibrahim, 398
Abdesselam, Robert, 3254
Abdinoor, Elias, 9
Abdinoor, George, 9
Abdlhamid I, 2726
Abdou Diouf, 3378
Abd Rabb Enabi Hafex, 2655
Abduh, Muhammad, 9
Abdul Ali, Mir, 887
Abdul-Aziz, 2875, 1647
Abdülaziz, (Ottoman Empire, d.1876), 3242
Abdulaziz, Faisal Bin Musaed Bin, (Saud.
    pr. 1976), 3257
Abdul Aziz Bouteflika, 2675
Abdul Hamid, 2088, 3507
Abdul Hamid II, 355, 1099
Abdul Kader Auwda, 2288
Abdul Khalliq, 2275
Abdullah, 3252, 3255, 3257
Abdullah al-Hejiri, 3504
Abdullah, Dzaiddin, 741
Abdullah Fattah Enayat, 2835
Abdullah Hami, 2835
Abdullah, Mohammed, 9-10, 398
Abdullah Salah, 2894
Abdullah, Sameer Mohammed, 1081
Abdul Malik, 2096
Abdul Wahhab Kayali, 3519
Abdur Rasul Sayaf, 3522
Abednego, 2733
Abel, 10, 1101, 3237 king
Abel, Ferdinand "Gus", 596

Abelard, Peter, 522
Abellanosa, Santos, 3230
Abello Silva, Joseph, 3397
Abercromby, James, 10
Aberdeen Witches, 10
Abergavenny, 1970
Aberholt, Orville, 3375
Abernathy, Ralph, 1862
Abetz, Heinrich Otto, 10, 3538
Abeyta, Agapito, 3544
Abimelech, 10, 3232
Abinger, Edward, 10, 2226
Ablay, Alfred, 1743
Ablay, Jules, 1742
Ableiges, Jacques d', 10
Ables, John, 3564
Abner, 10, 3232
Abner, John, 1453
Abokka, 10
Abolitionist Riot, 10-11
Abood, Charles, 2713
*About the Murder of the Clergyman's
    Mistress*, 11
Abraham, Jack, 1805
Abraham, John D., 1178
Abraham, Mortado, 1393
Abrahams, 11
Abrahams, A.L., 1328
Abram, Donald, 3452
Abramowitz, Rose Simons, 657
Abrams, Albert, 11-13
Abrams, Henry, 3349
Abrams, Hiram, 847
Abrams, Hyman, 3379
Abrams, Michael, 13, 3294
Abrams, Robert, 480
Abrams, Sam, 13
Abrams, Stuart, 175, 2272
Abreu e Silva, Antonio Carlos de, 3333
Abrial, Jean Marie, 3538
Abscam, 13-14
Abshier, George Johnson, 3459, 1176
Absolom, 14, 109, 3232
Abu Abbas, 140, 3321, 3529
Abu Bakr, 3015, 3236
Abu Daoud, 3329, 3498
Abud Zaid, 3520
Abu Eain, Ziyad, 14
Abu Hanifah, 14
Abu Iyad, 3521
Abu-Jamal, Mumia, 3453
Abu Jihad, 3528
Abu Khaled, Nasser Mohammed Ali, 14
Abu Mousa, 140, 3529
Abu Nidal, 3176, 3334, 3474, 3501, 3505,
    3523, 3525, 3527, 3529, 3530
Abu Nidal Faction, 3529
Abu Walid, 3526
Acao Libertadora Nacional (ALN) 3327,
    3328, 3482, 3485, 3529
Accardi, Settimo, 14-15, 3401
Accardo, Anthony Joseph "Big Tuna", 15-
    18, 44-45, 73, 131, 283, 525, 613, 616,
    665, 745, 1034, 1153, 1306, 1410, 1491,
    1555, 1980, 2339, 2529, 2574, 2396,
    2688, 3226, 3380, 3382, 3384-3385
Accetturo, Anthony, 18, 3401
Accolti, Benedetto, 18
Accoramboni, Vittoria, 18, 3139
Accorso, Francesco, Sr., 18
Accorso, Francesco, Jr., 18
Ace, Kid Boots, 3326
Acevedo, Louis, 18
Acheson, Kenneth John, 3272, 3511
Achew, James, 18-19
Achey, John Henry, 19

Achillas, 3234
Acid Bath Murders, 19
Acker, George, 19
Acker, Jean, 3027
Ackerman, 19
Ackerman, Bradley, 19
Ackerman, Frederick P., 3380
Ackerman, Harold, 18
Ackerman, James Waldo, 19
Ackerman, Martha, 2025
ACLU, 2554
Acosta, Cristobal, 3291
Acosta, Miguel, 3464
Acosta, Pedro, 3249
A. Cowen & Co., 3289
Action Directe, 3261, 3280
Action Organization for the Liberation of
    Palestine, 3529
Action pour la Renaissance de la Corse,
    3529
Acton, Thomas, 19-20
Acton, Thomas C., 2318
Actor's Blood, 20
Acturk, Barin, 1098
Acua, Chile Mapocho, 2894
ad-Dawlah, Nasir, 3236
Adachi Mineichiro, 20
Adair, William, 2445
Aldabero, 30
Adalbero "The Old Traitor", 20
Adaloald, 20, 3236
Adam, Antonio-Edmund, 20
Adam, Fred J., 1816, 1931
Adam, Isobel, 2472
Adam, Juliette, 20
Adam, Quirin François Lucien, 20
Adam, Sam, 2838
Adam, Yekotiel, 3260, 3523
Adami, John George, 20
Adamic, Louis, 20
Adamo, Joseph, 3396
Adamo, Michael, 2542
Adamo, Momo, 3396
Adamov, Oleg, 2177
Adams, Agnes, 1508
Adams, Albert J., 20-22, 2765, 3401
Adams, Arthur, 2776
Adams, Aubrey, 3447
Adams, Caleb, 22
Adams, Charles, 3544
Adams, Charles Francis, 3388
Adams, Charles Wayne, 3428
Adams, Clifford Leroy, Jr., 2026
Adams, Curtis, Jr., 1920
Adams, Dan, 3343
Adams, Dick, 22
Adams, E.C. (U.S. pr.1940s), 1425
Adams, Eddie, 22-25, 583
Adams, Edith, 722
Adams, Fanny, 215
Adams, Francis W.H. (U.S. pr.1950s), 1803,
    3425
Adams, Frank (U.S. d.1813), 1722
Adams, Frank (U.S. pr.1892), 1194
Adams, Frank (U.S. pr.1927), 1908
Adams, Franklin P. (U.S. pr.1930s), 1659
Adams, Gene, 722
Adams, George, 25
Adams, Gerry, 3261
Adams, Grover, 550
Adams, Hal W., 2026
Adams, Harry F., 3424
Adams, Hattie, 2413
Adams, Henry, 2052

Adams, J. Emory, 1994
Adams, J.H., 3544
Adams, Jake, 1175
Adams, James, 25, 3447
Adams, Jani, 25-26
Adams, Jesse Fairchild, 95
Adams, Joe, 376, 3246, 3414
Adams, John (Brit. pr.1789) 2270
Adams, John (Brit. 1760-1829) 26
Adams, John Bodkin, 26
Adams, John Quincy, 26, 205, 334, 355, 492,
    726, 765, 813, 815, 884, 1236, 1713, 1493,
    1556, 1917, 1963, 2130, 2209, 2795, 2989,
    3097, 3178
Adams, John Truslow, 2911
Adams "Judge", 3562
Adams, Katharine, 2198
Adams, Kenneth, 3161
Adams, Kitty, 26, 3380, 3383
Adams, Larry, 3452
Adams, Lionel, 812
Adams, Lizzie, 215
Adams, Louis, 26-27
Adams, Maria, 2965
Adams, Mark, 26
Adams, Mary, 27
Adams, Mel, 1714
Adams, Michael, 3338
Adams, Millicent, 27
Adams, Moses, 27
Adams, Nick, 27-28
Adams, Paul, 1493
Adams, Phyllis, 3380
Adams, Randall Dale, 28
Adams, Red, 2032, 3380
Adams, Reddrick, 3347
Adams, Robert, 658
Adams, Roger, 3296
Adams, Ron, 1248
Adams, St. Clair, 812
Adams, Samuel (U.S. 1700s), 447, 2837,
    3355
Adams, Samuel (U.S. 1800s), 759
Adams, Simon, 3352
Adams, Spencer, 908
Adams, Steve, 1500, 2066
Adams, Sylvester, 3454
Adams, Terry, 1208
Adams, Thomas, 3453
Adams, Victor, 3346
Adams, Washington, 3368
Adams, Wayne, 1091
Adams, William Nelson, 28
Adamson, Blossom, 3354
Adamson, Carl, 1278, 2181, 3553
Adamson, John, 3447
Adamson, John Harvey, 28-29, 424, 3270
Adamson, Joy, 29, 1079, 1080
Adamson Mushala, 3526
Adanandus, Dwight, 3454
Adan, Richard, 7-8
Adcox, Keith, 3448
Adcox, Robert, 29
Addams, Jane, 552, 2833
Addicks, John Edward O'Sullivan, 29
Addington, Sir Anthony, 29-30, 406
Addison, Jack, 30
Addonizio, Hugh J., 30-31, 896, 3401
Adega Fresneda, Juan, 3472
Adelaide, 181
Adelasia, 1099
Adelchis, 3236
Adel, Frank F., 74, 2529
Adel Najin Abu-Asi, 3498
Adenauer, Konrad, 2291, 3252, 3253
Aderholt, Orville F., 287, 3246
Adham, Burhan, 2090
Adherbal, 3234
Ad Hoc Committee to End Political

Suppression, 3481
Adib, Hojatoleslam Nematollah, 3259,
    3516
Adivar, Halidé Edib, 1420
Adkins, Carl Wayne, 3454
Adkins, David, 176, 3553
Adkins, George, 363
Adkins, Harry, 391
Adkins, Orville, 436, 3326
Adkins, Ricky, 3447
Adkins, Ryland, 687
Adler, Friedrich "Fritz", 31, 3243, 2873
Adler, Jakie, 3386
Adler, John, 31, 3380
Adler, Lou, 3331
Adler, Lydia, 31
Adler, Pearl, 31
Adler, Polly, 31-32, 3401
Adolphus, A., 416
Adomeit, Kurt, 32, 2580
Adomeit, Ursula, 32
Adonijah, 3232
Adonis, Joseph, 1-2, 32-34, 35, 104, 111,
    117, 178, 525, 591, 604, 608, 616, 623,
    794, 1034, 1295, 1296, 1491, 1555,
    1892, 1895, 2002, 2004, 2114, 2138,
    2218, 2252, 2336, 2689, 2702, 2974,
    3140, 3226, 3393, 3401, 3408
Adrian VI, 2087
Adshade, Michael, 1382
Adshead, John, 35-36, 104
Adwan, Kamal, 36, 3256
Aegidi, Ludwig Karl, 36
Aelfthryth, 3237
Aemilia, 1749
Aeronauts in the New York *World*, 36
Aethelberht, 662
Aethelheard, 36
Aethelred II, 1052, 3237
Aethelstan, 36
Aétius, 36, 3025, 3235, 3303
Aetius, Flavius, 36
Afanaseyev, Yuri N., 1769
Afer, Domitius, 36
Affaire des Poisons, L', 36-37
Affre, 2751
Affre, Denis Auguste, 3241
Afong, Abram Henry, Jr., 3104
Afra, Saint, 37
Africa, Birdie, 2236
Africa, Charles Sims, 2236
Africa, Delbert Orr, 2236
Africa, Edward Goodman, 2236
Africa, Janet Hallaway, 2236
Africa, Jeneane Phillips, 2236
Africa, John, 2236
Africa, Merle Austin, 2236
Africa, Michael Davis, 2236
Africa, Ramona, 2236
Africa, William Phillips, 2236
African National Congress, 3260, 3261,
    3271, 3274, 3276-3278, 3280, 3281,
    3507, 3509, 3515, 3516, 3521-3523,
    3525, 3527, 3528
Africanus, Leo, 1931, 3291
Afrikaner-Broederbond, 37
Afro-American Liberation Army, 3494,
    3529
Afro-American Society, 3480, 3481
After House, The, 37
After the Fact, 37
Aga Khan, 866, 1915
Agan, James, 3449
Agar, Edward, 37, 1367, 3457
Agar, James, 3303
Agca, Mehmet Ali, 3257, 3258, 3510, 3512
Agede, Abate, 3255
Agelof, Sylvia, 2994
Agenda Murder, The, 37

Agesilaus, 2958, 3233
Aggeler, William Tell, 3001
Agha, Ghulum, 3246
Agha Mohammad Khan Qajar (Per.
    pr.1794), 1991
Agha, Zara, 844
Agnello, Carmine, 3401
Agnew, James, 631
Agnew, John, 1581
Agnew, Joseph, 455
Agnew, Spiro T., 37, 896, 1312, 3101
Agone, Joseph, 3401
Agostini, Antonio, 37-39
Agostini, Linda Platt, 37-39
Agra Double Murder, 39
Agrippa, Herod I, 2450
Agrippa, Marcus Vipsanius, 2485
Agrippina, 493, 580, 727, 3234
Agrippina the Elder, 39
Agrippina the Younger, 39-40, 2007, 2305
Agrippina, Vipsania, 39, 1029, 2724
Agro, Salvatore, 1394
Agron, Evsei, 3401, 3408
Aguayo, Robert, 40, 3396
Agueci, Albert, 40, 3380
Agueci Brothers, 40, 112
Agueci, Vito, 40, 3380
Aguelari, Epeminto, 3553
Aguero Echeverria, Carlos, 3270, 3504,
    3510, 3512
Aguesseau, Henri Francois d' (Daguesseau),
    40
Aguiar Rodriguez, Miguel, 3472
Aguiar Rodriguez, Roberto, 3472
Aguilar, Ceberiano, 3553
Aguilar, Donaciano, 3553
Aguilar, Frank, 166
Aguilar, Miguel Angel, 322
Aguilar, Oscar, 3246
Aguilar, Reymundo, 3553
Aguilar, Robert Peter, 40
Aguillan, Felix, 3553
Aguinaldo, Emilio, 429, 2021
Aguirre, Jermin, 3553
Aguirr, Martin, 2224
Aguiyi, J.T.V. Ironsi, 3255
Agustin, Antonio, 40
Agustin Esquivel Medrano, 3467
Agustin I, 2679
Ahab, 330, 1717
Ahala, C. Servilius, 3232
Ah Ann, 3253
Ah Anong Ti, 3340
Ahaziah, 41, 175, 3232
Ah Chai 40-41, 3327
Ahearn, Daniel Francis, 41, 1894, 3060
Ahenobarbus, Domitius, 39
Ahern, Bob, 1465
Ahern, F., 3426
Ahern, Frank, 577
Ahern, James, 936
Ahern, Michael (U.S. pr.1946), 1511
Ahern, Michael J. (U.S. pr.1925) 131
Ahithophel, 14
Ah Kum, 1031
Ahlden, Princess of, 2816
Ahle, Charles, 2104
Ahlers, Nicolaus Emil Herman Adolph, 41
Ahlstedt, Gustave, 41, 1000
Ahlstrom, Edwin, 2973
Ahmada, 41
Ahmada Mohammad Ali, 1766
Ahmad Assaf, 3522
Ahmad Baba, 41
Ahmad Khan, Sir Sayyid, 41
Ahmad Khomeini, 3523
Ahmad Raza Kasuri, 356
Ahmed I, 1844
Ahmed Kassim, 1767

Alfano, Pietro, 2473, 3381
Al Fatah, 36, 91, 140, 198, 2275, 2397, 3256-
    3260, 3266-3268, 3270, 3271, 3276, 3484,
    3490, 3491, 3494-3496, 3498, 3505, 3506,
    3513, 3520, 3522, 3529, 3530
Alfonso, 627, 1850, 2551
Alfonso II, 91, 3238
Alfonso IV, 656, 896
Alfonso V, 3055
Alfonso VI, 938
Alfonso XII, 600
Alfonso XIII, 194, 1152, 3216
Alfonso of Aragon, 91
Alfonso, Roberto, 2408
Alford, George, 3553
Alford, William, 91
Alfred, 91
Algano, Lorenzo, 3381
Algarron, Jacques, 1867
Alger, Cyrus, 92
Alger, Horatio, 321, 595, 603, 1657
Algernon, Wilfred Jones, 1336
Algirdas, 1806-1807
Algren, Nelson, 646
Alhambra, the, 3414
Ali Abu Nuwar, 2090
Ali, Drew, 397
Ali, El-Amin Ahmad, 3453
Aliens of America, 3500, 3529
Ali Hajem, 3259
Ali Hassan Salemeh, 2536
Ali ibn Abi Talib, 92
Ali, Kamal Hasan, 3509
Ali Mamoud, 3018
Alingal, Godfredo, 3512
Ali Osseiran, 3334
Alioto, John, 3398
Alioto, Joseph, 702
Ali Pasha, 92
Ali, S., 3247
Ali, Sayed, 1048
Ali, Sayyid Amir, 113
Alito, Samuel A., Jr., 1816
Aliwoli, Jamaljah, 92
Ali, Zakiah, 807
Al Jihad Al Mudaddas Front, 3276, 3520,
    3529
Alkmund, 1070
All-African People's Revolutionary Army,
    3529
All-India Communist Party, 3519, 3529
Allah, 397
Allaire, Anthony J., 1044, 1666
Allaire, Frank, 2039
Allal, Said, 3253
Allan, David, 2034
Allan, E., 2943
Allan, Jane Louise, 928
Allan, John, 2346, 2479
Allan, John Frederick, 882
Allan, Rachel, 1112
Allard, Alain, 3466
Allard, Georges, 1905
Allard, Leon, 1905
Allard, Pierre, 918, 3049
Allaway, Edward Charles, 92
Allaway, Thomas Henry, 92-93, 191, 579,
    725
Allbee, James R., 3472
Allectus, 3235
Allee, Alfred Y., 93, 788, 3544, 3557
Allegra, Mechiore, 2085
Allegret, Marc, 405
Allegretti, Jimmie "The Monk", 162, 978,
    3381-3383
Allen, A.D., 1203, 2870
Allen, A.W., 1909
Allen, Abe, 3544
Allen, Alfred, 3092

Allen, Anthony, 2409
Allen, Arthur L., 2764
Allen, Barry, 1329
Allen, Betty, 1191
Allen, "Big Time" Charlie, 3295
Allen, Bill, 1594, 3553
Allen, "Bladder," 3553
Allen, "Bull Run," 1458
Allen, Brenda, 93
Allen, Brown, 2270
Allen, Charles (U.S. pr. 1910s), 93, 3348,
    3412, 3553
Allen, Charles (U.S. pr. 1970s), 1584
Allen, Clarence R., 3448
Allen, Claude, 94
Allen, Donald, 2089
Allen, Edward H.B., 93
Allen, Elisha (U.S. d.1793), 1239
Allen, Elisha Hunt (U.S. 1804-83), 93-94
Allen, Emily, 2570
Allen, Ezra, 3138
Allen, Florence Ellinwood, 94
Allen, Floyd, 94-95, 3458
Allen, Frank, 3553
Allen, Frank Ely, 1722
Allen, Frederick Lewis, 2911
Allen, Gary, 3453
Allen, George, 3338
Allen, George Charles, 522, 3197
Allen, George E., 95
Allen, George W., 438, 2423
Allen, Henry, 3343
Allen, Howard, 3451
Allen, J.A., 1702
Allen, J. Wesley (U.S. pr.1901), 1877
Allen, Jack (U.S. pr.1882), 1996
Allen, James (Brit. b.1783), 1524
Allen, James (U.S. d.1967), 1511
Allen, James (Brit. pr.1911), 3304
Allen, James (U.S. d.1894), 3345
Allen, James (U.S. pr.1880s), 3553
Allen, James S., 98
Allen, Joe, 2181
Allen, John, 95-96, 3401, 3553
Allen, John C., 3453
Allen, John Edward, 96
Allen, John R., 804
Allen, Joseph (U.S. d.1899), 3350
Allen, Joseph (U.S. d.1909), 96, 2181,
    3353, 3359
Allen, Julia, 1436
Allen, Kathleen, 1875
Allen, Kenneth, 96-97, 3451
Allen, Larry, 2719
Allen, Laura, 3128
Allen, Lewis, 2812
Allen, Lizzie, 97, 804, 1115, 3381, 3383,
    3385
Allen, Louise Jane, 1900
Allen, Mal, 3553
Allen, Margaret, 97-98, 1348
Allen, Mary, 1472
Allen, Moony, 3355
Allen, Ned, 98, 3414
Allen, O.K., 1982, 1984
Allen, Paul B., 789
Allen, Peggy, 98
Allen, Peter Anthony, 98
Allen, Raymond, 1191
Allen, Rich, 3357
Allen, Richard (U.S. d.1899), 3350
Allen, Richard (U.S. pr.1981), 3511
Allen, Roderick, 2128
Allen, Roger, 98
Allen, Roy, 2737
Allen, Shang, 1174
Allen, Sidna, 94, 95
Allen, Sloan, 3344
Allen, Stanley, 3450

Allen, Stuart Buckner, 98
Allen, T.A., 2818
Allen, Thomas (U.S. d.1911), 3361
Allen, Thomas (U.S. d.1899), 3351
Allen, Thomas (Brit. pr.1650s), 1558
Allen, Thomas (U.S. pr.1940s), 2866
Allen, Timothy, 3453
Allen, Timothy Charles, 1631
Allen, Todd, 515
Allen, Victor, 95
Allen, W.H., 3554
Allen, W. Stooks, 2212
Allen, Walter, 3354
Allen, Wanda Jean, 3453
Allen, Mrs. Wesley, 2735
Allen, William (U.S. pr.1932), 1482
Allen, William (U.S. pr.1979), 1543, 2301,
    3014, 3357
Allen, William (U.S. pr. 1927), 2301
Allen, William (U.S. pr.19th Cent.), 3014
Allen, William (U.S. d.1906), 3357
Allen, William E., 1143, 1188, 3426
Allen, William Joshua, 98
Allen, William O'Meara, 98-99
Allen, William Pitt, 2136
Allen, Wilma Frances, 504, 3327
Allen, Woody, 1189, 1900
Allende Gossens, Dr. Salvador, 99, 3256
Allende, Hortensia Bussi, 99
Allende, Salvador, 1942, 3377
Allers, Katherine, 99, 3228
Allerton, Mary, 2733
Allesandron, Eugene, 1944
Allevato, Dominic J., 3393
Alley, Henry, 3363
Alley, Leavitt, 99
Alley, Sedley, 3454
Alliance of the Lao Reactionary Group
    Fronts, 3523, 3529
Alligood, Clarence, 1971
Allingham, Dan, 1884
Allingham, Margery Louise, 99
Allins, Andrew, 2668
Allison, Charles, 99, 3544, 3565, 3567, 3553
Allison, Dave, 3544, 3545
Allison, Isaac, 167, 3263
Allison, James, 99
Allison, John, 101, 3356
Allison, Joseph, 159
Allison, Robert A. Clay, 99-102, 742, 743,
    1385, 3546, 3547, 3553, 3559
Allison, Thomas N., 3342
Allison, Watson, 3448
Allison, William Stafford, 1601
Allman, James, 2091
Allman, James P., 3424
Allnach, Kay-Werner, 3475
Allnutt, William Newton, 102
Allou, 2751
Allred, A.M., 508
Allred, C.W., 3077
Allred, James V., 102
Allred, Rulon C., 1914
Allridge, James, 3454
Allridge, Ronald Keith, 3454
Allsop, Thomas, 2280, 2282
All the King's Men, 102
All This and Heaven Too, 102
Allums, Ernest, 3361
Allweiss, David, 102
Allwhite, Louis, 3356
Almagro, Diego de, 2472, 2527, 3238
Almaneih, Naser, 3272, 3506
Alman, John E., 2827
Almarez, Stella Delores, 102
Almazan, Juan Andreu, 3249
Almdijk Case, 102-103
Almeida, Jose, 3246
Almeida, Louis, 3381

Anderson, Bernard, 3544
Anderson, Bill (U.S. d.1878), 3556
Anderson, Bill (U.S. pr.1860s), 3567
Anderson, Billy Dean (U.S. c.1944-79), 122
Anderson, Boston Pete, 1355, 2984
Anderson, C. Michael, 3452
Anderson, Charles, 136, 3360
Anderson, Charlie, 2569
Anderson, Clifford, 122
Anderson, Clinton, 809
Anderson, Damon, 2248
Anderson, David L., 122
Anderson, Dick, 2936
Anderson, Don Benny, 123, 3334
Anderson, Edward, 1050
Anderson, Elly Hope, 1088
Anderson, Emily Hope, 1088
Anderson, Evelyn, 658
Anderson, Fordy, 273
Anderson, George "Dutch" (U.S. d.1926), 683-685
Anderson, George (Brit. pr.1954), 334
Anderson, George (U.S. pr.1906), 1402
Anderson, George Weston (U.S. 1861-1938), 123
Anderson, Grant, 3339
Anderson, Ham, 1449, 3553
Anderson, Harry, 123
Anderson, Hugh, 123, 359, 1447, 2026, 2315, 3305
Anderson, J., 3247
Anderson, J.E., 3544
Anderson, James (U.S. d.1898), 3350
Anderson, James (U.S. d.1896), 3348
Anderson, James (Brit. pr.1840s-50s), 1724
Anderson, James (U.S. pr.1881), 2144
Anderson, Jim (U.S. d.1860s), 3553
Anderson, John (U.S. d.1898), 3350
Anderson, John (U.S. d.1891), 3340
Anderson, John (Scot. pr.1840s), 1315
Anderson, John (U.S. pr.1920s), 2068
Anderson, John (U.S. pr.1876), 3546
Anderson, Johnny Ray, 3454
Anderson, Joseph, 123
Anderson, Joshua, 3354
Anderson, Judith Mae, 123
Anderson, Kirk, 3331
Anderson, Larry Norman, 3454
Anderson, Leroy Gene, 123
Anderson, Levi E., 123-124
Anderson, Lucious, 124
Anderson, Margaret, 1332
Anderson, Mary, 1676
Anderson, Matilda, 2521
Anderson, Maxwell, 3177
Anderson, Moses, 3351
Anderson, Mylette, 1837
Anderson, Noah, 3346
Anderson, Nyborg, 3329
Anderson, Owen, 3338
Anderson, Percy Charles, 124
Anderson, Perry L., 3425
Anderson, Perry L. Jr. 124
Anderson, Peter, 2576
Anderson, Reese, 124, 3553
Anderson, Richard, 3449
Anderson, Richardson, 3364
Anderson, Robert (Fr. pr.1900s), 124
Anderson, Robert (Scot.), 635, 3188
Anderson, Robert Palmer (U.S. 1906-78), 124
Anderson, Scott L., 124, 3553
Anderson, Simon, 3359
Anderson, Stephen, 3448
Anderson, Terry, 124, 3334
Anderson, Terry A., 1865, 1914
Anderson, Thomas C., 2862, 2863
Anderson, Thomas Weldon, 124-125
Anderson, Tom (U.S. pr.1910s) 3399, 3400

Anderson, Tom (U.S. pr.1890s), 155
Anderson, William (U.S. d.1864), 125-126
Anderson, William (U.S. d.1891), 3340
Anderson, William (U.S. d.1892), 3342
Anderson, William (U.S. d.1897), 3349
Anderson, William (U.S. d.1906), 3357
Anderson, William "Bill" (U.S. pr.1873), 1997, 3553
Anderson, William "Bloody Bill" (U.S. pr.1837-64), 125-126, 2519
Anderson, William C. (U.S. pr.1820s), 3424
Anderson, William H. (U.S. d.1878), 126, 3544
Anderson, Wilson, 1988
Anderson, Winfield, 2432
Anders, Ted, 929
Andolino, Simone, 3401
Andrade, Gonzalo Freyere de, 322
Andrade, Guillermo de, 322
Andrade, Richard, 3447
Andrassy, Edward, 731, 986
Andre, Jean-Louis, 3428
Andre, John, 126, 161
Andréa, John, 184
Andreev, Leonid Nikolaevich, 127
Andreski, Mitchell, 3504
Andress, Ray, 1337
Andrew, Hauk, A., 1478
Andrew, Philip, 869
Andrew, Robert, 126, 3544
Andrew, Ruth Ann, 869
Andrews, Byron, 1272
Andrews, Dana, 436, 3135
Andrews, Dorothy Ann, 126
Andrews, Sir Edmund, 1111
Andrews, Hank, 3553
Andrews, Herbert, 245
Andrews, Herschel, 2399
Andrews, James, 2130
Andrews, Jay, 3036
Andrews, Jennette, 2844
Andrews, Jesse J., 3448
Andrews, John (U.S. 1980s), 1207
Andrews, John (U.S. 1810s), 1166
Andrews, John U., 2316, 2319, 2325
Andrews, Joseph, 126
Andrews, Kathleen, 2847
Andrews, L.Y., 3249
Andrews, Loraine, 494
Andrews, Lowell Lee, 126-127
Andrews, Lucius, 3340
Andrews, Capt. M., 3544
Andrews, Mary, 127
Andrews, Maurice, 3454
Andrews, Milton Franklin, 127
Andrews, Nathan, 3341
Andrews, Norman, 1917-1918, 3461
Andrews, Original, 3388
Andrews, Robert, 3349
Andrews, Samuel M., 127
Andrews, Shang, 3381
Andrews, Stephen, 2672
Andrews, Terry, 126
Andrews, Thomas, 127
Andrews, William (U.S. pr.1974), 2464
Andrews, William (U.S. pr.1988), 3456
Andreyev, Leonid Nikolayevich, 127
Andriensen, Maryn, 1044
Andrieux, Louis, 349
Andronicus I Comnenus, 127, 3237
Andronicus II, 1181, 2173, 3237
Andros, Sir Edmund, 127, 772, 1031, 2304
Andry, John N., 390
An Du Hi, 1820
Andujar, Emilio Jaime, 3194
Anekuelo, Ben, 2139
Angarita, General, 354
Ange, Pere, 3292

Angel, 127
Angel, Miriam, 1969
Angel, Ron, 1838
Angela Pompilia, Francesca Camilla Vittoria, 1208
Angelescu, M., 3246
Angeles, Felipe, 2077
Angelina, James, 3401
Angelini, Donald, 3381, 3383, 3390
Angelino, Aurelius, 1110
Angell, Joseph Kinnicutt, 127
Angelo, Carlo De, 3401
Angelo, Fra, 1207
Angelo, Gertrude, 1759
Angelos, Anthony G., 127
Angelus, Issac, 127
Anger, Lou, 148, 150
Anger, Roger, 127
Angersika, John, 3392
Angersola, Fred, 3392
Angersola, George, 3392
Angersola, John, 1949, 3392
Angetter, Vit, 3464
Angieli, Helen, 2830
Angier, Samuel, 1972
Angiers, Michele, 703
Angiulo, Gennaro J., 127-128, 3379
Anglade, Gaby, 2820
Anglesey, Marquis of, 1285
Anglin, Arthur L., 3061
Anglin Brothers, 56
Anglin, Clarence, 68, 3428
Anglin, Francis Alexander, 128
Anglin, John, 68
Anglin, Joseph, 3428
Anglin, Thomas, 68, 3251
Angry Brigade, 128, 3265
Angry Merchants, 3277, 3529
Angry Metallurgists, 3524
Ang Tie Cho, 3464
Anguilar, Martinez, 46
Anguita, Maria del Carmen Lopez, 3271
Angus, Earl of, 1695
Anile, Francisco, 3469
Animal Rights Militia, 3279, 3526, 3529
Anjou, Charles of, 766, 3237
Anjou, Duke of, 2872
Anjou, Victoriano, 3343
Ankney, Gorden, 1096
Anleu, Julio Cesar Difuentes, 3333
An Lu-shan, 128, 3205, 3236
Ann, Alicia, 424
Ann Arbor Murders, 128
Anna, Santa, 594
Anne (Brit. 1665-1714), 127, 1227
Anne (Brit. 1950-   ), 221, 3330
Anne of Cleves, 1627
Anne, Duchess d'Etampes, 927
Anne, Henrietta, 1517, 3239
Anne, Princess, 3330
Annear, Thomas, 1459
Annee, Paul A., 128, 3425
Annenberg, Moses L., 128-129, 178, 616, 796, 1584, 1663, 2529, 3381, 3390, 3392
Annenberg, Walter, 129, 1189
Annerino, Sam, 1980
Annesley, James, 129
Annesley, Richard, 129
Annett, Wiley, 3355
Annie, Battle, 1342
Annixter, Julius "Lovin Putty", 756, 3381
Anno, 129, 3237
Annunziata, Joseph, 129
Ansaldi, Marius, 129
Ansara, Brian, 768
Ansara, Pete, 1391
Anschutz, Willie, 1823
Ansegisus, 129
Ansel, James, 3086

Arena, Joanne, 1321
Arensdorf, John, 154
Aretino, Ludovico 870
Arevalo y Veitia, Juan, 3252
Argentine Anticommunist Alliance, 3529
Argentine Political Violence, 154
Argentinian Revolutionary Workers Party,
    3529
Argento, Arthur, 1040
Argilagos, Jose, 1769
Argimiro Gabaldon Revolutionary
    Command, 2335
Argo, Henry, 3367
Argoll, Joan, 1139
Argone, Joseph, 3401
Argov, Shlomo, 3260
Arguello, A., 3553
Arguello, Patrick, 3468, 3486
Argueta, Manuel Colom, 3506
Argyll, Archibald Campbell, 1356
Argyll, Earl of (Scot. pr.1865), 2569
Argyll, Ninth Earl of (Scot. 1629-1685),
    1083, 2569
Argyll, Tenth Earl of (Scot. 1651-1703), 593
Arias, Arnulfo, 2344
Arias, Paramo, 3253
Arias, Roberto, 3255
Arias Dávila, Pedro, 1151
Arias Espinosa, Ricardo, 2566
Ariberto da Antimiano, 154
Arikan, Kemal, 3259, 3520
Arindell, William, 1179
Arinori, S., 3242
Ariobarzanes III, 3234
Ariola, Michael, 3014
Aristides, 2926
Aristippus, 1874
Aristobulus (Hasmonaean, d.6 B.C.), 133-
    134, 154, 1726, 3234
Aristobulus III (Hasmonaean, d.35 B.C.),
    154, 3234
Aristogiton, 154
Aristophanes, 70
Aristotle, 521, 584
Ariya Dhamma Thera, 1900
Ariyoshi, George, 1138
Ariza, Carlos B., 3246
Arizona Jack, 3553
Arizona Rangers, 108, 154-155, 2782
Arjun Dass, 3261
Arjun Mal, 155
Arkansas Bill, 3553
Arkansas Tom, 155, 3549
Arkill, Gustave, 41, 1000
Arkinson, William, 3343
Arkle, Thomas, 1435
Arlacchi, Pino, 2473
Arledge, Jimmy, 458
Arlen, George V., 1930
Arlen, Michael, 1512
Arline, Sam, 3361
Arlington, Jim, 3381
Arlington, Josie, 155-156, 2862, 3398
Arlosoroff, Chaim, 156, 3247
Armadale, 156
Armagnac, Bernard VII d', 156
Armah, William, 354
Armas Peréz, Ramón, 354, 3254
Armato, Dominic, 3381
Armed Commandos of Liberation, 3487,
    3529
Armed Communist Formations, 3270, 3504,
    3529
Armed Communist League, 3494, 3504, 3529
Armed Forces of National Liberation of
    Puerto Rico, 1228, 3501, 3529
Armed Forces of National Resistance, 3529,
    3530
Armed Nationalist Reactionary Group,

3277, 3523, 3529
Armed Nuclei for Popular Autonomy,
    3529, 3532
Armed Proletarian Cells, 3532
Armed Proletarian Nuclei, 2553, 3529,
    3532
Armed Revolutionary Nuclei (NAR),
    3271, 3507, 3526, 3529, 3532
Armed Revolutionary Vanguard-Palmares,
    3529
Armed Revolution Squads, 3508, 3529
Armed Struggle, 3526, 3529
Armed Vanguard of the Proletariat, 3504,
    3529
Armee de Liberation Quebecois (ALQ)
    3476, 3529
Armellini, Angela, 3330
Armellino, John R., 30
Armenian Orly Group, 3276, 3520, 3529,
    3533
Armenian Secret Army for the Liberation
    of Armenia, 3271, 3277, 3278, 3280,
    3506, 3523, 3525, 3529
Armenia, Tiridates of, 2460
Armenta, Anthony, 1067
Armenteros, Jesus, 3465
Armes, Monroe "Blackie", 3192
Armes, Tony, 3192
Armijo, Luis E., 2087
Arminius, 3234
Armistead, Norma Jean, 156
Armitage, Robert, 3252, 3253
Armitage, William H., 1048
Armone, Joseph, 3401
Armor, William, 3342
Armour, Edward, 395
Armour, J.A., 1826
Armour, John Douglas, 156
Armour, Joseph, 156
Armstrong, Anne, 3103
Armstrong, Benjamin, 3079
Armstrong, Charles, 3544
Armstrong, Dwight Allan, 1159
Armstrong, Eliza, 2846
Armstrong, George, 1228
Armstrong, Glen, 408
Armstrong, Herbert Rowse, 156-157, 849,
    871, 1236, 3023
Armstrong, Jack, 3553
Armstrong, Janet, 158
Armstrong, John (Brit. pr.1956), 157-158
Armstrong, John (Brit. pr.1528), 157
Armstrong, John (U.S. pr.1877), 3559
Armstrong, John Barclay (U.S. 1850-1913),
    158-159, 1449, 1722, 3544
Armstrong, John M., 1644
Armstrong, Karelton Lewis, 159, 1159,
    3266
Armstrong, Katherine, 156-157
Armstrong, Katherine Mary, 2830
Armstrong, Louis, 2862
Armstrong, Terese, 2568
Armstrong, Thomas Jefferson, 159-160
Armstrong, V.S., 3252
Armstrong, William, 691
Armwood, George, 159, 3367
Army for the Liberation of Lesotho, 3275,
    3518
Army Mathematics Research Center, 3289
Army of God, 3334
Arnall, Ellis, 553
Arnas, 160
Arndt, Charles Coatsworth Pinckney, 3055
Arnegunde, 3291
Arnet, Richard, 159, 227, 1494
Arnett, James, 3447
Arnold, A.C., 95
Arnold, Andrew J., 159
Arnold, Benedict, 126, 159, 160-161, 2035

Arnold, Betty Jean, 2806
Arnold, Clement Harisse, 1881
Arnold, Dorothy Harriet Camille, 161-162,
    705, 2805
Arnold, Francis, 161, 162
Arnold, H.M., 1846
Arnold, J.C., 3424
Arnold, John, 3454
Arnold, Joseph, 162, 463, 1109, 3381
Arnold, Keith, 3329
Arnold, Louise, 162
Arnold, Marvin, 2805
Arnold, Morris S., 562
Arnold, Phillip, 162-163, 871
Arnold, Quilt, 404, 554
Arnold, Reuben, 1222
Arnold, Roger, 3011
Arnold, Samuel B. (U.S. pr.1864), 163,
    1954
Arnold, Stephen, 163
Arnold, Thurman Wesley, 163
Arnold, Tom, 3086
Arnold, W.J., 2028
Arnold, William, 1712
Arnott, Charles E., 1283
Arnoul II, 3158, 3236
Arnstein, Jules W., 163-166
Arnstein, Nicky, 3015
Arnstein, Peter, 3394
Arocena, Eduardo, 3257
Aronowitz, Joseph, 166
Aronstein, Joseph, 1759
Arpels, Claude, 166
Arquello, David, 3553
Arquilla, Bernard, 2549
Arra, Frank, 3401
Arraj, Alfred Albert, 166
Arran, Earl of, 2853
Arran Murder, 166
Arrarista, Carolino, 3250
Arras Witches, 166
Arreaga, Ernesto M., 3255
Arregui Izaguirre, Jose Ignacio, 3509
Arrhidaeus, 166, 2444,2457
Arria, 166
Arriaga, Manual Jose de, 166
Arridy, Joseph, 166-167
Arrington, Chester, 3143
Arrington, Curtis, 1428, 3171
Arrington, George W., 167, 3544
Arrington, Marie Dean, 167, 1740
Arrington, Stephen, 909
Arrington, Willis, 3553
Arrison, William, 167-168, 3263
Arroyo, Miguel, 168
Arroyo Quintero, Alberto, 3466
Arrue Martinez, Jose, 3468
Arsenault, Henry, 168
Arses, 168, 207, 3233
Arsinoë III, 168, 3233
Arsinoë IV, 168, 3234
Arsitogiton, 3232
Artabanus, 168, 3200, 3232
Artabanus III, 1350
Artaphernes, 1564
Artavasdes III, 168, 3234
Artaxerxes, 153, 168
Artaxerxes I, 168, 584, 2926, 3200, 3232
Artaxerxes II, 168, 2958
Artaxerxes III, 153, 168, 207, 3233
Artaxerxes IV, 354, 3233
Artbanus, 2162
Artegian, Rodney, 3169
Artery, John, 956
Arthes, Billy, 1339
Arthur, 168, 1794
Arthur, Duke of Brittany, 544
Arthur, Cecelia, 2713
Arthur, Charles (Brit. pr.1911), 168

B

Barrow, Ronald, 3451
Barrow, William, 3362
Barrow Gang, 52, 1186
Barrowman, Mary, 2776
Barrows, Ralph Edward, 263-264
Barrows, Samuel June, 264
Barry, Arthur, 182, 264
Barry, Chevalier Jean du, 1030
Barry, Edith, 1764
Barry, Guillaume du, 1030
Barry, James, 1080
Barry, Jeanne du, 264, 3240
Barry, John Brooks, 2176
Barry, Marie Jeanne Bécu Du, 906, 1030
Barry, Marion, 264, 1809
Barry, Mary Ann, 264
Barry, Patrick J., 3425
Barry, Sir Redmond, 264
Barry, Richard, 264-265
Barry, Richard J. 74
Barrymore, Ethel, 1668
Barrymore, John, 756, 1251
Barrymore, Lionel, 2195, 2725
Barrymore, Maurice, 596
Barshay, Hyman, 1069
Barsi, Jozsef, 265
Barsi, Judith, 265
Barsimantov, Yacov, 3259, 3521
Barstow, Ralph Gordon, 265
Barstow, S.T., 320
Bart, Jean, 265
Bartelemy, Georges, 3250
Bartels, John, 560
Bartels, John R., Jr., 265, 984, 1027, 3426
Barter, Richard, 265-266, 3554
Barthel, Joan, 2560-2561
Barthélemy, Emmanuel, 3305
Barthélemy, Emanuel, 266
Barthelet, Jean, 3250
Barthou, Jean Louis, 75, 76, 78, 266, 3022, 3248
Bartle, Thomas, 693
Bartlett, Adelaide, 266-269
Bartlett, Ara, 269
Bartlett, Betty Jean, 2842
Bartlett, Charles, 266
Bartlett, Edwin, 266, 268, 269
Bartlett, Helen, 269
Bartlett, Ichabod, 403
Bartlett, John Calvin, 421
Bartlett, Josiah, 269-270
Bartlett, Linda Joy, 584
Bartlett, Marion, 2840, 2842
Bartlett, Minnie, 1853
Bartlett, "Soup", 394, 3381
Bartlett, Velda, 2840
Bartlett, William, 270
Bartlett, Wright, 269
Bartley, Alvis R., 270
Bartley, C.C., 3544, 3550-3552
Bartolomei, Susan, 475
Bartolus, 270
Barton, Andrew, 270
Barton, Bert, 270
Barton, Charles, 3544
Barton, Elizabeth, 270-271
Barton, Harry, 797
Barton, Henry, 3567
Barton, Ian, 1470
Barton, James Lyon Walker, 1473
Barton, James R., 1181
Barton, Jerry, 3554
Barton, John Browning, 2781
Barton, John Evert, 271
Barton, John J., 3044
Barton, "Kid", 3554
Barton, Leila, 3398
Barton, Luie Loveday Walker, 1473
Barton, Mary, 271

Barton, Reddish, 3354
Barton, Robert, 611, 2973
Barton, Russell, 545
Barton, Sir Edmund, 270
Barton, Sylvester, 3119
Barton, William, 1137
Barwell, Sir Henry Newman, 271
Barwick, Charles, 271
Barz, Ingeborg, 199, 3475
Barzani, Mullah, 3256, 3491
Bas, Laurent, 2117
Bas, Marvin, 3381
Bas, Marvin J., 271-272
Basa, Teresita, 2750
Basaritchik, G., 3246
Basasiri, al, 272
Basch, Victor, 3251
Bascone, Vito, 1292, 3381
Basdorf, Clemens, 871
Basemore, William, 3453
Basham, Tucker, 1704, 3554
Bashford, Celia, 1596
Bashold, Jack, 272
Bashold, Joanne, 272
Bashold, Peg, 272
Basil, 2765
Basil I, 3236
Basil II, 2328
Basil the Macedonian, 233, 2176
Basile, Emanuele, 3300
Basile, James "the Duke", 2689
Basile, James, 3381
Basile, Tobia, 272
Basin Street, 3398-3400
Basketball Scandal, 272-273, 547
Baskin, Roland, 2040
Basque Fatherland and Liberty Group, 3509, 3529
Basque Nationalists, 3529
Basque Witches, 273-274
Bass, Andrew, 274
Bass, Brad Lee, 1361
Bass, Charles William, 3447
Bass, L. Joe, 1844
Bass, Outlaw, 2058, 3548
Bass, Samuel, 174, 246, 274-277, 878, 884, 1014, 1426, 1940, 1997, 2048, 2259, 2920, 2931, 3457, 3549-3552, 3554, 3556, 3557, 3560-3563
Bassam Shaka, 3507
Bassendawah, Ahmed, 3255
Bassenge, 906
Basset, Harry, 3554
Bassett, Charles, 277, 1056
Bassett, Charles E., 3544
Bassett, Charlie, 1794, 2144, 2749, 2955
Bassett, Herbert, 3456
Bassett, James Eugene, 2800
Bassett, Marcus, 3283, 3459
Bassi, Pietro, 3505
Bassi, Ugo, 277-278
Bassin, Victor Kaire, 3333, 3524
Bassity, Jerome, 3414, 3415
Basso, Hamilton 102, 2877
Bassot, Henri, 1317
Bass-Smith, Matthew, 1069
Bassville, Nicolas-Jean Hugou de, 278, 3240
Basta, Giörgio, 278, 2176, 3239
Bastard Verdict, 278
Bastendorf, Severin, 278, 981
Bastian, Sharon, 763
Bastianini, Giovanni, 278
Bastien-Thiry, 902
Bastille, 278, 492
Basto, Frank, 3401
Bastwick, John, 278-279
Bat Masterson, 3544, 3549, 3551
Bataan Death March, 279, 280

Batasuna, Herri, 3511
Batavia Street Gang, 3401, 3409, 3412
Batcheller, George Sherman, 280
Batchelor, Charles T., 3424
Batelme, Mary, 3036
Bateman, Charles, 280
Bateman, John, 280, 281
Bateman, Mary, 280-281
Bates, Albert, 210, 281, 1784, 1786
Bates, Clara "Cad", 1754
Bates, Clyde, 3264
Bates, Daniel, 213
Bates, Dutch Charley, 3556
Bates, Edward, 281
Bates, Frank, 3360
Bates, George, 2400
Bates, Joseph, 765, 766, 3460
Bates, Karl, 3381
Bates, Marlene Mary, 1086
Bates, Ruby, 2714, 2716
Bates, Sanford 182
Bates, Sidney, 878
Bates, Thomas, 3342
Bates, W.L., 3039-3040
Bates, Wayne Lee, 3451, 3454
Bates, Willard, 1228
Bates, William, 1837
Batho, Robert, 3293
Bathory, Elizabeth, 281-282
Bathory, Gabriel, 3239
Bathtub Murder, The, 282
Bathurst, Benjamin, 282
Bathurst, Earl, 282
Batie, Cecil, 226
Batista, Amarilo, 1880
Batista, Fulgencio y Zaldivar, 103, 118, 282-283, 796, 1100, 1397, 1399, 1895, 2006, 2835, 3041, 3253, 3264, 3393, 3465
Batt, Jethro, 3209
Battaglia, Alfredo, 283, 3332
Battaglia, Anthony J., 3381
Battaglia, Charles, 3396, 3413
Battaglia, Frank J., 283, 3424
Battaglia, Giuseppe, 283
Battaglia, Samuel, 283, 854, 1410, 3381, 3388, 3389
Batten, Elsie, 560
Battenfield, Billy, 3453
Batters, Joe, 283
Battersbey, Roland, 797
Battey, John, 1154
Batthyány, Lajos, 283, 3241
Battice, Earl Leo, 283-284
Battistella, Annabella, 2951, 2952
Battistella, Eduardo, 2951
Battistelli, Mathieu, 1915
Battisti, Amleto, 2696
Battisti, Cesare, 284
Battisti, Frank J., 1737
Battle, Jaime, 544
Battle, Thomas, 3452
Battle Annie, 3401
Battle of Beecher Island, 3143
Battle Row Ladies's Social and Athletic Club, The, 1342
Batto, James, 936
Batton, Jack, 361
Battus, John, 284
Baud, Linda, 1674
Baudelaire, Charles, 3293
Bauder, Otto, 3030
Bauer, Arch, 3350
Bauer, Christian, 1745
Bauer, Conrad, 2052
Bauer, Edward G., 3067
Bauer, Gustav Adolf, 245
Bauer, Mary A., 1585
Bauer, Otto, 988
Bauer, Thomas J., 1605

Beckett, Henry, 310-311
Beckett, Mary, 311
Beckett, Moses, 311
Beckett, Rose, 311
Beckett Sisters, 311
Beckford, William, 311
Beckham, J.C.W., 1326
Beckley, Gil, 3394
Beckley, John Ernest, 881
Beckman, Martin, 840
Beckner, Frederick, 3544
Beckstead, Don, 1376
Beckwith, Byron De La, 1117
Beckwith, Henry, 1734, 3554
Beckwith, J.A., 2485
Beckwith, Jennings, 311
Beckwith, John (U.S. pr.1910s), 1100
Beckwith, John, 3544, 3554
Beckwith, John H. (U.S. d.1879), 311, 1739
Beckwith, Oscar F., 311
Beckwith, Robert W., 311, 364, 3544, 3554
Beckwourth, James, 311-312, 2803, 3168
Bedami, Angelo, 3394
Bed Bug Row, 3381, 3386
Beddia, Pietro 179
Beddingfield, Ann, 312
Beddingfield, John, 312
Bede, "Sukie", 312
Bede, Bearcat, 828
Bede, Bill, 312
Bede, Elijah, 828
Bede Gang, 292, 312
Bede, Jeff, 292, 828
Bede, Jesse, 312, 3097
Bede, Pitt, 2778
Bede, Poley, 312, 3097
Bede, Ron, 828
Bede, Sherrod, 312, 3097
Bede, Sherwood, 312
Bedell, Joshua, 312, 3334
Bedell, Penn, 312
Bedford, Bit, 2543-2544
Bedford, Duke of (Brit. 1389-1435), 3185
Bedford, Duke of (Brit. 1792-1878), 2737
Bedford, Gunning, Jr., 312
Bedford, J.S., 3342
Bedford, Joseph, 2410
Bedford, Michael, 3449
Bedford Hills Correctional Facility, 312-313
Bedloe, William, 313
Bednarski, Richard Lee, 313
Bedraja, 313, 2282
Bedreddin, 313
Bedstead Suffocations, 313
Beebe, Abner, 3371
Beebe, Chick, 306
Beebe, Lucius, 2231
Beebe, William, 1251
Béeche Argüello, Octavio, 313
Beecher, Henry Ward, 313-314, 2039, 2895,
    2956, 2981, 3009, 3184
Beecher, Lyman, 313, 3019
Beeding, Francis, 893, 2824
Beehler, Sarah, 1200
Beeker, Clifford, 314, 3424
Beekman, Azariah, 1430
Beeler, Daniel, 3337
Beeler, Rodney, 3448
Beeman, Gary L., 314
Beer, Petrus Cornelius de, 894
Beer Hall Putsch, 2251
Beers, George, 3038
Beers, Philip, 2136
Beery, Wallace 31
Beeson, Ben, 652
Beets, Betty Lou, 3454
Beets, Edward, 3452
Beg, Toghrul, 272
Begeron, John F., 3345

Beggar's Opera, The, 314
Begin, Menachem, 2653
Begley, David, 456
Beha, Lorenzo, 2936
Behan, John, 314-315, 481, 482, 719, 810,
    1056, 1594, 2583, 3544, 3545, 3550
Behan, William, 1822
Beheshti, Ayatollah Muhammad, 315
Behesti, Hojatoleslam Seyyed Hasan,
    3260, 3273, 3515
Behr, Ferdinand, 1216
Behre, Friedhelm, 436
Behrend, Henry, 853
Behringer, Earl, 3454
Behrman, Martin, 2863
Behsharat, Muhammad Taki, 3259, 3519
Beidler, Jacob, 3381
Beidler, John X., 315, 1254
Beierman, Sigurd, 789
Beige, Frank, 3381
Beigel, Alvin, 3298
Beihl, Eugen, 315, 3328, 3487
Beiliss, Mendel, 315
Bein, Samuel, 999
Beirne, William, 2355
Beit, Alfred, 3283, 3500
Bejarano, John, 3452
Bela, Nograde, 3339
Belachheb, Abdelkrim, 315316
Beland, Charles, 316
Beland, J.H., 316
Beland, Joseph, 316
Beland, Lucy, 316
Beland, Ma, 316
Beland, Willie, 316
Belasco, David, 1631, 2198
Belaúnde, General, 1493
Belbenoit, René, 932, 3427
Belcastro, James "King of the Bombers",
    316, 393, 3263, 3381
Belcher, E.A., 2736
Belcher, Emory Allen, 316-317
Belcourt, L.J., 462
Belden, V., 3242
Beldock, Myron, 646
Belesme, Robert of, 317
Belew, George Lester, 317
Belfast Riots, 3378
Belin, Jean, 2878
Belin, John, 3350
Belki, Johannes, 3058
Belknap, Myrta, 2242
Belknap, William Worth, 317
Bell, Alexander, 3342
Bell, Alexander Graham, 2139
Bell, Arthur, 3363
Bell, Bob, 3544
Bell, C.S., (U.S. prom.1869), 1514, 3554
Bell, Camille, 3166
Bell, Charles U., 1743
Bell, Sir Charles, 317
Bell, Charlotte Jane, 820
Bell, "Choctaw", 3554
Bell, Ed, 3356
Bell, Edward J. (U.S. pr.1960s), 3425
Bell, George Joseph, 317
Bell, Griffin Boyette, 317, 669, 1771, 3166
Bell, Hamilton, 317, 3544
Bell, Henry, 3358
Bell, Herman, 317, 396, 449
Bell, J.W., 318, 366, 3427
Bell, James A.H., 1113
Bell, James E., 317-318
Bell, James W., 3544
Bell, John, 318, 2840
Bell, John S., 3426
Bell, Joseph, 1014, 1016,1602, 2202
Bell, Larry Gene, 318, 3329, 3334, 3454
Bell, Margaret Hawkesworth, 2686

Bell, Martin, 1543
Bell, Mary Flora, 318-319
Bell, Mary Hayley 127
Bell, Norma, 318, 319
Bell, Peter, 3338
Bell, Randy, 3447
Bell, Roger Morris, 3454
Bell, Ronnie, 3448
Bell, Shirley, 319
Bell, Sydney, 319-320
Bell, Terry, 3353
Bell, Thalia, 2142
Bell, Thomas Frederick, 2476
Bell, Tom, 320-321, 1391, 3554
Bell, Walter, 3454
Bell, William (U.S. d.1894), 3345
Bell, William (U.S. d.1898), 3350
Bell, William (U.S. d.1924), 3366
Bell, William H., 3454
Bell, Willie, 1300
Bell, Yusef, 3166
Bella, A. Ben, 3255
Bellacosa, Joseph, 2057
Bellamy, Charles, 321
Bellamy, Dennis, 1283
Bellamy, George Anne, 321
Bellamy, Samuel, 321
Bellanca, Benny 179
Bella Union, 3414, 3415
Bellavia, Charles, 1655
Bellavia, Joanne, 1655
Belle, Earl, 321
Bellenden, Sir John, 321
Bellenger, Etienne, 2157
Belleville Katzenbach, Nicholas de, 1769
Belli, Melvin, 25, 321, 1178, 1748, 1799
Bellinger, Charles Byron, 321
Bellingham, John, 321-322, 522, 2443, 3232,
    3240
Bellmar, Percy, 1250
Bellmore, Larry, 3451
Bello, Ahmadu, 3255
Bello, Alfred P., 645
Bello, Carlos, 3449
Bello, Clemente Vazquez, 322
Belloc-Lowndes, Marie, 700, 1689, 1722
Bellomont, 1814
Bellson, Samuel, 1436
Belmont, August 163, 3305
Belmont, Courtney, 3554
Belmont, Dick, 3554
Belmont, Frankie, 3398
Belmont, Lillian, 2801
Belmont, Oliver, 2104
Belmontes, Fernando, 3448
Belon, Christian, 3467, 3483
Belot, Françoise, 322
Belser, David G., 3173
Belshaw, Ethel, 2811
Belshaw, William, 1777
Belt, Richard, 1906
Belteton, Edwin Paz, 3333
Belton, Oliver, 2414-2415
Beltran-Lopez, Mauricio, 3449
Beltran, Noe, 3454
Béluche, Ren, 1872, 3398
Belushi, Jim, 322
Belushi, John, 2782, 3301
Belvin, Paul Augustus, 322
Belyeu, Clifton, 3454
Belzú, Manuel Isidoro, 3241, 3255
Belzaire, Ovide, 3346
Bembenek, Laurie, 322
Bembenek, Lawrencia, 322-323
Bemis, Charley, 323
Bemis, China Polly, 323
Bemis, H.V., 1805
Benahmed, Ali, 3255
Benaiah, 3232

Blanquet, Aureliano, 2077
Blanqui, Auguste, 407
Blanqui, Louis-Auguste, 1152
Blanther, Joseph, 407
Blanton, John, 1827
Blanton, Johnny Y., 518
Blanton, Luther, 1827
Blanton, Ray, 407
Blasi, Dominic "Butch", 1306, 3382
Blasi, Raffaele de, 3522
Blasier, Ollie, 1241, 1414
Blaskowitz, Johannes, 407-408, 3538
Blastares, Matthew, 408
Blatchford, Samuel Milford, 408
Blattman, Aaron, 2941
Blau, Thomas, 3345
Blaubergs, Maija, 975
Blaudins, Giovanni, 2044, 3382
Blaul, William, 3030
Blavat, Jerry, 3412
Blay, Hannah, 2682
Blaylock, Celia "Mattie", 1061
Blazak, Mitchell, 3447
Blazcik, Tony, 2456
Blazek, Frank, 408
Blazer, Emil, 486
Blazes, Albert, 408, 3366
Bleackley, Horace, 2740
Bleak House, 408
Bleakley, William F., 2859
Blease, Cole L., 3361
Blee, Mr., 348
Blee, Thomas, 1789, 2928
Bleicher, Hella, 709
Blémant, Robert, 408, 1397, 3393
Blemer, Ethel, 1748
Blemer, John, 1748
Blennerhassett, Harman, 408, 555
Blevins, Andy, 408, 1361
Blevins, Charles, 408
Blevins, Hampton, 408, 2919, 2999
Blevins, John, 408, 3554
Blevins, M., 3554
Blevins, Richard, 761
Blevins, Sam Houston, 408
Blevins Family, 408
Blewett, George, 725
Bligh, Timothy, 2508
Bligh, William, 2022, 2269-2270
Blin, George, 408-409
Blind Joe, 3554
Blind Mahoney, 3402
Blish, John N., 2935
Bliss, Clarence, 1791
Bliss, Cornelius, 3025
Bliss, George Miles, 409
Bliss, Thomas 19, 20
Blitz, Barnett "Barney", 2814
Blitzstein, Marc, 3255
Bliven, Bruce, 2907
Blixt, Claus, 1499
Blobel, Paul, 2291, 3538
Bloch, Lazare, 1440
Bloch, Robert, 2510
Block, Cheryl, 2759
Block, Howard, 2894
Block, Johanna, 1074
Block, William, 3382
Block, William D., 1950
Blocks, David M., 3424
Blodgett, Rush, 2436
Blodgett, Wilson A., 1380-1381
Blódox, Erik, 1101
Blomberg, August W., 37, 469
Blome, Kurt, 3538
Blondel, 409
Blondel, Guillaume, 1125
Blonger, Lou, 2344
Blonger, Louis, 409

Blood, James Harvey, 3184
Blood, Janet, 2533
Blood, Thomas, 409-410, 840, 3170, 3457
Blood Brotherhood, 1660
Bloods, 3396
Blood Tubs, 1082
Bloody Angle, 3402
Bloody Sunday Massacre, 410, 3375
Bloom, David, 410-411
Bloom, Ike, 411, 3382, 3384
Bloom, Lloyd, 1227, 3086, 3414
Bloom, Robert S., 3448
Bloom, William, 623
Bloomberg, George, 2059
Bloomingdale, Alfred, 2403
Bloomington, Ind., Racial Violence, 3375
Bloomquist, Paul Abel, 200, 3267, 3493
Blore, Alfred, 2577
Blossner, Robert, 1676
Blot, Henri, 352, 411
Blot, Robert, 928
Blount, Andy, 3343
Blount, James Henderson, 411
Blount, John, 2818
Blount, William, 1375
Blow, Harry, 2711
Blowes, John, 2980
Bloyd, Dale, 3448
Blue, Michael, 3454
Blue Book, 3398
Blue Cross, 3289
Blue Duck, 411-412, 2843, 3554
Bluestone, Jesse, 412
Bluffstein, Sophie, 412
Blum, Dominick, 1942
Blum, Herald H., 3472
Blum, Léon, 1024, 2450, 3248
Blum, Robert, 412
Blum, Zita, 3231
Blume, Johanna Maria Louisa, 488
Blume, Walter, 3538
Blumen, Julius, 412-413
Blumen, Leopold, 412
Blumenfield, Harry, 3402
Blumenfeld, Isadore "Kid Cann", 238, 413, 1951
Blumenthal, Alan, 1135
Blumenthal, Albert Howard, 343
Blumenthal, W. Michael, 648
Blumer, Fred J., 413, 3325
Blumner, Charles, 3545
Blun, Kenry, 3554
Blundell, James, 1457
Blunk, Ernest, 960
Blunt, Charles R., 1680
Blunt, George W., 3356
Blunt, Harry, 2223
Bluntschli, Johann Kaspar, 413
Bly, Elias, 2717
Bly, Nellie, 1333
Blydenstein, B.W., 1366
Blye, John, 2666
Blystone, Scott, 3453
Blyth, Ellen, 2249
Blythin, Edward, 2742
Boal, William, 1371
Boardley, Warren, 1393
Boarini, Mark, 902
Boarman, James, 56, 62
Boasso, Theodore J., 413
Boatright, Buck, 413
Bob, Charles V., 413-414
Bobadilla, Francisco de, 414
Bobbitt, Angus A., 96, 2181, 3545, 3549, 3554, 3564
Bobek, Emil, 928
Boberg, U.R., 207
Bobermin, Hans, 3538
Bobo, Tony L., 3454

Bobrikov, Nikolai Ivanovich, 414, 3243
Boca, Steve 193
Bocarmé, Hippolyte de, 414
Boccacio, 3291
Bocchini, Anthony, 765, 3460
Bocchino, Joe 118
Boccia, Ferdinand "The Shadow", 414-415, 1296, 3402, 3406
Bocking, Diana, 843
Böcking, Eduard, 415
Boclair, Stanley, 3451
Bocognani, Roger, 3393
Bocskay, István, 415, 3239
Bodasse, Désir, 3059
Bodawpaya, 415, 3240
Boddy, Albert, 415
Bodeker, Fred J., 1154
Boden, Margarete "Marja", 1557
Boden, Wayne Clifford, 415
Bodenan, Francois, 3465
Bodenham, Anne, 415
Bodenheim, Maxwell, 1333
Bodenschatz, Karl, 1574
Bodia, O.K., 1426
Bodian, Helen, 1676
Bodin, Jean, 415
Bodine, Andrew, 416
Bodine, Joseph Lamb, 415
Bodine, Mary, 415-417
Bodine, Polly, 416-417
Boding, Alma, 2423
Bodkin, Archibald, 417, 1523, 1667, 2070, 2089
Bodkin, Dominick, 417
Bodkin, John, 417
Bodkin, Oliver, 417
Bodley, Hugh S., 3045
Bodmin Jail Riot, 417
Body, John, 2489
Body Snatchers, The, 417
Boe, Nils Andreas, 417-418
Boe, William Thomas De, 894
Boeck, Renata, 583
Boehmer, Elise, 2437
Boesak, Allan, 1926
Boesky, F. Ivan, 418, 3089
Boethius, 3235
Boethius, Anicius Manlius Severinus, 47, 418, 2891
Boettcher, Charles, II, 418, 1784, 2678, 3326
Boettcher, Charles K., Sr. 418
Boettger, Macklin, 654
Boettiger, John, 3382
Bofors, Lena, 1414
Bogan, Dan, 3555
Bogard, Delia, 769
Bogard, J.J., 467
Bogart, Humphrey, 396, 1547, 2454
Bogatko, Marian, 3249
Bogdanoff, Alexander, 1395
Bogdanovich, N.M., 3243
Bogen, Guenter, 3149
Boger, Wilhelm, 418-419, 3538
Boggess, Holt, 3454
Boggie, Clarence Gilmore, 419
Boggs, Eli, 419, 1494
Boggs, Henry, 3344
Boggs, J., 265
Boggs, John, 3449
Boggs, Lillburn W., 1478
Boggs, Richard, 3456
Boggs, Thomas O., 3555
Boghdady, Gowad Khalid, 2894
Bogle, Helen McDermott, 419
Bogle, James H., 419-421, 462
Bogolepov, Nicholai Parlovich, 3242
Bogolyubsky, Andrey Yuryevich 126
Bogoslausky, M., 3243

Boot, Joe, 1468-1469
Boot, Joseph, 3555, 3560
Bootan, Barry, 3463
Booth, Anna, 473-474
Booth, Arnett, 436, 3326
Booth, Ballington, 437
Booth, Bramwell, 2846
Booth, Brindley James, 2558
Booth, Byron V., 3466
Booth, David, 3467
Booth, Edwin, 1954, 1964, 1965, 2038
Booth, Elizabeth, 2664
Booth, Ernest, 436-437
Booth, George, 880, 2766
Booth, Henry, 437
Booth, Herbert, 1973
Booth, John, 3452
Booth, John Wilkes, 513, 782, 1953, 1954,
    1956, 1958, 1963-1965, 2320, 2503, 3241
Booth, Junius Brutus, 1954, 2965
Booth, Newton, 1147
Booth, William, 1690
Booth-Clibborn, Catherine, 437
Boothroyd, Charles, 2875
Bootle, William Augustus, 437, 473
Booze, Eugene P., 437
Boozer, D.G., 3156
Bopp, Franz, 48, 677, 1508, 1560
Boppart, Herman, 3457
Borah, William Edgar, 437, 1500, 2066
Borchard, Edwin, 437
Bordaberry, Juan M., 3256, 3499
Bordeaux, Duc de, 1650
Bordelon, Abbé Laurent, 1883
Borden, Abby Durfee Gray, 437-438, 440
Borden, Andrew Jackson, 437
Borden, Emma, 437, 440
Borden, Lizzie, 437-440, 479, 595, 1923,
    1973, 1987, 2113, 2207, 2456, 2433, 2338,
    2681
Borden, Sarah Morse, 437
Border, Peter, 773
Border Gang, 3402
Bordin, Burton, 3484
Boreham, Leslie, 2880
Borelli, Frank, 2785, 3297
Borelli, Gene, 440
Borelli, Laverne, 440, 1076
Borelli, Patsy, 3402
Boreman, Herbert Stephenson, 440
Boreman, Jacob Smith, 440-441
Boren, Roger W., 1884
Borenstein, Morton P., 2768
Borge, Toms, 2200
Borgeaud, Henri, 3253
Borger, Texas, 441
Borgia, Alfonso, 441
Borgia, Cesare, 441-442, 658, 1316, 2455,
    3238
Borgia, Francis, 441
Borgia, Giovanni, 442
Borgia, Lucrezia, 442, 658
Borgia, Rodrigo, 441-442, 658
Borgia Family, 441-442
Borgio, Rosario, 442-443, 3392
Boring, Floyd, 2997
Boris, 2568
Boris III, 1074, 3245, 3249, 3250
Bork, Robert, 1794
Bork, Robert H., 3100
Borland, O.E., 2022
Borland, Sam, 2749
Bormann, Martin Ludwig, 443-444, 2348,
    3538
Born, Dutch Henry, 2145, 3555
Born, Jorge, 444, 2204, 3330
Born, Juan, 444-445, 2204, 3330
Born, Ronald Joseph, 445
Bornancini, Raul, 3329, 3497

Borne, Henry, 1044
Borno,
    Louis-Eustache-Antoine-François-Jose
    ph, 445
Bornstein, Irwin, 2747
Borom, Mildred, 1282
Borosky, George, 3065
Borotra, Jean, 2954
Borowiec, Matthew, 709
Borowsky, Walter 73
Borquez, Israel, 3259, 3518
Borradaile, Mary Tucker, 1943
Borrelli, Joseph, 345
Borrins, Stephen, 2782
Borroto, Abbie C., 2675
Borroto, Reginald, 2675
Borrow, George, 445
Borrowski, Lorraine, 1288
Borsiard, 3237
Borsos, Robert L., 1285
Borst, Billy, 827
Borstein, Sydney, 2691
Borthon, Marie 186
Borum, Alfonso, 2129
Borynski, Henry, 445
Borzewski, Alexis, 2291
Bosak, William P. 96
Bosanquet, John, 3081
Bosch, Orlando, 445, 3041
Boschetti, Enzo, 445, 3327
Boscosel de Chastelard, Pierre de, 690
Böse, Wilfried, 1098, 3475
Bosely, Henry, 2436
Bosford, William, 1466
Boshears, Willis Eugene, 445-446
Boshoff, E.A., 1046
Bosola, Daniel de, 870
Bosque, George, 3463
Bosroger, Esprit de, 1994
Boss Crawford, 2118
Bosse, François, 674
Bosse, Marie, 674, 917
Bossert, Liselette, 2165
Bossert, Wolfram 2165
Bostock, Lyman, 2798
Boston, 446
Boston, Marshall, 3345
Boston, Mary, 3139
Boston, Patience, 446
Boston, Riley, 3545
Boston Anti-Impressment Riot, 3371
Boston Bread Riot, 3370
Boston Brothel Riot, 3370, 3373
Boston *Globe* Hoax, 446
Boston Joe, 124, 2048, 3553
Boston Massacre, The, 446-447, 3371
Boston Police Strike, 447, 3375
Boston Strangler, 1803
Boston Tea Party, The, 447-448, 3371
Bostwick, Ann, 3362
Boswell, Alexander, 2872
Boswell, Aubrey, 1656
Boswell, Bushrod, 3305
Boswell, James, 1663
Boswell, John, 3305
Boswell, N.K., 652, 1987
Boswell, Willa Jean, 1656
Bosworth, Eugene J. 127
Bosworth, Mary, 2855-2856
Botelho, Sandra Ann, 2309
Botha, C., 1046
Botha, D.H., 1903
Botha, Louis, 2854, 3130
Botha, P.W., 2101, 2736, 3281
Bothwell, Albert J., 187, 3555
Bothwell, Earl of (Scot. c.1535-78), 2768
Bothwell, Earl of (Scot. pr.16th Cent.),
    3179
Bothwell, Earl of (Brit. pr.1567), 872

Bothwell, Fourth Earl of, 448
Botkin, Cordelia, 157, 322, 448-449, 505,
    3536
Botkin, Eugene, 2333
Botkin, Welcome A., 448
Botnick, Adolph, 1117
Bott, Jean, 1177
Bott, Matilda, 1177-1178
Bottaro, Angelo, 449, 3415
Böttcher, Herbert, 3538
Botting, James, 449
Bottom, Anthony, 317, 396, 449
Bottom, John T., 1521
Bottomley, Horatio William, 360, 449-453,
    1124
Bottomley, William King, 449
Bottoson, Linroy, 3449
Botts, Bryan, 1392
Bouchard, Conrad, 3380
Bouchard, Gaetane, 3061
Bouchard, Jean Guy, 3061
Bouchard, Wilfrid, 3061
Boucher, Anthony, 650
Boucher, Billy, 1643, 3555
Boudes, Abbé, 453
Boudia, Mohammed, 3256, 3268, 3497
Boudin, Kathy, 453, 489, 1771, 3107
Boudin, Leonard, 453
Boudin, M., 2658-2659
Boudreau, Lou, 2054
Boudreau, Marjorie, 2136
Boudreau, Sharyn, 2054
Boughton, Theodosius, 818, 999
Bougrat, Pierre, 453
Bouguereau, Robert, 1549-1550
Bouhler, Philipp, 3538
Bouillon, Godfrey of, 1324
Bouisson, Jean, 3250
Boulanger, Georges Ernest Jean Marie,
    453-454, 1181, 1324, 2523, 3305
Boulay, Louis, 2912
Boullé, Thomas, 1994
Boulogne, Henri, 454
Boulton, Robert, 454
Boumedienne, Houari, 3256
Boumethoka, A., 3245
Bounds, Patra Mae, 2724
Bouquillon, Moise, 629
Bouras, Chelsais "Steve", 1149, 3412
Bouras, Steve, 3413
Bourassa, Robert, 1897
Bourbon, Cesar de, 454
Bourbon, Charles Ferdinand de, 454, 3240
Bourbon, Charles Louis de, 894-895
Bourbon, Duc de, 877
Bourbon, Duchess de 877
Bourbon, François, 454
Bourbon, Henri, 454
Bourbon, Louis-Alexandre-Stanislas de,
    1877
Bourbon, Louis-Auguste de, 454
Bourbon, Louis de, 2121
Bourbon, Louis Joseph de, 2656
Bourbon-Parme, Xavier de, 2450
Bourbon-Condé, Louise-Bénédicte de, 454
Bourdais, Marie, 520
Bourdette, Philip, 899
Bourdon, Jean, 191
Bourg, Frank, 454
Bourget, Paul 126
Bourgot, Pierre, 3041
Bourguiba, 3378
Bourguiba, Habib, 1668
Bourguiba, Habib ibn Ali, 3254, 3255
Bourguignon, Louis Dominique, 647
Bourignon, Antoinette, 1953
Bourke, Patrick, 454-455
Bourke, Richard Southwell, 455
Bourne, George, 406

Bourne, Peter, 3300
Bousfield, William, 455
Bousquet, Pierre, 455
Bouterse, Desi, 2913
Bouton, Bessie 127
Bouvier, John, 455
Bouvier, Léone, 455
Bouvier, Louise, 520
Bouvier, Maurice, 2170
Bouyer, Lester, 455
Bouza, Anthony V., 455-456, 3425
Bove, James V., 1140
Bowdach, Gary, 3402
Bowden, Jerome, 3447
Bowden, John, 456
Bowden, Roosevelt, 3449
Bowdre, Charlie, 122, 364, 366, 368, 486,
    1277, 1278, 2462, 2717, 3547, 3555
Bowe, Alice Atte, 456
Bowe, Martin, 3402
Bowen, Charles Synge Christopher, 456
Bowen, Charley, 456
Bowen, George, 456
Bowen, Jane, 1448
Bowen, John "Chick", 2164
Bowen, John (U.S. pr.1983), 1677
Bowen, Joseph, 1363
Bowen, Keith, 3338
Bowen, Nancy, 456
Bowen, Otis, 1974
Bowen, Perry T., Jr., 836
Bowen, Seabury W., 438
Bowen, Thomas, 3346
Bowencamps, Ernest, 2035
Bowens, James, 3347
Bower, Benjamin, 3326
Bower, Elias, 500
Bower, Elliot, 456-457
Bower, Fanny, 456-457
Bower, Lester L., 3454
Bowerbank, Hannah, 724
Bowerman, Robert, 843
Bowers, Annie, 1442
Bowers, Bill, 2697
Bowers, Donald, 2180
Bowers, Edward G., 3545
Bowers, Ellis, 558
Bowers, George, 3555
Bowers, Harry, 457
Bowers, Herb, 805
Bowers, J. Gordon, 1323
Bowers, J. Milton, 457, 975
Bowers, Jacob, 3364
Bowers, Joe 53
Bowers, Martin L., 457
Bowers, Mickey, 2785
Bowers, Sam H., Jr., 457-458
Bowers, Teresa, 457
Bowery Boys, 889, 1025, 3402, 3403, 3405,
    3408, 3409
Bowery Gangs, 698
Bowery Indians, 3402
Bowie, Benito, 3453
Bowie, Jim, 2675
Bow Kum, 458, 2967, 3402, 3407
Bowler, Tom, 458-459
Bowles, Charles, 426, 1949
Bowles, Frank, 459, 705
Bowles, Homer, 459
Bowles, Tom, 739
Bowles, William, 3366
Bowlsby, Alice Augusta, 459
Bowman, Ed 25
Bowman, Euday, 3009
Bowman, Hattie, 3360
Bowman, John B., 3242
Bowman, John H., 1732
Bowman, Margaret, 540
Bowman, Mason T. 100

Bowman, Nathaniel, 3352
Bowman, Thyra, 211
Bowman, Walter, 1581
Bowman, Wess, 708
Bown, Asa, 3337
Bowrey, Thomas, 3292
Bowron, Fletcher, 787, 1261
Bowser, William, 3373
Bowsher, Perry, 459
Bow Street Runners, 205, 391, 424, 459-
    460, 499, 503, 543, 3039
Bowyer, Linda, 2866
Bowyer, Thomas, 1686
Box, Jack, 2572
Box, John M., 3250
Boxely, Joe, 3367
Boxer Rebellion, 460
Boxers, The, 460, 2328
Boy, Sorley, 931
Boyard, Cyril, 956
Boyce, Arthur Robert, 460, 1492
Boyce, Henry, 460
Boyce, Mart, 3555
Boyce, Newt, 506
Boyce, Reuben H., 3555
Boyd, Arthur Martin, 3453
Boyd, Barbara, 461
Boyd, Charles, 3454
Boyd, Cleveland, 461
Boyd, Donald, 494
Boyd, Frank R., 2942
Boyd, Jabez, 460
Boyd, James Edmund, 460
Boyd, Jorge Eduardo, 460
Boyd, Juan, 3448
Boyd, Kenneth, 3453
Boyd, Kimberly, 1515
Boyd, Marion Speed, 460
Boyd, Michael Joe, 3454
Boyd, Murray Allen, 461, 3380
Boyd, Payne, 461
Boyd, Percy, 255, 262
Boyd, Richard K., 3465
Boyd, Robert M., 1233
Boyd, Ronald Lee, 3453
Boyd, Russell, 3451
Boyd, Stephen, 3521
Boyd, Thomas (U.S. pr.1933), 2185
Boyd, Thomas (U.S. d.1895), 3345
Boyd, Thomas M. Jr. (U.S. pr.1880s),
    3555
Boyd, Tom (U.S. pr.1930s), 1161
Boyd, William, 3447
Boyd, William C., 461
Boyd, William H., 1626
Boyd, Willis, 3351
Boyde, Richard, 3448
Boydstun, Glan, 771
Boy-Ed, Karl, 2159
Boyer, Brian, 1443
Boyer, Carl, 459
Boyer, Charles 102, 3209
Boyer, Edward L., 1730
Boyer, Elizabeth, 1022
Boyer, Ernie, 461-462
Boyer, Father, 930
Boyer, Marie, 3057
Boyer, Nancy, 1166, 2161
Boyes, Nellie, 2229
Boyet, Johnny, 1063
Boyington, Charles R.S., 462
Boykin, Edward, 692
Boylard, Janice, 2800
Boyle, Andrew, 3555
Boyle, Benjamin, 3454
Boyle, Charles Edmund, 462
Boyle, D.A., 1544
Boyle, Emmet, 1736
Boyle, Helen, 3325

Boyle, James, 1775
Boyle, John (U.S. pr.1889), 1902
Boyle, John (U.S. pr.1874), 3212
Boyle, Johnny (Brit. pr.1950), 462
Boyle, Kay, 832
Boyle, Patricia Jean Ehrhardt Pernick, 462,
    1945
Boyle, Richard, 462
Boyle, Robert H., 3555
Boyle, "Sport", 3555
Boyle, Tom 180
Boyle, Tony, 462
Boyle, "Umbrella Mike", 2780
Boyle, Victor James, 462
Boyle, William Anthony, 462-463
Boyles, Odell Carlysle, 463
Boyles, Sue Zachary, 463
Boynton, Charles A., 463
Boynton, Edward, 463
Boynton, James, 463, 3465
Boynton, Nathan, 1203
Boynton, Thomas, 133
Boyog, George Albert, 3460
Bozelli, Gloria, 463
Bozeman, David, 3462
Bozkurtlar, 3530, 3531
Bozydaj, Wasyl, 1189
Bozzeli, Peter, 463
Braasch, Clarence E., 463-464
Brabham, John, 3079
Brabourne, Doreen Lady, 2235
Bracciano Orsini, Duca di, 18
Brace, Philander, 464, 1528, 3050, 3336
Bracey, Edward, 464
Bracey, Joan, 464
Bracey, William, 3447, 3451
Brach, Helen Voorhees, 464
Brack, Viktor, 3538
Bracken, J.W., 3545
Bracken, Katherine, 309
Brackenbury, Robert, 464
Brackett, H.H., 3425
Brackett, Harold, 2927
Brackett, Lillian Rich, 2927
Brackett, Winslow, 3425
Bracton, Henry de, 464
Bracy, William, 1609, 3382
Bradberry, F.T., 254
Bradburn, George, 2745
Bradburn, Richard, 658
Bradbury, Mary, 2669
Bradbury, Thomas, 2256
Bradbury, William, 2256
Bradd, Ann, 1069
Bradfield, Christine Catherine, 220
Bradfield, John, 220
Bradford, Bill (U.S. pr.1980s), 3448
Bradford, Billie (U.S. pr.1923), 1822
Bradford, Clyde, 1250
Bradford, Edward, 3426
Bradford, Edward Green, 464
Bradford, Edward Ridley Colborne, 464-
    465
Bradford, Gayland, 3454
Bradford, John (Brit. 1510-55), 465
Bradford, John Young, Jr. (U.S. 1927-80),
    465
Bradford, Jonathan (Brit. pr.1700s), 465
Bradford, Lowell, 5
Bradford, Margaret, 2863
Bradford, Priscilla, 465
Bradford, Robert, 3518
Bradford, William (U.S., 1755-95), 465
Bradford, William (U.S. d.1627) 2231, 2432
Bradford, William (U.S. d.1911), 3361
Bradinham, Robert, 1812
Bradlaugh, Charles, 353, 450, 465
Bradley, Arthur D., 645
Bradley, Cyrus Parker, 1749, 2130, 3424

Bradley, Danny Joe, 3447
Bradley, Edward E., 465
Bradley, Fred, 3263
Bradley, Gerard, 3275
Bradley, James (Brit., pr.1861), 465-466
Bradley, James (U.S., d.1982), 466
Bradley, James (U.S. d.1982), 3301
Bradley, Jim (U.S. pr.1869), 1447
Bradley, John M., 3336
Bradley, Joseph P., 466
Bradley, Magda, 466, 3327
Bradley, Margaret, 3372
Bradley, May, 3277
Bradley, Shequila, 3173
Bradley, Solomon, 2964
Bradley, Stephen Leslie, 466
Bradley, Tom, 1182 3459
Bradley, Washington, 3356
Bradshaw, Ford, 1186, 3460
Bradshaw, Fred, 3015
Bradshaw, George 154
Bradshaw, Jack, 466
Bradshaw, John, 466, 828
Bradshaw, Rufus, 1823
Bradstreet, Agnes, 1372
Bradstreet, Anne, 1602
Bradstreet, John, 2669
Bradwell, 1730, 1788
Brady, Al, 466-467
Brady, "Big Bob", 210, 260, 1186, 3015, 3427, 3460
Brady, Charles A., 435
Brady, David, 3275, 3519
Brady, Denny, 3402
Brady, George William, 3462
Brady, Harold S., 2757
Brady, Ian, 2212, 3327
Brady, Jack, 3555
Brady, James, 3258, 3511
Brady, James E., 3353
Brady, James S., 2549
Brady, John, 467
Brady, Joseph, 660, 2134
Brady, Mary (U.S. pr.1889), 467-468
Brady, Mary Jane 2533
Brady, Matthew, 468
Brady, Patrick (Aust. 1893-1965), 468, 2839
Brady, Warren, 2953
Brady, William (U.S. d.1878), 363-364, 506, 739, 1112, 1235, 1559, 1734, 3544, 3545, 3547, 3548, 3555, 3564
Brady, William, 1966, 1986, 2149, 2177, 3071
Brady, "Yakey Yake", 3402
Brady Gang, 3382
Braeseke, Barry, 468-469
Braeuer, Gertraude "Sisi", 1607, 2699
Braga, Archbishop of, 896
Bragg, Bertha, 2858
Bragg, Braxton, 469
Bragg, Thomas, 469
Brahm, John, 1442
Brain, George, 469, 1642, 3196
Brain, Russell, 3297
Braisted, John M., Jr., 2337
Brajnovic, Norma, 537, 2029
Brake, Bud, 3351
Brake, Joseph, 3356
Braker, Daniel J., 2903
Bram, Thomas Mead Chambers, 37, 469-470
Bramah, Ernest, 470
Braman, Ella F., 517
Bramble, Clifford, 470, 3228
Brame, Benjamin, 3359
Brame, Lex, Jr., 470
Bramwell, George William Wilshere, 470
Bramwell, Henry, 470
Brancata, Dominick, 3382
Brancati, Charles, 470, 3325

Brancato, Anthony, 3396
Brancato, Joseph, 3402
Brancato, Peter J., 423, 1441
Brancato, Rose, 1905, 1906
Branch, Elizabeth, 470-471
Branch, Mark, 471
Branch, Mary, 470
Branch, Spencer, 3343
Branchaud, Gary, 1322
Branco, Suput, 3282
Brâncoveanu, Constantin, 471
Brand, Christian Pieter, 471
Brand, Elizabeth, 471-472
Brand, Maria Adriana Griffiths, 471
Brand, Samuel, 472
Brandebury, Lemuel G., 472
Brandegee, Frank, 2908
Brandeis, Louis Dembitz, 472, 2894
Brandenburg, B.F., 3424
Brandenburg, Leopold, 3297
Brandenburg, Leopold William August, 472, 2457
Brandes, 908
Brandino, Joseph, 2262
Brandl, John H., 472
Brandler, Mark, 1151
Brando, Marlon, 1513, 1646, 1828, 2481
Brandon, Dorelle C., 1515
Brandon, Duke of, 1009
Brandon, Gregory, 472-473, 920
Brandon, Howard, 2169
Brandon, Isaac, 3341
Brandon, Karen, 1142
Brandon, Mark, 472-473
Brandon, Richard, 472-473
Brandreth, Jeremiah, 473
Brands, Jennie, 1387
Brandsness, David 25
Brandstater, Samuel, 1370
Brandstatter, N.L., 473
Brandstein, Howard, 2811
Brandt, Heinz, 1574
Brandt, Karl, 3538
Brandt, Ludwig, 2174
Brandt, Rudolf, 3538
Brandt, Wayne F., 2936
Brandt, Willy, 199, 1081
Brani, Roland, 714
Braniff, Anthony, 3517
Brank, Robert M., 3305
Brann, William Cowper, 473, 3555
Brannagan, Michael, 1074
Brannan, George, 3348
Brannan, Joshua, 473, 2306
Brannan, S., 1719
Brannan, Samuel, 3050
Branson, 1842
Branson, Edith May Olive, 2467
Branson, George Arthur Harwin, 473, 1562, 3195
Branson, William, 473-474
Brantley, Howard, 1103
Brantley, Jeffery David, 3450
Brantley, John, 474, 1629
Brantley, Mineempainrva, 1104
Brantley, Minerva, 474
Bras Coupé, 474-475
Brasco, Donnie, 2473
Brassfield, George, 1876
Bratt, Mary Alice, 1074
Bratten, Florence Umberhocker, 2552
Brattle, Thomas, 475
Bratz, Albert, 3382
Brauer, Robert, 1753
Braun, Anna, 212
Braun, Bernhard, 3475
Braun, Dorothy, 212
Braun, Eva, 444, 1572, 1580
Braun, Thomas Eugene, 475

Braund, William, 865
Braune, Werner, 2291, 3538
Braunsdorf, Eugene, 475-476
Braunsdorf, Virginia, 475
Braunsteiner, Hermine, 3149
Braunsteiner-Ryan, Hermine, 3538
Bravata, Joseph 182
Braverman, William, 2059
Bravin, George, 2855
Bravo, Charles Delauny Turner, 476
Bravo, Florence Ricardo, 476-479, 2347
Bravo, Joseph, 476
Bravo, Nicolas, 479
Bravo Cervantes, Manuel, 586
Bravo-Murillo, Juan Gonzalez, 479
Bravos, George, 479-480, 3382
Brawley, Tawana, 480
Bray, Elizabeth, 2825
Bray, Neil, 557
Bray, Reginald, 3132
Bray, Reginald More (Brit. 1842-1923), 480
Braya, John, 2955
Braydee, William, 3348
Brayne, H.G., 1544
Brazee, Andrew Washburne, 480
Brazel, Wayne, 3555
Brazelton, William, 3555
Brazier, Nicola, 480
Brazil Riots, 3375
Brazil, Wayne, 1278
Brazilian Carnival Murders, 480
Brazilian Death Squad, 480-481
Brazilian Prison Riot, 3378
Brazilian Unemployment Riots, 3378
Brazza Savargon, Contessa di, 231
Bread Riot, 481
Breadalbane, 857
Breakenridge, William M. "Billy", 481-482, 495, 1058, 1644, 3133, 3545, 3151, 3555, 3560, 3567
Breakiron, Mark, 3453
Breaks, Harriet Elsie "Kitty", 1604
Breakthrough, 3495, 3530
Breaux, David, 3448
Brecheen, Robert, 3453
Brecht, Bertolt, 979
Breckinridge, John (U.S., 1760-1806), 482
Breckinridge, John Cabell (U.S., 1821-75), 482
Brécourt, Jeanne Amenaide, 482-483
Bredell, Baldwin S., 483, 1692-1693, 2899
Bredius, Abraham, 3032, 3034
Breeding, Judy, 1668
Breedlove, McArthur, 3449
Breeds, John, 483-484
Breene, James, 1180
Breeze, Dean, 382
Breeze, James L., 2723
Breezy, Daniel, 3007
Breguet, Bruno, 3520
Brehm, Walter E., 484
Breidenstine, 1307
Breitel, Charles, 1136
Breitenstein, Jean Sala, 484
Breitzke, Philip, 2338
Brekke, Carstein, 484
Breland, J.J., 891
Bremard, Julia, 2812
Brembar, Nicholas, 484
Brembre, Nicholas, 2345
Bremer, Adolph, 240
Bremer, Arthur, 3256, 3493
Bremer, Arthur Herman, 3080, 3081
Bremer, Edward G., 238, 240, 1764, 1766, 3326
Bren, Alfred, 3344
Brenda, Marion Kay, 3027
Brennan, Allan, 2034
Brennan, Ben, 485

Broms, Allan, 2765
Broncato, Tony, 1376
Bronco Bill, 107
Bronco Charlie, 3555
Bronfman, Edgar M., 2016
Bronfman, Samuel, 3330
Bronfman, Samuel, II, 497, 2016
Bronson, Charles, 2566
Bronson, E.C., 2866
Bronson, George, 3345
Bronson, Joseph, 3361
Bronson, S. Jerome, 724
Brönte, Robert, 1032
Bronzich, Connie Jo, 2810
Brook, John, 497, 3462
Brook, Maggie, 1947
Brooke, Charles W., 530, 1973
Brooke, F., 3244
Brooke, Henry, 1560
Brooke, Philippa, 585
Brooke, Ralph, 472
Brookes, Mabel, 2279
Brookhart, Smith W., 2160
Brookings, Wilmot W., 497
Brookins, A.B., 2818
Brookins, Louis Dwight, 497, 2027
Brooklier, Dominick, 1018, 1228, 3396, 3397
Brooklyn Museum of Arts and Sciences'
    Sargent Theft, 498
Brooklyn Refinery Robbery, 498
Brooks, Allen, 3352
Brooks, Annie, 2400
Brooks, Charles, 498, 3447
Brooks, Cynthia, 1356
Brooks, David Owen, 785
Brooks, Donald, 498-499
Brooks, Edmund, 1032
Brooks, Emma, 549
Brooks, Fisher, 2676
Brooks, Flossie, 499
Brooks, Gene Edward, 499
Brooks, George, 3451
Brooks, Henry, 3364
Brooks, Henry L., 903
Brooks, Henry M., 499
Brooks, Holland, 3360
Brooks, Hugh M., 499
Brooks, J.R., 2108
Brooks, Jack Edward, 123
Brooks, Jake, 3366
Brooks, James (U.S. pr.1744), 499
Brooks, James (U.S. pr.1872) 814
Brooks, James (U.S. d.1899), 3338
Brooks, James Abijah (U.S., 1855-1944),
    499, 3545
Brooks, James J. (U.S. pr.1869) 1465
Brooks, James J. (U.S. 1876-88) 2314, 3426
Brooks, Joe, 3385, 3386
Brooks, John, 3346
Brooks, Joseph "Dynamite", 2529
Brooks, Larry F., 3466
Brooks, Louis E., 2161
Brooks, Louise, 595, 2404
Brooks, Pierce, 1378, 3166
Brooks, Preston "Bully Boy", 499-500, 509,
    513, 3241
Brooks, Simon, 3351
Brooks, Thomas, 3363
Brooks, Virginia, 2858, 2918, 3382
Brooks, William (U.S. d.1894), 3344
Brooks, William (U.S. d.1901), 3353
Brooks, William (Brit. pr.1778), 2832
Brooks, William L. "Buffalo Billy", 500,
    3545, 3546, 3555
Broome, William, 500
Broomell, Jeanne, 1644
Broomell, Ron, 1644
Brophy 99, 136, 154
Brophy, Hank, 3555

Brosin, John, 3354
Brostron, Curtis, 500-501, 3426
Brotherhood of Aleppo, 3509, 3530
Brothers, James, 1764
Brothers, Dr. Joyce, 2234
Brothers, Leo Vincent, 501-503, 561, 616,
    959, 1074, 2660, 3382, 3384, 3386
Brothers, William V., 2071
Brotherton, Eric, 503
Brouard, Alfred, 905
Brouckère, Suzanne de, 10
Brough, Alfred, 2457
Brougham, Henry, (Brit. pr.19th cen.),
    503
Brougham, Henry Peter (Brit. pr.1820s),
    503
Broughton, Henry John Delves, 503
Broughton, Joseph, 3124
Broughton, William, 503-504
Broun, Heywood, 2652
Brower, George E., 2942
Brown, A.W., 3545
Brown, Aaron Venable, 504
Brown, Abe, 3351
Brown, Addison, 504, 2338
Brown, Adrienne, 508
Brown, Agnes, 692
Brown, Albert, 3448
Brown, Albert N., 3425
Brown, Andrew, 730
Brown, Angus, 504, 3545
Brown, Anthony Silah, 504
Brown, Arthur (Peru, pr.1849), 107
Brown, Mrs. Arthur Ross, 504
Brown, Arthur Ross (U.S., 1925-56), 504-
    505, 3327
Brown, Barry Austin, 505
Brown, Benjamin, 505, 3354
Brown, Beresford, 706
Brown, Bettie, 1373
Brown, Billy, 3555
Brown, Bob (U.S. d.1978), 1739
Brown, Bob (U.S. pr.1900), 1037, 2854,
    3555
Brown, Bobby Ray, 3453
Brown, Bradford, 505
Brown, Bruce, 505
Brown, Caesar, 1001
Brown, Calvin, 3340
Brown, Carrie, 323
Brown, Charles (U.S. d.1892), 862
Brown, Charles (U.S. pr.1896), 37, 469-
    470
Brown, Charles (U.S. d.1897), 3348
Brown, Charles E. (U.S. pr.1890-1910s),
    1101
Brown, Charles T. (U.S. pr.1920), 505
Brown, Charlie (U.S. pr.1870s), 1054,
    2216
Brown, Clarence, 515
Brown, Conrad, 505
Brown, Cornelius, 3453
Brown, Curtis, 3354
Brown, D.C. 23
Brown, David, 3453
Brown, David Junior, 3453
Brown, David Paul, 1601
Brown, Debra, 743, 3334, 3451
Brown, Dennis, 314
Brown, Donna, 331
Brown, Echo, 3351
Brown, Edmund G., 5, 1239, 3118
Brown, Edward (U.S. d.1899), 3351
Brown, Edward (U.S. d.1902), 3354
Brown, Elizabeth A., 461
Brown, Erastus, 3349
Brown, Eric, 3264
Brown, Ernest, 505-506, 1202, 1642, 3228
Brown, Ernest W., 3426

Brown, Fat Moe, 304
Brown, Finis Arthur, 388
Brown, Fiona, 3333
Brown, Florence, 2006
Brown, Frances, 1510, 3460
Brown, Frank (U.S. d.1900), 3352
Brown, Frank (U.S. d.1903), 3355
Brown, Frank (U.S. d.1905), 3357
Brown, Frank (U.S. pr.1900), 3015
Brown, Fred, 3567
Brown, Frederick (Brit., prom.1951), 514,
Brown, Fredric (pr.1940s), 2716
Brown, Gary Leon, 3447
Brown, Gene, 3365
Brown, George (Brit. pr.1902), 2544
Brown, George (U.S. d.1819), 506
Brown, George (U.S. d.1881), 2554
Brown, George (U.S. d.1894), 1335
Brown, George (U.S. d.1864), 3336
Brown, George (U.S. pr.1970s), 3470
Brown, George N. (U.S. pr.1880s), 804
Brown, George S. (pr.1880s), 3545
Brown, Grace "Billie", 113, 1313
Brown, H. Rap, 507, 3478, 3484, 3491, 3534
Brown, H.S., 1451
Brown, Hannah, 1375
Brown, Harold, 3369
Brown, Harvey, 2322
Brown, Harvey K., 3263
Brown, Hazel, 221
Brown, Helen, 3001
Brown, Henry (U.S., pr.1865), 1460
Brown, Henry Billings, 506
Brown, Henry Newton "Hendry", 364, 486,
    506-507, 1559, 2717, 3071, 3545, 3551,
    3555, 3566, 3567
Brown, Holmes, 1586
Brown, Holy Eleanora, 2475
Brown, Irving F., 507
Brown, J.B., 508-509
Brown, James (U.S. 1928-), 507-508
Brown, James (U.S. d.1971), 1376
Brown, James (U.S. pr.1867), 507
Brown, James (U.S. d.1901), 3015
Brown, James W. (U.S. d.1901), 508
Brown, Jeff, 3364
Brown, Jerry, (U.S. pr.1944), 284
Brown, Jerry, (U.S. pr.1970s-80s), 1738
Brown, Jerry (U.S. pr.1890s), 3343
Brown, Jessie, 2862
Brown, Jim (d.1878), 2056
Brown, Jim "General" (d.1982) 3382
Brown, JoAnne, 509
Brown, Joe, 729
Brown, John (Scot. 1627-85), 509, 1357
Brown, John (U.S. 1800-59), 509-514, 1457,
    1954, 1963, 1965, 2289, 2412, 2468, 2793,
    3374
Brown, John (U.S. d.1890), 3339
Brown, John (U.S. d.1891), 3340
Brown, John (U.S. d.1903), 3355
Brown, John (pr.1883) 3293
Brown, John (U.S. pr.1988) 3448
Brown, John (U.S. pr.1988) 3451
Brown, John C. (U.S. pr.1932), 1850
Brown, John G. (U.S. pr.1988), 3447
Brown, John Whelan (Aus. 1933-), 514
Brown, Joseph "Brownie" (U.S. pr.1914),
    1726
Brown, Joseph (Brit. 1918-51), 514
Brown, Joseph (pr.1987), 3283
Brown, Joseph (d.1909), 3359
Brown, Kenneth, 671
Brown, Kitty, 1268
Brown, L.W., 3424
Brown, Larry, 3449
Brown, Lawrence, 3348
Brown, Lee (U.S. d.1895), 3345
Brown, Lee (U.S. pr.1970s-80s), 3166

Brown, Lee Patrick, 514-515
Brown, Leslie, 515, 1970
Brown, Lucretia, 1662
Brown, Mack Edward, 3454
Brown, Margaret, 593, 733, 2113
Brown, Mark, 3340
Brown, Martin George, 318
Brown, Mary, 923
Brown, Maud, 1335
Brown, Maude, 2025
Brown, Melody, 3138
Brown, Michael, 3463
Brown, Morton, 473
Brown, Nathan, 3363, 3450
Brown, Nathaniel, 1097
Brown, Neal, 1794, 2749, 3545
Brown, Nichol, 515
Brown, Nolan, 3290
Brown, O.S., 467
Brown, Owen, 509, 3209
Brown, Pat, 577
Brown, Paul A., 3449
Brown, Peter, 509
Brown, Prentiss Marsh, 515
Brown, Raymond, 645, 1712, 3447
Brown, Reese B., 515-516
Brown, Richard J., 743
Brown, Rob (d.1897), 3348
Brown, Robert (pr.1590s), 1379
Brown, Robert (U.S. d.1891), 3340
Brown, Robert (pr.1979), 3388
Brown, Robert C. (pr.1900s), 3555
Brown, Robert J. (pr.1943), 2726
Brown, Ronald, 516
Brown, Rube, 2901
Brown, Sam, 516, 3555
Brown, Samuel (U.S. d.1818), 1741
Brown, Samuel (U.S. pr.1980s), 453, 489
Brown Sisters, 519
Brown, Stanley, 2284, 2926, 3427
Brown, Stephen (U.S. d.1916), 3364
Brown, Steven (U.S. pr.1976), 3462
Brown, Thaddeus, 2436, 2963, 3425
Brown, Thomas, (Scot. d.1705), 2472
Brown, Thomas (U.S. d.1890), 3339
Brown, Thomas (U.S. d.1902), 3354
Brown, Thomas Jack, 3453
Brown, Thomas Mathieson, 516
Brown, Thomas Watson, 1645
Brown, Tom (Brit prom.1890), 2092
Brown, Tom (U.S. pr.19th Cent.), 3399
Brown, Tony, 1192
Brown, Vernon, 3452
Brown, Vivienne, 2113
Brown, W.E., 3555
Brown, Walter Folger, 516
Brown, Washington, 3338
Brown, Waverly, 489
Brown, William (U.S. d.1891), 3339
Brown, William (U.S. d.1900), 3352
Brown, William (U.S. d.1906), 3357
Brown, William (Brit. pr.1900s), 801
Brown, William Adams, 664
Brown, William C., 3001
Brown, Willie, 3453
Brown, Willis, 1473
Brownback, Garrett A., 1618
Browne, Carl, 803
Browne, Frederick Guy, 516-517, 1207, 3262
Browne, George (pr.1930s-40s), 371, 591,
    622, 3382, 3402
Browne, George (pr.1943), 866
Browne, George (pr.1940), 2573
Browne, H. Huffman, 517-518
Browne, Robert, 518
Browne, Thomas, 3346
Browne, William George, 518
Brownell, George W., 2191

Brownell, Herbert, Jr., 35, 518
Brownell, Sarah Elizabeth, 1919
Browning, Elizabeth Barrett, 1605, 1645
Browning, James Robert, 518
Browning, John Moses, 518
Browning, Matthew, 518
Browning, Orville Hickman, 518
Browning, Paul Lewis, 3452
Browning, Paul Louis, Jr., 518
Browning, Radford, 806
Browning, Robert (Brit. 1920s), 618, 813,
    1605, 2182
Browning, Robert (U.S. 1920s), 2068
Browning, Robert (Brit. pr.1868-69), 2584
Browning, Russell, 1778
Browning, William, 3555
Browning, William Lacy, 919
Brownlee, John, 518, 3345
Brownlee, Johnny, 2048
Brownlee, Joseph, 2023
Brownlee, Thomas, 3346
Brownlee, Virgil Lee, 3447
Brownlee, Walter, 3362
Brownlow, William, 292, 312
Brownmiller, Roy E., 518
Brownrigg, Elizabeth, 518-519
Brownrigg, James, 518-519
Broyles, Nash R., 503
Broz, Josip, 2837
Brozishewski, Barnett, 353
Bruccola, Philip, 127, 3379, 3380
Bruce, Henry, 75, 3344
Bruce, J.T., 1230
Bruce, Kirk, 3452
Bruce, Robert (Scot. pr.1932), 2534
Bruce, Robert (U.S. pr.1910), 3360
Bruce, Robert (Scot. pr.1300s), 763, 1071
Bruce, W.H., 519
Bruce, William Cabell, 519
Brucioli, Antonio, 519
Bruckner, Wilbur, 426
Brückner, Wilhelm, 519
Brudenell, James, 725
Brudenell, James Thomas, 519, 2999, 3305
Brudenell-Tuckett Duel, 519-520
Brudos, Jerry, 520
Bruegel, Pieter, 2098
Bruffey, Ed, 580
Bruggemann, Hardy, 2832
Brugh, Peter, 405
Brühne, Vera, 520
Bruin, Peter, 555
Brumit, Lucille, 1544-45
Brumm, Frank, 2827
Bruncher, George, 1388
Brunder, Wilfred, 3402
Brundige, Harry Thompson, 29
Brune, Guillaume Marie Anne, 520, 3240
Bruneau, Albert, 520, 3228
Bruneau, Emile, 3398
Brunell, Alan, 1770
Bruner, Heck, 3545
Brunet, Leon, 2536
Brunette, Arlene, 520
Brunette, Harry, 520-521
Brunhilde, 521, 1257, 2759, 3236
Brunkella, Jay, 1718
Brunner, Alois, 3538
Brunner, Heinrich, 521
Brunner, Linda Mae, 3331
Brunner, Neal, 3545
Bruno, Angelo, 104, 521, 755, 2574, 2746,
    2918, 3395, 3412, 3413
Bruno, Anthony, 2975
Bruno, Eugene, 423
Bruno, Giordano, 521
Bruno, John J. "Big Joe", 521, 3248
Bruno, Karl, 521, 3538
Bruno, Michael, 3449

Bruno, Phillip, 521
Bruno, Sam, 3396
Bruns, Morten, 2524
Bruns, Neils, 2524
Bruns, Richard, 2693
Bruns, Robert, 1678
Bruno, Saint, 521
Brunskill, Frank, 3425
Brunskill, William, 522, 730, 914, 926, 1324,
    1596, 1890, 2880
Brunswick, Caroline of, 633-634
Brunswick, Duke of, 2737
Brunt, John, 658, 2929
Brunton, "Tex", 3555
Brushrod, Raymond, 3349
Brussel, James A., 2172
Brussels Church and King Riot, 3372
Brust, Albert, 522, 3329
Brust, Joseph A., 2812
Brust, Julius, 1095
Brutus, Marcus Junius, 570-571, 2490, 3232,
    3234
Bruxton, Howard Barnes, Jr., 912
Bruys, Peter of, 522, 2452
Bryan, A.S., 1679
Bryan, Albert V., Jr., 1899
Bryan, Anthony, 3449
Bryan, Harry John, 522-523, 3197
Bryan, John Henry, 3197
Bryan, Joseph Francis, Jr., 523
Bryan, Michael Neely, 3428
Bryan, Pearl, 1679-1680
Bryan, Stephanie, 4-6, 3327
Bryan, William Jennings, 523, 874, 876-877,
    2708, 2709
Bryan, Willie, 3367
Bryant, Anthony G., 3466
Bryant, Betty, 2577
Bryant, Carolyn, 2178
Bryant, Charles "Black Face Charley", 523,
    860, 3555
Bryant, Charlotte, 322, 523-524
Bryant, Ed, 3545
Bryant, Eugene F., 2686
Bryant, Frederick, 524
Bryant, J.E., 2713
Bryant, J.J., 3414
Bryant, James, 3453
Bryant, John, Jr. 2178
Bryant, Kenneth, 524
Bryant, Lige, 647
Bryant, Robert, 3449, 3355
Bryant, Robert Pernell, 3453
Bryant, Roy, 2178
Bryant, Thomas, 1513
Bryant, William Cullen, 919
Bryant, William Perkins, 524
Bryce, James, 524
Brynder, J.E., 3250
Bryning, Isaac, 2156
Brynmore, John Edward, 792
Bryon, Robert, 3085
Bryson, Andy, 1427
Bryson, Christopher, 340
Bryson, William, 2980
Bryukhanov, Viktor P., 524
Brzeczek, Richard, 524, 3424
BTK Strangler, 524-525
Bua, Nicholas, 2683
Bua, Nicholas John, 472, 525
Buback, Siegfried, 203, 525, 2528, 3257,
    3504
Bublik, Josef, 1531
Buccieri, Fiore "Fifi", 283, 525, 2969, 3382,
    3396
Buccieri, Frank, 525, 3396
Buccolo, Anthony, 3460
Buchalsky, "Izzy the Rat", 3382
Buchalter, Louis "Lepke", 1, 32, 34, 111-

Burgos, Violeta, 2838
Burgoyne, Johnny 161
Burgreen, Robert W., 3426
Burgunder, Robert Marcus, Jr., 544-545, 2821
Burgunder, Robert Marcus, Sr., 544-545
Burgundy, Duchess of, 3090
Burgundy, Philip of, 1724
Burgundy, Sigismund of, 701
Burial of the Fruit, 545
Burk, Homer, 3361
Burk, Richard, 2118
Burk, Wayne, 545
Burke, A.F., 3545
Burke, Billy "The Kid", 1355, 2019, 2020
Burke, Charles (U.S., d.1933), 545
Burke, Charles (U.S. pr.1921), 2040
Burke, Charles F. "Dink" (U.S., pr.1890), 1506
Burke, David Augustus, 545
Burke, David P., 3471
Burke, Dell, 545
Burke, Dennis, 523
Burke, Edmund, 1475
Burke, Edward, 2528
Burke, Ella, 545
Burke, Elmer, 545-546, 3379
Burke, Frank, 1111, 2555
Burke, Fred R. "Killer", 296, 546-547, 614, 1002, 1074, 2044, 2660, 3176, 3414
Burke, George, 3338
Burke, Harold P., 547
Burke, Mrs. Harvey, 396
Burke, J.S., 2732, 3545
Burke, James, 547
Burke, James E., 3011
Burke, Jerry, 3348
Burke, John (Brit., pr.1839), 586
Burke, John (U.S., pr.1860), 1540
Burke, Katherine, 730
Burke, Kenneth, 2261
Burke, Lloyd Hudson, 547
Burke, M., 3426
Burke, Margaret, 1134
Burke, Redmond, 3344
Burke, S., 1252
Burke Sales Co., 3289
Burke, Sarah A., 1458
Burke, Steve, 531, 3556
Burke, Thomas (Can. pr.1877-78), 2069
Burke, Thomas (Brit. pr.1931), 2912
Burke, Thomas (Brit. pr.1926), 3295
Burke, Thomas Henry, 660-661, 1662, 3242
Burke, Trigger, 546
Burke, William, 417, 547-549, 1498
Burke, Wood, 3362
Burkett, Jesse, 1920
Burkitt, William, 549
Burkley, Bluitt, 549-550
Burkley, Thurman, 549
Burks, Curtis C., 1183
Burks, David, 2851
Burks, Harold Finnon "Arkansas", 1520
Burks, John, 3454
Burleigh, 218
Burleigh, Cornelius Alverson, 550
Burleson, Pete, 3555, 3560
Burley, Benjamin D., 3424
Burley, Garfield, 3354
Burley, Simon, 550
Burlison, John, 3333
Burmeister, F.H., 1194
Burmese Civil Riots, 550
Burmese Riots, 3378
Burnell, Freda, 1737
Burnes, Alexander, 550, 1752
Burnet, Gilbert, 550, 1420
Burnet, William, 1385
Burnett, Alfred, 805

Burnett, Benjamin, 2393
Burnett, Ernie, 3009
Burnett, John, 550-551
Burnett, Joseph, 1781
Burnett, Melvin, 551
Burnett, Thomas, 3359
Burnett, W.R., 1547
Burnett, William (Brit. pr.1862), 1388
Burnett, William (U.S. pr.1892), 3342
Burnett, William Riley (U.S. 1899-1982), 551
Burney, Charles, 3070
Burnham Abbey Farm, 3227
Burnham, George, 1138
Burnham, Josiah, 551
Burning Court, The, 551
Burns, Alfred, 551
Burns, Anthony, 551
Burns, Arnold I., 2162
Burns, Bill, 399, 495, 2205
Burns, Charles, 1184
Burns, Daniel, 3449
Burns Detective Agency, 2287
Burns, Eddie, 1254
Burns, Ellen Bree, 551
Burns, George (U.S. 1896-), 681, 1178, 1903
Burns, Haywood, 458
Burns, J.E., 3425
Burns, James (U.S. pr.1899), 1693
Burns, James Milton (U.S. 1924-), 551
Burns, Jeannette, 3125
Burns, Jerry, 2719
Burns, John, 551
Burns, Joseph, 951
Burns, Kit, 95-96, 1174, 3402
Burns, Louis Henry, 551
Burns, Michael, 1235
Burns, Mildred, 2029
Burns, Nat, 3518
Burns, Owen McIntosh, 551
Burns, Rex, 2796
Burns, Richard, 1698
Burns, Robert (U.S. pr.1930s), 1183
Burns, Robert (Brit. 1759-96), 2852
Burns, Robert Easton, 1826
Burns, Robert Elliott (U.S. 1890-1955), 551-553
Burns, Thomas, 3363
Burns, Tommy, 1729
Burns, Vincent, 1490
Burns, Viola, 2866
Burns, William (U.S. pr. 1980s), 3454
Burns, William (U.S. pr.1891), 3014
Burns, William (U.S. pr.1907), 3358
Burns, William (U.S. pr.1907), 3550
Burns, William J., 213, 483, 553-554, 628, 1143, 1144, 1189, 1220, 1479, 1534, 1612, 2062, 2159, 2213, 3426
Burns, William Thomas "Sleepy Bill", 399
Burns, Zura, 635
Burnstine, Kenneth, 3299
Burnworth, Edward, 554
Burr, Aaron, 161, 408, 424, 554-556, 881, 888, 1892, 1917, 2534, 2130, 3112, 3158, 3178, 3303, 3304
Burr, Charlie, 3449
Burr, Jim, 1507
Burr, John, 3358
Burr, William S., 2271
Burrel, Dennis, 3350
Burrell, Albert Ronnie, 3451
Burrell, Berry B., 96, 2181
Burrell, D.B., 3359
Burres, Swan, 3338
Burris, Gary, 3451
Burris, J.A., 3342
Burrough, John "Peanuts", 1956
Burroughs, Ada L., 600

Burroughs, Adonirum J., 1462
Burroughs, George, 556, 2667, 2668
Burroughs, Stephen, 556
Burroughs, W.H., 3545
Burroughs, William S., 2347
Burrow Brothers Gang, 495
Burrow, James Buchanan, 557
Burrow, Jim, 556-557
Burrow, Reuben Houston, 556-558, 3555
Burrowes, William, 458
Burrows, Albert Arthur, 2738
Burrows, Albert Edward, 558
Burrows, Erskine Durrant, 558, 2893
Burrows, George, 2395
Burrows, James Buchanan, 3555
Burrows, Jean, 322
Burrows, Joseph, 3451
Burrows, Reuben Houston, 556-558, 3555
Burrows, Warren Booth, 558
Burrus, Sextus Afranius 558, 727, 2728
Burse, Nathaniel, 911
Bursum, Holm O., 3545
Burt, Cyril Lodowic, 558, 1739
Burt, Frank, 583
Burt, Leo, 1159
Burt, Sam, 3555
Burton, Andre, 3448
Burton, Desiree, 1740
Burton, George, 3350
Burton, Harold Hitz, 558
Burton, James, 1285
Burton, Lee A., 558-559, 3326
Burton, Lucille, 1981
Burton, Magnolia, 2463
Burton, Martha, 2296-2297
Burton, Murray, 3361
Burton, Reginald, 271
Burton, Richard, 3364
Burton, Robert, 3292
Burton, Sarah, 1998
Burton, Scott, 3359
Burton, Theodore Elijah, 559
Burton, Thomas Henry, 643
Burton, Walter William, 559
Burton, William (U.S. pr.1939), 1981
Burton, William Walter, 1193, 2581, 2984
Burts, Matthew, 559, 3545, 3555
Burts, William, 3351
Burundi Africa Massacre, 559, 3378
Burwell, Charles, 3346
Burwell, W.M., 3545
Bury St. Edmunds Witches, 559
Bury, William Henry, 559
Busacca, Florence, 559-560
Busacca, Thomas F., 559-560
Buscetta, Tommaso, 560, 1372, 1952, 3301, 3415
Busch, Joseph A., 1125
Busch, Niven, 1032
Buse, Deanna, 475
Buse, William, 560
Buselitch, Abbe, 3251
Busembaum, Hermann, 560
Bush, Edwin Albert, 560
Bush, George, 1436, 1623, 2220, 3259, 3275, 3301, 3517
Bush, George C., 2827
Bush, Horace W., 695
Bush, John Earl, 660, 3449
Bush, Mary, 1709
Bush, Robert, 560
Bush, Sam, 3343
Bushaw, Elaine, 693
Bushnell, Bennie, 1314
Bushnell, John, 1702
Bushnell, William D., Jr., 654
Bushrod Washington, 218
Bushyhead, E.W., 3426
Busic, Julienne, 560, 3471

Busic, Zvonko, 560, 3471
Buskin, Robby, 3359
Buss, Timothy D., 561
Busse, Fred, 798
Bussey, Frank "Monk", 2862
Bussey, William de, 924
Bussey, Willie "Cajun", 2862
Bussi, Aurelio, 1317
Bussy-d'Amboise, Louis de Clermont de, 561, 3239
Bustamante, Anastasio, 1397, 2679, 3241
Bustamente, Antonio Garate, 792
Bustamente, Pablo, 1828
Busteed, William, 3402
Buster, John, 3555
Buswell, Harriet, 558, 561, 2234
Butcher, Christine, 181, 561
Butcher, Susan, 1338
Butcher, William, 3346
Butchill, Elizabeth, 561
Bute, Earl of, 2804, 3157
Bütefisch, Heinrich, 3538
Butkovich, John, 1248
Butler, Allen, 3343
Butler, Andrew Pickens, 499
Butler, Benjamin Franklin, 163, 561, 1702, 1727
Butler, Charles (Brit., 1750-1832), 561
Butler, Charles (U.S. pr.1896), 2093
Butler, Charles C. (U.S., pr.1911), 1521
Butler, Cleon, 883
Butler, Cleveland, 3366
Butler, Edward, 1774
Butler, Eleanor, 720
Butler, Harry Linton, 561-562, 3460
Butler, Horace, 3454
Butler, James (Brit. c.1688-1716), 562
Butler, James (Ire. 1420-61), 562
Butler, Jerome, 3447, 3454
Butler, Jesse, 3355
Butler, John, 422
Butler, John L., 3425
Butler, Josephine Elizabeth, 562
Butler, Louise, 562
Butler, Norman 3X, 2095
Butler, Patrick, 1713, 2324
Butler, Pierce, 562
Butler, R.A., 710, 2134
Butler, Richard Girnt, 562-563
Butler, Robert, 563, 3457
Butler, Steven, 3454
Butler, William (Brit., d.1910), 563
Butler, William (Brit., pr.1938), 563
Butler, William (U.S., 1822-1909), 563
Butler, William (U.S., pr.1882), 826
Butler, William (Brit. pr.1909), 3282
Butler, William (U.S., pr.1893), 3343
Butler, William H. (U.S. pr.1853), 3092
Butler, William J. (U.S., pr.1928), 1201
Butt, Edwin, 264
Butt, Isaac, 563
Butte, George Charles, 563
Butterfield 8, 564
Butterfield, Alexander P., 3100
Butterfield, Jane, 563
Butterfield, Neale Allen, 563-564
Butterworth, Jane, 471
Buttner, A.F., 3545
Buttons, Pearl, 1635, 3409
Buttrum, Janice, 3450
Butts, Charles "Reggi", 3331
Butts, Delmire, 353
Butts, Joyce, 2764
Butts, Thomas, 564
Butts, Vernon, 429
Buus, Mrs. Paul, 2860
Buvée, Barbara 186
Buxbaum, Ferdinand, 3382
Buxton, Charles Roden, 564

Buxton, Edward, 564
Buxton, John H., 1846
Buxton, Lawrence, 3454
Buxton, Thomas Fowell, 564, 2312
Buyoya, Pierre, 559
Buys, Christiaan, 1392
Buys, Maria, 1392
Buys, William de, 474
Buzhardt, J. Fred, 3100, 3101
Buzzard, Abe, 564
Buzzard Brothers, 564
Buzzard, Joe, 564
Buzzard, Mother, 564
Bybee, Hilton, 259
Byblius, Philo, 3068
Byck, Samuel J., 3470
Byers, Herbert, 1353
Byers, John, 3558, 3560
Byers, Josie, 1507
Byers, Martha, 457
Byers, Mortimer, 654, 2052, 2205
Byers, Walter, 3564
Byington, Zebulon, 3424
Byles, 3170
Byles, Andrew, 691
Byng, John, 564, 2683
Byng, Julian Hedworth George, 565, 2683, 3426
Bynum, John, 2764
Byrd, Arthur, 3462
Byrd, Don A., 3424
Byrd, Harry 95
Byrd, Maurice, 3452
Byrd, Milford, 3449
Byrd, Richard, 414
Byrd, Walter, 3361
Byrd, Wesley, 769
Byrne, Anthony, 565
Byrne, Dominic P., 497, 2016-2017, 3330
Byrne, Edward (U.S. pr.1988), 2025
Byrne, Edward (U.S. d.1988), 3447
Byrne, Ethel, 2677
Byrne, Garret, 565, 3324
Byrne, Jane, 524, 2233
Byrne, Joe, 1779
Byrne, John, 3508
Byrne, Laurence Austin, 565
Byrne, Patrick Joseph, 565
Byrne, William D., 1226
Byrne, William Matthew, Jr., 565
Byrnes, Frank, 1666
Byrnes Hotel Burglary Gang, 566
Byrnes, James Francis, 565-566
Byrnes, Joseph, 216, 2131
Byrnes, Thomas (U.S. d.1866), 566
Byrnes, Thomas F. (U.S. 1842-1910), 323, 409, 566, 1170, 1290, 2041, 2289, 2876
Byrns, Joseph Wellington, 566
Byron, Emma, 566-567
Byron, George de Luna, 567
Byron, George Gordon, 1906, 2069
Byron, Kitty, 939
Byron, Robert, 288, 3085, 3451
Byron, William, 567
Byrski, Martin, 1134-1135
Bywaters, Frederick, 579, 849, 2469, 2933
Bywaters, Thompson, 3126

C

Caamaño, José Maria Plácido, 568
Caballero, Guadalupe, 568, 3555
Caballero, Juan, 3451

Cabassa, Lisa, 1113
Cabbarus, Jesus, Jr., 2119
Cabestant, Guillaume de, 568
Cabey, Darrell, 1329
Cable, Chester M., 952
Cables, Mariano Avila, 3472
Caboche, Simon, 568
Cabral, Amilcar, 568, 3256
Cabranes, Jose Alberto, 568
Cabrera, Luis, 568
Cabrera, Ramón, 568
Cabrera, Rene, 3254
Cabrerra, Benito, 1323
Cabrinovic, Nedeljko, 1212
Caccavale, Anthony, 3298
Caccina Paetus 166
Caceres, Luis M., 3254
Cacheu, Paul, 2437
Caci, Vincent Dominic, 2178
Cada, Joseph, 3382
Caddell, Dr. George, 568
Cade, Clyde, 3447
Cade, Jack, 3185
Cade, John, 3238
Cadek, Louis J., 568
Cadelli, Nicolas, 2021
Cadière, Marie Catherine, 568-569
Cadieux, Cynthia, 928
Cadle, Z.C., 3355
Cadman, Josiah, 569
Cadon, Albert, 3465
Cadore, Norm, 3362
Cadoudal, Georges, 569, 3240
Cadwalader, John, 569, 3303
Cadwallader, Dorothy, 1229
Cady, Dick, 1741
Cady, John P., 2071
Cady, William, 569
Caecina, 569
Caedwalla, 569, 3236
Caelius, 569
Caepio, Quintus Servilius, 569
Caerularius, Michael, 569
Caesar, Arthur, 2103
Caesar, Augustus, 1749, 2460
Caesar, Drusus, 1029
Caesar, Gaius Julius, 569-571, 714
Caesar, Julius, (Brit., 1558-1638), 571
Caesar, Julius (Roman, 100-44 B.C.) 580, 902, 985, 1029, 1245, 2118, 2470, 2485, 2490, 2510, 2979, 2985, 3227, 3232, 3234, 3303
Caesarea, Pamphilus of, 2402
Caesarion, 2510
Caeser, Paul G., 912
Caesonia, 581
Caetini, Don Gelasio, 2987
Caetti, Andrien, 3393
Cafaro, Vincent, 2670
Caffee, Peggy, 2458
Caffee, William, 572
Caffey, Francis Gordon, 572
Caffrey, Jimmy, 1758
Caffrey, Raymond, 1590, 1613, 1756
Caffrey, Regina, 1758
Caffrey, Thomas, 660
Cage, Tommy, 3451
Caglio, Anna Maria, 2204
Cagliostro, Count Alessandro di, 572-574
Cagney, James, 240, 1969, 2230, 2293, 2984
Cagoule, La, 574
Cahill, Bob, 2548
Cahill, Clyde, 574
Cahill, Frank P., 363
Cahill, Joseph, 3166
Cahill, Laura, 1470
Cahill, Pete, 1322
Cahill, Thomas, 577, 3426
Cahill, Tim, 3173

Cahill, Wilford, 1470
Cahill, William, 2656
Cahn, George, 741
Cahn, William, 574
Cahoon, Robert, 2795
Cahoon, Sam, 960
Cahoon, W.B., 1066
Caiaphas, Joseph, 575
Caicedo, Edison, 1711
Caicedo, Gilberto, 1711
Caifano, Marshall Joseph, 575, 577, 1005, 1895, 1980, 3382, 3384
Caillaux, "Haughty" Henriette Claretie, 575-576, 3243
Caillaux, Joseph, 575, 576
Caillol, Alain, 576, 1030, 1093, 3331
Cain, 576
Cain, Frank, 1108
Cain, James M., 1008
Cain, John, 576
Cain, Marcus, 3208
Cain, Melanie, 1693
Cain, Neil, 812
Cain, Paul, 537, 2029
Cain, Richard, 1980, 3382
Cain, Richard B. (U.S. 1924-73), 44, 576-577, 1306
Cain, Russell, 3454
Cain, Tracy, 3448
Caire, Celia "Sally", 1253
Cairns, Hugh McCalmont, 577
Cairns, Ralph, 577, 3247
Cairoli, Benedetto, 1639
Caius, Marcus, 577
Caius Memmius, 3234
Cajetan of Thiene, 577
Calabaza, Ariz., 577
Calabrese, Frank James, 3382
Calabriese, Joseph, 3382
Calamia, Leonard, 577, 3414
Calamity Jane, 277, 388, 412, 577, 595, 1469, 1537, 1539, 1540
Calamy, Edmund, 577
Calandra, John, 3392
Calandra, Joseph, 578
Calandra, Salvatore R., 1189
Calas, Jean, 578, 3061
Calas, Marc Antoine, 578, 3061
Calbeck, Lorene, 578
Calcraft, William, 249, 348, 578-579, 1182, 1207, 1532, 2134, 2157, 2932, 2934, 3107, 3126
Caldarone, Thomas J., Jr., 3097
Caldclough, James, 579
Caldecote, Thomas Walker Hobart Inskip, 579
Calder, Ritchie, 705
Calderazzo, Vincent, 3014, 3402
Calderon, Ismael, 1321
Calderon, Rodrigo, 579
Calderon, Zosimo, 1152
Calderon Forero, Jairo Alberto, 3254
Caldwell, Andy, 3338
Caldwell, Arthur, 579
Caldwell, Charles, 579
Caldwell, Diana, 503
Caldwell, Henry Clay, 579
Caldwell, Isaac, 826
Caldwell, James (U.S. d.1770) 446
Caldwell, Jim (U.S. pr.1980s) 1419
Caldwell, John, (Can., pr.1934), 518
Caldwell, John (Scot., 1926-,), 579
Caldwell, Leland, 1161
Caldwell, Marjorie, 579
Caldwell, Mary, 1021
Caldwell, Richard, 3454
Caldwell, Rickie Tim, 3454
Caldwell, Roger, 579-580, 1913
Caldwell, William, 3346

Cale, Guillaume, 580
Cale, Louis D., 3470
Cale, Melvin C., 3470
Caleaway, James, 3352
Caleb Powers, 3242
Calef, Robert, 2145, 2669
Calero, Gilberto Cables, 3472
Calevacca, Vincent 162
Calextus III,, 658
Calhoun, Eben, 3358
Calhoun, James, 3452
Calhoun, John (U.S., 1806-59), 580, 3365
Calhoun, John Caldwell (U.S., 1782-1850), 580, 3108
Calhoun, Nelson, 3346
Calhoun, Patrick, 580, 3305
Calhoun, R.N., 3558
Calhoun, William James, 580
Calhoun-Williamson Duel, 580
Cali, John, 910
Cali, Renee, 910
Calico Jim, 580, 3414
California Department of Justice, 3289
Caligula, 36, 39, 580, 581, 669, 727, 730, 2170, 2470, 3234
Calinescu, Armand, 581, 3249
Calippus, 3233
Calise, Ralph, 1120
Calkins, William Henry, 581
Call, Charles, 2686
Call, George, 3351
Call, The, 3529
Calla, Caesar, 581
Calla, Salvatore, 1751
Callabi, Giuseppe, 2987
Calladine, Hannah, 558
Callaghan, E., 1689
Callaghan, Jeremiah, 1300-1301
Callahan, Bill, 583
Callahan, Dan, 698
Callahan, Edward, 581, 1453
Callahan, Gerald Michael, 581-582, 3382
Callahan, Harvey G., 3426
Callahan, J.H., 2334
Callahan, Jack, 582
Callahan, James, 836, 3324, 3447
Callahan, John, 22-23, 25, 582-583
Callahan, Michael, 583
Callahan, Paul M., 2957
Callahan, Raymond G., 904
Callahan, William H., 583-584
Callahan, William Washington, 2716
Callahan, Willis, 3246
Callan, Harry, 2723
Callan, Mary, 2959
Callanan, John, 3459
Callaway, Anderson, 3358
Callaway, Austin, 3368
Callaway, Dennis, 584
Callehan, William, 1800
Calleja, Félix, 3240
Callemin, Francois, 432
Callender, Alex, 221
Callender, James Thompson, 584
Calles, Plutarco Elias, 1589, 2356, 3246, 3248
Calley, William, 3489
Calley, William J., 2161
Calley, William Laws, Jr., 584, 2272
Callias, 584
Calligan, Sam "The Bully Boy", 2316
Callister, Marion Jones, 584
Callisthenes, 584-585
Callistratus, 585
Callistus III, 441
Calloway, John, 3350
Calloway, Joseph, 1520
Calloway, Willie, 585
Calls, Gams, 3350

Calman, 2030
Calmette, Gaston, 575, 3243
Calotescu, Corneliu, 3538
Calpurnius Bestia (Roman pr.100 B.C.), 585
Calpurnius Bestia, Lucius (Roman pr.63 B.C.), 585
Cals, Pierre, 1920
Calton, James, 3357
Calvarez, Alvaro, 896
Calverley, Walter, 585-586
Calverly, Bob, 651
Calvert, Arthur "Arty", 1678
Calvert, George, 223
Calvert, Mrs. Louie, 586
Calvert, Marie, 3327
Calvert, Mary, 1909
Calvert, Milt, 3353
Calvert, William, 586
Calvi, Robert, 2118
Calvin, Clarence W., 1969
Calvin, James Russell, 2309
Calvin, John (U.S. d.1895), 3346
Calvin, John (Fr. pr.1500s), 806
Calvin, R.H., 3015
Calvo, Escolastico, 3255
Calvo, L., 3251
Calwell, Arthur, 3255
Calwell, Jimmy "Speckled Jimmy", 2474
Camacho, Jacqueline, 545
Camacho, Olga, 2213
Camarda, Emile, 2102, 3402
Camarena Salazar, Enrique, 107, 229, 586-587, 634, 792, 1104, 1147, 1192, 1255, 1651, 1834, 2523, 2248, 3397, 3398
Camb, James, 587-588, 654, 1550
Cambacérès, Jean Jacques-Régis de, 588
Camberg, John F., 588
Cambon, Alfredo, 3328, 3490
Cambon, Pierre-Joseph, 588
Cambri, Susanna, 2202
Cambridge, Godfrey 115
Cambyses, 3232
Cambyses I, 3232
Cambyses II, 588, 2510, 2781
Camelford, Lord, 3304
Cameron, Andrew, 3555
Cameron, Archibald, 588, 3003
Cameron, Benjamin Franklin, 589
Cameron, Donald, 741
Cameron, Duncan, 589
Cameron, Elsie, 2830, 2939
Cameron, Everett L., 3428
Cameron, Herbert, 2747
Cameron, Hugh, 1357
Cameron, James, 671
Cameron, John (Brit. pr.1950s), 1345
Cameron, John (Scot. d.1625), 589, 3545
Cameron, John Hillyard, 1826
Cameron, Mary, 249
Cameron, Mathew Crooks, 2069
Cameron, Maude Eileen, 1426
Cameron, Richard, 623
Cameron, Theodore, 3382
Camil, Scott, 1249
Camilla, Frank, 606, 758
Caminada, Jerome, 2416
Cammerata, Frank, 3392
Cammillieri, John, 3380
Cammisano, William, 589, 3395
Camomile, James, 1884
Camorra, The, 272, 392-394, 589-591, 2080, 2217
Camp Claxton, 3344
Camp, Elizabeth Annie, 591
Camp, Eugene J., 591, 3426
Camp, Martha, 2403
Camp, Reese (U.S. d.1893), 3343
Camp, Reese (U.S. d.1898), 3350

Campagna, Louis "Little New York", 15, 42,
  591, 611-612, 617, 866, 1306, 3381, 3382
Campana, Giampietro, 591
Campanella, Tommaso, 591-592
Campanello, Frank, 3402
Campbell, Alex, 3340
Campbell, Alexander, 1775
Campbell, Archibald, 1083
Campbell, Bertram, 592, 2928
Campbell, Betty 147
Campbell, Billy, 1997
Campbell, Calif., Post Office Burglary, 592
Campbell, Caryn, 538, 540
Campbell, Cecil, 592
Campbell, Charles, 3456
Campbell, Charles E. (Can. pr.1950s), 518
Campbell, Colin, 592-593, 2853
Campbell, Daniel, 1172
Campbell, Don, 593
Campbell, Edward (U.S., pr.1840) 319
Campbell, Edward Francis (Brit., pr.1950),
  486
Campbell, Gary Lee, 593
Campbell, Harry, 238, 1764, 3326, 3460
Campbell, Henry Colin, 592-593
Campbell, Ian James, 2796
Campbell, J.E, 3545
Campbell, James (Brit. pr.1690), 1735, 2061,
  3449
Campbell, Jimmy Lee, 2343
Campbell, John (Brit. 1779-1861), 593
Campbell, John (Scot. 1635-1716)), 593
Campbell, John (U.S. pr.1907), 3358
Campbell, John Archibald (U.S. 1811-89),
  593
Campbell, John Henry ((U.S. 1868-1928),
  593
Campbell, John Ross, 1475
Campbell, John W. (U.S. 1848-1918), 593,
  3423
Campbell, John Wilson (U.S. 1782-1833),
  593
Campbell, Joseph, 287
Campbell, Joseph, Jr., 2042
Campbell, Judith, 1121
Campbell, Kenneth, 3454
Campbell, Kevin, 1515
Campbell, Larry, 286
Campbell, Marcus B., 654
Campbell, Marie, 1110
Campbell, Melville, 593
Campbell, Mungo, 2853
Campbell, Nancy, 3327
Campbell, Patrick (U.S. pr.1930) 501
Campbell, Patrick K., 2835
Campbell, Pauline, 2218
Campbell, Peter, 593
Campbell, Richard, 733
Campbell, Sarah, 3010
Campbell, Sonny, 2785
Campbell, Tom, 2205
Campbell, W.E., 2744
Campbell, William (U.S., pr. 1878), 366,
  2149, 3353, 3555
Campbell, William (U.S. pr.1950s), 1119
Campbell, William (U.S. pr.1950s), 2566
Campbell, William Joseph, (U.S. b.1905),
  594, 1110
Campbell, Willy, 3354
Campden, Viscountess of Gloucestershire,
  2448
Campden Wonder, The, 594
Campell, Jim, 3527
Camper, Franklin Joseph, 3511
Campi, Michel, 594
Campion, Albert 99
Campion, Edmund, 594, 2416
Campione, Frank, 394, 621, 3382
Campisciano, Ignazio, 1287

Campise, Jasper, 1109, 2812
Campisi, Joseph, 3393
Campos Salles, Manuel Ferraz de, 594
Camp Pendleton Attack, 594
Camps, Francis, 891
Camps, F.E., 2512
Camps, Francis, 706, 1092
Campus, Giocanni, 3327
Camus, Albert, 1256
Canaan, Keith, 3451
Canadian Hungarian Freedom Fighters
  Federation, 3491
Canale, Salvatore, 3382
Canale, William Vincent, 916
Canalejas y Méndez, Jose, 594, 3243
Canales, Daniel, 72
Canalizo, Valentin, 594
Canal Street, 594, 3380, 3400
Canape, Richard, 3452
Canaris, Wilhelm Franz, 594-595
Canary, Martha Jane, 577
Canary Murder Case, The, 595
Canazzi, Robert, 595
Canby, Edward Richard Sprigg, 595, 619
Cancel, Linda Louise, 595
Candaules 1411
Candelaria, Jose, 3557
Candelaria, Nev., 595
Candidus, 2153
Candra Gupta II, 595
Canfield, Julia, 596
Canfield, Richard Albert, 595-598, 1432,
  1723, 3402, 3408
Canfield, William, 595
Cangiano, Cosmo, 3402
Cangro, Joseph, 2535
Canham, John, 361
Canida, Innocencio, 3256
Canipe, Guy, 1823
Cann, William, 3500
Cannaday, John Eli, 598
Cannarozzo, Steven, 3380
Cannary, Martha Jane, 577
Cannella, John M., 15, 2121, 2671
Cannicott, William, 598-599
Cannidy, Lola, 2293
Canning, Elizabeth, 599
Canning, George, 599, 2688, 2854
Canning, Gertrude, 599
Canning, Joseph, 362, 600
Cannino, Giuseppe, 600
Cannon, Anne, 1598, 1600
Cannon, Dan, 1547
Cannon, Elizabeth, 2307
Cannon, Esther Marie, 2102
Cannon, Frank, 2026
Cannon, George Quayle, 600
Cannon, Howard W., 1005, 1323, 1980,
  2907, 3165, 3387
Cannon, Jack, 1746
Cannon, James, Jr., 600
Cannon, John, 2307
Cannon, Joseph F., Jr., 463
Cannon, Joseph J., 3454
Cannon, Randy, 3453
Canon, W.O., 3060
Canovas del Castillo, Antonio, 600
Cant, George, 600
Cantalupo, Joseph, 3402
Cantazaro, Robert, 1897
Cantellops, Nelson, 1250, 3402
Cantelupe, Walter de, 600
Canter, Jack, 600
Canterbury, Thomas, 1397, 3303
Cantero, David, 601
Cantero, Jonathan Eric, 601
Cantero, Patricia, 601
Canton, Frank H. (U.S. pr.1880s), 1734,
  2555

Canton, Frank M. (U.S. pr.1880s), 187-189,
  601-602, 675, 1038, 3545, 3555
Cantoni, Aldo, 3246
Cantor, Louis, 602
Cantor, William, 3341
Cantrell Cleaners, 3229
Cantu, Domingo, 3455
Cantu, Ruben, 3455
Canty, Troy, 1329
Canute (Denmark pr.1017), 1052, 1109,
  3237
Canute (Brit. d.1035), 2854
Canute II, 3237
Canute IV, (Den. c.1043-86) 602, 3237
Canute V, (Den. d.1157) 602, 3237
Canute VI, (Den. 1163-1202) 3024
Canute the Great (Den. 995-1035) 1052
Canute Lavard, (Den. 1094-1131) 602, 3237
Cao Thi Nguiet, 1939
Capasso, Carl A., 602-603, 2271
Capasso, Nancy, 2272
Capasso, Vincenzo, 2573
Capdeville, Jean, 534, 3398
Capeau, Louise, 45
Capehart, Gregory, 3449
Capehart, Tom, 3555
Capel, Arthur, 603
Capelle, Marie Fortunée, 1871
Capello, Bianca, 603
Capet, Hugh, 20
Capetillo, Alonso, 3246
Cape Town Race Riots, 3376
Capezio, Anthony, 3382
Capise, Jasper, 3382
Caplan, Alan, 1513
Caplan, David, 2064
Capocci, Giuseppe, 2574
Capon, Paul, 2729
Capone, Alphonse "Al", 16, 18, 31, 42, 43,
  50, 52, 54, 70, 71, 106, 110, 111,
  128-130, 132, 178, 179, 183, 184, 211,
  225, 316, 342, 345, 371, 411, 413, 427,
  435, 501, 503, 525, 528, 546, 551, 582,
  591, 603-617, 618, 630, 634, 634, 655,
  866, 882, 933, 959, 1002, 1018,
  1026-1028, 1065, 1098, 1105, 1123, 1124,
  1174, 1198, 1226, 1243, 1270, 1292-1294,
  1296, 1298, 1305, 1397, 1410, 1480, 1492,
  1511, 1584, 1613-1614, 1641, 1644, 1663,
  1664, 1735, 1758, 1775, 1788, 1793, 1820,
  1847, 1895, 1901, 1926, 1976, 1979, 2002,
  2004, 2006, 2014, 2015, 2037, 2043-2044,
  2070-2071, 2085, 2102, 2114-2115, 2125,
  2183, 2213-2215, 2230, 2254-2255, 2260,
  2269, 2301, 2307, 2339-2340, 2351, 2354-
  2355, 2466, 2476, 2503, 2505, 2513, 2529,
  2564, 2567, 2571, 2573, 2657, 2659, 2660,
  2662, 2673, 2705, 2720, 2739, 2747, 2757,
  2780, 2831, 2852, 2891, 2896, 2914, 2916,
  2937, 2970, 2972, 2974, 2976, 3015, 3016,
  3028, 3119, 3120, 3121, 3139, 3140, 3148,
  3171, 3176, 3202, 3203, 3204, 3223, 3226,
  3228, 3245, 3248, 3263, 3326, 3381-3391,
  3395-3397, 3404, 3412, 3414
Capone, Ermino John, 3382
Capone, Frank, 613, 614, 617-618, 714, 3382
Capone, Louis, 1, 111, 112, 528, 2254-2255,
  2563, 3003, 3402, 3409
Capone, Matt, 575
Capone, May, 50
Capone, Ralph "Bottles", 105, 616, 618,
  1410, 3382
Caponi, Gabriel, 603
Caponi, Teresa, 603
Caponigro, Antonio, 3412, 3413
Caponsacchi, 618
Caponsacchi, Giuseppe Maria, 2584
Capote, Truman 6
Capotorto, James "Big Jim", 3299

651, 653, 1807, 1817, 1920, 3545, 3546,
3550, 3555, 3556
Cary, Steven, 3463
Casado, Angel Lugo, 3469
Casale, Michael, 3298
Casalini, Armando, 3245
Casalino, Mike, 3458
Casander, 648
Casanova, Carlos Eugenio Vides 73
Casanova, Eduardo, 648, 3331
Casanova, Giovanni Giacomo de Seingalt,
648
Casares, Jose Hilario, 648
Casas, Karen, 2860
Casas, Rail, 2860
Casas, Roxanne, 2860
Casasus, Antonio, 905
Casaubon, Meric, 2216
Casca, 570, 571
Cascioferro, Vito, 648-647, 2222, 3402, 3415
Case, Jerry Douglas, 3453
Case, William, 649
Case Book of Jimmy Lavender, The, 649
Case of Clyde Griffiths, The, 650
Case of the Solid Key, The, 650
Casebolt, Crawford, 649
Casella, Louis, 649
Casella, Martin "Motts", 2105
Casella, Peter, 3297, 3412
Casement, Roger, 397, 649-650, 1085, 2786,
2875
Caserio, Santo Geronimo, 632, 650, 732,
3242
Casey, Gerald E., 3471
Casey, James P., 780, 781, 2677, 3336
Casey, Joe (U.S. pr.1880s), 3556
Casey, John Edward, 650
Casey, John P., 3556
Casey, Joseph (U.S. d.1879), 650
Casey, Joseph E. (U.S. d.1973), 650, 3426
Casey, May, 1474
Casey, Michael, 1980
Casey, Robert, 1559, 3568
Casgrain, Philippe Baby, 650
Cash, Bailey, 650
Cash, Edward, 3344
Cash, James Bailey, 3326
Cash, James Bailey, Jr., 2023
Cash, Jonathan, 2149
Cash, Leland, 2830
Casharago, James, 3556
Cashel, Judi, 2864
Cashiere, Catherine, 650
Cashman, John (Brit. d.1817), 650
Cashman, John (U.S. pr.1970s), 1298
Casimir, Calipe, 331
Casimir-Périer, 632, 650-651
Casino Internacional, 3393
Caskey, Samuel Alan Victor, 3321, 3522
Casler, Abraham, 651
Casner, Ray "Tommy" 24
Cason, John, 701
Cass, Lewis, 651, 793
Cass, Mark R., 3455
Cassander, 910, 3233
Cassel, Ernest, 1009
Cassells, James Dale, 651, 1206, 2088, 2410,
2415
Casserley, Georgina May, 681
Casserley, Percy, 681
Cassese, Vincent, 3402, 3405
Cassibry, Fred James, 651
Cassidy, Albert 182
Cassidy, Butch, 176, 487, 647, 651-653, 704,
848, 1442, 1591, 1807, 1817, 1909, 1920,
1922, 1977-1979,, 2025, 2468, 2688, 3011,
3078, 3123, 3457, 3458, 3545, 3556, 3559,
3561-3564, 3567

Cassidy, Charles, 3398, 3399
Cassidy, David, 2989
Cassidy, Francis, 2583
Cassidy, Harold B., 968
Cassidy, James P., 2056
Cassidy, John F., 654
Cassidy, Mike, 647, 651
Cassidy, Raymond, 1028
Cassidy, William "Red", 936, 1099, 1624
Cassini, Dennis, 3081
Cassini, Samuel de, 654
Cassity, John H., 2433
Cassius, 144, 154, 190, 3234
Cassius, Avidius, 654, 3235
Cassius Longinus, 654
Casswell, Joshua David, 588, 654, 1505,
1991, 2544
Castagna, John F., 3379
Castaing, Edmé Samuel, 654
Castalas, Louis, 654-655
Castanedo Reyes, Rafael A., 3472
Castel, Oscar, 3329, 3497
Castellammarese War, 655, 1296, 3402,
3405, 3407-3411
Castellano, Paul, 136, 655, 908, 1251, 1259,
1351, 1889, 2670, 3402, 3403-3405,
3411, 3412
Castellano, Peter, 1259
Castellanos, Candelario, 1711
Castellito, Anthony, 2508
Castelnau, Peter of, 2452, 3237
Castiglione, Dante di, 3303
Castiglione, Guy, 1513
Castiglioni, Eros, 665, 666
Castile, King of, 2481
Castilla, Miguel Hidalgoy, 655
Castillano, Jose Demas, 1267
Castillo, Angela, 655
Castillo Armas, Carlos, 656, 3253
Castillo, Candido, 3556
Castillo, David Allen, 3455
Castillo Hernandez, Enrique, 3465
Castillo, Louis, 1265
Castillo, Manuel, 3556
Castillo Morales, Juan, 2213
Castillo, Ramón S., 655, 1828
Castillo, Richard, 655-656
Castle, Florence Thompson, 2340
Castle, Kit, 3545
Castle, Latham, 656
Castle, Mary Crittenden Scott, 688
Castlereagh (Robert Stewart), 460, 2854,
2929, 3304
Castleton, Kate, 1084
Castlin, Alfred, 2226
Castner, Ralph, 1183, 2180
Casto, William T., 3305
Castor, Marvin, 3451
Castrejon Diez, Jaime, 3491
Castro, Bernard, Jr., 656
Castro, Carlos, 3428
Castro Cruz, Miguel I., 3466
Castro, Edward, 3449
Castro, Fidel, 133, 282, 656, 755, 1120,
1306, 1397, 2122, 2983, 3041, 3394,
3397, 3464, 3504, 3514, 3530, 3532
Castro, Iñez de, 656, 896
Castro, John, 3453
Castro, Julie Ann, 656
Castro, Lorenzo Groztiza, 2663
Castro, Orlando, 3472
Castro, Rosendo G., 3251
Castronovo, Carlo, 3415
Castronovo, Francesco, 3415
Castronovo, Frank, 3402, 3408
Castucci, Richard, 755, 3379, 3394
Casula, Joseph, 423
Casuse, Larry Wayne, 656

Caswell, Alex, 2056
Catalano, Angelo "Julie", 2254
Catalano, Anthony Joseph, 976, 977
Catalano, Salvatore, 2473, 3402, 3407
Catalbi, Anthony, 1602
Cataldo, Anthony, 3379
Cataldo, Domenico, 231
Catalino, Julie, 3402
Catania, Joseph, 3402
Catena, Gerardo Jerry, 136, 1251
Catena, Gerardo Vito, 3394
Cater, Nathanial, 3167
Catesby, Robert (Brit. 1553-1605), 656,
1140, 1405
Catfish Kid, 3556
Cathala, Pierre, 3250
Cathars, 657
Cathcart, Earl of, 639
Cathcart, Vera, 638, 639
Cather, John, 657
Catherine I, 2166
Catherine II, 657, 1671
Catherine of Aragon (Brit. 1485-1536),
3181
Catherine of Alexandria, 657
Catherine of Braganza (Brit. 1638-1705)
3074
Catherine the Great (Rus. 1729-96), 379,
657, 1671, 2426, 2451-2452, 2492, 2511,
2774, 3240
Catherman, Robert, 2783
Cathey, J. Lee, 2719
Catiline, Lucius, 585, 666
Catlen, Bud, 3351
Catlos, Josef, 3538
Cato, 657
Cato Street Conspiracy, The, 658
Cato Street Conspirators, 2929
Cato, William, 3356
Catoe, Jarvis Theodore Roosevelt, 657-658
Caton, Daniel David, 1159
Catone, Anthony 1
Catron, Jim, 3556
Catron, John, 658
Catroni, Pepi, 3380
Cattanei, Vanozza dei, 658
Catterall, John Bernard, 1782
Cattle Annie McDougal, 3545, 3556, 3562
Cattran, Michael, 2337
Catuara, James, 3382
Catullus, 569
Caturla, Alejandro Garcia de, 3249
Cauble, Rex, 3301
Cauce, Cesar Vicente, 2795
Cauchon, Pierre, 1724
Cauchy, Eugène-François, 658
Caudle, Joan, 2127
Caudle, Rayford Maynard, 2795
Caudle, Theron Lamar, 1664, 3163
Caulfield, Frederick, 658-659
Caulfield, Henry A., 2834
Caulfield, Henry Stewart, 546
Caulfield, John J., 3099
Caulfield, Michael, 996
Caumont La Force, Antonin-Nompar de,
659
Caupolicán, 659, 3239
Causeret, 866
Cauty, Bill, 659
Cauvin, Louis, 659, 2176, 2177
Cavaignac, Jean Baptiste, 659-660
Cavalieri, Sam, 3402
Cavallaro, Charles, 2189, 3392
Cavallaro, Louis, 3382
Cavallot, Guy, 3522
Cavallotti, Felice Carlo Emmanuele, 660,
3305
Cavanaugh, James, 2210, 3011

Cavanaugh, Patrick, 3174, 3452
Cavataio, Dominic, 3393
Cavataio, Julian, 3393
Cavataio, Peter, 3393
Cavatajo, Michele, 3415
Cave, Alphonso, 660, 3333, 3449
Cave, Frank, 181
Cave, George, 660
Cavendish, Lady 2526
Cavendish, Frederick Charles, 660-662, 1662, 2134, 2465, 3242
Cavendish, John, 662
Cavendish, Thomas, 662
Caverly, John, 874
Caverly, John R., 712, 1938
Cavilli, Hugo, 290
Cawley, Brian, 662
Cawley, Donald F., 3425
Cawley, Frank, 3382
Caxias Alves de Lima y Silva, Luis Duque de, 107
Caylus, 916, 2151, 3303
Cayson, Doyle, 662, 3249
Cayson, Jesse, 662, 3249
Cazenave, Jean, 2282-2283
Ceawlin, 662
Cebelak, Anton, 976
Cebellos, Martin, 3397
Cecco III, 3238
Cecco d'Ascoli, 662
Cecconi, Patrick, 3041
Cecere, Daniel "Red", 3402, 3412
Cecil, Sir Robert (Brit. pr.1600s), 585, 1083, 1140, 1405
Cecil, William, 662, 2135
Cedarholm, Eugenia, 662-663
Cedeno, Pedro Livio, 3254
Cedillo, Saturnillo, 3249
Ceja, Jose, 3447
Celani, Frederick George, 370
Celestine I, 2419
Celestine III, 1655
Celestine, Willie, 3447
Celestius, 663
Celles, Henry, 2659
Cellini, Benvenuto, 663
Cellini, Dino, 755, 3393
Cello, John, 463
Cellules Communistes Combattantes, 3280, 3530
Cellura, Leo, 1949, 3393
Celso de Assis Figueiredo, 663
Celsus, Publius Juventius, 663
Cem, 663
Cenci, Beatrice, 663
Cenci, Francesco, 663
Centanni, Paul, 3283
Center, Richard, 3341
CENTO, 3266, 3267
Central Fidelity Bank, 3289
Central Gang, 236
Centralia, Wash., Riot, 663
Centry, Henry, 3340
Ceol, 662
Cepeda, Dolores, 357
Cepola, Bartolommeo, 663
Ceracchi, Giuseppe, 3240
Cerchi, Vieri dei, 663
Cerden Calixto, Enrique, 3516
Cerdini, André, 233
Cereno, Joseph, 3351
Cermak, Anton Joseph, 249, 618, 663-664, 1781, 2015, 2016, 2091, 2937, 3247, 3389
Cermiak, Helmut, 3464
Cermiakova, Hana, 3464
Cernak, Matus, 3253
Cerny, Dorothy, 492
Cerny, Wenzel, 664
Cero, Gangi, 664, 1255, 1256

Cerone, Frank, 664-665, 3382
Cerone, John Philip "Jackie the Lackie", 15, 525, 625, 664, 665, 1153, 1249, 1323, 1897, 1980, 2812, 3382, 3383
Cerrito, Joseph, 3414, 3415
Cerro, Luis Sanchez, 665, 2402
Cesar, Thane, 3396
Cesare Terranova, 1952
Cesario, Charles, 1654
Cesario, Kristal, 3156
Cesario, Nan, 665
Cesario, Salvatore, 3379
Cesario, Sam, 665
Cesaroni, Enrico, 665-666
Cethegus, Gaius Cornelius, 666
Cevdet Pasa, Ahmed, 666
Cezanne, Paul, 2390
Chabanel, Noël, 666
Chabannes, Antoine, 666
Chabas, Paul, 763
Chabert, Paul-Emile, 3254
Chabot, François, 666
Chabot, Saul, 666
Chabukiani, Vakhtang M., 2906
Chacha, Joseph, 3338
Chack, Paul, 666, 3538
Chaco, Icnacio, 3556
Chacón, Augustin, 154, 666-667, 2234, 3556
Chacon, Juan, 2998
Chaconas, John, 576
Chaddick, Mrs. Harry, 3332
Chadee, Edward, 2096
Chadwell, William "Happy Bill", 1700, 1702, 1704, 3212, 3556, 3563
Chadwick, Constance Cassandra, 667-669
Chadwick, Leroy, 667
Chadwick, Marshall, 3350
Chadwick, Nancy Ellen 97
Chadwick, William, 1134
Chaerea, Gaius Cassius, 581, 669
Chafee, Zechariah, 669
Chaffee, Jonathan, 3454
Chaffers, Alexander, 669
Chaffin, James D., 2764
Chafin, Ed, 475
Chaflin, Tennessee, 314
Chagall, Marc, 2098, 2847
Chagas, Joao, 3243
Chagra, Elizabeth, 1458
Chagra, Jamiel Alexander, 669-670, 1457
Chagra, Joseph Salim, 669, 1457
Chain, Ernst Boris, 670, 1181
Chairman, Alice Mary Heinrich, 670
Chai Swee Sang, 3253
Chait Singh, 670
Cha Ji-Chul, 711
Chaka, 670
Chakir, Hedi, 3252
Chakravarty, Chandra Kanta, 677, 1508, 1560
Chalcraft, J., 670, 692
Chalden, Jack H., 2549
Chalinder, Jean, 670
Chalker, Edward Poole, 670
Chalkley, Thomas, 670-671
Challe, Maurice-Prosper-Félix, 671
Challoner, William, 671
Chalmer, E. Lawrence Jr., 2390
Chalmers, George, 671, 1663
Chalmers, James, 671
Chalmers, Mackenzie Dalzell, 671
Chalon, Renier, 1201
Chaman, Joseph, 2408
Chamand, Jocelyne, 492
Chamberlain, Alice Lynne, 671-672
Chamberlain, Clyde, 1967
Chamberlain, Frank, 2060
Chamberlain, Frederick, 3346

Chamberlain, Henry Barrett, 696, 3382
Chamberlain, Houston Stewart, 1566
Chamberlain, Joseph 43
Chamberlain, Lindy, 671, 672
Chamberlain, Michael, 671, 672
Chamberlain, Neville, 1573
Chamberlain, R.R. St. C., 514
Chamberlain, Sir Robert, 672
Chamberlain, Samuel E., 3556
Chamberlain, Thora, 2060
Chamberlin, John F., 596
Chambers, Albert, 741
Chambers, Alick, 212
Chambers, Ann, 1182
Chambers, Annie Lou, 3366
Chambers, Arthur, 672, 1340, 2526
Chambers, Clifton, 674
Chambers, Ernest John, 672
Chambers, Gus, 531
Chambers, Henry, 3102
Chambers, Isaiah, 672-673
Chambers, James (U.S. d.1801), 3304, 3452
Chambers, Jerome, 2714
Chambers, Karl, 3453
Chambers, Kurt, 3343
Chambers, Leon, 673
Chambers, Lon, 122, 673, 1277
Chambers, Melissa, 674
Chambers, Morgan, 3360
Chambers, Robert, 673
Chambers, Robert K., 673-674
Chambers, Ronald, 3455
Chambers, Wayne, 1630
Chambers, Whittaker, 674, 1563
Chambers, William, 3351
Chamblers, Christopher, 3342
Chamblit, Rebekah, 674
Chambon, Louis, 2680
Chambre Ardente Affair, 674-675
Chamfort, Sébastien-Roch Nicolas, 675
Chamorro, Pedro, 3257, 3505
Chamoun, Camille, 3256
Champen, Roger 180
Champier, Symphorien, 654
Champion, Dudley, 675, 2748
Champion, Nathan D., 601, 602, 675, 1084, 1734, 1977, 1979, 2555, 2748, 2803, 3556
Champion, Steve, 3448
Champlain, Samuel de, 1047
Chanan Singh, 3247
Chance, John Henry, 675-676
Chancy, Harrison, 676
Chandler, Albert B., 913
Chandler, Charles R., 3256, 3480
Chandler, Douglas, 354, 676, 870, 1312
Chandler, Fayette, 3364
Chandler, Florence, 676
Chandler, Frederick, 881
Chandler, Hariette, 3205
Chandler, J.L., 3353
Chandler, James, 3449
Chandler, John, 3361
Chandler, Karen, 540
Chandler, Mark, 3451
Chandler, Maurice, 676
Chandler, Raymond Thornton, 676-677, 1438, 1565, 3296
Chandler, Samuel, 3346
Chandler, Stephen, 771
Chandler, Susan, 843
Chandler, William (U.S. d.1895), 3346
Chandler, William Eaton (U.S. d.1917), 677
Chandless, Odell, 254
Chandra, Ram, 677, 1560
Chaney, Anthony, 3447
Chaney, James, 457, 3368
Chaney, Lon, 2658
Chang Ching-Yao, 3247
Chang Chipu, 3496

Chang Duk Soo, 3252
Chang H. Hsie, 3090
Chang Han-Yen, 3249
Chang, Henry, 2139
Chang Hsi-Fu, 3251
Chang Hsiao-lin, 3249
Chang Hsien-chung, 677
Chang Hsueh-liang, 677-680, 696
Chang-Jen, Tjou, 678
Chang, John M., 711, 3253
Chang Ju-ch'eng, 3243
Chang Soo Lee, 678-679
Chang Taik Sang, 3251
Chang Tso-lin, 677-680, 1970, 3205, 3246,
    3264
Chang Wen-hsiang, 3241
Chang Yee Sing, 2179
Channel Islands Witchcraft, 680
Channell, Sir Arthur Moseley, 680
Channon, Paul, 2402
Chantrelle, Elizabeth, 680
Chantrelle, Eugène Marie, 680
Chao Anou, 680
Chao Chi, 680
Chao Huan, 680
Chao Kao, 680, 1970, 3233
Chao Nan, 680
Chao Phraya Chakki, 2894
Chapar, 1291
Chapel, Jean, 3253
Chapel, Martha, 680
Chapelle, Fernand Bonnier de la, 3250
Chapelle, William, 680
Chaperau, Albert Nathaniel, 680-681
Chaperau, Nathaniel, 1903
Chapin, Charles, 681
Chapin, Dwight L., 3100
Chapin, Harry Lorenzo, 1416
Chapin, Kenneth R., 681
Chaplin, Charles Spencer, 143, 144, 681,
    1309, 1310, 1661, 1849, 2202, 2904, 3093,
    3283
Chaplin, Edward, 2026
Chaplin, Edward Royal, 379, 681-682, 1642
Chaplin, J.P., 3020
Chaplin, Ralph, 1152
Chapman, Abraham, 3414
Chapman, Annie, 682, 1921
Chapman, Charles, 2984
Chapman, Christian, 3259, 3518
Chapman, Clyde R., 640
Chapman, George (Brit. pr.1903), 2, 3, 417,
    682-683, 1084, 1363, 1689
Chapman, George (U.S. pr.1893), 2723
Chapman, Gerald, 683-685, 3458, 3459
Chapman, H.J., 3557
Chapman, Henry, 685
Chapman, Huston, 366, 2149
Chapman, Jack, 1035
Chapman, James, 2088
Chapman, James A., 3263
Chapman, John T. (U.S. b.1832), 651, 685,
    884
Chapman, Joseph, 297
Chapman, Lucretia, 2187
Chapman, Mark David, 685-686
Chapman, William, (Brit. prom.1944) 2112
Chapman, William, (U.S. prom.1831) 2187
Chappell, George Shepard, 686
Chappell, Holly, 3398, 3399
Chappell, William, 3455
Chapple, William, 3006
Chappleau, Joseph Ernst, 686
Chapwan, Andrew, 3361
Charafeddine, Mohammad, 686
Charbeneau, Jaimi Dean, 3451
Charbonnet, J. Arthur, 1463
Chardin, Jean, 3292
Charee, Jacob, 498

Charette de la Contrie, Francois-Athanase,
    686
Charlemagne, 129, 1390, 2672, 3074
Charles I (Brit. pr.1600), 278, 279, 285,
    409, 466, 469, 473, 577, 680, 686, 727,
    767, 810, 828, 850, 880, 887, 1082,
    1158, 1330, 1348, 1381, 1465, 1517,
    1522, 1527, 1558, 1648, 1903, 1940,
    1972, 2530, 2575, 2090, 2130, 2203,
    2206, 2260, 2452, 2501,2510, 2659,
    2725, 2869, 3054, 3082, 3087, 3097,
    3126, 3131
Charles I of Spain, 229
Charles II (Brit., pr. 1600s), 206, 212, 280,
    410, 542, 603, 623, 686, 797, 801, 803,
    840, 1031, 1047, 1151, 1285, 1330,
    1348, 1411, 1517, 1597, 1649, 1716,
    1970, 2034, 2048, 2090, 2220, 2712,
    2735, 2891, 3074, 3170, 3457
Charles II (Sp., pr. 1680), 2122
Charles II, (Hung. d.1386), 3238-3240
Charles II the Bald, (Ger. pr.1840s),
    1066
Charles III (Fr. pr.1650s), 2150, 3324
Charles III (Brit.), 2448
Charles III (Spain pr.1759), 2815
Charles III, (Naples-Hung. d.1386), 686,
    1204, 1724, 3238
Charles III, Duke of Savoy (Switz.
    pr.1500s), 349
Charles IV (Hung.), 2759
Charles IV (Spain pr.1780s), 2121
Charles V (Fr. pr. 1380), 278, 413, 669,
    686-687, 870, 1099, 1153, 1362, 1398,
    1726, 1898, 2114, 2531
Charles V (Neth. pr. 1567) 2206
Charles V (Brit.), 2481
Charles V (Neth.), 3158, 3181
Charles VI (Fr.), 10, 156, 278, 346, 568,
    1726, 1898, 3238
Charles VII (Fr.), 2816, 3030
Charles VII (Swed. d.1167), 687, 740,
    1724, 1726, 3237, 3238
Charles VIII (Fr. 1470-98) 762, 2732, 3090
Charles VIII (Swed. c.1408-70) 2850
Charles IX (Italy pr.1400s), 3303
Charles IX (Fr. 1550-74), 687, 745, 746,
    1517, 1726
Charles X, 348, 454, 877, 1193
Charles XI, 2216
Charles XII (Swed. d.1718), 1349, 2419,
    2469, 3240
Charles, 3148
Charles of Anjou, 1517
Charles of Prussia, 2737
Charles the Bad, 2117
Charles the Bold, 223
Charles the Good (Bruges d.1127), 3237
Charles, Arthur, 3255
Charles, Dauphin, 2117, 3238
Charles, Earl, 687
Charles, Ernest Bruce, 687
Charles, Eula, 3363
Charles, Flossie Mae, 687
Charles, Gomer, 1208
Charles, Henri, 687
Charles, Jane, 494
Charles, Landgrave, 2658
Charles, Noel, 3251
Charles, Prince 1348, 3273, 3275
Charles, Mrs. Tom 136
Charles, Weymouth,, 940
Charles, William, 2008
Charles-Louis, (Napoleon III), 293
Charles Louis of Baden, 1491
Charles Phillipe, 877
Charleston Slave Revolt, 3374
Charlestown Anti-Catholic Riots, 3373
Charlesworth, Violet, 687-688

Charley the Cripple, 3402, 3407, 3412
Charley, Bogus, 619
Charley, Dutch, 1741
Charlie, Bonnie Prince, 589, 1995
Charlie Chopoff Slayings, 688
Charlotte, 3175
Charlton, John B., 3545
Charlton, Paul, 688
Charlton, Porter, 688
Charlton Street Gang, 688, 3324, 3402,
    3410
Charmers, Robert, 3347
Charmoy, Jacques-Bonaventure Collet de,
    688
Charnock, Anne, 1195
Charnock, Robert, 688, 1195, 3240
Charpentier, August, 918
Charrette, Jean P., 3466
Charrier, Jacques Mecislas, 688
Charrière, Henri-Antoine, 932, 688-689
Charteris, Francis, 689
Charteris, Leslie, 2195
Chartists, The, 689, 736
Chartrand, Richard, 689, 3265
Chase, Charles, 689
Chase, Clinton, 3196
Chase, Earl, 3363
Chase, Edith Irene, 1884
Chase, Fletcher, 1304
Chase, Fred, 2918
Chase, Harrie, 689
Chase, John Glenn, 3160
Chase, John Paul, 52, 689-690, 2302, 2304
Chase, Matthew, 3359
Chase, Richard Trenton, 690
Chase, Salmon Portland, 690, 1955, 1965,
    2870
Chase, Samuel, 690
Chase, V., 3241
Chasles, Michel, 2002
Chassot, René, 729
Chasteen, Terry Lee, 1748, 3332
Chastelard, Pierre de Boscosel de, 690
Chasteuil, François Galaup de, 674
Chateaubriant, Françoise de, 690, 927
Châteauneuf (Fr. pr. 1500s), 690, 3303
Châteauneuf, Alphonse (Fr. pr.1885), 2166
Château Roussillon, Raymond of, 568
Châteigneraie, de la, 3303
Châtel, Jean, 690
Chatelard, Du 1030-1031
Chater, Daniel, 1827, 2897
Chatfield, Andrew Gould, 690
Chatfield, Virginia, 2150
Chatham, Linwood, 1732
Chatterton, Thomas, 690, 2098
Chattopadhya, 1301
Chaucer, Geoffrey, 690-691, 3324
Chaumette, Pierre-Gaspard, 691
Chaumont, De, 3303
Chauncey, Dr. Henry, 691
Chautemps, Camille, 2845
Chautemps, Pierre, 2407
Chauveau-Lagarde, Claude François, 691
Chauvet, Lewis, 3371
Chauvigny, de, 3304
Chaves, Juan, 3556
Chaves, Paz, 3556
Chavette, Eugène, 1353
Chavez, Antonio, 3556
Chavez, Bernardino, 3555
Chavez, Carlos, 3556
Chavez, Fernando, 3556
Chavez, Francisco, 3545
Chavez, Josefito, 3556
Chavez, Judy, 691
Chavez, Manuel, 3264
Chavez-Ortiz, Ricardo, 3470
Chavez, Patrick, Jr., 3148

Christensen, Karen, 3069
Christensen, Steven F., 1587
Christensen, Ward, 3329
Christensen, William Dean, 702-703
Christenson, F.J., 3252
Christgen, Eric, 1476, 2571
Christi, Frank, 703
Christian (1599-1626), 703
Christian II, 703, 1051, 1406, 2990
Christian IV, 703, 2724
Christian V, 1386
Christian VII, 634, 703, 2871
Christian X, 1230
Christian, Almeric Leander, 703
Christian, Edward, 3360
Christian, Elizabeth Ann, 2910
Christian, Fletcher, 2269
Christian, Frank, 3414
Christian, George, 2910
Christian, Will "Black Jack" (U.S. d.1897), 703, 1012, 1037, 1498, 1545, 3545, 3547, 3553, 3556, 3558, 3560, 3564, 3568
Christian, William (Brit. 1608-63), 703
Christiana Affair, 703-704, 3373
Christiansen, Carl C., 967
Christiansen, Leonard, 1908
Christianson, Willard Erastus, 651, 704, 3545, 3556
Christie, 3305
Christie, Agatha, 704-705, 1259, 1995, 2460
Christie, Archibald, 704, 705
Christie, Avril, 705
Christie, Balm, 705
Christie, Ernest, 706
Christie, Ethel, 706
Christie, Hank, 705
Christie, Harold, 911
Christie, Isham Thomas, 459, 705
Christie, John Reginald Halliday, 397, 705-708
Christie, Ned, 708, 1654, 3545, 3556
Christie, Sammy, 705
Christie-Scott Duel, 708
Christina (1626-89), 709, 2200, 3239
Christison, Robert, 709
Christman, Earl, 238, 239, 2286, 3459
Christman, Jacob, 2887
Christmas, Annie, 709
Christ Miracle Healing Center and Church, 709-710
Christner, K.O., 630
Christodolides, C.P., 2426
Christodulas, George, 2953
Christoff, Nicholas, 3300
Christofferson, C., 1404
Christofi, Stavros, 709
Christofi, Styllou, 709-710
Christoph, Johann, 1077
Christophe, Henri, 710, 926, 3240
Christopher, William, 3449
Christos, Eftihia, 710
Christov, Dmitri, 3538
Christy, Lawrence, 3453
Chryostomos, 3246
Chrysostom, John, 2927
Chu Wen, 714, 3236
Chua, Jose, 2750
Chua, Remimbas, 2750
Chuang, Marilyn, 1021
Chubb, Edith, 710
Chubin, Bahram, 1619, 3236
Chuck, Lee, 1192, 1921
Chuculate, Perry, 1819
Chudleigh, Elizabeth, 710-711, 804
Chudzinski, Rose, 1287
Chu Gain, 2012
Chu Hou-Chao, 711
Chu Hou-tsung, 711
Chukaku-Ha, 3530

Chu Kichol, 711
Chulalongkorn, 2729
Chun, 3260
Chun Doo Hwan, 1648, 2818, 3280, 3508
Chung, Harry C.C., 1137
Chung-Hee, Park, 711
Chungking Fire, 711
Chung Yi Miao, 711-712, 1642, 1816
Chun Kyung Hwan, 1648
Chun Mal Soon, 3181
Church, Bill, 2941
Church, Carl, 2505
Church, Harvey, 712
Church, John, 3111
Church, Maple, 712
Church, Richard J., 712-713
Churchill, Adelaide B., 438
Churchill, Charles, 1512
Churchill, Deborah, 713
Churchill, Frederick, 844
Churchill, Ida, 678
Churchill, James, 1476
Churchill, John, 713
Churchill, Lawrence, 678, 679
Churchill, May Vivienne, 713, 1396, 3282, 3457
Churchill, Robert, 156, 168, 247, 265, 460, 517, 599, 715, 865, 881, 1066, 1832, 1874, 2429, 2455, 2495, 3084, 3135, 3262
Churchill, Sarah, 2664, 2666, 2667
Churchill, Winston L., 713-714, 1009, 1527, 2226, 2268, 2758, 2834, 2875, 3252, 3425
Churchill-Coleman, George, 2064
Churmtyev, 1671
Chu Yuan-Chang, 3140
Chu Yü-chien, 692, 714, 3239
Chu Yu-cho, 3113
Chu Yü-lang, 714, 3239
Chu Yun-Fung, 3246
Chy Kong, 3255
Ciaculli Massacre, 3415, 3416
Ciallella, Maria, 360
Ciancaglini, Joseph, 3412
Ciancutti, Thomas A., 3413
Ciano, Edda Mussolini, 2266
Ciano, Galeazzo, 647, 1297
Ciappina, Ugo, 665, 666
Cibuku, Gazi, 714
Cicaria, R.P., 3245
Cicchini, Nicolas, 3380
Ciccio, Don, 1952
Ciccu, V., 3415
Cicero (Rom. pr. c. 48 AD), 2186, 2214
Cicero, Frank, 342, 1832
Cicero, Ill., 617, 714, 2102, 2142, 2190, 2198-2199, 3382, 3387
Cicero, Ill., Race Riot, 714-715
Cicero, Marcus, 714, 902, 1157, 1931, 2672, 2759, 2877, 3227,
Cicippio, Joseph, 1914
Cicotte, Eddie, 399
Cider Queen, 702
Cideville Case, 715
Cienski, Ludomir, 715, 1475, 1642
Cieplenski, Robert, 1816
Cieslik, Arthur J., 2711
Ciganovic, Milan, 1212
Cigrand, Emeline, 2244
Cihal, Charles, 1669
Cilley, Jonathan, 3305
Cimber, Tillius, 571
Cimerman, Adrian, 1140
Cimini, Anthony, 3393
Cimo, Tony, 3368
Cinchonero Popular Liberation Movement, 3525
Cincinnati Race Riot 1841, 715, 3373,

Cinderella, Dominic, 2044, 3382
Cinema Trust, 715-716
Cinna 134
Cinna, Cornelius, 571
Cinna, Helvius, 571
Cinna, Lucius, 570
Cino, Stephen, 2178
Cinotti, Raffaele, 3511
Cinq-Mars, Marquis de Henri Coffier de Ru'ze, 716
Cinquin, Francois, 3250
Cioppa, Elio, 716
Cipriani, Amilcare, 716, 2263
Cipriani, Franceschi, 2279
Circella, Nick, 575, 622
Circular Jack, 3403
Circus Gang, 607, 617, 716, 2073, 2972, 2974, 3382, 3387
Cirencester, Richard of, 351
Cirillo, Ciro, 2683, 3333, 3512
Cirillo, Gaetano, 2670
Cirillo, Louis, 716-717, 3298
Cirillo, Nicholas, 2670
Cirofici, "Dago" Frank, 307, 1931, 3403, 3410
Ciro Lai, 3508
Ciro Terranova, 2002
Cirotta, Ray, 1014
Cirrincione, Lela, 2127
Cirrongone, Joseph, 182
Cirvelo, Pedro Sanchez, 717
Cisneros, Antonio, 3246
Cisneros, Rosa Judith, 3259, 3516
Cisternino, Pasquale, 3392
Ciszewski, John, 1443
Citizen's Commission to Investigate the FBI, 3488, 3492
Citron, Anna, 178
Ciucci, Vincent, 717, 3229
Civella, Anthony, 717
Civella, Carl, 717
Civella, Nicholas, 219, 589, 717, 1322, 3166, 3395, 3396
Civello, James, 136
Civello, Joseph, 3393
Civiletti, Benjamin R., 2128
Civil Rights Violence, 3376
Clabourne, Scott, 3447
Claffey, Bill, 1874
Clafin, Dora, 3382
Claflin, Tennessee, 3184
Claiborne, Billy, 719, 1058, 1060, 1940
Claiborne, Harry E., 717
Claiborne, W.C., 1872
Claiborne, William "Billy the Kid" (U.S. d.1882), 717-718, 719
Claiborne, William C.C., 3304
Claiborne, William F., 3556, 3562
Claimant, Tichborne, 222, 456
Clair, Kenneth, 3448
Clair, Kittie, 1474
Clair, Pierre, 2817
Clam, Mercier du Paty de, 1023
Clan-na-Gael, 718, 828, 1148
Clanachan, Patrick, 718
Clancy, Frank, 454
Clancy, John, 3556
Clancy, John W., 2247
Clancy, Joseph, 3340
Clanton, Earl, 3447
Clanton, Ed Newt, 3460
Clanton, Finneas "Finn", 718, 719, 1056
Clanton, Joseph Isaac "Ike", 718, 719, 810, 1594, 2855, 3556
Clanton-McLowery Gang, 494, 718-720, 1450, 1593, 1594, 1643, 1822
Clanton, Newman H. "Old Man", 718, 1056, 1061, 1931, 2855, 3556

Clegg, Ellen, 3403
Cleitus, 733
Clem, Nancy E., 728-729
Clemenceau, Georges, 346, 1024, 3244
Clemens, Flavius, 996
Clement III, 1518
Clement V, 2197
Clement VI,, 271
Clement VII, 631, 663, 1153, 3181
Clement, A., 3250
Clément, Charles, 729
Clement, Jacques, 1518, 3239
Clement, James, 2857
Clement, Robert, 765-766, 3460
Clement, William, 3348
Clementis, Vladimir, 729
Clements, Amy Victoria Burnett, 730
Clements, Arch, 2519, 2521
Clements, Robert George, 730
Clements, Emanuel, Jr., 729, 3545, 3556
Clements, Emanuel, "Mannen" Sr., 729,
     1314, 1447-1449, 2181, 2584, 3556
Clements, George, 1111
Clements, Hillary, 2673, 3383
Clements, James, 1596, 3556
Clements, Joe 2181
Clements, John Gibson, 3556
Clements, Joseph, 3556
Clements, Kenneth W., 3448
Clements, Mark, 729-730, 3230
Clements, Rudolph, 3354
Clements, W.T., 3545
Clemm, Maria, 2479
Clemm, Virginia, 2479
Clemmons, Abel, 730
Clemmons, Eric, 3452
Clemons, Chandler, 3452
Clench, Martin, 730
Clenche, Andrew, 1465
Clendennin, W.S., 3242
Clenet, Émile, 455
Cleomenes I, 730
Cleon, 730, 1650
Cleopatra I, 2510
Cleopatra II, 2510
Cleopatra III, 2510
Cleopatra VII, 730, 2510, 3234
Cleopatra Selene, 730
Cleopatra Thea, 133, 168, 341, 570, 571, 574,
     730, 3233, 3234
Cleophon, 730
Clerc, Jean Pierre, 730
Clercq, Jacques du, 166
Clere, Henry, 2054
Clere, Judy, 2054
Clermont de Bussy-d'Amboise, Louis de,
     3239
Clermont-Tonnerre, Stanislas Marie
     Adélaide de, 730, 3240
Clesson, Neta, 3187
Clesson, Paul, Jr., 3187
Clesson, Paul, Sr., 3187
Cleveland, George, 3556
Cleveland, Grover, 98, 135, 228, 232, 321,
     348, 370, 411, 462, 488, 594, 624, 785,
     800, 895, 1240, 1458, 1515, 1613, 1678,
     1719, 1746,1876, 1884, 1982, 2021, 2027,
     2157, 2227, 2414, 2434, 2483, 2491, 2495,
     2511, 2802, 3074, 3131, 3138, 3374
Cleveland, Jack, 2477
Cleveland, Stephen Grover, 730-731
Cleveland Butcher Murders, 731
Cleveland May Day Riot, 731-732
Clevenger, Frank M., 2052
Clever, Charles P., 3545
Clever, Daniel, 732
Cleves, Anne of, 828
Cleves, William of, 3130
Clewes, Thomas, 1514

Clichy Uprising, 732
Click, Franklin, 732, 1974, 3327
Cliff, Henrietta, 3187
Cliffe, Adam, 611, 2973
Clifford, George, 3383, 3389, 3391
Clifford, John David, Jr., 732
Clifford, John de, (Brit. d.1461) 732
Clifford, Lord de, (Brit. pr.1920's) 849
Clifford, Mary, 519
Clifford, Nathan, 732
Clifford, Sarah, 1303
Clifford, William, 3358
Clift, Martha, 768
Clifton, Alice, 732
Clifton, Daniel "Dynamite Dick", 732-733,
     1003, 2732, 3556
Clifton, Madge, 1837
Clifton, W.C., 3355
Clinch, Tom, 733
Cline, Alfred Leonard, 733, 1076
Cline, Delora Krebs, 733
Cline, Herman, 2725
Cline, Royal C. 54
Clines, Hoyt, 3448
Clingman, Thomas L., 3305
Clinton, Bill, 2764
Clinton, Charles C., 1177
Clinton, Clifford, 787, 2736
Clinton, DeWitt, 733, 769, 1892, 3304
Clinton, George, 733, 1892
Clinton, Linton, 3364
Clinton Prison Riot, 181, 182, 733
Clisby, Willie, 3447
Clitherow, Margaret, 733
Clitus, 733
Clive, Robert, 395, 733, 2190
Clodianus, 996
Clodius, 1245, 2470, 2511
Clodius, Karl, 3538
Clodius, Publius, 570, 733, 3227
Clohessy, Michael J., 3425
Cloots, Jean-Baptiste du Val-de-Grace,
     733, 2394
Close, Henry Colin, 733
Close, J.B., 3118
Close, Louis, 3098
Close, Sylvestor C., 3205
Closset, Nicholas, 2239
Closter, Ronald, 2392
Clotilde, Marguérite Eléonore, 3030
Cloud, Richard 134
Clough, Joel, 733-734
Clough, Jonathan, 734
Clouser, John William, 3327, 3428, 3461
Clouthier, Manuel, 1524
Clover, Billie Lee, 734
Clover, Sam, 675
Clover, Vernon J., 772
Clovis, 701
Clovis Dominici, 995
Clowsen, Jane Maria, 2488
Cloyce, Sarah, 2669
Clozza, Albert, 3456
Clum, John P., 1058, 3556
Clute, Mary, 3041
Clutter, Bonnie, 1534, 1535
Clutter, Herbert, 1534, 1535
Clutter, William, 734
Cluverius, Thomas J., 734-735, 2459
Clyde, Charles, 3556
Clynes, John Robert, 3179
Coakley, Abe, 981, 1941, 2019
Coakley, Daniel, 2419
Coakley, J. Frank, 1787
Coakley, J. Fred, 5
Coal Heavers' Riot, 3371
Coal Oil Jimmie, 3556
Coalson, Doug, 3545
Coastes, Fred, 601, 675

Coates, Edward, 735
Coates, Gwendolyn, 2312
Coates, Lew, 3556
Coats, Linda Jean, 1365
Coax, Elmer, 3348
Cobb, Denniss, 3341
Cobb, Gail A., 735
Cobb, Howell, 735
Cobb, James, 3365
Cobb, John (Brit. pr.1500s), 270
Cobb, John R. (U.S. pr.1850s), 735
Cobb, Matt, 2211
Cobb, Samuel, 317
Cobb, Scott, 2026
Cobb, Seth, 3352
Cobb, Silas T., 1959
Cobb, Ty, 1885
Cobb, Wayne L., 1982
Cobbett, William, 735
Cobbin, William, 2034
Cobby, John, 1827
Cobham, Reginald, 424, 2533
Cobham, Eleanor, 424, 735, 1745
Coble, John, 1619, 1620
Cobos Moscoso, Jose Roberto, 1990
Cobras, 3383
Coburn, Camden, 2205
Coburn, George, 1632
Cocceius, Nerva, 735
Cocceji, Baron Samuel, 735
Cocchiaro, Carmelo, 3403
Cochise, 709, 735, 3324
Cochran, A.L., 1471
Cochran, Alexander, 1315
Cochran, Bob, 3190
Cochran, Christina, 1315
Cochran, Ernest Ford, 735
Cochran, Garland, 735
Cochran, James, 3447
Cochran, W. Bourke, 308
Cochran, W.S., 3136
Cochran, Willie Grady, 735-736, 3327
Cochrane, Charles, 689, 736
Cochrane, Harry 60
Cochrane, Henry S., 736-737, 1459, 3282
Cochrane, Thomas, 737
Cock, George, 737
Cock, Nicholas, 2430-2432
Cockburn, Alexander James, 353, 737,
     2062, 2400, 3071
Cockburn, Henry Thomas, 737, 2061
Cocke, Mary, 692
Cockerill, Tilton, 3556
Cocklain, Matthew, 737
Cockle, James, 737
Cocklin, John J., 2783
Cockling, James, 3347
Cocklyn, Thomas, 737, 1868
Cockran, William Bourke, 737
Cockrane, Kilso, 737
Cockrane, Thomas, 3556
Cockrell, James, 1452-1453
Cockrell, Lee, 737
Cockrell, Tom, 1452-1453, 2119
Cockrill, T., 3426
Cockrum, John, 3455
Coco, Ettore, 3403
Coco, Francesco, 488, 737-738, 2552
Cocozza, Joseph, 1134
Codarre, Edwin, 738
Codd, Michael J., 1069, 3425
Codding, William, 2176
Coddington, Herbert James, 738, 3334
Coddington, John, 3563
Codère, Georges, 738, 1193, 2673
Codgo, 284
Codlin, William, 738
Codog, Eustaquio, 1828
Codreanu, Cornelius Zelea, 738-739, 1030

Collier, John Payne, 749
Collier, Mimms, 3348
Collier, Robert, 2104, 3450
Collier, W.W., 3545
Collier, William, 2534
Collier, William Miller, 749
Colligan, Thomas, 3567
Collin, Frank, 749-750, 3271
Collings, Benjamin P., 750
Collings, Jack, 750
Collington, John, 750, 3227
Collingwood, Percy, 750-751
Collins, Addie Mae, 3264
Collins, Ben (U.S. d.1906), 751, 3350
Collins, Benjamin F. (U.S. pr.1928), 751
Collins, Bill, 126, 3544
Collins, Burkitt, 2041
Collins, C. Wesley, 2565
Collins, Clarence, 2724
Collins, Curly, 1424
Collins, Dapper Dan 3015
Collins, W. Maunsell, 753
Collins, Ed, 751
Collins, Ellen, 1679
Collins, Francis Dignan, 751
Collins, George, 3457, 3556, 3565
Collins, George D., 751
Collins, George Edward, Jr., 751, 3327
Collins, Henry, 3556
Collins, Isaac, 3363
Collins, J., 2447
Collins, J.C., 3362
Collins, James, 3343
Collins, James Thomas, 751-752, 1492
Collins, Jennie, 3363
Collins, Joel (U.S. d.1877), 126, 274, 275,
    884, 1997, 3557, 3562
Collins, John, 3545
Collins, John Baptist, 752
Collins, John M., 3424
Collins, John Norman, 752
Collins, Joseph, 1128
Collins, Kenneth, 3452
Collins, Lawrence (U.S. pr.1930s), 225
Collins, Lawrence Grey (U.S. pr.1970s),
    1331
Collins, Leonora, 2202
Collins, LeRoy, 1377
Collins, Marshall, III, 3470
Collins, Maude, 2399
Collins, Melvin, 752
Collins, Michael (Brit. pr.1922), 3172, 3245
Collins, Morgan A., 610, 2352, 2973, 3203,
    3383, 3424
Collins, Omester, 1967
Collins, Paralee, 3363
Collins, Richard, 231
Collins, Robert, 3344
Collins, Robert Frederick, 752
Collins, Robert J., 1736
Collins, Roger, 3450, 3451
Collins, Roger Lee, 1609, 3383
Collins, Roosevelt, 752-753
Collins, Sam, 1335
Collins, Shirley, 753
Collins, Thomas, 3363
Collins, Walter, 2345
Collins, Wilkie, 156, 1016, 1804, 2209
Collins, William, 752, 3346, 3556
Collinson, Amy, 1499
Collinson, William Robert, 753
Collinsworth, Willion, 753
Collison, Merle, 2842
Colliva, Domenico, 3303
Collot d'Herbois, Jean Marie, 753
Collyer, Arthur, 1596
Colman, Ronald, 2960
Colman, William T., 753-754
Cologne, Archbishop Ferdinand of, 754

Cologne Witch Trials, 754
Colom Argueta, Manuel, 3257
Colombo, Anthony, 3403
Colombo, Carlo, 3331
Colombo, Joseph A., Sr., 223, 427, 428,
    754-755, 1256, 1259, 1730, 2012, 2046,
    2087, 2689, 3402, 3403, 3406
Colombo, Louis J., 1988
Colombo, Marc, 755
Colon, Cristobal, 3261, 3281
Colonial Office Bombing, 755
Colontuono, Emile, 3403
Colony Sports Club, 755, 3395
Colorado State Prison Riot, 755
Colosimo, James "Big Jim", 31, 130, 176,
    394, 411, 604, 617, 755-759, 1098, 1105,
    2002, 2033, 2214, 2475, 2970, 3203,
    3382, 3383, 3385, 3388, 3390
Colosimo, Luigi, 755
Colosky, Morris Eugene, 2566, 3471
Colpitts, Frances, 1532
Colquhoun, Patrick MacChombaich de,
    759, 2921
Colquitt, Oscar Branch, 791
Colquitt, Symeon, 1282
Colquitt, Walter Terry, 759
Colson, Charles W., 575, 3081, 3100
Colson, David, 759
Colson, Forrest Ray, 759
Colson, Peter, 3154
Colston, Abithal, 3346
Colt, John Caldwell, 759-760, 2966, 3227
Colt, Samuel, 759, 760, 3227
Coltart, William, 2429
Colter, Velma, 1400
Coltman, Justice, 1582
Colton, George, 3424
Colton, Harold, 975, 3403
Colton, John, 2338
Colton, Walter, 3352
Columbia University Riots, 3376
Columbo, Frank, 760, 761
Columbo, Joseph, 3402
Columbo, Mary, 761
Columbo, Michael, 761
Columbo, Patricia, 760-761
Columbus, Christopher, 414, 3281
Colvert, Robert, 2840
Colville, James, 3556
Colvin, A.J., 1471
Colvin, Eugene, 3452
Colvin, Harvey Doolittle, 2032, 3383
Colvin, Ralph, 1755
Colvin, Russel, 436
Colwell, Jack, 1845
Colwell, Martin, 761
Colyer, Nathaniel, 1728
Comando da Libertacao Nacional, 3530
Comans, James, 806
Combat Zone, 3379
Combe, George, 2834
Combe, Michael, 761
Combes, Marc, 727
Combettes, Cécile, 427
Combs, Lee, 3249
Combs, Lewis, 3249
Comeans, William, 761
Comeaux, Adam, 3451
Comeaux, James, 3362
Comédie Humaine, 3049
Comer, Jack ("Spot"), 761-762, 1556, 3395
Comer, Robert, 3447
Comerford, James, 59
Comfort, Robert Anthony, 762, 3462
Comines, Philippe de, 762
Comings, Adeline T., 762
Comings, William Freeman, 762
Comiskey, Charles, 399
Comité Argentino de Lucha

Anti-Imperialista, 3267, 3493
Comito, Nicholas, 1718
Comitz, Lorenzo, 1516
Commanche Tony, 1701
Commando Boudia, 3530
Commandos Armados de Liberacion, 3530
Commission to Demilitarize Industry, 3492
Commito, Angelo, 762-763
Committee for Afro-Asian Solidarity, 3257
Committee for Socialist Revolutionary
    Unity, 3331
Committee of One Hundred, 3398
Commodus, 2448, 3235
Commodus, Lucius Aelius Aurelius, 763
Communards, 3242
Communist Armed Nuclei, 3514, 3530
Communist Front for Counter-Power,
    3230, 3277, 3524, 3530
Communist Groups for Proletarian
    Internationalism, 3275, 3518, 3530
Communist Sedition Trial, 763
Comnenus, Isaac, I, 2176
Comodeca, Frank, 2456
Comodeca, Joseph, 2456
Compaoré, Blaise, 3261
Comparini, Pietro, 1208
Comparini, Violante, 1208
Compton, Betty, 1791, 3076, 3077
Compton, Louis, 474
Compton, W.W., 1054
Compulsion, 763
Computer Liquidation and Hijack
    Committee, 3271
Computeristics, Inc., 3289
Comso, James, 3339
Comstock, Anthony, 314, 763, 1551, 2570,
    2677, 2765, 3184
Comstock, Nehemiah, 1478
Comus, 2231
Comyn, John, 763, 3238
Comyn, Peter, 763, 3227
Conaboy, Richard Paul, 763
Conaway, Asbury Bateman, 763
Concannon, Jack, 763-764
Concha, Perez, 3333, 3509
Conceicao, Raimundo Alves da, 3474
Condon, Charles M., 2768
Condon, John F., 1480, 2699
Condon, John, 3383, 3388
Condon, Kate, 2711
Condon, Lottie, 1389
Condon, William, 766
Condorcet, Marquis de, 764
Condout, Alex, 3349
Cone, Fred P., 662
Cone, Gary, 3454
Cone, Patrick, 1517
Coneys, Theodore Edward, 764
Confalonieri, Federico, 764
Confederate Underground, 3264
Confessions of Artemus Quibble, The, 764
Confessore, Alfonse, 764
Conforte, Joseph, 3396
Conforti, John, 717
Conforti, Marie, 966, 967
Congden, Robert, 764-765
Congdon, Elisabeth, 579
Congdon, Thomas, 579
Conger, Edward, 765
Conger, Everton Judson, 765, 782, 1960
Conine, Phyllis, 732, 1974
Conkle, Ellen, 1187
Conklin, A.M., 3553, 3554
Conklin, Charles, 3545
Conklin, Fay, 2024
Conklin, Robert, 3450
Conkling, Alfred, 765
Conkling, Roscoe, 765, 1271
Conley, Dick, 3337

Conley, Ed, 3545
Conley, Frank, 846
Conley, Harold, 2258
Conley, Jim, 553, 1218-1220, 1222-1224
Conley, Mary, 3364
Conley, Sam, 3364
Conley, Stanley, 2395
Conley's Patch, 3383
Conlin, Charles William, 765
Conlisk, James B., Jr., 765, 1443, 3424
Conlisk, James B., Sr., 765
Conlon, Frank, 3383
Conlon, George, 1149
Conlon, L. (U.S. pr.1935), 2704
Conlon, Leo (U.S. c.1915-45), 3028
Conlon, Loretta (U.S. pr.1932), 3209
Conlon, Luke, 1592
Conly, Henry, 3365
Conn, Jolyne Lou, 2566
Connally, John, 1796, 3143, 3161, 3255
Connaughton, Edward M., 1501
Conneally, Joyce, 1643
Connecticut Witches, 765
Connell, Ed, 3545
Connell, John A., 2394
Connell, Nancy, 2557
Connell, William (U.S. d.1895), 3346
Connell, William (U.S. d.1897), 3349
Connelly, Alice Mary, 3174
Connelly, Charles T., 765, 863, 3545
Connelly, Frank, 3383
Connelly, John Patrick, 848
Connelly, Joseph, 703
Connelly, Matthew J., 1664
Connelly, Patrick, 2190
Connelly, Thomas, 1028
Connelly, William C., 765-766
Connelly, William H., 3460
Conner, Eugene "Bull", 1231
Conner, Julia, 2244
Conner, Kevin, 3451
Conner, Martin Sennett, 892
Conner, P., 3245
Connery, Sean, 807
Connick, Harry, 2889
Connington, J.J., 3010
Connolly, Al, 3383
Connolly, Ann, 2834
Connolly, "Baboon", 3403
Connolly, Charles, 1782
Connolly, Genevieve, 767
Connolly, John, 3275
Connolly, John B., 295
Connolly, Mary, 767
Connolly, Maurice E., 766, 2717
Connolly, Mick, 1421
Connolly, Patrick, 2022
Connolly, Peter, 2031
Connolly, Richard, 3007
Connolly, Robert, 767
Connolly, "Slops", 3147, 3403
Connolly, Thomas, 495
Connor, Al, 3556
Connor, Bill, 3556
Connor, Eugene, 3014
Connor, Fred, 3556
Connor, Jacqueline, 2444
Connor, John, 3556
Connor, John Wayne, 3450
Connor, Josephine, 2675
Connor, Ned, 320
Connor, Ronnie, 3447
Connor, Thomas, 2464
Connor, William, 2902
Connor, Willis, 3556
Connors, Babe, 766
Connors, Charles "Ice Wagon" (U.S. pr.1933), 766, 3460
Connors, Chuck, 3403

Connors, David, 766
Connors, Dorsey, 3331
Connors, Felicity, 1770
Connors, Jimmy, 2491, 3025
Connors, Pete, 1322
Connors, William, 2761
Conole, Irene Marion, 2869
Conoley, Simeon, 2035
Conover, Daniel D., 2482
Conrad II 154
Conrad, "Curly", 2001
Conrad, Fritz, 766
Conrad, Joseph, 2221
Conrad, Paul, 1993
Conradi, Sandra, 2768
Conradin, "Conrad the Younger" 766, 3237
Conring, Herman, 767
Conritez, Loretto, 3339
Conroy, Ed J., 3425
Conroy, John, 767
Conroy, Patsy, 767, 981, 1286, 3402, 3404-3406, 3409, 3411, 3412
Conroy, Stanley, 493
Conroy, Teresa Miriam, 767
Conroy, Thomas, 767
Consalvo, Carmine, 3403
Consalvo, Frank, 3403
Considine, Robert, 713
Consolidated Edison, 3289
Conspiracy of London, The, 767
Constable, Jean Sylvia, 445
Constable, William, 767
Constans, 767, 1139
Constans I, 2087, 3235, 3236
Constans II Pogonatus, 767, 2087, 3236
Constant, Benjamin, 1868
Constant, Tiffin P., 1510
Constantine, (Ital. c.322), 1949, 2154, 2195
Constantine, (Rus. pr.1820s), 2186
Constantine, 3235-3237, 3240
Constantine I, 767, 3235
Constantine II, 1139, 3235
Constantine III, 767-768
Constantine III Heraclius, 3236
Constantine IV, 768
Constantine VI, 1663, 2926, 3236
Constantine VII, 768, 3236
Constantine VIII, 2328
Constantine IX Monomachus, 2176
Constantine the Great, 767, 825, 1139
Constantine, Yvette, 646
Constantine Asen, 768, 3237
Constantine Phaulkon, 3240
Constantine-Silvanus, 768
Constantius, 768
Constantius Chlorus, 976
Constantius II, 36, 1139, 1257, 1624, 3235
Constanza, Frank, 2230
Constanzo, Frank, 1111
Conte, Bertrand, 427
Content, Harry, 2686
Conterno, Dominic, 2118
Conti, Samuel, 1513
Continental Revolutionary Army, 3501, 3503, 3530
Continental Trailways, 3321
Contopoulos, Christos, 3251
Contorno, Salvatore, 3415
Contreras Brothers, 2721, 2722
Contreras, Fernando de, 898
Contreras, Francisco Orlando, 72
Contreras, Juan, 2721, 2722, 3398, 3400
Contreras, Manuel, 1942
Contreras, Rafe, 2721, 2722
Contreras Castro, Carlos Antonio, 1760
Contrie, François-Athanase Charette de la, 686

Contrino, Calogero, 1996
Conventionists, 3052
Converse, Frank, 1373, 3457
Convin, Morton, 1445
Conway, Albert, 1545
Conway, Godfrey, 768
Conway, John, 768, 2572, 3095, 3324
Conway, M.F., 3242
Conway, Michael 130
Conway, Michael J., 3095
Conway, Thomas, 569, 768, 3303
Conwell, Chic, 768
Cony, Avice, 692
Cony, Joan, 692
Conybeare, Frederick, 2774
Conyers, James, 768
Coo, Eva, 768
Coogler, Ovida "Cricket", 768-769
Cook, Annie 97
Cook, Anthony, 3455
Cook, Barry 123
Cook, Bascom, 3345
Cook, Bill, 3559, 3562, 3564
Cook, Carroll, 449, 3042
Cook, Charles, 769
Cook, Daniel Wayne, 3447
Cook, David, 2262, 3449
Cook, David J., 769
Cook, DeWitt Clinton, 769
Cook, Edgar, 3428
Cook, Ethel Marie Workman, 2719
Cook, Frederick A., 769, 803
Cook Gang, 1654
Cook, George, 3359
Cook, H.E., 461
Cook, Isaac, 3339
Cook, J., 3426
Cook, J.H., 204
Cook, James (Brit. 1811-32), 769-770
Cook, James (U.S. pr.1894), 1335
Cook, James S. (U.S. d.1906), 1038
Cook, Japhet, 770
Cook, Jesse B., 2251
Cook, Jim, 3557, 3559
Cook, John (Brit., pr.1692), 1465
Cook, John Clarence (U.S., pr.1968-70), 1601
Cook, John E., 513
Cook, John Parsons, 2400
Cook, Julian, Jr., 979
Cook, Kerry Max, 3455
Cook, Margaret, 1374
Cook, Peter, 770
Cook, Ralph G., 2149
Cook, Robert, 3453
Cook, Robert Lee, 903
Cook, Ronald, 899
Cook, Thalis T., 770, 1314, 3545, 3559
Cook, Thomas, 358
Cook, Tobe, 3342
Cook, William Edward, 770-771, 3327
Cook, William Tuttle, 218, 771-772, 1335, 1345, 3557
Cooke, Ann, 293
Cooke, C.G., 3545
Cooke, C.L., 1161
Cooke, Dan, 2782
Cooke, Elisha, 772
Cooke, Ernest, 741
Cooke, Jewey, 772
Cooke, Joseph Cottin, 3041
Cooke, Judith, 1119
Cooke, Mordecai Cubitt, 3293
Cooke, Thomas N., 1791
Cooks, Cornell, 3453
Cooks, J. Bernard, 1463
Cooks, Jesse Lee, 398, 3218
Cooks, Tony, 772
Cooks, Vincent, 3455

Davidson, William (U.S. pr.1982), 1596
Davies, "Parson", 3383
Davies, Alfred T., 312
Davies, Mrs. Elrich, 1419
Davies, Evan "Skip" (U.S. pr.1947), 373
Davies, Evan Thomas (Brit. d.1941), 881
Davies, Fox, 311
Davies, Frederick Stanley, 2711, 2712
Davies, Gerald, 881
Davies, Gwendoline Edwards, 880
Davies, Idris, 881
Davies, Jack, 2957
Davies, John (Brit. 1569-1626), 881
Davies, John (Brit. pr.1980s) 493
Davies, John Michael (Brit. 1933-,) 881-882
Davies, Louis Henry, 882
Davies, Marion, 151, 152, 1132
Davies, Moll, 801
Davies, O. Mytton, 2464
Davies, Richard, 882
Davies, Rodger P., 3257
Daviess, Samuel, 882
Davila-Jimeno, Raul, 2163
Davin, Guy, 882
Da Vinci, Leonardo Da, 3282
Davis, "Diamondfield" Jack, 1550
Davis, "Dinky", 3403
Davis, "Lucky", 3557
Davis, Alfred, 3344
Davis, Allen, 3449
Davis, Angela Yvonne, 882, 3492
Davis, Anthony, 3357
Davis, Arthur, 3359
Davis, Barton, 885
Davis, Benjamin Jefferson, Jr., 1525
Davis, Bette, 102, 583
Davis, Billy Wayne, 814
Davis, Bruce A., 882-883
Davis, Bud, 3353
Davis, Charles (U.S. d.1901), 3353
Davis, Charles (U.S. pr.1932), 2140
Davis, Charles (U.S. pr.1933), 952
Davis, Charles (U.S. pr.1980s), 3453
Davis, Charles E. (U.S. d.1920), 3366
Davis, Charlie (U.S. pr.1881), 2554
Davis, Charlie (U.S. pr.1933), 672
Davis, Chich, 3351
Davis, Chloe, 885
Davis, Clarence, 2889
Davis, Clifford, 3252
Davis, Curfew, 3450
Davis, Curtis, 3462
Davis, Dan, 3361
Davis, Danny, 380, 3333
Davis, Darnell, 3463
Davis, David, 883
Davis, Debbie Dudley, 2826
Davis, Delteena, 2985
Davis, Doc, 3342
Davis, Don M., 2671
Davis, E.J., 1514
Davis, E.K., 3546
Davis, Ed (U.S. pr.1933), 210, 3427
Davis, Edward (Aus. d.1841), 883
Davis, Edward (U.S. d.1964), 168
Davis, Edward (U.S. prom. 1688-92), 883
Davis, Edward Lee, 883
Davis, Edward M., 883, 3425
Davis, Eliza, 883
Davis, Eugene, 3453
Davis, Frank (U.S. d. 1908) 3359
Davis, Frank (death row) 3451
Davis, Gene, 1465
Davis, George (U.S. d.1892), 3341
Davis, George (U.S. pr.1870s), 3557
Davis, George (U.S. pr.1925), 853
Davis, George (U.S. pr.1939), 1750
Davis, George (U.S. pr.1980s), 3450

Davis, George Breckenridge (U.S. 1847-1914), 883
Davis, George James (Brit. d.1830), 883
Davis, Girvies, 3451
Davis, Gregory, 883, 3451, 3452
Davis, Harold, 1180
Davis, Harvey, 395, 396, 890, 3393
Davis, Henry (U.S. d.1890), 495, 508, 3338
Davis, Henry (U.S. d.1907), 3358
Davis, Henry (U.S. pr.1980s), 3449
Davis, Hog, 3557
Davis, Howard, 3363
Davis, Howell, 737, 883-884
Davis, I.J., 2009
Davis, J. Richard "Dixie" (U.S., pr.1930s), 1561
Davis, J.W., 3425
Davis, Jack (U.S. d.1898), 3349
Davis, Jack (U.S. pr.1870s), 274, 275, 685, 884, 3557
Davis, Jacob, 3343
Davis, James (U.S. d.1906), 3357
Davis, James (U.S. pr.1936), 493
Davis, James (U.S. pr.1969), 1443
Davis, James Carl Lee, 3455
Davis, James E. (U.S. pr.1930s), 2736, 3425
Davis, James Edgar "Two Gun" (U.S., pr.1927), 1534
Davis, James J. (U.S. pr.1930s), 884
Davis, James T. (U.S. pr.1986-87), 3426
Davis, Jeff, 1514
Davis, Jefferson, 331, 481, 865, 1876, 1954, 1963-1965, 2519, 2571, 3374
Davis, Jeffrey, 1131
Davis, Jim (U.S., d.1887), 104
Davis, Jim (U.S., pr.1887), 1424
Davis, Jimmy Wayne, 3447
Davis, John (Brit. d.1721), 2527
Davis, John, (U.S., b.1876), 884
Davis, John (U.S. d.1889), 3338
Davis, John (U.S. d.1902), 3354
Davis, John (U.S. pr.1920s-30s) 3398-3399
Davis, John A. (U.S., 1761-1847), 884
Davis, John Chandler Bancroft, 884
Davis, John Michael, 3450
Davis, John W. (U.S. 1870-71), 3424
Davis, John W. (U.S. b.1782), 884-885
Davis, John Warren (U.S. 1867-1945), 885, 3090
Davis, Jose, 3332
Davis, Joseph, 3359
Davis, Joseph L., 1787
Davis, Julius Richard, 885, 3403
Davis, Ken "Stinky", 885
Davis, Kenneth, 3447
Davis, King, 3361
Davis, Larry Ronald, 885
Davis, Lem, 2084
Davis, Levi, 3546
Davis, Lewis, 531, 532, 3555
Davis, Lois Ann, 1428, 3171
Davis, Lolita, 885
Davis, Louis, 2543
Davis, Lucky, 531, 532, 3557
Davis, Malcolm, 254
Davis, Mark (U.S. d.1907), 3358
Davis, Mark (U.S. pr.1980s), 3449
Davis, Mary, 1715
Davis, Mattie, 2968
Davis, Maude, 1787
Davis, Mendel J., 2546
Davis, Michael, 3447
Davis, Mildred, 1750
Davis, Mrs. J.C., 3353
Davis, Nelson Grant, 2889
Davis, Peter, 3361
Davis, Phillip, 3356
Davis, Ralph, 3452

Davis, Ralph Orin, 885
Davis, Randy, 2314
Davis, Raymond Charles, 3076
Davis, Rennie, 697, 698
Davis, Richard, 3343
Davis, Robert (U.S. d.1900) 3352
Davis, Robert (U.S. d.1906), 3357
Davis, Robert (U.S. pr.1981-83), 2048
Davis, Robert Earl (U.S. pr.1987), 1311
Davis, Rose Beck, 1288
Davis, S.F., 891
Davis, Sammy, Jr., 1829
Davis, Samuel, 1364
Davis, Sandra, 2236
Davis, Sarah Eliza, 329
Davis, Sol, 959
Davis, Stephen, 3357
Davis, Sterling Black "Cooter", Jr., 885, 1156
Davis, Sterling Black, 885, 1156
Davis, T.E., 473, 3555
Davis, T.O., 1033
Davis, Thomas Cullen, 885-886, 1498
Davis, Timothy, 3447
Davis, Tramell, 1086, 1199
Davis, Vincent, 886
Davis, Volney, 236, 238, 2286, 3459
Davis, W.E., 2920
Davis, Walker, 3355
Davis, Wallace B. (U.S. pr.1930s), 1913
Davis, Wallace, Jr. (U.S. 1952-,), 886
Davis, Walter, 2935
Davis, Warren, 1674
Davis, William (Brit. 1635-89), 886-887
Davis, William (Brit. pr.1744), 499
Davis, William (Brit. pr.1773), 2534
Davis, William (U.S. d.1901), 3353
Davis, William (U.S. d.1913), 3362
Davis, William E. (U.S. pr.1863), 2320
Davis, William L. (U.S. d.1971), 2719
Davis, William Prince, 3455
Davison, William, 887
Davitt, Michael, 887
Davria, Govind Narayen, 887
Davy, Gloria, 2822
Davys, John, 887
Dawani, 887
Dawda Kairaba Jawara, 3515
Dawes, Charles G., 3326
Dawes, Sophie, 1992
Dawi, Kamel 14
Dawkins, Iris, 887
Dawkins, Sam, 3471
Dawson, Ann, 1837
Dawson, Charles "Charley", 1339, 3559
Dawson, Charles (Brit. d.1916), 887
Dawson, Charles I. (U.S. 1881-1969), 887
Dawson, Daniel (Brit. d.c.1811), 887
Dawson, Daniel (U.S. d.1895), 3346
Dawson, David T., 3449, 3452
Dawson, Dee, 3359
Dawson, Donald L., 2552
Dawson, Francis Warrington, 2035
Dawson, Frank Albert, 3055
Dawson, Hen-y, 3452
Dawson, James "Jimmy", 887, 2979
Dawson, John, 887
Dawson, Kenny, 1339
Dawson, Leroy, 3118
Dawson, Lillian, 1131
Dawson, R.W., 3346
Dawson, Robert, 3353
Dawson, Sie, 887-888
Dawson, William L. 73
Dawud Mu'Min, 2250
Day, Alexander, 888
Day, Alfred, 888, 3557
Day, Alice, 3071
Day, Benjamin Henry, 1975

Day, Charles, 1000
Day, Christopher, 3448
Day, Daniel A., 3425
Day, Doris, 2110, 3209
Day, Edward Denny, 883
Day, Ethel, 624
Day, Gertie, 1155
Day, J.H., 3345
Day, Jack, 888
Day, James, 886
Day, James E. (U.S. pr.1936), 888, 1938
Day, John, 2964
Day, Luke, 2737
Day, Mary Anne, 509
Day, O.L., 2289
Day, P., 1978
Day, Raymond, 888
Day, Sylvester, 1112
Day, William L., 888
Day, William Rufus, 562, 888
Dayal, Har, 1301, 1446
Dayan, Moshe, 2021
Daybreak Boys, 888, 2681, 3403, 3406, 3407,
    3409-3411
Days, Glenco, 3356
Dayson, Curtis, 771, 3557
Dayton, Alston Gordon, 888
Dayton, John, 1730
Dayton, Jonathan, 555, 888-889
Daza, Hilarión, 889
Dazeley, Sarah, 889
Dazeley, William, 889
D'Azevado, Maria Luiza Jacobetty, 2562
Dazevedo, Frank, 445
Dazzele, Joseph, 3347
de Abreu e Silva, Antonio Carlos, 3333
Deacon Brodie; or, The Double Life, 889
Deacon, Thomas, 2979
Dead Man's Alley, 889, 3383, 3384
Dead Man's Tree, 889
Dead Rabbits Gang, 698, 889-890, 1025,
    1174, 3403, 3407
Dead Rabbits Riot, 889-890
Deadshots, The, 370, 3383
Deák, Ferenc 890
Deakin, Alfred, 890
de Almagro, Diego, 2527, 3238
de Almeida Garrett, Joao Baptista da Silva
    Leitao, 1276
Deal, Pony, 2584
Deal, Robert, 3031
DeAmato, James F., 3203, 3383
Deamen, Frederick, 3124
Dean-Siddel, Elizabeth, 892
Dean, Archibald, 233
Dean, Arthur, 3361
Dean, Charles, 2128
Dean, Cyrus B., 890
Dean, Dan, 890
Dean, Dayton, 396, 890-891, 3393
Dean, Delos, 948
Dean, Dickie, 1424
Dean, Dovie, 891
de Andrade, Gonzalo Freyere, 322
de Andrade, Guilllermo, 322
Deane-Tanner, Dennis, 2903, 2906
Deane-Tanner, William Cunningham, 2903
Deane, Doris 151
Deane, Mary, 3346
Deane, Mrs. Joshua, 448
Deane, Silas, 892
Dean, Frank, 298
Dean, Gavin, 3514
DeAngelis, Anthony "Tino", 892
De Angelo, Carlo, 3401
DeAngelo, Pietro, 892
Dean, Geoffrey 70
Dean, Harold, 2547
Dean, Henry Clay, 1700

Dean, James, 2840
Dean, John (U.S. pr.1879), 1175
Dean, John Gunther, 3258, 3510
Dean, John Wesley, 896, 3044, 3099, 3100
Dean, Julia, 3399
Dean, Lawrence Michael, 891
Dean, Lucinda, 768
Dean, Margie, 891, 3458
Dean, Robert, 703
Dean, Sarah Ruth, 891-892
Dean, Silas, 1551
de Antiquis, Alec, 1300, 3084, 3461
de Antonio, Emile, 3107
de Antrade, Leopoldo, 322
Dean, Warren, 3343
Dean, William, 2343
de Araluce, Juan Maria 141
Dearborn, Mich., Massacre, 892, 3375
de Arcos, Duque, 2135
Dearie, Raymond, 2107
Dearing, Christopher, 2504
Dearnley, Albert Edward, 892-893
Dear Old Gentlemen, The, 893
de Arriaga, Manual Jose 166
Dearth, Clarence W., 856
Deary, Welton, 645
Deason, Cecil, 2422
de Assis Figueiredo, Celso, 663
Death Angel, 3498
Death Corner, 893, 3383, 3390
Death in the Deep South, 893
Death, John, 2249
Death Walks in Eastrepps, 893
Deát, Marcel, 3249, 3250
Deaton, Jason P., 3449
Deaton, Walter, 3249
de Austria, Don Carlos, 627, 3239
de Avala, Don Juan Manuel 47
Deavall, Ralph, 3101
Deaver, Bascom Sine, 893
Deaver, Michael K., 893
de Avila Pedrarias, Pedro Arias, 1104
de Azevedo, Coutinho, 3246
de Baer, Philip, 1159
de Bailol, Edward, 1010
de Balboa, Vasco Núñez, 217, 1104, 2435,
    2348
de Baliol, John, 763
de Balsham, Inetta, 893
de Balzac, Honore, 3292
de Baquendano, Angel de Saavedra
    Ramirez, 2649
Debar, Ann O'Delia Diss, 893-894, 2672
de Bassville, Nicolas-Jean Hugou, 278,
    3240
de Beauchamp, Richard, 293
de Beauharnais, Alexandre Vicomte, 293
de Beauharnais, Hortense, 293
de Beaumont, Gustave, 2960
de Beaumont, Robert, 293
de Beaurepaire, Quesnay, 594
de Beauvallon, Rosamond, 894, 3305
de Beer, Petrus Cornelius, 894
Debeler, Shelby, 3452
de Belleville Katzenbach, Nicholas, 1769
De Benedictis, Joseph 30
de Bergerac, Savinien de Cyrano, 852,
    3303
de Bernardy, Sigoyer, 346
de Berry, Charles Ferdinand Duc, 348,
    454, 898
de Beruyère, Scipion du Roure 47
Debevoise, Dickinson Richards, 894
DeBiase, John, 3383
de Biencourt de Poutrincourt, Jean, 1047
Deblanc, David Wayne, 3455
de Blasi, Raffaele, 3522
de Bobadilla, Francisco, 414
de Bocarmé, Hippolyte, 414

DeBoer, Frank, 894
De Boe, William Thomas, 894
de Boisdeffre, R.C.F., 1023
de Boissieu, Alain, 902
de Bolea, Abarca, 1
DeBoni, Frank, 1063
de Bonneville, Nicolas, 431
De Bono, Emilio, 894, 2264, 2266
De Bono, Giardio, 2148
de Bordeaux, 1650
de Boscosel de Chastelard, Pierre, 690
de Bosola, Daniel, 870
de Bosroger, Esprit, 1994
Deboue, Thomas, 3451
de Bourbon-Condé, Louise-Bénédicte, 454
de Bourbon-Parme, Xavier, 2450
de Bourbon, Cesar, 454
de Bourbon, Charles Louis, 894-895
de Bourbon, Charles Ferdinand, 3240
de Bourbon, Duc, 877
de Bourbon, Duchess, 877
de Bourbon, Louis-Alexandre-Stanislas,
    1877
de Bourbon, Louis-Auguste, 454
de Bourbon, Louis, 2121
de Bourbon, Louis Joseph, 2656
de Bracton, Henry, 464
Debray, Regis, 3277, 3524
de Brigue, Jehenn, 2409
de Brinon, Fernand, 895
de Brinvilliers, Antoine, 491-492
de Brinvilliers, Marie, 37, 491, 551
de Brogile, Jean, 497
de Brogny, 497
de Brouckère, Suzanne 10
de Bruys, Pierre, 522
Debry, Jean, 3240
Debs, Eugene Victor, 731, 872, 876, 877,
    895-896, 1393, 2064, 2207, 2511
Debs, Kathleen, 896
de Burgh, Hubert, 544
de Bussey, William, 924
Debus, Sigurd, 3272, 3509, 3512
de Bussy-d'Amboise, Louis de Clermont,
    561, 3239
Debussy, Claude, 1994
de Buys, William, 474
de Cabestant, Guillaume, 568
de Cambacérès, Jean Jacques-Régis, 588
de Campos Salles, Manuel Ferraz, 594
de Cantelupe, Walter, 600
de Carillac, Madame, 877
de Caritat, Marie-Jean-Antoine-Nicolas,
    624
DeCarlo, Angelo "Gyp", 30, 104, 896, 3403,
    3412
Decarnelles, Paul, 896
Decarnelles, Suzanne, 896
de Carranza, Bartolomé, 636
de Carvalho, Elenil Avles, 480
de Cassini, Samuel, 654
de Castro, Countess Iñez, 896
de Castro, Inés, 656
Decatur-Barron Duel, 897-898
Decatur Incident, 3373
de Caturla, Alejandro Garcia, 3249
Decatur, Stephen, 896-897, 3305
de Caumont La Force, Antonin-Nompar,
    659
Decavalcante, Samuel Rizzo, 898, 3403,
    3407, 3409
de Caxias Alves de Lima y Silva, Luis
    Duque, 107
Decazes, Elie, 898
Decelle, Martin, 2194
December 29-ETA, 3332
Decembrist Plot, 898
de Champlain, Samuel, 1047
de Charmoy, Jacques-Bonaventure Collet,

de la Cueva, Alfonso, 843
de Lacy, Hugh (Brit. d.1186), 1870
de Lacy, Hugh (Brit. pr.1204), 799
de Lafayette,, 1875, 2115
De La Fontaine, Peter, 1193
de la Gasca, Pedro, 1282
Delagi, Michael N., 164
Delahanty, James, 2549
Delahanty, Thomas, 3258
De La Hoz, Licenciada M. 905
de la Huerta, Adolfo, 2356
Delahunty, James, 2223
Delaitre, Pierre-Joel, 905
De Lally, Thomas Arthur, 1875
de la Madrid Hurtado, Miguel, 792, 1524,
	1651
De Lamar Clayton, Henry, 728
Delamare, Eugene, 800
de la Mare, Gertrude, 905
de la Mare, Gertrude 905
Delamare, Louis, 905-906, 3259, 3516
de la Maza, Antonio, 2995, 3254
de la Maza, Ernesto, 3254
de la Maza, Octavio, 2995, 3253
de Lamballe, Marie-Thérèese-Louise, 1877,
	3240
de Lamballe, Prince 1877
de la Meurthe, Antoine Jacques Claude
	Joseph Boulay, 454
de Lamoriciere, Louis Christophe Léon
	Juchault, 1880
de Lamotte, Comptesse, 573, 906
de Lamotte, Etienne Saint-Faust, 920
de La Motte, Francis Henry, 2234
de la Motte Guyon, Jeanne-Marie, 1409
De Lancey, James, 906
de Lancre, Pierre, 273, 1883
Delaney, "Crooked Neck", 3206, 3399
Delaney, Daniel (Brit. pr.1911-13) 906
Delaney, Daniel (U.S. d.1865), 287
Delaney, Denis W., 906, 3163
Delaney, Dolores, 1764
Delaney, Joseph A., 1641
Delaney, Mike, 409
Delaney, Patrick, 660
Delaney, Robert Augustus, 906-907
Delaney, William E. "Mormon Bill", 380,
	867, 907, 1504, 3557, 3558
Delangle, Claude-Alphonse, 2751
Delano, Columbus, 907
DeLansy, Peter, 1926
de la Parra Urbaneja, Luis, 3258, 3514
de la Paz, Santiago Gonzalez, 3518
Delap, David, 3449
DelaPlace, Jose, 3250
de la Pole, Edmund, 2481
de la Pole, Michael 2932
De la Pommerais, Edmond, 907
de Lara, Enrique, 907
de la Reynie, Nicholas, 674, 924
De La Riviere, Bureau, 1898
de la Roca, Victoria, 3230, 3333, 3519
de la Rochefoucauld, Armand, 832
De La Roche, Harry, Jr., 907-908
de la Roche, René, 1363
de la Rosa, Jesse, 3447
de la Rouvillire, Michel, 3038
Delarue, James, 1582
de la Sel Korsatko, Herman Diez, 3333
de la Serna, Roberto Guevara, 3518
De La Torre, Lillian, 1339
de la Torre, Miguel, 1636
de la Torriente, C., 3247
de la Torriente, Jose, 3500
de la Tour d'Auvergne, Henri 2164
de la Tremouille, Adelaide Blanche, 266
de Laubardemont, Jean, 1362
de Launay, Bernard Rene Jordan, 1903
Delaunce, François, 1399

DeLaurentis, Frank, 2673, 3383
Delaurentis, Salvatore, 1654
De Léautaud, Marie, 1871
de Lauzun, Duc, 2206
de la Vega, Artura Lasso, 3246
Delaware, Sandra, 1288
Delay, Dallas Ray, 908
Del Bono, Frank, 3383
Delbos, Yvon, 908
Del Carlo, Eugene H., 848
del Castillo, Enrique Alvarez, 1147
de Leeuw, Huibrecht Jacob, 908
de Lenclos, Anne, 1929
de León Toral, José, 2356, 3246
DeLeonardis, Tony, 2427
DeLeon, Leoncio "Jello", 107, 1075
DeLeon, R., 3245
de Lerma, Duque, 579
de Lesseps, Charles Aimée, 1942
de Lesseps, Ferdinand Marie de, 1942,
	3074
Delfau, Denise, 3539
Delgado Chalbaud, Carlos, 908, 3252
Delgado, Humberto, 1258
Delgado, José Matias, 908
Delgado, Leonei Carias, 3275, 3517
Delgado, Manny, 3463
Delgado, Nicasio M. Cadahia, 3466
DelGado, Pete, 2737
Delgado Villegas, 3256
Del Gaudio, Nick, 590
DelGiorno, Thomas, 3412
Del Gracio, August "Little Augie", 3296
DelGrasio, August "Augie the Wop", 1726
Delhomme, Eugénie, 3023
de Lima y Silva, Luis Duque de Caxias
	Alves, 107
de Liniers, Santiago Antonio Maria, 1968
Delin, Richard C., 1234
Delk, Monty Allen, 3455
Dell'Osso, Tom, 2057
Dellacroce, Aniello, 655, 908, 1259, 1350,
	3394, 3403, 3409
Dellacroce, Armond, 3403
della Maggiore, Michelle, 2087
de Llano, Queipo, 1990
Dellarusso, Anthony, 3379
della Vigna,Pietro, 2465
Dell, Floyd, 1333
Dellinger, David, 698
Delling, M.G., 3546
DelliSanti, Richard, 910
Dell, John, 3360
DeLloyd, Salustio, 3246
Dell, Paul F., 432
Dellums, Ronald, 3207
Dell, William, 835
Dellwo, Karl-Heinz, 203, 2163, 3476
Delmas, Delphin, 2924
Delmatius, 3235
Delmonico, Fred, 1136
Delmont Montgomery, Bambina Maude,
	144, 146-148, 150, 151
Deloach, Tom, 3557
de Lobel, Paul, 1628
Deloncle, Eugène, 574
Deloney, Nina Lee, 3103
Delong, G.B., 3245
DeLong, Robert, 1230
Delong, Wayne, 3456
Delony, Lewis S., 908, 3546
De Lopez, Blanca A. Uriarte, 3298
DeLorean, John, 3301
De Lorean, John Zachary, 908-909
Delorme, Abbé J. Adelard, 909-910
Delorme, Marion, 910, 1929
Delorme, Raul, 909
de Lorraine, Charles, 1991
de Lorraine, François, 1991, 3239

de Lorraine Guise, Henri I, 687, 745, 1398-
	1399, 1991, 3239
de Lorraine, Louis II, 1991
de Los Santos, Ceferino, 2260
De Los Santos, George, 910
de Louvois, François Michel Le Tellier,
	3227
Del Petrarca, Robert, 910
del Pino Pacheo, Emilia, 552
del Riego y Nuñez, Rafael, 2581
del Rio, Dolores, 2266
del Rosario Murray, Esther, 2260
Delsanter, Anthony, 3392
Deltag, Joan, 144
Del Toro Cuevas, Emilio, 910
DeLuca, Frank (U.S. 1938-,) 760-761
Deluca, Frank (U.S. b.1898), 910
Deluca, Joseph, 910
Deluca, Mariano, 3414
DeLuca, Victor, 2574
de Lucerno, Alitea, 2002
De Lucia, Felice, 15
DeLucia, Felice, 2573-2574
DeLucia, William, 910
de Lucy, Richard, 293, 2007
Delude-Dix, Elizabeth, 2402
de Luna, Alvaro, 2012
DeLuna, Carl, 219, 717, 1323, 3395
de Luna, Carlos, 3447
de Luna, Countess, 567
de Lussatz, Gaetan, 620, 2831, 3393
DeLutro, Charles, 3403
Deluzy-Desportes, Henriette, 918
Delvalle, Eric Arturo, 2344
Del Vecchio, George, 3462
Delvecchio, George, 3451
Demades, 910
Demakos, Thomas A., 1942, 2026
de Malet, Claude François, 2096
Demandolx, Madeleine de, 45
DeMange, George Jean "Big Frenchy", 31,
	629, 1141, 2700, 2704, 3325
Demara, Ferdinand Waldo, Jr., 910-911
Demaree, Luther W., 759
Demaret, Jean, 3250
DeMaria, Judith Lynne, 849
DeMaria, Luciano, 665, 666
deMarigny, Alfred Marie de Fouguereaux,
	911
DeMarinis, Thomas J., 1918
Demaris, Ovid, 1228
DeMaro, Audrey, 2435
DeMaro, Michael, 2435
de Martino, Francesco, 3324
Demascio, Robert Edward, 911
de Masel, Madame, 911
DeMasi, Donna, 345
De Mau Mau Gang, 911-912
de Maupassant, Guy, 1454
DeMayo, Frank "Chee Chee", 2085
DeMayo, Thomas, 2752, 3396
Demba Diop, 3255
de Médici, Catharine, 631, 745, 864, 1398,
	2134
Demean, John, 3343
de Meath, Petronilla, 1866
de Medici, Ferdinand, 603
de Medici, Francesco, 603
de Medicis, Marie, 2122
de Melcy, Gérard, 2164
DeMelker, Clarence, 912
DeMelker, Daisy Louisa Cowle Sproat,
	912, 2941
DeMello, Debra Perry Greenlaw, 2309
de Mendoza, Abelardo, 665
de Mendoza de Eboli, Ana, 1066
de Mendoza, Don Garcia Hurtado, 659,
	3239
de Mendoza, Teresa Nunez, 3466

de Saint Pierre, Georges, 482, 483
DeSalvo, Albert Henry, 207, 921-923, 1646
DeSalvo, Michael, 2670
de Sanchez, L. Torres, 3248
Desanti, Mark, 3253
Desantis, Stephen, 3448
De Saulles, Bianca, 3026, 3027
De Saulles, Jack, 3027
Descamisados Peronistas Montoneros, 3495
Descamps, Édouard Eugène François, 923
Deschamps, Etienne, 923-924
Descharner, L.N., 3341
DeSciscio, Richard "Bocci", 2105
de Scotiney, Walter, 924
de Seingalt Casanova, Giovanni Giacomo,
648
de Seliverstoff, Michael, 2726
De Serval, Luis, 3248
Desfargues, Jean (U.S. d.c.1815), 1873, 3399
des Gachons, Peyrot, 928
Desgrandchamps, Charles, 535, 924
Desha, Isaac B., 924
Desha, Joseph, 3305
Deshayes, Catherine, 37, 674, 675, 924-925,
2206
DeShazor, Robin, 1356
Deshields, Kenneth, 3449
de Sillé, Gilles, 2531
De Silva, Charles Percival, 925
DeSimone, Frank, 1018, 1948, 3396, 3397
De Simone, John, 2127
DeSimone, Thomas, 547, 2009
DeSimone, Vincent, Jr., 645
de Siqueira Torres, Joaquim Antônio, 1880
de Sixt, Ducros, 594
Desjardens, Louvina, 1899
Deslauriers, Georges, 2170
Desmettre, Louis, 925
Desmettre, Pierre, 925
Desmond, Jeffrey Paul, 3483
Desmond, John, 881
Desmoulins, Camille, 278, 925, 1123, 1204,
3240
Desnoyers, Guy, 925-926
de Soto, Benito, 926
de Sotomayor, Alonso, 3303
Desouches, Thierry, 926
de Sousa, May, 798
de Souto, Jorge, 1258, 3321
Despard, Edward Marcus, 926, 1298, 1299,
3240
Despenser, Hugh 926
Despenser, Hugh le, 926, 3238
Despenser, Thomas, 926
de Sperati, Giovanni, 2828
de Sperati, Jean, 926
Des Pres, Terrence, 7
Dessalines, Jean-Jacques, 710, 926, 3240
Desslain, M., 3250
d'Estaing, Valéry Giscard, 497, 3272, 3512
de Stamir, Victor, 926
D'Estange, Chaix, 457
DeStefano, Mario Anthony, 926-927
DeStefano, Mike, 927
DeStefano, Rocco Nicholas, 1943, 3383
DeStefano, Sam, 283, 926, 927, 2829
De Stefano, Sam, 3380
Destree, Rose, 3125
d'Estrées, Gabrielle, 927
De Strobel, Pellegrino, 2118
de Sucre, Antonio José, 2875
de Suso, Andreas Gonzalez, 3258, 3512
de Tavarez, Minerva Mirabel, 3254
de Tejada, Sebastian Lerdo 1939
d'Étampes, Anne 927
d'Etaples, Jacques Lefevre 1922
DeTell, Hugh, 927
Deters, Bernard, 25
de Thouars, Catherine, 2530

de Thuin, Raul, 927-928
de Tingry, Madame, 674
Detlavs, Karlis, 928, 3539
de Toledo, Fernando Alvarez 107
de Toledo, Francisco, 3002, 3239
Detollenaere, Jean-Baptiste, 928, 3457
de Torquemada, Tomás, 1657, 2969
de Tourville, Henri, 928, 3228
DeTraux, Jean, 191
de Tristan, Jane, 2247
de Tristan, Marc, 2247, 3326
de Tristan, Marc, Jr., 2150, 2247
Detroit Brothel Riots, 3374
Detroit Child Murders, 928-929
Detroit Government Corruption Scandal,
929
Detroit Race Riot (1943), 929, 3376
Detroit Race Riot (1967), 929-930, 3376
Deubler, Josie, 155
Deubler, Peter, 155
Deuel, Joseph M., 2104
Deukmejian, George, 2770
Deupree, Jim, 930
de Uribe, Arboleda, 3253
Deurwaerder, Louis de, 899
Deutscher, Albert, 930, 3539
Deutsch, Julius, 988
Deutsch, William, 1934
Devadetta, 3232
de Valdivia, Pedro, 659
de Valdés, Juan, 631
de Valence, William, 924
de Valencia, Jerónimo, 3303
DeValkenaere, Albert, 340
de Valle, Richard, 1866
Devall, John, 2534
Devall, William, 3175
de Valois, Charles, 3029
de Valois, Marguerite, 687, 927
de Valverde, Vincent 173
Devaney, June Anne, 1388
Devann, Patrick, 930
de Varga, Pierre, 497
de Varigny, Henri, 3065
de Vaudreuil, Pierre Cavagnial de Rigaud,
3038-3039
Deveaux, Jean-Marie, 930
De Vecchi, Cesare Maria, 2264
de Vega, Lope, 870
de Veil, Thomas, 98, 459, 1156
Devens, Charles, 930
Deventer, Conrad Theodor von 930
Deveny, Eleanor, 3179
Deveraux, Walter 931
Devereaux, Jules, 3400
Devereaux, Walter, 3239
Devereaux, William, 1087
De Vere, Pearl, 930
de Vere, Robert, 2236, 2932, 3041
Devereux, Arthur, 1084, 2581
Devereux, Robert, 930-931, 2817
Devereux, Walter, 931
Devers, Frank, 1832
de Verteuil, F.J., 1409
Devert, Thomas, 3365
Dever, William Emmet, 608, 618, 714,
2070, 2352, 2937, 2972, 3347
Devery, William S. "Big Bill", 21, 302,
2018, 2413, 2876, 3403
de Viau, Thophile, 3044
Device, Alison, 1882
Device, Elizabeth, 1882
de Vidil, Alfred John, 931
de Vidil, Alfred Louis Pons, 931
Devier, Darrell, 3450
Devieux, Samuel, 3253
Devil's Acre, 3414
Devil's Island, 931-932
de Villemessant, Hippolyte-Auguste

Delaunay, 931
de Villiers, Etienne, 3035
de Villiers, H.C., 2032
De Villiers, Jacob, 931
de Villiers, James Arthur, 931
De Villiers, John Henry, 931
Devil Man, The, 931
Devine, James, 3337, 3557
Devine, John J., 1384
Devine, Johnny, 3414
Devine, Michael, 3274, 3378, 3516
Devine Securities Theft, 932
Devine, William J., 1136, 3425
Devinish, Fritz, 3403
De Vita, Antonio, 3514
Devitt, Edward James, 932
de Vlaera, Eamon, 245
Devlin, Edward Francis, 551
Devlin, Frank "Blubber", 936
Devlin, Henry, 348, 932
Devlin, John E., 3182
Devlin, Justice Sir Patrick Arthur, 26, 932,
1033, 1501
Devlin McAliskey, Bernadette, 3258
Devol, George, 932, 1741, 3399, 3400
DeVol, Larry, 209, 210, 236, 238, 239, 1763,
2286, 3459, 3460
Devorsetz, Irving, 2295
DeVoss, James T., 927
De Vries, John, 3295
Dev Sol, 3473, 3513, 3520, 3530
de W. Connaught, Peter, 805
de Wagner Wehrborn, Eloise Bosquet,
1251
Dewar, J.M., 563
Dewar, Leroy, 180
de Warville, Jacques-Pierre, 691
Dewberry, Emily, 1773
Dewerchin, Beruardo, 3524
De Wet, Christiaan Rudolph, 932, 3130
de Wet, F.P., 3035
Dewey, Al, 1534
Dewey, John, 2987
Dewey, Robert, 771
Dewey, Thomas Edmund, 112, 117, 184,
526, 528, 932-933, 976, 1140, 1297, 1346,
1561, 1854, 2004, 2112, 2254, 2467, 2687,
2689, 2702, 2734, 2928, 3006, 3120, 3146,
3166, 3187, 3407
Dewhurst, Lily, 3294
DeWinton, R.W.M., 3251
DeWit, Paul, 933
De Witt, Cornelius, 933-934, 3239
DeWitt, Jan, 3370
De Witt, John, 933-934, 3239
Dewitt, Mary, 883
Dewley, Ernest, 3354
De Wolf, Orrin, 934
Dewster, H., 1562
Dewster, Joseph, 1562
Dew, Walter, 820, 822, 824, 2879
Dexter, 3383
DeYoung, Robert, 2393
Dezman, Leona, 4
Dezman, Otto, 4
Dharmavamsa, 934
d'Herbois, Jean Marie Collot, 753
Dhiliyiánnis, Theódoros, 934, 3243
Dhingra, Madar Lal, 107
Dhlomo, Sicelo Godfrey, 934
Diagoras, 934
Dial-A-Porn Case, 934
Dial, J.I., 3557
Dial, Preston, 785
Diamant, Manos, 1077
Diamond, Alice, 935, 938
Diamond, Eddie, 2734
Diamond, Edward, 934, 936
Diamond, Frank, 2071, 3120, 3383

Diamond, Gladys, 846
Diamond, Henry, 1112
Diamond, Jack "Legs", 111, 526, 748, 794, 838, 934-938, 1099, 1124, 1295, 1546, 1624, 1650, 1894, 2004, 2072, 2085, 2700, 2734, 2917, 3282, 3295, 3403, 3404, 3405, 3406, 3409, 3458, 3459
Diamond, John (Brit. pr.1740s), 1827
Diamond, John, Sr. (U.S. pr.20th Cent.) 934
Diamond, May, 2425-2426
Diamond, Morris, 3403
Diamond, Patrick J. 34
Di Angelo, James, 3403
Di Angelo, Thomas, 3403
Diapoulas, Peter "Pete the Greek", 1256, 3403
Dias Bandaranaike, Solomon West Ridgeway, 3254
Dias Gomide, Aloysio, 3002, 3486
Diaz, Aldolfo, 938, 3246
Diaz, Alvin Ross, 1942
Diaz, Anacleto, 938
Diaz, Angel, 3449
Diaz Claro, Jose, 3466
Diaz de Solis, Juan, 938
Diaz de Vivar, Rodrigo, 938
Diaz, Hector Arturo 142
Diaz Herrera, Roberto, 2344
Diaz, Juan Tomas, 2995, 3254
Diaz, Modesto, 3254
Diaz, Porfirio, 636, 637, 792, 1269, 1282, 1844, 1940, 2074, 2078, 2355-2356, 3050
Diaz, Robert R., 938, 3448
Dibble, Gisela, 3221
Dibble, Ilka, 3221
Dibble, Theodore, 899
DiBella, Dominick, 3384
DiBella, Thomas, 3403, 3412
DiBenedetto, Dennis, 805
DiBenedetto, Ernest, 2835
DiBeneditto, Stephen J., 1609
DiBernardo, Robert, 3403
DiBiasio, John, 3403
Diblanc, Marguerite, 938-939
di Bracciano Orsini, Duca 18
di Brazza Savargon, Contessa, 231
Dibrell, John L., 3546
di Cagliostro, Count Alessandro, 572-574
DiCarlo, John, 3403
DiCarlo, Joseph J., 1949, 3380
DiCaro, Martha, 1875
DiCarpo, Frank, 1752
di Castiglione, Dante, 3303
Dice, Howard, 421
Diceto, Ralph of, 1172
Dicey, Albert Venn, 939
Dickason, Isaac Q., 3546
Dickens, Charles, 43, 408, 436, 476, 566, 636, 914, 939, 1052, 1173, 1644, 1972, 1980, 2105, 2106, 2433, 2965, 3056, 3070, 3109
Dickens, Henry Fielding, 566, 939
Dickenson, A.V., 3035
Dickens, William, 2986
Dickerson, Benjamin, 3362
Dickerson, Elinor, 423
Dickerson, Richard, 3356
Dick, Evelyn Maclean White, 939
Dickey, Douglas A., 3466
Dickey, Jacob, 2135
Dickey, Orange C., 939-940, 1297
Dick, Frank, 939
Dickinson, A.V., 1039
Dickinson, Charles Monroe (U.S. 1842-1924), 940
Dickinson, Charles (U.S. pr.1806), 1681, 3304
Dickinson, Howard Carter, 2708, 3460
Dickinson, John, 379
Dick, Jack, 939

Dick, Joe, 1000
Dick, John, 939
Dickman, John Alexander, 745, 940, 2000, 3458
Dickman, William, 3384
Dick, Robert Paine, 939
Dicks, Daniel, 3348
Dicks, Jeffrey, 3454
Dickson, "Dic", 3353
Dickson, Bennie, 1666, 3460
Dickson, Christopher, 940
Dickson, Clarence, 3425
Dickson, Noah, 3337
Dickstein, Samuel, 1854
DiCocco, Paul, Sr., 940-941
Di Cristina, Giuseppe, 941
DiCristina, Paul, 193
Di Cristina, Paul, 393, 941-942, 2084
Didato, Dominick, 526
Diderot, Denis, 942
Diderot, Pantophile, 942
Didier, Paul, 3252
Didius, Julianus, 942
Di Donne, Theodore, 423
Diecidue, Frank, 3394
Dieguez, Manuel, 3245
Diehl, Bill "Pony", 135, 136, 3557
Diel, John, 345
Diels, Rudolph, 2560
Diemont, Marius, 2525
Diener, George Edward, 942
Diener, Richie, 942
Dier, Richard A., 942
Diesbach, Niklaus von 942
Dies Committee Investigation, 942
Dies, Martin, 942
Diessl, Gustav, 2404
Diestel, Schuett, 2543
Dieter, Norman, 967
Diether, Herbert, Jr., 264
Dietl, Judy, 942
Dietl, Marilyn, 942
Dietrich, Joseph "Sepp", 942, 1531, 2097, 3251, 3539
Dietrich, Noah, 1665
Dietrich, Otto, 3539
Dietrich, Walter, 947, 950, 951, 1834, 3459
Dietrich, Wolfgang, 2543
Dietz, Hugo, 3250
Dietzler, George, 561
Diez, Jaime Castrejon, 3328
DiFede, Jean, 793
DiFede, Joseph, 793
Di Filippi, Joseph, 2542
di Flor, Roger, 1181
DiFonzo, Luigi Michael "Lou", 2512
DiFronzo, John "No Nose", 625, 942-943, 3382, 3384
Difuentes Anleu, Julio Cesar, 3514
Digby, Everard, 943, 1140
Digby, John, 2530
diGenova, Joseph, 264
Diggens, Buster, 1470
Digges, Dudley, 943
Diggs, Andrew, 3355
Diggs, Charles C., Jr., 943
Diggs, Frank, 3480
Diggs, Ira, 2128
DiGiacomo, Biagio, 3379, 3380
DiGilio, John, 3403
Di Giovanino, Peter, 3395
di Giovanni, 742
di Giovanni, Domenico, 994
di Giovanni, Eduardo, 3509
DiGiovanni, Joseph "Scarface", 393, 2085, 3395
DiGiovanni, Peter "Sugarhouse Pete", 393, 2085
Digital Equipment Corp., 3289

diGrazia, Robert J., 3424
DiGrigorio, Gasperino, 224, 3403, 3412
Dikko, Umaru, 943, 3334, 3527
Dikler, Mahmut, 3258, 3509
DiLeonardi, Joseph G., 1440, 3424
Dilion, Jerry, 3557
Dilke, Charles, 943
Dillard, E.H., 943
Dillard, George L., 461
Dillard, James, 3354
Dillard, Norman, 943
Dillard, Skip, 943
Dillard, Whit, 3350
Dillen, Bob, 943
Diller, J., 2545
Dilling, Elizabeth, 2137
Dillinger, Audrey, 944, 947, 948, 964, 972
Dillinger, Elizabeth, 948
Dillinger Gang, 52, 182, 239, 257, 260, 2056
Dillinger, John Herbert, 183, 211, 235, 250, 252, 260, 263, 338, 432, 466, 503, 551, 582, 817, 943-973, 1144, 1182, 1186, 1187, 1547, 1612, 1613, 1707, 1764-1766, 1834, 2056, 2103, 2154, 2302, 2454, 2513-2514, 2913, 3282, 3427, 3459, 3460
Dillinger, John Wilson, 944
Dillinger, Mollie, 944
Dillingham, Bill, 2018
Dillingham, Jack, 3357
Dillingham, Jesse, 3344
Dill, Jimmy, 3447
Dill, John, 2997
Dillman, Bradford, 763
Dillman, John, 2889
Dillon, J.F. (U.S. pr.1903), 457
Dillon, James (U.S. pr.1890s), 668
Dillon, John Blake, 1033
Dillon, Raymond F., 3425
Dillon, Robert S., 3021
Dillon, William, 973
Dillulio, Albert, 1759
Dill, Victor Robert Colquhoun, 1208
Dilma, "Commander", 3465
Dilma, Olga, 3465
DiLorenzo, Ross, 1899
Dilworth, Dwight, 973, 3458
DiMaggio, Joe, 2201
Dimahilig, Carlito, 2119
Dimaio, Frank, 2082
di Melikoff, Concordia, 3296
Dimenstein, Jean, 1282
Dimes, "Italian Albert", 761
Dimes, Albert, 3395
di Mino, Bartolomeo, 2552
Dimitriev, Radko, 980, 3244
Dimitrijevic, Dragutin, 75, 81, 84, 394, 973-974, 1210, 3243
Dimitroff, Alexander, 3244
Dimitrov, Georgi Mikhailovich, 974, 1498
Dimmick, Walter, 974-975
Dimmig, John, 457, 975
Dimmock, Emily Elizabeth, 2464, 3183
Dimock, Edward J., 2433
di Modrone, Luchino Visconti, 1839
Dimond, Anthony Joseph, 975
di Montelara, Luigi Rossi, 1952
Dimou, Sophia, 3523
Dimpna, 1051
Dimsdale, Thomas J., 975, 3050
Dinan, J., 3426
DiNapoli, Vincent, 975, 3404
di Nardi, Nicolletta, 975
Dindarte, Marie, 274
Dineen, Joseph F., 491
Dine, Harvey Van, 3457
Dines, Courtland S., 2906
Dingaan, 975, 2570, 3241
Dingbat Oberta, 3383, 3390
Ding Dong, 3404

Dingfelder, Johannes, 1568
Dingley, Charles, 3371
Diniso, Oupa Moses, 2736
Dinivan, Walter, 3163
Dinky Quan, 3391
Dinnan, James A., 975
Dinneen, Joseph F., 975-976
Dinos, Yiorgalli, 1692
Dinsdale, Peter, 1917
Dinsmore, Robert, 1012
d'Instruction, Juge, 1836
Di Nuccio, Carmela, 2202
Diocletian, 37, 976, 2007, 2118, 2153, 2437,
     2719, 3055
Diodotus II, 976, 3233
Diogenes, 976, 1874
Dioguardi, John, 526, 2582, 2849
Dio, Johnny, 526, 976, 1018, 2913, 3404
Dion, 976, 3233
Dionysius Cassius Longinus, 1987
Dionysius the Younger, 976
Diori, Hamani, 3255
D'Iorio, Ernest, 976
Dio, Tommy, 976, 3404
Diouri, Mustapha, 3253
DiPalermo, Charles, 3404
DiPalermo, Joseph, 976, 1974, 3404
DiPalermo, Pete, 1974
DiPasquale, Anthony Louis, 976-977
DiPasquale, Diego, 1252, 1253
DiPiazza, Salvatore, 3399
DiPietro, Robert A., 3379
Dipley, Walter, 1864
Dipo Negoro, Pangeran, 977
Dippolito, Charles, 3397
Dippolito, Joseph, 3397
Direct Action, 3275, 3278, 3279, 3517, 3518,
     3525, 3529, 3530
Directoria General de Inteligencia, 3530
Direly, William, 805
di Rienzi, Cola, 2582
Dirksen, Everett 73
Dirksen, Lawrence, 561
Dirks, Ray, 1331
DiRobbio, Emil, 645
Di Rocco, Ennio, 3524
DiRosa, Steve, 2700
Dirr, Raymond, 3250
Dirty Face Jack, 3404
di Santarosa, Santorre, 2679
Disco, David, 1424
Di Sema, 1905
DiSessa, Louis, 1771
Dishman, E.F., 3425
Dishonored Lady, 978
DiSimone, Frank, 136, 223, 427, 754, 978,
     3397
Disintegrating Checks, Case of 978
Disraeli, Benjamin, 476
Distafano, Ralph P., 978
Distant Shore, The, 978
Distefano, Luigi, 1252, 1253
Distleman, Harry, 2099
Disto, Betty, 1508
Dittmeyer, Edward, 341
di V. Nahum, Jack, 2261
DiVarco, Joseph Vincent, 463, 978, 1109,
     3384
DiVarco, Joseph Vincent, 3384
Divens, Emmett, 3346
Diver, Jenny, 850, 978-979
Divivo, John, 3468
Divver, Paddy, 2876
Dix, Dorothea Lynde, 979
Dix, Enoch George Wilfred, 979
Dix, Gertrude, 2863, 3399
Dixie Davis, 2700
Dix, John, 1737, 2421
Dixon, Billy, 1054, 1449

Dixon, Bob, 1921
Dixon, Carl R., 1190, 3283, 3462
Dixon, Charles, 1732, 1921
Dixon, E.M., 3558
Dixon, Fred Michael, 979
Dixon, Gene, 2952
Dixon, Harold, 1676
Dixon, Herbert B., Jr., 2221
Dixon, James, 979
Dixon, Lee, 743, 2979
Dixon, Margaret, 979-981
Dixon, Melvin, 227
Dixon, Philip, 3452
Dixon, R. (Ire. d.1919), 3244
Dixon, Richard (U.S. d.1904), 3356
Dixon, Richard F. (U.S. pr.1972), 3469
Dixon, Sam, 1940, 3342
Dixon, Simp, 1447, 1921
Dixon, Thomas, 3364
Djalawi, Abdul Aziz Ben Saud, 3255
Djemal Pasha, Ahmed, 980
Djurhuus, K., 3253
Dlamini, Jacob Kuzwayo, 2736
d'Medici, Catherine, 687
Dmitri, 980, 1324
Dmitri I, 980
Dmitri II, 980
Dmitri III, 980
Dmitri IV, 980
Dmitriev, Radko, 980, 3244
Dnawy, Kadir el, 398
Dönitz, Karl, 3539
Doak, August, 2986
Doan, Joe T., 2052
Doane, Abe, 980
Doane Gang, 980
Doane, Levy, 980
Doane, Moses, 980
Dobbert, Ernest, 3447
Dobbin, James, 2527
Dobbs, Hannah, 278, 980, 981
Dobbs, Johnny, 767, 980-981, 1941, 1942
Dobbs, L.S., 1218
Dobbs, Wiley, 3450
Dobell, Charles Joseph, 981
Dobie, Armistead Mason, 981
Dobkin, Harry, 565, 981, 3196
Dobkin, Rachel, 981
Dobler, Johann, 990
Dobson, Bill, 320
Dobson, James, 319
Dobson, Margaret Jane, 1609
Docherty, "Dutch", 981
Docherty, Mary, 548
Do Chuc, 2272
Dock Rats, 3404
Dockery, John, 1427
Dockery, Octavia, 2169
Dockett, Ronald, 2726
Dockney, Austin Henry, 1721
Doctors' Riot, 981-983, 3371-3373
Dodd, Frank, 3364
Dodd, Jeff, 983
Dodd, William, 914, 983
Dodds, John, 3557
Dodge, Beth, 3156, 3157
Dodge City Gang, 3108
Dodge, David, 1805, 3333, 3524
Dodge, F.S., 214
Dodge, Franklin L., Jr., 2567
Dodge, George H. 163
Dodge, William C., 932, 1561
Dodington, George Bubb, 877, 1512
Dodrill, Carl, 1339
Dodsin, Gerald, 983, 1581
Doe, Charles, 983
Doe, Mark, 558, 2893
Doe, Samuel K., 2964, 3258, 3261, 3515
Doeberl, Frank A., 1229-1230

Doeg, John, 2954
Doelitzsch, Fritz, 983-984
Doellen, Michael, 1265
Doenitz, Karl, 984, 1558, 1576
Doerfler, Samuel, 1751
Doering, Charles, 2054
Doerner, Doris, 2392
Doetsch, Alexander, 984
Doetsch, Catherine, 984
Doetsch, Gunter, 984
Doetsch, Joyce, 984
Doggett, Caroline, 267
Dogin, Cynthia, 985
Dogin, Henry S., 984-985, 1027, 3426
Doheny, Edward L., 1130, 2910
Doheny, Michael, 1147
Doherty, Charles Joseph, 985
Doherty, Edward P., 782, 1960
Doherty, Henry Latham, 2686
Doherty, Hugh, 1774
Doherty, James J. "Red", 110, 608, 1026,
     2070, 3384, 3387
Doherty, John, 3544, 3546
Doherty, Kieran, 3514, 3515
Doherty, Martin, 3030
Doherty, Peter, 3515
Dohrn, Bernadine Rae, 985, 1771, 3107,
     3508
Doihara Kenji, 3539
Doiron, Adrian, 1363
Dokyo, 985
Dolabella, Publius Cornelius, 985, 2985
Dolan, Dandy John, 3147
Dolan, Edmund "Eddie", 847
Dolan, Elizabeth, 2504, 3355
Dolan, Elmer, 1422
Dolan, James J., 363, 366, 486, 739, 985,
     1966, 2149, 3557
Dolan, Johnny, 985
Dolan, Josephine, 1437
Dolan, Patrick, 3328, 3546, 3548, 3551
Dolan, Terrance, 1715
Dolben, William, 1195
Dolden, Kenneth Stuart, 985-986
Dole, Robert, 3270
Dole, Sanford Ballard, 986
Dolet, Étienne, 986
Dolezal, Frank, 731, 986-987
Dolezel, Oldrich, 3464
Dolgoruki, Pëtr Vladimirovich, 987
Dolinsky, Raymond, 3449
Dollar, James, 1940
Dollfuss, Engelbert, 987-994, 1093, 1573,
     2266, 3247, 3248
Dollfuss, Josepha, 987
Dollinger, Isidore, 2133
Dollman, William, 1351
Dolphin, Particia, 2437
Dolz, Ricardo, 322
Dom Pedro, 896
Domat, Jean, 994
Dombkiewicz, Peter, 994
Domblewski, Philip, 1280
Domby, Victor, 994
Domela, Harry, 994
Domenech, Maria, 870
Domenech, Virginia, 870
Domenico di Giovanni 994
Domes, Hans, 990, 994
Domingo, Anton, 3358
Domingo Crespo, Santiago, 816
Dominguez, Frank 150
Dominguez, Rodolpho, 638, 3330
Domini, Sara, 3324
Dominici, Gaston, 995-996
Dominici, Gustave, 995
Dominicki, Agnes, 2695
Dominique, Robert, 996
Dominique You, 1872

Dominiquez, Orin, 996
Domitian, 996, 2306, 3235
Domitilla, Flavia, 996
Domitilla, Vespasian, 996
Domitius, 2728
Donadieu, Alfredo-Hecktor, 996-997
Donahoe, Jack, 390, 997
Donahoe, Marcus, 3390
Donahoe, Thomas, 1001
Donahue, Cornelius, 997, 3546
Donahue, Florencio 100
Donahue, John Xavier, 997-998
Donahue, Maurice H., 998
Donald, Alexander, 998
Donald, Beulah Mae, 1498
Donald, Jeannie Ewen, 43, 998
Donald, John, 558
Donald, Michael A., 1068, 1498
Donald, Samuel M., 3348
Donald, T.S., 3251
Donaldbane, 1035
Donaldson, Allen, 2096
Donaldson, Archibald, 1030
Donaldson, Bert, 3246
Donaldson, Bill, 2054
Donaldson, Esther, 1601
Donaldson, Francis A., III, 93
Donaldson, Ivanhoe, 264
Donaldson, Margaret, 1385
Donally, James, 998
Donati, Corson, 663
Donato-Martin, Ramon, 3465
Dondone, John, 998
Donegan, Edward, 998-999
Donegan, Joe, 3009
Donella, Schuyler, 483
Donellan, John, 818, 999
Donelly, Andrew, 1680
Donelly, James P., 1000
Donero, Robert, 1513
Dongan, Thomas, 999
Dongarro, Charles, 3404
Donigan, George, 3359
Donkin, R., 3248
Donlan, Harry E., 3175
Donley, Ed, 3546
Donlon, Charles, 1544
Donne, Charles, 1740
Donne, Theodore Di, 423
Donnell, Richard, 999
Donnellan, George L. 103, 1038, 2119, 2478
Donnelly, Bridget, 641, 1000
Donnelly, "Buck", 1775
Donnelly, Edward, 999
Donnelly, Jack, 3512
Donnelly, James (Can. d.1880), 641, 999-1000
Donnelly, James (U.S. pr.1900), 1000
Donnelly, James (U.S. pr.1934), 576, 1131
Donnelly, James P. (U.S. d.1858), 1000
Donnelly, Johannah, 641, 999
Donnelly, John, 1000
Donnelly, Michael, 421
Donnelly, Nell Quinlan, 919, 3325
Donnelly, Robert, 3342
Donnelly, Thomas, 641, 1000
Donner, George, 1806
Donner, Jacob, 1806
Donner, Tamsen, 1806
Donnor, Kid, 2955
Donogan, Patrick, 1478
Donoghue, William, 1000
Donohue, Alice, 41, 1000
Donohue, Daniel, 41, 1000
Donohue, John, 1000
Donohue, Thomas, 1000-1001
Donohue, "Yellow Jack", 1775
Donovan, Arthur, 631
Donovan, Conrad, 1001, 2464

Donovan, David W., 3468
Donovan, Edward, 464
Donovan, George Thomas, 877, 1001, 2785
Donovan, James, 3259, 3275
Donovan, James, 3519
Donovan, James J., 1001
Donovan, Jean, 73
Donovan, Mike, 2399
Donovan, Mildred, 1722
Donovan, Raymond J., 1001, 2167
Donovan, "Stink Bomb", 3384
Donovan, Terence, 2248
Donovan, William (U.S. d.1876), 1165
Donovan, William Joseph (U.S. 1883-1959), 1001-1002, 2483
Donovan, "Wreck", 767, 3404
D'Onston, Roslyn, 1689
Doody, William, 1002
Doolan, James, 2093
Doo Lew, 1002
Dooley, Alvin, 1002, 1073, 3249
Dooley, Rafer, 1002, 3176
Dooley, Robert, 2817
Doolin Gang, 384, 403, 404, 1654, 2931, 3544, 3545, 3547, 3549
Doolin, William M. "Bill", 24, 403, 404, 523, 732, 733, 860, 862, 863, 878, 1002-1004, 1038, 1720, 2463, 2530, 2732, 2931, 2955, 3069, 3070, 3128, 3129, 3551, 3557
Dooling, John Francis, Jr., 1004
Dooling, Maurice Timothy, 1004
Doolittle, Jeanette, 2733
Doolittle, Mrs. Clinton, 2733
Dooly, James, 1178
Dopierla, Rochelle Clifford, 2309
Doran, Joseph W., 3426
Doran, S.A., 3399, 3400, 3557
Doran, Verne, 1074, 1626
Doran, William, 1180, 1808
Dorans, Ralph, 3358
Dorbell, Tom, 1004-1005
Dorcy, Joseph M., 3147
Dorfman, Allen, 1005, 1228, 1980, 3166, 3384
Dorfman, Benny, 775, 776
Dorfman, Paul "Red", 3384
D'Orgenay, Francis J.L., 3546
Doria, Andria, 1157, 3238
Doria, Gianettino, 1157, 3238
Dorion, Antoine Aimé, 1005
Dorislaus, Isaac, 1005, 3239
Dorji, Jigme P., 3255
d'Orléans, Duc, 2678
d'Orléans, Gaston, 716, 2206
d'Orléans, Henri-Eugene-Philippe-Louis, 1992
d'Orléans, Jean Louis Phillipe, 877, 1871, 3303
d'Orleans, Marie Louise, 2122, 3240
Dorman, Bobbie Louise, 1225
Dorman, Frank, 358, 359
Dormer, Pat, 2066
Dormoy, René Marx, 1005
Dorn, Albert Edward, 2209
Dorn, Christine, 2209
Dorn, Roosevelt F., 772
Dornan, Robert, 3207
Dorner, Dalia, 912
Dorothea, Sophia, 1842
Dorotheus, 1005
Dorr, David L., 2118
Dorr, Thomas Wilson, 1005
Dorran, Paddy, 2545
Dorrego, Manuel, 1005, 3240
Dorrier, Elizabeth, 1863
Dorset, Earl of, 764
Dorset, Marquis, 1383

Dorsey, Charles, 1005, 2423
Dorsey, Frank, 812, 1945
Dorsey, George, 3368
Dorsey, Hugh Mason, 1219, 1223
Dorsey, John, 3545, 3557
Dorsey, Richard, 1005-1006
Dorsey, Tommy, 115, 2217
Dorylaeum, Eusebius of, 1110
Dos Passos, John, 102, 2348, 2652
DOSAAF, 1006
Dos Santo, Francisco, 1006
dos Santos, Joao, 3292
dos Santos, José Ferreira, 1880
Dos Santos, Machado, 3244
Dosoo, Alex, 2276
Doss, Nannie, 1006
Doss, Samuel, 1006
Dossena, Alceo, 1006-1007, 1138
Dossett, Dan, 7
Dossett, Moses, 3358
Dost Mohammad Khan 1007
Dostler, Anton, 1007, 3539
Dostoevsky, Fëdor Mikhailovich, 248, 1007, 1868
Dózsa, György, 1017
Dot, King, 595
Dothard, E.C., 3081
Doto, Guiseppe Antonio, 32, 35
Doto, Joseph "Joe Adonis", 1775, 2535
Doto, Joseph, 1
Dotort, David, 545
Dotson, Clint, 1007, 1178
Dotson, Consuela, 2236
Dotson, Gary, 1007
Dotson, Oliver, 1007, 1178
Doty Affair, 1008
Doty, Bennet J., 1008
Doty, Sile, 1007-1008
Doty, Susan, 885
Doty, William, 3424
Douat, Vital, 1008
Double Indemnity, 1008
Doucett, Jeffrey Paul, 2475
Doudet, Célestine, 1008-1009
Dougal, Samuel Herbert, 1009, 1084, 1312, 2195, 3195
Dougan, Jacob J., 3449
Dougherty, Harry M., 2160
Dougherty, Johnny, 105
Doughty, Jack, 1009
Doughty, John, 3282
Douglas, Alfred, 1009, 3154, 3155
Douglas, Archibald Stewart, 1036, 1524, 1695
Douglas, Bill, 3408
Douglas, Catherine, 1694
Douglas, David, 1009, 1010
Douglas, Dorothy, 2885
Douglas, Douglas Sholto, 332
Douglas, Earl (Scot. 1426-88), 1695
Douglas, Earl (Scot. d.1440), 1009
Douglas, Fred Berre, 3448
Douglas, George Frederick, 1299
Douglas, Howard, 3449
Douglas, J.S. (Sing. pr.1960), 1544
Douglas, James (Brit. pr.1712), 3303
Douglas, James (Scot. c.1516-81), 1009
Douglas, James (Scot. pr.1596), 2853, 2871, 3239
Douglas, Janet, 1009-1010
Douglas, Jasper, 3359
Douglas, Jean, 1010
Douglas, John, 1010, 1903
Douglas, Joseph, 3129
Douglas, Margaret, 2853
Douglas-Pennant (WRAF) Enquiry, 849
Douglas, Philip, 1010
Douglas, Richard, 1010
Douglas, Rickey, 3453

Douglas, Sawney, 1010
Douglas, Stephen Arnold, 500, 513, 883, 1010, 1954, 1964
Douglas, T., 3344
Douglas, Wallace, 3340
Douglas, William (Scot. 1327-84), 1010
Douglas, William (Scot. 1423-40), 1010
Douglas, William (Scot. 1425-52), 1010
Douglas, William, 1010
Douglas, William Lewis, 676
Douglas, William Orville, 5, 872, 1010-1011, 1200, 2123, 3056
Douglas, York, 3347
Douglas-Mahun Duel 1009
Douglass, E. Wingfield, 772, 2032
Douglass, Howard V., 3449
Douglass, Joseph, 3324
Douglass, Lewis L., 1989
Douglass, Robert, 1011
Douglass, Robyn, 2203
Doulder, Howard C., 402
Doumer, Paul, 1011, 3247
Doumergue, Gaston, 2846
Douthwaite, Arthur Henry, 26
Do Van Nang, 3252
Dove, Daniel, 3358
Dove, Frank, 1011
Dove, Fred, 1011
Dove, William, 1011-1012
Dover, Thomas, 1012
Dover, Wendell, 1410
Dow, E.A., 3546
Dow, Harriet, 2825
Dow, J. Leslie, 3546, 3558
Dow, Leslie "Les", 1012, 1791, 3548, 3561, 3562
Dow, Luke, 3546
Dow, Neal, 1012
Dowd, Daniel, 380, 3558
Dowd, John (U.S. pr.1912), 2223
Dowd, John F. (U.S. pr.1930s), 1012-1013
Dowd, Tim, 345
Dowdall, James, 853, 1013
Dowdall, Michael Douglas, 1013
Dowe, Anne, 1013
Dowe, Robert, 2310
Dowie, John Alexander, 3060
Dowling, Delphine, 296
Dowling, Elmer Sylvester "Dutch", 3192
Dowling, Oscar, 3295
Downes, J.M., 3305
Downes, John Tilston, 219
Downes, Olin, 1848
Downey, Chrissie, 1390
Downey, Francis, 1944
Downey, John (Aus. pr.1950s), 1390
Downey, John (Brit. pr.1900s), 1013
Downey, Laurence James, 3473
Downey, Lesley Ann, 2212, 3327
Downey, Samuel B., 1692-1693
Downey, William H., 2803
Downing, Edward, 2324
Downing, Melvin Douglas, 3462
Downing, R.R., 2031
Downing, William, 1013-1014, 2094, 3546, 3558
Downs, Bobbie Lee, 3449
Downs, Elizabeth Diane, 1014
Downs, Ernest, 3449
Downs, Thomas, 74
Downshire, Lady, 2578
Dowry Murders, 1014
Dowse, Margaret, 1014
Dowsing, John, 701
Doxsee, Tom, 1014
Doyle, Arthur Conan, 704, 1014-1017, 1068, 1392, 1602, 1690, 2244, 2710, 2777, 3188
Doyle, Austin J., 3424
Doyle, Bobby, 2115, 2138

Doyle, Charles, 1014
Doyle, Danny, 3449
Doyle, Dorsey, 3147
Doyle, Drury, 509
Doyle, James (Brit. pr.1925), 1017
Doyle, James (U.S. d.1856), 509
Doyle, James E. (U.S. pr.1982), 1617, 3425
Doyle, James Edward (U.S. 1915-,), 1017, 1159
Doyle, Jeane Lecki, 1017
Doyle, Jess, 238, 239, 1442, 2286, 3459
Doyle, Jimmy, 526
Doyle, John (U.S. d.1856), 509
Doyle, John (U.S. d.c.1860), 2775
Doyle, Lady Conan, 855
Doyle, Martin, 1017
Doyle, Mary, 1014
Doyle, Michael J., 1775, 1781, 2034
Doyle, Patrick, 3373
Doyle, Patsy, 2072, 3404
Doyle, Simon, 1455
Doyle, William, 509, 1199
Doze, Grace, 1017
Dozier, Denise, 3177
Dozier, James Lee, 2553, 2683, 3333, 3519
Dr. Jekyll and Sister Hyde, 981
Dr. Moon, 981
Drabing, Michael Edward, 1017-1018
Drachman, Louis, 1018
Draco, 1018
Dracula, 3058
Draga, 3243
Dragna Family, 1019
Dragna, Jack I., 426, 978, 1018, 1019, 1895, 1948, 2085, 3396, 3397
Dragna, Louis Tom, 1018-1019, 2178, 3397
Drago, Luis Maria, 1019
Drago, Orazio, 1979
Dragon Flower Sacred Religious, 3391
Dragoti, Stan, 1019
Draighton, Erik, 3454
Drain, Dorothy, 167
Drake, Charles (U.S. d.1956), 1202, 2870
Drake, Charles Daniel (U.S. 1811-92), 1019
Drake, David H., 1891
Drake, Elijah, 3354
Drake, F.P., 1090
Drake, Francis, 662, 1019-1020, 1083, 1471
Drake, Frank, 1676
Drake, Leroy, 1020
Drake, P.H., 3243
Drake, Philip, 1020
Drake Swindle, 1020
Drake, Thomas Jefferson, 1020
Draper, John, 858
Draper, Morris, 3328, 3485
Draper, Shang, 21, 1020, 1666, 1941, 1942, 3084, 3404, 3406
Draper, Simeon, 889
Draper, William, 1020, 2872
Draskovic, Milorad, 3244
Draughon, Martin, 3455
Drause, Fred, 607
Drautman, Adolphina, 1749
Draw, Derrick, 1020-1021
Drax, Don Felipe, 1020
Drayton, Frank, 2093
Drayton, John, 1021
Drayton, Leroy, 3454
Drayton, William (U.S. 1732-90), 1021
Drayton, William Henry (U.S. 1742-79), 1021
Dreamer, Mary, 1021
Dreamer, Robert, 1021
Dreesman, Agnes, 1021
Dreesman, John, 1021
Dreesman, Robert, 1021

Dreher, Thomas, 1021-1022, 1915
Dreiser, Theodore, 113, 1158, 1255, 1313, 2958, 3206
Drenovac, Martin, 1901
Dressen, Mary, 2174
Dreux, Louise, 2165
Drew-Bear, Edith, 124
Drew, Bernard, 2291
Drew, Charles, 1022
Drew, Daniel, 1022, 1167, 1171, 1351, 1352
Drew, Donald, 1976
Drew, Dorthy Louise, 1406
Drew, Gerald A., 3253
Drew, Joseph, 1022
Drew, Marlin, 1405, 1406
Drew, Marvin, 1022
Drew, Pearl, 1022
Drew, Robert, 3455
Drexler, Anton, 1568
Drey, Frederick, 2227
Dreyer, Anna Elizabeth, 1490
Dreyfus, Alfred, 351, 931, 1023-1024, 1040, 1138, 1223, 1868, 2523, 2649, 2652, 3074
Dreyfus, Aurelia, 1822
Dreyfus, Louise, 2863
Dreyfus, Mathieu, 1023
Driggs, George, 3337
Drinan, John Albert, 1024-1025, 1416
Drinkard, Jimmy, 2046
Drinkard, Richard, 3455
Driscoll, Alfred E., 2739
Driscoll, Barbara, 2723
Driscoll, Daniel, 1025, 3147
Driscoll, Joseph, 3031
Driscoll, Robert, 3452
Driscoll, Tom, 3555
Driver, Samuel Marion, 374, 1025
Drogo de Hauteville 1025
Droner, Willy, 2532
Dropsie, Moses Aaron, 1025
Drossner, Charles Jean, 1025
Droubi Pashda, 3244
Droubin, Jeanne, 1316
Drouet, Jean-Baptiste, 1025, 2117
Drousiotis, John, 3078
Drover, Abby, 1493, 3331
Drown, Carolyn, 2149
Drown, Ruth, 1025-1026
Drucci, Cecilia, 1027
Drucci, Vincent "The Schemer", 110, 130,, 606, 1026-1027, 1293, 1294, 2044, 2213, 2350, 2673, 2972, 3016, 3119, 3384
Drucker, Charley, 2032
Drucker, Jack, 2254, 2868
Drude, Thomas Edward, 1046
Drug Enforcement Agency, 1027, 3289
Druggan, George, 3384
Druggan-Lake Gang, 105, 1027-1028
Druggan, Terry, 104, 607, 966, 1027, 1028, 1586, 3028, 3384, 3406
Druitt, Montague John, 1689
Drukman, Samuel, 1638
Drumm, Maire, 1028, 3504
Drummond, A.E., 3426
Drummond, A.L., 736
Drummond, Edward, 2061-2062, 3241
Drummond, Elizabeth, 995
Drummond, Jack, 995, 3252
Drummond, Margaret, 1028
Drummond, William, 1028
Drummond, William Wormer, 1028
Drury, Charles Marshall, 784
Drury Lane, 1919
Drury, William, 271, 1028, 3384
Druscovich, Nathaniel, 1008
Druse, John, Jr., 1029
Druse, John, Sr., 1028-1029
Druse, Mary, 1028
Druse, Roxana, 1028-1029

Drusilla, Julia, 581
Drusilla, Livia, 1029
Drusus, 1029, 3234
Drusus Caesar, 1029, 2724, 3234
Drusus, Marcus Livius, 1029
Drusus, Tiberius Claudius, 581, 726
Dryden, John, 14, 1029
Drysdale, Alexander 1029
Drysdale, Peter, 1470
Drzewiecki, Paul, 356
du Barry, Chevalier Jean, 1030
du Barry, Guillaume, 1030
du Barry, Jeanne, 264, 3240
Du Barry, Marie Jeanne Bécu, 906, 1030
du Bois, Henri Pene, 1994
Du Bois, W.E.B., 2833
Du Chatelard, 1030-1031
du Clercq, Jacques 166
du Guesclin, Bertrand, 1397, 3303
Dulcino of Novara 1034
du Parcq H., 1501, 2745
du Plessis, Andries Stephanus, 1039
Du Plessis, Dirkie Cathrina, 2346
Du Ponceau, Pierre Étienne, 1039
Dupont de l'Evre, Jacques Charles 1039
du Pr Labouchre, Henry 1868
du Richelieu, Armand-Jean, 1048, 1220, 1238
Du Rose, John, 1691, 2000
du Tilb, Arnold, 1045
Du Toit, Petrus Hendrik, 1045-1046
Dutrevil de Rhins, Jules Léon 1046
du Val-de-Grace Cloots, Baron Jean-Baptiste, 733
Du Vergier de Hauranne, Jean, 1048
Duane, Charles P., 3414
Duane, James, 1029
Duane, William (U.S. 1760-1835), 1029
Duane, William John (U.S. 1780-1865), 1029
Duarte, José Napolen, 3334
Duarte, Juan Pablo, 1029-1030
Duarte, Maria Eva, 2445
Dubarry, Albert, 2846
Dubesseneff, Kilko, 1336
Dubinski, Rachel, 981
Dublano, Nicholas, 3354
Dublin, Aldred, 3361
Dublin, Dell, 3558
Dublin, Richard Dick, 1313, 3361, 3547, 3558
Dublin Riots, 3378
Dubof, Yourka, 2758
Dubois, Aline, 1125
Dubois, Frank, 1030
Duboise, E. Leon, 3558
Dubonnet, Paul, 1830
Dubost, Charles, 691
Dubrin, David, 1275
Dubrock, Melvin, 1030
Dubs, Adolph, 3257, 3506
Dubuisson, Pauline, 1030
Duca, Jon, 738, 1030, 3247
Ducas, Theodore, 2452
Duchateau, Daniel, 1030
Duchowski, Charles, 1031
Duck, Aug Tai, 1031
Duck, Mock, 3404, 3412
Ducket, Laurence, 456
Duckett, George, 558, 2893
Duckett, James, 3449
Duckett, Robert E., 2733, 3453
Duckworth, Jim, 3568
Ducore, Moe, 2006
Ducre, Yvonne, 646
Duddy, Norman, 3521
Dudley, Ambrose, 1031
Dudley, Andrew, 3356
Dudley, Benjamin W., 3305
Dudley, Bert, 3364

Dudley, Carl, 3364
Dudley, Deborah Johnson, 1508
Dudley, Earl, 2767
Dudley, Edmund, 1031, 1093
Dudley, Florence, 1618
Dudley, Frank, 1827
Dudley, Guildford, 1031, 1383
Dudley, J.W., 3424
Dudley, James, 3340
Dudley, John (Brit. 1502-53), 1031, 1383
Dudley, Joseph, 772, 1031
Dudley, Nathan Augustus Monroe, 364, 3558
Dudley, Richard, 1031-1032
Dudley, Robert W., 2552
Dudley, Thomas, 1032
Dudzech, de, 1032
Duel in the Sun, 1032
Duell, William, 1032
Duer, John, 1032
Duer, Robert 159
Duer, William (U.S. 1747-99), 1032
Duer, William Alexander (U.S. 1780-1858), 1032
Duest, Lloyd, 3449
Duff, Adolph W., 409, 1243, 2344
Duff, David, 596
Duff, Edmund, 840, 1032
Duff, Grace, 840, 1032
Duff, James H., 1461
Duff, John, 1001
Duff-Smith, Markham, 1033, 3455
Duffey, Steven, 3454
Duffield, Austin Christopher, 1032-1033
Duffield, Gordon, 3325
Duffield, Milton B., 3546
Duffin, Mike, 288
Duffue, Jacobus Johannes, 471
Duffy, Broadway Bill, 629, 2072
Duffy, Charles Gavan, 1033
Duffy, Charley, 3400
Duffy, Clinton T., 321, 1033
Duffy, Daniel B., 92
Duffy, Frank Gavan, 1033
Duffy, Gavan, 2811
Duffy, George B., 370
Duffy Hills, 3404
Duffy, Kevin Thomas, 1033, 1771, 1771, 1775, 3089
Duffy, Martin, 2337
Duffy, Mickey, 620, 3412
Duffy, Renee, 932, 1033
Duffy, Thomas "Red" (U.S. pr.1920), 608, 2070, 3384, 3404
Duffy, Thomas (U.S. d.1881), 3108, 3558
Duffy, Thomas, (U.S. pr.1890), 2082
Duffy, Tom, (U.S. pr.1985), 2056
Duffy, William P. "Big Bill", 1141
Dufour, Donald, 3449, 3452
Dufrene, Roosevelt A., 1609
Dugan, Eva, 1033
Dugan, J.W., 806
Dugaot, Alda, 2862
Dugar, Troy, 3451
Dugdale, Bridget Rose, 3283, 3500
Dugdale, Richard Louis, 1033, 1748
Dugdale, Rose, 1254
Duggan, Andrew, 3523
Duggan, Eugene, 435
Duggan, Harry, 1774
Dugger, Thomas E., 1033-1034
Duggins, Albert, 1175
Dugi, Giovanni, 3558
Duguet, Désiré 190
Duguet, Sophie, 3328
Duguit, Leon, 1034
Duhamel, Emile Pierre, 3455
Dujarier, Alexandre Henri, 894, 3305
Dukakis, Michael, 1623

Duke, Benton, 1617
Duke, Charles Thomas, 880
Duke, Frank, 3558
Duke, John, 3364
Duke, Nell, 1592
Duke, Thomas S., 328
Duke, William M., 3305
Duke, Winifred, 278, 1874, 2773
Duke's Restaurant, 1034
Dukes, John, 3368
Dukes, N.L., 2348
Dulany, Lloyd, 3303
Dulcie September, 3528
Dulfer, Bill, 1198, 3386
Dulin, William, 1034
Dull, Judy Ann, 1321
Dullea, C., 3426
Dullea, Charles, 1074, 1722
Dulles, Allen, 2010
Dulles, John Foster, 1034, 1316
Duly, Bell, 3354
Dumais, Joseph, 390
Dumas, Alexander, 1871, 3292
Dumas, Bernalyn, 2517
Dumas, L.C., 3343
Dumas, René François, 1034
Dumas, Roy, 2517
Dumini, Amerigo, 1034, 2148, 2149
Dummett, R.E., 892
Dumollard, Marie, 1034
Dumollard, Martin, 1034
Dumont, William A., 3180
Dun, Thomas, 1034-1035
Dun, Timothy, 1035
Dunavey, Nick, 2405
Dunavan, C.T., 3546
Dunbar, Daniel, 2145
Dunbar, Mary, 2087
Dunbar, Reuben A., 1035
Dunbar, Ronald Patrick, 1035
Dunbar, Tony, 2913
Duncalf, William, 777
Duncan I, 1035, 3237
Duncan II, 1035, 3237
Duncan, Anita, 2568
Duncan, Bob, 1036
Duncan, David, 3454
Duncan, Dick, 3558
Duncan, Elizabeth (U.S. 1904-62), 1035-1036
Duncan, Elizabeth (U.S. d.1955), 1664
Duncan, Gilly, 2345
Duncan, Goebel, 1664
Duncan, Harry, 3357
Duncan, Henry, 3343
Duncan, Henry Earl, 3448
Duncan, J.C., 1036
Duncan, Jack, 2770
Duncan, James, 1450
Duncan, John, 3338
Duncan, Joseph Cecil, 3447
Duncan, Mamie, 1664
Duncan, Mary, 248, 3457
Duncan, Olga, 1036
Duncan, Patrick, 1036
Duncan, Peter, 658
Duncan, Raymond, 1664
Duncan, Robert Morton, 1036
Duncan, Tom, 917
Duncan, Utt, 3354
Duncan, Victor, 3253
Duncan, W.S., 1194
Duncan's Saloon, 1036
Duncomb, Lydia, 2095
Dundas, Robert, 1036
Dunegan, Manuel, 3346
Dunfee, S., 3246
Dunford, Peter Anthony, 1036
Dungee, George, 1036-1037, 3428

Dunham, James C., 1037
Dunham, Sterling, 3356
Dunham, Walter L., 2552
Dunk, George Montagu, 3198
Dunkel, Blanche, 2784
Dunkins, Horace Franklin, Jr., 1037, 3447
Dunkle, Jon S., 3448
Dunlap, Cal, 1195
Dunlap, Jack, 1037, 2854
Dunlap, Jimmy, 3457
Dunlap, Leon A., 1037
Dunlap, Max 29
Dunlevy, Elsie, 1037
Dunlevy, John, 1037
Dunley, Mond, 3347
Dunlop, Arthur, 236
Dunlop, Arthur V., 238
Dunlop, James, 1037
Dunlop, John, 3558
Dunlop, John Colin, 1037
Dunman, William Hickman, 3546
Dunmark, Althea, 311
Dunn, Alice McQuillan, 2553
Dunn, Amasa G., 3546
Dunn, Beverly Wyly, 1037, 3263
Dunn, Bill, 602, 1003, 1038
Dunn, Bob, 2734
Dunn, Francis, 171, 3326
Dunn, Frank "Sunny", 2553, 2972
Dunn, Harvey J., 3414
Dunn, Jack, 1038
Dunn, James, 3134
Dunn, Jere, 3384
Dunn, John M. "Cockeye", 1038, 1977, 2743, 2785
Dunn, Kenneth D., 3455
Dunn, Penny, 1038
Dunn, Pete, 2212
Dunn, Reginald, 2738
Dunn, Rosa, 2309
Dunn, Sonny, 3384
Dunn, Stanley, 2113
Dunn, William W., 239, 3346
Dunne, Ben, 3333, 3517
Dunne, Billie, 838
Dunne, Edward, 1030
Dunne, Larry, 3300
Dunne, Michael, 3301
Dunne, "Old Man", 3384
Dunne, Reginald, 3172, 3245
Dunne, Robert, 3301
Dunne, Shamie, 3301
Dunnigan, Jimmy, 1670, 2197
Dunnigan, John, 1038
Dunnigan, Madeline Green, 1038
Dunning, Elizabeth, 448
Dunning, John Presley, 448
Dunsdon Brothers, 1038
Dunstan, 1038, 1069
Dunstance, Norman Jackson, 1038-1039
Dunster, Henry, 1039
Dunton, Alvin R., 1468
Dunton, R.F., 1468
Duny, Amy, 559, 843, 1039
Duong Van Minh, 2327
Dupaquet, Jules, 1209
Duparinof, L., 3245
Duperrault, Arthur, 1472
Dupin, André Marie Jean Jacques, 1039
Duplantier, Adrian Guy, 1039
Duplessis, Lucille, 925
Dupocher, Michael A., 3449
Dupont, John, 3558
Dupont, Norma, 1039
Dupont-Fournier Duel, 1039
Duport, Adrien-Jean-François, 1039
Dupré, Jacqueline, 790, 791, 2465
Dupre, George, 1039-1040
Dupree, Frank, 3355

Dupree, Franklin, Jr., 912
Dupree, Lewis 17X, 1040
Dupree, Ronald, 885
DuPugh, Robert Bolivar, 2189, 3532
Dupuy, Charles-Alexandre, 632, 650, 1040
Duquette, Michael, 471
Duran, Desidario, 1636
Duran, Rosa, 1469
Durand, Charles, 3305
Durand-Deacon, Henrietta Helen Olivia Robarts, 1417
Durand, Earl, 1040-1041
Durand, Guillaume, 1041
Durani, Ahmad Shah, 3335
Duranquet, Father, 1542
Durant, Henry Fowle, 1041
Durant, Jack, 1041
Durant, Thomas, 814
Durbin, Walter, 3546
Durden, Harry P., 1177
Durden, Munroe, 3363
Duren, David, 3447
Durent, Edmund, 843
d'Urfe, Marquis, 648
Durfee, Joseph, 3363
Durfee, Minta, 143
Durfort, Louis de, 2712
Durgan, Bridget, 1041
Durham, George P., 3546
Durham, Monte, 1200
Durham, Plato, 1860
Durill, Grover, 3459
Duringer, Rudolph "Fats", 838, 839
Durk, David, 1834, 2728
Durkheim, Emile, 1041
Durnan, Robert J., 1041
Durnford, George A., 182
Durocher, Michael, 3449
Duroux, Mimiche, 1316
Durrah, Edward, 311
Durrant, Theo, 1041
Durrant, Thomas, 247
Durrant, William Henry Theodore, 1041-1043
Durrell, Grover, 1755, 1819, 3427
Durrell, Lawrence, 1724
Durrill, Grover, 2283-2284, 2926
D'Urso, Giovanni, 3332, 3507, 3508
Durso, Natale, 3384
Durso, Thomas N., 3298, 3384
Durst, E.B., 3132
Durst, S.O., 3546
Durston, Charles F., 1790
Durvez, P., 3249
Duryée, Abram, 1043, 2966
Dusenbury, Charles, 2480
Dussert, Max, 191
Dustin, Hannah, 1043
Dutartre, Judith, 1043
Dutartre, Peter, 1043-1044
Dutch Bill, 3384
Dutch Frank, 3384
Dutch Henry, 445, 510, 1044
Dutch Joe, 209
Dutch John, 320
Dutch Mob, 1044, 3404, 3406, 3407, 3410
Dutch Riot, 3370
Dutch West India Company, 1044-1045
Dutoy, René, 902
Dutra, Eurico Gaspar, 1046
Dutthagamani, 1046
Dutton, Ralph, 699
Dutton, Stephen, 1046
Dutton, Thomas, 1688
Duval, Claude, 1046-1047
Duval, Emma, 3384
DuVal, Harvie, 2234
Duval, Jack, 2577
Duval, Jean, 1047

Duval, Pierre, 2453
Duval, William Pope, 1047
Duvalier, Eric, 1419
Duvalier, François "Papa Doc", 1047, 2968, 3256
Duvalier, Jean-Claude "Baby Doc", 1047, 2968
Duvall, Gabriel, 233, 1047-1048
Duvall, J.B., 2739
Duvall, James, 1048
Duvall, John L., 1048
DuVall, Perry, 362, 3554, 3568
Duvall, Richard, 2682
Duvall, William Potts, 1048
Duvalle, John, 3453
Duver, Leo, 1301
Dvila, Pedro Arias, 2348
Dwe, San 1048
Dwevi, Hindawy, 2288
Dwight, Theodore William, 1048
Dwight, Walton, 1048-1049
Dwindle, Charlie, 3558
Dwinelle, Samuel, 1126
Dworecki, Reverend Walter, 1049
Dworecki, Wanda, 1049
Dwyer, Billy (U.S., d.1850s), 1458
Dwyer, Donald, 3425
Dwyer, Edward, 2784
Dwyer, John G., 649
Dwyer, Paul Nathaniel, 640
Dwyer, R. Budd, 1049
Dwyer, Richard, 1739
Dwyer, William (U.S. pr.1988), 2335
Dwyer, William Vincent "Big Bill", 360, 526, 794, 935, 1049, 1050, 1141, 1049-1050, 1295, 1546, 1894, 3403
Dyal, Har, 677, 1560
Dyar, Oliver 95
Dyatlov, Anatoly S., 524
Dyck, William, 1846
Dye, Joseph, 3341
Dye, Lewis William, 3010
Dye, Russell, 979
Dye, Troy, 1050
Dye, William M., 3426
Dyer, Albert, 319, 1050
Dyer, Alfred, 3448
Dyer, Amelia Elizabeth, 1050
Dyer, David Patterson, 1050
Dyer, Eliphalet, 1050
Dyer, Ernest, 1050-1051
Dyer, Harold, Jr., 983
Dyer, James, 1051
Dyer, Laura Lillian, 1158
Dyer, Mary, 1051
Dyer, Reginald Edward Harry, 1051
Dyer, Stephen, 219
Dyke, Stewart, 1187
Dykes, James, 3249
Dykes, John, 3364
Dylan, Bob, 3107
Dymoke, Thomas, 1051
Dympna, 1051
Dyon, John, 1051
Dyon, William, 1051
Dyson, Albert, 1412
Dyson, Arthur, 2430-2432
Dyson, Donald, 2349
Dyson, Frank, 3424
Dyson, George, 266, 268, 269
Dyson, John William, 2031
Dyson, Katherine, 2430
Dyveke, 1051
Dzerzhinski, Feliks Edmundovich, 1051

E

Eades, Isom, 508
Eadric Streona, 1052, 3237
Eadwig, (Brit. pr.955-57), 1038
Eadwig the Fair, 1069
Eady, Muriel, 706
Eagan, James, 1789
Eagan, John, 3427
Eagan, Rexford, 3118
Eagan, W.F. "Dad", 246, 274, 275
Eagels, Jeanne, 1304
Eagles of National Unity, 3493, 3530
Eagles of the Palestinian Revolution, 3321, 3498, 3530
Eagle Warrior Society, 3501, 3530
Eaker, George I., 3304
Eakins, Leo "Red", 954
Ealy, Silas, 3358
Eames, Edmund, 1365
Eames, Rebecca, 2669
EAN, 3496
Earhart, Amelia Mary, 1052-1053
Earhart, Bill, 1053, 2583
Earhart, Edwin Stanton, 1052
Earhart, James, 3455
Earhart, William, 3558
Earl, Debbie, 1382
Earl, Dick, 1382
Earl, J.B., 225
Earl, Thomas, 2527
Earl, Wanda, 1382
Earle, George Howard, III, 518
Earle, Willie, 1053, 1645, 3368
Earls, Catharine, 1053
Earls, John, 1053
Early, Jubal A., 1993
Earnshaw, Joseph 139
Earp Brothers, 1060, 1062, 2059, 2144
Earp, James, 1053
Earp, Josie, 1061
Earp, Morgan, 842, 1056, 1060-1063, 1594, 1729, 1822, 2059, 2855, 3546, 3551, 3555, 3566
Earp, Newton, 1053
Earp, Nicholas, 1053
Earp, Virgil W., 494, 495, 718-720, 1053, 1056, 1058, 1060-1062, 2059, 2584-2585, 2855, 3546, 3547, 3550, 3551
Earp, Virginia, 1053
Earp, Warren, 1061-1063, 1729, 2059
Earp, Wyatt Berry Stapp, 101, 277, 314, 315, 369, 388, 482, 494, 495, 507, 542, 718, 719, 729, 769, 799, 810, 812, 842, 1053-1063, 1450, 1451, 1499, 1539, 1593-1595, 1729, 1794, 1941, 1996, 1997, 2548, 2579, 2585, 2059-2060, 2144-2145, 2462, 2477, 2717, 2727, 2748, 2749, 2855, 2933, 2936, 2955, 3067, 3108, 3544, 3546, 3548, 3550, 3555-3557, 3560, 3563, 3566
Earth to Ashes, 1063
Earullo, Fred, 1063
Earvin, Harvey, 3455
Easley, Elbert, 3448
Easley, Ike, 3451
East, Clay, 2817
East, Wayne, 3455
East, William 116
East, Winifred, 1063
East Berlin Riot, 3376
Eastburn, Gary, 1517
Eastburn, Kathryn, 1517
East Coast Conspiracy to Save Lives, 3491
Easter, Mary Ann, 1891
Easter Commandos, 3530
Eastland, James, 3356
Eastman, Edward "Monk", 164, 298, 301, 813, 1063-1065, 1172, 1652, 2004, 2876,

2970, 3147, 3218, 3224, 3225, 3403, 3404, 3407, 3410-3412
Eastman, Robert, 1065-1066
Eastman Gang, 1652
Easton, Francis J., 2423
Easton, Jane, 1431
Easton, Rufus, 1066
East St. Louis, Ill. Race Riot (July 2, 1917), 1066, 3375
East St. Louis, Ill., Race Riot (May 28, 1917), 1066, 3375
East Side Crashers, 3404
East Side Dramatic and Pleasure Club, 3404
East Side White Pride, 2773
Eastwood, Clint, 1329
Eastwood, Edwin John, 3328, 3331
Eastwood, John Francis, 1066
Eatman, Robert, 2127
Eaton, Charles, 24
Eaton, Cyrus, 1658
Eaton, Dennis W., 3456
Eaton, Helen Spence, 1066
Eaton, Nathaniel, 1066
Eaton, Richard, 547
Eaton, Robert, 807
Eaton, Winthrop, 3451
Eaves, Walter Musker, 220
Ebbets, William R., 1048
Ebbo of Reims 1066
Ebeid Pasha, 3250
Ebel, Johann Wilhelm, 1066
Eberhardt, Fred O., 1066
Eberhardt, Susan, 2821
Ebermayer, Ludwig, 1066
Ebersold, Frederick, 3424
Ebert, Friedrich, 3086
Ebert, Paul, 2250
Eberwein, C., 3248
Ebner, Esther, 1066
Ebner, Gerald, 1400
Eboli, Ana de Mendoza de, 1066
Eboli, Louis, 2405, 3384
Eboli, Ralph, 3298
Eboli, Thomas "Tommy Ryan", 427, 1066-1067, 3299, 3404
Eccles, R.G., 2527
Ecevit, Bulent, 912
Echazabal, Rodriguez, 3254
Echevarria, Carlos Aguero, 3530
Echeverria, Esteban, 1067
Echeverria, José Marie, 1395
Echeverry, Gloria Lara de, 3260, 3524
Echezarreta-Cruz, Modesto, 2163
Echols, Samuel, 3346
Eckart, Dietrich, 1568
Eckdohl, E. Carl, 1236
Eckel, John, 846
Ecker, Lewis C., II, 1067
Eckert, Thomas, 1962
Eckes, Christa, 3475
Eckles, Delena R., 1067
Ecklund, Edward, 1067
Eclanum, Julian of, 1749
Economidou, Artemis, 3147
Ed-Dawlah, Solat, 3248
Edalji, George, 294, 1016, 1067-1068
Edalji, Shapurji, 1067
Edd, G.W., 3361
Edde, Emile, 3250
Edde, Raymond, 1068
Eddleman, Dick, 2744
Eddmonds, Durlyn, 3451
Eddowes, Catherine, 1685, 1690
Eddy, Mary Baker, 1662
Ede, Dewey, 2941
Edel, Frederick W., 1068
Edelbacher, Peter, 3448
Edelmann, Johann Christian, 1068

Edelson, Mitchell, Jr., 1068
Edelstein, David Norton, 411, 1068
Edelstein, W.N., 2480
Eden, Charles, 388
Eden, Robert Anthony, 3251
Eden, Sir William, 1629
Edens, Lloyd, 1331
Edens, William, 3337
Ederle, Gertrude, 1977
Edgar, Jimmy L., 1068-1069
Edgar, Johnny, 1068-1069
Edgar, Nathaniel, 2930
Edgar the Peaceful, 1069
Edgecombe, John, 2506
Edgell, C.W., 1632
Edgerly, James A., 2684
Edgerton, Alonzo Jay, 1069
Edgerton, Henry White, 1069
Edgerton, Sidney, 1069
Edghill, Carlos Antonio, 1069
Edglin, John, 3082
Edinburgh, Duke Alfred of 91-92
Edinburgh Mock Battle Death, 1069
Edison, Thomas A., 1245, 1657
Editor Shannan, 3564
Edlestein, Edward, 1328
Edmands, Violet, 2579
Edmier, John L., 2549
Edmonds, Ann, 1069
Edmonds, Dana, 3456
Edmonds, Dorothy, 3085
Edmonds, Edmund, 1069
Edmonds, Jeanette, 1069
Edmonds, John W., 417
Edmondson, Mary, 1069-1070
Edmund, (Brit. pr.841-70), 1070
Edmund I, (Brit. pr.922-46) 1038, 1070, 3236, 3248
Edmund II Ironside, 1052
Edmund of Woodstock, 2229
Edmund, Franz Creffield, 2191
Edmund, Jarecki, K., 618
Edmund, William, 3030
Edmunds, Christiana, 1070
Edmunds, George Franklin, 1070
Edmunds, Mabel Jennings, 1723
Edmunds, N.B., 2707
Edmunds, Peter, 221
Edmunds, William Charles, 1070
Edmundson, Calvin Jerome, 1070
Edrington, W.R., 639
Edward (Earl of Warwick), 1071
Edward (The Martyr), 1109, 1070-1071
Edward, Prince of Wales, 3238
Edward I, 763, 1071, 1434, 2120, 2271, 3081
Edward II, 917, 926, 1071, 1171, 1286, 1882, 2229, 2236, 2930, 3238,
Edward III, 41, 858, 1361, 2229, 2534, 2576, 2932, 3198
Edward IV, 464, 720, 1031, 1051, 1071, 1200, 2308, 2576, 2748, 2836, 2852, 2958, 3012, 3090, 3185, 3238
Edward V, 464, 720, 1071, 1518, 2979, 3238
Edward VI, 567, 1096, 1268, 1383, 1630, 2731, 2765
Edward VII, 683, 1071, 1690, 2157, 2433
Edward VIII, 426, 1071, 2058, 2235, 3248
Edward of Norwich 1071
Edward the Black Prince, 3324
Edward, Mrs. Albert Vonderahe, 2721
Edward, Anderson,, 1050
Edward, Charles, (Scot. pr.1725-61), 1083, 1086, 2034
Edward, James, 2154
Edward, William, 3352
Edwardh, Marlys, 2413
Edwards, Augustus, 2569
Edwards, Bob, 2052, 3548
Edwards, Buster, 1371, 1372

3558, 3564, 3566
Evans, Christopher, 1111
Evans, Connie Ray, 3447
Evans, Dan, 3558
Evans, Daniel R., 3331
Evans, David (Brit. prom 1700s) 1111
Evans, David (U.S. prom. 1981), 231
Evans, Donald C., 840
Evans, E. Gerald, 1472
Evans, Edward, 2212
Evans, Elizabeth, 1803
Evans, Evan, 1111-1112
Evans, Franklin B., 1112
Evans, Gary, 493
Evans, George (Brit. pr.1965), 1301
Evans, George (U.S. 1890s), 1230
Evans, Gwynne Owen 98
Evans, Haydn Evan, 1112
Evans, Henry, 1112
Evans, Herbert, 2128
Evans, Hiram Wesley, 1858
Evans, Ingvelde, 234
Evans, J.C., 3368
Evans, James, 1952, 3166
Evans, James T., 848
Evans, Jasper, 1298
Evans, Jerome, 1331
Evans, Jerry, 3359
Evans, Jesse, (U.S. pr.1870s), 311, 363, 368,
    486, 507, 1112-1113, 1361, 1554-1555,
    2149, 2717, 2727, 3544, 3545, 3547,
    3549-3551, 3553-3555, 3557, 3558, 3559,
    3560
Evans, Jesse, (U.S. d.1897), 3348
Evans, John, (Brit. pr.1722), 1113
Evans, John, (U.S. d.1913), 3363
Evans, John, (U.S. deathrow), 3447
Evans, Johnnie Lee, 3451
Evans, Jonathan, 3454
Evans, Joseph, 3546
Evans, Larry Dean, 1113
Evans, Lila May, 2941
Evans, Lou, 2512
Evans, Mary, (Brit. prom. 1909), 1627
Evans, Mary (U.S. 1957-), 1113
Evans, Mary, (Brit. b.1813), 2966
Evans, Michael, 1113
Evans, Michael Wayne, 3447
Evans, Nat "Brown", 399
Evans, O.P., 2917
Evans, Orinda Dale, 1113
Evans, R.D., 3060
Evans, Rees W., 1113-1114
Evans, Robert, 3300
Evans, Rut, 3546
Evans, Spencer, 3365
Evans, Terence T., 219
Evans, Thomas, 3019
Evans, Timothy John, 705, 1946
Evans, Vernon, 3452
Evans, Walter E., 1114
Evans, Walter Howard, 1114
Evans, Wilburt, 3456
Evans, William, 1111-1112
Evans, Winifred, 1532
Evans Gang, 3545, 3547, 3549-3551
Evarts, Robert, 3344
Evarts, William Maxwell, 1114
Evatt, Herbert Vere, 1114
Eve, Mother, 691
Evelyn, Gladys, 2155
Everdeane, Margaret, 2072
Everest, Wesley, 663
Everett, Charles, 3341
Everett, John, 1114
Everett, Madeline, 1050
Everett Massacre, 1114
Everett, Melba, 1050
Everett, Ronald James, 1300-1301

Everett, William Meade, Jr., 2097
Everhard, Lydia, 1501
Everhart, Jeffery L., 2827
Everingham, Paul, 671
Everington, James W., 3425
Everitt, Frank (Brit. 1890-1946), 1114-
    1115, 1392
Everleigh, Ada, 18, 1115, 2970, 3384
Everleigh, Minna, 97, 1115, 2970, 3384
Everleigh Sisters, 758, 804, 1115-1117,
    3102, 3121
Evers, Medgar W., 1117, 3255
Eversole, Joseph, 1234, 1235
Every, Henry, 1117-1119
Evetts, J.H., 3546
Evil-Merodach, 1717
Evinrude, Ralph, 660
Evola, Natale "Joe Diamond", 136, 2542,
    3294, 3404
Evrard, Simmone, 2117
Ewald, George, 2717
Ewald, George F., 811
Ewart, Hamilton Glover, 1119
Ewart, William, 1119
Ewart-Biggs, Christopher, 1119, 1664,
    3257, 3270, 3504
Ewen, B.J., 2119
Ewing, Robert, 3517
Ewing, Russ, 1551, 3173
Ewing, Thomas C., 2521
Ex parte Milligan, 3106
Executive Committee for the Liberation of
    Palestine, 3468, 3483
Executive Securities Corp., 3289
Exner, Dan, 1120
Exner, Judith Campbell, 1119-1120, 1306,
    1614
Expansion Committee, 3481
Experius, 2153
Exxon Corp., 3289
Eyadema, Etienne, 3256
Eye, Dr. Charles, 956
Eyler, Larry, 3451
Eyler, Larry W., 1120-1121
Eyman, David L., 1121
Eyraud, Michel, 1121-1122
Eystein, 2759
Eyton, Charles, 2903, 2904
Ezaki Katsuhisa, 1122
Ezekiels, Alexander, 3546
Ezzeddine, Hassan, 1433

F

Faber, Abraham, 2179
Faber, Charles, 101, 3546
Faber, Frederick, 1742
Faber, Horace, 494
Fabian, Lillian, 2299
Fabian, Robert, 349, 715, 1226, 1300,
    1415, 2057, 2089, 2658, 2710
Fabiano, Sandra, 1123
Fabre d'Eglantine, 1123
Fabrizi, Nicola, 1123
Fabrizius, Paula, 2305
Facq, Louis, 926
Facta, Luigi, 2264
Factor, Jerome, 1124, 1125
Factor, John "Jake The Barber", 225,
    1123-1125, 1642, 2976, 3326, 3326
Fadallah Abu Mansur, 3215
Fadell, Fred, 1842
Fagan, Michael, 661, 1125, 3283

Fagard, Edmond, 1125
Faget, M., 3249
Fagin, Michael, 3301
Fagler, John, 3356
Fagner, Richard, 1730
Fahey, Eileen, 2432
Fahey, Francis, 2433
Fahey, Helen, 2826
Fahmy Bey, Prince Ali Kamel, 1125
Fahmy, Marie-Marguérite, 1125-1126, 1424
Fahner, Ty, 3011
Fahringer, Herald Price, 1189
Fahy, Henry, 3454
Fahy, William, 1126
Failla, James, 3404
Failla, Louis R., 3379
Fain, Grover C., 3367
Fain, John W., 1798
Fain, William, 3546
Fainer, Joseph, 2737
Fair, Emma, 3343
Fair, Laura (U.S. 1837-1919), 1126
Fair, Laura (U.S. d.1870), 1312
Fair, Laura D., 3241
Fair, May, 737
Fair, William D., 1126
Fairall, William, 1827
Fairbank, Robert, 3448
Fairbanks, Douglas, 1849
Fairbanks, Jason, 1126-1127
Fairbanks, Ronnie, 2073
Fairchild, Barry, 3448
Fairchild, Charles, 3007
Fairchild, Richard, 829
Fairchild, Thomas Edward, 1127
Fairchild, Wiley, 2340
Fairfax, Thomas, 2530
Fairlie, Walter, 1127
Fairris, Bethel, 1127
Fairris, Hurbie Franklin, Jr., 1127
Fairris, Iwana, 1127
Fairstein, Linda, 673
Faisal, 1127-1128, 2753, 3252, 3253, 3257
Faisal Bin Musaed Bin Abdulaziz, 1127-
    1128
Faisal II, 1128, 1767
Faisans, Georges, 3378
Faisst, Ray L., 2713
Faithfull, Stanley, 1128
Faithfull, Starr, 564, 1128-1130, 3296
Fakhr al-Din II, 1130, 3239
Fakkak, The, 1130
FAL, 3328
Falangists, 3512, 3530
Falcén, Alberto Sicilia, 2147, 2663
Falco, Thomas "Big Tony", 762
Falcon, Sicilia, 3393, 3397
Falconde, M., 3248
Falconieri, Francesco, 2222
Falconieri, Michelangelo, 3415, 3416
Fales, Elizabeth, 1126, 1127
Falieri, Marino, 1130
Falk, Arno, 2403
Falk, Cats, 1414
Falkenberg, Peter, 436
Falkenstein, Julius, 917
Falkirk Cat Burglar Case, 1130
Falkis, Nicholas J., 1195
Falkland, Richard, 318
Falkner, Frederick, 3558
Fall, Albert Bacon, 554, 1130, 1204, 1451,
    1612, 2908, 2911, 3549, 3552, 3558, 3564,
    3567
Fall, James, 3305
Fall, Philip, 3546, 3558
Fall River Legend, 1132
Falla, Raul, 3513
Fallaci, Oriana, 1811
Fallen, Horace, 2433

Fregonese, Hugo, 2103
Freiberg, Solly, 411
Freidgood, Dr. Charles E., 1233-1234
Freidgood, Sophie, 1234
Freidland, David, 1234
Freihage, Florence, 2717
Freiheit, Heike, 1987
Freihoff, William, 1234
Freisler, Roland, 1234, 1577, 1578, 3539
Freisner, Isidore, 598
Freita, Joao de, 3243
Freitas, Joseph, 3121
Freitas, Michael de, 2096
Frelinghuysen, Frederick Theodore, 1234
Fremont, John C., 1838, 3168
French, A.H., 1204
French, Alfred, 2190
French, Fulton, 1234-1235
French, G.P., 1235
French, George Arthur, 1235
French, Harry, 1235
French, J.B., 259
French, James, 3558
French, Jeanne, 390
French, Jim, 364, 771, 1235, 1559, 1654,
    3071, 3228
French, John Denton Pinkstone, 3244
French, Mary Rae, 2693
French, R.A., 1235
French, Roy, 3379
French, Thomas, 424
French-Algerian Riots, 3376
French Anti-Clerical Riots, 3375
French Bread Riots, 3371, 3372
French Corn Riots, 3371
French Draft Riots, 3371
French Financial Riots, 3370
French Food Riots, 3370, 3371
French Labor Riot, 3372
French Quarter, 3398-3400
French Revolution of 1848, 3373
French Revolutionary Brigades, 3277, 3531
French Riviera Gang Wars, 1235
French School Riots, 3375
French Silk Weavers Riot, 3373
French Spinners Riot, 3372
French Student Riots, 3378
Freneau, Philip Morin, 1235-1236
Frente Argentino de Liberacion, 3530, 3531
Frente Revolucionario AntiFascista y
    Patriotica, 3531
Frente Sandinistande Liberacion Nacional
    (FSLN), 3468, 3487, 3504, 3531
Frente Urbana Zapatista, 3531, 3535
Frerichs, Friedrich Theodor von, 1236
Frescan, Cesario, 3558
Freschi, John J., 1399
Frese, Luis A., 3466
Fresina, Carmelo, 2466
Fresno State College, 3289
Fretwell, Bobby Ray, 3448
Freud, Sigmund, 3293
Freund, Christine, 345
Freund, Valentin, 1967
Frey, Clifford, 2278
Frey, Eric, 1096
Frey, Gerard, 1285
Frey, Roderick, 3454
Frey, Saundra, 1096
Frey, Willi, 1236, 3539
Frey, William, 1223
Freyer, John, 3292
Friar, Art, 1636
Friar, Jubel, 1636
Frick, Henry Clay, 343, 344, 598, 1138, 1332,
    1606
Frick, Wilhelm, 1236, 3040, 3539
Fricke, Charles, 694
Fricke, Charles W., 2739

Friday Market, 1236
Friderichs, Hans, 1877
Frieake, Edward, 3071
Fried, Arthur, 1399
Fried, Hugo, 1399
Friedberg, Lesser, 3384, 3388, 3390
Friede, William, 853
Friedenberg, Hans Georg von, 3539
Friedman, Abraham, 3404
Friedman, Arthur, 3296
Friedman, Charles, 3394
Friedman, Daniel, 906
Friedman, Harold, 3392
Friedman, Isadore, 3403
Friedman, Maurice, 776
Friedman, Solly, 3384
Friedman, Walter "Good Time Charley",
    629
Friedman, Zeev, 1081, 1143
Friedson, Annete, 1231
Friend, Emmanuel "Manny", 2939
Friend, Harry J., 1722
Friend, Hugo, 1885
Friend, John, 1562
Friend-Smith, Ernest, 1001
Friend, Wilbert Felix, 1236
Frierson, Lavell, 3448
Fries, John (U.S. 1750-1818), 1236
Frink, D.B., 3558
Frink, John, 2416
Frink, John B. (U.S. pr.1840s-60s), 21,
    1236-1237
Frisbee, Willard, 1876
Frisby, Royal, 3340
Frisco Sue, 1237
Friser, Ingram, 2126
Fristoe, Leonard T., 1237
Fritchey, Clayton, 568
Frith, John, 810, 1237
Frith, Mary, 850
Frith, William Powell, 853
Fritsch, Freiherr Werner von, 1573
Fritsch, Moritz, 2119
Fritsch, Theodor, 2543
Fritz, Gretchen, 2693
Fritz, Ursula, 295
Fritz, Wendy, 2693
Fritz, Will, 550
Fritzsche, Hans, 1237, 3539
Friuli, Duke of, 1390
Friuli, Marquis of, 1877
Frobish, Harold, 107, 3302
Frobisher, John, 586, 1678
Frobisher, Martin, 1424
Froehling, Lucille, 1478
Froehling, Walter Otto, 1478
Frog Hollow Gang, 2699
Frog Hollows, 3404
Froines, John, 698
Fromant, Kenneth Joseph, 2934
Frome, Nancy, 1237
Frome, Weston G., 1237
Frome, Mrs. Weston G., 1237-1238
Fromentin, Eligius, 1238
Fromm, Friedrich, 1576
Fromme, Lynette Alice "Squeaky", 1195,
    3257, 3502
Frommer, Fritz, 3114
Fronckiewicz, Mark, 3455
Fronde, The, 1238
Frondizi, Arturo, 1077, 3254
Front de Liberation de la Bretagne-Armee
    Revolutionnaire Bretonne, 3530, 3531
Front de Liberation du Quebec (FLQ),
    1238, 1897, 3264, 3265, 3328, 3477,
    3485, 3530, 3531
Front de Liberation National, 3476, 3530,
    3531
Front de Liberation of Algeria, 3530, 3531

Front for Counter Power, 3277, 3278
Front for the Liberation of Lebanon From
    Foreigners, 3274, 3276
Front for the Liberation of Lebanon, 3516,
    3517, 3531
Front for the Liberation of Occupied South
    Yemen, 3530, 3531
Front Line, 3531
Front Line and Fighting Communist
    Formations, 3505
Front Page, The, 3089
Frosh, Stanley B., 2030, 2164
Frost, Clattie, Jr., 504
Frost, David, 1623
Frost, George William, 1238
Frost, John, 1238
Frost, Nathaniel, 462
Frost, Richard Percival Bodeley, 1346
Frost, Samuel, 1238-1239
Fruett, David Mark, 3456
Frugoni, E., 3249
Fry, Elizabeth, 1239, 2310
Fry, Jack, 3328, 3484
Fry, John, 1239, 3346
Fry, Peggy Ann, 1127
Fry, Ralph A., 3295
Fry, Sir Edward, 1239
Fryatt, Charles Algernon, 1239
Frye, Edward, 307
Frye, Jerry G., 3448
Fryer, Lucy, 3364
Frykowski, Voyteck, 2111
Fu-ch'i, 3243
Fu Hsiao-an, 3249
Fu Siau-En, 3249
Fu Su, 1970
Fuad I, 1135
Fuca, Patsy, 3404
Fucaloro, Anthony, 1134-1135
Fucceri, Louis, 3404
Fuchs, Bernard, 1239
Fuchs, Ernst, 1239
Fuchs, Roy, 3327
Fuchsberg, Jacob D., 1819
Fudge, Keith, 3448
Fuenta Argentino de Liberation, 3484
Fuentes, Jose, 3448
Fuerst, Ruth, 706, 708
Fuerst, Walter, 1302
Fuerzas Armadas de Liberación Nacional,
    1132, 3269, 3270, 3276, 3500-3503, 3505,
    3521, 3527
Fuerzas Armadas Peronistas (FAP), 3483,
    3498
Fuerzas Armadas Rebeldes (FAR), 3265,
    3479, 3483, 3484, 3491, 3497, 3499, 3507,
    3520
Fuerzas Armadas Revolucionarias de
    Colombia, 3531
Fuerzas Revolucionarias Armadas del
    Pueblo, 3531
Fugate, Caril Ann, 2840, 2842
Fugiwara, Kamatari, 2812
Fugmann, Karl, 3181
Fugmann, Michael, 1239, 1841
Fujiwara Sumitomo, 1239
Fujui, Y., 3251
Fuk Yee Hing Triad Society, 3391
Fukuda, M., 3245
Fukunaga, Myles Yutaka, 1239-1240
Fulcher, Alice, 267
Fulda, Abbot of, 754
Fulgam, James, 3547
Fulkerson, Samuel Cole, 1240
Fullam, Augusta Fairfield, 1240
Fulle, Floyd, 1240
Fuller, A., 2237
Fuller, Aaron, 3455
Fuller, Albert, 2422

Gallegos, Nestor, 3559
Gallegos, Pantaeleon, 3559
Gallegos, Rómulo, 908
Galleshaw, Frankie, 3332
Galleshaw, Tammy, 3332
Galletti, Anna, 2575
Gall, Eugene, 3451
Gall, Franz Joseph, 579, 1254
Galley, William, 1827, 2897
Galli-Curci, Amelita, 756
Gallichan, David, 2337
Gallichio, Anthony, 516
Gallico, Paul, 629
Gallighen, Mona, 1829-1830
Galliher, Carl, 2180
Gallinari, Prospero, 2223
Gallo, Albert, 1257, 3405
Gallo Brothers, 754, 755, 1256, 2046
Gallo Gang, 2
Gallo, Joseph "Crazy Joe", 2, 116, 120, 245,
     754, 1256, 1651, 1730, 2012, 3401, 3402,
     3403, 3405, 3407, 3408, 3253
Gallo, Lawrence, 120, 3405
Gallo-Profaci War, 1257
Gallo, Samuel, 664, 1255-1256
Gallo, William, 414, 1296
Gallogly, Richard Gray, 1257
Gallop, Captain (Brit., pr.1759), 1432
Gallory, Richard, 1466
Gallostra, Jose, 3252
Galloway, Alexander, 3425
Galloway, Joseph, 1257
Galloway, Kerry, 1312
Galloway, Richard, 3362
Galloway, Robert, 1257
Gallows Garden, The, 1257
Gallus, Caesar, 1257
Gallus, Gaius Vibius Trebonianus, 1257,
     3235
Gallus Mag, 1257, 3405
Gallwey, Patrick, 2337
Galman, Rolando, 140
Galmot, Jean, 3246
Galoui, Si Hadi Thami, 3252
Galswintha, 521, 1257, 2759, 3236
Galsworthy, John, 2652
Galt, Judge, 1728
Galt, Thomas, 1826
Galton, Francis, 1138, 1257-1258, 1519, 3065
Galton, Paul, 644
Galton, Thomas, 351
Galvaligi, Enrico, 3258, 3507
Galvao, Henrique, 1258, 3321
Galvez, José, 1258
Galvez, Marion, 1828
Galvez, Orlando, 3301
Galvez, Roberto, 3329, 3497
Galvin, John, 3559
Galvin, Lillian, 374
Galvin, Marjorie, 2803
Galvin, Tom, 1258
Gam, Wiley, 3354
Gama, Stephen Ferrera de, 1083
Gamarra, Agustin, 2663
Gambardella, Dominic, 1134
Gambetta, Léon-Michel, 1258
Gambino, Anthony Peter, 3399
Gambino, Carlo, 32, 116, 118, 120, 136, 223,
     427, 655, 754, 797, 908, 1018, 1099, 1250,
     1251, 1253, 1256, 1259, 1306, 1350, 2085,
     2087, 2138, 2505, 2574, 3399, 3401-3405,
     3412
Gambino, Emmanuel, 3405
Gambino, Frank "Don Chick", 109, 1292
Gambino, Giuseppe, 3405
Gambino, Manny, 1350
Gambino, Paolo, 3405
Gambino, Philip "Fat Fungi", 2012
Gambino, Thomas, 3403, 3405

Gambi, Vincent, 1258, 1872, 3399
Gamble, A.E., 562
Gamble, John, 3344
Gamblers Row, 3385
Gambola, John, 3351
Gambrell, Roderick Dhu, 1435
Gambrill, Bill, 1235
Gambrill, Henry, 789, 1259-1260
Gamelin, Maurice Gustave, 1261
Game, Philip Woolcott, 1260-1261, 3426
Games, James, 3451
Gamson, Benny, 1261
Ganci, Giuseppe, 2473, 3405
Gancia, Vittorio Vallarino, 488, 2552
Gandhi, Indira, 226, 1261, 2442, 3258,
     3261, 3378, 3512, 3527
Gandhi, Mohandas Karamchand, 426,
     1051, 1261-1264, 1324, 1823, 2101,
     2297, 2418, 2683, 3252
Gandhi, Rajiv, 2442, 3220, 3261
Gandia, Giovanni of, 1316
Gandil, Arnold "Chick", 399
Gandillon, Antoinette, 1264
Gandillon, Georges, 1264
Gandillon, Perrenette, 1264
Gandillon, Pierre, 1264
Gandolfe, Jeanne, 1264
Gandolfo, James V., 2692
Gandy, Gene, 1821
Ganeff, M., 3248
Ganev, Gantscho, 3093
Ganey, James Cullen 1264
Gangy, Paul W., 1264-1265
Gannon, Tommy, 238
Ganse, Anderson, 3351
Gans, Lillian, 1835
Gans, Sydney, 1835
Gant, Hugh, 1645
Gant, Riley, 1645
Gant, W.C., 1265
Gantt, John M., 1218, 1219
Gantz, John, 1344
Gantz, Richard, 3462
Ganz, Jacob, 2452
Gapacini, Albert, 2951
Gapolan, 2547
Gapon, George, 410, 2328
Garabedian, David, 1265
Garand, John Cantius, 1265
Garat, Dominique Joseph, 1265
Garat, Joseph, 2845
Garber, Anna 121
Garber, Conrad 121
Garber, Jerome, 3228
Garceau, Robert, 3448
Garces, Sardi, 3253
Garcia, Alredo R., 3245
Garcia, Amado, 2997, 3254
Garcia, Antonio, 422
Garcia, Bartole, 3558
Garcia, Benigno, 3520
Garcia, Carlos, 2969
Garcia, Demas, 3565
Garcia, Emmett, 656
Garcia, Enrique, 3449
Garcia, Fernando, 3333, 3455, 3465
Garcia, Francisco, 475, 3498
Garcia, Henry, 3449
Garcia, Ignacio, 1363, 3512
Garcia, Iñiguez, 1265
Garcia, Inez, 1265
Garcia, Isabel 46
Garcia, Javier, 1455
Garcia, Joaquin, 3465
Garcia, John Abbes, 354
Garcia, Jose Guillermo, 3508
Garcia, Joseph, 3228
Garcia, Joseph, Jr., 1266

Garcia, Joseph, Sr., 1266
Garcia, Juan, 1181
Garcia, Luis, 1266
Garcia, Manuel "Three-Fingered Jack",
     1266-1267, 2256, 3414
Garcia, Manuel Philip, 1267
Garcia, Manuel Vigil, 3245
Garcia, Maria Jose, 3514
Garcia, Nelson, 3158
Garcia, Nicanor, 3558
Garcia, Otto Walter, 3258, 3512
Garcia, Percy, 1267
Garcia, Ramino, 3465
Garcia, Ramon, 3466, 3480
Garcia, Rolando, 2408, 3449
Garcia, Samuel Ocaa, 3398
Garcia, Suarez, 3480
Garcia Guerrero, Amado, 3254
Garcia Landaeta, Ivan G., 3469
Garcia Leyva, Jose, 3299
Garcia Lorca, Federico, 1267, 1990
Garcia Menocal, Mario, 1267, 3245
Garcia Meza, Luis, 3301
Garcia Moreno, Gabriel, 1267, 3242
Garcia Ramirez, Garcia, 1651
Garcia Zurita, Juan Francisco, 3466
Gard, Edward, 272, 2814
Gard, George E., 3425
Gardelle, Theodore, 1267-1268, 3003
Garden, James, 3358
Garden, Mary, 756
Gardiner, Alexander, 597, 598
Gardiner, Bishop 465, 2117
Gardiner, Faikai, 312
Gardiner, Frank, 1268, 1421
Gardiner, John, 1814
Gardiner, Lord 3258, 3514
Gardiner, Stephen, 1268
Gardiner, William George, 939, 1268, 1906,
     3150
Gardner, 2108
Gardner, Archibald K., 1268-1269
Gardner, Billy Conn, 3455
Gardner, "Chicago Jack", 2174
Gardner, David, 3455
Gardner, Deo, 1084
Gardner, Eric, 563
Gardner, Erle Stanley, 212, 419, 585, 1269,
     1452
Gardner, Henry, 3358
Gardner, John, 3453
Gardner, Joseph, 3463
Gardner, Larrie, 1908
Gardner, Laurene, 1386, 1387
Gardner, Margery, 1504, 1505
Gardner, Mark, 3448
Gardner, Raymond Hatfield, 3547
Gardner, Rheta, 3198
Gardner, Ronnie Lee, 3456
Gardner, Roy, 52, 224, 1269-1270
Gardner, Wilson, 3362
Gardstein, George, 1625, 2758
Gareis, Hans J.K., 1279
Gareis, William B., 1528
Garesio, Antonio, 1270
Garesio, Gian Battista, 1270
Garfias, Pete, 3559
Garfield, James Abram, 765, 814, 1270-
     1275, 1794, 2071, 2150, 3232, 3242
Garfield, John, 2028
Garfield, Samuel, 871
Garfinkle, David, 3029
Gargan, Bridie, 2022
Gargani, Giuseppe, 818
Gargan, Thomas J., 3424
Gargano, Michael, 3298
Gargotta, Charles, 370
Gargullo, Merlita, 2822
Garibaldi, Giuseppe, 660, 1123, 2288, 2455,

2504, 3305
Garibay, Robert, 40
Garippo, Louis B., 1440, 2990
Garland, Augustus Hill, 1275
Garland, Bonnie, 1525
Garland, Joan, 1525
Garland, John, 1072
Garland, Wallace Graydon, 1275
Garlick, Edward Donald, 1275
Garlick, Elizabeth, 765
Garlick, R.R., 3247
Garmire, Bernard, 3425
Garner, Elmer, 2137
Garner, John Nance "Cactus Jack", 1278
Garner, Ralph H., 2793
Garner, S.G., 3364
Garner, Samuel, 3338
Garner, Stanley, 1275
Garner, Vance, 1275
Garness, L.A., 1328
Garnet, Mark John, 778
Garnett, Clarence, 3353
Garnier, Gilles, 1275-1276
Garnier, Pierre, 432
Garnsey, Sir Gilbert, 1477
Garofalo, Frank, 136, 3405
Garofalo, Vincent, 3405
Garozzo, Fred, 2998
Garr, E.S., 914
Garrecht, Francis Arthur, 1276
Garret, James, 2857
Garret, Katherine, 1276
Garret, Thomas, 1276
Garretson, William, 2111
Garrett, Billy, 2315
Garrett, Buck, 3547
Garrett, Daniel, 3455
Garrett, Della, 3353
Garrett, Dorcas, 1826
Garrett, George Nathaniel, 3394
Garrett, James, 1507
Garrett, Joao Baptiste da Silva Leitao de
     Almeida, 1276
Garrett, Joe, 3559
Garrett, John, 531
Garrett, Johnny F., 3455
Garrett, Oliver B., 847, 3379
Garrett, Oliver H.P., 1998
Garrett, Patrick Floyd, 96, 122, 205, 318,
     366, 369, 486, 507, 673, 775, 1276-1279,
     1920, 1966, 2046, 2052, 2181-2182, 2462,
     2727, 3049, 3427, 3544, 3545, 3547-3550,
     3553-3555, 3559, 3562-3565
Garrett, Rebecca, 735
Garrett, Richard, 1960
Garrett, Richard P., 782
Garrett, Silas, 2422
Garrett, William, 2024
Garrette, Simeon, 3339
Garrick, David, 321
Garrick, George, 3303
Garrick, Luke, 2102
Garris, John, 1279
Garrison, Barnett Wade, 2234
Garrison, David Lloyd, 3373
Garrison, Donald Graham, 1279-1280
Garrison, James, 1632
Garrison, Richard, 3448
Garrison, William Lloyd, 1298, 2934
Garrity, Breezy, 1025, 3147
Garrity, John J., 606, 3424
Garrity, Leona, 3385
Garrity, Wendell Arthur, Jr., 1280
Garr, Jack, 914
Garr, Roy, 914
Garrow, Robert, 1280
Garry, Charles, 1265, 1739
Garside, William, 693, 1280
Garsson, Henry M., 1280

Garsson, Murray, 1280
Gartner, Frank, 2939
Gartside, John Edward, 1280
Garvan, Francis Patrick, 1280
Garvard, Elmo, 3359
Garvey, James J., 2990
Garvey, Marcus Aurelius, 1280-1281, 3295
Garvey, Mike, 1281
Garvie, Maxwell, 2919
Garvie, Mervyn, 1281
Garvie, Sheila Watson, 2919
Garvin, Edward Louis, 1281
Garvin, Sandra, 1356
Garwood, Robert R., 1281-1282
Gary, "Red", 3385
Gary, Carlton, 1282, 3450
Gary, Elbert Henry, 1282, 2910, 3021
Gary, Ind., Police Department, 1282
Gary, Joseph Easton 106, 1497
Garza, Catarino, 1282, 3559
Garza, Isuaro, 1282
Gasca, Pedro de la, 1282
Gascoigne, Richard, 2133
Gascoigne, William, 1282
Gascoyne, Crisp, 599
Gas House Gang, 1283, 1724, 3405, 3407
Gash, Stanton, 1282-1283
Gaskins, Donald Henry "Pee Wee", 1283,
     3454
Gaskins, Larry, 1513
Gasoline Trust, 1283
Gasperi, Alcide De, 3251
Gasperoni, Antonio, 1283-1284
Gasre, Iran Prison Escape, 1284
Gass, Carl, 2227
Gassell, Mandel, 3405
Gassmann, F.L., 2238
Gassowski, Paul, 3250
Gaston, George, 573
Gaston, Ike, 1860
Gaston, Lucy Page, 3385
Gaston, William, 1284, 2159
Gastonia Communists, 1498
Gatch, Charles A., 1958
Gates, Daryl F., 1284, 3425
Gates, Harry, 3354
Gates, Horatio, 569, 768, 3158, 3303
Gates, Johnny Lee, 3450
Gates, John W. "Bet-a-Million", 597, 1115
Gates, Oscar, 3448
Gates, Rick L., 1284
Gates, Samuel, 3365
Gates, Thomas, 2583
Gates, William (U.S. d.1897), 3348
Gates, William (U.S. d.1891), 3340
Gathers, Demetrious, 3454
Gathers, Philip, 3366
Gatley, Clement Carpenter, 1284
Gatlin, Alma Petty, 1284
Gatti, Salvatore, 1284-1285
Gattucio, Jasper, 3060
Gattuso, John, 1109, 2812, 3385
Gauchet, Georges, 1285
Gaudry, Nathalis Mathieu, 482-483, 1363
Gaufridi, Louis 45, 396
Gauguin, Paul, 2098
Gaule, John, 1618
Gaulle, Charles de, 232, 671, 901-902, 903,
     2235, 2450, 2663, 2820, 3251, 3254,
     3255
Gault, Julian, 1285
Gault, M.B. "Manny", 262
Gaumata, 588
Gaumer, Catherine de, 45
Gaumer, Jacques, 1363
Gaumer, Monique, 1363
Gaunt, Elizabeth, 1285
Gauntlett, Roger A., 1285
Gauntt, Jean, 2690

Gautama Buddha, 3232
Gauthe, Gilbert, 1285-1286
Gauthier, Monique Huguette, 3511
Gautier, Pierre Jules Theophile, 3292
Gautier, Théophile, 1869
Gautschi, Arthur, 2898
Gauvin, Jacques, 2174
Gaveis, Karl, 3244
Gaveston, Piers, 1286, 1882, 2930
Gavin, John, 586
Gavin, Larry, 3385
Gavin, Michael, 618
Gaviria Escobar, Pablo, 1147
Gaviria, Pablo Escobar, 2161
Gavis, Julia, 3463
Gavrel, Gus, 886
Gavre, Prince of, 1075
Gavriloff, Mirailo, 3246
Gavriloff, Risto, 3246
Gavrush Sarkisya, 2680
Gawden, Elizabeth, 1592, 1593
Gawler, Henry, 3304
Gawthrop, John, 1041
Gaxiola, Angel, 3244
Gay, Benjamin, 3348
Gay, Bill, 1665
Gay, Clestell, 3004
Gay, Daniel, 320
Gaydon, Jonathan, 1286
Gaye, Marvin, 1286
Gay, George, 3366
Gayhart, Tom, 1235
Gay, Jean-Baptiste-Sylvère, 1286
Gay, John, 314, 1445
Gay, Kenneth, 3448
Gayles, Joseph, 767, 1286
Gay, Marvin Pentz, Sr., 1286
Gaynor, "Tom", 1474
Gaynor, William Jay, 304, 307, 309, 370,
     1284, 1286-1287, 2013, 2021, 3075, 3243
Gazaway, Doyle, 3460
Gazell, Jiggs, 2055
Gazzera, Franco, 3249
Gbrurek, Tillie, 1287
Geagan, Michael V., 489
Geale, Eunice Mercel, 1622
Geaquenta, Mack, 1105
Gearish, Anthony, 1287
Gear, William, 3154
Geary, Charles Russell, 1287
Geary, John S., 1287
Geary, Percy, 2107
Gebbia, Leonardo, 1287-1288
Gebbia, Nicolina, 1288
Gebelain, Richard, 2392
Gebhardt, Fritz, 2439, 2869
Gebhardt, Hans Kurt, 3329, 3497
Gebhardt, John, 324
Gebhardt, Karl, 1557, 3539
Gebhart, Joseph, 3338
Gecht, Robin, 1288
Geddes, Eric Campbell, 536
Gedeon, Joseph, 1666, 1667
Gediminas, 1806
Gedney, Bartholomew, 2665
Gee, Charlie, 1288
Gee, David, 1092
Gee, Dorothy, 1288-1289
Gee, Harry, 3296, 3405
Gee, Timothy, 1092
Geelof, Anne, 1086
Geer, Louis Gerhard de, 1289
Geers, William, 2062
Geetere, Frans de, 830
Gehr, Herbert, 1289
Gehrke, Chris, 712
Geidel, Paul, 1289
Gein, Edward, 1289-1290, 1564, 2510
Gein, Henry, 1289

Goins, Jimmy D., 641
Goins Brothers, 1330
Gold Accumulator Swindle, 1330-1331
Gold, Charles, 1073
Gold, Frederick, 1922
Goldbaum, Hy, 3396
Goldberg, Arthur J., 920, 1200, 1331, 2229
Goldberg, Bernard, 681
Goldberg, Jay, 2272
Goldblum, Stanley, 1331, 3289
Goldenberg, Abraham, 1331
Goldenberg, Jack, 1331-1332
Goldenberg, Mark, 1332
Golden, Bertha, 2863
Golden, Isador, 150
Golden, James P., 222, 3554
Golden, John, 3559
Golden, Sadie, 412
Goldenson, Alexander, 1332
Golden, Welcome, 3341
Golde, Stanley, 468
Golding, Anthony, 1336
Goldman, Abraham, 1332
Goldman, Daniel Jesse, 3327
Goldman, Emma, 341, 343, 344, 1188, 1332-
    1333, 1610, 1616, 2051, 2207, 2554
Goldman, Louis, 3297
Goldman, Maurice, 794
Goldman, Murray, 1441
Goldner, Abe, 2689
Goldsborough, Fitzhugh Coyle, 1333-1334
Goldsborough, Robert, 1334
Goldsborough, Thomas Alan, 1334
Goldsby, Crawford, 771, 1334-1335, 1654,
    3559
Goldschmidt, Lena, 650
Goldsmith, Elsie Alice, 2398
Goldsmith, Jack, 2814
Goldstein, Abraham "Bummy", 110, 3385
Goldstein, Al, 1936
Goldstein, David, 2394
Goldstein, George S., 688
Goldstein, Grace, 1764, 1766
Goldstein, Ira, 1803
Goldstein, Isadore, 2765
Goldstein, Louis, 3028
Goldstein, Martin "Bugsy", 112, 117, 2252,
    2563, 3003, 3405, 3410
Goldstein, Michael, 1146
Goldstein, Morris, 1896
Goldstein, Robert, 2336
Goldstein, Sam, 3460
Goldstein, Stuart, 1335-1336
Goldstone, Charles Joseph, 1336
Goldstone, Linda, 3162, 3331
Gold, Vivian, 2785
Goldwater, Barry M., Jr., 372, 3207
Golkar Party, 3230
Golkowski, Johann, 1336
Goll, George, 546
Gollancz, Sir Victor, 1336
Golovnin, A.V., 85
Goluneff, Paul, 1336
Gomes, Gilberto, 480
Gomet, Allen, 3332
Gometz, Randy, 2762
Gomez, Anthony, 2279
Gomez, Arnulfo, 3342
Gomez Carrasco, Fred, 638
Gomez, David, 899
Gomez, Eustaquio, 3248
Gomez, Jose F., 3245
Gomez, Juan, 3559
Gomez, Luis Arce, 3397
Gomez, Maximiliano, 3015
Gomez, Pauline, 3331
Gomez, Roberto Surez, Sr., 2874
Gomide, Aloisio Mares Dias, 3328
Gomide, Dias, 3486

Gompers, Samuel, 553, 816, 2064
Gompers v. the United States, 1602
Gonatas, Antigonus, 2460, 3233
Goncia, Vittoria Vallarina, 847, 3330
Goncourt, Comtesse de 1981
Gondorf, Charley, 1336, 1337, 2032
Gondorf, Fred, 1336, 1337, 2032
Gondorf Brothers, 1336-1337
Gonse, Charles-Arthur, 1023
Gonsky, Paul M., 44, 3385
Gontaut, Armand de, 1337
Gontaut, Charles, 1337
Gontaut Biron, Charles de, 379
Gonzaga, Tomaz Antônio, 1337
Gonzales, Edward E., 1337
Gonzales, Frank, 1337
Gonzales, Joaquim, 3298
Gonzales, Juan, 2857, 3551, 3566
Gonzales, M., 3244
Gonzales, Marcus, 3559
Gonzales, Patricia Mirabel de, 3254
Gonzales, Pedro, 2256
Gonzales, Ralph, 3470
Gonzales, Thomas A., 103, 1161, 1337
Gonzales, Walter, 2706
Gonzalez, Abraham, 3243
Gonzalez, Adolfo Suarez, 141
Gonzalez, Charles, 2460
Gonzalez, Daniel de Jesus Rivera, 3473
Gonzalez, Ireno L., 3343
Gonzalez, Jesse, 3448
González, Jesús, 791
Gonzalez, Jose Alejandro, Jr., 1337
Gonzalez, Mario Estebes, 3301
Gonzalez, Martin, 3448
Gonzalez, Mike, 1074
Gonzalez, Octavio, 743
Gonzalez, Otilio, 3246
González, Pablo, 637
Gonzalez, Rodolfo, 3256
Gonzalez, Rosario, 3156
Gonzalez, T.A., 1338
Gonzalez, Thomas, 834
Gonzalez, Virgilio R., 3099
Gonzolez, Gabriel, 3559
Gonzolez, Juan, 3559
Gonzalez de Suso, Andres, 1363
Gonzalez Medina, Jose, 3467
Gonzalez Piloto, D., 3251
Gonzalez Sanchez, Rigoberto, 3471
Gonzalez Valenzuela, Delfina, 1338
Gonzalez Valenzuela, Maria de Jesús,
    1338
Gonzolez y Blea, Manuel, 3559
Gonzolez y Blea, Martin, 3559
Gooch, Arthur, 1338, 3326
Good, Daniel, 1338
Good, Earl, 2828
Good, Franklin, 3459
Good, Isham, 3559
Good, John H., 1053, 1338-1339, 1920,
    2666, 3550, 3559, 3565
Good, Lee, 3559
Good, Margaret, 948
Good, Millard, 1339
Good, Old Molly, 1338
Good, Sarah, 2666, 2667
Good, Thomas, 3242
Good, Walter, 1339, 1920, 3559
Good, William, 1918
Goodale, Robert, 1339
Goodbye, Miss Lizzie Borden, 1339
Goodchild, George, 893
Goodchild, Pamela, 1159
Goode, Arthur Frederick, III, 1339, 3447
Goode, Eliza, 3350
Goode, Washington, 1339
Goode, Wilson, 2236
Goodell, Francis M, 3470

Gooden, Albert, 3368
Gooden, Lorene P., 3462
Goodere, John Dinelly, 1339
Goodere, Samuel, 1339
Gooderidge, Alice, 871
Goodie, Ed, 1942
Goodin, Carl V., 3424
Gooding, Florence, 1339-1340
Gooding, Frank R., 2066
Gooding, Rose Emma, 1340, 2885
Goodlet, Bill, 3547, 3559
Goodloe, William Cassius, 1340
Goodmacher, Marks, 1340
Goodman, Andrew, 457, 3368
Goodman, Annie, 1826
Goodman, Augustus, 3357
Goodman, Esther, 2545
Goodman, John, 1340
Goodman, Leopold, 2545
Goodman, Louis E., 487, 694
Goodman, Michael, 3455
Goodman, Thomas M. 125
Goodman, William, 3559
Goodnight, Charles, 100, 3547, 3559
Goodpasture, Ernest William, 1340
Goodrich, Arthur, 618
Goodrich, B.W.F., 40
Goodrich, William, 143, 151
Goodspeed, Edgar J., 2195
Goodwin, Alfred Theodore, 1340
Goodwin, Alvin, 3455
Goodwin, Ann, 2463
Goodwin, Bessie, 2979
Goodwin, Doris Kearns, 2868
Goodwin, Edward, 3351
Goodwin, Francis H., 3547
Goodwin, Henry K., 1340
Goodwin, Jack (Brit. d.1706), 672, 1340
Goodwin, James, 1340
Goodwin, Joel, 2833
Goodwin, John, 579
Goodwin, Joyce, 1340-1341
Goodwin, Marvin Clyde, 1341
Goodwin, Paul, 1341
Goodwin, Ralph, 1478
Goodwin, Ralph L., 3469
Goodwin, Solomon, 1341
Goody, Douglas, 1371
Goody, Gordon, 1370, 3461
Goo Goo Knox, 1342
Goold, Honora, 794
Goolde, Maria Vere, 700, 1341
Goolde, Vere, 1341
Goolsie, Kirby, 3365
Goosby, John, 3351
Goosenby, David, 3345
Goozee, Albert, 1341
Gopher Gang, 794, 1140, 1141, 1341-1342,
    1348, 1634, 1635, 1652, 3401, 3402,
    3404-3409
Gorby, Thomas, 3454
Gordel, Dominic, 1342
Gordianus I, 1342
Gordianus II, 1342
Gordianus III, 3235
Gordianus, Marcus Antonios III, 1342,
    2154
Gordon, Al, 2312
Gordon, Alec, 1973
Gordon, Alex, 2963
Gordon, Aloysius "Lucky", 2506, 2508
Gordon, Annie, 1342-1343
Gordon, Arthur (U.S. d.1929), 691
Gordon, Arthur J. (U.S. pr.1935), 976
Gordon, Benita, 1376
Gordon, Blanche, 1474
Gordon, Clara, 1343
Gordon, Clifford, 3349
Gordon, Cosmo, 3303

Gordon Dick, Anthony, 1071
Gordon, Duchess of, 2057
Gordon, Edgar, 800
Gordon, Eugene Andrew, 1343
Gordon, Galner, 3354
Gordon, George (Brit. 1751-93), 1102, 1343, 1347, 1348, 2069, 2585, 3371
Gordon, George (Brit. pr.1592), 3239
Gordon, George (Scot. b.1649), 1343
Gordon, George (U.S. pr.1901), 3352
Gordon, George (U.S. 1911-), 3413
Gordon, Harry "Shorty" (U.S. pr.1910s), 1726
Gordon, Harry (U.S. pr.1987), 228
Gordon, Harry W. (U.S. 1905-41), 1343
Gordon, Henry, 3355
Gordon, Herman Hy, 1601
Gordon, Iain Hay, 1343-1344
Gordon, Isaac 19
Gordon, James, (U.S. d.1861), 1535
Gordon, James, (U.S. pr.1860), 1344
Gordon, James Gay, 1944
Gordon, Jennie, 2158
Gordon, John (Scot. d.1945), 636
Gordon, John (U.S. d.1845), 1344
Gordon, John B. (U.S. pr.1900), 802
Gordon, John Williams (Brit. 1931-), 1344-1345
Gordon, Joseph, 3359
Gordon, Judah Leib, 1345
Gordon, Keith, 3300
Gordon, Kennedy, 3353
Gordon, Lauden, 1345
Gordon, Leroy, 2258
Gordon, Lewis, 3341
Gordon, Lockhart, 1345
Gordon, Lon, 771, 1345, 3559
Gordon, Mary, 1662
Gordon, Matt, Jr., 389
Gordon, Mike, 1593, 3559
Gordon, Nathaniel, 1345
Gordon, Patrick, 3448
Gordon, Peyton, 1345-1346, 3090
Gordon, Ralph, 1662
Gordon Riots, 1347-1348, 2310, 2312, 3371
Gordon, Tom, 3559
Gordon, Vivian, 1346, 1376, 3041
Gordon, Walter A., 1346
Gordon, "Waxey," 1346, 2004, 2072, 3225, 3401, 3405, 3409
Gordon, William (Brit. d.1733), 1346
Gordon, William (Scot. d.1716), 1346
Gordon-Baille, Mary Ann, 1346
Gordon-Gordon, 1346-1347
Gordon-Lennox, Ellen, 3034
Gordon-Lennox, George St. Leger, 3034
Gore, David, 3449
Gore, Verne, 182
Gorelov, V., 2177
Goremykin, Ivan Longinovich, 1348, 3243
Gorgulov, Paul, 1011
Gorham, David, 3449
Gorhanson, Charles, 1192
Gorillas, 1342, 1348, 3405
Goring, Charles B., 1348
Goring, George, 1348
Göring, Hermann, 984
Gorky, Maxim, 3201
Gölitz, (Countess of Darmstadt), 1348
Gorman, Benjamin, 3355
Gorman, James, 3355
Gorman, Joseph, 1443
Gorman, Louis, 2399
Gorman, Mary, 2814
Gorman, R.N., 380
Gorman, Sam, 534
Gorman, William, 1348
Gormon, John W., 1440
Goron, François M., 911, 1121

Goron, Marie-François, 2878
Gorrell-Barnes, Henry, 1630
Gorringe, Esther, 1348
Gorringe, Jack, 1348
Gorringe, Phyllis, 1348
Gorsky, Jacob, 2042
Gorsuch, Edward, 703, 3373
Gortari, Carlos Salinas de, 1524
Gorton, Samuel, 1348
Gosch, John David, 1349
Gosch, Lesley Lee, 3455
Gosch, Noreen, 1349
Gosier, Harry, 3451
Goslett, Arthur Andrew Clement, 1349, 2738
Goslett, Evelyn, 1349
Gosling, Frederick, 514
Gosling, Harold L., 1349, 3547
Gossage, Amy, 1349
Gossage, Eben, 1349-1350
Gossage, Howard, 1349
Goss, Cornelius, 3455
Gosselin, Ambroisine, 1350
Gossens, Salvador Allende 2469
Gosse, Philip, 1350
Gossert, Jacob, 3424
Goss, Winfield S., 3014, 3227
Gotarzes II, 1350
Gotha, John, 2939
Gotlieb, Matthias, 1350
Goto Shojiro, 1350
Gotschall, Glenn, 723
Gottfried, Gesina Margaretha, 1350
Gotthardt, Minnie Mae, 221
Gotti, Gene, 1350, 2105, 3405
Gotti, John "The Dapper Don", 655, 908, 1350-1351, 1889, 2085, 2105, 3401-3406, 3408, 3409, 3411
Gotti, John A. Jr., 3405
Gotti, Peter, 3405
Gotti, Richard, 3405
Gottlieb, Harry, 3006
Gottschalk, Louis, 2115
Gottschkov, 86
Gottwald, Klement, 3251
Gotzman, Leo, 988
Goucher, Allen, 1351
Goudie, Thomas Patterson, 1351
Gouffé, Toussaint-Augustin, 1121
Gough, Bill, 2766
Gough, Elizabeth, 1804
Gough, John, 1351
Gough, William, 926
Gouin, Lomer, 1351
Gould, Barbara, 772
Gould, Frank, 772
Gould, Gidfrey, 3348
Gould, Harry, 1462
Gould, Honora, 3324
Gould, Inc., 3290
Gould, Jacob, 868
Gould, Janice Irene, 465
Gould, Jay, 1022, 1167, 1171, 1347, 1351-1352, 1495, 2434, 3007, 3009
Gould, John Franklin, 772
Gould, Morton, 1132
Gould, Richard, 1352
Gould, Robert, 2484
Gould, Sarah Jane, 1081
Gould, Wesley, 3350
Gould, William (Brit. d.1867), 98
Gould, William (U.S. pr.1908), 1352
Goulter, Sidney Bernard, 1352
Gounares, Demetrios, 1352
Gourbin, Emile, 1353
Gourgues, Dominique de, 1353
Gourier, Pere, 1353
Gourlay, William, 854
Gourley, Wallace S., 2692

Gouzenko, Igor Sergeievitch, 2348
Governor, Jimmy, 1353
Govind Singh, 1353
Gow, Betty, 1479, 1480, 1482
Gow, Douglas W., 2235
Gow, John, 1353-1354
Gowdie, Isobel, 1354
Gowen, Franklin, 1781
Gower, William, 981
Gozalez, Dario, 174
Gozman, Maria Teresa Mirabel de, 3254
GPU, 1354
Graber, Roland H., 1354
Grabez, Trifko, 1212
Grabiner, Joseph "Jew Kid", 394, 758, 3385
Grabowski, Klaus, 1354-1355
Grabowsky, Peter, 3539
Gracchus, Gaius Sempronius, 1174, 1355
Gracchus, Lucius, 620
Gracchus, Tiberius Sempronius, 1355
Grace, Charles, 2741
Grace, Frank "Parky", 1355
Grace, Mike, 135
Grace, Ross, 1355
Gracial, Roberto Romero, 3466
Grady, Arthur, 167
Grady, Daniel C., 2030
Grady Gang, 1355
Grady, John (U.S. pr.1866), 1355
Grady, John D. "Traveling Mike" (U.S. pr.1860s), 1355, 3405
Grady, John Francis (U.S. 1929-), 644, 1355, 1443, 2127, 2513
Grady, Michael, 2352
Grady, Richard, 1475
Grady, Thomas, 1064, 3559
Graeff, Donal, 391
Graf, Conrad, 1929
Graf, Herbert, 3247
Graff, Aaron A., 2009, 3325
Graff, Joann, 923
Graff, William De, 902
Graffenreid, Edna de, 2727
Graham-Tewksbury Feud, 1361
Graham, Adam, 1355
Graham, Albert, 1361, 3559
Graham, Archibald, 1006
Graham, Barbara, 694, 1355-1356
Graham, Bob, 25, 2128, 2876
Graham Brothers, 1361
Graham, Carson, 1622
Graham, Cecil, 3518
Graham, Charles, 1361, 3559
Graham, Dayton, 1356, 2782, 3547
Graham, Dollay, 1361, 3559
Graham, Eric Stanley George, 1356
Graham, Fred, 697
Graham, Gary, 3455
Graham, George E., 1356
Graham, Gloria, 1359, 1360
Graham, Harold, 956
Graham, Harrison, 1356, 3454
Graham, Henry, 1356
Graham, Jack Gilbert, 3264
Graham, James (Brit. pr.1844), 2684
Graham, James (Brit. 1745-94), 1357
Graham, James (Brit. pr.1632), 3078
Graham, James (Scot. 1612-50), 1356-1357
Graham, James (U.S. d.1814), 1357
Graham, John (Brit. 1800s), 1357
Graham, John (Scot. 1648-89), 509, 857, 1357
Graham, John (U.S. pr.1880), 2919
Graham, John D. (U.S. d.1887), 3559, 3567
Graham, John Gilbert (U.S. 1932-57), 1145, 1357-1361
Graham, Julius, 1823
Graham, Lady 216,
Graham, Madge, 1414

Green, Dwight, 1250, 1659, 2092
Greene, Albert Gorton, 1376
Greene, Alejandro, 3245
Greene, Carlos, 3245
Greene, Daniel, 3392
Greene, Danny, 1948, 1949
Green, Eddie (U.S. pr.1934), 962-964, 972, 2284, 2302, 2304
Green, Edward Hamilton (Brit. pr.1872), 1366
Green, Edward W. (U.S. 1833-66), 1373, 1696, 3457
Greene, Francis V., 3425
Greene, Gary, 3453
Greene, George, 3127
Greene, Harold, 1809
Greene, Lorne, 175
Greene, Miriam, 3127
Green, Ernest, 3368
Greene, Thomas, 3405
Green, Everett D., 1373, 3229
Greene, Ward, 893, 1827, 2927
Greene, William, 1376
Greene, William H., III, 3470
Greenfield, Alfred, 2034
Greenfield, Anna, 1376
Greenfield, Edward J., 317
Greenfield, James, 128
Greenfield, Jerry, 1376
Greenfield, Louis, 1376-1377
Green, Fred, 2785
Green, G.W., 3455
Green, George (Brit. d.1789), 916
Green, George (U.S. pr.1907), 3547
Green, George W. (U.S. d.1855), 1373
Green, Georgia, 3001
Green, Gilbert, 1155
Green, Harry, 1068
Green, Harvey Lee, 3453
Green, Henry G., 1373-1374
Green, Hershey, 2123, 2124
Green Hills Club, The, 1377
Greenhill, Theodora, 2988
Greenhut, Zoltan, 915
Green, Israel, 513
Green, Jack, 3348
Green, James, 2039, 3357
Green, John, (Brit. pr.1768) 3371
Green, John, (U.S. pr.1950) 3461
Green, John (U.S. pr.1726) 1188
Green, Jonathin F., 3000
Green, Joseph 133, 2669
Green, Joyce, 1374
Green, June, 37, 2414
Green, King, 3359
Green, Larry Craig, 398, 3218
Greenleaf, Simon, 1377
Greenlease, Bobby, 1145, 3211
Greenlease, Brady, 2798
Greenlease, Robert, Sr., 1421, 1422
Greenlease, Robert C., Jr., 1421-24, 1482, 3327, 3391
Greenlee, Charles, 1377, 1665
Green, Leo, 3340
Green, LeRoy, 1375
Green, Leslie, 1374, 3461
Green, Martha, 3346
Green, Mary, 2818
Green, Maurice, 1027
Green, Michael (U.S. pr.1990), 3453
Green, Michael S. (U.S. pr.1972) 3470
Green, Nate, 3366
Green, Nathan, 3121
Green, Nelson, 2854
Greeno, Edward, 2000
Green Ones, The, 843, 1377
Green Pang, 3391
Green, Pincus, 2575
Green, Raymond, 2854

Green, Rita, 1374
Green River Killer, 1378
Green, Robert (Brit. d.1679), 1374
Green, Robert (Brit. pr.1700s), 1432
Green, Roosevelt, 3447
Green, Sam, 3006, 3357
Green, Samuel, 1374-1375, 1860
Green, Samuel Lee, 3454
Green, Sarah, 744
Greensmith, Mother, 765
Greens, Soup, 3411
Green, Stephen, 1374
Green Street Gang, 3385
Green, Teddy, 3428
Green, Terry A., 2768
Greenthal, Carrie, 164
Green, Thomas (d.1878), 3559
Green, Tillman, 3344
Green, Tom (pr.1870s), 3559
Green, Tom (U.S. pr.1938), 3368
Green, Tormut, 2014
Greentree, Ethel, 2990
Greenup, Wilson P., 3305
Greenville, Henry, 1188
Greenwald, Emil, 3124
Greenwald, Irving, 264
Greenwalt, Morris, 2825
Greenway, Herman, 1224
Greenway, Richard H., 3447
Green, Willard, 1801
Green, William (U.S. pr.1940), 2687
Green, William (U.S. pr.1931), 2926
Green, William (U.S. pr.1915), 1222
Green, William (U.S. pr.1770), 446
Green, William S. (U.S. 1920-), 1375
Green, Willie, 3363
Green, Winona, 1375
Greenwood, David, 175, 1378
Greenwood, Harold, 157, 278, 1378-1379, 1424, 2229, 2738
Greenwood, John, 1379
Greenwood, Robert, 3344
Greenwood, Vaughn Orrin, 1379
Greer, Arthur, 3132
Greer, Frederick Arthur, 1379
Greer, Horace A., 2906
Greer, John, 320
Greer, Lillian, 3221
Greer, Ray, 1551
Greer, Ray C., 3463
Greer, Thomas, 3042
Greer, William, 1798
Gregg, Troy Leon, 1300
Gregg, William, 1379
Gregg, William H., 2519
Gregory V, 1379, 3237
Gregory VI, 1379
Gregory VII, 1518
Gregory IX, 2969
Gregory X, 429, 1041, 2173
Gregory XI, 3198
Gregory, Arthur John Peter Michael Maundy, 1379-1380
Gregory, David, 498, 3367
Gregory, Dick, 1971
Gregory, Elizabeth, 2443
Gregory, Floyd, 3341
Gregory, James, 2682
Gregory, Lampson, 3344
Gregory, Maurice, 3298
Gregory, Menas, 2228, 3127
Gregory, Ronald, 2880
Gregory, S.L., 2052
Gregory, Sharon, 471
Gregory, Thomas Watt, 1380, 1610
Gregory, Walter, 3547
Gregson, Harry, 2862
Gregson, John, 3362
Gregsten, Michael John, 1444

Greguski, Kenneth, 901
Greifelt, Ulrich, 3539
Greifeneder, Johann, 991
Greigo, Francisco, 3547
Greig, Rodney, 1380
Greil, Hans, 1586-87
Greiser, Artur, 3539
Greissing, Raoul Bidegain, 3002
Grell, Charles, 489
Grellet, Stephen, 1380
Grenfell, T. Remington, 1380-1381
Grenier, Jean, 1381
Grenières, Deniselle, 166, 1381
Grennan, Barry, 560
Grenville, George, 1381
Grenville, Richard, 1381
Grenville, William, 1205
Grer, Walter, 3361
Grese, Irma, 1381-1382, 1839, 1846, 2212, 3539
Gresham, Walter Quintin, 1382, 1884
Gresheimer, Fred, 1382
Gretzler, Douglas, 1382, 3447
Greving, August, 1455
Grévy, François Paul Jules, 632
Grey, Alice, 1382-1383
Grey, Arthur, 1383
Grey, Catherine, 2730
Grey, Charles, 1383
Grey, Dick, 3559
Grey, Dora May, 1383
Grey, Fanny, 1997
Grey, George, 1383, 3195
Grey, Henry, 1383
Grey, Jane, 691, 1031, 1171, 1383, 2135, 2581, 2731, 2902, 2979
Grey, John de, 1383
Grey, Lady de, 169
Grey, Leonard, 1383-1384
Greylord Judicial Investigation, 1384
Grey, Susan, 2430
Grey, Thomas, 1383
Grey, William, 1383
Grey Wolves, 3261, 3528, 3530, 3531
Grey, Zane, 52
Gribanov, Oleg, 903
Gribble, Kenneth, 1384-1385
Gribble, Leonard, 2106
Gribble, Timothy, 3455
Gribetz, Kenneth, 453
Griboedov, Aleksandr Sergeevich, 1385
Gridley, Jeremiah, 1385
Grieco, Joseph, 1654
Grieco, Julius, 665
Griego, Francisco Pancho, 100, 1385, 3559
Grier, Eric J., 3454
Grier, Robert Cooper, 1385
Grier, Roosevelt, 1801
Grierson, Alan James, 1385
Grierson, Isobel, 1385
Grier, William, 3363
Griesa, Thomas P., 2397
Grieve, Elizabeth, 1385-1386
Griffenburg, Elizabeth, 223
Griffen, Charles, 3340
Griffenfeld, Peder Schumacher, 1386
Griffey, Willis, 3345
Griffin, Anthony Patrick, 3331
Griffin, B.G., 1698
Griffin, Charles, 3363
Griffin, Cynthia, 2276
Griffin, Cyrus, 1386
Griffin, D.B., 3563
Griffin, Dennis, 3141
Griffin, Donald, 3448
Griffin, Elmer H., 1171
Griffin, Farrell, 463
Griffin, Frank, 1698, 2207, 3338, 3449
Griffin, George, Jr., 2434, 3559

Griffin, Gerald, 2687
Griffin, Henry, 1386, 2673, 3356, 3451
Griffin, Jane, 1386
Griffin, Jeffery, 3455
Griffin, Kenneth, 3449
Griffin, Larry, (Mo. death row inmate), 3452
Griffin, Larry, (U.S., pr.1870s), 3405
Griffin, Lawrence, 1111
Griffin, Lloyd, 313
Griffin, Milton, 3452
Griffin, Nolan, 2129
Griffin, Oscar, 1107
Griffin, Presto, 3363
Griffin, Reginald, 3452
Griffin, Richard, 2920
Griffin, Rodney, 3454
Griffin, Sarah, 1032
Griffin, Walter, 3356
Griffin, Wayne, 551
Griffin, William, 1386, 1971, 2137
Griffith-Jones, Mervyn, 1092, 2287
Griffith, Almira, 329
Griffith, Ben, 3559
Griffith, Christina, 1387
Griffith, David Wark, 144, 1856
Griffith, Elizabeth Ford, 1386-1387
Griffith, George, 479
Griffith, Griffith J., 1387
Griffith, John Ike, 1637
Griffith, Katie May, 1387
Griffith, Lewis, 805
Griffith, Michael, 1942
Griffith, Robert F., 773
Griffith, Roy, 1987
Griffith, Samuel Walker, 1387
Griffith, Stiles H., 1387-1388
Griffith, Walter L., 1186
Griffith, William, 1387-1388, 3345
Griffith, William M., 3547
Griffiths, George Edward, 3070
Griffiths, Isabella, 2047
Griffiths, James (Brit. pr.1862), 1388
Griffiths, James (Scot. 1935-69), 1388
Griffiths, John Lewis, 2872
Griffiths, Martha, 585
Griffiths, Mena, 2811
Griffiths, Peter, 1348, 1388-1389, 2336
Griffiths, Thomas, 1351, 1378
Griggard, Henry, 3341
Griggs, Ethel, 1389
Griggs, James, 1497
Griggs, John William, 1389
Griggs, Ronald Geeves, 1389
Grigor, John, 3293
Grigoryants, Sergei I., 1389
Grigsby, Stanley Thomas, 1336
Grigson, James, 28
Grillandus, Paulus, 396, 1389
Grills, Caroline, 1389-1390
Grimaldi, Gianluca, 3332, 3507
Grimball, William A, 2489
Grim, Edward, 310
Grimes, A.C., 3547
Grimes, Barbara, 1390
Grimes, Ellis, 246
Grimes, Hoke, 276
Grimes, Joseph, 1390
Grimes, Patricia, 1390
Grimes, Timothy, 1942
Grimes, William, 3549
Grimm, Baltazard, 1390
Grimm, Gustav, 826
Grimm, Paul, 3257
Grimoald I, 1390, 3236
Grimoald III, 1390
Grimshaw, George, 1300
Grimshaw, George Stanley, 3205
Grimwood, Eliza, 1391

Grin "Louis de Rougemont," 1391
Grinder, Martha, 1391
Grinevitsky, Ignaty, 88
Grinling, Henry, 3084
Grinnan, W.L., 3305
Gripson, Adam, 3343
Grisafe, Joseph, 3385, 3387
Griscom, George, 161
Gristeller, Harry, 643
Gristy, Bill, 320, 1391
Griswald, J.F., 2521
Griswold, Ephraim, 3091
Griswold, M.V.B., 2768
Gritz, Jennie, 647
Gritzmacher, Charles, 3425
Grivas, George, 1452
Grizzard, Alfred, 3337
Grizzard, Joseph, 1370, 1391
Groake, James, 1391
Groake, Patrick, 1391
Groat, David, 2426
Groat, Gerald W., 722
Grobbelaar, Petrus, 1046
Grobler, N.J., 3035
Groce, Bunt, 1391-1392
Groesbeck, William Slocum, 1392
Groesbeek, Gerhard, 1392
Groesbeek, Maria, 1392
Groff, S.H., 3298
Grogan, Barney, 3385
Grogan, Daniel, 421
Grogan, Steve, 2111
Groggard, Ephraim, 3341
Grohan, Zachioli, 3339
Groh, Henry "Heinie", 1556
Grohmann, 2697
Grondkowski, Marian, 828, 1115, 1392
Gronouski, John, 2129
Gronwall, Eris, 2052
Groom, Joseph, 222
Grooms, W.J. "Red", 1755
Grooms, William, 3425
Grootens, Anthony, 341
Groot, Huigh, 1392
Groover, Tommy, 3449
Gropper, Oscar H., 1038
Groseclose, William, 3454
Grosinger, Adam, 1836
Grosolé, Hilarión, 889
Gross, Albert, 3547, 3559
Gross, Charles (U.S. d.1952), 942
Gross, Charles E. (U.S. pr.1933), 950
Gross, Diana, 697
Gross, Ernst William, 1392
Gross, Hans, 1392
Gross, Harry, 1392, 2259
Gross, John, 1112
Gross, Louis, 1392-1393
Gross, Martin (Aust.-Hung. pr.1882), 3058-3059
Gross, Martin (U.S. b.c.1891), 3120-3121
Gross, P., 1826
Gross, Reginald R., 1393
Gross, William, 1392, 1393
Grosscup, Peter Stenger, 1393
Grosser, Alexander P., 3470
Grossman, Israel G., 1393
Grossman, Martin Edward, 3449
Grossmann, George, 1393
Grosso, Daniel, 2888
Grosvenor, Lady, 1520
Grotefend, Georg, 3068
Groth, Daniel, 1443
Grotius, Hugo, 1392, 1393-1394
Grounds, Billy, 482
Grounds, Bob, 1003
Groundy, Thomas, 1334
Groupe de Liberation armee de la Martinique, 3507, 3531

Groupe de Liberation armee de la Guadeloupe, 3272, 3507, 3531
Grouslsby, William, 3353
Grousset, Paschal, 428
Grouteau, Inspector, 1519
Grove, Donald, 3329, 3494
Grove, M., 3248
Groves, George S., 1394
Groves, Jimmy, 53
Groves, Wallace, 1394, 3393
Grove, William Robert, 1394
Growden, Gerald, 1394
Groza, Alex, 273
Groza, Lou, 273
Grubbs, Ricky Lee, 3452
Gruber, Emanuel Henry, 1394
Gruchy, Michael de, 1438
Gruebert, Frederick, 1394
Gruenawald, Peter, 547
Grufein, Murray, 2687
Gruhn, Erna, 1573
Grumbach, Wilhelm von, 1394
Grumet, Jacob, 2748
Grundmann, Wolfgang, 199, 3475, 3475
Grundy, Felix, 1394
Grundy, Sidney, 1311
Grunebaum, Ernest, 175
Grunewald, Henry, 1664
Grunspavnin, Nikolas, 2884
Grunwald, O., 3250
Grupen, Peter, 1394-1395
Grusdat, Eric, 3475
Grynszpan, Herschel, 3062, 3249
Grzechowiak, Stephen, 1395
Gsellman, George, 1416
Guacci, Tocco, 3339
Guadalajara-Mexico City Express Massacre, 1395
Guadalupe Canyon Massacres, 1395
Guadeloupe Liberation Army, 3272, 3508, 3509
Guadeloupe Riots, 3378
Guadet, Marguerite Élie, 1395
Guajardo, Jesus, 3244
Gualtiere, Carmine, 3405
Gualto, Pito, 2117
Guardado, Facundo, 3508, 3333
Guardian Angels, 1395
Guardino, Johnny "Two-Gun", 1292
Guardiola, Santos, 1395, 3241
Guarella, Eddie, 3393
Guarna, Domenico, 283
Guarnieri, Anthony F., 3405, 3412
Guatemalan Committee of Patriotic Unity, 3520, 3531
Guatemalan Labor Party's National Directorate Nucleus, 3520, 3531
Guatemalan National Revolutionary Unity, 3520, 3531
Guatemalan Work Party, 3512, 3531
Guatemotzin, 1395-1396
Guay, Albert, 1396, 3264
Guay, Rita Morel, 1396, 3264
Guayama, P.R., Prison Riot, 3378
Gubow, Lawrence, 1396
Gucciardo, Thomas, 1942
Guccione, Bob, 1189
Guderian, Heinz, 1557
Gudermaine, Margery, 1082
Gudino, Cordova, 1990
Guelphs, Luccan, 1305
Guenther, Rudolph, 115
Günther, William, 2543
Guenzel, Guel Sultan, 1396
Guer, James, 3352
Guerin, Eddie, 713, 1396, 3282, 3457
Guerin, Gabriella, 2154
Guerin, Joseph, 1396-1397
Guerin, Michel, 3250

Guerin, Webster, 2031, 2033
Guillaume de Hauteville, 1398
Guérini, Antoine, 408, 1397, 3393
Guérini, Barthélemy, 1397
Guérini, "Mimi", 1235
Guérini, Pascal, 1397
Guerra, Arturo, 1337
Guerra, Geraldo, 3472
Guerra Jimenez, Eduardo, 3471
Guerra, Juan M. Borges, 3469
Guerra, Rámon, 3052
Guerra, Raul, 3328, 3490
Guerra, Ricardo, 3455
Guerra Valdez, Santiago M., 3469
Guerrazzi, Francesco Domenico, 1397
Guerre, Martin, 1045
Guerrero, Vicente, 1397, 2679, 3241
Guerrilla Army of the Poor, 3273, 3506,
    3515, 3520, 3525, 3531
Guerrilla Party, 3525, 3531
Guerrilleros Del Cristo Rey, 3531
Guertner, Franz, 1570
Guesclin, Bertrand du, 1397, 3303
Guest, Anthony, 3451
Guest, Frederick, 1052
Guevara, Ernesto "Ché", 1397, 3002, 3256,
    3269, 3467, 3498, 3518
Gueydan-Caillaux, Berthe, 575
Gufler, Max, 1397
Guggenheim, Isaac, 2104
Guglielmi, Rudolpho, 3025, 3026
Gugliemetti, Matthew, Jr., 3379
Guibal, Inspector, 2467
Guida, Vincenzo, 3324
Guide, William, 2127
Guidice, Joseph, 3461
Guidroz, Edward, 1901
Guidry, Gilbert, 3365
Guifoyle Gang, 1397
Guild, Leo, 144
Guile, Michael, 3331, 3462
Guilen, Carlos, 3350
Guilford, Howard, 1397-1398, 1951, 1767
Guilfoyle, Martin, 607, 1397, 2972, 3385
Guiliani, Rudolph W., 2542, 2575
Guiliano, Giorgio, 3300
Guillard, Pierre, 1398
Guillaume Iron Arm, 1025
Guillemenot, Adolphe, 121, 3283
Guillen, Antonio Arias, 1398
Guillen, José, 1398
Guillet, Lucien, 1885, 1886
Guillo Lara, Jaime, 3301
Guillotin, Joseph Ignace, 1398
Guillotte, J. Valsin, 413
Guimares, Alberto Santos, 1821
Guinan, Frank, 3452
Guinan, Mary Louise Cecilia, 1141
Guinan, Texas, 31, 1366
Guiney, Eric, 3321
Guin, Junius Foy, Jr., 1398
Guinness, Walter Edward, 1398, 3251
Guinn, Neal, 3367
Guinta, Francisco, 2264
Guinta, Joseph "Hop Toad", 131, 614
Guise, François, 1398
Guise, Henri I de Lorraine, 1398, 1517
Guisseppone, Peter, 2150
Guiteau, Charles Julius, 1271, 1275, 2071,
    3242
Guiteau, John, 1274
Guiteras, Antonio, 1399
Guitierrez, Gavino Tierra, 2566
Guittar, Lewis, 1399
Guizado, José Ramon, 2566
Gula, Demetrius, 1399
Gula, Denis, 1399
Guldensuppe, Willie, 2939
Gulick, Jim, 2326

Gullett, "Chicken Harry", 394, 758
Gulley, Tom, 1924
Gull, William Whithey, 2, 476, 1921, 1399-
    1400, 1690, 2252
Gully, James Manby, 476
Gulumian, Pierre, 3524
Gumble, M.G., 3344
Guminger, E., 3245
Gumm, Eugene P., 1184
Gump, Emily, 380
Gump, Frederick B., 2924
Gump, Jean, 1400
Gump, Joseph, 1400
Gunderman, Stacey, 1400
Gundhus, Staale, 3524
Gundimar II, 1400
Gundlacht, Charles, 486
Gundobad, 1400
Gunduz, Orhan R., 3260, 3522
Gungor, Kani, 3259, 3522
Gungunhana, 1400
Gunn, Curt, 3385
Gunn, Raymond, 1400, 3367
Gunn, Robert, 1131
Gunnell, Bertram Clive, 1085
Gunness, Belle, 1400-1405, 1885, 3228
Gunness, Peter, 1400-1405
Gunpowder Plot, 742, 1405
Gunsby, Donald, 3449
Gunson, Roger, 2481
Gunter, Anne, 2443
Gunter, Brian, 2443
Gunter, "Pop", 1022
Gunter, Thomas, 1405-1406
Gunther, James Lee, 3455
Gúnther, Rolf, 3539
Gurdjieff, George Ivan, 1406
Gurfein, Murray Irwin, 1406
Gurga, Jeffrey, 1406
Gurgel, Haroldo, 1406
Gurholdt, Henry, 1404
Gurino, Vito, 1, 2254, 3405
Gurion, David Ben, 3481
Gurley, J. Ward, 2018
Gurley, Wilson, 3447
Gurney, Joseph John, 1406
Gurrero, Sebastian, 2814
Gürtner, Franz, 1406
Guru Arjun, 1453
Gusciora, Stanley H., 489
Guse, Michele, 1467
Gusenberg, Frank, 110, 606, 614, 1293,
    2044, 2214-2215, 2350, 2352, 2660,
    2973, 3119, 3385
Gusenberg, Peter, 42, 606, 612, 2044,
    2214-2215, 2350, 2660, 3119, 3385
Guseva, Kionia, 2541
Gush, Howard, 1837
Gushi, Peter J., 2512
Gussler, Eva, 3139, 3385
Gustaafsdotter, Elizabeth, 1684
Gustav IV, 121
Gustav, Karl Hulten, 565
Gustavson, Nicholas, 1704
Gustavus I, 1406
Gustavus II Adolphus, 1153, 3082, 3239
Gustavus III, 1406-1408, 2240, 2833, 3240
Gustavus Vasa, 1406, 1407
Gustloff, Wilhelm, 1408, 3248
Gust, Sidney, 3348
Guswelle, Arthur, 1096
Guswelle, Barbara, 1096
Guswelle, Ron, 1096
Guswelle, Vernita, 1096
Guszkowski, Joseph, 1287
Guterma, Alexander L., 379, 871, 1408-
    1409
Gutfreund, Yosef, 1081, 1143
Guthrie, Charles John, 1409

Guthrie, Colon, 3447
Guthrie, Jane, 1084
Gutierrez, Ruben, 3218
Gutierrez, T. Monje, 3251
Gutierrez Obregon, Samuel Rodolfo, 3259,
    3517
Gutkind, Johann, 1409
Gutlich, Philip, 3181
Gutteridge, George W., 517, 3262
Gutwirth, Leisir, 1370, 1391
Guyader, Alain, 1653, 2403
Guy, Bridget, 1409
Guy, Thomas, 1409
Guylee, Edward Harold, 1409
Guyon, Jeanne-Marie de la Motte, 1409
Guyon, Melvin Bay, 1409-1410
Guyon, Walter, 721
Guy, Ralph B., Jr., 1409
Guyse, Buck, 3547, 3559
Guyton, Walter, 3462
Guzek, Randy, 3453
Guzik, Harry, 606, 756, 1511, 3385
Guzik, Jake "Greasy Thumb", 71, 73, 178,
    371, 606, 607, 613, 616, 617, 756, 1034,
    1298, 1306, 1410, 1555, 1775, 2529, 2673,
    3139, 3226, 3384-3386
Guzman, Dominic, 657
Guzman, Gary, 3448
Guzmán, Jacobo Arbenz, 1397
Guzman, Jos Valds, 1990
Guzman, Rene Adolfo, 1410
Guzman, Tayo, 583
Guzman y Pimental, Gaspar de, 1410
Guzzi, Ercole, 3247
Guzzino, Sam, 3385
Gwin, William M., 1410, 3305
Gwin-McCorckle Duel, 1410-1411
Gwinner, Else, 1410
Gwinnett, Button, 2046, 3303
Gwyer, Maurice Linford, 1411
Gwyn, Ronce, 3356
Gwynne, Nell, 801, 1411, 2357
Gyges, 1411, 3234, 3236
Gylam, Jack, 1622
Gylippus, 1411

H

Haag, Randy, 3454
Haag, Siegfried, 3475
Haaga, Wilhelmina "Billie", 732, 1974
Haakon I, 1101
Haakon IV, 2805, 3237
Haakon VII, 1412, 2542
Haarman, Fritz, 1412
Haas, Adolph, 3392
Haas, Arthur D., 3253
Haas, Benjamin, 2888
Haas, Hermann C.A., 1582
Haas, Leonard, 1220
Haas, Maria, 2584
Haas, Sam, 3392
Haas, Wilhelm, 3250
Haas, William, 2127
Haase, Herman, 492
Haase, Hugo, 3244
Habash Front, 3265, 3269, 3465-3469,
    3481-3483, 3495, 3499, 3500, 3507, 3514,
    3531
Habash, George, 2518, 3522
Haberman, Chris, 899
Haberstroh, Richard, 3452
Habib, Jacob, 1601

Herrick, William A., 1230
Herrin Mine Massacre, 1525, 3375
Herrin, Richard, 673, 1525
Herring, Bob, 3560
Herring, Charles, 914
Herring, John, 652, 936
Herring, Johnny, 3078
Herring, Marshal, 1260
Herring, Robert, 1525-26
Herring, Ted, 3449
Herriot, Edouard, 1526
Herron, Jim, 1721
Herron, L.J., 2030
Herron, Robert, 3337
Herrschaft, William, 19481
Hersch, Charles H., 2457
Herschel, Anneliese, 295
Herschel, F., 1881
Herschel, John, 1975
Herschel, William, 351, 1519, 1526, 3065, 3306
Herschel, William John, 1526
Herschko, David, 3058-3059
Herschler, Ed, 1694
Hersey, George Canning, 1526
Hersh, Seymour, 2344
Herter, Christian Archibald, 1896, 2010
Hertford, Countess of, 2682
Hertford, Lord, 1629
Hertogs, Robert, 1135
Hertz Corporation, 1526-27
Hertz, Emanuel, 1525
Hertz, Martin, 848
Hertzer, John, 817
Hertzog, James Barry Munnik, 1527, 2275
Hervouet, Pierre, 19151
Herwegh, Georg, 1527
Herz, Alfred, 347
Herz, George Washington, 1717
Herzen, Aleksandr Ivanovich, 2470
Herzog, Marianne, 3475
Heselden, John, 1759
Hesilrige, Arthur, 1527
Hesketh-Wright, Millicent, 1650
Heslin, Patrick E., 1547, 3325
Heslin, Peter, 1527
Hesp, Hazel, 1433
Hess, John, 3547
Hess, Julia May, 2676
Hess, Lorraine, 646
Hess, Rudolf, 443, 984, 1583-1584, 2336, 3539, 3540
Hess, W. Dale, 2100
Hess, Walter, 805, 806
Hess, Walter Richard Rudolf, 1527, 1568, 1570, 1580
Hess-Kassel, Frederick of, 1349
Hessberger, George L., 1527
Hessberger, Marie, 1527
Hesse, Countess of, 1041
Hesse, Edwin B., 3426
Hesse, Hermann, 1256
Hesse-Darmstadt, Alexander of, 87
Hessel, 1715
Hester, Hubert, 1224
Hester, Pat, 1775
Hester, Robert, 2676
Hester, Robert S., 3334
Hester, Willie, 814
Heston, Charlton, 1119
Hestor, Patrick, 1001
Hetenyi, George Paul, 1527-28
Hetenyi, Jean G.R. Gareis, 1527
Heth, Joice, 1528
Hetherington, Joseph, 464, 1528, 3050, 3336, 3560
Hetman, Tanka, 3223
Hetrick, William Morgan, 909
Hett, Thomas, 2831

Hettinger, Karl, 2796
Hetzer, Ludwig, 1528
Heughebaert, 414
Heusinger, Adolf, 1574
Heuston, Peter, 2330
Hevens, Samuel, 3363
Heward, Francis, (U.S. pr. 1855) 1205
Hewart, Gordon, 220, 1528, 1604, 2157
Hewell, Virgil, 3299
Hewett, Jack, 1528, 2738
Hewey, Vergil, 19861
Hewicker, John A., 1236
Hewitt, Abraham S., 827
Hewitt, Abram Stevens, 3405
Hewitt, Estelle, 1529
Hewitt, Joseph, 245
Hewitt, Martin, 2226
Hewitt, Marvin, 1528-29
Hewitt, Patricia Anne, 19011
Hewitt, W.A., 720
Hewlet, Thomas, 1324
Hewlett, James, 3399
Hewling, John, 1679
Hews, John, 1772, 1908
Hext, John, 805
Heyda, James, 156
Heydrich, Reinhard Tristan Eugen, 1076, 1659, 1529-32, 1557, 1558, 1754, 1852, 2266, 2695, 3061, 3250, 3539
Heyer, Adam, 614, 2660, 3385
Heyman, Marcus, 2056
Heyman, Peter, 1399
Heymann, Phillip, 2834
Heymann, Robert L., 1532
Heymann, Walter M., 1532
Heyns, Garrett, 585
Heys, Arthur, 1532
Heyward, Edward, 3305
Heywood, C.W., 2707
Heywood, David George, 3329, 3498
Heywood, Greta, 846
Heywood, Joseph Lee, 1704, 3212
Heywood, Peter, 2270
Hezbe Islami, 3333
Hezbollah, 686, 3531
Hibbler, Poe, 3365
Hibner, Esther, 578, 1532
Hickey, George, 3242
Hickey, Henry, 3242
Hickey, James, 718
Hickey, John Joseph, 1532
Hickey, Michael C., 3424
Hickey, Mike, 3547
Hickey, William F., Jr., 2547
Hickling, John, 446
Hickman, Millard, 1722
Hickman, Sophia, 1532
Hickman, Tom, 3547
Hickman, William Edward, 1532-34, 2984, 3325
Hickock, Richard Eugene, 1534-35
Hickok, James Butler "Wild Bill", 101, 542, 577, 719, 740, 769, 1054, 1448, 1500, 1535-40, 1672, 1940, 1988, 1997, 2023, 2748, 2802, 2864, 3547, 3545, 3556, 3561, 3567
Hickok, Polly Butler, 1535
Hickok, William Alonzo, 1535
Hicks, A., 3344
Hicks, Albert E., 1540-43, 3406
Hicks, Charles, 3363
Hicks, David, 3455
Hicks, Dick, 19771
Hicks, Earl, 2340
Hicks, Edward L., 227, 1543
Hicks, Elizabeth, 1544
Hicks, Helga, 1544
Hicks, James, 1619, 2023
Hicks, John, 19701

Hicks, Larry, 1543-44
Hicks, Lucy, 1544
Hicks, Lutien Roy, 1544
Hicks, Mary, 1544
Hicks, Milt, 3560
Hicks, Robert Karl, 3366, 3450
Hicks, Xenophen, 1544
Hickson, Joe, 3554, 3567
Hicswa, Joseph, 1544
Hidalgo, Miguel, 2217
Hidalgo y Costilla, Miguel, 1544, 3240
Hiednik, Gary, 3454
Hiempsal I, 1544, 3234
Hier, Marvin, 19691
Higashiyama Hirosato, 3261
Higdon, Lloyd, 1544-45
Higginbotham, Aloyisus Leon, Jr., 1545
Higginbotham, Ellwood, 3368
Higginbotham, Patrick Errol, 1545
Higginbotham, Solomon, 799
Higginbottom, Albert James, 1545
Higginbottom, Harry, 1545
Higginbottom, Henry James, 1545
Higginbottom, Mary Louisa, 1545
Higgins, Buff, 3385
Higgins, Carlisle, 1600
Higgins, Erma, 435
Higgins, Frank, 2421
Higgins, Frank Wayland, 115
Higgins, Fred, 3547
Higgins, Fred R., 1498, 1545
Higgins, Harry, 3385
Higgins, James W., 1545, 2803
Higgins, Jean, 1546
Higgins, John (Scot., d.1911), 1546
Higgins, John Calhoun Pinckney "Pink" (U.S. 1848-1914), 244, 1545, 1621-22, 2838, 3192
Higgins, Louis, 3358
Higgins, Mark H., 3254
Higgins, Otto, 642, 1545-46, 3396
Higgins, Patrick, 1546
Higgins, Pink, 244
Higgins, Thomas J., 1186, 1758
Higgins, Vannie, 748, 794, 838, 935, 1546, 1894
Higgins, William (Scot., d.1911), 1546
Higgins, William R., 1547, 1865, 1914, 3425, 3532
Higginson, Thomas Wentworth, 510, 513
Higgs, Mary, 423
High, George, 1453
High, Jose, 3450
High Sierra, 1547
Highfill, George, 257
Hightower, Bobby Ray, 3453
Hightower, Jacinto, 3452
Hightower, John, 3450
Hightower, Peggy, 1547
Hightower, Rudy, 1547
Hightower, William, 3325
Hightower, William A., 1547-49
Hiker Slayings, 1549
Hilaire, Marcel, 1549-50
Hilaire, Odette, 1549
Hilarin Daza, 3242
Hilbery, Malcolm, 1550
Hilbruner, William J., 3426
Hilburn, Nathaniel G., 373
Hildebrand, Sam, 1701
Hildebrandt, Big Bill, 3296
Hildebrandt, Richard, 3539
Hildebrant, Alex, 3464
Hildegard, Evelyn, 1550
Hildegard, Percy, 1550
Hilderman, George, 3560
Hildreth, Peter, 3557
Hildreth, William, 3547
Hildwin, Paul, 3449

Hoagland, John, 3508
Hoal, W.G., 3035
Hoar, Dorcas, 2670
Hoar, Ebenezer Rockwood, 1581
Hoar, Patrick J., 2803
Hoard, Dudley, 2857
Hoare, Samuel, 2312
Hoban, Dennis, 2879
Hoban, Peter, 3229
Hobart, Henry, 1182
Hobbes, Thomas, 1581
Hobbs, Abigail, 2668
Hobbs, Augusta, 2469
Hobbs, B.T., 1435
Hobbs, Deliverance, 2667
Hobbs, James (U.S. pr.1692), 2668
Hobbs, James (U.S. pr.1830s), 3168
Hobbs, Leonard, 1490
Hobbs, Ricky, 227
Hobbs, William (U.S. prom. 20th Cent.), 1581
Hobbs, William Cooper, (Brit. pr.1919-38) 1581, 2314
Hobday, Stanley Eric, 1581-82, 2894
Hobel, Hans, 3250
Hobert, Leonard T., 1561
Hoboken Anti-German Riot, 3373
Hobson, Eric, 3247
Hobson, James, 2880
Hobson, Valerie, 2506
Hoch, Caroline, 1582
Hoch, Johann Otto, 1582
Hochberg, Alan, 1582
Hochmuth, Amandus, 1488, 1489
Hochstein, Peter, 3452
Hock, John, 3338
Hock, Otto, 1180
Hocke, Theodore 169
Hocker, Thomas Henry, 1582
Hocking, Clarence, 789
Hocking, Frederick, 588
Hockinsmith, Clark, 2521
Hocum, Lori, 3333
Hocum, Ronald, 3333
Hodapp, Jacob Frederick, 1583
Hoddenbach, Keith, 1583
Hodel, 3242
Hodge, Benny Lee, 3451
Hodge, Dennis, 2349
Hodge, E.D., 374
Hodge, Fred, 493
Hodge, Louis, 3339
Hodge, Orville Enoch, 1583, 3192
Hodge, Walter Hartman, 1583
Hodges, Frank, 2059
Hodges, Frederick, 778
Hodges, George M., 3449
Hodges, James, 3359
Hodges, Mary, 2474
Hodges, Thomas (U.S. 1944-76), 445
Hodges, Thomas (U.S. pr.1856), 1391
Hodges, W.O., 1583
Hodges, William, 3359
Hodgson, Arthur, 1977
Hodgson, Edward, 3254
Hodja, Nasreddin, 3291
Hodzic, Shefka, 1583
Hoel, Halvor Nielsen, 1583
Hoepner, Erich, 1574
Hoeppel, John Henry, 1583
Hoeppel, Charles J., (1583
Hoerster, Daniel 1320, 2137
Hoes, George, 3341
Hoess, 3540
Hoets, May Overton, 1968l
Hoey, James F., 2706
Hofacker, Cäsar von, 1574
Hofer, Andreas, 1584, 3240
Hoff, Dierk Ferdinand, 200

Hoff, John P., 952
Hoff, Max "Boo-Boo" 178, 1584, 3412, 3413
Hoff, Sonja Lillian, 9
Hoffa, James Riddle "Jimmy", 294, 534, 781, 857, 896, 908, 976, 1005, 1018, 1173, 1584-85, 2498, 2508, 2513, 2574, 2582, 2906, 3161, 3166, 3219, 3220, 3254, 3330, 3384, 3391-3393, 3404
Hoffert, Emily, 819
Hoffman, Abbie, 697, 698, 1585
Hoffman, Barry, 3449
Hoffman, Carol, 102
Hoffman, Charles, 25
Hoffman, Richard, 815
Hoffman, Dustin, 3090
Hoffman, Etta, 1585
Hoffman, Fred, 3197
Hoffman, Harold Giles, 1585, 3226
Hoffman, Harry L., 1585
Hoffman, Heinrich, 3540
Hoffman, J., 3252
Hoffman, J.H., 426
Hoffman, James Timothy, 909
Hoffman, Jerome D., 1585-86
Hoffman, John Thompson, 1586, 1715
Hoffman, Julius (U.S. prom. 1930s), 1159
Hoffman, Julius Jennings, 698, 979, 1586, 1862, 1945
Hoffman, K., 3250
Hoffman, Maxwell, 3451
Hoffman, Ogden, 2489
Hoffman, Peter (U.S. pr.1920s), 1020, 1506, 1586, 2972, 2976, 3088
Hoffman, Peter B., 3386
Hoffman, Robert, Sr., 2762
Hoffman, Sydney J., 775
Hoffman, Victor Ernest, 1586
Hoffman, Walter Edward, 1586
Hoffmann, Calvin, 2126
Hoffmann, Heinrich, 1572
Hoffmann, Karl-Heinz, 1841
Hoffmann, Susan, 2812
Hoffner, Anna, 1586-87
Hoffner, Louis, 1587
Hofheinz, Roy, 3297
Höfle, Anton, 245
Höfle, Hans, 3540
Höfle, Hermann, 3540
Hofman, Charles, 333
Hofman, Mark W., 1587
Hofman, Mayme, 333
Hofmann, Albert, 3296
Hofmann, Kuno, 1587
Hofmann, Melchior, 1587-88
Hofmann, Otto, 3540
Hofner, Harry, 3361
Hofrichter, Adolph, 1588
Hofstaedter, Ephraim, 2442
Hogan, Barbara Ann, 1588
Hogan, Danny, 1588
Hogan, Dominick, 1776
Hogan, Ed, 1468
Hogan, Edward, 1776
Hogan, Ernest, 3375
Hogan, Frank (U.S. d.1927), 1037
Hogan, Frank S. (U.S. Pr.1940s), 273, 379, 1034, 1038, 1588
Hogan Gang, 2466
Hogan, John, 417
Hogan, Kenneth, 3453
Hogan, Martin, 1384
Hogan, Mary, 1289, 1290
Hogan, Michael J., 1588
Hogan, Michael Ray, 3452
Hogan, Robert, 1940l
Hogan, Tom, 1500
Hoges, Henry, 3560
Hogg, Caroline Gwinnell, 1588, 1589

Hogg, Clara, 3133, 3134
Hogg, Douglas McGarel, 1588
Hogg, Frank, 2433, 3133
Hogg, Mary Anne, 1588-89
Hogg, Phoebe, 2433, 3133
Hogg, Quintin, 494
Hogue, Beatrice, 1792
Hogue, Ed, 812, 2933
Hogue, Jerry, 3455
Hohberg, Hans, 3540
Hohenau, Walter, 1589
Hohensee, Adolphus, 1589
Hohfer, Frank, 1301
Hohimer, Francis L., 2444
Hohmann, Arthur C., 3425
Hohne, Harold, 2056
Hojatoleslam Ali Ghodussi, 3516
Hojo Yoshitoki, 2959
Hoke, David, 3424
Hoke, Robert, 1680
Hoke, Ronald Lee, 3456
Holahan, Joseph R., 1652
Holbach, Helen, 3458
Holbach, Joseph, 3458
Holbert, Kenneth, 2150
Holbert, Luther, 3356
Holbrook, Buck, 3386
Holbrook, Elizabeth, 2155
Holbrook, Ernest, Jr., 1589-90
Holbrook, Mollie, 3386
Holcomb, Joe, 2763
Holcomb, S.B., 3425
Holden, Alan, 1590
Holden, David, 3505
Holden, Frank, 1590
Holden, George, 3366
Holden, James Stuart, 1590
Holden, "Judge", 3560
Holden Gang, 235
Holden-Keating Gang, 1755
Holden, Russell, 3453
Holden, Thomas, 209, 235, 236, 238, 728, 1454, 1590-91, 1756, 1784, 2183, 2284, 2286, 2513, 3117, 3427, 3459
Holden, William, 170, 1591
Holder, Cale James, 1591
Holder, D.F., 641
Holder, Luther, 1591
Holder, William, 3470
Holderman, James F., 463, 1135, 2811
Holdson, James, 2126
Hole-in-the-Wall (U.S. pr.1890s-1900s), 1442, 1591, 1619, 1920, 1977, 1978
Hole-in-the-Wall Gang, 3548
Hole-In-The-Wall Saloon (U.S. pr.1850s-70s), 1591
Holeman, Jacob H., 3305
Holford, John, Jr., 1524
Holford, John, Sr., 1524
Holiday, Billie, 3297
Holiday, Dallas, 3450
Holinshed, 1383
Holladay, Glenn, 3447
Hollan, Alexander, 3244
Holland, Anne, 1591
Holland, Camille Cecile, 1009, 1084
Holland, David Lee, 3455
Holland, Gerald, 3452
Holland, Henry Edmund, 1591
Holland, James, 3456
Holland, James Buchanan, 1591
Holland, Joe, 3557
Holland, John, 1591
Holland, Kenneth Raymond, 1591-92
Holland, Mary, 1664
Holland, Robert, 1715
Holland, Tom, 1592
Holland, Walter, 3351
Holland, William, 3454, 3555

Hollander, Eugene, 343
Hollander, Xaviera, 700
Holle, Edward, 1592
Holles, (Baron) Denzil, 1592, 1650
Hollest, George Edward, 1473, 1592
Holley, Carroll, 958
Holley, Lillian, 958, 962
Hollick, Frederick, 3293
Holliday, Anderson, 3345
Holliday, Bertram Redvers, 1592
Holliday, Billie, 1076, 2192
Holliday, Christopher, 1355
Holliday, John Henry "Doc", 314, 315, 482,
    495, 718-720, 842, 1056, 1058, 1060-1062,
    1593-95, 1708, 1729, 2059, 2144, 2727,
    2749, 2777, 3547, 3550, 3556, 3560, 3565
Holliday, John (Brit. d.1700), 1592-93
Holliman, Richard, 1609
Hollings, W.H., 1595
Hollingsby, George, 1303
Hollingsworth, C.L., 862
Hollingsworth, James, 159
Hollins, Jess, 1595
Hollins, John, 3355
Hollins, Lawrence Henry, 1595-96, 2097
Hollinshead, T.W., 3348
Hollis, David Lee, 1596
Hollis, Debbie, 1596
Hollis, Herman, 972, 1187, 1613, 2304, 2514
Hollister, Burr C., 509
Hollister, Cassius M. "Cash", 1596, 3547
Holloway, Duayne, 3448
Holloway, Emmett, 3455
Holloway, Jerome, 3329
Holloway, John (Brit. d.1807), 1324, 1596
Holloway, John William (Brit. 1806-31),
    1596
Holloway, Joseph, 1596-97
Holloway, Russ, 3560
Holloway, William (Brit. d.1712), 1597
Holloway, William Judson, Jr. (U.S. 1923-),
    1597
Holly, Sean M., 2551, 3015, 3328, 3483
Holly, William H., 876
Hollyday, William, 1597
Holm, Celeste, 583
Holman, George, 1597, 3228
Holman, Jesse Lynch, 1597
Holman, Joseph, 3346
Holman, Libby, 1597-1601, 3196
Holman, Nat, 273
Holman, Robert, 3346
Holman, Tafford, 3451
Holmberg, John, 1722
Holmer, Hans, 2398
Holmes, Alexander William, 1601
Holmes, Annie, 1622
Holmes, Bill, 135
Holmes, Cornelius, 127
Holmes, David, 2866
Holmes, Gardner "Pop", 2039
Holmes, H.H., 903
Holmes, H.L., 1300
Holmes, Henry (U.S. d.1890), 3338
Holmes, Henry (U.S. d.1914), 3363
Holmes, Inie, 468
Holmes, J.A., 3246
Holmes, James W., 3448
Holmes, Janice Anne, 1717
Holmes, Jimmy Jack, 1601
Holmes, John (Brit. pr.1870s), 1601
Holmes, John (U.S. d.1933), 1243
Holmes, John A. (U.S. pr.1900s), 441
Holmes, John Haynes, 1602
Holmes, John Maurice (U.S. pr.1933), 1601-
    02, 1606, 2949, 3326, 3367
Holmes, Leonard, 687, 1602
Holmes, Nathan, 2260
Holmes, Nathaniel, 1602

Holmes, Oliver Wendell, Jr., 472, 895,
    1000, 1016, 1222, 1563, 1602, 3147,
    3293
Holmes, Oliver Wendell, Sr., 1602
Holmes, Peggy Agnes, 1602
Holmes, Phillips, 113, 1600
Holmes, Ralph, 1600
Holmes, Reginald, 468, 2839
Holmes, Robert, 2691
Holmes, Robert B., 1240
Holmes, Sherlock, 1602-03, 1684, 1690,
    1691, 1935, 2202, 2244, 2252, 2410,
    2468, 2777, 2787, 2830
Holmes, Taylor, 1600
Holmes, Thomas, 3350, 3425
Holmes, W.A., 3547
Holmes, Warren D., 2738
Holmes, Wayne, 841
Holmes, William, 725, 1603
Holmes, William Henry, 2716
Holmyard, William John, 725, 1603
Holofernes, 3232
Holohan, James B., 1560
Holohan, William V., 1652
Holovko, Tadeusz, 3247
Holoway, Arnold, 3454
Holroyd, Michael, 1603
Holroyd, Susannah, 1603
Holschuh, John David, 1603
Holsinger, Maurice Paul, 1603
Holsoe, George, 3123
Holst, Minnie, 1180
Holstein, Sim, 2902
Holt, Alfred, 3348
Holt, Alice, 1603
Holt, Anatol, 775
Holt, Becky, 775, 3327
Holt, Cindy, 1605
Holt, Emory, 1603-04
Holt, Everett L., 3469
Holt, Frederick Rothwell, 1379, 1424,
    1604
Holt, George, 3386
Holt, George Chandler, 1604
Holt, Jane, 1139
Holt, John, 1604
Holt, Joseph, 1604
Holt, Len, 19081
Holt, Lucius, 3344
Holt, M.P., 1127
Holt, O.T., 2420
Holt, P., 3246
Holt, Preston, 828
Holt, Sam, 1604-05, 3351
Holt, Thomas H., 3305
Holt, Thomas J., Jr., 1605
Holt, William, 3351
Holtier, Jane, 600
Holtman, Robert, 3146
Holton, Mrs. E.S. 2242
Holton, Mrs. W.E., 3346
Holton, Rudolph, 3449
Holtslag, Joe, 1476
Holtz, "Curly", 526, 3406
Holtz, David, 2293
Holtz, Hyman "Little Hymie", 526
Holtz, K.F., 3249
Holtz, Max, 3247
Holtz, Michael, 1776
Holtzendorff, Franz von, 1605
Holtzman, Elizabeth, 169, 2056
Holtzoff, Alexander, 544, 1605, 3119
Holwell, Robert, 2990
Holy Child Orphanage Case, 1605
Holy Track, Paul, 3349
Holyoake, Elizabeth, 450
Holyoake, George, 450
Holyoake, Jacob, 450
Holzapfel, Floyd Albert "Lucky", 2435

Holzberger, John, 2039
Holzer, Franz Joseph, 3024
Holzhay, Reimund, 1605, 3560
Holzheimer, William Andrew, 1605
Holzman, Alfred, 1597, 1598
Holzman, Rachel Workum, 1597
Holzman, Ross, 1598
Holzweber, Franz, 990, 991
Holzworth, John, 1890l
Homann, Peter, 3475
Hombogen, Alfred W., 1301
Home Counties Riots, 1606
Home, Daniel Dunglas, 1605-06
Home, George (Brit. pr.1611), 1606
Home, George K. (U.S. b.1879), 1606, 3425
Home, Henry, 1606
Home-Stake Case, 1606
Homecoming, 1606
Homer, John Arthur, 1336
Homestead (Pa.) Strike, 1606
Homestead Steel Riot, 3374
Homick, Steven, 3452
Homma Masaharu, 279, 1606-07, 3540
Homme, Robert O. 9
Honduran Death Squads, 1607
Honduran National Agrarian Institute,
    3513
Honduran Peasant Riot, 3378
Hone, William, 3074
Honecker, Erich, 3260
Honeycutt, Mildred Kay, 621
Honeymoon Gang, 1607, 3406
Honeywell, 3289
Hong Chow-Ling, 3245
Hongisto, Richard, 1607
Honka, Fritz, 1607-08
Honore Palmer, Bertha, 2104
Honorius, Flavius, 174, 663, 1522, 2855,
    3235
Hontvet, Maren, 3069
Hoobler, Ray L., 3426
Hood, Elizabeth, 320
Hood, Harry, 1131
Hood, James A., 3080
Hood, John T., 1520
Hood, Linda, 1608
Hood, Michelle, 1608
Hood, Robin, 634, 647, 684, 817, 3050
Hood, Thomas, 142
Hood, Vera, 1608
Hoody, Albert C., 2879
Hooe, William F., 1608
Hoogh, Pieter de, 3032, 3034
Hoogling, John, 1399
Hooijaijers, Frans, 1608
Hook Gang, 1608-09
Hooker, Cameron, 1608
Hooker, Horace, 247
Hooker, Janice, 1608
Hooker, John, 3453
Hookers, The (U.S. pr.1850s-60s), 3406,
    3408
Hooks, Benjamin L., 1329
Hooks, Joseph, 3447
Hooley, Ernest Terah, 1609
Hoolhouse, Robert, 1609
Hooper, Emma, 3364
Hooper, Harney E., Jr., 1609
Hooper, Harold, 3449
Hooper, Jack, 828
Hooper, John (Brit. d.1555), 1609
Hooper, John (Brit. pr.1700s), 1609
Hooper, Louise, 317
Hooper, Murray, 1609, 3386, 3448, 3451
Hooper, Warren G., 3251
Hoorn, Count, 1075
Hoos, William, 461
Hooton, Earnest A., 1609-10
Hoover, Ann (Scheitlin), 1610

Hoover, Charles V., 2871
Hoover, Dickerson, 1610
Hoover, George M., 1054
Hoover, Herbert, 72, 425, 434, 435, 572, 614,
  621, 784, 1114, 1198, 1581, 1612, 1618,
  1636, 1729, 1793, 1820, 1835, 1980, 2046,
  2192, 2336, 2662, 2781, 3125, 3148, 3166,
  3175, 3198, 3246, 3326
Hoover, J.(ohn) Edgar, 37, 48, 50, 52, 69,
  132, 171, 183, 209, 211, 225, 235, 238,
  243, 263, 344, 348, 359, 398, 428, 507,
  521, 528, 554, 617, 620, 654, 796, 817,
  845, 855, 896, 933, 954, 966, 967, 970,
  973, 1062, 1143, 1188, 1189, 1224, 1333,
  1399, 1610-17, 1660, 1758, 1764-1766,
  1777, 1786, 1798, 1801, 1823, 1826, 1834,
  1976, 1980, 2284, 2287, 2304, 2306, 2340,
  2398, 2412, 2513-2514, 2554-2555, 2678,
  2710, 2718, 2720, 2964, 2994, 3086, 3262,
  3299, 3326, 3426
Hoover, Tuck, 1617
Hop Sings, 2967, 3414
Hope, Alexander Augustus, 1476
Hope, Alexander W., 3425
Hope, Anthony, 78
Hope, Bob, 1829
Hope, Charlie, 1709, 1711
Hope, Edgar, 1617
Hope, James "Jimmy", 981, 1054, 1617-18,
  1941, 2211
Hope, Johnny, 2019
Hope, William, 3334
Hopkins, Arthur A., 3547
Hopkins, Edward, 3424
Hopkins, Gilbert W., 3547
Hopkins, Harry, 3386
Hopkins, James, 3349
Hopkins, James D., 915
Hopkins, Mark, 3193
Hopkins, Mary Frances Sherwood, 3193
Hopkins, Matthew, 534, 1133, 1604, 1618
Hopkins, Moses, 3193
Hopkins, Richard Joseph, 1618
Hopkins, Samuel, 1206
Hopkins, Sterling A., 2916
Hopkins, Tighe, 661
Hopkins, W., 2801
Hopkins, W.S.B., 695
Hopkins, William, 3355
Hopkins, William Seeley, 1618
Hopkinson, Alfred, 1498
Hopkinson, Joseph, 1618
Hopkinson, Mark, 3456
Hopley, Elizabeth, 720
Hopp, James, 3343
Hoppe, Werne, 198, 3475, 3476
Hopper, Abigail, 1307
Hopper, Edward, 410
Hopper, Isaac Tatem, 1307
Hopper, James, 144
Höppner, Erich, 3540
Hopps, William, 3338
Hopson, Howard Colwell, 1618
Hopson, Stephen, 3413
Hopwood, Edward, 191, 1618
Hora, Nicolae, 1618-19
Horan, James, 1002, 1073
Horan, John, 3560
Horan, Robert, 1759
Horgan, Edward, 865
Horgas, Joseph, 2826, 3037
Hormizd III, 1619, 3235
Hormizd IV, 1619, 1811, 3236
Horn, Adam, 1619
Horn, Henry, 2227
Horn, Johnny, 2990
Horn, Philip de Montmorency, 1619
Horn, Thomas, 3547, 3551, 3560, 3565
Horn, Tom, 135, 189, 1619-20, 1922, 2028,

2164, 2748
Horn, Willie Berle, 737
Hornberger, Freda, 380
Horne, Brian, 1620
Horne, Carlton, 1620
Horne, J.W.C., 3241
Horne, Percy, 1227
Horne, Robert, 2221
Horne, Thomas, 849
Horne, William Andrew, 1620-21
Horner, Fred, 777
Horner, Freda, 2072
Horner, George, 2327
Horner, Henry, 426
Horner, Joe, 601
Horner, John, 3425
Horner, Nannie, 2327
Horner, Nicholas, 1621
Hornig, Frank, 1621
Hornigold, Benjamin, 321, 1621
Hornik, Josef, 3464
Hornik, Mrs. Josef, 3464
Hörnlein, George, 1835
Hornung, Ernest William, 1621
Horowitz, Abe, 2562
Horowitz, David, 2782
Horowitz, Flo, 2189
Horowitz, Gloria, 915
Horowitz, Harry "Gyp the Blood", 304,
  794, 1931, 3218, 3406, 3407, 3410
Horowitz, Jay, 2313
Horowitz, Martin, 9
Horowitz, Moe, 2189
Horrall, C.B., 93
Horrall, Clarence B., 3425
Horrell, Ben, 1621-22, 3003
Horrell, John, 1621-22
Horrell, Martin, 243, 244, 1621-22, 2838,
  3192
Horrell, Matt, 3567
Horrell, Merritt, 243, 1621-22
Horrell, Sam, 243, 244, 2838, 3003, 3192,
  3560
Horrell, Tom, 243, 1621-22
Horrell Brothers, 243
Horrell-Higgins Feud, 244, 1621-2, 1739,
  3548, 3550
Horridge, Thomas Gordon, 1622
Horry, George Cecil, 1622
Horschoot, Van, 866
Horseman, Harriet, 2059
Horseman, William, 1175
Horsewell, Philip, 1154
Horsey, D.T., 1622
Horsfall, Frank, 846
Horsford, Walter, 362, 1622
Horsley, Edward, 3447
Horsley, William, 881
Horsley, William Watts, 2864
Horst, Terri M., 2836
Hortado, Mary, 2672
Hortense, Queen, 2279
Horthy, Miklos, 78, 3176
Horton, Black, 1676
Horton, Charles "Big Man", 107, 1075
Horton, Elta, 1623
Horton, Floyd, 1622-23
Horton, George, 3547
Horton, James, 3448, 3450
Horton, James E., 2716
Horton, John, 738
Horton, Kenneth, 1623
Horton, Margaret Weaver, 3072
Horton, Smith, 736
Horton, W. Banks, 1656
Horton, Wayne Donald, 3462
Horton, William Robert, 1623
Horwood, William Thomas Francis, 1623,
  2683, 3426

Hory, Elmyr de, 902
Hose, Samuel, 3351
Hosein, Arthur, 1623-24, 2047, 3328
Hosein, Nizamodeen, 1623-24, 2047, 3328
Hoshea, 3232
Hoshen, 1624
Hoshino, Kanehiro, 3202
Hosius, 1624
Hosking, Gladys, 19311
Hosni, Mohammed Salem, 3276, 3521
Hosni Mubarak, 2654
Hospodar, Steve, 1654
Hossack, Kenrick, 19981
Hossbach, Friedrich, 1557
Hossius, 2676
Hossler, Franz, 3540
Hosten, Theophil, 1137
Hosteny, Joseph N., 1146
Hoth, Hermann, 3540
Hothan, Lois Ann, 2489
Hotson, J.E.B., 3247
Hotsy Totsy Club, 1624
Hotte, Eunice, 2308
Houchard, Jean Nicolas, 1624
Houck, Charles Weston, 1624
Houdaz, John, 3367
Houdini, Harry, 880
Houdremont, Eduard, 3540
Houdson, Arthur, 2180
Houet, Germaine, 866
Hough, Benson W., 1624
Hough, Kevin, 3451
Hough, Luke, 3353
Houghton, Alanson, 1245
Houghton, Charles, 1624, 2888
Houghton, Hugh, 1624-25
Houghton, Joab, 1625
Houghton, Thomas, 1625
Houghton, Troy, 2189
Houillon, Florence Mary Doris, 1251
Houk, J. Spencer, 2741
Houk, Kenneth, 960
Houk, Seely, 2526
Hounds, 1625, 3414, 3415
Houndsditch Murders, 1625
Houphouet-Boigny, Felix, 3255
Hourigan, John, 19431
Housden, Charles, 1626
Housden, Jane, 1625-26, 1733
Housden, Nina, 1626
House, A.L., 18881
House, Aline, 638
House, Alma, 3365
House, Derrick, 3451
House, Eddie, 3560
House, Fred, 2886
House, James Arthur, 1626
House, Maggie, 3365
House, Paul Gregory, 3454
House, Thomas Jefferson, 3560
House in Queen Anne Street, The, 1626
House Of All Nations, 1626
House of Rest for Weary Boatman, 1626
Household, David, 2057
Housel, Tracey Lee, 3450
Houseman, Ann, 505
Houseman, Emeline, 416, 417
Houseman, George W., 416
Houseman, Polly, 415, 416
Houseman, Richard, 141
Houser, Charles, 3209
Housman, Nathan S., 1626-27
Houston, Betty Jean, 286
Houston, Cynthia, 1617
Houston, Hoyt, 3086
Houston, John, 3566
Houston, Richard, 3454
Houston, Robert, 1738
Houston, Sam, 2023, 2559, 2679, 2920,

Hurley, "Pugsy", 767, 3406
Hurley, Tom, 1775
Hurley, William J., 1646
Hurok, Sol, 920, 3267, 3492
Hurson, Martin, 3514
Hurst, Billy E., Jr., 3469
Hurst, Cecil James Barrington, 1646
Hurst, Charles G., Jr., 911
Hurst, George, 3344
Hurst, Lloyd, 2831
Hurtado, Camilo Martin Walter, 3473, 3523
Hurtado de Mendoza, Diego, 1646
Hus, Jan, 497, 1723
Husain Jawad 3236, 3247
Husayn, 3240
Husband, Pat, 3358
Husbands, Hermon, 1646
Huscar, 3238
Huáscar, Prince, 1634
Huser, Tom, 2714
Huseyin Inan, 2442
Husham Dabbas, 2091
Husham Mohammed Rajih, 3512
Huss, John, 1646
Hussein (Jor. 1935-), 140, 1646, 2275, 2518,
    3256, 3257, 3492, 3501
Hussein, Kamal, 3260, 3277, 3523
Hussein, Saddam, 1811, 2518
Hussein, Sharif, 1127
Hussein Abbas Muhammad, 2654
Hussein Ali Hariri 3474
Hussein ali Montazeri, 3520
Hussein Avni Pasha, 1647
Husseini, Fawzi, 3251
Hussey, Charles, 1647
Hussey, Eleanor, 854
Hussey, James, 1371
Hussmann, Karl, 1647
Hussmann, Maria, 2695
Hustead, Thomas E., 3463
Hustion, Eugene, 3386
Huston, Angelica, 2481, 3299
Huston, Felix, 3305
Hutchens, Augustus, 2965
Hutcheson, Charles Sterling, 1647
Hutchings, Harvey, 1647
Hutchins, Harry Burns, 1647
Hutchins, James, 3447
Hutchins, Louise, 1523
Hutchins, Robert Maynard, 1647
Hutchinson, Amy, 1647
Hutchinson, Anne, 1647-48, 3134, 3177
Hutchinson, Carl, 2859
Hutchinson, Francis, 1648
Hutchinson, George, 2, 1688
Hutchinson, John (Brit. 1615-64), 1648
Hutchinson, John (Brit. d.1750), 1647
Hutchinson, Jonas, 234
Hutchinson, Lottie, 374
Hutchinson, St. John, 1581, 1648
Hutchinson, Thomas, 1648, 2838
Hutchinson, William, (U.S. pr. 1630s) 1647
Hutchinson, William, (U.S. pr. 1880s) 374
Hutchison, Barbara, 3330, 3500
Hutchison, Charles, 1648
Hutchison, Harvey Macleary, 1648
Hutchison, John James, 1648
Hutson, Tip, 3351
Hutten, Philipp von, 1648
Hutton, Barbara, 1309
Hutton, F.A., 1837
Hutton, John, 508
Hutton, Peregrine, 1648
Huuf, William, 3351
Huxley, Aldous, 2228, 3297
Huyck, Emery E., 1775
Huyler, Joseph, 3364
Huynh Phu So, 1648
Hwan, Chun Kyung, 1648

Hwang Fu, 3247
Hyatt, "Crazy" Jack, 3376
Hyatt, Frank, 99, 3553
Hyatt, Jack, 2817
Hyatt, Ralph, 890
Hyde, Bennett Clarke, 333, 1648-49
Hyde, Charles Cheney, 1649
Hyde, Edward, 1649
Hyde, Fanny, 1649-50
Hyde, Frances, 1649
Hyde, H.H., 2558
Hyde, Henry, 1650
Hyde, Nicholas, 1650
Hyde de Neuville, Jean-Guillaume, 1650
Hyde Park Riots, 1650
Hyderabad Massacre, 1650
Hyderabad, Nizam of, 3252
Hydes, Robert, 2880
Hyer, Tom, 2488, 2682, 2964
Hyers, Gus, 2223
Hyland, "Chick", 2072, 3406
Hyland, Jim, 1254
Hyland, Keith, 2212
Hyland, Martin, 3424
Hyland, Ray, 376, 378, 3414
Hylton-Foster, Harry, 543
Hyman, Cap, 793, 2835, 3386, 3390
Hynes, Charles, 343, 1582
Hynes, Jack, 1199, 2219
Hynes, James, 1650
Hypatia, 1650, 3235
Hyperbolus, 1650, 3233
Hyperides, 1650, 3233
Hyrcanus, John, II, 3234
Hyun Hui Kim, 1820

I

I Pong-chang, 3247
Iacovetti, David, 3406
Iamascia, Danny, 2700
Iannarella, Francis Jr., 3412
Iannece, Charles, 3412
Ianniello, Matthew "Matty The Horse",
    1651, 3298, 3406
Iannone, James, 3397
Iannone, Salvatore, 2752
Iavarone, Jean, 3327
Ibarra, Leon, 3246
Ibarra Herrara, Manuel, 587, 1651, 3391
Iberia, Anthimus of, 133
IBM, 3289
Ibn al-Abbar, 1651
Ibn al-Baytar, 3291
Ibn al-Jawzi, 1651
Ibn-Hanbal, 1651
ibn Jabr, Rahmah, 1651
Ibn Khallikan, 1651
Ibn Saud, 1127
Ibn Shaddad, 1651
Ibn-Tamas, Beverly Ann, 1651-1652
Ibn Taymiyah, 1652
Ibn Wahshiyah, 3291
Ibrahim I, 1844
Ibrahim, Abu, 3266
Ibrahim el Fayeb, 2288
Ibrahim Lodi, 1652
Ibrahim, Said Zaghloul Pasha ibn, 3245
Ibrahimovic, Emin, 1583
Ibraimov, 3258, 3507
Ibsen, Jense Albert, 3250
Icardi, Aldo Lorenzo, 1652
Ichiwa-kai, 3395

Ickes, Harold, 1200
Ida, Horace, 2139, 2140
Ida, Joseph, 136, 3412
Ida The Goose, 1652
Ida The Goose War, 1652
Ide, Henry Clay, 1652
Ideman, James, 1151
Iden, Alexander, 3238
Idi Amin, 2054
Idone, Sando, 3412
Idris Senussi I, 2518
Idriss, Moulay, 3252
Iggulden, George William, 1652
Iglesias, José Maria, 1652
Iglesias, Julio, 3332
Iglesias, Santiago, 816
Ignacio Novo, 1942, 1943
Ignatiev, Countess, 2538
Ignatovich, Nicolai Ivanovich, 2177
Igoe, Michael Lambert, 1652
Igor, 1652
Ihn, Max Otto, 3540
Ikonomoff, M., 3246
Ilah, Abdul, 3250, 3253
Ileo, Joseph, 2010
Iles, Francis, 141, 169
Iles, John, 2980
Ilgner, Max, 3540
Iliano, Frank "Punchy", 1256, 3406
Ilic, Danilo, 1212
Illingworth, Hallie, 1652
Illingworth, Monty, 1652-1653
Illinois Anti-Abolition Violence, 3373
Illinois Driver Registration Bureau, 3289
Illmer, Harold, 1019
Ilsley, Agnes Boeing, 812
Ily, Nicole, 1653, 2403
Im Sook Pin, 2466
Imad Mughniyah, 1914
Imam Moussa Sadr, 3473
Imbert Berrera, Segundo, 3254
Imbert, Jacques "Tomcat", 1235
Imbert, Peter Michael, 1653, 3426
Imbler, Paul Kern, 1653
Imbriani, Michael, 2107
Imbrie, Robert W., 1653, 3245
Imbruglia, Frank, 3379
Imlay, Alice, 1631
Impastato, Nicolo, 1653, 3406
Impelliteri, Vincent, 1136, 2002
Imperial Chemical Industries, Ltd., 3289
Imperial, R., 3251
Imperiale, Sebastien, 742
Impey, Elijah, 1653
Imposimato, Ferdinando, 3519
Imredy, Béla, 1653, 3540
In Ho Oh, 2129
In Ki Wish, 3345
In Muffled Night, 1656
Inadi, Joseph, 3413
Inagawa-kai, 3395
Inagawa Kakuji, 1653-1654, 3395
Inaros, 3232
Incardona, Bastiano, 2082, 3399
Ince, George, 497, 3462
Ince, Wallace, 870
Indelicato, Alphonse "Sonny Red", 1943,
    3406
Indelicato, Anthony "Bruno", 2448, 2670,
    3406
Independence, Liberation, Resistance
    Organization, 3268, 3494, 3531
Inderlied, Herman, 1270
Indian Charley, 842
Indian Hindu-Muslim Riots, 3378
Indian, John, 2664
Indian Marxist Communist Party, 3524
Indian Riots, 3378
Indian Territory, 1654

Jacobs, Stephen, 3339
Jacobs, Timothy, 3334
Jacobs, William M., 483, 1692-1693, 3228
Jacobsen, David, 1914
Jacobson, Benjamin, 3386
Jacobson, Harry, 2875
Jacobson, Herbert, 2770
Jacobson, Howard "Buddy", 1693
Jacobson, Jacob, 1693
Jacobson, Leslie, 1461
Jacobson, Samuel, 319
Jacobson, Walter, 2390
Jacobus, 471, 535, 1693, 1745
Jacoby, Henry Julius, 1693, 2336, 2512
Jacquemain, Claude, 3333, 3516
Jacques I, 926
Jacques, Paul, 2273
Jacquier, Nicholas, 1693-1694
Jael, 3232
Jager, Miemie Magdalena Josina de, 1903
Jäggli, Margaret, 2452
Jagiello, 1807, 3238
Jaglowski, Gregory, 1515
Jagusch, August, 1694
Jahan, Shah, 1453
Jahangir, Emperor, 155, 1453
Jahn, Ray, 669
Jahnke, Deborah, 1694
Jahnke, Kurt, 2119
Jahnke, Maria, 1694
Jahnke, Richard C., 1694
Jahnke, Richard J., 1694
Jahoda, William, 3386
Jakaby, Joseph, 3464
Jake Fleagle Gang, 338
Jakobson, Barbro, 484
Jalal-ad-Din, 3237
Jalal-ad-Din Mingburnu (d.1296), 1694
Jalal-ud-Din Firuz Khalji (d.1231), 1694, 3237
Jalandoni, Rafael, 2523
Jalovec, Richard, 1443
Jamaat al Takfir wal Hijira, 3215
Jamal, H.A., 3496
Jamali, Hojatoleslam Nasser, 3259, 3516
Jamericco, Numio, 2044, 3386
James I (Brit. 1566-1625), 585, 656, 680, 686, 742, 810, 872, 1140, 1154, 1188, 1405, 1453, 1628, 1629, 1694-95, 2090, 2135, 2345, 2443, 2444, 2533, 2796, 2817, 2819, 3054, 3104, 3180
James I (Scot. 1394-1437) 1694, 3238
James II (Brit. 1600s), 280, 550, 713, 754, 775, 887, 999, 1285, 1716, 1926, 2034, 2350, 2712, 3238
James II (Scot. 1430-60), 1009, 1010, 1695
James III (Scot. 1452-88), 2852
James III (Brit. pr.1715), 1199, 2145
James IV, 270, 290 , 1028, 1695
James V (Scot. 1512-42) 157, 1010, 1695, 2134, 2853
James VI (Scot. 1566-1625) 2853, 2871
James, Albert T., Sr., 1695
James, Alexander Franklin (U.S. 1843-1915), 862, 1196, 1695, 1706, 2519, 3009, 3212, 3457, 3561
James, Ann, 3177
James, Antonio, 3452
James, Davidson, 3450
James, Francis, 1695
James, Frank (U.S. d.1896), 3348
James, Frank (U.S. 1843-1915), 862, 1196, 1695, 1706, 2519, 3009, 3212, 3457, 3561, 3568
James, Fullarton, 1202
James Gang, 3457
James, Gomer, 1775
James, Henry (Brit. 1828-1911), 943, 1695, 1923

James, Henry (U.S. pr.1928), 2235
James, Jesse Woodson, 125, 235, 236, 254, 256, 275, 277, 292, 363, 369, 557, 558, 857, 858, 862, 864, 962, 1182, 1186, 1195-1197, 1565, 1590, 1613, 1695-1709, 1781, 2283, 2468, 2519, 2740, 2801, 3009, 3212, 3214, 3457, 3554, 3557, 3558, 3560-3562, 3568
James, John (Brit. pr.1700s), 1491
James, John (U.S. d.1905), 3357
James, John (U.S. pr.1700), 1709
James, Mrs. John (U.S. d.1929), 3367
James, John H., 3350
James, John Towers (U.S. pr.1900s), 329
James, Johnny, 3455
James, Joseph, 3348
James, Lee, 3343
James, Lester, 316
James, Lydia Ruth, 1709
James, Martha, 1191
James, Perry, 1194
James, Reuben, 897
James, Richard (U.S. d.1920), 3366
James, Richard (U.S. pr.1970), 3406
James, Richard F., 1191
James, Robert (U.S. d.1850), 1695
James, Robert (U.S. d.1942) 1709-1711
James, Robert Jacques (Brit. pr. 1805), 1628
James, Roy, 1371
James, "Saint", 1695
James, Steven, 3448
James Street Gang, 2970, 2973
James, T.J., 592
James, Terrence, 3453
James, Thomas Lemuel, 1711
James, William (U.S. pr.1864), 1602
James, William (U.S. pr.1874), 1701
James, William (U.S. d.1906), 3357
James, William Reginald, 2872
James, Zee, 1196, 1701, 1706
James, Zeralda, 1196
James-Younger Gang, 2468, 2764
Jameson, Edwin Cornell, 600
Jameson, Forest, 3351
Jameson, James, 1711
Jameson, Jean, 148, 150
Jameson, Leander Starr, 1711
Jameson, Tom, 2463
Jameson, William James, 1711
Jameson-Carr, George, 1128
Jamie, Daft, 548
Jamieson, Alexander, 1227
Jamieson, Elizabeth, 2036
Jamieson, Frederick W., 1239
Jamieson, George, 3561
Jamieson, Gill, 1239, 3325
Jamieson, James, 2953
Jamison, Arnett, 899
Jamison, Valerie, 1356
Jamkodjian, Madiros, 3274
Janda, Leslie, 2434
Jandezjak, Frank, 498
Janecka, Allen Wayne, 1033
Janeff, Sotir, 3250
Janega, Rudolph, 2027
Janes, John, 3561
Jannaeus, Alexander, 1726
Janney, Edith, 1877
Janowski, Daniel, 2893
Jansen, A. Elmer, 3426
Jansen, C.J., 340, 2871
Jansen, Cornelis Otto, 1048, 2523
Jansen, Heinrich, 3475
Janson, H.A., 2732
Janssen, Albertus, 1632
January 1st Popular Front, 3520
January 31 Popular Front, 3512, 3531
Janus, Adam, 3011

Janus, Christopher G., 1711
Janus, Stanley, 3011
Janus, Theresa, 3011
Januszewski, Judith, 1113
Japanese Red Army, 3281, 3330, 3531, 3533
Jaquez-Diaz, Ismael, 3298
Jarallah, Ahmad, 3261
Jaramillo, Anibal, 1711
Jaramillo, Heraldo, 985
Jardine, Edward, 2324
Jarecki, Edmund, 714
Jarmain, Peter Joseph, 1711
Jarman, George B., 1711
Jarman, James, Jr., 1798
Jarnac, Guy Chabot de,, 3303
Jarnac-Châteigneraie Duel, 1711-1712
Jarnette, John Kinchloe De,, 902-903
Jaroslawicz, Pinchos, 2894
Jarosz, Andor, 3540
Jarrell, David A., 1300, 3450
Jarrell, Sanford, 1712
Jarrells, Jonathen, 3450
Jarrett, Cato, 3355
Jarrett, Floyd, 1177
Jarrett, Rebecca, 2846
Jarrett, Ronald, 516
Jarrett, Walter R., 1784
Jaruzelski, Wojciech, 1853
Jarvis, Fred, 1630
Jarvis, Washington, 3355
Jascalevich, Mario E., 1712
Jasper, Alfred, 3454
Jasso, Mauro, 1524
Jaudon, Anza, 3366
Jaunutis, 1806
Jauregui, Alfredo, 2404
Jauregui, Antonio, 3246
Jaureguy, Juan, 3159
Jaurès, Jean-Joseph-Marie-Auguste, 3243
Jaurès, Jean Léon, 1024, 1712-1713
Javits, Jacob, 1896
Jaw, Bull Donohue, 646
Jawad, Muhammad Ali, 3249
Jawarski, Paul, 3459
Jaworski, Leon, 544, 3100
Jay, Jerry, 3143
Jay, John (U.S. 1745-1829), 982, 1086, 1713
Jay, Peter, 2337
Jayanagara, 1250
Jaybird-Woodpecker War, 1713
Jayne, George, 1713, 1714
Jayne, Marion, 1713, 1714
Jayne, Silas, 464, 1713-1714
Jean, René, 1905, 3458, 3459
Jeanneret, Marie, 1714
Jech, Anton, 295
Jeckeln, Friedrich, 3540
Jee, Alan, 1199, 1463
Jeffcott, John, 1714, 3305
Jeffcott-Hennis Duel, 1714-1715
Jefferds, Charles, 1715
Jefferies, Christopher, 1715
Jefferies, Elizabeth, 2931
Jefferies, Joseph, 1205
Jeffers, Jimmy, 3448
Jeffers, William J., 625
Jefferson, Albert, 3447
Jefferson, Burtell M., 3426
Jefferson, Dunk, 3548
Jefferson, Eddie, 1715
Jefferson, Edward, 2464
Jefferson, Larry, 2349
Jefferson, Lawrence, 3450
Jefferson, Lenny, 3352
Jefferson, Leroy, 1715, 3297, 3397, 3406
Jefferson, Lewis, 3347
Jefferson, Mack, 2349
Jefferson, Robert, 3365
Jefferson, Thomas, 205, 424, 482, 555, 584,

690, 897, 1020, 1029, 1066, 1519, 1734,
1805, 1892, 1944, 1965, 1973, 2410 ,2743,
2832, 3178
Jeffery, Henry Edward, 1715
Jeffrey, Francis, 1716
Jeffrey, Henry, 3154
Jeffrey, William, 405
Jeffreys, Alec, 2471
Jeffreys, Francis, 1716, 3304
Jeffreys, George, 280, 285, 1716, 2891
Jeffreys-Moore Duel, 1716
Jeffries, Edward, 426
Jeffries, Elizabeth, 1716
Jeffries, George, 1195
Jeffries, Jim, 1269
Jeffries, Mary, 1716
Jeffries, Patrick, 3456
Jeffries, William, 2556
Jeffs, Amelia, 1716
Jeffs, Doreen, 1716-1717
Jeffs, Frederick Walter, 1717
Jeffs, Linda, 1717
Jegado, Hélène, 1694, 1717
Jehoiachin, 1717
Jehoram, 175, 1717, 3232
Jehu, 41, 1717, 3232
Jelaleddin, 1291
Jelf, Arthur Richard, 1717, 1907
Jelinek, Harry, 960
Jelke, Mickey, 379
Jelke, Minot F., 1717
Jellison, Leo C., 3155
Jem, 1717
Jenco, Lawrence Martin, 1914
Jenecka, Allen, 3455
Jenkerson, Francis C. 134
Jenkin, William Thomas Francis, 1717
Jenkins, Allison, 1717-1718
Jenkins, Anne Katherine, 3327
Jenkins, Billy, 814
Jenkins, Bruce, 1226
Jenkins, Carrie Lee, 1718
Jenkins, Charles, 2316
Jenkins, Charles Harry, 1300, 3461
Jenkins, Daniel (U.S. d.1935), 3367
Jenkins, Daniel (U.S. pr.1983), 3448
Jenkins, David, 1718
Jenkins, E.B., 1718
Jenkins, Edward, 3344
Jenkins, Elizabeth, 1458
Jenkins, Ferguson, 1718
Jenkins, George, 951
Jenkins, Harold, 2875
Jenkins, Harry (U.S. pr.1957), 1718
Jenkins, Harry (Brit. pr.1910), 3084
Jenkins, Huntley, 1597
Jenkins, J.B., 3247
Jenkins, James (U.S. pr.1930s), 948, 951,
3427
Jenkins, James Gilbert (U.S. 1834-64), 1719,
3561
Jenkins, James Graham (U.S. 1834-1921),
1719
Jenkins, Joe Ben, 723
Jenkins, John, 1719, 2677, 2888
Jenkins, John James (U.S. 1843-1911), 1719
Jenkins, Lawrence Hugh, 1719
Jenkins, Leon V., 3425, 3426
Jenkins, Lonnie, 1719
Jenkins, Neville, 2735
Jenkins, Ruby, 1600
Jenkins, Sam, 3011
Jenkins, Sam F., 1978
Jenkins, Thomas (Brit. pr.1953), 2676
Jenkins, Thomas (Brit. pr.1869-1955), 2062
Jenkins, Thomas James, 1506
Jenkins, Tom (U.S. d.1826), 3138
Jenkins, Tom (U.S. pr.1907), 3561
Jenkins, Walter, 1200

Jenkins, William, 3349
Jenkinson, Arthur, 1083
Jenks, Albert Ernest, 1101
Jenks, Edward, 1720
Jenks, Thomas L., 3424
Jennings, Alphonso J., 857, 858, 1720-
1721, 3561
Jennings, Augustus Otis, 1721
Jennings, Bernard, 1759
Jennings, Bryan, 3450
Jennings, Charles, 3365
Jennings, Dora, 1722
Jennings, Ed, 1720, 3560
Jennings, Edgar S. 182
Jennings, Frank, 1720, 1721, 3561
Jennings, George Augustine, 1721
Jennings, Glenn, 1721
Jennings, Henry, 1721
Jennings, J.D.F., 1720
Jennings, James, 3340
Jennings, James Brandon, 1721-1722
Jennings, Jasper, 1722
Jennings, John (Brit. pr.1798), 1722
Jennings, John (U.S. pr.1890s), 1720
Jennings, John H., 3470
Jennings, Michael, 3448
Jennings, Napoleon Augustus, 1722, 3548
Jennings, Newell, 1908
Jennings, Newton M., 1722
Jennings, Robert M., 3455
Jennings, Wilbur, 3448
Jennings Gang, 812, 1916, 3128, 3548
Jennsen, Adolph, 3030
Jenny Newstead, 1722
Jenrette, John W., Jr., 13
Jensen, Benton Franklin, 3252
Jensen, Bettilou, 3222
Jensen, Carl Kruse, 484
Jensen, Christian, 1919
Jensen, Gordon, 2117
Jensen, James, 2472
Jensen, John P., 3425
Jensen, Max, 1314
Jensen, Robert, 2842
Jensen, Thomas Peter, 1722
Jenzer, John, 855
Jeppesen, Louise, 1722
Jerkins, Jacob T., 1460, 3425
Jermyn, Edmund Beson, 1722
Jermyn, Frederic, 3454
Jernegan, Prescott Ford, 1330, 1722
Jernigan, Joseph, 3455
Jeroboam I, 3232
Jerome of Prague, 1723
Jerome, William Travers, 597, 598, 1460,
1722-1723, 2104, 2924, 3402
Jerrell, Henry, 2569
Jerviswood, Baille of, 212
Jerwa, Rabeh, 3259, 3333, 3519
Jeskewitz, Richard, 1969
Jesse, F. Tennyson, 2469
Jesse, Frederick, 2248
Jesse, Frederick William Maximilian, 1723
Jessie, Willis, 3465
Jessop, Mary, 728
Jessup, Brother, 1723
Jessup, Charles, 1723
Jessup, Georgia, 2690
Jessup, Rose, 1723
Jessy, John, 3342
Jesus Christ, 134, 193, 575, 1195, 1695,
2098, 2450, 2466, 2774
Jesús Gonzalez Valenzuela, Maria de,,
1338
Jesus Marquez Monreal, Jose de, 3253
Jesus Marrero Otero, Manuel de, 138
Jesus Rivera Gonzalez, Daniel de, 3519
Jett, Curtis, 1453, 1723, 2119
Jette, Louis Amable, 1724

Jetton, White, 3356
Jeune, Francis, 2712
Jewbach, Al, 1726
Jewbach, Moe, 1867
Jewel, Will, 30
Jewell, Joseph, 2093
Jewell, Margaret, 3162
Jewell, Stephen, 1724
Jewett, John G., 2672
Jewish Armed Resistance, 3491, 3503, 3504,
3523, 3531
Jewish Defense League (JDL), 3229, 3259,
3266-3269, 3274, 3276, 3328, 3482, 3483,
3485-3493, 3497, 3499, 3500, 3501, 3503,
3516, 3518, 3520, 3522, 3523, 3531, 3532
Jewish Underground Army, 3503, 3531
Jewitt, Jonathan, 456
Jezebel, 3232
Jeziorski, Frank, 943
Jiang Qing, 3272
Jibral (Jibril) Front, 3267, 3268 ,3469, 3483,
3488, 3492, 3494, 3531
Jibril, Ahmed, 2402
Jihad Command, 3473, 3510, 3511
Jimenez, Fernando, 905
Jimenez, Jesus, 3448
Jimenez, Tucapel, 3259, 3521
Jimenez, Victor, 3452
Jimerson, Aaron, 3365
Jimerson, Lila, 456
Jimerson, Verneal, 3161, 3451
Jiminez, Juan, 1266
Jimison, Tom P., 287
Jimmerson, Silas, 3362
Jimmy Curley Gang, 1724, 3402, 3406, 3407
Jim the Penman, 1724
JIN, 3503
Jines, Jenkin, 1681
János Zápolya, 3127
Joab, 10, 14, 109, 3232
Joachim, 2879
Joachim, Paul, 3254
Joan (Italy pr.872-82), 1724
Joan I, 1993
Joan of Arc, 2530-2532
Joan of Navarre, 1725
Joanna I, 686, 1724, 3238
Joanna II, 1724
Joash, 110, 175, 3232
Joasmis, 1725
Jobe, Jonathon, 1836
Jobes, Marigray, 3119
Jobin, Gaston, 543, 1725
Jobin, Marie, 543-544, 1725
Jobin, Paul, 544, 1725
Jocker, Harry, 1229, 1725
Jodl, Alfred, 1573, 1574, 1725, 3540
Joe the Greaser Gang, 1725-1726
Joe the Mumper, 548
Joel, Collins, 3556
Joel, Solly, 1865
Joel, Woolf, 1865, 3064
Joglar, R.D., 3251
Jogues, Isaac, 1726
Johannes, Mike, 3425
Johansson, Erik, 1406
John I (Brit. 1400s), 1149
John I (Port. 1357-1433), 1931
John I (Spain 1379-1416), 1149
John II (Spain pr.1400s), 1149, 1726, 2012
John II (Fr. 1393-1458), 3324
John III, 1726
John IV the Valiant, 168, 2164
John V, 1725, 1731
John VI, 2177
John VIII, 1724
John IX, 2728
John X, 3236
John XI, 2127, 2728

John XIV (Brit. d.c.984) 1726, 3237
John XIV (Brit. 1715) 1726
John XXIII, 1723
John of Gloucester, 1519
John of Lancaster, 1726
John of Leiden, 1726
John of Nepomuk, 1726
John of Wesel, 1727
John the Constant, 1726
John the Fearless, 3238
John the Parracide, 47, 3238
John, Cobby, 2897
John, Cordeiro, 2762
John, Cullen, 2747
John, Don, 1066
John Hyrcanus II, 1726
John, Lenora, 742
John, Pelham, 495
John, Percy Malcolm, 1881
John, Schonchin, 619
John Bar Quorsos, 1726
John Birch Society, 3503
John Paul II, 1727, 2118, 2692, 3258, 3260,
    3272, 3321, 3334, 3509, 3510, 3512, 3523,
    3528
Johns, Cloudsley, 2207
Johns, Foster, 2725
Johns, Joe, 253
Johns, John, 3379
Johns, Margaret, 1532
Johns, Stephen, 3452
Johns, Walter, 3178
Johnson, Abe, 3358
Johnson, Alan Godfrey, 775
Johnson, Alex, 3358
Johnson, Alexander, 3350
Johnson, Alice Hannah, 2940
Johnson, Alva, 1005
Johnson, Andrew, 385, 408, 507, 690, 849,
    1020, 1114, 1392, 1554, 1604, 1625, 1727-
    28, 1837, 1955, 1962-1965, 2313, 2824,
    2838, 2852, 3105, 3162
Johnson, Andrew (U.S. pr.1988) 3451
Johnson, Anne, 2153
Johnson, Anthony, 1621, 3348
Johnson, Anthony Keith, 3447
Johnson, Armstead, 3337
Johnson, Arthur, 726
Johnson, Ban, 402
Johnson, Becky Lou, 504
Johnson, Benjamin (U.S. d.1889), 3305
Johnson, Benjamin (U.S. d.1895), 3346
Johnson, Bill (U.S. pr.1833-53), 2681
Johnson, Bill (U.S. pr.1898), 2688, 3561
Johnson, Bill (U.S. d.1881), 845
Johnson, Billy Ray, 2349
Johnson, Bonnie Louise, 1732
Johnson, Brian, 2509
Johnson, Bumpy, 1728
Johnson, Bunk, 2862
Johnson, C.S., 2210
Johnson, Carl, 1728, 3455
Johnson, Carl E., 3425
Johnson, Carol Sue Boling, 814
Johnson, Cassidy Marie, 1131
Johnson, Ceasar L., 3453
Johnson, Charles (U.S. pr.1930s), 813
Johnson, Charles (U.S. pr.1902), 3354
Johnson, Charles (U.S. pr.1892), 3548
Johnson, Charles O. (U.S. d.1923), 879
Johnson, Charles S. (U.S., 1854-1906), 1728
Johnson, Chas, 3561
Johnson, Christopher, 1728
Johnson, Claude, 3364
Johnson, Claude F., 1728, 3424
Johnson, Clyde, 68
Johnson, Clyde M., 2078
Johnson, Collins, 3365
Johnson, Cortland A., 1002, 1073

Johnson, Corwin, 2733
Johnson County War, 1619, 1620, 1734,
    3553, 3555, 3568
Johnson, Courtland C., 1728
Johnson, Curtis, 3455
Johnson, D.C., 3365
Johnson, Dan, 1453, 3561, 3564
Johnson, Darlenia Denise, 1233
Johnson, David H., 3426
Johnson, DeWitt C., 3561
Johnson, Diane, 3326
Johnson, Dick, 2432
Johnson, Donnie Edward, 3454
Johnson, Dorsie, 3455
Johnson, Doyle, 254, 3459
Johnson, E.G., 3242
Johnson, E. Lynn, 1517
Johnson, Ed, 3357
Johnson, Eddie, 3455
Johnson, Edward, 3363
Johnson, Edward Earl, 1728, 3447
Johnson, Edwin, 1728
Johnson, Elijah, 3367
Johnson, Ellsworth, 1728
Johnson, Emma, 2863, 3399
Johnson, Enoch L. "Nucky", 178, 1728-
    1729
Johnson, Erskine Leroy, 3454
Johnson, Eugene, Sr., 692
Johnson, F.O., 3344
Johnson, Florence, 2340
Johnson, Frank (U.S. 1947-), 1733
Johnson, Frank (U.S. d.1897), 3349
Johnson, Frank (U.S. pr.1906), 3544,
    3549-3552
Johnson, Frank M. (U.S. pr.1967) 3478
Johnson, Frank Minis, Jr. (U.S. 1918-),
    1729
Johnson, Fred, 3365
Johnson, Gary, 3455
Johnson, George (U.S. d.1882), 1729, 3337
Johnson, George (U.S. d.1908), 3359
Johnson, George (U.S. d.1909), 3359
Johnson, George (U.S. d.1935), 3367
Johnson, George (U.S. pr.1904-15), 2343
Johnson, George (U.S. pr.1935), 2963
Johnson, George E.Q. (U.S. 1874-1949),
    1729
Johnson, George J., 3347
Johnson, George W., 3557
Johnson, Gordon, 3425
Johnson, Grant, 3353
Johnson, Gregory Scott, 3451
Johnson, Gus, 3348
Johnson, Harold, 1160
Johnson, Hazel, 658
Johnson, Henry "Kerley" (U.S. pr.1893),
    1676, 1729
Johnson, Henry (U.S. d.1890), 3339
Johnson, Henry (U.S. d.1901), 3353
Johnson, Henry (U.S. d.1902), 3355
Johnson, Henry (U.S. d.1907), 3358
Johnson, Henry (U.S. d.1908), 3282
Johnson, Hensley, 3355
Johnson, Hiram Warren, 1729, 1744
Johnson, Hudson, 3338
Johnson, J. (U.S. d.1903), 3030
Johnson, J.E. "Dobe", 3563
Johnson, J.V., 3357
Johnson, Jack "Turkey Creek" (U.S.
    pr.1870-80s), 842, 1061, 1729, 3548,
    3558, 3561
Johnson, Jack (U.S. pr.1912), 1729
Johnson, Jack (U.S. pr.1953), 840
Johnson, Jack (U.S. pr.1910), 1864
Johnson, Jack R., 3471
Johnson, James (U.S. 1780-1811), 1729
Johnson, James (U.S. pr.1983), 3448
Johnson, Jasper (U.S. pr.1946), 3003

Johnson, Jed, 1521
Johnson, Jeffrey, 2405
Johnson, Jerome A., 754, 1256, 1259, 1730,
    3403, 3404, 3406
Johnson, Jerry (U.S. d.1895), 3346
Johnson, Jerry (U.S. d.1907), 3358
Johnson, Jerry (U.S. pr.1982), 3097
Johnson, Jim (U.S., pr.1901), 508
Johnson, Jim (U.S., pr.1981), 621
Johnson, Joe (Brit. pr. 1704), 3148
Johnson, Joe (U.S. pr. 1988), 3448
Johnson, John (Brit. d.1760), 1152
Johnson, John (U.S. d.1892), 3342
Johnson, John (U.S. d.1893), 3343
Johnson, John (U.S. pr.1880s), 1730
Johnson, John (U.S. pr.1896), 1419
Johnson, John (U.S. pr.1977), 3331
Johnson, John (U.S. pr.1870-80), 1730, 3548
Johnson, John A. (U.S. pr.1911), 1730
Johnson, John C., 3368
Johnson, John R. (U.S. 1941-), 1730
Johnson, John V., 3386
Johnson, Johnnie (Can. pr.1880), 1728
Johnson, Johnnie L. (U.S. pr.1980), 1300
Johnson, Johnny (U.S. 1919-53), 1730
Johnson, Joseph (U.S. d.1894), 3345
Johnson, Joseph (U.S. d.1916, 3364
Johnson, Joseph, Jr. (U.S. 1938-,), 1312
Johnson, Julia, 862, 863
Johnson, Karen (U.S. pr.1980s), 1946
Johnson, Karen (U.S. pr.1968), 264
Johnson, Kathleen, 2941
Johnson, Kenn, 1311
Johnson, Kitty, 3399
Johnson, Larry Joe, 3450
Johnson, Laura, 1730-1731
Johnson, Laverne, 3448
Johnson, Lawrence, 3346
Johnson, Lee, 1773
Johnson, Leonard, 3360
Johnson, Lillian, 3175
Johnson, Louis P., 3350
Johnson, Lyndon Baines, 644, 651, 725,
    728, 744, 753, 779, 978, 1017, 1072,
    1090, 1108, 1127, 1151, 1146, 1200, 1224,
    1280, 1302, 1331, 1343, 1396, 1463, 1471,
    1478, 1532, 1545, 1597, 1616, 1636,
    1769, 1796-1799, 1828, 1877, 1884, 1909,
    1990, 2037, 2060, 2108, 2129, 2130, 2154,
    2247, 2308, 2328, 2471, 2571, 2836, 2896,
    2939, 3063, 3134, 3135, 3208, 3216, 3229,
    3298
Johnson, Maggie, 2087
Johnson, Malcolm, 3453
Johnson, Mark (U.S. 1979), 1636
Johnson, Mark (U.S. pr.1986), 1913
Johnson, Mark (U.S. pr.1988), 3451
Johnson, Marvin, 3450
Johnson, Mary (Brit. pr.1912), 1731
Johnson, Mary (U.S. d.1648), 765, 1731,
    3208
Johnson, Mary Mae, 1924
Johnson, Maurice, 2509
Johnson, Michael, 446
Johnson, Milton, 1731, 3451
Johnson, "Mushmouth", 1731, 3388
Johnson, Nathan, 3406
Johnson, Nelson F., 3425
Johnson, Noble Jacob, 1731
Johnson, Noel, 1311
Johnson, Norma, 505
Johnson, Nubry, 3352
Johnson, O.T., 3002
Johnson, Oma, 2001
Johnson, Otter, 3561
Johnson, Pat, 2982
Johnson, Paul B. (U.S. pr.1940s), 1591
Johnson, Paul Beasley (death row), 3450
Johnson, Peggy, 1731

Jones, George (U.S. pr.1963), 115
Jones, George (U.S. pr.1971) 1443
Jones, Gladys, 1379
Jones, Graham, 2872
Jones, Gregory M., 3452
Jones, Gus, 3548
Jones, Gus T., 210
Jones, Harllel, 1737
Jones, Harold (Brit. 1906-), 1737
Jones, Harold (U.S. pr.1925), 1740
Jones, Henry, 3340
Jones, Henry Earl, 721
Jones, Howard, 2065
Jones, Hugh, 3359
Jones, J. Edward, 1095
Jones, J. Walter, Jr., 37
Jones, J.P., 3248
Jones, James (Brit. b.c.1826) 1473
Jones, James (U.S. d.1895), 3346
Jones, James (U.S. d.1898), 3349
Jones, James (U.S. pr.1988), 3454
Jones, James Lee, 3454
Jones, James McHall (U.S. 1823-51), 1737
Jones, James Warren (Guyana 1931-78),
    671, 1737-1739
Jones, Jane, 1338
Jones, Jeff, 3107
Jones, Jeffrey, 3448
Jones, Jennifer, 2954
Jones, Jeremiah, 1739
Jones, Jessie, 3343
Jones, Jim (U.S. d.1900), 1742, 2192, 2793
Jones, Jim (U.S. pr.1918), 3365
Jones, John (Brit. d.1789), 868, 916
Jones, John (Brit. pr.1842), 1739
Jones, John (U.S. d.1900), 1742
Jones, John (U.S. pr.1870s), 311, 364, 1739
Jones, John (U.S. pr.1870s), 3561, 3567
Jones, John (U.S. d.1890), 3339
Jones, John (Brit. pr.1700), 3292
Jones, John B. (U.S. 1834-81), 276, 1622,
    1739, 3192, 3545, 3548, 3557
Jones, John B. (U.S. pr.1816), 793
Jones, John Gale (Brit. pr.1810), 543, 3548
Jones, John P., 1775, 1781, 2034
Jones, Jon, 3356
Jones, Joseph, 3351
Jones, "Judge", 3360
Jones, Julius "Babe", 1834
Jones, June, 645
Jones, Kernard, 3425
Jones, Leo, 3450
Jones, Leslie, 3450
Jones, M. Ashby, 1860
Jones, Mabel Theresa, 3035
Jones, Marshall, 3352
Jones, Martin, 1466
Jones, Marvin, 3452
Jones, Mary (Brit. 1700-40), 850
Jones, Mary (Brit. 1765), 519
Jones, Mary (Brit. pr.1756), 1815
Jones, Mary (Brit. pr.1760), 1791
Jones, Mary (Brit. pr.1771), 1739-1740
Jones, Mary (U.S. 1884-1947), 1740
Jones, Mary (U.S. pr.1925), 3325
Jones, Maurice P., 1354
Jones, Michael, 1740
Jones, Michael Gordon, 3328, 3486
Jones, Michael Steven, 3455
Jones, Milton E., 2764
Jones, Moll, 1740
Jones, Mose, 3366
Jones, Moses (U.S. d.1892), 3342
Jones, Moses (U.S. d.1899), 3351
Jones, Nat B., 3548
Jones, Nathaniel Raphael, 1740
Jones, Newton, 3344
Jones, Noel (U.S. pr.1964-670, 1740, 3425
Jones, Owen, 3339

Jones, Palmer, 744
Jones, Patricia B., 1828, 3453
Jones, Paul Roland, 3393
Jones, Payne, 1698
Jones, Peter, 1740
Jones, R.L., 3424
Jones, Randall Scott, 3450
Jones, "Ranger", 3561
Jones, Raymond, 3455
Jones, Rebecca, 1195
Jones, Red Bill, 1175
Jones, Reginal, 1740
Jones, Rena Radcliff, 1742
Jones, Rex Harvey, 1740
Jones, Richard, 3455
Jones, Robert (U.S. d.1908), 3359
Jones, Robert (U.S. d.1911), 3361
Jones, Roger Lee, 1740-1741
Jones, Ronald, 3451
Jones, Ronnie Lee, 3450
Jones, Roy, 3384, 3386
Jones, Sam, 3348
Jones, Sam H., 1520
Jones, Samuel Milton, 1741
Jones, Slim, 208, 209
Jones, Solomon, 3351
Jones, Somerset, 1472
Jones, Stanton T., 2188
Jones, Taneka, 1743, 1820
Jones, Thomas (Brit. pr.1682), 1195
Jones, Thomas (Brit., pr.1733), 1466
Jones, Thomas (U.S. d.1824), 1741
Jones, Thomas (U.S. d.1902), 3354
Jones, Thomas (U.S. d.1908), 3359
Jones, Thomas (Brit. d.1885), 2557
Jones, Thomas (U.S. pr.1988), 3454
Jones, Thomas (U.S. pr.1900), 3457
Jones, Thomas R., 3425
Jones, Thomas V., 3101
Jones, Tom (Brit. c.1672-1702), 1741
Jones, Tom (U.S. pr.1973), 494
Jones, Tom (U.S. pr.1800s), 3561
Jones, Townes, 3173
Jones, Troy, 3448
Jones, Twentyman, 2032
Jones, Virgil, 3359
Jones, W.D., 252, 3459
Jones, W.R. (U.S. pr.1899), 1978
Jones, W.R., 652
Jones, Walter (U.S. pr.1880s), 2865
Jones, Walter (U.S. pr.1913), 3362
Jones, Walter (U.S. pr.1887), 3548
Jones, Walter (U.S. pr.1978) 644
Jones, Waverly M., 317
Jones, Wesley Livsey, 1741
Jones, Wilfred, 2247
Jones, Wilfred Algernon, 1336
Jones, Will (Brit. 1667-93), 1741
Jones, Will (Brit. d.1697), 1597
Jones, William "Canada Bill" (U.S. d.1877),
    1741-1742, 3561
Jones, William (pr.1850s-60s), 3399, 3406
Jones, William (U.S. d.1870), 1252
Jones, William (U.S. d.1897), 3349
Jones, William (U.S. d.1898), 3350
Jones, William (U.S. d.1909), 3360
Jones, William (U.S. d.1913), 3362
Jones, William (U.S. d.1914), 3363
Jones, William (U.S., draftee, pr.1863),
    2316
Jones, William (U.S., mur. vic. pr.1863),
    2320
Jones, William (Mo. death row), 3451,
    3452
Jones, William Blakely (U.S. 1907-79),
    1742
Jones, William Daniel (U.S. pr.1930s), 253
Jones, William G. (U.S. pr.1944), 1898
Jones, William Lloyd (Brit. pr.1840), 1238

Jones, William Q., 3453
Jones, Willie (U.S. 1952-77), 1742
Jones, Willie Lee (U.S. b.1952), 1742
Jones, Willie Leroy, 3428, 3456
Jones, Zmable, 3244
Jones Brothers, 1742
Jong, Adrianus M. De,, 3250
Joniaux, Henry, 1743
Joniaux, Marie Thérèse, 1742-1743
Jonson, Ben, 2981
Joop Den Udyl, 2818
Joplin, Janis, 2192
Jordaan, Phillipus Johannes, 3089
Jordan, Arthur, 891
Jordan, Chester, 1743
Jordan, Clayton, 1743, 1820
Jordan, Daniel Ben, 1914, 1915
Jordan, Dawson, 3361
Jordan, Don, 620
Jordan, Dorca, 1139
Jordan, Francisco, 3561
Jordan, Frank (U.S. d.1906), 3036, 3357
Jordan, Frank M. (U.S. pr.1986), 1743,
    3426
Jordan, Gilbert Paul, 1743
Jordan, Henderson, 262
Jordan, Honora, 1743
Jordan, James E., 458
Jordan, Jean Bernadette, 2879
Jordan, Jerry, 1149
Jordan, John, 3386
Jordan, John Maurice, 3229
Jordan, Joseph M., 3424
Jordan, Kirk, 500
Jordan, Mary Ann, 2822
Jordan, Raymond, 3462
Jordan, Richard, 3452
Jordan, Theodore, 1743-1744
Jordan, Theresa, 1675
Jordan, Thomas, 1744
Jordan, Vernon, E., Jr., 1225, 1744, 3258
Jordano, Frank, 193, 1744
Jordano, Iolando, 1744
Jorden, Edward, 2443
Jordon, Harry, 3347
Jordon, John, 2584
Jordon, Josiah, 2834
Jordon, Robert, 3342
Jorgensdatter, Siri, 1744
Jorgensen, Christine, 1289
Jorgensen, Jorgen, 1744
Jorgensen, Martin, 1501
José de Sucre, Antonio, 3241
Josaphat Kuncewicz, 1744
Joscelyn, Ralph John, 1507
Jose, Simao, 2562
Josef, Franz, 407, 866, 974, 987
Joseph I, 3240
Joseph II, 2237
Joseph, A.W., 3362
Joseph, Charles, 1622
Joseph, Edward L., 453, 489
Joseph, Francis, 1194, 1210, 1212, 1214
Joseph, Fred, 423
Joseph, French, 3404, 3411
Joseph, Geoffrey, 1091
Joseph, Martin, 3561
Joseph of Volokolamsk, 2154
Joseph, Sarah, 3029
Josephine, 1203
Joshua, 2191
Josiane, 654
Jost, Heinz, 3540
Jotham, 10
Jouannet, Doris, 846
Joubert, John J. (U.S. pr.1988), 1744, 3452
Joubert, Petrus Jacobus, 1745
Jouffroy, Jean, 166
Jourdan, Maggie, 2735

Kaplan, Fanny Roid, 1929
Kaplan, J.M., 1760
Kaplan, Jacob, 498
Kaplan, Joel David, (U.S. pr. 1971) 1759-1760, 3428
Kaplan, Louis Nathan "Kid Dropper" 526, 935, 1295 1760-1762, 1894, 1867, 2821, 3406, 3410, 3411
Kaplan, Morris "The Mock", 1726
Kaplan, Sam, 1762
Kaplan, Solomon, 1974
Kaplan, Veronica, 935
Kaplan, William, 498
Kaplany, Geza de, 903-904
Kaplany, Hanja de, 903
Kapnist, Kyra, 1193
Kapodistrias, Ioannis Antónios, 1762, 2153, 3241
Kapp, Wolfgang, 1762, 2543
Kappler, Anneliese, 1762
Kappler, Herbert, 1762, 3540
Kapuuo, 3257, 3505
Karabaghi, Khan, 3260
Karageorge, 1762, 3240
Karageorgevic, Alexander, 3248
Karakhan, Lev Mikhailovich, 1762-1763
Karakinikas, John, 2188
Karakozov, Dimitri, 84
Karalis, Michael Thomas, 3463
Karam, Max, 983
Karamanlis, Constantine, 2483
Karamba, Floyd, 1763
Karamba, Terrence, 1763
Karami, Rashid, 1763, 3254, 3261, 3228, 3281
Karayigit, Kadir, 1396
Kardiner, Abraham, 3127
Kardy, Leonard T., 1312
Karenski, Ana, 2449
Karis, James, 3448
Karkare, Vishnu, 1262
Karl, Harry, 776
Karlebach, Edith, 1198
Karloff, Boris, 1764, 2012
Karmel, David, 2261
Karnes, Etta, 1446
Karnes, John, 1449
Karnes, Quill, 3548
Karnes, Samuel, 1446
Karnopp, Merle, 2842
Karny, Dean, 1643
Karos, Zdzislaw, 3520
Karow, Juliette, 780
Karpach, Joe, 374
Karpis, Alvin "Creepy", 50, 52, 54, 210, 211, 225, 236, 238-240, 242, 243, 583, 617, 962, 973, 1144, 1590, 1612, 1613. 1763-1766, 2041, 2215 2284, 2286-2287, 2304, 3139, 3282, 3326, 3459, 3460
Karpis, Anna, 1763
Karpis, John, 1763
Karpowicz, Raymond Alvin, 1763
Karry, Heinz Herbert, 3258, 3512
Karume, Abeid Amani, 1766-67, 3256
Karvosky, Ronald J., 674
Karwinsky, Erwin, 990
Kasabian, Linda, 2110, 2111
Kasallis, Rose, 1328
Kasavubu, Joseph, 1436, 2010, 3254
Kasche, Siegfried, 3540
Kaseman, George A., 3548
Käser, Anna, 1077
Kasherman, Arthur, 1398, 1767, 1951
Kashiwa, Shiro, 1767
Kashmiri Liberation Army, 3334
Kashney, Roland, 1767
Kasper, Frank J., 1550
Kasper, Ingrid, 1767
Kasper, Karl, 1767

Kasravi, Ahmad, 3248
Kassab, Alfred, 2032
Kassar, Liliane, 2951
Kassel, Max, 3042
Kasselo, A., 3245
Kassem, Abdul Karim, 1767, 3253-3255
Kassim, Ahmed, 1767
Kassow, Raymond, 1733
Kastalli, Chedly, 3252
Kastel, Philip "Dandy Phil", 796, 1491, 1767-1768, 1874, 1895, 1984, 2702, 3399
Kasten, Walter, 1017
Kasten, William, 886
Kastin, Elissa Teresa, 356
Kastner, Rudolf, 3540
Katanic, Jason, 3463
Kately, Henry George, 1208
Katharane, Nicholas, 3406
Kathov, Arkady, 3334
Katist-Chen, 1768
Katt, William, 285
Kattan, Isaac, 3300
Kattar, George, 3379
Katterfelto, Gustavus, 1768
Katyn Massacre, 1768-1769
Katz, Arthur, 1769
Katz, Craig, 1718
Katz, Gene B., 3473
Katz, George, 14
Katz, Michael, 3325
Katzen, Morris, 1769
Katzenbach, Nicholas, 3080
Katzenberg, Yasha, 526, 1769
Katzmann, Frederick, 2650
Katzmann, Fritz, 3540
Kauffman, Julian, 3386
Kauffman, Paul, 1769
Kaufman, Frank Albert, 1769, 2684
Kaufman, George S., 2113
Kaufman, Irving Robert, 1769
Kaufman, Louis, 372, 3386
Kaufman, Ronald, 3490, 3491
Kaufman, William, 1769-70, 1351, 3185
Kaunda, Kenneth, 3302
Kaur, Sarabjit, 2769
Kaurish, Jay, 3448
Kavadh II, 1811, 3236
Kavaja, Nikola, 3471
Kavale, Ronald, 1845
Kavanagh, F.B., 895
Kavanagh, Paul, 3275
Kavinsky, Gerald, 1770
Kavolick, Philip, 3406
Kawakami, Jotaro, 3254
Kawakita Tomaya, 1770
Kawananakoa, David Kalakaua, 1770
Kay, Fanny, 1369
Kay, Jean, 2820
Kay, Jim, 3561
Kay, Peter, 2212
Kayali, Abdul Wahhab, 3257
Kaye, Emily, 2088, 2830, 3306
Kaye, Herman, 1770
Kaye, Mary Steele, 1900
Kaye, Violette, 2099-2100
Kaye, William Henry, 43
Kayira, Andrew, 3277
Kays, Henry, 2565
Kayser, Otto, 1770-1771
Kazakov, I.N., 3201
Kazan, Elia, 435
Kazel, Dorothy, 73
Kazem Mohaman Tavakolian, 3300
Kazner, Hyman "Hymie", 111
Kazuko Konno, 1840
Kazuo, Nakanishi, 3395
Kazuo, Taoka, 3202, 3203, 3395
Keach, Benjamin, 1771

Keane, Morris, 2037, 3384
Keane, Thomas, 3381, 3386
Kearnes, Henry, 2315
Kearney, Aloysius, 3386
Kearney, Dennis, 915
Kearney, Frank (U.S. pr.1924), 1771
Kearney, Frank (U.S. pr.1881), 3561
Kearney, Harry, 853
Kearney, Jack, 2021
Kearney, John J., 1771-1772
Kearney, Kent, 1278
Kearney, Lawrence, 1307
Kearney, Patrick (U.S. pr.1881), 1272
Kearney, Patrick (U.S. pr.1920s), 113
Kearney, Patrick Wayne (U.S. pr.1977), 1772
Kearney, "Woolley", 3414
Kearns, J.J., 972
Kearse, Hannah, 3347
Kearse, Isom, 3347
Kearsley, John, 3371
Kearsley, William, 3177
Keating, Francis, (U.S. pr.1933) 209, 235, 236, 238, 728, 1454, 1590-91, 1756, 1784, 2284, 2286, 2513, 3117, 3427, 3459
Keating Gang, 235
Keating, James, 2142
Keating, Lawrence, 1335
Keating, Mary, 1772
Keating, Thomas, (U.S. pr. 1856) 1522
Keating, Tom, (Brit. pr. 1979) 1772
Keating's Saloon, Battle of, 1772-1773
Keatley, John Henry, 1773
Keaton, Buster, 151, 2960
Keaton, David Roby, 1230
Keaton, Diane, 359
Keaton, Pierce, 1773, 3561
Keats, John, 690, 3072
Keck, Ira, 658
Keech, Henry, 2315
Keech, Mary Ann Newton, 2315
Keedy, David, 1081
Keegan, David Daniel, 3461
Keele, Polly Hamilton, 968
Keele, Richard, (Brit. 1681-1713) 844, 1773, 1999
Keeler, Christine, 2506-2508
Keeler, George, 2785
Keeler, Leonard, (U.S. pr. 1920s) 3061
Keeler, Leonarde, (U.S. 1903-49) 1773, 2091
Keeley, Leslie, 3293, 3294
Keeley, Pat, 3206
Keeling, Frederick, 1773
Keeling, Walter Angus, 1773
Keely, John E. Worrell, 1773-1774
Keen, Edward, 646
Keen, Michael Scott, 3450
Keen, Moses W., 1774
Keen, Ruby, 2859
Keenan, Barry W., 115, 3327
Keenan, Brian Paschal, 1774
Keenan, Fannie, 1056
Keenan, John F., 2272
Keenan, Joseph B., 2041
Keenan, Maurice, 3448
Keenan, Rosemary, 345
Keene, John (U.S. d.1865), 1774
Keene, John (U.S. pr.1906), 1774
Keene, Laura, 1956, 1958
Keene, Lawrence, 2785
Keene, Paul, 2785
Keene, William, 430
Keeney, John, 3005
Keep, Judith N., 1513
Kees, Derrick, 1199
Kees, Willie, 3368
Keet, Lloyd, 3325, 3375
Keeton, James, 1376

Kipley, Joseph, 864, 1516, 3424
Kipnik, Erich, 2656, 2657
Kipp, Martin, 3448
Kirby, Andrew, 3561
Kirby, Emily Francis, 765
Kirby, George, 1828-1829
Kirby, Harry, 813
Kirby, James, 1829
Kirby, M.W., 3424
Kirby, Richard, 1095
Kirby, Thomas, 765
Kircher, Athanasius, 3196
Kirchner, Karl, 3548
Kirchwey, George Washington, 1829
Kiritsis, Anthony G., 1829, 3331
Kirk, Buck, 3245
Kirk, Dana, 1829
Kirk, George, 3561
Kirk, James, 1829-1830
Kirk, Paul L., 5
Kirk, Taylor, 3351
Kirk, William T., 1113
Kirkaldie, Douglas A., 3470
Kirkealdy, William (Scot. d.1573), 1830
Kirkealdy, William (Scot. pr.1546), 292
Kirker, James, 1830, 3168
Kirkes, Leonard, 1830
Kirkhan, Said, 3247
Kirkland, Alfred Y., 807, 1110
Kirkland, Dick, 738
Kirkland, Haywood T. (U.S. pr.1969), 1732
Kirkland, Walter, 644
Kirkland, Willie, 3367
Kirkpatrick, E.E., 1786
Kirkpatrick, F. (U.S. pr.1878), 3426
Kirkpatrick, Frederick (U.S. pr.1988), 3452
Kirkpatrick, William Huntington, 1830, 3448
Kirksey, Jimmy, 3452
Kirkwood, James Boyd, 1830
Kirov, Sergei Mironovich, 1830, 2837, 3221, 3248
Kirschner, Leo, 159
Kirtanananda Swami Bhaktipada, 3302
Kirwan, Andrew Donaldson, 1830-1831
Kirwan, John Stanley, 1830
Kirwan, Peter, 2209
Kirwan, Thomas, 1831
Kirwan, William Bourke, 1831
Kiser, Joseph, 3349
Kiser, W.H., 1175
Kish, Alexander, 1229
Kishi Nobusuke, 1820, 1831, 1841, 3254
Kiss, Bela, 1831-1832
Kiss, Gabor, 3464
Kissinger, Henry A., 405, 1899, 3257
Kistayya, Pahwa Shankar, 1262
Kita, Ikki, 1831
Kitamura, L., 2117
Kitchell, John E., 3428
Kitchen, George, 1832
Kitchen, James, 1832
Kitchen, John Joseph, 1832
Kitchener, Horatio Herbert, 1231
Kitchener, 1301
Kitchens, Elizabeth, 3366
Kitchens, William, 3455
Kitcherman, William, 2965
Ki Tsuyoshi Inukai, 3247
Kitt, George, 3561
Kittakachorn, Thanom, 3255
Kitte, Butch, 304
Kitterman, Robert, 908
Kittle, Hub, 2725
Kittler, Teddy, 1752, 1753
Kitto, Michael, 1420-21
Kittrell, Braxton, Jr., 1498
Kivel, John, 2684
Kivlen, John C., 3471
Kiykendall, Ruth, 3143

Kjeldgaard, Andreas, 2489
Kjeldgaard, Franklin, 2489
Kjellstrom, Albert, 3567
Klapman, Sander, 1608
Klapprott, August, 2137
Klar, Gabriel, 342, 1832
Klarsfeld, Serge, 232
Klaske, John, 1031
Klass, Louis, 1832
Klaus, Annie, 1770, 1771
Klaus, Herman, 983
Klaus, Martin, 408
Klausener, Erich, 1573, 3248
Klausman, Alfred, 1104
Klawes, David, 593
Kleber, Jean-Baptiste, 1832-1833, 3240
Kleberg, Richard, 1827
Kleberg, Robert, 1827
Klein, Allen, 1833
Klein, Arnold, 3065
Klein, Arthur Jack "Harry", 936, 1124
Klein, Benjamin, 3018
Klein, Christine, 1863
Klein, Elizabeth Hannah, 733
Klein, Fritz, 3540
Klein, Hans-Joachim, 3475
Klein, Harold, 1275
Klein, Ignatz, 3058-3059
Klein, Jack, 426
Klein, Jacob, 3335
Klein, Johann, 1833
Klein, Kenneth D., 1676
Klein, Morris, 3396
Klein, Nelson, 249
Klein, Nicholas, 2207
Klein, Peter (Ger. pr.1923), 1863
Klein, Peter N. (U.S. d.1926), 1031
Klein, Philip (U.S. pr.1949), 166
Klein, S. Philip (U.S. pr.20th Cent.), 1847
Klein, William (U.S. pr.1975), 3299
Klein, William (U.S. pr.1923), 811
Kleiner, Kathy, 540
Kleinhaus, Maurice, 1299
Kleinman, Edward, 3392
Kleinman, Morris, 2689, 3392, 3413
Kleinschmidt, Black Lena, 2101, 3406
Kleinz, Henry, 1650
Kleist, Ewald von, 3540
Kleist, Heinrich von, 1833
Kleist, Karl, 2079
Klement, Rudolf, 1833, 2992
Klemfuss, Harry C., 3027
Klemm, Herbert, 3540
Klemt, P., 3467
Klenha, Joseph Z., 618, 714
Klerk Lee, Jan de, 1919
Klevenhagen, John, 939
Klevkoff, Sapria, 3250
Klieger, Bernie, 1899
Kliendienst, Richard Gordon, 896, 1833, 3099, 3101
Klier, Freya, 1847
Klimek, Anton, 1287
Klimek, Dagmar, 2485
Klimetz, Paul, 2191
Klimowicz, Antoni, 2921
Klinck, Earl, 2850
Kline, Charles H., 1833
Kline, Henry, 703
Kline, Marvin (U.S. pr.1939), 1767
Kline, Marvin L. (U.S. pr. 1950s), 1842
Kline, Michael, 3526
Klinefelter, Marion, 1152
Klineman, Kent M., 1606
Kling, David, 845
Kling, Florence, 2907
Kling, Richard, 3205
Klingelöfer, Waldemar, 3540
Klingenfuss, Karl Otto, 3540

Klinghoffer, Leon, 140, 2199, 3321
Klisz, Louis, 1063
Klman, 1754
Kloeb, Frank Leblond, 1833
Kloehr, John Joseph, 863, 3561, 3565
Kloklec, Victor, 3450
Klopfer, Gerhard, 3540
Klosowski, Severin Antonionvitch, 2, 682, 1689
Klotz, Louis Lucien, 1833
Kludt, Bertha, 373
Kludt, Beverly June, 373
Klug, George, 2567
Kluge, Guenther von, 1574, 1578
Klukofsky, Eli, 1833, 2814
Klutas, Jack, 951
Klutas, Theodore "Handsome Jack", 1833-1834
Kmiecek, Kenneth, 904
Knapp Commission, 1834-1835, 1943, 1947
Knapp, George, 1834
Knapp, Harold, 1312
Knapp, John Francis, 839
Knapp, Joseph, 839
Knapp, Roger, 1834
Knapp, Whitman, 1834, 2728
Knappen, Loyal Edwin, 1835
Knatchbull, Nicholas, 2235
Knau, Jobst, 1835
Knauf, Elton G., 3254
Knecht, Charles, 1674
Knee, C.A., 258
Kneebone, William, 2741
Kneilands, Anne, 2113
Kneissl, Annie Laurie, 3062
Knetzer, Robert L., 1835
Knevet, Edmund, 1835
Kniffen, Luther, 1239
Kniffin, John W., 1249
Knight, Alice, 1070
Knight, Arthur B., 1732
Knight, C. (Mex. d.1927), 3246
Knight, Clarence (U.S. pr.1985), 1608
Knight, Curtis (U.S. d.1987), 1836
Knight, Deetta, 1836
Knight, E.G., 3424
Knight, Frances, 1472
Knight, Goodwin J., 5, 1236
Knight, H. Stuart, 3426
Knight, James R., 123
Knight, Jill, 3258
Knight, Jim, 3561
Knight, John, 1835
Knight, Jourdan, 3561
Knight, Kevin, 1836
Knight, Martha, 1440
Knight, Mary, 1835
Knight, Phillip, 2408
Knight, Ricky, 1835
Knight, Roger, 1835
Knight, Thomas (U.S. pr.1974), 1835, 3450
Knight, Thomas Edmund, Jr. (U.S. pr.1936), 2716
Knight, Tobias, 388
Knight, Virgil, 1835-1836
Knighten, Greg, 1836
Knighton, Ernest, 3447
Knighton, William, 1836
Knights of Mary Phagan, 1856
Knights of the White Camelia, 1855
Knipperdolling, Bernhard, 1836
Knipschild, William, 1836
Knisely, Ella, 1511
Knobloch, Kurt, 3327
Knochen, Helmuth, 2355, 3540
Knodt, Manuela, 1852
Knolding, Sarah, 2578
Knoll, Michael, 3505
Knollys, Charles, 1836

Lamon, James, 766
Lamon, Ward Hill, 1151, 1879
Lamonaco, Philip, 2107
Lamond, James, 3425
Lamont, Anne, 1879
Lamont, Blanche, 1043
Lamont, Daniel, 2814
La Montagne, Montaigu, 1879-1880
La Montagne, Morgan, 1879
La Montagne, René, Jr., 1879
La Montagne, René, Sr., 1880
La Montagne, William, 1879
LaMonte, Frank, 3393
Lamonti, Charles, 2137
Lamoriciere, Louis Christophe Léon
    Juchault de, 1880
Lamorie, Richard, 180
Lamothe, Bessie, 2862
Lamotte, Comptesse de, 573, 906
Lamotte, Etienne Saint-Faust de, 920
Lamp, Jacqueline Leah, 383
Lamphere, Ray, 1402, 1404
Lampião, 1880
Lampugnani, Gian Andrea, 2732
Lamson, Allene Thorpe, 1881
Lamson, David Albert, 282, 1880-1881
Lamson, George Henry, 1881
LaMunyon, Richard, 525, 1160
LaMunyon, Sharon, 1160
Lanahan, Michael, 1881-1882
Lancashire Weavers Riot, 1882
Lancashire Witches, 1882
Lancaster, Duke Henry of, 695, 3227
Lancaster, Earl of, 2229, 2236
Lancaster, Harry, 1394
Lancaster, John of, 1726
Lancaster, Roscoe, 891, 3458
Lancaster, Thomas, 1882
Lancaster, Val Edwin, 1882
Lancaster, William Newton, 1882-1883
Lance, Myron, 1776, 3327
Lancelin, Genevieve, 1291, 2407
Lancelin, Madame, 2407
Lancelin, Ren, 2407
Lancey, John, 1883
Lancia, Joseph "Jumbo", 546
Lancleve, Julius, 3561
Lancre, Pierre de, 273, 1883
Land, Alfred, 1883-1884
Landau, Abe, 346, 2700, 2702, 3410
Landers, Ann, 1390
Landers, Loeb, 3342
Landers, Paul T., 3470
Landesman, Jeanette, 2660
Landfried, Friedrich, 3541
Landini, Silvio, 1549
Landis, Abraham Hoch, 1884
Landis, Frederick, 1884
Landis, James, 1884
Landis, James M., 1224, 1393
Landis, John, 1884
Landis, Kenesaw Mountain, 402, 1884-1885
Landis, M.D., 1885
Land, James M., 1492
Land, Leo, 1031
Land, Marvin J., 2466
Landon, Alfred M., 488, 1161
Landregan, Bridget, 2469
Landress, Cindy, 3451
Landreth, Ted, 2032
Landru, Henri Desiré, 903, 1564, 1885-1888,
    1995, 2202, 2460, 2732, 2778, 2878, 3062
Landrum, James David, 3548
Landrum, Samuel B., 735
Landry, Raymond, 3447
Landry, Robert, 3343
Landsteiner, Karl, 1888
Landusky, Pike, 1977
Landwehr, Ken, 525

Landy, G.W. "Dad", 3459
Lane, Brant, 1888
Lane, Chief Justice Lord, 1083
Lane, Constance, 1417
Lane, David, 341
Lane, Ed, 1888
Lane, Floyd, 273
Lane, George "Clubfoot", 1254, 1514,
    3049, 3337, 3562
Lane, Harold, 3455
Lane, Harriet Louisa, 3071
Lane, Henry, 3161
Lane, James, 1889 (U.S. d.1817)
Lane, James H., 2521
Lane, Jim, (U.S. pr.1860) 1535
Lane, Mary Ann, 2183
Lane, Rudd, 3364
Lane, Thomas, 3093
Lane, Van, 3548
Lane, Vicky, 2293
Lane, Wendy, 2225
Laney, Dan F., 1283
Laney, Thomas Gerald, 3454
Lanford, Newport, 1219
Lang, Ann, 933
Lang, Bill, 3562
Lang, Charles, 3368
Lang, Donald, 1889
Lang, Edward, 3364
Lang, Ervin, 2784
Lang, Evelyn, 1253
Lang, Fritz, 263, 1243
Lang, G.W., 966
Lang, Howard "Howie", 1889
Lang, Irving, 8
Lang, Jrg, 3475
Lang, Kenneth, 3448
Lang, Mark, 1382
Langdale, Marmaduke, 2530
Langdell, Christopher Columbus, 1889
Langdoll, Gerhard, 2163
Langdon, Oscar, 613
Lange, Frank, 714
Lange, Martin, 493
Lange, Otto, 3541
Lange, T., 2505
Langella, Gennaro "Gerry Lang", 1889-
    90, 2448, 2670, 3406
Langemier, Else, 2917
Langer, William, 1890
Langevin, Theodore C., 3290
Langfeldt, Philipini, 407
Langford, Frances, 660
Langford, Nathaniel Pitt, 3050, 3548
Langford, Terry, 3452
Langiewicz, Marjan, 1890
Langley, Andrea Locke, 102, 1969
Langley, Edmund of, 1071
Langley, Gilbert, 1890
Langley, Gus Colin, 1890
Langley, John (Brit. 1766-1817), 650, 730,
    1890
Langley, John W. (U.S. pr.1921), 1890-
    1891
Langley, Robert, 3453
Langmaid, Josie, 1897
Langsner, Maximilien, 435
Langston, Frank, 1891
Langston, Sarah, 1891
Langston, Sell, 3562
Langston, William S., 1891
Langton, Catherine, 1891
Langton, John, 1158
Langton, Jonathan, 1891
Langton, Pauline, 1095
Langtry, Joyce, 1511
Langtry, Lily, 289, 1320
Languille, Henri, 1891
Langulet, Antoine, 1891

Langworthy, Charles, 3562
Lanham, Harry, 1891
Lanier, Angel, 3166
Lanier, Arthur Ray, 3452
Lanier, Mitchell, 2768
Lanihan, Jerry, 1537
Lanihan, Peter, 1537
Lanjus, Countess, 1214
Lankester, Gordon, 2799
Lankford, Brian, 3451
Lankford, Mark, 3451
Lannen, George, 2735
Lannen, Gordon, 1891-1892
Lanner, Josef, 1848
Lansing, John, 1892
Lansky, Jake, 1894, 2689
Lansky, Max, 1892
Lanksy, Meyer, 18, 32, 34-35, 43, 103-104,
    117-118, 120, 128-129, 132, 138, 178 229,
    282, 283, 345, 346, 372, 394, 415, 428,
    525, 526, 528, 617, 620, 634, 655, 741,
    748, 755, 758, 780, 786, 857, 911, 933,
    938, 1018, 1034, 1050, 1100, 1259, 1295,
    1297, 1311, 1346, 1375, 1410, 1491,
    1892-1896, 1980, 1986, 2002-2006, 2085,
    2183, 2217-18, 2252, 2254-2255, 2268,
    2505, 2513,, 2657, 2689, 2702,2307,
    2336, 2340, 2561, 2564, 2573, 2705, 2734,
    2753, 2757, 2771, 2814, 2829, 2834, 2835,
    2868, 2870, 2877, 2891, 2974, 2983, 3120,
    3122, 3225, 3226, 3299, 3379, 3389, 3390,
    3393-3397, 3405-3408, 3412, 3413
Lansky, Yetta, 1892
Lantier, Germain, 3541
Lantier, Ike, 1545
Lanza, James J., 3414
Lanza, Joseph "Socks", 1896, 2006, 3406
Lanz, Hubert, 3541
Lanzillo, Carmello, 1896
Lanzillo, Luigi, 1896
Lanzo of Milan, 1896
Laodice, 133, 3233
Laohavichairat, Supol, 3299
Lapa, Frank Albert, 1896
LaPage, Joseph, 1896-1897
Lapansee, Armour, 501
La Passionaria, 2076
Lapella, Florence, 1474
Lapierre, Emile, 913
Lapierre, Imelda, 1605
La Pietra, Angelo, 516, 665, 1897, 3396
LaPietra, James, 1897, 3386
Lapiparo, Tony, 3414
LaPlaca, Joseph, 1714
Laplace, Basil, 3351
LaPoint, Richard, 3469, 3488
LaPorte, Frank, 3386, 3387
LaPorte, George, 966
Laporte, Pierre, 835, 1238,1897, 3328, 3486
Lappeus, James H., 3425
La Prade, Arthur T., 545
LaPrade, J. Wallace, 1771
LaPrade, Paul, 2023
La Presta, Lawrence, 2044
Larabee, Paula, 533
Lara Bonilla, Rodrigo, 3301
Larach, Jacobo Ramon, 3333, 3520
Lara, Daniel, 1424
Lara, Enrique de, 907
Lara, Mario, 3450
Lara, Ruperto, 3562
Lara, Victor, 1424
LaRasso, Louis, 3406
la Raviere, Raymond, 2546
L'archeveque, Sostenes, 3562
Lardino, John, 3386
Lardner, Ring, 402, 756
Larette, Anthony, 3452
Large, Georgia, 2181

le Scrope, Henry (Brit. c.1376-1415) 2716
le Scrope, Richard, 2236, 2716
le Scrope, William, 2716
Lesher, Harvey, 1281
Leshhart, Charles, 291
Lesko, John, 3454
Leslie, Alexander, 1940
Leslie, "Buckskin" Frank, 718-720, 1058,
    2584-85
Leslie, David, 1356
Leslie, Foreman,, 1692
Leslie, George Leonidas, 566, 981, 1941-
    1942, 2019, 3282, 3402-07,3409, 3457
Leslie, Harald, 2113
Leslie, Harry (U.S. pr. 1939) 947
Leslie, John, 1942, 3238
Leslie, Sir John, 1206, 3327
Leslie, Nashville Franklin, 1940-1941, 3551,
    3556, 3558-60, 3562
Leslie, Norman, 292, 3228
Leslie, Stephen, 3327
Lesobre, Raymond, 3113
Lesotho Liberation Army, 3321, 3516, 3528,
    3532
Lespinasse, Paul, 3250
Less, Isaiah W., 449
Lesseps, Charles Aimée Marie, 1942
Lesseps, Ferdinand de, 3074
Lesseps, Ferdinand Marie de, 1942
Lesser, Henry, 2407
Lesser, Louis, 3565
Lessing, Gotthold, 2240
Lessing, T.S., 3032
Lessing, Theodor, 1942
Lester, Betty, 2739
Lester, David L., 1035
Lester, Jon, 1942
Lester Kills On Top, 3452
Lester, Stephen V., 1035
Lester, William, 1525
Lestocq, Johann Hermann von, 1943
LeStrange, Joseph E., 1801, 3425
Le Strange, Terry, 1608, 3407
Lesuere, Rufus, 3356
Les Vivants, 3472
Leta, Ethal, 3461
Letcher, John, 481
Letelier, Orlando, 99, 1942-1943, 3257
Leternee, Karl, 1396
Letterman, David, 2547
Lettie, W. Reed, 309
Lettiere, Robert, 29
Letty Lynton, 1943
Leuci, Robert, 1943
Leuenberger, Nikolaus, 1943
l'Eure, Jacques Charles Dupont de, 1039
Leval, Pierre Nelson, 1943, 2473
Le Van, Benjamin, 1287
Le Van, Kathryn, 1287
Le Van, Orlando, 1287
Levangie, Michael, 2650
Le Van Vien, 1943
Levee, the, 3386
Levenson, Alfred Percival, 1336
Levenson, Robert, 508
Leventon, L.W., 508
Leventon, Robert, 508
Levenson-Gower, John, 1944
Leveque, 924
Lever, E.F., 517, 1207
Leverson, Philip, 1943
Leverson, Sarah Rachel Russell, 1943-1944
Leveson-Gower, Granville, 2443
Levey, Friedman, 3138
Levey, Harry, 545
Levick, Alice, 1944
Levi, Dr. Joseph (U.S., pr.1858), 1470
Levi, Edward Hirsch, 1944
Levi, Joe (Brit., pr.1910), 1625

Levi, Lincoln, 1944
Levi, Lyle, 3349
Levin, Dan, 673
Levin, Emma Erika, 700, 1341
Levin, Fred, 1331
Levin, Glen, 1989
Levin, I., 3251
Levin, Jacob, 1742
Levin, Jennifer, 573
Levin, L.G., 3201
Levin, Meyer, 763
Levin, Ronald G., 1643
Levin, Seymour, 1944
Levine, Abraham "Pretty", 2254
Levine, Abraham (Brit. d.1949), 2735
Levine, Abraham (U.S. pr.1930s), 2868
Levine, Ave, 1394
Levine, Bruce, 899
Levine, Dennis, 418, 1944
Levine, Herman, 2583
Levine, Hymie, 3386
Levine, Jacob, 3080
Levine, Manuel, 1416
Levine, Max "Maxie", 2188
Levine, Murray, 1944
Levine, Peter David, 1944, 3326
Levine, Samuel "Red", 1296, 1894, 2115
Levinsky, Benjamin, 1969, 3407
Levinsky, Johnny, 3402, 3412
Levinson, Ed, 3396
Levinson, George, 1261
Levinson, Harry, 1944-1945
Levinson, John, 1934
Levinstein, Edward, 3293
Levison, Philip, 1943
Levison, Sarah Rachel Russell, 156
Levitan, Benjamin, 517
Levitsky, Asher, 2237
Levitt, Jules, 3394
Levy, Abraham, 2423
Levy, Charles, 1002
Levy, Frederick, 720
Levy, Henry, 1945
Levy, Jack, 166
Levy, Jim, 3562
Levy, John Goodman, 2718
Levy, John J., 416
Levy, Joseph, 1945
Levy, Lisa, 540
Levy, Norma, 1877
Levy, Norman, 1899
Levy, Philip, 544
Levy, R.F., 1522
Levy, Robert Surez, 2874
Levy, Sally, 3399
Levy, Sam, 2019
Lev, William, 283
Lewandowski, James, 1175
Lewelling, L.G., 1191
Lewens, Curtis, 595
Lewinski, 3541
Lewis, Al "Junior", 1945
Lewis, Alfred Henry, 2038
Lewis, Andre, 3455
Lewis, Anna, 419
Lewis, Art (U.S. pr.1973), 1331
Lewis, Arthur (Ire. pr.1953), 1344
Lewis, Austin, 2207
Lewis, Benjamin (U.S. d.1963), 1228,
    1945, 3289
Lewis, Bill, 1731, 3562
Lewis, Callie, 1450
Lewis, Charles, (U.S. d.1863), 1945
Lewis, Charles (U.S. d.1909), 3360
Lewis, Charles (U.S. pr.1980s), 264
Lewis, Charles (U.S. d.1918), 3365
Lewis, Charles (U.S. d.1911), 3361
Lewis, Charles E. (U.S. d.1939), 1040
Lewis, Charles H. (U.S. pr.1960), 916

Lewis, Columbus, 3350
Lewis, Cylone, 3224
Lewis, "Dago" Frank (U.S. pr.1900s), 3386
Lewis, David (Brit. d.1925), 1025
Lewis, David (Brit. d.1947), 1973
Lewis, David Lee, 3455
Lewis, Edward, 3357
Lewis, Elizabeth Hunt, 733
Lewis, Elmer "The Slaughter Kid", 812,
    1945, 3557, 3562
Lewis, Eva, 891
Lewis, Frank (U.S. pr.1895), 1945-1946,
    3106
Lewis, Frank "Jumbo" (U.S. pr. 1918), 891
Lewis, George, 2513, 3338
Lewis, George F., 3393
Lewis, George Henry, 1946
Lewis, Harlan C., 2817
Lewis, Harrison, 3346
Lewis, Harry, (Brit. 1923-46), 1946
Lewis, Harry, (U.S. pr.1922), 99
Lewis, Helynn R., 1946
Lewis, Howard Henry, 1227, 2133
Lewis, Hubert, 515
Lewis, Jackson, 3356
Lewis, Jake, 1334
Lewis, James, 3011
Lewis, Jeffery, 3270
Lewis, Jennifer, 2956
Lewis, Jerry, 2194
Lewis, Jim (U.S. d.1881), 3562
Lewis, Jim (U.S. d.1918), 3365
Lewis, Jimmy "Baby Face", 3298
Lewis, Jimmy, 2306
Lewis, Joan, 827
Lewis, Joe E., 2044
Lewis, John, (U.S. d.1760), 1946
Lewis, John (U.S. d.1819), 506
Lewis, John (U.S. pr.1980), 2711
Lewis, John D. (U.S. pr.1942), 319
Lewis, John L. (U.S. pr.1947), 3056
Lewis, Joseph, 3386, 3407
Lewis, Joseph R., 1946
Lewis, Kid, 2079
Lewis, Lawrence, 3450
Lewis, Leo, 182
Lewis, Lon, 3548
Lewis, Mercy, 2664-2667
Lewis, Michael B., 938
Lewis, Milo F., 1471
Lewis, Monroe, 3363
Lewis, Morgan, 1946
Lewis, Reginald, 3454, 3462
Lewis, Robert (U.S. d.1892), 3342
Lewis, Robert (U.S. pr.1988), 3448
Lewis, Robert E., 1459
Lewis, S.C., 1180
Lewis, Samuel, 3346, 3386
Lewis, Sanford, 3361
Lewis, Sherman, 3338
Lewis, Sinclair, 2907, 3062
Lewis, T., 3347
Lewis, T.G., 1137
Lewis, T. Hubert (Brit. pr.1953), 1458
Lewis, Tobe, 3363
Lewis, Tom, 2748, 2794
Lewis, Vach "Cyclone Louie", 3407, 3409
Lewis, W.W., 3548
Lewis, Warren, 3366
Lewis, Watkins, 3363
Lewis, Whitey, 3427
Lewis, Wilfred Hubert Poyer, 1946
Lewis, William (U.S. d.1891), 3340
Lewis, William (U.S. d.1894), 3344
Lewis, William (U.S. d.1819), 1946
Lewis, William O., 2851
Lewisohn, Kate, 1675
Lewisohn, Mrs. Walter, 1088
Lexow, Clarence, 1946

Lexow Committee, 1946-1947
Ley, Hugo, 3143
Ley, James, 1947
Ley, John, 1947
Ley, Robert, 1947, 3541
Leyba, Marino, 3562
Leydet, Auguste, 2849
Leyes, David, 1947
Leyra, Camilo Weston, Sr., 1947
Leyra, Camilo Weston, Jr., 1947-1948
Leyra, Catherine, 1947
Li, M. (China d.1938), 3249
Li, Mi (Burma pr.1950s), 3214
Li Ang, 1948
Liang-pi, 3243
Liao Chang-Shin, 1948
Liao Chung-k'ai, 1948, 3245
Liaquat Ali Khan, 1948
Libberton, Lawrence, 3448
Libelt, Karol, 1948
Liberace, Wladziu Valentino, 1948
Liberation Army of Martinique, 3272
Liberation Tigers of Tamil Eelam, 2242,
    3280, 3281, 3532
Liberatore, Anthony, 3392
Liberius, 1948, 3018
Liberman, Samuel, 917
Liberto, Frank, 1825, 3399
Liberto, Salvatore, 3399,
Liberty Athletic Club, 3407
Libow, Julius, 1150
Librero, Salvator, 3353
Libyan Riots, 3378
Licata, Carlo, 3397
Licata, Nicholas, 1018, 1948, 3397
Licata, Pietro, 3402, 3407
Licata, Victor, 3296
Li Causi, Girolamo, 3058, 3416
Licavoli, Dominic, 3393
Licavoli, Jack, 2178
Licavoli, James, 1228, 3392
Licavoli, James T. "Blackie", 1948-1949, 2990
Lacavioli, Thomas "Yonnie", 1949, 3219,
    3393
Licavoli Mob, 1183, 1186, 1764, 1949
Licavoli, Peter, 242, 1183, 3392-93, 3413
Licavoli, Peter Joseph, Sr., 1949
Li Chao-liu, 3251
Lichtenstein, Perry L., 2433
Licinius, Valerius Licinianus, 1949, 3224,
    3235
Licio Giorgieri, 3528
Liddell, Dick, 1196, 1565, 1704, 1706, 3560,
    3562
Liddell, James Andrew, 3562
Liddy, G. Gordon, 575, 3098, 3099
Lie, Jonas, 3541
Lieb, Joseph Patrick, 1950
Liebenhenschel, Arthur, 3541
Lieber, Francis, 1950
Lieberman, Brad, 1950
Liebestruth, Johanna, 342
Liebknecht, Karl, 1950, 3040, 3244
Liebknecht, Wilhelm, 1950
Liebler, Anthony, 1717
Liebowitz, Barney, 1039
Liebowitz, Essie, 1039
Liebscher, William, Jr., 1950-1951, 3461
Liege, Bishop of, 1951
Lierman, Arthur Francis, 2022
Lieser, Kurt, 3221
Lietke, Andrew, 1005
Liffey, Pasha, 1951
Ligammari, Giovanni, 3407
Liger, Jean, 1951
Liggett, Edith, 1951
Liggett, Walter, 413, 1398, 1767, 1951
Liggins, Herbert, 1250
Liggio, Luciano, 1951-1952, 3416

Lightbourne, Ian, 3450
Lightbourne, Wendell Willis, 1953
Lightfoot, James, 1953
Lightfoot, William, 1953
Light, Harry J., 2885
Light, Ronald Vivian, 649, 1622, 1952-
    1953
Light, Zachary, 3546, 3558, 3562
Li Hsiu-Cheng, 1953
Lihuang, Wei, 3214
Li Hung Chang, 2967, 2988
Likens, Jennie, 226, 227
Likens, Sylvia, 226, 227
Li Kung-p'o, 3251
Lilburne, John, 1953
Liles, Mark, 3453
Liles, Panta Lou "Pat", 3001
Lilian, Gertrude, 1127
Lilinokalani, 411, 777, 2949
Lillard, Thomas, 3342
Lille Novices, 1953
Lilli, Amedeo, 874
Lillie, Beatrice, 1598
Lillie Dab, 2760
Lillie, Fred William, 1776
Lilly, J. Joseph, 264
Lillywhite, Harry, 642
Lima, Anthony, 3415
Lima y Silva, Luis Duque de Caxias Alves
    de, 107
Limann, Hilla, 3519
Limburger Roarers, 3407
Limerick, Tom, 53, 63
Li Mi, 3214
Limone, Peter, 3379
Linabary, Orville, 1040
Linam, Gina, 1821
Linarducci, Joseph, 1134
Lincecum, Kevin, 3455
Lincoln, Abraham, 218, 269, 281, 513, 536,
    579, 782, 883, 1010, 1017, 1020, 1046,
    1069, 1151, 1155, 1165, 1232, 1271,
    1322, 1345, 1447, 1525, 1604, 1629,
    1633, 1678, 1727, 1731, 1794, 1815,
    1854, 1879, 1953-1965,, 2031, 2103,
    2188, 2235, 2240, 2248, 2288, 2315,
    2467-68, 2503, 2518-2319, 2326, 2719,
    2824, 2857, 2864, 2870, 2887, 2896,
    3052, 3081, 3157, 3160, 3173, 3185,
    3193, 3232, 3241
Lincoln, Benjamin, 2738
Lincoln, C. Eric, 397
Lincoln County War, 311, 363, 366, 368,
    369, 481, 486, 506, 507, 1966-1967,
    1986-87, 3544, 3545, 3548-51
Lincoln, Duane, 1734
Lincoln, Edward, 1954
Lincoln, Evelyn, 1120
Lincoln, Isaac, 3343
Lincoln, Levi, 1965, 2832
Lincoln, Mary Todd, 1462
Lincoln, Nancy Hanks, 1954
Lincoln, Natalie Sumner, 1965
Lincoln, Robert Todd, 1962-1963
Lincoln, Thomas, 1954
Lincoln, Warren, 1965-1966
Lincoln, William, 1954, 3241
Lindauer, Hilmar C., 1181
Lindbergh, Anne Morrow, 1479-90, 2227
Lindbergh, Charles Augustus, Jr., 1239,
    1479-90, 3326
Lindbergh, Charles Augustus, Sr., 849,
    1052, 1017, 1479-90, 1841, 2410, 2986,
    3208, 3324, 3326
Lindbloom, Olaf, 1404
Lindboe, Thomas, 1404
Lindemann, Fritz, 1578
Linden, Robert, 3189
Linderfeld, Wolfe, 1967

Linderfelt, Karl E., 3228
Linderman, Max, 3463
Linder, Sonia Jacobs, 1967
Lindet, Jean Baptiste Robert, 1967
Lindet, Nathaniel, 1967
Lindh, Aaron, 1967
Lindholm, Harry, 3425
Lind, John E., 2182
Lindley, George, 3338
Lindley, Marion, 1627
Lindley, Monaei, 1394
Lindley, Walter C., 1283
Lindley, William Marvin, 1967
Lindon, Jimmie "The Wolf", 208
Lindow, Kurt, 3541
Lindörfer, Friedrich, 1967
Lindörfer, Lina, 1967
Lindquist, Mildred, 3113
Lindsay, Alexander, 1967
Lindsay, Coutts, 3135
Lindsay, John V., 781, 1040, 1834, 2271,
    2714, 2728, 2896
Lindsay, Sandra, 1508
Lindsay, Wayne, 228
Lindsey, Benjamin Barr, 1967
Lindsey, Bryon, 1967-1968
Lindsey, David, 2836
Lindsey, Horace "Buster", 1341
Lindsey, Michael, 3447
Lindsey, R.L., 2042
Lindsey, Seldon T., 1968
Lindsey, Tyronne, 3452
Lindwall, Richard, 1968
Line, Anne, 1968
Lineveldt, Gamat Salie, 1968
Linevill, Abraham, 3118
Linfold, Alice Isobel, 2418
Ling, David W., 1968
Lingfelter, Jean, 2800
Lingar, Stanley, 3452
Lingard, Anthony, 1968
Lingg, Louis, 106, 1497, 3263
Lingle, Alfred "Jake", 501, 503, 616, 617,
    798, 959, 1074, 1511, 2660, 3223, 3382,
    3386
Lingler, Roscoe, 950
Lingley, Bill, 619, 3408
Lingo, Leonard, 1653
Linguet, Simon Nicolas Henry, 1968
Liniers, Santiago Antonio Maria de, 1968
Link, Frank J., 1968
Link, George, 3271
Link, Karen Glabe, 1968
Link, Mitchell, 1968, 1320
Link, Theodore C., 1969
Linkomies, Edwin,, 3541
Linkowski, John, 139
Links, George, 3367
Linnaeus, Carl, 3292
Linnas, Karl, 1969, 3541
Linn, Charlie "Buck", 2548
Linn, James, 670, 1515
Linnell, Avis, 2579
Linse, Walter, 3327
Linstedt, Dreyer, 2560
Linstedt, Henry, 2560
Linthicum, William A., 1312
Linton, George, 3345
Linton, Henry, 3348
Linton, Mary, 960
Linton, Thomas, 3351
Lin Tse-hsu, 1969
Linwood, Robert, 3425
Lionberg, Lawrence, 3161
Lionel, 858
Lion Is in the Streets, A, 1969
Lionhood, Richard, 1695
Lipa, Jonathan, 1969
Lipa, Peter, 1969

716, 864, 924, 934, 1406, 1407, 1517, 2154, 2899
Louis XV, 426, 454, 648, 865, 906, 1030, 1992, 2045, 2096, 2656, 2658, 3240, 3370
Louis XVI, 230, 454, 569, 573, 569, 573, 574, 588, 660, 688, 869, 877, 894, 1025, 1082, 1650, 1992, 2096, 2115, 2394, 2678, 2845, 3162
Louis XVII, 1992
Louis XVIII, 266, 348, 454, 1992
Louis Francis Albert Victor Nicholas, 3257
Louis Henri Joseph, 1992
Louis of Flanders, 1993
Louis of Tarant, 1992
Louis the German, 1066
Louis, Joe, 629, 631, 929, 3296
Louis, Marcus, 598
Louis, Charles, 1210
Louis, Duc d' Orléans, 1726
Louise, 3240, 3246
Louise, Marie, 1993
Louisiana Lottery, 1993, 3399
Louisiana Slave Revolt, 3372
Louisiana State University Scandal, 1993
Louisiana Sugar Strike, 1994, 3374
Louisiana Sugar Uprising, 1994
Louis le Debonnaire, 129
Louis-Napoléon, 2751, 2960, 2979
Louis Philippe, 917, 919, 1157
Louisville (Ky.) Anti-German Riots, 3374
Lourdes, Woody, 498
Lourie, David, 784
Loutrel, Pierre, 179
Loury, Glenn C., 1994
Louvel, Jean Pierre, 348
L'Ouverture, Toussaint, 710, 926, 2583
Louvois, François Michel Le Tellier de, 3227
Louw, Eric, 3043
Louw, Reginald, 931
Louwage, F.E., 1659
Louys, Pierre, 1994
Lovat, Lord (Simon Fraser), 1994
Lovat, Twelfth Baron of, 1227
Lovato, Ricardo, 3559
Love, Bird, 3347
Love, David, 1305
Love, H.M. (U.S. pr.1899), 3548
Love, Harry (U.S. pr.1853), 1266, 2256
Love, Harry (U.S. pr.1850s), 3548, 3562, 3564
Love, Jennie, 234
Love, Joe, 3367
Love, John, 258
Love, Martin, 3338
Love, Thomas D. (U.S. pr.1895), 771
Love, Tom (U.S. pr.1881), 2744
Lovejoy, Elijah P., 3373
Lovejoy, Rose, 3387
Lovejoys, John, 2668
Lovelace, Carrie, 2860
Lovelace, Terry, 3361
Loveland, Judge, 1332
Lo Verde, Toto, 3407
Lovering, Clara A. 2240
Lovering, Georgianna, 1112
Lovesay, Joseph John, 844
Lovett, "Wild Bill", 3407, 3412
Lovett, George, 1740
Lovett, Red, 1182
Lovett, Robert, 3362
Love, W.H., 652
Loving, Dwight J., 3456
Loving, Frank, 277, 3562
Loving, Oliver, 100
Lo Voi, Gioacchino, 2222
Low, Dick, 537, 1425
Low, Frank, 1036
Low, George, 792

Low, Seth, 1560
Lowber, Robert W., 3182
Lowden, Frank O., 698, 2907
Lowe, Eliza, 3340
Lowe, Frederick, 2047
Lowe, Harriet (U.S. d.1918), 192, 1744
Lowe, Hudson, 2857
Lowe, James, 3545, 3562
Lowe, Joseph "Rowdy Joe", 3548, 3554, 3562
Lowe, Kate, 291
Lowe, Linda, 316
Lowe, Margaret, 845
Lowe, "Rowdy" Joe, 126, 291
Lowe, Ramona Jean, 2489
Lowe, Richard, 3360
Lowe, Robert, 72
Lowe, Willis, 3340
Lowell, James, 813
Lowell, Samuel, 1331
Lowenfield, Leslie, 3447
Lowenstein, Allard, 2887
Lowenstein, Martha, 2119
Lowenthal, William, 2746
Lowery, Chris, 1628
Lowery, Curtis, 2127
Lowery, Della, 1442
Lowery, James, 3451
Lowery, Terry, 3451
Lowes, Elizabeth, 2185
Loweth, Margaret, 2172
Low Hee Tong, 458, 3407
Lowie, O. Franklin, 979
Lowman, Bertha, 3367
Lowman, Demon, 3367
Lowman, Francis, 3247
Lowman, Francis, 3247
Lowndes, Marie Belloc, 2456, 3131
Lowrey, William, 3304
Lowrie, William, 2154
Lowry, 3259, 3521
Lowry, Eva, 3387
Lowry, Henry, 3366
Lowry, Joseph, 2784
Lowry, Samuel G., 309
Low Sing, 2967
Lowther, James, 3303
Lowther, William, 844
Loxton, Diana, 372
Loxton, Samuel, 372
Loya, Angelina, 1524
Loyd, Alvin, 3452
Loyd, Thomas J., 3337
Loy, Myrna, 971, 2103
Lozano, Richard, 41
Lozier, Doctor, 3548
Luang Bipul Songram, 3248
Luard, Charles Edward, 37
Lubin, Dr. Martin, 1590
Lubinga, Godfrey, 3302
Lucan, Veronica of, 370, 938, 2860
Lucan, Lady, 370
Lucania, Charles, 603
Lucas, Cecil, 3454
Lucas, Charles, 3305
Lucas, Cissie (U.S. d.1945), 3210
Lucas, David A., 3448
Lucas, Elmer "Chicken", 771, 3562
Lucas, Eudore, 2139
Lucas, Frederick (U.S. d.1945), 3210
Lucas, Harold, 3450
Lucas, Henry Lee, 3358, 3455
Lucas, Jim, 53
Lucas, John, 3451
Lucas, Larry, 3448
Lucas, Red (U.S. pr.1890s), 2732
Lucas, Roosevelt, 3451
Lucas, T.G. (Brit. pr.1924), 2658
Lucas Garcia, Fernando Romeo, 3513

Lucchese, Frances, 3405
Lucchese, Joseph, 3407
Lucchese, Thomas "Three-Finger Brown", 223, 528, 427, 525, 528, 547, 655, 754, 781, 975, 1296, 1491, 2085, 2087, 2114-2115, 2138, 2189, 2505, 2891, 3401, 3403, 3405, 3406-3411, 3407, 3409, 3410
Lucchinacci, François, 790, 2102, 2216, 2465
Lucciani, Toto, 595
Lucente, Anthony, 1249
Lucerno, Alitea de, 2002
Lucero, Aban, 3562
Lucero, Cecilio, 3343, 3562
Lucero, Cesario 108
Lucero, Francisco, 3562
Lucero, Philip, 3448
Lucero, Quinia, 3562
Lucero, Sostenes, 3562
Lucero, Tomas, 3562
Luce, Timothy, 475
Lucey, Nathan, 3361
Lucheni, Luigi, 1083
Lucia, Felice De, 15
Luciana, Salvatore, 3025
Luciano, Anthony, 941
Luciano, Charles "Lucky" 2, 18, 31-32, 35, 43, 103, 111, 120, 128, 132, 178, 179, 229, 345, 346, 402, 415, 427, 428, 525, 526, 528, 591, 603, 616, 623, 634, 655, 779, 786, 932, 935, 941, 976, 1018, 1124, 1174, 1226, 1250, 1295, 1307, 1311, 1346, 1491, 1555, 1561, 1588, 1613, 2085, 2102, 2114, 2138-2139, 2215, 2217-2218, 2252, 2254-2255, 2269, 2657, 2686, 2700, 2734, 2757, 2771, 2814, 2834, 2835, 2868, 2870, 2884, 2891, 2963, 2969, 2974, 2983, 3120, 3139, 3226, 3294-3296, 3390, 3394, 3401, 3403, 3404, 3407, 3408, 3411, 3412, 3416
Luciano, Dominic, 1252, 1253
Luciano, Frank, 3407
Lucido, Salvatore, 3393
Lucie-Smith, John, 3252
Lucier, Phillip, 3485
Lucius Aelius Sejanus, 3234
Lucius Appuleius Saturnius, 3234
Lucius Calpurnius Piso, 1110
Lucius Cornelius Cinna, 3234
Lucius Cornelius Sulla, 3234
Lucius Septimius Severus, 3014, 3235
Lucius Sergius Catiline, 3234
Luckett, George, 2509
Luckman, Harry, 1638
Luckman, Meyer, 1638
Lucky, Darnell, 3448
Luc Levasseur, Patricia Gros, 2107
Lucretia, 2898
Lucusta, 2007
Lucy, Saint, 2007
Lucy, Reggie, 704
Lucy, Richard de, 293, 2007
Lucy, Thomas, 2007
Ludberg, H., 3250
Luddites, 2007
Ludendorff, Erich von, 1569
Luderitz, Wolf, 994
Ludin, Hans Elard, 3541
Lüdke, Bruno, 2007
Ludlam, Ned, 3372
Ludlow, Colo., Strike, 2007, 3375
Ludlow, Fitzhugh, 3293
Ludlow, Justice, 1442
Ludlum, Lou, 2032, 3387
Ludwig I, 2204, 2672
Ludwig the Bloodsucker, 383
Ludwig, Frederick, 1506, 2397
Luen Group, 3391
Luer, August, 3326
Luetgert, Adolph Louis, 2007

Luff, Arthur Pearson, 2829
Luff, Gladys Isobel, 3084
Luflore, Joseph, 3351
Lufthansa Robbery, 2008
Lugar, Richard G., 713
Lugazy, John, 2009
Lugeon, Micheline, 2784
Luggle, Jeff, 3344
Lugo, Diego, 2009
Lugo, Freddy, 445
Lugo Alencia, Rena, 3467
Luhman, Mrs. George B., 915
Luis, 3243
Luisa, Maria, 2121
Lujan, Martiniano, 3562
Luke, Johnny, 3447
Lukens, Albert B., 2009
Lu Lien-k'ui, 3249
Lull, Louis J., 1702, 2468, 3212, 3568
Lully, Raymond, 2009
Lumdy, Richard, 3339
Luminoso, Sendero, 3281, 3521, 3525, 3335
Lumley, Mrs. J.V., 2432
Lumpkin, Dan, 3360
Lumpkin, Walter R., 3208
Lumumba, Patrice Hemery, 1436, 3254, 2010-2012
Luna, Alvaro de, 2012
Luna, Carlos de, 3447
Luna, Countess de, 567
Luna, Juan Martin, 3527
Luna, Melchior, 3562
Lunacharski, Anatoli Vasilievich, 2012
Lundberg, Eveline, 1390
Lundberg, John, 1389
Lundberg, William, 899
Lunde, Donald, 3137
Lundgren, Signe, 484
Lundien, Kenneth, 3428
Lundin, Fred "the Poor Swede", 874, 2937
Lundin, Oscar, 613
Lundy, Benjamin, 2012
Lundy, Richard, 3341
Lundy, William D., 2091
Lung, Leong, 2012
Lungren, E.A., 1177
Luongo, Alfred, 2685
Luparelli, Joe, 2012
Lupino, Ida, 2960
Lupino, Stanley, 2960
Lu Po-hung, 3248
Lupo, Ignatz "The Wolf", 2217
Lupo, Salvatore, 345
Lupporini, Cavaliere, 3245
Lü Puwei, 2012
Lured, 2012
Lurie, Charles, 3332
Lurie, Reuben, 1013
Lurton, Horace H., 1000, 2894, 2012
Lurye, Willie, 2012
Lusco, Joe, 3395
Lu Sing-pan, 2012
Lusk, Bobby, 3450
Lusk, Dianthe, 509
Lusk, George, 1685
Lusk, Grace, 2012-2013
Lussatz, Gaetan de, 620, 2831, 3393
Luster, 3338
Lustgarten, Edgar, 2830, 3306
Lustgarten, William, 2013
Lustig, Henry, 2013
Lustig, Victor "The Count", 2013-2015, 2978, 3105
Lustig, William, 1726
Luter, A.A., 3246
Lutes, George W., 3145
Luther, Angela, 200, 202, 3475
Luther, Hans, 3247
Luther, Martin, 246, 508, 1435, 1588, 2413,

2458
Luther, Mills, 3341
Luther, Paul, 2509
Luther, Seth, 2015
Lutherland, Thomas, 2015
Luttig, Elizabeth, 805
Lutton, Maurice, 3511
Luttrell, Charles (U.S. pr. 1880) 3562
Luttrell, Colonel (Brit. pr. 1773) 1156
Lutt, Terrence, 1199, 1463
Lutz, B.J., 3425
Lutz, Emma, 347
Lutz, Philip, 962
Luvaas, John, 1340
Luxembourg, Duke of, 674
Luxemburg, Rosa, 3040, 3244
Luynes, Duke of, 3239
Luzi, Frank, 3387
Lwin, Sein, 550
Ly Bon, 3236
Ly, Cam, 3454
Lych, G.W., 3365
Lyell, William Darling, 1626
Lyle, John H., 16, 1410, 1511, 2214
Lyle, W.O., 583
Lyle, Walter, 1484
Lyman, Abe, 2960
Lyman, Levi, 1528
Lyman, Tommy, 3009
Lyman, William, 247, 2679
Lynch, Barry, 3399
Lynch, Charles, 3336
Lynch, Cornelius, 182
Lynch, Gregory, 3453
Lynch, Helen, 1419
Lynch, James, 2093
Lynch, John J. "Jack", 3325
Lynch, Joseph (U.S. d.1940), 3187
Lynch, Joseph (Ire. d.1981), 3513
Lynch, Kevin, 3281, 3515
Lynch, Margaret, 1418
Lynch, Mel Patrick, 497, 3330
Lynch, Robert, 2092
Lynch, Roche, 3068
Lynch, Thomas, 1724, 2092
Lynch, William, 3336
Lyng, Stephanie, 3331
Lynn, Frederick, 3447
Lynn, Joseph, 3513
Lynn, Karen, 584
Lynn, Samuel, 3093
Lynn, Wylie, 2955, 3551
Lyon, Charles, 2714
Lyon, Donner, 3328, 3485
Lyon, Elizabeth, 2740
Lyon, James E., 1091
Lyon, Katherine, 3330
Lyon, Mabel Dana, 282
Lyon, Montague, 320
Lyon, Nelson, 2782
Lyon, Robert, 3173
Lyons, Anthony, 1436
Lyons, Dan, 1025, 3147, 3404
Lyons, Emma, 1357
Lyons, Frank, 3206, 3399
Lyons, Harry, 647
Lyons, Hayes, 1254, 3337
Lyons, Haze, 3049, 3562
Lyons, Jack, 3399
Lyons, James, 2025
Lyons, John, 1181, 1514
Lyons, Lawrence "Pat", 731
Lyons, Marcus, 856, 857
Lyons, Ned, 1617, 3407
Lyons, Ronald L., 3471
Lyons, Sherman, 374
Lyons, Sophie, 2101, 2468, 3407
Lyon, Stephanie, 3330
Lyons, William, 1352

Lysander, 1411
Lysias, 133, 3233
Lysicles, 171
Lysimachus, 2510, 2725
Lytle, James, 3341
Lyton, Edward Bulwer, 476
Lyttelton, Neville, 3172

M

Ma Chan-shan, 2045
Ma Hsin-i, 3241
Ma You-Feing, 3249
Maag, Arthur, 1641
Maalot Massacre, 2021
Maas, Peter, 2728
Mabini, Apolinario, 2021
McAdams, Louis, 3352
McAdoo, Anthony LaQuin, 2930
McAdoo, William, 183, 1139, 2021, 2454, 3425
McAfee, Henry, 3352
McAliskey, Bernadette Devlin, 3508
McAlister, Elizabeth, 348
McAlister, Jock, 1621
McAllister, Bill, 2403
McAllister, C.L., 2660
McAllister, Hill, 1460
McAllister, Matthew Hall, 2021
McAlmon, Robert, 832
McAlpin, J.S., 3558
McAlpin, William, 3355
McAlroy, Patrick H., 3469
McAnarney, John, 2650
McAnarney, Thomas, 2650
McAndrew, William, 2937
Macapagal, Diosdado, 3255
MacArdle, Harold John, 2021
MacArthur, Charles, 756, 1438, 1505, 1586, 3087, 3088, 3089
MacArthur, Douglas, 279, 434, 1563, 1607, 2725, 2963, 3025, 3161, 3204, 3375
MacArthur, Douglas II, 3328, 3487
Macarthur, John, 2021-2022
MacArthur, Malcolm, 2022
Macartney, 3303, 3304
McAtee, Joseph G., 2022, 3425
McAtee, Leon, 983
Macaulay, James Buchanan, 2819
McAuley, Harry B., 856
McAuliffe, Cynthia, 2472
McAuliffe, Deborah, 2472
McAuliffe, James S., 3160
McAuliffe, Joseph Herbert, 2022
McAuliffe, Robert, 2472
McAuliffe, Susan, 2472
McAvoy, Frank, 1230
McAvoy, Thomas J. 91
Macbeth, 2022, 2094, 3237
McBratney, James, 1350, 3405
McBride, Arthur B., 3392
McBride, Bill, 3465
McBride, Bob, 2878
McBride, Lillie, 254
McBride, Linda, 1678
McBride, Michael, 3455
McBride, Sebastian, 3356
McCabe, John, 2022
McCabe, William, 3407
Maccabees, Jonathan, 2022, 3233
Maccabees, Simon, 2022, 3233
McCafey, Therese, 3387
McCafferty, James, 566, 1193

McCaffrey, John P., 75
McCaig, James, 456
McCain, William Rufe, 54, 3427
McCain, Willie B., 2940
McCall, Edward L., 2022, 3448
McCall, Franklin Pierce, 2023, 3326
McCall, Gerald F., 646
McCall, Jack, 577, 1537, 1539, 1672, 2864, 3545, 3547
McCall, Jim, 3562
McCall, John, 2023, 3562
McCall, Thomas P., 2023, 3548
McCall, Willis, 1377, 1665
McCallum, McNeill Francis, 2023
McCambridge, Mercedes, 2125
McCandles, David C., 1535, 3547, 3562
McCann, E. Michael, 904
McCann, Edward C., 3387
McCann, Frances, 329
McCann, John, 3098
McCann, Joseph A., 3124
McCann, Reddy, 2856
McCann, Robert, 3010
McCann, William, 3566
McCann, Wilma, 2879
McCardie, Henry Alfred, 855, 2023, 2094
McCarney, Fred, 1307
McCarthy, Andrew, 2679
McCarthy, Bill, 3562, 3563
McCarthy, Carol, 2233
McCarthy, Cowlegged Sam, 2681
McCarthy, Daniel, 2746
McCarthy, Edward, 3425
McCarthy, George, 1556
McCarthy, Jack L., 3425
McCarthy, James P., 2417
McCarthy, James William, 2023
McCarthy, John (U.S. 1942-), 107, 1075
McCarthy, John (U.S. d.1866), 761
McCarthy, John (U.S. pr.1880s), 1025
McCarthy, John, 3147
McCarthy, John J., 2024, 3426
McCarthy, John P. (U.S. pr.1940s), 929
McCarthy, Joseph Raymond, 942, 2024,2098, 3123
McCarthy, Justin William, 2024, 3461
McCarthy, Kittie, 1474
McCarthy, Marcella, 867
McCarthy, Sam, 888
McCarthy, Thomas, 2024, 3258, 3556, 3562, 3563
McCarthy, William, 2829, 3379
McCarthy, William T., 2024
McCartney, Edward, 2897
McCartney, George, 1559
MacCartney, James, 2087
McCartney, Linda, 2024
McCartney, Paul, 2024, 3300
McCartney, Thomas Peter, 2024
McCarty, Bill, 651, 652, 2025
McCarty, Blanche, 2025
McCarty, Fred, 2025
McCarty, George, 704
McCarty, Henry, 3563
McCarty, John, 3305
McCarty, Patrick Henry, 363
McCarty, Tom, 651, 704, 2025, 3545
McCarty Brothers, 2025
McCarver, Ernest, 3453
McCaskie, Sonja, 290
McCaskill, Hamby, 2025
McCauley, Arthur, 3354
McCauley, Hamp, 3563
McCauley, James, 3348
McCauley, Joseph, 2800
McCauley, W.J., 218
McCauley, William, 3548, 3560
McCawley, Daniel, 1353
Macchiarole, Pasquale "Paddy Mac", 1250,

3407
McClachlan, Jessie, 1656
McClain, John, 1698
McClain, Leonard, 333
McClary, David, 2025-2026
McClatchey, John, 3521
McClatchy, Frank A., 3326
McClaughry, Robert W., 3424
McClease, Jim, 3563
McClease, Samuel M., 480
McCleester, Country, 3403
McClellan, 2021
McClellan, George B., 370, 2468
McClellan, George P. 163
McClellan, Glenn H., 2803
McClellan, John, 1584
McClelland, Andrew, 174
McClelland, Hugh, 174, 175
McClements, W.J., 625
McClendon, John, 841
McClendon, Otis, 842
McClennon, Walter, 3353
McClernand, John Alexander, 2026
Macclesfield, Anne, of, 2682
Macclesfield, Earl of, 2026
McClinton, J.H., 3354
McCloskey, Andy, 3563
McCloskey, James, 910, 3078
McCloskey, Sam, 3563
McCloskey, William, 364, 2061, 2717
McCloud, Andrew, 3367
McCloud, Jim, 1620
M'Cloud, Peter, 2026
McClung, Alexander Keith, 3305
M'Clure, Alexander Logan, 2026
McClure, Bob, 218
McClure, George Buchanan, 2026
McClure, Robert, 3548
McClure, Vance, 3345
McClurkin, James, 2489
McCluskey, Joe, 298
McCluskie, Arthur, 123, 2026, 3305
McCluskie, Mike, 123, 2026
McClusky, Francis, 3525
McClusky, George W., 566
McCly, Jerry, 3344
McCollom, John, 1384
McCollum, Edward, 3355
McCollum, Ruby, 2026
McConaghy, Andrew, 2967
McConaghy, Robert, 2026
McConkey, Joseph, 2026
McConnel, M., 3241
McConnell, Andrew, 2027, 2802
McConnell, Brian, 221
McConnell, Brice, 1181
McConnell, Diane Linn, 1550
McConnell, J.R., 2027
McConnell, William B., 2027
McCook, Alexander McDowell, 3177
McCook, Barney, 2713
McCook, Edward Moody, 3177
McCook, Edwin S., 3177, 3242
McCool, Len, 602
McCorckle, Joseph, 1410
McCord, Gerald, 2027
McCord, Gloria, 2027
McCord, J.B., 3454
McCord, James W., Jr., 3099
McCord, Myron, 3548
McCord, William, 480
McCorkle, Joseph, 3305
McCormac, Hugh, 3527
McCormick, Andrew Phelps, 2027
MacCormick, Austin Harbutt, 2027, 3123
McCormick, Charles, 825
McCormick, Harold, 2104
McCormick, James, J., 2027
McCormick, John, 756

McCormick, Ken, 585
McCormick, Michael, 2719, 3454
McCormick, Robert Rutherford, 1398
McCormick, Sammy, 3521
McCormick, William, 1137
McCormick, William, Sr., 2027-2028
McCorquodale, Timothy W., 1300, 3447
McCortele, Jess, 3364
McCory, Arthur, 1701
McCotter, R.D., 3242
MacCowan, Robert Henry, 3183
McCoy, Frank, 3407
McCoy, Garfield, 3355
McCoy, Green, 3338
McCoy, Harmon, 1477
McCoy, Horace, 3354
McCoy, Houston, 3143
McCoy, John B., 3242
McCoy, Joseph, 2028, 3348
McCoy, "Old Dick", 2028
McCoy, "One-Legged-Jim", 3563
McCoy, Paris, 1477
McCoy, Pharmer, 1477
McCoy, "Rabbit Bill", 3359
McCoy, Randall, 1477
McCoy, Richard Floyd, 2028, 3470
McCoy, Russell, 537, 2029
McCoy, Sam, 1477
McCoy, Stephen, 3433, 3434, 3437, 3438, 3447-3450, 3452, 3453, 3455
McCoy, T.J., 3055
McCoy, Tolbert, 1477
McCoy, Tom, 2028
McCoy, Walter, 2407
McCoy, William, 2029
McCracken, Claude L., 1235
McCracken, Henry, 2029
McCracken, W.H., 2029
McCrae, James, 3450
McCrary, Carolyn, 2029-2030, 3462
McCrary, Danny, 2029, 3462
McCrary, Sherman, 2029, 3462
McCrary Family, 2029
McCray, Edward, 3407
McCray, Michael J., 1113
McCray, Warren T., 1676
McCrea, Duncan Cameron, 929
McCready, Dorothy, 898
McCready, Ray, 968, 972
McCree, Arleigh, 2228
McCreery, John S., 3467, 3482
McCreesh, Raymond, 3513
McCreight, Emory, 2052
McCrory, David, 886
McCrory, Phil, 842
McCrotty, W.F., 326
McCrystal, Thomas, 1516
Maccubbin, Samuel T., 412
McCue, Fannie, 2030
McCue, J. Samuel, 2030
McCue, "Rags", 3387
McCue, Richard J., 3037
McCue, William, 3351
McCuiston, O.W., 3548
McCullagh, John H., 1020
McCullen, Edward J., 2433
McCulley, David J., 910
McCulloch, Ben, 2920
McCulloch, Noel, 3522
McCullom, Phillip, 3451
McCullough, Green, 3563
McCullough, John, 101, 3413
McCullough, Robert, 2071, 3387
MacCumhaill, Finn, 1147
McCune, Edward, 3326
McCurdy, Alex, 3345
McCurley, A.D., 1410
McCurry, Lynn, 1037
MacCurtain, T., 3244

McCusker, Harold, 3521
McCutcheon, Peter M., 2030
McCutcheon, Sam, 3001
McCutcheon, William, 550
McDade, Edward, 584
McDade, Wendy, 583
McDaniel, Jim, 363
McDaniel, John, 3354
McDaniel, Stephen, 2928
Macdaniel, Stephen, 348
McDaniels, "Bootjack", 3368
McDaniels, Bud, 2030
McDaniels, J. (U.S. pr.1880s), 3563
McDaniels, Jim (U.S. pr.1870s), 3563
McDaniels, Lee, 3342
McDaniels, William, 3563
McDermott, Frederick Lincoln, 2030
McDermott, Michael F., 342
McDevitt, H.A., 2692
McDevitt, Harry S., 361
McDonagh, Pat "Paddy", 2031
McDonagh, Terence, 2031
MacDonagh, Thomas, 2031
MacDonald, A.B., 2429
MacDonald, Alexander, 687, 2034
MacDonald, Arthur, 2031
McDonald, Bill, 3562
MacDonald Clan Massacre, 2034
McDonald, Daniel, 1167
McDonald, David, 2031
MacDonald, David Rowland, 2031
McDonald, Dennis, 3332
McDonald, Dora Feldman 2031, 2033
MacDonald, Ewan, 2031
McDonald, Eddie, 1131
McDonald, Elizabeth, 689
McDonald, Errol, 6
McDonald, Floyd, 840
McDonald, Frank, 1464
McDonald, George, 1339, 3190, 3559
McDonald, Harry D., 1114
MacDonald, Harry J., 72
MacDonald, Hugh, 560
McDonald, J., 3563
McDonald, J.H., 2027
McDonald, James, 2437
MacDonald, Jayne, 2879
MacDonald, Jeffrey, 265, 2032
McDonald, Joe, 936
Macdonald, John, 646
McDonald, John, 2208
M'Donald, John, 385
McDonald, John Edward, 2032
Macdonald, John Hay Athole, 2032 sir
Macdonald, John Sandfield, 2032
McDonald, Joseph, 3349
MacDonald, Lynda Anne, 1252
McDonald, Michael Cassius "Big Mike",
   1464, 2031-2033, 2475, 3383, 3384,
   3386-3390
McDonald, Miles, 1392, 2259, 2505
McDonald, Peter Alexander, 1632, 2033
MacDonald, Ramsay, 1475
M'Donald, Robert, 2804
McDonald, Roland, 2033
McDonald, Sam, 3452
McDonald, Tom, 3206
McDonald, Victor, 2033
McDonald, W.J., 812
McDonald, Walter, 3563
McDonald, Wilbur, 2033-2034
Macdonald, William, 2034
M'Donald, William, 2804
McDonald, William Jesse, 3548
McDonel, France, 1164
Macdonell, Alastair Ruadh, 2034
McDonnell, Calvin, 3341
McDonnell, Clifford, 1084
McDonnell, Florence, 2125

MacDonnell, George, 1366
McDonnell, James, 2034
McDonnell, Joe, 3378, 3514
McDonnell, John J., 1384, 2034
McDonnell, Michael, 3453
MacDonnell, Randal, 2034
M'Donoghy, Peter, 1478
McDonough, James, 2034, 3426
McDougal, "Cattle" Annie, 2955
McDougal, Helen, 547, 548
McDougal, John, 340
Macdougal, Nell, 547
McDougald, Anthony, 3452
McDougald, Daniel A., 2035
MacDougall, Alexander, 2035
MacDougall, Colin, 3123
McDougall, Hugh, 2738
McDougall, John, 2677
McDougall, Mike, 3453
McDow, Thomas Ballard, 2035
McDowell, Charles, 3448
McDowell, Jack, 864, 2035, 3557, 3563
McDowell, Jacob, 3359
McDowell, John, 3357
McDowell, Lacene, 185, 3264
MacDowell, Malcolm, 2956
McDowell, William, 1700
McDuffie, Arthur, 2128
McDuffie, Henry, 3342
MacDuncan, Malcolm III, 2094
Mace, Cal, 3563
Macé, Gustave, 483, 2878, 3059
Mace, John, 3563
MacEarlane, Frankie, 3389
Macedon, Philip of, 733, 2414
Macedonian Revolutionary Organization,
   3245
McEhanie, Bill, 860
Macek, Richard, 2186
McElligot, Thomas, 3387
McElree, J. Paul, 2174
McElroy, Henry F., 183, 642, 1186, 1545,
   2036, 3009
McElroy, Kenneth Rex "Kenrex", 2035
McElroy, Mary, 183, 1186, 2036, 2041,
   3326
McElwaine, Seamus, 3281
McElway, John, 2036
McElway, Marita, 2036
McEnery, Samuel D., 413
McEntee, Edward Matthew, 2037
Maceo, Rose, 2162
Maceo, Sam 2162
McErlane, Frank, 128, 608, 610, 2037,
   2673, 2972, 3119, 3386, 3387, 3388
McErlane, Vincent, 3387
McEvoy, James, 3424
McEwan, P.R., 3249
McEwen, Janet, 1227
McEwen, Mervin Clare, 2037
McFadden, Charles W., 2943
McFadden, George, 3344
McFadden, Jerry, 3455
McFadden, Richard, 2036
McFaddin, "Buckskin Bill", 3336
McFall, Daniel, 608, 2037, 3387
M'Farlane, Sarah, 857
McFarland, Daniel, 2037-2039
McFarland, Earl, 2039
McFarland, Frank, 3455
McFarland, James, 3372
McFarland, Mary, 3011
McFarland, Russell, 498
McFarlane, James, 3135
MacFall, John Edward, 3082
MacFarland, Ruth, 2039
MacFarland, William Allison, 2039
Macfarline, George J., 24
McFatton, Duncan, 3342

McGahee, Earl, 3447
McGahey, Ozias, 3347
McGale, Charles, 3427
McGann, Patrick, 360
McGannon, William H., 2040
McGarigle, William J., 1464, 3387, 3424
McGarr, Frank James, 1068, 1361, 2040
McGarry, Dennis William, 2040
McGarry, Kevin Arnold, 2441
McGeary, James, 359
McGee, Andrew Fergus, 1674
McGee, Eddie, 2040
McGee, George, 2036
McGee, Harry, 3351
McGee, Isaac, 3348
McGee, Jewel R., 3455
McGee, John, 593
McGee, Patrick, 3325
McGee, Rosetta, 2041
McGee, Thomas D'Arcy, 2040
McGee, Walter, 183, 2036, 2041, 3326
McGee, Willie, 2041
McGeesey, John, 3350
McGeoahegan, Daniel, 3387
McGerald, Fig, 3147, 3407
McGhee, Beulah, 2744
McGhee, Richard, 2784
McGhie, Isaac, 3366
McGill, S.D., 673
M'Gillavrae, Alexander, 1357
McGinley, John C., 2105
McGinnis, Art, 956, 959
McGinnis, Blaine, 2185
McGinnis, David, 3158
McGinnis, Harry L., 255
McGinnis, Joseph F. "Big Joe", 489, 3461
McGinnis, Mollie, 2185
McGinnis, Tom, 1731
McGinniss, Joe, 265, 2032
McGinty, Thomas Jefferson, 2689, 3392
McGirl, Francis, 2235
McGivern, Gary, 843
McGlane, Jeremy, 2041
MacGlegno, 2055
McGloin, Michael, 2041, 3147
McGloon, J.C., 712
McGlory, Billy, 3405
McGlue, Charles, 848
McGlynn, Joseph B., 1181
McGohey, John F.X., 2042
McGough, James, 3028
McGovern, Chauncey, 1547
McGovern, George, 3080
McGovern, Hughey "Stubby", 1028, 3387
McGovern, Walter, 1681
McGowan, A. Russell, 1037
McGowan, Brian, 1254
McGowan, Emma, 2953
M'Gowan, James, 1711
McGowan, Margaret, 1691
McGowan, Wilder, 3368
McGowen, Roger Wayne, 3455
McGown, Kitty, 3147
McGrady, Tobe, 3347
MacGranahan, Mary Horvath, 3106
McGrand, Ed, 3563
McGranery, James Patrick, 2042
McGrath, A.G., 2035
McGrath, E.J., 3407
McGrath, J. Howard, 1664, 3163
McGrath, James, 2042
McGrath, James H., 2042
McGrath, James Patrick, 2042
McGrath, Price, 596, 2042, 3399, 3400
McGrath, Stephen, 182
McGrath, Violet, 2042
McGraw, Alice Marie, 2042
McGraw, Bill, 3387
McGraw, John, 1132

3401, 3404, 3406-3409, 3411
Madden, "Punk", 3407
Madden, Robert, 3455
Madden, Sow, 888, 2681, 3407
Maddocks, Henry, 454
Maddox, Allen R., 3549
Maddox, Alton H., Jr., 480
Maddox, Claude, 15, 607, 716, 2073, 2972, 3382, 3387
Maddox, Corinne, 2073
Maddox, Dick, 3556
Maddox, Jerome, 3556
Maddox, Kathleen, 2108
Maddox, Thomas H., 2675
Maddux, Murphy, Jr., 1723
Maddux, Ronald, 2073
Maddux, Wanda Gibson, 2073
Madeiros, Celestino, 2652
Madej, Gregory, 3451
Madeleine, 2073
Madeleine Graham, 2073
Mader, Prussian Charley, 3206
Mader, Richard, 1588
Madera, Juan, 3349
Madero, Evarista, 2073
Madero, Francisco I., 636, 637, 2073, 2077-2078, 3050, 3052, 3243
Madero, Gustavo, 2076-2077, 3243
Madero, Rául, 3050
Madero, Sara, 2077-2078
Madia, Josep, 3248
Madia, Miguel, 3248
Madigan, Harry, 2071, 3387
Madigan, Paul, 56, 403, 2078
Madison, Daryl, 3455
Madison, Fannie Lillian, 734
Madison, J.C., 1066
Madison, James, 1021, 1047, 1171, 1632, 2410, 2480, 2858, 2864, 2989, 3012, 3178
Madison, Roger, 1073
Madison, William, 3356
Madonia, Benedetto, 648, 941, 2217
Madonna, Matthew, 2078
Madsen, Andrew, 2079
Madsen, Christian, 404, 1003, 1627, 2078, 2931, 2955, 3197, 3549, 3568
Madsen, Yvette, 2079
Maebara, Issei, 2079
Maelbaethe, 3237
Maelzel, Johann Nepomuk, 2079
Maelzer, Kurt, 3541
Maerth, Gaby Kiss, 3334
Maes, Alejandro, 3562
Maes, Juanito, 3563
Maes, Patricio, 3555, 3563
Maes, Pete, 568
Maes, Zenon, 3563
Maesa, Julia, 1080, 1749
Maestas, German, 3563
Maetzu y Whitney, Ramiro de, 2079
Maeys, Alvin, Jr., 2828
Maffetore, Anthony "Dukey", 112, 2254, 3003
Maffia, Tony, 1724
Maffie, Adolph "Jazz", 489, 491
Mafia, 206, 219, 223, 224, 229, 245, 272, 283, 295, 340, 357, 368, 370, 372, 391-394, 398, 402, 414, 415, 421, 424, 426-428, 434, 442, 449, 454, 501, 521, 528, 533, 534, 546, 554, 560, 2072, 2079-2087, 2102, 2105, 2112, 2114-2115, 2117, 2137-2138, 2147, 2215-2218, 2222-2223, 2255, 2260, 2264, 2268-2269
Mafia Diaries, The, 2086
Mafia Induction Oath, 3398
Mag, Gallus, 1591
Magaddino, Antonio, 3380
Magaddino, Gaspare, 3380
Magaddino, Peter, 3380

Magaddino, Stefano "Steve", 40, 223, 427, 754, 1491, 2086-2087, 2114, 3380, 3403
Magagna, Giuseppe, 3513
Magagna, Paula, 2125
Magee, Carl C., 2086
Magee, Harry, 2929
Magee, Patrick, 3281
Magee, Port, 3342
Magee, Richard, 3342
Magee, Ruchell, 882
Magee, Tom, 3415
Magee, Walter, 240
Magee Island Witch Trial, 2087
Magellan, Ferdinand, 3291
Magendie, François, 2087
Magers, Patrick F., 938
Maggie: A Girl of the Streets, 2087
Maggio, Antonio, 3243
Maggio, Joseph, 192
Maggio, Mrs. Joseph, 192
Maggiore, Michele della, 2087
Maggs, William, 2821
Magid al-Molqi, 2199
Magine, Paul, 2189
Magliocco, Ambrose, 3407
Magliocco, Giuseppe, 3401
Magliocco, Joseph, 136, 223, 427, 655, 754, 1491, 2087, 3407
Magliulo, Julie, 3334
Magloire, Gabriel, 3342
Magna, Maria T., 1190
Magnabosco, Marco, 3387
Magnentius, 767, 3235
Magnentius, Flavius Popilius, 2087
Magness, Ray, 2719
Magnetic Peripherals, Inc., 3290
Magnier, Louis-Bernard, 2087
Magnus I, 378
Magnus III, 2087, 3237
Magnus IV, 2087
Magnus Clemens Maximus, 3235
Magnus the Strong, 602, 1455, 3237
Magnus, Johannes, 2087
Magnuson, John, 2088, 3263
Magoon, Seymour "Blue Jaw", 117, 2252
Magruder, Billy, 723
Magruder, Jeb Stuart, 575, 3099, 3100
Magruder, Lloyd, 1628
Magruder, Michael L., 3472
Maguid, Carlos, 142
Maguin, André, 2847
Maguire, Andy, 1698
Maguire, Elizabeth, 777
Maguire, Sam, 3172
Magwood, Billy Joe, 3447
Magwood, Kenneth, 3447
Mahady, Frank, 3215
Mahaffey, Jerry, 1551, 3451
Mahaffey, Reginald, 1551
Mahan, Margaret, 3326
Mahan, William, 855, 856, 3075, 3326
Mahaney, Jack, 1670, 2088
Mahar, Maureen, 902
Maharaj, Krishna, 3450
Maharg, Billy, 399
Mahdi, Imam al-Hadi, 3484
Mahdi Mohammed Ahmed, 2777
Mahendra, 3254
Maher, Edward, 1104-1105
Maher, John C., 2658
Mahew, Susan, 3207
Mahidol, Prince, 116
Mahieu, Johan, 493
Mahir Pasha, Ali, 2088
Mahl, Phyllis, 288
Mahler, Emil, 3097
Mahler, Horst, 198, 202, 3475
Mahmoud, Ben, 3254
Mahmoud Mansour Bey, 2237

Mahmud, 2733
Mahmud II, 92, 2269, 3240
Mahmud, Masood, 356
Mahmud Sevket, 1099
Mahmud Shevket Pasha, 2088
Mahn Ba Khaing, 3251
Mahoin, Marie, 2437
Mahomet IV, 3220
Mahon, Eldon Brooks, 2088
Mahon, Francis J., 2417
Mahon, Guy, 2171
Mahon, John J., 2742
Mahon, Patrick Herbert, 191, 651, 849, 2088, 2830, 3306
Mahone, Cathy Phelps, 3334
Mahone, Lauren, 3334
Mahoney, Arthur James, 1066
Mahoney, Barbara, 1356
Mahoney, Blind, 1670
Mahoney, Bum, 1286, 3407, 3412
Mahoney, Edward, 420
Mahoney, James, 3091
Mahoney, James E., 2089
Mahoney, James "Jim", 2089
Mahoney, John, 3282, 3563
Mahoney, Mary, 300
Mahoney, Peter P., 1249, 3251
Mahorn, Tom, 3549
Mahrländer, Alfred, 3475
Mahseredjian, Suzy, 3508
Maia, Mario, 1258
Maikovskis, Boleslavs, 3541
Mailer, Norman, 6-8, 1189, 1314, 2089, 2868
Maillart, Jean, 3238
Maillat, Loyse, 421
Maillefert, Arthur, 799
Maillert, Jean, 2117
Main, Andrea, 2508
Main, Robert C., 916, 2508
Mainardi, Paolo, 2203
Maine, Henry James Sumner, 2089
Maine, Leonard, 475
Maine State Prison, 2089
Mainwaring, Gerald, 2089
Mainwaring, Henry, 2090
Maione, Harry "Happy", 1, 111, 117, 2090, 2252, 2255, 2702, 2868, 3003, 3401, 3404, 3408, 3410
Mais, Robert, 2990, 3413
Maisel, Ernst, 1578
Maison Coquet, 2090, 2097
Maita, Filippo, 3415
Maitland, Frederic William, 2090
Maitland, Thomas, 1315
Maitland, William, 2090
Maitreya, 3140
Majali, Hazza, 2090, 3254, 3264
Majczek, Helen, 2091
Majczek, Joseph, 2091-2092
Majczek, Tillie, 2091
Majczek, Vera, 2091
Majed Abu Sharar, 3259
Majeski, William, 7
Major, Arthur, 2092
Major, Ethel Lillie, 379, 2092
Major, John H., 2228
Majorian, 2092
Majoros, Janos, 3464
Majors, Abe, 2092-2093
Majors, Archie, 2093
Majors, Dudley, 23, 582
Majors, Lloyd L., 2092-2093
Majors, Ray, 23, 582
Majors, Robert (U.S. pr.1880s), 3547, 3560, 3563
Majors, Sank, 3357
Majuri, Frank, 3407
Mak Kwan Fai, 2093, 3456
Mak Shui, 1288

Makarios III, 3256
Makarios, Archbishop, 1452
Makinen, Marvin William, 2094
Makino, 3248
Makley, Charles "Fat Charley", 947, 951,
   952, 954, 964, 3427, 3460
Makoto Saito, 3248
Maksimowski, Piotr, 2094
Makume, John, 2094
Malaga, Sam, 2673
Malaquais, Jean, 7
Malarkey, Stumpy, 1341, 3407
Malasauskas, Victor, 3510
Malatesta, Enrico, 2987
Malatesta, Gianciotto, 2094, 2481
Malaysian Race Riots, 3377
Malchow, Frederick, 2444
Malcolm I, 1070
Malcolm III MacDuncan, 2094, 2236, 3237
Malcolm, Douglas, 1642, 2094
Malcolm, George Arthur, 2094
Malcolm, Roger, 3368
Malcolm, Sarah, 1609, 2094-2095
Malcolm, Vance, 463
Malcolm X, 397, 398, 1040, 2095-2096, 3255,
   3476, 3496
Malder, Theodore, 1471
Maldon, Charles, 898
Maldonado, Manuel, 3563
Male, Mary, 2855
Maledon, George, 2096, 3549
Malesherbes, 2678
Malet, Claude Françoise de, 2096
Malik, A.S., 3260, 3526
Malik, Mustaq, 3302
Malik ibn-Anas, 2096
Malin, Jan, 383
Malinowski, Bronislaw Kasper, 2096
Malinowski, Henry, 828, 1115, 1392
Malins, June Florence, 1194
Mallalieu, Richard Louis, 2096-2097
Malki, Andan al-, 3253
Mallard, John, 2414
Mallard, Robert, 3368
Mallarmé, Stéphane, 3293
Mallary, Rollin C., 133
Mallery, Caleb, 880
Mallett, Jerome, 3452
Mallick, George, 3193
Mallinson, William, 2875
Mallock, George, 3297
Mallock, John, 3297
Mallon, John, 661
Mallon, Kevin, 1254, 3330
Mallon, Peter J., 2966
Mallory, James H., 3169
Mallory, L.P., 3563
Mallory, Wyatt, 3353
Mallowan, Max, 705
Malloy, Everett Baily, 2097
Malloy, Mike, 2123, 2124
Malloy, Snapper Johnny, 2032
Malmed, Erwin S., 2236
Malmedy Massacre, The, 2097
Malmgren, Camille, 624
Malone, Cavan John, 2098
Malone, D., 3355
Malone, Daniel, 3338
Malone, Don V., 2505
Malone, Dorothy, 3196
Malone, Edmund, 1663, 2098
Malone, Hazel, 2098
Malone, James H., 3425
Malone, James "Shooey", 178, 3563
Malone, Kelvin, 3448, 3452
Malone, Vivian J., 3080
Maloney, Daniel, 1546
Maloney, Edward, 1142
Maloney, George, 3387, 3389

Maloney, James, 2098
Maloney, James J., 3426
Maloney, Kathleen, 706
Maloney, Reuben, 2916, 3415
Maloney, Thomas (U.S. pr.1983), 1406,
   1609
Maloney, Tom (U.S. d.1936), 1239
Maloney, William P., 427
Malory, Thomas, 2098
Malott, Jim, 621
Malskat, Lothar, 2098
Maltby, Cecil, 2098, 2177
Maltby, L.U., 596
Maltese, Frank, 2098
Maltese, Stephen, 3407
Malvy, Louis-Jean, 2099
Maly, Ella, 3222
Maly, Lillie, 3222
Mamaea, Julia, 2099
Mamby, Henry, 3563
Mamedzi, Shifulaso, 2099
Mamertinus, Claudius, 2099
Mamesi, Salvatore, 3298
Mammoliti, Saverio, 1304, 3416
Mammoliti, Vincenzo, 1304, 3416
Mamun al, 114, 3236
Man, John, 642
Man in the Attic, 2103
Man Made Anggry, 2104
Man Who Came to Dinner, The, 2113
Mances, 1351
Manchester Gangster Plot, 2099
Manchester Martyrs, 2099
Mancillas, Oscar, 3299
Mancini, Antonio, 2099
Mancini, John, 590
Mancini, Pasquale Stanislao, 2099
Mancini, Tina, 1681
Mancini, Tony, 473, 651, 2062, 2099-2100
Manco Inca Yupanqui, 2100, 3002
Mancusi, Vincent, 180
Mancuso, Antonio, 1304
Mancuso, Rosario, 3407
Mancuso, Thomas, 3407
Mancy, Mitchell E., 3563
Mandame, Mary, 2100
Mandani, Assodollah, 3259, 3274, 3516
Mandel, Georges, 3250
Mandel, Martin, 37
Mandel, Marvin, 2100
Mandel, Robert W., 1069
Mandela, Nelson Rolihlaha, 2101, 2158,
   2197
Mandelbaum, Fredericka, 2101
Mandelbaum, Marm, 1355, 1631
Mandell, John, 516
Mandeville, Alexis, 2101, 2232
Mandeville, Henry, 2101, 2232
Mandeville, Walter, 2101, 2232
Mandic, Karen, 357
Mandin, H.A., 3338
Mandique, M., 3249
Mandroyan, Claude, 1397
Mandusa, 699
Maneri, Salvatore, 3297
Manes, Harlan F., 1182, 3459
Manfield, H.H., 3068
Manfra, Frank, 3215
Manfredi, Tony, 443
Mangan, Hilary R., 1544
Mangano, Angelo, 3416
Mangano, Benjamin, 3407
Mangano, James V. 34
Mangano, John, 3408
Mangano, Lawrence, 2102, 3387, 3389
Mangano, Philip "Philly", 111-112, 118,
   1259, 2102, 3408
Mangano, Vincent, 111, 118, 178, 1259,
   2102, 3140, 3408

Mangham, Arthur, 2102
Mangham, Leonard, 2102
Mangope, Lucas, 3334
Mangovin, Leo, 3383
Manguin, André, 2102
Mangum, Minnie, 2102
Mangunkusumo, Tjipto, 2103
Manhattan Island Sale Swindle, 2103
Manhattan Melodrama, 2103
Maniaci, August, 2960
Maniatis, James "Jimmy the Greek", 2512
Manin, Daniele, 2103
Manina, Robert, 3506
Maning, Frederick Edward, 2103
Manion, Isaac, 3346
Manion, Thomas L., 210
Manipur, 3532
Manipur Liberation Army, 3522
Manisty, 1075
Mankato Massacre, 2103
Mankiller, Smoker, 3563
Mankowitz, George, 3176
Manley, George, 2103
Manley, Robert, 390
Manlius Capitolinus, Marcus, 2104
Manlius Imperiosus Torquatus, Titus, 2104
Mann, Alonzo, 1223
Mann, Anthony, 3453
Mann, Bernard, 2034
Mann, Carl, 1537
Mann, Conrad Henry, 884
Mann, Edward Ames, 2104
Mann, Fletcher, 3455
Mann, Henry, 2104
Mann, Jack, 1253
Mann, James, 412, 3029
Mann, James Robert, 2104
Mann, Jim, 158-159, 1450
Mann, Larry, 3450
Mann, Lynda, 2470, 2471
Mann, Matthew D., 2051
Mann, Michael, 551
Mann, Simranjit Singh, 1261
Mann, William d'Alton, 2104, 2105
Manna, Louis Anthony, 2105, 3408
Mannarino, Gabriel, 136, 3413
Mannichen, David, 2412
Manning, A.B., 1704
Manning, A.E., 3212, 3563
Manning, Alphonse, Jr., 1225
Manning, Carol, 2107
Manning, Clyde, 3168
Manning, Doc, 2106
Manning, Frederick George, 2105
Manning, George "Doc", 2864
Manning, Henry, 2861
Manning, James "Jim", 845, 2106
Manning, James, 2864, 2865, 3546, 3563
Manning, John, 2107
Manning, Laura, 3215
Manning, Maria, 408, 2778
Manning, Thomas William, 2107
Manning, Warren, 3454
Manning, William, 2106
Manningham-Buller, Reginald, 26, 158
Mannlicher, Ferdinand von, 2107
Manno, Patrick, 3387
Manno, Thomas, 3387
Mannoia, Francesco Marino, 3416
MANO, 3328
Mano Blanco, 3532
Manoel, Prince, 626, 627
Manos, John, 2107
Manos, Steve "The Greek", 435
Manotoc, Tommy, 3333
Manrique, Fray Sebastien, 3292
Mansberg, Marvin, 1097
Manse, Castle, 3350
Mansell, Alvin, 2108

Mansfield, Billy, 2056, 2108
Mansfield, Helen Josephine "Josie", 1170, 1352
Mansfield, Katherine, 1406
Mansfield, Lord, 983
Mansfield, Margaret, 159
Mansfield, Walter Roe, 2108
Mansker, Jim, 3563
Manson, Charles, 534, 1195, 1379, 1564, 2032, 2108-2112, 2481, 3257
Manson, Donna Gail, 538
Manson, Lena, 1414
Manson, Rose, 3387
Mansour, Hassan Ali, 3255
Mansour, Shafik, 2835, 3245
Manstein, Fritz Erich von, 2112, 3541
Mansueto, Simone, 2112, 3416
Mansur, Fadlallah Abu, 3252
Mansur, May, 3281
Mantell, Dominic, 2746
Mantia, Robert, 1617
Manton, Bertie, 2710
Manton, Caroline "Rene", 2112
Manton, Horace William, 2112
Manton, Martin Thomas, 526, 2112
Mantua, Mary of, 716
Mantz, Paul, 1052
Manuel, King, 166
Manuel, Peter Thomas Anthony, 2113
Manuel, William, 3359
Manuel Rodriguez Patriotic Front, 2469, 3530, 3532
Manuel Sanchez, 3562
Manufacturing Data Systems, Inc., 3289
Manzanas, Militon, 3256
Manzella, Cesare, 3416
Manzella, John, 1654
Manzi, Vincenzo, 1
Manzie, Frederick, 3387
Manzur, Abul, 3258
Mao Tse-Tung, 678, 702, 3246, 3253
Maple, Frank, 2114
Maples, Dan, 3556
Maples, Horace, 3356
Maples, Sam, 708
Mapp, Mary, 3166
Maquehue, Moises Carril, 3333
Maquer, Chevalier, 2114
Maquiera, Jose, 3450
Mar, Countess of, 2852
Mar, Earl of, 864, 2852, 2853
Mar, Sixth Earl of, 1199
Mara, Carlos, 3244
Mara, Richard, 516
Maraghi, Mustapha El, 3245
Marandel, J. Patrice, 2390
Marangello, Nicholas, 3408
Marangoni, Luigi, 3258, 3510
Marano, 572
Maranzano, Salvatore, 34, 117, 178, 427, 526, 591, 655, 1259, 1295, 1296, 2085, 2102, 2114-2115, 2138-2139, 2217, 3024, 3380, 3402, 3407, 3408, 3410, 3411
Marat, Jean-Paul, 691, 2115, 2117, 3240
Marbeck, John, 2117
Marbury v. Madison, 3100
Marcais, Jacques, 2453
Marcantonio, Vito, 2714
Marceddu, Giovanni, 3520
Marceddu, Tiziana, 3520
Marcel, Etienne, 2117, 3238
Marcel, Louise, 3023
Marcelino, Julian, 2117
Marcella, Anthony, 357, 3412
Marcelle, Joseph P., 3163
Marcello, Anthony, 3297, 3397, 3399
Marcello, Carlos, 104, 282, 454, 634, 1491, 1653, 2085, 2117-2118, 3393, 3398-3400
Marcello, Joseph Jr., 3399

Marcello, Nicholas, 3399
Marcello, Pasquale, 3399
Marcello, Peter, Sr., 3399
Marcello, Peter, Jr., 3399
Marcello, Salvadore, 3399
Marcello, Sam, 3387
Marcello, Vincent, 3399
Marcellus, 1029
Marcellus I, 2118
Marcellus, Marcus Claudius, 2118
Marcelt, Bruno, 1452
Marcepoil, 1291
Marchand, Clothilde, 456
Marchand, Henri, 456
Marchant, Peter A., 2118
Marchena, Joseph, 2681
Marchese, Antonio, 2082
Marchese, Aspero, 2082
Marchese, Carmela, 1105
Marchese, Paulo, 393, 941, 3399
Marchese, Richard, 3413
Marchese, William J., 645
Marchesi, Antonio, 1516, 3339
Marchesi, Asperi, 3399
Marchman, L.C., 3362
Marchone, Pasqualino, 3387
Marcian, 171
Marciniak, John, 1031
Marcinkiewicz, Theodore, 2091
Marcinkus, Paul C., 2118
Marco, Albert, 721, 2118
Marconi, Guglielmo, 663, 1667
Marconi, Michela, 3331
Marcos, Ferdinand Edralin, 139-140, 1152, 2118, 2119, 3054, 3256, 3258, 3333, 3508
Marcos, Imelda Romualdez, 2119, 3256
Marcucci, Noël, 228
Marcum, James B. (U.S. d.1903), 581, 1453, 1723, 2119
Marcum, Thomas, 1453
Marcus Antonius, 3234, 3235
Marcus Antonius Gordianus III, 3235
Marcus Atilius Regulus, 3233
Marcus Aurelius Antoninus, 3235
Marcus Aurelius Carausius, 3235
Marcus Aurelius Numerianus, 3235
Marcus Aurelius Probus, 3235
Marcus Caelius Rufus, 3234
Marcus Claudius Marcellus, 3234
Marcus Claudius Tacitus, 3235
Marcus Clodius Pupienus Maximus, 3235
Marcus Didius Julianus, 3235
Marcus Junius Brutus, 3234
Marcus Licinius Crassus, 3234
Marcus Livius Drusus, 3234
Marcus Otho, 2953
Marcus Perperna, 3234
Marcus Tullius Cicero, 3234
Marcus Valerius Messala Barbatus, 2170
Marcus, Bernard K., 2119
Marcus, David, 1482
Marcus, James L., 781
Marcus, Leonard, 3387
Marcus, Sam, 3387
Marcuso, Angelo, 3348
Marcy, Marvin, 3020
Marcy, William Learned, 2119
Mardian, Robert C., 3100, 3101
Mardirosian, Robert, 1265
Mardonius, 3200
Maréchal, Nanette, 1363
Maréchal, René, 1363
Mare Island Explosion, 2119
Mare Island Mutiny Case, 2119
Marek, Anton, 990
Marek, Emil, 2120
Marek, Ingeborg, 2120
Marek, John R., 3450

Marek, K., 3473
Marek, Martha Lowenstein, 2119
Mares, Hilario, 3563
Marescot, Nicole, 2810
Maret, Hugues Bernard, 2120
Margaret of Anjou, 2120, 2229, 3324
Margaret (Scot. 1240-1275), 2120
Margaret (Scot. 1283-1290), 2120
Margerison, George Frederick, 2120
Marginals, 1635, 3408, 3409
Margiotti, Charles J., 521, 1400
Margolies, Irwin, 2120
Margolies, Madeleine, 2120-2121
Margolis, Henry, 2121
Margolis, Jeremy, 3011
Margrove, Stephen, 2121
Mari, Frank, 3408
Maria, Henrietta, 880, 1348, 2510, 2517
Maria Christina, 2969
Maria Luisa, 2121, 3018
Mariani, Angelo, 3294
Mariani, Paul, 2121, 2122
Marianne the Hasmonaean, 154, 2121
Mariano, Gene, 1049
Marie, Juliane, 2871
Marie Antoinette, 2237
Marie de Medici, 2122
Mariel, Francisco P., 637
Marielitos Riots, 2122
Marighella, Carlos, 2122, 3532
Marigny, Enguerrand de, 2122
Marillac, Louis, 2122
Marin, Jose, 3465
Marin, Therese, 3264
Marina, Fernando, 3246
Marinelli, Giovanni, 2148, 2149
Marinelli, Gualterio, 1663
Marino, Angelo, 3415
Marino, Antonio, 2123
Marino, Arthur, 2123
Marino, Frank, 3463
Marino, Gino, 3416
Marino, James, 2115, 3408
Marino, Joseph "Pepe", 3462
Marino, Lewis, 1654
Marino, Salvatore, 3415
Marino, Tony, 2123-2124, 2256
Marion, J., 3250
Marion, P., 3250
Mariotta, John, 3112
Mariotti, Ignace, 383
Mario Velasquez Fonseca, 3465
Maris, Herbert L., 2124
Maritas, Theodore, 975
Maritz, Salomon Gerhardus, 2124
Marius, 47, 129, 134
Marius, Gaius, 620, 1174, 2729, 2877
Marius Plateau, 3245
Marja, 2124
Marjeram, Albert Edward, 2124
Mark, Reuben, 1041
Mark, Robert, 2124, 3426
Mark, W.J.E., 867
Markert, Louis, 806
Market Streeters, 3387
Market Street Gang, 2124, 2125
Markey, Morris, 1130
Markgraf, 1031
Markham, Baird H. Jr., 2984
Markham, W.F., 3567
Markievicz, Constance Georgine, 2125
Markland, Cliff, 1140
Markle, Fletcher, 2125
Markle, John, 2125
Markov, Georgi, 2125, 3537
Markowitz, Paul, 3458
Markowitz, Rubin, 1146
Markowski, Joseph Edward, 2125
Marks, Ben, 2159

Marks, Charles, 2096
Marks, Claude Daniel, 3169
Marks, Jason, 2434
Marks, Jonathan, 686
Marks, Laurie, 1351
Marks, Lawrence, 2125
Marks, Thomas Albert "Ginger", 1301
Marks, Willie, 179, 614, 2037, 2215, 2660
Marks-Moritz, Leslie, 2782
Markus, Edward Jules, 2125, 3034
Marlborough, Duke of, 689, 713, 1593, 2429
Marley, Kemper, Sr., 29
Marlow, Charles, 2126
Marlow, James, 3448
Marlow Brothers, 3563
Marlowe, Boone, 2126
Marlowe, Christopher, 2126
Marlowe, Epp, 2126
Marlowe, G., 1498
Marlowe, Hugh, 3451
Marlowe, Stephen, 2256
Maroc, Richard, 494
Marochel, Josef, 1018
Maroney, Nathan, 2126
Maroney, Richard, 180
Marovich, George, 763, 2168
Marovitz, William, 2127
Marozia, 3236
Marques, John, 3467
Marquett, Jack, 362, 2127
Marquette, Richard, 2127
"Marquette 10", 2127
Marquez, Alfredo Chavez, 2127
Marquez, Gonzalo, 3448
Marquez, Howard, 3453
Marquez, Mario, 3455
Marquez, Raymond, 3408, 3409
Marquis of Argyll, 2260
Marquis, André, 3541
Marquis, Arthur, 2127
Marr, Robert H., 924
Marr, Timothy, 3162, 3163
Marrera, Ralph R., 2512
Marrero, Alex, 2128
Marriner, J.T., 3249
Marriott, Iris, 806
Marris, Herbert L., 1460
Marritt, John, 3348
Marro, P.F., 1131
Marroto, Rafael, 2469
Marrs, Robert, 2062
Mars, Florence, 458
Marschall, Carl, 134
Marschall, Theresa, 134
Marsden, Crosby, 3549
Marsden, Mary Ann, 1008
Marseilles, Bishop of, 45
Marsh, Asa, 890
Marsh, Elizabeth, 2128
Marsh, F.H., 1312
Marsh, Fred, 2835
Marsh, Frederick H., 3424
Marsh, Ike, 536, 1513, 3189
Marsh, Irving, 273
Marsh, James, 2128, 2509, 3536
Marsh, Luther R., 893, 2672
Marsh, Maud, 682
Marsh, Ngaio, 2128
Marsh, O.C., 1638
Marsh, Randy, 3283
Marsh, Thomas, 2128
Marsh, Thomas John, 1422
Marsh, William, 2129
Marshal, W.A., 24
Marshal, William, 3084
Marshal, Willie, 2129
Marshall, A.P., 179
Marshall, Archie, 710
Marshall, Chadwick, 3349

Marshall, Charles C., 914, 3563
Marshall, Constance, 2130
Marshall, Consuelo Bland, 2129
Marshall, David, 1544
Marshall, Doreen, 1505
Marshall, Douglas, 3207
Marshall, Doyle C., 3068
Marshall, Franklin, 2129
Marshall, Frederick, 2764
Marshall, Gene, 3361
Marshall, George, 3448
Marshall, Grahame James, 1467
Marshall, Harry, 2395
Marshall, Henry, 1108, 2129, 3086
Marshall, Humphrey, 2396, 3304
Marshall, J.E., 236
Marshall, James, 2129
Marshall, Janet, 191
Marshall, Jerome, 3454
Marshall, Jerry J., 3454
Marshall, John (Brit. pr.1806) 1515
Marshall, John (U.S. pr.1807), 555, 1734, 2130, 3097
Marshall, John E. (U.S. pr.1901), 508
Marshall, Lavergne, 3106
Marshall, Leroy, 3462
Marshall, Lindsay Howitt, 2130
Marshall, Matthew, 3450
Marshall, Mattie, 3399
Marshall, Prentice Henry, 1640, 1711, 2130, 2417, 2421, 3165
Marshall, Robert, 3452
Marshall, Ryan, 3448
Marshall, Sam, 3448
Marshall, Thomas F, 3304, 3305
Marshall, Thurgood, 25, 1377, 1665, 2130, 2795, 3090
Marshland, Steve, 3337
Marsin, Daniel Joseph, 3327
Mars-Jones, W.L., 644
Marson, John, 802
Marsowsky, 3176
Marston, Sidney, 3206
Marston, Thomas K., 3469
Mart, John, 1083
Mart, Tom, 3003
Marteinn, 143
Martell, Clark Reid, 2773
Martelletti, Augustin, 2912
Martelli, Lodovico, 3303
Marten, Henry, 2130
Marten, Maria, 783
Martens, Frédéric Frommhold de, 2130
Martens, Peter, 2130
Martenson, Richard, 1146
Martin I, 767
Martin, Albert-Alexandre, 2130, 3337
Martin, Aubrey Wayne "Buddy", 462
Martin, Augustus P., 3424
Martin, Big Jim, 15
Martin, Billy, 551
Martin, Bonnie Lee, 3164
Martin, Boyce Ficklen, Jr., 2131
Martin, Burke, 3338
Martin, Caroline Wardlaw, 3094
Martin, Célestine Camille, 2131
Martin, Charles, 3351, 3563
Martin, Claude, 846
Martin, Cora, 2158
Martin, Cy, 1384
Martin, David, 114, 3447, 3455
Martin, Dennis, 3339
Martin, Fomit, 3347
Martin, François Xavier, 2131
Martin, Gary, 3512
Martin, Genevieve Wren, 596
Martin, Grau San, 2164
Martin, H.B., 1638
Martin, Hymie, 2131, 3394

Martin, Ian, 3329, 3497
Martin, Ida, 1474
Martin, J., 3426
Martin, J.B., 1192
Martin, Jack, 1054
Martin, James, 3351, 3447
Martin, James Loren, 2131
Martin, James Robert, Jr., 1646
Martin, Jim, 2744
Martin, Joe, 3206
Martin, John (d.1886), 216, 2131, 2964, 3356
Martin, John (pr.1900), 3094
Martin, Joseph, 3424
Martin, Julie, 2700
Martin, Kimberly Diane, 357
Martin, Lee Roy, 899, 2131
Martin, LeRoy, 1515, 2132, 3424
Martin, Luis, 3211
Martin, Maria, 597
Martin, Marie, 2708
Martin, Marius, 2132
Martin, Mary Lou, 2132
Martin, Max, 3259, 3520
Martin, May, 2860
Martin, Maybelle "Mabs", 738, 3334
Martin, Michael, 2132, 2999
Martin, Morris, 3387
Martin, Nicholas, 768
Martin, Nina, 2860
Martin, Nollie, 3450
Martin, Oscar, 3364
Martin, Oswald Norman, 157
Martin, Paris T., 421
Martin, Patrick, 3513
Martin, Paul, 2920
Martin, Pete, 1310
Martin, R.A.C., 1700
Martin, Rene, 3461
Martin, Robert (U.S. pr.1879) 3563
Martin, Robert (pr.1960), 887
Martin, Robert H., 2132
Martin, Romeo, 3428
Martin, Ronald Everett, 2052
Martin, Samuel, 2133, 3303, 3338
Martin, Sarah, 2975
Martin, Sherri, 2029
Martin, Susanna, 2666
Martin, Tony, 776
Martin, V., 3248
Martin, White Pine, 3381
Martin, William (U.S. 1858-85), 732
Martin, William (U.S. pr.1930s), 54
Martin, William, 3427
Martin, William G., 3349
Martin, William J. (U.S. pr.1978) 1532
Martin, William "Wild Bill", 3555, 3563, 3564
Martin Diaz, Juan, 2132
Martineau, John E., 2432
Martinelli, Peter, 3379
Martinetti, Paul, 820
Martinetti, Mrs. Paul, 820
Martinex, Candido, 3245
Martinez, Alfredo, 3248, 3558
Martinez, Ana Maria, 3333, 3520
Martinez, Anthony, 2132
Martinez, Antonio, 3343
Martinez, Atanacio, 3563
Martinez, Benizno, 3562
Martinez, Bob, 871
Martinez, Eugenio R., 3099
Martinez, Felix, 3353
Martinez, Francisco, 3565
Martinez, Gilberto, 1525, 3453
Martinez, José Maria, 330
Martinez, Juan, 1622
Martinez, Luis, 2814
Martinez, M., 3467

Martinez, Raymond, 3455
Martinez, Romero, 3143
Martinez, Romulo, 3549
Martinez, Rudy W., 3328
Martinez, Santos, 1583
Martinez de Escobar, Rafael, 3246
Martinez de la Rosa, Francisco de Paula, 2132
Martinez Fernandez, L.J., 3251
Martinez-Villareal, Ramon, 3448
Martinis, Gareth, 2132
Martinis, Joseph A., 1676, 2133
Martins Bank, Ltd., 2133
Martins Bank Robbery, 2133
Martinsen, Carl, 3251
Martinsen, Larry, 2023
Martinson, Oscar, 3425
Martinsville Seven, 2133
Martin-Trigona, Anthony R., 2133
Martinucci, Ivy Winifred, 2133
Martinucci, Piero Maria, 2133
Martinus, 535, 1693, 2133
Martinuzzi, Györgi, 2133, 3238
Martin-Wilkes Duel, 2132, 2133
Martirosoff, Reuben, 1115, 1392
Marti y Perez, José, 1109
Martland, Harrison, 1592
Martorano, George "Cowboy", 3413
Martorano, Raymond, 1149, 3413
Martyn, Wyndham, 2133
Marvell, William, 2133
Marvin, Horace, Sr., 2133
Marvin, Horace, Jr., 2133, 3325
Marvin, L.P. Waldon, 1670
Marvin, Lee, 1513
Marwood, Ronald Henry, 2134
Marwood, William, 348, 579, 2134
Marx, Eileen, 2030
Marx, Groucho, 1178, 2963
Marx, Gustave, 3030-3031, 3387, 3457
Marx, Hugo, 3179
Marx, Joseph, 1625
Marx, Karl, 6, 425, 1610, 2836
Marx, Zeppo, 776
Mary I, 1096, 1151, 2135, 2828, 2864, 2865, 3181
Mary, Queen, 448, 465, 571, 691, 799, 810, 1522, 1609
Mary, Queen of Scots, 872, 887, 930, 1030, 1031, 1083, 1209, 1383, 1405, 1434, 1435, 1522, 1627, 1629, 1630, 2134-2135, 2090, 2427, 2443, 2444, 2768, 2839, 2852, 2853, 2942, 3084, 3239
Mary of Guise, 2853
Mary, Jean, 453
Mary Edward St. George, 3019, 3020
Mary John, 3019
Mary Magdalene, 3019
Mary, Jean, 453
Marymont, Marcus, 2135
Marymont, Mary Helen, 2135
Marzano, Pasquale Charles "Patsy", 2135, 2512
Marzano, William Anthony "Tonye", 2512
Marzek, Sonia, 976
Marzook, Mustafa, 3260, 3523
Mas, Radames, 3408
Masada, Action and Defense Movement, 3267, 3494, 3532
Masaharu, Homma, 3204
Masahisa Takenaka, 3301, 3395
Masaniello, 2135
Masao, Hori, 3395
Masaryk, Jan, 3251
Masaryk, Tomás Garrigue, 2652
Masatoshi Tashiro, 3289
Mascarenas, Richard J., 3471
Mascolino, Sal, 463
Masefield, John, 594

Masferrer, Rolando, 3503
Mashburn, Wiley, 3209
Mashin, Alexander, 81, 973
Mashin, Draga, 75, 78, 80, 81, 82, 84, 395, 973, 1018, 1210
Masih, Tara, 356, 2135
Maskas, Richard, 2990
Mason, Alexander Campbell, 1207, 2135, 2248, 2888
Mason, Alfred, 3132, 3243
Mason, Armistead T., 3305
Mason, Arnold Caverly, 1275
Mason, Barney, 1277, 3549, 3563
Mason, C. Mason, 480
Mason, Carlton, 2136
Mason, Charles, 2136
Mason, David, 3448
Mason, Dolly, 1549
Mason, Ebenezer, 2136
Mason, Mrs. Elizabeth, 186
Mason, Elizabeth, 2136
Mason, Francis Van Wyck, 2136
Mason, Frank, 3357
Mason, George, 3371
Mason, Howard "Pappy", 2025
Mason, Jack, 2184
Mason, James (U.S. d.1894), 3345
Mason, James (U.S. d.1895), 3346
Mason, Jeremiah, 2136
Mason, Joan, 773
Mason, John Archibald Campbell, 2136
Mason, John Young, 2136
Mason, Lewis Jr., 2025
Mason, Morris, 3447
Mason, Noble B., 3466
Mason, Oscar, 3450
Mason, Pamela, 773
Mason, Samuel, 2136, 3400
Mason, William, 735
Mason, Winnie, 3132, 3243
Mason County War, 2137
Mason v. Haile, 3097
Mason y Serrate, Jesus, 3464
Masri, Zafr al-, 3261
Mass, Cecil Wallace, 1336
Massacer, John, 2819
Massachusetts Convent Burning, 3373
Massachusetts State Police, 3289
Massagee, George, 3563
Massei, Joseph, 3392, 3393
Masselli, William P., 1001
Masseria, Giuseppe "Joe the Boss", 32, 34, 117, 120, 178, 427, 591, 655, 1259, 1295, 2085, 2114, 2217, 2137-2139, 3024, 3025, 3402, 3404, 3405, 3407, 3408, 3411
Massers, Emilio, 3027
Massett, Louise, 362, 2139
Massey, Jim, 1473
Massey, R.J., 1372
Massey, Robert L., 2390
Massie, Robert, 3448
Massie, Thalia, 2139, 2140, 2142
Massie, Thomas, 1200, 2139, 2140, 2142, 3375
Massie, Thornton L., 94, 3458
Massie, William Rodney, 1537
Massina, Joseph, 3408
Massinbach, Christian von und du, 2137
Massinissa, 3233
Massiva, 3234
Massotta, Thomas, 3408
Massouemi, Anselme, 3255
Mass Sedition Trial, 2137
Massu, J., 3253
Mast, Dannielle Tyece, 2142
Mast, Harold, 113
Mast, Milton, 3545, 3549
Mast, Randi, 113

Master, Karen, 886
Masterberg, Hugo, 2396
Masters, Alan, 2142
Masters, Alex, 2721
Masters, Dianne G., 2142
Masters, Eugene, 2842
Masters, Paul, 1149
Masters, Robert, 1457
Masterson, Catherine, 2143
Masterson, Edward J., 2143, 2144, 3544, 3549, 3563
Masterson, James, 878, 1056, 2143, 2144, 2732, 3549, 3563
Masterson, Mike, 621
Masterson, "Paddy", 3387
Masterson, Robert, 3549, 3563
Masterson, Thomas, 2143
Masterson, William Barclay "Bat", 277, 315, 317, 720, 799, 1044, 1056, 1627, 2143-2146, 2399, 2727, 2748, 2749, 2795, 2855, 2864, 2933, 2936, 3544, 3549, 3551, 3556, 3563, 3566, 3567
Mastocciolo, Joseph A., 1229-1230
Mastrian, Norman, 2935, 2936
Mastriana, Louis "the Doctor", 3175
Mastrotaro, Carlo, 3379
Mast Tree Riot, 2145, 3370
Masud, Muhammad, 3252
Masuku, Lookout, 3521
Mata, Luis, 3448
Mata, Ramon, 3455
Mataino, Giuseppe, 2080
Matanic, Peter, 560, 3471
Matarello, Caspar, 892
Match King, The, 2145
Matecki, Wayne, 844
Matera, Pietro, 2145
Mates, Ian, 3508
Matesi, Francesco, 941
Mathenia, Charles Lee, 3452
Mather, Cotton, 475, 559, 2124, 2145, 2146, 2445, 2664, 2666-2668, 2670
Mather, Dave H., 2145, 2146
Mather, Emily, 900
Mather, Increase, 2146, 2672, 3227
Mather, Mysterious Dave, 3067
Mathers, David, 3549, 3563
Mathers, Jimmy Lee, 3448
Mathers, Joanna, 3511
Matheson, Duncan, 150
Matheson, Herbert, 2146
Mathewe, William, 1642
Mathews, Charles, 894, 2146, 2712
Mathews, Clifton, 2146
Mathews, John M., Jr., 3469
Mathews, Ralph, 2422
Mathews, Robert, 2146, 2147, 2150
Mathias, Oscar, 3563
Mathis, Columbus, 2147
Mathis, Darlene, 2147
Mathis, Emile E.C., 3460
Mathis, James, 3450
Mathis, James H., 2147
Mathis, James R., 2147
Mathis, Jean, 3027
Mathis, Louis, 1190, 3283, 3462
Mathis, Mary, 1356
Mathis, Preston, 1409
Mathis, R. William, 1549, 2480
Mathu, Eliud, 2152
Matilda, 2147
Matilda, Caroline, 2871
Mationg, Florencio Lopez, 2147
Matisse, 2098
Matlick, Jack, 464
Matos Guerra, Gregrio de, 2147
Matranga, Anthony "Tony", 2082, 2147, 3400
Matranga, Charles "Millionaire Charlie",

634, 1516, 2082, 2147, 3398, 3400
Matras, Jean, 2122
Matricon, 1746
Matrisciano, George, 394, 3387
Matsell, Baron, 802
Matsokota, Lazare, 3255
Matson, Jesse, 3360
Matson, John, Jr., 3455
Matson, Mark, 522, 3329
Matson, Michael, 3454
Matsuba-kai, 3395
Matsuda-gumi, 3395
Matsui Iwane, 3541
Matsukichi Tsumaki, 2998
Matt, Frank, 1307
Matta Ballesteros, Juan Ramón, 1147, 1651,
   2147, 3397
Mattar, Nazeh, 3523
Mattas, Donald James, 3198
Matteotti, Giacomo, 1034, 2124, 2148, 2264,
   3245
Mattern, William K., 2246
Matthau, Walter, 2989
Mattheis, Valorus, 2149
Matthews, Billy, 2177, 3071
Matthews, Blanche Mary, 1070
Matthews, Burnita Shelton, 484
Matthews, C.J., 2049
Matthews, Charles, 290, 566, 1523, 1597
Matthews, David Wayne, 2795, 3451
Matthews, Dorothea, 1289
Matthews, Earl, 3454
Matthews, Edward, 773
Matthews, Frank "Pee Wee", 3298, 3299,
   3549
Matthews, George, 1366
Matthews, Harold, 2459
Matthews, Henry, 2156
Matthews, J.B., 364
Matthews, Jacob B., 2149, 3549, 3563
Matthews, John W., 1715
Matthews, Jonathan, 2249
Matthews, Kevin, 3454
Matthews, Mabel, 2489
Matthews, Robert (Brit. pr.1955), 1344
Matthews, Robert (U.S. d.1910), 3360, 3361
Matthews, Robert (U.S. d.1984), 341
Matthews, Rod, 2149
Matthews, Stanley, 485, 2150
Matthews, T.S., 2975
Matthews, Warner, 814, 3352
Matthews, William, 366
Matthias, Peter, 1745
Matthias, Vivian, 2183
Mattio, Thomas, 3298
Mattioli, Ercole Antonio, 2150
Mattison, Carl, 762, 763
Mattox, Jon, 2150
Mattox, Ursula, 465
Mattson, Charles, 2150, 3326
Mattson, Michael, 3448
Mattson, W.W., 2150
Mattu, Salvatore, 2261
Matulla, John, 2150
Matulla Murders, 2150
Matura, Gregory F., 92
Mature, Victor, 2234
Matuschka, Sylvestre, 2150
Matusek, Joseph, 2822
Matusek, Patricia, 2822
Matuska, James, 1415
Matyalana, Douglas, 1046
Matysek, Stanley, 3014
Mau Mau, 2151-2153, 2261
Maude, John Cyril, 1000, 1310, 2151
Maudsley, Henry, 2151
Maugerin, 3303
Maugerin-Riberac Duel, 2151
Maugham, Somerset, 838

Maul, Franklin C., 891
Maulden, Charles, 3450
Maulding, Reginald, 1585
Maule, A.C., 3252
Maumovic, Colonel, 81, 82
Maunders, Cyril Edward, 2153
Maung Maung, 415, 3240
Maupin, Joseph, 2028
Maura y Montaner, Antonio, 1152
Maurer, Robert, 3245
Mauriac, Franois, 2450
Maurice, Emil, 1572
Maurice, William, 2153
Mauricius, 2153, 3236
Mauriot, Nadine, 2203
Mauro, Vincent, 3297
Mauro Hoyos, Carlos, 1633
Maurras, Charles, 2475, 3541
Maury, Harry, 3305
Mauser, Peter Paul, 2153
Maverick, Samuel, 446
Mavor, Osborne Henry, 120, 2778
Mavromichalis, Petros, 2153
Maw, Will, 2153
Mawbey, John, 1353, 1426
Mawer, Peter, 3170
Mawson, Pieter, 1079
Maxentius, 657, 2118, 2153
Maxey, George W., 1400
Maxey, John, 3359
Maxfield, W.J., 3364
Maxim, Hiram Percy, 1098, 2153
Maxim, Hiram Stevens, 2153
Maxim, Hudson, 2153
Maximian I, 167, 205, 767, 976, 2077,
   2153, 2163, 2189, 2932, 3090, 3235,
   3241
Maximilian, Duke of Bavaria, 3227
Maximiliano Hernandez Martinez, 3255
Maximinus, Gaius Julius Verus, 2154,
   2485
Maximo Mena Command, 3267
Maximus, 996, 1364, 2154, 3235
Maximus Daia, 3235
Maxon, Joe, 1404
Maxon, Leroy J., 2931
Maxwell, Andrew, 3451
Maxwell, Bill, 2782
Maxwell, Bloody, 3382
Maxwell, Bobby Joe, 2154
Maxwell, C.G., 253
Maxwell, C.L., 3077
Maxwell, Chester, 3450
Maxwell, David, 1418
Maxwell, Deluvina, 368
Maxwell, Edith, 2154
Maxwell, Fred, 3454
Maxwell, Gunplay, 651
Maxwell, Jacqueline, 774
Maxwell, John (Scot. 1586-1612), 2154
Maxwell, John Crawford, 3498
Maxwell, Mary, 2154
Maxwell, Peter Menard, 1278, 2235, 3554,
   3563
Maxwell, Robert Earl, 2154
Maxwell, Walter Lennox, 499
Maxwell, William, 2154
Maxwell Street Police Station, 2154
May, Andrew Jackson, 1280
May, Boone, 388, 3554, 3563
May, Catherine, 2941, 2942
May, Clayton, 2154
May, Dorothy, 1675
May, Elvira, 1239
May, Frederick, 807, 3305
May, George, 1539
May, Jeannette, 2154
May, John, 614, 2660, 3387
May, Justin Lee, 3455

May, Keith Joseph, 3331
May, Leonard, 2719
May, Louis, 1193
May, Luke S., 800
May, Robert, 694
May, Robert Earl, Jr., 2155
May, Shauna, 1549, 2480
May, Stephen, 2154
May Arab Movement for the Liberation of
   Palestine, 3273, 3274
May Day Riots, 3375
Maybaum, Charles, 3387
Maybaum, Julius, 3387
Mayberry, David F., 2155
Mayberry, Harvey, 3347
Mayberry, Martin, 3340
Maybrick, Edwin, 2156
Maybrick, Florence Elizabeth, 2155-2157,
   2850, 3536
Maybrick, James, 2155, 2156
Maybrick, Michael, 2156, 2157
Maycotte, Fortunato, 3245
Mayer, Earl, 2800
Mayer, Edwin Justus, 699
Mayer, George, 3166
Mayer, Julius, 1333, 2157
Mayer, Lucien Joseph, 461, 3380
Mayer, Mabel, 2157
Mayer, Max, 1369, 1391, 1659
Mayer, Norman, 3279, 3301
Mayer, Robert, 2157
Mayer, Wilhelm, 294
Mayes, Ed, 3353
Mayes, Richard "Dic", 3343, 3353
Mayeski, John, 1463
Mayfair Playboys, 2157
Mayfield, Demetrie, 3448
Mayfield, Dennis, 3448
Mayfield, I.D., 3355
Mayfield, John, 158
Mayfield Road Mob, 3392
Mayhall, Ward, 954
Mayhue, Fred, 3454
Maynard, Anson, 3453
Maynard, Curtis, 1589
Maynard, Edward, 2157
Maynard, Sam, 2185
Maynard, Thomas, 2157
Maynard, William A., 2157
Maynard, William John, 2158
Mayne, Mary, 3090, 3091
Mayne, Richard, 2710, 3426
Maynor, Alex, 3107
Mayo, Asey, 2902
Mayo, Joseph, 481
Mayo, Randy, 3455
Mays, Fannie, 734
Mays, Nobel, 3455
Mazarei, Alimaghi Bahman 3300
Mazarin, 454, 910, 1238,
Mazarin, Duchess of, 3180
Mazepa, Ivan Stepanovich, 2158
Maze Prison, 1664
Mazer, Richard, 1513
Mazin, Max, 3257
Mazin Abu Khalil, 3257, 3468
Mazuera, H.J., 3252
Mazur, J.R., 378
Mazzanars, Lawrence "Tiny", 435
Mazzara, Gaetano, 3408
Mazzella, Chris, 3156
Mazzen, John, 3452
Mazzie, Rocco, 3408
Mazzini, Giuseppe, 2158
Mazzoli, Frank, 1655
Mazzoli, Mike, 1655
Mazzoli, Pearl, 1655
Mazzoli, Theresa, 1655
Mazzone, A. David, 2158

Mazzotti, Cristina, 3330
Mazzurco, Salvatore, 2473, 3408
Mbeki, Govan, 2158
Mboya, Tom, 3256
Meacham, Albert B., 619
Meacham, Craig, 3208
Meacham, Jeremiah, 2158
Meachum, Joseph, 2158
Mead, Cowles, 555
Mead, Elmer, 2158, 2159
Mead, George, 2158, 3457
Mead, Henry, 2866
Mead, Simeon, 889
Mead, William Elmer, 1243, 2158
Meade, P., 3244
Meade, Thomas, 2159
Meade, William Kidder, 3549, 3563
Meador, John, 2884
Meadows, Alberta, 2458
Meadows, Alice, 331, 332
Meadows, "Buck", 562
Meadows, Catherine, 981, 1236
Meadows, Evelyn, 711
Meadows, George, 3337
Meadows, John, 3350
Meager, Michael, 1054
Meagher, John, 2744
Meagher, Mike, 2159, 2744
Meagher, Thomas Francis, 2159
Mealey, Michael, 3425
Mealli, Michael, 2217
Meanes, James R., 3455
Meaney, Thomas, 1000, 2053
Means, Bevo, 389
Means, Gaston Bullock, 554, 1144, 1479,
    1612, 2159, 2911
Means, Russell, 3500, 3502
Means, Colonel Thomas, 3563
Mears, P., 1544
Mecham, Evan, 2160
Mechelin, Leo, 2160
Mechene, Merritt Cramer, 2160
Medad M'Kay, 2047
Medalie, George Z., 932, 2686
Medeiros, Jose, 2762
Medeiros, Virgilio, 2762
Medellin Murders, 2161
Meders, Jimmy F., 3450
Medici, Alessandro, 2161, 3238
Medici, Catherine de, 1517
Medici, Giuliano, 3238
Medici, Lorenzino, 2161, 3238
Medill, Joseph, 1464
Medina, Carlos, 3211
Medina, Ernest L., 207, 2161, 2272-2273
Medina, Harold R., 763
Medina, Javier, 3455
Medina, Mrs. Mario, 3063
Medina, Pedro, 3450
Medina, Teofilo, 3449
Medina Perez, Luis, 3279, 3465
Medley, Joseph Dunbar, 1166, 2161
Medlock, John, 3563
Medran, Florentino, 3563
Medrano, Angel, 3448
Mee, John Lester, 2695
Meeghan, George, 2037, 3382, 3387
Meehan, Colm, 3523
Meehan, Dinny, 3140, 3408, 3412
Meehan, Eamon, 3523
Meehan, G. Thomas, 709
Meehan, Leslie, 2795
Meehan, Martin, 981
Meehan, Red Shay, 3408
Meehan, W.J., 3425
Meek, Howard, 2161
Meeker, Nathan Cook, 2162
Meekins, Frank, 1123
Meeks, Alexander H., 3158

Meeks, Bob, 652
Meeks, Douglas, 3450
Meeks, Henry Wilbur, 3563
Meeks, Ira D., 3468
Meenahan, Joseph, 1250
Meese, Edwin, III, 2162, 3112
Meetze, Dub, 3343
Meff, John, 2162
Megabyzus, 2162
Megna, Joe, 1181
Megna, Mike, 2162
Mehaffy, Pat, 2162
Meharg, William, 3278
Mehdawi, Omran el-, 3258
Mehemaet Ali Pasha, 2162
Mehmed II, 41, 663
Mehmed IV, 2251
Mehmed, Emin, 1091
Mehmedbasic, Mohammed, 1213, 1214
Mehmet Ali Agca, 3334
Mehrtens, William, 463
Meier, John, 1666
Meier, Louis, 560
Meigs, Return Johnathan, 2162
Mein, John Gordon, 3327, 3479
Meinhof, Ulricke Marie, 195, 196, 199,
    202, 525, 3475, 3476, 3483, 3493, 3501,
    3502, 3504, 3505, 3508, 3516, 3529
Meins, Hölger Klaus, 198, 200, 202, 1750,
    3475
Meinster, Robert Jay, 2163, 2475
Meir, Golda, 1081, 1225, 3497
Meiraki-gumi, 3395
Meir of Rothenburg, 2163
Meiselas, Susan, 3508
Meisner, Michael, 1512
Meisonnier, Ottilie, 294
Mejia, Marcelos, 3246
Mejia, Tomás, 2163, 3241
Mejia Milian, Fluvio Alirio, 3512
Mekler, Michael, 2163
Melanchthon, Philipp, 2458
Melando, Mary, 2198
Melbourne, Lord, 844
Melcher, Terry, 2110
Melcher, Tommy R., 2699
Melchers, Paulus, 2163
Melchert, Peter, 2163
Melchione, John, 2123
Melchiorre, Gene, 273
Melcy-Castlereagh Duel, 2164
Meldrum, Bob, 2164
Mele, Charles, 919
Mele, Stefano, 2202
Melendez, George, 107, 1075
Melendez, Juan Roberto, 3450
Melford, Charles, 1715
Melgar, José, 665
Melgarejo, Luis, 3467
Meli, Angelo, 3393
Meli, Frank, 3393
Meli, Salvatore Angelo, 3393
Meli, Vincent, 3393
Melia, Aloysius J., 343, 1040, 1676
Melke, Gary Dean, 2767
Melker, Robert, 3368
Mella, Julio Antonio, 3246
Mellant-Lenfant Duel, 2164
Mellen, Jim, 3107
Mellett, Don R., 1398, 3246
Mellis, Teresa, 2097
Mellon, Andrew W., 616, 1679
Mellon, Arthur, 2160
Mellor, David, 1655
Melmine, Bill, 234
Melo, Francisco Manuel de, 2164
Melock, Robert, 3451
Meloy, Francis, Jr., 3257
Melson, Hugh, 3454

Melton, Ernest, 771, 1335
Melton, James, 3449
Melton, Lydia, 1459
Melton, Tracy, 2164, 3300
Melton, Wash, 3348
Melton, William, 2164, 3300
Meltzer, Harold, 3397
Melville, Andrew, 2164
Melville, Herman, 2221
Melville, Sam, 3482, 3483
Melville, William, 2415
Melvin, Charley, 582
Melvin, E.M., 3364
Melvin, William, 1353
Membre, Zenobius, 2164
Memorial Day Massacre, 2164, 3375
Memro, Harold, 3449
Mena, Luis, 3246
Mena Prez, Julio L., 3467
Menasci, Cesare, 3333, 3513
Mencher, Bruce S., 1651
Menchine, W. Albert, 1312
Mencken, August, 3178
Mencken, H.L., 676, 876, 1549
Menczer, Augustus, 3563
Mendelsohn, Dave, 306
Mendenhall, Edward J., 793
Mendez, A.M. Garcia, 3249
Mendez, Ernesto V., 3246
Mendez, Francisco, 783
Mendez, Ricardo, 3333, 3524
Mendez, Roquelino Recinos, 3333, 3516
Mendez Lopez, Carlos Humberto, 3258,
    3513
Mendez Montenegro, Mario, 3255
Mendez-Vargas, Radhames, 3465
Mendieta, Carlos, 1399, 2164, 3248
Mendival, Salvador, 1253
Mendizabal, Manuel Aristimuno, 3511
Mendleson, Anna, 128
Mendola, Guy, 576
Mendoza, Benjamin y Amor, 2427, 3256
Mendoza, Manuel, 3449
Mendoza de la Cerda, Ana, 2164
Mendoza Viera, Irardo, 3466
Mendés-France, Pierre, 2164
Mendyk, Todd, 3450
Menéndez, Bernardo, 3249
Menendez, G., 3242
Menendez, Jose P., 3464
Menesclou, Louis, 2165
Ménétret, Elodie, 2166
Mengele, Dieter, 2166
Mengele, Josef, 2165-2166, 3148, 3541
Mengistu Haile Mariam, 3257
Meng Shen, 3291
Menifee, John, 3305
Menken, Adah Bertha 2166
Menndez de Avils, Pedro, 2165
Mennini, Luigi, 2118
Menocal, Garcia, 2164
Menominee Warrior Society, 3501, 3504,
    3532
Menoni, Hector, 3328, 3493
Menotti, Ciro, 2166
Mensinger, George, 1084
Menten, Pieter, 2166
Mentot, Philibert, 3041
Menzies, Ralph W., 3456
Mephistopheles, 1731
Meppen, Adele, 3176-3177
Meras, Nica, 3563
Mercado, Rosa, 2997
Mercado, Ruth Rita, 1321
Mercer, George "Tiny", 3447
Mercer, George, IV, 1456
Mercer, William, 3350
Merchant, George, 175
Merchant, Jay, 849

Mihalache, Ion, 2177
Mihelich, Kristine, 929
Mika, Daniel, 2674
Mikasevich, Gennadiy, 2177
Mike, Sheeney, 1044
Mikell, William, 3454
Mikenas, Mark, 3450
Mikhailoff, P., 3245
Mikhailov, Timofey, 88
Mikhailovich, Nikolai, 3244
Mikhaylovsky, Nikolay Konstantinovich, 2178
Milam, J.W., 2178
Milam, Jim, 1237
Milan Bank Robbery, 2178
Milan, Duke of, 2732
Milan, King, 78, 80-83
Milani, Joseph Harry, 2178
Milani, Paul, 2178
Milano, Anthony, 3397
Milano, Antonio, 2483, 3392
Milano, Bobby, 2178
Milano, Carmen, 2178
Milano, Eugene, 3412, 3413
Milano, Frank, 857, 2483, 3392
Milano, Gaetano J., 3379
Milano, Jerry, 3392
Milano, Joseph, 2056
Milano, Nicholas, 3413
Milano, Peter John, 2178, 3397
Milano, Tony, 857
Milanoff, Elena, 1336
Milanoff, Steffy, 1336
Milas, Wilhelm, 990
Milazzo, Frank, 2178
Milazzo, Gaspar, 2086, 3219
Milburn, John G., 2051
Milburn, Mary, 1249
Milch, Eberhard, 3541
Mileff, N., 3245
Miles, A.F., 946
Miles, Albert, 3257
Miles, Clyde, 23-24, 583
Miles, Edward, 2179
Miles, Frank, 1689
Miles, Hod, 3549
Miles, John, 3359
Miles, John L., 3009, 3122
Miles, Julia Branch, 2904
Miles, Moses, 2027, 2802
Miles, Nellie, 23-25, 583
Miles, Nelson, 1730, 2143, 3133, 3192, 3556
Miles, P.C., 806
Miles, Reginald, 2048
Miles, Robert, 562
Miles, Sydney, 3461
Miles, Tom, 3361
Miles, Vivian, 2463
Miles, Wendell Alverson, 2179
Miles, William, 3347
Milescu, Nicolae, 2179
Miley, Greg, 429
Miley, James, 3348
Milgazo, F.F., 2179
Milgram, Arthur, 2179, 3408
Milian, Fluvio Alirio Mejia, 3333
Milic, Jan, 2179
Militant Jewish Defense League, 3520, 3532
Military Sports Group Hoffman, 3532
Milk, Harvey, 3137, 3257, 3377
Milken, Michael R., 418
Milkovic, Captain, 82
Milkowski, Zygmunt, 2179
Millain, Jean Marie, 535, 2179
Millain, John, 2179
Milland, Ray, 2812
Millard, Frederick William, 2869
Millard, George, 3549
Millard, Zoe, 3387

Millen, Irving, 2179
Millen, Murton, 2179
Millen, Norma Brighton, 2179
Miller, Adrian H., 2179
Miller, Alice, 3212
Miller, Amos, 3341
Miller, Andrew, 2180
Miller, Andrew Galbraith, 2180
Miller, Arthur, 2201
Miller, Beth, 222
Miller, Bill "The Killer", 1183, 2180
Miller, Bob, 3387
Miller, Bruce, 820, 822
Miller, Charles (U.S. pr.1960s) 1240
Miller, Charles (U.S. pr.1896) 2180, 3341, 3343, 3357
Miller, Charles H. (U.S. pr.1920s), 378
Miller, Charles P., 3400, 3408
Miller, Charlotte, 2180
Miller, Clark, 1021
Miller, Clell, 1700-1702, 1704, 3212, 3564
Miller, Cleona, 2862
Miller, Craig, 1255
Miller, C.W. "Jake", 465
Miller, David, 3454
Miller, Davy "Yiddles", 2218, 3387
Miller, Donald, 3449, 3455
Miller, Doris Denise, 1467
Miller, "Dutch Gus", 713
Miller, Ed (U.S. pr.1870s), 1700, 1701, 1704, 1706
Miller, Eddie (Can. pr.1950), 1363
Miller, Eddie Lee, 3448
Miller, E.J., 60
Miller, Eli, 3564
Miller, Emily, 28
Miller, Eugen 2180
Miller, Florence, 2990
Miller, Frank, 2180, 3407, 3413
Miller, Fred, 1500
Miller, Frederick Alvah, 704
Miller, Garry, 3455
Miller, Gene, 1440, Gene, 2738
Miller, George (pr.1875), 2180, 3387
Miller, George (pr.1925), 2213
Miller, George (pr.1933), 952
Miller, Gertrude, 1282
Miller, Gordon E., 2182
Miller, Heinrich "Big Heinie", 1027, 3382, 3387
Miller, Helen, 391
Miller, Henry, 1302, 2186
Miller, Herbert J., 893
Miller, Herschel "Hershie", 2230
Miller, Hilda, 2180
Miller, Horace H., 3046
Miller, Howard, 1164
Miller, Irene, 1136
Miller, Jack, 425
Miller, Jack Jr., 3332
Miller, Jacqueline, 1510
Miller, James (Brit. pr.1876), 244
Miller, James (U.S. pr.1870s), 1054
Miller, James Alfred, 3520
Miller, James B., 2181, 3545, 3547, 3549
Miller, James P., 3564
Miller, J.B., 3359
Miller, J.H., 3197
Miller, Jean, 2708
Miller, Jesse, 3341, 3564
Miller, Jim "Deacon" (U.S. pr.1890s), 1204, 1229, 1278, 3553, 3559
Miller, Jim "The Killer", 96, 729, 751, 2181, 2727
Miller, Joaquin, 2182
Miller, Joe, 500, 3461
Miller, John (U.S. pr.1858), 1679, 2182, 3246, 3549
Miller, John (U.S. pr.1921), 24

Miller, Captain John, 3564
Miller, Johnson, 3353
Miller, Joseph, 623, 3408
Miller, Judas, 3344
Miller, Judith Lynn, 356
Miller, Justin, 2182
Miller, Kathryn, 869
Miller, "Kid", 2032, 3387
Miller, Lee, 221
Miller, Lillian, 3332
Miller, Lloyd Eldon, Jr., 2182
Miller, Lucille, 2182
Miller, Magdalene, 2467
Miller, Marguerite, 2182
Miller, Mary, 3387
Miller, Mary Jo, 3197
Miller, May, 806
Miller, Mayshe, 3363
Miller, Michael, 3450
Miller, Myra, 1164
Miller, Norman, 2252
Miller, Otis, 3348
Miller, Richard, 1036
Miller, Robert, 25
Miller, Robert Ingersoll, 2182
Miller, Robert John, 2404
Miller, Robert Lee, 3453
Miller, Robin, 1734
Miller, Ruby, 813
Miller, S.C., 3564
Miller, Samuel "Gameboy", 506, 3392
Miller, Samuel Freeman, 2182
Miller, Samuel R., 3424
Miller, Squint, 183
Miller, Susie, 407
Miller, T.O., 2048
Miller, Theodore G., 884
Miller, Thomas, 133
Miller, Thomas W., 2911
Miller, Vernon C., 183, 209, 239, 1186, 1545, 2182-2183, 2440, 3396, 3459
Miller, Wallace, 3360
Miller, Walter, 2183
Miller, "Wild Bill", 3564
Miller, William (b.1799), 2183
Miller, William (pr.1920), 2805
Miller, William (d.1909), 3359
Miller, William A., 58, 62, 63, 66
Miller, William F., 115
Miller, William Franklin, 2184, 2486
Miller, William Henry Harrison 2184
Miller, Winifred, 1675
Miller-El, Thomas Joe, 3455
Millet, Jean Francois, 1398
Millie, Joseph, 422
Milligan, Lambdin P., 2887
Milligan, Ronnie Gayle, 3452
Milligan, Rosa, 1001
Milliken, John T., 2421
Milliken, Paul M., 3424
Millin, Sarah Gertrude, 2941
Millington, Frank C. 2184
Millington, Mary 2184
Million, Roger, 3113, 3114
Millman, Harry, 2254, 2868
Millner, Booker T., 2133
Millot, Michael G., 2408
Mills, Alexander H., 3564
Mills, Ballard, 2185
Mills, Charlotte, 1431
Mills, Cope, 3360
Mills, Dorothy, 2184
Mills, Eleanor Reinhardt, 1428-31
Mills, Ellen, 1388
Mills, Fred, 2185
Mills, George, 3351
Mills, Gregory, 3450
Mills, Herbert Leonard, 2184
Mills, Jacqueline Smith, 2395, 2440

Montgomery, Richard, 161
Montgomery, Robert, 2205-2206
Montgomery, Robert Morris, 2206
Montgomery, Samuel, 3509
Montgomery, T.H., 2206
Montgomery, Ulece, 3451
Montholon, Charles Tristan de 2206
Monti, James, 870
Montiel, Richard, 3449
Montieth, Robert, 649
Montieth, William, 656
Montjeau, Louis, 3560
Montmorency, Anne Marie Louise d'Orlans, 2206
Montmorency, Filips van 2206
Montmorency, Henri II de 2206
Montmorency-Bouteville, François-Henri de 2206
Montone, Nicholas, 2686
Montoneros, Juan Jose Valle, 3532
Montos, Nick George, 2206
Montoya, Alfred, 2147
Montoya, Cypriano, 3566
Montoya, Harold, 2147
Montoya, Irineo, 3455
Montoya, Jose F., 3564
Montoya, Narciso, 3564
Montoya, Ramon, 3455, 3564
Montrose, James Graham, 2206, 3335
Montrose, Marquis of, 1356, 1357
Montúfar y Rivera Maestre, Lorenzo, 2206
Montvoisin, Antoine, 2206
Montvoisin, Catherine, 2206
Monument, John, 658
Monvoisin, Antoine, 924
Monvoisin, Marguerite, 925
Monzer Soleiman Khalifa, 2894
Monzingo, B.B., 259
Monzon, Telesforo, 315
Moo, John, 1402, 1404
Moodie, Anita, 2206
Moodie, Duncan, 2206-2207
Moody, Anne Maria, 2261
Moody, Bill, 2979, 3567
Moody, Daniel, 441, 2049, 3181
Moody, Gideon Curtis, 2207
Moody, James, 1715
Moody, John, 3353, 3455
Moody, Samuel, 3339
Moody, W. Osborne, 2411
Moody, William Henry, 2207
Moon, Edward, 865
Moon, Jim, 3564
Moon, Larry Eugene, 3450
Moon, Norman, 2207
Moon, Sun Myung 2207
Moon, Susan, 891
Moon, William, 3424
Moonen, Mary, 192
Moonen, Matthias, 192
Mooney, Bernard, 2207
Mooney, Bob 1255
Mooney, Mary, 2207
Mooney, Michael, 1559
Mooney, Nelson W., 3455
Mooney, Rena, 2208
Mooney, Thomas Jeremiah, 1498, 2207-2209, 3263
Mooneyhon, W.J., 3355
Moonlight Murderer, 2209
Moonstone, The, 2209
Moony, Gayle, 3331
Moor, Charles, 1462
Moore, A. Harry, 1431
Moore, Albert, 183
Moore, Alfred (Brit., 1915-52), 2209
Moore, Alfred (U.S., 1755-1810), 2209
Moore, Alvin, 3447
Moore, Alvin, Jr., 1321

Moore, Andrew M., 3424
Moore, Andrew W., 3424
Moore, Arch A. Jr., 1339
Moore, Arthur C., 3424
Moore, Belle, 2209
Moore, Bob, 3029
Moore, Bob, Jr., 1637
Moore, Bobby James, 3455
Moore, Brian Keith, 3451
Moore, Brian Steven, 2209
Moore, Carey, 3452
Moore, Carzell, 3450
Moore, Cecil, 634
Moore, Charles (Brit. b.1817), 340, 2209-2210
Moore, Charles (pr.1980s), 3449
Moore, Cory C., 2210
Moore, Curt, 398
Moore, David, 3352
Moore, Dennis Albert Reginald, 2210
Moore, Dewey, 3453
Moore, Donald P., 840
Moore, Edward, 3388
Moore, Elizabeth, 1048
Moore, Emmanuel A., 1239
Moore, Ernest, 2698
Moore, Eugene, 253
Moore, Eugenia, 860, 862
Moore, Flossie, 849, 2210, 3388
Moore, Fred, 2650, 3367
Moore, Freddy, 3367
Moore, Frederick, 3350
Moore, Gallow May, 594
Moore, George (Brit. d.1854), 266
Moore, George (U.S. pr.1901), 1030
Moore, George (U.S. pr.1930s), 716
Moore, George (pr.1980s), 3453
Moore, George Curtis, 3256, 3495
Moore, Georgina, 2428
Moore, H. Paul, 1093, 1095
Moore, Hutchie T., 2210, 3261
Moore, Irene, 1731, 2210
Moore, J.E. "Screwy", 716
Moore, Jack, 2059
Moore, Jack Carlson "Clayton", 3208
Moore, James E., 3173
Moore, James Vernell, 2210
Moore, Jeff B., 3549
Moore, Joe, 421
Moore, John (d. 1695), 2210
Moore, John (d. 1906), 3357
Moore, John (d. 1911), 3361
Moore, John (pr.1896), 3549
Moore, John Bassett, 2210
Moore, Joseph, 3361
Moore, Kenneth, 3425
Moore, Kit, 1636
Moore, La Verne, 2211
Moore, Langdon W., 2210-2211
Moore, Leonard Page, 2211
Moore, Lester, 3564
Moore, Lloyd J., 2211
Moore, Lucy, 1167
Moore, Manuel, 398, 3218
Moore, Martha, 423
Moore, Mary Adelaide, 3206
Moore, Matthew M., 123
Moore, Mattie, 2745
Moore, Mollie, 3388
Moore, Morris, 246, 276
Moore, Oliver, 3367
Moore, Orlando, 3408
Moore, Polly Ann, 2920
Moore, "Pony", 3388, 3457
Moore, Randolph, 3452
Moore, Raymond, 3460
Moore, Richard, 3451
Moore, Roger, 2211
Moore, Roy, 1359

Moore, Samuel Leon, 3452
Moore, Sandra L., 2211
Moore, Sara Jane, 1195, 3257, 3503
Moore, Scott Lee, 3453
Moore, Sid, 3566
Moore, Stephen, 2428
Moore, Susanna, 1535
Moore, Thomas (pr.1806), 1716, 3304
Moore, Thomas (pr.1878), 3564
Moore, Tyrone, 3454
Moore, W.C., 3564
Moore, Walter, 3091
Moore, Wayne, 23
Moore, William (pr.1860), 1715
Moore, William (U.S. 1928-63), 2211
Moore, William (d. 1889), 3338
Moore, William C., 3426
Moorehead, James, 3553
Moorehouse, Ward, 1600
Moores, Charles, 2100
Moorhouse, Anthony, 2211
Moorhouse, Francis, 2211
Moorman, Edward, 3343
Moorman, Richard, 3343
Moorman, Walter H., 1312
Moorman, Watt, 3336
Moormann, Robert Henry, 2211-2212, 3448
Moors Murders, The, 2212
MoPoCo, 3497, 3532
Mora, Frederico, 2213
Moradabad Riots, 2213
Morain, Alfred, 285
Morale, John, 3408
Morales, Agustin, 2213, 3242
Morales, Francisco Kraus, 771
Morales, Herberto, 536
Morales, Juan Castillo, 2213
Morales, Michael Angelo, 2213, 3449
Morales, Ricardo "Monkey", 3300
Morales, Salvador, 3454
Morales, William, 1133
Moran, Edward, Jr., 911
Moran, Eugene, 936, 2169
Moran, Frank, 767
Moran, George "Bugs", 15, 42, 128, 130, 179, 435, 501, 546, 591, 606, 613, 614, 962, 1026, 1027, 1293, 1296, 2037, 2044, 2073, 2213-2215, 2230, 2659, 2660, 2662, 2673, 2761, 2972, 2973, 3016, 3119, 3223, 3282, 3382, 3385-3387, 3388, 3389-3391, 3458, 3460
Moran, James B., 2757, 2829, 3333
Moran, James J., 2215
Moran, Jose C., 3246
Moran, Joseph P. "Doc", 242, 2215
Moran, Michael, 3229
Moran, Richard, 3452
Moran, Thomas, 2042
Moran, Thomas B. "Butterfingers", 2216
Moran, W. Herman, 483
Moran, Willard, 3413
Moran, William H., 3426
Moran Gang, 42, 110, 131, 178
Morano, Pellegrino, 590, 2217
Morantz, Paul, 899
Morath, Kathy, 2693
Moravec, E., 3251
Mora Witches, 2216
Moray, Mormaoe of, 3237
Mora y del Rio, José, 1395
Morazan, Francisco, 2216
Morazzini, Jacques, 790, 2216, 2465
Morcar, 1052
Morco, John "Happy Jack", 1054, 2216
Mordaunt, Charles, 2216
Mordaunt, Mary, 2940
Mordechai Gur, 2021
More, Henry, 2216
More, Thomas, 270, 1172, 2979

Muhangi, Joseph, 3512
Muhlenbroich, Jakob, 2150
Muhlenbroich, Wilhelm Jakob, 2247, 3326
Muhly, Doug, 899
Muir, D. Erskine, 1174, 1656
Muir, Francis Adolphus, 1099
Muir, P.B., 826
Muir, Richard, 332, 451, 1194, 1209, 2094,
    2248, 2867, 2869, 3126, 3186, 3195
Muir, Ruth, 1236
Muir, William, 2248
Muirhead, William, 385
Mujaheddin, 3531, 3532
Mujahedeen Khalq, 3276, 3504, 3514-3520,
    3522, 3524, 3525
Mujahedeen Saff, 3516
Mulcahey, James, 2230
Mulcahy, Catherine, 846
Mulder, Doug, 28
Muldoon, Cathy, 2839
Muldoon, Eileen, 1265
Muldowney, Dennis George, 2248
Mulheren, John Jr., 418
Mulherin, Doyle, 1425
Mulholland, Eugene, 3517
Mulholland, Winifred Virginia, 1100
Mullarkey, Thomas, 2941
Mullen, Francis "Bud" (U.S. pr.1981-85),
    1027, 1651
Mullen, Francis, 3301
Mullen, Francis M., Jr., 2248, 3426
Mullen, George, 1474
Mullen, Horace, 2484
Mullen, Jimmy, 3521
Mullen, Louis, 3348
Mullen, Mary, 921
Mullen, Robert R., 847
Mullen, Rodney, 899
Mullen, Terence, 2248
Mullendore, E.C., III, 2248-2249
Mullendore, Gene, 2249
Mullendore, Linda Vance, 2248
Mullens, John, 246, 3341
Mullens, Nat, 3352
Mulleono, Frank, 784
Muller, Carl, 2174
Muller, Dora, 1102
Müller, Eduard, 2249
Müller, Franz, 222, 2249
Müller, Gerhard, 199, 3475
Muller, Henry, 271
Muller, Horace, 3354
Muller, Johannes Pieter, 472
Muller, Ralph, 2439
Mullet, James, 660
Mulligan, Billy, 2249
Mulligan, Charles, 3340
Mulligan, Joseph, 3447
Mulligan, Thomas, 3246
Mullin, Herbert William, 2249-2250
Mullinen, Joseph, 2250
Mullins, Christie Lynn, 628
Mullins, Edward, 2747
Mullins, James, 2250
Mullins, Kenneth, 205
Mullins, Patrick, 2250, 3228
Mulock, William, 2250
Mulraney, Happy Jack, 1342
Mulrooney, Edward P., 811, 1480, 2941,
    3131, 3425
Mulveron, William, 408
Mulvey, Bill, 1537, 3547
Mulvihill, Martin C., 3223
Mulvihill, Terrence, 2236
Mumford, Jane, 2400
Mumford, Thomas, 481
Mumfre, Joseph "Doc", 193, 1744, 2250
Mu'Min, Dawud, 2250-2251
Mumit, Abdullah Hakim El-, 3452

Mummenthey, Karl, 3541
Mummius, Lucius, 2251
Muncaster, 169, 3324
Munch, Hans, 2166
Munda, Roland, 894
Munday, William, 563, 3457
Mundell, William A., 1560
Mundy, Marc, 826
Mundy, Peter, 3292
Mundy, Sue, 723
Müneccimbasi, Ahmed Dede, 2251
Munger, A.S., 2251, 3425
Munhangi, Joseph, 3258
Muni, Paul, 552
Munich Putsch, 2251
Municipal Brothel, 2251
Munif, Dejelal, Bey, 3244
Muniz, Pedro Cruz, 3455
Munk, K., 3250
Munk, Kaj Harald Leininger, 2251
Münnich, Burkhard Christoph von, 2251
Munnick, Jan Willem Hendrik, 2251
Munoman, Eleanor, 2251
Munoz, Carlos, 3356
Munoz Echaniz, Jose Miguel, 3522
Munro, Ernest A., 3256, 3479
Munro, Irene Violet, 1155
Munro, Peter, 869
Munro, Robert, 2425
Munroe, Charles Edward, 2251
Munroe, Thomas, 2251
Munson, Adolf, 3453
Munson, Bub, 2744
Munson, Daniel, 1552
Munson, Henry, 771, 1345, 3564
Munson, William H., 1253
Munter, Carl, 2251, 2252
Munter, Judith Marie, 2251-2252
Munz, Adolfo, 3363
Murad IV, 2252
Murad V, 1647
Muralto, Onuphrio, 3084
Murat, Joachim, 620, 2252
Muratore, Giorgio, 3416
Muravyov-Apostol, Mikhail Nikolayevich,
    2252
Muravyov-Apostol, Sergey Ivanovich, 2252
Murchison, Ivan, 3549
Murchison, John, 841
Murdaugh, John, 3158
Murden, Jesse, 3079
Murder By Decree, 2252
Murder, Inc., 1-2, 34-35, 111-112, 117-118,
    120, 342, 345, 370, 525, 526, 528, 529,
    545, 940, 976, 1294, 1297, 1310, 2086,
    2090, 2102, 2252-2256, 2868, 3139,
    3187, 3396, 3401-3403, 3405-3412, 3414
Murder in the Basement, 2256
Murder is My Dish, 2256
Murder Stable, 2657
Murder Stones, 2256
Murder Takes the Stage, 2256
Murderer's Alley, 3408
Murdoch, Anna, 1623, 2047
Murdoch, Rupert, 1623, 2047, 3328
Murdock, Ready, 3345
Murdock, Roger E., 3425
Muren, Anders, 484
Muren, Randi, 484
Muret, Ernest Arthur, 2695
Murguia, Francisco, 3244
Murieta, Joachim, 320, 1266, 1267, 2256-
    2258, 3414, 3415, 3564
Murietta, Procopio, 3564
Murietta, Tex, 1737
Murillo, Zeke, 3564
Murlas Commodities, 2258
Muromtsey, Sergei Andreevich, 2258
Murphy, Angus, 2258

Murphy, Anne, 978
Murphy, Anne-Marie, 3281
Murphy, Archie, 3399, 3400
Murphy, Bill, 635
Murphy, C., 3425, 3426
Murphy, Charles (U.S. pr.1907), 1561
Murphy, Charles (U.S. b.1887), 2258-2259
Murphy, Christian, 2259
Murphy, Clarence, 2940
Murphy, Craig, 3454
Murphy, Daniel, 2851
Murphy, David, 2123-2124
Murphy, Deacon, 2189
Murphy, Dennis, 2225
Murphy-Dolan, 3555, 3557, 3558, 3565
Murphy-Dolan Gang, 1739
Murphy, Edward, 2803
Murphy, Emily F., 3295
Murphy, Ernest, 3343
Murphy, Ervin Edward, 2414
Murphy, Frances, 3113
Murphy, Frank (U.S. 1890-1949), 2123,
    2259, 3204
Murphy, Frank (U.S. pr.1987), 3527
Murphy, Frederick George, 2259
Murphy, Gerald Lester, 1253, 2995
Murphy, H.A., 3113
Murphy, H.D., 262
Murphy, Henderson, 276
Murphy, J. Reginald, 3499
Murphy, Jack (pr.1964), 2259
Murphy, Jack (pr.1988), 670
Murphy, James (d.1886), 2259
Murphy, James (pr.1893), 2397
Murphy, James (pr.1980s), 3456
Murphy, James W., 276
Murphy, Jeffrey W., 3471
Murphy, Jeremiah, 2966
Murphy, Jim, 246, 275-277, 2259
Murphy, John (S.Afri. pr.1932), 472
Murphy, John (U.S. pr.1989), 1384
Murphy, John (U.S. pr.1905), 3564
Murphy, John Brady (U.S. d.1953), 1730
Murphy, John M. (U.S. pr.1980), 13
Murphy, John Reginald "Reg", 3167, 3330
Murphy, Joseph, 2805
Murphy, Kid (U.S., pr.1887), 1424
Murphy, Lawrence Gustave, 363, 486, 985,
    2149, 3563, 3564
Murphy, Logan, 3342
Murphy, Mallet, 1341
Murphy, Michael, 2886
Murphy, Michael C., 3425
Murphy, Michael J., 3425
Murphy, Patrick, 3166
Murphy, Patrick V., 3112, 3425
Murphy, Peter (Brit. pr.1879), 1074
Murphy, Peter (U.S. 1705-31), 355
Murphy, Ralph, 3330
Murphy, Richard D., 360
Murphy, Robert, 3505
Murphy, Roger, 1384
Murphy, Thomas, 1563, 2259
Murphy, Thomas F., 3425
Murphy, Timothy D., 2259-2260, 3458
Murphy, Walter P., 999
Murphy, William, 3347
Murray, A.W., 3425
Murray, Andrew, 3508
Murray, Anthony, 19
Murray, Billy, 2180
Murray, Brian, 560
Murray, Bud, 3461
Murray, Charlie, 2260
Murray, Daniel, 1583, 2767
Murray, David, 2260
Murray, Edith, 2260
Murray, Edna "The Kissing Bandit", 238
Murray, Edwin, 3085, 3086

Murray, Esther del Rosario, 2260
Murray, Felicia, 3022
Murray, Frank J., 1465
Murray, George, 2780
Murray, George C., 2260
Murray, Grenville, 2260
Murray, Grizel, 1364
Murray, James, 1730
Murray, John (Brit. pr.1830s), 567
Murray, John (pr.1877), 2069
Murray, John (Scot. d.1642), 2260
Murray, John A. (U.S. pr.1873), 596
Murray, John Robert (U.S. d.1980), 722
Murray, John Wilson (Can. pr.1880s), 372, 429, 1728
Murray, Mae, 3026
Murray, Major William, 2260
Murray, Maud, 2180
Murray, Mick, 2260
Murray, Nora, 3269, 3497
Murray, Paddy, 613, 3120
Murray, Patrick, 3388
Murray, Robert "Tony", 3452
Murray, Robert, 2260
Murray, Robert V., 3426
Murray, Tom, 2182
Murray, Veronica, 1013
Murray, William (Brit. 1705-93), 2260
Murray, William (Brit. 1820-1907), 2260-2261
Murray, William H. "Alfalfa Bill", 239, 1184
Murray, William J., 959
Murrel, John A., 2261, 3400
Murrell, Andrew, 3340
Murri, Tullio, 430
Murry, H., 2718
Murry, Paul, 3447
Murry, Robert A., 3299
Mursilis I, 2261, 3232
Murtagh, Dennis Patrick, 2261
Murtagh, Derek, 2261
Murtagh, John, 943
Murti Vanya, 2258
Murtishaw, David, 3449
Murton, Tom, 2999
Musa, 2197, 3234
Musa, Achmet, 844
Musajiro, I., 3241
Muscarella, Angeline, 1545
Muscau, Andrea, 2170, 2261-2262
Musetto, Carmela, 780
Musey, George, 724, 742, 1588, 2162, 2262, 2475
Musgrave, Vernon Cecil Ellingham, 2262
Musgrove, Donnis, 3447
Musgrove, Lee H., 769, 2262
Mushala, 3514, 3526
Mushala, Adamson, 3260
Mushala Gang, 3532
Musica, Arthur, 2263
Musica, Philip, 134, 2049, 2262-2263
Musico, Joseph, 898, 899
Muskgrove, George, 3564
Muskgrove, L.H., 3564
Muskgrove, M., 3564
Muskie, Edmund, 3080
Muslim Brotherhood, 3215, 3252, 3274, 3507, 3509, 3517, 3520, 3532
Mussa Kheyyabani, 3259
Mussabini, Sampson, 2846
Mussachio, Salvatore, 3408
Mussato, Albertino, 2263
Mussay, Washington, 3358
Mussert, Anton, 3541
Mussolini, Alessandro, 2263
Mussolini, Benito Amilcare Andrea, 78, 347, 434, 631, 647, 738, 818, 894, 940, 987, 1034, 1153, 1250, 1297, 1309, 1573, 1576, 2080, 2087, 2148-2149, 2222, 2263-2264,

2266, 2268-2269, 2415, 2472, 2488, 2652, 2681, 2849, 2850, 2974, 3057, 3117, 3245-3247, 3250, 3251, 3402, 3415
Mussolini, Bruno, 2266
Mussolini, Vittorio, 2266
Musson, Barry, 2269
Mustafa IV, 2269, 2726, 3240
Mustafa, Guylam, 356
Mustafa, Mustafa Ali, 3261
Mustasim, al, 2269, 3237
Musto, William V., 2269
Musty, Carole, 2767
Musulman, Habibollah Asghar Owladi, 3260
Musumeci, Joseph, 1256, 3408
Musunge, Kamawe, 2488
Mutawak-kil, Yahya Mahmud al (Yemen, d.1948), 2269, 3252
Mutawakkil al- (Baghdad, d.861), 1651, 3236
Mutch, Lawrence, 951
Muth, Freddie, 3325
Mutillo, Giuseppe, 3061
Mutiny on the Bounty, 2269-2270
Muto Akira, 3541
Muto, Silvano, 2204
Mutsuhito, 2662
Muzziotti, Dominique, 1198, 2270
MVD, 1354
Mwanga, 2270
Mwari, 699
My Lai Massacre, 2272-2273
Myda, Joseph, 3326
Myers, Allen, 430
Myers, Arthur Elliott, 1275
Myers, Dan, 2218
Myers, Eugene Arter, 2163, 2475
Myers, Gustavus, 999
Myers, Homer T., 3228
Myers, John, 3425
Myers, Kim, 899
Myers, Mary, 1614
Myers, Michael, 13
Myers, Rodes E., 914
Myers, Samuel S., 2271
Myers, Stanley, 1665
Myers, T.M., 3356
Myers, Twymon, 3498
Myers, Venson, 3449
Myers, Virginia, 2270-2271
Myers, William J., 2270
Myers, William R., 2270-2271
Myerson, Bess, 602, 2271-2272
Myles, Jerry, 2273
Myrick, W.F., 3388
Myrtal, Héra, 354, 2273-2274
Mystery of Marie Roget, The, 2274
Mytovich, Mary, 1550, 1551

N

Naan, Michael, 3508
Nabih Berri, 3529
Nabinger, Harry, 768
Nabis, 2275
Nabonidus, 2275
Nabors, Kit, 3352
Naceur, Ridoub Amar Ben, 3253
Nachmann, Werner, 2275
Naciri, Mohamed, 3253
Nack, Augusta, 2939
Nacken, Ulrich, 3065

Nacrelli, John, 3413
Nâdasdy, Ferencz, 281
Nadel, Bernard, 2233
Nader, Jacob, 3359
Nadeua, Armand, 3460
Nadir Shah, 2275
Nadjari, Maurice, 1899
Nafte, Jaerl, 2275
Nagata Tetsuzan, 2275, 3248
Nagel, Kurt, 3329, 3498
Nagelstock, Dr. Walter, 988
Nagi, Mohammed, 3255
Nagle, David, 3549
Nagle, Liz, 675
Nagle, Mamie, 1836
Nagy, Esther, 2136
Nagy, Imre, 2275, 2955
Nahman, Moses Ben,, 2233
Naif, Abdul Razak al-, 3257
Nail, William, 3350
Naim, Sardar Mohammed, 3254
Nairn, Second Viscount Finlay of, 1160
Naisbitt, Carol, 2464
Naisbitt, Cortney, 2464
Najjar, Mohammed Yusif, 36, 2275-2276
Nakaoka Konichi, 1445
Naka Sakai, 1316
Nakasone Yasuhiro, 2276
Naldi, Nita, 3027
Naldi, Pio, 430
Nalepa, Patrick, 2778
Nalls, Gabe, 3345
Nalls, R.L., 964
Nalls, Ulyssess, 3345
Nally, Margaret Ellen, 2276
Nally, William, 2276
Nalo, Sam, 762
Namari, Michel, 3261
Namba, Daisaku, 3245
Namphy, Henri, 1419
Nana Sahib, 2276
Nance, Allen, 3364
Nance, James, 3348
Nandakumar, 2276
Nanders, G., 3246
Nangle, John F., 2998
Nango, El, 1103
Nangway, Charles, 3564
Nani, Sebastiano, 577, 3408
Nanjing Riots, The, 2276-2277
Nannery, James, 2277
Nannie, Williams, 2244
Nanys, Estelle, 585
Naosuke, Ii, 3241
NAP, 2553
Napetoff, P., 3247
Napier, Carl, 3455
Napier, Jimmy, 1190
Napier, Lowell, 463
Naples Church and King Riots, 3372
Napoléon I, 219, 234, 282, 362, 422, 428, 454, 555, 563, 569, 588, 737, 1025, 1199, 1203, 1205, 1832, 1833, 1872, 1905, 2070, 2096, 2120-2121, 2216, 2252, 2268, 2277-2279, 2282, 2319, 2656, 3047, 3103, 3240, 3401, 3536
Napoléon III, 85, 86, 266, 293, 428, 594, 836, 1140, 1210, 1258, 1628, 1871, 1880, 1940, 2174, 2206, 2279-2282, 2990, 3241
Napoli, Alexander, 435, 2123
Napoli, Anthony, 2670
Napoli, James, 3408
Napoli, Joseph, 699
Napoli, Vincent, 3408
Napolitano, Anthony, 3297
Napolitano, Dominick, 3408, 3410
Napolitano, Joey, 755, 3395
Nara, Giuliano, 737

Nelder, A., 3426
Nelles, John Hamilton, 2980
Nelles, Mary, 3327
Nelles, Susan, 2298
Nelligan, Thomas, 584
Nellis, Preech, 3362
Nellist, 1334
Nelme, Samuel, 102
Nelms, John W., 802
Nelson, Barry, 2055
Nelson, Bill, 3034
Nelson, Bob, (U.S. pr.1939) 1040
Nelson, Bob, (U.S. pr.1800's) 3564
Nelson, Carl R., 1240
Nelson, Charles, (U.S. pr.1944) 1884
Nelson, Charles, (U.S. d.1902) 3356
Nelson, Charles L., (U.S. pr.1946) 3425
Nelson, Dale Merle, 2298-2299
Nelson, David, 3447
Nelson, Doris Lee, 902
Nelson, Earle Leonard, 352, 871, 1564, 2299-
    2301, 2929, 3427
Nelson, Ernest "Pop", 3299
Nelson, Fred, 3486
Nelson, G., (Mex. d.1927) 3246
Nelson, Gary, (U.S. pr.1988) 3450
Nelson, George "Baby Face", 204, 235, 252,
    689, 817, 948, 962, 966, 972, 973, 1144-
    1145, 1186-1187, 1612, 1613, 2301-2304,
    2913, 3459
Nelson, Harry, 1030
Nelson, Helen, 2304
Nelson, Horatio, 619, 1299
Nelson, Jackie, 3208
Nelson, James, (U.S. d.1897) 3348
Nelson, James, (U.S. pr.1980) 644
Nelson, John, (U.S. 1654-1734) 2304
Nelson, John, (U.S. 1794-1860) 2304
Nelson, John B., (U.S. d.1838) 885
Nelson, Laura, 3361
Nelson, Lord, 1357
Nelson, Marlin, 3455
Nelson, Mart, 3564
Nelson, Martlick, 2978, 3427
Nelson, Mary, 722
Nelson, Peter D., 3455
Nelson, Rita, 706
Nelson, Roger, 2304
Nelson, Ronald (U.S. 1950-1969), 1302, 2347
Nelson, Ronald (U.S. pr.1988), 461
Nelson, Samuel, 2304
Nelson, Steve, 3119
Nelson, Teddy, 2304-2305
Nelson, Thomas, 3296
Nelson, Trenton, 3332
Nelson, Victor F., 2305
Nelson, Walter, 3208
Nemechek, Francis Donald, 2305
Nementh, John, 901
Nemiken, Raisa, 1132
Nenni, Pietro Sandro, 2305
Neocleous, Loucas, 1692
Neo-Fascist Democratic Idealist Turkish
    Association, 3510
Neponuck, Joseph, 234
Nepos, Julius, 1323
Nero, 39, 40, 134, 493, 558, 571, 577, 581,
    654, 699, 726, 727, 782, 996, 1029, 1251,
    2001, 2007, 2282, 2305-2306, 2319, 2450,
    2470, 2681, 2728, 2941, 3227, 3234, 3235
Nerone, Giuseppe "The Cavalier", 1026,
    1292, 1293
Nerone, Joseph, 3388
Nershbred, William, 3345
Nerva, Marcus Cocceius, 996, 2306
Nerva Cocceius, 2306
Nesbit, Evelyn, 1723, 2922, 2924, 2926, 3295
Nesbit, John Innes, 940, 3458
Nesbit, Mary, 2299

Nesbit, William Raymond, 2306
Nesbitt, Alma, 3165
Nesbitt, Bronston, 2306
Nesbitt, Bull, 2306
Nesbitt, Elbert "Eb", 2306
Nesbitt, George, 3164
Nesbitt, Louisa, 3164
Nesbitt, Sally, 2306
Nesbitt, Suzanne, 2306
Nesbitt-Talbot Feud, 2306
Nesmith, George, 3562
Ness, Eliot, 593, 2306-2307, 2340
Nesselrode, Karl, 1762
Nesset, Arnfinn, 2307
Nestead, Stephen, 3453
Nestorius, 1110, 2307
Netherland, Clarence, 2549
Netherland, Robert, 2307
Nethery, Stephen, 3455
Neto, António Agostinho, 2307
Nettles, Joshua, 2307
Nettleton, Edith, 2012
Neu, Kenneth, 2307-2308
Neu, S. Gustave, 3196
Neubacher, Hermann, 3541
Neubeck, Richard, 3388
Neuberger, Fred, 3112
Neufeld, Billy, 2308
Neumann, Lawrence, 844, 3388
Neupert, Gregory, 2048
Neurath, Konstantin von, 3541
Neuring, Otto, 3244
Neuschafer, Jimmy, 3452
Nevares, Jaime Herrera, 2147
Nevil, John, (Brit. d.1794) 2128
Nevill, Charles L., (U.S. pr.1880's) 3549
Neville, Charles, (Brit. 1543-1601) 2308
Neville, Charles, (Ire. d.1982) 3275, 3518
Neville, George, 2308
Neville, John, (Brit. pr.1966) 2873
Neville, John, (U.S. pr.1794) 3135
Neville, Philip, 2308
Neville, Ralph, 2576
Neville, Richard, (U.S. pr.1987) 1515
Neville, Richard, (Brit. 1400-1460) 2308,
    3185
Neville, Seymour, 3344
Nevin, Robert Reasoner, 2308
Nevins, Sam, 3211
Nevison, William, 2308
Nevius, Thomas, 3452
Nevsky, St. Alexander 85
New, J.N., 3564
New Africa Organization, 3377
Newall, Billy, 104
Newall, Frank, 104
Newaye, Germane, 3254
New Bedford (Mass.) Serial Murders,
    2308-2309
Newberry, Ted, 179, 614, 2037, 2215, 2350,
    2660, 3388, 3389
Newberry, Truman Handy, 2309
Newbery, Frederick, 1124
Newbery, George, 2861
New Bethel African Methodist Church,
    2309
Newbold, Thomas Gray, 2309
Newby, Norma, 1465
Newcastle, Duke of, 2429
Newcomb, George "Bitter Creek", 860,
    1003, 1038, 2309-2310, 2463, 2732,
    3070, 3564, 3565
Newcomb, Indian Ed, 651
Newcomb, J.D., Jr., 1425
Newcomb, Walter C., 2803
Newcombe, Arthur, 3156
Newcombe, Edmund Leslie, 2310
Newcomen, John, 362
Newcomer, Clarence Charles, 2310

New Dawn Collective, 3504, 3530, 3532
Newel, Fred, 59
Newell, Arthur L., 2393
Newell, Henry, Jr., 628
Newell, J. Benson, 3549
Newell, John, (Scot. prom.1923) 2310
Newell, John T., (U.S. d.1889) 3337
Newell, Stub, 2310
Newell, Susan, 2310
Newell, William C., 1638
Newfield, Jack, 2056
Newgate, 2310-2312
Newhall, James T., 3549
Newhouse, Mrs. Russell, 2859
Ne Win, 550, 3378
Newitt, Harvey K., 483, 1692-1693
New Jersey Tenant Riots, 2312, 3371
Newkirk, Frank, Sr., 2664
Newland, Robert, 3450
Newlon, Rayfield, 3452
Newman, Art, 376, 378
Newman, Bud, 1773, 2312, 3564
Newman, Carolyn Ann, 2001
Newman, Clara, 2299
Newman, Ernest, 1848
Newman, Eugene Francis, 3461
Newman, H.S., 2856
Newman, James, (Brit. pr.1758) 1520
Newman, Jay, 967, 2304
Newman, Jim, (U.S. pr.1860's) 3549, 3564
Newman, John, 2312
Newman, Jon Ormond, 2312
Newman, Julia St. Clair, 2312
Newman, Kenneth, 2312, 3426
Newman, Merrit, 2312
Newman, Monte, 2312
Newman, Mrs. Ursula, 1731, 1732
Newman, Oliver, 2312-2313
Newman, Paul, 1279, 2561
Newman, Ralph G., 2313
Newman, Sarah Jane, 2774
Newmark, Benjamin "Jew Ben", 606, 2780
Newmark, Meyer, 2941
New Mexico State Prison Riot, 2313, 3377
Newnham, Susan, 807
New Order, 309, 398, 488
New Organization, 3273, 3513, 3532
New Orleans Anti-Mafia Riot, 2313, 3374
New Orleans Race Riot, 2313
New Orleans Rebellion, 2313-2314
New Orleans Whisky Ring, 2314
New People's Army, 2314, 3272, 3473, 3507,
    3526, 3528, 3532
Newsom, Robert P., 3426
Newsome, Leroy, 1363
Newsome, Ray, 3366
Newstead, Norman Lee, 3453
Newto, Edward Clanton, 1186
Newton, Anne, 1603
Newton, Arthur, 2314
Newton, Daniel, 3359
Newton, Mrs. Donald, 192
Newton, Florence, 2314
Newton, Frances, 3455
Newton, George, 2854
Newton, Henry, 668
Newton, Huey P., 398, 3478, 3529
Newton, Isaac, 2115
Newton, J.O., (U.S. prom.1907) 3549
Newton, John, (Brit. prom.1830) 2679
Newton, Lee, 3354
Newton, Montague "Monty" Noel, 1581,
    2314-2315
Newton, Robert, 20
Newton, Theodore, Jr., 2147
Newton, William, 2315
Newton General Massacre, 2315
Newton-John, Olivia, 2291
Newton Keech, Mary Ann 2315

Nobling, Karl, 3157
Nobunaga, Oda, 170, 2341, 3239
Nobusuke, Kishi, 3203
Nobuya, Giga, 679
Nodder, Frederick, 379, 1501, 2341-2342
Nodin, Henri, 3023
Nodot, François, 2681
Noe, James H., 985, 3147
Noe, Joey, 936
Noe, Mark, 3209
Noel, Anne, 1287
Noel, Cleo A. Jr., 140, 3256, 3495
Noel, Harrison, 2342, 3325
Noel, William, 2342
Nofziger, Lyn, 3112
Nogaret Guillaume de 2342
Nogent-Saint-Laurens, 2751
Nogi, 2851
Noguchi, Thomas T., 2782
Noguera, Willaim, 3449
Noir, Victor, 428
Nokes, Alice, 692
Nol, Lon, 2483
Nol, Oude, 3222
Nolan, Bob, 171
Nolan, Charles, 2342
Nolan, Dan, (U.S. pr.1982) 1378
Nolan, Daniel, (U.S. pr.1906) 2342
Nolan, Edward D., 2208
Nolan, Eugene, 3400
Nolan, Francisco, 3564
Nolan, Gerald, 521
Nolan, Mary, 2342
Nolan, Samuel W., 3424
Nolan, Stella Darlene, 1073
Noland, John, (U.S. pr.1892) 2342
Noland, John, (U.S. pr.1988) 3453
Noles, Henry, 3353
Noles, "Piggy", 3408
Nolte, Elizabeth, 380, 2342-2343
Nolte, Frederick, 855
Nolte, Michael, 3453
Nolting, Anton, 1744
Nolting, Frederick, 3255
Noon, E.E., 1829
Noonan, Fred, 1052, 1053
Noonan, Gregory Francis, 2343
Noonan, Mary, 2031, 2033, 3388
Noor, Marvin Dean, 2343
Nootbar, Max, 3388
Nopwasky, Gladys Keen, 2250
Noraid, 3527
Noranjo, Aristotle, 3564
Norbregas, Leslie, 3464
Norcross, Frank Herbert, 2343
Nordberg, John, 578
Nordeen, William, 2347
Norden, Peter, 2695
Nordhus, Alf, 2307
Nordlund, Elmer C., 3425
Nordlund, Herman, 2343
Norek, Fran, 1305
Norfleet, J. Frank, 409, 1243, 2343-2344,
    3564
Norfolk, Duke of, 423, 828, 931, 1004, 2940
Norfolk, Earl of, 3086
Norgle, Charles, 1458
Noriega Morena, Manuel Antonio, 2344-
    2345, 3302, 3511
Norman, Beverly, 3221
Norman, William, 3362
Normand, Mabel, 143, 2903, 2904, 2906,
    3296
Norodom, 2176, 2345
Norris, Al "Maniac", 1135
Norris, Charles D., 1822
Norris, Charles S., 1089, 1337
Norris, Clarence, 2714, 2716
Norris, Edward, 2927

Norris, Frank, 426
Norris, Harold, 164
Norris, Jean Hortense, 2717
Norris, Melissa, 2345, 2489
Norris, Michael, 3455
Norris, Robert, 443
Norris, Roy Lewis, 383
Norris, Sterling E., 1208
Norry, August, 383, 384
Norse, T., 3250
North, Edward, 153
North, Frank P., 2549
North, John, 2345
North, Lord, 1385
North, Oliver, 2344
North Berwick Witches, 2345
Northampton, John de   2345
Northcott, Gordon Stewart, 2345
Northcott, John, 2031
Northcott, Sarah Louise, 2345
Northcutt, Elliott, 2345
Northern, Earl, 950
Northern India Riots 3377
Northern Ireland Riots, (1979), 3377
Northern Ireland Riots (1981) 3378
Northey, I.M., 3304
Northrup, John E., 728
Northumberland, Duke of, 1031
Northumbria, Edwin of, 2439
Northumbria, Oswald of, 2439
Northumbria, Oswy of, 2439
Northwest Mounted Police, 2345-2346
Nortje, Anna, 2346
Nortje, Jan Christian, 2346
Norton, Brocky Jack, 642
Norton, Charles, 3565
Norton, Fletcher, 142
Norton, George, 1698
Norton, Heber, 2346
Norton, J.W., 1054
Norton, Ken, 273
Norton, Paul M., 2030
Norton, Roger, 2211
Norton, Ruth, 3001
Norton, Samuel, 2346
Norton, Stephen Allen, 1081
Norvell, Randal, 2346
Norway, Duke of, 1942
Norwich, Edward of, 1071
Noseda, Alfredo, 1854
Nosenko, Yuri, 2346
Noske, Gustav, 2347, 3541
Notarbartolo, Emanuel, 2080
Notarbartolo, Leopoldo, 2080
Notaro, Joseph, 3408
Notaro, Tony, 590
Nothing But the Night, 2347
Not Sufficient Evidence, 2347
Nott, Abraham, 2347
Nott, Charles, Jr., 1561, 1762
Nott, John, 3276, 3521
Nott, Thomas, 1446
Nott-Bower, John Reginald Hornby, 2347,
    3426
Noury, Christian, 2470
Nova, A.I., 231
Novack, Josef, 1842
Nova Express, 2347
Novak, Franz, 3541
Novara, Dulcino of, 1034
Novarro, Fats, 2192
Novarro, Ramon, 1150
Novello, Ivor, 1976, 2456
November 17, 2347, 3532
Noverraz, Abram, 2278
Novick, Hyman David, 2347
Novo, Guillermo, 1942, 1943
Novotny, Josef, 1531
Novyky, Grigori Efimovich, 2536

Nowak, John, 2049
Nowell, Roger, 1882
Nowhir, John E., 3349
Nowitzke, Frederick, 3450
Nowling, Joe, 3364
Noyes, Berry, 3365
Noyes, John Humphrey, 2347
Nozière, Violette, 2347
Nuccio, Dominick, 3388
Nuccio, Richard L., 1302, 2347
Nuckols, Kenneth, 3453
Nuclei Armati Proletari, 3532
Nuestra Familia, 3503
Nueva Organizacion Anticommunista, 3532
Nugent, Carol, 27
Nugent, John (U.S. pr.1878), 1618, 1941
Nugent, John (U.S. pr.1906), 1500
Null, William, 3346
Number One, 2304, 2348
Numeiri, al-, 3256
Nunan, Joseph D., Jr., 1664, 3163
Nunez de Balboa, Vasco 2348
Nunez Vela, Blasco, 2348
Nunn May, Alan, 2348
Nunn, Sam, 560, 3402
Nunziata, Joe, 1943
Nunzio, Judge, 1428
Nuoro (Sardinia) Kidnappings, 2338
Nuremberg Trials, 984, 2348
Nuri-el-Said, 1128
Nurse, Rebecca, 2666, 2670
Nussbaum, Harald, 1767
Nussbaum, Hedda, 2847
Nussbaum, Irwin, 915
Nute, Tracy Leroy, 1208
Nutt, James, 2348
Nutt, Lizzie, 2348
Nuttall, G.H.F., 1754
Nuzum, Jerry, 768
Nyaose, Petrus, 3260, 3277
Nyerere, Julius, 3473, 3521
Nypen, Lisbet, 2348
Nypen, Ole, 2348
Nys, Ernest, 2348

O

Oakes, Betty, 2229
Oakes, Gregory, 2349
Oakes, Sir Harry, 911
Oakes, Jerry, 2349
Oakes, John Howard, 2349
Oakes, Phyllis, 2229
Oakey, James, 1384
Oakland County Murders, 2349
Oakley, Frederick William, 2349, 2491
Oakley, K.P., 887
Oakley, Paul M., 262
Oaks, Louis D., 3425
Oates, Presley, 3349
Oates, Reginald Vernon, 2349
Oates, Titus, 313, 1324, 2219, 2349-2350,
    3074
Oatley, Evelyn, 845
Oats, Sonny Boy, 3450
Obando, José Maria, 2350
O'Bannion, Charles Dion "Deanie", 42,
    104-105, 128, 129, 132, 501, 606, 608,
    756, 1002, 1026, 1028, 1079, 1292, 1294,
    1980, 2044, 2073, 2124, 2213, 2350-2355,
    2563, 2659, 2972, 3119, 3203, 3282, 3381,
    3384, 3386-3388, 3391, 3412, 3458
O'Bannion, Viola, 2354

Ogilvie, Richard B., 576, 745, 2549
Ogilvie, Thomas, 1874
Ogle, Miles, 2025, 2569
Oglethorpe, James Edward, 2365
Ogorzov, Paul, 2365
Ogotai, 1291
OGPU, 1354, 2365
O'Grady, Brandt, 3352
O'Grady, Edward, 489
O'Grady, James E., 2365-2366, 3010, 3424
O'Grady, John, 3549
O'Guinn, Kenneth W., 3454
O'Hagan, Thomas, 2366
O'Hair, John, 2409
O'Halloran, Xiomara, 1399
O'Hara, Birdie, 1691
O'Hara, Danny, 370
O'Hara, John, 564
O'Hara, Patrick, 3378, 3513
O'Hara, Ronald E., 2421
O'Hare, Edward J., 616, 848, 3388
Ohern, Michael, 2366
O'Higgins, Bernardo, 638
O'Higgins, Kevin Christopher, 2366, 3246
Ohio Doctors' Riot, 3373
Ohio Gang, 2907, 2908, 2910-2912
Ohio State Penitentiary, 2366
Ohlendorf, Otto, 2291, 3541
Ohliger, Rosa, 1863
Ohlson, George E., 292
Ohmura Ichiro, 2366
Ohnesorg, Benno, 195, 1750
Ohta, Victor, 1229
Ohta, Virginia, 1229
Oi, John, 2927
Ojeda Perez, Uriel, 3470
O.K. Corral, 314, 495
Okada Keisuke, 3248
Okamoto Kozo, 1143, 2552
Okanda, S., 3249
Okao, Zeb, 3259, 3520
Okawa Shumei, 2366, 3541
OK Corral, 2366-2367
O'Keefe, Albert J., 848
O'Keefe, Jennie, 1020
O'Keefe, John, 1020
O'Keefe, Joseph James "Specs", 489, 546, 3461
Okhrana, 691, 2331, 2367
Okinawa Anti-U.S. Riots, 3377
Okinawa Treaty Riots, 3377
Okito, Joseph, 3254
Oklahoma State Prison Riot, 2367
Okonski, Augusto, 2449
Okotie-Eboh, Festus, 3255
Okrimiuk, E.R., 3333, 3516
Okubo, Toshimichi, 2367
Okuchi Nobuo, 3328, 3484
Okudaira Junzo, 2367, 3281
Olah, Susanna, 1142
Olander, Nellie, 1404
Olarte, David, 3467
O'Laughlin, Jimmy, 3564
O'Laughlin, Michael, 1954
O'Laughlin, Pearl, 2367
Olbricht, Friedrich, 1574
Olcay, Cezmi, 3509
Old Bailey, 2367-2368
Old Brewery, 2368
Oldcastle, John, 2368
Oldenbarnevelt, Johan van, 2368
Oldfield, George, 2879
Old Flaherty, 3408
Oldham, George, 24
Oldoini, Virginia, 2368
Old Parish Prison, 2082, 2084
Old Polk, 2998
Olds, Reuben, 2832
Old Shakespeare Case, 2368-2369

Oldys, Valentine, 2069
O'Leary, Arthur, 968
O'Leary, Bart J., 977
O'Leary, Daniel, 3413
O'Leary, James, 2369, 3388
O'Leary, Katherine, 697
O'Leary, Matthew, 2986
Olen Lebby, 1915
Olesiewicz, Anna M., 359, 360
Oleson, Ole, 2357
Oley, Francis, 2107
Oley, John 2107
Ole Yantis, 1003
Olgiati, Girolamo, 2732, 3238
Olguin, Jesús Maria, 175, 1737
Olid, Cristóbal de, 2369
Olinger, Perry, 3451
Olinger, Robert (Bob) 318, 366, 1739, 3427, 3564
Olinger, Wallace, 1734, 3564
Oliphant, Charles, 1664, 3163
Oliphant, Ethelbert, 2369
Oliphant, Laurence, 1463
Oliphant, Nathaniel, 3337
Olitsch, Kurt, 3250
Olive, Clive, 1513, 2209
Olive, Ison Prentice, 2369-2370
Olive, Marlene, 2370
Oliver, Alfred, 1177, 2370
Oliver, Andrew, 2370
Oliver, Arthur, 2837, 2838
Oliver, Constance, 1352
Oliver, Fanny, 2370
Oliver, Frank Miles, 2785-2786
Oliver, George, 687
Oliver, Hannah, 1968
Oliver, James, 645
Oliver, John, 2229
Oliver, John T., 3166
Oliver, John Wesley, 3453
Oliver, Johnnie L., 1409
Oliver, Kenneth, 2509
Oliver, Mary, 2229
Oliver, Michael, 3388
Oliver, Paul Ambrose, 2370
Oliver, R. Spencer, 3099
Oliver, Rowland Giffard, 454, 2370
Oliver, Tony, 3209
Oliver, William, 3349
Olivera, Norberto C., 3246
Oliverio, Antonio, 936
Olivero, Louis, 393
Olivié, Roger 184
Olivier, C.J.B., 1919
Olivotto, Guglielmo, 1898
Olliver, Richard, 3350
Olmstead, Roy, 2370-2371
Olney, Cyrus, 2371
Olney, Peter B., 2101
Olney, Richard, 2371, 2511
O'Loughlin, James, 3154
Olofsson, Clark, 2371
Olozaga, Salustiano, 2371
Olsen, Hans Jacob, 3338
Olsen, Jack, 785, 2864
Olsen, Jens, 1853
Olsen, Richard E., 1246, 2434
Olshausen, Justus von, 2371
Olson, Clifford, 2371
Olson, Culbert Levy, 493, 1627, 2209
Olson, Floyd B., 347
Olson, Frank, 2150
Olson, Harold, 130
Olson, Henry, 2371
Olson, James B.E., 3163
Olson, Jennie, 1402, 1404
Olson, Leo, 963
Olson, Raymond Lee, 2149
Olson, Roger L., 2453

Olson, Vincent, 1902
Olson, Sigurd, 1404
Olson, Wayne, 1384
Olsson, Jan-Erik, 2372
Olympias, 166, 648, 3233
Olympio, Sylvanus, 2370, 3254, 3255
O'Mahoney, John, 1147
O'Malley, Dominick, 1516
O'Malley, Grace, 2372
O'Malley, James, 2372
O'Malley, Jack, 2065
O'Malley, John, 3388
O'Malley, Joseph F., 2247
O'Malley, Morris, 1720
O'Malley, Pat, (U.S. pr.1890s), 1720
O'Malley, Patrick, (U.S. pr.1900s) 3388
O'Malley, William Patrick (U.S. 1891-1934), 958, 968
Oman, John B., 1049
Oman, Lee, 3340
Oman, Sultan of, 3276
O'Mara, Daniel J., 1020, 1528
O'Mara, Elizabeth, 944
Omar I, 2372
Omar al-Mokhtar, 2518, 3236
O'Meally, William John, 2441
O'Meara, Francis, 1913
O'Meara, Stephen, 3424
Omega 7, 3257
Omelus, Ulrick, 3450
Omichund, 2372
Omohundro, John B., 3564
O'Neal, Abe, 3365
O'Neal, Belton, 2372
O'Neal, John B., 1453
O'Neal, John J., 2372, 3425
O'Neal, Lee, 1100
O'Neal, Ransom, 3355
O'Neal, Robert, 3452
O'Neal, William M., Jr., 1443
O'Neall, Darren, 2372-2373
One-Eyed Jack, 422
Oneida Creek, 2347
O'Neil, Abram, 1678
O'Neil, Eugene, 1670
O'Neil, Jack, 2372
O'Neil, John, 3449
O'Neil, Thomas, 3360
O'Neill, Cornelius J., 1001, 2053
O'Neill, E.A., 1031
O'Neill, Eugene, 1255
O'Neill, Francis, 3424
O'Neill, Hugh, 3514
O'Neill, John H. "Jack", 3549
O'Neill, Joseph F., 3425
O'Neill, Michael, 3273, 3513
O'Neill, Oona, 2954
O'Neill, Patrick, 755
O'Neill, Thomas, (U.S. pr.1974) 2990
O'Neill, Thomas, (U.S. pr.1800s) 3564
O'Neill, William, 3520
1J4, 2995
Onesto, Anthony, 1875
Oneto, Tulio, 3331
One Year Tim, 3415
Ongania, Juan Carlos, 142
On Leong, 2967, 3294
Onlu, Ed, 3343
Ono, Yoko, 686
Onomacritus, 2373
Onorta, 2373
On the Spot, 2373
Ontiveros, Gilberto, 3398
Onufrejczyk, Michael, 2373
Opalka, Adolf, 1531
Opdyke, George, 2319
Opendorfer, George, 1416
Operation Phocus, 2373-2374
Operation Greylord, 1135

Operation Quack Quack, 2374
Opietress, Owen, 3345
Opimius, 1355
Opium Bob, 3556
O'Posen, Sam'l, 849
Oppenheim, E. Philips, 1688, 2467
Oppenheim, S. Chesterfield, 246
Oppenheimer, Jacob, 2374
Oppenhof, Franz, 3251
Opper, Johann, 3180
Opperman, Gertrina Petrusina, 740
Opposition United Front of the Revolution
    Party, 3257
OPRA, 3520
OPR-33, 3328
OP Riots, 2374
Optimius, Lucius, 620
Optimum Services, Inc., 3289
Oquendo, Wilfredo Roman, 2374, 3465
Oradour-sur-Glane Massacre, 2374-2375
Oram, Thomas F.D. 2957
Orange, Leroy, 3451
Orange, William of, 437, 643, 713, 857, 934,
    1075, 1357, 1712, 1716, 2439, 2718
Orange Blossoms, 2375
Orange Riots, 2375
Orbach, Jerry, 1256
Orbilius Pupillus, 2375
Orbis, Heinz, 3245
Orchard, Harry, 872, 877, 1500, 1552, 2066,
    2375, 2554, 2851, 3094, 3243, 3263
Orcutt, P.D., 24
Orczy, Emmuska Magadalena Rosalia Marie
    Josepha Barbara, 2375
Ordeal by Glory, 2376
Ordelaffi, Pino III, 2376, 3238
Order, The, 2376, 3532
Order of Our Lady of Mercy, 2376
Order of the Assassins, 2376-2377, 2654,
    2655, 3237
Order of the White Rose, 1855
Ordine, 3269
Ordonez, Francisco Paredes, 1828
Orduno, Manuel Burgueno, 2663
Ordzhonikidze, Grigori Konstantinovich,
    2377
O'Regan, Brian, 2377
O'Reilly, Alexander, 2377
O'Reilly, John Boyle, 2377
O'Reilly, Pat, 420
Orejuela, Gilberto Rodriguez, 3398
Orejuela, Jorge Rodriguez, 3398
Oreman, Samuel, 353
Orendorff, Max, 184
Orenic, Michael A., 186, 1731, 2393
Orestes, 1650, 2377, 3235
Orfila, Mathieu Joseph Bonaventure, 1871,
    2377
Organization for Black Unity, 3483
Organization for Victims of Zionist
    Occupation, 3492, 3532
Organization of Struggle Against World
    Imperialism, 2456
Organization of the National Confrontation
    Front, 3333, 3511, 3532
Organization of the Oppressed on Earth,
    3532
Organization of the Popular Revolution-33,
    3490, 3532
Orgen, Jacob "Little Augie", 526, 935, 1295,
    1867, 1892-1894, 2004, 2377-2378, 2734,
    3406, 3409
Orgeron, Paul, 2378
Oribasius, 3291
Oribe, Berro, 3328, 3488
Oriental Saloon, 2378, 2748, 2749
Oriol y Urquijo Antonio Maria de, 2378
Oritz, Gerald, 3462
Orkney, Duke of, 448

Orkney, Earl of, 689
Orlandi, Emanuela, 3334
Orlandino, Marcantonio, 3297
Orlando, Andrew, 3388
Orlando, Ignazio, 3297
Orlando, Samuel, 1546
Orlando, Tony, 521
Orleans, Duke of, 2378
Orleans, Louis I, 2378-2379
Orleans, Louis Philippe Joseph, 2379
Orleans, Louis Philippe Robert, 2379
Orloff, Michael A., 2379
Orlov, Alexis Aleksei, 3240
Orlov, Grigory Grigoryevich, 657, 2451
Orlova, Gay, 31, 2006
Orly Group, 3529, 3533
Ormento, John, 136, 1974, 3294, 3297,
    3409
Ormento, Thomas, 3409
Ormesher, Margaret, 2379
Ormesher, May, 2379
Ormiston, Kenneth G., 2068
Ormonde, Dougal, 2379
Ormonde, James, Duke of, 409, 2379
Ormonde, James, Earl of, 1171, 2379
Ormsby, Jonathan, 890
Ormsdorf, Peter, 1175, 2988
Ornano, Philippe Antoine d', 2379
Orndorff, Michael, 3448
Orodes II, (Parthia d.36 B.C.) 2193, 2379,
    2460, 3234
O'Rourke, Anthony, 2379
O'Rourke, Johnny, 2379, 2584
O'Rourke, Michael, 3448
Orozco, Pascual, 2076-2078, 2355, 2406
ORPA, 3230, 3508-3510
Orpet, William, 2379-2380
Orr, Emma, 99
Orr, John, 3564
Orr, John Wellesley, 2380
Orr, Leon, 3347
Orr, Ronald, 3454
Orr, Thomas, 214, 215
Orr, William Edwin, 2380
Orrechio, Michael, 898
Orrick, Thalia, 2380
Orrick, William, 1513
Orrock, Thomas Henry, 2380
Orsini, Felice, 1140, 2279, 2282, 3241
Ortega, Fernando, 2380
Ortega, Hortense, 1524
Ortega, Manuel, 2969
Ortega, Ricky, 2213
Ortega Gasset, Eduardo, 3248
Orthwein, Adolphus Busch, 3325
Ortin Gil, Constantino, 843, 2380
Ortiz, 830
Ortiz, Carmen, 3332
Ortiz, Ignacio, 3448
Ortiz, Jessie, 1424
Ortiz, Lorna, 2380
Ortiz, Tommy, 3462
Ortiz, William, 180
Ortiz-Acosta, Jairo, 3465
Ortiz-Rubio, Pascual, 3246
Ortlepp, Reinhold Johannes, 908
Orton, Arthur, 222, 456, 737, 1492, 2380-
    2382
Orton, Dick, 3551
Ortona, Egidio, 1316
Ortuno, Rene Barrientos, 3255
O'Ryan, John F., 3425
O'Ryan, John J., 2357
Oryema, E.W., 114
Orysiak, Chester, 182
Orzoco, Martin Aguirre, 2663
Osadchey, Edward P., 3396
Osama Abd al-Hayy, 3279
Osana, Kenji, 2382

Osband, Lance, 3449
Osborn, Albert, (Brit. pr.1901) 2711, 2712
Osborn, Albert S., (U.S. pr.1940s) 498,
    3012
Osborn, Frank, 2382-2383
Osborn, Henry, 2456
Osborn, John Marion, 2383
Osborn, Thomas, 324
Osborn, William S., 3549
Osborne, Alberta, 2383
Osborne, Carl, 2383
Osborne, Daniel, 2446
Osborne, Deborah, 360
Osborne, Ellen, 722
Osborne, Ethel, 2383
Osborne, George O., 2383
Osborne, Harry, 1471
Osborne, J.J., 1453
Osborne, James W., 530, 1177, 2104, 2198
Osborne, John E., 3337
Osborne, Merle, 181
Osborne, Sarah, 2667
Osborne, Thomas, (Brit. 1631-1712) 2383
Osborne, Thomas Matt, (U.S. 1859-1926)
    223, 1906, 2305, 2383
Osborne, William M., 3424
Osceola, 2384
Osceola, John, 2384
Osgood, Suzanne, 2384
O'Shaughnessy, William, 3292
O'Shea, Kitty, 2414
O'Shea, Ronald, 3454
O'Shea, William Henry, 2414
Oshima Hiroshi, 3541
Osio, Gian Paulo, 2384
Oskilko, Radziwill, 3246
Osman Digna, 2384
Osman, Sülün, 2384
Osmena, Sergio, III, 2119
Osmond, Marie, 2291
Osorio, Julio, 1640
Osseiran, Adel, 1320
Osseiran, Ali, 1320, 3528
Osselin, Gerard, 3047
Ossietzky, Carl von, 2384
Oster Gang, 2384
Osterman, Andrei Ivanovich, 2384
Ostrom, E.N., 3251
Ostrowsky, Steven, 878
O'Sullivan, Joseph, 3172, 3245
O'Sullivan, Patrick, 828, 2385
O'Sullivan, Richard, 2385
O'Sullivan, William J., 530
Osuna, Duke of, 2523
Osuna, Pedro Téllez y Girón, 2385
Oswald, Barbara A., 2385, 2983, 3471
Oswald, Gerd, 2716
Oswald, H.R., 815
Oswald, Henry P., 932, 1832
Oswald, Lee Harvey, 330, 1302, 1616, 1796,
    1799, 1800, 2346, 2438, 3236, 3255, 3398
Oswald, Robyn S., 2385, 2983, 3471
Oswald, Russell G., 180, 2048
Oswiu, 3236
Oszkandy, Dorothy, 1266
Otano, Fidel Rego, 3473
Otano, Rogelio Vincente, 3473, 3522
Otano, Vincente Rego, 3473
Otero, Celestino, 205
Otero, Charles, 524
Otero, Joseph, 524
Otey, Harold, 3452
Othman, 2385, 3236
Otho, Marcus Slavius, 2385, 3235
Otis, Arlene, 2385
Otis, Harrison Gray, 872, 2062, 2207, 3243
Otis, William, 3351
O'Toole, Avis Mary, 1426
O'Toole, Betty Doreen, 1426

Patterson, Raymond, 3454
Patterson, Robert (U.S. pr.1846), 3305
Patterson, Robert (U.S. pr.1988), 869
Patterson, Robert Porter (U.S. b.1891) 2425
Patterson, Roger, 1884
Patterson, Thurston M., 3014
Patterson, Wade, 3361
Patterson, William (Can. pr.1927), 2299
Patterson, William (U.S. pr.1958), 1203, 2870
Patterson, William (U.S. pr.1988), 2020
Patterson, William (U.S. d.1898), 3350
Patterson, William J. (U.S. pr.1973), 1249
Patti, Adelina, 820, 1177
Patti, D., 2425
Pattinson, Joseph Colin, 2425-2426
Pattison, Granville Sharp, 2425
Pattison, Robert E., 564
Pattle, Eliza, 3074
Pattmore, May, 2426
Patton, D.R., 2831
Patton, Dorothy, 670
Patton, E.J., 964
Patton, George S., 434, 2422, 3295, 3375
Patton, James, 3342
Patton, Lawson, 3359
Patton, Richard E., 789
Patton, Wesley, 460
Patz, Etan, 2426
Patz, Stanley, 2426
Patzke, Thomas, 505
Paul I, 334, 2426, 3240, 3251
Paul III, 663, 870, 1152, 1157, 1165 pope
Paul IV, 577, 631
Paul V, 631, 1134
Paul VI, 2426-2427, 2553, 3505, 3256
Paul, Bob, 103, 810, 1058, 1594, 1931, 3556
Paul, Dr. Charles, 867
Paul, David, 2410
Paul, Frederick James, 3169
Paul, Isadore, 110
Paul, Jerry, 1971
Paul, John V., 3549
Paul, Philip "Pinchy", 1726, 3409
Paul, Prince, 78
Paul, Rene, 2427
Paul, Robert H., 3549
Paul, Sidney George, 171, 1066, 1642, 2427
Paul, W. Brady (U.S. pr.1930), 2698
Paul, William (Brit. pr.1900s), 1336
Paul, William, (U.S. pr.1822), 3044
Paulden, Thomas, 2530
Paulding, Hiram, 2325
Paule, Kevin, 3076
Paulet, Amias Paulet, 2427
Paulet, John, 2427
Pauli, Johann, 1289
Pauli, Louis, 3549
Paulina, Lollia, 39
Paulino, Dom, 762
Paulson, Belle, 1400
Paulson, Michael, 2427
Paulus, Julius, 2730, 2427-2428
Paulus, Lucius Aemilius, 1749
Pausanias, 2457, 3233
Pavarno, Margaret, 2428
Pavelic, Ante, 76-78, 169, 2428, 3021, 3248, 3541
Pavesi, Ernest, 182
Pavlick, Richard P., 1794
Pavlides, Vassos, 1865
Pavlik, Edward, 461
Pavone, Tommaso, 2204
Pavón Reyes, Jorge Armando, 586, 634
Pavy, Benjamin, 1984
Pavy, Yvonne, 1984
Pawlak, Steve, 182
Paxton Boys, 2428
Paxton, Harry, 1521

Paxton, Kenneth W., 3453
Paxton, Louis, 3565
Paxton Riots, The, 2428, 3371
Pay, Charles, 2428
Pay, Esther, 2428
Payne, A.D. (U.S. d.1930), 2429, 3264
Payne, Alfred Augustus (Brit. b.c.1862), 2429
Payne, Clyde, 1446
Payne, Daniel, 1541
Payne, E.W., 506
Payne, Edward, 3455
Payne, Frederick, 2429
Payne, George, 3304
Payne, Jesse James, 3368
Payne, Jimmy Ray, 3167
Payne, John Barton, 2801
Payne, Joseph, 3456
Payne, Larry (U.S. pr.1980s), 2941
Payne, LeRoy (U.S. pr.1970s), 2719
Payne, Nickoli "Dick", 1917
Payne, Pervis, 3454
Payne, Philip, 639, 1431
Payne, Randy Joe (U.S. pr.1980s), 3453
Payne, Ransom (U.S. pr.1890s), 3549
Payne, Richard, 803
Payne, Zebadiah, 2429
Payson, Herta, 1136
Payton, Barbara, 2293
Payton, William, 3449
Paz Belteton, Edwin, 3513
Paz Estenssoro, Victor, 3253
Paz, Federico, 3451
Pea y Pea, Manuel de la, 2439
Peabody, Irving, 1743
Peabody, Mrs. M.A., 3243
Peabody, Mrs. Richard Rogers, 829
Peabody, Nelson J., 2188
Peace and Freedom Fighters, 3533
Peace, Charles, 142, 397, 931, 1412, 1492, 2134, 2190, 2429-2432
Peach, Arthur, 2432
Peach, Phillip, 1636-37
Peacher, Paul D., 2432
Peacock, A.J. 2144
Peacock, Lewis, 1732, 1921, 2432, 3565
Peacock, Linda, 1493
Peacock, Ruth Pearce, 1328
Peacock, Silber C., 1328
Peak, Duane, 2575, 3266
Peak, Junius, 246, 275, 3424, 3549
Peak, Pat, 2546
Peake, Ephraim, 2432
Peake, Rebecca, 2432
Peakes, Bayard Pfundtner, 2433
Pearce, Derek, 2470-2471
Pearce, Dorothy, 1953
Pearce, Phyllis, 2781
Pearce, William, 2433
Pearcey, Mary Eleanor, 2433, 2778, 3133
Pearcy, Gladys, 271
Peare, William, 2433
Pearl, Cora, 836
Pearl, William S., 3565
Pearlman, Mark David, 3258, 3507
Pearlman, William, 274
Pearlstein, Charles, 2433
Pearse, Peter, 805
Pearson, Alice, 2434
Pearson, Drew, 634
Pearson, Ed (U.S. d.1906), 3357
Pearson, Edmund Lester (U.S. 1880-1937), 2421, 2433
Pearson, Elizabeth, 2433
Pearson, Emaline, 1677
Pearson, Hesketh, 2433
Pearson, Jeannine, 1406
Pearson, Kathleen, 1406
Pearson, Larry, 340
Pearson, Mabel, 146

Pearson, Mary, 3350
Pearson, Moses, 2433-2434
Pearson, Sarah, 2434
Pearson, William, 2410, 3457
Pearson, Yvonne, 2879
Peary, Robert Edwin, 769, 1853
Pease, Ben, 1494
Pease, J. Loren, 1150
Pease, L.M., 1201
Peavey, Henry, 2903, 2904, 2906
Peavy, Banjo, 3355
Pecce, Edward A., 923
Pecella, Daniel, 1845
Pecho, Eleanor, 2434
Pecho, Walter A., 2434
Peci, Patrick, 3515
Peci, Roberto, 3515
Peck, Benjamin, 1767
Peck, Bernard, 3252
Peck, Catherine, 3072
Peck, Clara, 3072
Peck, Cortez L., 3425
Peck, Ellen, 2434
Peck, Erastus, 1902
Peck, George R., 1048
Peck, John E., 3072
Peck, Katherine, 2259
Peck, Percy, 3072
Peck, Richard W., 2434
Peck, Steven, 2293
Peckham, George, 3132
Peckham, Robert, 1739
Peckham, Rufus Wheeler, Jr., 161, 2434-2435
Peckham, Wheeler Hazard, 2434-2435
Pecock, Reginald, 2435
Pecora, Ferdinand, 297, 418, 2435, 2685
Pecora, Nofio J., 3400
Pecorara, Rose, 110
Pecoraro, John, 3451
Pecoraro, Michael, 2435, 3409
Pedachenko, Dr. Alexander, 1688
Peddan, Robert, 1385
Peddie, James, 3247
Pedote, Frank, 1841, 2435
Pedrarias, 2435
Pedraza, J., 3248
Pedro Bautista, 2427
Pedro Chavez, 3551
Pedro el Cruel, 896, 2435, 3238
Pedulla, Joseph, 2574
Peede, Robert, 3450
Peeff, Jordan, 3249
Peek, David, 3450
Peekskill Riot, 2435, 3376
Peel, Fanny, 2435
Peel, Joseph, Jr., 2435
Peel, M.C., 1643, 3560
Peel, Sir Robert, 391, 460, 1156, 1606, 2061-2062, 2435-2436, 2684, 2709, 2928, 3046, 3124, 3241
Peeler, Oscar, 2181
Peers, Rosanna, 1173, 3404, 3409
Peete, Lofie Louise, 2436
Peete, Richard, 2436
Pegler, Westbrook, 2687
Pegram, George B., 2433
Pegram, Thomas E., 1406
Pehrson, Ella, 1752
Peichev, Lubomir, 3470
Peifer, Jack, 238, 239, 1758, 1763
Peiper, Joachim, 2097, 2436-2437
Peisistratus, 1562
Pekahia, 3232
Pekowsky, Robert, 1967
Pekwek, Frank, 3337
Pel, Albert, 2437
Pelaez, J. Fernandez, 3250
Pelagia of Antioch, 2437

Pelagius (Roman. d.420), 1749, 2437
Pelagius I (Italy d.561), 2437
Pelham, John, 495
Pelham, William, 1171
Pelke, Ruth, 777
Pelke, William, 777
Pell, Henry, 3565
Pell, Max, 2218
Peller, Sam, 613, 3120, 3388
Pellerano Albantosa, Rafael Fredesvindo, 3473, 3511
Pelletier, Lawrence, Jr., 2437
Pelletier, Nicolas-Jacques, 2437
Pelletier, Sir Charles Alphonse Pantalon, 2437
Pellew, Edward, 3304
Pelley, Douglas, 372
Pelley, William Dudley, 488
Pellham, Steven, 1475
Pellicano, Anthony J., 2437-2438
Pellico, Silvio, 2438
Pelligrini, David, 3452
Pelligrino, Rocco, 3409
Pellizioni, Serafino, 2196, 2438
Pelosi, Giuseppe, 2438
Pelsey, Thomas, 1268
Peltier, Leonard, 2438
Peltz, Greta, 2439
Peltzer, Armand, 2439
Peltzer Brothers, 126, 2439
Peltzer, Léon, 2439
Pelzer, Kevin, 3454
Pemberton, Sir Francis, 1195, 2439
Pemberton, J.C., 3294
Pembroke, Duke of (Brit. pr.1470), 2836
Pembroke, Lord (Brit. pr.1670s), 1324
Pena, Augusto, 3246
Pena, Joseph, 2127
Pena Soltren, Luis A., 3466
Pencovic, Francis, 2439
Penda, 2439, 3236
Pendegast, Lyle, 3425
Pendergast, James, 2439, 2440, 3009
Pendergast, John, 208
Pendergast Machine, 23, 183, 184, 2439-2440
Pendergast, Thomas J., 183, 208, 370, 642, 842, 1377, 1545, 1755, 2036, 2259, 2286, 2439-2440, 2696, 3009, 3121, 3396
Pendlebury, Frank E., 73
Pendleton, Allen, 3357
Pendleton, Edmund (U.S. 1721-1803), 2440
Pendleton, Edward (U.S. d.1858), 1431-32, 2395, 2440-2441
Pendleton, William H., 1088
Pendola, Teddy, 3409
P'eng Chia-chen, 3243
P'eng Teh-huai, 3253
Penlez, Bosavern, 2441
Penn, D.B., 2313
Penn, James, 3450
Penn, John, 2428
Penn, William, 1285, 2441
Penner, George, 3339
Pennetta, Ricardo, 666
Pennington, Elizabeth, 448
Pennington, Frank, 3452
Pennington, John, 3353
Pennsylvania Brothel Riot, 3373
Pennsylvania Negro Riots, 3372
Pennsylvania Steel Strike, 3375
Penny, John, 1425
Peñoran, Jos Miquel, 405
Penruddock, Charles Wadham Wyndham, 2441
Penry, John (Brit. 1559-93), 2441
Penry, Johnny Paul (U.S. pr. 1957), 2441, 3455
Pensendorfer, Joseph, 2441
Pensinger, Brett, 3449

Penson, Richard, 1457
Pentagon Anti-War Protest, 3376
Pentagon Papers, 3098
Pentecost, David, 3450
Pentecost Riot, 2441
Pentenza, Rocco, 3388
Pentridge Prison Escape, 2441-2442
Penwell, E.S., 3549
Penycate, John, 2047
Peoples, Clint, 1108
Peoples, John, 1166, 3447
People's Army, 3532, 3533
People's Fedayeen Movement, 3512
People's Forces Unit IX, 3533
People's Front 31st January, 3520, 3533
People's Liberation Army, 2442, 3488, 3492, 3515, 3519, 3533, 3534
People's Liberation Forces, 3271, 3506, 3533
People's Liberation Front, 2442
People's Party, 3485, 3486, 3502
People's Redemption Council, 3259, 3507, 3515, 3533
People's Revolutionary Armed Forces, 3329, 3496, 3533
People's Revolutionary Army (Zero Point), 3496, 3529, 3532, 3533
People's Revolutionary Army, 2442-2443
People's Revolutionary Front, 3266, 3331, 3533
People's Revolutionary Party, 3533
People's Savings Bank, 3289
People's Will, 3263
Peparo, Michael Anthony, 3466
Pepe, Carmine, 716
Pepe, Guglielmo, 2443, 2479
Pepin I, 3074
Pepitone, Emanuel, 3079
Pepitone, Michele, 193
Pepitone, Mrs. Mike, 1744
Pepitone, Pietro, 193, 393
Pepitone-Albano, Michele, 2250
Pepper, Augustus Joseph, 2829
Peppin, George, 365, 1986, 2149, 3549, 3565
Peppott, George, 836
Pepwell, Agnes, 2443
Pepwell, Mary, 2443
Pepys, Samuel, 12, 2443, 2712
Pequot Tribe Massacre, 2443
Peralta, Daniel, 3246
Peralta, Miguel A., 3246
Peralta, Pedro de, 2443
Perault (Italy pr.16th Cent.), 3303
Perceval, Spencer, 522, 2443, 3232, 3240
Percey, James William, 1251
Perchand, Charles, 1877
Percy, Charles, 1336, 2444, 3388
Percy, Edward, 1870, 1901, 2190, 2879
Percy, Sir Henry (Brit. c.1532-85), 2443
Pecy, Sir Henry (Brit. 1564-1632), 1491, 2443
Percy Orlando Rush, 2393
Percy, Sir Thomas (Brit. c.1344-1403), 2443-2444
Percy, Sir Thomas (Brit. 1528-72), 2444
Percy, Sir Thomas (Brit. 1560-1605), 1140, 1405, 2444
Percy, Valerie, 1336, 2444
Perdgen, Wes, 3452
Perdicaris, Ion, 2532, 3325
Perdiccas, 910, 2444, 3233
Perdomo Osorio, Modesto, 595
Perdue, Donald, 1249
Perdue, Frank, 655
Perdue, L.W., 3347
Peredeo, 3236
Pereira Reverbel, Ulysses, 3002
Pereira, Sebastiao, 1880

Perenze, Antonio, 1319
Perera, Manuel, 90
Peretti, Aniello, 590
Perez, Alberto M., 1337
Perez Alonso, Carlos, 3515
Perez, Amodio, 3002
Pérez, Antonio, 1083, 2165, 2444
Perez, Carlos Alonzo, 3333
Perez, Domingo, 3451
Perez, Jesus, 1801
Perez, José, 444
Perez, Leonara M., 2282
Perez, M., 3245
Perez, Manuel J., 3455
Pérez, Mariana, 1204
Pérez, Orlando, 3472
Perez, Sara, 2074
Perez Lazono, Julian, 3244
Perez Perez, Crecencio, 3472
Perez Rodriguez, Juan, 3257
Perfect Park Home Garden Society, 3487
Pericles (Gr. pr.430 B.C.), 70, 171, 1524
Pericles Paxinos (S.Afri. pr.1930s), 1039
Perigo, Rebecca, 281
Perigo, William, 281
Perillo, Emilio, 2573-2574
Perillo, Pamela, 3455
Perini Corporation, 2444
Perivolidis, Arthur, 234
Perkins, Anthony, 2510
Perkins, Benjamin D., 2444
Perkins, Charles, 1146
Perkins, Dorothy, 2508
Perkins, Elisha, 2444
Perkins, Emmett, 1356
Perkins, Josephine Amelia, 2444
Perkins, Louis, 3565
Perkins, Mrs. Ben C., 3353
Perkins, R.S. (U.S. pr.1854), 3425
Perkins, Rudolph (U.S. 1949-,), 2444-2445
Perkins, Simon, 509
Perkins, William (Brit. 1555-1602), 2445
Perkins, William (U.S. pr.1865), 2569
Perkins, Willis, 3362
Perley, D.W., 2916
Perley Poore, 2441
Perlowin, Bruce J., 2445
Perna, Anthony, 3380
Perna, Michael, 18
Pernell, Julian, 3301
Pernotte, Louis, 1316, 3536
Peroff, Frank P., 3409
Perón, Isabel, 445, 1102, 2445, 3499
Perón, Juan Domingo, 142, 1077, 1397, 2445, 2674, 3252, 3253, 3256, 3270, 3463, 3494, 3499
Perone, John, 1488
Perone, Sam, 428
Peronist Armed Forces, 3266
Perot, H. Ross, 1284
Perovsky, Sophia, 88
Perperna, Marcus, 2729
Perreau, Daniel, 914, 2445
Perreau, Jeanne, 695
Perreau, Robert, 914, 2445
Perrin, Richard, 1827
Perrin, Robert, 314
Perris, "Worcester" Sam, 1941, 2019
Perritt, Henry, 3399, 3400
Perrone, Pauline, 3393
Perrone, Santo, 3393, 3394, 3409
Perrot, Sir John (Brit. c.1527-92), 2445
Perrot, Marc, 2522
Perrott, John (Brit. 1723-1761), 2445-2446
Perrott, Samuel V., 3424
Perry, Arthur, 2446, 3452
Perry, B.F., 2246
Perry, C.C., 771
Perry, Calvin D., III, 2446

1157, 2193, 2729
Pompey the Great, 2485, 3234
Pompey, Maurice, 1135
Pompez, Alexander, 3409
Pompidor, Abbé, 185
Pompilia, 618
Pompilj, 3245
Pomroy, Karen Ann, 622
Ponce, Noratto, 422, 2228, 2485
Ponce, Ramiro, 3525
Poncet, Antonin, 633
Pond, Augustus, 3345
Pond, George, 3345
Pond, George R., 20011
Pond, Sheldon, 2485
Ponder, Andrew, 1753
Ponder, Edward, 508
Ponder, Ernest, 3368
Poniatowski, Michel, 497
Pons-Gerard, Michel, 3047, 3048
Pontani, Albert, 3413
Ponte, Kenneth C., 2309
Pontelli, Mike, 2102
Ponti, Carlo, 19901
Ponti, Phil, 3396
Pontiac, Chief, 2485
Pontian, 2485 saint
Ponticelli, Anthony, 3450
Pontius, Maria, 1299
Pontius, Roland, 314
Ponto, Jürgen, 203,2528, 3257, 3331, 3505,
    3508
Pony Deal, 3549
Ponzi, Cavaliere, 648
Ponzi, Charles, 1843, 2485-2486, 2488, 2845
Ponzinibio, Gianfrancesco, 654, 2488
Pook, Edmund Walter, 2488
Pook, Hermann, 3542
Poole, Alice, 692
Poole, Becky, 890
Poole, Bill "the Butcher", 2291, 2488, 2682,
    3401
Poole, Calvin, 562
Poole, Charles, 396, 890
Poole, Derek Alan, 2488
Poole, Felix, 3343
Poole, Gus T., 772
Poole, Harry, 2736
Poole, J.P., 2485
Poole, James, 2156 sir
Poole, Peter Harold, 2488
Poole, Serjeant, 1520
Poole, William, 2488
Poore, Ben, 2395
Poore, Joseph, 3331
Poorman, Sean, 2414
Pop, Eugene Lewis, 2489
Pope Alexander VI, 2462
Pope, Alexander, 1445, 1901
Pope, Bill, 3042
Pope, Carlton, 3456
Pope, Duane Earl, 2489
Pope, Ephreim, 3356
Pope, Ervin, 2489
Pope, Henry C., 3305
Pope Innocent VIII, 2462
Pope, Jimmie, 3453
Pope, John, 2103
Pope, Joyce, 2345, 2489
Pope, Nathaniel, 2489
Pope Paul VI, 2426-2427
Pope Zosimus, 2437
Pope, Thomas Dewey, 3450
Popelka, Viktor, 3464
Popham, Sir John, 2489
Popieluzsko, Jerzy, 3334
Popik, Paula, 2990
Popillius, 714, 3234
Popish Plot, 2349

Pople, G.T., 2489-2490
Popolo, John, 1049
Popovic, Cvetko, 1213
Popovitch, V., 3247
Popp, Georg, 2692
Poppe, Hank, 273
Popular Democratic Front For the
    Liberation of Palestine, 2397, 3533
Popular Forces of April 25, 3273, 3512,
    3533
Popular Front For the Liberation of
    Palestine, 2397, 2402, 2456,
    3265-3268, 3481, 3483, 3490, 3493,
    3533
Popular League, 3533, 3534
Popular Liberation Forces, 648, 3272,
    3506, 3511, 3533
Popular Resistance Group, 3493, 3533
Popular Revolutionary Bloc, 3331, 3332,
    3505, 3506, 3530, 3533
Popular Revolutionary Resistance Group,
    3267
Popular Revolutionary Struggle, 3230,
    3512, 3533
Popular Revolutionary Vanguard, 2490
Popular Struggle Front, 3484, 3485, 3533
Porat, Tirza, 2490
Porcari, Luciano, 3471
Porch, Edith Mary, 621
Porcherot, 2465
Porcia, 2490
Porcino, Antonio, 1880
Porello, Angelo, 3392
Porello, James, 3392
Porello, Joseph, 3392
Porello, Raymond, 3392
Porello, Rosario, 3392
Poret, Clifton Alton, 18671
Poretto, Joseph Albert, 3399, 3400
Porpora, Nicola, 1848
Porsena, Lars, 2685
Porst, Lee, 19081
Port Stockton, 2857
Portales, Diego José Victor, 2490, 3241
Portalier, Victor, 3023
Portch, Daniel, 3086
Porteous, John, 2490-2491
Porteous, Tom, 1190
Porter, Albert S., 228
Porter, Alice, 1143
Porter, Anne, 3165
Porter, Anthony, 3451
Porter, Austin, 3342
Porter, Barry, 3258, 3273, 3512
Porter, Billy, 1666, 3084
Porter, Carrie May, 733
Porter, Daniel, 1280
Porter, Derrick, 1199
Porter, Donald James, 2491
Porter, Elizabeth, 2390
Porter, Ernest, 3454
Porter, Fannie, 653, 1978
Porter, Fitz-John, 2491
Porter, Frank, 3565
Porter, George, 3450
Porter, Henry, 3111
Porter, Henry Martinez, 3447
Porter, Ian, 1692
Porter, J. Robert, 2098
Porter, James, 3347
Porter, James W. (U.S. pr.1930s), 1735
Porter, Jimmy (U.S. pr.1874), 1742
Porter, Joseph, 2314
Porter, Katherine Ann, 1080, 2652
Porter, Laura, 3360
Porter, Preston, 3352
Porter, Raleigh, 3450
Porter, Ray, 3340
Porter, Robert, 3111

Porter, Roger, 3453
Porter, Samuel Lowry, 2491
Porter, Sarah, 3165
Porter, Solomon, 3118
Porter, Thomas, 2785
Porter, Warren, 2224
Porter, William Howard, 3453
Porter, William Sydney, "O. Henry", 1426,
    1721, 2195, 2491, 2762
Porter, William Wood, 2491
Porterfield, Sidney, 3454
Porterie, Gaston Louis Noel, 2491
Porterie, J.A., 3550
Portis, Bill, 723
Portis, Sidney, 3463
Portland Whorehouse Riot, 2491, 3373
Porto, Pietro, 3389
Portsmouth Square, 3415
Portugal, Edward of, 1149
Portugal, Ferdinand of, 1149
Portugal, Maria of, 627
Porus, 2492, 3233
Posada, José Guadalupe, 2492
Posada-Carriles, Luis, 445
Posey, Billy Wayne, 458
Posey, "Dock" 3358
Posey, Joseph, 2492
Posner, Arthur L., 848
Pospechil, Zvonimir 76
Pospichal, E.J., 3251
Posse Comitatus, 3502, 3533
Post, Charles N., 508
Post, Edwin Main, 2104
Post, Emily, 2104
Post, Garnetta, 1415
Post, George, (U.S. pr.1980s) 1415, 3389
Post, George W., (U.S. pr.1880s), 2032
Post, J.D., 1037
Post, Louis F., 2555
Post, Melville Davisson, 2492
Post, Robert, 3290
Post, Vaudrey, 1415
Postell, Charles, 1300
Postell, Judi, 1300
Posthuma, F.E., 3250 dr.
Postlethwaite, Graham, 493
Postley, Clarence A., 2723
Postman Always Rings Twice, The, 2492
Postumus, Marcus Cassianius Latinius,
    2492
Potamitis, Christos, 2492
Potashes, The, 435, 1635, 3409
Potemkin, Grigori Aleksandrovich, 657,
    2492
Potenza, Rocco, 3389
Potenza, Vincent, 3409
Potkonjac, Vjekoslav, 3065
Potocki, Andreas, 3243
Potocki, Stanislaw, 2492
Potoriek, Oskar, 1213
Potter, Andrew Jackson, 3565
Potter, Andrew P., 2492
Potter, Bruce, 2492
Potter, Charles, 3562
Potter, Charles H., 3091
Potter, Dell, 3550
Potter, George D., 551
Potter, Henry Codman, 2492
Potter, John S., 2420
Potter, Thomas, 1512
Potter, William, 3361
Potter, William E., 2131
Pottinger, Frederick, 1268
Pottinger, J. Stanley, 1771
Potts, Helen, 529, 530, 1459
Potts, Jack Howard, 2492, 3450
Potts, Larry, 3451
Potts, Robert, 3485
Potz, Ignatz, 2780

Rafeedie, Edward, 107, 587
Raffaelo, Roberto, 2123, 2528
Raffanti, Sonjia, 3064
Rafferty, Anthony, 2528
Rafferty, John, 1701
Raffield, George, 1836
Rafsanjani, Ali Akbar Hashemi, 1811, 3260
Raft, George, 32, 755, 3393, 3395
Rag, Isaac, 1035
Ragan, James, 2421
Ragen, Frank, 2529, 3389
Ragen, James M., 128, 1028, 1775, 2529
Ragen, James, Sr., 3382, 3388, 3389, 3391
Ragen, Joseph E., 2529
Ragen's Colts, 2529, 2972, 3387, 3389, 3390,
Rag Gang, 3409
Ragged Bill, 3544
Ragged Stranger, The, 3087, 3088, 3089
Raghunath Rao, 2529
Ragon, Heartsill, 2529
Ragone, Antonio, 2985
Ragsdale, Edward, 3450
Ragtime, 3075
Ragucci, Anthony, 3389
Rahim, Tariq, 3510
Rahmah ibn Jabr, 1651
Rahman, Mujibur, 2529, 3257
Rahman, Ziaur, 3258
Rahn, Arthur, 2986
Rahn, Peggy, 3328
Rahoumi, Ahmed, 3255
Raidler, William, 1003, 2529-2530, 2955,
  3565
Raies, Jeanne, 2530
Raikes, Dandy, 503
Raikes, St. John, 2262
Railroad Strike, 3374
Raimondi, Harry, 109
Raimundo Benavides, Oscar, 3247
Rain, Harold K., 2530
Rainbow, Elizabeth, 425
Rainey, Andrew, 3355
Rainey, John, 2218
Rainey, Lawrence, 458
Rainge, Willie, 3161
Rains, Claude, 2927
Rainsborough, Thomas, 2530
Rainsey, Arthur, 3341
Rainsford, E.G., 1837
Rainulf, 1398
Rainwater, Houston, 3394
Rais, Ben, 3252
Rais, Gilles de, 2530-2532
Raisuli, 2532, 3325
Raitch, Yvan, 76
Raiton, Ronald, 3413
Rajagopalachari, Chakravarti, 3251
Rajai, Ali, 315
Rajai, Mohammed Ali, 3259, 3516
Rajakowitsch, Erich, 2532
Rajavi, Massoud, 906, 3259, 3520
Raji, Mohammed Ali, 3274
Rajk, Laszlo, 2532
Rakeshi Okudeira, 2552
Rakoczy, Mark, 1120
Rakosi, Matyas, 2532
Rakovski, Georgi Sava, 2533
Rakovsky, J. Andressy 3244
Rakovsky, Khristian Georgiyevich, 2533
Rakovsky, Melchoir, 3240
Rale, Antonio, 3565
Raleigh, Walter, 423, 585, 742, 930, 2489,
  2533, 2979, 3291
Ralent, Evan, 3360
Raley, David, 3449
R. Almada, Octavio, 3246
Ralph, Edward, 2533
Ralph, Ronald E., 3471
Ralston, Annie, 1702

Ralston, Henry, 3362
Ralston, William C., 162
Rama I, 680
Rama VII, 1811
Rama VIII, 3251
Ramadier, Paul, 3251
Ramashamola, Theresa, 2736
Ramb, Christine, 1582
Rambova, Natacha, 3027
Ram Chandra, 677
Rameau, Jaquette, 2533
Ramensky, Johnny, 2533
Ramey, Irving, 3451
Ramey, Richard, 1063
Ramirez, Anthony Richard, 3449
Ramirez, Carlos, 3455
Ramirez, Diego, 3469
Ramirez, Patrick, 2533
Ramirez, Raul Anthony, 2533
Ramirez, Richard, 3449
Ramirez Castaneda, Ramirez, 3466
Ramirez Ortiz, Antulio, 3465
Ramirez Razo, Samuel "El Samy", 1255
Ramirez Sanchez, Illich, 3521, 3522
Ramm, Geraldine, 1511
Ramon, José, Jr., 2566
Ramón Mercader del Rio Hernandez,
  Jaine, 2994
Ramorino, Girolamo, 2533
Ramos, Graciliano, 2533
Ramos, Marcelino, 3449
Ramos, Maria Elena, 2523
Ramos Cobas, Jesus, 3468
Ramos Lopez, Leonardo, 1410
Ramp, James, 2236
Rampino, Anthony, 3409
Ramsay, Allan, 1903
Ramsay, George, 3304
Ramsay, John, 2533
Ramsay, William, 3359
Ramseur, James, 1329
Ram Singh, 677
Ramsperger, Charles, 317
Ramus, Petrus, 2533
Rancourt, Susan, 538
Rand, Ayn, 2336
Rand, Greedy Jake, 2984
Rand, Jake, 1355, 3409
Rand, Sally, 1076, 2533-2534
Rand, Tamara, 3397
Rand, William, 2423
Randaccio, Federico, 3380
Randall, Alvin C., 340
Randall, Amos, 3355
Randall, Andrew, 1528
Randall, Otis, 3389
Randall, Tom, 2534
Randall, William, 3565
Randazzo, Anthony, 3394
Randazzo, Gaspar, 901
Randazzo, Vincenzo, 3416
Rande, Frank, 3565
Randella, Snooks, 2863
Randolph, Mrs. David Meade, 1245
Randolph, Edmund Jennings, 2534
Randolph, Jennie, 2299
Randolph, John, 3305
Randolph, Richard, 3450
Randolph, Thomas, 2534
Randolph-Clay Duel, 2534
Ranelagh, 1943
Raney, James, 2349, 2534
Raney, W.J., 1787
Rangel, Jose, 2461
Rankin, Andrew, 1472
Rankin, Gilman D., 2656
Rankin, Hezekiah, 3340
Rankin, John, 942, 3550
Rankin, Quinten, 3359

Rann, John, 914, 2534-2535
Ransdell, Joseph E., 1982
Ransom, Charles, 596, 2535
Ransom, Florence, 2535
Ransom, Harry, 3143
Ransom, John, 3342
Ransom, Kenneth Ray, 3455
Ranston, Thomas, 3358
Rao, Baji, II, 2276
Rao, Charles, 583
Rao, Eleanor, 583
Rao, Joseph, 2535, 2700, 3124, 3409
Rao, Narayan, 2529
Rao, Vincent John, 3409
Raoul, Clair, 2535, 3047, 3048
Raoul, Court M., 2535
Rape, Charles, 3428
Raper, Millicent, 2535
Raper, Pamela, 2535
Raphael, 2672
Raphael, Sylvia, 2536
Raphel, Arnold, 3220
Raposo, Victor, 2762
Rapp, Mabel, 144
Rappe, Virginia, 143-152, 1437
Rardon, Gary, 2536
Rasberry, Jerry, 2192
Rasch, Otto, 3542
Rasche, Karl, 3542
Raschig, Sigmund, 3542
Rascoe, Burton, 639
Rascon, Eugenio, 3565
Rash, Matt, 1619
Rasiewicz, Barbara, 2536
Rasiewicz, William, 2536
Rasin, Alois, 2536, 3245
Raspail, François Vincent, 2536
Raspberry, M.W., 312
Raspe, Jan-Carl, 200, 525, 2528, 3475, 3505
Rasputin, Gregori Efimovich, 1688, 2098,
  2331, 2536-2541, 3214, 3243
Rassouli, 2532, 3325
Rasta-Coptic Smuggling Network, 2541
Rastell, William, 2542
Rastelli, Philip "Rusty", 2542, 2670, 3405,
  3406, 3409, 3411
Rataj, Maciej, 3249
Ratanji, Hakim Bakhtyar Rustonji, 2542
Ratburi, Prince of, 2827
Ratchitch, Punica, 2527
Ratcliff, Henry, 3352
Ratcliff, Leo, 954
Ratcliffe, George, 3351
Ratcliffe, John, 766
Ratelwacht, 2542
Rath, Maurice, 399
Rathbone, Basil, 1995
Rathbone, Henry Riggs, 1956
Rathel, Otis, 2822
Rathenau, Walther, 2542-2543, 3245
Rathlev, Ray, 504
Ratliff, Marshall, 2543
Ratmat, Elmar, 3124
Ratoff, Gregory, 2234
Ratsey, Gamaliel, 2544
Ratsimandrava, Richard, 3257
Rattenbury, Alma, 828, 2544
Rattenbury, Francis Mawson, 2544
Rattenbury-Stoner Case, 1914
Rattigan, Terence, 3177
Rattler, John, 3346
Rau, Benegal Narsing, 2544
Rau, Gustav, 2544, 3042
Rauch, John O., 2327
Rauff, Walter Herman Julius, 2545
Raulerson, James, 3447
Raulin-Laboureur, Ede, 3252
Raul Lopez Alvarez, 3334
Rauls, Edward, 3425

Reed, Sam, 3353
Reed, Stanley, 3146
Reed, Stanley Forman, 2557
Reed, Thomas, 3304
Reed, Walker, 2833
Reed, William, 3363
Reed, Wilmot, 2669
Rees, Alt, 3357
Rees, Melvin David, 2557
Rees, Rees T., 2557
Reese, Albert, 3359
Reese, Bessie, 2577
Reese, Donald, 3452
Reese, Freeman, 2558
Reese, Guy, 3425
Reese, James, 3565
Reese, John, 3357
Reese, Lawrence, 1225
Reese, Louis, 1113
Reese, Walter, 2558
Reese, William, 1410
Reeve, Arthur B., 2759
Reeve, Arthur Benjamin, 2558
Reeve, Tapping, 2558
Reeves, Albert L., 2440
Reeves, David, 3277, 3523
Reeves, Frank, 3353
Reeves, Gene, 1189
Reeves, John, 1821
Reeves, Louise, 678
Reeves, Randolph, 3452
Reeves, Ruth, 726
Reeves, Sandy, 3365
Reeves, Thomas, 1469
Refai, Najeeb Sayeb, 3260, 3525
Reffett, Randall, 1248
Reform League Riots, 2558
Regan, Jane, 641
Regan, John H., 1669
Regan, Leonard, 2558
Regan, Mick, 1865
Regent, Robert, 3050
Reggettz, Paul, 2558
Reggettz, Vanessa, 2558
Reggio, Tony, 998
Reggione, Michael "Little Apples", 2870
Reginald of Chtillon, 2559
Reginault de Saint-Jean d'Angely, Michel-
    Louis-Etienne, 2559
Rego, Victor, 558, 2893
Rego Otano, Fidel, 3522
Regulators, 2748, 2803
Regulator War, 2559
Regulus, Marcus Atilius, 2559
Rehlinger, Ludwig, 1847
Rehm, Jacob, 1749, 3424
Rehnquist, William H., 381, 1189, 2559
Reich, Susan, 2747
Reichstag Fire, 974, 1748, 2559-2560
Reickles, John H., 2560
Reid, Addie, 883
Reid, Andrea, 1329
Reid, C.S., 1547
Reid, David, 646
Reid, Ed, 2564
Reid, F.J., 3550
Reid, Frank R., 2192
Reid, James, 3350
Reid, James W., 3367
Reid, John H., 1208, 2978
Reid, Patrick, 2560
Reid, Richard, 785
Reid, Robert Threshie, 2560
Reid, Sharon, 1343
Reid, Wallace, 144, 3295
Reid, William H., 2466
Reid, Willie, 3368
Reida, Kevin, 724
Reida, William, 724

Reifel, George, 2560
Reifel, Henry, 2560
Reilley, James F., 2552
Reilley, M.F., 3404
Reilleys, Terry, 3411
Reilly, Ben, 174
Reilly, Charles, 1527
Reilly, Edward J., 1488, 1841
Reilly, James, 72
Reilly, John, 1287
Reilly, Mark, 3449
Reilly, Oliver, 3339
Reilly, Pat, 964, 966
Reilly, Peter, 2560-2561
Reilly, Philip J., 2174
Reilly, Robert, 3425
Reilly, Robert E., 2561, 3044
Reilly, Terrence, 182
Reily, Jim, 2315
Reimer, Jean, 3333
Reims, Ebbo of, 1066
Reina, Gaetano, 2114, 2138, 3409
Reina, Tom, 2561
Reina Barrios, José Maria, 2561, 3242
Reinders, Ralf, 202, 3475
Reinecke, Hermann, 3542
Reinemann, Eugenia, 2213
Reiner, Mary, 3011
Reinfeld, Joseph H., 3409
Reingold, Gail, 3461
Reingold, Moe, 3461
Reinhardt, Hans, 3542
Reinhardt, Kathe, 3180
Reinhardt, Rudolf, 2898
Reinier, Gertrude M., 948
Reinman, June, 1080
Reinstein, Samuel, 2561
Reiper, Honora Mary, 1638
Reiper, Pauline Yvonne, 1638
Reis, Arthur Virgilio Alves, 2562
Reis, Maria Luiza Jacobetty D'Azevado,
    2562
Reischauer, Edwin, 3255
Reiser, Charles "The Ox", 2562, 3282
Reiser, Martin, 1299
Reiser Safecracking Gang, 3282
Reiss, Ignace, 2563
Reissfelder, George, 2563
Reisz, Karel, 2336
Reles, Abraham "Kid Twist", 1, 35, 111,
    112, 117, 342, 1289, 620, 2090, 2252,
    2255, 2563-2564, 2689, 2702, 3003,
    3120, 3187, 3401, 3404, 3407, 3408,
    3409, 3410, 3411
Relkin, Marie, 1372
Relphe, Linn, 2357
Rembrandt, 2098, 3032
Remedios, Patricio, 2564
Remeliik, Haruo, 2671
Remeta, Daniel, 3448, 3450
Remine, Richard, 3565
Remington, Eliphalet, 2564
Remington, Henry, 3360
Remiro, Joseph, 1502, 2889
Remley, Charles, 2565
Remling, Dale Otto, 2565, 3428
Remón, José Antonio, 2566, 3252
Remus, George, 1141, 2566-2567
Remy, 2988
Remy, Nicholas, 2567
Remy, William H., 1048, 1676
Renata, Maria, 2567
Renato Curcio, 3533
Renczi, Vera, 2567
Rendall, Charles, 532
Rendall, Martha, 2568
Rendel, George William, 2568
Render, Rose, 1085
Rendigs, Charles, 1132

Rendleman, Carroll, 2568
Rendrick, Courtney, 3348
Rendulic, Lothar, 3542
Rene of France, 2568
Renfroe, John W., 802
Rengo Sekigun, 3533
Renick, William, 2568
Rennels, Robert R., 2568
Rennels, Troy, 2568
Renner, Karl, 987
Rennick, "Cowboy" Bob, 2548
Rennie, Margaret, 2042
Renno, Donald, 516
Rennyson, Archie, 1463
Reno Brothers, 152, 1701, 1707, 2468, 2568,
    3457
Reno, Frank, 2568-2569, 3457
Reno, Gus, 426
Reno, Janet, 2577
Reno, Jim Bill, 2052
Reno, John, 2568-2569, 3457
Reno, Marcus, 1111, 2282
Reno, Ralph, 2568
Reno, Simeon, 2568-2569
Reno, Simon, 3457
Reno, William, 2568, 3457
Renoir, 2098
Renoux, Cécile, 1390
Renowden, William P., 2093
Rension, Patrick, 2152
Rentoul, Gervais, 2569, 2721
Rentschler, William H., 2569
Renwick, James, 2569
Renwood, Minnie, 2723
Renya, Mudaguchi, 279
Renzulli, Thomas "Crunch", 1513
Reppert, Eugene C., 1545, 1758
Repsold, Herbert, 3427
Republic of New Africa, 3481, 3490, 3491,
    3533
Requier, Augustus Julian, 2569
Rera, George, 521
Rert, Nai, 2827
Reschny, Hermann, 990
Resnick, Samuel L., 1679
Resnover, Gregory, 3451
Resquena, Andres, 1253
Restell, Ann, 2569
Restell, Madame, 1200
Restifo, John A., 1240
Restivo, Albert, 2157
Restrepo, Fabio Ochoa, 2358
Retief, Pier, 975
Retief, Pieter, 2570, 3241
Retrosi, Enzo, 3513
Retz, Cardinal de, 2570
Reuben, "Calico Jim", 3324
Reubens, Marks, 2570
Reubens, Morris, 2570
Reuf, Abe, 3414, 3415
Reuland, Phil, 2671
Reuter, Ida, 1863
Reuther, Dutch, 399
Reuther, Victor, 3252
Reuther, Walter, 425, 3252
Réveillon Riot, 3372
Revel, Powel, 226
Revel, Richard, 1373
Revelli-Beaumont, Luchino, 3331
Revels, Thomas, 1230
Revere, Joseph Warren, 2570
Revere, Paul, 2725
Revilla, Daniel, 3453
Reville, Anne, 2429
Reville, E.B., 2570, 3330
Reville, Hezekiah, 2429
Reville, Jean, 2570
Revolutionare Zellen, 3533, 3534

Richardson, Charles Wilson (Brit. pr.1956-67), 2576-2577, 3395
Richardson, Christopher, 3166
Richardson, Damon, 3455
Richardson, "Dude", 208
Richardson, Eddie, 3395
Richardson, Edmund, 1500
Richardson, Edward, 2576-2577
Richardson, Edward Michael, 3258
Richardson, Elliot Lee, 2577, 3099, 3100
Richardson, Floyd, 3451
Richardson, George, 2833
Richardson, Gerald, 2730
Richardson, Grace, 724
Richardson, Grant, 3360
Richardson, H.L., 1424
Richardson, Harriet, 2844
Richardson, Herbert Lee, 3447
Richardson, Irene, 2879
Richardson, Jacqueline, 1951
Richardson, James, 2577, 3455
Richardson, Jeffrey, 1017
Richardson, Jimmy, 389, 787
Richardson, John, 2577
Richardson, Joseph, 2578, 3362
Richardson, Leonard, 2578
Richardson, Leslie, 2297
Richardson, Levi, 277, 1996, 2579, 3562
Richardson, Louis B., 1233
Richardson, Miguel A., 3455
Richardson, Robert, 3565
Richardson, Samuel Q., 3094, 3305
Richardson, Scovel, 2579
Richardson, Thomas F., 489
Richardson, Virgil, 2579
Richardson, William (U.S. pr.1856), 207, 780, 3228
Richardson, William H. (U.S. pr.1888), 3305
Richelieu, Cardinal, 293, 454, 592, 716, 1362, 2206, 2122
Richeson, Clarence V.T., 2579
Richetti, Adam "Eddie", 183, 1186, 1758, 2286, 2440, 3326, 3396, 3459
Richey, Charles Robert, 2579
Richey, Larry, 1612, 2454
Richier, Jean, 2579-2580
Richier, Xavier, 2579
Richley, Daryl, 3448
Richman, Fred, 1247
Richman, Harry, 31, 2349
Richmond, Earl of, 1518, 2229
Richmond, Frederick W., 3207
Richmond, King, 3364
Richmond, Thomas, 2175
Richmond, Va., Bread Riot, 3374
Richmond, William, 2236
Richmond, Willie Lee, 3448
Richter, Georg, 2580
Richter, George, 32
Richter, Robert, 2580
Richter, Ursula, 32, 2580
Richter, William, 911
Rick, Harman, 2919
Rickard, Christopher, 2580
Rickard, Tex, 812
Rickards, Byron Dague, 291, 2402
Ricker, Craig, 2463
Ricker, Darci, 2463
Ricker, Mary, 2463
Rickets, Thomas, 695
Rickman, Ronald, 3454
Rickover, Hyman, 2229
Rickson, William, 2580
RICO, 3380, 3398, 3406, 3408, 3409
Ricord, Auguste, 3299, 3393
Ricord, Dennis, 3350
Riddell, George, 3303
Ridder, Daniel, 19
Riddle, Ernest, 3454

Riddle, Franville, 3455
Ridenhour, Richard, 2273
Rideout, Greta, 2580
Rideout, John, 2580
Rider, Donald L., 3470
Rider, Jim, 2878
Rider, Theodore, 283
Ridge, Charles Field Williams, 1436
Ridgley, Elizabeth, 1501, 2580-2581
Ridgly, D.B., 3305
Riding, Joe, 523
Ridley, Caleb A., 1860
Ridley, Edward (Brit. 1843-1928), 2581
Ridley, Edward Albert (U.S. 1845-1933), 2581
Ridley, Nicholas, 2581
Ridolfi, Roberto, 2581
Riebel, David, 628
Riechmann, Dieter, 3450
Rieck, John J., Jr., 1973
Riedel, Erna, 2698
Riederer, Albert, 340
Riego y Nunez, Rafael del, 2581
Riehl, Arthur M., 1431
Riehl, Phil, 467
Riehle, George, 90
Riekhaff, H.F., 3424
Riel, Caroline, 938
Riel, Charles D., 3449
Riel, Louis, 2346, 2935
Riembauer, Franz Sales, 2581
Riemeck, Renate, 196
Riemenschneider, Tilman, 2582
Rienzi, Cola di, 2582
Ries, David, 1384
Riesel, Victor, 976, 2582, 2913, 3253
Rieth, Dr. Kurt, 988
Rievers, Olivia, 2880
Rifai, Zaid, 3256, 3491
Rifkin, Edward, 463
Rifkin, Stanley Mark, 2582, 3283, 3289, 3462
Riga, Michael, 2583
Rigaud, 2979
Rigaud, André, 2583
Rigaut, Pierre, 3400
Rigdon, Robert M. (U.S. d.1858), 789, 1260
Rigdon, Terrell, 3550
Riggi, John Sr., 3409
Riggi, Salvatore, 2195
Riggins, David, 3452
Riggins, John, 3363
Riggins, Margaret, 1767
Riggs, Barney, 2583, 3565
Riggs, Bobby, 2954
Riggs, David, 1037
Riggs, Elisha Francis, 2583, 3248
Riggs, Glenn E., 3469
Riggs, Lawrason, 3424
Riggs, Lyndsey, 1013
Riggs, Robert, 1184
Rightists, 3509, 3511, 3524
Rignall, Jeffrey, 1247
Rigney, Dale, 459
Riina, Salvatore, 3416
Riis, Jacob August, 2584
Rijke, Sjef, 2584
Riles, Hollis, 3368
Riles, Raymond, 3455
Riley, Bob, 1739
Riley, Bush, 3356
Riley, Chime, 3365
Riley, Elbert T., 789
Riley, Irish Tom, 1652
Riley, Irvin George, 211, 3334
Riley, James "Butt", 2584
Riley, James (Del. death row inmate), 3449

Riley, James (pr.1870s), 3415
Riley, James (U.S., pr.1878), 739
Riley, James (U.S., pr.1981), 7
Riley, James H., 1966
Riley, Joe, 297
Riley, John, 2342
Riley, John H., 2149
Riley, John Henry, 3565
Riley, Joseph, 163, 3359
Riley, Michael Lynn, 3455
Riley, Noah, 1040
Riley, Pat, 1764
Riley, "Rags", 3409
Riley, Razor, 3405, 3409
Riley, Steven, 2168
Riley, Thomas, 798, 2584
Riley, Wardell, 3450
Rimbaud, Arthur, 3294
Rimerman, Ronald A., 3471
Rimes, Terri, 2192
Rimmer, Beatrice, 551
Rincon, J., 3252
Rinedollar, John Wesley, 2290
Rinehart, Frank, 1720
Rinehart, Mary Roberts, 37, 470, 2584
Rinehart, Nancy Christine, 899
Rinehart, Stanley Marshall, 2584
Riner, John Alden, 2584
Ring and the Book, The, 2584
Ring, Elias, 3113
Ring, Elizabeth, 2941, 2942
Ring, Robert, 2880
Ringe, Richard, 312
Ringer, Gordon, 1286
Ringgenberg, Inez Marie, 2733
Ringgold, Johnny, 1058
Ringling, John, 1778
Ringo, Daniel, 2584
Ringo, John, 718, 719, 729, 773, 1058, 1320, 1395, 1450, 2584, 3554, 3555, 3560, 3562, 3565, 2137
Rinhalter, Gottlieb, 826
Rintelen, Anton, 988, 990
Rio, Antonio Blanco, 3253
Rio, Frank, 131, 178, 612, 614, 616, 2071, 2214, 2976, 3389
Riordan, Frank, 354
Riordan, James, 2012
Riordan, James J., 3098
Riordan, Joseph, 3427
Riordan, M., 3426
Riordan, Michael, 1331
Riorton, Dennis, 495
Rios, Joe, 3455
Rios Cruz, Jose, 3466
Riot Act, 3370
Riots of London, 2585
Ripan, Alexander, 2585
Ripepi, Antonio, 3413
Ripley, Beulah, 155
Ripley, Charles, 600
Ripley, Charles E., 2277
Ripley, Garnett, 1326
Ripley, James, 208, 3459
Rippetoe, Ken, 1400
Rip Raps, 1082
Risberg, Charles "Swede", 399
Riscio, Tina Marie, 3156
Risely-Pritchard, John, 3175
Rish, Nancy D., 1071-1072
Risner, Joseph, 2585
Risner, Mark, 2585
Risner, Susan, 2585
Ristovitch, V., 3246
Ritavouri, Heikki, 2585, 3244
Ritchie, Albert Cabell, 159
Ritchie, Charles, 2980
Ritchie, Clara, 1442
Ritchie, Emma, 3389

Robinson, Aubrey E., Jr., 2235, 2595
Robinson, Billy, 692
Robinson, Bishop L., 3424, 2595
Robinson, Charles (Brit. pr.1919), 1581, 2314
Robinson, Charles (U.S. pr.1866), 3352
Robinson, Christopher, 2595
Robinson, D.S., 3550
Robinson, David, 523, 3327
Robinson, Duncan, 803
Robinson, Dwight, 3453
Robinson, Eddie, 3453
Robinson, Edward, 2430
Robinson, Edward G., 52, 1431
Robinson, Emma, 2073, 3139
Robinson, Esau, 3367
Robinson, Eugene, 1769
Robinson, Eugene C., 1351, 3185
Robinson, Florence Maud, 1581, 2314
Robinson, Fred, 3448
Robinson, George, 3358, 3367
Robinson, George D., 440, 695
Robinson, George Frederick, 2595-2596
Robinson, George T., 1959
Robinson, Gertrude, 1953
Robinson, Greg, 1739
Robinson, Harvey, 822
Robinson, Henrietta, 2596
Robinson, Herbert, 1596-97
Robinson, Ida P., 3469
Robinson, J.E., 3337
Robinson, Jack, 2862
Robinson, James (U.S. d.1894), 3344
Robinson, James (U.S. pr.1912-20), 3425
Robinson, James (Brit. 1866), 798
Robinson, Jesse, 2775
Robinson, Jill, 929
Robinson, Jim, 1827
Robinson, Jim R., 3550
Robinson, Joan, 1553
Robinson, Joe, 2393
Robinson, John (Brit. b.1764), 170
Robinson, John (Brit. pr.1817), 1591, 1642
Robinson, John (U.S. pr.1902), 1007
Robinson, John (U.S. pr.1892), 2888, 3341
Robinson, John, 2596
Robinson, Johnny J., 3450
Robinson, Joseph, 3347, 3348
Robinson, Joseph T., 1984
Robinson, Josephine, 657
Robinson, Kent 1899
Robinson, L. Vern, 1425
Robinson, Lewis, 1729, 3357
Robinson, Margaret, 1426
Robinson, Mary, 1476, 1477, 2596-2597
Robinson, Mervyn Basil, 3513
Robinson, Nellie, 1998
Robinson, Noah, 1086, 2597
Robinson, Norman Wesley, 2597-2598
Robinson, Pearl Lowenberg, 3283
Robinson, Peter, 2598, 3259, 3520, 3521
Robinson, Philo, 819, 822
Robinson, Quinton, 2598
Robinson, Rich, 3357
Robinson, Richard, 3357, 2598-2601
Robinson, Rose Ada, 1991
Robinson, Sarah Jane, 2601
Robinson, "Sugar" Ray, 561
Robinson, Thelma, 1821
Robinson, Thomas H., 2601, 3465
Robinson, Thomas H., Jr., 3326
Robinson, Timothy, 3450
Robinson, Van Bering, 2601-2602
Robinson, Victor, 3294
Robinson, Virgil, 2602
Robinson, William, (U.S. d.1909), 3360
Robinson, William (U.S. d.3362
Robinson, William, 3455
Robinson, Willis, 3365

Robison, James, 29
Robison, Larry, 3455
Robison, Olan Randle, 3453
Robitaille, Marie-Ange, 1396
Robitzsch, Felton, 2025
Robledo, Luis, 2408
Robledo, Martin, 791
Robles, J.A., 3244
Robles, June, 3326
Robles, Richard, 819, 2602
Roblick, Frieda, 1607
Robsart, Amy, 2603
Robson, Annie, 2603
Robson, Frank, 703
Robson, Mary Ann, 797
Rocchia, Anita Venza, 577
Rocco, Alfredo, 2603
Rocco, Alphonse, 2603
Rocco, Michael, 3379, 3380
Rocha, William, 3332, 3506
Roche, Alexander Adair, 2603
Roche, Berthe, 3059-3060
Roche, Edward, 2603-2604
Roche, Eleanor, 2534-2535
Roche, John Francis, 2604
Roche, Justice, 765
Roche, Phillip, 2604-2605
Roche, Walter, 3007
Rochefort, Henri, 428
Rochelle, Fred, 3353
Rochester, Gundulf of, 2979
Rochester, Lord, 1225
Rochester Race Riot, 3376
Rochet, Gary, 1073
Rochetti, Francisco, 3346
Rochford, James M., 2605, 3424
Rochfort, William Henry, 3171
Rockburn, Walter, 2942
Rockefeller, John Davison, 2605
Rockefeller, Nelson, 181, 343, 754, 1167, 2198, 3265, 3376, 3482
Rockmam, Milton, 665, 1323, 1980, 2605, 3392
Rock Springs Massacre, 2605, 3374
Rockwell, Frederick Kress, 2605
Rockwell, George Lincoln, 3256, 3478
Rockwood, Edward, 2605
Rodden, James, 3452
Roddy, George S., 2862
Roderick, Audrey, 2605-2606
Roderick, Ike, 2973, 3389
Roderty, G.A., 3242
Rodey, Bernard Shandon, 2606
Rodez, Bishop of, 453
Rodgers, Alva, 3389
Rodgers, Alva Johnson, 1980
Rodgers, Dick, 3557
Rodgers, Edward Bell, 505
Rodgers, Harry W. III, 2100
Rodgers, Jessie, 505
Rodgers, Jim, 359, 1447
Rodgers, Joe, 3368
Rodgers, John, 3344
Rodgers, Julius, 1971
Rodgers, Richard, 1598
Rodgers, William A., 2100
Rodgers, Woodes, 3031
Rodiguez, Antonio, 3360
Rodney, Caesar Augustus, 2606
Rodriguez, A., 3245
Rodriguez, Alredo, 3246
Rodriguez, Carlos, 2606
Rodriguez, Comacho, 2562
Rodriguez, Edward, 3470
Rodriguez, Felipe, 3211
Rodriguez, Felix, 3249
Rodriguez Francia, José Gaspar, 1209
Rodriguez, Frank, 3449
Rodriguez Gacha, José Gonzalo, 3397,

3398
Rodriguez, Jesus, 3565
Rodriguez, José (Spain pr.1939), 250
Rodriguez, José (U.S. d.1852), 1198
Rodriguez, Jose, 3449
Rodriguez, Luis, 3449
Rodriguez, Manuel, 1251
Rodriguez, Michael, 3360
Rodriguez, Ramón Milian, 2345
Rodriguez, Rodolfo, 3300
Rodriguez, Rolando, 2276
Rodriguez, Santos, 2606
Rodriguez Diaz, Antonio, 3464
Rodriguez Gacha, José Gonzalo, 2606
Rodriguez Orejuela, Gilberto, 2606-2607, 3398
Rodriguez Orejuela, Jorge, 2606-2607, 3398
Rodriguez Orejuela, Miguel Angel, 3398
Rodriguez Rodriguez, Moises, 3466
Rodriquez, Benjamin, 3409
Rody, Fred, Jr., 3023
Roe, Clifford, 1298
Roe, Ralph, 53, 3427
Roe, Ruth, 2956
Roe, Theodore, 3382
Roed, O. Jimmy, 3426
Roeder, Erwin, 27
Roediger, Frtiz, 2607-2608
Roehl, Frank, 2397
Roehl, Klaus, 196
Roehm, Ernst, 942, 990, 1101, 1325, 1557, 1568, 1569, 1572, 1573, 1576
Roerig, Peter, 1058
Roerk, Peter, 810
Roeski, Emil, 3030-3031, 3389
Roettinger, Sebastien, 1929
Rogatsch, Johann, 2608
Roger, Louis Emory, 1451
Rogers, Adam, 658
Rogers, Albert, 3356
Rogers, Annie, 3565
Rogers, Ben, 3208
Rogers, Ben T., 3366
Rogers, Bill, 2833
Rogers, Bob, 3565
Rogers, "Buckshot", 739
Rogers, C.L., 3550
Rogers, David, 3447, 3449, 3565
Rogers, Dayton, 2608-2609, 3453
Rogers, Dick, 3557, 3562, 3565, 3567
Rogers, Earl, 91, 872, 1309, 1387, 2609-2610
Rogers, Ernest, 3550
Rogers, Erskine C., 915, 916
Rogers, Francis J., 2610
Rogers, George White, 2610
Rogers, Henry, 3253
Rogers, Hunter Charles, 2610
Rogers, Ike, 3550
Rogers, Irene, 2610
Rogers, Isaac "Ike", 1335
Rogers, J.H., 3550
Rogers, James, 3451
Rogers, Jeffrey, 2811
Rogers, Jerry Layne, 3450
Rogers, Jim, 2878
Rogers, Joe, 2981
Rogers, John (Brit. 1627-1665), 2610, 3339
Rogers, John (Brit. 1648-1721), 2610
Rogers, John (Brit. 1940-), 2610-2611
Rogers, Joshua, 1112
Rogers, Kenneth Paul, 2611
Rogers, L.T., 3550
Rogers, Mark, 3452
Rogers, Mary, 1541, 2569-2570
Rogers, Mary Cecilia, 2274, 2479, 2611-2612, 2958
Rogers, Michael, 2569
Rogers, Patrick, 3167, 3455
Rogers, R.T., 3357

Rose, Pete, 402
Rose, Vincent, 1581
Rosebberg, Ethel, 1738
Rosebrook, Marjorie Patricia, 207
Roseburg, Charles, 1301
Roselli, John 372, 1120, 1306, 2620, 2983, 3396, 3397
Rosemond, Janice Denice, 1086
Rosen, Benjamin, 975
Rosen, Bernard J., 2228
Rosen, Charles, 272, 1582
Rosen, Edward, 2583
Rosen, Joseph, 528, 2254, 2564, 3120, 3402, 3409
Rosen, Marty, 1900
Rosen, Morris, 1375
Rosen, Nig, 178
Rosenbaum, Edward, 3394
Rosenbaum, Joseph H., 2551
Rosenbaum, Wilhelm, 3542
Rosenberg, Alan, 3389
Rosenberg, Alfred, 1557, 1568, 2543, 2620-2621, 3542
Rosenberg, Edward, 1180
Rosenberg, Ethel, 1010, 3056
Rosenberg, Frank, 3135
Rosenberg, Julius, 1010, 1738, 3056
Rosenberg, Louis "Lefty Louie", 307, 1931, 3218, 3410
Rosenberg, Moe, 3389
Rosenberg, Willie, 485
Rosenblatt, Mimi, 1636
Rosenblum, Jacob J., 1326
Rosencrantz, Lulu, 2700, 3406
Rosene, Charles, 793
Rosenfeld, Nathan, 3328, 3486
Rosenfeld, Jimmy, 2621
Rosenfeld, Sigmund, 306
Rosengolz, A.P., 3060
Rosenhaus, Jerome, 342
Rosenheim, A., 3425
Rosenheim, Julius, 3389
Rosenman, Samuel Irving, 2621
Rosenstein, Fred, 687
Rosenstein, Max, 687
Rosenstein, Myra, 687
Rosenstrach, Milton, 1806
Rosensweig, Joseph " Joe the Greaser", 1725, 1867, 2621, 3409, 3410, 3411
Rosenthal, Charles Marvin, 3325
Rosenthal, Chuck, 1902
Rosenthal, Frank, 1322, 3396
Rosenthal, Herman "Beansie", 298, 302-304, 306, 308, 553, 1330, 1931, 1947, 2876, 3075, 3401, 3403, 3406, 3410
Rosenthal, Matthew, 768
Rosenthal, William, 3550
Rosenwald, Julius, 1934
Roseque, Jesus Anaya, 3466
Rosetti, John, 537
Rosewaine, Edward, 1603
Rosi, Ermenegildo, 666
Rosier, Dr. Peter, 2621
Rosin, Allen, 1384
Rosling, George, 1239
Rosner, Edmund, 1943
Rosoff, Samuel, 2555
Ross, Abraham, 1388
Ross, Barnaby, 1919
Ross, Barney, 2229
Ross, Bobby Lynn, 3453
Ross, Charles B. "Charley", 263, 837, 2621-2623, 3098, 3129, 3282, 3324, 3404, 3408
Ross, Charles, Ray, 2623
Ross, Charles S., 2717, 3326
Ross, Charles, William, 2623-2624
Ross, Christian, 3129
Ross, Colin Campbell, 2624
Ross, Craig, 3449

Ross, David, 1166, 2527
Ross, Diane, 2674
Ross, Donald, 121, 3283
Ross, Donald Roe, 2624
Ross, Eddie Lee, 3451
Ross, Elizabeth, 2624
Ross, Ezra, 2832
Ross, Harold, 1222
Ross, Josephine Alice, 1510, 3460
Ross, Michael, 3449
Ross, Michael B., 2624
Ross, Norman, 515
Ross, Perry Dean, 2624-2625
Ross, Rachel, 1388
Ross, Robert, 3227
Ross, T.M., 3550
Ross, Tony, 612
Ross, W.E., 2022
Ross Case, 1738
Rosse, Brigate, 737
Rosse, Edith, 1380, 2625
Rosse, Henry, 1182
Rosselin, Bernard, 3252
Rossen, Robert 102
Rosser, Luther Z., 1219
Rossi, Alfredo, 3380
Rossi, Cesare, 2148, 2149
Rossi, Maurizio, 1304
Rossi, Pellegrino, 2625, 3241
Rossi, Richard, 3448
Rossignol, Joseph, 2708
Rossimus, Frank, 3340
Rossin, Michael, 3300
Rossner, Bernard, 2163
Rossner, Bernd Maria, 203, 3475
Rossouw, Marthinius, 2625
Rostock, Max, 1531
Roswell, Isaac, 1737
Rosyk, Bill, 435
Roszkowski, Stanley J., 127
Rotaeche, Ramon Romero, 3258, 3510
Rotariu, Anna, 613
Rotch, Josephine Noyes, 832
Rote Armee Fraktion, 3281, 3533, 3534
Roth, Al, 273
Roth, Annie, 774
Roth, Bruce, 1384
Roth, Fred, 2717, 3565, 3566
Roth, Karl Heinz, 3475
Roth, Michael, 774
Roth, Murray David, 2625
Roth, Philip, 2561
Roth, Robert, 3107
Roth, Stephen John, 2625
Roth, Steven, 2625
Rothari, 2625
Rothaug, Oswald, 3542
Rothe, Theodore, 2273
Rothenberger, Curt, 3542
Rother, Stanley, 3515
Rothko, Kate, 1973
Rothko, Mark, 1973
Rothkopf, Bernard, 3396
Rothkopf, Louis, 178, 2625-2626, 2689, 3392, 3396
Rothman, David M., 2444
Rothman, Harry, 2626
Rothrock, Joseph, 846
Rothschild, Abe, 881
Rothschild, Charles Paul, 1203, 2626, 2870
Rothschild, Evelyn, 2154
Rothschild, Julia, 1082
Rothstein, Arnold "Big Bankroll", 163, 164, 178, 302, 304, 399, 402, 470, 811, 934, 936, 1064, 1065, 1100, 1132, 1295, 1346, 1546, 2014, 2626-2628, 2689, 2734, 2881, 2930, 2978, 3131, 3225, 3296, 3407, 3409, 3410
Rothstein, Robert, 2719

Rothwel, Frerickl Holt, 1528
Rothwell, John, 3158
Roti, Bruno, 647
Roti, Fred, 647, 3389
Rotramel, Nora, 699
Rotramel, Robert, 699
Rottman, Arthur, 2629
Rottura, Concetta, 3415, 3416
Roubatis, Yiannis P., 2483
Roubeaux, James, 3453
Rouchomowski, Israel, 2629
Rougeau, Paul, 3455
Rough Riders, 3410
Rough Skins, 1082
Rougier, Hilary, 1940, 2629
Roulet, Jacques, 2629
Roumeguere, Pierre, 3056
Round Back Rangers, 3410
Roundtree, Dovey, 841
Roundtree, Oscar J., 3550
Roupell, William, 2629
Rousch, Harvey L., 3228
Rous, Francis Peyton, 2629
Rouse, Alfred Arthur, 379, 1063, 2629, 2894
Rouse, Bruce, 2630
Rouse, Fred, 3366
Rouse, John, 3074
Rousell, Louis, 3400
Roush, Harvey L., 2630
Rousseau, André, 1924
Rousseau, Anibal, 3455
Rousseau, Jean Baptiste, 2630
Rousseau, Jean-Jacques, 942, 3074, 3084
Rousseau, Minnie, 649
Rousseau, Roger, 3254
Rousseau, Rosella, 2630
Rousseau, William, 649
Roussel, Mathurin, 2522
Rouster, Gregory, 3451
Rout, Daniel, 3365
Rout, Jerry, 3365
Routledge, Jeanette, 38
Routly, Daniel, 3450
Routt, Cora, 2723
Roux, Jacques, 2630
Rover, Leo, 484
Rovner, Ilana D., 1030
Rovold, Hans, 3522
Rowan, Archibald, 848
Rowan, Carl, 2041, 2630
Rowan, Charles, 3426
Rowan, Dan, 1306
Rowan, John, 498, 3304-3305
Rowan, Julie, 2895
Rowan-Chambers Duel, 2631
Rowand, James, 1945
Rowbottom, Harry Ephraim, 2631
Rowder, Berry, 3341
Rowder, James, 3341
Rowe, Alleen, 2693
Rowe, G. Edward, 2552
Rowe, Gary Thomas, Jr., 2631
Rowe, Gordon, 1150
Rowe, Simon, 883
Rowe, Thomas, 1287
Rowe, William Garfield, 2418, 3147
Rowell, Dale, 1154
Rowell, Earle, 3296
Rowell, Edwin C., 3470
Rowell, Robert, 3296
Rowland, Bud, 3352
Rowland, Dick, 3002
Rowland, Ferrin, 2631
Rowland, Guy Kevin, 3449
Rowland, John, 460, 1736
Rowland, Robert, 1458-59
Rowland, Thomas, 3339
Rowland, Tom, 2631

S

Sandeman, Condie, 1827
Sander, Hermann N., 2675-2676
Sander, Phil, 583
Sanders, Ab, 311, 583, 739, 1734, 1986, 2061
Sanders, Albert, 2676
Sanders, Clindell, 3452
Sanders, David "Battleship Dave", 1726
Sanders, David Lee, 3451
Sanders, Deborah Lynn, 2741
Sanders, George, 771, 2012, 3566
Sanders, Harold, 20
Sanders, Henry, 3339
Sanders, Howard L., 2676, 3425
Sanders, James, 3367
Sanders, John, 3352
Sanders, Lindberg, 2676, 3334
Sanders, Nicholas, 2676
Sanders, Norell, 2741
Sanders, Reginald, 3449
Sanders, Ricardo, 3449
Sanders, Robert, 1720, 2676
Sanders, Ronald, 3449
Sanders, Stanley, 3453
Sanders, Wilbur Fisk, 3050
Sanders, William, 3364
Sanderson, G.D., 3249
Sanderson, Henry, 3351
Sanderson, Ricky Lee, 3453
Sandhoe, P., 3251
Sandhoff, Roberto Rischer, 3331
Sandhu, Suchnam Singh, 2769
Sandiford, Cedric, 1942
Sandinistas, 2676
Sandino, Augusto César, 2676, 3247
Sandlin, Robert L., 133, 3466
Sandobal, Juan, 3566
Sandoval, Alfred, 3449
Sandoval, Anastacio, 3566
Sandoval, Remigio, 3566
Sandrucci, Renzo, 3333, 3515
Sands, Bobby, 1664, 3277, 3511, 3512
Sands, Gertrude Sheldon, 3144
Sands, Gulielma Elmore (Elma), 3112
Sands, Hope, 3112
Sands, "Icie", 2894
Sands, John, 2099
Sands, Stafford, 3393
Sands, The, 2676-2677, 3389
Sandusky, Henry, 715
San Dwe, 1048
Sandwich, Earl of, 1010
Sandwich, Lord, 1413
Sandys, Edwin, 2677
Sandys, Thomas, 801
Sanez, Doroteo, 3566
Sanford, Edward S., 2126
Sanford, Edward Terry, 2677
Sanford, John F.A., 2711
Sanford, John L., 1326
San Francisco Anti-Squatter's League, 2677
San Francisco Race Riot, 3376-3377
San Francisco Vigilance Committee, 2677, 3415
Sang, David, 1628
Sanger, George, 777
Sanger, Margaret, 2677
Sanger, Tom, 1775
Sanger, William W., 2677
Sangerman, Joseph, 394, 3387, 3389
Sangret, August, 2677-2678
Sangwala, 116
Sanjar, 2678
Sankey, Joann, 885
Sankey, John, 2678, 3132
Sankey, Verne, 2678, 3326
Sankodigian, Mardiros, 3273
San Martin, Ramón Grau, 2662, 2696, 3247
Sanna, François, 1915
Sanoja, Juan Manuel, 354

Sans, South, 497
Sansanese, Daniel, 3380
Sanson, Charles, 2678
Sanson, Charles-Henri, 2678
Sanson, Charles Jean Baptiste, 2678
Sanson, Clement-Henri, 2679
Sanson, Henri, 2678-2679
Sanson, Louis-Charles-Martin, 688
Sanson Family, 2678-2679
Santa Anna, 2679
Santa Clara, 2663
Santa Cruz, Marta, 2679
Santana, Carlos, 3455
Santana, Frank, 2679
Santana, Lloyd A., 910
Santana, Pedro, 1030
Santander, Francisco, 428
Santangelo, Giuseppe, 3273, 3514
Santarosa, Santorre di, 2679
Santerre, Antoine-Joseph, 2679
Santiago Mencia, 2696
Santiago, Radames, 3158
Santiago, Rafael, 3462
Santiago, Salvadore, 3454
Santiapichi, Severino, 2223
Santin, Antonio, 3251
Santini, Donald Michael, 2679
Sant Jarnail Singh Bhindranwale, 3473
Santle, Curly, 208
Santleben, August, 3566
Santo Mauro, Duke of, 3249
Santo Trafficante, 2689
Santore, James, 3297
Santoro, Salvatore "Tom Mix", 2448, 2670, 3410
Santos, Carlos, 3450
Santos, Francis A., 804
Santos, Jack, 1356
Santos, Mary Rose, 2309
Santowski, Donald, 2848
Santucci, Girolamo "Bobby Doyle", 2115, 2138, 3410
Santucci, John J., 644
Santucho, Robert, 3504
Sanxay, Edmund, 563
Sanyal, H.N., 3255
Sao Sam Heun, 3251
S.A.O. Terrorists, 3534
Sapatorra, 2256
Saperstein, Louis, 896
Sapieha, Leon, 2679
Sapp, Robert, 3368
Sapphine, Sam, 3228
Sapronov, Timofey Vladimirovich, 2679
Sapru, Tej Bahadur, 2679
Sapwell, William, 2679
Saraga, "Luger Moe" 2556
Saragossa, 2675
Saratkin, Miriam, 2125
Sarber, Jess, 952, 958, 3427
Sarber, Lucy, 952
Sardan, Hugo Carlos, 3257, 3504
Sardar Mohammad Daud Khan, 3253, 3257
Sardini, Peter, 2145
Sardinian Shepherds, 2679-2680, 2692
Sardou, Victorien 36
Sargent, John Garibaldi, 2680
Sargent, John Singer, 410, 498, 2235
Sargent, Peter, 2665
Sargon II, 2728
Sarit Thanarat, 2680
Sarjeant, Marcus Simon, 1083, 3514
Sarkiyev, Ilyas, 2680
Sarno, Albert, 942
Sarraut, Maurice, 3251
Sarrazin, Rosalie, 1717
Sarret, Georges, 1418
Sarris, Tom, 2546

Sartain, Albert E., 2680-2681
Sartan, Robert G., 2671
Sartawi, Issam, 3260, 3527
Sartawi, Marwan Muhammed, 3520
Sarti, Lucien, 3393
Sartor, William, 1825
Sartrain, Albert E., 2567
Sartre, Jean-Paul, 691, 1256, 1291, 18671, 3056
Saruco, Charles, 2680-2681
Sary, Ieng, 2484
Sasakawa Ryoichi, 2681
Sasaki, A., 853
Sasdy, Peter, 1441
Sassaman, William, 2009
Sassone, Regina, 998
Satan's Circus, 2895, 2913, 3405, 3406, 3410
Satan's Mile, 3383, 3389
Satan Was a Man, 2681
Satchell, Michael, 2952
Satsuma, 2662
Satterlee, Peggy La Rue, 1310
Satterwhite, John, 3455
Sattiewhite, Vernon, 3455
Satur, 996
Saturnino, José, 1880
Satyricon Hoax, 2681
Sauber, Werner, 3475
Sauckel, Fritz, 2681, 3542
Saudi Arabian Riots, 3378
Sauerbrey, Siegfried, 3114
Saul, 10, 1093
Saul, Nicholas, 888, 2681-2682, 3407, 3410
Saulet, B., 3241
Saulque, Leo B., 2860
Saulsbury, Ross, 3389
Sault, David, 445
Saumeraz, Gerald, 3085
Saun, John, 3564
Saunders, Evelyn, 213
Saunders, George, 3361
Saunders, Howard Donald, 2682
Saunders, J.W., 3550
Saunders, John, 2534, 2693
Saunders, Kevin Patrick, 3297
Saunders, Newt, 3358
Saunders, Norman, 3302
Saunders, Patty, 543
Saunders, Phillip, 3425
Saunders, Raymond "Scissors", 2682
Saunders, William, 3350, 3566
Saunders, Willie "Smokey", 2690
Saupe, William, 3471
Saupp, John, 3410
Saurraut, Albert, 2456
Sauvageot, Serge, 121, 3283
Savage, Arthur William, 2682
Savage, Daniel, 670, 2466
Savage, James, 3450
Savage, John, 3481
Savage, May, 2953
Savage, Richard, 2682
Savage, Roy, 3452
Savage, Sterling, 3347
Savage, Thomas, 2682
Savage, Tristram, 1591
Savama, 3258
Savanoff, Vera, 2696
Savard, Ernest, 1501
Savarkar, Vir Vinayak Damodar, 2682-2683
Savary, Henry, 2683
Savasta, Antonio, 2683
Savastano, Salvatore, 3332
Save Our Israel, 3504
Savery, Paul Walcott, 2561
Savides, Christ, 2683
Savidge, Irene Marjory, 2683
Savidge Affair, 2683
Savigny, Friedrich Karl von, 2683

Scipio Nasica, Publius Cornelius, 2708
Scire, Anthony, 3452
Sclafani, Joseph, 3410
Scoby, Alpheus, 2816
Scola, Sam, 3396
Scoot, Jerry, 3567
Scoperto, Charles, 3410
Scopes, John Thomas, 523, 876, 1498, 2708-2709
Scopo, Ralph, 2448, 2670, 3410
Scoppetta, Nicholas, 1943
Scorgins, John, 3566
Scorsese, Martin, 1675
Scosta, Piero, 3331
Scot, Reginald, 1133
Scotford, James O., 2816
Scotland, James VI, 1405
Scotland Yard, 2658, 2663, 2673, 2676, 2679, 2683, 2687, 2695, 2709-2710, 2711, 2718, 2721, 2731, 3104
Scots, Queen Mary of, 204, 321, 423, 448, 497, 529, 622, 690, 1694, 1695
Scott, A.A., 1310, 2954, 3179
Scott, A.D., 557
Scott, Abron, 3450
Scott, Andrew George, 2710-2711
Scott, Andy, 1731
Scott, Barret, 3345
Scott, Ben, 2816, 3349
Scott, Bill, 467
Scott, Bradford, 3339
Scott, Bradley, 3450
Scott, Claughton, 2869
Scott, Clem, 3358
Scott, D., 3426
Scott, Don, 2713
Scott, Dred, 403, 593, 658, 848, 866, 1731, 2304, 2711, 3106
Scott, E., 3566
Scott, E.E., 1166
Scott, Edgar E., 3102
Scott, Edward Burke, 2711
Scott, Elliot Nathaniel, 2711
Scott, Ethelbert D., 759
Scott, Evelyn, 2712
Scott, Francis, 2711
Scott, Garvin, 2096
Scott, George, 3350
Scott, George M., 192
Scott, Gester, 3342
Scott, H.E., 2686
Scott, Harold Richard, 2711, 3426
Scott, Harry, 1219, 3426
Scott, Hazel, 1826
Scott, Henry, 2711-2712, 3344, 3366
Scott, Ira, 185, 3264
Scott, James, (Scot. 1649-85) 280, 2164, 2712, 2940
Scott, James, (U.S. d.1891) 3340
Scott, James, (U.S. pr.1980s) 1113, 3449
Scott, James T., 3366
Scott, Jeremy L., 3450
Scott, Jerry, 243, 3003
Scott, Jim, 3251
Scott, John, (Brit. c.1630-96) 2712
Scott, John, (Brit. d.1821) 3305
Scott, John, (Brit. d.1883) 3549, 3566
Scott, John, (U.S. pr.1957) 2557
Scott, John Paul, (U.S. pr.1960s) 69, 403
Scott, Judy, 461
Scott, Larry, 3451
Scott, Leonard Ewing, 2712
Scott, Leslie, 228
Scott, Ligon, 3365
Scott, Lindsey, 2712-2713
Scott, Margaret, 2669
Scott, Marie, 3363
Scott, Paul, 2713, 3450
Scott, Ray, 374

Scott, Ronald Allen, 2713
Scott, Thomas, 2713
Scott, Todd, 2026
Scott, Transou, 1600
Scott, W.M., 1826
Scott, Walter, 3076
Scott, Sir Walter, 1052, 1501
Scott, Walter H., 3471
Scott, William, (Brit. 1745-1836) 2713
Scott, William, (U.S. pr.1880s) 667
Scott, William J., (U.S. pr.1894) 2246
Scott, William J., (U.S. 1927-) 2713
Scott, William Lester, (U.S. pr. 1931) 2713-2714
Scott, Willie, 2714
Scott, Winfield, 28, 173, 2395, 2679
Scott-Elliott, Walter Travers, 1420
Scotten, Ed H., 3550
Scottish Food Riot, 3373
Scottish National Liberation Army, 3521, 3534
Scotto, Anthony M., 2714
Scottoriggio, Joseph R., 780, 2714, 3251
Scottsboro Boys, 562
Scottsboro Case, 1498, 2714-2716
Scott v. Sanford, 3106
Scovia, L., 3031
Screaming Mimi, The, 2716
Scribano, Mildred, 2131
Scribner, John C., 2716
Scribonius, 39
Scripps, E.W., 2064
Scriver, Peter, 2663
Scro, Vincent, 3380
Scroggs, Paul, 3343
Scroggs, William, 2716, 3074
Scrope, Henry le, (Brit. pr.13th Cent.) 2716
Scrope, Henry le, (Brit. c.1376-1415) 2716
Scrope, Richard le, 2716
Scrope, William le, 2716
Scruggs, Robert, 3354
Scrutton, Thomas Edward, 2716
Scudder, Isaac Williamson, 2021
Scull, Jesus, 3450
Scuotto, Antonio, 3061
Scurlock, Josiah G. "Doc", 486, 2716-2717, 3566
Scutari, Richard, 341
Scylla, 2170
Scythia, 2460
Seaborn, J.C., 404, 732, 1003
Seaborn, Joe, 2530
Seaborn, Oscar, 2530
Seabright, Thomas, 3357
Seabrook, Sara, 1972
Seabury, Samuel, 308, 2717, 3025, 3077, 3410
Seabury Investigation, 1947, 2413, 2717
Seacey, Thomas, 3356
Seadlund, John Henry, 2717-2718, 3326
Seager, George, 2718
Seal, Barry, 1103
Seale, Bobby, 398, 698, 1862, 3529
Seale, James, 3550
Sealock, John, 849
Seaman, Carey, 863, 3566
Seaman, Roger, 1384
Seaman, William, 2718
Seamore, Rodium, 3364
Searcy, Charles J. "Texas Jack", 2718
Searle, J.N., 2940
Sears, Barnabas Francis, 1443, 2718-2719
Sears, George M., 1236, 3426
Sears, Gradwell, 716
Sears, Harry, 3044
Sears, John, 3390
Sears Roebuck, 3289
Seaton, Dan, 1175

Seaton, David, 2345
Seaton, Ronald H, 3449
Seaton, Terry, 2719
Seattle Urban League, 3480
Seaver, Frank, 298
Seavey, Valorious A., 3424
Seay, Abraham Jefferson, 2719
Seba, Yusuf, 3505
Sebastian, 2719
Sebastian, Charles E., 3425
Sebastian, James, 996
Sebastiani, Fanny, 917
Sebe Barnes, 3561
Sebeille, Edmond, 995
Sebestyen, Rosalie, 1142
Sebring, Jay, 2111
Seburn, Irma, 3001
Secchi, Dr. Carlo, 430
Sechrest, Ricky, 3452
Second of June Movement, 2528, 3257, 3534
Second New York City Orange Riot, 3374
Secor, John B., 358
Sécretain, Francoise, 421
Secret Anti-Communist Army, 3534
Secret Army for the Liberation of Armenia, 3506-3508, 3510, 3522, 3523, 3525, 3529, 3534
Secret Army Organization, 3491, 3493, 3494, 3534
Secret Cuban Government, 3489, 3490, 3492, 3496, 3498, 3534
Secret Service Agency, 2719-2720
Secrist, Ronald, 1331
Security Pacific National Bank, 3289
Seddon, A., 3344
Seddon, Frederick Henry, 536, 1424, 1506, 2720-2721
Seddon, Margaret Ann, 2720, 2721
Seddon, Mary Ann, 536
Seder, James, 436, 3326
Sedgwick, Ellery, 2188
Sedillo, Dan, 769
Sedley, Bill, 2721-2722, 3398
Sedlmeier, Hans, 2166
Sedotto, Anthony, 3410
Sedov, Lev Lvuvich, 2722
Sedway, Moe, 1375
See, James, 3566
See, Leon, 629
See, Lloyd, 537, 2029
See, Louise 2029
Seebode, Marjorie, 2392
Seefeld, Adolf, 2722
SEEK, 3480
Seeley, Herbert Barnum, 2722
Seeley, Louise, 448
Seeley, Milton, 2180
Seeley Dinner Scandal, 2722-2723
Seemler, Harland, 3346
Sefatsa, Reginald, 2736
Sefholic, Marie, 1474
Segal, Harry, 3410
Segal, Martin, 2561
Segal, Vivienne, 1791
Segar, Joseph, 3241
Segar, William, 472
Segars, Mack, 3344
Segee, Robert Dale, 2723-2724
Segouia, Fernando, 3245
Segret, Fernande, 1886
Segretti, Donald H., 3101
Segura, Jose, 3566
Sehested, Hannibal, 2724
Seibers, Phyllis, 2040
Seibert, Frank, 2042
Seibert, Willi, 3542
Seidel, Catherine, 358
Seiden, Richard, 1738

Seidensahl, Joe, 1679
Seidenschmer, Jacob "Whitey Lewis", 307, 1931
Seidl, Siegfried, 3542
Seidlitz, Bertram, 3289
Seidman, L. William, 3193
Seifer, Wayne, 1014
Seifert, Daniel, 1980
Seiff, Teddy, 3256
Seigel, Sheldon, 920
Seigler, Hoyle, 1829
Seimsen, John, 853
Seipel, Ignatz, 3245
Seipel, Johannes, 3181
Seitz, Amy Sue, 1224
Seiv, Harold, 3499
Sejanus, Lucius Aelius, 1029, 2724, 3234
Sekiguchi Eiji, 1820
Sekou Odinga, 453, 489
Sekoyan, Henrik, 3465
Sekul, John N., 3180
Selas, M., 3245
Selassie, Haile, 2266, 2268, 2541
Selaya, Lorenzo, 2984
Selby, Dale Pierre, 3447
Selby, Joseph Franklyn, 2724
Selby, Norman, 1808, 2724-2725
Selby, Wilma, 2724
Selcuk, Timur, 3510
Selden, J.W., 374
Selden, John, 2725
Seldes, Gilbert Vivian, 2725
Sele, Baron, 3238
Seleucus I, 2510, 2725, 3233
Seleucus IV, 2725, 3233
Seleucus V, 2725, 3233
Self-Defense Against All Authority, 3271, 3507, 3534
Selfridge, Edward, 3138
Selfridge, Thomas O., 2725
Selhurst, John, 2725
Selig, Lucile, 1218
Seligman, Henry, 163
Seligman, Joseph, 2725
Seligman, Stanley, 2055
Selik, Mike, 3251
Selim I, 230, 2726
Selim III, 2269, 2726
Selina, 3415
Selinger, Rudolph, 988
Selivanov, Kondrati, 2774
Seliverstoff, Michael de, 2726
Selkirk, Alexander, 1012
Sellard, William, 1715
Sellers, Brad, 3086
Sellers, Charles, 3361
Sellers, Frederick Aked, 2726
Sellers, James, 3349
Sellers, Johnny, 1283
Sellers, Sean, 3453
Sellers, Willie Foster, 2726
Sellis, Joseph, 2726
Sellman, Dorothy, 2726
Sellman, Edward Leon, 1233, 2726-2727
Selman, John, Sr., 1450, 1451, 1539, 1595, 1898, 2058, 2180, 2556, 2688, 2727, 3549-3551, 3559, 3566
Selman, John, Jr., 3550
Selman, Tom, 2727
Seltzer, Louis B., 2742
Selvage, John Henry, 3455
Selvester, Tom, 1558
Selvig, Monica, 2825
Selz, Ralph Jerome Von Braun, 2727
Selznick, David, 2193, 2954
Semnacher, Al, 144, 146, 150
Semple, Robert, 2068
Semyon Ter-Petrosyan, 425
Sena, George, 3550

Sena, Jose D., 3550
Sena, Shiv, 3276
Sena y Baca, Jesus Maria, 3550
Sendero Luminoso, 3534
Senderowitz, Steven, 2757
Sendic, Raúl, 3002
Seneca, Lucius Annaeus, 2305, 2728, 3234
Senecal, Charles, 3256 or 3265
Senegal, Louis, 3347
Senegalese Election Riots, 3378
Seng, Marvin, 878
Senghor, Léopold Sédar, 3255
Senn, Nicholas, 1419
Sennacherib, 2728, 3232
Sennanedj, Roger Mardothée, 1915
Sennett, Mack, 143, 144, 150, 152
Sens, Uwe Rusch, 2203
Senteney, Margaret, 1830
Senzani, Giovanni, 3519
Seoane, Juan, 665
Sepala Ekanayaka, 3301
Sepe, Alfonso C., 1778
Sepoy Mutiny, 2276
September, Dulcie, 3261
September 23 Communist League, 3330, 3534
Septimus Bassianus Caracalla, 3235
Sepulveda Fernando Pinto, 3249
Seqenenre, II, 2728
Sequero, Francisco R., 3254
Sequine, B., 3426
Serafima, 2728
Serajulddin, Sayyed, 3260, 3523
Seraphine, Danny, 2692
Seraw, Mulugeta, 2177
Serfling, Aubrey G., 2885
Sergeant, Jonathan Dickinson, 2728
Sergey Aleksandrovich, 2684
Sergius, 2987
Sergius I, 2417
Sergius III, 2127, 2728
Serhant, Robert B., 2728
Serido, John, 3460
Series, Alice, 2229
Sérini, Jean, 618, 2200
Serlin, J., 3250
Serna, John, 3448
Serot, Andre, 3252
Serota, Joseph, 2814
Serpa, Salvatore, 2990
Serpe, Diane, 1329
Serpico, Bonnie, 1230
Serpico, Francisco Vincent, 1834, 2728-2729
Serpico, John, 1897
Serra, Salvatore, 3394
Serrano, Francisco R., 2356, 3246
Serrate, Leonard, 3464
Serritella, Daniel, 2529, 3390
Sertorius, Quintus, 2729
Serturner, Friedrich, 3537
Servan, Joan, 3276, 3520
Servano, Alfredo, 1265
Servetus, Michael, 2729
Servius Tullius, 3232
Servizzi, Julius, 380
Sesa, A., 3248
Session, James, 3455
Sessions, William Steele, 560, 669, 1145, 2729, 3426
Sessoms, Gilliam, 1830
Setrabutra, Panep, 2729
Settembrini, Luigi, 2729
Setten, Bill, 2137
Setty, Diane, 2729
Setty, Stanley, 1641
Seuffer, James, 3451
Sevan, Pearl, 628
Seven Rivers Crowd, 311

Seventh Passenger, The, 2729
Seventh Suicide Squad, 3497, 3534
Severbrinik, M.A., 1414
Severtson, Rich, 2812
Severus, Alexander, 1749, 2154, 2428, 3235
Severus, Galerius, 3235
Severus, Lucius Septimius, 619, 942, 1080, 1303, 2336, 2407, 2729-2730, 3235
Severyns, William, 1426
Sevillano, Emilio, 3253
Sevket Pasa, Mahmud, 2730
Sewall, Samuel, 2145, 2665, 2669, 2730
Seward, Augustus, 1959
Seward, Fanny, 1959
Seward, Frederick, 1958
Seward, William Henry, 408, 1232, 1233, 1955, 3241
Sewell, Dallas, 3366
Sewell, Douglas, 2730
Sewell, Ethel Jean, 2730
Sewell, Frederick Joseph, 2730, 3462
Sewell, James, 1467
Sewell, Martha Ann, 1348
Sewell, Nathaniel, 1226
Sewer Gang, 2409
Sexton, Clarence, 2827
Sexton, John, 1206
Seydel, Eugen, 992
Seye, Blaise Ferrage, 2730
Seyffardt, Hendrik Alexander, 3250
Seymour, Allen, 3363
Seymour, Brian, 2730
Seymour, Charles, 835
Seymour, Digby, 2560
Seymour, Edward, (Brit. c.1500-52) 2730
Seymour, Edward, (Brit. c.1539-1621) 2730
Seymour, Ernest J. Cox, 769, 803
Seymour, Florence, 2046
Seymour, Golney, 2730-2731
Seymour, Henry Daniel, 2731
Seymour, Horatio, 2324, 2326, 2731
Seymour, J., 3426
Seymour, Jane, 423
Seymour, John, 1230
Seymour, Melin, 1653
Seymour, Thomas, 2731
Seymour, Walter, 2731
Seymour, Whitney North, Jr., 716, 893
Seymour, William, 2871
Seyss-Inquart, Arthur, 994, 2731, 3542
Seznec, Guillaume, 2731-2732
Seznec, Jeanne, 2732
Sforza, Carlos, 3251
Sforza, Galeazzo Maria, 2732, 3238
Sforza, Giovanni, 442
Sforza, Lodovico, 2732
Sgelirrach, Frank, 2455
Sgroi, Alfonso "The Butch", 590
Shabat, Michael, 2418
Shabazz, James, 3497
Shachori, Ami, 2732, 3256, 3267, 3494
Shackart, Ronald, 3448
Shaddy, Gregory, 2732
Shadley, Lafe, 1003,1627, 2732-2733
Shadow and the Web, The, 2733
Shadrach, 703, 2733
Shadur, Milton, 2689
Shaeffer, Daniel, 2733
Shafer, Russell F., 2733
Shaffenburg, M.A., 3550
Shaffer, Charles, 3100
Shaffer, Clarence Lee, Jr., 466, 467
Shaffer, George "Sombrero Jack", 363
Shaffer, Howard, 2733
Shaffer, James, 1465
Shafford, Alfred, 3337, 3338
Shafizadeh, Abraham, 2894
Shaftesbury, Anthony Ashley Cooper, 2733
Shaftesbury, Earl of, 1975

Siebert, Wayne, 1731
Siebolt, Anton, 3340
Siedenschner, Jacob, 3218, 3410
Sieff, Joseph Edward, 2456, 3499
Sieg, Harvey W., 1275
Siegal, Robert, 3463
Siegel, Benjamin "Bugsy", 32, 34, 111, 117,
     655, 741, 786, 796, 1018, 1019, 1100,
     1295, 1296, 1310, 1376, 1491, 1555, 1556,
     1892, 1893, 1894, 1895, 1900, 1901, 2004,
     2005, 2006, 2114, 2138, 2252, 2254, 2529,
     2561, 2828, 2753-2757, 2835, 3225, 3396,
     3406, 3408
Siegel, Joseph E., 2757
Siegel Trading Company, 2757-2758
Siege of Sidney Street, 2753, 2758-2759
Siegl, Peter, 3522
Sieker, Edward A., 3551
Sieker, Frank, 3551
Sieker, Lamartine P., 174, 3551
Sieker, Tom, 3551
Siena, Catherine of, 569
Siepmann, Ingrid, 3475
Sierra, G.R.G., 3252
Siers, David S., 2759
Sietsome, Mary, 2299
Sievers, Wolfram, 3542
Sievier, Robert S., 2759
Sieys, Emmanuel-Joseph, 2394
Sifton, Charles Proctor, 2759
Sifton, Winfield, 1830
Sigebert I, 521, 700, 2759, 3236
Sigebert II, 2759, 3236
Sigeferth, 1052
Sigel, Elsie, 2012
Sigh, M., 3473
Sighibuldi, Cino dei, 2759
Sigismund, 1400, 1646, 2759
Sigismund, John, 3235, 3238
Sigler, Susan, 1589
Sigmond, John, 3338
Sigonius, Charles, 2759
Sigsby, Bob, 2999
Sigurd I, 1455
Sigurd II, 2759, 3237
Sihanouk, Norodom, 3254
Sihtricson, Olaf, 1070
Sikh, 3240, 3249, 3259, 3261
Siko, Albert R., 913
Silagy, Charles, 2759, 3451
Silberbauer, Karl, 3149
Silberman, Samuel H., 1791
Silberrad, Rupprecht, 1410
Silberstein, Alexander, 1153
Silent Bullet, The, 2759
Siler, Eugene Edward, Jr., 2759
Silesi, Joseph Albert, 3394, 3410
Silius, Caius, 727, 2282
Silks, Mattie, 1500, 2399, 2759-2760
Silkwood, Karen, 2760-2761
Silles, Florence Alice Bernadette, 1618
Silliman, Benjamin, Jr., 1091
Siloa Valente, Alvaro, 627
Sils, Alfred, 2012
Silva, Antônio José da, 2761
Silva, Benjamin, 3449
Silva, Carlos, 3244
Silva, Flavius, 339
Silva, Henry, 2079
Silva, Jos Abello, 3397
Silva, Mark J., 2324
Silva, Mauricio, 3449
Silva, Robert, 2762
Silva, Vicente, 568, 919, 2761, 3551, 3553,
     3555-3557, 3559, 3560, 3566, 3567
Silva, Vincente, 2761
Silva Xavier, Joaquim José da, 2761
Silvela, Francisco, 2761
Silver, Frankie, 2761

Silver, Gertrude, 2707
Silver, James, 2061
Silver, Norm, 2761
Silvera, Martha, 2761
Silvera, Vincent, 2761
Silverberg, Albert I., 2312
Silver Gang, 3410
Silverius, Saint 2761
Silverman, Leon, 418
Silverman, Max, 722
Silverman, Samuel J., 2133
Silverman, Simon, 1370, 1391
Silverman, Sydney, 778, 2394
Silverosa, George, 877, 1636, 3196
Silvers, Louis, 3394
Silvers, Phil, 776
Silvers, Rachel, 2761-2762
Silvers, Robert 7
Silver Shirts, The, 2762
Silverstein, Jack, 772
Silverstein, M., 3263
Silverstein, Thomas, 2762
Silver Tip, 651
Silvestri, Aguazio, 1290
Silvia, Daniel, 2762-2763
Silvino, Antonio, 1880
Siman, Teofilo, 3333, 3512
Simaniuk, George, 2763
Simants, Erwin Charles, 2763
Simard, Francis, 1238, 1898
Simard, Jacques, 1898
Simececk, James, 2763
Simenon, Georges, 2763
Simeone, Mike, 2830
Simering, Mary, 2008
Simic, Slobodan, 3065
Simmon, Gerd, 295
Simmons, Beoria, 2763, 3451
Simmons, Charles, 3003
Simmons, Daniel T., 2733
Simmons, Del, 1003, 2732
Simmons, Dennis, 3362
Simmons, G.W., 463
Simmons, Henry, 3366
Simmons, Hurbert, 3356
Simmons, Isaac, 3368
Simmons, James Douglas, 1451
Simmons, Jesse, 213
Simmons, John, 213, 3264, 3339
Simmons, Lee, 260, 262
Simmons, Ronald, 3448
Simmons, Ronald Gene, 2763-2764
Simmons, Rush, 1126
Simmons, Theodore, 185, 2764, 3264
Simmons, Thomas, 3448
Simmons, Tommie Bernard, 1233, 2726
Simmons, Tuillie, 3359
Simmons, Walter, 2879
Simmons, William J., 1134, 1220, 1223,
     1856
Simmons, Zachariah, 20, 2764-2765, 3410
Simms, Billy, 1165
Simms, Darryl, 3451
Simms, David, 3357
Simms, Henry, 2765
Simms, Lee, 3362
Simms, Michelle Denise, 1981
Simms, Nathaniel, 2133
Simms, Pink, 3551
Simms, Sam, 3357
Simms, W.H., 3566
Simms, William, 3350
Simnel, Lambert, 721, 2765
Simon, 2765
Simon, Arlette, 2845
Simon, Carleton, 2765
Simon, Edward H.H., 3144
Simon, Ford, 3357
Simon, Gustav, 3542

Simon, J.C., 398, 3218
Simon, Jeanne, 2522
Simon, Jocelyn, 1472
Simon, John Allsebrook, 1071, 2094, 2765
Simon, Michael, 1655
Simon, Richard, 3454
Simon, Stanley, 3112
Simon, Viscount, 2099
Simone, John, 3413
Simone, Nicola, 3259, 3519
Simone, William, 665
Simonelli, Joe, 3380
Simonelli, Neil 129
Simonet, Guy, 497
Simonetti, Anthony, 2107
Simons, Arthur "Bull", 1284
Simons, Ellis, 1944
Simons, Hannah, 1232
Simons, John, 2287
Simons, Jules, 2037
Simonsen, David, 3453
Simonson, Archie, 1225
Simpkins, Jack, 1500
Simpkins, Lloyd, 542
Simpson, Abigail, 548
Simpson, Alexander, 1287
Simpson, Arthur, 2885
Simpson, Charlie, 2765-2766
Simpson, Edward, 2766
Simpson, Floyd, 2211
Simpson, Frank, 3347
Simpson, Gordon, 2098
Simpson, Jane, 826
Simpson, John, 3426
Simpson, John Richard, 2766, 3426
Simpson, Jonathan, 2766
Simpson, Joseph, 2766-2767, 3359
Simpson, Keith, 494, 981, 2729
Simpson, Lenox, 3247
Simpson, Nelson, 3352
Simpson, Palmer, 3350
Simpson, Patrick, 3166
Simpson, Perrie Dyon, 3453
Simpson, Ray, 2025
Simpson, Simmons, 3338
Simpson, T.S., 3023
Simpson, Varnado, 2273
Simpson, William, 1608, 3410
Simpson, Willie Joe, 2767
Simpton, John, 3336
Sims, Allen G., 3469
Sims, David, 2767, 3341
Sims, Frank, 2990
Sims, James, 3340
Sims, John, 3341, 3354
Sims, Loyie, 2767
Sims, Marlene, 226
Sims, Michael, 2767
Sims, Mitchell Carleton, 2767-2768, 3449,
     3454
Sims, Mosely, 3341
Sims, Richard M., 3118
Sims, Robert, 3341
Sims, Ruben, 3356
Sims, Terry, 3450
Sims, W.D., 3365
Sims, Walter Lee, 1113, 1860
Sims, William, 2933
Sinacola, Joseph, 3390
Sinai, Stuart, 1173
Sinatra, Frank, Jr., 115, 3211, 3327
Sinatra, Frank, Sr., 115-116, 896, 1097,
     1119, 1189, 1228, 1491, 2194, 2217, 2835,
     3396, 3409
Sin City Disciples, 3479
Sin Foo 2768
Sinclair, Alexander John Maum, 485
Sinclair, George, 2768
Sinclair, Harry, 399, 554, 1130, 1612, 1657,

2910
Sinclair, James, 2682
Sinclair, John, 2474
Sinclair, Joseph, 3283
Sinclair, Stephen, 2337
Sinclair, Sydney, 1415
Sinclair, Upton, 12, 13, 446
Sinclair, Walter, 927
Sindicic, Vinko, 2847
Sindona, Michele, 2768
Sindone, Frank, 3412, 3413
Singapore Jibril Front, 3494
Sing Dock, 3415
Sing Low, 3415
Singer, Fred, 2144
Singer, Herbert, 2119
Singer, John Timothy, 2886
Singer, Joseph, 843
Singer, Louis, 2561
Singer, Maurice 1409
Singer, Saul, 1849, 2119
Singer, Vickie, 2886
Singh, Atinder Pal, 1261
Singh, Balbir, 1261
Singh, Beant, 1261
Singh, Boysie, 2768-2769
Singh, Dalip Lutchmie Persad, 2769
Singh, Darbara, 3260
Singh, Dilip, 1261
Singh, Govind, 1353
Singh, Gurbax, 3473
Singh, Hardayal, 3261
Singh, Hari, 1581
Singh, Jarnail, 3517
Singh, Kalyan, 1854
Singh, Kehar, 1261
Singh, Mithileshwar, 3334
Singh, Ram, 1560
Singh, Satwant, 1261
Singh, Udham, 176, 3249
Singh Sandhu, Suchnam, 2769
Sing Lee, 2769
Single, Albert, 1027
Single Hearted Celestial Principles, 3391
Singleton, Charles, 287, 3448
Singleton, Claud, 3365
Singleton, Cornelius, 3447
Singleton, Edgar, 946
Singleton, Fred, 3454
Singleton, John Edward, 2769
Singleton, Lawrence, 2769-2770
Singleton, Man, 3351
Singleton, Ray, 1192
Singleton, Sherry Lynn, 2048
Sing Sing Prison Riot, 3378
Sinha, Satyendra Prasanno, 2770
Sinistrari, Ludovico Maria, 2770
Sinks, Judy, 2770
Sinks, Theodore P., 2770
Sinn Fein, 1148
Sinzinger, Adolf, 988
Siola, Uberto, 3258, 3513
Sioux Indian Massacre, 2770-2771
Sipiagin, Dimitri Sergeevich, 3243
Siple, Frank E., 2771
Sippy, Benjamin, 3551
Siqueiros, David Alfaro, 2771, 2992
Siracusa, Pepino, 3410
Siragusa, Charles, 2771, 3297
Siraj-ud-daula, 2190, 2771
Sirani, Elisabetta, 2964
Siratka, Julius, 73
Sireci, Henry, 3450
Sirgo, Louis, 1106
Sirhan, Sirhan Bishara, 776, 1801-1803, 3256, 3479, 3497
Sirica, John J., 3099, 3100, 3101
Sirikul, Taweeyos, 2771
Siringo, Charles Angelo, 652, 1979, 2771-

2772, 3551, 3566
Siripongs, Jaturun, 3449
Sirk, Douglas, 2012, 3196
Sirkorski, Wladyslaw, 3250
Sirocco, Jack, 308, 1725, 1726, 3218, 3411
Sirr, H.C., 1092
Sisera, 3232
Sisk, T. Edward, 2772
Sisk, Thomas, 407
Sisneros, Dionicio, 3566
Sisson, Robert N., 2772
Sisson Documents, 2772
Sister's Row, 3411
Sisti, Mark, 674
Sitgreaves, John, 2772
Sitters, Joe, 3551
Sitting Bull, 2772, 3192, 3242, 3293
Sitting Crow, Jesse, 1322
Sittler, Thomas M., 1356
Siu, Alvin Antonio, 3474
Sivak, Lacey, 3451
Si Votha, 2772
Siward the Strong, 2094, 2772
Siwik, Edward R., 1788
Six, Franz, 3542
Sixpence Temba, 2275
Sixteen-String Jack, 870
Sixtus II, 1906, 2772
Sixtus IV, 126, 1657, 2772, 2969
Sizemore, James, 1776
Sjahrir, Sutan, 2772
Skaar, Eugene, 3187
Skaggs, David, 3451
Skaggs, Elijah, 2772-2773
Skapp, William, 3340
Skar, Manny, 2773, 3390
Skarbek, Christine, 2248
Skeen, Orel, 212
Skelba, Edward, 712
Skelhorn, Norman, 158
Skelly, Charles, 546
Skelly, John, 684
Skelton, John, 3455
Skene, George, 2773
Skepper, Donald, 2297
Skeres, Nicholas, 2126
Skerritt, Joseph, 2096
Skerritt, Nicholas, 1940
Skewes, Jeanne R., 1709
Skidmore, William, 2673, 2973, 3381, 3382, 3390
Skillern, Doyle, 3447
Skillman, W. McKay, 585
Skin for Skin, 2773
Skingle, Arthur, 2773
Skinheads, 2773-2774, 3534
Skinner, Albert W., 1527
Skinner, Cyrus, 265, 2774, 3337
Skinner, George, 265
Skinner, John, 2070
Skinner, John K., 3425
Skinner, Kenneth, 2774, 3228
Skinner, Leslie, 3248
Skinner, Mary, 835
Skipwith, J.K., 2774
Skivington, George J., 1528
Skobline, Nadine Plevitskaia, 2774
Skobline, Nicholas, 2774
Skog, John Albert, 2774
Skolnick, Albert, 2191
Skoptzy, 2774
Skorzeny, Otto, 1372, 1576, 1577, 2266
Skou Tour, 3256
Skull, George, 2775
Skull, Sally, 2774-2775
Skurlock, J.G., 364
Skwierawski, Michael, 323
SLA, 3330, 3334, 3500-3502
Slack, Anne, 1179

Slack, John, 162
Slade, Dolly, 1507
Slade, Gerald, 1746
Slade, Haddon, 1434
Slade, Jack, 2775, 2776
Slade, James A., 3337
Slade, Joseph Alfred, 2775-2776, 3566
Slade, Joshua, 2776
Slade, Tim, 2910
Slaney, Sidney, 2776
Slanning, Andrew, 801
Slánsky, Rudolf Salzmann, 2776
Slapik, Theodore, 3427
Slark, Tom, 2776
Slater, A.R., 1837
Slater, Arthur, 2746
Slater, Frances Julia, 660, 3333
Slater, Harry, 1774
Slater, Oscar, 43, 1016, 1068, 1409, 2026, 2776-2777, 2867
Slater, Phil, 3366
Slater, Sidney, 3411
Slater, William, 1404
Slatin Pasha, Rudolf Anton Karl von, 2777
Slaton, John M., 554, 1224
Slaton, Lewis, 692, 3167
Slatter, Herbert Shorland, 2680
Slaughter, Gabe, 2884, 2901, 2902
Slaughter, John, 108, 718, 2048, 2309
Slaughter, John Horton, 3544, 3547, 3551, 3556, 3558, 3566
Slaughter, P., 3344
Slaughter, Tom, 204
Slaughter, Warren, 1908
Slaughterford, Christopher, 2777-2778
Slaughter Housers, 3411
Slavenburg Bank, 3290
Slavin, Mark, 1081, 1143
Slavin, Pat 3555
Slawson, Linda, 520
Slawter, James, 3451
Slayman, Dorothy, 1764
Slayton, Elmo, 2778
Slayton, Jesse, 3347
Slayton, John, 865
Slayton, Rosie, 2895
Slayton, Roy, 2778
Sleeping Clergyman, A, 2778
Sleeping Sphinx, The, 2778
Slesers, Anna, 921
Slick, Sam, 1420
Slick, Thomas W., 2778
Slivinski, Emanuel 676
Slivinski, Lillian, 676
Sliwa, Curtis, 1395
Sliwinski, Evelyn, 2690
Sliwka, Tadeusz, 2778
Sloan, Jeffrey, 3452
Sloan-Kettering Cancer Center, 3290
Sloat, E.C., Jr., 3245
Slobbery Jim, 888, 3409, 3411
Slocum, Bill, 95
Slocum, Frances, 2778
Sloss, Albert, 3351
Sloss, John, 2212
Sloss, William, 419
Slotnik, Barry I., 1329, 3463
Slough, John P., 3241, 3565
Slovak, John, 3363
Slovak, Miroslav, 3464
Slover, Enoch A., 3425
Slovik, Edward Donald, 2778-2779
Slow, John, 3118
Sly, Albert "Bertie", 1506
Sly, Don, 1739
Slyter, George B., 2779
Smaldone, Clarence, 2779
Smaldone, Clyde, 2779
Smaldone, Eugene, 2779, 3412

Sylvester, David Joseph, 2889
Sylvester, George, 3206, 3400
Sylvester, Richard, 3426
Sylvester, Stanley, 3328, 3489
Symbionese Liberation Army, 1464, 1502-03, 2889-2891, 3330, 3498-3500, 3502, 3534
Syme, Sydney, 679
Symes, Ellen Ann, 531
Symes, J. Foster, 2891
Symes, Tommy, 906
Symington, Charles J., 2580
Symmachus, Quintus Aurelius Memmius, 47, 2891, 3235
Symmonds, Thomas, 446, 1432
Symmons, Justice, 1043
Symonds, Yvonne, 1504
Symons, Bill, 2872
Sympson, Bernard, 917
Sympson, George, 1559
Sympson, Thomas, 2891
Syndicate, The, 2891-2892
Sypher, Pearl, 3029
Syracuse, Charles, 184, 185
Syracuse, Dionysius of, 2460
Syrian National Socialist Party, 3280
Syzmanklewicz, Joseph, 2827
Szabo, John, 3451
Szabo, Mrs. Ladislaus, 1142
Szalai, Andras, 2532
Szehsien, Wen, 1605
Szendi, Maria, 1142
Szentes, Dorotta, 281
Szilagyi, Linda, 2990
Szinswaska, Sonia, 1090
Szálasi, Ferenc, 2892, 3543
Szonyi, Tibor, 2532
Sztaray, Countess, 1082, 2046
Sztojay, Döme, 3543
Szuchon, Joseph, 3454
Szurma, Sonia, 2880
Szyc, John, 1248
Szymankiewicz, W., 3467

T

Taafee, Bernard "Barney" P., 3426
Tabinshwehti, 2893
Tabor, James, 3360
Taborsky, Albert, 2893
Taborsky, Joseph, 2893
Tabram, Martha, 1682, 1684, 1688
Taby, Arpad, 2893
Taccetta, Michael, 18
Tacitus, Marcus Claudius, 2893
Tacklyn, Larry Winfield, 558, 2893
Taewon-gun, 2893
Tafel, Monika, 1852
Tafero, Jessie J., 1967, 3450
Taffe, G.A., 3424
Tafoya, Donaciano, 3555
Taft, Alphonso, 2893
Taft, Charles Sabin, 1958
Taft, Henry Waters, 2893
Taft, Robert A., 2853
Taft, William Howard, 230, 523, 583, 593, 624, 888, 910, 1084, 1524, 1636, 1719, 1816, 1839, 1852, 1884, 2012, 2046, 2069, 2076, 2157, 2160-2161, 2206, 2228, 2262, 2407, 2471, 2494, 2893-2894, 3006, 3029, 3030, 3035, 3138, 3148, 3180, 3208, 3215
Taggart, Alyce O., 3102, 3103
Taggart, Frank, 3566

Taglianetti, Louis, 3380
Tagliercio, Giuseppe, 3333, 3513
Taha, Sami, 3251
Tahmasp II, 2275, 2733, 3240
T'ai-ch'ang, 3239
Taijo, Assem, 3254
Tailford, Hannah, 1691
Taini, Reno, 2480
Taira, 2187
Taisho, 1445
Tait, Charles, 3343
Tait, Sydney D., 2894
Taitel, Morris, 2981
Takaakira Kato, 392, 3245
Takai, David, 2139
Takaji Wachi, 279
Takamori Saigo, 3242
Takashi Hara, 1445, 3244
Takasugi, Robert, 909
Takejiro Onishi, 3543
Takenaka Masahisa, 3395
Takfir Wal-Hajira, 2654, 3534
Taki, 790
Taksin, 2894
Takuma Dan, Baron, 3247
Tal, Schlomo, 2894
Tal, Wasfi, 1143, 2894, 3256, 3491
Talaat, Yousef, 2288
Talat Pasha, Mehmed, 2894
Talavera, Norman Ramirez, 2399
Talbert, Dorothea, 2827
Talbert, James, 3342
Talbot, Acie, 2306
Talbot, Ben, 285, 2895
Talbot, Bess, 459
Talbot, George John, 2894-2895
Talbot, Jim, 2159
Talbot, Julie, 2895
Talbot, Len, 2895
Talbot, "Lug", 285, 2895
Talbot, Lura Lee, 459
Talbot, Sims, 1237
Talbot, Thomas, 3338
Talbot, Thurgood, 2306
Talbot, William, 3175
Talbott, Albert, 2895
Talbott, Charles E., 2895
Talbott, Salome, 284
Talfourd, Thomas Noon, 2895
Talib, Taha, 3259
Taliercio, Giuseppe, 2683, 3260, 3514
Talley, Harriet, 3346
Talley, John, 3362
Tallien, Jean Lambert, 2895
Tally, U.G., 3364
Talmadge, Eugene, 553, 1223
Talmadge, T. DeWitt, 2895
Talow, Michael, 3253
Talty, Francis, 2742
Tambo, Oliver, 2101, 2197
Tambone, Peter, 3411
Tamburello, Peter, 717
Tamechika Okada, 3241
Tameleo, Enrico Henry, 3379, 3380
Tameleo, Henry, 2419
Tamerlane the Great, 2895-2896
Tamil Eelam Liberation Organization, 3534
Tamkin, Edward, 361
Tamlyn, Dorothy, 598
Tamm, Edward Allen, 801, 2896
Tammanend, 2896
Tammany, Bill, 2072
Tammany Hall, 2288, 2326-2327, 2896, 3401-3407, 3410-3412
Tan Shu-Kuei, 3250
Tanaka Kakuei, 1841, 1975, 2276, 2896
Tanassi, Mario, 1975
Tancl, Eddie, 608, 2070, 3390

Tandogan, Nevzat, 3251
Tandy, John, 1740
Taney, Roger, 690, 849
Taney, Roger Brooke, 2711, 2870, 2896
T'ang, Prince of, 692, 714
T'ang Shao-i, 3249
Tang Yu-Jen, 3248
Tanguay, Germaine, 1605
Tanis, Hazel, 645
Tankosic, Major, 974
Tannehill, Robert J., 3462
Tannenbaum, Albert "Tick Tock", 117, 620, 1310, 2252, 2255, 3410, 3411
Tannenbaum, Benjamin, 3411
Tannenbaum, Gershon, 1239
Tannenbaum, Harold, 3400
Tanner, Adam, 2699
Tanner, Bertha, 883
Tanner, J.H., 3424
Tanner, John, 2897
Tanner, M.F., 3350
Tanner, Tobias, 1302
Tanner, Väinö, 3543
Tanner, William, 2249, 3207
Tansey, John, 2897
Tantis, B.D., 3353
Tantleff, Jules, 2849
Tanuma Okitsugu, 2897
Taoka Kazuo, 2681, 2897, 3395
Tao Shan-Chen, 3249
Tapia Barraza, Carlos, 3514
Tapia, José Carrasco, 2469
Tapley, Colin, 641
Tapner, Benjamin, 1827, 2897-2898
Tappan, Arthur, 10, 11, 3373
Tappan, Bob, 705
Tappan, Lewis, 3373
Tappenier, J.C., 380
Tarabya, 3094
Tarafa, 2898
Taranto, Louis of, 1993
Tarbouriech, Edith, 1291
Tarbuck, Joseph Q., 504
Tarditi, Adolphe, 3297
Tardy, Mary Louise, 1827
Tariq, Abu, 3259
Tarkington, Booth, 2452
Tarlentino, Anthony, 3297
Tarling, Dorothy, 1968
Tarnower, Herman, 1461
Tarnowska, Marie, 2291
Tarolino, Salvatore, 3411
Taron, Luc, 1923
Tarquin the Proud, 3232
Tarquinius, Sextus, 2898
Tarrant, Thomas Albert, 3265
Tarricone, Alphonse, 3411
Tartamella, John, 3411, 3413
Tarter, Alvis, 704, 2898
Tarter, Bing, 285, 2898
Tarter, Sammy, 2898
Tarter-Coffelt Feud, 2898
Taruc, Luis M., 2523
Tarun, Robert W., 1532
Tarver, Bobby, 3447
Tarver, Robert Lee, 3447
Tascarella, Michael, 3380
Taschereau, Henri Elzear, 2898
Taschereau, Henri Thomas, 2898
Tassin, Robert, 3452
Tatad, Francisco S., 2119
Tatar khan Tokhtamysh, 3037
Tate, Albert, Jr., 2898
Tate, Auguster, Sr., 709
Tate, Gene, 2150
Tate, Georgia, 709
Tate, Jackson R., 1244
Tate, Kenneth, 3453
Tate, Mary, 390

Towhidi, Hojatoleslam, 3259, 3516
Towne, John, 3359
Towneley, Francis, 2979
Towner, Milton M., 1439
Towner, Samuel, 3362
Townes, Richard, 3456
Townes, Roosevelt, 3368
Townley, Edmund, 2261
Townley, George, 2979, 3195
Townley, Michael Vernon, 1942
Townley, Vera, 2261
Townsend, E.H., 3197
Townsend, Eleanor, 1967
Townsend, Everett E., 3551
Townsend, Harry, 2980
Townsend, Jean, 2980
Townsend, Joe, (U.S. pr.1887), 729
Townsend, Joe, (U.S. pr.1970), 1230
Townsend, Johnny, 3451
Townsend, Kate, 2888
Townsend, Pink Earl, 1822
Townsend, Smith, 1274
Townsend, Thompson, 3139
Townsend, William, 2980
Townsend, Winfield, 3352
Townshend, Charles, 2825
Townsley, Bob, 3551
Townsley, Forest, 3551
Townsley, James, 510
Toyama Mitsuru, 391, 2980-2981, 3202
Toyoshi Nakamura, 3459
Toyotomi Hidetsugo, 2981
Toyotomi Hideyori, 2964
Toyotomi Hideyoshi, 1842, 2964, 2981
Tozzini, Gualtiero, 1652
Turkish People's Liberation Army (TPLA),
    3328, 3470, 3488, 3492
Turley, Orville, 3428
Trabucco, Joseph Jerome, 1881
Trabzon, Eugenius of, 3200
Tracey, Frank J., 2981
Tracey, Joseph Robert, 2191
Tracey, Kid, 1864
Tracey, Walter, 2981
Trackenburg, Max, 2981
Tracy, Ann Gibson, 2981
Tracy, Benjamin Franklin, 2981
Tracy, Christopher, 810
Tracy, Edward Austin, 1914
Tracy, George, 3346
Tracy, Harry, 2981-2982, 3427, 3563, 3567
Tracy, J.A., 3133
Tracy, Martha, 2982-2983
Tracy, Mary, 2095
Tracy, William, 310
Traeger, William, 2068
Trafficante, Sam Cacciatore, 3394
Trafficante, Santo, Sr., 2085, 2983, 3393,
    3394, 3407
Trafficante, Santo, Jr., 136, 282, 1251, 1491,
    1990, 2983, 3394
Trafton, Richard S., 2426
Trafton, Stanley, 2426
Trahina, Charles, 1516, 3339
Train, Arthur, 764, 2983
Traina, Giuseppe, 3411
Trainor, Jack, 2656
Trainor, Patrick, 3519
Trajan, 138, 3536
Trajetto, Duchess of, 230
Trammel, C.W., 3424
Trammell, Park, 508
Tramunti, Carmine, 3411
Tran, Andrew, 233
Tran, Heck Van, 3454
Tranalone, John, 3380
Traore, Boubacar, 2276
Trapani, Emanuela, 3028
Trapia, Francisco, 2983

Trapnell, Garrett Brock, 2983-2984, 3469,
    3471
Trapnell, John Graham, 2984
Trapped, 2984
Trask, Christiane, 2666
Trask, John, 2665
Traubner, Ed, 3209
Trausch, Clarence P., 461
Travaglia, Michael, 3454
Traveling Mike Grady Gang, 2984
Travers, George, 2984
Travers, Moll, 3153
Travis, Charles M., 1618
Travis, Herbert, 1190
Travis, John, 436, 3326
Travis, Joseph, 3004, 3373
Travis, William, 2319
Trawick, Gary, 3450
Traxler, Roy "Pete", 2984
Trayer, Bruce J., 3471
Traylor, Caroline, 1916
Traynor, Nick "Chaw Jimmie", 208
Treadaway, Jonathan C., 2984
Treadway, Mary L., 3331
Treadwell, Sophie, 2045
Treager, A., 936
Treager, William T., 2355
Treanor, John, 505
Trease, Edward J., 2984
Trébert, Guy, 2985
Trebonius, Gaius, 2985
Tree, Beerbohm, 3183
Trefethen, James, 2985
Treffene, Phillip John, 2985
Trefton, Nellie, 1670
Tregillis, Mary Ann, 2902
Tregillis, William, 2902
Tregle, Bernard, 3400
Tregoff, Carole, 776, 1158, 1310
Treleaven, R.W., 2022
Treloar, James Gray, 2985
Trelstad, Laura, 390
Tremaine, Harry, 1165
Tremamunno, Donato, 2985
Tremoglie, Joe, 179
Tremont, Fred, 3390
Tremont, Peter, 3390
Tremont, Tom, 3390
Trench, John, 2776
Trench, William Crosby, 3125
Trenchard, Hugh Montague, 2985, 3426
Trenchard, Thomas Whitaker, 1488
Trenck, Baron Franz von der, 2985
Trendle, Kathleen, 1551
Trenkler,, Walter, 90
Trent, Betty Lou, 2986
Trent, Lindbergh, 2985-2986
Trent, Shepherd, 3365
Trentham, Charles, 3551, 3567
Trenton Prison Riots, 2986
Trepoff, Dmitri Feodorovich, 2986-2987,
    3243
Trepov, Fyodor Fyodorovich, 85, 3242
Tresca, Carlo, 1250, 2987-2988, 3250, 3411
Tresckow, Henning von, 1574, 1577
Tresham, Francis, 656, 2988
Tresham, Robert, 2204
Tresp, Nicholas, 211
Trest, J.T., 1728
Treves, Prince-Archbishop of, 1175
Treves Witch Trials, 2988
Trevino, Jose Mario, 3455
Trevino, Pancho, 3297
Trevino, Ramon, 3245
Trevor, Dorien Harold, 171, 565, 2988
Trevor-Roper, Hugh, 1580
Trew, Nellie, 1378
Triad Society, 2988-2989
Tribonian, 1005, 1750, 2989

Tric, M., 1886
Trice, Andrew, 3358
Trice, Eddie, 3453
Tricker, Chick, 1652, 3218, 3408, 3411
Trickers, The, 1652
Tricot, Renée, 3114
Trieber, Jacob, 2989
Trifa, Valerian, 3543
Trifon, Peter, 1587
Triglia, Joseph, 3394
Trilby Gang, 3390
Trillo, Miguel, 3052
Trimble, David, 3304
Trimble, James, 3452
Trimble, Robert, 2989
Trimble, Tommy Lee, 313
Trimble, William, 2989
Trimmell, John, 791
Trimmer, Frank, 2984
Trimmer, Wayne, 3171
Trinchera, Dominick, 3406, 3411
Trinder, Stanley, 1014
Triplett, Ezra, 686
Triplett, June, 686
Tripoli, Mimi, 3397
Tripp, Glenn Kurt, 2989, 3472
Tripp, Grace, 2989
Trippet, Robert S., 2989-2990
Tripps, Peter, 705
Tripps, Roy, 3042
Tri-State Gang,, 2990
Triton, William, 141
Trivulzio, Luigi, 3249
Tro, Emilio, 2662
Trochu, Louis-Jules, 931
Troia, Vincenzo, 3411
Trojanoff, Christo, 1074
Troland, Thomas E., 998
Trolia, John, 2990
Trolle, Gustav Eriksson, 2990
Trombino, Anthony, 3397
Trompin, Katherine, 2872
Tronkiewitz, M., 3244
Tronolone, John "Peanuts", 2990, 3392
Troop, William, 2733
Tropea, Orazio "The Scourge", 1292, 1294,
    3390
Troppman, Jean-Baptiste, 1901, 2990-2992
Trossman, Robert, 869
Trot, Benjamin, 446
Trot, Nicholas, 431
Trotman, Daniel, 744
Trotsky, Leon, 535, 1213, 1469, 1610, 1833,
    1929, 2292, 2333, 2517, 2563, 2722, 2836,
    2987, 2992-2994, 3244, 3249
Trott, Nicholas, 1119
Trott, Peter, 1227
Trotter, Charles, 3076
Trotter, Clarence, 2994
Trotter, George J., 3305
Trotter, Melvin, 3450
Troup, George M., 885
Trousdale, David A., 1817, 3458
Trout, John B., 2025
Troutsdale, David A., 295
Trowbridge, C. Pfeiffer, 660
Trowbridge, Edmund, 2994
Trowell, Nicholas, 1692
Troxwell, Flash, 828
Troy, Christopher, 1159
Troy, Jack, 3356
Troy, N.Y., Brothel Riot, 3373
Truber, Manfred, 2994-2995
Trudeau, Pierre, 835
True, James, 2137
True, John L., 1356
True, Ronald, 1693, 2995
Trueblood, Michael, 3451
True Blue Americans, 3411

Truen, Jerome, 2671
Truesdale, Louis, 3454
Truitt, Alben W., 3466, 3480
Truitt, James, 2192
Truitt, Kenneth, 1821
Trujillo, Adelado S., 3471
Trujillo, Antonio Maria, 3567
Trujillo, Esteban, 3559
Trujillo, Joseph, 3185
Trujillo, Julian, 3567
Trujillo Molina, Rafael Léonidas "Ramfis", 354, 1253, 2995-2997, 3254
Truly, Roy, 1798
Truman, Harry S., 102, 286, 347, 381, 551, 644, 702, 724, 732, 749, 777, 847, 848, 906, 975, 1025, 1068, 1190, 1192, 1200, 1319, 1441, 1469, 1470, 1544, 1551, 1605, 1607, 1664, 1679, 1731, 2024, 2042, 2064, 2177, 2189, 2297, 2343, 2439, 2462, 2551, 2844, 2896, 2940, 2964, 2997, 3056, 3194, 3212, 3252
Trumbo, William, 2964
Truong Dinh Tri, 3251
Trupiano, Matthew M., Jr., 2997-2998
Truscott, Steven Murray, 2998
Trussell, George, 793, 3383, 3386, 3389, 3390, 3391
Trutt, Fran Stephanie, 3281
Truxton, Olli, 3339
TRW Credit Data, 3289
Tryforos, Lynne, 1461
Tryggvesson, Olaf, 1109
Tryphon, 2022, 3233
Tsai-feng, 3243
Tsang Hou, 3244
Tsankoff, Alex, 3245
Tsankoff, Danoso, 3245
Tsantes, George, 3261
T'sa Tsu, 1973
Tschentscher, Erwin, 3543
Tse-ne-gat, 2998
Tse-ven Soong, 3247
Tshombe, Moise, 1436, 3465, 3478
Tsiganovic, Major, 974
Tsironis, Vassilies, 3467
Tso, Jack B., 2768
Tsong Ing Van, 3090
Tsuji, Masanobu, 279
Tsumaki, Matsukichi, 2998
Tsuneo Mori, 2552
Tsung, Jen, 1133
Tsuruoka Masajiro, 1654
Tsuyoshi Okudaira, 1976
Tuam, Archbishop of, 1178
Tubbs, Frank, 1672
Tubman, William Vacanarat Shadrach, 2998, 3253
Tuccello, John, 3390
Tucholker, Alexander, 182
Tucillo, John, 1105, 2673
Tuck, Mark, 2998
Tucker, Barbara, 1838
Tucker, Charles Louis, 2998-2999
Tucker, Clara, 152, 153
Tucker, Cyril Grigg, 3035
Tucker, Donald, 1676
Tucker, Felix, 2999
Tucker, Frederick, 1746
Tucker, Garson, 3392
Tucker, George, 3551
Tucker, Henry St. George, 2999
Tucker, Jeffery, 3455
Tucker, Jesse, 3356
Tucker, Jim, 3567
Tucker, Karla Fay, 3455
Tucker, Kevin, 3425
Tucker, Michael, 3453
Tucker, Minnie Margaret, 2999
Tucker, Nathaniel Beverley, 2999

Tucker, Oscar, 3356
Tucker, Richard (U.S. pr.1930) 335
Tucker, Richard, 3447
Tucker, Samuel, 2689, 3392, 3393
Tucker, Sophie, 756, 2725
Tucker, Susan M., 2826
Tucker, Tom, 2919, 2999, 3551, 3567
Tucker, William Boyd, 3447
Tucker Prison Farm, 2999
Tuckers, John, 3400
Tuckett, Harvey Garnett Phipps, 520, 2999, 3305
Tuckett-Brudenell Duel, 2999
Tuckfield, Charles, 1242
Tuckhorn, Sime, 3390
Tudor, Elizabeth, 2134
Tudor, Mary, 1075, 1096, 1171, 1383
Tudor, Owen, 2999
Tuer, Angus McDougall, 2999
Tuer, William Franklin, 2999
Tufts, Henry, 2999-3000
Tufverson, Agnes, 2478
Tufverson, Selma, 2478
Tufverson, Olive 2478
Tugendhat, Christopher, 3258, 3507
Tuggle, Lem, 3456
Tuggle, Lem, Jr., 3428
Tuilaepa, Paul, 3449
Tuit, Tommy, 3389
Tuite, Gerald, 3517
Tuite, Patrick, 2811
Tuka, Vojtech, 3543
Tuke, Samuel, 1521
Tukhachevsky, Mikhail, 2837, 3000
Tulay, George, 312
Tulio, Marco, 3513
Tullar, D.S., 2013
Tuller, Brice, 3000, 3470
Tuller, Charles A., 3000, 3470
Tuller, Jonathan, 3000, 3470
Tullis, Aaron M., 1050
Tulloch, Marshall E., 915
Tullock, William, 1020
Tully, Grace, 533
Tully, Jim, 1564, 2195, 2655, 3001
Tully, Pat, 1775
Tully, Samuel, 3000-3001
Tully, Thomas Alton, 3001
Tulsa Bludgeonings, 3001
Tulsa Race Riot, 3002
Tumanyan, Serge, 3465
Tumilson, Joe, 1449
Tuminaro, Angelo, 3297, 3411
Tumlinson, Old Joe, 2884
Tumminello, Vincenzo, 3518
Tumpowski, Louis, 3030
Tumulty, Joseph P., 895
Tung Cheh, 3012
Tung Cho, 3002, 3235
Tung Fook, 3353
Tung Group, 3391
Tunisian Food Riots, 3378
Tunk, Jarvis, 2306
Tunk, Mary Ellen, 2306
Tunnel Gang, 3403, 3404, 3411
Tunney, Gene, 629
Tunstall, Charles, 3355
Tunstall, John H., 311, 363, 486, 739, 1112, 1276, 1554, 1555, 1559, 1966, 2060, 2149, 2177, 3071, 3554-3557, 3559-3561, 3563-3565, 3567, 3568
Tupac Amarú (Peru d.1572), 2964, 3002
Tupac Amarú (Peru 1742-81)
Tupac Amarú Revolutionary Movement (MRTA), 3532, 3534
Tupamaros-Movimiento de Liberacion Nacional (MLN) 3002, 3266, 3283, 3328, 3481, 3485-3488, 3498, 3532, 3534

Tupper, Jack, 1693
Turan-Shah, 3002, 3237
Turano, Giuseppe, 1251
Turgenev, Ivan, 2992
Turgenev, Nikolay Ivanovich, 3002
Turgot, Anne-Robert-Jacques, 942
Turilli, Rudy, 858
Turkis, Burton B., 3411
Turkish-Islamic Underground Organization, 3513
Turkish People's Liberation Army (TPLA) 3266, 3488, 3489, 3506, 3534, 3543
Turkish People's Liberation Front (TPLF) 3489, 3506, 3534
Turkish People's Liberation Party, 3505
Turkish Political Riots, 3377
Turkish Revolutionary Left Group, 3534
Turkmen, Dogan, 3257
Turko, Teresa, 28
Turks, Tameka, 744
Turkus, Burton B., 1, 118, 2255, 2564, 3002-3003
Turley, Preston S., 3003
Turlis, Thomas, 914, 3003
Turman, Helen, 870
Turman, James, 870
Turnblazer, William, 463
Turnbo, L.S., 3551, 3555
Turnbull, William A., 520
Turner, Aaron "Treetop", 3003
Turner, Andrew F., 2870
Turner, Anne, 1628
Turner, Belle, 820
Turner, Ben, 3003-3004, 3567
Turner, Bernard, 3
Turner, Carlton, 3301
Turner, Claude, 3453
Turner, Dick, 409
Turner, Donna M., 1109
Turner, Eddie, 124
Turner, Ellen, 3074
Turner, Emily, 2547
Turner, Ezekiel B., 3004
Turner, Felton, 3368
Turner, G.D., 877
Turner, George Arthur, 1622, 3551
Turner, Glenn W. 208, 3004
Turner, Harald, 3543
Turner, Hayes, 3365
Turner, Isaac, 2251
Turner, J.W., 2860
Turner, James, 2488
Turner, Jesse, 1914, 3334
Turner, Jessel, 3455
Turner, John (Brit. pr.1811), 3163
Turner, John (U.S. pr.1870s-80s), 3382, 3384, 3389, 3390
Turner, John (U.S. pr.1874) 1656
Turner, John (U.S. d.1889), 3338
Turner, John (U.S. d.1903), 3355
Turner, John (U.S. d.1979), 3187
Turner, John Virgil (U.S. d.1930), 3004
Turner, Joyce, 3004
Turner, Julia Jean Mildred Frances, 3004
Turner, Kevin, 3452
Turner, Lana, 741, 807, 809, 1310, 2928, 3397
Turner, Louisa, 2547
Turner, Lucille, 2221
Turner, Marion, 364, 3551, 3561, 3567
Turner, Mark, 2037
Turner, Mary, 3365
Turner, Maurice T., Jr., 3004, 3426
Turner, Melvin, 3449
Turner, Mildred, 809, 3004
Turner, Nat, 475, 1246, 3004-3005, 3373
Turner, Oscar, 3356
Turner, Richard (U.S. d.1976), 3005
Turner, Richard (U.S. pr.1980s) 3449

U

Urbane, Robinson, 1640
Urbano, Gilbert, 3455
Urbien Orbegozo, Jesus, 3511
Urdaneta, I., 3248
Urdaneta, Rafael, 2350
Urdaneto, Magdalena, 2198
Ure, Alexander, 2777
U'ren, Milton, 150
Uren, William, 1775
Uriah the Hittite, 2066
Uribe, David, 3246
Urich, Heinz Karl Gunther, 3018
Urich, Liliane, 3018
Urieta, Leandro, 3567
Uris, Harold, 762
Uritsky, Moisay S., 1929, 3244
Urquhart, David, 3293
Urschel, Charles F., 52, 209, 211, 1784, 2041,
     3326
Ursins, Marie-Anne de La Trémoille des,
     3018
Ursinus, 3018
Ursinus, Sophie, 3018
Urso, Joseph, 1120, 1718
Ursula, Saint, 3018
Ursuline Convent Riot, 3018-3021
Ury, John, 2297
US, 3480, 3481, 3482, 3499
U Saw, 185, 3251
U.S. Cultural Organization, 3534
U.S. Embassy Bombing, 3021
U.S. Nazi Riot, 3375
U.S. Race Riots, 3376
U.S. Steel Strike, 3021
Usefof, Joseph, 2056
U Sein Lwin, 3378
Usher, Cornelius, 3021
Usher Gahagan, 1249
Uskoks, 3021
Ustacha, The, 76-78, 2428, 3021-3022
Ustinov, Peter, 1261
Utica, Cato of, 2490
U Tin Tut, 3251, 3252
Utley, Ronald, 1254
Utley, Ruben, 2550
Utley, Teresa "Dusty", 1365
Utrillo, Maurice, 2098
Utt, Mary Lee, 1592
Utter, Charles, 3567
Utter, Earl Ray, 3022
Utterbach, F.W., 1751
Utting, Charles, 3551
UVF, 3491, 3502, 3503
Uzziah, 3232

V

Vaccarelli, Paolo Antonini, 1174, 2876, 2970,
     3225
Vaccarizi, Raymond, 3023
Vaccaro, John, 3023
Vacco, Carmen, 2354
Vachell, Charles Francis, 3023
Vacher, Joseph, 3023-3024
Vacko, Pavel, 3024
Vadala, Anthony, 3411
Vadala, Becky, 2959
Vadala, Betty, 2959
Vaden, John, 867
Vadino, Frank, 3413
Vadis, Arthur, 2351
Vaglica, Anthony B., 1190, 3283, 3462
Vahid-Dastgerdi, 3239, 3274

Vail, Theodore, 843
Vaillancourt, Norma, 415
Vaillant, Auguste, 632, 650, 1040, 3024
Valachi, Joseph Michael 40, 136, 427, 560,
     590, 793, 898, 976, 1226, 1228, 1259,
     1295-1297, 1307, 2085, 2114, 2138,
     2392, 2503, 2505, 2561, 2751, 2834,
     2870, 3024, 3282, 3297-3298, 3380,
     3389, 3398, 3404, 3409-3411, 3459
Valade, Sandra, 773
Valazquez Rivera, R., 3249
Valcik, Josef, 1531
Val-de-Grâce, Jean Baptiste du Cloots,
     3024
Valdemar II, 3024
Valdemaras, Augustine, 3024
Valdès, 3024
Valdespino y Diaz, Ignazio, 1395
Valdez, Alberto, 3455
Valdez, Antonio Jose, 919, 3551, 3567
Valdez, David H., 1337
Valdez, Geraldo, 3453
Valdez, Rose G., 2340
Valdivieso, Conchita, 1399
Valencia, Joaquin, 2256
Valens, 1364, 2926
Valente, Dino, 2960
Valente, Francis L., 1717
Valente, Sam, 2044, 3392
Valenti, Frank Joseph, 3380, 3411
Valenti, Jody, 344
Valenti, Umberto "Rocko", 2137-2138,
     3024-3025, 3411
Valentine, Benjamin, 1650
Valentine, Edward, 122, 3365
Valentine, Jimmy (U.S. fiction), 2491,
     3025
Valentine, Jimmy (U.S. pr.1930s), 2704
Valentine, Lewis Joseph, 2357, 2868, 3025,
     3425
Valentine, Patricia Graham, 645
Valentine, Rene, 2674
Valentinian I, 1364, 3018
Valentinian II, 3235
Valentinian III, 36, 3025, 3235
Valentino, Rudolph, 32, 152, 2044, 3130,
     3025-3027, 3375
Valenzuela, Carol, 538
Valenzuela, Delfina Gonzalez, 1338
Valenzuela, José, 3398
Valeri, Robert, 2685
Valerian, 852
Valerio, John, 3452
Valestra, John M., 909
Valis, Adolfo, 3027
Valjean, Jean, 551
Vallance, Gabriel, 1310
Vallandigham, Clement Laird, 3027
Vallanzasca, Renato, 3027-3028
Vallat, Xavier, 3543
Valle, Juan Jos, 142, 3328
Valle, Manuel, 3450
Vallejo, Daniel, 1072
Vallejo Corona, Juan, 788-789
Valletutti, John, 3028
Valley, Frank, 3567
Valley Boys, 3415
Valley Gang, 104, 105, 607, 2972, 2974,
     3028, 3382, 3384, 3386, 3387, 3389,
     3390
Valliga, 2142
Valline, John, 3371
Vallinsky, Harry, 303
Vallint, Miles, 3028
Vallisi, Patrizia, 3028-3029, 3331
Vallon, Harry, 303, 306
Valois, Catherine of, 2999
Valois, Charles de, 3029
Valois, Elizabeth of, 627

Valpy, Elizabeth, 1452
Valukas, Anton, 618, 1384, 2034, 2811
Vambre, 2122
van Agt, Andreas, 2818, 3333
Van Amburgh, Betsy, 163
Van Amburgh, Charles J., 1669
Vanartsdalen, Donald West, 3029
Van Asche, Henri, 191
Van Berkensham, M. Harman, 3303
van Beuningen, D.G., 3034
Van Bever, Julia, 3029, 3390
Van Bever, Maurice, 756, 1298, 3029, 3387,
     3390
VanBrunt, John, 3347
Van Buren, Martin, 561, 866, 1674, 2049,
     2180, 2532, 2935, 3138, 3175, 3184
Van Buren Long, Elisha, 1982
Van Buskirk, John, 958
Van Buuren, Clarence Gordon, 3029
Vance, C.H., 2525
Vance, John, 28
Vance, Philo, 335, 3195
Vancil, Ralph, 3059
Van Cleave, Greg, 3451
Van Cleve, D.M., 328
Vancy, Eugene, 3347
Van Dam, Philip, 1173
van de Corput, Piet, 3029
Vandenburg, B.C., 3551
Vandenbush, Merle, 520
Vandenkerchove, Jacques, 1743
Vanderah, the, 3415
Van Denton, Earl, 3448
Van de Panne, Jan. J., 3329, 3494
Vanderbilt, Cornelius (U.S. pr.1870s), 1022,
     1167, 1347, 1351, 3079, 3184
Vanderbilt, Cornelius, Jr. (U.S. pr.1940s),
     1658
Vanderbilt, George, 232
Vanderbilt, Jimmy, 3455
Vanderbilt, William K., 2104
Vanderbourg, Charles, 3030
van der Kemp, Gérald, 3283
van der Linde, Christopher, 1925
van der Linde, Susanna, 1925
Vanderlip, Verner V., 2827
van der Lubbe, Marinus, 1572, 2559-2560
Van Der Meersch, Jean-André, 2162
van der Merwe, Dorothea, 3030
Van der Noot, Henri, 2162, 3062
Vanderook, Simon A., 311
Vanderpoel, Edward S., 2318
Vanderveen, Linda, 1917
Vandervoort, Louis, 2052
Vandervoort, Melinda Freeland, 1826
Van der Poel, J., 3255
Van Devander, Mat, 2572
Van Devanter, Willis, 384, 2894, 3030
van Deventer, Conrad Theodor, 930
Van Dine, Harvey, 3030-3031, 3390
Van Dine, S.S., 335, 595
Vandiver, William, 3447
Van Doren, Charles, 3031
Van Druten, John, 1914
Van Duyn, Owen M., 1500
Van Dyk, H.P., 1588
Van Dyke, Chris, 2674
Van Dyke, John, 1515
Van Dyke, Mona, 3085
Van Dyke, W.S., II, 2103
Vane, Charles (Int'l. d.c.1719) 2104, 3031
Vane, Sir Henry, 3031
Vanek, David, 2298
van Erpe, Thomas, 2735
Van Every, Edward, 2271
Van Fleet, William Cary, 1560, 3031
Van Gelder, Clifford, 3134
Vangilder, G.W., 2558
van Gogh, Vincent, 2098, 3034, 3463

van Graaf, Egmond, 2206
Vanguard, 3504, 3534
Vanguarda Armada
    Revolucionaria-Palmares, 3483, 3529,
    3534
Vanguarda Popular Revolucionaria (VPR),
    3256, 3328, 3480, 3484, 3485, 3534
van Heerden, Cornelius Johannes Petrus,
    3032
Van Hoorne, 107
Van Housen, Mary, 1467
Van Houten, Leslie, 2110, 2111
Vanhuile, Joseph, 2394
Van Ieperen, Robert, 2028
Vanilli, Roxie, 3390
van Jaarsveld, Jacobus Frederick, 1903
Van Kirk, Herbert, 915
Van Lam, Tran, 3252
Van Lear, Thomas, 1398
van Linschoten, John Huyghen, 3291
Van Loon, Orrin, 1858
Van Lynseele, Marie, 669
van Meegeren, Anna, 3032
van Meegeren, Han, 1328, 3032-3034
van Meegeren, Henricus, 1328, 3032-3034
Van Meter, Chet, 1596
Van Meter, Homer, 947, 959, 962, 964, 972,
    1186, 2302
van Montmorency, Filips 2206
Vann, Sherman, 1335
Van Natta, Isabell, 733
Vannear, Charles, 2327
Van Nest, John G., 1232, 1233
Van Niekerk, Andries, 3034
van Niekerk, Maria, 1919
Vannier, Ren, 2465
Van Noorloos, Gerrit, 2799
Vannoy, J.F., 254
Van Nuys, Senator, 856
Van Orsdel, Josiah Alexander, 3034
Van Pelt, Aure, 2104
Van Pelt, James, 1299
Van Poyck, William, 3450
Van Raalte, William, 894
Van Ravenzwaai, C., 3250
van Rem, Mathijis, 3034
van Rensburg, Smartryk Johannes Jacobus
    Jansen, 3034-3035
Van Rensselaer, John, 2315
Van Rensselaer Crosby, Stephen, 829
van Riebeeck, Jan, 3292
Van Roosevelt Solomon, 3447
Van Schaik, Al, 1189
Van Schaik, Roger, 96
Van Scoyk, Grace, 576
van Sickles, Henry, 516
Van Stenlandt, Albrecht, 3250
Van Stovall, 2860
van Strijvesande, Rienstra, 3034
Van Tassel, Wright, 358
Van Tienhoven, Cornelius, 1044
Van Tilburgh, Peter, 2297
Van Tran, Han, 2461
Van Valkenberg, Herber, 951
Van Valkenburgh, Arba Seymour, 3035
Van Valkenburgh, Elizabeth, 3035
Van Van, Tran, 3255
Van Vechten, Carl, 3295
Van Vliet, George, 891
Van Wie, Francis, 3035
Van Woudenbert, Sammy, 3453
Van Wyk, Stephanus Louis, 3035
Vanzetti, Bartolomeo, 446, 517, 1224, 1498,
    2216, 2649-2652, 2926, 3284, 3458
van Zyl, H.S., 3035
Van Zyl, J.P.C., 1046
Vaquier, Jean Pierre, 849, 1424, 1475, 2778,
    3035-3036
VAR-Palmares, 3467, 3534

Varain, Leland, 104
Varas Flores, Pedro, 3467
Varchetti, Joe, 1106
Varchetti, Ralph, 1106
Varchetto, Joseph A., 3462
Varecha, Frank, 3036
Varecha, James, 3036
Varela, Marcos, 3567
Varelli, John "the Bug", 2692
Varenhorst, Gerrit Hendrick, 3036
Varesanin, Marijan, 974, 1212, 3036
Varga, Carol, 2260
Varga, Maria, 1142
Vargas, Anastacio, 3036
Vargas, Getúlio Dornelles, 1046, 3036-
    3037, 3249, 3334
Vargas, Lazaro, 3295
Vargas, Miguel, 3218
Vargas Agueros, Manuel, 3466
Vario, Paul, Sr., 547, 3411
Varius Avitus Bassianus, 1080
Varley, Cromwell, 2532
Varley, Joseph., 1336
Varnell, Harry, 3390
Varnes, Blair, 2338
Varoteaux, Marcel, 3250
Varotta, Adolpho, 2528
Varotta, Joe, 2528
Varotta, Salvatore, 2528
Varriale, Carmine, 3411
Varriale, Pasquale, 3411
Varrier, Maria, 3465
Varsalona, Paolo, 3057
Vasa, Gustav I, 703, 2087
Vasil, George T., 3037
Vasily I, 3037
Vasily III, 1670
Vasily Shuysky, 3037
Vasisko, Vincent, 136
Vasquez, Camilo, 248
Vasquez, David, 2827, 3037
Vázquez, Franciso, 2074
Vasquez, Horacio, 2995
Vasquez, Ramon, 3218
Vásquez, Tiburcio, 422, 1460, 3037-3038,
    3564, 3567
Vassallo, Giuseppe, 1952
Vasser, Pamela, 3037
Vassileva, Nina, 1625, 2758
Vathana, Savang, 3255
Vaudreuil, Pierre Cavagnial de Rigaud,
    Marquis de, 3038-3039
Vaughan, George, 3039
Vaughan, H. (U.S. pr.1940), 519
Vaughan, Helen Rau (U.S. pr.1965), 1225
Vaughan, James Clayton, Jr., 1225
Vaughan, James Clayton, Sr., 1225
Vaughan, Jerry, 3039
Vaughan, May, 1455
Vaughan, Noemi, 3039
Vaughan, Richard William, 3039
Vaughan, Thomas, 3039
Vaughan, Tom, 1356, 2782
Vaughn, J.S., 3558
Vaught, Millard, 3039-3040
Vaught, Red, 3394
Vause, W. Bernard, 2205
Vaux, James Hardy, 3040
Vaux, Roberts, 3040
Vawter, Vernon, 2671
Vaz, Ruben Florentino, 3252
Vazquez, Judy, 3466
Veale, Geoffrey, 1035, 3174
Veale, R.R., 2706
Vealey, Claude, 462
Vease, John, 3361
Vecchioni, Sergio, 3520
Vece, Carmen, 2027
Vega, Anibal, 3253

Vega, Cruz, 100, 1385, 3567
Vega, Evelyn, 2437
Vega, Luis, 100
Vega, Martin, 3455
Vegnaduzzi, Andre, 3040
Vegter, Robert, 1543
Vegvary, Robert, 1694
Vehme, 3040
Veiling, Joseph, 1790
Vela, Filemon Bartolome, 3040
Velasco Alvarado, Juan, 3040
Velasco Ibarra, Jose, 3252
Velasques, Miguel Mayor, 3466
Velasquez, Jose, 168
Velcich, George, 2417
Velez, Ignacio, 142
Velez, Luis S., 3040
Velgo, Jan, 664
Velgo, Marie Havlick, 664
Vella, Joseph, 3040-3041
Velleff, Randy, 3041
Vellota, Giuseppina, 3061
Velo, Jose, 1258, 3321
Velásquez, Diego, 2283
Venable, Shelby Jean, 2557
Venditti, Anthony, 3405
Venegas, Juan, 3041
Venizelos, Eleutherios, 3041, 3247
Venta, Krishna, 2439
Vento, Joseph, 3411
Ventura, Dominique, 790, 2216
Ventura, Peter, 3450
Venturini, Marco Antonio, 1209
Ver, Fabian, 140
Vera Gerard Case, The, 3041
Vera Serafin, Aldo, 3041
Vercingetorix, 570, 3041
Vercoe, William J., 3383, 3390
Verdi, Tullio Suzzaro, 1958
Verdier, Jean, 3250
VerDow, Jason, 1339
Verdugo-Urquidez, René Martin, 107, 587,
    3398
Verdung, Michel, 3041
Vere, Robert de, 3041
Verenseneckockockhoff, Albert Frederick
    George, 3041-3042
Verge, Richard, 3361
Verge, Sam, 3361
Verger, Jean-Louis, 2751, 3042, 3241
Vergès, Euphémie, 1869
Verges, Jacques, 9
Vergil, Polydore, 3012
Vergniaud, Pierre Victurnien, 3042
Vergo, Crispin, 3264
Vergue, Patricio F. Degach, 3467
Vergura, Antonio, 2390
Verilla, John A., 3414
Verlaine, Paul, 832, 3294
Verlynde, Pierre, 493
Vermaak, Herbert Vincent, 1759
Vermeer, Jan, 3032, 3034
Vermeille, Constant, 688
Vermeulen, René, 1924
Vermillion, Joseph, 3338
Vermillion, Texas Jack, 1061
Vermilye, Claudius I., 3042
Vern Kills On Top, 3452
Verne, Jules, 718
Vernet, Alexandrine, 185
Verney, Francis, 3042
Verney, Harry Lloyd, 3283
Vernitchy, Ivan, 2804
Vernon, Caroline, 3175
Vernon, Hazel, 930
Vernon, James, 322
Vernon, Ralph, 1656
Vernon, Roger, 3042
Vernon, Tom, 3459

Vernotico, Anna Petillo, 1295
Vernotico, Gerard, 1295, 3411
Veronica Mutineers, 3042-3043
Verota, Giuseppi, 2123, 3325
Verres, Gaius, 714, 3043
Verri, Alessandro, 429
Verrill, Sidney, 640
Vertis, Jennie, 1442
Vertress, John J., 3242
Verwoerd, Hendrik Frensch, 2735, 3043, 3254-3255
Verzeni, Vincent, 3043
Vesalius, Andreas, 3043
Vesco, Robert Lee, 1657, 3043-3044, 3299, 3301
Vesey, Denmark, 3044, 3372
Vesey, Harry, 936
Vesey Uprising, 3044
Vespasian, 569, 654, 735
Vesper, Bernard, 195
Vespucci, Amerigo, 938
Vetsera, Marie, 1210
Vettari, Stanislaus, 3346
Vettel, Ronald, 314
Vetter, Donna Lynn, 1439
Vetterli, Reed E., 1755-1756, 2286
Veverka, Charles R., 2128
Veza, Daniel T., 3044, 3425
Vialpando, J.M., 3567
Vialpando, Juan de Dios, 3567
Vian, Shirley, 524
Viana, Charles of, 1726
Viana, F. Melo, 3246
Viana, Nicholas, 394, 621, 3391
Viau, Théophile de, 3044
Vicars, A., 3244
Vicars, Henry Edward, 3044-3045
Vicars, John, 3045
Viccei, Valerio, 3045
Vice Lords, 3391
Vicente, Vincente Sanchez, 3511
Vickers, Robert (U.S. pr.1988), 3448
Vickers, Robert (U.S. pr.1972), 3493
Vickery, Mary, 853
Vicksburg Gamblers, 3045
Vicksburg Race Riot, 3045-3046, 3374
Victor, Albert, 465
Victor, Prince Albert, 1400
Victor, Clarence, 3452
Victor, Claude, 3046
Victor Emmanuel II, 590, 1639, 2264
Victor Emmanuel III, 2148, 2149, 3249
Victor, Sara M., 3046
Victor, William, 3454
Victoria, 169, 465, 476, 669, 718, 1008, 1041, 1152, 1400, 1460, 1681, 1685, 1690, 1691, 1918, 1921, 1943, 2106, 2153, 2157, 2249, 2328, 3035, 3046-3047, 3054, 3085, 3096, 3232, 3241-3243, 3263, 3511
Victoria, Camillo, 2080
Victoria, Guadalupe, 479
Vidal, Achille, 2731
Vidal, Carlos A., 3246
Vidal, Eugene, 1052
Vidal, Ginette, 3047
Vidal, Gore, 1052, 1189
Vidal, Luis Melchior, 1760
Vidarrauzaga, Gaston, 2469
Videla, Jorge, 1102
Vidocq, Eugene François, 1454, 2535, 2658, 2659, 2878, 3047-3049
Viebrock, John Albert, 654
Viede, Marshal, 75
Vieira, Ana Gloria, 1253
Vieira, Joseph, 2762, 2763
Viennese Church and King Riot, 3372
Vientemilla, José, 568
Vieques Group, 3523, 3534

Viera, Jose Rodolfo, 3258, 3507
Vietnam Moratorium Day, 3377
Viett, Inge, 3475
Vifiades, Markos, 2483
Viger, Denis Benjamin, 3049
Vigil, Lorraine, 1321
Vigilance Committee, 1685, 1719, 3399, 3400, 3414, 3415
Vigilantes' Executive Committee, 3049
Vigilantes of Montana, 3049, 3050
Vigilantes of San Francisco, 3050
Vigilius, 2437, 2761
Vigneault, Donald L., 3455
Vignon, Henri, 3050
Vigoreux, La Dame, 674
Vigouroux, 1868
Vilas, William F., 1656, 3050
Vilcko, Stephanie, 520
Viles, Larry, 234
Viljoen, Christoffel Johannes Botha, 1046
Viljoen, P.J., 908
Villa, Alessandro, 1854
Villa, Pancho, 93, 636, 637, 791, 1075, 2074, 2076-2078, 2355-2356, 3050-3054, 3244, 3245, 3458, 3459
Villa Arce, Jose, 3246
Villaboas, J., 3248
Villafuerte, Jose, 3448
Villagra, Annabella, 2951
Villagran, Dovie Beams, 3054
Villagran, Sergio, 3054
Villain, Raoul, 1712, 3243
Villalobos, Gerardo Wenceslao, 3044
Villalobos, Señor, 1395
Villalobos-Rico, Aristides, 3465
Villamor, Ignacio, 3054
Villapando, James, 1134-1135
Villar, Jorge, 2128
Villard, Henry, 2038
Villard, Jacques, 3054
Villareal, Antonio, 2076, 3054
Villaroel, Gualberto, 3251
Villarreal-Valdez, Manuel, 3299
Villegas, Delgado, 3488
Villegas, Nestor, 2404
Villiers, George, 1082, 3054-3055, 3239
Villiers, Harry, 3055
Villiers, J.E., 2032
Villiers, Jeanette, 1428
Villipique, Henry J., 3364
Villon, François, 812
Vincent, Saint, 3055
Vincent, Blanche, 1675
Vincent, Gaius Tom, 3055
Vincent, Sir Howard, 2959, 3055
Vincent, Larry J., 3463
Vincent, Mary Bell, 2769-2770
Vincent, Mordel, 3246
Vincentello d'Istria, 3055
Vinci, Francesco, 2202
Vinci, James, 3391
Vinci, Michele, 1252
Vinci, Salvatore, 2202
Vinci, Sebastiano, 3514
Vincileoni, Charles, 1915
Vindiola, Bernard, 3055
Vindiola, Christina, 3055
Vindiola, Eddie, 3055
Vine, Irving, 3391
Vine, Richard, 3044
Viner, Charles, 3055
Vines, Ellsworth, 2954
Vines, Mack M., 3424
Vineyard, James R., 3055-3056
Vinh Le Quong, 1939
Vinocur, Barry Allan, 3056
Vinogradoff, Paul Gavrilovitch, 3056
Vinson, Charles, 3346

Vinson, Frederick Moore, 3056, 3096, 3136
Vinson, Samuel, 3346
Vinson, Willie, 3368
Vintaloro, James, 3411
Vintenon, François, 3056
Viola, Giuseppe, 1034
Violante, Raymundo, 3246
Violante, Robert, 345
Violet, Thomas Norman, 2931
Viramontes, Kathryn, 156
Virchow, Rudolf, 2394
Virgil, 1903
Virgilio, Nicholas, 3413
Virginia Slave Revolt, 3371, 3372
Viriathus, 3233
Viscaino, Fernando, 3244
Visconti, Carlo, 2732
Visconti, Filippo Maria, 628
Visconti, Gian Galeazzo, 3056
Visconti, Gianmaria, 3056
Visconti, Girolamo, 3056
Viscotti, John, 3449
Vishinksky, Andrei, 1234, 3543
Vishnefsky, Yetta, 1675
Vision, Solly, 3391
Visser, A.J.C., 2887
Vitaco, John, 3391
Vital, Thomas, 3353
Vitale II Michiel, 3237
Vitale, Albert H., 811, 2717
Vitale, John Joseph, 3057, 3414
Vitale, Paul, 3394
Vitale, Peter, 3394
Vitale, Vito, 3394, 3416
Vitalis (Roman. d.c.286), 2153
Vitalis, Leon (Fr. pr.1877), 3057
Vitellius, Aulus, 569, 3235
Vitrano, Salvatore, 818
Vitry, 3239
Vittorio Emanuele III, 3057
Vitu, Auguste-Charles-Joseph, 931
Vitzizai, Guiseppe, 3330
Vivaldi, Antonio, 1848
Vivian, James, 2135
Vizetelly, Albert, 633
Vizzard, Fred, 2030
Vizzini, Calógero, 2006, 2222, 3057-3058, 3416
Vlad Dracul, 3058
Vlad Tepes, 3058
Vladimirescu, Tudor, 3058
Vlanton, Elias, 2483
Vlasic, Mark, 560, 3471
Vlok, Adriaan, 934
Vlught, Leona, 1380
Vogel, Amsel, 3058-3059
Vogel, Edward, 435, 3391
Vogel, Henriette, 1833
Vogel, Jacob, 2758
Vogel, Wolfgang, 1847
Vogt, Milo F., 3059
Voight, Ralph A., 29
Voight, Wilhelm, 3059, 3458
Voigt, Elizabeth, 738
Voigt, R., 3251
Voikoff, Peter, 3246
Voirbo, Pierre, 3059
Voisin, Louis Marie Joseph, 725, 3059-3060
Voisine, William, 891
Voison, La, 674
Voiss, Peter, 3060
Vojkov, Peter Lazarevitch, 3060
Vokes, Charles P., 695
Voldemaras, Augustinas, 3060
Voliva, Wilbur Glenn, 3060
Volk, Adam, 3060-3061
Volk, Leo, 3543
Volk, Robert, 960

W

Watts, Tony R., 3450
Watts, Walter, 3105
Watts, William (U.S. pr.1935), 2015, 3105
Watts, William (Brit. d.1830), 883
Watts Race Riots, 3105-3106, 3376
Watzl, Ernest, 3106
Waugh, Dennis, 3280
Waugh, Evelyn, 247
Wawzynak, Helen, 2301
Waxworks, 3106
Way, Fred, 3450
Way, Jean, 415
Way, William, 3360
Waye, Alton, 3106, 3447
Wayland, Cecil, 3347
Wayman, John E.W., 1100, 3391
Wayne, James Moore, 466, 3106
Wayne, John, 2293, 2337
Wayne Tobin, 2959 dr.
Wayne, Tom, 3242
Way of Eternal Bliss, 3506, 3534
Wayt, Fred, 364
Weadcock, Jack, 958
Weaker Sex, The, 3106
Weallans, Clifford Alexander, 3106, 3228
Weare, Meshech, 3106
Weare, William, 693, 2949, 3457
Wearn, Walter, 225
Weart, James Brennan, Jr., 3106-3107
Weatherall, Albert, 2442
Weatherall, Edward Christopher, 3107
Weatherall, Florence Jean, 3107
Weatherbee, Walter O., 2420
Weatherby, Candace Grace, 2233
Weatherill, Miles, 3107
Weatherly, Eugene T., 2698, 3424
Weatheroff, Nelson, 3346
Weather Underground Organization
    (Weathermen), 1133, 1145, 1771, 3107,
    3265, 3266, 3269, 3270, 3482, 3483,
    3484-3488, 3490, 3491, 3493, 3496, 3498,
    3499-3503, 3506, 3518, 3533-3535
Weaver, A.E., 2015
Weaver, Bill "Lapland Willie", 238, 239, 240,
    3452, 3459, 3460
Weaver, Edward, 3356
Weaver, Elmer E., 1511
Weaver, G.H., 2920
Weaver, George "Buck", 399
Weaver, James, 1001
Weaver, Joseph, 3107
Weaver, Moses, 3356
Weaver, Rilla, 3350
Weaver, Robert, 3339
Weaver, Ward Francis, 3449
Weavers Riots, 3371
Webb, Alfred Charles Bertram, 2852
Webb, Calvin, 701
Webb, Charles, 1449
Webb, Clifton, 1598
Webb, Daniel K., 463, 2127
Webb, Dennis, 3449
Webb, Duncan, 2171
Webb, Edwin Yates, 3107
Webb, Freddie, 3455
Webb, George H. (U.S. pr.1861), 1715
Webb, George W. (U.S. pr.1914), 3107,
    3325
Webb, Gilbert, 3567
Webb, Isaac, 3358
Webb, James W., 3305
Webb, John Joshua, 1593, 3108, 3551, 3561,
    3566, 3567
Webb, Madeline, 2747
Webb, Nathan, 3108
Webb, Seward, 2104
Webb, Teddy, 1506
Webb, Wiley (U.S. d.1892), 3341
Webb, Wilfred (U.S. pr.1880s), 3567

Webb, William B. (U.S. pr.1860s), 3426
Webb, Willie (U.S. d.1913), 3362
Webbe, James, 233
Webbe, Peter, 3414
Webber, John D., Jr., 3256, 3479
Webber, Louis Bridgie, 303, 304, 306
Weber, Adolph, 3108
Weber, Bill, 901
Weber, C.M., 3296
Weber, Edward J., 1150
Weber, F.H.L., 1845
Weber, Frank, 2284
Weber, Gunther, 3065
Weber, Hugo, 3114
Weber, J.J., 1205
Weber, James, 536
Weber, Jeanne, 3108
Weber, Julius, 3108
Weber, Lieselotte, 461
Weber, Randolph Henry, 3108
Weber, Rosa, 681, 1903
Weber, Thomas, 2978
Webster, Alonzo B., 2144, 2868
Webster, Andrew, 10
Webster, Daniel (U.S. 1782-1852), 551,
    580, 848, 1092, 1167, 2395, 3108
Webster, Daniel (U.S. pr.1860s), 2968
Webster, Daniel R. (U.S. pr.1977), 3108-
    3109
Webster, Elvin, 1718
Webster, Freddy, 2676
Webster, James Mathewson, 2342
Webster, John (Brit. 1610-82), 870, 3109,
    3139
Webster, John Stanley (U.S. 1877-1962),
    3109
Webster, John White, 2737, 3078, 3109-
    3111
Webster, Kate, 2134, 2778, 3111, 3449
Webster, Richard, 1906
Webster, Robert, 3111-3112
Webster, William Hedgcock, 669, 1145,
    2248, 3112, 3426
Weckler, Kristina, 356
Wedderburn, Alexander, 3112
Wedderburne, T. Webster, 3112
Wedderburne-Stanhope Duel, 3112
Wedra, Dennis, 716
Wedtech Scandal, 356, 3112
Weed, Stephen, 1501, 1502, 2889
Weed, Thurlow, 1892
Weeks, Mrs. C.L., 3351
Weeks, Lemuel, 3364
Weeks, Levi, 3112-3113
Weeks, Nathaniel, 403
Weeks, Varnell, 3447
Weems, Charles, 2714, 2716
Weems, Frank, 3368
Wegener, Ulrich, 2456
Weger, Chester, 3113
Weggeland, Diane Marie, 2059
Wehde, Albert, 3113
Weichs, Maximilian von, 3543
Wei Chung-hsien, 3113
Weick, Charles, 3113
Weidemann, Fritz, 3543
Weidmann, Eugene, 3113-3114, 3326
Weigand, Richard, 1512
Weightman, Hiram, 3348
Weihofen, 1072
Weil, Asher, 3118
Weil, Joseph "Yellow Kid", 413, 533, 1095,
    2015, 2033, 3114-3118
Weil, Levi, 3118
Weill, Ruby, 2994
Wein, Edward Simon, 3118
Wein, George, 916
Weinbaum, Sidney, 3118
Weinberg, Abe "Bo", 1546, 2700

Weinberg, George, 1561, 2700, 3412
Weinberg, Israel, 2208
Weinberg, Joseph W., 3119
Weinberg, Mel, 13
Weinberg, Morris, Jr., 2575
Weinberg, Moshe, 1081, 1143
Weinberg, Paul S., 2399
Weinberger, Beatrice, 1876
Weinberger, Harry, 341
Weinberger, Morris, 1876
Weinberger, Peter, 1876, 3327
Weiner, Alexander S., 2108
Weiner, Benjamin "Chippy", 485
Weiner, Bertha, 3119
Weiner, J.E., 887
Weiner, Herman, 2698
Weiner, Irwin S., 3391
Weiner, Lee, 698
Weiner, Ludwig, 3119
Weinfeld, Edward, 716
Weinge, Charles A., 3470
Weinger, Mitchell, 3119
Weinglass, Leonard, 453, 698
Weinhold, Henry 59
Weininger, W.W., 3325, 3459
Weinkamper, William, 3331, 3505
Weinshank, Albert, 614, 2660, 3391
Weinstein, David, 1275
Weinstein, Jack B., 1159, 1987
Weinstein, Joseph, 354
Weinstein, Lee, 2581
Weipert, Lee, 2934
Weir, Benjamin, 1914
Weir, Jane, 3119
Weir, Jean, 3291
Weir, Thomas, 3119
Weirman, John, 2042
Weis, Annette Kathryn, 382
Weisberg, Leonard, 1104
Weisberger, George, 23
Weisel, William, 1803
Weisenberg, Nate, 3392
Weisenthal, Simon, 444, 2532
Weisgal, Fred, 2349
Weiss, Aimee, 3121
Weiss, Allen, 3121
Weiss, André, 3119
Weiss, Carl Austin, 1984, 1986, 3248
Weiss, Earl "Hymie", 105, 130-131, 501,
    606, 608, 1026, 1293, 1492, 1493, 2044,
    2213, 2230, 2350, 2354, 2563, 2659, 2673,
    2972, 3016, 3119-3120, 3282, 3386, 3388,
    3391,
Weiss, Ed (U.S. pr.1900s-20s), 3121
Weiss, Ed (U.S. d.1926), 3391
Weiss, Emmanuel "Mendy", 526, 528, 112,
    2254-2255, 2563, 2702, 3003, 3120, 3187,
    3410, 3412
Weiss, George, 868
Weiss, Jacqueline, 1178
Weiss, Jeanne Daniloff, 3120
Weiss, Joseph (U.S. pr.1941), 1280
Weiss, Joseph J. (U.S. b.1897), 3120-3121
Weiss, Louis, 3391
Weiss, Margaret, 3139, 3391
Weiss, Morris, 3121
Weiss, Seymour, 1993
Weiss, Theodore S., 2433
Weiss, William, 3412, 3413
Weissbecker, Thomas, 3475
Weiss Club, 3121
Weiss Gang, 3139
Weissman, Solly "The Terrible", 183, 1377,
    1758, 2440, 3009, 3121-3122
Weissman, William, 1758, 3121
Wei Tao-Ming, 3122
Weitzman, David, 882
Weitzman, Howard, 909, 2782
Weitzman, Irving, 3122-3123

Weitzman, Louis J., 3122
Weizsäcker, Ernst von, 3543
Welborn, Clint, 1591
Welby, John Robson, 98
Welch "Rebecca" Riots, 3373
Welch, Albert, 3123
Welch, Bernard Charles, Jr., 3123
Welch, David E., 3449
Welch, Ed, 3123
Welch, Harry, 443
Welch, J.M., 3424
Welch, Johanna, 2671
Welch, John, 3551
Welch, Joseph Nye, 3123
Welch, Nellie, 3391
Welch, Robert, 1302, 1371
Welcome, Herbert, 3452
Welcome, Mary, 3167
Welcome, Verda, 3255
Weld, Aaron Davis, 829
Weld, William F., 2162
Weldon, Dana, 3454
Weldon, Rose, 3084
Weldon, W.H., 3242
Welfare Island Prison Scandal, 3123-3124
Welfeld, Jack A., 2759
Welham, Edward George, 3124
Weller, Lee, 170
Weller, Michael, 26
Welles, Justus P., 3551
Welles, Orson, 190, 763
Wellesley, Arthur, 1158, 3124, 3305
Wellesley–Finch-Hatton Duel, 3124
Wellings, Edward, 1636-37
Wellington, Duke of, 1606, 3171, 3124
Wellington, Harold, 1158
Wellington, Lillian Dorothy, 1158
Wellington, Norma Gwendolyn, 1158
Wellman, Edward John, 3124
Wellman, Frances L., 530, 1460
Wellman, George, 3562
Wellman, Horace, 1535
Wellman, William Mason, 3124
Wellnitz, Fred, 951
Wells, Alfred, 3124-3125
Wells, Billy, 3126
Wells, Carolyn, 3125
Wells, Charles (Brit. pr.1924-26), 3125
Wells, Charles Knox Polk (U.S. pr.1880s), 3567
Wells, David Raymond, 3125
Wells, Edmund William, 3125
Wells, Elijah, 3355
Wells, Floyd, 1534
Wells, Frederick, 1155
Wells, George, 3303
Wells, Green, 3340
Wells, H.G., 2652, 2956
Wells, Harold (U.S. pr.1980), 3463
Wells, Harry, 954, 3125, 3460
Wells, Ida Bell, 3125
Wells, Ira Kent, 3125
Wells, J.J., 1558
Wells, James (U.S. d.1896), 1037
Wells, Jane, 1303
Wells, Jean, 3125
Wells, Jeff, 2675
Wells, Littleton, 3305
Wells, Luther, 3452
Wells, Nicholas, 3125
Wells, Robert William, 3126
Wells, Samuel L., 2675, 3212
Wells, Susannah, 599
Wells, Thomas, 3126
Wells, Violet, 3125
Wells, William, 3138
Wells Fargo Bank of San Francisco, 3289
Wells Street, Chicago, 3126
Welly, Grant, 3352

Welsby, Joseph, 3346
Welsh, D., 1544
Welsh, Leila, 3126
Welsh, Richard S., 3257
Welsh, Thomas Vaughan (Brit. pr.1961), 656
Welsh, Tom (U.S. pr.1884), 3567
Welty, Bert, 811
We Must Do Something, 3499
Wenceslaus IV, 1726
Wenceslaus, 1646
Wendel, John Gottlieb, 2226
Wendel, Marie, 1547
Wendel, Paul, 2410
Wendt, Kenneth, 1343
Wendt, Molly, 473
Wene, Elmer, 3226
Wenham, Jane, 3126
Wen I-to, 3251
Wenner-Gren, Axel Leonard, 2834
Wensley, Frederick, 1625, 2226, 2570, 2758, 3060, 3126
Wentely, Alex, 3342
Wentworth, Alexander, 2866
Wentworth, Asa, 3126
Wentworth, Cora, 1507
Wentworth, Henry T., 3126
Wentworth, Horace, 3126
Wentworth, John (U.S. pr.1850s), 2677, 3374, 3389, 3391
Wentworth, John Page (U.S. pr.1958), 3253
Wentworth, Thomas, 462, 2866, 2869, 3126-3127, 3140
Wentz, Arthur Philip, 3127
Wentz, Elsie, 3127
Wentzel, Gerald C., 3127
Wenzel, Lloyd Wallace, 789
Wepman, Dennis, 1207
Wepman, Joseph, 2800
Werbell, Mitchell L., 1189
Werboczi, István, 3127, 3238
Werckle, Louis, 1941
Were, Martin, 713
Werewolf of Paris, The, 3127
Wergin, Kate Martha, 1478
Wergin, Otto Richard, 1478
Wergin, Wolfgang, 1478
Werner, Frederick, 1749
Werner, Karl, 3127
Werner, Katherine, 1550
Werner, Louis, 547, 2008
Werner, Mrs. Matt, 2338
Werner, Sophie, 1749
Werner, Walter, 919
Wernett, John, 3551
Wertham, Frederic, 681, 3127-3128
Wertheimer, Mert, 104, 3394
Wertz, Guy, 25
Wertz, William, 1899
Wesel, John of, 1727
Wesizwe, Umkonto, 3523
Wesley, Cynthia, 3264
Wesley, Jefferson, 1968
Wesley, John, 277, 359, 369, 506, 3567
Wesley, Joseph, 3354
Wesley, Ronald, 3447
Wesley, Thomas, 3337
Wesolowski, Theodore, 715
Wessel, Ferne Redd, 1827
Wessel, Horst, 195, 992, 994, 2290, 3128, 3246
Wessel, Ulrich, 203, 2163, 3475
Wesson, Daniel Baird, 3128
Wesson, Harry E., 508
West, Allen, 3339
West, Andrew, 1801
West, Benny, 1753
West, Charles A., 2272

West, Duval, 3551
West, Eugene, 3128
West, Everett C., 2222
West, Frank, 3351
West, Henry, 952
West, Jack "Zip", 330, 1097
West, James (U.S. pr.1880), 3567
West, James (U.S. pr.1911), 3361
West, Jesse, 96, 2181, 3359, 3555
West, John (U.S. pr.1884), 3425
West, John (U.S. pr.1922), 3366
West, John Alan (Brit. pr.1964), 98
West, John Coulter (U.S. d.1948), 867
West, Joseph B., 464
West, Joseph P., 1528
West, Lawrence, 3351
West, Linda, 1524
West, Linette, 492
West, Lottie, 1756
West, Mary, 785
West, Millard F., 1890
West, Paul, 3451
West, Richard "Little Dick", 1003, 1720, 3128-3129, 3567
West, Robert W., 3455
West, Roland, 2960, 2963
West, Ronald Eugene, 3129
West, Sam (U.S. d.1901), 3353
West, Samuel H. (U.S. 1872-1938), 1626, 3129
West, Steven, 3454
West, Mrs. T.J., 3347
West, Thomas (Neth. 1577-1618), 3129
West, Thomas (U.S. pr.1980s), 3448
West, Thomas Edward (U.S. pr.1928), 3129
West, Velma, 3129
West, Walter, 1501
West, William (U.S. d.1892), 3341
West, William (U.S. pr.1903), 3129
West, William (U.S. pr.1979), 2437
West, Willie (U.S. pr.1903), 3129
West Bank Riots, 3377
West Bengal Riots, 3377
Westbury, James Lawson, 2039
Westenhaver, David C., 3129
Westermann, Butcher (Japan pr.1933), 2898
Westermann, François Joseph (Fr. 1751-94), 3129
Westervelt, William, 3129, 3324
Westfall, Robert, 314
Westfall, William, 1704
Westies, 3403, 3404, 3412
Westinghouse, 3289
Westlake, John (Brit. 1828-1913), 3129
Westlake, John (Can. pr.1913), 1846
Westley, Anthony Ray, 3455
Westminster, Abbot of, 924
Westmoreland, Earl of, 286, 1432
Westmoreland, William, 2272, 3347, 3492
Weston, Benjamin, 2061
Weston, George, 3129-3130
Weston, J., 3252
Weston, John D., 1998
Weston, Joseph, 3129-3130
Weston, Parker, 3551
Weston, Richard, 1224-1225, 1628
Westphalen, Jules, 646
Westphalia, King Jerome of, 428
West Tyrone Brigade, 3523
Westwood, Billy, 3130
Westwood, John, 3130
Westwood, Sarah, 3130
Westwood, William John, 3130
We the People, 3130
Wet, Christiaan Rudolf de, 3130
Wetherell, Charles, 493
Wethern, George, 1513
Wetzel, Cecil, 2247

Wilson, Minor, 3351
Wilson, Nathaniel, 3174
Wilson, Norah, 3172, 3174
Wilson, Ocie, 3174-3175
Wilson, Orlando W., 3424
Wilson, Orville, 1482
Wilson, Otto Stephen, 3175
Wilson, Philip Morrel, 3175
Wilson Rangers, 3401
Wilson, Ray, 662
Wilson, Red Bill, 1255, 1972
Wilson, Robert (Brit. pr.1800s), 503
Wilson, Robert (U.S. pr.1954), 911
Wilson, Robert (U.S. pr.1986), 2683
Wilson, Robert (U.S. d.1896), 3347
Wilson, Robert (U.S. d.1898), 3449
Wilson, Roland, 2040
Wilson, Rufus Rockwell, 2396
Wilson, Samuel Fell, 3175
Wilson, Sarah, 3175
Wilson, Scott, 3175
Wilson, Shepp, 3447
Wilson, Tammy, 1365
Wilson, Terence, 493
Wilson, Thomas, 3357
Wilson, Thomas Stokeley, 3175
Wilson, Todd, 1311
Wilson, Tug, 3175
Wilson, Vernon Coke, 3552
Wilson, Vernon D., 1121
Wilson, Wilbur, 1184
Wilson, William (U.S. d.1898), 3351
Wilson, William (U.S. pr.1920), 3391
Wilson, William A., 901
Wilson, William "Buffalo Billy", (U.S.
    d.1911), 3552, 3568
Wilson, Willie, 3451
Wilson, Woodrow, 37, 123, 217, 346, 425,
    447, 470, 472, 523, 637, 694, 725, 728,
    743, 763, 801, 885, 895, 896, 998, 1004,
    1097, 1098, 1109, 1134, 1165, 1281, 1553,
    1605, 1648, 1728, 2007, 2070, 2077, 2094,
    2112, 2208, 2452, 2462, 2480, 2870, 2894,
    3054, 3103, 3113, 3129, 3172
Wilson, Zachary, 3454
Wilson-Lyon Duel, 3173
Wilstach, John, 3015
Wilt, Dawnette Sue, 3156
Wiltgen, Thomas C., 3472
Wiltshaw, Alice, 1374, 3461
Wiltshaw, Cuthbert, 1374
Wiltshire, Benjamin, 1309
Wiltshire Weavers Riot, 3370
Wimsey, Peter, 2685
Winch, Claude, 915
Winch, Joel C.C., 3175-3176
Winche, Paul, 3176
Winchell, Terri, 2213
Winchell, Walter, 528, 809, 942, 1141, 1614,
    1616
Winchelsea, Earl of, 3124
Winchester, Bishop of, 635
Winchester, Earl of, 926
Winckler, Otto, 1321
Windell Bank Fraud, 849
Windell, D.S., 1667
Windgrodzki, Piotr, 3473
Windham, Thomas R., 3176
Windisch-Graetz, Alfred Candidus, 3176
Windisch-Graetz, Ludwig, 3176
Windred, Robert, 340
Windsor, B.P., 3243
Windsor, Claire, 2903
Windsor, Harvey, 3447
Windsor, Thomas, 1298
Wine, Dawn, 1837
Wine, Karen, 1838
Wineiger, W.W., 1177
Winfield, Joseph, 1275

Winfrey, R.L., 3424
Wing, Francis Joseph, 3176
Wing, George C. (U.S. pr.1874), 1998
Wing, George Chew (U.S. 1904-37), 3176
Wingard, Samuel Cyrus, 3176
Wingate, George Wood, 3176
Winge, Al, 1397, 3385
Wingfield, E., 3035
Wingfield, Wesley, 3346
Wingo, Dorcey, 1884
Wingo, Jimmy, 1321, 3447
Winheld, Oscar, 3176
Winifred, Countess of Nithsdale, 2154
Winker, Sharon, 3076
Winkle, Frank F., 1632
Winkler, F. (Aust. pr.1932), 3247
Winkler, Franz, 988
Winkler, Gus, 238, 1002, 3176, 3391
Winkler, Max, 3543
Winkler, Peter, 3176
Winn, A.M., 2834
Winn, Alexander, 3366
Winne, Walter, 898
Winner, Jessie, 3348
Winnickes, Sonia, 2168
Winnik, Abraham, 3176-3177
Winningham, George, 260
Winograd, Alvin C., 2757
Winrod, Gerald B., 2137
Winslow, Angela, 3177
Winslow, "Big Susan", 3186, 3391
Winslow Boy, The 3177
Winslow, Forbes Benignus, 3177
Winslow, Milton, 3425
Winslow, Thomas, 3177
Winsor, Charlotte, 3177
Winstanley, Elijah, 3177
Winston, 3037
Winston, Henry, 1155
Winston, John, 3361
Winter, Dale, 606, 758
Winter, David, 2509
Winter, James, 1353
Winter, Thomas (Brit. pr.1604), 1140,
    1405
Winter, Thomas (Brit. pr.1749), 2185
Winter, Willie, 3177
Wintermute, Peter P., 3177, 3242
Wintermute, Phebe, 1048
Winters, Evelyn, 390
Winters, Jim, 1977, 1978
Winters, John, 3177
Winters, O.T., 2934
Winters, Shelley, 1309
Winterset, 3177
Winterstein, Ralph, 1036
Winthrop, David, 2987
Winthrop, John, 3177-3178
Winthrop, Wait, 2665
Winton, Earl of, 802
Winzel, Kittie, 1474
Wire, William, 762, 763
Wirt, William, 3178
Wirth, Karl Joseph, 2543
Wirz, Henry, 3081, 3178
Wisbey, Thomas, 1371
Wisborg, Bernadotte af, 346
Wischnewski, Nikolai, 3471
Wise, Glenn, 3428
Wise, Henry, 513
Wise, Joe, 3456
Wise, John, 3354
Wise, Martha Hasel, 3178
Wise, Olive Catherine, 3178-3179
Wise, Raymond, 2690
Wisecarver, Ellsworth C. Jr., 3179
Wisehart, Mark, 3451
Wiseman, Lorraine, 2068, 2346
Wiseman, Thomas, 2040

Wishart, George, 292, 1830, 3179, 3238
Wishart, Janet, 10
Wisliceny, Dieter, 3543
Wisner, George, 1975
Wisniewski, Steve, 105, 2230, 3119
Wisotsky, Sandra, 1717
Wissinger, Hans, 3179
Wissner, Nathan, 775, 2549, 2847
Witchey, Arthur, 1763
Witherall, Gladys Julia, 3325
Witherall, Leonidas, 2902
Witherell, George, 3345
Withers, Beta, 2299
Withers, Bush, 3360
Withers, Jack, 3179
Withers, Robert W., 2018
Withers, William, Jr., 1956
Witherspoon, William, 3179-3180
Witherups, Abraham, 3354
Withfield, Jerome, 3366
Withrington, Jack, 3180
Withrington, Thomas, 3180
Witmer, Charles B., 3180
Witt, Cornelis, 3180
Witt, Franz, 1559
Witt, Herman, 1394
Witt, Johan de, 3180
Witt, Johnny Paul, 3447
Witt, Richard D., 3468
Witte, Christina Regina, 3018
Witte, Sergius, 410, 2328
Wittelsbach, Otto of, 2510
Wittenberg, Solomon, 87
Witthaus, Rudolph, 530
Wittman, G., 3426
Wittman, Manfred, 3180
Wittmer, Arthur, 1251
Wittrock, Frederick, 3180, 3457
Witzke, Lothar, 2119
Witzleben, Erwin von, 1574
Witzler, Margarete, 3180-3181
Wivallius, Lars, 3181
Wiwatowski, Jean, 2417
Wladyslaw II, 1807
Wo Group, 3392
Wobblies, 3263
Wochele, Julius, 1583
Woerman, Samuel R., 1632
Wogan, Lawrence, 1439
Wöhler, Otto, 3543
Wohlfahrt, Joanna, 134
Wohlfahrt, Johan, 134
Wohrle, John, 3546, 3552, 3568
Wojciechowaki, Joseph, 182
Wojtasik, Gerald, 3181
Wolchak, Samuel, 3077
Wolcott, Frank, 601, 1734, 2555
Wolcott, Major Frank, 3568
Wolcott, Margaret, 2854
Wolf, Arch, 708
Wolf, August, 3181
Wolf, Emma, 1180
Wolf, Geoffrey, 830
Wolf, James P., 1829
Wolf, Jerome W., 3181
Wolf, Susie, 1180
Wolf, Walter E,, 3181
Wolf, William, 3296
Wolfe, David M., 74
Wolfe, Gerald Bennett, 1512
Wolfe, James R., 2767
Wolfe, Joan Pearl, 2677
Wolfe, Tom, 418
Wolfe, William "Cujo", 1503
Wolfe, William, 2891
Wolfenberger, John, 3337
Wolff, Jerome B. 37
Wolff, Karl, 3543
Wolff, Leslie, 1943

Wolff, Mariette, 2849
Wolfgang, Prince, 1041
Wolfson, Dean, 1135
Wolfson, Jo-Anne, 1969
Wolfson, Louis, 1200, 2893
Wolimer, Henri, 3328, 3489
Wolin, Alfred, 3078
Wolinsky, Moey "Dimples", 528, 3394, 3412
Wollenberg, Albert C., 2937
Woller, Douglas, 2396
Wolosky, David, 3412
Wolseley, Lord, 1009
Wolsey, Thomas, 246, 828, 1268, 2747, 3012, 3181,
Wolter, Albert W., 3181
Wolter, Peter, 2869
Wolters, Jacob F., 441, 3181
Wolverton, Edwin, 3085
Wolz, Charles, 3568
Womack, Alan, 1092
Womack, John, 3365
Womack, Melvin, 3368
Womack, William, 3357
Wombacker, Katherine, 3103
Women's Social and Political Union, 2875
Wondra, Gerald R., 3290
Wong Gee, 1999, 2000
Wong Get, 3412
Wong Io, 3464
Wong, John, 3297
Wong Lau Deu Ts, 702
Wong, Nellie, 2000
Wong Shing Kong, 3299
Wong, T.H., 3244
Wong, T.T., 3090
Wong, Walter, 3527
Woo Bum Kong, 3181-3182
Woo, Roh Tae, 2818
Wood, 3342
Wood, Alfred, 1016
Wood, Ben, 596
Wood, David, 3182
Wood, Donald, 741
Wood, Elmer, 497
Wood, Fernando, 596, 2481, 3182, 3374
Wood, Fred V., 1787
Wood, Frederick H., 716
Wood, Fremont, 1500
Wood, George, 1175, 2327
Wood, Harlington, Jr., 3182
Wood, Horace, 3193
Wood, Ira, 3424
Wood, Isaac, 3182-3183
Wood, Ivy Lydia, 290
Wood, John (U.S. pr.1979), 1457
Wood, John, 1906, 2121
Wood, John H., Jr., 669, 3257
Wood, Kathryn, 2851
Wood, Laura, 938
Wood, Lum, 3346
Wood, Mayor, 890
Wood, Moses, 550
Wood, Nicholas L., 3424
Wood, Percy A., 3271
Wood, Peter, 2441
Wood, Robert, 28
Wood, Robert William Thomas Cavers, 3183
Wood, Roland Wayne, 2795
Wood, Samuel, 3344
Wood, Sidney, 3183-3184
Wood, Sidney Grant, 3187
Wood, Thomas, 558, 1493, 1494
Wood, Walter, 348
Wood, Will (Brit. pr.1895), 1680
Wood, William Foristal, 2161
Wood, William V., 3426
Wood, William Westley (U.S. pr.1960s), 115
Woodard, Alonzo, 1515

Woodard, Brenda Denise, 1233
Woodard, Robert Roy, 3463
Woodbridge, Benjamin, 3303
Woodburn, Catherine, 2986
Woodburn, Shirley Ann, 2985, 2986
Woodburne, John, 742
Woodbury, Levi, 3184
Woodbury, Willie, 243
Woodcock, Sarah, 223
Woodfield, Lawrence, 228
Woodfield, Mary Outland, 2131
Woodfield, Randall Brent, 3184
Woodhouse, Elinor Drinkwater, 1624
Woodhouse, Joan, 3184
Woodhouse, Martha Gordon, 1624
Woodhull, Canning, 3184
Woodhull, Victoria, 314, 3184
Woodill, Edith May, 1065
Woodland, J.W., 2834
Woodley, Roberta, 2764
Woodman, Eliza Ellen, 1731
Woodman, James, 3357
Woodman, Terence David, 882
Woodmansee, Ernest, 3184-3185
Woodray, Alan, 493
Woodruff, David, 3453
Woodruff, Kathleen, 1282
Woodruff, Len, 3561, 3567, 3568
Woods, A.S., 762
Woods, Andrew, 3515
Woods, Arthur, 1098, 3412, 3425
Woods, Barbara, 2413
Woods, Benjamin, 3361
Woods, Billy, 1286
Woods, Billy Joe, 3456
Woods, Cassius Clay, 144
Woods, David, 3451
Woods, Denis, 2413
Woods, Dorothy, 3185
Woods, Edward, 2984
Woods, Frank, 1351, 1769, 3185
Woods, Fred, 3331
Woods, Frederick Newhall, 3185
Woods, George, 2554
Woods, James, 1535
Woods, John, 1217, 2025, 2655, 3185
Woods, Joseph, 2512
Woods, Mag, 2554
Woods, Mark, 493
Woods, Morris, 3412
Woods, Ronald, 3450
Woods, Rose Mary, 3100
Woods, Tony, 3086
Woods, William Burnham, 3185
Woodson, Edward, 3365
Woodstock, Thomas of, 1171, 2481, 2932, 3041, 3238
Woodville, Elizabeth, 720, 3012
Woodville, John, 3185
Woodville, Richard, 3185
Woodward, Arthur, 2998, 3357
Woodward, Sir Arthur Smith, 887
Woodward, Bob, 2782, 3099
Woodward, Charles, 3354
Woodward, Daniel, 1154
Woodward, Garry D., 1425
Woodward, Harold E., 848
Woodward, Harry, 1770
Woodward, Joanne, 2561
Woodward, John, 3354
Woodward, Jonathan, 3180
Woodward, Kathleen Diana Lucy, 96
Woodward, Len, 700, 3556
Woodward, Lester B., 3067
Woodward, Paul, 3452
Woodward, Raymond L. Jr., 3185-3186
Woodward, Ronald, 200
Woodward, Talcum, 3357
Woodward, Thomas, 1492, 3339

Woodward, Walter, 672
Woodward, William, 3352
Woodward, William Carroll, 3186
Woodworth, Oliver, 22
Woody, Bill, 3546
Woody, Loretta, 1829-1830
Woodyard, H.F. "Woody", 2558
Woofter, Dorothy, 721
Woofter, Emery, 721
Wooldridge, Charles, 222
Wooldridge, Clifton Rodman, 123, 234, 405, 494, 551, 696, 722, 792, 849, 880, 889, 890, 943, 1000, 1030, 1134, 1171, 1194, 1249, 1312, 1330, 1436, 1474, 1516, 1634, 1729, 1730, 1772, 1782, 1788, 1888, 1920, 2154, 2022, 2024, 2342, 2706, 2745, 2783, 2801, 2804, 2860, 3186
Wooldridge, Ellen, 3186
Wooldridge, N.B., 766
Woolem, Mamie, 806
Wooley, Avis, 1769
Woolfe, George, 3186
Woolfolk, Charles, 658
Woolfolk, Thomas, 3186
Woollcott, Alexander, 306, 2113
Woolliscroft, Angela, 1467
Woolls, Randy, 3447
Woolman, Jacob, 1420
Woolmington, Reginald, 2984, 3186
Woolmington, Violet, 3186
Woolridge, Charles Thomas, 3186-3187
Woolsey, John Munro, 1326
Woolworth, Jessie, 2685
Woomer, Ronald, 3187, 3447
Wooten, Dick, 2571
Wooton, Richard, 2759
Woratzeck, William, 3448
Worcester, Earl of, 1031
Worden, Bernice, 1290
Worden, Edna, 2340
Worden, Frank, 1290
Wordsworth, William, 3070
Worel, Richard, 2580
Workers Army of the Welsh Republic, 3279, 3526, 3534
Workers Autonomy, 3529, 3534
Workers Self-Defense, 3259, 3275, 3517, 3534
Workman, Charles "The Bug", 112, 2254, 2563, 2702, 2705, 3120, 3187, 3412
Workman, Dena, 3187
Workman, Hubert, Jr., 2719
Workman, Julian, 47
Workman, Karen Mae, 2719
Workman, Phillip, 3454
Workman, Raymond, 3187
Workman, Wendell, 3453
Workman, William, 3187
Workmaster, George, 592, 2928
World's Fair Bombing, 3187
Worley, Captain, 3187-3188
Worley, Claude M., 3188, 3424
Worley, Henry, 3344
Worley, James, 693
Worley, John, 772, 2137, 3557
Worley, Joseph, 3264
Worley, Newnham, 1953
Worley, Richard, 3188
Worls, Jack, 1066
Worms, Pamela Lee, 3188
Woronzow, Elizabeth, 2451
Worrall, Samuel, 217
Worrell, Ed, 1072
Worsley, Franklin, 956
Worten, Jesse, 333
Worth, Adam, 536, 1016, 1602, 2468, 3188-3191, 3282, 3457
Worth, John, 3190
Wortham, Quintin, 3191

Yaras, David, 3391
Yarborough, Ralph, 1107, 1796
Yarden, Oron, 3332
Yarham, Samuel, 3205
Yarnowsky, Charles, 3403, 3412
Yarris, Nicholas, 3454
Yarros, David, 479, 2421
Yarrow, Ann, 1136
Yarrow, Don, 1136
Yasin, Ali, 3257, 3505
Yasin, Jamal, 14
Yasko, Claudia, 3010
Yasukata Oku, 2851
Yates, Dale Robert, 3454
Yates, Eddie, 1281
Yates, Gertrude, 2995
Yates, James, 1665
Yates, Lonnie, 3205
Yates, Nenomoshia, 1233
Yates, Robert, 3205
Yates, Silas Barnwell, 1283
Yates, Steve, 2096
Yavitz, Sheldon, 1838
Yawkey, Thomas, 762
Yazdegerd I, 3205
Yazdegerd II, 3205
Yazdegerd III, 3205, 3236
Yazdi, Hojatoleslam Mortraza Ayatollahi
    Tabataba, 3259, 3516
Yazid, 3236
Yazid ibn al-Muhallab, 3205
Ybarra, Robert, 3452
Yeager, Dick, 384
Yeakel, John, 2783
Yeats, William Butler, 3294
Yee Toy, 3415
Yeh T'ing, 3205
Yehonatan Netanyahu, 1099
Yeiser, John O., 1100
Yelder, George, 562
Yeldham, Elsie, 3205
Yeldham, James, 2738
Yeldham, William James, 725, 3205
Yellow, Marjorie, 3206
Yellow Beards, 3391
Yellow Hand, 2078
Yellow Henry Gang, 3206
Yellow Long, 3091
Yellow Turban Rebellion, 3206
Yellowlees, Henry, 1418, 2459
Yellowwolf, John, 3354
Yemelyanov, Ivan, 88
Yen Yuen, 1921
Yenzer, James, 2435
Yerbury, Jerry, 405
Yerevan Bank Robbery, 3206
Yerguz, Mehmet, 3514
Yerkes, Charles Tyson Jr., 1158, 2958, 3206-
    3207
Yerly, Gene, 3357
Yerman, J., 3246
Yesh, Robert, 3207
Yessler, Charles, 1136
Yesukai, 1291
Yeswit, Joey, 901
Yezhov, Nicolai, 343
Yiorgalli, Dinos, 1692
Yip Chow, 3176
Yip Yee Tak, 702
Ylvisaker, William Wendell, 3301
Yo Fei, 700, 3207
Yoakum, Benjamin, 1098
Yoas, Bravo Juan, 1037, 2854
Yodice, Peter, 838
Yong Am Pin, 2466
Yonker, Bronco Sue, 1338
Yoritomo, 3207
York, A.M., 325
York, Angel, 1288

York, Duke of, 1716, 2120, 2312, 2328,
    2443, 2475, 2712, 2733, 3074, 3090,
    3185, 3238
York, Duke Richard of, 233, 280, 464,
    633, 720, 725, 865, 870, 1071, 1166
York, George Ronald, 1901-1902
York, Ina Mae, 1372
York, Jimmy, 1372
York, Moses, 3352
York, William, 325, 3207
Yorke, Charles, 1520
Yorke, Kid, 3406
Yorke, Philip, 3207
Yorke, Rose, 1159
Yorty, Sam, 3106
Yoshida, Shigeru, 3395
Yoshimitsu, 3207-3208
Yoshimura, Wendy, 1464, 2891
Yoshio Kodama, 1831, 3202, 3203, 3208,
    3395
Yoshitsune, 3207
Yoshuyiki Yasuda, 1976, 2552
Yoske, Nigger, 3402, 3407, 3412
Yost, Gilbert, 1941
You, Dominique, 3401
Youmans, A., 3344
Youmans, Frank A., 3208
Yound, Kevin D., 3454
Young, A.L., 24
Young, Ab, 3367
Young, Alse, 3208
Young, Andy, 3339
Young, Arline, 3210
Young, Art, 952
Young, Arthur, 3366
Young, Bob, 3208
Young, Brigham, 600, 1918, 2798, 2805,
    2901, 3211
Young Brothers, 3209
Young, C.C., 2860
Young, Charles, 3354, 3355, 3363
Young, Cheryl Lynn, 2305
Young, Chester, 2453
Young, Clement Calhoun, 1114, 1192,
    1281
Young, Clyde, 1021
Young, Cole, 3568
Young Croatian Republican Army, 3503,
    3535
Young, Curtin, 3350
Young, Daniel E., 3347
Young, Danny Jerome, 3208
Young, David, 3450, 3456
Young, Don John, 3208
Young, E. Merl, 2551
Young, Earl, 3208
Young, Edward Louis III, 3208-3209
Young, Elaine, 3209
Young, Filson, 2721
Young, Francis Thomas "Caesar", 2423
Young, Fred, 3363
Young, Fred A., 1587
Young, George, 1453, 2054, 2254, 3209
Young, Gig, 3209
Young, Graham, 3209
Young, Guy William, 2305
Young, Harry, 3209-3210, 3354
Young, Helen Abbey, 1166
Young, Henry (U.S. d.1918), 54, 3357,
    3427
Young, Herbert J., 3210
Young, Herschel, 2552
Young, Hugh, 2092
Young, Iva, 1021
Young, J.D., 3209
Young, Jacob, 728
Young, James, 3210, 3424
Young, Jane, 2777, 2778
Young, Jennings, 3210

Young, Jerry, 1718
Young, John (Brit. d.1750), 3210
Young, John (U.S. pr.1985), 3447
Young, John (Brit. pr.1954), 710
Young, John Louis (U.S. pr.1987), 3210
Young, John Riley (Brit. d.1954), 3210
Young, Joseph (U.S. pr.1980s), 3454
Young, Joseph Louis, 3210
Young, Kenneth, 3210-3211
Young, Kevin, 2442
Young, Kevin D. (U.S. pr.1980s), 3454
Young, Lauretta, 2551
Young Lords, 181, 3483, 3535
Young, Mabel H., 2469-2470, 3129
Young, Margaret Irene, 2480
Young, Mary, 978
Young, Merl, 2551-2552
Young, Merlin, 422
Young, Moses, 3452
Young, Myrtle, 296
Young, Nancy J., 728
Young, Nim, 3344
Young, Olive, 2995
Young, Oscar, 3210
Young, Paul, 3210
Young, Perry, 3347
Young, Philip, 825
Young, Richard, 3354
Young, Robert, 3211
Young, Rodney, 1393
Young, Ruby, 3183
Young, S. Glenn, 3211
Young, S. Grant, 901
Young, Sam, 3350
Young Socialist Alliance, 3479
Young, Stephen, 423
Young, Thelma, 1021
Young, Tom, 214
Young Turks, 2466, 2561, 2573
Young, Vinita, 3209
Young, Wes, 3358
Young, William (U.S. pr.1988), 3451
Young, William (U.S. pr.1910s), 3426
Young, William, (U.S. pr.1870s), 3211, 3568
Young, William Hooper, 3211
Youngblood, Dr. B., 860
Youngblood, Herbert, 960, 3427
Youngblood, John, 3355
Youngblood, Rufus, 1798
Youngdahl, Luther Wallace, 3211-3212
Younger, Adeleine, 858
Younger, Bill, 1224
Younger, Bob, 1702, 3212
Younger Brothers, 236, 858, 860, 862, 878,
    1182, 1197, 1613, 1695, 1696, 1698, 1700,
    1704, 1707-1709, 3212-3214, 3457, 3566
Younger, Cole, 1696, 1698, 1700-1702, 1704,
    1707, 1708, 2283, 2519, 25212556, 2843,
    2844, 3212, 3457, 3563, 3567
Younger, George, 3357
Younger, James, 3568
Younger, Jim, 1702, 3212
Younger, John, 3212, 3568
Younger, Lawrence, 3345
Younger, Pearl, 2844
Younger, Robert, 3568
Younger, Thomas Coleman, 3568
Youngman, William Godfrey, 3214
Yount, Benjamin, 1440
Yountis, Oliver, 3568
Youssef, Salah Ben, 3254
Youth Action Group, 3270, 3501, 3535
Youth Council, 3478, 3535
Youth in Action, 3491
Youth League to Crush the Y and P
    System, 3535
Youtsey, Henry, 1326
Ypres, Earl of, 2746
Ysmet, Irving, 2847

Yu Chien, 3214
Yu Ching-man, 3214
Yu Kikumura, 3281
Yuan Shin-k'ai, 3243
Yuckman, Robert, 3299
Yuet Tung Society, 3391
Yugoslavian Riots, 3378
Yuh Sueh-Chung, 3247
Yui Shosetsu, 3214
Yukl, Charles, 3214
Yuko Hamaguchi, 3247
Yum Kee, 3556
Yung-yen, 3214
Yuran, Hyman, 3412
Yurka, Blanche, 1598, 1600
Yurovsky, Jacob, 2333
Yurrita, Gonzalvo, 3510
Yurubi Toledo, Miguel, 3472
Yury Otrepyev, 3239
Yushchinsky, Andrei, 315
Yusuf Ahmad Saad, 2199
Yusufi, Wali, 3260
Yusupov, Felix, 2538, 3214, 3243
Yusupov, Irina Alexandrovna, 3214
Yuzo Kawachi, 1316
Yves of Brittany, Saint, 3214
Yzurdiaga, John, 772

Z

Zablocki, Jennie, 976
Zabolio, Trudy, 1033
Zaccaro, John A., Jr., 3215
Zacharias, Louis, 2836
Zachary, Bob, 687, 3337
Zacher, Martine, 1304
Zachery, Bob, 2774
Zaffarano, Michael, 427, 3412
Zagame, Joseph, 2236
Zagel, James, 3011
Zaghlul Pasha, Saad, 3215
Zagorski, Edmund, 3454
Zagorski, Wlodzimierz, 3246
Zahaby, Mohammed Hussein, 3215
Zahedi, Ardeshir, 1809
Zahir Khan, 2275
Zahir Shah, Muhammed, 878
Zahle, Carl Theodor, 3215
Zahn, Bertha, 1394
Zahn, Melvin, 3329
Zaim, Husni, 3215, 3252
Zakharin-Koshkin, Anastasia Romanovna, 1671
Zakrewski, Vadislav, 1845
Zaleucus, 3215
Zaluski, Andrzej, 3215
Zambelli, Giuseppe, 3458
Zambino, Luigi, 3215
Zambrana Family, 1525
Zambrana, Jesus, 1525
Zambriano, Dagoberto, 3279
Zammit, Joseph, 1086
Zammuto, Joseph, 3391
Zamora, Francisco, 1739, 3568
Zamora, Rufus, 1246
Zamora y Torres, Niceto Alcala, 3215-3216
Zamot, Emilia, 283
Zamp, Jerome, 355
Zampano, Robert Carmine, 3216
Zamparelli, Paolo, 666
Zanati, Maher Bakri, 3215
Zande, Richard, 2149
Zandt, Johann, 2988

Zane, Charles Shuster, 3216
Zangara, Joseph, 664, 3247
Zangareh, Abdul Hamid, 3252
Zangarra, Anthony, 3412
Zanghi, Anthony, 2990
Zannino, Ilario, 127, 3379, 3380
Zantzinger, Jane, 3216
Zantzinger, William Devereux, 3216
Zapas, Gus, 3391
Zapata, Emiliano, 475, 636, 637, 791, 2076-2078, 2355, 3050, 3052, 3216-3218, 3244
Zapata Urban Front, 3535
Zapatista, 3531, 3535
Zapien, Conrad J, 3449
Zappi, Ettore, 3412
ZAPU Patriotic Front, 3521, 3535
Zaradel, Francine "Zaza", 1317
Zaragosa, Ruben, 3448
Zarate-Albarran, A., 3250
Zarkesh, Ali, 3522
Zarkovich, Martin, 958, 968, 970-972, 1187, 2514
Zarvos, Nicholas, 3081
Zasulich, Vera Ivanovna, 86, 2986, 3242
Zavatt, Joseph Carmine, 3218
Zayas, Fernando, 3218
Zebra Killings, 3218
Zechariah, 3218, 3232
Zedekiah, 2295, 3218
Zeev, Israel, 3218
Zeglicky, Tadeusz, 3251
Zehner, Wilhelm, 990
Zeid, Charles, 3413
Zeigler, Tillie, 1790
Zeigler, William, 3450
Zeime, Claes, 2398
Zeinati, Emir Mohammed, 3251
Zeitoun, Fanny, 1340
Zeitvogel, Richard, 3452
Zekerman, Andrew, 2051-2052
Zelig, Jack "Big Jack" 21, 301, 303, 307, 813, 1064, 1145, 2189, 3218-3219, 3403, 3408, 3411
Zelmanowitz, Gerald, 3412
Zelwanski, Leon, 3486
Zemenides, Angelos, 1066, 2455
Zengakuren, 3535
Zenge, Mandeville, 3219
Zenger, John Peter, 1434, 2804, 3219
Zenner, Albert, 3219
Zenobia, 185, 1987
Zenogalache, 135
Zerajdic, Bogdan, 974, 1212, 3036
Zerash, 3223
Zerbst, Fred, 2407
Zerilli, Anthony, 3394
Zerilli, Joseph, 1948, 3219-3220, 3393, 3394
Zero, 3496, 3500, 3535
Zerr, Christopher Leroy, 2767
Zertuche, Antonio R., 3246
Zettlemoyer, Keith, 3454
Zetzer, Al, 1766
Zeugous, John, 3251
Zevaco, Raoul, 3254
Zevallos, Hector, 123, 3334
Zevi, Sabbatai, 3220
Zevin, Marvin, 560
Zeyad Mahmond Badran, 2894
Zhdanov, Andrei, 1849, 3543
Zhelyabov, Andre, 87
Zia, 3300
Zia ul-Haq, Mohammed, 356, 3220, 3378, 3510, 3528
Ziani, Sebastiano, 3220
Zic, Frank, 2456
Zic, Mike, 2456
Zicarelli, Joseph, 3412

Zickefoose, S.W., 23
Ziegfeld, Florenz, 639, 1382, 1821
Ziegler, Elaine, 2108
Ziegler, George W., 3424
Ziegler, Otto, 1901, 1902
Ziegler, Ronald L., 3099
Ziegler, Shotgun, 2660
Ziegler, William, 3354
Zielinski, Victoria, 2783
Ziemba, Cheryl, 184
Ziemba, Christopher, 184
Ziepke, Rudolf, 2543
Zigic, Bogdan, 3464
Zillman, Bertha, 3220
Zimbabwe African National Union, 3275, 3501
Zimbabwe Missionary Massacre, 3220
Zimbardo, Philip, 391
Zimisces, John, 2328, 3236
Zimmerly, Harry C., 3220
Zimmerman, Blanche, 2161
Zimmerman, Ernest, 3280
Zimmerman, Felton, 3246
Zimmerman, Howard, 2179
Zimmerman, Isidore, 3220
Zimmerman, Leroy S., 1049
Zimmerman, Matt, 3554
Zimmerman, Paul C., 2869
Zimmermann, Ernst, 3261
Zimmermann, Jack, 1902
Zimri, 1080, 3232
Zind, Ludwig, 3220-3221
Zingara, Joseph, 3412
Zinger, Elliot R., 2417
Zinn, Herbert D., 3221
Zinoviev, Grigori, 1830, 1929, 2836, 2992, 3221
Zinoviev Letter, 3221
Zinzendorf, Nikolaus Ludwig von, 3221
Zinzigk, Perry, 3221
Zion, Eddie, 110
Zirpins, Walter, 3543
Zirpoli, Alfonso Joseph, 3221
Zisser, Maria, 2692
Zito, Benito, 3413
Zito, Frank, 136, 3221, 3414
Zivkovic, Lieutenant, 82
Ziyad Al Hilu, 3268
Zizzio, Domenick, 423
Znidar, Thomas F., 3221
Zoccollo, Carmine, 3461
Zodiac Killer, 3221-3222
Zoe, 3222
Zog I, 3247
Zola, Emile, 1024
Zola, James E., 3452
Zoldoske, Rose, 3222
Zoll, Glen "Big Foot", 950
Zolotucho, R., 3467
Zomar, Abdel Osama el-, 3275
Zon, Hans von, 3222
Zonis, Marvin, 1811
Zoot-Suit Riot, 3222-3223, 3376
Zotow, Eugen, 2804
Zouche, Richard, 3223
Zowkowski, John, 3223
Zrinyi, Peter, 3223
Zuaiter, Wael, 3256
Zuazo, Hernn Siles, 2874, 3334
Zubresky, Andrew, 2357
Zucker, Joseph, 3392
Zuckerman, Benjamin, 3391
Zukor, Adolf, 150, 151, 847, 2903, 2904
Zulfikar Ali Bhutto, 2135
Zumati, Adel, 3260
Zumbach, André, 1674
Zumbach, Charles, 1674
Zumbach, Marie, 1674
Zummo, Thomas, 3412